BIRTH I… THEIR KARMIC P…

Your karm… Simply find… in which y… both a nam…

YEAR	BIRTH DATE	KARMIC PATH NUMBER	KARMIC PATH NAME	PAGE
1952	January 1–May 11	21	Revelation	364
	May 12–September 30	20	Consideration	348
	October 1–December 31	19	Release	332
1953	January 1–February 18	19	Release	332
	February 19–July 10	18	Freedom	316
	July 11–November 29	17	Electricity	300
	November 30–December 31	16	Mastery	284
1954	January 1–April 19	16	Mastery	284
	April 20–September 8	15	Articulation	268
	September 9–December 31	14	Consolidation	252
1955	January 1–January 28	14	Consolidation	252
	January 29–June 18	13	Expression	236
	June 19–November 7	12	Amplification	220
	November 8–December 31	11	Inspiration	204
1956	January 1–March 27	11	Inspiration	204
	March 28–August 16	10	Responsibility	188
	August 17–December 31	9	Reform	172
1957	January 1–January 5	9	Reform	172
	January 6–May 26	8	Influence	156
	May 27–October 15	7	Introspection	140
	October 16–December 31	6	Intention	124
1958	January 1–March 6	6	Intention	124
	March 7–July 25	5	Awareness	108
	July 26–December 14	4	Instruction	92
	December 15–December 31	3	Compassion	76
1959	January 1–May 4	3	Compassion	76
	May 5–September 23	2	Discipline	60
	September 24–December 31	1	Artistry	44
1960	January 1–February 12	1	Artistry	44
	February 13–July 2	48	Grounding	796
	July 3–November 21	47	Solution	780
	November 22–December 31	46	Structure	764
1961	January 1–April 12	46	Structure	764
	April 13–August 31	45	Trust	748
	September 1–December 31	44	Confidence	732
1962	January 1–January 20	44	Confidence	732
	January 21–June 10	43	Resolve	716
	June 11–October 30	42	Study	700
	October 31–December 31	41	Versatility	684
1963	January 1–March 21	41	Versatility	684
	March 22–August 9	40	Seduction	668
	August 10–December 29	39	Originality	652
	December 30–December 31	38	Tenderness	636
1964	January 1–May 19	38	Tenderness	636
	May 20–October 7	37	Enchantment	620
	October 8–December 31	36	Experience	604
1965	January 1–February 26	36	Experience	604
	February 27–July 17	35	Translation	588
	July 18–December 6	34	Liberation	572
	December 7–December 31	33	Modulation	556
1966	January 1–April 27	33	Modulation	556
	April 28–September 15	32	Innocence	540
	September 16–December 31	31	Grace	524
1967	January 1–February 4	31	Grace	524
	February 5–June 26	30	Satisfaction	508
	June 27–November 14	29	Empowerment	492
	November 15–December 31	28	Discovery	476
1968	January 1–April 4	28	Discovery	476
	April 5–August 24	27	Individuation	460
	August 25–December 31	26	Wonder	444
1969	January 1–January 12	26	Wonder	444
	January 13–June 3	25	Passion	428
	June 4–October 23	24	Transcendence	412
	October 24–December 31	23	Devotion	396
1970	January 1–March 13	23	Devotion	396
	March 14–August 2	22	Extension	380
	August 3–December 21	21	Revelation	364
	December 22–December 31	20	Consideration	348
1971	January 1–May 12	20	Consideration	348
	May 13–October 1	19	Release	332
	October 2–December 31	18	Freedom	316
1972	January 1–February 19	18	Freedom	316
	February 20–July 10	17	Electricity	300
	July 11–November 29	16	Mastery	284
	November 30–December 31	15	Articulation	268
1973	January 1–April 19	15	Articulation	268
	April 20–September 8	14	Consolidation	252
	September 9–December 31	13	Expression	236
1974	January 1–January 28	13	Expression	236
	January 29–June 18	12	Amplification	220
	June 19–November 7	11	Inspiration	204
	November 8–December 31	10	Responsibility	188
1975	January 1–March 28	10	Responsibility	188
	March 29–August 17	9	Reform	172
	August 18–December 31	8	Influence	156
1976	January 1–January 6	8	Influence	156
	January 7–May 26	7	Introspection	140
	May 27–October 15	6	Intention	124
	October 16–December 31	5	Awareness	108
1977	January 1–March 6	5	Awareness	108
	March 7–July 25	4	Instruction	92
	July 26–December 14	3	Compassion	76
	December 15–December 31	2	Discipline	60
1978	January 1–May 4	2	Discipline	60
	May 5–September 23	1	Artistry	44
	September 24–December 31	48	Grounding	796
1979	January 1–February 12	48	Grounding	796
	February 13–July 3	47	Solution	780
	July 4–November 22	46	Structure	764
	November 23–December 31	45	Trust	748
1980	January 1–April 12	45	Trust	748
	April 13–August 31	44	Confidence	732
	September 1–December 31	43	Resolve	716
1981	January 1–January 20	43	Resolve	716
	January 21–June 10	42	Study	700
	June 11–October 30	41	Versatility	684
	October 31–December 31	40	Seduction	668
1982	January 1–March 21	40	Seduction	668
	March 22–August 9	39	Originality	652
	August 10–December 29	38	Tenderness	636
	December 30–December 31	37	Enchantment	620
1983	January 1–May 20	37	Enchantment	620
	May 21–October 8	36	Experience	604
	October 9–December 31	35	Translation	588
1984	January 1–February 27	35	Translation	588
	February 28–July 17	34	Liberation	572
	July 18–December 6	33	Modulation	556
	December 7–December 31	32	Innocence	540
1985	January 1–April 27	32	Innocence	540
	April 28–September 15	31	Grace	524
	September 16–December 31	30	Satisfaction	508
1986	January 1–February 4	30	Satisfaction	508
	February 5–June 26	29	Empowerment	492
	June 27– November 14	28	Discovery	476
	November 15–December 31	27	Individuation	460
1987	January 1–April 5	27	Individuation	460
	April 6–August 25	26	Wonder	444
	August 26–December 31	25	Passion	428
1988	January 1–January 13	25	Passion	428
	January 14–June 3	24	Transcendence	412
	June 4–October 23	23	Devotion	396
	October 24–December 31	22	Extension	380
1989	January 1–March 13	22	Extension	380
	March 14–August 2	21	Revelation	364
	August 3–December 21	20	Consideration	348
	December 22–December 31	19	Release	332
1990	January 1–May 12	19	Release	332
	May 13–October 1	18	Freedom	316
	October 2–December 31	17	Electricity	300
1991	January 1–February 19	17	Electricity	300
	February 20–July 11	16	Mastery	284
	July 12–November 30	15	Articulation	268
	December 1–December 31	14	Consolidation	252
1992	January 1–April 19	14	Consolidation	252
	April 20–September 8	13	Expression	236
	September 9–December 31	12	Amplification	220
1993	January 1–January 28	12	Amplification	220
	January 29–June 18	11	Inspiration	204
	June 19–November 7	10	Responsibility	188
	November 8–December 31	9	Reform	172
1994	January 1–March 28	9	Reform	172
	March 29–August 17	8	Influence	156
	August 18–December 31	7	Introspection	140
1995	January 1–January 6	7	Introspection	140
	January 7–May 27	6	Intention	124
	May 28–October 16	5	Awareness	108
	October 17–December 31	4	Instruction	92
1996	January 1–March 6	4	Instruction	92
	March 7–July 25	3	Compassion	76
	July 26–December 14	2	Discipline	60
	December 15–December 31	1	Artistry	44
1997	January 1–May 4	1	Artistry	44
	May 5–September 23	48	Grounding	796
	September 24–December 31	47	Solution	780
1998	January 1–February 12	47	Solution	780
	February 13–July 3	46	Structure	764
	July 4–November 22	45	Trust	748
	November 23–December 31	44	Confidence	732
1999	January 1–April 13	44	Confidence	732
	April 14–September 1	43	Resolve	716
	September 2–December 31	42	Study	700
2000	January 1–January 21	42	Study	700
	January 22–June 10	41	Versatility	684
	June 11–October 30	40	Seduction	668
	October 31–December 31	39	Originality	652
2001	January 1–March 21	39	Originality	652
	March 22–August 9	38	Tenderness	636
	August 10–December 29	37	Enchantment	620
	December 30–December 31	36	Experience	604
2002	January 1–May 20	36	Experience	604
	May 21–October 8	35	Translation	588
	October 9–December 31	34	Liberation	572
2003	January 1–February 27	34	Liberation	572
	February 28–July 18	33	Modulation	556
	July 19–December 7	32	Innocence	540
	December 8–December 31	31	Grace	524
2004	January 1–April 27	31	Grace	524
	April 28–September 15	30	Satisfaction	508
	September 16–December 31	29	Empowerment	492
2005	January 1–February 4	29	Empowerment	492
	February 5–June 26	28	Discovery	476
	June 27–November 14	27	Individuation	460
	November 15–December 31	26	Wonder	444
2006	January 1–April 5	26	Wonder	444
	April 6–August 25	25	Passion	428
	August 26–December 31	24	Transcendence	412
2007	January 1–January 13	24	Transcendence	412
	January 14–June 4	23	Devotion	396
	June 5–October 24	22	Extension	380
	October 25–December 31	21	Revelation	364
2008	January 1–March 13	21	Revelation	364
	March 14–August 2	20	Consideration	348
	August 3–December 21	19	Release	332
	December 22–December 31	18	Freedom	316
2009	January 1–May 12	18	Freedom	316
	May 13–October 1	17	Electricity	300
	October 2–December 31	16	Mastery	284
2010	January 1–February 19	16	Mastery	284
	February 20–July 11	15	Articulation	268
	July 12–November 30	14	Consolidation	252
	December 1–December 31	13	Expression	236
2011	January 1–April 20	13	Expression	236
	April 21–September 9	12	Amplification	220
	September 10–December 31	11	Inspiration	204
2012	January 1–January 29	11	Inspiration	204
	January 30–June 18	10	Responsibility	188
	June 19–November 7	9	Reform	172
	November 8–December 31	8	Influence	156
2013	January 1–March 28	8	Influence	156
	March 29–August 17	7	Introspection	140
	August 18–December 31	6	Intention	124
2014	January 1–January 6	6	Intention	124
	January 7–May 27	5	Awareness	108
	May 28–October 16	4	Instruction	92
	October 17–December 31	3	Compassion	76
2015	January 1–March 7	3	Compassion	76
	March 8–July 26	2	Discipline	60
	July 27–December 15	1	Artistry	44
	December 16–December 31	48	Grounding	796
2016	January 1–May 4	48	Grounding	796
	May 5–September 23	47	Solution	780
	September 24–December 31	46	Structure	764
2017	January 1–February 12	46	Structure	764
	February 13–July 3	45	Trust	748
	July 4–November 22	44	Confidence	732
	November 23–December 31	43	Resolve	716
2018	January 1–April 13	43	Resolve	716
	April 14–September 1	42	Study	700
	September 2–December 31	41	Versatility	684
2019	January 1–January 21	41	Versatility	684
	January 22–June 11	40	Seduction	668
	June 12–October 31	39	Originality	652
	November 1–December 31	38	Tenderness	636
2020	January 1–March 21	38	Tenderness	636
	March 22–August 9	37	Enchantment	620
	August 10–December 29	36	Experience	604
	December 30–December 31	35	Translation	588
2021	January 1–May 20	35	Translation	588
	May 21–October 8	34	Liberation	572
	October 9–December 31	33	Modulation	556

THE SECRET LANGUAGE OF
DESTINY

THE SECRET LANGUAGE OF
DESTINY

A PERSONOLOGY GUIDE
TO FINDING YOUR LIFE PURPOSE

GARY GOLDSCHNEIDER

JOOST ELFFERS

VIKING STUDIO

ACKNOWLEDGMENTS

Editor: Marie Timell
Contributing Editor: Teresa Kennedy
Crystal Consultant: Miranda Ryan
Editorial Assistance: Martha Craig, Cliff Corcoran, David Chalfant

Photo Research: Linda Pilgrim
Photo Research Assistance: Radha Pancham

Art Direction: Marie Timell
Design: Betty Lew
Production Layout: Susan Lusk
Karmic Path Symbol Design: Joost Elffers
Symbol Design: Iwan Baan

Managing Editor, Viking Penguin: Victoria Klose
Production Director, Viking Penguin: Roni Axelrod
Art Director, Viking Penguin: Jaye Zimet

Astronomical data courtesy of Astro Communications Services

Thanks to Isaac Brilleman and to Alex Moore at Corbis/Bettmann

VIKING STUDIO
Published by the Penguin Group
Penguin Putnam Inc., 375 Hudson Street,
New York, New York 10014, U.S.A.
Penguin Books Ltd, 27 Wrights Lane, London W8 5TZ, England
Penguin Books Australia Ltd, Ringwood, Victoria, Australia
Penguin Books Canada Ltd, 10 Alcorn Avenue,
Toronto, Ontario, Canada M4V 3B2
Penguin Books (N.Z.) Ltd, 182–190 Wairau Road,
Auckland 10, New Zealand

Penguin Books Ltd, Registered Offices
Harmondsworth, Middlesex, England

First published in 1999 by Viking Studio,
a member of Penguin Putnam Inc.

3 5 7 9 10 8 6 4 2

ISBN 0–670–88597-5
CIP data available

Printed in the United States of America

Illustration credits appear on pages 823-824.

Gary Goldschneider and Joost Elffers extend special thanks to Marie Timell
whose editorial skills and astrological expertise have been indispensable to
the *Secret Language* series.

To Berthe Meijer

How To Use This Book

The description of your life purpose is outlined by one of the forty-eight karmic paths presented in this book. Your karmic path is based on your birthday. Turn to the chart located at the front or back of this volume, find your birth year, then locate the period in which your month and day of birth fall. You will find the name of your karmic path, its number, and the page on which the text describing your karmic path begins. For ease of reference each karmic path has been numbered from one to forty-eight; they appear in this volume in numeric order.

Turning to the page that begins the section on your karmic path, you will find four pages of main text on your path. Read this section very carefully. This is the core description of your karmic path. It is followed by information on how the forty-eight possible positions of the sun in the personology system might work with that karmic path. Those familiar with the previous volumes in this series are likely to know their personology period. Turn to page 12 for a brief overview of personology and to the table on page 14 to determine your personology period if you don't already know it. Brief descriptions of all the personology periods begin on page 17.

Contents

Introduction

1

An Overview of Personology

11

The Personology Periods

17

The Karmic Paths

43

Index of Notables

813

"The Dance of the Zodiac"

Introduction

A person's fate or destiny can be described as a unique and wholly personal thread woven into the fabric of the universe. Thus it is both interconnected with the destiny of many others yet also distinct unto itself, making its own unique contribution to the whole cloth. When viewed from this perspective, it is easy to see why a person's destiny—a single thread in the divine plan—though equally as important as the whole, may be difficult to discern. It is human nature to wonder about the greater meaning of life, both life in general and one's own life in particular. Throughout the centuries human beings have gazed heavenward and asked themselves, "Why am I here? What is the purpose of my life?" Deep within all of us lies the certainty that there is something more to life and to ourselves—a purpose that transcends the physical plane and gives our lives meaning in the context of a greater, more beautiful whole.

Who among us hasn't pondered the mystery of our destiny? And why must it be mysterious in the first place? Lucky is the man who has a sense of the purpose of his life. And is there anything more pitiable than a lost soul—someone who yearns to understand himself and his role in the world but is, as yet, unknowing and confused? The questioning and yearning for answers are part of the process of discovering why we are here. Our life purpose is meant to unfold and our understanding of it to deepen, broaden, and ripen with maturity and wisdom. Pondering your life purpose is integral to finding and manifesting it. If you are reading this book, then you are engaged in the process of fulfilling your destiny; by seeking meaning, you are creating it. The purpose of *The Secret Language of Destiny: A Personology Guide to Finding Your Life Purpose* is simple: to give you some of the answers to your questions so that you may find and understand your life purpose. If you receive even a brief moment of insight into the larger plan for your life as you read this book, then we, the authors, have succeeded in our task—and our own life purposes. The threads of our lives have meshed with yours as the fabric of the universe continues to unfold.

The *Secret Language* series, of which *The Secret Language of Destiny* is a part, provides its audience with esoteric astrological information in an easily accessible format. *The Secret Language of Destiny* continues the progression of the first two books in the *Secret Language* series. *The Secret Language of Birthdays,* a book about the self, describes an individual's personality and his or her strengths and weaknesses. *The Secret Language of Relationships* discusses the manner in which we relate to others and how our energies combine with theirs to predict the kinds of relationships we will form. *Destiny* expands the topic further to discuss an individual's relationship with the universe, or the world at large, and his or her place in it. Its perspective is more spiritual, and implicit in the text is the idea that the soul is eternal and comes into each lifetime with a mission for growth.

Like its predecessors, *Destiny* works with both astrology and personology, to reveal what an individual came into life to achieve, what lesson to learn, what goal to embrace. It deals with issues of the growth of the self or soul. In *Destiny*, we address the issue of life purpose by sharing with a broader audience a secret that astrologers have always known: on the day of your birth, it is possible to identify two symbolic points in space known as the nodes of the moon that together indicate the direction a person's life is fated to take. Like an arrow, the line between the two nodes points the way to a person's destiny. Consider it a pathway that each person must walk, each in his own way and time. Esoteric astrologer Dane Rudhyar called it a "destiny axis," though he also credited the term to Marc Edmund Jones. The journey from the south to the north node is, in essence, one's life purpose. By studying the placement of these points, an astrologer can tell a client what, on a spiritual level, he or she is meant to achieve in the course of his or her present lifetime. *The Secret Language of Destiny* calculates these points and interprets their meaning for you.

What Are the Karmic Paths?

A karmic path can be likened to a bridge from the past to the future, one that spans and takes up the present. *The Secret Language of Destiny* presents forty-eight karmic paths, each representing a spiritual journey with a starting point—complete with a person's innate talents and abilities—and a destination that signifies what a person came here to learn or do. It is our destiny to move from one point to the other. A karmic path is based on a person's birthday and is the straight line drawn between the positions of the two opposite nodes of the moon on that day. Each karmic path has a south node position—the beginning of the path—and a north node position—the destination of the path. Unique to this volume, however, is the fact that the nodal positions are interpreted according to personology's unique forty-eight periods. In this manner the information contained in this volume differs significantly from traditional astrology, which delineates just twelve possible nodal positions, one for each sign of the zodiac. (A brief discussion of the *Secret Language* personology system can be found on page 12.)

Each karmic path is described in detail in text that discusses what can enhance progress along the path, one's gifts, and how best to approach achieving one's ultimate goal. Each path has a name that describes the main process or journey involved in moving from the starting point to the destination. For ease of reference, a number from one to forty-eight has been assigned to each of the karmic paths. The description of the forty-eight karmic paths begins on page 43 of this volume with the Pisces–Aries cusp at the south node position, since this is the spring equinox and so represents the start of the astrological year. This karmic path, which ends at its astrologically opposite position in the personology system, the Virgo–Libra cusp, is called "The Way of Artistry" and is Karmic Path 1 (KP 1). Proceeding from the Cusp of Rebirth (Pisces–Aries) to the Cusp of Beauty (Virgo–Libra), this karmic path calls those on it to invoke a kind of artistry as they move from an approach to life that is natural, direct, perhaps even primitive to one that embodies elegance and aesthetic discernment. This requires quite a metamorphosis, one that might be likened to the spiritual transformation described by early alchemists and symbolized by the process of turning lead into gold. Not all of the karmic paths require such a startling change; many of them call for only subtle shifts in perception or mode of thought or feeling. Your own karmic path, however, represents the growth or spiritual development that is your particular purpose or goal in this lifetime. Whether you actually entertain this growth, thereby taking your destiny into your own hands, or not is up to you. If you do not, however, your spirit may languish and its evolution may be slowed. These lines from Shakespeare's *Julius Caesar* come to mind:

> There is a tide in the affairs of men,
> Which, taken at the flood, leads on to fortune;
> Omitted, all the voyages of their life
> Is bound in shallows and in miseries.

Not only is it in our own best interest to be carried along on the tide of destiny, but it would seem to behoove us to do so consciously, to use our free will as a rudder to steer our course. But of course, much like any traveler, it would help us to have a map or star to steer by. The forty-eight karmic paths in *The Secret Language of Destiny* are such celestial guides, tailor-made for you.

The Moon's Nodes

There are a number of important astronomical points in Western astrology charts that, like the moon's nodes, are not planets but are considered by astrologers to have significance. Such points occur in pairs and represent related concepts—for example, self/other and home/career—all connected in some way to one's place in the world. The moon's nodes are such points, and their calculation involves the sun's seeming revolution around the earth and the orbit of the moon. From a symbolic viewpoint, it seems quite fitting that the interaction of these celestial bodies should have something to do with destiny since the sun represents our individual will while the moon has long been associated by metaphysicians with the soul and its mission. In fact, like the soul, a portion of the moon always remains hidden from view. It is interesting to note that the south and north nodes are exalted in Gemini and Sagittarius, both signs that rule matters of learning and travel. The nodes are a rich source of creative potential. The journey from one to the other, if undertaken consciously, will challenge you to operate at your highest level both creatively and spiritually. However, it is the integration of both nodes into your life that will contribute to your greatest growth and success.

There are two nodes, south and north, directly opposite each other in the heavens. The south node is called the tail of the dragon while the north is its head. They have also been called the tail and head of the serpent. In Hindu astrology these points are known as Ketu and Rahu. While in the West the primary dragon myths involve the slaying of a dragon by an intrepid hero, in East Asia dragons are symbols of happiness and long life. The differing mythologies extend to differing views on

How to Find Your Karmic Path

Using this book is extremely simple. First consult the charts printed on the endpapers of this volume. Affixed to the front and back covers, the endpapers are printed with a table of dates. By finding your birthday on this table, you will find your karmic path, both its name and number, and the page where it is described in this book. The forty-eight karmic paths delineated in *The Secret Language of Destiny* have been given numbers for ease of reference. Your karmic path is not your sun sign. Like your sun sign it is determined by your date of birth, but it is based on an astronomical calculation rather than the position of the sun on the day of your birth. In this book, your karmic path has been determined for you. Read the four pages of text that describe your karmic path. Then turn to the page in the section on your karmic path that predicts how someone with your personology period might negotiate that karmic path. The description of each karmic path also contains a table of the birth dates that apply to that path.

fate as well: in the West fate is something to be feared and fought, while in the East, if one enters into the proper relationship to fate, it confers immortality. Because of a snake's ability to shed its skin, serpents have been taken to symbolize transformation and the cycle of death and rebirth. Moreover, serpents are also a symbol of kundalini, the spiritual power that yogis say resides at the base of the spine and that, when uncoiled and allowed to move freely up the spine, releases one from material attachments and opens one to higher states of awareness. Based on their symbols alone, one can have little doubt that the nodes are of great spiritual import.

The South Node: Where You Come From

The south node is said to represent the past, more specifically behavior patterns from the past. Commonly, astrologers think of these patterns as having originated in past lives. Alternatively, one could think of these patterns as the effects of psychological conditioning in early childhood or heredity, whether in the form of social conditioning or genetics. Usually, we exhibit the behaviors of the south node early in life. These behavior patterns operate like a well-worn groove in our lives. We tend to stay in such patterns because they are automatic for us. We may have adopted these behaviors, talents, and skills in past lives and resort to them now in the present lifetime because they are what come easily to us. By acting out our south nodes, we are following the path of least resistance. This is not problematic per se, as the south node provides us with certain innate talents and gifts. It quite often explains those people who try something and quickly become adept at it or are "naturals." If we could only see into the past, we would undoubtedly perceive all the hard work that they put into learning that skill or talent in another lifetime. Though usually individuals have no memory of their past lives, the residual effects of such lives can be identified by the position of the south node. It is said that one's past karma comes into this lifetime through the south node. People tend to identify with their south node. It often symbolizes character traits of which they are most proud. For example, people with a south node in Aries, the sign of the warrior, may think of themselves as take-charge, courageous people with leadership abilities, people who are willing make tough decisions.

One problem is that the south node is a bit too habitual. Habits give people a sense of security, and so most individuals stick to what they know. This is especially true during times of stress. People tend to go scurrying back to the behavior sets of their south node when tired, ill, unhappy, or frightened. However, a man's reach must exceed his grasp, and in order to grow, we are called on to break out of the ruts in which we love to wallow and to learn something new or approach life in a different way. Moreover, often because the behavior set associated with the south node is so unconscious, people exhibit the less desirable sides of the energy, usually without even thinking about it. An individual with the south node in the sign Aries, continuing the example above, may actually be rather tyrannical in his approach to others or at least extremely bossy and perhaps even rash in his decision making. It is the behaviors represented by the south node that are most often is examined and discussed when people are in psychotherapy or counseling.

The North Node: Where You Are Going

The north node is the opposite of the south node. It is what one is working toward; it can be thought of as the destination of one's life journey. The sign in which the north node is found delineates the set of skills, qualities, or character traits that we have come into this lifetime to learn. Often it represents our own unexpressed vision of life for ourselves. Deep down we know this is what we are supposed to be doing. But it doesn't come easily; it requires some work. We aren't too good at the areas of life represented by the north node yet, and we need to go easy on ourselves because working on the north node can entail some frustration. When we awaken the potentials that lie sleeping at the north node, much like the sleeping dragon in fairy tales, we may have to do battle to learn to work from that place rather than from our old behavior sets and patterns. Ultimately, however, as you do the work of incorporating the north node into your repertoire of life skills, your reward will be a great deal of satisfaction. As we overcome the obstacles presented by the north node, our consciousness expands and we move toward higher awareness. Sometimes, when presented with their north node, astrology clients find that it represents an area they are quite good at. How can this be? It may be that by the time they learn about their north node, they have already spent a portion of their life working on it!

The Karmic Journey: Life's Purpose

While an individual's life purpose is to move from the south to the north node, the south node should not be left behind entirely. This would be like throwing out the baby with the bathwater. People aren't supposed to rid themselves of all the attributes of the south node but to bring them into balance with the newfound ones of the north node. Religion and myth are filled with paradigms of the union of opposites into a new synthesized third entity. As you evolve on your life journey, you will learn to identify which behaviors or patterns associated with your south node must be released and which can be used

---

The Nodes of the Moon

A Brief Note

The karmic paths delineated in *The Secret Language of Destiny* are based on the zodiac positions of the moon's nodes on the day of a person's birth. What are the moon's nodes? They are not planetary bodies but symbolic representations of points in the heavens. They are the points formed by the intersection of the orbit of the moon with the ecliptic, or the apparent path traced by the sun around the earth as measured against the backdrop of fixed stars. The point at which the moon in its orbit touches the ecliptic as it moves into the Northern Hemisphere is called the north node, whereas the place where it touches the ecliptic when it moves into the Southern Hemisphere is known as the south node. The south and north nodes are always 180 degrees apart; thus there is a theoretical axis or straight line between them. Some astrologers consider that the south node has an influence akin to that of the planet Saturn while the influence of the north node is more like that of the planets Jupiter and Venus.

The lunar nodes wiggle backward and forward, but on the whole their direction of travel is backward through the zodiac, traveling, for example, from 22 degrees of Cancer on a given day back to 1 degree of Cancer and then into Gemini over the course of several months. For the purposes of this book, we have used the mean nodal positions to identify the karmic paths since the mean node smoothes the effect of the wiggle. It takes approximately eighteen and a half years for the nodes to travel through all the astrological signs or personology periods. A node remains in a sign a little more than a year and a half and in a personology period for roughly four and a half months. Thus, individuals born around the same time in a given year share the same karmic path.

along the journey. As on any trip, deciding what to pack to bring along is all-important. Learning to release outworn south node attributes can teach us a profound lesson about surrender and release in general. Moving toward the north node may involve learning how to shift your perception. Often we find north node behaviors and qualities difficult only because, being new to us, they appear to be that way. Working with the power of our minds to effect change through intention is a crucial part of the process. Actually, we receive quite a lot of help from our guides and teachers when we are working toward our north node, and once we choose to make the effort, it comes more easily to us than we expected. That's because it is our destiny. The secret is knowing and accepting that this is where you want to be.

The Secret Language of Destiny may help you start the process because it articulates what you already know: what it is you came here to do. A general rule of thumb is that when you're feeling dissatisfied or unfulfilled you are probably stuck in your south node. We have a lot of expectations, even fantasies, in the areas governed by the south node. When we are operating more in accordance with our north node, we experience a feeling of empowerment—not willfulness as much as a deep sense of inner authority. The north node is a more realistic or detached place; when you are aligned with your north node, people don't disappoint you or let you down as much. The north node can teach you important lessons about the value of detachment in general. Detachment enables us to rise above the pain of emotion and conflict. Not infrequently, people view the north node as "boring." The south node holds a lot of drama for us and thus seems more exciting. But what could truly be more boring than acting out the same old behavior sets or attachments to excitement over and over again? Ultimately, both nodes must be integrated into and balanced in the personality. Though they represent opposite energies, they must be turned into complements. Each can aid the other to enhance your overall awareness and success.

Working with the Karmic Paths

Each of the forty-eight karmic paths is presented in a detailed text of four pages. Your karmic path is based on your birthday.

The Nodes and Eclipses

An interesting fact about the nodes is that the ancients probably first noticed their position due to the occurrence of eclipses. These powerful celestial events always occur in astrological degrees and signs close to the positions of the nodes of the moon. As is widely known, eclipses occur at either the new or full moon. An eclipse occurs when the earth blocks the sun, thus casting a shadow on the moon (lunar eclipse, at the full moon), or the moon blocks the sun, thus casting a shadow on the earth (solar eclipse, at the new moon). Eclipses have long been considered mysterious, even feared events. We note their connection to the nodes purely as a matter of interest.

Turn to the charts located at the front and back of this book and find your birth year. Then find the period during which the month of and day of your birthday fall. You will find the name of your karmic path, its number, and the page number where the description of your karmic path begins. Read this description of your path very carefully. It contains much valuable information. You may wish to reread it at once or read it again later as the information contained in the text may resonate with your understanding in different ways at different times. The main text provides a detailed description of your south and north nodes and what they have to say about your life purpose. It is followed by a discussion of three individuals born to that karmic path and how their lives reflect that karmic path.

Each karmic path description is accompanied by highlighted information pertaining to that specific karmic journey. The core lesson of each path is a skill, characteristic, or quality that must be assimilated in order to move along the path. The goal of your path is, in essence, what will fulfill your destiny—what you must work to achieve. Usually the core lesson and the goal work together, the goal being more spiritual or esoteric. Keep in mind that this is your true self or soul's goal. The core lesson is more rooted in the mundane world and is thus seemingly more practical or direct. It is, however, what will help you get to your goal. Consider this to be a major theme of your inner growth. Situations having to do with this lesson will crop up again and again in your life until the lesson is learned.

Interestingly, each karmic path seems to confer certain talents or gifts. These are natural or innate and can be thought of as characteristics or qualities that can help us along our journey. The gifts of the path come easily to those on the path and help one to move along it. Using your gifts is so free-flowing and natural to you that you may not even be aware of how easy they are. Moreover, you gift others with these traits, often using them to help or serve those around you. The pitfalls of a path are modes or patterns of behavior that we also slip into easily but that we should try to avoid. They represent less positive behaviors that we exhibit either when being stubborn or stuck out of fear or when we go overboard as we move forward toward the destination of the path. When we find ourselves acting in the manner described by the pitfalls of the karmic path, it is time to take stock of ourselves and redress any imbalances—of body, mind, or spirit—that may be present in our lives.

Finding balance is key to the success of any karmic journey. Grappling with the challenges of life often means that we have to reconcile conflicting energies. Each of the karmic paths seems to require finding the middle ground between two concepts that often appear to be unrelated or mutually exclusive. Resolving this paradox is part of the journey. The text describing each karmic path highlights these two points. For example, on Karmic Path 5, the Way of Awareness, the balance that needs to be struck is between Love and Power. Though the idea that integration between these two can occur may at first seem illogical or impossible, recall that in Zen Buddhism students are given seemingly impossible koans upon which they are to meditate. Working with a paradox causes one to move outside the framework of ordinary perceptions or notions of logic and can bring the student to new levels of awareness.

For those spiritual seekers who are open to crystals, *The Secret Language of Destiny* provides a suggestion as to what kind of crystal may be useful for each of the karmic paths. Often the choice of crystal is directly related to the balance point described in the preceding paragraph. Sitting quietly and holding the crystal may result in achieving significant insights or may help you attune yourself to the energies of your path. Those wishing to work with the suggested crystals can use their intuitive wisdom as to the best way to work with them.

As your understanding of your evolution deepens, you may find that the description of your karmic path becomes more and more clear to you. The purpose of the main text that describes your karmic path is to bring you to a better understanding of both the challenges and the opportunities you encounter in your life. Use the material presented in the description of your karmic path as you reflect upon the recurring themes of your life. Usually, those situations that seem to repeat themselves are precisely those from which we have the most to learn. For example, individuals born on the Way of Revelation (KP 21) are called upon to develop better discernment and judgment about other people. It may be inevitable that they will experience betrayals of their trust. However, these experiences, as painful as they may be, will teach them better judgment. Ultimately, they will choose people as intimates who are worthy of their trust. And the experience of being able to truly trust others and to feel secure in that trust will be a kind of blessing

in the end. It is important to develop the objectivity to gather the fruits of the lessons as you encounter them. Otherwise life may seem meaningless or, worse, hopeless. The highlighted material called "Release/Reward" speaks to such an objective viewpoint.

Usually, in order to be more aware as we travel our karmic paths, each of us needs to release our own specific perceptive flaw. Highlighted in the main text as "Release," this may be a chronic need for approval, an unconscious need to suffer, overdependence on others, or a refusal to admit mistakes because of a need to be infallible, to name a few. Practice removing such tendencies from your repertoire or changing your point of view, and often you will notice that your thinking becomes clearer and your ability to see the larger view of your life expands. Changing your perspective in this manner while also evolving in accordance with your karmic path can lead you to find your joy. Rarely is your joy what you would expect. This joy is what is highlighted in the main text as "Reward"—and what better reward can there be?

Personology Periods on the Karmic Paths

Always remember that your sun sign or, in the system used in the *Secret Language* series, your personology period is different from your karmic path. The sun sign or personology period in astrology symbolizes how we express our will in the world; it may be thought of as our character, creativity, and impetus in life. Obviously, it will greatly influence how each of us approaches the journey of our karmic path and the choices we will make along the way. In order to personalize the karmic paths, *The Secret Language of Destiny* provides brief predictions of how each personology period may fare on each path. These descriptions are presented in the pages that follow the main text of each karmic path. Those already familiar with the *Secret Language* series will know their personology period. To find your personology period, turn to the table on page 14. In addition, pages 17 to 41 contain abbreviated descriptions of the personology periods for your reference.

How does a specific personology period relate to a karmic path? For example, do Aries II's, with all the strengths and weaknesses of that period, fare as well on the Way of Compassion (KP 3) as Cancer III's? In this example, Aries II's may find it more difficult to put the good of the group above their own needs, the core lesson of the Way of Compassion, since they tend to be more self-involved. Cancers are naturally feeling-oriented and nurturing. Thus, one could expect that

Cancer III's would have an easier time learning their karmic lessons on this path than Aries II's. Highlighted in the section on the sun's personology periods on the karmic path are the key challenge and the greatest fulfillment for each personology period on that path. To continue the example above, the greatest challenge for Cancer III's on the Way of Compassion is to be sure to nourish their spirit by pursuing a spiritual path as they work on behalf of others. Meanwhile, Cancer III's will experience fulfillment as their work on behalf of others bears fruit.

Notables on the Karmic Paths

In addition to its foundation in astrology, as is typical of personology, the information contained in this book is based on the observation of a database of 7,500 notable individuals. For the reader, the tables of birth dates go as far back as 1880 and as far into the future as 2021, but notables from periods even further back in time were included in the database. Throughout the text of this book, famous individuals born to each of the forty-eight karmic paths are noted. First, in the main text on each karmic path, three notables are discussed whose lives appear to have embodied the successful negotiation of destiny. In a few cases, notables were selected because they don't seem to be fulfilling the calling of their karmic path. Notables are also highlighted throughout each section, together with their birthdays and their personology period.

It is extremely interesting to study the notables on a given karmic path. At first glance they may seem to have little in common with one another or the path. Upon reflection, however, one can discern the themes of the karmic path running through their lives like a thread. Of course, destiny or life purpose is an extremely private, if not wholly personal and inner, matter. It may be difficult to detect the karmic theme in the life of someone we barely know other than by published reports, but it is there. Although it is not for us to judge another, sometimes one gets the sense that someone is choosing not to do the work of his karmic path. Other times it is obvious that a notable individual is, whether consciously or unconsciously, fulfilling her destiny.

The Secret Language of Destiny is about one's role in the world. The nodes of the moon that are the basis of this book have also long been associated with matters of the collective and the public. Often it is through our position in the world, our career, our service activities, or the public roles we take on that we fulfill our life purpose. It can be predicted, then, that moving through one's life in accordance with one's destiny will bring a certain degree of success or even public recognition. Based on our work on this book, this appears to be true. The notables on each karmic path are, on some level, walking it successfully; otherwise they wouldn't be notables. This turned out to be particularly true for those paths that are more worldly in orientation. It is interesting to note that there are fewer notables in the database on the karmic paths that are more internal in orientation. Not infrequently, the database failed to contain a notable for a specific personology period on a specific path. This is of considerable interest since one could make the generalization that that particular combination may be a bit more challenging.

In addition, it frequently happens that fulfilling one's life purpose is meant to be an inner-directed process, one that may not require outer manifestation. For example, people on the Way of Introspection are supposed to become more self-aware, to spend time looking inward to better understand themselves and their own workings. Someone might do this delivering letters as a postal worker, inputting information into a computer as a data processor, or writing a novel. Even an internal process, however, will change how we interact with the world. Moreover, it would seem that successfully negotiating a karmic path is apt to make people "known"—even if only within their own circle or profession.

Other Points to Keep in Mind: Connections on the Karmic Paths
Because the energies represented by the two poles of your karmic path can be considered significant for you, you may find it interesting to notice when the personology periods of your friends, family, and associates fall on either pole. For example, if your karmic path is the Way of Articulation, which begins at Cancer II and ends at Capricorn II, you might ask yourself if you know anyone born in the Cancer II or Capricorn II periods. If you do, it may be that these individuals have some involvement in your destiny. A Capricorn II friend, for example, will possess some of the energies that you are trying to embody on your journey and thus may, quite indirectly, serve as a teacher to you. It is our experience that individuals born in the personology period represented by the destination on your karmic path tend to enjoy a free-and-easy give-and-take with you. You receive a lot from these people without even realizing it. Meanwhile, Cancer II people may somehow be influencing you to remain stuck in your south node roots. Sometimes such individuals may seem to drain you or be a bur-

den in some way. Positively, by examining these people in your life closely, you may learn quite a bit about yourself by finding, in them, sides of yourself that you didn't know existed.

Another fascinating point is when you find yourself involved with individuals whose karmic path is opposite your own. This means that the poles of their karmic path are the mirror image of the poles of your karmic path. Suppose your path is the Way of Study (KP 42), which begins at Aquarius I and ends at Leo I. You may fall in love with someone who is on the Way of Freedom (KP 18), which begins at Leo I and ends at Aquarius I. (This situation occurs with karmic paths that are twenty-four paths apart.) The point is that you have come into this lifetime with quite a lot of Aquarius I energy and you are trying to learn about Leo I energy. Meanwhile, your partner knows all about Leo I energy since this is what he or she has dealt with in the past. Your partner, in turn, is striving to learn about what you know, Aquarius I. Thus you have much to teach each other, and this could be considered quite a "karmic" relationship. Keep in mind that individuals with karmic paths opposite yours will be roughly nine to ten years, twenty-seven to twenty-eight years, even forty-six to forty seven years older or younger than

you. Obviously, a significant relationship such as this can easily occur with a beloved parent or grandparent. Thus, the table of birth dates at the beginning and end of this volume begins as far back as 1880 so that you can ascertain the karmic paths of grandparents and other older relatives

Similarly, you may find that there are people in your life who have the same karmic path as you. It could be said that since you share a similar destiny, you are travelers on a similar road. You may find that you and your friend are unusually compatible or comfortable with each other or see things the same way. You are working toward the same goal, and though each of you must do so in your own way, it may be a source of comfort to you to share your experiences with someone who is encountering similar life lessons. Such people will be born in the same four-month span of time as you, such as school chums, or will be eighteen to nineteen years, thirty-seven to thirty-eight years, or fifty-six to fifty-seven years older or younger than you. The table of all the birth periods in each karmic path is provided in the body of the main text on each of the karmic paths, thereby enabling you to quickly determine who shares your karmic path with you.

Destiny and Karma: A Conceptual Framework

What Is Destiny?

Are our lives preordained? The concept of fate postulates as much. Since *The Secret Language of Destiny* is a book about fate, it is important to examine how this book uses that word. The word "fate" comes from the Latin *fatum*, meaning, "what has been spoken." In ancient times, pronouncements were considered to be law even if unwritten. People's fate was also usually seen to be immutable, as if the plan of their lives had been decided and written in some large book that had existed since the beginning of time with a text that could never be changed or rewritten.

In *The Secret Language of Destiny*, we do not argue about whether a divine plan exists for us. Rather, this book is based on the notion that there is indeed a larger spiritual context to everyone's life and that this context can be viewed as a divine plan. However, no entity or law outside ourselves forces this plan on us. We are beings who possess free will. It is with our free will that we engage in and help to create the plan for our lives. Such a plan is one that we, on a soul level, have chosen in cooperation with our Creator or the universe, if you will. As cocreators of our own destiny, we are responsible for it, and thus we ourselves determine how it will unfold.

Some esoteric astrologers believe that what can be seen or read about a person's destiny in an astrological chart is a symbolic representation of that individual's own choices. This leads to the next question: Since you are

usually unaware of having made the choices that may be read in your astrological chart, who or what has made the choices? It is the part of you that is your true Self or soul, the part that is at one with all there is. *The Secret Language of Destiny* is about the growth and expansion of this Self and your inner life, and it is based on reincarnation as a core premise.

Many religions and spiritual traditions embrace the notion that human beings consist of a Self or soul, separate from the personality, that is eternal, living past physical death in one lifetime to be born anew in another. The primary purpose of such rebirths is the evolution of the soul through experience on the earth plane. Birth into a new lifetime gives the soul the opportunity to learn and to grow through its interactions with gross matter on the physical plane. Such growth is by nature action-oriented and requires a direction—and indeed, a direction exists. Thus our life purpose is our own personal path of evolution. The soul itself determines the lessons that will be learned in each lifetime. Sometimes many lifetimes are required before the skills, insight, or knowledge embodied by certain lessons is learned. The ultimate goal of each lifetime is the continued evolution of our consciousness to develop ever-increasing levels of awareness.

In our goal-oriented society, it is important to keep in mind that, in truth, life purpose is really more a process of becoming. What are we becoming? Our highest and best self. Of course, the ultimate goal is to align the soul to ever-higher awareness in order to return to the source or Creator. Think of the evolutionary journey as an upward-moving spiral. In a single lifetime, one may work on a single issue, thus remaining on the horizontal plane of the spiral for a while. Then, with a jump in consciousness that may take lifetimes to achieve or that may occur several times in a single lifetime, one moves to a higher rung on the spiral. The process is ongoing, and what appears to be a destination only leads us on to the next level.

What is the role of free will in all of this? Given that each human being has free will, the gift of choice, any individual may or may not choose in any particular lifetime to pursue his chosen lessons or destiny, to make the effort to grow or learn in accordance with his own divine blueprint. Free will—whether our own or someone else's—can alter our fate. Perhaps we should think of fate as simply the architectural plan of our potential. It is up to each individual to decide what kind of edifice he or she will build. Sometimes, people seem to fall into their destiny, learning their lessons easily without any apparent effort. Quite often, spirit guides and other teachers in many forms assist people along their paths. If someone doesn't wish to evolve further in a lifetime, that is his or her choice. It is said that there are "resting lifetimes." But it is a human being's nature to constantly seek to better himself, to find perfection within himself, and such is the nature of the soul's calling. Whether we are aware of it or not, we are all evolving in accordance with our own chosen and perfect plan.

What Is Karma?

Karma, a term adopted from Hindu philosophy, has been interpreted in a number of ways. Many writers on the topic have used the following quote from the Bible to explain karma: "Whatsoever a man soweth, that shall he also reap." (Galatians 6:7) At the simplest level, this means that our actions generate equal reactions. Thus karma is also commonly likened to Newton's law of cause and effect. A single action creates a necessary reaction, and many such actions over time build up a huge sum of necessary responses, this being karma. Karma is both the action that creates a result and the sum of the necessary results. Therein lies the often-overlooked importance of free will and choice. Each choice a person makes may either create new karma or burn existing karma. Karma is neither good nor bad, it is neutral. But an individual's interpretation of karma and its effects may result in its classification as good or bad.

Karma is considered a universal law. As such, it promises that we will *always* be confronted with what we have created. And karma is patient—it has all of your eternal life to find you. So even if you escape with impunity the effect of an action in this lifetime, you will encounter it in some other lifetime. Karma exists and must be addressed. Thus, in any given lifetime, your destiny may include the necessity of answering to your karma both in the form of unresolved karma accumulated from past lives in ad-

dition to any new karma you create in this lifetime. Perhaps this is the reason destiny has so often been viewed as immutable. Yet your soul determines what karmic issues it will choose to work with in a given lifetime. As an example, say you were married to someone in a past life and it was a contentious, strife-filled relationship. Perhaps this current lifetime is the one in which your soul has decided to work through the karma of that time. One would expect, then, that the theme of your present lifetime may revolve generally around relationships and more specifically around developing the capacity to forgive. Will you encounter your partner of old again? Perhaps, perhaps not. You may find and marry that soul once more, or you may encounter him or her in the form of a parent or workmate. Alternatively, someone previously unknown to you may step in to work with you on this lesson. Perhaps your lessons in forgiveness will be more abstract or simply involve learning to forgive yourself. In any event, it is our belief that you will choose a personality and set of circumstances for this lifetime that reflects your choice to resolve this issue. You will select for yourself the character traits that will help you. Such a life direction can often be predicted or interpreted from the symbols present in astrological charts.

How Can Astrology Help?

If you are conscious of the desire to evolve, it is desirable to attune your actions and intentions to your spiritual blueprint. Learning what that blueprint is, however, presents a challenge. Though nothing can replace soul-searching and turning within for the answers to one's spiritual questions, there is no doubt that astrology can also prove helpful. Since the time of the ancients, astrology has been used to illuminate a portion of the divine plan for human beings, to provide answers to more metaphysical questions. Paramahansa Yogananda writes in *Autobiography of a Yogi*, "A child is born on that day and at that hour when the celestial rays are in mathematical harmony with his individual karma. His horoscope is a challenging portrait, revealing his unalterable past and its probable future results." And Rabbi David A. Cooper writes in *God is Verb*, his excellent treatise on the Kabbalah, "In Jewish mysticism fate is often referred to as *Mazzal*, which is usually translated as luck, but which also means 'the stars of the zodiac.'" Do the stars ordain our fate? This question is impossible to answer. But there does appear to be a mysterious correlation between the position of the planets at the moment of one's birth and as they continue to revolve in their orbits, and the events of one's life. The great contribution of astrology is its capacity to pierce the veil of mystery that shrouds the plan of our lives. Astrology provides guidance that may be either heeded or ignored. We do not defend astrology here, but rather offer up some of its secrets to those who might benefit from them.

An Overview of Personology

A Brief Overview of Personology

The Grand Cycle of Life

Symbolically, much in life can be conceived of as one grand cycle, and human life, nature, and astrology can be studied and compared within such a circular framework. For humans, the circle may represent a lifetime, from birth to death; for nature, the inexorable succession of the seasons throughout a year; in astrology, the zodiac, depicting the signs and their positions. The circle on which these three worlds are based is divided by two axes: one horizontal, one vertical. To travel through a cycle, one need only begin at the left endpoint of the horizontal axis, in astrology known as the

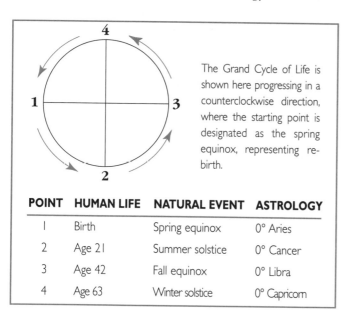

The Grand Cycle of Life is shown here progressing in a counterclockwise direction, where the starting point is designated as the spring equinox, representing rebirth.

POINT	HUMAN LIFE	NATURAL EVENT	ASTROLOGY
I	Birth	Spring equinox	0° Aries
2	Age 21	Summer solstice	0° Cancer
3	Age 42	Fall equinox	0° Libra
4	Age 63	Winter solstice	0° Capricorn

ascendant, and proceed in a counterclockwise direction until one arrives back at the beginning.

The horizontal axis marks an important division of the cycle of life into upper and lower halves. The lower half of the circle, or first half of the life cycle, represents objective, outward growth in both human and natural terms (birth to age forty-two, spring to fall). During this period, dramatic physical growth takes place that transforms both the individual and the landscape. The upper half of the circle, or second half of the life cycle, represents subjective, inward growth in human and natural terms (ages forty-three to eighty-four, fall to spring). During this period, in both nature and the human psyche,

deepening and maturation take place beneath the surface of life. Thus, the second half of the cycle is the reverse of the first.

The four most important points on the circumference of the circle are where the two axes touch it. These points mark the summer and winter solstices (ends of the vertical axis) and spring and fall equinoxes (ends of the horizontal axis). Marking the longest day/shortest night (June 21) and the shortest day/longest night (December 21), the solstices show maximum polarity. In the *I Ching* (Book of Changes), these extremes or poles represent the most *yang* and *yin* points of the year, respectively. The equinoxes, on the other hand, mark points of maximum movement either toward (March 21) or away from (September 23) the sun and demonstrate a perfect day-night balance.

These four points also mark the boundaries of the four quadrants into which the 360-degree circle of life is divided by the two axes. In the average human lifetime of eighty-four years, each of these quadrants represents a period of twenty-one years; in the yearly cycle of nature, a season; in astrology, a group of three signs (the order of which is invariably cardinal, fixed, and mutable). In addition, each of these quadrants may be associated with a mode of apprehending the world:

I Intuition	III Sensation
II Feeling	IV Thought

Because personology is based on a distinctly earth-oriented system, the two equinoxes and solstices occupy a position of central importance in demarcating the Grand Cycle of Life. In this respect, the traditionally heavenly oriented astrological

As the diagram clearly shows, aside from the summer and winter solstices, there is no time in the year that is not either waxing or waning. Thus, at any point on the circle, there is movement toward increasing light or darkness.

view is given a shift of emphasis to the here and now of our daily life: the eternal cyclical progression of the seasons and life periods, the rhythms of existence we experience year after year on our home planet.

The Forty-eight Personology Periods

This book is based on personology, a theory that posits that there are forty-eight distinct periods in the year, each associated with specific personality characteristics. The forty-eight periods, made up of twelve cusps and thirty-six "weeks," are each six to nine days in length. Personology predicts the characteristics or basic energies associated with these periods. Much like astrology, personology recognizes the original twelve heavenly constellations—and the signs derived from them—that form the band called the zodiac, which encircles our earth. However, personology goes further by concentrating first on the overlapping area between two signs called the cusp and second on individual periods within the signs.

Like traditional astrology, personology predicts personality characteristics based on date of birth. However, in the personology system, the position of a person's birthday in the grand cycle of the year is emphasized to a greater degree, resulting in more specific and nuanced conclusions about character.

Personology begins with the idea that cusps are points of considerable energy and as such must be accorded their own unique place in an astrological system. Thus, in personology, there are cusp personalities such as Gemini–Tauruses and Virgo–Libras. Those born during these and the other ten cusp periods of six to seven days each will share certain personality traits. In other words, there is such a thing as a distinct cusp personality. Cusp people are different from others not only because they embody a blend of the sharply contrasting traits of two adjacent signs (such as Aries and Taurus or Gemini and Cancer), but also because their individuality is determined not by a major sign of the zodiac but frequently by something more indefinable. The personology system, based on the empirical observation of thousands of individuals, also considers that periods within signs have significant effects on personality and thus create important differences among people born within one sign of the zodiac. In those astrological periods of about a month between cusps, traditionally known as signs, we find different representations of personality based on where a week or period falls in the month. In personology, these months or signs are further divided into three "weeks." For example, Libra I's are Libras in orientation but have certain

traits that are unique from and that differentiate them from those of Libra III's.

Looking at each of the astrological signs from this point of view, we find five principal types of people for each sign: two on either side of the sign at the two cusps that demarcate it and three born within the three approximately week-long periods at its center. Thus, for example, instead of there being a "Virgo" personality, as presented in the sun-sign astrology system, in personology there are five types of Virgos: Leo–Virgo Cusp (August 19–25, the Cusp of Exposure), Virgo I (August 26–September 2, the Week of System Builders), Virgo II (September 3–10, The Week of the Enigma), Virgo III (September 11–18, the Week of the Literalist) and finally, Virgo–Libra Cusp (September 19–24, the Cusp of Beauty). Of course, since each cusp is shared by two signs, this last cusp is also the first period of the five different kinds of Libras. For this reason, while a sun-sign astrologer speaks about an Aries, a Scorpio, or a Capricorn, a personologist may refer to an Aries II, a Scorpio–Sagittarius, or a Capricorn III.

Personology's focus on the twelve cusps proceeds from the importance that the four major cusp periods have on life as it is lived here on earth, since the spring equinox, the summer solstice, the fall equinox, and the winter solstice mark the boundaries of the seasons. Spring, summer, fall, and winter succeed one another in an orderly rhythm, for the most part, and structure life on the planet along with the unvarying diurnal changes of day and night. In terms of the signs, in the Northern Hemisphere these cusps are Pisces–Aries (spring equinox), Gemini–Cancer (summer solstice), Virgo–Libra (fall equinox), and Sagittarius–Capricorn (winter solstice). In personology the names of these cusps are the Cusp of Rebirth, the Cusp of Magic, the Cusp of Beauty, and the Cusp of Prophecy, respectively.

It is recommended that readers get to know their own particular period since the section describing the karmic paths in this book also contains information on how someone born within a particular period or week might fare on that path. Though your personology period and your karmic path are determined by your birthday, they are not the same thing. The sun sign or personology period symbolizes how we express our will in the world; it can be thought of as our character, creativity, and impetus in life. Obviously it will have a lot to do with how we choose to journey along our karmic paths. Thus, in the pages that follow, we summarize the forty-eight personology periods.

The 48 Periods and Cusps

Personology divides the year into forty-eight periods, each associated with distinct personality characteristics typical of people born during these periods. The essence of these traits is represented by the name of each period. Personology's forty-eight periods and their names are listed here.

PISCES–ARIES CUSP
MARCH 19–24
The Cusp of Rebirth

ARIES I
MARCH 25–APRIL 2
The Week of the Child

ARIES II
APRIL 3–10
The Week of the Star

ARIES III
APRIL 11–18
The Week of the Pioneer

ARIES–TAURUS CUSP
APRIL 19–24
The Cusp of Power

TAURUS I
APRIL 25–MAY 2
The Week of Manifestation

TAURUS II
MAY 3–10
The Week of the Teacher

TAURUS III
MAY 11–18
The Week of the Natural

TAURUS–GEMINI CUSP
MAY 19–24
The Cusp of Energy

GEMINI I
MAY 25–JUNE 2
The Week of Freedom

GEMINI II
JUNE 3–10
The Week of New Language

GEMINI III
JUNE 11–18
The Week of the Seeker

GEMINI–CANCER CUSP
JUNE 19–24
The Cusp of Magic

CANCER I
JUNE 25–JULY 2
The Week of the Empath

CANCER II
JULY 3–JULY 10
The Week of the Unconventional

CANCER III
JULY 11–18
The Week of the Persuader

CANCER–LEO CUSP
JULY 19–25
The Cusp of Oscillation

LEO I
JULY 26–AUGUST 2
The Week of Authority

LEO II
AUGUST 3–10
The Week of Balanced Strength

LEO III
AUGUST 11–18
The Week of Leadership

LEO–VIRGO CUSP
AUGUST 19–25
The Cusp of Exposure

VIRGO I
AUGUST 26–SEPTEMBER 2
The Week of System Builders

VIRGO II
SEPTEMBER 3–10
The Week of the Enigma

VIRGO III
SEPTEMBER 11–18
The Week of the Literalist

VIRGO–LIBRA CUSP
SEPTEMBER 19–24
The Cusp of Beauty

LIBRA I
SEPTEMBER 25–OCTOBER 2
The Week of the Perfectionist

LIBRA II
OCTOBER 3–10
The Week of Society

LIBRA III
OCTOBER 11–18
The Week of Theater

LIBRA–SCORPIO CUSP
OCTOBER 19–25
The Cusp of Drama and Criticism

SCORPIO I
OCTOBER 26–NOVEMBER 2
The Week of Intensity

SCORPIO II
NOVEMBER 3–11
The Week of Depth

SCORPIO III
NOVEMBER 12–18
The Week of Charm

SCORPIO–SAGITTARIUS CUSP
NOVEMBER 19–24
The Cusp of Revolution

SAGITTARIUS I
NOVEMBER 25–DECEMBER 2
The Week of Independence

SAGITTARIUS II
DECEMBER 3–10
The Week of the Originator

SAGITTARIUS III
DECEMBER 11–18
The Week of the Titan

SAGITTARIUS–CAPRICORN CUSP
DECEMBER 19–25
The Cusp of Prophecy

CAPRICORN I
DECEMBER 26–JANUARY 2
The Week of the Ruler

CAPRICORN II
JANUARY 3–9
The Week of Determination

CAPRICORN III
JANUARY 10–16
The Week of Dominance

CAPRICORN–AQUARIUS CUSP
JANUARY 17–22
The Cusp of Mystery and Imagination

AQUARIUS I
JANUARY 23–30
The Week of Genius

AQUARIUS II
JANUARY 31–FEBRUARY 7
The Week of Youth and Ease

AQUARIUS III
FEBRUARY 8–15
The Week of Acceptance

AQUARIUS–PISCES CUSP
FEBRUARY 16–22
The Cusp of Sensitivity

PISCES I
FEBRUARY 23–MARCH 2
The Week of Spirit

PISCES II
MARCH 3–10
The Week of the Loner

PISCES III
MARCH 11–18
The Week of Dancers and Dreamers

The Grand Cycle of Life

The Personology
Periods

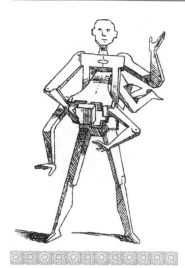

ZODIAC POSITION

**APPROXIMATELY
27° PISCES–4° ARIES**

ELEMENTS

WATER/FIRE

RULERS

NEPTUNE/MARS

SYMBOLS

THE FISH/RAM

Pisces–Aries Cusp

THE CUSP OF REBIRTH
March 19–24

Those born on the Pisces–Aries cusp are basic, elemental individuals, unusually direct in their approach to life. The puzzling thing is that although they think that they view life in a simple, unclouded way, those who know them well often describe them as unrealistic dreamers, unable to get a handle on the harsh realities of the world. Their direct and dynamic facade often belies a sensitive, emotionally complex, even troubled inner life. Thus Pisces–Aries are doers as well as dreamers.

The directness of Pisces–Aries people inevitably arouses antagonism. Outspokenness can make them alternately admired or misunderstood. Impulses, hunches, and relying on instinct are important to Pisces–Aries. Ultimately, they must learn to weigh alternatives carefully before speaking or acting. Once they learn the value of thoroughness and preparation, the logic of their arguments can be remarkably persuasive and compelling. This means that they win a good deal of the time. However, dealing with outright failure can be particularly difficult for those born on the Cusp of Rebirth; it is not really in their vocabulary. In relationships, family can be surprisingly important to these highly independent souls, but family in the larger sense, including friends and associates as well as kin. They can love deeply and passionately, giving a great deal of attention to their love object, but they are not always monogamous. Since they are not overly self-aware, do not dig too deeply into their motives, try to analyze their personalities, or urge them to explain themselves.

STRENGTHS:	**STRAIGHTFORWARD, INTUITIVE, PASSIONATE**
WEAKNESSES:	**MISUNDERSTOOD, IMPATIENT, UNREALISTIC**

PISCES–ARIES CUSP NOTABLES: Holly Hunter, Glenn Close, William Shatner, Bruce Willis, Matthew Broderick, Spike Lee, Pat Riley, Johann Sebastian Bach, Andrew Lloyd Weber, Stephen Sondheim, Gary Oldman, Akira Kurosawa, Joan Crawford

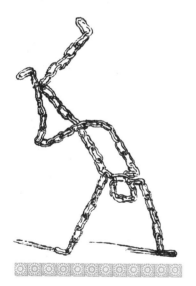

ZODIAC POSITION

**APPROXIMATELY
3–13° ARIES**

ELEMENT

FIRE

RULER

MARS

SYMBOL

THE RAM

Aries I

THE WEEK OF THE CHILD
March 25–April 2

Because Aries I's show the frank and open demeanor of children, they are sometimes accused of having a naïve or superficial view of life. But this so-called naïveté is the expression of the awe and wonder they experience in response to the world around them—a wonder they need to share with others. Because it is vitally important to them that others regard them as mature and responsible, Aries I's dislike being reminded of their childlike demeanor. Often, their childhood is characterized by periods of isolation as they retreated from repeated criticism and misunderstanding. This pattern carries through in their tendency to retreat from the world at frequent intervals, to some safe haven of their own making. To Aries I's, this haven is inviolable. Highly energetic and individualistic people, Aries I's rarely respond to societal pressures.

Although Aries I's tend to spend time alone when away from work, their careers inevitably involve group or team endeavors. Those involved with Aries I's must be sensitive to their moods or risk seeing them fly off the handle, usually resulting from their feeling that they have been misunderstood, and must be willing to give them the freedom to act and to be themselves. In any kind of relationship with Aries I's, knowing when to back off is essential. Their love relationships tend to the unusual, since they can be extremely unrealistic in their choice of partners, and may at times be suffused with a sense of unreality or a fairy-tale quality.

STRENGTHS:	**FRANK, SPONTANEOUS, DYNAMIC**
WEAKNESSES:	**NAÏVE, TRANSGRESSIVE, OVERIDEALISTIC**

ARIES I NOTABLES: Leonard Nimoy, Diana Ross, Eric Clapton, Vincent Van Gogh, Albert Gore, Jr., Aretha Franklin, Sandra Day O'Connor, Tennessee Williams, Sarah Vaughan, Quentin Tarantino, Joseph Campbell

Aries II

THE WEEK OF THE STAR
April 3–10

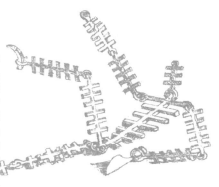

Aries II people need to be at the center of things. They often feel lonely, even in the middle of a crowd, and, consequently, they rarely allow themselves to be alone. Born in the Week of the Star, they must have satellite planets revolving around them: admirers, supporters, co-workers. These individuals may seem self-centered, but many are able to let go of their ego to a surprising degree by giving themselves fully to a project, cause, movement or religion. Those born during the Aries II period are highly goal oriented. Extreme behavior and a tendency to excess—basically not knowing when to stop—can land Aries II's in hot water again and again. Transferring their abundant energy into hard work is often the solution sought by Aries II's. Consequently, one real way to relate to them is to get right in there with them, to work side by side with them and share their frustrations and joys.

Aries II's make themselves indispensable, since they need others to need them. This is ironic, since at heart they want to be free to act, to move, to decide, without the encumbrance of familial or societal responsibilities. Their love relationships often burn out quickly, like shooting stars. Aries II's have a real problem opening up at a deep level and rarely let others into their inner world. Those best for them are those who patiently hang in there, encouraging them to express and discuss their feelings.

ZODIAC POSITION
APPROXIMATELY
12–21° ARIES

ELEMENT
FIRE

RULER
MARS

SYMBOL
THE RAM

STRENGTHS:	**SUCCESS ORIENTED, COURAGEOUS, ENERGETIC**
WEAKNESSES:	**ALOOF, IRRITABLE, EXCESSIVE**

ARIES II NOTABLES: Marlon Brando, Billie Holiday, General Colin Powell, Eddie Murphy, Maya Angelou, Francis Ford Coppola, Bette Davis, Spencer Tracy, Gregory Peck, Ravi Shankar, Harry Houdini

Aries III

THE WEEK OF THE PIONEER
April 11–18

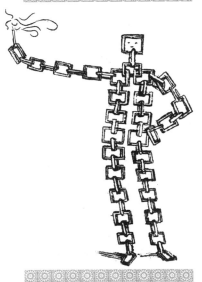

Aries III's are quite uncharacteristic of the more self-centered, egotistic Aries types; much more social in nature, they must interact dynamically and regularly with their fellow humans. Often true leaders, more concerned with doing good for others than with their own glory, these pioneers are idealistic types who follow their visions fearlessly and who frequently choose the path of sacrifice—a path their family or social group is usually expected to share. Needless to say, they cannot exist side by side for long with another dominant personality. Because they can be generous with their resources, these giving individuals can easily be taken advantage of.

Aries III's do not do well living alone. They need to surround themselves daily with children, family, and social groups, which they invariably seek to infuse with their dynamic idealism. Yet at the same time they find it difficult to give themselves easily to simple one-on-one conjugal relationships. The principal problem of Aries III's is their habit of forcing their ideas on others, putting abstractions ahead of personal considerations. Another problem for intimates of Aries III's is that, due to their intensely positive attitude, although these individuals are usually ready to listen, they have little ability to understand or empathize and have no patience for nagging or complaining. On the positive side, however, Aries III's have much to teach and also convey a nobility and a depth of conscience and commitment that are highly admirable.

ZODIAC POSITION
APPROXIMATELY
20–29° ARIES

ELEMENT
FIRE

RULER
MARS

SYMBOL
THE RAM

STRENGTHS:	**PROTECTIVE, GENEROUS, FEARLESS**
WEAKNESSES:	**UNREALISTIC, UNYIELDING, SELF-SACRIFICING**

ARIES III NOTABLES: Leonardo da Vinci, Loretta Lynn, Charlie Chaplin, David Letterman, Thomas Jefferson, Evelyn Ashford, Bessie Smith, Nikita Khrushchev, Merce Cunningham, Buddha, Kareem Abdul-Jabbar

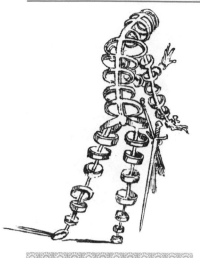

ZODIAC POSITION
**APPROXIMATELY
27° ARIES–4° TAURUS**

ELEMENTS
FIRE/EARTH

RULERS
MARS/VENUS

SYMBOL
THE RAM/BULL

Aries–Taurus Cusp
THE CUSP OF POWER
April 19–24

Those born on the Aries–Taurus cusp temper and ground the fiery dynamism of Aries through the solidity and earthiness of Taurus, causing them to strive for power in their daily lives. Their preoccupation with power reflects their view that their birthright is nothing less than the best that life has to offer. Yet they generally know how to pursue their goals without arousing antagonism in others. Because they are powerfully persuasive, it is easier and more advantageous to agree with them than to disagree. They know the value of money, how to get it, and how to use it. Blessed with a superb sense of timing, and of *kairos*—knowing the right time to act and not to act—Aries–Tauruses don't care whether it takes a long or a short time to achieve their ends, as long as they get there.

Those involved with them must understand that their careers will always be at least as important to them as their relationships. However, once they have fixed their sights on someone the matter is settled. Aries–Tauruses can be long-suffering, hanging in there not only because they are faithful but also, more important, because they have a hard time admitting to failure. Aries–Tauruses must learn to give up a certain amount of their power and to replace it with a degree of sharing, cooperation, and acceptance. Love has a softening effect on those born on the Cusp of Power, and they shine most brightly when this love involves unconditional giving on their part.

STRENGTHS:	**SOLID, POWERFUL, LAVISH**
WEAKNESSES:	**BLUNT, MERCENARY, LAZY**

ARIES–TAURUS CUSP NOTABLES: Vladimir Ilyich Lenin, Queen Elizabeth II, Barbra Streisand, William Shakespeare, Shirley MacLaine, Adolf Hitler, Jack Nicholson, Daniel Day-Lewis, Luther Vandross, Ryan O'Neal, Don Mattingly

ZODIAC POSITION
**APPROXIMATELY
3–13° TAURUS**

ELEMENT
EARTH

RULER
VENUS

SYMBOL
THE BULL

Taurus I
THE WEEK OF MANIFESTATION
April 25–May 2

Those born in the Week of Manifestation are hardheaded pragmatists and among the most dominant individuals of the year. When seized by an idea or plan, they will not let it rest until it is implemented. Their forte is manifesting or giving shape to a concept. A feeling for structure, particularly of a hierarchical kind, comes naturally to Taurus I's. Technically oriented, they love to find out how and why things work, never hesitating to take something apart and put it back together again. Intensely sensitive physically—sex, food, comfort, and sports and recreation of all kinds are important to their mental and physical well-being—they have a pronounced desire for harmony in their environment. The Taurus I boss stresses employees' needs to get along with each other and to work as a team. Their role at work often mirrors that at home: they are protectors and nurturers.

In relationships with Taurus I's, head-on confrontation should be avoided. Among the most stubborn of all the Tauruses, they are impossible to convince of the need for change. Unfooled by their cool, often gruff exterior, those who know them well know how emotionally vulnerable they are. Since Taurus I's like to run the show, shouldering huge burdens all day at work, they feel that a peaceful home environment is worth protecting at all costs. Thus the desire of Taurus I's for peace and quiet, together with their resistance to change, can become oppressive, even stifling, to those who live with them.

STRENGTHS:	**PRODUCTIVE, PHYSICAL, TENACIOUS**
WEAKNESSES:	**STUBBORN, SMUG, EXAGGERATING**

TAURUS I NOTABLES: Oskar Schindler, Michelle Pfeiffer, Duke Ellington, Al Pacino, Ella Fitzgerald, Andrei Agassi, Bianca Jagger, Saddam Hussein, Jerry Seinfeld, Coretta Scott King, Willie Nelson, I. M. Pei, Ann-Margret

Taurus II
THE WEEK OF THE TEACHER
May 3–10

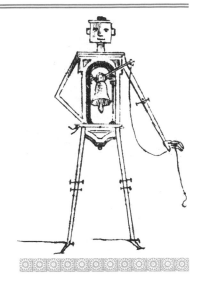

Those born in the Week of the Teacher are mainly involved in the development of ideas and techniques. It can be said they have a calling for imparting information and, more important, presenting it in a manner that others can understand. Verbalizing their ideas and observations, generating discussion, and leading by example are all Taurus II's favorite activities. Those born in the Taurus II period are movers and shakers. Excellent entrepreneurs, they can set up and run both businesses and families. The moral stance of the Taurus II, with firm ideas about right and wrong, is unusually strong, even unyielding. They tend to side with the underdog and to feel all forms of unfairness and discrimination keenly. Physical activity, whether dance, sports, music or fitness training, comes naturally to Taurus II's, yet they do not convey the impression of being earthy, sensuous types.

It's not surprising that Taurus II's have a strong need for teacher-student–type interactions. Interracial or cross-cultural relationships are common for Taurus II's. Although excellent bosses, parents, and teachers, Taurus II's are not always the easiest people to be involved with day to day as mates, lovers, or friends since they can be very demanding and critical, making their dislikes known sharply and incisively. Taurus II's often have a host of admirers. Those who relate best to Taurus II's understand their need to be left alone rather than to be fussed over or spoiled. Taurus II's like their partners to be strong and dignified above all.

STRENGTHS:	**ENTERPRISING, FAIR, MAGNETIC**
WEAKNESSES:	**DEMANDING, CRITICAL, INFLEXIBLE**

TAURUS II NOTABLES: Orson Welles, Eva Perón, Sigmund Freud, Karl Marx, Sugar Ray Robinson, Golda Meir, Audrey Hepburn, Roberto Rossellini, Willie Mays, Candice Bergen, Fred Astaire, Peter Ilyich Tchaikovsky

ZODIAC POSITION
**APPROXIMATELY
12–21° TAURUS**

ELEMENT
EARTH

RULER
VENUS

SYMBOL
THE BULL

Taurus III
THE WEEK OF THE NATURAL
May 11–18

Taurus III's are spontaneous, fun-loving, zany individuals who insist on being free to express themselves as directly and naturally as they wish. They do not react well when others try to correct, reform or change their basic habits. They are drawn throughout their lives to the natural world, in part due to the freedom it represents. A duality between a natural impulsiveness and a need for stability can be the key factor in the lives of Taurus III's. Thus, many born in this week who might have been satisfied with an easygoing, freedom-oriented life (and better suited to it as well) are often driven onward in their careers by their own quest for security, the goal frequently being financial. However, while in the end money can bring independence or freedom, at what price? Taurus III's are, above all, people who create their own challenges. Successful Taurus III's are those who are able to give form to their fantasy, to embody it in a product, service, or artistic activity.

In relationships, rebelliousness against authority can haunt Taurus III's their whole life long. Craving action and excitement, and often unable to keep their strong opinions of those around them to themselves, they can easily get into trouble. Emotionally volatile and easily bored, Taurus III's often change their friends, lovers, and generally their entire scene. An eternal fascination with the oddball, unusual aspects of life will always threaten to remove them from steadier and more stable situations and individuals.

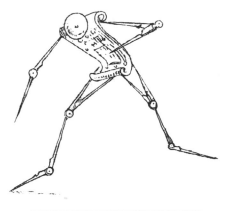

STRENGTHS:	**FUN LOVING, ADVENTURESOME, IMAGINATIVE**
WEAKNESSES:	**OBSESSIVE, REBELLIOUS, FRUSTRATED**

TAURUS III NOTABLES: Dennis Hopper, Martha Graham, Salvador Dalí, George Lucas, Pope John Paul II, David Byrne, Jiddu Krishnamurti, Henry Fonda, Katharine Hepburn, Stevie Wonder, Harvey Keitel, Debra Winger

ZODIAC POSITION
**APPROXIMATELY
20–29° TAURUS**

ELEMENT
EARTH

RULER
VENUS

SYMBOL
THE BULL

Taurus–Gemini Cusp

THE CUSP OF ENERGY
May 19–24

Those born on the Taurus–Gemini cusp see themselves more as forces than as people. Not particularly self-aware, they forge from an early age a role in life that is active rather than passive, dynamic rather than static. Interested as children in everything around them, those born on the Cusp of Energy often fly every which way in their search for stimulation. Despite their considerable energy, they do not always manifest an endurance equal to their desires and impulses. Learning about the creation of structure and the value of limitations is essential to the growth of a Taurus–Gemini. Moreover, it is essential for these people to learn the value of patience, planning, introspection, and soul searching. While it may not come easily to a Taurus–Gemini, in the long run it will save much pain and hardship.

Taurus–Gemini's abundant energy, keen interest in the world around them, and charm tend to draw innumerable friends and lovers. However, intimates may come to feel that their only role is to watch or listen to the Taurus–Gemini perform. Taurus–Geminis may spend their time heading off after the newest exciting prospect while their counterpart deals with the mundane tasks of home management. The best partners for them are often those who are strong enough to maintain their own individuality. Sharing the many interests of Taurus–Geminis is not nearly so important, however, as respecting and appreciating them.

STRENGTHS:	VERSATILE, ACTIVE, BRILLIANT
WEAKNESSES:	GARRULOUS, COMPULSIVE, HASTY

TAURUS–GEMINI CUSP NOTABLES: Grace Jones, Malcolm X, Cher, Bob Dylan, Arthur Conan Doyle, Mary Cassatt, Laurence Olivier, Nicole Brown Simpson, Priscilla Presley, Socrates, Ho Chi Minh, Peter Townshend, Jimmy Stewart

ZODIAC POSITION
**APPROXIMATELY
27° TAURUS—4° GEMINI**

ELEMENTS
EARTH/AIR

RULERS
VENUS/MERCURY

SYMBOLS
THE BULL/TWINS

Gemini I

THE WEEK OF FREEDOM
May 25–June 2

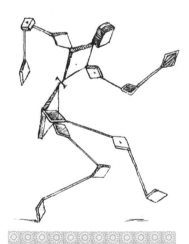

The Gemini I period takes freedom as its central image. Gemini I's balk at restrictions and aim to maintain their freedom at all costs. Generally on the side of the individual, they hate oppression and exploitation, opposing them both in theory and in practice. Gemini I's will not usually back down from a fight. Naturally combative, they stick up for what they believe is right and will not hesitate to attack wrongdoing in any form. One of their strongest weapons is laughter or ridicule, which they do not hesitate to pull out of their formidable verbal arsenal. Bright, perky, and alert but also a tad abrasive, Gemini I's are high-speed players who become impatient with the slower responses of other people. Given this low threshold of irritation, they become unhinged easily, and stress can cause them to lash out with irony or sarcasm. They are constantly dreaming up new plans and schemes, perhaps at the expense of pressing matters that need attention and leave behind enough unfinished projects to occupy a dozen human beings.

Family life can have a grounding influence, causing a relatively rootless Gemini I to blossom. Those born in the Week of Freedom are both emotionally volatile and not at all shy about verbalizing any discontent they may have. Moreover, they are not above emotional manipulation. In fact, they rarely hesitate to turn on their considerable charms in order to get their way. They are highly seductive and few can resist them. Considering their emotional volatility and changeability, they are surprisingly loyal partners.

STRENGTHS:	WITTY, CHARISMATIC, TECHNICALLY GIFTED
WEAKNESSES:	TYRANNICAL, MANIPULATIVE, COMPLAINING

GEMINI I NOTABLES: Marilyn Monroe, John Fitzgerald Kennedy, Walt Whitman, Clint Eastwood, Henry Kissinger, Sally K. Ride, Jim Thorpe, John Wayne, Miles Davis, Morgan Freeman, Brooke Shields

ZODIAC POSITION
**APPROXIMATELY
3–13° GEMINI**

ELEMENT
AIR

RULER
MERCURY

SYMBOL
THE TWINS

Gemini II

THE WEEK OF NEW LANGUAGE
June 3–10

The Gemini II period takes New Language as its central image. Gemini II's have a strong desire to communicate their thoughts and feelings verbally. Yet their means of expression are highly personal, to the point that they tend to develop and speak their own unique language. This leads to all kinds of problems, tensions, and frustrations since others frequently misunderstand them. Moreover, what they are trying to say often gets lost in the shuffle since some Gemini II's use a barrage of words, relying on quantity over quality to win the day. Entertaining and witty, these people know how to dazzle. Though primarily verbal, Gemini II's have a great need for physical expression, and their body language can be a powerful addition to their well-developed vocabulary.

Secretly fascinated by the dark side of life, Gemini II's frequently summon it up in the form of a lover or friend. While they are tempted to choose people from radically different backgrounds, in reality they often relate more successfully to those from the same city, neighborhood, ethnic background, or economic stratum since sharing associations and idioms makes communication much easier in the long run. The defensiveness of those born in this week can easily get out of hand, causing them to engage their rapier wit and often leaving scars. Much of it is due to their fear of appearing foolish. Learning to be more accepting of their inadequacies and coming to terms with their own dark side can bring them a long way toward happier and more fulfilling relationships.

ZODIAC POSITION
APPROXIMATELY
12–20° GEMINI

ELEMENT
AIR

RULER
MERCURY

SYMBOL
THE TWINS

STRENGTHS:	**COMMUNICATIVE, COMPETITIVE, INNOVATIVE**
WEAKNESSES:	**MISINTERPRETED, FLAKY, DISORGANIZED**

GEMINI II NOTABLES: Judy Garland, Allen Ginsberg, Frank Lloyd Wright, Paul Gauguin, Cole Porter, Barbara Bush, Johnny Depp, (TAFKA) Prince, Laurie Anderson, Federico Garcia Lorca, Spaulding Gray

Gemini III

THE WEEK OF THE SEEKER
June 11–18

The primary drive of a Gemini III is to go beyond the limitations imposed by society and nature. Gemini III's are never happier than when they are on the move: probing, testing, tasting, and exploring the most interesting things life has to offer. Not afraid to take chances, those born in the Week of the Seeker are attracted to risk and danger. Adventurers in every sense of the word, Gemini III's are restless types. Life is never dull with a Gemini III around. However, those born in this period do not necessarily have to travel to far-off lands to explore or to find challenge—for them, all of life is an adventure. Many Gemini III's are surprisingly good with money since it symbolizes freedom to them. Their overall style is to remain free to progress as far as possible. They like to keep others guessing as to their next move.

Love and affection are important to Gemini III's but are not usually given top priority. With an undeniable tendency to please others through charm, they can be powerfully controlling and persuasive in a subtle manner. Sometimes warm and giving, other times quite cool and detached, they are accused of blowing hot and cold, and with justification. Gemini III's may move from one partner to another. Even those who establish a well-grounded primary relationship are constantly tempted away from it by a career, a hobby, or another person, although they'll stay put if given enough room to breathe.

ZODIAC POSITION
APPROXIMATELY
19–28° GEMINI

ELEMENT
AIR

RULER
MERCURY

SYMBOL
THE TWINS

STRENGTHS:	**EXPLORATORY, RISK TAKING, MONEY WISE**
WEAKNESSES:	**EMOTIONALLY VOLATILE, DISILLUSIONED, IMPATIENT**

GEMINI III NOTABLES: Margaret Bourke-White, William Butler Yeats, Barbara McClintock, Anne Frank, Paul McCartney, Jacques Cousteau, Isabella Rossellini, Vince Lombardi, Courtney Cox, Donald Trump

Gemini–Cancer Cusp

THE CUSP OF MAGIC
June 19–24

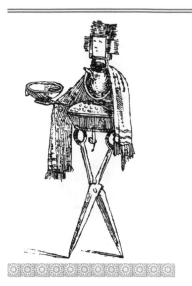

Those born during the magical cusp of the summer solstice can be defined as falling under the spell of enchantment. Romantic and inspirational, Gemini–Cancers often put their talents and energies in service to a higher purpose, be it family, religion, philosophy, arts, or political or social causes. Gemini–Cancers appear mild, even self-effacing, but they can also enchant others; their sweetly innocent charm can be seductive. Although possessed of a certain magnetism, Gemini–Cancers can be remarkably cool customers. They have a useful objectivity, and their reasoning powers make an effective foil to their deep emotions. They are an interesting blend of logic and feeling.

Gemini–Cancers are capable of a wide range of personal interaction, from acquaintanceship and friendship to full-blown passion. Tending to be private people, they do not often grant access to their inner world. If they do, it implies a sacred trust. Their special needs as sensitive individuals can impose heavy demands on their friends and intimates. Nothing is more important to Gemini–Cancers than love; they see love as the primary reason to live. But no matter how deeply in love they fall, they remain masters of their emotions. Listen to them carefully, for although they can give their hearts fully, the fact that they are spending time with you is no guarantee that they have done so. As much as they have a deep capacity to give love, they are equally capable of withholding it.

ZODIAC POSITION
**APPROXIMATELY
27°GEMINI–4° CANCER**

**ELEMENTS
AIR/WATER**

**RULERS
MERCURY/THE MOON**

**SYMBOLS
THE TWINS/CRAB**

STRENGTHS:	**AFFECTIONATE, SEDUCTIVE, OBJECTIVE**
WEAKNESSES:	**ISOLATED, SELFISH, DEMANDING**

GEMINI–CANCER CUSP NOTABLES: Aung San Suu Kyi, H. Rider Haggard, Meryl Streep, Jean-Paul Sartre, Nicole Kidman, Billy Wilder, Errol Flynn, Prince William, Lou Gehrig, Bob Fosse, Kris Kristofferson

Cancer I

THE WEEK OF THE EMPATH
June 25–July 2

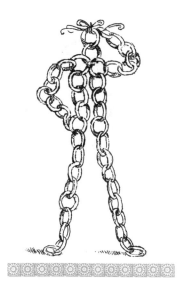

The Cancer I period takes the Empath as its central image due to the psychic sensitivity of those born during this time. Because of the depth, diversity, and fluctuating nature of their feelings, Cancer I's are hard to figure out. Empathic, Cancer I's are quick to pick up on, or even to absorb, the emotions of others—often even subconsciously acting them out. Do not assume, however, that Cancer I's are wishy-washy characters out of touch with practical realities. They can be very clever in getting their way and are particularly good with money. In fact, their makeup includes a natural aggressiveness that they can have difficulty channeling into positive expression. Too often they swing from angry outbursts to seething repression, which often leads them into melancholia.

Cancer I's are capable of withdrawing from the world for months or even years in order to protect themselves from the feelings of those around them. However, through sheer guts and determination, they are often able to overcome their own sensitivity and put it to work in the service of their fellows. Patience is obligatory for those desiring a successful relationship with these individuals, especially when they bottle up their feelings or enter into their self-imposed isolation. Those who persevere, however, are rewarded; Cancer I's have a great deal to offer in a relationship: financial astuteness, a good managerial sense, and, most important, the ability to truly understand.

ZODIAC POSITION
**APPROXIMATELY
3–11° CANCER**

**ELEMENT
WATER**

**RULER
THE MOON**

**SYMBOL
THE CRAB**

STRENGTHS:	**FINANCIALLY ASTUTE, SENSITIVE, TECHNICALLY PROFICIENT**
WEAKNESSES:	**AGGRESSIVE, FEARFUL, NEEDY**

CANCER I NOTABLES: Helen Keller, Herman Hesse, Lady Diana Spencer, Mike Tyson, George Orwell, Carl Lewis, Jerry Hall, Ron Goldman, Lena Horne, John Cusack, Pamela Anderson, George Michael, Sidney Lumet

Cancer II

THE WEEK OF THE UNCONVENTIONAL
July 3–10

Born in the Week of the Unconventional, Cancer II's appear quite normal, occupying ordinary positions in the work world. However, the unusual and the bizarre irresistibly attract them. While few colleagues and associates are granted access to their secret world, their intimates come to realize, often only after years of association, how closely their fascination with all that is strange and curious mirrors their own inner selves. Whether dreaming of far-off lands or romance, vivid fantasies are always a part of their secret inner lives. This imaginative landscape may actually give rise to commercially lucrative ideas, though Cancer II's are rarely good at manifesting them. It takes another person or persons to recognize and implement the inventions of Cancer II's. Becoming enmeshed in their own fantasies is a danger for them. Obsession is a real risk since it is hard for them to control their desires. It is important for them to learn nonattachment and how to separate fantasy from reality.

Interactions with unusual friends allow them to share their wilder side and to act out unconscious fantasies. Cancer II's share their lives best with others who value privacy and with whom they can share their personal vision—finding such people is key to their overall happiness. Lavish in their expenditures, they will go to extraordinary lengths to make their living space flamboyant. Often the zaniness, sense of fun, and sensitivity of Cancer II's can earn them a valued position in the lives of others.

STRENGTHS:	**FANTASY-RICH, FUN, PSYCHOLOGICALLY ASTUTE**
WEAKNESSES:	**SELF-DESTRUCTIVE, OBSESSIVE, EMBARRASSSING**

CANCER II NOTABLES: Tom Hanks, Franz Kafka, Frida Kahlo, Gustav Mahler, Marc Chagall, Tom Cruise, Anjelica Huston, Kevin Bacon, Geraldo Rivera, Sylvester Stallone, Ringo Starr

ZODIAC POSITION
APPROXIMATELY
10–19° CANCER

ELEMENT
WATER

RULER
THE MOON

SYMBOL
THE CRAB

Cancer III

THE WEEK OF THE PERSUADER
July 11–18

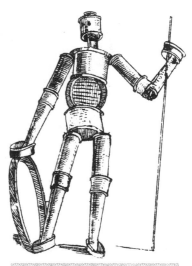

Cancer III people know how to convince others to do their bidding. Powerful manipulators of their environment, they often manifest great drive and determination. The underlying dynamic of their ambition, however, is a need for the security that it represents rather than a need for power. They rarely fall victim to blind ambition, preferring to invest in themselves rather than indulge in materialism or ego tripping. Cancer III's know how to wait, watch, and listen. Observant of what goes on around them, they are good at reading the signs of the times and knowing when to act. Their ability to persuade and convince others is supported by a solid bedrock of observation and on having facts and results at their fingertips.

Passionate people, Cancer III's are no strangers to the depths of human emotion. However, part of the personal power of Cancer III's comes from their ability to control their own needs. In relationships, for example, they would sooner be alone than enter a dubious or unstable partnership. They generally require few luxuries and can efficiently order their lives without interference from others. The other side of the coin, however, is the tendency of Cancer III control to devolve into excess. While their directness may prove too threatening to others, as friends and family members Cancer III's can be giving, sharing, and affectionate. Left alone to go ahead with their work and plans, however, which they usually see as intended for the good of the group, they are content, peaceful, and even quiet in demeanor.

STRENGTHS:	**ENTERPRISING, PERSUASIVE, OBSERVANT**
WEAKNESSES:	**EXCESSIVE, MANIPULATIVE, INSECURE**

CANCER III NOTABLES: Bill Cosby, Nelson Mandela, Saint Mother Cabrini, Julius Caesar, Henry David Thoreau, Harrison Ford, James Cagney, Richard Branson, Rembrandt, Cesar Chavez, Ginger Rogers

ZODIAC POSITION
APPROXIMATELY
18–26° CANCER

ELEMENT
WATER

RULER
THE MOON

SYMBOL
THE CRAB

ZODIAC POSITION
**APPROXIMATELY
26° CANCER–3° LEO**

ELEMENTS
WATER/FIRE

RULERS
THE MOON/SUN

SYMBOLS
THE CRAB/LION

Cancer–Leo Cusp
THE CUSP OF OSCILLATION
July 19–25

Of all twelve cusp personalities, Cancer–Leo exhibits most distinctly the influence of two signs—the feeling orientation of Cancer and the fiery, aggressive characteristics of Leo. When integrated, these contrasting characteristics can produce a highly balanced and creative personality. When they compete with each other, however, the result can be wide swings of mood, causing great psychic stress. Cancer–Leos have a dynamic side—they bore easily, hanker for excitement, and love to be on the edge of innovative projects and activities—that attracts them to risk taking and danger, which occasionally can manifest as megalomania. They possess calm under fire, and their moral courage stands them in good stead in crises and emergencies. Perhaps out of fear of their own wildness, they may impose restrictions on themselves that produce frustration, causing them to be emotionally blocked from time to time, and resulting in depression and an inability to feel.

In relationships, those born on the Cusp of Oscillation are interested in a wide variety of people. It is not that they are promiscuous; rather, they have a wide palette of emotional and sexual expression. The dramatic changes of affect of those born on the Cusp of Oscillation can make it hard for others to know how to approach them. In their dealings with others, they do best with people who are of even disposition and can promote a peaceful and constant environment in day-to-day relations. Steady jobs, steady relationships, and a dependable mate are important in evening out their contrasting moods.

STRENGTHS:	**MORALLY COURAGEOUS, EXCITING, DAUNTLESS**
WEAKNESSES:	**MANIC-DEPRESSIVE, ADDICTIVE, EMOTIONALLY BLOCKED**

CANCER–LEO CUSP NOTABLES: Amelia Earhart, Ernest Hemingway, Rose Fitzgerald Kennedy, Woody Harrelson, Iman, Robin Williams, Natalie Wood, Edgar Degas, Bob Dole, Zelda Fitzgerald, Tom Robbins, Gregor Mendel

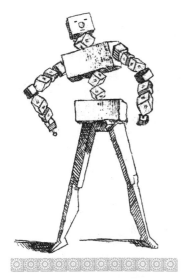

ZODIAC POSITION
**APPROXIMATELY
2° –11° LEO**

ELEMENT
FIRE

RULER
THE SUN

SYMBOL
THE LION

Leo I
THE WEEK OF AUTHORITY
July 26–August 2

Among the most powerfully authoritative of the year, Leo I's are intense, hard-driving individuals. They are dedicated primarily to their own personal activities—developing their own strengths and abilities, growth, and development. Asserting themselves and being taken seriously are what appeals to them. They believe in higher authorities, the abstract truths and principles embodied in the practice of their principal endeavor. Many Leo I's can be highly competitive and geared toward coming out on top. Others don't really care that much for worldly success, being more interested in bettering their own personal best. Their capacity to dominate is often greater than their capacity to lead.

Being involved with such individuals is rarely an easy task. Their standards for themselves are extremely high, and they too often expect the same from others. They may interact most easily with people who have been drawn to them as admirers, students, or disciples. Though Leo I's can make loyal and faithful friends, most of those born in the Week of Authority would do well to work on their treatment of their fellow human beings, particularly in terms of kindness, patience, and understanding. Anyone involved with these tough customers must themselves be prepared to show these traits in abundance. Trying to get the undivided attention of Leo I's can be frustrating since they are often intensely preoccupied. Those who can seduce them away from their work or interests will play important roles in their lives and will benefit from the best that Leo I's have to offer.

STRENGTHS:	**TRUTH LOVING, LOYAL, PASSIONATE**
WEAKNESSES:	**FRUSTRATED, DEMANDING, EGOTISTICAL**

LEO I NOTABLES: Carl Jung, Jacqueline Kennedy Onassis, Marcel Duchamp, Stanley Kubrick, Emily Brontë, Jerry Garcia, Mick Jagger, Arnold Schwarzenegger, Michael Spinks, Herman Melville, Benito Mussolini

Leo II

THE WEEK OF BALANCED STRENGTH
August 3–10

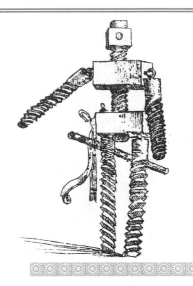

The Leo II period takes Balanced Strength as its central image. Solid and tough, Leo II's do not back down from challenges; in fact, they thrive on them and are often at their best when facing problems or difficulties. Leo II's generally exercise tremendous powers of concentration. Gifted with endurance and tenacity, Leo II's hang in there for the duration. This has a downside, however, since it is very difficult for them to change. Moreover, their single-mindedness may cause them to lose their peripheral vision and forget their best assets—that is, their intuitive strength, capacity for hunches, and timing. They certainly can be their own worst enemies and exhibit a streak of masochism—a tendency, for example, to suffer while trying to hold a romance, marriage, or business together. Learning not to push themselves too hard and to live a balanced life are crucial to their overall well-being.

For the most part Leo II's are extraordinarily faithful people. Being straightforward and unpretentious themselves, Leo II's often dislike people who put on airs. They see themselves as champions of the downtrodden and protectors of the weak. In their toughness, Leo II's are able to withstand many disappointments. They usually weather the storm and win out through knowing how to wait—"having the long breath." Those involved with Leo II's know that those born in this week must not be pushed or prodded when in a negative frame of mind; rather, they must be left alone to work things out for themselves.

STRENGTHS: DEVOTED, TRUSTWORTHY, PHYSICAL

WEAKNESSES: MASOCHISTIC, DEPRESSED, GUILTY

ZODIAC POSITION
APPROXIMATELY
9–18° LEO

ELEMENT
FIRE

RULER
THE SUN

SYMBOL
THE LION

LEO II NOTABLES: Whitney Houston, Patrick Ewing, John Huston, Andy Warhol, Percy Bysshe Shelley, Melanie Griffith, Dustin Hoffman, Martin Sheen, Martha Stewart, Courtney Love, Neil Armstrong, Lucille Ball

Leo III

THE WEEK OF LEADERSHIP
August 11–18

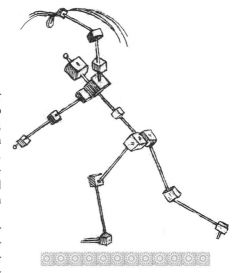

Leo III's often assume a commanding role. Action comes naturally to these dynamic individuals. Their main impulse is to lead, but not necessarily to dominate or rule. Good planners, they are able to organize a strategy and see it through. All Leo III's have a heroic view of themselves. Aggressive, they know what they want and how to get it. In the process, they may arouse antagonism since they can be inconsiderate, often choosing to ignore what others are feeling in order to achieve their own aims. But they may also inspire tremendous loyalty, respect, and love in others who overlook their self-centeredness. The creativity of Leo III's runs high. While they are often narrow or selfish in their personal dealings, in their careers their imagination, philosophical perspective, and wide range of expression often result in artistic, financial, and social rewards.

Because Leo III's are not very approachable, working shoulder to shoulder with them is the best way of getting close to them and can result in deep ties that last a lifetime. Other strong personalities inevitably clash with Leo III's, and such relationships are likely to be stormy unless the other party compromises or backs down. Leo III's are not unaware of their charisma. As long as they are honored and respected, they will be generous and kind, but they will not hesitate to end a relationship if they feel they haven't been accorded their due. Equally often, their partners, unwilling to live with double standards, may drop them suddenly in disgust, amazing the more unaware Leo III's—just when things were going so well!

STRENGTHS: COMMANDING, HEROIC, CREATIVE

WEAKNESSES: DICTATORIAL, SELFISH, INSENSITIVE

ZODIAC POSITION
APPROXIMATELY
17–26° LEO

ELEMENT
FIRE

RULER
THE SUN

SYMBOL
THE LION

LEO III NOTABLES: Napoleon Bonaparte, Madonna, Magic Johnson, Julia Child, Angela Bassett, Sean Penn, Alex Haley, Steve Martin, Robert De Niro, Alfred Hitchcock, Fidel Castro, Robert Redford, Kathleen Battle

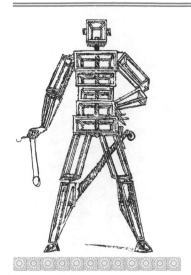

ZODIAC POSITION
APPROXIMATELY
27°LEO–3°VIRGO

ELEMENTS
FIRE/EARTH

RULERS
THE SUN/MERCURY

SYMBOLS
THE LION/VIRGIN

Leo–Virgo Cusp
THE CUSP OF EXPOSURE
August 19–25

Those born on the Leo–Virgo cusp are an interesting blend of introvert and extrovert. Leo–Virgos combine the practical, earthy qualities of Virgo with the more intuitive, fiery traits of Leo, producing quietly inspired individuals who keep their light within. They tend to conceal the truth about themselves and not show their real inner selves until they get where they are headed, socially or professionally. But though they may hide certain personal qualities or facts about themselves for years, their inner flamboyance will break out periodically. The more they try to hide, the more the world seems to take notice of them. Leo–Virgos use information, whether concealing or revealing it, as a tool. Usually it is information they themselves have gathered. Those born on the Cusp of Exposure are often outstanding observers and judges of character. Further, they are often good at recording their impressions in thought or word. Others often come to depend on their memory, judgment, and objectivity.

Leo–Virgos do not easily show their passion and affection, but when they do they are dependable and reliable friends. People who like mysteries and detective work will like Leo–Virgos—although they do not deeply need appreciation, kudos, or flattery, they cry out for understanding. Trust is a big issue—they must be able to trust their friends and lovers to keep their secrets and be faithful. Those who continue to love them even after they fully reveal themselves become lifelong friends and partners.

STRENGTHS:	**SELF-CONTAINED, OBSERVANT, FLAMBOYANT**
WEAKNESSES:	**NARCISSISTIC, SECRETIVE, NONSHARING**

LEO–VIRGO CUSP NOTABLES: Bill Clinton, Gabrielle "Coco" Chanel, Sean Connery, Orville Wright, Deng Xiaoping, Cal Ripken, Jr., Leonard Bernstein, Lola Montez, Wilt Chamberlain, Elvis Costello, Connie Chung

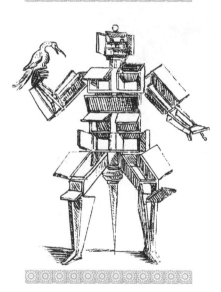

ZODIAC POSITION
APPROXIMATELY
2–10° VIRGO

ELEMENT
EARTH

RULER
MERCURY

SYMBOL
THE VIRGIN

Virgo I
THE WEEK OF THE SYSTEM BUILDER
August 26–September 2

Structure is the major theme in the lives of Virgo I's. Gifted with great objectivity and powers of concentration, they are able to order their world accordingly, frequently creating elegant decision trees or inescapably logical forms. This capacity makes Virgo I's extremely valuable to a company or family. Underlying their drive for order, however, is a need to limit the number of decisions they have to make. Plagued by indecision, Virgo I's feel safest when given no choice. They suffer greatly when unable to think clearly due to emotional pressure. Particularly upset by chaos, building an effective daily routine, a practical home, or an efficient work space is essential to their mental health. Inflexibility, rigidity, or the imposition of too many rules on others can be the possible result of such structuring. Their objectivity does not extend to themselves and their own needs and feelings, which are often given short shrift, causing them to suffer from acute nervous instability and depression.

Interestingly, Virgo I's are often involved in service—perhaps because they so clearly see what others need. However, this also means they tend to attract dependent, needy types who drain their energies and exhaust their capacity to give. They must learn how to free themselves from the constant demands of others if they are to develop their own expressive, creative, and financially productive side. Since learning to loosen up is essential for Virgo I's, their best relationships are often with those with whom they can just let go and have a good time.

STRENGTHS:	**STRUCTURED, DEPENDABLE, SERVICE ORIENTED**
WEAKNESSES:	**RIGID, EMOTIONALLY UNAWARE, SELF-DESTRUCTIVE**

VIRGO I NOTABLES: Ingrid Bergman, Johann Wolfgang von Goethe, Edwin Moses, Michael Jackson, Charlie Parker, Mary Shelley, Gloria Estefan, Yasir Arafat, Maria Montessori, Geraldine Ferraro, Richard Gere

Virgo II

THE WEEK OF THE ENIGMA
September 3–10

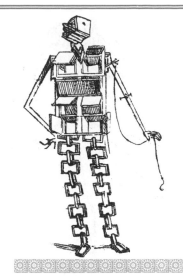

Virgo II's are puzzling individuals, often proving difficult to figure out. Sphinxlike, their faces do not reveal what they are thinking; indeed, showing emotion can be difficult for them. Virgo II's will go to great lengths to avoid revealing who they are, and they are not above creating elaborate defenses to throw people off track. They sternly resist attempts to analyze them. However, just because they cultivate an air of mystery doesn't mean that they are devious. They are true believers in doing the right thing and they are highly ethical individuals. Many Virgo II's are kind, thoughtful, considerate people who see no need to bother those around them with their difficulties. Asking for help may be a real problem for them. Luckily, those born during this week are blessed with great inner strength and so are able to work out their problems on their own. Communicative and quick, they love humor in many forms—even the most dour Virgo II has a zany side.

Discriminating types who pride themselves on their good taste, they have extremely high standards, which can lead people to reject them as overly picky. Their social circle consequently tends to be small. Finding that special individual with whom they can be intimate is often the first step toward unlocking their deepest sources of self-expression. Although they have no real need to live with others, it is only through daily interaction, at home or work, that Virgo II's will learn acceptance, sympathy, and how to open up.

STRENGTHS:	**TASTEFUL, PRACTICAL, THOUGHTFUL**
WEAKNESSES:	**GUARDED, OVEREXACTING, DETACHED**

VIRGO II NOTABLES: Grandma Moses, Peter Sellers, Sonny Rollins, Leo Tolstoy, Joseph P. Kennedy, Otis Redding, Raquel Welch, Charlie Sheen, Jane Curtin, Buddy Holly, Freddy Mercury, Patsy Cline

ZODIAC POSITION
**APPROXIMATELY
9–18° VIRGO**

ELEMENT
EARTH

RULER
MERCURY

SYMBOL
THE VIRGIN

Virgo III

THE WEEK OF THE LITERALIST
September 11–18

The willful individuals born during the week of Virgo III generally persist until they get their way. Their mental willpower is so strong that their goals are tangible to them, which means they can't even imagine not attaining them. Sometimes they are so convinced of an outcome that they do not hesitate procrastinating before getting there. Those born in the Week of the Literalist place a great deal of emphasis on practicality, and they have a talent for shrewd evaluations. Elegant constructions and the mastery of craft are what they admire most. They see irrationality or emotional displays, particularly public ones, as a sign of ostentation and a lack of self-control. Virgo III's also dislike phoniness and pretension. Literalists, they like to tell it as they see it, uncovering the truth and revealing it to the world. On the other hand, Virgo III's do not like trouble or unpleasantness, and feel that a modicum of courtesy is demanded in almost any human situation. They are sometimes torn, then, between their love of truth and their need for harmony.

In relationships, Virgo III's are highly demanding, expecting the very best for themselves. Extremely capable, they can keep troubled or problematic relationships alive for years through their perseverance and dedication. Results are important to these pragmatic personalities, who are likely to ultimately lose interest or walk away when their work on a relationship fails to bear fruit. Those born in this week must be careful not to succumb to selfish and manipulative drives.

STRENGTHS:	**COMPOSED, NURTURING, CAPABLE**
WEAKNESSES:	**SENSATIONALISTIC, JUDGMENTAL, RUTHLESS**

VIRGO III NOTABLES: H. L. Mencken, Greta Garbo, D. H. Lawrence, Agatha Christie, Lauren Bacall, O. Henry, Oliver Stone, Tommy Lee Jones, Claudette Colbert, Jesse Owens, Roald Dahl, Margaret Sanger, B. B. King

ZODIAC POSITION
**APPROXIMATELY
17–26° VIRGO**

ELEMENT
EARTH

RULER
MERCURY

SYMBOL
THE VIRGIN

Virgo–Libra Cusp
THE CUSP OF BEAUTY
September 19–24

Those born on the Virgo–Libra cusp are fatally taken up with the pursuit of an ideal. Because they are attracted to physical, sensuous beauty, whether in art objects, nature, or people, the lure of color, shape, form, texture, and the intriguing sound of music or a voice pushes all their emotional buttons and brings them creative inspiration. They require a highly aesthetic environment both at home and at work. Virgo–Librans pride themselves on being up to date and aware of the latest trends in fashion, design, art, and technology, and their sixth sense for current developments in their fields stands them in good stead. Often seen as superficial or glitzy, Virgo–Librans, in fact, have a dark side, and concomitant addictive tendencies may surface, representing their sensuous nature at its most self-destructive. Sooner or later in their lives, these individuals will have to address spiritual matters, for they usually discover at some point that their love of externals is inadequate preparation for an encounter with the more unpleasant side of life.

Those born on the Cusp of Beauty usually require that the people with whom they choose intimate involvement are very good-looking. Although Virgo–Librans periodically need to indulge their sense of touch, they may appear removed or untouchable themselves and may allow physical contact only at special times. They have a tendency to isolate themselves in an ivory-tower situation in which they can avoid arguments, confrontations, and unpleasantness in general. Many born on this cusp are content to admire beauty from a distance.

STRENGTHS:	AESTHETIC, SENSUOUS, HARMONIOUS
WEAKNESSES:	SNOBBISH, ADDICTIVE, UNSETTLED

VIRGO–LIBRA CUSP NOTABLES: Ray Charles, Sophia Loren, Stephen King, John Coltrane, H. G. Wells, Ricki Lake, Leonard Cohen, F. Scott Fitzgerald, Bruce Springsteen, Jason Alexander, Linda McCartney, Jim Henson, Cass Elliot

---

ZODIAC POSITION
**APPROXIMATELY
26° VIRGO–2° LIBRA**

ELEMENTS
EARTH/AIR

RULERS
MERCURY/VENUS

SYMBOLS
THE VIRGIN/SCALES

Libra I
THE WEEK OF THE PERFECTIONIST
September 25–October 2

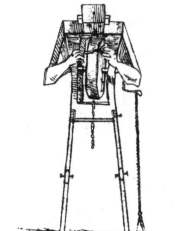

Libra I's have perfectionist tendencies. Every area of their lives is infused with a desire to find out what's wrong and to try to fix it. The theme of putting things right reflects their knowledge and technical know-how, and also their conviction that they know what's best for those around them. Libra I's are highly prone to applying their often mercilessly high standards equally to themselves and others. Their wry sense of humor and often biting wit express themselves in many forms but are usually designed to make others think. They are often torn by indecisiveness, and insecurity drives those born in this week to be overachievers. Their hunger for perfection sometimes results in their becoming obsessive and compulsive, which can lead them to adopt overly rigid routines. Libra I's are intense personalities, extremely thorough in carrying out their plans and capable of great achievements.

They are often highly attractive personalities, yet they are not overly social ones, needing to spend quite a lot of time alone. Emotionally complex, they can give an impression of coolness that masks a maelstrom of inner emotions. Mastery of their emotions is usually such a high priority for them that there's a real danger they will chronically repress their true feelings, which may ultimately prove debilitating to any relationship. Those involved with Libra I's would do best to keep feelings out in the open from the start, even to the point of insisting that those born in this week vent their emotions.

STRENGTHS:	ATTRACTIVE, EXACTING, COOL
WEAKNESSES:	INDECISIVE, SCATHING, REPRESSED

LIBRA I NOTABLES: Glenn Gould, Brigitte Bardot, Groucho Marx, George Gershwin, William Faulkner, Sting, Heather Locklear, Bryant Gumbel, Jimmy Carter, Truman Capote, Mahatma Gandhi, Christopher Reeve, Annie Leibovwitz

---

ZODIAC POSITION
**APPROXIMATELY
1–10° LIBRA**

ELEMENT
AIR

RULER
VENUS

SYMBOL
THE SCALES

Libra II

THE WEEK OF SOCIETY
October 3–10

The paradox of those born during this week is that although their social skills are highly developed, they are really loners by nature. Gifted with exquisite aesthetic taste, their knowledge of current events, fashions, and matters concerning lifestyle is impressive, and family and friends usually consult them on how to do almost anything in the most tasteful way possible. Generally well liked and constantly in demand as confidants and counselors, Libra II's often have difficulty finding time for themselves and at some point must learn how to limit the time and energy they give others. They inspire others to trust them, but, while fair, just, and agreeable in most situations, Libra II's can also be extremely sharp and critical. Usually their insights are dead-on correct, which means their criticism stings all the more. A tendency toward emotional mood swings may be their biggest single problem. Changing affect is frequently the result of an ever-present tendency for these imaginative individuals to indulge in fantasy. As a result, there is too often a glaring discrepancy between what Libra II's think they want and what they truly need.

Libra II's are highly valued by their friends, not least for their light and fun-loving manner. They are often good conversationalists. Those born in this week may blunt their own desires by not taking them seriously. Self-deception can lead to disastrous choices of partner and professional blunders. Lacking a clear view of themselves, they cannot make cogent personal choices and are constantly landing in hot water.

ZODIAC POSITION
**APPROXIMATELY
9–18° LIBRA**

ELEMENT
AIR

RULER
VENUS

SYMBOL
THE SCALES

STRENGTHS:	**UP TO DATE, FAIR, INSIGHTFUL**
WEAKNESSES:	**COMPLACENT, SEVERE, SELF-DECEIVING**

LIBRA II NOTABLES: Jesse Jackson, Susan Sarandon, John Lennon, Buster Keaton, Armand Assante, Vaclav Havel, Jackson Browne, Thelonious Monk, Helen Hayes, Giuseppe Verdi, Sigourney Weaver, Juan Perón, Bob Geldof

Libra III

THE WEEK OF THEATER
October 11–18

If "all the world's a stage," as Shakespeare wrote, then Libra III's are some of the finest players upon it. Acting out the drama of their own lives is their specialty. Keenly aware of the value of image, Libra III's spend a lot of time crafting how best to present themselves on center stage. Worldliness is perhaps the greatest strength of Libra III's; their know-how, knowledge, and experience give them the confidence to meet any challenge. With highly developed leadership ability, they typically find themselves at the head of a social group or business. Hardheaded, Libra III's may stick to the same course for years, whether it is right for them or wrong. Their mistakes can consequently be big ones since they tend to give their all once they commit to something—although all too frequently this happens without adequate analysis or planning. Libra III's who have faced great disappointment may become cynical.

Libra III's are not terribly interested in other people or in their feelings, and although they suffer exceedingly when misunderstood, they seldom go out of their way to understand others. They are uncomfortable when heavy emotional expectations are put on them. They see themselves as serious, responsible, and ethical, but they may relate more immediately to what others are thinking about than to what they are feeling. Their detachment, even coolness, may sometimes irritate or infuriate those around them, but it is misleading, for it is merely an act achieved with years of rehearsal—Libra III's are actually very emotional people.

ZODIAC POSITION
**APPROXIMATELY
16–25° LIBRA**

ELEMENT
AIR

RULER
VENUS

SYMBOL
THE SCALES

STRENGTHS:	**WORLDLY, HARD DRIVING, KNOWLEDGEABLE**
WEAKNESSES:	**UNHEEDING, BLAMING, OVERCONFIDENT**

LIBRA III NOTABLES: Luciano Pavarotti, Margaret Thatcher, Eugene O'Neill, Eleanor Roosevelt, Arthur Miller, Oscar Wilde, Mario Puzo, Martina Navratilova, Sarah Ferguson, Rita Hayworth, Chuck Berry, George C. Scott

Libra–Scorpio Cusp
THE CUSP OF DRAMA AND CRITICISM
October 19–25

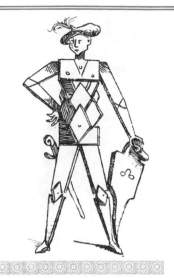

ZODIAC POSITION
APPROXIMATELY
26° LIBRA–3° SCORPIO

ELEMENTS
AIR/WATER

RULERS
VENUS/PLUTO AND MARS

SYMBOLS
THE SCALES/SCORPION

Big personalities, those born on the Libra–Scorpio cusp may prove too much for anyone to handle. These are charismatic and intellectual individuals, with ideas that are well thought out and highly developed. Libra–Scorpios usually have something to say on almost any subject—and they say it fervently. Their penchant for preaching from the pulpit makes them natural teachers. Those born on this cusp meld the airy (mental) nature of Libra and the watery (emotional) characteristics of Scorpio. These two aspects of their personality are often at war, with the head guiding and the heart denying, or vice versa. The tensions and disappointments of life can at times prove too much for them, such that they retreat into isolation. Their mental orientation appears as perceptiveness and sharp insightfulness, but these also contribute to a sense of personal infallibility and a tendency to be overcritical.

As responsible as many Libra–Scorpios seem in many areas of everyday life, they have an undeniably wild, unpredictable side. The private lives of Libra–Scorpios may include many love affairs, charting a path strewn with broken hearts. Sensuousness and passion, expressed in a love of beauty, are important themes in the lives of those born on the Cusp of Drama and Criticism. Those involved romantically with Libra–Scorpios must beware addictive tendencies in such relationships. However, if both parties can retain their own identities and maintain healthy boundaries, a marriage characterized by both deep love and friendship is possible with a Libra–Scorpio.

STRENGTHS:	**SENSUOUS, CHARISMATIC, ARTISTIC**
WEAKNESSES:	**OVERCRITICAL, ADDICTIVE, RIGID**

LIBRA–SCORPIO CUSP NOTABLES: **Sarah Bernhardt, Evander Holyfield, Pablo Picasso, Peter Tosh, Catherine Deneuve, Johnny Carson, Dizzy Gillespie, Carrie Fisher, Benjamin Netanyahu, Arthur Rimbaud, Mickey Mantle**

Scorpio I
THE WEEK OF INTENSITY
October 26–November 2

ZODIAC POSITION
APPROXIMATELY
1–11° SCORPIO

ELEMENT
WATER

RULER
PLUTO (CO-RULER: MARS)

SYMBOL
THE SCORPION

Scorpio I's are demanding personalities who have few equals in attention to detail and applying their powers of concentration to the task at hand. Those born in the Week of Intensity are extremely discriminating, possibly to the point of being judgmental. In matters of fairness and ethics, they are likely to evaluate people more for their motives than for their actions, refusing to accept excuses for, say, lateness since to them everything has a meaning. Thus it is difficult for Scorpio I's to forgive, and it is almost impossible for them to forget slights. More than most, Scorpio I's have a charged, polarized personality with two sides—one sunny, one dark. Their sunny side gives them a radiance and a seductive charm—even the mildest of them has more than a touch of the performer; Scorpio I's are often excellent mimics. Their dark side is destructive and when out of control can inflict serious damage. Their virtuoso energies in either direction are often manifestations of a needy side—a craving for approval and affection that also makes them thin skinned when it comes to criticism.

Scorpio I's are highly selective; their friends may be few, their contacts with family carefully controlled, their relations with co-workers limited. Once selected as intimates, however, most friends of these interesting and attractive folks feel honored and can attest to the highs of relations with them. Of particular note is their sense of humor—they can keep those around them rolling around on the floor.

STRENGTHS:	**TRUTHFUL, DISCERNING, SINGLE-MINDED**
WEAKNESSES:	**HURTFUL, STERN, SELF-DESTRUCTIVE**

SCORPIO I NOTABLES: **Dylan Thomas, Hillary Rodham Clinton, Bill Gates, Sylvia Plath, François Mitterrand, Julia Roberts, Christopher Columbus, Jan Vermeer, John Cleese, Teddy Roosevelt, Daniel Boone**

Scorpio II
THE WEEK OF DEPTH
November 3–11

Profundity in all forms is an irresistible attraction of Scorpio II's. Shunning superficiality, those born in the Week of Depth take a serious view of life, both at work and at home. This is not to say that they don't like to have fun—far to the contrary. But even in pursuing their hobbies, pastimes, and lighter activities, they show full-bodied intensity and concentration. Because they are highly competitive, jealousy and envy are naturally close to their passionate core. Scorpio II's are extremely empathic, for they know what it is to suffer. They will feel tragedy deeply—so deeply, in fact, that it can leave them devastated. Often, they repress their shadow side by various means of escape, such as retreating to a safe haven, switching off, or indulging in substance abuse. To allay anxiety and because they are aware of the power of money, Scorpio II's need to be good earners, and rarely will they knowingly put themselves at any economic disadvantage.

It can be difficult to get Scorpio II's to open up and talk about whatever may be bothering them. Even a trusted life partner or dear friend must pass all kinds of roadblocks. Any deep bond formed with such an individual obviously cannot be taken lightly; not everyone is ready for such heavy commitment. Though tending to the secretive and controlling, Scorpio II's generally make steadfast friends and faithful lovers and are unusually kind, giving, and even sentimental.

STRENGTHS:	**SERIOUS, STEADFAST, SEXUAL**
WEAKNESSES:	**DEPRESSIVE, WORRYING, ESCAPIST**

SCORPIO II NOTABLES: **Marie Curie, Hedy Lamarr, Fyodor Dostoyevsky, Yanni, Robert Mapplethorpe, Bonnie Raitt, Sally Field, Roseanne, Richard Burton, Will Rogers, John Philip Sousa, Maria Shriver, Mike Nichols**

ZODIAC POSITION
APPROXIMATELY
10–20° SCORPIO

ELEMENT
WATER

RULER
PLUTO (CO-RULER: MARS)

SYMBOL
THE SCORPION

Scorpio III
THE WEEK OF CHARM
November 12–18

Realists first and foremost, Scorpio III's rarely overreach themselves. Gifted with trustworthy judgment and keen assessment, they have a realistic view of themselves and others. Those born in this week do well in administrative positions or as leaders of a social group or working team, roles in which their evaluative, organizational, and practical abilities can come to the fore. Because some things come so easily to them, they may become complacent or perhaps self-satisfied. The most successful Scorpio III's are often those who have dared to strive toward realizing their most impossible dreams. Unusually passionate individuals, Scorpio III's are equally adept at control. The charming or inscrutable facade that they present to the world often hides tremendous inner conflict. Addictions of all sorts, broken only with difficulty, plague them. However, such compulsions, once mastered, are rarely readopted.

Scorpio III's who are able to show or at least discuss a small part of their feelings for another person will be closer to realizing success in relationships. Charming and seductive, Scorpio III's rarely are at a loss for lovers or friends. Anyone who wants to make friends with Scorpio III's must keep in mind their aversion to those looking for a free ride. People born in this week are often attracted to self-sufficient individuals with something unusual to offer. Scorpio III's rarely kid themselves about their romantic lives. They are rarely found hanging on to relationships that have proved unproductive or detrimental.

STRENGTHS:	**TOGETHER, CHARMING, RESOURCEFUL**
WEAKNESSES:	**DEFENSIVE, COMPLACENT, CONTROLLING**

SCORPIO III NOTABLES: **Grace Kelly, Whoopi Goldberg, Prince Charles, Claude Monet, Neil Young, Demi Moore, Joseph McCarthy, Boutros Boutros-Ghali, Charles Manson, Georgia O'Keeffe, Danny DeVito, Martin Scorsese**

ZODIAC POSITION
APPROXIMATELY
19–27° SCORPIO

ELEMENT
WATER

RULER
PLUTO (CO-RULER: MARS)

SYMBOL
THE SCORPION

Scorpio–Sagittarius Cusp
THE CUSP OF REVOLUTION
November 19–24

The combination of the emotionally deep, serious, and secretive Scorpio and the intuitive, outwardly directed, freedom-loving Sagittarius yields revolution. Not all revolutionaries are wide-eyed, bomb-throwing idealists; within the souls of many freedom fighters lurk secret autocrats. The revolt that engages the Scorpio–Sagittarian is the fight against sloppiness, bad taste, ineffectualness, stupidity, and old-fashioned, outworn attitudes. They are capable of exploding old myths, true, but they are equally capable of reviving and preserving myths that they view to be useful; those born on this cusp are secret traditionalists at heart. With a disdain for middle-of-the-road policies and middle-class ethics, most Scorpio–Sagittarians would rather be very rich or very poor. This hankering after extremes leads many to indulge in excess. Making plans for the future, dreaming up elegant new schemes, and guiding a decent percentage of them to fruition are all characteristic of Scorpio–Sagittarian imagination and determination.

Goal and result oriented, those born on this cusp may pursue a friend or life partner with unrelenting zeal. They use sarcasm and derision, but do not take kindly to being talked down to or derided themselves, seeing such teasing as an attempt to humiliate them. Moral questions are important to them. They strive to be honest, but they may tell only part of the truth. However, their undeniable charm and their well-meaning, faithful, and loyal attitudes usually lead those who love them to forgive them.

STRENGTHS:	ECSTATIC, LOYAL, GUTSY
WEAKNESSES:	AUTOCRATIC, DERISIVE, WILD

SCORPIO–SAGITTARIUS CUSP NOTABLES: Robert Kennedy, José Orozco, Nadine Gordimer, Jodie Foster, George Eliot, Charles De Gaulle, Voltaire, Goldie Hawn, Ken Griffey, Jr., Billie Jean King, Henri de Toulouse-Lautrec, Ted Turner, Jeane Kirkpatrick

---

ZODIAC POSITION
**APPROXIMATELY
26° SCORPIO–3° SAGITTARIUS**

ELEMENTS
WATER/FIRE

RULERS
PLUTO AND MARS/JUPITER

SYMBOLS
THE SCORPION/ARCHER

Sagittarius I
THE WEEK OF INDEPENDENCE
November 24–December 2

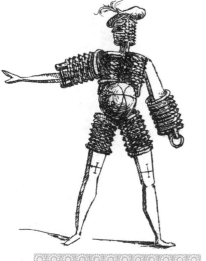

In many ways the most independent people of the year, Sagittarius I's must feel free to act on their impulses and intuition. Even though they try to project an air of self-assurance and confidence, behind this facade there often lurks a sensitive and even insecure individual. Sagittarius I's have a thing about fairness. Honor and trust are high on their list of priorities; without these, they feel, life reverts to the law of the jungle. Because Sagittarius I's possess enormous willpower, loyalty is a matter not only of principle or of emotion but also of stubbornness; sticking to their guns is a character trait. Sagittarius I's can be unreasonable, and winning is essential to their highly competitive nature, but they are usually open to discussion. Actually, these quick, witty individuals thoroughly enjoy verbal repartee and debate.

Many born in the Week of Independence have a greater need to give than to receive. While there are also those who are not at all bashful about making demands, when Sagittarius I's respect their spouse or living partner, they will cooperate, sharing their feelings and dividing chores. Sagittarius I's generally have only one or two people with whom they feel close enough to share their innermost thoughts. Such soulmates know those born in this week as highly ethical individuals who value integrity and character above all, except, perhaps, their freedom. Those who want to spend time with Sagittarius I's usually have to be able to keep up with them by sharing the fast pace they set, whether in sports, travel, work, or hobbies.

STRENGTHS:	HONORABLE, INTUITIVE, RESPONSIBLE
WEAKNESSES:	OVERCOMPETITIVE, IMPULSIVE, TEMPERAMENTAL

SAGITTARIUS I NOTABLES: Bette Midler, Woody Allen, Tina Turner, Winston Churchill, Maria Callas, Mark Twain, Richard Pryor, Jimi Hendrix, Bruce Lee, William Blake, Joe DiMaggio, Adam Clayton Powell, Jr., Caroline Kennedy Schlossberg, John F. Kennedy, Jr.

ZODIAC POSITION
**APPROXIMATELY
2–11° SAGITTARIUS**

ELEMENT
FIRE

RULER
JUPITER

SYMBOL
THE ARCHER

Sagittarius II

THE WEEK OF THE ORIGINATOR
December 3–10

Sagittarius II's are different and are not afraid to show it. Among the more unusual people of the year, even the most apparently normal of them may come to seem a tad peculiar once you get to know them better. They rarely consider doing anything in any way but their own. In consequence, Sagittarius II's commonly encounter rejection. Those born in this week are often clever—good with their hands, quick with their minds, technically proficient in their principal pursuit. Perhaps out of an inner drive to show people who they really are, Sagittarius II's can sometimes let aggression run riot, whether it be territorial, intellectual, sexual, or emotional. Many success-oriented Sagittarius II's will push to get ahead and rise to the top at any cost; this may be a result of their tremendous need to be accepted. Strangely enough, it is often only when they forget about success that they suddenly achieve it—as if by accident and usually by cashing in on their own wacky way of seeing and doing things.

In general Sagittarius II's will save themselves and others a great deal of agony by seeking out people who will appreciate their uniqueness and avoiding the effort to impress or be accepted by those who will not. They usually become dependent on one or two close friends or family members for acceptance and emotional support. Those born in this week are liable to give their all for love and to get hurt in the process.

ZODIAC POSITION
**APPROXIMATELY
10–19° SAGITTARIUS**

ELEMENT
FIRE

RULER
JUPITER

SYMBOL
THE ARCHER

STRENGTHS:	**UNUSUAL, ARDENT, TALENTED**
WEAKNESSES:	**PECULIAR, IRRESPONSIBLE, REJECTED**

SAGITTARIUS II NOTABLES: Walt Disney, Emily Dickinson, Wassily Kandinsky, Kenneth Branagh, Jean-Luc Goddard, Sinead O'Connor, John Malkovich, Jim Morrison, Redd Foxx, Tom Waits, Sammy Davis, Jr., Kim Basinger, Willa Cather

Sagittarius III

THE WEEK OF THE TITAN
December 11–18

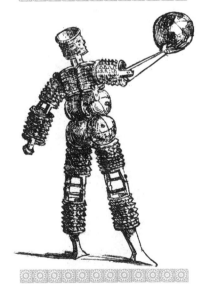

Born in the Week of the Titan, Sagittarius III's think on a grand scale. Geared to big projects, whether planning a family get-together or mapping out a business strategy, they reach for the stars but keep both feet on the ground. Big-hearted, Sagittarius III's give shamelessly but are realistic enough to expect something in return. Drawn to magical and ecstatic experiences, they love the impossible challenge and to pull off miracles. Yet these Titans cannot be called competitive; from where they sit no real competition exists. That outlook may seem egotistical, but it gives some idea of the self-confidence and assurance of Sagittarius III's. And yet behind the massive bulwark of their personality lurk insecurity and a lack of self-awareness—a high price to pay for peace of mind.

Those involved with these powerful individuals will have to learn to play a subordinate role. There are moody and disturbing elements to the Sagittarius III personality that may strain their relationships. Sagittarius III's actually find these dark moods an essential way to withdraw and chew things over. Extremely thoughtful, they can ruminate over a problem or plan for weeks. It is best to leave them alone to do so. The most successful lovers and mates of those born in the Week of the Titan are often those who can weave a magical spell around them, after first lulling them into letting their guard down. Sagittarius III's actually enjoy being enchanted by those who can lighten their ponderous workload or their crushing personal responsibilities.

ZODIAC POSITION
**APPROXIMATELY
10–19° SAGITTARIUS**

ELEMENT
FIRE

RULER
JUPITER

SYMBOL
THE ARCHER

STRENGTHS:	**BIG-HEARTED, SELF-ASSURED, ASPIRING**
WEAKNESSES:	**SELF-UNAWARE, SECRETLY INSECURE, FUSSY**

SAGITTARIUS III NOTABLES: Alexander Solzhenitsyn, Steven Spielberg, Liv Ullmann, Ludwig van Beethoven, Frank Sinatra, Dick Van Dyke, Margaret Mead, William Safire, Michael Ovitz, Teri Garr, Dionne Warwick, Fiorello LaGuardia

Sagittarius–Capricorn Cusp

THE CUSP OF PROPHECY
December 19–25

ZODIAC POSITION
APPROXIMATELY
26° SAGITTARIUS–4° CAPRICORN

ELEMENTS
FIRE/EARTH

RULERS
JUPITER/SATURN

SYMBOLS
THE ARCHER/GOAT

Sagittarius–Capricorns are influenced by both Jupiter and Saturn. The energies of these two planets are diametrically opposed: Jupiter stands for expansion, jollity, and optimism, Saturn for contraction, seriousness, and realism. A kind of push-pull effect is at work in the personalities of the unusual individuals born on this cusp—they may want to have fun but may be too serious to do so. But this combination also produces highly developed faculties of intuition and sensation; consequently, those born on this cusp are at their best when trusting their hunches. Ultimately, the development of extrasensory abilities, or even a single sixth sense, is often the most unique and remarkable quality that those born on the Cusp of Prophecy can offer to the world. Masters of the art of silence, Sagittarius–Capricorns have no need for speech to get their point across. Whether happy, seductive, threatening, or punishing, Sagittarius–Capricorns make their moods known very unambiguously.

Cassandra-like, those born on the Cusp of Prophecy do not expect to be liked by other people. Being independent of the approval of others gives Sagittarius–Capricorns a power and freedom that many lack. Only a few individuals manage to get close to them, and their friends and lovers understand their need to be alone, gaining great satisfaction from sharing a private or secluded life with them. Partners of the more outgoing Sagittarius–Capricorns, on the other hand, often provide a link between them and the world, and bring them out of their shell.

STRENGTHS:	PSYCHIC, INSCRUTABLE, INTENSE
WEAKNESSES:	FRUSTRATED, ANTISOCIAL, OPPRESSIVE

SAGITTARIUS-CAPRICORN CUSP NOTABLES: Florence Griffith Joyner, Edith Piaf, Joseph Stalin, Nostradamus, Diane Sawyer, Ismail Merchant, Cicely Tyson, Frank Zappa, Jane Fonda, Howard Hughes, Robert Bly, Ava Gardner, Annie Lenox

Capricorn I

THE WEEK OF THE RULER
December 26–January 2

ZODIAC POSITION
APPROXIMATELY
3–13° CAPRICORN

ELEMENT
EARTH

RULER
SATURN

SYMBOL
THE GOAT

Highly dependable, Capricorn I's assume many of the responsibilities of life without complaint. Running their family, business, or social organization is their forte, and they are excellent at delegating responsibility, seeing that things run smoothly, and utilizing their special genius for efficiency. When Capricorn I's speak, they expect others to listen. Their high opinions of their own ideas may, in extreme cases, approach authoritarianism. Many Capricorn I's, of course, are not tyrants at all. Shrewd calculators, they can have an instinct for turning a profit. Overall, they have a very healthy respect for tradition and are more oriented toward making improvements in a given system than in tearing it down. Ironically, their honesty and sense of fairness may undercut their own ambitions by hindering them from reaching the top of their profession.

Acceptance of attitudes or approaches other than their own does not come easily to Capricorn I's. It is not that they are bigoted or prejudiced—quite the contrary, they oppose injustice fearlessly. It is just that they see their way as the best way—and it usually is, reflecting values of hard work and excellence of achievement. They are stern taskmakers, and not all mates are willing to accept Capricorn I rule. The best solution is usually a division of labor. Emotional expression does not come easily to those born during this week; often creatures of deep feeling, they can get all wrapped inside a cocoon of repressed emotion. Associates of those born in this week know them as caring, concerned, and trustworthy individuals.

STRENGTHS:	CAPABLE, HARD WORKING, CONCERNED
WEAKNESSES:	DOGMATIC, BOTTLED UP, TYRANNICAL

CAPRICORN I NOTABLES: Marlene Dietrich, Henry Miller, Mao Zedong, Henri Matisse, Louis Pasteur, Denzel Washington, Anthony Hopkins, Ted Danson, Patti Smith, Bo Didley, Mary Tyler Moore, John Denver, Betsy Ross, Paul Revere

Capricorn II
THE WEEK OF DETERMINATION
January 3–9

Those born in the Week of Determination often have the drive and ambition necessary to reach the top of their profession. Capricorn II's are strivers, like the mountain goat that seeks out the highest crags. Once they embark on a course of action, they are extremely difficult to dissuade. No matter how great or modest their gift, Capricorn II's make the most of their abilities and stretch their talents to the outer edge of the envelope. Generally pictured as hardheaded, down-to-earth thinkers, those born in the Week of Determination are also often interested in theoretical, even metaphysical, religious or spiritual subjects and practices. Nor are their ideas in these areas at all conservative; they may, in fact, be rather radical. Capricorn II's often appear tough and aggressive, but most are highly sensitive underneath. They usually despise weakness in almost any form, and admitting failure is not really a possibility for them.

In their personal lives, Capricorn II's are happiest when they have a partner with whom to share the joys and sorrows of everyday life. Work comes first with these individuals, and friends of Capricorn II's are often colleagues. Their loyalty enables them to hang in there for years trying to make a difficult or even somewhat undesirable relationship work out; in this they are motivated less by sympathy for their partner than by a refusal to admit failure. As realistic as they are, Capricorn II's are often seen as idealistic and even at times naïve. Naïveté, in fact, can be considered their Achilles' heel.

STRENGTHS: **RESILIENT, RESOURCEFUL, THEORETICAL**

WEAKNESSES: **NAÏVE, ARMORED, WORKAHOLIC**

CAPRICORN II NOTABLES: **Richard Nixon, Simone de Beauvoir, Alvin Ailey, Elvis Presley, Isaac Newton, Louis Braille, Steven Hawking, Diane Keaton, Mel Gibson, Umberto Eco, Jimmy Page, Kahlil Gibran**

ZODIAC POSITION
**APPROXIMATELY
11–20° CAPRICORN**

ELEMENT
EARTH

RULER
SATURN

SYMBOL
THE GOAT

Capricorn III
THE WEEK OF DOMINANCE
January 10–16

Born in the Week of Dominance, many Capricorn III's do not need to rise to the top of their field, or even to lead, as long as they can express their dominance within the day-to-day dynamic of their family, work, or social group. With tremendous diligence and dedication, they are able to stick to the path they have set for themselves without being sidetracked. A strongly moral attitude and a tendency to divide the world into good and evil means that they need to learn not to judge themselves or others harshly or be extreme in their views. Self-confidence is extremely important to the psychic well-being of Capricorn III's. A secret inferiority complex plagues them such that they need to prove to themselves that they are worthwhile. As long as they are not beset by worry or do not expect too much of themselves, they function well. Also, there is an undeniable streak of eccentricity in many Capricorn III's—though they don't try to be outrageous, they often wind up like that anyway.

The happiest Capricorn III's are those who can take people as they are. Capricorn III's can be severe in dealing with those close to them, notably their mates and families. Yet they can be counted on for honest opinions and good advice. Capricorn III's value service highly, but their giving attitudes may make them too self-sacrificing. Years of devotion to a needy family member can drain them of their energy, deprive them of time for themselves, and also cause the buildup of tremendous frustrations.

STRENGTHS: **PROFESSIONAL, SURMOUNTING, MAINTAINING**

WEAKNESSES: **UNHEEDING, OUTRAGEOUS, SELF-SACRIFICING**

CAPRICORN III NOTABLES: **Faye Dunaway, Aristotle Onassis, George I. Gurdjieff, Martin Luther King, Jr., Albert Schweitzer, George Foreman, Joan of Arc, Howard Stern, Julia Louis-Dreyfus, Jack London, Kirstie Alley**

ZODIAC POSITION
**APPROXIMATELY
19–27° CAPRICORN**

ELEMENT
EARTH

RULER
SATURN

SYMBOL
THE GOAT

Capricorn–Aquarius Cusp

THE WEEK OF MYSTERY AND IMAGINATION
January 17–22

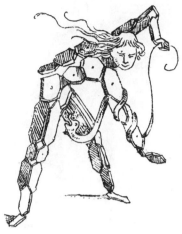

The electric individuals born on the Capricorn–Aquarius cusp generate excitement wherever they go. Unable to keep out of the action for long, they make their presence dramatically felt immediately upon entering a room. Capricorn–Aquarians have a tremendous interest in bettering the lot of the poor and disadvantaged, never hesitating to contribute time, money, or energy to help anyone less fortunate. At the same time, they have little sympathy for those they see as freeloaders or parasites, able to pull their own weight but refusing to do so.

Capricorn–Aquarians can get pretty wild. The influence of Capricorn lends them structure and a sense of responsibility, but the unpredictable energy of Uranus (ruler of Aquarius) threatens to break this order apart at any moment. They can appear sensible and reasonable one moment, uncontrolled the next. These chaotic energies can produce tremendous unrest in the lives of those born on this cusp. They lead a kind of Walter Mitty existence, with few guessing the extent of their interior life or the degree of their inventiveness. Capricorn–Aquarians love to tell and play jokes. Their mates, friends, and family must understand and appreciate this quality. Moreoover, they can fully respect only people who share daily chores and duties fairly. Capricorn–Aquarians often seek hard-working, dependable mates, though those who live alone may learn the greatest lesson by dealing with the most difficult and elusive customer they have ever met—themselves.

STRENGTHS:	**EXCITING, ENTERTAINING, LIGHTHEARTED**
WEAKNESSES:	**CHAOTIC, DIFFICULT, ERUPTIVE**

ZODIAC POSITION
APPROXIMATELY
26° CAPRICORN–3° AQUARIUS

ELEMENTS
EARTH/AIR

RULERS
SATURN/URANUS

SYMBOLS
THE GOAT/WATER BEARER

CAPRICORN–AQUARIUS CUSP NOTABLES: **Muhammad Ali, Janis Joplin, Federico Fellini, Benjamin Franklin, Al Capone, Humphrey Bogart, Geena Davis, Jim Carrey, Dolly Parton, Chita Rivera, Placido Domingo, Rasputin, Jack Nicklaus**

Aquarius I

THE WEEK OF GENIUS
January 23–30

Although Aquarius I's may not necessarily be more intelligent than others, they generally learn quickly, often arousing other people's amazement, and also jealousy, due to the speed and ease with which they pick things up at the first go. Exhibiting an alert, even high-strung demeanor, they do not count patience as one of their virtues. Like thoroughbreds, they are hot-blooded types, usually champing at the bit to get on with it. Although it is true that Aquarius I's are easily bored, they are quite capable of perseverance when they feel it is warranted. They believe that experience is the best teacher and are often self-taught types. The lure of worldly excitement will often entice them away from the classroom, and travel to foreign lands can have a particular fascination for them.

In their careers, those born in this week rarely do well in jobs where they are told what to do or have too much social contact. Self-employment suits them better since they need the freedom to make their own choices and plans and to follow their instincts and be true to what they believe. Their impulsiveness can easily bring them into conflict with authority figures. They can be emotionally unstable and at times can appear distracted, wired, and self-absorbed, and they can be easily upset. In matters of love, Aquarius I's insist that their mates understand their need for freedom. They will not be tied down to fixed routines and schedules. Aquarius I's will rarely accept restrictions.

STRENGTHS:	**PRECOCIOUS, UNIQUE, SELF-TAUGHT**
WEAKNESSES:	**RECKLESS, DISTRACTED, STRESSED OUT**

ZODIAC POSITION
APPROXIMATELY
2–11° AQUARIUS

ELEMENT
AIR

RULER
URANUS

SYMBOL
THE WATER BEARER

AQUARIUS I NOTABLES: **Wolfgang Amadeus Mozart, Oprah Winfrey, Franklin Delano Roosevelt, Lewis Carroll, Paul Newman, Mikhail Baryshnikov, John Belushi, Sharon Tate, Viriginia Woolf, Greg Louganis**

Aquarius II

THE WEEK OF YOUTH AND EASE
January 31–February 7

The Aquarius II period takes Youth and Ease as its central image. "No hassles" could be the motto of most Aquarius II's. They value their happiness highly, asking only to be left alone to travel their own path with as little interference as possible. Those born in this week have a tendency to virtuosity in their makeup. Whether in the office, the laboratory, the building site, or the kitchen, they display a mastery of their medium and a pronounced craftsmanship. Although they give the impression of performing their tasks effortlessly, years of hard work may have gone into perfecting their technique. Youthfulness of all kinds (physical, mental, emotional) is a characteristic of Aquarius II's. They often look and act far younger than their years. Not surprisingly, those born in the Week of Youth and Ease are sometimes accused of emotional immaturity and superficiality.

Aquarius II's tend to be so well liked and admired that one might wonder what their problems are. But the popularity that is their strength can also be their undoing. They can become hooked on other people's applause, or they may isolate themselves for fear of failing to live up to others' expectations. More out of choice than necessity, Aquarius II's may like to keep their relationships light. Paradoxically, they often are magnetically drawn to deep, profound, even troubled people. One wonders if the happy-go-lucky image these individuals seek to convey is really as accurate as it appears.

ZODIAC POSITION
APPROXIMATELY 10–19° AQUARIUS

ELEMENT
AIR

RULER
URANUS

SYMBOL
THE WATER BEARER

STRENGTHS: **ACCOMPLISHED, ADMIRED, REFINED**

WEAKNESSES: **IMMATURE, TORTURED, CUT OFF**

AQUARIUS II NOTABLES: **Anna Pavlova, Clark Gable, Bob Marley, James Joyce, Betty Friedan, Babe Ruth, Natalie Cole, Jackie Robinson, Langston Hughes, Ronald Reagan, William S. Burroughs, Gertrude Stein**

Aquarius III

THE WEEK OF ACCEPTANCE
February 8–15

The theme of acceptance is strong in the lives of Aquarius III's. Some of them are not open to unusual ideas and must learn to become tolerant. Others are overly accepting from an early age and allow themselves to be taken advantage of by those more selfish. The challenge for Aquarius III's is to remain open while at the same time learning discernment and the ability to screen out harmful influences. Disliking those who put on airs, pretending to be something they are not, Aquarius III's make a specialty of poking holes in other people's balloons. Resourceful individuals, Aquarius III's are rarely at a loss for new ideas—especially when it comes to extricating themselves from the difficult or challenging situations they get themselves into. Rarely at rest for long, Aquarius III's love activity and movement.

Due to their lively, affectionate nature, unusual demeanor, and colorful language, they are often sought out by others. Humor, irony, and wit are theirs in abundance. Though craving love, it is apparently hard for them to find a stable partnership. They need a wide variety of experiences, bore easily, and tend to remain unattached. The danger is that they remain the eternal butterfly, flitting from one delicious flower to the next. This nonattachment is not in itself a negative trait—on the contrary, it is a lesson that all of us have to learn sooner or later. For Aquarius III's, however, the lessons that need to be learned are those of constancy, consistency, application, and dedication.

ZODIAC POSITION
APPROXIMATELY 18–27° AQUARIUS

ELEMENT
AIR

RULER
URANUS

SYMBOL
THE WATER BEARER

STRENGTHS: **LIVELY, INVENTIVE, AFFECTIONATE**

WEAKNESSES: **IRRITATED, VULNERABLE, NEEDY**

AQUARIUS III NOTABLES: **Alice Walker, James Dean, Mia Farrow, Abraham Lincoln, Galileo, Charles Darwin, Susan B. Anthony, Thomas Edison, Bertolt Brecht, Bill Russell, Roberta Flack, Peter Gabriel, Chuck Yeager**

ZODIAC POSITION
**APPROXIMATELY
26° AQUARIUS–4° PISCES**

ELEMENTS
AIR/WATER

RULERS
URANUS/NEPTUNE

SYMBOLS
THE WATER BEARER/FISH

Aquarius–Pisces Cusp

THE CUSP OF SENSITIVITY
February 16–22

Those born on the Cusp of Sensitivity are often success-oriented individuals who give top priority to their career. They are usually fighters, an attitude sometimes based on underlying insecurity and the need to prove themselves. A chip-on-the-shoulder attitude in many Aquarius–Pisces individuals makes them aggressive toward others and belligerent when attacked. A great personal challenge, then, is for them to rediscover and acknowledge their inner makeup and to break down some of the barriers they have built up. The tough, even aggressive exterior belies the sensitive personality inside. Since Aquarius is the most universal sign and Pisces one of the most intimate, many born on this cusp orient themselves to one or two extremes: either the most far-out, idealistic pursuits or the most inner, deep, profound ones. Combining such essentially unlike attitudes may be extremely difficult, and many born on this cusp swing from one to the other. In their work, for example, they may deal with abstract concerns, or with attempts to surpass objective limitations while in their private lives they delve into the world of feelings, people, and human affairs.

In relationships, fear of rejection figures prominently and may lead to exhibitions of negativity or pessimism. Such a facade is designed to preclude any deep involvement. By working on interpersonal relationships, Aquarius–Pisces people will widen their humanity and ease feelings of being isolated and misunderstood. Finding the courage to be vulnerable is their greatest lesson.

STRENGTHS: **SUCCESS ORIENTED, CONCERNED, CARING**

WEAKNESSES: **INSECURE, PESSIMISTIC, ISOLATED**

AQUARIUS–PISCES CUSP NOTABLES: **Frédéric Chopin, Toni Morrison, Michael Jordan, Yoko Ono, Amy Tan, Ansel Adams, Sidney Poitier, Charles Barkley, John Travolta, Matt Dillon, Milos Forman, Edward M. Kennedy, Sonny Bono**

ZODIAC POSITION
**APPROXIMATELY
3–12° PISCES**

ELEMENT
WATER

RULER
NEPTUNE

SYMBOL
THE FISH

Pisces I

THE WEEK OF SPIRIT
February 23–March 2

Those born in the Week of Spirit live in the nonmaterial side of life. Whether engaged in the arts or finance, religion or administration, Pisces I's generally approach their work devotionally, elevating it to an idealistic plane. They are not without strong physical drives or a love of the pleasures of the table and the bed. But a blend of the spiritual and the sensual is at the heart of their personalities. Spirited, Pisces I's are often lively and entertaining people. They have a youthful air that can belie their age. A desire to do good, in the sense of leaving the world a bit of a better place at the close of a career or a life, is characteristic of those born in the Week of Spirit.

The service-oriented side of Pisces I's may make them the prey of more selfish individuals, who see them as an easy touch. They often make big-hearted offers to others and then come to regret or resent these promises, thus sending mixed signals. They have an intense emotionality, wearing their hearts on their sleeves. Imagining themselves to be on a higher plane than those around them and presenting a know-it-all attitude frequently create antagonism in others. Rather than living in a world of expectations, concepts, and ideas most of the time, Pisces I's would do well to accept the responsibility of simple everyday tasks and chores that will ground them in the here and now.

STRENGTHS: **SPIRITUAL, SENSUAL, TRANSPARENT**

WEAKNESSES: **EMOTIONAL, IRRESPONSIBLE, CATASTROPHIC**

PISCES I NOTABLES: **Elizabeth Taylor, Linus Pauling, Mikhail Gorbachev, W. E. B. Du Bois, George Frederick Handel, Tom Wolfe, John Irving, Lou Reed, Bernadette Peters, George Harrison, Joanne Woodward, Harry Belafonte**

Pisces II

THE WEEK OF THE LONER
March 3–10

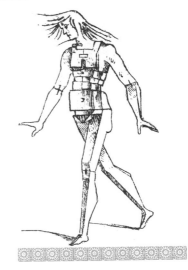

ften living in a private world of their own, Pisces II's make their home a retreat from the vicissitudes of life. Possessing a strongly soulful side, apparent in their love of music and in their empathy for all forms of human suffering, they are great admirers of beauty, particularly in people and paintings, and their homes and surroundings generally show some kind of special touch. Grace, honesty, and an unassailable aesthetic and moral code prevent them from acting underhandedly or, in particular, hurtfully. They generally believe that life is not just there to be enjoyed, and that one must in some way pay one's dues with a certain amount of suffering. Rarely will those born in this week escape at least one severe trauma in their lives. In the workplace, they do well as freelancers or operating outside the office.

Generally speaking, Pisces II's ask only one thing from the world, and that is to be accepted as they really are. To comfort themselves, and to shield themselves from disappointment and rejection, they may surrender to the pursuit of money or retreat to a fantasy-full interior life. Those born in the Week of the Loner usually have few friends. In love, they are more prone than others to be snagged by a pretty face, sensuous voice, or alluring body. Friends and mates of a practical nature tend to bring them down to earth. Meanwhile, children will help them share their sense of wonder and awe at the natural world.

ZODIAC POSITION
APPROXIMATELY
11–21° PISCES

ELEMENT
WATER

RULER
NEPTUNE

SYMBOL
THE FISH

STRENGTHS:	**SOULFUL, INTIMATE, GRACEFUL**
WEAKNESSES:	**RECLUSIVE, DISAPPOINTED, SUFFERING**

PISCES II NOTABLES: **Bobby Fischer, Alexander Graham Bell, Jackie Joyner-Kersee, Gabriel García-Márquez, Michelangelo, Aidan Quinn, Piet Mondrian, Cyd Charisse, Ornette Coleman, Raul Julia, Cyrano de Bergerac**

Pisces III

THE WEEK OF DANCERS AND DREAMERS
March 11–18

he Pisces III period takes Dancers and Dreamers as its central image. Strongly philosophical, Pisces III's often spend time contemplating the intricacies of the universe. Their minds roam freely over areas that many would find daunting or at least mysterious. They start wondering about the meaning of life early on, and, indeed, these issues can become the driving force behind their careers and lifestyles. Although visionary in thought, Pisces III's have an intensely practical side and, often, well-developed technical or scientific skills. They may seem quite down-to-earth, pragmatic, even ordinary types, yet their achievements at times border on the miraculous or the paranormal. They may manifest clairvoyant or telepathic abilities, often at an early age.

Pisces III's must beware appearing too glib and learn when to speak on a given subject. Their omniscient manner can antagonize people. Developing humility and admitting mistakes will only add to their credibility. To an unusual degree, however, their lives are ruled by fate. Yet curious wanderlust or impermanence in their lifestyles can make for frequent moves. Although Pisces III's usually seem very independent, they need to feel that they count. The need to be needed may be one of their most vulnerable points. Pisces III's can be unstable and unrealistic in their romantic relationships and often get involved with the wrong partner. Yet if they make the commitment to a love that is positive and nurturing, they are quite capable of making loyal and devoted spouses.

ZODIAC POSITION
APPROXIMATELY
19–28° PISCES

ELEMENT
WATER

RULER
NEPTUNE

SYMBOL
THE FISH

STRENGTHS:	**PHILOSOPHICAL, HELPFUL, MIRACLE WORKING**
WEAKNESSES:	**INEFFECTUAL, IMPERMANENT, DEPENDENCY FOSTERING**

PISCES III NOTABLES: **Nat King Cole, Liza Minnelli, Albert Einstein, Ruth Bader Ginsburg, Jerry Lewis, Quincy Jones, Rudolph Nureyev, Billy Crystal, Michael Caine, Diane Arbus, Bernardo Bertolucci, Kate Greenaway, Wilson Pickett**

The Karmic
Paths

The Way of Artistry

PISCES–ARIES CUSP TO VIRGO–LIBRA CUSP
Rebirth to Beauty

Those on the Way of Artistry are destined to discover for themselves the nature of beauty and what, at the deepest levels of their hearts, they truly value. To do this, they must become more acute observers and appreciators of the world around them. In the process of doing so, individuals on this karmic path often recognize an ideal or ideal form of beauty and make it their guiding light, their polestar, that becomes the very ground of their being. Though not necessarily artists themselves, they have the task of sharpening and shaping their aesthetic sensibilities and putting them at the service of their inspirational ideals and visions, whether with regard to the arts, to political and economic structures, or in other life areas.

The search for such ideal forms or ideas involves a process not only of enhancing their physical senses and perceptions (these individuals have a strongly sensual nature) but also of developing an incisive mentality. By becoming more discriminating, they will more easily be able to discern what it is they treasure. Developing a capacity for analysis is crucial for people on this karmic path since without it they will be unable to hone their concept of the ideal to the proper level of perfection. Once these concepts are reworked, those on this path are ready to follow them to the ends of the earth, but such a quest inevitably arouses a welter of chaotic passions that must be tamed if a cool, detached vision of their ideal is to

be maintained. Some born to this karmic path will find the discovery of an idealized form of beauty more difficult and spend years in search of it. Others will find or formulate it rather early in life but will have problems keeping their interest and devotion from flagging. Whichever the case, it will be hard or impossible for most of these individuals to accomplish their transformation until such an ideal is manifested in their lives.

Those who tread the Way of Artistry come into this lifetime as creatures of instinct, with more natural, spontaneous, and open energies than most people. Their life process may demand a total transformation since, in pursuing their dream, they tend to re-create themselves and in a sense become the creator of their own self-invention. Their new persona is usually one that admits them to more sophisticated levels of aesthetic and social interaction. However, their innate primal power should not be downplayed but harnessed as a force for spiritual and psychological growth.

Those on this karmic path must learn to ground themselves in the here and now in order to put their idealized visions to work for them. It is not enough for them simply to have an ideal—they must also be able to live that ideal and watch it in action. Thus, career endeavors are frequently the principal arena in which their life issues are worked out. Not surprisingly, they will often find themselves in the world of the arts—whether music,

---

> **CORE LESSON**
>
> Establishing aesthetic values through discrimination and analysis

> **GOAL**
>
> To manifest one's idealized vision

GIFTS
Passionate, Sensitive, Committed

PITFALLS
Superficial, Chaotic, Devious

film, painting, literature, or other creative areas. Others born to this karmic path become appreciators of the simple beauties offered by everyday life, and their creative energies find expression in pursuing leisure-time pursuits at home, raising offspring or pets, traveling to photograph exotic or unspoiled natural settings, collecting objects, or taking an interest in styles of dress and behavior. Since many of the foregoing processes entail shifting the emphasis from Pisces–Aries passion to Virgo–Libra sensuousness, some take place when the individual is a bit older and therefore in more mature personal or social settings.

Several pitfalls may materialize along the Way of Artistry. Unfortunately, attempting to transform the instinctual into the sophisticated may involve a certain amount of superficiality—even dishonesty or deviousness—which may be at variance with the very idealism that motivates such behavior. Excessive idealism can also be a big problem here, making it difficult or impossible for these individuals to be effective at practical matters such as running a family or business, particularly if their ideal becomes an overly stern taskmaker. Moreover, a more realistic approach to everyday life can be compromised by a fruitless yearning for perfection. The key here is to let the goal remain an ideal, a vision of perfection, that one *attempts* to live up to while, at the same time, recognizing that life is im-

perfect. Remembering to forgive oneself and others is important on this karmic path.

On the other hand, some on this path may latch onto a single ideal that is unattainable and therefore suffer a great deal of frustration. Years may pass before they are able to admit that they will never reach their goal, and much energy can be wasted in this manner. Frequently impatient and unrealistic, those on this karmic path may get mired down in such attitudes and find themselves unable to manifest even simple ideas on a daily basis. Finally, friends and family may well get upset if they see the straightforward, honest approach of these primal individuals changing to one that is more snobbish and neglectful of basic responsibilities.

Other people may not always agree on whether those on this karmic path are rough individuals or refined ones. It is often the case that folks from simpler backgrounds see the men and woman on the Way of Artistry as pretentious and those from more sophisticated ones may view them as upstarts. In fact, the individuals who will be of the most help and support to those on the Way of Artistry are friends and lovers who understand their passion and can offer assistance in the form of introductions to the more harmonious approaches to life—teaching them, for example, the social graces or the fine art of diplomacy. Being

---

RELEASE

The attraction to the more primitive aspects of life

REWARD

The joy of loving something for its own sake

SUGGESTION

Focus on what you truly respect. Observation will help you find your ideal.

helped to come to grips with and master their tumultuous personalities and become more patient and realistic about their abilities and the world itself is what those on this karmic path really need. On the other hand, anyone who excites or arouses them to ever more unsettling experiences should be avoided, since in this case the urge for sheer excitement will be self-defeating.

Some of the destiny issues for these individuals will involve relationships. Born with an innate aversion to being held down or trapped in any way, those on the Way of Artistry will seem to ever slip from the grasp of friends and lovers. Two major relationship problems will be encountered on this karmic path. The first is that these individuals tend to overidealize the role of spouse, friend, teacher, or mate, thus setting themselves up for disappointment as mere mortals fail to live up to their idealized roles. The second is that in their search for the perfect relationship, these individuals may fail entirely at the art of commitment for fear of relaxing their standards and "settling." But it is the men and women on the Way of Artistry who will benefit the most from the taming influence of intimate involvement. The happiest individuals of this configuration will aim high, work hard to honor their interactions by adhering to high moral standards, and learn to forgive much.

Obviously, what is best for those on this karmic path is people and experiences that will nourish their idealistic search without arousing their excitable nature. Reaching a peaceful plateau emotionally by eschewing the ups and downs of their psyche is essential to their well-being. Through yoga, meditation, or other balancing regimens, not the least of which is following a healthful diet, those on the Way of Artistry may well discover spiritual values that will contribute to their personal development. Another part of their challenge is to develop a good sense of timing, particularly concerning when to will what they want into being and when to simply let them happen. By developing a feeling for *kairos,* the right time for events to unfold, they will limit the stress in their lives and promote the well-being that comes from being in sync with their soul's journey. Moreover, although the Way of Artistry is the fate of those who move from a humble and often uncultured social background to one of greater refinement, the most successful of these individuals are those who can draw on their basic, elemental personalities and life experiences for inspiration and support.

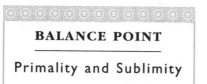

BALANCE POINT

Primality and Sublimity

Perhaps the Way of Artistry can best be likened to a newly mined, rough, precious stone that must be patiently ground and polished into a rich, lustrous gem before its facets and fine geometrical shapes are revealed. The process by which this is accomplished is part craft, part inspiration—a magical melding of hard work and imagination. Ultimately, moving from rebirth to beauty may be likened to renouncing the natural in favor of the artificial and exchanging the animal for the angelic, the human for the divine.

CRYSTALS AND GEMSTONES

Snowflake Obsidian stimulates primal energies to connect with the sublime. This stone protects the physical body and inspires the spirit to traverse the realms of imagination.

NOTABLES ON THIS KARMIC PATH

Born into poverty as Archie Leach in Bristol, England, **Cary Grant** surmounted his humble origins to become one of Hollywood's most witty and sophisticated actors. Following his highly inauspicious debut touring with an American acrobatic troupe, Grant tried his hand at musical

CARY GRANT

comedy before turning his attention to film. As is typical of many on this path, Grant pursued an ideal of beauty for most of his life and was successful in reinventing himself as a model of this aesthetic.

PAUL GAUGUIN

Paul Gauguin was a painter who sacrificed everything in his quest for beauty. In 1883, after forsaking his Parisian life as a stockbroker and leaving his wife and five children, Gauguin lived a solitary life of poverty in order to fully pursue his artistic vision. When he finally departed Europe to work in Tahiti, he relinquished his cultural heritage to create some of the most strikingly original paintings of his time.

Breaking with the Impressionists to follow his primitive ideal, Gauguin isolated himself from Western civilization and died penniless.

Representative of many on the Way of Artistry, **Bob Dylan** was fired by his turbulent passions to embrace a placid aesthetic vision. Dylan objectified and manifested his ideals through his poetry and music, elevating folk to new-found heights, at first as a sophisticated poet and later as a vi-

BOB DYLAN

brant rock musician. Never afraid to follow his ideal, Dylan was invariably at the center of controversy. His political statements fired up an entire generation and in the process transformed his own person.

Other Notables: Maya Ying Lin, Carlos Montoya, Joseph Campbell, Ann-Margret, George F. Will, Richie Valens, Paul Winfield, Ed Bradley, Pierre Cardin, Louis B. Mayer, Norman Lear, Percy Bysshe Shelley, G. W. Pabst, H. G. Wells, Arthur Penn, Sarah Ferguson, Wassily Kandinsky, Florence Griffith-Joyner, Alexander Hamilton, George Balanchine, Nastassja Kinski, Greg Louganis, Louis Comfort Tiffany, Jimmy Dorsey, Dr. Seuss

BIRTHDAYS ON KARMIC PATH 1

April 11, 1885–August 29, 1885 | November 22, 1903–April 11, 1904 | July 3, 1922–November 21, 1922

February 12, 1941–July 2, 1941 | September 24, 1959–February 12, 1960 | May 5, 1978–September 23, 1978

December 15, 1996–May 4, 1997 | July 27, 2015–December 15, 2015

KARMIC PATH
1

March 19–24

REBIRTH
PISCES–ARIES CUSP

These souls are blessed with a primal energy that makes them survivors in the highest sense. Strongly bound to their origins, however, they may find it difficult to get out of the starting gate in order to pursue their higher inspirations and inclinations. Pisces–Arians give a whole new meaning to the phrase "rugged individualist." They would rather "do" than teach or be taught and may resent the efforts of those who try to tone them down or smooth their rougher edges. Over time, however, they become more discerning and better able to distinguish between the quiet certainty of true instinct and the passion of the moment. Making peace with their parents will serve them well in life, as will learning to regulate their sometimes wild mood swings. When they succeed in tapping into a larger moral code or ideal, these warrior/philosophers are always involved and forever honest, and their considerable passion can serve as a beacon of inspiration to others when their energies are directed to larger, less personal goals.

JOHN J. SIRICA
Judge of Watergate case

3/19/1904
Pisces–Aries Cusp

CHALLENGE: **LEARNING PATIENCE**
FULFILLMENT: **SHARING THEIR VISION WITH OTHERS**
NOTABLE: **WYATT EARP (GUNFIGHTER)**

March 25–April 2

THE CHILD
ARIES I

Aries I's on the Way of Artistry may well spend much time feeling like the proverbial bulls in a china shop. Frank, even blunt, at times, they are drawn to the more sophisticated and refined side of life yet are not always confident about their ability to "fit in." Spontaneous and even naive, they have a yearning for cultural enrichment that may give rise to deep feelings of insecurity. Subject to an overriding idealism, they can find themselves undergoing all sorts of conversions as the newest passion or fashion captures their never-lingering attention. It is important for these dynamic people to cultivate inner stability and a sense of personal worth. With their great willingness to learn, a love of the finer things can take them on a grand adventure in this life during which they may invent and reinvent themselves several times over. Most Aries I's will go farther than they ever dreamed possible once they learn the gentler arts of playing fair, not overwhelming others, and discovering the strength to be found in giving.

CHALLENGE: **BEING CAUTIOUS OF SUPERFICIAL ATTRACTIONS**
FULFILLMENT: **RAISING SELF-ESTEEM**
NOTABLE: **CHARLOTTE FORD (SOCIALITE)**

April 3–10

THE STAR
ARIES II

The bad news for Aries II individuals is that the Way of Artistry can easily manifest itself in narcissism and that their search for beauty may begin and end with themselves. The good news is that Aries II's are capable of great leadership and vision, of carrying others along on the tide of their tremendous energy. The image they project to the world means a great deal to them, and they can spend those energies in a never-ending search for self-improvement and style. In this group can be found bodybuilders, fashion mavens, and trendsetters of every ilk. And here is where can also be found snobs and social climbers who live for "keeping up with the Joneses." At best, Aries II individuals will use their sense of beauty and passion for style to shape the tastes, fashions, and ideals of entire generations. Either way, they are capable of generating tremendous excitement in others as they quest for aesthetic savvy. Those born during the Week of the Star hunger for technical knowledge and will doubtless develop into true experts in their chosen field of endeavor.

JOSEPH CAMPBELL
Mythologist
and educator

3/26/1904
Aries I

CHALLENGE: **PURSUING LASTING SPIRITUAL VALUES**
FULFILLMENT: **IMPROVING THEMSELVES NEARLY TO THE POINT OF PERFECTION**

April 11–18

THE PIONEER
ARIES III

The enthusiastic, pioneering spirit of the Aries III individual cannot help but be drawn to the groups, causes, and social activities that the Way of Artistry demands. Perhaps their greatest danger is that of overenthusiasm, for this is the position of the saint, the zealot, and even the dictator. Still, attachment to an ideal, a goal, or a cause is these people's lifeblood, and they are not above extracting an ounce or two of the same from those brave enough to follow as they forge a path to their goal. Yet their ultimate success may be determined by how well they learn to roll back the more personal frontiers of human relationships. Aries III's do need others but may suffer quite a shock when they realize that others may not need them, especially when their natural idealism and strength of conviction harden into rigidity or lack of tolerance. Nonetheless, their tireless capacity for work, passionate convictions, and talent for diplomacy will surely help them along this karmic path.

CHALLENGE: **REMAINING FLEXIBLE ENOUGH TO PURSUE NEW AVENUES OF BEAUTY**
FULFILLMENT: **WATCHING OTHERS DEVELOP ARTISTICALLY**
NOTABLE: **ROBERT DELAUNAY (FRENCH PAINTER)**

KARMIC PATH
I

April 19–24

POWER
ARIES–TAURUS CUSP

A good feeling for aesthetic matters is usually found in Aries–Taurus individuals, and their natural passion and sensuousness can become real hands-on creativity. Those born on the Cusp of Power are more than capable not merely of admiring beauty but of manifesting their love of refinement in material ways. Here we find artists whose creations serve some practical purpose while being highly aesthetic at the same time. Aries–Tauruses also make fine collectors or curators. These people do have a possessive side, however, and may fail to share their interests or possessions with others. Also, they can become snobbish or overbearing if their search for beauty becomes a manifestation of personal power and prestige. Their material side can be quite demanding. Here is the proverbial "champagne taste, on a beer budget." Whatever this individual's personal tastes, though, they are likely to have good taste indeed, and if they combine that good taste with good sense, their success on this karmic path is ensured as long as spiritual values are not neglected.

ANN-MARGRET
Performer/actress

4/28/1941
Taurus I

CHALLENGE: **AVOIDING COVETOUSNESS AND MATERIALISM**
FULFILLMENT: **CREATING BEAUTIFUL SURROUNDINGS**
NOTABLE: **RYAN O'NEAL (ACTOR)**

April 25–May 2

MANIFESTATION
TAURUS I

Taurus I's are generally quite happy on the Way of Artistry and able to bring great satisfaction to those they meet along the path. Their pronounced love of beauty sensitizes them to the extent that they are able to find beauty in almost anything, and their openness to new experiences can take them to often exotic places and pursuits. The danger is that they may forget their humbler beginnings or, worse, sentimentalize them beyond all recognition. Either way, they may slip into a state of chronic self-satisfaction and cut themselves off from the power of their own intuitions. And it is that inner intuition and inspiration that guide them to their goals. Without it, their natural stubbornness can become complacency and they may be unable to progress. Nonetheless, those born during the Week of Manifestation are blessed with a profound sense of beauty, finely honed instincts, and the practical good sense necessary to see almost any endeavor as a platform on which to build "the good life" for themselves.

CHALLENGE: **ESCHEWING SENTIMENTALITY AND COMPLACENCY**
FULFILLMENT: **BRINGING AESTHETIC SATISFACTION TO OTHERS**

May 3–10

THE TEACHER
TAURUS II

Natural teachers, Taurus II's may undertake a life journey that enables them to share their sense of the aesthetic by educating others about matters of beauty and refinement. Their main problem is that they may become too didactic or bossy when they feel they have the inside track on just what constitutes aesthetic value and what does not. Taurus II's might do well to remember the maxim that "one man's trash is another man's treasure" and that beauty exists ultimately in the eye of the beholder and is not a moral standard to which they must somehow make the rest of the world conform. Still, their sense of what is beautiful will serve them well in the realization of their artistic goals. Taurus II individuals make passionate collectors and educators and can be wonderful preservationists or historians as well. As long as their impulse to moralize on aesthetic matters is kept under control, this will be a relatively trouble-free karmic journey, and the transformation of their primal energies into more sophisticated, refined ones is almost certain.

RICHIE VALENS
Early rock singer,
La Bamba

5/13/1941
Taurus III

CHALLENGE: **AVOIDING BOSSINESS AND MORALIZING**
FULFILLMENT: **EDUCATING OTHERS ON MATTERS OF IMPORTANCE TO THEM**
NOTABLE: **GEORGE F. WILL (JOURNALIST)**

May 11–18

THE NATURAL
TAURUS III

The great naturalness and spontaneity of Taurus III's on the Way of Artistry may very well lead them to fields of endeavor where they can pursue their aesthetic goals and values in a natural environment. Taurus III's are great lovers of the unspoiled and may derive tremendous satisfaction as gardeners, naturalists, or environmentalists or by working with animals. Their primary problem is that their great love of the natural world may lead them away from more sophisticated social pursuits and into an isolated, even lonely lifestyle, free of the demands of the outside world. Taurus III's may also fail to acquire the necessary balance to function in a world of more restrained and regulated emotion. Great appreciators of beauty, Taurus III personalities can combine their love of the natural world with a sense of beauty to create things that will inspire us all. Quite capable of becoming artists themselves, Taurus III's are especially suited to the visual worlds of painting, sculpture, and film.

CHALLENGE: **NURTURING THEIR NEED FOR SOLITUDE WITHOUT BECOMING ISOLATED**
FULFILLMENT: **DEVELOPING A FULL AWARENESS OF THE NATURAL WORLD**
NOTABLE: **OTTO KLEMPERER (CONDUCTOR/COMPOSER)**

May 19–24
ENERGY
TAURUS–GEMINI CUSP

Taurus–Geminis on this karmic path will encounter nothing if not variety in their search for aesthetic values. Highly active and at times even aggressive, those born on the Cusp of Energy may very well overwhelm others with their natural showiness and need for self-assertion. Unfortunately, it is those very qualities that others may find off-putting, and these souls may find themselves excluded from the very clubs they want desperately to join as they search for greater refinement and sophistication. Their love of beauty can manifest in mere flashiness or, worse, a tendency to take outrageous risks simply for the fun of shocking the establishment. And while these powerhouses may indeed generate considerable energy, there is an equal danger that they will burn out unless they save their considerable energies for the longer haul. If these personalities can cultivate more endurance and depth and commit themselves to a larger ideal, however, their sparkling energy can serve as a beacon of inspiration for those they meet along the way.

PAUL WINFIELD
Film actor, *Sounder*

———

5/22/1941
Taurus–Gemini Cusp

CHALLENGE: **TEMPERING THEIR OUTRAGEOUSNESS**
FULFILLMENT: **STICKING TO A COMMITMENT TO A LARGER IDEAL**
NOTABLE: **BOB DYLAN (FOLK/ROCK SINGER/SONGWRITER)**

May 25–June 2
FREEDOM
GEMINI I

These freedom lovers will go far in life as long as their aspirations involve a break with the structures and strictures of the past. Whatever their roots or family situation, Gemini I's will almost certainly make some significant departure from them at some point in their lives. Yet it is equally true that the relationships they establish with others will do much to help or hinder them on their life's journey. This is one instance where who one knows may indeed be more important than what one knows. And these people will generally know a great deal. Gemini I's are unusually bright and apt pupils in almost any subject, and their need for beauty and yearning for cultural enrichment are not likely to remain undernourished. Yet they will gain much personal stability from the people around them, and if they cultivate their ability to tend to unfinished business and see their myriad of projects and inspirations through to conclusion, their success is ensured whatever their chosen field of endeavor.

CHALLENGE: **ESTABLISHING RELATIONSHIPS THAT EXPAND THEIR SOCIAL NETWORK**
FULFILLMENT: **GAINING STABILITY FROM OTHERS**
NOTABLE: **JOHNNY PAYCHECK (COUNTRY SINGER)**

June 3–10
NEW LANGUAGE
GEMINI II

Brilliant communicators all, Gemini II personalities on the Way of Artistry are sure to make significant contributions to their world in the fields of writing, speaking, and communication of all kinds. The principal danger of this configuration is that they will fail to attach themselves to a larger ideal or goal. It is important for those born during the Week of New Language to feel themselves understood, and they will go to great lengths to make sure that they are. But all that verbalization can be a turnoff for others, and the Gemini II personality would do well to learn when to be quiet and let someone else do the talking. Their competitive spirit is strong, giving them considerable energy as they reach for their personal star. They can make formidable public speakers of all kinds, and their skill with language can be truly inspirational. Gemini II's can become enraptured with the sheer beauty of ideas and would do well to remember that those ideas, well expressed and articulated, can awaken the intuitions and inspirations of a wide and willing audience.

STACY KEACH
Actor

———

6/2/1941
Gemini I

CHALLENGE: **LEARNING TO BE QUIET**
FULFILLMENT: **EXPRESSING THEMSELVES TO A WIDER AUDIENCE AND FEELING UNDERSTOOD**
NOTABLE: **PAUL GAUGUIN (PAINTER)**

June 11–18
THE SEEKER
GEMINI III

Seekers on the Way of Artistry can find themselves caught up in any number of adventures, even in the most ordinary circumstances. Gemini III individuals are restless by nature and leave their origins with hardly a backward glace. If the most important part of a journey is the first step, Gemini III's will never have much trouble beginning a trip. They seem continually on the move, testing and probing their limits in their search for higher ideals. Indeed, these are people for whom the best life has to offer may never seem good enough. Unwilling to commit in the classic sense, they may well resist the demands of dedicating themselves to the world of relationships and responsibilities; at their worst, they may cut themselves adrift in a sea of unrealistic dreams and plans, never testing their validity in the real world. Though Gemini III's are unlikely to be pinned down to any single cause or ideal, their dogged determination, ambition, and natural subtlety will doubtless smooth many of the rougher stretches of this karmic path.

CHALLENGE: **REMAINING GROUNDED AND REALISTIC**
FULFILLMENT: **FINDING AN IDEAL BY WHICH THEY CAN LIVE**

June 19–24

MAGIC
GEMINI–CANCER CUSP

Gemini–Cancers on the Way of Artistry have a good chance of success, due simply to the fact that they display a natural attraction to devotional causes almost from the moment of birth. Whether the field be religion, philosophy, the arts, or any number of other political or social causes, Gemini–Cancers will devote themselves to it wholeheartedly. The principal danger of this configuration is simply that they can be much too romantic and idealistic, and unable to recover completely from any great disillusion or disappointment. Gemini–Cancer individuals often show a natural inclination toward self-sacrifice and ought to take care that their ideals do not lead them into situations where they are exploited or otherwise unappreciated. Possessed of considerable charm and magnetism, they will easily gain entrance to refined and sophisticated circles. Blessed also with formidable intelligence, they will never have a problem discerning real quality from its cheaper imitations.

ED BRADLEY
TV journalist, *60 Minutes*

6/22/1941
Gemini–Cancer Cusp

CHALLENGE: **DEALING WITH AND LEARNING TO OVERCOME DISAPPOINTMENT**
FULFILLMENT: **BEING RECOGNIZED FOR THEIR REFINED SENSIBILITIES**

June 25–July 2

THE EMPATH
CANCER I

Those born during the Week of the Empath are blessed with considerable sensitivity, depth, and diversity, to the extent that they are capable of turning feeling itself into a kind of art. Natural actors and psychologists, their principal pitfall is that harsh conditions early in life may cause them to retreat permanently behind an impenetrable shell. Alternatively, they may feel deprived of adequate mothering or nurturing and be emotionally demanding of others all their lives. Their great sense of beauty may express itself in more personal ways, such as gorgeously decorated homes. In any event, possessions will always be important to them, and they are likely to spend wisely on the items that they value most. Often they will prove to have some investment potential. However, Cancer I's are at their best when they can express their highly emotional nature by means of some artistic endeavor, and their natural empathy can serve as the Muse for the creative endeavors of others.

CHALLENGE: **OVERCOMING THEIR DESIRE TO BE PROTECTED AT ALL COSTS**
FULFILLMENT: **SATISFYING THEIR DESIRE FOR THE BEAUTIFUL**
NOTABLE: **STOKELY CARMICHAEL (RADICAL ACTIVIST)**

July 3–10

THE UNCONVENTIONAL
CANCER II

The Way of Artistry will no doubt hold some strange twists and turns for these flamboyant, fantasy-prone, unconventional souls. Passionately attracted to the unusual and sometimes even bizarre aspects of artistic expression, Cancer II's will have little problem with creative expression and may gain a certain notoriety simply by virtue of their knack for being in the right place at the right time. The conditions of their early lives may have a great deal to do with how they manifest their ideals, and in most cases the salient characteristic of their upbringing was an insistence on conformity. The danger is that they may bear some guilt over not being "normal" that can keep them from reaching beyond a boring desk job or other mundane, and ultimately creatively unfulfilling, pursuit. In that event, their need for an ideal may be confined to a vivid fantasy life, dark obsessions, or secret addictions. Ideally, though, their need for the unusual and exotic will win out and take them to far-off lands, unusual friends, and imaginative and rewarding careers.

LOUIS B. MAYER
Cofounded MGM studios

7/4/1885
Cancer II

CHALLENGE: **RESISTING THE LURE OF OBSESSION**
FULFILLMENT: **PUTTING THEIR FANTASY WORLD TO CONSTRUCTIVE USE**
NOTABLE: **PIERRE CARDIN (DESIGNER)**

July 11–18

THE PERSUADER
CANCER III

The great drive and determination of the Cancer III personality on the Way of Artistry are almost certain to manifest themselves first in the professional arena and second in the personal sphere. Highly observant, these individuals are unusually well organized and capable of choosing the perfect opportunity to make their mark on the world. Passionate and involved, Cancer III's are idealistic yet capable of the solid, practical application of their goals and ideals. Their sense of beauty is innate, even though they may never feel a need to own or possess beautiful things for themselves. Perhaps the principal pitfall of this configuration is a tendency to steamroll others in an effort to realize their larger goals or to overindulge in what they might consider the "finer things," which, in this case, are usually aesthetic experiences. Ideally, though, people with this configuration will transform their dreams into reality quite easily and leave this world much better than they found it.

CHALLENGE: **NOT REPRESSING OTHERS**
FULFILLMENT: **SEEING THEIR AESTHETIC IDEALS MANIFESTED IN FORM**

July 19–25
OSCILLATION
CANCER–LEO CUSP

Though they must fight a tendency to overemotionalism throughout their lives, the key to success for those born on the Cancer–Leo cusp will surely be their unique ability to work well with others. These people have a great talent for being both able to lead and able to follow, as a situation demands. However, something in their egos requires possession, so it is difficult for them to share their aesthetic sensibility or discoveries with those around them. Learning to share things of beauty and value will raise their spirits and ultimately boost their sometimes shaky egos as their sense of the sublime is validated. Cancer–Leos are frequently parsimonious and can take their natural appreciation of the arts to something more resembling solitary worship. These souls will doubtless have an easier time than many, though, simply by virtue of their natural expansiveness and passionately caring spirit. If they are able to surround themselves with people who can steady the roller coaster of their emotions, they are sure to realize their heart's desires.

CHALLENGE: **DEVELOPING GENEROSITY OF SPIRIT**
FULFILLMENT: **SHARING THEIR DELIGHT IN WHAT THEY CONSIDER TO BE BEAUTIFUL**

NORMAN LEAR
TV producer,
All in the Family

7/27/1922
Leo I

July 26–August 2
AUTHORITY
LEO I

Whatever the aesthetic goals and ideals of Leo I's, their journey will be highly original, deeply felt, and certainly intense. Their early life may well have set them on the road to success, for no matter how humble their origins, they are blessed with drive and a fine competitive spirit that rarely settles for less than it has to. Though Leo I's may choose to work alone toward developing a personal aesthetic, they function equally well on a team. Intense and high-minded, Leo I's can fall victim to disillusion when it becomes clear that not all people share their standards. Equally, they may fail to connect with some larger spiritual ideal and end up spending their prodigious energies on personal issues, often becoming megalomaniacal in their need to control. Still, if they can learn to accept the limitations of other people and resist the temptation to worship false gods, their karmic path will be paved with not mere glitter but true gold.

CHALLENGE: **NOT PERMITTING DISILLUSION IN THEMSELVES OR OTHERS**
FULFILLMENT: **REALIZING A SPIRITUAL IDEAL WITH WHICH TO LEAD**
NOTABLE: **BLAKE EDWARDS (DIRECTOR; PLAYWRIGHT)**

August 3–10
BALANCED STRENGTH
LEO II

The naturally balanced energies of the Leo II personality will serve them well in that they are not as likely to suffer the extremes of emotion often experienced by those on the Way of Artistry. These people have a certain toughness, a solidity of character, that was likely forged by their early childhood conditions. Though their yearning for artistic and cultural enrichment may be strong, there is a danger that their logical, cut-and-dried way of thinking will keep them tied to a stoic, no-frills sort of lifestyle in the name of realism. It's difficult to get them to change their minds, especially in the name of ideals. Nonetheless, they are quite romantic underneath, and their sensitivity to the finer things in life is bound to surface at some point. The danger is that their amazing capacity for concentration may lead them to obsession and even paranoia. When Leo II's succeed in attaching themselves to a higher cause or ideal, however, no one is stronger, more committed, or more able to protect and uplift the downtrodden.

CHALLENGE: **OVERCOMING STUBBORNNESS AND OBSESSION**
FULFILLMENT: **UPLIFTING THE DOWNTRODDEN IN THE SERVICE OF SOMETHING GREATER**

PERCY BYSSHE SHELLEY
Poet; expelled from
Oxford; friend of Byron;
drowned

8/4/1792
Leo II

August 11–18
LEADERSHIP
LEO III

Enthusiasm and experience come together in Leo III's, who are more than capable of attaining the heights of success. Though they can be self-centered and even selfish, they are wonderful leaders, able to restructure and reorganize people and organizations for the larger good. Marvelous managers and creative administrators, their amazing energy and single-mindedness bless them with the ability to be successful in almost any endeavor they undertake. Rising from harsh early conditions should not be a problem, yet later in life Leo III's may show an unwillingness or inability to "lower" themselves to more menial tasks. It is on the more personal level that their search for value and beauty will prove to be problematic, since they are curiously indecisive about deciding what it is they want for themselves. However, if they can manage to avoid the pitfalls of elitism and the illusion of their own infallibility, their chances of success are very high indeed.

CHALLENGE: **DISCOVERING WHAT IS VALUABLE OR BEAUTIFUL TO THEM ON A PERSONAL LEVEL**
FULFILLMENT: **USING THEIR LEADERSHIP ABILITY FOR A GREATER CAUSE OR GOOD**
NOTABLE: **SHELLEY WINTERS (ACTRESS)**

KARMIC PATH
I

August 19–25

EXPOSURE
LEO–VIRGO CUSP

Woe betide those in this group who seek to conceal their humbler origins or the secrets of their past. It is likely that the book of their lives will be opened at some point, usually as a result of their having given themselves away. Leo–Virgos can be rather late starters when it comes to moving up in the world, yet once they have discovered a personal ideal, they will move toward it with a great deal of determination and tenacity. Naturally passionate and idealistic, their principal danger is that they may somehow fail to direct that passion toward a cause or issue. While they are astute observers, many prefer to remain on the periphery, hesitant to reveal their true thoughts and feelings. Still, once they have achieved emotional maturity, they make charismatic leaders with enormous staying power. Their sense of beauty is not as pronounced as is their feeling of the importance of service, and they will dedicate themselves tirelessly to an ideal or cause—providing, of course, that they are surrounded by a select group of individuals they know they can trust.

RENÉ LEVESQUE
Canadian government
official, sought
independence for Quebec

8/24/1922
Leo–Virgo Cusp

CHALLENGE: **DIRECTING THEIR PASSION TOWARD AN IDEAL**
FULFILLMENT: **TAKING JOY IN SERVING**

August 26–September 2

SYSTEM BUILDERS
VIRGO I

The Virgo I personality may struggle a bit along the Way of Artistry, simply because their need to impose order on the world is often at odds with the chaos of their emotional life. The harshness of their early childhood conditions more than likely involved their shouldering great responsibility early on, and many grow to adulthood harboring a great deal of resentment. Unresolved emotional issues can plague them, and some shut down entirely, taking refuge in the comfort of self-imposed limitations and the order of a daily routine. Sometimes prone to a lack of self-awareness, Virgo I's are nonetheless highly aware of others and are keen observers and evaluators, able to expertly articulate the dynamics of individuals and groups. The realization of their aesthetic goals may have much to do with surrounding themselves with more flexible, laid-back, and creative personalities. Virgo I's learn by example, and if they are surrounded by freethinking types, they are sure to blossom.

CHALLENGE: **ALLOWING THEIR AWARENESS TO GO BEYOND MUNDANE DETAIL TO THE GREATER WORLD OF FORM**
FULFILLMENT: **THE EXPRESSION OF CREATIVITY THROUGH CRAFTSMANSHIP**
NOTABLE: **GENTLEMAN JIM CORBETT (BOXER)**

September 3–10

THE ENIGMA
VIRGO II

Good taste and high standards are two hallmarks of Virgo II's on the Way of Artistry. Sensitive and discriminating, they will likely have little trouble rising beyond their origins. Still, Virgo II's are unlikely to share the details of their upbringing with anyone, preferring to keep their personal business private. Highly ethical, they should have no problem attaching themselves to higher causes and ideals, and some of them will be attracted to organized religion or spiritual or philosophical studies. In any event, their sense of destiny is quite pronounced, for they sincerely believe that self-improvement is always and only the result of personal moral effort. Their principal danger is that their insistence on self-reliance may make them fail to form meaningful relationships with others. At times quite guarded, Virgo II's may appear to others as cold, calculating, or simply disinterested. Yet underneath that daunting exterior is a passionate, sensitive soul who longs for closeness and the attainment of romantic ideals.

SID CAESAR
TV comedian,
Your Show of Shows

9/8/1922
Virgo II

CHALLENGE: **TAKING CARE NOT TO BE OVERLY DETACHED**
FULFILLMENT: **WORKING ON SELF-IMPROVEMENT OR THEIR VISION OF AN IDEALIZED SELF**
NOTABLE: **CARL VAN DOREN (WRITER; CRITIC)**

September 11–18

THE LITERALIST
VIRGO III

Virgo III's are marked by a truly formidable willfulness, and whatever they want, they are likely to get. They have a natural dislike of undue displays of drama and emotion yet may be quite capable of throwing a tantrum if they think it will be effective. Still, for all their seeming passion in youth, they have a cool, calculating streak, and they are more than capable of keeping their heads when all around them are losing theirs. Their love of beauty and refinement will more than likely manifest itself in learning a craft, and they will doubtless master it over time. Disappointed or disillusioned Virgo III's may flounder, for integrity is paramount to them and once betrayed, they do not recover easily. Their principal danger is that they may promote full-scale revolution when a simple change would do or embark on any number of rebellious crusades in the name of morality. In fact, they will display more fire in the name of an ideal than they will about an individual and would do well to nurture the more personal side of their deeply caring natures.

CHALLENGE: **PLAYING DOWN THEIR DESIRE FOR REBELLION**
FULFILLMENT: **MASTERING A CRAFT**
NOTABLE: **JEAN SYLVAIN BAILLY (MAYOR OF PARIS; ASTRONOMER)**

September 19–24
BEAUTY
VIRGO–LIBRA CUSP

These people can really shine when placed on the Way of Artistry, for Virgo–Libra individuals live for beauty in all its forms. In fact, lack of harmony in their immediate physical environment can prove quite damaging to their psyches, and, depending on the exact conditions of their early life and upbringing, their impulse to rise above their origins can border on the obsessional. Sensuous and sensitive, those born with this configuration may nevertheless content themselves with superficial glitz and glamour. Virgo–Libras may become snobs or ivory-tower idealists, going to great lengths to avoid the more unpleasant aspects of reality. They may seek escape in the darker realms of fantasy and addiction. At worst, their love of the ideal is something of a fatal attraction, and they may become neurotic and possessive in pursuit of a goal. At best, however, those born on the Cusp of Beauty are destined to make the world an easier place to live in, for their presence can serve to remind us all of how truly beautiful life can be.

H.G. WELLS
Writer, *The Time Machine* and *War of the Worlds*

9/21/1866
Virgo–Libra Cusp

CHALLENGE: **BEWARING OF OBSESSION**
FULFILLMENT: **BEING SURROUNDED BY OBJECTS OF BEAUTY**

September 25–October 2
THE PERFECTIONIST
LIBRA I

These emotionally complex people may fight the scars of childhood throughout their lives. It is likely that Libra I's suffered the undue domination or influence of an incompatible parent, and they may spend far too much energy in trying to right the sometimes unrightable mistakes of the past. Though their impulse toward perfection will surely cause them to improve greatly upon their childhood conditions, they may carry excess emotional baggage on their quest for the ideal. Though well suited to the more refined side of life, Libra I's are likely to marry someone in order to change them or to expend enormous amounts of energy in similarly unproductive ways. Further, they may demonstrate a tendency to inner instability. Their inner turmoil may make them indecisive, and their inability to make decisions due to their perfectionism may in turn contribute to this. Yet they may experience a rebirth in the course of their lifetime, for once they have undertaken the business of personal transformation, they are unlikely to fail at it.

CHALLENGE: **LETTING GO OF CHILDHOOD PROBLEMS**
FULFILLMENT: **FEELING SATISFIED WITH THE LEVEL OF THEIR OWN REFINEMENT**

October 3–10
SOCIETY
LIBRA II

With their finely honed social sense and great feel for diplomacy, Libra II's will function well on the Way of Artistry. Others seem to naturally trust them, and the gentle Libra II's are usually more than worthy of that trust. However, they may have learned early on that their feelings and impulses were not to be relied upon, and the result is that the principal pitfalls of this configuration are twofold: simple inertia and self-deception. Having an overly developed level of impulse control, they can fail to act when the moment is right. However, Libra II's have a healthy dose of worldly ambition, making them inclined to take their own needs and desires seriously. As they mature, their innate sense of justice can serve to guide them, and they make excellent crusaders or reformers if they don't fall victim to complacency. Their natural creativity and sense of beauty can manifest in almost any fashion, and if they cultivate the ability to follow things through, assert themselves, and ask for more of what they want from life, success can be theirs.

SARAH FERGUSON
Ex-wife of Duke of York

10/15/1959
Libra III

CHALLENGE: **FIGHTING THEIR INERTIA**
FULFILLMENT: **CONTRIBUTING TO THE CREATION OF BEAUTY**
NOTABLE: **MAYA YING LIN (ARCHITECT; DESIGNED VIETNAM WAR MEMORIAL)**

October 11–18
THEATER
LIBRA III

Unlike many traveling on the Way of Artistry, Libra III's will be less likely to struggle with the tumult of their emotions. Their unique ability not to take things too personally can serve to insulate them from many of the world's harsher aspects but at the same time can prove frustrating and even infuriating to those close to them. Those born during the Week of Theater are blessed with natural savvy and, whatever their origins, were doubtless well aware of the possibilities of bettering themselves from an early age—their principal danger being that, having arrived, they can easily fall victim to a kind of chronic cynicism. The ability to connect on an intimate level is very important to them, yet it is precisely in the area of personal relationships that they may encounter their greatest difficulties. Always ready to learn and to embrace new concepts and ideologies, Libra III's can use their attraction to the world of ideas and ideals to tap into truly transformative energies. But to fully experience the beauty demanded by the Way of Artistry, their task is to apply those energies toward their deeply personal relationships.

CHALLENGE: **TAKING CARE NOT TO LET THEIR NATURAL CYNICISM INTERFERE WITH THEIR SEARCH FOR THE IDEAL**
FULFILLMENT: **EMBRACING THE BEAUTY OF INTIMACY**
NOTABLE: **MARIE OSMOND (ENTERTAINER)**

October 19–25

DRAMA AND CRITICISM
LIBRA–SCORPIO CUSP

These powerhouses are charismatic and can be unpredictable. At once emotional and intellectual, Libra–Scorpios want to be noticed and are very good at getting whatever message they have across. They should do quite well on the Way of Artistry, for they are usually gifted in some creative area. Their impulse toward transformation is quite strong, and, whatever the circumstances, they are capable of rising above even the most outrageous turns of fortune. Their principal danger is their tendency to be overcritical of those who are not as strong, as talented, or as passionate as they are or to succumb to dark-side attractions at the expense of higher values. This position is especially appropriate for actors, preachers, and teachers of all kinds, yet their sense of the aesthetic may also be manifested in other ways. Their relationships with others may work on them like a drug; they can easily forfeit objectivity in the interest of emotional extremes, substituting sensation for sensitivity. If these individuals can learn the fine art of compromise and not indulge in self-pity, they are sure to make their mark.

CHALLENGE: **NOT EXPECTING TOO MUCH OF OTHERS**
FULFILLMENT: **HAVING OTHERS SHARE THEIR VISION**
NOTABLE: **JACK ANDERSON (JOURNALIST)**

CHARLES BRONSON
Tough-guy actor

11/3/1922
Scorpio II

October 26–November 2

INTENSITY
SCORPIO I

Scorpio I's are well suited to working on matters of the spirit, since the business of transformation and rebirth is in no way at odds with their natural inclinations. However, the Way of Artistry may prove problematic for them, since they are marked by a certain polarization in their emotional makeup that may keep them from developing the detachment necessary to identify a spiritual or aesthetic ideal. Possessors of a passion for material things, Scorpio I's spare no expense when it comes to the acquisition of quality goods. However, they would do well to evaluate whether they are being discerning or merely acquisitive. And while they might demonstrate a tendency to social climbing or piling up riches for their own sake, their principal danger is that they may find themselves unable to attach themselves to a larger ideal or cause. Though their sense of justice is highly developed, their natural suspicion can degenerate into paranoia if not kept under control.

CHALLENGE: **DEVELOPING THE CAPACITY TO STEP BACK AND VIEW THINGS MORE OBJECTIVELY**
FULFILLMENT: **APPLYING THEIR POWERS OF ANALYSIS AND DISCRIMINATION IN THE SERVICE OF A HIGHER IDEAL**
NOTABLE: **BARBARA BEL GEDDES (ACTRESS, *DALLAS*)**

November 3–11

DEPTH
SCORPIO II

Cultivating a rapport between the conscious and unconscious will prove especially important to Scorpio II's. Otherwise, they may find themselves tossed about on some very rough emotional waters or at the mercy of subconscious impulses that appear to defy all understanding. Though Scorpio II's are well equipped with both the strength and energy necessary to rise above even the harshest of childhood conditions, their love of beauty and sense of the finer things may express itself in pretension, snobbishness, or self-indulgence. Their tendency to escapism is quite pronounced, and if they do not cultivate what might best be called "emotional management," there is a danger of violent emotional outbursts, depression, and self-defeating patterns of behavior. Still, they are sure to go far in worldly terms and will doubtless improve their material and financial standing as they mature. Scorpio II people have naturally fine tastes and make tireless administrators, managers, and leaders of all kinds; their perceptions of others' motives and strengths are without equal.

CHALLENGE: **BRINGING THE CONSCIOUS AND UNCONSCIOUS INTO SYNC**
FULFILLMENT: **CULTIVATING THE FINER THINGS IN LIFE**
NOTABLE: **KURT VONNEGUT (AUTHOR, *SLAUGHTERHOUSE FIVE*)**

DR. SUN YAT-SEN
Father of the Chinese
Republic; medical doctor;
revolutionary

11/12/1866
Scorpio III

November 12–18

CHARM
SCORPIO III

The winning ways of Scorpio III's are sure to serve them well on the Way of Artistry. Those born during the Week of Charm will have less trouble than some in managing their emotional ups and downs, and they are blessed with a realism and good judgment that will be invaluable as they strive to reach even the most unreachable star. Scorpio III's will have little trouble improving their material lot in life, for they have a fine work ethic and a knack for going into profitable careers. The principal danger for these primal individuals is their attraction to sensual pleasures. No strangers to desire, Scorpio III's may retreat into lust or addiction at the expense of their soul's growth. A failure to take responsibility for their own behavior can sometimes lead them to believe that they are victims of forces beyond their control. Still, their charming exterior conceals a tough, resourceful soul that is able to overcome almost any self-imposed obstacle in the search for transformation.

CHALLENGE: **OVERCOMING AND TEMPERING THEIR MORE PRIMAL URGES**
FULFILLMENT: **HAVING EMBRACED A SPIRITUAL IDEAL, FEELING VALUED FOR HAVING DONE SO**
NOTABLE: **BOUTROS BOUTROS-GHALI (FORMER U.N. SECRETARY GENERAL)**

November 19–24
REVOLUTION
SCORPIO–SAGITTARIUS CUSP

The early environment of Scorpio–Sagittarians doubtless imbued them with a sense of being different from other people. Whatever their childhood domestic situation, a strong desire to re-create themselves will take them far from home. Their natural attraction to causes and ideals, if directed toward aesthetics, will assist them along the Way of Artistry. Their principal danger is that they may embrace change simply for its own sake or that their natural courage may manifest in a kind of "more guts than brains" approach to life. Alternatively, a rough exterior may serve to conceal their sensitivity and belie their true refinement. In some instances Scorpio–Sagittarians may indeed be the kind who can "dish it out but not take it." Those born on the Cusp of Revolution will find that their greatest potential for transformation lies in their ability to cultivate empathy and to choose their battles wisely, for this is one configuration that is attracted to extremes of all kinds. Nonetheless, their great sense of humor and love of freedom are sure to make their progress along the Way of Artistry a fine adventure indeed.

CHALLENGE: **CULTIVATING EMPATHY**
FULFILLMENT: **GAINING REFINEMENT**
NOTABLE: **MAXWELL CAULFIELD (ACTOR)**

WASSILY KANDINSKY
Abstract artist, leader of
"Der Blaue Reiter" group

12/4/1866
Sagittarius II

November 25–December 2
INDEPENDENCE
SAGITTARIUS I

Regardless of their early origins, Sagittarius I's often assert their independence early and may strike out on their own before getting a clear picture of just who and what they are declaring independence from. Still, the Way of Artistry is well suited to these honorable souls, whose sense of the finer things is intimately bound up with their ideals of fairness, justice, and defense of the weak. Their love of beauty will doubtless be manifested in a deep love of nature, and their independent spirit is sure to carry them to "where the wild things are." Inherent to this karmic path is the ability to connect with and pursue larger ideals, not merely to move from one challenge to the next or to embrace the beauty of chaos. Stubbornness can also be a problem, though the same energy, properly directed, can give Sagittarius I's enormous willpower. If Sagittarius I's take care to cultivate their natural generosity and expansive spirit, the transformation promised here will surely be realized.

CHALLENGE: **LEARNING TO WORK WITHIN A VALUE SYSTEM RATHER THAN RUN FROM IT**
FULFILLMENT: **APPLYING THEIR LOVE OF THE NATURAL WORLD TO OTHER AREAS OF THEIR LIVES**

December 3–10
THE ORIGINATOR
SAGITTARIUS II

The need for refinement and artistic ideals is sure to find some form of original expression in the Sagittarius II personality. Naturally eccentric and sometimes a bit on the wacky side, these folks are well suited to a variety of cutting-edge forms of artistic expression and would make fine visual or performance artists. Alternatively, Sagittarius II's have a knack for manual dexterity and the kind of technical aptitude that make for inventors and innovators. Sagittarius II's have a great need to be accepted, and they may flounder if they fail to deal with their childhood conditions psychologically. Perhaps their greatest pitfall is that their love of beauty may lead them to spread themselves too thinly, embracing one ideal or concept after another without mastery or a true sense of commitment. Too, Sagittarius II's can sometimes be quite overbearing in their need to express themselves adequately. Yet the conscious cultivation of their spiritual and artistic nature, and their ability to turn their prodigious energies to community or humanitarian causes, will serve them well.

CHALLENGE: **REALIZING THAT NOT EVERYTHING HAS TO BE ORIGINAL TO BE VALUABLE**
FULFILLMENT: **MAKING A COMMITMENT TO AN IDEAL**

ERSKINE CALDWELL
Writer, *Tobacco Road*

12/17/1903
Sagittarius III

December 11–18
THE TITAN
SAGITTARIUS III

The schemes and plans of Sagittarius III's on the Way of Artistry will be grand in scope, for this is the configuration of dynasty builders, corporate moguls, and larger-than-life achievers. Perhaps the character of these titans was forged in some way by the harshness of their early childhood conditions, but wherever they come from, they will go places and not stop until they get there. The pitfall of individuals on this karmic path is that the bigger they are, the harder they tend to fall. Their brash self-confidence can be eroded by fears and insecurities, and they can get stuck in trying to right the mistakes of the past or bear unreasonable grudges. Sagittarius III's should take special care to cultivate emotional balance and ensure that their self-assurance does not degenerate into megalomania or a chronic sense of entitlement. Ideally, their love of beauty and need for cultural enrichment will find expression on a grand and glorious scale, providing they are not seduced into believing that bigger is better or might makes right.

CHALLENGE: **CULTIVATING EMOTIONAL BALANCE**
FULFILLMENT: **REALIZING THEIR IDEALS ON A GLORIOUSLY LARGE SCALE**
NOTABLE: **CARLOS MONTOYA (FLAMENCO GUITARIST)**

KARMIC PATH
1

December 19–25
PROPHECY
SAGITTARIUS–CAPRICORN CUSP

Those born on the Sagittarius–Capricorn cusp can be plagued by deep insecurities and chronic shyness, yet time and maturity are the keys to their advancement. These individuals are highly sensual, and their love of beauty is easily nurtured, though they must take care not to descend to a path that consists of worship of the flesh. The ability to cultivate intuition will be key to their success, and they should take special care to educate themselves in alternative traditions in religion, science, and the arts. Though there is a danger that they may delude themselves into believing that their humbler origins have somehow marked them for life, nothing could be further from the truth. Rather, it is their own hesitancy to reach for things they know they want that tends to keep them tied to less-than-satisfying people, places, and things. Still, their great natural kindness, depth, and understanding can create tremendous growth and the attainment of considerable material comfort here.

CHALLENGE: **RELEASING THEIR THIRST FOR PHYSICAL BEAUTY IN FAVOR OF THE INTANGIBLE**
FULFILLMENT: **CULTIVATING ALTERNATIVE SPIRITUAL TRADITIONS**
NOTABLE: **FLORENCE GRIFFITH JOYNER (TRACK STAR)**

MICHAEL STIPE
Lead singer for the band
R.E.M.

1/4/1960
Capricorn II

December 26–January 2
THE RULER
CAPRICORN I

Dependable and reliable, Capricorn I's may have had more than their share of responsibility as children. Though there is a danger that Capricorn I's will never move much beyond their origins to attain their higher goals and ambitions, it is equally possible that those same early responsibilities imbued them with a sense of energy and ambition that will be hard to beat. These strongly ethical people are blessed with a practical streak that will serve them well on the Way of Artistry, and whatever their form of expression, their sense of the finer things will manifest in some tangible, practical, and possibly lucrative fashion. The pitfall here is that their moral and ideological sensibility may be so entrenched that they can fall victim to a kind of tunnel vision, refusing to expand their sphere of influence or to accept that it is sometimes possible to change the world simply by changing one's mind. Still if Capricorn I's manage to stay flexible, their integrity and honesty are sure to strike a chord of response in the world of beauty and collective ideals.

CHALLENGE: **OVERCOMING THEIR TENDENCY TO GET STUCK**
FULFILLMENT: **WORKING FOR A GREATER CAUSE**
NOTABLES: **TRACY ULLMAN (COMEDIAN); VAL KILMER (ACTOR)**

January 3–9
DETERMINATION
CAPRICORN II

Deeply attuned to the intuitive, spiritual side of their own natures, Capricorn II's on the Way of Artistry nonetheless also have a sense of drive and ambition in the material side of life. This combination of factors can link them strongly to the collective unconscious, and whatever their artistic or professional achievements, they are likely to find beauty in the smaller details or practical matters of everyday life. Individuals born during the Week of Determination may overthink and overstudy a particular problem to the extent that they render themselves incapable of solving it. Unwisely administered, their sensuality can be expressed in addictions. They would do better to cultivate their formidable intuition and allow it to guide them to the discovery of their own lodestar rather than try to reason themselves into it. Extraordinarily resilient and resourceful, Capricorn II's have enormous potential for the growth called for by the Way of Artistry; as long as they tap into their ability to see the beautiful, they will succeed in applying it in their own lives.

CHALLENGE: **TAKING RISKS**
FULFILLMENT: **INCORPORATING A DAILY DOSE OF BEAUTY INTO THEIR LIVES**

ALEXANDER HAMILTON
Cowrote *Federalist Papers*

1/11/1755
Capricorn III

January 10–16
DOMINANCE
CAPRICORN III

Overattachment to a parent can hamper the development of Capricorn III's on the Way of Artistry, keeping them too strongly bound to their origins and causing the frustration of their own innermost needs and desires. Capricorn III individuals can find it difficult to say no, and they often retreat into rich fantasy lives or unrealistic imaginings as a result of their tendency to self-sacrifice. Nonetheless, they are blessed with an eccentric sense of humor, and their sensual nature is deeply attracted to the world of beauty and finer things. Though mood swings and tempestuous emotions can be a problem, Capricorn III's will always retain the ability to back up and put things into perspective. Their sense of beauty is sure to find expression in a rare kind of personal charisma. Naturally dominant, Capricorn III's can rise to the top of their chosen fields of endeavor, and their attraction to and comfort in being part of a team or group will aid them in achieving their karmic goals.

CHALLENGE: **AVOIDING THE TENDENCY TO OVERINDULGE IN FANTASY**
FULFILLMENT: **DEVELOPING PERSONAL CHARISMA**
NOTABLE: **RAY BOLGER (ACTOR, *THE WIZARD OF OZ*)**

January 17–22
MYSTERY AND IMAGINATION
CAPRICORN–AQUARIUS CUSP

Those born on the Cusp of Mystery and Imagination will doubtless enjoy some wild and exciting times along the Way of Artistry, providing they learn the finer art of keeping their personal demons in check. Emotionalism is almost certain to be something of a problem, as these individuals are especially prone to the mood swings and the roller-coaster ride of feelings associated with the Way of Artistry. The danger is that they may fall prey to the pursuit of sensation for sensation's sake or succumb to self-destructive tendencies in an attempt to discover their own limits. It is important for them to avoid the pitfall of self-pity and to cultivate objectivity. In truth, Capricorn–Aquarians are well suited to the Way of Artistry, having the gifts of a fine imagination, tremendous energy, and formidable creative talent at their disposal. Controversial and quite dramatic, they can be inspirational figures once connected to a cause and will always be in the thick of the action.

GREG LOUGANIS
Gold medal Olympic diver

1/29/1960
Aquarius I

CHALLENGE: **BALANCING THEIR MOODS AND FEELINGS**
FULFILLMENT: **BEING GIVEN THE CHANCE TO INSPIRE OTHERS**
NOTABLES: **CARY GRANT (FILM ICON); GEORGE BALANCHINE (CHOREOGRAPHER, NEW YORK CITY BALLET)**

January 23–30
GENIUS
AQUARIUS I

Thinkers, teachers, and performers of all kinds can be found here. Aquarius I's have a wonderful opportunity for spiritual growth on the Way of Artistry. It is likely that whatever their origins, high expectations were placed on them in childhood. There is a self-taught quality about these souls, and whatever their ideals or ambitions, their style is likely to be bold and original. Though impulsiveness and rebelliousness can be problems, their principal danger is that they may exhaust their potential for transformation in trying to refine or better others rather than themselves. Those born during the Week of Genius have a deep need to attach themselves to higher ideals and causes but should take care not to exercise their creative natures in a series of disappointing Pygmalion-like personal relationships. Still, Aquarius I's are capable of imprinting any number of creative and ideological pursuits with the stamp of their own personal style, and the Way of Artistry should prove quite smooth.

CHALLENGE: **TEMPERING THEIR IMPULSIVENESS AND CULTIVATING THOUGHTFULNESS**
FULFILLMENT: **EXPRESSING THEIR ORIGINALITY THROUGH ARTISTIC PRODUCTIONS**
NOTABLE: **NASTASSJA KINSKI (ACTRESS)**

January 31–February 7
YOUTH AND EASE
AQUARIUS II

Aquarius II's placed on the Way of Artistry may turn out to be crowd pleasers of the highest caliber. Indeed, it can sometimes seem that they have the curious knack of being able to please "all of the people, all of the time." Though there is little chance that they will get stuck in any of the traps of early childhood, they will doubtless look back fondly at the people and places of their youth for most of their lives. Technique and craftsmanship are important to this group, their principal danger being that, having established a certain virtuosity in a given realm of endeavor, they will never move beyond what works for the moment in order to connect with a higher goal. Though they are natural performers, self-satisfaction and even a measure of conceit can be problems here, as can the challenge to go beyond what is merely popular to that which will endure. At best, Aquarius II's on the Way of Artistry are quite uplifting, for they have the enviable knack of making even the most difficult of life's endeavors look easy.

BELLE STARR
Bandit queen;
immortalized in popular
literature

2/5/1848
Aquarius II

CHALLENGE: **EMBRACING VALUES OF A MORE LASTING NATURE**
FULFILLMENT: **RE-CREATING ONESELF**
NOTABLE: **S. J. PERELMAN (WRITER, *THE NEW YORKER*)**

February 8–15
ACCEPTANCE
AQUARIUS III

The tendency to engage in an ongoing struggle to gain objectivity about the harsher realities of their childhoods may hamper Aquarius III's in their search for higher ideals. Having learned early on to accept the limitations of youth, they can sometimes fail to move beyond their family of origin to reach for their personal star. Once these individuals learn to release the past and to overcome their poor self-image, they are ideally suited to championing the rights of the downtrodden or exalting a personal ideal. In fact, Aquarius III individuals become far more open and tolerant as they progress in life, and exposure to the world of beauty and culture will do much to dispel their prejudices. Those born during the Week of Acceptance would do well to cultivate self-awareness and avoid projecting their fears and weaknesses onto others. The challenge here is to avoid tantrums and grudges. When Aquarius III's absorb the lessons of personal detachment in the interest of connecting with a universe of higher aspirations, the Way of Artistry will open and their artistic and creative efforts will expand.

CHALLENGE: **LETTING GO OF NEGATIVITY**
FULFILLMENT: **EXALTING THEIR PERSONAL IDEALS**
NOTABLE: **BRIAN HOLLAND (SONGWRITER)**

KARMIC PATH
I

February 16–22
SENSITIVITY
AQUARIUS–PISCES CUSP

Though Aquarius–Pisces individuals are deeply sensitive to the world of beauty and refinement, their impulse toward cultural enrichment may never find an adequate foothold on the Way of Artistry until they learn to be more practical or grounded. Subject to extremes of emotion and at times hypersensitive, they have an enormous potential for artistic and idealistic expression. Aquarius–Pisces people are very success-oriented and may give top priority to their career path, often at the expense of more personal relationships and interests. Some, though, may retreat behind a curtain of fantasies and fears, disguising their sensitive natures under a tough, aggressive exterior. Strongly intuitive, those born on the Aquarius–Pisces cusp are blessed with a fine sense of style and can be quite bold and original in their creative expression, once they abandon their innate fear of rejection. Still, if they cultivate the more social and lighter sides of their sensitive natures, their natural empathy and caring will provide the necessary energy for true spiritual rebirth.

CHALLENGE: **ABANDONING THEIR CHRONIC FEELINGS OF REJECTION**

FULFILLMENT: **DEVELOPING A PERSONAL STYLE**

NOTABLE: **LOUIS TIFFANY (GLASSMAKER; DESIGNER)**

DR. SEUSS
a.k.a. Theodor Geisel; authored award-winning children's books

3/2/1904
Pisces I

February 23–March 2
SPIRIT
PISCES I

Well suited to the Way of Artistry, Pisces I's are naturally gifted in the areas of art, culture, religion, and philosophy. The greatest problem here is that these finer impulses may never be given adequate expression in the material world. Pisces I's are subject to overidealism as a rule, and their sensitive natures give rise to all sorts of upsets and setbacks. Still, when operating in the material universe, they are capable of the great devotion and service to larger causes and connections that the Way of Artistry demands. Generous and spiritual, Pisces I's have a great need to improve the world and will doubtless improve themselves as they go about pursuing their goals. Staying grounded in the here and now is essential to the success of those with this configuration. True connection, for these spirits, demands involvement at the soul's deepest levels, and if these people can overcome their tendency to avoid confrontation with the seamier, more practical side of life, they are sure to flourish.

CHALLENGE: **BEING MATERIALLY GROUNDED**

FULFILLMENT: **MAKING A CONNECTION TO A HIGHER IDEAL**

NOTABLES: **GLENN MILLER (BANDLEADER, "IN THE MOOD"); JIMMY DORSEY (BANDLEADER)**

March 3–10
THE LONER
PISCES II

Naturally graceful, spiritual, and refined, Pisces II's placed on the Way of Artistry face the challenge of finding beauty in connecting with others. They have a pronounced tendency to retreat into a private world of their own making. Sensual and soulful, Pisces II's can drift in the stormy seas of their own emotions. In fact, they can have a masochistic approach to emotional pain, and many of them prefer to believe that suffering is a necessary prelude to transformation. Yet they are blessed with a great capacity to recover from even the most extreme disasters, even when mired in depression or deep-seated feelings of unworthiness. Addiction to drugs or alcohol can also be a problem, as they often find it necessary to tune out their intuitions and deaden their extreme sensitivity to external sensory stimuli. Still, if they can consciously acknowledge their need for the company of others and control their more strident escapist impulses, the Way of Artistry holds considerable promise for those of this group able to connect with a higher, more social ideal.

CHALLENGE: **LETTING GO OF THE NEED TO SUFFER**

FULFILLMENT: **ACHIEVING SOCIAL SUCCESS**

NOTABLE: **GEORGE GAMOW (PHYSICIST WHO HELPED FORMULATE BIG BANG)**

BARBARA FELDON,
seen here with Don Adams. TV actress, *Get Smart*

3/12/1941
Pisces III

March 11–18
DANCERS AND DREAMERS
PISCES III

Chances are, Pisces III souls on this karmic path will find the journey one of utmost ease and high accomplishment. Indeed, many of them seem destined for a particular career or artistic pursuit from a very early age, and, providing those impulses are not squelched or their spirits crushed by harsh childhood conditions, these dreamers of dreams are destined to travel far into the worlds of beauty and refinement. Deeply spiritual and great appreciators of beauty in its myriad forms, these people must nevertheless guard against a tendency to waffle in their decision making or to content themselves with restless movement in lieu of real accomplishment. Many of them are blessed with the innate ability to turn the proverbial sow's ear into a silk purse, no matter what the situation or circumstance. Their principal challenge is not to be at the mercy of their own sometimes scattered energies. Further, they must cultivate a measure of stability. Properly applied, however, the great gifts of this configuration can work miracles.

CHALLENGE: **UNIFYING THEIR MANY TALENTS IN PURSUIT OF AN IDEAL**

FULFILLMENT: **PUTTING THINGS TO THEIR BEST USE**

NOTABLE: **MIKE LOVE (BEACH BOYS)**

The Way of Discipline

ARIES I TO LIBRA I
Child to Perfectionist

The life purpose of those on the Way of Discipline is to develop a sufficient level of detachment to be able to comment on the lives of those around them, thereby lending insight into the workings of their society. Individuals on this path are born with a desire to illuminate, correct problems, and right wrongs. Indeed, such work is their destiny. Their karmic path is to discover their unique ability to observe, analyze, and reflect on others—both their intimates and their community—thereby lending insight into the psychology or sociology that is at work in various situations; once adequately articulated, this will guide and inspire. However, before the skills needed to achieve such results can be developed, those on this karmic path must learn to temper a sometimes overzealous and childlike enthusiasm that can hinder the kind of impartial analysis needed if they are truly to influence the world around them. No matter how difficult developing the necessary detachment may be, those on the Way of Discipline must labor unceasingly on themselves to develop greater self-discipline and impose healthy structures on their own lives in order to do this work. These socially conscious individuals will spare neither time nor energy in their struggle to reveal the truth.

Those born to the Way of Discipline tend to have an innate sense of and need for perfection. In this context, perfection can be defined as excellence whether in design or in application, such as the perfection of the workings of a business, political, or social structure, the adherence to a moral or legal code, or the inner workings of the individual. The men and women on the Way of Discipline love efficiency! This sense, of course, lends itself to spotting imperfection. Thus, these individuals will tend to see all that requires fixing, improving, or changing around them. The problem, however, is that they tend to rush into situations with the best of intentions, only to act much like a bull in a china shop. Thus, before these individuals can truly become effective they must learn to stand back and observe and in a detached state outline problems and plan the appropriate courses of action or solutions. Imposing such restraint on their minds and emotions is never easy for them, since their overall approach to life is rather childlike and often overly direct. However, they are born with the capacity to be thoughtful, and the development of this thoughtfulness and other mental disciplines will enable them to proceed along their path.

It is important for these individuals to remind themselves to be in the world but not of it; in other words, to take an active role in society but to stand somewhat outside and unto themselves as well. Once they have developed such a relatively mature understanding of life, they will be able to contribute their substantial views on the world around them. They can then go about the business of correcting

CORE LESSON

Cultivating the discipline of emotional detachment

GOAL

To share their keen observations in a gentle, helpful manner

GIFTS
Enthusiastic, Thoughtful, Persistent

PITFALLS
Foolhardy, Compulsive, Excessive

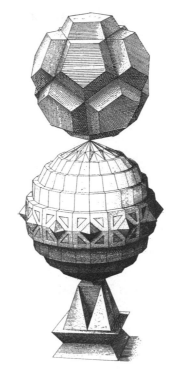

society's ills. On a smaller scale, they can often provide psychological and spiritual insight to friends and colleagues, frequently giving those around them the opportunity to enjoy aspects of existence that had seemed out of their reach. They are also surprisingly good at dispensing practical advice, whether financial or otherwise. Thus, those on this karmic path bring hope and inspiration to those around them but are also adept at sounding the warning bell when urging friends, family, colleagues, and the wider public to wake up to any problems, deceptions, or follies that may be lurking around the next corner.

Though the gifts given to those on the Way of Discipline are those of dynamism and spontaneity, their life process requires them to learn to become ever more exacting, calculating, and demanding. Since a part of the personality of those on the Way of Discipline is decidedly childlike, preferring spontaneous action and complete freedom to explore the world around them, this perfectionistic process challenges them to drop their naïvcté and become better controlled without being too repressed or indecisive. Such individuals' substantial natural curiosity will help them accomplish this. The satisfaction of this curiosity inevitably requires some sort of training or education, and ultimately these individuals come to realize the value of self-discipline. Although it would seem

RELEASE

The overly high standards set for either oneself or others

REWARD

The joy of effecting positive change

that a teacher or role model would be of great help in such a process, those on this karmic path are more often than not self-taught. Frequently, those on the Way of Discipline are even more demanding of themselves than they are of others. Their ultimate goal is to utilize the powers of observation their curiosity gives them, combine it with a system of thought or action, and take advantage of this formidable arsenal in righting the wrongs they see around them or simply in providing information to others.

The family often proves to be the arena in which life lessons are learned and worked out. Should those on this karmic path have conflicts with a strict parent or other family member in early childhood, they will usually rebel strongly against such influence. Later, in adulthood, they may project this figure onto a boss or employer since their innate need for freedom may pose problems. Also, by internalizing this figure in symbolic fashion deep within the psyche, they may become overstrict—with both themselves and others—or even tyrannical as they grow into late adulthood and old age. At first glance, most individuals fated to tread the Way of Discipline seem to have a great need for fame and success, since they appear to be workaholics, putting in long hours and giving their all to projects. Interestingly, it is not so much the approval of others they crave but the perfection of their creations. In fact, it would be

SUGGESTION

More can be achieved through planning than through bluster.
Learn to overlook inefficiency and imperfections.

healthy for them to apply a bit of discipline to their own impossibly high standards by keeping them in check. Thus, those on this karmic path will inevitably face great stress in their careers. If warning signs are not heeded, mental or physical breakdowns, or both, may occur. Colleagues may also fear their irrepressible childlike energy and see them more as wild cards than as serious contenders. Because of this, they should avoid those who refuse to treat them as mature individuals or to take them seriously.

These individuals must take care that their Aries I frankness is not transformed into Libra I scathing indictment when things do not go their way. Another pitfall is that, once they have learned to become more detached emotionally, they may exchange their rather endearing brand of naïveté and openness for an uncaring coolness. The most successful of those on this karmic path will succeed in becoming attractive personalities who draw others to them due to the objectivity and wisdom of their views. However, in both private and professional spheres, they must learn not to transgress the boundaries of others. Also, by midlife these individuals tend to have developed a strict moral code, and they must be careful not to impose this code on others. Some friends and family members may view those on the Way of Discipline as highly capable individuals with valuable advice to offer but hold back from consulting them because they are afraid of their controlling or overly moralistic attitudes.

In relationships, no matter how cool those on the Way of Discipline may appear, they have a great capacity to give and receive affection, and their relationship with a lover or mate may assume extraordinary significance in their life. A great challenge for these individuals is to apply some discipline to their own love of freedom so that they can more comfortably enter into a longer-term or more committed relationship. They must also put their perfectionistic attitudes aside; otherwise, potential mates may never measure up! Trust is a key issue in the choice of a partner, one that will make or break any relationship they have. Recognition is the food that feeds those on this karmic path, and nothing is more important to them than feeling valued by an individual whom they love or respect; if they are, they will blossom. However, all forms of false flattery are anathema to them. They are good judges of character and will usually reject those who attempt to manipulate them through praise. Also, being acknowledged as an important part of an organization and being sufficiently rewarded will guarantee continued dedication and hard work on their part.

BALANCE POINT

Passion and Detachment

This destiny axis seems to demand maturity and growth, since it moves from the Aries I child to the Libra I perfectionist. However, though the child within those born on the Way of Discipline must agree to grow up, it must also be nurtured and kept alive; otherwise, a cranky, rigid pedant may well be the result of this life process. The image that comes to mind here is that of an immaculately kept fruit tree that each year brings forth a new and delicious harvest. Although unmistakably mature and neat in appearance, the tree's eternal youth is evident in the quantity and quality of its annual yield.

CRYSTALS AND GEMSTONES

Pietersite dispels layers of illusion, assisting one to perceive the bigger picture. This stone illuminates through loving guidance without judgment and holds a vibration of leadership.

Children's author **Beatrix Potter** painstakingly developed both her written and illustrative styles through the

BEATRIX POTTER

books that immortalized characters such as Peter Rabbit. In designing her tiny volumes (which she originally self-published), she kept in mind the little hands that would hold them. Using her analytic abilities in a manner typical of the Way of Discipline, Potter utilized her four-footed friends to allegorically comment on the world around her, creating tales that could teach as well as delight her young readers and listeners.

As a paleontologist, **Louis Leakey** discovered the meaning of discipline in his examinations of the most obscure fossil remains of our human ancestors. Because he displayed the directness that is typical of his karmic path, Leakey did not always endear himself to fellow scientists. By pushing back the date of mankind's appearance on the planet, disputing human ancestry, and identifying the Olduvai Gorge as the cradle of life,

LOUIS LEAKEY

Leakey flew in the face of established tradition. Combining spontaneity and objectivity in a manner unique to the Way of Discipline, Leakey blazed a trail for future investigators of human origins.

As is typical of those on the Way of Discipline, **Judy Garland** had a great desire for fame and success, and was willing to put in the long hours necessary to achieve these goals. The outcome of this ambition is apparent in her successful portrayal of Dorothy in *The Wizard of Oz,* where her childlike Aries I origins are clearly visible. However, this juvenility hindered Garland's attempt to survive in an increasingly hos-

JUDY GARLAND

tile adult world where, unfortunately, she could not achieve the mental-emotional balance she so beautifully portrayed on the screen. Eventually, the stress encountered on this path proved too much for Garland and resulted in several tragic breakdowns.

Other Notables: Thomas More, Jerry Lee Lewis, Barry Moser, John Gotti, James Burrows, Eileen Ford, Kingsley Amis, Anne Sullivan, Randy Travis, P. T. Barnum, Earvin "Magic" Johnson, John Lennon, Terry Gilliam, Bruce Lee, Frank Zappa, Faye Dunaway, Plácido Domingo, James Watt, Neil Diamond, Aaron Neville, Helen Gurley Brown, Yitzhak Rabin, Isak Dinesen, Michael Milken, Irving Stone

BIRTHDAYS ON KARMIC PATH 2

November 20, 1884–April 10, 1885 | July 3, 1903–November 21, 1903 | February 12, 1922–July 2, 1922

September 23, 1940–February 11, 1941 | May 5, 1959–September 23, 1959 | December 15, 1977–May 4, 1978

July 26, 1996–December 14, 1996 | March 8, 2015–July 26, 2015

KARMIC PATH
2

March 19–24

REBIRTH
PISCES–ARIES CUSP

The key to success for these souls on the Way of Discipline is learning the fine art of when to speak and when to keep quiet. Sensitive and caring, these individuals may be required to take a few steps back into their family histories before they feel free to move forward. The principal danger of this configuration is a lack of objectivity, and these types can misapply their considerable communicative skills in being hypercritical of others, indulging in all manner of displays of temperament, or in simply refusing to acknowledge that there are two sides to every story or situation. Though Pisces–Arians will undoubtedly mellow a bit with age, they would do well to remember that the rest of the world does not always move as fast as they do and that the impulse toward reform is frequently a projection of an impulse toward self-improvement. Nevertheless, these forceful, dynamic souls have a powerful intuition, and if they can apply their sense of personal justice to less personal areas of endeavor, they can do much to change and improve their world.

CARL REINER
Comedian, actor, writer,
Dick Van Dyke Show

3/20/1922
Pisces–Aries Cusp

CHALLENGE: **LEARNING TO THINK BEFORE THEY SPEAK**
FULFILLMENT: **APPLYING THEIR OWN BRAND OF JUSTICE**
NOTABLE: **JOSEPH PULITZER (JOURNALIST/PUBLISHER; ESTABLISHED PULITZER PRIZE)**

March 25–April 2

THE CHILD
ARIES I

This group is marked by a naive, impulsive nature. Sometimes neglecting to look before they leap or speak, Aries I's nevertheless have a fine sense of wonder and curiosity that they will carry with them all their lives. They may experience undue amounts of criticism or misunderstanding as children, causing them to unconsciously internalize those same rigid, perfectionistic attitudes as they mature. Equally, this group can refuse the challenge of this karmic path and try to retreat into Peter Pan's Never-Never Land, where games and playing at life become a substitute for the real thing. Nonetheless, Aries I's have a high code of ethics and can establish whole new ways of thinking about social issues. Providing that their impulses for change are not expressed as chronic complaining and their need for improvement is not turned inward in a neurotic preoccupation with their physical lives, these exciting, inspired souls have an excellent chance of success as team leaders, coaches, and star players of all kinds.

CHALLENGE: **LETTING GO OF THEIR CHILDHOOD DREAMS**
FULFILLMENT: **ADOPTING A CODE OF ETHICS AND LIVING BY IT**
NOTABLE: **ELI LILLY (PRESIDENT AND CHAIRMAN, LILLY PHARMACEUTICAL CO.)**

April 3–10

THE STAR
ARIES II

Aries II's are likely to flourish on the Way of Discipline. Impelled by their need to be at the center of action, they nevertheless have the inborn ability to be fair and are capable of putting their ego aside in the interest of a larger good. They can, however, be alarmists and should take some care that their impulse toward perfection is not expressed in pickiness, impatience, or rage. Those born during the Week of the Star sometimes walk a fine line and must be careful that their will to succeed and improve themselves not manifest itself as intolerance or a lack of empathy for others. Many in this group will experience a number of tempestuous family and love relationships in which rejection will force them to turn their energies inward in an effort at self-examination. Successfully managed, however, these situations will cause Aries II souls to recognize and improve upon their own flaws, nurture their capacity for deep and lasting partnerships, and relieve them of the necessity to take center stage.

ANNE SULLIVAN,
seen here with Helen Keller.
Teacher of Helen Keller;
lifelong companion; the
real "Miracle Worker"

4/14/1866
Aries III

CHALLENGE: **PUTTING ASIDE EGO ISSUES FOR THE GREATER GOOD**
FULFILLMENT: **FINDING THE EMPOWERMENT THAT WORKING ON THEMSELVES WILL GIVE THEM**
NOTABLE: **WILLIAM BOOTH (BRITISH FOUNDER OF SALVATION ARMY)**

April 11–18

THE PIONEER
ARIES III

Highly social in nature, Aries III's will find a wide arena of possibilities on this karmic path. Group efforts are important to these people, and they will doubtless spend many hours, days, and years trying to correct society's ills. In fact, their social sensitivities can be so highly developed that their ideals manifest themselves in extremes of self-sacrifice. The Aries III soul on this path would do well to back up from time to time in order to better examine whether their sacrifices are genuine or simply a means of avoiding confrontation with their problems. Aries III's will also have to take care not to force their ideas, opinions, and systems on others or to insist that improvement can be attained only through strict and rigid adherence to a narrow path. Still, these people are blessed with both the fearlessness and the energy necessary to accomplish even the most daunting feats, and if they avoid the pitfalls of overly controlling attitudes, their natural magnetism is sure to draw many fans.

CHALLENGE: **BACKING OFF SOMETIMES BY NOT TAKING ON TOO MUCH**
FULFILLMENT: **PIONEERING EFFORTS AT IMPROVING PROBLEM SITUATIONS**
NOTABLE: **EMMA THOMPSON (ACTRESS; WON OSCAR FOR BEST SCREENPLAY)**

KARMIC PATH
2

April 19–24
THE CUSP OF POWER
ARIES–TAURUS CUSP

Powerful and practical, this group may find the Way of Discipline an unusually smooth karmic path. Those born on the Aries–Taurus cusp are quite likely to see the seeds of their improvements bear considerable fruit in the course of their lives, and whatever their field of endeavor, they are likely to flourish. The childlike enthusiasm that marks this path is tempered here by practical instincts. Thus, Aries–Tauruses are quite capable of proving to themselves and others that slow and steady can indeed win even the most arduous race. The principal challenge of this configuration is that the impulse toward improvement and perfection may get stalled somewhere along the way, and that they will be unwilling to jeopardize their own power and influence in the interest of righting a wrong. Yet with their natural dignity, curiosity, and capability, they can do much to cure society's ills in highly tangible ways, for they are well aware how difficult it is to think of heaven on an empty belly.

CHALLENGE: **NOT BEING SO FEARFUL OF JEOPARDIZING THEIR POWER**
FULFILLMENT: **CONTRIBUTING TO MAKING LIFE AS GOOD AS IT CAN BE**
NOTABLE: **CLINT HOWARD (ACTOR; BROTHER OF RON)**

JACK KLUGMAN
Actor, *The Odd Couple*

4/27/1922
Taurus I

April 25–May 2
MANIFESTATION
TAURUS I

Taurus I's are bound to find a sure footing on the Way of Discipline. They love to give shape to structures and systems, and their natural knack for implementation and improvement is sure to find expression with this configuration. Not only can Taurus I's perceptively identify problems and trouble spots, they can fix them, too. Nurturing and protective by nature, they may encounter some difficulty in personal relationships simply because they will forever be trying to improve or otherwise uplift those who become close to them, regardless of whether their loved ones themselves feel the same need. Thus, their good intentions can frequently be misinterpreted, for they are often more concerned with implementing their plans than they are with explaining them to anyone. Still, if they are careful not to become too rigid or inflexible in the sphere of personal morality and learn to apply their considerable diplomatic talents in the world of relationships, they are likely to attain a fortunate, comfortable position in life.

CHALLENGE: **AVOIDING FIXING OTHERS**
FULFILLMENT: **IMPLEMENTING THEIR PRAGMATIC PLANS**

May 3–10
THE TEACHER
TAURUS II

RANDY TRAVIS
Country music
singer/songwriter

5/4/1959
Taurus II

On the Way of Discipline, whatever the message of Taurus II's, someone is going to hear about it. Natural educators, Taurus II individuals are quite at home in the world of ideas and during their lives will do much to spread their ideas. Self-made and self-taught for the most part, there is some danger that these folks can become too rigid or pedantic, so sure of themselves that others' views hold little fascination for them. Further, their sense of perfection and need for improvement may exist at odds with their need to explore other societies and cultures, for this is a configuration that would love to tour the slums of Calcutta, for example, but only if they are cleaned up first! Still, if those born in the Week of the Teacher allow their natural sense of justice and moral integrity to prevail, their inner needs to learn and to teach should shine in a personality that is capable of fighting the good fight against the perennial wrongs of unfairness, discrimination, and injustice.

CHALLENGE: **SOFTENING THEIR MORAL STANCE SOMEWHAT**
FULFILLMENT: **IMPARTING THEIR VIEWS ON PRACTICAL APPLICATIONS TO OTHERS**

May 11–18
THE NATURAL
TAURUS III

Creative and independent, Taurus III individuals may find that the Way of Discipline demands constant refining and redefining of their natural talents. Though some in this group may experience difficulties in family relationships that, they feel, will "tie them down" or otherwise threaten to repress their exuberant natures, others of this group will probably find themselves so caught up in an ideal or cause that in order to accomplish their purpose, they will have to adjust their behavior to better conform to society's rules. With their "love me, love my dog" approach to the world, this is an ideal configuration for environmentalists, animal rights activists, and social workers of all kinds. If Taurus III's rise to the challenge of better integrating their personal ideals with those of society as a whole, they are likely to go far.

CHALLENGE: **ALLOWING OTHERS TO COMMENT ABOUT THEM—AND LISTENING!**
FULFILLMENT: **DEVELOPING THE ABILITY NOT TO VIEW EVERYTHING AS AN AFFRONT TO THEIR FREEDOM**
NOTABLE: **KLEMENS FÜRST VON METTERNICH (AUSTRIAN STATESMAN; NEGOTIATED NAPOLEON'S MARRIAGE)**

May 19–24

ENERGY
TAURUS–GEMINI CUSP

These versatile, direct people may come on strong, then "fall apart in the stretch" when it comes to family and social relationships. Born attention getters, Taurus–Geminis may fail to delve beneath the surface of their ideal of the moment, and though they are perfectly capable of applying themselves, their raucous, energetic approach to problem solving can turn to pickiness and downright irritability when they fail to achieve instant gratification of their needs or desires. Still, when Taurus–Geminis are willing to meet the simple challenge of slowing down long enough to understand and reflect upon other's points of view, they can be sparkling diplomats and fund-raisers and inspirational champions of a better way of doing things. The Way of Discipline is bound to be a bit rocky for them at times, yet if they cultivate their talent for real accomplishment, then use their accomplishments to support their sometimes shaky egos, the road will smooth considerably, as this is one group that rarely needs to learn the same lesson twice.

CHALLENGE: **OPENING THEMSELVES TO OTHER PERSPECTIVES**
FULFILLMENT: **BECOMING A MOVER AND SHAKER**
NOTABLE: **JUDITH CRIST (FILM CRITIC)**

**NICOLE BROWN
SIMPSON**
Ex-wife of O.J.;
murdered

5/19/1959
Taurus–Gemini Cusp

May 25–June 2

FREEDOM
GEMINI I

These freedom lovers are likely to flourish on the Way of Discipline, providing they do not allow their considerable verbal talents to be used solely for criticizing and fault finding. In fact, while a sense of justice and social conscience is highly developed in Gemini I's, there is a tendency to engage in rebellion for its own sake. Highly moral and natural fighters, Gemini I's with this configuration may not, however, have the patience to see their projects and causes through to a satisfying conclusion. They also have a tendency to promise a great deal more than they can actually deliver and may falter on this karmic path as a result of failing to assimilate the maxim that "God is in the details." Still, they will do well to cultivate relationships with people who feed their intellectual energies and who allow them to flourish within the structure of a family or other social unit without tying them down to mundane tasks or boring routines.

CHALLENGE: **QUASHING THEIR PROPENSITY TO USE RIDICULE AS A WEAPON**
FULFILLMENT: **APPLYING THEIR TECHNICAL VIRTUOSITY TO GOOD EFFECT**

June 3–10

NEW LANGUAGE
GEMINI II

Gemini II's are intent upon understanding and being understood, and the Way of Discipline will hold ample opportunity for them to work that out. In both social and personal relationships, Gemini II's on this karmic path will doubtless find the venue for self-expression they so desire. Still, they will also have to learn the wisdom of occasional silence, since those with this configuration often form relationships with people less verbally skilled and articulate than themselves. There is also a danger that Gemini II's on this path will do themselves and others great injustice through their need to win an argument at all costs. Though verbally gifted enough to be able to do so, they may win such battles at the expense of losing the war. Often their tendency to be hypercritical is the projection of a poor self-image. Yet over time, as they work to refine and perfect themselves as required by the Way of Discipline, Gemini II's will be rewarded with the affection and understanding of others that they so desire.

CHALLENGE: **DEPERSONALIZING THEIR MODE OF COMMUNICATION ENOUGH TO RELATE TO OTHERS**
FULFILLMENT: **IMPROVING THE QUALITY OF THEIR ASSOCIATIONS**
NOTABLE: **JUDY GARLAND (SINGER; FILM STAR)**

ROCKY GRAZIANO
Middleweight champ

6/7/1922
Gemini II

June 11–18

THE SEEKER
GEMINI III

Testing the limits of relationships and social structures will be paramount to Gemini III's on the Way of Discipline. Those born during the Week of the Seeker are blessed with the ability to go far beyond ordinary boundaries in their quest for perfection and equally blessed with the determination and ambition to do just that. Their fascination with the truth will doubtless require that more than once in their lives they will have to get to the bottom of things before they rise to the top. The Way of Discipline sometimes demands greater depth from these interesting, entertaining people, and they may have to learn the lessons of thoroughness and practical application before they can truly progress. Gemini III's can also be hampered by an inability to break entirely free from their parents or communities of origin. Still, with their keen intellects, fine insight, and subtle charm, the Way of Discipline holds great promise and infinite variety for these knowledge-hungry souls.

CHALLENGE: **BEING EVER CONSCIOUS OF THEIR OWN ABILITY TO BE MANIPULATIVE**
FULFILLMENT: **SPURRING THEMSELVES TO GO EVEN DEEPER IN THEIR SEARCH FOR THE TRUTH**
NOTABLE: **MORRIS UDALL (POLITICAL FIGURE)**

KARMIC PATH
2

June 19–24
MAGIC
GEMINI–CANCER CUSP

While there is a chance that Gemini–Cancers may withdraw from the challenges of the Way of Discipline by retreating into a private universe, there is an equal possibility that they will direct their natural concern for others and great capacity for love toward any number of social and personal causes. Religious, philosophical, and artistic crusades will repeatedly present themselves to Gemini–Cancers on this karmic path, and over time they will learn to weigh the importance of larger social issues against their need for privacy. Too, there is a danger that their pet ideas and inspirations may go untested in reality, resulting in a kind of chronic frustration with the way their lives are as opposed to how they might have been. Still, if these gentle, sensitive people can remain grounded in practical reality while at the same time allowing their romantic and imaginative natures to inspire those around them, the Way of Discipline will prove both fruitful and rewarding.

ELEANOR PARKER
1940s film actress

6/26/1922
Cancer I

CHALLENGE: **DETACHING SUFFICIENTLY FOR THINGS TO WOUND THEM LESS**
FULFILLMENT: **APPLYING THEIR ROMANTIC VISION IN REAL TERMS**
NOTABLE: **AAGE NIELS BOHR (NOBEL WINNER, PHYSICS)**

June 25–July 2
THE EMPATH
CANCER I

When those born in the Week of the Empath tread the Way of Discipline, it will be extremely important for them to gain objectivity and learn to separate the head from the heart. Their impulse to identify with others can manifest in a need to reform or change people and situations, and their strong emotionality can sometimes make it difficult for them to see when such situations are unproductive or even hopeless. Thus, Cancer I's can sometimes find it difficult to "let go and let God" and may invest too much of their ego and self-image in successful outcomes. Though Cancer I's can misuse their energies, their natural affinity for technical projects and systems can do much to offset their emotional nature. Grounding themselves in systems and organizations that work toward the larger good will show them how it is possible to help others without necessarily having to "save" them first.

CHALLENGE: **UNDERSTANDING THAT IT IS NOT USUALLY WITHIN THEIR POWER TO RESCUE EVERYONE**
FULFILLMENT: **CONTRIBUTING TO THE IMPROVEMENT OF ORGANIZATIONS OR SYSTEMS ON A LARGER SCALE**
NOTABLE: **DAN ROWAN (COMEDIAN, *LAUGH-IN*)**

July 3–10
THE UNCONVENTIONAL
CANCER II

When placed on the Way of Discipline, Cancer II individuals have a strong impulse to put the stamp of individuality on any situation or relationship, and they may experience some conflict as to whether they want to gain personal recognition for their efforts or to "raise the class average" as a whole. Responsible and kind, Cancer II's are nevertheless quite capable of asserting themselves as the situation requires and in some instances may be perceived as quite demanding. These people gain a great deal of security and satisfaction by seeing their projects come to fruition, though they may stall on the way when they discover that reality is rarely as perfect or orderly as their ideals. Though Cancer II's may fight the tendency, their attraction to the unconventional and untried will serve them well on the Way of Discipline, for it is sure to be exotic people, places, and things that will inspire them to expand their horizons.

P.T. BARNUM
seen here with Tom Thumb.
Circus promoter,
"Greatest Show on Earth"

7/5/1810
Cancer II

CHALLENGE: **TAKING CARE TO CHANGE THINGS FOR THE BETTER, NOT JUST TO HOW THEY WANT THEM TO BE**
FULFILLMENT: **SEEING ONE OF THEIR MORE INVENTIVE IDEAS TAKE HOLD IN A PRACTICAL FORM**
NOTABLE: **JOHN SINGLETON COPLEY (ARTIST, PORTRAIT OF PAUL REVERE)**

July 11–18
THE PERSUADER
CANCER III

Well grounded in the facts and figures necessary to implement their ideals, the Way of Discipline holds great promise for these passionate, powerful people. Blessed with the ability to get things done, Cancer III's may, however, become too caught up in the details of carrying out their plans to be able to view their own larger purposes accurately. Principles are very important to those with this configuration, and Cancer III's may take the world a little too personally when things don't go according to their plans. Perhaps the main danger here is that they may be as hard on the people around them as they are on themselves. By educating themselves in the ways of tolerance, patience, and the natural give-and-take of relationships, those born in the Week of the Persuader will learn to be more accepting of themselves, gaining a great deal of confidence and wisdom in the process. Still, these dynamic people will make their mark here, and the world will be the better for it.

CHALLENGE: **BEING LESS HARD ON THEMSELVES AND OTHERS**
FULFILLMENT: **USING THE POWER OF PERSUASION TO MAKE CHANGES FOR THE BETTER**
NOTABLE: **SUZANNE VEGA (SINGER/SONGWRITER)**

July 19–25
OSCILLATION
CANCER–LEO CUSP

Cancer–Leos on this karmic path will doubtless come to experience the truth of the adage "To rule is to serve" at some point in their lives. In truth, Cancer–Leos make fine rulers and managers of all kinds, yet there is an equal possibility that they will become so caught up in their internal dramas and conflicts that they fail to successfully develop the detachment necessary to negotiate this path successfully. There is a danger that they will fall prey to the tyranny of their own emotions from time to time, making others the unwilling victims of and participants in dramas of their own making. Yet it is precisely by dedicating themselves to a larger ideal or social system and working for the good of all that those born on the Cusp of Oscillation will free themselves. Nonetheless, these dynamic individuals are blessed with the kind of moral conviction and courage that can make them truly fearless leaders and administrators. And those qualities, combined with their natural wisdom, can be pressed into the service of collective, rather than personal, needs and goals.

CHALLENGE: **BEING OBJECTIVE IN ALL MATTERS**

FULFILLMENT: **ADHERING TO THEIR MORAL CONVICTIONS AS THEY WORK FOR A LARGER IDEAL**

ROSANNA ARQUETTE
Actress,
Desperately Seeking Susan

8/10/1959
Leo II

July 26–August 2
AUTHORITY
LEO I

Commanding, expansive, and naturally sincere, Leo I's will nevertheless have to be mindful of their tendency to overassert their authority. When placed on the Way of Discipline, those born in the Week of Authority may have to overcome great odds and suffer many personal disappointments before coming to terms with the fact that the way of success lies outside the sphere of personal needs and gratification. Naturally assertive, Leo I's generally have no trouble in getting others to do what they want them to, yet the limitations of their authority will become obvious if they neglect other people's desires in the process. They have a tendency to be rather overbearing or even downright dictatorial as they try to implement their vision of what is right. Still, these powerful people's natural attraction to the larger ideals and causes of humanity will never be entirely neglected, and providing they temper their personal needs with objectivity, they are sure to achieve much on the Way of Discipline.

CHALLENGE: **TRAINING TO BE MORE SOCIALLY CONSCIOUS**

FULFILLMENT: **BEING ABLE TO IMPOSE SOME OF THEIR STANDARDS ON THE WORLD AT LARGE**

NOTABLE: **BEATRIX POTTER (CHILDREN'S BOOK AUTHOR/ ILLUSTRATOR, *PETER RABBIT*)**

August 3–10
BALANCED STRENGTH
LEO II

Naturally tough, individuals born during the Week of Balanced Strength should have little trouble rising to the challenges presented by the Way of Discipline, and whatever their choices along the road, they are likely to be well informed and carefully considered. Idealistic, socially inclined, and very loyal by nature, Leo II's are inspired enough to "dream the impossible dream" but wise enough not to expect the dream to materialize in reality. Thus, they are usually able to work toward the highest goals and aspirations without having to endure too much in the way of disillusion or disappointment. Leo II's do well to be aware of the dangers of trying to do everything themselves, however. For this karmic path also demands the willingness to work with others and to form meaningful relationships with those able to help them along the way. Still, if Leo II's cultivate their need to share and learn to relinquish control to the larger designs of fate, they are likely to find this quite an easy road.

CHALLENGE: **NOT BEING TOO MASOCHISTIC IN THEIR SEARCH FOR PERFECTION**

FULFILLMENT: **FINDING THEMSELVES IN A SOCIAL MILIEU WHERE HONESTY IS THE NORM**

NOTABLE: **LOUIS B. LEAKEY (ARCHEOLOGIST; PHYSICAL ANTHROPOLOGIST)**

EARVIN "MAGIC" JOHNSON
U.S. basketball player for Los Angeles Lakers; retired after testing positive for HIV

8/14/1959
Leo III

August 11–18
LEADERSHIP
LEO III

Faith in themselves and in others makes Leo III's with this configuration more than likely to succeed in any chosen field of endeavor. Natural leaders, Leo III's are attracted to systems and organizations dedicated to improving the world, and these popular personalities are likely to rise to the top of many such groups in the course of their lives. Providing Leo III individuals do not succumb to the dangers of hubris and a preoccupation with more egocentric views of the world, they will doubtless go far indeed. They do well to choose partners and associates whom they consider their equals and who are capable of working side by side with them or even taking the reins from their hands. In fact, the issue of equality in relationships may well be an important one, for Leo III's do not give up control easily and sometimes find it difficult to view other people's efforts with the same degree of confidence and appreciation that they do their own. Still, if they allow the feelings of others to serve as a barometer of how well they're doing, they are likely to do very well indeed.

CHALLENGE: **BECOMING A BETTER ANALYZER OF DATA**

FULFILLMENT: **WORKING SIDE BY SIDE WITH OTHERS TO BETTER A PROJECT, SYSTEM, OR CAUSE**

August 19–25

EXPOSURE
LEO–VIRGO CUSP

Leo–Virgos on the Way of Discipline will doubtless experience more than a little conflict among their close relationships and the world of larger social responsibilities. Whatever their childhood environment, they were probably imbued with a sense of ambition that can be hard to reconcile with the ideals of service and discipline. Thus, their conflicts may manifest as lackluster careers that are offset by colorful personal lives or vice versa. The Way of Discipline demands greater integration of their sometimes opposing tendencies and inclinations. Still, as they mature, their natural honesty and sense of integrity will drive them to greater degrees of perfection and set them on the path of higher standards of behavior. Those born on the Cusp of Exposure are excellent judges of character and objective observers of society. If they can manage to reconcile their personal conflicts, they will be free to work on the greater needs of humanity with diligence, loyalty, and dedication.

LOUIS XVI
Executed following
French Revolution

8/23/1754
Leo–Virgo Cusp

CHALLENGE: **DEMANDING A LITTLE LESS PERFECTION FROM THEMSELVES AND OTHERS**
FULFILLMENT: **EXPOSING INEFFICIENCY OF ALL KINDS**
NOTABLES: **JIM MCMAHON (FOOTBALL PLAYER); THEODORE PARKER (MINISTER; ANTISLAVERY LEADER)**

August 26–September 2

SYSTEM BUILDERS
VIRGO I

Those born in the Week of System Builders are likely to find themselves extremely happy on the Way of Discipline, as long as they do not become so preoccupied by details and structure that they lose sight of their larger, more idealistic goals. Still, this configuration is likely to manifest itself in some manner of service, whether it be in their family, in social organizations, or in their professional lives. Virgo I's are rather businesslike by nature, and some of their friends and family might find their mania for self-improvement rather off-putting or cold. It may be a challenge for the Virgo I's on this karmic path not to attempt to shore up their self-image by turning inward in an increasingly exacting fashion or to impose their sometimes rigid beliefs on others. Still, if Virgo I's on the Way of Discipline work to combine their natural modesty and dependability with greater flexibility and tolerance, success will come quite easily for them.

CHALLENGE: **NOT DRIVING THEMSELVES CRAZY WITH THEIR NEED FOR EVERY DETAIL TO BE PERFECT**
FULFILLMENT: **FINDING THAT BEING DISCIPLINED GIVES THEM A SENSE OF COMFORT AND SAFETY**
NOTABLE: **ARTHUR GODFREY (RADIO/TV ENTERTAINER)**

September 3–10

THE ENIGMA
VIRGO II

High standards and a strict moral code tend to characterize Virgo II individuals, and they are destined for success on the Way of Discipline, providing they learn the necessary lessons in the sphere of interpersonal relationships. Though they can be quite loving, it may be difficult for them to express their personal needs and vulnerability adequately. Their natural reserve and dislike of emotional displays can be misinterpreted as aloofness, and they must be careful not to isolate themselves or shut down emotionally when love does not come easily. Too, those born in the Week of the Enigma can become so preoccupied with what others may think of them that they neglect to think about others at all. Yet if they cultivate their natural talent for communication in their personal relationships, remember not to take themselves too seriously, and keep in mind that they are here to learn that, indeed, "no one is an island," their progress on the Way of Discipline is ensured.

CAPTAIN WILLIAM BLIGH
Commander of
HMS *Bounty*

9/9/1754
Virgo II

CHALLENGE: **LETTING GO OF THEIR PICKINESS WHEN CHOOSING A PARTNER**
FULFILLMENT: **PUTTING THEIR FINE DISCRIMINATION AND ANALYTIC ABILITY TO WORK**

September 11–18

THE LITERALIST
VIRGO III

Those born in this week who travel the Way of Discipline are likely to have a fine instinct for getting to the heart of things and zooming in on what matters most in practical efforts. Still, they have a tendency to go overboard at times and should guard against the dangers of becoming too didactic or narrow-minded in their view of how things should be done. Though their innate dislike of conflict and confrontation can make them rather manipulative, it is equally likely that they will be able to get their ideas across with an attitude that is both polite and no-nonsense. Their high standards will serve them well, however, and their natural capability, keen sense of observation, and diligence in getting a job done make them destined for success on this karmic path. Whatever their calling, they can be counted upon to tell the truth, solve problems, and get results, whether it makes them popular or not.

CHALLENGE: **OFFSETTING A DEMANDING ATTITUDE TOWARD OTHERS WITH GREATER GENEROSITY OF SPIRIT**
FULFILLMENT: **FINDING JOY IN SEEING THEIR SHREWD EVALUATIONS PROVE TO BE CORRECT**
NOTABLE: **ROY ACUFF (COUNTRY MUSIC SINGER; FIDDLER)**

September 19–24
BEAUTY
VIRGO–LIBRA CUSP

Blessed with great idealism and sensitivity, those born on the Cusp of Beauty may find their communicative talents put to the test in the sphere of personal relationships. Often Virgo–Libras will fall under the domination of a more stable and stalwart love partner or family member, and despite their keen perception of social issues and their knack for sounding necessary alarms, they may ignore the challenge of this karmic path and fail to speak up for either their own or other people's rights. Indeed, they can get mired in their desire to please all the people all the time and experience decidedly mixed results when their natural diplomacy is used to mask the real issues. It's important for Virgo–Libras to develop real standards and to cultivate their highest sense of right and wrong. Still, if they make an effort to use their talents for harmony in the service of tangible goals, they will find—to their great delight—that it is possible to be both popular and respected.

PAUL WILLIAMS
Songwriter-turned-counselor

———

9/19/1940
Virgo–Libra Cusp

CHALLENGE: **RELEASING THEIR NEED TO BE POPULAR IN ORDER TO MAKE TOUGH CHOICES**

FULFILLMENT: **APPLYING THEIR FINELY CULTIVATED AESTHETIC SENSIBILITY**

September 25–October 2
THE PERFECTIONIST
LIBRA I

For those born in the Week of the Perfectionist, the principal challenge of the Way of Discipline will be to learn when and how to "go with the flow." Perfectionists by nature, Libra I's can go overboard when placed on this karmic path and become difficult, cranky, and "holier than thou." Much of their insistence on perfection, however, arises from an inner need for security, and they should keep in mind that it is not always necessary to have their physical environment in order before they allow themselves to grow and expand spiritually. Libra I individuals would do well to cultivate the kind of intimate relationships that don't make them feel as though they are somehow "not good enough." On the other hand, many Libra I's make the mistake of choosing inappropriate or unequal partners and associates simply to make themselves feel more important, competent, educated, and so forth. Still, if they make an effort to cultivate flexibility and tolerance, their natural sense of fairness and humanity will triumph.

CHALLENGE: **NURTURING THEIR INNER CHILD**

FULFILLMENT: **USING WIT TO POINT OUT INEFFICIENCY**

NOTABLE: **JERRY LEE LEWIS (MUSICIAN, "WHOLE LOTTA SHAKIN' GOIN' ON")**

October 3–10
SOCIETY
LIBRA II

With individuals born in the Week of Society, social issues and causes may be exalted at the expense of more intimate relationships, and though they are likely to do well on the Way of Discipline, they will probably have to face challenges from the more personal side of life, generally in the area of family relationships. Natural reformers and crusaders, Libra II's can neglect the needs of their nearest and dearest in the interest of larger issues. Equally, their great need for peace can cause them to retreat from conflicts and problems, so that they fail to take up the challenge of this karmic path and employ their considerable communicative talents to make the world a better place. Libra II's on this path need to get in touch with the simple fact that what they want is usually not so very different from what everyone else wants. That realization will allow them to unite with others in such a way that they can use their special diplomatic and verbal gifts in the pursuit of humanity's highest goals.

JOHN LENNON
Songwriter, member of The Beatles; shot by fan in 1980

———

10/9/1940
Libra II

CHALLENGE: **WORKING ON THE QUALITY OF THEIR MOST INTIMATE RELATIONSHIPS**

FULFILLMENT: **HONING THEIR POWERS OF OBSERVATION TO EXCEL AT SPOTTING LARGER SOCIETAL TRENDS**

NOTABLE: **THOMAS MORE (AUTHOR, *CARE OF THE SOUL*)**

October 11–18
THEATER
LIBRA III

Those born in the Week of Theater have worldly personalities and may encounter some degree of adventure on the Way of Discipline, though they will likely have a sense of drama in even the most ordinary circumstances. Keenly sensitive to injustice in any form, Libra III's may nevertheless get mired in a chronic need for attention and acceptance before turning their considerable intellectual and spiritual talents to the larger world. It is likely that whatever their chosen field of endeavor, they will invent or reinvent themselves several times over, changing careers, locales, lifestyles, friends, and love interests many times. Libra III's do well to cultivate stable relationships with people who ground them a bit. Confidence and experience will do much to mellow their rather tumultuous view of life, however, and if they are careful not to become overly caught up in life's little soap operas, their perception, insight, and objectivity will serve them well.

CHALLENGE: **NOT BECOMING EMBROILED IN THEATRICAL DISPLAYS**

FULFILLMENT: **BEING VALUED FOR THE STRENGTH OF THEIR VIEWPOINTS DUE TO THEIR ORIGINATION IN HARD DATA**

NOTABLE: **BARRY MOSER (BOOKMAN; ILLUSTRATOR; ENGRAVER)**

October 19–25

DRAMA AND CRITICISM
LIBRA–SCORPIO CUSP

Charismatic and communicative in the extreme, those born on the Libra–Scorpio cusp have a curious knack not only for knowing when they are right but for being able to convince others of it as well. Perhaps the principal danger here is that inner conflict will express itself in difficult personal and family relationships, for these people can see other people's patterns of behavior much more easily than their own. As a result, Libra–Scorpios can become overcritical and demanding, using their considerable verbal talents to point out the failings of others or the world at large without the concomitant self-examination that is necessary. Too, they are somewhat scornful of more conventional morality and may set decidedly different standards of behavior for themselves than for their loved ones. Nevertheless, if Libra–Scorpios can discipline themselves to remain aware of their own inner motivations without abusing their power to motivate others, their path to success is ensured.

JOHN GOTTI
New York crime boss

10/27/1940
Scorpio I

CHALLENGE: **SOFTENING THE EXPRESSION OF THEIR OPINIONS**
FULFILLMENT: **SENSING THAT THEIR INSIGHTFULNESS IS VALUED**
NOTABLE: **BOBBY KNIGHT (BASKETBALL COACH)**

October 26–November 2

INTENSITY
SCORPIO I

Scorpio I's can be very hard on themselves when placed on the Way of Discipline. Blessed with a highly developed conscience and sense of morality, they are well suited to the demands of the Way of Discipline yet can become too judgmental or preoccupied with details. Guilt can also be a stumbling block for Scorpio I individuals, and they can hang themselves up by refusing to be more tolerant of their own and others' failings. Whatever the job at hand, however, Scorpio I will get it done and done well. Responsibility comes quite naturally for them, and they will never pass the buck or shirk their duties for some lighter diversion. In fact, those born in the Week of Intensity would do well to remain aware of the dangers of taking oneself too seriously. Yet if they can cultivate a lighter approach to the world and its foibles and avoid the tendency to develop a sort of tunnel vision regarding their causes, they will find themselves more able to persuade others to adopt their ideals.

CHALLENGE: **LETTING UP ON THE INTENSITY OF THEIR DRIVE FOR PERFECTION**
FULFILLMENT: **PERFECTING THEIR TALENTS AND APTITUDES TO THE POINT OF HIGH ART**

November 3–11

DEPTH
SCORPIO II

Though Scorpio II individuals are likely to succeed in worldly and material terms, they can falter on the Way of Discipline if they are not careful to cultivate their more spiritual side. It is important for those born in the Week of Depth to connect with individuals and social systems that will steer them away from self-absorption and toward a larger good. Escapist tendencies may also prove a problem, as may a tendency to mood swings. The area of personal relationships will prove especially instructive for those born in the Week of Depth as they learn to put their own needs aside and share with partners or family members. Too, they may form relationships with those who awaken their spiritual selves, whether for good or for ill. Still, if they avoid the pitfalls of jealousy, possessiveness, and too frequent emotional outbursts, the Way of Discipline will be a path to both material success and spiritual integration.

WALKER EVANS
American photographer

11/3/1903
Scorpio II

CHALLENGE: **LETTING GO OF RESENTMENT IN FAVOR OF A "LIVE AND LET LIVE" ATTITUDE**
FULFILLMENT: **KNOWING THAT THEY HAVE BETTERED THE LIVES OF THEIR LOVED ONES**

November 12–18

CHARM
SCORPIO III

Blessed with the relatively rare combination of both realism and charm, Scorpio III's are likely to do wonderfully well when placed on this karmic path. Their considerable verbal skills and talents will likely manifest themselves in a high degree of diplomacy, a gracious manner, and considerable insight into situations in which they find themselves. The principal challenge here will be to put their own interests aside as a means of accomplishing some greater purpose. And whether that challenge manifests itself in the larger social arena or in that of purely personal relationships, it is likely to be a challenge indeed. Some on this path may have experienced emotional or material deprivation early on, and their resulting sense of insecurity can retard their spiritual development. Still, if they learn to distinguish between sensible self-interest and simple selfishness and to utilize their communicative talents in an open, truthful, and responsible manner, the Way of Discipline holds great promise for them.

CHALLENGE: **LEARNING TO BE DIRECT RATHER THAN INDULGING IN CHILDISH MANIPULATION**
FULFILLMENT: **FEELING THAT THEY HAVE A GREATER PURPOSE IN LIFE**

November 19–24

REVOLUTION
SCORPIO–SAGITTARIUS CUSP

Scorpio–Sagittarians are all but assured of experiencing the improvements and transformations promised by the Way of Discipline. Their natural empathy has a universal quality, and even if they encounter their karmic lessons in personal relationships alone, they are likely to be able to apply that knowledge in larger, more universal ways. Fearless fighters, those born on the Cusp of Revolution will connect with larger ideals and purposes yet they may experience a number of revolutions in their personal lives as well. Conflicts in family relationships may force them to reevaluate their roots, and their need for freedom may cause them to make a complete break with their past. Overidealism can be a problem and exist at odds with the attention to detail demanded by this karmic path. Still, these inspirational, imaginative people should find great success on the Way of Discipline, especially when they learn to temper their sometimes sarcastic communicative talents with wisdom and humor.

BRUCE LEE

Actor; martial-arts expert

11/27/1940
Sagittarius I

CHALLENGE: **KNOWING WHEN TO DETACH FROM THEIR OWN IDEAS**

FULFILLMENT: **SEEING THEIR IDEAS FOR REFORM TAKE SHAPE**

NOTABLE: **TERRY GILLIAM (COMEDIAN; DIRECTOR, MONTY PYTHON)**

November 25–December 2

INDEPENDENCE
SAGITTARIUS I

While those born in the Week of Independence are blessed with a highly developed sense of honor and fairness that will lead them to connect with the larger social causes and ideals demanded by the Way of Discipline, their intense need for freedom may prove problematic on this path. Blessed with a childlike enthusiasm, they may find it difficult to learn to control their tempers, and they may also have a tendency to bowl others over with histrionics when a well-thought-out, quieter presentation would do. Many Sagittarius I's are not nearly as confident as they appear, and they can become overly defensive when their views and opinions are challenged to any degree. Nonetheless, they are honorable in the extreme and when working toward a greater good will find and apply the discipline demanded by this karmic path.

CHALLENGE: **NOT FEELING CONTROLLED BY OUTSIDE FORCES**

FULFILLMENT: **USING THEIR OBSERVANT MINDS AND VERBAL ACUITY TO CONVINCE OTHERS OF THE NEED FOR CHANGE**

December 3–10

THE ORIGINATOR
SAGITTARIUS II

It may be something of a struggle for these sometimes eccentric souls to find themselves on the Way of Discipline. Though Sagittarius II's will doubtless do their best to rise to the top of any profession or chosen field of endeavor, their more unusual and even exotic qualities and inclinations may serve as a distraction from their impulse to perfect themselves. In a word, Sagittarius II's can be far more passionate in thinking about a particular subject or cause than in actually being involved with it. The same idealism can spill over into their personal relationships as well, and they will often put an interesting or unusual partner on something of a pedestal as a means of avoiding greater intimacy. It may be quite some time before Sagittarius II's mellow enough to be able to slow down and develop the more introspective, spiritual sides of their natures. Yet once they do, they will be rewarded with a depth of perception and experience that only a few can imagine.

RICHARD PRYOR

Controversial
comedian/actor; struggled
with drug addiction

12/1/1940
Sagittarius I

CHALLENGE: **WARMING TO GREATER INVOLVEMENT WITH OTHERS**

FULFILLMENT: **ORIGINATING OPERATING IMPROVEMENTS AT WORK**

December 11–18

THE TITAN
SAGITTARIUS III

For Sagittarius III individuals to face the challenges presented on the Way of Discipline, they must develop a greater awareness of what makes them and others tick. Though quite generous and big-hearted by nature, those born in the Week of the Titan can nonetheless be plagued by a troublesome instability that can prove a real stumbling block to their spiritual and, in some cases, material progress. Sagittarius III's must develop greater empathy and subdue, or at least better manage, their need for approval. Inner anxieties can also make this group rather fussy, and they can obsess over the details of projects and plans to the point where they frustrate themselves and everyone else. Still, Sagittarius III's have a kind of larger-than-life quality, and if they use it for the benefit of others, rather than simply to dominate or subdue their detractors, they are likely to rise in the world, accompanied by a faithful and devoted following of friends, family, and fans.

CHALLENGE: **GIVING UP ALL THEIR SECRET MEANS OF SELF-PUNISHMENT**

FULFILLMENT: **IMPLEMENTING LARGE-SCALE PLANS FOR THE EFFICIENT OPERATION OF THEIR HOME OR WORK ENVIRONMENT**

NOTABLE: **TOM HAYDEN (ACTIVIST; LEGISLATOR)**

December 19–25

PROPHECY
SAGITTARIUS–CAPRICORN CUSP

This is a road fraught with both danger and blessings, for though Sagittarius–Capricorns are well suited to the demands of this karmic path, these personalities can experience no small amount of conflict as they work to reconcile their urge for perfection in the details of their lives with their impulse toward expansion. The resulting tension can manifest itself in a kind of "sky is falling!" mentality, and they may squander their gifts of foresight and insight in anxiety. Hurts and frustrations in the personal sphere can further cause them to withdraw and refuse to take responsibility for events that they would like to believe are outside their control. Still, this path much improves their talents at communication, and if those born on the Sagittarius–Capricorn cusp work to express themselves in a such a way as not to alarm or alienate those around them, their considerable extrasensory and spiritual gifts will come to the fore, and they will achieve great recognition for their efforts.

CHALLENGE: **BECOMING LESS FOOLHARDY AND IMPULSIVE IN THE EXPRESSION OF THEIR VIEWS**
FULFILLMENT: **HAVING A FIRM HAND ON THE REINS OF MANAGERIAL OR ADMINISTRATIVE CONTROL**

JOAN BAEZ
Leading American folk-singer

—

1/9/1941
Capricorn II

December 26–January 2

THE RULER
CAPRICORN I

Capricorn I's on this path are sure to show genuine, heartfelt concern for those around them. Gifted with a fine talent for leadership and dogged determination, those born in the Week of the Ruler should, however, guard against a tendency toward tyranny in their dealings with others. In the field of family and social relationships, their great need for love and connection may be hidden under a tough, demanding exterior, and they can be quite exacting and dogmatic when it comes to dealing with spouses, children, and friends. For those reasons, Capricorn I's do well to make a genuine effort to get in touch with their spiritual and emotional side and not to be afraid to show some vulnerability. Still, when it comes to making a better life for themselves, their families, and society as a whole, there are none who work harder, longer, or with more determination to succeed.

CHALLENGE: **NOT BEING TOO EXACTING A TASKMASTER TO THEIR INNER CHILD**
FULFILLMENT: **MANAGING AN ENTERPRISE WHERE THEY CAN DIRECTLY IMPACT THE BOTTOM LINE**
NOTABLES: **JAMES BURROWS (DIRECTOR, *CHEERS*); PHIL SPECTOR (RECORD PRODUCER)**

January 3–9

DETERMINATION
CAPRICORN II

For Capricorn II's, the Way of Discipline is likely to manifest itself in a demand that their religious or philosophical theories be put into practice in the interest of a larger good. Some Capricorn II's may be overly sensitive and retreat from the challenge of this configuration into cynicism and personal touchiness, while others may preoccupy themselves with trying to reform an unworthy partner and neglect themselves in the process. Maturity is likely to improve their judgment about people and things, freeing them from the need for approval and blessing them with a unique sense of humor and perspective on the world. As sound as their advice and insights can be, they must take care not to resist the suggestions of others out of sheer stubbornness or fear of change. When those born in the Week of Determination learn that self-improvement is necessary to all growth and not evidence of some personal insufficiency, they are likely to flourish and gain the necessary confidence to reach for their personal star.

CHALLENGE: **SOFTENING THEIR HARDHEADED APPROACH TO SEEING THEIR WILL PREVAIL**
FULFILLMENT: **PUTTING THEIR DOWN-TO-EARTH THEORIES OF ORGANIZATIONAL BEHAVIOR INTO PRACTICE**

FAYE DUNAWAY
Won Oscar for *Network*

—

1/14/1941
Capricorn III

January 10–16

DOMINANCE
CAPRICORN III

Both great saints and terrible sinners can be found with this configuration, for whatever Capricorn III's do, they are unlikely to do it halfway. When placed on the Way of Discipline, they have a great tendency to become self-sacrificing in the extreme. Thus, here is where quite a number of hair shirt wearers and doomsayers are found, for Capricorn III's can be quite pessimistic about the future of those less interested in reformation than they are. For these individuals, who are highly physical but not especially sensual, the need for self-improvement may also manifest itself in the adoption of a strenuous exercise regime or, in extreme cases, problems such as eating disorders. The key to success here is turning their formidable determination outward and connecting with a social cause or system that will absorb their attention without narrowing their focus. Once they are so connected, those born in the Week of Dominance will prove invaluable in their dedication, their strong sense of morality, and their loyalty to a cause.

CHALLENGE: **CONNECTING TO A LARGER SOCIAL CAUSE OR PURPOSE**
FULFILLMENT: **IMPOSING THEIR OWN MANAGEMENT STYLE**
NOTABLE: **CAPTAIN BEEFHEART (MUSICIAN)**

KARMIC PATH
2

January 17–22

MYSTERY AND IMAGINATION
CAPRICORN–AQUARIUS CUSP

The individuals born in the Week of Mystery and Imagination are exciting people likely to flourish on the Way of Discipline, as long as they do not become too excitable or uncontrolled in their attempts to alert the rest of us to the problems of the world. Naturally vivid and expressive, Capricorn–Aquarians are very much at home on this path, for they are blessed with a great sensitivity to the causes of the downtrodden and have an inborn need to make the world a better place. Yet there is a danger that in grappling with the issues at hand, they may set themselves up as both judge and jury, failing to take into account the infinite variables that come to bear when different personalities work together for a common goal. Whether they realize it or not, these highly independent people need others as much as others need them. Yet if they take care to cultivate relationships with those who will steady them without boring them to tears, their natural humor, sense of duty, and truly creative approach to problem solving will serve them well.

CHALLENGE: **TAMING THEIR OFTEN FRENETIC ENERGIES**
FULFILLMENT: **HELPING THOSE LESS FORTUNATE**
NOTABLES: **BOBBY GOLDSBORO (SINGER); JAMES WATT (INVENTOR OF STEAM ENGINE)**

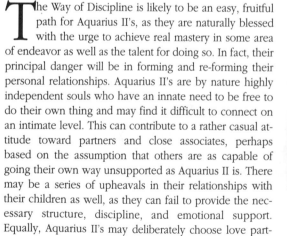

PLÁCIDO DOMINGO
Leading opera tenor

1/21/1941
Capricorn–Aquarius Cusp

January 23–30

GENIUS
AQUARIUS I

The gifted, futuristic Aquarius I people on this karmic path are likely to succeed in almost any area of endeavor, providing they manage to connect with the more personal sides of life. Though Aquarius I's are blessed with natural humanitarianism and a keen sense of justice, they are nevertheless quite capable of detaching emotionally and viewing people and situations more as abstractions than as realities. However impartial their sense of justice, it will remain blind until they sensitize themselves to others' motives and emotions. In family and personal relationships, Aquarius I's should also work to steer clear of personal touchiness, for they can also be self-centered at times. Thus, the great challenge for those on this karmic path will be to hone their expressive talents in such a way that their messages to the world can be absorbed on a personal rather than purely intellectual level. Then their ideals are sure to resonate in us all.

CHALLENGE: **LEARNING TO ANALYZE THEIR INTIMATE ENDEAVORS LESS**
FULFILLMENT: **WORKING FROM OUTSIDE CORPORATE OR SOCIETAL STRUCTURES TO IMPROVE THEM**
NOTABLES: **NEIL DIAMOND (SINGER); AARON NEVILLE (SINGER, THE NEVILLE BROTHERS)**

January 31–February 7

YOUTH AND EASE
AQUARIUS II

The Way of Discipline is likely to be an easy, fruitful path for Aquarius II's, as they are naturally blessed with the urge to achieve real mastery in some area of endeavor as well as the talent for doing so. In fact, their principal danger will be in forming and re-forming their personal relationships. Aquarius II's are by nature highly independent souls who have an innate need to be free to do their own thing and may find it difficult to connect on an intimate level. This can contribute to a rather casual attitude toward partners and close associates, perhaps based on the assumption that others are as capable of going their own way unsupported as Aquarius II is. There may be a series of upheavals in their relationships with their children as well, as they can fail to provide the necessary structure, discipline, and emotional support. Equally, Aquarius II's may deliberately choose love partners who appear to require of them far more than they are prepared to give. Still, their easygoing ways should serve them in good stead on this path, and with a modicum of self-awareness, they should find the deepest happiness.

CHALLENGE: **NOT TAKING THE PATH OF LEAST RESISTANCE**
FULFILLMENT: **MASTERING A CRAFT OR OTHER SKILL**
NOTABLE: **JOHANN ALBRECHTSBERGE (COMPOSER)**

SINCLAIR LEWIS
Journalist/writer; first American to win Nobel Prize in literature

2/7/1885
Aquarius II

February 8–15

ACCEPTANCE
AQUARIUS III

Blessed with a fine sense of justice and social conscience, those born in the Week of Acceptance are likely to become staunch champions of a variety of social causes and expressive and passionate spokespeople for the rights of all. The Way of Discipline will doubtless demand that they let go of many early attitudes and prejudices and turn loose some of the baggage carried from childhood. Thus transformed, they will lose many of their more temperamental aspects and become creative and useful problem solvers in almost any field. Their principal challenge will again be in the area of family relationships, since these people's public image is often at odds with their private selves. Aquarius III's can be overly critical of their nearest and dearest and they should take great care not to alienate loved ones with their sometimes picky, demanding behavior. Still, their chances of success are very high, and as they mellow a bit over time, the dramas of the moment should fade rather nicely to color the tapestry of their larger life experience.

CHALLENGE: **MELLOWING SOME OF THEIR OPINIONS OR PREJUDICES**
FULFILLMENT: **EMBRACING A BROADER SET OF PROBLEMS**
NOTABLE: **BESS TRUMAN (FORMER FIRST LADY)**

February 16–22
SENSITIVITY
AQUARIUS–PISCES CUSP

Properly embraced, the challenge of this configuration provides Aquarius–Pisces cusp people the greatest opportunity for success and achievement. The demands of the Way of Discipline will doubtless afford these complex and sometimes contradictory people a wonderful avenue for reconciling the extremes of their natures through social connections and contacts. Through their relationships with others, they can more fully explore the middle ground between the universal and the intimate. The chief problem here is that Aquarius–Pisces individuals may seek out extremes in their associates and partners or view even the mildest interactions in highly dramatic terms. For here is a person who can imagine whole worlds of sex and passion, marriage, divorce, and even death over a single cup of coffee. Still, if they learn to relax a bit and allow themselves to experience some of the infinite variety possible in human relationships, they can learn to find the middle ground called for by this karmic path.

HELEN GURLEY BROWN
Feminist, writer/editor of
Cosmopolitan

———

2/18/1922
Aquarius–Pisces Cusp

CHALLENGE: **NOT PERMITTING THEIR UNDERLYING INSECURITY TO GET THE BETTER OF THEM**

FULFILLMENT: **BECOMING MORE ATTUNED TO THE COOLLY RATIONAL WORLD OF FACTS AND FIGURES**

February 23–March 2
SPIRIT
PISCES I

Philosophical, sensitive, and perceptive, Pisces I individuals may nevertheless find a few stumbling blocks on the Way of Discipline. They tend to be rather thin-skinned as a rule, and their extreme sensitivity may manifest itself in their withdrawing or refusing to connect with the larger social ideals demanded by this karmic path. Equally, the world of personal relationships may prove troublesome, and Pisces I's may find themselves running through quite a number of love partners in the search for an "ideal" relationship. Still, they are blessed with wonderful empathy and a fine sense of humanity that is sure to be expressed in ways that will strike a chord for us all. When Pisces I's speak, they do so from the heart. If they work to cultivate their more practical side and do not place unrealistic expectations upon themselves and others, their intense commitment to righting social wrongs will become evident.

CHALLENGE: **RECOGNIZING THEIR TENDENCY TO TRY TO FIX TOO MANY THINGS—PARTICULARLY PEOPLE**

FULFILLMENT: **ALLOWING THEIR MORE EXPRESSIVE SIDE TO ACT ON BEHALF OF RIGHTING SOCIAL WRONGS**

NOTABLE: **YITZHAK RABIN (LATE ISRAELI PRIME MINISTER; WINNER OF NOBEL PEACE PRIZE; ASSASSINATED)**

March 3–10
THE LONER
PISCES II

Extremes of isolation may plague Pisces II souls placed on this path, for though they are in fact quite comfortable in their private world, they are likely to be troubled by the unfinished business that surrounds their personal and social relationships. These people's soulful quality yearns for sharing and connection, yet they may be unwilling or unable to seek out those connections for themselves. The resulting isolation can manifest itself in self-pity, depression, and extremes of personal touchiness when they are emotionally moved by outside people and events. The need to control can be strong in those born in the Week of the Loner, and they may choose partners over whom they feel they can exert an almost Svengali-like influence. Equally, many Pisces II's will withdraw into pedantic or abstract social studies or try to exert their need to improve and perfect the world while ignoring the more personal side of life. Still, if Pisces II's make the necessary effort to express their views, their influence is likely to be widely felt.

CHALLENGE: **DISPENSING WITH THE NEED FOR SELF-PITY**

FULFILLMENT: **DISCOVERING THAT THEIR OPINIONS AND INSIGHTS ARE CONSIDERED WISE BY OTHERS**

NOTABLES: **RING LARDNER (WRITER; JOURNALIST); JOHN HERSCHEL (ENGLISH SCIENTIST AND ASTRONOMER)**

JACK KEROUAC
Beat writer, *On the Road*

———

3/12/1922
Pisces III

March 11–18
DANCERS AND DREAMERS
PISCES III

These practical yet visionary people have a strong possibility for the highest achievement when placed on the Way of Discipline. Though others may view them as unrealistic or even downright childish, the wonderfully expressive qualities of Pisces III's are sure to touch the hearts and minds of many. However grave a situation, they can imbue their partners and associates with a high degree of hope and inspiration for its improvement. Keenly sensitive, they should take care not to appear too glib or high-handed for fear of alienating those who might help them the most. Too, an air of self-importance can surround Pisces III individuals, and though they are quite sensitized to the needs of others, they can give the impression of carelessness or superficiality. The Way of Discipline will doubtless demand much in the way of personal growth and spiritual expansion from them. Yet if they heed their inner voice and make real contributions to the lives of those around them, they are unlikely to stray far from the path of fulfillment.

CHALLENGE: **TRYING TO BE A LITTLE MORE REALISTIC OR GROUNDED IN THEIR APPROACH**

FULFILLMENT: **SEEING THE SOLUTION TO ANY PROBLEM**

The Way of Compassion

ARIES II TO LIBRA II
Star to Society

It is the destiny of those on the Way of Compassion to learn to mute their own ego drives so that they can become a part of what goes on around them rather than forever demanding to be at the center of things. Those on this karmic path are here to develop a greater commitment to, understanding of, and concern for others. Because these individuals are gifted with the ability to implement their visions, by developing a deeper compassion they have the potential to help create a better world by working toward a greater good—whether for their own families, their community, or society in general. Learning selflessness is an extremely difficult assignment for these individuals, entering the world as they do with a radiant energy that attracts attention and inspires admiration. However, in order to grow spiritually, they must learn to direct the spotlight away from themselves and onto the more important concerns, ideas, or causes of others. Instead of being a single star at the center of their own solar system, those on the Way of Compassion must learn to become one of many in a whole social galaxy.

The most successful of those on this path will firmly set aside their selfish aims to work tirelessly for the common welfare and good. The core lesson for those on this path is that the best interests of a group can be congruent with their own self-interest and that by advancing the cause of their coworkers, family, political group, municipality, country, or humanity as a whole, they are, in fact, advancing their own cause as well. First, however, those on the Way of Compassion must have the capacity to understand what the common good actually is. Assisting such an identification process is the innate visionary ability of those born to this karmic path. The trick for these energetic, on-the-go individuals is stopping long enough in their busy lives to broaden their vision enough to understand those around them. Those who begin the journey at the Aries II point will transform themselves by using their considerable energies selflessly in defense of an entire group.

Unavoidably, these individuals must learn about the nature of compassion. Involving both empathy and sympathy, compassion requires the ability to place oneself in someone else's shoes: to feel as they feel, to see as they see, and to care what happens to them. For those starting out as a Star, both of these skills will need some significant further development. Often they will be confronted by some important lessons involving loss or suffering that will ultimately give them the ability to relate to those less fortunate than themselves. These lessons can take many forms: suffering due to addiction; struggling with their own illness or that of a loved one; money problems, such as undergoing bankruptcy; or the death of near family members. They may also occur on a smaller, less traumatic scale, simply as part

---

CORE LESSON

Placing the good of the
group ahead of self-interest

GOAL

To be worthy of the
trust of others

GIFTS
Goal-oriented, Courageous,
Idealistic

PITFALLS
Overly Emotional, Critical, Petty

of the wounds of everyday life. But it is how the individuals on this karmic path deal with their own personal misfortunes that is significant. Will they devolve into self-pity, or will they rise above it all and perceive that they are not alone; that because of their own experience they have something to offer others? Often it is personal misfortune that sinks the well of compassion into the hearts of these men and women.

The predominant area of challenge for individuals on the Way of Compassion will be the social sphere. Any activity that draws them into contact with their fellow human beings on an equal footing will help them on their way. First, those on this karmic path with be forced to hone their social skills to a fine edge. Despite their tendency to remain aloof, this path will force them to mix with a wide variety of people from all walks of life—whether they like it not. By discovering the ways in which people are alike rather than different, these individuals will finally be able to begin their life's work. This will prove to be a challenge since others are often put off by them and tend to view them, at least initially, as haughty and superior. A positive side effect of this process of forced social interaction is that those on this path will learn much more about the ways of the world, becoming much better informed and plugged into the latest trends. Frequently, the most evolved people on this path will actually become social commentators and critics, successfully overcoming their own narrow perspective of self-interest for the public good.

A hurdle for those on the Way of Compassion is learning actually to give of themselves. They may become irritable when called upon to share, whether their time, their money, or even their personal feelings. All too often those on the Way of Compassion will give generously up to a point and then pull back, particularly if they get little acknowledgment in return. In other cases, the success orientation of those starting out as a Star may be successfully harnessed to a company or other group, but their need to keep the group in the spotlight will be only a thinly disguised extension of their own abnormal need to receive reflected glory, whatever the cost. Obviously, unless those on this karmic path take the time to build a strong set of human values or a moral code, they will be easily lured away from their spiritual path onto the byways of egoism.

People who initially view those on the Way of Compassion as self-centered, narcissistic, or haughty may welcome the transformation in their personality toward more empathy, warmth, and sharing. Naturally, those on this karmic path should avoid sycophants who build them up through fake admiration; most often such dependent individuals are just looking for a source of power they can latch onto. Rather, these individuals would do well

RELEASE

The need for vanity and
ego affirmation

REWARD

The joy of giving of oneself

SUGGESTION

Develop a moral code, and live by it. Find some way to serve others, and stick to it.

to seek out socially skilled people who can introduce them to other groups and individuals engaged in the kinds of humanitarian efforts that will help these travelers progress. Any service activity will help this goal. It is quite possible for those on this karmic path to do a complete turnaround and to begin to live for others, in a healthy sense, rather than needily attracting attention.

Choosing a partner with more of a social conscience may help these individuals; however, their true challenge may be in child rearing. Having children can prove an excellent test for those coming into this lifetime with Aries II energy because they will have to acknowledge the daily needs of others and be forced to serve them but also to discover to what extent their selfishness has dissolved. Every bit of ego they are able to drop in this process should bring fulfillment and reward. Here, it is hoped, they will be compelled to learn how to sacrifice their own needs for the needs of their own children or other children for whom they are responsible. If this particular lesson is not learned, dire consequences are the inevitable result. It may actually be the destiny of those on this karmic path to have unusually talented or special children who require even more attention, time, or care than is typical. Among loved ones, disabilities, illnesses, and accidents will all test the ability of these individuals to give of themselves unselfishly and compassionately.

BALANCE POINT

Personal Needs and
Societal Needs

What is best for those on this karmic path is life situations that challenge them to find a balance between their own personal needs and the needs of those who are near and dear to them. It may be crucial for them to discover the best balance between career and family life if they are truly to do the soul work of putting the interests of others before their own. Making promises and keeping them, giving unconditionally, and fulfilling obligations without feeling resentment will do a great deal to build the moral fiber and character of these individuals. However, it may not hurt if, every once in a while, those on the Way of Compassion totally indulge themselves, since by doing so they will get the desire to do so out of their systems while perhaps realizing how empty pure selfishness can be. A renewed sense of commitment to others might even ensue.

The Way of Compassion might be likened to an individual looking into a mirror admiringly, only to watch her image dissolve and reassemble into a kaleidoscopic of smaller images, each representing various individuals in her life, past and present. This image of a multiplicity of forms making up a single one serves as a reminder that we are all connected and that even the most isolated individual is rarely alone. As the once narcissistic individual gazes admiringly into the glass, the love of self is transmuted into the love of humanity.

CRYSTALS AND GEMSTONES

Rhodonite *assists mastering love of self so the focus shifts from the personal to the universal.*
It helps the individual understand how the many come together to create the one.

BENJAMIN SPOCK

Like most successful individuals on this karmic path, **Dr. Benjamin Spock** worked unceasingly for the common good of mankind. Spock's commonsense approach to child rearing, which stresses firmness and understanding, became a dominant influence on several generations of parents, and his books have been read by millions of people around the world. However, despite his mainstream popularity, Spock was no stranger to controversy, and he was convicted of counseling draft evasion during the Vietnam War. His social involvement led him to run for president in 1972 as a candidate for the pacifist People's Party.

Like others on the Way of Compassion, singer-songwriter **Fiona Apple** has been touched by suffering. Though challenged by a traumatic childhood, she has triumphed through her courage, radiant energy, and driving ambition to become a youthful example of how to rise above personal misfortunes. Socially conscious, she is a committed vegetarian. As she further evolves on this karmic path, Apple must continue to develop her talents, putting her star

FIONA APPLE

qualities in service of her ever-growing audience and her causes.

Humanitarian **Eleanor Roosevelt** was known as the First Lady of the World because of her involvement in many worthy causes both at home and abroad. Roosevelt's life journey typified the process of the Way of Compassion as she transformed herself from a withdrawn girl born to privilege into a worldly, mature woman involved in the plight of the disadvantaged. Though many initially viewed her as haughty, ultimately they were won over

ELEANOR ROOSEVELT

by her concern for others. Roosevelt was particularly dedicated to the issues of racism, child care, and unemployment, and helped draft the Universal Declaration of Human Rights in 1948.

Other Notables: Brian "Kato" Kaelin, Irene Cara, Susan Faludi, Bernard Shaw, George Orwell, Jesse Helms, Jr., David Mannes, Cyril Arthur Pearson, Bob Hope, Lou Gehrig, Mariette Hartley, Al Hirschfeld, Ginger Baker, Valerie Harper, Jim Brady, Raquel Welch, Frankie Avalon, Jim McKay, Yves Montand, Rodney Dangerfield, Françoise Gilot, Rudyard Kipling, Catherine Booth, Lawrence Taylor, Edgar Bergen, John McEnroe, Anaïs Nin

---

BIRTHDAYS ON KARMIC PATH 3

July 1, 1884–November 19, 1884 | February 12, 1903–July 2, 1903 | September 23, 1921–February 11, 1922

May 4, 1940 September 22, 1940 | December 15, 1958–May 4, 1959 | July 26, 1977–December 14, 1977

March 7, 1996–July 25, 1996 | October 17, 2014–March 7, 2015

KARMIC PATH
3

March 19–24
REBIRTH
PISCES–ARIES CUSP

The feelings and reactions of others should prove an important indicator to those born on the Pisces–Aries cusp of just how well they're doing on the Way of Compassion. Pisces–Aries individuals may experience any number of episodes in which their best intentions are misunderstood, causing them to withdraw into a sulky or high-handed refusal to dedicate themselves to the common good. Their principal challenge is to utilize their considerable intuition to better attune themselves to the group dynamic and further develop their capacity to love and work with others. It is very important for Pisces–Arians to avoid the traps of indulging in self-pity and taking events too personally. Yet, curiously, these people will find that many of their lessons come through conflict. Pisces–Aries individuals are frequently so misunderstood themselves that conflict can serve as their impetus to better understand, interpret, and comment on the world and its social dynamics.

MATTHEW MODINE
Film actor
_____
3/22/1959
Pisces–Aries Cusp

CHALLENGE: **REALIZING THE OPPORTUNITY FOR GROWTH IN CONFLICT**
FULFILLMENT: **MOVING AWAY FROM AN ORIENTATION OF SELF-INVOLVEMENT TO ONE OF COMPASSION**
NOTABLE: **MALCOLM MUGGERIDGE (WORLD WAR II COUNTER-INTELLIGENCE SPY; WRITER)**

March 25–April 2
THE CHILD
ARIES I

Marked by a childlike openness and spontaneity, Aries I individuals may encounter some difficulty on the Way of Compassion, if only because they may not be as aware as others. They may fail to adequately understand their fellows, preferring to move ahead alone in a constant, restless search for attention and sensation. Sooner or later, though, Aries I's will find the social connection indicated by this path, if only because their lively minds and strong sense of idealism demand it. The challenge for these souls will be to relinquish their need for personal approval and to tackle some larger, more worldly issues. Otherwise, Aries I's might well find themselves skating on the surface of life, all appearance and little substance underneath. Still, their frankness, idealism, and natural appeal will serve them well, providing the child within them is encouraged to grow—not merely spoiled by too much attention.

CHALLENGE: **DEEPENING THEIR INVOLVEMENT WITH OTHERS**
FULFILLMENT: **OVERCOMING THE SCARS OF THEIR CHILDHOOD BY HELPING OTHERS**
NOTABLE: **RUDOLF SERKIN (DIRECTOR, CURTIS INSTITUTE)**

April 3–10
THE STAR
ARIES II

The Way of Compassion holds enormous potential for those born in the Aries II period, providing they can rise to the challenge of overcoming vanity and the tendency to consider themselves at the center of the universe. Still, rising to challenges is what these folks do best, and Aries II's will doubtless rise in the world. Passionate and even inspirational at times, they have a capacity to fire and inspire the hopes and imaginations of others that is sometimes quite formidable, and they make excellent spokespeople and champions for any number of social issues and causes. If those born in the Week of the Star take care to cultivate the necessary objectivity, avoid the tendency to be too demanding or overbearing, and turn their attention outward rather than trying to draw attention to themselves, they will discover a universal connection with others and will be rewarded with great success in return.

CLARE BOOTH LUCE
Playwright; journalist;
public official
_____
4/10/1903
Aries II

CHALLENGE: **TURNING THEIR FOCUS ON THEIR SURROUNDINGS RATHER THAN LOOKING TO THEM AS A KIND OF MIRROR**
FULFILLMENT: **GAINING THE SERENITY THAT NO LONGER BEING EGO-DRIVEN CAN BRING**
NOTABLES: **BUTCH CASSIDY (OUTLAW); DAVID HYDE PIERCE (ACTOR)**

April 11–18
THE PIONEER
ARIES III

The drive to learn and explore is strong in Aries III's, and this drive can serve them well on this karmic path. Those born in the Week of the Pioneer will have to cultivate moderation in their approach to life, however, and rising to the challenge of becoming successful, energetic social workers and commentators will sometimes require that they alter their often drastic views and recommendations. Still, Aries III's are fired by the inner conviction that they want only what's good for the rest of us, and much of the time they're quite correct. Their keen sense of social issues and their desire to make a better life for us all are quite strong. If Aries III's do not allow their ideals and fearless crusades to become tainted by too much in the way of ego issues or the need for personal recognition, they can experience the greatest success in the media, in communications, and as cutting-edge social reformers.

CHALLENGE: **DEVELOPING GREATER COMPASSION FOR THE INTIMATES WHO RESIDE IN THEIR INNER CIRCLE**
FULFILLMENT: **LEARNING TO TRULY PUT THEMSELVES INTO ANOTHER'S SHOES**
NOTABLE: **SUSAN FALUDI (FEMINIST WRITER)**

April 19–24
POWER
ARIES–TAURUS CUSP

Aries–Tauruses on the Way of Compassion are certain to become a force to be reckoned with in the social arena. Those born on the Cusp of Power have an inborn talent for pursuing their own goals, yet more often than not, what they want for themselves can be beneficial for the rest of us as well. Perhaps their principal challenge will be not to fail to make the necessary distinctions between real social needs and personal agendas. Since Aries–Tauruses are naturally powerful, commanding people, they should also take care to surround themselves with people of integrity who will not be afraid to steer them right when they get off course or to oppose them if necessary. Greed and a certain mercenary quality can be pitfalls here, since Aries–Tauruses know the value of money and are well aware of its power. Still, if they cultivate a broader vision and stay attuned to the needs of society, their natural generosity will allow them to experience the real joy of nonattached giving.

ELIOT NESS
Head of "Untouchables,"
fought organized crime

4/19/1903
Aries–Taurus Cusp

CHALLENGE: **GIVING UP AN EGO-DRIVEN POWER ORIENTATION FOR ONE DRIVEN BY LOVE**
FULFILLMENT: **USING THEIR POWER TO ADVANCE THE CAUSE OF THOSE MORE UNFORTUNATE**
NOTABLE: **GREGOR PIATIGORSKY (RUSSIAN CELLIST)**

April 25–May 2
MANIFESTATION
TAURUS I

Gifted with a keen desire for the ideal and the necessary pragmatism to develop it, Taurus I's are likely to flourish on the Way of Compassion. Their natural diplomacy and sensitivity to structure can make them formidable commentators and social reformers, as they have the ability not only to discern social problems and ills but to put into place methods and systems that can cure them. It's important for Taurus I's to guard against feeling unappreciated or unrecognized for their efforts and to learn to take their satisfaction from seeing their plans come to fruition in group endeavors instead. Personal touchiness can also be a problem. Still, if those born in the Week of Manifestation use their impulses toward expansion to gain greater knowledge of people and cultures outside their immediate experience, they are likely to be blessed with a unique and thoroughly useful perception of society that they will in turn pass on to others along this path.

CHALLENGE: **CONVINCING THEMSELVES THAT THEY NEED TO MAKE CHANGES IN THEMSELVES**
FULFILLMENT: **WORKING ON BEHALF OF OTHER CULTURES**
NOTABLE: **BENJAMIN SPOCK (PHYSICIAN; AUTHOR ON CHILD CARE)**

May 3–10
THE TEACHER
TAURUS II

Gifted with a natural sense of fairness and an extraordinary sense of social justice, Taurus II personalities are likely to attain great achievements on the Way of Compassion. Their natural magnetism is sure to gain them much in the way of applause and personal admiration, yet they will rarely be content with applause alone. Though vanity can be a problem—as Taurus II's have big egos and a strong sense of dignity—their more important challenge will be to learn to bring their acute vision to bear in a group dynamic. Their sense of self is so strong that they often feel that if they want something done, they have to do it themselves. Still, if those born in the Week of the Teacher are careful to cultivate the necessary flexibility in their approach to people and things and to avoid a tendency to be corrupted by close associates, these dynamic, energetic personalities will surely make their mark on the world with a lasting legacy of good works and improved moral standards.

JAMES L. BROOKS,
seen here with his
children. TV producer,
Cheers; director,
As Good As It Gets

5/9/1940
Taurus II

CHALLENGE: **KNOWING THAT SOMETIMES TRUE EMPATHY INVOLVES THE ABROGATION OF JUDGMENT**
FULFILLMENT: **TEACHING THEIR MORAL APPROACH TO THEIR FELLOW HUMAN BEINGS**
NOTABLE: **PETER BENCHLEY (AUTHOR, *JAWS*)**

May 11–18
THE NATURAL
TAURUS III

The Way of Compassion can have a certain aura of adventure for those born in the Week of the Natural, and their search for social improvement may take them far from their origins in a quest to gain perspective and insight. Perhaps the chief stumbling block with this configuration is their tendency to travel far and wide without stopping long enough to absorb their experiences, analyze what they mean, or help anyone else along the way. Thus, Taurus III's can waste their energies in instability and aimlessness. The key here will be to gravitate to causes and social issues that will allow them to become truly involved and committed without becoming obsessive or overly rebellious in their quest to make the world a better place. If Taurus III's allow their naturally fine instincts to serve as their guide, finding a middle ground on the Way of Compassion will prove enlightening and fruitful indeed.

CHALLENGE: **LEARNING HOW TO TRULY BE THERE FOR OTHERS, NOT JUST CHARM THEM**
FULFILLMENT: **DISCOVERING THE SERIOUSNESS OF PURPOSE THAT WORKING FOR THE GOOD OF OTHERS CAN GENERATE**
NOTABLE: **MARIA THERESA (ARCHDUCHESS OF AUSTRIA)**

May 19–24
ENERGY
TAURUS–GEMINI CUSP

Those born on the Taurus–Gemini cusp have a great gift for making a splash on the social scene and are likely to be attention getters, whatever their chosen field. Yet the Way of Compassion does not come easily to hard-driving Taurus–Geminis. There is an inherent danger of narcissism or, at the very least, a preoccupation with appearances at the expense of deeper experience and investigation. Their principal lesson, then, will be learning to set aside their tendency toward selfishness and to work on their analytical skills. Since Taurus–Geminis do not turn inward easily, they do best when surrounded by those who demand a higher level of performance and integrity than they might require of themselves. However, Taurus–Geminis are blessed with natural brilliance, and if they use their talents to gain attention for causes other than their own, the Way of Compassion holds considerable promise for these lively, curious souls.

CHALLENGE: **SLOWING DOWN ONCE IN A WHILE TO TAKE STOCK OF WHERE OTHERS ARE**

FULFILLMENT: **CREATING AND NURTURING A FAMILY OR A CLOSE CIRCLE OF INTIMATES**

NOTABLE: **BERNARD SHAW (JOURNALIST; ANCHOR, CNN)**

BOB HOPE
Beloved entertainer and comedian; known for USO tours
———
5/29/1903
Gemini I

May 25–June 2
FREEDOM
GEMINI I

These freedom lovers will likely respond well to the challenges of the Way of Compassion, but that response may exist more in theory than in actual practice. Since it is the nature of Gemini I's to balk at restriction in any form, making the necessary social contacts and connections in order to see their best impulses through to fruition may be somewhat difficult. Perhaps their principal challenge will be to find the level of commitment required for real social analysis and to put aside their touchiness and frustration with slower-witted people and bureaucratic machines. Still, Gemini I individuals are often blessed with astonishing technical as well as verbal gifts, and if they can apply those talents to taking a harder and more in-depth look at just what makes the world go around, and providing they cultivate the patience and understanding to follow things through, they are likely to proceed with ease and brilliance along this karmic path.

CHALLENGE: **DISCOVERING THAT RIDICULE IS NOT COMPASSIONATE**

FULFILLMENT: **COMING TO A DEEP PERSONAL UNDERSTANDING OF WHAT FREEDOM MIGHT MEAN TO ANOTHER**

NOTABLES: **HONEY RUSSELL (COLLEGE BASKETBALL PLAYER AND COACH); LEVON HELM (MEMBER, THE BAND)**

June 3–10
NEW LANGUAGE
GEMINI II

The key to success for Gemini II's placed on the Way of Compassion will more than likely be their ability to learn that they do not always or automatically know what's good for others. Those born in the Week of New Language are highly verbal personalities and have a quick grasp of people and situations, yet they need to be aware that their first take on any given issue is not always the whole story. Gemini II's can sally forth in order to convey a message on behalf of the masses only to find that their interpretation of things does not represent the real situation at all. They are marvelously adept socially, however, and can be counted upon to find a way out of any number of diplomatic disasters should the need arise. Their charm, humor, and lightning wit can ease many a crisis, and, properly applied, their energetic, expressive approach to solving the world's problems will find great response in society at large.

CHALLENGE: **KNOWING THAT BEING SOCIAL IS NOT THE SAME AS BEING PERSONAL**

FULFILLMENT: **LEARNING NOT ONLY TO BE UNDERSTOOD BUT TO UNDERSTAND**

NOTABLES: **TOM JONES (SINGER); NANCY SINATRA (SINGER)**

GALE SAYERS
4-time all-pro running back, Chicago Bears
———
5/30/1940
Gemini I

June 11–18
THE SEEKER
GEMINI III

Gemini III's may be somewhat hampered on the Way of Compassion by their restless, irrepressible spirits. Though those born in the Week of the Seeker are blessed with a great and unique love of learning and truth, they may sometimes fail to connect with the social side of life, preferring to pursue their own interests in their own way and time. As a result, Gemini III's can remain aloof and distant from the more troubled aspects of human affairs. Nevertheless, they are for the most part deeply caring people, and though their spiritual natures may be awakened by personal suffering, it is unlikely that they will totally ignore the demands placed on them by the Way of Compassion. By nature excellent critics and commentators, they will truly blossom when their astute observations and insights are tempered by the necessary measure of humanity.

CHALLENGE: **REALIZING THAT OTHER HUMAN BEINGS ARE NOT PUPPETS FOR THEIR ENTERTAINMENT**

FULFILLMENT: **DISCOVERING THE MANY FACETS OF THEIR FELLOW HUMAN BEINGS**

June 19–24
MAGIC
GEMINI–CANCER CUSP

Always able to bring a touch of magic to others, there is something special about the individuals born on the Gemini–Cancer cusp when placed upon the Way of Compassion. Their deep sensitivity blesses them with a key ingredient of this karmic path: a natural empathy for others. In fact, Gemini–Cancers can be so sensitive that they tend to isolate themselves from the world and its problems, perhaps out of fear of overloading their minds and hearts with the needs of others. Thus, the principal challenge of this configuration will be to find the balance between working for the needs of others and seeing to their own. Gemini–Cancers will doubtless be invited to experience true commitment to a cause or social structure, one that will encourage them to deepen their sometimes superficial involvements. Still, if Gemini–Cancers work to cultivate their capacity for love and fight the pull of fantasy, their success is ensured.

LOU GEHRIG
Baseball great; afflicted
with disease named
after him
___
6/19/1903
Gemini–Cancer Cusp

CHALLENGE: **LEARNING THAT FEELING DEEPLY IS NOT THE ISSUE; TAKING ACTION IS**

FULFILLMENT: **FINDING DEEP PERSONAL FULFILLMENT IN GIVING TO OTHERS**

NOTABLES: **MARIETTE HARTLEY (TELEVISION PERSONALITY); AL HIRSCHFELD (CARICATURIST)**

June 25–July 2
THE EMPATH
CANCER I

The Way of Compassion holds considerable promise for those born in the Week of the Empath, providing they can work to keep their emotions in hand. Highly sensitive and caring, Cancer I's nonetheless have a tendency to believe that they alone are responsible for the world's ills and they alone are capable of solving the world's problems. The danger here is of developing a hypervigilant and overly responsible attitude. Cancer I's should take care to establish some boundaries between themselves and others, for it is only by releasing control that they will be able to discover the joy of giving and working for the larger, less personal goals of life. Nevertheless, Cancer I's are deeply attracted to spirituality and have a natural affinity for the kind of moral code found in many world religions. Thus, they do wonderfully well as ambassadors and spokespeople for the higher good and a better way of life for all humankind.

CHALLENGE: **WORKING HARD TO ESTABLISH BOUNDARIES AND TO KEEP THEM**

FULFILLMENT: **LEARNING THE LESSON THAT THEY ARE CAPABLE OF PARTICIPATING FULLY IN THE WORLD**

NOTABLE: **GEORGE ORWELL (AUTHOR, *1984*)**

July 3–10
THE UNCONVENTIONAL
CANCER II

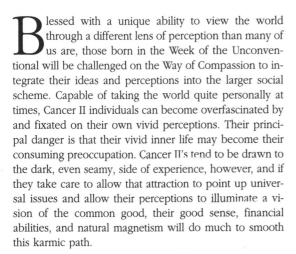

Blessed with a unique ability to view the world through a different lens of perception than many of us are, those born in the Week of the Unconventional will be challenged on the Way of Compassion to integrate their ideas and perceptions into the larger social scheme. Capable of taking the world quite personally at times, Cancer II individuals can become overfascinated by and fixated on their own vivid perceptions. Their principal danger is that their vivid inner life may become their consuming preoccupation. Cancer II's tend to be drawn to the dark, even seamy, side of experience, however, and if they take care to allow that attraction to point up universal issues and allow their perceptions to illuminate a vision of the common good, their good sense, financial abilities, and natural magnetism will do much to smooth this karmic path.

RINGO STARR
Drummer for The Beatles
___
7/7/1940
Cancer II

CHALLENGE: **LEARNING NOT TO APPLY THEIR MORE IMAGINATIVE SCHEMES TO OTHERS**

FULFILLMENT: **KNOWING THEIR ATTRACTION TO THE UNCONVENTIONAL GIVES THEM A BROADER BASE OF COMPASSION**

NOTABLE: **JAMES BAILEY (CIRCUS COFOUNDER)**

July 11–18
THE PERSUADER
CANCER III

Gifted with the ability to persuade others to do most anything as well as being excellent manipulators of their environment, Cancer III's are destined to be confronted by any number of opportunities to make the world a better place. These folks can be powerful and effective, both behind the scenes or in front of a crowd. Cancer III's have considerable energy, passion, and commitment to bring to almost any cause or social issue. There is a danger, however, of general excess in their approach to life, as well as one of allowing their own successes to make them lazy or self-satisfied as time goes on. While learning to have few needs themselves, Cancer III's can discount the neediness of others. Still, Cancer III's have a great depth of understanding of their fellows as well as the capacity to make things happen. Given their naturally spiritual bent, Cancer III's will evolve quite rapidly on the Way of Compassion.

CHALLENGE: **PURSUING A SPIRITUAL PATH TO HELP THEM SUSTAIN THEIR COMMITMENT TO OTHERS**

FULFILLMENT: **SEEING THEIR HARD WORK ON BEHALF OF OTHERS BEAR FRUIT**

NOTABLES: **PATRICK STEWART (ACTOR, *STAR TREK: THE NEXT GENERATION*); JOE TORRE (MANAGER, NEW YORK YANKEES)**

July 19–25

OSCILLATION
CANCER–LEO CUSP

Gifted with the convictions needed to literally "take on the world," those born on the Cancer–Leo cusp can accomplish great things when placed on this karmic path. The passions of these bright, sometimes impulsive people run strong, and they will prove to be real champions in the fight against injustice. They have a tendency to become obsessive, however, and they should approach their crusades with a degree of objectivity, in order to ensure that their passions and convictions do not degenerate into mania. Letting go of ego will also be difficult for Cancer–Leos, for they are more than capable of seeking out challenges and conflicts for the pure joy of the fight. But if these folks learn to nurture their analytical skills, put aside the demands of ego, and occasionally meditate on the truth of the maxim "still waters run deep," their natural moral courage and their ability to fight for what is right will serve them well.

CHALLENGE: **RECOGNIZING THEIR TENDENCY TO CREATE EMERGENCIES AND CRISES FOR THE SAKE OF THE EXPERIENCE**

FULFILLMENT: **INTEGRATING THEIR FEELING AND ACTION SIDES**

NOTABLE: **DON IMUS (RADIO PERSONALITY)**

ALEX TREBEK
TV host, *Jeopardy*

7/22/1940
Cancer–Leo Cusp

July 26–August 2

AUTHORITY
LEO I

The impulse to work toward larger and higher causes is strong in those born in the Week of Authority, and this karmic path and its tasks will doubtless do much to help them overcome their natural tendency toward introversion or isolation from the world and its problems. Gifted with a natural detachment, Leo I's have a pronounced ability to back up and objectively analyze problems and situations, yet they may exhibit a tendency to be overcritical or insensitive as a result. In this instance, the Way of Compassion will require them to give their knowledge and love of learning back to the world in some form, either as teachers or commentators or through the written word. Social contact of all forms will be critical to their success, however, and Leo I's will have to work to overcome an attitude of snobbishness, whether in a sense of moral or intellectual superiority. Still, their love of truth, combined with their desire to share their worlds of knowledge, will forge their spiritual destiny as they travel the Way of Compassion.

CHALLENGE: **DEVELOPING GREATER KINDNESS, PATIENCE, AND UNDERSTANDING TOWARD THEIR FELLOWS**

FULFILLMENT: **TAKING THEIR FOCUS OFF WORK**

August 3–10

BALANCED STRENGTH
LEO II

Tough and realistic, those born in the Week of Balanced Strength will doubtless rise to the challenges presented by this karmic path. Attracted to causes and crusades for the weak and downtrodden, Leo II individuals will relish the struggle and commitment required to work for the common good. There is a danger that their causes will remain rather common, however, since they are somewhat scornful of ideas and ways of life that they do not consider grounded firmly in the here and now. It is therefore important for Leo II's to avoid the tendency to be too judgmental and high-handed when dealing in the areas of ideology or religion, as well to overcome the conviction that they simply know better than anyone else. Still, their natural magnetism and "get it done" dynamic will be a tremendous advantage, providing they recognize the value of inspiration as well as perspiration when it comes to group effort.

CHALLENGE: **REALIZING THAT IF THEY PERMIT THEMSELVES TO SUFFER, THEY CAN BE OF LITTLE USE TO OTHERS**

FULFILLMENT: **LIVING WITH A BALANCE OF SELF-INTEREST AND GIVING**

MARTIN SHEEN
Stage/film actor,
Apocalypse Now

8/3/1940
Leo II

August 11–18

LEADERSHIP
LEO III

Those born in the week of Leo III make truly creative and inspirational leaders whose potential to succeed on the Way of Compassion may nevertheless involve a number of personal setbacks. It is of the utmost importance for Leo III's to learn and relearn the value of being sensitive to the feelings of others, for they can be quite demanding and even gaudily selfish at times. They have the almost naive conviction that their goals ought to be everyone else's goals too and are likely to receive quite an education in that area before they discover the real meaning of the words "group dynamic." Energetic and positive, Leo III's do need to slow down and consider the views and needs of others before forging ahead. Still, they are capable of bringing great forces to bear in the interests of improving life on earth, and if they are careful to set their own needs aside and sublimate their sometimes childish need for ego reinforcement and approval, their path to enlightenment will be considerably eased.

CHALLENGE: **CONSIDERING THE FEELINGS AND NEEDS OF OTHERS MORE**

FULFILLMENT: **USING THEIR CHARISMA AND STRATEGIC SKILLS IN A GOOD CAUSE**

August 19–25

EXPOSURE
LEO–VIRGO CUSP

Sharing, whether of themselves, their time, or their personal resources, does not come naturally to Leo–Virgos, but their impulse to serve humankind is nonetheless quite strong. They are particularly suited to exploring and exposing the corruption and irresponsibility that are responsible for much of the world's ills and injustice. Personal vanity can be something of a sticky point for Leo–Virgos, however, and they do best when they form comradeships with those who will admire them for their considerable accomplishments while at the same time being willing to turn a blind eye when they prove touchy or irritable. As truly gifted observers of life, Leo–Virgos' analytic and verbal skills can be formidable. If they take care to learn the fine art of turning the spotlight on issues rather than themselves, their accomplishments on the Way of Compassion will gain them much in way of the admiration they so require.

GINGER BAKER
Drummer for rock
group Cream

8/19/1940
Leo–Virgo Cusp

CHALLENGE: **KNOWING THAT ALL THAT ONE GIVES COMES BACK IN ANOTHER FORM**

FULFILLMENT: **USING THEIR POWERS OF INFORMATION AS A TOOL FOR THE IMPROVEMENT OF SOCIAL CONDITIONS**

NOTABLE: **VALERIE HARPER (ACTRESS, *THE MARY TYLER MOORE SHOW*)**

August 26–September 2

SYSTEM BUILDERS
VIRGO I

Blessed with the rare gift of being able to put systems and structures into place, Virgo I individuals can really shine on this karmic path. Dedicated and hardworking, they have enormous powers of concentration that will doubtless express themselves in service to the world, their families, or higher spiritual causes. The gifts of Virgo I's can be diminished, though, when they retreat into isolation or go overboard with a preoccupation with detail. Still, their capacity to observe, identify, and analyze makes them extremely valuable to any cause to which they might attach themselves. In fact, Virgo I's might very well find themselves rather reluctantly beckoned out of the shadows and into the spotlight at more than one juncture in their lives. How they deal with the resulting attention will do much to determine the quality of their lives and spiritual expansion along this karmic path.

CHALLENGE: **NOT PERMITTING THEMSELVES TO RETREAT INTO THE SAFETY OF A TASK, RATHER THAN PEOPLE, ORIENTATION**

FULFILLMENT: **BEING KNOWN AS THE COMPASSIONATE PEOPLE THEY ARE**

NOTABLE: **JIM BRADY (GUN CONTROL ACTIVIST; FORMER PRESS SECRETARY TO PRESIDENT REAGAN)**

September 3–10

THE ENIGMA
VIRGO II

Here, the Way of Compassion manifests itself primarily in the areas of personal and social communication. Highly moral and naturally ethical people, those born in the Week of the Enigma may have to work hard to make themselves and their views recognized, if only because they are somewhat hesitant to step up to the podium when it comes time for them to be heard. In fact, social skills in general can be difficult for them to acquire, as they find it difficult to relate or to share with more extroverted and emotional beings. Too, they can find many worthy causes unworthy of their attention if becoming involved in them means compromising their high and often rigid standards. Nonetheless, Virgo II's are blessed with great conviction when it comes to doing the right thing, and if they don't become too preoccupied with appearances to go out on a limb in the interest of a cause or larger social good, they will find that the Way of Compassion holds great rewards for them.

RAQUEL WELCH
Actress; considered one
of the world's great
beauties

9/5/1940
Virgo II

CHALLENGE: **DROPPING THE NEED TO BE MYSTERIOUS AND JUST ROLLING UP THEIR SLEEVES TO WORK**

FULFILLMENT: **GRADUATING FROM "SOCIAL CONSCIOUSNESS 101"**

September 11–18

THE LITERALIST
VIRGO III

Practical and shrewd, those born in the Week of the Literalist have the capacity to do great things along the Way of Compassion, providing they do not remain aloof from those around them or insensitive to their needs. Virgo III's work best with tangible goals and concepts, and though they have considerable intellectual powers, chances are their destiny will be expressed in material terms. They may raise money for people in need, build houses for the homeless, help ship blankets and food to hurricane survivors. Well able to control their emotions, Virgo III individuals do not have much patience for others who aren't and can sometimes stumble when they are forced to recognize that passions can run high in even the most worthy causes. Thus, it is important for Virgo III's to cultivate sympathy and empathy. The resulting enlightenment should help them as they confront the kind of complex challenges in which the best thing to do for others is not always the most "right" or obvious path.

CHALLENGE: **OPENING THEMSELVES TO SOME OF THE MESSIER ASPECTS OF THE HUMAN PSYCHE**

FULFILLMENT: **FINDING THE TRUTH IN THE HUMAN CONDITION**

NOTABLES: **BRIAN DE PALMA (FILM DIRECTOR); MERLIN OLSEN (FOOTBALL PLAYER; SPOKESPERSON)**

September 19–24

BEAUTY
VIRGO–LIBRA CUSP

Virgo–Librans' need for beauty and harmony can work against them on the Way of Compassion, as they may turn away from the difficulties, miseries, and needs of the less fortunate in the interest of pursuing a "higher" or less realistic ideal. Those born on the Cusp of Beauty don't especially care for "getting down and dirty" in any event, and they may falter on this karmic path if they fail to allow their hearts to be touched by the plight of those in need. Too, it may take Virgo–Librans some time to develop a truly moral code, for they have a chameleon-like quality that sometimes makes them only as good as the associates they choose. However, their natural diplomatic gifts and personal charms can do much to further a cause. Though there is some danger that narcissism will hamper their spiritual development, it can also work to their advantage when they recognize that it is those who have a healthy dose of self-love that are most capable and effective when it comes to loving others.

JIM McKAY
TV sports journalist
___
9/24/1921
Virgo–Libra Cusp

CHALLENGE: **GROUNDING THEIR HIGHER IDEALS IN THE REALITY AROUND THEM**
FULFILLMENT: **FINALLY FINDING A MORAL CODE THAT THEY CAN BE PROUD OF**

September 25–October 2

THE PERFECTIONIST
LIBRA I

Those born in the Week of the Perfectionist are well equipped to deal with life along the Way of Compassion. Their natural attractiveness, social sense, and gift for putting things right will all prove to be wonderful tools in the construction of their personal destinies. The biggest stumbling block for Libra I individuals will be their need for perfection, which can sometimes stand in the way of growth. Libra I's can become preoccupied with their perceptions of a problem, when in fact their challenge is to successfully connect with a larger good or greater need. They must be careful not to expend their considerable energy in less-than-worthy enterprises and pursuits, but rather to be willing to expand their vision and relinquish control. "Don't sweat the small stuff" is a phrase Libra I's might do well to learn to live by. When they do, they will recognize that things don't need to be perfect before they can improve and that fairness and justice are the result not of flawless systems but of worthy ideals.

CHALLENGE: **BELIEVING THAT PEOPLE ARE PERFECT JUST AS THEY ARE**
FULFILLMENT: **KNOWING THAT THEY HAVE THE CAPACITY TO MAKE A DIFFERENCE**
NOTABLE: **JAMES WHITMORE (CHARACTER ACTOR)**

October 3–10

SOCIETY
LIBRA II

Individuals born in the Week of Society are blessed with a formidable sense of social acumen and the kind of good judgement and discernment that is necessary to success on this karmic path. Excellent counselors, Libra II's have the knack of getting to the heart of almost any problem or situation and inspiring the trust of others, seemingly without much effort. There is a danger with this configuration, however, that these souls will fail to attach in a meaningful way and develop a sense of connection with and compassion for their fellow human beings. For all their social talents, Libra II's can be loners, and it will be important to their growth to experience some form of apprenticeship in religious, physical, or spiritual disciplines as a means of grounding their sometimes unstable energies. Connecting to a cause is only half the battle here—the other half will be in implementing and sticking to a course of action in order to achieve their goals.

YVES MONTAND
Actor/singer, protégé of
Edith Piaf
___
10/13/1921
Libra III

CHALLENGE: **GIVING MORE OF THEMSELVES TO OTHERS THAN TO SOCIAL NICETIES**
FULFILLMENT: **MAKING A COMMITMENT TO CREATING CHANGE**

October 11–18

THEATER
LIBRA III

Sometimes seeming as though they were born sophisticated, these worldly souls face the challenge of developing their higher spiritual values when placed on the Way of Compassion. Ambitious and often driven, Libra III's can frequently appear cynical, world-weary, or simply self-involved. It may require quite a bit of work for Libra III's to attune themselves to the needs of other people, for as astute and perceptive as they are, their viewpoint is often a rather abstract one that fails to take into account the human emotions involved. Equally, they can fail to analyze their own motivations and discover their own emotional side. Still, Libra III's will blossom in groups, families, and other social units of all kinds, and if they can translate their need to be at center stage to a talent for being at the center of the action, their success and achievement on this karmic path are certain.

CHALLENGE: **UTILIZING THEIR WORLDLINESS AND LEADERSHIP ABILITY ON BEHALF OF THE LESS FORTUNATE**
FULFILLMENT: **FINDING OPPORTUNITIES TO DEEPEN THEIR EXPERIENCE OF HUMANITY**
NOTABLES: **ELEANOR ROOSEVELT (FORMER FIRST LADY); JESSE HELMS (U.S. SENATOR)**

KARMIC PATH
3

October 19–25

DRAMA AND CRITICISM
LIBRA–SCORPIO CUSP

Dominant and charismatic, those born on the Libra–Scorpio cusp will nevertheless be faced with the challenge of operating within the social, professional, and personal structures available. Libra–Scorpios are blessed with a fine moral sensibility for the most part and will likely have a talent for airing their views as well. They can be overly opinionated, hypercritical, and subject to extreme stress, however, and will do well to learn when to back off from a particular issue and let someone else take the reins. Isolation can also be a problem, since Libra–Scorpios have little patience or tolerance for the more humdrum side of human existence and often prefer to be alone. Selfishness can prove a burden to their development as well. Yet if Libra–Scorpios can bring their sense of drama and justice to bear in the arena of social improvement, as well as in the realm of spiritual growth, they can rest assured they have been gifted with a voice that is sure to be heard.

JOHN ADAMS
2nd president of the
U.S., was vice-president;
framer of Constitution

10/30/1735
Scorpio I

CHALLENGE: **EXTRAPOLATING WHAT THEY HAVE LEARNED INTO A GREATER DEPTH OF FEELING FOR OTHERS**
FULFILLMENT: **RECOGNIZING THE BEAUTY IN THE HUMAN HEART**

October 26–November 2

INTENSITY
SCORPIO I

The key to success for Scorpio I's placed on the Way of Compassion will be their ability to overcome self-interest. Though blessed with keen perception and considerable sensitivity, Scorpio I's sometimes fail to understand the interconnectedness of human experience. Perhaps it is due to the fact that those born in the Week of Intensity are usually so willing to assume responsibility for themselves and their actions that they presume that others are, in some similar way, responsible for their own misfortunes. Still, for all their sometimes unbending attitudes, Scorpio I's are blessed with a powerful conscience and a fine sense of right and wrong. If they allow it to speak for the needs of the many as well as their own, they will doubtless be well guided along their path. Another gift to Scorpio I's is a powerful analytic ability that will require expression at some point as their views of the world come into clearer focus. For the Scorpio I soul will not stand idly on the sidelines and allow his fellowman to continue to make what he considers to be stupid mistakes.

CHALLENGE: **DEMANDING LESS OF OTHERS**
FULFILLMENT: **CHANNELING THEIR DESTRUCTIVE ENERGIES INTO CONSTRUCTIVE PURPOSES**

November 3–11

DEPTH
SCORPIO II

To ensure their spiritual development, Scorpio II's must not only empathize with the plight of the less fortunate but also avoid being overwhelmed by it. Sensitive and caring for the most part, Scorpio II's can nevertheless give in to depression and hopelessness when they feel that circumstances are beyond their control. Once connected with an issue or a cause, they are likely to stay connected, to the benefit of all. Though there is a danger of their becoming somewhat overbearing, especially in later years, Scorpio II's are blessed with a fine sense of purpose and the ability to do whatever they set out to do. If they can overcome their less generous impulses and avoid their tendency toward escapism, they are likely to discover that the Way of Compassion will offer them great fulfillment and considerable opportunity in both the personal and professional areas of life.

CHALLENGE: **MANAGING DEPRESSION BY LEARNING TO CALL ON A HIGHER POWER IN TIMES OF DISTRESS**
FULFILLMENT: **FEELING THE SENSE OF PURPOSE CREATED BY WORKING FOR A GREATER GOOD**
NOTABLE: **HERMANN RORSCHACH (PSYCHIATRIST; DEVELOPED INK-BLOT TEST)**

November 12–18

CHARM
SCORPIO III

Passionate and often inspirational, those born in the Week of Charm are likely to shine when placed on this karmic path. Realistic and blessed with acute powers of perception, Scorpio III's are difficult people to fool and unlikely to expend their considerable energies on unworthy or unachievable goals. There is a danger of stalling on this path if they fail to bring their powers and talents to bear in the interest of improving the lives of those around them. Scorpio III individuals are capable of extremes of both sacrifice and philanthropy, however, and if their passionate sense of conviction is awakened, their resourcefulness and resilience in the face of adversity can really be something to see. Blessed with fine communicative and diplomatic talents, Scorpio III's have the ability to sway the world to their own opinions, and as charmed as their lives can sometimes seem, they will be faced with the greater challenge of bringing that charm to bear on the lives of others.

BRIAN KEITH
Actor

11/14/1921
Scorpio III

CHALLENGE: **RECOGNIZING THAT MANIPULATION IS NOT CARING**
FULFILLMENT: **AWAKENING THE PROFOUND SENSE OF COMPASSION THAT LIES DORMANT WITHIN THEM**

November 19–24

REVOLUTION
SCORPIO–SAGITTARIUS CUSP

Whatever the cause or issue those born on the Cusp of Revolution might discover on the Way of Compassion, they are likely to breathe some new and much-needed energy into it. Scorpio–Sagittarians have a revolutionary streak, and though they might be sometimes tempted to stir things up just for the joy of seeing the pot boil over, they usually confine themselves to a more structured approach to accomplishing their goals. In fact they are highly results-oriented, and whatever they begin, they will see through to a satisfying conclusion. For this reason alone, Scorpio–Sagittarians tend to be successful. Striving for higher causes, the larger goals, and the greater good comes naturally for these folks, who are blessed with tremendous loyalty, courage, and an inborn morality. If Scorpio–Sagittarians take care not expend their gifts and energies in overzealousness or a tendency to be autocratic, they can do a great deal to change the world.

RODNEY DANGERFIELD
Comedian and actor,
"I get no respect"
———
11/22/1921
Scorpio–Sagittarius Cusp

CHALLENGE: **TEMPERING THEIR WELL-DEVELOPED DISDAIN FOR ALL THEY CONSIDER AESTHETICALLY TASTELESS**

FULFILLMENT: **FINDING A DEEPER SPIRITUAL VIEWPOINT FROM WHICH TO LOOK AT OTHERS**

NOTABLE: **JOHN V. LINDSAY (FORMER NEW YORK CITY MAYOR)**

November 25–December 2

INDEPENDENCE
SAGITTARIUS I

Blessed with a strongly nurturing nature and a keen sense of fairness, Sagittarius I individuals are well disposed to success on the Way of Compassion. It may take some time, however, for them to successfully connect with the social structures that will aid them on the journey, for as keen as their sense of justice can be, it is matched by an equal need for independence and personal freedom. Generous to a fault, they must cultivate their analytical powers, for they tend to leap before they look. Too, they can be so excitable that they fail to take a broad enough view of a situation to really understand what it is they're fighting for. Still, if Sagittarius I's avoid the pitfall of overaggression and work to develop a deeper understanding of their fellows, their courage and enthusiasm will ensure them a great journey.

CHALLENGE: **BEING WILLING TO GIVE OF THEIR MOST PRECIOUS COMMODITY: THEIR FREEDOM**

FULFILLMENT: **LEARNING ABOUT THE REWARDS OF CONTRIBUTING TO THE LIVES OF OTHERS**

NOTABLE: **FRANÇOISE GILOT (COMMON-LAW WIFE OF PABLO PICASSO; PALOMA'S MOTHER)**

December 3–10

THE ORIGINATOR
SAGITTARIUS II

The intricacies of social structure may be a bit difficult for Sagittarius II's to navigate when placed on this karmic path, and they may encounter no little amount of resistance to their sometimes peculiar or extreme ways. Natural individualists, those born in the Week of the Originator may retreat into isolation or escapism when things don't go their way and they fail to find the acceptance they so desire. Alternatively, they may fall into the trap of becoming more and more extreme as a means of gaining if not the acceptance of others, then at least their attention. As difficult as this configuration might sometimes seem, Sagittarius II's would do well to keep in mind that it is precisely the challenge to connect with others in the interest of the larger good that will serve to depersonalize their conflicts and allow them broader vision. Humanitarian efforts will enable them to grasp the simple truth that on a very basic level we are all brothers and sisters.

JIM GARRISON
New Orleans district
attorney
———
11/20/1921
Scorpio–Sagittarius Cusp

CHALLENGE: **REFUSING TO REJECT OTHERS WHEN ENCOUNTERING REJECTION THEMSELVES**

FULFILLMENT: **NORMALIZING THEIR RELATIONS WITH THEIR FELLOW HUMAN BEINGS**

NOTABLE: **DEANNA DURBIN (ENTERTAINER)**

December 11–18

THE TITAN
SAGITTARIUS III

Blessed with a larger-than-life persona and a great deal of charismatic charm, Sagittarius III individuals may find the Way of Compassion a bit difficult. Though their spirits are naturally generous, it may take some time for them to successfully attach to the idea of working for the larger good of society, for there is a danger of self-absorption here. Moodiness and emotional instability can be real stumbling blocks for those born in the Week of the Titan, and they would do well to cultivate greater objectivity. This promises the opportunity to work for the kind of humanitarian effort that will free them from their insecurities and increase their awareness. Finally, Sagittarius III's have a kind of star quality that will serve them well, for they are capable of bringing people together in a common cause or challenge under an inspiring and even heroic leadership. When they join forces with those of like mind and heart, they are sure to work miracles.

CHALLENGE: **RUMINATING LESS ON THE HUMAN CONDITION AND ACTING MORE**

FULFILLMENT: **DISCOVERING THE ENCHANTMENT OF BRINGING LARGE NUMBERS OF PEOPLE TOGETHER IN A CAUSE**

December 19–25
PROPHECY
SAGITTARIUS–CAPRICORN CUSP

Time will prove a great friend to Sagittarius–Capricorns when placed on the Way of Compassion, for with it they will doubtless improve on their ability to articulate and comment on the world around them in meaningful ways. Earlier in life, Sagittarius–Capricorns may struggle a bit with the challenges of this road, for their impulses toward generosity and helpfulness to others may exist at odds with a kind of inborn pessimism. Self-pity or a tendency to withdraw from the world and its problems can also be a stumbling block with this configuration. Socialization will be extremely important for Sagittarius–Capricorns, and they will do best when they are surrounded and befriended by those who encourage their unique and occasionally precognitive abilities and nurture their ease of expression. Once those born on the Cusp of Prophecy gain confidence in their unique abilities and perceptions and learn to share them with the rest of us, all will be better for the experience.

STEVE ALLEN
Comedian/TV host,
The Tonight Show

12/26/1921
Capricorn I

CHALLENGE: **BANISHING A "WHAT'S THE POINT" OR PESSIMISTIC ATTITUDE**
FULFILLMENT: **GLORYING IN THE SPIRIT OF THE HUMAN RACE**
NOTABLE: **MAUDE GONNE (IRISH NATIONALIST)**

December 26–January 2
THE RULER
CAPRICORN I

Dependable and responsible, Capricorn I individuals are likely to be quite happy on the Way of Compassion, though they will have to develop greater patience and flexibility on the social scene. Those born in the Week of the Ruler have a special genius for reorganizing things and are at their best when their causes and crusades involve improving efficiency or the like. Their deep-seated sense of tradition may be severely challenged on this karmic path, however, and they will doubtless be forced to discard old ways of life and outdated prejudices as they work to increase their awareness and understanding of the world around them. There is a real danger here of becoming too dogmatic and even tyrannical when they find their principles challenged. Yet if Capricorn I's work to utilize their great love of ideas to stay in tune with humanity's larger goals, the Way of Compassion will give them ample opportunity to shine.

CHALLENGE: **TAKING ON EMOTIONAL RESPONSIBILITY ONCE IN A WHILE**
FULFILLMENT: **TAKING CHARGE OF A PROJECT OR ORGANIZATION THAT PROVIDES SOME KIND OF SERVICE TO OTHERS**
NOTABLE: **RENATA TIBALDI (OPERATIC SOPRANO)**

January 3–9
DETERMINATION
CAPRICORN II

Individuals born in the Week of Determination are destined for great fulfillment when placed on the Way of Compassion. Gifted with natural determination and ambition, Capricorn II's are also blessed with an inborn sense of the deeper spiritual needs of humankind and will likely be sensitive to any challenges that present themselves here. If there is a danger, it is that they don't know when to quit and may find it difficult to admit when they've made a mistake. For that reason, they must be careful to choose their friends and crusades with discretion, or they could wind up wasting their energies in unworthy pursuits. Though social skills do not always come easily to them, they are wonderfully persuasive people, and once they break out of their early shells, their influence on the world is likely to last for a long time to come.

RUDYARD KIPLING
British writer, born in
India; *Jungle Book*; won
Nobel Prize

12/30/1865
Capricorn I

CHALLENGE: **TAKING CARE NOT TO LET EGO DRIVES TAKE OVER, EVEN THOUGH THEY ARE WORKING ON BEHALF OF OTHERS**
FULFILLMENT: **FINDING A PARTNER WITH WHOM THEY CAN FEEL EMPATHY**

January 10–16
DOMINANCE
CAPRICORN III

The self-sacrificing, generous attitudes that characterize Capricorn III's will be of tremendous aid on the Way of Compassion, yet they must take care that they don't take them too far. In the social sphere, Capricorn III's will be faced with the challenge of learning when and to whom they must say no. Also, their tendency to take themselves too seriously can impair their empathy for others, and they may occasionally collapse into bouts of self-pity and hopelessness. Capricorn III's will benefit greatly from cultivating their social contacts and skills, and their ability to share with others on a personal level will in turn nurture their ability to share with the world. Still, their great thoughtfulness, fine analytic ability, and wonderful sense of humor will doubtless make them popular, admired figures, providing that they bring those talents to bear in commenting on issues at hand.

CHALLENGE: **CHECKING ON THEIR CLOSER INTIMATE RELATIONSHIPS TO EVALUATE WHETHER THEY SMACK OF CODEPENDENCY**
FULFILLMENT: **FEELING THE BOOST TO THEIR SELF-CONFIDENCE THAT COMES WHEN OTHERS TURN TO THEM FOR THEIR CARING ADVICE**
NOTABLE: **SADE (POPULAR SINGER)**

January 17–22

MYSTERY AND IMAGINATION
CAPRICORN–AQUARIUS CUSP

The humanitarian disposition of those born on the Capricorn–Aquarius cusp will be of great benefit to them on the Way of Compassion, yet it is not always predictable just how their love of humankind will be expressed. Capricorn–Aquarians are likely to be controversial figures in any event and may encounter some quite explosive social situations on their journey. They may also do a great deal of wrestling with their personal demons and should take care that their considerable energies are not burned out by restlessness, mood swings, and extremes of irritability. While causes and crusades may hold a great attraction for them, they will also be challenged to cultivate more meaningful personal relationships, and learning to join forces with others and work with them on a day-to-day basis will doubtless occur. Nevertheless, their considerable empathy and natural talents as observers will be a great blessing, providing they do not fall into the traps of displays of emotional immaturity.

ROBERT HOLLEY
Shared 1968 Nobel Prize for medicine with Khorana for genetic code

1/28/1922
Aquarius I

CHALLENGE: **RECOGNIZING THEIR OWN CAPACITY FOR THE LESS SAVORY ASPECTS OF THE HUMAN TEMPERAMENT**
FULFILLMENT: **EXPANDING THEIR CAPACITY TO GIVE**
NOTABLES: **SUSANNAH HOFFS (LEAD SINGER, THE BANGLES); PAUL SCOFIELD (STAGE AND SCREEN ACTOR)**

January 23–30

GENIUS
AQUARIUS I

Striking a balance between social commitment and personal independence may cause some problems for Aquarius I's, since at the bottom line, they just don't like being told what to do. Individuals born in the Week of Genius are, however, blessed with a unique understanding of how the world works and an equally unique perspective on how to make it a better place. Whatever their projects or passions, they are sure to excite the imaginations and intellects of all around them, yet they may find it in their best interest to leave the detail work to someone else. They therefore make wonderful teachers and commentators, providing they cultivate the patience necessary to get their ideas across. Analysis and social consciousness come easy for Aquarius I's, but fulfillment will come through the expression and sharing of their views.

CHALLENGE: **NOT PERMITTING THEMSELVES TO INDULGE IN CHRONIC EMOTIONAL UPSETS OVER THE PLIGHT OF OTHERS**
FULFILLMENT: **PERSEVERING FOR THE RIGHT PERSON OR CAUSE, EVEN FACING FAILURE, DISASTER, OR WORSE**

January 31–February 7

YOUTH AND EASE
AQUARIUS II

Those born in the Week of Youth and Ease can become real masters of the social scene, since they are blessed with popularity and a rare kind of appeal. Aquarius II's may find it difficult to separate from their own star quality, however, and may falter in their development due to a certain tendency to allow other people's opinions of them to shape their opinion of themselves. For that reason they may withdraw from the challenge of social issues, preferring to avoid controversy in the interest of maintaining their image. They can in fact be so well socialized that they adopt the values and mores of those around them without proper analysis. It's critical for these people to work on their moral code and develop a set of beliefs that will allow them to grow past their core insecurities. Once they do, their natural talents and social sensitivities will provide them with the necessary tools to accomplish great things on the Way of Compassion.

LAWRENCE TAYLOR,
seen here with Mark Bavaro; former NY Giants football player

2/4/1959
Aquarius II

CHALLENGE: **BURDENING THEMSELVES WITH MORE SOCIAL OR COMPASSIONATE TASTES ONCE IN A WHILE**
FULFILLMENT: **EXPERIENCING THE GROWING EMOTIONAL MATURITY THAT CARING BRINGS**
NOTABLE: **PATRICK MacNEE (ACTOR, THE AVENGERS)**

February 8–15

ACCEPTANCE
AQUARIUS III

Aquarius III individuals will surely be challenged to overcome old prejudices when placed upon this karmic path. Indeed, all forms of social interaction are learning experiences for them, and the development of a more tolerant attitude toward people on both the personal and larger social levels will be critical to their spiritual expansion. Somewhat touchy by nature, Aquarius III's run the risk of expending their energies in an excess of aggression and will benefit enormously from greater objectivity. Joining themselves to humanitarian efforts and larger social concerns will free Aquarius III's from the demands of ego and enable them to rise above many of the day-to-day annoyances that tend to plague their personal lives. Yet with their fine sense of the future, their affectionate and hopeful natures can wage the battle for a better world with passion, courage, and conviction.

CHALLENGE: **LEARNING TO RESPECT THE HUMANITY EVEN OF THOSE THEY CONSIDER TO BE SUPERFICIAL OR EGOTISTICAL**
FULFILLMENT: **FURTHER DEVELOPING THE BROAD TOLERANCE THAT IS THEIR NATURE**
NOTABLE: **WILLIAM HENRY HARRISON (9TH U.S. PRESIDENT; DIED AFTER ONE MONTH IN OFFICE)**

February 16–22
SENSITIVITY
AQUARIUS–PISCES CUSP

This socially oriented karmic path will help Aquarius–Pisces cusp personalities find a middle road between far-out idealism and profound inner exploration. All forms of social interaction and concern will illuminate both the inner reality for these highly sensitive people as well as their larger ideals, and they should take care to cultivate their social inclinations at every opportunity. They are blessed with a natural concern and caring for their fellow human beings, and if they can overcome their personal insecurity and fear of rejection to air their views and join forces with those of like mind, they will find that the walls they have built around themselves will come tumbling down, affording them great freedom of expression. As a reward, their work for the larger good will never lose its touch of essential humanity and their sensitivity will never lose sight of the larger goal.

**EDGAR BERGEN &
CHARLIE MCCARTHY**
Ventriloquist, shown with
Charlie McCarthy;
Candice Bergen's father
———
2/16/1903
Aquarius–Pisces Cusp

CHALLENGE: **DEVOTING SOME OF THE TIME THEY GIVE TO THEIR CAREERS TO DOING GOOD WORKS**
FULFILLMENT: **DISCOVERING THE CARING—THOUGH USUALLY SUPPRESSED—SIDE OF THEIR PSYCHES**
NOTABLES: **FRÉDÉRIC CHOPIN (POLISH PIANIST/COMPOSER); DAVID MANNES (FOUNDER OF MUSIC SCHOOL); JOHN MCENROE (TENNIS PLAYER)**

February 23–March 2
SPIRIT
PISCES I

Pisces I individuals are born with a natural ability to rise above many of the pettier concerns of life, yet they may on occasion rise so high that they are brought back down to earth with something of a jolt. Their starlike quality will serve them well on this path, providing they are careful not to shirk the social responsibilities that go with it. Blessed with a deep concern for their fellows, Pisces I's may nevertheless turn their backs on suffering, believing themselves unable to be of any great assistance in the hands-on aspects of making the world a better place. Still, the social opportunities of this configuration cannot be ignored, and their destinies will surely beckon them into a position of prominence that will enable them to fight for the highest good. If Pisces I's take up the challenge, their diplomatic abilities, combined with their generous dose of personal appeal, will ensure their success on this journey.

CHALLENGE: **OPENING THEIR EYES TO SUFFERING BEFORE THEY ARE MADE TO LEARN FIRSTHAND**
FULFILLMENT: **SERVING IN SMALL, EVERYDAY WAYS**
NOTABLES: **HERBERT DOW (FOUNDED DOW CHEMICAL CO., 1900); CYRIL ARTHUR PEARSON (PUBLISHER; FOUNDER, *PEARSON'S WEEKLY*)**

March 3–10
THE LONER
PISCES II

Pisces II souls on the Way of Compassion may find that their struggles center around issues of basic connection and socialization. Those born in the Week of the Loner do not take to others easily and can be downright timid when it comes to joining forces for a common cause. Relationships will have to be formed and re-formed with considerable regularity here, as Pisces II's believe on some level that they can figure out the secrets of social interaction and commitment without necessarily having to participate. How the world works can become a major preoccupation for them. Still, they are highly intelligent and crave being able to communicate their ideas. If they are careful to devote their energies to concrete concerns and socially stable professions and institutions, the good Pisces II's can do for others is considerable in the areas of the written word, teaching, psychology, and service.

AIDAN QUINN
Film actor
———
3/8/1959
Pisces II

CHALLENGE: **FORCING THEMSELVES TO INTERACT SOCIALLY, EVEN IF ONLY SUPERFICIALLY**
FULFILLMENT: **FEELING THAT THEY ARE CARD-CARRYING MEMBERS OF THE HUMAN RACE**
NOTABLES: **BRIAN "KATO" KAELIN (NOTED HOUSEGUEST AND PERSONALITY); TOM ARNOLD (COMEDIAN/ACTOR)**

March 11–18
DANCERS AND DREAMERS
PISCES III

The Way of Compassion holds every promise for Pisces III individuals. Gifted with the philosophical and empathetic qualities required, those born in the Week of Dancers and Dreamers also have enormous personal appeal and will have little trouble with many of the social stumbling blocks presented to others on this karmic path. Finely attuned to the views and needs of mankind, Pisces III's may nevertheless become too subjective and lose sight of the larger picture. Alternatively, they may get caught up in theory at the expense of practical considerations, and their ability to do good may be compromised as a result. Pisces III's need to work on developing a solid moral code and avoid their tendency to drift with the tide of current fashions and social concerns. Otherwise they run the risk of helping the homeless one week and joining a cult the next. Still, if they cultivate stability and a solid work ethic, they can apply their considerable gifts in a way that can reveal the truths that are common to us all.

CHALLENGE: **CENTERING THEIR EFFORTS FOR OTHERS ON ONE PATH AND TAKING IT ONE STEP AT A TIME**
FULFILLMENT: **FINDING A DEEPER MEANING IN LIFE**
NOTABLES: **LAWRENCE WELK (BANDLEADER; TELEVISION PROGRAM HOST, 1951–1971); DOROTHY SCHIFF (FIRST WOMAN PUBLISHER IN U.S., *NEW YORK POST*)**

The Way of Instruction

ARIES III TO LIBRA III
Pioneer to Theater

Those who find themselves on the Way of Instruction are destined to share or impart some unique expertise or experience with others—sometimes simply the wisdom achieved by living. Thus, one finds these individuals acquiring or developing a system of knowledge or a skill early in their lives. Their journey, however, does not stop there. Those on the Way of Instruction must learn to share their expertise with others. Inherent in the character of these people is a natural leadership ability. They truly have a desire to lead but must work hard to develop the skills to do so. Rising to the top of a profession or social system may not come easily to them. Once they have arrived, however—and they always do—their mission is to learn how to teach what they know without falling prey to their inborn didacticism.

The core lesson of the Way of Instruction is the development of a real desire to share what one knows with others, while allowing them to have their own thoughts, ideas, and theories. Anyone on this path eventually discovers the truth in the well-worn saying "Knowledge is power." Thus, in their long, hard struggle to become top dog, one of their weapons may be withholding information and keeping what they know to themselves. But it is the destiny of those on this karmic path to overcome this tendency, difficult as it may be. Another problem is that since this journey begins at the Pioneer, there exists

CORE LESSON

Discovering that the best leaders are also teachers and that the best teacher guides a student to the student's own conclusion

GOAL

To lead and teach democratically while also considering the feelings of others

---

GIFTS
Positive, Diplomatic, Sacrificing

PITFALLS
Didactic, Self-pitying, World-weary

---

an ingrained habit of forcing one's ideas on others. Part of the lesson of the Way of Instruction is to actively encourage students to draw their own conclusions; in other words, not to lecture so much as query, allowing students to formulate their own views. Individuals on this karmic path are prone to be gentle tyrants. It is best for them to keep the attitude that, on any spiritual path, instructors can learn as much—if not more—from their students as their students learn from them. Interestingly, those on the Way of Instruction have many spiritual lessons to learn.

These individuals have a certain fearlessness, one that permits them to attain great heights. Is it any surprise that many with this configuration become political leaders? Highly idealistic, they are born with a pioneering spirit that, when harnessed, can be transmuted into an extraordinary capacity for leadership. Donning such a mantle, however, does require the development of greater sophistication in the ways of the world. Though these individuals are gifted natural diplomats, they are by nature also rougher, more outspoken types, who tend to approach others on a "take me or leave me" basis and are certainly not willing to change or soften themselves for anyone. If these trench soldiers are to become generals, they must learn more about social niceties or "spit and polish."

It's lonely at the top, and usually those on this path would rather be surrounded by loved ones. Thus, once

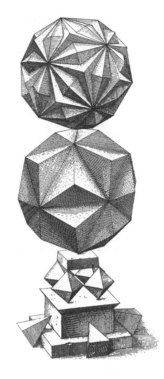

they achieve a position of ruler-ship, they are apt to struggle with feelings of loneliness and depri-vation. Luckily, their intimacy needs are dependent not on deep connections with others but rather on numerous ones. They just like to have a lot of other people around them. Thus, there is a danger that people on the Way of Instruction will surround themselves with sycophants or groupies. These types of people, unfortunately, are unlikely either to stand up to those on the Way of Instruction or to challenge them to see other points of view, something that is sorely needed for their development.

Those traveling the Way of Instruction must learn that a certain amount of theatricality should go into the edu-cational process; that is, entertainment can be one of the greatest ways of making a point. Generally serious in outlook, individuals on the Way of Instruction would do well to learn to take themselves less seriously and to incorporate more playful or expressive quali-ties into their nature. However, once the worldliness and success they work so hard to achieve comes to them, they are apt to relax and the rest of their journey will fall into place. They will mas-ter the grand gesture and the ability to command an au-dience, and ultimately, they will have a desire to share the fruits of their hard-won wisdom.

Obviously, the arena of life that is most fated for those on the Way of Instruction involves career or social

standing. Meetings of all types—whether business, club, aca-demic, recreational, parental, or other—will acquaint those on this karmic path with the social skills needed to lead such groups. Thus, those on this path are urged to seek out and participate in social organizations of all kinds. However, patience is war-ranted, as many years of maturing in such contexts may be required before those on this karmic path are ready to exert effective leadership. A major mistake would occur if their natural thirst for ide-alism and leadership causes them to lunge headfirst into an attempt to take over the reins of power in a group. Doing this before establishing a constituency of support by others will only succeed in making others angry. Al-ternatively, feeling insecure in their ability to lead, they may lock themselves into a self-sacrificing situation of perpetually remaining in the role of foot soldier. Once in a leadership role, they may also be-come tyrannical, expecting others to blindly, unquestioningly, and loyally follow them to their ulti-mate goal—without ever telling anyone what that goal is.

The ability of those on this karmic path to lead and to teach is heavily dependent on how their constituency sees them. Should others see them as wide-eyed idealists or monomaniacal, obviously only the more unstable of their followers will continue to be will-ing to learn. Thus, it is important for them to express their goals and outline their agenda clearly. Holding

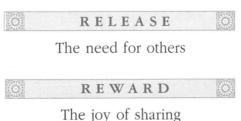

RELEASE

The need for others

REWARD

The joy of sharing
what one knows

SUGGESTION

*Be open to all ideas; any one could prove useful. Assuage feelings
of loneliness by developing a relationship with spirit.*

back information or being secretive will always engender suspicion and hostility. The best leaders are often those who also serve by squarely placing their support behind others rather than blindly following an ideal at all costs. Strong bonds with leaders of other groups, whether professional, leisure-time, or family, will provide them with examples to learn from and identify with and create open channels of communication for learning. Having even one such individual from whom advice can be sought is essential to remaining objective.

Because those on this path have little time for a personal life, they tend to give up more intimate personal relationships in favor of worldly action. Their lovers, mates, friends, and family members will often suffer from feelings of neglect. Those on the Way of Instruction, who have a strong need for close intimates, may periodically suffer from having to sacrifice their relationships to a greater cause. A danger exists here: these individuals are usually gifted with a healthy, if not powerful, sexuality. It is imperative for them to learn to rein in their passions as they adjust to leading a more solitary life. Otherwise the combination of their lustiness together with a tendency to rationalize could prove to be a lethal combination. Sexual peccadillos are the minefields on this karmic path and could prove to be their undoing.

Partners of those on this path must be independent types who can also be flexible. Those on the Way of Instruction come to spiritual fruition only later in life. In the meantime, husbands, wives, and lovers will have to learn to live with the absence and workaholic tendencies of their mates. Moreover, the these individuals' inherent idealism means that they expect quite a lot from their partners, given that they feel they themselves are sacrificing so much, and tend to want what they want when they want it.

These people do not always know what is best for them. Their drive for success may mean that they neglect their own needs or health. They may wish others to follow them around, attending to their every need, but in fact this is not what is good for them. They need people who will point out when they are wrong or misguided. And they must learn not to oscillate between their career and personal lives so rapidly. Finding the balance between work and play is key here. Learning to delegate responsibility, to develop others to take on duties and share power—in other words, to teach what they know—is what the Way of Instruction is all about. It is the key to their long-term success, health, and prosperity. Ultimately, they will discover that the pleasure of sharing knowledge is the real reward.

The image that comes to mind for those on this karmic path is a productive fruit tree that stands alone, permitting birds to nestle in its branches, giving shade to animals and humans, shedding its leaves to fertilize the ground, below, and ultimately giving freely of its yield for all to enjoy.

BALANCE POINT

Education and Learning

CRYSTALS AND GEMSTONES

Carnelian activates the mind and stimulates initiative that can lead an individual to positions of power. This regal stone inspires openness, patience, and clear communication.

NOTABLES ON THIS KARMIC PATH

MADONNA

Following the Way of Instruction, **Madonna** has not been content to be solely a rock star despite her meteoric rise to fame. Instead, she has shown an acute need to share her experience with others and to teach by example. Her prominent public stances have been interpreted in many ways; some see her as an important feminist, others as a spokesperson for her generation. Like many on this path, Madonna is both idealistic and pioneering, but her outspokenness seems to land her in hot water now and then. However, as she has matured she has developed the more refined social skills that will ensure her continued success on the Way of Instruction.

Star Trek creator **Gene Roddenberry** shared his unique vision of the future with millions of people around the world. A true pioneer, Roddenberry not only learned the attributes of his karmic destination of Libra III theater, he also excelled at conveying his ideas, and his use of the grand gesture succeeded in capturing the imagination of his viewers. Roddenberry's desire to lead is reflected in his alter ego, Captain Kirk. Through the appeal of this character and the corre-

GENE RODDENBERRY

sponding success of *Star Trek,* Roddenberry was truly able to go "where no man has ever gone before." Doubtless Roddenberry, like Kirk, also learned to delegate responsibility and build a most effective team.

JACK NICKLAUS

The domination of any major sport is a destiny reserved for a select few. Champion golfer **Jack Nicklaus** has achieved this distinction in his long and successful career. Simultaneously, he has built an impressive following for both himself and his sport. Many who otherwise would have shown little interest in the game have been attracted, even mesmerized, by Nicklaus's skill, dedication, and stamina. His charismatic persona has also played a large role in the assumption of a prominent leadership role in this profession. Truly an "instructor" who has taught by example, Nicklaus stands in our time as an outstanding model of a golf player.

Other Notables: Alan Jackson, Tom Brokaw, Barney Frank, Charles Scribner, Jr., Jack Valenti, Alice Tully, Smokey Robinson, Al Pacino, Harry S. Truman, Dante Gabriel Rossetti, Andrei Sakharov, Philip Mountbatten, Joseph Papp, Liv Tyler, Nancy Reagan, Angela Bassett, Alex Haley, Jacqueline Susann, Ben Bradlee, Ethan Coen, Ed Sullivan, Jamie Lee Curtis, Kit Carson, Thomas Alva Edison, Nick Nolte, Alexander Graham Bell

BIRTHDAYS ON KARMIC PATH 4

February 11, 1884–June 30, 1884 | September 23, 1902–February 11, 1903 | May 4, 1921–September 22, 1921

December 15, 1939–May 3, 1940 | July 26, 1958–December 14, 1958 | March 7, 1977–July 25, 1977

October 17, 1995–March 6, 1996 | May 28, 2014–October 16, 2014

KARMIC PATH
4

March 19–24

REBIRTH
PISCES–ARIES CUSP

Learning to rise above personal slights and misunderstandings is paramount for those born on the Pisces–Aries cusp, and the challenges presented by this karmic path will ensure that they improve their powers of communication in order to better impart their unique brand of knowledge. Pisces–Aries individuals tend to have something of an obsessive quality, however, and may find it difficult to relinquish the personal in favor of the universal. Since this path demands that individuals work in groups while at the same time learning to live independently, this karmic path may well lead to a life of wandering in environments where excellent social skills are demanded and expected but personal relationships are not so important. Still, if Pisces–Aries individuals remain open to new horizons and cultivate the love of knowledge for its own sake, the Way of Instruction will abound with opportunities to share that knowledge with the world.

CHALLENGE: **MINIMIZING THE INSTINCTUAL IN FAVOR OF THE RATIONAL**

FULFILLMENT: **MOVING INTO A POSITION OF AUTHORITY FROM WHICH THEY CAN ULTIMATELY SHARE WHAT THEY KNOW**

WALTER HUSTON
(on right), seen here with John Huston; won Oscar for son John's *Treasure of the Sierra Madre*

4/6/1884
Aries II

March 25–April 2

THE CHILD
ARIES I

Aries I's approach the Way of Instruction with admirable enthusiasm and excitement, though there is some danger that they will be viewed as overzealous or childish in their need to communicate their latest discoveries. Those born in the Week of the Child do well to cultivate more depth and avoid the temptations of greener pastures and wider skies. Proper amounts of time alone, with adequate opportunities for introspection, will help Aries I's absorb their experience in a way that they can translate to others. Passionate and excitable, they can get mired in a need for approval and may waste their energies by clinging to the notion that their egos are inseparable from their need to instruct. Still, Aries I's are gifted with a taste for exploration and an open, willing heart. If they apply those qualities to their quest for expertise and take care to return that knowledge to the world, they will travel far indeed.

CHALLENGE: **BALANCING THEIR NEED TO STRIVE IN THE WORLD WITH THEIR NEED TO BE ALONE**

FULFILLMENT: **IMPARTING THEIR CHILDLIKE ENTHUSIASM FOR THEIR METIER TO OTHERS**

NOTABLES: **BARNEY FRANK (DEMOCRATIC CONGRESSMAN); ASTRUD GILBERTO (BRAZILIAN SINGER)**

April 3–10

THE STAR
ARIES II

Individuals born in the Week of the Star are likely to do well on the Way of Instruction, since they are naturally attracted to groups and group dynamics. Though Aries II's crave center stage, that is not always a disadvantage on this karmic path, since their starlike qualities give them a fine opportunity to impart their knowledge and experience. There is some danger that their need for attention will spill over into their personal lives and that they will surround themselves with the kind of superficial associations and personal satellites they would be better off without. Aries II's are perfectly capable of misleading others as to the level of their personal commitment and can break any number of hearts before they come to recognize and own the nature of their destiny. Still, their need for success, personal charisma, and ability to give themselves fully to a profession, movement, or cause will serve them well on the Way of Instruction.

CHALLENGE: **OCCASIONALLY RELINQUISHING CENTER STAGE TO THOSE THEY TEACH**

FULFILLMENT: **RELISHING THE POSITION OF ELDER STATESMAN OR SCHOLAR**

NOTABLE: **JOHN HAVLICEK (BASKETBALL PLAYER)**

HERBIE HANCOCK
American jazz musician

4/12/1940
Aries III

April 11–18

THE PIONEER
ARIES III

Blessed with true nobility of character, Aries III individuals are sure to flourish on the Way of Instruction. Generous of themselves and protective of others, Aries III's will likely rise to the level of expertise and social comprehension demanded by this karmic path. Those born in the Week of the Pioneer are gifted with the ability to motivate others to their dynamic ideas and ideals, and that talent is sure to find full expression in the course of their lives. Perhaps the real pitfall here is a tendency to force others to their way of thinking and bend less sturdy types to their will. Too, they may experience some difficulty in giving up the more personal side of life in favor of some larger calling, for they do not like to be alone. Still, if they remember that teaching, by its very nature, is a give-and-take of ideas, and if they are careful not to become rigid or isolated by a set of inflexible beliefs, their success on this path is all but ensured.

CHALLENGE: **GIVING OF THEMSELVES IN ONE-ON-ONE INTIMATE RELATIONSHIPS**

FULFILLMENT: **SHARING THEIR CONSCIENCE AND COMMITMENT WITH OTHERS**

NOTABLES: **JULIE CHRISTIE (ACTRESS); MARGARETHE II (QUEEN OF DENMARK)**

April 19–24
POWER
ARIES–TAURUS CUSP

Personalities with this configuration are blessed indeed, for over the course of time they will not only enjoy an ongoing sense of discovery but will also put their full powers into play. Natural leaders, these hardworking, dynamic people are gifted with a unique sense of timing that will prove of the utmost importance on their personal journey. Though Aries–Tauruses can get mired in repetitive or even compulsive behaviors that keep them from discovering a broader range of knowledge, their yearning for expertise can impart a whole new meaning to the phrase "Knowledge is power." For those born on the Cusp of Power, the two are one and the same. Even though they will doubtless be asked at some point to relinquish a share of their personal power in order to impart their considerable understanding to the world, they are almost sure to accept that opportunity with the grace and dignity demanded by the Way of Instruction.

CHALLENGE: **LEARNING HOW TO LET GO OF THE REINS OF POWER AND SHARE WITH OTHERS**
FULFILLMENT: **REAPING THE REWARDS OF THEIR EVOLUTION TO TEACHER**
NOTABLE: **LEE MAJORS (ACTOR, SIX MILLION DOLLAR MAN)**

AL PACINO
Film actor, Scarface
————
4/25/1940
Taurus I

April 25–May 2
MANIFESTATION
TAURUS I

Taurus I's may experience a bit of a struggle when placed upon this karmic path, if only because their attachment to creature comforts may exist at odds with the need to develop a broader vision called for by this path. Still, they have a great deal going for them with this configuration, and though they may be confirmed workaholics and quite stubborn, they are likely to do well in groups and will thrive in the spotlight, providing they can rouse themselves for the performance. Though a real tendency to self-indulgence is present here, Taurus I individuals make fine leaders who can keep their fingers on the pulse of the many in highly practical and efficient ways. Cultivating the ability to share along every step of the way will be important for these sturdy souls. Yet, if Taurus I's do so and further leave themselves open to a lively exchange of ideas and strengths, they will have found their truest calling.

CHALLENGE: **BECOMING MORE DISCRIMINATING IN THE SATISFACTION OF THEIR PHYSICAL DESIRES**
FULFILLMENT: **ASCENDING, AFTER A LONG AND PATIENT CLIMB, TO A SEAT OF LEADERSHIP**
NOTABLE: **WILHELMINA COOPER (FOUNDED MODELING AGENCY)**

May 3–10
THE TEACHER
TAURUS II

Taurus II personalities will doubtless find themselves wonderfully suited to the Way of Instruction. Though those born in the Week of the Teacher can be quite demanding on a personal level and do best when they limit or at least moderate their relationships, their impulse to share and to instruct others is sure to outweigh any possible disadvantages of this configuration. Taurus II's have the necessary energy to place themselves at the center of the action. If they cultivate the empathy to tune in to the needs and wishes of their audience, their nurturing, protective side will blossom. With time they will develop the patience and perseverance necessary to ensure that their body of knowledge is shared for the collective benefit of mankind. For Taurus II's are blessed with the ability not only to teach but also to show others how to teach by their example. Thus, their influence can be boundless.

CHALLENGE: **NEGOTIATING THE INTRICACIES OF THEIR CLOSEST RELATIONSHIPS**
FULFILLMENT: **KNOWING THAT THEY HAVE EXCELLED, TAUGHT, AND HELD TRUE TO THEMSELVES**
NOTABLE: **JEAN HENRI DUNANT (SHARED FIRST NOBEL PEACE PRIZE)**

HARRY S. TRUMAN
33rd U.S. president;
"the buck stops here"
————
5/8/1884
Taurus II

May 11–18
THE NATURAL
TAURUS III

An ability to integrate with their environment will be critical to the success of Taurus III individuals on the Way of Instruction. Their fascination with the natural world is sure to manifest in the acquisition of some expertise in that area, and they would do well to pass their insights along. Those born in the the Week of the Natural may be largely self-taught and self-made, as they have something of an aversion to structure and discipline. But their yearning for freedom will get in their way only if they allow it to interfere with their commitment to society. The only real danger is that they may neglect to develop any necessary expertise and retreat into a kind of self-imposed isolation where the wealth of their knowledge is squandered in obsessive frustration or missed opportunities to connect with the world.

CHALLENGE: **LEARNING HOW TO BE A STUDENT THEMSELVES**
FULFILLMENT: **ENJOYING THE SECURITY THAT SUCCESS AND THE RESPECT OF THEIR PEERS AND THEIR STUDENTS BRING THEM**
NOTABLES: **DANTE GABRIEL ROSSETTI (POET; PAINTER); FARLEY MOWAT (WRITER)**

May 19–24
ENERGY
TAURUS–GEMINI CUSP

Those born on the Cusp of Energy are blessed with a keen interest in the world around them, and their impulse to broaden and expand their horizons will be evident at a very early age. Despite their tremendous energies, however, they may fail to slow down long enough to acquire the depth of experience and expertise demanded by this path. Taurus–Geminis have a rather charmingly unselfconscious approach to life, but it can hold them back if they fail to develop a thorough knowledge of themselves. Gifted performers, they can sometimes lose their audience through displays of temper or by insisting on their own way at the expense of the larger group objective. Still, these individuals are destined to harness their energy over time, and their ability to slow down, to focus, and to give themselves to the world as teachers, artists, and experts will ensure their success.

ANDREI SAKHAROV
Helped develop Soviet H-bomb; became a dissident; won Nobel Peace Prize

5/21/1921
Taurus–Gemini Cusp

CHALLENGE: **FOCUSING THEIR ENERGIES ON THE DEVELOPMENT OF ONE AREA OF EXPERTISE**

FULFILLMENT: **LEARNING TO RELEASE, THROUGH INSTRUCTION, ALL THE KNOWLEDGE THEY SPENT YEARS GATHERING**

May 25–June 2
FREEDOM
GEMINI I

Witty and charismatic, individuals born in the Week of Freedom have truly formidable gifts, for it is essential to their natures to express themselves openly and to stick up for what they believe in. Still, the road to honing their verbal talents to a diplomatic fine edge may be difficult, and they will doubtless have many struggles and disappointments over their tendency to "spill the beans" or say too much, too soon. Unfinished business and undeveloped talents may also be a problem, since this configuration lends itself to dilettantism and the scattering of one's energies. As leaders, Gemini I's can excel, as long as they delegate responsibility for detail work to somebody else. Naturally social, Gemini I's are capable of meeting the demands of this karmic path, providing they allow themselves the time to mature and cultivate determination and commitment. Blessed with considerable problem-solving ability and great powers of reason, the Way of Instruction will be good to them, imparting an ability to share their hard-won wisdom.

CHALLENGE: **CULTIVATING PATIENCE WITH SLOWER-WITTED COLLEAGUES, STUDENTS, AND FRIENDS**

FULFILLMENT: **ENJOYING THE VERBAL REPARTEE INHERENT IN THE TEACHING PROCESS**

NOTABLE: **HAL DAVID (LYRICIST)**

June 3–10
NEW LANGUAGE
GEMINI II

Gifted with the ability to communicate in unique ways, Gemini II's will really start to flower once they come to the understanding that their immediate social circle may provide them with the best audience they could hope for. As highly personal as the verbal expression of those born in the Week of New Language can sometimes be, they are not always readily understood by others. It may therefore be something of a struggle for them to forgo the larger adventure in order to convey a greater message and teaching—for in this case the Way of Instruction may well begin in their own backyard. The mantle of leadership, too, will not come easily, as Gemini II's dislike the feeling of being overburdened with responsibilities. Still, if they choose their areas of endeavor well and work hard to cultivate the strength of purpose required by this configuration, Gemini II's are sure to rise to the wealth of opportunities for self-expression presented by this karmic path.

CHALLENGE: **FINDING GROUPS, ASSOCIATIONS, AND FRIENDS WITH WHOM THEY CAN FEEL AT HOME**

FULFILLMENT: **SHARING THEIR UNIQUE MODE OF THOUGHT WITH EVEN JUST A HANDFUL OF PEOPLE**

NOTABLE: **PRINCE PHILIP MOUNTBATTEN (QUEEN ELIZABETH II'S HUSBAND)**

June 11–18
THE SEEKER
GEMINI III

Gifted with nearly boundless curiosity, Gemini III's will struggle against many of the limitations imposed by the Way of Instruction, for if ever there were a group of individuals willing to argue with the dictates of fate, it is these seekers. Though they are restless and independent, their thirst for knowledge will serve them in good stead, and if they accept the restrictions of responsibility imposed on them by this karmic path, they can attain great success as educators, leaders, diplomats, and philosophers of all kinds. Part of their destiny may require them to bear the responsibility of tearing down old social orders in favor of new ways of thought or government, and many will find themselves thrust into far-off lands and unusual circumstances in their quest for progress. Still, Gemini III's are unlikely to suffer much from the lessening of personal involvement indicated here and will flourish in the acquisition of more worldly ways and tastes.

NELSON RIDDLE
Musician and bandleader

6/1/1921
Gemini I

CHALLENGE: **ESTABLISHING A WELL-GROUNDED CAREER AS A BASE OF OPERATIONS**

FULFILLMENT: **LEARNING TO ENJOY THE GIVE-AND-TAKE OF THE EDUCATIONAL PROCESS**

June 19–24
MAGIC
GEMINI–CANCER CUSP

Destined by both inclination and disposition to put their natural talents to the service of a higher cause, those born on the Gemini–Cancer cusp are likely to accomplish a great deal when placed on the Way of Instruction. Though they can sometimes project an image of innocent charm, they are nevertheless well grounded, hardworking people who can inspire those around them with their knowledge, considerable insight, and almost magical grasp of human dynamics and events. Gemini–Cancers have little or no problem stepping into a role of leadership, though they may experience difficulty with the more personal side of this path, especially if it requires them to let go of their deepest emotional attachments. Still, Gemini–Cancers will find some way to impart their knowledge to the rest of us, probably through their ability to strike the universal chords of feeling that run through us all.

JOSEPH PAPP
Stage producer; founded NY's Shakespeare in the Park

6/22/1921
Gemini–Cancer Cusp

CHALLENGE: **GRAPPLING WITH THEIR INTIMACY NEEDS, THEIR NEED FOR SOLITUDE, AND THE SOCIAL REQUIREMENTS OF THIS PATH**
FULFILLMENT: **GIVING OF THEMSELVES TO OTHERS**
NOTABLE: **JANE RUSSELL (FILM ACTRESS)**

June 25–July 2
THE EMPATH
CANCER I

Gifted with tremendous empathy and fine managerial talents, Cancer I individuals may be quite happy on the Way of Instruction, providing they avoid the tendency to get tripped up by their own emotions. At some point in their lives, they will doubtless be faced with the lesson of learning to focus their energies away from the personal and toward the universal. Yet time will be kind to Cancer I's, for as they grow away from emotional dependency they will discover a wealth of personal and executive strengths. They would do well to cultivate their social contacts and inclinations, for they have a great need to put their experience and understanding to the service of their fellows. Though those born in the Week of the Empath may indeed have "greatness thrust upon them," if they avoid isolation and their tendency to nurse old hurts and beat dead horses, they will shine on this karmic path.

CHALLENGE: **DISCERNING WHO THEIR MOST TRUSTWORTHY ASSOCIATES ARE AND THEN SHARING ALL WITH THEM**
FULFILLMENT: **DISCOVERING THEIR OWN ABILITIES AS EXECUTIVES AND "ELDER STATESMEN"**
NOTABLE: **LIV TYLER (FILM ACTRESS)**

July 3–10
THE UNCONVENTIONAL
CANCER II

The Cancer II personality on the Way of Instruction is more or less assured of having an exciting time of it. Naturally flamboyant, their charisma is sure to spark the imaginations of many along the road. Blessed with a fine sense of honesty and generosity, Cancer II's will be attracted to the social side of life and are the kind of people who can make giving seem the best adventure of all. Further, they are capable of shouldering great responsibilities in the interests of the larger social good though are usually hampered somewhat since they rarely take the traditional routes to success. Once they find their venue, they may well have to sidestep issues of narcissism—or at least the tendency to fall for their own press releases—but they will find that the real mirror of character is their audience. Still, if they take care to cultivate the solid traits of character that lie beneath their impressive facades, they will do well on the Way of Instruction.

JOHN GLENN
Astronaut and senator; 2nd American and the oldest man in space

7/18/1921
Cancer III

CHALLENGE: **SUBSTITUTING A NONTRADITIONAL ROUTE FOR A MORE TRADITIONAL PATH**
FULFILLMENT: **TEACHING OTHERS WHO SHARE THEIR PERSONAL VISION**
NOTABLE: **NANCY REAGAN (FORMER FIRST LADY)**

July 11–18
THE PERSUADER
CANCER III

Irresistibly attracted to the corridors of power, those born in the Week of the Persuader will find this karmic path an easy road to travel. Blessed with the ability to bring others around to their way of thinking as well as a great ability to control their own needs, Cancer III's make formidable, responsible leaders. However, they have a tendency to take themselves rather too seriously and will doubtless be confronted with the reality that, in order to get people to do their bidding, they must sometimes first lighten their hearts. If the true measure of leadership is in the conviction that the good of the group is at stake, the Cancer IIIs are unlikely to be plagued by self-doubt. Thus, if they can avoid being too manipulative and work against their need to surround themselves with those unwilling to challenge their sometimes ironclad opinions, their directness, goals, and plans will serve them well.

CHALLENGE: **SOFTENING THEIR APPROACH TO LIFE**
FULFILLMENT: **HAVING SPENT YEARS INVESTING IN THEMSELVES, OPENING UP THE VAULT AND BLOWING THE WAD**
NOTABLE: **CHARLES SCRIBNER, JR. (PUBLISHER, SCRIBNER BOOK CO.)**

July 19–25

OSCILLATION
CANCER–LEO CUSP

The passion, conviction, and considerable measure of moral courage that characterize Cancer–Leos promises great success on the Way of Instruction. The pitfalls here are primarily of a personal nature, and those born on the Cusp of Oscillation must cultivate a greater awareness of their predisposition to promiscuity, immediate gratification, and overdramatization of situations and circumstances. Learning emotional control is important, as is realizing that Cancer–Leos exist for the good of their audience and not the other way around. Still, their ability to handle crises, their dauntless approach to problems, and their fine intuitive sense of what the right thing to do is will serve them well. If Cancer–Leos are careful to dissociate from their own passions and at the same time nourish their playful, expressive side, they are sure to become the socially effective leaders and teachers called for by this karmic path.

ANGELA BASSETT
Film actress, played
Tina Turner

8/16/1958
Leo III

CHALLENGE: **RAISING THEIR LOW BOREDOM THRESHOLD BEFORE IT CREATES A DISASTER**
FULFILLMENT: **FORMING A BOND OF COMMONALITY WITH THEIR STUDENTS, ADMIRERS, AND ASSOCIATES**

July 26–August 2

AUTHORITY
LEO I

Maintaining a social network is extremely important for Leo I's with this configuration, as contact with a variety of people and situations will be essential to their development of the tolerance required by the Way of Instruction. Individuals born in the Week of Authority are generally very demanding of both themselves and others, yet they must absorb the lesson that in order to be effective teachers, they will have to cultivate the qualities of kindness, patience, and understanding. Later in life, they will also need to be aware of their tendency to withdraw from society into a personal ivory tower, thereby depriving themselves of the opportunity to grow through further social exposure. Still, Leo I's are blessed with dogged determination and are likely to become true experts in more than one area of endeavor. Born to impart their knowledge to the world, if they can avoid the pitfalls of excessive egotism and learn that service to humankind through leadership is perhaps the ultimate expression of generosity, their success is ensured.

CHALLENGE: **STAYING OUT OF THE IVORY TOWER**
FULFILLMENT: **REAPING THE REWARDS OF THEIR AMBITION BY FINDING OPPORTUNITIES TO SHINE**
NOTABLE: **KATE BUSH (POPULAR SINGER; MUSICIAN)**

August 3–10

BALANCED STRENGTH
LEO II

For the most part, Leo II's are blessed with the social skills necessary for real success along the Way of Instruction. Altruistic by nature, they also have an unpretentious quality that enables them to strike a chord of response in a wide variety of audiences. Well suited to this karmic path, Leo II's may nevertheless get mired in a tendency to be rather too self-sacrificing or to refuse to admit failure. Extreme loyalty in relationships and a certain unwillingness to be alone can also be problems. Still, they are gifted with an extraordinary and steady determination that gives them strength for the long haul. Though those born in the Week of Balanced Strength may occasionally find the Way of Instruction quite a long one before they are given their opportunity to shine, their sense of timing is usually faultless, and when the opportunities come, they are unlikely to miss them.

ALEX HALEY
Wrote biography of
Malcolm X (as dictated
by him) and *Roots*

8/11/1921
Leo III

CHALLENGE: **NOT NEGLECTING THEIR INTUITIVE SIDE**
FULFILLMENT: **ENJOYING A WELL-DESERVED REST AFTER THEIR LONG HAUL TO THE TOP**

August 11–18

LEADERSHIP
LEO III

Those born in the Week of Leadership have an almost heroic vision that can give them some difficulty in finding a footing on the Way of Instruction, for they would rather accomplish a mighty task themselves than impart their knowledge of how to do so to others. Impressive as they are, Leo III's are not especially fond of "giving away their magic" and may collapse into selfishness or a dictatorial attitude as a result. Learning to work well with others is paramount for them, as is being able to delegate and regulate their responsibilities. These are naturally powerful personalities whose commanding presence and creative approach in any social context are sure to win them attention. Gifted with the ability to win an audience, Leo III's will nevertheless have to be careful to complete their journey by sharing the knowledge and experience they have gained with others. When they do, they will find themselves an open channel for the love of the universe.

CHALLENGE: **BEING WILLING TO SHARE WHAT THEY HAVE LEARNED**
FULFILLMENT: **INDULGING THEMSELVES IN THE HONOR AND RESPECT OF OTHERS**
NOTABLES: **MADONNA (SINGER; ACTRESS); BELINDA CARLISLE (SINGER, THE GO-GOS)**

August 19–25

EXPOSURE
LEO–VIRGO CUSP

Blessed with a combination of practicality and idealism, individuals born on the Cusp of Exposure will doubtless do quite well on the Way of Instruction, as they have the capacity both to develop practical expertise and to expand ideologically. Leo–Virgos may struggle with the central task of sharing, however, since these rather secretive and even reclusive personalities tend to withhold information as a means of broadening their personal power base. Too, they will have to find the balancing point between self-interest and service to others. Still, Leo–Virgos are blessed with an admirable inclination to work for the larger social good. If they use their natural flamboyance to gain the audience necessary to accomplish their larger objectives, they will find themselves blessed with rare opportunities to become socially effective forces in the world.

JACQUELINE SUSANN
Actress-turned-novelist,
Valley of the Dolls

8/20/1921
Leo–Virgo Cusp

CHALLENGE: **FIGHTING THEIR INCLINATION TO STOCKPILE INFORMATION RATHER THAN SHARE IT**
FULFILLMENT: **RECORDING WHAT THEY KNOW AS A MEANS OF SHARING IT**
NOTABLE: **GENE RODDENBERRY (CREATOR, *STAR TREK*)**

August 26–September 2

SYSTEM BUILDERS
VIRGO I

Naturally a bit reticent when it comes to worldly affairs and inclinations, Virgo I's may find life full of sometimes unwelcome surprises when placed on the Way of Instruction. Though they are blessed with their own brand of social gifts, Virgo I's will have to fight their inclination to be rather too self-sacrificing. Too, many of them will find the limelight an unwelcome intrusion on their private world, and many will struggle with their natural shyness when offered opportunities to share their unique knowledge with the world. As a result, their teaching legacy may be admittedly grand but somewhat impersonal systems or structures. Still, whatever their area of endeavor, the work of Virgo I's will have a practical purpose, a social impact, and the mark of highly individual wisdom.

CHALLENGE: **OVERCOMING SHYNESS IN ORDER TO BECOME LEADERS**
FULFILLMENT: **BEING IN A POSITION TO SHARE WHAT THEY KNOW WITHOUT DEMANDS**
NOTABLES: **MICHAEL JACKSON (POPULAR SINGER/DANCER); SCOTT HAMILTON (FIGURE SKATER; OLYMPIC GOLD MEDALIST, 1984)**

September 3–10

THE ENIGMA
VIRGO II

While it is rather unlikely that Virgo II's will indulge in the flamboyant personal presentation of many others on this karmic path, they will nevertheless make their mark in an impressive manner. Highly socially conscious and with a pronounced executive ability, they can be quite capable of stepping in and taking charge when a situation requires it. Though Virgo II's may struggle with the high expectations that others place upon them, these souls will nevertheless rise to their opportunities with a great deal of dignity and a minimum of fuss. They should, however, avoid the tendency to take things too seriously or to become preoccupied with their worldly image to the extent that it impairs their social effectiveness. Whatever their chosen social milieu, this path will demand of them that they learn to share their feelings in a very personal way in order to effect their purposes. Thus, if they can learn to open up, their progress on the road will be rapid indeed.

BEN BRADLEE
Publisher *Washington Post*, writer-journalist

8/26/1921
Virgo I

CHALLENGE: **RECOGNIZING THAT THEY MAY IN FACT NEED ONE OR TWO CLOSE RELATIONSHIPS**
FULFILLMENT: **TEACHING OTHERS ABOUT THE FINER THINGS IN LIFE**
NOTABLE: **JACK VALENTI (PRESIDENT, MOTION PICTURE ASSOCIATION)**

September 11–18

THE LITERALIST
VIRGO III

Virgo III's on this karmic path are sure to bring their considerable evaluative and communicative powers into play. Highly attracted to tangible goals, they can nevertheless be fired by true idealism. On the social scene, however, they will be faced with many lessons revolving around the development of greater tolerance of and empathy for their fellows. Too, they may get mired in their own ideologies and moral crusades and fall into the trap of deciding that they know what's good for everybody else. Dependency issues may abound in their relationships until they come to terms with the fact that they are better off unencumbered by problematic or burdensome companions. Still, if they are careful to avoid a certain ruthlessness in themselves and keep their selfishness under control, they will be blessed with the rare experience of passing their insight on to others.

CHALLENGE: **NOT BECOMING SO MIRED IN THE DETAILS THAT IT HINDERS RISING IN THEIR CAREER**
FULFILLMENT: **RESTING IN THE PEACE OF MIND THAT BEING AN AUTHORITY FIGURE BRINGS THEM**
NOTABLE: **OREL HERSHISER IV (BASEBALL PLAYER)**

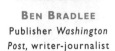

September 19–24
BEAUTY
VIRGO–LIBRA CUSP

Climbing down from the ivory tower of ideals and learning how to put theory into practice will figure prominently in the lives and destinies of Virgo–Libra individuals. Their need for harmony and beauty can lead many of these men and women into rather sheltered or unrealistic environments, and their ability to go out and meet some of the harsher realities will be tested here. Others may be unwilling to deal with dependency issues in the area of personal relationships and may be forced to spend time alone, if only to convince themselves that they are capable of doing so. Still, Virgo–Libras have a great potential to attract people and resources to their cause, as well as a fine sense of social trends and directions. If those born in the Week of Beauty use their natural charm as the instrument for delivering knowledge to the world, they are likely to be blessed with a large and willing audience.

ED SULLIVAN
Hosted long-running
eponymous variety show

9/28/1902
Libra I

CHALLENGE: **BECOMING HARDER DRIVEN AND LESS SELF-INDULGENT**
FULFILLMENT: **SHARING THEIR EXPERIENCES OF AESTHETIC FULFILLMENT WITH OTHERS**
NOTABLE: **ETHAN COEN (FILMMAKER)**

September 25–October 2
THE PERFECTIONIST
LIBRA I

Libra I's on the Way of Instruction are certain to develop the expertise demanded by this karmic path, yet not as certain to complete their journey by then sharing their knowledge with the world. Social contacts can be troublesome for these exacting and perfectionistic souls, and they will need to move in a variety of circles before they can truly feel comfortable with their ability to adjust to new circumstances. There is much about this configuration that indicates that Libra I's would much prefer to strike out on their own in their search for perfection, but their destiny path will nevertheless demand that they turn their attention from details to the bigger picture. Still, if these individuals cultivate flexibility and calm without becoming rigid or didactic in their attitudes toward others, and take some care to strike a balance between the personal and professional areas of their lives, opportunities for growth on the Way of Instruction will abound.

CHALLENGE: **RELAXING THEIR HIGH STANDARDS**
FULFILLMENT: **USING HUMOR TO MAKE OTHERS THINK**
NOTABLE: **SHAUN CASSIDY (SINGER)**

October 3–10
SOCIETY
LIBRA II

Libra II's on the Way of Instruction are likely to find themselves quite content. Blessed with formidable social skills, they nevertheless have a certain detachment regarding the personal relationships necessary to this path. Many can devote themselves fully to their profession or area of expertise yet be largely untroubled by more personal demands. Still, those born in the Week of Society must learn to take their own needs and desires more seriously, especially in the area of their emotions. Too much repression can contribute to a lack of self-awareness, making them subject to mood swings and occasional bouts of depression. Also, they should avoid the tendency to become isolated or self-absorbed. They should also take care to establish boundaries in personal relationships, for they can become too self-sacrificing, sometimes without being aware of it. Nevertheless, they are beautifully suited to the Way of Instruction, and with time their talents are sure to find their truest expression.

RAY KROC
Founder of McDonald's

10/5/1902
Libra II

CHALLENGE: **DEVELOPING ENDURANCE FOR THE LONG HAUL**
FULFILLMENT: **FINDING THEMSELVES AT THE PINNACLE OF ACHIEVEMENT, SURROUNDED BY THEIR MANY STUDENTS**
NOTABLE: **TANYA TUCKER (COUNTRY AND WESTERN SINGER)**

October 11–18
THEATER
LIBRA III

These dynamic, flamboyant souls are sure to get their message across, whatever the medium. The problem with this configuration is that Libra III individuals may not be capable of monitoring their audience before delivering that message. By and large, they find it somewhat difficult to understand people and positively loathe the prospect that their ideas may be lost in the vagaries of others' emotional reactions. Naturally cool and quite sophisticated, they may become cynical when disappointed or disillusioned. Libra III's can also be somewhat hypercritical and fail to really connect with others' needs. Overconfidence or a tendency to dwell in the realm of pure abstraction can be problematical for those placed on this path, for delivering a message is not quite the same as sharing it. Those born in the Week of Society would do well to keep in mind that teaching often demands an emotional commitment in order for the teacher to be truly effective.

CHALLENGE: **TAKING OFF THEIR WORLD-WEARY MASK ONCE IN A WHILE IN ORDER TO CONNECT WITH OTHERS**
FULFILLMENT: **ACTING OUT THE DRAMA OF THEIR LIVES**
NOTABLE: **ALICE TULLY (SINGER; PHILANTHROPIST)**

October 19–25
DRAMA AND CRITICISM
LIBRA–SCORPIO CUSP

Dramatic and intense, those born on the Cusp of Drama and Criticism are attention getters, whatever their area of endeavor. Well suited to the demands of this karmic path, they may, however, falter a bit as they swing between personal and professional obsessions. It will be extremely important for them to strike a balance between those areas of life and to avoid addictive behavior in any form. Whatever their chosen field, they are intellectually and creatively gifted, blessed with the ability to master almost anything. Their minds are indeed "terrible things to waste," and they should be careful to steer clear of too much indulgence of their sensual and sexual natures for fear of letting those minds go underdeveloped. In fact, they simply have too much to give the world to ignore the lessons of the Way of Instruction. If Libra–Scorpios dedicate themselves to the universal good by sharing the wealth of their knowledge and experience in a larger social context, this road will hold many rewards for them.

CHALLENGE: **TONING DOWN THEIR PROPENSITY TO PREACH**
FULFILLMENT: **FLESHING OUT THEIR THINKING WITH OTHERS**

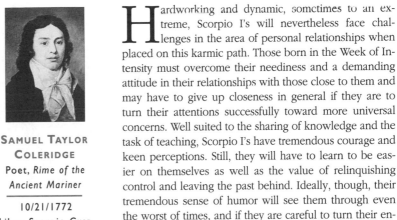

SAMUEL TAYLOR COLERIDGE
Poet, *Rime of the Ancient Mariner*

10/21/1772
Libra–Scorpio Cusp

October 26–November 2
INTENSITY
SCORPIO I

Hardworking and dynamic, sometimes to an extreme, Scorpio I's will nevertheless face challenges in the area of personal relationships when placed on this karmic path. Those born in the Week of Intensity must overcome their neediness and a demanding attitude in their relationships with those close to them and may have to give up closeness in general if they are to turn their attentions successfully toward more universal concerns. Well suited to the sharing of knowledge and the task of teaching, Scorpio I's have tremendous courage and keen perceptions. Still, they will have to learn to be easier on themselves as well as the value of relinquishing control and leaving the past behind. Ideally, though, their tremendous sense of humor will see them through even the worst of times, and if they are careful to turn their energies outward rather than inward, they will attain the highest success.

CHALLENGE: **NOURISHING THEIR CAPACITY TO FORGIVE**
FULFILLMENT: **GAINING THE ATTENTION AND RESPECT OF A SELECT GROUP OF FOLLOWERS**
NOTABLES: **WARREN G. HARDING (29TH U.S. PRESIDENT); ELSA LANCHESTER (ACTRESS)**

November 3–11
DEPTH
SCORPIO II

Serious, dedicated, and gifted with considerable powers of concentration, individuals born in the Week of Depth will have little trouble developing the practical expertise demanded by the Way of Instruction. Scorpio II's may, however, experience a number of problems when it comes to sharing their knowledge in a larger social context, for it is their natural inclination not necessarily to expand but rather to go into things deeply, with attention and awareness. Thus they can get mired in overattention to detail, worry, and workaholic habits that can separate them from their truest calling. Still, Scorpio II individuals are gifted with a natural empathy for others that will serve them well in social situations, and if they fight their tendency to be suspicious and hypercritical, they are sure to win both the hearts and the attention of the larger world.

CHALLENGE: **BALANCING THEIR RELATIONSHIP NEEDS WITH THE DEMANDS OF THEIR AVOCATION**
FULFILLMENT: **MAKING A DIFFERENCE IN THE LIVES OF OTHERS**

TIM ROBBINS
Actor, *Shawshank Redemption*

10/16/1958
Libra III

November 12–18
CHARM
SCORPIO III

The mantle of leadership will come quite naturally to Scorpio III individuals, and they will rarely fail either in the development of their skills or in the sharing of those skills for the larger social good. Blessed with keen insight and considerable courage and understanding, those born in the Week of Charm have a knack for knowing what people need and when they need it. Though they rarely shirk responsibility, they can become overly controlling and will need to allow the input of others to freshen their insights and expand their knowledge. Capable of the self-sufficiency demanded by this karmic path, Scorpio III's will nevertheless have to monitor their tendency to use others for their own selfish ends. Cultivating spirituality will be crucial for these souls, as turning from purely material objectives in order to connect with universal themes will be the key that unlocks their ability to share their experiences with the world.

CHALLENGE: **DEFENDING AGAINST THEIR TENDENCY TO BE CONTROLLING**
FULFILLMENT: **UTILIZING THEIR CONSIDERABLE CHARMS TO HELP OTHERS GROW**

November 19–24

REVOLUTION
SCORPIO–SAGITTARIUS CUSP

Well meaning and attuned to the social context, Scorpio–Sagittarians will doubtless flourish on the Way of Instruction, providing they cultivate the necessary practical skills to accomplish their goals and objectives. These freewheeling individuals may be hampered in their development by a tendency to extremes not appropriate to general social mores. Those born on the Scorpio–Sagittarius cusp will do well to remember that their answers are not to be found in all work or all play but somewhere in the middle. Still, they are charismatic characters, and if they take care to solicit the opinions of others from time to time, they will doubtless find those opinions quite educational in the long run. In fact, Scorpio–Sagittarians have a natural affinity for the realms of education and philosophy, and as the years progress, they are likely to be blessed with the ability to share on an increasingly universal level, for the betterment of all.

STROM THURMOND
Conservative Democrat-
turned-Republican senator
from South Carolina
———
12/5/1902
Sagittarius II

CHALLENGE: **SUPPRESSING THEIR MORE ANARCHISTIC LEANINGS BY KEEPING THEIR EYE ON THEIR LONG-TERM GOALS**
FULFILLMENT: **CREATING A REVOLUTION IN THE THINKING OF OTHERS**
NOTABLE: **JAMIE LEE CURTIS (ACTRESS)**

November 25–December 2

INDEPENDENCE
SAGITTARIUS I

Those born in the Week of Independence will find their destiny on the Way of Instruction in both a love of, and a need for, travel to far-off places. They are likely to find their life's work taking them far from their nearest and dearest, yet their urge to merge with the larger social structure will ensure that their need to give supersedes their need for reinforcement and fulfillment in the realm of personal relationships. Blessed with a natural integrity and sensitivity to those things common to us all, they will nevertheless have to work hard at cultivating diplomatic skills and avoid their tendency to overcompetitive behavior and their love of debate at the expense of the exchange of ideas. Still, if Sagittarius I's are careful to give back to the world, in some fashion, the wealth of knowledge and understanding they glean in their far-flung quests, their path to success will be one of great adventure and rare comprehension.

CHALLENGE: **TAKING ON A SUFFICIENT LEVEL OF RESPONSIBILITY TO BE A LEADER**
FULFILLMENT: **REALIZING THAT WINNING REALLY HAPPENS WHEN EVERYONE GAINS**

December 3–10

THE ORIGINATOR
SAGITTARIUS II

Highly original and blessed with a fearless sense of their own originality, these individuals will do well on the Way of Instruction, providing they do not succumb to feelings of rejection and frustration. As closely tied as they can sometimes be to only one or two close associates, Sagittarius II's on this path first must develop a broader education in the ways of the world and, second, share their knowledge with those around them in an ever-widening circle. Though these independent souls may see the demands of this karmic path as rather severe, they will nevertheless benefit from the acquisition of social skills and sensibilities. Embracing those skills will in turn free them from many of their more self-conscious or even downright peculiar inclinations and groom them to be the teachers and givers this path demands they become. Their highly original talents will ensure a ready audience for shared expertise, and attuning themselves to the needs of the crowd will surely help them along the way.

LIV ULLMAN
Actress,
Private Confessions
———
12/16/1939
Sagittarius III

CHALLENGE: **NOT RETREATING TOO FAR INTO THEMSELVES WHEN THEY ENCOUNTER REJECTION**
FULFILLMENT: **DEVELOPING THE DAILY INVENTIVENESS NECESSARY TO THE TEACHING PROCESS**
NOTABLE: **MARGARET HAMILTON (ACTRESS, *THE WIZARD OF OZ*)**

December 11–18

THE TITAN
SAGITTARIUS III

Those born in the Week of the Titan and placed on the Way of Instruction will doubtless live life on a kind of cutting edge of aspiration. Blessed with big dreams and big plans, they will achieve much but will nevertheless be faced with the tasks of learning how to share what they have learned with others, particularly in the realm of their chosen profession. Sagittarius III's are people whose darker side may cause them to want to keep what they know to themselves. But the Way of Instruction requires that somehow they pass their knowledge on. Sagittarius III's may be encumbered in their search for growth by the demands of ego and personal relationships and may often be hampered by tying themselves to partners and associates who protect them from the everyday aspects of living. Still, they are naturally charismatic and gifted with a philosophical turn of mind that will see them through any number of turns of fortune, providing they retain a proper perspective.

CHALLENGE: **NOT STORING UP ALL THEY HAVE LEARNED IN THE EVENT OF A RAINY DAY**
FULFILLMENT: **BECOMING CAPTAINS OF THEIR OWN SHIP AND CHARTING A COURSE FOR OTHERS**

KARMIC PATH
4

December 19–25

PROPHECY
SAGITTARIUS–CAPRICORN CUSP

The integration of energy will be of great importance to those born on the Cusp of Prophecy when placed on the Way of Instruction. They are at once expansive and introverted and will be faced with the task of learning how to channel their energies in such a way that they can be shared and expressed. And sharing will not come easily to Sagittarius–Capricorns, for they tend to hesitate and second-guess themselves to the point where the significance or timeliness of their teaching can be lost. Still, they have a fine ability to attune themselves to the needs of the many and are capable of shouldering great responsibility without complaint. If Sagittarius–Capricorns allow themselves to relax a bit and lose their more self-conscious qualities through social connections to others, their insights and worldly perceptions will be of benefit to us all.

KIT CARSON
American guide, trapper,
and soldier

12/24/1809
Sagittarius–Capricorn
Cusp

CHALLENGE: **LEARNING TO TRUST OTHERS AS MUCH AS THEY TRUST THEIR OWN INSTINCTS**

FULFILLMENT: **ARTICULATING HOW OTHERS CAN TAP INTO THEIR INTUITIVE SIDES**

December 26–January 2

THE RULER
CAPRICORN I

Capricorn I's are sure to thrive on the Way of Instruction, for they are blessed with natural leadership, the ability to concentrate, and a heartfelt interest in the social fabric of existence. Strongly traditional, Capricorn I individuals believe in structure and are truly concerned with the general welfare. Though they will have to guard against workaholic tendencies, they are capable of the self-sufficiency indicated by this path and may do quite well leading a more solitary existence. Their principal danger is that they may neglect to cultivate a social network that provides for the lively and necessary exchange of ideas and become too dogmatic and set in their ways. Still, their ability to wait for the right opportunity and then rise to a position of responsibility without letting it go to their heads is extraordinary and will serve to ensure that those born in the Week of the Ruler will not only succeed but exceed the usual goals.

CHALLENGE: **BROADENING THEIR CAPACITY TO ACCEPT VIEWPOINTS DIFFERENT FROM THEIR OWN**

FULFILLMENT: **SETTING THINGS UP SO THAT DELEGATING RESPONSIBILITY AND TEACHING BECOME ONE AND THE SAME**

NOTABLE: **JIM BAKKER (EVANGELIST)**

January 3–9

DETERMINATION
CAPRICORN II

It is likely that for many Capricorn II's, the Way of Instruction will require them to expand their awareness of metaphysical and spiritual matters. Gifted with natural practicality and the ability to apply themselves to almost any task, their journey will nonetheless involve some movement toward the higher and more universal aspirations of humankind. For though they are extraordinarily hardworking, they are philosophers and thinkers at heart. If there is a danger with this configuration, it is simply that they do not always know when to give up or admit failure and may thus waste their prodigious energies in unproductive pursuits and relationships. Still, once those born in the Week of Determination allow their personal experience to illuminate larger social concerns, their insights and leadership abilities will come to the fore, to the betterment of their world.

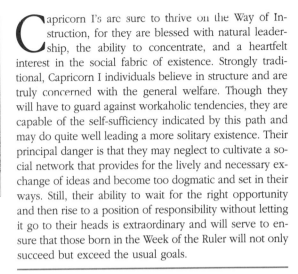

W. E. GLADSTONE
British prime minister

12/29/1809
Capricorn I

CHALLENGE: **GRAPPLING WITH ANY REGRETS AT HAVING MISSED OUT ON MORE INTIMATE RELATIONSHIPS**

FULFILLMENT: **HAVING RISEN UP THE LADDER OF SUCCESS, BECOMING A MENTOR FOR OTHERS**

January 10–16

DOMINANCE
CAPRICORN III

Proper socialization and connections will be very important to Capricorn III's placed on the Way of Instruction, since their contacts with worldly ways and means will do much to nourish their self-confidence. Well suited to the demands of this karmic path, Capricorn III's will nevertheless have to guard against their tendency to be too self-sacrificing and overinvolved, especially in the area of personal relationships. Too, they will doubtless be asked to divest themselves of a measure of their naïveté along the journey, and it may take them some time to truly flower. Avoiding extremes in their perceptions and finding a balance point between the personal and professional sides of life will be essential to their success. Though not necessarily extroverts by nature, Capricorn III's are nonetheless quite charismatic, and their sense of responsibility and justice will make them wise and willing leaders.

CHALLENGE: **INVOLVING THEMSELVES SUFFICIENTLY IN GROUPS AND ASSOCIATIONS TO OVERCOME THEIR FEELINGS OF INFERIORITY**

FULFILLMENT: **ATTAINING A ROLE OF PROMINENCE AND RESPECT**

NOTABLES: **TREVOR NUNN (STAGE DIRECTOR, CATS); BARBARA HEPWORTH (BRITISH SCULPTOR)**

January 17–22

MYSTERY AND IMAGINATION
CAPRICORN–AQUARIUS CUSP

Certain to draw the attention of their society, individuals born on the Capricorn–Aquarius cusp have a way of generating excitement wherever they go. Still, there is a danger that they will settle for mere excitement and fail to develop the depth of knowledge and understanding indicated by this path. Mismanagement of their energies will be a lifelong issue for many Capricorn–Aquarians, and they will have to work especially hard not to swing between the extremes of hard work and hard play. Still, they are blessed with a genuine and heartfelt interest in their fellow human beings that is more than theoretical, and they may be quite generous in terms of their time, money, and resources. Through their often controversial views and dramatic presentations, Capricorn–Aquarians can serve to stimulate both the hearts and the imaginations of us all in the search for a better world.

TALLULAH BANKHEAD
Stage and film actress

1/31/1903
Aquarius II

CHALLENGE: **TRANSFORMING THEIR MORE ECCENTRIC ENERGIES INTO AN ABILITY TO GENERATE EXCITEMENT IN OTHERS**
FULFILLMENT: **FEELING THE PLEASURE OF HELPING OTHERS LEARN**
NOTABLES: **JACK NICKLAUS (CHAMPION GOLFER); JOHN HURT (ACTOR)**

January 23–30

GENIUS
AQUARIUS I

Brilliant and inventive, those born in the Week of Genius will nevertheless have to strive to develop greater practicality when placed on the Way of Instruction. Blessed with a natural love of learning and new ideas, perhaps their only real pitfall will be their tendency to develop a superior attitude toward the social fabric of life or believe that sharing their learning would be tantamount to casting pearls before swine. Too, Aquarius I's may retreat into an ivory-tower world of theory and speculation and fail to make the practical human connections required along their life journey. Though they are quite socially adept, they are unlikely to experience much trouble as they detach from personal relationships to become more self-sufficient and will doubtless excel as teachers and leaders in almost any realm of endeavor.

CHALLENGE: **FINDING A CAREER THAT WILL ALLOW THEM TO BE SELF-EMPLOYED, THOUGH NOT ISOLATED**
FULFILLMENT: **BRINGING THEIR INVENTIVE APPROACH TO TRANSFORMING THE EDUCATION PROCESS ITSELF**
NOTABLE: **ROBERT GWATHMEY (ARTIST)**

January 31–February 7

YOUTH AND EASE
AQUARIUS II

Lively and quite popular, Aquarius II's are likely to find the Way of Instruction a bit of a rocky road, unless they take some care to develop greater depth and practical expertise in their chosen area of endeavor. Sensitive and highly attuned to the social side of life, those born in the Week of Youth and Ease may nonetheless have to struggle with the commitment to sharing required by this configuration. Further, they be fearful of risking their personal image to speak out against social ills and problems. If they take care to ground themselves a bit and apply their considerable talents without succumbing to the temptation to scatter their energies, their natural magnetism is sure to gain them a rapt and attentive audience for their ideas. Aquarius II individuals thrive on lively and interesting exchanges of information and are blessed with the humanity required by this path. If they cultivate depth and practicality, their success will be ensured.

THOMAS ALVA EDISON
Invented phonograph,
light bulb; held over
1,000 patents

2/11/1847
Aquarius III

CHALLENGE: **TAKING THE HARDER ROAD OF BECOMING AN AUTHORITY FIGURE**
FULFILLMENT: **PUTTING ON VIRTUOSO PERFORMANCES WHILE EDUCATING**
NOTABLES: **TOM BROKAW (NBC ANCHOR); FRAN TARKENTON (FOOTBALL PLAYER)**

February 8–15

ACCEPTANCE
AQUARIUS III

Lessons of tolerance and increased understanding will doubtless occur for those born in the Week of Acceptance when placed on the Way of Instruction, and they will almost certainly be faced with the task of accepting others to the same degree that others are willing to accept them. Blessed with considerable wit and a healthy sense of irony to color their exchange of ideas, Aquarius III individuals are be popular, influential figures, providing they avoid displays of excessive nervous energy and the pitfalls of self-absorption. The practical application of knowledge will also be something of an issue, since it is sometimes difficult for them to settle down long enough to master a task, situation, or area of expertise. Still, they have great potential for success, and if they are careful to cultivate a stable network of friends, comrades, and business associates, they are sure to go far.

CHALLENGE: **GROUNDING THEMSELVES TO PURSUE A SINGLE PATH OR VOCATION**
FULFILLMENT: **OPERATING IN AN ENVIRONMENT OF OPENNESS AND DISCERNMENT**
NOTABLE: **TED KOPPEL (TV JOURNALIST; HOST, NIGHTLINE)**

February 16–22

SENSITIVITY
AQUARIUS–PISCES CUSP

Good socialization and the ability to grow beyond early emotional attachments will be of paramount importance to these sensitive personalities placed on the Way of Instruction. Breaking down personal barriers and overcoming insecurity in order to truly connect with others are themes that will run through the whole of their lives. Yet those born on the Cusp of Sensitivity can nevertheless do well on this karmic path, providing they ground themselves in practical realities while at the same time allowing themselves freedom of emotional and intellectual expression. The lessening of personal attachments required by this karmic path may cause them to retreat into isolation without connecting to larger, more worldly concerns and pursuits. Still, if these men and women are careful to reach beyond the bounds of the personal and into the broader social milieu, they can be assured of a warm, willing welcome.

ALEXANDER GRAHAM BELL
Invented telephone

——————

3/3/1847
Pisces II

CHALLENGE: **EXTENDING THEMSELVES IN SOCIAL SITUATIONS**
FULFILLMENT: **FIGHTING THEIR WAY INTO A POSITION WHERE THEY CAN RELATE TO OTHERS AS EQUALS**

February 23–March 2

SPIRIT
PISCES I

Whatever the area or field chosen by Pisces I's, there is likely to be a touch of the spiritual about their approach to the subject. For these are folks who can find God in ditch digging or while checking out at the grocery store. The big stumbling block here is that those born in the Week of Spirit may fail to stay grounded in practical reality and retreat into a fantasy world. Pisces I's have the capacity to bring a unique, universal, perspective on life to a larger social network, and if they take care to stay connected, they are destined for real success. Blessed with a natural sensitivity to others and a generous spirit, they will nonetheless be challenged to channel their emotional energies away from the personal and toward the universal in order to become truly effective. Once freed, they will doubtless surprise themselves with their capacity to enjoy their own company and their depth of commitment to giving back to the world.

CHALLENGE: **DEALING IN THE SPECIFIC LONG ENOUGH TO DEVELOP AN EXPERTISE OR SKILL**
FULFILLMENT: **LEAVING THE WORLD A BETTER PLACE FOR HAVING SHARED WHAT THEY HAVE LEARNED**
NOTABLES: **MARIO ANDRETTI (RACE CAR DRIVER); DAME ELLEN TERRY (BRITISH ACTRESS)**

March 3–10

THE LONER
PISCES II

Blessed with tremendous empathy, Pisces II individuals may nonetheless have some trouble developing the necessary worldliness to share in the larger human experience. In fact, those born in the Week of the Loner can be rather blatantly antisocial at times and will have to work to allow others into their private worlds. Likely to develop real expertise in some artistic or aesthetic area, Pisces II's are further gifted with great concentration and depth when it comes to mastering a particular field or profession. Though they will always require at least a modicum of time alone, they will nevertheless make fine leaders, for they are gifted with a great sense of morals and ethics, as well as the strength to put them into practice. In return for their commitment to social action, the world will reward them with a deep sense of connection to their fellows and the necessary nourishment for both mind and soul.

BERNARDO BERTOLUCCI
Italian film director

——————

3/16/1940
Pisces III

CHALLENGE: **OVERCOMING FEELINGS OF BEING MISUNDERSTOOD**
FULFILLMENT: **DISCOVERING THAT THEY HAVE MUCH TO GIVE TO OTHERS**
NOTABLES: **RAUL JULIA (ACTOR); DAVID RABE (PLAYWRIGHT)**

March 11–18

DANCERS AND DREAMERS
PISCES III

Though individuals born in the Week of Dancers and Dreamers are blessed with many talents and gifts, they will face the task of developing greater seriousness of purpose and practicality when placed on the Way of Instruction. Naturally flamboyant and able to inspire others, they may nevertheless find themselves exploited by others for self-interested purposes. Pisces III's can appear to be quite giving yet turn out to be less than generous on closer inspection. Too, they can be marked by a certain emotional neediness not in keeping with this karmic path. Yet their sense of destiny is certainly pronounced, and they are unlikely to miss the opportunities for larger commitments that this path requires. If they take care to avoid a tendency toward superficiality or to coast along on the strength of their charms alone, their perseverance, talents, and gift for philosophy are sure to exert a lasting and considerable influence on society.

CHALLENGE: **STRIVING TO APPEAR LESS GLIB AND MORE WORLDLY**
FULFILLMENT: **BECOMING A VISIONARY OR LEADER IN THE ARTS**
NOTABLES: **AL JARREAU (POPULAR/SOUL SINGER); PHIL LESH (MEMBER, GRATEFUL DEAD)**

The Way of Awareness

ARIES–TAURUS CUSP TO LIBRA–SCORPIO CUSP
Power to Drama and Criticism

Born with a powerful nature that needs to assert itself and control most situations, individuals on the Way of Awareness are here to gain insight into how power works and to learn how to use it in the most intelligent manner. Although their need to express power is usually unconscious rather than calculating, this karmic path teaches that the possession of conscious awareness and the insights gained from it are more powerful than all the brute force in the world. Power is only one type of energy in the universe, and the preoccupation that these individuals have with it can severely limit their life experience. If they can open themselves to the world more fully and with heightened awareness, experiencing its enchantment in their daily lives, they may learn that an appreciation of beauty is more valuable than power. By bringing this awareness to those around them, whether by words or example, they will encourage others to raise their own consciousness.

In order to progress from power to consciousness, those on this path must be convinced by their life experience that such a raised consciousness is not only desirable but necessary. Individuals with gift of power rarely give up easily, adhering forcefully to their own point of view. Most often only an epiphany or peak experience will reveal the truth to them, often in a moment of breakthrough that shatters their current worldview and broadens their vision. Usually, they reach such a point in their lives only after repeatedly butting up against other potent individuals. Because they constantly attract energy similar to their own, they will be forced to look into the face of power and may find themselves at its mercy over and over again. Gradually they will come to understand that power is not what is most important in life. In some cases, such individuals may find that they have been disempowered by substance abuse or relationship addictions. However, their struggle with such experiences may lay the groundwork for personal transformation.

When the final breakthrough in consciousness occurs, the doors of perception will open and truth will inevitably be revealed to them. Whether through a monumental event in sports, a deep emotional experience, or a brilliant revelation, such an occurrence will reorient the perspective of those on this path. Such an ecstatic process metaphorically entails being pushed out of body to view life from a more objective place. Through opening their perspective to more mystical or spiritual energies, these individuals can come to realize how puny their former notions of power were and leave them behind. Moreover, those born to this path are so accomplished at standing their ground that, once transformed, they rarely return from whence they came. Once opened by such experiences, individuals on the Way of Awareness will encounter more and more periods in their lives when, through heightened awareness, they find they are

---

CORE LESSON

Falling in love with the beauty
of life and communicating it to others

GOAL

To develop a full consciousness
of the world around them

GIFTS
Charismatic, Creative,
Persuasive

PITFALLS
Overcritical, Addictive,
Manipulative

existing purely in the moment—simply being with no thought of past, present, or future. As these times become more frequent, those born to the Way of Awareness can come to create an ongoing dialogue with and sense of enchantment about the world.

Those on the Way of Awareness are also called to another task, that of communicating their newfound consciousness to others. This, however, will not be difficult since once they have tasted the fruits of greater awareness, these men and women will be likely to want to share their experiences with anyone who will listen. They are aided in this process by their natural gift of persuasion, compounded by an innate likability, which they often develop into such scintillating charm that they fascinate others with their allure. Yet their real goal is to help others, whether by work or example, to be a bit more conscious as well. Perhaps this can best be accomplished simply by asking pointed or rhetorical questions or sharing, in as gentle a manner as possible, their views on some of the more unconscious actions of their fellows. These individuals may also work with others to help them give up abusing substances that keep them from being fully present. Whatever the forum, opening others to the beauty of life will be their task. Those who begin at the Aries–Taurus cusp come into this lifetime with an ability to coerce only to transform this natural talent into the ability to seduce. The most successful of those on this

path share their message by tapping into a more primal level in others, working, for example, through symbolism such as a story or an image. Frequently, they will be found in the arts, such as theater, film, poetry, and music. These individuals overcome their own ego drives to share their love of beauty with others in a noncoercive manner.

One danger is that their transformation can lead to an addiction with life itself. Should they wax rhapsodic on the wondrous nature of the world and their own transformation, they run the risk of appearing preachy or worse and thereby alienate their audience through overly romantic and unrealistic attitudes. Remaining aware of such tendencies requires constant vigilance. Furthermore, they have an undeniable tendency to alter the truth to fit their needs and thus may find it easy to justify a white lie for the sake of their mission. Another problem can be overreaching in search of their goals and becoming increasingly overcritical, rigid, and impatient with those who have yet to see the light. Moreover, they can alienate family members and friends by giving the impression that they are the only ones who know the truth about life. Most often those on this karmic path will attract whoever is ready to learn what they have to share, and thus there is no need for them to beat the bushes for disciples. Maintaining a good sense of humor and learning not to take themselves too seriously or insist that every element of

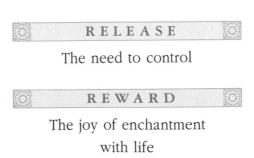

RELEASE

The need to control

REWARD

The joy of enchantment
with life

SUGGESTION

Open your eyes to all that exists around you. Power is just one form of energy in the universe. Learn to express what you feel. Always reflect on the power of truthfulness.

life be mercilessly held to the light of consciousness will help on their journey. Last, they must not let up in their vigilance to detect and root out stubborn power drives and ego trips in themselves and others.

Such attractive individuals are not often fated to have only one partner in life. Many of their important life lessons will be learned in the realms of love, sex, and romance. Although promiscuity may be the norm for them, others should not be quick to condemn such behavior since it often results in a painful yet necessary educational process for those on this karmic path. Yet family and children can be caused great heartbreak by the inability of these individuals to remain faithful to their mate. Having a close circle of friends within which a rich palette of emotions can be expressed may be a partial solution. Nonetheless, some on the Way of Awareness may feel victimized by poor choices of partners throughout their lives, not realizing that they may in fact have created the perfect environment for their own spiritual education.

Because of their addictive tendencies, what is best for those on this karmic path is not usually what they most desire, despite the sincerest commitment to spiritual and psychological growth. An understanding parent, friend, or psychologist can be most helpful by carefully reminding them that what is best may be precisely the opposite of what makes them feel good. Awareness is the key to discovering what keeps them healthy and rejecting the whole gamut of dependency-producing drugs, relationships, and sex. Self-discipline complements greater consciousness and should be practiced studiously. Also, surrounding oneself with others who are also actively working toward greater consciousness and spirituality will prove invaluable. Often friends of this type will be voices of reason when slipups occur. Finally, those on the Way of Awareness should never completely cut themselves off from their subconscious side but should feed it in healthier ways, for example, by indulging in deep sleep, daydreaming, relaxation, periodic laziness, and generally just letting go. Any program of prayer or meditation can help create the quiet time needed for looking inward and developing the "quiet witness" of the self and the capacity for focusing and being in the moment that is necessary for heightened awareness and expanded consciousness.

BALANCE POINT

Power and Love

Moving from a power orientation to consciousness calls to mind the image of a warrior putting down his weapon and adopting a method of strategic defense that can outwit the enemy. Such a tactic might involve using the enemy's strength to work against it or even making the enemy into a friend or comrade. Ultimately, however, those on this path will discover the value of surrender, so that the war can be left behind and both sides can go home.

CRYSTALS AND GEMSTONES

Ruby is the stone of passionate devotion and is excellent when seeking a balance between love and power. It encourages gentleness and inspires a deep respect for life.

NOTABLES ON THIS KARMIC PATH

Like many on the Way of Awareness, **Leni Riefenstahl** influenced others using strong symbolic forms and imagery, communicating much through her work. Her early preoccupation with power is apparent in her creation of Nazi propaganda films. During this time, Riefenstahl also made a film of the 1938 Olympic Games that even detractors acknowledge as an exemplary testament to the beauty of the human

LENI RIEFENSTAHL

form. Later in life, Riefenstahl applied her discerning eye to the exploration of the medium of photography, producing *The Last of the Nuba* and *The People of Kau*. These works, featuring the people of Africa, visually describe the human figure in terms of exalted physical glory.

ALFRED, LORD TENNYSON

Despite the struggles he faced throughout his life, **Alfred, Lord Tennyson,** the great Victorian poet, left a distinguished legacy. Born the fourth of twelve children to a family plagued by epilepsy and mental illness, Tennyson fought early on to gain a sense of power over his health and financial straits. Though he periodically contended with depression, the poet achieved a position of prominence through his writing, and was named poet laureate in 1850. Through works such as *The Lady of Shallot* and *The Charge of the Light Brigade,* Tennyson evoked an atmosphere of such dramatic and haunting beauty that his poems are still widely admired today.

Both in his paintings and murals, Mexican artist **Diego Rivera** expresses a strong awareness of his people. Whether he is depicting farm or factory workers, capitalists or conquistadors, Rivera turns the fierce headlight of criticism on power and graphically illustrates its inner workings. Aesthetic revelations dot the landscape of his tumultuous life, at times causing him to be swept away by his own creative process. The rhapsodic nature and intense social realism of Rivera's art increased the public's awareness of the plight of the masses.

DIEGO RIVERA

Other Notables: Drew Carey, Robert James Waller, Oksana Baiul, Mario Lanza, Henrik Ibsen, Meyer Lansky, Terrence McNally, Thomas Elmer Braniff, Gary Oldman, Simone Signoret, Sugar Ray Robinson, Dolley Madison, The Artist Formerly Known as Prince, Nancy Lieberman, Kevin Bacon, Jimmy Smits, Michael Flatley, Peter Bogdanovich, William Friedkin, Lily Tomlin, George Westinghouse, Lee Harvey Oswald, Grace Slick, Lee Trevino, Jaleel White, Paul Revere, Lloyd Bentsen, Jr., Hugh Downs, Betty Hutton, Sharon Stone

---

BIRTHDAYS ON KARMIC PATH 5

September 22, 1883–February 10, 1884 | May 4, 1902–September 22, 1902 | December 14, 1920–May 3, 1921

July 26, 1939–December 14, 1939 | March 7, 1958–July 25, 1958 | October 16, 1976–March 6, 1977

May 28, 1995–October 16, 1995 | January 7, 2014–May 27, 2014

March 19–24
REBIRTH
PISCES–ARIES CUSP

Unique in their ability to transform themselves, those born on the Cusp of Rebirth are gifted with considerable power and energy. Nevertheless, Pisces–Aries individuals have a tendency to give in to sheer aggression when they don't get their way. These diverse and interesting people will doubtless garner the attention of a wide variety of admirers during the course of their lives, yet they may fall into the trap of making others' opinions of them their personal barometer of success. Still, disappointments and disillusions will doubtless give them occasion to meditate on the idea that might doesn't necessarily make right. If they take care not only to cultivate the more sensitive side of their naturally expressive natures but to learn to take the risk of exposing their vulnerability to others, they are sure to be rewarded not only in the material world but in the higher spiritual realms as well.

HOLLY HUNTER
Film actress; won Oscar
for *The Piano*

3/20/1958
Pisces–Aries Cusp

CHALLENGE: **AVOIDING AGGRESSIVE BEHAVIOR**
FULFILLMENT: **DISCOVERING THAT THEIR SENSITIVITY HAS A PLACE IN THE WORLD**
NOTABLES: **GARY OLDMAN (ACTOR); HENRIK IBSEN (PLAYWRIGHT, *THE DOLL'S HOUSE*)**

March 25–April 2
THE CHILD
ARIES I

Gifted with a strong and nearly dauntless sense of self, these individuals will nevertheless have a bit of a struggle if they are to reach the mature perspective demanded by this karmic path. Fortunately, Aries I's tend to enjoy solitude, and the long periods they spend alone will only encourage the reflection necessary to master the deeper awareness demanded by this karmic path. The key to success for these people will come with the realization that power simply isn't enough, nor is mere material reward. For Aries I's, awareness is usually about realizing that they are actually not as tormented as they perceive themselves to be. If they manage to absorb this truth without giving in to their impulse to strike out for new frontiers or broaden their power base in ever-expanding attempts to avoid the obvious, they will doubtless progress as their personal sophistication, worldliness, and enthusiasm expand in a widening perspective in both the visible and invisible realms of experience.

CHALLENGE: **TRYING TO BALANCE THEIR EMOTIONS AND AVOID OUTBURSTS**
FULFILLMENT: **RELEASING THE PAST AND ITS BAGGAGE**
NOTABLES: **BART CONNOR (GYMNAST; OLYMPIC GOLD MEDALIST); SIMONE SIGNORET (FRENCH ACTRESS)**

April 3–10
THE STAR
ARIES II

Aries II individuals may be faced with unexpected limitations in physical reality that will turn out to be blessings in disguise. Whatever their talents, these people must learn not to rage against such limitations nor to blame them on other people, external conditions, or circumstances beyond their control. Instead, they will have to learn to go within in order to overcome their immediate environment. They may also experience a wealth of material and sensual opportunities, only to find them ultimately limited. Once they make this discovery, they will find themselves confronted with a wealth of opportunities to broaden their experience beyond the reach of their previous imaginings. If they cultivate the fine art of learning not to obsess over bad breaks and missed chances or attempt to escape in addictive and destructive behaviors and relationships, they will find themselves transformed along the path of higher and more sophisticated awareness.

ALEC BALDWIN
Actor and political
activist

4/3/1958
Aries II

CHALLENGE: **CULTIVATING HUMILITY BY DESTROYING ANY IMPULSES TOWARD BECOMING A KIND OF GURU**
FULFILLMENT: **REDEFINING WHAT WINNING MEANS TO THEM**

April 11–18
THE PIONEER
ARIES III

True leaders and pioneers, Aries III's may find themselves in the curious position of becoming the unintended victims of their own ideals as they journey along the Way of Awareness. Blessed with the natural sense of conviction to assure themselves that many of their actions and intentions are indeed based on "the right thing to do," they may nonetheless need a considerable amount of education as to what "right" actually is. Their wonderful impulse to be at the center of the action may, for example, relegate them to the sidelines for a time, or their desire to help others may result in their being taken advantage of, sometimes greatly. Equally, an impulse to sensual, rather than ideological excess is present in this configuration, and they would do well to cultivate physical discipline. Still, if they work to grow beyond their own perspective, not only will they be blessed with friends, lovers, and associates who are also pursuing a spiritual path, but they will help others with their unique perspective.

CHALLENGE: **REDEFINING THEIR MORAL CODE**
FULFILLMENT: **CREATING A SPIRITUAL FAMILY**

April 19–24
POWER
ARIES–TAURUS CUSP

Those born on the Aries–Taurus cusp who are placed on the Way of Awareness will surely be educated rather early as to the ways and means of wielding power. Inevitably, it seems, they will have to learn those lessons all over again as they grow into power of their own. Materially blessed and quite capable, they will nevertheless have to be on guard against a tendency to overindulgence and even lavishness in their worldly and sensuous forms of expression. They may overidentify with a powerful parent, only to realize later in life that their birthright is falling far short of their expectations. Still, these persuasive, magnetic people are sure to realize some of their fondest dreams, providing they take the time to cultivate the necessary self-awareness to learn that they are not living out a legacy to which they have ceased to be attached. If they nurture their capacity for the subtler forms of persuasion, ultimately their power will be their own.

CHALLENGE: **DIVESTING THEMSELVES OF DEPENDENCY ON THOSE IN AUTHORITY**
FULFILLMENT: **UNDERSTANDING THAT ONE CAN OWN ONE'S OWN POWER**
NOTABLE: **ANDIE MCDOWELL (ACTRESS)**

KEITH HARING
Popular artist

5/4/1958
Taurus II

April 25–May 2
MANIFESTATION
TAURUS I

Stubborn and tenacious, often to an extreme, those born in the Week of Manifestation will find that their success lies in how well they handle their own intense physicality. Prone to sensual extremes, they can sometimes refuse to give up addictions to sex, food, alcohol, or drugs out of sheer stubbornness or the inner conviction that whatever the problem, they can "handle it." Taurus I's are people who prefer to hold on to what they've got, rather than to reach out into the unknown in the interest of personal and spiritual growth. As a result, for these individuals to become more aware they may need to experience any number of revelations or personal epiphanies that are designed to open their eyes to a world of larger possibility, while at the same time limiting their opportunities in the world of their own making. Still, their innate practicality can be of enormous benefit to them, and if they work to stay sensible and generous to others rather than to themselves, the Way of Awareness holds great promise.

CHALLENGE: **MANAGING THEIR SENSUAL DESIRES**
FULFILLMENT: **COMPLETING A PROJECT WHOLLY BORN OF SPIRIT**
NOTABLE: **SATYAJIT RAY (INDIAN FILM DIRECTOR)**

May 3–10
THE TEACHER
TAURUS II

These unique personalities are blessed with the ability and need to instruct others, no matter what the specific character of their experience. Curiously, they may not fully realize how much they have been changed or transformed along the Way of Awareness until they begin to express their knowledge to others, especially in the personal sphere. It is through the articulation of their revelations and peak experiences that they will truly begin to understand just how far they have come along the path of spiritual growth. Creative and charismatic, Taurus II's are blessed with the kind of charm that attracts others, yet they will have to work to wean themselves away from their need for constant one-on-one validation and steer clear of their tendency to become hypercritical. If they realize that their truest powers lie not necessarily in who they are but in what they know, they experience a blossoming of awareness and consciousness.

CHALLENGE: **OPENING THEIR HEARTS AND MINDS TO NEW IDEOLOGIES**
FULFILLMENT: **ARTICULATING PERSONAL EXPERIENCE**
NOTABLE: **DAVID O. SELZNICK (MOVIE EXECUTIVE RESPONSIBLE FOR *GONE WITH THE WIND*)**

RICHARD DALEY, SR.
Chicago mayor

5/15/1902
Taurus III

May 11–18
THE NATURAL
TAURUS III

Changing environments can be as easy for Taurus III's as changing clothes. Restless and easily bored, they can sometimes lack the patience to deal with the demands of this karmic path and may see themselves as unfairly fettered on the road of life. Yet once they begin to truly understand that though they can indeed run, they can't always hide from the world and its complexities, they will begin to understand the restrictions of civilized life more objectively. Once that truth is revealed, they can reorient themselves with surprising alacrity. If they do not become mired in purely physical pursuits at the expense of higher interests and cultivate their formidable communicative powers in such a way that they can win others to their cause with words, not force, they will have the relatively rare experience of "beating their swords into plowshares" and finding true peace in the course of their productive lives.

CHALLENGE: **STAYING THE COURSE**
FULFILLMENT: **DISCOVERING THE ENTERTAINMENT AFFORDED BY AN ONGOING DIALOGUE WITH THE MYSTICAL**

May 19–24
ENERGY
TAURUS–GEMINI CUSP

Natural energy and great power come together here in a rather volatile mix. Those born on the Cusp of Energy seem to come into the world convinced that they can have it all and do it all, sometimes at the expense of their spiritual growth. In this instance, their considerable charm and talent for salesmanship can make them seem rather untrustworthy, but in fact they would rather risk a reputation for spreading themselves too thin than be tied to the same old routines and people. The fact that boredom is anathema to these personalities may put them into a position of failing to deliver on their many promises—for Taurus–Geminis are perfectly capable of making a pitch that is far better than the actual product. The challenge of this karmic path requires not so much that they diminish their expectations of life but that they increase their awareness of the things that constitute real value in both their relationships and their professions.

CHALLENGE: **TEMPERING THEIR COMPULSIVE OR FRENETIC ENERGIES**

FULFILLMENT: **DEVELOPING THE ABILITY TO ENCHANT OTHERS**

NOTABLES: **DREW CAREY (ACTOR; COMEDIAN); DOLLEY MADISON (POPULAR FIRST LADY); NICHOLAS II (LAST CZAR OF RUSSIA)**

THE ARTIST FORMERLY KNOWN AS PRINCE
Well-respected musician

6/7/1958
Gemini II

May 25–June 2
FREEDOM
GEMINI I

Brilliant and charismatic communicators, Gemini I's have something of a combative streak that they will have to monitor carefully on the Way of Awareness. As they are naturally impatient, many of their life's lessons will involve the need to slow down, curb their abrasiveness, and avoid the tendency to test their powers in the art of seduction. Still, they are often irresistible and magnetic and may be destined for more than one marriage or partner. These personalities are truly "quick studies," and perhaps they would be wisest to occasionally turn their formidable talent for communication inward—that is, to get in touch with their inner voice and listen to its messages. The fact is, Gemini I's don't always know what's good for them, and they would do well to find out before venturing forth to convince others of the validity of their many ideas and opinions.

CHALLENGE: **TOLERATING THOSE WHO HAVE YET TO BECOME MORE AWARE**

FULFILLMENT: **DISCOVERING THAT FREEDOM IS JUST A STATE OF MIND**

June 3–10
NEW LANGUAGE
GEMINI II

Once fully engaged in their work on the Way of Awareness, Gemini II's are likely to be blessed not only with great understanding but also with the ability to communicate their knowledge to others and be understood. Perhaps their principal danger is becoming too glib or merely skimming the surface of a subject or issue, in which case they will be confronted with their lack of comprehension later, often to the detriment of their personal or professional reputation. Physical discipline and health consciousness may also be important in their lives, and they would do well to establish and stick to healthful diet and exercise routines that will help to balance their natural nervousness and excitability. Still, Gemini II's on this path have great things going for them, providing they avoid the tendency to egotism and power tripping. They would do well to remember that wars may be fought with words alone, but the wrong words can make enemies of even the closest friends and supporters.

CHALLENGE: **BEING FULLY AWARE OF WHAT THEY ARE SAYING AND HOW THEY ARE SAYING IT**

FULFILLMENT: **SEEING THE EFFECTS OF THEIR COMMUNICATIONS ON OTHERS**

NOTABLE: **FREDERICK COOK (EXPLORER, NORTH POLE AND MT. MCKINLEY)**

WILLIAM BUTLER YEATS
Poet and playwright; won 1923 Nobel Prize for Literature

6/13/1865
Gemini III

June 11–18
THE SEEKER
GEMINI III

Naturally thirsty for a broader experience of life, those born in the Week of the Seeker are likely to rise quite easily to the challenges of this karmic path, if only because their inquiring minds will present them with any number of opportunities to increase their personal awareness. Their challenge will be to internalize what they are learning in such a way as to result in genuine self-awareness, rather than allowing their knowledge to exist as abstraction, resulting in a kind of "do as I say, not as I do" attitude toward experience. Not as much at risk of physical addictions or problems as some others on this karmic path, they can, however, collapse into disillusionment and cynicism in the face of life's disappointments. Too intense a need for change may express itself in a number of sexual and romantic partners, to the despair of those who try to get close to them. Nevertheless, if they can cultivate their natural sophistication, they are sure to flourish.

CHALLENGE: **STICKING TO A STRUCTURE FOR FOLLOWING A SPIRITUAL PATH**

FULFILLMENT: **EXPANDING THEIR UNDERSTANDING BEYOND THEIR WILDEST DREAMS**

NOTABLE: **ERIK ERICKSON (PSYCHOANALYST); ERIC HEIDEN (SPEED SKATER; OLYMPIC GOLD MEDALIST)**

KARMIC PATH
5

June 19–24
MAGIC
GEMINI–CANCER CUSP

Alluring and quite romantic, those born on the Gemini–Cancer cusp are a step ahead of the game on the Way of Awareness. Here the lesson is less to discover the enchantment of the everyday—something they already know how to do—but rather to come to increased consciousness in the realm of sensuality and personal relationships. They exert power over others with a naturally seductive charm and can be quite the Casanovas on the romantic scene, moving from one partner to another with sometimes astonishing speed. However, their gifts of conquest can serve to conceal a rather cool heart, and they may fail to truly connect with their partners with the degree of consciousness required by this karmic path. Alternatively, they may close themselves off in a private and inaccessible inner world, shutting out the love they desire. Still, their capacity for seeing the beautiful in life can serve them well, and their potential for success is great indeed.

CHALLENGE: **VIEWING THEMSELVES MORE OBJECTIVELY IN RELATIONSHIPS**
FULFILLMENT: **MAKING A PERFECT MELD OF WHO THEY ARE AND THEIR FATE**
NOTABLES: **GUY LOMBARDO (BANDLEADER); ROBERT HENRI (U.S. PAINTER)**

RICHARD RODGERS
Pulitzer Prize-winning songwriter; wrote music for 40 Broadway musicals including *Oklahoma!* and *The Sound of Music*

6/28/1902
Cancer I

June 25–July 2
THE EMPATH
CANCER I

These emotionally complex people are promised a rich, diverse life's journey when placed on the Way of Awareness. Naturally powerful, Cancer I's will nevertheless have to find an outlet for some of their more aggressive tendencies. Constructive physical and emotional outlets such as sports, creative projects or hobbies, and the like can serve to release bottled-up feelings and reveal much about themselves—to themselves. Highly materialistic, these souls will have to struggle a bit with the requirements of this karmic path and may amass considerable wealth and possessions before they reassess their spiritual values. In addition, a desire for escape or retreat from the world and its problems may result in unfortunate addictive or even physically dangerous behaviors. Yet if they recognize the facts that aggression often exists to mask fears, all will go well for them.

CHALLENGE: **RECOGNIZING THE ROLE THAT FEAR PLAYS IN THEIR LIVES**
FULFILLMENT: **HAVING THE KIND OF AWARENESS THAT CAN WORK MIRACLES**
NOTABLES: **NANCY LIEBERMAN (BASKETBALL PLAYER); JOHN DILLINGER (GANGSTER)**

July 3–10
THE UNCONVENTIONAL
CANCER II

Natural psychologists and explorers, Cancer II's are likely to blossom on the Way of Awareness. As they are gifted with considerable insight and tolerance, their consciousness will surely increase in the course of their life experience. Perhaps their principal pitfall is the danger of developing obsessions and compulsions or letting their fascination with the darker side of human experience lead them down some unsavory, and ultimately unnecessary, trails. They may have a misleading sense of their own personal power, causing them to have an unfounded idea of their own infallibility. Alternatively, they can retreat from the challenges of this karmic path into a private, and impenetrable world. Yet if by acting out their impulses they purse sometimes extreme situations or people, the ultimate result can be a sense of balance, fairness, and a greater awareness of things things are valued by us all, and in that case this karmic path will provide a rare life adventure.

CHALLENGE: **MISTAKING SUBSTANCE-INDUCED EXPERIENCES FOR TRUE AWARENESS**
FULFILLMENT: **LIVING AN AUTHENTIC, ORIGINAL LIFE BY WALKING A SPIRITUAL ROAD**
NOTABLES: **KEVIN BACON (ACTOR, *FOOTLOOSE*); HENRY CABOT LODGE (U.S. SENATOR); JIMMY SMITS (ACTOR)**

WILLIAM WYLER
Director-producer, *Ben-Hur*

7/1/1902
Cancer I

July 11–18
THE PERSUADER
CANCER III

At once observant and passionate, Cancer III's with this configuration are indeed the kind of people who can sell ice cubes to the Eskimos. Born with the power of persuasion, they will face a number of challenges as they learn to regulate that power in the interest of the higher good. Enterprising and often excessive, they must take care not let their desires get out of hand, for they can be rather controlling when preoccupied with getting their own way. Still, they possess a considerable talent for inspiring others by generously sharing their own hard-won insights. This, combined with their great depth of understanding, is sure to win them some fans. They are blessed with the gift of being able to exert considerable self-control and if they learn to relinquish their impulse toward power in the interest of greater critical study and analysis, their gifts for observation and concentration will stand them in good stead on the Way of Awareness.

CHALLENGE: **TRYING NOT TO IMPOSE ON OTHERS WHAT THEY THINK IS GOOD FOR THEM**
FULFILLMENT: **KNOWING THAT, BY EXAMPLE, THEY HAVE INFLUENCED OTHERS TO GROW IN CONSCIOUSNESS**
NOTABLE: **RICHIE SAMBORA (GUITARIST, BON JOVI)**

July 19–25
OSCILLATION
CANCER–LEO CUSP

Cancer–Leos may experience any number of highs and lows as they make their journey along the Way of Awareness. Possessing great courage and the ability to rise to almost any occasion, Cancer–Leos can nevertheless fail to find the perspective required and may expend their energies in a whirlwind of experience that remains devoid of real understanding. Egos are big with this configuration, and the tendency to surround themselves with willing, if unworthy, associates is rather pronounced. Alternatively, Cancer–Leos can become mired in a sense of contest and may put themselves into physical danger in order to increase their spiritual awareness; some of them seem forever to be trying to "live on the edge." Still, they have an undeniable magnetism that, properly channeled, can serve to draw to them the people and experiences they most require. If they cultivate calm and a good sense of humor, their success on this path is ensured.

CHALLENGE: **AVOIDING ANYTHING THAT MIGHT THROW THEM OUT OF BALANCE**
FULFILLMENT: **ENHANCING THEIR PSYCHIC ABILITIES**
NOTABLE: **ERIC HOFFER (WRITER; LONGSHOREMAN-PHILOSOPHER)**

PETER BOGDANOVICH
Film director,
Last Picture Show
—————
7/30/1939
Leo I

July 26–August 2
AUTHORITY
LEO I

Marked by great intensity, these hard-driving souls may find the Way of Awareness a bit of a wild ride. Fearless and gifted with great authority, Leo I's may nevertheless get mired in purely personal pursuits that fail to afford the proper outlets and opportunities for their spiritual growth. It is more than likely, however, that they will discover that the ability to dominate others isn't everything and that while confrontations and the search for peak experiences may be exciting, such activities lose their luster with the passage of time. Still, their love of the truth and their admirable loyalty will help them avoid many of the pitfalls of this configuration, and if they are careful to channel their prodigious energies into greater understanding, not merely greater force, the revelations produced along the Way of Awareness will be welcomed and embraced with great joy.

CHALLENGE: **LEARNING TO SEE BEYOND NARROW SELF-INTEREST**
FULFILLMENT: **FINDING JOY IN NURTURING OTHERS**
NOTABLE: **ROBERT JAMES WALLER (AUTHOR, *BRIDGES OF MADISON COUNTY*)**

August 3–10
BALANCED STRENGTH
LEO II

Blessed with natural strength and courage, Leo II's personality on the Way of Awareness will nevertheless have to work to not become their own worst enemies. It is likely that the major challenge of those with this configuration will be avoiding the extremes of physical activity to which they are prone and resisting the temptation to abuse their power on the battlefields of life. Though this type can well become high-handed or even overbearing as they exercise their power over others, their didacticism will doubtless mellow with time and increased understanding. In their struggles, they will do well to cultivate diplomacy and remember to go easy on themselves, for a loss of self-control only aids their opponents. Though their energies can easily get out of control, their ability to balance those energies will nevertheless always remain within their reach—and the effort to do so could prove to be the source of many spiritual revelations.

CHALLENGE: **LOOSENING THE SINGLEMINDEDNESS OF PURPOSE THAT HOLDS THEM IN ITS GRIP**
FULFILLMENT: **ENJOYING A QUIETER, MORE PEACEFUL TYPE OF STRENGTH—SERENITY**
NOTABLE: **TOMMY AARON (GOLFER)**

GEORGE HAMILTON
Film actor
—————
8/12/1939
Leo III

August 11–18
LEADERSHIP
LEO III

Leo III's on the Way of Awareness will have an easier time of it than most, providing they do not allow their natural talent for command to degenerate into dictatorship or simple bullying. Having a profound faith in their own abilities, they must nevertheless learn the art of when and how much faith to put in others. Socially gifted, they can fall into the trap of egotism if they are seduced by illusions of their own infallibility and will doubtless receive some education in that area along the Way of Awareness. Still, their creativity is considerable, their energies are prodigious, and their gifts of understanding and awareness are in place. If they do not squander those gifts through emotional storms, selfish aims, or petty confrontations, their path to success is all but ensured as they travel this karmic path with charm, authority, and the strength to make great transformations.

CHALLENGE: **HAVING A CLEAR VIEW OF THEIR OWN INTIMATE INTERACTIONS**
FULFILLMENT: **ASSUMING THE ROLE OF QUIET HERO TO OTHERS ON THE INWARD JOURNEY**

August 19–25

EXPOSURE
LEO–VIRGO CUSP

Here the challenge presented by the Way of Awareness is for Leo–Virgos to learn to wield power in an intelligent, effective fashion without manipulating it to their own ends. These personalities are gifted with a knack for knowing when to take a backseat and when to come forward, but they will nonetheless have to avoid the traps of secrecy and sensationalism in order to truly progress. Earthy and sensual, they are greatly attracted to the physical side of life and may expend their energies unwisely, to the detriment of both their physical and emotional health. The revelatory nature of this configuration will doubtless manifest itself in the exposure of some rather uncomfortable secrets. Yet if these individuals deal with those secrets with the grace, charm, and deeper awareness that are all gifts of this karmic path, they will rise above their trials and sorrows with a new perspective and increased knowledge.

CHALLENGE: **OVERCOMING THEIR PROPENSITY TO USE INFORMATION AS A TOOL**

FULFILLMENT: **FINDING THE COURAGE TO SHOW THE WORLD WHO THEY ARE**

NOTABLE: **LENI RIEFENSTAHL (GERMAN FILMMAKER AND PHOTOGRAPHER)**

WILLIAM FRIEDKIN
Film director, *The Exorcist*

8/29/1939
Virgo I

August 26–September 2

SYSTEM BUILDERS
VIRGO I

Many Virgo I's may find themselves at the mercy of unconscious drives and seemingly inexplicable behavior until they rise to the challenges of the Way of Awareness. Here a preoccupation with power may manifest itself mainly as a compulsive need for control, physical disorders, or a neurotic attention to the dramas and details of daily life. Exercise such as yoga or tai chi may be especially beneficial for this group, though some may overdo it in an effort to perfect in themselves what they are not always able to control in others. In relationships, those with this configuration may be hampered by their choice of partners and the tendency to foster dependency in others. Still, they can achieve a great deal on the Way of Awareness, providing they cultivate their abilities to relax, to indulge both themselves and others, and to offer their insights without giving in to the temptation to criticize or complain.

CHALLENGE: **REFUSING TO BOX THEMSELVES IN WITH RIGID THINKING**

FULFILLMENT: **DEVELOPING AN AWARENESS AND UNDERSTANDING OF THEIR OWN NEEDS**

September 3–10

THE ENIGMA
VIRGO II

Gifted with natural discernment and good taste, these individuals will have little trouble separating the wheat from the chaff when placed on the Way of Awareness and will be quick to discover the advantages of a greater consciousness of life. Formidably persuasive and clearly responsible, they will nonetheless discover that self-expression will be the key to their highest success and attainment. Because Virgo II's are alternately quite emotional and completely detached, perhaps their only real danger is repressing their real motivations and subconscious drives. As much as they are enigmas to others, this group runs the risk of also remaining enigmas to themselves and of becoming rigid and defensive when challenged or increasingly cynical and uncaring as life goes on. Still, if they nurture the qualities of dependability, thoughtfulness, and grace with which they have been blessed, they will move along the Way of Awareness with an ever-widening sense of humanity and tolerance.

CHALLENGE: **CONVINCING THEMSELVES THAT SECRETIVENESS OR MYSTERY IS NOT AN ADVANTAGE**

FULFILLMENT: **HAVING SEEN THE LIGHT, SHARING IT WITH OTHERS**

NOTABLES: **DANIEL HUDSON BURNHAM (ARCHITECT; CITY PLANNER); DARYL ZANUCK (FILM EXECUTIVE)**

LILY TOMLIN
Actress/comedian; won Tony for *Search for Signs of Intelligent Life in the Universe*

9/1/1939
Virgo I

September 11–18

THE LITERALIST
VIRGO III

Highly intellectual in orientation, Virgo III's can do very well on the Way of Awareness. First they must expand their sometimes narrow view of what is "real." Their "show me" approach to life is thus apt to be challenged repeatedly by encounters with the more spiritual and metaphysical side of existence. Willful and sometimes quite stubborn, these people will have to exercise great care as they expand and wield their personal power, for they can become quite ruthless and demanding. Alternatively, their need for harmony may cause them to retreat from the challenges of this karmic path, and they may fail to add their support to even the worthiest pursuit if it entails personal risk or conflict. Ultimately, however, Virgo III souls are likely to flourish on this path. They relish the rewards of discipline, education, and personal triumph. Their quest for greater awareness, then, is likely to be very productive as long as they do not waste their energies defending ideas that have lost all meaning.

CHALLENGE: **RELEASING THEIR ATTACHMENT TO MATERIAL REALITY AND ITS FORMS**

FULFILLMENT: **CREATING A NEW, MORE INSPIRED AND INSPIRING CONSTRUCT FOR LIVING**

NOTABLE: **DAVID SOUTER (U.S. SUPREME COURT JUSTICE)**

September 19–24
BEAUTY
VIRGO–LIBRA CUSP

Blessed with a love for the finer things, Virgo–Libras may find this path to be difficult at first, but ultimately it will reward them with a deeper, more meaningful definition of what is beautiful. Deeply attracted to sensuous pursuits and driven by a need for harmony, they can go off the deep end in their search for an escape from unpleasant or difficult realities. Addictions in relationships, substance abuse, and self-destructive behavior can all be real problems here, since Virgo–Libras are not always the best judges of what is good for them. Still, their sense of fun and free-spirited ways will free them from the necessity of taking themselves too seriously. If they are careful to nurture their capacities for stability and caring and to employ their charm and fine communicative talents for other than selfish purposes, their journey promises rich and varied rewards.

CHALLENGE: **DEVELOPING THE DESIRE TO LOOK BEYOND THE SUPERFICIAL**
FULFILLMENT: **FINDING A MORE PROFOUND VIEWPOINT FROM WHICH TO LOOK AT THE WORLD**
NOTABLE: **JOHN HOUSEMAN (ACTOR; DIRECTOR OF *THE PAPER CHASE*)**

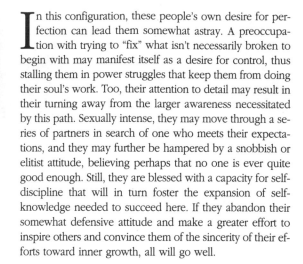

GEORGE WESTINGHOUSE
Engineer and inventor, gas meter
———
10/6/1846
Libra II

September 25–October 2
THE PERFECTIONIST
LIBRA I

In this configuration, these people's own desire for perfection can lead them somewhat astray. A preoccupation with trying to "fix" what isn't necessarily broken to begin with may manifest itself as a desire for control, thus stalling them in power struggles that keep them from doing their soul's work. Too, their attention to detail may result in their turning away from the larger awareness necessitated by this path. Sexually intense, they may move through a series of partners in search of one who meets their expectations, and they may further be hampered by a snobbish or elitist attitude, believing perhaps that no one is ever quite good enough. Still, they are blessed with a capacity for self-discipline that will in turn foster the expansion of self-knowledge needed to succeed here. If they abandon their somewhat defensive attitude and make a greater effort to inspire others and convince them of the sincerity of their efforts toward inner growth, all will go well.

CHALLENGE: **OVERCOMING THEIR DESIRE TO "FIX" THE SPIRITUAL SHORTCOMINGS OF OTHERS**
FULFILLMENT: **BEING FULLY CONSCIOUS OF THE INHERENT PERFECTION IN THE UNIVERSE**
NOTABLE: **JOHN ROSS (LED EASTERN CHEROKEES TO OKLAHOMA, EARLY 19TH C.)**

October 3–10
SOCIETY
LIBRA II

Popular and in demand, these souls are blessed with a natural understanding of the subtler forms of power and how to use it. On the Way of Awareness, then, they will need to be careful. Their approach to power is so nuanced and subtle, they may hardly know they are activating their own power drive. Too much external pressure can send them in search of relief from their internal conflicts and into dependencies on alcohol, tranquilizers, or the like. Meanwhile, their startling capacity for self-deception can cause such problems to go untreated or unaddressed for long periods of time. Alternatively, they may get rather lazy or downright complacent when it comes to issues of consciousness raising or the challenge of developing a higher awareness. Still, if they reach beyond what works for the moment and into the realms of what will work for all time, they are likely to achieve great things on this karmic path.

CHALLENGE: **TAPPING INTO AND RECOGNIZING THE WAYS IN WHICH THEY USE POWER**
FULFILLMENT: **SHARING ALL THAT THEY HAVE LEARNED ABOUT CONSCIOUSNESS WITH OTHERS**
NOTABLE: **PAUL HOGAN (AUSTRALIAN ACTOR)**

LEE HARVEY OSWALD
Assassin of President Kennedy
———
10/18/1939
Libra III

October 11–18
THEATER
LIBRA III

Ambitious, hard-driving, and blessed with a fine understanding of worldly ways, Libra III's are generally successful on the Way of Awareness. There is, however, a danger of heedlessness and bad planning with this configuration, and a certain overconfidence on this karmic path may manifest in accidents and even the odd, unanticipated disaster that will shake them off a poorly chosen course of action. Naturally quite sophisticated and provocative, these souls should take care to avoid becoming world-weary or jaded at the expense of a developing a more spiritual outlook and many will find that even their highest triumphs will turn to ashes until they look beyond the limits of their personal ambitions. Still, the Way of Awareness holds enormous potential for these personalities for to them increased knowledge and the exercise of power exist in a reciprocal and unusually harmonious relationship.

CHALLENGE: **COMBATING A TENDENCY TO BE WORLD-WEARY**
FULFILLMENT: **VIEWING LIFE FROM A HIGHER PERSPECTIVE**
NOTABLES: **RALPH LAUREN (DESIGNER; FASHION EXECUTIVE); MIKE DITKA (FOOTBALL PLAYER; BEARS COACH)**

KARMIC PATH
5

October 19–25

DRAMA AND CRITICISM
LIBRA–SCORPIO CUSP

Integration of the mental and emotional aspects of these charismatic leaders will be the key to their developing the awareness demanded by this karmic path. Blessed with a keen sense of responsibility and fine social skills, those born on the Cusp of Drama and Criticism may nevertheless become overbearing and downright preachy at times, to the detriment of their own further development. Alternatively, they may turn away from others and become isolated in cynicism. In many ways, they need to open and broaden the channels of communication between their conscious and unconscious drives and work to find the balance point between them. Destiny has provided them with a wide stage on which to act out their fates and a willing audience with whom to share their views of the world. If they are careful to keep those views fresh and their performance genuine, these gifted actors on the stage of life will be rewarded with rare insight and a fine understanding of the eternal verities.

JOHN CLEESE
Member of Monty
Python's Flying Circus,
actor
————
10/27/1939
Scorpio I

CHALLENGE: **GOING INTO THEIR OWN GREAT RESERVES OF STRENGTH TO FIND THE COURAGE TO TRANSFORM THEMSELVES**

FULFILLMENT: **ACTIVATING THEIR PASSION THROUGH A MORE SPIRITUAL CONNECTION TO THE WORLD**

October 26–November 2

INTENSITY
SCORPIO I

The influence and power of Scorpio I's on the Way of Awareness are likely to be felt keenly, whatever their area of endeavor. Blessed with great discernment and sophistication, they have much of the "iron hand in the velvet glove" about them, and they will no doubt be keenly aware of the fact that sometimes the surest evidence of real power is the ability to know when not to use it. Charming and persuasive, these people will rarely run the risks associated with merely skimming the surface of issues and problems. They will nevertheless have to be on guard against a tendency in themselves to get mired in rigidity, possessiveness, or just plain heartlessness in their dealings with others. Too, they have a dark side that can manifest in unhealthy and self-destructive behaviors, as these are the kind of people who are quite capable of leading a secret life. Still, their radiant and seductive charms, and their need for both spiritual and material connections will be of great benefit.

CHALLENGE: **FACING THEIR OWN SHADOWS AND BRINGING THEM INTO THE LIGHT OF CONSCIOUSNESS**

FULFILLMENT: **DISCOVERING THAT CONSCIOUSNESS SETS THEIR SENSE OF HUMOR FREE**

November 3–11

DEPTH
SCORPIO II

The quest for profound experience is sure to be given full expression by Scorpio II's, though they may be misled by clinging to the trappings, rather than delving into the workings, of worldly power. Serious and dedicated, these personalities are survivors, capable of rising, phoenixlike, from the ashes of their misadventures. Blessed with keen financial gifts, they may become too materialistic and preoccupied with a sense of their own "worth." Some may refuse the challenges offered by this karmic path, squandering their gifts in escapist pursuits and any number of sexual peccadilloes. They run the risk of obsession in any event and must take care not to exhaust themselves in bouts of worry and depression, which in turn deprive them of opportunities to broaden their vision. Letting go of their unduly defensive and destructive attitudes will do much to unburden them, however, and impart the greater awareness promised by this karmic path.

CHALLENGE: **LEARNING THAT SERIOUSNESS AND CONSCIOUSNESS ARE NOT THE SAME THING**

FULFILLMENT: **REALIZING THAT THERE IS A GREATER PURPOSE BEHIND THEIR SUFFERING**

NOTABLE: **TERRENCE MCNALLY (PLAYWRIGHT)**

GRACE SLICK
Model-turned-singer;
cofounder of
Jefferson Airplane
————
10/30/1939
Scorpio I

November 12–18

CHARM
SCORPIO III

The charm and magnetism of Scorpio III's are matched by a rare realism, and the resulting combination promises great success in almost any area. Still, these gifted souls will have to fight the tendency to become entrenched in their personal power base or remain too complacent to acquire the greater consciousness demanded by this karmic path. Keeping in touch with their own vulnerabilities is a healthy pursuit for them, and an ability to admit their weakness will do much to increase their understanding of themselves and others. It may come as no surprise that it will periodically become necessary for Scorpio III's to give up bad habits, unworthy associates, and crippling relationships. As difficult as those changes may be, these individuals will nevertheless realize that the ability to master one's demons is the real test of power and the ultimate key to exercising power over others in a responsible and thoughtful manner.

CHALLENGE: **RECOGNIZING WHEN SOMETHING IS UNHEALTHY**

FULFILLMENT: **FREEING THEMSELVES FROM THEIR DEMONS**

NOTABLES: **BRENDA VACCARO (ACTRESS); OKSANA BAIUL (FIGURE SKATER; OLYMPIC GOLD MEDALIST)**

November 19–24

REVOLUTION
SCORPIO–SAGITTARIUS CUSP

There is a nearly mythological quality about the journey of Scorpio–Sagittarians on the Way of Awareness, and this karmic path will doubtless require that they get in touch with both their personal myths and the universal models common to us all. There is much of the revolutionary about these people, and if they are not careful, they may get what they wish for, only to witness the destruction and waste that even the best-meant revolution can create. Moderation in both behavior and ideology will be important, if only to save them from the hazards of false conversion experiences or even becoming addicted to God. Still, they have a capacity for real depth and a fine philosophical perspective on the world. If they use their communicative talents to persuade rather than incite, they have the potential to be instrumental in a veritable revolution in consciousness.

LEE TREVINO
Golf champion

12/1/1939
Sagittarius I

CHALLENGE: **REALIZING THAT ALL THAT HAS GRIPPED THEM IS ONLY TEMPORAL**

FULFILLMENT: **EXPERIENCING A MOMENT OF EPIPHANY**

November 25–December 2

INDEPENDENCE
SAGITTARIUS I

Blessed with great generosity of spirit and a fine sense of independence, these people may nevertheless fall victim to the sense that they are "above the law" when it comes to wielding power. Hard to control at best, Sagittarius I's have a need for power that can manifest itself in a thoroughly autocratic attitude, resulting in the resentment of those under their domination, when in fact it is approval and love that Sagittarius I's truly desire. Honorable and responsible, they can nevertheless be competitive in the extreme, and unless their impulse to win is curbed by integrity, these fighters may see some bloody battles indeed. On the more personal front, they may experience similar struggles as they seek validation through any number of sexual partners and ardent admirers. Cultivating depth and learning to accept defeat and acceptance, as demanded by this karmic path, will help them to succeed when meeting their greatest challenge.

CHALLENGE: **FINDING THE INNER PEACE THAT WILL ALLOW THEM TO LOOK WITHIN**

FULFILLMENT: **TRANSCENDING PHYSICAL AND EMOTIONAL LIMITATIONS**

NOTABLES: **NIKOS KAZANTZAKIS (AUTHOR, *ZORBA THE GREEK*); JALEEL WHITE (TELEVISION ACTOR, "URKEL")**

December 3–10

THE ORIGINATOR
SAGITTARIUS II

Power over others can manifest itself in an unusual or even quite capricious fashion here, and these people will have to learn to broaden their admittedly original but sometimes unwieldy ideas to include a wider range of people and situations. A more humanitarian approach will be of great benefit to them on the Way of Awareness, but only if their concepts include a real understanding of what others need. Prone to a certain irresponsibility and even a destructive tendency in personal relationships and interactions, they may strike out against others for fear of losing or becoming hurt. A kind of "get them before they get me" attitude can color their perceptions and cut them off from a broader vision. Still, if they abandon their more defensive attitudes and control their need to prove themselves in a purely aggressive fashion, their ability to turn inward will be rewarded with the expanded and improved understanding that is the promise of the Way of Awareness.

JAMES GALWAY
Flautist; plays gold flute

12/8/1939
Sagittarius II

CHALLENGE: **UNDERSTANDING THAT THEIR SENSE OF UNIQUENESS IS LESS ABOUT SELF-AWARENESS THAN ABOUT EGO**

FULFILLMENT: **NO LONGER HAVING TO PROVE THEMSELVES**

NOTABLES: **THOMAS BRANIFF (FOUNDER, BRANIFF AIRWAYS); DIEGO RIVERA (MEXICAN PAINTER)**

December 11–18

THE TITAN
SAGITTARIUS III

Sagittarius III's can do very well on the Way of Awareness, as they are gifted with a thoughtful, philosophical turn of mind. Self-assured and naturally expansive, they will nevertheless have to defend against the sense of entitlement that goes with this configuration. Sometimes plagued by secret insecurity, these personalities will often be driven to bigger and bigger displays of power in an attempt to prove themselves. They will have to avoid the traps of rising to impossible challenges and reaching for unreachable stars and thereby losing sight of more authentic goals. Moodiness and extremes of behavior can also be problems, though it is unlikely that any of their more unfortunate behaviors will be deliberately self-destructive. Rather, such tendencies are better viewed as symptoms of unawareness, best treated with time, introspection, and an increased consciousness of themselves and their true place in the grander scheme.

CHALLENGE: **WARDING OFF ANY TENDENCIES TO EXERT THEIR POWER AUTOCRATICALLY**

FULFILLMENT: **SEEING THE LARGER PICTURE**

December 19–25
PROPHECY
SAGITTARIUS–CAPRICORN CUSP

Undoubtedly the fiercest battle these people will face is within themselves. Blessed with more than a modicum of charm and good communicative skills, Sagittarius–Capricorns will nonetheless be masters of the art of knowing when to keep their powers to themselves and hold their cards close to the chest. Above all, these souls need to acquire a greater awareness of the actual source of their own best hunches and instincts and learn to trust themselves and others. They have a tendency to self-doubt and suspicion that can sometimes put them at the mercy of suppressed feelings and pent-up resentments. Still, their more militant aspects will be given full play in this configuration, and if they direct their conflicts into constructive actions they are sure to be educated in the ways and means of power beyond their wildest imaginings. Success may come late for these people, but when it does come, it will serve to affirm a sense of themselves that was doubtless present all along.

PAUL REVERE
Patriot and silversmith;
famous ride to Lexington
in 1775

1/1/1735
Capricorn I

CHALLENGE: **GRAPPLING WITH THE UNREST THAT THEIR OWN CHAOTIC ENERGIES GENERATE**

FULFILLMENT: **STEPPING FULLY INTO A PROPHETIC ROLE**

December 26–January 2
THE RULER
CAPRICORN I

Gifted with a natural genius for efficiency, Capricorn I's will do quite well on the Way of Awareness, providing they do not allow their administrative powers to degenerate into autocracy. While it is true that these souls usually demand no more of others than they do of themselves, the rest of the world may not always see it that way. Stern taskmasters, those born with this configuration are gifted with considerable charm yet are capable of cutting through the fluff and getting a job done. Though they will doubtless struggle with issues of authority, they have a tendency to get bottled up and repress their emotions, often leading to extremes of behavior or tantrums of sheer frustration. Thus balance will be important. Capricorn I's can afford to relax a bit and allow the social side of their natures greater expression; if they do, they will be rewarded with the ability to trust others as much as others are prone to trust them.

CHALLENGE: **NOT USING THEIR CRITICAL THINKING AS A VEILED TOOL OF POWER**

FULFILLMENT: **EXPRESSING THEIR CONCERN FOR OTHERS**

NOTABLE: **MAURICE UTRILLO (PAINTER, PICTURE POSTCARD VIEWS OF PARIS)**

January 3–9
DETERMINATION
CAPRICORN II

Well versed in the ways of power, Capricorn II's on the Way of Awareness will certainly be blessed with a wealth of opportunities to make their marks in the world. Quite interested in money generally, they may misuse their power to amass a fortune in the material world, to the detriment of their higher consciousness. Yet the principal danger is that they may employ their natural charms and communicative skills in underhanded or manipulative ways. For these are people who quite readily believe that the end justifies the means, and they are not above trying to fool all of the people, all of the time or taking advantage of others just because they can. Still, if they use their inborn interest in things metaphysical and theoretical as stepping-stones for spiritual development, they are unlikely to stray far from the Way of Awareness.

SIR ISAAC NEWTON
Physicist/mathematician;
discovered law of gravity

1/4/1642
Capricorn II

CHALLENGE: **ELIMINATING JUDGMENTALNESS FROM THEIR PSYCHOLOGICAL MAKEUP**

FULFILLMENT: **FEELING THEIR SPIRITUAL SIDE FLOWER**

January 10–16
DOMINANCE
CAPRICORN III

Blessed with a confidence in their own abilities that does not always require a display of power, these people are likely to be quite content on the Way of Awareness. They are naturally professional and quite competent; the key to their success, however, will be in their ability to control their tendency to worry or to obsess, which in turn can lead them down some wrong paths as they search for relief from their anxieties. A regular program of physical exercise or training in some sport or outdoor activity will help them build a positive self-image and "get them out of their own heads" in a positive fashion. This configuration holds a number of possibilities for peak experiences, and these people are likely to have the relatively rare opportunity to expand their awareness in a sudden or even shocking epiphany at some point. Once their spirituality is thus awakened, it is unlikely that it will be ignored.

CHALLENGE: **WORRYING LESS ABOUT CAREER CONCERNS**

FULFILLMENT: **STUDYING METAPHYSICS**

January 17–22

MYSTERY AND IMAGINATION
CAPRICORN–AQUARIUS CUSP

These people have the potential for great progress and attainment on the Way of Awareness, yet they may need to regulate their own behavior before they can enjoy the rewards of this karmic path. Prone to disregard their health, these people can push too hard and too fast, and, though blessed with great strength, they can nevertheless burn themselves out or develop chronic physical problems. Too, they may externalize their personal demons and wind up wasting their energies in paranoia or any number of trick wars and false crusades. They can become addicted not so much to specific substances but to a search for the "ultimate highs and lows" of experience, pushing the limits of what they can endure beyond good sense and into the realms of active self-destruction. If Capricorn–Aquarians learn early on how to express their creative power and control their anger, their road will be smoothed considerably.

JEAN FELIX AND AUGUSTE PICCARD
Twin brothers; oceanographer/balloonist

1/28/1884
Aquarius I

CHALLENGE: **NOT GOING OVERBOARD IN A KIND OF CONVERSION "EXPERIENCE"**
FULFILLMENT: **FINDING THAT THEY ARE NOT QUITE AS ALONE AS THEY BELIEVED THEMSELVES TO BE**

January 23–30

GENIUS
AQUARIUS I

Though Aquarius I's are quite definite about wanting to have things their own way, it is more an expression of their personal need for freedom than a need to dominate others. For that reason alone, they can do quite well on the Way of Awareness. Their principal danger is one of instability; they can be so self-assured that they become reckless, and their vulnerability to external stress can make them prone to search for often unhealthy forms of escape. On this karmic path they will also be required to cultivate a greater sensitivity to others and learn about the emotional bonds that unite us all. Otherwise they can become quite careless of other people's affections, alienating those close to them without quite knowing how or why. Still, if they do not abuse their considerable power by becoming overcritical of the elitism, rigidity, or lack of personal direction of others, their unique style and formidable intelligence will serve them well.

CHALLENGE: **ELIMINATING THE UNHEALTHIER FORMS OF ESCAPE FROM THEIR LIVES**
FULFILLMENT: **TASTING THE TOTALITY OF EXISTENCE IN A SINGLE MOMENT OF PERCEPTION**
NOTABLE: **DONNA REED (TV ACTRESS, *THE DONNA REED SHOW*)**

January 31–February 7

YOUTH AND EASE
AQUARIUS II

Social, popular, and charming in the extreme, Aquarius II's may nevertheless turn away from the challenges of this karmic path in a refusal to cultivate spiritual values and understanding. Many of them will retreat into a kind of chronic shallowness in their view of the world, while others may succumb to rigidity, unfounded prejudices, and a lack of tolerance for their fellows. In any event, they can get quite addicted to their own popularity and would do well to keep a watchful eye on their need for approval. Here, the Way of Awareness is all but sure to manifest itself in a need to develop a set of values and beliefs that are tied to universal concerns. If they delve beneath the surface of life in a search for truth, their rewards on this karmic path will include maturity, perspective, and the ability to administrate power with rare grace and refinement.

BETTY FRIEDAN
NOW founder, feminist leader; *Feminine Mystique*

2/4/1921
Aquarius II

CHALLENGE: **ATTEMPTING TO GO DEEPER INTO THEMSELVES AND OTHERS**
FULFILLMENT: **LIVING IN THE MOMENT**
NOTABLES: **JOHN M. PRITCHARD, SR. (CHIEF CONDUCTOR, BBC SYMPHONY ORCHESTRA); MARIO LANZA (OPERA SINGER)**

February 8–15

ACCEPTANCE
AQUARIUS III

Though not exactly famous for their willingness to change their minds and habits, those born in the Week of Acceptance will be asked to do just that when placed on the Way of Awareness. Too, these people must learn to regulate aggression and express themselves diplomatically or run the risk of eroding their power base through tantrums, emotional displays, and hypercriticism. Too, this karmic path may require them to slow down and avoid scattering their energies. Yet underneath they are quite sensitive to the thoughts and opinions of others, and if they can learn to glean the value of ideas without taking disagreements too personally, all will go well. Finally, these souls are wonderfully inventive, able to synthesize enormous amounts of information into truly unique ideas for improving and motivating others. Blessed with such inspiration, they are likely to travel far on the way of awareness.

CHALLENGE: **DETACHING COMPLETELY FROM THEIR VIEWS**
FULFILLMENT: **BEING INSPIRED TO MOTIVATE OTHERS**
NOTABLES: **LLOYD BENTSEN (FORMER U.S. SENATOR AND SECRETARY OF THE TREASURY); EVA GABOR (TELEVISION ACTRESS, *GREEN ACRES*); JULES VERNE (WRITER; "FATHER" OF SCIENCE FICTION)**

KARMIC PATH
5

February 16–22

SENSITIVITY
AQUARIUS–PISCES CUSP

The simple tendency to overreact may be an ongoing issue for those with this configuration, as their powerful exteriors may exist at odds with their sensitive, emotional interior lives. Cultivating a greater awareness of their own emotional habits will be paramount to their success. Otherwise, those born on the Aquarius–Pisces cusp may waste the gifts of this path in a kind of chronic "off with their heads!" response to challenges to their authority. Highly success-oriented, they are unlikely to settle for less than the best when it comes to the realization of either their personal or professional goals. Their communicative talents will do much to alleviate their potential for being misunderstood, and if they are careful to use their sensitive natures to attune themselves to an awareness of the deeper issues and larger concerns of life, rather than to retreat into an isolated world of old grudges and injured egos, they are certain to excel.

GIULIETTA MASINA
Film actress, *La Strada*

2/22/1921
Aquarius–Pisces Cusp

CHALLENGE: **TRANSFORMING THEIR EMOTIONAL SENSITIVITY INTO A SENSITIVITY TO BEAUTY**

FULFILLMENT: **SURPASSING OBJECTIVE LIMITATIONS**

February 23–March 2

SPIRIT
PISCES I

Blessed with the ability to understand the spiritual as part of their personal power, Pisces I's are likely to shine on the Way of Awareness. While they live a great deal in their own hearts, they have considerable communicative talents, making them fine politicians, diplomats, and spokespeople with a shrewd and effective ability for administration. Their danger is that, in traveling this path, they may become so overinvolved that they narrow their focus from the broader perspective required by it. Alternatively, they may retreat into dreaminess and sensuality, thus dissipating their powers for the larger good. Finally, they can be just plain lazy when it comes to the spiritual path—enjoying the positive energy without doing the work to remain conscious. Still, their spirituality is part and parcel of their makeup; if they dedicate themselves to channeling their energy into meeting larger and more important needs than their own and cultivating the self-discipline needed to broaden their awareness of the ways and means of power, they are likely to reap a rich reward.

CHALLENGE: **DISCIPLINING THEMSELVES TO DO THE WORK OF BEING CONSCIOUS**

FULFILLMENT: **LIVING FROM THEIR HEARTS**

NOTABLE: **ERNST HAAS (PHOTOJOURNALIST)**

March 3–10

THE LONER
PISCES II

Pisces II's run the risk of holding themselves aloof from the challenges of the Way of Awareness by their tendency to turn away from a broader perspective and into a world of their own making. Still, they are blessed with a rather primal sort of insight into how power works on both the personal and worldly levels. Their search for an ideal may lead them to a variety of sexual encounters that can fail to satisfy, as they may resist connection in the interest of control. Yet the principal problem with this configuration will be emotional instability; they are at once highly sensitive as far as their own needs and image are concerned and astonishingly insensitive to the needs of others. Yet if they take care not to narrow their vision in an attempt to protect themselves or adopt an overly defensive attitude toward the world, their fine intellect, considerable understanding, and genuine need to connect with higher spiritual consciousness will surely be seen along the Way of Awareness.

SHARON STONE
Actress, *Basic Instinct*

3/10/1958
Pisces II

CHALLENGE: **RECOGNIZING THAT AWARENESS DOES NOT NECESSITATE SUFFERING**

FULFILLMENT: **FINDING THE UNIVERSAL IN THE BEAUTIFUL**

March 11–18

DANCERS AND DREAMERS
PISCES III

Born with an innate ability to make astonishing quantum leaps in consciousness, these souls may make great strides along the Way of Awareness. Possessing great charisma and a sometimes nearly magical charm, Pisces III's may nevertheless have a tendency to use others or to be plagued by a certain shallowness in their perceptions and interactions with others. Displays of temperament and a myriad of complaints about life's harsher realities may show up here, and they must guard against the tendency to throw up smoke screens as a means of disguising their own inadequacies. However, it's unlikely that they will abuse their considerable powers for long, for they have naturally helpful impulses and a genuine concern for the greater welfare. If they cultivate their capacity for depth and their ability to cope with sometimes unpleasant realities, they will find their powers increasing to impressive proportions.

CHALLENGE: **CULTIVATING HUMILITY**

FULFILLMENT: **MAKING THEIR DREAM A REALITY FOR OTHERS**

NOTABLE: **GORDON MacRAE (ACTOR)**

The Way of Intention

TAURUS I TO SCORPIO I
Manifestation to Intensity

Those born to the Way of Intention are here to learn how to concentrate fully on any matter at hand, to eliminate the superfluous from their life and work, and to acquire greater mastery. While these thoroughly practical men and women have an innate ability to focus, too often this ability is more sporadic than consistent in nature. While they are already able to concentrate in short, intense spurts, these individuals are here to learn how to focus over the long haul. For this to occur, those on this karmic path must learn to set an intention and hold it. The development of such a capacity for intention is, in essence, about harnessing one's own mind for a specific purpose. For the individuals on this path, who are easily knocked off balance and blown off course, this is far more difficult than it may seem.

At first glance, these individuals often appear to be the epitome of the natural man. Highly sensuous, they enjoy life and its pleasures with the greatest of gusto. A core lesson for those on this karmic path is how not to be sidetracked, whether by the latest pleasure or the latest gizmo, scheme, or plan, all of which usually offer only short-term rewards. In fact, much of the journey for these sybaritic individuals involves learning how to tame these urges in order to focus on more important areas of life: work, health, home life, or relationships with spouses, friends, or children. These voluptuous men and women can easily re-

CORE LESSON
Developing the self-mastery not to permit distraction at any cost

GOAL
To remain focused over the long term

main ensconced in their pleasures, yet by doing so would stagnate intellectually, psychologically, morally, and spiritually. Apt to be content with the status quo, they tend to avoid anything that requires discipline and attention, thus stymieing their ability to move forward to greater achievements. Therefore, this karmic path must literally force them to pull themselves out of the proverbial Eden and move onward.

It may be easy to spot these individuals on the street; they are the ones who are meandering along enjoying the life around them with a gently sexual swagger to their stride, occasionally stopping to peer intently at whatever catches their fancy. Their destiny, however, is to learn how to move resolutely toward a goal by firmly setting their intention on reaching and keeping it. Scorpio I energy is often more concerned with intention than results, and thus those on the Way of Intention must teach themselves to be less pragmatically involved in details—which usually bog them down—and more morally driven. That is, they need to have the moral courage to think always of the long-term goal and the greater good by cutting away all that does not contribute to those aims.

The struggles of those on the Way of Intention can be substantial, for these individuals are born with a great deal of stubbornness and resistance to change. Only when they have succeeded in eliminating a certain laziness from their character will they free their hands to grapple with the

GIFTS
Practical, Technical, Stubborn

PITFALLS
Single-minded, Lusty, Fixed

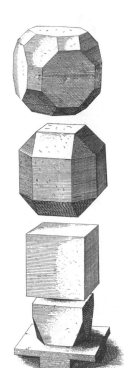

world. While their tenacity can help them along this path, they often use it instead to merely cling to the status quo, often staying in the same rut year after year, whether it is good for them or not, and never freeing themselves from the old habits that are so deeply ingrained in their personality. Moreover, their emotional vulnerability to the approval and disapproval of others can hold them back. Moving toward a more truthful, single-minded, and dynamic approach requires letting go of a kind of smug self-satisfaction. In order for the core lessons of focusing and intending to be learned, those on this karmic path must keep their eyes firmly on an object they desire, not be sidetracked, and acquire a somewhat compulsive attitude that will not compromise or let up in its intensity.

The primary area in which their struggle takes place and the lessons of their karmic path will be achieved is first and foremost within themselves. Before they accomplish a psychological and spiritual turnaround, they will be unable to proceed effectively in their professional or personal activities. In early years, family and school may be the arenas of such training, which could well involve strict parents and teachers who plant the first seeds of an uncompromising approach to chores and study habits. Sooner or later, those on this karmic path will see that a hard choice must be made between present pleasures and future goals if anything meaningful is to be accomplished. Of course, the ability to enjoy themselves must not be impaired or even crushed in childhood, or the result may well be a workaholic or puritanical attitude, which could cripple all real spiritual growth and prevent any lasting happiness.

Obviously, the extremes on this karmic path are problematical. Those proceeding from the energy of Taurus I manifestation always risk getting bogged down in their own sensuality and procrastination. Since they can so easily slip back, they must be ruthless in blocking out their tendency just to hang out and relax. However, the opposite problem, that of Scorpio I intensity taking over and creating unbearable tensions and an inability to take it easy, must also be dealt with. A pattern of hard work and reward is undoubtedly the best kind of program. In such a scenario, having proceeded to home in on a problem and solve it with the laserlike focus of Scorpio I, the Taurus I sensuous side can kick in to provide great satisfaction in the ensuing rest period.

Above all, those on the Way of Intention have a fascination for the simple pleasures, for nature and natural living. If they can lead a simpler life, their goal of avoiding distractions may be more easily achieved. Thus, it is highly recommended that these individuals live a more rural lifestyle that will help them avoid the many amusements that larger cities offer. In nature, it is far easier for these individuals to see the bigger picture and to stick to

RELEASE

The attraction to
short-term amusements

REWARD

The joy of accomplishment

SUGGESTION

*It's often not enough to have a goal in mind; usually
one must also have the intention to achieve it.*

their goals. What is perhaps best for those on the Way of Intention is to have a "normal" lifestyle, in which family and neighborhood responsibilities must be discharged regularly. By forming bonds with their neighbors and taking pride in their home, these individuals will have a greater chance for domestic happiness. Also, in the process a middle ground can be forged between the excessive physicality of Taurus I and the spartan attitudes of Scorpio I. Parties, dinners with friends, holiday celebrations, and family get-togethers are all venues that encourage self-expression and sharing.

In relationships, a danger exists that the stubborn, tenacious qualities of Taurus I will overlie and meld with an overly stern or hurtful Scorpio I attitude, thus creating an unforgiving attitude toward others that can survive for years or even decades. Learning to let go of resentments and blame, which can easily provide a source of distraction for years, is imperative for the men and women on the Way of Intention, who find it easy to be overpossessive, even codependent, in their relationships. This can be gratifying to the object of their affections, their intended, or a mate who is made to feel needed and appreciated, but it can also cause them to feel trapped or at least hemmed in. Moreover, this sort of attention to relationship is apt to keep those on the

Way of Intention from focusing on more important, longer-term goals. Therefore, the best mates for those on this karmic path are strong, dedicated individuals who are able to withstand their partner's intensity without giving up their own individuality. Mates, friends, and lovers who are weak and overly dependent will only arouse the wrong kind of protective energy or demand too much attention, holding back the development of those on the Way of Intention. A good partner for these individuals is pragmatic enough to help them keep their focus while also having the capacity to see the big picture, helping to broaden their loved one's focus.

The Way of Intention can be personified by a sculptor who crafts his vision from a piece of marble. Chipping away day after day, the sculptor rids his work of all extraneous material, ultimately revealing the beautiful form within the stone. Focused and always keeping the image of his finished piece in mind, the artist does not allow anything to come between him and his creation. Thus, those on this karmic path are challenged to keep their passion for their goal alive through both thick and thin, until the last piece falls into place and the desired outcome is achieved; otherwise, their creative intensity might flag, their resolve weaken, and their vision fade.

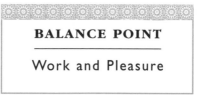

BALANCE POINT

Work and Pleasure

CRYSTALS AND GEMSTONES

Lodestone facilitates reaching and maintaining a deep state of meditation. This practice will assist the individual to be disciplined and to concentrate on long-term goals.

NOTABLES ON THIS KARMIC PATH

CHARLIE PARKER

Lifelong problems with intoxicants often kept jazz musician **Charlie Parker** from focusing on his work. Like many on the Way of Intention, Parker was an intense personality and over-indulged in drugs, alcohol, and other forms of escape. Despite these weaknesses, his mastery of the alto saxophone places him among the greats of jazz. Unfortunately, Parker burned out at an early age and died young from a sudden heart attack. Parker exemplifies the gifts and the pitfalls possessed by those on this path.

Anthropologist **Margaret Mead's** amazing ability to focus on her work epitomizes the concentration possessed by those on the Way of Intention. Early on, Mead's travels to the South Sea islands piqued her interest in the social activities of native cultures. These studies played an important role in her professional life, and by writing about her numerous field trips she was able to focus her energies. Mead later extended her anthropological observations to her own culture, publishing *And Keep Your Powder Dry: An Anthropologist Looks at America.*

MARGARET MEAD

In her roles as a curator at the American Museum of Natural History and as a professor at Columbia and New York universities, Mead further realized the significant achievements that would fulfill her destiny.

Though he is often credited with introducing the theory of evolution, **Charles Darwin** did not in fact originate the idea. However, it was through his field work on the Galápagos Islands and the resultant book *On the Origin of Species* (1859) that the theory gained recognition. This success was due particularly to Darwin's stubbornness and resistance to change, drawbacks typical of those on this path, that he turned to his advantage. Only after years of aggressive effort was this single-minded scientist able to convince straitlaced Victorian society to accept the likelihood of their animal origins.

CHARLES DARWIN

Other Notables: Art Monk, Matt Lauer, John Steinbeck, Judy Chicago, Helen A. Thomas, Marvin Gaye, David Frost, Judy Carne, Judy Collins, Gerald Levin, Harvey Keitel, Dixie Carter, Peter Carl Fabergé, Franz Kafka, Hunter S. Thompson, Maureen O'Hara, Ray Bradbury, William Rutherford Mead, Christopher Robin Milne, Alicia Silverstone, Mario Puzo, Henri Toulouse-Lautrec, Marlene Dietrich, Andrew Johnson, Ellen DeGeneres, Charles Lindbergh, Abraham Lincoln, Ansel Adams

BIRTHDAYS ON KARMIC PATH 6

May 3, 1883–September 21, 1883 | December 14, 1901–May 3, 1902 | July 25, 1920–December 13, 1920

March 7, 1939–July 25, 1939 | October 16, 1957–March 6, 1958 | May 27, 1976–October 15, 1976

January 7, 1995–May 27, 1995 | August 18, 2013–January 6, 2014

KARMIC PATH
6

March 19–24
REBIRTH
PISCES–ARIES CUSP

Pisces–Arians on the Way of Intention will have something of a struggle because they have an impulse to oversimplify their lives and habits that is at odds with the complexity of their creative urges. Blessed with formidable intuition and the ability to "do" as well as to dream, they can nevertheless become mired in an emotional vulnerability that keeps them from taking necessary risks. Alternatively, they may become preoccupied with other people's motivations and perceptions and fail to be true to themselves. Those with this configuration will nevertheless find great reward and satisfaction in those they consider family, including friends, love interests, and especially children. If they are careful not to turn their eyes from the future or to turn the energy of focusing inward, they will receive great rewards and accomplish great things.

CHALLENGE: **WADING THROUGH THE COMPLEX OF THEIR EMOTIONS TO FIND A FOCUS**
FULFILLMENT: **BEING FULLY PREPARED FOR ALL THAT MAY COME THEIR WAY**
NOTABLES: **THOMAS E. DEWEY (FORMER GOVERNOR OF NEW YORK STATE; PRESIDENTIAL CANDIDATE); BRIAN MULRONEY (CANADIAN POLITICAL LEADER)**

MARVIN GAYE
Soul/pop singer;
killed by his father

4/2/1939
Aries I

March 25–April 2
THE CHILD
ARIES I

To a great extent, these people's success on the Way of Intention will be largely a result of their early education and experience. As long as their joy in discovering the world has not been repressed or subjected to too much discipline, resulting in an uncompromising or even puritanical approach to their work habits, and as long as their considerable energy is balanced between hard work and hard play, they are likely to do quite well. Dynamic and even temperamental at times, they nonetheless possess an openness to new experience and a love of challenge—even when the challenge is something to be overcome in themselves. Though they face some danger of misusing their energy in resentments, feuds, and all manner of grudge matches, they are nevertheless equal to the tasks of refining and redefining their characters and letting go of outdated habits and unproductive behaviors. If they take care to nurture their own sense of potential and set clear and realistic goals for themselves, their natural passion and enthusiasm will serve them well.

CHALLENGE: **REMEMBERING THEIR NEED FOR PLAY**
FULFILLMENT: **REAPING THE REWARDS OF THEIR SOLITARY AND DETERMINED APPROACH**
NOTABLE: **PHIL NIEKRO (BASEBALL GREAT)**

April 3–10
THE STAR
ARIES II

A tendency to extremes in both behavior and life experience is all but sure to confront Aries II's on the Way of Intention. Driven by a need to be at the center of the action, these people can be rather compulsive at times. Too, they may face many challenges that involve turning their attention toward the future and its rewards, for this is one configuration for whom the "bird in the hand" is far more important than the one in the bush. Possessiveness in all its forms can be a problem, and these people are likely to experience some difficulty with issues of jealousy, envy, or outright greed before they learn the gentle art of letting go. Alternatively, they can fail to focus and may become too dependent on the approval or disapproval of others at the expense of their own capacity for development. Nevertheless, their dynamic, single-minded approach imparts great powers of concentration, wonderful stamina, and the necessary energy to accomplish great things in almost any area of endeavor.

CHALLENGE: **NOT BEING DISTRACTED BY THE APPROVAL OR DISAPPROVAL OF OTHERS**
FULFILLMENT: **GIVING THEMSELVES FULLY TO A PROJECT, CAUSE, OR GOAL**
NOTABLE: **JOHN SCULLEY (BUSINESS EXECUTIVE)**

SIR DAVID FROST
Broadcaster and
businessman, *That Was
the Week That Was*

4/7/1939
Aries II

April 11–18
THE PIONEER
ARIES III

Blessed with fine social skills and a great capacity for leadership, these people will certainly flourish on the Way of Intention. They are gifted with a passion and dedication that inspire others, and their optimism and positive attitudes are certain to be of great help along this karmic path. They may be prone to ignore their own faults or put them on some spiritual back burner, however, and can resist the need for self-examination for alarmingly long periods of time. Alternatively, they may be encumbered by an overly judgmental or overbearing attitude that seeks to control rather than inspire. These souls may therefore have some rude awakenings when it comes to issues of character or spiritual development. In the end, whatever the challenges of this karmic path, Aries III's are likely to meet them fearlessly and with an admirable depth of commitment to a more enlightened future.

CHALLENGE: **LOOKING INWARD ONCE IN A WHILE**
FULFILLMENT: **SACRIFICING FOR A GREATER GOOD**
NOTABLE: **LOUISE LASSER (TELEVISION ACTRESS, *MARY HARTMAN, MARY HARTMAN*)**

KARMIC PATH
6

April 19–24
POWER
ARIES–TAURUS CUSP

Powerful and productive, these souls have lavish tastes that can easily get out of hand. Sensualists all, these personalities see material things as expressions of personal power and will likely have a great talent for supporting their opulent inclinations. Their love of wealth and sensuality can manifest itself in mercenary tendencies, however, or in the mistaken attitude that "too much is never quite enough." Too, the tendency to wield their material power over others is pronounced here. Alternatively, they may become downright lazy—enmeshed in physical pleasure at the expense of spiritual expansion and awareness and forever tied to the same old routines, associates, and activities. Still, if they are careful to avoid the dangers of smugness and self-satisfaction and not to measure their personal worth by worldly standards, their success on the Way of Intention is ensured.

WALTER GROPIUS
Bauhaus architect and
educator, designed
Pan Am building

5/18/1883
Taurus III

CHALLENGE: **CONTROLLING THEIR MYRIAD SENSUAL AND PHYSICAL DESIRES**
FULFILLMENT: **PICKING THE CORRECT TIME TO FULFILL THEIR INTENTIONS**

April 25–May 2
MANIFESTATION
TAURUS I

Highly protective and nurturing, sometimes in the extreme, these people can turn the challenges provided by the Way of Intention into opportunity. Perhaps the principal pitfall with this configuration is the tendency of Taurus I's to stagnation and stubbornness. Many of them on this karmic path will be forced to repeat the same lessons time and again, if only because they fail to make necessary changes in themselves or their habits. This is not because they don't get the message the first time but rather because of their insistence on the need to make their own mistakes in the name of "realism." Still, this path should provide them with a wonderful family life, a secure and profitable career, and the ability to hang in for the long haul. If they take care not to allow their tenacity to harden into rigidity or seek to control their nearest and dearest with "smother love," the Way of Intention will provide them with an ever-widening scope of rewarding possibilities.

CHALLENGE: **BREAKING PATTERNS BORN OF STUBBORNNESS AND RESISTANCE**
FULFILLMENT: **ONCE SET, SEEING THEIR INTENTIONS MANIFESTED BY ACCOMPLISHMENTS**
NOTABLE: **JUDY COLLINS (FOLKSINGER)**

May 3–10
THE TEACHER
TAURUS II

Astute and enterprising, these people are blessed with a natural fairness and sense of truth that will be of enormous benefit to them on the Way of Intention. Though they do run the risk of becoming quite demanding and inflexible as they realize success in worldly affairs, their need to impart their acquired expertise and to nurture those close to them is likely to balance their more self-interested side. They will doubtless acquire great dignity as they move along this karmic path, for this is a configuration that is bound to manifest itself in the need not only for recognition but for respect. These people like to work and are quite comfortable with the idea that they must exert themselves in order to realize both material and spiritual rewards. If they bring that dynamic to bear on their need for wider horizons and a broader range of possibilities for fulfillment, they are likely to soar above the obstacles and realize their fondest dreams.

CHALLENGE: **NOT ALLOWING THEMSELVES TO GET TOO BOGGED DOWN IN FIGURING OUT HOW THINGS WORK**
FULFILLMENT: **SEEING OTHERS BENEFIT FROM THEIR DETERMINATION**
NOTABLE: **GERALD LEVIN (BUSINESS EXECUTIVE; CHAIRMAN, WARNER ENTERTAINMENT)**

May 11–18
THE NATURAL
TAURUS III

It will be truly important for these personalities on the Way of Intention to be well socialized. Determined for the most part to march to the beat of their own drum and attune themselves to the world of nature, they will nevertheless benefit enormously from love interests and family members who will keep them from retreating into a self-imposed, comfortable isolation. Taurus III's must struggle to become more worldly, especially in the areas of commerce, money, and ambition. Once they understand that they might indeed want more out of life, they may widen their fields of endeavor and activity considerably. Still, they are unlikely to lose their protective attitude toward all living creatures, especially those less conscious than themselves. If they work to raise their own level of insight and expand their horizons beyond their immediate environment, they will be rewarded with the ability to see well beyond the trees and gain a more accurate picture of the forest.

HARVEY KEITEL
Film actor, *Smoke*

5/13/1939
Taurus III

CHALLENGE: **TAKING CARE NOT TO SUBCONSCIOUSLY REBEL AGAINST THEIR OWN GREATER GOALS**
FULFILLMENT: **GAINING SECURITY BY WORKING TOWARD LONGER-TERM GOALS**

May 19–24
ENERGY
TAURUS–GEMINI CUSP

Cultivating the ability to concentrate their considerable forces in a particular field or area of endeavor will be critical to the success of these dynamic souls when placed on the Way of Intention. This karmic path could prove to be either their greatest blessing or their worst curse. Until they rid themselves of the need to always grab the spotlight or to be performers who must always be "on," there can be somewhat less of substance to their personalities than that which meets the eye. They would do well to remember, therefore, that the ability to garner admiration is quite another thing from the quality of character required to command respect. Still, if they take care not to content themselves with the glamour of the moment and to carefully ground themselves in real, rather than superficial, relationships, their great versatility and natural brilliance are sure to guide them toward fulfillment.

DOUGLAS FAIRBANKS
Silent film actor

5/23/1883
Taurus–Gemini Cusp

CHALLENGE: **CULTIVATING THE AWARENESS TO KNOW WHETHER OR NOT THEY ARE ACCOMPLISHING THEIR GOALS**
FULFILLMENT: **GAINING THE SELF-RESPECT THAT COMES FROM SEEING SOMETHING THROUGH**

May 25–June2
FREEDOM
GEMINI I

Though unlikely to get mired in the complacency that is one of the pitfalls of this karmic path, these souls will nevertheless be faced with a number of challenges and distractions along the Way of Intention. Simple restlessness can be a problem, as can the tendency to attract and discard any number of fair-weather friends. Further, they are quite able to misdirect the energies of this path in displays of tyranny and temperament, to say nothing of their capacity to be downright manipulative if it suits their purposes. Mastering a specific craft or area of technical expertise will allow them to direct their considerable energy in a constructive fashion as well as provide them with a sense of both security and accomplishment on the Way of Intention.

CHALLENGE: **MANAGING STRESS**
FULFILLMENT: **MASTERING A HOBBY, SKILL, OR CRAFT**
NOTABLES: **DIXIE CARTER (ACTRESS, *DESIGNING WOMEN*); PETER CARL FABERGÉ (GOLDSMITH AND JEWELER); BRENT MUSBERGER (TELEVISION SPORTS JOURNALIST)**

June 3–10
NEW LANGUAGE
GEMINI II

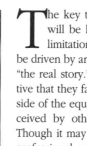

Blessed with a nearly limitless potential for success in fields that involve communication and innovation, these personalities will nevertheless have their share of ups and downs along the Way of Intention. Of primary importance will be the ability to buckle down to the task at hand and become organized enough to accomplish tangible goals. These people are rather easily sidetracked by what they consider to be the darker side of human existence, and they can waste valuable resources in less-than-savory activities, associates, and sensual pursuits. Surrounding themselves with stable people who will aid them on both personal and professional levels will be important here, as will the development of steady work habits. Still, if they avoid the pitfalls of aloofness, hypercriticism, and simple overkill when it comes to communicating their ideas to the world, their unique gifts are sure to be recognized and rewarded.

AL UNSER, SR.
Race car driver

5/29/1939
Gemini I

CHALLENGE: **TAKING CARE NOT TO ALLOW THEIR DARKER PROCLIVITIES TO INTERFERE WITH THEIR GOALS**
FULFILLMENT: **FOCUSING ON THE QUALITY RATHER THAN QUANTITY OF THEIR EFFORTS**
NOTABLES: **MARGARET DRABBLE (WRITER); MARIAN WRIGHT EDELMAN (CIVIL RIGHTS ACTIVIST; CHILDREN'S ADVOCATE)**

June 11–18
THE SEEKER
GEMINI III

The key to the success of Gemini III's on this path will be learning to distinguish between focus and limitation. Restless and curious, these people can be driven by an inner need to get to the truth and uncover "the real story." In fact, they can sometimes be so objective that they fail to take in the more emotional or human side of the equation. As a result, they are likely to be perceived by others as smug, aloof, and even heartless. Though it may be difficult to tie them down to family or professional responsibilities, they are more than willing to bond with people who can give them intellectual and spiritual nourishment. If they are careful not to allow themselves to build up resentments or to become unduly disillusioned in their search for greater knowledge, their talents for financial success, spiritual expansion, and true emotional connection are all sure to appear.

CHALLENGE: **DISCOVERING THAT THE BEST WAY TO ANSWER THE BIGGER QUESTIONS IS TO PICK ONE PATH AND FOLLOW IT TO THE END**
FULFILLMENT: **FINDING THE FREEDOM THAT SUCCESS CAN BRING**

June 19–24

MAGIC
GEMINI–CANCER CUSP

Naturally caring and protective, these people are nonetheless an interesting blend of logic and emotion. Their often mellow, laid-back exteriors can, however, disguise very private people who may be somewhat hesitant to allow others into their inner worlds. These individuals should make every effort to examine and reexamine old baggage, if only to ensure that they are not hanging on to unnecessary emotional problems and issues that can stand in the way of their further expansion and development. Issues of dependency and codependency can be problems. Alternatively, they can be quite demanding of others and misuse the energies of this karmic path in insisting on a variety of proofs or guarantees before dedicating themselves fully to a widening of their perspective. Ultimately, in learning to let go and avoid possessiveness, their natural curiosity and their capacity for "emotional intelligence" will serve them well on the Way of Intention.

CHALLENGE: **NOT BEING DISTRACTED BY THEIR INVOLVEMENTS WITH OTHERS**
FULFILLMENT: **SETTING THEIR MINDS ON CLEARING A PATH THROUGH EMOTIONAL ENTANGLEMENTS**

FRANZ KAFKA
(portrait by H. Fronius)
Czech novelist,
Metamorphosis

7/3/1883
Cancer II

June 25–July 2

THE EMPATH
CANCER I

Blessed with a fine capacity for hard work as well as a natural sensitivity to others, Cancer I's on the Way of Intention may nevertheless struggle as they seek to find the balance between personal comfort and the need for a broader perspective. In fact, they can get so preoccupied with emotional matters that they lose sight of the larger rewards promised by this karmic path. Controlling their impulse to withdraw will be of paramount importance, as will avoiding their tendency to indulge—or rather, overindulge—in sensual pursuits. Alternatively, greater experience and exposure may harden them somewhat and manifest itself as an aggressive and unduly controlling attitude in both the personal and professional spheres. Still, if Cancer I's take care to maintain a meaningful social life and loving family relationships, they and all those with whom they are associated will benefit from their astute financial gifts, fine technical talents, and comforting and truly understanding presence.

CHALLENGE: **ERECTING PSYCHIC BOUNDARIES BETWEEN THEMSELVES AND OTHERS**
FULFILLMENT: **THE WORLDLY SUCCESS THAT SINGLE-MINDEDNESS OF PURPOSE CAN GIVE THEM**

July 3–10

THE UNCONVENTIONAL
CANCER II

These unconventional, imaginative people may do very well when placed on the Way of Intention, providing they are able to direct their rich fantasy lives in such a way as to color and enhance the more ordinary aspects of existence. Quite lavish in their tastes and with a fondness for creature comforts, they may face a number of financial challenges before they come to understand the danger of living beyond their means or overspending on impractical items. Too, Cancer II's may run the risk of becoming obsessive and even greedy in their search for material pleasure and can fail to address the more fun-loving side of their natures. Nevertheless, family and domestic life, especially having children, will doubtless bring out the best in these people, as such interactions will serve to broaden their perspective away from self-interest while indulging their more playful, imaginative sides.

CHALLENGE: **DEVELOPING FINANCIAL DISCIPLINE**
FULFILLMENT: **TURNING AN INVENTION OR INNOVATION INTO A COMMERCIALLY VIABLE PRODUCT**
NOTABLE: **FRED SAVAGE (TELEVISION ACTOR, CHILD STAR OF *THE WONDER YEARS*)**

HUNTER S. THOMPSON
"Gonzo" journalist,
author of *Hell's Angels*
and *Fear and Loathing in
Las Vegas*

7/18/1939
Cancer III

July 11–18

THE PERSUADER
CANCER III

Highly materialistic, sometimes in the extreme, Cancer III's are likely to have great success on the Way of Intention. Their workaholic tendencies will have to be kept in careful check, however, since they can go overboard in their desire to achieve their goals. Stubborn and enterprising, these people are unlikely to miss their chance when opportunity knocks, yet they can become quite obsessive about work and professional issues. The key here will be to take special care to nourish the more social and creative aspects of their personalities and, in a word, learn when to take a vacation. Meaningful and lively social lives will provide them with valuable input and help them to avoid the perils of "all work and no play." Taking care to broaden their horizons and avoid the tendency to tunnel vision or overly controlling behaviors will ensure that they will realize the intensity, success, and celebratory aspects of life promised by the Way of Intention.

CHALLENGE: **RELAXING LONG ENOUGH TO REJUVENATE THEMSELVES OR CONSIDER OTHER POINTS OF VIEW**
FULFILLMENT: **THE MANIFESTATION OF THEIR CREATIVE IDEAS IN PHYSICAL FORM**
NOTABLE: **MAURITZ STILLER (FILM DIRECTOR; "DISCOVERED" GRETA GARBO)**

KARMIC PATH
6

July 19–25
OSCILLATION
CANCER–LEO CUSP

Blessed with a natural ability to balance the nurturing and aggressive sides of their natures, Cancer–Leos may nevertheless have some difficulty bringing those talents to bear on the Way of Intention. On the one hand, there is a danger that they will get mired in the more sensitive, nurturing sides of their natures, thus becoming tied to familiar environments and pleasures at the expense of necessary self-examination. Also, they may indulge in intensity and emotional drama, thereby forfeiting stability and productive activity. Thus, life on the Way of Intention should prove quite a juggling act for these volatile personalities. Once grounded in solid domestic and family relationships, they will doubtless do very well and may truly blossom when they undertake the task of raising or working with children. Still, if they can channel their great energy into a productive profession that will allow them full play of their charisma, creative talents, and spontaneity, their journey along the Way of Intention will prove not merely exciting but truly profitable and rewarding.

CHALLENGE: **BALANCING THE CONTRADICTORY SIDES OF THEIR NATURE**
FULFILLMENT: **MAKING A COMMITMENT TO FAMILY**
NOTABLE: **JUDY CHICAGO (ARTIST)**

BENITO MUSSOLINI
Dictator of Italy during WWII; arrested and shot

7/29/1883
Leo I

July 26–August 2
AUTHORITY
LEO I

Blessed with a natural sense of authority and a dynamic, sensual side, these personalities will nevertheless face their share of challenges along the Way of Intention. Tenacious and opinionated, often in the extreme, they will be faced with some big lessons in the necessity for change and adaptation in their professional and personal endeavors. Authoritarian and hardworking, they can easily rise to great levels of achievement yet may just as easily back down from the prospect of making necessary adjustments for the prospect of future rewards. The tendency to self-satisfaction is especially strong with this configuration, and an intense preoccupation with inflexible standards can be their undoing. Yet their great honesty, sense of fairness, and natural largesse will all be of benefit on the Way of Intention. Taking care to exercise their considerable staying power on behalf of greater progress will ensure that they will avoid some of the more obvious pitfalls on this karmic path.

CHALLENGE: **BUDGING FROM THEIR POSITIONS ONCE IN A WHILE**
FULFILLMENT: **SETTING THEIR GOALS TO ALIGN WITH THEIR HIGHER PRINCIPLES**

August 3–10
BALANCED STRENGTH
LEO II

Learning to trust their own hunches will be important for Leo II's on the Way of Intention. Though they are gifted with amazing powers of concentration, they can nevertheless become entirely too wrapped up in their own reality and fail to heed their best instincts. Extremes of physicality can manifest themselves, and their tremendous energies can run amok in bouts of overindulgence or a preoccupation with the pleasures of the moment. By the same token, Leo II's sometimes find it hard to let go of their past mistakes and may withdraw into long periods of guilt and depression that compromise their ability to enjoy the world. Still, if they can channel their talent for extremes into a structured lifestyle that includes hard work followed by rest and reward, their accomplishments will result in the spiritual evolution indicated by this karmic path.

CHALLENGE: **SUFFERING THE DISTRACTIONS OF RELATIONSHIP WOES**
FULFILLMENT: **LIVING LIFE AS STRAIGHTFORWARDLY AS POSSIBLE**
NOTABLE: **HELEN THOMAS (UPI WHITE HOUSE BUREAU CHIEF)**

MAUREEN O'HARA
Actress, *Rio Grande* with John Wayne

8/17/1920
Leo III

August 11–18
LEADERSHIP
LEO III

Likely to experience great worldly and material gifts on the Way of Intention, Leo III's will nevertheless have to avoid a tendency to become self-satisfied and overly entrenched in a narrow, materialistic view of life. Too, they are capable of manipulating others through their financial powers and may encounter challenges and struggles revolving around their attempts to control the lives of other people through money or worldly goods. As they progress, they may need to refine their commanding approach to life and its responsibilities and educate themselves in the ways and means of subtler forms of power. The demands of this karmic path may acquaint them with issues of mortality and spirituality beyond that which can be controlled or manipulated through worldly means. Still, whatever the challenges of the Way of Intention, these commanding, creative people will doubtless meet them with a fearless, forceful faith in their own abilities that will in turn inspire and uplift the hearts of those around them.

CHALLENGE: **WALKING A MORAL HIGH ROAD IN RELATIONSHIPS**
FULFILLMENT: **ACHIEVING THEIR AIMS**
NOTABLE: **CHARLES BUKOWSKI (POET; WRITER)**

August 19–25

EXPOSURE
LEO–VIRGO CUSP

The dispositions of Leo–Virgo's are unlikely to allow them to simply hang out and ignore the challenges implicit on the Way of Intention. If anything, these souls can become positively Machiavellian as they explore the myriad ways they can expand their worldly base of power. Highly observant and perceptive, they may nevertheless find themselves confronted with a truly unmanageable level of intrigue as time goes by. Issues of trust and understanding are likely to figure prominently in the lives of those on this journey and should they develop complacency or too much self-satisfaction, it's doubtful that the universe will allow them to linger there for long. Thus, self-expression will be the key to remaining connected with the higher aspirations of this karmic path. If they are careful to be honest and avoid the tendency to manipulate or manage information at the expense of the truth, their travels on this karmic path will be considerably eased.

CHALLENGE: **LEARNING WHOM TO TRUST AS THEY PROGRESS TOWARD THEIR GOALS**
FULFILLMENT: **KEEPING THE LONG VIEW IN SIGHT TO HELP THEM OVERCOME TEDIOUS MOMENTS**
NOTABLE: **JOSEF STRAUSS (CONDUCTOR; WALTZ COMPOSER)**

RAY BRADBURY
Science fiction writer,
The Martian Chronicles

————

8/22/1920
Leo–Virgo Cusp

August 26–September 2

SYSTEM BUILDERS
VIRGO I

Highly structured and utterly dependable, Virgo I people with this configuration can nevertheless become imprisoned in a system of their own making. Certain to be highly successful and unlikely to waste their talents in overindulgence or material excess, they can falter on this karmic path if they neglect their spiritual expansion in the interest of maintaining a safe, secure environment. However, they may be confronted with emotional pressures that beckon them out of their detachment. Alternatively, their need to be of service to others is highly pronounced, and they may expend their energies on dependent or needy people who take advantage of them. The key to success for these travelers will be climbing out of their safe routines and taking up the reins of their own power. If they are careful to avoid rigidity and surround themselves with those who can support rather than hinder their travels along this karmic path, they are sure to excel.

CHALLENGE: **REFUSING TO WORRY ABOUT EVERY DETAIL**
FULFILLMENT: **RECOGNIZING THAT THEY NEED NOT BE MERELY DRONES OF THE SYSTEM**
NOTABLE: **CHARLIE "BIRD" PARKER (JAZZ VIRTUOSO)**

September 3–10

THE ENIGMA
VIRGO II

"Never let them see you sweat" might well be the motto for those born in this week who travel the Way of Intention. Whatever the specific challenges involved, these capable and thoughtful individuals will take care of business—whether that business is of a material or spiritual nature. Diligent and goal-oriented for the most part, they will nevertheless have to be on guard against a stubborn and even quite didactic streak in themselves that can hamper their vision of future rewards. They can get so caught up in the tasks and duties of the moment that they fail to adequately grasp the connections between cause and effect. However, they are more than capable of handling the need for focus and care demand by this path. As long as they are careful not to become overly detached or to lose their connection with a sense of the greater design for their development, they will surely succeed.

CHALLENGE: **EXPRESSING THEIR BROADER PLANS OR DESIGNS, IF ONLY TO SET THEM MORE FIRMLY IN THEIR OWN MINDS**
FULFILLMENT: **ADHERING TO THE HIGH STANDARDS THEY SET**
NOTABLE: **CRAIG CLAIBORNE (FOOD EDITOR, *NEW YORK TIMES*)**

MARGARET SANGER
Birth control advocate,
cofounder of Planned
Parenthood

————

9/14/1883
Virgo III

September 11–18

THE LITERALIST
VIRGO III

Persistent, tenacious, and practical are all adjectives frequently applied to those born in this week. Yet as they embark on their journey along the Way of Intention, it is those same qualities that can hold them back as they reach for greater opportunity, wider vision, and worldly success. A certain intensity comes naturally to Virgo III's, yet they may be forced out of otherwise comfortable circumstances and routines before it can be truly acknowledged and utilized for achievement. Born with a great need for harmony and the finer things of life, they may refuse to rock the boat by working toward a goal, sometimes at the cost of struggle or other problems. If they can avoid acquisitiveness, a preoccupation with constancy, and a tendency to turn their backs on the broader opportunities indicated by this karmic path, all will go well.

CHALLENGE: **GETTING A GRIP ON THEIR TENDENCY TO PROCRASTINATE**
FULFILLMENT: **ENJOYING THE FRUITS OF THEIR EFFORTS**

September 19–24
BEAUTY
VIRGO–LIBRA CUSP

Physical and sensuous by disposition, those born on the Cusp of Beauty who travel the Way of Intention may nonetheless stumble a bit along the way. Prone to a certain laziness when it comes to taking personal inventory, they may misuse the inherent and considerable blessings of this configuration by retreating to a world of cushy comforts and elitist attitudes. Rather prone to extremes of self-indulgence and self-absorption, Virgo–Libras face the challenge of cultivating a more mature vision of themselves and their own needs, as well as avoiding the myriad of material toys and distractions that will doubtless become available to them over time. Real self-knowledge and awareness are nevertheless sure to develop along their journey, providing they work to discover their own talents and begin to view the world in terms not of what the world can give them but of what they can give the world.

CHALLENGE: **DISCOVERING THEIR OWN ABILITIES AND DECIDING TO INVEST IN THEM**
FULFILLMENT: **FEELING THE MORE THAN SUPERFICIAL SENSE OF ACCOMPLISHMENT GAINED FROM HARD WORK**
NOTABLE: **MICKEY ROONEY (MUCH-MARRIED HOLLYWOOD STAR)**

LOUIS JEAN LUMIÈRE
Pioneer filmmaker; invented film projector with brother Auguste

10/5/1864
Libra II

September 25–October 2
THE PERFECTIONIST
LIBRA I

Those born in the Week of the Perfectionist who travel the Way of Intention will have to grapple with the likelihood that they will overdo on this karmic path. Though not too prone to excessive sensuous self-indulgence, their cool, collected exteriors can sometimes mask a wealth of emotional conflicts. They will have to get in touch with some of their inner workings before they can realize the wealth of more worldly blessings promised by this karmic path. The tendency to nurse old grudges and hold on to resentments is pronounced in this configuration, and these individuals will receive a clear education in the fine art of simply letting go when people and events don't accord with their exacting standards. Alternatively, many of these souls will find greatest fulfillment in adopting a less materialistic and more spartan approach to worldly pleasures, finding that their greatest achievement lies not in monetary or material rewards but in the mastery of a particular craft or profession that will exalt their talent for perfection.

CHALLENGE: **OVERLOOKING SMALLER IMPERFECTIONS IN FAVOR OF KEEPING THINGS MOVING FORWARD**
FULFILLMENT: **LEARNING TO BE DECISIVE**
NOTABLE: **WALTER MATTHAU (ACTOR, *THE ODD COUPLE*)**

October 3–10
SOCIETY
LIBRA II

These imaginative, somewhat romantic people will have to avoid a tendency to scatter their energies along the Way of Intention. Popular and quite insightful, they have a bit of a lazy streak when it comes to applying their considerable talents in a professional arena and can be chronic underachievers in material terms. The key to their advancement along the Way of Intention will lie in their ability to zoom in on themselves and the things they really want out of life and avoid self-deception and procrastination when it comes to working toward those goals. Yet if they take care to surround themselves with highly motivated associates and not to give in to the occasional temptation to bite off more than they can chew, they will find themselves freed from undue distractions and more than prepared to rise to the challenge of greater expansion and awareness indicated by the Way of Intention.

CHALLENGE: **INTEGRATING THEIR ENERGIES TO WORK TOWARD A SINGLE GOAL**
FULFILLMENT: **LIVING A SIMPLER, MORE DIRECTED LIFE**
NOTABLES: **ALICIA SILVERSTONE (ACTRESS, *CLUELESS*); FRANK HERBERT (SCIENCE FICTION WRITER, *DUNE* SERIES)**

MARIO PUZO
Novelist and screenwriter, *The Godfather*

10/15/1920
Libra III

October 11–18
THEATER
LIBRA III

Dramatic and flamboyant, Libra III's on the Way of Intention will be quite a force on this path. These ambitious individuals certainly have the knack for worldly success. They do run the risk of becoming mired in self-admiration or a sense of overconfidence. Gifted with a magnetic and entertaining charm, they will nevertheless have to regulate a disposition to excess in terms of both sensual indulgence and emotional displays. Part of what it would behoove them to divest in their search for higher consciousness and greater focus may be their tendency to "ham it up" or exaggerate hurts and slights, as well as their tendency to be rather lazy and do only what they have to in order to get by. For all of their flair, they may be a bit uncomfortable with others' expectations of them. Yet as they mature, they will discover in themselves an ability to commit and a capacity for depth that will make them provocative, formidable characters indeed.

CHALLENGE: **KNOWING WHEN TO GIVE UP**
FULFILLMENT: **HAVING THEIR EFFORTS BRING THEM INTO THE SPOTLIGHT**

October 19–25

DRAMA AND CRITICISM
LIBRA–SCORPIO CUSP

These cusp personalities will doubtless be faced with the challenge of creating greater harmony within themselves as they travel the Way of Intention. Though they may often appear larger than life and extravagant in their interactions with the world, this karmic path will nevertheless require them to turn their energies inward from time to time in an effort to create greater balance between their intellectual and emotional proclivities. Libra–Scorpios run the risk of believing in their own infallibility and may fall for the idea that they can do no wrong as long as others believe that. Alternatively, they can become quite rigid and dictatorial when they do make mistakes, perhaps believing that they can still impose their will on lesser beings, no matter what the circumstances. Still, their great talents will doubtless be at the service of their great ambitions and produce even greater rewards as they move toward the refinement and savoir faire required by the Way of Intention.

TIMOTHY LEARY
Author; advocate of LSD
in the 60s; hippie guru
———
10/22/1920
Libra–Scorpio Cusp

CHALLENGE: **ACHIEVING THE SERENITY NECESSARY FOR ANY LONG-TERM INVOLVEMENT**

FULFILLMENT: **TRANSFORMING THEIR CONSIDERABLE PASSION INTO FUEL FOR THEIR ACHIEVEMENTS**

October 26–November 2

INTENSITY
SCORPIO I

Scorpio I's may have difficulty in managing their own levels of intensity on this karmic path. The ability to learn to relax will be of paramount importance, as will the lessons of learning to forgive and forget, for it is easy for these men and women to become so focused on their goals that they lose sight of the feelings of others. Highly likely to become a master of their profession or in any endeavor, they are also sure to achieve the material success that goes hand in hand with achieving a level of virtuosity in one's vocation. However, these highly emotional people may never be entirely satisfied with themselves or others and will do best when they surround themselves with a select group of family and friends whose more tolerant and indulgent attitudes will encourage Scorpio I's to exercise their wonderful sense of humor and learn to laugh at themselves.

CHALLENGE: **REMEMBERING TO LET THEIR SUNNIER SIDE SHINE THROUGH ONCE IN A WHILE**

FULFILLMENT: **ATTAINING A VIRTUOSO-LIKE LEVEL OF SKILL IN THEIR CHOSEN MÉTIER**

NOTABLES: **HELMUT NEWTON (EROTIC PHOTOGRAPHER); JAMES J. KILPATRICK, SR. (JOURNALIST)**

November 3–11

DEPTH
SCORPIO II

The Way of Intention will doubtless entail some profound experiences for those born in this week. Blessed with great energy and powers of concentration, they have the innate ability, on the one hand, to home in on the essentials of any problem or situation and discover the underlying truths. On the other hand, they may also have a pronounced inability simply to "lighten up" and thereby avoid the dangers of obsession or fixation that are part of their makeup. In addition, they may ignore the development of higher spiritual awareness often demanded by this karmic path and get stuck in a strictly material approach to life and success. For these are individuals who can come to believe that the dollar is indeed almighty. Yet there is enormous potential for success with this configuration, and if they take care to let down their personal barriers and open themselves to a larger universe of possibility, the spiritual hunger that is part of this destiny is sure to be satisfied.

LYLE LOVETT
Country singer/
songwriter
———
11/1/1957
Scorpio I

CHALLENGE: **DIVESTING THEMSELVES OF THEIR MATERIALISTIC STREAK**

FULFILLMENT: **TAKING PLEASURE IN FULLY CONCENTRATING ON ANY MATTER**

NOTABLE: **JELLYBEAN BENITEZ (RECORD PRODUCER)**

November 12–18

CHARM
SCORPIO III

Those born in this week are sure to have an easy time on the Way of Intention. Blessed with a knack for living the good life, they nevertheless have a realistic vision of what they bring to a wide variety of social contacts and professional situations. These charming people can fall victim to their own passions, however, and should be careful to avoid a tendency to become distracted by indulging in sensual and sexual excesses. Over-possessiveness and jealousy in relationships can show up here, and many on this path will struggle with "the green-eyed monster." For all of the charm and talent that go with this configuration, their generally excellent insight can be less than objective, and they can fall victim to complacency and stagnation when their material lives get a little too comfortable. Still, if they are careful to nurture even a modicum of ambition, they will find themselves moving beyond comfort and into the realms of spiritual and personal fulfillment. On this path, then, they are sure not only to dream the impossible dream but to reach that seemingly unreachable star.

CHALLENGE: **NOT WASTING THEIR ENERGIES IN SEARCHING FOR THE SATISFACTION OF PHYSICAL NEEDS**

FULFILLMENT: **KNOWING THAT THEY ARE CONTENDERS**

November 19–24
REVOLUTION
SCORPIO–SAGITTARIUS CUSP

The individuals born in this week who travel the Way of Intention run the risk of squandering their great energies in an excess of idealism and zealotry. For these are the people who chase windmills and do battle with all kinds of largely imaginary foes. Keeping a sense of proportion and perspective will be critical to their success, and much of what this karmic path requires will be for them to turn their energy inward in a greater effort at self-examination. Still, those born on the Cusp of Revolution possess enormous potential for realizing their fondest dreams, and if they are careful to ground themselves in the stabler energies of those close to them, they can learn to control their more volatile impulses and direct their energy in laserlike focus toward the tasks and goals at hand.

HENRI TOULOUSE-LAUTREC

French artist, Moulin Rouge poster designer

11/24/1864
Scorpio–Sagittarius Cusp

CHALLENGE: **CHOOSING THEIR BATTLES CAREFULLY**
FULFILLMENT: **GUIDING THEIR SCHEMES TO FRUITION**
NOTABLES: **STAN MUSIAL (BASEBALL OUT- AND INFIELDER); GENE TIERNEY (ACTRESS)**

November 25–December 2
INDEPENDENCE
SAGITTARIUS I

Sagittarius I's on the Way of Intention may find themselves chafing at the restrictions and challenges presented by this karmic path. Though gifted with enormous willpower and "stick-to-itiveness," the Way of Intention may be problematic for these free spirits to some extent, if they view it as limiting their energy rather than channeling it. Equally, they may abuse their gifts and get mired in a need to win at any cost. Stubbornness, fixations, and obsessions with less-than-worthy causes or ideals can all be obstacles to their development, as can their tendency to be demanding and autocratic in the exercise of their natural authority. In the end, if they are careful to nurture their social gifts and ground their considerable energies in workable routines, these souls will shine on the Way of Intention.

CHALLENGE: **FINDING PARTNERS TO SHARE THEIR FOCUS AND ENROLLMENT ENTHUSIASM**
FULFILLMENT: **ACHIEVING THEIR OWN UNIQUE AIMS WITHIN THE RULES OF MORE CONVENTIONAL SOCIETY**
NOTABLES: **CAROLINE KENNEDY SCHLOSSBERG (AUTHOR); RICARDO MONTALBAN (TELEVISION ACTOR, FANTASY ISLAND)**

December 3–10
THE ORIGINATOR
SAGITTARIUS II

Whatever natural inclination Sagittarius II's may have toward complacency, self-satisfaction, or stagnation, careful work on the Way of Intention will ensure that such tendencies are not indulged for long. In fact, this configuration may manifest itself in a kind of "overnight success" phenomenon in which the unique or even peculiar ideas of these individuals are suddenly brought into the spotlight, to great acceptance and material rewards. It will be important for these individuals to maintain their avant-garde perspective in the face of such acceptance and not lose their creative edge in smugness, self-satisfaction, or a kind of chronic "I told you so," attitude toward the world. The focus and refinement that are the lessons of this karmic path are absolute necessities if they are to follow up on the opportunities generated by Sagittarius II originality, though, and they will doubtless come to realize that without the necessary follow-through, even the best ideas are only ideas.

DAVE BRUBECK
Legendary jazz pianist

12/6/1920
Sagittarius II

CHALLENGE: **NOT LETTING THEIR FEAR OF REJECTION DISSUADE THEM**
FULFILLMENT: **CRAFTING A FULLY CONSCIOUS PATH FOR THEIR INNER DRIVE**
NOTABLE: **ART MONK (FOOTBALL PLAYER)**

December 11–18
THE TITAN
SAGITTARIUS III

The Way of Intention may be a bit difficult for the self-assured souls born in this week, and they may struggle along the road to find a footing in a profession or the right direction for their careers. Multitalented, they will nevertheless face the lesson of settling down to a single occupation or pursuit in the interest of developing greater expertise and even a certain level of mastery. Further, they can have a tendency to overthink problems and situations and may retreat from pressing realities as a result. Too, the demands of the material world and practical realities may require more of their attention than they would like to give. As their focus increases, however, Sagittarius III's may face down some personal demons or grapple with issues of depression, since eventually circumstances will demand that they regulate their mood swings and displays of temper before they can realize the success they truly desire.

CHALLENGE: **NOT DREAMING UP SUCH BIG SCHEMES THAT THEY SET THEMSELVES UP FOR FAILURE**
FULFILLMENT: **BEING THE MASTER OF THEIR DOMAIN**
NOTABLE: **MARGARET MEAD (CULTURAL ANTHROPOLOGIST)**

December 19–25

PROPHECY
SAGITTARIUS–CAPRICORN CUSP

The Way of Intention is likely to lead these souls toward a more spiritual and even metaphysical approach to reality. Blessed with both practical and psychic insight, they are likely to shine on this karmic path. The task of creating an intention and keeping it comes quite naturally to these individuals, and as long as they take care not to turn their backs on the social side of life nor to isolate themselves to the extent that their unique talents and insights are lost to the world, they can achieve the highest level of success. Unusual and gifted, they will nevertheless have to avoid an overly suspicious or even paranoid attitude toward others. Greed and a preoccupation with money can also be issues here. Still, those born on the Cusp of Prophecy are naturals on this karmic path, and this combination promises much indeed as it provides the right mix of inclination, passion, material ambition, and spiritual depth for real success.

ANDRÉ KOSTELANETZ
Maestro who popularized classical music in the 20th century
———
12/22/1901
Sagittarius–Capricorn Cusp

CHALLENGE: **REINING IN THEIR TENDENCY TO TREAT INDULGENCE IN SENSUAL OR SEXUAL PLEASURES AS A REWARD**
FULFILLMENT: **PLAYING THE ROLE OF ACHIEVER**

December 26–January 2

THE RULER
CAPRICORN I

Those born in the Week of the Ruler who travel the Way of Intention are likely to be single-minded creatures indeed. Capable of displaying an astonishing dedication to their own personal dreams and ambitions, they nonetheless do manage to remain concerned with and connected to others. Perhaps their principal danger is that their single-mindedness may become narrow-mindedness and their natural administrative talents degenerate into high-handed dictatorship. Eventually, they may be required to release their bottled-up emotions and frustration in such a way that they are freed from the boundaries of self. Learning to regulate their work habits, delegate responsibility, and cultivate a more "hands-off" management style will doubtless be of benefit here. If Capricorn I's invest in their more spiritual side, allowing it to shine through their material demands, they are likely to be bright lights indeed.

CHALLENGE: **KEEPING IN MIND THE NEED TO NURTURE THEIR SPIRITUAL CORE**
FULFILLMENT: **ATTAINING A ROLE OF PROMINENCE AND INFLUENCE**
NOTABLES: **ANDREW JOHNSON (1ST U.S. PRESIDENT TO BE IMPEACHED); MATT LAUER (COANCHOR, *TODAY* SHOW)**

January 3–9

DETERMINATION
CAPRICORN II

The spiritual expansion and increased awareness promised by developing the capacity for intention will no doubt require Capricorn II's to really stretch their talents and beliefs about who they are and what they can do. Often plagued by insecurities and self-doubts, they will be required to release much of their hesitancy and hardheadedness about what is and is not possible. The nuance here is that intending something implies partnering with something greater than oneself, rather than indulging in sheer force of will, as is the wont of Capricorns II's. However, the theoretical and metaphysical leanings of these personalities are very pronounced, and if they nurture their talent for broader vision and expanded awareness, they will open up new frontiers of consciousness and life experience that will effectively combine the practical and spiritual aspects of existence.

MARLENE DIETRICH
German actress and singer
———
12/27/1901
Capricorn I

CHALLENGE: **DEVELOPING A RELATIONSHIP WITH A HIGHER POWER**
FULFILLMENT: **DISCOVERING THE MAGIC IN MIND-SET RATHER THAN WILL**

January 10–16

DOMINANCE
CAPRICORN III

Capricorn III's will doubtless enjoy great success both professionally and personally as they do the work of the Way of Intention, provided they do not ignore the need to grow or allow themselves to become mired in safe routines and ideas. It is most difficult to get these people to change their minds about anything once they are set on a course of action, and they will doubtless face the lesson of learning to distinguish the difference between focusing on a goal and simply setting one's attention on something and going through life with blinders on. Their need to dominate those in their immediate circle will prove to be a challenge, and they are likely to experience some struggle as those close to them question their sense of authority or ways of doing things. Still, if they cultivate within themselves the gentle art of going with the flow, they will have a great potential for both material success and spiritual reward.

CHALLENGE: **BOWING TO THE DEMANDS OF THE TIME**
FULFILLMENT: **HAVING FAITH THAT EVERYTHING WILL TURN OUT AS IT SHOULD**
NOTABLE: **ALFRED TARSKI (MATHEMATICIAN; AUTHOR OF *ORDINAL ALGEBRA*)**

January 17–22
MYSTERY AND IMAGINATION
CAPRICORN–AQUARIUS CUSP

Marked by a kind of electric and magnetic energy, Capricorn–Aquarians who travel the Way of Intention may be in for some wild times indeed. Though they may find themselves at decided odds with the lessons and challenges indicated on this path, they can nevertheless excel, sometimes in startling ways. The element of unpredictability and even luck will play a role in the destinies of these individuals, and the Way of Intention may require them to abandon previous notions of how things work, rehaul their relationships, or even win the occasional lottery in order to reorient them to a truer sense of their destiny. At worst, Capricorn–Aquarians will fritter their energies away in a less-than-serious attitude toward life and its responsibilities. At best, they will rise to the unusual set of challenges presented by this karmic path with grace, humor, and a sense of real excitement about what the future may hold.

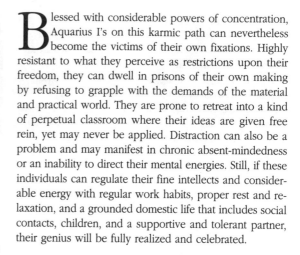

EDGAR ALLAN POE
Poet, writer, journalist, editor, master of symbolism, *The Raven*
───
1/19/1809
Capricorn–Aquarius Cusp

CHALLENGE: **STAYING THE COURSE EVEN IN THE FACE OF TWISTS AND TURNS**

FULFILLMENT: **DISCOVERING THE MANY OPPORTUNITIES THAT ARISE FROM STAYING TRUE TO THEIR INTENTIONS**

January 23–30
GENIUS
AQUARIUS I

Blessed with considerable powers of concentration, Aquarius I's on this karmic path can nevertheless become the victims of their own fixations. Highly resistant to what they perceive as restrictions upon their freedom, they can dwell in prisons of their own making by refusing to grapple with the demands of the material and practical world. They are prone to retreat into a kind of perpetual classroom where their ideas are given free rein, yet may never be applied. Distraction can also be a problem and may manifest in chronic absent-mindedness or an inability to direct their mental energies. Still, if these individuals can regulate their fine intellects and considerable energy with regular work habits, proper rest and relaxation, and a grounded domestic life that includes social contacts, children, and a supportive and tolerant partner, their genius will be fully realized and celebrated.

CHALLENGE: **PRYING THEMSELVES LOOSE FROM THEIR OLD GAMES**

FULFILLMENT: **MAKING A MARK ON THE WORLD**

January 31–February 7
YOUTH AND EASE
AQUARIUS II

Aquarius II's placed on this karmic path may fall victim to sheer laziness. Though gifted with a naturally relaxed attitude and lighthearted approach to life, they will have to work hard to cultivate the stable habits and mental discipline required to excel in their chosen field. Perhaps they will do best when they cultivate relationships with those less laid back and more ambitious than themselves, those who will not allow them to shirk responsibility or distract them from their goals. Though they may be hampered by a certain immaturity or unwillingness to grow up, these people are nevertheless gifted with a natural capacity to make themselves and others happy. They would do well to expand their definition of what happiness means, and then apply a little willpower to getting it.

ABRAHAM LINCOLN
16th U.S. president, the "Great Emancipator"
───
2/12/1809
Aquarius III

CHALLENGE: **NOT RESTING ON THEIR LAURELS**
FULFILLMENT: **PERFECTING A CRAFT OR SKILL**
NOTABLES: **LANGSTON HUGHES (AUTHOR OF *SHAKESPEARE IN HARLEM*); CHARLES LINDBERGH (AVIATOR)**

February 8–15
ACCEPTANCE
AQUARIUS III

Issues of tolerance and temperament will always be themes in the lives of Aquarius III's. The cutting loose of old habits and opinions will prove to be very important on the Way of Intention, and Aquarius III's must be careful not to resist the changes afforded by this karmic path. The saving grace of this configuration is the simple fact that these individuals tend to bore easily, and, hopefully, they can utilize this characteristic to get themselves unstuck from even the deepest ruts. Alternatively, a risk is that they may misdirect their gifts and exhaust their potential in seeking approval and assuming values that are not their own. Even so, tremendous changes are likely to be experienced by Aquarius III's when they take the necessary care to absorb, refine, and distill the variety of their experience in meaningful ways. Then the rewards of becoming focused will be a sense of mastery and control over their own lives and destinies.

CHALLENGE: **DIRECTING THEIR PENCHANT FOR MOVEMENT IN A FORWARD DIRECTION**
FULFILLMENT: **DISCOVERING THE REWARDS OF DEDICATION**
NOTABLES: **CHARLES DARWIN (DEVELOPED THEORY OF EVOLUTION); CYRUS MCCORMICK (INVENTED THE REAPER)**

February 16–22
SENSITIVITY
AQUARIUS–PISCES CUSP

Overemotionalism and hypersensitivity can mark the journeys of these cusp personalities on the Way of Intention. Thus, in trying to escape them they may gravitate toward those things and places that appear to restore their equilibrium and sense of comfort, yet in doing so they risk failing to rise to the challenges of this karmic path. As a result, their travels on the Way of Intention may result in a kind of "two steps forward, one step back" dynamic until they learn to how to focus their attention away from personal issues and ground themselves in a sense of professional achievement. Mastery of a career or craft will do much to stabilize these people, and they should take care early on to develop a routine that requires study and self-discipline, and gives the appropriate measure of reward. Such habits will do much to allay their fears of rejection and serve to help them avoid the pitfalls of insecurity and isolation. When they are successfully grounded in the tangible, Aquarius–Pisceans can easily progress toward the spiritual with a lightened heart.

CHALLENGE: **WORKING TO BECOME OPTIMISTIC**
FULFILLMENT: **SUCCESSFULLY NEGOTIATING THEIR OWN SENSITIVITY**

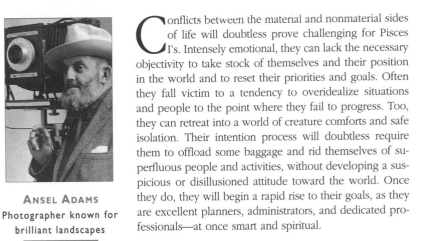

ANSEL ADAMS
Photographer known for brilliant landscapes
—————
2/20/1902
Aquarius–Pisces Cusp

February 23–March 2
SPIRIT
PISCES I

Conflicts between the material and nonmaterial sides of life will doubtless prove challenging for Pisces I's. Intensely emotional, they can lack the necessary objectivity to take stock of themselves and their position in the world and to reset their priorities and goals. Often they fall victim to a tendency to overidealize situations and people to the point where they fail to progress. Too, they can retreat into a world of creature comforts and safe isolation. Their intention process will doubtless require them to offload some baggage and rid themselves of superfluous people and activities, without developing a suspicious or disillusioned attitude toward the world. Once they do, they will begin a rapid rise to their goals, as they are excellent planners, administrators, and dedicated professionals—at once smart and spiritual.

CHALLENGE: **DIVESTING THEMSELVES OF ALL THAT DOES NOT FURTHER THEIR GREATER GOALS**
FULFILLMENT: **OPERATING FROM A BASIS OF FAITH IN THEMSELVES**
NOTABLES: **BUFFALO BILL (COWBOY; SCOUT; ENTERTAINER); PAULA ZAHN (TELEVISION JOURNALIST)**

March 3–10
THE LONER
PISCES II

The material side of existence is likely to offer these people considerable opportunity as they travel the Way of Intention, though there is some danger that they will focus first, last, and always upon themselves. The fact is, these souls do not require very much by way of social contact or acceptance and may retreat from the challenges of this karmic path into a world of their own making. Thus, they can be in for some rude awakenings as the universe intrudes in an effort to encourage them to broaden their perspective and fields of endeavor. Still, if they take care not to collapse into pure self-interest nor to retreat into nonchallenging efforts geared toward creating security, their spiritual and professional potential can combine in ways that will provide great fulfillment along this karmic path.

CHALLENGE: **LEARNING NOT TO BURY THEIR HEADS IN THE SAND**
FULFILLMENT: **KNOWING THAT THEY HAVE THE DETERMINATION TO FULFILL SOME OF THEIR FONDEST DREAMS**
NOTABLE: **ANDY GIBB (POPULAR SINGER)**

NEIL SEDAKA
Singer/songwriter,
"Laughter in the Rain"
—————
3/13/1939
Pisces III

March 11–18
DANCERS AND DREAMERS
PISCES III

Pisces III people who travel the Way of Intention will have to learn to delve beneath the surface of their dreams or philosophies in an attempt to unravel the way to fulfill them in the world. Though they may certainly struggle with issues of laziness and instability, once they come to terms with their own ambitions and set their minds on it success, success is quite likely for them. Overemotionalism can be a problem, as can a tendency to dramatize and fret over inconsequentials. Gifted with any number of highly creative talents as well as the ability to delve into the real meaning of life, their capacity for success may manifest in some miraculous turns of fortune. Providing they cultivate in themselves a preparedness to rise to the occasion, follow their opportunities through with dedication and hard work, and never lose their unique empathy for their fellows, the Way of Intention will make for a truly remarkable life's journey.

CHALLENGE: **RELEASING THE PROPENSITY TO WORRY NEEDLESSLY**
FULFILLMENT: **MAKING MIRACLES HAPPEN**

The Way of Introspection

TAURUS II TO SCORPIO II
Teacher to Depth

Those on the Way of Introspection are here to explore the deeper aspects of themselves and others fearlessly and fully. Because they are naturally attracted to social involvements and causes, they must periodically withdraw from the world in order to touch base with their unconscious, reflect on its workings, and use what they learn in the development of a greater understanding of their fellow human beings. Only then will they be able to renew their societal contacts in a more meaningful fashion. Born with a naturally helpful nature, those on this path too often neglect themselves and their own personal development by devoting themselves to others. At some point they must learn to place themselves first and to put their energy in service of their own spiritual growth. Introspection can be an extremely painful and difficult process for those on this karmic path. However, it is usually only after they learn how to do battle with their inner demons and to periodically check in on their inner life that they can unlock the true source of spiritual power within themselves.

These individuals can be characterized as rigid in their viewpoints. They tend to be didactic, and much of the way they approach others takes the form of expressing strictly held opinions rather than engaging in an easy give-and-take or an exchange of ideas or feelings. The core lesson for those on the Way of Introspection is to broaden their own views and opinions and to become less judgmental of others and, most important, themselves. Otherwise they will tend to become self-condemning as soon as they begin to examine their own inner workings. Loosening up is imperative for these men and women, since it is important for them to get in touch with their own humanity in order to accept differences in others. Both the Taurus II origin and Scorpio II destination carry an inflexibility, and therefore those on this karmic path must strive to remain open to change. Standing steadfast must not be confused with refusing to acknowledge other viewpoints. Ultimately, those on the Way of Introspection will learn that truly caring for others is less about imparting what one considers to be the truth than it is about taking the time to peer into the depths of someone else's being in order to understand what might be true *for them*.

Another important lesson that must be learned by those on the Way of Introspection is how to take the time to be alone and to key into a quiet, meditative state. In addition, these individuals must actually discover and believe in the value of such a process. Divesting themselves of social contact is not easy for those coming in with Taurus II energy. They love surrounding themselves with others, not only to partake with them of all the good things life has to offer but to use them as an audience, as a medium through which they can express their ideas. These people are happiest seated at a

---

CORE LESSON

Surrendering judgments that prevent opening to one's inner life

GOAL

To develop a deeper understanding of one's own inner process and that of others

---

GIFTS
Studious, Steadfast, Caring

PITFALLS
Rigid, Didactic, Pleasure-seeking

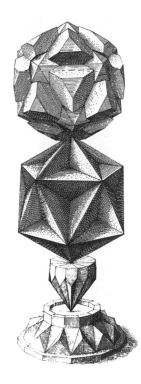

crowded, noisy dinner table consuming the finest food and wine and enjoying a lively debate. Natural teachers and lecturers, those on this karmic path must learn to be their own teachers, to teach themselves what they need to know. This knowledge, locked within their hearts, can be revealed only in the peace and quiet of solitude. This struggle to turn the teaching process around will lead to self-knowledge, of course, but also to the ability to tune in to the hearts of others and to learn from them. One of their great gifts is their propensity for reading and study, as well as physical self-discipline and sports. All these activities serve to encourage those on this karmic path to spend more time alone.

Those on the Way of Introspection tend to be interested not only in causes, both political and social, but also in cultures different than their own. Often, those who become mired in their preoccupation with the plight of others will have difficulty proceeding further in their spiritual development since focusing on someone else is far easier and more comfortable than turning the spotlight on themselves. This, however, should not be confused with gaining a deeper understanding of others. Frequently, these men and women can spend their lives wrapped up in one involvement after another—without giving it too much thought. Often, only a crisis such as an illness, the death or loss of a loved one, or some other serious disap-

pointment or rejection will throw them back onto themselves, forcing them to look to their inner resources for answers. However, they are strong and can withstand much, so ultimately they always emerge from any dark night of the soul more self-assured and fulfilled. But for these individuals one major life experience of going deeply within is not enough. Once they have gotten to know themselves, continuing to touch base with their deepest self is imperative, and so periods of solitude becomes a necessary part of their lives.

The home is usually the arena in which the process of introspection takes place. Only here can these individuals find the serenity they need for this soul work. Should their domestic situation in early life be chaotic, or their parents or siblings unduly repressive, they will either fight to establish their own private space or wait until a bit later in life when they are able at last to establish privacy. In school or at work, those on the Way of Introspection initially tend to become involved in teams, projects, and other group endeavors and because of their gifts can achieve substantial social success. At some point, however, they will feel the call to turn away from these activities and find a quiet place where they can be alone. Perhaps only one single friend will prove to be their link to the world, often an outgoing type of person who is sensitive to the needs of those on this karmic path.

RELEASE

The need for an audience

REWARD

The joy of a deeper viewpoint
from which to see others

SUGGESTION

Open yourself to all that resides within not with fear but with love.
Once there, reserve all judgment.

Although some see those on the Way of Introspection as quite serious individuals, others may view them as riotous types who love to have fun. Humor is their saving grace here and those on this karmic path usually prefer to spend time with lighthearted types. However, these are exactly the people who will seduce those on this karmic path away from the work they need to do. Thus, not only must those on the Way of Introspection learn to be alone, they must also learn not to indulge their more fun-loving or superficial friends. Cultivating friends who are more sensitive, spiritual, or involved in psychology is important. These individuals will often play the role of a sounding board or mirror when those on the Way of Introspection run into a rough patch in their spiritual process. However, care must be taken to be sensitive to the viewpoints of such friends. Usually those beginning as teachers haven't much patience with what those who are unlike them have to say, particularly if it contradicts their already established worldview. They must learn to accept the help of such friends gracefully, with full consideration for the feelings of others.

A family that can understand the need of these individuals to be alone can be particularly helpful for those on the Way of Introspection, but even more helpful would be one individual, perhaps an aunt or uncle, cousin, or grandparent, who is sensitive and responsive to the needs of those on this karmic path. When those on this path have a large or energetic family of their own, often the workplace can be the place of retreat they require. Choosing a life partner is something that those on this karmic path do not jump into quickly, particularly once their process of introspection has begun. They do not trust easily and know enough about themselves to be extremely careful about choosing a partner.

What is generally best for those on this karmic path is to find a life activity that can absorb them totally. Such work not only complements this oftimes lonely path but also allows them to make productive use of its more solitary nature and, ultimately to emerge as an expert in a field—something that will also satisfy their need to teach. Whether through academia, the arts, writing, product development, or other business endeavors, those on this karmic path will be able to use what they have taught themselves to become highly influential members of society. Therefore, those on this path would do well to specialize and avoid going into too many areas of interest or spreading their energy too thin.

BALANCE POINT

Social Life and Solitude

The Way of Introspection brings to mind the butterfly, which must isolate itself from its fellows and create a cocoon within which its metamorphosis can take place. Only after its successful emergence will it again be free to take part in the life around it. Inevitable as it is, this process cannot be rushed or hurried in any way since without undergoing it and giving it the necessary time, no real development is possible. Likewise, although it is highly restrictive, the Way of Introspection ultimately leads to greater freedom, strength, and self-sufficiency.

CRYSTALS AND GEMSTONES

Aventurine *supports healing of the heart by gently clearing deep-seated fears and resentments.*
Considered the stone of psychotherapy, aventurine inspires the path of self-knowledge.

NOTABLES ON THIS KARMIC PATH

Through a horrendous accident and an amazing comeback, pop singer **Gloria Estefan** explored the deeper

GLORIA ESTEFAN

aspects of herself to gain self-understanding. As a result of this experience, Estefan learned to use her energy for her own spiritual growth. Through this inner fulfillment, she is now able to give even more to her audience than she did previously. Estefan's approach to life after her recovery is also characterized by a deepening seriousness, a change that results from her searching meditation following her injury.

By encouraging his admirers to become more meditative and less attached to the material, poet, philosopher, and painter **Kahlil Gibran** utilized his energies to deepen spirituality. In a slim volume called *The Prophet,* Gibran spoke of nonpossessive love, urging his readers to regard their children not as belongings but as entities who "come through you" rather than being "of you." As a result of their contact with his

KAHLIL GIBRAN

uplifting ideals, his many readers were given a taste of the bliss that comes from understanding universal love.

Watching her perform, few would guess that expressive singer **Tina Turner** is a practicing Buddhist. Yet without the strength gained from this introspective religion, Turner may never have taken her career to its current plateau of success. By shedding external values and finding a quiet meditative place within (as is characteristic of this karmic path) Turner acquired the self-assurance to cast off the psychological and physical bondage that disrupted her early growth. Now, through her concentration

TINA TURNER

on inner nourishment, this energetic performer has developed into a person of tenacity and dedication.

Other Notables: Eleuthère Irénee DuPont, Frances McDormand, Germaine Greer, John Reed, Pamela Harriman, Howard Cosell, Toshiro Mifune, Jack Webb, Richard Strauss, David Brinkley, Kelly McGillis, Jon Lovitz, Louis Armstrong, Melanie Griffith, Fran Drescher, Marlo Thomas, Walt Disney, Dyan Cannon, Maury Povich, Sal Mineo, Roberta Flack, Peter Fonda

---

BIRTHDAYS ON KARMIC PATH 7

December 13, 1882–May 2, 1883 | July 25, 1901–December 13, 1901 | March 6, 1920–July 24, 1920

October 16, 1938–March 6, 1939 | May 27, 1957–October 15, 1957 | January 7, 1976–May 26, 1976

August 18, 1994–January 6, 1995 | March 29, 2013–August 17, 2013

KARMIC PATH
7

March 19–24
REBIRTH
PISCES–ARIES CUSP

Those born on the Cusp of Rebirth are likely to experience a great deal of personal transformation when traveling the Way of Introspection, providing they are able to cultivate the necessary skills for turning inward. Blessed with considerable unconscious knowledge, they will need to bring that wisdom forth through training in meditation, religion, or other spiritual disciplines. Their key to success along this path will be increasing their awareness of the subtler aspects of existence, cultivating the ability to examine their own actions and motivations, and learning to weigh alternatives carefully before making decisions. Though retreating from the hubbub of daily life will not always come easily for these people, they will nevertheless derive enormous benefit from developing a particular skill or hobby that allows them the freedom to be alone with their thoughts, while at the same time occupying their highly physical side.

HOWARD COSELL
Legendary sportscaster
known for coverage
of boxing and
Monday Night Football
───
3/25/1920
Aries I

CHALLENGE: **WORKING WITH THEIR MANIA FOR PHYSICAL ACTIVITIES, TO LEARN TO BE INTROSPECTIVE AS THEY INDULGE IN THEM**
FULFILLMENT: **COMING TO A BETTER UNDERSTANDING OF THEMSELVES AND HOW OTHERS VIEW THEM**
NOTABLE: **PAMELA HARRIMAN (DIPLOMAT; SOCIALITE)**

March 25–April 2
THE CHILD
ARIES I

Aries I's on the Way of Introspection will doubtless create a safe haven where they can retreat from the demands of the world, indulge in their pursuits, and truly be themselves. Blessed with great energy and curiosity, Aries I's may nevertheless have to work hard to turn that energy inward. At the same time, these personalities must learn to regulate their emotions so that their periods of introspection do not turn into depression or simple moodiness. Still, if they do not neglect their personal development or retreat into a never-never land of unrealistic dreams and expectations, these personalities will doubtless enjoy the great freedom promised by this path. Providing they cultivate and apply their passion in a consuming profession or other area of expertise, they are sure to experience a rare and fruitful life's journey, marked by both spontaneity and ever-evolving wisdom.

CHALLENGE: **CURBING EMOTIONAL OUTBURSTS**
FULFILLMENT: **SPENDING TIME IN THEIR FAVORITE RETREAT OR HAVEN**
NOTABLE: **JACK WEBB (TELEVISION ACTOR/DIRECTOR/PRODUCER, *DRAGNET*)**

April 3–10
THE STAR
ARIES II

The challenges of the Way of Introspection may prove difficult for Aries II's, since their makeup demands that they be in the center of the action. These souls must further be aware of their tendencies to make themselves indispensable to others and become overly involved in the dramas of daily life or pet personal causes, to the detriment of their higher development. Their energy and courage will work for them, though, once they cultivate the knack of self-observation and make an effort to avoid "doing for doing's sake." Still, the promise of the greater discovery of their inner world is great, and if they seek a professional or personal environment that allows them to shine, yet provides for needed periods of retreat and self-examination, they will succeed in avoiding the "all-or-nothing" attitude that often goes with this configuration. Solitude will help them on their spiritual journey, and if they are careful to set aside some time in their day for quietude, they will face the world with renewed energy and a keener perception of their true spiritual destiny.

TOSHIRO MIFUNE
Japanese film actor
───
4/1/1920
Aries I

CHALLENGE: **LEARNING WHEN NOT TO GO OVERBOARD**
FULFILLMENT: **DISCOVERING THE FREEDOM THAT COMES FROM LOOKING WITHIN**
NOTABLES: **RAVI SHANKAR (INDIAN SITARIST OF WORLD RENOWN); ARTHUR HAILEY (AUTHOR OF *AIRPORT*)**

April 11–18
THE PIONEER
ARIES III

Those born in this week must be especially aware of the danger of becoming too involved in teamwork or group activity. Naturally social and quite dynamic, they will nevertheless encounter periods in their life's journey where they are "thrown upon themselves" and forced to reexamine their goals and direction. Marked by a positive attitude and great optimism, they will nevertheless have to avoid viewing the seeming setbacks in their lives as frustrations and instead see them as opportunities to explore the frontiers of their lively inner world. Though introspection does not come naturally to those born in the Week of the Pioneer, they will find the rewards more than worth the effort. If they keep in mind that self-knowledge is the best road to real independence and personal freedom, their fearlessness and dedication will serve them well as they work to establish themselves not only in the eyes of the world but in their own.

CHALLENGE: **NOT SURROUNDING THEMSELVES WITH PEOPLE SIMPLY TO AVOID BEING ALONE WITH THEMSELVES**
FULFILLMENT: **DEVELOPING THEIR DEPTH OF CONSCIOUSNESS**
NOTABLE: **IMOGEN CUNNINGHAM (EXPERIMENTAL PHOTOGRAPHER)**

April 19–24
POWER
ARIES–TAURUS CUSP

The task of becoming their own best teacher will be somewhat difficult for those born on the Cusp of Power, as their earthy energy and fiery dynamism are at odds with the turning inward required by this karmic path. As a result, they face the danger of becoming bogged down in sensual and material pursuits at the expense of spiritual awareness and psychological development. Alternatively, these personalities can misuse their gifts in emotional obsessions, possessiveness, and envy. Still, there is enormous potential for professional and material success here, and if they rise to the challenge of fully dedicating themselves to becoming experts in their chosen field of endeavor, they are sure to realize a wealth of material and spiritual rewards. They would also do well to cultivate a personal or domestic environment that can serve as a haven from the demands of the world. When they are thus removed from mundane concerns, their spirituality will blossom in a way that reveals their true destiny.

HARRY CHANDLER
Made career with
LA Times, greatly
increased circulation

5/17/1864
Taurus III

CHALLENGE: **WORKING UNCEASINGLY TO BE KIND**
FULFILLMENT: **RECOGNIZING THAT THE SOURCE OF TRUE POWER IS NEVER THE EGO**
NOTABLE: **JOHN PAUL STEVENS (U.S. SUPREME COURT JUSTICE)**

April 25–May 2
MANIFESTATION
TAURUS I

Those born in the Week of Manifestation face the task of overcoming what might at first appear to be their "better" natures as they travel the Way of Introspection. Since these souls thrive on social contact and possess a great deal of empathy and concern for their fellows, it may not at first be easy for them to divest themselves of their causes and crusades in the interest of expanding their spiritual life. Yet if they remember the simple truth that we are all teachers and the things we teach are the things we must learn for ourselves, their path to success will be greatly clarified. A routine of physical discipline and domestic peace will be important for them, as will any activity that requires quality time alone and in deep concentration. No strangers to the need for solitude, for these souls the struggle is less about being alone and more about what they will do once they get there. and true calling.

CHALLENGE: **DIVESTING THEMSELVES OF THE FEAR OF CHANGE**
FULFILLMENT: **GAINING THE INSIGHTS BORN OF QUIET REFLECTION**

May 3–10
THE TEACHER
TAURUS II

For those born in this week, the Way of Introspection is bound to manifest in a lifelong fascination and perhaps struggle with the issues of learning and teaching. It is therefore essential for these souls to avoid those who would seek them out in the interest of personal or professional education, since it is the destiny of those with this configuration to relinquish the role of teacher in the material world in order to become a student of the spiritual. The journey may be especially difficult for those born in this week, so this path may require their having to confront a number of personal losses, rejections, or even mortality issues before they begin to look for answers in themselves. Staying flexible and open will be critical to their success and enable them to come to grips with the fact that sometimes it's not what you know that counts but your consciousness of the things you have yet to learn.

POPE JOHN PAUL II
Head of Roman Catholic
Church from 1978 to
the present

5/18/1920
Taurus III

CHALLENGE: **TRAVERSING TIMES OF LIFE CHALLENGE IN CONSCIOUSNESS**
FULFILLMENT: **APPLYING THEIR NATURAL CURIOSITY AS TO HOW THINGS WORK TO THEMSELVES**

May 11–18
THE NATURAL
TAURUS III

The privacy and solitude required by those on the Way of Introspection will come quite easily for those born in this week, and they are likely to find themselves quite happy establishing a private niche in a natural setting. Staying close to the rhythms of the earth is important for these souls, and therefore enjoying the solitude of the country or even the wilderness will greatly aid them on this life's journey. Though many with this configuration may become preoccupied with money and material success, it is important for them to realize that one of the great benefits of the Way of Introspection is that material security comes quite easily, so that the soul can be free to complete its mission of self-knowledge and discovery. Thus, if these individuals are careful to control their sense of restlessness and embark on the adventure of self-discovery, they are sure to find the freedom and sense of personal liberation promised by this karmic path.

CHALLENGE: **ASKING THEMSELVES THE QUESTION "WHAT IS THE TRUE VALUE OF THIS?"—AND ASKING IT OFTEN**
FULFILLMENT: **SPENDING TIME IN NATURE**

May 19–24
ENERGY
TAURUS–GEMINI CUSP

Self-discipline and focus will be key to the success of those born on the Cusp of Energy who travel this destiny path. Blessed with tremendous natural curiosity and keen perception, they must nevertheless adjust to the knowledge that limitations and structure have considerable value as they work to both refine and expand their awareness. Drawn to the world of ideas and metaphysical pursuits, they will nevertheless have to fight the temptation to spread themselves too thin on the one hand or to succumb to worry, escapism, or nervous complaints on the other. Still, the development of a hobby or profession into which they can pour their energy and enthusiasm will do much to focus their sometimes scattered attention. If Taurus–Geminis are careful to turn the ambition that goes with this configuration into a sense of self that includes an area of expertise and authority, their travels along this karmic path will be considerably eased.

TIMOTHY BUSFIELD,
seen here with Patricia
Wettig, TV actor,
thirtysomething

6/12/1957
Gemini III

CHALLENGE: **CULTIVATING TRUE PEACEFULNESS OF SPIRIT WITHIN THEMSELVES**
FULFILLMENT: **ENCOURAGING THEIR INQUISITIVE MINDS TO TRAVEL FAR INTO METAPHYSICAL REALMS**

May 25–June 2
FREEDOM
GEMINI I

Truly rare individuals, Gemini I's born on the Way of Introspection will derive great benefit from cultivating a family or domestic environment that allows them to be completely themselves. "Turning off" their heads and listening to their hearts will be of paramount importance for these people, as their minds tend to work so quickly that they often neglect or ignore their intuition. Though it may take some time for these freedom lovers to take up the challenges of this karmic path and settle down enough to be able to turn inward, once they begin the process they will doubtless make up for lost time. Developing an area of technical aptitude or expertise will help them learn how to focus their attention. Once these analytic and intelligent souls are grounded by a settled and fulfilling domestic environment and the confidence that comes with professional achievements, self-knowledge and higher awareness are likely to come easily to them. Quick studies all, their efforts at introspection promise to be well and richly rewarded.

CHALLENGE: **TURNING OFF THEIR "MENTAL MONKEY"**
FULFILLMENT: **FOCUSING AND DIRECTING THEIR VERBAL ACUITY**

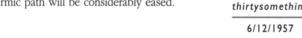

June 3–10
NEW LANGUAGE
GEMINI II

Many of the brilliant communicators, such as Gemini II's, who travel the Way of Introspection will find that their greatest fulfillment lies in writing, scholarship, or research, as such endeavors will allow them to exercise their communicative gifts yet indulge in the periods of thoughtful introspection and solitude required by this configuration. Though there is some danger here of developing an overly defensive or even paranoid attitude toward the world, as well as of succumbing to their darker side through escapism or substance abuse, their formidable capacity for analysis, properly controlled, can work to their great advantage. Gifted with clarity of both vision and communication, they have a rare ability to articulate their inner processes in a way that is beneficial both to themselves and to humanity as a whole.

RICHARD STRAUSS
Composer: opera, song,
and orchestral works

6/11/1864
Gemini III

CHALLENGE: **NOT BECOMING CAUGHT UP IN THEIR SHADOW QUALITIES AS THEY TURN INWARD**
FULFILLMENT: **THROUGH UNDERSTANDING, COMING TO TERMS WITH WHO THEY ARE**
NOTABLE: **L. A. REID (R & B SONGWRITER AND PRODUCER)**

June 11–18
THE SEEKER
GEMINI III

Preferring as they do to look almost exclusively outward rather than inward, those born in the Week of the Seeker may chafe a bit at the limitations suggested by this karmic path. Proper grounding in both material and personal reality will be critical to their success, as will the ability to withdraw when they feel themselves victims of information overload. They should also work hard to overcome their tendency to try to please others and attend to the task of pleasing themselves. Being alone does not come naturally for these highly social people, yet they will benefit greatly when grounded by a stable home environment or a trusted friend or companion. Activities such as keeping a journal, analyzing their dreams, or connecting with some study of religion or philosophy will greatly aid their quest for spiritual awareness, as will establishing a routine of meditation and physical exercise that will help to control their highly strung natures, while at the same time serving to expand the frontiers of personal awareness.

CHALLENGE: **TRANSFORMING THE DIRECTION OF THEIR ATTENTION FROM OUTWARD TO INWARD**
FULFILLMENT: **FORGIVING THEMSELVES**

June 19–24
MAGIC
GEMINI–CANCER CUSP

Those born on the Cusp of Magic who travel the Way of Introspection are likely to be fortunate people indeed. These souls possess an almost enchanted vision and an intuitive awareness of their own destinies; thus, they will take quite easily to the demands of this path, providing they are willing to divest themselves of some of their more romantic notions and attachments. Relinquishing their great need for love and personal relationships may prove the central challenge of this configuration, and some will suffer rejection or some other form of personal loss in this area that will reorient them to the rewards of self-reliance and greater spiritual depth. Still, they are likely to emerge from their periods of personal travail more self-assured than ever and blessed with a deep, abiding knowledge of what it means to both give and receive the love of the universe.

CHALLENGE: **EMBRACING THE PRINCIPLE OF NONATTACHMENT**
FULFILLMENT: **DISCOVERING THE ROLE OF LOVE IN THEIR LIVES**
NOTABLES: **ELEUTHÈRE IRENÉE DuPONT (INDUSTRIALIST); FRANCES McDORMAND (ACTRESS; WON OSCAR FOR *FARGO*)**

DAVID BRINKLEY
TV journalist
───────
7/10/1920
Cancer II

June 25–July 2
THE EMPATH
CANCER I

Blessed with great psychic and extrasensory gifts, those born in the Week of the Empath are likely to flourish on the Way of Introspection. Though these individuals will probably express a lifelong fascination with spiritual and philosophical pursuits, for some this configuration will lead to great material and/or monetary success. Either way, they are likely to become experts in their chosen fields of endeavor. Though their principal pitfall is one of overidentification with others at the expense of their own development, they have perhaps an equal tendency to bottle up or repress their feelings in the interest of self-protection. Still, they have a natural need to withdraw from the demands of the world that will greatly benefit them on their journey, especially if they get into touch with their deepest feelings and insights, which in turn will liberate and exalt their higher natures.

CHALLENGE: **DISENTANGLING THEMSELVES FROM ALL FORMS OF CODEPENDENCY**
FULFILLMENT: **REAPING THE REWARDS OF EMOTIONAL CLARITY**
NOTABLES: **LEONA HELMSLEY (HOTEL/REAL ESTATE MOGUL); EUNICE KENNEDY SHRIVER (FOUNDER, SPECIAL OLYMPICS; ADVOCATE FOR THE MENTALLY DISABLED)**

July 3–10
THE UNCONVENTIONAL
CANCER II

The secret inner world of those born in the Week of the Unconventional is likely to hold quite a few strange and even bizarre revelations as these individuals undertake the process of gaining self-awareness and exploring themselves. Some may retreat into a Walter Mitty–like fantasy world, while others will find that their quest takes them down some dark and even dangerous psychic avenues. Obsessions of all kinds are to be avoided, as they will ultimately prove to be mere distractions from the real work of developing self-awareness. Still, this configuration implies considerable material blessings, even wealth, and with the proper channeling of their unusual energies into crafts, hobbies, or other activities that require a hands-on approach to creativity, these individuals can live comfortably in the material universe while at the same time exploring the worlds of imagination, fantasy, and their higher spiritual natures.

CHALLENGE: **DISCERNING THE DIFFERENCE BETWEEN A CONSCIOUS INNER LIFE AND FANTASY**
FULFILLMENT: **ACCEPTING THEIR OWN MORE UNCONVENTIONAL ASPECTS**
NOTABLE: **PATTY SMYTH (POPULAR SINGER, "THE WARRIOR")**

YUL BRYNNER
Actor, *The King and I*
───────
7/11/1920
Cancer III

July 11–18
THE PERSUADER
CANCER III

Cancer III's who travel the Way of Introspection are likely to find a rare degree of personal fulfillment. Though possessed of a social and gregarious side, they are nonetheless quite content with their own company and able to control their more material or physical needs in the interest of expanded awareness. Though there is some danger that their periods of withdrawal may devolve into sensual excess or escapism, it is more likely that they will attune themselves to the watery, intuitive energy of this karmic path, resulting in deep insight and great personal transformation. Their relationships are likely to be highly selective, and when they do find love, it is will doubtless be a lasting relationship marked by depth and soulful understanding. A happy domestic life will be very important for these souls, and their homes or other places of personal and spiritual retreat will doubtless be marked by rare beauty and great comfort.

CHALLENGE: **NOT PERMITTING THE DEMANDS OF THEIR WORK TO INTERFERE WITH THEIR SPIRITUAL JOURNEY**
FULFILLMENT: **DISCOVERING THE ENDLESS FASCINATION OF THEIR OWN AND OTHERS' INNER WORKINGS**
NOTABLE: **CAMERON CROWE (FILM DIRECTOR/WRITER)**

July 19–25

OSCILLATION
CANCER–LEO CUSP

The individuals born on the Cusp of Oscillation who travel this karmic path may have some difficulty getting their footing. Though blessed with a fine sense of moral courage and a keen interest in the world around them, they may have difficulty with the degree of self-examination and evaluation that this destiny requires. Emotional ups and downs are likely to contribute to their spiritual awareness, however, and they are capable of learning a great deal from their own extremes. Staying grounded by stable partners and peaceful environments will do much to help them stay balanced and in control of their passions. The key to success for these souls lies first in cultivating a measure of objectivity, then in learning how to apply that objectivity to the process of self-discovery. Chances are they will surprise themselves with their own strength, courage, and endurance as their spiritual path widens into a wealth of opportunity for greater understanding.

CHALLENGE: **FINDING THEIR FOOTING WELL ENOUGH TO BELIEVE IN SOMETHING**
FULFILLMENT: **EXPERIENCING THE GREAT CALM THAT COMES FROM BEING CENTERED**
NOTABLES: **ISAAC STERN (VIOLINIST); BELLA ABZUG (U.S. REPRESENTATIVE; CIVIL RIGHTS ATTORNEY)**

RUDY VALLEE
Bandleader and singer,
first "crooner"

7/28/1901
Leo I

July 26–August 2

AUTHORITY
LEO I

Those born in this week may find themselves somewhat resistant to the challenges presented on the Way of Introspection. Naturally tough customers, they may get mired in inflexibility or their innate need to exercise a certain level of power or authority over others. Still, if they can develop the self-control required by this karmic path and turn their passion for expertise into a consuming professional pursuit or avocation, they are likely to find their way with ease. Overcoming egotism and the need for recognition and devotion may be especially difficult, and it will be very important for them to cultivate a sense of peace with the idea of being alone. Yet if they learn to love their tasks for their own sake, maintain their sense of humor, and undertake the voyage of self-discovery with the same enthusiasm and high standards that mark their dealings with the outside world, their struggles will reveal greater strength and a more positive sense of self than they might have otherwise believed possible.

CHALLENGE: **RELAXING THEIR NEED TO BE IN CONTROL**
FULFILLMENT: **GAINING THE STRENGTH THAT COMES FROM SELF-KNOWLEDGE**

August 3–10

BALANCED STRENGTH
LEO II

Blessed with tenacity and endurance, Leo II's are likely to realize great success on the Way of Introspection, providing that their periods of withdrawal and self-evaluation do not devolve into depressive binges or "pity parties." There is a rather masochistic side to many of these folks, and they will have to exercise a great deal of self-control in order not to confuse the process of introspection with simple suffering. Still, they respond quite naturally to the periods of privacy demanded by this karmic path. If they work to expand their intuitive and extrasensory capacities through meditation techniques, strenuous exercise, and productive routines, they will succeed in releasing much of the tension and sense of preoccupation that seem to go with this configuration. Finally, the simple ability to stay flexible will do much to broaden their inner horizons and ultimately reveal that true self-awareness is much different from self-absorption.

CHALLENGE: **MANAGING THEIR THINKING AND GUIDING IT TOWARD THE POSITIVE**
FULFILLMENT: **CULTIVATING THEIR TREMENDOUS CAPACITY FOR CONCENTRATION THROUGH MEDITATION**
NOTABLE: **LOUIS "SATCHMO" ARMSTRONG (JAZZ MUSICIAN)**

MELANIE GRIFFITH
Film actress

8/9/1957
Leo II

August 11–18

LEADERSHIP
LEO III

Individuals born in the Week of Leadership may find the Way of Introspection a bit of a rocky road, as their naturally commanding persona can make them somewhat hesitant to divest themselves of the social contacts and causes that make up their power base. Still, they are not always the most approachable of people, and others may find them to be distant or even exuding a forbidding aura of authority. These individuals will nevertheless respond well to cultivating the degree of expertise and self-reliance indicated by this karmic path, and their wide areas of interest in creative and philosophical pursuits will doubtless lead them to acquire the professionalism and passion for their work that is part of this karmic path. If they remain flexible and open to new ideas and willing to delegate responsibility to others, their success on the way of introspection could well assume heroic proportions.

CHALLENGE: **FINDING THE COURAGE TO LOOK AT THEIR OWN SHADOWS**
FULFILLMENT: **CHANNELING GREATER SELF-AWARENESS INTO ARTISTIC EXPRESSION**
NOTABLES: **DAVID HWANG (DRAMATIST); ARTHUR C. KELLER (INVENTED STYLUS, MAKING HI-FI POSSIBLE)**

August 19–25

EXPOSURE
LEO–VIRGO CUSP

These cusp personalities will doubtless experience a number of ups and downs along the Way of Introspection. A curious combination of secrets and revelations will doubtless contribute to their need to be alone and to set aside time for private thought and the process of going inward. Though they will respond well to the need to be self-contained and "masters of their own fate," the more they struggle to withdraw, the more the world will take notice of these frequently flamboyant people. It will be doubly important, therefore, for them to establish an inviolable personal retreat where they can go to get away from it all or to find a select partner or friend with whom they can establish real trust. Nevertheless, they will respond well to the professional challenges of this path and are likely to find a consuming vocation through which their minds become more focused, their skills can be refined, and their true destiny can be revealed.

DANIEL STERN
Actor and voice-over
artist
—————
8/28/1957
Virgo I

CHALLENGE: **BEING CONSCIOUS OF WHEN, THROUGH DENIAL, THEY ARE KEEPING SECRETS EVEN FROM THEMSELVES**
FULFILLMENT: **LEARNING TO TRUST WHO THEY ARE**

August 26–September 2

SYSTEM BUILDERS
VIRGO I

The destiny issues of Virgo I's on the Way of Introspection are not easy to predict or identify. On the one hand, they are possessed of great objectivity and analytic abilities, while on the other, they often have difficulty applying those same skills to the process of self-awareness and the self-examination. They run the risk of withdrawing to the point of depression and even paranoia, and they would do well to cultivate emotional balance. Some of them will find themselves experiencing a great deal of difficulty disconnecting from their notion of service to others in order to go inward. Generally, they will do best when they establish a regular routine of exercises in meditation or yoga and learn to see such routines as both healthy and self-fulfilling. Structure is important to them in any event, and if they seek to combine their talent for creating ordered systems with a real and enthusiastic quest for higher spiritual awareness, they are likely to blossom on this karmic path.

CHALLENGE: **RECOGNIZING THE CONNECTION BETWEEN THEIR PHYSICAL AND EMOTIONAL SIDES**
FULFILLMENT: **GAINING FREEDOM FROM THEIR OWN RULES**
NOTABLE: **GLORIA ESTEFAN (POPULAR SINGER)**

September 3–10

THE ENIGMA
VIRGO II

Those born in the Week of the Enigma are likely to do very well indeed on this karmic path. Professional expertise and developing an absorbing interest in a hobby or profession will come very naturally to these people, and early training in their particular talents will serve them quite well in the long run. Naturally discriminating, they will have little trouble divesting themselves of an excess of social involvements or other distractions from their truer calling, yet they may nevertheless get a bit sidetracked in a preoccupation with money and worldly acquisition. Still, if they apply their gifts in such a way that their material success better enables them to attend to the business of expanding their spiritual awareness rather than piling up material goods as a barrier against the world, they are likely to flourish on the Way of Introspection, getting in touch with their real feelings and discovering their true motivations in the process.

HAROLD CLURMAN
Director, theater critic
—————
9/18/1901
Virgo III

CHALLENGE: **REVEALING THEMSELVES TO OTHER PEOPLE**
FULFILLMENT: **OPENING TO THE LIGHT OF CONSCIOUSNESS SIDES OF THEMSELVES THAT MIGHT HAVE REMAINED HIDDEN**
NOTABLE: **DONALD BAILEY (INVENTED BAILEY BRIDGE FOR ARMY TROOPS)**

September 11–18

THE LITERALIST
VIRGO III

It will be rather too easy for Virgo III's to misdirect their willfulness along the Way of Introspection. It's difficult for them to change their minds in any event, and they will have to watch for a tendency in themselves to cling to outdated patterns of behavior or ways of thinking, simply because they are the way they always done things or because they are reluctant to undergo much in the way of soul-searching. There is a danger that they may become too judgmental of people and situations, while failing to evaluate themselves with the same stringency. Still, they are blessed with a wonderful ability to "call 'em as they see 'em." If these people can cultivate in themselves a willingness to turn inward and apply that same gift to expanding their inner world, they are likely to discover that they are capable of greater awareness and more depth of understanding than they had expected.

CHALLENGE: **LEARNING TO LOOK PAST THE OBVIOUS**
FULFILLMENT: **GAINING A FULLER UNDERSTANDING OF THEIR OWN TRUTH**

September 19–24
BEAUTY
VIRGO–LIBRA CUSP

Virgo–Librans are likely to be somewhat unprepared for the challenges presented by the Way of Introspection. Sensitive and quite attracted by aesthetic and refined externals, they will from time to time nevertheless be confronted with the vicissitudes of life and forced to go beneath the surface of both circumstances and their own personalities in an effort to develop greater understanding. There is some danger that they may overdo their withdrawal from the world in an attempt to flee reality, and they would do well to realize that isolation and escapism (perhaps even substance abuse) are not the same things as true introspection and honest self-evaluation. However, if they can keep their sensuousness under control while at the same time exalting their love of beauty in their search for spiritual understanding, they are likely to lead quite a comfortable material existence whose true function is to enable them to broaden that understanding.

CHALLENGE: **GOING DEEPLY INTO THEIR OWN EXPERIENCE OF LIFE**

FULFILLMENT: **FORMULATING THEIR OWN CONCEPT OF WHAT INNER BEAUTY MEANS**

ENRICO FERMI
"Father" of the
atomic bomb

9/29/1901
Libra I

September 25–October 2
THE PERFECTIONIST
LIBRA I

Gifted with a great impulse toward personal and professional achievements, those born in the Week of the Perfectionist who travel this karmic path are likely to realize great fulfillment. Perhaps the principal danger of this configuration is a tendency to be obsessive, and they will doubtless have occasion to confront the truth that spiritual laws rarely operate in a way that can easily be pinned down. It will be important for these personalities to "let it be" from time to time and further to disallow the notion that their private world is a place where they exercise ultimate control. Still, most of these people will do very well on the Way of Introspection, providing they understand that while God may indeed be in the details, too much preoccupation with details can sometimes hinder the search for God.

CHALLENGE: **FORGIVING THEIR OWN FOIBLES**

FULFILLMENT: **WATCHING THE STORM OF THEIR OWN EMOTIONS RECEDE ON ITS OWN**

NOTABLES: **BILL PALEY (FOUNDER, CBS); BETH HEIDEN (OLYMPIC SKATER)**

October 3–10
SOCIETY
LIBRA II

Libra II's who make their way along this destiny path are likely to have an easy road. Though blessed with formidable social skills, most of these personalities nevertheless have a private side and will really require the periods of private thought and peaceful seclusion indicated by this karmic path. Though there is some danger that they will fail to establish necessary boundaries and create quality time for themselves, their natural gifts of observation and analysis can usually be applied to the business of increased self-awareness and spiritual expansion without much trouble. Nonetheless, it will be important for them not to get mired in emotional instability or overwhelmed by negative emotions such as envy, possessiveness, or a tendency to become hypercritical. Thoughtful periods of rest and introspection will do much to "mellow them out," however, as will training in spiritual, religious, or physical routines that allow them to be grounded yet deepen their awareness of the soul and its mission.

CHALLENGE: **BECOMING AS INSIGHTFUL ABOUT THEMSELVES AS THEY ARE ABOUT OTHERS**

FULFILLMENT: **MAKING PEACE WITH THEIR FEELINGS**

EVEL KNIEVEL
Motorcycle stunt
performer

10/17/1938
Libra III

October 11–18
THEATER
LIBRA III

Those born in this week will find that, as they spend more time alone or with their own thoughts, they will achieve a high level of speciality or expertise in an area that will in turn result in great material reward. Worldly and hardheaded, they will nevertheless also need to utilize their "downtime" to develop a greater awareness of their own inner processes and motivations or run the risk of having success "turn to ashes" in their search for fulfillment. While their need to take center stage may be at odds with their need to withdraw into an inner universe, most of these personalities will discover the balance necessary to indulge both the public and private sides of their natures. Though much of this destiny path will manifest itself in a high degree of professional commitment, such behaviors will operate to the soul's advantage here as they will serve to separate Libra III's from an overabundance of connection and enable them instead to turn their attention to the search for higher spiritual awareness.

CHALLENGE: **TRANSLATING SELF-UNDERSTANDING INTO UNDERSTANDING OTHERS**

FULFILLMENT: **WATCHING THE CAST OF CHARACTERS ON THEIR INNER STAGE**

October 19–25

DRAMA AND CRITICISM
LIBRA–SCORPIO CUSP

The challenge for Libra–Scorpios who travel the Way of Introspection will doubtless involve reining in their forceful personalities from time to time and carefully moderating the influence they have over others. These people can quite literally not know their own strength and may have their limits tested from time to time along this karmic path as they define and redefine their notions of integrity. Charismatic and flamboyant, they will nevertheless have to work to develop the depth of character and objective self-evaluation skills called for here. Some of this type may have to struggle to emerge from a labyrinth of negative emotions or conditioning, and much of their private time may involve analyzing and reanalyzing their destructive patterns of behavior. However, if they can learn to combine their passion with flexibility and not fall victim to sensuous overindulgence, rigidity, or manipulative power plays, their chances for success are much improved.

RALPH BAKSHI
Cartoonist,
Lord of the Rings

10/26/1938
Scorpio I

CHALLENGE: **BECOMING CONSCIOUS OF THE WORKINGS OF THEIR EGOS**
FULFILLMENT: **REMOVING THE VEILS FROM THEIR PERCEPTION**
NOTABLE: **GEORGE GILLETT, JR. (BUSINESS EXECUTIVE)**

October 26–November 2

INTENSITY
SCORPIO I

Extreme single-mindedness of purpose may be the biggest stumbling block for those born in the Week of Intensity who travel the Way of Introspection. A tendency to overfocus on the outer aspects of their lives means that they will have to work hard to open the doors to higher awareness. The abilities to relinquish control, to trust others, and to maintain their sense of privacy without degenerating into a sort of neurotic insistence on self-sufficiency will all be keys to success on this karmic path, as will a stable grounding in a happy domestic environment. Some with this configuration will be further challenged by paranoia, emotional problems, or other self-destructive tendencies that must be evaluated and discarded over time. Yet there is promise of great transformation with this configuration and if Scorpio I's learn to manage their own energies, battle their own demons, and nurture their capacity to be happy, their prospects for material and spiritual expansion are almost limitless.

CHALLENGE: **FORCING THEMSELVES TO STOP RUNNING FROM THEIR DARK SIDE**
FULFILLMENT: **DISCOVERING THAT THEY CAN BE HAPPY**

November 3–11

DEPTH
SCORPIO II

Opening the channels between the conscious and unconscious will prove especially important for those with this configuration. Blessed with a natural depth and inner understanding of themselves and the world, these souls will nonetheless have to work hard to bring that knowledge to the fore and integrate their intuitions in such a way that will color their conscious experience. Highly competitive by nature, they must nevertheless work to avoid chronic feelings of jealousy that can erode their sense of self-confidence. Conversely, these souls can get mired in the need for material comfort and sensual pursuits and become rather spiritually lazy when their material needs are satisfied. Still, they are quite likely to develop the level of specialty and expertise called for by this path, and if they are careful to augment their material lives with spiritual explorations in religion, meditation, hypnosis, or other alternative disciplines, they are likely to find great content and personal fulfillment on the Way of Introspection.

LEE STRASBERG
Director of the Actors
Studio

11/17/1901
Scorpio III

CHALLENGE: **ALLAYING THEIR ANXIETY**
FULFILLMENT: **RECOGNIZING THE PURPOSE OF SUFFERING IN THEIR LIVES**

November 12–18

CHARM
SCORPIO III

Both realistic and aware of themselves and the world around them, Scorpio III's will doubtless prosper on the Way of Introspection. Cultivating a private space filled with beloved personal objects can be especially important, since for these souls possessions are a means of staying connected to spiritual realities in a tangible fashion. They will face the challenge of resolving some significant inner conflicts, however, often involving attachments to things they know aren't good for them. Ultimately, they will learn, through the acquisition of real self-confidence, to show a more authentic and genuinely emotional face to the world. Still, if they take care that their private space is not invaded by the demons of addiction, compulsions, or escapism, their world will open up in a universe of revelation and possibilities for real spiritual discovery and expansion.

CHALLENGE: **APPLYING THEIR KEEN ASSESSMENT TO THEIR BLIND SPOTS**
FULFILLMENT: **LEARNING THE VALUE OF BEING OPEN**
NOTABLE: **GORDON LIGHTFOOT (FOLKSINGER/SONGWRITER)**

November 19–24
REVOLUTION
SCORPIO–SAGITTARIUS CUSP

It may well be difficult for the Scorpio–Sagittarius personality to cultivate a liking for the peace and privacy dictated by the Way of Introspection. Blessed with great energy and something of a talent for tearing down old systems, they may nonetheless have difficulty with the earthy and watery energies associated with this karmic path. Loneliness or a sense of isolation may well prove a factor in their early family environment, yet if they use this early experience to become comfortable with themselves and their own company, they will lay valuable groundwork for the future exploration of their adult identity. Gifted with a fine sense of personal direction and the ability to dream big dreams, the structure of their professional lives will do much to direct and mitigate their tendency to extremes. Naturally philosophical and blessed with a great sense of humor, these personalities will surely go far as long as they do not lose the capacity to step back and laugh at themselves.

CHALLENGE: **NOT VIEWING THEIR PSYCHOLOGICAL TENDENCIES OR COMPLEXES AS SACRED COWS**

FULFILLMENT: **EXPLODING THEIR EGOS ONCE IN A WHILE**

NOTABLES: **DICK SMOTHERS (COMEDIAN, *THE SMOTHERS BROTHERS SHOW*); MARLO THOMAS (ACTRESS, *THAT GIRL*)**

TED TURNER
CNN founder; owner of Atlanta Braves baseball team

———

11/19/1938
Scorpio–Sagittarius Cusp

November 25–December 2
INDEPENDENCE
SAGITTARIUS I

Sagittarius I's who travel the Way of Introspection will benefit greatly from their ability to attract and cultivate a stable relationship with a friend or soul mate who can serve as their principal conduit to the outside world. These freedom lovers are likely to respond well to the challenges of this karmic path, yet the need for connection and groundedness will doubtless have to be addressed as they undertake the challenges of becoming their own best teachers. Though they may chafe at the restrictions implied by cultivating a speciality or profession into which they can pour their energies and enthusiasm, the freedom provided by their achievements will do much to shore up their sometimes shaky egos and calm their insecurities. Whatever the seemingly reckless pace of their lives, Sagittarius I's are at their best when at home, surrounded by stability, peace, and a partner with whom they can share their inner world.

CHALLENGE: **OVERCOMING THEIR STUBBORN REFUSAL TO LET GO OF THEIR INSECURITIES**

FULFILLMENT: **BECOMING THE RECIPIENT OF THEIR OWN WISDOM**

NOTABLES: **TINA TURNER (POPULAR SINGER); RICH LITTLE (COMEDIAN, IMPERSONATOR)**

December 3–10
THE ORIGINATOR
SAGITTARIUS II

The originators who travel the Way of Introspection are likely to be rather unusual people who will nevertheless find themselves quite happy on this road. Often perceived as eccentric or peculiar, they will have to overcome a somewhat defensive attitude before they can truly settle down to the business of developing their unique talents. The ability to recognize and nurture their inner lives may prove to be more problematic, however. These individuals are not known for their awareness, particularly regarding feelings of anger or rejection. For that reason, they must be on guard against the tendency to complacency, stubbornness, or a rather lazy attitude toward the Way of Introspection. Refining their skills and honing their discipline for conscious awareness of their emotions will be paramount. Sagittarius II's who are able to develop greater introspection may ultimately find themselves pursuing a home-based business or enterprise, usually involving some level of technical proficiency, thereby melding spiritual and professional achievement.

CHALLENGE: **GRAPPLING WITH SUPPRESSED ANGER**
FULFILLMENT: **PEACEFULLY GOING THEIR OWN WAY**
NOTABLE: **ELIOT PORTER (WILDLIFE PHOTOGRAPHER)**

WALT DISNEY
Animation genius, originator of Mickey Mouse

———

12/5/1901
Sagittarius II

December 11–18
THE TITAN
SAGITTARIUS III

Blessed with a naturally philosophical turn of mind, those born in the Week of the Titan who travel this destiny path will nevertheless have to work at narrowing their focus such that their imaginative schemes and plans can be realized. Ambitious and generous, sometimes to a fault, they run the risk of overextending themselves to the point where they do not create the alone time necessitated by this karmic path, and can quite literally "lose themselves" in the process. Confronting their inner selves will impart real confidence to these souls and do much to assuage their secret insecurities. Studies of religious and spiritual subjects will prove very beneficial to many of them and enable them to gain greater perspective on their place in the universe. Yet perhaps the greatest benefit to those with this configuration will be in using their periods of study and introspection to better learn self-control. Once their darker sides are regulated and disciplined, their light will shine forth with confidence.

CHALLENGE: **STRUCTURING TIME TO BE ALONE WITH THEMSELVES**

FULFILLMENT: **GAINING THE PERSPECTIVE OF A LARGER PICTURE OF THEMSELVES**

NOTABLES: **ZOLTAN KODÀLY (HUNGARIAN COMPOSER); CONNIE FRANCIS (POPULAR SINGER)**

December 19–25
PROPHECY
SAGITTARIUS–CAPRICORN CUSP

The challenge for these cusp personalities will doubtless revolve around developing and honing their intuitive and extrasensory skills. Not always the most confident of souls, Sagittarius-Capricorns will nevertheless have a fairly easy time on the Way of Introspection. Blessed with great independence and self-reliance, they will have little trouble with the more private, secluded aspects of this karmic path and will establish their need for private time and space quite early. Though there is some danger that they may become controlling and rigid as they go on in life, it is far more likely that their unique sense of self will truly blossom through the acquisition of spiritual skills such as meditation or other mental and physical disciplines. Though professional success may not come until somewhat later in life, they can be assured of material prosperity with this configuration, and whatever their particular field, they will imbue their endeavors with a unique blend of insight and foresight.

BOBBY HULL
Hockey left wing, 3-time
NHL scoring leader

1/3/1939
Capricorn II

CHALLENGE: **COMBATING THEIR TENDENCY TO DEPRESSION**
FULFILLMENT: **FINDING HOW MUCH THEIR CAPACITY FOR SILENCE HAS TO TEACH THEM**
NOTABLE: **MATTY ALOU (BASEBALL PITCHER)**

December 26–January 2
THE RULER
CAPRICORN I

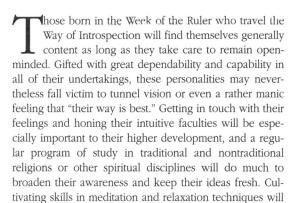

Those born in the Week of the Ruler who travel the Way of Introspection will find themselves generally content as long as they take care to remain open-minded. Gifted with great dependability and capability in all of their undertakings, these personalities may nevertheless fall victim to tunnel vision or even a rather manic feeling that "their way is best." Getting in touch with their feelings and honing their intuitive faculties will be especially important to their higher development, and a regular program of study in traditional and nontraditional religions or other spiritual disciplines will do much to broaden their awareness and keep their ideas fresh. Cultivating skills in meditation and relaxation techniques will also help them avoid the tendency to workaholic patterns of behavior and serve to remind these dedicated people of the limitations of material success.

CHALLENGE: **CHALLENGING THEIR RIGID VIEW OF HOW THINGS WORK**
FULFILLMENT: **APPLYING THEIR RIGOROUS HONESTY TO THEMSELVES**

January 3–9
DETERMINATION
CAPRICORN II

Though gifted with considerable ambition and the ability to strive for seemingly impossible goals, Capricorn II's will doubtless find themselves presented with a more metaphysical set of challenges as they travel the Way of Introspection. These personalities are gifted with a more theoretical disposition than many others who travel this karmic path and will doubtless enjoy the periods of solitude and going inward that are indicated here. Though it is likely that their profession or particular area of expertise will come first in their lives, they will nevertheless derive great benefit from a select partner or soul mate with whom they can share their spiritual journey as well as their material success. A rare combination of realism and idealism permeates this configuration, and if these personalities are careful to strike a balance between the two through a process of going inward in search of spiritual expansion, they are likely to shine.

SAL MINEO
American actor

1/10/1939
Capricorn III

CHALLENGE: **NOT PERMITTING THEIR FEAR OF BEING HURT TO DETER THEIR INNER QUEST**
FULFILLMENT: **INVESTING IN THEIR METAPHYSICAL SIDE**
NOTABLES: **KAHLIL GIBRAN (POET; PAINTER; AUTHOR OF THE PROPHET); MAURY POVICH (TELEVISION JOURNALIST AND HOST); CAROLINA HERRERA (FASHION DESIGNER)**

January 10–16
DOMINANCE
CAPRICORN III

Naturally authoritarian and blessed with great dedication, those born in the Week of Dominance who travel the Way of Introspection may find themselves in a bit of a quandary. On the one hand, they will respond quite well to the periods of solitude and grounded domestic life required by this karmic path, while on the other, they may be quite resistant to the spiritual expansion that is also necessary. Capricorn III's tend to view the world and its issues in terms of black and white or good and evil, sometimes without the shadings required to gain a clearer perspective. As a result, many on this path may find themselves confronted with less-than-obvious issues and situations that require deeper consideration and greater tolerance. Still, if they face the challenge not to judge others too harshly, they will be blessed with the ability to go easier on themselves, resulting in greater confidence and increasing their happiness on the Way of Introspection.

CHALLENGE: **SEEKING OUT A MIDDLE GROUND**
FULFILLMENT: **LEARNING TO STOP JUDGING THEMSELVES**

January 17–22

MYSTERY AND IMAGINATION
CAPRICORN–AQUARIUS CUSP

The restless, energetic personalities born in this week who travel the Way of Introspection may find themselves a bit uncomfortable with the challenges presented here. It will doubtless be important for them to retreat to their lively, imaginative inner worlds throughout their lives, but it will be difficult for them to stay out of the action for extended periods of time. A peaceful home and a grounded domestic life will help them along the road, as will mastering meditation and relaxation techniques. They should also be aware of their tendency to overextend themselves in the service of a cause or organization, as too much in the way of self-sacrifice will ultimately prove distracting to their mission of gaining greater self-awareness. Still, if they cultivate the ability to take their dreams and fantasies more seriously, they will find much to learn simply by traveling the frontiers of their own imaginations.

WOLFMAN JACK
Syndicated rock DJ

1/21/1939
Capricorn–Aquarius Cusp

CHALLENGE: **GIVING VOICE TO THEIR TREMENDOUS SENSITIVITY**
FULFILLMENT: **WEAVING A PATH OF UNDERSTANDING THROUGH THE TUMULT OF THEIR INNER ENERGIES**
NOTABLE: **PHIL EVERLY (POPULAR SINGER/SONGWRITER, THE EVERLY BROTHERS)**

January 23–30

GENIUS
AQUARIUS I

Those born in the Week of Genius who travel the Way of Introspection are likely to be quite happy with the self-taught and self-instructive aspects of this karmic path. They will need to cultivate serenity, however, and many of their spiritual challenges will doubtless revolve around the ability to cultivate greater patience with both themselves and others. Still, they are likely to do very well, especially if they go into a profession where they can avoid too much social contact. Drawn to the theoretical and intellectual areas of life, they should also work to educate themselves in the spiritual. Exercise routines and relaxation techniques will benefit their high-strung natures enormously and help key them into the meditative state demanded by this karmic path. They may also respond well to hands-on hobbies and creative activities. Thus, a home workshop or quiet space where they can putter around undisturbed will do much to channel their energies and turn their attention inward.

CHALLENGE: **OWNING UP TO THE IDEA THAT IRRITABILITY IS NOT KIND**
FULFILLMENT: **ACHIEVING PEACE OF MIND**
NOTABLE: **GERMAINE GREER (FEMINIST, AUTHOR, *THE FEMALE EUNUCH*)**

January 31–February 7

YOUTH AND EASE
AQUARIUS II

Aquarius II's who travel the Way of Introspection may be in for a rocky time, especially if they allow themselves to be swept along on the tide of other opinions and values without first developing a firm code of beliefs for themselves. Turning inward will not be easy for many of these personalities and some may get mired in complacency or material comfort to the detriment of their higher nature. Still, if they allow themselves to be drawn to a deeper, more profound relationship with a particular soul mate, they will find their natural popularity less troublesome. Gifted with the ability to master their chosen medium, they will focus much of their energy on their vocation or speciality, often with spectacular success. If they can also master the art of turning inward as they pursue their talents, all will be well.

EUBIE BLAKE
Composer and pianist

2/7/1883
Aquarius II

CHALLENGE: **MATURING THEIR VIEW OF WHO THEY ARE**
FULFILLMENT: **BEING LEFT TO PROGRESS AT THEIR OWN PACE**
NOTABLES: **MIKE FARRELL (TELEVISION ACTOR, *MASH*); JOHN S. REED (BUSINESS EXECUTIVE)**

February 8–15

ACCEPTANCE
AQUARIUS III

Letting go and learning the art of acceptance will be somewhat difficult for Aquarius III's who travel the Way of Introspection. While they are likely to have little difficulty with the detachment and periods of solitude required by this karmic path, there is a danger that their periods on introspection may find them nursing old hurts and bearing useless grudges. Gifted with keen perception, these souls will nevertheless face the challenge of getting in touch with their more emotional and intuitive energies and remaining open to new ideas. Disciplining their lively minds will be especially important, and they should work to combine their natural love of learning with stable study habits and good mental discipline. Once they have mastered the art of self-control, their impulse to control others will diminish and these souls will find themselves considerably freed from the wealth of complaints and irritations that can often color their lives.

CHALLENGE: **LEAVING THE PAST BEHIND AS THEY LOOK TO THE FUTURE**
FULFILLMENT: **FINDING THE INNER CALM THAT COMES WITH ACCEPTING THINGS AS THEY ARE**
NOTABLE: **JOHN GARNET CARTER (INVENTED MINIATURE GOLF)**

February 16–22

SENSITIVITY
AQUARIUS–PISCES CUSP

Those born on the Cusp of Sensitivity who travel this karmic path are likely to be quite happy, as long as they are careful to channel their energies into the mastery of a fulfilling profession or craft. Unencumbered by a need for much in the way of social contact or connection, these souls will be at peace with the degree of solitude indicated here, though they would do well to monitor their own inner journeys and emotions so that they do not get stuck in pessimism, isolation, or undue self-involvement. Alternatively, some may lose their way in false ideas of self-sacrifice or a kind of chronic victimhood. Still, the huge majority of these people are gifted with a natural aptitude for the Way of Introspection and will likely be blessed with a rare combination of material success, professional achievement, and profound spiritual experience as they make their way along this karmic path.

ROBERTA FLACK
Pop/soul singer

2/10/1939
Aquarius III

CHALLENGE: **BREAKING THE CHAINS OF INSECURITY**
FULFILLMENT: **FINDING A PLACE IN THEIR LIVES FOR THEIR SPIRITUAL LEANINGS**

February 23–March 2

SPIRIT
PISCES I

Pisces I's are likely to face the challenges of reconciling the material and nonmaterial sides of life on the Way of Introspection. Naturally spiritual and gifted with the ability to devote themselves completely to a task, person, or cause, they do run the risk of becoming too self-sacrificing and idealistic and will have to cultivate a healthy degree of self-interest before they can truly progress. Some of them may be confronted with the demands of material reality and struggle with a excess of physical drive, sensuousness, or overindulgence, while others may learn through the management or mismanagement of money and material resources. Grounding themselves in the simple pleasures of domestic life will be especially beneficial for Pisces I's, as will learning to accept professional responsibility gracefully. Yet if they do not allow their periods of solitude and meditation to degenerate into escapism and worry, their life's journey promises fulfillment and peace.

CHALLENGE: **LEARNING TO PROTECT THEIR HEARTS**
FULFILLMENT: **BRINGING THEIR SPIRITUAL AMBITIONS TO ATTAINABLE LEVELS—ONE DAY AT A TIME**

March 3–10

THE LONER
PISCES II

Loners who travel the Way of Introspection run the risk of becoming too isolated from reality. Though they are likely to be untroubled by the demands for solitude and introspection of this karmic path, their reclusive natures can go overboard with this configuration, resulting in a narrow perspective devoid of needed input from others. Too, they can become suspicious of others who could serve as trusted advisers and friends and come to resent even minimal social contact as an intrusion into their private universe. Still, if they are careful to stay grounded with a select partner or friend of a practical, easygoing disposition and surround themselves with the beauties of nature, their deeper needs and higher aspirations will be illuminated. Once they gain the confidence of true spiritual identity, it will serve to pave the way for the world to accept them as they really are.

PETER FONDA
Actor, *Easy Rider*

2/23/1939
Pisces I

CHALLENGE: **DEALING WITH RATHER THAN DENYING TRAUMA**
FULFILLMENT: **KNOWING THAT ALL ARE ONE IN SPIRIT**
NOTABLE: **PAULA PRENTISS (ACTRESS)**

March 11–18

DANCERS AND DREAMERS
PISCES III

Those born in this week who travel the Way of Introspection may fall victim more than once to their need to be needed. Helpfulness is the hallmark of many of these personalities and they would do well to discipline and educate themselves to the point where they are not so easily taken in. Yet many of these souls will realize amazing success on their life's journey, providing they can ground their unique energies in practical ways and train their talents in productive ways. Turning inward may not come easily for them, yet their spiritual progress demands that they cultivate greater depth to color their natural understanding. Highly sensitive, they will doubtless come to appreciate the need to remove themselves from the demands of the world in order to rest themselves and refresh their resources. As they cultivate mental, spiritual, and physical tools to manage their own magic better, they will certainly prosper along the way.

CHALLENGE: **LOOKING LESS TO WHAT THEY WANT AND MORE TO WHAT THEY HAVE FOR FULFILLMENT**
FULFILLMENT: **COMING TO BELIEVE THAT GOODNESS AND HONESTY WILL PREVAIL**
NOTABLE: **ELAINE DEKOONING (ARTIST; WIFE OF NOTED PAINTER)**

The Way of Influence

TAURUS III TO SCORPIO III
Natural to Charm

On the Way of Influence, a path of steadily increasing maturity, individuals are called to work on developing the character traits that will enable them to take on a mantle of quiet authority. Ultimately, those born on the Way of Influence are to become leaders of others not by rule but by example. Thus, those born to this path must learn to have more self-control by subduing or taming their passions and to develop the qualities in themselves that will engender respect: trustworthiness, sound judgment, resourcefulness, and calm under pressure. In this way, they will influence those around them in an objective, purposeful fashion. This path tends to be a relatively easy one since it is a path of steady evolution, not necessarily one that creates inner conflict or struggle. This is because though opposites, the goal of the Way of Influence, Scorpio III Charm, is simply a higher octave of the origin, Taurus III, the Natural; thus this process is one more of maturation than of transformation. Rather than being called on to learn a whole new set of skills, individuals on this karmic path must learn how to use their gifts more consciously and capitalize on them to achieve their goals. To earn the societal success they secretly yearn for, those on the Way of Influence must temper the pull of their own desire for freedom, a desire that frequently gets them into hot water. Too often these individuals behave like teenagers when they should be working on being adults. It is only when they choose to be grown-ups that they can utilize their naturally vibrant, imaginative, and charming personalities to be a source of inspiration to others.

Learning to be more grounded and content in who they are, without losing their spontaneity and natural appeal, is the core lesson for the individuals on this karmic path. Born with a certain sense of insecurity and a great fear that others will quash their natural enthusiasm, they are extremely sensitive to criticism. Rarely will they listen to what others have to say for fear that it will somehow control them. But if they can recognize and own up to their very real need for achievement and recognition, and realize that their natural wildness is only hurting them, perhaps they can begin to impose some limitations on themselves. Ultimately they will be happier for it. Once they are more comfortable with who they are, they will succeed in attracting many friends, associates, and acquaintances to them and before long will find themselves amid a circle of admirers who respect their views and trust their judgment. Gifted with a sixth sense or outright psychic ability, those on this karmic path often anticipate the wishes or concerns of others, and, being naturally sympathetic to their fellow humans, they want to fulfill them. But it is the destiny of the men and woman on this path not simply to be popular but to become a bit larger than life

> ### CORE LESSON
> Becoming fully centered in and content with who they are
>
> ### GOAL
> To evolve gracefully in order to take on a mantle of authority

> ### GIFTS
> Imaginative, Intuitive, Resourceful
>
> ### PITFALLS
> Rebellious, Controlling, Insecure

in order to spread their example to a fairly large circle. Learning to be more centered and measured in their responses is crucial for these individuals, since any sort of erratic behavior will certainly put people off. Moreover, personal integrity is of the utmost importance. One moral misstep could result in an irreparable loss of faith on the part of their fellows.

The primary area in which life lessons will be learned on this karmic path is usually social or career interactions of an everyday sort. It is here that these individuals will learn to tone down their more extreme tendencies. By observing themselves in interaction with others, they will begin to pay closer attention to the example they set and the effect they have. Learning to take greater care in what they say, they will speak less in generalities and offer information less freely. As they learn to rein themselves in, these individuals will become increasingly trusted and thus more influential. Eventually, they will stop chasing after adventure or exciting individuals, and others will seek them out for their indispensable qualities, particularly their resourcefulness. It is nearly ensured that these men and women will rise to prominence as they develop their ability to positively influence their group, business, or organization as it develops. At some time or other in their lives, those on this karmic path will likely become leaders of

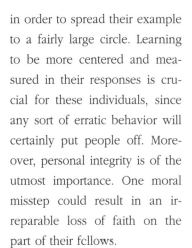

RELEASE

The attraction to the
wild side of life

REWARD

The joy of gaining the
respect of others

their social group or bosses, positions that suit them well and the attainment of which will be the barometer of their developmental progress.

As they achieve the prominence for which they are destined, individuals on the Way of Influence must grow increasingly cautious of the workings of their egos. For more than anything else, the ego trips can ruin all that these individuals have worked to attain. Any behavior remotely resembling a tantrum, a need to control, or a holier-than-thou attitude will irreparably harm the influence they have achieved. It is precisely their humility that is their most attractive feature. Sometimes self-destructive behavior is merely their old pattern of rebelliousness rearing its ugly head. The need to rebel can also manifest itself as a kind of archconservatism, specifically as a defensive attitude that will not acknowledge mistakes or consider better ways to do things. Another pitfall for those on this path is the misuse of power. These individuals are seductive in the extreme, but any attempt to seduce others for amoral purposes of their own will result in nothing short of disaster. The same goes for any bending of the truth: even the hint of a lie can damage the hard-won reputations of those on this path. Scrupulous honesty is necessary, not simply to remain influential but to protect the individual's soul.

People tend to see these individuals as a bit wild in

SUGGESTION

Convince yourself that the rewards of a mature, measured approach far outweigh fantasies of freedom or lost youth.

youth, perhaps uncontrollable, and, as they evolve, less and less rough around the edges. Their more unsettling energies tend to stabilize as the years go by, and the need to seek "kicks" to alleviate boredom will gradually disappear. However, some family members and friends may exhibit a certain nostalgia about these individuals when they were younger and more vibrant and come to resent their controlling attitudes as they grow older. Not everyone will react positively to their increasing authority or charm, since some may see this as only a thinly disguised tool for manipulation. Furthermore, as their influence over others, in particular people in positions of greater power, grows, those on this karmic path will inevitably arouse envy in others, particularly in the workplace. Due to their irrepressible charm, the individuals on this path are completely capable of the task of managing and defusing the jealousy of others, but being aware that it exists is the first step.

Once the individuals on the Way of Influence move toward an increasing seriousness of purpose and the ownership of their own authority in their lives, some friends, lovers, and, perhaps, even their mate might be left behind. New partners, often people who share their more mature perspective, will inevitably emerge. Generally speaking, those on the Way of Influence would do best to seek out more self-sufficient people to spend their time with as they themselves take on more responsibilities. Relationships firmly based on a balance of

BALANCE POINT

Youthfulness and Maturity

power nourish the growth of those on this karmic path. There is no denying that these people will attract many hangers-on, and it is important for them not to permit others to become overdependent on them or to use them. Their attitude toward children and therefore their children's attitude toward them will also change, usually allowing them to become better parents, since they will grow out of their early reactivity and obsessiveness and become more authoritative, aloof, and wise.

The best thing for those on this karmic path is to have a close circle of friends. Few value friendships or enjoy them as fully as those on the Way of Influence. No matter what difficulties and disappointments those on this path encounter in relationships, particularly with family, mates, or colleagues, they will always be able to fall back on their friends for sympathy and support in time of need. In turn, they offer their friends some of their best qualities. In the long run, affection and empathy are better for them than turbulent romance.

The journey of the individuals on this path can be likened to that of a wild horse that has been captured and tamed. Though the horse must be broken to accept the saddle, if it is done properly, it doesn't lose its heart. Lovingly transformed from its wild state to one of domesticity, it ultimately develops a symbiotic relationship with its master. Even though tame, such a horse can exhibit a pride, stature, or bearing that commands not only respect or affection but reverence.

CRYSTALS AND GEMSTONES

Garnet adjusts the flow of energy within the inner pathways of the spinal column. This alignment "smooths" deep passions and convictions, allowing expression to be full, refined, and sound.

NOTABLES ON THIS KARMIC PATH

SPIKE LEE

Being born on the Way of Influence has meant that film director **Spike Lee** must confront the challenge of taming his passionate side and imposing limitations on himself. Through his films, Lee has effectively channeled his own rebellious spirit into highly nuanced, accurate, and creative visions of everyday life and, in the case of *Malcolm X,* the history of his people. As is typical of many on this karmic path, Lee has become increasingly serious in his artistic purpose and has therefore been taken more seriously by others.

Tiger Woods has emerged as one of the youngest individuals in golf to achieve world renown. Combining diligent training and unflappable calm, Woods exhibits the steady growth that is characteristic of this path. Aided by his natural skill, this maturation has brought him quickly to the top of his profession without great struggle or conflict. With his ease, modesty, and charm, Woods demonstrates how those on the Way of Influence can achieve their goals in a graceful and adult fashion.

TIGER WOODS

Extremely well grounded, Tiger Woods has been an influential example of a true champion.

Today show host **Katie Couric** has dazzled a generation with the combination of youthfulness and maturity that is the balance point of this karmic path. As is typical of many successful individuals on the Way of Influence, Couric combines spontaneity with sound judgment, and has exerted a tremendous influence on many Americans through her positive yet unforced approach. The public, in return, has shown great admiration for her courage in dealing with the tragic loss of her husband. Couric has emerged from this sorrowful process with a still deeper understanding of life's infinite meaning.

KATIE COURIC

Other Notables: Barbara Cartland, Vince Gill, "Coco" Chanel, Sue Mengers, Daniel Day-Lewis, Michele Pfeiffer, Gary Cooper, Frederick Loewe, Fanny Burney, Joyce Carol Oates, Barry Goldwater, Jr., Natalie Wood, Peter Jennings, Sam Goldwyn, Kenny Rogers, James Fenimore Cooper, Kate Winslet, John Dean, Bela Lugosi, N. C. Wyeth, Isaac Asimov, Alfred Stieglitz, Fernando Lamas, Mario Van Peebles, Federico Fellini, Princess Caroline of Monaco, Vanna White, Nicolas Copernicus, Eamon De Valera

BIRTHDAYS ON KARMIC PATH 8

July 24, 1882–December 12, 1882 | March 6, 1901–July 24, 1901 | October 16, 1919–March 5, 1920

May 27, 1938–October 15, 1938 | January 6, 1957–May 26, 1957 | August 18, 1975–January 6, 1976

March 29, 1994–August 17, 1994 | November 8, 2012–March 28, 2013

KARMIC PATH
8

March 19–24
REBIRTH
PISCES–ARIES CUSP

Learning the fine arts of tact and diplomacy will doubtless prove important as these individuals travel the Way of Influence. Blessed with great sensitivity and intuition, their goal will be to allow their empathy to better inform their manner of expression and presentation. Ultimately, this configuration will offer them greater steadiness and do much to allay the antagonism these souls can sometimes evoke with their overly straightforward approach to people and problems. If they can take up the task of managing their passions without succumbing to rigidity or the tendency to become tyrannical, these action-oriented souls can accomplish a great deal on this karmic path, that will manifest itself in material prosperity, considerable evolution toward a higher consciousness, and a fine integration of their physical, emotional, and intellectual aspects.

AMANDA PLUMMER
Daughter of Christopher Plummer; actress

3/23/1957
Pisces–Aries Cusp

CHALLENGE: **LEARNING TO OVERCOME THEIR OWN BRUSQUE MANNER**
FULFILLMENT: **FEELING THAT THEY ARE WELL LIKED**
NOTABLE: **SPIKE LEE (FILM WRITER/DIRECTOR)**

March 25–April 2
THE CHILD
ARIES I

These souls will doubtless confront their core issue of better managing their sometimes wild imaginations when traveling the Way of Influence. As children, they are likely to have a vivid, active fantasy life that should be channeled early on into creative, productive outlets. Though many of them will resist the maturation process required by this path, most will find themselves quite happy on this life's journey, provided they match their natural spontaneity with the ability to empathize and share with others. Too, a need to cultivate and appreciate a sense of timing is indicated, as these personalities are quite likely to "rush in where angels fear to tread." The impulse of Aries I's to isolate themselves or withdraw from society should be avoided, as too much time alone will interfere with their steady evolution. Still, this karmic path can do much to ground their fiery energies in practical reality, and if they take up the challenge of toning down their more extreme impulses, they can excel in careers that involve team effort and social interaction.

CHALLENGE: **EMBRACING MATURITY IN ALL ITS ASPECTS**
FULFILLMENT: **DISCOVERING THAT THEY ARE APPRECIATED**
NOTABLE: **WHITTAKER CHAMBERS (JOURNALIST/WRITER; SOVIET AGENT; LATER AN ANTI-COMMUNIST)**

April 3–10
THE STAR
ARIES II

The Way of Influence will do much to help fulfill the needs of those born in the Week of the Star, as it will doubtless put these personalities into life situations where they are afforded a wealth of attention and interaction. As a result, these souls are sure to learn how and why to refine their rougher edges from exposure to a wide variety of social and professional contacts. Likely to be highly successful and materially blessed, they will nonetheless encounter a bit of a struggle with issues of self-centeredness or selfishness and will have to work hard to develop the empathy and sympathy required by this karmic path. Still, there is little doubt that others will seek them out and be drawn to their energy, resources, and increasingly good business and creative sense. If they are careful to relish the attention without becoming tyrannical, complacent, or ego-centered in the extreme, these stars will truly shine brightly when traveling the Way of Influence.

PAUL REISER
Comedian, writer, actor, *Mad About You*

3/30/1957
Aries I

CHALLENGE: **RESISTING THE DEMANDS OF THEIR EGOS**
FULFILLMENT: **REFINING THEIR SOCIAL SKILLS**
NOTABLE: **MELVYN DOUGLAS (ACTOR)**

April 11–18
THE PIONEER
ARIES III

A rare combination of sociability and dynamism pervades the personalities of those born in this week, making their journey along the Way of Influence a pleasant one. Gifted with a natural generosity and empathy for others, they will nonetheless have to curb their tendency to become domineering as their influence grows. These pioneers will do well to develop a real degree of self-knowledge as early in life as they can or run the risk of succumbing to nostalgia and an increasing sense of detachment as time goes by. Passionate and provocative, these people will doubtless see their personal stars shine early in life as they conquer the frontiers of their chosen vocations. In fact, there is something of a *Wunderkind* aspect to this configuration, and the challenge for these souls will be to build on their early success while at the same time working to refine and augment their social and administrative skills in such a way that their influence continues to build.

CHALLENGE: **WORKING HARD TO OVERCOME THEIR DOMINEERING TENDENCIES**
FULFILLMENT: **CREATING A BROAD SOCIAL CIRCLE WITH THEMSELVES AT ITS CENTER**
NOTABLE: **VINCE GILL (COUNTRY SINGER/SONGWRITER)**

April 19–24

POWER
ARIES–TAURUS CUSP

Those born on the Cusp of Power who travel the Way of Influence are likely to consider themselves fortunate indeed. Gifted with a natural sense of timing, these people seem to know when to act and when not to act, and much of their journey will take place in the career area, resulting in considerable and sometimes even phenomenal success. They would do well, however to avoid an overemphasis on professional interests and take care to nurture the more personal sides of their passionate natures. Forming deep and lasting friendships with peers will prove especially beneficial to their higher spiritual awareness and help serve to protect them from the envy of others that this configuration can sometimes cause. Equality in relationships will prove important in any event, and Aries–Tauruses should take special care to choose only partners and close associates who are capable of the same potential for growth and success as themselves.

EMPEROR HIROHITO
Emperor of Japan

4/29/1901
Taurus I

CHALLENGE: **LEARNING TO DEAL WITH OTHERS' ENVY**
FULFILLMENT: **DEVELOPING THE ROLE OF QUIET DYNAMO BEHIND ANY VENTURE**
NOTABLE: **DANIEL DAY LEWIS (ACTOR; WON OSCAR FOR MY LEFT FOOT)**

April 25–May 2

MANIFESTATION
TAURUS I

Those born in the Week of Manifestation who find themselves on this karmic path will have the rare life experience of seeing their fondest hopes and dreams come to fruition. Yet along with their great potential for success, they will have to monitor themselves carefully for complacency, stubbornness, and the tendency to get increasingly lazy as their ambitions are fulfilled. Too, they may attract hangers-on or less-than-productive relationships. As their influence and charm mature, they can find themselves wasting their resources on people who don't contribute anything to their development or higher growth. A mistaken sense of loyalty should therefore be avoided, but not at the expense of personal compassion. Still, if Taurus I's can cultivate the necessary flexibility to guide their natural strength, their chances for both professional and personal success on this karmic path are excellent.

CHALLENGE: **TAKING EVERY PRECAUTION AGAINST BECOMING AN IMMOVABLE OBJECT AS OPPOSED TO A QUIET AUTHORITY**
FULFILLMENT: **ENJOYING THE ROLE OF MENTOR-MENTEE**
NOTABLE: **MICHELLE PFEIFFER (FILM ACTRESS)**

May 3–10

THE TEACHER
TAURUS II

The unique communication skills of those born in the Week of the Teacher will doubtless figure into their success. Highly attracted to the world of concepts and ideas, these individuals will almost certainly attain greater maturity and influence as they take up the challenge of refining and honing their ability to impart ideas. Though in youth, as they attempt to get their ideas across, they may put others off by a tendency to come on too strong or be too blunt, with time and experience they will gain a much better sense of how to share their views in such a way that they are not only readily understood but welcomed by a willing audience. Likely to rise to the pinnacle of success through entrepreneurial effort or the hierarchy of a business or educational organization, they may nonetheless find it difficult to develop and keep a network of loyal peers and trusted friends. They will have to make a special effort to avoid their tendency to view relationships with both love partners and children through a lens of Pygmalion-like superiority.

GARY COOPER
Film actor, *High Noon*
and *Sergeant York*

5/7/1901
Taurus II

CHALLENGE: **DEVELOPING RELATIONSHIPS BASED ON EQUALITY**
FULFILLMENT: **LEADING BY EXAMPLE**
NOTABLES: **PHIL MAHRE AND STEVE MAHRE (TWIN BROTHERS; OLYMPIC SKIERS)**

May 11–18

THE NATURAL
TAURUS III

Taurus III's on the Way of Influence may find themselves with a nostalgia for simpler times or ways of living that they in fact may never actually have experienced. As a result, they are likely to struggle a bit with the constraints and challenges presented on their life's journey and get mired in frustration or rebellion against the rules and means of developing a more complex or mature lifestyle. It will be best for them to balance their professional interests with participation in outdoor sports or hobbies such as gardening, which will give them the sense of staying connected to the natural world without hindering their advancement or professional goals. Finally, cultivating the ability to better deal with authority will be especially important, as this karmic path will surely demand that they themselves assume leadership roles as they progress along the road.

CHALLENGE: **RELEASING THEIR NOSTALGIC LONGING FOR THEIR YOUTH**
FULFILLMENT: **OVERCOMING INSECURITY AS THEY ACHIEVE SUCCESS BY FOLLOWING SOCIETY'S MORE TRADITIONAL RULES**

May 19–24
ENERGY
TAURUS–GEMINI CUSP

Those born on the Cusp of Energy will have to be careful on the Way of Influence not to burn themselves out during a truly reckless youth. Dynamic and even aggressive at times, they will have to work to manage their energy in such a way as to time their actions for the greatest efficacy or even to avoid action altogether in the interest of attaining longer-term objectives. Cultivating good work habits will do much to augment their potential for success, as will applying their naturally brilliant intellects to a study of structure and perhaps management theories and planning systems. Once the importance of such concepts has been grasped and, hopefully, applied to their goals and pursuits, these quick studies may very well experience an almost meteoric rise to a position of influence and recognition. Maintaining that position, however, will require patience, a sense of timing, and continuing contact with a select group of loyal friends and advisers who can help to guide them along this most interesting journey.

CHALLENGE: **REINING IN THEIR MORE EXCESSIVE IMPULSES**
FULFILLMENT: **DEVELOPING THE ENDURANCE TO ACHIEVE THEIR AIMS**

JEFFERSON DAVIS
President of the
Confederate States of
America 1861–65

6/3/1808
Gemini II

May 25–June 2
FREEDOM
GEMINI I

Boredom is not likely to be a problem for Gemini I's who find themselves on the Way of Influence. Though they may chafe at the demands and responsibilities imposed by this karmic path, they will nonetheless enjoy the journey more than most. Yet if they are to realize their full potential, they must work at toning down their sometimes abrasive personae and cultivating empathy for those with whom they work and play. Irritability and a low frustration threshold may fire their rebellious side, and they should be aware of their tendency to "shoot first and ask questions later," especially since their weapons are chosen from a well-stocked verbal arsenal. Still, they will doubtless rise in the world, especially when they apply their natural charms to the task of achieving tangible goals and objectives and avoid employing those same charms for manipulative or selfish ends.

CHALLENGE: **DISCOVERING THE INNER FREEDOM THAT COMES WITH MATURITY AND COMMITMENT**
FULFILLMENT: **APPRECIATING THE GROUNDEDNESS OF A LIFE LIVED RESPONSIBLY**
NOTABLE: **PETER YARROW (FOLKSINGER, PETER, PAUL, AND MARY)**

June 3–10
NEW LANGUAGE
GEMINI II

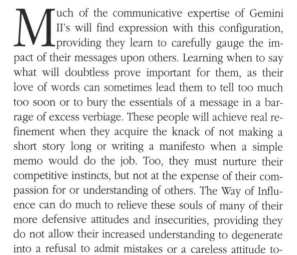

Much of the communicative expertise of Gemini II's will find expression with this configuration, providing they learn to carefully gauge the impact of their messages upon others. Learning when to say what will doubtless prove important for them, as their love of words can sometimes lead them to tell too much too soon or to bury the essentials of a message in a barrage of excess verbiage. These people will achieve real refinement when they acquire the knack of not making a short story long or writing a manifesto when a simple memo would do the job. Too, they must nurture their competitive instincts, but not at the expense of their compassion for or understanding of others. The Way of Influence can do much to relieve these souls of many of their more defensive attitudes and insecurities, providing they do not allow their increased understanding to degenerate into a refusal to admit mistakes or a careless attitude toward their own achievements.

CHALLENGE: **ATTEMPTING TO COMMUNICATE ALONG MORE TRADITIONAL LINES**
FULFILLMENT: **HAVING A COMMANDING PHYSICAL PRESENCE**
NOTABLE: **FREDERICK LOEWE (COMPOSER OF BRIGADOON)**

FANNY BURNEY
Novelist, diarist

6/13/1752
Gemini III

June 11–18
THE SEEKER
GEMINI III

Blessed with natural subtlety and considerable charm, those born in the Week of the Seeker who travel this karmic path will doubtless have a far easier time of it than most. Perhaps the only real danger of this configuration lies in a tendency to become too controlling and manipulative as time goes by. Whatever their professional or career area, these souls must work to develop their more compassionate side and take care to stay in touch with others' needs, for their ability to grow into effective managers and move into positions of authority may well depend on it. Though many of these souls may at first resist the restrictions that the Way of Influence seems to place on their sense of personal freedom, they should find the material and spiritual rewards of this configuration well suited to their natural sense of adventure and their unique ability to push beyond their limits in their quest for personal success and spiritual expansion.

CHALLENGE: **STICKING TO THE TASK AT HAND**
FULFILLMENT: **HAVING THE INFLUENCE TO SHARE THEIR BROADER VIEWS**
NOTABLE: **JOYCE CAROL OATES (POET; WRITER)**

June 19–24

MAGIC
GEMINI–CANCER CUSP

Gemini–Cancers are likely to flourish on the Way of Influence, as they will find it relatively easy to tap into the watery and often seductive energies of this karmic path. Their ability to attract and even enchant others with their unique blend of logic and feeling will serve them especially well, and they are likely to find considerable success in almost any area of endeavor. Their tendency to selfishness can become pronounced as time goes on, however, and they would do well to stay in touch with others' needs. Some of these people may hold themselves back from higher development by refusing to let go of outmoded relationships in both the personal and professional arenas, while others will have to confront lifelong issues surrounding the overidealization of a parent before they can successfully assume the mantle of authority or become parents themselves.

CHALLENGE: **LETTING GO OF A CERTAIN AMOUNT OF ROMANTICISM IN ORDER TO MATURE**

FULFILLMENT: **DEVELOPING THE CAPACITY TO ENCHANT OTHERS**

NELSON EDDY,
seen here with
Jeanette MacDonald;
popular baritone

6/29/1901
Cancer I

June 25–July 2

THE EMPATH
CANCER I

Cancer I empaths can be in for a bit of a rough ride early in life and may have to go through a considerable process of maturation before they conquer their sense of frustration and rebelliousness. Cultivating objectivity and setting boundaries will be critical to their success; too often their extreme sensitivity will prove something of a liability until they gain the necessary perspective and sophistication to be able to manage people and problems effectively without becoming too emotionally involved. Still, this configuration is likely to lead to a great deal of material success and recognition, as it will provide these souls with many opportunities to exercise their keen financial sense, especially in the investment area. If they can control their aggression and avoid their tendency to try to fulfill their emotional needs through material means, they are likely to go far.

CHALLENGE: **FORCING THEMSELVES TO EMERGE FROM THEIR SELF-IMPOSED COCOON AND BE IN THE WORLD**

FULFILLMENT: **ACHIEVING CAREER SUCCESS**

July 3–10

THE UNCONVENTIONAL
CANCER II

These unconventional people will doubtless have a fascinating journey along the Way of Influence, especially in the areas of spiritual and extrasensory exploration. Gifted with great psychic ability, they should nevertheless be careful that their attraction to the darker side of existence does not subsume their other priorities. They are likely to be quite rebellious early in life; their adult identities may be shaped by unfortunate or even bizarre events, and they will have to avoid lapsing into emotional instability and an increasing sense of isolation as a result. Still, if they channel their energies into productive habits and allow their imaginative and creative lives to interact with the workaday world, their karmic path can take some surprising and successful turns.

CHALLENGE: **PUTTING THE BRAKES ON THEIR WILD SIDE**

FULFILLMENT: **AS THEIR INFLUENCE GROWS, SHARING THEIR DREAMS WITH OTHERS**

NOTABLE: **BARBARA CARTLAND (PROLIFIC BRITISH ROMANCE NOVELIST)**

JERRY RUBIN
Activist and author, anti-
war organizer, "Yippie"
founder

7/14/1938
Cancer III

July 11–18

THE PERSUADER
CANCER III

Blessed with a natural sense of timing and keen powers of observation, these gifted personalities are sure to find considerable, even phenomenal, success on the Way of Influence. These souls already know how to get others to do their bidding and will readily assume the positions of authority and leadership promised by this karmic path. Further, they are well suited to the kind of everyday social contacts and commitments that are part of life. These hard-driving, ambitious souls will, however, have to be on guard against a tendency to become ruthless or overly manipulative as they rise in the world, as well as a propensity to isolate themselves in service to their sense of position. Close friends, family, and trusted advisers will be especially important here, as they will both provide the necessary emotional connections and serve to remind Cancer III's that all work and no play can make them dull boys and girls indeed.

CHALLENGE: **BEING CONTENT WITH EXERTING BEHIND-THE-SCENES INFLUENCE**

FULFILLMENT: **HAVING THE OPPORTUNITY TO USE THEIR NATURAL GIFTS OF PERSUASION**

July 19–25

OSCILLATION
CANCER–LEO CUSP

Cancer–Leos who find themselves on the Way of Influence will be gifted with a greater sense of personal and emotional stability than many of their fellows born on this cusp and will doubtless enjoy personal recognition and a degree of material security as well. The key will be to find the specific means of grounding their excitable natures early on and to avoid the pitfalls that go with a youthful sense of rebellion. In any event, extremes in mood and behavior will show up from time to time, and these souls will have to work hard to regulate their emotions to the point where they do not put others off, thus interfering with their ambitions and goals. As they learn to relinquish the need to chase after adventure or excitement and instead allow the excitement to come to them, they will relish the attention and increasing sense of personal power that are part of this karmic path.

NATALIE WOOD
Film actress; drowned

7/20/1938
Cancer–Leo Cusp

CHALLENGE: **REGULATING THEIR MOOD SWINGS AND OTHER ERRATIC BEHAVIOR**
FULFILLMENT: **EXPERIENCING THE SECURITY THAT MATURITY BRINGS**
NOTABLES: **JANET RENO (U.S. ATTORNEY GENERAL); DIANA RIGG (ACTRESS)**

July 26–August 2

AUTHORITY
LEO I

Learning to distinguish the subtle difference between leadership and domination will prove critical to the success of Leo I's on the Way of Influence. These individuals have a pronounced tendency to become preoccupied with their personal goals and ambitions, and many of them will have to learn, through trial and error, the various repercussions of riding roughshod over others in both the personal and professional areas of life. It's more than likely that these driven individuals will realize many of their dreams and ambitions, if only because they are willing to work harder than anyone else to attain them. Yet this karmic path will also demand that they develop compassion and empathy for others, as well as the ability to express their authority in a more refined or seductive way. Should these tough customers fail to take up that challenge, they may see their influence dissipate with alarming speed.

CHALLENGE: **GIVING UP THEIR HARD-DRIVING APPROACH IN FAVOR OF ONE THAT IS MORE SUBTLE**
FULFILLMENT: **WINNING THE RESPECT AND ADMIRATION OF OTHERS**
NOTABLES: **ALBERTO FUJIMORO (PRESIDENT OF PERU); HERBERT IVES (PHYSICIST; HELPED DEVELOP TELEVISION)**

August 3–10

BALANCED STRENGTH
LEO II

Though Leo II's are capable of rising to almost any challenge, those who travel the Way of Influence may nevertheless have to face down a number of personal demons before they can experience the degree of success and recognition for their efforts that is promised by this karmic path. Many of them will resist the challenge of developing a greater degree of sophistication and charm, believing such efforts to be pretentious or unnecessary, while others may choose to exercise their influence in a narrow sphere or content themselves with being a "big fish in a little pond," to the detriment of their higher development and their greater potential. Fiercely loyal, they must also avoid a tendency to be rather masochistic or to tie themselves to overdependent or unworthy associates out of a misguided sense of fidelity. Nonetheless, their chances of success are considerable, and with time, training, and a willingness to relinquish their stubbornness, Leo II's can flourish on this life's journey.

PETER JENNINGS
TV anchorman;
Canadian born

7/29/1938
Leo I

CHALLENGE: **CONVINCING THEMSELVES THAT IT'S NOT A CRIME TO LET A RELATIONSHIP RUN ITS COURSE**
FULFILLMENT: **ALLOWING THEMSELVES TO BE LOVED ONCE IN A WHILE**
NOTABLE: **CONNIE STEVENS (ACTRESS)**

August 11–18

LEADERSHIP
LEO III

Leo III's are likely to find themselves well suited to the demands and challenges of the Way of Influence. Blessed with a good sense of timing and perspective as regards their personal goals and ambitions, they are willing to wait for the right moment of opportunity. Their tendency to overaggression or rebelliousness will doubtless abate with time and experience, freeing them to channel their energies into highly productive, creative, and often financially rewarding careers. Charismatic and well respected as a rule, they must take care not to go overboard or to become rigid or dictatorial as their influence increases. Though they have a pronounced disposition to be rather selfish, the scope of their dreams can more than make up for any lack of deep personal ties. Once they have formed friendships, however, they are intensely loyal and able to channel not just their own energies but those of others into extraordinarily productive group efforts.

CHALLENGE: **LETTING GO OF SELF-CENTEREDNESS**
FULFILLMENT: **DONNING THE MANTLE OF AUTHORITY THEY ALWAYS KNEW WAS THEIR DUE**
NOTABLES: **SAM GOLDWYN (COFOUNDED MGM STUDIOS); DASH CROFTS (SINGER, MUSICIAN, SEALS AND CROFTS)**

KARMIC PATH
8

August 19–25

EXPOSURE
LEO–VIRGO CUSP

Some interesting revelations should serve to color the lives and careers of Leo–Virgos on the Way of Influence. Cultivating a sense of timing as regards the telling of their own and others' secrets will doubtless be called for on this karmic path. They may have much to learn about the management of information before the recognition and position of influence promised by this path becomes available to them. Too, they may experience some unpleasant or uncomfortable confrontations with the specters of their own past experiences, especially if their youthful rebellion manifested itself in questionable activities or associations. Still, being someone of quiet authority suits them well. If they take care to cultivate a willingness to trust and to make themselves worthy of trust in return, their natural charisma and flamboyance will prove great assets on this life's journey.

**LUDWIG II,
KING OF BAVARIA**
King; patron of
composer Wagner

8/25/1845
Leo–Virgo Cusp

CHALLENGE: **CULTIVATING A NEAR-PERFECT SENSE OF TIMING
THEIR REVELATIONS**
FULFILLMENT: **BEING KNOWN FOR STRENGTH OF CHARACTER**
NOTABLE: **KENNY ROGERS (COUNTRY SINGER)**

August 26–September 2

SYSTEM BUILDERS
VIRGO I

Unlikely to be troubled by the youthful wildness that plagues many fellow travelers on the Way of Influence, Virgo I's will nevertheless face their share of challenges on this karmic path. Stubbornness can be a problem, as can rigidity or a tendency to ultraconservatism as they progress in years. Nonetheless, these often introverted types can really expand in confidence and the ability to share as their concentrated and disciplined efforts are recognized and they gain the influence promised by this path. Accordingly, gaining financial rewards and assuming a role of authority will renew their confidence and sense of self, resulting in a wider vision and greater perspective on the patterns and systems that give structure to our lives. If they are careful to cultivate a select social circle of loyal friends with whom they can indulge their considerable sense of humor and zanier impulses, they can achieve a fine balance between work and play and find great fulfillment on their journey.

CHALLENGE: **MATURING BY MANAGING THEIR EMOTIONAL
NEEDS TO BETTER EFFECT**
FULFILLMENT: **HAVING A VOICE IN HOW THINGS ARE DONE**
NOTABLES: **SUE MENGERS (HOLLYWOOD AGENT); MAXINE
WATERS (U.S. REPRESENTATIVE); ELLIOT GOULD (ACTOR)**

September 3–10

THE ENIGMA
VIRGO II

Those born in the Week of the Enigma are likely to find themselves beautifully suited to the demands and challenges of this karmic path. Blessed with natural dignity and a sense of refinement, they will not have to work very hard to smooth their rougher edges and may even leave home early, particularly if such a move puts them into better touch with the finer things in life. Yet they may encounter some difficulty with issues of flexibility and their own high standards once they assume a leadership role, for not many can live up to their high expectations. The daily social contact and interaction required by this karmic path will be of great benefit to these people, however, and as they gain confidence and influence, their exposure to others will afford them great opportunities to cultivate empathy, compassion, and the ability to open themselves to others.

**JAMES FENIMORE
COOPER**
Early American fiction
writer

9/15/1789
Virgo III

CHALLENGE: **LOWERING THEIR STANDARDS TO MORE MAN-
AGEABLE LEVELS**
FULFILLMENT: **USING HUMOR TO WIN OTHERS OVER**
NOTABLE: **CARYL CHURCHILL (DRAMATIST)**

September 11–18

THE LITERALIST
VIRGO III

Virgo III's who find themselves on this karmic path may have a great deal to wrestle with as they come to reconcile their own stubborn, willful side with their need to expand and exert their power. On the one hand, inflexibility can hinder their chances for success, while on the other, a preoccupation with preserving harmony can erode their influence. Their tendency to become judgmental or even suspicious of others may increase over time, and these folks will benefit greatly from tempering their shrewdness with a measure of compassion. Further, some will have to avoid a tendency to keep troubled relationships alive out of a misplaced sense of loyalty and learn to gently offload those who would impede their progress. Still these practical, bottom-line people can go far on this road, providing they learn to distinguish adequately between refinement and pretension, as well as to grasp the fine art of learning to accept their own success with grace and élan.

CHALLENGE: **ACCEPTING THAT NOT ALL TRUTHS NEED TO BE
TOLD**
FULFILLMENT: **CREATING MORE HARMONY IN THEIR LIVES**
NOTABLE: **GAYLORD PERRY (AMERICAN LEAGUE BASEBALL
PITCHER)**

September 19–24

BEAUTY
VIRGO–LIBRA CUSP

Those born on the Cusp of Beauty who travel this karmic path are likely to be blessed creatures indeed. Their natural sense of beauty and refinement can lend a whole new meaning to the phrase "a charmed life," and if they are careful to avoid the complacency that sometimes comes with success, their influence can spread far and wide. The gifts of this path can ground their idealism in practical realities, while the goals of their life's journey will doubtless serve to illuminate and enhance their self-knowledge and spirituality. Though there is some danger that they will collapse into an excess of sensuality or come to depend solely on others to convey them to their higher destinations, there is a far greater probability that their natural style, ease of expression, and great sensitivity will find tasteful, creative outlets, resulting not only in material security but in the admiration of a host of devoted followers.

REX REED
Film critic

10/2/1938
Libra I

CHALLENGE: **CULTIVATING A MORE MATURE VIEWPOINT**
FULFILLMENT: **KNOWING THAT OTHERS DO NOT VIEW THEM AS SUPERFICIAL**

September 25–October 2

THE PERFECTIONIST
LIBRA I

Intense frustration can mark the passages of Libra I's on the Way of Influence until they relinquish their compulsion to seek out and fix the problems of the world and grasp the wisdom of the adage "Never borrow trouble." These people will almost certainly struggle with issues of authority for much of the early part of their lives, yet their early rebellions may only be a smoke screen for indecisiveness or deep-seated insecurity. Still, if they can harness their intensity and make a concerted effort to channel it toward the achievement of realizable goals, they can make considerable strides in whatever field they choose and gain respect as true achievers— even overachievers—in that field. Once their need for control is assuaged by their increasing influence over others, they can begin to exert their powers in more productive, less critical ways.

CHALLENGE: **DEVELOPING THE MATURITY TO ACCEPT IMPERFECTION**
FULFILLMENT: **BEING ABLE TO EFFECT CHANGE**

October 3–10

SOCIETY
LIBRA II

Those born in the Week of Society who find themselves on this karmic path are blessed indeed. They are all but sure to find an easy road to its promised rewards, even though they may struggle at times with a tendency to spread themselves rather thin or to become preoccupied with matters of taste, sensual issues, or an overemphasis on appearances, to the detriment of deeper awareness and development. Still, this configuration imparts considerable practicality to Libra II's, and though they may turn their backs on their early environment without so much as a backward glance, their talent for diplomacy, conversational skills, and natural compassion will serve them well. If they avoid the dangers of self-deception and learn to both trust and hone their intuitive skills, their chances for success are considerable.

KATE WINSLET
Film actress, *Titanic*

10/5/1975
Libra II

CHALLENGE: **TEMPERING THE EXPRESSION OF THEIR OFTEN SHARP AND CRITICAL INSIGHTS**
FULFILLMENT: **FILLING THE ROLE OF CONFIDANT**
NOTABLE: **ROBERT GODDARD ("FATHER" OF MODERN ROCKETRY)**

October 11–18

THEATER
LIBRA III

The life journey of the personalities who travel this karmic path is likely to bring some considerable notoriety, along with the potential for personal and spiritual fulfillment. Though they may be quite driven at times, their natural ambition will doubtless find an outlet as they assume the roles of authority and leadership promised by this path. They must take care, however, not to overemphasize the role of image in their rise to positions of influence, as more than any other karmic path, this one demands that the authority granted be backed by real talent. Those born in the Week of Theater will relish the attention, as well as the chance to wield their influence over others. If they take care not to become ego-centered and learn to admit their mistakes, they are sure to respond beautifully to both the challenges and the promises of this karmic journey.

CHALLENGE: **NOT OVEREMPHASIZING IMAGE OR THE SUPERFICIAL**
FULFILLMENT: **OPERATING ON A LARGER STAGE**
NOTABLE: **JOHN DEAN (COUNSEL TO PRESIDENT NIXON; JAILED FOR ROLE IN WATERGATE)**

KARMIC PATH
8

October 19–25

DRAMA AND CRITICISM
LIBRA–SCORPIO CUSP

Libra–Scorpios who travel the Way of Influence are gifted with both unusual brilliance and the ability to express themselves with an often stunning clarity. They will, however, have to cultivate and control their wilder side if they are to achieve the heights of influence and recognition promised by this karmic path. Sensuous and often passionate, these personalities will blossom in the spotlight but may manifest a certain carelessness with others, especially lovers and mates. Promiscuity or a string of broken relationships can result as these souls search for equality and growth potential in their associates. Still, if these remarkable and gifted individuals can form a strong network of reasonable and understanding friends and coworkers who can serve as a support system, they will be able to avoid the dangers of alienation or misanthropy and learn to wield their special powers with sureness, clarity, and wisdom.

BELA LUGOSI
Stage/film actor, *Dracula*

10/20/1882
Libra–Scorpio Cusp

CHALLENGE: **STRUGGLING TO TAME THEIR WILDER SIDE**
FULFILLMENT: **BEING GIVEN A PULPIT FROM WHICH THEY MAY SHARE THEIR VIEWS**
NOTABLE: **DORIS LESSING (AUTHOR)**

October 26–November 2

INTENSITY
SCORPIO I

Blessed with formidable powers of concentration and self-discipline, Scorpio I's are likely to find themselves quite happy on the Way of Influence. Yet a certain suspicion and tendency to become judgmental may color their life experience and prevent them from realizing the full potential of this configuration. Frustration can be a stumbling block, and they will have to work hard to integrate patience and compassion into their dealings with others or run the risk of becoming dictatorial and even tyrannical as they get older. These souls could well find themselves in the unenviable position of commanding respect yet failing to evoke the love or concern of their peers, their associates, and perhaps even their children. Yet this configuration will do much to help mellow their sometimes difficult, demanding natures, and if they are careful to cultivate their sense of humor along with their natural virtuosity, their potential for success is limitless.

CHALLENGE: **LEARNING TO BE LESS JUDGMENTAL EVEN AS THEY LEARN TO TAKE CRITICISM THEMSELVES**
FULFILLMENT: **DEVELOPING THEIR SEDUCTIVE CHARM TO THE POINT OF HIGH ART**
NOTABLE: **N. C. WYETH (PAINTER, BOOK ILLUSTRATOR)**

November 3–11

DEPTH
SCORPIO II

It's difficult to gauge just how far the influence of these profound personalities will go as they travel this karmic path, but it is likely to be considerable. Blessed with great understanding and the tenacity necessary to achieve both spiritual and material goals, they may nevertheless have to work beyond their feelings of jealousy and envy, perhaps only to have them return once they have realized their fondest dreams. Serious and success-oriented, these steadfast souls are unlikely to find any obstacle insurmountable in their quest for greater worldly power, yet they should devote equal concern to finding and maintaining a close circle of intimates with whom they can share their innermost feelings and insights. Positions of authority and leadership will come quite naturally to these fine administrators, yet they will nevertheless find that their greatest power rests in their ability to touch the hearts and minds of their admirers and associates on a deep, even subliminal level.

SHAH OF IRAN
Iranian leader; exiled in 1979 when Khomeini came into power

10/26/1919
Scorpio I

CHALLENGE: **LETTING GO OF THE MANY CHIPS ON THEIR SHOULDERS**
FULFILLMENT: **ACHIEVING A GREAT EARNING POTENTIAL THROUGH INFLUENCE**

November 12–18

CHARM
SCORPIO III

Great good fortune awaits those born in the Week of Charm who find themselves on this karmic path. Blessed with a strong sense of who they are and where they want to go, Scorpio III's will doubtless reach their personal destinations with flair and flawless timing. The principal danger of this configuration is a tendency to rest on their laurels or to fail to realize their true potential, simply because things have a way of coming to them easily. Some in this group may have to resolve their inner emotional conflicts or addictive patterns of behavior before they can free themselves to reach their highest levels of achievement. Still, the promise of material, spiritual, and intellectual fulfillment is clear, and it is doubtful that these powerful souls will take many wrong turns along the way.

CHALLENGE: **HOLDING ON TO SPONTANEITY AND NATURALNESS OF APPROACH**
FULFILLMENT: **RISKING REVEALING THEMSELVES TO OTHERS**
NOTABLE: **JOSEPH WAPNER (JUDGE, TELEVISION PERSONALITY, *THE PEOPLE'S COURT*)**

November 19–24

REVOLUTION
SCORPIO–SAGITTARIUS CUSP

Rebelliousness and an inherent fondness for stirring things up will have to be kept in careful check by those born in the Week of Revolution who travel this spiritual road. At their most constructive, they will prove to be dynamic, resourceful people who are capable of taking the helm of almost any business or entrepreneurial endeavor. At their worst, they can get mired in an explosive, often abrasive attitude that will alienate those who could do them the most good. Still, these goal- and success-oriented people derive real delight from seeing their dreams and plans come to fruition and are promised no little achievement on this karmic path, provided they keep in mind that there is little point in tearing down the traditions of the past unless one has a plan for the future.

EVELYN KEYES
1940s film actress

11/20/1919
Scorpio–Sagittarius Cusp

CHALLENGE: **DEVELOPING THE MATURITY TO RESIST TURNING EVERYTHING ONTO ITS SIDE**
FULFILLMENT: **HAVING THE INFLUENCE TO EXPLODE MYTHS AND CHANGE STRUCTURES FOR THE BETTER**

November 25–December 2

INDEPENDENCE
SAGITTARIUS I

Issues of loyalty and fairness can be real sticking points for Sagittarius I's when placed on the Way of Influence, and they will doubtless face the sometimes painful reality of having to let go of misplaced alliances before they can realize the true potential of this karmic path. Learning to slow their pace and adequately measure the responses of others will serve them well, as will strengthening their intuition and timing their actions accordingly. While extending their circle of influence beyond one or two intimates may prove difficult for them, society will be better off for having been exposed to their special brand of loyalty and honor. Still, as they learn to curb their natural impulsiveness and cultivate a wide range of social and professional contacts, their perspective will broaden in such a way as to augment their sense of freedom, while at the same time gaining them an in-depth, sophisticated sense of values.

CHALLENGE: **STAYING PUT RATHER THEN RUNNING WHEN THEY FEEL INSECURE**
FULFILLMENT: **SHARING THEIR VALUE SYSTEMS WITH A BROADER AUDIENCE**
NOTABLE: **ANN COX CHAMBERS (U.S. AMBASSADOR TO BELGIUM, 1977–1981)**

December 3–10

THE ORIGINATOR
SAGITTARIUS II

Blessed with stunning originality and a sense of adventure, these souls can truly change the world as they travel the Way of Influence, provided they don't fail to take up the challenges of this karmic path. They will have to work hard to learn the value of refining their presentation in order to get their ideas across better, but once they do, the result will be astonishing. Their ability simply to "do their own thing" will be a great asset, though they will have to take some care to cultivate a stronger sense of confidence and personal identity and not to act out of needing to impress. Frustration and a rather wild streak can show up here, yet if Sagittarius II's can master the art of channeling their passions into a particular talent or professional endeavor, their spiritual, financial, and personal rewards will be quite surprising both to themselves and to everyone else.

ARCHDUKE FRANZ FERDINAND
His assassination precipitated WWI

12/18/1863
Sagittarius III

CHALLENGE: **OVERCOMING THEIR FEAR OF BEING REJECTED FOR BEING DIFFERENT**
FULFILLMENT: **BEING COMPLETELY COMFORTABLE IN THEMSELVES**

December 11–18

THE TITAN
SAGITTARIUS III

Those born in the Week of the Titan who travel the Way of Influence are blessed with a capacity not only to dream the impossible dream but to bring that dream to realization. Sometimes taking on too much, these individuals would do well to allow themselves to be spontaneous once in a while. This truly fortunate configuration promises success of blockbuster proportions, but only if these personalities first succeed in conquering the tendency to agonize about or overwork problems to the point where the solutions cease to be relevant, resulting in missed opportunities and frustrations of all sorts. Increasing their self-awareness will be important to realizing their biggest dreams and plans, as will the ability to choose their friends and associates carefully, for Sagittarius III's are destined to learn much about the ways of charm and seduction from those to whom they give their hearts.

CHALLENGE: **GRAPPLING WITH THEIR DARKER MOODS**
FULFILLMENT: **SEEING THE FRUITION OF THEIR PROJECTS**

December 19–25

PROPHECY
SAGITTARIUS–CAPRICORN CUSP

These personalities will most likely experience a number of personal transformations on this karmic path. Fun-loving and unconstrained in their early years, they will doubtless grow more serious and more self-possessed as they grow older. Well suited to the demands of the Way of Influence, those born on the Cusp of Prophecy are sure to attain their highest goals and aspirations, provided they do not succumb to frustration or their tendency to be high-handed and even autocratic once they have assumed the position of authority promised by this karmic path. Getting in touch with their deepest needs and exploring the resources of their own intuition will be critical to developing their sense of timing. Yet these remarkable people will benefit greatly by maintaining a select and discriminating group of friends who can guide them along their journey, nurture their social side, and give them the measure of support and love they require to attain their personal best.

CHALLENGE: **AVOIDING BECOMING TOO SERIOUS OR EVEN OLD BEFORE THEIR TIME**
FULFILLMENT: **UTILIZING THEIR INTUITION AS THEY INFLUENCE OTHERS**

ISAAC ASIMOV
Science fiction author

1/2/1920
Capricorn I

December 26–January 2

THE RULER
CAPRICORN I

Natural leaders and administrators, Capricorn I's are blessed indeed. Remarkably shrewd and honest to a fault, these individuals are sure to flourish with this configuration and are not likely to be encumbered by the issues of wildness or restlessness that can plague some of their fellow travelers on this karmic path. Though frustration and a tendency to get mired in tradition at the expense of expansion and growth can be problems, it is likely that Capricorn I's will spend their time more wisely than most, first in the development of professional skills and acumen, then in the ability to await opportunities for advancement and recognition in quiet certainty. Once they assume mantle of authority indicated by the Way of Influence, it is likely to be a fine fit, resulting in a handsome income, wonderful efficiency, and a highly developed sense of justice and responsibility.

CHALLENGE: **DISTINGUISHING BETWEEN BEING A RULER AND BEING A LEADER**
FULFILLMENT: **MASTERING THE SKILLS NEEDED TO SERVE AS AN EXAMPLE TO OTHERS**
NOTABLE: **TIGER WOODS (GOLFER)**

January 3–9

DETERMINATION
CAPRICORN II

An aura of spirituality can color even the most mundane business dealings of Capricorn II's. Well prepared with the breadth of vision and self-sufficiency necessary to this karmic path, these ambitious people nevertheless have a theoretical turn of mind that allows them to see beyond the constraints of the moment. Thus, issues of frustration and rebelliousness are not likely to be especially troublesome, though these souls must nevertheless guard against allowing an excess of personal sensitivity or becoming mired in a sense of disillusionment and disappointment when things don't go their way. A refusal to admit their own mistakes can also be a real stumbling block. Yet once they master the distinction between true ideals and naïveté, their progress along this karmic path will be swift and sure, populated with loyal friends, staunch admirers, and loving families.

CHALLENGE: **DEVELOPING THE CAPACITY TO MOVE ON IN RELATIONSHIPS**
FULFILLMENT: **BEING IN A POSITION TO TEST THEIR SOMETIMES RADICAL IDEAS**
NOTABLE: **KATIE COURIC (TELEVISION JOURNALIST, COANCHOR OF *TODAY* SHOW)**

ALFRED STIEGLITZ
Photographer/curator;
promoted photography as
fine art

1/1/1864
Capricorn I

January 10–16

DOMINANCE
CAPRICORN III

Family issues that revolve around a parent may figure prominently on the life journey of Capricorn III's as they navigate the Way of Influence. Early rebelliousness against a strict or dominant upbringing may manifest itself here, only to be replaced by resentment or even envy of those early repressors as Capricorn III's come into their own. Their tendency to be overly self-sacrificing to the detriment of their higher development should be studiously avoided, and many of these personalities will benefit greatly from learning to set boundaries, sometimes with professional help. As they mature, though, these personalities may work hard to enhance their ability to accept people as they are, thereby avoiding the danger of being too demanding of themselves and others. As a result of taking up these challenges, they will likely experience both worldly success and the higher spiritual gift of having made peace with themselves.

CHALLENGE: **OVERCOMING THEIR NEED TO PROVE THEY ARE WORTHY**
FULFILLMENT: **DEVELOPING SELF-CONFIDENCE**
NOTABLE: **MARIO VAN PEEBLES (WRITER/DIRECTOR/ACTOR)**

January 17–22
MYSTERY AND IMAGINATION
CAPRICORN–AQUARIUS CUSP

FEDERICO FELLINI
Italian film director
――――
1/20/1920
Capricorn–Aquarius Cusp

Prone to generating a certain amount of excitement, these sometimes eccentric souls may have something of a wild ride when placed on the Way of Influence. At worst, their rebelliousness may manifest in a chronic tendency to shoot themselves in the foot before they can realize their goals or to seize on boredom or frustration as an excuse to abandon even their best-laid plans. At best, however, they can learn to regulate and mediate their sometimes chaotic energies in such a way as to breathe new life into projects, structures, and organizations and radically change the way other people think about even mundane situations and problems. Friends and close associates may be their salvation, as social contacts and concerns will certainly bring out the best in Capricorn–Aquarians and serve to stabilize and smooth their life's journey.

CHALLENGE: **MARSHALING THEIR CHAOTIC ENERGIES**
FULFILLMENT: **SEEING HOW THEIR INFLUENCE BENEFITS OTHERS**
NOTABLES: **GEENA DAVIS (OSCAR-WINNING ACTRESS); DeFOREST KELLY (TV ACTOR, "BONES" IN** STAR TREK**)**

January 31–February 7
YOUTH AND EASE
AQUARIUS II

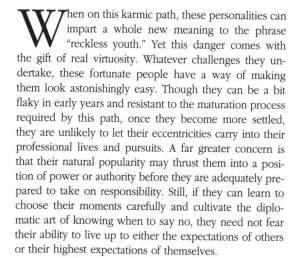

AN WANG
Wang computer founder
――――
2/7/1920
Aquarius II

When on this karmic path, these personalities can impart a whole new meaning to the phrase "reckless youth." Yet this danger comes with the gift of real virtuosity. Whatever challenges they undertake, these fortunate people have a way of making them look astonishingly easy. Though they can be a bit flaky in early years and resistant to the maturation process required by this path, once they become more settled, they are unlikely to let their eccentricities carry into their professional lives and pursuits. A far greater concern is that their natural popularity may thrust them into a position of power or authority before they are adequately prepared to take on responsibility. Still, if they can learn to choose their moments carefully and cultivate the diplomatic art of knowing when to say no, they need not fear their ability to live up to either the expectations of others or their highest expectations of themselves.

CHALLENGE: **CULTIVATING THE ABILITY TO HANDLE RESPONSIBILITY**
FULFILLMENT: **MASTERING THEIR MEDIUM**

January 23–30
GENIUS
AQUARIUS I

Those born in the Week of Genius who travel this karmic path are likely to go far and wide in the search for intellectual and spiritual expansion and will surely relish the opportunities and challenges of the Way of Influence. Though boredom and restlessness may be problems for these high-strung people, their ability to seek out and discover real value is highlighted with this configuration, and they are far less likely than some to scatter their energies or squander their talents in unproductive ventures. As they mature into the higher octaves of development, they will assume authority gracefully, to the benefit of everyone involved. They should, however, be aware of their tendency to inspire envy in others and strictly avoid high-handedness or impatience in their dealings with slower people or cumbersome organizations. Still, these souls are destined for success along this path, and they are sure to imbue this path with the touch of genius that characterizes all their undertakings.

CHALLENGE: **CENTERING OR GROUNDING THEMSELVES**
FULFILLMENT: **RELISHING THE WISDOM THAT MATURITY BRINGS**
NOTABLE: **PRINCESS CAROLINE OF MONACO (DAUGHTER OF GRACE KELLY)**

February 8–15
ACCEPTANCE
AQUARIUS III

This configuration will add some much-needed stability and groundedness to the life journey of those born in the Week of Acceptance, and if they can learn the necessary self-discipline, they are likely to make fine progress on the Way of Influence. There is, however, a danger that they may lapse into complacency and rigidity as they get older, and their tendency to resurrect outdated beliefs and prejudices must be cast aside or they will run the risk of becoming didactic, dictatorial, and chronically irritable as they assume the roles of leadership and authority promised by this karmic path. Indeed, there are times when Aquarius III's can appear to have a downright capricious management style, and only through the cultivation of empathy and compassion for others will they free themselves to rise to the levels of mature understanding and sophisticated evaluation required.

CHALLENGE: **THROWING OFF THE PREJUDICES OF THEIR YOUTH**
FULFILLMENT: **REMAINING OPEN YET GROUNDED IN REALITY**
NOTABLE: **LANA TURNER (HOLLYWOOD ACTRESS)**

February 16–22

SENSITIVITY
AQUARIUS–PISCES CUSP

Destined to rise to the top of their profession, these scrappy yet sensitive souls will nevertheless face their share of challenges along the Way of Influence. Career-oriented to a fault, they will have to face down their demon of personal insecurity and feelings of inadequacy before they will be able to really enjoy the fruits of their success. Naturally distrustful, these personalities would do well to nurture their friendships, as caring contact and camaraderie will help shore up their shaky sense of self without the attendant stresses of professional responsibility. Too, they may hold themselves back from realizing their true potential through a fear of rejection. Yet if they work to integrate the often disparate facets of their personalities, cultivate faith in their own abilities, and avoid the tendency to degenerate into paranoid or Machiavellian manipulations to protect their authority, they are promised great rewards and success.

CHALLENGE: **TEMPERING THEIR OVERLY SENSITIVE AND BELLIGERENT SIDE**
FULFILLMENT: **FINDING SUCCESS IN THEIR RELATIONSHIPS**
NOTABLE: **VANNA WHITE (TELEVISION PERSONALITY)**

NICOLAS COPERNICUS
Founder of modern
astronomy

2/19/1473
Aquarius–Pisces Cusp

February 23–March 2

SPIRIT
PISCES I

The Way of Influence does much to ground the ideals of Pisces I's in practical reality, yet whatever their chosen career, it is likely that their endeavors will always be tinged with high ideals and a sense of spiritual values. The key to their success, however, will be working through their tendency to allow others to take advantage of their generous natures or to give away their hard-won expertise for free. Too, they may fail to take up the challenge of this karmic path and retreat into a kind of perpetual immaturity that refuses to deal with the practical and material side of existence. Yet sensual Pisces I's will enjoy the creature comforts that are promised by this karmic path and as they mature will doubtless develop the discipline, responsibility, and shrewdness that will enable them to bring their dreams to fruitful and profitable reality.

CHALLENGE: **RECOGNIZING WHEN OTHERS ARE PREYING UPON THEM**
FULFILLMENT: **USING THEIR INFLUENCE TO ACCOMPLISH GOOD WORKS**

March 3–10

THE LONER
PISCES II

Loners may struggle on the Way of Influence, especially as regards the development of the more social and worldly sides of their sensitive natures. Financial considerations and issues may be a real stumbling block for these people until they make the connection between sharing their expertise and professional talents and gaining material rewards. Because they tend to pursue ideals of beauty rather than material goods, they will need to cultivate a more objective, less idealistic approach to professional success. As they develop the necessary sophistication to navigate the Way of Influence, they may refuse the recognition offered by this karmic path and retreat into misanthropy. True friends and soul mates of a practical sort will keep them connected. If these souls work to release the ghosts and traumas of the past, they can rest assured that the future will be brighter than they might have dared to dream.

CHALLENGE: **FIGHTING THEIR DESIRE TO WITHDRAW FROM THE WORLD**
FULFILLMENT: **HAVING WORKED HARD TO CULTIVATE A CIRCLE OF INTIMATES, DISCOVERING THAT THEY ARE ACCEPTED FOR WHO THEY ARE**

TONY RANDALL
Actor/director,
The Odd Couple

2/26/1920
Pisces I

March 11–18

DANCERS AND DREAMERS
PISCES III

Visionary and gifted, Pisces III's may nonetheless be blissfully unaware of their power over others. On the Way of Influence, part of the task for these souls will be learning the lesson that with influence go responsibility and commitment. The key to their success will be their ability to set aside their more childish ways and their almost naive view of the universe. Once they do, their achievements on this karmic path will be of a nearly miraculous character, both drawing heartfelt adulation from and creating bitter envy in those they meet along the way. Yet if they can learn to admit their own mistakes and apply themselves to the ideal of lifelong achievement rather than flash-in-the-pan success, the recognition and success promised by this karmic path offer truly delightful prospects for both spiritual and worldly advancement.

CHALLENGE: **TAMING THEIR INDULGENCE IN FANTASY WHILE GROUNDING THEIR VISIONS IN THE PRESENT**
FULFILLMENT: **IMPARTING THEIR DREAMS TO OTHERS**

The Way of Reform

TAURUS–GEMINI CUSP TO SCORPIO–SAGITTARIUS CUSP
Energy to Revolution

The tremendously energetic individuals born on the Way of Reform came to this lifetime to overthrow established systems and institute new ways of viewing or doing things. On this karmic path reform has many meanings. In one respect it represents a revolutionary toppling of existing mores or organizations. However, it can also mean a return to a more traditional approach, sometimes after an extended period of innovation. Moreover, it also implies "re-creation," an act of creativity that gives something a new or more vital form. The individuals who find themselves on this karmic path will be called to involve themselves in all the aforementioned aspects of reform. In order to do this, they must first deeply involve themselves in the status quo, for only by understanding the traditions of the past and present can they make revolutionary corrections that will be of benefit to all. In this respect, the reformers on this path are both masters of tradition and potent forces for change. Finally, as much as they would prefer otherwise, those on the Way of Reform must not be content to merely change society but are also fated to learn how to reform their own moral and value systems.

The dynamic individuals on the Way of Reform are passionately enthusiastic in leading the charge in any of their many causes or battles. Unfortunately, however, their level of energy is so wide-ranging and unsettled that it is rare for them to follow through on their endeavors. All too often, they will lead the rallying call for change only to be nowhere to be found when push comes to shove. This is in part due to the wide diversity of their interests; no sooner have they focused their energy on something than some other cause or matter grabs their attention, and off they go in another direction. Thus, the core lesson for the men and women on this karmic path is to involve themselves fully in one cause or project and finish it before going on to the next. These individuals are often accused of an inability to see things through, and this path calls on them to form real commitments. Moreover, before they become involved with any cause, it would be wise for them to set their priorities straight and consciously choose the battles they will fight. All the rewards attendant to having an impact on the world can be theirs as long as they stick to their guns.

The struggles that those on the Way of Reform are fated to undergo are prodigious, since any notion of reform implies going against the status quo. Difficulties and barriers of all types must be surmounted, whether poverty, physical handicap, prejudice, childhood deprivation, or their own deeply ingrained patterns of behavior. Ultimately, the men and women on this karmic path learn not only how to handle opposition but how to thrive on it, since it is difficult to imagine them achieving their goals without a good fight. Though they do not always win their battles, those on this karmic path are born with the ability to

---

CORE LESSON
Committing fully to a cause, project, or even another human being

GOAL
To be a catalyst for change

GIFTS
Gutsy, Original, Brilliant

PITFALLS
Amoral, Compulsive, Flighty

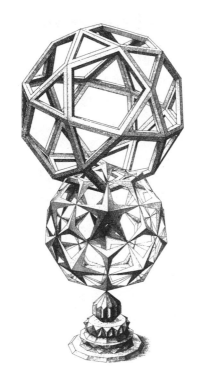

pick themselves up even after back-to-back defeats, dust themselves off, and keep on going. This does not mean that they enjoy such difficulties; on the contrary, they would like nothing better than to have a steady diet of pleasurable experiences and skim over life superficially but pleasantly. However, if they do, they will not proceed far in their spiritual development and risk living quite a dissipated life. Digging in and taking a stand are essential for them to progress, and by doing so they will actually free themselves from their flightiness, put down roots, and allow real growth to take place.

The primary arenas of the kinds of reforms necessitated by this path may be social, cultural, or political. As revolutionaries, the individuals on this karmic path will home in on the systems, institutions, or modes of thought in society that appear to them to be outdated or, worse, dangerous. Once engaged, they tend to have extreme views, and often they will express a disdain for anything that smacks of the middle way. Developing a more balanced approach will certainly help them to succeed. Part of their task, too, is to learn how to use the arts of war—strategy and planning—to achieve their aims. Too often they will suffer the consequences of being too hasty and consequently not thorough enough in what they do. On the career path, these individuals are very achievement-oriented but must learn the diffi-

cult lesson that quality is to be preferred to quantity. Moreover, they should not allow their work to get out into the world or even be seen by others unless it is of the highest merit.

Generally speaking, these individuals' battleground is the world rather than their own individual psyche (though no small amount of reform will also be needed there). Should they be successful in their crusades or otherwise make it to the top, they will have to guard against autocratic tendencies. A loss of humility and the adoption of an arrogant or haughty attitude can turn others against them and ultimately sabotage their quest for supremacy in their chosen field or endeavor. Cultivating modesty and guarding against hubris are life lessons they must learn. They will inevitably encounter individuals who represent the projection of their own psychological issues, and by successfully dealing with such people, they will also work out key personal issues. Though not wholly comfortable when engaged in deeper involvement with others, they will find that these experiences will encourage the growth of greater self understanding or self-realization, which can occur in sudden epiphanies.

Others may view these individuals as versatile and charming but will generally feel wary of them and have a sense that they are not always to be trusted. This is not surprising, given their anarchistic approach to life.

RELEASE

The use of seduction
as a tool

REWARD

The joy of changing other
people's lives for the better

SUGGESTION

Work to be less polarized in your viewpoints, and don't give in to paranoia.
Try to operate within the rest of the world's rules once in a while.

Moreover, in relationships, though they are moral, they may have trouble living up to their own or society's standards of behavior. To gain the trust of others and to accomplish the metamorphosis required for their evolution, these individuals often take on heavy responsibilities, possibly more than they can handle. If they are not careful, they may prematurely take too much on their shoulders and self-destruct. While early in life they should avoid frivolous people who may distract them from their causes, in later life, once they have formed a commitment to something greater than themselves, it often does these individuals good to attract lighter, more fun-loving associates who can seduce them away from their serious dedication.

Passions run high in those born to the Way of Reform, and satisfying their natural desires often entails cataclysmic pairings and tearing scenes. As the lovers of these individuals will attest, such relationships can involve rather large doses of both pleasure and pain. Those on this karmic path can be highly loyal but not particularly faithful as they exhibit a considerable inability to commit to one person. When they are finally mature enough to make such a commitment, they may find themselves surprisingly happy and content. Before such an event can occur, a significant reform of their sexual and moral sides needs to occur. As they are capable of deep transformation, this is not entirely out of the question. Until that time, their partners must be extremely understand-

ing and be willing to stick with them despite the tumultuous quality of their lives.

While on an intimate level they may be viewed by some as cads, on a societal level they want nothing more than to help improve the conditions of their fellow human beings. Because of their intense need to get involved in and reform what they see around them, one of their essential requirements is to actually see the fruit of their labor and to know that their efforts have had a positive effect. Likewise, satisfying their sensuality with good food and drink, physical companionship, and the joys of art, film, or music will keep them happy, but they will remain healthy only as long as they indulge themselves in moderation. Although this is true for us all, it is particularly true of those on the Way of Reform that precisely what they like most may be the worst for them, particularly in large doses.

In some ways these individuals can be compared to a biological catalyst, a substance that simply by its presence causes important life functions to occur. Although traditionally a catalyst is not itself changed in the process, the real challenge for those on the Way of Reform is to break this natural law and allow themselves to undergo a metamorphosis during this process. Thus, by changing others they will also be changed and perhaps equipped even better to catalyze the environment around them the next time, at an even higher level.

BALANCE POINT

Love and Passion

CRYSTALS AND GEMSTONES

Ammonite motivates individuals to instigate revolutionary systems that will inspire society to embrace new perspectives. This fossil inspires a return to evolutionary origins as a means of understanding the present.

NOTABLES ON THIS KARMIC PATH

MARTINA NAVRATILOVA

Like many on the Way of Reform, tennis champion **Martina Navratilova** has thrived on challenge both on and off the court. With her gutsy style and calculating skill, Martina was able to intimidate her competitors and control the game like few before her. By validating the role of female athletes and publicly supporting gay rights, she acted as a true catalyst for change. Through these actions, Martina was clearly a reformer of considerable influence during the many years that she dominated her sport.

Typifying the tendency of those on this karmic path to effect change, **Henry Ford** is credited with both the widespread introduction of the automobile into American society and the implementation of radically new methods for producing cars. By assigning employees specialized

HENRY FORD

tasks and manufacturing vehicles through an assembly-line process, Ford drastically cut the time needed to construct automobiles. Although it has been said that Ford acted amorally at times (as those on the Way of Reform are wont to do), it cannot be denied that he bettered the lives of many, thus fulfilling his destiny.

Called "the man who freed music," **Ludwig van Beethoven** broke with the tradition of his time, wherein composers were supported by the aristocracy. Through his desire to be independent, Beethoven became the first truly self-sufficient composer; instead of collecting a salary from a single controlling benefactor, he accepted commissions and was paid by publishers. Beethoven was an important initiator of change in the art of composition as well. After mastering the classical forms of Haydn and

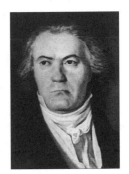

LUDWIG VAN BEETHOVEN

Mozart, Beethoven diverged from strict construction in favor of Romantic freedom, sacrificing form to feeling. Beethoven was a true revolutionary, and was able to put his gift of tremendous energy in service of his inspirational muse.

Other Notables: Etta James, Sigrid Undset, Richard Scarry, Iris Murdoch, Edvard Munch, John Guare, Ali MacGraw, Jerry Brown, Leopold Stokowski, Maxim Shostakovich, Georges Braque, Susan Strasberg, William Kunstler, Malcolm Forbes, Georg Wilhelm Friedrich Hegel, David Copperfield, Debby Boone, Carrie Fisher, Margaret Mitchell, Larry Bird, Betsy Ross, Nancy Lopez, Clark Gable, Sherman Hemsley, Rudolf Nureyev, Charlie Pride

---

BIRTHDAYS ON KARMIC PATH 9

March 5, 1882–July 23, 1882 | October 15, 1900–March 5, 1901 | May 27, 1919–October 15, 1919

January 6, 1938–May 26, 1938 | August 17, 1956–January 5, 1957 | March 29, 1975–August 17, 1975

November 8, 1993–March 28, 1994 | June 19, 2012–November 7, 2012

KARMIC PATH
9

March 19–24

REBIRTH
PISCES–ARIES CUSP

Pisces–Arians who travel the Way of Reform are likely to find themselves well suited to its challenges. Gifted with great passion and considerable energy, their sensitivity and natural depth will enable them to delve into problems and situations with greater understanding and a fine intuitive sense of what needs to be done in order to effect change. They will have to work hard to cultivate thoroughness, however, and may experience a great deal of difficulty before they learn to put their talents and energies to work in a clear, concentrated way. Some with this configuration may need to work on problems from childhood that could lead to uncontrolled aggression and a sense of "me against the world." Others may content themselves with skimming the surface of life, to the detriment of their more spiritual, sensitive side. These tough, talented souls are likely to do well on this path, provided they allow their sensitivity and good sense to guide them.

CHALLENGE: **DEVELOPING THE AWARENESS TO PERMIT SELF-REFORM**

FULFILLMENT: **WORKING ON BEHALF OF A LARGER, MORE GLOBAL FAMILY**

JERRY BROWN
California governor
1975–82,
mayor of Oakland

4/7/1938
Aries II

March 25–April 2

THE CHILD
ARIES I

Aries I's often ignore the need for deeper exploration and involvement on this karmic path and thus are apt to get mired in a tendency to squander their energies on a preoccupation with appearances or an otherwise superficial view of life. They would do well to cultivate their need for variety yet at the same time work to increase their stamina for the grind of detail work. A sense of context and the desire to educate themselves in matters of tradition and where they came from will give them a better sense of where they are going and how to get there. Many of these souls experience some really rough beginnings, yet the secrets of childhood will provide them with needed clues as to the workings of their own psyches. Once freed from the demons of the past, they will be liberated from unproductive patterns and relationships and able to achieve the success they so desire.

CHALLENGE: **DEALING WITH THE UNRESOLVED ISSUES OF CHILDHOOD**

FULFILLMENT: **SHARING THEIR SENSE THAT ANYTHING IS POSSIBLE**

NOTABLES: **ALI MacGRAW (FILM ACTRESS, *LOVE STORY*); LEONARD STERN (BUSINESS EXECUTIVE)**

April 3–10

THE STAR
ARIES II

The Way of Reform may hold some interesting twists and turns for those born in this week, though they may have to overcome some unfortunate early conditioning before they can realize their true potential not only to change their lives but to change the world. These attention getters will doubtless face the lesson of learning to perfect their work before bringing it to public attention or facing some unfortunate consequences of their failure to do so. Further, their tendency to excess and extreme competitiveness can hinder their potential for higher development, as they seem deliberately to place themselves in the middle of crises where they have to put out the "small fires" of their existence. However, their potential for transformation is quite remarkable, and, properly handled, the trials, joys, sorrows, and triumphs of these rather public personalities can serve to both delight and inspire those around them.

CHALLENGE: **RECOGNIZING THAT OVERINVOLVEMENT OF THEIR EGOS IN A CAUSE MAY PROVE TO BE A DETRIMENT**

FULFILLMENT: **FULLY INDULGING THEIR WILL TO WIN**

NOTABLES: **BARTLETT A. GIAMATTI (YOUNGEST PRESIDENT OF YALE AND BASEBALL COMMISSIONER); DON MEREDITH (FOOTBALL PLAYER)**

LEOPOLD STOKOWSKI
Longtime conductor with
Philadelphia Orchestra

4/18/1882
Aries III

April 11–18

THE PIONEER
ARIES III

Fearless and visionary, those born in the Week of the Pioneer who travel the Way of Reform are sure to have an impact on their world and times. Blessed with a highly developed social sense, these dynamic leaders like nothing better than to revolutionize ways of thinking and doing things. They may, however, have to learn to back up a bit now and then and examine their own mistakes before they realize that in some cases, at least, progress can be made only by the smallest of degrees and that sometimes when they find fault with the world, the problem actually resides in themselves. Still, these achievement-oriented people are likely to go far and will find a great deal of fulfillment on this path. In the end, their commitment and dedication to their ideals can very well develop in ways that will benefit us all.

CHALLENGE: **NOT BECOMING AUTOCRATIC OR, WORSE, UNCONCERNED ABOUT OTHER PEOPLE'S DEEPER FEELINGS**

FULFILLMENT: **LEADING THE CHARGE ON THE WAY OF REFORM**

April 19–24
POWER
ARIES–TAURUS CUSP

Aries–Tauruses who make their way along this karmic path will doubtless do very well. While their groundedness means that it is unlikely that they will confront the issues of flightiness or superficiality that will trouble some of their fellow travelers, they will have to be on guard against their tendency to become autocratic or to succumb to purely selfish ambition at the expense of a commitment to a higher sense of responsibility. Moderating their own needs will be important, as these sensual people may grapple with problems of excess along the road. Passionate and powerful, these personalities will likely attract any number of admirers, yet they will do best when their wild oats are sown and they can commit to a partner who shares both their ambition and their social involvement at a deep and abiding level.

CHALLENGE: **KEEPING A GOAL IN SIGHT, GIVING UP A PREOCCUPATION WITH POWER, AND WORKING TOWARD GREATER COOPERATION**

FULFILLMENT: **DISCOVERING THE ROLE LOVE CAN PLAY IN THEIR EFFORTS**

NOTABLE: **BETTY CUTHBERT (AUSTRALIAN TRACK ATHLETE)**

MAXIM SHOSTAKOVITCH
Led USSR symphony; interpreted father Dmitri's work; defected

5/10/1938
Taurus II

April 25–May 2
MANIFESTATION
TAURUS I

Gifted with hardheaded practicality, Taurus I's will likely flourish on the Way of Reform, as they are considerably more grounded in realistic goals and expectations than some others on this karmic path. Though some may be troubled by a highly unstable early environment that will cause them to turn their backs on higher ideals in the interest of security, it's far more likely that they will have the tenacity to find their way through even the toughest problems and situations. Above all, these souls will understand the value of work and experience little difficulty in focusing their energies on a productive and rewarding career. Though they may resist the need for change that is the key to this karmic path and get mired in staid, stuffy habits of mind or worldviews, once they rise to the challenge and take a stand in the interest of needed change or reform, there is no one who will fight with greater dedication or deeper commitment.

CHALLENGE: **MOVING OUT OF THEIR PREEXISTING ORIENTATION**

FULFILLMENT: **SEEING THEIR HARD WORK INITIATE CHANGE**

NOTABLE: **GEORGE MIFFLIN (COFOUNDER OF HOUGHTON MIFFLIN)**

May 3–10
THE TEACHER
TAURUS II

These teachers are likely to travel far and wide in their search for the personal and professional transformations indicated by this karmic path. Taurus II's are imbued with the right combination of idealism and practical application required for any real success at reform. Some on this path may find themselves deeply committed to working in other countries or in interracial or cross-cultural environments, while others may find that their life's work takes a more entrepreneurial turn. Though they must be aware of the dangers of overburdening themselves with an excess of responsibility or overly rigid perceptions of right and wrong, these magnetic, caring individuals are nevertheless blessed with keen perception, unusual intelligence, and the ability to convey abstract ideas and concepts to any number of productive and truly rewarding endeavors.

CHALLENGE: **RESISTING THE CALL OF THEIR SENSUALITY**

FULFILLMENT: **FULLY EMBODYING THE ROLE OF "MOVER AND SHAKER"**

GEORGES BRAQUE
Cubist painter

5/13/1882
Taurus III

May 11–18
THE NATURAL
TAURUS III

Those born in the Week of the Natural who find themselves on the Way of Reform may be in for a rude awakening or two before they learn the value of restraining their need for personal freedom in the interest of taking a stand. Marked by a tendency to be rather too easygoing and fun-loving, some with this configuration may fail to take up the challenge implied here, only to live superficially or be content to "let sleeping dogs lie" even when their consciences would have them do otherwise. For others, security issues may take precedence over more moral values. Still, if they cultivate the necessary measure of self-discipline and refuse to allow the passions of the moment to shape their visions of the future, they will doubtless be blessed with a most unusual experience on this road and may even find an odd kind of freedom as well.

CHALLENGE: **NOT TAKING THE PATH OF LEAST RESISTANCE**

FULFILLMENT: **FINDING AN OUTLET FOR THEIR NATURAL REBELLIOUSNESS**

NOTABLE: **LEO STEIN (ART COLLECTOR/CRITIC; GERTRUDE'S BROTHER)**

May 19–24

ENERGY
TAURUS–GEMINI CUSP

These dauntless, dynamic souls may have a great deal to overcome when navigating the Way of Reform. Early obstacles, childhood deprivation, or other problems may have contributed to their dynamism, yet those born on this cusp will nonetheless have to learn to slow down and go into things with greater depth before they realize the kind of progress promised by this karmic path. Good intentions may be hindered by poor execution with this configuration, and learning to plan carefully will prove a great asset in their quest for advancement and greater maturity. Blessed with the ability to deal with trouble in an active, versatile fashion, they may succeed brilliantly, especially in professions that require them to have a finger on the pulse of their times. Provided they cultivate greater self-awareness, endurance, and the ability to make peace with the hardships of their pasts, the promise for their future is great indeed.

CHALLENGE: **LETTING GO OF THEIR NEAR ADDICTION TO EVER NEW FORMS OF STIMULATION**
FULFILLMENT: **FEELING THE SELF-ESTEEM THAT COMES FROM LEAVING ONE'S MARK**
NOTABLE: **TOMMY CHONG (COMEDIAN, CHEECH AND CHONG)**

WILLIAM KUNSTLER
Attorney who fought for constitutionality of flag burning

6/7/1919
Gemini II

May 25–June 2

FREEDOM
GEMINI I

The freedom lovers born in this week make for truly independent thinkers when placed on the Way of Reform. Yet for all their formidable evaluative talents and shrewd judgment, they will have to avoid becoming the "rolling stones who gather no moss" or squandering their considerable energy in fly-by-night schemes and confidence games. Highly seductive and blessed with amazing charm, they may become increasingly manipulative as they mature and may also fall victim to hubris when it comes to getting what they want. Alternatively, they may become mired in early patterns that make them too excitable or even downright abrasive when things don't go according to one of their many plans. Still, it is unlikely that these souls will want for ideas or inspiration. And if they augment their natural gifts of technical expertise and keen analysis with thorough training, a sense of realism about their goals, and modesty about their own abilities, they will realize great success.

CHALLENGE: **RAISING THEIR IRRITATION THRESHOLD**
FULFILLMENT: **FIGHTING FOR THE RIGHTS OF OTHERS**

June 3–10

NEW LANGUAGE
GEMINI II

These are the people to call when there's a need to put a new spin on information. Brilliant and versatile, these communicators can nevertheless fall victim to superficiality or fail to address the real issues in both the personal and professional arenas. Gifted with shrewd evaluative instincts in addition to their unique communicative talent, they know how to dazzle others and even to pull the wool over their eyes. Cultivating honesty and integrity will be critical to their success, as will countering their tendency to project their darker impulses and motivation onto others. Further, some early problems and obstacles may give them a rather defensive attitude toward the world that must be relinquished before they can experience the evolution indicated by the Way of Reform. Once they take a stand and dedicate themselves to larger ideals of future progress rather than self-interest, their fulfillment is ensured.

CHALLENGE: **RECOGNIZING THAT THEY THEMSELVES CONJURE UP ALL THE STURM UND DRANG IN THEIR RELATIONSHIPS**
FULFILLMENT: **CONTRIBUTING TO A NEW VOCABULARY FOR THEIR TIMES**
NOTABLE: **RICHARD SCARRY (CHILDREN'S BOOK WRITER/ ILLUSTRATOR)**

IGOR STRAVINSKY
Russian conductor and composer, *The Rake's Progress*

6/17/1882
Gemini III

June 11–18

THE SEEKER
GEMINI III

Seekers who travel the Way of Reform will usually rise to its challenges. Since it is their nature to press beyond the limitations imposed by both the social order and the world of nature, these personalities will doubtless relish the energy and excitement generated along this karmic path and take delight in applying their talents to any number of causes, challenges, and personal crusades. Though their involvement may not always be total, Gemini III's must nevertheless have the freedom to move among a variety of ideologies until they gain the experience to select higher goals more consciously. Genuinely loyal, they may struggle against those who would tie them down or smother their curiosity with an excess of emotional demands. Yet once they have received the information necessary to take a stand and commit themselves to a cause, a relationship, or a field of endeavor, they will doubtless find themselves quite content, secure in the knowledge that their involvements are the result of their own choosing.

CHALLENGE: **FINDING SOMETHING THEY CAN COMMIT TO**
FULFILLMENT: **EXPERIENCING THE ADVENTURE OF THE REVOLUTION**
NOTABLE: **UTA HAGEN (STAGE ACTRESS; TEACHER)**

June 19–24
MAGIC
GEMINI–CANCER CUSP

Those born on the Cusp of Magic who travel the Way of Reform are likely to experience considerable happiness and success, provided they avoid the dangers of excessive sensuality or romantic delusion. Deep involvement and dedication come quite naturally to these types, though they would do well to develop greater discrimination and keener judgment or risk "casting their pearls before swine." Too, this configuration can manifest in extremes of passion and emotional expression that can place heavy demands on those with whom they become involved; these individuals will do best with those who can stay calm even in the midst of the emotional storms that they sometimes generate. Still, they are very likely to gain greater confidence as they mature and to become considerably less needy as time goes by. If they cultivate realism and avoid taking on too many burdensome responsibilities, they will be free to enjoy the fruits of their evolution and to find a universal love.

LOUIS JOURDAN
French film actor, *Gigi*

6/19/1919
Gemini–Cancer Cusp

CHALLENGE: **NOT PERMITTING THE STORMINESS OF THEIR ROMANTIC LIVES TO INTERFERE IN THEIR WORK**
FULFILLMENT: **HELPING TO BRING MAGIC TO THE MOST MORIBUND TRADITIONS**
NOTABLE: **PAULINE KAEL (FILM CRITIC; AUTHOR)**

June 25–July 2
THE EMPATH
CANCER I

The depth, diversity, and great sensitivity that mark the personalities of Cancer I's will find considerable expression on the Way of Reform. Though they may be prone to ignore or at least discount their considerable intuitive and psychic capabilities early in life, they will nevertheless come to appreciate these qualities as they mature, using them to augment their fine managerial skills and astute financial sense. The principal challenge of this configuration will be channeling their highly emotional energies into productive patterns and positive expression. Extremes of all sorts are especially to be avoided, as Cancer I's are apt to squander their talents in emotional excess on the one hand or withdraw from calls to involvement by stubbornly and rather sulkily refusing to participate. Though these personalities may take some time to settle down to the tasks of this karmic path, once they do, maturity will bring considerable wisdom, financial success, and a high degree of personal fulfillment.

CHALLENGE: **RESISTING THE TEMPTATION NOT TO PARTICIPATE DUE TO HURT FEELINGS**
FULFILLMENT: **OFFERING THEIR CONSIDERABLE SKILLS FOR THE BETTERMENT OF THE WORLD AT LARGE**

July 3–10
THE UNCONVENTIONAL
CANCER II

Cancer II's appearances can be deceptive, for their seemingly ordinary lives and circumstances can belie seething emotional passions, dark addictions, and vivid fantasies of all kinds. Blessed with considerable imagination and a unique way of looking at the world, their primary task on this karmic path will be to better integrate their inner gifts with their outer circumstances and literally channel their visions into the kind of practical tasks that effect lasting change. Early hardships may have forged their imaginative natures, yet many of them do not give themselves credit for having overcome serious obstacles and may thus hold themselves back from the level of involvement required by this path through escapism, fickleness, or a wildly protective attitude toward their inner world. Still, they are blessed with the resources necessary to live lucrative, marvelously fulfilling lives, provided they avoid the dangers of obsession and defensiveness and channel their best ideas into concrete goals with practical and purposeful ends.

IRIS MURDOCH
Irish author

7/15/1919
Cancer III

CHALLENGE: **LETTING GO OF THEIR DARKER OBSESSIONS**
FULFILLMENT: **MANIFESTING THEIR UNCONVENTIONAL VISION IN THE WORLD**

July 11–18
THE PERSUADER
CANCER III

The key to success for Cancer III's who find themselves on the Way of Reform will be their ability to accurately perceive and manipulate their power over others. Early on, these highly persuasive people will employ their talents in overcoming personal obstacles and environmental disadvantages, yet they may get mired in their continuing need to manipulate others for reasons of personal security. Attached as they are to the traditions and methods of the past, it may be hard at first for them to identify what, if anything, needs reforming. Still, the depth of their empathy for others will doubtless beckon these souls to greater levels of involvement in service or other causes, and eventually they will seek out the situations and companions who promise to fulfill their emotional and material needs. Providing they do not sink into sensual or emotional excess, such involvements will free them to experience the fruits of their dedication and the joy of discovering their own considerable ability to effect positive change.

CHALLENGE: **ESCHEWING THEIR NEED TO CONTROL THE ACTION**
FULFILLMENT: **USING THEIR POWER OF PERSUASION TO CHANGE THE LIVES OF THOSE AROUND THEM**

July 19–25
OSCILLATION
CANCER–LEO CUSP

Though the early lives of Cancer–Leos who travel the Way of Reform may be characterized by a high degree of psychic stress, they can nevertheless rise to a significant degree of personal and spiritual evolution on this karmic path. Though they can fall into the trap of dishonesty or a tendency to try to please all of the people all of the time, they are nevertheless capable of drawing on the more grounded energies of this configuration and channeling their volatile natures into the innovation of exciting projects and pursuits. Blessed with a fine intuitive sense of what's hot and what's not, they will do best in careers that demand dedication and structure but at the same time give full play to their creative talents. Controlling their moods and avoiding depression will prove important, as will surrounding themselves with more practical and emotionally steady people. Finally, these souls must fully acknowledge their natural moral courage. Properly guided by their innate sense of right and wrong, their path to greater commitment will doubtless become clear with time.

CHALLENGE: **NOT QUESTIONING EVERY STEP THEY TAKE**
FULFILLMENT: **REVELING IN THE BROAD CHANGES EFFECTED BY FATE**

WILLIAM CLARK
Soldier, explorer, better known as half of Lewis & Clark
———
8/1/1770
Leo I

July 26–August 2
AUTHORITY
LEO I

Those born in the Week of Authority who travel the Way of Reform are likely to be hard-driving individuals who may not always have the best awareness of what needs reforming since often they are more concerned with themselves than with others. Gifted with the ability to lead and inspire others, these people may not always know what is best for those they lead or what is most pertinent to their spiritual and material advancement. Though unlikely to merely skim the surface of issues, they must nevertheless be on guard against the tendency to become autocratic or tyrannical about maintaining the status quo. Deeply loyal, Leo I's on this path are apt to fight for maintaining the traditions of the past or even returning to them. Still, their standards are extremely high; if they can bring their innate sense of what is right to bear on their involvements and their commitment can be awakened, they promise to make a lasting contribution to their society.

CHALLENGE: **INCREASING THEIR UNDERSTANDING OF ABSTRACT TRUTHS AND PLACING THEM IN THE SERVICE OF REFORM**
FULFILLMENT: **DEFENDING THEIR PRINCIPLES**
NOTABLE: **HENRY FORD (AUTOMAKER; INDUSTRIALIST)**

August 3–10
BALANCED STRENGTH
LEO II

Blessed with a truly phenomenal level of energy and natural endurance, those born in this week who navigate the Way of Reform will nevertheless have to cultivate a broader vision of themselves and the world around them before they can become more involved. Though these personalities are by nature champions of the downtrodden, they can nevertheless be single-minded to a fault and truly unable to "see the forest for the trees." As a result, their powers of concentration and determination can sometimes stand in the way of the progress to which they aspire. Learning to lighten up and take a longer view of their goals for reform will prove extremely valuable. As they mature and get into touch with their shrewder, more objective side, they will doubtless flourish, blessed as they are with the passion, trustworthiness, and endurance to overcome any of the battles that this life's journey can throw their way.

CHALLENGE: **BROADENING THEIR VIEW OF THE ISSUE AT HAND**
FULFILLMENT: **INVOKING THEIR NATURAL FIDELITY IN THE SERVICE OF CHANGE**

DINO DE LAURENTIIS
Italian film star/producer
———
8/8/1919
Leo II

August 11–18
LEADERSHIP
LEO III

Gifted with the ability not only to develop plans but to see them through to a fruitful and satisfying conclusion, those born in the Week of Leadership who involve themselves in reforms of all kinds will doubtless find much happiness and success. For these people, involvement will surely mean having to assume a role of authority or leadership, and they may have to cultivate the qualities of patience, endurance, and diplomacy before they can find their way to where they can do the most good and gain the recognition and freedom to achieve what they most desire. Ego issues can be a problem, as can an excess of passion and sensuality. Still, if they take care to channel their formidable talents and energies into an appropriate professional area and avoid the dangers of overpersonalizing problems and situations, they are likely to make quite a mark on the world.

CHALLENGE: **PUTTING THE GOAL AT HAND ABOVE THE CONSIDERATIONS OF THEIR EGO**
FULFILLMENT: **OFFERING THEIR GIFT OF LEADING TO A TRULY WORTHY CAUSE**
NOTABLE: **MICHAEL KIDD (CHOREOGRAPHER, GUYS AND DOLLS)**

August 19–25

EXPOSURE
LEO–VIRGO CUSP

Natural reformers, those born on the Cusp of Exposure who find themselves on this karmic path will doubtless encounter any number of tricky situations involving cover-ups, intrigues, or infighting. Though they are likely to know the secrets of just about anybody with whom they work or play, they will nonetheless face the challenge of learning real integrity and developing a sense of honesty in their dealings with the world. Their ability to manipulate others through information is profound, yet they are likely to face some public battles that will force them to reveal their true colors and take a stand for what they believe is right or risk having their own secrets compromised into the bargain. Developing trustworthiness and calmness will serve them well on this karmic path, and their success will doubtless be measured by the loyalty they inspire along the way.

CHALLENGE: **NOT BECOMING TOO BOGGED DOWN IN SKIRMISHES AT THE EXPENSE OF THE WAR**

FULFILLMENT: **EXPRESSING THEIR SECRET FLAMBOYANCE**

NOTABLE: **MALCOLM FORBES (FOUNDER, *FORBES* MAGAZINE)**

GEORGE C. WALLACE
Segregationist governor
of Alabama; shot and
paralyzed in 1972

8/25/1919
Leo–Virgo Cusp

August 26–September 2

SYSTEM BUILDERS
VIRGO I

Virgo I's who travel the Way of Reform are likely to be quite happy and successful, since this karmic path will surely lead them along the way of service. While happy to work for reform, Virgo I's may lack the broader vision or originality of thought to know what may be needed. However, in following others they will be invaluable in setting up the systems to effect change. A certain emotional instability, fits of temper, and emotional dramas can trip them up in unexpected ways and hamper their development and their progress toward their goals. Still, they are blessed with the powers of concentration needed to succeed in almost any area of endeavor, and if they avoid the dangers of rigidity, hypervigilance, and the tendency to cling to outworn or outmoded traditions, their success will be ensured.

CHALLENGE: **REMAINING UNDAUNTED IN THE FACE OF EMOTIONAL PRESSURE**

FULFILLMENT: **WORKING IN SERVICE OF A GREATER GOOD**

NOTABLE: **ALFRED BEACH (BUILT PNEUMATIC SUBWAY UNDER BROADWAY IN NEW YORK CITY, 1868)**

September 3–10

THE ENIGMA
VIRGO II

Those born in the Week of the Enigma are blessed with both endurance and natural discrimination. Their choices as regards their own advancement are likely to be good and their judgments of others quite sound. Their calm, collected exteriors can, however, hide a passionate, seething emotional life that may be exacerbated on the Way of Reform. Thus, they would do well to better integrate their "hot" and "cold" aspects or risk developing a kind of Jekyll-and-Hyde approach to their personal lives. Isolation can also be a problem, as will their tendency to become increasingly manipulative or intolerant as they grow older. Still, the promise of success is very strong with this configuration, and if they allow themselves the luxury of honest self-expression and an understanding group of associates with whom they can let their hair down, they will make great strides forward.

CHALLENGE: **SEARCHING FOR THAT SPECIAL INDIVIDUAL TO WHOM THEY CAN MAKE A COMMITMENT**

FULFILLMENT: **CALLING ON THEIR ETHICS TO TEMPER THE REVOLUTIONARY ZEAL OF THEIR ASSOCIATES**

**GEORG WILHELM
FRIEDRICH HEGEL**
Idealist philosopher

8/27/1770
Virgo I

September 11–18

THE LITERALIST
VIRGO III

Gifted with amazing willpower as well as the abilities to develop tangible goals and to focus their energies in all the right ways, Virgo III's who travel the Way of Reform are likely to really shine. Results-oriented, they like nothing better than to see tangible rewards for their efforts in both the personal and professional areas of life and will work with great dedication to that end. Still, they run the risk of becoming increasingly entrenched as they mature and will have to guard against their tendency to avoid change of any kind. Personally, their passions may lead them astray, as they have a sensationalistic streak that may be hard to manage, especially in youth, and may cause their efforts at reform to go astray. Later on, they may become the kind of people who use others for their own ends, then drop them like the proverbial hot potatoes if their plans fail to come to fruition.

CHALLENGE: **LOOSENING THEIR NEED FOR HARMONY ENOUGH TO MAKE ROOM FOR CHANGE**

FULFILLMENT: **SEEING THE RESULTS OF THEIR DEDICATION AND PERSEVERANCE**

NOTABLE: **DAVID COPPERFIELD (MAGICIAN)**

September 19–24
BEAUTY
VIRGO–LIBRA CUSP

Virgo–Libras who travel the Way of Reform may find that their higher sensibilities will need considerable grounding before they can make real progress at the level of commitment demanded by this karmic path. It will be difficult for these personalities to focus their energies, but if they overcome a certain early flakiness and direct their talents toward a profession or pursuit that demands a measure of self-discipline, yet nurtures their need for beauty, they will doubtless succeed. Though some early hardships may manifest themselves in self-destructive tendencies or problems with excess, these souls are blessed with the ability to rise from even the worst experiences. Careers that involve innovation in the arts and fashion will doubtless be pursued by these individuals, but so will those of con men and hustlers. Cultivating honesty will be especially important, as will learning to take a stand. Still, if these souls recognize early the value of taking an ethical line, all will go well.

DEBBY BOONE
Singer

9/22/1956
Virgo–Libra Cusp

CHALLENGE: **DEVELOPING THE DEPTH TO CARE PASSIONATELY ABOUT SOMETHING**
FULFILLMENT: **CONTRIBUTING TO THE SETTING OF NEW TRENDS**

September 25–October 2
THE PERFECTIONIST
LIBRA I

Born with the impulse to set things right, Libra I's will feel very much at home on the Way of Reform. The main pitfall here is falling prey to a lifestyle that depends too much on appearances. Some Libra I's on this karmic path may keep back their progress by holding on to resentments, slights, or the feeling that they just can't get a break. Obviously, they will have to make many of their own breaks, but when they begin to focus their attention less on details and more on the larger picture, their direction will become clear and their paths to achievement in innovative and interesting formats widened. Venting their emotions to a trusted group of peers will be important as will the ability to offload too much personal or professional responsibility. Once they learn to control the more demanding side of their nature and find a good balance between work and play, their dedication to their cause is sure to be unflagging.

CHALLENGE: **LETTING GO OF INDECISIVENESS AND TAKING ACTION**
FULFILLMENT: **CHANGING THINGS FOR THE BETTER**
NOTABLE: **ALFRED VAIL (MANUFACTURED TELEGRAPH)**

October 3–10
SOCIETY
LIBRA II

Characterized by a remarkable aesthetic sense, those born in the Week of Society who travel this karmic path will nevertheless have to avoid the dangers of superficiality. Blessed with a good sense of what's topical and fashionable, these tasteful, astute people run the risk of never delving beneath the surface or of refusing to challenge the status quo. They may also fail to develop the commitment and dedication demanded by this path. Thus, while they easily inspire trust in others, they may not always be trustworthy themselves. Alternatively, some of this type may give too much too soon and too often, and need to learn to offload less-than-desirable responsibilities, overly dependent associates, and fair-weather friends. Still, once they learn to take their own needs a bit more seriously and apply their energies in a direction that will lead to realistic and tangible rewards, their ability to generate the reforms necessary to their professions and social milieu will result in rewards.

TOM HARMON
Football star/sportscaster

9/28/1919
Libra I

CHALLENGE: **REMAINING EVER VIGILANT AGAINST THEIR TENDENCY TO SELF-DECEPTION**
FULFILLMENT: **UTILIZING THEIR LASERLIKE INSIGHTS TO EFFECT CHANGE**
NOTABLE: **STEPHANIE ZIMBALIST (TELEVISION ACTRESS)**

October 11–18
THEATER
LIBRA III

Image-conscious, sometimes in the extreme, those born in the Week of Theater who find themselves on the Way of Reform are likely to find themselves blessed with an exciting, fulfilling journey. If they can avoid the dangers of being merely actors who play their parts in life without the level of deeper commitment called for by this configuration, they are likely to exceed even their own expectations of happiness and success as leaders of a veritable revolution. Though their overinvolvement in image can risk forcing them to fight to the bitter end for the reforms they feel are important, as they mature, they may well maintain and augment their involvement in causes, especially volunteer efforts or even politics. Such ongoing involvements will fuel their life force and help them to avoid the dangers of isolation and cynicism.

CHALLENGE: **FOCUSING LESS ON SUPERFICIALITIES AND MORE ON RESULTS**
FULFILLMENT: **BRINGING THE FULL WEIGHT OF THEIR WORLDLINESS TO BEAR ON THEIR COMMITMENTS**
NOTABLE: **MARTINA NAVRATILOVA (TENNIS CHAMPION)**

October 19–25

DRAMA AND CRITICISM
LIBRA–SCORPIO CUSP

Unusually capable revolutionaries, these larger-than-life personalities can give a whole new meaning to the phrase "sowing their wild oats." When younger, they can get themselves into and out of some pretty spectacular scrapes and misadventures in the search for drama and excitement. As they mature, however, they will doubtless gain the knowledge needed to apply their energies in a more constructive fashion, and their hard-driving qualities will find greater focus and refinement. Passionate and inspiring, these souls will nevertheless benefit from learning to lighten up a bit and moderate their behavior. Controlling a promiscuous and colorful private life through the formation of a mutually respectful and ambitious partnership will also help in their search for direction and enable these hard-driving individuals to maintain their independence, realize their dreams, and give full play to their profound range of emotion.

MARGARET MITCHELL
Writer; won Pulitzer for
Gone With the Wind

11/8/1900
Scorpio II

CHALLENGE: **TAMING THEIR PRIVATE LIFE**
FULFILLMENT: **UTILIZING THE STRENGTH OF THEIR IDEAS TO CREATE REAL REFORM**
NOTABLE: **CARRIE FISHER (ACTRESS; WRITER/NOVELIST)**

October 26–November 2

INTENSITY
SCORPIO I

Those born in the Week of Intensity are likely to find themselves quite happy on the Way of Reform, though this configuration will nevertheless present some unique personal challenges. Critical to their success will be nurturing their sense of a higher purpose in all their endeavors and steering clear of the kind of byzantine intrigues and petty personal vendettas that will obscure their sense of commitment. In any event, they have a pronounced tendency to take things personally, and suspicious Scorpio I's will have to struggle a bit to stay both honest and open on this path. Blessed with great discernment and a natural disposition to intense involvement, these souls will prove fortunate indeed as they channel their virtuosity into productive outlets. By maintaining high personal and ethical standards and growing beyond self-interest, a real blossoming will occur.

CHALLENGE: **ALWAYS KEEPING HIGHER SPIRITUAL VALUES IN MIND**
FULFILLMENT: **FINDING THEMSELVES CATALYSTS FOR CHANGE**
NOTABLES: **HORACE SMITH (INVENTED REPEATING PISTOL, SMITH & WESSON); ELLSWORTH SLATER (ESTABLISHED HOTEL CHAIN)**

November 3–11

DEPTH
SCORPIO II

These serious, soulful people are likely to do quite well on the Way of Reform, provided they draw on their profound resources to overcome some early challenges. Childhood will not have been especially easy for these personalities and many will bear some scars that can prevent them from doing their life's work until they learn to discriminate between suffering in the interest of a higher ideal and suffering for its own sake. Highly competitive, they will have little difficulty applying their energies in a practical, concentrated fashion but will nevertheless have to avoid the dangers of envy, pretentiousness, and the use of less-than-ethical means to accomplish their ends. Passionate and emotionally demanding, they will do best when they learn to unbend and open up a bit, even if it means creating a few chinks in their well-constructed armor.

AARON COPLAND
Composer, *Appalachian Spring*

11/14/1900
Scorpio III

CHALLENGE: **REFORMING THEIR PSYCHOLOGICAL PATTERNS**
FULFILLMENT: **FIGHTING THE GOOD FIGHT FOR THEIR CAUSE**

November 12–18

CHARM
SCORPIO III

Tough, realistic, and very together, those born in the Week of Charm who travel the Way of Reform may nevertheless have to work to overcome self-interest in order to realize their higher goals and dreams. Security issues from early life may be a problem, and many will succumb to their childhood demons, refusing to risk greater advancement or involvement in the interest of not making waves or simply protecting their own immediate interests. Blessed with keen judgment, considerable diplomatic power, and fine work skills, they are highly effective at generating reform from within a structure. Their realism can also be their undoing if it is not fired by passion and inspiration and devolves into cold calculation or manipulation of others to do or be what they themselves dream of. Still, they are quite capable of great innovation, in any number of areas, once they nurture their creative and spiritual aspects by giving greater credence to all that is possible and less to what is merely probable.

CHALLENGE: **OVERCOMING A TOO REALISTIC APPROACH AND BELIEVING IN THE POSSIBILITY OF CHANGE**
FULFILLMENT: **WORKING WITHIN AN ORGANIZATION TO ACHIEVE INNOVATION AND REFORM**
NOTABLE: **KATIE SAGAL (ACTRESS, *MARRIED WITH CHILDREN*)**

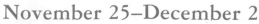

November 19–24

REVOLUTION
SCORPIO–SAGITTARIUS CUSP

Naturally rebellious and free-spirited, Scorpio–Sagittarians are sure to blossom on the Way of Reform. They will have to choose their milieux with some discretion, however, and take time to slow down and carefully evaluate what they want before the right opportunities will present themselves. Chances are, these gutsy risk takers will be found on the cutting edge of business, culture, and the arts. As talented as they are at getting on with the new, however, they may have a pronounced tendency to "throw out the baby with the bathwater," only to be forced to return and reassess the value of some things they may have cast aside in their breakneck pursuit of ideals. Still, these unique, passionate people are likely not only to see some excitement along this life's journey but to generate more than their share. Gifted commentators on, willing participants in, and champions of the future and all its possibilities, they will doubtless find the nuances of meaning in the ancient saying "May you live in interesting times."

BO DEREK
Model/actress, *10*
———
11/20/1956
Scorpio–Sagittarius Cusp

CHALLENGE: **MARSHALING THEIR FORCES, AS OPPOSED TO ALLOWING THEIR DISSIPATION**

FULFILLMENT: **DETONATING A FEW WELL-PLACED BOMBS**

November 25–December 2

INDEPENDENCE
SAGITTARIUS I

Sagittarius I's have the capacity to make significant contributions to the reformation of matters both small and large, provided they can learn to distinguish between their need for real change and their tendency to act out of simple frustration or rebelliousness. Gifted with a high moral sense and a genuine concept of what it means to be fair, they will nevertheless have to struggle a bit to express their ideals. These dauntless personalities would do well to cultivate practicality and focus as they are prone to scatter their energies, resulting in the proverbial "jack of all trades, master of none." Too, they can be prone to poor impulse control and an overcompetitiveness that can hinder their further development. Still, success will be theirs when they allow themselves to be guided by their considerable intuition and keep their passions in check by reminding themselves of the wisdom of the saying "Temperament is the last refuge of the amateur."

CHALLENGE: **OVERCOMING INSECURITY TO PARTICIPATE FULLY IN A BATTLE**

FULFILLMENT: **LIVING A LIFE BASED ON THEIR PRINCIPLES**

NOTABLE: **CHARLES RINGLING (CIRCUS FOUNDER)**

December 3–10

THE ORIGINATOR
SAGITTARIUS II

Originators are likely to enjoy the fate that the Way of Reform bestows on them. The key to their success will be their unique capacity for original thought. Not only can these innovators think big, they can implement their grand schemes as well. They would do well to keep their low frustration threshold and their more aggressive tendencies in check, as these may erode their support system. Self-control and the ability to rise above the squabbles of the moment will bring out the creativity inherent in these gifted people and increase their confidence in their mission, as well as help them to garner the acceptance from those around them. Maturity is sure to refine some of their more difficult aspects, and if they do not turn away from the challenges of this karmic path in isolation, rejection, or the refusal to give of themselves, their chances for personal and spiritual fulfillment are impressive indeed.

LARRY BIRD
Basketball MVP
———
12/7/1956
Sagittarius II

CHALLENGE: **NOT FRITTERING AWAY THEIR ENERGY IN FRUSTRATION OR AGGRESSION**

FULFILLMENT: **WITNESSING THE REVOLUTIONARY EFFECT THEY HAVE ON THE WORLD AROUND THEM**

NOTABLE: **RICHARD W. SEARS (MERCHANT; COFOUNDER OF SEARS, ROEBUCK)**

December 11–18

THE TITAN
SAGITTARIUS III

These expansive personalities may have a few growing pains when placed on the Way of Reform. Blessed with great generosity of spirit, they can nevertheless become quite skittish at the prospect of commitment and shy away from having to develop the moral integrity required by this karmic path. In short, some with this configuration are far more comfortable when sought out by others for their leadership and charisma than they are in generating the revolution called for here. Settling down and applying themselves may also prove to be something of a problem, and they may squander their talents in exhibitionism at the expense of élan. Still, they are blessed with a thoughtful and philosophical turn of mind that will serve them well, as they are always able to put things into a larger perspective. That, together with their great sense of humor, will serve to strengthen their resolve, expand their minds, and buoy their hearts.

CHALLENGE: **NOT EXPECTING ANYTHING IN RETURN FOR THEIR EFFORTS**

FULFILLMENT: **SEEING SOME OF THEIR OWN LARGER-THAN-LIFE INNOVATIONS TAKE FORM**

NOTABLES: **LUDWIG VAN BEETHOVEN (COMPOSER/MUSICIAN); EDVARD MUNCH (EXPRESSIONIST ARTIST)**

December 19–25
PROPHECY
SAGITTARIUS–CAPRICORN CUSP

Sagittarius–Capricorns who travel this karmic path may find themselves gifted with an almost supernatural sense of what is to come. The future, both in the abstract and in its particulars, is sure to be something of a preoccupation for these people. Grounded and basically quite sure of themselves, these souls may definitely march to the beat of a different drummer. Torn between tradition and revolution, they will have to strike a careful balance between security and their vision of progress. Cultivating sociability will be important for them, since a connection to others will help them maintain a balanced perspective and remind them that they are not alone. Still, these brilliant and sometimes forbidding people may have a surprising and intriguing passage. They would do well to keep their frustrations in check, however, and learn to evaluate both the past and the present in their search for self-realization. Otherwise, like many visionaries, they may lead a revolution—only to lose their heads.

BETSY ROSS
Early American patriot, seamstress; possibly made first U.S. flag

1/1/1752
Capricorn I

CHALLENGE: **BALANCING THEIR LOVE OF TRADITION WITH THEIR DESIRE FOR PROGRESS**
FULFILLMENT: **QUIETLY OBSERVING THE RESULTS OF THEIR REFORMS**

December 26–January 2
THE RULER
CAPRICORN I

Evaluating and reevaluating their sense of tradition and personal mythology will doubtless play a prominent part in the lives of Capricorn I's who travel the Way of Reform. Blessed with a fine sense of loyalty and trustworthiness, they may nevertheless find themselves having to take a second look at any number of their sacred cows along the way. Accepting the beliefs and traditions of others will not come easily to them, however, and they will doubtless be faced with the challenge of cultivating greater tolerance along with increasing their charm or running the risk of becoming rather staid, stodgy, and stale in their belief systems. Still, these hard workers' prospects for achievement are phenomenal and the blessings of this path very much in keeping with their personal talents and ambitions.

CHALLENGE: **DISCERNING WHICH TRADITIONS ARE THE MOST IMPORTANT**
FULFILLMENT: **CHANGING THE LIVES OF PEOPLE AROUND THEM THROUGH THE JUDICIOUS USE OF AUTHORITY**

January 3–9
DETERMINATION
CAPRICORN II

Gifted with the ability to go into matters of personal importance with more than the usual depth of perception, those born in the Week of Determination will likely travel far on this karmic path. Still, their capacity for concentration and application may prove to be their undoing, should they fail to cultivate a broader vision or collapse in self-interest or even greed. Too, their natural sense of loyalty can be misplaced, and they will have to learn to off-load too heavy responsibilities and unproductive relationships in their travels along this karmic path. Realistic, sometimes to a fault, they must learn not to view change with suspicion and give full play to the philosophical and intuitive side of their nature. Once they integrate higher aspirations with their natural ambition, their progress in making changes is ensured.

FULGENCIO BATISTA
Cuban dictator overthrown by Castro in 1959

1/16/1901
Capricorn III

CHALLENGE: **ACCEPTING THAT NOT ALL THEIR IDEAS ARE CORRECT**
FULFILLMENT: **EFFECTING REFORMS BASED ON THEIR SENSE OF FAIRNESS**
NOTABLE: **NANCY LOPEZ (GOLFER; LPGA PLAYER OF THE YEAR 4 TIMES)**

January 10–16
DOMINANCE
CAPRICORN III

Somewhat rigid in their attitudes toward the world and its problems, those born in this week will nevertheless have to cultivate a greater degree of tolerance and depth of understanding in order to realize their fondest dreams and ambitions. They can put people off with their severe, autocratic attitudes and require quite a bit of softening up before they realize the promise of this karmic path. It is therefore important for them to cultivate self-awareness and perhaps even indulge their wilder, more impulsive side from time to time. Once they develop a greater degree of tolerance for their own mistakes, tolerance for others will follow. While on the Way of Reform, Capricorn III's will do well to educate themselves in a new version of the three R's: relating, relaxing, and reevaluating their sometimes narrow approach to all that is possible.

CHALLENGE: **BECOMING MORE OPEN TO VIEWPOINTS OTHER THAN THEIR OWN**
FULFILLMENT: **GIVING EXPRESSION TO THEIR MORE OUTRAGEOUS SIDE**
NOTABLE: **JACK JONES (POPULAR SINGER)**

January 17–22
MYSTERY AND IMAGINATION
CAPRICORN–AQUARIUS CUSP

Early along this karmic path, Capricorn–Aquarians will doubtless face the challenge of learning to control their wilder side. Still, the peaks and valleys these souls experience will contribute to their sense of the real and serve to enhance their instincts not only for getting what they want for themselves but for applying their talents to improve the lot of others. Though their involvement with personal causes and crusades may be quite intense, it may also prove short-lived as their curious and passionate natures spur them onward. Still, if they are careful to tone down their approach, not overwhelm others with their demands, and not torture themselves with their extremes of mood, their prospects for success and achievement in improving both their own lives and the lives of those around them are considerable.

CLARK GABLE
Film actor,
Gone With the Wind

2/1/1901
Aquarius II

CHALLENGE: **KEEPING THEIR REVOLUTIONARY ENTHUSIASM IN CHECK SO AS NOT TO OVERWHELM OTHERS**
FULFILLMENT: **APPLYING THEIR FERTILE AND IMAGINATIVE MINDS TO THE WORLD AROUND THEM**

January 23–30
GENIUS
AQUARIUS I

Aquarius I's will take quite naturally to the Way of Reform, provided they can focus their energies and apply them in a steadier fashion than might at first seem natural to them. Restless and high-strung, they can succumb to simple rebelliousness and hamper their own progress by an extremely low frustration threshold. The demands of this karmic path will doubtless manifest themselves by drawing them away from their personal preoccupations and into the larger social arena. Though they may struggle a bit with the reality that they can't accomplish their highest goals without help and the development of more refined people skills, these quick minds will readily adjust to a broader vision and a commitment to higher ideals. Seeing the wealth of their plans and ideas put to use in practical ways will doubtless prove satisfying for these personalities, and though they can become quite calculating as they mature, they are unlikely to lose their sense of commitment to the larger world.

CHALLENGE: **ACCEPTING THE HELP OF OTHERS**
FULFILLMENT: **USING THEIR ORIGINAL THINKING TO INNOVATE**
NOTABLE: **ALLEN DuMONT (PIONEER IN THE DEVELOPMENT OF TELEVISION)**

January 31–February 7
YOUTH AND EASE
AQUARIUS II

Those born in this week who travel the Way of Reform may falter a bit, as their great need to be accepted by and to accept others may preclude their developing higher spiritual values and the ability to dig in their heels and take a stand. Though not naturally indecisive, these souls prefer not to make waves if they can help it. Thus, the demands of this destiny path may manifest in their experiencing any number of pricks and prods to their consciousness, putting them face-to-face with the less fortunate, the unscrupulous and the unfair until they stand up and stop trying merely to belong. Their chameleonlike tendencies can also be their undoing if they content themselves with skimming the surface of problems or frittering their energies away in admittedly pleasurable but ultimately unproductive enterprises. Still, their natural talents may prove enough to take them to the top of a chosen profession or enterprise. Nonetheless, it will be their own efforts that keep them there.

JASCHA HEIFETZ
Considered greatest
violinist of all time

2/2/1901
Aquarius II

CHALLENGE: **OVERCOMING FEAR IN ORDER TO TAKE A STAND**
FULFILLMENT: **FINDING THAT THEIR WILDER SIDE CAN BE USED TO ADVANTAGE**
NOTABLE: **JOHN GUARE (DRAMATIST, *THE HOUSE OF BLUE LEAVES*)**

February 8–15
ACCEPTANCE
AQUARIUS III

The Way of Reform may throw those born in this week a number of curveballs in an effort to increase their levels of tolerance and understanding. Blessed with gifts of humor, wit, and liveliness that will buoy them along this path, they will nevertheless confront and struggle with issues of prejudice, tolerance, and acceptance as their world order and personal mythology are overturned and subsumed by new values. To what extent they contribute to those far-reaching changes will be an issue in their lives. Easily bored and often irresponsible, they may refuse the challenge of this path by turning away from greater commitment and interaction. Alternatively, they may retreat into rigidity, irascibility, and cynicism. Still, their potential for success is great, providing they cultivate the greater discernment and increased compassion that are part of this life's journey.

CHALLENGE: **TEMPERING THEIR PROCLIVITY FOR IRRITATION AND OVERALL GRUMPINESS**
FULFILLMENT: **BEING PART OF A GREATER CAUSE OR MISSION**
NOTABLES: **STELLA ADLER (ACTRESS; ACTING TEACHER); JUDY BLUME (AUTHOR); ANDY STEWART (PUBLISHER)**

February 16–22

SENSITIVITY
AQUARIUS–PISCES CUSP

Career-oriented and ambitious, Aquarius–Pisceans may have to find a balance between personal touchiness and the abstractions of social interaction. They may well get mired in a belligerent, rebellious attitude toward the world, and their aggressive tendencies may be their undoing until maturity affords them the perspective and patience to apply their talents and ambitions in a steady, realistic fashion. Yet the potential for deep and sensitive involvement is surely present, though it may manifest itself in a purely personal set of circumstances, such as a commitment to family, friends, or a soul mate. However, if these personalities work to integrate the personal and professional sides of their lives, as well as to break down the psychological barriers and crippling traditions and outworn myths that hold them back from higher development, their success on the road and in the world is ensured.

CHALLENGE: **REMOVING A FEW OF THE CHIPS FROM THEIR SHOULDERS**
FULFILLMENT: **FEELING A SENSE OF DEEP COMMITMENT AND CONNECTEDNESS TO OTHERS IN A CAUSE**
NOTABLE: **CHARLES MCBURNEY (PHYSICIAN; SURGICAL PIONEER)**

RUDOLF NUREYEV
Ballet superstar

3/17/1938
Pisces III

February 23–March 2

SPIRIT
PISCES I

Pinning themselves down to practical realities may be difficult for those born in this week as they make their way along the Way of Reform. Blessed with a natural spirituality, they may nevertheless resist the challenges presented by it and squander their energies and talents in feel-good escapism or perpetual naïveté. Too, they may become rather overburdened with irksome tasks and responsibilities, as their desire to do for others may hold them back in developing a greater sense of their own needs. Yet these talented, sensitive individuals can find real success as historians and philosophers and through the exploration of religious and spiritual disciplines of all kinds. If they control their generosity, harness their imaginations, and surround themselves with those who will support rather than burden them, all will go well.

CHALLENGE: **HARNESSING THEIR IMAGINATIONS RATHER THAN SEEKING REFUGE IN ESCAPISM**
FULFILLMENT: **EMPLOYING THEIR ORIENTATION TOWARD SERVICE**
NOTABLE: **LINUS PAULING (CHEMIST, NOBEL PRIZE WINNER FOR WORK ON MOLECULAR STRUCTURE)**

March 3–10

THE LONER
PISCES II

The loners who travel the Way of Reform will do well to channel their assets into areas of more abstract, rather than purely personal, areas of commitment. Gifted with natural empathy, their more self-protective instincts may exist at odds with this karmic path's call to greater involvement in the world and its affairs. Dedicating themselves to a career or profession that will serve to boost their self-confidence and yet allow them periods of rest and retreat will be important, as will the steady support of a trusted, select group of friends who can educate them in the ways of personal involvement. Should they be fortunate enough to have children, they make wonderful parents, dedicated to nurturing yet blessed with the ability to exercise the right combination of authority and wisdom. If they do not allow themselves to be seduced by ephemeral and abstract concerns at the expense of their own comfort and quality of life, they can find enviable success and standing on this karmic path.

CHALLENGE: **LEARNING TO LOOK AT REALITY**
FULFILLMENT: **EFFECTING REFORMS ON BEHALF OF THEIR NEAREST AND DEAREST**

CHARLIE PRIDE
Country music singer

3/18/1938
Pisces III

March 11–18

DANCERS AND DREAMERS
PISCES III

Practical issues of all kinds can be a real sticking point for Pisces III's who travel the Way of Reform. They have a pronounced tendency to skim the surface of problems and issues, they souls will have no small struggle in their quest for stability. Still, this karmic path is sure to aid them, as its responsibilities will keep these souls grounded in the here and now of career issues and nurture their considerable talents through its call to increased focus and application. Their broader view of life and their fine philosophical perspective will be an invaluable asset on this life's journey, affording them both an insight into tradition and the creativity necessary to initiate far-reaching change. If they can cultivate a measure of personal strength and trustworthiness, they have the potential for a truly phenomenal rise in a chosen profession.

CHALLENGE: **LEARNING TO LOOK AT PROBLEMS DIRECTLY**
FULFILLMENT: **APPRECIATING THEIR PERSONAL STRENGTH**
NOTABLE: **DOROTHY BRUNSON (BROADCASTING EXECUTIVE)**

The Way of Responsibility

GEMINI I TO SAGITTARIUS I
Freedom to Independence

The individuals born to this karmic path are destined to learn the lessons of responsibility. Coming into this life with a nature that is freedom-loving and rebellious, these individuals rail against all limitations. Thus it is their nature to avoid responsibility. However, it is precisely the duty and accountability deriving from the acceptance of responsibility that will fulfill their destiny and lead them to a true sense of Sagittarius I independence. Often these individuals have a kind of manic fear of being controlled by others. But those born to this path must learn not only to free themselves from such control but to realize that an ongoing negative reaction to authority is itself a form of being controlled. Having no reaction at all to authority may be the real freedom for these men and women. Moreover, this path demands that those born to it not only throw off the yoke of their self-imposed fear of restriction but also give birth to an inner sense of responsibility through discipline.

Such are the subtleties of destiny that these individuals are here to learn a lesson on the nature of freedom. Moving from Gemini I freedom to Sagittarius I independence involves a shift of emphasis rather than a complete turnaround in approach, since the origin and goal of this karmic path are similar in that both are concerned with issues of liberty. However, on this karmic path freedom is found in responsibility. Until those born to this path are able to

---

CORE LESSON
Knowing that fighting limitations can itself be a form of limitation

GOAL
To develop self-control and discipline through the acceptance of responsibility

---

GIFTS
Honorable, Expansive, Fair

PITFALLS
Volatile, Tyrannical, Impulsive

---

form their own value system and learn how to accept structure—often in the form of self-imposed limits—and how to work within it, their desire to break free of restraint will dominate them. Being willing to take on responsibility, they will at last be able to begin assuming the kind of maturity that leads to real spiritual growth and, ultimately, to inner freedom.

Those who tread the Way of Responsibility are often extremely sensitive to the injustices in the world around them and feel it deeply. But these individuals are here to learn that fighting society's ills often only adds to their power by giving them energy. These individuals do much better when they change their viewpoint from one that obsesses in a cynical, ironic manner on all that is wrong, to one that, like that of Sagittarius I's, is more thoughtful, hopeful, and philosophical. Part of the process of transforming the fight for freedom into true independence involves living according to a larger principle and finding spiritual freedom in it. An example is Mahatma Gandhi, who gained freedom for his people but adhered to a nonnegotiable, overreaching principle: nonviolence. Such pioneers succeed in battling injustice and prejudice by refusing to acknowledge their existence and instead accepting the responsibility of being the best they can be in their chosen field. This standpoint then becomes both their message and their weapon.

One key area in which the life lessons of this karmic

path are experienced is the family. Classically, these individuals have authority problems and may lash out against parents or relatives. Usually only in young adulthood do they start to take a broader view and observe who their parents actually are, thus beginning to understand some of the reasons for their behavior. In this way, the individuals on the Way of Responsibility have the first glimmerings of truth about their origins. At this point they may begin to see how their rebelliousness has forced them always to take the opposite view but, in doing so, has formed a set of values that have always been negative in nature. Adopting a stance that is truly their own, as opposed to simply being a reaction to someone else's, will lead them to real independence.

These people have a marked tendency toward rootlessness. Thus it is imperative for them to establish a base of operations of some kind. Often, more mature individuals find that building a family of their own is just the ticket for helping them do their karmic work. There are few things as rewarding as taking on duties out of love. Though taming these freedom lovers will be no easy task and their naturally volatile natures are bound to challenge their loved ones, committing to another person and building a life and family with them will take these men and women far on their spiritual journey. Out of deference to those they share a life with, they would do well to put some hard work into developing the willpower to keep in check any erratic emotional responses that might either hurt the feelings of loved ones or otherwise keep them from fulfilling their responsibilities.

Those on the Way of Responsibility must learn to control themselves in more ways than one. If they revel in their own glibness and sarcasm, they may become mired in denigrating attitudes. Overly aggressive in their approach, they have a tendency to act preemptively. Thus, these individuals often risk becoming that which they themselves despise: tyrannical and manipulative. The key here is to adopt deeply human values that do not permit putting oneself above others. Those on the Way of Responsibility can gradually give up their need to order others about but must also beware of not going too far in the other direction by refusing to impose the limits that others may need.

Many who are involved with those born on this karmic path will view them more as their Gemini I side—irresponsible freedom lovers—than as the honorable, independent thinkers (Sagittarius I) they believe themselves to be and are working to become. This may sometimes be because striving for freedom is too often done selfishly, at someone else's expense. In fact, history has shown that one person's gaining freedom may be predicated on another being enslaved or victimized. Earning true independence, on

RELEASE

The fear of domination

REWARD

The joy of feeling secure in
one's inner authority

SUGGESTION

Drop the obsession with life's flaws and believe in its possibilities;
there you will find true freedom.

the other hand, often entails encouraging others to achieve independence of spirit as well or gladly sharing the rewards of liberty with others. This mature approach is the reason that other people tend to view more highly evolved individuals on the Way of Responsibility as being really independent, rather than just struggling to be free. It is best, therefore, for those on this karmic path to avoid those who fancy themselves to be rebels (especially *without* a cause!) and develop relationships with independent individuals who are freethinkers but are also willing to operate within the norms of society.

In their professional life, those on the Way of Responsibility are often mavericks and do best when granted independence of action within a corporate or other structured setting. Once they give up fighting the system and learn to work within it, these individuals are often trailblazers who set new standards or break new ground. Within the family, those on the Way of Responsibility tend to be close to their parents and children, as well as to a few very dear friends. Ultimately, this karmic path encourages individuality rather than group involvement, necessitating more solitude. Although a series of brief love affairs may characterize the romantic lives of such people, finding a life partner is more grounding since it teaches the core lesson of how to be responsible to another person. Those who wish to be deeply involved with those on this karmic path should be prepared to be

BALANCE POINT

Freedom and Restriction

honest and open and never to go back on their given word, since integrity and ethics are of primary importance to them. Those with whom an easy give-and-take can be established will become true friends of these somewhat difficult, discriminating individuals.

Contact with nature in its many manifestations is essential for those on this karmic path. Not only do they desire and need it because it calms their often volatile emotions, it has another salutary effect on them as well: it is in the silence and simplicity of nature that those on the Way of Responsibility can find the greater truths that will be their polestars. The insights gained when they are exposed to the natural world help those on this karmic path develop the perspective to realize that much of what they struggle with is not really all that important. Having pets, living in the country or at least spending vacations in unspoiled areas, adopting a vegetarian or other healthy diet, and participating in ecological activities are all salutary for those on the Way of Responsibility.

Perhaps an image that could represent this karmic path is one taken from the Bible: ". . . and they shall beat their swords into plowshares." The anger and rebellion associated with a battle for freedom are transmuted into the energy needed to accomplish the work of peace, in particular leading a good and responsible life. Thus, though those on the Way of Responsibility may first revolt, ultimately they will win the battle by transmuting this energy into a productive, creative force.

CRYSTALS AND GEMSTONES

Amethyst washes away feelings of limitation and encourages the individual to understand that any external burden or chain is an opportunity to focus, strengthen, and free the self.

 NOTABLES ON THIS KARMIC PATH

WILLIAM RANDOLPH
HEARST

As portrayed in Orson Welles's film *Citizen Kane,* newspaper magnate **William Randolph Hearst** fell into a classic trap for those on this path. Seeing himself as a warrior crusading against political evil, he himself came to embody the very tyranny against which he strove. Although Hearst was unable to trade his personal agenda for human values, he did succeed in revealing, through his journalism, information hidden from the public eye. And though his gigantic estate in San Simeon, California, stands as a monument to himself, it is also a beautiful public edifice enjoyed by tens of thousands each year.

Eva Duarte de Perón (or Evita, as she was known in Argentina) felt a deep responsibility for the disadvantaged of her land. By becoming an advocate of the working classes while married to the country's dictator, she was able to effect much reform; her Eva Perón Foundation established many schools and hospi-

EVA DUARTE DE
PERÓN

tals as well as other charitable institutions. Working within the structure of the government for her own independent agenda, Evita was a maverick who achieved a balance between freedom and restriction, thereby finding karmic success. Controversial even in death, her body was stolen and moved first to Italy, then Spain, and finally home to Argentina.

Film actress, political activist, and exercise guru **Jane Fonda** appears to have succeeded in learning an important lesson of this path: lashing out at society's ills is less effective than adopting an attitude of philosophical hopefulness. By building a stronger sense of inner authority, she has been able to shed much

JANE FONDA

of her revolutionary and anarchic angst. Fonda's choice of spouses is fully indicative of this change; though once married to activist-politician Tom Hayden, Fonda is now wife to media mogul Ted Turner. In recent years she has established herself as an individual who remains committed to her causes, albeit within the restrictions of society.

Other Notables: Patricia Cornwell, James Hilton, Henry John Heinz, Michael Landon, Yaphet Kotto, Andy Garcia, Pete Seeger, Margot Fonteyn, Bjorn Borg, Joe Montana, Jerry Hall, Delta Burke, Anita Hill, Patti Scialfa, Robert Redford, Helen Hayes, Pablo Picasso, Leonardo DiCaprio, Anthony Hopkins, Andy Rooney, A. A. Milne, Franklin D. Roosevelt, Virginia Woolf, James Joyce, Jackie Robinson, Drew Barrymore, Nat King Cole

---

BIRTHDAYS ON KARMIC PATH 10

October 14, 1881–March 4, 1882 | May 26, 1900–October 14, 1900 | January 6, 1919–May 26, 1919
August 17, 1937–January 5, 1938 | March 28, 1956–August 16, 1956 | November 8, 1974–March 28, 1975
June 19, 1993–November 7, 1993 | January 30, 2012–June 18, 2012

**KARMIC PATH
10**

March 19–24
REBIRTH
PISCES–ARIES CUSP

Extreme emotional volatility will be hard to regulate for the Pisces–Arian who travels the Way of Responsibility. Their natural forthrightness need not be a liability, however, if they refuse to allow their many emotional buttons to be pushed. They will need to learn to speak out only when they have examined an issue in detail and are sure of their stand. Stunningly logical, these people are capable of careful, astute analysis; once they free themselves from their petty obsessions, they can set a fine grasp of the bigger picture. Yet they may squander their considerable energy in futile rebellion or the need to win at all costs. Still, these souls can do surprisingly well on this path, especially when grounded in good partnerships and family relationships. If they take care not to engage in needless railing against authority nor to "split" their own personality by seeking freedom in escapist fantasies, they can act as a force for change and considerable accomplishment.

CHALLENGE: **FINDING PRINCIPLES BY WHICH THEY CAN LIVE THEIR LIVES**
FULFILLMENT: **FEELING THE SATISFACTION OF KNOWING THAT THEY ARE TRULY INDEPENDENT AGENTS**

SIR FREDERICK HENRY ROYCE
Engineer; founded Rolls-Royce

3/27/1863
Aries I

March 25–April 2
THE CHILD
ARIES I

Marked by a sense of wonder and spontaneity, those born in the Week of the Child who travel the Way of Responsibility may have quite a time before coming to an understanding of their truest destiny. Early childhood issues may make them quite phobic as regards societal or personal pressure to "stay within the lines" or "get with the program." Still, their natural maturity and generosity of spirit will serve them well with this configuration, providing they do not allow a preoccupation with their disappointments and disillusionments to cause them to withdraw into isolation or a cynical disregard for their higher development. Once they gain the knack of imbuing their daily lives with a few healthy restrictions and gracefully assume the responsibilities they want others to believe them capable of taking on, they are likely to make fine and fast progress along this karmic path.

CHALLENGE: **LETTING GO OF THE IDEA THAT THEIR PARENTS WERE TYRANTS**
FULFILLMENT: **MOVING THROUGH THEIR LIVES AND RESPONSIBILITIES UNFETTERED BY FEARS**
NOTABLE: **MCGEORGE BUNDY (SPECIAL ASSISTANT TO PRESIDENTS KENNEDY AND JOHNSON ON NATIONAL SECURITY)**

April 3–10
THE STAR
ARIES II

Aries II's who are born to the Way of Responsibility may wrestle a bit with issues precipitated by their need to be at the center of the action. As much as they feel the need to be the stars of their own worlds, they will find they draw considerable pressure and restriction to them as a result of their charisma. Though able to handle challenges that others would find quite daunting and more than willing to take them on, they will nonetheless have to step back and reevaluate their own need for attention from time to time. Blessed with great ambition and an unshakable confidence in their talents and abilities, they will doubtless rise to the top of their chosen field or profession. Yet they can undermine their own efforts through a profound insensitivity to or, in extreme cases, contempt for their own best fans and supporters. Once they adapt to the demands of this karmic path through the acceptance of and responsibility for all those admirers and satellites they draw to them, their success is ensured.

CHALLENGE: **KNOWING THAT THEY CREATE THE CIRCUMSTANCES OF THEIR OWN LIVES**
FULFILLMENT: **MAKING BETTER CHOICES FOR THEMSELVES**
NOTABLE: **FRANCES PERKINS (ACTRESS)**

MERCE CUNNINGHAM
Dancer, choreographer

4/16/1919
Aries III

April 11–18
THE PIONEER
ARIES III

Aries III's who travel the Way of Responsibility will doubtless find themselves quite happy on the journey, blessed as they are with a pioneering spirit and the ability to detach from the wealth of petty concerns and personal dramas that can plague some of their fellows. Still, they ought to take considerable care to cultivate depth of vision along with breadth of the same and avoid the tendency to overwhelm or overpower others with their inspirational style. Many on this road will find themselves tripped up or halted altogether until they learn the lessons of limitation, and some of the more restless of this type will have will have occasion to ponder a line from an old song: "Freedom ain't worth nothing if it ain't free." Yet if they can channel their energies into social awareness, a broader philosophical perspective, and personal discipline, they can consider themselves fortunate indeed.

CHALLENGE: **RECOGNIZING THEIR RESPONSIBILITIES TO THEIR FAMILIES OR LOVED ONES**
FULFILLMENT: **FEELING THAT THEY ARE WORKING FOR A GREATER CAUSE**
NOTABLES: **ANDY GARCIA (ACTOR); ERIC ROBERTS (ACTOR)**

April 19–24
POWER
ARIES–TAURUS CUSP

Aries–Tauruses on this karmic path must learn to temper their keen perception and formidable ambition with a larger sense of the world and its workings. The pursuit of their own goals can cause these souls to put blinders on and hinder their effectiveness through narrowed vision or a preoccupation with material concerns, thus crippling the versatility that is part of this configuration. Still, it is precisely their knack for making and appreciating the value of money that will serve them in good stead, since theirs is a pursuit that values money not just for its own sake or even for its power over others but for the freedom and independence an adequate income can provide. These personalities would, however, do well to keep in mind that their personal freedom should not be purchased at the price of others' unhappiness. Still, as they cultivate the philosophy, philanthropy, and expansiveness that this karmic path demands, their progress will be both easy and rewarding.

LIBERACE
Flamboyant pianist and entertainer

5/16/1919
Taurus III

CHALLENGE: **RESOLVING TO FREE THEMSELVES FROM THEIR ATTACHMENT TO POWER**

FULFILLMENT: **USING THEIR SUBSTANTIAL STRENGTH TO HELP OTHERS TO BECOME INDEPENDENT**

April 25–May 2
MANIFESTATION
TAURUS I

Those born in the Week of Manifestation who travel this karmic path may have their hardheadedness softened a bit along the way. Throughout their lives, these personalities will address issues of structure and system, at once embracing the stability that organizations and established methods can provide yet resisting them for the restrictions they represent. Contact with nature in the form of activities such as gardening, outdoor hobbies, or a rural lifestyle will be especially beneficial to these souls, for it will put them in touch with a larger view of the universe and its workings while at the same time nourishing and comforting their more physical side. Taurus I's will doubtless respond well to the call to responsibility of this karmic path and are unlikely to shirk their duties in the interest of rootlessness. With time and perspective, they will doubtless acquire the inner sense of authority and joy of responsibility that are their reward.

CHALLENGE: **FREEING THEMSELVES FROM THEIR RIGIDITY**
FULFILLMENT: **FINDING PROFUNDITY IN NATURE**
NOTABLE: **WILLIAM RANDOLPH HEARST (PUBLISHING MOGUL; SUBJECT OF *CITIZEN KANE*)**

May 3–10
THE TEACHER
TAURUS II

Those born in the Week of the Teacher who travel the Way of Responsibility may find their issues with authority evaporating as if by magic through their exposure to other cultures and traditions. Though these high-powered intellects are well suited to the demands indicated by this karmic path, they may nevertheless turn away from the challenges indicated here and succumb to the sort of restlessness and rootlessness that indeed widens horizons, but to the benefit of no one—not even themselves. Still, their appreciation for the world of ideas and their extraordinary ability to convey those ideas to others will be of great benefit here, and if they are careful to turn their attention away from perceived restrictions, hypercriticism, or a jaded worldview and to nurture a sense of greater independence through ongoing intellectual and spiritual education, their journey along this path will be a truly "mind-bending" experience.

MARGOT FONTEYN
British ballerina

5/18/1919
Taurus III

CHALLENGE: **NOT GETTING BOGGED DOWN IN TRYING TO FIGHT EVERY INJUSTICE**
FULFILLMENT: **EMBRACING AND TEACHING NOBLER PRINCIPLES**
NOTABLES: **EVA PERÓN (ARGENTINIAN CULT FIGURE; SUBJECT OF *EVITA*); PETE SEEGER (FOLKSINGER/SONGWRITER, "IF I HAD A HAMMER")**

May 11–18
THE NATURAL
TAURUS III

Negative reactions to authority may send these souls off into the wilderness with hardly a backward glance, never to be heard from again. Yet taking such action is not in keeping with the demands of the Way of Responsibility, and circumstances will doubtless beckon them back from their "noble savage" inclinations and into the larger society. Many of these people will explore issues of environmental concerns by going back to nature or fighting the good fight against planetary pollution. Others will learn the value of limitation in more personal ways through commitment to a business, partnership, or marriage. Yet those with this configuration are promised great progress as their fears and phobias of the so-called establishment give way to a more enlightened perception of the good human beings can do when banded together and the power organizations can wield in the interests of reform and progress.

CHALLENGE: **REALIZING THAT THEY HAVE NOTHING TO PROVE**
FULFILLMENT: **GIVING THEMSELVES PERMISSION TO LIVE A MORE NATURAL, FREER LIFE**
NOTABLE: **SUGAR RAY LEONARD (CHAMPION BOXER)**

May 19–24

ENERGY
TAURUS–GEMINI CUSP

Taurus-Geminis who travel the Way of Responsibility will doubtless have an easier time if they learn to control both their tongues and their tempers. Blessed with amazing energy, they will nonetheless have a harder row to hoe if they do not first learn to settle and channel themselves into activities that require depth of perception. Some in this group may have a hair-trigger temper, and that, combined with their formidable ability to articulate their feelings, can alienate some of the less verbal and less volatile people they meet. As a result, their striving for freedom will come to naught unless they learn to focus better and avoid preemptive action. The development of a less cynical, reactive, and rebellious attitude will serve them well and enable them to liberate themselves from the hidden spiritual chains that often bind them.

JAY SILVERHEELS
Actor, played Tonto on television program
The Lone Ranger

5/26/1919
Gemini I

CHALLENGE: **LEARNING TO RESTRAIN THEIR TEMPERS AND THEIR TONGUES**
FULFILLMENT: **EXPERIENCING THE EMPOWERMENT THAT COMES FROM MATURING GRACEFULLY**

May 25–June 2

FREEDOM
GEMINI I

The fear of domination can be a real sticking point for those born in the Week of Freedom, and they may engage in any number of mind games or intellectual contests with those who would steer them toward a more relaxed and accepting approach to ordinary duties and obligations. These personalities can misuse their energies in verbal tirades, mental restlessness, or exercises in cynicism that keep them from reaching their higher goals. Still, their sheer intellectual power and fascination with the world of mental challenges and ideals will stand them in fine stead with this configuration, and if they ground themselves with stable relationships, obligations that remind them of the growth that is possible through raising children, or deep love relationships, they may well be able to slow down long enough to "catch up with themselves" and integrate their worldview in a way that is productive for all.

CHALLENGE: **KNOWING THAT THEIR INTOLERANCE OF STRESS AND IRRITABILITY IS ITS OWN KIND OF THRALLDOM**
FULFILLMENT: **DEVELOPING A MORE IDEALISTIC VISION OF LIFE**
NOTABLE: **LISA HARTMAN-BLACK (ACTRESS)**

June 3–10

NEW LANGUAGE
GEMINI II

Gemini II's who travel the Way of Responsibility may have quite a time with bosses or other professional authority figures. As they have very little trouble saying precisely what's on their mind, it may well be their verbal skills that trip them up as they struggle to come to terms with issues of power and accountability. Often, their simple ability to articulate the truth may be perceived as insubordinate or rebellious, and their witty, sarcastic style can contribute to a wealth of misunderstandings and misinterpretations. Too, they may summon up their darker side in the form of partners or authority figures and repeat unfortunate or nonproductive personal and professional patterns until they gain in self-understanding. Still, once they learn to imbue their discourses and analyses with a measure of kindness and a broader philosophical perspective that takes into account the reality that no one individual or circumstance is perfect, they will find their work relationships considerably eased and their path to success much clearer.

CHALLENGE: **TEMPERING THEIR EXPRESSIVENESS**
FULFILLMENT: **CHOOSING TO SETTLE DOWN WITH A TRUSTED FRIEND WHO UNDERSTANDS THEM**
NOTABLES: **PATRICIA CORNWELL (BESTSELLING AUTHOR); BJÖRN BORG (SWEDISH TENNIS CHAMPION)**

June 11–18

THE SEEKER
GEMINI III

JOE MONTANA
Quarterback, won four Super Bowls with the 49ers

6/11/1956
Gemini III

Seekers who travel the Way of Responsibility may have a difficult time settling down to the demands of the workplace or a stable relationship. Attracted to all sorts of risks and even a measure of danger now and then, they can engage in a certain amount of "bear baiting" when it comes to coping with authority figures, sometimes with unfortunate results. A deeper understanding of the issues and workings of the system will enable them to become more diplomatic and political players and thus avoid many of the pitfalls that go with their love of variety and stimulation. Still, as they mature they will have to work on their tendency to be manipulative. Once they come into their own, they are likely to realize great accomplishments as they come to terms with the fact that true independence is rarely a question of external circumstances but something that is ultimately realized in the mind.

CHALLENGE: **OWNING THAT SOME LIMITATION IS HEALTHY— OTHERWISE WHAT WOULD THEY HAVE TO TRANSCEND?**
FULFILLMENT: **KNOWING THAT THE FREEDOM THEY SEEK IS WITHIN**

KARMIC PATH
10

June 19–24

MAGIC
GEMINI–CANCER CUSP

Deeply sensitive to the injustice and inequity in the world around them, Gemini–Cancers are likely to flourish on the Way of Responsibility. The energies of this configuration will manifest for some as placing themselves quite willingly in the service of a higher cause or purpose, while for others, conflicts with authority or their fear of being controlled will drive them into a private world that is all but inaccessible. In any event, it may be difficult to determine what these people really think, for as able as they are to express their feelings or air their grievances, they can play their cards quite close to the chest in an effort to avoid confrontation or to manipulate circumstances to their own advantage. At worst, these people will be highly verbal, emotionally demanding, and quite prone to complain. At best, their sensitivity will be fired with energy and inspiration and their capacity for love widened to include the larger needs of humankind.

JERRY HALL
Supermodel; married
Mick Jagger

7/2/1956
Cancer I

CHALLENGE: **CRAVING INDEPENDENCE FOR THEMSELVES**
FULFILLMENT: **FINDING THEIR FREEDOM IN FIGHTING ON BEHALF OF OTHERS**

June 25–July 2

THE EMPATH
CANCER I

Though the Way of Responsibility can imbue Cancer I's with a highly useful objectivity and a somewhat thicker skin than they might otherwise have, chances are that many of these souls will stumble a bit before finding their footing on this karmic path. The need for freedom and independence that goes with this configuration, combined with their extreme sensitivity, can drive many of them to withdraw from the world and into a self-imposed isolation that may well prove more limiting than the circumstances they are trying to avoid. Others will manifest a sort of manic or aggressive self-reliance that is at decided odds with their deeper impulse toward emotional bonding and connection. Nurturing their sometimes subdued willpower will be important, yet once they apply their formidable understanding to discovering what they truly want out of life and settle down to the tasks at hand, financial and spiritual success is certain.

CHALLENGE: **ERECTING PSYCHIC BOUNDARIES THAT WILL FREE THEM FROM THE TYRANNY OF OTHERS' FEELINGS**
FULFILLMENT: **OPERATING FROM PRINCIPLE RATHER THAN EMOTION**
NOTABLES: **LOUIS EARL OF MOUNTBATTEN (LAST VICEROY OF INDIA; ASSASSINATED); CHRIS ISAAK (POPULAR/COUNTRY SINGER; MUSICIAN)**

July 3–10

THE UNCONVENTIONAL
CANCER II

Those born in the Week of the Unconventional who find themselves on the Way of Responsibility may be in for a wild and woolly time of it as they struggle to first confront, then vanquish the conflict between accountability and independence. Some of them will refuse the challenges offered and retreat into an admittedly fantasy-rich yet unrealistic or unstable emotional life, while others will act out their rebellions, usually with the help of unsavory associates. Too, they may obsess over the flaws and imperfections in their lives and circumstances and use some of their more unfortunate perceptions as an excuse for sidestepping the tasks at hand. However, they are quite capable of acquiring the deeper human values and broader philosophical perspective required by this karmic path, and if they are careful to cultivate a measure of optimism and view the glass as half full rather than half empty, they are likely to find great success.

ANTOINE DE SAINT-EXUPÉRY
Airman and writer,
The Little Prince; lost in
WWII

6/29/1900
Cancer I

CHALLENGE: **NOT CONFUSING INDULGENCE IN FANTASY WITH FREEDOM OF THOUGHT**
FULFILLMENT: **HARNESSING THEIR CREATIVITY AND PUTTING IT TO PRODUCTIVE USE**

July 11–18

THE PERSUADER
CANCER III

Those born in the Week of the Persuader who travel the Way of Responsibility may be a bit too charming for their own good. Able to convince people of the wisdom of their plans and schemes, they often bite off more than they can chew in the way of responsibility and take on too much for their own good. On the other hand, ambition may cause them to retreat from the challenges of this karmic path into selfish and egocentric modes of behavior, to the detriment of their higher spiritual goals. Still, in the fight against society's ills and inequities, they are likely to come out the winners—provided they can control their often excessive desires in the interest of accomplishing a larger, more enduring good.

CHALLENGE: **BEING RESPONSIBLE FOR THEIR OWN NOURISHMENT AND WELFARE**
FULFILLMENT: **ACTING WITHOUT RESTRICTION TO FULFILL PLANS THEY VIEW AS BEING FOR THE GOOD OF ALL**

July 19–25
OSCILLATION
CANCER–LEO CUSP

These cusp personalities may find themselves torn in any number of directions as they navigate this karmic path. Sensitivity may war with selfishness, cynicism with enthusiasm, and moral courage with indecision or sheer impulsiveness. Yet once they begin to understand that much of their fear of restriction and their issues with authority are but projections of their inner turmoil and indecision, their path will be considerably smoothed. Nevertheless, they will discover ample and often delightful opportunities to indulge a wide spectrum of emotions, any of which may keep them from doing the work on the Way of Responsibility. If Cancer–Leos are careful to acquire and maintain the broader philosophical perspective indicated here and to adhere to the simple spiritual law of "doing unto others," both self-realization and considerable accomplishment can be theirs.

ANITA HILL
Law professor; provoked
sexual harassment issue
in Supreme Court
nomination hearing
———
7/30/1956
Leo I

CHALLENGE: **BECOMING FREE OF MOOD SWINGS**
FULFILLMENT: **ENJOYING THE PLEASURES OF FAMILY AND HOME**

July 26–August 2
AUTHORITY
LEO I

Those born in the Week of Authority may have a bit of a rough ride on this karmic path until they get a handle on just who's in charge. More than likely, those born with this configuration will be highly resistant to anyone or anything bold enough to imply that the person running the show is anyone other than themselves, and they may have to get a diploma from the school of hard knocks before they begin to broaden their understanding. Passionate and truth-loving, they can nevertheless be aggressive and competitive in the extreme, and their highly volatile tempers will have to be kept in careful check if they are to be taken as seriously as they desire. Still, they have a capacity to develop and embrace some necessary limitations. If these souls are careful to temper their sense of command with a measure of humanity and a true understanding of their fellows, the heights of success are within their reach.

CHALLENGE: **BEING RESPONSIBLE ENOUGH TO GIVE OTHERS THEIR FREEDOM**
FULFILLMENT: **LIVING OUT THEIR BELIEF IN HIGHER TRUTHS**
NOTABLES: **DOROTHY HAMILL (OLYMPIC GOLD MEDAL FIGURE SKATER); CHARLES MORTIMER (INDUSTRIALIST)**

August 3–10
BALANCED STRENGTH
LEO II

Honing and developing their intuitive side may be the biggest struggle for Leo II's on the Way of Responsibility, as a capacity for introspection is rarely their greatest strength. Impulsive and often reckless in the extreme, these rather touchy personalities may expend needless energy in excitability, irritability, and generally making mountains out of molehills. Erratic emotions and an unpredictable temper will doubtless be their biggest pitfall, and they would do well to develop objectivity, a personal philosophy, and above all the ability to laugh at themselves if they want to find success on this karmic path. Blessed with great empathy and a need to employ their talents in the service and protection of the downtrodden, they can find great fulfillment, providing they develop the knack of knowing when to get out of their own way.

THOMAS SCOPES
Teacher who taught
Darwinism, defended in
1925 "Monkey Trial"
———
8/3/1900
Leo II

CHALLENGE: **NOT HIDING FROM FREEDOM UNDER A LOAD OF DUTY**
FULFILLMENT: **DEVOTING THEIR STRENGTH TO A HIGHER CAUSE**
NOTABLE: **ELIZABETH, THE QUEEN MOTHER**

August 11–18
LEADERSHIP
LEO III

Learning to value and work within a system will be paramount to the success of Leo III's who travel the Way of Responsibility. Working their way up through the hierarchy of a company or organization may be a necessary prelude to their assuming the mantle of leadership that comes so naturally to them. Though these dynamic people thrive on challenge, they will need to develop greater discernment and learn to choose their battles carefully. Selfishness and a certain insensitivity can be their greatest flaws, and they may wind up quite angry at themselves and everyone else when their plans go awry through the simple failure to anticipate others' real needs or understand their true motivations. Still, their promise of success is loud and clear, and if they rise to the challenge of greater responsibility and learn that the respect and honor of their fellow travelers must first be earned, all will go well.

CHALLENGE: **BEING FULLY HONEST ABOUT THEIR NEED FOR INDEPENDENCE**
FULFILLMENT: **LEADING BY EXAMPLE**
NOTABLE: **ALAN DUNN (CARTOONIST, *THE NEW YORKER*)**

August 19–25
EXPOSURE
LEO–VIRGO CUSP

Keeping their plans, schemes, and activities on the up-and-up will be crucial to the success of Leo–Virgos who travel the Way of Responsibility. Their need for freedom may manifest itself in the development of a fantasy-ridden or escapist secret life or by merely paying lip service to the rules—until, of course, the proverbial chickens of accountability come home to roost. Though well equipped to deal with the challenges offered by this karmic path, these will nevertheless have to cultivate a highly moral attitude in their dealings with the world. Blessed with fine perception, great powers of observation, and considerable communicative talents, they will doubtless find ways to turn almost any system to their own advantage, and most will realize considerable success, providing they develop the deeper human values called for and never fall into the trap of holding themselves above either human or spiritual law.

CHALLENGE: **ACCEPTING THAT NEVER TRUSTING ANYONE IS NOT THE SAME AS BEING FREE**

FULFILLMENT: **BEING VIEWED AS DEPENDABLE, EVEN IN THE FACE OF THEIR OWN DRIVE FOR INDEPENDENCE**

JAMES HILTON
Author,
Goodbye, Mr. Chips

9/9/1900
Virgo II

August 26–September 2
SYSTEM BUILDERS
VIRGO I

Virgo I's who travel this karmic path will find themselves quite contented with its general scheme, though they may experience a measure of conflict, as their need for structure and safety can exist at decided odds with the demands of independence. Still, it is unlikely that they will experience much of the rootlessness or rebellion some of their fellows on this path do, and though there is a danger that they will sink into cynicism, hypercriticism, or simple pessimism, it is far more possible that they will accept the demands of this path with grace and dependability. Cultivating a higher degree of self-awareness is crucial and will help them avoid much of the acting out or self-destructive behaviors that can appear as they come to terms with both personal and societal issues of authority.

CHALLENGE: **CONVINCING THEMSELVES OF THEIR NEED FOR INDEPENDENCE**

FULFILLMENT: **STRUGGLING AGAINST INJUSTICE ON BEHALF OF OTHERS**

NOTABLE: **TOMMY SANDS (SINGER)**

September 3–10
THE ENIGMA
VIRGO II

Those born in the Week of the Enigma who travel the Way of Responsibility are likely to find considerable success and happiness. Highly observant and perceptive, they are unlikely to be troubled much by the issues of rebellion and temperament that plague many of their fellow travelers along this path, though they will have to work to avoid the dangers of cynicism. Although there is a danger that they will become the victims of their own sometimes impossibly high standards, thus isolating themselves from the social concerns and larger moral values that are part of this karmic path, they are likely to respond quite well to assuming greater obligations, which, combined with their natural discernment, fine management skills, and highly developed ethical sense, will smooth their passage to self-realization and success.

CHALLENGE: **TAKING CARE NOT TO LOSE THEIR FREEDOM OF MOVEMENT IN A MAZE OF IMPOSSIBLY RIGID STANDARDS**

FULFILLMENT: **PURSUING THE MOST ETHICAL PATH**

NOTABLE: **RICHARD TRENCH (NOTED PHILOLOGIST; POPULARIZED STUDY OF LANGUAGE)**

CLAUDE PEPPER
U.S. senator/
representative, pro-labor
liberal

9/8/1900
Virgo II

September 11–18
THE LITERALIST
VIRGO III

Virgo III's who travel the Way of Responsibility may very well resist the demands of this karmic path until they have been shown some practical reasons why changing their minds might very well change their lives. Though these personalities are generally quite well equipped to deal with the more pragmatic aspects of responsibility to others, they may stumble a bit as they learn that taking responsibility (especially for one's own actions and behavior!) can be quite different from taking on additional jobs, duties, and obligations. Thus, some of the subtler challenges of this path may be lost on this rather hardheaded group. Though their hearts may be in the right place, they may take a while for them to develop the broader philosophical perspective and higher sense of ethics necessitated by this karmic journey and avoid the selfishness and manipulative tendencies that can crop up there.

CHALLENGE: **FIGURING OUT THE DIFFERENCE BETWEEN A PRINCIPLE AND AN ELEGANT CONSTRUCTION**

FULFILLMENT: **CONTACTING NATURE FOR A SENSE OF BOTH GROUNDEDNESS AND FREEDOM**

September 19–24
BEAUTY
VIRGO–LIBRA CUSP

Those born on the Cusp of Beauty who travel this karmic path may well accomplish great things, provided they allow their idealism to broaden into a deeper understanding of moral and ethical values. Many on this path will manifest their destiny by simply striving to become the very best they can be, without wasting much thought or energy on vain struggles with those who might be blocking their progress. Others will hinder their own advancement and higher spiritual development through a series of highly volatile relationships with unduly dominant or repressive authority figures, whether in the personal or professional areas of life. Still, if they take care to raise their search for truth and meaning to the same level as their quest for beauty, their progress on this destiny path is ensured.

HELEN HAYES
Stage/film actress

10/10/1900
Libra II

CHALLENGE: **TEMPERING THEIR SENSUOUS EXCESSES WITH A DOSE OF SELF-DISCIPLINE**
FULFILLMENT: **FEELING A GREATER SENSE OF POWER THAT THE ACCEPTANCE OF RESPONSIBILITY BRINGS THEM**

September 25–October 2
THE PERFECTIONIST
LIBRA I

Libra I's who travel the Way of Responsibility are likely to find great success and accomplishment, as a disposition for working within a system or organization is part of their gift. Yet they should take care not to "bite the hand that feeds them" as they work out their authority issues and would do well to cultivate both the philosophical perspective and deeper human values that are part of this destiny, rather than wasting their energy and keen perceptions on petty or irrelevant concerns. Too, a great deal of finger-pointing and tongue wagging can go on until they learn to accept their own capacity to make mistakes. Some Libra II's must also avoid overloading their lives with an excess of mere "busyness" and activity. Still, if those around them can understand that their sense of integrity is deeply bound to their attention to details and give them rein to progress toward their higher dreams and ambitions, their lives will run much more smoothly.

CHALLENGE: **DEVELOPING A GREATER CAPACITY TO LAUGH AT THEMSELVES**
FULFILLMENT: **BLAZING A TRAIL**

October 3–10
SOCIETY
LIBRA II

Blessed with a natural and abiding sense of fairness, Libra II's are unlikely to get into too much trouble on the Way of Responsibility. Providing they do not fritter away their energies in skimming the surface of life's deeper issues and attempt to cultivate a sense of values that is tied to more than their impulse to please, they are more than likely to arrive at great independence of spirit. Marked by considerable communicative and conversational talents, Libra II's will find their insight on this karmic path increasing through interaction with others. Though some may well succumb to the dangers of a sarcastic style of criticism, others will learn that, in putting their ideas out to the world, they will catch more flies with honey than with vinegar. Though settling down to one partner, career, or personal ambition may take some time, once they do, their success and progress along this life's journey are all but ensured.

THOMAS WOLFE
Writer/playwright, *You Can't Go Home Again*

10/3/1900
Libra II

CHALLENGE: **WORKING TO BALANCE THEIR ETHICS WITH THEIR CRITICAL SIDE**
FULFILLMENT: **ATTAINING A SUFFICIENTLY SENIOR PROFESSIONAL ROLE TO GIVE THEM INDEPENDENCE**

October 11–18
THEATER
LIBRA III

Though these dynamic and often inspiring people can make some pretty big mistakes on the Way of Responsibility, this added risk means that they also have a greater potential for success. Natural leaders, they will inevitably encounter some lessons in authority, usually by having it imposed on them. How they handle it will in large measure determine their success on this karmic path. Naturally glib, they can fall victim to overconfidence from time to time and will do well to study situations and circumstances thoroughly so as to avoid the pitfalls of premature or preemptive action. Too, they may fail to master the more universal or principled understanding required by this path, but if they can channel and refine their passions into a passion for truth and a higher sense of justice, they will doubtless find great liberation along this life's journey.

CHALLENGE: **GRAPPLING WITH AUTHORITY ISSUES**
FULFILLMENT: **LIVING LARGE, BUT ALSO WITH LARGE IDEALS**
NOTABLE: **HENRY JOHN HEINZ (FOUNDED H. J. HEINZ CO.)**

October 19–25

DRAMA AND CRITICISM
LIBRA–SCORPIO CUSP

Perceptive and insightful, sometimes to an uncomfortable degree, Libra–Scorpios can have their share of ups and down on the Way of Responsibility, especially when it comes to clashes and issues with those in authority. Their need for freedom can sometimes drive these personalities far outside the norm, and their refusal to allow others to dominate them can manifest in some large displays of temper and poor decisions. Yet for all their theatrics, Libra–Scorpios are a highly responsible lot and will have little trouble acquiring the sense of perspective and higher ethical standards required by this karmic path. Though their personal lives may be fraught with passionate, short-lived, and generally messy interactions, maturity will help them rethink their place in the scheme of things, mellow their critical streak, and enhance their sense of independence.

PABLO PICASSO
Cubist; dominating figure
of early 20th-century art

10/25/1881
Libra–Scorpio Cusp

CHALLENGE: **RECOGNIZING THEIR TENDENCY TO PLAY THE ROLE OF OPPRESSOR, BOTH EMOTIONALLY AND INTELLECTUALLY**

FULFILLMENT: **OPERATING FROM A POSITION OF RESPONSIBILITY**

NOTABLES: **ALAN LADD, JR. (PRODUCER); SARAH BERNHARDT (FRENCH ACTRESS)**

October 26–November 2

INTENSITY
SCORPIO I

As darkly intense and downright difficult as Scorpio I's on the Way of Responsibility can be, they will nevertheless be marked by a superb sense of humor and a finely tuned grasp of the ironic. A real feel for the truth goes with this configuration, and once they believe they have gotten to the bottom of a particular issue or personality, it may be extremely difficult to change their minds. Thus, their work on issues of responsibility and accountability will not so much be bound up with higher integrity as revolve around their development of greater single-mindedness and dedication. Since the notion that greater responsibility will bring freedom is difficult for these men and women to grasp, they must look at situations from the viewpoint of fairness: in fairness they will shoulder more of a burden, and then in fairness they will find that the burden is lifted from them.

CHALLENGE: **REALIZING THAT ONLY FORGIVENESS CAN RELEASE THEM**

FULFILLMENT: **SHARING ANOTHER PERSON'S LOAD**

NOTABLE: **MICHAEL LANDON (ACTOR/WRITER/PRODUCER, *THE LITTLE HOUSE ON THE PRAIRIE*)**

November 3–11

DEPTH
SCORPIO II

Those born in the Week of Depth who travel this karmic path are likely to realize considerable success and accomplishment, providing they do not allow their competitive sense to get in the way of their own best interests. The abiding need to achieve and to excel can put them head-to-head with those in positions of authority, and these personalities will have to be careful to do their homework before going out on a limb or taking undue risks in the interests of personal advancement. On the other hand, Scorpio II's on the Way of Responsibility can also retreat from its challenges into escapist or addictive behaviors in an attempt to avoid or mitigate their sense of responsibility. However, the formation of deep and lasting emotional bonds will ultimately prove liberating, since the burdens taken on in such relationships will prove to be joyful ones. Thus they also offer these profound people the chance to open themselves to a world spiritual transformation.

LEONARDO DiCAPRIO
Actor, *Titanic*

11/11/1974
Scorpio II

CHALLENGE: **ARRESTING ATTEMPTS TO EVADE RESPONSIBILITY THROUGH ESCAPISM**

FULFILLMENT: **DEVELOPING THE BINDING TIES OF FAMILY**

NOTABLE: **MARY TRAVERS (SINGER, PETER, PAUL, AND MARY)**

November 12–18

CHARM
SCORPIO III

Those born in this week who travel the Way of Responsibility will doubtless face the problem of getting others to take them as seriously as they take themselves. Though their natural charms can often mask steely ambitions, others may perceive these personalities as less than substantial, only to find out later that they have been seductively manipulated. Thus, assuming responsibility for their own often rather selfish motives and less-than-honest methods may prove part of the challenge here, as will the ability to cultivate honesty and reliability in their dealings with the world. Finally, Scorpio III's will fulfill the promise of this destiny path when they come to terms with the limitations of self-satisfaction and self-indulgence by turning their attention to the larger achievements and goals of humankind.

CHALLENGE: **OPERATING IN THE WORLD MORE OPENLY AND HONESTLY**

FULFILLMENT: **ENJOYING THE RESPECT ACCORDED THEM WHEN THEY BECOME MORE RESPONSIBLE**

NOTABLE: **YAPHET KOTTO (ACTOR)**

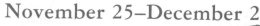

November 19–24

REVOLUTION
SCORPIO–SAGITTARIUS CUSP

Scorpio–Sagittarians who travel the Way of Responsibility have every possibility for success, providing they can at some point find and learn the value of the middle of the road. Gifted with natural sincerity and a genuine desire to free the world of all that is foolish, useless, and ineffectual, these volatile people may scatter their energies in a chronic tendency to take offense prematurely or get involved in high-flown, poorly conceived plans and ideas. Getting a handle on authority will also be something of a problem, and they would do well to apply their analytic and objective talents to examining the value of an individual or system before exploding in torrents of reactive and emotional rhetoric. Above all, they will have to relinquish their anger before they can become truly productive. Still, these progressive people can make enormous strides, provided they learn to abide within some necessary limits and don't attempt to do away with the old unless their plans for the new are well designed and firmly in place.

ROBERT GUILLAUME
Actor, *Benson*

11/30/1937
Sagittarius I

CHALLENGE: **ACCEPTING RESPONSIBILITY FOR STIRRING THE POT**

FULFILLMENT: **UPHOLDING TRADITIONS HONESTLY AND EFFECTIVELY**

November 25–December 2

INDEPENDENCE
SAGITTARIUS I

The acquisition of an inner sense of authority will be critical to the success of those born in this week who navigate the Way of Responsibility. Yet just how they go about that task will be as varied and unpredictable as these individuals themselves. Depersonalizing their sense of injustice will be an important first step, however. Also, these individuals must learn that much of their restlessness and resistance to responsibility are only misplaced anxiety about their own abilities. Becoming more self-confident and immersing themselves in a study of philosophy, the law, or spiritual disciplines will imbue them with a larger sense of perspective and serve to nurture the sense of adventure that is part of this path. Whatever their professional choices, they will doubtless discover their highest potential through their generosity of spirit and their pronounced need to give to others. Once those qualities are given full play, they will be able to assume their rightful roles in a productive and wonderfully fulfilling journey.

CHALLENGE: **SLOWING DOWN THEIR PACE AND LIVING A MORE GROUNDED LIFE**

FULFILLMENT: **DEBATING AND DEFENDING THEIR PRINCIPLES, THUS BECOMING ROLE MODELS**

NOTABLE: **KARL FRIEDRICH BENZ (AUTOMAKER; ENGINEER)**

December 3–10

THE ORIGINATOR
SAGITTARIUS II

Managing aggression can be the key to success for Sagittarius II's on the Way of Responsibility since they tend to become fearful and angry if they sense that their freedom, particularly their independence of thought, is being encroached upon. Yet they may fail to see their many ideas come to fruition until they discover the value of harnessing their ideas or displaying their talents in a more structured way. A sense of rejection can drive these souls far outside the parameters of the workaday world, and some will find their truest calling in a setting that is close to nature. For others, however, this karmic path will lead them to set aside their insecurities and employ their considerable communicative talents to bring their ideas to the attention of an organization or business. Positively, on the Way of Responsibility, many of their rougher edges will be smoothed, as will their ability to present themselves in a beneficial light.

BOBBY ALLISON
Stock car racer; 3-time Daytona 500 winner; winner of 1983 Winston Cup

12/3/1937
Sagittarius II

CHALLENGE: **MANAGING THE FEAR THAT THEIR IDEAS WILL BE RIDICULED OR QUASHED**

FULFILLMENT: **TAKING THE RESPONSIBILITY OF SEEING THEIR IDEAS THROUGH TO FRUITION**

December 11–18

THE TITAN
SAGITTARIUS III

Powerful and magnetic, many born in the Week of the Titan may have to learn to curb their impulse to bite off more than they can chew when placed on the Way of Responsibility. Others may be blessed with more than their share of natural charm yet fritter away their energies in irresponsible behavior and fits of temper. These personalities may in fact be blessed with so many talents that it is difficult for them to apply themselves to any one area of endeavor, and some will cling to the belief that they can do anything for so long that they fail to accomplish much in the end. However, if they consciously discipline themselves to the point where they can focus on the dailiness of human experience and avoid a never-ending pursuit of the ecstatic, they will find miracles unfolding quite regularly before them.

CHALLENGE: **NOT PERMITTING THE SHEER MAGNITUDE OF THEIR ENDEAVORS TO OPPRESS THEM**

FULFILLMENT: **GAINING A LARGER NOTION OF INDEPENDENCE OF SPIRIT.**

NOTABLES: **TYCHO BRAHE (SWEDISH ASTRONOMER); MAX BORN (NOBEL PHYSICIST)**

December 19–25

PROPHECY
SAGITTARIUS–CAPRICORN CUSP

The Way of Responsibility enhances the ßability and desire of Sagittarius–Capricorn's to express themselves, and these unusual people will doubtless find quite a large measure of personal fulfillment along this life's journey. Nevertheless, they may have their share of struggles with authority figures and may have to overcome their tendency to cultivate secret or escapist inclinations at the expense of their larger ambitions. Still, they are blessed with a natural and quite unassailable sense of independence that springs from an inner sense of self. If they take care to nurture and educate their intuitive skills and express their insights in the interest of the higher good, they are destined for fulfillment, no matter what their outer circumstances.

SIR ANTHONY HOPKINS
Actor; won Oscar for
Silence of the Lambs

12/31/1937
Capricorn I

CHALLENGE: **FINDING A WAY TO MAKE GREATER COMMITMENTS IN THEIR RELATIONSHIPS**
FULFILLMENT: **FEELING THE SATISFACTION OF MATURING WELL**
NOTABLES: **BRANCH RICKEY (BASEBALL MANAGER AND EXECUTIVE; FOUNDED "FARM" SYSTEM); JANE FONDA (ACTRESS; ACTIVIST; PHILANTHROPIST)**

December 26–January 2

THE RULER
CAPRICORN I

Highly dependable and gifted with considerable insight, those born in the Week of the Ruler who travel the Way of Responsibility are likely to find a great sense of inner freedom, providing they do not allow their sense of authority to run riot in expressions of irresponsible autocracy. This position enhances their natural concern for their fellows, and some may get mired in assuming too much in the way of responsibility or develop an overactive conscience as they attempt to cure all the world's ills. Too, their high opinions of their own ideas may get them into hot water with people in positions of power. Still, if they temper their personal ambitions with a broader perspective, they are likely to realize rich rewards and a high degree of spiritual advancement.

CHALLENGE: **ASSUAGING ANY WILD IMPULSES FOR FREEDOM BY TAKING A LONG LOOK AT WHO IS DEPENDING ON THEM**
FULFILLMENT: **FINDING THE JOY OF INDEPENDENCE THROUGH ACCEPTANCE**

January 3–9

DETERMINATION
CAPRICORN II

Those born in the Week of Determination are likely to find considerable happiness and fulfillment on the Way of Responsibility. Generally quite dependable, they are blessed with the broader perspective necessary for success with this configuration. Their natural attraction to the spiritual, philosophical, and metaphysical will be of great benefit here, and their interests in these areas will enable them to truly blossom on this karmic path. Most of them have a rather radical streak that may not be readily apparent, yet if they are careful not to expend their energies carelessly or in needlessly railing against authority and to apply their broader understanding in the interests of improving and innovating new means of raising the general consciousness, they will doubtless experience great support and fellowship.

ANDY ROONEY
Essayist; humorist; TV
journalist, *60 Minutes*

1/14/1919
Capricorn III

CHALLENGE: **ADMITTING TO THEIR EXCESSES**
FULFILLMENT: **LOOKING AFTER OTHERS**
NOTABLES: **JUAN CARLOS I OF SPAIN; DANICA MCKELLAR (ACTRESS, *THE WONDER YEARS*)**

January 10–16

DOMINANCE
CAPRICORN III

Developing a sense of inner authority should prove quite easy for Capricorn III's, and they are likely to realize wonderful fulfillment on the Way of Responsibility. Gifted with a strongly moral attitude, they may nevertheless have to avoid the pitfalls of narrow-mindedness or a holier-than-thou attitude in order to realize the broader perspective and greater tolerance promised by this karmic path. Considerably less serious and more fun-loving than many of their fellow Capricorn III's, most will find wonderful contentment in staying in touch with nature and the outdoors. Regular exercise and relaxation will help temper their tendency to take on too much too soon or burn themselves out with excessive worry and nervous nit-picking. Still, developing tolerance will add greatly to their happiness, and they will doubtless find the Way of Responsibility an easy and productive one.

CHALLENGE: **FREEING THEMSELVES FROM THEIR INNER DEMONS**
FULFILLMENT: **LEADING A BALANCED, UPSTANDING LIFE**
NOTABLES: **ROBERT STACK (ACTOR; TELEVISION HOST); "STRETCH" MCCOVEY (BASEBALL PLAYER)**

January 17–22

MYSTERY AND IMAGINATION
CAPRICORN–AQUARIUS CUSP

Capricorn–Aquarians who navigate the Way of Responsibility may have to face down the demons of rebellion before they can find fulfillment and success along this karmic path. Blessed with the impulse to serve humanity, they may nevertheless resist the challenge to tie themselves down or to accept restrictions they don't feel are in their best interest. Still, their great mental versatility will be of benefit here, prompting them to explore the very issues that confront them, and their acceptance of necessary structure will aid them in the search for understanding. If they can keep their unpredictable side under control or at least acknowledge that the need for change should not necessarily always be indulged, they can make wonderful progress along this path, especially in fields that value the rich and varied contribution they can make to a business, educational institution, or organization.

A. A. MILNE
Writer, *Winnie-the-Pooh*

1/18/1882
Capricorn–Aquarius Cusp

CHALLENGE: **LEARNING TO STAY THE COURSE AND TAKE A LONGER VIEW**

FULFILLMENT: **CONTRIBUTING TO SOCIAL ACTION OR SERVICE**

January 23–30

GENIUS
AQUARIUS I

Those born in the Week of Genius will have to deal with some difficult and cumbersome authority issues before they can liberate themselves from undue distractions and the tendency to be swept off their course by whims. The rich and varied world of ideas is their lifeblood, yet they may fail to see their richest inspirations and innovations bear fruit until they learn to limit and focus themselves, and to apply their considerable energies to the pursuit of their goals. Self-discipline will be highly important, as will the ability to remove themselves from the wealth of interesting distractions they may encounter along this path in both the professional and personal realms. Self-employment will also be an attractive option. Yet whatever their goals, they will doubtless learn that no matter what the arena, without rules there is only chaos.

CHALLENGE: **REINFORCING THEIR ABILITY TO PERSEVERE**

FULFILLMENT: **HOLDING A POSITION OF RESPONSIBILITY IN A NONTRADITIONAL OCCUPATION**

NOTABLES: **SARA GILBERT (ACTRESS, *ROSEANNE*); VIRGINIA WOOLF (NOVELIST, *THE WAVES*)**

January 31–February 7

YOUTH AND EASE
AQUARIUS II

These people's happy-go-lucky persona may well get in the way of their getting down to business on the Way of Responsibility, as people will be somewhat reluctant to take them seriously. As a result, they may not be asked to be particularly accountable. However, the issue of how they are viewed by others is one they will have to face. Despite their relaxed attitudes, they can avoid many of the pitfalls of this karmic path simply by cultivating a high ethical standard and refusing to "pass the buck." A deeper sense of responsibility need not be the result of hard lessons or disappointments. Rather, greater discipline and awareness can be found in the mastery of a craft, a restful routine, or the study of ancient traditions. Thus, if they release the fear of losing their own considerable popularity, Aquarius II's can reach the liberation of consciousness indicated here, sometimes simply by realizing that the knowledge and understanding they seek can be theirs for the asking.

CHALLENGE: **COUNTERING THE VIEW OF OTHERS THAT THEY ARE NOT TO BE TAKEN SERIOUSLY**

FULFILLMENT: **DEVELOPING A PHILOSOPHY OF LIFE**

NOTABLES: **JACKIE ROBINSON (FIRST AFRICAN AMERICAN MAJOR LEAGUE BASEBALL PLAYER); JAMES JOYCE (IRISH AUTHOR OF *ULYSSES*)**

FRANKLIN D. ROOSEVELT
32nd U.S. president; New Deal economics; WWII

1/30/1882
Aquarius I

February 8–15

ACCEPTANCE
AQUARIUS III

Developing tolerance for their fellow creatures will be critical to the success of Aquarius III's who travel the Way of Responsibility. Though not unusually resistant to the more practical demands of this path and often more than willing to shoulder their share of the work at hand, some of them may still fail to cultivate the broader understanding that is part of their destiny. Others will find themselves too easily swayed by the opinions or prejudices of others and will have to work to develop a higher code of ethics than might be the norm. Cultivating stable partnerships will prove enormously beneficial, as will grounding themselves in the peace and tranquillity of the outdoors, for the world of nature will do much to offset their more irritable tendencies.

CHALLENGE: **ATTEMPTING TO FIND STABILITY IN RELATIONSHIP RESPONSIBILITIES**

FULFILLMENT: **BETTER DISCERNING WHAT THEY CAN TOLERATE AND THUS TAKING RESPONSIBILITY FOR THEMSELVES**

NOTABLE: **JOHN BARRYMORE (ACTOR; MEMBER OF ACTING DYNASTY)**

February 16–22

SENSITIVITY
AQUARIUS–PISCES CUSP

Getting rid of their resentments for past hurts may prove especially challenging for those born on the Cusp of Sensitivity who travel this karmic path. Though they may expend a great deal of energy in resisting those in positions of authority, it's equally likely that they will find success in their chosen fields of endeavor, for there is a part of Aquarius–Pisceans that relishes the security of a good job and a responsible position in a well-run organization. Ambitious and often single-minded, they must get in touch with their more sensitive side and employ it in the search for improved understanding. Once they broaden their scope to include the needs of mankind as well as their own and realize that much of their challenges arise not from authority nor from external circumstances but from their own impulse of self-protection, their path to a sense of inner freedom will be ensured.

DREW BARRYMORE
Youngest of Barrymore
clan; actress,
E.T., Ever After

2/22/1975
Aquarius–Pisces Cusp

CHALLENGE: **OVERCOMING PAST HURTS IN ORDER TO COMMIT TO TODAY**
FULFILLMENT: **ACHIEVING CAREER SUCCESS**

February 23–March 2

SPIRIT
PISCES I

Those born in this week who travel the Way of Responsibility are likely to trip themselves up when they fall into the traps of unrealistic expectation or "living in the never-never." Yet these highly spiritual people can nevertheless find great success on this karmic path, providing they do not succumb to the temptations of ignoring obvious practical realities or give in to the impulse to take flight when the going gets rough. Blessed with a natural understanding of and empathy for those in need, their failures in life may come more through excessive idealism than through selfishness. Yet if they cultivate the strength to withstand the "slings and arrows of outrageous fortune" and work to develop a thicker skin, they will find themselves desensitized to the petty and more personal side of human affairs and more in touch with the issues and answers that truly matter to us all.

CHALLENGE: **COMMITTING TO A SPECIFIC SPIRITUAL PATH**
FULFILLMENT: **INVOLVING THEMSELVES IN CHARITIES AND UNDERTAKING OTHER FORMS OF SERVICE**
NOTABLE: **JENNIFER JONES (FILM ACTRESS)**

March 3–10

THE LONER
PISCES II

Pisces II's who travel the Way of Responsibility may have to fight their tendency to be their own worst enemies when it comes to the issues of authority and responsibility that dominate this karmic path. Fighting those in positions of power may prove a dangerous game for them, since they are unlikely to garner much support from their comrades. Too, they may do no small amount of shadowboxing or purely emotional reacting before they learn which are real issues and which are merely projections of their own fears. Accepting responsibility for their own weaknesses and mistakes may come especially hard for this group, since they have a tendency to "spiral downward" when something goes wrong. Still, if they are careful to pursue a course of universal compassion, increased optimism, and practical grounding in everyday reality, they can realize great progress and amazing self-fulfillment.

NAT KING COLE
Singer and performer

3/17/1919
Pisces III

CHALLENGE: **ACKNOWLEDGING THE ROLE THEY PLAY IN THEIR OWN UNHAPPINESS**
FULFILLMENT: **LOOKING AFTER SOMEONE THEY LOVE**
NOTABLE: **HARRIET TUBMAN (LED SLAVES TO SAFETY)**

March 11–18

DANCERS AND DREAMERS
PISCES III

The war between that which is possible and that which is actual may prove a real battleground for Pisces III's on this karmic path. At best, these people have a magical streak that can cause them to work miracles in even the most limited circumstances. At worst, their chronic resistance to accepting responsibility for their own mistakes and failings can make them freeloaders, moochers, and parasites on the efforts of others. Being blessed with the gift of being able to "charm the birds from the trees" can in fact contribute to their more irresponsible attitudes. Yet if they nurture their sensitivity and compassion into a higher sense of moral and ethical responsibility, their prospects of finding success and a wider philosophical understanding will be manifested beautifully.

CHALLENGE: **NOT ALLOWING THEIR IMPRACTICAL NATURE TO PREVENT THEM FROM TAKING ON CHORES**
FULFILLMENT: **BELIEVING THAT THEY MATTER TO ANOTHER PERSON**

The Way of Inspiration

GEMINI II TO SAGITTARIUS II
New Language to Originator

Those on the Way of Inspiration are here to use their naturally expressive energies to give rise to a unique form of creativity. The individuals born to this karmic path are gifted with a facility of mind that manifests itself in a quick wit, the enjoyment of language, and technical proficiency. It is their task to put these skills to some extraordinary and productive use, to put their ideas into action so that they may contribute something original to the world. They must learn to hear their inner voice of inspiration, their intuition, and to act upon it. When it speaks to them, they know it in their hearts, and it is for this that they truly live. Feeling spirit moving through them, they become their most authentic and are best able to ignore their ego's demands.

To accomplish this rather lofty aim, the men and women on the Way of Inspiration must learn how to become a channel for ideas or creativity that is greater than themselves. This level of inspiration comes from only one place: they must learn how to communicate directly with the divine. Ultimately, they will never feel fully satisfied or happy until they find a way to do so. Gifted as they are, they may churn out all that they know over and over again, doing everything the same old way. However, it is their fate to express new or possibly untried approaches, whether in the arts, politics, education, or even simple everyday tasks; for example, when fixing the plumbing or mending an article of clothing. A truly inspired thought is the one never before experienced.

The trouble is that those on the Way of Inspiration tend to be very restless, hardly able to contain themselves, much less sit still. They have a tremendous need for physical activity. For those on this path, beginning as they do with Gemini II energy, there appears to be a direct correlation between satisfying their need for physicality and staying quiet long enough for their minds or hearts to be filled with creative information. If they are ever to open themselves to the inspiration that can be their destiny, they must learn to center and ground themselves—that is, to be quiet. Whatever their inspirational process may be—whether meditation, prayer, walking in nature, or simply quiet contemplation before embarking on a project—it is important for them to find one. Sometimes this may require setting up routines or set times for exercise programs such as jogging, swimming, yoga, or tai chi to help them stay centered or when they need to break through their creative blocks or barriers.

Given that those on this karmic path have a tendency to bore easily and never stick to anything, a danger exists that they may be content merely to copy others or otherwise be derivative in their thinking. Brilliant at imitation, they may take this route rather than digging to find or express true originality. Though it can be argued that much of the creative process lies in

CORE LESSON
Developing a means of communicating directly with spirit

GOAL
To operate from an authentic source of inspiration

GIFTS
Mentally Facile, Witty, Technically Proficient

PITFALLS
Fearful of Criticism, Prone to Dissemble, Restless

derivation, should those on the Way of Inspiration engage in their talent for imitation only to produce a derivative end result, they will suffer from it as their inner voice will always whisper the truth. A pitfall here is the innate confidence that those on this path have in their ability to express themselves in writing, speech, or body movement. Because of this facility, they may opt for the path of least resistance and be satisfied with their most superficial efforts—which, it should be noted, usually impress others—or spend more time talking about what they could do with some of their more inspired ideas rather than actually putting them to some productive use. A good strategy could be initiating a project using ideas from other sources and then formulating a new way to use them, look at them, or present them so that imitation becomes the springboard for a unique contribution in a field or creative endeavor.

Unfortunately, because they have such a strong need for recognition, these individuals may revel in their more obvious talents and not really push their striking originality to its outer limits out of fear of rejection. Their greatest fear is that their unusual personalities will be unpalatable to others or will be written off as peculiar. Thus, those on the Way of Inspiration often wrap their true feelings inside elaborate deceptions that frequently involve not telling the truth or stretching it beyond acceptable limits. Their attempts to craft the way others view them are based in a deep-seated sense of chronically being misunderstood or unfairly criticized. In this way, their talent for dissembling can work against their gaining greater artistic rewards. Taking gambles and daring to fail are vital if these individuals are to reach the peak of their creative expression. The men and woman on this karmic path face the task of learning to trust their inner genius enough to present themselves to the world as they are.

Career and romance are the two main areas in which the life lessons of this karmic path are likely to play out. In both areas, the individuals here can be tremendously inspirational to others, colleagues and lovers alike—even though at work, due to their confidence and love of freedom, they may have great difficulty dealing with powerful individuals whom they perceive as wanting to make decisions for them or control them. To be successful, they must learn the lessons of compromise and cooperation. Rejection is extremely difficult for these men and women to handle, as are most forms of criticism. Both of these facts indicate that their self-confidence may not run as deep as they think it does. When those on the Way of Inspiration are able to let bouts of envy and other negativity slip away without provoking a reaction, they will know they have come a bit further in their spiritual journey.

A curious blend of introvert and extrovert, those on this karmic path often lead an incredibly private personal

RELEASE

The need for recognition

REWARD

The joy of channeling
original ideas

SUGGESTION

*Actively develop physical routines to help you center
and ground yourself. Make time for quietude.*

life while at the same time shamelessly flaunting their ideas, talents, clothes, or good looks before the world. Not surprisingly, others often do not see those on the Way of Inspiration as they really are. Many view them as wholly unique characters, entertaining and lively if not complete originals. As gregarious as they appear to be, these individuals may possess a dark, moody side, one that is readily apparent to the friends, family, and lovers who successfully penetrate their shield. They have tumultuous personalities, and their feelings cry out for expression. One challenge of their soul journey is to learn to control their very short emotional fuse and tendency to explode in anger. Should their energies be frittered away in egotistic and indulgent displays of emotion, they will lose a marvelous opportunity for insight and self-discovery.

Socially, those on this karmic path frequently make a strict separation between their public and personal life. Such a split is not objectionable in itself, but it may be prompted by fear or shame, a desire to hide a secret life, or an inability to make a connection between personal and social matters. Not infrequently, those on the Way of Inspiration attract and are attracted to troubled individuals, who may be projections of the emotional elements of their own internal struggle. Passionate feelings are no stranger to those on this path, and by grappling with the problems of their stormy lovers, those on the Way of Inspiration frequently become sidetracked from their creative endeavors.

Although inspiring to others and inspired by them in turn, these individuals must learn that what is best for them is a steady dose of self-inspiration. The process of looking inward for such a source—and ultimately finding it—is the real reward of this karmic path. Neither rejection nor recognition is sufficient to give meaning to life, since they come from outside and not from a living, vital source within. Feeling peculiar, misunderstood, irresponsible, or disorganized may be the product of old scripts that have been playing since childhood. Rooting out this negativity, much like weeding a garden, is essential to health. Flatterers, hangers-on and admirers are the worse kind of companions for those on this karmic path.

BALANCE POINT

Introversion and Extroversion

Much like Hans Christian Andersen's ugly duckling, what these individuals really need is to find an accurate self-image. As long as they rely on the observations and values of others, they are likely to flounder. However, by unlocking their internal mystery, freeing themselves in peace and quiet to hear the call of their spirit, and finding out who they really are, they will succeed in allowing their creativity to be fully, rather than only partially, expressed. Paradoxically, when those on the Way of Inspiration finally forget about trying to achieve popularity and success and begin to look within, it is precisely at this time that they begin to truly inspire others to admire them. But by then it's too late, and their unique creative achievement is all they really need.

CRYSTALS AND GEMSTONES

Apophyllite clears the channels of receptivity and allows the individual to tap into high realms of inspiration. This crystal leads one to experience the unspeakable.

NOTABLES ON THIS KARMIC PATH

Few would have guessed that an underprivileged child from the north Philadelphia ghetto would have succeeded in becoming one of the highest paid and most famous entertainers in America. Yet widely loved performer **Bill Cosby** was able to use his wit and creativity to rise beyond these humble beginnings, forming an original comic mix that appeals to people of all ages and racial backgrounds. Like many successful followers of this path, Cosby was able to channel his own internal mystery, then soar on the wings of inspiration through it.

BILL COSBY

CECIL B. DEMILLE

It could be argued that **Cecil B. DeMille** did not successfully meet an important challenge on this path, that of releasing an exaggerated need for recognition. Yet despite this shortcoming, he was able to pursue his unique vision to its fruition and develop films of great power and striking originality. Preoccupied with amassing wealth and promoting his career, DeMille drove himself relentlessly and thus had little time to develop his contemplative side. Unfortunately, his tumultuous personality frequently alienated him from his co-workers and resulted in debilitating displays of anger and ego.

Coming from the Gemini II origins of New Language, **J. D. Salinger** developed a unique style and wrote two highly original books, *The Catcher in the Rye* and *Franny and Zooey*. Characteristic of this path, Salinger is a curious blend of introvert and extrovert: despite his high name recognition, his personal life has absorbed him for many years and removed him from the public eye. Like his celebrated character Holden Caulfield, Salinger has struggled to make the connection between social and personal matters and in fighting his demons has gotten sidetracked from more creative endeavors. Although inspirational to others, this unusual writer may have failed to inspire himself.

J. D. SALINGER

Other Notables: Paula Zahn, William Edward Boeing, Warren Beatty, Paul Verlaine, Colin Powell, Billy Dee Williams, Jack Nicholson, George Carlin, Mary Cassatt, Morgan Freeman, Derek Jeter, Tom Stoppard, Dustin Hoffman, Ted Williams, Paul Harvey, Rita Hayworth, Billy Graham, Billy Idol, Madeleine L'Engle, Alexander Solzhenitsyn, Mel Gibson, Robert E. Lee, Mimi Rogers, Luis Buñuel

BIRTHDAYS ON KARMIC PATH 11

May 25, 1881–October 13, 1881 | January 5, 1900–May 25, 1900 | August 17, 1918–January 5, 1919

March 28, 1937–August 16, 1937 | November 8, 1955–March 27, 1956 | June 19, 1974–November 7, 1974

January 29, 1993–June 18, 1993 | September 10, 2011–January 29, 2012

KARMIC PATH
11

March 19–24
REBIRTH
PISCES–ARIES CUSP

Pisces–Arians who find themselves on the Way of Inspiration will likely be highly volatile types blessed with both dynamism and enormous sensitivity. They may well experience some of the "ugly duckling" syndrome associated with this configuration, however, and will have to hone their communicative talents in such a way that their ideas can be expressed and understood. Some of them will be characterized by a brash, know-it-all sort of style, while others may conceal their best dreams, innovations, and insights out of a fear of being rejected. However, these unique people have a profound store of energy and an abiding desire to win. Thus they are unlikely to be cowed by even the worst mishaps; with time their sensitivity and passion will integrate in such a way as to smooth their easily ruffled feathers, and they will find themselves transformed into the swans promised by this karmic path.

CHALLENGE: **GROUNDING THEIR IDEAS IN PRACTICAL REALITY**
FULFILLMENT: **GIVING BIRTH TO VISIONS OF THEIR INNER WORLD**
NOTABLE: **JEAN JOLIOT CURIE (NOBEL PRIZE WINNER FOR PHYSICS)**

MERLE HAGGARD
Country music singer
4/6/1937
Aries II

March 25–April 2
THE CHILD
ARIES I

Lack of inspiration, ideas, and enthusiasm will never be a problem for those born in the Week of the Child who travel this karmic path. Rather, their challenges are likely to revolve around their ability to get down to business and transform those ideas into reality. They are also marked by a certain naive quality that must be overcome or at least further refined before their creative work can attain the level of real originality indicated here. Impressionable and verbal, their quick wits and facile minds may lead them to live more superficially until they acquire real discipline and training in a particular career or craft. Their early environment will be especially important, as poor conditioning may lead to any number of problems with authority figures later in life. Still, their potential for success is pronounced, and if they remain receptive to their own best hunches, they will likely make great progress along the road.

CHALLENGE: **RELEASING THEIR FEAR OF CRITICISM**
FULFILLMENT: **SHARING THEIR NATURAL ENTHUSIASM WITH OTHERS**
NOTABLES: **PAUL VERLAINE (FRENCH POET; COMPANION OF RIMBAUD); WARREN BEATTY (ACTOR/PRODUCER/DIRECTOR, REDS, DICK TRACY)**

April 3–10
THE STAR
ARIES II

Aries II's on the Way of Inspiration are destined to make a unique mark on their world, providing they can manage their creativity to the point where the success of their ideas is totally divorced from their ego issues. For many of these personalities that might be a harder task than it sounds, for they thrive on the affection, attention, and admiration of others, and their desire to "go with what works" may well override their more original inspirations. On this karmic path, they may face the challenge of developing the courage to take the risk of bringing their ideas to the attention of the public, and many will experience their share of ups and downs before they find real acceptance. Restlessness and a tendency to overdo can also be problems, and they would do well to channel their highly physical energies into the kind of constructive activity that will clear their rather crowded minds, yet allow their channels of intuition to open wide.

CHALLENGE: **SLOWING DOWN LONG ENOUGH TO LISTEN TO THE VOICE OF INSPIRATION**
FULFILLMENT: **ENJOYING THE SPOTLIGHT THAT INSPIRING OTHERS BRINGS**
NOTABLES: **COLIN POWELL (FORMER CHAIRMAN OF JOINT CHIEFS OF STAFF); SPENCER TRACY (OSCAR-WINNING ACTOR)**

DENNIS BANKS
Cofounder of American Indian Movement
4/12/1937
Aries III

April 11–18
THE PIONEER
ARIES III

The Pioneers who travel the Way of Inspiration are likely to have a fine time of it, as their impulse to forge ahead into new and untried territories can meld quite nicely with the energies of this karmic path. Cultivating a sense of timing may prove important, however, as some with this configuration may be driven to barge ahead before their ideas have really taken shape. Intense optimism can be both a blessing and a curse for them. On the one hand, it will give them the necessary energy to strive for realization and success no matter what the odds, yet at the same time it can serve to make them the victims of their own overconfidence. They would do well to consider the lesson of the myth of Icarus: However inspired, in the end, an idea is only as good as its execution.

CHALLENGE: **LEARNING HOW TO BE ALONE AND TUNE IN TO THEIR THOUGHTS**
FULFILLMENT: **INSPIRING OTHERS AS THEY FOLLOW THEIR OWN VISION**

KARMIC PATH
11

April 19–24

POWER
ARIES–TAURUS CUSP

Those born on the Cusp of Power who navigate the Way of Inspiration have considerable resources at their disposal. Their innovation and creativity are grounded in a more practical approach, yet their tendency to be blunt or overbearing can prove their undoing. Technically proficient and mentally adept, these gifted people must nevertheless learn that there are far more ways to play the game than by simply making up their own rules. Learning to compromise and cooperate will be critical to their success, as will the ability to align their personal goals and ideas with a larger, more universal sensibility. Once they do, the creative products that are promised by this karmic path will doubtless bear a touch of the divine—both larger than life and better than dreams.

JACK NICHOLSON
Film actor, *Chinatown*,
The Shining; recently won
Oscar for
As Good as It Gets
___
4/22/1937
Aries–Taurus Cusp

CHALLENGE: **GIVING UP THEIR PREOCCUPATION WITH POWER IN FAVOR OF MORE SPIRITUAL IDEALS**
FULFILLMENT: **FINDING THEIR IDEAS ARE LARGER THAN LIFE**

April 25–May 2

MANIFESTATION
TAURUS I

Blessed with the ability to make their plans take shape in the world, those born in the Week of Manifestation who travel the Way of Inspiration are likely to realize amazing success. Though their inspirations and ideas may not have the avant-garde qualities that characterize the work of some others on this path, there is something eminently and ultimately useful about the ideas and inspirations of Taurus I's, and they are likely to have a unique talent for seeing ordinary things or circumstances in entirely new ways. In fact, their biggest problem will probably be convincing themselves that innovation or change is necessary at all. Yet their technically oriented intellects will doubtless keep ideas coming, and if they can give themselves the necessary boost to put those ideas into play, all will go well on this most interesting and productive life journey.

CHALLENGE: **DIGGING SO DEEPLY WITHIN THAT THEY FIND THEIR MUSE**
FULFILLMENT: **DEVELOPING TECHNICAL INNOVATIONS**
NOTABLE: **CHARLES RICHTER (INVENTOR OF RICHTER SCALE TO MEASURE EARTHQUAKES)**

May 3–10

THE TEACHER
TAURUS II

Teachers who are born to the Way of Inspiration may find that their biggest problem lies in finding students, apprentices, or an audience that is able to keep up with the breakneck speed of their flow of ideas. Real movers and shakers, these enterprising types may nevertheless have to struggle with issues of compromise and cooperation, since at times they can be convinced that they are not only a great deal smarter but considerably more efficient than everyone else. Though that may well be the truth, Taurus II's will nevertheless need to learn the value of slowing down and allowing themselves to open up to the worlds of larger knowledge with which they might not yet be familiar in order to realize the higher forms of inspiration and originality that are promised by this path. Cultivating flexibility will be important, and they would do especially well to study alternative or cross-cultural religions as a way of both stimulating their formidable intellects and accessing and nurturing their intuitive side.

CHALLENGE: **TEACHING THEIR OWN IDEAS, RATHER THAN THOSE OF OTHERS**
FULFILLMENT: **SEEING THEIR IDEAS APPLIED IN A PRACTICAL WAY**
NOTABLE: **FRANKIE VALLI (SINGER)**

May 11–18

THE NATURAL
TAURUS III

These fun-loving, restless souls can find considerable food for thought on the Way of Inspiration, providing they do not squander their gifts in rebelliousness, dilettantism, or undue impulsiveness. Their unique gifts enable them to go directly to the core of an idea, problem, or situation in order to ferret out the essentials, yet they are equally able to ignore or postpone the necessity to put their inspirations into practice for alarmingly long periods of time. Too, their easygoing attitudes can turn them into perennial "wannabes"—always talking about what they might accomplish but rarely doing anything about it. Yet when their restlessness and craving for excitement threaten to get in the way of a more ordered approach to creativity, they would do well to remind themselves of the implications of the poet's phrase "The saddest are these: 'It might have been.' "

GEORGE CARLIN
Controversial comedian,
actor
___
5/12/1937
Taurus III

CHALLENGE: **NO LONGER RUNNING FROM THE CALL OF THEIR INNER SELVES**
FULFILLMENT: **FEELING THE SELF-CONFIDENCE THAT COMES FROM GIVING A WHOLLY ORIGINAL IDEA TO THE WORLD**
NOTABLE: **BROOKS ROBINSON (ONE OF THE BEST 3D BASEMEN IN BASEBALL)**

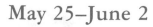

May 19–24
ENERGY
TAURUS–GEMINI CUSP

For those born on the Cusp of Energy, life can be a never-ending search for stimulation. Yet if stimulation fails to bring enlightenment in its wake, these dynamic souls may well stumble on the Way of Inspiration. Many of these people learn by imitation, and much of the image they present to the world may be a hodgepodge of characteristics, costumes, and witticisms culled from those they admire most. Still, they run the risk of never developing much more than an image if they do not slow down from time to time and delve beneath the surface. Quite clever and often very gifted when it comes to matters of style, fashion, and presentation, they make wonderful performers, public speakers, and harbingers of fashion. Yet if they are to realize the fulfillment promised by this path, they will also have to learn that the real excitement of creative endeavor lies in the joy of becoming a channel for the divine, not in the admiration or attention of others. Once they go beyond their own personae to explore the spirit that is the ground of being, they are likely to be well and generously rewarded on this life journey.

MARY CASSATT
American painter;
lived in France

5/22/1844
Taurus–Gemini Cusp

CHALLENGE: **FINDING A WAY TO CALM THEIR HYPERKINETIC ENERGIES**
FULFILLMENT: **OPENING TO THE DIVINE**

May 25–June 2
FREEDOM
GEMINI I

Gemini I's born in the Week of Freedom who travel the Way of Inspiration may find that their degree of progress along this karmic path exists in direct proportion to the number of unfinished projects that clutter up their closets, attics, basement, offices, and even the secret recesses of their minds. In fact, learning to finish what they start may be the biggest stumbling block for these brilliant yet often rather scattered people. However, they will derive much satisfaction from integrating their mental energies with physical activity. A useful exercise would be exploring hobbies or pursuits that are highly creative yet yield tangible results and products. Crafts of all kinds such as sewing, knitting, and such activities as potting or painting all demand a focus of concentration yet allow for mental and spiritual quiet time. Once these people allow themselves necessary and productive interludes, they will be opened to the higher forms of creative thought and inspiration promised by this karmic path.

CHALLENGE: **SEEING PROJECTS THROUGH TO COMPLETION**
FULFILLMENT: **STANDING UP FOR WHAT THEY BELIEVE IN**

June 3–10
NEW LANGUAGE
GEMINI II

"Silver-tongued devils" is the phrase that comes to mind when considering those born in the Week of New Language who travel this karmic path. Powerful communicators, they have creative gifts that may well extend beyond the use of language into more abstract forms of personal expression, especially music. Frequently misunderstood by their contemporaries and compatriots, they may feel frustrated and rebellious, yet it is just as likely that they will use such feelings to further fuel their creative fires and expand the boundaries of the possible in their field. Since they are usually prolific in addition to being powerfully expressive, many of them receive their recognition not for individual works or efforts but rather for a body of work that is the product of a lifetime. Thus, they will do well to cultivate a long view. A useful meditation would be concentrating on the truth that if one is not bound to the gratification of recognition, one is also freed from the fear of rejection.

MORGAN FREEMAN
Actor, *Shawshank Redemption*

6/1/1937
Gemini I

CHALLENGE: **NOT RELYING ON THEIR MENTAL FACILITY ALONE**
FULFILLMENT: **GRASPING ONE OF THEIR MANY IDEAS AND GROUNDING IT IN THE HERE AND NOW**

June 11–18
THE SEEKER
GEMINI III

Creative talents combine with a sense of adventure in the lives of those born in this week who travel the Way of Inspiration, yet cultivating their unique talents may not prove as important to them as finding, exploring, and learning from the work of others. Still, however far their search may take them, they will doubtless have to confront the issue of their uniqueness at some point in their lives and turn their energies away from the quest and into the application of knowledge. Though issues of authority may be a problem for these freedom-loving souls, they will likely take more delight in keeping their superiors guessing than they will in direct confrontation. Positively, their prospects of great success are pronounced, and if they can avoid the pitfalls of playing mind games and refusing to take themselves and their talents seriously, all is likely to go well.

CHALLENGE: **COMING TO TERMS WITH OTHERS' REJECTION OF THEIR IDEAS**
FULFILLMENT: **STRIVING FOR THE METAPHYSICAL**
NOTABLE: **WAYLON JENNINGS (COUNTRY MUSIC STAR)**

June 19–24

MAGIC
GEMINI–CANCER CUSP

Gemini–Cancers who travel the Way of Inspiration are likely to be endowed with some very special gifts. Possessed of a formidable yet lucid imagination as well as the intuitive talents necessary to success on this karmic path, Gemini–Cancers are likely to find themselves quite contented with their lot. Perhaps the principal pitfall for these romantic people will be a tendency to dissemble in the interest of preserving their fantasies or to view the world through rose-colored glasses as a means of avoiding the necessity for self-direction and self-discipline. The Way of Inspiration bodes well for them, since their considerable verbal and communicative talents will offer them a wide range of interaction and opportunity. Further, their creative efforts and inspirations are likely to have a wonderfully personal touch that will doubtless elicit a response in the hearts and minds of a devoted following of personal and professional admirers.

CHALLENGE: **COMBATING THEIR SHYNESS IN ORDER TO REVEAL THEIR OWN MIGHT**

FULFILLMENT: **DISCOVERING THE DEVOTION THAT TRUE INSPIRATION GIVES THEM**

RICHARD PETTY
Race car champion

7/2/1937
Cancer I

June 25–July 2

THE EMPATH
CANCER I

Able to attune themselves to and then articulate the myriad of feelings, frustrations, and flights of fancy of those around them, Cancer I's who find themselves on the Way of Inspiration may nevertheless have a bit of trouble in coming to terms with just where others' ideas stop and their own begin. Cultivating uniqueness and originality will come easier for them when they consciously separate themselves from an overabundance of contact with the outside world and learn to explore what is happening inside their own heads. Putting their considerable sensitivity to work in the interest of a creative project or endeavor will nonetheless be very healing for those on this karmic path and help them avoid their tendency to be pulled in too many directions at once. Blessed with a fine financial sense, they have the unique ability to manage their creativity in a business environment, and that skill alone is likely to contribute a great deal to their success on this life journey.

CHALLENGE: **DEVELOPING A PSYCHIC SELF-DEFENSE SYSTEM, USUALLY THROUGH PHYSICAL ACTIVITY**

FULFILLMENT: **PUTTING THEIR IDEAS TO WORK IN A BUSINESS SETTING**

NOTABLES: **DEREK JETER (BASEBALL PLAYER); MARABEL MORGAN (ANTIFEMINIST AUTHOR)**

July 3–10

THE UNCONVENTIONAL
CANCER II

Cancer II's are likely to be rather wildly unconventional when placed on the Way of Inspiration. Whatever they do and wherever they go, there will doubtless be a touch of the bizarre about these personalities that simply refuses to be kept under wraps. Thus, they may prove to be a thorns in the side of any number of authority figures, especially those who favor conformity. And though it's not necessarily their fault, there are any number of Cancer II's who aren't above using their very uniqueness to ruffle the feathers or shock the sensibilities of more pedestrian types. Controlling their vivid fantasies will be important here, as will the ability to distinguish between fantasy and genuine creative inspiration. If they avoid the tendency to squander their energy in petty rebellions and make sure to access their considerable stores of creativity, they can find the highest fulfillment on this karmic path with creative contributions that are likely to be unique, lucrative, and stunningly original.

CHALLENGE: **DEALING WITH FAILURE WHEN THEIR WORK DOESN'T FIND PUBLIC ACCEPTANCE**

FULFILLMENT: **TOUCHING OTHERS BY CAPTURING THEIR IMAGINATIONS**

NOTABLE: **NED BEATTY (ACTOR, DELIVERANCE)**

TOM STOPPARD
Playwright; won Tony for
*Rosencrantz and
Guildenstern Are Dead*

7/3/1937
Cancer II

July 11–18

THE PERSUADER
CANCER III

Another of the group of "silver-tongued devils" who travel the Way of Inspiration, Cancer III's can put any number of politicians, orators, and snake-oil salesmen to shame when it comes to capturing the imagination of an audience with words. Ambitious, these are the people who can indeed sell ice cubes to Eskimos or air conditioners in Antarctica if it suits their purposes to do so. They can push emotional buttons with words, and their communication is marked by a curiously intimate and even seductive style. Still, creative as their presentations can be, real creativity may receive awfully short shrift as Cancer III's pursue their purely personal needs and goals. Coming to terms with issues of rejection and security will be especially important for them, as will the need to control their tendency to physical excesses of all kinds. Ultimately, their real gifts will come to the fore if they avoid deceiving others and themselves with the convenient notion that the end always justifies the means.

CHALLENGE: **RECOGNIZING THE WAYS IN WHICH INSECURITY INTERFERES WITH TRUE ORIGINALITY**

FULFILLMENT: **DISCOVERING THE JOY OF INSPIRING OTHERS IN THE SERVICE OF TRUTH**

NOTABLE: **BILL COSBY (COMEDIAN; ACTOR; AUTHOR)**

July 19–25

OSCILLATION
CANCER–LEO CUSP

Tremendous restlessness can be something of a stumbling block for Cancer–Leos who travel the Way of Inspiration, since it makes it difficult for them to access the higher channels of creativity and innovation that are part of their destiny. Too, these verbally gifted people can be rather touchy when it comes to others' input or opinions, and they may become quite alienated if their ideas are not met with the recognition they feel they deserve. They may also manifest their natural uniqueness in a kind of megalomania, refusing to admit their mistakes or accept the rejections that are part of the price of being different. Cultivating real self-confidence will be an issue here, and many of these people will find that their highest creative expression is manifested only when they learn the superiority of silence to speech and of peace to the excitement of battle.

SIR ALEXANDER FLEMING
Discovered penicillin; shared 1945 Nobel Prize for this accomplishment

8/6/1881
Leo II

CHALLENGE: **CENTERING THEIR CONFLICTING ENERGIES AND DEVELOPING GRACE OF MOVEMENT**

FULFILLMENT: **LEARNING HOW TO TAP INTO THEIR CONSIDERABLE INTUITION**

July 26–August 2

AUTHORITY
LEO I

A certain self-centeredness may afflict those born in the Week of Authority who travel this karmic path and that may well interfere with their spiritual and worldly advancement. Though they are certainly gifted with the capacity to channel the higher energies of the universe and connect with the realm of spirit, they will first have to come to terms with the notion that there actually are forces greater than themselves. Most people with this configuration will adhere to an extremely high set of standards and thus can be rather difficult and exacting in their approach, especially to professional or career matters. Cultivating flexibility and the art of compromise is important, as is avoiding the tendency to overconfidence. Still, once they learn the lesson of how to yield to an authority higher than themselves, their steady progress along this karmic path is ensured.

CHALLENGE: **RECOGNIZING THAT THEIR NEED TO DOMINATE INTERFERES WITH THEIR SPIRITUAL GROWTH**

FULFILLMENT: **ROUSING OTHERS TO ADHERE TO HIGHER STANDARDS OF INTEGRITY**

NOTABLE: **ALFONSE D'AMATO (FORMER U.S. SENATOR)**

August 3–10

BALANCED STRENGTH
LEO II

Blessed with a broader perception and a greater degree of flexibility than many others born in the Week of Balanced Strength, Leo II's who travel the Way of Inspiration are likely to find considerable success. The key to that success, however, will be their ability to nurture and cultivate their own intuitive and spiritual capacity, which will keep them informed about the wrong turns that can be taken along this karmic path. Egotism in general can be their principal failing, since they are especially susceptible to those who would flatter them, thus causing them not to push themselves to ever-greater levels of creative fulfillment. Provided they apply their sense of integrity to their creative products and develop a degree of immunity to the need for approval or adulation, they are likely to find happiness and a great sense of accomplishment on this life journey.

DUSTIN HOFFMAN
Actor; won 2 Oscars, *Tootsie*

8/8/1937
Leo II

CHALLENGE: **NOT BELIEVING THEIR OWN PRESS RELEASES**

FULFILLMENT: **INVOKING THEIR EXCELLENT SENSE OF TIMING IN THE IMPLEMENTATION OF THEIR IDEAS**

NOTABLE: **LOUELLA PARSONS (GOSSIP COLUMNIST)**

August 11–18

LEADERSHIP
LEO III

This configuration bodes especially well for success in some artistic or financial field. Leo III's have a unique ability to strategize, plan, and implement their best ideas into practical activities that will serve them extremely well on the Way of Inspiration. Often blessed with good verbal skills or even oratorical talent, they can easily persuade others to accept their pet causes, ideas, or projects, and this ability to spark the imaginations of their coworkers and colleagues will serve them especially well. In general, their creative products and brilliant ideas have a touch of the mythic about them, though these souls must take care not to allow success to go to their heads or to become overly possessive of their inspirations. They would do well to view their talents with a necessary touch of humility and to remember that in the end, no commodity is in greater abundance than good ideas; what matters is seeing them brought to fruition.

CHALLENGE: **NOT GIVING IN TO HUBRIS**

FULFILLMENT: **LEADING OTHERS IN A MAGNIFICENT CAUSE**

NOTABLE: **CECIL B. DEMILLE (FILM DIRECTOR, *THE TEN COMMANDMENTS*)**

August 19–25

EXPOSURE
LEO–VIRGO CUSP

August 26–September 2

SYSTEM BUILDERS
VIRGO I

These socially and creatively adept individuals may nevertheless be quite deceptive, presenting a rather light, witty facade that serves to conceal a more serious and sometimes even sinister interior life. In any event, those born on the Cusp of Exposure are likely to be quite brilliant, difficult to fathom, and even harder to fool. Issues of trust may abound for them, since they may be unwilling to reveal their best ideas, inspirations, or creative endeavors to those they feel are unworthy or unable to understand. Too, their fear of rejection may be quite pronounced. Yet when they cultivate a measure of ease and compliance with their unique abilities, their more self-protective qualities will fall away to reveal brilliantly creative, inspiring individuals whose grasp of the higher truths may surprise even themselves.

TED WILLIAMS
Baseball great,
outstanding hitter

8/30/1918
Virgo I

The impulse to impose order upon one's creative life may cause those born in the Week of System Builders to falter a bit along this karmic path. Indeed, they may find themselves entirely resistant to many of its challenges. One day, spurred on perhaps by their sense of frustration with the way things are done, they will be forced to come to terms with the fact that they are here to make things better through their own original work—not merely to keep existing systems and structures in reasonably good working order. Provided they develop the confidence that they are capable of original thinking, and once they establish the necessary connection with a greater source of inspiration, their ability to translate their ideas into entirely new and useful methods and systems will truly be unparalleled.

CHALLENGE: **OVERCOMING THEIR FEAR OF HOW OTHERS VIEW THEM**
FULFILLMENT: **SEEKING THE SOURCE OF INSPIRATION WITHIN THEMSELVES**
NOTABLE: **LEONARD BERNSTEIN (COMPOSER/CONDUCTOR)**

CHALLENGE: **GENERATING A MORE ACCURATE SELF-IMAGE**
FULFILLMENT: **ELABORATING THEIR PLANS INTO A REALITY THAT IMPROVES THE LOT OF OTHERS**
NOTABLES: **ALAN JAY LERNER (LYRICIST, *MY FAIR LADY*); MARTHA MITCHELL (WIFE OF JOHN, CONVICTED ATTORNEY GENERAL DURING WATERGATE)**

September 3–10

THE ENIGMA
VIRGO II

September 11–18

THE LITERALIST
VIRGO III

The most striking thing about Virgo II's on the Way of Inspiration is that they are often marked by an extraordinary sense of humor. Though their lightning-fast wits and amazing verbal talents may go a bit over the heads of some slower people, watching them observe and comment on the world around them can be an uproarious and enlightening experience. They will rarely overstep the bounds of good taste, however, and their wittier side can serve to disguise a rather cynical yet highly ethical view of the world. Learning to display their creative and original talents without fear of rejection or reprisal may be their principal task, for their emotional life is intimately tied to their sense of inspiration, and self-protective Virgo II's will not risk revealing either easily.

PAUL HARVEY
Radio journalist, known
for distinctive delivery
style

9/4/1918
Virgo II

The practicality and creativity of Virgo III's make for an interesting mix for those who travel the Way of Inspiration. Still, the gifts of this karmic path make them far more flexible than they might otherwise be, and their inspirations, creative productions, and other innovative ideas will have more than a touch of the practical about them. Their creative side is expressed not in high-flown theories or brilliant and beautiful ephemera, but rather in discovering newer, easier, and more useful ways of doing ordinary things. They may, however, hide their lights under the proverbial bushel basket, and their fear of rejection may cause them to retreat from the challenges indicated here. If they allow themselves periods of quiet contemplation and find avenues for practical expression of their creative inspirations, they are likely to find great fulfillment on this karmic path.

CHALLENGE: **REVEALING THEMSELVES TO THE WORLD**
FULFILLMENT: **DISCOVERING THAT HUMOR AND INSIGHT ARE OFTEN GENUINELY DIVINE**

CHALLENGE: **LEARNING THAT IT'S OKAY TO BELIEVE IN MAGIC**
FULFILLMENT: **UNCOVERING TRUTH AND REVEALING IT TO THE WORLD**
NOTABLES: **ETTORE BUGATTI (LUXURY AND RACE CAR MANUFACTURER); CLIVE BELL (PAINTER; ART CRITIC)**

KARMIC PATH
11

September 19–24
BEAUTY
VIRGO–LIBRA CUSP

Those born on the Cusp of Beauty who travel the Way of Inspiration are likely to be extraordinarily gifted yet may fail to find the grounding necessary to adequately explore and express their own unique talents. Their sense of the aesthetic is quite pronounced and sometimes even extreme, causing them to set impossible standards for both themselves and the rest of the world. Some may refuse the challenges indicated here and retreat into glibness, cynicism, or elitism of the most superficial kind. Yet their potential for higher awareness and spiritual connection is very strong, and if these people take care not to become unduly isolated, their originality and unique brand of the divine spark will find their fullest expression.

RITA HAYWORTH
Movie actress; died of Alzheimer's

10/17/1918
Libra III

CHALLENGE: **FORGETTING THAT THEY WANT TO BE POPULAR**
FULFILLMENT: **LOOKING WITHIN TO FIND THEIR OWN BEAUTY**

September 25–October 2
THE PERFECTIONIST
LIBRA I

The author Albert Camus once wrote about a writer who never completed his novel because he kept rewriting the opening sentence. Such may be the fate of Libra I's when placed on the Way of Inspiration, unless they can successfully master the ability to go with the creative flow. These individuals can be difficult and exacting, their more inspired impulses may get lost in the search for perfection, and they would do well to learn the art of being easier on themselves before taking up the task of criticizing others. Opening themselves to the realm of spirit will prove especially healing, however, and their periods of retreat from society will reveal much about their own emotional workings. Once their inner lives become more ordered, their perceptions of their environment will fall into place, and they will acquire the personal and creative freedom promised by this life journey.

CHALLENGE: **LOOSENING THE RIGIDITY OF THEIR VIEWPOINTS**
FULFILLMENT: **CREATING ENOUGH QUIET TIME TO MUSE**
NOTABLES: **WILLIAM BOEING (FOUNDED BOEING AIRCRAFT); PHIL RIZZUTO (BASEBALL PLAYER; SPOKESMAN)**

October 3–10
SOCIETY
LIBRA II

Scattered energy may be the principal stumbling block for those born in the Week of Society who travel this karmic path. Light, fun-loving, and highly social, they have a pronounced sense of fairness that may not extend to themselves. Thus, they may bend over backward trying to please or entertain others without giving due respect to their own talents and needs. Creating time and space for themselves is especially important, as is the ability to channel their innate good taste and fine sense of the aesthetic into creative and productive endeavors. Finding an accurate self-image will be critical to their success, for until they do, they may find themselves slaves to fashion or otherwise preoccupied with the new and trendy. Provided they keep in mind that originality and uniqueness need not be a curse but a blessing, they can find great fulfillment along this karmic path.

ROBERT WALKER,
seen here with his sons; film actor, *See Here, Private Hargrove*

10/15/1918
Libra III

CHALLENGE: **ALLOWING TIME FOR THEIR OWN SPIRITUAL PRACTICES**
FULFILLMENT: **RECOGNIZING THEIR UNIQUE ABILITY TO INSPIRE OTHERS**
NOTABLES: **ALLEN LUDDEN (GAME SHOW HOST, *PASSWORD*); E. HOWARD HUNT (JAILED FOR HIS PARTICIPATION IN WATERGATE; AUTHOR)**

October 11–18
THEATER
LIBRA III

Those born in the Week of Theater who travel the Way of Inspiration may have to divorce themselves from the demands of their own image before they can realize the high degree of creative fulfillment that is promised. Truly brilliant communicators and wonderful actors, they may be seduced by their very worldliness and fail to access the deeper source from which their talents spring. Overconfidence in their own abilities is pronounced, and some will doubtless experience the truth of the maxim "The bigger they are, the harder they fall" at some point in their life. Still, if they do not succumb to the impulse to blame others for their own shortcomings or wallow in a sense of being misunderstood or unappreciated, they can make an indelible mark on the world with their rare and original gifts.

CHALLENGE: **NOT EXPECTING EVERY IDEA TO BE A BIG ONE**
FULFILLMENT: **FINDING THE CONFIDENCE TO TAP INTO THEIR OWN BRILLIANCE**
NOTABLE: **JEROME ROBBINS (DANCER/CHOREOGRAPHER)**

KARMIC PATH
11

October 19–25

DRAMA AND CRITICISM
LIBRA–SCORPIO CUSP

Until they come to terms with their deepest inner calling, life can be a very unpredictable business for Libra–Scorpios who travel the Way of Inspiration. It will be essential for them to turn their sharply evaluative and discriminatory instincts inward from time to time and think less about the world and more about their place in the grander scheme of things. Emotional insecurity and a poor self-image may contribute to a tendency to be hypercritical of others, and these people should avoid building themselves up by tearing others down. Nevertheless, they are gifted with a pronounced sense of beauty that will serve them well along this karmic path, and their impulses to teach, to inspire, and to uplift those around them are likely to find full expression.

AUGUST LUMIÈRE
With brother Louis Jean
invented film projector;
pioneer filmmaker

10/19/1862
Libra–Scorpio Cusp

CHALLENGE: **TEMPERING THEIR HARD-DRIVING INTENSITY LONG ENOUGH FOR MOMENTS OF SPIRIT TO SEEP IN**
FULFILLMENT: **SHARING THEIR PASSION FOR BEAUTY WITH OTHERS**
NOTABLE: **JOHANN STRAUSS (VIOLINIST; CONDUCTOR/COMPOSER, *DIE FLEDERMAUS*)**

October 26–November 2

INTENSITY
SCORPIO I

Blessed with virtuoso talents and abilities, Scorpio I's are likely to do extremely well when navigating the Way of Inspiration, as they have a strongly spiritual side that will doubtless come forth during this life journey. Their ability to articulate their judgments and air their grievances can stand in the way of their success however, especially since what they may perceive as the "truth" is often the reflection of a narrow and rather suspicious worldview. While channeling their more creative impulses into useful activity will not be difficult, coming to terms with their need for approval and affection will be hard. Yet once they emerge from their cocoon of self-protection and secrecy, they will find themselves at last able to soar to the heights of achievement that they have always sensed was their true and rightful place in the world.

CHALLENGE: **RELENTING IN THE INTENSITY OF THEIR FOCUS**
FULFILLMENT: **FINDING THE UNIQUE INSPIRATION THEY DRAW FROM ROMANCE**
NOTABLE: **RAY WALSTON (TV ACTOR, *MY FAVORITE MARTIAN*)**

November 3–11

DEPTH
SCORPIO II

Not likely to be prey to the superficiality that can plague some of their fellow travelers along the Way of Inspiration, Scorpio II's are likely to exert a lasting influence in their chosen spheres of activity, extending, in some cases, beyond the span of their own lifetime. Secrecy can nevertheless be a problem for these people, who are rather prone to play things close to the chest, and they may thus miss out some important opportunities for creative self-expression. For Scorpio II's, the chance to connect with higher spiritual sources may be benumbed by substance abuse or escapism. On the Way of Inspiration, they have the opportunity to channel their more profound energies into creative and productive endeavors, allay their insecurities by managing their incomes and finances, and develop the self-confidence to open themselves to some of the highest sources of inspiration available.

ART CARNEY
Actor, comedian,
The Honeymooners

11/4/1918
Scorpio II

CHALLENGE: **AVOIDING THE TENDENCY TO WALLOW IN THE DARKEST DEPTHS OF FEELING**
FULFILLMENT: **DIRECTING THEIR PASSION TO ALL THAT IS LIGHT**
NOTABLES: **SPIRO AGNEW (1ST U.S. VICE PRESIDENT FORCED TO RESIGN); BILLY GRAHAM (EVANGELIST)**

November 12–18

CHARM
SCORPIO III

The seductive charm and sociability of Scorpio III's, combined with the verbal skills of those born on the Way of Inspiration, can prove both their greatest blessings and their greatest stumbling blocks. In general, it can be said that, thanks to the gifts of this path, things, especially material things, will come quite easily to them. However, it is also precisely because of their facility to please others that they may fail to develop their spiritual side and may become preoccupied with material gain, personal appearance, and superficial values. Yet Scorpio III's are possessed of the ability to dream big dreams, and this will prove to be their salvation. Their most creative and innovative impulses will find fullest expression only when they realize that their truest destiny lies not in the material rewards of a given enterprise but in the spiritual gifts of the varied and multifaceted acts of creation.

CHALLENGE: **NOT RELYING ON THEIR EASY CHARM**
FULFILLMENT: **REALIZING SOME OF THEIR MOST MAGICAL DREAMS**

November 19–24

REVOLUTION
SCORPIO–SAGITTARIUS CUSP

To describe those born on the Cusp of Revolution who travel this karmic path as innovative is something of an understatement. Scorpio–Sagittarians can be both well ahead of their times and well ahead of themselves when it comes to enthusiasm and zeal in pursing their creative ideals. The problem is that they will have to work hard to channel their tremendous gifts into useful and productive avenues of expression. Many of them will have to exert great personal effort not to succumb to the frustration, rejection, and approval seeking that so often are the lot of those born to this karmic path. Still, they will doubtless have a distinct view of the world, a highly ethical and moral standard of behavior, and fine creative talents, all of which will stand them in fine stead along their life's exciting, if arduous, journey

BILLY IDOL
British rock star

11/30/1955
Sagittarius I

CHALLENGE: **FINELY TUNING THE ART OF SELF-DISCIPLINE**
FULFILLMENT: **WATCHING THEIR IDEAS HAVE AN IMPACT ON THE WORLD AROUND THEM**
NOTABLE: **CHARLES I OF ENGLAND**

November 25–December 2

INDEPENDENCE
SAGITTARIUS I

Once they come to terms with the fact that truly independent people care very little for others' opinions of their efforts, Sagittarius I's are likely to find considerable fulfillment on the Way of Inspiration. Though some of them may squander their energies in needless or unimportant run-ins with authority, most others will pursue their inner calling with tremendous willpower, sustained effort, and amazing endurance. Sticking to a specific course of action often amounts to a moral issue for these souls, and it is that quality that will lend integrity to their creative pursuits, though they must learn to regulate their levels of activity and slow their pace from time to time to place themselves at the disposal of the higher source of inspiration. It is important for Sagittarius I's to avoid the tendency to be seduced into too much debate, excess verbiage, or the simple need to win at any cost. If they do, their success is all but ensured.

CHALLENGE: **BALANCING PHYSICAL AND CREATIVE ACTIVITY**
FULFILLMENT: **ENJOYING TRUE INDEPENDENCE OF THOUGHT**
NOTABLE: **MADELEINE L'ENGLE (WRITER, *A WRINKLE IN TIME*)**

December 3–10

THE ORIGINATOR
SAGITTARIUS II

Not only do these people march to the beat of a different drummer, chances are they wrote the song, made the drum, and carved the sticks themselves. Indeed, there is an almost manic need for self-sufficiency that goes with this configuration, yet some of their best ideas, contributions, and inspirations may fail to see the light of day unless they can resist their impulses to withdraw and to hoard their ideas. Blessed with real insight into their truest gifts, they nevertheless crave understanding and acceptance and may collapse into feelings of rejection or worthlessness when criticized or made to conform. Yet when they can release such negative energies without allowing them to affect their sometimes shaky self-image, they will be well on their way to the attainment of their highest dreams.

ALEXANDER SOLZHENITSYN
Nobel Prize-winning Russian writer,
Gulag Archipelago

12/11/1918
Sagittarius III

CHALLENGE: **ACKNOWLEDGING AND MANAGING THEIR AGGRESSION**
FULFILLMENT: **LEARNING HOW TO BE A FULLY OPEN CHANNEL FOR CREATIVE INSPIRATION**

December 11–18

THE TITAN
SAGITTARIUS III

Those born in the Week of the Titan who travel this karmic path may encounter no small struggle in facing down ego-related issues and opening themselves to the world of possibilities that await them. Both powerful and gifted, they may nevertheless fall victim to a sense of their own infallibility, and should take care to plan carefully and thoroughly before presenting their ideas to the public. Conversely, these folks have a guarded side and may withhold their finest ideas or innovations out of insecurity, contenting themselves with derivative or hackneyed approaches to creative thought and effort. Still, these people have the potential for huge success, providing they can compromise and cooperate with others and open themselves to others' opinions and input as well as to their own stores of inner knowledge.

CHALLENGE: **NOT GIVING IN TO THEIR DARKER MOODS**
FULFILLMENT: **CREATING ECSTATIC MOMENTS IN EVERYDAY LIFE**

December 19–25
PROPHECY
SAGITTARIUS–CAPRICORN CUSP

There may be something of the Zen master about those born on the Cusp of Prophecy on this karmic path. Their ideas, innovations, and creations will be notable not just for their originality but for their simplicity. These people have something of a knack for "discovering" what has always been there yet what others may have failed to grasp or overlooked. Gifted with formidable intuition and powerful insight, they will also have greater talents and inclinations for personal expression than many others born on this cusp, yet they are unlikely to waste that energy in excess verbiage or in trying to win the favor of others. Though some will withdraw from the challenges presented by this karmic path by failing to cultivate the deep spiritual qualities that are their truest gifts, most others will find the highest achievement, acclaim, and liberation as they attempt to draw in others on what is a truly inspired life journey.

ANWAR SADAT
Egyptian president;
shared Nobel with Begin;
assassinated

12/25/1918
Sagittarius–Capricorn
Cusp

CHALLENGE: **NOT SUCCUMBING TO A DOUR OR OVERLY SERIOUS VIEW OF LIFE**

FULFILLMENT: **WORKING FOR THE GREATER GOOD**

NOTABLE: **HELMUT SCHMIDT (FORMER CHANCELLOR OF GERMANY)**

December 26–January 2
THE RULER
CAPRICORN I

The Rulers who are born to the Way of Inspiration are blessed with lighter hearts and more expansive tendencies than many of their Capricorn compatriots, yet they will nevertheless encounter some obstacles along this journey. Though their potential for finding practical and useful applications for their innovations and creative impulses is great, they may resist coming to the knowledge that they are "different" or uniquely gifted for many years before they come into their own. Still, maturity will tinge their creative efforts with lasting value, and if they do not cling quite so stubbornly to tradition, they will make tremendous strides along the way. The highly physical Capricorn I's will do best on this life's journey when they choose to expend some of their energy in activities such as exercise or athletics. The calming effects of such endeavors will clear away their creative blocks and open them to the higher worlds of possibility offered by this karmic path.

CHALLENGE: **CONVINCING THEMSELVES THAT THEY ARE ALLOWED TO BE INSPIRED AND OPEN**

FULFILLMENT: **EXPRESSING THEIR IDEAS IN FULL PUBLIC VIEW**

NOTABLE: **J. D. SALINGER (AUTHOR, *THE CATCHER IN THE RYE*)**

January 3–9
DETERMINATION
CAPRICORN II

These people's struggle to conform can exist at decided odds with their inner knowledge of their own uniqueness, and many of those born in the Week of Determination will falter a bit on this karmic path before they free themselves of their need to be like everybody else and accept and encourage their own talents and abilities. It is part of their destiny to try new things and new approaches, and as much as they or others might resist those challenges, chances are that simple practicality will lead them to that result in the end. In short, many of them will find it far easier to explore their uniqueness than not to. Once they integrate their interest in philosophical and metaphysical issues with their naturally down-to-earth approach, the spiritual doors will swing wide, revealing in an abundance of both creative gifts and material reward.

MEL GIBSON
Actor, director; won
Oscar for *Braveheart*

1/3/1956
Capricorn II

CHALLENGE: **ACCEPTING THAT THEY ARE ALLOWED TO WALK THE BEATEN PATH**

FULFILLMENT: **EXPRESSING THEIR MORE SENSITIVE SIDE**

NOTABLE: **RICHARD HALLIBURTON (EXPLORER)**

January 10–16
DOMINANCE
CAPRICORN III

Generally untroubled by the issues of boredom and restlessness that can plague some others who travel the Way of Inspiration, those born in the Week of Dominance are likely to find no small degree of fulfillment on this karmic path. Able to apply their energies with diligence, they are unlikely to be sidetracked from their creative endeavors and will doubtless see their efforts well rewarded. Blessed with a higher degree of tolerance and a more developed sense of values than some, they will almost certainly relish their prospects and will take considerable delight in seeing their ideas and plans brought to fruition. This path imbues them with some necessary self-confidence, and if they are able to cultivate the necessary measure of expansiveness required, they will be able to avoid the pitfalls of mere eccentricity and develop their creative gifts to a level of real originality and achievement.

CHALLENGE: **CULTIVATING A GREATER FACILITY OF MIND**

FULFILLMENT: **FINDING THAT THEIR ECCENTRICITY CAN WORK FOR THEM**

NOTABLE: **EZRA CORNELL (FOUNDED WESTERN UNION)**

January 17–22

MYSTERY AND IMAGINATION
CAPRICORN–AQUARIUS CUSP

The principal pitfall for Capricorn–Aquarians on this karmic path is that they may be unable to stay out of the action long enough to access their higher creative impulses. Characterized by a great need for excitement and activity, these restless individuals may fail to anchor their gifts in reality. Blessed with a theoretical and conceptual turn of mind, they will doubtless find unique outlets for their unusual brand of creative expression, yet there is an equal possibility that they will squander their energies in an abundance of talk or theorizing backed up with very little in the way of substantive effort. Still, their spiritual unrest may well point them in the right direction. If they make time for quiet, for going inward and exploring the worlds of mind and spirit available to them, the expression of their inspirations will come naturally, and their efforts will become almost effortless as they work to turn their dreams into reality.

ROBERT E. LEE
Commanded Confederate
Army in Civil War

1/19/1807
Capricorn–Aquarius Cusp

CHALLENGE: **QUIETING THE ELECTRICITY OF THEIR THOUGHTS**
FULFILLMENT: **FINDING A USE FOR THEIR INVENTIVENESS**
NOTABLE: **DAVID LLOYD-GEORGE (FORMER BRITISH PRIME MINISTER; REMOVED LORDS' VETO)**

January 23–30

GENIUS
AQUARIUS I

Lightning-quick minds characterize this group when placed on the Way of Inspiration, and whatever their specific area of endeavor, those born in the Week of Genius are likely to have be interested in a huge variety of subjects. Yet these highly independent people care so little for the opinions of others that they may well isolate themselves in an ivory tower and fail to find practical or realistic applications for their plans and theories. Lack of focus may be a big problem, since they have little patience for detail work and even less for the red tape of businesses and bureaucracies. Still, if they can conquer the demon of their own disorganization and learn to finish at least some of their projects and plans before undertaking the next intellectual or spiritual odyssey, they are likely to find this life journey both rewarding and remarkable.

CHALLENGE: **GENERATING A DESIRE TO UNDERSTAND THE MORE SPIRITUAL OR RELIGIOUS AREAS OF LIFE**
FULFILLMENT: **SEEING THEIR IDEAS TAKE FORM AND BECOME LUCRATIVE**
NOTABLES: **MIMI ROGERS (ACTRESS); HYMAN RICKOVER ("FATHER" OF ATOMIC SUBMARINE)**

January 31–February 7

YOUTH AND EASE
AQUARIUS II

Blessed with considerable charm and a rather laid-back attitude toward life's vicissitudes, those born in this week who find themselves on the Way of Inspiration may have a bit of trouble with the fact that the most innovative, creative, and useful ideas or plans are not always the most popular. Thus they may content themselves with admittedly charming, but often superficial pursuits, associates, or activities and fail to mine for the gold of genuine creative impulse. Cultivating a real sense of self will be critical for Aquarius II's on this karmic path, as will a willingness to forfeit personal popularity in the interest of genuine accomplishment. Provided that they make an effort to connect with the higher and more authentic forms of inspiration and enlightenment, they can find great fulfillment and spiritual expansion.

KONSTANTIN STANISLAVSKY
Method acting of
Strasberg's Group Theater
based on Stanislavsky

1/17/1863
Capricorn–Aquarius Cusp

CHALLENGE: **GOING AS DEEPLY AS POSSIBLE INTO THE HEART OF THINGS**
FULFILLMENT: **FINDING A FORM OF SPIRITUALITY THAT WORKS FOR THEM**
NOTABLES: **NATHAN LANE (FILM AND BROADWAY ACTOR); JOHNNY ROTTEN (SINGER, SEX PISTOLS)**

February 8–15

ACCEPTANCE
AQUARIUS III

Not blessed with the finest judgment of either themselves or others, these individuals will doubtless struggle with the issue of reconciling their highest creative ideals with practical reality. Often stubborn and oddly rigid in their thinking, they will need to avoid their tendencies both to slack off when a situation demands that they strive and to turn judgmental and critical when a situation begs for understanding. Their lively curiosity and affectionate natures will serve them well with this configuration, however, and help to keep them open to their innermost knowledge. Once they come to terms with the idea that their intolerance of others may amount to nothing more than an uneasy relationship with their unique gifts, their direction will be considerably clarified and they will gain the confidence to express and inspire others with a myriad of innovative and inventive thoughts, perceptions, and creative products.

CHALLENGE: **FREEING THEMSELVES OF THE IDEA THAT THEY HAVE TO ENGAGE IN A TRADITIONAL LINE OF WORK**
FULFILLMENT: **LEARNING THE LESSONS OF CONSTANCY AND APPLICATION**
NOTABLE: **JOHN "HONEYFITZ" FITZGERALD (FORMER BOSTON MAYOR; ROSE KENNEDY'S FATHER)**

February 16–22
SENSITIVITY
AQUARIUS–PISCES CUSP

Fear of rejection will be the bogeyman for those born on the Cusp of Sensitivity who travel the Way of Inspiration. Though attuned to the world of spirit and its creative gifts, they may choose to ignore the bounty available to them and squander their energies in a belligerent fashion. Though they seem to be quite sure of themselves, their confident facade can hide considerable inner torment. This karmic path may manifest itself in far-out idealism and truly original concepts or in a highly spiritual and deeply profound inner life. The trick for these people will be to integrate their spirituality to the extent that it is allowed to better inform their talents, inspirations, and creative efforts, and then to bring their unique offerings into the larger world.

**HENRY WADSWORTH
LONGFELLOW**
Poet

2/27/1807
Pisces I

CHALLENGE: **UNLEASHING THEIR HIDDEN SENSITIVITY**
FULFILLMENT: **ACHIEVING TRADITIONAL SUCCESS IN NON-TRADITIONAL WAYS**
NOTABLES: **LUIS BUÑUEL (SPANISH FILM DIRECTOR); LUCIEN PISSARRO (PAINTER)**

February 23–March 2
SPIRIT
PISCES I

Pisces I's on the Way of Inspiration are likely to find quite a bit of success and acceptance of their creative talents and abilities. Inclined to take themselves and their attributes quite seriously, they will doubtless approach their life's work and calling with considerable idealism. Yet they will encounter some struggles with the practical application of their talents and may face challenges in the area of practicalities. Finding financing for their projects, seeing them to conclusion, and establishing needed priorities and schedules may all be problems. Learning to regulate their level of expectation to better conform to their rate of production and understanding that their laurels will come only when they have produced a solid body of creative work will ensure that all goes well.

CHALLENGE: **PLANTING THEIR FEET MORE FIRMLY ON THE GROUND**
FULFILLMENT: **ENLIVENING OTHERS WITH THEIR NOVEL AND SPIRITED IDEAS**
NOTABLE: **KURT WEILL (COMPOSER)**

March 3–10
THE LONER
PISCES II

Gifted with an admirable aesthetic sense and an innate understanding of the creative process, those born in the Week of the Loner who travel this karmic path may nevertheless falter a bit and retreat from the challenges offered. Despite the great blessings of this configuration, isolation, fear of rejection, and failure to connect with the world of spirit can all be stumbling blocks. These souls can live quite easily with their own uniqueness, yet at the same time may rely on their sense of being different to justify all sorts of antisocial activities as well as a lack of substantive creative or spiritual effort. In fact, they can often be quite self-defeating, making excuses and choosing to believe that their nonconformity and originality are the curses that stand in the way of their success. Yet their need for self-expression is likely to override many of their fears, and the challenges presented by this karmic path will doubtless do much to draw them out of their shells and into a higher and more liberated worldview.

JAMES MADISON
4th U.S. president;
authored *The Federalist
Papers* with John Jay

3/16/1751
Pisces III

CHALLENGE: **NOT SHIELDING THEMSELVES FROM LIFE AT THE EXPENSE OF A SENSE OF SPIRIT**
FULFILLMENT: **SHARING THEIR SENSE OF WONDER WITH OTHERS**

March 11–18
DANCERS AND DREAMERS
PISCES III

Visionary and creatively talented, sometimes to an extreme degree, these souls will nevertheless encounter their share of ups and down along the Way of Inspiration. Plagued by what may be a lifelong inability to settle down and direct their creative efforts in a productive fashion, they may indeed inspire others yet fail to come to terms with their own true calling. Their verbal powers may be quite astonishing, yet they may have any number of conflicts with those in power due to their rather high-handed style. They will need to release their secret belief that they are somehow better or more gifted than the rest of us (though it may well be the truth!). Yet establishing a good connection with a higher source of inspiration and creativity will doubtless imbue these talented people with the necessary measure of humility, and if they are careful to apply themselves and their talents in such a way that their gifts can be enjoyed by everyone, they are likely to realize lasting and profound success.

CHALLENGE: **NOT PERMITTING THEMSELVES TO BE SIDE-TRACKED BY ROMANCE**
FULFILLMENT: **TRUSTING THEIR OWN INNER CALLING**
NOTABLE: **NIKOLAI RIMSKY-KORSAKOV (POST-ROMANTIC COMPOSER)**

The Way of Amplification

GEMINI III TO SAGITTARIUS III
Seeker to Titan

The life purpose of those on the Way of Amplification is to choose a path and live it large—to live out loud. To do this, they must learn to think for the long term and see the big picture, rather than wasting their energy flitting from one project, interest, or person to another. Individuals on the Way of Amplification are asked to create a life that is greater than who they think themselves to be or even the sum of their parts. These individuals come into the world as Seekers and thus naturally exhibit a desire to learn about larger or more universal concepts and issues. On this karmic path, they will eventually learn to live according to such higher, broader, more expansive views. Born with a pragmatic orientation, those on the Way of Amplification must take care not to be bound down or tethered by the mundane details of life but rather to dare to dream and to reach for the stars. Of course, the hardheaded, commonsensical attitude that is their blessing is a fine gift and should never be abandoned, particularly in financial matters. But unless those on this karmic path are ready to go for greatness when the opportunity arises, they will sell themselves short and fail to achieve what they are capable of.

Interestingly, amplification is not mere expansion. These individuals can easily expand their lives in many directions all at once in a rather willy-nilly fashion. Amplification requires the selection of some particular aspect of self or some cause—preferably a higher cause—that is worthy of cultivation and growth. After making such a choice, these men and women must apply the focus necessary to guarantee productivity and to create growth. It is this single-mindedness of focus and care that results in greatness. And it is this focus that is the core lesson of the Way of Amplification. As much as they may be distracted by amusements or other passions, by keeping their minds fixed on one true thing in their lives the men and women on the Way of Amplification will, in a mysterious way, actually amplify and propel themselves into a mythic realm.

Many of those on this karmic path will put their energy in the service of a higher cause. By abandoning a series of immediately gratifying but ultimately unproductive actions and instead making a significant contribution to large-scale projects, they will increase their soul's growth exponentially. The first step in accomplishing this is redefining their self-image, specifically seeing themselves not so much as struggling individuals but as part of a larger whole, be it a cause, group, or team. This reorientation of their viewpoint may actually have rewards in the form of a rise in rank within a group over time. Typically, they will experience a great sense of relief if they proceed along such lines, since moving upward also means moving away from an operation's day-to-day concerns. By doing so, those on this karmic path may at last be able to occupy themselves

CORE LESSON
Developing the ability to focus one's attention to cultivate growth

GOAL
To live a life that is greater than the sum of its parts

GIFTS
Exploratory, Risk Taking, Aspiring

PITFALLS
Insecure, Nit-picking, Flighty

with higher thoughts and expansive plans and leave the worry about petty details to others.

Finding the right moment for action is essential. Blessed with excellent intuition, these individuals would do well to cultivate it and listen to it. Although the core energy here is exploratory and risk-taking, this does not by any means guarantee a good sense of timing. Both impatience and fussiness must be guarded against, since the former will lead to striking too soon, the latter too late. Overshooting the mark is, of course, a danger on any karmic path as expansive as this one. Part of the problem is that these individuals may not even be aware that they have made a miscalculation because they have a real problem acknowledging failure. After all, picking yourself up, dusting yourself off, and proceeding ahead demand the recognition that you have fallen down in the first place! In this respect, having an objective friend, mate, or relative who can be totally honest is often lifesaving.

For those on the Way of Amplification, the arena in which this process manifests itself most clearly is their career. Often these individuals are destined for an out-of-the-ordinary level of career success and are likely to become leaders. Moving up through the ranks and growing in confidence and stature as part of an organization are often typical of those on the Way of Amplification. While those on this karmic path always have a bit of insecurity

inside, this tends to give them the push they need to get to the top. Once they arrive at an executive level, they often face two choices. One is to take over the leadership of their company with enthusiasm, vigor, and vision. The other is to leave corporate life and go off on their own, ultimately establishing themselves as consultants, entrepreneurs, writers, performers, or other authorities in their field. No matter what their choice may be, those who successfully travel the Way of Amplification always leave a mark. It should also be noted that such careers do not develop along traditional paths but tend to grow out of some passion or leisure-time activity.

Although others may be awed by the drive and vision of those on the Way of Amplification, this is not necessarily positive. Once the process of growth has been undertaken, the life path chosen, and the core lesson of focus learned, those involved with these individuals may feel slighted when they apply themselves to their own great cause. Understandably, such individuals do not always have the time, energy, or inclination to invest in building friendships, marriages, or abiding love affairs. It is really not necessary or advantageous for those on the Way of Amplification to seek out other high-minded and bighearted individuals, who may in fact contribute to the risk of overexpansion of thought, word, and deed that characterizes

RELEASE

The belief in their unworthiness

REWARD

The joy of living life
on a grand scale

SUGGESTION

Learn to release all that is petty or small within yourself.
Always remember that your destiny is larger than your concerns.
Never forget that your myth is not who you really are.

some of those on this karmic path. A steady, solid mate, one who has patience and understanding in abundance and a large dose of practicality besides, will prove to be the most beneficial. Ultimately, however, this may prove to be a tall order, since potential partners may find it difficult to live in the shadows of their larger-than-life companions.

The most successful relationships for those on the Way of Amplification are in the family and professional spheres. This is mainly because family members and colleagues are those who are likely to see them the most and also are usually the only ones the individuals on this karmic path feel comfortable turning to in time of need. Proud to the extreme, they find it difficult to acknowledge neediness. They will usually prefer to suffer rather than ask outright for assistance. An understanding family member or colleague may be able to give help in a subtle manner without either party acknowledging it as such. Family life is generally good for these people, since it is often a training ground in leadership. A word of warning: The children of those on this path may feel neglected or extraneous, so those on this karmic path may want to think carefully about having children at all.

What is best for them, and perhaps even essential to their journey, is having the elbow room to move and grow. Being involved with a family, partner, school, or other organization that blocks this process can have disastrous consequences. Since little can contain them, those on the Way of Amplification will usually overcome any obstacle. However, understanding parents, teachers, and bosses will make the process less painful and more productive for all concerned. As adolescents and young adults, these individuals will have a special need for professional tools that must be satisfied, whether special cameras, computers, design materials, or other tools they need to express their visions. Usually money spent on such items is well invested for the future.

The image that best describes the Way of Amplification is from the fairy tale "The Seven-League Boots." So large and deep was this pair of boots that when worn they allowed their wearer to take gigantic strides. In a sense, all those on the Way of Amplification must find a symbolic set of such shoes. It is the discovery of their vehicle that enables these souls to really take off. Secretly, those whose origin is the Gemini III Seeker want nothing more than to become the Sagittarius III Titan, but often, lacking focus, become disillusioned by their daily life. Finding the right pair of boots will set them on their path and enable them to become the giants they always imagined themselves to be.

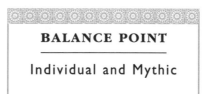

BALANCE POINT

Individual and Mythic

CRYSTALS AND GEMSTONES

Copper *conducts electrical impulses and magnifies the energy an individual transmits.*
This mineral works to inspire awareness of the magnificence of nature and humanity.

NOTABLES ON THIS KARMIC PATH

The incredible life of **Nelson Mandela** illustrates beautifully the Way of Amplification. While his larger-than-life journey from prisoner to president of South Africa is amazing, more impressive is his ability to put aside whatever personal hatred he might have felt to place his energies in service of a higher

NELSON MANDELA

cause. Acting for the benefit of his fellow South Africans, Mandela effected drastic reform in his torn country. His greatest achievements include the exorcism of apartheid and the return of South Africa to its original inhabitants. Consistently refusing to compromise his beliefs despite years of personal suffering, Mandela succeeded in surmounting all obstacles and becoming the father of freedom for his people.

BILL GATES

Said to be the world's richest businessman, **Bill Gates** found the suitable outlet for his drive and vision with the creation of Microsoft, a company that touches the lives of people all over the world. Gates's identification with his firm fulfills his destiny despite the fact that he hardly fits the conventional image of a business tycoon. In fact, his somewhat nerdy style has redefined the look

of success. Currently under fire from antitrust regulators, Gates maintains that he encourages competition and creates jobs. Like other successful individuals on this path, he has given himself room to move and grow.

The story of how a little-known teenage actress achieved overnight fame to become a musical icon with both critical and commercial acclaim is already history. Certainly a risk taker, **Alanis Morissette** and her ambitious first effort, the album *Jagged Little Pill,* characterize those on the Way of Amplification who dare to dream and reach for the stars. Alanis was able to harness feelings of insecurity, giving her the push she needed to rise to the top of her profession. Her single-mindedness also certainly

ALANIS MORISSETTE

contributed to her huge success. It remains to be seen if in the future she will triumph or fall prey to the flightiness that plagues those on this karmic path.

Other Notables: Pierre Teilhard de Chardin, Theodore Von Karman, Marcus Wallenburg, Sam Walton, Betty Ford, Ella Fitzgerald, Jack Paar, Mike Wallace, Jewel, Ingmar Bergman, Iman, Billy Bob Thornton, O. Henry, Yo Yo Ma, Maria Shriver, Lou Rawls, Noel Coward, Mary Tyler Moore, Lord Byron, Humphrey Bogart, Jorge Luis Borges, Vanesssa Redgrave, Boris Spassky, Anna Pavlova, Arthur Schopenhauer, George Washington, Nancy Wilson

BIRTHDAYS ON KARMIC PATH 12

January 4, 1881–May 24, 1881 | August 16, 1899–January 4, 1900 | March 28, 1918–August 16, 1918
November 7, 1936–March 27, 1937 | June 19, 1955–November 7, 1955 | January 29, 1974–June 18, 1974
September 9, 1992–January 28, 1993 | April 21, 2011–September 9, 2011

KARMIC PATH
12

March 19–24

REBIRTH
PISCES–ARIES CUSP

Those born on the Cusp of Rebirth who travel this karmic path may prove impressive personalities indeed, marked by both a dreamy idealism and the ability to get things done. This path gifts Pisces–Arians with a greater awareness of their own hunches and intuition, and once they embark upon a course of action or area of professional interest, they will likely cut a rather wide swath, to the everlasting chagrin of their detractors. Being able to admit their failures and shortcomings may well be a problem for these individuals, as will learning to exercise a degree of diplomacy and to play their cards a bit closer to the chest. Given their remarkable ability to control and direct their large dreams and sense of ambition, they are likely to find the greatness for which they are destined by the Way of Amplification.

PEARL BAILEY
Singer and actress

―――

3/29/1918
Aries I

CHALLENGE: **RECOGNIZING WHEN THEY HAVE FAILED**
FULFILLMENT: **APPLYING A SIMPLE APPROACH TO LIVING LARGE**

March 25–April 2

THE CHILD
ARIES I

Bighearted and marked by perennial enthusiasm for any number of plans and projects, those born in the Week of the Child who travel the Way of Amplification will doubtless do best when they learn to follow their hearts. If they do, they may build something very big indeed. Gifted with a passion for living, they may have to face the challenge of coming to terms with the fact that not everyone in the world is as fearless as they are. The discipline of "paying their dues" within an organization, business, or profession will be especially useful for these people, as such training will improve their sense of personal timing and help them to avoid taking preemptive action. Once they have a degree of experience and refinement, their talents are likely to find fullest and grandest expression along this road.

CHALLENGE: **RELENTING IN THEIR FOCUS ON CAREER ONCE IN A WHILE**
FULFILLMENT: **EXPANDING ON THEIR NATURAL SENSE OF WONDER**
NOTABLES: **BÉLA BARTÓK (COMPOSER; MUSICIAN); ARISTIDE BRIAND (FORMER FRENCH PRIME MINISTER); FRANZ JOSEPH HAYDN (AUSTRIAN COMPOSER; INFLUENCED MOZART AND BEETHOVEN)**

April 3–10

THE STAR
ARIES II

Those born in the Week of the Star who travel this karmic path are sure not to disappoint their staunchest supporters and greatest fans. Hardworking and often driven—sometimes excessively—they are not likely to let anyone or anything stand in their way. Though some may be hampered by an ongoing battle with personal insecurity, shoring up their egos with too many people and too many projects or making themselves indispensable in order to stay at center stage, most will find the necessary freedom to explore a higher set of dreams and ambitions. Defining their self-image is important, as is the ability to turn their attention away from petty cares and woes and toward their considerable talents in the service of a higher cause, goal, or dream. Still, their sense of destiny on this karmic path will rarely fall short of their expectations, as these Stars will inevitably shine larger than life.

SAM WALTON
Retail executive; founded Wal-Mart; 1991 richest man in U.S.

―――

3/29/1918
Aries I

CHALLENGE: **EXTENDING THEIR VISION BEYOND THE NARROW VIEW OF THE SELF AND ITS NEEDS**
FULFILLMENT: **GIVING THEMSELVES FULLY TO A GRAND SCHEME, PROJECT, OR MOVEMENT**
NOTABLE: **BETTY FORD (FORMER FIRST LADY; FOUNDED THE BETTY FORD CLINIC)**

April 11–18

THE PIONEER
ARIES III

Unhampered by many of the more ego-centered issues that can trip up others of their sign, Aries III's who travel the Way of Amplification are likely to connect with an almost mythic or archetypal sense of destiny. Dominant and extremely well informed, these people can make considerable spiritual and personal progress along this road, as its challenges are already very much in keeping with Pioneers' expansive outlook. Though they may encounter problems by being unable to know where their own happiness lies or by believing that "the grass is always greener," even a modest measure of self-awareness should see them over the rough spots and guide them to the realization of even their most impossible dreams.

CHALLENGE: **PRUNING BACK ON THEIR OFTEN OVERLY EXPANSIVE IDEAS**
FULFILLMENT: **ADOPTING A LARGER-THAN-LIFE PERSONA**
NOTABLE: **WILLIAM HOLDEN (ACTOR, *SUNSET BOULEVARD*, *NETWORK*)**

KARMIC PATH
12

April 19–24

POWER
ARIES–TAURUS CUSP

Lavish and exciting personalities are apparent in those born on the Cusp of Power who travel the Way of Amplification. Blessed with a profound sense of ambition, once they learn how to place it within the context of a bigger picture or a larger concept, they may enjoy tremendous career success. This will be due in large measure to their rare capacity for prediction, particularly regarding matters of money and investment. In short, they have an ability to analyze what people want and when they want it and in addition can usually even tune into what people will want five or ten years down the road. They are also impervious to the concerns of others and would do well to cultivate the common touch. Tending to immerse themselves in the world of their careers, they may close themselves off from personal and family connections, however, and run the risk of isolating themselves in a world of avarice, thus hindering their higher development. Still, their impact on the world is assured and they are not likely to be soon forgotten.

ELLA FITZGERALD
Singer, "Mother" of
American jazz singing

4/25/1918
Taurus I

CHALLENGE: **SOFTENING THEIR APPROACH IN RELATIONSHIPS**
FULFILLMENT: **STEPPING INTO A LEADERSHIP ROLE IN THEIR CAREERS**

April 25–May 2

MANIFESTATION
TAURUS I

A willingness to take the good with the bad will mark the ambitions of Taurus I's on this karmic path. Indeed, they are blessed with a strong and unflappable sense of self that informs their dreams and show a marked ability to "keep their heads when all about them are losing theirs." That quality will serve them well, enabling them to steer their ship of fate along a smooth, steady course. Perhaps the principal danger of this configuration is that they may become bogged down or mired in the more mundane details of their enterprises, causing them to overplan and miss important opportunities. Although they sometimes employ structure as a restraint upon creativity, they are bound eventually to engage their intuitive and imaginative skills to inform their sense of structure, thereby freeing up their life for the amplification called for by this karmic path.

CHALLENGE: **LOOSENING UP THEIR ROUTINES AND RITUALS**
FULFILLMENT: **WITNESSING THE SCALE ON WHICH THEIR IDEAS TAKE SHAPE**
NOTABLES: **JACK PAAR (ORIGINAL HOST OF *THE TONIGHT SHOW*); PIERRE TEILHARD DE CHARDIN (HELPED DISCOVER PEKING MAN; ATTEMPTED TO RECONCILE EVOLUTION WITH CATHOLIC DOCTRINE)**

May 3–10

THE TEACHER
TAURUS II

Those born in the Week of the Teacher who travel the Way of Amplification are often possessed of a brilliance and communicative ability that is hard to match. The problem with this configuration is that they tend to be overly oriented toward the search for new ideas and concepts and rather weak in the area of seeing their plans to completion and fruition. Cultivating a greater sense of adventure is important for those on this karmic path if they are ever to broaden their view and achievements. Taurus II's must be careful to divest themselves of flatterers, groupies, and hangers-on and concentrate on relationships that provide mutual reinforcement, intellectual stimulation, and the freedom necessary to manifest their desires and dreams. Especially suited to the development of artistic activities, services, and creative and intellectual products, they are likely to flourish on this path.

MIKE WALLACE
Radio/TV journalist,
adversarial interviewer,
60 Minutes

5/9/1918
Taurus II

CHALLENGE: **RELEASING SOME OF THEIR INFLEXIBILITY AND RISK AVOIDANCE**
FULFILLMENT: **ENGAGING THEIR ENTREPRENEURIAL SIDE**

May 11–18

THE NATURAL
TAURUS III

The greatest difficulty for the freedom lovers born in the Week of the Natural on this path may be knowing which aspects of their varied personalities are most worth nourishing and enhancing. Otherwise, their truest talents may get lost in the shuffle, or they may squander their resources in needless rebellions or conflicts with authority. Still, they are blessed with an easygoing quality that enables them to seek out and find real freedom and great satisfaction in the expansion of the particular and well-loved goal. If they then embrace it with spiritual and heartfelt dedication, their progress along this karmic path is ensured.

CHALLENGE: **FORCING THEMSELVES TO BE LESS ORIENTED TOWARD FINANCIAL SECURITY**
FULFILLMENT: **FINDING THE FREEDOM THAT EXPANDING THEIR NARROW VIEW BRINGS THEM**
NOTABLES: **DANIEL BAIRD WESSON (GUNSMITH, INVENTED BREECH LOADING RIFLE; SMITH & WESSON); THEODORE VON KARMAN (AERONAUTICAL ENGINEER)**

May 19–24
ENERGY
TAURUS–GEMINI CUSP

As they try to expand their personal horizons, these amazingly energetic yet curiously analytical personalities will be blessed with a fine sense of trend and style. Yet critical to their progress along the Way of Amplification will be applying that ability to a wider world of knowledge and understanding, rather than in mere image seeking or off-the-wall avant-garde fashion statements. They will doubtless find great excitement on this life journey, however, and that is likely to please them no end. If they can cultivate the necessary perspective to mine the gold of their most creative and important inspirations and not be content to be swept up in the tide of current impulses, their natural sense of style and unique ability to keep their finger on the popular pulse should lead them to great achievements and some truly inspired moments.

JEWEL
Folk/pop singer

5/23/1974
Taurus–Gemini Cusp

CHALLENGE: **CALMING THEIR TENDENCY TO FLIT FROM ONE THING TO ANOTHER**

FULFILLMENT: **FINDING THE PEACE OF MIND THAT EMBRACING A SINGLE PATH CAN BRING**

May 25–June 2
FREEDOM
GEMINI I

Though loath to sacrifice their freedom in the interest of pursuing a larger plan Gemini I's who travel this karmic path will find that their passionate intellectual and spiritual curiosity will ultimately encourage them to amplify their goals. What they will have to watch, however, is their extraordinary verbal ability and marked tendency to "shoot first and ask questions later." Getting in touch with their kinder, gentler twin will be most beneficial here. Also, they would do well to cultivate the spiritual art of turning the other cheek when they would most like to blow away the competition with a barrage of well-chosen words, as this will prove to be the key to their advancement. If they keep in mind that knowledge of one's real talents and gifts is both the key to success and the best use of power, they are likely to find considerable success.

CHALLENGE: **CONTROLLING THEIR TENDENCY TO BECOME EASILY UNHINGED**

FULFILLMENT: **TRANSFORMING THEIR WELL-KNOWN LOYALTY INTO DEDICATION**

NOTABLE: **ALANIS MORISSETTE (POPULAR ROCK SINGER/SONGWRITER)**

June 3–10
NEW LANGUAGE
GEMINI II

Born with the desire to express their perceptions of life's big concepts and issues in new and sometimes startling ways, Gemini II's who travel the Way of Amplification may prove to be the spokespeople of their generations. Gifted with unusual verbal and writing talents, they may also manifest their destiny in other methods of communication, such as computer programming, creating advances in technology, and the like. Failing to find a voice for their larger-than-life ideas could prove to be their greatest frustration. Their biggest stumbling block for these personalities will be displays of petulance because of being misunderstood. Fussiness or overattention to detail can also cause them to lose sight of their higher objectives and dreams. Yet whatever their chosen areas of endeavor, their unique ability both to perceive the big picture and to articulate it for the rest of us will play an enormous part in their success.

FRANCE MODIGLIANI
Won 1985 Nobel Prize
for theories of savings,
corporate finance

6/18/1918
Gemini III

CHALLENGE: **NOT ALLOWING THEMSELVES TO GIVE UP IN THE FACE OF BEING MISUNDERSTOOD**

FULFILLMENT: **DAZZLING OTHERS WITH THEIR UNIQUE TAKE ON WHAT REALLY MATTERS**

June 11–18
THE SEEKER
GEMINI III

Resisting limitation and yearning for growth may engage many of these souls in a constant battle with self. Mentally and spiritually restless, they may fail to meet the challenges of this path through moving constantly or seeking out immediate forms of gratification at the expense of larger, more complex goals. Sparkling and witty, these risk takers will nonetheless be gifted with a practical streak, as well as an ability to perceive the larger patterns in both their own and others' behavior. Yet they will have to control their very versatility and cultivate greater depth before they can realize many of the more substantive rewards promised by this karmic path. These seekers will be forced to choose one particular life area to amplify. If they ground their fickleness with faithfulness and their inspirations with determination, all is likely to go well.

CHALLENGE: **SETTLING ON ONE THING TO DEVOTE THEMSELVES TO**

FULFILLMENT: **EXPERIENCING THE INNER PEACE THAT COMES FROM CREATING SOMETHING**

June 19–24

MAGIC
GEMINI–CANCER CUSP

Those born on the Cusp of Magic who find themselves on the Way of Amplification are likely to be enchanting, inspirational people. The greatest pitfall with this configuration will be focusing on love and romance such that they become overblown in their hearts and minds, to the exclusion of all else. They are prone to being on a perpetual search for the "right" lover, soul mate, or business partner at the expense of fulfilling their tasks or developing an identity apart from other people's. Applying their natural objectivity to themselves and their own personalities may come hard for some of them, yet on the whole they are likely to find considerable success, especially when in the service of higher and less personal causes, crusades, and projects. Cultivating greater intellectual discipline is important, and their innate knowledge of the human condition will be a fine aid as they apply their special talents toward finding a higher level of aspiration and a broader vision of love.

CHALLENGE: **NOT BECOMING ENMESHED IN ROMANTIC YEARNINGS**
FULFILLMENT: **LEARNING TO EXIST IN A FIELD OF LOVE RATHER THAN FOCUSING ON ONE PERSON**

ABIGAIL VAN BUREN & ANN LANDERS

Twin sisters; advice columnists, *Dear Abby/ Ann Landers*

7/4/1918
Cancer II

June 25–July 2

THE EMPATH
CANCER I

The Empaths who travel the Way of Amplification may need to do quite a bit of work to establish personal boundaries before they discover the particular aspect of themselves or area of endeavor that is worthy of nurture and growth. Highly prone to taking on other people's problems, petty disputes, and even personality traits, they may need to undergo a learning process of sifting and winnowing before they realize that their deepest needs have gone unsatisfied or their truest callings unfulfilled. An ability to back up from the dramas of the moment, put their famous business acumen to work, and get in touch with the bigger picture will be essential, and they would do especially well to cultivate greater objectivity and self-reliance. Still, they are blessed with the sheer guts and determination to see them through the rougher spots on their life journey and are likely to develop a highly realistic view of themselves that is neither overly positive nor utterly negative as they face down their personal demons. Once they do, they will enjoy great personal, financial, and creative success along this karmic path.

CHALLENGE: **LETTING GO OF RESENTMENTS**
FULFILLMENT: **SUCCEEDING IN BUSINESS**
NOTABLE: **ROBERT SARNOFF (NBC EXECUTIVE)**

July 3–10

THE UNCONVENTIONAL
CANCER II

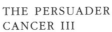

Those born in the Week of the Unconventional who travel the Way of Amplification personify a sentiment once expressed by the comedian Stephen Wright. "I spend a lot of time in my own little world," he remarked, "but it's okay, they know me there." Blessed with the ability to view their quirks with a measure of tolerance and understanding, these people will attract more than their share of the unusual and even bizarre along this life journey. Yet there is a danger of overindulgence in fantasy, idealism, and escapism. Finding a broader audience or more public forum for their quirky viewpoints would be just the thing to keep these Cancer II's happy.

CHALLENGE: **RESISTING THE TEMPTATION TO HIDE OUT**
FULFILLMENT: **CREATING AND DECORATING A LAVISH HOME ENVIRONMENT**
NOTABLE: **AMY WALLACE (WRITER)**

INGMAR BERGMAN

Swedish film and stage director

7/14/1918
Cancer III

July 11–18

THE PERSUADER
CANCER III

In a word, these personalities know how to get others to do what they want, and hence it follows that they would do well to have a thorough knowledge of just what their wants are. The Persuaders who travel the Way of Amplification will doubtless manifest their personal destiny in a charismatic and even enviable fashion. The danger of settling for lesser goals than they might achieve or seeking out instant forms of gratification may be a stumbling block for these essentially powerful people. Too, they may give way to any number of excesses and overindulgences in the process of trying to identify their higher needs and may go in search of any number of spiritual "fixes." Still, their special gifts give them the ability to garner great forces in their quests, and if they avoid becoming overly nit-picking, they are apt to inspire many and, for themselves, find great success, especially when wending their ways through the sometimes byzantine structures of politics or corporations.

CHALLENGE: **PERMITTING THEMSELVES A MORE LUXURIOUS OR EXPANSIVE LIFESTYLE**
FULFILLMENT: **DISCOVERING THEIR NATURAL ABILITY TO TIME THEIR ACTIONS PERFECTLY**
NOTABLES: **NELSON MANDELA (SOUTH AFRICAN LEADER); GUSTAV KLIMT (PAINTER)**

July 19–25

OSCILLATION
CANCER–LEO CUSP

P ride may indeed go before the fall with Cancer–Leos on this karmic path, for they are likely to exalt themselves in the areas where they should be humble and to humble themselves in the areas they should most exalt. Their more egotistic impulses may obscure their intuition and hinder them, as may their tendency to engage in melodrama. While the amplification here of such displays, histrionics and even tantrums may at times allow them to turn a situation to their advantage, they should keep in mind that merely getting things off one's chest does not guarantee access to the deeper areas of the hearts and minds of others. Still, they are blessed with a consuming curiosity that will allow them to transcend their own insecurity, belligerence, or just plain bad timing. They would do well to meditate from time to time on the statement: "Seek, and ye shall find."

IMAN
Model; married to
David Bowie

7/25/1955
Cancer–Leo Cusp

CHALLENGE: **FOCUSING LESS ON THEIR OWN MOODS AND MORE ON THINGS OUTSIDE THEMSELVES**

FULFILLMENT: **DISCOVERING THE EXCITEMENT OF EXPANDING THEIR WORLDVIEW**

July 26–August 2

AUTHORITY
LEO I

B elieving in higher principles and abstract truths, those born in The Week of Authority who travel this karmic path may well bowl others over with their exuberant confidence, powerful intellect, and sheer dynamism. Whatever their inclinations, interests, or avocations, they are likely to make a real mark and to see their endeavors brought to fruition. The main danger is that these personalities may see themselves as being at the center of their universe and become so enmeshed in their personal pursuits that they fail to cultivate the broader vision demanded by this karmic path. The ability to manifest a deeper and more abiding sense of humanity will therefore be of great benefit to Leo I's since they tend to set very high standards for others. Once they apply their keen perception and practical talents to a larger cause or higher purpose, their place in the grand scheme of things will become clear.

CHALLENGE: **REDUCING THEIR EXPECTATIONS OF OTHERS**

FULFILLMENT: **ASSUMING THE MANTLE OF AUTHORITY TO WHICH THEY WERE BORN**

August 3–10

BALANCED STRENGTH
LEO II

B lessed with the ability to thrive on almost any challenge that fate might throw them, those born in the Week of Balanced Strength who travel this karmic path will doubtless experience a rare level of personal and spiritual transformation as their intuitive gifts reach a peak. In fact, the only real pitfall of this configuration is that they may attach themselves too tenaciously to unproductive ventures or causes. They take such great pride in their ability to endure that they may waste their energies through a refusal to admit their mistakes or an inability to give up on something that fails to conform to their expectations. Being endowed with greater objectivity and perspective than they might otherwise have had means that they will prosper and expand on this path as they work to focus and amplify what really matters to them.

BILLY BOB THORNTON
Film actor and writer;
won Oscar for best
screenplay, *Slingblade*

8/4/1955
Leo II

CHALLENGE: **ALWAYS REMEMBERING TO CHECK IN ON THEIR EXCELLENT INTUITION**

FULFILLMENT: **WATCHING THEIR DREAMS SLOWLY TAKE FORM**

August 11–18

LEADERSHIP
LEO III

H ighly creative and at times breathtakingly dynamic, Leo III's on the Way of Amplification are sure to make a big splash. Whatever their special talents, they will doubtless possess the ability to see their projects and dreams through to fruition. There are the makings of not a few heroes here, and whatever their area of endeavor, they are likely to find enormous success. However, ego issues can be something of a problem, not necessarily because they think so highly of themselves but because they tend not to think of others at all. As a result, they may fail to build necessary support because comrades and coworkers view them as conceited or selfish. And when Leo III's fail to garner respect, their sense of identity can suffer. This karmic path blesses those born in the Week of Leadership with both a finer social sense and a higher grasp of human needs than they might otherwise have had. If they are careful to amplify those qualities and mute the demands of their egos, they are likely to flourish on this life journey.

CHALLENGE: **CONSIDERING THE FEELINGS OF OTHERS**

FULFILLMENT: **RECEIVING THE RESPECT OF THOSE THEY LEAD**

NOTABLE: **NAPOLEON BONAPARTE**

August 19–25

EXPOSURE
LEO–VIRGO CUSP

Those born on the Cusp of Exposure have been blessed with a certain ability to keep their best ideas and qualities to themselves until they feel the time is right for them to shine. Thus, they are apt to do wonderfully well on the Way of Amplification. Intensely analytical and naturally flamboyant, they must nonetheless avoid the temptation of indulging in forms of immediate gratification shoring up their egos by being content to be merely a big fish in a small pond. Though especially gifted in the areas of written and spoken communication, they may have to watch their tendency to waste their energies through a failure to settle down and apply their talents productively. If these charismatic people can channel their expansiveness into areas that demand informed leadership, their grasp of the larger issues and fine sense of the quirks and unpredictability of the human heart will enable them to travel far and wide.

JORGE LUIS BORGES
Argentine writer

8/24/1899
Leo–Virgo Cusp

CHALLENGE: **REVEALING THEIR INNER LIGHT MORE CONSISTENTLY**

FULFILLMENT: **LETTING THEIR FLAMBOYANT SIDE HAVE FREE REIN ONCE IN A WHILE**

NOTABLES: **GEORGES CUVIER (ORIGINATED SYSTEM OF ANIMAL CLASSIFICATION); WILLIAM C. PROCTER (MANUFACTURER, PROCTER & GAMBLE)**

August 26–September 2

SYSTEM BUILDERS
VIRGO I

Those born in this week who travel the Way of Amplification are likely to be a bit uncomfortable with a number of its challenges. Possessed by a great need to keep the world in order and to bring reality into better alignment with their need for logic, they may suffer a number of rather unpleasant consequences when they refuse to expand their vision or to "go with the flow." However, they have been gifted with greater versatility than many, and this should serve them well in their quest for spiritual development. They must, however, learn to zealously guard against fussiness and overattention to detail on this karmic path, though they can make enormous strides if they place themselves in the service of some worthy cause or organization that will benefit from their unique ability to structure and plan. When they find their special niche, they are quite likely to rise in the ranks and will doubtless also enjoy the rewards of greater powers of leadership, perception, and vision than anyone might have believed possible.

CHALLENGE: **WORKING HARD NOT TO GET BOGGED DOWN IN DETAILS**

FULFILLMENT: **SERVING OTHERS FOR A GREATER GOOD**

NOTABLES: **CHARLES BOYER (FRENCH ACTOR); EDWIN MOSES (OLYMPIC HURDLER)**

September 3–10

THE ENIGMA
VIRGO II

The Enigmas who travel the Way of Amplification will likely relish its call to craft a higher life purpose, yet may resist relinquishing their sense of pride and structure to live more in the moment. Since they are not natural risk takers, they may struggle a bit with the idea of amplifying and developing their special talents in a way that puts them in a more prominent position or in the public eye. Nevertheless, they are likely to be quite tasteful and self-assured and run little risk of developing any of the blowhard or superegoistic tendencies others on this karmic path must guard against. The principal risks and greatest rewards will doubtless revolve around defining and redefining their sense of personal identity. Once they have released their need to be an island of self-sufficient effort and join with others in the interest of accomplishing some higher purpose, their capacity for creative self-expression is likely to be liberated and their high standards affirmed.

O. HENRY
Short story writer

9/11/1862
Virgo III

CHALLENGE: **STRUGGLING TO MOVE THEIR PERSONAL QUESTS TO A LARGER ARENA OF ACTION**

FULFILLMENT: **WEAVING AN EVER-LARGER WEB OF MYSTERY ABOUT THEMSELVES**

NOTABLE: **BILLY ROSE (ENTERTAINMENT ENTREPRENEUR)**

September 11–18

THE LITERALIST
VIRGO III

The Literalists who find themselves on the Way of Amplification may really seem like ducks out of water. And indeed, many of these hard-driving, practical people may go through a real "ugly ducking" phase until they face the challenge of going within and redefining their sense of identity. Practical in the extreme, they may well resist the call to a more philosophical orientation or expanded vision of themselves. Virgo III's on this karmic path are apt to raise everyday details or objects to the level of the sublime; the question is whether others will "get it." Though plagued by a secret insecurity that can manifest itself as fussiness, ruthlessness, or even megalomania, they are likely to rise within the ranks of any number of organizations. Once they learn to believe in themselves more, an expanded and more tolerant vision of the rest of the world is likely to follow and they will find their travels along this road considerably eased.

CHALLENGE: **GETTING THEMSELVES NOT TO OVEROBSESS ABOUT PRACTICAL DETAILS**

FULFILLMENT: **RELEASING THE CHAINS THAT BIND THEM TO THE MUNDANE**

NOTABLE: **HAL WALLIS (MOTION PICTURE PRODUCER)**

September 19–24

BEAUTY
VIRGO–LIBRA CUSP

Those born on the Cusp of Beauty who travel the Way of Amplification will doubtless have to find ways to ground themselves long enough to find outlets for self-expression and creativity. There is a danger that these somewhat unstable people will fail to attach themselves to a higher sense of purpose and will waste their energies in a never-ending cycle of sensation and immediate gratification. Though gifted with a sense of the aesthetic, they will have to develop the necessary inner strength to give shape and substance to their ideas and inspirations. Real spirituality will be at issue here, for their astonishing versatility may well fail to find adequate expression or outlet until they cultivate the capacity for greater focus and depth. Yet once they set their minds on answering the call to a higher purpose, their special gifts will blossom, especially in the areas of the performing, written, and spoken arts.

JASON ALEXANDER
Actor; known for role of
George in *Seinfeld*

9/26/1955
Libra I

CHALLENGE: **NOT PERMITTING THEIR YEARNING FOR THE SUB-
LIME TO TURN AGAINST THEM IN SELF-DESTRUCTIVE WAYS**
FULFILLMENT: **FULLY EMBODYING THEIR PURSUIT OF AN IDEAL**
NOTABLE: **LOUISE NEVELSON (SCULPTOR)**

September 25–October 2

THE PERFECTIONIST
LIBRA I

This karmic path grants a rather more easygoing aspect to Libra I's than some others born in this week have. The Way of Amplification will help them achieve great success, providing they do not succumb to their own mercilessly high standards. An ability to back up and see the big picture and then to embrace it will be something Libra II's will have to develop; once it is developed, they will also have to learn to relinquish some of their pet obsessions in the interest of the greater good. Some with this configuration may be unduly restless or flighty, moving from one project or plan to the next with an odd sort of anxiety and being unable to locate themselves in a larger scheme or structure. Still, if they can master their resistance to risk taking and learn the fine art of practicing a bit more of what they preach, they will be rewarded with a better ability both to assume and to delegate responsibility. Freed from the stress and strain of attending to the world of detail, they will be released to enjoy the rewards promised by this karmic path.

CHALLENGE: **TRANSFORMING THEIR DESIRE TO FIX THINGS
INTO A TALENT FOR MAKING THEM GROW**
FULFILLMENT: **ADOPTING A MASTER PLAN**
NOTABLE: **LORRAINE BRACCO (ACTRESS, *THE SOPRANOS*)**

October 3–10

SOCIETY
LIBRA II

Self-knowledge and the ability to separate from others in order to better explore their own needs and gifts will be of particular importance to those born in the Week of Society who travel this karmic path. Popular and well liked, this is a talkative group whose talent for conversation and daily interactions may distract them from focusing on a higher set of goals. Though much in demand, Libra II's must learn to demand more from themselves if they are to find the self-realization promised by this karmic path. Too, they have a pronounced tendency to procrastinate or simply to refuse to make choices when it is are most required. Yet if they come to terms with their own deep need to lead and inspire others through creative, practical, or personal efforts, Libra II's on the Way of Amplification will gain a greater knowledge of just what's best for them and, freed from the restraints that result from self-neglect, will see their fondest dreams come true.

YO YO MA
World's most celebrated
cellist

10/7/1955
Libra II

CHALLENGE: **LIMITING THEIR SOCIAL ACTIVITY**
FULFILLMENT: **SEEING THAT SOME OF THEIR FANTASIES CAN
ACTUALLY COME TRUE**
NOTABLES: **DAVID LEE ROTH (ROCK SINGER); MARCUS
WALLENBURG (SWEDISH DIPLOMAT; RESCUED JEWS IN
WORLD WAR II)**

October 11–18

THEATER
LIBRA III

No matter who they are, Libra III's are likely to be noticed as they travel the Way of Amplification. Uniquely suited to the development of a larger-than-life attitude, those born in the Week of Theater will surely find their calling by expanding on something important in life. Able to step into the role of leader with aplomb, these theatrical individuals have the confidence to pick a course and stick to it. What may be an Achilles heel is whether they can actualize their plans in a way that is also spiritually inspiring. While living large suits them, they may fail to heed the higher purpose that beckons. Their hard-driving intensity may desensitize them to the needs of others, and their own destiny may suffer for it. Success isn't worth much if it comes solely at others' expense.

CHALLENGE: **REMEMBERING THAT LIVING LARGE MEANS
LIVING BY PRINCIPLE**
FULFILLMENT: **ACTING OUT THE LARGER DRAMA OF THEIR
LIVES**

KARMIC PATH
12

October 19–25

DRAMA AND CRITICISM
LIBRA–SCORPIO CUSP

These people tend to seem a bit larger than life, even from earliest childhood. Indeed, they have a hunger for experience that can leave lesser types in the dust as they make their breakneck journey along the Way of Amplification. What they will doubtless learn is the relatively simple lesson that more is not always better, and they must learn to regulate their considerable passions in the interest of greater refinement. In some cases this karmic path may require them to exalt a particular ability for talent at the seeming expense of others. But their biggest challenge will be to develop a sense of greater humility and a more compassionate understanding of their fellows, since they tend to be overly critical and patronizing. Overall, they are well suited to selecting a cause or mission and nurturing it to its largest possible form.

CHALLENGE: **RECOGNIZING WHEN THEIR PASSION DETRACTS FROM THEIR GOAL**

FULFILLMENT: **LEAVING THEIR MARK ON THE WORLD**

NOTABLES: **WILLIAM MORRIS, JR. (FOUNDED TALENT AGENCY); EDDIE BAUER (FOUNDED SPORTING GOODS COMPANY)**

MARIA SHRIVER
TV journalist

———

11/6/1955
Scorpio II

October 26–November 2

INTENSITY
SCORPIO I

Blessed with the single-mindedness of purpose needed to realize the rewards of the Way of Amplification, those born in the Week of Intensity will nonetheless learn to control their emotions before they can realize their highest goals. Though this karmic path gifts them with greater versatility and a somewhat lighter attitude than Scorpio I's normally possess, they may nevertheless turn those very qualities into liabilities through an excess of worry or self-abnegation. Still, their great empathy will likely be their greatest asset along this life journey, for their fearless ability to look into every corner of the human heart will lead them to a higher understanding. If they expand their vision beyond the constraints of personal power and turn their search for the mythic to the larger universe of thought and inspiration, they are sure to blossom.

CHALLENGE: **TAKING CARE THAT THEIR JUDGMENTAL TENDENCIES DO NOT CLOUD THEIR BROADER VISION**

FULFILLMENT: **RADIATING THEIR SENSE OF PURPOSE**

NOTABLE: **BILL GATES (CHAIRMAN, MICROSOFT CORP.)**

November 3–11

DEPTH
SCORPIO II

Unlikely to be troubled much by the restlessness or attraction to the superficial that can plague many of those who travel the Way of Amplification, Scorpio II's can realize their fondest dreams and highest aspirations, providing they do not shun the larger sense of responsibility and purpose required. Indeed, they have a great sensitivity to others, and if they take care to nurture their expansiveness, generosity, and broader vision, they can realize astonishing success and acceptance of their special talents and gifts. However, their very steadfastness may be their undoing, especially if their ambitions are stubbornly attached to purely material goals or issues of personal security. They may find taking risks to be difficult, yet risks that are taken in the interest of greater accomplishment offer the greatest and most consistent rewards.

CHALLENGE: **TAKING CARE NOT TO AMPLIFY THEIR PROBLEMS**

FULFILLMENT: **ENJOYING THE CAREER SUCCESS THIS KARMIC PATH AFFORDS**

NOTABLE: **EDWARD GIBSON (ASTRONAUT)**

EUGENE ORMANDY
Conductor, Philadelphia
Orchestra

———

11/18/1899
Scorpio III

November 12–18

CHARM
SCORPIO III

Those born in the Week of Charm who travel the Way of Amplification are likely to achieve a great deal, providing they do not remain content with a superficial vision for themselves or succumb to the tendency to cultivate a rather narrow sense of ambition. Many of those born in this week are attracted to the world of wealth and power yet squander their resources in a preoccupation with appearances and acquisition by failing to tap into a mythic symbolism or larger purpose. Perhaps their inborn passions will provide the greatest clues to where their truest success lies, and if they learn to nurture their enthusiasms into a real joie de vivre and to be willing to take the risks associated with "going for broke" in order to achieve their higher dreams, life on the Way of Amplification will rarely disappoint them.

CHALLENGE: **NOT ALLOWING THEIR PRACTICALITY TO PREVENT THEM FROM GOING FOR BROKE**

FULFILLMENT: **ENJOYING THE SELF-CONFIDENCE THAT CAREER SUCCESS BRINGS**

November 19–24
REVOLUTION
SCORPIO–SAGITTARIUS CUSP

Being able to perceive themselves in the role of instrument rather than instigator will be critical to the success of Scorpio–Sagittarians who travel the Way of Amplification. Living large will come easily to these sometimes extreme personalities, yet they will need to develop greater self-control and a sense of focus in order to realize their fondest ideals and ambitions. Their tendency to be autocratic can hamper their progress, and they would do well to remember that while "the squeaking wheel gets the grease," there is another side to that quality in the story of those who perpetually cry wolf. However well intentioned they are, part of their life journey will doubtless demand that they disassociate themselves from extraneous or nonproductive pursuits and turn their attention to a larger sense of accomplishment. On the Way of Amplification, Scorpio–Sagittarians would do well to remember that though it may be thrilling to win a battle, the possibility always looms of losing the larger war.

LOU RAWLS
Popular blues and soul
singer
———
12/1/1936
Sagittarius I

CHALLENGE: **CONSIDERING THEIR OPTIONS MORE CAREFULLY BEFORE TAKING ACTION**
FULFILLMENT: **INITIATING LARGE-SCALE CHANGES IN THEIR ENVIRONMENT OR SOCIETY**
NOTABLES: **DICK CAVETT (TELEVISION HOST); DON DELILLO (AUTHOR, WHITE NOISE)**

November 25–December 2
INDEPENDENCE
SAGITTARIUS I

Well suited to the demands of the Way of Amplification, those born in this week may nevertheless resist the challenge of focusing on those aspects of themselves that require careful nurturing and encouragement to growth. Fearing, perhaps, that the refinement of their talents and abilities may somehow limit their independence and curiosity, they may flounder a bit by pursuing excess rather than excellence. Provocative people, Sagittarius I's are unlikely to stick to the straight and narrow when larger plans or projects or a sense of higher purpose is at stake. While some may be limited by a restrained, uncertain, or otherwise inhibited view of themselves and their talents, if they nurture their great sense of freedom, they will doubtless find the strength to rise above a false or limited perception and will then be able to claim the rewards of this karmic path.

CHALLENGE: **REMAINING FOCUSED ON FINER POINTS**
FULFILLMENT: **FINDING A GRAND WAY TO SHARE THEIR LARGESSE WITH OTHERS**
NOTABLE: **ABBIE HOFFMAN (1960s POLITICAL ACTIVIST)**

December 3–10
THE ORIGINATOR
SAGITTARIUS II

The Originators who travel the Way of Amplification are likely to achieve considerable success, providing they do not retreat into a defensive attitude toward the world or resist the challenges of this karmic path by contenting themselves with being square pegs in round holes. Controlling aggression will be something of a problem for them, as will setting aside any preoccupation with success and concentrating on nurturing their talents and abilities. Though many of these people crave recognition and acceptance and may go to great lengths to get others' attention, unless their efforts to be noticed are backed up by substantive achievements and a real sense of passion and commitment, they may come to naught. What is required is to release the insecurities that often come with possessing originality or talent or simply being different and to concentrate not so much on acceptance into the mainstream as on the respect and honor of those whose opinions are of real value.

SIR NOEL COWARD
Actor and composer,
Private Lives
———
12/16/1899
Sagittarius III

CHALLENGE: **DISCERNING WHAT IS WORTH AMPLIFYING**
FULFILLMENT: **APPLYING THEIR ORIGINALITY TO BIGGER PLANS AND SCHEMES**
NOTABLE: **DAVID CARRADINE (ACTOR, KUNG FU)**

December 11–18
THE TITAN
SAGITTARIUS III

Those born in the Week of the Titan will doubtless find the Way of Amplification very much to their liking. Titans like to think on a grand scale and will doubtless find any number of opportunities to express their bighearted and generous side. Still, for all their considerable resources, they may fail the challenges of this path if their considerable self-assurance is not backed up by substantive efforts or their largesse devolves into excess and braggadocio. Cultivating greater self-awareness will be critical to their success, especially when choosing their avenues of professional and personal expression. Yet if they manage to avoid having a sense of infallibility and sacrifice their self-involvement to a higher spiritual awareness and sense of gratitude for their gifts, they can leave quite a mark on the world.

CHALLENGE: **BEING WILLING TO ACKNOWLEDGE FAILURE**
FULFILLMENT: **SENSING THE HINT OF ECSTASY IN FEELING THEMSELVES TO BE WONDER WORKERS**

December 19–25
PROPHECY
SAGITTARIUS–CAPRICORN CUSP

Those born on the Cusp of Prophecy who find themselves on this karmic path may be a bit uncomfortable with some of its challenges. Gifted with a rare ability to focus their talents and to hone in on the aspects of themselves that require greater cultivation, they may nonetheless become frustrated when their efforts at expansion aren't met with instant acceptance or approval. Feelings of unworthiness or insecurity can cause them to withdraw from or question their own best impulses and intuitions. Yet they are blessed with a natural sense of independence that promises to serve them quite well on this life journey, and if their great curiosity, considerable intellect, and strong spiritual sense are employed in the service of a larger purpose or ideal, they are capable of a rare and single-minded effort that will be untroubled or distracted by the opinions of others.

ISMAEL MERCHANT
Successful film producer,
A Room with a View

12/25/1936
Sagittarius–Capricorn
Cusp

CHALLENGE: **CONTROLLING THEIR NATURAL INCLINATION TO CONTRACTION**
FULFILLMENT: **AMPLIFYING AND GIVING VOICE TO THEIR SIXTH SENSE**
NOTABLES: **HECTOR ELIZONDO (TELEVISION ACTOR); HUMPHREY BOGART (ACTOR, *CASABLANCA*)**

December 26–January 2
THE RULER
CAPRICORN I

The spiritual quest of those born in the Week of the Ruler who find themselves on the Way of Amplification may involve some curious and unexpected turns. Gifted with the ability to focus their talents and energies on a path of genuine and lasting achievement, these people will nonetheless wrestle with issues of expansion. Thus they may find themselves confronted by a host of opportunities, blessings, and turns of fortune for which they are unprepared. In fact, many of these people keep themselves rather tightly controlled or bottled up, and they may undertake any number of contortions as the blessings of this karmic path shower down on them in an attempt to get them to open up, let their hair down, and enjoy what life has to offer. However, if they relinquish their feelings of guilt and still their overactive consciences with philanthropical, educational, or other humanitarian endeavors, they can experience great rewards on this life journey.

CHALLENGE: **LEARNING TO CONSIDER OTHER METHODS OF DOING THINGS AS THEY BUILD THEIR EMPIRE**
FULFILLMENT: **REVELING IN THE PHILANTHROPY THAT SUCCESS ON THIS PATH AFFORDS**
NOTABLE: **XAVIER CUGAT (BANDLEADER; LATIN MUSICIAN)**

January 3–9
DETERMINATION
CAPRICORN II

Capricorn II's are likely to resonate with the challenges and promises offered by the Way of Amplification. Natural strivers, they will have little trouble rising to the height of achievement in any number of professional or personal pursuits, yet at the same time they may have difficulty cultivating the generosity of spirit called for by this karmic path. Capable of stretching their resources to the limit, they are often curiously troubled by insecurity and a lack of self-confidence, and what the source of such anxiety may be calls for further scrutiny and reevaluation. Though surprising, their capacity for hard work and their gutsy determination to reach their goals may prove to be their undoing. Should they fail to nurture their interest in spiritual, metaphysical, and theoretical matters, they may go through life like a good plow horse—useful, but hardly worthy of the race.

MARY TYLER MOORE
TV/film actress,
Mary Tyler Moore Show

12/29/1936
Capricorn I

CHALLENGE: **GRAPPLING WITH ANY OUTSTANDING ISSUES OF INSECURITY OR LACK OF SELF-ESTEEM**
FULFILLMENT: **CREATING A PHILOSOPHICAL OR SPIRITUAL VIEWPOINT**

January 10–16
DOMINANCE
CAPRICORN III

Those born in the Week of Dominance are impressive characters indeed, and on this karmic path their natural sense of dignity, leadership, and authority may well be augmented. In any event, they are blessed with the ability to set a course for success that they will navigate with diligence and savoir faire. Yet for all of their obvious virtues, these people may shy away from the higher challenges of this karmic path. Redefining their sense of self and facing down an inferiority complex may present a big opportunity for growth to these worthy people, as will a willingness to open themselves to the larger world of understanding, tolerance, and enlightenment that awaits. Getting in touch with their philosophical leanings and more humanitarian aspect will serve them especially well and enable them to avoid the dangers of pettiness or a hesitancy to reach for the gusto and greatness that is the promise of this life journey.

CHALLENGE: **LEARNING HOW NOT TO SUBDIVIDE THEIR WORLDVIEW BASED ON PETTY JUDGMENTS**
FULFILLMENT: **DEDICATING THEMSELVES TO THEIR LARGER PROFESSIONAL GOALS**
NOTABLE: **COLE YOUNGER (BANDIT)**

January 17–22

MYSTERY AND IMAGINATION
CAPRICORN–AQUARIUS CUSP

Possessed of an aura of drama that follows them wherever they go, those born on the Cusp of Mystery and Imagination who find themselves on this karmic path will either do spectacularly well or very poorly, depending on their ability to channel their impulses into substantive creative effort. Though it may often seem as if they have more ideas than one mind can safely hold, they nevertheless have a fine grasp of larger issues, should they care to address them. Many with this configuration will wrestle with issues of rebellion and aggression or have a pronounced inclination to taking somewhat wild or just plain stupid risks. However, as a rule, they like to live life on the edge; if they can successfully ground their chaotic energies through concentration, meditation, and a more focused application of their talents and abilities, they can make great progress.

LORD GEORGE BYRON
Romantic poet, *Don Juan*

1/22/1788
Capricorn–Aquarius Cusp

CHALLENGE: **TAMING THEIR ENERGY SWINGS IN ORDER TO FOCUS BETTER**
FULFILLMENT: **WEAVING THE WEB OF THEIR PERSONA INTO AN EVER-LARGER AND MORE MYTHIC ENERGY FIELD**
NOTABLE: **JOSEPH WAMBAUGH (AUTHOR)**

January 23–30

GENIUS
AQUARIUS I

Aquarius I's on the Way of Amplification will doubtless succeed in finding wonderful avenues for the expression of their biggest plans and highest ideals. The problem is that they may often be too distracted to notice when such opportunities present themselves and may ignore the necessity of attending to their own best interests. In fact, the joys of teamwork may be more a theoretical dream than a working reality for these people, who tend not to function well under authority. Still, the call of deeper values and larger issues will be very attractive to these ethical people, and if they can successfully place themselves in the service of a cause, creative effort, or philosophically based organization whose goals benefit humankind, their contributions will be important and long-lasting.

CHALLENGE: **DEVELOPING A BETTER SENSE OF TIMING**
FULFILLMENT: **EXPERIENCING A BROADER WORLD THROUGH THE TRAVEL THIS PATH PROMISES**
NOTABLES: **VANESSA REDGRAVE (ACTRESS); BORIS SPASSKY (CHESS PLAYER)**

January 31–February 7

YOUTH AND EASE
AQUARIUS II

Superficiality and a pronounced disposition to "go with the flow" will be at the heart of the struggle for those born in this week who travel the Way of Amplification. Still, their capacity for virtuosity should do much to clarify their choices here and pave the way for a remarkably successful and rewarding journey. Coming to terms with their real values, cultivating greater depth, and aligning themselves with the higher goals of humanity are all in the stars for these fortunate people. If they can avoid the tendency to get hooked on the applause and attentions of others, avoid flatterers, groupies and hangers-on, and attend to the business of true soul growth, they will doubtless make huge strides along their spiritual road.

ANNA PAVLOVA
Ballerina, choreographer

1/31/1881
Aquarius II

CHALLENGE: **FOCUSING THEIR ATTENTION LESS ON SUPER-FICIALITIES AND MORE ON SPIRITUAL TRUTHS**
FULFILLMENT: **CRAFTING A LARGER-THAN-LIFE WAY OF LIVING**
NOTABLES: **DON EVERLY (SINGER); SUZANNE PLESHETTE (FILM/TELEVISION ACTRESS)**

February 8–15

ACCEPTANCE
AQUARIUS III

Aquarius III's on the Way of Amplification may initially have some difficulties, only later to enjoy great success and acquire real power along the road. Sometimes colorful, those born in the Week of Acceptance may have to cultivate greater constancy and consistency to enjoy the ultimate benefits of this path, and settling upon a course of action or career may be a real problem for some. While initially their fear of superficiality may hold them up, they will doubtless discover a quality and depth of experience that satisfies their needs in a way that mere quantity cannot. Depending on their individual talents, they would do well to commit themselves to the acquisition of particular tools, lessons, or equipment that will allow them to focus without tying them down to petty or overly personal constraints and concerns. As they redefine their self in terms of identity rather than simple inclination, all is likely to go quite beautifully.

CHALLENGE: **RECOGNIZING THAT LIVING LARGE DOES NOT PRECLUDE BEING REAL—OR HUMBLE**
FULFILLMENT: **DEVELOPING OPENNESS AND GENEROSITY OF SPIRIT**

February 16–22

SENSITIVITY
AQUARIUS–PISCES CUSP

February 23–March 2

SPIRIT
PISCES I

The single-mindedness of focus required by the Way of Amplification is likely to cause Aquarius–Pisceans no little trouble as they travel this karmic path. Torn between the desire to take aggressive and dynamic action in the world of ideals and the need to cultivate a profound inner experience, they may try to go in several directions at once in their search for fulfillment. Career choice will be especially important for these people and will allow them to define, redefine, and enlarge their identities through cultivating their talents, abilities, and accomplishments. Their fine pragmatic side will, in any event, allow them to apply their talents in the kind of profession that speaks to their ideals and keeps them connected to the world of the larger good. Ultimately, they will find themselves released from pessimism and insecurity and are likely to find great happiness.

JERRY O'CONNELL
Film actor
—
2/17/1974
Aquarius–Pisces Cusp

CHALLENGE: **TRANSFORMING NEGATIVITY**
FULFILLMENT: **PURSUING THEIR MORE IDEALISTIC VISIONS**
NOTABLE: **ARTHUR SCHOPENHAUER (PHILOSOPHER, REJECTED HEGEL)**

Those born in the Week of Spirit who travel the Way of Amplification may be in for an unusual time. Whatever their individual responsibilities and talents, they are likely to approach them in an idealistic and even devotional fashion, yet they will have to do greater work on themselves before they can develop the necessary discrimination to know just what aspects of their multifaceted natures require greater growth and which are best discarded. Failure to ground themselves in useful activity can be a real problem, since their conception of the larger picture is already so tinged with spirituality and idealism that they may refuse the challenge of developing to their highest potential in more ordinary ways and thus get lost in their sense of the grander scheme. Still, if they are careful to cultivate greater practicality and dwell a bit less in the realms of the theoretical, they can make fine progress along this karmic path.

CHALLENGE: **STAYING GROUNDED EVEN AS THEY DWELL IN THE MORE MYTHIC REALMS**
FULFILLMENT: **FINDING GREATNESS IN SERVING OTHERS**

March 3–10

THE LONER
PISCES II

March 11–18

DANCERS AND DREAMERS
PISCES III

Those born in the Week of the Loner on this karmic path may be a bit bewildered by its challenges. Possessed of a formidable intellect and great curiosity, they may move from one obsession or consuming passion to the next, yet fail to connect with the sense of higher social purpose and the urge to expand required by this karmic path. They have a great sense of beauty that may well be their truest compass. If they can allow themselves to expand their world of relationships and connections and avoid their natural tendency to withdraw into misanthropy, they will be rewarded with the kind of acceptance, recognition, and sense of personal worth that is their heart's desire.

GEORGE WASHINGTON
1st U.S. president;
commanded army in
American Revolutionary
War
—
2/22/1732
Aquarius–Pisces Cusp

CHALLENGE: **CULTIVATING A BIGGER SENSE OF SELF WITHOUT SLIPPING INTO FANTASY**
FULFILLMENT: **FINDING THE ACCEPTANCE THAT THROWING OFF ALL THAT KEEPS THEM SMALL BRINGS**
NOTABLE: **IVAN BOESKY (CONVICTED WALL STREET INVESTMENT BANKER, INSIDER TRADING, 1986)**

Marked by wanderlust and a sense of adventure, those born in this week who travel the Way of Amplification can find great reward, if only they can be persuaded to stay in one place long enough to put down some roots. Scattered energy is a big problem, as is their habit of disconnecting from demanding situations. One of the hallmarks of these extraordinarily talented souls is their seeming ability to work miracles. They can do themselves a great disservice on this path, however, if they fail to recognize the fact that acting on opportunities for expansion and growth also implies taking on greater responsibility. However, there is the potential for them to become real legends in their own time, if only they will not turn away from the leadership, responsibility, and level of commitment of which such legends are generally made.

CHALLENGE: **PLACING THEIR SEARCH FOR THE MEANING OF LIFE IN THE HERE AND NOW**
FULFILLMENT: **FEELING THAT THEY SERVE A PURPOSE AS PART OF A GREATER WHOLE**
NOTABLE: **HOWARD GREENFIELD (SONGWRITER)**

KARMIC PATH
12

The Way of Expression

CANCER–GEMINI CUSP TO SAGITTARIUS–CAPRICORN CUSP
Magic to Prophecy

Individuals on the Way of Expression come into this lifetime with spiritual faculties that allow them to look into the hearts and minds of others. Not only are they highly empathic, but their intuitive and even psychic abilities are so well developed that one may ask, What were they up to in previous incarnations? Blessed with many magical gifts, the individuals on this karmic path are fated not only to be in touch with unseen realms but to express their visionary views. Though the fact that their intuitive side is highly developed means they could easily withdraw from the world into religious retreat, it is their destiny to participate fully in the world through the full and positive articulation of their gifts. Those on the Way of Expression are called to be prophets of a sort. However, the most successful prophets are perhaps those who do not make elaborate calculations or inspired guesses but rather create the future through their own actions, thus ensuring the success of their prophecies.

Often found in the arts, these people must learn to manifest the unseen as the seen, to tap into spiritual realms, draw from them, and create an end product for others to share. The core lesson the individuals on this karmic path must learn is how to take the abstract and make it concrete. Surely this in itself is a great achievement, as well as one of the tasks involved in pursuing a spiritual path. Embarking on this journey requires being ready to cross

boundaries of space and time. Should those on this path accept the karmic task of being prophets of their time, they must hone their intuition to razor sharpness and summon the kind of courage needed to speak to the public at large. Although this can be done with words, those on this karmic path may also find a form of physical expression for themselves. It is their destiny to become a spiritual medium or channel for the benefit of society as a whole.

Although many wonderfully romantic and imaginative energies swirl around those on the Way of Expression, this path necessitates diving fearlessly into the more dark and perilous areas of their own psyches, as well as those of the collective. To accomplish such a highly personal journey and to plug into alternate forms of energy, they will need to spend a great deal of time alone. Letting in the light of spirit through meditation and prayer and maintaining a positive attitude, while at the same time developing the strength and willpower to contact the shadow side when they choose to do so is critical to survival, since care must always be taken whenever other energy forms are released.

There is a pronounced tendency to magnify some of the pitfalls of both of the poles of this path, as Gemini–Cancer isolation and selfishness can easily develop into antisocial, frustrated Sagittarius–Capricorn traits, severely impeding the evolution of these individuals. It may be easy for these men

---

CORE LESSON

Taking the unseen forces of spirit and giving them creative form or manifestation

GOAL

To fully and in detail express their experience of the numinous

---

GIFTS
Prophetic, Charismatic, Affectionate

PITFALLS
Intense, Withdrawn, Dangerous

and women to become stuck in darker states such as depression, self-pity, or fatalism. In order to avoid getting bogged down this way, those on the Way of Expression must develop the ability to walk the fine line of their psychic and psychological energies, learning to mine the gems while throwing out the dross. One peril is believing that one has no freedom of will in the face of larger forces, thus declining to choose to be the master of one's destiny and leaving oneself open to fate. Gambling addiction may be a risk for these people. Any program that reinforces positive thinking would be of benefit on this karmic path.

As much as the individuals on this karmic path would like to withdraw totally from the outside world, it is usually their destiny eventually to emerge from their periods of going inward to share what they have experienced with the world at large. As they are naturally shy, this may prove difficult at first. Fearful of others' disapproval while yearning for their approval, these individuals are apt to sidestep the issue of how to relate more effectively. Rather than articulating directly what they know, they will create metaphors to express themselves; poetry, language, dance, even rhetoric will be used to share but not to reveal their innermost selves. Therefore, it behooves their audience to pay extremely close attention to them, since they may thereby catch a glimpse of a whole other reality. However, the more direct and well articulated

the message these souls have to share, the further they will progress along their karmic path, so they should be given every encouragement to open themselves more fully to others.

Because they really prefer to be on their own a great deal, it is the irony of their fate to attract many friends and admirers. In this way, life is quietly ensuring that they will fulfill their karmic task. (If one is alone, is one truly expressing oneself, or is one missing out on the alchemical reaction that occurs between performer and audience?) These individuals need to have someone to express themselves to in order to transform. In addition, their personalities are of such a seductive and affectionate nature that they will almost never be at a loss for lovers or other admirers. Constantly surrounded by adoring fans who subconsciously are seeking to touch that which these souls connect with on a regular basis, those on this path may find it difficult to have as much alone time as they need. Thus, early in life they will need to develop the willpower to isolate themselves periodically, while later, when they are a little more mature and further along on their path, they will need to force themselves to go out into the glare of the public spotlight. In their social, professional, or family group they are likely to establish high standards and over the years guide the development of the groups to which they belong in matters of taste and advanced thought.

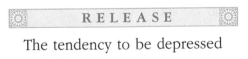

RELEASE

The tendency to be depressed

REWARD

The joy of bringing
magic to others

SUGGESTION

Remember to focus on the positive. Know that the light of truth eliminates all darkness.

People do not see those on this path very clearly, largely because of the charismatic aura that surrounds them. They do tend to attract the wrong sort of people and must particularly beware of flatterers and even worshipers. Surrounding themselves with admirers is a bit like putting themselves in a hall of mirrors—their self-image may come to resemble what others reflect back to them. This can have disastrous consequences and take them completely out of touch with their real inner selves. It comes as no surprise that while the professional arena is an important one in which these individuals can express themselves to the world at large, it will be to their more intimate friends that they will be most likely to reveal who and what they truly are. Due to the emotional, psychological, and emotional depth of their spirits, others may not understand them easily. Thus, a few close, discerning, and empathetic friends with whom they can be themselves will be crucial to their development. In love, their sexual experiences may prove to be so deeply transformative both for themselves and for their partners that problems with sex and love dependencies may develop. Many partners may be available to them, but fidelity is not necessarily their forte. Moreover, they do tend to disappear on their loved ones frequently—to go either within, to their inner lives, or outside, to their adoring public. Perhaps those on this karmic path would do well to forgo marriage, except

that they love the magic of love and with each new partner are convinced that this is "the one." Because of the importance of their prophetic drives and their fate to be spokesmen or icons for those in their group or profession, they may find it necessary to make a strict separation between their private and personal lives. In most cases, keeping their turbulent feelings under control can be a full-time job in itself.

The Way of Expression is akin to Pandora's box, opened perhaps out of curiosity but perhaps also out of a need to see the truth. Two problems emerge once it is opened: how to close it again and how to deal with the wild spirits that have been released into the world. Those on the Way of Expression must have not only the courage to face what is inside the box but also the strength to deal with it once the box is opened. In many ways such individuals are our representatives, and we are spared the exalted agonies they endure for us. One may think of some lines from Coleridge's *Kubla Khan:*

> And all should cry, Beware, Beware,
> His flashing eyes, his floating hair!
> Weave a circle round him thrice,
> And close your eyes with holy dread,
> For he on honey-dew hath fed,
> And drunk the milk of Paradise.

BALANCE POINT

Public and Private Life

CRYSTALS AND GEMSTONES

Celestite grounds vibrations from angelic realms and unerringly brings light to any cloud of fear. This stone strengthens awareness that mystical revelations truly fit into the scope of "reality."

NOTABLES ON THIS KARMIC PATH

Immensely expressive, **Fred Astaire** displayed effortless sophistication in both his dancing and acting. By dedicating many solitary hours to developing his talent, Astaire was able to cultivate his signature style and then (as is typical of those on the Way of Expression) share his magical gift with his admirers. Astaire deftly maintained a strong separation between his private and public life, thereby reaching the balance point of this karmic path. Hardly at a loss for adoring fans, this dancer carved out a unique niche for himself in show business.

FRED ASTAIRE

British science fiction writer **Arthur C. Clarke** has certainly used his prophetic gifts with striking effectiveness. Clarke conjured images of the future, predicting the advent of satellite communication twenty years ahead of time and mapping a vision of interplanetary travel in his space odyssey books. Though he shared the world of his imagination with his public, Clarke lived reclusively on the

ARTHUR C. CLARKE

island of Sri Lanka, where he indulged in his favorite pastimes—skin diving and photography. Clarke is perhaps best known for his book *2001: A Space Odyssey,* the basis for the outstanding futuristic film by director Stanley Kubrick.

Through her authorship of beautiful love poems, **Elizabeth Barrett Browning** brought expressive romance to the lives of others. Perhaps her greatest achievement was *Aurora Leigh,* a romantic melodrama in verse with great popular appeal. Unfortunately, Browning did succumb to some of the pitfalls on the Way of Expression, including depression and antisocial behavior. Yet despite these problems, she was true to the core lesson of her path, showing great interest in exploring spiritual matters, sharing her insights with others, and manifesting this inspiration in her daily life.

ELIZABETH BARRETT BROWNING

Other Notables: Vaclav Havel, John Grisham, George Dewey Cukor, A. S. Byatt, Don Cornelius, Reba McEntire, Duke Ellington, Roseanne Cash, Sandra Bernhard, Kris Kristofferson, E. B. White, Ernest Hemingway, Elizabeth Dole, Alfred Hitchcock, Wilt Chamberlain, Jim Henson, Louis Jacques Daguerre, Indira Gandhi, Arsenio Hall, Greg Norman, Kelsey Grammer, Gary Sinise, Albrecht Dürer

BIRTHDAYS ON KARMIC PATH 13

August 15, 1880–January 3, 1881 | March 27, 1899–August 15, 1899 | November 7, 1917–March 27, 1918

June 18, 1936–November 6, 1936 | January 29, 1955–June 18, 1955 | September 9, 1973–January 28, 1974

April 20, 1992–September 8, 1992 | December 1, 2010–April 20, 2011

KARMIC PATH
13

March 19–24
REBIRTH
PISCES–ARIES CUSP

The Way of Expression blesses the individuals born in this week with a much higher degree of insight and self-realization than they might otherwise have had, and most of those with this configuration are likely to do amazingly well on this karmic path. Despite some seemingly rough edges and an often overwhelming appetite for life, they may have a curious store of a special kind of elemental wisdom at their disposal. Indeed, they come into this journey so poised for transformation that they may well be able to take some surprising shortcuts to their goals. Though their tendency to succumb to the need for approval is pronounced, these people nevertheless have an advantage when it comes to dealing with the slings and arrows of outrageous fortune, and if they are careful to keep the channels between the inner and outer worlds open, they will experience an unusual and exciting passage.

BRUCE WILLIS
TV/film actor,
Moonlighting, Die Hard

3/19/1955
Pisces–Aries Cusp

CHALLENGE: **DELVING INTO THEIR DARKER IMPULSES**
FULFILLMENT: **EXPRESSING THEIR SENSITIVITY**
NOTABLE: **PAUL JENNINGS (LABOR UNION OFFICIAL)**

March 25–April 2
THE CHILD
ARIES I

A tendency to view the world through rose-colored glasses is a pronounced character trait of those born in the Week of the Child who travel this karmic path. These individuals will further cultivate their inborn sense of wonder and awe as they make this life journey and are more than likely to be blessed with a unique ability to draw others into their enthusiastic and even magical perception of life. Though with this configuration there is a danger of withdrawing into either isolation or approval seeking, the Way of Expression blesses Aries I's with such a multitude of gifts that it is unlikely such tendencies will be much of a problem. Far more important will be their ability and willingness to adapt and respond to the social pressures of this karmic path, for in order to realize their greatest potential, they will at times have to struggle to stay connected with their audience.

CHALLENGE: **NOT RETREATING INTO THEMSELVES SO MUCH AS TO BECOME ANTISOCIAL**
FULFILLMENT: **SHARING THEIR SENSE OF WONDER**
NOTABLES: **DANA CARVEY (ACTOR/COMEDIAN); REBA MCENTIRE (COUNTRY WESTERN SINGER/ENTERTAINER)**

April 3–10
THE STAR
ARIES II

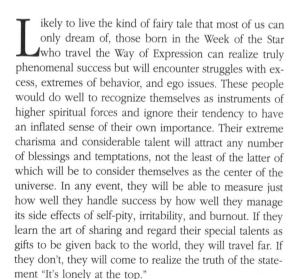

Likely to live the kind of fairy tale that most of us can only dream of, those born in the Week of the Star who travel the Way of Expression can realize truly phenomenal success but will encounter struggles with excess, extremes of behavior, and ego issues. These people would do well to recognize themselves as instruments of higher spiritual forces and ignore their tendency to have an inflated sense of their own importance. Their extreme charisma and considerable talent will attract any number of blessings and temptations, not the least of the latter of which will be to consider themselves as the center of the universe. In any event, they will be able to measure just how well they handle success by how well they manage its side effects of self-pity, irritability, and burnout. If they learn the art of sharing and regard their special talents as gifts to be given back to the world, they will travel far. If they don't, they will come to realize the truth of the statement "It's lonely at the top."

GLORIA SWANSON
Film actress, played character based on herself in
Sunset Boulevard

3/27/1899
Aries I

CHALLENGE: **DEVELOPING BETTER DISCERNMENT WHEN VIEWING BOTH THEMSELVES AND OTHERS**
FULFILLMENT: **BEING AT CENTER STAGE**

April 11–18
THE PIONEER
ARIES III

Those born in the Week of the Pioneer who travel the Way of Expression are likely to be gifted with both considerable insight into their own processes and a unique vision of the future. Fearless without being reckless, they have the ability to inspire others in almost any area of endeavor. This karmic path gives them a much more highly developed sense of empathy for their fellows than might otherwise be the case, and they will doubtless strike willing chords of response and support as they put themselves and their ideas before the public. Too, they are more positive by nature than some others on this karmic path, and their natural high spirits and intrepid approach to problems will allow them to transcend almost any obstacles they may encounter along the way.

CHALLENGE: **TAKING CARE WHOM THEY ATTRACT INTO THEIR CIRCLE**
FULFILLMENT: **REGULARLY INTERACTING WITH OTHERS**

April 19–24
POWER
ARIES–TAURUS CUSP

Those born on the Cusp of Power who travel this karmic path can be downright dangerous when it comes to getting what they want. The key to success for these dynamic people will be keeping themselves tied to issues and concerns beyond their immediate sphere of influence and staying connected to the higher spiritual forces from which their power flows. Gifted with tremendous instincts and dynamic energy, they will find it easy to control their immediate environment but not so easy to control their own deeper or darker urges. Thus, learning to relinquish their sense of control in order to nurture and expand their talents will prove especially important. Otherwise, they may encounter difficulties, especially if they remain bound to purely material and monetary endeavors.

VLADIMIR NABOKOV
Russian writer, *Lolita*

4/22/1899
Aries–Taurus Cusp

CHALLENGE: **LEARNING HOW TO EXPRESS WHAT THEY KNOW ONLY PSYCHICALLY**

FULFILLMENT: **COMING TO UNDERSTAND THAT TRUE POWER RESIDES OUTSIDE THE SELF**

NOTABLE: **MICHAEL O'KEEFE (ACTOR)**

April 25–May 2
MANIFESTATION
TAURUS I

Protective and nurturing, Taurus I's on the Way of Expression may wrestle with the need to release some security issues before they can successfully navigate this karmic path. Taking risks is not in their usual repertoire, and they may repress a great deal of creativity, inspiration, and imagination as they attempt to impose structure on the unpredictable world of their impressions. While most will successfully rise to the challenges presented by this karmic path by turning their inspired abstractions into concrete reality, a sense of fatalism will cause others born in this week to retreat into laziness or the belief that luck controls their personal destiny. Yet if they can shake themselves up a bit and cultivate the ability to become true spiritual and worldly self-starters, all is likely to go well.

CHALLENGE: **RELEASING THEIR FIXITY IN ORDER TO BETTER EMBRACE A SENSE OF MAGIC**

FULFILLMENT: **SATISFYING THEIR LOVE OF ALL THINGS VENUSIAN**

NOTABLE: **FIRST DUKE OF WELLINGTON (BRITISH GENERAL AND PRIME MINISTER; DEFEATED NAPOLEON AT WATERLOO)**

May 3–10
THE TEACHER
TAURUS II

The Teachers who travel the Way of Expression are likely to lead a rather charmed life, for they have a unique ability to turn even the most far-out concepts, ideas, and inspirations into comprehensible and accessible material for a wide and varied audience. Charismatic and sensual, they will doubtless manifest the gifts of this karmic path in special talent for the more physical arts, including dance, athletics, and especially music. Yet these demanding people may resent its challenges and retreat into isolation or selfishness. Impatience can be a big problem as well. But if they are careful to fulfill their promise by attuning themselves to the world of larger ideas and inspirations and then finding a way to convey that knowledge to the world, they will have all the qualities needed for a sweet and successful journey along the Way of Expression.

DUKE ELLINGTON
Composer, conductor, musician, *Take the A Train*

4/29/1899
Taurus I

CHALLENGE: **AVOIDING THEIR TENDENCY TO RETREAT INTO SELF-INDULGENCE AND FANTASY**

FULFILLMENT: **EXPRESSING THEMSELVES PHYSICALLY**

NOTABLE: **FRED ASTAIRE (ACTOR/SINGER/DANCER; HOLLYWOOD LEGEND)**

May 11–18
THE NATURAL
TAURUS III

Though the Way of Expression provides those born in this week with much of the freedom from mundane concerns they so desire, it also presents a rare set of challenges. Finding the right outlet for their romantic and imaginative energies will be critical to their success, as will the ability to cope with the unique pressures presented by their tendency to attract throngs of willing admirers and supporters. Though many of them will retreat from the larger world to be alone with their thoughts and attune themselves to some higher form of energy, others will find themselves literally thrust into the spotlight in order to better spread their messages abroad. Whatever the specific manifestations, however, Taurus III's are likely to do quite well on this path, providing they do not deny themselves access to the world of nature or to the sense of personal freedom from which they draw their strength.

CHALLENGE: **MAKING SURE THEY SPEND ENOUGH TIME IN NATURE TO REPLENISH THE WELLSPRINGS OF THEIR CREATIVITY**

FULFILLMENT: **BEING ABLE TO EXPRESS THEMSELVES FREELY**

NOTABLE: **DEBRA WINGER (FILM ACTRESS)**

May 19–24
ENERGY
TAURUS–GEMINI CUSP

Naturally talented performers, those born on the Cusp of Energy who travel this karmic path will doubtless draw the attentions of others like a magnet. Gifted with considerably more insight into both themselves and others than they might otherwise be, these people will nevertheless face the challenge of regulating their brilliance and versatility in the interest of maintaining their connection to higher spiritual forces. Taurus–Geminis have a peculiarly driven quality, and on this karmic path they may expend considerable energy trying to outrun, avoid, or evade their responsibility to their higher self or others due to glitziness, superficiality, or just plain sleaziness. No matter how gifted they are, these people may have a rather uneasy relationship with their own talents—enjoying and embracing them on the one hand while resisting and diminishing them on the other.

SANDRA BERNHARD
Comedian and actress

6/6/1955
Gemini II

CHALLENGE: **GROUNDING THEMSELVES SUFFICIENTLY TO ACT AS A CONDUIT FOR HIGHER FORCES**
FULFILLMENT: **ENJOYING THE PEACE OF MIND THAT THE ARTICULATION OF THEIR FEELINGS BRINGS**
NOTABLE: **ROSEANNE CASH (SINGER/SONGWRITER)**

May 25–June 2
FREEDOM
GEMINI I

Articulate and communicative in the extreme, those born in the Week of Freedom who navigate the Way of Expression will doubtless be quite happy, providing they grace their keen insights with a measure of charm and regulate their razor-sharp wit so as not to cut so close to the bone. Irritability and stress can be big problems for those born with this configuration, and their delicately wired sensibilities may suffer when they channel their energies away from higher concerns and concepts and into sensationalism and thrill seeking. Such daredevil tendencies may gain them the attention they crave, yet over time they may only escalate them to provide greater satisfaction for their audience. Cultivating the will to be alone and get in touch with the forces of spiritual life through such activities as prayer and meditation will be especially useful, as will an ability to focus their considerable and seductive charm on matters of lasting import rather than the concerns of the moment.

CHALLENGE: **ESTABLISHING SET ROUTINES FOR CONNECTING WITH SPIRIT**
FULFILLMENT: **LEARNING THAT WHAT THEY SAY HAS A LARGER IMPORT OR BROADER MESSAGE**
NOTABLE: **IRVING THALBERG (MGM FILM EXECUTIVE)**

June 3–10
NEW LANGUAGE
GEMINI II

Learning to channel their unique communicative talents into some form of artistic and creative expression will be paramount to the success of Gemini II's who navigate the Way of Expression. For those born in the Week of Freedom, there is a tendency to become distracted or even quite confused by intimate or personal relationships when others fail to understand their unique communications, but they should never lose sight of the fact that this karmic path promises them bigger fish to fry. If they can avoid the pitfalls of approval seeking and defensiveness and develop their rare talents for accessing and communicating more universal truths, their success on this karmic path is ensured, especially in the areas of writing, public speaking, music, journalism, or the more futuristic forms of multimedia.

JOHN ROEBLING
Brooklyn Bridge engineer

6/12/1806
Gemini III

CHALLENGE: **AVOIDING THE PITFALL OF BEING OVERLY CONCERNED ABOUT WHAT OTHERS THINK OF THEM**
FULFILLMENT: **FULLY ARTICULATING THEIR DEEPLY PERSONAL BRAND OF COMMUNICATION**

June 11–18
THE SEEKER
GEMINI III

Gemini III's will have little problem jumping the traces of convention when traveling this karmic path. Those born in the Week of the Seeker like nothing better than to transcend the limits of reality, and some will be gifted with the kind of perception that will enable them to "go where no one has gone before." Natural risk takers, these people may indulge the intuitive gifts of this path through a tendency to gamble, not only in traditional games of chance but in a number of other areas as well. Romance, the stock market, and even skydiving may all be manifestations of their restless and often careless inclinations. Yet if they can balance their unique brand of personal expression with an equal capacity to listen—both to others and to "the still small voice within"—they will doubtless find the adventure they crave.

CHALLENGE: **NOT SQUANDERING THEIR GIFTS ON GET-RICH-QUICK SCHEMES**
FULFILLMENT: **TAPPING INTO THE NUMINOUS AND EXPERIENCING IT FULLY**

June 19–24
MAGIC
GEMINI–CANCER CUSP

The special endowments of those born on the Cusp of Magic who travel the Way of Expression may be far more obvious to others than to themselves. Gemini–Cancers may, however, get a bit mired down along the way if they take their talents for granted and refuse the greater opportunities for expression offered by this karmic path. Their greatest danger is that they may become overly absorbed in purely personal pursuits and preoccupations and fail to rise to the higher, more transcendental purpose of their life journey. Staying aware of and connected to spiritual forces and directing their considerable energies to some broader purpose will be paramount to their success. Intellectual discipline will help to balance their romantic natures, and cultivating greater objectivity will allow them to avoid the pitfalls of oversensitivity and depression when their higher talents are required.

KRIS KRISTOFFERSON
Songwriter/singer/actor, wrote "Me and Bobby McGee"

6/22/1936
Gemini–Cancer Cusp

CHALLENGE: **NOT BEING SWAMPED BY THEIR PSYCHIC IMPRESSIONS AND RETREATING FROM LIFE**

FULFILLMENT: **RECOGNIZING THEIR UNIQUE TALENT FOR TOUCHING OTHERS ON A DEEP LEVEL**

June 25–July 2
THE EMPATH
CANCER I

The Empaths who travel the Way of Expression may seem downright spooky in their ability to attune themselves to unseen forces. These highly psychic people may manifest their gifts from an early age and may be found doing anything from ghost busting to channeling entities from Alpha Centauri. The problem is that they may become so caught up in acting out the myriad of feelings, vibrations, and fluctuations of the invisible world that they fail to adequately connect with this one or even with themselves. Thus, a solid grounding in self-knowledge will be the key to their success along this karmic path, as will establishing and maintaining some necessary boundaries. Nevertheless, they are blessed with a measure of determination that will balance them on the road to higher development, and if they are careful always to consider the true source from which an inspiration springs, they are unlikely to be sidetracked along the way.

CHALLENGE: **GRAPPLING WITH THEIR OWN FEAR OF THEIR GIFTS**

FULFILLMENT: **CONNECTING WITH AND CHANNELING THE LIGHT OF INSPIRATION**

NOTABLE: **CHARLES LAUGHTON (STAGE/FILM ACTOR)**

July 3–10
THE UNCONVENTIONAL
CANCER II

Whatever destiny may have in store for Cancer II's who travel the Way of Expression; chances are it will involve a reconciliation between their private world of fantasy and their public life and self. Many of these wildly romantic souls will lead a sort of double life, projecting a public image very different from their personal reality or absorbing themselves in some profession or job far removed from their dreams for success. The principal danger is that they may succumb to own darker impulses and lose themselves in a world of sensation, depression, addiction, or even self-destructive tendencies. Yet if they allow their phenomenal intuition and insight to better inform their sense of the future and then express those insights to others without fearing rejection or misunderstanding, they can attain great success along this road.

E. B. WHITE
Writer/editor, *New Yorker* essayist, *Stuart Little, Charlotte's Web*

7/11/1899
Cancer III

CHALLENGE: **RECOGNIZING THAT THEIR FRIENDS HAVE A TREMENDOUS IMPACT ON THEIR EMOTIONAL BALANCE—FOR BOTH GOOD AND ILL**

FULFILLMENT: **FINDING A FORUM FOR EXPRESSING THEIR SECRET INNER WORLD**

NOTABLE: **GEORGE CUKOR (FILM DIRECTOR, *MY FAIR LADY*)**

July 11–18
THE PERSUADER
CANCER III

Blessed with a rare ability to invest in themselves and their sense of the future, Cancer III's who travel the way of Expression are likely to find considerable success. Their communicative talents will be put to good use on this karmic path, and they may well have a truly mesmerizing presence as they bring their talents and insights into the public eye. Though a tendency to excess or overconfidence may be present, overindulgence in either will only serve to mute their connections to the higher spiritual forces at work in their lives. Yet if they can come to terms with their security issues and display a readiness to transform their most inspired plans into concrete reality and the larger sphere of public acceptance, these souls are likely to find wonderful fulfillment.

CHALLENGE: **STRUGGLING WITH THEIR TENDENCY TO DEPRESSION**

FULFILLMENT: **USING THEIR PERSUASIVE TALENTS IN ARTICULATING THEIR HIGHER VISION OR SPIRITUALITY**

NOTABLE: **JIMMY CAGNEY (SHOWMAN; FILM ACTOR, *YANKEE DOODLE DANDY*)**

July 19–25
OSCILLATION
CANCER–LEO CUSP

July 26–August 2
AUTHORITY
LEO I

Once they grasp that taking on the challenges of the Way of Expression will provide them with both necessary grounding and a measure of passionate inspiration, Cancer–Leos will do very well on this karmic path. Likely to be especially gifted and creative, they may well have a clearer sense of vocational direction than many of their fellows. Delicately wired as a rule, they will nevertheless have to guard against the dangers of excitability or even megalomania, as they pursue their fondest plans and dreams. Emotional blockages of all kinds may be a special sticking point, and they may swing from extremes of hyperactivity to periods of shutting down completely. Their love of innovation and invention will complement their call to prophecy and transcendence, and if they discipline themselves to manage their more extreme inclinations better, they will find themselves beautifully aligned with the spiritual and creative forces at their disposal.

ERNEST HEMINGWAY
Author and literary
great, *A Farewell to Arms,
For Whom the Bell Tolls*

7/21/1899
Cancer–Leo Cusp

Leo I's will doubtless relish the prospect of public attention implied by this path but may have to work to divest themselves of their need for ego stroking and approval before they can fulfill their truest callings and highest aspirations. The search for higher truth and permanent values will surely figure prominently in their lives, and their naturally lofty standards will serve to ensure that their talents and abilities are combined with a rare degree of integrity, since "selling out" in the interest of commercial acceptance or public acclaim is not generally in their vocabulary. But perhaps the greatest strength of this very promising karmic path is that it gifts those who travel it with considerably more insight and empathy than those born in the Week of Authority might otherwise possess. If they can employ that empathy and integrate it with their leadership, creativity, and passion, they are promised great fulfillment along this journey.

CHALLENGE: **PRYING THEMSELVES OUT OF THEIR EMOTIONAL AND CREATIVE BLOCKS**
FULFILLMENT: **INSPIRING OTHERS WITH THEIR PROPHETIC IDEAS**
NOTABLE: **DON DRYSDALE (HALL OF FAME BASEBALL PITCHER)**

CHALLENGE: **NOT ALLOWING THEIR HIGH STANDARDS TO PREVENT THE SELF-EXPRESSION THAT IS THEIR KARMA**
FULFILLMENT: **STEPPING INTO THE ROLE OF ARTICULATOR OF LARGER CONCERNS OR VISIONS**
NOTABLES: **ELIZABETH DOLE (PRESIDENT OF AMERICAN RED CROSS); YVES SAINT LAURENT (FASHION DESIGNER)**

August 3–10
BALANCED STRENGTH
LEO II

August 11–18
LEADERSHIP
LEO III

Strength of character and an ability to endure will doubtless mark the passage of Leo II's who travel the Way of Expression. Though it may take some time for them to come into their own and get in touch with their own sources of intuition and inspiration, they have a rare ability to turn their dreams into reality through hard work, tenacity, and concentration. They must be careful, however, not to fail to take up the challenges of this karmic path by being single-minded or withdrawn. Depression and a feeling of self-pity can distract them from their truest purpose and cloud their vision. Yet it is likely that their expressive talents and their strong sense of being the champion of less fortunate souls will combine to create a person who not only can see the future but feels compelled to do something about it.

SIR ALFRED HITCHCOCK
Film director, *Psycho*

8/13/1899
Leo III

The larger-than-life energies of those born in this week who travel the Way of Expression will doubtless find wonderful opportunities for expression. Blessed with a marked ability to tap into archetypal ideas and concepts, these people will nevertheless have to work hard so that their more aggressive tendencies do not overpower their empathy with or compassion for others. Selfishness or, at the very least, self-centeredness will prove the biggest barrier to their success, and it will be only when they broaden their vision to include other people's viewpoints that their talents and abilities will find their fullest expression. Nevertheless, artistic, creative, and financial rewards all beckon, and if they are careful to align themselves with the source from which those blessings flow, all will go well.

CHALLENGE: **RECOGNIZING WHEN TAKING ON THE BURDENS OF OTHERS WILL PREVENT THEM FROM DOING THE WORK OF THIS KARMIC PATH**
FULFILLMENT: **ACTIVATING AND MANIFESTING THEIR GREAT INTUITIVE ABILITY**

CHALLENGE: **CONSIDERING THE FEELINGS OF OTHERS**
FULFILLMENT: **PRESENTING THEIR LARGE AND EXPRESSIVE CREATIVE VISIONS**
NOTABLES: **ANTONIO SALIERI (COMPOSER; HAD FAMOUS RIVALRY WITH MOZART); JACOB SHUBERT (PRODUCER; THEATRICAL MANAGER)**

August 19–25

EXPOSURE
LEO–VIRGO CUSP

Leo–Virgos are difficult people to fool and will doubtless have an astonishing knowledge of the hearts and minds of those around them. Yet they will have to be careful not to use their amazing perceptions for purely personal or manipulative ends. Also, working to find the balance between public and private life is sure to figure prominently in their life journey as they navigate the Way of Expression, for many of them will experience special conflicts in that area. Their natural shyness may interfere with their desire for expression, just as their desire to withdraw will be at odds with their many opportunities to expand their audience of admirers. In any event, they are bound to have an interesting ride. If they do not allow their fears and darker fascinations to get the best of them and at the same time turn their attentions to issues of the larger good, they may well answer this karmic path's call to prophecy and transcendence.

BUDDY HOLLY
Pop/rock performer/
writer; died in plane crash

9/7/1936
Virgo II

CHALLENGE: **GETTING A GRIP ON THEIR SHYNESS AND TENDENCY TO WITHDRAW**

FULFILLMENT: **FINE-TUNING THEIR ABILITY TO REVEAL OR UNVEIL THEMSELVES AT PRECISELY THE RIGHT MOMENT**

NOTABLES: **WILT CHAMBERLAIN (BASKETBALL GREAT; 4-TIME MVP); A. S. BYATT (AUTHOR)**

August 26–September 2

SYSTEM BUILDERS
VIRGO I

Though the Way of Expression imbues Virgo I's with a greater sense of emotional awareness than they might otherwise have, these people will still have to struggle to rise to its challenges. Many of this configuration may in fact consciously relinquish a sense of control over their lives and destinies, preferring to defer decisions or to lay their conflicts in the lap of the gods. Yet they have a good potential for success, providing they are given the opportunity to superimpose a sense of structure and meaning on the expansive energies with which they will doubtless make contact. In fact, they are fine candidates for objectifying certain experiences and energies and will doubtless flourish as interpreters and analyzers who bring the tools of greater understanding to a wide audience. Vocations such as the clergy, psychology, art, and architecture will all appeal and will afford them a chance to reconcile their innate sense of order with a larger sense of purpose.

CHALLENGE: **FINDING THE RIGHT VALVE TO LET OFF THE PRESSURE OF EMOTIONAL STEAM**

FULFILLMENT: **CONVINCING OTHERS THAT THE UNIVERSE IS ORDERLY**

September 3–10

THE ENIGMA
VIRGO II

Puzzling to the point of being downright mysterious, those born in the Week of the Enigma who travel the Way of Expression will discover that their greatest strength is also their greatest weakness. Whatever their specific gifts, going within and cultivating greater intuition and understanding of life's bigger picture may come easily to them, yet applying that understanding to the workings of their own minds and psyches may prove more difficult. Capable of great objectivity and perception in the nonpersonal areas of life, these people tend to be well suited to assuming a more public role. Their natural discrimination and strong moral sense will be especially at ease in politics, fund-raising, and social leadership, and if they are drawn to the arts, they will bring a fine business sense to their endeavors, along with innate good taste.

CHALLENGE: **FORGOING THEIR IMPULSE TO THROW PEOPLE OFF TRACK**

FULFILLMENT: **FINDING THE STRENGTH TO EXPRESS THEIR ANALYTICAL AND INTUITIVE VIEWS FEARLESSLY**

NOTABLE: **LOUIS XIV (GREATEST MONARCH OF HIS AGE; "THE SUN KING")**

September 11–18

THE LITERALIST
VIRGO III

Though blessed with the ability to turn abstractions into concrete reality, Virgo III's may face a challenge when it comes to recognizing the abstractions of this karmic path. Their expressive talents are quite pronounced, and they are unlikely to have problems telling it as they see it. Yet the key to their development will be their willingness to delve into the worlds of the unseen and unexplored. Nevertheless, they are possessed of a fine talent for discerning the truth and are likely to seek it fearlessly and express it well. Once they come to grips with the fact that even truth is an abstraction, full of nuances and shades of gray, they will doubtless find that their lives become easier.

H. L. MENCKEN
Editor/writer/critic,
Baltimore Sun

9/12/1880
Virgo III

CHALLENGE: **NOT TAKING THINGS SO LITERALLY**

FULFILLMENT: **RELAXING THEIR OBJECTIVITY AS THEY OPEN TO THE MYSTICAL**

September 19–24

BEAUTY
VIRGO–LIBRA CUSP

Especially suited to the world of the arts and creative endeavors of all kinds, Virgo–Libras who travel the Way of Expression are likely to realize really splendid success. Cultivation of stamina and personal strength as well as the ability to eschew excess will be a critical factor in how long their success will last and how great that success will be. Some on this life journey will fail the challenges of this karmic path and misuse their energies in a selfish or self-destructive fashion, while others may ignore the higher spiritual calling indicated and become so preoccupied with ivory-tower aesthetics or a fantasy of how things "should" be that they ignore the dynamics that fuel their creativity, only to become blocked or stale. A willingness to relinquish their tendency to please others or to keep up appearances will help them in their journey, as will broadening their perspective to include both darkness and light.

CHALLENGE: **AVOIDING RELIANCE ON MERE GLITZINESS**
FULFILLMENT: **EXPRESSING A MORE PROFOUND SENSE OF BEAUTY THAN THEY EVER BELIEVED POSSIBLE**

JIM HENSON
Director/screenwriter/
puppeteer, created
Muppets

9/24/1936
Virgo–Libra Cusp

September 25–October 2

THE PERFECTIONIST
LIBRA I

Those born in the Week of the Perfectionist will doubtless produce any number of spectacular manifestations of their talents as they travel this karmic path. They must, however, be careful not to alienate those they meet along the way. Well able to express themselves and to "crack the whip" when they feel a situation calls for greater attention to detail or a higher level of craftsmanship, these people will likely be dauntless and untiring in their efforts to generate a little magic around them. But there is another side to this configuration, one that calls these people to rise above details and broaden their perspective to include passion, intuition, and insight into the problems not just of the moment but of the future. Once they acquire that broader vision and relinquish their need to control things down to the smallest detail, they will be rewarded with a richness of experience that will make even their most arduous efforts seem effortless, inspired, and even transcendental to those who behold them.

CHALLENGE: **RELAXING THEIR STANDARDS A BIT**
FULFILLMENT: **CASTING A MAGICAL SPELL ON THOSE AROUND THEM**
NOTABLES: **GWYNETH PALTROW (OSCAR-WINNING ACTRESS); WINNIE MANDELA (FORMER WIFE OF SOUTH AFRICAN PRESIDENT)**

October 3–10

SOCIETY
LIBRA II

Trying to please all the people all the time may well stand in the way of success for those born in the Week of Society who travel this karmic path. It will be essential for these talented, willing individuals to separate themselves from cares and daily concerns and rise above the wants and woes of others in order to nurture the creative energies within them. Otherwise, some of them may dissipate their considerable potential in sharp-tongued criticism or admittedly witty but ultimately pointless tirades, while others will become easy prey for sycophants and flatterers. Once they turn their attention to themselves, their creations, and the higher level of energy that is available to them and get in touch with the needs and experiences that are common to all of humanity, their purpose on this path will doubtless become clearer and their sense of the future will be better informed by insights of substance and duration.

CHALLENGE: **BEING MORE TO THE POINT WHEN EXPRESSING THEIR VIEWS**
FULFILLMENT: **UTILIZING THEIR UNIQUE TALENT FOR UNDERSTANDING OTHERS FOR A GREATER GOOD**

VACLAV HAVEL
Czechoslovakian premier;
former playwright

10/5/1936
Libra II

October 11–18

THEATER
LIBRA III

The ability to give their all to their art, a cause, or an idea is a pronounced characteristic of Libra III's who travel the Way of Expression, and they will pull out all the stops once they commit themselves to what they consider to be a higher purpose. They may, however, become preoccupied with image, and fail to cultivate the greater depth and sense of universality called for by this karmic path. Too, the more calculating of this type may have a tendency to resist the flow of creative ideas and allow such resistance to inform their career or personal choices. Nevertheless, the strength of their talents is likely to far outweigh the weaknesses of this configuration, and if they learn to accept the responsibility of their capacity to move others through emotion, they are likely to find considerable success and adulation.

CHALLENGE: **NOT SUCCUMBING TO THEIR MANY FLATTERERS AND SYCOPHANTS**
FULFILLMENT: **HAVING THE EARS OF THE WORLD**
NOTABLE: **ROBERT LIVINGSTON STEVENS (SHIPBUILDER; INVENTOR; INVENTED INVERTED T-RAIL FOR RAILROADS, 1830)**

October 19–25

DRAMA AND CRITICISM
LIBRA–SCORPIO CUSP

Gifted with a curious blend of passion and per-spective, Libra–Scorpios who travel the Way of Expression are likely to find a measure of fame in whatever their sphere of influence may be. Able to draw attention like a lightning rod, they are unlikely to go un-noticed for any long period of time. Furthermore, these sensuous, charismatic people seem to have their fingers on the pulse of the collective and will likely be able to speak to the needs of the many. Yet all that attention and admiration does have a downside: there is a pronounced tendency to become hypercritical that can interfere with the ability to tap into the unseen, and many Libra–Scorpios will discover that the more cynical, worldly, or over-confident they become, they less effective they will be. Still, their unshakable sense of beauty is likely to shine, serving as a guiding light for their travels along this road.

BOBBY SEALE
Cofounder of
Black Panthers

10/22/1936
Libra–Scorpio Cusp

CHALLENGE: **RECOGNIZING THEIR NEED FOR RETREAT WHILE LIMITING THEIR NEED TO RESORT TO IT**

FULFILLMENT: **SHARING THEIR WELL-CONCEIVED VIEWS WITH OTHERS**

October 26–November 2

INTENSITY
SCORPIO I

Scorpio I's who travel the Way of Expression are likely to have a rather polarized and extreme view of the world. Their journey will seem either wonderfully blessed or terribly trying, with very little in between. Yet for all their highly charged emotions, they have the seri-ousness and concentration necessary to carry out even their most impossible dreams. Their key to success, how-ever, will be an ability to cultivate greater empathy with-out becoming suspicious or cynical. Whatever they do, they are likely to be extremely good at doing it. When they channel their natural virtuosity and control their darker side, they make truly magical performers, actors, musicians, and public speakers, able to illuminate even the darkest corners of human experience with compas-sion, fairness, and deep understanding.

CHALLENGE: **BEARING THE RESPONSIBILITY OF SO MANY ADMIRERS**

FULFILLMENT: **PUTTING THEIR VIRTUOSO TALENTS ON DISPLAY**

November 3–11

DEPTH
SCORPIO II

Whatever the life choices of those born in the Week of Depth who travel the Way of Expres-sion, they will have to avoid a subconscious tendency to create serious and even tragic problems for themselves as a means of aligning with higher spiritual forces. There is a side to these individuals that may well believe that if something doesn't hurt, it isn't really a valid experience, and they are apt to romanticize their sense of suffering beyond all reason. Thus, depression may sap their energy and sway them from their higher purpose. Yet if they cultivate the ability to lighten up once in a while and nurture a more positive sense of their own place in the universe, this karmic path promises them rec-ognition, achievement, and financial success and security.

LOUIS JACQUES DAGUERRE
Photographic pioneer

11/18/1787
Scorpio III

CHALLENGE: **RESISTING THEIR IMPULSE TO ROMANTICIZE SUFFERING**

FULFILLMENT: **FINDING THEIR CREATIVE VOICE**

NOTABLE: **SIR JOHN RICHARDSON (NATURALIST; EXPLORER; SURVEYED CANADIAN ARCTIC COAST)**

November 12–18

CHARM
SCORPIO III

Scorpio III's on the Way of Expression will doubtless be blessed with considerable charisma and creative talent, as well as the ability to implement their fond-est dreams. On this path, those born in the Week of Charm have a rare awareness of just what it is that makes people's hearts beat faster, and their special brand of em-pathy and understanding is hard to resist. In fact, most things in life will seem to come quite easily to them, yet therein lies the challenge. Reaching beyond the obvious or the immediately accessible will be paramount to their higher development, as will developing an ability to delve beneath the surface and face down their personal demons long enough to realize that the self-sufficiency and re-sourcefulness they admire in others are qualities worth cultivating in themselves if they are to fulfill the highest goals of this karmic path.

CHALLENGE: **ADHERING TO A MORAL CODE IN THEIR ROMAN-TIC LIVES**

FULFILLMENT: **DISCOVERING THAT THEY HAVE THE CAPACITY TO MAKE A DIFFERENCE**

NOTABLE: **DAVID HELPERN (SHOE DESIGNER)**

November 19–24
REVOLUTION
SCORPIO–SAGITTARIUS CUSP

A pronounced taste for extremes and a phoenixlike ability to emerge from even the worst trials and tribulations will doubtless mark the passage of Scorpio–Sagittarians who travel the Way of Expression. Yet there is a danger that their wild and often conflicting energies may be wasted in a never-ending search for ever-escalating sensation or a tendency to romanticize their sense of the extreme. Some with this configuration may be reminiscent of the two-faced god Janus, who looked to both the past and the future. If these people find a way to manage their more extreme tendencies, find a productive channel for personal expression, and stay in touch with the larger forces at work in their lives, they can provide the world with a unique sense of both. If, on the other hand, they succumb to the temptations of sensationalism, autocracy, or alarmism, they will be in for a very bumpy ride.

INDIRA GANDHI
Daughter of Nehru;
Indian prime minister;
assassinated
──────
11/19/1917
Scorpio–Sagittarius Cusp

CHALLENGE: **TAKING CARE NOT TO USE THEIR CAPACITY TO INSPIRE MERELY TO FOMENT REVOLUTION**
FULFILLMENT: **FEELING INSPIRATION COURSE THROUGH THEM**
NOTABLE: **HOWARD DUFF (FILM ACTOR)**

November 25–December 2
INDEPENDENCE
SAGITTARIUS I

Those born in the Week of Independence who travel this karmic path may be happy indeed, for their energies entwine in a rare combination of strength, versatility, and intuition. Likely to be extraordinarily gifted, some Sagittarius I's may nevertheless resist their sense of a higher calling, especially if it threatens to tie them down or otherwise interfere with their need for freedom. In fact, many with this configuration will have a real talent for simply disappearing when things get ponderous and may give new meaning to the phrase "When the going gets tough, the tough get going." However, these individuals are likely to be able to call their own shots at some point in what promise to be highly productive careers, and if they can learn to temper their impulsiveness with insight and soften their more headstrong tendencies with higher forms of love, their lives are likely to go wonderfully well.

CHALLENGE: **OVERCOMING THEIR NATURAL SHYNESS**
FULFILLMENT: **INCORPORATING A VERSION OF THEIR CODE OF HONOR INTO THEIR EXPRESSIONS**
NOTABLES: **MONICA SELES (TENNIS CHAMPION); LEONARD WOOLF (PUBLISHER; WRITER; HUSBAND OF VIRGINIA)**

December 3–10
THE ORIGINATOR
SAGITTARIUS II

The Originators who travel this karmic path are assured of making a real mark on their world, whether in the areas of art or technology or in their ability to see the future in all its possibilities. Though they may experience their share of ups and downs along the road, it is unlikely that they will confront personal rejection. Indeed, they may be so charismatic, so thoroughly avant-garde, that they become a bit uncomfortable with their ability to draw the admiration of others. Still, success is sure to come to these complex personalities, for they have been gifted with the kind of unique talents that literally demand expression. If they are careful not to retreat from the challenges of this karmic path into self-pity, depression, or escapism, they will be able to return a gift to the world quite unlike any that has been given before.

OSSIE DAVIS
Actor, Joe Lewis Story
──────
12/18/1917
Sagittarius III

CHALLENGE: **RELEASING THEIR NEED TO PROVE THEMSELVES TO OTHERS**
FULFILLMENT: **STEPPING INTO THE ROLE OF PROPHET OF ALL THAT IS TECHNOLOGICAL OR INNOVATIVE**

December 11–18
THE TITAN
SAGITTARIUS III

The Titans who find themselves on the Way of Expression may come into this world with so many natural talents that they simply take them for granted. While that quality blesses these people with a remarkable confidence, it can also curse them with a sense of entitlement that is hard to overcome. Nevertheless, these generous and larger-than-life personalities have a thoughtful, introspective side that will work to their advantage along the road, providing they are careful to use their periods of introspection to align themselves with larger and more universal energies and steer quite clear of endless ruminations over personal slights, secret insecurities, and the fussier forms of fretting. Indeed, they may well develop something of an obsession over finding their place in the larger scheme of things. But when they do finally find it, the depth of knowledge and prophecy they are able to share with the world will shape the hearts and minds of generations to come.

CHALLENGE: **COMING TO TERMS WITH THEIR MOODIER OR MORE OMINOUS ELEMENTS**
FULFILLMENT: **REVEALING THE SHEER MAGNITUDE OF THEIR PROPHETIC VISION TO THE WORLD**
NOTABLE: **ARTHUR C. CLARKE (PROLIFIC SCIENCE FICTION AUTHOR, 2001)**

December 19–25

PROPHECY
SAGITTARIUS–CAPRICORN CUSP

A certain sense of irony may color the life passage of those born in this period who find themselves on the Way of Expression. Independent in the highest sense of the word, these sturdy and often quite serious personalities may care very little about the opinions or approval of others, yet will draw from them admiration and even adoration seemingly without effort. They may care even less for sharing their intense insights, gifts, or talents with the rest of us, yet they can rest assured that life will somehow ensure that their gifts are not lost to the world. It is important for them to nurture close and secure connections with a select group of friends or family with whom they can really be themselves and who will bolster their self-confidence in such a way as to make them equal to the demands of this unusual life journey. But perhaps the greatest gift they can to themselves is the cultivation of their ability to play their hunches. When they do so, very little can go wrong.

CHALLENGE: **RESISTING THE TEMPTATION TO LIVE IN SECLUSION**

FULFILLMENT: **ARTICULATING THEIR INTUITIVE INSIGHTS— AND HAVING THEM HEARD**

FRANK NELSON DOUBLEDAY
Publisher

1/8/1862
Capricorn II

December 26–January 2

THE RULER
CAPRICORN I

A chronic sense of being misunderstood may affect those born in the Week of the Ruler who find themselves on this karmic path, and they will doubtless face a number of obstacles in bringing their unique talents and perspectives before an audience. Furthermore, they may be encumbered by their high opinion of their own ideas; while the ability to have faith in oneself is admirable, their rigidity and authoritarianism are not. Nevertheless, there are a number of indicators of success with this configuration, especially if they can avoid their tendency to repress their emotions and instead use their deepest feelings to open the channels between themselves and a more universal perspective. Once they allow more eternal truths to inform and expand their vision, their progress along the Way of Expression is ensured.

CHALLENGE: **FREEING THEIR INNER LIFE FROM SELF-IMPOSED STRUCTURES**

FULFILLMENT: **SEEING THEIR NOTIONS BECOME NOT ONLY ACCEPTED BUT POPULAR**

January 3–9

DETERMINATION
CAPRICORN II

I nterest in the religious, the metaphysical, and the unseen worlds of experience will be more pronounced in those born in the Week of Determination who travel this karmic path than in others of the period, and they would do well to cultivate those leanings as a means of tapping into the higher energies available to them. Though they are gifted with a rather theoretical turn of mind, there is little danger that they will disappear into an ivory tower of pointless speculation, for at the core they are well grounded and practical. Thus, their manifestation and articulations of this path's special gifts will be grounded in real life, making their contributions all the more valuable for their usefulness and their prophecies, insights, and example all the more appreciated for their sensitivity.

CHALLENGE: **FORGOING SOME OF THEIR FAMOUS PRACTICALITY IN FAVOR OF MORE MYSTICAL MATTERS**

FULFILLMENT: **GIVING THEIR IDEALISTIC SIDE FREE REIN**

KATE MOSS
Model, connected to
Calvin Klein

1/16/1974
Capricorn III

January 10–16

DOMINANCE
CAPRICORN III

T hough many Capricorn III's will find themselves somewhat uncomfortable with the demands and challenges presented by the Way of Expression, there is a prospect of great success along the way. Yet how quickly that success will come will depend on their willingness to open themselves to a wider world of experience and to summon the courage to act as a spokesperson or icon. These roles may not sit easily with them, however, and it is possible that they will turn from the challenges presented by this karmic path and withdraw into a more ordered and private universe. Yet their willingness to face the truth and their highly ethical attitudes will serve them especially well, and it is likely that the strength of their convictions will provide them with the self-assurance they require to fully realize the promise of this life journey.

CHALLENGE: **SHORING UP THEIR COURAGE TO FACE THE DEMANDS OF THIS PATH HEAD-ON**

FULFILLMENT: **GIVING THEIR MORE ECCENTRIC SIDE POSITIVE EXPRESSION**

NOTABLE: **GAMAL ABDEL NASSER (EGYPTIAN PRESIDENT; NATIONALIZED THE SUEZ CANAL)**

January 17–22

MYSTERY AND IMAGINATION
CAPRICORN–AQUARIUS CUSP

Likely to be creative and artistic in the extreme, Capricorn–Aquarians who travel the Way of Expression will find great possibilities for the fulfillment of their highest dreams and ambitions. These are people who create their own excitement, provide their own entertainment, and generate a host of innovative ideas and concepts. Though settling on a focus for their talents and finding productive avenues for expression of their energies may prove more difficult, those born in this week are not likely to remain unnoticed for long. The principal danger of this configuration is a pervasive tendency to indulge in escapism, fantasy, and less-than-useful internal preoccupations or obsessions. Yet if they keep in mind that their unique gifts are meant to be given back to humanity and that their special brand of prophecy and insight can guide us all to a better world, they are likely to do well on this road.

EDITH WHARTON
Writer; 1st woman to
win Pulitzer Prize for
fiction

1/24/1862
Aquarius I

CHALLENGE: **TEMPERING SOME OF THE CHAOS OF THEIR INNER LIVES**
FULFILLMENT: **GENERATING FORMS OF EXPRESSION THAT CAN ELECTRIFY OTHERS**
NOTABLE: **RICHARD HENRY LEE (SIGNER OF DECLARATION OF INDEPENDENCE)**

January 23–30

GENIUS
AQUARIUS I

Those born in the Week of Genius who find themselves on the Way of Expression may well discover that their single greatest challenge lies in developing their ability to express to the rest of the world all the wonders their minds are capable of producing. Self-sufficient and self-taught, these rugged individualists may well become so wrapped up in their own ideas that they fail to connect with those who would most benefit from their special grasp of the eternal verities. Thus, settling down and staying connected with both the world of spirit and the world of social contact and connection will prove especially important to their success. As they possess a higher degree of empathy than many of their fellows, the gifts of this karmic path can only augment their already considerable talents.

CHALLENGE: **OVERCOMING THEIR TENDENCY TO BE BORED IN ORDER TO CREATE A BODY OF WORK**
FULFILLMENT: **ENJOYING THE PLEASURE OF CREATION**
NOTABLE: **SKITCH HENDERSON (BANDLEADER)**

January 31–February 7

YOUTH AND EASE
AQUARIUS II

Aquarius II's may do quite well on the Way of Expression, providing they can force themselves to be willing to delve into some of the darker areas of the human experience and avoid the tendency to content themselves with a perpetually shallow vision of life in general and their own talents in particular. Though things will come rather easily to them, and they are willing to work hard to master a craft or profession, they will face the challenge of cultivating greater depth of vision or run the risk of developing all sorts of creative blockages and barriers. Yet if they are careful to tap into the higher source of their inspiration and allow that contact to nurture they already considerable skills, they are likely to realize tremendous success and will establish both new modes of expression and new standards of virtuosity while on this life journey.

GREG NORMAN
Champion golfer and
golf course designer

2/10/1955
Aquarius III

CHALLENGE: **NOT SETTLING FOR SUPERFICIAL ANSWERS TO LIFE'S LARGER QUESTIONS**
FULFILLMENT: **BEING ADMIRED**
NOTABLE: **IDA LUPINO (FILM ACTRESS; DIRECTOR)**

February 8–15

ACCEPTANCE
AQUARIUS III

Aquarius III's are likely to realize considerable acclaim on the Way of Expression, for their special talents and gifts are very much in keeping with the energies of this karmic path. Independent to a fault, these restless souls may, however, resist some of its challenges and fail to cultivate the broader spiritual perspective that it demands. Too, their need for variety may distract them from their higher sense of purpose and result in a failure to find a focus for their many gifts. Though they will delight in their ability to bring joy to others, it will not be until they call upon their deepest resources that they will find the fulfillment promised by this karmic path. However, if they keep in mind that through their example others can learn to accept and adopt a higher and more tolerant set of human values, they will find great reward on this life journey.

CHALLENGE: **STAYING OPEN ENOUGH TO RECEIVE BIG IDEAS**
FULFILLMENT: **USING HUMOR AND IRONY AS FORMIDABLE WEAPONS IN THEIR ARSENAL OF EXPRESSION**
NOTABLE: **ARSENIO HALL (COMEDIAN; TELEVISION HOST)**

February 16–22
SENSITIVITY
AQUARIUS–PISCES CUSP

Integrating their great sensitivity and empathy into a means of expression will be especially important to Aquarius–Pisces individuals on this karmic path. They have a pronounced tendency not only to hide their light under a bushel but to allow themselves to be buffeted about on the tides of others' emotions to the extent that they fail to connect with their own. The principal danger of this configuration is that they will be so self-protective that they fail to develop the generosity to share their insights and ideas with the world, thus neglecting their best opportunities for worldly success. Nevertheless, their sense of the future and their natural idealism will serve them well along this life journey and, along with their willingness to transcend the usual limits of ordinary reality, promise great rewards.

CHALLENGE: **TEMPERING AND GROUNDING THEIR SENSITIVITY SO IT DOESN'T TEAR THEM APART**

FULFILLMENT: **DEVELOPING THE ABILITY TO ALLOW A FREE FLOW OF IDEAS AND FEELINGS**

NOTABLES: **JEFF DANIELS (ACTOR, *DUMB AND DUMBER*); KELSEY GRAMMER (ACTOR, *FRASIER*)**

STEVEN JOBS
Founded Apple
Computer, current CEO

2/24/1955
Pisces I

February 23–March 2
SPIRIT
PISCES I

Well suited to the demands of the Way of Expression, those born in the Week of Spirit are likely to have a fine time, providing they do not succumb to the temptations of escapism, introspection, and inability to deal with reality. Chances are, these personalities will be preoccupied with the realms of the metaphysical, philosophical, or even the paranormal yet may fail to adequately focus their insights in such a way that they can be shared with the larger world. It will be important for them to stay in touch with the more sensual side of their nature and use it as a means of maintaining connection to others. For those inclined to artistic pursuits, rigorous training and self-discipline may prove to be their greatest asset. Nevertheless, there is a possibility of considerable recognition, especially when they come to terms with the fact that even in the realms of the unseen, we are all ultimately connected to one another.

CHALLENGE: **TAKING CARE NOT TO BECOME OVERLY PRE-OCCUPIED WITH SEXUAL PLEASURES**

FULFILLMENT: **SEEING THE PRACTICAL CONSEQUENCES OF THEIR PREOCCUPATION WITH THE NONMATERIAL**

NOTABLE: **BOBBY RIGGS (TENNIS PLAYER; BET HE COULD BEAT ANY WOMAN; WAS DEFEATED BY BILLIE JEAN KING)**

March 3–10
THE LONER
PISCES II

Pisces II's may have a bit of a struggle when they find themselves on the Way of Expression, for the demands of developing a more public persona may be hard for these introspective souls. Though especially gifted in the areas of written and spoken communication, they may demonstrate unusual talents elsewhere, especially in music and musicianship. Many of their gifts may, however, be lost through their refusal or inability to connect to an audience that is part of the journey along this path. Pisces II's will have to delve deeply within themselves to find the resources that will allow them to display their most personal insights, experiences, and talents to the public. Yet on this life journey they may find that by "taking their act on the road" they are able to gain what they desire the most—acceptance of and recognition for who they really are.

CHALLENGE: **DEVELOPING THE COURAGE TO SHARE THEM-SELVES WITH AN AUDIENCE**

FULFILLMENT: **FULLY EXPRESSING THEIR SOULFUL SIDE**

NOTABLES: **ELIZABETH BARRETT BROWNING (POET); PENN JILLETTE (ILLUSIONIST)**

GARY SINISE
Actor, *Forrest Gump*

3/17/1955
Pisces III

March 11–18
DANCERS AND DREAMERS
PISCES III

Marked by a visionary streak a mile wide, Pisces III's are ideally suited to the Way of Expression and will seem to be blessed indeed. Here the sense of prophecy assumes almost clairvoyant aspects, and their insights into the human condition will doubtless be marked by a rare and complete understanding. Pisces III's are not without their blind spots, however, and one principal failing of this configuration is that they may refuse to discipline themselves to the point where they can develop accessible media for their messages. Yet if they are careful to avoid hubris and a sense of infallibility as regards their own particular talents, these progressive, insightful people are capable of restoring a sense of magic and transcendence to an often suffering world.

CHALLENGE: **DISCIPLINING THEMSELVES ENOUGH TO HONE A CRAFT**

FULFILLMENT: **EXHIBITING A KIND OF MAGICAL, DO-NO-WRONG ALLURE**

NOTABLE: **GLENNE HEADLY (ACTRESS, *DICK TRACY*)**

The Way of Consolidation

CANCER I TO CAPRICORN I
Empath to Ruler

Those on the Way of Consolidation are here to secure their sense of self and learn to stand firm in who they are. Those who travel this path must learn to be more grounded, operate from a core of strength, deal resolutely with their emotions, and toughen their egos in order to be fully in charge of their lives. Coming from a place of deep empathy and sensitivity, men and women on this karmic path may find themselves buffeted by the winds of feeling, their own as well as that of others. In fact, so impressionable and psychic are they that, like mirrors or pools, they reflect the feelings of those closest to them. Moreover, since they don't have a clear understanding of who they are to begin with, it is easy for them to confuse their own feelings or personality traits with those of others. Driven by an innate desire to please and a corresponding fear of rejection, it is common for them to become what others need them to be. Consequently, chameleon-like, their personality will adapt itself to that of anyone they spend much time with. The Way of Consolidation will force those born to this path to come to some conclusions about who they are, how they interact with others, and who exactly they want to be. Furthermore, it will then make them pull it all together in an act of consolidating who they are into a healthier whole. Above all, this path will teach them how to know their true self, how to nurture it, and how to defend it.

> ### CORE LESSON
> Establishing psychological and psychic boundaries
>
> ### GOAL
> To create a firm internal structure and identity

Obviously, the key lesson of this karmic path is for these sensitive individuals to learn how to establish and maintain psychological and psychic boundaries, thereby building, brick by brick and wall by wall, a firmer ego structure. Setting boundaries requires knowing and understanding one's own wants and needs and not confusing them with those of others. Moreover, a psychic boundary can protect against emotional vampires, those who spread their own energies around while drawing energy from others. Cultivating the abilities to know when others are infringing on one's rights or territory and, more than anything else, to say no, is crucial. Instead of looking at others to find out what they themselves should be, those who tread the Way of Consolidation successfully will go to meetings, appointments, and other encounters with a clear sense of who they are and what they want. In plain terms, if those on the Way of Consolidation can learn to be more guarded or detached, perhaps even sometimes a little emotionally cold, they will make progress; if not, they will continue to flounder until they learn to muster a tougher brand of objectivity. On this axis of destiny, being a Ruler implies learning to rule the fortress of self.

This karmic path demands that these individuals work steadily to develop self-understanding and a more philosophical view of life such that the drama and intensity of their emotional lives becomes more muted and

> ### GIFTS
> Empathic, Financially Astute, Caring
>
> ### PITFALLS
> Ruthless, Overly Structured, Miserly

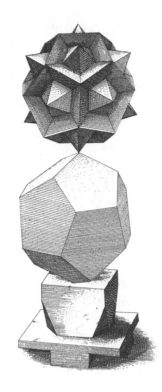

no longer threatens to swamp their sense of self. They must continuously and relentlessly cut away counterproductive tendencies and patterns, particularly that of sinking back into the shifting sands of feeling. Through self-understanding, they can build a strong base from which they can then better operate in the world and which will help them to stay in balance both emotionally and psychologically. It is important, however, for these individuals not to "throw the baby out with the bathwater"; that is, they should not try to excise their unique talent for feeling deeply with both compassion and empathy from their core nature. Repression of emotion is not the goal.

In establishing a firm identity for themselves, those on the Way of Consolidation will have to learn to identify and fearlessly express what they really believe and feel, sticking to their guns and refusing to vacillate when challenged. Taking responsibility for one's own feelings and being honest about them will lead to their learning more straightforward approaches to having their feelings acknowledged or honored. Their background is often such that emotional blackmail or manipulation is second nature to them. Here is a pattern that must be dealt with ruthlessly. These people tend to seek out people who will nurture them in a motherly fashion. Often, subconsciously, they mother others out of a feeling that they will be mothered in return. This often leads to disap-

pointment and anger when their own needs are not met.

Developing the ability to nurture themselves is crucial for those on the Way of Consolidation, as is the recognition that it is not up to others to fulfill their emotional needs. Once such inner work is accomplished, those on the Way of Consolidation will find that they are uniquely gifted at parenting—having clear boundaries and a choice in the matter—and bringing out the best in others. This talent can be applied not only to raising children but to managing others within a company or a team to create a product or service. Alternatively, in the service sector, Cancer I sensitivity can evolve into Capricorn I concern such that these individuals become unusually capable of championing the causes of those less fortunate than themselves.

Part of the life journey for the men and women on the Way of Consolidation may involve channeling their sensitivity into artistic expression. By redirecting it into a physical form and structuring it via the development of a skill or craft, these individuals may be able to operate in more practical terms. Usually, creativity can be both a method of managing feelings and an eloquent form of expression. Understanding will occur by virtue of the fact that creating art can be an act of detachment and objectivity.

Ultimately, whether in business, the arts, or service, the Way of Consolidation promises great career success.

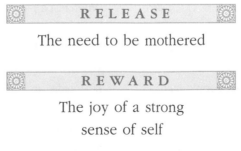

RELEASE

The need to be mothered

REWARD

The joy of a strong
sense of self

SUGGESTION

Develop a philosophy of life. Know that what you feel one moment may change the next. Create a sense of balance and wholeness within yourself and in your environment. Remember to nourish your soul by giving it what it needs.

Implicit in this life journey is a focus on the creation of structure, not just within individuals but also in the outer world. Once those on this karmic path have created a firm strong sense of self and determined what they want, they may be unstoppable. Combining their strong intuitive and psychic ability with their tremendous capacity to get things done, those who evolve successfully on this karmic path are sure to make their mark on the world. Though they may never become so ruthless that they strive to rise to the top of the corporate ladder, their projects will always achieve results. A certain financial astuteness comes with this karmic path, and anyone born to it will put this talent to good use—once their judgment is no longer clouded by their emotions.

As those on this karmic path evolve toward greater inner strength, family members and old friends may become alarmed as they witness these souls transform from "nice" to "tough"; feeling particularly threatened will be those who were able to manipulate such individuals in the past. Considerable pressure can be exerted by family members during the vulnerable times in which such a metamorphosis is taking place, and a struggle, of internecine proportions, may take place, particularly if a parent or old friend is determined to continue to control the other person's life. In general, this karmic path requires people on it to spend less time with family and friends, and more time making new contacts. To avoid being dragged down, they must avoid the types of relationship dependencies they fostered before they began to do the work required by this path.

BALANCE POINT

Self and Other

The best kinds of people for these individuals to spend time with are other strong-minded, independent souls who will strengthen their ego-building process. And despite becoming stronger in their sense of self, these men and women will still need to find a special someone to whom they can expose their more sensitive side. Thus, the choice of a partner is crucial and particularly difficult since their discrimination in this area is not good. Tending to be ruled by emotion and, in love, falling back into codependency, they will usually make a few disastrous choices before ultimately finding the right partner. More conscious or evolved friends, those who do not judge or take advantage and who understand the wonderfully broad palette of human psychology, are best for them. Ideally, their friends will point out their excesses and encourage these sensitive souls to stand up for themselves.

An image that comes to mind to describe this path is that of a liquid solution that appears clear but in fact is crowded with a high concentration of colliding, yet still soluble ions. When just a pinch more of the solid is added, the whole solution suddenly precipitates out. The Way of Consolidation is a bit like this process, bringing together the diverse, amorphous, and unrecognizable aspects of a personality into a single, strong, visible form. Although a return to the original state is possible, the new configuration will be strongly resistant to such reversion. Watery elements have been successfully transformed into earthy ones.

CRYSTALS AND GEMSTONES

Moonstone casts a gentle vibration of self-acceptance that clarifies the boundary between self and others. Even while in the mire of fluctuating emotions, this mineral provides a sense of wholeness.

NOTABLES ON THIS KARMIC PATH

Blind, deaf, and dumb, **Helen Keller** faced many seemingly insurmountable obstacles, though none was greater than the task of discovering and developing her own identity. As is common for those born on this path, due to heightened sensitivity, she frequently found herself drowning in a sea of feeling and overreacting to the emotions of those around her. Through the inspirational guidance of her teacher, Anne Sullivan, Keller overcame the limitations of her sensory deficiencies to become a symbol

HELEN KELLER

and champion for the indomitability of the human spirit. Triumphing, she earned a degree from Radcliffe College and became a renowned lecturer and writer, thus firmly consolidating her inborn abilities.

MONICA LEWINSKY

Throughout the probing public examination of her relationship with President Clinton, **Monica Lewinsky** was forced to adopt a tough brand of objectivity and build a firmer ego structure. Exchanging a seemingly eager desire to please for self-fulfillment, Monica has grown past her youthful impressionability and awe of power to become a woman in charge of her own life. In using her recent televised interview as a promotional tool for her new book, Lewinsky displays the financial astuteness so often possessed by those on this path.

Responsible for the first of the highly visible Live-Aid concerts watched by millions around the world on television, **Bob Geldof** emphasized the plight of the world's hungry in a highly dramatic fashion. By harnessing his innate empathy to help others, he suddenly pulled himself together (as those on this path often do). Given purpose, direction, and meaning, Geldof's life dramatically began to move in the right direction while

BOB GELDOF

gaining in structure and form. Though he attained success as a rock singer, Bob Geldof truly consolidated his sense of self by successfully championing the cause of those less fortunate.

Other Notables: Jean-Pierre Rampal, Sean O'Casey, Frank Serpico, Larry McMurty, William Wrigley, Jr., Ursula Andress, Leonardo da Vinci, Zubin Mehta, Bobby Darin, Dennis Hopper, Lena Horne, Andrew Wyeth, Thelonious Monk, Arthur M. Schlesinger, Jr., Ray Stark, Yanni, C. S. Lewis, Chris Evert, Annie Lennox, Joseph Smith, Denzel Washington, Phil Collins

---

BIRTHDAYS ON KARMIC PATH 14

March 26, 1880–August 14, 1880 | November 6, 1898–March 26, 1899

June 18, 1917–November 6, 1917 | January 29, 1936–June 17, 1936 | September 9, 1954–January 28, 1955

April 20, 1973–September 8, 1973 | December 1, 1991–April 19, 1992 | July 12, 2010–November 30, 2010

KARMIC PATH
14

March 19–24

REBIRTH
PISCES–ARIES CUSP

Those born on the Cusp of Rebirth who travel the Way of Consolidation will encounter their share of extremes in the quest for a more solid sense of identity. Agony and ecstasy, angels and demons, highs and lows will all serve to mark this unique passage. Yet it will be characteristic of this group that their greatest periods of personal and spiritual growth will occur in quantum leaps of consciousness, assorted epiphanies, and even the odd conversion experience, rather than through deep psychological delving or painstaking personal analysis. If they cultivate the ability to trust their passions and work to avoid squelching their considerable sensitivity through repression or disassociation, they will finally come to terms with the fact that in this case, at least, the impulse of the heart is the most direct route to discovery of the soul.

CHALLENGE: **STRIVING FOR GREATER DISCRIMINATION IN THEIR ROMANTIC ATTACHMENTS**

FULFILLMENT: **DEVELOPING GREATER CONFIDENCE AS THEY DEFEND THEIR INNER CORE**

NOTABLES: **URSULA ANDRESS (SWEDISH ACTRESS); MAI BRITT (SWEDISH ACTRESS; MARRIED SAMMY DAVIS, JR., INCURRING THE WRATH OF THOSE OPPOSED TO INTERRACIAL MARRIAGE)**

March 25–April 2

THE CHILD
ARIES I

Destined to develop a greater degree of self-knowledge whether they like it or not, those born in the Week of the Child who find themselves on this karmic path may be in for a struggle until they come to terms with the fact that only by separating themselves from the need to be needed can they free themselves from the perils of their own emotionalism. What this karmic path gives them is a much higher degree of empathy and understanding than they might have otherwise had, as well as a golden opportunity to assume the levels of responsibility and stability they so desire. Once they adjust to the idea that their sensitivity is nothing more or less than a means of self-discovery and a tool for the development of a spiritual vocabulary rather than an end in itself, they are likely to find great prosperity along this road.

LEONARDO DA VINCI
Painter/sculptor/engineer;
Mona Lisa

4/15/1452
Aries III

CHALLENGE: **DELVING INTO THEIR NEEDS AND FEELINGS**

FULFILLMENT: **DONNING THE MANTLE OF MATURITY THAT SUCCESS ON THIS KARMIC PATH CONFERS**

NOTABLE: **SEAN O'CASEY (IRISH DRAMATIST)**

April 3–10

THE STAR
ARIES II

Those born in the Week of the Star who travel the Way of Consolidation will face the challenge of learning to distinguish between the roles they play and the truer sense of self that beckons. They are likely to experience any number of problems through a tendency to emotional or physical excess and will have to work hard to learn how to remove themselves from action occasionally in the interest of cultivating greater objectivity. Though blessed with a naturally strong ego, they may need to get to the root of their desire to please, to be needed, and to otherwise make themselves indispensable to their families, businesses, and social organizations. Yet if they nurture their great sense of freedom and use it to create a stronger, less needy identity that is at the same time reliable, dependable, and efficient in bringing their goals to manifestation, they are likely to find success on this most interesting life passage.

CHALLENGE: **WEANING THEMSELVES FROM THEIR NEED TO BE NEEDED**

FULFILLMENT: **EXPERIENCING A SOLID GROUNDING IN AND UNDERSTANDING OF WHO THEY ARE**

HENRY JAMES
Writer and critic,
The Bostonians

4/15/1843
Aries III

April 11–18

THE PIONEER
ARIES III

Blessed with great positivity of outlook and considerable personal resources, Aries III's who travel the Way of Consolidation will nevertheless have to work hard to divorce themselves from the tendency to be overly self-sacrificing on the one hand, or smotheringly nurturing on the other. Learning to allow others to go their own way will doubtless be a big stumbling block for them, and they may become entirely too emotionally invested in their families, friends, and projects as a means of maintaining their sense of control—and self. Yet once they come to terms with the reality that the finest leaders and greatest administrators are able to take a backseat from time to time and learn to relinquish their authority without feeling a loss of personal power, they can realize great fulfillment along this path.

CHALLENGE: **RECOGNIZING THAT CONTROL OF OTHERS DOES NOT BRING WITH IT CONTROL OF SELF**

FULFILLMENT: **DEVELOPING A CAPACITY TO ENJOY THEMSELVES, EVEN "FAR FROM THE MADDING CROWD"**

NOTABLE: **FRANK SERPICO (NEW YORK CITY POLICE OFFICER; FOUGHT CORRUPTION; FILM OF STORY)**

April 19–24
POWER
ARIES–TAURUS CUSP

Those born on the Cusp of Power will doubtless face the prospect of defining and redefining their personal ambitions on this karmic path. In youth, they tend to be emotionally demanding and may resort to any number of tricks, devices, and emotional blackmail as a means of getting what they want. Yet at some point in their lives they will have to face the fact that real power emanates from within and is the result not of getting others to fulfill their desires but of finding fulfillment for oneself. Once that bridge has been crossed, these people are likely to turn their attention away from personal and ephemeral concerns and focus it upon more substantive effort. Financial endeavors, the arts, and corporate management are likely to be vocational choices here, and all promise great reward.

CHALLENGE: **TRANSFORMING THEIR IMPULSE TO MANIPULATE OTHERS INTO AN OBJECTIVE ASSESSMENT OF WHO THEY ARE**
FULFILLMENT: **ENJOYING THE PERSONAL POWER THAT CONSOLIDATING THEIR SENSE OF SELF BRINGS**
NOTABLES: **GLEN CAMPBELL (SINGER/SONGWRITER, "RHINESTONE COWBOY"); JILL IRELAND (ACTRESS)**

ZUBIN MEHTA
Born in Bombay;
conductor of L.A., N.Y.,
and Israeli Philharmonic
Orchestras

4/29/1936
Taurus I

April 25–May 2
MANIFESTATION
TAURUS I

Taurus I's are likely to flourish on the Way of Consolidation, since much of the groundwork for the successful passage of this life journey is in keeping with their natural inclinations and character. Blessed with a rare combination of empathy and practicality, these people are marked by a toughness and realism that are all the more formidable because of their emotional coloration. Thus, their plans and goals often benefit others as well as themselves. On the downside, they have a tendency to be overly nurturing upon occasion, and stubbornness can also be a problem. Yet if they are careful not to exploit the emotions of others for their own ends nor to overburden themselves with too much responsibility, they can make huge strides along this life journey.

CHALLENGE: **RELAXING THEIR KNEE-JERK TENDENCY TO DOMINATE FOR FEAR OTHERS WILL ATTEMPT TO DOMINATE THEM**
FULFILLMENT: **NURTURING PROJECTS AND PLANS TO COMPLETION**
NOTABLES: **MICHEL FOKINE (CHIEF CHOREOGRAPHER FOR BALLETS RUSSES); ALBERT LASKER (ADVERTISING EXECUTIVE)**

May 3–10
THE TEACHER
TAURUS II

The Teachers who find themselves on the Way of Consolidation may bring to mind a Henry Higgins or, in more extreme cases, a Svengali in their approach to their associates and fans. In any event, they have a strong tendency to cultivate teacher-student-type relationships, as well as to imbue those relationships with all sorts of hidden emotional agendas. At the very least, they not only will be fond of communicating their ideas and impressions but will be compelling and charismatic instructors, whatever their particular venue. At the same time, their particular challenges are to divorce their ego and self-image from the process of sharing knowledge and always to keep in mind that while one can control the messages and ideas one shares with the world, it is impossible to control how—or what—others bring away from that experience.

CHALLENGE: **KNOWING WHEN A FEELING OR IDEA IS REALLY THEIR OWN AND WHEN IT IS "BORROWED" FROM SOMEONE ELSE**
FULFILLMENT: **ENJOYING THE STABILITY OF KNOWING WHO ONE IS**
NOTABLES: **GIORGIO DI SANT'ANGELO (FASHION DESIGNER); ALBERT FINNEY (BRITISH ACTOR, MILLER'S CROSSING)**

BOBBY DARIN
Pop singer,
"Mack the Knife";
shown with Sandra Dee

5/14/1936
Taurus III

May 11–18
THE NATURAL
TAURUS III

The spontaneity of those born in this week who find themselves on the Way of Consolidation may interfere with their growth if they do not work hard to control their more emotional side. In fact, these people are quite capable of mistaking their more chameleon-like tendencies for genuine intimacy, while the prospect of real commitment may panicked them and have them heading for the hills. Thus, issues of both emotional and financial security will figure prominently in their lives, yet they may not experience real success until they learn to focus their more divisive energies in a way that gives form to their fantasies, especially through the development of a craft or artistic product. Once they learn that a sense of security is always and only to be found within the self, they will doubtless be rewarded with both the stability they crave and the adventure they require.

CHALLENGE: **NOT SUCCUMBING TO THE TENDENCY TO INDULGE IN ROMANTIC FANTASIES**
FULFILLMENT: **GENERATING A WEB OF MAGIC AROUND A STRONG SENSE OF AND BELIEF IN THEMSELVES**
NOTABLES: **GUY-PHILIPPE DE MONTEBELLO (DIRECTOR OF METROPOLITAN MUSEUM OF ART); DENNIS HOPPER (ACTOR, EASY RIDER); LINCOLN ELLSWORTH (EXPLORER; ENGINEER)**

May 19–24
ENERGY
TAURUS–GEMINI CUSP

Taurus–Geminis are likely to become involved in more than a few struggles on the Way of Consolidation until they learn the value of steadier habits and less convulsive emotions. In the course of this life journey, these naturally magnetic, energetic people will draw to them any number of admirers, detractors, and assorted basket cases who may well sap their energies until they learn to set some limits and learn just where they leave off and others begin. Not blessed with the best judgment regarding matters of character, they may make some spectacularly bad choices of mates, lovers, or business partners before they face the facts. Nevertheless, these dynamic, attractive people are versatile and gifted enough to pull themselves out of even the deepest dumps and to rise from even the most extreme circumstances. If they are willing to give themselves the respect they require from others, they are likely to travel far along the road.

CHALLENGE: **FORCING THEMSELVES TO LOOK INWARD AND BECOME MORE SELF-AWARE**

FULFILLMENT: **LEARNING TO ENJOY THEIR AUDIENCE RATHER THAN DEPEND ON IT**

MARTHA WASHINGTON
First First Lady;
did not enjoy the role

6/2/1731
Gemini I

May 25–June 2
FREEDOM
GEMINI I

Restless and brilliant, Gemini I's on the Way of Consolidation may find their natural inclinations to be at odds with its demands and challenges. However, they have the ability to allow their considerable intellect to inform their emotions, and if nothing else, their natural impatience will rarely allow them to become mired in the problems or emotions of others for long. Yet their short attention span can operate to their detriment if, in their restlessness, they fail to cultivate a sense of process, an ability to build for the long term, or the capacity to focus that are all required by this destiny path. If they can control their irritability, manage their tendency to manipulate others, and direct their considerable talent for technical expertise into a productive career or the creation of a useful product, they will find great fulfillment on this karmic path.

CHALLENGE: **CULTIVATING THE PATIENCE NEEDED TO BECOME ADEPT AT CONSOLIDATION**

FULFILLMENT: **GROUNDING THEIR IMPULSIVE NATURE**

June 3–10
NEW LANGUAGE
GEMINI II

These gifted communicators can find considerable success on the Way of Consolidation, providing they do not allow their strong verbalization and language talents to be counteracted by personal problems or permit the innumerable small dramas that affect their lives to serve as their principal preoccupation. Though perhaps no one is better qualified to articulate the often mysterious world of emotion, they will nevertheless find themselves inadequate to that task unless they develop a larger perspective and a firmer sense of identity. This will require coming to terms with their darker inclinations and releasing the insecurities and frustrations to which they are prone. Yet there they have the prospect of breaking new ground in the communicative arts, and if they can apply themselves and their talents to such activities as writing, multimedia, or psychology, they will enjoy considerable success and achievement.

CHALLENGE: **TAKING CARE NOT TO SUMMON UP THEIR DARK SIDE IN THE FORM OF UNHEALTHY INTIMACIES**

FULFILLMENT: **LEARNING TO UNDERSTAND THEMSELVES BETTER THROUGH ARTISTIC EXPRESSION**

NOTABLE: **LARRY McMURTRY (AUTHOR, LONESOME DOVE)**

BRUCE DERN
Actor

6/4/1936
Gemini II

June 11–18
THE SEEKER
GEMINI III

The Seekers who travel the Way of Consolidation are marked by a curious ability to all but transform themselves into their companions, mirroring their emotions and creating a sympathetic, synergistic aura that can be quite seductive to anyone fool enough to believe that their heart is truly involved. Better listeners than talkers, these people can be quite deceptive in their quest for increased understanding and may leave a trail of broken hearts and tattered friendships due to their ability to immerse themselves totally in the experiences of others, then withdraw just as totally. As emotions are not generally given first place in the Seekers' roster of priorities, they will likely rise nicely to the demands of this path, demonstrating an ability both to assert their identity and to manage their life from both the financial and creative points of view. If they are careful to avoid the pitfalls of cynicism and manipulation, they are likely to have a fine time on this life journey.

CHALLENGE: **RESISTING THE IMPULSE TO MERGE WITH OTHERS SIMPLY FOR THE SAKE OF EXPERIENCE**

FULFILLMENT: **FORMULATING THEIR OWN LIFE PHILOSOPHY**

NOTABLE: **OSAMI NAGANO (PLANNED ATTACK ON PEARL HARBOR)**

June 19–24
MAGIC
GEMINI–CANCER CUSP

A tendency to overromanticize the little hurts, slights, and problems of the world may well interfere with Gemini–Cancers' ability to rise above the personal and cultivate the stability needed to successfully navigate the Way of Consolidation. Love can make fools of these people, and they may have to experience a number of disappointments in that area before they learn that they are complete without a mate or partner—able to exist, function, and succeed on their own. Many of these highly sensitive people will demonstrate the objectivity and perspective needed to tap into a higher source of inspiration than the merely romantic and to share their knowledge in a wider arena through some artistic or even metaphysical pursuit. If they avoid the pitfalls of cynicism, selfishness, and ruthlessness in achieving their goals, they will find great prosperity and fulfillment.

CHALLENGE: **CONSOLIDATING WHO THEY BELIEVE THEM-SELVES TO BE**
FULFILLMENT: **BUILDING THEIR SELF-ESTEEM THROUGH PRO-FESSIONAL SUCCESS**
NOTABLE: **JULIETTE LEWIS (ACTRESS)**

LENA HORNE
Singer, actress,
"Stormy Weather"

6/30/1917
Cancer I

June 25–July 2
THE EMPATH
CANCER I

These psychic, intuitive people are blessed with considerable insight into both human and spiritual affairs, yet they the Way of Consolidation will force them to learn to distinguish between self-assertion and self-protection. Their desire to please is certainly pronounced, yet they may also have a curious way of "shooting themselves in the foot" or being their own worst enemies when it comes to getting what they want. Thus they can alienate others through neediness, clingyness, or smother-mothering in their search for attachment and security. Nevertheless, they are blessed with the determination, practicality, and sheer guts to overcome almost any obstacle, and if they allow themselves the freedom to grow into the individual their intuition tells them they can be, they are certain to build a greater sense of self.

CHALLENGE: **AVOIDING THEIR TENDENCY TO MOTHER OTHERS**
FULFILLMENT: **GIVING VOICE TO THEIR SENSITIVITY**
NOTABLES: **HELEN KELLER (AUTHOR; ADVOCATE FOR THE BLIND); BUDDY RICH (JAZZ DRUMMER; BANDLEADER); BARON KELVIN (MATHEMATICIAN/PHYSICIST; DEVELOPED ABSOLUTE TEMPERATURE SCALE)**

July 3–10
THE UNCONVENTIONAL
CANCER II

Cancer II's who travel the Way of Consolidation often have a fascination with the darker and more bizarre sides of human experience as a means of "numbing" their highly sensitive dispositions. Others will avoid extremes and seek ways to "turn off" the flow of emotions, impressions, and experiences, real or imagined, that threatens to overwhelm them. In any case, their propensity for emotional intensity can lead them through some rather dangerous waters and may end in a failure to establish adequate personal boundaries or the strong sense of self that is required by this karmic path. Thus, escapism, addiction, and obsession can all be problems for those with this configuration. Yet if they are careful to channel their more imaginative tendencies into creative and productive activities and careers, things are likely to go more smoothly. Especially suited to vocations in the arts, psychology, or investigative work, Cancer II's on the Way of Consolidation can find special happiness in their work.

CHALLENGE: **SUFFERING LESS GRIEVOUSLY WHEN OTHERS FAIL TO UNDERSTAND THEM**
FULFILLMENT: **ESTABLISHING A STRONGER SENSE OF IDENTITY**

ANDREW WYETH
Son of N.C.; painter,
Christina's World

7/12/1917
Cancer III

July 11–18
THE PERSUADER
CANCER III

Blessed with a greater sense of ambition and a stronger sense of identity than some fellow Cancerians, those born in the Week of the Persuader are likely to find considerable fulfillment along the Way of Consolidation. Though by no means less sensitive or emotional, they are a bit better at controlling their own needs in the interests of larger objectives and will likely be able to direct their considerable energy toward the achievement of an ambitious but thoroughly workable set of goals. They would do well, however, to guard against their tendency to become bottled up emotionally and fail to integrate their sensitivity adequately with their worldly ambitions. Yet their persuasive abilities are likely to be tinged with a sense of passion and inspiration. If they do not misuse that great strength, all will go well on this life journey.

CHALLENGE: **AVOIDING THEIR TENDENCY TO RESORT TO MAN-IPULATION**
FULFILLMENT: **FEELING THE SENSE OF SATISFACTION THAT COMES FROM CREATING A TALENT, PROJECT, OR BUSINESS FROM SCRATCH**
NOTABLES: **PHYLLIS DILLER (COMEDIAN); BRIAN AUSTEN GREEN (ACTOR); DOUGLAS EDWARDS (CBS NEWS CORRESPONDENT)**

July 19–25

OSCILLATION
CANCER–LEO CUSP

TEMPEST BLEDSOE
TV actress,
The Cosby Show

8/1/1973
Leo I

Chances are, the Way of Consolidation will provide these unusual people with more in the way of stability than they might otherwise have had, due to the fact that their highly developed intuition and sensitivity will give them a readier grasp of their own inner workings. Yet it is equally likely that they will divert a great deal of attention to searching for the kinds of friends, associates, and partners who can provide them with constancy and stability before they come to terms with the fact that inner equilibrium is something they have to develop for themselves. Some of them may easily achieve a sense of mastery over their own domains yet run the risk of becoming rather dogmatic or emotionally blocked. However, if they can find the excitement they crave in the slower building and solid achievements promised by this karmic path, they are likely to make considerable progress.

CHALLENGE: **DEVELOPING A SAFETY VALVE THEY CAN USE WHEN THEIR MOODS THREATEN TO OVERWHELM THEM**
FULFILLMENT: **CULTIVATING THE MORAL COURAGE TO BUILD SOMETHING GREATER THAN THEMSELVES**
NOTABLE: **MONICA LEWINSKY (WHITE HOUSE INTERN; WELL-PUBLICIZED AFFAIR WITH PRESIDENT)**

July 26–August 2

AUTHORITY
LEO I

Those born in the Week of Authority are likely to find great reward and stature on the Way of Consolidation. Leo I's like to be taken seriously and will doubtless respond quite well to the leadership and authority demands of this path, though they will have to be on guard against a tendency toward emotional melodrama on the one hand, and a demanding or authoritarian attitude on the other. Still, their high standards, love of hard work, and decisive approach to achieving their goals will serve them well on this karmic path. If they are careful to use their natural sensitivity to inform their sense of personal direction, they can realize tremendous success.

CHALLENGE: **TEMPERING THEIR NEED FOR APPLAUSE AND APPROVAL WITH A HEALTHY MEASURE OF SELF-LOVE**
FULFILLMENT: **PULLING TOGETHER ALL THE NECESSARY ELEMENTS WITHIN THEMSELVES TO ACHIEVE A GOAL**
NOTABLE: **CHARLOTTE CORDAY (FRENCH REVOLUTIONARY)**

August 3–10

BALANCED STRENGTH
LEO II

Gifted with a stronger ego structure and the ability to establish personal boundaries than many along the Way of Consolidation, those born in this week are likely to experience great fulfillment, providing they do not allow a pronounced sense of suffering or even a tendency to masochism to hinder their growth. While many of these people can be single-minded to a fault, their great sense of concentration is especially well suited to the slow building and solid goals demanded by this karmic path. They are also blessed with greater empathy than many born in this week and will doubtless be able to employ that strength in the wise administration and management of any number of personal or business empires, up to and including the domains of spirit.

CHALLENGE: **FAILING TO RELEASE UNHEALTHY RELATIONSHIPS DUE TO A MISGUIDED SENSE OF LOYALTY**
FULFILLMENT: **ENJOYING THE FINANCIAL AND ARTISTIC REWARDS OF CAREER SUCCESS**

ALEXANDER DUMAS
FILS
Writer, *Camille*

7/27/1824
Leo I

August 11–18

LEADERSHIP
LEO III

Wonderful planners and strategists, those born in the Week of Leadership are likely to flourish on the Way of Consolidation, providing they do not scatter their energies in personal touchiness, emotional hyperbole, or simple selfishness. Here their natural sensitivity and empathy are likely to inform a highly developed creative sense, which can result in artistic expressions and endeavors of truly universal import. The key to their success, however, will be the development of greater objectivity and the wider philosophical perspective that will come with the ability to remove themselves from unduly emotionally demanding people or situations. Yet with the great strength, love of hard work, and emotional sensitivity that are the gifts of this path, Leo III's are likely to find wonderful fulfillment.

CHALLENGE: **REINING IN THEIR EGO AS THEY DEVELOP A SOLID SENSE OF SELF**
FULFILLMENT: **FEELING THEMSELVES TO BE THE MASTER OF THEIR DESTINY**
NOTABLE: **CHRISTY MATHEWSON (BASEBALL PLAYER)**

KARMIC PATH
14

August 19–25
EXPOSURE
LEO–VIRGO CUSP

Those born on the Cusp of Exposure who travel this karmic path may encounter difficulties along the way, especially if their talent for the spotlight and public attention should appear before they can fully establish a sense of their own identities. These people may live life in a kind of fishbowl, subject to a certain amount of scrutiny, admiration, and censure as they undergo the processes mandated by this karmic path. Quite a few of the less controlled of this type will wind up making all their mistakes in public until they learn to manage their great sensitivity and stay out of the limelight until the time they are ready to shine. Especially suited for careers in the arts, politics, and the drama, they will nevertheless face the challenge of finding a personal identity that has little or nothing to do with their public image.

JOHN LEE HOOKER
American blues great

8/22/1917
Leo–Virgo Cusp

CHALLENGE: **DEFENDING THEMSELVES AGAINST EMOTIONAL MANIPULATION BY OTHERS**
FULFILLMENT: **THE EXPOSURE AND INTEGRATION OF SIDES OF THEMSELVES THEY DIDN'T KNOW EXISTED**
NOTABLE: **MEL FERRER (ACTOR)**

August 26–September 2
SYSTEM BUILDERS
VIRGO I

System Builders who travel the Way of Consolidation may enjoy themselves quite a bit, as its energies are very much in keeping with their natural disposition to order. Though gifted with a greater sense of objectivity than many others traveling this road, they will face the challenge of identifying and learning to own their own emotions, on the one hand, while avoiding the concomitant dangers of rigidity and inflexibility, on the other. Their highly structured sense of the world may exist at odds with a seething emotional life, resulting in depression, acting out, or obsessive behaviors. Yet their potential to integrate their sensitivity more healthily into their overall personas by creating structures and tools with which to navigate their deeper emotional waters is very pronounced, and they are likely to thrive.

CHALLENGE: **OVERCOMING THEIR TENDENCY TO WANT TO "DIVIDE AND CONQUER" IN MATTERS OF SELF-AWARENESS**
FULFILLMENT: **CREATING A CONSOLIDATED SENSE OF SELF**

September 3–10
THE ENIGMA
VIRGO II

Those born in the Week of the Enigma can realize wonderful fulfillment along the Way of Consolidation, as they are gifted with both a greater capacity for objectivity and a stronger sense of personal identity than many others traveling this karmic path. However, they will have to be willing to do a certain amount of delving into their own emotional workings in order to realize their promise. Their desire to please can hinder their higher development, as can their tendency to withdraw in the face of conflict and pretend that problems don't exist. Nonetheless, their sense of personal and psychic boundaries will doubtless serve them well, and that, coupled with their ability to direct their energies in a realistic and practical fashion, will result in professional endeavors marked by fine taste, high standards, and a deep artistic sense.

ISABEL SANFORD
Actress, *The Jeffersons*

8/29/1917
Virgo I

CHALLENGE: **ASSESSING THEMSELVES AS OBJECTIVELY AND COOLLY AS THEY ASSESS OTHERS**
FULFILLMENT: **TRUSTING THEMSELVES ENOUGH TO LET THEIR INNER LIGHT SHINE**
NOTABLE: **HENRY FORD II (CHAIRMAN OF FORD MOTOR CO., 1960–1980)**

September 11–18
THE LITERALIST
VIRGO III

The Literalists who find themselves on this karmic path may discover a tremendous capacity for personal denial when it comes to dealing with their own highly emotional energies. Self-awareness may not be high on their list of priorities, so it may be some time before they get down to the business of developing a sense of identity separate from those of their parents, professional associates, and peers. They can be rather suspicious of their own emotions and question their own best and most sensitive impulses; as a result, indecision can hamper their effectiveness. Alternatively, they may repress their emotions altogether, refusing to own their own sense of empathy and sensitivity in the interest of what they perceive as "the facts." Still, great accomplishment can be achieved with this configuration, especially in the financial arena and careers that involve channeling creativity into producing tangible goods and services.

CHALLENGE: **REALIZING THAT A RESULTS-ORIENTED APPROACH OFTEN DOESN'T WORK WHEN IT COMES TO ONE'S INNER WORKINGS**
FULFILLMENT: **ACHIEVING THEIR LARGER, MORE TANGIBLE GOALS**
NOTABLE: **FERDINAND MARCOS (PHILIPPINES PRESIDENT/DICTATOR)**

September 19–24
BEAUTY
VIRGO–LIBRA CUSP

Virgo–Libras who travel the Way of Consolidation may have to struggle to come to terms with their emotionalism. Blessed with fine artistic and aesthetic leanings, they may nevertheless have to toughen up and develop some objectivity before they can become truly effective forces in their chosen fields of endeavor. Waffling, indecision, and avoidance of confrontation can all be stumbling blocks for these people, who would often rather "switch than fight," even if the fight involves claiming some necessary space for their own further development. They may also overindulge in sensual or sensory input, as a means of anchoring their sensitivity in material reality. Their keys to success will be self-discipline, assertiveness, and the ability to channel their imaginative and emotional impulses into satisfying and aesthetically pleasing creations.

CHALLENGE: **DISCIPLINING THEMSELVES TO WORK ON THEIR OWN BETTERMENT**

FULFILLMENT: **IMPROVING THEIR CONCEPTION OF WHO THEY ARE**

RED AUERBACH
Legendary basketball coach of the Boston Celtics

9/20/1917
Virgo–Libra Cusp

September 25–October 2
THE PERFECTIONIST
LIBRA I

Libra I's can realize wonderful success along the Way of Consolidation, but they may have to endure a number of challenges and issues over just who they want to be "when they grow up." In fact, these people may waste the gifts of this karmic path by becoming overly preoccupied with problems, petty details, and personal dramas, and some may literally martyr themselves on the altar of their own emotions before they back up and develop some perspective. Thus, the ability to take personal risks, overcome touchiness, and avoid getting hung up on trivial issues will be paramount to their achievement. Nonetheless, their talent for structure and detail and their impulse to perfection can serve them quite well with, as long as they keep in mind that perfection is an ideal to strive for, not an interim goal to be achieved before moving on.

CHALLENGE: **MANAGING AND SCULPTING THE CHAOTIC MIX OF THEIR EMOTIONS**

FULFILLMENT: **CRAFTING A PERSONA AND A WAY OF LIFE**

NOTABLES: **WILLIAM WRIGLEY, JR. (FOUNDED CHEWING GUM COMPANY; BASEBALL EXECUTIVE); LOUIS AUCHINCLOSS (AUTHOR)**

October 3–10
SOCIETY
LIBRA II

The greatest challenge facing those born in the Week of Society who travel this karmic path will be learning to establish time and space for themselves. These popular people are usually blessed with a degree of understanding and compassion that is a cut above that of more ordinary sympathizers, and they may run the risk of becoming bleeding hearts, to the detriment of their higher objectives and potential for self-realization. Thus, their ability to cut themselves free from hangers-on will be important, as will cultivating emotional balance. Coming to terms with their own desires and talents will prove most rewarding, and their efforts to channel their emotional and aesthetic energies into sound and productive efforts promise to be well rewarded.

CHALLENGE: **REFUSING TO BE BUFFETED ABOUT BY THE DEMANDS OF OTHERS**

FULFILLMENT: **THE CONFIDENCE AND SOLIDITY THAT COME FROM A CLEAR SENSE OF SELF**

NOTABLES: **STEVIE RAY VAUGHN (VIRTUOSO BLUES GUITARIST); BOB GELDOF (SINGER; ORGANIZED LIVE-AID CONCERTS)**

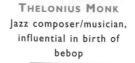

THELONIUS MONK
Jazz composer/musician, influential in birth of bebop

10/10/1917
Libra II

October 11–18
THEATER
LIBRA III

Those born in this week who travel the Way of Consolidation may be inclined to act out the drama of their own lives and personalities, but they will have to avoid the tendency to "ham it up" as they navigate this karmic path. Prone to overreaction, blowing things out of proportion, and floundering about in the ocean of their emotions, they may well exhaust themselves and others until they learn to tone things down a bit and substitute quality of experience for quantity. They would do well, therefore, to cultivate the ability to take refuge in everyday things and with calmer, less excitable people. Yet they can find great reward on this life journey, especially if they refuse to allow their perceptions to be shaped by the conflicts or ecstasies of the moment and learn to concentrate their energies on the life roles that enable them not just to shine but to cast a more enduring light.

CHALLENGE: **VALUING OTHERS' APPROVAL LESS AND SELF-UNDERSTANDING MORE**

FULFILLMENT: **REAPING THE REWARDS OF A STRUCTURED, MATURE APPROACH**

NOTABLES: **THOMAS GEOFFREY BIBBY (ARCHEOLOGIST; DEVELOPED CARBON DATING); ARTHUR M. SCHLESINGER, JR. (HISTORIAN; MEMBER OF KENNEDY AND JOHNSON ADMINISTRATIONS; WON 2 PULITZER PRIZES); RAY STARK (FILM PRODUCER)**

October 19–25

DRAMA AND CRITICISM
LIBRA–SCORPIO CUSP

Those born on the Cusp of Drama and Criticism who find themselves on this karmic path are gifted with a higher sense of discernment than many others traveling this road. Nevertheless, they are likely to have to struggle a bit with emotional excess. Too, their penchant for speaking their minds may get these volatile people into all kinds of hot water if they do not give themselves the necessary time and space to develop their ideas and concepts fully before airing their opinions. More highly emotional than many born in this week, they will need to nurture their more intellectual inclinations adequately. Yet they will doubtless develop the strong ego and sense of identity called for by this karmic path, and if they allow their fertile minds and formidable capacity for observation and analysis full play, they will certainly make their mark in the world through sustained effort, well-balanced emotions, and their flair for compassionate insights.

DIZZY GILLESPIE
Jazz musician, made first definitive bebop recordings

10/21/1917
Libra–Scorpio Cusp

CHALLENGE: **WASTING LESS TIME ON THEIR TEMPESTUOUS ROMANTIC ENTANGLEMENTS**
FULFILLMENT: **PULLING THEMSELVES TOGETHER AND DEVOTING THEIR CONSIDERABLE FOCUS TO ACCOMPLISHING SOMETHING**
NOTABLE: **JOAN FONTAINE (ACTRESS; FAMED RIVALRY WITH HER SISTER, OLIVIA DE HAVILLAND)**

October 26–November 2

INTENSITY
SCORPIO I

Those born in the Week of Intensity who travel the Way of Consolidation may have to fight a tendency to emotional extremes, yet in the end they are likely to win the battle for mastery of the self. Finding real direction and outlets for their natural intensity is especially important, and they will have to work hard to avoid getting entangled in suspicion, jealousy, and emotional possessiveness. Too, overattachment and even obsession may hinder their progress along the road, especially if they fail to realize that many of their dramas and traumas are but projections of their own deep-seated emotional needs. Still, they are gifted with the necessary focus and concentration to make this a highly successful passage, and if they can find the middle road that lies between the lighter and darker aspects of their own personalities, all will go brilliantly.

CHALLENGE: **ESTABLISHING FIRMER BOUNDARIES BETWEEN THEMSELVES AND OTHERS**
FULFILLMENT: **BEING STRONG ENOUGH TO WALK A SOLITARY PATH**

November 3–11

DEPTH
SCORPIO II

Scorpio II's who travel the Way of Consolidation would do well to stay in close touch with their personal source of power in order to make this a successful and rewarding passage. The sooner they formulate a clear idea of what they want out of life, the less risk they run of getting bogged down in a world of emotion or of exalting their own sense of suffering as a substitute for a clear sense of personal ambition. Setting well-defined goals and building real self-esteem will be especially important here, as will the ability to apply their considerable powers of concentration to career or financial endeavors. In any event, they would do well to avoid seeking means of escape through addictions, sexual overindulgence, or indulgence of their darker fantasies. Directing their emotional energies outward in sustained, substantive effort will prove most rewarding and will result in the sense of sureness, power, and control they so desire.

YANNI
Popular "New Age" musician and composer

11/4/1954
Scorpio II

CHALLENGE: **REMAINING FOCUSED ON THEIR GOALS**
FULFILLMENT: **BEING INDIFFERENT TO OTHERS' OPINIONS OF THEM**
NOTABLE: **ADAM ANT (BRITISH ROCK STAR)**

November 12–18

CHARM
SCORPIO III

Those born in the Week of Charm who travel this karmic path can find fulfillment along the way, providing they do not allow their natural empathy to overwhelm their more realistic side. Still, these somewhat secretive people may spend much more time exploring and examining others' emotions than they do their own and will have to come to terms with the fact that much of their interest in what makes others tick is really a desire for greater self-knowledge. In any event, these individuals will have to work especially hard to develop some boundaries, for their desire to be liked and accepted is especially strong. However, this karmic path promises great success, particularly if they allow their natural sensitivity and perception to combine with their practical gifts and avoid the tendency to manipulate others as a substitute for developing a more authentic sense of personal power.

CHALLENGE: **DELVING INTO THEIR MOTIVATIONS ON A REGULAR BASIS**
FULFILLMENT: **DEVELOPING THE SELF-ESTEEM THAT BUILDING A CAREER BRINGS**

November 19–24

REVOLUTION
SCORPIO–SAGITTARIUS CUSP

Those born on the Cusp of Revolution who travel the Way of Consolidation will doubtless have a wider conservative streak than many born on this cusp, but their natural excitability may interfere with this realization until they are somewhat further along the road. Their boundary issues are apt to manifest themselves as an absorption in struggles against established values and relationships. Their ability to analyze their own motives will be especially important, as will developing a greater sense of history and cultural context regarding their pet projects and causes. Yet along with the considerable empathy bestowed by this path, Scorpio–Sagittarians have a highly ethical and moral sense. When properly channeled, the synthesis of those two qualities can result in works and contributions of lasting value.

C. S. LEWIS
Writer/scholar,
The Chronicles of Narnia

11/29/1898
Sagittarius I

CHALLENGE: **RESOLVING THEIR BOUNDARY ISSUES BY REALIZING THAT THEY ARE THE ONES WHO HAVE TROUBLE WITH THEM**
FULFILLMENT: **WORKING THEIR OWN BRAND OF REFORM ON THEMSELVES**
NOTABLE: **RENÉ MAGRITTE (SURREALIST PAINTER)**

November 25–December 2

INDEPENDENCE
SAGITTARIUS I

The freedom-loving souls born in this week may need to wrestle with their impulses to self-sacrifice before they can successfully navigate the Way of Consolidation. Marked by an expansive and too-generous nature, they will have to choose their causes and companions carefully or run the risk of casting their pearls before any number of swine in their search for fulfillment. Too, they can become rather overly emotionally invested in some rather hopeless people or situations, and that, coupled with their highly competitive nature, can make it very difficult for them to admit failure. Yet if they avoid the pitfalls of a false sense of honor, on the one hand, and sheer temperament, on the other, they can realize great progress, especially when their energies are focused on and infused with the lasting sense of inspiration that is part of this karmic path.

CHALLENGE: **STOPPING RUNNING LONG ENOUGH TO ASSESS THEMSELVES REALISTICALLY**
FULFILLMENT: **TEMPERING THEIR IMPULSES AND SHAPING THEM INTO A COHERENT PLAN OF ATTACK**
NOTABLE: **JOEL COEN (FILM WRITER/DIRECTOR, *FARGO*)**

December 3–10

THE ORIGINATOR
SAGITTARIUS II

Emotional defensiveness and personal sensitivity will prove to be the particular stumbling blocks for those born in the Week of the Originator who travel the Way of Consolidation. Yet once they divorce themselves of their need for acceptance and approval and learn to go their own way, unfettered by a thirst for recognition or acceptance of their sometimes radical views, they will find great fulfillment. Blessed with a special genius for imbuing their projects and efforts with both creativity and sensitivity to the workings of the intuitive and emotional side of life, they can make some startling and innovative strides in their chosen field of endeavor. The key to their success will be an ability to cultivate greater detachment and recognize that this karmic path promises higher rewards than immediate emotional gratification or acceptance.

HENRY WELLS
Founded
American Express with
William Fargo

12/12/1805
Sagittarius III

CHALLENGE: **OVERCOMING THEIR NEED FOR APPROVAL**
FULFILLMENT: **ENJOYING THE INDEPENDENCE OF SPIRIT THAT FEELING STRONG IN THEIR SENSE OF SELF BRINGS**
NOTABLES: **ALFRED EISENSTAEDT (PHOTOJOURNALIST); ROBERT JEAN-EUGÈNE HOUDIN (FATHER OF MODERN CONJURING)**

December 11–18

THE TITAN
SAGITTARIUS III

Though gifted with a greater sense of self-assurance and a stronger ego than many of their fellow travelers along the Way of Consolidation, those born in the Week of the Titan will nevertheless have to face down the demons of emotional extremes and unveil some of their deepest secrets before they can find fulfillment. They will have to work hard not to allow others to reinforce a false sense of identity, for they are highly susceptible to flatterers and hangers-on. Too, personal touchiness and emotional volatility may be special stumbling blocks on this path until they develop greater self-awareness. Recognizing that true self-esteem is based not on what others think of one, but on what one thinks of oneself will do much to smooth this passage and reward them with the ability to employ their talents in such a way as to champion their causes and goals through charismatic and creative expression of their ideals and beliefs.

CHALLENGE: **ESCHEWING THEIR CAPACITY FOR MANIPULATION**
FULFILLMENT: **DEVELOPING GREATER STRENGTH OF CHARACTER AND TOUGHER MORAL FIBER**
NOTABLES: **ERASMUS DARWIN (POET; NATURALIST); CHRISTINA ONASSIS (HEIRESS; EXECUTIVE)**

December 19–25
PROPHECY
SAGITTARIUS–CAPRICORN CUSP

Those born on the Cusp of Prophecy who navigate the Way of Consolidation are likely to have a fine time, providing they do not disown their empathy or intuition. While most come into this journey already free of the need for approval or acceptance, they will face their share of challenges. Although considerable career and financial success is indicated here, avoiding workaholic tendencies, emotional and social shutdowns, and miserliness will be important. Blessed with extraordinary insight and even psychic ability, they will have to exercise greater care to share those insights with others. Otherwise, they will doubtless have occasion to meditate upon the ancient axiom "To deny a truth is to give it strength that is unendurable."

CHRIS EVERT
Tennis champion

12/21/1954
Sagittarius–Capricorn
Cusp

CHALLENGE: **MAKING THE TIME FOR QUIET REFLECTION**
FULFILLMENT: **DEVELOPING A FIRMER EGO STRUCTURE AND LESS POROUS SENSE OF SELF**
NOTABLE: **ANNIE LENNOX (POP SINGER)**

December 26–January 2
THE RULER
CAPRICORN I

Those born in the Week of the Ruler who navigate the Way of Consolidation are promised rich rewards and considerable success, especially when they apply their special genius for structure and efficiency to the world of the emotions and the realm of the spirit. They should have little trouble developing the sense of personal boundaries indicated by this karmic path, as their highly directed, goal-oriented nature allows for very little interference, even when it comes from their own emotions. As a result, they are likely to achieve pretty much whatever they want in worldly terms yet will run the risks of becoming rather dogmatic, frustrated, and quite shut down emotionally. Allowing their great sensitivity to inform their goals will be especially useful and will soften their enormous sense of responsibility with both empathy and a measure of wisdom.

CHALLENGE: **TAKING ADVANTAGE OF THE GREAT EMPATHY THIS PATH CONFERS**
FULFILLMENT: **FINDING SUCCESS AND CRITICAL ACCLAIM THROUGH HARD WORK AND DILIGENCE**
NOTABLE: **DENZEL WASHINGTON (ACTOR, *MALCOLM X*)**

January 3–9
DETERMINATION
CAPRICORN II

A rather sweet, self-effacing persona can disguise a steely streak in Capricorn II's who find themselves on the Way of Consolidation. Blessed with an astute perception of their own and others' often confusing motivations, these individuals will likely enjoy the journey along this karmic path, though they will have to avoid their tendency to hide their talents under the proverbial bushel or lapse into personal insecurity when things don't go the way they'd planned. Yet they are able to temper even the rockiest of emotional episodes with a measure of philosophical perspective, and if they take care that their natural impulses toward self-protection do not harden into armor, they will recognize the realization of some of their fondest dreams and aspirations along this life journey.

JOSEPH SMITH
Mormon religious
founder and leader

12/23/1805
Sagittarius–Capricorn
Cusp

CHALLENGE: **NOT TURNING THEMSELVES OFF TO OTHERS TOO TOTALLY**
FULFILLMENT: **MAKING THE MOST OF THEIR ABILITIES**
NOTABLES: **JEAN-PIERRE RAMPAL (RENOWNED FLAUTIST); CRYSTAL GAYLE (COUNTRY SINGER, "DON'T IT MAKE MY BROWN EYES BLUE")**

January 10–16
DOMINANCE
CAPRICORN III

Those born in this week who find themselves on the Way of Consolidation may have to come to terms with some interesting control issues. Many of them will struggle to suppress their own emotionalism and will have to cultivate a greater degree of self-awareness before they come to terms with the fact that their impulse to control or dominate their immediate environment and close associates may in fact arise from the impulse to eradicate their own suppressed passions. Owning and integrating their feelings will be especially important to their success, and they will have to take some long, hard looks at themselves in the interest of overcoming their tendencies to inflexibility. Yet if they allow their more emotional and intuitive side to nourish their tolerance of both themselves and others, they can realize great fulfillment.

CHALLENGE: **OWNING AND INTEGRATING THEIR OWN FEELINGS RATHER THAN PROJECTING THEM ONTO OTHERS**
FULFILLMENT: **FINDING THE PEACE OF MIND THAT SELF-CONFIDENCE GIVES**
NOTABLES: **KIRSTIE ALLEY (TELEVISION ACTRESS); FRANK JAMES (OUTLAW)**

KARMIC PATH
14

January 17–22
MYSTERY AND IMAGINATION
CAPRICORN–AQUARIUS CUSP

Though gifted with a bit more personal and emotional stability than some other Capricorn–Aquarians, these individuals on the Way of Consolidation will have to learn to channel their considerable natural energy and imagination into sustained productive efforts to realize the highest promise of this karmic path. Restlessness and instability may be problems, as may their tendency to disguise or repress their feeling side in fantasy or a sense of unrealistic expectation. Yet this position is especially well suited to artistic and creative efforts, and if these people take care to cultivate the necessary sense of personal discipline and remember to take the long view when it comes to realizing their fondest ambitions, they can achieve great accomplishment and even acclaim along this life's journey.

EDDIE VAN HALEN
Guitar legend of Van Halen; formed hammer-on style

1/26/1955
Aquarius I

CHALLENGE: **CONTROLLING THEIR WILDER ENERGIES AND MORE UNPREDICTABLE DISPLAYS OF EMOTION**
FULFILLMENT: **MANAGING THEIR LIVES AND RELATIONSHIPS FIRMLY**
NOTABLES: **KEVIN COSTNER (ACTOR/DIRECTOR, *DANCES WITH WOLVES*); AL CAPONE (CHICAGO GANGSTER)**

January 23–30
GENIUS
AQUARIUS I

Those born in the Week of Genius who travel the Way of Consolidation may experience a few difficulties as they attempt to integrate their emotions into their highly theoretical and idealistic personalities. Though not likely to be troubled by the need to establish firm personal or professional boundaries, some with this configuration may exhaust their energies in bouts of rather fevered imagination, a false sense of inspiration, or highly unrealistic or unworkable goals. Thus, setting limits for themselves may figure prominently in their quest for self-realization, as will an ability to identify their feelings adequately. When they have done the necessary groundwork and developed self-discipline, they can establish wonderfully rewarding careers, especially when they involve themselves in the kind of work that will allow their ideas, designs, or theories to find manifestation in material reality.

CHALLENGE: **COMBINING THEIR MANY DIVERGENT IDEAS AND FEELINGS INTO AN INTEGRATED WHOLE**
FULFILLMENT: **BRINGING THE VARIETY OF THEIR EXPERIENCES TO BEAR ON THE FULFILLMENT OF THEIR GOALS**
NOTABLE: **WILLIAM MCKINLEY (25TH U.S. PRESIDENT; ASSASSINATED)**

January 31–February 7
YOUTH AND EASE
AQUARIUS II

Aquarius II's who travel the Way of Consolidation will have to overcome their need for acceptance and personal recognition before they can claim the higher prizes offered by this karmic path. Their chameleon-like tendencies may be especially pronounced, and they will have to work hard to overcome their desire to please. Establishing a strong sense of ethics and personal values will be especially important to their success, as will a willingness to divorce themselves from those who would seduce or distract them from a higher sense of purpose. Yet many with this configuration will find their passage considerably eased if they exercise a particular talent or creative inclination. If they are careful to channel their energies by disciplining, developing, and nurturing their gifts, they are unlikely to miss their goals.

BURT REYNOLDS
Film actor, *Deliverance, Boogie Nights*

2/11/1936
Aquarius III

CHALLENGE: **BECOMING MORE DEMANDING OF THEMSELVES**
FULFILLMENT: **FREEING THEMSELVES FROM THEIR DEPENDENCE ON OTHER PEOPLE'S APPLAUSE**
NOTABLES: **FLETCHER HARPER (PUBLISHER); PHIL COLLINS (POP SINGER; MEMBER OF GENESIS)**

February 8–15
ACCEPTANCE
AQUARIUS III

Many of those born in the Week of Acceptance may have to overcome a pronounced tendency to "go with the flow," especially when the flow threatens to carry them away from the goals and aspirations of this path on a tide of emotion. While a number of those with this configuration will have to confront the fact that they are regularly taken advantage of in personal and professional situations, others may be plagued by inflexibility, rigidity, or emotional repression as they attempt to come to terms with issues of identity and personal boundaries. Either extreme is to be avoided. By far the biggest challenge of this configuration will be learning to settle down to the kind of slow building and conscientious application of their gifts that is required by this karmic path. Yet if these people work to cultivate emotional perspective, a sense of larger human values, and simple constancy, they will truly flourish.

CHALLENGE: **BECOMING MORE ADEPT AT EXTRICATING THEMSELVES FROM UNHEALTHY RELATIONSHIPS**
FULFILLMENT: **LEARNING THE LESSONS OF CONSTANCY AND CONSISTENCY**
NOTABLE: **JANE SEYMOUR (ACTRESS)**

February 16–22

SENSITIVITY
AQUARIUS–PISCES CUSP

The Way of Consolidation may well enhance some of the natural characteristics of those born on this cusp, resulting in both a heightened sense of emotional empathy and an equally heightened need for of aggressive self-protection. It will therefore be of paramount importance for those born to this karmic path to learn to set limits and to structure their lives according to their higher aims and aspirations. Personal achievement will never be an abstract for these people, and they may need quite a bit of material evidence of their success to reinforce their sense of identity. Yet if they can overcome their sometimes overwhelming fear of rejection and channel their intensity into steady efforts and realistic goals, they can recognize wonderful rewards here, especially in careers that will access their higher sense of human values, such as politics, the arts, or some form of entertainment.

BARBARA JORDAN
U.S.representative from Texas; member of the Watergate House investigating committee

2/21/1936
Aquarius–Pisces Cusp

CHALLENGE: **NOT BECOMING MIRED IN THEIR INNER QUEST FOR WHOLENESS**
FULFILLMENT: **REDIRECTING THEIR ENERGIES OUTWARD, NOT ONTO PEOPLE BUT ONTO GOALS FOR ACHIEVEMENT**
NOTABLES: **MONTGOMERY WARD (FOUNDED 1ST MAIL-ORDER COMPANY, 1872); C. V. WHITNEY (FOUNDED PAN AMERICAN AIRWAYS; COPRODUCED *GONE WITH THE WIND*)**

February 23–March 2

SPIRIT
PISCES I

Those born in the Week of Spirit who tread the Way of Consolidation may experience quite a bit of difficulty in discerning their own truest needs and ambitions, as opposed to the expectations of others. Tremendously empathetic and wonderfully kind, they may nevertheless flounder a bit before they get their bearings, especially if they have been unduly dominated by a parent or carefully controlled childhood environment. Yet their natural creativity can find its highest expression on this karmic path. If they can indulge their impulse to do good without allowing themselves to be exploited and balance their great insight with a measure of objectivity, they will realize great fulfillment and lifelong achievement, especially in the arts, finance, or more philosophical studies and pursuits.

CHALLENGE: **TEMPERING THEIR SELF-INDULGENCE**
FULFILLMENT: **FOCUSING ON CAREER OR SERVICE ENDEAVORS**
NOTABLES: **PATRICIA RICHARDSON (TELEVISION ACTRESS, *HOME IMPROVEMENT*); CHARLES BEST (CODISCOVERER OF INSULIN)**

March 3–10

THE LONER
PISCES II

Those born in the Week of the Loner will face the curious dilemma of being at once quite empathetic and attuned to the needs of those around them and distrustful of those who would encroach upon their very private personal domain. Yet the Way of Consolidation is uniquely positive for them, and they are apt to do quite beautifully on this karmic path, providing they establish some limitations without repressing their more intuitive and emotional natures. Many of this type strongly believe in paying one's dues, so it is likely that they will build the great career and financial success promised by this karmic path. If they can manage to toughen themselves without shutting down and come to terms with the need to both separate and unite with their fellows, they will realize great fulfillment.

F. W. DE KLERK
Former South African president; shared 1993 Nobel Peace Prize with Nelson Mandela

3/18/1936
Pisces III

CHALLENGE: **LOOKING THEMSELVES SQUARELY IN THE FACE AND MAKING A SEARCHING, FEARLESS PERSONAL INVENTORY**
FULFILLMENT: **DEVELOPING A TOUGHER SELF THAT IS ABLE TO DEAL WITH LIFE BETTER**
NOTABLES: **RICHARD (LEO) SIMON (PUBLISHER; COFOUNDER OF SIMON AND SCHUSTER); MARION BARRY (FORMER MAYOR OF WASHINGTON, D.C.)**

March 11–18

DANCERS AND DREAMERS
PISCES III

Issues of dependency, indecision, and hypersensitivity may figure prominently in the lives and personal challenges of those born in this week. Channeling their sense of inspiration into steady, productive, and highly creative efforts will be especially important for these talented people, as they may sometimes waste their resources by refusing to apply themselves or by getting bogged down in rather ordinary emotional melodramas. Too, their choice of a partner will prove especially important, though there may be a bit of trial and error as they undergo the required metamorphosis from emotional vulnerability to personal strength. Yet when they come to grips with the truth that a sense of trust will be achieved more easily if they first trust themselves to seek what's best for their happiness, all is likely to go well.

CHALLENGE: **APPLYING THEIR PRACTICALITY TO MATTERS OF LOVE AND ROMANCE**
FULFILLMENT: **DEVELOPING THE DISCIPLINE REQUIRED FOR LARGE-SCALE ACHIEVEMENTS**
NOTABLES: **ANTONIN SCALIA (U.S. SUPREME COURT JUSTICE); GEORG SIMON OHM (GERMAN PHYSICIST)**

The Way of Articulation

CANCER II TO CAPRICORN II
Unconventional to Determination

Those on the Way of Articulation are here to make a commitment to their unusual thinking or way of doing things by articulating it and bringing it to the attention of a broader audience. Highly observant, they have a unique talent for seeing things in a different way, and their resulting opinions and insights are always original, to say the least. Frequently, the singular viewpoints of those on this karmic path are brilliant, and, once others are convinced, they will surely come to share them. Too often, the trouble is that individuals on the Way of Articulation keep their quirkier ideas to themselves for fear of being viewed as strange. However, if they can learn to be more secure in their approach and make a commitment to doing things their way, they will be propelled to the heights of career success. This karmic path does entail some struggle, however, since those who travel it must learn to employ their considerable determination, as well as some patience, if they are ultimately to achieve the recognition they so sorely desire. Remaining true to themselves at the same time means they will have to work all the harder to get it. In fact, one of the requirements of this karmic path is that these often rather shy and retiring types must learn to articulate their goals clearly to themselves so they can remind themselves of their destination when they hit the rockier parts of the road. Luckily, these determined individuals rarely give up once they have begun.

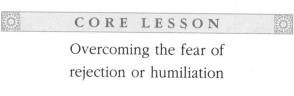

CORE LESSON
Overcoming the fear of rejection or humiliation

GOAL
To dare to be different

GIFTS
Freethinking, Financially Astute, Determined

PITFALLS
Hubristic, Fearful, Tyrannical

If they are to find success on this path, those on the Way of Articulation must overcome their fear of being rejected because of their unusual ideas. Otherwise they will never muster the courage to reveal themselves as individuals who walk to the beat of a different drum. Nor will they succeed in persuading others of their views. The world always needs a few courageous souls who will stand up and announce that the emperor has no clothes. Often they become harbingers of social change and create small revolutions in the social and intellectual milieux of their time. But to do so they must dare to be different, not just in the privacy of their own homes but out in public view. Acquiring self-confidence is crucial to this process, though it may take a number of years to grow to effective proportions. As much as they would like to keep their thoughts to themselves, those who walk this karmic path must take the risk of showing the world who they are and what they think. This is no small task, since being humiliated is one of their deepest fears. Essentially, the men and women on this karmic path are somewhat conservative, even old-fashioned, types who find that they just can't help what their brains seem to dream up. So, unlike certain others who enjoy rebelling against systems or organizations, these individuals are secretly ashamed of their own eccentricity. Learning to speak out no matter what the cost will go a long way toward consolidating their sense of self, particularly as the promise of this

karmic path is fulfilled and they ultimately discover that they are not ridiculed for their unique views but rather rewarded—often financially.

Usually career-oriented, those who travel the Way of Articulation need to turn what they once perceived to be a liability—their unconventionality—into an asset. Their attraction to all that is unusual or bizarre may confound their parents and friends, but ultimately, they will have the last laugh when the very thing that fascinates them takes off in popular culture, reaping rewards for the people traveling this road, who will then be celebrated as prescient when they were merely being true to their own unusual selves. Their eccentricities can take many forms, whether singing in a near croak to collecting rocks from around the world to having a new vision for the world order. One day their ship will come in, and that croak or those rocks or that vision will suddenly be of great value to others. Fortunately, these men and women are gifted with tremendous financial and business acumen. In truth, they can do quite well plodding along in any typical job. Far greater and more satisfying, however, is the success that will be theirs when they risk being different. And when their unusual idea starts to take off, they will have the talent and financial acumen to ensure that it turns a profit. Never, however, is money their primary goal. Until the time of their success, they will surely encounter some rejection, particularly as they start out on their career path. Thus they will be forced to develop the dogged determination that is the gift of this karmic path in order to realize their dreams of traditional success. Even in the face of early difficulties, they must learn to persist against long odds.

Those who walk the Way of Articulation must take care, however, that their determination to stick to their guns does not become a quest for success that overwhelms all other considerations. As they work toward their goals, they may fall prey to a tendency to be highly inconsiderate of others; in fact, they may ignore the rights of other individuals in their quest for power. Meanwhile, their sensitivity to rejection may become transformed into overweening pride and such a strong attachment to their way of doing things that their personalities become crystallized or rigid. Frequently, because their life struggle demands enormous self-discipline, those on this karmic path may be seen as a tad ruthless in applying their considerable willpower not only to their own lives but to those of others as well. Coworkers and family members may see them as having changed from modest, slightly kooky people into purposeful, relentless individuals who have forgotten their true friends. But this is not usually the case, since those on this path rarely forget their origins, even though they are not above using others for their own purposes. Another danger is

RELEASE
The attraction to the darker side

REWARD
The joy of celebrating one's unique view of the world

SUGGESTION

Focus on what you enjoy and let life take care of the rest.
Believe in yourself and honor what you believe.

that in order to get ahead, those on the Way of Articulation may become amoral. Moreover, because their fascination for the unusual extends to the darker or seamier aspects of life, even bordering on criminality, they must be careful that the shadow side of their inner lives does not get out of hand later in life. Thus, those on this karmic path must proceed along ethical lines or ultimately risk their own downfall.

The drama of this karmic path will be enacted whenever those who travel it become involved in any ambitious effort, whether in school, professional life, sports, or social activities. Since, at their core, those on the Way of Articulation are often retiring, quiet individuals who live in their own little world, sometimes they need to be shaken up, have their desire aroused, and be given the courage to go for the gold. In their professional life, those on the Way of Articulation may work for a period of time at quite insignificant jobs where they try to appear normal or are able to hide from the world, but once they embark on their karmic process and leave their Cancer II shyness behind, they are usually prepared to move forward and upward with no regrets.

The life partners of those on this karmic path will have to be extremely understanding of their need to spend most of their time with friends or colleagues who may share or understand their unusual points of view. It is also important for the intimates of those on the Way of Articulation to be extremely accepting, open individuals since the men and women on this path need to feel completely safe before they will reveal their more unusual side. Any hint of disapproval will cause them to scurry back to their friends or colleagues for comfort. Moreover, their mates need to encourage these souls to talk about what they think in an effort to help them articulate better. The best friends and associates for those on this karmic path will have the patience both to draw them out and to wait while they strive to achieve success. What is best for those on the Way of Articulation is recognition, but generally not by the public at large. Those on this karmic path need professional approval and acknowledgment by their peers that their work, methods, and concepts are of top quality. Ultimately, however, the most powerful of these individuals will become extremely suspicious of compliments and will come to rely on their own inner judgment for self-approval.

Perhaps an individual on the Way of Articulation may be compared to someone who finds the pot of gold at the end of the rainbow, symbolizing their spiritual, worldly, or personal goal. Initially they only dream of the rainbow, fearing to share their dream with anyone else. However, one day, seized by the sense that they must share their vision with others, they find the determination to articulate what they see in their mind's eye. As they exert themselves in this effort through many trials and tribulations, they will find the end of the rainbow and their rich reward.

BALANCE POINT

Popular and Private
Viewpoints

CRYSTALS AND GEMSTONES

Aquamarine strengthens and clears the throat, empowering the individual to speak the truth. This mineral helps to simplify and organize the complexities of the mind.

NOTABLES ON THIS KARMIC PATH

I. M. PEI

Chinese-American architect **I. M. Pei** certainly shared his unusual vision with others. Although it took him many years to build his career, Pei doggedly persisted in articulating his unique architectural style. By using strong geometrical shapes and uncommon materials, he has made a powerful impression on both colleagues and the lay public and left a lasting impression on his field. Having built his personality on a strong bedrock of self-confidence, Pei was able to survive in his competitive profession and distinguish himself internationally as a skilled and sophisticated practitioner of his craft.

JOHN FITZGERALD KENNEDY

One of the most articulate of all U.S. presidents, **John Fitzgerald Kennedy**'s concise verbal acuity left little doubt about his message. Whether countering Richard Nixon or Nikita Khrushchev, Kennedy was a formidable opponent and a born fighter. Viewed by some as ruthless and possessing a dark side, Kennedy not only displayed the positive, but also the negative qualities of this karmic path. This youngest U.S. president certainly dared to be different, often arousing animosity in those he opposed. There is no doubt, however, that his determination contributed to many of the nation's achievements, including putting a man on the moon.

JERRY SEINFELD

Even in his early days as a stand-up comic, **Jerry Seinfeld** and his eccentric brand of comedy and determination marked him as treading this karmic path. Widely known for his starring role in the sitcom bearing his name, Seinfeld found success for creating a "show about nothing." With this unusual idea, he and his show's quartet held up a mirror to the peculiarities of 1990s' society and with a fine blend of silliness and insight were able to articulate and satirize many of the values of their peer group. Prevailing where many others before him have failed, Seinfeld managed to nearly dominate his field.

Other Notables: Amy Heckerling, Irving Penn, M. C. Escher, Katharine Graham, Erich Maria Remarque, Jean Jacques Rousseau, Elvis Costello, Alexander Calder, George Washington Carver, Amelia Earhart, Henry Moore, James Cameron, Patrick Swayze, Johann Wolfgang von Goethe, Preston Sturges, Ken Kesey, Julie Andrews, George Gershwin, Johnny Mathis, Luciano Pavarotti, Leon Trotsky, Woody Allen, Cal Ripken, Sr., Sandy Koufax, Douglas MacArthur, Dinah Shore

---

BIRTHDAYS ON KARMIC PATH 15

June 17, 1898–November 5, 1898 | January 28, 1917–June 17, 1917

September 9, 1935–January 28, 1936 | April 20, 1954–September 8, 1954 | November 30, 1972–April 19, 1973

July 12, 1991–November 30, 1991 | February 20, 2010–July 11, 2010

KARMIC PATH
15

March 19–24

REBIRTH
PISCES–ARIES CUSP

Initially at least, reaching for their personal star may be a bit of a conundrum for Pisces–Arians on this karmic path. Though blessed with considerable courage and the ability to get to the heart of any number of issues, their strong intuitive sense may well be at war with their innate fear of being rejected or misunderstood. And in some instances, the more aggressively they try to convince others of the validity of their aims and aspirations, the more misunderstood they tend to be. Thus, the Way of Articulation may not be an entirely easy passage for them. Yet if these dauntless souls work to smooth some of their rougher edges, constantly refine and define their presentation skills, and make peace with their own passions, they will realize great fulfillment along the way, as their personal fascinations have a unique way of coinciding with those of the collective spirit.

CYRUS VANCE
Lawyer; former secretary
of state

3/27/1917
Aries I

CHALLENGE: **BREAKING THROUGH THE COMPLEXITY OF THEIR INNER LIFE**

FULFILLMENT: **ENJOYING THE LOGIC OF THEIR ARGUMENTS**

March 25–April 2

THE CHILD
ARIES I

Those born in the Week of the Child who find themselves on the Way of Articulation have a unique and enthusiastic vision to share with the rest of us, yet they may have to develop a modicum of self-restraint before they can get their particular message across. Emotional sensitivity and a rather temperamental attitude can send them into any number of tailspins, until they learn to release their sense of personal frustration along with their need for approval. They will doubtless be blessed with a cutting-edge sensitivity to what's new, what's exciting, and what's sure to spark the imaginations of those around them. If they can learn the value of expressing their kookier inspirations and ideas without becoming too attached to outcomes and of developing a greater sense of personal security, they will have a fine and truly rewarding journey.

CHALLENGE: **OVERCOMING THE PAIN OF CHILDHOOD CRITICISM**

FULFILLMENT: **FINDING WITHIN THEMSELVES THE FREEDOM TO BE WHO THEY ARE**

April 3–10

THE STAR
ARIES II

Those born in this week who navigate the Way of Articulation are natural-born extremists who can nonetheless recognize considerable fulfillment along this karmic path. Their need for attention can serve them well, ensuring them a dedicated following for their inspirational and unconventional ideas. The fear of rejection may, however, manifest itself in a tendency to excess, especially emotional excess, resulting in some rather unfortunate emotional displays. Alternatively, their sense of ambition may result in their having a ruthless attitude toward others as they steamroll toward their goals. Yet these success-oriented individuals can indeed dare to be different in the manner indicated by this karmic path, and once they learn not to take the ups and down of their emotional lives quite so seriously and not to be afraid to have fun, they are likely to achieve great things.

QUEEN FREDERIKA
of Greece

4/18/1917
Aries III

CHALLENGE: **NOT PERMITTING THEIR LONELINESS TO REINFORCE THEIR FEAR OF REJECTION**

FULFILLMENT: **STANDING CENTER STAGE AND EXPRESSING THEMSELVES**

April 11–18

THE PIONEER
ARIES III

The Pioneers who tread the Way of Articulation are likely to realize considerable fulfillment on this karmic path, since their best ideas, goals, and ambitions will likely be tinged with both originality and inspiration. These adventuresome types are capable of bringing great forces to bear in their quest for success, and their passionate natures will serve to inspire others in a highly constructive manner. Though many may label them as unrealistic, their unique visions will be built on the kind of solid and informed foundation that makes for real progress. If they take care not to force their ideas on others, thereby circumventing the possibility of having their feelings hurt feelings and being rejected, all is likely to go beautifully for them.

CHALLENGE: **REALIZING THE FINE LINE BETWEEN ARTICULATING THEIR VIEWS AND BEING PEDANTIC**

FULFILLMENT: **SHARING WHAT THEY HAVE TO SAY WITH OTHERS**

April 19–24
POWER
ARIES–TAURUS CUSP

Those born on the Cusp of Power who travel the Way of Articulation can be counted on to reach the pinnacle of personal achievement and success but will doubtless have to learn to value their own uniqueness better before it will happen. Daring to be different can be a bit hard for these individuals, and they may struggle a bit in the course of developing and embracing their more unique impulses and ideas. However, they are likely to be helped along this journey by a great psychological astuteness that will make them formidable judges of character and worldly conditions. That, coupled with their great sense of timing, can make for wonderful rewards. If they are careful not to abuse their considerable power in ruthlessness and relentlessness, on the one hand, or complacency and laziness, on the other, all is likely to go well and they will reap the rewards promised by this karmic path.

CHALLENGE: **REMEMBERING TO ENJOY THEMSELVES ONCE IN A WHILE**

FULFILLMENT: **DISCOVERING THAT THERE IS A PATH OF LEAST RESISTANCE**

JERRY SEINFELD
Comedian/writer,
hit TV show *Seinfeld*

4/29/1954
Taurus I

April 25–May 2
MANIFESTATION
TAURUS I

Those born in the Week of Manifestation who travel the Way of Articulation may experience their greatest difficulties when they refuse to take their quirkier inclinations seriously. This karmic path will lend these rather practical people a greater degree of imagination than they might otherwise have had, yet they will have to do a certain amount of work to stay open to their greatest sources of inspiration. Too, their need for acceptance and approval may be pronounced, and some may have a great reluctance to rock the boat. Yet if they develop the discrimination to take on only those responsibilities that will further their own aims and ambitions and take care to develop their more playful side, their formidable financial sense, great energy, and fine work ethic will lead to great personal, professional, and material success.

CHALLENGE: **NOT ALLOWING THEIR NEED FOR HARMONY TO PREVENT THEM FROM FULLY REVEALING THEMSELVES**

FULFILLMENT: **BREAKING WHOLLY NEW GROUND IN ANY FIELD OF ENDEAVOR**

NOTABLE: **I. M. PEI (CELEBRATED ARCHITECT)**

May 3–10
THE TEACHER
TAURUS II

The Teachers who navigate the Way of Articulation are likely to have a wonderful time, for this karmic path demands the greater articulation and expression of a personal vision or passion. Since these people like nothing better than to share their ideas, they are unlikely to offer much resistance to the demands of this karmic path. Though they may not be everyone's cup of tea, these intrepid characters aren't apt to care too much about what others may think and are likely to produce any number of startling insights. Their entrepreneurial sense will come in especially handy here, and if they can channel their unconventional attitudes into a productive professional enterprise, they are unlikely to miss the summons when opportunity comes knocking.

CHALLENGE: **TAKING CARE NOT TO ALLOW THEIR STRONG MORAL STANCE TO LEAD THEM TO DARK OR EXTREME JUDGMENTS**

FULFILLMENT: **PRESENTING THEIR IDEAS IN A CLEAR AND EASILY UNDERSTOOD MANNER**

AMY HECKERLING
Director, *Fast Times at Ridgemont High*

5/7/1954
Taurus II

May 11–18
THE NATURAL
TAURUS III

Taurus III's who find themselves on the Way of Articulation can get pretty far out indeed, yet they would do well to keep in mind that much of their wildness and unconventional behavior may in fact be a manifestation of a quest for security. In any event, they may rank among the freest spirits on the planet as they pursue their destiny, and will not they don't recoil from the higher demands of this karmic path. While there is a risk that they will refuse to accept the challenge to stand up for what they truly believe in or to share their unique brand of knowledge with others, they can realize great rewards. If they can truly commit to their own unique visions, lifestyles, and insights, they are likely to pursue them fearlessly, untroubled by others' opinions or restrictions. Curiously, this configuration can also result in the accumulation of considerable material wealth, perhaps as fate's means of easing the passage of these truly unique souls.

CHALLENGE: **NOT CONFUSING MERELY GENERATING DRAMA WITH STANDING UP FOR WHAT THEY BELIEVE IN**

FULFILLMENT: **EXPERIENCING THE FREEDOM OF SPEAKING OUT ON THEIR OWN BEHALF**

NOTABLE: **MARY KAY (FOUNDER OF MARY KAY COSMETICS)**

May 19–24
ENERGY
TAURUS–GEMINI CUSP

Whatever Taurus–Geminis' personal attraction to the unusual or bizarre, it is unlikely to stay hidden for long on this karmic path. Wonderfully adventuresome personalities, those born on the Cusp of Energy will doubtless have to come to terms with the necessity to develop the strength of their convictions at some point or run the risk of failing the demands of this karmic path by flitting from one cause to another due to their eternal search for stimulation. Often intellectually brilliant, they are unlikely to be unduly troubled by the shyness and sensitivity that can plague others on this road yet will have to work to channel their considerable energy into productive effort. When they discover that their ability to draw others to them by virtue of their uniqueness carries with it a measure of responsibility, life with this configuration can indeed be the proverbial bowl of cherries.

M.C. ESCHER
Artist, known for optical illusions

6/17/1898
Gemini III

CHALLENGE: **GROUNDING THEIR OPINIONS IN A MORAL CODE AND THEREBY TRANSFORMING THEM INTO CONVICTIONS**
FULFILLMENT: **DISCOVERING THAT OTHERS VALUE WHAT THEY HAVE TO SAY**

May 25–June 2
FREEDOM
GEMINI I

Sticking to their guns and standing up for what they believe in will come quite naturally to those born in the Week of Freedom who travel the Way of Articulation, yet they will have to regulate their tendency to antagonize people before they can fully realize the promise of this karmic path. Their highly intellectual nature and often razor-sharp wit may prove both their greatest blessings and their greatest curses, and they will doubtless have to work a bit to refine their powers of expression to become more effective. Moreover, emotional volatility and a tendency to scatter their energies will be rather pronounced. Yet if they pursue their ideals fearlessly and explore their attraction to the unusual thoroughly, their experience can synthesize in highly progressive and useful manifestations of their ideas.

CHALLENGE: **TEMPERING THEIR ATTRACTION TO THE DARK SIDE**
FULFILLMENT: **APPLYING THEIR CONSIDERABLE INTELLECT TO PRODUCING CLEAR AND COGENT ARGUMENTS IN FAVOR OF THEIR CONVICTIONS**
NOTABLE: **JOHN F. KENNEDY (35TH U.S. PRESIDENT; "CAMELOT"; ASSASSINATED)**

June 3–10
NEW LANGUAGE
GEMINI II

Undue personal sensitivity and an inability to adequately come to grips with issues of personal relationship may be the principal stumbling blocks for those born in the Week of New Language who find themselves on the Way of Articulation. Too, these people may hinder their progress along this karmic path through a fascination with the darker side of experience and would do well to temper their impulses in this area, especially when those impulses result in bad relationship choices. Yet despite their early defensiveness and even shyness about being who they truly are, time will doubtless give them greater strength as well as a more integrated sense of self. Aided by the power of their communicative and innovative talents, they may not find journey especially easy, but it will doubtless be interesting in the extreme.

KATHARINE GRAHAM
Washington Post publisher

6/16/1917
Gemini III

CHALLENGE: **GIVING UP TOO EARLY IN THEIR QUEST FOR UNDERSTANDING**
FULFILLMENT: **OVERCOMING THE CHALLENGE OF THEIR HIGHLY PERSONAL COMMUNICATION STYLE TO BECOME ARTICULATE**
NOTABLE: **HARVEY FIERSTEIN (ACTOR)**

June 11–18
THE SEEKER
GEMINI III

Gemini III's may find that their search for expanded knowledge takes some strange turns along the Way of Articulation, yet they are likely to reap great rewards, not to mention considerable entertainment, on this karmic path. Since they are gifted with a unique sense of adventure, they are likely to thoroughly enjoy the journey, whether it results in travels to far-off and exotic places or takes place within their own backyard. Either way, progress is likely to be the bottom line. Gifted with a pronounced knack for making and administering money, they are likely to find this a materially rewarding journey, especially when they find within themselves the strength and focus required to fearlessly apply their considerable skills to the achievement of their fondest dreams and most innovative ideas.

CHALLENGE: **STOPPING LONG ENOUGH IN THEIR SEARCH FOR MEANING TO DISCOVER IT WITHIN**
FULFILLMENT: **APPLYING THEIR HARD-WON KNOWLEDGE IN MATERIALLY REWARDING WAYS**
NOTABLES: **DEAN MARTIN (ACTOR/SINGER); IRVING PENN (FASHION PHOTOGRAPHER); JIM BELUSHI (ACTOR/COMEDIAN)**

June 19–24

MAGIC
GEMINI–CANCER CUSP

Those born on the Cusp of Magic who travel the Way of Articulation will first and foremost be inclined toward some rather unusual romantic choices and inclinations and may choose partners that are the despair of their more conservative parents, friends, or associates. Love and romance may well be the principal foci of their more unconventional ideas until they come to grips with the fact that they need not depend upon others for stimulation, approval, spiritual exaltation or even to act out their own more bizarre sides. They can indeed shine brightly on their own, especially when they place themselves in the service of some higher cause, and they will rarely lose their aura of romantic idealism. If they can develop the courage to stand up for even their most bizarre ideas, chances are their expressions of self will be met with warm approval and genuine collective appreciation.

FREDDIE PRINZE
TV actor,
Chico and the Man
———
6/22/1954
Gemini–Cancer Cusp

CHALLENGE: **OVERCOMING THEIR SENSITIVITY TO CRITICISM OR DISAPPROVAL**

FULFILLMENT: **EXPRESSING THEIR OWN UNIQUE CHARACTER RATHER THAN BECOMING INVOLVED WITH MORE BIZARRE OR UNUSUAL PEOPLE**

NOTABLE: **ERICH MARIA REMARQUE (NOVELIST, *ALL QUIET ON THE WESTERN FRONT*)**

June 25–July 2

THE EMPATH
CANCER I

Emotional neediness can hinder the higher progress of Empaths who travel the Way of Articulation, especially when their need for approval manifests itself in a passive-aggressive style that has them advancing toward their goals, then withdrawing in the face of conflict or disapproval. Yet they will be encouraged in this passage as their vision matures and they learn to appreciate their own quirkier inclinations more. The key to their success will be the ability to channel their empathic and intuitive insights into clearly articulated verbal or written forms of communication. This may be easier if they work not to be so hard on themselves as well as to allow themselves greater freedom of thought and action. Yet they have the innate strength of character to make it through even the toughest periods of this passage, and their financial aptitude, hard-won sense of authority, and unique vision should combine to create a truly rewarding career.

CHALLENGE: **CULTIVATING THE STRENGTH OF CHARACTER TO BE TRUE TO THEIR CONVICTIONS**

FULFILLMENT: **SUCCEEDING IN ARTICULATING WHAT THEY KNOW IN THEIR GUTS TO BE TRUE**

NOTABLES: **WILLIAM MAYO (COFOUNDED MAYO CLINIC); JEAN-JACQUES ROUSSEAU (POLITICAL PHILOSOPHER; INFLUENCED FRENCH REVOLUTION)**

July 3–10

THE UNCONVENTIONAL
CANCER II

Though it's entirely possible that these people may live out their lives in the uncomfortable position of being square pegs in round holes, they are bound to have more than their share of fun along the way. Finding the strength to flaunt convention may prove somewhat difficult for them, but sooner or later the secrets of their unconventional inclinations will leak out. In fact, controlling their fantasies may be their biggest problem, especially in childhood. Yet they have a curious knack for psychological insight and are rarely afraid to apply their insights to themselves when the going gets tough. If they can manifest their attraction for the unusual in productive rather than destructive ways and learn that being different is an asset rather than a liability, they will doubtless earn a valued position in the hearts and minds of those around them.

GEORGE WASHINGTON CARVER
Chemist/educator/botanist;
invented peanut butter
———
7/12/1864
Cancer III

CHALLENGE: **MONITORING THE REAL REASONS BEHIND WHY THEY CHOOSE THEIR FRIENDS**

FULFILLMENT: **IMPLEMENTING THE MORE UNUSUAL IDEAS THAT THIS PATH DENOTES**

July 11–18

THE PERSUADER
CANCER III

Though those born in the Week of the Persuader who find themselves on the Way of Articulation may indeed march to the beat of a different drum, chances are they will manifest their destiny more in the manner of a Pied Piper as they draw others to their views and causes with considerable and sometimes even startling power. In fact, they are not always above using others to achieve their own purposes and will have to guard not only against developing an amoral or cynical outlook but also against their tendency to test the limits of their power over others with all sort of games and darker manipulations. If they can manage to avoid the dangers of excess, on the one hand, and a rather autocratic and workaholic obsession, on the other, they will be rewarded with financial success and professional recognition of an enduring quality.

CHALLENGE: **RELEASING THEIR ATTRACTION TO THE MURKIER ELEMENTS OF LIFE**

FULFILLMENT: **BACKING UP THEIR CONSIDERABLE POWERS OF PERSUASION WITH THE STRENGTH OF THEIR CONVICTIONS**

NOTABLES: **BERENICE ABBOTT (AMATEUR PHOTOGRAPHER); ALEXANDER BROOK (PAINTER)**

July 19–25
OSCILLATION
CANCER–LEO CUSP

AMELIA EARHART
Aviator; 1st woman to
cross the Atlantic

7/24/1898
Cancer–Leo Cusp

Cancer–Leos who navigate the Way of Articulation will be exciting, courageous, and often downright wild. Personal sensitivity can be a big stumbling block for these generally fearless people, yet their tendency to rush in where calmer souls might fear to tread can get them into trouble from time to time, especially when the quest of the moment involves parental approval or acceptance by a lover or friend. The barest breath of rejection can send them into paroxysms of dramatic suffering, and they may expend a great deal of energy fretting over where they went wrong. Yet their affinity for the unusual and bizarre can also rescue them from some of their more manic tendencies and widen their perspective in some very interesting ways. Still, this path blesses them with perhaps a greater degree of stability than some of their fellows, and once they channel their energies into a plan for success, they can find great fulfillment.

CHALLENGE: **OVERCOMING THEIR OVERDEPENDENCE ON APPROVAL**
FULFILLMENT: **CHANNELING THEIR INTUITIVE ENERGIES INTO SOME FORM OF CREATIVE EXPRESSION**
NOTABLES: **ALEXANDER CALDER (SCULPTOR/PAINTER); HERBERT MARCUSE (PHILOSOPHER)**

July 26–August 2
AUTHORITY
LEO I

Blessed with a greater ability to assert themselves than many others on this karmic path, those born in the Week of Authority who travel the Way of Articulation are likely to find it a relatively easy trip. They bring a flair for the dramatic and unusual to their lives, and whatever the specific results of their destiny, they are likely to command attention wherever they go. Translating that attention into personal ambition will prove almost effortless, providing they do not allow their ego issues or fear of rejection to hamper their higher development. Too, they have a great empathy for others, in these personalities, and as long as they keep in mind that they must employ that empathy in an effort to control their more demanding side, they can reach the heights of personal and professional excellence.

CHALLENGE: **ESCHEWING MERE DRAMA IN FAVOR OF A TRUTHFUL PRESENTATION OF WHO THEY ARE**
FULFILLMENT: **FURTHERING OF THEIR CHARACTER DEVELOPMENT THROUGH CAREER ENDEAVORS**
NOTABLES: **HENRY MOORE (SCULPTOR); ALEXIS, COMTE DE TOCQUEVILLE (AUTHOR, *DEMOCRACY IN AMERICA*)**

August 3–10
BALANCED STRENGTH
LEO II

Those born in this week who travel the Way of Articulation will experience something of an emotional roller-coaster ride, aided, of course, by their fascination for unusual people and situations, until they learn to balance themselves better. Their fight against their tendency to be too self-sacrificing or masochistic will figure prominently in achieving that sense of balance, however, as will the need to divorce themselves from more conservative or careful individuals who threaten to hold them back from accomplishing their ambitions. Yet they are likely to cut a dramatic figure, and if they develop the knack for controlled and sustained effort, as well as the ability to tell their detractors where and when to get off, they will realize great progress along this karmic path.

CHALLENGE: **LETTING GO OF THE CORE BELIEF THAT THEY ARE NOT ENTITLED TO BE WHO THEY ARE**
FULFILLMENT: **INVOKING THEIR CONSIDERABLE DETERMINATION AS THEY ACHIEVE SUCCESS**

JAMES CAMERON
Film director, *Titanic*

8/16/1954
Leo III

August 11–18
LEADERSHIP
LEO III

Leo II's will doubtless do wonderfully well on the Way of Articulation, providing they focus their dreams and ambitions and refuse to allow defensiveness or fear of ridicule to hinder their higher development. Though it may take some time for them to get their footing, their taste for the unusual is sure to fuel the fires of their highly creative talents. Overcoming egotism in its most negative aspect—fear—and employing it in its highest aspect—self love—will figure prominently in their quest for success. Yet in seeking the approval and approbation of others, they would do well to secure their sense of self-respect before attempting to command respect from others.

CHALLENGE: **OVERCOMING THEIR HUBRISTIC NEED FOR APPROVAL**
FULFILLMENT: **ARTICULATING THEIR PERSONAL VISION NO MATTER WHAT THE COST**
NOTABLE: **PATRICK SWAYZE (ACTOR, *DIRTY DANCING, GHOST*)**

August 19–25

EXPOSURE
LEO–VIRGO CUSP

August 26–September 2

SYSTEM BUILDERS
VIRGO I

ELVIS COSTELLO
British pop star

8/25/1954
Leo–Virgo Cusp

Those born on the Cusp of Exposure who travel the Way of Articulation may well be inclined to keep their inner light under wraps or hide their more unusual inclinations. Yet on this karmic path they will discover that the harder they try to toe the line, the more likely they are to draw attention to themselves. Thus, making peace with who they are will involve making a few waves whether they like it or not. Using their powers of observation to arrive at strong convictions and beliefs will be especially important. However, when they come to terms with the fact that their attraction to the unusual, the bizarre, or the unconventional in friends, interests, or associates is more than likely an expression of their own flamboyance and a manifestation of some truth about themselves, their travels along this karmic path are likely to get much easier.

CHALLENGE: **LOOSENING THE RIGIDITY THAT REPRESENTS NOTHING MORE THAN A FEAR OF THEIR OWN INCLINATIONS**
FULFILLMENT: **HEARING THE APPLAUSE THAT THE REVELATION OF THEIR SECRETLY FLAMBOYANT SIDE BRINGS**
NOTABLE: **AUGUST BOURNONVILLE (DANCER/ CHOREOGRAPHER)**

System Builders who travel the Way of Articulation may not have an entirely easy time until they learn to integrate their sensitivity better and get at the roots of what can sometimes be an overriding need to conform. Also, these people can be rather self-effacing and keep their best ideas and inspirations under wraps, to the detriment of their higher development and success. Once free to tell it as it is, these analytical individuals will prove to be some of the most articulate of their group. Thus, while daring to be different will not come easily, once they build a strong and unassailable fortress of self that is untroubled by the need for approval, and apply their incisive minds in presenting their views, they will achieve great success.

CHALLENGE: **LETTING GO OF THEIR NEEDS FOR SAFETY AND SECURITY IN MAKING CHOICES**
FULFILLMENT: **UTILIZING THEIR CAPACITY FOR ANALYSIS IN EXPRESSING THEMSELVES**
NOTABLES: **PRESTON STURGES (FILM WRITER/DIRECTOR); SHIRLEY BOOTH (ACTRESS, *HAZEL*)**

September 3–10

THE ENIGMA
VIRGO II

September 11–18

THE LITERALIST
VIRGO III

JOHANN WOLFGANG VON GOETHE
Poet/dramatist

8/28/1749
Virgo I

Those born in the Week of the Enigma who make this life's passage along the Way of Articulation will have an interesting journey. These people tend to be very private souls, hesitant to allow others into their private inner worlds, and that quality may be especially pronounced, given their sometimes unconventional inclinations. Thus, there may exist quite a discrepancy between their public and private selves, though each will doubtless be marked by the typically high standards and discrimination of Virgo II's. Yet the better integrated of them will eventually allow their true nature to shine forth, often through a particularly zany sense of humor. Capable of developing great strength of conviction, they may nevertheless require some time to dare to be truly different, especially in public. Yet when they do, they can shine forth with a special light.

CHALLENGE: **FIGHTING THEIR TENDENCY TO CULTIVATE AN AIR OF MYSTERY AT THE EXPENSE OF HAVING AN OPINION**
FULFILLMENT: **USING HUMOR TO EXPRESS THEIR IDEAS**
NOTABLES: **ADELE ASTAIRE (SISTER AND EARLY PARTNER OF FRED); CORBIN BERNSEN (ACTOR)**

Gifted with the strength and concentration to achieve even the most unlikely goals, Virgo III's who travel the Way of Articulation will have little trouble focusing their attention on a vocation or career. What will prove a stumbling block, however, is coming to terms with their innate unconventionality, since they may often resist or discount some of their own original or innovative ideas, especially if they think those ideas are colored by emotion. Yet their talent for determining the truth will find expression, even if it means living a lie for a time in order to discover what is true about themselves in the end. If they work to integrate their instincts and attractions with their often astute financial and vocational talents and maintain a clear sense of who they are, they can take great strides along this path.

CHALLENGE: **GRAPPLING WITH THEIR FEAR OF BEING DIFFERENT**
FULFILLMENT: **LIVING A LIFE FREE OF PHONINESS AND PRETENSION**
NOTABLES: **KEN KESEY (AUTHOR, *ONE FLEW OVER THE CUCKOO'S NEST*); BEN SHAHN (PAINTER/PHOTOGRAPHER; DOCUMENTED SACCO-VANZETTI CASE)**

September 19–24

BEAUTY
VIRGO–LIBRA CUSP

This configuration is sure to manifest itself in a truly extraordinary sense of the innovative and original, especially in areas of aesthetics, taste, and fashion. Virgo–Libras may, however, be reluctant to make waves and may content themselves with a rather humdrum lifestyle, as long as it provides them with security or material comfort. Moreover, they will have to struggle a bit with their tendency to detach themselves emotionally or physically from situations that demand more than they are willing to give. Thus, they would do well to concentrate on developing greater self-awareness and a surer sense of conviction. Aided by their aesthetic sensitivity, they are capable of achieving great success, providing they apply their talent for innovation in disciplined and substantive effort. When they learn to rely on themselves more than others, they will realize both the spiritual depth and material rewards promised by the Way of Articulation.

CHALLENGE: **NOT SUCCUMBING TO THEIR ATTRACTION TO DARKER, MORE ESCAPIST SIDES OF LIFE**

FULFILLMENT: **HAVING THEIR VIEWS HEARD AND ADMIRED BY OTHERS**

NOTABLE: **SIR HOWARD FLOREY (PURIFIED PENICILLIN FOR MEDICAL USE; SHARED NOBEL PRIZE)**

JULIE ANDREWS
Singer/actress,
Victor/Victoria, Mary Poppins

10/1/1935
Libra I

September 25–October 2

THE PERFECTIONIST
LIBRA I

Those born in this week who find themselves on the Way of Articulation may have to come to terms with both their emotional vulnerability and their unconventionality before they can make real progress. Their sometimes overwhelming fear of rejection may lead them to strike out at others on occasion or project their worst fears about themselves onto the rest of the world. As a result, they may sometimes be darkly paranoid, on the one hand, and entirely too demanding or didactic, on the other, and this can result in a rather a gloomy worldview. Yet despite some early difficulties, these people are blessed with the kind of dogged determination that will enable them to find real fulfillment and should face no problem that cannot overcome. If they can control their more exacting energy and the expression of their true feelings and, in particular, their views of what merits attention or exaltation, they are apt to find that their exquisite taste is shared by all.

CHALLENGE: **NOT REJECTING THEMSELVES BY BEING OVERLY DEMANDING OR PICKY**

FULFILLMENT: **EXPRESSING TECHNICAL VIRTUOSITY**

NOTABLES: **GEORGE GERSHWIN (PROLIFIC COMPOSER, "RHAPSODY IN BLUE"); JOHNNY MATHIS (POPULAR SINGER)**

October 3–10

SOCIETY
LIBRA II

Those born in the Week of Society who navigate the Way of Articulation may have to work hard to control their tendency to indulge in emotional outbursts, mood swings, and a preoccupation with fantasies or darker imaginings. Furthermore, they have a tendency to try to please others, sometimes at the expense of their own needs and desires, resulting in an even greater sense of personal frustration. On the plus side, however, these people have a rare and unique sense of original style and an almost sixth sense of what will be popularly embraced especially in aesthetic matters and current events. When they drop some of their more cumbersome emotional baggage in order to get a better handle on their goals and ambitions, their vision and insight are sure to lead to considerable personal success and wonderful material rewards, just by virtue of their having found the courage to be who they really are.

CHALLENGE: **REALIZING THAT THEY OFTEN SEEK APPROVAL FROM OTHERS**

FULFILLMENT: **STAYING TRUE TO THEIR PERSONAL VISIONS ONCE ARTICULATED**

LUCIANO PAVAROTTI
Operatic tenor, one of
"The Three Tenors"

10/12/1935
Libra III

October 11–18

THEATER
LIBRA III

The talented people born in this week who travel the Way of Articulation will not have much trouble expressing their originality. Projecting a competent and compelling personal image will doubtless be important to them, and that effort alone will eliminate many of the secret fears that plague some of those who find themselves on this karmic path. They will have to delve a bit deeper than mere image, however, if they are to successfully navigate the twists and turn of this road. Some of them will discover that embracing their love of the unconventional and innovative, then manifesting their beliefs in the world, is much easier when they have learned the folly of laying blame upon others for their own weaknesses or insecurities, while others will have to avoid the dangers of blind ambition. Yet all can realize great fulfillment here, as the demands of this karmic path are very much in keeping with their more dramatic inclinations.

CHALLENGE: **COMING TO TERMS WITH THEIR OWN SHADIER ACTIONS**

FULFILLMENT: **INDULGING IN THEIR FLAIR FOR THE DRAMATIC AS THEY PRESENT THEMSELVES, THEIR IDEAS, OR THEIR TALENTS**

NOTABLE: **PETER BOYLE (ACTOR)**

October 19–25

DRAMA AND CRITICISM
LIBRA–SCORPIO CUSP

Those born in this period who find themselves on the Way of Articulation can be characterized as having "glass egos," or a fragility of their sense of self. More specifically, these big and charismatic people may have such a fear of rejection that the smallest slight can shatter their sense of identity beyond all proportion. Nevertheless, their worldly orientation and ambition are quite strong, and once they release the notion that they must conform in order to succeed, they can realize an often astonishing level of success. Buoyed in their journey by their love of beauty, astute evaluative skills, and naturally charismatic and compelling spirit, they must nevertheless avoid the tendency to become overbearing as time goes on. Yet, all things being equal, these dramatic, artistic people are likely to leave a highly personal mark on their world.

ROY SCHEIDER
Film actor, *Jaws*

———

11/10/1935
Scorpio II

CHALLENGE: **TEMPERING THEIR SENSE OF PERSONAL INFAL-LIBILITY**

FULFILLMENT: **FULLY INHABITING THEIR OWN LARGE PERSON-ALITIES BY EXHIBITING THE VIRTUOSITY OF THEIR IDEAS**

NOTABLE: **MARIO BUATTA (INTERIOR DECORATOR)**

October 26–November 2

INTENSITY
SCORPIO I

Those born in the Week of Intensity who travel the Way of Articulation are likely to find great success, providing they can get a grip on some of their more fearful and suspicious tendencies and learn to regulate their emotions better. Extreme sensitivity and a fear of rejection, coupled with their natural inclination toward the unconventional, can lead these individuals down some pretty dark avenues from time to time. Scorpio I's are best advised always to accentuate the positive. There can often be quite a discrepancy between the face they present to the world and the one they wear in private, though their facade will often break down in the face of criticism or disapproval. However, there is a particular promise of financial success on this karmic path, and whatever their professional inclinations, they are likely to make a considerable income. If they don't allow their darker sides to get the best of them, they will find great promise and fulfillment.

CHALLENGE: **NOT LETTING THEIR MOODIER OR DARKER SIDE RUN RAMPANT**

FULFILLMENT: **APPLYING THEIR FULL POWERS OF DISCRIMI-NATION AND CONCENTRATION**

NOTABLE: **GARY PLAYER (SOUTH AFRICAN GOLFER)**

November 3–11

DEPTH
SCORPIO II

Naturally self-possessed and often poised, the calm and serious exteriors of Scorpio II's who travel the Way of Articulation may belie a profound and even seething emotional life. It is important for them not to get mired in their fears and passions, especially if those fears include a dread of rejection or humiliation. Should either of those things appear in their lives, as they no doubt will, they would do well to learn the value of release and forgiveness, if only to free their sense of self and forge a less cautious and constrained identity. Daring to be different may not come easily for some with this configuration, while the more advanced of this type may become eccentric indeed as they realize their own unique powers.

CHALLENGE: **BANISHING THEIR CHIP-ON-THE-SHOULDER ATTITUDE ALONG WITH THEIR DESTRUCTIVE BRAND OF DEFENSIVENESS**

FULFILLMENT: **PERFORMING, IN ANY CAPACITY, TO ACCLAIM**

NOTABLES: **ALAIN DELON (FRENCH ACTOR); LEON TROTSKY (LENIN'S CHIEF LIEUTENANT DURING RUSSIAN REVOLUTION)**

KING IBN TALAL HUSSEIN
King of Jordan

———

11/14/1935
Scorpio III

November 12–18

CHARM
SCORPIO III

Those born in this week who navigate the Way of Articulation may have to make peace with their own desires both to please others and to manipulate them by using their considerable charm. Until they cultivate a truer sense of identity that is unconcerned with public opinion, these people may hide their best ideas, inspirations, and original work behind a facade of congenial and less-than-honest conformity. Yet at their core, Scorpio III's on this karmic path are really quite realistic and even shrewd. As life teaches them to honor their own uniqueness more and to be less manipulative, they will become free to channel their considerable financial, creative, and organizational talents into a clear path to a success made all the sweeter by virtue of its authentic and innovative style.

CHALLENGE: **LEARNING TO LOOK WITHIN, RATHER THAN FOREVER LOOKING TO MIRROR OTHERS**

FULFILLMENT: **TURNING THEIR UNIQUE TALENTS INTO LUC-RATIVE ASSETS**

November 19–24
REVOLUTION
SCORPIO–SAGITTARIUS CUSP

Scorpio–Sagittarians who travel the Way of Articulation are likely to be untroubled by some of the emotional baggage that goes with this configuration and are unusually well suited to answer the call of this karmic path to honor their eccentricities. Strength of conviction comes quite naturally to these often reckless people, and early in life they may well prove the despair of conservative parents, teachers, or associates. Such early experiences will doubtless do much to shape their rather mixed feelings about authority in general and contribute to their need to tear down old and outdated structures to make way for new ones. Yet they should be careful not to throw out the baby with the bathwater or attempt to erect their plans and ambitions on unstable foundations. Yet the Way of Articulation does impart a greater sense of stability than these people might otherwise have, and if they can channel their energy appropriately, these revolutionary people may find themselves truly making a difference.

CHALLENGE: **NOT BECOMING OVERLY RIGID IN THEIR VIEWPOINTS**

FULFILLMENT: **FINDING A POSITIVE OR CREATIVE MEANS OF EXPRESSION FOR THEIR MORE EXTREME IDEAS**

WOODY ALLEN
Director/writer/actor/
comedian, *Annie Hall*
———
12/1/1935
Sagittarius I

November 25–December 2
INDEPENDENCE
SAGITTARIUS I

Unencumbered by the shyness and insecurity that can plague many others on the Way of Articulation, these dauntless, independent people will likely have an easy trip along this karmic path. Since freedom and independence are essential to them, they should experience little trouble with the call to honor their eccentricities and recognize their unique abilities as assets, rather than liabilities. Though some early repression may set them people back a bit in their search for independence or tie them down from time to time in old patterns or a need to please, it's unlikely that they will suffer fools gladly or for very long. As long as they are careful to realize that their high sense of honor, usually used to bolster their self-respect, should be used to serve others as well, they are unlikely to stumble along the way.

CHALLENGE: **HOLDING THEMSELVES TO THE SAME CODE OF HONOR TO WHICH THEY HOLD OTHERS**

FULFILLMENT: **DISCOVERING THE MYRIAD FORMS THAT EXPRESSING THEIR GENUINE LIKING OF THEMSELVES CAN TAKE**

December 3–10
THE ORIGINATOR
SAGITTARIUS II

The Originators who tread the Way of Articulation will do so rather lightly and easily, given that they often have little choice but to embrace their own eccentricities. In fact, some of them can be downright odd, and life will doubtless give them an early education in the folly of trying to fit in. Yet this karmic path gifts them with a keener intuition and understanding of others than they might otherwise have had, and thus they will find it much easier to overcome the sense of rejection or personal touchiness that often plagues their fellows. As a result, following their own stars, dreaming their own dreams, and inventing new and ever-evolving ways to be themselves more fully will all be second nature to these free spirits. If they set their sights high, garner their forces, and work to manifest their ongoing love affair with the wacky, they are promised a great deal of fun and adventure along this karmic path.

CHALLENGE: **TEMPERING THEIR MORE AGGRESSIVE APPROACHES TO PUTTING FORTH THEIR IDEAS**

FULFILLMENT: **PURSUING THEIR INTERESTS WITH ABANDON**

NOTABLES: **CHARLES PILLSBURY (INVENTED METHOD TO PROCESS FLOUR MORE QUICKLY); GUNNAR MYRDAL (NOBEL PRIZE-WINNING ECONOMIST); IRA GERSHWIN (LYRICIST TO BROTHER GEORGE)**

CAL RIPKEN, SR.
Player/manager for the
Baltimore Orioles
———
12/17/1935
Sagittarius III

December 11–18
THE TITAN
SAGITTARIUS III

The eccentricities of those born in the Week of the Titan who travel the Way of Articulation are likely to manifest themselves as a fascination with magical, ecstatic, or peak experiences of all kinds. In fact, these people may have a bit of trouble following the ordinary rules and conventions, which may contribute to some early insecurities and a fear of rejection. Cultivating self-awareness as opposed to self-consciousness will contribute greatly to their development, as will finding the courage to simply divorce themselves from less visionary people, careers, and endeavors. If they do not waste their considerable gifts in neediness and egotism, they will be blessed with the inner resources to realize even their most impossible dreams and will find great adventure and fulfillment on this karmic path.

CHALLENGE: **NOT PERMITTING FRUSTRATION TO MANIFEST ITSELF IN TEMPER TANTRUMS OR OTHER DISPLAYS OF EGO**

FULFILLMENT: **DISCOVERING THE ENCHANTMENT OF PURSUING THEIR FANTASTIC VISIONS**

NOTABLE: **ROBERT KOCH (BACTERIOLOGIST; DISCOVERED TB; WON 1905 NOBEL PRIZE)**

December 19–25
PROPHECY
SAGITTARIUS–CAPRICORN CUSP

The Way of Articulation blesses these often serious people with a lighter, zanier side than they might otherwise have had, and this will do much to buoy them along their journey. Too, they may well have have an extraordinary ability to detect patterns and portents of the future, to the extent that their highly developed intuitive faculties may contribute to their sense of being decidedly out of the mainstream. Their early psychic talents may have been rigorously suppressed, and their spiritual side may have to undergo a rediscovery or reawakening before they can realize their highest potential. Yet they are blessed with all of the strength of character needed to accomplish great things on this life journey, and if they don't take their natural disdain for other's opinions too far, they can lend their special talents to the realization of a better life and an infinitely better world.

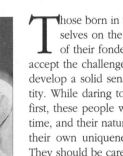

PHIL DONAHUE
TV talk show host
───────
12/21/1935
Sagittarius–Capricorn
Cusp

CHALLENGE: **NOT ALLOWING THEIR NEED FOR PRIVACY TO DEVOLVE INTO INDULGENCE IN DARK OR AMORAL ACTIVITIES**

FULFILLMENT: **DEVELOPING THE CAPACITY TO ARTICULATE THEIR OFTEN PROPHETIC FEELINGS OR IDEAS**

NOTABLE: **JOSEPH STALIN (MARXIST REVOLUTIONARY; LATER DICTATOR OF USSR)**

December 26–January 2
THE RULER
CAPRICORN I

Those born in the Week of the Ruler who find themselves on the Way of Articulation can realize some of their fondest dream on this path, provided they accept the challenge to greater leadership and the call to develop a solid sense of personal and professional identity. While daring to be different may not come easily at first, these people will find their footing in the course of time, and their natural courage to stand up for and honor their own uniqueness will doubtless come to the fore. They should be careful, however, not to go overboard, as the pitfalls of this position may include ruthlessness, amorality, and emotional repression. Yet their flair for the different will find great expression and manifest itself in a unique sense of self-respect that will command the respect and admiration of others.

CHALLENGE: **ACCEPTING ALL SIDES OF THEMSELVES**

FULFILLMENT: **PUTTING THEIR CAPACITY FOR LEADERSHIP IN THE SERVICE OF THEIR HIGHER CONVICTIONS**

NOTABLES: **SIDNEY GREENSTREET (ACTOR, *CASABLANCA*); DAVID BAILEY (BRITISH FASHION PHOTOGRAPHER)**

January 3–9
DETERMINATION
CAPRICORN II

Those born in the Week of Determination who travel the Way of Articulation may take some time to shine, perhaps due to early feelings of rejection or personal setbacks they find hard to surmount. Yet the gifts of this karmic path will allow them to explore their uniqueness with great freedom and the assurance that they are allowed to experience a measure of real fun along the way. These people will find that many of their weirder inclinations draw them to the outer edges of spiritual understanding, and some will be able to translate their experiences into embracing new belief systems or alternative religions. The key to their success and happiness will be to divest themselves from those who would hold them back or tie them down in the name of tradition. This may not be easy, but their ability to draw upon huge resources of personal and spiritual strength in order to come into their own is sure to have a positive effect in the course of their often unusual lives.

SANDY KOUFAX
One of the greatest left-handed pitchers of all time, played for the Dodgers
───────
12/30/1935
Capricorn I

CHALLENGE: **ACKNOWLEDGING AND FORGIVING THEIR OWN SENSITIVITY**

FULFILLMENT: **DISCOVERING THAT THEIR DETERMINATION IS A UNIQUE AND VALUABLE QUALITY**

NOTABLE: **TOM MIX (FILM ACTOR; MOSTLY SHORTS)**

January 10–16
DOMINANCE
CAPRICORN III

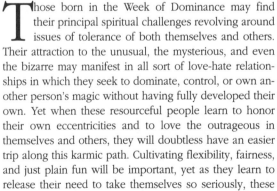

Those born in the Week of Dominance may find their principal spiritual challenges revolving around issues of tolerance of both themselves and others. Their attraction to the unusual, the mysterious, and even the bizarre may manifest in all sort of love-hate relationships in which they seek to dominate, control, or own another person's magic without having fully developed their own. Yet when these resourceful people learn to honor their own eccentricities and to love the outrageous in themselves and others, they will doubtless have an easier trip along this karmic path. Cultivating flexibility, fairness, and just plain fun will be important, yet as they learn to release their need to take themselves so seriously, these powerful people will realize wonderful rewards in almost any area of endeavor they might choose.

CHALLENGE: **HEALING THE SCARS OF CHILDHOOD REPRESSION**

FULFILLMENT: **UNCOVERING AND EMBRACING THEIR ECCENTRIC STREAK**

January 17–22
MYSTERY AND IMAGINATION
CAPRICORN–AQUARIUS CUSP

Another of the wilder configurations, those born on the Cusp of Mystery and Imagination who navigate the Way of Articulation will be blessed with innumerable opportunities for self-expression, expansion, and adventure. Their fear of humiliation or rejection can make them rather touchy or difficult at times, however, and their volatile emotions will boil to the surface in periodic eruptions of volcanic proportion. Yet time is bound to ameliorate their more chaotic energies and channel their inspirations into more productive paths. Their biggest challenge will be not living in a rich fantasy world while enduring a drab and uninspired existence in material reality. Thus, their willingness to use their fantasies to inform and inspire their life choices will be crucial to their happiness, as will gathering the strength to take some risks and gamble on themselves.

CHALLENGE: **CONTROLLING THEIR ERUPTIVE TEMPER RATHER THAN JUSTIFYING IT AS A FORM OF SELF-EXPRESSION**
FULFILLMENT: **RABBLE-ROUSING ON BEHALF OF THOSE LESS FORTUNATE**
NOTABLES: **STONEWALL JACKSON (CONFEDERATE GENERAL DURING U.S. CIVIL WAR); MACK SENNETT (FILM DIRECTOR/ACTOR/PRODUCER OF SILENT FILMS; KEYSTONE KOPS)**

W.C. FIELDS
Early film comedian

1/29/1880
Aquarius I

January 23–30
GENIUS
AQUARIUS I

Those born in the Week of Genius who find themselves on the Way of Articulation are likely to achieve great success, as they are naturally gifted with a fine sense of independence and the relative freedom to march to their own unique rhythms. Thus they will likely have little trouble flying in the face of convention or freeing themselves from fears of rejection or humiliation, at least in the personal sense. In the professional arena, they may have a harder time hitching their wagons to a star, however, and may act out some personal insecurities in issues and conflicts with people in positions of authority. Underachievement in general can be a problem, yet with time and increased confidence, these rugged individualists will surely forge some highly innovative and inspired trails.

CHALLENGE: **APPLYING THEIR DETERMINATION TO ACHIEVE THEIR GOALS OR CAREER SUCCESS, EVEN IN THE FACE OF THEIR IMPULSIVENESS**
FULFILLMENT: **HAVING THE ARTICULATION OF THEIR IDEAS BE LAUDED AS BRILLIANT**
NOTABLES: **ALAN ALDA (TELEVISION/FILM/STAGE ACTOR, MASH; ART); TROY DONAHUE (ACTOR, SURFSIDE SIX)**

January 31–February 7
YOUTH AND EASE
AQUARIUS II

Aquarius II's on the Way of Articulation will doubtless wrestle with the twin demons of approval and acceptance that are so much a part of this configuration. They will sometimes be too forgiving of their own weaknesses and may succumb to complacency or a rather laissez-faire attitude toward personal and spiritual development. Nevertheless, they will always be free spirits at heart, and their innate fascination with the unusual will stand them in fine stead, especially when it leads them to explore and develop some truly virtuoso talents. When they allow their gifts to synthesize with a more refined and mature sense of identity, they will surely make their presence felt in any number of extraordinary creative efforts.

DOUGLAS MACARTHUR
Five-star general in WWII and Korea

1/26/1880
Aquarius I

CHALLENGE: **COMBATING THE TENDENCY TO BE SO ACCEPTING OF THEMSELVES THAT THEY FAIL TO PUSH THEMSELVES TO ACHIEVE**
FULFILLMENT: **ACCEPTING THE RESPONSIBILITY OF MAKING SOMETHING OF THEMSELVES**

February 8–15
ACCEPTANCE
AQUARIUS III

Aquarius III's who make their way along this karmic path may manifest their fascination with the unusual through any number of far-flung pursuits and spiritual or intellectual wanderings. Though many of them will have a needy side, their innate love of the new and their inventiveness will rarely allow them to become unduly bogged down in their fears or hampered in their need for greater freedom. The call to develop greater strength of conviction may also appear as a desire to champion the causes of the weak or downtrodden, even at the risk of being humiliated or derided. Once they access a higher set of principles, it will serve to reinforce their sense of identity in such a way that they will experience a rare level of personal fulfillment on the Way of Articulation, as well as a stimulating and adventuresome journey.

CHALLENGE: **BALANCING THEIR TENDENCY NOT TO BECOME INVOLVED WITH THEIR COMMITMENT TO THEIR CONVICTIONS**
FULFILLMENT: **DEDICATING THEMSELVES TO NURTURING AND FULFILLING ONE OF THEIR INNOVATIVE IDEAS**

February 16–22

SENSITIVITY
AQUARIUS–PISCES CUSP

Personal sensitivity will be a big stumbling block for those born in this week who travel the Way of Articulation, yet they are nevertheless gifted with the kind of gritty determination to overcome even the most overwhelming obstacles to their higher development. Most pronounced will be their tendency to shut down emotionally and concentrate on their career interests, and they may sometimes develop a harsh or even ruthless attitude toward others as they armor themselves against intrusions on their inner worlds. As a result, they often have interior lives that are far removed from their worldly or vocational interests. Their great challenge will be to risk articulating their intuitive and idealistic insights in the interest of integrating their own personalities better. When their sense of the unusual becomes detached from their egos and celebrated, they will know they have finally arrived.

DINAH SHORE
TV/radio host and singer

3/1/1917
Pisces I

CHALLENGE: **GRAPPLING WITH THEIR COMMITMENT PHOBIA**
FULFILLMENT: **FINDING THE COURAGE TO BE VULNERABLE**

February 23–March 2

SPIRIT
PISCES I

Pisces I's who navigate the Way of Articulation may well find that their fascination for the unusual leads them on some rather bizarre quests in the search for a firmer sense of self and stronger convictions. Indeed, some of them may become spiritual or religious groupies, attaching themselves to all sorts of cults and movements before they have a clear idea of what they personally are about. Others may take the lower road and bury their more unconventional aspirations in an excess of sensual indulgence or escapism. Too, their tendency to be too self-sacrificing and the fact that they allow themselves to be taken advantage of by sturdier souls may stunt their potential for expansion. Yet it is likely that their spirituality will prove to be their greatest strength, and if they allow themselves the freedom to find the god that dwells within, the rest is bound to be easy.

CHALLENGE: **WORRYING LESS ABOUT THE ARTICULATION OF BIG IDEAS AND FOCUSING MORE ON THE EXPRESSION OF MUNDANE ONES**
FULFILLMENT: **SHARING THEIR IDEAS ON SERVICE WITH OTHERS**
NOTABLES: **ROBERT LOWELL, JR. (POET, *NOTEBOOK*); DESI ARNAZ (SINGER/ACTOR/PRODUCER, *I LOVE LUCY*); LYTTON STRACHEY (BRITISH BIOGRAPHER; BLOOMSBURY CROWD)**

March 3–10

THE LONER
PISCES II

Those born in the Week of the Loner who travel the Way of Articulation may have little trouble daring to be different but may neglect the higher demands of this karmic path by failing to celebrate and share their uniqueness with others. Their fear of rejection or humiliation can be quite pronounced, and many of them will have to do some serious internal work before they can release the past and move forward. Still, their unique vision may propel them in ways that they may not have counted on, and their more soulful qualities are likely to be especially useful on this karmic path as they search for a firmer and more unassailable sense of identity. Yet on this path more than any other, these returning souls may find the courage to be themselves, only to be blessed with the acceptance of who they are by the rest of us.

JAMES IVES
Publisher,
Currier and Ives

3/5/1824
Pisces II

CHALLENGE: **EMERGING FROM THEIR PERSONAL RETREAT LONG ENOUGH TO ARTICULATE SOMETHING ABOUT THEMSELVES**
FULFILLMENT: **LEARNING TO ACCEPT OTHERS**

March 11–18

DANCERS AND DREAMERS
PISCES III

The Dancers and Dreamers who travel the Way of Articulation are likely to be unusual indeed. Their natural gifts and talents are often so well developed that it may be hard for them to hold themselves back or, in any other way, to consciously hinder their own development. They will experience their share of ups and downs, however, especially if they neglect to nurture their interest in the spiritual side of life and content themselves with appearing "normal" when in fact they are anything but that. On the other side of the coin, smugness or a rather high-handed attitude toward less developed souls can set them back greatly. Whatever the specific manifestations of this configuration, however, these individuals will doubtless be called to strengthen their faith in the unseen workings of the universe and can take comfort in the knowledge that they may well be the favorites of some beneficent god.

CHALLENGE: **NOT FEELING SO SELF-CONFIDENT THAT THEY FAIL TO REVEAL THEMSELVES TO OTHERS**
FULFILLMENT: **SHARING THE WEALTH OF SPIRITUAL INSIGHT THEY SEEM TO ABSORB—ALMOST VIA OSMOSIS!**

The Way of Mastery

CANCER III TO CAPRICORN III
Persuader to Dominance

Those on this karmic path are here to lay claim to an area of expertise and make it their own. Although money and ambition are attractive to those on the Way of Mastery, their orientation is not necessarily materialistic. Rather, their goal is to develop a talent or skill to a level of mastery. Achieving such a lofty aim often requires these people to renounce or sacrifice other desires or interests in order to give all their energy to their prime focus. A strange blend of idealist and realist, reserve and extroversion, and the serious and comic, they are able to focus on their goal with savage intensity. Those who get in their way are likely to be trampled underfoot, usually unintentionally. However, once they perfect themselves in their chosen skill or master a particular talent, these individuals have an even more difficult task, since true mastery requires manifesting a unique vision or utilizing their talent in a unique way. Thus, ideas, ideals, and creative vision are important since they must be made into solid reality or utilized as a philosophical backdrop for the individuals on this karmic path to create form from purpose or concept. Their souls come from a place of deep subconscious awareness of the imaginal realms, the waters of life from which all creativity springs. Their task is to mold or craft such an oceanic perspective into a practical one by dispensing with the emotion attached to it, engaging only the core ideas that they fish out of those waters, and applying them to a practical end.

Honing a skill to the level of craft requires that those on the Way of Mastery embark on a path that can be likened to the artisan guilds of yore, beginning one's education in a specific field, first apprenticing oneself to a master, then graduating to more and more responsibility, and ultimately becoming a master oneself. Although the guild system is no longer operative, it serves as a model of education for those on the Way of Mastery. Once the individuals on this karmic path select an area of study, it behooves them to find a mentor akin to the masters of yore and to learn their skill from them. Searching for, engaging, and interacting with such an individual is a necessary basis of learning the mastery called for by this karmic path. Coming into this lifetime with the skills of observation and persuasion, these men and women will need to enlist both to find the best teacher for them. First, by keeping their eyes open, they will need to discover who in their circle has the talent and the capacity to serve as a mentor. Then they will have to engage their gift of persuasion to talk that particular person into taking them on and, in so doing, sharing all the secrets that they possess of their profession or field.

For the men and women who travel it, this karmic path also means that, once expertise is acquired, the apprentice must eventually leave the mentor behind in order to move on to make his or her own mark in the field. Patience is key, for it will often take years to master a craft. Thus, com-

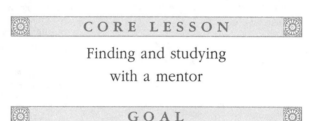

CORE LESSON
Finding and studying
with a mentor

GOAL
Mastering a craft or art

GIFTS
Diligent, Persistent, Persuasive

PITFALLS
Domineering, Insecure,
Solitary

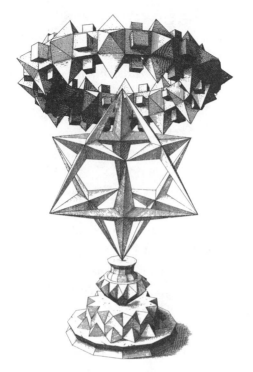

ing into one's own on this path usually requires the ability to have the "long breath." Fortunately, those on the Way of Mastery come into this life blessed with tremendous diligence and dedication. Part of the process over the longer haul is for them to transform their self-image from one of student to one of a mature master. No matter how long it takes, when the time comes for them to go out on their own, they will know it. They will also know precisely how to put their hard-won craft to the best use.

Once they have mastered their craft by working humbly with an older and wiser person, negotiated the delicate process of leaving their mentor behind, and hung out their own shingle, so to speak, those on this karmic path will proceed smoothly and successfully in cultivating professional success. Having the native talent to persuade others, they will be good at marketing themselves. However, they are less interested in using their persuasiveness to manipulate opinion and more in presenting their work or product in the best light, letting its quality speak for itself. The next stage of maturity for these individuals may be tapping into their own Cancer III roots by learning how to return to the well of creative inspiration in order to replenish their supply of ideas. Those who walk this karmic path will come to understand what they were taught when they were young, that is, that craft is just one part of the process required for

RELEASE

The tendency to workaholism

REWARD

The joy of perfecting
one's craft

success and fulfillment; the other is finding a unique expression of that craft.

At their Cancer III root, these individuals are often stimulated by an underlying insecurity that pushes them to achieve—or overachieve. However, the Capricorn III desire for success is fueled by a different force, that of a need to overcome obstacles. Thus, implicit in this karmic path is an urge to dominate. Those on the Way of Mastery must beware of allowing the negative aspects of their insecurity to overwhelm their personality. One lesson that must be learned by those on this karmic path is how to proceed with grace and dignity and to mature calmly in the knowledge that they will reach their goal. Otherwise, their insecurity may express itself as an overblown ego, putting off those who might help them on their way. As much as those on the Way of Mastery may love to dominate their field, this is not a path of leadership. The more successful of them will restrict their professional efforts to objective pursuits, whether commercial or artistic, that do not necessarily involve directing other people. They are much more successful at perfecting their own techniques and methods than telling others what to do, except in exceptional circumstances. The best thing for them is to work on their own. These men and women are able to challenge themselves over and over again and have no need for external stimulation to urge them forward. It is likely that in later

SUGGESTION

Try to be kinder to yourself by occasionally lowering your standards. Remember to indulge in fantasy and to cultivate your imagination once in a while.

years they will themselves become teachers or mentors, thereby completing a karmic circle by sharing what was given to them early in their lives.

Those on this path generally set very high standards, not only for themselves and the quality of their work but also for others. Thus, their interpersonal relationships are often fraught with overly high expectations. They do best when attracting others of equal ability with whom they can work on their projects. Although many will place those on the Way of Mastery on a pedestal, rarely will this go to their heads, since they have a need to prove themselves again and again in their own eyes and those of their associates. They thrive not only on the responsibility of being a role model but also on demonstrating their ability to give of themselves in a warmhearted manner. They will always be acutely aware of how they appear to others and will cherish their image highly. The importance of their commitment to the standards of their craft and life is one that they gradually realize on their path; they value it highly, and it often becomes the cornerstone of their existence. Probably the hardest thing for them is being thought badly of by others or having accusations of shoddy

BALANCE POINT

Craft and Inspiration

workmanship or underhanded or immoral methods leveled against them.

A social forum for their ideas or work, whether comprised of professional colleagues or just plain friends, is just the ticket for these work-oriented individuals. In fact, in some cases it is a basic requirement for their happiness and fulfillment. They do have a rather charming "common touch" that often grants them the ability to make others laugh, or at the very least smile, at their characterization of human foibles. It is undeniable that those on the Way of Mastery will rarely surrender their need to focus their all on their work. Thus, they may give up on meeting one single life partner. So much of their energy is shared with colleagues, friends, and followers that the dynamics of such relationships can often satisfy their social and personal needs fully.

The image that best describes this karmic path is that of a student and a Zen master. The student tries to attract the master's attention and gain his approval, but to no avail. Only the student himself can achieve enlightenment, after being guided by the master or awakened by a sharp intuitive slap. Subsequently, the student takes the master's place.

CRYSTALS AND GEMSTONES

Fluorite dispels ambivalence and encourages the individual to joyfully strive for mastery. This crystal helps one to move beyond the limits of perfectionism to experience the bliss of the mind/heart connection.

 NOTABLES ON THIS KARMIC PATH

Epitomizing the best in broadcast journalism for a generation, **Walter Cronkite** was a true master in his field. Hardworking to a fault like many on the Way of Mastery, he managed to be on top of practically every breaking news story during his long career. In front of the camera, Cronkite's pitch was at once

WALTER CRONKITE

friendly and forceful, containing just enough aloofness to preclude any appearance of personal interest or prejudice. His unique blend of idealism and realism, the serious and comic endeared him to viewers. Crafting his reporting to perfection, Cronkite persuaded millions due to the amicable objectivity and adherence to high standards that are typical of this path.

FREDERICK THE GREAT

Having established Prussia as a strong and modern German state in the eighteenth century, **Frederick the Great** has been considered by many to be a master of the art of war. However, he was also a commentator on society and culture; his works and letters fill numerous volumes, attesting to his intellectual abilities, and his close relationship with the Bach family displays his love of music. Early on, Frederick turned to books for education and inspiration, rejecting the authority of his father. Due to this initiative, Frederick was able to develop the diverse skills possessed by an enlightened ruler, allowing him to preside over Prussia for forty-eight years.

Though he seemed to make one of the most surprising comebacks in film history due to the success of *Pulp Fiction,* in truth **John Travolta** spent many years perfecting his craft. From his early days as an actor on the television show *Welcome Back, Kotter* to his success as a disco dancer on *Saturday Night Fever* to *Look Who's Talking,* he diligently worked his way through all manner of roles to emerge in the nineties as a major star. As is character-

JOHN TRAVOLTA

istic of successful individuals on this path, he was able to focus his talent, and, by winning roles of increasing depth, display the growing maturity of his acting ability.

Other Notables: Ludwig Bemelmans, Vernon Jordan, Alexandra David-Neel, Hans Christian Andersen, Paul Robeson, Golda Meir, Bennett Cerf, Norman Vincent Peale, Federico García Lorca, Christo, Frieda Lawrence, Cameron Diaz, Roald Dahl, James Herriot, François Mitterrand, Kim Basinger, Betty Grable, Howard Stern, Oprah Winfrey, Matt Groening, Alfred North Whitehead, Ron Howard, Rudolf Steiner

---

BIRTHDAYS ON KARMIC PATH 16

January 27, 1898–June 16, 1898 | September 8, 1916–January 27, 1917

April 21, 1935–September 8, 1935 | November 30, 1953–April 19, 1954 | July 11, 1972–November 29, 1972

February 20, 1991–July 11, 1991 | October 2, 2009–February 19, 2010

KARMIC PATH
16

March 19–24
REBIRTH
PISCES–ARIES CUSP

Those born on the Cusp of Rebirth who travel the Way of Mastery are afforded a fine opportunity for success, as this karmic path gifts them with a greater practical sense and a more stable outlook than they might ordinarily have had. Though they will still have to work to regulate their tendency to emotional excess and may chafe a bit at the restrictions and discipline required, the slow development and painstaking craftsmanship called for by this karmic path is bound to serve them well as they turn their dreams into tangible reality. While they will have to work to avoid bluntness or tactlessness in any number of situations as well as to cultivate greater refinement, they can do especially well in careers that involve group endeavors, and in many cases this karmic path will lead to their stepping into a leadership role after years of dedication to a family business or traditional craft.

CHALLENGE: **FINDING A SOCIAL FORUM FOR THEIR WORK**
FULFILLMENT: **WORKING TO PERFECT ONE CRAFT OR TALENT**
NOTABLE: **GEORGE ALPERT (RAILROAD EXECUTIVE)**

HANS CHRISTIAN ANDERSEN
Writer, known for children's tales, *The Ugly Duckling*

4/2/1805
Aries I

March 25–April 2
THE CHILD
ARIES I

Those born in the Week of the Child who travel the Way of Mastery will be aided in their quest for personal and spiritual advancement by their boundless curiosity. Settling down and focusing their considerable energies may pose a problem for some of them, though time will be on their side. Too, Aries I's crave respect and greater stature, as well as responsibility. On this karmic path, they will be able to realize those aspirations, and once they have established themselves in a chosen field, they will have little trouble breaking away from the security of a larger organization or particular individual in order to pursue their vocation. If they can temper their great idealism with practical knowledge, they will achieve much on this life journey.

CHALLENGE: **TEMPERING THEIR DISPLAYS OF TEMPER, PARTICULARLY IN THE WORKPLACE**
FULFILLMENT: **PARTICIPATING IN PROFESSIONAL ORGANIZATIONS**
NOTABLE: **CURTIS SLIWA (SOCIAL ACTIVIST; FOUNDED GUARDIAN ANGELS, 1979)**

April 3–10
THE STAR
ARIES II

The Stars who find themselves on the Way of Mastery may find it difficult to adjust to the need to take a backseat from time to time, gain greater knowledge, and simply pay their dues. The road to the top may not be entirely comfortable for them, yet they will respond to the promise of respect and authority that beckon. While some on this journey may content themselves with being big fish in relatively small ponds or in focusing their considerable powers on trying to make other people execute their plans and schemes, most will rise to the greater challenge and direct their talents and energies with an eye to the bigger prizes offered by this karmic path. Success-oriented, sometimes in the extreme, Aries II's will realize fine fulfillment here, providing they don't demand too much too soon.

CHALLENGE: **BEING WILLING TO WORK UNDER A MASTER**
FULFILLMENT: **PUTTING THEIR ENERGY INTO HARD WORK AND REALIZING ITS REWARDS**
NOTABLES: **DENNIS QUAID (ACTOR, *THE BIG EASY*); HENRY R. LUCE (*TIME, LIFE* PUBLISHER)**

PAUL ROBESON
Actor/singer/activist, blacklisted as Communist

4/9/1898
Aries II

April 11–18
THE PIONEER
ARIES III

Those born in the Week of the Pioneer who find themselves on the Way of Mastery are blessed with the natural inclination to fire even their most mundane endeavors with passion, dedication, and enthusiasm. Whatever their specific calling, they will be well suited to the social demands of this karmic path, and will doubtless approach their period of apprenticeship with openness and a willingness to draw on the wisdom and talents of those who are able to guide them toward greater independence. In fact, they would do well not to go overboard in a tendency to make themselves indispensable, thus failing to further their development. Yet their intensely positive attitude is sure to buoy them over some of the rougher spots on this journey, and if they are careful to exercise good timing, all will go brilliantly.

CHALLENGE: **NOT SACRIFICING THEIR FURTHER DEVELOPMENT BECAUSE THEY FEEL NEEDED**
FULFILLMENT: **GOING OUT ON THEIR OWN WHEN THE TIME COMES**

April 19–24
POWER
ARIES–TAURUS CUSP

Those born on the Cusp of Power who travel the Way of Mastery are wonderfully blessed, as the energies involved on this karmic path can synthesize in sometimes extraordinary ways. Their natural sense of timing and their ability to wait for what they want while quietly honing and enhancing their skills are especially pronounced. However, there is a danger that they may expend all their energies on career interests to the detriment of their higher development, and they would do well to stay in close touch with the considerable subconscious energy and guidance that are part of their spiritual endowment. Too, an inclination to be rather mercenary or even downright greedy may manifest itself. As a result, some of them will encounter a number of opportunities to learn or study that are less than financially rewarding, yet ought not to be overlooked in the grander scheme of their long-term aspirations.

LUDWIG BEMELMANS
Writer, *Madeline*
children's stories

4/27/1898
Taurus I

CHALLENGE: **KEEPING A WEATHER EYE ON THEIR MORE MER-CENARY TENDENCIES**
FULFILLMENT: **ENJOYING THE SELF-ASSURANCE THAT MAS-TERY BRINGS**

April 25–May 2
MANIFESTATION
TAURUS I

Taurus I's who navigate the Way of Mastery are likely to find it an especially fulfilling journey. Tenacious in the extreme, they are blessed with a unique ability to get wherever it is that they want to go, though their way of doing so will doubtless be in the manner more of the tortoise than of the hare. Yet there is a danger that these protective, nurturing people will do themselves a disservice by getting caught up in the wants or needs of others and fail to get adequately in touch with the necessity for self-realization. Too, their rather rigid adherence to tradition may cause them to fail to take the necessary risks in the quest for greater independence and fulfillment. Yet all other things being equal, they will realize considerable security and material reward along this path.

CHALLENGE: **LEARNING HOW TO SHARE THE WORKLOAD**
FULFILLMENT: **MANIFESTING OR GIVING SHAPE TO A BODY OF WORK**
NOTABLE: **PEHR GYLLENHAMMAR (CHAIRMAN VOLVO AB)**

May 3–10
THE TEACHER
TAURUS II

If the saying that what we teach is what we have to learn is true, it was never more so than it is for Taurus II's who travel the Way of Mastery. Enterprising by nature, they will nevertheless have to learn to cultivate considerable depth in a specific area in order to realize their highest potential. Moreover, they are infinitely more comfortable in the role of teacher than student, yet if they set aside issues of ego and personal insecurity and actively seek out the tutelage they need to become the experts they want to be, their passage will be eased considerably. Concentrating their energies away from the purely theoretical and onto the realm of tangible products and results will also be helpful, as will an ability to control the demands they tend to make on others.

GOLDA MEIR
Israeli prime minister

5/3/1898
Taurus II

CHALLENGE: **RELAXING THEIR STANDARDS AND WORKING TO BE LESS CRITICAL OF THEMSELVES AND OTHERS**
FULFILLMENT: **LEADING BY EXAMPLE**
NOTABLE: **DANIEL GERBER (INVENTED STRAINED BABY FOOD, 1928; BUSINESS EXECUTIVE)**

May 11–18
THE NATURAL
TAURUS III

Those born in the Week of the Natural who travel the Way of Mastery may find it somewhat difficult to get their bearings, and a number of perpetual students can be found among those with this configuration. Yet success is definitely possible, providing they can find not only the right teacher or mentor but the right environment in which to display and enhance their gifts. Though rebelliousness can be a special sticking point, these people bring a great sense of fun and adventure to this karmic path, and if they are careful not to resist its restrictions, nor to scatter their energies in less-than-productive activities, they can acquire a level of knowledge and understanding that will far surpass their expectations.

CHALLENGE: **REFUSING TO GIVE IN TO THEIR TENDENCY TO CHAFE UNDER AUTHORITY**
FULFILLMENT: **FINDING MASTERY IN AN ENTREPRENEURIAL FIELD**
NOTABLES: **FELIPE ALOU (BASEBALL MANAGER); ARTHUR SEYMOUR SULLIVAN (COMPOSER; GILBERT AND SULLIVAN)**

May 19–24

ENERGY
TAURUS–GEMINI CUSP

Those born on the Cusp of Energy who find themselves on this karmic path will doubtless have the necessary charm, persuasive talents, and personal charisma to attract the mentors and teachers they need to find fulfillment but will experience a number of difficulties when it comes to finding the focus they need for real success. Perhaps their greatest challenge will be to accept that the Way of Mastery has endowed them with great endurance and to stop resisting that quality in themselves. Slowing down and cultivating patience and inner calm will be especially beneficial, as will adapting themselves to some degree of limitation in the interest of their long-term objectives. yet if they can avoid the temptations of perpetual studenthood, dilettantism, or the need to be the center of attention before they have fully prepared themselves to assume the roles and responsibilities of mastery, their diligence will be rewarded with some memorable achievements.

CHALLENGE: **DEVELOPING THE CAPACITY TO FOCUS OVER THE LONG HAUL**

FULFILLMENT: **LEARNING ABOUT THE VALUE OF STRUCTURE**

NORMAN VINCENT PEALE
Religious leader/author,
Power of Positive Thinking

5/31/1898
Gemini I

May 25–June 2

FREEDOM
GEMINI I

Those born in the Week of Freedom may find the Way of Mastery a bit rocky at times. Yet they bring a fine gift for technical proficiency and considerable intelligence to this life journey, and if they are careful to control their sometimes combative natures with discipline, focus, and simple patience, they can ease their passage to a great degree. Also, their inventive minds have a tendency to send them off on any number of tangents, and they may experience quite a number of ups and down until they learn to finish what they start. Yet the Way of Mastery will doubtless gift them with a greater degree of tenacity than they might otherwise have had. As long as they apply that energy to their own higher development and accept that task as their only real preoccupation, time will reward them with both the perspective and the patience required for genuine material and spiritual accomplishment.

CHALLENGE: **OVERCOMING THEIR TENDENCY TO TURN ON THE CHARM TO GET OUT OF RESPONSIBILITY**

FULFILLMENT: **FINDING THE RIGHT MEDIUM FOR THEIR TALENT**

NOTABLE: **BENNETT CERF (COFOUNDED RANDOM HOUSE)**

June 3–10

NEW LANGUAGE
GEMINI II

The uniquely personal perspective of Gemini II's who find themselves on the Way of Mastery is bound to manifest itself in some communicative art or calling. Curiously, the energies here can be quite compatible, providing they don't allow themselves to become mired in purely emotional, mundane, or petty concerns and direct their talents to their own higher challenges and development. Restricting themselves to more objective concerns and pursuits, will be essential, as it will free them from their chronic need to feel that they are understood and afford them opportunities to "do their own thing" without being overly concerned about what others may think or say about it. As a result, they will make better journalists than poets, metaphorically speaking, though perhaps their greatest challenge will be attaining the level of expertise in their chosen field, where facts can be presented with poetic elegance or poetry with the clarity of truth.

CHALLENGE: **TAKING CARE NOT TO INDULGE IN A SOLITARY KIND OF INSECURITY**

FULFILLMENT: **HONING THEIR TALENT FOR COMMUNICATION**

NOTABLE: **FEDERICO GARCÍA LORCA (POET; ASSASSINATED)**

GENE WILDER
Actor/comedian,
Willy Wonka and the Chocolate Factory

6/11/1935
Gemini III

June 11–18

THE SEEKER
GEMINI III

Though many born in this week who travel the Way of Mastery may chafe at the sense of restriction this life journey may represent, they will possess an instinct for enlightenment that will stand them in excellent stead. In fact, getting to the bottom of things or ferreting out the truth or essence of a particular subject or calling may be something of an obsession for them. If they can only focus their energies on a single topic and strive to deepen their understanding of it, their karmic task will have been achieved. Hooking up with a mentor or mentors is second nature to many of them, yet they will have to cultivate patience and personal discipline in order to make those relationships work for any length of time. Yet if these souls do not succumb to the belief that their road to success lies in their ability to "talk a good game" and accept that mastery requires thoroughness, diligence, and dedication, they can find fulfillment here.

CHALLENGE: **CULTIVATING A MORE EXACTING APPROACH TO A TOPIC**

FULFILLMENT: **BROADENING THE UNDERSTANDING THAT COMES WITH MASTERY**

NOTABLE: **CHRISTO (ARTIST WHO WRAPS BUILDINGS, LANDMARKS)**

June 19–24

MAGIC
GEMINI–CANCER CUSP

Those born on the Cusp of Magic who travel the Way of Mastery will have a genius for attracting the people and situations they need in order to find fulfillment along the way. Yet as gifted as these people can be at getting what they want out of life, they will almost certainly discover that there is a difference between magic and real mastery. Therein lies the rub for these rather remarkable people. Like the sorcerer's apprentice, they can sometimes become distracted or unduly enchanted by their ability to manifest their inner aspirations. Yet they will be required to learn to exercise a degree of control and self-discipline in the interest of developing a higher level of wisdom and development. If they turn their energies into the search for the right teacher and away from the seduction of believing that natural talent is the same thing as expertise, they will make marvelous progress along this road.

PETE HAMILL
American journalist

6/24/1935
Gemini–Cancer Cusp

CHALLENGE: **NOT BEING SIDETRACKED BY ROMANCE**
FULFILLMENT: **BECOMING INVENTIVE ONCE THEY HAVE MASTERED A TOPIC OR SKILL**

June 25–July 2

THE EMPATH
CANCER I

Life is likely to be kind to Cancer I's who travel the Way of Mastery, especially when their education in the profession or field of their choice begins early. A willingness to discipline their natural sensitivity and emotionalism and channel their energies in less personal and more objective ways will prove especially necessary for these individuals, as they can waste time and effort by becoming overly wrapped up in the cares and woes of the world. Learning to value their sense of ambition and make hard choices in the interest of success are skills they can gain in their period of apprenticeship, though many with this configuration may find it especially hard to break away from a favorite teacher, mentor, or boss in order to give full expression to their powers. Once they do, however, they are likely to go far, as long as they don't go overboard with repressed emotions, aggression, and a rather tyrannical or domineering attitude toward those under their protection.

CHALLENGE: **TAKING CARE THAT WHEN THEY WITHDRAW, IT IS TO WORK, NOT TO HIDE**
FULFILLMENT: **FOSTERING THEIR BUSINESS ACUMEN**

July 3–10

THE UNCONVENTIONAL
CANCER II

Whatever the obstacles on their path toward higher development and a sense of mastery, Cancer II's are likely to overcome them in a unique fashion. In fact, these people can bring a real sense of fun to this life journey and will doubtless be possessed of a lighter heart and generally less dour attitude toward achievement than many of their fellow travelers on this karmic path. Their natural affinity for unconventional people will lead them to find the right person to aid them in their development, but the circumstances that will bring them together with a mentor may be marked by a confluence of unusual circumstances, events, or conflicts. Personal discipline and proper training will aid them in turning their often wild ideas and fantasies into tangible reality, yet they may not be marked for material abundance and reward until they bite the proverbial bullet and tough out a few lean years.

DIAHANN CARROLL
Actress/singer,
Julia and *Dynasty*

7/17/1935
Cancer III

CHALLENGE: **FEEDING THEIR NEED TO ESCAPE BY STRUCTURING REGULAR, PERIODIC VACATIONS**
FULFILLMENT: **DEVELOPING A FEW CLOSE ASSOCIATIONS WITH THOSE IN THEIR FIELD OR A SIMILAR ONE**
NOTABLES: **OTTORINO RESPIGHI (ITALIAN COMPOSER; PROFESSOR); STEVE LAWRENCE (SINGER)**

July 11–18

THE PERSUADER
CANCER III

As good as they are at getting people to do what they want them to do, Cancer III's on the Way of Mastery may not achieve real success until they relinquish their considerable powers of persuasion in the interests of learning to achieve for themselves. "God bless the child that's got his own" may turn out to be a sort of spiritual anthem for these individuals, as they will discover not only fulfillment but a degree of self-realization and even a sense of dominance on this karmic path. As observant as they are, Cancer III's will have little trouble finding the mentor called for. Moreover, if they can set aside their personal needs, these powerful personalities will be able to focus sufficiently to attain the mastery that is their destiny.

CHALLENGE: **SETTING ASIDE THEIR MORE SENSITIVE SELVES**
FULFILLMENT: **UTILIZING THEIR POWERS OF OBSERVATION**
NOTABLE: **ALEX KARRAS (FOOTBALL PLAYER-TURNED-ACTOR)**

July 19–25

OSCILLATION
CANCER–LEO CUSP

This life journey may be rather bumpy for Cancer–Leos, until they learn to distinguish between a sense of personal frustration and a healthy dose of self-imposed structure. Though these dynamic and often ambitious people may see the path to their success quite clearly and undertake their educational and material tasks quite willingly, the resulting restrictions may cause inner conflicts that are difficult to handle. These volatile people may become impatient with themselves or their teachers and may do themselves a disservice through emotional meltdowns that only serve to delay their progress and development. Curiously, the less they repress or bottle up their emotions in the course of their apprenticeship, allowing themselves to blow off steam once in a while, the more likely they are to find the sense of control and mastery they crave, for this is one instance where the occasional small fire can offset the danger of larger, more destructive conflagrations.

CHALLENGE: **GROUNDING THEIR CRAVING FOR EXCITEMENT THROUGH SELF-DISCIPLINE**

FULFILLMENT: **PROPELLING THEMSELVES INTO INNOVATIVE FORMS OF THEIR CRAFT**

BEN AFFLECK
Actor/writer,
Good Will Hunting

8/15/1972
Leo III

July 26–August 2

AUTHORITY
LEO I

Blind ambition may prove the principal pitfall for those born in the Week of Authority who find themselves on the Way of Mastery. Though clearly destined for success and a high level of achievement, Leo I's may well resist the call to the more methodical development of their talents called for by this karmic path. Also, they may misuse their gifts not by dominating but by domineering over others. Still, they are blessed with a deep respect for authority, and that is sure to aid them in their search for the right teacher or mentor to aid their development. Though they will occasionally have to swallow their considerable pride as they navigate this karmic path, they are sure to realize great progress.

CHALLENGE: **REINING IN ANY PROPENSITY TO DISPLAYS OF EGO**

FULFILLMENT: **CHALLENGING THEMSELVES TO ACHIEVE THEIR PERSONAL BEST**

NOTABLE: **ALFRED MARSHALL (FOUNDER OF NEOCLASSIC ECONOMICS)**

August 3–10

BALANCED STRENGTH
LEO II

Marked by an often extreme single-mindedness, Leo II's who find themselves on the Way of Mastery may indeed achieve great things. The discipline and focus required to attain real expertise are very much in keeping with their natural gifts and strengths, yet they will have to moderate their sense of personal ambition to the extent that they occasionally allow themselves to stop and smell the roses. If they don't, they may well become experts of a rather insufferable variety, unable to function in any area but their own narrow field of interest. Interaction with their mentor of choice can do much to mellow these individuals, however, and if they can somehow manage to acquire their professional education within the context of a more personal relationship, so much the better.

CHALLENGE: **NOT NEGLECTING THEIR INTUITIVE SIDE IN THEIR QUEST FOR DOMINANCE**

FULFILLMENT: **BEING TRUE TO THEMSELVES AND THEIR GOALS**

FRIEDA WEEKELY
Married to D .H. Lawrence

8/11/1879
Leo III

August 11–18

LEADERSHIP
LEO III

The impulse toward leadership may sometimes exist at odds with the journey toward the simple mastery of a profession called for by this karmic path. Leo III's on the Way of Mastery may have to work rather hard to reconcile themselves to the plain necessity of paying their dues before they can realize this journey's rewards. These people may well experience several periods of defining and redefining their expectations of success as they make their way along this road, and some may have to learn to content themselves with less in the short term in order to realize a higher level of reward further down the line. Though that will not come easily for these dynamic people, their education will be well worth their investments in time and patience and may result in the kind of expertise and authority that are all the more valuable for their humble wisdom.

CHALLENGE: **RECOGNIZING AND RESPECTING THEIR BETTERS**

FULFILLMENT: **KNOWING THAT THEIR EXPERTISE HAS BEEN EARNED THE HARD WAY**

NOTABLES: **ETHEL BARRYMORE (ACADEMY AWARD-WINNING ACTRESS); VERNON JORDAN (ADVISER TO PRESIDENT CLINTON)**

August 19–25

EXPOSURE
LEO–VIRGO CUSP

These people are a study in contrasting personality traits. Both introvert and extrovert, idealist and realist, the Leo–Virgos who find themselves on the Way of Mastery are assured of an interesting passage. Curiously enough, individuals with this configuration may find one level of professional success early on, then abandon that area of interest completely in order to apprentice themselves in an entirely different field, often to the dismay of friends, families, or close associates. Yet if life is about process and becoming more completely who one is, Leo–Virgos will rarely fail to rise to that challenge, and whatever their changes or choices, they will remain self-assured, even if they must, on occasion, stand alone.

CAMERON DIAZ
Actress, *There's Something About Mary*

8/30/1972
Virgo I

CHALLENGE: **LEARNING HOW TO ACKNOWLEDGE WHAT THEIR REAL PLANS FOR THEMSELVES ARE**

FULFILLMENT: **SUCCESSFULLY DEVELOPING A MENTOR-MENTEE RELATIONSHIP, OR EVEN SEVERAL OF THEM**

NOTABLES: **KING LUDWIG I OF BAVARIA (PATRON OF COMPOSER WAGNER); ANNIE PROULX (AUTHOR)**

August 26–September 2

SYSTEM BUILDERS
VIRGO I

System Builders who navigate the Way of Mastery may well experience a truly rewarding passage, as they like nothing better than exerting sustained effort and applying their talents in a practical way. In fact, the principal danger is that they may settle into a specific career area without having first sought out the necessary education or mentor to aid them in their development. As a result, their progress may be delayed a bit, but progress they almost certainly will. On the other side of the coin, however, they are service-oriented by nature and may fail to make the necessary break from the security of a boss or mentor in order to manifest their own unique vision. Yet, all things being equal, their journey along the Way of Mastery should prove to be an easy one.

CHALLENGE: **BREAKING FREE FROM THE YOKE OF APPRENTICESHIP AT THE RIGHT TIME**

FULFILLMENT: **SATISFYING THEIR DRIVE FOR TECHNICAL ACHIEVEMENT**

NOTABLES: **SEIJI OZAWA (LONGTIME CONDUCTOR OF BOSTON SYMPHONY); JOHN PHILLIPS (SINGER, THE MAMAS AND THE PAPAS); FRANK ROBINSON (BASEBALL PLAYER/MANAGER); GERALDINE FERRARO (VICE-PRESIDENTIAL CANDIDATE)**

September 3–10

THE ENIGMA
VIRGO II

Virgo II's who travel the Way of Mastery are earmarked for considerable rewards and achievement. Gifted with a knack for knowing the right thing to do in almost any circumstance, their high standards and innate moral and ethical sense will stand them in good stead as they move toward the upper echelons of mastery—whether of themselves, their careers, or their immediate environment. They are so self-contained, however, that they may fail to ask for help when they need it most, and they may have to sacrifice some of their false pride before they can find the proper guide. Nonetheless, these practical and thoughtful people are blessed with all the natural resources to achieve their fondest dreams and ambitions, and if they recognize early that they don't necessarily have to go it alone, their path to success is ensured.

ROALD DAHL
Writer, *Charlie and the Chocolate Factory*

9/13/1916
Virgo III

CHALLENGE: **KNOWING WHEN TO ASK FOR HELP**

FULFILLMENT: **PUTTING THEIR HIGH STANDARDS TO WORK IN THE MANIFESTATION OF THEIR TALENTS**

NOTABLE: **CAROL LAWRENCE (SINGER/ACTRESS, STAGE VERSION *WEST SIDE STORY*)**

September 11–18

THE LITERALIST
VIRGO III

The Literalists who journey along the Way of Mastery have both time and natural persistence on their side, yet they will have to make some strides in overcoming their tendency to be too demanding before they can realize the promise of this karmic path. Though they will almost certainly be quite nurturing, they may neglect their personal ambitions and higher sense of aspiration in the interest of keeping any number of unproductive relationships alive. Objectifying their point of view will be most beneficial, as will developing the ability to assert themselves in the interest of personal ambition and advancement. Practical and patient, these people can realize all their fondest dreams with this configuration and are especially suited to the levels of elegant craftsmanship, tangible products, and expert vocations and avocations that are elements of this karmic path.

CHALLENGE: **REMEMBERING TO NOURISH THEIR CREATIVITY AND MORE SOULFUL SIDE**

FULFILLMENT: **PURSUING THEIR CRAFT ALONE**

NOTABLE: **FRIEDRICH VON STEUBEN (GERMAN-BORN SOLDIER IN AMERICAN REVOLUTION; PREPARED STILL-USED MANUAL OF TACTICS FOR ARMY)**

September 19–24

BEAUTY
VIRGO–LIBRA CUSP

High idealism may mark the ambitions of the people born this week who travel the Way of Mastery, yet many of them will experience some difficulty in bringing their ambitions down to the level of practical application that is required. As a result, they may flounder a bit until they successfully attach themselves to a master or expert in their chosen field. Even then, it may prove difficult for them to break away and pursue their own work, especially when the presence of a mentor or teacher serves to ground them in a comforting sense of security. Yet many of them will realize progress and accomplishment on this life journey, as long as they keep in mind that even the most pleasant of ivory towers can seem like a prison if one's spirit is unnourished or one's deepest needs are unsatisfied.

CHALLENGE: **NOT BEING SATISFIED WITH EASY OR GLOSSED-OVER APPROACHES TO THEIR WORK**

FULFILLMENT: **MANIFESTING THEIR UNIQUE VISION OF BEAUTY**

September 25–October 2

THE PERFECTIONIST
LIBRA I

The Perfectionists who travel the Way of Mastery will find themselves quite happy and fulfilled along this life journey, providing they channel their knack for detail work into a sense of higher aspiration and accomplishment. Likely to be very vocal, especially when it comes to voicing their complaints and dissatisfactions, they will do themselves a disservice if they alienate those who can help them the most along the road through pickiness, standoffishness, or a secret belief that they know more than their teachers. Cultivating humility in the face of mastery and using that knowledge to nurture their sense of standards, rather than allowing those standards to frustrate their deepest desires, will be of great benefit, as will a willingness to back up and take a longer, more objective look at the world and its eccentricities.

CHALLENGE: **MANAGING THEIR OFTEN NEGLECTED EMOTIONS BY INDULGING IN FANTASY OR PLAY NOW AND THEN**

FULFILLMENT: **WORKING WITH A TEACHER WHOM THEY TRULY RESPECT**

JAMES HERRIOT
Veterinary surgeon, *All Creatures Great and Small*

10/3/1916
Libra II

October 3–10

SOCIETY
LIBRA II

Whatever the life choices for those born in the Week of Society who travel the Way of Mastery, they are likely to be tinged with a high degree of creative instinct and intuitive knowledge. Though some on this path may falter until they learn to take themselves and their ambitions more seriously, once they have chosen a particular area of endeavor they are likely to do very well, as long as they do not allow themselves to be distracted from their heart's calling by the needs of others. In fact, many with this configuration can really blossom by virtue of association with the right teacher, though the relationship may hit some rough spots if they allow their direction to be changed or their progress stalled by an overly dominant mentor.

CHALLENGE: **KEEPING A WARY EYE ON THEIR TENDENCY TO SELF-DECEPTION—ESPECIALLY IN THEIR CHOICE OF A TEACHER**

FULFILLMENT: **ENJOYING THE SOLITARY PURSUIT OF THEIR AESTHETIC GOALS**

October 11–18

THEATER
LIBRA III

Those born in the Week of Theater who travel the Way of Mastery may feel as though their talent for leadership, along with their natural charisma, have them "all dressed up with nowhere to go." Indeed, it may be quite difficult for them to align themselves with the demands of this karmic path and cultivate the slow, patient attitude that is necessary for success. Yet Libra III's are blessed with the hardheadedness, worldly knowledge, and cool detachment that are useful on the Way of Mastery. Thus, these naturally confident people will realize great success if they are careful not to succumb to the pitfalls of recklessness, ruthlessness, and their general tendency to be overbearing when they would do better to be modest and kind.

CHALLENGE: **ACCEPTING THE BURDEN OF EXPECTATION THAT A MENTOR IS LIKELY TO PLACE ON THEM**

FULFILLMENT: **APPLYING THEIR HARD-DRIVING BRAND OF AMBITION TO MASTERY IN THEIR FIELD**

GRANT HILL
Basketball player,
Detroit Pistons

10/5/1972
Libra II

October 19–25

DRAMA AND CRITICISM
LIBRA–SCORPIO CUSP

These individuals may be possessed of a sense of overriding ambition that subsumes all other considerations, and their large personalities may have a bit of trouble fitting into the narrow spheres of influence indicated by the Way of Mastery. The key to their success will be their ability to turn their formidable powers of observation and calculation away from ego-oriented issues and onto the longer view and larger scheme of things. Too, their formidable persuasive talents will serve them well in their quest for advancement. This is one configuration where mentors and teachers may well be found in the context of love affairs, marriages, or partnerships, and if Libra–Scorpios allow their hearts to be captured by older, wiser, or more educated individuals from whom they can learn, their life journey will be considerably eased.

FRANÇOIS MITTERRAND
President of France;
leader in the Socialist
Party

10/26/1916
Scorpio I

CHALLENGE: **PRYING THEMSELVES AWAY FROM THEIR EMO-TIONAL ENTANGLEMENTS**

FULFILLMENT: **STEPPING INTO THE ROLE OF MENTOR**

NOTABLE: **JEAN DAUSSET (NOBEL PRIZE WINNER FOR PHYSI-OLOGY, GENETICS)**

October 26–November 2

INTENSITY
SCORPIO I

Those born in the Week of Intensity who navigate the Way of Mastery are blessed with a single-mindedness of purpose and a purity of intent that will work to their great advantage here. These individuals have little problem keeping their eyes on the prize of personal achievement, and whatever their goals may be, they are likely to reach them. Though they have a tendency to become mired down in emotional concerns, especially those of suspicion, defensiveness, and other distrustful attitudes, they nevertheless have a rather shrewd and calculating streak, that, properly and objectively applied, will serve their ambitions. If they are careful not to merely use their teachers and mentors but to cultivate real respect for genuine mastery, they can achieve wonderful success.

CHALLENGE: **APPRECIATING THOSE WHO GUIDE THEM RATHER THAN DISTRUSTING THEM**

FULFILLMENT: **FEELING THE SENSE OF ACCOMPLISHMENT THAT INTENSIVE EFFORT GIVES**

NOTABLES: **JENNY MCCARTHY (ACTRESS); FRANÇOIS MITTERRAND (FRENCH PRESIDENT; WW II VETERAN)**

November 3–11

DEPTH
SCORPIO II

Whatever their area of study or inclination, Scorpio II's who travel the Way of Mastery are likely to approach their subject with a rare intensity and depth. Blessed with the kind of steadfastness that makes for real success, these individuals are more than likely to find avenues to fully develop and express their particular vision, as giving material form to the wealth of their subconscious knowledge is very important to them. Though they have a pronounced tendency toward ruthlessness and a rather mercenary attitude that may evolve into an obsession with financial and material concerns, if they do not allow issues of personal security to stand in the way of their higher development, all will go brilliantly for them.

WILL ROGERS
Humorist/actor

11/4/1879
Scorpio II

CHALLENGE: **KNOWING WHEN THEY HAVE GONE OVERBOARD IN THEIR WORKAHOLIC TENDENCIES**

FULFILLMENT: **ENJOYING THE DEPTH OF THE TEACHER-STUDENT RELATIONSHIP THAT THIS KARMIC PATH PROMISES**

NOTABLE: **WALTER CRONKITE (LONGTIME ANCHORMAN FOR CBS; TELEVISION JOURNALIST)**

November 12–18

CHARM
SCORPIO III

Those born in the Week of Charm are likely to find the Way of Mastery to be an extraordinarily happy and fulfilling journey. This path gifts Scorpio III's with a knack for turning their inspirations and insights into tangible assets and achievements. Moreover, they have the added advantage of being able to add the extra spice of seduction to their already formidable power of persuasion. Attracting the right teachers and mentors will prove no problem at all, though they will have to take care not to use the knowledge and expertise of others merely for their own ends and to dedicate themselves fully and humbly to the learning process. A real awareness of their own motives in every situation will prove especially beneficial in their progress toward their goals, as will an ability to objectify and absorb constructive criticism.

CHALLENGE: **AVOIDING THE IMPULSE TO JUMP FROM TEACHER TO TEACHER IN HOPSCOTCH FASHION**

FULFILLMENT: **DARING TO REALIZE THEIR DREAMS**

November 19–24
REVOLUTION
SCORPIO–SAGITTARIUS CUSP

Those born on the Cusp of Revolution may have considerable difficulty in absorbing the life's lessons offered by the Way of Mastery. These individuals tend to create havoc when they should stay calm and to tear down structures when they ought to be building them. However, if they get in touch with their secret sense of tradition and refuse to allow their emotions to direct their choices, their journey will be eased considerably. The period of apprenticeship required by this karmic path will almost surely involve their willingness to ally themselves with someone who speaks to their sense of idealism and can show them more effective ways to manifest their dreams and desires. Yet when they have found the right master, these quick studies can absorb knowledge and expertise in record time.

KIRK DOUGLAS
Actor, Van Gogh in
Lust for Life, Spartacus

12/9/1916
Sagittarius II

CHALLENGE: **BECOMING CONVINCED THAT THE ROLE OF APPRENTICE HAS A LONG AND HONORABLE HISTORY**
FULFILLMENT: **DISCOVERING THE FULFILLMENT INHERENT IN BUILDING STRUCTURES RATHER THAN TEARING THEM DOWN**

November 25–December 2
INDEPENDENCE
SAGITTARIUS I

Those born in the Week of Independence who make their way along this karmic path may find it a difficult road until they come to terms with the fact that their quest for mastery must involve a real commitment to a mentor or teacher with whom they can share their innermost selves. Their sense of independence may lead them to resist that level of commitment, however, and many of them may take refuge in a rather misplaced sense of idealism or fits of temperament until they face the fact that there will always be more to learn. They will find this a more comfortable journey if they take their lessons or increase their expertise within the context of a more personal relationship. Many with this configuration will marry their boss, date their professor, or become best friends with the chairperson of their corporation. In any case, they will find life much improved if they create an environment of instruction that is not threatening to them.

CHALLENGE: **APPLYING THEIR CODE OF HONOR AND HIGH STANDARDS TO THEIR EDUCATION**
FULFILLMENT: **SETTING THEIR OWN PACE IN WHATEVER FIELD OF ENDEAVOR THEY PURSUE**

December 3–10
THE ORIGINATOR
SAGITTARIUS II

Finding the right outlet for their unique talents and abilities may not be the easiest thing in the world for those born in the Week of the Originator on this karmic path, but they can rest assured that once they do, their journey will be most rewarding. It is especially important for these people to objectify their own emotions and set aside issues of personal rejection if they are to give substance to their dreams. At the same time their sense of personal ambition may well be founded on their need for acceptance. Clearly, they will have to do a great deal of soul-searching before they come to terms with the fact that being different is not a liability but an asset. Finding the right guide or teacher could prove to be crucial, since whoever takes them on will likely provide the acceptance Sagittarius II's crave and will help guide their more peculiar traits onto the straight and narrow path.

JOHN MALKOVICH
Actor, *Dangerous Liaisons*

12/9/1953
Sagittarius II

CHALLENGE: **CONTROLLING THEIR COMPETITIVENESS**
FULFILLMENT: **ESTABLISHING A LONG-TERM RELATIONSHIP WITH SOMEONE WHO UNDERSTANDS THEM ENOUGH TO GUIDE THEM**
NOTABLES: **KIM BASINGER (OSCAR-WINNING ACTRESS); DIANE SCHUR (JAZZ SINGER)**

December 11–18
THE TITAN
SAGITTARIUS III

The Titans who travel the Way of Mastery may find this an uncomfortable passage, since they will probably have to learn to swallow their considerable pride before they can find the education and enlightenment they seek. Moodiness and a pervading sense of isolation can be problems, and they may have to do a great deal of work before they learn not to take the world so personally. Cultivating humility and real respect for the talents and abilities of others will do much to ease their passage, however. If they can learn to approach the task of turning their fondest dreams into tangible reality while maintaining an attitude of reverence for themselves and their teachers, they will realize great progress.

CHALLENGE: **NOT OVERBURDENING THEMSELVES WITH TOO CRUSHING A LOAD OF EXPECTATIONS**
FULFILLMENT: **REALIZING THE NOBLESSE OBLIGE OF BEING A MASTER**
NOTABLE: **BETTY GRABLE (ACTRESS; PINUP GIRL)**

KARMIC PATH
16

December 19–25
PROPHECY
SAGITTARIUS–CAPRICORN CUSP

The individuals born in this period who travel the Way of Mastery may have an unusual journey, since in many respects their challenge will be twofold: first, to access and develop their considerable intuitive and psychic insight and, second, to somehow turn their unique vision into some tangible reality, craft, or vocation. In fact, this is a configuration that will make for any number of professional mystics, psychics, and soothsayers as these individuals come to terms with the challenge to develop their remarkable gifts. The power of the subconscious is especially strong in these individuals, however, and they are unlikely to be led astray by undue emotionalism, insecurity, or a need to throw their weight around. If they can learn to access the source of their considerable power, all will go brilliantly.

CHALLENGE: **OVERCOMING THEIR PROPENSITY TO DOMINATE THROUGH SILENCE**
FULFILLMENT: **MANIFESTING THEIR CAPACITY FOR SERIOUSNESS OF PURPOSE**

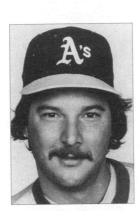

TOM UNDERWOOD
Journeyman pitcher for 6 major league teams 1974–1984
———
12/22/1953
Sagittarius–Capricorn Cusp

December 26–January 2
THE RULER
CAPRICORN I

Those born in the Week of the Ruler who find themselves on the Way of Mastery may well be blessed with a fine sense of who they are and where they want to go. Yet once they achieve a specific set of goals or even a position of authority, many of them will change direction, profession, or even their entire spiritual perspective in the quest for a more genuine sense of accomplishment. In any event, their essential dependability will serve them well as they work to study, refine, and redefine the goals and personal objectives that shape their lives. In fact, they are blessed with so secure a sense of personal identity that their their need for a teacher or mentor may take them somewhat by surprise. Yet if they accept their opportunities for higher development with good grace and a willingness to learn, their life journey can hold great promise and considerable reward.

CHALLENGE: **MAKING SURE THEY ATTACH THEMSELVES TO THE RIGHT PERSON'S COATTAILS**
FULFILLMENT: **STAYING TRUE TO THEIR SENSE OF FAIRNESS**

January 3–9
DETERMINATION
CAPRICORN II

These determined souls will doubtless have a relatively easy and generally rewarding journey along the Way of Mastery. Once they have set a specific goal or chosen a path of development, they are unlikely to be swayed from their course for any great length of time and will be aided in their quest by their talent for practical application and study and their patience. Also, their considerable sensitivity is combined with a tough, resilient nature that is not always obvious to their associates and peers. Though they can blend quite nicely into the background at times, it would be a mistake to write these people off as unambitious, unaware, or unwilling to get the best and most out of any circumstance in which they find themselves.

CHALLENGE: **LEARNING TO PICK PARTNERS WHO WILL ACCEPT THAT THEIR WORK COMES FIRST**
FULFILLMENT: **STRIVING FOR THEIR OWN PROFESSIONAL PEAK BY STRETCHING THEIR TALENTS TO THE LIMIT**

HOWARD STERN
Popular syndicated radio host; often criticized for vulgarity
1/12/1954
Capricorn III

January 10–16
DOMINANCE
CAPRICORN III

Those born in this week who navigate the Way of Mastery may be powerful people indeed. Yet with that power comes the danger that the Capricornian urge to dominate will supersede their quest for mastery and higher development. Ruthlessness and rigidity of character may also stand in the way of their success here, especially when their innate sensitivity is shut down, turned off, or otherwise suppressed in the face of more practical and pressing matters. Alternatively, they may be prone to creating their own obstacles or otherwise make trouble for themselves. The key to their success will thus lie in their willingness to surrender some of their considerable power and worldly standing in order to place themselves in the service of higher development.

CHALLENGE: **FINDING THEIR SOFTER, MORE FEMININE SIDE FOR THE INTUITIVE AND IMAGINATIVE GIFTS IT IMPARTS**
FULFILLMENT: **INJECTING A BIT OF INNOVATION OR INGENUITY INTO THEIR AREAS OF EXPERTISE**

January 17–22
MYSTERY AND IMAGINATION
CAPRICORN–AQUARIUS CUSP

Extraordinarily high or unrealistic expectations and attitudes may mark the journey of Capricorn–Aquarians who navigate the Way of Mastery. Crucial to their development will be their willingness to allow their considerable sensitivity and imagination to inform their vision, craft, spiritual, or professional interests, rather than considering the world of practical matters and the world of imagination and creative activity to be mutually exclusive. While they may chafe a bit at the seeming restrictions of this karmic path and allow restlessness or excitability to get in the way of their plans for achievement, they have the potential to make wonderful progress, and they are bound for a journey enlivened by a lighthearted enthusiasm for what the future may hold.

OPRAH WINFREY
TV host/actress

———

1/29/1954
Aquarius I

CHALLENGE: **LATCHING ON TO THE RIGHT MENTOR TO HELP TEMPER THEIR WILDER IMPULSES**
FULFILLMENT: **HAVING FOCUSED ON ONE AREA, DEVELOPING A VIRTUOSO LEVEL OF EXPERTISE**
NOTABLE: **BETTY WHITE (TELEVISION ACTRESS)**

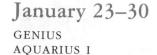

January 23–30
GENIUS
AQUARIUS I

Though it may prove somewhat difficult for these highly intelligent and gifted individuals to settle on a single skill or goal, Aquarius I's who navigate the Way of Mastery have considerable potential and resources at their disposal to find contentment and fulfillment on this karmic path. As long as these unique people seek out a venue or particular talent that will allow them to continue to transform themselves and their products and continually evolve, thereby avoiding the dangers of frustration, boredom, and recklessness, they can be self-made men and women in the very best sense of the term. As they are blessed with considerable insight and sensitivity, much of their genius will manifest itself in the kind of common touch that is at once in tune with collective needs and an inspiration to those who would better themselves.

CHALLENGE: **OVERCOMING THEIR INSISTENCE TO BE SELF-TAUGHT**
FULFILLMENT: **DISCOVERING THE AUTONOMY OF BEING A CRAFTSPERSON**
NOTABLE: **ERNEST BORGNINE (TELEVISION AND MOVIE ACTOR, *POSEIDON ADVENTURE*)**

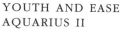

January 31–February 7
YOUTH AND EASE
AQUARIUS II

Developing virtuosity and mastery may not be difficult for those born in the Week of Youth and Ease, yet there is a significant danger that they may happen into comfortable circumstances without first coming to terms with what they really want or with the necessity to develop a uniquely personal vision. Though these popular people will have little trouble attracting any number of teachers, mentors, and masters, they may fail the higher challenge of this karmic path and absorb their training in such a way that their end product is derivative of what has gone before, rather than a full-blown, independent effort. Yet if they cultivate the personal strength to get through occasional conflicts in order to clarify their values and vision, the Way of Mastery will indeed be the high road for them.

SOLOMON R. GUGGENHEIM
Philanthropist; founded Solomon R. Guggenheim Museum

———

2/2/1861
Aquarius II

CHALLENGE: **GRAPPLING WITH THEIR DESIRE TO BE A PERPETUAL STUDENT OR EVEN A DILETTANTE**
FULFILLMENT: **ROLLING UP THEIR SLEEVES AND SETTLING IN FOR THE LONG HAUL**
NOTABLE: **CHRISTY BRINKLEY (MODEL)**

February 8–15
ACCEPTANCE
AQUARIUS III

Those born in the Week of Acceptance who navigate the Way of Mastery may experience their share of ups and downs until they absorb the lesson that this is one case where acceptance of certain restrictions and limitations will prove the road to salvation. Letting go of their high expectations or rigid standards is essential, as is developing a willingness to open themselves to the instruction of a gifted mentor and apply themselves to a subject with discipline. Also, accepting the commitment inherent in such a relationship may prove a bit difficult for these generally gregarious, engaging personalities. Yet if they keep their eyes on the higher spiritual and material prizes that beckon, their unusual demeanor, colorful character, and inspired visions will find full expression along this life's journey.

CHALLENGE: **FACING DOWN THE CHALLENGE OF BECOMING A TRUE MASTER**
FULFILLMENT: **FREEING THEMSELVES FROM SECRETLY BELIEVING THEMSELVES TO BE INADEQUATE**
NOTABLES: **BERTOLT BRECHT (GERMAN PLAYWRIGHT/ SCREENWRITER, *THREEPENNY OPERA*); MATT GROENING (CARTOONIST, CREATOR OF *THE SIMPSONS*); ALFRED NORTH WHITEHEAD (MATHEMATICIAN; IDEALIST PHILOSOPHER)**

February 16–22

SENSITIVITY
AQUARIUS–PISCES CUSP

Cultivating greater objectivity is crucial to the successful negotiation of the Way of Mastery for those born on the Cusp of Sensitivity. These people may struggle with emotional extremes, unrealistic expectations, and outright pessimism on this life journey, and they will have to work hard to set aside their more cumbersome psychic baggage before they can find fulfillment. Nonetheless, this karmic path gifts them with a stronger awareness of their intuitive workings than they might otherwise have possessed, and if they are careful to limit their ambitions in order to focus their talents and gifts better, they will find real rewards along the way. By keeping their attention off more abstract notions of success and personal ambition and concentrating on the work in front of them, they will find great pleasure in the process of learning, developing, and ultimately mastering a task for its own sake.

RENE RUSSO
Film actress, *Get Shorty*

2/17/1954
Aquarius–Pisces Cusp

CHALLENGE: **SHUTTING UP AND LISTENING TO OTHERS ONCE IN A WHILE**
FULFILLMENT: **TAKING PRIDE IN THEIR WORK**
NOTABLES: **JOHN TRAVOLTA (ACTOR, *SATURDAY NIGHT FEVER*); PATTY HEARST (KIDNAPPED HEIRESS)**

February 23–March 2

SPIRIT
PISCES I

Those born in the Week of Spirit who find themselves on the Way of Mastery will derive their greatest fulfillment from the less material aspects of this configuration. Though this journey may demand a more practical and tangible manifestation of their gifts and talents than they might otherwise be inclined to produce, it also gifts them with a measure of stability and groundedness that can be a great asset in their search for fulfillment. Though unrealistic or overly idealistic expectations of themselves and their relationships may prove to be a problem, Pisces I's will nevertheless approach the tasks at hand with great devotion and a sort of mystical concentration that, properly applied, can result in near miracles of achievement despite some formidable odds.

CHALLENGE: **NOT ALLOWING THEMSELVES TO BE TAKEN ADVANTAGE OF BY THOSE WHO TEACH OR GUIDE THEM**
FULFILLMENT: **DEVELOPING A ZEN-LIKE ATTITUDE TO THEIR UNDERTAKINGS**
NOTABLE: **RON HOWARD (ACTOR, *HAPPY DAYS*; TURNED FILM DIRECTOR, *COCOON*)**

March 3–10

THE LONER
PISCES II

Those born in the Week of the Loner who travel the Way of Mastery can find great contentment and fulfillment, especially as they achieve the stature and experience to break away from the protection of a teacher or organization and really come into their own. Though that process will require time and effort, the years of apprenticeship and training are well suited to their essentially studious, solitary nature. As they release their fears of personal rejection through contact with wiser people who are better versed in the ways of the world, they will be able to set their personal needs aside in the interest of larger and more permanent achievements. If they are able to avoid the dangers of depression, self-negation, and a tendency to withdraw in the face of tougher choices or challenges, their life's work and experience will synthesize into rewarding achievements of truly lasting value.

RUDOLF STEINER
Austrian philosopher, founded Anthroposophical Society, spirituality as independent of senses

2/27/1861
Pisces I

CHALLENGE: **MAINTAINING A POSITIVE ATTITUDE IN THE FACE OF EDUCATIONAL CHALLENGES**
FULFILLMENT: **MASTERING A PROFESSION, TRADE, OR CRAFT**
NOTABLE: **CHOU ENLAI (LEADER OF COMMUNIST CHINA)**

March 11–18

DANCERS AND DREAMERS
PISCES III

Though there are a number of chronic underachievers, dilettantes, and perpetual students among those born with this configuration, there are an equal number of gifted and tenacious souls who are capable of attaining the highest levels of spiritual and material success. The key to these people's success will be their ability to cultivate humility and a certain reverence for the guides and instructors they meet along the way. At the same time, they may be led or misled into codependent patterns with their mentors and teachers and will have to work hard to develop the personal strength and solid sense of identity necessary to truly come into their own. Practicality may be their biggest stumbling block, yet once they come to see it as a tool rather than an annoyance, they will be able to give form and substance to even their most high-flown aspirations and ambitions.

CHALLENGE: **DEVELOPING GREATER HUMILITY**
FULFILLMENT: **FOCUSING ON THEIR TECHNICAL AND SCIENTIFIC SKILLS**
NOTABLES: **DOROTHY GISH (FILM ACTRESS; KNOWN FOR PANTOMIME AND LIGHT COMEDY IN SILENT FILMS); REGINALD MARSH (ILLUSTRATOR)**

The Way of Electricity

CANCER–LEO CUSP TO CAPRICORN–AQUARIUS CUSP
Oscillation to Mystery and Imagination

Serving in a capacity akin to a lightning rod, those on the Way of Electricity are here to bring crackling energy down from the heavens, to ground it in the here and now, and, in so doing, to generate a kind of excitement and enthusiasm that will infect all those who come in contact with them. Whether serving as a public icon for their time or as a behind-the-scenes instigator, those on the Way of Electricity will always make their influence felt. These individuals have been brought into this life to stir things up, serving as a catalyst to impart new ideas, modes of thought, or revolutionary concepts to their society, whether for good or ill. Movers and shakers, these people lend spice and verve to family gatherings and other social events. Born with a love of all that is innovative, the men and women on this karmic path are blessed with a gift for sensing what will be the next wave to hit their culture. Technological in approach, their interest is not in changing or modifying tradition but rather in embracing all that is new. By tapping into their highly developed intuitive ability, those on this karmic path instinctively sense what will be of interest to others and then, by propelling those around them into the trend, are responsible for many success stories, both their own and their partners'. This karmic axis has an inherent dynamism, and by working it properly, utilizing its intuitive strengths to the fullest, and encouraging others, individuals on this karmic path will leave a legacy that will last for generations.

Both Cancer–Leo and Capricorn–Aquarius can be somewhat schizophrenic in their orientation, each carrying two nearly diametrically opposed energies. Learning to generate the solar electricity of the Leo/Aquarius side of the lineup without falling into the more depressive lunar and Saturnian aspects of the Cancer/Capricorn side will be the tricky part of this journey. The core lesson for these individuals is to learn to honor and nurture both sides of themselves so that their personalities and moods do not swing wildly in either direction. Obviously blessed with many gifts, those on the Way of Electricity run the risk of falling out of balance emotionally or psychologically so that they slip into either a manic phase or a depressive phase. Although this karmic path calls for a significant level of upbeat, positive, and charismatic activity, learning to respect their need for peace and quiet, structure, and routine will help keep these individuals on a more balanced path. Though one side is more subdued and emotional, this more feminine aspect actually provides the deep intuitive awareness that enables those on the Way of Electricity to discern which new products, forms of entertainment, or scientific breakthroughs can actually establish a foothold. Moreover, it is the taskmaster in the Capricorn part of the equation that permits these people to know how to make a new concept work in the practical realities of the world. Thus, even though

---

CORE LESSON

Replenishing their personal electricity by honoring their feminine, intuitive side

GOAL
To generate excitement for new ideas in others

GIFTS
Brilliant, Innovative, Charismatic

PITFALLS
Moody, Depressive, Fantasy Prone

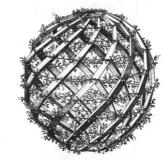

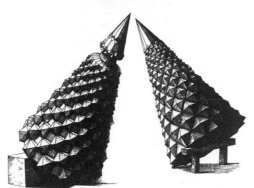

others do not see the darker side of these individuals when they are out invigorating everyone, this side is hard at work and must be honored by those on this karmic path, for it is what nourishes and sustains their famous electric appeal.

Early in life these individuals often lead an introverted existence, one in which fantasy may play a prominent role. Already as children they want to partake of anything that is exploratory or new. The often undisclosed secret about those who walk this karmic path is that they possess a profound yearning for the divine or formless. A drive to understand the infinite or at the very least to challenge any limitations imposed on them is highly characteristic. Deep within them is a desire to transcend the human form. Often this is apparent in their interest in astronomy or space exploration, technical innovations that lead humankind onward, or even a kind of mysticism. Escaping may become a preoccupation for such individuals. To achieve the transcendence they seek, the pursuit of a religious or other spiritual path is highly recommended. Certainly a great pitfall for those on the Way of Electricity is getting lost in their fantasies or developing patterns of substance abuse in an effort to achieve the release they crave.

Part of the reason the individuals on the Way of Electricity are so taken with infinitude is that they have a rare capacity to tap into it or perceive it. They are blessed with brilliant, lightning-quick minds that observe and intuit so rapidly that they are able to take in a great expanse in one glance without even realizing that they are processing its details with lightning speed. These people cut a wide swath. The moment they enter a party or other gathering, an electric current seems to spread throughout the room and all eyes are riveted on them. Moreover, in an instant, those on this path size up the space and everyone in it and usually make a beeline for the very person who can help them in their latest scheme. These charismatic individuals do not persuade others so much as transmit their own excitement about something. Receiving such a jolt of energy can make others feel as though they are part of something bigger than themselves—in essence, that they are playing a part in making history.

When viewed objectively, those on the Way of Electricity are not really interested in taking a lot of passengers along for the ride. Yet it is their destiny to act as purveyors of change, and they are often Svengali-like in their influence on others—it is not unusual for them to completely alter the course of someone's destiny. Although their charisma would seem to indicate that they will have many followers and groupies, generally those on this karmic path are not comfortable with more intimate forms of relationship. Often they spend much of their time wrapped up in their own thoughts and emotions, areas that are rarely accessible to their mates or even their friends. However,

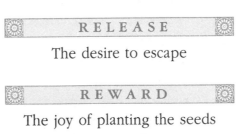

RELEASE

The desire to escape

REWARD

The joy of planting the seeds of positive change

SUGGESTION

Engage in physical routines to stay in balance. Work to build communication pathways to those you love. Pursue a spiritual path with rituals and routines that calm the mind.

they do need to be able to share their inner life. Many of them will need to learn how to build solid bridges of understanding between themselves and others. Great diversity exists in the way people view those on this karmic path: some see them as conservative, others as liberal. This may be because they are open in expressing their views, which may be reactionary or radical, but at the same time quite accepting of human weakness. Because they are rather high strung, people who get on their nerves can bring out their disruptive and violent impulses almost instantaneously. Unfortunately and often fated, these are often just the family members who are nearest and dearest to them.

These individuals are not particularly well suited for family life, but they frequently find themselves at the center of such a group, which can mean a rough ride for all concerned. Coming from a place where emotional oscillation is the norm, those on this path must struggle for evenness and normality in their relationships, particularly in matters of the heart. Often the best partners for these individuals are quiet, stable people who have their own agenda but can also be an appreciative audience. In their professional life they are capable of sticking with jobs that are less than ideal, but the temptation is always strong for them to leave what they are doing and move on to something else. Thus, al-

though it may be part of their life task to generate the energy to buoy others up, they must learn to regulate these energies so as to keep their own cataclysmic personality on an even keel and under control. They are not known for having a calming influence on others, and this can cause problems, especially if they acquire a reputation as troublemaker. Usually, the very thing those on the Way of Electricity want most—excitement—is just the opposite of what they need—peace and quiet. As they themselves have a hard time knowing what is best for them, dedicated family members or friends may sometimes be required to act to keep them from going over the edge into burnout, particularly where alcohol or other drugs are concerned.

Television and its advent into society are apt symbols for those on the Way of Electricity. Upon its advent, this new technology permanently changed the nature of entertainment, how information is transmitted to the public, the fabric of society, even the structure of the family and how it conducts itself. However, its technology consists of a series of dots of color that create a whole that transcends its individual elements. What viewers see is exciting images that invigorate their imaginations and take them on a journey to a world far from their everyday existence. Like the energy of the Way of Electricity, television irresistibly pulls everything else along in its wake.

BALANCE POINT

Lightning and Ground

CRYSTALS AND GEMSTONES

*Meteorites in any form, but especially **Gibbeon,** ground energy originating in outer space. This gift from the heavens links individuals to other dimensions as a source of inspiration and information.*

NOTABLES ON THIS KARMIC PATH

ALBERT EINSTEIN

Like many on this path, theorist, inventor, and physicist **Albert Einstein** contributed revolutionary ideas to society, advancing knowledge and understanding. Due to the power of his intellect and highly developed capacity for thought, Einstein literally brought energy down from the heavens. From his theory of relativity to his explanation of Brownian motion and photoelectric effect, as well as his contribution to atomic physics, Einstein's influence on twentieth-century physics cannot be measured. Despite his scientific beliefs, mystical yearnings often characterized his quest. Einstein searched for the underlying order behind the universal void and saw the hand of God everywhere.

Music legend **Elvis Presley** certainly possessed an electric excitement that affected those who came into contact with him. A real mover and shaker, the King's innovative style strongly influenced the rock and roll of his time. By stirring things up, Elvis was a catalyst for a number of the social changes that came about in America during the 1950s. Unfortunately, Elvis fell prey to the pitfalls characteristic of the Way of Electric-

ELVIS PRESLEY

ity. Increasingly moody and depressed, he slipped deeper and deeper into the addiction that ended his life. Yet so powerful was Elvis's music and personality that even his death could not disband his loyal following.

Cher's onetime husband **Sonny Bono** proved successful in many areas. After achieving renown through music and television, Bono (like Ronald Reagan) applied his show business sense to the world of California politics. With the charisma typical of this path, Sonny pushed himself to the limits of his talent, surprising

SONNY BONO

those who doubted him early on in his career. Sonny's early influence on ex-wife Cher typifies the Svengali-like role many on this path adopt. Like many on the Way of Electricity who do not grant access to their inner lives, his greatest challenge was building a solid bridge of understanding between himself and others.

Other Notables: Keith Hernandez, Judi Dench, Herb Alpert, Edward Steichen, Loretta Lynn, Erich von Daniken, Yehudi Menuhin, Anthony Quinn, Glenn Ford, Harold Robbins, Robert McNamara, Gustav Mahler, John Quincy Adams, Annie Oakley, Ingrid Bergman, William Faulkner, Elijah Poole Muhammed, Paul Joseph Goebbels, Benjamin Disreali, A. J. Foyt, Sam Cooke, Wilhelm Grimm, Shaquille O'Neal

BIRTHDAYS ON KARMIC PATH 17

September 7, 1897–January 26, 1898 | April 19, 1916–September 7, 1916
November 30, 1934–April 19, 1935 | July 11, 1953–November 29, 1953 | February 20, 1972–July 10, 1972
October 2, 1990–February 19, 1991 | May 13, 2009–October 1, 2009

KARMIC PATH
17

March 19–24

REBIRTH
PISCES–ARIES CUSP

Individuals born in this week who travel the Way of Electricity might find themselves spending a great deal of time and energy exploring the question "Why me?" until they come to terms with their own power. Until that time, however, they may tend to feel victimized or overwrought by their ability to act as a catalyst within their personal and professional environments. Thus, going within and coming to terms with their own needs will prove especially important to their success and advancement along this karmic path, as will actively seeking out validation for the kind of knowledge and understanding they intuitively possess. Once they comprehend that emotional sensitivity and intuition do not necessarily preclude or exclude a craving for excitement, a dynamic approach to life, or a need to explore the boundaries and test the limits of more ordinary reality, they can find great enlightenment and fulfillment on this life journey.

CHALLENGE: **BALANCING THE MANY FORCES WITHIN THEM**
FULFILLMENT: **EXPLORING THEIR ROLE AS CATALYSTS WITHIN THEIR SOCIAL CIRCLE**

March 25–April 2

THE CHILD
ARIES I

Those born in the Week of the Child who travel the Way of Electricity are high-voltage personalities whose magnetic charm may prove a lot for them to handle. Blessed with amazing energy and enormous reserves of enthusiasm, they will doubtless discover that their road to self-realization will in some way involve them in group efforts and activities directed toward the achievement of some innovative or even futuristic vision. Though it may be important for them to withdraw from the pressures of group involvement from time to time in order to cultivate calm and greater emotional balance, they will discover that fulfillment lies not so much in the realization of their personal ambitions as in their ability to bring out the best in others. In a word, a great deal of personal happiness is promised by this karmic path, providing they don't take their ups and down too seriously.

CHALLENGE: **BREAKING THE PATTERNS OF ISOLATION AND RETREAT FORMED IN CHILDHOOD**
FULFILLMENT: **PARTICIPATION IN TEAMS GEARED TOWARD TECHNOLOGICAL, ARTISTIC, OR OTHER FORMS OF INNOVATION**
NOTABLES: **RICHARD CHAMBERLAIN (ACTOR, *SHOGUN*); EDWARD STEICHEN (PHOTOGRAPHER, *VOGUE; VANITY FAIR* CHIEF)**

HERB ALPERT
Musician; founder of
A&M Records

3/31/1935
Aries I

April 3–10

THE STAR
ARIES II

Those born in the Week of the Star who navigate the Way of Electricity may have more personal charisma than they quite know what to do with. Yet most of them will find themselves quite happy on this karmic path, for in addition to their ability to draw the attention of others, they are gifted with extraordinary insight and intuition as to the newest and most important developments on the cultural and collective scene. Some of them may, however, become preoccupied with a purely personal focus, and become obsessed with issues of image, fashion, and physical appearance to the detriment of the higher development demanded by this karmic path. Yet when they come to understand that their real role in the grander scheme of things is involved in collective rather than individual progress, all will go well.

CHALLENGE: **NOT SHORTING THEMSELVES OUT IN A BURST OF EGO-DRIVEN SELF-AGGRANDIZEMENT**
FULFILLMENT: **TRANSLATING THEIR ABUNDANT AND ELECTRICAL ENERGY INTO THE FUEL FOR NUMEROUS AND VARIED ACHIEVEMENTS**
NOTABLE: **BOSS TWEED (CORRUPT NEW YORK POLITICAL BOSS)**

April 11–18

THE PIONEER
ARIES III

The Pioneers who navigate and explore the Way of Electricity are likely to be truly inspirational characters whose effects on others may appear in a highly polarized fashion. In short, people will either love them or hate them, but their dreams, visions, and inspiration will generate a certain amount of controversy. Perhaps the greatest challenge for those with this configuration will lie in their ability to successfully attune themselves to a deeper and more lasting source of inspiration and to resist the temptation to be swept up in the passions and causes of the moment. Moreover, they would do well not to turn too far inward and succumb to emotional orgies of self-examination when their passions and convictions are frustrated by practical considerations. The ability to step down, back up, and think long term will prove to be a great advantage, as will aiming at with realistic and achievable objectives.

CHALLENGE: **FINDING OUTLETS FOR THEIR FRUSTRATIONS**
FULFILLMENT: **INTERACTING WITH OTHERS REGULARLY AND DYNAMICALLY**
NOTABLES: **FREDERIC MELCHER (PUBLISHER; R. R. BOWKER EXECUTIVE); ERICH VON DANIKEN (AUTHOR, *CHARIOTS OF THE GODS?*); LYLE WAGGONER (ACTOR, *WONDER WOMAN*)**

LORETTA LYNN
Country music singer

4/14/1935
Aries III

KARMIC PATH
17

April 19–24
POWER
ARIES–TAURUS CUSP

Those born on the Cusp of Power who find themselves on the Way of Electricity are fortunate indeed, for they are clearly marked to have a considerable impact on their times. In fact, their principal danger is that they may use their power to achieve purely personal goals and objectives and fail to make the higher social and collective connections required by this karmic path. Thus, cultivating simple philanthropy will be of enormous benefit to their higher development. Yet these rare individuals bring to the Way of Electricity a greater measure of stability and a somewhat broader perspective than might otherwise have been the case. If they keep in mind that power is neither good nor evil except as it is wielded by individuals, they not only will reach a rare level of self-realization but will leave a lasting legacy that will shape the future in ways as yet unknown.

ANTHONY QUINN
Actor, *Zorba the Greek*

4/21/1916
Aries–Taurus Cusp

CHALLENGE: **PUTTING A SEVERE LIMIT ON THEIR MORE MERCENARY TENDENCIES**
FULFILLMENT: **ALLOWING THEMSELVES TO BE A SOURCE OF POWER FOR POSITIVE CHANGE**
NOTABLES: **YEHUDI MENUHIN (VIOLINIST); DUDLEY MOORE (ACTOR, *ARTHUR*; 10)**

April 25–May 2
MANIFESTATION
TAURUS I

This configuration may produce some truly Renaissance men and women. The practicality and sensual, physical side of Taurus I's do much to ground the highly charged energies present here on the Way of Electricity, while the demands of this karmic path will do much to uplift and broaden their perspective and help them avoid getting mired down in day-to-day pursuits and concerns. Thus, the combination can synthesize into powerful manifestations of ambition and vision. Perhaps the principal pitfall for those on this unusual life journey will be the fact that they are bound to have truly awful tempers and may indulge in confrontations that, even though infrequent, can do serious and even irreparable damage to the parties involved. Yet greater self-awareness will do much to offset these dangers and passions, and if they take care simply to count their blessings, they will find it quite a time-consuming task.

CHALLENGE: **TAKING CARE NOT TO THINK TOO MUCH ABOUT INSPIRATION AS IT FLOWS THROUGH THEM; OTHERWISE, CONFUSION MAY ENSUE**
FULFILLMENT: **IMPLEMENTING THEIR BROADER VISIONS OR INNOVATIONS**
NOTABLE: **HENRY HOUGHTON (PUBLISHER, HOUGHTON, MIFFLIN)**

May 3–10
THE TEACHER
TAURUS II

Taurus II's traveling the Way of Electricity can find considerable happiness and fulfillment, as they are blessed with a truly charismatic and magnetic personality through which to display their gifts and explore their quests. In fact, the principal danger for those with this configuration will be their tendency to become too obsessed with abstract pursuits and concerns and lose their audience in a preoccupation with the theoretical. Nonetheless, they can be highly provocative and innovative visionaries with well-developed communicative talents. If they are careful not to allow their ideas to become too morally or ethically polarized and to stay in touch with collective needs, they can realize great rewards, especially in the areas of philosophical, religious, academic, or spiritual endeavors.

GLENN FORD
Actor, *Blackboard Jungle*

5/1/1916
Taurus I

CHALLENGE: **WARDING OFF THE TENDENCY TO POLARIZATION ON ALL FRONTS**
FULFILLMENT: **PRETENDING TO BE TEACHERS WHEN THEY ARE REALLY PROVOCATEURS**

May 11–18
THE NATURAL
TAURUS III

Those born in the Week of the Natural may be in for a rather wild ride on the Way of Electricity. Gifted with some truly formidable instincts and intuitions, they may dissipate those those qualities can nevertheless by giving in to mood swings, overemotionalism, and irresponsibility until they learn to calm down a bit and focus their energies. One way or another, they will be revolutionary rather than innovative in their outlook, and will experience any number of problems with authority and limitations, real or imagined, to their freedom. Yet if they learn to tap into the things that are common to human experience and learn the value long-term and even visionary goals, they can make wonderful progress along this road, if only by virtue of the fact that they can make even the most difficult and daunting task look easy. And that may be the greatest inspiration to us all.

CHALLENGE: **RETREATING TO NATURE TO GROUND THEMSELVES ONCE IN A WHILE**
FULFILLMENT: **APPLYING THEIR TALENT FOR EMBODYING UNUSUAL IDEAS FOR THE BETTERMENT OF THE LIVES OF OTHERS**

May 19–24
ENERGY
TAURUS–GEMINI CUSP

No matter what the specific careers, life goals, or personal visions of Taurus–Gemini's who travel the Way of Electricity, they are likely to have a real genius for tapping into what's hot, what's happening, and what's next. Though living on the cutting edge is not always a comfortable or secure position, these trendsetters will be blessed with both the resilience and the versatility to change direction and turn on the proverbial dime when things don't pan out. Yet they must also cultivate depth and breadth of vision if they are not to burn themselves out or fail to follow up on their inspirations in more practical ways. If they keep in mind that the working out of one's destiny is a lifelong journey and not merely a race to a finish line, they can realize considerable success and happiness.

HAROLD ROBBINS
Writer, *The Carpetbaggers*

5/21/1916
Taurus–Gemini Cusp

CHALLENGE: **THE TENDENCY TO MOVE MANIACALLY FROM ONE PROJECT TO THE NEXT BEFORE COMPLETING ANY**
FULFILLMENT: **DEVELOPING A GREATER INTUITIVE OR FEMININE AWARENESS WITH WHICH TO SOOTHE THEIR JANGLED NERVES**
NOTABLES: **LADY NANCY ASTOR (FIRST WOMAN IN BRITISH HOUSE OF COMMONS); LORD WALDORF ASTOR (BRITISH POLITICIAN; PROPRIETOR OF *THE OBSERVER*)**

May 25–June 2
FREEDOM
GEMINI I

A higher social and spiritual sense and an ability to tap into collective experience are very pronounced in those born in the Week of Freedom who travel the Way of Electricity. Though there is a real danger of scattering their energies, on the one hand, or resisting the responsibilities of the revolutionary, on the other, Gemini I's are blessed with a real social and collective conscience that will stand them in good stead. Curbing their natural excitability and somewhat abrasive streak in order to become more effective will be essential, as will being willing to cultivate greater calm and tie into the larger psychospiritual reality. In short, great reward and achievement are possible on this karmic path, providing they pause from time to time to reflect upon the words of St. Augustine: "The reward of patience is patience."

CHALLENGE: **GRAPPLING WITH THEIR INBORN DESIRE TO LOSE ONESELF IN SPIRITUAL TRUTH**
FULFILLMENT: **REAPING THE REWARDS OF GIVING UP A MEASURE OF PERSONAL FREEDOM IN FAVOR OF SERVING OTHERS**
NOTABLE: **VANESSA BELL (PAINTER; DECORATIVE DESIGNER)**

June 3–10
NEW LANGUAGE
GEMINI II

Turning their intuition, inner resources, and inspirations outward in effective and innovative forms of communication will be one of the principal tasks for those born in the Week of New Language who navigate this karmic path. This configuration makes for a truly interesting mix, though it may take some time for these people to settle on a specific set of goals and ambitions. In fact, they may end up so far ahead of the pack that they will have to slow down to allow the rest of us time to catch up. They have a highly personalized view of the world that was doubtless formulated by their early attempts (and failures) to convey their understanding and knowledge in a unique style. Yet if they learn to accept the technical value of such early lessons without attempting to carry the emotional baggage that often goes along with them, they will achieve amazing success as they gain the confidence to stir things up and to use their natural gift for all forms of communication to strike the chords of the collective response.

ROBERT McNAMARA
Secretary of defense during Vietnam War

6/9/1916
Gemini II

CHALLENGE: **CONTROLLING THEIR MOODIER OR MORE DEPRESSIVE TENDENCIES**
FULFILLMENT: **COMMUNICATING IN A BRILLIANT OR TRULY SCINTILLATING WAY**
NOTABLE: **FRANCIS CRICK (CODISCOVERER OF DNA)**

June 11–18
THE SEEKER
GEMINI III

Those born in this week who travel the Way of Electricity will have little problem taking up a banner or fighting the good fight against all that is restrictive, oppressive, or limiting. In fact, they have something of an obsession with a quest for the "truth." Thus, some of them may travel far and wide in search of broader, more inspiring horizons, while others will turn inward in search of enlightenment. Yet their highly intellectual orientation may well hinder them along this life journey, since they may have little patience to share their discoveries with other more ordinary mortals. Their sense of adventure will also be an asset, and whatever the course they choose to follow on their search for higher development, it is likely not to be smooth, boring, nor bland but heavily seasoned with a fine sense of fun and the spice of life itself.

CHALLENGE: **REGULATING THEIR OVERLY EMOTIONAL OR EVEN MANIC BEHAVIORS**
FULFILLMENT: **LIVING LIFE ON THE MOVE**

KARMIC PATH
17

June 19–24

MAGIC
GEMINI–CANCER CUSP

Those born on the Cusp of Magic who navigate the Way of Electricity may experience any number of ups and downs, especially in the area of learning to regulate and control some rather manic tendencies and emotional excesses. The key to their success will be their ability to distinguish fact from fantasy and to control their escapist side. At their best, they will have the gift of being able to imbue even the most adverse setbacks and circumstances with an element of graceful romanticism or mystical import. At their worst, they may allow their darker and more depressive side to gain the upper hand and become enchanted with "slipping the surly bonds of earth" in any way they can—through substance abuse, daredevil antics, or martyring themselves to a cause. The road to their destiny is wide open, and both great saints and terrible sinners can be found along the way.

CHALLENGE: **GETTING A GRIP ON THEIR PROPENSITY TO ESCAPISM BY PURSUING A SPIRITUAL PATH**

FULFILLMENT: **PUTTING THEIR CONSIDERABLE ENERGIES INTO THE SERVICE OF HIGHER PRINCIPLES OR A MORAL AGENDA**

GUSTAV MAHLER
Composer,
"Song of the Earth"

7/7/1860
Cancer II

June 25–July 2

THE EMPATH
CANCER I

Extreme sensitivity can be both the biggest blessing and the biggest curse of those born in this week who travel the Way of Electricity. In any event, they will have to learn to objectify their views and cultivate a measure of distance in order to successfully rise to the challenges of this karmic path. Too, a tendency to cling to the values and traditions of the past may interfere with their higher development, and some will display an almost maudlin preoccupation with old hurts, slights, and personal losses. Still, progress is possible once they learn to broaden their perspective while at the same time allowing their intuition to inform their worldview more. If they can learn to embrace conflict as a creative tool rather than a destructive force and to divest themselves of the fear of abandonment, they will make a rapid and even joyful journey toward enlightenment.

CHALLENGE: **ALLOWING THE NEARLY ELECTRICAL CURRENT OF INSPIRATION TO COURSE THROUGH THEM WITHOUT BEING SPOOKED BY IT**

FULFILLMENT: **USING THEIR INSPIRATIONS TO HELP OTHERS**

NOTABLE: **OLIVIA DE HAVILLAND (ACTRESS; OSCAR WINNER, *GONE WITH THE WIND*)**

July 3–10

THE UNCONVENTIONAL
CANCER II

There are some real characters born in the Week of the Unconventional who travel the Way of Electricity, and their impact upon their immediate circle is bound to be lasting. Though they may not at first appear to be the type to take up the banners of revolution, reform, and spiritual progress, once they find their niche and the torch is passed, they will relish the opportunity to tear down the old and get on with the new. Their principal dangers will be indulging in escapism or conjuring up their darker side through consorting with unsavory associates. Their tendency to retreat into fantasy rather than cope with reality may also be a stumbling block. Yet they will doubtless have a great concern for the less fortunate and sympathy for those who dare to break the rules. If they can muster the strength to break out of their mold in the interest of some large idea or noble cause, their efforts will meet with approval and renown.

CHALLENGE: **TEMPERING THEIR DESIRE TO ESCAPE TO FAR-OFF LANDS**

FULFILLMENT: **SHARING THEIR ZANINESS AND SENSE OF FUN WITH A VALUED PARTNER—WHOSE LIFE THEY CHANGE IN THE BARGAIN**

JOHN QUINCY ADAMS
6th president of the
United States

7/11/1767
Cancer III

July 11–18

THE PERSUADER
CANCER III

Those born in the Week of the Persuader who navigate the Way of Electricity are likely to fare quite well and may well become icons of their time. They will, however, have to guard against their tendency to be ruled by passion, and would do well not to allow their natural zealotry to get out of hand. Otherwise the more revolutionary aspects of this configuration could manifest in a chronic "off with their heads!" approach to problem solving. In fact, avoiding excess in any form in favor of a more detached and intellectual attitude will be most important to both their worldly and higher spiritual development. If they cultivate their formidable powers of observation and reinforce their genuine desire to help others, they will truly flourish and will have a great influence and impact upon the lives of those around them.

CHALLENGE: **RELAXING THEIR NEED TO BE IN CHARGE LONG ENOUGH FOR DESTINY TO WORK THROUGH THEM**

FULFILLMENT: **PARTICIPATING IN, EVEN BEING THE CATALYST FOR, A CULTURAL REVOLUTION**

NOTABLE: **LEON SPINKS (HEAVYWEIGHT BOXER)**

July 19–25
OSCILLATION
CANCER–LEO CUSP

Cancer–Leos on this karmic path are gifted with the energy and resilience to conquer the world and its problems, but they will first have to learn the difference between being a catalyst for change and merely being cataclysmic. Emotional dramas may be a way of life until they learn to cultivate greater objectivity, and many of them have the ability to quite literally drive themselves crazy with worry, overextension, and frustration. Nonetheless, one of their highest endowments is their great moral courage. If they see a wrong, they will not rest until they have done something about it. On the other side of the coin, they may overspend their energies in a chronic need for excitement that is forever in search of satiation. Intellectual pursuits, physical exercise, and a regular routine of meditation or relaxation will be especially useful as outlets for their dynamic and forceful energies.

CHALLENGE: **GRAPPLING WITH THE PSYCHIC STRESS OF OSCILLATING TOO WILDLY IN THEIR MOODS**
FULFILLMENT: **BEING THE QUIET DYNAMO AT THE CENTER OF THE STORM**
NOTABLES: **ALPHONSE MUCHA (DESIGNED ART NOUVEAU POSTERS); LIZZIE BORDEN (ALLEGED MURDERESS); MARCEL CERDAN (BOXER)**

KATHY LEE GIFFORD
TV host
———
8/16/1953
Leo III

July 26–August 2
AUTHORITY
LEO I

Those born in the Week of Authority who journey along this karmic path are likely to make swift and sure progress in their development, providing they refuse to succumb to self-interest and their tendency to be entirely too domineering. Giving up the purely personal in the interest of some larger good may not come so easily to these people, who tend to resist change in any event. Though many of them will turn away from the greater humanitarian and moral challenges presented by this karmic path through an inability to see the bigger social picture, an equal number will wield their natural authority with grace and considerable élan. The key to their success will be their commitment to others: if they can lift their heads and look toward some future vision, they will in turn be a focal point for change and a wonderful role model for those who would travel along with them.

CHALLENGE: **TREATING THEIR DISCIPLES WITH GREATER COMPASSION**
FULFILLMENT: **ENJOYING THE ATTENTION THAT THEIR BRAND OF ELECTRICITY GENERATES**
NOTABLES: **ELIZABETH HARDWICK (AUTHOR; CRITIC); ROBERT GRAY (SONGWRITER; GUITARIST); DAVID BROWN (PRODUCER, *THE STING, JAWS*)**

August 3–10
BALANCED STRENGTH
LEO II

Leo II's who travel the Way of Electricity are highly social animals, blessed with a knack for making connections between themselves and others. Though some with this configuration will prove highly resistant to the more spiritual level of challenge presented by this karmic path, even more of them will employ their considerable strength and vision to instigate needed changes. At their best, these individuals will lead with flair; they are well equipped to build bridges to a better world. At their worst, however, they are easily overtaken by depression, masochism, and a highly irritable approach to their responsibilities. Yet their hunches can see them through the worst stretches, and if they can avoid the need to be belligerent or to make trouble for its own sake, they will find wonderful fulfillment.

CHALLENGE: **NOT OVEREXTENDING THEMSELVES IN THEIR EFFORTS TO PROMOTE CHANGE OR SHIFT ENERGY**
FULFILLMENT: **HAVING THE OPPORTUNITY TO WORK THEIR BEST ASSETS: INTUITION AND TIMING**
NOTABLE: **BARBARA COONEY (ILLUSTRATOR; CHILDREN'S BOOK AUTHOR, *OX-CART MAN*)**

ANNIE OAKLEY
Markswoman/rodeo performer, subject of *Annie Get Your Gun*
———
8/13/1860
Leo III

August 11–18
LEADERSHIP
LEO III

Dynamic and action-oriented, Leo III's who travel the Way of Electricity may have to work hard to slow down and consider their own motivations as they travel this karmic path. Blessed with great strength of character and an unusually well developed moral sense, they will nonetheless have to manage their marked fondness for putting the match to powder kegs and baiting bears. These souls can also be somewhat cantankerous when it comes to taking responsibility for their actions, and may can find it rather tough to hang in for the longer haul. Yet if they can manage to translate some of their more heroic fantasies into real efforts for change and a workable plan for the future, their vision and leadership will combine in a character that is almost certainly legendary and sometimes even godlike in its influence on the lives of others.

CHALLENGE: **CULTIVATING GREATER EMPATHY, ALTRUISM, OR COMPASSION IN THEIR DEALINGS WITH OTHERS**
FULFILLMENT: **ELECTRIFYING THEIR ENVIRONMENT WITH THEIR MANY CREATIVE IDEAS**

August 19–25

EXPOSURE
LEO–VIRGO CUSP

Though this configuration is likely to result in people with a charismatic and dynamic presence, it is far more likely that they will become the instruments of change or catalysts for reform than it is that they will assume the burdens of leadership or the mantle of authority or serve as the role models for revolution. In fact, they will be prone to playing their cards pretty close to the chest; they are the kind of people who can be found quietly dropping the right word or planting the right seed in the fertile ground of the thoughts and imaginations of the public rather than those who light the fires of revolution. As a result, they can be manipulative in the extreme and may turn into the kind of power brokers who are all but invisible as they work their way through the world. Yet that invisibility will never last for long, especially if their vision, execution, and ideas are not in strict accord with the highest moral and spiritual standards.

INGRID BERGMAN
Film and stage actress

8/28/1916
Virgo I

CHALLENGE: **BUILDING BETTER SYSTEMS OF COMMUNICATING WITH THEIR INTIMATES**
FULFILLMENT: **WENDING THEIR WAY THROUGH THE CORRIDORS OF POWER**
NOTABLE: **PETER HORTON (ACTOR, *THIRTYSOMETHING*)**

August 26–September 2

SYSTEM BUILDERS
VIRGO I

It may be rather uncomfortable for Virgo I's to ride the waves of change when navigating this karmic path. Though extremely technically gifted and blessed with a greater degree of natural analytic ability than some on this road, they will have to work hard to overcome their predisposition to worry, frustration, or getting lost in details. Thus, they may well resist some of their best inspirations and visions and become chronically unable to see the forest for the trees. Nonetheless, their hearts are sure to lead them in some service-oriented direction, and if they cultivate a sense of peace and a greater ability to trust, not only will their journey will go more smoothly but they will experience far greater joy in connecting with the infinite plan—if only by planting a single seed of positive, far-reaching change.

CHALLENGE: **COMING TO TERMS WITH THEIR EFFECT ON OTHERS**
FULFILLMENT: **BELIEVING THAT THEIR EFFORTS ARE ON BEHALF OF A HIGHER PRINCIPLE**
NOTABLES: **MARCIA CLARK (PROSECUTOR, O. J. SIMPSON TRIAL); MARTHA RAYE (ENTERTAINER; KNOWN FOR USO TOURS)**

September 3–10

THE ENIGMA
VIRGO II

The Way of Electricity may do quite a bit to "jazz up" the lives of those born in this week, while the high moral standards, natural discrimination, and analytical approach to people and problems that Virgo II's bring to the equation will do a great deal to assist their progress along this life journey. In a word, their greatest problem or challenge will be developing the willingness and ability to close the gap between their deepest needs and highest aspirations and to give themselves the proper credit for their own creativity. Nonetheless, these rather steely people are made of sterner stuff than any number of their fellows on the Way of Electricity, and if they do not allow their more rigid attitudes, buried fears of rejection, or need to keep up appearances to interfere with their higher challenge to raise and inspire the collective consciousness, they will take fine and distinguished, if somewhat measured, strides along this karmic path.

GRANDMA MOSES
Painter, started in her late 70s

9/7/1860
Virgo II

CHALLENGE: **WORRYING LESS ABOUT APPEARING FORMIDABLE**
FULFILLMENT: **COMING TO ENJOY BEING A MOVER AND SHAKER**
NOTABLES: **AMY IRVING (ACTRESS, *YENTL*); EDWARD FILENE (MERCHANT; ESTABLISHED 1ST CREDIT UNION)**

September 11–18

THE LITERALIST
VIRGO III

The natural gifts of Virgo III's may at first glance appear to be at odds with the challenge and promise of the Way of Electricity, yet there is the possibility of great advancement along this karmic path. Among their natural gifts and blessings is the ability to apply themselves and to see their pet projects and plans through to conclusion in a practical fashion. Yet among their chief failings is the refusal to give proper reverence and acknowledgment to their higher intuitions, aspirations, and the collective need. Too, their knack for serving as a catalyst may work for either good or ill, depending almost entirely on whether they choose to assume a reactionary, protective, and rigid approach to innovation or whether they instead take the high road and serve as the champions of talented and inspired individuals who may not be blessed with quite the same ability to draw the hearts and minds of the collective and public consciousness.

CHALLENGE: **REALIZING THAT TO PROD OTHERS ALONG THEY THEMSELVES CANNOT AFFORD TO PROCRASTINATE**
FULFILLMENT: **UNCOVERING TRUTH**
NOTABLE: **DAVID SHINER (MIME)**

September 19–24
BEAUTY
VIRGO–LIBRA CUSP

Those born on the Cusp of Beauty who navigate the Way of Electricity may find that instability and moodiness are their greatest liabilities. Yet their chief challenge on this karmic path will be not so much learning to divest themselves of instability but rather learning to go with the flow by aligning themselves with deeper spiritual and creative forces. Indeed, the struggle to become established, credible, and ensconced in the hearts and minds of those around them may well be their principal preoccupation until they learn that all that glitters is not necessarily gold and that real power lies not so much in the ability to fit in, conform, or allow oneself to be dominated by popular wisdom as it does in taking the necessary risks involved in being different, standing up for what one believes in, and championing the causes of the less fortunate. In general, tapping into a larger sense of human values, rather than being entirely dependent upon their image, will be essential to their success.

CHALLENGE: **COUNTERING THEIR CAPACITY TO BECOME MIRED IN UNSAVORY ACTIVITIES**

FULFILLMENT: **BEING AT THE FOREFRONT OF CURRENT DEVELOPMENTS IN FASHION, MEDIA, OR THE ARTS**

WILLIAM FAULKNER
Writer; 1949 Nobel Prize
winner for literature
——
9/25/1897
Libra I

September 25–October 2
THE PERFECTIONIST
LIBRA I

Those born in this week who travel the Way of Electricity may have a bit of a rough ride until they get into tune with higher forces and relinquish their need for control. Though it can be said that these exacting and often demanding people have the collective good at heart, it is equally true that they may use their talent for homing in on injustice and sounding the alarms in public life as a means of avoiding their own deeply personal issues. In fact, Libra I's may be uncomfortable with many of the challenges of this karmic path until they learn to avoid the dangers of compulsion, excitability, and finger-pointing. Until they develop the confidence to let their hair down, relax, and stop putting barriers between themselves and their subconscious, they will be in for a rather rocky passage. All in all, they will do best to meditate frequently upon the axiom "Sufficient unto the day are the troubles thereof."

CHALLENGE: **WORKING LESS ON TRYING TO FIX MUNDANE DETAILS AND MORE ON OPENING OTHER PEOPLE'S EYES**

FULFILLMENT: **PERMITTING THEIR FEELING SIDE TO NOURISH THEIR INSIGHT AND CONVICTIONS**

NOTABLE: **WILLIAM STOKES (MODERN EUROPEAN DOCTOR; LED DUBLIN SCHOOL OF ANATOMICAL DIAGNOSTICS)**

October 3–10
SOCIETY
LIBRA II

These people may well be marked by a love-hate relationship with society and its rules of behavior. On the one hand, they may feel compelled to perform for others or become preoccupied with and mired in others' opinions and needs. On the other, they may have a clear and rather exalted vision of what needs to be done in the name of collective progress, yet find themselves lacking in sufficient strength to do anything about it. Still and all, it is highly likely that they will serve as catalysts for change—whether they choose to embrace that aspect of themselves or not. If they do, they will find great fulfillment and advancement along this life journey. If they don't, they may well have to content themselves with serving as an inspiration to others.

CHALLENGE: **CONTROLLING THE ONSLAUGHT OF PEOPLE INTO THEIR LIVES IN ORDER TO KEEP THEIR EMOTIONS BALANCED BETTER**

FULFILLMENT: **ENERGIZING OTHERS FOR POSITIVE CHANGE**

NOTABLE: **ELIJAH (POOLE) MUHAMMAD (CONTROVERSIAL BLACK MUSLIM LEADER)**

VICTORIA TENNANT
Actress/writer
——
9/30/1953
Libra I

October 11–18
THEATER
LIBRA III

Those born in the Week of Theater who navigate the Way of Electricity will doubtless relish the attention, excitement, and challenges they meet along the way, yet they may find it difficult to focus on higher spiritual objectives. Their worldliness and natural savoir faire may prove to be great assets, yet if these highly sophisticated people become too preoccupied with worldly matters, they will most likely fail to achieve their more spiritual objectives. One way or another, their challenge will be to attune themselves to a more human set of values and release their need for approval. However, if they can find the strength, skill, and constancy to overcome their need to ride the tide of public opinion and instead learn to employ their knack for creating controversy in such a way as to serve as an inspiration for others, all will go brilliantly for them.

CHALLENGE: **REFRAINING FROM PROJECTING A KNOW-IT-ALL ATTITUDE**

FULFILLMENT: **POSITIONING THEMSELVES AT THE CENTER OF THE ACTION**

NOTABLE: **JOHN WILKES (ENGLISH SOCIAL REFORMER)**

October 19–25

DRAMA AND CRITICISM
LIBRA–SCORPIO CUSP

The energies here can combine in such a way that the dramatic presence of Libra–Scorpios is exalted to nearly heroic proportions. However much dynamism and charisma they may have, however, they will need to take care to avoid developing a sense of entitlement or the idea that they deserve an award simply for showing up. Thus, the ability to follow through on their best ideas, inspirations, and observations will be especially important, as will the ability to release hurts, slights, and rivalries. Too, their high-voltage personalities may cause them to take refuge in addictions or substance abuse as they attempt to calm themselves down. Yet they have the possibility for great achievement if they find more constructive outlets for their amazing energy and employ their considerable powers of observation to construct a vision of lasting value. If they succeed in doing so, their efforts will have a lasting impact upon the world, especially in artistic and cultural areas.

KEITH HERNANDEZ
Baseball player, NY Mets

10/20/1953
Libra–Scorpio Cusp

CHALLENGE: **GRAPPLING WITH A NEED TO RETREAT THAT OFTEN MANIFESTS ITSELF AS DEPRESSION**
FULFILLMENT: **HAVING THE WORLD'S EAR**

October 26–November 2

INTENSITY
SCORPIO I

Though Scorpio I's who travel the Way of Electricity will find this life journey highly unpredictable, one thing is certain: sooner or later they will develop a deeply spiritual orientation. How these individuals go about finding their god will be as varied as the individuals themselves, yet it's a safe bet that both extreme worldliness and extreme escapism will figure into the journey. Blessed with an ability to thrive on pressure, they have a highly charged, intense character that can mesh well with the energies of the Way of Electricity, and if they do not allow their desire for the extreme to manifest itself in self-destructive tendencies, they will discover within themselves a capacity for real transcendence and extraordinary vision on this breathtakingly polarized life journey.

CHALLENGE: **NOT ALLOWING THEMSELVES TO SLIP INTO EXTREMISM**
FULFILLMENT: **SHOWING THEIR SOLAR BRAND OF ELECTRICITY TO OTHERS**
NOTABLE: **PAUL JOSEPH GOEBBELS (POWERFUL NAZI LEADER)**

November 3–11

DEPTH
SCORPIO II

Any number of mystics and moguls can be found among the Scorpio II's who navigate the Way of Electricity. These are people who are prone to take life seriously and are blessed with the ability to turn even the most far-out vision into reality. Though there is some danger that some of them will fail the higher challenges of this karmic path by refusing to connect with its humanizing and futuristic aspects, others will embrace the call to a more deeply spiritual or religious orientation with an open heart. Though these people will have to work hard to overcome their predisposition to emotional extremes and rather negative and pessimistic outlook, they can nevertheless find considerable success and progress, providing they allow themselves to release the purely personal and embrace the universal in their search for higher truth and greater fulfillment.

DENNIS MILLER
Actor/political comedian;
started on
Saturday Night Live

11/3/1953
Scorpio II

CHALLENGE: **NOT DEVOLVING INTO ENVY, COMPETITIVENESS, OR VENGEFULNESS**
FULFILLMENT: **UTILIZING THEIR UNIQUE BRAND OF HUMOR TO INFLUENCE OTHERS**
NOTABLES: **KATE CAPSHAW (ACTRESS); MABEL NORMAND (SILENT FILM ACTRESS)**

November 12–18

CHARM
SCORPIO III

Truly formidable manipulators of public and private opinion, these people can find wonderful success along the Way of Electricity. Savvy and sophisticated, they may become preoccupied with matters of taste and image to the extent that they fail to grasp the higher promise and greater spiritual challenges of this karmic path. Yet their natural sense of realism is sure to aid them along the way, and they will derive great enjoyment and fulfillment from seeing their carefully laid plans come to fulfillment through either their own efforts or those of the people around them. At best, they will do wonderfully well working behind the scenes, networking and bringing a sense of alchemy to their plans and projects. At worst, they will be overly controlling, determined to gain credit for their accomplishments, and complacent about making progress toward a higher set of values.

CHALLENGE: **CONTROLLING THEIR MORE PASSIONATE SIDE**
FULFILLMENT: **DISCOVERING HOW KEEN THEIR DISCERNMENT IS AND HOW EASILY THEY ARE ABLE TO CHARM OTHERS INTO DOING THEIR BIDDING**

November 19–24
REVOLUTION
SCORPIO–SAGITTARIUS CUSP

Scorpio–Sagittarians who navigate the sometimes treacherous terrain of the Way of Electricity may really have to watch their footing on this road. Yet the highest level of attainment is possible for them if they will only turn away from petty and emotional concerns, concentrate on their ability to embrace the new, and set their sights on clear and specific goals and results. There may be something of the iconoclast about them, however, and they would do well to avoid their tendency to change things simply for the sake of changing them and to control their own excitability. Otherwise they may exhaust themselves and everyone else with their extremes of attitude and behavior. Yet the capacity to gain a great perspective on the human condition exists in all of them, and if they channel their vision and energy into a broader sense of collective values, they will find not only validation for what is new but the security that comes from aligning oneself with the eternal.

JOAN DIDION
Novelist/*Vogue* editor

12/5/1934
Sagittarius II

CHALLENGE: **HOLDING THEMSELVES TO A MORAL COMPASS**
FULFILLMENT: **APPLYING THEIR UNRELENTING ZEAL IN THE PROMOTION OF CHANGE OR INNOVATION**

November 25–December 2
INDEPENDENCE
SAGITTARIUS I

The ability to distinguish between mere impulse and genuine intuition may prove essential to the success of those born in this week who travel the Way of Electricity. Otherwise, they may make this journey at breakneck speed, obsessed with independence yet hampered by their inability to set themselves tangible goals and higher objectives. Though they will doubtless seek out those environments that will afford them free range of their ideas and self-expression, they would do well to learn the value of slowing down, going into their visions with greater depth and awareness, and, looking before they leap. Yet if they learn to rely on their great sense of fairness, highly developed ethics, and genuine generosity of spirit, they will realize wonderful success along this road as they fight for greater freedom not just for themselves but for others.

CHALLENGE: **REMEMBERING TO SLOW DOWN AND LOOK INWARD IN QUIET REFLECTION NOW AND THEN**
FULFILLMENT: **FIGHTING FOR JUSTICE**
NOTABLE: **CYRIL RITCHARD (ACTOR/DIRECTOR, *PETER PAN*)**

December 3–10
THE ORIGINATOR
SAGITTARIUS II

Those born in this week who travel the Way of Electricity may find themselves quite happy on this life journey, as its challenge to explore the new, the avant-garde, and the latest in innovative trends and techniques is very much in keeping with their natural dispositions and inclinations. Never afraid to be different, these people can derive great personal delight from their ability to stir things up and draw attention to their latest ideas. However, they have a tendency not to follow through and see their ideas and inspirations brought to a satisfying conclusion, and this may prove to be their principal failing. Yet if they can manage to overcome their tendency to scatter themselves in superficial efforts and avoid plunging into emotional depths in the face of rejection, they are likely to leave a lasting impression in the hearts and minds of all those with whom they come into contact.

JUDI DENCH
British actress;
Oscar and Tony winner

12/12/1934
Sagittarius III

CHALLENGE: **NOT DEGENERATING INTO AGGRESSION OR OTHER EXTREME BEHAVIORS**
FULFILLMENT: **FINDING THEMSELVES TO BE THE PIED PIPERS OF THEIR SOCIAL SET**
NOTABLE: **MARCUS DALY (BUSINESS EXECUTIVE; FOUNDED ANACONDA MINING CO.)**

December 11–18
THE TITAN
SAGITTARIUS III

The search for excellence and ecstatic experience may mark the journey of the people born in this week who find themselves on the Way of Electricity. Blessed with considerable self-assurance and a rather devil-may-care attitude toward public opinion, they may nevertheless have to guard against the dangers of hubris and unrealistic expectations while on this life journey. Too, they will have little stomach for slights and disappointments, and their big hearts are sometimes overshadowed by by even bigger egos. Thus, they would do well to tread this karmic path lightly and not to take their own or other people's follies too seriously. Yet at bottom, these people have an awe-inspiring belief in life that can serve as a beacon of passion and inspiration for those they meet along the way.

CHALLENGE: **NOT INDULGING OR ACTING OUT THEIR MOODIER OR DARKER SIDES**
FULFILLMENT: **WEAVING A MAGICAL, ELECTRICAL SPELL AROUND OTHERS**
NOTABLE: **RICHARD ZANUCK (FILM EXECUTIVE/PRODUCER, *JAWS*, *DRIVING MISS DAISY*)**

December 19–25

PROPHECY
SAGITTARIUS–CAPRICORN CUSP

Those born on the Cusp of Prophecy who travel the Way of Electricity have an almost eerie knack for pinpointing the latest in trends and developments. In fact, this quality of observation and prediction can be so great that they garner more than their share of attention and interest. Yet they may care very little for the opinions of others, preferring to withdraw into a world of study and contemplation rather than take a more active role in instigating change or reform. Though personal sensitivity may get the best of them early in life, the indications of greater and more highly developed spirituality are very strong, and some with this configuration may lean toward organized or alternative religions and lifestyles, especially as they slow down with the passage of years.

BOB DENVER
TV actor, *Gilligan's Island*

1/9/1935
Capricorn II

CHALLENGE: **CULTIVATING THEIR SOLAR, OR MORE SOCIAL, SIDE**
FULFILLMENT: **IMPARTING THEIR HUNCHES AND NEARLY PSYCHIC INSIGHTS TO OTHERS**
NOTABLE: **BENJAMIN DISRAELI (BRITISH NOVELIST; PRIME MINISTER)**

December 26–January 2

THE RULER
CAPRICORN I

The innate need of Capricorn I's for stability, dependability, and tradition may be at odds with the more unsettled and explosive energies of the Way of Electricity. Yet as inflexible and even authoritarian as these people can sometimes be, this karmic path is sure to offer a great education in the ways and means of effective change. If they are careful to weigh their options, hear all sides, and make decisions based on their inner conviction of right and wrong, they are unlikely to stray very far from the road to higher development. This karmic path will imbue their lives with more excitement than they might be entirely comfortable with, yet they will bring stability and a sense of lasting values to its often explosive energies. The combination can make for a volatile mix, yet if they work to open the channels between the practical and the infinite, they will live the kind of legend of which most of us can only dream.

CHALLENGE: **REMAINING MORE OPEN TO NEW IDEAS OR APPROACHES**
FULFILLMENT: **GENERATING THE KIND OF CHARISMA THAT MAKES FOR EFFECTIVE LEADERSHIP**
NOTABLES: **TOM JARRIEL (ABC NEWS CORRESPONDENT); MAGGIE SMITH (ACTRESS; OSCAR FOR *CALIFORNIA SUITE*)**

January 3–9

DETERMINATION
CAPRICORN II

Those born in the Week of Determination who make their way along the Way of Electricity may lose their footing from time to time, yet will find that their salvation lies in their predisposition toward and inclination to study higher spiritual and metaphysical matters. They will doubtless find themselves quite happy on this karmic path, and though it may take a number of years for them to discover their real talent for innovation and invention, they are blessed with an innate down-to-earth quality that will serve them well even as they explore their highest-flown ambitions and aspirations. Getting in touch with their radical side will be the real key to their happiness, however, and once they leave the burdens of the past behind and turn their eyes toward the future, they will be able to instigate and effect far-reaching and important changes, both in their own lives and in the lives of those around them.

A. J. FOYT
Auto racer

1/16/1935
Capricorn III

CHALLENGE: **OVERCOMING THEIR MORE SERIOUS OR NEGATIVE ATTITUDES**
FULFILLMENT: **BEING INSPIRED TO PURSUE MORE UNUSUAL TOPICS**
NOTABLES: **ELVIS PRESLEY (THE "KING" OF ROCK 'N' ROLL); CAPUCINE (FRENCH ACTRESS, *WHAT'S NEW, PUSSYCAT?*); FLOYD PATTERSON (BOXING CHAMP)**

January 10–16

DOMINANCE
CAPRICORN III

Those born in the Week of Dominance who navigate the Way of Electricity can be rather cantankerous and difficult personalities until they develop the necessary self-confidence to become the movers and shakers they really want to be. In fact, many of these people have a really outrageous side to their characters, though many will keep it carefully under wraps in their dealings with all but their nearest and dearest. Too, they may become rather unsettled by their ability to attract attention, as others will often pick up on their more passionate energies without quite knowing why, intuitively responding to them with a kind of "where there's smoke, there's fire" reaction. Yet once they begin to direct their talents toward broad goals and trends, they can bring their visions to satisfying and tangible manifestation through solid efforts and grounded ambition. If they can avoid their temptations to authoritarianism, emotional repression, and flat-out tyranny, all can go brilliantly here.

CHALLENGE: **SETTING ASIDE THE PESSIMISTIC BELIEF THAT THEIR LIVES ARE FATED**
FULFILLMENT: **BEING ABLE TO INDULGE THEIR ECCENTRICITY SAFELY**
NOTABLES: **KRESKIN (THE AMAZING KRESKIN; PSYCHIC ENTERTAINER); WILLIAM JAMES (PHILOSOPHER; PSYCHOLOGIST)**

January 17–22
MYSTERY AND IMAGINATION
CAPRICORN–AQUARIUS CUSP

It may seem to some that Capricorn–Aquarians who find themselves on the Way of Electricity have gotten far more than their fair share of the divine spark, for when it comes to inspiration, innovation, and the ability to fire the public imagination, they are blessed with an almost magical ability to make the world see things their way. The problem is that they may not be able to settle down to the extent that they can appreciate or develop their own gifts, much less direct them in any productive fashion. The chaotic and difficult aspects of this configuration may result in any number of emotional and even mental problems. Yet for all their struggles to regulate and moderate their emotional extremes, they will be blessed with an equal measure of inspired genius. Thus, if they can turn inward and cultivate the self-discipline required to engage in activities such as meditation, relaxation, and prayer, they will find what they need on the Way of Electricity.

CHALLENGE: **MELDING THE VARIETY OF THEIR DIVERSE ENERGIES INTO A SOOTHING BLEND**

FULFILLMENT: **CHANNELING AND GROUNDING ALL FORMS OF INSPIRATION**

NOTABLE: **TIPPI HEDREN (ACTRESS, *THE BIRDS*)**

SAM COOKE
Soul singer,
"You Send Me"

1/22/1935
Capricorn–Aquarius Cusp

January 23–30
GENIUS
AQUARIUS I

Those born in the Week of Genius who find themselves journeying along the Way of Electricity will be blessed with a real sense of what's on the next horizon. They will also find that they are able to divest themselves of much of their emotionalism and tendency to extremes, and as a result will set their sights quite high when it comes to personal and social achievements. Though recklessness and a tendency to start much more than they can ever finish can work to their detriment, it is more than likely that they will successfully overcome such inclinations, especially when their minds are fired by the vision of a new concept, a new invention, or even a whole new world. If they can cultivate personal discipline and the study and work habits necessary to hone their fine minds to a cutting edge, they will encounter few obstacles to achieving great rewards.

CHALLENGE: **GUARDING AGAINST A DOMINEERING OR TYRANNICAL SIDE**

FULFILLMENT: **DISCOVERING THEIR VIRTUOSO CAPACITY TO "WORK A ROOM"**

NOTABLES: **RANDOLPH SCOTT (ACTOR; WESTERNS); BOB UECKER (FORMER BASEBALL PLAYER; SPORTSWRITER; ACTOR)**

January 31–February 7
YOUTH AND EASE
AQUARIUS II

First and foremost, Aquarius II's who travel the Way of Electricity are bound to be blessed with a refreshingly lighthearted and easygoing approach to people and problems. These people, however reckless, restless, or downright distracted they may be, are unlikely to sweat the small stuff or become too tightly bound to the dramas and details that occupy some others traveling this karmic path. In fact, perhaps their chief downfall will be their sheer popularity or their tendency to live up to others' expectations rather than their own. Yet if they go within to develop and explore their higher spiritual awareness and sources of personal strength and conviction and take time out to cultivate the quiet moments of inspiration that are essential to us all, they will bring their knowledge and special grasp of new ideas to a wide and willing audience.

CHALLENGE: **RESISTING THEIR TEMPTATION TO REMAIN LOCKED IN THE FANTASY LAND OF THEIR CHILDHOOD**

FULFILLMENT: **BEING A CATALYST IN THEIR SOCIAL GROUP**

JANE WAGNER
Actress, writer, director,
*The Search for Intelligent
Life in the Universe*

2/2/1935
Aquarius II

February 8–15
ACCEPTANCE
AQUARIUS III

The unusual characters born in this week who travel the Way of Electricity may turn out to be inspiring figures indeed, providing they do not allow some of their more fixed or inflexible attitudes to cloud their better judgment or their intuitive sense of what's in the interest of the collective good. In fact, they may be truly progressive in their approach to what needs to be done yet hampered by an attitude that is either overly accepting and laissez-faire or intolerant and overly resistant to change. Yet if they keep in mind that all change begins not in the outside world but within the self, they can realize great advancement along this road, especially when they concentrate their energies upon planting seeds rather than counting the harvest.

CHALLENGE: **MELLOWING THEIR REACTIONARY SIDE**

FULFILLMENT: **EXPERIENCING THE VARIETY THIS PATH AFFORDS**

February 16–22
SENSITIVITY
AQUARIUS–PISCES CUSP

The great sensitivity that is the the hallmark of those born in this week will be even more heightened on the Way of Electricity, though they will have a greater sense of personal detachment and objectivity than might otherwise be evident. The most successful of these people will have the knack of using their intuition in abstract ways and will display a gift for synthesizing old knowledge in new ways. Their innovative and far-reaching concepts and ideas may impact the world for generations to come. Yet for many this karmic path will not always be an easy one to travel, especially if they allow eccentricity, escapism, or runaway fantasies to disturb their rather delicate emotional balance. If they work to overcome the dangers of pessimism and insecurity, however, they will be able to find the courage to reach for seemingly impossible goals, and the results will likely benefit us all.

CHALLENGE: **TEMPERING THEIR TENDENCY TO GO TO EXTREMES**

FULFILLMENT: **FINE-TUNING THEIR INTERPERSONAL STYLE**

NOTABLE: **SONNY BONO (ACTOR; ENTERTAINER, SONNY & CHER; POLITICIAN)**

WILHELM GRIMM
Folklorist,
Grimm's Fairy Tales

2/24/1786
Pisces I

February 23–March 2
SPIRIT
PISCES I

Those born in the Week of Spirit who navigate the Way of Electricity may be blessed with a rare and genuine spirituality that is not frequently found on terra firma. Likely to have rich imaginative and often psychic talents, they will nonetheless have to work to overcome their hypersensitivity while at the same time struggling to maintain and sustain their rather fragile emotional balance. It is unlikely that simple grounding is the answer, for these people find ordinary stability rather stifling. Instead, they should concentrate their energies in some direction where they can better explore and expand on their desire to do good and to leave the world a better place than they found it. When their energies are so directed, they will find their passage much smoother and themselves better able to appreciate the progress, attention, and pleasures they attract along the way.

CHALLENGE: **COMING TO TERMS WITH THEIR YEARNING FOR THE DIVINE**

FULFILLMENT: **INVOLVING THEMSELVES IN ART, LITERATURE, OR OTHER AESTHETIC FIELDS**

NOTABLE: **ROBERT CONRAD (ACTOR, *WILD WILD WEST*)**

March 3–10
THE LONER
PISCES II

Going within to honor the spiritual aspects of existence may come naturally to those born in the Week of the Loner who travel the Way of Electricity, yet by the same token these astute and highly intelligent individuals will have a natural knack for worldly affairs. This combination can make for quite an interesting and diverse mix of inclinations and aspirations, and many Pisces II's will go through quite a process of soul-searching before they can sort out their lives. Mood swings and fits of depression may be their biggest problems, and even in the best of times they can have a tendency to "fall off the wagon" and into the depths of despair, escapism, and substance abuse. Yet the fact that they continue to survive does much to boost their self-confidence, and as they age and leave the burden of uncertainty somewhere by the side of road, they will find the Way of Electricity a progressively happier journey.

CHALLENGE: **RECONCILING THEIR PREFERENCE FOR A SOLITARY LIFE WITH THEIR UNIQUE ELECTRIC APPEAL TO OTHERS**

FULFILLMENT: **EMBRACING THE POWER OF POSITIVE THINKING**

SHAQUILLE O'NEAL
Basketball star, Lakers
center; recording artist

3/6/1972
Pisces II

March 11–18
DANCERS AND DREAMERS
PISCES III

High idealism and good practical instincts are a truly formidable combination on this karmic path, especially when Pisces III's concentrate their energies more on the general human condition and less on their personal goals. An ability to back up, detach themselves, and cultivate a broader spiritual perspective will be especially useful and will help these sometimes troubled people divest themselves of the emotional burdens they bear. Getting into touch with a more universal sense of the patterns and rhythms that rule our lives will be important, as will seeking out professions and avocations that allow them the free range of their ideas. Perhaps, however, these people will come to discover that their greatest talent lies not in specific goals or achievements but in their unique ability to touch the lives of others in ways that effect far-reaching and significant change.

CHALLENGE: **GROUNDING THEIR PERIPATETIC ENERGIES**

FULFILLMENT: **SHARING THEIR FORMIDABLE DREAMS OR IDEAS WITH OTHERS**

NOTABLES: **JUDD HIRSCH (ACTOR, *TAXI*); STÉPHANE MALLARMÉ (SYMBOLIST POET, *A DICE THROW*); ALBERT EINSTEIN (NOBEL PRIZE-WINNING PHYSICIST; THEORY OF RELATIVITY)**

The Way of Freedom

LEO I TO AQUARIUS I
Authority to Genius

The feisty individuals on this karmic path strive to do things their own way. Often, those on the Way of Freedom come into life with a strict set of standards or codes of behavior to which they feel themselves compelled to adhere. Freeing themselves of such principles, traditions, and modes of thought is the requirement of this karmic path. The individuals here are called to unfetter themselves from societal pressure and to have the courage either to be different or to think differently. Particularly fated individuals, those on the Way of Freedom are often required to leave the safety of known quantities behind and strike off on their own, following a path that depends more on learning from experience rather than learning from established educational institutions. The lure of the unusual or exotic is strong, and thus travel and its broadening effect on one's perspective will always entice those on the Way of Freedom. This karmic path can engender brilliant breakthroughs in thinking since those following it will learn that they need not be limited by the way others see things. Such a metamorphosis is not easily accomplished, particularly for these people, who like to feel secure within the protective womb of an established system of social philosophy, religion, or family morals.

The core lesson for those on the Way of Freedom is to be true to themselves. Unfortunately, in order for these men and women to be who they are, they are often forced to make a break with their family of origin or social group. These individuals arrive in this life with a fear of change and are inclined to cling to the rules with which they were brought up. It is interesting that if they are unable to create the inner assurance to believe in themselves enough to find a way to work within the system, the system or their family seems to reject them and spit them out. Certainly many on this karmic path are able to step into the fullness of their true selves and live authentically without undergoing the trauma of a separation from family, friends, or society. However, if they are unable to achieve such a inner break by truly accepting themselves, their social milieu may create the conditions that will teach them this lesson once and for all.

The individuals on this path will have a great respect for tradition yet will never really feel that it belongs to them. In childhood they tend to be oddballs or outcasts, frequently wishing or yearning to belong to a club that doesn't want them as a member. Sometimes these men and women spend their whole lives trying to prove themselves worthy of fitting in, often struggling to impress what are really only shadows from the past. A preoccupation with being popular can mark these people for life, when in truth they are loners. It is also their early and formative experiences that cause them to be unusually concerned about fairness and other democratic values. They may exhibit a real passion for the downtrodden masses and will often work tirelessly on behalf of those less fortunate

CORE LESSON
Being true to oneself by living an authentic life

GOAL
To experience full freedom

GIFTS
Democratic, Freethinking, Ingenious

PITFALLS
Dogmatic, Fearful, Reckless

than themselves. Moreover, as they mature and come to believe in their own right to be free, they will begin to fight for the rights of others. For those on this karmic path, freedom is not a concept, it is a religion.

Sometimes the freedom these individuals find is simply a mental one. Breaking taboos and societal norms isn't really up their alley, since they never truly rid themselves of their belief in higher principles. They find great joy in liberating their mental processes from having to be used in any particular way or adhering to any system of thought. This enables them to embark on any endeavor with a fresh approach, thereby allowing them to make substantial creative contributions to any field. The best education for them is learning through trial and error. Destiny seems to be their most important educator, and it will usually serve them just the diet they need but hardly expect. Prematurely being let go from a job or relationship may launch them into unknown waters—but also into new learning experiences. In fact, they seem destined to learn most things pretty much on their own. Because of this, and since they tend to be radical thinkers, they must take great care when presenting their ideas to the world. Thorough preparation and solid presentation are essential for those on the Way of Freedom, since when ill prepared they are easily knocked off their feet and can become frustrated or depressed.

More than any other karmic path, this one holds the

RELEASE

The need to be popular

REWARD

The joy of being oneself

greatest danger for individuals on it who become stuck or unable to grow. Coming in at Authority, those on this path may succumb to the fear of acknowledging the truth of who they are and of what familial or societal disruptions would result were they to truly reveal themselves to others. The result can be a profoundly unconscious and unquestioning adherence to rules or higher principles, accompanied by extreme dogmatism. Projecting their fears and their own shadow qualities onto others, they will often exhibit prejudice and intolerance. Even more troublesome is that they are fairly stubborn, even immovable or domineering when they want to be. Once set on a dogmatic course, they may be unable to awaken to the truth and their soul's calling

Although these people possess the capacity to be authority figures or leaders, their karmic journey necessitates breaking away from such tendencies and being free to follow one's own impulses. Leading confers an obligation to those one leads and to the rules of the group. To pursue the Way of Freedom, those on this karmic path must guard against the temptation to take on responsibility or a mantle of authority. Another pitfall is that the freer these men and women become, the more they show a disturbingly reckless or distracted side. On the whole, however, these individuals are not apt to stray too far outside society's rules. What is perhaps best for them, in the long run, is finding a healthy

SUGGESTION

Realize when you are replaying old scripts or projecting fears onto others.
Embrace who you are, and you'll find that others begin to accept you.

balance between freedom and responsibility. Fulfilling set requirements, domestic or otherwise, on a daily basis while leaving large blocks of time free for themselves will help keep them on an even keel.

In matters of career, those on the Way of Freedom usually do best when self-employed or working in an independent capacity. They are not really social by nature. Though they like to be well thought of by their colleagues, they need to stay out of the pack in order to keep their thought processes and methods untainted by outside influences. A number of the lessons of this path will be learned in work or career. Often it is here that those on the Way of Freedom will have to fight to walk to the beat of a different drum. Because of their battles with the world, such individuals usually need to periodically retreat, meditate, and recharge before reemerging into the fray.

It may be difficult for those on this karmic path to maintain steady relationships, since it is not human contact they are interested in as much as a given field of study, whether scientific, technological, artistic, or economic. The lives of those on the Way of Freedom rarely follow a straight line. In fact, it may be many years before they are able to settle down long enough to devote themselves to one field. The choice of an intimate partner can be problematic for them. Although unassuming and stable individuals would seem to be best for them, they do bore easily and often demand someone who is as unusual as they. Their partner will have to show great tolerance, since they have a tremendous need to become involved with other people (frequently the wrong ones) and chafe at any form of restraint. Sudden, sharp, and somewhat painful breaks in relationships seem to be the norm. For example, those on this karmic path are often forced to cut ties with their relatives in their struggle for freedom.

Since fate takes such a strong hand in guiding their experiences, others often see them as flitting from one thing to another, spending their time tasting the pleasures that life has to offer. However, these people rarely allow themselves to be consistently happy since they find contentment a rather boring state. The upside of such instability, however, is that not only do people find them to be fascinating individuals, they also admire their constant searching and refusal to be conventionally satisfied. Because of their nervous tendencies, those on this karmic path are best off avoiding unstable individuals, who will feed their own reckless fire. What will benefit those on the Way of Freedom is grounding themselves with exercise and earthy foods, and creating a quiet home base. Like a boat cut adrift, those on the Way of Freedom must learn to surrender themselves to the flow, trusting that they will arrive at their destination in full possession of who they really are.

BALANCE POINT

Acceptance and Rejection

CRYSTALS AND GEMSTONES

Tiger Eye connects individuals to their power. This stone fosters the courage to be free as its inner light clarifies and brings order to confused, shadowy aspects of the mind.

NOTABLES ON THIS KARMIC PATH

French chanteuse **Edith Piaf** possessed the feisty individuality that drives those born on this path to strike out on their own and learn from experience rather than schooling. Piaf was forced to learn the lessons of releasing the past as well as the pain of the present. From her early days as a child living on the streets of Paris to later struggles with illness and tragedy, misfortune seemed to dog her. Through it all, Piaf stayed true to herself, focused on her art, and gave adoring audiences her all, creating a devoted following around the world.

EDITH PIAF

Ophthalmologist Richard Raskin's decision to become **Rene Richards** through a highly publicized sex change operation exemplifies the determination of those on this path to embrace their true identity. Through this public self-acceptance, Richards became a living symbol for thousands who felt unfairly trapped in a corporeal prison of the wrong gender. By disregarding strict societal codes of behavior, finding the courage to be herself, and drastically altering her ap-

RENE RICHARDS

pearance to visibly bare her true person, Richards fulfilled her destiny.

As a fierce individualist, seventh U.S. president **Andrew Jackson** (known as Old Hickory) is characteristic of those on the Way of Freedom. Jackson often acted as a maverick, striking off on his own path rather than following the established way of doing things. Awkward as a politician and really a military man, Jackson achieved office his own way, becoming the first of a new breed of presidents who rose to power through the people instead of through affiliation with political parties or Congress.

ANDREW JACKSON

Jackson was also the first president to come from a territory west of the Appalachians.

Other Notables: Charles Kuralt, Gunther Gebel-Williams, Midori, Horton Foote, Gregory Peck, Tony Blair, Frank Capra, Cyndi Lauper, George Sand, Giorgio Armani, Barbara Eden, General H. Norman Schwarzkopf, Roger Maris, Leonard Cohen, Sophia Loren, Brigitte Bardot, Soon-Yi Previn, Winona Ryder, Carl Sagan, Frank Sinatra, William Masters, Jackie Gleason

---

BIRTHDAYS ON KARMIC PATH 18

April 18, 1897–September 6, 1897 | November 30, 1915–April 18, 1916

July 11, 1934–November 29, 1934 | February 19, 1953–July 10, 1953 | October 2, 1971–February 19, 1972

May 13, 1990–October 1, 1990 | December 22, 2008–May 12, 2009

KARMIC PATH
18

March 19–24
REBIRTH
PISCES–ARIES CUSP

Those born on the Cusp of Rebirth who travel the Way of Freedom may go through some spectacular personal and professional transformations in their quest for higher development, though many of them will have to reach a point where the still, small voice within has shouted itself hoarse before they can find the wherewithal to do what they must. Perhaps their major problem will be their tendency not to take their hunches and flashes of inspiration seriously enough or to believe themselves more of an authority on something than they really are. Yet they will doubtless make fine progress along this karmic path, especially if they break with their early origins and pursue the passions that make them feel most completely alive.

WILLIAM JENNINGS BRYAN

U.S. political leader; orator; prosecutor at Scopes monkey trial

3/19/1860
Pisces–Aries Cusp

CHALLENGE: **FEELING LESS TROUBLED WHEN OTHERS FAIL TO UNDERSTAND THEM**

FULFILLMENT: **RELYING ON THEIR IMPULSES, HUNCHES, AND INSTINCTS**

March 25–April 2
THE CHILD
ARIES I

Those born in the Week of the Child who navigate the twists and turns of the Way of Freedom can profit from this karmic path's success and greater awareness, but they will encounter some rough spots, especially if they were subjected to unduly strong or restrictive early conditioning. Though they may replay old scripts with astonishing regularity or cling to rather childish notions of what constitutes conformity or acceptable behavior, much of their passage will be governed by subconscious motivations until they learn to delve within and gain a better understanding of just what makes them tick. Yet if they don't retreat into isolation, hurt feelings, or sense of entitlement, they can make enormous strides in their personal and spiritual evolution, and eventually gain the freedom they crave.

CHALLENGE: **OVERCOMING THE SCRIPTS OF CHILDHOOD**

FULFILLMENT: **GENERATING THE SELF-AWARENESS TO BE A FREETHINKER**

NOTABLES: **EUGENE MCCARTHY (FORMER PRESIDENTIAL CANDIDATE; U.S. SENATOR); CHRISTIAN ANFINGEN (CHEMIST; NOBEL PRIZE FOR RESEARCH ON ENZYME RIBONUCLEASE)**

April 3–10
THE STAR
ARIES II

Those born in the Week of the Star who travel the Way of Freedom may find their growth a bit stunted until they turn loose their inherent need to be admired and appreciated. For all the many satellites, family members, and social contacts with whom they surround themselves, their key to progress along this road will be the sense of loneliness that lies at the bottom of the Aries II heart. Though these people will find it difficult to go through the necessary process of introspection in order to better examine their feeling of isolation, chances are they will find that it springs from their failure to find truly kindred spirits with whom they can share their innermost selves. Yet if they realize that their many solitary journeys and their dedication to their craft or work are in fact symbols of their search for freedom, it could prove to be the beginning of a new era of self-understanding and karmic reward.

SIRIMAVO BANDARANAIKE

Sri Lankan prime minister; first female PM in world

4/17/1916
Aries III

CHALLENGE: **RECOGNIZING THE SYNCHRONISTIC PATTERNS IN THEIR LIVES**

FULFILLMENT: **KNOWING THAT DEEP DOWN, THEY DON'T REALLY WANT TO TAKE THE TRADITIONAL PATH**

NOTABLES: **GREGORY PECK (ACTOR; OSCAR FOR *TO KILL A MOCKINGBIRD*); RENÉ LALIQUE (ART NOUVEAU JEWELER)**

April 11–18
THE PIONEER
ARIES III

Aries III's may find the Way of Freedom rather difficult until they relinquish their need to force their ideas on others and divest themselves of their admittedly positive, yet unrealistic view of their responsibilities. Too often, they are prone to making themselves indispensable, serving as a kind of linchpin for their family, an organization, or the place where they work. Though they may handles this role quite well, this karmic path requires that, sooner or later, they learn honor their own needs and follow their own star in an effort to become more truly who they are. Curiously, enlightenment may come more easily as they attune themselves better to the complaints and dissatisfactions of others. By cultivating greater empathy, they may find many of their questions both raised and answered by the Way of Freedom.

CHALLENGE: **BREAKING FREE OF THEIR RESPONSIBILITIES TO OTHERS ONCE IN A WHILE**

FULFILLMENT: **WORKING ON BEHALF OF JUSTICE AND FAIRNESS FOR OTHERS**

NOTABLE: **ALFRED S. BLOOMINGDALE (DEVELOPED DINER'S CLUB CREDIT CARD CO.)**

KARMIC PATH
18

April 19–24
POWER
ARIES–TAURUS CUSP

Those born in this period who find themselves on the Way of Freedom may misuse its energies by refusing to release their goals of worldly power in the interest of personal freedom. In a curious way, many of them may stubbornly cling to the belief that power, specifically material power, *is* freedom, which may well be an attitude forged by their parents or early authority figures. Yet in maintaining such an attitude, they will only hold themselves back from growing spiritually and broadening their perception. Nevertheless, they have a great potential for success, especially when they answer the higher call of this karmic path and relinquish power in the interest of sharing, acceptance, and personal development. Overcoming their tendency to be overbearing will be a good first step, as will the ability to accept setbacks not as failures but as opportunities for escape.

CHALLENGE: **QUESTIONING THEIR NOTIONS OF JUSTICE AND FREEDOM**

FULFILLMENT: **RELYING MORE FULLY ON THEIR SENSE OF TIMING, OR** *KAIROS*

NOTABLE: **ERIC BOGOSIAN (ACTOR; PLAYWRIGHT,** *DRINKING IN AMERICA***)**

TONY BLAIR
British prime minister

5/6/1953
Taurus II

April 25–May 2
MANIFESTATION
TAURUS I

Those born in the Week of Manifestation who travel the Way of Freedom may indeed live in a "house divided" until they become less resistant to change. However solid, practical, and pragmatic these hardworking personalities may appear, such qualities may disguise a soul who yearns for greater freedom of action, thought, and inquiry. In fact, many of them may be prone to choose free-spirited life or professional partners who speak to these inner needs in an attempt to quell their more radical inclinations or otherwise "own the magic." The result may be a number of marriages or business associations "made in hell" until they come to terms with the idea that change itself is a necessary and integral part of existence and realize that many times a house divided is in fact the home of the self.

CHALLENGE: **TAKING CARE NOT TO ATTRACT, IN THE FORM OF FATE, THE VERY EXPERIENCES OR LESSONS THEY ARE MOST RESISTANT TO LEARNING**

FULFILLMENT: **GIVING FORM TO THEIR MORE FREE-SPIRITED OR INGENIOUS IDEAS**

NOTABLE: **J. FRED COOTS (SONGWRITER, "SANTA CLAUS IS COMIN' TO TOWN")**

May 3–10
THE TEACHER
TAURUS II

Those born in the Week of the Teacher who navigate the Way of Freedom may have an easier time than some others on this karmic path, yet they will have to do a certain amount of soul work to discover and perhaps dissect their need to express themselves within the context of student-teacher-type relationships. Though well suited to the call to higher intellectual ideals and pursuits, they may get mired in their need to assert their authority or their insistence on being "experts" in their chosen fields. Indeed, that dynamic may spill over into their personal relationships, and they will have to struggle a bit to overcome a know-it-all attitude or a tendency to foster dependency in others. Yet they have the possibility of great success on the Way of Freedom, simply because their fine minds and intellects will be illuminated by the beacon of freedom. Thus, challenging boundaries, breaking molds, and learning to teach themselves as well as they have taught others will all come naturally to them.

CHALLENGE: **FREEING THEMSELVES FROM INTELLECTUAL CONSTRUCTS THAT MAY HAMPER THEIR THINKING**

FULFILLMENT: **GENERATING AND PARTICIPATING IN THE FREE FLOW OF IDEAS THROUGH DEBATE OR DISCUSSION**

NOTABLE: **SIR JAMES MATTHEW BARRIE (AUTHOR,** *PETER PAN***)**

FRANK CAPRA
Film director,
It's a Wonderful Life

5/18/1897
Taurus III

May 11–18
THE NATURAL
TAURUS III

Those born in the Week of the Natural will doubtless find great fulfillment along the Way of Freedom, for there are few configurations where the higher spiritual challenges of a karmic path are so much in keeping with inborn inclinations. Yet these people may have to set their sights a bit higher than they would ordinarily be inclined to in order to achieve the transcendence and broader perspective that beckons them. Too, fighting a sense of entitlement and personal frustration may take up more of their time than it should, and they may become preoccupied with mundane issues in an effort to avoid the terrors of getting what they really want. Yet whatever the obstacles, there lurks a rugged individualist within the heart of everyone born in this week. If they find the strength to believe that this path affords them the opportunity to integrate and express that person, divested of the need for anger or rebellion, all will go well here.

CHALLENGE: **TRUSTING THEMSELVES ENOUGH TO FOLLOW THEIR HEARTS**

FULFILLMENT: **KNOWING THAT BEING TRUE TO THEMSELVES IS THEIR BIRTHRIGHT**

NOTABLES: **ELLEN AXSON (FIRST LADY OF WOODROW WILSON); GEORGE BRETT (HALL OF FAME BASEBALL PLAYER, KANSAS CITY ROYALS)**

May 19–24
ENERGY
TAURUS–GEMINI CUSP

There are such formidable energies created when those born on the Cusp of Energy travel the Way of Freedom that there is little anyone can do to contain these individuals. However, their personal declarations of independence may take place with such regularity that they may put others in mind of the boy who cried wolf as they make their way along this karmic path. Indeed, there is something about these individuals that is so preoccupied with breaking free that they may fail to adequately assess just what it is they are trying to get away from or where it is they are trying to go. As a result, their quest for greater freedom and higher truth may be a rather shallow pursuit. Too, they may fail to approach their intellectual infatuations with seriousness and depth and hence may suffer the consequences of ill-formed plans and poor preparation. Yet when they come to terms with the fact that the road to freedom and personal growth must always be paved with more than good intentions, they can make great progress here.

DONALD CUSHING McGRAW
Publisher, McGraw-Hill
Publishing Company

5/21/1897
Taurus–Gemini Cusp

CHALLENGE: **CHANNELING THEIR URGE FOR FREEDOM INTO PRODUCTIVE ACTIVITIES**
FULFILLMENT: **FINDING OPPORTUNITIES TO BROADEN THEIR PERSPECTIVE AND, THUS, THEIR PROSPECTS**
NOTABLE: **FRANK SHEED (PUBLISHER)**

May 25–June 2
FREEDOM
GEMINI I

Freedom's ring being such a resounding theme of this karmic path, Gemini I's are likely to be quite happy on the journey, as their temperaments are well suited to its demands and challenges. In fact, their principal danger here will be their tendency to be rather aggressive or combative or to throw their weight around in situations where they have no real vested interest in the outcome. They are blessed with a certain lightness of heart that will protect them against some of the more unpleasant surprises their journey may hold and are unlikely to be overly troubled by the baggage of fear or early conditioning. If they take care that their fine minds and tremendous curiosity receive the proper nurturing, they will find great advancement, personal growth, and spiritual awareness along the road.

CHALLENGE: **TAKING CARE NOT TO IMPINGE ON THE FREEDOM OF OTHERS THROUGH BEING IMPATIENT**
FULFILLMENT: **FEELING THAT BEING WHO THEY ARE IS IN ACCORD WITH THEIR DESTINY**
NOTABLE: **NORMA TALMADGE (ACTRESS)**

June 3–10
NEW LANGUAGE
GEMINI II

Gemini II's have a fine potential for success and self-realization on the Way to Freedom yet may have to do a bit of work to avoid getting mired in the struggle to make themselves understood. In fact, many of them have a nearly unshakable faith in their ability to communicate and may get stuck replaying old scripts and old scenarios as they cling to the belief that any communication problems are somehow their fault. Yet if they don't retreat into a wounded ego or a feeling of being misunderstood and work to overcome what may be a deep-seated fear of rejection, they can make wonderful progress and gain considerable confidence on this karmic path, especially when it requires them to break free of their origins and early ties and present their special message to the larger world.

TIM ALLEN
Comedian/actor,
Home Improvement

6/13/1953
Gemini III

CHALLENGE: **NOT LETTING FREEDOM DEVOLVE INTO RECKLESSNESS**
FULFILLMENT: **RESTING IN THE PEACE OF MIND THAT ACCEPTING THEMSELVES AS UNIQUE CAN BRING**
NOTABLE: **DUCHESS TATIANA (RUSSIAN ROYALTY)**

June 11–18
THE SEEKER
GEMINI III

Those born in the Week of the Seeker who find themselves on this karmic path are likely to have a fine time, though they will need to get their chameleon-like tendencies under control before they can rise to the larger challenges indicated here. Their tendency to please others through charm, combined with the natural sense of authority that is part of the endowment of this karmic path, may make them quite sought after, yet the result may be that they cultivate some rather superficial contacts or fair-weather friends to the ultimate detriment of their own deeper needs. However, it is likely that their natural sense of excitement and adventure will prove a great asset, and if they can combine it with their love of learning, formidable powers of observation, and pervading sense of fun, they will discover that real success and achievement are natural by-products of being true to oneself.

CHALLENGE: **LEARNING THE ART OF CUTTING UNPRODUCTIVE TIES**
FULFILLMENT: **RELEASING THE NEED TO CONTROL OTHERS**

June 19–24

MAGIC
GEMINI–CANCER CUSP

Those born on the Cusp of Magic who journey along the Way of Freedom may have to work to objectify some of their more emotional tendencies before they can realize the level of fulfillment promised by this karmic path. Specifically, the fear of rejection can be so strong in these individuals that they may become entangled in their ideas of what they think others want them to be. Moreover, they may get mired in a tendency to apply their considerable gifts to solving problems when they would be better served by merely leaving the problems behind and broadening their horizons. Making some necessary breaks with the past or their early conditioning may be difficult for them as well. Yet if they come to terms with the fact that only through the process of finding the freedom to be who we are will we be drawn to the love we need, they will flourish on the Way of Freedom.

CYNDI LAUPER
Pop singer of the 80s
———
6/22/1953
Gemini–Cancer Cusp

CHALLENGE: **OVERCOMING THEIR FEAR OF BEING REJECTED FOR WHO THEY ARE**
FULFILLMENT: **FREELY REVEALING THEIR OWN PARTICULAR BRAND OF MAGIC TO THE WORLD**
NOTABLE: **BENAZIR BHUTTO (PAKISTANI PRIME MINISTER)**

June 25–July 2

THE EMPATH
CANCER I

Those born in the Week of the Empath may have to struggle a bit with issues of personal boundaries and learning to distinguish where others leave off and they begin. The quest for a stronger sense of identity may figure prominently in their journey, as will the impulse toward higher intellectual and spiritual development. Though some of the sudden changes, losses, or breakups that are typical of this karmic path may send them reeling in search of comfort and explanation, they will be better served by cultivating both a sense of humor and philosophical detachment. Too, selfishness and a tendency to be rather demanding in their dealings with others may work to their detriment. Yet if they can find the strength to withdraw from time to time in search of the answers they need, their prayers for liberation are not likely to go unanswered.

CHALLENGE: **CARING LESS ABOUT HURTING OTHERS' FEELINGS AND MORE ABOUT EXPRESSING THEIR OWN FREELY**
FULFILLMENT: **COMING INTO A SENSE OF THEIR OWN POWER**
NOTABLE: **GEORGE SAND (WRITER, *INDIANA*)**

July 3–10

THE UNCONVENTIONAL
CANCER II

Learning to channel their highly imaginative side into material manifestation will figure prominently in the life journey of those born in this week who travel the Way of Freedom. Blessed with vivid dreams, unconventional inclinations, and great psychological insight, they will nevertheless have to find the strength to become more truly who they want to be. In fact, there may be a rather wide gap between the image they present to the world and the person who lives inside their head and heart. Their destiny will doubtless involve narrowing that gap, and they will have to make a number of leaps of faith in their efforts toward greater self-realization. Letting go of their self-protective instincts will be important to their success, as will an ability to avoid obsession. Still, if they can get in touch with their more radical side and educate themselves to the distinction between real thought processes and simple fantasy, all will go brilliantly for them.

GIORGIO ARMANI
Italian fashion designer
———
7/11/1934
Cancer III

CHALLENGE: **DISTINGUISHING BETWEEN PERSONAL FREEDOM AND MERE ESCAPISM**
FULFILLMENT: **FEELING FREE TO BE WHO THEY ARE**
NOTABLE: **SIR JOHN GILBERT (PAINTER/ILLUSTRATOR)**

July 11–18

THE PERSUADER
CANCER III

Those born in this week may be so good at controlling their needs that they fall entirely out of touch with their deeper motivations and inclinations, thereby failing to achieve the sense of personal freedom demanded by this karmic path. In addition, a certain fearfulness can characterize this journey, causing them to adhere rather strictly to tradition or their own brand of morals in an attempt to avoid the possibility of risk or rejection. Yet they possess a spiritual side, as well as natural curiosity, so that when personal liberation comes to them, they will manage to shake off the chains that have bound them. It can be a truly awe-inspiring experience as they make a headlong break for freedom in answer to the higher needs of their soul's true calling.

CHALLENGE: **NOURISHING RATHER THAN NEGLECTING THEIR DEEPER NEEDS**
FULFILLMENT: **HAVING THE AUTONOMY TO PEACEFULLY GO ABOUT ACHIEVING THEIR GOALS AND FULFILLING THEIR PLANS**
NOTABLES: **DONALD SUTHERLAND (ACTOR, *MASH*); WOLE SOYINKA (AUTHOR; 1ST BLACK PERSON TO WIN NOBEL PRIZE FOR LITERATURE); VAN CLIBURN (PIANIST; 1ST AMERICAN TO WIN TCHAIKOVSKY PRIZE)**

July 19–25

OSCILLATION
CANCER–LEO CUSP

These people can do very well along the Way of Freedom, providing they do not allow others to convince them that it is somehow inappropriate to want what they want, to feel what they feel, or to take the risks necessary to get where they want to go. Thus, though this life journey may be characterized by a marked tendency to "political incorrectness" they can find great fulfillment. Early encouragement of their talents and gifts will prove especially important, but so will their ability to know when it's time to move on. They would do well to apply their intuition to the task of cultivating a better sense of timing and their considerable intellect to the process of embracing their more radical inclinations without fear of rejection or reprisal. They would also do well to remember that they have within them the simple moral courage necessary to do what they must in their quest to live a more authentic life.

LOUISE FLETCHER
Actress, *One Flew Over
the Cuckoo's Nest*

———

7/22/1934
Cancer–Leo Cusp

CHALLENGE: **BOGGING DOWN IN MOOD SWINGS**
FULFILLMENT: **UNCOVERING THEIR COURAGE AND USING IT
ON THEIR OWN BEHALF**

July 26–August 2

AUTHORITY
LEO I

Leo I's who travel the Way of Freedom will be marked by great vitality, personal charisma, and the ability to get things done. Yet their very intensity may sometimes get in the way of their higher objectives here, and they would do well to learn when to back off and let things take their course. Nevertheless, they have a fine predisposition to abstractions and intellectual explorations of all kinds that will serve them well as they navigate the twists and turns of this life journey; sheer intellectual curiosity may prove to be their salvation. Essential to their finding the sense of freedom to become more authentically themselves will, however, lie in their ability not to care about others' expectations, to forget about rules, and to cut themselves adrift in the oceans of life experience that await them.

CHALLENGE: **NOT BECOMING SLAVES TO TRADITION**
FULFILLMENT: **ACCEPTING THE CHALLENGE OF BEING THE
BEST THEY CAN BE**

August 3–10

BALANCED STRENGTH
LEO II

Those born in this week who find themselves traveling along the Way of Freedom may find that their very tenacity is their undoing. In fact, their tendency to single-mindedness may make this journey a rather difficult one unless they apply their talents in such a way that they acquire expertise in a specific field of study, research, or endeavor and thus create opportunities for the brilliant breakthroughs promised by this karmic path. Though their considerable efforts are sure to pay off in the long run, they should always take care to develop themselves beyond their particular set of gifts, or their dedication may only stand in the way of their higher development. Too, it is likely that fate will lend a hand from time to time by creating just the kind of disruptive, surprising, and sometimes unwelcome changes they need to get themselves off the treadmill and back onto the spiritual track.

TADEUSZ REICHSTEIN
Chemist; Nobel Prize for
work on hormones

———

7/20/1897
Cancer–Leo Cusp

CHALLENGE: **BREAKING FREE OF THE DEPENDENCIES THAT
OTHERS HAVE ON THEM**
FULFILLMENT: **EXHIBITING THEIR WILLINGNESS TO STAND UP
ON THEIR OWN BEHALF**

August 11–18

LEADERSHIP
LEO III

Those born in the Week of Leadership who travel the Way of Freedom have a considerable chance to find fulfillment and success, provided that their more dominant qualities are not too tied up with personal issues or the need to be liked. Leo III's are blessed with a truly secure sense of identity that will serve them well here. The key to their further self-realization will, however, lie in their ability to evaluate their own growth and teach themselves some new tricks from time to time, rather than succumbing to feelings of complacency or even allowing themselves to stagnate as a way of maintaining their sense of control. Too, they may find it difficult to break with people and things that hold them back from higher development. Yet their natural strength will stand them in good stead, and this configuration holds the promise of achievement for those aware enough to heed its call.

CHALLENGE: **FEARING CHANGE SO MUCH THAT THEY BECOME
DOGMATIC OR TYRANNICAL**
FULFILLMENT: **APPLYING THEIR WIDE RANGE OF CREATIVE
EXPRESSION TO MAKING THEIR LIFE RUN THE WAY THEY
WANT IT TO**

August 19–25

EXPOSURE
LEO–VIRGO CUSP

Those born on the Cusp of Exposure who navigate this karmic path may assume a worldly image that is at odds with the person they are inside. Likely to be quite talented and even brilliant in many respects, they may nevertheless trip themselves up through an unwillingness to come to terms with who they are and what they truly want out of this life. In fact, this karmic path may manifest itself in any number of surprise public disclosures about them that they might have preferred go unnoticed. Yet for all the upheaval that follows, they can use these strange twists of fate to forge a more authentic and better-integrated sense of self, rather than withdrawing into hurt feelings or a sense of being victimized. Thus, success and fulfillment can be theirs, providing they do not give their secrets undue power to rule their lives and take the risks involved in revealing themselves to the world.

BARBARA EDEN
Actress, *I Dream of Jeanie*

8/23/1934
Leo–Virgo Cusp

CHALLENGE: **COMING TO TERMS WITH THE WAY FATE EXPOSES THEIR EVERY FOIBLE**

FULFILLMENT: **FEELING FREE OF THE FEAR OF EXPOSURE**

NOTABLES: **RENE RICHARDS (TENNIS PLAYER); GENERAL H. NORMAN SCHWARZKOPF (GENERAL IN GULF WAR); REGIS PHILBIN (TV HOST)**

August 26–September 2

SYSTEM BUILDERS
VIRGO I

System Builders who travel the Way of Freedom may find themselves somewhat ill at ease on this karmic path, since they are by nature rather resistant to the changes, choices, and sense of personal or professional liberation that it requires. Hence, they may expend a good deal of energy trying to impose order on the outer world, only to have to confront chaos and disorder in their most private thoughts and feelings. Developing increased self-awareness and overcoming their tendency to be dogmatic, inflexible, or unconscious in their adherence to the rules and regulations of ordinary living will serve them well. And if they consider the fact that even the most elegant and formidable structures are ultimately only as solid or durable as the foundations upon which they are built, enlightenment and freedom are sure to follow. Thus, finding a way to express their need for structure within the context of a renewed sense of identity and commitment will be the key that unlocks the doors of success for those who make this journey.

CHALLENGE: **RELEASING THEIR FEAR OF FREE-FALLING**

FULFILLMENT: **BUILDING A SENSE OF FAITH OR SPIRITUALITY TO SUPPORT THEM**

September 3–10

THE ENIGMA
VIRGO II

Authenticity may take a while to manifest itself in the lives of those born in the Week of the Enigma who find themselves on this karmic path. While they may present a flawless, unflappable facade to their cohorts, colleagues, family, or friends, they may find that their high standards for themselves become restrictive to the point of strangulation. Thus, a they will constantly need to evaluate and reevaluate their innermost and private goals and learn to let down both their hair and their guard in the interest of spiritual and intellectual advancement. Yet if they do not seek to maintain the mores and standards of a stifling existence but find within themselves the ability to reach beyond the obvious and into the infinite realm of possibility, all will go well for them.

ROGER MARIS
Baseball player; broke Babe Ruth's homerun record with 61

9/10/1934
Virgo II

CHALLENGE: **FREEING THEMSELVES FROM THE NEED TO BE INSCRUTABLE**

FULFILLMENT: **UTILIZING THEIR INGENIOUS MINDS TO DREAM UP GROUNDBREAKING THEORIES, IDEAS, AND PLANS**

NOTABLES: **CHARLES KURALT (CBS NEWS REPORTER); ANTONÍN DVOŘÁK (COMPOSER, *NEW WORLD SYMPHONY*)**

September 11–18

THE LITERALIST
VIRGO III

Those born in the Week of the Literalist will have a rather rough time of things on this karmic path until they reach a point where they feel confident in releasing their sense of tradition and going beyond the obvious and into the realms of the invisible. However, experience is likely to be a great teacher, and if they can open themselves to the idea that there is more to life than toeing the line, they will make great strides along this karmic path. Blessed with a more grounded energy than some who travel this road, they will nevertheless have to avoid the tendency to become obsessed with getting others to see things their way. Yet they have a fine sense of truth and a dislike of pretension that will serve them well, providing they allow their instincts to be their guide. Otherwise, they may have occasion to meditate upon the truth of the phrase "Experience is what you get when you didn't get what you wanted."

CHALLENGE: **RELAXING THEIR NEED FOR EVERYTHING TO GO SMOOTHLY**

FULFILLMENT: **REVEALING THE TRUTH OF WHO THEY ARE TO THE WORLD**

NOTABLE: **GUNTHER GEBEL-WILLIAMS (ANIMAL TRAINER)**

September 19–24
BEAUTY
VIRGO–LIBRA CUSP

Virgo–Librans who find themselves on this karmic path are likely to have a fine time, as long as they refuse to allow themselves to have their desires dictated by others or to become dominated by their need for acceptance and popularity. Indeed, learning to march to the beat of a different drum may be the principal struggle for those with this configuration. Though they may be great espousers of the doctrine of personal freedom, the realities of their lives may tell a much different story, especially if they develop dependencies upon mundane jobs or dominant partners or cling to outworn conditioning or parental values. Yet freedom is theirs for the asking. If they cultivate the courage and strength to strike out in search of enlightenment, enlightenment is sure to follow.

SOPHIA LOREN
Italian actress, *Two Women*

9/20/1934
Virgo–Libra Cusp

CHALLENGE: **RECOGNIZING THAT SUPERFICIAL EGO MATTERS ARE NO SUBSTITUTE FOR BELIEVING IN ONESELF**
FULFILLMENT: **EXPERIENCING DEEPER AWARENESS OF SELF**
NOTABLES: **LEONARD COHEN (SINGER/SONGWRITER; POET; NOVELIST); UPTON SINCLAIR (SOCIAL REFORMER; NOVELIST, THE REFORMER); BRIAN EPSTEIN (MANAGED THE BEATLES)**

September 25–October 2
THE PERFECTIONIST
LIBRA I

Perfectionists who travel the Way of Freedom will have to avoid the tendency to become enmeshed in the actions, mistakes, and foibles of others and get in touch with its calling to fulfillment. For these people, that will be easier said than done, for they have some rather fixed and often inflexible tendencies that may require greater scrutiny before they can answer the call to liberation. Letting go of their fears and insecurities will prove especially important to their higher development, as will learning the simple art of self-acceptance. If they can learn to leave others to their own business and apply their higher standards and fine intellects to personal liberation, self-instruction, and creative application of their gifts and talents, their resulting sense of renewed and re-fashioned identity will surely be reinforced by an approving universe.

CHALLENGE: **LETTING GO OF JUDGMENT AS MEANINGLESS IN THE FACE OF FREEDOM**
FULFILLMENT: **FINDING AN IDEA OR CAUSE FOR WHICH THEY ARE WILLING TO BREAK THE RULES**
NOTABLES: **GREG MORRIS (ACTOR, MISSION IMPOSSIBLE); WILFORD BRIMLEY (ACTOR, COCOON)**

October 3–10
SOCIETY
LIBRA II

Those born in the Week of Society who navigate this karmic path may encounter quite a number of fate's interventions. Though blessed with a great sense of fairness, a fine capacity for observation, and a keen sense of empathy, these souls will experience quite a few personal upheavals until they learn to release themselves from the demands of the group and take up the task of becoming their own person. Finding time for themselves and learning to take their own needs seriously will prove especially important, as will the ability to recognize that the approval or rejection of others is of little consequence if one does not have self-esteem or self-respect. Getting in tune with their own more surprising and even radical thoughts and feelings will be the key to their higher development, as somewhere within their own impulses lies the secret to self-knowledge and fulfillment.

BRIGITTE BARDOT
French actress

9/28/1934
Libra I

CHALLENGE: **ACCEPTING THAT OLD WOUNDS CAN'T BE UN-DONE—OR REVENGED**
FULFILLMENT: **MAKING THEIR OWN ROAD THROUGH LIFE**
NOTABLE: **SOON-YI PREVIN (ADOPTED DAUGHTER OF MIA FARROW; MARRIED WOODY ALLEN)**

October 11–18
THEATER
LIBRA III

The Way of Freedom may present those born in the Week of Theater with wonderful fulfillment, providing these individuals take care not to allow the roles and masks of personal image to dominate or control their sense of identity. Though they are gifted with great creativity and versatility, as they move in society they may get lost in their sense of performance until they begin to acquire the more authentic sense of self that is required by this karmic path. They may also have difficulty letting go of their own capacity for leadership and hence find themselves overwhelmed by responsibilities, duties, and obligations—until they learn to relinquish their need to be in charge. Yet when they allow themselves to surrender to the curiosity, intellectual expansion, and adventure that await them on this life journey, they will make any number of discoveries, not the least of which is the discovery of self.

CHALLENGE: **KNOWING WHEN TO STEP AWAY FROM A COURSE OF ACTION THAT ISN'T WORKING**
FULFILLMENT: **HAVING THE SELF-CONFIDENCE TO PURSUE THEIR PERSONAL DREAM**

October 19–25

DRAMA AND CRITICISM
LIBRA–SCORPIO CUSP

Brilliant and creative in the extreme, these people are likely to have little choice but to answer their soul's call to personal liberation as required by the Way of Freedom. Indeed, most of them will be especially well suited to the promises and challenges of this karmic path, gifted as they are with a rare combination of a strong mental orientation together with an equal measure of passion. Those qualities will make for a rare mix and result in some rare and wonderful adventures along the Way of Freedom. If they take care not to become enamored of their capacity for authority and leadership and instead learn to strike out on their own in search of personal satisfaction and fulfillment, they will truly find their heart's desire.

WINONA RYDER
Actress, *Reality Bites*

10/29/1971
Scorpio I

CHALLENGE: **NOT CONFUSING FREEDOM WITH WILDNESS**
FULFILLMENT: **PURSUING INTELLECTUAL FREEDOM NO MATTER WHAT THE COST**
NOTABLES: **TONY WALTON (SET AND COSTUME DESIGNER); MIDORI (VIOLINIST; CHILD PRODIGY)**

October 26–November 2

INTENSITY
SCORPIO I

Scorpio I's who navigate the Way of Freedom are blessed with a discerning sense of what is in their own best interests that will serve them well, though they may struggle a bit to reconcile the darker and lighter aspects of personality that go with this configuration and will have to learn to nurture and cultivate a more cohesive sense of self, rather than reeling from their highly developed sense of the extreme. Yet their sense of independence and love of truth will prove their salvation, for no matter how tough the road or how uncertain the outcome, Scorpio I's have the strength of character to break out and declare their freedom. Like the mythical phoenix, which arises from its own ashes, these are people by whom the opportunity to reinvent the self will doubtless be relished and warmly embraced.

CHALLENGE: **LOOSENING, IF NOT DISREGARDING, THEIR PRE-CONCEPTIONS**
FULFILLMENT: **HAVING THE COURAGE TO BE AUTHENTIC**

November 3–11

DEPTH
SCORPIO II

The search for a more authentic or original existence may prove to be primarily an inner journey for those born in this week who travel the Way of Freedom. These serious, intense individuals will be aided in their quest for self-realization by their fine intelligence and penetrating insight, and many with this configuration will bear the mark of real genius. Able to focus their energies and talents as well as to apply themselves to the task at hand, they can make substantial and creative contributions to almost any field of endeavor. They will have to guard against a tendency to be rather too calculating, however, and release their need to control others through manipulation and their tendency to become cynical with the passage of time. Yet they can find real success here, and if they are careful to cultivate the ability to use their past experiences to inform their sense of the future, rather than clinging to old hurts and slights, their search for self will surely be rewarding even if somewhat relentless.

CARL SAGAN
Astronomer/author,
Cosmos, Contact

11/9/1934
Scorpio II

CHALLENGE: **GRAPPLING WITH THE DARKER CONSEQUENCES OF PURSUING A PATH OF FREEDOM**
FULFILLMENT: **SOARING, UNFETTERED, WITHIN THEIR OWN MINDS**

November 12–18

CHARM
SCORPIO III

Those born in the Week of Charm who journey along the Way of Freedom may wrestle a bit with issues of conformity versus those of independence. In fact, they may well conceal their more radical inclinations under a calm, easygoing exterior, and the image they present to the world may reveal very little of what they are really about. Too, complacency or a preoccupation with material comforts may hamper their higher development until they gain a greater grasp of what it is they really want and find the courage to leave their former ideas of success and achievement by the wayside. Yet they are gifted with great resourcefulness and resiliency, and if their sense of ambition is truly attuned to their inner needs and desires, there is very little that can hold them back or tie them down.

CHALLENGE: **NOT BATTLING THE SHADOWS THEY PROJECT ON OTHERS**
FULFILLMENT: **LAYING TO REST THE INNER CONFLICT THAT PLAGUES THEM**
NOTABLES: **GARRY MARSHALL (TV PRODUCER, *HAPPY DAYS*); CHARLES MANSON (CULT LEADER OF "THE FAMILY"; INVOLVED IN NOTORIOUS MURDERS)**

November 19–24
REVOLUTION
SCORPIO–SAGITTARIUS CUSP

Those born on this cusp are characterized by a rather fearless and radical attitude, and thus have a natural talent and disposition for realizing the rewards promised by the Way of Freedom. Gifted with a natural talent for intellectual and philosophical pursuits, they will nonetheless have to be on guard to control themselves against a tendency to become autocratic and hypercritical of the systems and machines that make the world go around, on the one hand, and an overidealistic vision, on the other. If they recognize that such excessive attitudes will only erode their sense of mental freedom, they can make wonderful progress. Aided by their sense of adventure, they may embark on world travel, political careers, or any number of moral crusades that serve the larger interests of humankind.

CRISTINA APPLEGATE
Actress, *Married with Children*

———

11/25/1971
Sagittarius I

CHALLENGE: **RECOGNIZING THAT ALL TRUE REVOLUTIONS OCCUR WITHIN**
FULFILLMENT: **FEELING THAT THEY ARE GUIDED BY SOMETHING GREATER THAN THEMSELVES**

November 25–December 2
INDEPENDENCE
SAGITTARIUS I

Those born in the Week of Independence who travel the Way of Freedom are fortunate indeed, for there are few configurations where temperament and karmic task fit together better than they do here. In fact, their only real danger will be their need to have to prove to themselves and others just how unfettered they are by the conventions and mores that serve the interests of civilization. In fact, they may be pretty wild until they learn to control their energies and direct them toward the development of a broader intellectual and spiritual perspective. Until then, they may be real loose cannons on both the personal and professional fronts, and their low frustration level may actually instigate any numbers of upsets, separations, and anxieties that could have been avoided. Yet fate will doubtless take a hand here, and if they take care to maintain their natural honesty and moral courage, they are unlikely to stray far.

CHALLENGE: **NOT THROWING OUT THE BABY WITH THE BATHWATER**
FULFILLMENT: **EXISTING WITHIN SOCIETY, YET OUTSIDE IT**
NOTABLE: **ADOLPH GREEN (WRITER, HOLLYWOOD AND BROADWAY MUSICALS)**

December 3–10
THE ORIGINATOR
SAGITTARIUS II

The Way of Freedom promises great achievement and self-realization for Sagittarius II's. The key to their success will be their willingness to release their early conditioning and their fear of rejection. Daring to be different and live outside the norm will characterize their search for higher development, and their often stunning and highly radical approach to their talents, gifts, and fields of endeavor can manifest itself in truly rare creativity. If they can broaden and nurture the gifts within and learn to give up on those who reject them for being who they are, they will find the highest spiritual and personal fulfillment on this path. If they don't, they may sentence themselves to a life journey on which they expend their energy in forever knocking on heaven's door, refusing to acknowledge that the keys to fulfillment are within easy reach.

FRANK SINATRA
Singer/actor; only singer to have hit records in five consecutive decades; "My Way"

———

12/12/1915
Sagittarius III

CHALLENGE: **NOT HANGING ON TO PERSONAL SLIGHTS OR CHILDHOOD REJECTIONS**
FULFILLMENT: **REVELING IN THEIR ORIGINALITY**
NOTABLE: **ELI WALLACH (ACTOR, *THE MISFITS*)**

December 11–18
THE TITAN
SAGITTARIUS III

Naturally drawn to some seemingly impossible challenges, the Titans who travel the Way of Freedom are well suited to its tasks and rewards, though they will have to do some work in the area of ego-related issues and approval seeking before they can realize its higher levels of success and fulfillment. Their big hearts and expansive attitude will serve them well, but their personal insecurity may cause them to get caught up in "beating dead horses" or trying to solve insoluble problems, to the detriment of their truest selves and highest aspirations. Freeing themselves of their need to be needed will be important, as will an ability to admit mistakes and move on toward better and brighter horizons. If they can manage their innate urge to always be in control and learn to chuck their responsibilities in the interest of being true to themselves once in a while, they will be put in touch with their visionary, philosophical, and creative aspects and will find the Way of Freedom a much easier passage.

CHALLENGE: **LOWERING THEIR EXPECTATIONS OF THEMSELVES**
FULFILLMENT: **SEEING THE BIGGER PICTURE OF WHO THEY ARE AND THE BROAD MEANING OF THEIR LIVES**
NOTABLE: **ARANTXA SANCHEZ-VICARIO (TENNIS PLAYER)**

December 19–25
PROPHECY
SAGITTARIUS–CAPRICORN CUSP

Those born in this period who navigate the Way of Freedom may have quite a few battles with their inner demons along the way. In fact, they will have to relieve themselves of their idea that restriction is necessary to development and let go of early conditioning that may have taught them that conformity is preferable to the terrors and uncertainty of being different. Learning self-trust may prove the principal task of those with this configuration, who may have to do a great deal of soul-searching before they can allow their intuitive side the acknowledgment it deserves. In any event, they will have a real gift for perceiving the bottom line and getting to the heart of any number of matters. If they allow that talent full play, it will be an important step toward attaining the level of mental and emotional freedom promised by the Way of Freedom.

CHALLENGE: **TRUSTING WHAT THEIR HEARTS TELL THEM**
FULFILLMENT: **TRANSFORMING THEIR FIGHT FOR FREEDOM INTO COMPASSION FOR THOSE LESS FREE**
NOTABLE: **EDITH PIAF (LEGENDARY FRENCH SINGER)**

December 26–January 2
THE RULER
CAPRICORN I

Those born in the Week of the Ruler may have to work hard to release their natural managerial and leadership qualities in the interest of greater personal freedom and development. In fact, this is one of the configurations where fate will play a huge part in educating them about the necessity of personal liberation and enlightenment, and for that reason alone, this combination is bound to make for an interesting life experience. Though many of these people will find it especially hard to break with families, jobs, or communities in the interest of higher development, the enlightenment such experiences bring in their wake will prove more than worthwhile. If they keep in mind that there is more to life than fitting in, assuming responsibility, and paying lip service to outmoded traditions and ways of thinking, the Way of Freedom will reward them with some important revelations.

CHALLENGE: **BREAKING WITH THE PAST OR TRADITIONAL APPROACHES**
FULFILLMENT: **ENJOYING INTELLECTUAL FREEDOM**

WILLIAM H. MASTERS
Sex therapist,
Masters & Johnson

12/27/1915
Capricorn I

January 3–9
DETERMINATION
CAPRICORN II

Those born in this week who navigate the Way of Freedom may require some time to get out of the starting gate, perhaps due to unfortunate early circumstances or conditioning. Still, it is those very circumstances that will serve to forge much of their sense of mental freedom and personal resilience. Gifted with a natural interest in intellectual, philosophical, and spiritual pursuits, these individuals would do well to concentrate their energies in these areas and away from approval seeking and a preoccupation with personal insecurity or feelings of unworthiness. One of their especially pronounced qualities is the ability to learn from experience. Thus, if they take care to break out of restrictive or otherwise inhibiting circumstances in search of such experience, their efforts at achievement, liberation, and self-realization will be well rewarded.

CHALLENGE: **ADMITTING FAILURE AND BEING WILLING TO START OVER**
FULFILLMENT: **DEVELOPING A PERSONAL SPIRITUAL PHILOSOPHY**

LOUIS PASTEUR
Chemist, developed
pasteurization

12/27/1822
Capricorn I

January 10–16
DOMINANCE
CAPRICORN III

Capricorn II's who travel the Way of Freedom may find this an awfully uncomfortable journey until they come to terms with the fact that many of their natural inclination do not always serve their own best interests. Though their life may be well ordered, materially rewarding, and quite calm, these individuals will suffer from psychic and spiritual unrest or a sort of mental claustrophobia as they struggle to come to terms with their own needs. Thus, this configuration may manifest itself in emotional problems, especially depression, until they learn to jump the traces, divest themselves of tiresome or enervating responsibilities, and go after their higher dreams. Though risk taking does not always come naturally to these stalwart souls, they will learn that there are worthy gambles to be taken in the interest of higher spiritual development.

CHALLENGE: **NOT REPLAYING THE NEGATIVE VOICES OF THEIR CHILDHOOD**
FULFILLMENT: **FULLY OWNING THEIR ECCENTRIC SIDE**
NOTABLES: **MATHEW BRADY (AMERICAN PHOTOGRAPHER; FAMOUS FOR LINCOLN PORTRAIT); SUNE KARL BERGSTROM (SHARED NOBEL PRIZE FOR PROSTAGLANDINS RESEARCH)**

January 17–22
MYSTERY AND IMAGINATION
CAPRICORN–AQUARIUS CUSP

The electric and often unpredictable personalities born in this week who travel the Way of Freedom are likely to find wonderful adventure and fulfillment along this karmic path, particularly since they are apt to make any number of startling personal transformations along the way. Though it may seem to these individuals that any number of these changes are due to circumstances outside their immediate control, they are able to put their faith in a higher power without too much argument. Perhaps the principal pitfall for those born with this configuration is their tendency to become too caught up in wild or unrealistic ideologies or to become too self-sacrificing in the course of championing the causes and crusades of the less fortunate. Yet their talent for invention and innovation and their sheer intellectual curiosity will serve them well along this road. If they take care to nurture these higher impulses and to integrate their gifts for inspiration and imagination, life will be a fine adventure for them.

CHALLENGE: **CALMING THEIR CHAOTIC ENERGIES THROUGH A MIND-BODY PRACTICE SUCH AS YOGA OR TAI CHI**
FULFILLMENT: **FINDING FREEDOM AS THEY FIGHT FOR OTHERS**
NOTABLE: **FRANCIS PICABIA (PAINTER; EDITOR; COFOUNDER OF DADA)**

VICTOR MATURE
Actor
———
1/29/1916
Aquarius I

January 23–30
GENIUS
AQUARIUS I

Those born in the Week of Genius who navigate the Way of Freedom are in for a fine time, providing they can avoid the tendencies to become overly fixated on pet theories on the one hand and too reckless or distracted on the other. Curiously, it is the rather fixed nature of Aquarius I's that can prove their undoing, and many of them can be found taking the path of *most* resistance, especially when they tie themselves to routine jobs, spouses, or responsibilities in the interest of so-called stability and thus have to expend considerable energy in trying to manage their resulting sense of frustration. Yet their fine minds, unique capacity for self-education, and curiosity will all serve them well, especially when they develop the self-confidence to abandon the plebeian in a quest for greater excitement, freedom of thought and expression, and the sheer adventure of being alive.

CHALLENGE: **COMING TO TERMS WITH THEIR SECRET YEARNING FOR THE DIVINE**
FULFILLMENT: **EXPERIENCING THE EXCITEMENT OF BEING SELF-TAUGHT**

January 31–February 7
YOUTH AND EASE
AQUARIUS II

The ability to learn on their own and avoid a tendency simply to patch together their beliefs and ideas from other sources will prove essential to the success of those born in this week on the Way of Freedom. In fact, these gifted personalities may be "kicked out of paradise" any number of times until they absorb the lessons that they are here to cultivate real uniqueness and make a bit more personal effort than simply going with the flow. Their very popularity could prove to be a rather hollow and lackluster experience until they answer the higher call to awakening and development demanded by this karmic path. On the other hand, irresponsibility will prove equally unsatisfying. Yet if they can find energy to seek out what freedom means to them, they will have the experiences they need in order to learn the art of coming into their own.

CHALLENGE: **FREEING THEMSELVES FROM THEIR NEED TO BE POPULAR OR WELL THOUGHT OF**
FULFILLMENT: **LEARNING HOW TO LIVE IN THE MOMENT**

SPENCER FULLERTON BAIRD
Developed methods for field study used by botanists and zoologists
———
2/3/1823
Aquarius II

February 8–15
ACCEPTANCE
AQUARIUS III

Cultivating faith may prove the biggest challenge for those born in the Week of Acceptance who travel the Way of Freedom. While some with this configuration will struggle with issues of tolerance, prejudice, and negative belief systems, others will have to fight against having a rather lackadaisical attitude toward personal development and being content to merely accept things pretty much as they are. Either set of beliefs is bound to be challenged, and both types would do well to heed the often disruptive call to evaluate and reevaluate just where they stand. If they can begin by accepting that there are none among us destined for failure in the search for enlightenment and then put their faith in the invisible forces that intervene in all our lives, they can find all their answers on the Way of Freedom.

CHALLENGE: **TAKING A GOOD, HARD LOOK AT THEIR BELIEF SYSTEMS**
FULFILLMENT: **EMBRACING THEIR BIRTHRIGHT AND, WITH IT, TRUE SELF-ACCEPTANCE**

February 16–22

SENSITIVITY
AQUARIUS–PISCES CUSP

Those born on the Cusp of Sensitivity who travel this karmic path may have to relinquish a certain chip-on-the-shoulder attitude toward higher development and to release their need for self-protection before they can open themselves to the higher challenges it offers. In fact, getting in touch with their deepest needs and desires may involve divesting themselves of a preoccupation with personal issues and settling down to a given field of study or area of endeavor. This is one instance where the development of an area of expertise or speciality may serve to illuminate many of the more hidden aspects of the soul. If these people can open themselves to enlightenment and avoid the pitfalls of distrust and pessimism as they tough out some of the rougher parts of their journey, they will learn much of the ways and means of true transcendence.

JACKIE GLEASON
TV actor/comedian,
The Honeymooners

2/26/1916
Pisces I

CHALLENGE: **TEARING DOWN THE BARRIERS THAT PREVENT THEM FROM KNOWING WHO THEY ARE**
FULFILLMENT: **PURSUING A DEEP INWARD SEARCH**

February 23–March 2

SPIRIT
PISCES I

Those born in the Week of Spirit who find themselves on this karmic path are well suited to the challenge of greater freedom and the call to live a more authentic life. Nevertheless, they may struggle with any number of rejections and disappointments along the way until they learn to release such patterns and rewrite the script for their personal fulfillment. Conversely, some with this configuration will have to avoid working against their admittedly spiritual but rather dogmatic attitude toward what does and what does not constitute higher development and release their rather smug or holier-than-thou approach to spiritual education and enlightenment. In fact, these individuals have a tremendous need for other people that may exist at odds with their need for greater freedom. As a result, they may maintain relationships of a sometimes superficial quality or misuse their considerable gifts through irresponsibility, recklessness, or flat-out flakiness.

CHALLENGE: **DESENSITIZING THEMSELVES TO THE CRITICISM OF OTHERS**
FULFILLMENT: **CONNECTING TO THE DIVINE WITHIN THEMSELVES**

March 3–10

THE LONER
PISCES II

Though the individuals born in this week who travel the Way of Freedom may be blessed with more than a modicum of self-knowledge, they may get stuck in feelings of rejection and disappointment until they come to terms with the fact that gaining self-knowledge is only half of their soul's journey and that the other half is learning that true liberation will result when they find the courage to reveal themselves to others, rather than merely expecting to be understood and accepted even though they conceal much of their innermost selves from the world. In the event that they can overcome their tendency to withdraw in the face of conflict and come to terms with the fact that being unique does not preclude the asking for support and acceptance, the resulting expansion in their worldview will do much to buoy them along the way.

MICHAEL BOLTON
Pop singer

2/26/1953
Pisces I

CHALLENGE: **STANDING UP FOR THEMSELVES**
FULFILLMENT: **FINDING SELF-ACCEPTANCE**
NOTABLES: **JOHN DYKES (COMPOSER; CLERGYMAN); EMILIO ESTEFAN, JR. (MIAMI SOUND MACHINE FOUNDER)**

March 11–18

DANCERS AND DREAMERS
PISCES III

Blessed with a uniquely philosophical approach to life's vicissitudes, these soulful people can do quite well on the Way of Freedom but will have to avoid the dangers of irresponsibility, a sense of omniscience, or perennial immaturity. In fact, their avenues to liberation are wide open here and may manifest themselves any number of ways, and they are likely to explore a variety of far-out philosophies and go on wild tangents in their quest for experience and education. One thing is likely, though, and that is that even though these people may view themselves as authorities on free-spiritedness, they will have to come to terms with the fact that real freedom is often found within the bounds of responsibility. Otherwise, they run the risk of becoming mere sycophants, buffeted about by the tides of life, with neither the rudder of identity nor a sense of achievement to guide their passage.

CHALLENGE: **NOT LETTING FREEDOM DEVOLVE INTO RECKLESSNESS**
FULFILLMENT: **FINDING SENSE OF FREEDOM AFFORDED BY THE EXOTIC, TRAVEL, AND WIDE-OPEN SPACES**
NOTABLES: **ANDREW JOHNSON (17TH U.S. PRESIDENT; 1ST TO BE IMPEACHED); HORTON FOOTE (SCREENWRITER, *TENDER MERCIES*)**

The Way of Release

LEO II TO AQUARIUS II
Balanced Strength to Youth and Ease

Born with the tendency to hang on to habits, people, and things, those on this karmic path are here to learn how to release all that has outworn its usefulness. Learning how to release is a highly individual, finely nuanced art. It is one that is not easily acquired by these somewhat fixed and often long-suffering people. However, the rewards of releasing the burdens of self-imposed negativity, worry, and crushing responsibilities are considerable since it results in a lightening of the spirit and an easing of the soul. More than many, this is a progressive path, one that must be taken one step at a time. Each instance of release is a small victory and often will lead to another, so that over time the process becomes easier and the person's psychological load lighter. Ultimately, these individuals will transform themselves and, discovering the capacity to break the ties that bind them to the earth, spread their wings to soar unfettered as they live in the moment. With a newfound joyfulness and sense of freedom, those on this karmic path will come to influence those around them positively. However, focusing on their own metamorphosis must take precedence over any other considerations.

Achieving a lightening of spirit by teaching oneself how to let go of what doesn't serve one's highest and best self isn't as simple as it may sound. It usually requires spending some time looking deeply within and, with discrimination, determining what character traits or relationships may be unhealthy or may not serve the greatest good of the individual. Making such an objective approach to oneself is never easy, particularly when others are involved, but it is the necessary first step. The second is determining to free oneself of what one has identified as having outworn its usefulness—no matter what the cost. Such unflinching self-assessment is difficult for the men and women born to the Way of Release, but it is their core lesson. While they do possess the ability to look at themselves squarely and can be quite aware of their own limitations, they also possess quite a capacity for rationalization. Their elaborate justifications for why they should hang on to something can border on the hilarious, whether they are applied to mementos that clutter their cupboards, so-called old friends who were never particularly nice to them, bad habits such as smoking or overspending, or less-than-ideal moral traits.

It is particularly difficult for the individuals on this karmic path to be objective when it comes to others in their lives. After all, these are people who routinely shoulder the burdens of their fellows, and they pride themselves on being there for them. It takes a lot of heartache before they even begin to consider that someone might not be good for them. The idea that they might have to let a person or a relationship go or let someone down is anathema to them. So they are apt to concoct elaborate reasons for why they shouldn't do so.

CORE LESSON

Practicing unflinching and objective self-assessment

GOAL

To let go of all that does not serve the highest and best in oneself

---

GIFTS
Courageous, Hardy, Realistic

PITFALLS
Masochistic, Long-suffering, Fixed

Often, hanging on to their bad habits or outworn patterns causes these individuals a certain amount of genuine suffering. For example, their inability to release their pride may cause any number of temperamental flare-ups that only hurt themselves in the long run. Another example is failing to leave an abusive spouse or boss or a bad situation out of a misplaced sense of loyalty. It's really rather odd that these individuals don't seem to consider that they deserve better or that life can and should be easier. In fact, it seems at times that the men and women on this karmic path do not really believe that they deserve happiness. Unhappiness is customary—and often comfortable—to them. They, like Hamlet, would sooner "bear those ills they have than fly to others that they know not of." As they progress along this path, one day they will finally find the courage to release their attachment to unhappiness itself, not merely the source of that unhappiness. Sometimes this is prompted by a single peak experience or a flash of insight or inspiration. In an instant, the foolhardiness of holding on to their suffering is revealed, and even at the risk of hurting others, the recognition of the possible rewards of letting it go galvanizes them into action.

Positively, those on the Way of Release are gifted with tremendous powers of concentration and a kind of craftsmanlike approach to any matter at hand. Once they turn their attention inward and honestly begin to assess their negative patterns or problems, they will chip away at them diligently for many years in an attempt to perfect themselves. Applying even a small dose of their own heroic temperament to fighting on their own behalf will reap rich rewards. Initially, they may take on this process of self-improvement somewhat intensively. They may also become overly focused or concentrated on a single character trait that they wish to transform. Such an approach may prove a bit counterproductive, since concentrating too fully on something sometimes inadvertently reinforces it. All this will become clearer through the process of trial and error. As they mature and grow, those on the Way of Release will learn to flow with their process in a more easygoing manner.

In relationships, the main arena where many of the lessons of this karmic path are apt to take place, those on the Way of Release will have to guard against feelings of both guilt and misplaced loyalty. Either may prevent them from making the best decisions about their relationships. A healthy dose of self-interest or selfishness is required to keep them moving ahead. In fact, it may be an absolute necessity since at some point on their journey, as they try to adjust, transform, or release some of their existing relationships or their patterns, it is likely that family members, old friends, or partners will try to manipulate them into remaining where they are. This is apt to take the form of tapping

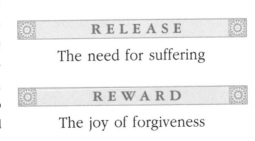

RELEASE

The need for suffering

REWARD

The joy of forgiveness

SUGGESTION

Work with a professional to review your strengths, weaknesses, and other patterns of behavior. Be objective, but do not condemn yourself; problems can be opportunities for growth. Forgive and forget.

into their propensity to feel guilty and of withholding recognition and approval—something those on this karmic path especially crave. Fortunately, these individuals do possess the ability to step back and detach emotionally. Doing so in charged situations such as those mentioned will help them to know when others have a valid point or are merely attempting to control them. Such detachment can also help them maintain the strength of purpose to stick to their guns. Given that this karmic path's origin in the Leo II period means that those born to it tend to nurse old hurts and grudges, they would do well to remember that dealing effectively with relationships that aren't healthy is not about revenge. Hurting someone should never be the goal. Rather, in many, many ways, the secret of release is learning how to forgive both oneself and others.

While the history of their relationships may cause them to be a bit gun-shy, those on the Way of Release will come to believe that personal relationships can be both bountiful and nurturing and will eventually see the benefit of admitting others into their life in a more unconditional way. Working with a therapist, psychologist, spiritual teacher, or counselor can provide untold benefits by teaching these individuals how to hold a mirror to themselves and their lives, and such work can speed their growth exponentially. Later, the development of healthy friendships with people on a spiritual path of their own can also serve a similar, though more limited,

function. Having children of their own and building a family, or living with or near others with whom they can share the joys and sorrows of everyday existence, can bring them a great deal of happiness and fulfillment.

Once they learn how to disengage themselves from nonproductive or hurtful relationships, as well as from their bad habits, negative psychological patterns, and what may be a subconscious need to suffer, those on this karmic path will begin to taste the fruits of living in a freer, more relaxed manner. As they learn to let go, forgive, and lighten their spirits, they will begin to flow with life, accept its abundance, and become more joyful, trusting, and lighthearted. In fact, old friends, when meeting these individuals later in life, after they have, it is hoped, done the work called for by this karmic path, may find them something of a wonder to behold since their transformation can have a startling effect on their appearance.

BALANCE POINT

Retention and Release

An image comes to mind that may describe an individual on this path: Seated in a posture of meditation, the care, worry, and pain of this world left behind, the spirit moves freely to leave the body and soar aloft. Experiencing the bliss of higher worlds, an objective view of the seated figure is attained as the observer becomes the observed. After a time, the spirit returns to the body, which now arises renewed, relieved, and refreshed and more fully able to enjoy what life has to offer.

CRYSTALS AND GEMSTONES

Malachite helps transform one's thinking. This mineral assists in the release of negativity that in turn allows the individual to express the highest aspect of their being.

NOTABLES ON THIS KARMIC PATH

For actress **Shirley MacLaine**, treading the Way of Release has involved an intense quest for spirituality and meaning in life. Not completely fulfilled by Hollywood stardom, MacLaine began a search for her true self, recounted in best-selling books *Out on a Limb* and *Dancing in the Light*. This pursuit led her on an exploration of reincarnation and the examination of her past lives, allowing her to release baggage she had carried around for centuries.

SHIRLEY MACLAINE

Through this transformation, MacLaine learned how to break ties with the earth and soar unfettered, successfully fulfilling her destiny.

BILL MOYERS

Legendary broadcast journalist **Bill Moyers** has experienced quite a transition from his early days as a Baptist preacher. He served as a special assistant and later press secretary for President Lyndon Johnson, became publisher of *Newsday,* then joined public television, where he has produced numerous critically acclaimed and award-winning programs, many on the exploration of man's consciousness and spirituality.

It was his series with mythologist Joseph Campbell that seemed to have the most impact on Moyers personally. Since then, he has explored diverse topics from mysticism to addiction, but a common theme seems to be the concept of release.

ROSEANNE

Portraying a decidedly unglamorous housewife for ten years on her eponymous television sitcom may have won **Roseanne** fame and fortune, but she has certainly struggled to attain inner peace. On the Way of Release, Roseanne has publicly grappled with myriad personal problems as she has attempted to heal the wounds of her past and her tumultuous present. Today, the host of her own talk show, she seems to have released her demons and her spirit appears considerably lightened as a result.

Other Notables: Mark Wahlberg, Noah Wyle, David Halberstam, Emma Goldman, Tom Petty, Gloria Steinem, Jane Goodall, John James Audubon, Tupac Shakur, Gregor Mendel, Ring Lardner, Jr., Jada Pinkett Smith, Arthur Miller, Bill Walton, Georges Seurat, Gelsey Kirkland, Marion Davies, Anton Chekhov, Sir Henry Morton Stanley, Bobby Unser, Oliver Wendell Holmes, Jr.

BIRTHDAYS ON KARMIC PATH 19

November 28, 1896–April 17, 1897 | July 11, 1915–November 29, 1915

February 19, 1934–July 10, 1934 | October 1, 1952–February 18, 1953 | May 13, 1971–October 1, 1971

December 22, 1989–May 12, 1990 | August 3, 2008–December 21, 2008

KARMIC PATH
19

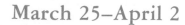

March 19–24
REBIRTH
PISCES–ARIES CUSP

Pisces–Aries individuals who take up the tasks and challenges indicated by the Way of Release are destined for some astounding transformations and a high degree of personal enlightenment, provided they force themselves to take take the first steps along the road by learning to let go of their touchy personal sensitivity and a certain affection for their own suffering. In fact, many of these personalities may well adhere to a sort of "no pain, no gain" attitude that is contrary to the higher promise of this journey, believing, perhaps, that suffering has a refining aspect or that they are somehow unable to advance without the attendant challenge of overcoming some self-inflicted obstacles first. For that reason alone, it is likely that their transformations along this road will be largely determined by peak experiences of an ecstatic or relevatory nature, augmented by slow and steady progress.

CHALLENGE: **LETTING GO OF A NEED TO SUFFER**
FULFILLMENT: **WAKING UP ONE DAY TO DISCOVER THAT THEY'VE UTTERLY TRANSFORMED THEMSELVES**
NOTABLE: **PRINCESS EUGENIE (DAUGHTER OF PRINCE ANDREW AND SARAH FERGUSON)**

GLORIA STEINEM
Writer/feminist/
performer; founded
Ms. magazine
———
3/25/1934
Aries I

March 25–April 2
THE CHILD
ARIES I

Those born in the Week of the Child whose spiritual path winds along the Way of Release are likely to have a fine time, providing they nurture their capacity for wonder and spontaneity and do not get mired in a misplaced sense of responsibility or living up to what others view as "adult" behavior. Nonetheless, this journey will require them to cultivate a greater sense of self-awareness and knowledge of the subconscious factors that may be inhibiting their higher development. Many of this type may be tied to early childhood issues or an especially restrictive upbringing that was at odds with their dynamic and spontaneous energy. However, they will have to take particular care that the professionals they may summon along the way offer real assistance and do not merely stand in the role of overbearing or restrictive parents. Yet whatever their specific stumbling blocks, these people are blessed with both the courage and the idealistic vision to fuel their life's explorations to the fullest.

CHALLENGE: **EXAMINING CHILDHOOD ISSUES AND RELEASING THEM**
FULFILLMENT: **ENJOYING THE FULL-BLOWN ENTHUSIASM OF THEIR APPROACH TO LIFE ONCE THEY ARE SECURELY ON THIS KARMIC PATH**
NOTABLE: **SHIRLEY JONES (ACTRESS, *THE PARTRIDGE FAMILY*)**

April 3–10
THE STAR
ARIES II

Defining and redefining just what is in their own best interests will doubtless figure prominently in the lives of Aries II's who travel the Way of Release. These individuals have a marked tendency to become rather overly involved and emotionally invested in certain unfortunate patterns and behaviors. In a way, overconfidence may be their undoing, as they may be highly resistant to the challenge of letting go—of people, professions, or behavioral patterns—until they learn just when to stop, back up, and take stock of what is motivating their need to succeed at all costs. Thus, this life journey can be fraught with no end of struggles with false pride, fake challenges, and "trick wars" until they release the baggage of outworn emotions, ego issues, and excess responsibility and embrace the sense of freedom that lies at the heart of their desires.

CHALLENGE: **CONSIDERING THE SOURCE OF THEIR COMBATIVENESS**
FULFILLMENT: **FREEING THEMSELVES FROM THEIR NEED TO HAVE OTHERS DEPEND ON THEM**
NOTABLE: **DAVID HALBERSTAM (WRITER OF POP CULTURE)**

JANE GOODALL
Famous chimpanzee
researcher
———
4/3/1934
Aries II

April 11–18
THE PIONEER
ARIES III

Those born in this week who travel the Way of Release can find great success and happiness, as they are aided in their journey by a naturally expansionist outlook, along with any inborn ability to broaden their physical, emotional, and spiritual horizons. Since these personalities tend to do best in a group environment, it is sure that their involvements with others will do much to buoy them along this karmic path, especially as long as they take care to keep an open mind and not to impose their ideas on others in the interest of increasing their sense of power or authority. In a curious way, their propensity for abstraction and idealism can be of great benefit, as it will enable them to objectify their problems and personal issues greatly. That, coupled with their generally optimistic outlook, will do much to free them from old emotional baggage and ensure that they travel lightly along the Way of Release.

CHALLENGE: **TAKING CARE TO TEMPER THEIR EXCESSIVE LOYALTY**
FULFILLMENT: **WATCHING AS THEIR RELATIONSHIPS ARE FREED OF EXPECTATIONS—BOTH THEIR OWN AND OTHERS'**
NOTABLE: **CARL BRAESTRUP (SCIENTIST; AMONG FIRST TO REALIZE DANGERS OF RADIATION)**

April 19–24
POWER
ARIES–TAURUS CUSP

These souls can achieve great things and garner tremendous personal recognition along the Way of Release, yet they will have to do a great deal of soul work to overcome their innate tendency to be long-suffering or martyred or unable to admit failure, especially in the area of personal relationships. Both their need for power and their rather lavish and purely materialistic tendencies need to be examined and, if necessary, released before they can reach for the higher level of fulfillment promised by this karmic path. Yet if they work to change their old habits and ways of thinking and embrace the future with a hope and confidence that is grounded not necessarily in earthly values but in a joyous vision of the future, all will go well for them.

JOHN JAMES AUDUBON
Roseate Spoonbill painted by artist/naturalist; founded Audubon Society

4/26/1785
Taurus I

CHALLENGE: **LETTING GO OF THEIR PREOCCUPATION WITH POWER**
FULFILLMENT: **FINDING THEMSELVES BECOMING SHARING, ACCEPTING, EVEN LOVING**
NOTABLE: **SHIRLEY MacLAINE (AUTHOR; ACTRESS; OSCAR FOR** *TERMS OF ENDEARMENT***)**

April 25–May 2
MANIFESTATION
TAURUS I

Those born in the Week of Manifestation who journey along the Way of Release may encounter a number of issues and problems that center around their personal idea of practicality versus the need for change. It may thus take some time for them to find adequate footing on this karmic path, as most are quite resistant to giving up the old in favor of abstractions such as greater personal liberation or growth. As a result, they may be subjected to some tumultuous experiences in the course of their development and may be asked to endure some personal trauma or sacrifice that will in fact pave the way for their higher spiritual development. Finding the balance between openness and complacency will prove especially important, as will the ability to let go of old hurts in the interest of nurturing their capacity for happiness.

CHALLENGE: **PRYING THEMSELVES LOOSE FROM THEIR INGRAINED HABITS AND NEGATIVE PATTERNS OF BEHAVIOR**
FULFILLMENT: **IMPROVING THEIR PHYSICAL WELL-BEING AS THEY LEARN TO RELEASE EMOTIONAL WOUNDS**

May 3–10
THE TEACHER
TAURUS II

Cultivating the knack of turning their fine intellects and talent for information inward in a quest for greater objectivity and understanding will immeasurably aid those born in the Week of the Teacher to find fulfillment along the Way of Release. Yet they will have to watch their tendency to be hypercritical and demanding of others and especially of themselves. Their evaluative skills may backfire when they go within, and the results may be a tremendous loss of self-confidence, an inability to make decisions, or an overdependency on others in their quest for greater awareness. Yet if they keep in mind that mistakes, by definition, are merely unintended outcomes and learn to trust and to take their desires for fulfillment seriously, they can make great progress.

LIONEL BARRYMORE
Actor

4/28/1878
Taurus I

CHALLENGE: **LEARNING TO BE LESS CRITICAL**
FULFILLMENT: **FINDING RELATIONSHIPS WITH OTHERS EQUAL TO THEM**
NOTABLE: **GUSTAV STRESEMAN (GERMAN STATESMAN; SHARED 1926 NOBEL PEACE PRIZE)**

May 11–18
THE NATURAL
TAURUS III

Blessed with the courage and lightness of spirit necessary for success on the Way of Release, the personalities born in the Week of the Natural have great potential for fulfillment on this karmic path. Nonetheless, they may have to give up any number of old patterns and obsessions along this journey or run the risk of wasting that potential in a series of never-ending and rather pointless rebellions and frustrations. Too, some of this group may get mired in self-pity or even outright misanthropy, believing, perhaps, that the demands of civilization as we know it are simply too great an infringement on their freedom-loving spirits. Yet if they cultivate a broad range of friends, lovers, and professional endeavors that speak to their love of the unusual and unconventional, and at the same time work to put their money where their mouth is as to issues of personal freedom and higher development, they can find the release they seek.

CHALLENGE: **RECOGNIZING THAT OTHERS ARE NOT WHAT'S MAKING THEM FEEL RESTRICTED**
FULFILLMENT: **TRANSFORMING INWARDLY SUCH THAT THEY FIND PEACE WITH THEMSELVES**
NOTABLE: **DWAYNE HICKMAN (ACTOR,** *THE MANY LIVES OF DOBY GILLIS***)**

May 19–24

ENERGY
TAURUS–GEMINI CUSP

The lessons of the Way of Release may be a bit tricky for those born in this period, as they may become entangled in merely acting out their anxieties, compulsions, and emotional burdens until they find the time and strength to turn their energy inward in the interest of cultivating greater objectivity. Once discovered and properly evaluated, however, they are less likely than some to hold on to unfortunate patterns or to replay unproductive scripts, and they may well find that the release promised by this karmic path comes in the form of peak experiences or epiphanies of understanding. Too, if they can free themselves of their need to surround themselves with those who may well admire their talents yet nevertheless hold them back with guilt or mind games or by convincing them that they are simply too scattered to truly succeed, Taurus–Geminis will find this a most interesting and highly unusual journey.

ISADORA DUNCAN
Dancer

5/27/1878
Gemini I

CHALLENGE: **REALIZING THAT NOT ALL LIMITATIONS NEED TO BE RELEASED**
FULFILLMENT: **CREATING, THROUGH OBJECTIVITY AND DISCRIMINATION, A CIRCLE OF GOOD FRIENDS**
NOTABLES: **ROBERT A. MOOG (CREATED THE MOOG SYNTHESIZER); JIM LEHRER (TV JOURNALIST, *MACNEIL/LEHRER REPORT*)**

May 25–June 2

FREEDOM
GEMINI I

Those born in the Week of Freedom who journey along the Way of Release are likely to find considerable success as they are blessed with a natural objectivity and the keen evaluative skills necessary to realize its promise. Key to their higher development, however, will be a willingness to abandon nonproductive behaviors, specifically their tendencies toward combativeness. Many of them will have an overly emotional attitude toward their personal causes and crusades that will operate to their detriment until they summon up some needed objectivity. On the other side of the spiritual coin lies the danger of indulging in all manner of highly manipulative games, as they are not above controlling others through charm or any other weapons drawn from their well-stocked verbal arsenal. Yet if they can cultivate greater emotional control in the interest of simply going with the flow, they will discover that they can raise their spirits in more ways that they might have imagined.

CHALLENGE: **DEVELOPING THE OBJECTIVITY TO THINK BEFORE THEY SPEAK**
FULFILLMENT: **CALMING THEIR INNATE EMOTIONAL VOLATILITY**
NOTABLE: **PAT BOONE (SINGER)**

June 3–10

NEW LANGUAGE
GEMINI II

These souls may find the work of the Way of Release more difficult than some others traveling this karmic path, simply by virtue of the fact that it may take them no small amount of time to come to terms with their own darker side. Somewhat hampered by defensiveness and the fear of appearing foolish, some of them will experience quite a bit of discomfort, rejection, and misunderstanding until they embrace the opportunities for growth that will doubtless present themselves. They must avoid feeling victimized by the process, however, and should cultivate strategies to cope with depression. Gifted with the extraordinary communicative talents that are the hallmark of Gemini II's, they would do well to cultivate and expand the qualities of humor, philosophical detachment, and an understanding of the fact that the issues that preoccupy them are in fact common to us all.

CHALLENGE: **RECOGNIZING WHEN THEY ARE SUMMONING UP THEIR OWN DARK SIDE IN THE FORM OF A LOVER OR FRIEND**
FULFILLMENT: **EXPRESSING THEMSELVES WITH THE EASE OF SOMEONE WHO HAS FOUND INNER FREEDOM**
NOTABLES: **BILL MOYERS (PRESS SECRETARY TO LBJ; PBS JOURNALIST); MARK WAHLBERG (SINGER; ACTOR, *BOOGIE NIGHTS*); NOAH WYLE (ACTOR, *ER*)**

June 11–18

THE SEEKER
GEMINI III

Gemini III's who find themselves on the Way of Release can find considerable fulfillment and success on this karmic path, providing they avoid the dangers of cynicism and superficiality that can sometimes be part and parcel of this combination. In fact, these souls may spend a great deal of time avoiding rather than confronting their personal issues and problems and may turn outward in an ever-expanding search for fulfillment, rather than inward in such a way as to come to better terms with who they really are. Yet once they focus their attention and natural intellectual acumen on self-analysis and let go of their resistance to commitment and fear of being controlled, they are sure to embrace the lightness of spirit and easygoing attitudes that are the higher calling of this karmic path.

TUPAC SHAKUR
Rap/hip hop star

6/16/1971
Gemini III

CHALLENGE: **STAYING PUT LONG ENOUGH TO LOOK INWARD**
FULFILLMENT: **EXPERIENCING A SENSE OF INNER RELEASE TO MATCH THEIR OUTWARD ADVENTUROUSNESS**
NOTABLE: **CHRISTOPHER LEHMANN-HAUPT (*NEW YORK TIMES* BOOK REVIEWER)**

June 19–24

MAGIC
GEMINI–CANCER CUSP

Those born in this period who navigate the challenge and promise of the Way of Release can realize wonderful progress, but they will first have to embark on a rather comprehensive voyage of self-discovery. Paramount to their fulfillment will be to let go of people, patterns, and behaviors that imbue them with a sense of security yet at the same time prove stifling to their higher development. Indeed, many of these people may become romantically attached to their depressiveness, content to founder in rather chaotic emotions or to hold themselves back with the conviction that they are somehow destined for a life of suffering. Indeed, nothing could be further from the truth. If they take a hard look at their more demanding or selfish tendencies and learn to embrace people, partners, and circumstances without romanticizing or idealizing the situation, they can discover a capacity for happiness that will no doubt surprise them.

GENA ROWLANDS
Actress

6/19/1934
Gemini–Cancer Cusp

CHALLENGE: **RELEASING THEIR NEED FOR DEPENDING ON OTHERS FOR EMOTIONAL SECURITY**
FULFILLMENT: **LEARNING THE FINE ART OF SELF-INTEREST, PARTICULARLY WHEN IT COMES TO LETTING GO OF PEOPLE**
NOTABLE: **MARTIN LANDAU (ACTOR, *ED WOOD*)**

June 25–July 2

THE EMPATH
CANCER I

Cancer I's who travel the Way of Release will be especially well served on this life's journey by cultivating practical strategies for coping with their often tumultuous emotions. In fact, they may spend a great deal of time and energy devoting themselves to the emotional needs of others without first adequately coming to terms with their own feelings and motivations. Highly sensitive and even psychically gifted, they may project their own negative patterns or conditioning onto others quite readily, since having a strong sense of boundaries has never been their strong point. Yet they have the natural determination and strength to overcome almost any obstacle, and if they work to use their sense of devotion and dedication to serve the larger needs of humankind, they will no doubt find new ways to serve their own.

CHALLENGE: **DEVELOPING GREATER EMOTIONAL OBJECTIVITY**
FULFILLMENT: **RELEASING THE NEED TO BE LOYAL TO THE POINT OF MASOCHISM**
NOTABLE: **EMMA GOLDMAN (ANARCHIST)**

July 3–10

THE UNCONVENTIONAL
CANCER II

Those born in this week will doubtless experience a highly interesting series of personal transformations along the Way of Release. Aided in their development by a natural inclination toward unusual people, places, and things, they can learn a great deal about themselves by examining their more unconventional relationships. It will be important, however, for them to view these with a degree of objectivity; otherwise they may retreat from the higher challenge of gaining psychological insight into a world of fantasy or empty imaginings. Nonetheless, these individuals have a real gift for psychological analysis and interpretation. If they turn that gift inward in a search for increased self-knowledge and insight, they will experience the singular delight of learning to be comfortable within one's own skin.

KRISTI YAMAGUCHI
American figure skater, shown after winning the gold in Albertville, 1992

7/12/1971
Cancer III

CHALLENGE: **RELEASING THEIR DEPENDENCE ON FANTASY**
FULFILLMENT: **BEING FREE TO MOVE FULLY**
NOTABLE: **GEORGE M. COHAN (THEATRICAL COMPOSER, "YANKEE DOODLE DANDY," "OVER THERE")**

July 11–18

THE PERSUADER
CANCER III

Those born in the Week of the Persuader who travel the Way of Release may spend more time and energy than necessary in attempting to impose their will, needs, and desires on others than in cultivating the degree of acceptance, tolerance, and understanding of self demanded here. Emotional volatility and a sense of being victimized or martyred can be a danger since Cancer III's often give much but also look for a return on their investment. Yet true transformation is possible for these determined souls, providing they seek the help they need to adequately analyze the labyrinth of self and avoid the tendency to merely repeat old patterns or to move from one parental substitute to another in an attempt to resolve old issues. If they can learn to embrace the freedom that comes with relinquishing the need for security, they will experience true enlightenment along this road.

CHALLENGE: **HAVING THE COURAGE TO WORK OUT THEIR ISSUES IN A THERAPEUTIC RELATIONSHIP**
FULFILLMENT: **FINDING THEMSELVES FREE TO ENJOY THEIR PASSIONS RATHER THAN BE RULED BY THEM**
NOTABLES: **PHILIP GRAHAM (PUBLISHING MOGUL); KRISTI YAMAGUCHI (OLYMPIC ICE SKATER)**

July 19–25
OSCILLATION
CANCER–LEO CUSP

Emotional blockage may prove the principal issue of those born on this cusp who travel the Way of Release, and some on this karmic path may find themselves plagued by any number of seemingly inexplicable problems or psychosomatic symptoms until they come to terms with what lies at the bottom of them all. Indeed, the self may remain something of a mystery for many of these people until they summon the necessary courage to both identify and release their fears of their wilder side. They will also benefit greatly from allowing themselves to sample from the banquet of emotions available to them, in order to better nourish the renewed sense of identity that will doubtless emerge with the passage of time. Though they may never live life on what others may see as an even keel, this journey is likely to be interesting in the extreme.

CHALLENGE: **KNOWING WHEN THEY ARE INDULGING IN THEIR TASTE FOR RISK TAKING**

FULFILLMENT: **DISCOVERING THEIR COURAGE AS THEY NAVIGATE THEIR INNER LIVES**

GREGOR MENDEL
Biologist/botanist; father
of modern genetics

7/22/1822
Cancer–Leo Cusp

July 26–August 2
AUTHORITY
LEO I

Those born in the Week of Authority who journey along the Way of Release may have to do a great deal of work before they realize that the higher level of development that beckons will result from their ability to release the baggage, issues, and unresolved conflicts of the past. In fact, these tough customers may come to realize that pride indeed goeth before the fall, especially when they misuse their great strength when they believe that merely ignoring obstacles and problems will remove or resolve them. Yet by and large, these people are blessed with a wonderful ability to be comfortable in their own company and pursue their own interests. If they utilize that gift in the interest of higher spiritual development and greater tolerance and acceptance of both themselves and others, life on the Way of Release will prove to be a real education.

CHALLENGE: **REALIZING THAT CLINGING TO A PRINCIPLE OR TRADITION MAY NOT BE IN THEIR BEST INTEREST**

FULFILLMENT: **ACCEPTING THEMSELVES**

NOTABLE: **ABRAM STEVENS HEWITT (INDUSTRIALIST)**

August 3–10
BALANCED STRENGTH
LEO II

Leo II's who journey along this karmic path can find wonderful fulfillment along the way, providing they do not allow themselves to fall prey to rigidity or the inability to change. On the one hand, they may harbor some rather pronounced masochistic and depressed tendencies that will require scrutiny and objective evaluation. On the other, they may go overboard in learning to release their emotional problems and wind up devoid of a solid set of personal values or at the mercy of their own popularity. Still, if they take care to expend their more single-minded energies into the development of some virtuoso talent or skill, and at the same time learn to leave the burdens of insecurity and guilt by the side of the road, these personalities can find real spiritual release along the way.

CHALLENGE: **NOT ADHERING SO RIGIDLY TO ALL THAT IS KNOWN AND COMFORTABLE TO THEM**

FULFILLMENT: **FINDING THAT OLD WORRIES AND TENSIONS SIMPLY FLOAT AWAY**

NOTABLE: **VISCOUNT WILLIAM HOWE (COMMANDER BRITISH TROOPS, AMERICAN REVOLUTION)**

PETE SAMPRAS
Tennis champion

8/12/1971
Leo III

August 11–18
LEADERSHIP
LEO III

Leo III's who travel along the Way of Release make inspiring and popular leaders and authority figures, yet they will have to take care that their responsibilities do not subsume the broader view and more personal higher challenges of their lives. Though they may find it difficult to seek out the professional help they may require to cope with and release their emotional problems, they are unlikely to shrink from the task of self-scrutiny or to cling to old patterns once they have been identified. For that reason, they may experience quite a lot of upheaval on this karmic path, especially in the area of personal relationships, and may have to be especially watchful of their tendency to project their own failings or ambitions onto others, particularly their children. Too, their need for respect and appreciation is quite strong; if they come to terms with the fact that the ability to inspire the respect of others arises naturally from a sense of self-respect, they can travel far along this karmic path.

CHALLENGE: **ALLOWING SOMEONE ELSE INTO THEIR INNER WORLD LONG ENOUGH TO HELP THEM**

FULFILLMENT: **GENERATING A SENSE OF SELF-ADMIRATION AND SELF-RESPECT**

August 19–25

EXPOSURE
LEO–VIRGO CUSP

Those born on the Cusp of Exposure who find themselves on the Way of Release will likely do quite
well on this life journey, as they are gifted with a
high degree of objectivity and the kind of keen psychological insight that is of great benefit here. Though they
will be inclined to examine others' issues more than their
own, the demands of this karmic path will require them
to expose any number of their secrets to the light of day,
if only in the interest of freeing them from the power such
secrets may have over their lives. If these flamboyant and
popular people can develop the necessary degree of trust
in those who truly want to understand them, they may
discover that the greatest worldly recognition cannot compare with the intimacy that results from being able to reveal oneself to others, unencumbered by fear.

RING LARDNER, JR.
Screenwriter, *M*A*S*H**

8/19/1915
Leo–Virgo Cusp

CHALLENGE: **REFUSING TO HIDE THEIR MORE UNSAVORY
QUALITIES FROM THEMSELVES**
FULFILLMENT: **EXPERIENCING GREATER EASE OR FLOW AS
THEY GO THROUGH LIFE**

August 26–September 2

SYSTEM BUILDERS
VIRGO I

Virgo I's on the Way of Release may encounter any
number of struggles arising principally from their
lack of self-evaluation as well as a certain disposition toward suffering. Though they perceive others'
needs clearly, they are often unable to identify and satisfy their own desires and may be further hampered by
feelings of guilt or inadequacy. Indeed, emotional pressure of any kind can send them into a tailspin of denial
and defensiveness. For that reason, they should seek
counselors or therapists whose approach is based on analytical rather than confrontational interaction. Yet it is
important to remember that no one is ever challenged
without being equipped to answer that challenge, and
though the Way of Release will demand much of Virgo
I's it will also manifest itself in some highly creative talents, greater self-expression, and relationships that offer
them the opportunity to loosen up and become more
truly who they are.

CHALLENGE: **LETTING GO OF THEIR DEPENDENCY ON
STRUCTURE**
FULFILLMENT: **LOOSENING UP AND MORE FULLY BEING WHO
THEY ARE**
NOTABLE: **NATHAN PRITIKIN (DIRECTOR, LONGEVITY RE-
SEARCH INSTITUTE)**

September 3–10

THE ENIGMA
VIRGO II

Gifted with real inner strength and a natural sense
of discrimination, these souls can find considerably more success along the Way of Release than
many of their fellow travelers. Though they have a tendency to want to work out their problems on their own
and thereby avoid revealing the more personal side of
their natures to anyone else, they would do well to put
aside their pride and seek the help they may require to
rise to this karmic path's challenge of objective self-
evaluation. Though letting go will not be entirely easy,
they are nonetheless blessed with the necessary stamina
to cope with even the most traumatic events and setbacks,
even if coping means taking things one step at a time. Yet
as they come to recognize and appreciate their ability to
endure, they will develop the ability to tear down the barriers to happiness and fulfillment. For once a problem or
unfortunate pattern is identified, it is unlikely to be repeated by those born in the Week of the Enigma.

HENRY THOMAS
TV/film actor, *E.T.*

9/9/1971
Virgo II

CHALLENGE: **NOT ALLOWING THEIR RATIONALIZATIONS TO
CARRY THE DAY**
FULFILLMENT: **NOT BEING ENSLAVED BY THEIR HIGH STAN-
DARDS**
NOTABLE: **IONE SKYE (ACTRESS)**

September 11–18

THE LITERALIST
VIRGO III

Those born in the Week of the Literalist who find
themselves on the Way of Release are likely to
make considerable progress along the way. These
personalities have a unique and often quite admirable gift
for "calling a spade a spade," even when the spade in
question happens to be one of their own psychological
quirks. Yet they will have to overcome their tendency to
be entirely too self-sacrificing or to otherwise misplace
their loyalties and will doubtless have to come to terms
with their need to avoid confrontation and unpleasantness. Still, there is a possibility for real happiness and personal liberation with this configuration, especially when
they cultivate a greater degree of tolerance, humanity, and
sheer affability while at the same time learning to give up
the relative security of the so-called real world in order to
better acknowledge and honor the world of invisible
knowledge and understanding available to us all.

CHALLENGE: **FINDING THE WHEREWITHAL TO LET GO OF
TROUBLED RELATIONSHIPS**
FULFILLMENT: **REVELING IN THE SIMPLICITY THAT RELEASE
AFFORDS**
NOTABLES: **JADA PINKETT SMITH (ACTRESS MARRIED TO WILL
SMITH); FREDERICH A. PRAEGER (PUBLISHER)**

September 19–24

BEAUTY
VIRGO–LIBRA CUSP

Those born on this cusp who embrace the challenge and promise of the Way of Release may find that their great sense of beauty gets rather short shrift until they learn to off-load old values, habits, and unfortunate behavior patterns. In fact, many of these men and women may find themselves in the unenviable position of acting out an endless array of old scripts or trying to "fix" past disappointments through an assortment of codependent relationships until they summon the courage to go within and take a long, hard look at just what they've been doing and why they've been doing it. Though they may well be great espousers of personal freedom and tolerance, they may nevertheless find themselves in highly restrictive or domineering relationships, perhaps due to their tendency to be indecisive. Taking time to be alone and becoming comfortable with their own company will provide them with an opportunity to discover their spirituality, as will the experience of having children and its attendant joys of rediscovering unconditional love.

CHALLENGE: **EVALUATING THEIR VALUE SYSTEM ON A REGULAR BASIS**
FULFILLMENT: **CULTIVATING HEALTHY RELATIONSHIPS**

September 25–October 2

THE PERFECTIONIST
LIBRA I

Repression of emotion may prove the principal stumbling block to the higher spiritual awareness offered by the Way of Release for Libra II's born in this week, as they may have an especially hard time learning to kick back, relax, and simply accept others for who they are. Indeed, trying to perfect or refashion others into what Libra I's believe they ought to be can occupy far too much of their time and energy, and they have a pronounced tendency to nurse old grudges or seek revenge. Yet simple mastery of the emotions is a high priority for these souls. If, in their quest for higher standards, they come to comprehend that real mastery is not so much a question of mere control or repression as of going within to cultivate a greater understanding of the problems, joys, and sorrows that are common to us all, they can realize great fulfillment.

ETHEL ROSENBERG
Half of husband/wife
team executed for treason

9/28/1915
Libra I

CHALLENGE: **LETTING OTHERS BE WHO THEY ARE**
FULFILLMENT: **COMING TO IDENTIFY WITH THE PERFECTION OF THEIR OWN NATURE**

October 3–10

SOCIETY
LIBRA II

The great mutability of those born in the Week of Society who travel the Way of Release will serve them especially well on this road, providing they don't use their unique brand of social skills to disguise or otherwise obscure their personal issues. Indeed, many of them can get a bit lost in trying to fulfill others' needs at the expense of their own higher development and would do well to carve out niches of time and space for themselves in order to smooth their passage along this karmic path. Yet discovering the simple truth that in order to unite, one must first learn to separate and go within will prove especially useful to these highly social people. In short, there is a great promise for success and happiness here, as these personalities, once they have embarked on the journey, are unlikely to cling for long to the "truths" that have ceased to serve higher development, greater understanding, and truly spiritual awareness.

CHALLENGE: **CARVING OUT THE NECESSARY TIME TO BE ALONE AND LOOK INWARD**
FULFILLMENT: **DEVELOPING A GREATER CLARITY ABOUT WHO THEY ARE**
NOTABLE: **RUTHERFORD B. HAYES (19TH U.S. PRESIDENT)**

October 11–18

THEATER
LIBRA III

Until these rather hardheaded personalities discover the value of greater flexibility, they may find the journey along the Way of Release something of a trial. Learning to change their course from time to time in the interest of expanding their personal repertoire of emotions and experience will prove especially useful on this karmic path. In any event, they will be prone to give their all, even when giving considerably less may prove the wiser course. Nevertheless, some with this configuration will make some pretty spectacular mistakes along the way, simply by virtue of the fact that they stick to a particular course of action even after the warning flags go up. Yet if they keep in mind that such episodes are perhaps the universe's way of freeing them from the ties that bind them, the people who restrict them, or the habits of mind that hold them back from true fulfillment, they can make wonderful progress.

ALFRED DREYFUS
French army officer,
defended in *J'accuse*

10/9/1859
Libra II

CHALLENGE: **LOOSENING THEIR LOVE OF DRAMA, PARTICULARLY WHEN IT IS USED TO HIDE THE REAL ISSUES**
FULFILLMENT: **INHABITING THEIR OWN SKINS FULLY AND EASILY**
NOTABLE: **ARTHUR MILLER (PLAYWRIGHT; PULITZER FOR *DEATH OF A SALESMAN*)**

October 19–25

DRAMA AND CRITICISM
LIBRA–SCORPIO CUSP

Those born on the Cusp of Drama and Criticism who travel the Way of Release may spend no small amount of time at war within themselves and everybody else until they learn the fine art of integrating their intellect and emotions. Gifted with a dramatic and often quite compelling persona, these people have a gift for airing their views and opinions, though the linchpin of their philosophy might well be "Do as I say and not as I do" until they come to terms with their own problems. Though rigidity and an overcritical attitude may well hinder their progress along this karmic path, personal transformation will always be somewhere on their agenda, and they will be unlikely to shrink from the quest for the kind of self-knowledge required to free them from outworn habits and old emotional baggage.

TOM PETTY
Rock musician, Tom Petty
and The Heartbreakers

10/20/1952
Libra–Scorpio Cusp

CHALLENGE: **PRACTICING WHAT THEY PREACH**
FULFILLMENT: **CULMINATING THEIR WORK ON THEMSELVES BY ENTERING INTO A HEALTHY, BALANCED RELATIONSHIP**
NOTABLES: **JEFF GOLDBLUM (ACTOR, *JURASSIC PARK*); PATTI ANN DAVIS (DAUGHTER OF RONALD REAGAN)**

October 26–November 2

INTENSITY
SCORPIO I

An attitude of chronic and self-imposed negativity may well hinder the higher development of those born in the Week of Intensity who navigate the Way of Release. Yet these personalities are characterized by a phoenixlike quality that ensures that they will emerge from even the worst trials and setbacks to soar to heights of spiritual awareness and personal achievement. For these souls, however, the trick will be to recognize that it is not always necessary to burn to ashes first. In fact, learning to move from release to release, one step at a time, rather than storing up rage, indignation, and emotional trauma to the point of spontaneous combustion will prove most valuable for these people, as will educating themselves in the art of integrating their sometimes highly polarized natures. After all, light and dark aspects of the personality can coexist without necessarily blending into a dull, uninspired gray.

CHALLENGE: **COMING TO BELIEVE THAT RELEASE IS POSSIBLE**
FULFILLMENT: **DISCOVERING THAT THEIR DARK SIDE HOLDS NO POWER OVER THEM**

November 3–11

DEPTH
SCORPIO II

There are a number of roadblocks to the higher awareness of the Way of Release for the deep and soulful personalities born in this week, not the least of which may be their unwillingness to share their problems with others or even to allow anyone into the secrets of their private worlds. Excessive worry can be a problem, especially when their emotional burdens become too much to bear and they seek addictive and even dangerous avenues of escape. Too, they will have to cultivate a willingness to forgive and forget that is not always readily evident in the makeup of Scorpio II's. There is nonetheless the promise of truly astonishing personal transformation and success on this karmic path, providing they exalt their objectivity and develop the necessary tolerance to learn to love themselves better.

BILL WALTON
Basketball center

11/5/1952
Scorpio II

CHALLENGE: **LEARNING HOW TO FORGIVE AND FORGET**
FULFILLMENT: **REALIZING THAT MASOCHISM NEEDN'T BE A WAY OF LIFE**
NOTABLES: **ROSEANNE (ACTRESS; COMEDIAN; TALK SHOW HOST); SARGENT SHRIVER (1ST HEAD OF PEACE CORPS)**

November 12–18

CHARM
SCORPIO III

Those born in the Week of Charm who find themselves on the Way of Release are likely to have a fine and fulfilling life journey, as they bring to this karmic path many of the qualities necessary to the self-realization that beckons. Many things come easily to these often gifted people, yet they will have to do a certain amount of soul work to find the higher fulfillment and promise of this karmic path, specifically in the area of personal relationships. They may have a tendency to project their needs, desires, and even deficiencies onto others that results from a capacity for self-deception until they come to a better psychological and spiritual understanding of their own patterns and habits. Too, letting go does not come easily to Scorpios in general. Yet at their heart, they are realistic souls, and that quality alone will ensure their progress along this path. If they allow that progress to blossom into a quest for real happiness, so much the better.

CHALLENGE: **INVOKING SPIRITUALITY AS SITUATIONS WARRANT**
FULFILLMENT: **WAKING UP ONE DAY TO DISCOVER THAT WHATEVER WAS TORMENTING THEM IS GONE**

November 19–24

REVOLUTION
SCORPIO–SAGITTARIUS CUSP

Whatever the personality quirks, foibles, and follies of those born in the Week of Revolution who journey along this karmic path, they will surely undergo some transformation. These souls can thus find no end of fulfillment here, though that fulfillment will probably not manifest itself as the more usual sense of placid contentment found elsewhere. Yet tearing down the old to make way for the new is pretty much a way of life for these cusp personalities, and they are unlikely to hang on to cumbersome emotional baggage or allow others to hold them back. Though finding their way to the middle of the road may prove as difficult for these impatient people as it will be to master the step-by-step process necessary for development, they can rest assured that the joy and transformation that beckons will be more than worth the trip.

MANDY PATINKIN
Singer/actor

11/30/1952
Sagittarius I

CHALLENGE: **DIGGING DEEPER INTO THEIR OWN PSYCHES EVEN THOUGH THEY THINK THEIR WORK IS DONE**
FULFILLMENT: **ERECTING A NEW, MORE COMFORTABLE SELF**
NOTABLES: **BILLY THE KID (OLD WEST OUTLAW AND MURDERER); WILHELM FRIEDMANN BACH (COMPOSER; OLDEST SON OF J. S. BACH); BILLY STRAYHORNE (JAZZ COMPOSER, "TAKE THE A-TRAIN")**

November 25–December 2

INDEPENDENCE
SAGITTARIUS I

Though it may well prove important for those born in the Week of Independence to take some hard looks at just what factors are fueling their more impulsive actions, they are gifted with the necessary willpower, forthrightness, and sense of principle to rise to the demands and challenges of this karmic path. In fact, their high degree of idealism may well provide the key to their personal transformation, as they are unlikely to get mired in the need to play out old scripts or rerun old problems when there are frontiers of thoughts and insight yet to be conquered. In short, their attraction to the renewed sense of freedom and identity that are the goal of the Way of Release is likely to far outweigh any attachment they might have to unproductive patterns or cumbersome baggage that might impede their progress along the way.

CHALLENGE: **CASTING A WEATHER EYE ON THEIR NEED TO GIVE**
FULFILLMENT: **RENEWING THEMSELVES THROUGH RELEASE ON A PERIODIC BASIS**
NOTABLES: **ROD LA ROCQUE (PRODUCER; SILENT FILM ACTOR); CHRISTIAN DOPPLER (ENUNCIATED THE PRINCIPLE OF THE DOPPLER EFFECT); BROWNIE McGHEE (SOUTHERN BLUES MUSICIAN)**

December 3–10

THE ORIGINATOR
SAGITTARIUS II

Going within in order to acquaint themselves with their motivations may come naturally to the souls born in this week who travel the Way of Release. Many on this karmic path will embark quite fearlessly on the voyage of self-discovery required and will likely apply their unique insights, views, and techniques to solving any number of personal problems. The resulting transformation may be quite startling and original, and some of them will have something of the rebel or outlaw about them as they make their way along this road. The impulse to show others who they truly are runs quite strong in this group, and for that reason alone, they are assured of great success and will serve as an inspiration to those they meet along the way.

GEORGES SEURAT
Painting detail by French artist, pointillist style

12/2/1859
Sagittarius I

CHALLENGE: **OVERCOMING THEIR TENDENCY TO REMAIN ATTACHED TO THOSE WHO DON'T APPRECIATE THEM**
FULFILLMENT: **FINDING THEMSELVES UNFETTERED FROM EXPRESSING THEMSELVES**
NOTABLES: **SUSAN DEY (ACTRESS, *THE PARTRIDGE FAMILY*, *LA LAW*); CHRISTINA ROSSETTI (POET)**

December 11–18

THE TITAN
SAGITTARIUS III

Those born in the Week of the Titan like nothing better than to pull off the occasional miracle, yet when they find themselves on the Way of Release, that miracle will doubtless involve a personal transformation of no small proportions. In fact, they will be faced with no less a task than to overcome, once and for all, the fussiness and personal insecurity that often lie at the heart of their extravagant approach to life and to develop the unassailable sense of self that is the higher calling of this karmic path. Just how that may manifest itself in the lives of these often heroic people will be as varied as the individuals themselves, yet one can rest assured that whatever the smaller steps involved, there will be at least one great and inspiring leap in consciousness that few will ever experience but many will doubtless envy.

CHALLENGE: **CHOOSING TO SEE THE TREES WITHIN THE FOREST OF THEIR PSYCHES**
FULFILLMENT: **ALLOWING OTHERS TO LIGHTEN THEIR LOADS ONCE IN A WHILE**
NOTABLES: **JAMES DOOLITTLE (AVIATOR); CATHY RIGBY (GYMNAST)**

December 19–25
PROPHECY
SAGITTARIUS–CAPRICORN CUSP

The personalities born on this cusp who tread the Way of Release will make wonderful progress along this road, especially when they allow themselves to be guided by their special navigational tools of prescience and spiritual insight. They will, however, need to come to terms with their tendency to rationalize their behavior or to discount their special psychic gifts, and the burdens of worry, pessimism, and negativity may all hamper their development, as may a willingness to stay tied to less gifted souls in the interest of self-sacrifice. Yet sooner or later, these people are likely to find the release, transformation, and freedom that are promised by this karmic path, if only out of the need to reconcile their inner natures with the outer world. Thus, though this may not prove the happiest of life journeys, it will no doubt prove one of the most profound.

GELSEY KIRKLAND
Ballet dancer

12/29/1952
Capricorn I

CHALLENGE: **REFUSING TO SACRIFICE THEMSELVES FOR OTHERS**
FULFILLMENT: **FINDING SECURITY WITHIN THE SELF**
NOTABLE: **LEONARD HOBBES (DEVELOPED J-57 GAS TURBINE ENGINE POWERING 1ST AMERICAN JETS)**

December 26–January 2
THE RULER
CAPRICORN I

If they take care to avoid their tendency to hang on to outdated ways of thinking or outworn emotional and behavioral patterns in the name of tradition, those born in the Week of the Ruler who tread the Way of Release can find wonderful success and achievement. Well suited to the step-by-step process of self-realization required by this journey, they may find that their biggest obstacle will be their unwillingness to make the first critical steps toward greater fulfillment. Though the process of releasing the past and embracing the future may give them pause, and though it may well take considerable time for them really to begin the work of the Way of Release, they will be aided in this journey by their abiding need to be all they can be, and for that reason alone Capricorn I's can be assured of progress along this karmic path.

CHALLENGE: **STRUGGLING WITH THEIR DIFFICULTY IN BEING ACCEPTING**
FULFILLMENT: **APPLYING THEIR CONSIDERABLE DETERMINATION TO THEIR GROWTH**
NOTABLES: **RAY KNIGHT (BASEBALL PLAYER; PLAYED MOSTLY WITH THE REDS); ROGER SESSIONS (COMPOSER; WON PULITZER)**

January 3–9
DETERMINATION
CAPRICORN II

If they are careful that their natural naïveté does not manifest in a perennial ignorance of their problems or an unfamiliarity with the inner working of their personalities, those born in the Week of Determination can realize some truly amazing transformations along the Way of Release. Cultivating greater self-esteem will prove paramount to their success, however, as these somewhat retiring people have a tendency to retreat into the belief that they are somehow undeserving of the happiness, ease, and fulfillment available to others. A curious aspect of this configuration is that Capricorn II's have a pronounced interest in the metaphysical, spiritual, and philosophical aspects of life. It is therefore likely that their predisposition to these areas will open the avenues to the self-realization, acceptance, and freedom that are all promised by this karmic path.

MARION DAVIES
Actress

1/3/1897
Capricorn II

CHALLENGE: **ACKNOWLEDGING THEIR INSECURITIES**
FULFILLMENT: **FREEING THEMSELVES FROM GUILT AND MISPLACED LOYALTY**

January 10–16
DOMINANCE
CAPRICORN III

The road to spiritual fulfillment can be a rocky one for those born in the Week of Dominance who tread the Way of Release. They will have to work hard to redirect the qualities of diligence and dedication that are their natural endowments in such a way that they serve their own higher natures and not the needs and demands of others. Too, these people can be awfully hard on themselves, and they will need to learn to develop a higher degree of tolerance and understanding before they will be able to realize the higher promise of this karmic path. Perhaps the best advice for these souls will be to consciously cultivate their more eccentric side and embrace a broader, less secure range of experience. Ultimately, however, their task will be to relinquish their need for control, recognizing that it arises out of a sense of inferiority rather than one of confidence and freedom.

CHALLENGE: **RECOGNIZING THAT A PROPENSITY FOR WORRY SHOULD AND CAN BE RELEASED**
FULFILLMENT: **BELIEVING THEMSELVES ENTITLED TO ABUNDANCE**

January 17–22

MYSTERY AND IMAGINATION
CAPRICORN–AQUARIUS CUSP

Learning to view their problems, trials, and personal tribulations more realistically will lie at the heart of Capricorn–Aquarians' quest for fulfillment as they travel the Way of Release. In fact, many of these personalities have a playful side that will serve them especially well on this karmic path, as long as they do not retreat into superficiality or immaturity in the interest of maintaining their lightheartedness. Though there are some with this configuration whose sense of self will forever remain elusive, they have the possibility of great success as they are more prone than most to having life experiences of a peak, unexpected, or revelatory nature that will show them the way to greater happiness. Providing they learn to take the experience of happiness as seriously as they sometimes take their woes, all will go well for them.

ANTON CHEKHOV
Playwright,
The Cherry Orchard
———
1/17/1860
Capricorn–Aquarius Cusp

CHALLENGE: **LETTING GO OF THEIR ATTRACTION TO THE CHAOTIC**

FULFILLMENT: **ENJOYING THE PEACE OF MIND THAT INNER FREEDOM BRINGS**

NOTABLE: **DESI ARNAZ, JR. (SON OF LUCILLE BALL AND DESI ARNAZ)**

January 23–30

GENIUS
AQUARIUS I

Those born in the Week of Genius who travel the Way of Release can realize tremendous success and achievement, providing they can come to understand that flexibility and changeability are inherent in all emotional lives. Though they are blessed with amazing intellectual comprehension, it may take time for their knowledge to filter down into a deeper level of understanding, as these souls have a tendency to view some very human situations and experiences in unduly abstract terms. As a result, they may cling to old behavior or outworn patterns, being well aware of the facts yet believing perhaps that they are somehow unchangeable. Too, they may undertake the business of solving their problems in ways that may be quite thorough and systematic yet fail to take into account the variables of other people's nature, much less their own. In a word, cultivating simple people skills will be of tremendous help, as will grounding their more intellectual approach in the simple routines of domestic life, child rearing, and one-on-one relationships.

CHALLENGE: **MODERATING THEIR OVERALL APPROACH TO LIFE**

FULFILLMENT: **KNOWING THAT THEY ARE FREE TO MAKE POSITIVE CHOICES**

January 31–February 7

YOUTH AND EASE
AQUARIUS II

Grounding their generally happy-go-lucky personalities in a sense of self and an unassailable set of values will be especially important for the souls born in this week who travel the Way of Release. Indeed, simple immaturity will prove the principal stumbling block for many of these people, as they may have a kind of Peter Pan approach to responsibility and dedication. Moreover, there will be a pronounced need to release the need to live up to others' expectations and take the risk of striking out on one's own in order to discover who they really are and what they really want out of this life experience. Yet they have the possibility for great personal transformation and many will develop an identity that is both tolerant and wise. If they do not ignore their Leo II origins of strength and devotion by retreating into a kind of prolonged adolescence, they have the potential to really shine.

SIR HENRY MORTON STANLEY
Explorer and journalist
———
1/28/1841
Aquarius I

CHALLENGE: **WORKING ON THE ESTABLISHMENT OF A STRONG VALUE SYSTEM AND SENSE OF SELF**

FULFILLMENT: **FREEING THEMSELVES FROM THEIR ATTRACTION TO TROUBLED PEOPLE**

February 8–15

ACCEPTANCE
AQUARIUS III

Though there are some born in this week who travel the Way of Release for whom the principal lessons will revolve around letting go of old prejudices or an intolerant attitude, there are others who will have to delve deep within in order to reemerge with the ability to establish where their boundaries are, especially in the area of self-sacrifice or their tendency to feel victimized by external circumstances. In any event, these lively and affectionate souls are blessed with all the resources they require to navigate this karmic path successfully, as they are already disposed to embrace movement and activity and have a pronounced love of new concepts, ideas, and ways of thinking that will serve them especially well here. If they can be careful not to allow such enthusiasms to degenerate into superficiality by trying to merely outrun their problems, this will doubtless prove a rich and satisfying life passage.

CHALLENGE: **TOLERATING THEIR OWN CRYING NEED TO LOOK WITHIN**

FULFILLMENT: **LIGHTENING THEIR SPIRIT AND TRANSFORMING THEIR LIVES**

NOTABLE: **MARY STEENBURGEN (ACTRESS, *MELVIN AND HOWARD*)**

February 16–22

SENSITIVITY
AQUARIUS–PISCES CUSP

Those born on the Cusp of Sensitivity who find themselves on the Way of Release will surely be faced with a number of issues that revolve around the need to reconcile their tougher, more aggressive tendencies with their deeply emotional inner worlds. While the need for self-protection may prove invaluable in their early years, ultimately they will have to do no small amount of work to release their insecurity and find the courage to be more truly themselves. Yet the personal metamorphosis promised by this karmic path is sure to occur, and if they keep in mind that they have already been gifted with the strength necessary to overcome whatever obstacles may present themselves and keep in mind that the level of our expectations can do much to shape the quality of our lives, they can find the highest attainment and enlightenment.

BOBBY UNSER
Race car driver
_____
2/20/1934
Aquarius–Pisces Cusp

CHALLENGE: **RELEASING THE PATTERNS SET IN CHILDHOOD**
FULFILLMENT: **OPENING UP TO THEIR OWN TENDERNESS**

February 23–March 2

SPIRIT
PISCES I

Individuals born in the Week of Spirit may find the Way of Release a bit of a rocky road until they come to terms with the need to ground their energies in responsibility, a more practical approach to problem solving, and a striving toward maturity. Blithe spirits though they may be, these men and women may nevertheless become mired in resentments from the past that may cause them to retreat into a rather childlike resistance to the part they play in shaping their own destinies. Too, they will have to avoid emotional neediness as well as the tendency to be taken advantage of by more calculating or selfish people. Yet if they work to transcend their personal sensitivity or sense of victimhood in the interest of developing a higher sense of happiness than merely immediate gratification, they can travel quite far along the Way of Release.

CHALLENGE: **GRAPPLING WITH RESENTMENT AND SENSITIVITY**
FULFILLMENT: **PURSUING THEIR DREAMS UNFETTERED BY EMOTIONAL BAGGAGE**
NOTABLE: **MAX LINCOLN SCHUSTER (PUBLISHER; COFOUNDED SIMON AND SCHUSTER)**

March 3–10

THE LONER
PISCES II

Pisces II's who travel the Way of Release will find that many of their life's lessons are played out in the arena of personal relationships. Many of these souls will have a marked tendency to venture forth to bond with others, then retreat into reclusive misanthropy, pessimism, and self-pity at the first sign of conflict. Indeed, they may have to divest themselves of a measure of unrealistic fantasy about just how relationships ought to be before they can navigate this karmic path successfully. Further, there is a strong possibility that they may have to go into some early traumas in detail, sometimes with professional help, until they gain the necessary insight into how such events might still be shaping their attitudes or worldview. Yet whatever the problems associated with this configuration, they can serve as the springboards to greater happiness and true personal liberation, just as soon as Pisces II's gather the strength to dive.

OLIVER WENDELL HOLMES, JR.
Jurist and Supreme Court justice
_____
3/8/1841
Pisces II

CHALLENGE: **BEING WILLING TO LOOK AT THEMSELVES OBJECTIVELY**
FULFILLMENT: **SURRENDERING THEMSELVES TO THEIR OWN HIGHER GOOD**
NOTABLE: **YURI GAGARIN (RUSSIAN COSMONAUT; 1ST MAN IN SPACE)**

March 11–18

DANCERS AND DREAMERS
PISCES III

These philosophical individuals who find themselves on the Way of Release may have a bit of difficulty settling down long enough to face themselves and get to the bottom of their problems, as they tend to have much better instincts for solving others' problems than their own. In fact, they may be somewhat hampered in their higher development by an omniscient or holier-than-thou attitude toward human woes, as well as a tendency to scatter their energies by refusing to focus on the tasks at hand. Too, there are some who will find themselves plagued by an inability to choose a course of action and stick to it, and a number of them may become therapy "junkies" as they run from themselves in an ever-widening search to become "fixed." Yet they have the potential for great spirituality, and, if they can learn to harness that power in the interest of illuminating some of the darker corners of their psyches, the transformation and liberation that occur may be remarkable indeed.

CHALLENGE: **ADOPTING A MORE HUMBLE APPROACH IN ORDER TO ASSESS THEMSELVES MORE REALISTICALLY**
FULFILLMENT: **TRANSCENDING THEMSELVES**
NOTABLES: **SAM DONALDSON (TV JOURNALIST; WHITE HOUSE CORRESPONDENT); JOHANN STRAUSS (COMPOSER, VIENNESE WALTZ)**

The Way of Consideration

LEO III TO AQUARIUS III
Leadership to Acceptance

The individuals on this karmic path are here to develop consideration for the feelings, viewpoints, and lifestyles of others. The type of understanding or sensitivity implied by the Way of Consideration is more than a onetime ability to have empathy for another. What is important is continuity; that is, the development of an ongoing capacity to think of others from moment to moment. First one must become open to, and accepting of, views or feelings other than one's own. Second, one must consider these views or feelings in one's dealings with people, whether one agrees with or understands them or not. Such a process requires a certain detachment, since it requires a thoughtful or contemplative regard of another as a prelude to understanding. Moreover, developing the art of reflection will aid those born to this karmic path to see their own actions and their effects more objectively, thus enabling them to think before they act more and more frequently over time.

Cultivating a more open and accepting point of view toward others rather than judging them is the first step toward regarding them with consideration, compassion, and thoughtfulness. The core lesson for the individuals on this karmic path is to free themselves from making ego-related judgments. It is judging a person's actions, goals, opinions, or feelings as right or wrong that often leads to a lack of consideration. This is because most people do not value or take into account anything they have once invalidated or dismissed. Moreover, judgmental tendencies often come from an attitude of superiority that is ego-driven. The men and women on the Way of Consideration would do well to guard against such a stance, as they do possess such a commanding manner and have such a self-assured approach that they tend to dominate those around them, if not ride roughshod over them. This karmic path requires those born to it to give up their rather larger-than-life egos, in particular their tendency to believe themselves to be infallible. None of this is very easy to accomplish, since deep inside, those on the Way of Consideration believe themselves worthy of kingship, and they act this out by attempting to rule—handing down judgments and meting out punishments. As they struggle with the core lesson of this karmic path, they may even go so far as to believe that their brand of "justice" is actually in the best interests of others. Obviously, their struggle with ego and judgmentalism may take some time, and patience may be required before humility begins to emerge in these souls.

Developing a greater ability to detach and reflect is also necessary. The men and women on the Way of Consideration are born with a headstrong, passionate approach to life and love. Burning with emotional intensity, they often rush headlong into situations without fully considering the results. Moreover, these individuals are especially sharp-tongued

CORE LESSON
Releasing the ego's need to judge

GOAL
To develop an ongoing, thoughtful consideration of others

GIFTS
Heroic, Affectionate, Inventive

PITFALLS
Domineering, Insensitive, Judgmental

and have a propensity to be hurtful in their directness. Prickly pears, they have an extreme sensitivity to anything that smacks of criticism, and this causes them to go on the attack, often verbally. What's more, they have an uncanny ability to really "stick in the knife and turn it" in others' most vulnerable spots. However, learning to stop and think before they speak and becoming more aware of the effects of their words or actions on others will occur over time. It is ironic, however, that such individuals as these should place such a high premium on being accorded honor and respect yet find it so difficult to accord others the same. Of course, they never see it this way. Ultimately, these powerful individuals will release their need to dominate and to inflict their opinions on others at all costs and will learn to use their considerable charm and facility for wit or humor to spare the feelings of others or to deflect situations that might otherwise be hurtful, helping others over rough spots or making up for their own mistakes or omissions. A good strategy for those on this karmic path is to acquire sufficient objectivity to shift their view of themselves as being at center stage and to take on the perspective of one who is standing on the sidelines and watching the action, thus enabling them to see what the other players may need and their own role in the action.

Of considerable benefit to the men and women born to this karmic path are their innate heroism and sense of justice. Truly wanting to do the right thing by the people in their lives, they are often pained when shown the ways in which they have been thoughtless. If they can develop sufficient objectivity to recognize, without judgment, and understand the needs, desires, and greater goals of those around them, they may, in fact, become everyday heroes for others, offering kindness, thoughtfulness, and small, continuous doses of caring. The great potential here is for Leo III's fiery passion to be transmuted into a kind of compassionate love of humanity that is of the universal kind. The great creativity that is innate in those on this karmic path can be put to use to serve others in a myriad of inventive ways.

Ultimately, those on this karmic path will open to the notion that they are in fact part of something much larger, not just a greater social whole but also a universal oneness. Luckily, the idea that all human beings are equal is not anathema to them. They are exceedingly democratic in many ways, though they may not be aware that, deep down, they believe that they and they alone are superior to the rest of the human race. As their development progresses and they learn to accept and tolerate others, it is not unusual for them to become champions of the underdog or fighters of injustice in any form. They may involve themselves in humanitarian efforts, charity, or other forms of service. These somewhat extreme personalities must, however, take care that their propensity for judgmentalism does

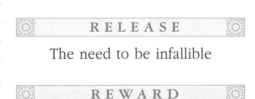

RELEASE
The need to be infallible

REWARD
The joy of being there for another

SUGGESTION

*Realize that we are all one and that hurting another only hurts yourself.
Try to remember that needing to do things your own way is only
your ego's way of asserting itself. Think before you speak.*

not take another form so that they begin to go overboard when defending the rights of others, pointing a finger at anyone they feel is not sufficiently compassionate or thoughtful—in other words, becoming bullies but justifying such shaming of others as caring for those less fortunate.

It is in the realm of relationships that most of this karmic path's processes will be experienced. Often those on the Way of Consideration find that fate places them in the company of a wide variety of people, particularly those whom they find especially difficult to accept or even intolerable. It is typical for those on this karmic path to be born into families or to give birth to children who are totally different from them in temperament and outlook. Here, in the bosom of family, is the crucible of many difficult lessons. Their children in particular, thanks to the fierce love that those on the Way of Consideration feel for their progeny, will help teach those on this karmic path about acceptance.

Other important lessons will include setting aside selfishness and self-centered aims in favor of learning how to give others what they need. Those intimately involved with individuals on the Way of Consideration are apt to go through some considerable trials by fire as their loved ones, walking this karmic path, vacillate between aggressive and passive behavior, one moment ruling with a heavy and often ruthless hand, only to exhibit awareness and kindness the next. In addition, mates of these individuals may have to wait quite a while before

BALANCE POINT

Acceptance and Rejection

their husbands, wives, or lovers realize that a double standard is not exactly considerate. Those on this karmic path may lose those they love due to their overbearing attitudes, intolerance, or inconsideration before they learn the lesson, "Do unto others as you would have them do unto you."

By transferring their belief in themselves into a belief in others and universal laws, those on the Way of Consideration will grow spiritually and find that their moral values have matured. Many will also find that the workplace provides a source of growth. These powerful individuals often achieve positions of authority; thus, their struggle to deal with their autocratic tendencies and to understand, support, and appreciate their coworkers will fall neatly into the work of this karmic path. They do enjoy working side by side with others. It is important for those involved with these souls to remember that, try as they may, they will never truly rid themselves of their ego's needs. Thus, giving them a certain amount of acknowledgment and appreciation when they have made the effort to be considerate will go a long way in helping them along their karmic path.

A symbol of this karmic path might be that of the Tin Man from *The Wizard of Oz*. Lacking a heart, he joined with his fellow travelers to search for the wizard, a symbol of the power of greater consciousness. In the end, by overcoming his fears and allowing himself to be more vulnerable, he reveals his humility, his love, and his heroism and discovers that he has a heart after all.

CRYSTALS AND GEMSTONES

Rose Quartz is said to possess the vibration of unconditional love. Holding this stone shifts the focus from the judgment of the mind to the empathy of the heart.

NOTABLES ON THIS KARMIC PATH

The cinematic Everyman of our time, actor **Tom Hanks** conveys the understated heroism required of those following the Way of Consideration. Using his screen roles as a vehicle for promoting the qualities of kindness, thoughtfulness, and caring, Hanks exhibits the core values of this karmic path. As a

TOM HANKS

champion of the underdog and a fighter against injustice, Hanks's low-key characters have found their way into the hearts of moviegoers everywhere. Able to strike a common chord with audiences, Hanks shines in roles that echo such popular protagonists as Jimmy Stewart and Gary Cooper.

Not only has **Marianne Williamson** learned many of the lessons of this path, but she has also taken the responsibility of passing her knowledge along to others. Since

MARIANNE WILLIAMSON

1983, Williamson has been sharing her understanding of the importance of consideration through *A Course in Miracles,* teaching her pupils that we recognize that much of our thinking is fear based and can be transformed by love. Embodying the quality of acceptance and believing that it is possible to heal both self and others, she emphasizes the need to find peace first in our own hearts. By making this her life's work, Williamson typifies the tendency of this path to transmute Leo III fire into compassionate love of humanity.

Actor and comedian **Robin Williams** has allowed his energies to move with his destiny. Not only has he put the wide mood swings characteristic of those born in his personology period, the Week of Oscillation, to work in his manic comedic riffs, but he has also embraced his karmic path, the Way of Consideration. Through Comic Relief, the organization he cofounded, he has helped the home-

ROBIN WILLIAMS

less. It is interesting to note that among his many film successes, including *The World According to Garp, Mrs. Doubtfire, Dead Poets Society,* and *Awakenings,* he has played characters of unusual compassion. It was his role as a caring psychologist in the film *Good Will Hunting* that won him an Oscar.

Other Notables: Frederick Law Olmsted, Billie Holiday, Ulysses S. Grant, Orson Welles, George Strait, Sir Arthur Conan Doyle, Saul Bellow, Liam Neeson, David Rockefeller, Dan Aykroyd, Cheryl Ladd, Jean Piaget, Jimmy Connors, Paul "Pee-Wee Herman" Reubens, Christopher Reeve, Ruth Gordon, Auguste Rodin, Carl Sandburg, Mary J. Blige, Henry "Hank" Aaron, Nolan Ryan

---

BIRTHDAYS ON KARMIC PATH 20

July 9, 1896–November 27, 1896 | February 19, 1915–July 10, 1915

October 1, 1933–February 18, 1934 | May 12, 1952–September 30, 1952 | December 22, 1970–May 12, 1971

August 3, 1989–December 21, 1989 | March 14, 2008–August 2, 2008

KARMIC PATH
20

March 19–24

REBIRTH
PISCES–ARIES CUSP

This will doubtless prove an interesting and educational life journey for those born on this cusp who travel the Way of Consideration, though they may have to work hard to overcome a rather passive-aggressive approach to their own development and enlightenment. Gifted with extraordinary sensitivity and intuition, these individuals will nevertheless have to come to terms with their more defensive and domineering attitudes in order to utilize their considerable instincts better. Though they do have a huge capacity for love, they may also have little faith in their ability to share that love with others, and the resulting frustration may manifest itself in rage, argumentativeness, and a conflicted and difficult emotional life. Still, they can make wonderful progress, providing they learn to set aside their often shaky egos and replace the chips on their shoulders with an attitude that combines both forgiveness and objectivity.

BILLIE HOLIDAY
Jazz singer; subject of
Lady Sings the Blues

4/7/1915
Aries II

CHALLENGE: **GETTING THEIR PASSIONS UNDER CONTROL**
FULFILLMENT: **SURROUNDING THEMSELVES WITH A FAMILY OF FRIENDS**

March 25–April 2

THE CHILD
ARIES I

Those born in the Week of the Child who navigate the challenges and demands of the Way of Consideration may have a difficult passage until experience, time, and greater enlightenment endow them with the necessary degree of empathy to set aside ego issues and develop greater consistency. Yet these souls have been gifted with a fine sense of wonder and enthusiasm that will do much to pave the way to better socialization, causing them to reach out to others in an effort to share. Thus, they will learn about many of the nuances and finer points of human interaction from those they meet along the way. Providing they do not retreat into isolation or unrealistic expectations and remain open to the world of possibilities available through contact, compassion, and caring for others, they can find great fulfillment.

CHALLENGE: **OVERCOMING THEIR TENDENCY TO SELF-CENTEREDNESS**
FULFILLMENT: **ACCEPTING THE PAST**
NOTABLES: **JACK JOHNSON (U.S. HEAVYWEIGHT BOXER); EWAN MCGREGOR (ACTOR, *TRAINSPOTTING; STAR WARS: THE PHANTOM MENACE*)**

April 3–10

THE STAR
ARIES II

Gifted with abundant energy and the ability to get things done, those born in the Week of the Star who travel the Way of Consideration can realize great success and accomplishment along this life journey, providing they release their ego attachment to the idea that there are "right" and "wrong" ways of doing things. The ability to give themselves fully is quite pronounced, and as long as these individuals do not perceive their natural dedication as something deserving of personal reward, they will find considerable fulfillment. Too, they will have to avoid extremes and to try to be more consistent in their relationships with others, as they have a tendency to overpower those who oppose them with temper tantrums, emotional displays, and simple theatrics. While much of the work of this karmic path will doubtless be played out in family and romantic relationships, they would do well to seek out higher causes, movements, and projects that exalt their sense of tolerance and illuminate collective values.

PICABO STREET
Olympic skier,
gold medalist

4/3/1971
Aries II

CHALLENGE: **ACKNOWLEDGING THAT THEIR WAY MAY NOT ALWAYS BE THE RIGHT ONE**
FULFILLMENT: **GIVING THEIR TIME AND CONSIDERATION TO OTHERS**

April 11–18

THE PIONEER
ARIES III

For the personalities born in the Week of the Pioneer, the challenges and demands of the Way of Consideration will doubtless manifest themselves in their having to reevaluate their considerable leadership abilities in order to discover the broader range of human interaction. In fact, these people are gifted with a generosity of spirit that is very much in keeping with the higher purposes of this karmic path, yet they will have to work to overcome their notion that they know what's good for everybody else. Too, their high degree of idealism will surely cause some of them to develop some shockingly judgmental attitudes that will give them no end of trouble and may serve only to alienate those they would most like to have on their side. Yet if they channel their dynamic idealism in constructive ways that speak to the needs of the many and not just of the few, they will take impressive strides along this road.

CHALLENGE: **REALIZING THE VALIDITY OF OTHER VIEWPOINTS**
FULFILLMENT: **NURTURING AND SUPPORTING THEIR LOVED ONES**

April 19–24
POWER
ARIES–TAURUS CUSP

Those born on the Cusp of Power who find themselves on the Way of Consideration will time and again confront situations in which the needs of others exist at decided odds with their own sense of driving ambition. Many of these individuals are, in fact, so focused on what they want and where they're going that their objectives may far outweigh personal considerations, to the detriment of the needs of those around them. Yet the Leo III origins of this karmic path will endow them with the sense of devotion and dedication required to sensitize themselves better to others. If they become willing, in the course of their lives, to relinquish part or all of their power base to bond with loved ones and family members in a spirit of caring, sharing, and acceptance, they will realize tremendous progress and fulfillment.

ULYSSES S. GRANT
18th U.S. president;
commanded Union Army
in Civil War
―――――――
4/27/1822
Taurus I

CHALLENGE: **OVERCOMING THEIR MERCENARY TENDENCIES**
FULFILLMENT: **UTILIZING THEIR POWER IN AID OF THOSE LESS FORTUNATE THAN THEMSELVES**
NOTABLES: **CATHERINE THE GREAT (EMPRESS OF RUSSIA; KNOWN FOR HER MANY AFFAIRS); EDWARD BARNES (ARCHITECT, PREFABRICATED ALUMINUM HOUSE); MADAME DE STAËL (WRITER; FAMOUS FOR ROMANTIC NOVEL CORINNE)**

April 25–May 2
MANIFESTATION
TAURUS I

The qualities of dominance and leadership may combine in a formidable way in the personalities born in this week who travel the Way of Consideration, and they may find it hard to reconcile their truly powerful personae with the spiritual demands of this karmic path. Yet along with their more dominating side they have a nurturing aspect that will serve them well. Since confrontations and difficulties over personal issues tend to cause Taurus I's to dig in their heels and simply refuse to change, they would do well to cultivate greater detachment and a higher understanding, rather than allowing relationship issues to push them into their emotional hot spots of the fear of their own vulnerability and of being hurt. Yet they are quite well suited to the kind of quiet and reflective development required by the Way of Consideration and will surely flourish in domestic and professional surroundings that allow their caring natures to emerge in an atmosphere of quiet strength and wisdom.

CHALLENGE: **EXPOSING THEIR SOFTER SIDES**
FULFILLMENT: **ACTING IN THE ROLE OF CHAMPION OR PROTECTOR**
NOTABLES: **BRUCE HENDERSON (BUSINESS STRATEGY CONSULTANT); FREDERICK LAW OLMSTED (PLANNED CENTRAL PARK IN NEW YORK CITY)**

May 3–10
THE TEACHER
TAURUS II

Those born in the Week of the Teacher who navigate this karmic path may well encounter their share of ups and downs until they come to terms with their tendency to consider their own point of view as omniscient or infallible. Steering away from playing out the more authoritarian side of their natures in their role as mentor will prove especially useful to their higher development, as will refusing to surround themselves with flatterers or "groupies" who indulge their need to display their knowledge and opinions. Perhaps the best measure of their progress along the Way of Consideration will lie in their inclinations and educational interests. If they lean toward greater exploration of social concerns such as democracy and freedom, they will do fine. If, on the other hand, they find themselves inclining toward morally rigid or unduly critical attitudes, they will run the risk of getting stuck in a tiresome and didactic pomposity.

ORSON WELLES
Actor/director,
Citizen Kane
―――――――
5/6/1915
Taurus II

CHALLENGE: **TEMPERING THEIR SOMETIMES OVERLY CRITICAL NATURES**
FULFILLMENT: **INTERACTING WITH INDIVIDUALS FROM ALL WALKS OF LIFE AND CULTURES**
NOTABLES: **DENNIS THATCHER (HUSBAND OF MARGARET); BETTY COMDEN (LYRICIST, ON THE TOWN)**

May 11–18
THE NATURAL
TAURUS III

The interesting, unusual people born in this week who find themselves on the Way of Consideration may flounder a bit in the process of establishing greater empathy or compassion for their fellow human beings until they cultivate a more detached and reflective way of thinking about the world. In fact, the demands of this karmic path may call many of them to retreat from stressful or high-pressure situations and into a more secluded lifestyle or environment to gain a better understanding of their role in the grander human scheme. While sheer emotionality and a rather volatile temper may hinder their steps along the way, in general these individuals can make great emotional and spiritual progress on this life journey as they will surely be aided in the quest for enlightenment by their attraction to the unique, their ability to be flexible, and their innate empathy for the world of nature and the rights of all beings who dwell here.

CHALLENGE: **LEARNING HOW TO COMMIT IN RELATIONSHIPS**
FULFILLMENT: **MATURING INTO THE ROLE OF STEADY FRIEND, SPOUSE, OR LOVER**
NOTABLES: **GEORGE STRAIT (COUNTRY MUSIC SINGER); PIERCE BROSNAN (ACTOR); PAUL SAMUELSON (ECONOMIST; AUTHOR)**

May 19–24

ENERGY
TAURUS–GEMINI CUSP

The highly proactive approach that Taurus–Geminis have to life in general can be a great asset on the Way of Consideration, providing they direct their energy toward gaining a better perception of the world around them and place less emphasis on personal struggles, superficial obsessions, and augmenting their already formidable egos. The principal pitfall for those with this configuration will be their tendency to place themselves at the center of the action to such an extent that they deprive themselves of needed moments for reflection and reevaluation. Their headstrong approach to human interaction may leave a trail of broken hearts (including their own) until they learn to make the connection between their highly self-centered style and its consequences. Though "doing unto others" may be a hard-learned lesson, Taurus–Geminis are blessed with the brilliance necessary to ensure that that lesson will be taken to heart here.

SIR ARTHUR CONAN DOYLE
Writer, created
Sherlock Holmes

—————
5/22/1859
Taurus–Gemini Cusp

CHALLENGE: **CONSIDERING THAT THE PURPOSE OF THE PEOPLE IN THEIR LIVES IS NOT MERELY TO BE THEIR AUDIENCE**
FULFILLMENT: **TRANSFORMING THEIR NATURAL CURIOSITY ABOUT OTHERS INTO A CAPACITY TO UNDERSTAND THEM**
NOTABLES: **MOSHE DAYAN (ISRAELI GENERAL); FREDERIC PASSY (ECONOMIST; SHARED 1ST NOBEL PEACE PRIZE)**

May 25–June 2

FREEDOM
GEMINI I

Souls born in the Week of Freedom can do quite beautifully on the Way of Consideration, as the challenges, demands, and higher promise of this karmic path are very much in keeping with their natural inclinations. In fact, their biggest stumbling block is likely to be their unwillingness to develop the sensitivity and caring it calls for. Empathy is an idea that is easily grasped intellectually but much harder to put into practice in the sphere of daily human interaction. Too, they may experience problems with developing a sense of continuity, and their bursts of caring or sharing may have a rather haphazard or sporadic quality as a result. Yet if they cultivate their more affectionate side and take care not to spend their energies in rebellion or unduly manipulative tactics, they are sure to rise along the way.

CHALLENGE: **DEVELOPING GREATER PATIENCE**
FULFILLMENT: **LEARNING HOW TO USE THEIR CONSIDERABLE WIT NOT TO RIDICULE BUT TO COMFORT**

June 3–10

NEW LANGUAGE
GEMINI II

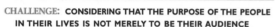

Those born in the Week of New Language will have to address the issues of learning to communicate more effectively with those who may not be able to understand their unique manner of expressing themselves. Otherwise, the task of developing greater empathy can often seem overwhelming for these souls, and they will experience any number of ups and downs, especially in relationships, until they learn when to stop asserting their points of view and simply shut up and listen. Also, competitiveness may be a particular problem for these rather insecure people, and their need to dominate interactions of all kinds can really get in the way of their higher understanding. Yet if they develop the necessary detachment to grasp the notion that differences of semantics and styles of expression are not nearly as important as the unspoken ties of universal experience that bind us all together, they can take some significant strides along the way.

ISABELLA ROSSELLINI
Actress; daughter of
Ingrid Bergman

—————
6/18/1952
Gemini III

CHALLENGE: **KNOWING WHEN CERTAIN RELATIONSHIPS ARE SERVING IMPORTANT PURPOSES**
FULFILLMENT: **COMING UP WITH UNUSUAL FORMS OF COMMUNICATION TO TRULY CONNECT WITH OTHERS**
NOTABLES: **SAUL BELLOW (AUTHOR; WON NOBEL AND PULITZER PRIZES); LIAM NEESON (ACTOR, *STAR WARS: THE PHANTOM MENACE*)**

June 11–18

THE SEEKER
GEMINI III

Emotional volatility may be the principal stumbling block for those born in the Week of the Seeker who tread the Way of Consideration, and they may manifest a marked impatience with the more mundane and everyday aspects of experience that will send them hurtling off in search of ever-widening horizons. Though these intelligent, curious souls may find much to discover in the course of their adventures, they are likely to remain dissatisfied with it all until they come to terms with more personal issues of empathy and consideration. Rather judgmental, they are nevertheless gifted with a natural detachment and some highly evaluative instincts that will doubtless be warmed by a wide variety of relationships and emotional growth with the passage of this life journey.

CHALLENGE: **CULTIVATING A GREATER DEPTH OF COMPASSION WITHIN THEMSELVES**
FULFILLMENT: **EXPANDING THEIR UNDERSTANDING AS THEY OPEN TO THE VIEWPOINTS OF OTHERS**
NOTABLES: **DAVID ROCKEFELLER (BANKER; PHILANTHROPIST); CAROL KANE (ACTRESS, *TAXI*)**

June 19–24
MAGIC
GEMINI–CANCER CUSP

Those born on the Cusp of Magic can expect some wonderful rewards and accomplishments along the Way of Consideration, providing they protect their empathetic and emotional side from becoming wounded. Though the tendency to play out the destiny of this karmic path in the arena of purely personal issues is highly pronounced in this configuration, Gemini–Cancers would do well to develop a broader and more all-embracing attitude in which love of one's fellowman does not get short shrift in the face of their pursuit of personal fulfillment or romantic idealism. Too, some on this journey will fail its higher calling to detach and open to others in a more objective fashion by allowing themselves to dominate those around them by purely emotional means. Nevertheless, there is a prospect of great reward and fulfillment along this life journey, and if all goes well, they will find ample opportunity to explore their immense capacity for love.

CHALLENGE: **DISENTANGLING THEMSELVES FROM THEIR RO-MANTIC NOTIONS OF RELATIONSHIPS**

FULFILLMENT: **LEARNING HOW TO LOVE IN THE BROADER, MORE HUMANITARIAN SENSE**

NOTABLE: **JOHN GOODMAN (ACTOR, ROSEANNE)**

June 25–July 2
THE EMPATH
CANCER I

Those born in the Week of the Empath who navigate this karmic path will find themselves considerably buoyed on this life journey by the fact that they come into it endowed with more natural strength and endurance than they might otherwise have had. Yet the key to their soul's further development will lie in their willingness to view things more objectively and not to make judgments or assessments of their fellows based on prejudice or intolerance operating in the name of "instinct" or "psychic impression." Too, they will have to avoid their tendency to withdraw to such an extent that they isolate themselves from the world of everyday interaction that is part of the calling of this karmic path and avoid exercising their more aggressive tendencies in personal vendettas, revenge, and assorted grudge matches. With time, however, they can move from a purely personal viewpoint to the more universal attitude required by this karmic path.

CHALLENGE: **BEING AWARE THAT SOMETIMES THEIR BRAND OF "CONSIDERATION" IS MERELY MANIPULATION**

FULFILLMENT: **SERVING THEIR FELLOWS THROUGH CHARITY OR OTHER GOOD WORKS**

NOTABLES: **CHERYL LADD (ACTRESS, CHARLIE'S ANGELS); JEAN STAFFORD (WRITER; WON PULITZER)**

DAN AYKROYD
Comedian/actor/writer,
The Blues Brothers

7/1/1952
Cancer I

July 3–10
THE UNCONVENTIONAL
CANCER II

The higher calling of the Way of Consideration will require those born in the Week of the Unconventional to kick over the traces of narrow egotism and self-absorption and play out their richly imaginative ideas in the arena of the larger world. Though the demands of this karmic path will in some way require that they avoid hiding their intuitive and imaginative side under the proverbial bushel basket, they are sure to relish its opportunities for learning easygoing acceptance and tolerance of their fellows. Until they embrace those opportunities, however, these souls may be prone to finger-pointing and tongue wagging, particularly at those who are seemingly unable to stick to the rules. Yet if they come to terms with the fact that such objections are only the soul's way of calling them to reveal and express their own wackier side, these personalities are promised a highly interesting life journey.

CHALLENGE: **NOT INDULGING IN WHAT THEY CONSIDER TO BE HARMLESS GOSSIP**

FULFILLMENT: **COMING TO ACCEPT THEMSELVES AS THEY LEARN TO ACCEPT OTHERS**

NOTABLES: **MARIANNE WILLIAMSON ("COURSE IN MIRACLES" TEACHER; AUTHOR); TOM HANKS (OSCAR-WINNING ACTOR, PHILADELPHIA, FORREST GUMP)**

July 11–18
THE PERSUADER
CANCER III

Those born in the Week of the Persuader who navigate the challenge and promise of the Way of Consideration may be forced to look at themselves and their craving for greater personal recognition. Passionate and intense, these men and women may expend entirely too much energy in attempting to throw their weight around or otherwise demand satisfaction, until they free themselves from ego involvement and develop a degree of detachment. However, their inborn talent for observation gives them a leg up on this karmic path, since recognizing the needs of others is often a prelude to considering them. As long as they invoke their leadership abilities in service of others rather than as a way of dominating, their tendency to work for the good of the group will play well. Blessed with the ability to control their own needs, great empathy, and a real understanding of the issues that shape all our lives, they will make great progress.

CHALLENGE: **NOT EXPECTING RECOGNITION**

FULFILLMENT: **UTILIZING THEIR CONSIDERABLE PSYCHOLOGICAL INSIGHT IN SERVICE OF A GREATER GOOD**

NOTABLES: **DAVID HASSELHOFF (PRODUCER/STAR, BAYWATCH); NICOLETTE LARSON (SINGER); SIDNEY JAMES WEBB (BRITISH SOCIAL REFORMER)**

JOHN TESH
Musician; former cohost
Entertainment Tonight

7/9/1952
Cancer II

July 19–25
OSCILLATION
CANCER–LEO CUSP

Developing greater emotional consistency will no doubt play a huge part in the higher development of those born on the Cusp of Oscillation who navigate the challenge and rewards of this karmic path. Yet they bring to this journey a measure of moral courage and a love of humanity, in particular children, that will surely serve them well. In fact, the principal pitfall for those born with this configuration may be that their own emotional oscillations or blockages will stand in the way of the awareness of the needs of others that is demanded. Thus, going deeply within the self in order to understand their own feelings better will pave the way for smoother, more fulfilling relationships. If they absorb the lesson that their rewards will be found not so much in the pursuit of a quantity of relationships as in a search for quality and develop an easier attitude with the dynamics of everyday give-and-take, they will be able to find great happiness.

CHALLENGE: **BECOMING AWARE OF THE EFFECTS OF THEIR MOODS ON THOSE AROUND THEM**

FULFILLMENT: **TRANSLATING THEIR INTEREST IN A WIDE VARIETY OF PEOPLE INTO A CONCERN FOR THEM**

NOTABLES: **ROBIN WILLIAMS (ACTOR, *DEAD POETS' SOCIETY*, *GOOD WILL HUNTING*); SAMUEL AUGUSTUS MAVERICK (RANCHER; HELPED ESTABLISH TEXAS)**

JEAN PIAGET
Psychologist, leading
child development expert

8/9/1896
Leo II

July 26–August 2
AUTHORITY
LEO I

Those born in the Week of Authority who tread the Way of Consideration may have to learn to lighten their steps a bit before they make real progress along this karmic path. They have a tendency both to dominate and to try to manipulate others with their own passions and sense of conviction, sometimes without adequately tuning in to the core of others' real needs, thoughts, and feelings. Thus (and most especially), with partners and children they may project their own feelings to such an extent that they are continually deciding what's best for everyone without first considering the myriad of variables involved. Gifted with a generous, expansive nature, they may falter a bit until they back up a bit and learn greater empathy and objectivity. Though they may indeed get a chance to "rule the world," it may prove a rather hollow affair unless they can divest themselves of ego issues and learn what it means to live and let live.

CHALLENGE: **AVOIDING THE TENDENCY TO MERGE THEIR IDENTITY WITH THOSE OF THEIR LOVED ONES**

FULFILLMENT: **STOPPING TO APPRECIATE THEIR RELATIONSHIPS ONCE IN A WHILE**

August 3–10
BALANCED STRENGTH
LEO II

Gifted with the admirable qualities of endurance, tenacity, and inborn strength, the souls born in this week may nevertheless have a rather hard row to hoe on the Way of Consideration. Indeed, single-mindedness and a refusal to change may be the biggest sticking points for the individuals who travel this karmic path, for once they have decided on a specific course of action, it may prove nearly impossible to dissuade them from that course. Thus, setting their sights high above the realms of personal ambition and fulfillment will prove particularly important on this karmic path, as will being willing to grow. Still, they are blessed with the ability to "keep their heads when all around them are losing theirs," and if they properly channel that capacity into a deeper understanding of what those around them need and then meet those needs in a consistent and reliable fashion, their generosity, caring, and natural compassion are unlikely to go unrewarded or unrecognized.

CHALLENGE: **REMEMBERING TO TAP INTO THEIR INTUITIVE AWARENESS OF THE NEEDS OF OTHERS**

FULFILLMENT: **EXPRESSING THE FULL PALETTE OF THEIR STEADFASTNESS AND LOYALTY**

J. P. WARBURG
Businessman/
philanthropist/author

8/18/1896
Leo III

August 11–18
LEADERSHIP
LEO III

These naturally inspirational, commanding personalities may need to study the meaning of the word "hero" a bit more closely before they can find success and fulfillment on the Way of Consideration. Indeed, they will doubtless spend a fair amount of time needlessly asserting their authority or attempting to get others to fall into line with their views and opinions, until they release their tendency to self-absorption and allow themselves to face the needs, emotions, and objectives of the larger human community. Whether that scenario is played out in the realms of family, partnerships, or business dealings will be largely up to them, yet being able to rise above the personal and reach into the collective will prove essential to their search for higher development. Yet once they reach the understanding that in order to rule in any given situation, we are first required to serve, all will go well.

CHALLENGE: **RECOGNIZING THAT THERE IS LITTLE ROOM FOR DOUBLE STANDARDS ON A SPIRITUAL PATH**

FULFILLMENT: **TAKING POSITIVE ACTION ON BEHALF OF OTHERS**

NOTABLE: **GERTY TERESA CORI (SHARED NOBEL PRIZE FOR MEDICINE)**

KARMIC PATH
20

August 19–25

EXPOSURE
LEO–VIRGO CUSP

Though gifted with the powers of observation and perception needed to take tremendous strides along the Way of Consideration, those born on the Cusp of Exposure may find it a rather tricky and difficult journey until they learn not only how to cultivate compassion and caring but also how to display them in their interactions and relationships with others. In fact, these souls may know a great deal more about the need of others than they are willing to let on, and their rather secretive and nonsharing side may get in their way until they allow themselves to manifest their higher natures in a consistent, dependable fashion. Yet once they come to terms with the fact that getting to the bottom of others' concerns will serve to put them in touch with their own, they can realize wonderful success, as long as they are willing, from time to time, to wear their hearts on their sleeves.

PAUL "PEE-WEE HERMAN" REUBENS
Actor/comedian,
Pee Wee's Playhouse

8/27/1952
Virgo I

CHALLENGE: **OVERCOMING THEIR TENDENCY NOT TO REACH OUT TO OTHERS FOR FEAR OF REVEALING TOO MUCH OF THEMSELVES**

FULFILLMENT: **TAKING ACTION ON BEHALF OF OTHERS BASED ON THEIR INTUITIVE UNDERSTANDING OF THEIR NEEDS**

August 26–September 2

THE SYSTEM BUILDERS
VIRGO I

Virgo I's who tread the Way of Consideration may find their journey marked by a rather deconstructionist approach to human interaction that is somewhat at odds with the calling of this karmic path. Their need for structure and secure hierarchies of behavior means that though the heart of these service-oriented souls may well be in the right place and they may be well aware of others' needs, they are a bit leery of any situation that requires too much of them or threatens their sense of security with emotional demands. Thus, some will fail their soul's higher calling through a refusal to rise to the challenge of greater awareness, since that awareness may run them up against their fears. Others will indeed come to terms with sometimes needing to give more in relationships. If they can channel their devotion and expand their innate capacity to know what others need, things will become much clearer for them.

CHALLENGE: **WORKING AGAINST THEIR TENDENCY TO DIVIDE THE WORLD INTO ABSOLUTES**

FULFILLMENT: **COMING TO A PLACE WHERE THEY ARE ABLE TO GIVE WITHOUT FEARING HOW MUCH IT WILL COST THEM**

NOTABLE: **JIMMY CONNORS (TENNIS CHAMPION)**

September 3–10

THE ENIGMA
VIRGO II

The modest, elegant, and discerning people born in the Week of the Enigma who find themselves traveling this karmic path are likely to find wonderful success, providing they do not sacrifice a deeper understanding of human values to their notions of worldly image. With this configuration there is something of a tendency to rigidity that may manifest itself as a refusal to recognize their own impact, on the one hand, and a dislike of or intolerance for messy emotional displays, on the other. Yet if they turn their keen powers of observation and evaluation toward personal rather than worldly affairs and come to accept the part their own behaviors may play in the rebellions, inconsistencies, and emotional reactions of others, they will gain a measure of self-knowledge and realization that will far outweigh the risks and rockier stretches of the Way of Consideration.

ELSA SCHIAPARELLI
Fashion designer, utilized
surrealist designs

9/10/1896
Virgo II

CHALLENGE: **BECOMING CONSCIOUS ENOUGH TO KNOW WHEN TO DROP THEIR ENIGMATIC APPROACH OR OVERLY HIGH STANDARDS**

FULFILLMENT: **OPERATING FROM THE BASIS OF THEIR OWN ETHICS**

NOTABLE: **LUTHER CROWELL (INVENTED SQUARE-BOTTOM GROCERY BAG)**

September 11–18

THE LITERALIST
VIRGO III

It can safely be said that those born in the Week of the Literalist may alienate quite a few of their closest associates and compatriots on this life journey—that is, until they make an inward journey. Due to a certain unconsciousness of the effect they have on others, these personalities tend to refuse to acknowledge others' complaints or dissatisfaction with the assortment of defenses that they engage in—usually revolving around a "You're just imagining things" kind of counteraccusation. Yet if they can find the courage and detachment that will allow them not so much to admit when they are wrong as to admit when others are right, the resulting maturity and increased sense of tolerance and acceptance will prove more than worth the cost.

CHALLENGE: **NOT RATIONALIZING THEIR BEHAVIOR WITH ELEGANT ARGUMENTS THAT SERVE ONLY TO PATRONIZE OTHERS**

FULFILLMENT: **TAKING ON THE ROLE OF PROTECTOR**

NOTABLE: **SAM ERVIN (CHAIRED U.S. SENATE'S INVESTIGATING COMMITTEE OF WATERGATE BREAK-IN)**

September 19–24

BEAUTY
VIRGO–LIBRA CUSP

The souls born on this cusp are characterized by a headlong and passionate rush toward winning the objects of their desire that exists at decided odds with the calling to deeper empathy and personal detachment required by this karmic path. Though the Way of Consideration blesses them with a measure of authority and strength that is lacking in many of their fellows, Virgo–Librans would do themselves a great disservice by manifesting that strength in selfishness, neediness, or a high-handed attitude toward others. Yet somewhere at the core of these personalities lies both a sense of fairness and a sense of service. If they can cultivate those qualities and avoid the dangers of poor planning and the self-centered pursuit of pleasure, the resulting enlightenment will greatly aid them in their quest for spirituality and fulfillment.

F. Scott Fitzgerald
Writer, *The Great Gatsby*

9/24/1896
Virgo–Libra Cusp

CHALLENGE: **TAKING THEIR MINDS OFF THE PURSUIT OF THE IDEAL LONG ENOUGH TO SEE THE REALITY OF THOSE NEAR TO THEM**
FULFILLMENT: **EMBRACING A LOVE OF HUMANITY**
NOTABLE: **JOSEPH PATRICK KENNEDY III (CONGRESSMAN)**

September 25–October 2

THE PERFECTIONIST
LIBRA I

Though Libra I's who journey along the Way of Consideration may indeed be blessed with a real sense of fairness and equality, it may take them some time to relinquish the idea that while we are all created equal, they may just be a little bit better than anyone else. Often the victim of their own mercilessly high standards, they will have to do a measure of soul work in order to discover the relationship between their exacting behavior and its effect on others. Yet they bring to this karmic path a natural desire to get to the bottom of problems, as well as some fine analytical skills. If they turn their need for time alone into a quest for a greater sense of personal security, their anxieties, barriers, and tendency to repress emotion will give way to an increased understanding of and tolerance for their own faults and foibles that in turn will translate into greater empathy for those around them.

CHALLENGE: **RELEASING PICKINESS AND JUDGMENTALISM**
FULFILLMENT: **DISCOVERING THAT A SMALL AMOUNT OF TOLERANCE AND CONSIDERATION GOES A LONG WAY**
NOTABLE: **THOMAS NAST (EDITORIAL CARTOONIST; HELPED UNDO BOSS TWEED)**

October 3–10

SOCIETY
LIBRA II

Highly considerate as a rule, those born in the Week of Society who find themselves on the Way of Consideration can realize great fulfillment, providing they do not succumb to the tendency to project their own values, desires, or frustrations onto others. As long as they cultivate their objectivity enough to be clear about what others may be going through or require, these social souls need only guard against their inclination to put the needs of others before their own. Otherwise, they may go so overboard in their tolerance and protection of those they feel secretly ashamed of, or somehow uncomfortable with, having had their own needs met. Indeed, they may appear maddeningly wishy-washy about asking for what they want, which in turn causes others to undervalue them. Thus, learning to gain a better sense of where they are in the more universal scheme will surely work to their advantage, as will developing an ability to be as fair to themselves as they are to others.

Christopher Reeve
Actor, *Superman*; injured in horseback riding accident

9/25/1952
Libra I

CHALLENGE: **DISCERNING MORE CLEARLY THE DIFFERENCE BETWEEN THEIR OWN NEEDS AND THOSE OF OTHERS**
FULFILLMENT: **TRANSFERRING THEIR EFFORTS ON BEHALF OF OTHERS FROM PERSONAL TO UNIVERSAL CONCERNS**
NOTABLES: **HEINRICH DOVE (DEVELOPED LAW OF GYRATION); MICHAEL KORDA (FAMED EDITOR)**

October 11–18

THEATER
LIBRA III

Those born in this week who find themselves faced with the challenges and tasks of the Way of Consideration will have an interesting journey, providing they learn to relinquish some of their natural leadership in the interest of higher self-development. Many of these individuals are marked by a rather pervasive disinterest in others and their feelings. Developing greater empathy and understanding, even on a more universal level, will therefore be the key to their successful passage. It is likely, however, that their worldliness will lead them into situations and circumstances where issues of injustice and intolerance cannot be ignored. If they rise to the challenges presented to them without becoming cynical and at the same time allow a more mature set of moral values to blossom, they will make tremendous progress in both personal and worldly spheres of endeavor.

CHALLENGE: **ENGAGING IN AN EQUALITY OF GIVE-AND-TAKE IN MORE INTIMATE RELATIONS**
FULFILLMENT: **WORKING ON BEHALF OF HUMANITY FOR A HIGHER CAUSE**
NOTABLE: **LILLIAN GISH (FILM ACTRESS; "FIRST LADY OF THE SILVER SCREEN")**

KARMIC PATH
20

October 19–25

DRAMA AND CRITICISM
LIBRA–SCORPIO CUSP

Though these individuals may have a natural ability to blow their opposition out of the water with their imposing presence and sharp-tongued ways, they may be thrown back upon themselves more than once as they travel the Way of Consideration. Indeed, this configuration may well produce some intense and even traumatic situations until they gain a better handle on their own power and the objectivity necessary to adequately assess their impact on others. Too, they may resist the more mundane and everyday aspects of this passage and go in search of larger and more worldly arenas in which to display their talents. Yet if they cultivate their considerable charm and diplomacy and translate it into a genuine understanding of the needs and feelings of others, they may well find that they can become the sort of personal hero or role model they believed themselves to be all along.

CHALLENGE: **LEARNING TO THINK BEFORE THEY SPEAK**
FULFILLMENT: **TAKING A CALMER, MORE DETACHED APPROACH TO THEIR RELATIONSHIPS**

RUTH GORDON
Actress,
Harold and Maude

10/30/1896
Scorpio I

October 26–November 2

INTENSITY
SCORPIO I

If Scorpio I's avoid the tendency to turn their talent for finding and telling the truth into a weapon of either aggression or defense, they can make wonderful progress along the Way of Consideration. In short, the key to success for these intense, discerning individuals will be their willingness to utilize their talents in a quest for higher and more universal values and transcend their fear of being dominated and their suspicion of others' actions. In fact, they may have a real gift for ferreting out when others are dissembling, but not why. Expanding their great psychological insight into an understanding of what motivates others will take them a lot further along this karmic path, while allowing them to relax a bit. Thus, releasing themselves from the idea that they are somehow at the center of things will be especially enlightening, as will developing a willingness to accept others simply for who they are, rather than rejecting them on the basis of unfounded and often unfair suspicions.

CHALLENGE: **DETACHING THEMSELVES FROM THEIR VIEW OF A SCENE**
FULFILLMENT: **FREEING THEMSELVES FROM PARANOIA THROUGH THE DEVELOPMENT OF TRUST**
NOTABLE: **WALLACE POOLE MUHAMMAD (MUSLIM LEADER; SON OF ELIJAH)**

November 3–11

DEPTH
SCORPIO II

Those born in the Week of Depth who navigate the Way of Consideration are likely to have a rather blessed passage, as they come to this life journey with the qualities of empathy, understanding, and steadfast devotion firmly in place. The key to their success will be their willingness to release some highly controlling attitudes, on the one hand, and to trust others more by revealing their more emotional side, in the form of neediness and vulnerability, on the other. Though they do possess the tendency to be judgmental without necessarily being fair, this will surely come under scrutiny as they come to a better understanding of the challenges and demands of this karmic path. If they cultivate their finer qualities of simple kindness and generosity, they will find their efforts well rewarded.

CHALLENGE: **TEMPERING THE MORE PASSIONATE SIDE OF THEIR NATURES**
FULFILLMENT: **GIVING OF THEMSELVES TO OTHERS**
NOTABLE: **MICHAEL DUKAKIS (FORMER GOVERNOR OF MASSACHUSETTS; PRESIDENTIAL CANDIDATE)**

AUGUSTE RODIN
Sculptor, *The Thinker*

11/12/1840
Scorpio III

November 12–18

CHARM
SCORPIO III

Awakening to the existence of higher and more universal moral values may take some time for those born in the Week of Charm. These rather self-satisfied people have quite a capacity for fully understanding and accepting the broad palette of human needs but an equal capacity to manipulate those needs to their own benefit as they "look out for number one." In addition, ego issues are especially prominent, and these seductive individuals have a marked tendency to attract flatterers and sycophants whose attentions may well boost their egos, but only at great cost to their self-respect. Yet if they actively seek to increase their knowledge of spiritual matters, universal laws, and issues relating to the good of mankind, they can exert a powerful and lasting influence that will do much to shape the values and opinions of others, bringing all to a greater sense of human values.

CHALLENGE: **DEVELOPING A FIRMER SET OF MORAL VALUES**
FULFILLMENT: **EXPERIENCING THE SATISFACTION OF UNCONDITIONAL GIVING**
NOTABLE: **MAMIE EISENHOWER (FORMER FIRST LADY)**

November 19–24

REVOLUTION
SCORPIO–SAGITTARIUS CUSP

The life journey of those born on this cusp who travel the Way of Consideration will doubtless involve a fair amount of commitment to the rights and causes of the less fortunate. Nevertheless, they will have to come to terms with the fact that beneath their lofty goals there can lurk some secret dictatorial or autocratic tendencies, for here are to be found precisely those personalities who strive to gain freedom from persecution only to turn around and persecute others. Above all, Scorpio–Sagittarians need to back up and develop greater detachment in order to better discern the underlying dynamic of their relationship patterns. Yet if they refuse to allow their moral sense to degenerate into authoritarianism and remember to keep the iron hand of leadership always within the velvet glove of consideration and caring, they can be a tremendous force for good.

LARRY KING
TV/radio journalist
and host

———

11/19/1933
Scorpio–Sagittarius Cusp

CHALLENGE: **SIDELINING THEIR ICONOCLASTIC TENDENCIES WHEN IT COMES TO THE SACRED COWS OF THEIR NEAR AND DEAR**

FULFILLMENT: **PLACING THEIR WORK IN THE CONTEXT OF A GREATER MEANING**

November 25–December 2

INDEPENDENCE
SAGITTARIUS I

Those born in the Week of Independence can realize considerable fulfillment on the Way of Consideration, providing their sense of honor and fairness is not allowed to degenerate into stubbornness, an insistence on getting their own way, or a rather overcompetitive attitude in their relationships with others. Indeed, they have a greater need to give than to receive, and their natural generosity of spirit and philosophical leanings will buoy them greatly along this karmic path. In fact, their principal pitfall is likely to be sheer stubbornness, and there will doubtless be a number of times in their lives when they stick to their guns long after their ammunition is gone. Yet if they divest themselves of their need to wage an assortment of "holy wars" and maintain the consistent clarity of vision required to manifest their love for others in quieter ways on a daily basis, they can enjoy the best of times on this life journey.

CHALLENGE: **RELAXING THEIR NATURAL COMPETITIVENESS**
FULFILLMENT: **LIVING A LIFE THAT IS IN ACCORD WITH THEIR INTEGRITY AND SENSE OF ETHICS**
NOTABLE: **ROBERT GOULET (STAGE/SCREEN ACTOR)**

December 3–10

THE ORIGINATOR
SAGITTARIUS II

Providing they do not allow the complaints, demands, and dissatisfactions of others to translate into feelings of rejection, personal defensiveness, or touchiness, those born in the Week of the Originator who negotiate the Way of Consideration can expect a highly rewarding, interesting passage. Unencumbered by much of the stubbornness and authoritarian tendencies of some of their fellows on this journey, these interesting people are likely to be blessed with a unique philosophical perspective that will serve them well along the road. The wide variety of people they will encounter will do much to expand their personal horizons and serve to nourish their talents and interests. As they gain the self-knowledge and experience required for the development of genuine empathy and learn to let go of their more defensive attitudes, they will truly blossom.

FLIP WILSON
Actor/comedian,
The Flip Wilson Show

———

12/8/1933
Sagittarius II

CHALLENGE: **CONTROLLING THEIR SENSITIVITY OR TOUCHINESS**
FULFILLMENT: **ENJOYING A BROAD AND VARIED SOCIAL LIFE**
NOTABLE: **MARY, QUEEN OF SCOTS (QUEEN OF SCOTLAND; EXECUTED FOR TREASON)**

December 11–18

THE TITAN
SAGITTARIUS III

Coming to terms with the need for consistency in their consideration of their fellows indicated by this karmic path may prove something of a struggle for those born in this week. They possess the capacity to take others into account; it's just that their attention is easily sidetracked by their grand schemes. Rugged individualists, they may also do a fair amount of wrestling with issues of commitment versus freedom and caring versus control as they tread this karmic path. Indeed, these rather heroic types may do a great deal of soul-searching in the process of discovering just what it is that others expect of them, for they are possessed of such a degree of confidence that they are often quite bewildered when things fail to go according to plan. Yet if they exalt their more thoughtful side and turn inward in the search for greater enlightenment, they are sure to find the answers necessary to enjoy a fruitful and expansive journey.

CHALLENGE: **PLACING OTHERS IN POSITIONS OF EQUALITY TO THEMSELVES**
FULFILLMENT: **ENGAGING IN ACTIVITIES OF MORE UNIVERSAL CONSEQUENCE FOR HUMANITY**

December 19–25

PROPHECY
SAGITTARIUS–CAPRICORN CUSP

Though it is likely that the souls born on this cusp who travel the Way of Consideration will need to grapple with their rather troubling passive-aggressive approach to human relationships, they can nevertheless realize great fulfillment along the way. The key to their success, however, will be coming to terms with the idea that at some level, at least, they are not at all indifferent to what others may think and that in the larger scheme we all have responsibilities to one another. Yet if they take the time to get in touch with the unconscious impulses, hunches, and intuitions that are so much a part of their makeup, the resulting knowledge will do much to illuminate the more universal themes of human experience. More than many, these individuals must come to understand that no one is an island and share that special understanding with others in a spirit of generosity and empathy.

CICELY TYSON
Actress, *Roots*

12/19/1933
Sagittarius–Capricorn
Cusp

CHALLENGE: **COMING TO AN UNDERSTANDING OF THEIR MORE AMBIVALENT FEELINGS AND THEIR CONSEQUENCES IN RELATIONSHIPS**
FULFILLMENT: **USING THEIR GIFT OF PROPHECY TO HELP OTHERS**

December 26–January 2

THE RULER
CAPRICORN I

Overcoming some rather domineering and inflexible tendencies in the interest of developing greater empathy and understanding of their fellowman may prove somewhat difficult for Capricorn I's who journey along the Way of Consideration. In fact, they may have real problems learning to accept and tolerate the ways of others, not so much because they are innately intolerant but because they are convinced that their own way of doing things is best. Yet for all their seeming rigidity, the hearts of these individuals are usually in the right place. They oppose injustice in all its forms, and if they keep in mind that developing a wider and significantly more detached perspective will enable them to embrace a higher level of sensitivity while not necessarily lessening the strength of their own values and convictions, they may well learn to live and let live.

CHALLENGE: **REALIZING THAT BEING DEPENDABLE IS NOT THE SAME AS BEING CONSIDERATE**
FULFILLMENT: **OVERCOMING THEIR FEAR OF EXPOSING THEIR EMOTIONAL VULNERABILITY**

January 3–9

DETERMINATION
CAPRICORN II

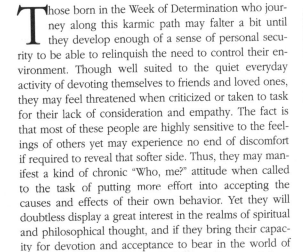

Those born in the Week of Determination who journey along this karmic path may falter a bit until they develop enough of a sense of personal security to be able to relinquish the need to control their environment. Though well suited to the quiet everyday activity of devoting themselves to friends and loved ones, they may feel threatened when criticized or taken to task for their lack of consideration and empathy. The fact is that most of these people are highly sensitive to the feelings of others yet may experience no end of discomfort if required to reveal that softer side. Thus, they may manifest a kind of chronic "Who, me?" attitude when called to the task of putting more effort into accepting the causes and effects of their own behavior. Yet they will doubtless display a great interest in the realms of spiritual and philosophical thought, and if they bring their capacity for devotion and acceptance to bear in the world of human, rather than theoretical, values, they can make a fine go of things.

CARL SANDBURG
Poet/writer/folklorist;
won Pulitzer Prize for
Lincoln biography

1/6/1878
Capricorn II

CHALLENGE: **APPLYING A LITTLE LESS IDEALISM AND A LITTLE MORE REALISM TO THEIR INTERACTIONS**
FULFILLMENT: **INTEGRATING THEIR QUIET SPIRITUALITY INTO THEIR RELATIONSHIPS**

January 10–16

DOMINANCE
CAPRICORN III

Somewhat hampered by their tendency to divide the world into good and evil, black and white, and any number of variations on those same dichotomies, these individuals will have a rather rough time of things until they learn the higher lesson of tolerant acceptance that is called for by the Way of Consideration. Their soul work may first entail the development of a more secure sense of identity in the form of greater tolerance for their own failings. This will, in turn, enable them to embrace others with greater empathy. Since they tend to be rather hard on themselves, their priority will be to learn to be a bit more relaxed in their need for perfection and achievement. Yet they bring to this karmic path honesty and a natural impulse to nurture. Once they learn that consideration comes down more to a question of what others really need than to what Capricorn III's think is good for them, all can go well, if not entirely easily, on this path.

CHALLENGE: **RELAXING THEIR PROPENSITY TO JUDGE OTHERS AND THEMSELVES TOO HARSHLY**
FULFILLMENT: **INDULGING THEMSELVES IN SELF-ACCEPTANCE**
NOTABLES: **MARY J. BLIGE ("QUEEN OF HIP HOP SOUL"); JUDITH CAMPBELL EXNER (FAMOUS AFFAIRS WITH JFK AND SAM GIANCANA); BERTHE MORISOT (ARTIST; IMPRESSIONIST)**

January 17–22

MYSTERY AND IMAGINATION
CAPRICORN–AQUARIUS CUSP

The personalities born on this cusp who travel the Way of Consideration are likely to have an interesting ride, as they are blessed with a natural empathy for the less fortunate and a strong belief in the moral rights of others. Though many of their life's lessons may be played out in a worldly arena rather than the more personal side of human affairs, they will find that their sense of humor is their biggest asset in either area. Though many will criticize these individuals for their often difficult temperaments and wide emotional swings, they can develop a measure of objectivity to temper their more passionate side and with time and experience will learn to choose their battles more carefully and to mine the gems of understanding and empathy that enrich their highly imaginative natures, finding great satisfaction in the process.

CHALLENGE: **BALANCING THEIR EMOTIONS**

FULFILLMENT: **WORKING TO BETTER THE LOT OF THE POOR OR DISADVANTAGED**

NOTABLES: **GRAHAM KERR (CHEF, *THE GALLOPING GOURMET*); SHARI LEWIS (VENTRILOQUIST/ENTERTAINER; PUPPET LAMB CHOP); BILL BIXBY (TV ACTOR, *MY FAVORITE MARTIAN*)**

HENRY "HANK" AARON
Baseball player, home run king, Braves

2/5/1934
Aquarius II

January 23–30

GENIUS
AQUARIUS I

Those born in the Week of Genius who travel the Way of Consideration may well go a bit overboard when it comes to the detachment and objectivity called for by this karmic path. Great problem solvers and wonderful thinkers, they will nevertheless have to come to terms with the reality that the laws of emotions and empathy do not always correspond to their often inspired, yet ultimately scientific or systematic way of thinking. In short, the lessons of this karmic path may be forced on them through any number of conflicts with authorities, partners, and colleagues until they discover that many of their seemingly detached solutions to the problems of human interactions are based on their own highly involved, yet often neglected emotional side. Thus, they are destined to work out the challenges of this karmic path through first learning to acknowledge their sense of principle and then to integrate it with their sense of humanity.

CHALLENGE: **CULTIVATING A GREATER UNDERSTANDING OF THE RANGE OF HUMAN FEELING**

FULFILLMENT: **WORKING ON BEHALF OF OTHERS—AT A DISTANCE**

January 31–February 7

YOUTH AND EASE
AQUARIUS II

Aquarius II's have excellent prospects for enlightenment when they find themselves on the Way of Consideration. Yet they will have to work at developing a stronger code of honor to guide their interactions or run the risk of being buffeted about by the winds of their own flightiness. In short, learning how to make a commitment and stick to it is called for. Also, they tend to relate to others solely on the basis of what they think others may want of them. On the other hand, they are so well liked and accepted by others that they may not come to terms with the need to develop consideration or accountability, preferring perhaps to dominate their small social sphere and do what is safe or easy. Forcing themselves to take on larger issues of sharing, spiritual connection, and social consciousness will help them develop a more sincere form of empathy. It is important that they take the work of this karmic path seriously, since the importance of kindness should never be underestimated.

CHALLENGE: **LEARNING HOW TO STICK TO SOMETHING**

FULFILLMENT: **JUGGLING THE VARIETY OF RELATIONSHIPS THAT THIS KARMIC PATH BRINGS THEM**

NOTABLE: **MINNIE DRIVER (ACTRESS, *A CIRCLE OF FRIENDS*)**

BILL RUSSELL
5-time NBA MVP; 1st African American coach in the NBA; seen here with Wilt Chamberlain

2/12/1934
Aquarius III

February 8–15

ACCEPTANCE
AQUARIUS III

These charismatic and rather commanding personalities will need to develop the ability to reveal their more vulnerable side as they travel the Way of Consideration. Though they may possess a high degree of understanding of and commitment to the rights of others, they may experience quite a bit of discomfort should that commitment amount to no more than lip service or an occasional donation to the cause of the moment. In short, once they realize that real kindness is a function more of the spirit than of the ego and that principles are formed more from detached and long-range observation than they are from ideas and abstraction, they will do very well on this karmic path. On it they will find both moral courage and the ability to take on the big issues due to the broadness of vision that beckons.

CHALLENGE: **STEPPING DOWN FROM THE REALM OF AIRY IDEALS TO ROLL UP THEIR SLEEVES AND GET DOWN TO WORK**

FULFILLMENT: **FINDING THE CORRECT AVENUE OF EXPRESSION FOR THEIR ACCEPTING AND TOLERANT VIEWS**

NOTABLES: **FLORENCE HENDERSON (ACTRESS, *THE BRADY BUNCH*); TINA LOUISE (ACTRESS, *GILLIGAN'S ISLAND*); MARY QUANT (FASHION DESIGNER; MOD LOOK)**

February 16–22

SENSITIVITY
AQUARIUS–PISCES CUSP

These individuals can do beautifully on the Way of Consideration, though they may required to come to terms with the reasons for their aggressiveness first. Personally, they are likely to have little trouble developing the compassion for others that is called for by this karmic path, yet professionally they may have to learn to release an attitude of combativeness and belligerence. Though blessed with an ability to accurately assess relationship issues and the needs of others, they will have to work hard to balance their emotional extremes if they are to become more considerate. Still, if they release their fear of rejection and the pessimistic outlook that so often marks them by cultivating more laid-back and accepting attitudes, their progress will be ensured.

CHALLENGE: **RECOGNIZING THE NEGATIVE CONSEQUENCES OF THEIR OVERLY AGGRESSIVE STYLE**
FULFILLMENT: **LEARNING HOW TO BE VULNERABLE**
NOTABLE: **SIR FRANCIS GALTON (SCIENTIST-EXPLORER)**

ERYKAH BADU
R&B vocalist, winner of
2 Grammies

2/26/1971
Pisces I

February 23–March 2

SPIRIT
PISCES I

Those born in the Week of Spirit who travel the Way of Consideration will doubtless express considerable idealism and a rather uniquely spiritual outlook along this road. Perhaps the only real danger for those born with this configuration will be their tendency to go overboard, becoming so service-oriented and thoughtful that they neglect their own needs; giving rise to self-pity or other negative feelings. Yet they have such a strong desire to leave the world a better place than they found it that they are likely to become very involved with the plight of the less fortunate, anxious to contribute their unique brand of service and emotional support to the lives of those around them. However, in order to sustain such efforts, they would do well to cultivate a support group of their own, perhaps through their church or spiritual community.

CHALLENGE: **NOT NEGLECTING THEIR OWN NEEDS**
FULFILLMENT: **WORKING DEVOTIONALLY ON BEHALF OF OTHERS**

March 3–10

THE LONER
PISCES II

Pisces II's may have to endure a fair amount of soul-searching and personal effort before they come to terms with the fact that their deep and abiding need for acceptance is not precisely the same thing as having consideration for others. More than many, those born in the Week of the Loner would benefit from developing greater detachment and objectivity, particularly about themselves. Moreover, there is a danger that they will become overly defensive and involved with their own processes to such an extent that larger issues regarding others, such as consideration, consistency, and expressions of support, will go all but unnoticed by them. Yet at heart, they possess a genuine capacity for empathy, the impulse to help others, and an unassailable moral code. If they do not collapse into neediness or a sense of disappointment when faced with the many ups and downs of personal interactions, their great sensitivity will find a place to shine.

CHALLENGE: **BECOMING MORE OBJECTIVE ABOUT THEMSELVES**
FULFILLMENT: **SURRENDERING TO THEIR RESPONSIBILITIES TO OTHERS**

ZERO MOSTEL
Actor/singer/artist,
Fiddler on the Roof

2/28/1915
Pisces I

March 11–18

DANCERS AND DREAMERS
PISCES III

These inspirational, creative individuals can work their special brand of magic on the Way of Consideration, providing they do not hold themselves above the fray in an attitude of lofty superiority or maintain a patronizing stance toward those who venture to criticize their inconsistencies. Though cultivating a sense of detachment will come rather easily for these people, they also possess the capacity to take it too far and thus refuse responsibility for their own behavior. In fact, learning the fine art of admitting to their mistakes will be very important, as will developing greater humility in general. While some with this configuration will exhibit extremes of tiresome and cloying emotional neediness, most of these souls have a wonderfully expansive and spiritual side that, if consistently shared, can be a real inspiration to those around them.

CHALLENGE: **BALANCING THEIR WANDERLUST WITH THE NEED TO BE THERE FOR OTHERS**
FULFILLMENT: **APPLYING THEIR DEPTH OF UNDERSTANDING AND SYMPATHETIC MANNER TO HELPING OTHERS**

The Way of Revelation

LEO–VIRGO CUSP TO AQUARIUS–PISCES CUSP
Exposure to Sensitivity

Sensitive, though often closed and secretive, the individuals on the Way of Revelation are here to break down the emotional barriers that keep them from sharing their feelings, ideas, or concerns with others. Coming into this lifetime with a talent for shrouding themselves in mystery, those born to the Way of Revelation can be so adept at hiding their true natures that they may not be sure of who they really are or what they really feel. Thus, the process of revelation necessitates that the men and women born to this karmic path go within and become reacquainted with themselves. Often those on the Way of Revelation nurse pain and resentment over wounds inflicted in the past and possess elaborate defense mechanisms that are carefully crafted to protect themselves from pain. Developing a sense of hope and trust will allow these souls to heal their scars and, ultimately, to reveal themselves openly to others. It is essential for those on the Way of Revelation to cultivate their social skills and practice interpersonal interaction. However, this cannot be attempted until they begin to strip away the armor that holds them back from meaningful contact with their fellow human beings.

The endpoints of the Way of Revelation, Leo–Virgo and Aquarius–Pisces, both denote great emotional sensitivity as well as a tendency to be secretive and self-protective and to keep one's inner light from being revealed to others.

> **CORE LESSON**
> Learning to trust
>
> **GOAL**
> To strip away the defenses built up to protect their sensitive natures and reveal who they are to both themselves and the world

Often the men and women on this karmic path go beyond simple guardedness and actually set up smoke screens to hide the truth of their essential nature or motivations. Easily wounded, they have a depth of emotional sensitivity that alone is sufficient reason for their caution, but when it is combined with the likelihood that they underwent some significant emotional scarring in their early lives, often as a result of wounds inflicted by an overbearing parent or authority figure, the result is that they have become a virtual fortress of defense mechanisms. Difficult people to get to know, they have, by adulthood, made sure that their interactions with others are kept to a limited or superficial level, so that they generally live rather isolated lives.

Having once been hurt, these individuals are often found on the sidelines of human relations in the role of observers who are as interested in keeping their own behavior secret as they are with guardedly watching others in order to protect themselves from being hurt again. Part of this attitude is justified since they have a considerable knack for seeing the proclivities of people and the less-than-savory sides of humanity clearly. More than many, those born on the Way of Revelation understand what shadow qualities are at work in men and women and the dangers they can represent to others. However, their self-protective stance, combined with a feeling that the good

> **GIFTS**
> Observant, Sensitive, Diligent
>
> **PITFALLS**
> Prickly, Secretive, Nonsharing

things in life are passing them by while going to less deserving individuals, often gives rise to feelings of resentment, jealousy, rivalry, and an overall chip-on-the-shoulder attitude. This, of course, makes them rather unappealing to others and results in a kind of self-fulfilling prophecy such that they find themselves left alone. Mistrusting others, they in turn become mistrusted by them.

The unqualified lesson for the individuals on the Way of Revelation is learning to trust. First, the individuals on this karmic path must learn to put their faith in something greater than themselves, perhaps simply trusting life or whatever their personal notion of the divine may be; for example, to protect them when they take a risk or catch them when they fall. Hopefully, this type of trust will encourage these gentle souls to begin to open themselves more frequently to others and, as their trust is rewarded, to cause them to develop greater trust in people as well. Sometimes what these souls need is to trust themselves enough to believe that they won't make the same mistakes again or repeat negative patterns. Ultimately, having the ability to trust will cause them to drop the jealousy, resentment, and mistrust that too often keep them lonely. Moreover, as their trust creates a new attitude of openness and sharing, their insecurities and defenses will begin to fall away as if by magic.

Though the Way of Revelation is an outward-directed path requiring that those on it ultimately direct their en-

ergies toward the world at large, there are aspects of this life journey that require a healthy dose of inner work and self-review. These individuals must develop a stronger sense of self by looking at their own strengths and weaknesses, truly acknowledging and dealing with their feelings, and examining the kinds of mechanisms they have used to keep themselves defended. As a spiritual path, the Way of Revelation requires consciousness; that is, the revelation of the self to the self. In order for the individuals on this karmic path to communicate their feelings or concerns authentically, they must first develop the habit of being rigorously honest with themselves and combine it with a willingness to grow. Self-understanding will lead to the development of the kind of courage necessary to reveal oneself to others. A great gift of those on the Way of Revelation is their intuitive ability to see what is going on in the inner lives of others, including what they are feeling and why, and what is motivating them. Turning such a gift inward will bear them rich fruit in the form of greater self-awareness.

What usually brings the men and women on this karmic path to the point where they have no choice but to do something about themselves? Usually, it involves some career slight or setback. Extremely career- and success-oriented, workaholism runs rampant in those on the Way of Revelation, both because it provides the ideal excuse to avoid deeper or more intimate relationships and because usu-

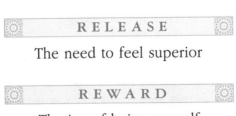

RELEASE

The need to feel superior

REWARD

The joy of being oneself

SUGGESTION

Observe yourself more closely and notice the reasons behind your superior attitudes and judgments of others. Develop a relationship with and trust in spirit.

ally those on the Way of Revelation have a strong work ethic that includes focus, diligence, and a hardheaded, if not stubborn, willpower. These men and women are quietly inspired individuals who possess quite a bit of creative fire, invention, and general inspiration, much like Daedalus, the mythological Greek inventor. However, the tale of Daedalus's son is applicable to these individuals as well. Icarus, flying with the help of the magical wings made by his father, allowed his ego to get the better of him and flew too close to the sun so that the wax holding the wings together melted, causing him to fall to his death. Often the ego defenses of the individuals on this karmic path cause them to "crash and burn" time and again in the workplace—sometimes due to sudden, unfortunate, or damaging revelations but most often simply because they don't seem to know how to connect to others or get their views across. Eventually, their ambitions will get the better of them and they will resolve to address their problems. If successful, they will develop the courage to show themselves and their creative talents, ideas, or products to the world. Otherwise, years of hard work and dedication may go unnoticed or unrewarded.

Though it may well be career considerations that prompt those on this karmic path to do its work, the end result will be a significant improvement in their interpersonal relationships. Should those on the Way of Revelation develop a sufficiently trusting nature to enter into more intimate involvements, these are apt to be few. Having found one or two important people to share themselves with, they may become quite dependent on or possessive of such relationships. Invariably, those on this karmic path exhibit possessive attitudes or jealousy toward those with whom they are involved, prompting sometimes painful lessons on nonattachment.

Despite their general closedness, those on this karmic path are sometimes viewed as extremely attractive by others, due to the appeal of their cloaked manner and enigmatic ways, which permits others to project onto them—though usually with disastrous consequences. Those on this path should try to gravitate toward people who encourage them to be more open, sharing, and direct in their approach. Slowly building a circle of valued friends to whom they can reveal themselves is highly beneficial for those on the Way of Revelation. Often this will occur first through their career or chosen field, since the structure of the workplace and its implicit taboos on deeper involvements provide a safe arena for them to practice the lessons of this path. Once they have a taste of being appreciated and acknowledged for who they are, they are apt to open themselves to others more and more.

BALANCE POINT

Safety and Risk

An individual on the Way of Revelation can be likened to someone standing on the sidelines of life in the most elaborate of costumes, thinking that those passing by in everyday garb do not notice him. The costume effectively isolates the person and prevents any true interaction. Believing that, through disguise, he has convinced others of a false identity, he in fact becomes dependent on it, perhaps even lost in it. Only by removing and discarding the costume can the true self be revealed, even to the individual himself. By taking the risk of showing others the sensitive nature that resides inside the costume, the individual opens himself to the possibility of living an authentic life.

CRYSTALS AND GEMSTONES

Peridot reveals the difference between detrimental boundaries that cause an individual to shut out life and healthy boundaries that offer security and ultimately lead to a deep trust in life.

PETER ILYICH
TCHAIKOVSKY

Genius composer **Peter Ilyich Tchaikovsky** experienced a difficult adolescence due to his mother's death and his own repressed homosexuality. Extremely sensitive, like many on this path, he nursed great pain and resentment and through his music was able to heal old wounds and reveal himself more openly to others. In fact, he has been accused of pinning his heart on his sleeve in his ostentatious compositions. Although he continually dealt with romantic difficulties compounded by a disastrous marriage, the beauty of his work redeemed his suffering. Tchaikovsky most successfully let down his guard with Madame von Meck, his patroness and close friend.

Welshman **Dylan Thomas** devotedly followed his creative lodestar but ultimately succumbed to its demands. Best known for his highly original but obscure poems, his collections include *18 Poems* and *25 Poems*. Obviously, Thomas struggled to understand and reveal his true nature, but was unable to negotiate the pitfalls of his karmic path. Though he

DYLAN THOMAS

created works of unquestionable beauty, he was eventually overcome by the dark side of his enormous talent, finally dying of acute alcohol poisoning at the age of thirty-five.

The love that King Edward VIII of England felt for **Wallis Warfield Simpson** was so strong that he relinquished his throne to marry her. Despite the enormous publicity this decision inspired, the pair retired from public life to become the Duke and Duchess of Windsor. The extremely private life she led with her husband, necessitated

WALLIS WARFIELD
SIMPSON

by the enormous publicity surrounding Edward's abdication, in some ways hindered her progress on this path. However, the intimacy of Simpson's relationship with the duke allowed her the openness and freedom of expression called for on the Way of Revelation.

Other Notables: John Elliot Bradshaw, Thor Heyerdahl, Eli Whitney, Thomas Merton, Kenneth Grahame, Bob Costas, Joan Collins, Ralph Waldo Emerson, F. Lee Bailey, Jerzy Kosinski, Jerry Falwell, Roman Polanski, River Phoenix, Conway Twitty, Zoe Caldwell, Matt Damon, Jackie Coogan, Jonas Salk, Claude Monet, Giacomo Puccini, Lorne Greene, Claudio Abbado, Gustave Flaubert, Thomas Hardy

---

BIRTHDAYS ON KARMIC PATH 21

February 18, 1896–July 8, 1896 | October 1, 1914–February 18, 1915

May 12, 1933–September 30, 1933 | December 22, 1951–May 11, 1952 | August 3, 1970–December 21, 1970

March 14, 1989–August 2, 1989 | October 25, 2007–March 13, 2008

KARMIC PATH
21

March 19–24

REBIRTH
PISCES–ARIES CUSP

The souls born on this cusp who travel the Way of Revelation are likely to do wonderfully well, as their natural energies are very much in keeping with the gifts, tasks, and promise of this karmic path. In fact, though they may be more personally defensive than some others along the way, they are also likely to be less secretive about who they really are and where they want to go in life. Too, this karmic path endows them with a greater measure of natural dedication and the ability to prepare their plans and schemes better. Yet it will be especially important for them to ground their often divisive energies in family and close personal relationships. Once they have established an emotional base that allows them to feel safe, they will be free to explore both their worldly options and their considerable emotional depth within the context of this most winning combination.

BOB COSTAS
TV sports personality

3/22/1952
Pisces–Aries Cusp

CHALLENGE: **RELEASING THEIR FEAR OF EMOTIONAL VULNER-ABILITY**

FULFILLMENT: **FINDING A BETTER UNDERSTANDING OF THEMSELVES**

March 25–April 2

THE CHILD
ARIES I

Aries I personalities who find themselves on the Way of Revelation will doubtless have an interesting and expansive life's journey. These personalities may be somewhat less inclined to maintain the privacy and self-protection indicated by this path due to their frank and spontaneous nature. Nevertheless, they will have tend to exhibit the more aggressive aspects of this configuration in their quest to reveal themselves more fully to the world. Yet this karmic path will gift them with a fine ability to tap into their own motivations and feelings, one that will surely be an asset in their quest for success and fulfillment. If they avoid the pitfalls of touchiness and operating from a fear of being hurt, and keep in mind that the personal barriers they may have erected are sometimes best removed stone by stone rather than by a single explosion, they will realize both great social and professional advancement.

CHALLENGE: **HAVING THE COURAGE TO RETURN TO THEIR CHILDHOODS IN ORDER TO HEAL THE WOUNDED CHILD WITHIN**

FULFILLMENT: **OPENING THEMSELVES TO NEW FRIENDSHIPS**

NOTABLES: **OSCAR MAYER (FOUNDED MEAT COMPANY, 1883); WALLACE BEERY (ACTOR)**

April 3–10

THE STAR
ARIES II

Individuals born in this week who find themselves on the Way of Revelation can expect an exciting and fulfilling passage, as long as there does not develop too great a gap between their private lives and public personae. In fact, many with this configuration may feel plagued by chronic loneliness, even in the midst of a crowd, until they go inward and develop sufficient insight into their own character and its motivations. Often they will realize that the reason they are not getting what they need from others is because they are not revealing what it is they need. Though likely to be success-oriented in the extreme, they will find that their real fulfillment lies not in worldly recognition for their efforts but in the mysterious and ineffable laws that bring people together in intimacy.

E. Y. "YIP" HARBURG
Lyricist, "Over the Rainbow"

4/8/1896
Aries II

CHALLENGE: **NOT INDULGING THEIR WORKAHOLIC TENDENCIES IN AN EFFORT TO ESCAPE INTIMACY**

FULFILLMENT: **ALLOWING OTHERS INTO THEIR INNER WORLD**

NOTABLE: **MARILU HENNER (ACTRESS, *TAXI*; AUTHOR ON HEALTH AND STRESS)**

April 11–18

THE PIONEER
ARIES III

The pioneering personalities born in this week may spend more time going outward in search of validation through group efforts and endeavors than they do turning inward in the search for enlightenment and the degree of self-knowledge called for by the Way of Revelation. Though they will be blessed with the rare gift of true insight into the motivations of others, enabling them to be highly effective in almost any chosen field of endeavor, they may nevertheless find themselves rather disillusioned by what they consider their colleagues' and partners' "insensitivity" to their needs. The resulting frustration may be somewhat difficult to bear for these self-sacrificing souls, since they are often not unduly tied to personal considerations. Yet their depth of commitment and intensely positive attitude will surely come to the rescue, and if they are careful to stay realistic, their secret dreams and wishes will be fulfilled here.

CHALLENGE: **RECOGNIZING THAT THEY ARE UNHAPPY LIVING ALONE**

FULFILLMENT: **DEEPENING THEIR RELATIONSHIPS THROUGH SELF-REVELATION**

April 19–24

POWER
ARIES–TAURUS CUSP

Aries–Tauruses may find themselves hindered rather than helped along the Way of Revelation by their preoccupation with the workings of power and rather pronounced superiority complex. Though gifted with an amazing capacity for work that will doubtless leave even their most serious competitors in the dust, they may be too well blessed materially to bother much about what may be lacking in their personal lives and interactions. Thus, in this passage, fate may intervene to force them into giving up a measure of security in the interest of exploring their inner landscapes and getting in tune with their own emotional needs. Finally, the self-protective aspect of this configuration may produce the kind of person who needs to realize that it is one thing to be a formidable adversary, quite another to be a formidable friend.

CHALLENGE: **COMING TO BELIEVE IN THE POWER OF LOVE**
FULFILLMENT: **PUTTING THEIR TRUST IN OTHERS**

PETER ILYICH TCHAIKOVSKY
Russian composer,
The Nutcracker
──────
5/7/1840
Taurus II

April 25–May 2

MANIFESTATION
TAURUS I

Stubbornness can serve to disguise a shocking degree of emotional vulnerability for those born in this week who travel the Way of Revelation, and they will doubtless have to do quite a bit of soul work before they find the necessary courage and imagination to divest themselves of their emotional armor. Yet work is what Taurus I's like best, and if they apply their energies in such a way as to uncover some of the darker corners of their psyche, they are likely to find the resulting exposure at least productive, if not entirely comfortable. Yet if they employ their need for peace and stability in such a way that it expands and refreshes their outlook, their sense of responsibility, hard work, and considerable insight will not go unrewarded for long.

CHALLENGE: **KNOWING WHEN THEIR STUBBORNNESS IS HURTING THEM**
FULFILLMENT: **REVELING IN THE POWER OF UNCONDITIONAL GIVING**

May 3–10

THE TEACHER
TAURUS II

Those born in the Week of the Teacher are likely to do fine on the Way of Revelation, since they are inclined to its worlds of ideas, concepts, and abstractions. Especially well suited to ideological pursuits, they may experience greater difficulty in the arena of interpersonal relationships, hiding behind a remote or inaccessible exterior or subduing their more emotional and caring impulses under a mask of superiority. Yet their considerable empathy and insight will do much to smooth this sometimes volatile passage, and if they employ their great curiosity in searching for who they truly are and work to unlock the mysteries of their own hearts before they go analyzing, criticizing, or otherwise poking around in the inconsistencies and failings of others, they will flourish in rather remarkable ways.

CHALLENGE: **NOT LOCKING THEMSELVES UP IN AN IVORY TOWER**
FULFILLMENT: **LEARNING TO IMPART INFORMATION ABOUT THEMSELVES**

MARGARET SULLAVAN
Actress
──────
5/16/1896
Taurus III

May 11–18

THE NATURAL
TAURUS III

For the individuals born in this week who travel the Way of Revelation, success may well be defined as the ability to garner enough monetary or material resources to eventually be able to spit in the eye of the establishment. And though these motivated individuals will likely do well on this karmic path from that perspective, successful interpersonal relationships may prove more difficult for them to grasp. For all that these people may tout the virtues of personal freedom, they may have a number of disturbing hidden agendas in their dealings with others, not the least of which is that their refusal to be tied down may be a smokescreen for their defensiveness and vulnerability. Still, the ability to transcend those issues is always within their power, and if they are careful to seek out relationships with people whose ideas and philosophies are interesting or unusual enough to spark their sense of adventure without tripping their defense mechanisms, life will become much easier.

CHALLENGE: **NOT HIDING THEIR FEAR OF EXPOSURE BEHIND THEIR NEED FOR FREEDOM**
FULFILLMENT: **CREATING STABILITY IN A RELATIONSHIP**

May 19–24

ENERGY
TAURUS–GEMINI CUSP

Likely to be gifted with a greater measure of diligence and dedication than many of their fellow Taurus–Geminis, the individuals born on this cusp who find themselves on the Way of Revelation may nevertheless encounter a number of frustrations in their search for higher development. In a word, they may not be especially interested in higher development, nor in cultivating the necessary degree of self-awareness that will enable them to understand their own motivations better. Thus, their natural emotional sensitivity may get mired down in personal touchiness, high-handedness, or an inability to bond. Yet for all of that, these people will respond well to the world of ideas, abstractions, and creative inspiration that beckon here, and, gifted as they are with a unique ability to take some necessary risks, they will surely make real progress on this life journey.

JOAN COLLINS
Actress, *Dynasty*
—————
5/23/1933
Taurus–Gemini Cusp

CHALLENGE: **SITTING STILL LONG ENOUGH TO BECOME ACQUAINTED WITH THEMSELVES**
FULFILLMENT: **LETTING DOWN THEIR GUARD ENOUGH TO SHARE AT LEAST INTELLECTUAL CAMARADERIE**

May 25–June 2

FREEDOM
GEMINI I

Protecting their privacy and sense of personal freedom may become something of a neurotic preoccupation for those born in this week who navigate the Way of Revelation, as they are naturally highly resistant to the kind of intense personal scrutiny that they apply to others. In fact, interacting with these personalities may feel rather like being put under a microscope as they attempt to analyze and deconstruct all manner of human motivation, then move on to the next prospect or puzzle without so much as a backward glance. And while they may have formidable insight and considerable charm, empathy and sentimentality will never be high on the list of their priorities until they develop a more comprehensive understanding of their own emotions and motivations. Yet when their quest for adventure and stimulation reveals itself to be an impulse to identify not with the facts but with the mystery, it will prove to their advantage to answer the call.

CHALLENGE: **EXAMINING THEIR NEUROTIC NEED TO MAINTAIN THEIR SUPERIORITY THROUGH RIDICULE**
FULFILLMENT: **OWNING UP TO THEIR EMOTIONAL NEEDINESS**

June 3–10

NEW LANGUAGE
GEMINI II

Though these people are troubled by a pronounced tendency to hide their light under a bushel or keep to themselves in a defensive attitude of self-protection, it is unlikely that their special gifts and highly creative nature will be kept under wraps for long. There may be some who stumble on this path by refusing to embrace trust and holding onto their darker impulses and the relative safety to be found in addiction, it is unlikely that their secrets will be their undoing. For these people are almost sure to be blessed with some unique ability or talent that seeks expression in much the same way that their capacity for love seeks fulfillment. Thus, unless they work actively to prevent the process of enlightenment, it will surely unfold for them.

RALPH WALDO EMERSON
Essayist/poet/philosopher
—————
5/25/1803
Gemini I

CHALLENGE: **REALIZING THAT THEIR SECRET FASCINATION FOR THE SEAMIER ASPECTS OF LIFE IS KEEPING THEM ISOLATED**
FULFILLMENT: **REVEALING THEIR UNIQUELY CREATIVE FORM OF EXPRESSION TO THE WORLD**
NOTABLE: **F. LEE BAILEY (FAMED ATTORNEY, O. J. SIMPSON AND PATTY HEARST TRIALS)**

June 11–18

THE SEEKER
GEMINI III

Though they may be somewhat preoccupied with material success and the freedom it can bring, these hardworking and often calculating people will eventually come around to confronting the more obvious realities of interpersonal relationships along the Way of Revelation. It is not that they do not care about love, it is only that love may not rate as high as some other things on their list of priorities. Gifted with formidable intelligence, mental clarity, and verbal ability, they will nevertheless have a certain tendency to "be as sounding brass" until they come to better terms with the things that make up the life of the spirit, more specifically, their own. Yet it is their nature to embrace challenge; if they can apply that quality to the search for a more cohesive and enlightened sense of self, their sensitivity and intuition are sure to be easily integrated with their mental faculties, resulting in a considerably enriched and rewarding life journey.

CHALLENGE: **NOT ALLOWING THEIR OUTWARD SEARCH TO PRECLUDE AN INNER ONE**
FULFILLMENT: **FINDING THAT THE ANSWERS TO MANY OF THEIR QUESTIONS LIE WITHIN**
NOTABLES: **JERZY KOSINSKI (AUTHOR, *THE PAINTED BIRD*); WALTER JACOBS (FOUNDED HERTZ RENT-A-CAR)**

June 19–24

MAGIC
GEMINI–CANCER CUSP

Those born on the Cusp of Magic who travel the Way of Revelation may find themselves devoting their energies to the search for a soul mate or idealized relationship in a thinly veiled attempt to find themselves. Indeed, they are capable of learning more from falling and being in love than almost anyone on this karmic path, yet with that potential comes the caveat that they will have a measure of difficulty in revealing their truest selves to another. Thus, this life journey may be quite frustrating until these individuals learn to avoid the pitfalls of fantasy and work to bring their vision to reality. Alternatively, some of them will bury their more romantic side under a mountain of professional responsibility in an attempt to protect themselves from romantic disappointment. In any event, they will do best when they maintain a willingness to grow and seek the universal truths and experiences that will exalt their spirits without breaking their hearts.

JOHN ELLIOT BRADSHAW
Writer, *Championing Your Inner Child*

———
6/29/1933
Cancer I

CHALLENGE: **OWNING THEIR TRAITS RATHER THAN PROJECTING THEM ONTO SOMEONE ELSE**
FULFILLMENT: **FINDING A SOUL MATE TO WHOM THEY CAN ENTRUST THE SECRET OF THEIR TRUE SELVES**
NOTABLES: **DANNY AIELLO (ACTOR); WALLIS WARFIELD SIMPSON (DUCHESS OF WINDSOR)**

June 25–July 2

THE EMPATII
CANCER I

Often self-protective in the extreme, those born in the Week of the Empath may have some difficulty navigating the challenge and promise of the Way of Revelation, until they come to understand that their extreme sensitivity is neither a liability of character nor an inherent weakness that should be overcome. Indeed, learning to let go of old hurts and refusing to allow disappointments to shape their worldview may prove especially challenging to these individuals. Yet for all of their intuition and sensitivity, they are blessed with the personal strength and powers of observation needed to make their way successfully in the world. If they do not withdraw or isolate themselves and remember to meditate occasionally upon the words of the absurdist Samuel Beckett, who claimed that "nothing is funnier than unhappiness," life will take a number of turns for the better.

CHALLENGE: **OVERCOMING THEIR PROPENSITY TO BE WITHDRAWN AND SHY**
FULFILLMENT: **THROWING OFF THE SHACKLES OF THEIR SECRETS**

July 3–10

THE UNCONVENTIONAL
CANCER II

"The me that nobody knows" is the phrase that comes to mind when considering the personalities born in the Week of the Unconventional who find themselves on this karmic path. Indeed, many with this configuration will be inclined to lead rather ordinary lives, content with less-than-glamorous jobs, lives, and pursuits. Yet somewhere along this karmic path the secrets of their richly quirky inner lives will certainly be revealed, probably as the result of a buildup of frustration with the more mundane aspects of existence. Thus they may experience unpredictable and even catastrophic changes in their circumstances when the ability to be oneself becomes a question not merely of choice but of necessity. If they avoid the darker pitfalls of addiction, evasion, and self-destruction and embrace a higher sense of spiritual laws, the resulting revelations can benefit us all.

JOHN PAUL JONES
Naval officer/American Revolution hero

———
7/17/1747
Cancer III

CHALLENGE: **TAKING CARE NOT TO BECOME STUCK IN THEIR FANTASIES**
FULFILLMENT: **CULTIVATING THE KINDS OF FRIENDSHIPS THAT ALLOW THEM TO BE THEMSELVES**

July 11–18

THE PERSUADER
CANCER III

Those born in the Week of the Persuader who make their life journey along the Way of Revelation may find that their personal identity is rather consistently repressed under the cloak of some highly developed management skills. Career-oriented in the extreme, they will frequently avoid the necessity of exploring deeper interpersonal relationships and may well have a rather suspicious attitude toward their own needs into the bargain. Yet these psychologically astute individuals have considerable potential for development, as they are, in the end, no better at fooling themselves than they are at allowing others to fool them. If they recognize that their impulse to control their needs is merely a strategy for avoiding hurt, and open themselves to the possibility of the higher spiritual connections that exist between individuals, all will go smoothly for them.

CHALLENGE: **FORCING THEIR WORKAHOLIC TENDENCIES TO THE BACK BURNER IN FAVOR OF INNER PERSONAL DEVELOPMENT**
FULFILLMENT: **HAVING THE COURAGE TO SHOW OTHERS THEIR PROFOUND SENSITIVITY**
NOTABLE: **YEVGENY YEVTUSHENKO (RUSSIAN POST-STALINIST POET)**

July 19–25
OSCILLATION
CANCER–LEO CUSP

Though likely to be plagued on this life journey by a measure of psychic stress resulting from the division between the tremendous power of their intuition and their more active or dynamic side, the individuals born on the Cusp of Oscillation who find themselves on the Way of Revelation can expect considerable fulfillment. Once they understand that it is a part of their nature to venture outward, then inward, then outward again, they will succeed in gaining a great insight into their personal and spiritual rhythms that should ease their life journey considerably. Though there are many who will actively attempt to repress their more emotional side and and may fall out of touch altogether with their real motivations, many more will use the gifts of this karmic path in far more constructive and rewarding ways. Likely to be neither consistent nor complacent, these personalities are nevertheless sure to find the excitement and passion they need to make great strides along the way.

JERRY FALWELL
TV preacher

8/11/1933
Leo III

CHALLENGE: **BEING CAREFUL NOT TO HIDE JUST ONE SIDE OF THEMSELVES, THEREBY CREATING AN IMBALANCE**
FULFILLMENT: **INVOKING THEIR RISK-TAKING ABILITY IN ORDER TO REVEAL THEMSELVES TO OTHERS**

July 26–August 2
AUTHORITY
LEO I

The individuals born in the Week of Authority who travel the Way of Revelation will have to take care that they don't fall victim to their own high standards. In short, these people are likely to have had a rather rough start in life and may carry the burdens of early rejection for many years. In fact, they may be quite suspicious of others and prone to any number of knee-jerk reactions when their emotional buttons are pushed. Alternatively, some with this configuration will shrink from the higher challenges of this karmic path and retreat into self-interest, chronically hedging their emotional bets. It behooves them to come to terms with the fact that their impulse to dominate or control others may in fact arise from their refusal to face down the demons of insecurity. Moreover, one day their preoccupation with work and professional matters just might give way to a softer side that can prove positively cuddly as the lions residing within them are tamed.

CHALLENGE: **RELEASING LONG-HELD RESENTMENTS AND SUSPICIONS**
FULFILLMENT: **ALLOWING CREATIVE EXPRESSION TO SOFTEN THEM**
NOTABLE: **DOM DELUISE (ACTOR/COMEDIAN)**

August 3–10
BALANCED STRENGTH
LEO II

Leo II's can do quite well on the Way of Revelation, providing they do not turn their natural toughness into a badge of honor and force themselves to endure more by way of emotional suffering than is necessary. There is much about these personalities that will be prone to testing the limits of others, whether physical, moral, or emotional, and it's likely that only those blessed with a rare degree of understanding will realize that such exercises are more designed to reveal the inner qualities and limitations of Leo II's than those of their partners, lovers, or colleagues. Until these souls come to understand that much for themselves and learn to assimilate and share that knowledge, they are likely to experience a fair amount of guilt when their various games and psychosocial experiments go haywire. Still, when they come to understand that spirituality arises not from the need to establish limits but from the need to transcend them, they will be considerably enriched and rewarded.

ROMAN POLANSKI
Director, *Rosemary's Baby*, *Chinatown*

8/18/1933
Leo III

CHALLENGE: **DROPPING THE MASK OF THEIR TOUGH AND GRUFF PERSONA ONCE IN A WHILE**
FULFILLMENT: **SPENDING SOME TIME ALONE WITH THEMSELVES ON A REGULAR BASIS**

August 11–18
LEADERSHIP
LEO III

Not as likely to withdraw or to hide their lights as some on this karmic path, Leo III's who find themselves on the Way of Revelation are likely to experience great reward and achievement, providing they cultivate the impulse to go within in search of greater self-knowledge and understanding. There is, however, a danger that these rather charismatic types may present a commanding yet false facade to the world that crumbles upon closer scrutiny, and many with this configuration may manifest its conflicts as did the Wizard of Oz, by perpetuating the illusion of power even when there is no real strength behind it. Yet even when the curtain is pulled aside and the truth revealed, Leo III's are certain to rise to the occasion, buoyed along this life journey by their qualities of fierce loyalty and courage, tremendous insight, and a heart that is open to everyone.

CHALLENGE: **NOT HIDING BEHIND SCRUPULOUS MORALS IN AN EFFORT TO CONCEAL THEIR VULNERABILITY**
FULFILLMENT: **BASKING IN THE RESPECT OF OTHERS**
NOTABLE: **MALCOLM JAMAL WARNER (ACTOR, *THE COSBY SHOW*)**

August 19–25

EXPOSURE
LEO–VIRGO CUSP

Though they may never entirely be able to gain from others the same level of understanding they offer to the world, these remarkable personalities should take care to respect their own special brand of insight and resist the impulse to second-guess their best hunches or turn on themselves when they encounter rejection or disapproval. Though they may be self-conscious in the extreme, these individuals have a tremendous need to gain acceptance and approval through well-timed self-revelation. If properly acknowledged and not discounted as mere neediness, that quality will help them rise above the narrower restrictions of self and into the world of spirit. The ability to put themselves, their ideas, and their talents on view in areas such as teaching, the performing arts, or other public pursuits will prove especially rewarding, as these will be the areas where they will best be able to combine and employ their special gifts in a way that benefits all.

CLAUDIA SCHIFFER
Supermodel

8/25/1970
Leo–Virgo Cusp

CHALLENGE: **LEARNING TO TRUST THEIR INTUITIVE UNDER-STANDING OF OTHERS**
FULFILLMENT: **PUTTING THEIR UNIQUE TALENTS ON PUBLIC DISPLAY**
NOTABLE: **RIVER PHOENIX (ACTOR, *STAND BY ME*)**

August 26–September 2

SYSTEM BUILDERS
VIRGO I

Virgo I's may find the Way of Revelation something of an uneasy journey, as they are often quite reluctant to sacrifice their sense of order to the risks of greater self-exploration. Indeed, these personalities are frequently self-sacrificing in the extreme, and it may take quite a bit of time before they are ready to acknowledge their own needs. Even then, they may have to wrestle with feelings of chronic indecision, personal unworthiness, and emotional pressure. Yet it is their very impulse to impose rules and structures upon others that may blow up in their faces with some regularity. As upsetting as these problems and confrontations may be, however, they are likely to put them in better touch with their truest feelings. If they can then utilize their great objectivity in self-assessment and come to a sense of higher forgiveness and release, their rewards are ensured.

CHALLENGE: **FINDING SOURCES OF RELEASE FOR THE BUILD-UP OF EMOTIONAL PRESSURE**
FULFILLMENT: **HAVING COME TO A BETTER UNDERSTANDING OF SELF, RELAXING WITH IT**
NOTABLE: **CHARLES STEWART ROLLS (COFOUNDED AUTO-MOTIVE COMPANY)**

September 3–10

THE ENIGMA
VIRGO II

Those born in the Week of the Enigma are well suited to the challenges and promise of the Way of Revelation, providing they do not shrink from the task of learning to be more truly themselves with others or allow their natural good taste and discrimination to turn into a of high-handed feeling superiority. Exacting taskmasters and gifted with a phenomenal capacity for hard work, some with this configuration may be characterized by an aloof or even imperious attitude, while others may be self-effacing to the point of invisibility. Either way, these personalities are bound to have an oddly magnetic quality that will serve to draw others' attention. When they come to better terms with the idea that image isn't everything and may, in fact, be rendered unimportant when the opportunity to bond with others presents itself, they will realize great fulfillment.

CONWAY TWITTY
Country music singer

9/1/1933
Virgo I

CHALLENGE: **TEMPERING A PICKY OR CRITICAL MIND-SET THAT MAY DRIVE OTHERS AWAY**
FULFILLMENT: **UNFOLDING THEMSELVES SLOWLY OVER TIME IN A LOVE RELATIONSHIP**
NOTABLE: **MATTHEW BOULTON (STEAM ENGINE MANUFAC-TURER)**

September 11–18

THE LITERALIST
VIRGO III

This karmic path gifts these individuals with a greater sensitivity and insight into others' motivations and feelings than they might otherwise have had, but those born in this week may nevertheless have to work hard to overcome a rather naturally suspicious or defensive attitude toward interpersonal relations. Highly resistant to others' attempts to analyze them, it will doubtless fall to these individuals to face the task of mining their own feelings, psyches, and spirits for the gems of spiritual and social reward promised by this karmic path. Generally, such psychological mining is anathema to Virgo III's, but considerable courage and objectivity are associated with this configuration. If these souls can apply those same qualities to self-evaluation, then turn outward to share their truths with others, they will likely find great response and acceptance.

CHALLENGE: **BELIEVING IN THE BENEFITS OF SELF-STUDY AND ANALYSIS**
FULFILLMENT: **ALLOWING THEMSELVES A BIT OF AN OSTEN-TATIOUS DISPLAY ONCE IN A WHILE**
NOTABLE: **ZOE CALDWELL (STAGE ACTRESS; KNOWN FOR ROLE AS MARIA CALLAS)**

September 19–24
BEAUTY
VIRGO–LIBRA CUSP

Those born on the Cusp of Beauty who tread the Way of Revelation may experience a number of difficulties and obstacles to growth when they allow their conflicts to hinder their search for greater self-awareness and self-realization. Though the quest for spiritual context ought to figure prominently in these lives, it may take them longer than some to find their answers, since they tend to be distracted by superficial worldly or romantic pursuits. Yet at the heart of their quest is the impulse to align themselves with more universal concepts, ideas, and laws. If they can summon the courage to go within and to face down the demons of fear, inadequacy, and the need to submerge their own identities in unhealthy relationships with others, they will find a rare and surprising beauty that need not stay hidden within the confines of their own hearts.

CHALLENGE: **NOT BECOMING TOO ENAMORED OF THEIR OWN FALSE FRONT**
FULFILLMENT: **ALLOWING THEMSELVES THE OCCASIONAL HISSY FIT, IF ONLY BECAUSE IT REVEALS A CRACK IN THEIR ARMOR**
NOTABLES: **DAVID McCALLUM (ACTOR, *MAN FROM U.N.C.L.E.*); RICHARD OLDENBURG (DIRECTOR OF MUSEUM OF MODERN ART IN NEW YORK CITY)**

THOR HEYERDAHL
Anthropologist/author,
Kon-Tiki

10/6/1914
Libra II

September 25–October 2
THE PERFECTIONIST
LIBRA I

Those born in the Week of the Perfectionist who tread this karmic path can realize great progress, once they loosen the grip of some of their more obscure emotional impulses and become better friends with the person they are inside. In fact, these rather exacting personalities may be faced with the necessity of developing greater tolerance and somewhat less objectivity before they can come to terms with the simple fact that emotional impulses and human feeling do not always operate according to what is generally thought of as rational laws. Yet even though their impulse toward perfection may serve to disguise deeper insecurities, these souls can recognize great achievements along the Way of Revelation, especially when they allow themselves the luxury of occasionally letting down their barriers and letting the heart rule the head.

CHALLENGE: **UNDERSTANDING THAT THE REPRESSION OF THEIR FEELINGS WREAKS HAVOC ON THEIR EMOTIONAL LIVES**
FULFILLMENT: **ADOPTING A MORE EASYGOING APPROACH TO LIFE BY CARING LESS WHAT OTHERS THINK**

October 3–10
SOCIETY
LIBRA II

Those born in the Week of Society who find themselves on this karmic path may be subject to any number of distractions from the call of their own brand of spirituality until they come face-to-face with the fact they they frequently allow their own needs and emotions to become entirely subsumed by others'. In fact, they may be possessed of some chameleon-like qualities that will have to be adequately addressed before they are able to understand that real empathy consists not in making oneself over to please or advise others but in being able to respond to others on the basis of common experience. In short, self-deception may be their particular sticking point, especially when it masks itself as the latest trend, the latest friend, or the latest in devotional fads or fancies.

CHALLENGE: **INVESTING A GOOD BIT OF TIME IN THE EFFORT TO GET TO KNOW THEMSELVES**
FULFILLMENT: **PUTTING THEIR FAITH LESS IN THE SUPERFICIAL OR TRANSITORY AND MORE IN THE ETERNAL**
NOTABLES: **VIRGINIA GILDERSLEEVE (DEAN OF BARNARD COLLEGE, 1911–1947); BRENDAN GILL (CRITIC; AUTHOR)**

MATT DAMON
Actor, *Good Will Hunting*

10/8/1970
Libra II

October 11–18
THEATER
LIBRA III

Those who combine the Week of Theater with the Way of Revelation may well go through life as truly consummate actors, willing to play the roles and parts necessary to get ahead. Yet there will be a rather hollow quality to these varying performances until they come to a greater understanding of the soul's calling and realize that this life experience comes down to more than a question of learning one's lines or picking up one's cues. Until that time, however, life will seem to them to be a series of missed opportunities, might-have-beens, and "woulda, coulda, shoulda" events. Marked by a seeming overconfidence that may well disguise their inner impulses and needs, they will have to decide whether to turn inward in a search for greater self-realization or to content themselves with forming an identity based on the rather ill-informed impressions of those around them.

CHALLENGE: **GUARDING AGAINST THEIR PRODIGIOUS CAPACITY FOR SELF-DECEPTION**
FULFILLMENT: **CHOOSING TO ENGAGE FULLY IN LIVING THEIR OWN LIVES**
NOTABLE: **JERRY SIEGEL (CREATOR OF SUPERMAN)**

October 19–25

DRAMA AND CRITICISM
LIBRA–SCORPIO CUSP

The highly charismatic, compelling individuals born on this cusp who find themselves on the Way of Revelation will have rather a hard time keeping their light under wraps, no matter what defense mechanisms they may have in place. Indeed, they may encounter some difficulty in understanding just why it is that others are always in their faces or in their business until they come to realize that in many fundamental ways, their own personal dramas and secrets are linked to those of the collective. Nonetheless, this can prove a highly rewarding passage, providing they do not allow their rather overly developed critical faculties to serve as a defense against other people's attempts to reach their innermost hearts. Too, addictions of all kinds are to be avoided, especially when the individuals in question erect their own bad habits as yet another wall in the way of enlightenment and love.

CHALLENGE: NOT USING THEIR PERCEPTIVENESS AS A WEAPON IN THE WAR TO SHUT OTHERS OUT

FULFILLMENT: RETAINING THEIR IDENTITIES IN WELL-ROUNDED AND BALANCED RELATIONSHIPS

October 26–November 2

INTENSITY
SCORPIO I

The souls born in the Week of Intensity who make their way along this karmic path may be somewhat hampered in their search for enlightenment and connection by a suspicious and calculating attitude toward others that may, at times, border on the paranoid. Indeed, their obsession with privacy may be acted out in a way that may be quite damaging to all concerned. Especially susceptible to feelings of jealousy, envy, and greed, they will do best when they release their preoccupation with the "real" motivations of those around them and turn their attention inward in an effort to discover just why it is that they became so obsessed with privacy and secrets in the first place. When they turn their investigative talents toward the work of self-realization and discovery, however, they will find that their deepest fears will evaporate and the road to enlightenment will widen and smooth.

CHALLENGE: BEING LESS HARD ON BOTH THEMSELVES AND OTHERS

FULFILLMENT: DELVING INTO THEIR DARKER SIDE AND SHINING A LIGHT ON IT

NOTABLES: JACKIE COOGAN (ACTOR, "THE KID"); DR. JONAS SALK (DEVELOPED VACCINE AGAINST POLIO); CAPTAIN JAMES COOK (EXPLORER)

ROBERT FULTON
Inventor, built first commercially successful steamboat in America

11/14/1765
Scorpio III

November 3–11

DEPTH
SCORPIO II

CLAUDE MONET
Painter, father of Impressionism, *Water Lilies*

11/14/1840
Scorpio III

Learning to trust will not come easily to those born in the Week of Depth who find themselves on the Way of Revelation. Indeed, it may be a lifelong quest. Too often, these rather profound personalities will fall short of the understanding that embarking on personal relationships or other ventures with the idea that others must somehow prove their worthiness is an exercise in futility that results only in disappointment and cynicism. Indeed, they will have to face the facts that their defensive barriers are hindering, rather than ensuring, their happiness and that their fear of betrayal is essentially a self-fulfilling prophecy. And while these souls are almost certain to realize considerable financial and professional success along this karmic path, personal fulfillment will come only through the ability to open their hearts.

CHALLENGE: LEARNING THE ART OF RELEASING THEIR RESENTMENTS, JEALOUSIES, AND GRUDGES—THROUGH FORGIVENESS

FULFILLMENT: EXPLORING THE DEEPER AND MORE INTIMATE STATES OF HUMAN RELATIONS

NOTABLES: ETHAN HAWKE (ACTOR, *GATTACA*; AUTHOR); YITZHAK SHAMIR (ISRAELI PRIME MINISTER)

November 12–18

CHARM
SCORPIO III

Those born in the Week of Charm who navigate the challenge and promise of the Way of Revelation are somewhat more socially inclined and better able to trust than some of their Scorpio cousins who share this journey. Nonetheless, these individuals have a decidedly calculating streak, and they will be much inclined to want others to jump through all sorts of hoops to prove their devotion. Yet at their core, Scorpio III's are realists who are well able to face down the demons of personal distrust and defensiveness. If they can augment that realism with a desire to transcend the boundaries of what they consider their own strengths and weaknesses and place greater faith in their ability to realize a higher set of ambitions, they will doubtless make their mark.

CHALLENGE: BEING MORE DIRECT, HONEST, AND OPEN WITH OTHERS

FULFILLMENT: ADMITTING THEIR DREAMS TO THEMSELVES AND DARING TO ACHIEVE THEM

NOTABLE: TONYA HARDING (DISGRACED ICE SKATER)

November 19–24
REVOLUTION
SCORPIO–SAGITTARIUS CUSP

Perhaps the saving grace of the personalities born on the Cusp of Revolution who find themselves on this karmic path is a rather irreverent streak that, among other things, will free them from taking their own and others' failings too seriously. Though self-review and objective assessment may not be their strong suit, these individuals will discover much in their volatile natures that will require closer scrutiny as they make their way along this life journey. In fact, their biggest pitfall will be a tendency to build up resentments that result in explosive and often destructive displays of temper. Too, this configuration can manifest in some shockingly judgmental tendencies and a hypercritical streak. Yet when they come to understand that many of their more obvious problems are not so much the result of bad intentions as the products of poor planning and presentation, these revolutionaries may indeed discover the avenues through which they can reach the hearts and minds of the multitude.

CHALLENGE: **APPLYING A BIT OF THEIR ICONOCLASM TO THEIR OWN CAREFULLY CONSTRUCTED MYTHOLOGY**

FULFILLMENT: **PERMITTING THEMSELVES THE OCCASIONAL SHOW OF VULNERABILITY OR NEEDINESS**

DOROTHY LAMOUR
Actress

12/10/1914
Sagittarius II

November 25–December 2
INDEPENDENCE
SAGITTARIUS I

The formidable intuitive capacity of those born in the Week of Independence who make their life journey along the Way of Revelation will do much to protect them from those who would do them wrong. In fact, honor and trust rate quite high on their list of priorities, and they will rarely be found associating with people whose standards are not so elevated. Yet they may have certain problems, specifically those of using the need for freedom as a defense against personal interaction or commitment and a certain superior attitude that will only serve to isolate these often misunderstood people even further. Still, these individuals are quite social at their core and are likely to do the soul-searching necessary to find and form satisfying relationships in both the personal and professional spheres.

CHALLENGE: **RECOGNIZING THAT THEIR FEELING OF BEING MISUNDERSTOOD PERPETUATES BEING MISUNDERSTOOD**

FULFILLMENT: **SETTING ASIDE THEIR FREEDOM-LOVING WAYS LONG ENOUGH TO OPEN UP TO SOMEONE**

NOTABLE: **JOE DIMAGGIO (LEGENDARY YANKEE, "JOLTIN' JOE")**

December 3–10
THE ORIGINATOR
SAGITTARIUS II

Building bridges to satisfying careers and relationships may prove a bit difficult for those born in this week who find themselves on the Way of Revelation. It is likely that part of their rather defensive attitude toward the world was shaped by an early environment that did little to encourage their creativity and originality, which in turn may have caused them to form rather shaky opinions of both themselves and those who would be close to them. Yet if they do not shrink from the challenge of this karmic path by becoming reclusive, isolated, or otherwise peculiar in their outlook and attitude and come to terms with the fact that to be different is not necessarily to be suspect, their highly original flair, unique brand of creativity, and talent for innovation are bound to shine.

CHALLENGE: **GRAPPLING WITH THEIR TENDENCY TO AGGRESSIVENESS AND RESENTMENT**

FULFILLMENT: **DARING TO SHOW THE WORLD WHO THEY ARE, IF ONLY THROUGH A DISPLAY OF THEIR CREATIVITY**

NOTABLE: **MANNE SIEGBAHN (WON NOBEL PRIZE FOR X-RAY SPECTOGRAPHY)**

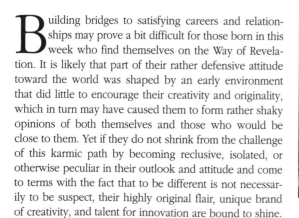

ELI WHITNEY
Invented cotton gin

12/8/1765
Sagittarius II

December 11–18
THE TITAN
SAGITTARIUS III

The Titans who travel the Way of Revelation may be marked by a deceptively open, "what you see is what you get" kind of attitude that can belie a welter of dark impulses and secret insecurities. Nevertheless, they are likely to do quite well, providing they do not indulge the workaholic tendencies of this path, thereby fulfilling the saying "it is lonely at the top." Perhaps their greatest defense mechanism is their tendency to overburden themselves with people and responsibilities in such a way that real intimacy becomes impossible. Too, they may take their inclination to ruminate over slights, problems, and personal direction to extremes, to the point where they become isolated and inaccessible to those who could be of help to them. Still, there is a promise of great success, and with time they will realize great influence and impact.

CHALLENGE: **NOT LETTING THEIR PURSUIT OF GREATER PLANS OR SCHEMES INTERFERE WITH THE JOB OF BECOMING ACQUAINTED WITH THEMSELVES**

FULFILLMENT: **ARRIVING AT A POINT IN THEIR LIVES WHERE THEY FEEL SECURE ENOUGH TO LET DOWN THEIR GUARD**

December 19–25
PROPHECY
SAGITTARIUS–CAPRICORN CUSP

Those born in this period who journey along the Way of Revelation are likely to be startling individuals whose gifts of insight and understanding can reach surprising proportions. Yet there is a danger that these souls will fail to answer the higher calling of this karmic path, and will refuse to share their unique brand of insight, vision, or extrasensory talents with others. In fact, they may cling to their sense of isolation in the belief that they simply don't care what others may think of them, and this configuration may produce a number of recluses, hermits, and misanthropes. Yet there is no heart so closed that it cannot be opened, and no secret that cannot be eventually revealed in a spirit of trust and hope. If they allow their psychic nature to illuminate the mysteries of their hearts, these prophets can do much to shape their own future, as well as that of those around them.

GIACOMO PUCCINI
Operatic composer,
Madame Butterfly
———
12/22/1858
Sagittarius–Capricorn
Cusp

CHALLENGE: **NOT ALLOWING THEMSELVES TO BECOME IM-PRISONED BY THEIR SENSITIVITY**

FULFILLMENT: **CULTIVATING FRIENDSHIPS AMONG OTHERS WITH PSYCHIC POWERS WITH WHOM THEY CAN SHARE THEIR GIFTS**

December 26–January 2
THE RULER
CAPRICORN I

The judgmentalism and sense of superiority of Capricorn I's may stand in the way of the higher development and understanding of the self required by the Way of Revelation. In fact, these rather stubborn, inflexible personalities may have a number of difficulties, not the least of which will be a tendency to bottle up their emotions under a rigid facade of discipline and inflexibility. Their workaholic tendencies are also especially pronounced, and while those with this configuration will doubtless enjoy a great deal of material success and achievement, they have an equal potential for loneliness, isolation, and abandonment. Yet if they allow themselves to be guided by their keen psychological insight and intuitive capacity, they will find themselves less inclined to be hard on others and, more especially, on themselves.

CHALLENGE: **TAKING CARE NOT TO BELIEVE THAT THEIR CAPACITY TO MAKE MONEY IS THE JUSTIFICATION OF THEIR EXISTENCE**

FULFILLMENT: **ACCEPTING BOTH THEMSELVES AND OTHERS MORE**

January 3–9
DETERMINATION
CAPRICORN II

Those born in the Week of Determination who journey along the Way of Revelation will be aided in their spiritual development by their often secret need to connect with their psychic intuition or spirituality. Holding on to the hurts of the past means they are only too ready to remain on guard with others. On this karmic path, their admirable capacity for work will do much to support their many career aspirations, though they tend to be too modest when it comes to garnering appreciation for their efforts. Though it may take some time for these resilient and resourceful people to release themselves from some emotional issues that have been standing in the way of their real growth, at heart they are essentially realistic people who are unlikely to encumber themselves with too much self-protection when the time for self-protection is past and the rewards of revelation become obvious.

BERT PARKS
Television host known
for emceeing the
Miss America Pageant
———
12/30/1914
Capricorn I

CHALLENGE: **NOT BEING ASHAMED OF THEIR METAPHYSICAL OR SPIRITUAL SIDE**

FULFILLMENT: **REALIZING THAT TRUSTING IN OTHERS IS REALLY ABOUT TRUSTING IN THE DIVINE**

NOTABLE: **CARRIE CHAPMAN CATT (WOMEN'S SUFFRAGE LEADER)**

January 10–16
DOMINANCE
CAPRICORN III

A secret inferiority complex may be the most important thing for Capricorn III's to deal with on the Way of Revelation, but until they do, these individuals may experience quite a few conflicts in working out the higher challenges of this karmic path. In fact, they may do themselves a disservice by assuming a worldly persona that is highly dependable, truly responsible, and accepting of being overlooked while inside they build up great levels of frustration and resentment over the failure of others to perceive the great potential underneath. Too, they have a marked tendency to place obstacles in the path of their own success, if only to give themselves something tangible to overcome. Still, the right partners and family relationships can do much to relax them and reveal that the way to Heaven can often be found in the things of Earth and that love of oneself can sometimes best be realized through the love of another.

CHALLENGE: **DEALING WITH A FEW OF THEIR MORE BASIC ISSUES BEFORE THEY PRESENT THEMSELVES TO THE WORLD**

FULFILLMENT: **DISCOVERING THE JOY OF BEING THEMSELVES**

NOTABLE: **ALAN LOMAX (MUSICOLOGIST)**

January 17–22

MYSTERY AND IMAGINATION
CAPRICORN–AQUARIUS CUSP

Try as they might to hide their light, it is unlikely that these personalities will be able to keep themselves hidden for any real amount of time on the Way of Revelation. In fact, they may be prone to draw more attention to themselves than they are comfortable with. In a word, this life journey will be characterized by a number of unpredictable events and developments resulting from fate's insistence that they emerge from their self-imposed isolation and get back into the world of action. Ironically, it is that very quality of uncertainty that gives rise to the sense of insecurity and distrust that is part of this life journey. Yet once they realize that even the best of us are neither entirely prepared nor entirely qualified for what life throws at us, their sense of distrust will give way to a broader perspective and a higher faith in the often hidden, but nevertheless revealing, language of destiny.

CHALLENGE: **LEARNING TO FLOW WITH THE OFTEN CHAOTIC ENERGIES THAT SWIRL AROUND THEM**

FULFILLMENT: **SUCCEEDING IN NAILING DOWN A SENSE OF THEIR OWN IDENTITY**

NOTABLES: **FRANCIS BACON (PHILOSOPHER; STATESMAN); LARRY FORTENSKY (EX-HUSBAND OF ELIZABETH TAYLOR)**

THOMAS MERTON
Trappist monk; poet

1/31/1915
Aquarius II

January 23–30

GENIUS
AQUARIUS I

Likely to be rather uninterested in many of the issues of safety, trust, and intimacy that are prominent for some others on this karmic path, those born in the Week of Genius who travel the Way of Revelation may nevertheless have to contend with the fact that their barriers to higher development may be erected on the otherwise lofty concepts of personal freedom, intellectual expansion, and the ability to stick to principles. In a word, with this group defensiveness may take the form of preoccupation, absent-mindedness, or ivory-tower intellectualism. Thus, becoming better acquainted with their emotions will be especially important for this group, and they would do well to cultivate concern for others and a greater capacity for intimacy. On this karmic path, steady partnerships, good friends, and child rearing will prove to be the avenues through which they come to discover the real meaning of faith and higher spirituality.

CHALLENGE: **RECOGNIZING THAT THEIR NEED FOR FREEDOM MAY MASK THEIR FEAR OF REJECTION**

FULFILLMENT: **INSISTING LESS ON BEING UNENCUMBERED AND MORE ON UNDERSTANDING OTHERS**

NOTABLES: **ROBERT MOTHERWELL (ABSTRACT IMPRESSIONIST PAINTER); MARK GOODSON (GAME SHOW PRODUCER)**

January 31–February 7

YOUTH AND EASE
AQUARIUS II

This is another of the configurations that can result in an often disastrous split between one's public and private self. Those born in the Week of Youth and Ease who make their way along this karmic path are nevertheless promised great achievement, popularity, and personal recognition, providing they overcome their rather immature attitude toward emotional problems and attune themselves to the need for higher awareness. They should also take care that their popularity and magnetism don't go to their heads and manifest in a prima donna attitude toward those who would like to be closer to them. Nevertheless, they are fortunate people, gifted with the capacity for both hard work and diligence, as well as discriminating and objective self-assessment. If they can bring these qualities to bear, they will travel far.

CHALLENGE: **TAKING THE TROUBLE TO APPLY THEIR PERCEPTIVENESS TO THEMSELVES**

FULFILLMENT: **BEING ADMIRED NOT FOR WHO THEY PRESENT THEMSELVES TO BE BUT FOR WHO THEY ARE**

NOTABLE: **HAVELOCK ELLIS (PHYSICIAN; WRITER ON SEX)**

LORNE GREENE
Actor, *Bonanza*

2/12/1915
Aquarius III

February 8–15

ACCEPTANCE
AQUARIUS III

Interesting and often highly attractive, Aquarius III's who travel the Way of Revelation may do themselves a considerable disservice if they allow their more intolerant attitudes to stand in the way of forming deeper bonds with others. Alternatively, the blithe spirits with this configuration may appear quite easygoing yet have any number of hidden agendas that prevent greater closeness or intimacy. In either case, they will do best when they go within in order to develop a greater understanding of and tolerance for their faults and failings. Once they overcome the need for self-deprecation and defense, their insecurities will fall away and be replaced with a sense of self-worth that will in turn manifest itself in easier and more rewarding interactions with others.

CHALLENGE: **ADMITTING THAT THEY CRAVE LOVE AND AFFECTION**

FULFILLMENT: **GENERATING GREATER PEACE OF MIND BY GROUNDING THEMSELVES IN THE HERE AND NOW**

NOTABLES: **AUNG SAN (BURMESE GENERAL); LOUIS XV (FRENCH KING; LOST COLONIES IN AMERICA AND INDIA)**

February 16–22

SENSITIVITY
AQUARIUS–PISCES CUSP

Getting to the heart of their underlying feelings of unworthiness or inadequacy may prove the central issue for the individuals born on the Cusp of Sensitivity who travel the Way of Revelation. In fact, many of them are so well defended that no one will be able to overcome their barriers and establish greater closeness, so it is likely that these individuals will have to face the necessity of tearing down their own defenses before they can realize the closeness they so desire. In fact, fear of rejection may be their principal stumbling block, leading to a self-defeating attitude that in turn alienates those who reach out to them. Yet underneath their rather crusty and even aggressive exterior there beats a heart of gold. If they can find the courage to reveal their treasure, they will be treasured by others in return.

AMY TAN
Author, *The Joy Luck Club*
───
2/19/1952
Aquarius–Pisces Cusp

CHALLENGE: **PUTTING SOME EFFORT INTO WORKING OUT THEIR CORE ISSUES**
FULFILLMENT: **DEVELOPING A SENSE OF HOPE AND TRUST**

February 23–March 2

SPIRIT
PISCES I

Those born in the Week of Spirit who find themselves on the Way of Revelation can realize the highest achievements on this karmic path, providing they are willing to cultivate the capacity to take greater responsibility for their behavior and to exorcise their emotional blockages and barriers. In fact, this configuration may manifest as a sense of being victimized, underrated, or chronically underappreciated, all of which will stand in the way of higher consciousness until they apply their intuitive faculties and keen perceptions to the task of finding out just what it is that stands in the way of their fulfillment. Too, they may retreat from the interpersonal development required by this karmic path by developing a superior attitude or the belief that no one is ever quite good enough to meet their often unrealistic expectations. Yet their potential for success far outweighs their chances of stagnation, and for that reason alone, they can expect some truly wonderful developments along this life journey.

CHALLENGE: **NOT NEGLECTING TO DEAL WITH THEIR CORE ISSUES AS THEY PURSUE A SPIRITUAL PATH**
FULFILLMENT: **PLACING THEIR FAITH IN SOMETHING GREATER THAN THEMSELVES**

March 3–10

THE LONER
PISCES II

Though this will doubtless be a challenging life journey for those born in the Week of the Loner, it promises some amazing opportunities for growth and increased consciousness. The struggle to form relationships may assume some truly archetypal proportions, and while such attempts may not always prove successful, they will surely be educational and spiritually enlightening. There is a danger that the Pisces II's on the Way of Revelation may shrink from the challenge of this karmic path in sulky or temperamental gestures of refusal, thus failing to bond with others in the interest of licking old wounds or nursing old hurts. However, if these Loners succeed in stepping into the light to reveal who they are in relationships, they can rest secure in the knowledge that they have successfully off-loaded the karma not just of this journey but of a number of lifetimes spent alone.

LYNN SWANN
Football player,
Pittsburgh Steelers
───
3/7/1952
Pisces II

CHALLENGE: **SETTING ASIDE THEIR SENSITIVITIES IN FAVOR OF THE GREATER GOAL OF SELF-REALIZATION**
FULFILLMENT: **FINDING SELF-ACCEPTANCE**

March 11–18

DANCERS AND DREAMERS
PISCES III

Though there may be a few shrinking violets associated with this configuration, the majority of those born in the Week of Dancers and Dreamers can realize the highest level of spiritual progress along this road. Perhaps their principal danger is that they will exalt their sensitivity to the point where it interferes with their more grounded and objective talents for self-assessment, miring them in an unrealistic vision of how things ought to be rather than the facts of what they are. Yet they have a unique ability to give form to their most inspired ideas and talents that will find a response in the collective minds and hearts of the public. If they do not succumb to the purely personal need to protect themselves from injury and instead aspire to the higher goal of revealing their special gifts to the world, they can lead rather blessed and fortunate lives.

CHALLENGE: **TRANSFORMING THEIR OMNISCIENT MANNER INTO ONE OF GREATER HUMILITY**
FULFILLMENT: **PRESENTING THEMSELVES AND THEIR TALENTS ON THE WORLD'S STAGE**

The Way of Extension

VIRGO I TO PISCES I
System Builders to Spirit

The life purpose of those on the Way of Extension is to take their talent for structuring their ideas, work, and lives and to extend it beyond mundane concerns and average thinking into the structuring of universal or spiritual ideas or inspirations. Moreover, it is their calling to teach their theories to others so that they can be put to practical use. To do this, those born on the Way of Extension must learn to orient themselves to the metaphysical. No matter how practical or down-to-earth they may be, it is their destiny to strive toward the higher realms of consciousness. Transcending barriers of space and time, such individuals must push their powers of discrimination to the maximum so that they can perceive a kind of order in the chaotic realms of spirituality, philosophical or political ideas, even conceptual systems. Sometimes this process requires a period of retreat or reflection to gather ideas followed by a return to everyday life with an understanding of higher concepts in tow. At such a point the individuals on the Way of Extension can share their unique system of thought with the world. On this karmic path, even the most earthbound or practical individuals, those who embrace little or no spiritual or religious belief system, will engage in meditation on what larger forces are at work in the world. Whether they want to or not, they must apply their analytical minds to such musings to extend their

CORE LESSON

Overcoming their propensity to seek emotional security in the small details and routines of everyday life

GOAL

To structure metaphysical or theoretical ideas into a format easily understood and used by others

---

GIFTS
Devoted, Practical, Spiritual

PITFALLS
Rigid, Insecure, Self-sacrificing

---

need for structure outward, much like a lasso, to rope in and tame such ideas for the benefit of all.

Proceeding along this karmic path does not entail a metamorphosis or turnaround as much as a steady outward thrust from the earthly to the spiritual. The main challenge for the individuals born to the Way of Extension will be learning to overcome themselves and their own predilections. Here the ability to systematize is both a curse and a gift. Far too often, those coming into a lifetime with Virgo I energies become bogged down with a preoccupation with the details of their lives, failing to see the proverbial forest for the trees. These individuals feel safest when boxed in by schedules, routines, and modes of thought. The problem is, these rather persistent and stubborn individuals actually like the way they have ordered their own—and often everyone else's—life. A more process-oriented or "go with the flow" approach causes them virulent anxiety born from a fear of being out of control. But if they are to tap into deeper levels of meaning or larger concepts, the core lesson for those on this karmic path will be to release their need for the safety of being limited by structures of their own making. In the end, they will come to realize that the theoretical and spiritual are simply natural extensions of the physical and will become just as comfortable rearranging these more ethereal sides of life in better-designed, more useful ways as

they are with ordering their physical world.

If they are successful, what those on the Way of Extension will offer the world is an easier grasp of larger concepts or ideas, often spiritual or at least collective. The men and women on this karmic path can make the big picture accessible and useful to the "little guy." Whether they are involved in the creation of a theory of past lives and how reincarnation works, the application of economic concepts in the real world, the explication of how high finance really operates, or merely the embodiment of concepts such as feminism or democracy as a role model, those on the Way of Extension can make a large mark on the world. And almost always their ideas, systems of thought, and practical applications of theory are not designed for their benefit alone but for that of average men and women. As a result, those on this karmic path are apt to be embarrassed to discover themselves the objects of the affection and veneration of a large and welcoming audience of fans and devotees.

In their hearts, those born on the Way of Extension make the unlikeliest of gurus. But this is what they must become, for this karmic path requires that they learn to share their conceptual systems with others. Humble in the extreme, these souls are perhaps just the ones we others need to teach us a thing or two, since they are unlikely to succumb to ego inflation and all its unsavory side effects. All of the gifts

RELEASE

The fear of what you can't control

REWARD

The joy of giving understanding to others

given to these individuals from the outset (their feeling for structure, their dependability, and their service orientation) can be magnificent springboards for their life's work. The individuals on the Way of Extension are some of the most devoted in the Grand Cycle of Life. Frequently, it is their very devotion that causes them to move beyond themselves, since their first forays into spiritual realms or more universal ideas or philosophies often occur as a result of extending themselves on behalf of others.

The giving and sacrificing side of those born on the Way of Extension can, however, be their downfall. Too often they push themselves too hard in trying to serve their fellows or allow others to drain them of energy or otherwise take advantage of them. A healthy dose of looking out for number one is called for if these souls are to "go the distance" and truly make a mark on the world. They are, in fact, sensual people and must take care of their physical needs both for pleasure and in terms of their health. Moreover, as much as others want to cling to them, they need to be strict about setting aside a sufficient amount of time to be alone, as it is in solitude that they recharge and do their work. The demands of others can keep them locked in the mundane workings of life and prevent them from moving their minds and hearts into other realms. The irony is that to protect themselves, these individuals must often rely on the very routines or

SUGGESTION

Know your own self-imposed limitations and realize that they can be overcome.
Be aware of when you retreat into structure for safety. Protect your health.

structures this karmic path requires that they ultimately transcend! There is a subtle but important point, however: daily physical routines can be utilized to erect protective boundaries, but rigid structures of the mind and rote modes of thought must be overcome. Often with these men and women, an overly strict adherence to physical routines simply mirrors a crystallization of thinking and a dependence on mental structures. Once these individuals break their reliance on mental routines, the physical holds no more power and can safely be used as a tool to create health and well-being.

Since mental orientation is so crucial for these people, it is important for them to receive some form of guidance early in life on how to expand their worldview or thinking into more theoretical or creative paths. Of course, on this karmic path there is the potential to overreach, or even to be led astray by false doctrines, overly ambitious teachers, or illusory experiences. Those who intend to seek a full-blown religious or spiritual experience may have to remember to engage their practicality and healthy propensity for doubt. However, the Way of Extension is usually experienced in a highly personal or more solitary fashion. Joining formal religious or spiritual groups may occur, even with good results, but usually such organizations serve only a temporary purpose. The best companions or mates for those on this karmic path are like-minded others who strive for a broader or more spiritual experience in life. What is best for those on the Way of Extension is the

steady love and support of a few close associates with strong boundaries who will not be dependent or needy. Those on the Way of Extension must be free to experiment and to soar in the rarified atmosphere of their highly personal visionary experience. In return, their associates will have a devoted and generous friend or mate who provides them with a whole new way of seeing things.

Career crises are not uncommon on the Way of Extension. At some point in their lives, these men and women may be forced to confront their assumptions about the nature of fame, wealth, and power. Scaling back or even discarding their ambitions may be necessary for their continued spiritual growth. Eventually, a balance can be reached between the satisfaction of their material and spiritual needs. Participating in study and discussion groups is most beneficial to the men and women on the Way of Extension, since it will keep their thinking open to new ideas and concepts. Examining doctrines, weeding through theories, and discarding useless concepts while integrating others are all necessary on an ongoing basis if those on this karmic path are to distill and perfect their hard-won vision or theories.

BALANCE POINT

Physical and Spiritual

The image that comes to mind to describe the Way of the Extension is a tree. With its root system grounded deep within the earth, it orients its branch and leaf structures toward the life-giving energy of the sun. Simply by being alive, the tree converts sunlight and carbon dioxide into something everyone can use, life-giving oxygen.

CRYSTALS AND GEMSTONES

Moldavite stimulates the individual to consider realms beyond the mundane and, in fact, beyond this galaxy. This tektite assists in communicating complex ideas in a clear and accessible manner.

NOTABLES ON THIS KARMIC PATH

EDGAR CAYCE

Edgar Cayce remains one of America's most widely known and highly regarded psychics. His calling, like many on the Way of Extension, was to bring the metaphysical into daily life so it could be understood by everyone. Cayce did more than fourteen thousand individual psychic readings, many on health, that were recorded and catalogued. These are still being studied today, long after his death. Because of Cayce's work, difficult concepts such as reincarnation and prophecy were elucidated in a direct and simple way. His humble origins on a Kentucky farm gave him the grounded quality that others trusted so firmly when consulting him.

German novelist and poet **Hermann Hesse** shared his intense spirituality with the world through his numerous published works, thereby fulfilling the goal of his karmic path to structure metaphysical or theoretical ideas into a format easily understood by others. Rebellious and difficult in his youth, he rejected formal instruction in favor of self-education. Emerging from this experience with a new-found inner clarity, Hesse learned that periods of introspection can produce inspiration. In 1911,

HERMANN HESSE

Hesse applied this principle to his life, departing from his work and family to explore India and the subcontinent's shrouded mysticism. Hesse took his early immersion in Eastern philosophy and penned *Siddhartha*. Notable among Hesse's other works are *Steppenwolf, The Journey to the East,* and *The Glass Bead Game.*

Christian Science founder **Mary Baker Eddy** became divinely inspired when she was miraculously healed from chronic spinal disease after reading the New Testament. Eddy shared her personal experience of faith by training successful healers, writing books, holding public meetings, and founding both her own school and church. As a result, her message has reached countless individuals, and her *Christian Science Monitor* is one of the leading newspapers in America. By building a structure to reach out to others and spread her spiritual ideas, Eddy fulfilled her life purpose.

MARY BAKER EDDY

Other Notables: Beck, Chrissie Hynde, Queen Latifah, Dave Winfield, Sanford I. Weill, Philip Roth, Juan Perón, Theodore Roosevelt, George Burns, Yoko Ono, Mariah Carey, Queen Noor, Samuel Johnson, Jack LaLanne, Sting, John Cougar Mellencamp, Michael Caine, Quincy Jones, Uma Thurman, Louis Farrakhan, Naomi Campbell

---

BIRTHDAYS ON KARMIC PATH 22

September 30, 1895–February 17, 1896 | May 12, 1914–September 30, 1914

December 21, 1932–May 11, 1933 | August 3, 1951–December 21, 1951 | March 14, 1970–August 2, 1970

October 24, 1988–March 13, 1989 | June 5, 2007–October 24, 2007

KARMIC PATH
22

March 19–24

REBIRTH
PISCES–ARIES CUSP

Though gifted with more of an ability to formulate structure and implement their personal plans and ideals than they might otherwise have had, those born on the Cusp of Rebirth who travel this karmic path will have to take care that their structures do not become prisons nor their plans so ironclad that they are devoid of inspiration. In short, they have the potential for enormous success, but they will have to lose their all-or-nothing outlook for that potential to be fully realized. They should avoid the impulse to swing from intuitive inspiration to military decisiveness and discipline and instead seek to open the channels between the self and the divine through service to others. When their dreams start coming true, they will know they've got it right.

MARIAH CAREY
Pop singer
———
3/27/1970
Aries I

CHALLENGE: **TAPPING INTO THE MORE ELEMENTAL SIDE OF THEIR PERSONALITIES TO SERVE AS A GUIDE**
FULFILLMENT: **ENJOYING THEIR FLASHES OF INTUITIVE INSIGHT**
NOTABLE: **PHILIP ROTH (AUTHOR, *PORTNOY'S COMPLAINT*)**

March 25–April 2

THE CHILD
ARIES I

Embracing a sense of structure as a personal safety net may well be the principal pitfall for those born in the Week of the Child who navigate the challenge and promise of the Way of Extension, though they may also have a pronounced inclination to remain in a never-never land of overidealism and misplaced faith. Yet these individuals are essentially well suited to the challenges of this karmic path, especially when they turn their talents and energies to group endeavors or efforts. If they take care to bring the sense of inspiration, awe, and wonder that is so much a part of their spirituality to the creation of systems, structures, and methods that are readily understandable by others, their efforts will remind us that a sense of spirit can be accessed through even the most ordinary human efforts. And through that single gift, these personalities can transform the lives of those around them.

CHALLENGE: **ONCE IN A WHILE EMERGING FROM THEIR IVORY TOWERS LONG ENOUGH TO TEACH OTHERS**
FULFILLMENT: **ENGAGING IN DISCUSSION GROUPS**
NOTABLE: **EMILE ZOLA (FRENCH NOVELIST; INVOLVED IN DREYFUS AFFAIR)**

April 3–10

THE STAR
ARIES II

Those born in the Week of the Star must take special note of their own tendencies to frustration, loneliness, and emotional repression when they find themselves on the Way of Extension. In fact, these rather volatile people can misspend much of their energy in self-centered pursuits or trying to reach the top while ignoring the host of opportunities for development that present themselves along the way. Yet many of them will show a rare gift for service and more devotional pursuits and can successfully mute the demands of ego by giving themselves fully to a cause, project, movement, or religion. In fact, if they don't avoid the higher calling of this karmic path by getting mired in details, making themselves indispensible, or taking refuge in mere material order when a larger universe of fulfillment awaits them, they will reap great rewards.

ELIZABETH MONTGOMERY
Actress, *Bewitched*
———
4/15/1933
Aries III

CHALLENGE: **CULTIVATING GREATER HUMILITY OR DEVOTION**
FULFILLMENT: **GIVING THEMSELVES TO A CAUSE**

April 11–18

THE PIONEER
ARIES III

Those born in the Week of the Pioneer who travel this karmic path are destined to work out many of its challenges within the context of groups, family, or social organizations. Though a bit less modest than some others traveling this karmic path, in fact they do have quite a knack for bring order out of chaos. Providing they don't use their gift for creating structure as a means of imposing their ideas on others or as evidence of their moral superiority, they can realize great success. They are sure to develop the hopefulness called for, since their uniquely positive attitudes do much to offset some of the more narrow or pessimistic tendencies of this karmic path, while their inspirational style can serve to restore a sense of the spirit to others in even the most difficult or trying circumstances.

CHALLENGE: **CARVING OUT ENOUGH TIME TO BE ALONE**
FULFILLMENT: **SHARING THEIR IDEAS OR THEORIES WITH OTHERS**

April 19–24
POWER
ARIES–TAURUS CUSP

Those born on the Cusp of Power who find themselves traveling this karmic path may indeed have greatness thrust upon them in the course of their highly productive lives. Likely to be quite self-contained, responsible individuals, they will nevertheless have to work hard to avoid the dangers of self-satisfaction and complacency. Yet there is much to like about this configuration, especially in the areas of worldly service, spiritual devotion, and an innately honorable attitude toward larger and more universal themes. Though the arena of career and professional interests is likely to be the place where these personalities will work out the details of their destiny, others are bound to learn and be inspired by their example as their life path unfolds.

UMA THURMAN
Actress, *Pulp Fiction*

4/29/1970
Taurus I

CHALLENGE: **RECOGNIZING WHEN THEY HAVE BECOME A ROLE MODEL**
FULFILLMENT: **SENSING THE PERSONAL POWER THAT EXTENDING THEMSELVES BRINGS THEM**

April 25–May 2
MANIFESTATION
TAURUS I

Those born in the Week of Manifestation who travel the Way of Extension are likely to have a fine time. Blessed with the unique ability and talent to turn their visions into concrete reality, these personalities are likely to make great progress and enjoy substantial achievements on this life journey. Indeed, they have the formidable analytical gifts, fine minds, and patient hearts necessary for real success. In fact, there is likely to be very little that will hold them back, and as long as they do not retreat from the larger challenges of this karmic path by becoming involved in elaborate personal rituals, getting mired in boring routines, or being preoccupied with pinning down details at the expense of their own spiritual awareness, they will find both happiness and a sense of liberation.

CHALLENGE: **NOT BOGGING THEMSELVES DOWN WITH A STUBBORN INSISTENCE ON STICKING TO THE RULES**
FULFILLMENT: **GIVING SHAPE TO A LARGER CONCEPT**
NOTABLES: **ANDRÉ AGASSI (TENNIS PLAYER); CAROL BURNETT (ACTRESS/COMEDIAN, *THE CAROL BURNETT SHOW*); JEROME LIEBER (SONGWRITER); ALICE B. TOKLAS (COMPANION TO GERTRUDE STEIN)**

May 3–10
THE TEACHER
TAURUS II

Those born in the Week of the Teacher who find themselves treading the Way of Extension are likely to have a fine and fulfilling journey, especially when they employ their talent for analysis and discrimination and use it to illustrate and illuminate larger and more universal themes. Yet their highly critical natures, as well as their tendency to be demanding, can make them rather prickly characters, especially when their methods are challenged. Thus, an ability to cultivate modesty in the interest of achieving greater understanding and empathy for others will be especially important. Still, there is the promise of much success for these intrepid souls, especially when they learn to release their tendency to be self-protective or even pedantic in the interest of developing spiritual awareness.

JOE LOUIS
Boxing heavyweight champion, held longest reign

5/13/1914
Taurus III

CHALLENGE: **TEMPERING THEIR TENDENCY TO BE PATRONIZING**
FULFILLMENT: **EXPLAINING THEIR IDEAS TO OTHERS**
NOTABLES: **JOHNNY UNITAS (FOOTBALL PLAYER); WILLIAM HENRY VANDERBILT (RAILROAD DEVELOPER AND FINANCIER)**

May 11–18
THE NATURAL
TAURUS III

Those born in the Week of the Natural who travel the Way of Extension are likely to find great comfort and fulfillment along the way. Considerably less frustrated and rebellious than some born in this week, they will do best when they can apply their sense of system and structure in more tangible and less abstract ways. Thus, working with their hands, working with the land, and allowing their lives to unfold in environments where they can best make contact with important universal themes in the natural world will be especially beneficial. Likely to be less inclined to wrestle with issues of authority than many of their fellows, yet blessed with dauntless energy and a fine capacity for hard work, they can realize great contentment, peace, and achievement on this life journey.

CHALLENGE: **PLACING LESS EMPHASIS ON CAREER AND MORE ON MAKING A CONTRIBUTION**
FULFILLMENT: **PURSUING THE CHALLENGE OF EXTENDING THEIR IDEAS BEYOND ORDINARY LIMITS**
NOTABLES: **STEWART ALSOP (REPORTER/COLUMNIST); LOUIS FARRAKHAN (MUSLIM LEADER)**

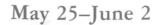

May 19–24
ENERGY
TAURUS–GEMINI CUSP

The feisty, energetic individuals born on this cusp who travel the Way of Extension may find it a somewhat uncomfortable fit until they reconcile their need for attention with the calling to higher spiritual understanding. Though admittedly more modest than some born in this week, they can nevertheless experience any number of conflicts, not the least of which is their resistance to the notion of anything that threatens their sense of independence. Too, they may be of the type whose plans are much discussed but rarely implemented, especially when they become preoccupied with telling others what to do or how to do it. If, however, they subsume their more egotistical energies through an awareness of others' needs, they will find that much of their personal insecurity falls away in the face of increasing higher awareness. Though they will always have a tendency to get hung up on rather petty concerns, cultivation of their intellectual and objective talents will ensure their success.

NAOMI CAMPBELL
Supermodel
———
5/22/1970
Taurus–Gemini Cusp

CHALLENGE: **DITHERING TOO MUCH OVER THE FINER POINTS**
FULFILLMENT: **DEVELOPING BETTER STRUCTURES FOR IMPLEMENTING THEIR IDEAS**
NOTABLE: **RICHARD GRANT WHITE (FATHER OF SANFORD)**

May 25–June 2
FREEDOM
GEMINI I

The individuals born in the Week of Freedom who find themselves on the Way of Extension may also find that their need for independence is at odds with the higher demands of this karmic path. Thus, a willingness to reconcile themselves to certain restrictions will be important to their soul's expansion and development. And, as with the character George Bailey in the classic film *It's a Wonderful Life*, there will be some rather difficult choices to make regarding the issues of personal freedom and responsibility. Nevertheless, their talent for keen analysis, formidable powers of observation, and fine common sense will stand them in wonderful stead. If they employ those powers to tap into the universal concepts and themes of this karmic path, they can serve as inspiring teachers, role models, and examples of personal fulfillment as they learn to bring practical systems to bear in the search for universal truths.

CHALLENGE: **APPLYING A BIT OF PRACTICALITY TO THEIR WEAKER PLANS OR SCHEMES**
FULFILLMENT: **DABBLING IN ALL MANNER OF HIGHER CONCEPTS AND THEORIES**

June 3–10
NEW LANGUAGE
GEMINI II

Though likely to to be much better organized and considerably less flaky than many of their fellows born in the Week of New Language, individuals with this configuration may have a difficult time coming to terms with its higher challenges. Thus, they may become mired in an increasing sense of insecurity or being misunderstood until they realize that the crux of their spiritual challenge is to help others comprehend themselves better. Gifted scholars and intellectuals, they can expect particular success in fields such as psychology, criticism, or the law, all of which will allow them to display and exercise their special verbal skills within established systems and structures. Though they may not be the brightest stars in their chosen spheres, they can nevertheless be among those who shine the longest as they journey along the Way of Extension.

LILLI PALMER
Actress,
The Boys from Brazil
———
5/24/1914
Taurus–Gemini Cusp

CHALLENGE: **BUILDING BETTER BRIDGES TO OTHERS FOR COMMUNICATING THEIR IDEAS**
FULFILLMENT: **PUTTING ON A BIT OF A SHOW WHEN THEY DESCRIBE THEIR IDEAS TO OTHERS**
NOTABLE: **RAOUL DUFY (FAUVIST PAINTER)**

June 11–18
THE SEEKER
GEMINI III

The individuals born in this week bring an admirable sense of adventure to the Way of Extension. Gifted with the ability to find truth in simplicity and to discover the gods who inspire spirituality in even the most ordinary circumstances, Gemini III's can make great progress along this karmic path, as long as they cultivate their greatest asset—an open mind. Nevertheless, their talent for system and structure may be expressed through good money management, thrift, and a high degree of personal efficiency. Since they are blessed with both the mental orientation and the yearning to overcome limitation that are in keeping with the higher challenges of this karmic path, they can find great success, providing they do not overreach themselves or fall victim to the notion that the grass is always greener somewhere else.

CHALLENGE: **NOT FORGETTING THAT DETAILS MATTER TOO**
FULFILLMENT: **ROAMING THE LOFTIER REALMS OF THEORY**

June 19–24

MAGIC
GEMINI–CANCER CUSP

The Way of Extension is likely to gift the souls born on this cusp with a greater degree of objectivity and personal perspective than they might otherwise have had, and its propensity for systems and structure may manifest itself in some highly developed management skills. Yet it is unlikely that these individuals will ever lose their aspirations toward higher understanding and universal acceptance. In fact, many with this configuration may manifest this path through devotion to religion, social service, and an almost mystical fascination with the impact of limits on our lives. In fact the principal danger is one of isolating themselves from others in the interest of maintaining their personal security. Though they may never be able to lessen their great sensitivity, if they allow their objectivity to assist them in the search for greater education and higher answers, their ability to rise beyond the mundane and into the realms of the divine will prove to be its own reward.

CHALLENGE: **REACHING OUT TO OTHERS TO SHARE WHAT THEY KNOW**

FULFILLMENT: **DEVOTING THEMSELVES TO SPIRITUALITY OR METAPHYSICS**

BABE DIDRICKSON ZAHARIAS
Golf legend, won 82 tournaments including 3 U.S. Women's Opens

6/26/1914
Cancer I

June 25–July 2

THE EMPATH
CANCER I

Those born in the Week of the Empath who travel the Way of Extension can make marvelous progress, providing they don't succumb to the demons of personal insecurity and chronic, or even neurotic, self-protection. Though some with this configuration may have to struggle to overcome extremes of sensitivity, shyness, or generally unmanageable and unstable emotions, they are gifted with greater objectivity and critical skills than they might otherwise have had. Thus, if they exalt their reasoning powers in higher learning and use their emotions to illuminate a larger sense of structure, they can make great progress along this life journey. It will, however, be especially critical for them to avoid codependent or unhealthy relationships and to cling only to those who would see them expand, rather than contract, their quest for transcendence.

CHALLENGE: **NOT GOING OVERBOARD AS THEY GO WITH THE FLOW**

FULFILLMENT: **COMBINING ANALYSIS WITH THEIR EMPATHIC ABILITIES**

NOTABLES: **CHRIS O'DONNELL (ACTOR, *SCENT OF A WOMAN*); LESTER FLATT (BLUEGRASS MUSICIAN, FLATT AND SCRUGGS)**

July 3–10

THE UNCONVENTIONAL
CANCER II

The souls born in the Week of the Unconventional who travel the Way of Extension may add some interesting wrinkles to its more ordinary modes of existence. In fact, these intriguing personalities can have quite a split between the quiet and unassuming face they present to the world and their rich, imaginative inner lives. Yet if they keep in mind that their more fantastic yearnings and aspirations represent a unique ability to contact the world of universal themes, spiritual reality, and higher consciousness, their journey is likely to be rich and well rewarded, especially when they gather the courage to show their truest colors through highly systematized presentations, well-thought-out plans, and elegantly executed designs.

CHALLENGE: **GUARDING AGAINST INVOLVING THEMSELVES WITH TOO MANY HANGERS-ON**

FULFILLMENT: **CALLING TO MIND ALL MANNER OF IMAGINATIVE LANDSCAPES AND THEN GIVING THEM FORM**

NOTABLES: **FRANZ BOAS (ANTHROPOLOGIST); WANDA LANDOWSKA (HARPSICHORDIST, TEACHER, REVIVALIST)**

BECK
Singer/songwriter,
Odelay

7/8/70
Cancer II

July 11–18

THE PERSUADER
CANCER III

The highly observant and powerfully persuasive individuals born in this week who travel the Way of Extension will nonetheless have to do a great deal of soul work to overcome their deep-seated feelings of insecurity and learn to transcend their sense of their own limitations as well as those of the people around them. In fact, many on this karmic path may be prone to adopting an overly moral attitude or displaying a pronounced tendency to be holier than thou. Still, if they relinquish some of their more manipulative aspects in the interest of higher awareness, they can offer the world a means of accessing the divine through a systematized approach to the powers of prayer, religious worship, and social work or other innovative and holistic philosophies that enable even the humblest person's natural power to access the eternal spiritual truths.

CHALLENGE: **NOT FALLING VICTIM TO AMBITION**

FULFILLMENT: **APPLYING THEIR CONSIDERABLE MANAGEMENT ABILITIES TO THE PRACTICAL APPLICATION OF THEIR IDEAS**

NOTABLES: **MARY BAKER EDDY (FOUNDER OF CHURCH OF CHRIST, SCIENTIST); HARRIET NELSON (ACTRESS, *OZZIE AND HARRIET*)**

July 19–25
OSCILLATION
CANCER–LEO CUSP

The souls born on this cusp who find themselves on the Way of Extension are gifted with a much higher degree of stability, fondness for structure, education, and discipline than they might otherwise have had. Thus they can make considerable progress, especially when they learn to consistently apply their passion to the search for higher systems of thought and greater self-realization. Though there are some whose principal limitation may consist of unruly or unmanageable emotions, extremes of temperament, or an inability to make decisions, far more will discover within themselves the ability to transcend even the worst of trials and tribulations and access the realms of higher awareness, free of insecurity and doubt. In fact, many of these people will hit upon new methods of managing their own extremes and, in doing so, will be able to systemize their approach to personal problems in such a way that the resulting knowledge can serve as a benefit to all.

CHALLENGE: **RECOGNIZING HOW THEIR NEED FOR SECURITY MAY INTERFERE WITH THEIR LIFE'S WORK**

FULFILLMENT: **CHALLENGING THEMSELVES TO GO TO THE NEXT STEP IN THEIR ENDEAVORS**

JENNIFER LOPEZ
Actress, *Selena*

7/24/1970
Cancer–Leo Cusp

July 26–August 2
AUTHORITY
LEO I

Those born in the Week of Authority who wend their way along this karmic path can experience wonderful fulfillment and enlightenment, providing they can overcome their tendency to be judgmental, inflexible, or unduly rigid in their dealings with others. The more service-oriented aspects of this configuration may prove a bit difficult for these naturally commanding personalities, however, and they will have to set aside issues of ego and personal gratification before they can realize the promise of this karmic path. Yet they have the potential for considerable success, especially when they cultivate their inner need to transcend the limits of ordinary reality in search of a higher cause or purpose. In short, their love of truth, moral courage, and natural faith in a higher set of authorities than their own will prove their key to fulfillment and enlightenment.

CHALLENGE: **TAKING CARE NOT TO ADHERE TOO RIGIDLY TO THEIR RULES OR PRINCIPLES**

FULFILLMENT: **ENJOYING THE CHALLENGE OF GROWING OUTWARD**

August 3–10
BALANCED STRENGTH
LEO II

If they take care that their tremendous powers of concentration, endurance, and tenacity do not allow them to lose sight of their higher goals and more spiritual aspirations, those born in the Week of Balanced Strength who travel the Way of Extension can find considerable happiness and fulfillment. In fact, their principal danger is that they may allow their need for established systems and structures or routines to become prisons of their higher self and obscure their view of more universal patterns and common experiences. Too, they have something of a masochistic tendency that can interfere with the development of personal security that is so necessary to their higher development, as they are capable of enduring a great deal with little reward but then collapsing into self-pity when rewards are not forthcoming. Yet if they can cultivate greater self-trust and work to counteract their more defensive habits, they can realize the promise of this karmic path and will doubtless enjoy any number of times when they contact the luminous by means of simple reverence and sincerity.

CHALLENGE: **OVERCOMING THEIR RIGIDITY**
FULFILLMENT: **HONING THEIR INTUITIVE CAPABILITIES**

PAUL RAND
Professor of graphic design at Yale, wrote *Thoughts on Design*

8/15/1914
Leo III

August 11–18
LEADERSHIP
LEO III

Excellent strategists and wonderful thinkers, the commanding personalities born in this week may nevertheless encounter a few stumbling blocks when placed on the Way of Extension. The modesty and adaptability called for by this karmic path are, however, very much at odds with their rather dictatorial tendencies, which are often coupled with an often rather narrow philosophical perspective. As they are gifted with rich administrative talents and a naturally expansive disposition, rising beyond their self-imposed limitations will generally come quite easily to them. The trick will be their ability to perceive and evaluate limitations first and to face facts squarely when they fail. Yet Leo III's can travel far on the Way of Extension as long as they do not allow their egos to stand in the way of their progress.

CHALLENGE: **NOT SLIPPING UP BY TAKING ON THE ROLE OF GURU OR OTHER SUPERIOR ASPECT**

FULFILLMENT: **PLAYING THE HERO BY GOING OUT INTO THE COSMOS ON BEHALF OF HUMANITY**

August 19–25

EXPOSURE
LEO–VIRGO CUSP

This is a configuration where the individuals involved will no doubt have greatness, or at least a measure of recognition for their efforts, more or less thrust upon them, and Leo–Virgos who travel the Way of Extension are therefore likely to have an interesting time. Yet the energies associated with these often secretive personalities and this karmic path are likely to prove quite compatible. If they are careful not to keep their light to themselves or to suppress their special gifts for perception of the inner systems and structures that govern all our lives, they can make great progress. Perhaps their single biggest danger is that they may retreat into the safety of their personal routines and rituals to such an extent that their impulse to expand or to transcend the ordinary falls by the wayside. Thus it will be important for them to keep in mind that service to others is the avenue by which they can successfully overcome their fears of the unknown. Once they understand that, they can serve as shining examples of spiritual generosity and personal achievement.

CHALLENGE: **BEING LESS RIGID IN THE WAYS THEY BELIEVE THEY MUST PUT THEIR IDEAS ACROSS**
FULFILLMENT: **PUTTING THEIR PERCEPTIVENESS TO WORK IN SERVICE OF A GREATER CAUSE**

QUEEN NOOR
Wife of King Hussein of Jordan

8/23/1951
Leo–Virgo Cusp

August 26–September 2

SYSTEM BUILDERS
VIRGO I

The highly efficient, well-organized individuals born in this week who travel the Way of Extension can realize commanding success along this life journey once they come to understand that not all structures are of their own making and that we are all, to some extent, dependent on the larger designs of the universe. The trick to attaining that higher level of realization will no doubt be their willingness to tap into the hidden forces at work in all of our lives. Thus, overcoming their natural skepticism and replacing it with a measure of faith will figure prominently in this journey, as will an ability to set aside the need to impose their beliefs on others and to use their special abilities to systematize knowledge in such a way that it illuminates, rather than obscures, the qualities of the divine.

CHALLENGE: **TACKLING THE ISSUE OF THE SOURCES OF THEIR ANXIETY**
FULFILLMENT: **ENJOYING THE ROLE OF TEACHER**
NOTABLE: **WILLIAM IV (KING OF ENGLAND; LAST MONARCH TO DISMISS A MINISTRY)**

September 3–10

THE ENIGMA
VIRGO II

If they can learn to distinguish between physical systems, designs or structures, and systems of thought, those born in the Week of the Enigma who travel the Way of Extension can realize great happiness and fulfillment. The trick will lie in learning that the laws of physical reality do not necessarily operate with the same predictable regularity or scientific precision as those that rule the realms of the unseen. Their spirituality may develop as an outgrowth of their affinity for beauty and sincere appreciation of the finer human characteristics. If these individuals build on their natural inclinations to integrity, discernment, and refinement, chances are that their efforts will result in increased spirituality and a belief system that is at peace with the idea of a larger design, while at the same time providing for the nuances of free will, growth, and ever-developing clarity.

CHALLENGE: **OVERCOMING THEIR DESIRE TO BE CRYPTIC**
FULFILLMENT: **GIVING VOICE TO BRAND-NEW CONCEPTS OR APPROACHES**
NOTABLES: **JULIE KAVNER (ACTRESS; VOICE OF MARGE SIMPSON ON THE SIMPSONS); DIXY LEE RAY (ZOOLOGIST; DEMOCRATIC GOVERNOR OF WASHINGTON); CHRISSIE HYNDE (ROCK SINGER, THE PRETENDERS)**

SAMUEL JOHNSON
English lexicographer/
author/critic/publisher

9/18/1709
Virgo III

September 11–18

THE LITERALIST
VIRGO III

Stubbornness can be the biggest downfall for those born in this week who make their way along this karmic path. Characterized by a kind of "show me" attitude toward the subtler forms of belief, they may become mired in a restrictive material reality until faith steps in to take a hand and illuminate the bigger picture and larger process. Thus, though there may be quite a few shake-ups along this road, all will serve to widen Virgo III's perceptions and open their hearts to the worlds of meaning that lie just outside the schedules, routines, and ironclad set of rules that often make up their lives. In fact, much of their seeming intransigence actually disguises sensitivity, indecision, and just plain fear of the unknown. Yet if these literal-minded people can learn to live in the moment and go with the flow, happiness will surely be theirs.

CHALLENGE: **DEVELOPING GREATER TOLERANCE AND OPEN-MINDEDNESS**
FULFILLMENT: **APPLYING THEIR SHARP INSIGHT AND KEEN DISCRIMINATION TO BROADER ISSUES**
NOTABLES: **ALLEN FUNT (PRODUCER/HOST, CANDID CAMERA); CLAYTON MOORE (TELEVISION ACTOR, LONE RANGER)**

September 19–24

BEAUTY
VIRGO–LIBRA CUSP

Chronic indecision may plague those born on this cusp who find themselves on the Way of Extension. Their need for structure, systems, and dependable routines can manifest itself in a preoccupation with appearances, the development of some rather superficial values, and an unwillingness to go within to get at the real reasons for their dependence on rules. Alternatively, they may resist the higher challenge of this karmic path and retreat into an ivory tower of isolation and a superior attitude toward the world and its vicissitudes. Yet at their core, these souls are quite inclined to spiritual pursuits, and if they do not allow their yearning for transcendence to manifest as mere escapism and at the same time remain alert to their tendency to erect false gods or worship false principles, they will find the right combination of transcendence and practical application that beckons along this life journey.

STING
Pop/rock singer/
songwriter, originally
with The Police

10/2/1951
Libra I

CHALLENGE: **TAKING THEIR EGOS TO TASK SO THEY CAN EXHIBIT THE DEVOTION CALLED FOR HERE**

FULFILLMENT: **PRIDING THEMSELVES ON THE ELEGANT CONSTRUCTIONS OF THEIR ARGUMENTS OR THEORIES**

September 25–October 2

THE PERFECTIONIST
LIBRA I

Those born in the Week of the Perfectionist who tread the Way of Extension will doubtless experience a lifelong struggle with obsession, compulsion, and a rather alarmist attitude toward those who dare to do things differently. In fact, many of these individuals feel disproportionately threatened by those who go outside the norm, and they will have to work hard to overcome their deep-seated insecurities or run the risk of becoming imprisoned by their own rigid standards. Greater tolerance and a more relaxed attitude will arise once they realize that their criticisms of others may well be a projection of their own fears of inadequacy. Their very thoroughness can enable them to realize tremendous achievement and rewards, especially when they allow their highest aspirations to unfold within the security of well-made, practical plans.

CHALLENGE: **NOT BECOMING A PRISONER OF THEIR OWN HIGH STANDARDS**

FULFILLMENT: **MEASURING THEIR WORDS TO BEST EXPRESS THEIR MORE METAPHYSICAL IDEAS**

NOTABLES: **MARK HAMILL (ACTOR, *STAR WARS*); JACK LALANNE (EARLY PROPONENT OF FITNESS; TV PERSONALITY)**

October 3–10

SOCIETY
LIBRA II

The individuals born in the Week of Society who travel the Way of Extension will have to take care that the road to their personal hell is not paved with good intentions. These folks can rather easily become overscheduled, overtaxed, and overextended as the result of their personal network and can quite easily fall victim to those who would take advantage of their better natures. Thus, many of those born in this week will need to withdraw from their many friends, family connections, and social interests to recharge and replenish their dissipated energies, go inward, and answer some of the higher challenges of this karmic path. Yet they have the potential for great success, especially when they find the delicate balance between adhering to established physical routines that allow for their growth, health, and development and freeing their minds to search for a set of higher truths and values.

JUAN PERÓN
Argentinean soldier and
president

10/8/1895
Libra II

CHALLENGE: **TAKING THE TIME TO ENGAGE IN SOLITARY MUSING**

FULFILLMENT: **DISCOVERING HIGHER REALMS OF CONSCIOUSNESS**

NOTABLES: **JOHN COUGAR MELLENCAMP (POP/ROCK SINGER); DAVE WINFIELD (BASEBALL OUTFIELDER); BUSTER KEATON (SILENT FILM STAR)**

October 11–18

THEATER
LIBRA III

Though considerably more modest and unassuming than many of their fellows born in this week, the charismatic personalities who populate the Week of Theater are no less multifaceted or complex. In fact, they will face the task of training and disciplining their many gifts, talents, and interests in order to obtain the higher level of realization promised by this karmic path, and may have to make a conscious decision to cultivate one aspect or gift at what may appear to be the expense of other interests. Inclined to be overcritical and rather demanding, they may misspend their energies in insisting that others do things their way before they have adequately established just what that consists of, and some may refuse responsibility altogether in an immature attempt to free themselves from their sense of limitation. Nevertheless, they have a great potential for achievement, for it is likely that their sheer talent and creativity will give them the tools they require to build a bridge to a higher sense of self.

CHALLENGE: **FOCUSING THEIR AREA OF INTEREST**

FULFILLMENT: **USING THEIR LEADERSHIP ABILITY TO TAKE A STAND OR MAKE A CONTRIBUTION**

NOTABLES: **DORIS HUMPHREY (MODERN DANCE PIONEER); TERRY MCMILLAN (AUTHOR, *WAITING TO EXHALE*)**

KARMIC PATH
22

October 19–25

DRAMA AND CRITICISM
LIBRA–SCORPIO CUSP

Providing they don't fall victim to the conceit that theirs is the only way of doing things, those born on the Cusp of Drama and Criticism can realize great happiness and success on this karmic path. Blessed with keen powers of observation, strong mental powers, and a formidable measure of horse sense, these souls not only can accurately perceive what needs to be done but will waste little time doing it. Talented and often creative in the extreme, they will doubtless find ways to express their special gifts in systematic and productive ways. In fact, their only real danger is that they will allow their talents and perceptions to become stale, uninspired, or otherwise mired down through a simple refusal to grow and embrace the opportunities that a bountiful universe is forever throwing in their direction.

CHALLENGE: **TEMPERING THEIR SENSE OF PERSONAL INFALLIBILITY**

FULFILLMENT: **REACHING INTO THE OTHER AND DRAWING OUT SOMETHING WHOLLY INNOVATIVE**

DESIDERIUS ERASMUS
Dutch scholar and leading humanist of Renaissance era

10/28/1466
Scorpio I

October 26–November 2

INTENSITY
SCORPIO I

Scorpio I's who travel the Way of Extension may have a rather rough ride until they release some of their more suspicious tendencies and find the road to higher awareness through devotion and service to others. Though they may often seem selfish, Scorpio I's nevertheless have a great capacity for empathy and are quite sensitive to the plight of the less fortunate. Also possessed of a surprising degree of intuition, they can anticipate others' needs and desires to a surprising degree, then address them in an often unassuming yet practical manner. Thus, they make truly devoted friends and lovers, and though they may never entirely free themselves from the expectation of reward, some with this configuration will discover that the path to transcendence will come as a result of aligning themselves with intensely personal relationships, religious activities, or deeply committed social pursuits.

CHALLENGE: **GRAPPLING WITH THEIR FEELINGS OF INSECURITY AND SUSPICION**

FULFILLMENT: **SURRENDERING THEMSELVES TO SOMETHING GREATER**

NOTABLE: **JULIAN SCHNABEL (NEOEXPRESSIONIST ARTIST)**

November 3–11

DEPTH
SCORPIO II

The profound and intriguing personalities born in this week who travel the Way of Extension may be a curious combination of personal humility and undue fanaticism. In any event, these people have a well-defined moral code and rather strict standards of behavior, and once the rules have been transgressed by others, it's unlikely they will be inclined to either forgive or forget. Yet their very rigidity can be their downfall, and these souls would do well to cultivate a willingness to change. At the same time, there exists with this configuration an all-or-nothing attitude that can result in their being bound to unhealthy addictions, on the one hand, and escapism, on the other. In any event, these personalities will have to work hard to find the balance point between acceptable structure and too much freedom. For all that, they are likely to move beyond themselves through devotion to others. When illuminated through love and being loved in return, these souls can realize tremendous fulfillment.

CHALLENGE: **EXAMINING THEIR ADDICTIONS, INCLUDING THAT TO WORK**

FULFILLMENT: **BEING GIVEN THE CHANCE TO SHOW WHAT THEY KNOW**

NOTABLES: **LOU FERIGNO (BODY BUILDER; ACTOR); ELIJAH PARISH LOVEJOY (JOURNALIST; ABOLITIONIST)**

THEODORE (TEDDY) ROOSEVELT
26th U.S. president; conservationist

10/27/1858
Scorpio I

November 12–18

CHARM
SCORPIO III

Highly organized and efficient, those born in the Week of Charm who travel the Way of Extension are likely to be at their best when working behind the scenes, inspiring others, and contributing their unique, graceful, and rather elegant concepts of system and structure to their homes, families, and business organizations. One way or another, these people are bound to have a better plan and be better at implementing that plan than almost anyone else. Perhaps their only real sticking point will be their inability or unwillingness to face their own feelings, which in turn may give rise to some rather pointless and self-destructive preoccupations until they face the emotions that lie at the root of their discontent. Yet once they comprehend the higher task of employing their unique administrative and organizational abilities to build the bridge to higher consciousness and greater faith in universal law, they can find great happiness.

CHALLENGE: **BREAKING THEIR STUBBORN PERSISTENCE IN THEIR BAD HABITS**

FULFILLMENT: **FLOWING, QUITE PEACEFULLY, WITH LIFE**

November 19–24
REVOLUTION
SCORPIO–SAGITTARIUS CUSP

Those born in this period who navigate this karmic path are in for an interesting process of development. In fact, the revolution they create with this configuration may well be their own—quiet and personal, perhaps, but no less a revolution for its profound impact on the individuals involved. Blessed with a greater sense of structure and better organizational abilities that many of their fellows, these personalities may nevertheless have to get in touch with their need to be free, and the resulting choices may well result in some astonishing transformations in lifestyle, relationships, and career choices. Otherwise, they face the danger of becoming rigid, inflexible, or simply stuck in traditions and habits not their own. Thus, higher education, philosophical expansion, and faith in their own sense of the future will allow them to objectively evaluate the limitations of the past in order to face the future with renewed hope.

CHALLENGE: **FREEING THEMSELVES FROM THEIR PECULIAR BRAND OF PETTY TYRANNY**

FULFILLMENT: **DREAMING UP SCHEMES AND PLANS THAT WILL "ROCK THE WORLD"**

BUCKY DENT
Baseball player, New York Yankees

———

11/25/1951
Sagittarius I

November 25–December 2
INDEPENDENCE
SAGITTARIUS I

Though much better able to cope with the restrictions and limitations imposed by ordinary life than some of their fellow Sagittarians, these souls will have to come to terms with the fact that their need for freedom and transcendence is an asset rather than a liability as they make their way along this karmic path. Too often, insecurity may cause them to discount many of their own better impulses, and the resulting sense of frustration or of "life's passing them by" can have unfortunate repercussions on their further development. Simple stubbornness is the biggest fault of many of these individuals, and it will be important for them to remain open to the world of expanded possibilities that beckon. Still, their ability to cooperate, to observe, and to hitch their wagon to the proverbial star will serve to buoy them along this life journey.

CHALLENGE: **FINDING THE MIDDLE GROUND BETWEEN FREEDOM AND RESPONSIBILITY**

FULFILLMENT: **RECOGNIZING PATTERNS IN CHAOS OR CONFUSION**

NOTABLE: **BUSBY BERKELEY (CHOREOGRAPHER AND FILM DIRECTOR; KNOWN FOR MUSICALS)**

December 3–10
THE ORIGINATOR
SAGITTARIUS II

Practical and useful application of spiritual knowledge will likely come easily to Sagittarius II's who travel the Way of Extension. Yet they will have to work extremely hard to overcome their feelings of inferiority and insecurity if they are to function at their most effective levels. Gifted with great intelligence and originality, they will doubtless specialize in finding new approaches to old problems or putting an entirely different spin on information that others take for granted. Cultivating greater objectivity will therefore be especially useful, as will the ability to release their fears of being rejected or misunderstood. These individuals will work out their destiny within a relatively secure and manageable context as long as they do not become overly dependent on those they trust and love. They can make great progress along this karmic path, especially when they display their gifts in a technical, scientific, or research-oriented environment.

CHALLENGE: **TEMPERING ANY RESENTMENT OF OTHERS' DEMANDS**

FULFILLMENT: **ORIGINATING A NEW WAY OF LOOKING AT SOMETHING**

NOTABLES: **GARY ROSSINGTON (LYNARD SKYNARD GUITARIST); ANNA FREUD (PSYCHOANALYST; DAUGHTER OF SIGMUND)**

GEORGE VI
King of England during WWII

———

12/14/1895
Sagittarius III

December 11–18
THE TITAN
SAGITTARIUS III

Though likely to be blessed with a higher degree of realism, a more down-to-earth attitude, and a better sense of planning than some others born in this week, the souls born in the Week of the Titan who find themselves on this karmic path will nevertheless have to face down the demons of personal insecurity, an overriding need for recognition, and hubris before they can operate at their most effective. Though likely to be quite dependable and nurturing, they may nevertheless manifest the restrictions of this karmic path by refusing to adapt to more ordinary lives and conditions, power tripping, or having a tendency to chronic fussiness. Still, they have the philosophical inclinations and generosity of spirit to aspire to transcendence and a higher level of understanding, whatever the circumstances of their lives. As long as they do not seek to overcome their limitations by overwhelming others or forcing issues, they have the ability to serve with an open heart and an open mind.

CHALLENGE: **TAKING CARE NOT TO BE LED ASTRAY BY FALSE DOCTRINES**

FULFILLMENT: **WRAPPING THEIR PRODIGIOUS MENTAL ABILITIES AROUND LARGE CONCEPTS**

December 19–25

PROPHECY
SAGITTARIUS–CAPRICORN CUSP

Those born on the Cusp of Prophecy can make an indelible mark on the Way of Extension, yet they will have to work hard to overcome their innate fear or suspicion of what be may in fact be their greatest asset: their intuition. Though many with this configuration may retreat from the higher challenges of this karmic path through refusing to come to terms with their own extrasensory gifts and engage in a never-ending effort to superimpose structure on their lives at the expense of their higher spiritual awareness, many others will successfully establish routines and personal rituals that allow them to feel safe and at the same time encourage the further development of their talents. Too, the process of emerging from the self-protective shell that surrounds these people may take years of encouragement. Yet when they do emerge, they will doubtless be able to share not only their special brand of insight but a number of methods for the practical application of extrasensory talent.

CHALLENGE: **COMING TO TERMS WITH THEIR AMBITION**
FULFILLMENT: **SHOWING OTHERS HOW TO USE THEIR INTUITION OR EXTRASENSORY PERCEPTION**

SUSAN SONTAG
Influential contemporary
American critic/novelist

———
1/16/1933
Capricorn III

December 26–January 2

THE RULER
CAPRICORN I

Those born in the Week of the Ruler who travel the Way of Extension are likely to be quite happy on this life journey. Dependable, pragmatic, and reliable in the extreme, they are capable of organizing their emotions and spiritual impulses in highly efficient and effective ways. There is a danger, however, that their need for safety and self-protection will manifest itself in some highly intolerant attitudes and an unwillingness to leave themselves open to the wider world of experience. Repressed emotion may also be something of a problem. Yet it will doubtless be the impulse to get in better touch with what makes them tick that will spark their search for higher spiritual truths, concepts, and realities. At their best, these people will have a profound understanding of the human condition that exalts the strengths of the common man yet tolerates his weaknesses. At their worst, they will be inflexible, demanding, and uninterested in anything that fails to provide for their own protection and safety.

CHALLENGE: **GRAPPLING WITH EMOTIONAL BLOCKAGES THAT KEEP THEM FROM MOVING OUT OF THEMSELVES**
FULFILLMENT: **RECOGNIZING THAT THERE IS MORE THAN MEETS THE EYE IN EVERYDAY REALITY**
NOTABLE: **JOE ORTON (BRITISH DRAMATIST)**

January 3–9

DETERMINATION
CAPRICORN II

Those born in the Week of Determination who find themselves navigating the challenge and promise of the Way of Extension are likely to realize great progress and considerable achievement. Reaching for the heights, overcoming obstacles, and transcending the limits of the ordinary in the interest of contacting higher dreams and higher realms come quite naturally to these dauntless, dependable souls. Too, they are gifted with a strong inclination toward theoretical and metaphysical concerns that will stand them in wonderful stead. Able to share the joys and sorrows of daily existence in a spirit of sustained effort and quiet understanding, they will doubtless realize great achievement, sincere appreciation of their efforts, and wonderful progress on this life journey.

JOHN DOS PASSOS
Novelist and war
correspondent

———
1/14/1896
Capricorn III

CHALLENGE: **OVERCOMING THEIR DEPENDENCE ON PHYSICAL ROUTINES**
FULFILLMENT: **DARING TO REACH FOR THEIR HOPES AND ASPIRATIONS**
NOTABLE: **ANDRÉ MASSON (SURREALIST ARTIST)**

January 10–16

DOMINANCE
CAPRICORN III

Blessed with tremendous diligence and dedication, those born in the Week of Dominance who find themselves on the Way of Extension can realize much personal expansion and higher awareness, providing they do not succumb to their need to control their circumstances and those of the people around them through ironclad rules or inflexible standards of behavior. Conversely, they have a tendency to sacrifice their own needs in service to others, and many on this karmic path may find their energies drained and their strengths sapped by overly needy friends and family members who claim to be unable to get by without their strong shoulders to lean on. At some point along the way, their sense of frustration may provide the springboard they need to open themselves up to enlightenment. If they can rise to the challenge, the resulting enlightenment will cause them to move beyond themselves and make necessary, if rather systematic, forays into the world of the infinite.

CHALLENGE: **SACRIFICING THEIR HARSHER JUDGMENTS OR STANDARDS FOR A HIGHER CAUSE**
FULFILLMENT: **EXPRESSING THEIR MORE RADICAL VIEWS**

January 17–22

MYSTERY AND IMAGINATION
CAPRICORN–AQUARIUS CUSP

Try as they may to control their wilder and more unpredictable side through stifling routines, boring personal rituals, or an ironclad set of personal standards, those born on the Cusp of Mystery and Imagination who travel the Way of Extension will nevertheless be unable to resist the urge to fly in the face of conventional wisdom and seek contact with the higher level of spiritual awareness that is already so much a part of their makeup. Should they resist that impulse, however, they may encounter disruptive influences at work in their lives. While the element of unpredictability may cause them to distrust their own judgment, it should instead be embraced as the avenues of greater spiritual awareness open up for them. If Capricorn–Aquarians make an effort to stay in touch with their richly imaginative side and understand that occasionally, at least, personal upsets are the harbingers of growth, they can take great and impressive strides along the road.

GEORGE BURNS
Comedian/actor

1/20/1896
Capricorn–Aquarius Cusp

CHALLENGE: **NOT REQUIRING OTHER PEOPLE TO KEEP THEM IN LINE OR IN BALANCE**

FULFILLMENT: **INFUSING THEIR MORE ECCENTRIC VIEWS WITH A BIT OF DRAMA**

January 23–30

GENIUS
AQUARIUS I

Those born in the Week of Genius who find themselves on the Way of Extension have an enormous potential for success, happiness, and achievement, as this karmic path gifts them with stability and the capacity to stick to even the most painstaking tasks and routines. Yet there is a danger that they will become too fixed in their attitudes and fearful of change and thus fail to attach themselves to the larger issues and more universal human concerns that are part of the higher calling of this karmic path. Though blessed with a great sensitivity to the less fortunate, they may refuse all manner of personal responsibility or go overboard in their urge for transcendence, displaying a distaste for involvement in the day-to-day working out of their pet theories or practical application of their systems. Yet if they stay grounded in the here and now, and follow their star, they can find great fulfillment and reward.

CHALLENGE: **TAKING TIME OUT TO RELAX AND REFLECT**
FULFILLMENT: **CHANNELING THEIR LIGHTNING-QUICK ANALYSES INTO A COHERENT AND EASILY UNDERSTOOD FORM OF EXPRESSION**
NOTABLE: **LOUIS RUKEYSER (TELEVISION PERSONALITY; ECONOMIC COMMENTATOR)**

January 31–February 7

YOUTH AND EASE
AQUARIUS II

Quite a few ordinary heroes can be found among those born in this week who journey along the Way of Extension. Quite accomplished, naturally admired, and refined, these individuals nevertheless like to be left alone to do their own thing and make their own plans. Accomplished craftsmanship, extraordinary technique, and great proficiency will likely characterize most of their endeavors. Yet personal insecurity, defensiveness, and self-doubt can all serve to hinder their higher development, and some may become quite dependent on appreciation, popularity, or others' opinions of them. The most advanced of these souls will become neither preoccupied with a need to toe the line nor detached in a careless and irresponsible attitude toward the needs of others. If they don't retreat in unawareness or isolate themselves for fear of not living up to others' expectations, they will rank among not only the most popular but the most effective people on this karmic path.

CORAZON AQUINO
Philippine president

1/25/1933
Aquarius I

CHALLENGE: **NURTURING THEIR PHYSICAL NEEDS MORE**
FULFILLMENT: **OVERCOMING ALL FORMS OF LIMITATION WITH EASE**
NOTABLE: **ANASTASIO SOMOZA (NICARAGUAN DICTATOR; ASSASSINATED)**

February 8–15

ACCEPTANCE
AQUARIUS III

Inclined to activity, movement, and at least the trappings of variety, those born in the Week of Acceptance who travel the Way of Extension may be quite preoccupied, overly busy, and entirely too wrapped up in their own agenda to come to terms with some of the higher challenges of this karmic path. Though unlikely to become overly mired in routines, ironclad rules, or set regulations for their own behavior, they may seek to impose restrictions and ideas on others. The result can be highly prejudicial or intolerant attitudes that will need to be overcome in order for them to be truly effective. Yet their simple and unabashed curiosity is likely to be their saving grace. Their strong mental orientation, natural objectivity, and an openness to new ideas should be given full play in study, education, and discussion. The resulting exchange of ideas and concepts will feed their spirits and nourish their aspirations toward transcendence and a more concrete and practical notion of universal love.

CHALLENGE: **REMEMBERING ALWAYS TO KEEP AN OPEN MIND**
FULFILLMENT: **DEVOTING THEMSELVES TO THEIR "HIGHER EDUCATION"**
NOTABLE: **KIM NOVAK (ACTRESS, VERTIGO)**

February 16–22

SENSITIVITY
AQUARIUS–PISCES CUSP

These individuals may have to do a great deal of soul searching, restructuring, and rethinking before they can come to terms with the defensive attitudes that may be holding them back from higher understanding. Until that time, they may seek to submerge their own anxieties in work, obsessive love interests, or an excess of family responsibilities that may take up their time but do little to nourish their spirit. Too, there are some on this karmic path who may have to scale back their ambitions, their notions of success, and their expectations of others before they can realize true fulfillment. Yet if they don't succumb to the demons of pessimism, isolation, and chronic insecurity and develop the necessary objectivity to perceive the larger patterns of the universe and align themselves with higher ideas of spirituality, they can do much to surpass and release many of their self-imposed limitations.

YOKO ONO
Avant-garde artist;
married John Lennon

2/18/1933
Aquarius–Pisces Cusp

CHALLENGE: **UNTANGLING THE SOURCES OF THEIR ANXIETIES**
FULFILLMENT: **GOING AS FAR OUT AS THEY WISH IN THEIR THINKING, BUT ALSO REMEMBERING TO COME BACK AGAIN**

February 23–March 2

SPIRIT
PISCES I

Though considerably less earthbound than many of their fellows on the Way of Extension, Pisces I's will nevertheless have to avoid being irresponsible, on the one hand, or entirely too self-sacrificing, on the other. Many of these individuals have a pronounced tendency to promise much more than they can deliver and may turn their resulting feeling of failure back on themselves in a continuing cycle of self-negation, while others may be characterized by a high-handed or holier-than-thou attitude that serves as a very effective disguise for their deep-seated insecurities. Yet if they make a conscious effort to achieve a balance between their material and spiritual needs, they can recognize the highest level of achievement, fulfillment, and happiness and will serve as shining examples of just what it means to live well by doing good.

CHALLENGE: **NOT LETTING OTHERS TAKE ADVANTAGE OF THEM**
FULFILLMENT: **DEVOTING THEMSELVES TO SHARING WHAT THEY KNOW**

March 3–10

THE LONER
PISCES II

Though blessed with a deeply soulful side, a natural depth of understanding, and a highly spiritual nature, those born in the Week of the Loner who travel the Way of Extension may see their best insights go unrecognized and their best intentions unappreciated until they make a greater effort to emerge from their shell and share their wealth of knowledge with those most in need. Their tendency toward isolation, pessimism, and disappointment is quite strong, and many of these souls will become lost in their own sense of suffering before they come to terms with the true nature of their self-imposed limitation. Though needing to be accepted and gifted with a practical side that will stand them in good stead, they will have to come to terms with the idea that greater freedom is not only possible but necessary to their higher spiritual advancement.

QUINCY JONES
Songwriter/musician/
producer

3/14/1933
Pisces III

CHALLENGE: **NOT GETTING BOGGED DOWN IN DETAILS OUT OF FEAR OF THE BIGGER PICTURE**
FULFILLMENT: **LEARNING HOW TO GO WITH THE FLOW**

March 11–18

DANCERS AND DREAMERS
PISCES III

Those born in the Week of Dancers and Dreamers who travel the Way of Extension are likely to become preoccupied with the higher truths and universal mysteries that govern all of our lives. Their unique combination of vision and practicality creates a kind of alchemy that is hard to beat, though some with this configuration may fall victim to their own need to be needed and should take care that their more devotional qualities do not manifest in codependent, unhealthy, or otherwise addictive behaviors and relationships. Yet if these personalities can adjust themselves to the fact that it is through modesty and service that even the humblest of us will ultimately be exalted, their contributions to the world of higher thought, well-developed theory, and practical application of spiritual principles will have a far-reaching impact.

CHALLENGE: **NOT SUCCUMBING TO THEIR OWN WANDERLUST**
FULFILLMENT: **SPENDING TIME WITH THEMSELVES**
NOTABLES: **JOSEPH STOLLER (SONGWRITER; WROTE MANY OF ELVIS PRESLEY'S HITS); SANFORD WEILL (BUSINESS EXECUTIVE, SHEARSON/LEHMAN BROS., PRIMERICA CORP.); QUEEN LATIFAH (RAP STAR; ACTRESS)**

The Way of Devotion

VIRGO II TO PISCES II
Enigma to Loner

In some ways, the Way of Devotion is more of a calling than a karmic path. Those born to it must find someone or something to which they can devote their lives. Sacrifice is no stranger to those on this karmic path, since the devotion required of the individuals on it is uncompromising. The men and women born to the Way of Devotion tend to be somewhat enigmatic and solitary. Loners, they are fond of puzzling over conundrums or philosophies at length. Sometimes this is merely their way of sorting through what matters to them. Soulful and sensitive, the men and women on this karmic path may have to search far and wide for the object of their devotion before they find it. Once they do, they will spend the rest of their lives giving themselves unselfishly to their personal divinity. This can take many forms, and whether it be religion or devotion to a cause, an artistic muse, a principle, or another person, those born to the Way of Devotion must be resilient and courageous in their struggle to give their all to their choice. In addition, although they are some of the most solitary people in the Grand Cycle of Life, their single-minded attention to their cause and their consecration of themselves to the task at hand will inspire others, who will shower them with admiration and crown them with a kind of iconic or larger-than-life persona, so that they often become public figures.

> ### CORE LESSON
> Being able to hear what their hearts are telling them
>
> ### GOAL
> To find a person, cause, principle, or deity to which they can unreservedly devote themselves

> ### GIFTS
> Discriminating, Sensitive, Humorous
>
> ### PITFALLS
> Suffering, Overexacting, Fantasy-prone

While the process involved in following all of the karmic paths in this volume is symbolic of the archetypal hero's journey—one often involving a quest, a loss, and redemption—more than any other, the Way of Devotion embodies this archetype. For the men and women on this karmic path, progress on this path usually begins as they embark on a spiritual search, often prompted by the sense that something is missing from their lives. This karmic journey can be likened to that of Parsifal and his quest for the Holy Grail: he begins his journey seeking one thing, but the journey becomes the process, and in the end he finds something quite different. Any hero's saga involves two essential elements: first, that the hero be unique among his peers in some way, and second, that he undergo a significant struggle, all the while exhibiting strength, courage, and conviction. Unusual individuals, those on the Way of Devotion are well aware that they are different from those around them, and, not uncommonly, they suffer social rejection at some point in their lives. Meanwhile, struggle is built into the life fabric of those on this karmic path. Not only coping with everyday exigencies but also attempting to make sense of life itself is a constant occupation for these individuals.

Luckily, those born to the Way of Devotion are born with highly discriminating minds that will help them make the right choices as they make their way through life. However,

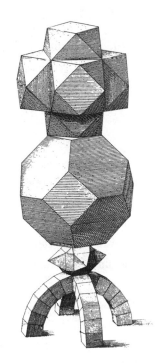

though discrimination can help them grapple with the practicalities of existence, it cannot give them the answers that they are, at bottom, seeking. Only by recognizing and acknowledging what it is that they love can those on this karmic path begin to apply the kind of devotion it calls for. Joseph Campbell wrote, "The hero is the man of self-achieved submission." "Submission to what?" one might ask. Answering this question is at the heart of the Way of Devotion. Ultimately, the answer should be "something of higher value." The core lesson for those on this karmic path is to discover and devote themselves to their heart's desire. Born worriers, they will analyze and ponder any issue ad infinitum. Living in their heads prevents them from acknowledging the most important thing of all: what their hearts are telling them. Only there does the secret of their life path reside; no amount of mental gamesmanship will reveal it. These are individuals who prefer not to look too deeply within for fear of what they might find. But it is only through such a process and by acknowledging their true feelings, that their path, their destiny, and their life's work will be revealed.

The struggles required by this karmic path, both inward and outward, are considerable. Initially, the inward struggle will demand that those on this path live a very private, even reclusive life for a time. During this period they will process their family-of-origin issues, reexamining childhood scripts that made them feel unwanted or

RELEASE

The tendency to self-pity

REWARD

The joy of following your heart

unloved, learn to drop self-critical attitudes, and free themselves of any negative thought patterns. Directing their energy toward inner psychological work and unraveling their personal problems can result in great self-knowledge. Their innate problem-solving ability will help them greatly in this phase of the journey.

Once the inner journey has been initiated and an object of veneration settled upon, those on the Way of Devotion can begin to make forays into the outside world. It is important for them to do so, as they can easily become stuck in their inner lives. When they do emerge, it is usually only because they must do so if they are to give themselves wholly to their cause—though even so it is likely that they will walk a rather solitary road. No strangers to sacrifice, they may be required to give up a great deal for their higher calling. Positively, humor comes easily to these souls and will be quite a comfort on this journey, particularly during times of suffering. Those on this karmic path know something about pain. This instills in them tremendous empathy for the suffering of others and is the reason so many of them are found serving the less fortunate or inspiring compassion in others. The main pitfall for those on the Way of Devotion is that an experience of suffering may devolve into self-pity. Less evolved souls risk becoming mired in this type of self-centeredness. Keeping a positive attitude and utilizing humor to lift one's spirits whenever possible are crucial.

SUGGESTIONS

Avoid worry. Learn to relax and let things be. Pay attention to your feelings. Acknowledge your mission.

Often, those on this karmic path are viewed by many as mysterious or as dreamers. Most people can't quite figure them out. Thus, others often project larger-than-life qualities onto them. Moreover, because the Way of Devotion is so closely aligned to the archetypal hero's journey, those who successfully navigate this karmic path often take on such mythic proportions in the minds of others that they come to be viewed as heroes themselves. What's more, this role of icon is not an entirely comfortable one for them. They never feel part of the mainstream, and, though they will grudgingly accept the type of hero worship that is directed toward them, will tend to keep themselves aloof and withdrawn interpersonally. Thus, friendships and a job that brings them into contact with their fellow human beings in more intimate ways can be of extreme importance to maintaining a healthy balance between their spiritual and more worldly concerns. They are born, however, with a certain tendency toward guardedness and mistrust, and should these gain the upper hand, they may be hopelessly precluded from normal social interaction.

Friends and lovers of those on the Way of Devotion can attest to their capacity for intimacy and the affection they are capable of lavishing on those they care for, since in more personal relations their devoted nature takes on a particularly beautiful form. However, sacrifice is part of this karmic path, and nothing pains those born

to it more than the need to put their cause, religion, or principles above their personal needs and the needs of others. Love affairs, marriages, and friendships that end in this way leave them deeply hurt and are likely to create a resolve not to get involved again at such a profound level, if only to protect those they love. They may come to rely heavily on parents, siblings, and other relatives to supply the affection and emotional support they so desperately crave. On rare occasions, those on the Way of Devotion will find their lives dedicated to another human being, such as when a spouse, child, or other family member suffers from a major illness or debilitating physical condition. Sometimes those on this karmic path will devote themselves to furthering the career or life purpose of another. Care should be taken to determine whether such a situation is a true "calling" or simply an unnecessary sacrifice of self.

Those on the Way of Devotion are not unlike Theseus, prince of Athens and a hero of Greek mythology, who had to go into the Cretan Labyrinth to face the Minotaur, much as those on this karmic path must face the puzzle of their own psyche and the monsters that reside therein. With the help of Ariadne, Theseus escaped from the Labyrinth, but he was forced to sacrifice his love for her as he continued on his quest. Theseus became known for fighting for democracy and against injustice and ultimately, through his devotion to his cause, united the city-states around Athens into a democratic union.

BALANCE POINT

Selfishness and Sacrifice

CRYSTALS AND GEMSTONES

Sugilite connects individuals to their reason for existence and supports the feeling of having a mission. This stone reveals methods of embodying the divine in human form.

 NOTABLES ON THIS KARMIC PATH

SALLY RIDE

Overachiever **Sally Ride** became the first American woman to venture into space. Though she withdrew from Swarthmore College to become a tennis professional, destiny later dictated that she continue her course of study at Stanford University. The devotion with which she then focused on her astrophysics curriculum was in many ways responsible for her being selected from thousands of applicants for space travel. Though initially misdirected, Ride (like many on this path) subsequently found her calling and gave herself to it totally.

GLENN GOULD

Canadian pianist **Glenn Gould** epitomized both the positive and negative aspects of this karmic path. Though he was often described as sensitive and funny (conductor George Szell dubbed him "a nut"), he preferred a solitary existence. Gould internalized the suffering associated with an exacting devotion, and through this concentration became a musical genius. Characteristic of this path, he eventually withdrew from public life and gave up performing for an audience. However, it was during this time that he recorded some of his most provocative and breathtaking work.

Ice cream gurus **Ben Cohen** and **Jerry Greenfield** have displayed considerable devotion to the quality of their product as well as to their employees and the environment. Beginning in a Vermont gas station, the childhood friends have succeeded against all odds in an overcrowded and highly

BEN COHEN & JERRY GREENFIELD

competitive market. Despite this success, these social activists have remained dedicated to their community and are still visible in local affairs. Ben and Jerry have discovered great joy in following their hearts' desire and have thereby achieved something of higher value.

Other Notables: Sean "Puffy" Combs, Octavio Paz, Stevie Wonder, Dorothea Nutzhorn Lange, Sir Alec Guinness, Charles Pierre Baudelaire, Janis Ian, Max Planck, Tyrone Power, Anatoli Karpov, Anjelica Huston, Huey Lewis, R. Buckminster Fuller, Alexandre Dumas Père, Peter O'Toole, Melvin Van Peebles, Antonia Fraser, Patsy Cline, Bobby Brown, Louis Malle, Friedrich Engels, Don King, Pablo Casals, Gypsy Rose Lee, William Burroughs, John Ford, Willy Brandt, Sir Richard Burton, Willa Cather, George I, Gurdjieff, Jiddu Krishnamurti

---

BIRTHDAYS ON KARMIC PATH 23

May 11, 1895–September 29, 1895 | December 21, 1913–May 11, 1914

August 2, 1932–December 20, 1932 | March 14, 1951–August 2, 1951 | October 24, 1969–March 13, 1970

June 4, 1988–October 23, 1988 | January 14, 2007–June 4, 2007

KARMIC PATH
23

March 19–24

REBIRTH
PISCES–ARIES CUSP

The personalities born on this cusp who find themselves on the Way of Devotion will no doubt make a remarkable journey along this karmic path. While they may experience some trepidation about looking inward to get in better touch with their deepest motivations, their search for greater self-awareness will be well worth the effort as they gain clearer insight into and better understanding of the higher symbolism at work in their lives. Though there is considerable risk that some of these people will become hopelessly alienated, misanthropic, or self-involved in the extreme, they are gifted with an overriding need to love and be loved in return that will almost certainly prove the crucible for their transformation and higher development.

SIR ALEC GUINNESS
Actor, *Bridge on the River Kwai, Star Wars*

4/2/1914
Aries I

CHALLENGE: **GRAPPLING WITH THEIR INNER CONFLICTS**
FULFILLMENT: **GOING THE DISTANCE ON BEHALF OF SOMETHING THEY CARE ABOUT**

March 25–April 2

THE CHILD
ARIES I

Those born in the Week of the Child who navigate the challenges and demands of the Way of Devotion may have a rather difficult time getting out of the starting gate. Deeply loving and naturally giving, they may have had early childhood experiences or traumas that left them feeling devoid of emotional support or unworthy of both giving and receiving the love and devotion to which they aspire. Some with this configuration will therefore become preoccupied with approval seeking, only to reject those who would approach them in greater intimacy. Too, self-pity and a tendency to make some unrealistic choices of love objects can interfere with their higher development and eventual attachment to a consuming quest. Yet if they are careful to avoid the dangers of isolation and oversensitivity, their natural enthusiasm, great curiosity, and idealism are sure to buoy them up along this karmic path.

CHALLENGE: **MAKING AN ATTEMPT TO BE A LITTLE MORE SOCIAL NOW AND THEN**
FULFILLMENT: **STEPPING INTO THE ROLE OF QUIET HERO**
NOTABLES: **OCTAVIO PAZ (MEXICAN POET/CRITIC/AUTHOR; EXPLORES THEMES OF LOVE AND DEATH); NORMAN BORLAUG (AGRICULTURIST; EXPERIMENTED WITH WHEAT)**

April 3–10

THE STAR
ARIES II

The souls born in this week who travel the Way of Devotion may hold themselves so aloof from contact and interaction with others that they are unable to establish the connections it requires. Though driven by a need to place themselves at the center of the action, they may hide a sensitive and rather fragile emotional nature under a carefully constructed worldly image. Opening up their lives, their hearts, and their souls and cultivating a more easygoing attitude will be especially important to their development, as will the willingness to drop their masks and reveal their truest selves to those they love. Though others may project larger-than-life qualities onto these charismatic and dynamic personalities, Aries II's on this karmic path may experience great loneliness and a less-than-satisfying life journey until they summon the courage to go within, explore themselves, and acknowledge their deepest levels and needs.

JANIS IAN
Folksinger,
"At Seventeen"

4/7/1951
Aries II

CHALLENGE: **TAKING CARE THAT THEIR CHOSEN FORM OF DEVOTION IS NOT MERELY TO THEIR OWN EGOS**
FULFILLMENT: **DISCOVERING WHAT IT IS TO GIVE UNCONDITIONALLY**
NOTABLE: **CHARLES BAUDELAIRE (POET PREOCCUPIED WITH THE MACABRE)**

April 11–18

THE PIONEER
ARIES III

The pioneering personalities born in this week who travel this karmic path are much more likely than some of their fellow Arians to realize the higher level of self-realization it requires. If they can overcome their tendency to be mistrusting and suspicious of others and consciously work on keeping their positive attitudes intact, their natural sense of adventure will jibe rather nicely with their higher spiritual quest. As they are equal to the task of submerging the self to some devotional calling, they will doubtless stumble but rarely collapse. If they do not suppress their empathy, sensitivity, and natural capacity for understanding due to the mistaken idea that such qualities weaken their resolve, nor suppress their strengths in the interest of isolation, aloofness, or a chronically superior attitude, they are wonderfully well qualified to make this hero's journey.

CHALLENGE: **NOT ALLOWING OTHERS TO TAKE ADVANTAGE OF THEM**
FULFILLMENT: **GIVING THEIR ALL TO THEIR CAUSE**

KARMIC PATH
23

April 19–24

POWER
ARIES–TAURUS CUSP

Early rejection may contribute to these individuals' preoccupation with power, and their worldly efforts may be motivated by the need to shore up a sometimes shaky sense of self. Yet they are blessed with a greater sense of direction than many on this karmic path and, though intelligent and naturally discriminating, will not be likely to succumb to overthinking their dilemmas or sinking into Hamlet-like quandaries on the nature of existence. In fact, their biggest weakness may lie in their inability to admit failure. For Aries–Tauruses, the more devotional aspects of this karmic path may manifest themselves in some rather smothering or overprotective qualities that they would do best to keep under strict control. Once they grasp the idea that true power lies not in our ability to get others to submit to us but in our ability to submit to the larger plans and designs at work in our lives, all will go well for them.

CHALLENGE: **COMING TO UNDERSTAND THE DIFFERENCE BE-
TWEEN SUBMISSION AND SURRENDER**

FULFILLMENT: **GIVING THEIR POWER OVER TO SOMETHING
GREATER THAN THEMSELVES**

NOTABLES: **MAX PLANCK (THEORETICAL PHYSICIST; WON
NOBEL FOR QUANTUM THEORY); TONY DANZA (ACTOR,
WHO'S THE BOSS?)**

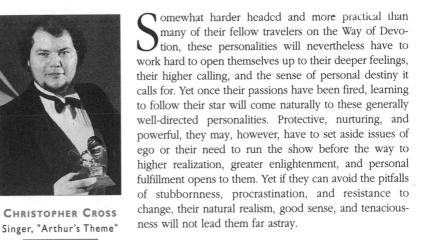

CHRISTOPHER CROSS
Singer, "Arthur's Theme"

5/3/1951
Taurus II

April 25–May 2

MANIFESTATION
TAURUS I

Somewhat harder headed and more practical than many of their fellow travelers on the Way of Devotion, these personalities will nevertheless have to work hard to open themselves up to their deeper feelings, their higher calling, and the sense of personal destiny it calls for. Yet once their passions have been fired, learning to follow their star will come naturally to these generally well-directed personalities. Protective, nurturing, and powerful, they may, however, have to set aside issues of ego or their need to run the show before the way to higher realization, greater enlightenment, and personal fulfillment opens to them. Yet if they can avoid the pitfalls of stubbornness, procrastination, and resistance to change, their natural realism, good sense, and tenaciousness will not lead them far astray.

CHALLENGE: **OPENING TO THE CALL OF THEIR HEARTS**

FULFILLMENT: **RETREATING TO A QUIET, PEACEFUL PLACE
WHERE THEY CAN PRACTICE THEIR DEVOTION**

May 3–10

THE TEACHER
TAURUS II

The astute, highly discriminating individuals born in the Week of the Teacher who travel the Way of Devotion may encounter some problems with the inward aspects of this life's journey. Likely to be more preoccupied with theories, ideas, and concepts than notions of personal passion, higher callings, and spiritual fire, they may fall into the traps of self-denial, aloofness, or the idea that who and what they love are not nearly so important as who loves them. This rather selfish attitude, or the need to make others jump through hoops to prove their worthiness, may cause them to alienate those whose affections they would most like to inspire. Yet if they allow their interactions with others to open their hearts to the wider world of possibilities and come to terms with the fact that what we know is not nearly as important as what we have yet to learn, all will go well on this life journey.

CHALLENGE: **NOT DEGENERATING INTO THE NEED TO BE THAT
WHICH OTHERS DEVOTE THEMSELVES TO RATHER THAN THE
DEVOTEE**

FULFILLMENT: **GOING ON A QUEST TO FIND THEIR HEART'S
DESIRE**

TYRONE POWER
Actor, Mr. Roberts

5/5/1914
Taurus II

May 11–18

THE NATURAL
TAURUS III

Those born in the Week of the Natural who travel the Way of Devotion are likely to be very unusual, even extreme individuals. Though there is some danger that they will shirk the higher spiritual tasks required by this karmic path and become reclusive, isolated, or otherwise withdrawn from the world and its problems, they have a deeply soulful quality, fine instincts, and a truly reverent attitude toward the causes, principles, and people that truly spark their heart's desire. In fact, many with this configuration work out its destiny as rugged individualists, eschewing the demands of social interaction to pursue a more solitary and contemplative life. Though somewhat more openly loving and certainly more adventurous than many of their fellow travelers on this karmic path, they will doubtless discover that following their truest selves will in some way require that they also follow their own need for greater freedom.

CHALLENGE: **KNOWING THE DIFFERENCE BETWEEN REBEL-
LING FOR THE RIGHT REASON AND REBELLING OUT OF FEAR**

FULFILLMENT: **SPENDING TIME IN NATURE TO HEAR THEIR
HEART SONG**

NOTABLES: **STEVIE WONDER (POP/SOUL SINGER, CHILD STAR);
ROBERT ZEMECKIS (FILM PRODUCER)**

May 19–24

ENERGY
TAURUS–GEMINI CUSP

Taurus–Gemini's who travel the Way of Devotion are likely to be blessed with self-awareness, personal depth, and soul quality. At the same time, they may be highly resistant to some of the demands of this karmic path due to a hesitancy to tie themselves down to a single quest, to devote themselves totally to a person, principle, or cause, or even to embark on the search for greater understanding of their life questions. They may have a pronounced tendency to play games among lesser evolved souls, and some may refuse to take life seriously enough until losses or upheavals bring them up short. Also, they may strive to be the center of attention, when a healthy dose of quiet observation, contemplation, and discrimination would stand them in better stead. Greater self-awareness will help bring their more devotional qualities to the fore. If they do not allow themselves to be distracted from what is truly important by that which is merely available, they can make great progress here.

CHALLENGE: **BEING STILL LONG ENOUGH TO SETTLE ON WHAT IT IS THEY LOVE**
FULFILLMENT: **FORGING A ROLE WHEREIN THEY FIGHT FOR THE RIGHTS OF OTHERS**
NOTABLES: **S. I. NEWHOUSE (MAGAZINE PUBLISHER, MOGUL); ANATOLI KARPOV (RUSSIAN CHESS CHAMPION)**

DOROTHEA LANGE
Documentary
photographer
(Her famous Depression-
era photo pictured above)

5/26/1895
Gemini I

May 25–June 2

FREEDOM
GEMINI I

Those born in the Week of Freedom who travel the Way of Devotion will have to come to terms with the fact that their personal salvation lies not so much in variety or quantity of experience as it does in their willingness to focus their attention, get in touch with their passion, and apply themselves to the things, people, principles, or causes that truly speak to the person they are inside. In fact, many of these personalities will take refuge in a superficiality that is quite out of place. Yet their lively minds, discerning sense of observation, and need for truth can do much to guide them successfully over the mountains and valleys of this karmic path. Though the level of commitment demanded by this karmic path may be somewhat difficult for these individuals to handle, once they summon the courage to reach for a higher love, they will find themselves rewarded with an increasing sense of fulfillment and self-realization.

CHALLENGE: **ACCEPTING THE IDEA THAT THEY ARE HEROES**
FULFILLMENT: **GIVING THEIR ALL TO THEIR CAUSE**
NOTABLES: **SAM SNEAD (CHAMPION GOLFER); SALLY RIDE (ASTRONAUT)**

June 3–10

NEW LANGUAGE
GEMINI II

The need to prove themselves, to communicate, and to feel themselves truly understood by others may characterize the life journey of Gemini II's who travel the Way of Devotion. In short, many of these individuals will have a highly defensive attitude, shaped no doubt by early life experiences that will require excavation, examination, and reevaluation before they can attain the sense of freedom and surety needed to embark successfully on their life quest. In fact, this configuration may be accompanied by quite a bit of emotional trouble, and they would do well always to remember that things will pass. Yet if these individuals can summon the levels of commitment, dedication, and simple reverence necessary to acknowledge and devote themselves to their heart's desire, they can make wonderful progress.

CHALLENGE: **HAVING THE COURAGE TO LOOK DEEPLY WITHIN THEMSELVES AND COME TO GRIPS WITH THE SHADOWS THERE**
FULFILLMENT: **SURRENDERING AND THE SELF-ACCEPTANCE IT BRINGS**

ROBERTO DURAN
Champion boxer

6/16/1951
Gemini III

June 11–18

THE SEEKER
GEMINI III

The individuals born in the Week of the Seeker who travel the Way of Devotion can realize much personal progress and spiritual expansion. Yet they will have to face down the demons of superficiality, restlessness, and disillusionment before they can answer some of its higher challenges. Though they are likely to do so vis-à-vis any particular set of goals or aspirations, their principal life focus may be coming to terms with a careless or superficial attitude regarding love and affection. Though the forming of a deep spiritual bond with another human being may seem quite out of character for these usually adventurous people, they may have occasion in their lives to face the facts of true love, if only in the interest of spiritual awareness.

CHALLENGE: **KNOWING WHEN THEIR SEARCH HAS BROUGHT THEM THE ANSWER**
FULFILLMENT: **DISCOVERING HOW WELL SUITED THEY ARE TO DEVOTION**
NOTABLE: **RICHARD THOMAS (ACTOR, *THE WALTONS*)**

KARMIC PATH
23

June 19–24

MAGIC
GEMINI–CANCER CUSP

Those born on the Cusp of Magic who travel the Way of Devotion are likely to have a rather singular life experience and spiritual journey along this karmic path. Yet reconciling their higher selves with deep emotional probing may prove the most difficult part of this journey, especially when their objectivity gets in the way of their instincts. In fact, for many of them it may prove to be a quite solitary process, as they may be quite reluctant to allow anyone into their inner worlds and resistant to the idea that their psyches could use a dusting off now and then to get rid of the cobwebs of insecurity and self-doubt. Yet their profound capacity for love is likely to be their salvation, and if they realize that part of their quest lies in simple progress and refuse to become mired in their losses, disappointments, and disillusionments, they may experience some magical transformations.

CHALLENGE: **BEING MORE CONSCIOUS OF THE WAYS THEY INSPIRE OTHERS**
FULFILLMENT: **CULTIVATING A SPIRITUAL FAMILY OF FRIENDS AND LIKE-MINDED OTHERS FOR SUPPORT ON THEIR LIFE JOURNEY**
NOTABLE: **JACK DEMPSEY (CHAMPION BOXER)**

ANJELICA HUSTON
Actress, *Prizzi's Honor*

7/8/1951
Cancer II

June 25–July 2

THE EMPATH
CANCER I

Those born in the Week of the Empath who find themselves on the Way of Devotion will likely have a very productive and enlightening life journey. Yet they will have to wrestle with the demons of self-doubt, a rather negative outlook or worldview, and an undue measure of personal sensitivity before they are free to realize its higher promise. Learning to distinguish between genuine passion and unrealistic or idealized romance may figure prominently in this process. Also, they will have to take special care not to isolate themselves in hurt feelings, chronic disillusionment, or the fear of loss and abandonment. They would do well to keep in mind that though the Way of Devotion requires many struggles, they are blessed with the natural strength, highly developed instinct, and sense of self required to enable them "to march into hell for a heavenly cause."

CHALLENGE: **TAKING CARE THAT THEIR CAUSE DOES NOT BECOME A CASE OF MISPLACED OR MISSPENT ROMANTIC ARDOR**
FULFILLMENT: **GIVING THEIR HEARTS FULLY**
NOTABLE: **OTIS SKINNER (ACTOR)**

July 3–10

THE UNCONVENTIONAL
CANCER II

The diverse personalities born in the Week of the Unconventional who find themselves on the Way of Devotion are likely to have an unusual and highly educational ride. Likely to be be viewed by others as rather mysterious or even downright eccentric, they can nevertheless realize enormous personal fulfillment and reward on this karmic path. Blessed with a greater sense of humor than many, they should nevertheless take care not to act out their unconscious or darker yearnings or replay old scripts that have outworn their usefulness. Perhaps the principal danger here is that these people will spend all of their time living in a kind of fantasy world and fail to adequately address the demands of practical reality. Yet if they can garner their strength and imaginative powers to access the truths and recurring themes of their fantasy lives, they will discover the powerful and archetypal energies needed for them to follow their personal star.

CHALLENGE: **KNOWING THE DIFFERENCE BETWEEN OBSESSION AND DEVOTION**
FULFILLMENT: **TAPPING INTO THE LARGER PICTURE OR ARCHETYPAL ASPECTS OF THEIR LIVES**
NOTABLES: **JEAN-CLAUDE DUVALIER ("BABY DOC"; DEPOSED HAITIAN DICTATOR); HUEY LEWIS (POP SINGER)**

STEVE WOZNIAK
Cofounder, Apple
computers

7/11/1951
Cancer III

July 11–18

THE PERSUADER
CANCER III

Those born in the Week of the Persuader who find themselves on the Way of Devotion are likely to have a rather satisfying life journey, providing they do not retreat into controlling behaviors in an attempt to protect their more sensitive, soulful side. In any event, they will have a pronounced tendency to worry and to concentrate upon details at the expense of the bigger picture. Thus, there are some who may fail the higher spiritual challenges of this karmic path, immersing themselves in external reality and thus ignoring their soul's calling. Nevertheless, if they learn to follow their hearts and not their heads and consciously undertake a search for their truest motivations, rather than looking outward in an attempt to control their reality, they are likely to find the union, affirmation, and spiritual identity promised by the Way of Devotion. They will have to be careful to remain open in all of their dealings or risk the possibility that their desire for privacy will become a prison of loneliness.

CHALLENGE: **BREAKING FREE FROM THEIR CALLING ONCE IN A WHILE TO SIMPLY BE**
FULFILLMENT: **APPLYING THEIR CREATIVE AND MANAGERIAL SKILLS TO FURTHERING THEIR CAUSE**
NOTABLES: **OSCAR HAMMERSTEIN II (LYRICIST OF RODGERS AND HAMMERSTEIN, *OKLAHOMA!*, *CAROUSEL*, *SOUTH PACIFIC*)**

July 19–25

OSCILLATION
CANCER–LEO CUSP

ALEXANDRE DUMAS, PÈRE

Novelist/playwright
———
7/24/1802
Cancer–Leo Cusp

The blessings of the Way of Devotion for these volatile and often uncompromising personalities can be great, as this karmic path affords those born on the Cusp of Oscillation a greater degree of natural stability, a more together attitude, and an emotional focus that they might otherwise have had. Likely to be quite magnetic, charismatic, and compelling to other people, they will nevertheless have to struggle with their tendency to be judgmental, overexacting, and uncompromising to the point that they take themselves out of the game. In fact, some among this group will retreat into an arbitrarily high sense of standard, an overly structured lifestyle, or a rather hollow sense of personal superiority rather than take up the challenge of getting in touch with their truest passions. Though the Way of Devotion will hold a number of peaks and valleys for Cancer–Leos, they can be sure that they will attain the highest heights if they are willing to explore their personal and spiritual depths.

CHALLENGE: **NOT BEING DIFFICULT MERELY BECAUSE THEY CAN BE**
FULFILLMENT: **UNFOLDING THE FULLNESS OF THEIR MORAL COURAGE FOR THE BENEFIT OF THEIR CALLING**
NOTABLE: **LYNDA CARTER (ACTRESS, *WONDER WOMAN*)**

July 26–August 2

AUTHORITY
LEO I

Those born in the Week of Authority who travel the Way of Devotion are likely to have a more introspective turn of mind than some of their fellows born in this week. Though much more likely to acknowledge their passion and allow their hearts to rule their heads, they may get rather mired in trying to figure out the larger design. They may submit themselves totally to the idea that we are all ruled by forces larger than ourselves, causing them to maintain rather fixed and uncomfortable attitudes. In short, they may waste much time waiting for circumstances, external events, or signs from the heavens to provide them with a sense of direction or calling when they would be better off simply following their own instincts. Though this configuration can carry with it a great deal of personal frustration, these individuals are blessed with the necessary strength, capacity for self-knowledge, and transformative energy to take themselves farther than they ever dreamed.

CHALLENGE: **FINDING WITHIN THEMSELVES A GREAT CAPACITY FOR KINDNESS AND PATIENCE**
FULFILLMENT: **ASSERTING THEMSELVES ON BEHALF OF A GREATER BELIEF OR PRINCIPLE**
NOTABLE: **LAMAR HUNT (FOOTBALL EXECUTIVE)**

August 3–10

BALANCED STRENGTH
LEO II

The forceful and steady personalities born in the Week of Balanced Strength who travel the Way of Devotion have a rare endurance and tenacity that will doubtless prove an asset on this karmic path. They should take care not to become too single-minded or obsessive, however, for critical to their success will be their ability to ignore their common sense or conventional wisdom from time to time in order to access their considerable stores of intuition, passion, and rather unique ability to play a hunch for everything it's worth. Though they would do well to be aware that they have some overly self-sacrificing tendencies and a somewhat romanticized sense of their own suffering, they can embark on their quest for greater happiness, fulfillment, and personal reward with confidence, capability, and the right spiritual attitude.

PETER O'TOOLE
Actor, *Lawrence of Arabia*
———
8/2/1932
Leo I

CHALLENGE: **LETTING THEIR HEARTS DO THE SPEAKING FOR THEM**
FULFILLMENT: **REALIZING THAT THE ONLY AND BEST THING TO GIVE THEIR LOYALTY TO IS THEMSELVES**
NOTABLE: **MEL TILLIS (COUNTRY SINGER)**

August 11–18

LEADERSHIP
LEO III

More inclined to a role of leadership than one of submission to larger spiritual forces, Leo III's may have something of a difficult passage along the Way of Devotion. Until they come to better terms with the issues of pride, egoism, plain selfishness, they may fail the higher challenges of this karmic path. Though temperamentally well suited to the pursuit of a personal ideology or divinity, they may run through any number of personal obsessions before their deepest needs and desires are revealed to them. Yet they can measure their success by the honor and respect awarded to them by others and the inspiration they bring to them. If they release their notions of reward and punishment and instead embrace the world of higher spiritual possibility, they will make great progress, though it will doubtless be in personal rather than more worldly terms.

CHALLENGE: **KNOWING THAT THE JOURNEY IS JUST AS IMPORTANT AS THE ARRIVAL**
FULFILLMENT: **EMBODYING THE ROLE OF EVERYDAY HERO**
NOTABLES: **RICHARD LAWLOR (SURGEON; PERFORMED 1ST SUCCESSFUL KIDNEY TRANSPLANT); BERT LAHR (ACTOR, "COWARDLY LION"); EYDIE GORME (SINGER/ENTERTAINER)**

August 19–25

EXPOSURE
LEO–VIRGO CUSP

Those born on this cusp who find themselves on the Way of Devotion may well discover a few secrets of the universe in their quest for self-realization. The pity is, they may well carry their secrets to their graves unless fate takes a hand and forces these often recalcitrant personalities into a position where they must share their hard-won knowledge with others, whether through service, personal intimacy, or public attention. Though they may well be in close touch with their passions and deepest needs, it is considerably harder for them to reveal themselves to others or to wear their heart on their sleeve. Yet if they can release their inclination to worry, overwork, or live in their heads, unable to open themselves to the possibility of attaining their fondest dreams, they can have a far-reaching impact and realize great accomplishment.

LADY ANTONIA FRASER
British historical writer

8/27/1932
Virgo I

CHALLENGE: **REVEALING WHO THEY ARE TO OTHERS ONCE IN A WHILE**

FULFILLMENT: **BEING PERCEPTIVE ENOUGH TO KNOW WHEN THEY'VE TOUCHED GREATNESS**

NOTABLES: **MELVIN VAN PEEBLES (WRITER/DIRECTOR); HOWARD JOHNSON (FOUNDED RESTAURANT CHAIN)**

August 26–September 2

SYSTEM BUILDERS
VIRGO I

System Builders are likely to have a more comfortable journey than some others on the Way of Devotion, yet they will have to struggle a bit to come to terms with the idea that it is necessary for them to transcend their tendencies to overanalyze, overwork, and overinvolve themselves with details in order to realize the higher challenge of this karmic path. Simply being emotionally unaware can prove their principal pitfall, and blockages of their deepest selfs may manifest themselves in all sorts of unhealthy and self-destructive behaviors of an especially obsessive variety. Their way to salvation will no doubt be found in their need to serve others. If they can hit upon a thing or person that arouses their passion, nurtures their creativity, and encourages a higher and more complete sense of self, their life journey will hold great contentment and an ever-increasing sense of accomplishment.

CHALLENGE: **WORRYING LESS AND ACCEPTING MORE**

FULFILLMENT: **UNDERSTANDING THAT THEY DESERVE TO FOLLOW THEIR HEART'S DESIRE**

September 3–10

THE ENIGMA
VIRGO II

Those born in the Week of the Enigma who travel the Way of Devotion have considerable potential for success, providing they do not isolate themselves in loneliness, a refusal to acknowledge higher spiritual realities, or a retreat into the darkness of worry, anxiety, or preoccupation with what others may think of them. Indeed, they may from time to time become the victims of their own high standards, and many of their life lessons will revolve around the issues of learning to relax, to go with the flow, and to realize that genuine passion rarely involves special planning. Thus, getting comfortable with spontaneity is especially important. More than anything, they will need to be able to let down their guard to the extent that they can ask others for help when help is what they need and reveal their true colors without being embarrassed or fearing reprisal.

PATSY CLINE
Country singer, "Crazy"

9/8/1932
Virgo II

CHALLENGE: **TAKING CARE THAT THEIR DEVOTION ISN'T THEIR UNDOING**

FULFILLMENT: **SUBMITTING TO THEIR FATE**

NOTABLES: **NIGEL BRUCE (BRITISH ACTOR); ISAAC KAUFFMAN FUNK (PUBLISHER, FUNK AND WAGNALLS COMPANY)**

September 11–18

THE LITERALIST
VIRGO III

Once the souls born in this week make the connection between that which they admire most in others and their own inner aspirations, they can realize great personal fulfillment on this karmic path. Yet for these personalities, the trick will be their ability to divorce themselves from the world of tangible reality and explore their inner worlds. Though many of these individuals will be highly resistant to that challenge and may retreat into negative or overly judgmental attitudes, their inclination to harmony and innate dislike of conflict will serve to guide them to the right life choices. Once they realize that some of their inner conflicts are manifesting themselves in outer conflicts, they will have taken the first steps toward enlightenment. Tending to be far more preoccupied with what they don't like than with what they do, they may find learning to take the path of least resistance to be their principal challenge on the Way of Devotion.

CHALLENGE: **KNOWING WHEN TO LET SOMETHING GO**

FULFILLMENT: **APPLYING THEIR WILLPOWER AND PRACTICALITY TO FURTHER THEIR CAUSE**

September 19–24
BEAUTY
VIRGO–LIBRA CUSP

Those born on this cusp who find themselves on the Way of Devotion can realize tremendous achievement, enlightenment, and acceptance, providing they eschew superficiality in all its forms and do not allow themselves to be seduced by shortcuts, self-indulgence, or mere lip service to their higher goals and ideals. Though some will be highly resistant to the process of going within in order to better discover and hopefully release some of their more self-destructive tendencies, it is likely that repeated patterns of rejection, dissatisfaction, or dependency on others will throw them back upon themselves for deeper self-evaluation. Yet following their hearts does come quite naturally to these highly discriminating and beauty-loving people, and if they do not allow themselves to be distracted from their quest for meaning by immediate gratification, they can realize rare enlightenment.

CHALLENGE: **KNOWING THE DIFFERENCE BETWEEN THE SUPERFICIAL AND THE SUBLIME**

FULFILLMENT: **FINDING THE GREATER MEANING IN THEIR QUEST**

NOTABLE: **INGEMAR JOHANSSON (SWEDISH BOXER)**

RICHARD HARRIS
Actor, *Camelot*; 2-time
Oscar nominee
___
10/1/1932
Libra I

September 25–October 2
THE PERFECTIONIST
LIBRA I

Libra I's who find themselves on the Way of Devotion may experience something of a rocky passage until they come to terms with the idea that their personal quest may well involve reaching beyond a rather narrow sphere of influence and into the world of higher possibility that awaits them. Indeed, many of these individuals have an almost evangelical streak that will manifest itself in a calling to expose or investigate the troubles of the world. Gifted with a natural talent for service, they will nevertheless have to take care that their striving for perfection is not allowed to run riot and that they do not alienate others with their never-ending impulses toward reform. Keeping the channel between their hearts and heads open is especially important, as is cultivating the ability to take action when the moment is right rather than expending their energies in worry, obsession, or the fear of taking risks.

CHALLENGE: **QUIETING THE ONGOING AND CRITICAL ANALYSES THAT FILL THEIR MINDS**

FULFILLMENT: **UNDERGOING THE SELF-REVELATION CALLED FOR ON THIS JOURNEY**

NOTABLES: **JOSEPH B. RHINE (PSYCHOLOGIST; COINED PHRASE "EXTRASENSORY PERCEPTION [ESP]"); GLENN GOULD (CANADIAN PIANIST)**

October 3–10
SOCIETY
LIBRA II

Those born in the Week of Society who navigate the challenge and promise of the Way of Devotion are likely to do quite well on this life journey, as this karmic path blesses them with more of a leaning toward solitary and contemplative pursuits than they might otherwise have had, thus freeing them from the possibility of becoming overly involved in the lives of others to the detriment of their own higher development. Yet their tendency to be too self-sacrificing will be quite pronounced, and they may have to learn to discriminate between truly being a saint and merely being a martyr. Too, there is a possibility of self-deception until these individuals come to terms with their deeper sense of passion and calling. Though this karmic path may meander a bit, Libra II's can expect some bountiful and promising turns along the way.

CHALLENGE: **GROUNDING THEIR DEVOTION IN PRACTICAL REALITY SO AS NOT TO OVERINDULGE IN FANTASY**

FULFILLMENT: **LEADING OTHERS IN A WORTHY CAUSE**

DICK GREGORY
Comedian; civil rights
activist
___
10/12/1932
Libra III

October 11–18
THEATER
LIBRA III

Those born in the Week of Theater who travel the Way of Devotion can realize tremendous enlightenment and spiritual development on this life journey, as they are well suited to the deep levels of commitment and dedication it requires. Passionate and sometimes quite demanding, they may have to work to set aside their pride from time to time in order to pursue their own deepest needs. Too, worldly distraction may delay their going within to explore the soul's regions, and some of them may content themselves with a rather hollow sense of ambition or earthly accomplishment until they are given cause to examine the reasons for their ennui. Yet the process of learning to submit their wills in search of greater meaning will be an education for them, and if they remain open and always willing to learn, they have everything it takes to find the greatest fulfillment.

CHALLENGE: **LETTING THEIR PASSION BE THEIR GUIDE ONCE IN A WHILE**

FULFILLMENT: **BELIEVING THAT THERE IS A "MASTER PLAN" AND THAT THEY HAVE A PLACE IN IT**

October 19–25

DRAMA AND CRITICISM
LIBRA–SCORPIO CUSP

Libra–Scorpios who travel the Way of Devotion may well dedicate their lives and selves to a particular creative talent, such as the pursuit of beauty, or a religious or devotional activity. Fired by a depth of passion and an expansive nature that is very much in keeping with their karmic tasks, they can realize wonderful success. The key to that success, however, will be an ability to avoid the dangers of addiction, self-criticism, rigidity, and intolerance, particularly given their propensity to be obsessive. Still, they have both the strength and the talent to reach for even the most unreachable stars, and, properly applied, that energy can serve to fuel the joy of following their heart's innermost desire.

CHALLENGE: **OVERCOMING EVEN THE SMALLEST HINT OF SELF-PITY**
FULFILLMENT: **ADOPTING A MORE FARSIGHTED AND PHILO-SOPHICAL APPROACH TO PURSUING THEIR DREAM**
NOTABLES: **ROBERT REED (ACTOR, THE BRADY BUNCH); BOBBY BROWN (POP SINGER); DAN DORFMAN (FINANCIAL WRITER)**

SYLVIA PLATH
Author/poet, The Bell Jar

10/27/1932
Scorpio I

October 26–November 2

INTENSITY
SCORPIO I

Those born in the Week of Intensity who journey along the Way of Devotion may experience a fair amount of rejection, misunderstanding, and suffering until they realize that perhaps the attitude of others toward them is but an outward manifestation of their own inner dissatisfaction. Undoubtedly soulful and certainly sensitive, these individuals will nevertheless have to undergo a process of coming to terms with what matters to them. Yet their natural mysticism will almost certainly come to the fore, and if they learn to release their feelings of being unloved and unwanted and work to unearth the more puzzling aspects of their own personality, the truths that are eventually revealed will certainly smooth their passage and guide their journey.

CHALLENGE: **STRUGGLING TO ENLIGHTEN THEMSELVES AND RELEASE THEIR DARKER SHADOWS**
FULFILLMENT:. **HONORING THEIR FEELINGS BUT, MUCH LIKE A GOOD PARENT, GUIDING OR CHANNELING THEM AS WELL**
NOTABLE: **LOUIS MALLE (FILM DIRECTOR)**

November 3–11

DEPTH
SCORPIO II

The Way of Devotion may manifest itself here in some unusual and even eccentric personalities. For those born in the Week of Depth who travel this karmic path, life can be a pretty serious business, and self-knowledge can be a god. Yet for all of their seeming intensity and profundity, these souls will also have to come to terms with the idea that submission of the ego's drives in service to others is part of their higher development. Thus, an ability to overcome selfishness, self-interest, and some of their more negative or suspicious attitudes toward humanity in general will prove essential. Once they conquer the demons of depression, worry, and obsession and understand that on a very deep level their attitudes are shaping their reality, whether for good or for ill, things will go more smoothly for them.

CHALLENGE: **GETTING RID OF THE NOTION THAT SUFFERING IS ROMANTIC**
FULFILLMENT: **EXPRESSING THEIR FULL INTENSITY FREELY THROUGH DEVOTION**
NOTABLE: **VACHEL LINDSAY (POET/AUTHOR)**

SEAN "PUFFY" COMBS
Rap singer/producer

11/4/1969
Scorpio II

November 12–18

CHARM
SCORPIO III

If they can rise to the higher challenges of the Way of Devotion and summon the courage and dedication necessary to pursue seemingly impossible dreams, the resilient and resourceful individuals born in the Week of Charm are apt to realize considerable success. Getting into their deeper motivations, passions, and feelings may, however, prove more difficult. It will therefore be especially important for these individuals to cultivate greater self-knowledge and avoid their tendency to denial, self-deception, or the need to keep up appearances. Yet they are highly discriminating, truly tasteful, and often quite charismatic. If they do not employ their charms solely in attempts to control others, they can discover strength, conviction, and new worlds of meaning on this most fascinating life journey.

CHALLENGE: **GRAPPLING WITH THEIR MORE MANIPULATIVE TENDENCIES**
FULFILLMENT: **FINDING SOMETHING TO BELIEVE IN**
NOTABLE: **PETULA CLARK (SINGER; FILM ACTRESS, GOODBYE, MR. CHIPS)**

November 19–24
REVOLUTION
SCORPIO–SAGITTARIUS CUSP

Though generally well suited to the challenge and promise of the Way of Devotion, those born on the Cusp of Revolution who travel this karmic path may have to avoid the dangers of fanaticism and zealotry in the pursuit of their personal divinity. Though this configuration makes for some unusual, heroic, and admirable people, it can also produce individuals characterized by chronic discontent, disdain for the rules, and a generally excessive approach to problems and reforms. Though many will perceive these people as unrealistic, fantasy prone, or ineffectual dreamers, the fact of the matter is that they are among those with the most potential for achieving the kind of heroic, mythological, and inspiring levels of self-evolution, discovery, and achievement available on this road of spiritual development.

JACQUES CHIRAC
Former French prime minister, president

11/29/1932
Sagittarius I

CHALLENGE: **REMEMBERING NOT TO LET THE ACT OF REBELLION ITSELF BECOME THE CAUSE**

FULFILLMENT: **MAKING A DIFFERENCE**

NOTABLES: **ROBERT VAUGHN (ACTOR, *MAN FROM U.N.C.L.E.*); KEN GRIFFEY, JR. (BASEBALL GREAT)**

November 25–December 2
INDEPENDENCE
SAGITTARIUS I

Characterized by genuine sensitivity, fine intuitive faculties, and a greater need to give than to receive, the men and women born in the Week of Independence who travel the Way of Devotion may struggle a bit with the idea of giving up some of their personal freedom in the process of rendering the necessary devotion, dedication, and diligence in the pursuit of their highest principles. A measure of regular interaction with others will enable them to weigh the pros and cons of their life options and help them make the correct choices. In fact, as they learn to follow their hearts and open themselves to greater intimacy, it is likely that they will discover the joy of attachment and a number of soul mates. Though part of their sacrifice will doubtless involve the giving up of certain competitive or impulsive leanings in the interest of making step-by-step progress along this karmic path, they can find great joy pursuing their heart's truest calling.

CHALLENGE: **KEEPING THEMSELVES FROM SUFFERING PERIODS OF INSECURITY ON THEIR OFTEN LONELY ROAD**

FULFILLMENT: **EMBARKING ON THE SPIRITUAL QUEST**

NOTABLES: **FRIEDRICH ENGELS (COLLABORATED WITH MARX ON *THE COMMUNIST MANIFESTO*); BENIGNO AQUINO (PHILIPPINE OPPOSITION LEADER ASSASSINATED BY MARCOS)**

December 3–10
THE ORIGINATOR
SAGITTARIUS II

Though they may feel themselves misunderstood, unappreciated, or otherwise outside the mainstream when placed on the Way of Devotion, those born in the Week of the Originator can nevertheless realize tremendous success and achievement on this karmic path. Yet they will have to work hard to overcome their deep-seated feelings of mistrust and alienation in order to succeed. In any event, they will have to avoid self-pity and keep up their sense of humor in the course of their personal evolution. Too, not controlling their feelings of aggression or allowing themselves to be driven by a need to be accepted rather than by a more authentic sense of self can hinder their higher development. Yet these souls will doubtless be aided in their quest by bonds of true intimacy with those they feel they can trust. And if they give their all for love, they will doubtless find themselves loved in return.

DON KING
Controversial boxing promoter

12/6/1932
Sagittarius II

CHALLENGE: **LOOKING WITHIN THEMSELVES TO ALLEVIATE THEIR FEELINGS OF ANXIETY OR LACK OF SELF-WORTH**

FULFILLMENT: **REMAINING TRUE TO THEIR HEART'S CALLING**

NOTABLES: **JACOB DYLAN (MUSICIAN, THE WALL FLOWERS; SON OF BOB); LITTLE RICHARD (FLAMBOYANT ROCK TROUBADOR, "TUTTI FRUTTI")**

December 11–18
THE TITAN
SAGITTARIUS III

Though they are likely to think on a rather grand scale, those born in the Week of the Titan who find themselves on the Way of Devotion may have to scale down their ambitions a bit in the search for greater meaning in their lives. Their visionary qualities doubtless led them to be pegged as unrealistic dreamers early on, which may have contributed to a rather shaky self-image and a wide streak of well-disguised insecurity. Yet whatever their faults or failings, these personalities are likely to have some rather evangelical leanings and may yearn for peak or ecstatic experiences. Conversely, many with this configuration will find themselves unable able to make the decisions or commitments needed to make real progress. Yet if they learn not to overthink or get too caught up in philosophical implications and follow their hearts in such a way that their process is not unduly complicated by mental games or the tendency to work things over ad infinitum, their lives can take on a great depth of meaning.

CHALLENGE: **DEVELOPING THE HUMILITY OF THE TRULY DEVOTED**

FULFILLMENT: **CASTING A MAGICAL SPELL AS THEY PURSUE THE OBJECT OF THEIR HEART'S DESIRE**

NOTABLE: **CHARLIE RICH (COUNTRY SINGER)**

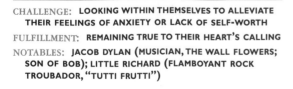

KARMIC PATH
23

December 19–25
PROPHECY
SAGITTARIUS–CAPRICORN CUSP

Those born on the Cusp of Prophecy who navigate the challenge and promise of the Way of Devotion are likely to do very well. Likely to be rather mysterious and intriguing personalities, they may nevertheless become alienated, isolated, or withdrawn to the extent that they are unable to make the necessary forays into the world that are part of the higher challenge of this karmic path. Yet they are gifted with an unusual degree of independence, a capacity for true self-knowledge, and an ability to look facts, whether spiritual, material, or extrasensory, squarely in the eye. If they can avoid the dangers of personal frustration, overcome their sense of rejection, and cultivate their sociability, there may well be more recognition, acceptance, and admiration than they ever dreamed possible awaiting them on the Way of Devotion.

PABLO CASALS
Cellist/conductor/
composer
———
12/29/1876
Capricorn I

CHALLENGE: **TRUSTING THEIR INNER VOICE ENOUGH TO KNOW ITS TRUTH**

FULFILLMENT: **DEVOTING THEMSELVES TO A SPIRITUAL PATH RATHER THAN A PATH OF PERSONAL AMBITION**

December 26–January 2
THE RULER
CAPRICORN I

The hardworking, capable individuals born in the Week of the Ruler who travel the Way of Devotion may have to discard a number of hierarchical notions before they can realize its promise. In fact, these people simply like to be in charge and may obscure their own higher calling and deeper emotional needs by trying to manage, control, or dominate others. As a result, this journey can take a number of turns that at first may seem surprising, unwelcome, or inconvenient. Yet if they keep in mind that these upheavals are often the universe's presentation of new opportunities for self-exploration and repeated calls from their innermost selves to a higher level of evolution and enlightenment, they can make great strides along this karmic path. Though the object of veneration that will prove the unifying force on this life journey is likely to be rather traditional, it will be no less powerful a force in their higher development.

CHALLENGE: **BEING WILLING TO ENDURE A RATHER SOLITARY WAY OF LIFE**

FULFILLMENT: **CONTRIBUTING HARD WORK AND DISCIPLINE TO WHAT THEY BELIEVE IN**

January 3–9
DETERMINATION
CAPRICORN II

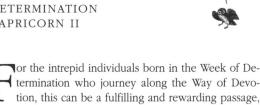

For the intrepid individuals born in the Week of Determination who journey along the Way of Devotion, this can be a fulfilling and rewarding passage, providing they do not bottle up their emotions to the extent that their higher evolution is put on the back burner in the interest of practical matters. Though a number of people with this configuration may present themselves to the world as hardheaded and even cynical, many of them have an interest in theoretical and metaphysical matters that will serve them well in their quest for a higher level of self-realization. These personalities have a streak of enthusiasm and hope that ought to be given full play, for though they may seem naive at times, it is among their fondest dreams and highest hopes to discover their heart's desire.

JANE WYMAN
Actress, *The Yearling*,
television's *Falcon Crest*;
won Oscar for *Johnny
Belinda*; 1st wife of
Ronald Reagan
———
1/4/1914
Capricorn II

CHALLENGE: **DARING TO DREAM BIG DREAMS**
FULFILLMENT: **GIVING FREE REIN TO THEIR IDEALISM**
NOTABLES: **JIMMY PAGE (SINGER/GUITARIST, LED ZEPPELIN); GEORGE REEVES (TELEVISION/FILM ACTOR; THE ORIGINAL *SUPERMAN*)**

January 10–16
DOMINANCE
CAPRICORN III

For the utterly sensible personalities born in the Week of Dominance who travel the Way of Devotion, there is a possibility of great success and considerable advancement. Though they will doubtless wrestle with issues of common sense, agonize over a course of action, and have to endure a certain amount of psychological excavation in order to realize their heart's truest calling, they are quite adaptable to the challenges of this karmic path. If they work to overcome their need for ritual and an overly structured existence, they will doubtless speed their progress along this road. Yet perhaps their biggest pitfall is their tendency to be too self-sacrificing. Gifted with tremendous empathy and natural compassion, they can do much to inspire those qualities in others. If only they can release their rather fearful attitudes toward higher spiritual awareness, they are more than capable of coping with both the practical and spiritual aspects here.

CHALLENGE: **STRUGGLING WITH THEIR SECRET FEAR THAT THEY AREN'T WORTHY OF LOVE**

FULFILLMENT: **EXPRESSING THEIR DEVOTION TO A CAUSE OR PRINCIPLE THAT ALSO ENRICHES AND NURTURES THEIR SPIRIT**

January 17–22
MYSTERY AND IMAGINATION
CAPRICORN–AQUARIUS CUSP

Those born on the Cusp of Mystery and Imagination who find themselves on the Way of Devotion will have to guard against a tendency to live in their heads to such an extent that they are unable to cope with practical reality. Indeed, many of these personalities can be too sensitive for their own good and may get buffeted about by their own chaotic energies. Yet as long as they take up the challenge to do their inner work, explore their own psychology, and stay in touch with their real motivations, they are more than capable of coming to terms with their sense of passion and devotion. Blessed with the inventiveness, lightheartedness, and resiliency needed to make a success of their lives, this will likely be an exciting passage, yet one that can be pursued with great enthusiasm and energy as these individuals educate themselves to the joy of following their personal star.

WILLIAM BURROUGHS
Writer/chief spokesman
of Beat movement,
Naked Lunch

2/5/1914
Aquarius II

CHALLENGE: **REALIZING THAT MUCH OF THEIR SUFFERING IS GENERATED BY THE CHAOS OF THEIR INNER TURMOIL**
FULFILLMENT: **FOLLOWING THEIR OWN UNIQUELY PERSONAL VISION**

January 23–30
GENIUS
AQUARIUS I

Aquarius I's who navigate the challenges and demands of the Way of Devotion may well find that many of their most cherished ideas, theories, and speculations will manifest themselves in concrete reality on this life journey. Indeed, many of these people have an almost starlike quality that is seemingly at odds with the more introspective and introverted aspects of this passage. Yet their very single-mindedness will serve them well along this road, for the fixed nature of Aquarius I's, once they are captured by an idea, a concept, or a dream, is unlikely to be swayed from their quest by any of the usual practical considerations or material distractions that present themselves. In a word, these souls are blessed with more than the usual measure of compassion. If they can get in touch and stay in touch with the deep reservoir of feelings that is part of the endowment of this karmic path, they are unlikely to go far astray in their quest for higher knowledge.

CHALLENGE: **SETTING ASIDE WHAT THEIR HEADS ARE TELLING THEM AND FOLLOWING THEIR HEARTS**
FULFILLMENT: **FIXING THEIR SIGHTS ON ONE SPECIAL GOAL**

January 31–February 7
YOUTH AND EASE
AQUARIUS II

Those born in this week who follow the Way of Devotion will be faced with an unique and enlightening journey. Strengthened in their quest for greater self-realization by an unusual measure of creative and intellectual talent, they should take some care to cultivate their virtuosity and not succumb to their need to be accepted. In fact, these souls may well have to endure some measure of self-imposed isolation in the interest of development, for here can be found the sort of prodigies and maestros who have little experience in social settings such as Little League due to the fact that they were composing sonatas at the age of seven! Later in life, that dynamic will of course become more complicated, and many of them will seek to expand their social horizons by denying their gifts or turning their backs on fulfillment. Yet if they can overcome their needier side and learn to take pride in that which affords them their greatest joy, the possibilities for formidable achievement are all firmly in place.

GYPSY ROSE LEE
Stripper/actress,
the movie *Gypsy* based on
her life

2/9/1914
Aquarius III

CHALLENGE: **NOT GETTING CAUGHT UP IN THEIR OWN HEROIC MYTH TO THE DETRIMENT OF THEIR SPIRITUAL PROGRESS**
FULFILLMENT: **FASHIONING A LIFE AROUND THEIR CALLING**

February 8–15
THE WEEK OF ACCEPTANCE
AQUARIUS III

Gifted with greater discernment, discrimination, and taste than they might otherwise have had, those born in the Week of Acceptance who travel the Way of Devotion may nevertheless experience something of a mythological journey as they make their way along this karmic path. Indeed, quite a few rather colorful characters have this configuration, leading to wide experience, far-flung travels, or a multifaceted and highly experimental inner journey. Though gifted with a finer sense of humor and a broader philosophical perspective than they might otherwise have had, they will have to work hard to cultivate the qualities of stability, diligence, and dedication required by this karmic path. While following their heart's desire will come quite easily to many of them, traveling the road of higher development with constancy, consistency, and dedication may prove more difficult.

CHALLENGE: **BOWING TO THEIR FATE AND ACCEPTING ITS CHALLENGES**
FULFILLMENT: **KNOWING THEIR LIFE'S PURPOSE**

February 16–22

SENSITIVITY
AQUARIUS–PISCES CUSP

Those born on this cusp who make their way along this karmic path may prove a curious combination of a deep, soulful emotionality and a cool, calculated, or even rather aggressive persona. Yet the sometimes disparate aspects of their personalities will come together in a more effective manner once they learn to understand and accept their underlying motivations. The danger, of course, is that they may become too caught up in the process of understanding their emotions and psychology and fail the higher challenge of this karmic path. In fact, there can be a rather narcissistic or overly contemplative aspect to this configuration, and they will do well to learn that introspection and self-awareness don't mean much unless the resulting revelations are complemented by action, dedication to newfound principles, and a willingness to sacrifice the ego to a higher sense of purpose.

RALPH ELLISON
Writer, *The Invisible Man*

3/1/1914
Pisces I

CHALLENGE: **NOT HIDING OUT TO PROTECT THEIR SENSITIVITY**
FULFILLMENT: **DEDICATING THEMSELVES TO THEIR KARMIC PATH AS FULLY AS POSSIBLE**

February 23–March 2

SPIRIT
PISCES I

Pisces I's who navigate the Way of Devotion are characterized by a rather elusive, mysterious, or even ethereal quality that can make life somewhat more difficult than it needs to be for these sensitive personalities. Yet this karmic path will no doubt gift them with a high degree of practicality to complement their spiritual side, and the result can be a truly winning combination. Chances are, however, that they will have to toughen up a bit and refuse to allow their desire to serve others and do good to lead them into situations where they can be taken advantage of or exploited. Yet they can realize all the promise of this karmic path, providing they do not slip into patterns of self-negation and learn to follow their passions with more commitment and less timidity.

CHALLENGE: **NOT BEING SIDETRACKED BY THE DEMANDS OF OTHERS**
FULFILLMENT: **GIVING FULL EXPRESSION TO THEIR SOUL'S DESIRES**

March 3–10

THE LONER
PISCES II

The Loners who find themselves on the Way of Devotion may be quite unusual people, characterized both by profound insight, soul, and spirituality and by some rather serious emotional problems. Though they will know something about suffering, and will likely bear the scars of loss, abandonment, or early trauma, they will be equally marked by a unique ability to transcend their trials, usually through their deep attachment to the world of art, refinement, or beauty. In fact, many of these personalities will experience no small amount of personal transformation along this road, and if they can avoid the tendency to self-defeating behaviors, chronic indecision, or the tendency to alienate those who might help them most, this can make for an inspiring and remarkable passage indeed.

CHALLENGE: **NOT GIVING IN TO FEELINGS OF HOPELESSNESS**
FULFILLMENT: **LETTING THEIR HEARTS BE THEIR GUIDES AND THEIR DEVOTION BE THEIR BEACON IN THE DARKNESS**
NOTABLE: **JOSEPH NICÉPHORE (ONE OF THE INVENTORS OF PHOTOGRAPHY)**

March 11–18

DANCERS AND DREAMERS
PISCES III

The gifted individuals born in the Week of Dancers and Dreamers who make their way along this karmic path may have to face down the demons of carelessness and superficiality before they can come to terms with its higher spiritual awakening. Though they will no doubt have many passions and be characterized by a tendency to wear their hearts upon their sleeves, they may scatter their energies through their tendency to become emotionally overextended. Thus, the idea of dedicating themselves to a single person, principle, or passion may seem a bit out of reach at first. Still, if they cultivate a deeper knowledge of themselves and commit themselves to those things that are at once positive and nurturing, their true calling will not remain a mystery for long.

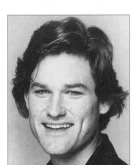

KURT RUSSELL
Actor, *Silkwood*

3/17/1951
Pisces III

CHALLENGE: **LEARNING HOW TO MAKE A COMMITMENT TO SOMETHING THEY LOVE**
FULFILLMENT: **GLORYING IN THE MORE MIRACULOUS ASPECTS OF THEIR JOURNEY**
NOTABLES: **ARTHUR OCHS (NEWSPAPERMAN); BEN COHEN AND JERRY GREENFIELD (FOUNDED SOCIALLY CONSCIOUS ICE CREAM COMPANY BEN & JERRY'S HOMEMADE, INC.)**

The Way of Transcendence

VIRGO III TO PISCES III
Literalist to Dancers and Dreamers

The destiny of those born to this karmic path is to learn how to transcend limitations, even if this means going beyond what ordinary conceptions of time and space may deem possible. Often, the limits these individuals must transcend exist only within their own minds. Those born to the Way of Transcendence tend to be hardheaded individuals firmly rooted in the here and now and the practicalities of daily life. Realists first and foremost, these sturdy men and women must learn to overcome their innate attachment to the tangible and to develop a belief in the impossible, for without such a viewpoint, none of the individuals on this karmic path would ever challenge their limitations. Their pragmatic orientation would prevent them from making any attempt to do so, and they would be unable to still the little voice in their heads that tells them, "It can't be done. It can't be done. It cannot be done!" While part of this karmic path is about breaking records or going beyond what anyone else has achieved in a field of endeavor, its underlying truth is that it calls the individuals on it to an awakening to and belief in the possibility of miracles and divine intervention. Once such beliefs are embraced by these men and women, there's no limit to their soul's growth. In fact, each soul born to the Way of Transcendence is offered the opportunity for the ultimate transcendence, that of overcoming the cycle of reincarnation itself.

If the men and women on this karmic path are to set themselves against limits in whatever form, they must first learn to develop a more positive outlook, and indeed this is the core lesson of this path. Prone to a debilitating brand of negativity, they are no strangers to depression. The causes of this are two. The first is their steely practicality. They generally know what works and what doesn't, but not always, since they rarely employ the secret ingredient of many success stories: faith. Second, they consider themselves to be infallible. Rarely do they doubt their estimation of what makes sense or is workable. Never questioning themselves, they will rarely try anything new, let alone take a leap of faith now and then. They tend to fall into comfortable grooves of routine, since repetition or the utilization of proven methods keeps their anxiety to a minimum, thus making them feel safe. Such self-imposed ruts eventually limit their personal growth and inadvertently create the basis of their depression as their souls begin to cry out for change and a more creative approach to life. Developing the capacity for faith and a positive, hopeful attitude toward the future is the key to success on this journey.

The men and women on the Way of Transcendence will find themselves immeasurably happier when they shake things up a bit and force themselves to take on new projects or goals. Initiating change more frequently can be essential. Once they start themselves moving in the right direction, their tremendous reserves of willpower become

---

CORE LESSON

Overcoming negativity to develop
a positive outlook

GOAL

To transcend the limits imposed
by their practical natures

GIFTS
Helpful, Practical, Spiritual

PITFALLS
Habit-forming, Stuck, Judgmental

KARMIC PATH
24

412

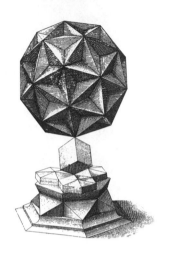

engaged so that they are able to achieve their goals and surmount every obstacle. A good plan of action for those on this karmic path may be to stop frequently during the course of the day or week and analyze whether what they are doing makes sense or is merely rote. Such a process can open their minds to new vistas and heretofore unseen possibilities. When tackling a problem or situation, while they will tend to want to apply whatever worked before in a similar situation, they must develop the capacity to forsake the lessons of history in favor of going beyond the limitations of their own experience. This may begin to change their thinking process from the linear and literal to one that is more creative or symbolic, moving from a masculine results orientation to a feminine process orientation.

Inherent in those on this karmic path is a need to be in control. If this trait is not dealt with, it can severely impair their prospects. Fundamentally fearful of anything they can't control, those on the Way of Transcendence cling to a literal interpretation of life because anything that is clearly defined makes them feel safe and provides them with emotional security. Dividing the world into absolutes is their forte, and this comes with concomitant traits of judgmentalism, argumentativeness, and a tendency to blame or condemn others. Transcending such attitudes requires dealing with their core issue, fear. Placing their trust in a

more benevolent and orderly universe will aid those on this karmic path to release their rigidity and need for control and allow them to flow with life.

Once the individuals on the Way of Transcendence overcome their literal-mindedness, they will begin to open to their imagination and creativity. Turning their attention to the many varieties of religious or spiritual experience will broaden their perspective and teach them a new outlook. Ultimately, they will learn that there is a way other than sheer strength of will to obtain results—that of engaging in a partnership with the divine. Prayer, intention, affirmation, and visualization will all become methods that those on the Way of Transcendence can use regularly to help them achieve their goals—many of which, by the way, will remain rooted in the practical and in everyday life. What can be expected of these always interesting individuals is the ability to accomplish wonderful things, even miracles, in both their own lives and those of others. Developing the capacity to dream and to believe in those dreams, no matter how impossible they may seem, is the main preoccupation of those on this karmic path. And very often, their dreams are fulfilled.

Striving to become more sensitive and better attuned to forces greater than themselves will require some hard work and resolve for these wonderfully stubborn, iconoclastic types. Though there is little likelihood that such well-grounded people will go overboard and become

RELEASE

The need to control

REWARD

The joy of transcending obstacles

SUGGESTION

Work to break outworn habits. Engage in a spiritual practice or study.
Learn how to believe with all your heart and soul. Trust.

lost in a fantasy world, this should still be guarded against. Once they are fully involved in more spiritual matters, others may begin to see those on the Way of Transcendence as slightly wacky individuals who have little time to waste on the ordinary tasks of daily life. Although it is true that their heads may be in the clouds a good deal of the time, they also have a practical side that can be good at handling money and getting jobs done. Once they undergo even a single transcendental experience, a fiery brand of iconoclasm may kick in and they may go overboard for a time, causing them to attempt to tear down structures, shock others, or otherwise behave badly. Reminding themselves to respect the viewpoints and dreams of their fellows and invoking their usually sound judgment when they pick fights may be necessary; otherwise they may forever be tilting at windmills.

Making a correct choice of partner can be difficult for those on this karmic path. To begin with, interpersonal relations are not really what this path is about. In fact, relationships may prove to be distractions to the matter at hand, which is their desire to transcend all limitations, whether in their work, lifestyle, or spiritual development. Too often they will suffer with a mate who is either too strong for them, finding themselves unable to meet such a partner's demands, or latch onto a weak individual whom they can never really satisfy and who drains their energy and holds them back, in fact becoming another form of limitation. In any event, their relationships frequently become just another thing for them

BALANCE POINT

Doubt and Faith

to overcome and release. Those on this karmic path rarely pursue a career for the sake of fame or power but more often for the opportunity it might present for achieving transcendence.

What may be best for those on the Way of Transcendence is putting themselves in service to a cause, whether organizational or personal. The philosophical fervor of such individuals is so strong that it can carry all before it, and such burning energy should be given an outlet. Constantly going beyond their own personal best or advancing their group's cause is at the heart of their need to transcend. Not only interested in gaining recognition in their own lifetime, they want badly to leave a legacy behind them. Perhaps their greatest desire is that they be granted immortality through the quality or influence of their work. For this to be possible, those on this karmic path must be given the chance to prove themselves, and such a break is usually bestowed on them only by fate and usually unexpectedly. Learning how to invoke fate may be their greatest challenge.

A person on the Way of Transcendence suggests a magician who has studied the forces of the universe and learned the mysterious art of calling things into being. Through a partnership with spirit, visions can be made manifest, amazing all observers. If no one in particular is served, however, such acts are mere sleight of hand. Only when it is placed in the service of a higher cause or greater good does the magician's craft become transcendental.

CRYSTALS AND GEMSTONES

Rainbow Obsidian brings the individual to the dark core of self-imposed limitations and inspires inner flight. This obsidian brings the light of transcendence into black holes of psychological despair.

NOTABLES ON THIS KARMIC PATH

Vibrant and talented **Debbie Reynolds** has faced her share of difficulties, including marital woes and financial

DEBBIE REYNOLDS

problems. First husband Eddie Fisher left her for Elizabeth Taylor, and her second husband left her deep in debt. Throughout it all, Reynolds has managed to overcome negativity and maintain a positive outlook, the core lesson of her karmic path. Thus she has achieved great success in a remarkably long career. With more than thirty-five films to her credit, most recently *Mother,* "unsinkable" trouper Debbie Reynolds has responded to challenges in her life with vigor and humor.

French journalist, playwright, novelist, and philosopher **Albert Camus** was the spokesman for a post war generation. His essay *The Myth of Sisyphus* typifies the Way of Transcendence, as the ancient hero overcomes his hard fate through mental attitude. Particularly interested in free will versus determinism, existentialist Camus posed crucial questions concerning the human condition. Grappling with the lack of meaning in an uncaring universe, Camus struggled to find

ALBERT CAMUS

some hope in an ever-darkening world. Through his writing he discovered an antidote to nihilism in moral imperatives and ethical values.

Ordained minister, singer, and television star **Della Reese** has lived an inspired life. Born on the Way of

DELLA REESE

Transcendence, she rose above tremendous difficulties through her faith and now attributes her success to God. Reese has in turn provided inspiration to many millions, most recently on her popular television show *Touched by an Angel,* and leaves no doubt concerning the power of following one's dreams and visions. Putting her

energy in the service of spirituality, this dynamic woman continues to touch the lives of many with hope and love.

Other Notables: Alberta Hunter, Dorothea Lynde Dix, Halston, John Candy, Modest Mussorgsky, Dane Rudhyar, Arthur Murray, Anthony Perkins, Elaine May, Casey Kasem, Mario Cuomo, Steffi Graf, Pier Angeli, John D. Rockefeller, Menachem Begin, Kenzo Tange, Jesse Owens, Jenny Lind, Jane Pauley, Vivien Leigh, Mary Martin, J. Edgar Hoover, Babe Ruth

BIRTHDAYS ON KARMIC PATH 24

December 20, 1894–May 10, 1895 | August 2, 1913–December 20, 1913

March 13, 1932–August 1, 1932 | October 23, 1950–March 13, 1951 | June 4, 1969–October 23, 1969

January 14, 1988–June 3, 1988 | August 26, 2006–January 13, 2007

KARMIC PATH
24

March 19–24
REBIRTH
PISCES–ARIES CUSP

Some extraordinarily diverse personalities are born with this configuration, yet they all have one important thing in common: in one way or another, they are poised on the brink of personal transformation. Thus, whether the individuals born on this cusp who navigate the Way of Transcendence are earthy, practical, and dynamic or appear to be more dreamy, idealistic, and detached, all will in some way be representative of the various and infinite possibilities for overcoming human limitation. Though the ways in which this karmic path unfolds will doubtless be as unique as the individuals themselves, all of these personalities can expect big things here and should rest assured that their lives hold the promise of transformation, rebirth, and reinvention of self in ways that not many people will ever experience.

ALBERTA HUNTER
Blues singer

4/1/1895
Aries I

CHALLENGE: **NOT LETTING THEIR SENSITIVITY BE AN EXCUSE FOR NOT GOING FOR IT**

FULFILLMENT: **APPLYING THEIR MOST DIRECT AND THOROUGH APPROACH TO OVERCOMING EVERY OBSTACLE**

NOTABLES: **MODEST MUSSORGSKY (RUSSIAN COMPOSER); DANE RUDHYAR (NOTED ASTROLOGER)**

March 25–April 2
THE CHILD
ARIES I

Aries I souls on the Way of Transcendence may well save themselves considerable time and frustration by reconciling themselves to the simple fact that "there are more things in Heaven and Earth than are dreamt of in their philosophies." Naturally frank and outspoken, they are drawn to the outer limits of their lives and experiences, yet are not always confident about their ability to overcome them. In fact, their yearning for transcendence and transformation may give rise to deep feelings of insecurity, on the one hand, or an overriding idealism, on the other. Thus, they may find themselves subject to any number of sudden conversion experiences as their newest passion captures their attention. It will be especially important for this dynamic group to cultivate inner stability and a sense of personal worth on which to base their higher aspirations. Yet with their great willingness to learn, this karmic path can take them on a grand adventure.

CHALLENGE: **TRANSCENDING THEIR CHILDHOOD AND FAMILY OF ORIGIN**

FULFILLMENT: **FINDING THE INNER FREEDOM THEY CRAVE**

NOTABLE: **DEBBIE REYNOLDS (FILM ACTRESS/SINGER/ ENTERTAINER, *TAMMY*)**

April 3–10
THE STAR
ARIES II

A certain tendency to excess is bound to manifest itself for those born in the Week of the Star who wend their way along the Way of Transcendence. Often driven by a need to be at the center of the action, these people can be rather compulsive at times as they try to find and overcome the limits that impede their higher development. Too, they may face many challenges that involve turning their attention away from practical matters and toward an expanded vision of what is possible. One of the personality types who regard the "bird in the hand" as far more important than the one in the bush, they may experience problems with possessiveness and even outright greed. Yet if they strive to develop a greater awareness of their own subconscious motivations and at the same time learn to place their faith in a higher set of rules, they can take great strides along this karmic path.

ARTHUR MURRAY
Dancer (shown with wife Katheryn)

4/4/1895
Aries II

CHALLENGE: **NOT DEVOLVING INTO AN EXCESSIVE FOCUS ON THE LIMITS IN LIFE OUT OF FRUSTRATION**

FULFILLMENT: **PUSHING PAST THE LIMITS OF THEIR EMOTIONAL WALLS**

NOTABLE: **DOROTHEA DIX (SOCIAL REFORMER; HELPED BUILD STATE HOSPITALS FOR THE INSANE)**

April 11–18
THE PIONEER
ARIES III

The individuals born in this week who travel the Way of Transcendence are likely to experience quite a bit of personal expansion and development, as their temperaments, leanings, and natural inclinations are all very much in keeping with their karmic tasks. In fact, many of this group are likely to spend a great deal of time in experimentation and adventure, yet will nonetheless be aided by a wider streak of practicality than they might otherwise have had. Too, they have a fine ability to surrender their egos in the service of a higher cause or set of principles. That quality alone is bound to open the doors to a more expanded belief system and even the occasional miracle as they journey along this karmic path.

CHALLENGE: **TRANSFORMING TRICKS INTO TRANSCENDENCE**

FULFILLMENT: **MYSTIFYING OTHERS WITH THEIR UNIQUE BRAND OF SLEIGHT OF HAND**

NOTABLE: **JOEL GREY (ACTOR, *CABARET*)**

April 19–24
POWER
ARIES–TAURUS CUSP

Natural leaders, the hardworking, dynamic people born on the Cusp of Power who find themselves on the Way of Transcendence may get mired in repetitive or even compulsive behaviors that keep them from discovering the broader range of knowledge, faith, and spiritual understanding it demands. At the same time, their yearning for power can play a big part in their personal redemption, especially when it comes time for them to acknowledge forces larger than themselves. Though this karmic path will demand that at some point they relinquish some of their worldly ambition in order to open themselves to a higher degree of understanding, they are almost sure to accept that opportunity with grace, dignity, and a sense of trust. In fact, once these people have fully comprehended the lessons involved in this life journey, they will impart a whole new meaning to the phrase "knowledge is power."

ELAINE MAY
Actress/director

4/21/1932
Aries–Taurus Cusp

CHALLENGE: **NOT FORGETTING THAT TRANSCENDENCE MUST INCLUDE LOVE**
FULFILLMENT: **APPLYING THEIR STRENGTH OF PURPOSE TO ACHIEVING THEIR AIMS**
NOTABLES: **FERNANDO BOTERO (ARTIST; SUBJECTS ARE PORTLY); HALSTON (FASHION DESIGNER)**

April 25–May 2
MANIFESTATION
TAURUS I

The practical, tenacious, and hardheaded individuals born in the Week of Manifestation who travel the Way of Transcendence can take some great strides along this road, but they will have to work hard to overcome a rather stodgy and complacent streak that may hinder their higher sense of calling and awareness. Rather more likely than some on this karmic path to get stuck in ruts of their own making, then justify their stagnation with issues of so-called practical reality, they will have to delve deep to unearth their fears and insecurities, bring them into the light of day, and set them aside. Yet as stubborn as these individuals can be, they can be equally dedicated and will surely display great devotion and strength of conviction as they come to acquire the higher sense of faith and awareness that beckons to them.

CHALLENGE: **DIGGING THEMSELVES OUT OF THEIR RUTS**
FULFILLMENT: **COMING TO BELIEVE IN A GREATER PURPOSE**
NOTABLES: **ANOUK AIMÉE (FRENCH FILM ACTRESS); LORENZ HART (LYRICIST, "MY FUNNY VALENTINE"); MEADOWLARK LEMON (BASKETBALL PLAYER, HARLEM GLOBETROTTERS)**

May 3–10
THE TEACHER
TAURUS II

The movers and shakers born in this week who travel the Way of Transcendence are likely to make a great success of things, providing they do not retreat into pedantry, an overly critical attitude, or a preoccupation with the letter of the laws that govern reality at the expense of a higher sense of meaning. Somewhat less likely than others on this karmic path to do things by rote or force of habit, these individuals will nevertheless experience a number of crossroads, and it will be important for them to keep a fresh outlook and an open mind in order to remain receptive to the good advice, spiritual strength, and transformative energy that is available through the establishment of a partnership with the divine. If they do not demand a guarantee of success before summoning the courage that will enable them, upon occasion, to leap empty-handed into the voids of the unknown, they are sure to experience a widening of their personal, spiritual, and intellectual frontiers.

CASEY KASEM
Syndicated DJ,
American Top 40

4/27/1932
Taurus I

CHALLENGE: **OVERCOMING THEIR NEED TO BE RIGHT**
FULFILLMENT: **ENGAGING THEIR OWN BRAND OF MYSTICISM ALONG THE ROAD**
NOTABLES: **BISHOP FULTON J. SHEEN (CATHOLIC PRELATE; ENTHRALLING SPEAKER; TV HOST); RUDOLPH VALENTINO (FAMOUS SCREEN LOVER, "THE SHEIK")**

May 11–18
THE NATURAL
TAURUS III

Though well suited to the challenges and demands of the Way of Transcendence, the individuals born in the Week of the Natural who navigate this karmic path may get stuck in their need for stability and security. Though inwardly they may be highly attracted to a freedom-loving lifestyle with no responsibility to anyone but themselves, they may hesitate to take the risks associated with overcoming limitations and practical concerns, staying stuck in boring jobs, unsatisfying relationships, or a rather stunted worldview. Yet their love of the natural world will figure prominently in their redemption. If they are able to turn their attention outward and allow themselves to become more receptive to the rhythms and cycles of life that govern nature, the resulting sense of affirmation and understanding should do much to broaden their outlook and raise their spirits. They must, however, take care that the challenges they create for themselves do not become insurmountable obstacles.

CHALLENGE: **WEANING THEMSELVES FROM THEIR NEED FOR SECURITY**
FULFILLMENT: **FINDING THE TRANSCENDENTAL IN THE NATURAL WORLD**

May 19–24
ENERGY
TAURUS–GEMINI CUSP

Those born on the Cusp of Energy who navigate this karmic path may experience their share of life's ups and downs, yet they are likely to be considerably less rigid than many of their fellow travelers on this road. Still, they may have to address some prominent control issues along the way and release their need not only to run the show, but to be the show. Applying themselves to a spiritual practice such as yoga, meditation, or visualization will be enormously helpful, as such disciplines will enable them to function within the confines of a structured routine yet at the same time serve to open their minds and imaginations to the world of higher possibilities that awaits their exploration. If they are careful not to content themselves with mere material acquisitions, achievements, and other tangible evidence of their place in the world, turning their attention instead to the development of greater sensitivity and idealism, they can expect wonderful things.

CHALLENGE: **GROUNDING THEIR ENERGIES SUFFICIENTLY TO FOCUS ON THEIR GOALS**

FULFILLMENT: **MOVING BEYOND ALL RESTRICTIONS**

May 25–June 2
FREEDOM
GEMINI I

The independent souls born in the Week of Freedom who travel the Way of Transcendence may display a rather difficult, iconoclastic side. Often rebellious in the extreme, they would do well to choose their battles more carefully and avoid their tendency to misspend their energies in endless debate, pointless arguments, and sarcastic commentary. Here is a configuration where these individuals may indeed have to face the fact that what they know will not ultimately prove as important as what they don't know. If they are careful to keep their minds more open than their mouths, release the need to win their arguments at any cost, and exalt and expand their capacity for belief in the infinite, their natural skepticism will fall by the wayside and be replaced by a joyful enthusiasm and interest in the worlds that extend beyond the visible and into the realms of the unseen.

PAUL EHRLICH
Biologist

5/29/1932
Gemini I

CHALLENGE: **TEMPERING NEGATIVE THINKING**

FULFILLMENT: **FINDING A STILL POINT FROM WHICH THEY CAN EXPAND THEIR UNDERSTANDING**

June 3–10
NEW LANGUAGE
GEMINI II

Those born in the Week of New Language who make their way along this karmic path may have to overcome a great deal of natural fearfulness, insecurity, and self-doubt before they can realize their higher potential. Getting stuck in a sense of frustration may be a lifelong pattern for some of these personalities, and the resulting defensiveness may hold them back from realizing any number of higher dreams and aspirations. Too, some early disappointments may have contributed to a rather negative outlook or worldview, causing them to become preoccupied with the need to be accepted or to impose their beliefs on others. Yet if they can learn to set aside their need to feel themselves understood in the interest of understanding others, the doors to greater joy and faith will swing open and their insecurities will be replaced by the confidence to move beyond ordinary experience and into the world of universal principles.

CHALLENGE: **BEING AWARE OF WHEN THEY RETREAT INTO THE SAFE STRUCTURES OF THEIR DEFENSIVENESS**

FULFILLMENT: **OVERCOMING COMMUNICATION BARRIERS**

NOTABLE: **JOHN DREW BARRYMORE (ACTOR)**

June 11–18
THE SEEKER
GEMINI III

Those born in the Week of the Seeker are blessed with a natural curiosity, sense of independence, and yearning for adventure that will doubtless serve them well on the Way of Transcendence. In short, pushing the envelope of ordinary life in the interest of expanding knowledge is very much in their line. Yet they will have to guard against a tendency to become rather iconoclastic, hyperbolic, or even chronically irritable in the effort to overcome their restrictions. In fact, these individuals may get stuck in the belief that they know all there is to know, and the resulting cynicism and disillusionment may lead them into self-imposed prisons of negativity and ennui. Such attitudes should not be allowed to interfere with their sense of higher development or disturb their faith in the future, for practical talents and spirituality can make for a winning combination.

STEFFI GRAF
Champion tennis player

6/14/1969
Gemini III

CHALLENGE: **NOT INSISTING ON FREEDOM TO THE DETRIMENT OF THEIR GREATER GOAL**

FULFILLMENT: **SETTING THEMSELVES SPECIFIC, MEASURABLE GOALS**

NOTABLES: **MARIO CUOMO (FORMER GOVERNOR OF NEW YORK); YASMIN BLEETH (ACTRESS, BAYWATCH)**

June 19–24

MAGIC
GEMINI–CANCER CUSP

Especially well suited to the higher calling of the Way of Transcendence, Gemini–Cancers may experience amazing degrees of inspiration and expansion. Yet they will have to work hard to break some less-than-useful habits of mind and develop faith in the larger design in order to realize their true potential and promise. Self-doubt and self-negation may be their most dangerous enemies, for the tendency of these men and women to second-guess themselves can reach truly destructive proportions. Too, they would do well to avoid a tendency to divide the world into the absolutes of reward and punishment, good and evil, or haves and have-nots and develop a more easygoing and receptive attitude toward the sacred. Able to combine objectivity and sensitivity in a rare and productive fashion, they will do especially well when they place themselves in the service of a higher cause. Properly channeled, their capacity for devotion will enable them to dwell in a more benevolent universe.

CHALLENGE: **NOT ALLOWING THEIR OBJECTIVITY TO TAKE OVER WHEN THEY ARE AFRAID**

FULFILLMENT: **FINDING ALL THE BEST REASONS TO BELIEVE IN SOMETHING GREATER THAN THEMSELVES**

NOTABLE: **PIER ANGELI (ITALIAN ACTRESS)**

DAVE THOMAS
Owner of Wendy's
fast-food chain

7/2/32
Cancer I

June 25–July 2

THE EMPATH
CANCER I

The Way of Transcendence imbues those born in this week with a higher degree of practical talent and considerably less personal sensitivity than they might otherwise have had. If they can find the balance between their intuitive powers and their practical application, the result will be great happiness and enlightenment. In fact, the principal danger here is that they will allow their fears of rejection to overtake them and manifest themselves in an unpleasantly aggressive, clingy, or demanding need to be needed. At the same time, they should be careful not to suppress their feelings or to concentrate solely on tangible reality, for that would close them off from some of their greatest assets and remove their potential for higher spiritual realization. Providing they don't succumb to depression or allow themselves to be unduly affected by others' negativity, they can expect a profound and rewarding life experience on this karmic path.

CHALLENGE: **TRANSCENDING THEIR SENSITIVITY**
FULFILLMENT: **ACHIEVING THEIR MORE WORLDLY GOALS**

July 3–10

THE UNCONVENTIONAL
CANCER II

On the Way of Transcendence, Cancer II's are likely to possess a rare combination of creative and imaginative talent. Gifted with the ability to generate unique concepts, fantasies and ideas, they are likely to put them into some practical form of application or manifestation on this karmic path. Thus, this will doubtless be an especially rewarding journey. They will, however, have to work hard to avoid the dangers of becoming emotionally armored, disillusioned, or isolated when things don't go their way. On the other side of the coin, becoming overwrought or obsessed can be a real risk since it is often hard for them to control their darker desires and fantasies. Yet if these individuals can employ their analytical skills and astute psychological sense in the acquisition of greater self-knowledge and make an effort to take a more creative approach to life, the resulting cohesion of their inner yearnings and outer experience will prove more than worth the trip.

CHALLENGE: **NOT BECOMING TOO LOST IN THE LANDSCAPE OF THEIR IMAGINATION**

FULFILLMENT: **PURSUING AND IMPLEMENTING THEIR VISIONARY GOALS**

NOTABLE: **DELLA REESE (MINISTER; SINGER; ACTRESS, TOUCHED BY AN ANGEL)**

JOHN D. ROCKEFELLER
Oil magnate

7/8/1839
Cancer II

July 11–18

THE PERSUADER
CANCER III

Those born in the Week of the Persuader who travel the Way of Transcendence may have a difficult time overcoming their need for control. Though quite capable of managing their own emotions and needs, they run the risk of becoming shut down to the world of larger possibility that awaits them. Too, they may be burdened with less-than-useful judgmental attitudes or misapply their considerable powers of observation to support a rather staid or unbending worldview. Yet beneath their sometimes ironclad exteriors, there lurks considerable passion and emotional power. If they allow their feelings to augment and inform their methods of administration, they are likely to be forces to be reckoned with and respected as they make their way along this karmic path.

CHALLENGE: **TEMPERING THEIR NEED TO BE IN CONTROL**
FULFILLMENT: **EXPANDING THE LIMITS OF THEIR INVENTIVE MINDS**
NOTABLE: **ROOSEVELT GREER (FOOTBALL PLAYER; ACTOR; MINISTER)**

July 19–25

OSCILLATION
CANCER–LEO CUSP

Those born in this period who travel the Way of Transcendence are likely to be gifted with a higher degree of stability and emotional calm than they might otherwise have had. Indeed, the practical gifts of this karmic path can make them highly effective individuals, providing they do not become overly dogmatic, rigid, or narrow-minded in their views. Though a certain amount of upheaval and a tendency to depression may accompany this configuration, Cancer–Leos have a dynamic side that is sure to urge them up from even the lowest nadirs of despair. Still, in order to realize the progress and promise of overcoming their limitations, they will first have to divest themselves of the fears of their own wilder side and perhaps get a bit more comfortable with who they are inside. Reaching beyond the constraints of conventional wisdom can come quite naturally to them, however, and if they are willing to take up the quest for higher realization, their efforts will not go unrewarded.

CHALLENGE: **CHANNELING THEIR RISK TAKING INTO GREATER INITIATIVE**

FULFILLMENT: **TRANSCENDING THE LIMITATIONS OF THEIR MOODS**

NOTABLE: **SIMON BOLÍVAR (VENEZUELAN REVOLUTIONARY; STATESMAN; "EL LIBERTADOR")**

MENACHEM BEGIN
Israeli prime minister

8/16/1913
Leo III

July 26–August 2

AUTHORITY
LEO I

The formidable personalities born in this week who make their way along this karmic path may prove to be their own worst enemies when it comes to developing the willingness to open themselves to the realms of the unseen, the invisible, or the infinite. Likely to be greatly preoccupied with issues of willpower, self-control, dominance, and the practicalities of life, Leo I's are rather prone to get stuck in ruts of personal habit or rituals and may wind up going through life wearing a rather uncomfortable set of blinders. They will have to work hard to counteract their impulse to fulfill others' expectations and instead turn their attention to their own higher development. Yet they are gifted with a capacity for belief that will stand them in good stead. Much attracted to abstract truths, higher principles, and the forces of spiritual life, at some point they will doubtless succeed in opening the channels between ordinary reality and the realms of the infinite.

CHALLENGE: **GOING UP AGAINST THEIR OWN PRECONCEIVED NOTIONS**

FULFILLMENT: **ADOPTING THE HOPEFUL, POSITIVE ATTITUDE CALLED FOR BY THIS KARMIC PATH**

NOTABLE: **MEIR KAHANE (RELIGIOUS LEADER; FOUNDED JEWISH DEFENSE LEAGUE)**

August 3–10

BALANCED STRENGTH
LEO II

Those born in the Week of Balanced Strength who travel the Way of Transcendence may have to struggle a bit to develop greater versatility and variety in their outlook before they can realize the higher promises of this path. In fact, though it is often an asset, on this path their single-mindedness can be their greatest enemy since it means that it is difficult for them to change their lives, habits, or beliefs no matter how much they recognize the necessity for such change. Thus, there are many with this configuration who will experience this life's journey as highly restrictive or unfulfilling until they open themselves up to their own spirituality. It will be especially useful for these souls to learn to focus their mental powers in prayer, meditation, or visualization. Once they grasp the relationship between intention and manifestation, life will doubtless take a turn for the better for them.

CHALLENGE: **NOT ENSLAVING THEMSELVES TO RIGID RULES OR CONCEPTS OF LOYALTY**

FULFILLMENT: **DISCOVERING THE POWER OF POSITIVE AFFIRMATION**

NOTABLE: **MATA HARI (DUTCH COURTESAN; SPY)**

CHRISTIAN SLATER
Actor,
Pump Up the Volume

8/18/1969
Leo III

August 11–18

LEADERSHIP
LEO III

Leo III's have a good chance for success and enlightenment on this karmic path, especially when they learn to submit to the forces outside themselves in the search for greater understanding. For these personalities, however, that may prove considerably more difficult than it sounds, and some with this configuration may have to endure a great deal of personal frustration arising from an often narrow or self-centered worldview. Thus, they would do especially well to expand their minds through the study of philosophy, religion, or alternative spiritual disciplines in an effort to unlock their own stores of subconscious understanding. Still, their creativity and power can help them develop wider philosophical perspective and a generally sunnier outlook, providing they resist the temptation to stick with the tried and true and set aside their selfishness by placing themselves in the service of a higher set of principles.

CHALLENGE: **BEING CAREFUL NOT TO STICK TOO NARROWLY TO THEIR PLAN**

FULFILLMENT: **EDUCATING THEMSELVES IN THE POWER OF THEIR THOUGHTS**

August 19–25

EXPOSURE
LEO–VIRGO CUSP

Those born on the Cusp of Exposure who find themselves on The Way of Transcendence will encounter a number of issues and situations where the facts may seem to exist at decided odds with the truth. These people are gifted with an extraordinary ability to dig beneath the surface and are likely to have a keen perception of others' secrets and motivations. Yet for all their powers of observation and investigation, they will have to learn to overcome the limits of intrigue, secretiveness, and their private sense of psychodrama in order to make real progress here. Facing the challenge of developing real integrity and developing a sense of honesty in their dealings with themselves and others will figure prominently in this life journey, as many of their pet beliefs and outworn dogmas will be put to the test. Many of this group will in fact face some very public battles that will force them to reveal their true colors and take a stand for what they believe is right, up to and including the admission that there is much they have yet to learn.

CHALLENGE: **RECOGNIZING THAT KEEPING SECRETS CAN BE A FORM OF RESTRICTION**
FULFILLMENT: **ENGAGING THEIR BURIED PASSION TO ACHIEVE AND SURPASS ANY GOAL**

KENZO TANGE
Contemporary Asian architect

9/4/1913
Virgo II

August 26

SYSTEM BUILDE
VIRGO I

System Builders may ~
ing challenges to their ~
they come to the end ~
Somewhat recalcitrant and ~ ~ese
personalities will have to do ~ ~ace the facts
when navigating the higher ~hallenges of this karmic path. Especially prone to get stuck in a rut or to try to impose their particular brand of structured beliefs on others, they will have to go within in search of the reasons for their reluctance to expand their views, not the least of which may prove to be the fear of making decisions. Yet they can make wonderful progress, and the most evolved of these personalities will be able to transcend their ego's limitations to grasp and embrace eternal truths.

CHALLENGE: **GRAPPLING WITH THE KIND OF DEPRESSION THAT COMES FROM FEELING OUT OF CONTROL**
FULFILLMENT: **DEVELOPING A MORE COMFORTABLE RELATIONSHIP WITH SPIRITUALITY**

Septemb
BEAUTY
VIRG

September 3–10

THE ENIGMA
VIRGO II

The souls born in this week who travel the Way of Transcendence will be inclined to pride themselves on their good sense, taste, and judgment. Yet they will have to take care that their discrimination and high standards do not become a form of limitation if they are to recognize the higher challenges here. In any event, this configuration may manifest itself in a highly internal sort of journey, as Virgo II's are not much inclined to share their questions, problems, or revelations with others. Taking up the study of alternative religions and philosophies will help to round out their view of the world, however, as will developing a willingness to engage in lively and stimulating debates and discussions in which all parties openly share their opinions. Too, their impulse toward service is very pronounced, and if they can allow themselves to follow their better nature, these personalities will enjoy considerable progress along this karmic path.

CHALLENGE: **DEALING WITH THEIR DEFENSE MECHANISMS IN ORDER TO CREATE AN OPENING WITHIN**
FULFILLMENT: **ENJOYING A QUIET SENSE OF ACCOMPLISHMENT FOR HAVING PUSHED BEYOND THEIR BOUNDARIES**
NOTABLE: **MICKEY COHEN (GANGSTER)**

JESSE OWENS
Olympic gold medal track star

9/12/1913
Virgo III

September 11–18

THE LITERALIST
VIRGO III

Those born in the Week of the Literalist may have to work hard to broaden their horizons and beliefs and to deepen their sense of faith if they are to make a success of this life journey. Though blessed with a character that is naturally indomitable, they will have to back up, lighten up, and detach themselves from their notions of truth from time to time, if only to gain some much-needed perspective. Once they come to terms with the fact that their unique ability to "call 'em as they see 'em" doesn't mean much if they remain all but blind to the larger picture, they can embark on a quest for self-realization. Ultimately, they will develop a capacity for reverence that will provide them with a greater sense of harmony and a feeling of alignment with the forces that govern the universe of individual and collective experience.

CHALLENGE: **RELEASING THEIR FEAR OF THE UNKNOWN**
FULFILLMENT: **INDULGING THEIR MORE ROMANTIC OR SPIRITUAL YEARNINGS**
NOTABLES: **PAUL "BEAR" BRYANT (LEGENDARY FOOTBALL COACH); SHERWOOD ANDERSON (WRITER/POET)**

r 19–24

–LIBRA CUSP

Much better grounded and more realistic than some of their fellow Virgo–Librans, those born on this cusp who find themselves on the Way of Transcendence can realize wonderful success, as they are both less inclined to be superficial on the one hand and more inclined to pursue spiritual matters on the other. Elegant and well organized, those born on the Cusp of Beauty will nevertheless have to avoid the danger of overconfidence or falling into repetitive negative behavior patterns without questioning what they're doing or why they're doing it. Though they have a tendency to be indecisive as well as rather self-indulgent, they are far more free-spirited than many on this road and are likely to rise above both their internal and external limitations in their search for beauty, truth, and a greater understanding of their place in the larger scheme.

GUNNAR AND MATTHEW NELSON
Twin sons of Ricky Nelson, band Nelson

9/20/1969
Virgo–Libra Cusp

CHALLENGE: **COMING TO TERMS WITH THEIR OWN DARKER OR MORE ADDICTIVE TENDENCIES**
FULFILLMENT: **REDEFINING THEIR NOTIONS OF BEAUTY FROM A SPIRITUAL PERSPECTIVE**

September 25–October 2

THE PERFECTIONIST
LIBRA I

Libra I's who travel the Way of Transcendence can realize great success and accomplishment, providing their own mercilessly high standards for achievement do not become the prison of their spirit. An ability to back up and see the big picture will be something they will have to develop almost from scratch, and they will also have to learn to relinquish some of their pet obsessions in the interest of increasing their awareness. Too, there are some with this configuration who may rise above a given set of limitations or restrictions only to develop an odd sort of flightiness, unable to ground themselves in one project or plan, yet equally unable to place themselves in the larger scheme or structure. Still, if they can master their resistance to risk taking and learn the fine art of embracing the unknown, they will be considerably freed from the stress of attending to the world of detail and will be able to open themselves up to the world of spiritual expansion that beckons to them.

CHALLENGE: **BEING LESS INCLINED TO FIX THINGS AND MORE INCLINED TO INITIATE THEM**
FULFILLMENT: **REPRESSING THEIR FEELINGS LESS AND OPENING TO THEIR SPIRITUAL SIDE**

October 3–10

SOCIETY
LIBRA II

Gifted with great insight and empathy, those born in the Week of Society who travel the Way of Transcendence are likely to take tremendous strides, providing they do not allow themselves to become stuck in unsatisfying routines, relationships, and habits of mind. Indeed, these souls are promised quite a bit of personal transformation and spiritual expansion, and, properly applied and directed, their natural energies will fall into a wonderfully comfortable alignment with those of this life journey. Though there is some danger that these individuals will refuse to take their own needs seriously enough or that they will shy away from the challenge to overcome the things that hold them back from greater self-realization, even their slightest efforts to rise above the ordinary should meet with resounding affirmation.

JENNY LIND
Operatic soprano

10/6/1820
Libra II

CHALLENGE: **DEVELOPING A CAPACITY TO SEE THEMSELVES MORE CLEARLY**
FULFILLMENT: **CIRCUMVENTING THE LIMITS OTHERS IMPOSE ON THEM**
NOTABLES: **TEMPLE FIELDING (FIELDING'S TRAVEL GUIDES); BRETT FAVRE (FOOTBALL GREAT)**

October 11–18

THEATER
LIBRA III

Those born in the Week of Theater who travel the Way of Transcendence can make some astonishing leaps in consciousness along the way, yet they may have to divest themselves of the restrictions of their rather exalted self-image before they can realize the higher degree of fulfillment it promises. Truly brilliant communicators, they may be seduced by their own success and worldliness and thus fail to access the hidden worlds of creativity, spirituality, and inspiration from which their impulse to excel springs forth. Marked by an overconfidence in their own abilities, these individuals may experience the truth of the maxim "The bigger they are, the harder they fall" at some point in their life journey. Still, if they do not succumb to the impulse to blame others for their own mistakes and concentrate their energies on rising above their trials and tribulations with a renewed sense of hope and understanding, they can take amazing strides along this karmic path.

CHALLENGE: **KNOWING WHEN TO ADMIT A MISTAKE AND START OVER**
FULFILLMENT: **REFRESHING THEIR ATTITUDE WITH A DOSE OF POSITIVE THINKING**
NOTABLE: **NANCY KERRIGAN (OLYMPIC ICE SKATER; WON SILVER MEDAL)**

October 19–25

DRAMA AND CRITICISM
LIBRA–SCORPIO CUSP

Libra–Scorpios who travel the Way of Transcendence are gifted with both an extraordinary intellect and the ability to express themselves with a sometimes uncomfortable clarity. While promised tremendous success and achievement on this path, however, they will have to cultivate a more intuitive sort of understanding and control their tendency to steamroll others in their attempts to get their points across. In fact, these are the type of people who may well cling to the very chains that bind them until they set aside their ego issues and align themselves more closely with their need to overcome their limitations, whether of the world or only in the mind. Sensuous, sometimes to an extreme, and often passionate, they will never suffer fools gladly and may manifest a certain carelessness with others, especially lovers and mates. Learning the fine arts of empathy and compassion will be especially important and will enable them to describe and then transcend the limits of their reality as they search for greater growth.

JANE PAULEY
TV journalist, former
cohost of *Today Show*

———

10/31/1950
Scorpio I

CHALLENGE: **TEMPERING THEIR FERVOR IN FAVOR OF A LARGER, MORE BALANCED PERSPECTIVE**

FULFILLMENT: **CULTIVATING AN ATTITUDE OF TRUST AND HOPE**

NOTABLE: **ROBERT CAPA (*LIFE* MAGAZINE PHOTOJOURNALIST)**

October 26–November 2

INTENSITY
SCORPIO I

Those born in the Week of Intensity who travel the Way of Transcendence may find that many of the limitations, restrictions, and boundaries they seek to overcome are ultimately self-imposed. Yet they have a possibility for great success, as they are likely to be talented, often brilliant, and very well organized. Many of their problems may arise from the refusal to acknowledge the disparity between the larger scope of their perceptions and their need to remain focused to such an extent that they make themselves unhappy. At the same time, their redemption will come from knowing that they have much to offer others and deep resources to draw upon in this life journey. If they can develop a higher degree of tolerance and avoid the tendency to be judgmental or extreme in their views, they will be able to overcome even the worst trials and setbacks and free to experience the levels of transformation, transcendence, and fulfillment that are all promised by this karmic path.

CHALLENGE: **LEARNING THE ART OF RELEASING THEIR MORE NEGATIVE ATTITUDES**

FULFILLMENT: **TAPPING INTO SOMETHING GREATER THAN THEMSELVES**

NOTABLE: **JOHN CANDY (ACTOR/COMEDIAN, *SPLASH*)**

November 3–11

DEPTH
SCORPIO II

Those born in the Week of Depth who make their way along this karmic path would do well to lighten up from time to time, increase their perspective, and cultivate the sense of humor and tolerance necessary to real success. Indeed, many of these individuals will struggle with the demons of depression, worry, or the insistence that theirs is the only way to think before they are able to jump the traces of their own self-imposed limitations and experience the levels of accomplishment and transformation promised by this karmic path. While many of these individuals will be very prone to deep-seated patterns of negative behavior, unfortunate addictions, and self-destruction, it will always remain within their power to rise from the depths and soar to the heights of higher development. If they can open their hearts and minds to a belief in miracles, the certainty of change, and the power of fate, God, or universal laws, they will be able to achieve their heart's desire.

BURT LANCASTER
Actor, *Elmer Gantry*

———

11/2/1913
Scorpio I

CHALLENGE: **REALIZING THAT THEIR BRAND OF NEGATIVITY KEEPS THEM FROM REALIZING THEIR DREAMS**

FULFILLMENT: **CONCENTRATING LESS ON THE LIMITATIONS OF EXISTENCE AND MORE ON THE NATURE OF THE ETERNAL**

NOTABLE: **VIVIEN LEIGH (ACTRESS, *GONE WITH THE WIND*)**

November 12–18

CHARM
SCORPIO III

Those born in the Week of Charm who navigate the promise and challenge of the Way of Transcendence are likely to have a rewarding journey, despite their tendency to become spellbound by or mired in their own opinions, perceptions of reality, and ways of doing things. Indeed, many of these individuals have a tendency to complacency, controlling behaviors, and a rather defensive attitude toward change that are all out of place on this karmic path. Yet if they go within and familiarize themselves with their own motivations and avoid distracting themselves with fair-weather friends or less-than-worthy associates, they can connect with higher laws, universal principles, and their own deeper convictions. The resulting revelations, combined with their own realism, will lead them to excellence, achievement, and a higher and more fulfilling level of personal development.

CHALLENGE: **CONTROLLING THEIR EXCESSES**

FULFILLMENT: **STRIVING TO REALIZE THEIR DREAMS**

NOTABLES: **WILLIAM PITT THE ELDER (ENGLISH STATESMAN; PRIME MINISTER); GRAHAM PARKER (PUNK ROCK MUSICIAN)**

November 19–24
REVOLUTION
SCORPIO–SAGITTARIUS CUSP

November 25–December 2
INDEPENDENCE
SAGITTARIUS I

Those born on the Cusp of Revolution who navigate this karmic path may experience the transformation and transcendence that beckon here, yet they will have to take care that they do not get mired in a sense of infallibility, undue aggression, or an entirely too literal interpretation of philosophical precepts and spiritual principles. In fact, many of the individuals on this karmic path will have little problem connecting to the world of larger ideals and universality that are part of its higher promise, yet they may defeat their effectiveness by becoming overly didactic, overly idealistic, or downright wacky in their view of the world. Likely to be honest in the extreme, they will always be interesting, though their sense of enlightenment and connection may well come and go.

MARY MARTIN
Stage/film actress,
Peter Pan, South Pacific
___
12/1/1913
Sagittarius I

Those born in the Week of Independence who travel the Way of Transcendence are likely to realize rare levels of excellence and accomplishment on this karmic path. Blessed on the one hand with a fine practical sense and on the other with vision, creativity, and imagination, they can take great strides. Yet they must be careful not to go overboard in the pursuit of their higher dreams and lose their effectiveness through either escapism or a high-handed or autocratic attitude toward those who oppose them. Indeed, they have a rather combative streak that will bear watching. Yet no matter what the realities of the present, these personalities are inclined to plan, dream, and keep an eye on the future in such a way that they are bound to overcome any obstacles that might stand in the way of their success.

CHALLENGE: **DEVOTING LESS TIME TO BATTLES AND MORE TO THE WAR**
FULFILLMENT: **UNDERSTANDING THAT WHAT THEY'RE REALLY TRYING TO DO IS OVERCOME THEMSELVES**
NOTABLE: **BENJAMIN BRITTEN (BRITISH SINGER/COMPOSER)**

CHALLENGE: **REALIZING THAT BELIEVING THAT THEY ARE FREE WILL MAKE IT SO**
FULFILLMENT: **FINDING THE FLOW IN LIFE SIMPLY BY MAINTAINING A POSITIVE OUTLOOK**

December 3–10
THE ORIGINATOR
SAGITTARIUS II

December 11–18
THE TITAN
SAGITTARIUS III

The unusual and often compelling people born in the Week of the Originator who find themselves on the Way of Transcendence are well suited to its challenges, though they may waste no small amount of time during this life journey trying to be someone they're not. In fact, their insistence on the letter of the law, certain codes of behavior, or the idea that material reality is all there is may be a form of trying to disguise or repress their better nature in an effort to be accepted by others. Once they have released their fear of rejection and allowed their creativity, technical proficiency, and natural brilliance to come to the fore, their courage and conviction are bound to meet with both visible and invisible affirmations from the larger universe.

JOSEPH CONRAD
Writer, *Heart of Darkness*
___
12/3/1857
Sagittarius II

The personalities born in this week who travel the Way of Transcendence are marked by an ability to think on a grand scale that will serve them extremely well. Thus, overcoming restrictions might seem a fairly easy for them. Yet that task might not prove as simple to master as it may sound, for at some point these individuals will have to come to terms with some deep-seated insecurities that hold them back from attaining their highest potential. Despite their bravado, depression can be a problem for many of them, journey, as they are burdened by some rather cumbersome philosophical quandaries and a tendency to chew on problems to the point that they render themselves ineffective. Yet if they can avoid exacerbating their natural irritability with unfortunate choices, let go of old grudges, and allow themselves to reach for the stars, even when they seem hopelessly out of reach, all will go well for them.

CHALLENGE: **NOT PERMITTING THEIR INSECURITY TO HOLD THEM BACK**
FULFILLMENT: **RISING TO THE TOP OF THEIR FIELD AND BEYOND**
NOTABLE: **JOAN ARMATRADING (SINGER)**

CHALLENGE: **ALLOWING THEMSELVES TO SURRENDER**
FULFILLMENT: **ENJOYING THE MAGIC OF LIVING IN A GRAND, EVEN TRANSCENDENTAL, SCALE**

December 19–25

PROPHECY
SAGITTARIUS–CAPRICORN CUSP

Those born on the Cusp of Prophecy who travel the Way of Transcendence are likely to experience a sense of connection with the larger forces in their lives that will be difficult, if not impossible, to ignore. Though some with this configuration will retreat from the larger challenges of this karmic path and stubbornly refuse to acknowledge the worlds that exist outside the narrow confines of ordinary perception, most will find themselves untroubled by ego demands, an insistence on their own viewpoint, or a need to control others. There is some danger, however, that the force of their intuitive and psychic powers may lead them rather too far, and they should take care to ground their remarkable sense of perception in healthy habits and the study of alternative philosophies, religions, and spiritual disciplines. Still, there is very little that can go seriously wrong for them, especially when they heed the call of their deepest needs and impulses.

CHALLENGE: **REMEMBERING THAT THEIR MORE WORLDLY OR AMBITIOUS SIDE NEEDS CHALLENGE, TOO**
FULFILLMENT: **FULLY LIVING FROM THEIR INTUITIVE POTENTIAL**

J. EDGAR HOOVER
Notorious head of F.B.I.

1/1/1895
Capricorn I

December 26–January 2

THE RULER
CAPRICORN I

Those born in the Week of the Ruler who find themselves on this karmic path may find their life journey fueled by a sense of destiny that may sometimes exist at odds with their sense of practical reality. Though they will be blessed with the strength of their convictions, part of their journey will doubtless involve discarding some pet theories or ideas in order to be able to pursue their sense of excellence and soar to the heights of ambition and achievement. Perhaps their principal pitfall will be simple stubbornness or an unwillingness to divest themselves of a limited set of opinions that holds them back from greater appreciation and understanding of others. Yet though their sense of integrity and honesty may be challenged from time to time along this karmic path, these personalities will emerge from the journey with renewed faith, wider perception, and a record of solid achievement.

CHALLENGE: **TURNING THEIR ATTENTION INWARD NOW AND THEN**
FULFILLMENT: **TRANSCENDING LIMITS IN CAREER OR OTHER ENDEAVORS**

January 3–9

DETERMINATION
CAPRICORN II

These dauntless, diligent souls who make their journey along the Way of Transcendence are well suited to its challenges and are likely to experience a truly satisfying life experience. As they are natural strivers, it is very much in keeping with their energies and inclinations to achieve and then surpass their own sense of personal best. Too, their interest in the philosophical and metaphysical will keep them from getting stuck in complacent routines or a tired set of opinions, and their sensitivity will do much to keep them attuned to their need for growth. In fact, only their sense of loyalty may bear examination and redefinition. For when it is misplaced, through ignorance, näiveté or undue self-sacrifice, it may lead these personalities down some unfortunate paths.

CHALLENGE: **NOT BOGGING THEMSELVES DOWN IN PRACTICAL DETAILS**
FULFILLMENT: **FREEING THEMSELVES TO PURSUE THEIR META-PHYSICAL SIDE**

LEROY RANDLE GRUMMAN
Founder/president
Grumman Aircraft

1/4/1895
Capricorn II

January 10–16

DOMINANCE
CAPRICORN III

Those born in the Week of Dominance who find themselves on the Way of Transcendence may find that they are in for a bit of a struggle until they learn to open themselves to the wider worlds of perception and accomplishment that await them. In any event, this is unlikely to be an easy passage, as they are particularly prone to some rather ostrichlike attitudes toward their own limitations and may well sacrifice their need for growth in the interest of maintaining their sense of self-confidence and security. Yet if they can find a way to place their wonderful organizational and administrative abilities in the service of some higher cause or sense of principle, they will find their fears falling by the wayside and replaced with strength, fortitude, and a wisdom that is all the more formidable for its tolerance of and openness to new ideas.

CHALLENGE: **GIVING UP THEIR DEPENDENCY ON ROUTINE**
FULFILLMENT: **SURMOUNTING THE CHALLENGES FATE PLACES IN THEIR PATH**

January 17–22

MYSTERY AND IMAGINATION
CAPRICORN–AQUARIUS CUSP

The often unpredictable characters born on this cusp who journey along the Way of Transcendence are unlikely to get mired in boring patterns or stifling lifestyles, yet they will have to be aware of some rather iconoclastic and even revolutionary tendencies within themselves. Though likely to be quite passionate and blessed with a rich interior life, they may refuse the higher challenges of this karmic path by misspending their emotional energies on unworthy or unproductive relationships or professional pursuits or succumbing to the mistaken belief that they will be more successful if only they can somehow make themselves just like everybody else. Yet it is unlikely that they will ever be able to fall completely out of touch with their unique brand of inspiration. If they stay open to the influences of their creative insights and channel their energies toward the pursuit of their highest ideals, very little will go awry for them.

CHARLES S. DUTTON
Actor, *Roc*

1/30/1951
Aquarius I

CHALLENGE: **WORKING ON DEVELOPING A GREATER SENSE OF TRUST**

FULFILLMENT: **BREAKING THROUGH THE ESTABLISHED ORDER**

January 23–30

GENIUS
AQUARIUS I

Those born in the Week of Genius who travel this karmic path may find themselves really pushing the envelope of ordinary reality as they make their way along this life journey. Blessed with more practical gifts and talents than some others born in this week, they will have a rare capacity to turn their best dreams, theories, and concepts into practical applications. For that reason, they can expect success and accomplishment, yet they should take care not to become too fixed in their attitudes or closed to the constant flow of inspiration and ideas available to them if they keep an open mind and an open heart. Thus, finding a balance between the strength of their convictions and respect for the opinions of others will be most beneficial.

CHALLENGE: **RELAXING THEIR NEED FOR CONSTANT STIMULATION AND LEARNING THE VALUE OF PEACEFULNESS**

FULFILLMENT: **INVOKING THE POWER OF THEIR CONSIDERABLE MINDS**

January 31–February 7

YOUTH AND EASE
AQUARIUS II

Those born in the Week of Youth and Ease who make their way along this karmic path can expect great things, providing they don't succumb to complacency or the fear that they won't be accepted or admired. Gifted with the ability to apply their creative talents in a highly practical fashion, they will doubtless be awarded appreciation and recognition for their efforts. In fact, this will be a relatively easy passage for them. Yet these personalities will benefit from the ability to develop the strength of their own set of values and convictions, without falling prey to an intolerance of or disdain for the ideas of others. Though emotional immaturity can often make them act like spoiled children when obstacles are placed in their path, if they can summon the strength to reach for their highest dreams and ideals and avoid the temptation to remain a big fish in small pond, all will go well for them.

BABE RUTH
Baseball legend; set numerous home run records; pictured at his final appearance at Yankee Stadium, 2 months before his death

2/6/1895
Aquarius II

CHALLENGE: **NOT TAKING THE EASE WITH WHICH THEY OVERCOME LIMITATIONS FOR GRANTED**

FULFILLMENT: **SETTING ASIDE THEIR NEED TO DO EVERYTHING WELL**

February 8–15

ACCEPTANCE
AQUARIUS III

The souls born in the Week of Acceptance who travel the Way of Transcendence may go from one extreme to another in their journey to higher development and self-realization. Likely to be rather colorful characters in any event, they may have a rather fixed set of views and opinions that will undergo an amazing transformation. Overcoming intolerance and developing greater discernment and a broader and better-informed view of the topics that preoccupy their minds will all figure prominently. Thus, however much they be convinced of their own views, they will doubtless encounter the things most necessary to transcending their limitations along this life journey. For here is a configuration where one can find former bigots marching for human rights, former priests extolling the virtues of high finance, and former atheists retreating to the convent—all in a quest to reach beyond the "surly bonds of Earth to touch the face of God"—or some close approximation thereof.

CHALLENGE: **BECOMING MORE TOLERANT AND OPEN**

FULFILLMENT: **INITIATING CHANGE**

KARMIC PATH
24

February 16–22

SENSITIVITY
AQUARIUS–PISCES CUSP

Those born on this cusp who navigate the challenge of the Way of Transcendence may have a rather crusty, belligerent, or downright aggressive persona that is at odds with a fearful, emotional, and rather shockingly sensitive soul. In fact, many of these personalities will have the rather unpleasant quality of becoming more entrenched in their views and habits, the more their inner insecurities grow. Thus, they may experience a number of difficulties, some of which can be successfully overcome only with the aid of dedicated friends, family members, or professionals. Yet there is no karmic path that does not endow those who travel it with the tools needed to rise above their trials to a higher level of consciousness and self-realization. If these individuals work hard to believe in that fact, all will go much more smoothly for them.

CHALLENGE: **GRAPPLING WITH THEIR SENSITIVITY AND THE WAYS IT HOLDS THEM BACK**

FULFILLMENT: **PURSUING THEIR IDEALISM**

MATTHEW BUNKER RIDGWAY
Army officer; one of the first to parachute in D-Day invasion of Normandy

3/3/1895
Pisces II

February 23–March 2

SPIRIT
PISCES I

Thankfully, the Way of Transcendence gifts the individuals born in this week with a higher degree of practical awareness and groundedness than they might otherwise have had. Even so, these ethereal and sensitive people will have to work a bit to overcome their tendency to excessive and rather superficial spirituality, on the one hand, or high-handed zealotry, on the other. Either way, the development of their powers of discernment and an insistence on getting all the facts before they sign away their inheritance to the latest guru will be especially helpful. Characterized by a certain disingenuousness and irresponsibility, they may have such a disdain for earthly affairs that they find themselves at the mercy of the landlord, the bill collector, or the tax authorities until they find the critical balance between faith in what is possible and commitment to what is necessary.

CHALLENGE: **LETTING GO OF THEIR EXPECTATIONS**

FULFILLMENT: **PURSUING A PATH OF DEVOTION OR SERVICE TO A CAUSE**

March 3–10

THE LONER
PISCES II

Those born in the Week of the Loner who travel the Way of Transcendence may become so preoccupied with their sense of idealism that they fail to make some necessary connections in the human sphere, and this group will doubtless have its share of recluses, hermits, and misanthropes. Too, their personal background may be such that they refuse to open themselves up to the idea of faith in a larger plan for fear of encountering another disappointment or disillusionment. Thus, this configuration may well hold its share of trials for them. Yet if they refuse to allow themselves to be defined by their losses and mistakes and cultivate an attitude of simple reverence for life itself coupled with a staunch refusal to be fooled again, they can take great strides along this road.

CHALLENGE: **TRANSCENDING THEIR SENSE OF SUFFERING**

FULFILLMENT: **DEVELOPING THE CAPACITY FOR HOPE**

NOTABLE: **HAROLD JOHNSON (VAUDEVILLIAN)**

JOHN UPDIKE
Writer/poet/critic,
Rabbit Run

3/18/1932
Pisces III

March 11–18

DANCERS AND DREAMERS
PISCES III

Quite a few miracles will abound along the life journey of those born in the Week of Dancers and Dreamers who make their way along this karmic path, but some of those miracles, at least, will be the attempts of more practical types to rescue them from their own folly. In short, these personalities are simply too easily swayed from their chosen course of action and will have to work hard to ensure that their sense of the infinite doesn't interfere with focusing on and enhancing their natural powers. Too, they may have a rather high-handed attitude that at once takes for granted their own abilities and discounts those of others. Yet if they come to terms with the fact that the real secret of magic is never to be so vain as to believe that one is more than the instrument of a larger force, they will doubtless fulfill their remarkable promise along the Way of Transcendence.

CHALLENGE: **QUESTIONING THE MOST PERVASIVE OF THEIR PRECONCEIVED IDEAS**

FULFILLMENT: **BELIEVING IN MIRACLES**

The Way of Passion

VIRGO–LIBRA CUSP TO PISCES–ARIES CUSP
Beauty to Rebirth

Those on the Way of Passion are here in this lifetime to let go of their preconceived notions of truth, goodness, and beauty and, by getting back to basics, to enjoy a fuller experience of life. The men and women on this karmic path are often born with highly refined, aesthetic sensibilities and a rather detached approach to life. However, such a point of view may hold them back from more full-bodied experiences. Often their ideas of what should be get in the way of appreciating what is. Thus, on this karmic path they are challenged to shed much of their idealistic baggage in order to grapple with life in its most real and unadulterated form. Those on this path are often somewhat emotionally numb: they live and love, but only according to the standards or rules set by others, rather than according to what they themselves feel. Frequently, they don't know what makes them truly happy; some may have even given up trying to find out. The Way of Passion calls for these individuals to throw away all their mental constructs and, by diving into life, fully experience everything that comes their way as though for the first time. Here they will open themselves to their own passion, indulge it, savor it, and learn from it as it gives them a more complete view of existence.

Too often those on the Way of Passion approach life from a mental orientation, living more in their heads than from their hearts. Rarely do they throw themselves into an experience without analyzing it first. Typically, while they are

doing something, there is an inner voice commenting on their actions and making judgments. It is difficult for these men and women to simply be with what is happening to them or around them. The detached approach of those on this path is often viewed by others as world-weary or even a bit jaded. But their "been there, done that" attitude only does them a disservice: it prevents them from generating any real enthusiasm or energy for anything or ever trying anything new. What's worse, when feeling any sort of strong emotion, those on the Way of Passion frequently run away from their feelings, back into the safety of a better-ordered or mental universe. Thus, the core lesson for these individuals, if they are to succeed on the Way of Passion, is to learn how to be in the moment by fully experiencing what they are feeling. The men and women on this karmic path must learn to approach each moment as though it were the first and only moment. They must give their all to whatever they do and, in so doing, fully explore every nuance of feeling it has to offer, including the rich variety of sensual experience attached to it. How juicy is the apple being bitten into? What is the subtle nuance of flavor that sets this variety apart from others? What delights more, having eaten it with, perhaps, cheese or chocolate? When cultivating the deeper awareness that being in the moment implies, how mundane the situation is or whether one has done it a thousand times before does not matter; what makes the difference is the attitude one

CORE LESSON
Learning to live each moment to the fullest

GOAL
To fully realize the experience of living

GIFTS
Sensuous, Direct, Intuitive

PITFALLS
Snobbish, Detached, Impatient

brings to it. Once those on the Way of Passion engage themselves in an exploration of life in this fashion, they will find ever-deeper layers of sensuality, pleasure, intrigue, and consciousness.

This karmic path calls those on it to seek out and indulge in a variety of experiences, new vistas, and avenues of excitement. An unintended consequence may be that they will be forced to reexamine most of their sacred cows and discard them, including their often fatal obsession with beauty. A lesson they must learn is that what is the most beautiful is not necessarily the purest, most honest, or truest. Usually, this occurs only through hard-won experience, not detached analysis. It may be difficult for these men and women to force themselves down from their ivory towers and allow their hearts to take the lead, but they must do so if they are to discover the greater truths of life. Too often, these people wrap themselves in idealistic concepts that have no real bearing on what life is all about. Considering themselves above all to be sophisticated, those on the Way of Passion will work hard to reveal their own more untutored sides and, above all, not to be ashamed of showing a more naive face to the world. The process is apt to be an upsetting one for them, preferring as they do the more peaceful, balanced, and detached Virgo–Libra state to the somewhat chaotic and contradictory emotions of Pisces–Aries energy.

Should they embark on a more fully realized experience of life, those on the Way of Passion will often have a sense of being reborn. Once awakened from a fantasy realm of superficial glitz to the teeming profusion of an alive and vibrant world, the men and women on the Way of Passion may feel inspired to share their passion with others and may prove quite eloquent in doing just that. One of the pitfalls that can arise is that they may go overboard and endlessly search for ever-newer and more outrageous experiences in an effort to find something they haven't done before. But becoming ever wilder, more shocking, or dangerous to themselves or others is not a positive activity. Another danger in going too far is that they may arouse their passionate nature to such a point that their lives become overly chaotic. In other cases, many regrets may surface when they leave the comfort and security of a well-ordered, idealistic system behind. There will be times when those on the Way of Passion are seized with regret and long to return to a life in which social acceptance is a given.

The arena in which the lessons of the Way of Passion occur is invariably the crucible of life experience. Those on this karmic path may be forced to put aside their love of books, films, videos, and music in order to break through to a more unaffected and basic existence. This may be necessary only for a time, however, until they learn their core lesson, for after that they may return to

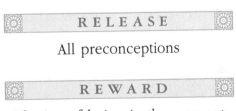

RELEASE

All preconceptions

REWARD

The joy of being in the moment

SUGGESTION

Stop overanalyzing. Make no assumptions. What you seek is within yourself, not in the next relationship. Develop a breathing practice.

the arts with a whole new way of looking at things. In their search for a truer reality, those on this karmic path may wish to travel to areas where people lead a more basic or unaffected life, since through such exploration they will come closer to discovering their own identity. A whole new library may emerge in the homes of such individuals, one with less emphasis on sophisticated art forms and more on primitive ones, such as folk art, less on modern architecture and more on tribal values and back-to-the-earth philosophies. Even a change of diet that emphasizes pure foods in place of haute cuisine may occur. The shift in emphasis from Virgo–Libra sensuousness to Pisces–Aries passion is also likely to occur in searing love affairs, which may very quickly put those on this path in touch with their basic instincts. Experiencing passion in one great, all-encompassing love affair isn't really the ideal way for those on this path to proceed, however. In fact, for some it can be destructive. It is healthier to explore one's passion through one's relationship to the world than to another person. Usually, though, it is through love that these rather frosty individuals are thawed out enough to set them on their way.

What is best for those on this karmic path in general is coming more closely into contact with their feelings. The Way of Passion may involve giving up snobbish traits and turning one's back on an overemphasis on knowing the right people and doing the accepted thing. Self-expression is the key here, and friends and associates who encourage those on this path to be true to themselves and honest about who they will be are an invaluable support. Family members may applaud their efforts to come to grips with themselves. It is these relatives who are often sought out when the going gets rough. Also, friendships previously rejected as those on this path attempted to climb upward on the social ladder may be reinvigorated. Often the most valuable individual to someone on the Way of Passion is someone who lives a more simple, natural, or basic lifestyle, reinforcing the process through their example. A series of affairs with people of this sort may be common as those on this path learn from one person and then another. Such relationships are apt to be searing in intensity and of short duration.

An image that comes to mind is that of a city dweller who, seized by the beauty of a primeval lake, sheds his or her clothes and plunges into the crystal clear, cold water. Diving to the bottom, he experiences a renewal of contact with nature and a feeling for the timelessness of existence. Emerging with a new sense of self, he is ready to return to the world renewed and energized—in a sense, reborn.

BALANCE POINT

Thinking and Doing

CRYSTALS AND GEMSTONES

Larimar encompasses the exquisite blue ray of the Caribbean Sea. Gazing upon this stone awakens the individual to the power and sacred ecstasy of the eternal now.

NOTABLES ON THIS KARMIC PATH

RICHARD BRANSON

Beginning with a mail-order business in discount records that led to a single record store in London, **Richard Branson** built an enormous empire, displaying his ubiquitous Virgin logo on CD's, shopping centers, and airplanes. Branson seeks out excitement wherever he goes, often indulging his special passion for transatlantic and around-the-world balloon jaunts. Despite the outrageousness of his public persona, he is very dedicated to his family as well as his many thousands of employees. Characteristic of many on the Way of Passion, Branson repeatedly seeks to challenge the high seas of life experience.

Passionate and beautiful film actress **Elizabeth Taylor** has been known for her searing romantic involvements both on and off the screen for decades. Her numerous marriages attest to her ability to overcome the emotional detachment so common to this karmic path, as do her humanitarian endeavors in the fight against AIDS. Achieving her first major success at age 13 in *National Velvet,* Taylor went on to captivate hearts in stylish movies such as *Cleopatra* as well as in serious roles in *But-*

ELIZABETH TAYLOR

terfield 8 and *Who's Afraid of Virginia Woolf* that won her two Academy Awards. Despite the personal trials she has endured, Taylor has come back again and again to surprise and delight her countless fans.

JACK LONDON

Though born to an astrologer father and a spiritualist mother, **Jack London** turned his back on the metaphysical to explore the core lesson of this path, living each moment to the fullest. Embracing this goal, London underwent several lifetimes worth of experience, and thus gained the material he needed to write his passionate short stories and novels. *Call of the Wild, Sea Wolf,* and *White Fang* have since become literary classics, defining man's struggle against both nature and his own instinctual self. The elegance of London's prose combined with this theme exemplifies the balance point of beauty and rebirth on this karmic path.

Other Notables: Wendy Wasserstein, Umberto Eco, Washington Irving, Oleg Cassini, Florence Nightingale, Anne Heche, Dorothy Kilgallen, Rodney Crowell, Bill Murray, Princess Anne of England, Gary Larson, Cathy Guisewite, e. e. cummings, Georges Bizet, Mike Nichols, Morley Safer, Dian Fossey, Paul Cezanne, François Truffaut, Jennifer Aniston, Edward Kennedy, Johnny Cash, Miriam Makeba, Andrew Jackson Young, Jr.

BIRTHDAYS ON KARMIC PATH 25

August 1, 1894–December 19, 1894 | March 13, 1913–August 1, 1913

October 23, 1931–March 12, 1932 | June 4, 1950–October 22, 1950 | January 13, 1969–June 3, 1969

August 26, 1987–January 13, 1988 | April 6, 2006–August 25, 2006

KARMIC PATH
25

March 19–24
REBIRTH
PISCES–ARIES CUSP

The souls born on the Cusp of Rebirth who travel the Way of Passion can experience great joy and fulfillment along this path so long as they avoid the tendency to "think themselves into a corner" with their inexorable brand of logic. Pisces–Arians must summon the courage to kick over the traces of convention, appearances, or a rather effete preoccupation with the "right" way of doing things before they can get what they want out of life. Moreover, many of these individuals are hampered by a number of emotional insecurities that may interfere with their ability to get a handle on what they really want in the first place. Nonetheless, possessors of a direct approach, intuitive strength, and a highly charged emotional nature, these individuals can shake themselves out of their revery on the Way of Passion and embrace the journey of experiencing life to the full.

CHALLENGE: **NOT BECOMING MIRED IN THEIR OWN LOGIC**
FULFILLMENT: **LOVING FROM THEIR OWN GREAT DEPTHS**

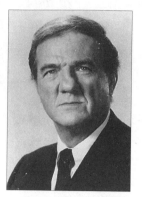

KARL MALDEN
Actor,
A Streetcar Named Desire

3/22/1913
Pisces–Aries Cusp

March 25–April 2
THE CHILD
ARIES I

Those born in this week are likely to have a wonderful time on the Way of Passion, as they will be aided by their great curiosity and natural enthusiasm, on the one hand, and gifted with idealism and refinement, on the other. Thus, there is very little that can go amiss here, unless they succumb to a superficial set of values or standards in lieu of accessing the deeper passions that motivate them. Becoming better acquainted with those passions and learning to balance them is key. If they avoid the seductions of the merely glamorous and the notion that all that glitters must be gold, they will find a rare freedom and renewed sense of identity.

CHALLENGE: **FORCING THEMSELVES NOT TO RETREAT WHEN CONFRONTED WITH CONFLICT**
FULFILLMENT: **EXPERIENCING THE FREEDOM THAT COMES FROM LETTING GO OF THEIR PRECONCEPTIONS**

April 3–10
THE STAR
ARIES II

If Aries II's on the Way of Passion can release their tendency to narcissism and their need to believe that the universe begins and ends with themselves, they can realize considerable success and achievement. Capable of great leadership and vision, they often carry others along on the tide of their tremendous energy. Yet their effectiveness may be hindered by their preoccupation with the image they project to the world—an image that is often based more on glitz than on substance. Also, they may wastefully spend their energy, to say nothing of their income, in supporting that image. Here is where one might find snobs and social climbers who live for "keeping up with the Joneses." At the least, appearances will be important to these people. At best, they will incorporate their sense of beauty with their considerable passion to shape not only their own lives but those of others.

CHALLENGE: **RELEASING THEIR NARCISSISTIC PREOCCUPATION WITH THEIR OWN IMAGE**
FULFILLMENT: **LEARNING, THROUGH PASSION, HOW TO OPEN THEMSELVES TO OTHERS**
NOTABLES: **WASHINGTON IRVING (AUTHOR, *RIP VAN WINKLE*); MAURICE DE VLAMINCK (ARTIST; INFLUENCED BY VAN GOGH)**

OLEG CASSINI
Fashion designer

4/11/1913
Aries III

April 11–18
THE PIONEER
ARIES III

The enthusiastic, pioneering spirit of Aries III's cannot help but be drawn to the kinds of people, causes, and situations that the Way of Passion demands. Gifted with a greater sense of refinement than they might have otherwise have had, they will nevertheless have to guard against an overriding or even obsessive idealism. Perhaps the greatest danger here is that they may become distracted by the newest fads or of becoming wannabes or groupies who flit from distraction to distraction without ever coming to terms with what makes them truly happy. They may also be overly attached to their pet ideals, goals, or causes and become so focused on those that they never allow themselves to experience much needed variety. Yet their ultimate success may well be determined by how well they learn to navigate human relationships. Their need to be needed may interfere with their higher development, and they may waste no end of time seeking answers from others, when in fact those answers must spring forth from themselves.

CHALLENGE: **NOT PUTTING ABSTRACTIONS OR IDEALS AHEAD OF PERSONAL CONSIDERATIONS**
FULFILLMENT: **INTERACTING DYNAMICALLY WITH OTHERS**
NOTABLE: **RACHELLE MUSSOLINI (WIDOW OF BENITO)**

April 19–24

POWER
ARIES–TAURUS CUSP

The individuals born in the Week of Manifestation who travel the Way of Passion will be gifted with a good feeling for aesthetic matters, natural passion, and a sensuousness that will serve to ground some of the more impractical aspects of this configuration. Capable of manifesting their love of refinement in material ways, they may, however, be materialistic and acquisitive in the extreme and at some point may have to come to terms with the idea that they do not own their possessions, their possessions somehow own them. Moreover, they may be snobbish or overbearing unless they learn to set aside some of their sacred cows. Thus there will be quite a few of these personalities who will give up powerful jobs, fine homes, and loving families for a life of poverty, poetry, or serendipity. Though such actions may cause them to be misunderstood or branded as completely self-centered, they are unlikely to be unhappy with their choice or the discoveries that lie just outside the norm.

CHALLENGE: **GIVING UP THEIR PASSION FOR MATERIAL THINGS**
FULFILLMENT: **PLUNGING INTO AN ALL-ENCOMPASSING EXPERIENCE OF LOVE**

April 25–May 2

MANIFESTATION
TAURUS I

Taurus I's may have something of a difficult passage on the Way of Passion, as their pronounced preoccupation with beauty may become an obsession. Not being entirely open to new experiences may also hinder their development. These individuals must periodically expend great effort to get out of their ruts and into interesting or exotic experiences if they are to awaken their truest sense of self. There is a real danger that they may slip into a state of chronic self-satisfaction that is at once neither satisfying nor truly of the self. Yet the power of their intuitions and inner inspirations will doubtless emerge at some point to shake up their natural complacency. If they take to heart one of the lessons of the *I Ching*, which reminds us that beauty is only the form and not the content of experience, their road will be considerably eased.

CHALLENGE: **NOT ALLOWING THEIR NEED FOR HARMONY TO INTERFERE WITH EXPERIENCING LIFE**
FULFILLMENT: **GETTING AWAY FROM SELF-IMPOSED ROUTINES TO GIVE THEMSELVES A TREAT—OF THE SENSUOUS VARIETY—NOW AND THEN**

WOODY HERMAN
Jazz musician

5/16/1913
Taurus III

May 3–10

THE TEACHER
TAURUS II

Natural teachers, Taurus II's on the Way of Passion may look to others for reinforcement or to help them get in touch with those things that make life worth living. Here their sense of the aesthetic and their highly developed mental constructs may get in the way of their ability to throw themselves into experience, the problem being that they may well fall in love with their own ideas before they fall in love with anything or anyone else. These souls would do well to not to confuse a sense of beauty with a moral standard to which they must somehow adhere. Still, their love for and sense of all that is beautiful are part of the gift of this journey and should be considered a liability only if it holds them back from developing a more complete view of life. If they are willing to assume the role of student of life, rather than that of teacher, control their tendency to impose their ideas on others, and not become stuck in a mental labyrinth, they will act on their heart's truest impulses.

CHALLENGE: **COMING DOWN OUT OF THEIR IVORY TOWERS NOW AND THEN**
FULFILLMENT: **REALIZING THAT THEIR STRENGTH LIES IN TAKING ACTION RATHER THAN GENERATING DISCUSSION**
NOTABLE: **STEWART GRANGER (ENGLISH FILM ACTOR)**

May 11–18

THE NATURAL
TAURUS III

Those born in the Week of the Natural who travel the Way of Passion are likely to have a fine time, as their energies and disposition are very much in keeping with its challenges and promise. They are gifted with a measure of intellectualism and detachment that they might not otherwise have had and that can make for a nice balance with their more impulsive or even eccentric side. Yet though they will doubtless walk on the wild side from time to time, there is little danger of their becoming stuck in a day-to-day routine or caught up in rarefied, unrealistic views. In any event, these sensual, fun-loving, and adventuresome people are sure to relish the call to live in the moment, divest themselves of tiresome social mores, and immerse themselves in the clarity, purity, and heightened sense of reality that true passion entails.

CHALLENGE: **NOT GOING OVERBOARD AS THEY SEEK EVER-NEW OUTLETS FOR THEIR PASSION**
FULFILLMENT: **UNDERSTANDING THAT THEY ARE FREE TO LIVE AS FREELY OR NATURALLY AS THEY WISH**

FLORENCE NIGHTINGALE
Hospital reformer, led 38 nurses in Crimean War

5/12/1820
Taurus III

May 19–24

ENERGY
TAURUS–GEMINI CUSP

Divesting themselves of superficial values and their need to conform socially will doubtless figure prominently in the life journey of those born on this cusp who travel the Way of Passion. They are dynamic and naturally inclined to savor the sweetness life has to offer; only their lack of self-awareness can stand in the way of their soul's calling. In short, they may become caught up in mental games, or even unduly aggressive patterns of behavior, without quite knowing why. Too, some of them will be rather chronically unaware of what makes them happy. As a result, some will move from job to job or partner to partner, ever searching for the things that lie only within themselves. Yet they are gifted with fearlessness and an ability to thumb their noses at stuffier, more conventional types that will stand them in excellent stead. If they give life all they've got, their efforts will be rewarded by the richness of their experience on this karmic path.

ANNE HECHE
Actress,
Six Days, Seven Nights

5/25/1969
Gemini I

CHALLENGE: **LEARNING TO RELY LESS HEAVILY ON THEIR CHARM TO GET BY**

FULFILLMENT: **KNOWING THAT PASSION CAN BE AS MUCH ABOUT DEPTH OF FEELING AS IT IS ABOUT EXCITEMENT**

May 25–June 2

FREEDOM
GEMINI I

Those born in the Week of Freedom who travel the Way of Passion are likely to enjoy a rich, rewarding life passage, providing they do not become enmeshed in a series of petty feuds or indulge in a tendency to argue endlessly over intellectual points at the expense of the further development of their emotions. In fact, an ability to get out of their heads and to avoid worry or chronic complaining will be especially important. Over-analysis of problems and situations can also be a stumbling block, as they tend to be more intellectually oriented than emotionally impelled. Yet they are quite capable of asking the right questions regarding their own need for freedom and greater satisfaction, and if that ability is matched with the courage to divest themselves of cumbersome relationships, social structures, or others' expectations, they will go far.

CHALLENGE: **NOT ALLOWING THEIR PASSION TO FUEL THEIR NATURAL COMBATIVENESS**

FULFILLMENT: **DEVELOPING A FULL-BLOWN PASSION FOR ONE THING**

NOTABLES: **TODD HUNDLEY (BASEBALL PLAYER, CATCHER); TONY ZALE (MIDDLEWEIGHT BOXER)**

June 3–10

NEW LANGUAGE
GEMINI II

Brilliant communicators all, the personalities born in the Week of New Language who travel the Way of Passion may become quite enraptured with the sheer beauty of ideas or words. Apt to get caught up in concepts of perfection that are not entirely their own, they will have to be willing to break more than a few rules in their quest to utilize their special abilities. The danger of this configuration is that they may become so attached to an ideal or goal that they fail to get in touch with the myriad experiences that await them. It is important for these people to feel understood, and they will go to great lengths to make sure that they are, yet they will have to understand themselves before they can really be effective. The competitive spirit is strong in these people, imparting energy as they reach for their personal star. They can find great satisfaction when they learn to express their ideas through a variety of creative mediums since they will find that they inspire and enchant a wide and willing audience.

RALPH EDWARDS
TV host, *This Is Your Life*

6/13/1913
Gemini III

CHALLENGE: **REALIZING THAT ENGAGING WITH PEOPLE FROM DIVERSE BACKGROUNDS IS NO SUBSTITUTE FOR DIRECT EXPERIENCE**

FULFILLMENT: **FINDING A PERSONAL VERNACULAR THROUGH THE EXPRESSION OF THEIR PASSION**

June 11–18

THE SEEKER
GEMINI III

The Seekers on the Way of Passion are gifted with the ability to find adventure in even the most ordinary circumstances. Restless by nature, they may become too caught up in moving around, whether from person to person or topic to topic, without turning inward long enough to get down to the nitty-gritty of their real desires. Given to testing limits, they will never have much trouble discarding outworn ideals or concepts that the world might still hold sacred. Yet, on the down side, these are the people for whom even the best life has to offer might never seem good enough. At their worst, they may drift in a sea of unrealistic dreams and plans. At their best, they will love life in the real world, embracing new experiences, people, and ideas with open arms. Their tremendous natural insight enables them to lead others with passion and foresight. If they can turn that insight inward in an examination of their own truest nature, their search will lead them to a passion for life itself.

CHALLENGE: **LETTING GO OF THEIR NEED TO PLEASE OTHERS**

FULFILLMENT: **ENGAGING FULLY IN ALL THE HIGH ADVENTURE LIFE HAS TO OFFER**

June 19–24
MAGIC
GEMINI–CANCER CUSP

Gemini–Cancer souls who travel the Way of Passion can experience great fulfillment, providing they overcome their tendency to sentimentalize certain ideals, structures, and patterns. Each of them has a strong attraction to religion, philosophy, and the arts. Thus, the principal danger of this configuration is that they may be entirely too romantic, causing them to throw caution to the winds as they indulge their more passionate longings. Many on this path will have to suffer any number of disillusions or disappointments before they are able to look reality squarely in the eye. Too, they often have a natural inclination toward self-sacrifice and must take care that their ideals do not lead them into situations in which they are exploited. However, they possess considerable charm and magnetism, which is sure to buoy them along this life's journey. Blessed also with a natural objectivity and formidable intelligence, they can rest assured they have the tools required to discern genuine passion from its impostors.

CHALLENGE: **BALANCING THEIR WILD SWINGS BETWEEN EMOTIONAL COLDNESS AND BEING OVERHEATED**

FULFILLMENT: **ENGAGING IN A MORE ELEMENTAL APPROACH TO LIFE**

DOROTHY KILGALLEN
Gossip columnist
in the 1930s

7/3/1913
Cancer II

June 25–July 2
THE EMPATH
CANCER I

These souls who travel the Way of Passion are blessed with considerable sensitivity, yet a greater depth of feeling may lie a bit out of reach until they develop the ability to separate from others and get into touch with their own motivations. Their principal downfall is that they may retreat permanently behind an impenetrable shell, unknown even to themselves. Alternatively, they may feel deprived of adequate mothering and nurturing and be emotionally demanding of others, drifting from partner to partner or friend to friend in an attempt to discover where their truest passions lie. Yet Cancer I's on this journey are never out of touch with the realities of life and would do well to encourage their more worldly orientation in an attempt to broaden their experience away from mere love affairs. At their best, though, they may express their highly emotional nature through true passion, then regulate it by taking life as it comes, rather than pining for the way things ought to be.

CHALLENGE: **FINDING A POSITIVE EXPRESSION FOR THEIR PASSIONATE SIDE**

FULFILLMENT: **RENEWING THEIR CONNECTION TO THEIR OWN LIFE FORCE**

July 3–10
THE UNCONVENTIONAL
CANCER II

Cancer II's can experience great satisfaction from this life experience, providing they do not hide their light or try to suppress their most creative and innovative ideas and inspirations. Though some with this configuration will be inclined to shy away from the task of going for broke or taking the big risks associated with engaging more fully in life, many more will find that their attraction to the unusual or unconventional is really their soul's urging them toward an expanded version of what is possible. Though their version of getting back to basics may not be everyone's cup of tea, there is a strong chance of real success here, providing they do not allow themselves simply to be content with their fantasies of a better life but get down to the business of making one.

CHALLENGE: **REEXAMINING SOME OF THEIR CORE BELIEFS OR SACRED COWS**

FULFILLMENT: **UNCOVERING THEIR WILDER SIDE**

NOTABLE: **WALTER KERR (AUTHOR/CRITIC, *NEW YORK TIMES*)**

RED SKELTON
Entertainer/radio-TV host

7/18/1913
Cancer III

July 11–18
THE PERSUADER
CANCER III

Passionate and involved, the individuals born in the Week of the Persuader who find themselves on the Way of Passion can make a great success of this journey, so long as they keep their attention on themselves and do not get caught up in trying to manifest their sense of passion through others. Highly idealistic, they are nevertheless capable of the solid, practical application of their talents and can take great comfort in a more back-to-basics lifestyle or scaled-down sense of ambition. Perhaps their principal pitfall here is their unique ability to control their own needs, and some will have to work hard to relinquish that sense of control and "go for the gusto" in the pursuit of happiness. Yet if they can successfully release their preconceptions of what ought to be and learn to relish what is, all will go well.

CHALLENGE: **LEARNING TO RELEASE THEIR SELF-CONTROL LONG ENOUGH TO TAKE A RISK**

FULFILLMENT: **BEING ENTERTAINED BY LIVING AS FULLY AS POSSIBLE**

NOTABLES: **GERALD R. FORD (38TH U.S. PRESIDENT); RICHARD BRANSON (FOUNDER AND PRESIDENT OF VIRGIN RECORDS); JOHANNES MULLER (FOUNDED MODERN SCIENCE OF PHYSIOLOGY)**

July 19–25
OSCILLATION
CANCER–LEO CUSP

The souls born in this week who travel the Way of Passion will doubtless have an easier time than many by virtue of their natural expansiveness and passionately caring spirit. Though this life journey will almost certainly produce quite a roller coaster of emotional ups and downs, they are likely to fare well when they stay on top of their feelings and do not surround themselves with people who preach of constancy, consistency, or steadier ways. Sampling a wide variety of people, places, and things will be important for these people, and they should indulge their risk-taking inclinations in an attempt to access their deeper sense of passion. Perhaps their principal danger is that they may become emotionally blocked in an effort to conform to a set of standards not their own. Yet though the volcano of passion within these personalities may lie dormant for some time, it is sure to erupt, eventually leading them to a much-transformed and better evolved sense of their heart's deepest desires.

CHALLENGE: **NOT GOING OVERBOARD AND TAKING FOOL-HARDY RISKS IN THEIR EFFORT TO LEAVE SECURITY OR ROUTINE BEHIND**

FULFILLMENT: **PUTTING THEIR PASSION BEHIND INNOVATIVE PROJECTS OR PERSONAL GOALS**

JUDGE LANCE ITO
Presided over
O. J. Simpson trial

8/2/1950
Leo I

July 26–August 2
AUTHORITY
LEO I

Whatever their aesthetic goals and ideals, Leo I's who navigate the Way of Passion will be blessed with a journey that is highly original, deeply felt, and intense. Though some on this karmic path may have difficulty extricating themselves from their preconceived notions of standards or principles, the chances are good that they will be able to transform their personal set of aesthetics or ideals into something personal, passionate, and functional. They are intense, and high-minded people; perhaps their principal danger is that they may fall victim to disillusionment when it becomes clear that not all people share their passions or inclinations. Equally, they can overdo things and turn their prodigious energies toward personal issues to such an extent that they become megalomaniacal in their need to fulfill their passionate inclinations. Still, if they can learn to accept the fact that part of this karmic path involves getting down to basics and resisting the temptation to control others, their path to realization will become obvious.

CHALLENGE: **RELEASING THEIR PRECONCEPTIONS**
FULFILLMENT: **PUTTING THE PEDAL TO THE METAL IN ORDER TO LIVE EACH MOMENT TO THE FULLEST**

August 3–10
BALANCED STRENGTH
LEO II

The naturally buoyant energies of Leo II's on the Way of Passion will serve them well as they are quite capable not only of discovering where their true passions lie but of going out and doing something about them. There is a certain toughness about this group, however, and their principal barrier to higher development might be their unwillingness to admit their mistakes or to let go of their attachment to structures or ideals—which, it should be noted, are usually not entirely their own. Their faithfulness is likely to hold them back on this karmic path, since it will make breaking out of the old dull routines all the more difficult. When combined with a single-mindedness that can be extreme, their loyalty, in particular to principles, will need to be overcome before they can allow themselves to unfold into the joy of living in the now.

CHALLENGE: **NOT ALLOWING HIGH-MINDED IDEALS TO RUN THEIR LIVES**

FULFILLMENT: **LIVING MORE FULLY FROM THEIR INTUITION**

NOTABLE: **RODNEY CROWELL (COUNTRY SONGWRITER AND PERFORMER)**

PRINCESS ANNE
Only daughter of Queen
Elizabeth II

8/15/1950
Leo III

August 11–18
LEADERSHIP
LEO III

Enthusiasm and experience come together in those born in this week who travel the Way of Passion, and they are more than capable of following their hearts wherever their passions may lead. In fact, they may go a bit overboard and to others will doubtless appear self-centered and even selfish as they pursue what's best for them. Though their yearning for greater freedom may be strong indeed, there is a danger that their logical minds will keep them tied to old notions and an unfortunately romantic conception of life. It's difficult to get them to change their minds in any event, especially if their creature comforts or personal rituals are disturbed. Nonetheless, they are quite passionate underneath, and if they can relinquish their notions of refinement to seek a more authentic lifestyle, they are bound to experience a transformation and redefinition of their goals on this life journey.

CHALLENGE: **COMING TO GRIPS WITH THEIR OVERLY RIGID ADHERENCE TO ROUTINES**

FULFILLMENT: **FREEING THEMSELVES TO LOVE FULLY**

NOTABLE: **GARY LARSON (CARTOONIST, "THE FAR SIDE")**

August 19–25
EXPOSURE
LEO–VIRGO CUSP

Though they may be rather late starters when it comes to climbing down from the ivory tower in search of a more authentic level of experience, Leo–Virgos who travel the Way of Passion are likely to do reasonably well. Once they have begun their quest for the "real" or have discovered that the way to enlightenment is by having enough sense of freedom to fully be oneself, they will move toward their objectives with a great deal of determination and tenacity. They are naturally passionate people; the principal danger of this configuration is that they may prefer to remain on the periphery of life, hesitant to reveal their true thoughts and feelings even to themselves. Selfishness may also be a problem, and others with this position may simply hedge their bets, presenting one face to the world while they privately pursue the people or things that make them happy. Still, once they have achieved a certain emotional maturity, their illusions will doubtless fall away and they will be ready to take life on its own terms.

AMY MADIGAN
Actress,
Places in the Heart

9/11/1950
Virgo III

CHALLENGE: **LEARNING HOW TO SHOW THE PASSION THEY REALLY FEEL**

FULFILLMENT: **TRUSTING THEIR OWN EXPERIENCE AND INTUITIVE INSIGHTS**

August 26–September 2
SYSTEM BUILDERS
VIRGO I

"Living in the moment" is not a phrase often found in the vocabulary of those born in the Week of System Builders, and many of them will find themselves uncomfortable as they journey the Way of Passion. Rather terrified of the often chaotic and contradictory emotions that passion implies, they may retreat from the higher challenges of this karmic path and become emotionally shut down or steadfastly unaware of what things might alleviate their burdens and give rise to a stronger, more confident sense of self. Too, their need for social acceptance may hold them back. However challenging this journey, Virgo I's are blessed with the resources, patience, and personal strength to overcome the obstacles to fulfillment. Once they catch on that many of those obstacles are in fact of their own making, life will become much sweeter.

CHALLENGE: **CIRCUMVENTING THEIR INNATE NEED FOR STRUCTURE**

FULFILLMENT: **BECOMING BETTER ACQUAINTED WITH THEIR FEELINGS**

September 3–10
THE ENIGMA
VIRGO II

Redefining their standards will not come easily to those born in the Week of the Enigma who find themselves on the Way of Passion. However, they have great powers of discernment at their disposal, and, if nothing else, their ability to be truthful with themselves will be of great assistance. At times quite guarded, they may appear to others as cold, calculating, or above it all. Yet underneath that daunting exterior is a passionate, sensitive soul who longs for closeness and the attainment of some truly personal goals. Being willing to jump the traces of social convention and constricting morals will be difficult but essential to their emotional health, as will an ability to open up to others. Yet most important of all will be an ability to go within in their search for answers and, when they have those answers, to strip away all that is irrelevant to their highest sense of fulfillment and satisfaction.

WILLIAM HOWARD TAFT
27th U.S. president; later Chief Justice of the Supreme Court

9/15/1857
Virgo III

CHALLENGE: **SPENDING SOME TIME TRYING TO FIGURE OUT WHAT TRULY MAKES THEM HAPPY**

FULFILLMENT: **FREEING AND REVEALING THEIR OWN ZANIER OR QUIRKIER APPROACHES TO LIFE**

NOTABLES: **ARTHUR FREED (PRODUCER, *THE WIZARD OF OZ*); CATHY GUISEWITE (CARTOONIST, "CATHY")**

September 11–18
THE LITERALIST
VIRGO III

Marked by a truly formidable willfulness, Virgo III's who find themselves on the Way of Passion are more than likely to get what they want, the trick, of course, being to discover where their deepest needs and desires lie and not to lose themselves in simple rebellion against the chains of tradition, pretension, or ideals that often bind them. Not as prone to either superficiality or undue idealism as some on this karmic path, they may nevertheless back down from some of its bigger risks and retreat into judgmentalism or didacticism. Often they will have to return to their origins to better discover (or rediscover) where their true passions lie. Still, for all their seeming passion in youth, Virgo III personalities have a cool, calculating streak. They would do well to nurture the more personal side of their deeply caring natures. If the need to shed some of their more undesirable qualities does not manifest itself as chronic self-criticism, happiness awaits them along this karmic path.

CHALLENGE: **LEARNING HOW TO GO WITH THE FLOW AND STOP ANALYZING EVERYTHING**

FULFILLMENT: **SEEING THE BEAUTY OF LIFE LESS IN ELEGANT CONSTRUCTIONS AND MORE IN WHAT LIES WITHIN THEIR GRASP**

September 19–24
BEAUTY
VIRGO–LIBRA CUSP

Sensuous and sensitive, those born on the Cusp of Beauty who travel the Way of Passion may struggle a bit for success. Some with this configuration may content themselves with superficial glitz and glamour, hesitant to scratch the surface of their sense of the ideal to discover what lies underneath. Gracious and naturally social, they may have an effete or snobbish side and may go to great lengths to avoid the more unpleasant aspects of reality until they are compelled to make the inward journey necessary to connect with what they really want out of life. In extreme cases, some of them may seek escape in the darker realms of fantasy and addiction. At worst, their love of the ideal is something of a fatal attraction and they may become, elitist, greedy, or pretentious in pursuit of a goal. At best, however, they will come to terms with what really matters and summon the independence and strength to set a new standard for freshness and breadth of vision that will strike a resounding chord in the hearts of those around them.

BILL MURRAY
Actor/comedian,
Caddyshack

9/21/1950
Virgo–Libra Cusp

CHALLENGE: **LIVING FROM THEIR HEARTS**
FULFILLMENT: **INDULGING THEIR SENSUOUS SIDE**

September 25–October 2
THE PERFECTIONIST
LIBRA I

A true rebirth and personal transformation can be experienced in the course of a lifetime for Perfectionists who travel the Way of Passion, for once they have undertaken the business of following their deepest impulses, they are more than likely to get what they want out of life. Though some may be hopelessly encumbered by or bogged down in emotional baggage or the quest to achieve unrealistic or unworkable goals of perfection, there are others whose personal obsessions will take a more constructive form. There is a danger that these indefatigable people will go overboard in the search for affirmation and enlightenment, resulting in indecision, self-righteousness, or a never-ending search for the kind of crisis that makes them feel more truly alive. However, most on this path will gradually let go of their more controlling impulses in such a way that they are able to become more accepting, more able to live in the moment, and more in touch with who and what they really are.

CHALLENGE: **BALANCING THEIR NEED TO MASTER THEIR EMOTIONS AND THEIR NEED TO EXPRESS THEM**
FULFILLMENT: **APPROACHING LIFE IN A MORE NATURAL, RELAXED MANNER**
NOTABLE: **RANDY QUAID (ACTOR, *THE LAST DETAIL*)**

October 3–10
SOCIETY
LIBRA II

Those born in the Week of Society who find themselves on this karmic path will more than likely have a relatively easy time of things, providing they are able to relinquish their need for social acceptance by breaking the mold or indulging in the taboo from time to time. Perhaps the greatest danger for these often pliable personalities is that they do not take their own needs seriously, as they are rather chronically self-deceptive. This journey will doubtless require them to rid themselves of a number of conventions, people, and outworn ideals in their search for what is truly important and get down to the basics of existence without distraction. They can find their answers if they realize that turning inward and facing themselves is critical to their soul's calling. In any event, they will have to work quite hard to avoid seeking passion through others or risk the loss of their higher self through scattered and sometimes quite dissipated energies.

WENDY WASSERSTEIN
Playwright; work details changes in modern women's lives

10/18/1950
Libra III

CHALLENGE: **NOT AMPLIFYING THEIR MOOD SWINGS BY POURING THEIR PASSION ONTO THEM**
FULFILLMENT: **FINDING A FORUM OR OBJECT OF AESTHETIC VALUE THAT THEY CAN FEEL PASSIONATE ABOUT**

October 11–18
THEATER
LIBRA III

A great deal of creative inspiration is part of the natural endowment of those born in this week who travel the Way of Passion, yet they will have to do a great deal of evaluating and reevaluating of their concepts of tradition in order to make an impact. In fact, many with this configuration will have to pay rather high dues before they come to terms with the idea that taking the risks associated with real creative genius is far preferable to channeling their energies and efforts into merely imitating their personal heroes or role models. Yet they have the capacity to give their all to something that will stand them in good stead, so long as they can divorce themselves from the demands of image and allow themselves to make choices based on their own inclinations rather than on what others may think.

CHALLENGE: **FORCING THEMSELVES TO CHANGE COURSE SOONER RATHER THAN LATER**
FULFILLMENT: **RELEASING THEMSELVES FROM THE ROLES THEY PLAY IN ORDER TO BE MORE VULNERABLE AND OPEN TO LIFE**
NOTABLE: **E. E. CUMMINGS (NOVELIST/POET, *TULIPS AND CHIMNEYS*)**

October 19–25

DRAMA AND CRITICISM
LIBRA–SCORPIO CUSP

Those born in this week who travel the Way of Passion are likely to have an inspiring and fulfilling journey, providing they recognize when the time has come to scale back and redefine their worldly preoccupations in the interest of self-evolution. Perhaps the principal danger of this configuration is the fact that they may avoid understanding what it is to live one's passion, seeking rather to discover it in endless liaisons, sexual peccadilloes, and short-lived love affairs. Too, they may be inclined to be overly critical or imbued with prima donna–like attitude that serves as a projection of their underlying fear of inadequacy or indecision. Yet they have the probability of great success and accomplishment, providing their are neither too impatient nor too unrealistic to apply themselves to the business of embracing life on its own terms.

DAN RATHER
TV anchor/journalist

10/31/1931
Scorpio I

CHALLENGE: **SIMPLIFYING THEIR LIVES BY OVERCOMING A PREOCCUPATION WITH SENSUOUS FORMS OF BEAUTY OR EXPERIENCE**
FULFILLMENT: **OPERATING FROM THE MOST BASIC AND ELEMENTAL LEVELS**
NOTABLE: **GEORGES BIZET (FRENCH COMPOSER)**

October 26–November 2

INTENSITY
SCORPIO I

Scorpio I's are well suited to the Way of Passion, as its higher challenges are very much in keeping with their natural inclinations. Whatever their personal background, these souls are blessed with an innate emotional maturity that enables them to take responsibility for their actions and their most passionate impulses. Too, Scorpio I's crave intensity and in fact are marked by a certain polarization in their emotional makeup that will be hard to hide as their passions run both light and joyful and dark and depressive. While, like most Scorpios, they can be as cold as ice on cue, there is the touch of the performer about them. This gives them the warmth and gusto to take big bites out of life. The main challenge for these intense individuals is not to get too caught up in their own ethics; otherwise, all will go well.

CHALLENGE: **TEMPERING THE DESTRUCTIVENESS OF THEIR DARKER SIDE**
FULFILLMENT: **ENGAGING THEMSELVES FULLY IN LIFE'S CHALLENGES**
NOTABLES: **RAND ARASKOG (PRESIDENT AND CEO OF ITT); JOHN KNIGHT (KNIGHT–RIDDER NEWSPAPER PUBLISHER)**

November 3–11

DEPTH
SCORPIO II

It will be especially important for those born in the Week of Depth to cultivate a rapport between the conscious and unconscious as they make their way along this life journey. Otherwise, they may find themselves navigating some rough emotional waters, seemingly at the mercy of subconscious impulses that defy all understanding. Though they are well equipped to stand up for what they truly believe in and go for what they really want, their love of beauty and sense of the finer things may express itself in pretension, elitism, or extreme selfishness. Curiously, however, their tendency to escapism is quite pronounced, and if they are open to the realization of their own best impulses, they are unlikely to be overly fearful or otherwise distressed by the changes that will inevitably come. If they can avoid the dangers of fruitless outbursts, chronic depression, and self-defeating patterns of behavior, they can expect great satisfaction along the road.

MIKE NICHOLS
Director, *The Graduate*

11/6/1931
Scorpio II

CHALLENGE: **ELIMINATING THE WORD "SHOULD" FROM THEIR VOCABULARY**
FULFILLMENT: **OPENING UP TO AND FULLY EXPRESSING THEIR REAL FEELINGS**
NOTABLES: **MORLEY SAFER (TV JOURNALIST, *60 MINUTES*); IKE TURNER (BANDLEADER WITH WIFE TINA)**

November 12–18

CHARM
SCORPIO III

Those born in this week may experience a bit of difficulty with the higher challenges of this karmic path, as they are a bit prone to complacency, manipulative behavior, and a certain timidity when it comes to reaching for a more authentic and passionate level of experience. Yet they are gifted with a naturally realistic approach to the world and are unlikely to be fooled by others. Nor are they able to fool themselves for very long. In addition, they have a rare ability to turn their backs on unproductive jobs, relationships, and endeavors without so much as a backward glance. Thus, if they can turn their natural savvy and keen perception inward in an attempt to reach their deepest feelings and learn to distinguish between passion and mere impulse, all will go well.

CHALLENGE: **NOT BEING AFRAID TO BE UNSOPHISTICATED**
FULFILLMENT: **DARING TO STRIVE TO ACHIEVE THEIR DREAMS**
NOTABLE: **ROBERTO C. GOIZUETA (CHAIRMAN OF COCA-COLA CO.)**

November 19–24
REVOLUTION
SCORPIO–SAGITTARIUS CUSP

A natural attraction to causes and ideals of all kinds will prove both a blessing and a curse to those born in the Week of Revolution who travel the Way of Passion. Though they are well equipped to divest themselves of outworn ideals, there is a danger that they may embrace change simply for its own sake, at the expense of getting in touch with the kind of lust for life required by this karmic path. Often a highly refined and sensitive exterior may conceal a secret impulse to get "down and dirty," and some may project those impulses onto others in elitism and snobbery. Thus, this group will do best to find the balance between change that is necessary and change for its own sake. Nonetheless, their great humor and sense of freedom, combined with a generous measure of what might be called the divine spark, are sure to make the Way of Passion a fine adventure for them.

CHALLENGE: **FIGHTING THEIR DESIRE TO BE EXCESSIVE OR OVERINDULGENT**

FULFILLMENT: **PURSUING THEIR IMAGINATIVE GOALS AND PLANS WITH GUSTO**

BROOKS ATKINSON
Drama critic; won
Pulitzer Prize

———

11/28/1894
Sagittarius I

November 25–December 2
INDEPENDENCE
SAGITTARIUS I

G ifted with a rebellious streak that can serve them well on the Way of Passion, Sagittarius I's will doubtless assert their independence early. They may, however, have to go back and reevaluate their ideals and beliefs a bit later in life, as they may strike out on their own without necessarily having a clear picture of just who and what they are declaring independence from. Still, they are generally well suited to this karmic path since they tend to give their all no matter what they do. Their love of beauty may manifest itself in a deep love of nature, and their independent spirit and sense of passion may well carry them to "where the wild things are." Yet the biggest tasks for those with this configuration will be not to allow their sense of passion to assume manic proportions and to remember that inherent to this path is the ability to connect to a more basic things that really matter, not merely to move from one challenge to the next.

CHALLENGE: **NOT LETTING THEIR INSECURITY KEEP THEM FROM INDULGING IN THE SIMPLER PLEASURES FOR FEAR OF SEEMING UNSOPHISTICATED**

FULFILLMENT: **ENGAGING IN ANY PHYSICAL ACTIVITY, PARTICULARLY OUTDOORS**

December 3–10
THE ORIGINATOR
SAGITTARIUS II

N aturally eccentric and often inspired, those born in the Week of the Originator who travel the Way of Passion can experience a wonderfully fulfilling passage, providing they do not lose themselves in their need to be accepted by others. Though blessed with both the creative and technical aptitude that make for inventors and innovators, their sometimes quirky facades can conceal a great personal insecurity that they will have to examine closely. Thus, they may flounder if they fail to assimilate their childhood conditions into their psychology, and part of their journey may involve coming to terms with feeling bad because they were made to feel different. Also, their love of beauty may lead them to spread themselves too thinly, embracing one ideal or concept after another without connecting to a true sense of what makes life real. Yet the conscious cultivation of self-knowledge will prove their salvation, and if they can go about immersing themselves in experience, devoid of doubt, all will go well.

CHALLENGE: **CARING LESS ABOUT WHAT OTHER PEOPLE THINK**
FULFILLMENT: **EXPERIENCING A FULLER SENSE OF SELF-EXPRESSION THROUGH PASSION**
NOTABLE: **T. V. SOONG (CHINESE CAPITALIST FIGUREHEAD)**

ARTHUR FIEDLER
Conductor, Boston Pops

———

12/17/1894
Sagittarius III

December 11–18
THE TITAN
SAGITTARIUS III

S agittarius III's who navigate the Way of Passion may face the karmic task of having to scale down their dreams, schemes, and plans in order to get more closely in touch with what they really want. Less inclined to the detachment and ivory-tower ideologies that can plague some on this road, these individuals may nevertheless worry themselves into incapacity when life fails to fulfill their expectations. The primary pitfall of this karmic path is that their brash self-confidence may be eroded by fears and insecurities, and they may get stuck in trying to right the mistakes of the past or bear unreasonable grudges. Yet if they take special care to cultivate and embrace their experiences without becoming too tied to their notions of outcome and if they remember to turn their sacred cows out to pasture, they will develop a renewed and improved sense of self.

CHALLENGE: **NOT BITING OFF MORE THAN THEY CAN CHEW**
FULFILLMENT: **BECOMING ABSORBED IN THE WONDER IN LIFE**

December 19–25
PROPHECY
SAGITTARIUS–CAPRICORN CUSP

Perhaps the biggest pitfall for those born on the Cusp of Prophecy who travel the Way of Passion will be a rather closed-minded or underappreciative attitude toward their truest talent: intuition. Likely to be rather hesitant to make the inward journey required by this karmic path, they will have to work hard to release their tendency to make the business of ideals and higher spiritual concepts someone else's problem and to come to better terms with their higher nature. Their need for social acceptance is very strong and may impede their development as they refuse to take the risks associated with living in the moment, including going against the status quo. Yet if they can manage their tendency to be rather results-oriented and instead learn to relish experience for its own sake, they will doubtless come to understand and embrace the wisdom of sentiments such as have been expressed in the song refrain "ain't nothin' like the real thing."

UMBERTO ECO
Italian author; background in semiotics

1/5/1932
Capricorn II

CHALLENGE: **GRAPPLING WITH THEIR FEAR OF BEING OSTRACIZED**

FULFILLMENT: **DIPPING INTO THEIR MORE PRIMAL IMPULSES NOW AND THEN**

December 26–January 2
THE RULER
CAPRICORN I

A big part of the challenge for those born in the Week of the Ruler who find themselves on the Way of Passion will be relinquishing a measure of their dependability and sense of control and learning to go with the flow. In fact, many of the souls on this road will come to the rather startling realization that in a very real sense, they are the flow, not merely a composite of goals, responsibilities, and duties. Yet whatever their struggles with control, responsibility, and worldly image, they have a wonderful "bottom-line" sense that will be of great benefit. As long as they remember to include their heart's truest impulses in their sense of what really matters, they have a great talent for getting back to basics and can realize great personal satisfaction in meeting the higher challenges of this karmic path.

CHALLENGE: **ACKNOWLEDGING THEIR FEELINGS**

FULFILLMENT: **REALIZING THEY CAN MAKE THEIR OWN RULES**

NOTABLE: **FRANK TORRE (FORMER BASEBALL PLAYER; BROTHER OF YANKEE MANAGER JOE)**

January 3–9
DETERMINATION
CAPRICORN II

The personalities born in this week who find themselves on the Way of Passion can realize great fulfillment, providing they can stay in touch with their own naïveté and avoid trying to conform to others' expectations. Too, they may be disinclined to kick over the traces of convention in their search for greater happiness and should further take care that their impulse toward self-sacrifice does not work to their detriment. Though many with this configuration are apt to take their time to dive into life, they will find that as their fears and preconceptions give way to a more developed sense of what is, rather than what should be, they are blessed with renewed hope, increased enthusiasm, and an infinitely more relaxed and trusting attitude toward happiness itself.

DIAN FOSSEY
Anthropologist; wrote *Gorillas in the Mist*; murdered by poachers

1/16/1932
Capricorn III

CHALLENGE: **SHEDDING THEIR MORE IDEALISTIC BAGGAGE**

FULFILLMENT: **ENJOYING THE CHALLENGE OF NEW EXPERIENCES**

NOTABLES: **RAISA GORBACHEV (WIFE OF USSR PRESIDENT MIKHAIL); CARLOS SAURA (SPANISH SCREENWRITER/FILM DIRECTOR)**

January 10–16
DOMINANCE
CAPRICORN III

Frustration of their innermost needs and desires can make this road something of a dead end until those born in the Week of Dominance take better control of their own lives and summon the courage to go for what they really want. This group can find it difficult to say no to their own sense of what is right. Thus, they often retreat into rich fantasy lives or unrealistic imaginings as a result of their tendency to self-sacrifice. Nonetheless, these souls are blessed with a rich and eccentric sense of humor, and their sensual nature is deeply attracted to the idea of a life that is unfettered by cumbersome ideologies and philosophical quandaries. If they work to become better acquainted with their own tempestuous emotions, they will find themselves able to back up and put things into perspective. Naturally dominant, they must first learn to master themselves, as the sense of direction that comes with self-knowledge will provide them with the self-confidence they require for happiness and success.

CHALLENGE: **FREEING THEMSELVES FROM THEIR OVERBLOWN SENSE OF AMBITION**

FULFILLMENT: **INDULGING IN LIFE'S SIMPLER OR MORE BASIC PLEASURES**

NOTABLE: **JACK LONDON (WRITER, *CALL OF THE WILD*)**

January 17–22

MYSTERY AND IMAGINATION
CAPRICORN–AQUARIUS CUSP

The souls born in this period who find themselves on the Way of Passion will doubtless enjoy an exciting, stimulating journey, providing they learn the difference between thinking and doing. Imagination can be something of a problem for them, as they are especially prone to overworking and overthinking things to the point where they lose sight of the real issues. Alternatively, these individuals may go overboard and fall prey to the pursuit of sensation for sensation's sake or succumb to self-destructive tendencies in an attempt to discover their own deeper emotions. It is especially important for those with this configuration to avoid the pitfall of seeking to have their passions fulfilled by others and to cultivate a measure of objectivity in their dealings that is at once analytical and involved. Yet they are especially well suited to this karmic path, having the gifts of energy, inspiration, and formidable creative talent, all of which will provide them with direction.

PAUL CÉZANNE
Self-portrait
postimpressionist
French painter

1/19/1839
Capricorn–Aquarius Cusp

CHALLENGE: **TEMPERING THEIR PROPENSITY TO BE OVER-ANALYTICAL OR CRITICAL**
FULFILLMENT: **CHANNELING THEIR PASSION INTO SIMPLY BEING IN EACH MOMENT**

January 23–30

GENIUS
AQUARIUS I

Those born in the Week of Genius who find themselves on the Way of Passion can enjoy extraordinary success and enlightenment, providing they do not become overly detached, completely theoretical, and simply too far out. Their tendency to retreat into ivory towers of pure speculation is especially pronounced, and they may become distracted, detached, or impervious to the richer variety of experience that life has to offer. Thus, much of the challenge of this karmic path will appear in the call to a less theoretical and more fully realized journey. For some of these personalities, that may mean they are called to immerse themselves in seemingly mundane details. For others, more open to its rewards, this life experience will ground them in a truly sensual, passionate, and compassionate sense of their life's true meaning.

CHALLENGE: **LEARNING TO LIVE NOT IN THEIR HEADS BUT IN THEIR HEARTS**
FULFILLMENT: **FINDING FULLNESS IN EACH MOMENT**

January 31–February 7

YOUTH AND EASE
AQUARIUS II

Though it can sometimes seem that they have the knack of being able to "please all of the people, all of the time," Aquarius II's on the Way of Passion will have to avoid the traps of popularity and learn to take a stand for what they truly believe. Self-satisfaction and even a measure of conceit can pose problems here, as can the challenge to go beyond what is accepted in search of what truly endures. Very prone to adopting the fashionable values and beliefs of the moment, they may turn away from the challenge to delve beneath the surface to discover their truer nature and innermost needs. At best, Aquarius II's on this karmic path are destined for real success and personal satisfaction. At worst, they will remain shallow, conventional, and imitative, suspended between the need to please others and the desire to please themselves—and somehow failing to do either.

CHALLENGE: **RECOGNIZING WHAT IS SUPERFICIAL AND WHAT HAS LASTING VALUE**
FULFILLMENT: **FREEING THEMSELVES FROM DEPENDENCY ON THE GOOD OPINION OF OTHERS**
NOTABLES: **FRANÇOIS TRUFFAUT (FRENCH NEW WAVE DIRECTOR); GAY TALESE (JOURNALIST, AUTHOR, THY NEIGHBOR'S WIFE); HERBERT SPENCER DICKEY (EXPLORER)**

JENNIFER ANISTON
Actress, *Friends*

2/11/1969
Aquarius III

February 8–15

ACCEPTANCE
AQUARIUS III

The personalities born in the Week of Acceptance may have to release a tendency to accept what is presented to them and take a hard look at some preconceived attitudes and prejudices as they travel the Way of Passion. Though some may fail to move beyond the limitations imposed by their pet theories and ideals to reach for their personal star, their tendency to greater tolerance and a renewed sense of values is pronounced, and most will realize both success and transformation in the search for life's deeper meaning. There are perhaps no others better suited to the higher promise of this karmic path, and once they come to understand the difference between theory and practice, they are bound to become far more open, tolerant, and accepting of the rich variety of experience that awaits them.

CHALLENGE: **IMMERSING THEMSELVES MORE FULLY IN EACH EXPERIENCE**
FULFILLMENT: **TAKING EACH DAY AS IT COMES, FULLY CAPITALIZING ON THE GROWTH IT AFFORDS**
NOTABLES: **JOSIAH GIBBS (MATHEMATICAL PHYSICIST); JOHN WILLIAMS (COMPOSER, STAR WARS)**

KARMIC PATH
25

February 16–22

SENSITIVITY
AQUARIUS–PISCES CUSP

Those born on this cusp may be highly resistant to the challenge of jumping in feet first and taking what life has to offer. Inclined to be overly sensitive at times, they often cultivate an attitude of extreme objectivity in the interest of self-protection and may suppress many of their own best impulses in the process. Though strongly attracted to the idea of passion, they may find it a somewhat elusive experience until they come to a better understanding of their inner workings. Yet they have a great potential for success, as their sensitivity, when properly channeled, enables them to experience the rich and subtle nuances of all that life has to offer. If they do, in fact, learn to jump in and not merely dip an occasional toe in the ocean of life, their courage and enthusiasm will be rewarded.

JOHNNY CASH
Country singer,
"The Man in Black"

2/26/1932
Pisces I

CHALLENGE: **NOT HIDING BEHIND PROTECTIVE WALLS OF IDEALISM OR ATTITUDES OF SUPERIORITY**

FULFILLMENT: **INDULGING THEIR PROCLIVITY TO FEEL AND LOVE DEEPLY**

NOTABLE: **EDWARD M. KENNEDY (U.S. SENATOR)**

February 23–March 2

SPIRIT
PISCES I

Prone to overidealism, those born in the Week of Spirit may find the Way of Passion challenging. Their sensitive natures give rise to all sorts of upsets and setbacks, which in turn may cause them to retreat into ivory towers of detachment and elitism. Though they will have to work hard to ground themselves in the material universe and summon the courage to connect with the nuts and bolts of their own deepest workings, they are capable of taking great strides here. Naturally generous and strongly spiritual, they have a great need to improve the world. If they can turn that impulse into reality by being willing to get their hands dirty in the pursuit of happiness, and learn to live more in the moment and less in the realms of the never-never, they are promised not only a rich and rewarding experience, but wisdom as well.

CHALLENGE: **GETTING BACK TO BASICS BY LIVING IN THE MUNDANE WORLD ONCE IN A WHILE**

FULFILLMENT: **DEVOTING THEMSELVES AND THEIR PASSIONATE SIDE TO SERVING OTHERS**

NOTABLE: **ELIZABETH TAYLOR (ACTRESS; 2-TIME OSCAR WINNER, *BUTTERFIELD 8*)**

March 3–10

THE LONER
PISCES II

Somewhat spiritual and refined, the souls born in this week who navigate the Way of Passion are rather less detached and theoretical than some, as this path endows them with more of an impulse to adventure, experience, and connection than they might otherwise have had. Thus, they may have a rewarding passage, providing they do not retreat from its higher challenges here by indulging in a timid streak that can hold them back from real happiness. Too, they have a pronounced tendency to retreat into a private world of their own making, unwilling to make too much contact with harsher realities. Sensual and soulful, they may drift in the stormy seas of their emotions at the expense of action. Yet they are blessed with a great capacity to recover from even the most extreme disasters, and if they can successfully circumvent depression or feelings of unworthiness and embrace the enormous variety of experience that beckons them, all will go well.

CHASTITY BONO
Daughter of Sonny and
Cher; spokeswoman

3/4/1969
Pisces II

CHALLENGE: **NOT CONFUSING PASSION WITH SUFFERING**

FULFILLMENT: **GROUNDING THEIR SENSE OF WHAT'S BEAUTIFUL IN WHAT'S PRACTICAL OR EVEN ATTAINABLE**

NOTABLES: **MIRIAM MAKEBA (SOUTH AFRICAN SINGER); KEELY SMITH (SINGER)**

March 11–18

DANCERS AND DREAMERS
PISCES III

Elitism and a tendency to worship false gods will both figure rather prominently in the lives of those born in the Week of Dancers and Dreamers who travel the Way of Passion. Yet by the same token, they may experience a rich and fulfilling journey, as they have a strong attraction to variety and adventure. If they take care that their adventures occur in the real world and get out of their heads and away from their fantasy lives, they will accomplish much. Yet their journey will first require them to get in touch with their own feelings to the extent that they become considerably more self-motivated than would ordinarily be the case. Though some with this configuration will go overboard and become too unrealistic in their search for life experience, most will find acceptance and enlightenment as they pass beyond the gates of social acceptance and into the realms of those things that have a deeper value.

CHALLENGE: **TAKING CARE NOT TO APPEAR TOO OMNISCIENT OR SUPERCILIOUS**

FULFILLMENT: **ADVENTURING INTO THE UNKNOWN WITHOUT FEAR**

NOTABLE: **ANDREW JACKSON YOUNG, JR. (CIVIL RIGHTS LEADER)**

The Way of Wonder

LIBRA I TO ARIES I
The Perfectionist to the Child

The goal for the individuals on the Way of Wonder is to let go of their exacting attitudes in order to approach life in a more open, relaxed manner, one that is defined by a childlike sense of awe at or delight in the world. Cultivating and experiencing wonder are the purpose of this path. This requires releasing an overemphasis on the details of life and a propensity to perfectionism in order to achieve a broader view. By being less critical and focused and by extending their vision behind the mundane, those on this karmic path will significantly enhance the quality of their lives and will become imbued with a sense of wonder as they get into touch with the larger forces at work in the universe. Awe is the natural by-product of such a process. Fairly cool customers emotionally, those born to this karmic path will usually need to become more familiar with their own feelings in order to become more spontaneous and fun. Play is the simple key to this path, as well as its core lesson. It is the fate of those on the Way of Wonder to slow down by putting the brakes on a bit and regularly take time to enjoy simple pleasures.

The individuals on this karmic path are born with a desire for order. They need to arrange their world in a fashion that feels right to them. Naturally, this requires quite a bit of management and organization. Their minds are taken up with all the little details of any situation or issue and with thoughts of how best to arrange them so that they form more beautiful or perfect relationships to one another. Efficiency is their god. As useful as this tendency may be, as anyone who has too much to do or worry about can attest, at a certain point the sheer volume of decisions required by such an exacting approach can be overwhelming. Stressed out, these individuals forget to see the bigger picture, to engage more openly or fully in the experience of living, or even to enjoy the end result of their labors. Sometimes they are so overinvolved in setting the details of their lives in the right order that nothing is good enough for them, causing them perpetual frustration and irritation.

The core lesson for those on this karmic path is quite simple: to nourish the child within through play. Teaching themselves how to engage in play and making sure that they give themselves enough playtime will help those on this karmic path to cultivate a sense of wonder.

Through play, those on this karmic path will forget to focus on everything they think needs to be done and begin to relax and allow things to go as they will. Of course, bills must be paid, daily tasks attended to, and provisions made for the future, but there is no reason why one cannot forget about work or chores for a while. The men and women on this path will discover that stress is largely something that they inflict upon themselves and that when they are able

---

CORE LESSON

Releasing themselves from an overemphasis on work and its many tasks and remembering to nourish a childlike need for play

GOAL

To cultivate an ongoing and inspiring sense of awe of the world and living

---

GIFTS
Charming, Frank, Dynamic

PITFALLS
Overly Exacting, Critical, Repressed

to put things out of their mind long enough to enjoy themselves, their general health and well-being improve dramatically.

Almost always, those coming into this lifetime with Libra I energies force themselves to assume a mature or overly responsible role. Often they are hard on themselves for not being perfect enough. Rarely satisfied, they drive themselves on toward greater and greater achievement in all areas of their life. Frequently, such a stance echoes an overly strict or critical parent or other authority figure from childhood. An underlying dynamic of this karmic path is that the individuals on it have a tendency to repress their feelings. Somewhere in the distant past, these men and women decided that mastering emotion was a high priority. This, combined with a dislike of anything that smacks of emotional messiness and a love of an efficient and well-ordered world, makes for people who are quite good at denying, stuffing, and blocking their feelings. They appear to be quite cool, even unemotional, but in fact they are quite complex on a feeling level. Developing any sort of spontaneity means that they must engage in the work of unlocking their emotional expression. While letting their real emotions out of the proverbial box may be fearful for them, ultimately they will discover how to balance feeling and rationality, contraction and expansion, expression and reticence. The child in them and its sense of wonder will begin to peek out and

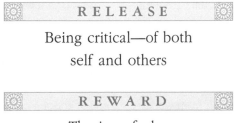

RELEASE
Being critical—of both self and others

REWARD
The joy of play

be heard only when their internal, and often critical, parent stops being so repressive. Moreover, they may find, as they rediscover their feelings, a kind of warmth and charm they never knew existed. They will know they are doing something right when they start to notice how many people seem to be attracted to them.

The men and women on the Way of Wonder are intense personalities, uniquely suited for tremendous achievements as long as they engage in the work of this karmic path and transform themselves into motivators rather than detractors of others. It is extremely unlikely that those born to this path will give up their discrimination or exacting tastes, but they must learn to keep them in balance with the rest of their personality and not allow them to dominate. Unusually critical people, they have a tendency to nitpick, be negative, or criticize others too severely based on their own high standards. They will always employ those standards to achieve the best results for their own and others' efforts, but when it comes to motivating others, learning to focus on the good and to ignore the less-than-perfect side of things (even though they will always see it pretty clearly) will reap them rich rewards in any field of endeavor. Relenting in this approach and becoming more accepting and forgiving will occur naturally as they do the work of this path and begin to relax and have more fun. Also, an important part of this

SUGGESTION

*Practice affirmations that remind you of your worth. Know that you deserve
to have pleasure. Realize that you are not responsible for fixing all of life's problems.
Try to be more spontaneous.*

process is that, following the development of a greater sense of wonder themselves, they will find that they are able to infect others with it. Moreover, they are possessed of a fierce, quick wit; once they learn to use it less to wound or to be critical and more simply to entertain, they will find that it is inordinately powerful as a form of engaging and charming people. Thus, they will be able to inspire others to great creative achievement.

This karmic path is likely to be worked out by these individuals on an internal or psychological level. Working on patterns in thinking and relating will be the main objective of this journey. Learning how to relax and drop one's critical attitudes is not as easy as it sounds to those who are not born to this path. The best approach is to attune oneself to the natural flow of things, letting things happen rather than attempting to make them happen. Since relaxation is so important here, those on this karmic path should spoil themselves more, particularly in the form of treating themselves to certain activities that will inevitably lead to removing tensions. Learning to enjoy themselves fully, without any feelings of guilt, is crucial to this process. Also, paying more attention to sleeping, eating, sex, and other natural functions will give their unconscious self more autonomy and free them from many strangling inhibitions.

What a relief it can be at last to back off from workaholic tendencies! Suddenly having more time on their hands and less work can lead those on this karmic path to make new friends and seek out whole new worlds of experience. In general, deemphasis on career and a focus on increasing interpersonal involvements are a

hallmark of progress on this path. Finding the right partner or partners will aid the process tremendously, and the joys of vacation, travel, affection, lovemaking, and in general just kicking back will steer the intense individuals on this path in a sensibly hedonistic direction. If they have children of their own, they will vicariously rediscover the joys of childhood through their own progeny. Also, having children provides them with a chance to become the loving, nonjudgmental parents that their own stern mother or father could never be. Attracting more free and open friends can exert a positive influence by fostering more fun-loving attitudes.

What is best for those on the Way of Wonder is to put aside more serious, intellectual, or demanding hobbies such as reading and discussion in favor of less cerebral and more active ones such as sports, dance, hiking, or biking. All outdoor activities should be pursued, since it is outdoors that a sense of wonder is truly fostered. Through really learning to enjoy themselves, even being silly and irresponsible from time to time, those on this karmic path will get into the habit of forgetting to be demanding and critical. Strange to say, for these people, who typically find it hard to reward themselves except with more hard work and responsibility, even the untrammeled pleasure of getting lost in the thorough enjoyment of a chocolate bar or a cartoon can represent a major spiritual breakthrough. Fulfillment on this path can be likened to a student's playing hooky from school. Removing himself from the reach of a critical or repressive teacher, he spends time on his own and simply indulges himself in the joy of a beautiful spring day.

BALANCE POINT

Work and Play

CRYSTALS AND GEMSTONES

Chrysoprase activates the individual to perceive the ordered chaos of the universe, resulting in the ability to let go and flow through the divine comedy of life.

NOTABLES ON THIS KARMIC PATH

Modern dance icon **Martha Graham** articulated a unique language of movement as both a dancer and a choreographer. Like many on this path, she reveled in physical expression, elevating play to a high aesthetic level. Prevented from going to dance school by her father, she enrolled upon his death. Through her interest in

MARTHA GRAHAM

a wide range of sources—the folk idiom, classical Greek drama, and various Asian styles—Graham was able to bring an unparalleled originality to the dance world. Performing as a soloist into her 90's, Graham refused to give up her highly demanding creative quest.

BOBBY MCFERRIN

Contemporary jazz vocalist **Bobby McFerrin** can sing Bach as easily as Bop. Though he has also employed his musical gift in conducting, it is his scat-like singing that has awarded him a unique position on today's music scene. His training and use of his voice perfectly represent the combination of precision and joy that is the hallmark of this path. Both intense and relaxed in his approach, he displays a bal-

ance between professionalism and playfulness that only the most successful on this path achieve. McFerrin's karmic journey may best be described by the title of his hit song, "Don't Worry, Be Happy."

Characteristic of those born to this path, **Danny Kaye** interwove a childlike joy into his stage, screen, and TV personas. Through hard work and perfectionism, Kaye developed a genius for mimicry and slapstick comedy that led him to a successful film career. In films such as *Hans Christian Andersen* and *The Inspector General,* Kaye used his non-threatening, foolish characters to engage audiences of all ages and share with them his sense of wonder, delight, and fantasy, bringing joy to the hearts of millions. In later years he devoted himself to charitable causes, in particular, UNICEF.

DANNY KAYE

Other Notables: Brendan Fraser, David Cassidy, Clarence S. Darrow, Jay Leno, Bernie Taupin, Aldous Huxley, Jerry Van Dyke, Edgar Rice Burroughs, Anthony Newley, Angie Dickinson, Will Smith, Barbara Walters, Mickey Mantle, Minnie Pearl, Gordon Parks, Roy Rogers, Sammy Sosa, Gillian Anderson, Richard Nixon, Debbie Allen, Lloyd Bridges, Rosa Parks, Susan B. Anthony, Peter Gabriel, Cybill Shepherd, Karen Carpenter, Vincente Minnelli

BIRTHDAYS ON KARMIC PATH 26

March 12, 1894–July 31, 1894 | October 22, 1912–March 12, 1913
June 4, 1931–October 22, 1931 | January 13, 1950–June 3, 1950 | August 25, 1968–January 12, 1969
April 6, 1987–August 25, 1987 | November 15, 2005–April 5, 2006

KARMIC PATH
26

March 19–24

REBIRTH
PISCES–ARIES CUSP

Pisces–Arians who navigate the challenges of the Way of Wonder can expect a rewarding life experience, though crucial to their spiritual development will be their ability to make the journey within in order to gain greater understanding of just why it is that they are so hard on themselves. In fact, many of these individuals may have to endure quite a lot of inner conflict and even suffering until they stop trying to suppress their sensitivity, learn to relax, and occasionally give themselves an even break. Though the ability to be kinder to themselves can be hard won for those born on the Cusp of Rebirth, the rewards of being able to relax the rules in order to experience the infinite are definitely worth the effort.

CLARENCE S. DARROW
Lawyer/social reformer;
defender in Scopes
"monkey" trial

4/18/1857
Aries III

CHALLENGE: **WORKING ON THEIR PSYCHOLOGICAL PATTERNS**
FULFILLMENT: **RELAXING IN THE GREAT OUTDOORS**
NOTABLE: **WILLIAM HURT (ACTOR; OSCAR FOR *KISS OF THE SPIDER WOMAN*)**

April 3–10

THE STAR
ARIES II

Aries II personalities are likely to flourish on the Way of Wonder, as they have an inborn ability to periodically set aside many of their hard-driving impulses and embrace pleasuring themselves. They may, however, be alarmists and should take care to avoid pickiness, impatience, and sarcasm. Though many on this path will have workaholic habits, they must take care that their will to succeed and improve themselves does not manifest itself as an obsession with detail and lack of enjoyment of life itself. These energetic people would do best to surround themselves with more laid-back, tolerant individuals who can help them overcome their sometimes explosive energies lest their efforts at self-examinations manifest as narcissism or a neurotic preoccupation with self-improvement. Learning to relax and let themselves off the hook will come quite naturally once they rid themselves of the fear of what others may think of them and learn instead to share their enthusiasm, passion, and awe of life itself.

CHALLENGE: **BEING LESS HARD ON THOSE AROUND THEM**
FULFILLMENT: **LETTING OFF SOME STEAM WITH THEIR FRIENDS ONCE IN A WHILE**
NOTABLES: **KEN GRIFFEY, SR. (BASEBALL PLAYER, MOSTLY WITH THE REDS); LAWRENCE BELL (AIRCRAFT MANUFACTURER)**

March 25–April 2

THE CHILD
ARIES I

The Way of Wonder should prove a relatively easy passage for those born in this week, providing they are willing to go through a process of introspection in order to dismantle the insecurities that hold them back from pursuing their own enthusiasms. Many of these personalities may have experienced undue amounts of restriction, criticism, or misunderstanding as children, causing them to internalize those same rigid and perfectionistic attitudes as they mature. Yet even as they undertake the excavation of the psyche that is necessary to understand just what motivates their inner drives, they will do well to take into account that each individual chooses what they learn. Equally, freeing themselves from the demands of their relentless inner taskmaster and opening themselves to the world of awe and wonder that awaits them will prove especially gratifying, particularly when they reach the point where they are able to share their enthusiasm with the kindred souls and spiritual playmates they are bound to encounter.

CHALLENGE: **NOT POURING ALL THEIR ENERGIES INTO WORK**
FULFILLMENT: **SPENDING SOME TIME ALONE, QUIETLY, BUT ENTHUSIASTICALLY ENJOYING THEIR FAVORITE ACTIVITIES**
NOTABLE: **TEDDY PENDERGRASS (POP/SOUL SINGER)**

April 11–18

THE PIONEER
ARIES III

The Way of Wonder holds many possibilities for Aries III's, providing they do not misdirect their considerable energies toward trying to correct everyone else's problems. Their impulses toward perfection can be so troublesome that their ideals manifest themselves in extremes of self-abnegation and denial. Thus, Aries III souls on this karmic path would do well to back up from time to time in an effort to slow down and get a better grasp of the big picture. Avoiding confrontation with their personal problems may be difficult, because unless they recognize the origins of their discontent, they may spend a lifetime trying to correct and perfect things that are better left alone. Still, these people are blessed with both the fearlessness and energy necessary to accomplish whatever they set out to do, and if they avoid the pitfalls of tyranny and overly controlling attitudes, their natural enthusiasm is sure to find expression and realization along the way.

CHALLENGE: **LETTING MORE CHAOTIC OR CREATIVE ENERGIES INTO THEIR RATHER ORDERED UNIVERSE**
FULFILLMENT: **EXPRESSING THEMSELVES MORE SPONTANEOUSLY BY CULTIVATING A SENSE OF HUMOR**
NOTABLES: **DAVID CASSIDY (ACTOR/SINGER, *THE PARTRIDGE FAMILY*); BESSIE SMITH (SINGER; "EMPRESS OF THE BLUES")**

NIKITA KHRUSHCHEV
Soviet prime minister;
denounced Stalin

4/17/1894
Aries III

April 19–24
POWER
ARIES–TAURUS CUSP

The individuals born in this period can find considerable success and happiness on the Way of Wonder, providing they can manage their pronounced workaholic tendencies and give in to the impulse to be a bit more relaxed and playful. Many of the lessons of this karmic path will revolve around learning to concentrate on what they have rather than what they don't. Though their development of the childlike enthusiasm that is the principal goal of this karmic path may be hindered by an overemphasis on practical matters, there is further a danger of overidentification with a restrictive or rigid parent or other role model that can hold them back from true fulfillment. The principal pitfalls of this configuration are that the impulse toward improvement and perfection may take over somewhere along the way and that these individuals may be unwilling to sacrifice a portion of their established power base in the interest of greater spiritual expansion and the simple experience of joy.

CHALLENGE: **RELEASING THEIR PREOCCUPATION WITH BEING IN CONTROL**
FULFILLMENT: **INDULGING THEMSELVES LESS IN GRAND EXTRAVAGANCES AND MORE IN SIMPLE PLEASURES**

JAY LENO
Comedian, host of
the *Tonight* show
———
4/28/1950
Taurus I

April 25–May 2
MANIFESTATION
TAURUS I

Those born in the Week of Manifestation who travel the Way of Wonder may encounter a few difficulties in overcoming their natural desire to establish order and feel in control in the interest of acquiring greater spontaneity. These individuals like nothing better than to impose structure and system on some of the more chaotic aspects of life, but they would do well to relinquish their impulses to dominate, especially in the arena of personal relationships. Yet they are naturally gifted with great sensuality and a need for creature comforts that, if judiciously indulged, can do much to nourish the child within. If they concentrate their energies a bit less on what is doable and a bit more on the worlds of wonder, joy, and spontaneity that await them on this life's journey, they will realize great expansion and contentment.

CHALLENGE: **THROWING OFF SOME OF THEIR SELF-IMPOSED RESPONSIBILITIES**
FULFILLMENT: **BECOMING MORE CHILDLIKE THEMSELVES RATHER THAN FOSTERING DEPENDENCIES FROM CHILDISH INDIVIDUALS**
NOTABLE: **THEO VAN GOGH (SUPPORTER AND BROTHER OF VINCENT)**

May 3–10
THE TEACHER
TAURUS II

Quite at home in the world of ideas, the self-taught souls born in this week who navigate the Way of Wonder nevertheless run the risk of becoming too rigid or pedantic. Naturally opinionated and rather hypercritical, many of those with this position are so sure of themselves that they may fail the higher challenge of this karmic path by failing to keep themselves open to new concepts or a real vision. Yet they are blessed with a need to explore other societies and cultures that should be indulged at every opportunity since it will help to generate the sense of awe called for by this karmic path. If they allow their natural sense of curiosity to prevail and channel their impulse toward perfection into a need for knowledge, they will realize great success and not a small measure of adventure.

CHALLENGE: **FREEING THEMSELVES FROM THE THRALL OF A HYPERCRITICAL INTERNAL PARENT**
FULFILLMENT: **INDULGING THEMSELVES IN MORE SENSUOUS PLEASURES**
NOTABLE: **JOHN WILKES BOOTH (ACTOR WHO ASSASSINATED PRESIDENT LINCOLN)**

MARTHA GRAHAM
Dancer, created
"choreography by
chance" movement
———
5/11/1894
Taurus III

May 11–18
THE NATURAL
TAURUS III

Those born in the Week of the Natural are well suited to the higher spiritual challenge of the Way of Wonder, as they are especially inclined toward the more relaxed and accepting worldview this passage confers. Perhaps the only real pitfall for the individuals with this position is that they may fail to take the journey inward in order to discover what gives rise to their insecurity and release issues that hold them back from a greater enjoyment of life. Too, they must avoid the tendency to overwork and would do well to meditate on Proust's caution about "those necessities that dull desire." Yet they have the possibility of wonderful success and personal happiness as they get into touch with the child within and free their independent spirits to rediscover the world enjoyment that awaits them.

CHALLENGE: **WEANING THEMSELVES FROM SELF-JUDGMENT AND INSECURITY**
FULFILLMENT: **FINDING FREEDOM IN PHYSICAL EXPRESSION AND BEING IN NATURE**

May 19–24
ENERGY
TAURUS–GEMINI CUSP

Born attention getters, those born in this period who travel the Way of Wonder are likely to have an exciting, rewarding journey, as they are quite capable of rushing in where angels fear to tread and of following their hearts at the drop of the proverbial hat. On the other hand, some with this configuration may have an overly energetic approach to problem solving that can turn picky, irritable, and downright difficult when they fail to achieve their objectives. Still, they have a fine sense of their own needs and desires, and when they are willing to meet the challenge of slowing down long enough to realize and reflect upon their more controlling impulses and their need to support their sometimes shaky egos with an excess of order, they can be sparkling and enthusiastic personalities, capable of such spontaneity and fun that they provide real inspiration to others.

CHALLENGE: **MUSTERING MORE ENDURANCE TO SEE THEIR PROJECTS THROUGH**

FULFILLMENT: **PURSUING THEIR LATEST ENTHUSIASM**

BERNIE TAUPIN
Lyricist and longtime collaborator with Elton John, "Your Song"

———
5/22/1950
Taurus–Gemini Cusp

May 25–June 2
FREEDOM
GEMINI I

The freedom lovers born in this week are likely to flourish on the Way of Wonder, providing they do not allow their considerable intelligence to manifest itself solely in criticism and faultfinding. Gifted with a fine sense of justice and social conscience, they have a highly developed tendency to engage in well-chosen rebellions that will serve them well. Though impatience can be a problem, as can self-criticism, if they take care to slow down and examine some of their deeper motivations and compulsions, they can take great strides. Nurturing their own lighter side, choosing their battles carefully, and encouraging their natural versatility and diversification will serve them especially well, as will the ability to cultivate a variety of relationships with people who feed their intellectual energies and who help them expand without tying them down to mundane tasks or rigid routines.

CHALLENGE: **HAVING CULTIVATED AWE OR WONDER, NOT ALLOWING IT TO TRANSMUTE INTO FANATICISM OR REBEL-LIOUSNESS**

FULFILLMENT: **REDEFINING WHAT FUN MEANS TO THEM**

NOTABLES: **JOSEF VON STERNBERG (DIRECTOR, *THE BLUE ANGEL*); BRIGHAM YOUNG (MORMON LEADER; COLONIZER OF UTAH)**

June 3–10
NEW LANGUAGE
GEMINI II

The individuals born in this week who travel the Way of Wonder can have a rich, rewarding passage, providing they find the courage to embrace life on its own terms. Though Gemini II's on this karmic path will doubtless find the venue for self-expression they so desire, they will also have to learn the value of giving up the rules and releasing their need to order the world before they feel safe enough to really be themselves. It is characteristic of those with this configuration to form relationships with people they want to change or reform. They will have to be aware of the tendency to do themselves harm through harboring somewhat defensive attitudes or needing to win arguments at all costs. Yet once they grasp that their tendency to be hypercritical is the projection of a poor self-image and learn to relax and embrace the great variety of people and experience that awaits them, they can relish the sense of awe that comes with greater understanding and truly spontaneous self-expression.

CHALLENGE: **GIVING UP THEIR FEAR OF APPEARING TO BE UNSOPHISTICATED OR FOOLISH**

FULFILLMENT: **LEARNING HOW TO IDENTIFY AND COMMUNICATE WHAT THEY FEEL**

DASHIELL HAMMETT
Detective writer,
The Thin Man

———
5/27/1894
Gemini I

June 11–18
THE SEEKER
GEMINI III

The souls born in the Week of the Seeker who travel the Way of Wonder are likely to have a fine time as long as they recognize and release their rather compulsive attitudes toward self-discipline and free themselves from the need to chase details rather than dreams. Though turning inward in order to understand the rigid or controlling attitudes that have held them back from true self-realization may prove difficult, chances are they will rise to the need for greater knowledge and experience and will have little trouble releasing the attitudes that stand in their way. Making time for play is essential to their mental health, as boring routines will surely stunt their emotional and psychological growth. Yet as long as they learn to manage stress, cultivate relaxation techniques, and recognize and indulge their own yearning for knowledge and adventure, they can find both inspiration and fulfillment on this karmic path.

CHALLENGE: **NOT PURSUING FUN AT THE EXPENSE OF SELF-UNDERSTANDING OR THE FEELINGS OF OTHERS**

FULFILLMENT: **ADDING A DOLLOP OF HUMILITY AND INNOCENCE TO HOW THEY PERCEIVE THE WORLD**

NOTABLE: **MARK VAN DOREN (POET/CRITIC; WON PULITZER, *THAT SHINING PLACE*)**

June 19–24

MAGIC
GEMINI–CANCER CUSP

Those born on the Cusp of Magic have a pronounced tendency to withdraw into a private world of rigid order and unrelenting self-discipline to assuage their intense need to feel safe. Since there is something of the zealot or the fanatic about some of these individuals, they will have to be careful that their impulses toward perfection are not allowed to run rampant in orgies of self-criticism or self-abnegation. Emotional failures can exacerbate these tendencies, and they will have to do a great deal of inner work to release many of the burdens of the past. Yet if they can learn to take off their hair shirts, set aside the whip, and slip into a more comfortable mind-set, they will further develop their innate sense of magic. Taking care to nourish and protect their sensitive inner child will help these romantic souls make wonder a way of life.

EDWARD VIII
King of England;
abdicated throne;
here with Wallis Simpson
———
6/23/1894
Gemini–Cancer Cusp

CHALLENGE: **BECOMING ENMESHED IN A PARTICULARLY COLD BRAND OF EMOTIONAL DETACHMENT**
FULFILLMENT: **KNOWING THAT THEIR CAPACITY FOR WONDER AFFIRMS WHO THEY ARE**
NOTABLE: **ALFRED KINSEY (SEXUALITY RESEARCHER; HELPED BRING ABOUT "SEXUAL REVOLUTION")**

June 25–July 2

THE EMPATH
CANCER I

Cancer I's on the Way of Wonder may spend a great deal of time trying to ignore, repress, or manage their own sensitivity before they can realize its higher fulfillment. Critical to this life journey will be their willingness to stop trying to order the world of emotion and to allow themselves to go with the flow, while at the same time maintaining their own identity. Their impulse to identify with others can manifest itself in a need to re-form or change people, and their strong emotionality can sometimes make it difficult to divest themselves of unproductive or otherwise draining situations and associates. Yet their innate ability to "let go and let God" will surely come to the fore with this position, and if they are willing to cultivate some spontaneity, unencumbered by fear, their energies, discernment, and instincts will do much to offset the poor emotional choices typical of them.

CHALLENGE: **BALANCING THE ROLES OF OVERLY STRICT OR DOMINATING PARENT AND IRRESPONSIBLE CHILD**
FULFILLMENT: **GIVING GREATER VENT AND EXPRESSION TO THEIR MORE SPIRITUAL IMPULSES OR SOULFUL FEELINGS**
NOTABLE: **IMELDA MARCOS (FILIPPINO FIRST LADY; KNOWN FOR EXTRAVAGANCE)**

July 3–10

THE UNCONVENTIONAL
CANCER II

Cancer II's who navigate the Way of Wonder will be marked by the need to place the stamp of perfection on any situation or relationship, and they may experience some conflict as to whether they want to gain approval for their efforts or encourage their deepest impulses toward originality and freedom. Many of those born in this week can become stuck in boring jobs and dull routines where they feel safe or capable of control, and this karmic path may force them into any number of awakenings in an effort to encourage greater spontaneity and childlike enthusiasm. Though naturally responsible, they will have to manage their tendency toward self-doubt, and though they may fight their attraction for the unconventional and untried, it will serve them well. For it will be exotic people, places, and things that will jumpstart their sense of awe and inspire them to expand their horizons to an acceptance of all that is possible.

LESLIE CARON
Actress/dancer,
An American in Paris
———
7/1/1931
Cancer I

CHALLENGE: **RECOGNIZING WHEN AWE OR WONDER IS LESS ABOUT LETTING THEIR FEELING RUN WILD AND MORE ABOUT SERENITY**
FULFILLMENT: **SURROUNDING THEMSELVES WITH FRIENDS WHO VALUE THEIR SENSE OF FUN**
NOTABLE: **DOROTHY THOMPSON (JOURNALIST; WROTE ANTI-NAZI PIECES)**

July 11–18

THE PERSUADER
CANCER III

The personalities born in this week may well become obsessed with the details, facts, and figures they feel are necessary for implementing their ideals, yet they would do better to release their more controlling and management-oriented energies and get in deeper touch with their more passionate side. Blessed with the ability to get things done, they may become entirely too caught up in the minutia of day-to-day life to be able to view their larger destiny accurately. Their sense of principle becomes outraged quite easily, and they are capable of taking the world all too personally when things don't go their way. Cultivating the ability to relax and take life as it comes and exploring the flowing rhythms of life will be especially beneficial, as will learning to be more accepting of themselves. Still, these dynamic people will make their mark on the Way of Wonder, providing they allow their more playful passions to guide them along the road.

CHALLENGE: **SLOWING DOWN, RELAXING, AND CULTIVATING FUN**
FULFILLMENT: **GIVING FREE REIN TO THEIR MORE PASSIONATE SIDE**
NOTABLE: **JOHN WANAMAKER (MAJOR RETAILER)**

July 19–25

OSCILLATION
CANCER–LEO CUSP

The personalities born in this period can have a truly rewarding passage along the Way of Wonder, providing they do the soul work necessary to discovering that there is a crucial difference between being childlike and merely childish. In any event, these individuals can be plagued by sometimes chaotic and conflicting emotional impulses that will require real evaluation. An ability to look within and discover just what lies at the heart of their need for discipline and control is critical here, as repression and denial can have devastating effects on their emotional health. Yet they are blessed with the strength and self-awareness to overcome even the worst obstacles and will surely be able to rediscover the sense of joy and spontaneity necessary to real happiness.

CHALLENGE: **NOT BEING OVERLY SELF-RESTRICTIVE SUCH THAT FRUSTRATION BOILS OVER INTO TEMPERAMENTAL OUTBURSTS**
FULFILLMENT: **STEADYING THEMSELVES BY KNOWING WHEN TO BALANCE WORK WITH PLAY**
NOTABLES: **WALTER BRENNAN (ACTOR); ARTHUR TREACHER (ACTOR; MERV GRIFFIN'S SIDEKICK)**

July 26–August 2

AUTHORITY
LEO I

Those born in the Week of Authority who travel the Way of Wonder are blessed with a natural generosity of spirit that will serve them well on this karmic path. As long as they can release many of their more controlling impulses and not succumb to the need to order their reality in elaborate personal rituals or rigid attitudes toward change, they can expect a rewarding experience. Though somewhat impelled by their need to assert themselves, they are equally capable of releasing their impulse toward control, such that much of this life journey will revolve around the issue of self-mastery rather than overinvolvement in the lives of others. Thus, though their selfishness may be extreme, they can imbue others with high ideals, fine standards, and great enthusiasm and as such will prove good parents, inspiring teachers and creative role models along this karmic path.

ALDOUS HUXLEY
Writer, *Brave New World*

7/26/1894
Leo I

CHALLENGE: **NURTURING THEIR INNER CHILD BY LOWERING THEIR STANDARDS FOR THEMSELVES**
FULFILLMENT: **SETTING ASIDE THEIR PREOCCUPATIONS LONG ENOUGH TO EXPERIENCE A SENSE OF AWE OF WHAT SURROUNDS THEM**

August 3–10

BALANCED STRENGTH
LEO II

Idealistic, social, and very loyal by nature, the personalities born in this week who travel the Way of Wonder are a nice blend of order and imagination. Thus, they may find this passage an easy road, as they are blessed with the ability to dream the impossible dream but wise enough not to feel as though they have to impose their dreams and beliefs on others. Generally able to work toward the highest goals and aspirations, they would do well to be aware of the danger of trying to do everything themselves. Their fixed energies can be rather troublesome, however, resulting in an obsession with order. For this karmic path also demands a willingness to cultivate greater spontaneity, relaxation, and inspiration. Still, if they learn to relinquish personal control to the larger cycles of life and develop a broader sense of the designs of fate, they are likely to find the Way of Wonder an inspiring highway.

CHALLENGE: **NOT OVERBURDENING THEMSELVES WITH TOO MUCH RESPONSIBILITY**
FULFILLMENT: **KEEPING THEIR SENSE OF HUMOR AND ABILITY TO LAUGH AT THEMSELVES HANDY SO THEY CAN PRODUCE THEM AT WILL**

August 11–18

LEADERSHIP
LEO III

If these confident and often controlling personalities can only develop the faith in others that they have in themselves, they can experience great reward along this life journey. Likely to be rather structured, they will have to work hard to open themselves to the world of broader experience that beckons. They are likely to be quite preoccupied with improving the world and may assume great responsibility before they learn to give up the reins and relax. Yet they have a unique ability to inspire others with their vision and perception, and if they employ their natural passion in a quest for greater fulfillment, broader vision, and the sense of wonder that comes with awakening to all that they have yet to learn and experience, their life will be rich indeed.

JERRY VAN DYKE
Actor, *Coach*

7/27/1931
Leo I

CHALLENGE: **NOT TRYING TO WILL THEMSELVES INTO A STATE OF RELAXATION OR HAVING FUN**
FULFILLMENT: **OPENING THEMSELVES TO THEIR IMAGINATION AND BENT FOR PHILOSOPHY AND SPIRITUALITY**
NOTABLES: **WILLIAM GOLDMAN (SCREENWRITER, *BUTCH CASSIDY AND THE SUNDANCE KID*); JANICE RULE (ACTRESS)**

August 19–25
EXPOSURE
LEO–VIRGO CUSP

If they are careful that their unique journey of secrets and revelation does not revolve solely around repressed emotions and personal frustrations, Leo–Virgos can do quite well on the Way of Wonder. The key to their development, however, will lie in their willingness to become more open and a bit less critical, though not necessarily less discerning, as they make their way along the road. While some with this configuration will project a cool, perfectionistic exterior, it may actually mask a whirl of conflicting emotions. Being preoccupied with details at the expense of a larger perspective will be especially troublesome, and they would do well to learn to relax if they are not to become the victims of their own intensity. Yet they have a great gift for service that will enable them to choose situations where they can best motivate others. As they learn to become less suspicious and self-protective, their inward journey toward self-realization is likely to reveal both a joyful heart and an open mind.

CHALLENGE: **KNOWING THE DIFFERENCE BETWEEN HIDING AND SUPPRESSING THEIR DEEPER, GENUINE FEELINGS**

FULFILLMENT: **FINDING A MEANS OF EXPRESSION FOR COMMUNICATING THEIR SENSE OF WONDER**

EDGAR RICE BURROUGHS
Writer, *Tarzan*

9/1/1875
Virgo I

August 26–September 2
SYSTEM BUILDERS
VIRGO I

Virgo I's may have a rather difficult journey along the Way of Wonder until they learn the fine arts of managing their sense of anxiety and letting the world go its own way. Though they may well be inclined toward hypercriticism and a rather shocking need to order events and people down to the smallest detail, perhaps their principal danger is that many of them will attempt to shore up their self-image by turning inward in an increasingly exacting fashion, resulting in the conviction that they are never quite good enough to live up to their own rigid standards. Still, if they work to combine their natural modesty and dependability with greater flexibility, tolerance, and openness, their success on the Way of Wonder is ensured, especially when they use their gifts to motivate, rather than intimidate, others.

CHALLENGE: **RECOGNIZING WHEN THEY HAVE BECOME TRAPPED BY THEIR MENTAL CONSTRUCTIONS AND THAT, PRECISELY THIS, WAS THEIR SECRET DESIRE**

FULFILLMENT: **ENJOYING FRIENDSHIPS THAT PULL THEM OUT OF THEIR WELL-ORDERED INNER WORLDS AND ALLOW THEM TO HAVE A GOOD TIME**

September 3–10
THE ENIGMA
VIRGO II

Those born in the Week of the Enigma can realize many of the higher goals of this karmic path, providing they do not allow themselves to become the victims of their own exacting morals and standards. Well suited to the demand of cultivating greater pleasure in life, they will need to take care not to impose their standards or beliefs on others unless a situation demands that their unique administrative talents come into play. Perhaps their principal risk is that they may insist on solving their own problems and thus stall on this journey by not seeking the help they may need. Yet they have a possibility of success, though they will have to get to know themselves a bit better first and be further willing to divest themselves of the tyrannies of a carefully cultivated worldly image or rigid patterns of thinking and behavior. Yet if they begin with the inner realization that no one is perfect, all can go well.

CHALLENGE: **RELAXING THEIR STANDARDS**

FULFILLMENT: **LETTING THEIR HUMOR AND ZANIER SIDE TAKE THE LEAD IN THEIR LIVES**

ANNE BANCROFT
Actress, *The Graduate*

9/17/1931
Virgo III

September 11–18
THE LITERALIST
VIRGO III

Getting in touch with their nurturing side will prove especially important for those born in the Week of the Literalist who find themselves on the Way of Wonder. Indeed, many of these personalities have a rather negative outlook that bears watching, as their critical faculties can get out of hand, especially when they refuse to make the necessary efforts at self-evaluation. In fact, self-control can be something of a god to these personalities, and repression in all its forms can consequently rank high on their list of personal demons. Yet at the heart of these concerned and caring people lies a need for harmony and fun that can find adequate expression, providing they let themselves and others off the hook from time to time and summon the courage and enthusiasm to motivate those around them with love and encouragement, rather than criticism and nit-picking.

CHALLENGE: **BEING AWARE THAT A DIRECT APPROACH IS MOST OFTEN A CRITICAL ONE**

FULFILLMENT: **ALLOWING THEMSELVES MORE TIME FOR RELAXATION**

NOTABLE: **GEORGE JONES (COUNTRY SINGER)**

September 19–24
BEAUTY
VIRGO–LIBRA CUSP

Blessed with great idealism and sensitivity, Virgo–Librans who travel the Way of Wonder are likely to do very well indeed, providing they don't fall under the domination of a rigid and controlling parent, partner, or family member and internalize attitudes that are not really their own. Gifted with greater organizational talents than they might otherwise have had, their keen perception, along with their knack for sounding the alarm when necessary, can cause them to ignore the challenge of this karmic path and lose their sense of wonder in a never-ending quest for greater emotional security. Indeed, they may get mired in tiresome details or the need to perfect themselves as a means of gaining approval. Yet they are gifted with a firmer set of standards than they might otherwise have had, and if they cultivate a high sense of beauty and combine it with an attitude of reverence and awe for life itself, they can expect great fulfillment.

CHALLENGE: **UNDERSTANDING THAT THEY DON'T HAVE TO MEASURE UP TO THEIR OWN AESTHETIC IDEALS**

FULFILLMENT: **CULTIVATING THE CAPACITY FOR WONDER SO THAT THEIR MANY PLEASURES HAVE MORE MEANING**

NOTABLES: **WILLIE SHOEMAKER (GREATEST WINNING THOROUGHBRED JOCKEY); LARRY HAGMAN (ACTOR, DALLAS)**

WILL SMITH
Actor/rap artist,
The Fresh Prince,
Independence Day

9/25/1968
Libra I

September 25–October 2
THE PERFECTIONIST
LIBRA I

For these souls, the principal challenge of the Way of Wonder will be to learn when and how to quell their impulse to fix things which are not necessarily broken in the first place. Exacting and sometimes difficult, they may become mired in their need for perfection and become chronically "holier than thou." Yet if they realize that much of their insistence on order arises from an inner need for security, things will get easier. They will benefit greatly from expanding their intellectual and social horizons, for acceptance of others will surely result in greater acceptance of themselves. Too, some of this group may go overboard and become increasingly careless or irresponsible or do quite a lot of "slumming" in their personal relationships in an attempt to discover or rediscover passions that might better be left alone. Yet if they make an effort to cultivate flexibility and openness to the world of ideas beyond their immediate sphere, their natural sense of joy is sure to blossom.

CHALLENGE: **LEARNING TO MANAGE THEIR EMOTIONS RATHER THAN MASTER THEM**

FULFILLMENT: **DISCOVERING THE FREEDOM OF BEING ABLE TO LAUGH AT THEMSELVES**

NOTABLES: **JAMES CRONIN (PHYSICIST; NOBEL PRIZE); ANGIE DICKINSON (ACTRESS, POLICE WOMAN)**

October 3–10
SOCIETY
LIBRA II

Paramount to the success of those born in the Week of Society who navigate the Way of Wonder will be learning to take their own desires and needs more seriously and not trying to quell their sense of passion or enthusiasm in endless responsibilities, unproductive relationships, or trying to reform others. Going within in order to get reacquainted with the child who dwells in all of us may prove quite an education for these souls, especially if it frees them from the rigid or overly exacting standards they have most certainly outgrown. Likely to be rather sharp-tongued and insightful, they would do well to keep their critical faculties under control and turn their attention to the task of developing a clearer vision of themselves and their place in the larger scheme. Thus, freed from self-deception, they can experience great happiness on this life journey.

CHALLENGE: **TAKING THEIR OWN NEEDS AND DESIRES MORE SERIOUSLY**

FULFILLMENT: **OPERATING FROM THEIR LIGHT, FUN-LOVING SIDE MORE OFTEN**

NOTABLE: **BISHOP DESMOND TUTU (NOBEL PEACE PRIZE WINNER FOR FIGHT AGAINST APARTHEID)**

BARBARA WALTERS
TV journalist/famed
interviewer, *20/20*

9/25/1931
Libra I

October 11–18
THEATER
LIBRA III

These worldly personalities may encounter quite a lot of adventure on the Way of Wonder, though whatever their circumstances, they will likely find a sense of drama in even the most mundane venues. They may nevertheless have a rather alarmist view of the universe and will have a pronounced tendency to get mired in a chronic need to air their complaints and concerns. Often brilliantly intellectual, they may nevertheless have to work to open themselves to a more enthusiastic and even naive view of the world. Yet it is likely that whatever their chosen field of endeavor, they will make a great impression through their thoroughness, dedication, and sheer style. Able to motivate others, they would do well to cultivate relationships with people who are willing to introduce them to the world of exciting possibilities that awaits them along this karmic path.

CHALLENGE: **NOT PLAYING THE ROLE OF A CHILD AS MUCH AS ENCOUNTERING THE CHILDLIKE PART OF THEMSELVES**

FULFILLMENT: **REALIZING THAT THEY WILL BE RESPECTED EVEN IF THEY PRESENT THEMSELVES AS LESS SERIOUS OR PONDEROUS**

NOTABLES: **ZIGGY MARLEY (REGGAE SINGER; SON OF BOB); EDGAR SELWYN (FORMED GOLDWYN PICTURES WITH SAM GOLDFISH)**

October 19–25
DRAMA AND CRITICISM
LIBRA–SCORPIO CUSP

Charisma and criticism may combine in a rather daunting combination in this group, for the personalities born on this cusp who travel the Way of Wonder have a knack for knowing when they are right and the communicative talents to convince others of almost anything. For that reason alone, they are bound to succeed on this karmic path yet may fail its higher spiritual challenge by refusing to release their more controlling and perfectionistic tendencies. Another danger is that their inner emotional conflicts may be expressed in any number of difficult relationships, for these individuals are much better at analyzing others' behavior than they are at seeing their own self-destructive patterns. Yet if they can learn to relax a bit and avoid the tendency to set different standards of behavior for others than they do for themselves, life along this road can prove a fine adventure, providing they do not abuse their power over others and learn to motivate, rather than manipulate.

CHALLENGE: **TRYING TO BRING A LEVEL OF MATURITY TO A RELATIONSHIP WITHOUT SUPPRESSING THEIR ROMANTIC IMPULSES**

FULFILLMENT: **SETTING FREE THEIR SENSE OF MISCHIEF**

NOTABLE: **MINNIE PEARL (COUNTRY MUSIC SINGER/ ENTERTAINER)**

MICKEY MANTLE
Baseball legend, Yankees
center fielder

10/20/1931
Libra–Scorpio Cusp

October 26–November 2
INTENSITY
SCORPIO I

Inclined to be very hard on themselves, this group may find the Way of Wonder a difficult journey at times. Gifted with a highly developed insight into others, they may nevertheless fall victim to their own exacting standards. Very much inclined to be a bit too judgmental and intense about details, they may find that many of their worries lessen as they go within and get to the bottom of some deep-seated feelings of guilt. They may further hinder their own development through refusing to be more tolerant of their own shortcomings. Learning to indulge themselves in simple pleasures will be most beneficial, as will keeping their feelings out in the open with those they can trust. Yet if they can cultivate a lighter approach to the world and its foibles and avoid the tendency to fearfulness and suspicion, they will find themselves more able to persuade and motivate others to their highest ideals.

CHALLENGE: **RESOLVING TO LIVE FROM THEIR LIGHTER SELVES WHILE ALSO GIVING EXPRESSION TO THEIR DARKER SIDE**

FULFILLMENT: **APPLYING SOME OF THAT FAMOUS FOCUS TO FINDING THE WONDERS THAT EXIST IN THE WORLD**

NOTABLES: **DALE EVANS (ENTERTAINER WITH HUSBAND ROY ROGERS); NICCOLO PAGANINI (VIOLIN VIRTUOSO); GORDON PARKS (PHOTOGRAPHER/WRITER/DIRECTOR)**

November 3–11
DEPTH
SCORPIO II

Though individuals born in the Week of Depth who travel the Way of Wonder are likely to succeed in material terms, they may falter on this karmic path if they do not take care to cultivate their sense of spirituality, wonder, and enthusiasm. Since this karmic path involves an inner journey, it will be important for these souls to connect with their curiosity and excavate some shutdown areas of their psyches in order to realize fulfillment. Personal relationships will prove especially instructive for these people as they learn to curb their critical tendencies and just go with the flow. Some in fact, will form strong bonds with those who awaken their spiritual natures or get them into touch with their inner child. Such combinations can work quite well if they avoid the pitfalls of jealousy or possessiveness, as this life journey can provide them an opportunity to motivate and inspire their nearest and dearest in such a way as to bring about both material success and greater spiritual integration.

CHALLENGE: **SLACKING OFF ON THEIR INTENSITY LEVEL ESPECIALLY WHEN IT COMES TO LEISURE-TIME PURSUITS**

FULFILLMENT: **SPENDING TIME WITH MORE LAIDBACK FRIENDS**

NOTABLE: **ROY ROGERS (ACTOR/SINGER/SINGING COWBOY)**

SAMMY SOSA
Baseball player, Chicago
Cubs, battled with Mark
McGwire for home run
record in 1998

11/12/1968
Scorpio III

November 12–18
CHARM
SCORPIO III

Those born in the Week of Charm who travel the Way of Wonder are likely to find the calling of this karmic path fairly easy to grapple with once they come to terms with some of their pressing inner issues. Quite capable of arranging reality more or less to their liking and pleasure, they will nevertheless find that a childlike sense of wonder is rather elusive for them until they get into touch with their spiritual side. Also, there is the danger that the playfulness called for by this karmic path will only mask an attempt to manipulate or seduce others. Though they may never acquire the degree of spontaneity that marks some others on this road, they can nevertheless expect great contentment along this karmic path since theirs is a nature given to enjoyment.

CHALLENGE: **DROPPING THE MASK TO REVEAL THE LITTLE KID INSIDE**

FULFILLMENT: **BEING TRUE TO THEIR FEELINGS AND SPIRITUAL IMPULSES**

NOTABLE: **BARBARA HUTTON (HEIRESS; SOCIALITE; "POOR LITTLE RICH GIRL")**

November 19–24

REVOLUTION
SCORPIO–SAGITTARIUS CUSP

Learning to choose their battles more carefully—or rather, to lay all weapons aside—may figure prominently in the life journey of those born in this period who find themselves on the Way of Wonder. In fact, those with this position have the potential for considerable transformation, though the revolutions experienced are likely to have more of a personal rather than worldly character. For this is a configuration that can appear in soldiers of fortune who turn into Buddhist monks and feminist CEOs who retire to raise their kids. In any event, many of these rather extreme personalities will have occasion to experience the truth of the adage "To rule is to serve." Yet they are promised a successful and rewarding journey, as they are gifted with the humor, natural wisdom, and fine sense of empathy that will prove among their greatest assets in the course of this life experience.

CHALLENGE: **WEANING THEMSELVES FROM A RATHER DEWY-EYED VIEW OF THEIR CHILDHOOD**
FULFILLMENT: **EXPERIENCING A SORT OF WONDER AT THEIR OWN ACHIEVEMENTS**
NOTABLES: **DORIS DUKE (SOCIALITE; PHILANTHROPIST); GEORGE ELIOT (EDITOR; AUTHOR, *MIDDLEMARCH*); GARSON KANIN (PLAYWRIGHT/DIRECTOR, *FUNNY GIRL*)**

GILLIAN ANDERSON
Actress, *The X-Files*

12/9/1968
Sagittarius II

November 25–December 2

INDEPENDENCE
SAGITTARIUS I

Those born in the Week of Independence who travel this karmic path can do especially well, as the sense of liberation that comes from divesting themselves of perfectionistic and workaholic habits is likely to be particularly sweet. Quite well suited to the challenge of becoming more relaxed and playful, these souls may nevertheless have to do quite a bit of internal searching before they can come to terms with some deep-seated insecurities. Yet they are gifted with an ability to share their innermost thoughts and feelings that few of their fellow travelers possess; if they can use that talent to release old baggage and at the same time employ their considerable wealth of creative inspiration to motivate those around them, they can expect wonderful success and accomplishment.

CHALLENGE: **NOT PERMITTING THEIR CODE OF HONOR TO TURN INTO A STRAITJACKET FOR THEM—OR ANYONE ELSE**
FULFILLMENT: **EXPLORING THE WORLD AROUND THEM AND THE FEELING OF AWE THEY HAVE FOR IT**
NOTABLES: **ELSIE PARSONS (SOCIOLOGIST; STUDIED NATIVE AMERICANS); ROBERT R. LIVINGSTON (MADE LOUISIANA PURCHASE)**

December 3–10

THE ORIGINATOR
SAGITTARIUS II

Those born in this week who navigate the challenge and promise of the Way of Wonder can experience a fine and rewarding passage, as these often eccentric souls are unlikely to suffer much from their perfectionistic tendencies. Though they will doubtless do their best to rise to the top of any profession or chosen field, their more unusual and even exotic qualities are sure to distract them from an overinvolvement in detail or nitpicking. In a word, these personalities are quite naturally ardent and adventurous, though the degree of passion they have for a particular subject is apt to be far greater than their degree of involvement with it. Thus, though their enthusiasms may come and go, they are likely to surround themselves with interesting and unusual people as a means of nurturing their higher selves. Though it may take time for them to set aside some of their defensive qualities and mellow out a bit, they can nevertheless develop a great capacity for joy along this road.

CHALLENGE: **OVERCOMING THEIR FEAR OF REJECTION AND NEED TO PROVE THEMSELVES**
FULFILLMENT: **INDULGING THEIR OWN WACKY WAY OF DOING THINGS**
NOTABLE: **LOUIS PRIMA (AMERICAN MUSICIAN)**

BRENDAN FRASER
Actor,
George of the Jungle

12/3/1968
Sagittarius II

December 11–18

THE TITAN
SAGITTARIUS III

The souls born in the Week of the Titan who make their way along this karmic path can realize the extremes of success and the depths of failure. In order to truly succeed, they will have to develop a greater awareness of what drives both themselves and others. Though blessed with great idealism, empathy is not their strong suit. Expansive and big-hearted by nature, they can ironically be plagued by an erosive and troublesome insecurity that can manifest itself in displays of temper, obsessive criticism of others, and rather unpleasant projections of their darker sides. They will have to work hard to subdue their anxieties or run the risk of obsessing over the details of their projects and plans to the extent that some of their best inspirations wither on the vine. Still, they have a kind of larger-than-life quality, and if they use their charisma to inspire and motivate others rather than to dominate or undermine their detractors, they are likely to rediscover any number of simple joys.

CHALLENGE: **SETTING ASIDE TIME FOR PLAY**
FULFILLMENT: **ADOPTING A LIGHTER APPROACH, ONE LESS BURDENED BY THE WEIGHT OF THE WORLD**
NOTABLES: **MOREY AMSTERDAM (ACTOR/COMEDIAN, *THE DICK VAN DYKE SHOW*); GENERAL BENJAMIN DAVIS, JR. (1ST BLACK WEST POINT GRADUATE)**

December 19–25

PROPHECY
SAGITTARIUS–CAPRICORN CUSP

Though well suited to the challenges presented on the Way of Wonder, Sagittarius–Capricorns will nevertheless experience a number of ups and downs along the road to their higher development. Basically, these personalities will experience no small amount of conflict as they work to reconcile their urge for perfection with their impulse toward enthusiasm and expansion. The resulting inner turmoil can manifest itself in an alarmist mentality, and they may squander their gifts of foresight, insight, and intuition in anxiety rather than hope. However, their inner journey is likely to be a rewarding one as they divest themselves of the need to reform the world and turn their attention to their own inner expansion. Once they accept that some events are outside their control, a renewed faith in the order of life will doubtless be followed by a deep reverence and understanding of their place in the universe. If they then complete the challenge of this karmic path by sharing their understanding with others, all will go beautifully.

RICHARD M. NIXON
37th U.S. president;
1st to resign due to
Watergate scandal

1/9/1913
Capricorn II

CHALLENGE: **ALLOWING OTHERS CLOSE ENOUGH TO SHARE SOME PRIVATE PLAYTIME**
FULFILLMENT: **LIVING MORE FULLY FROM THEIR MORE EXPANSIVE AND OPTIMISTIC SIDE**
NOTABLE: **LADY BIRD JOHNSON (LBJ'S FIRST LADY)**

December 26–January 2

THE RULER
CAPRICORN I

Those born in the Week of the Ruler who travel the Way of Wonder are bound for a rather difficult experience unless they learn the distinction between striving for perfection and exhausting oneself and one's energies in a never-ending series of responsibilities and details. Though they are likely to be well organized, these people can cause themselves and others no end of grief with their tyrannical insistence on order. It is essential for them to stay in touch with their earthier and more sensual inclinations and to make time for play. Too, part of their inner journey will involve coming to terms with the fact that they may have been denied the usual pleasures of childhood and weighed down with too much responsibility early on. Yet if they can bring themselves to enjoy the fruits of their considerable labors and adopt a more accepting attitude toward themselves and others, they can experience a major spiritual breakthrough.

CHALLENGE: **FORCING THEMSELVES NOT TO BE SUCH STERN TASKMASTERS**
FULFILLMENT: **REMEMBERING TO TAKE REGULAR BREAKS IN ORDER TO AWAKEN THEIR MORE FUN-LOVING SIDE**
NOTABLES: **WOODROW WILSON (28TH U.S. PRESIDENT); CHRISTY TURLINGTON (MODEL); MARTHA THOMAS (PRESIDENT, BRYN MAWR COLLEGE)**

January 3–9

DETERMINATION
CAPRICORN II

Some of this group may retreat from the challenge of the Way of Wonder and get mired in both cynicism and personal touchiness, while others may preoccupy themselves with futile efforts to reform others, to the detriment of their higher development. In any event, the tendencies to self-neglect and self-doubt will be pronounced. It will be essential to their success to free themselves from the need for approval and to embrace their own naive vision. Gifted with a unique sense of humor and perspective on the world, they will nevertheless have to stay open enough not to resist the advice and suggestions of others out of sheer stubbornness or fear of change. When they learn to take their own mistakes in stride and cultivate the sense of wonder and awe that awaits them in the discovery of wider worlds of thought and study, they are likely to flourish along this road and gain the necessary confidence to serve as a beacon of inspiration and motivation for others.

LLOYD BRIDGES
Actor; father of
Beau and Jeff

1/15/1913
Capricorn III

CHALLENGE: **NOT BEING ASHAMED OF THEIR NAÏVETÉ, RATHER CULTIVATING IT AS A GATEWAY TO WONDER**
FULFILLMENT: **SHARING THE JOYS OF LIVING WITH A SENSITIVE, PLAYFUL PARTNER IN PRIVATE**
NOTABLE: **LORETTA YOUNG (ACTRESS, *THE FARMER'S DAUGHTER*)**

January 10–16

DOMINANCE
CAPRICORN III

When born to the Way of Wonder, those born in the Week of Dominance may expend no small amount of energy in trying to make the rest of the world conform and reform to their own point of view. Thus, this road may be something of a struggle until these individuals gain a better grasp of their own often rigid attitudes and learn to go with the flow. They have a great tendency to become rather unhappily self-sacrificing or to turn their impulse to perfection inward in a relentless regime of self-improvement. These personalities can be quite pessimistic until they learn to leave the details to somebody else and have some fun. Highly physical but not especially sensual, their need for self improvement may also manifest itself in strenuous exercise regimes or, in extreme cases, psychological problems such as eating disorders. The real key to success is to turn their formidable energies inward in an effort to reawaken their spontaneous, childlike side.

CHALLENGE: **FREEING THEMSELVES FROM AN OVERLY RESPONSIBLE ATTITUDE AND EXCESSIVELY DEVOTED NATURE**
FULFILLMENT: **BELIEVING THEMSELVES ENTITLED TO MORE FUN AND EVEN A MORE SPIRITUAL POINT OF VIEW**
NOTABLE: **DEBBIE ALLEN (ACTRESS; CHOREOGRAPHER/DANCER)**

January 17–22
MYSTERY AND IMAGINATION
CAPRICORN–AQUARIUS CUSP

These stimulating, exciting people are likely to flourish on the Way of Wonder, as long as they keep their rather excitable natures under control. Much prone to the need to alert the rest of us to the problems of the world, they are equally capable of turning over the helm and allowing others to solve those problems. Thus, Capricorn–Aquarians can find quite a bit of fulfillment, though this journey will require them to turn their energies inward in an effort at sincere self-evaluation. Naturally vivid and expressive, they are unlikely to suppress their emotional conflicts to the point where they become damaging, and if their spontaneous side is given the fullest expression and encouragement, they will doubtless divest themselves of those attitudes that hinder their higher sense of fulfillment. If they recognize that one's first duty is, after all, to oneself, they can expect great satisfaction and considerable adventure.

CHALLENGE: **TAKING CARE NOT TO GO OVERBOARD BY SOBERLY PUTTING ON THE BRAKES**
FULFILLMENT: **FEELING FREE TO ALLOW THEIR CHILDLIKE INVENTIVENESS, ENTHUSIASM, AND SPONTANEOUS SELF-EXPRESSION TO BURST FORTH**
NOTABLES: **ANNE BRONTË (WRITER; GOVERNESS); DANNY KAYE (COMIC ACTOR, HANS CHRISTIAN ANDERSEN)**

ROSA PARKS
Civil rights activist, she would not give up her seat on the bus

2/4/1913
Aquarius II

January 23–30
GENIUS
AQUARIUS I

The gifted, highly individualistic personalities born in this week who navigate the Way of Wonder are likely to have an interesting passage, yet they will have to work hard to connect with the more intimate side of their own nature. Though blessed with natural humanity and a keen sense of justice, they are quite capable of detaching emotionally to the point where they cannot understand or comprehend either their own behavior or the negative reactions of those around them as they relentlessly pursue their ideals. Indeed, they may view people and situations more as abstractions than as reality. Curiously, they may manifest extreme touchiness and some rather temperamental qualities until they go within to find out what it is that motivates them and how such qualities can be manifestations of their own unaddressed emotional needs. Yet if they cultivate their humanity and avoid self-centeredness, they can realize great satisfaction.

CHALLENGE: **TEMPERING THEIR IMPATIENCE AND CULTIVATING SERENITY TO BETTER BE AWARE OF WHAT IS**
FULFILLMENT: **ENCOURAGING THEIR PENCHANT FOR TRAVEL AND ITS EXPANSION OF THEIR CAPACITY FOR AWE**

January 31–February 7
YOUTH AND EASE
AQUARIUS II

Those born in this week who find themselves on the Way of Wonder can have a truly rewarding passage, though they will have to learn to discern the difference between childlike playfulness and spontaneity and simple immaturity. Though they will doubtless make their share of mistakes, there is ultimately very little that can go wrong for them, due to the fact that their sometimes overextended energies are greatly strengthened by the self-discipline and organizational skill that are part of the endowment of this karmic path. At the same time, these personalities are blessed with more of a tolerant and accepting attitude than some of their fellow travelers on this karmic path, and the resulting combination is likely to make for a nice balance of work and play, expertise and openness, relaxation and personal reward.

CHALLENGE: **LEARNING TO STAY AWAY FROM MORE TROUBLED TYPES WHO WILL ONLY BRING THEIR EBULLIENT SELVES DOWN**
FULFILLMENT: **TRAVELING THEIR OWN PATH WITH AS LITTLE INTERFERENCE FROM OTHERS AS POSSIBLE**
NOTABLES: **MORGAN FAIRCHILD (ACTRESS); MARY LEAKEY (ANTHROPOLOGIST)**

PETER GABRIEL
Pop/world singer, founder of Genesis

2/13/1950
Aquarius III

February 8–15
ACCEPTANCE
AQUARIUS III

The Way of Wonder will demand that those born in the Week of Acceptance let go of many early attitudes and prejudices and turn loose some weighty psychological and emotional baggage carried from childhood. Yet their inward journey is likely to be well rewarded as they relinquish the impulse toward control in the interest of attaining greater personal peace and enjoyment of life. Thus relieved of many of their more temperamental aspects, they will prove themselves creative and useful problem solvers in almost any field. Since they may be overly critical of their nearest and dearest, they should take special care not to alienate loved ones with their sometimes rigid or demanding attitudes. Still, their chances of success are very high, and as these souls mellow a bit over time, they will be better able to enjoy the fruits of self-knowledge and gain the necessary sense of awe of the rhythms and design of life itself as they learn to live and let live.

CHALLENGE: **ACCEPTING THINGS THAT ARE LESS ORGANIZED OR EFFICIENT THAN THEY WOULD LIKE**
FULFILLMENT: **UTILIZING THEIR HUMOR, WIT, AND SENSE OF IRONY TO THE FULLEST**
NOTABLES: **WILLIAM SHERMAN (CIVIL WAR UNION GENERAL); SUSAN B. ANTHONY (WOMEN'S RIGHTS LEADER); JIMMY HOFFA (UNION BOSS)**

February 16–22

SENSITIVITY
AQUARIUS–PISCES CUSP

The ability to get out of their own heads and enjoy the wonders of the world around them will prove especially useful for those born on this cusp who travel this karmic path. In fact, there is a pronounced danger that once these souls turn inward in an effort to understand what motivates their own perfectionistic and rather fearful approach to life, they will fail the higher challenge by becoming preoccupied with self-improvement and excessive introspection. In extreme cases, these souls will be much prone to hypochondria, sleep disorders, and phobias until they gain a better grasp of their impulse toward self-protection. Inclined to be entirely too hard on themselves, they would do well to simply relax and forget the self, in the interest of connecting with and motivating others. Once they do, they will find the universe rewards their efforts and reconnects them with the sense of higher awareness and enthusiasm they so often seek.

CHALLENGE: **HEALING THEIR INSECURITY AND SELF-ESTEEM ISSUES BY WORKING WITH THEIR INNER CHILD**

FULFILLMENT: **TAPPING INTO THEIR MORE SENSITIVE OR SOULFUL SIDE**

NOTABLE: **CYBILL SHEPHERD (ACTRESS, *MOONLIGHTING*)**

JULIUS "DR. J" ERVING
Basketball legend

2/22/1950
Aquarius–Pisces Cusp

February 23–March 2

SPIRIT
PISCES I

Philosophical, sensitive, and perceptive, these souls may nevertheless encounter a few stumbling blocks along the Way of Wonder, for they tend to be rather thin-skinned and entirely too susceptible to their own fears. In fact, their extreme sensitivity and yearning for perfection may manifest themselves in some rather troublesome personal relationships, as many of these individuals may find themselves trying to reform loved ones or repeating unfortunate choices in the search for an ideal relationship. Still, if they can open their hearts and minds to the reality that at least a few of their disappointments were in fact of their own choosing, they are blessed with a fine sense of humanity and caring that, when properly directed, will do much to organize, motivate, and inspire others to the higher spiritual realities.

CHALLENGE: **CHANNELING THEIR RELIGIOUS FERVOR AWAY FROM TOO MUCH RESPONSIBILITY OR SELF-SACRIFICE TO JUST PLAIN JOYFULNESS**

FULFILLMENT: **FINDING THE FORM OF EXPRESSION THAT GIVES THEM JOY**

NOTABLES: **VINCENTE MINNELLI (FILM DIRECTOR, *GIGI*); JIM BACKUS (ACTOR; VOICE OF MR. MAGOO; *GILLIGAN'S ISLAND*)**

March 3–10

THE LONER
PISCES II

Extremes of isolation may plague Pisces II souls placed on the Way of Wonder, and they would do well to cultivate objectivity in assessing their true characters. Though they will undoubtedly be comfortable making the inward journey required by this karmic path, it can be a dangerous road unless they maintain contact with people who will offer them friendship and guidance without undue criticism. The soulful quality of these personalities yearns for sharing and connection, but they may suffer from such an extreme need for control that they are unable to make those connections. The resulting isolation can manifest itself in self-pity, depression, and extremes of self-abnegation. Equally, many of this group may withdraw into pedantic or abstract social studies while ignoring their own needs. Still, if they make an effort to express themselves, nourish their own deeper needs, and release the demons of self-doubt and self-deception, they will find a way to express their great love of and wonder at the beauty of this world.

CHALLENGE: **COMING TO UNDERSTAND THAT PAIN IS NOT A PREREQUISITE FOR HAPPINESS**

FULFILLMENT: **CULTIVATING MORE FRIENDS WITH WHOM THEY CAN SHARE RELAXATION AND FUN**

NOTABLE: **FRANCO HARRIS (FOOTBALL STAR)**

KAREN CARPENTER
Pop singer, "Close to You"; died of anorexia

3/2/1950
Pisces I

March 11–18

DANCERS AND DREAMERS
PISCES III

Though the souls born in this week who travel the Way of Wonder may have to guard against a tendency to go overboard with its higher challenge and become increasingly unrealistic over time, its unique combination of discipline and creative self-expression is likely to motivate and inspire many. They will have to take care not to manifest their talents in a high-handed or superior attitude, however, so as not to alienate those who can help them attain their highest ideals. A rather self-important worldview can serve to disguise some complex and conflicting emotions, and though they are quite sensitized to the needs of others, they may not be as well aware of their own. Yet if they make the necessary journey toward heightened awareness and take care to make real contributions and not just offer criticisms of those around them, they are unlikely to stray far from the path.

CHALLENGE: **DROPPING SOME OF THEIR PERFECTIONISTIC TENDENCIES**

FULFILLMENT: **DISCOVERING THAT WORK CAN BE FULFILLING, REWARDING, AND, YES, FUN**

NOTABLE: **BOBBY MCFERRIN (A CAPELLA SINGER, "DON'T WORRY, BE HAPPY")**

The Way of Individuation

LIBRA II TO ARIES II
Society to the Star

Those on this karmic path are here to shed their social orientation and to cause the radiant light of their unique individuality to shine forth. Individuation is the goal of this path, as those on it need to strengthen their sense of self and to identify and pursue their own unique form of fulfillment. To accomplish this, the men and women on this path must develop a

healthy dose of self-interest in order to slip away from the many who cling to them to pursue their own personal star. As those on the Way of Individuation embody all their best characteristics and talents, they are bound to attract attention and followers. Because of this, their fate is that they will find themselves at the center of a group either as a leader or role model. However, their karmic path requires them to do things "their way" without regard to others; if benefits to their family, circle, or society accrue, so much the better. Perhaps a key lesson here is that there is nothing wrong with putting oneself first, as long as social and moral values are maintained.

The individuals on this karmic path are born with the propensity to be blown about by the needs and desires of those close to them. Generally well liked and valued as friends and confidants, those on the Way of Individuation may one day look around and discover that a great number of people are dependent on them. The proof is that they are often bombarded by invitations, requests, and demands. Filling all these orders proves to be quite

---

CORE LESSON
Developing greater self-interest and self-awareness

GOAL
To fulfill themselves as individuals

GIFTS
Magnetic, Success-oriented, Caring

PITFALLS
Complacent, Irritable, Self-centered

---

a task. In fact, so preoccupied do they become with this social whirl that they often forget to look after themselves. Thus, the core lesson of this path is the development of a healthy dose of self-interest. By focusing their attention on themselves and their own needs and learning how to have firmer boundaries as regards others, those on the Way of Individuation will take the first step

toward their karmic goal. The thing these individuals must learn to guard most jealously is their time. Once they carve out sufficient time for themselves, they will be able to pursue their interests, goals, or dreams.

The Way of Individuation calls those on it to find their personal lodestar. Part of the journey on this karmic path is the creation of life goals, possibly involving career or other worldly ambitions. Often those on this path spend their early years without a sense of self or any personal ambition, perhaps even mired in complacency. Not knowing what they want, they may be swept along on others' coattails—for example, helping a mate pursue her goals,

doing what their friends do, or fulfilling their parents' expectations. Deciding on their own dream, no matter how unusual or silly it may seem, and going for it is the way of this path. Whether this involves a desire to pursue an art form, follow a spiritual path, set up one's own business, become a maverick in a particular field through innovation, or simply "go where no one has gone before," those on the Way of Individuation must find out

who they truly are and what they want. Then they must develop the self-assertion and initiative to demand it from the world so that they may implement their own visionary and courageous ideals.

The main pitfall of this karmic path is that self-interest may turn into self-centeredness or narcissism. Remaining self-aware and evaluating themselves and their actions from the perspective of their own keen sense of fair play should adequately counter this tendency. In fact, a healthy dose of ongoing self-criticism or analysis can only help these individuals. Excellent psychologists, those on the Way of Individuation have tremendous insight into the inner workings of others. Once they learn to apply their fine discernment and critical awareness to themselves and their own lives, not only will they be better prepared to man the helm of their ship of destiny, but they will avoid many of the pitfalls of this path and will be able to identify the goals or interests that can best help them achieve individuation.

The world loves a maverick, or anyone individualistic or fulfilled enough to go his own way. Should those on the Way of Individuation accomplish their karmic task, they will find themselves at the center of quite a bit of attention. Often fate calls those on this path to a leadership role. In such a capacity they can enjoy a marvelous blend of Libra II social concern with Aries II leadership and initiative for the great benefit of all. Stepping into the role of the Aries II Star in this manner implies becoming comfortable in the spotlight and accepting the attention or admiration of their fellows as they exude star power. Also, it requires setting aside time for solitude since the work of this path clearly calls those on it to pursue their dreams without getting bogged down by those who populate their lives. The secret is to understand that they needn't specifically cater to people; rather, as they individuate, their inner light will shine brighter and brighter until it is enough for others to bask in the glow of this light or simply to be present in their orbit.

Obviously, the arena in which the individuals on this karmic path undergo a transformation will be a social one, but also will often involve career. School or work will frequently be the stage for the discovery of one's talents and abilities. What is best for those on this karmic path is ongoing challenge, which is often best found in the workplace. Journeying along this path will imbue these individuals with an abundance of aggressive Aries II energy, which, if not channeled into self-realization, will only produce frustration and depression. Having well-defined goals that stand a good chance of being attained, or a string of moderate successes, will feed their inner fire. Cases where delusion causes the men and women on this path to overreact can only turn out positively since it will teach them how to deal with failure. Learning to dare to fail is an important lesson in itself.

RELEASE

The need to fill the expectations
of others

REWARD

The joy of personal growth
and challenge

SUGGESTION

Recognize when others have become too dependent on you. Strive to keep yourself challenged and energized. Avoid slipping into complacency. Know that it is not your job to take care of everyone else.

These people are apt to undergo some profound changes in their social lives as they proceed along this karmic path. Though participation in clubs, groups, or organizations will dominate their early years, over time and with age they will often pull back from such involvements in favor of the freedom to pursue more solitary interests. As those on this path embark on the process of discovering who they are, it is likely that their attitudes, beliefs, desires, or even political affiliations will change quite radically. Changing in such a manner may induce feelings of guilt. Sometimes those on the Way of Individuation will even refrain from doing the work of this path if they suspect that they are forsaking relationships or service to others in favor of mere egoism. It is also quite likely that people may reinforce such a view by telling those on the Way of Individuation that they have become selfish and self-centered. Many on the Way of Individuation must undergo a separation from their families, in particular their parents. A certain rebelliousness in their early years will prove beneficial to their process. Too often caught up in parental expectations, undergoing the psychological separation from the family of origin is necessary on the Way of Individuation and can provide good experience for separating from others later in life. This may be an inner process or take place physically as the individuals on this karmic path move far from home. Unlike on other karmic paths, however, this separation needn't be a permanent one as long as the job gets done and the people here wean themselves from the influence of their families.

The best partner for those on this karmic path may be a coworker or colleague, someone who can share a more dynamic lifestyle and keep up with their abundant energies. However, any partner, whether friend, lover, or mate, will have to be very patient with these individuals as they undergo a variety of experiences, all designed to provide greater awareness and reveal to them who they are. Although the right intimates can be wonderful mirrors, helping them to see themselves more clearly, ultimately those on this path must make this journey alone.

BALANCE POINT

Self-interest and
Others' Needs

Companions and life partners are not precluded by this path, but often those who marry young, before they have found out who they are, will outgrow their early loves and need to move past such formative unions.

A living symbol of the Way of Individuation might be a benevolent monarch. Subjects of such a ruler see that person as a figurehead, an embodiment of all their collective aspirations and dreams. The monarch has a strong bond with his or her subjects, a true love that goes far beyond mere ambition or a lust for power. But the monarch is also an individual person, and the best monarchs know this and are able to separate the public myth from the private reality.

CRYSTALS AND GEMSTONES

Fire Agate flashes a deep interior light that sparks from within a dark matrix. This stone encourages the spirit to shine forth and thrive in its individual expression.

NOTABLES ON THIS KARMIC PATH

Credited with introducing haute-cuisine to the American public, **Julia Child** exerted tremendous influence through both her wildly popular TV series and her book, *Mastering the Art of French Cooking.* Despite her lack of formal culinary training, Child's career took off when she became a success at the Cordon

JULIA CHILD

Bleu cooking school in Paris. Through her work she wedded her Libra II social needs to her drive to become an Aries II star. Unpretentious and down-to-earth, Julia Child followed her personal dream and implemented her vision with her own inimitably individualistic manner.

WALT WHITMAN

Regarded by many as America's greatest national poet, **Walt Whitman** revealed his inner feelings as few others have done, most notably in *Song of Myself.* Born to an illiterate mother and a Quaker carpenter, Whitman's early interest in literature and later support for gay rights marked him as a strong individualist. Whitman is perhaps best known for his small book of poems *Leaves of Grass,* which was first published at his own expense. Like many on this path, he felt a need to help others, at one point serving as a nurse to wounded Civil War soldiers. This experience on the front lines inspired Whitman to compose his beautiful elegy for Abraham Lincoln, *O Captain, My Captain.*

Bruce Springsteen, otherwise known as "The Boss," has definitely lived life his own way. A self-taught musician, he began playing guitar with a local high school group in 1965. For the next five years, he worked with a variety of musicians before assembling the E-Street Band and signing with Columbia Records.

BRUCE SPRINGSTEEN

His third album, *Born to Run,* was his most wildly successful. With his unique combination of folk and rock-and-roll, Springsteen's popular appeal has won him a wide range of admiring fans. Despite his high profile as a rock star, Springsteen, like many on the Way of Individuation, never forgot the common man or his working-class roots.

Other Notables: Elias Howe, Jack Kent Cooke, Bruce Jenner, William Shatner, Leonard Nimoy, Willie Mays, Lowell Weicker, Thomas Mann, Pamela Anderson, Woody Guthrie, Milton Friedman, Carl Jung, Herman Melville, Raoul Wallenberg, Gene Kelly, Richard Gere, Louis Sullivan, Sigourney Weaver, Bonnie Raitt, Whoopi Goldberg, Jeff Bridges, Teri Garr, Sissy Spacek, James Earl Jones, Gene Hackman, Norman Rockwell, Toni Morrison, Rupert Murdoch

---

BIRTHDAYS ON KARMIC PATH 27

October 21, 1893–March 11, 1894 | June 3, 1912–October 21, 1912

January 13, 1931–June 3, 1931 | August 25, 1949–January 12, 1950 | April 5, 1968–August 24, 1968

November 15, 1986–April 5, 1987 | June 27, 2005–November 14, 2005

KARMIC PATH
27

March 19–24

REBIRTH
PISCES–ARIES CUSP

Gifted with great sensitivity and compassion, those born in this period will nevertheless have to guard against a tendency to become overly involved with the feelings and reactions of others as they make their way along this karmic path. Somewhat prone to having their best intentions misunderstood or misinterpreted, their principal challenge will be to develop the ability to utilize their considerable intuition to better attune themselves to their own needs and to stop being quite so dependent on what others may think. It is very important for these individuals to avoid the trap of self-pity, on the one hand, or self-centeredness, on the other. Yet these personalities will find that many of their lessons revolve around letting go of conflicts and minor irritations and getting in touch with their own sense of identity. Once they begin to feel more secure within themselves, they will be able to be comfortable with the attention, independence, and recognition that beckon.

CHALLENGE: **COMING TO A BETTER UNDERSTANDING OF THEMSELVES**
FULFILLMENT: **BEING TRUE TO THEMSELVES**

WILLIAM SHATNER
Actor/director/author,
Star Trek

3/22/1931
Pisces–Aries Cusp

March 25–April 2

THE CHILD
ARIES I

Those born in this period who travel the Way of Individuation can experience great fulfillment and happiness, as their enthusiasm, sense of adventure, and love of a challenge will all serve them well. Rather irrepressible, they will be gifted with a natural buoyancy and good humor that is likely to win them any number of admirers along the way. So long as their process of stepping more fully into their individuality is not unduly hindered by their perception of others' needs or too much concern for what others may think they can expect great success. Providing they learn to access their own deepest sense of identity and do not succumb to a rather superficial attitude toward self-development or refuse to embrace more genuine ideals, all will go beautifully for them.

CHALLENGE: **FORGETTING THE PAST**
FULFILLMENT: **FORGING THEIR OWN PATH**

April 3–10

THE STAR
ARIES II

Though they are a curious combination of excessive energy and natural aloofness, those born in this week who travel the Way of Individuation can realize tremendous fulfillment and transformation, and many with this configuration will find themselves at center stage in some capacity for much of their lives. Thus, this path prompts those on it to indulge their need to be alone and turn inward in search of who and what they really are. Yet they have a tendency to delude themselves into thinking that such self-examination is unnecessary or to ignore their own needs in a never-ending search for popularity and approval. Since life will tend to be rather easy for these souls, it will be of the utmost importance for them to set their own highest goals and standards and always to reach for their most impossible dreams.

CHALLENGE: **AVOIDING THE NEED TO BE EVERYTHING FOR EVERYONE**
FULFILLMENT: **FINDING THAT THEY ARE ROLE MODELS**
NOTABLES: **PATRICIA ARQUETTE (ACTRESS, *ED WOOD*); DONALD BARTHELME (AMERICAN WRITER/JOURNALIST); PIERRE MONTREUX (FRENCH CONDUCTOR)**

LEONARD NIMOY
Actor/director/author,
Star Trek

3/26/1931
Aries I

April 11–18

THE PIONEER
ARIES III

The drive to learn and explore is much stronger here than it is for others on this path and the need of those born in the Week of the Pioneer to declare their independence and explore the frontiers of experience will serve them well. They will have to cultivate moderation in their approach to life, however, and learn to choose their battles more carefully. In theory, rising to the challenge of breaking free from established norms or social groups will be relatively easy for them, yet in practice, finding the time and freedom to be more truly themselves may be difficult, as they are prone to having large families, many friends, and a myriad of responsibilities. Still, these personalities are fired by the inner conviction that they know what's best; if they can delve a bit deeper to discover what's best for themselves, they can expect to accomplish great things. If they do not allow their quest for self-realization to become tainted by too many ego issues, they will experience the sweet reward of being who they know they truly are.

CHALLENGE: **MANAGING THE MANY PEOPLE IN THEIR LIVES**
FULFILLMENT: **STEPPING INTO THE SPOTLIGHT AND LEADING OTHERS BY DEFAULT**

KARMIC PATH
27

April 19–24
POWER
ARIES–TAURUS CUSP

The Aries–Taurus cusp personality on the Way of Individuation is certain to become a force to be reckoned with, both in the social and the personal arena. These charismatic individuals have an inborn talent for pursuing their own goals, yet will have to struggle with issues of complacency and conventionality along the way. Perhaps their principal challenge will be not to indulge themselves to the point where they abuse their power over others or fail to distinguish between their own and others' needs. Since they are naturally powerful, commanding personalities, they should also take care not to surround themselves with people who will be afraid to challenge them and their opinions. Yet if they cultivate the inner vision and clarity necessary to stay attuned to their own deepest needs, their natural generosity, administrative and organizational ability, and good sense will allow them to be truly formidable role models and sources of inspiration for many.

CHALLENGE: **BEING CAREFUL NOT TO LET THEIR PREOCCUPATION WITH POWER INTERFERE WITH THEIR INDIVIDUATION**
FULFILLMENT: **FEELING A SENSE OF EMPOWERMENT FROM BEING THEIR OWN PERSONS**
NOTABLE: **ASHLEY JUDD (ACTRESS; DAUGHTER OF NAOMI)**

JOHN MUIR
Explorer/naturalist;
founded the Sierra Club

———

4/21/1838
Aries–Taurus Cusp

April 25–May 2
MANIFESTATION
TAURUS I

The natural diplomacy and sensitivity to others that mark those born in the Week of Manifestation who travel the Way of Individuation can make it a bit difficult for them to discover the independence and identity that are at the heart of this karmic path. Likely to become quite entrenched in social structures and responsibilities, they must learn to guard against feeling unappreciated or unrecognized for their efforts and to take their satisfaction from their own sense of accomplishment. Too, many on this road are marked by personal touchiness and sensitivity to others' opinions. Yet if they make the necessary journey inward, divest themselves of some of their social baggage, and employ their impulse toward manifestation of their plans and dreams in an effort at solid accomplishment, all will go well.

CHALLENGE: **NOT SUCCUMBING TO THEIR NEED FOR HARMONY BY SACRIFICING THEIR NEED TO BE TRUE TO THEMSELVES**
FULFILLMENT: **FINDING THEMSELVES LEADING AN ORGANIZATION DEDICATED TO THEIR INNOVATIVE VISION**

May 3–10
THE TEACHER
TAURUS II

For those born in the Week of the Teacher who navigate the challenge of the Way of Individuation, life can be a richly rewarding experience, so long as they do not succumb to the notion that they know it all or otherwise fall for their own press releases. Their natural magnetism is likely to gain them much applause and personal adulation, yet they may find that they are not content with applause alone. It is important for them to distinguish between self-motivation and self-interest, for they have big egos and a strong sense of dignity. Their main challenge is to bring their considerable vision to bear, even if it means risking their careers, reputations, and worldly standing in order, to follow their personal star. Still, if they take care to cultivate their dreams and avoid being corrupted by flatterers and hangers-on, these dynamic and energetic personalities will surely make their mark, leaving the world a lasting legacy of popular and accessible inspiration.

CHALLENGE: **NOT TRYING TO FULFILL THEMSELVES THROUGH OTHERS, ESPECIALLY THOSE WHO ARE DIFFERENT FROM THEM**
FULFILLMENT: **HAVING FOUND THEMSELVES AND THEIR NICHE, SHARING IT WITH OTHERS**
NOTABLE: **TRACI LORDS (ACTRESS)**

WILLIE MAYS
Baseball legend, Giants
center fielder; the
"Say Hey" kid

———

5/6/1931
Taurus II

May 11–18
THE NATURAL
TAURUS III

The Way of Individuation can hold much adventure for those born in the Week of the Natural, for their search for self-knowledge may take them far from their origins in their quest to gain perspective and insight. Perhaps the chief stumbling block with this configuration is their tendency to travel far and wide without absorbing their experiences on an inner level or analyzing what they mean. Thus, a number of these souls may waste their energies in instability and aimlessness. The key here will be to seek their own sense of passion without pausing to second-guess themselves and to develop greater faith in their own judgment. If they allow their naturally fine instincts to serve as their guide, finding a middle ground between self-knowledge and social awareness on the Way of Individuation will prove enlightening and fruitful indeed.

CHALLENGE: **LETTING GO OF THEIR NEED FOR SECURITY IN FAVOR OF PERSONAL FULFILLMENT**
FULFILLMENT: **EXPERIENCING THE SECURITY OF KNOWING WHO THEY ARE**
NOTABLES: **ROBERT MORSE (ACTOR; TONY FOR *HOW TO SUCCEED IN BUSINESS WITHOUT REALLY TRYING*); LOWELL WEICKER (POLITICIAN)**

May 19–24
ENERGY
TAURUS–GEMINI CUSP

A tendency to superficiality or a preoccupation with appearances may prove to be the principal obstacles to individuation for those born on the Cusp of Energy who travel this karmic path. Though they will undoubtedly have a great gift for making a splash on the social scene and are likely to be attention getters, these hard-driving individuals may succumb to a kind of narcissism in lieu of deeper experience, self-exploration, or investigation. Not especially introspective by nature, their principal lessons may involve learning to go beneath the surface and refusing to allow themselves to be swept up in the latest trends. Yet if they cultivate their analytical skills and take care to surround themselves with those who demand a higher level of performance and integrity than they might expect of themselves, their blessings of natural brilliance, wonderful curiosity, and true charisma will take them far.

CHALLENGE: **CHOOSING A FEW OF THEIR MANY INTERESTS ON WHICH TO FOCUS MORE DEEPLY**

FULFILLMENT: **APPLYING THEIR PRODIGIOUS ENERGIES TO PURSUING A DREAM**

QUEEN VICTORIA
Queen of Great Britain,
1837–1901, Victorian Era

5/24/1819
Taurus–Gemini Cusp

May 25–June 2
FREEDOM
GEMINI I

Those born in the Week of Freedom who find themselves on the Way of Individuation can experience great fulfillment, providing they cultivate the necessary depth for true self-discovery. In fact, some of these likable people have a rather superficial attitude toward self-exploration and self-development and may pooh-pooh the idea of going deeper in order to find their challenges, strength, and dreams. Yet Gemini I's are gifted with above-average analytic abilities that will serve them well on this road. If they recognize that their need for freedom is an aspect of character and not just a quirk of fate and find the means to divest themselves of people and situations that would hold them back from following their personal star, they will doubtless realize the great fulfillment promised on this life journey.

CHALLENGE: **RELEASING THE TENDENCY TO RIDICULE OR CRITICIZE OTHERS**

FULFILLMENT: **CAPITALIZING ON THEIR INDIVIDUALISM BY FULLY EXPLORING THEMSELVES**

NOTABLES: **WALT WHITMAN (AMERICAN POET, *LEAVES OF GRASS*); GIOVANNI GENTILE (ITALIAN PHILOSOPHER); JULIA WARD HOWE (REFORMER; WRITER, "THE BATTLE HYMN OF THE REPUBLIC"); JOHN ROBERT SCHRIEFFER (SHARED NOBEL FOR SUPERCONDUCTIVITY)**

June 3–10
NEW LANGUAGE
GEMINI II

The souls born in the Week of New Language who find themselves on the Way of Individuation will likely have a fine and rewarding passage, providing they do not allow themselves to become preoccupied with what others may think of them or indulge an overriding need for approval and acceptance that keeps them tied to the concerns of others without adequately addressing their own. Critical to their success will be their ability to keep a firm handle on just how gifted they are in their unique ability to communicate and to follow their personal dream of success, no matter what the more immediate costs or obstacles. If they make some necessary breaks with tradition and do not get mired in structures, attitudes, or expectations not their own, their efforts will result in rare and original accomplishments of lasting value.

CHALLENGE: **NOT RELYING ON THE APPROVAL OF OTHERS**

FULFILLMENT: **STAYING TRUE TO THEIR NEED TO COMMUNICATE IN THEIR OWN WAY**

NOTABLE: **GUSTAVE COURBET (REALIST PAINTER, *BURIAL AT ORNANS*)**

THOMAS MANN
Novelist,
The Magic Mountain;
won Nobel Prize

6/6/1875
Gemini II

June 11–18
THE SEEKER
GEMINI III

Those born in the Week of the Seeker are likely to have a fine time on the Way of Individuation, providing they do not expend their energies in too many superficial contacts or undue flexibility. Learning occasionally to draw a line in the sand in order to guard their solitude will be very important for these personalities, as they have a tendency to get swept up in the ideas or issues of the moment and become overinvolved with a never-ending list of people to see and places to go. Thus, pulling in the reins and concentrating on their own emotional needs is especially important, as is developing a more secure sense of self. Yet, in the end, following a personal star and pushing beyond the limits of convention and social strictures will come rather easily for these personalities; it is only choosing which star is truly theirs that may take some time.

CHALLENGE: **REALIZING THAT TRYING TO CONTROL OTHERS IS MERELY TRYING TO LIVE THROUGH THEM TOO**

FULFILLMENT: **DISCOVERING THEMSELVES AS THEY SEEK**

June 19–24
MAGIC
GEMINI–CANCER CUSP

Those born on the Cusp of Magic who find themselves on the Way of Individuation will encounter any number of life lessons that revolve around the impulse to unite with others versus the impulse to separate from them. Yet as long as they keep in mind that they need not deny their caring and compassionate side to realize of their destiny, all can go brilliantly. The natural aloofness that characterizes many Gemini–Cancers will prove an asset, providing they don't go overboard and isolate or detach themselves completely. Too, they will have to learn to distinguish between the impulse toward self-fulfillment and the need for self-protection. Yet they are gifted with considerable intuition, deep insight, and a unique perspective on human affairs. If they allow themselves to apply that capacity in a voyage of discovery of their innermost identities, they can expect wonderful success and exciting levels of accomplishment.

CHALLENGE: **NOT ALLOWING LOVE OR THE YEARNING FOR IT TO INTERFERE WITH THEIR SELF-FULFILLMENT**

FULFILLMENT: **BRINGING SOME OF THEIR SECRET DREAMS FROM THEIR INNER WORLD TO THE OUTER ONE**

NOTABLES: **NORMAN COUSINS (EDITOR, *SATURDAY REVIEW*); MARY MCCARTHY (WRITER, *NATION, NEW REPUBLIC, PARTISAN REVIEW*)**

June 25–July 2
THE EMPATH
CANCER I

Learning to first make some necessary breaks with the past, then to challenge themselves to the heights of ambition and achievement, may make for a rather arduous journey for the gentle souls born in the Week of the Empath who find themselves on the Way of Individuation. Indeed, many of these personalities have a rather indistinct notion of what they truly want from life and are inclined to be so sensitive to the needs and feelings of others that it may take no small amount of time for them to come to terms with their own. Yet along with their great sensitivity, they are gifted with an equal measure of personal strength; if they can access that strength in the service of their convictions and higher sense of inspiration, they will experience tremendous personal satisfaction and achievement.

PAMELA ANDERSON
Model/actress/producer,
Baywatch, V.I.P.

7/1/1968
Cancer I

CHALLENGE: **DISCOVERING THE SOURCE OF THEIR OWN VERY PERSONAL STRENGTH**

FULFILLMENT: **FINDING THE RIGHT BALANCE BETWEEN THEIR OWN AND OTHERS' NEEDS**

July 3–10
THE UNCONVENTIONAL
CANCER II

Blessed with a unique ability to see the world a bit differently than most of us, Cancer II's who travel the Way of Individuation will not so much have to develop a stronger sense of self as to develop the courage to stand up and show the world what they're really made of. Blessed with astonishing powers of imagination, creativity, and psychological insight, they will have to avoid their tendency to please "all of the people all of the time" and learn to eschew the relative comforts of secure jobs, stable mates, and dull routines. Though there are undoubtedly any number of geniuses with desk jobs here, they would do well to understand that their higher challenge is to get out of their rut and make their dreams into reality. Too, there is a danger that their vivid inner life will become their consuming preoccupation and they will withdraw into eccentric or even rather dark fantasies. Yet even their more extreme tendencies are always balanced by good sense, fine financial ability, and natural magnetism.

CHALLENGE: **DISTINGUISHING THEIR DREAMS AND GOALS FROM THEIR FANTASIES**

FULFILLMENT: **GRANTING OTHERS ACCESS TO THEIR SECRET SELF**

NOTABLE: **ELIAS HOWE (PATENTED FIRST SEWING MACHINE)**

July 11–18
THE PERSUADER
CANCER III

Gifted with an excellent ability to manipulate their environment, Cancer III personalities who travel the Way of Individuation are destined for any number of fine opportunities to meet its higher challenges. For the most part, those born in the Week of the Persuader are powerful and effective both behind the scenes and in front of a crowd. Though they may have some difficulty breaking from accepted social codes to venture on a quest for greater self-fulfillment, they have the drive, energy, passion, and sense of commitment to achieve almost anything they set out to do. There is a danger, however, of taking a generally excessive approach to life, as well as of allowing their ambitions to become all-consuming. Alternatively, they may be content with achieving a certain level of competence and fail to challenge themselves adequately. Yet this is a configuration blessed with a certainty of success, and if they work to cultivate their ability to analyze and process their experiences, and at the same time avoid too much complacency, these souls will evolve quite rapidly.

WOODY GUTHRIE
Folk singer, "This Land Is Your Land"

7/14/1912
Cancer III

CHALLENGE: **NOT LETTING AMBITION GET IN THE WAY OF THEIR DEEPER SELF-UNDERSTANDING OR NEEDS**

FULFILLMENT: **HAVING ACHIEVED INDIVIDUATION, SHARING THEIR EXPERIENCE WITH OTHERS**

NOTABLE: **ART LINKLETTER (TV ACTOR/HOST/COMEDIAN)**

July 19–25

OSCILLATION
CANCER–LEO CUSP

A rare combination of natural courage, compassion for others, and the strength of conviction to literally "take on the world," these personalities can accomplish great things when placed on the Way of Individuation. Bright, ambitious, and sometimes overly impulsive, their passions run strong, and they will need to balance them out a bit in order to become most effective. Perhaps the principal danger is that they will bottle up their emotions or become so overly involved in the lives of others that they will fail to discover just what motivates them. Too, there is some danger that they may be overly aggressive, for they are inclined to attach themselves to issues not really their own or seek out challenges and conflicts for the pure joy of the fight. Yet they have much better analytical skills than many of their fellow Cancer–Leos, and if they can put aside their need to be accepted, they are in for an exciting ride.

CARL JUNG
Swiss psychiatrist, father
of analytical psychology

7/26/1875
Leo I

CHALLENGE: **NOT LETTING THE DEMANDS OF OTHERS INTERRUPT THEIR PROCESS OR THROW THEM OFF BALANCE**

FULFILLMENT: **FEELING THE FLOW OF THEIR ENERGIES AS THEY FREE THEIR INDIVIDUALITY**

NOTABLE: **JAMES GEDDES (ENGINEER; WORKED ON ERIE CANAL)**

July 26–August 2

AUTHORITY
LEO I

Those born in the Week of Authority who travel the Way of Individuation may appear to others to be rather shockingly self-absorbed, yet their intensity is usually bound up with a sense of their destiny that will be difficult to shake. In fact, once they've made some breaks with the past or their family of origin, some of these souls may manifest something approaching blind ambition as they make their way to the top of their chosen field of endeavor, guided by a specific idea of where they want to go in life and who they want to be. Their natural dynamism, passionate drive, and real determination will all serve them well. Likely to have a much stronger sense of self than some others on this path, Leo I's can expect real satisfaction and fulfillment, and though they doubtless have big egos and big plans, they also have the hearts to match.

CHALLENGE: **NOT ADHERING TO HIGHER AUTHORITIES OR CODES OF CONDUCT AT THE EXPENSE OF THEIR SELF-EXPRESSION**

FULFILLMENT: **INVESTING FULLY IN THEIR SELF-FULFILLMENT, THEN WATCHING OTHERS BENEFIT FROM IT**

NOTABLES: **MILTON FRIEDMAN (ECONOMIST; WON NOBEL PRIZE); HERMAN MELVILLE (WRITER, *MOBY-DICK*); VIVIAN VANCE (ACTRESS, *I LOVE LUCY*)**

August 3–10

BALANCED STRENGTH
LEO II

Naturally tough and thoroughly realistic, Leo II's who find themselves on the Way of Individuation can recognize great success as they rise to its challenges. Though naturally generous and sympathetic to the causes of the downtrodden, they are unlikely to allow themselves to be taken advantage of or to scatter their energies on unproductive pursuits. A great measure of personal ambition goes with this configuration, and there is a danger that they may bottle up their emotions or otherwise refuse to take their highest ideals seriously. It is important for them to feel needed, yet equally important for them not to allow their natural sense of fairness to degenerate into judgmental or high-handed snobbishness, on the one hand, or masochistic self-denial, on the other. Nevertheless, their natural magnetism and "just do it" approach is a tremendous advantage and is sure to aid them in their quest for even the most elusive prizes or seemingly impossible dreams.

RAOUL WALLENBERG
Swedish diplomat,
rescued Jews from the
Nazis in WWII

8/4/1912
Leo II

CHALLENGE: **CUTTING LOOSE THE NEEDIER PEOPLE WHO CLING TO THEM**

FULFILLMENT: **CHAMPIONING THE CAUSE OF THEIR OWN AMBITION OR FULFILLMENT**

NOTABLE: **CHARLES BULFINCH (1ST AMERICAN ARCHITECT)**

August 11–18

LEADERSHIP
LEO III

Those born in the Week of Leadership can realize wonderful personal satisfaction along the Way of Individuation, as their sense of self is likely to be strengthened, yet their more selfish tendencies mitigated, by the sociability and diplomacy that are part of the endowments of this karmic path. In fact, getting in touch with their own deepest needs and manifesting those needs in an almost mythic quest for fulfillment will come quite naturally to them. Charismatic in the extreme, they will nevertheless have little trouble establishing necessary boundaries between themselves and their many admirers. If they take care that their creative capacities are not squandered in derivative or unoriginal efforts to gain approval, they will be more than equipped to take their chances, marshal their forces, and do their own thing, no matter what that thing may be.

CHALLENGE: **NOT FALLING FOR THE SEDUCTION OF BEING AT THE CENTER OF A GROUP ONLY TO LOSE THEIR OWN CENTER**

FULFILLMENT: **FINDING THEIR CREATIVE AND SPIRITUAL OUTLET**

NOTABLES: **HALLE BERRY (ACTRESS); JULIA CHILD (CHEF; TV HOST); BEN HOGAN (GOLFER)**

August 19–25

EXPOSURE
LEO–VIRGO CUSP

The journey of those born in this period who travel the Way of Individuation is likely to be marked by periods of introspection in which they master their emotions alternating with periods of striving toward whatever goal they may have set for themselves. Thus, though it may appear to some as though Leo–Virgos on this karmic path take one step forward and two steps back, their capacity for self-awareness is sure to stand them in fine stead. Indeed, few configurations can match this combination of astute insight and energetic ambition. Unlikely to be overly concerned with the troubles of others, they have the ability to be sensitive and caring without allowing friends, family, or social concerns to interfere with their plans, schemes, and dreams.

GENE KELLY
Actor/dancer,
Singin' in the Rain

8/23/1912
Leo–Virgo Cusp

CHALLENGE: **PERMITTING THEIR SECRET FLAMBOYANCE TO BREAK OUT NOW AND THEN**

FULFILLMENT: **FEELING FREE TO REVEAL WHO THEY REALLY ARE**

NOTABLES: **ALLAN PINKERTON (FOUNDED PINKERTON DETECTIVE AGENCY); DURWARD KIRBY (ACTOR; COHOST** *CANDID CAMERA*); **GENE SIMMONS (FOUNDING MEMBER OF ROCK BAND KISS)**

August 26–September 2

SYSTEM BUILDERS
VIRGO I

The individuals born in this week who travel the Way of Individuation may have to overcome some powerful notions of responsibility, service, or just plain guilt before they can realize its higher promise. Indeed, many with this configuration will be held back by chronic avoidance of certain deep personal issues or who will fail to make the breaks with family, society, and convention that are necessary for them to set out on their quest for greater fulfillment. Refusing to realize that their destinies are ultimately in their own hands may make this life journey a difficult one, yet Virgo I's can realize success on this karmic path, especially when they free themselves from insecurity, find the courage to have some necessary confrontations with themselves and others, and use their talent for creating system and structure to build a bridge to their fondest dreams.

CHALLENGE: **NOTICING WHEN THEY ARE PLAYING BY A SET OF RULES EVEN AS THEY SEEK THEIR STAR**

FULFILLMENT: **KNOWING THAT BY SERVING THEMSELVES FIRST, THEY CAN BETTER SERVE OTHERS**

NOTABLES: **PRINCE ALBERT (PRINCE CONSORT TO QUEEN VICTORIA); RICHARD GERE (ACTOR,** *PRETTY WOMAN*)

September 3–10

THE ENIGMA
VIRGO II

There are any number of society mavens, social directors, and Florence Nightingales born in this week who travel the Way of Individuation, and these souls are gifted with a fine concern for others, as well as the rare ability to maintain a healthy degree of personal space and detachment. Yet they will have to unbend a bit and divest themselves of a sort of hyperawareness of public opinion in order to achieve the higher level of fulfillment promised by this karmic path. In fact, some will be quite preoccupied with what others may think of them and will guard their dreams and ambition so jealously that few other people will ever know what they're up to. Yet if they can rid themselves of their concerns over what the neighbors will think, they will be delighted with the personal rewards and public recognition available on this road.

LOUIS SULLIVAN
Chicago architect; father
of modernism, "form
follows function"

9/3/1856
Virgo II

CHALLENGE: **RELEASING THEIR PREOCCUPATION WITH SOCIETY AND WHAT PEOPLE THINK OF THEM**

FULFILLMENT: **PURSUING THEIR AESTHETIC VISION**

NOTABLES: **DAVID PACKARD (COFOUNDED HEWLETT-PACKARD); TOM WATSON (GOLFER)**

September 11–18

THE LITERALIST
VIRGO III

Gifted with considerably more sympathy and empathy than they might otherwise have had, Virgo IIIs who travel the Way of Individuation are likely to have a fine time, though they may stumble a bit along the way. Their single biggest problem will be their unwillingness to acknowledge their own dreams. Looking closely at themselves is not necessarily in their behavior patterns; thus, many will fail the higher challenge here of this karmic path to get in better touch with their own deepest self. In addition, some may be troubled by an overwhelming need to maintain harmony, regardless of the cost to their psychological health. Yet these hard-core realists are quite able to follow their star and see their plans through to completion, though their ambitions will likely manifest themselves in practical, attainable, and ultimately tangible goals.

CHALLENGE: **NOT EQUATING THEIR EXPECTATIONS OF THEMSELVES WITH SELF-UNDERSTANDING**

FULFILLMENT: **CHECKING TASKS OFF THEIR "TO DO" LIST**

NOTABLES: **ED BEGLEY, JR. (ACTOR,** *ST. ELSEWHERE*); **CLARA SCHUMANN (PIANIST)**

September 19–24
BEAUTY
VIRGO–LIBRA CUSP

These souls can realize considerable fulfillment and evolution along the Way of Individuation, yet they will have to overcome some rather hesitant or even wishy-washy tendencies in order to do so. Many of them will become overly involved in the lives and opinions of others, and their natural sensitivity and love of beauty may be something of a liability until they learn to seize the day and stop expecting others to either provide for their needs or solve their problems. Yet many on this path are blessed with a healthy dose of self-interest that can serve as a springboard for real achievement. If they can avoid the dangers of complacency, indecision, and superficiality, and find within themselves the courage and conviction necessary for true fulfillment, the road to individuation will prove a rich and rewarding journey.

TWIGGY
Model/actress/singer;
originated waif look

9/19/1949
Virgo–Libra Cusp

CHALLENGE: **REDEFINING THEIR VALUES TO ACCORD LESS WITH PREVAILING TRENDS AND MORE WITH THEIR OWN TRUTH**
FULFILLMENT: **EXPLORING THEIR DARKER INNER WORLD AND DISCOVERING THE TREASURE THERE**
NOTABLE: **BRUCE SPRINGSTEEN (ROCK STAR, "THE BOSS," *BORN TO RUN*)**

September 25–October 2
THE PERFECTIONIST
LIBRA I

Libra I's who travel the Way of Individuation can realize a high level of personal evolution and happiness, providing they do not allow themselves to get hung up on a myriad of details or refuse to acknowledge their innate need to march to the beat of their own drum. Though, on this karmic path, they are likely to be a bit less difficult and generally more accommodating than some of their fellow Perfectionists, they may get entangled in irritability, frustration, or a rather pessimistic outlook. Thus it is perhaps not so much self-knowledge that is at issue here, but the ability to take joy in small doses and gradual development as they make their way toward their goals. Learning not to repress their emotions will be especially helpful, as will the ability to give themselves enough credit for having the talent, determination, and ability to get to wherever they want to go.

CHALLENGE: **RELEASING OVERLY CRITICAL ATTITUDES AND OVERLY HIGH EXPECTATIONS OF THEMSELVES**
FULFILLMENT: **GIVING THEMSELVES PERMISSION TO HAVE THEIR FEELINGS**
NOTABLE: **JACK KENT COOKE (FORMER OWNER OF WASHINGTON REDSKINS)**

October 3–10
SOCIETY
LIBRA II

Those born in the Week of Society who find themselves on this path will have to face the necessity of taking a hard look at themselves and learning to take their own needs more seriously. Their ability to procrastinate when it comes to setting themselves goals and reaching for their higher potential is especially pronounced, as they are capable of coming up with any number of distractions, interruptions, and so-called reasons for not doing what they would truly like to. Too, they will have to free themselves from a sometimes misplaced sense of obligation and try to be clearer about the real reasons for their choices. Yet if they manage to divest themselves of the many people who cling to them and access the genuine idealism and sense of adventure in self-exploration that beckon, they will travel quite a distance in the search for the lodestar of personal destiny. In the end, they will return home to share their many treasures with others.

SIGOURNEY WEAVER
Actress, *Alien*

10/8/1949
Libra II

CHALLENGE: **FINDING ENOUGH TIME FOR THEMSELVES**
FULFILLMENT: **EXPLORING THEIR CREATIVE OR AESTHETIC SIDE**
NOTABLE: **ARMAND ASSANTE (ACTOR, *THE ODYSSEY*)**

October 11–18
THEATER
LIBRA III

Born sophisticates, the wise and worldly souls born in this week who travel the Way of Individuation are extraordinarily well suited to the challenges indicated here. Ambitious and quite driven, these personalities are perhaps a bit better attuned to the needs of other people than they otherwise would be, and the mix makes for a nice balance of natural compassion and healthy self-interest. They do have a tendency to objectify their own needs, however, for as accurate and perceptive as they can be, they are quite capable of distancing themselves from inner conflict or emotional need. Yet if they take care to cultivate true self-awareness as opposed to mere self-involvement and translate their desire to be at center stage into a lifetime of genuine achievement rather than a hankering after approval, they are in for some sweet rewards.

CHALLENGE: **FOCUSING LESS ON HOW THEY LOOK AND MORE ON HOW THEY FEEL**
FULFILLMENT: **MEETING AND OVERCOMING THE CHALLENGES ON THE WAY TO FINDING THEIR STAR**
NOTABLE: **DARYL HALL (POP SINGER, HALL AND OATES)**

October 19–25

DRAMA AND CRITICISM
LIBRA–SCORPIO CUSP

Those born in this period who travel the Way of Individuation can rest assured of considerable evolution, awareness, and advancement. Though many with this position are rather isolated from the mainstream, the sacrificing of superficial associates, dependable social structures, and idle contacts will be well worth the effort as they work to achieve a higher set of ambitions and aspirations. These are individuals who are unlikely to be daunted in their efforts to find out and express who they really are. Though overconfidence may result in a setback or two along the way, if they recognize that experience is only a teacher and time is only a friend, and do not allow themselves to be overwhelmed by disappointment or disillusionment, they are sure to attain recognition, reward, and the possibility of leaving a lasting legacy to the world.

BONNIE RAITT
Pop/rock/blues guitarist
and singer,
"Nick of Time"

11/8/1949
Scorpio II

CHALLENGE: **RESISTING THE TUMULT OF LOVE AND PASSION IN ORDER TO REMAIN FOCUSED ON FINDING THEMSELVES**
FULFILLMENT: **DISCOVERING THE KEY TO BALANCING THEIR ENERGIES**

October 26–November 2

INTENSITY
SCORPIO I

Scorpio I's who navigate the Way of Individuation are likely to enjoy a relatively smooth passage, providing they do not confuse the process of this karmic path with antisocial behavior for its own sake, selfishness, or indulgence in a blind or mercenary set of ambitions. Gifted with great sensitivity and empathy, they are quite capable of wasting energy nursing their wounds too long and plotting revenge too often. Thus, a tendency to extremes of behavior and attitude is very pronounced. Nevertheless, they have the natural objectivity and insight to be able to overcome almost any obstacle in their quest for self-actualization. If they do not fall prey to the demons of pessimism or self-doubt and take care to employ their insight in the evaluation of some of their more rigid attitudes, they will be more than equipped to achieve new heights of fulfillment and accomplishment.

CHALLENGE: **RECOGNIZING THAT INDULGING THEIR MORE VENGEFUL SIDE IS NOT INDIVIDUATION**
FULFILLMENT: **EXPRESSING THEIR VIRTUOSITY**
NOTABLE: **BRUCE JENNER (TRACK ATHLETE; 1976 OLYMPIC DECATHLON GOLD MEDALIST)**

November 3–11

DEPTH
SCORPIO II

Scorpio II's will doubtless find wonderful success and reward along this karmic path, though the pursuit of that success may take them far from their early origins. This configuration implies that a certain level of personal sacrifice will be necessary in order for them to refine their talents and special skills; these souls will nevertheless have to guard against a tendency to be rather too accommodating to those who might want to hitch their wagons to their stars. They will doubtless have a number of issues regarding their impulse to connect with others on a deep emotional level versus their need to follow their dreams. Yet if they can find the right balance between intimate involvement and healthy self-interest and ambition, they can expect tremendous personal satisfaction and the admiration of more than a few along this journey.

WHOOPI GOLDBERG
Actress/comedian,
Sister Act

11/13/1949
Scorpio III

CHALLENGE: **NOT BEING SIDELINED BY EMOTIONAL SETBACKS**
FULFILLMENT: **APPLYING THEIR SERIOUSNESS OF PURPOSE TO THE FULLEST MANIFESTATION OF WHO THEY ARE**
NOTABLES: **EDSEL FORD (SON OF HENRY); ANN REINKING (ACTRESS; DANCER/CHOREOGRAPHER)**

November 12–18

CHARM
SCORPIO III

Realistic and blessed with acute powers of perception and insight, these personalities may manifest the best of personal ambition and benevolent leadership. Seemingly, they are born role models, for they have an inspirational streak that is capable of striking deep chords of response in those around them. Indeed, it may well seem as though they have a "charmed" life as they journey along the Way of Individuation. Difficult people to fool, Scorpio III's are unlikely to expend their considerable energies on unworthy people or unachievable goals. Though there is some danger that they will stall on this karmic path if they become self-satisfied or complacent, provided they bring their passionate conviction, resourcefulness, and diplomacy to bear on the challenge of finding out who they are, they have the unique opportunity to step fully into their own spotlight. As long as they cultivate their purest feelings and analyze their deepest motivations, their way can be a fine way indeed.

CHALLENGE: **RELEASING THEIR ATTACHMENT TO CONTROLLING OTHERS**
FULFILLMENT: **KNOWING WHO THEY ARE**
NOTABLE: **LOUIS BRANDEIS (U.S. SUPREME COURT JUSTICE)**

November 19–24

REVOLUTION
SCORPIO–SAGITTARIUS CUSP

There is a promising life in store for those born in this period who travel the Way of Individuation, but they will be faced with the necessity of cultivating true self-knowledge and self-actualization before they can fulfill their desire to do good for others in the grander scheme. Indeed, these people may have their share of ups and downs along this road, as they are rather excitable as a rule and lacking in the discernment to see where their best choices lie. Thus, they should temper their tendency to take up with causes, cheerlead, or put matches to powder kegs until they've had a chance to properly evaluate whether they are truly involved or merely swept up in the cause of the moment. Yet once the process of defining themselves as individuals apart from a group is begun, it is likely that their journey of high ideals and deeply felt concerns will manifest itself in far-reaching and inspirational change.

CHALLENGE: **KNOWING THE DIFFERENCE BETWEEN SELF-ACTUALIZATION AND SIMPLE ICONOCLASM**

FULFILLMENT: **HAVING FOUND THEMSELVES, GRACEFULLY BECOMING A ROLE MODEL FOR OTHERS**

NOTABLES: **HARPO MARX (SILENT MEMBER OF THE MARX BROTHERS); AHMAD RASHAD (FORMER FOOTBALL STAR; SPORTSCASTER)**

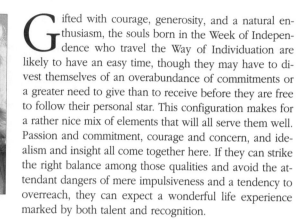

TERI GARR
Actress, *Tootsie*

12/11/1949
Sagittarius III

November 25–December 2

INDEPENDENCE
SAGITTARIUS I

Gifted with courage, generosity, and a natural enthusiasm, the souls born in the Week of Independence who travel the Way of Individuation are likely to have an easy time, though they may have to divest themselves of an overabundance of commitments or a greater need to give than to receive before they are free to follow their personal star. This configuration makes for a rather nice mix of elements that will all serve them well. Passion and commitment, courage and concern, and idealism and insight all come together here. If they can strike the right balance among those qualities and avoid the attendant dangers of mere impulsiveness and a tendency to overreach, they can expect a wonderful life experience marked by both talent and recognition.

CHALLENGE: **REMEMBERING TO BE AWARE OF THEIR EFFECT ON OTHERS**

FULFILLMENT: **EMBRACING INDEPENDENCE AND INDIVIDUALITY AS A WAY OF LIFE**

NOTABLES: **ALEXANDER GUDONOV (DANCER; ACTOR); PAUL SHAFFER (BANDLEADER FOR *LATE NIGHT WITH DAVID LETTERMAN*); GARY SHANDLING (ACTOR/COMEDIAN, *THE LARRY SANDERS SHOW*)**

December 3–10

THE ORIGINATOR
SAGITTARIUS II

Once they get the knack of using their talents to attract attention and stop trying to "fit in" in the classic social sense, those born in the Week of the Originator are in for a wonderful time on this life journey. But first they will have to overcome their deep-seated need to be accepted and learn instead just to "be." Until that realization occurs, however, a great many of these personalities will engage in any number of futile attempts to conform with their societal, social, and/or religious backgrounds, to the detriment of the adventure and self-expression that beckon. Endowed with great creative abilities, they should take care not to adopt a defensive or self-defeating attitude toward their unique talents. Yet if they can shake off the fetters of obligation or conformity in the process of self-actualization, they may well have the singular experience of having the world beat a path to their door.

CHALLENGE: **SHAKING THEIR INSECURITY**

FULFILLMENT: **GIVING THEIR ORIGINALITY FULL EXPRESSION**

NOTABLE: **JEFF BRIDGES (ACTOR, *THE FABULOUS BAKER BOYS*)**

EDWARD G. ROBINSON
Actor, famed 30s gangster movie villain, *Little Caesar*

12/12/1893
Sagittarius III

December 11–18

THE TITAN
SAGITTARIUS III

Though some with this configuration may run the risk of first embracing and then discarding some rather exaggerated ideas of what constitutes true fulfillment, they are likely to do quite well. In any event, they are bound to attract more than their share of people along the way and will have to guard against both getting too caught up in the need for acceptance as a safeguard against some secret insecurities and trying to impose their will on others without quite being sure of what it is they really want. Yet this karmic path holds some rather adventurous aspects for self-actualization, for these individuals have an innate yearning to get in touch with their own personal myth and live it to the utmost. Thus, given even half a chance, they can wind up with a whole dream come true.

CHALLENGE: **OFF-LOADING ENOUGH OF THEIR RESPONSIBILITIES TO ALLOW FOR SOME SELF-EXPLORATION**

FULFILLMENT: **REACHING FOR THE STARS WHILE KEEPING AN EYE ON OTHERS**

NOTABLE: **DON JOHNSON (ACTOR, *MIAMI VICE*)**

December 19–25
PROPHECY
SAGITTARIUS–CAPRICORN CUSP

Overcoming a certain mistrust of themselves will doubtless figure prominently in the life journey of those born on the Cusp of Prophecy who find themselves on the Way of Individuation. Yet they are gifted with a capacity for the kind of charismatic individualism called for, though this karmic path will nevertheless demand that they redefine some of their more conventional attitudes. Though more social than many born in this week, they will remain loners underneath and will do best when they separate themselves from the demands and responsibilities of daily life and make a concerted effort to determine what they really want in the calm of undisturbed contemplation. Once their inner guidance system of intuition and insight comes into full play, they are unlikely to be swayed from their course by irrelevant concerns or an overwhelming need for approval.

ROBERT RIPLEY
Illustrator/writer,
Believe It or Not
—————
12/25/1893
Sagittarius–Capricorn
Cusp

CHALLENGE: **AVOIDING THE RISKS OF NARCISSISM**
FULFILLMENT: **FINDING THEMSELVES BY BELIEVING IN THEIR OWN PROPHETIC VISION**
NOTABLES: **MAURICE AND ROBIN GIBB (FOUNDERS OF THE BEE-GEES); SISSY SPACEK (ACTRESS; OSCAR FOR *COAL MINER'S DAUGHTER*)**

December 26–January 2
THE RULER
CAPRICORN I

Gifted with a better sense of identity than some on the Way of Individuation, the powerful individuals born in the Week of the Ruler will nevertheless have to struggle a bit to discard outworn concepts, old rules, or attitudes that hold them back from the higher sense of self that beckons. Cultivating the ability to be flexible in the pursuit of their goals will prove especially important for souls with this configuration, as they may be much prone to blind ambition, on the one hand, and a tendency to overburden themselves with family, friends, and social responsibilities, on the other. Too, emotional expression does not come easily for many of this group, and at some point their repressed passions will surface. Yet when they meet the challenge to become more truly who they are and make a break with tradition and convention in order to realize their highest aspirations, no one will be able to stop them from getting where they want to go.

CHALLENGE: **TAKING CARE NOT TO DISCARD TOO MUCH OF THE PAST OR TRADITION AS THEY BREAK THE TIES THAT BIND**
FULFILLMENT: **SETTING UP AND LEADING A NEW ORGANIZATION BASED ON THE VISION BORN OF THEIR EXPERIENCE**
NOTABLE: **CHARLES GOODYEAR (DISCOVERED VULCANIZED PROCESS FOR RUBBER)**

January 3–9
DETERMINATION
CAPRICORN II

Marked by great insight and sensitivity, Capricorn II's who travel the Way of Individuation will nevertheless have to overcome their tendency to be somewhat too self-sacrificing or to submerge their own desires in an effort to reform or help others. In fact, here is a position where many of the individuals involved will find themselves quite literally liberated by the breakup of a long-term relationship, the death of a controlling parent, or the loss of a long-held job. Though such setbacks may at first present themselves as losses, Capricorn II's are more than capable of using such turns in life as opportunities for self-realization. Thus, though it may take them a while to embark on their quest to follow a long-held dream, the effort will not go unrewarded, nor the dream unfulfilled, for long as they travel this road.

MAO ZEDONG
Leader of Chinese
Communist revolution
—————
12/26/1893
Capricorn I

CHALLENGE: **NOT PERMITTING THEIR AMBITION OR LOYALTY TO INTERFERE WITH THEIR INDIVIDUATION**
FULFILLMENT: **MAKING THE MOST OF THEIR ABILITIES AND STRETCHING THEIR TALENTS**
NOTABLES: **JAKOB GRIMM (FOLKLORIST, *GRIMM'S FAIRY TALES*); JACQUES ETIENNE MONTGOLFIER (INVENTED HOT AIR BALLOON); TOM THUMB (ONLY 40 INCHES TALL; JOINED P. T. BARNUM'S SHOW)**

January 10–16
DOMINANCE
CAPRICORN III

Capricorn III's who travel the Way of Individuation will need to face the challenge of learning when and how to say no. Marked by a curious combination of deep sensitivity and the need to control their immediate environs, they may well be at the mercy of their own sense of convention or tradition until they make up their minds to acquire the surer sense of identity that arises from the pursuit of a dream. Too, many of these people will be strangers to their own passions, content to order a routine universe without thinking too much about whether it has any real meaning. Much inclined to love of material comfort, they will find it hard to take the risks associated with striking out on their own to follow something as ephemeral as a "star." Yet opportunity will knock loudly, and if they can release their concerns over the future, keep their sense of humor, and rouse themselves to answer the door, they can recognize great and truly lasting accomplishments.

CHALLENGE: **TEMPERING THEIR SENSE OF DEVOTION WITH SELF-INTEREST**
FULFILLMENT: **GIVING THEIR BURIED PASSIONS EXPRESSION**
NOTABLE: **THOMAS P. HOVING (DIRECTOR, METROPOLITAN MUSEUM OF ART IN NEW YORK CITY)**

January 17–22
MYSTERY AND IMAGINATION
CAPRICORN–AQUARIUS CUSP

The rugged individualists born in this week who find themselves on the Way of Individuation are likely to be controversial, charismatic figures capable of some truly startling leaps in personal development. Gifted with rather explosive energies, they may be at a loss to explain just how and why they always find themselves in the thick of things. They may also have to do a great deal of wrestling with personal demons and should take care that they don't burn themselves out in restlessness, mood swings, or irritability. As long as they remained focused, however, they can reach quite confidently for whatever brass rings might appeal to them. Their considerable empathy and natural insight will be especially useful, and as they undertake the process of breaking away from the pack, they will also break out of the traps of temperament and emotional immaturity.

GENE HACKMAN
Actor,
The French Connection

───────

1/30/1931
Aquarius I

CHALLENGE: **NOT CONFUSING WILDNESS OR DISRUPTIVE BEHAVIOR WITH EXPRESSING THEMSELVES**

FULFILLMENT: **LIVING OUT THEIR RICH INTERIOR LIFE**

NOTABLES: **JAMES EARL JONES (ACTOR; VOICE OF DARTH VADER IN *STAR WARS*); ROBERT MacNEIL (COHOST, *MacNEIL/ LEHRER REPORT*)**

January 23–30
GENIUS
AQUARIUS I

Since the individuals born in the Week of Genius who travel this karmic path are likely to be way ahead of the game in terms of being able to separate from convention or more accepted ideas, they will doubtless experience a fine and fulfilling passage. They just don't like being told what to and so will have little trouble striking out on their own to follow whatever dreams they have. Blessed with a greater empathy and understanding for others than they might otherwise have had, as well as a unique set of talents and abilities, whatever their projects and passions may be, they are sure to excite and inspire those around them. Though some with this configuration may prove themselves to be rebels without a cause, if they take care not to scatter their energies in too much responsibility, too much input, or too little focus on themselves, they may find that their way to fulfillment is connected with some form of innovation in the world of ideas and theories.

CHALLENGE: **HAVING A LITTLE MORE PATIENCE WITH THEIR ADMIRERS**

FULFILLMENT: **EXPLORING THE WORLD AND STUDYING ITS LESSONS FIRSTHAND**

January 31–February 7
YOUTH AND EASE
AQUARIUS II

Overcoming the need to be popular and accepted will prove the principal problem for those born in the Week of Youth and Ease who travel this karmic path. Likely to be quite entrenched in the social milieu, they are nevertheless gifted with a rare combination of personal appeal and genuine talent. They may find it difficult to separate from their established network in order to realize greater fulfillment, however, and may falter in their journey due to emotional immaturity and the fact that they frequently allow others' opinions of them to shape their opinion of themselves. Too, they may avoid some necessary confrontations in the interest of preserving their own position or sense of harmony. Yet if their formidable talents and abilities allow them to grow past their core insecurities and they can find the strength to challenge themselves even when no one else will, their personal fulfillment and happiness are ensured.

NORMAN ROCKWELL
Popular American
artist/illustrator, famed
for *Saturday Evening Post*
covers

───────

2/3/1894
Aquarius II

CHALLENGE: **PUSHING THEMSELVES TO FIND THEIR OWN IDENTITY**

FULFILLMENT: **BEING FREE OF THE BURDENS OF RELATIONSHIPS THAT SERVE ONLY TO ACT OUT THEIR OWN UNEXPRESSED SIDES**

NOTABLES: **ERNIE BANKS (HALL OF FAME BASEBALL PLAYER); RIP TORN (ACTOR)**

February 8–15
ACCEPTANCE
AQUARIUS III

The people born in this week who travel the Way of Individuation will doubtless encounter the necessity of letting go of outworn notions, ideas, or prejudices as they embark on their journey toward self-actualization. In fact, many of these souls will benefit from the gifts of this karmic path, as it will endow them with greater sensitivity, awareness, and insight into the larger patterns of behavior that govern all our lives. In short, they can often accept certain attitudes as truths without having to evaluate them too much. Yet they have an energetic, dynamic side that will beg for encouragement. If these personalities employ that natural energy in the quest for a higher set of ideals and pursue those ideals fearlessly, they have the strength of will, creative capability, and true idealism to make their own unique mark on the world.

CHALLENGE: **NOT MAKING SUCH A SPECIALTY OF NONATTACHMENT THAT THEY FAIL TO MAKE A COMMITMENT TO THEMSELVES**

FULFILLMENT: **INVESTING IN THEIR DREAMS**

NOTABLES: **LA DONNA HARRIS (SOCIAL REFORMER; COMANCHE INDIAN; FEMINIST); JACK BENNY (ACTOR/COMEDIAN); JAMES DEAN (ACTOR, *REBEL WITHOUT A CAUSE*)**

February 16–22

SENSITIVITY
AQUARIUS–PISCES CUSP

If they can overcome their personal insecurity and underlying fear of rejection, life holds any number of fascinating possibilities for those born in this period who travel the Way of Individuation. They will have to take care, however, to strike the right balance between their natural idealism and profound inner exploration or else run the risk of never seeing their fondest dreams take concrete form in real accomplishments. Too, they may manifest an overly rebellious or aggressive attitude as they embark on this journey and will have to temper their emotional extremes with realistic action. Yet their sensitivity to others is hard to ignore. If they don't allow their rebellious side to harden into alienation or their empathy into pessimism, they will be blessed with the natural charisma to see their dreams and plans through to a satisfying conclusion.

TONI MORRISON
Writer, *Beloved;* won
Nobel Prize

2/18/1931
Aquarius–Pisces Cusp

CHALLENGE: **GRAPPLING WITH A FEAR OF REJECTION THAT MAY KEEP THEM FROM SPREADING THEIR WINGS**

FULFILLMENT: **EDUCATING THEMSELVES ON WHAT THEY ARE TRULY MADE OF AND FINDING, TO THEIR SURPRISE, THAT THEY LIKE IT**

February 23–March 2

SPIRIT
PISCES I

Having a vision that is prone to be fixed on the stars will prove especially useful for Pisces I's on this karmic path, providing they are careful to develop the realism and strength necessary to pursue their dreams and see things through. Though gifted with considerable understanding and empathy, they have the capacity to rise above more mundane concerns in the pursuit of a set of higher goals. Challenging themselves will prove more difficult, however, since they are inclined to take the path of least resistance. Though some will fall prey to more aggressive or exploitative types, it is likely that fate will step in to lend a hand should Pisces I's stray too far from the path of fulfillment. If they take up the challenge to bring their fondest desires to tangible manifestation and avoid living in a world of expectation, their generous dose of personal appeal, combined with their natural talents, will ensure their success.

CHALLENGE: **EXTENDING SOME OF THEIR DEVOTION TO THEMSELVES**

FULFILLMENT: **SPENDING SOME QUIET TIME IN CONTEMPLATION OF WHO, WHAT, AND WHERE THEY ARE**

NOTABLES: **MIKHAIL GORBACHEV (LAST PRESIDENT OF USSR; KNOWN FOR PERESTROIKA); ROBERT NOVAK (JOURNALIST)**

March 3–10

THE LONER
PISCES II

Those born in the Week of the Loner who find themselves on this karmic path will doubtless be blessed with a higher degree of sociability than some of their fellows, yet will have little trouble retaining their sense of separateness as they embark on their journey of self-realization. Perhaps the principal danger here is that they will have to struggle to maintain a degree of realism as they find and follow their personal lodestar, for isolation may contribute to their capacity for self-delusion. On the other hand, disappointment can be especially hard for these sensitive people to bear, and they can easily become overwhelmed by pessimism or disillusion when things don't go as planned. Yet the world is not likely to overlook these unusual and rather extraordinary people, and real happiness can be theirs, providing they are careful not to throw it away.

RUPERT MURDOCH
Australian media mogul,
FOX

3/11/1931
Pisces III

CHALLENGE: **EXTRICATING THEMSELVES AWAY FROM THEIR OWN, RATHER UNREALISTIC, PRIVATE WORLD**

FULFILLMENT: **EXPERIENCING THE SELF-ESTEEM THAT COMES FROM STANDING FIRM IN WHO THEY REALLY ARE**

NOTABLE: **CARMEN DE LAVALLADE (DANCER)**

March 11–18

DANCERS AND DREAMERS
PISCES III

If the souls born in this week are careful not to allow others to become too dependent upon their special brand of help and insight, all can go exceedingly well for them. These personalities are frequently astonishingly gifted in some capacity and have the innate ability to dream big dreams and reach for even seemingly unattainable goals. They can do far more than just living in their heads, though, since their practical side is also well developed. They would do well to guard against the tendency to endlessly contemplate life's greater meaning when realistic effort is called for or otherwise delude themselves into believing that things will simply come their way. Taking fate into their own hands is their challenge; if they can do so, their journey will be remarkable indeed.

CHALLENGE: **DEALING WITH THEIR NEED TO BE NEEDED**

FULFILLMENT: **FINDING OUT WHAT LIFE MEANS BY LIVING IT**

NOTABLE: **LEE SHUBERT (BUILT POWERFUL BROADWAY THEATER EMPIRE WITH BROTHERS)**

The Way of Discovery

LIBRA III TO ARIES III
Theater to the Pioneer

It is the destiny of the individuals born to this karmic path to undergo a journey of exploration and discovery, one that often involves others. These men and women are called to follow their curiosity in order to reveal new knowledge or understanding, both for themselves and for society as a whole. The individuals on this karmic path are born with pioneering and leadership abilities that, when combined with their great breadth of vision and idealism, can result in some significant discoveries. Though accomplished in the art of diplomacy, those on this path have a number of lessons to learn about relating more intimately that will play themselves out in the group endeavors called for by this path. For this is the path not of a maverick but rather of one who works with others to accomplish an often lofty mission. Moreover, those on this path will enjoy using their excellent ability to think strategically and their dramatic flair when the time comes for them to share their discoveries with others.

Possessing a quiet brand of intellectualism and a subtly nuanced mode of thought, the men and women on this karmic path will use their talents more for the good of their cause than for self-aggrandizement, always seeking to bring something of value to others. The individuals on this path are born with an innate savvy that makes them quite worldly and even a bit dramatic. Their capacity to understand the politics of almost any situation is beyond compare. However, rather than allow themselves to become bogged down in intrigue or partisanship, those on this path must use this gift to help them accomplish their greater aim. Interestingly, what they place before the public at large is secretly geared toward educating themselves in some fashion, though this will never be obvious. In fact, the mission of those on the Way of Discovery, to give to their society something of benefit—for example, a scientific invention, an insight into or way of viewing life, a new art form, a medical breakthrough, or an innovation in the medical field—so compels them that they often sacrifice their own needs in order to answer their calling.

As skilled diplomats as they are and as vital as their mission is, those on the Way of Discovery do have a few lessons to learn in the area of interpersonal relations. Intimacy is not their forte. They are either playing to the crowd or, alternatively, looking off toward the horizon, dreaming of their goal and dropping everything to go find it. Apt to have many hangers-on, sycophants, and fans, these men and women must cultivate true friendships and intimacies. In a sense this involves a process of resocialization where more superficial forms of interaction with larger numbers of people are exchanged for fewer but deeper relationships. Part of the discovery process—and indeed their core lesson—is for those on this karmic path to learn how to relate on a deeper level. Learning the art of one-

---

CORE LESSON

Learning to relate to others more intimately

GOAL

To expand their own knowledge, and that of others, through exploration and discovery

---

GIFTS

Strategic, Hard-driving, Generous

PITFALLS

Unyielding, Self-sacrificing, Overly Independent

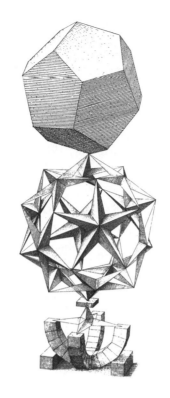

on-one interaction is essential because this path of destiny requires them to work closely with others. Developing greater empathy and understanding, as well as the ability to be available or present for others, will help those on the Way of Discovery fulfill their karmic task. For it is through collaboration with others that they will make their greatest advances.

The great joy of those on this karmic path is engaging in the process of discovery itself. Pushing back the frontiers in any field, going where others have not, following their theories down unexplored intellectual avenues—all are activities that provide them tremendous satisfaction. Often possessed of a visionary zeal, the crowning achievement for these hardy types is the "Eureka!" moment when they have attained their goal. Such an experience can occur in many fields, but this path does have a fair number of inventors on it. This moment can also be likened to the first staging of a play, the publication or reading of a written work, the presentation of a scientific paper, or making the speech of a lifetime. Often the vision of this moment can overwhelm all other considerations in the minds of these intrepid people, such that they are willing to give up everything, including home, family, even fame and wealth, for what they believe in. This is especially true when they are egged on by others of like mind. Such self-sacrificing tendencies must, however, be monitored and kept in check.

RELEASE

The need to do things themselves

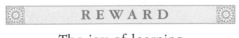

REWARD

The joy of learning

Many on this karmic path reach the pinnacle of success after long periods of anonymous work. Once-in-a-lifetime achievements are common among them. Having reached their goal, these individuals often experience a period of depression or letdown. However, once they go through this, they embark on another stage in their development in which they return to their dramatic roots. Sharing their discoveries with the public, educating them, or simply figuring out the best method for their presentation can provide them with enormous satisfaction. Indeed, they may even become teachers or educators later in life. Encouraging the process of discovery in others can be as rewarding as their own achievements. Further, their theatrical skills are so finely honed that many of them present their material in such a subtle manner that the members of their audience undergo a kind of discovery process themselves. Rather than making what they are teaching obvious, they utilize the power of subtlety, particularly when presenting a wholly new approach, and thus they will carefully plan and execute its presentation. These personalities are masters at creating slow realization in others.

A challenge and source of tension for those on this karmic path will be the question of how to balance their desire to go off exploring by themselves with their responsibility toward others. It is not enough that the byproducts of their karmic path will usually be of benefit

SUGGESTION

Slow down enough to realize others' value and worth. Learn the art of appreciation.
Don't pursue every idea. Find a confidant.

to society as a whole. These men and women must take others with them on the journey. Whether on an expedition of exploration, working in a laboratory with coworkers, engaging in collaborative efforts in dance or theater, or being involved with a muse as one creates, those on this path will not be alone—no matter how much they might wish to be. Moreover, it is not their destiny to be a distant manager or boss issuing orders from afar. Though they may lead, they must roll up their shirtsleeves and work shoulder to shoulder with others. As their interpersonal skills improve and they develop greater understanding, the men and women on this path will become more adept at bringing out the best in others. They are likely to develop a certain protectiveness, which may begin to resemble a paternal or maternal stance.

Sometimes those on the Way of Discovery will experience an epiphany and suddenly go out on their own to start a new venture or form their own organization. But those on this karmic path would do well to keep in mind that casting off for unknown shores on a perilous sea is best accomplished with a loyal crew. Alternatively, one of the greatest dangers for those on the Way of Discovery is that those who believe in them will follow them blindly or unquestioningly. Without involvement with people comfortable enough with them to question their methods, those on this path may end up at many a dead end or down a unrealistic or self-defeating byway as they hardheadedly pursue their visions. Also, allowing their pioneering spirit to turn into obsession may also turn off their followers so that they find themselves with an ever-diminishing number of co-

horts. Such overreaching tendencies may eventually correct themselves, however, particularly when these pragmatic individuals realize that they will soon be alone if they continue on their course.

In relationships, those on this karmic path will always be somewhat worldly souls, and they require a mate of like mind. The problem is that any life partner may take a dim view of the many close work relationships involved in the Way of Discovery or the long periods of devotion to a goal. Jealousy or possessiveness may then create intolerable friction. Family members may also feel particularly resentful toward the followers of those on this path, feeling that their position, particularly as son or daughter, has been usurped by protégés.

The degree of familial contentment of these individuals will depend heavily on how well they master the task of improving interpersonal skills.

The Way of Discovery calls to mind a schooner setting off on a voyage during the Age of Exploration. Before it can cast off, the crew must provision the ship for the long journey and correctly rig the sails. Proper preparation will enhance the safety of all concerned and allay many fears and anxieties. The captain of this vessel can be likened to an individual on this karmic path, responsible for leading the crew, having the foresight to consider all possible eventualities, charting the course, and holding the vision of the destination. Through it all, the captain works side by side with the crew and, ideally, inspires them. After the long journey, the ship returns to its port of call, laden with many treasures from distant shores for all to enjoy.

BALANCE POINT

Research and Teaching

CRYSTALS AND GEMSTONES

Labradorite leads to discoveries of ideas that hover just beneath the surface of the collective consciousness. The inner light of the stone assists in the articulation of new concepts with credence.

NOTABLES ON THIS KARMIC PATH

Considered the founder of psychoanalysis, and, like many on the Way of Discovery a pioneer in his field, Viennese physician **Sigmund Freud** was a hardworking empirical scientist. His personal experience as a therapist became the cornerstone of his psychological approach and led to his use of free association

SIGMUND FREUD

and dream interpretation to plumb the unconscious for data from childhood and other psychological clues. Alerting the public to the power of the unconscious and repressed sexuality, Freud came to receive professional acceptance and to be surrounded by disciples.

American children's writer and mythmaker **L. Frank Baum** is best known for his book *The Wonderful Wizard of Oz,* which later became a film classic, and aptly illustrates the theme of the Way of Discovery. Called a modern fairytale, this story follows Kansas farm girl Dorothy as she discovers a magical city in an alternate universe. Through this fantasy Baum illustrates a challenge of his own karmic path: balancing a desire to go off on one's own exploration and the need to fulfill one's responsibility to others.

L. FRANK BAUM

He continued this work throughout his life, producing numerous children's books with mystical themes as well as thirteen more books in the Oz series.

Characteristic of many on this path, **Dorothy Parker** put her intelligence to work for the advancement of meaningful causes. She began her career in New York working as a writer, editor, and critic, and her work appeared regularly in *The New Yorker*. While reporting on the Spanish Civil War, she was not

DOROTHY PARKER

afraid to stand up for her left-wing beliefs, even when they undermined her popular success. A true pioneer, she departed the New York literary scene (where she was a member of the Algonquin Round Table luncheon group) to pursue a career screenwriting in Hollywood. Parker is remembered for her malicious wit as well as the visionary zeal that is the hallmark of her path.

Other Notables: Vera Wang, Sara McLachlan, Wernher von Braun, Celine Dion, Lucy Lawless, Booker T. Washington, Billy Joel, Admiral Robert E. Peary, James Brown, Ken Follett, Meryl Streep, Nikola Tesla, Karl Menninger, George Bernard Shaw, Sean Connery, Ray Charles, Winston Churchill, John Wesley Hyatt, James Prescott Joule, Alvin Ailey, Albert Schweitzer, Daniel Webster, Lawrence Durrell, Maurice Ravel

BIRTHDAYS ON KARMIC PATH 28

June 2, 1893–October 20, 1893 | January 13, 1912–June 2, 1912

August 25, 1930–January 12, 1931 | April 5, 1949–August 24, 1949 | November 15, 1967–April 4, 1968

June 27, 1986–November 14, 1986 | February 5, 2005–June 26, 2005

KARMIC PATH
28

March 19–24

REBIRTH
PISCES–ARIES CUSP

Learning to nurture their capacity for personal inter-action and set aside some rather defensive attitudes will be paramount for the souls born in this period who travel the Way of Discovery. Yet the challenges presented by this karmic path will endow them with improved powers of diplomacy that will in turn help smooth the way toward the wealth of innovative accomplishments that are possible. Since this karmic path may demand that the individual work in groups, at the same time learning to cultivate a greater capacity for intimacy, this destiny may very well result in a life of working behind the scenes, where their unique skills are honed and appreciated by those with whom they come into contact but personal attention or recognition comes as a result of their discoveries rather than their personalities. Well suited to the role of explorer, Pisces–Arians on this karmic path will have an enhanced sense of vision, and that, in combination with their deep sensitivity, will create many possibilities for them.

WERNHER VON BRAUN
Developed German V-2
rocket

3/23/1912
Pisces–Aries Cusp

CHALLENGE: **CULTIVATING SUBTLETY IN INTIMATE RELA-TIONSHIPS**

FULFILLMENT: **GOING AFTER WHAT THEY ARE LOOKING FOR**

March 25–April 2

THE CHILD
ARIES I

If they take care to nourish their natural sense of ad-venture and enthusiasm, those born in this week are sure to do well on the Way of Discovery, providing they can overcome their tendency to feel misunderstood or unappreciated. Their impulse toward group efforts and endeavors is highly pronounced, and their natural dynamism is tempered with a more worldly, sophisticated perspective, all of which makes for a likable and rather inspiring mix. Thus, if they can employ their dramatic and creative talents in an effort to fulfill themselves with real originality and not as a means of vying for attention, they can use their rather naive yet wondrous vision to push themselves and others beyond the limits and toward the great frontiers of the unknown. As such, they are sure to break new and inspiring ground, whatever their chosen field of endeavor.

CHALLENGE: **NOT GOING OFF ON THEIR OWN BUT REMEM-BERING THAT EVERYONE NEEDS OTHERS**

FULFILLMENT: **ACTUALIZING A VISION**

NOTABLES: **CELINE DION (CANADIAN POP SINGER, "MY HEART WILL GO ON"); LUCY LAWLESS (ACTRESS, *XENA, WARRIOR PRINCESS*)**

April 3–10

THE STAR
ARIES II

Those born in the Week of the Star who travel the Way of Discovery have some truly splendid chances for success and development. Both diplo-matic and charismatic, they have a more or less assured worldly presence, yet they may struggle with issues surrounding their natural aloofness. It will be essential for these people to find the right balance of and venue for their efforts, one that involves both people and ideals. More than capable of forging ahead toward new frontiers, these inspiring personalities may find themselves without the necessary support for their inspirations unless they make the time and effort to cultivate warmer relationships with coworkers, family, and friends and not view those around them as mere satellites, sycophants, or minions. Capable of great dedication and hard work, they know how to get what they want; they must just be careful to take others along as they actualize their vision.

BOOKER T. WASHINGTON
Educator; born into
slavery; built Tuskegee
Institute

4/5/1856
Aries II

CHALLENGE: **TREATING THE MEMBERS OF THEIR TEAM LESS AS MINIONS AND MORE AS COLLABORATORS**

FULFILLMENT: **REACHING THE PINNACLE OF SUCCESS AND CELEBRITY AFTER MANY YEARS OF HARD WORK**

NOTABLES: **SONJA HENIE (ICE SKATER); JOHN OATES (POP SINGER, HALL AND OATES)**

April 11–18

THE PIONEER
ARIES III

Well equipped to forge ahead and to open new frontiers, the dazzling individuals born in this week who travel the Way of Discovery will nevertheless have to employ all their diplomatic and so-cial talents as they reach for their highest goals. Likely to be tempted to believe that they can do everything themselves or bend others to their will through the strength and drama of their presentation, Aries III's may face some hard lessons in the arenas of both personal relationships and group efforts. Yet if they can learn the value of at-tracting others to their causes through recognizing their effort, giving credit where credit is due, and seeking out support when necessary, these individuals will have little trouble tapping into the collective source of inspiration and carving out a new niche, icon, or ideology for the world to make its own.

CHALLENGE: **NOT SACRIFICING TOO MUCH OF THEMSELVES FOR THEIR PERSONAL QUEST**

FULFILLMENT: **BLAZING TRAILS IN ANY AREA**

April 19–24
POWER
ARIES–TAURUS CUSP

The personalities born on this cusp who travel this karmic path are blessed indeed, as they are endowed with subtlety and refined diplomatic talents. These, in combination with their great strength, will aid them in their quest to explore and expand the frontiers of their chosen fields of endeavor. Natural leaders, these hard workers have a great gift for working with other people toward a common goal. Given their dramatic sense of timing, they will enjoy considerable success, providing they do not attempt to impose their ideas on others by force or take their support network too much for granted. Though they may become mired in laziness or mercenary attitudes that keep them from discovering a broader vision, they are much more naturally adventurous than some of their fellow Aries–Tauruses, and by having the knack of knowing both when to lead and when to follow, they can accomplish much along the Way of Discovery.

CHALLENGE: **ALLOWING INTIMATE RELATIONSHIPS TO SOFTEN THEM**

FULFILLMENT: **KNOWING THE RIGHT MOMENT TO STRIKE**

NOTABLES: **JESSICA LANGE (ACTRESS, *TOOTSIE*); PATTI LUPONE (ACTRESS; SINGER, *EVITA*); PALOMA PICASSO (DESIGNER; DAUGHTER OF PABLO)**

BILLY JOEL
Singer/songwriter/pianist,
"The Piano Man"

5/9/1949
Taurus II

April 25–May 2
MANIFESTATION
TAURUS I

The individuals born in this week who travel the Way of Discovery may experience a bit of a struggle, because their attachment to creature comforts and personal security may exist at odds with the need to develop a broader vision and explore new frontiers. Still, Taurus I's have a great deal going for them with this configuration, as they are quite able to apply themselves to the kind of long-range commitment required by this karmic path. Though they may be confirmed workaholics and hence fail to become intimate with others, they are likely to do well in groups, providing they motivate themselves to do so. Yet if they can develop an interest in going beyond established boundaries and learn to enjoy the excitement to be found in reaching into the world of the unknown, they are more than capable of demonstrating their vision to the rest of us.

CHALLENGE: **TEMPERING THEIR STUBBORNNESS FOR THE GOOD OF THE CAUSE**

FULFILLMENT: **PURSUING THEIR VISION TO ITS MANIFESTATION**

NOTABLES: **JOYCE DEWITT (ACTRESS, *THREE'S COMPANY*); WINTHROP ROCKEFELLER (FORMER ARKANSAS GOVERNOR)**

May 3–10
THE TEACHER
TAURUS II

The individuals born in the Week of the Teacher who negotiate the challenges of the Way of Discovery will likely experience great satisfaction, as they are natural movers and shakers. Though they run the risk of scattering their energies by pursuing such a wealth of ideas that nothing ever quite gets accomplished, even a modicum of focus should provide them with great opportunities. Gifted with great leadership abilities, they may also have to readjust their views in the arena of human relationships and step back from their need to teach in order to join with others of like mind in the pursuit of a common goal. Yet they are always educational and often inspirational. If they can bring those strengths to bear in combination with the natural savvy and diplomatic grace of their Libra III origins, they will flourish.

CHALLENGE: **CULTIVATING GREATER OPEN-MINDEDNESS SO THAT THEY DON'T IGNORE AVENUES THAT MIGHT HAVE BORNE FRUIT HAD THEY BEEN EXPLORED**

FULFILLMENT: **TEACHING WHAT THEY HAVE DISCOVERED**

NOTABLE: **SIGMUND FREUD (FOUNDER OF PSYCHOANALYSIS)**

ADMIRAL ROBERT E. PEARY
Naval officer; 1st man to reach North Pole

5/6/1856
Taurus II

May 11–18
THE NATURAL
TAURUS III

The naturally rebellious, adventuresome souls born in this week who travel the Way of Discovery are likely to enjoy considerable success, as these freedom lovers are also gifted with a degree of worldliness and the diplomatic skill to get pretty much what they want out of life. Dramatic and often colorful characters, they can be held back only by a need for security that can exist at odds with the higher challenge of this karmic path. Equally, there are some who, due to an inborn complacency, will convince themselves that there are few frontiers left to conquer. Yet if they are careful to follow their vision, they are more than likely to give form to their unusual views or unique approach. Moreover, they are apt to take others along on a rather fun-filled journey.

CHALLENGE: **MARSHALING THEMSELVES TO ANSWER THE CALL TO EXPLORATION**

FULFILLMENT: **COMMUNICATING WHAT THEY HAVE LEARNED OR DISCOVERED IN THE SUBTLEST OF FASHIONS**

NOTABLES: **L. FRANK BAUM (AUTHOR, *THE WIZARD OF OZ*); ARCHIBALD COX (WATERGATE PROSECUTOR); PERRY COMO (POP SINGER OF 1940s AND 1950s)**

May 19–24
ENERGY
TAURUS–GEMINI CUSP

Amazingly dynamic, these interesting personalities who travel the Way of Discovery will doubtless be gifted with the ability to play a crowd. Sure to be well liked and much admired, they will nevertheless have to employ their ability to draw attention to themselves as a means of gaining support for their projects, plans, and explorations. In fact, a number of these personalities have the ability to come up with startling and what at first glance might appear rather extreme or far-out innovations in their chosen fields. Thus, they may well draw fire from more conservative types and will have to employ their diplomatic talents to keep their pet ideas on the drawing board or in the public eye. Yet if they don't get mired in a mere need to shock people and apply their considerable energy in such a way that it serves to excite rather than offend, they will take great strides along the way.

CHALLENGE: **GENERATING SUPPORT FROM OTHERS IN ORDER TO HELP THEM STAY FOCUSED ON THEIR GOAL**

FULFILLMENT: **DISCOVERING THE CAPACITY FOR PERSISTENCE WITHIN THEMSELVES**

NOTABLES: **SVEN DODINGTON (ENGINEER); JAMES BROWN (SINGER; "THE GODFATHER OF SOUL," "POPPA'S GOT A BRAND NEW BAG"); JOHN PAYNE (ACTOR, *MIRACLE ON 34TH STREET*)**

HANK WILLIAMS, JR.
Country singer

5/26/1949
Gemini I

May 25–June 2
FREEDOM
GEMINI I

There is much about these personalities that is cutting edge, charismatic, and shrewdly attuned to the politics of almost any situation in which they find themselves. Yet for all of their perception, sociability, and intellectual powers, many Gemini I's have a tendency to become caught up in intrigues and games at the expense of their impulse to break free and follow their own goals. In fact, many of them will be rather too social for their own good, while others may become so excited at the prospect of pushing back the frontiers and exploring their dreams that they scatter their energies and fail to generate the perspiration needed to carry through on their many inspirations. Yet they have the possibility of great success, and with a minimum of effort, they can expect a maximum of return.

CHALLENGE: **ENGAGING MUCH PATIENCE AND GENERAL STICK-TO-ITIVENESS**

FULFILLMENT: **HITTING UPON THE ANSWER TO A PROBLEM THEY HAVE WORKED ON FOR A LONG TIME**

NOTABLES: **JAMAICA KINCAID (WEST INDIAN AUTHOR); PAMELA JOHNSON (WRITER, *ON INIQUITY*); PHILIP MICHAEL THOMAS (ACTOR, *MIAMI VICE*)**

June 3–10
NEW LANGUAGE
GEMINI II

Inventive and innovative by nature, those born in the Week of New Language who set out on the Way of Discovery can expect great rewards along the way, as this karmic path gifts them with a greater measure of sophistication and style than they might otherwise have had. Thus these souls are rather more secure than some of their fellow Gemini II's and often quite sure of themselves. Yet they will have to be careful that their capacity to dazzle is not used as a tool to intimidate or to hide the lack of substance in their ideas. Equally, many of this type will chronically overreach themselves in their quest for the new and untried, and some may embark on some rather dark explorations in the attempt to push the limits. Yet if they recognize that concerted effort and joining with others to achieve a larger ideal is the path of fulfillment, they will in turn be rewarded with a wealth of opportunities to share their unique gifts and discoveries with the world.

CHALLENGE: **FIGURING OUT HOW TO EXPRESS WHAT THEY KNOW IN A LANGUAGE OTHERS WILL UNDERSTAND**

FULFILLMENT: **SHARING AN IDIOM, OUTLOOK, AND COMMON VISION WITH THEIR COWORKERS**

KEN FOLLETT
Author, spy novels,
Eye of the Needle

6/5/1949
Gemini II

June 11–18
THE SEEKER
GEMINI III

Those born in the Week of the Seeker who find themselves on the Way of Discovery are in for a fine time, since pushing the limits of exploration and innovation is very much in their psychic and spiritual vocabulary. Gifted with both great sophistication and a sense of adventure, most will do extremely well, providing they don't get mired in chronic restlessness at the expense of concerted effort. Picking and choosing among various options will prove especially important for these souls, as will an ability to cultivate closer personal relationships. Too, impatience and a rather volatile temper may be problems for them. They will have to employ their considerable charm in garnering the support they need to bring their fondest inspirations and innovations to manifestation in the real world. Yet if they can avoid manipulation and intrigue in their associations and keep their eye on the higher prizes that await them, their efforts will be well rewarded.

CHALLENGE: **STICKING TO ONE AREA OF STUDY OR EXPLORATION**

FULFILLMENT: **TESTING ANY LIMITS LIFE PRESENTS THEM WITH**

June 19–24

MAGIC
GEMINI–CANCER CUSP

Those born on the Cusp of Magic who navigate the challenges and demands of the Way of Discovery can experience great fulfillment. Yet they will have to take care to avoid the dangers of self-deception, since these rather romantic types can be a bit too willing to follow their hearts, even if that means relinquishing their good judgment. Nevertheless, they are well suited to the kind of concerted effort and group endeavor that beckon, and will in addition have an amazing grasp of how to inspire those around them to work toward a common goal. Though they may not be the most original or adventurous explorers on this road, they can nevertheless find great reward, both through their worldly achievements and in the arena of close personal relationships, as they are blessed with the capacity for both hard work and the development of deep and lasting emotional bonds.

CHALLENGE: **GRAPPLING WITH THEIR NEED FOR SECURITY AND A NUMBER OF THEIR FEARS**

FULFILLMENT: **DIVING INTO THE REALMS OF MAGIC, MYTH, OR FANTASY AND BRINGING TO THE WORLD THE RICHES THEY FIND THERE**

NOTABLES: **JOSÉPHINE DE BEAUHARNAIS (1ST WIFE OF NAPOLEON); LIONEL RICHIE (POP SINGER)**

MERYL STREEP
Actress, Oscar winner,
*Sophie's Choice, Out of
Africa*
_____
6/22/1949
Gemini–Cancer Cusp

June 25–July 2

THE EMPATH
CANCER I

Gifted with charisma, strength, tremendous empathy, and fine managerial talents, those born in this week who travel the Way of Discovery may be quite happy on this karmic path, providing they overcome some rather fearful attitudes and avoid their tendency to get entangled in emotional dramas. They will doubtless be faced with the lesson of learning to draw their energies away from purely personal issues and focus them on more universal themes and ideals. At some point in their lives, they are sure to be challenged to take greater risks and push the envelope of their experience, as well as to inspire others to do the same. Yet they have a great core of inner strength that will come into play, as well as the determination needed to accomplish whatever they set out to do. Often quite visionary, they have a truly inspired sense of all that is possible. If they are careful to nurture their sense of curiosity and augment it with their special brand of informed realism, all will go well.

CHALLENGE: **FORCING THEMSELVES NOT TO WITHDRAW WHEN THE URGE STRIKES**

FULFILLMENT: **UTILIZING THEIR MANAGERIAL ABILITIES IN SERVICE OF A GREATER VISION OR QUEST**

NOTABLE: **VERA WANG (WEDDING GOWN DESIGNER)**

July 3–10

THE UNCONVENTIONAL
CANCER II

Those born in the Week of the Unconventional who make their way along this karmic path can enjoy considerable reward and accomplishment, providing they are willing to take their own often far-out ideas and inspirations and see them through to realization. Their natural charisma is heightened on this karmic path and is sure to spark the imaginations of many along the road. Capable of shouldering great responsibilities in the interest of a higher ideal or larger good, they may have to cultivate greater depth of emotion before they can inspire or lead others to their cause. Though they may have to divest themselves of a rather narcissistic outlook as well as a tendency to try to do everything themselves, their attraction to the out-of-the-ordinary will prove their biggest asset along this road.

CHALLENGE: **GROUNDING THEIR IDEALISM AND EMPATHY WITH A MORE PRACTICAL APPROACH**

FULFILLMENT: **APPLYING THEIR UNIQUE BLEND OF LOGIC AND FEELING TO "SUSS OUT" THEIR DISCOVERIES**

NOTABLES: **DANIEL GUGGENHEIM (FINANCIER); SHELLEY DUVALL (ACTRESS, *POPEYE*)**

NIKOLA TESLA
Engineer, invented Tesla
coil
_____
7/9/1856
Cancer II

July 11–18

THE PERSUADER
CANCER III

Those born in the Week of the Persuader who travel the Way of Discovery may encounter some difficulty, as they may be so convinced of the rightness of their convictions that they fail to keep the degree of open-mindedness necessary to make new discoveries or explore untried methods, ideas, or frontiers. However, their skill at observation will be highly useful, as will their knack for persuading others of their views and inspiring them to follow their often visionary goals. This path is apt to suit their ambitious side, and their determination and drive will be put to good use for the benefit of all. Later, having achieved their goals, they may find particular fulfillment in their role as teacher, since they can then allow their inherent nurturing instincts to emerge. Since their ambition is less for themselves and more for their calling, those born in the Week of the Persuader will find a higher form of inspiration on this karmic path.

CHALLENGE: **CHALLENGING THEMSELVES TO BE LESS RIGID IN THEIR VIEWS**

FULFILLMENT: **INSPIRING AND EDUCATING OTHERS**

July 19–25

OSCILLATION
CANCER–LEO CUSP

July 26–August 2

AUTHORITY
LEO I

Those born on the Cusp of Oscillation who make their way along this karmic path will doubtless be able to generate the kind of excitement, energy, and enthusiasm required to forge into uncharted territory, yet they may stumble a bit when the situation calls for dedicated commitment to more routine tasks. They may be dramatic in the extreme and will have to control their tendency to fly into tantrums or histrionics when their plans do not work out. This is a journey that is likely to be marked by a number of peak experiences, followed by periods of letdown or depression; yet if they can form lasting bonds with those around them and avoid the tendency to believe they must bear the weight of the world on their shoulders, all will go brilliantly.

KARL MENNINGER
American psychiatrist;
cofounded the
Menninger Clinic

7/22/1893
Cancer–Leo Cusp

CHALLENGE: **KNOWING WHEN FORGING AHEAD IS ONLY A REFLECTION OF THEIR ATTRACTION TO DANGER**
FULFILLMENT: **BEING SURROUNDED BY A CORE GROUP OF SUPPORTIVE COLLEAGUES**
NOTABLE: **ALAN MENKEN (COMPOSER, DISNEY MOVIES, *THE LITTLE MERMAID*)**

The souls born in this week who find themselves on the Way of Discovery will have a rich and rewarding life experience, providing they can overcome some rather rigid attitudes and forge ahead. Though a high level of personal frustration sometimes goes with this configuration, they are more than capable of leading others on a great journey toward the unknown in an inspiring and uplifting fashion—their principal pitfall being that they often forget to include anyone else in their plans and schemes. Yet when their sense of passion is awakened and they apply themselves to the work and planning necessary to get to where they want to go, their journey will likely take on almost mythic proportions in the hearts and minds of those privileged enough to share in their discoveries, and their legacy to the larger world is not likely to be soon forgotten.

CHALLENGE: **PRACTICING LEADERSHIP RATHER THAN DOMINATION**
FULFILLMENT: **PUTTING THE RESULTS OF THEIR EXPLORATIONS ONSTAGE FOR PUBLIC CONSUMPTION—AND EDUCATION**
NOTABLE: **VIDA BLUE (BASEBALL PITCHER)**

August 3–10

BALANCED STRENGTH
LEO II

August 11–18

LEADERSHIP
LEO III

Modest and rather altruistic by nature, these personalities are likely to find great success along the Way of Discovery. Blessed with quiet and unpretentious dedication, they can make inspiring figures, able to draw others to them in a common effort. They may also, however, get mired in a tendency to be rather too self-sacrificing or refuse to admit failure, and many of these personalities will have such difficulty with their unwillingness to be alone that they are deaf to the calls to explore new worlds and new frontiers. Nevertheless, they are gifted with an extraordinary and steady determination that will impart great strength for the long haul. Though these souls may find the road quite long before they come across what they're looking for, the discoveries they make along the way are likely to be just as important as their ultimate goals.

GEORGE BERNARD SHAW
Playwright/essayist;
Pygmalion; won Nobel
Prize

7/26/1856
Leo I

CHALLENGE: **NOT PUSHING THEMSELVES TOO HARD**
FULFILLMENT: **REAPING THE REWARDS OF THEIR TOUGHNESS AND PERSISTENCE WHEN THEY REACH THEIR GOAL**
NOTABLE: **KEITH CARRADINE (ACTOR; SINGER)**

Many of the souls born in this week who travel the Way of Discovery have an almost heroic vision that will serve them especially well on this life journey, providing they are able to bring others into their process. Impressive as they are, sharing with others is not their greatest strength, and it is likely that any number of the lessons of this karmic path will be played out in the arena of personal relationships. Selfishness and a rather dictatorial attitude will be their principal stumbling blocks, for as inspirational and theatrical as they can be, they will have to learn to put ego aside in the interest of exploring new territory and making new discoveries. Learning to work well with others will be paramount, as will learning to delegate and regulate their responsibilities. Gifted with the ability to win an audience, they will nevertheless have to be careful to meet the higher calling of this karmic path by sharing the glory when it comes.

CHALLENGE: **MEDITATING ON THE DIFFERENCE BETWEEN PERSONAL GLORY AND COMMON WISDOM**
FULFILLMENT: **MAKING THEIR TEAMMATES A PRIORITY AND THEREBY WINNING THEIR RESPECT**

KARMIC PATH
28

August 19–25

EXPOSURE
LEO–VIRGO CUSP

Brilliant and sophisticated, the personalities born in this week who travel the Way of Discovery are likely to experience many breakthroughs. Some with this configuration may be formidable indeed, yet they will have to be careful that their sheer worldliness and insight do not manifest themselves in the kind of cynicism that leads them to distrust their impulses to forge ahead toward greener pastures, higher dreams, and new discoveries. Cultivating the art of sharing will prove especially beneficial, as these souls have a tendency to guard their inspirations and innovations quite jealously and may be confronted by some instruction in give-and-take along the road. Thus these souls must especially guard against their desire to forge ahead on their own. Yet if they take those lessons to heart, they will be able to scale new heights in both innovation and achievement.

SEAN CONNERY
Actor, James Bond films
———
8/25/1930
Leo–Virgo Cusp

CHALLENGE: **BEING WILLING TO SHARE WHAT THEY DISCOVER OR LEARN WITH OTHERS**
FULFILLMENT: **EXPLORING IDEAS AND UNRAVELING PROBLEMS OR PUZZLES**
NOTABLES: **DOROTHY PARKER (POET; WRITER, OFTEN FOR** *THE NEW YORKER*); **SHELLEY LONG (ACTRESS,** *CHEERS*); **RICK SPRINGFIELD (ACTOR; ROCK SINGER, "JESSIE'S GIRL")**

August 26–September 2

SYSTEM BUILDERS
VIRGO I

System Builders can be quite happy on the Way of Discovery, providing they keep themselves open to the new and avoid their tendency to stick their heads in the sand. They are gifted with great objectivity and a special kind of talent for sophisticated logic and are especially well suited to the kind of tireless research and careful structuring that are often necessary to pave the way to discovery. This may not always bode well, however, since others may find that they make better followers than leaders. Though their drive is indisputable, they may need to cultivate a broader vision to put before it. However, they are gifted with greater social skills and more charisma and natural modesty than they might otherwise have had, and those qualities are likely to open the doors to the acceptance of their special contributions.

CHALLENGE: **BROADENING THEIR VISION**
FULFILLMENT: **SERVING BY PURSUING A GOAL THAT COULD ULTIMATELY BENEFIT OTHERS**
NOTABLES: **BEN GAZZARA (ACTOR); HUEY P. LONG, JR. (GOVERNOR; SENATOR FROM LOUISIANA)**

September 3–10

THE ENIGMA
VIRGO II

Those born in the Week of the Enigma may struggle a bit with the challenge to exploration and innovation that beckons on this karmic path, due to the fact that they tend to bask in their own worldly image and become preoccupied with the risks involved in rocking what may be a rather comfortable boat. Too, they are prone to keeping their plans to themselves and may have to cultivate a willingness to take others along on their voyage of discovery. The ability to access their deepest feelings will open the doors to both intimacy and worldly accomplishment. Many of these personalities will find that the frontiers of self-exploration hold the most fascination and potential for development and discovery. Yet if they can avoid the tendency to be too self-sacrificing, on the one hand, or too self-sufficient, on the other, the Way of Discovery holds great promise for them.

SIR ALEXANDER KORDA
Film producer,
The Third Man
———
9/16/1893
Virgo III

CHALLENGE: **SPENDING LESS ENERGY ERECTING ELABORATE DEFENSES AND MORE ON SEEKING THE ANSWERS TO SOME OF LIFE'S TOUGHER QUESTIONS**
FULFILLMENT: **APPLYING THEIR TALENT FOR ANALYSIS TO DISCOVER THE TRUTH**
NOTABLE: **SONNY ROLLINS (JAZZ MUSICIAN; TENOR SAXOPHONIST)**

September 11–18

THE LITERALIST
VIRGO III

Likely to be greatly drawn to more tangible rather than idealistic types of discovery, those born in the Week of the Literalist can nevertheless be inspired by idealism along this karmic path, and their sense of innovation may well be motivated by a need to improve products or find new ways of doing things rather than strike out for parts unknown. Socially, they may be quite adept, though the intimate side of relationships will prove more elusive. Some with this configuration may fall into the trap of deciding that they know what's good for everybody else or try to force their ideas on others to the extent that they alienate their support network; others may be self-sacrificing to the extent that their best ideas are never given a chance to flower. Yet if they are careful not to demand too much in the way of results and instead nurture their capacity to learn for the love of learning itself, all will go well.

CHALLENGE: **TEMPERING A CERTAIN RUTHLESS STREAK**
FULFILLMENT: **INVOKING THEIR WILLFULNESS AND PERSISTENCE TO FIND THE ANSWERS OR REACH THE GOAL THEY SEEK**

September 19–24
BEAUTY
VIRGO–LIBRA CUSP

Likely to be blessed with some truly amazing creative gifts, Virgo–Libras will nevertheless have to resist the temptation to rest on their laurels and ignore the challenge to innovation and exploration presented by this karmic path. Inclined to be rather theoretical by nature, these personalities will also have to be careful of a tendency to be rather unrealistic in their quest for the ideal. Ivory-tower ideologies flourish among them and can serve to hinder both their personal relationships and their need to push the envelope of experience. Yet they have a rather unique and highly evolved vision of what is possible; if they can somehow reconcile that vision with reality and, with the help of others, bring it to life, their contribution to the world, especially the world of art or aesthetics, will serve as a revelation to us all.

CHALLENGE: **DEVELOPING A BETTER ABILITY TO DIG DEEPER**
FULFILLMENT: **PUSHING THEMSELVES PAST THE ENVELOPE OF SENSUOUS OR AESTHETIC REALMS**

RAY CHARLES
Singer/composer/pianist,
"Georgia on My Mind"

9/23/1930
Virgo–Libra Cusp

September 25–October 2
THE PERFECTIONIST
LIBRA I

Resisting the temptation to do everything themselves or to strike out on their own in search of a more perfect world will figure prominently in the lives of those born in this week who travel the Way of Discovery. Though they will be gifted with greater diplomatic skill than they might otherwise have had, these people will have to take care to avoid histrionics and an overly exacting attitude toward others, both of which can interfere greatly with their ability to draw others into their vision of what is possible. Too, some may struggle with indecision or a sense of insecurity regarding their need to venture into uncharted waters and may retreat into frustration or rigid thought patterns. Yet they are capable of tremendous achievement, and if they cultivate a love of learning and apply themselves to the good of their larger cause, they can expect great success.

CHALLENGE: **LETTING GO OF OVERLY STRICT ADHERENCE TO THEIR CONVICTIONS AND THEIR SELF-CRITICAL ATTITUDES**
FULFILLMENT: **BECOMING IMBUED WITH A VISION AND FOLLOWING IT, NO MATTER HOW MANY PROBLEMS OR INEFFICIENCIES THEY ENCOUNTER ALONG THE WAY**

October 3–10
SOCIETY
LIBRA II

Those born in the Week of Society who travel the Way of Discovery may kid themselves about where their truest impulses lie. Gifted with a great capacity for leadership and inspiration, they nevertheless have a tendency to detach themselves from their desires that will manifest itself in an inability to truly connect with others. Excellent diplomats and political players, they will nevertheless have to work hard to divest themselves of their tendency to submerge their own needs or stifle their curiosity about what lies around the next bend in the road. Interestingly enough, they have a rare knack for staying up to date on the latest developments and social trends: once they come to understand that this karmic path involves their taking that comprehension to a level where what is important is not the "now" but the new—that which is not yet accomplished, discovered, or dreamed—they are sure to make great strides along this road.

CHALLENGE: **BALANCING THEIR DESIRE TO GO OFF EXPLORING ON THEIR OWN WITH THEIR RESPONSIBILITIES TO OTHERS**
FULFILLMENT: **INVOKING THEIR SECRET DRAMATIC SIDE AS THEY PRESENT THEIR IDEAS TO OTHERS**

HAROLD PINTER
Playwright/director,
The Caretaker

10/10/1930
Libra II

October 11–18
THEATER
LIBRA III

Brilliant and often inspirational figures, those born in the Week of Theater who travel this karmic path will have to work hard to develop the personal responsibility and interpersonal skill that will enable them to achieve its higher promise. They may be a bit too charismatic for their own and everyone else's good and are capable of collecting any number of protégés, fans, and sycophants along the way. Thus, they will have to work hard to develop their talents for analysis and planning and avoid striking out for parts unknown without much idea of where they're going. Centering their attention on a cause or specific goal, even a theoretical one, will do much to harness their considerable energy in a productive fashion. Yet once they attune themselves to a sense of higher calling, the adventure, accomplishment, and discoveries they make along the way are bound to prove an education for us all.

CHALLENGE: **ADMITTING WHEN THEY HAVE VENTURED TOO FAR DOWN THE WRONG PATH**
FULFILLMENT: **FINDING THEMSELVES AT THE HEAD OF A BUSINESS OR ORGANIZATION DEVOTED TO INNOVATION, EXPLORATION, OR RESEARCH**
NOTABLE: **JIMMY BRESLIN (JOURNALIST; WON PULITZER PRIZE)**

KARMIC PATH
28

October 19–25

DRAMA AND CRITICISM
LIBRA–SCORPIO CUSP

Able to master any idea, task, or quest for discovery they undertake, the personalities born in this week who find themselves on this karmic path have a rather remarkable ability to break the mold, rise to new heights, and bring their discoveries to the world. They will, however, have to guard against an inclination to preach rather than teach, or otherwise to bring others to their cause through criticism or browbeating. Too, they may be possessed by a rather dangerous sense of their own infallibility that will bear watching, and they may love a challenge more than any tangible result or discovery. Yet if they are careful to nurture their love of learning and set aside their rather sizable egos in the interest of pursuing a larger goal or idea, they can bring a rare sense of adventure to this life's journey and will serve as role models for us all.

BIG BOPPER
Rock and roll star of 50s;
killed in plane crash

———

10/24/1930
Libra–Scorpio Cusp

———

CHALLENGE: **NOT PERMITTING THEMSELVES TO BE SIDE-TRACKED BY EMOTIONAL OR INTERPERSONAL ISSUES**

FULFILLMENT: **ENGAGING THEIR INSIGHTFULNESS AND PERCEPTIVENESS AS THEY EXPLORE THEIR FIELD**

October 26–November 2

INTENSITY
SCORPIO I

Though more social than many of their fellows, Scorpio I's who journey along the Way of Discovery will nevertheless face a few challenges, not the least of which will be their resistance to the idea of serving as a source of inspiration and education to others. In fact, many with this position will prove themselves far more adept at manipulating others than they are at actually inspiring them. Prone to emotional extremes, they have a hard time sharing and will have to work hard to overcome their distrust of others in order to bring their creations, innovations, and discoveries to the larger world. Yet they will be marked by brilliant intelligence, sophisticated views, and considerable subtlety. If they can keep themselves alert to what the *I Ching* refers to as "those things not yet in sight and those sounds not yet within hearing" and keep their suspicions to a minimum, all will go well.

———

CHALLENGE: **RELENTING, BY BEING A LITTLE LESS HARD ON PEOPLE—ESPECIALLY THOSE WORKING CLOSEST TO THEM**

FULFILLMENT: **FINDING A MEANINGFUL PURPOSE FOR THEIR INTENSITY, DISCRIMINATION, AND INSIGHT**

NOTABLES: **CLIFFORD BROWN (JAZZ TRUMPETER); MOBUTO SESE SEKO (PRESIDENT OF ZAIRE; HARSH DICTATOR)**

November 3–11

DEPTH
SCORPIO II

Though the Way of Discovery endows Scorpio II's with a more dramatic and intense personality than might be entirely comfortable for anyone, they in turn bring to this life journey a greater degree of empathy and sensitivity to others than many of their fellows on this road. Rather serious and dedicated by nature, they will nevertheless have to work against their tendency to be overly demanding of themselves and others and learn to actively inspire, rather than merely intimidate, those around them. Too, there is the possibility that they may employ their curiosity in less-than-constructive pursuits and find only new ways of escaping, rather than making the more substantial contributions and innovations called for by this karmic path. Nevertheless, they can truly flourish, especially in areas such as research, investigation, and scientific inquiry that absorb their attention without awakening their anxiety.

ABIGAIL ADAMS
First Lady to President
John Adams

———

11/11/1744
Scorpio II

———

CHALLENGE: **STRUGGLING WITH THEIR TENDENCY TO ENVY, RESENTMENT, AND JEALOUSY DURING THE "LEAN YEARS"**

FULFILLMENT: **PUTTING THEIR RESEARCH AND ANALYTICAL SKILLS TO GOOD USE IN ANY ENDEAVOR**

NOTABLE: **DERRICK ALBERT BELL, JR. (CIVIL RIGHTS LEADER)**

November 12–18

CHARM
SCORPIO III

Though expanding their horizons and forging into uncharted territory will not come easily to these worldly and self-confident people, the Way of Discovery will nevertheless hold a number of opportunities that even those born in the Week of Charm will find difficult to refuse. Though not as obviously adventurous as some others on this karmic path, these personalities will nevertheless experience considerable achievement, especially when they set aside their more selfish or egoistic inclinations and employ their considerable charisma as to inspire others. Though complacency may be something of a stumbling block, setting themselves unrealistic goals will not. Well organized, efficient, and generally rather sensitive to others' needs, these personalities can go far, as their considerable charm and social talents are here infused with a rare and dynamic idealism.

———

CHALLENGE: **NOT RESORTING TO CHARM OR MANIPULATION TO GET THEIR WAY**

FULFILLMENT: **EXPLORING THE DEPTHS OF THE HUMAN PSYCHE OR OTHER INNER WORLDS**

NOTABLE: **LISA BONET (ACTRESS, *THE COSBY SHOW*)**

November 19–24

REVOLUTION
SCORPIO–SAGITTARIUS CUSP

The powerful, persuasive personalities born in this week who travel the Way of Discovery may well have what it takes to change the world. Blessed with extraordinary perception and the skill to combine their idealism with diplomacy, there is little that can go wrong for them, with the possible exception of the fact that they are more than willing to go to extremes and perfectly able to take others to extremes as well. Still, though this can be a volatile mix, it is an unforgettable one. If these individuals can temper their zealotry with sensitivity and mix their inspiration with hard work and good planning, they are more than capable of bringing their followers to the threshold of a new age.

WINSTON CHURCHILL
British prime minister
during WWII

———

11/30/1874
Sagittarius I

CHALLENGE: **SPENDING LESS TIME EXPLODING OLD THEORIES AND MORE TIME INVENTING NEW ONES**
FULFILLMENT: **GOING OUT AND DISCOVERING NEW TERRAIN**
NOTABLE: **BORIS BECKER (TENNIS PLAYER)**

November 25–December 2

INDEPENDENCE
SAGITTARIUS I

Gifted with both a sense of adventure and a rare kind of moral integrity, those born in the Week of Independence who travel the Way of Discovery are in for enviable success. Inherent in this configuration is the kind of leadership ability that can open up whole new frontiers of discovery and innovation, and there is almost no one better equipped to garner social forces in the interest of a grand and glorious cause. A certain impulsiveness will have to be tempered with common sense, however, or they may run into problems, especially in the area of personal relationships. For though they are excellent partners, they are not above making some rather unreasonable demands, and they fully expect others to be endowed with the kind of willpower and determination they have themselves. In any event, they would do well to listen when the call to adventure and discovery sounds, for this a passage marked by an amazing sort of grace.

CHALLENGE: **SLOWING DOWN LONG ENOUGH FOR OTHERS TO JOIN THEM**
FULFILLMENT: **HEEDING THE CALL TO EXPLORE THE GREATER WORLD THROUGH TRAVEL AND ADVENTURE**
NOTABLES: **JOHN WESLEY HYATT (INVENTOR, PHOTOGRAPHIC FILM AND CELLULOID); G. GORDON LIDDY (WATERGATE FELON)**

December 3–10

THE ORIGINATOR
SAGITTARIUS II

The Originators who navigate the Way of Discovery are blessed with a fearless sense of the original and untried. Here these often insecure individuals are gifted with greater social skills and élan than they might otherwise have had, and the resulting mix may well be a recipe for success. Naturally compelling, they are unlikely to suffer overmuch from feelings of rejection, though they may well struggle with a certain amount of frustration as they seek to bring their rather avant-garde notions under the public eye. Too, the question of intimate relationships may not prove too much of a problem, since Sagittarius II's are quite inclined to cultivate one or two close confidants. Yet this karmic path will demand that they share their innovations and discoveries with others on a broader scale, and though they may well be resistant to the higher task of educating others, the rewards of daring to "think differently" are likely to be sweet indeed.

JEAN-LUC GODARD
French film director,
founder of New Wave
cinema, *Breathless*

———

12/3/1930
Sagittarius II

CHALLENGE: **COUNTERING ANY THOUGHTS OF GLORY OR ACCEPTANCE AS THEY PUSH TO THEIR GOAL**
FULFILLMENT: **ENJOYING THEIR OWN ORIGINAL BRAND OF PRESENTATION WHEN SHARING THEIR IDEAS**
NOTABLES: **MAXIMILLIAN SCHELL (ACTOR, *JUDGMENT AT NUREMBERG*); ANDY WILLIAMS (SINGER)**

December 11–18

THE TITAN
SAGITTARIUS III

The individuals born in this week who travel the Way of Discovery are likely to have a wonderful time, as they like nothing better than to boldly take up the challenge to forge into uncharted territory and lead others on a grand voyage of exploration. Yet there is a danger that their inspirations may fall a bit short of the mark due to their rather unrealistic attitude toward achievement. Working for long periods to achieve success will come rather hard for some of the more theatrical of this group, and their egos will have to be carefully controlled. Further, these seemingly dauntless people can alienate others through a rather high-handed attitude. Yet there is the possibility of some daring discoveries and crowning achievements along the way, for these visionary personalities will never long neglect their impulse to explore and expand.

CHALLENGE: **REMEMBERING THAT ALL DEPENDS ON A TEAM APPROACH**
FULFILLMENT: **SUCCEEDING IN IMPOSSIBLE CHALLENGES DESPITE ANY NAYSAYING BY OTHERS**
NOTABLES: **BILL BEUTEL (ANCHOR, WABC-TV); BOB GUCCIONE (PUBLISHER, *PENTHOUSE* MAGAZINE)**

KARMIC PATH
28

December 19–25
PROPHECY
SAGITTARIUS–CAPRICORN CUSP

Capable of shouldering great responsibilities and blessed with a fine sense of subtlety and insight, those born on the Cusp of Prophecy who journey along the Way of Discovery will doubtless have an interesting and often surprising passage. They have better-developed social skills than many of their fellow Sagittarius–Capricorns yet are unlikely to allow the opinions of others to interfere with the development of their sense of cause and purpose. Indeed, there may be much of the transcendental about these personalities' vision though the struggle to share that vision with others may be more problematic. Yet along with great insight, this path gifts them with great optimism and positivity. Thus, the call to new frontiers of achievement and discovery will find a dedicated, if somewhat calculated, response among them.

ALVIN AILEY
Choreographer/dancer

1/5/1931
Capricorn II

CHALLENGE: **JOINING WITH LIKE-MINDED OTHERS TO FULFILL THEIR VISION**
FULFILLMENT: **FOLLOWING THEIR SUPERB INTUITION TO THEIR GOAL**
NOTABLES: **ROBERT JOFFREY (BALLET DANCER/CHOREOGRAPHER); JAMES PRESCOTT JOULE (PHYSICIST)**

December 26–January 2
THE RULER
CAPRICORN I

The endowments of the Way of Discovery are likely to make the individuals born in this week a bit less ponderous than they might otherwise be, and that, along with increased enthusiasm, will greatly aid them. However reluctant they might be to the idea of far-flung explorations, once undertaken, in practice they can be extraordinarily competent. They are well suited to the higher challenges of this karmic path. If they can avoid the tendency to feel that they must do everything alone, being careful to cultivate an adequate professional and social support network, they will likely have little trouble seeking their fortune as they make their way along the road. Though some will resist the challenge to explore the unknown, preferring instead to leave well enough alone, others will rise to their inner need to expand their horizons and embrace the opportunities for learning, discovery, and real achievement that beckon.

CHALLENGE: **GRAPPLING WITH THEIR DESIRE TO EXPLORE THE WORLD, ON THE ONE HAND, AND THEIR NEED TO STAY HOME AND RULE THE ROOST, ON THE OTHER**
FULFILLMENT: **INJECTING ROOM FOR EXPLORATION INTO THEIR DAY-TO-DAY RESPONSIBILITIES**
NOTABLES: **CUBA GOODING, JR. (ACTOR; OSCAR FOR JERRY MAGUIRE); ODETTA (FOLKSINGER; GUITARIST)**

January 3–9
DETERMINATION
CAPRICORN II

Though the personalities born in this week who travel the Way of Discovery may be a curious mix of self-sacrifice and gutsy adventuresomeness, curiosity is nevertheless the key that will unlock the doors to their progress. These are the kind of people who have that rare brand of resourcefulness that will allow them to undertake seemingly impossible tasks simply because no one ever told them they couldn't be done or invent amazingly efficient tools or methods of doing things just because their ideas appear to be theoretically sound. Thus, they may experience considerable success along this road, as their often rather naive vision is fueled by pioneer courage, yet supported by the sophistication and insight of their Libra III origins. That, combined with Capricorn II's selfless dedication, resilience, and sheer hard work, are sure to be rewarded.

CHALLENGE: **DEFEATING THE FEAR THAT OTHERS WILL LAUGH AT THEM FOR THEIR NAÏVETÉ**
FULFILLMENT: **MOVING FEARLESSLY INTO UNCHARTED TERRITORY**
NOTABLES: **ROBERT DUVALL (ACTOR, THE APOSTLE); E. L. DOCTOROW (WRITER, RAGTIME)**

ALBERT SCHWEITZER
Missionary/physician, won
Nobel Peace Prize

1/14/1875
Capricorn III

January 10–16
DOMINANCE
CAPRICORN III

Those born in this week who travel the Way of Discovery may find it rather slow going until they come to terms with their need to dominate their immediate environment and employ their leadership abilities in such a way that they can inspire others to a cause or goal. Yet their self-confidence is likely to be greatly enhanced with this configuration and their curiosity much increased. Nevertheless, they have the kind of long-range diligence and natural dedication needed to make some tremendous and far-reaching discoveries, and if they can avoid their pronounced tendency to judge both themselves and others too harshly and learn to find joy in taking smaller steps, rather than great leaps, toward progress without losing sight of their objectives, their natural professionalism and protective attitude toward their associates will serve them well.

CHALLENGE: **RELEASING THEIR NEED FOR SECURITY IN ORDER TO EXPLORE UNCHARTED WATERS**
FULFILLMENT: **EMPLOYING THEIR DEVOTED NATURE IN SERVICE OF A HIGHER VISION**
NOTABLES: **LL COOL J (RAP STAR); CHAD LOWE (ACTOR)**

January 17–22
MYSTERY AND IMAGINATION
CAPRICORN–AQUARIUS CUSP

Though they will generate a certain amount of controversy with their grand ideas and imaginative concepts, those born on this cusp will have very little trouble drawing the support of others along the Way of Discovery. Generally speaking, they're just too exciting to ignore, and that quality alone is sure to draw others to them in the pursuit of the new and untried. Yet it is likely that most of their efforts at discovery will be made with an eye to improving the lot of humanity as a whole. Though they are marked by a tendency to extremes that can throw even their best-laid plans into chaos, if they take care not to scatter their energies in such a way that they chase after every idea that presents itself, they will realize amazing accomplishments through dedicated effort, honest expression, and inspired imagination of all that has yet to be learned.

D. W. GRIFFITH
Film director,
Birth of a Nation

1/22/1875
Capricorn–Aquarius Cusp

CHALLENGE: **QUELLING THEIR CHAOTIC ENERGIES IN THE INTEREST OF PEACEFUL COEXISTENCE WITH COWORKERS**
FULFILLMENT: **BETTERING THE LOT OF THE DISADVANTAGED THROUGH THEIR INVENTIONS OR DISCOVERIES**
NOTABLE: **DANIEL WEBSTER (U.S. SENATOR; ORATOR)**

January 23–30
GENIUS
AQUARIUS I

Those born in the Week of Genius and on the Way of Discovery may well take some really amazing strides, but they will have to take care that they learn to work closely with others in order to be at their most effective. Nevertheless, they are restless, curious, and inventive by nature and will have little trouble meeting the challenges of this karmic path. Though they have an attractive and compelling eccentricity, they run the risk of alienating others until they develop greater sensitivity and release their need to do everything alone. Yet there is real genius present with this position; if these unique individuals can focus their attention and power in concentrated effort, their accomplishments are likely to extend the boundaries of all that we previously believed possible. If they are careful to educate others along the way, their success, especially in the arts and sciences, is ensured.

CHALLENGE: **CULTIVATING THE PERSISTENCE AND PATIENCE NECESSARY TO MAKE BIG DISCOVERIES**
FULFILLMENT: **APPLYING THE FULL INTENSITY OF THEIR POWERFUL MINDS TO ANY PIONEERING EFFORT**
NOTABLES: **ED BURNS (DIRECTOR; ACTOR, *THE BROTHERS MCMULLEN*); SARAH MCLACHLAN (SINGER/SONGWRITER; FOUNDED LILITH FAIR)**

January 31–February 7
YOUTH AND EASE
AQUARIUS II

Rather too easygoing for their own good, those born in this week who travel the Way of Discovery are nevertheless gifted with a higher degree of curiosity and a greater sense of adventure than they might have otherwise. Yet many of their best inspirations and inclinations will never get full play until they release their need for approval, acceptance, and popularity and come to terms with their yearning to forge ahead. Though they will have no trouble finding others to take along on their voyage of discovery, it may take them a while to decide to make the trip. If they learn to focus on the tasks at hand and turn away from the limelight of others' opinions, they will find wonderful fulfillment and freedom.

BARBARA TUCHMAN
American historian;
winner of 2 Pulitzer prizes

1/30/1912
Aquarius I

CHALLENGE: **AVOIDING THE COMPLACENCY THAT MIGHT KEEP THEM FROM FORGING AHEAD**
FULFILLMENT: **EXPLORING THE INTERESTS OF THE YOUNGER GENERATION**
NOTABLES: **PAULY SHORE (COMEDIAN); ROBERTO ALOMAR (BASEBALL SECOND BASEMAN); EVA BRAUN (HITLER'S MISTRESS); LISA MARIE PRESLEY (ELVIS'S DAUGHTER)**

February 8–15
ACCEPTANCE
AQUARIUS III

The ability to turn inspiration and ideas into practical application and manifestation of knowledge will always be something of an issue for those born in this week who travel the Way of Discovery. They are not always the most open-minded of people, and may well back down from some of their own most intriguing challenges, since it is sometimes difficult for them to settle down long enough to focus their energies on a single quest and apply themselves to the business of doing what needs to be done in order for their inspirations to take shape in reality. They may also be chronically impatient or intolerant of others and will have to work on developing greater sensitivity if they are not to alienate those whose support they most require. Yet they will never be at a loss for inventive ideas, and, properly focused, their natural energies can lead them to some surprising discoveries.

CHALLENGE: **APPROACHING THEIR JOURNEY OF DISCOVERY WITH AN OPEN MIND**
FULFILLMENT: **SHARING THEIR WORK WITH A DEVOTED TEAM OF COLLEAGUES**
NOTABLES: **CHYNNA PHILLIPS (SINGER); JOHN RUSKIN (PRE-RAPHAELITE ARTIST AND CRITIC)**

February 16–22

SENSITIVITY
AQUARIUS–PISCES CUSP

The souls born in this week who find themselves on the Way of Discovery are likely to be gifted with considerably greater social skills than they might otherwise have had, and, aided by their great sensitivity and understanding, they may well be the kind of inventors and innovators who know what we need even before we need it. Real fighters for a cause or an idea, they may, however, become overly aggressive and will need to avoid overreaching themselves. Many of their ideas may well be considered too far-out or unrealistic to be taken seriously, a fact that may cause them no end of grief. Yet if they are careful to stay grounded and attuned to the valuable input and support that is available and avoid the dangers of both pessimism and isolation, they are sure to make an impact.

LAWRENCE DURRELL
Novelist/poet,
Alexandria Quartet

2/27/1912
Pisces I

CHALLENGE: **UNDERSTANDING THE REAL REASON FOR THEIR AMBITION: IS IT TO MAKE A DIFFERENCE OR TO PROVE THEMSELVES TO OTHERS?**
FULFILLMENT: **PURSUING THEIR IDEALISTIC VISIONS AND ABSTRACT CONCERNS**
NOTABLES: **PIERRE BOULLE (WRITER, *PLANET OF THE APES*); MURIEL HUMPHREY (WIFE OF HUBERT)**

February 23–March 2

SPIRIT
PISCES I

Likely to be gifted with a unique perspective, those born in the Week of Spirit who travel the Way of Discovery will have interesting and innovative perceptions on just what constitutes a frontier. Indeed, there may be something almost precognitive about their talents, and these personalities are likely to have their fingers on the pulse of the collective in sometimes astonishing ways. And there are few whose diplomatic talents can match those of an inspirational Pisces I. Though detail work will not be their forte, these people have a genuine desire to do good, and that, combined with their yearning to open the doors to discovery, can make for some breathtaking accomplishments on this life journey.

CHALLENGE: **TRUSTING THE RIGHT PEOPLE**
FULFILLMENT: **COUCHING THEIR DISCOVERIES WITHIN A BODY OF WORK INTENDED FOR MASS CONSUMPTION**
NOTABLE: **CLARA PETACCI (MUSSOLINI'S MISTRESS)**

March 3–10

THE LONER
PISCES II

Blessed with truly amazing powers of concentration and curiosity, the souls born in the Week of the Loner who travel the Way of Discovery can do much along this road, but they will have to work not to fail its higher challenge and to draw others into their voyage of discovery. This karmic path endows many of these individuals with a more positive attitude than they might otherwise have had, as well as better social skills. Yet the impulse to bond with others in order to work for a common goal may be lacking, and they may be characterized by a certain detachment that is hard to overcome. Yet they will show a truly astonishing depth and breadth of vision that will be hard to ignore. Though they may never be the warmest of people, they can be quite willing to give their society the benefit of their vision and will doubtless flourish.

MAURICE RAVEL
French impressionist
composer, *Bolero*

3/7/1875
Pisces II

CHALLENGE: **TEMPERING THEIR ALOOFNESS BY LEARNING A FEW PEOPLE SKILLS**
FULFILLMENT: **FINDING A WAY TO JOURNEY OR EXPLORE IN THE ARTS AND LETTERS**
NOTABLE: **PATSY KENSIT (ACTRESS)**

March 11–18

DANCERS AND DREAMERS
PISCES III

Though this configuration can make for some amazing accomplishments, the personalities born in this week who travel the Way of Discovery will have to learn to temper their enthusiasm with dedicated effort and their inspiration with a measure of realism before they can scale the heights of accomplishment that beckon. They may be so adept at bringing others to their cause, however, that they come to expect that their ideas will be brought to fruition not through concentrated effort on their own part but by work somehow done by other people. Yet they are more self-motivated than they might otherwise be, and Pisces sensitivity is here strengthened and illuminated by the fiery nature of Aries III. Though some on this path will struggle a bit with issues of humility, they can nevertheless leave a legacy of innovation, creation, and education that will be hard to ignore and even harder to forget.

CHALLENGE: **NOT SUCCUMBING TO SIMPLY DREAMING**
FULFILLMENT: **SATISFYING THEIR WANDERLUST THROUGH JOURNEYS AND EXPLORATIONS—WHETHER IN THE INNER OR OUTER WORLD**
NOTABLE: **PAT NIXON (FORMER FIRST LADY; RICHARD'S WIFE)**

The Way of Empowerment

LIBRA–SCORPIO CUSP TO ARIES–TAURUS CUSP
Drama and Criticism to Power

Those on this karmic path are here to learn how to unlock the sources of power within them. Blessed with charm, insight, and consciousness, those on the Way of Empowerment must learn to utilize their inner resources and believe in their own personal power. The individuals on this path can be described in one word: magnetic. They attract all manner of people and experiences to them. This capacity springs from the often unacknowledged potential of their power, which those born to this path will learn to harness. But first this journey often entails grappling with quite a bit of conflict, since it is the destiny of these individuals to encounter others who will attempt to assert their power or authority over them or suppress them in some fashion. It must be kept in mind that this is merely an outer reflection of an inner reality. Until those on this path begin to truly believe in themselves and their own strength, such lessons will continue to confront them, building their character until they do. Miraculously, once the individuals on this path step into fully owning their own power, such experiences and confrontations cease. The key is to set aside their self-judgment and criticism and learn how to love themselves.

The individuals on the Way of Empowerment are innately charismatic. They are both highly intellectual, possessing abundant taste and discernment, and passionate. Naturally and fundamentally attractive, they are also quite capable of utilizing their assets to manipulate others for their own reward. People are often magnetically drawn to them. Their love lives may be strewn with tempestuous romances and stormy scenes. Others might call them lucky since things seem to come their way magically. Their type of magnetism seems uniquely suited to tapping into one of the universal laws, that of attraction.

Ernest Holmes explored this in his seminal work *The Science of Mind*. And the mental power of these individuals is prodigious. However, as many good things as this capacity brings, it also comes with quite a bit of turmoil. Higher law states roughly that we attract what we are— or as within, so without. For example, if one burns with low-level anger, one finds others are often angry with one. Thus, until these men and women mature a bit and develop some emotional balance, they are apt to be confronted with quite a variety of sometimes distressing experiences before they reach a place of greater calm.

Those on the Way of Empowerment are highly discriminating and may even be a bit judgmental. But these insightful individuals are usually their own worst critics. So hard are they on themselves that often self-negation is second nature to them and they little realize how destructive this is for them. In large part, it is their self-critical attitudes that attract their more difficult experiences to them as mirrored in exterior circumstances, such that others may often be highly censuring of them. Early life,

---

CORE LESSON
Embracing themselves with self-love and self-respect

GOAL
To come to believe in their own strength and personal power

GIFTS
Charismatic, Formidable, Insightful

PITFALLS
Mercenary, Self-negating, Addictive

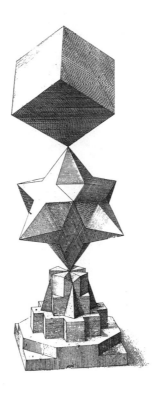

in particular, finds these men and women confronted with parents or teachers who are extremely exacting or stern or overly demanding. Problems with authority figures of all kinds plague them, not the least reason for which is their wilder side, with conflict the inevitable result. These individuals' karma appears to undergo a kind of trial by fire where others attempt to assert their power over them or manipulate them. This often reflects their weak ego structure and lack of feelings of self-worth. By being forced to confront such power plays over and over again, these individuals learn to stand up for themselves, thus slowly building their egos and healing some of their core issues—which often center around issues of self-worth.

These individuals must learn to love themselves more and criticize themselves less. Self-love is the core lesson for those on the Way of Empowerment. Approaching themselves with understanding, applying their great insight to seeing their own strengths, and accepting themselves will take them a long way toward self-empowerment. Once these men and women feel secure in who they are and what they have to offer, they will negotiate conflict better and will stand firm in their own defense. As they come to feel better about themselves inwardly, the outer world is bound to follow suit and the tensions of their lives—the conflicts, misunderstandings, and power struggles—will abate of their own accord.

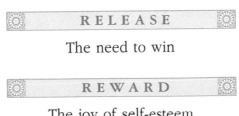

RELEASE

The need to win

REWARD

The joy of self-esteem

Once the individuals on this karmic path have become empowered through self-love and self-acceptance, they can begin to harness their enormous potential. As they learn to use their mental power as well as their magnetism, they will be able to invoke what they need to achieve their aims. These individuals can be found in many fields, but one thing is certain: when those on this path develop a greater degree of self-respect, there will be no stopping them. Moreover, engaging in as many battles as they surely will on this path, these people truly come to an understanding of how power works and, with a strong sense of self-worth in hand, will have the courage to go up against often daunting odds. Using a mixture of resolve and willpower, these individuals will inspire awe in even the most formidable of adversaries. Those on this path are apt to discover that when they combine their innate talents for persuasion and excellent sense of timing with their considerable charm, no one can resist them or fail to agree to their wishes and plans.

The most obvious danger for those on the Way of Empowerment is that their power urges or drives may run out of control. Unless governed by a strong moral imperative, those on this karmic path may inflict considerable pain on others in a misguided effort to secure a powerful position for themselves. Such overreaching inevitably leads to failure, leaving them angry and resentful, much to their own detriment and woe. En-

SUGGESTION

Remember the axiom "As within, so without." Try to analyze what your conflicts are telling you. Surrender to the source of all power. Know that in order to love others, one must first love oneself.

gaging in any kind of power mongering creates the risk of self-undoing, usually through a combination of hubris, overconfidence, and downright self-destructiveness. In addition, indulgence in sensuous pleasures is certainly a weakness for these people and can only lead to trouble. Thus, those on the Way of Empowerment, must develop vigilant self control, usually through mental reprogramming combined with adherence to a strict code of ethics.

Although it is within the arena of relationships—more specifically, one-on-one encounters—that many of the challenges of this karmic path take place, the area in which those on this path truly engage in its work is within their own psyches. Relationships are extremely important, because others will always act as a mirror for these individuals. Observing others and then reflecting on themselves is a large part of this process. The power these individuals achieve is never over others, but merely within themselves. Thus, many of their greatest life lessons and victories are psychological. Overcoming negative thinking or patterns, stilling the critical voice of an internalized parental figure, and recovering from addiction are some of the types of battles these individuals may be forced to wage. Some may also have to grapple with or overcome physical or mental handicaps. Winning through self-control results in greater emotional stability, inner peace, and self-esteem.

As those on this karmic path learn to love themselves better and give themselves a bit more credit, they will discover that their attitudes toward their fellows become similarly loving. An important realization that comes to many on this path is that giving up power can also be a powerful action, particularly when the desire to control others or to win is released and a path of kindness adopted. In recognizing the enormous power of love, those on the Way of Empowerment can temper their aggression and plug into universal values, which, after all, come from the ultimate power source—the divine. Those with religious values may choose to put their power into the service of God.

The choice of a partner is particularly crucial for these individuals. Sometimes it is through loving another that they learn to love themselves. If love is equated with sexual excitement, control, and competition, those on this karmic path can expect serious setbacks in their ability to relate. On the other hand, learning to share, empathize, listen, cooperate, and express kindness, consideration, and affection will tend to instill deeply human values that can guide their more ambitious drives in other areas of life. In this way, family, friendships, and married life can all function as a good moral proving ground for professional and career endeavors. What is best for those on the Way of Empowerment is a life in which a healthy balance can be maintained between maintaining a strong ego through active assertion and guiding it with equally powerful moral and loving attitudes.

For this karmic path, one can think of courageous souls everywhere who fight against oppression. At some point one member of an oppressed minority, strongly believing in his self-worth and human rights, refuses to bow to the authority of those in power. Some of the most effective instances of this have been when the oppressed refuse even to engage in battle with their adversaries. Mahatma Ghandi, Nelson Mandela, and even Rosa Parks are icons for this karmic path.

BALANCE POINT

Self-assertion and
Self-control

CRYSTALS AND GEMSTONES

Stibnite guides the individual to see how the outer world is a reflection of inner reality. This knowledge results in one taking responsibility to discipline the workings of the mind.

NOTABLES ON THIS KARMIC PATH

Born in the public eye and often criticized in the media, **Prince Charles,** heir apparent to the throne of England and Prince of Wales, is no stranger to the issue of personal power. His career and even marriage laid out for him, his ability to make his own life choices have been few. But like many on the Way of Em-

PRINCE CHARLES

powerment, he has maintained a certain dignity and has developed a kind of charismatic appeal while, doubtless, coming to understand how power works. Those born on this path are particularly prone to be hard on themselves. However, Charles has carved out a role for himself by embracing worthy causes including the Princes' Trust. Though he may have struggled with his destiny, he has succeeded in empowering himself and earning the respect of many.

With numerous hit singles and albums to her credit, singer **Natalie Cole** has come a long way from the time when she was known only as Nat King Cole's daughter. By believing in herself, she has built a solid, long-lasting career. Like many on this

NATALIE COLE

path, Cole has battled substance abuse but found the inner power to overcome her addictions. Her charm and

persuasiveness, as well as her timing and contemporary sensibility, have all helped her to reach great heights in the music world. Natalie's success in dealing with her father's legacy was underscored when she re-recorded Nat's hit "Unforgettable" as a posthumous duet with him.

Czech-born socialite **Ivana Trump** has made her mark not only with her jewelry and clothing lines but also through her personal appearances. Already a successful model and athlete when she met real estate mogul Donald Trump, she quickly rose to the executive ranks of his empire. After undergoing a messy

IVANA TRUMP

and public divorce from "The Donald," Ivana quickly moved on to new levels of personal success. As a woman who has empowered herself in the most dramatic manner, she shares practical advice in her book *The Best Is Yet to Come: Coping With Divorce and Enjoying Life Again.*

Other Notables: Toni Braxton, Lorraine Hansbury, Grace Mirabella, Mary Pickford, Jasper Johns, "Wild Bill" Hickok, Charles Augustus Lindbergh, Ross Perot, George Steinbrenner, Neil Armstrong, Deion Sanders, Frank Gifford, Princess Margaret, Harry Connick, Jr., Will Rogers, Jr., Mahalia Jackson, Julia Roberts, Martin Luther, Samuel L. Jackson, Barbara Mandrell, Donna Summer, George Foreman, Andy Kaufman, Sir William Golding

BIRTHDAYS ON KARMIC PATH 29

January 11, 1893–June 1, 1893 | August 25, 1911–January 12, 1912

April 5, 1930–August 24, 1930 | November 14, 1948–April 4, 1949 | June 27, 1967–November 14, 1967

February 5, 1986–June 26, 1986 | September 16, 2004–February 4, 2005

KARMIC PATH
29

March 19–24

REBIRTH
PISCES–ARIES CUSP

Though not as apt to being misunderstood or misinterpreted as some Pisces–Arians, those born in this week who find themselves on the Way of Empowerment will have to avoid a tendency to an excess of aggression or impatience when it comes to solving their own problems or those of the world. Yet they will be gifted with more insight into their own emotions than they might otherwise have had. Both dynamic and charismatic, they may find that things come rather easily, yet they will save themselves and their loved ones an enormous amount of struggle if they acquaint themselves with the fact that considerable sensitivity and a well-disguised soulful and intuitive side are the keys to their advancement along this road.

MARY PICKFORD
Actress, "America's Sweetheart"; cofounder of United Artists

4/9/1893
Aries II

CHALLENGE: **REALIZING THAT WINNING THE FIGHT DOESN'T MEAN THEY HAVE WON THE BATTLE**
FULFILLMENT: **EMBRACING THEIR OWN SENSITIVE SIDE**
NOTABLE: **RIC OCASEK (LEAD SINGER OF THE CARS)**

March 25–April 2

THE CHILD
ARIES I

Though many of those born in this week who navigate the promise and challenge of the Way of Empowerment may find it difficult to stop searching for the causes of their rather volatile experiences, there are others who will take advantage of the opportunities inherent in this configuration and learn to appreciate themselves for who they really are. In a word, establishing a solid core identity may be difficult for many of this group, as these highly spontaneous people are likely to be buffeted about by others' opinions of them. Yet they will show an overriding need to be taken more seriously; as soon they make a better connection between their own attitudes toward themselves and others' attitudes toward them, they will rise to both the challenge of and the opportunity for self-development.

CHALLENGE: **UNDERGOING SOME FORM OF THERAPY TO GRAPPLE WITH NEGATIVE PATTERNS LEFT OVER FROM CHILDHOOD**
FULFILLMENT: **FREEING THEMSELVES FROM THE PAST IN ORDER TO EMBRACE THE BEAUTY OF THE PRESENT**
NOTABLE: **RAY MAGLIOZZI (RADIO PERFORMER)**

April 3–10

THE STAR
ARIES II

The need to be at center stage can hamper the development of those born in this week until they come to terms with the fact that this life journey requires them to understand that they *are* the center—at least of their own spiritual lives. Likely to be extremely motivated to succeed, this journey will also require these individuals to divest themselves of their more sophisticated or worldly perspectives and enrich their experience through greater self-knowledge and understanding. Yet if they can avoid the dangers of excessiveness, irritability, and self-indulgence, and instead embrace the inner awareness that beckons, all will go well, although rather tempestuously, for them.

J. P. MORGAN
Financier; art collector; philanthropist

4/17/1837
Aries III

CHALLENGE: **BELIEVING IN THEIR OWN POWER ABSENT REINFORCEMENT FROM OTHERS**
FULFILLMENT: **INVOKING THEIR ABILITY TO CREATE GOOD FOR THEMSELVES**
NOTABLES: **IRENE CASTLE (ENGLISH CHAMPION BALLROOM DANCER); LESLIE HOWARD (ACTOR); ALGERNON SWINBURNE (POET; CRITIC)**

April 11–18

THE PIONEER
ARIES III

The pioneering personalities born in this week who travel this karmic path are likely to go far, especially when they turn their visionary talents inward in a search for greater understanding and empowerment. Though much more strongly personal than some of their fellow Aries III's, they will have to avoid a propensity to lose themselves in worldly or romantic distractions in order to realize the higher calling of this karmic path. There may be a pronounced temptation to assert authority over others, while a number of the setbacks they encounter are designed to set them on a more introspective course. If they can rise to the challenge of learning to love themselves more and accept even disappointment as part of their process, their accomplishments and generosity toward others will be well rewarded.

CHALLENGE: **UNDERSTANDING WHAT THEIR MANY CONFRONTATIONS ARE MEANT TO TEACH THEM**
FULFILLMENT: **DISCOVERING THEIR OWN STRENGTH AND USING IT TO STAND UP FOR OTHERS**
NOTABLES: **SIR JAMES ROSS (LOCATED MAGNETIC NORTH POLE); DEAN ACHESON (AMERICAN DIPLOMAT; LAWYER); TINY TIM (SINGER; ENTERTAINER)**

April 19–24
POWER
ARIES–TAURUS CUSP

Likely to be rather lavish and often remarkably self-indulgent, those born in this week who travel the Way of Empowerment may nevertheless expect to achieve great things. It is likely that these people will hold such sway over others, and things will come so easily to them, that going within in search of real self-esteem and understanding may present something of a last frontier. Well established, worldly, and wise, they may find their search for meaning and affirmation in earthly power, material goods, or authority over others to be a rather cumbersome set of responsibilities until they cultivate a matching strength of character. Until that time, they would do well to remember that tempestuous romances, lavish spending, and the like are only poor substitutes for inner peace, true self-awareness, and the comfort that comes from self-acceptance.

JOHN BROWN
U.S. slavery abolitionist

5/9/1800
Taurus II

CHALLENGE: **TAKING CARE NOT TO AROUSE ANTAGONISM IN OTHERS**

FULFILLMENT: **DISCOVERING THE ULTIMATE POWER: LOVE**

NOTABLES: **HAROLD LLOYD (ACTOR; "KING OF DAREDEVIL COMEDY"); SILVANA MANGANO (ITALIAN ACTRESS, *DEATH IN VENICE*)**

April 25–May 2
MANIFESTATION
TAURUS I

Those born in the Week of Manifestation who travel the Way of Empowerment can realize true fulfillment, providing they do not succumb to the dangers of overindulgence and materialism along the way. Blessed with a clear inner perspective, a kind of natural calm, and a keen insight that few can match, they will nevertheless have to shore up their own egos a bit and develop greater self-confidence before they can realize the kind of progress they dream about. Stubbornness and some rather bad tempers will show up here, however, and they will have to cultivate inner security regardless of their external circumstances. Yet if they understand that true empowerment is a process, rather than a single achievement or moment of epiphany, they can expect tremendous satisfaction.

CHALLENGE: **WEANING THEMSELVES FROM THEIR TENDENCY TO BE HIGHLY SELF-CRITICAL**

FULFILLMENT: **DISCOVERING THEIR POWER TO MAKE THINGS HAPPEN**

NOTABLES: **JAMES BAKER (U.S. SECRETARY OF STATE); ANITA LOOS (WRITER/PLAYWRIGHT, *GENTLEMEN PREFER BLONDES*)**

May 3–10
THE TEACHER
TAURUS II

The charismatic, gifted individuals born in this week who travel the Way of Empowerment will go through a number of changes as they make their way along the road. It is likely that they will encounter many of their life's lessons in the area of personal relationships, as they have a strong propensity for mentor-type encounters at both ends of the spectrum. Yet these relationships will always mirror some inner aspect of themselves that bears further analysis and examination. Nevertheless, if they can avoid the danger of hypercriticism of both themselves and others, and embrace the opportunities for the kind of inner freedom that comes with cultivation of character, all will go well for them.

JASPER JOHNS
Abstract expressionist painter

5/15/1930
Taurus III

CHALLENGE: **STILLING THE NEGATIVE AND CRITICAL VOICES OF AUTHORITY FIGURES, BOTH PAST AND PRESENT**

FULFILLMENT: **INVOKING THEIR STRONG SENSE OF SELF IN THEIR FIGHT AGAINST INJUSTICE**

May 11–18
THE NATURAL
TAURUS III

Rebellion and frustration may characterize the journey of those born in the Week of the Natural who travel the Way of Empowerment, and they may expend quite a bit of energy in trying to throw off the shackles of what they believe are external constraints before they take the first steps toward greater self-acceptance. Too, many on this path will ignore the challenge to embrace their own strengths and will instead immerse themselves in any number of material pursuits and achievements as they attempt to assuage their inner insecurities. Yet they will be gifted with a greater degree of worldly savvy and understanding than they might otherwise have had, and if they are careful to take the lessons of life's battles to heart as a means of self-realization, they can take great strides along this karmic path.

CHALLENGE: **COMING TO BELIEVE IN THEIR OWN WORTH**

FULFILLMENT: **USING THEIR PERSONAL MAGNETISM TO ATTRACT WHAT THEY NEED**

May 19–24
ENERGY
TAURUS–GEMINI CUSP

Likely to be somewhat resistant to making the kind of inner journey called for by the Way of Empowerment, Taurus–Geminis can nevertheless expect a measure of success, since they are not as inclined to self-criticism or a lack of confidence in their own abilities as some on this road. Certain to be dazzling and often quite brilliant, they may nevertheless scatter their energies in excess, displays of temperament, or compulsive behaviors. A wise choice of partner can do much to ease this road, and the right associates will not only serve to ground their often overwhelming energies but be as an important mirror for their development. Once they stop overreaching and learn the value of some necessary limitations (including and most especially their own), they can expect happiness and the kind of contentment that is neither too self-satisfied nor maniacally chasing rainbows.

LORRAINE HANSBURY
Writer, *A Raisin in the Sun*

5/19/1930
Taurus–Gemini Cusp

CHALLENGE: **LEARNING HOW TO LOVE THEMSELVES AND OTHERS TO BOOT**

FULFILLMENT: **APPLYING THEIR UNIQUE BLEND OF BRAIN-POWER AND CHARISMA TO ACHIEVING THEIR AIMS**

NOTABLE: **MARISOL (SCULPTOR/PAINTER, "WOMAN AND DOG")**

May 25–June 2
FREEDOM
GEMINI I

Those born in the Week of Freedom who find themselves on the Way of Empowerment are likely to experience quite a bit of personal transformation and success, providing they don't allow their more abrasive tendencies to get out of hand and keep a weather eye on some of their more autocratic or even tyrannical inclinations. Giving free rein to their aggressiveness may rob them of a necessary perspective on their own personalities. Likely to be the kind of individuals who will "talk you to death" to get their points across, Gemini I's are rather good at getting their way when traveling this road. Yet they will suffer from a tendency to question themselves as much as they question everyone around them and will have to learn to cultivate more calm and combat their distractibility in order to make a successful journey toward self-acceptance and greater inner security.

CHALLENGE: **TEMPERING THEIR TENDENCY TO ARGUMENTA-TIVENESS**

FULFILLMENT: **BELIEVING IN THEMSELVES AND THEIR IDEAS**

NOTABLES: **"WILD BILL" HICKOK (PIONEER; LAW ENFORCER); CLINT EASTWOOD (ACTOR/DIRECTOR, *DIRTY HARRY*); WASHINGTON ROEBLING (ENGINEER; CHIEF ON BROOKLYN BRIDGE)**

June 3–10
NEW LANGUAGE
GEMINI II

For those born in the Week of New Language who travel the Way of Empowerment, the need to be accepted by others can at times override the need to cultivate a stronger and more peaceful sense of self. In fact, learning to think before they speak can be paramount to their higher development, as many of these individuals will be endowed with such overwhelming communicative talents that they do far more talking than listening and far more complaining than accepting. Yet their innate creative capacity will serve them especially well on this road, and if they learn to go within to communicate with the source of their inspiration in activities such as writing, music, meditation, and the like, they will be rewarded with rare insight, a fine sense of personal timing, and an enhanced ability to achieve their heart's desires, unencumbered by uncertainty or self-doubt.

MARY-KATE AND ASHLEY OLSEN
Twin actresses, *Full House*

6/13/1986
Gemini III

CHALLENGE: **UNDERSTANDING THE SOURCE OF THEIR NEED FOR ACCEPTANCE**

FULFILLMENT: **FEELING THAT THEY ARE THE MASTERS OF THEIR OWN DESTINIES**

NOTABLE: **GRACE MIRABELLA (FASHION EDITOR)**

June 11–18
THE SEEKER
GEMINI III

Those born in the Week of the Seeker may not be especially interested in going within under any circumstances, least of all digging up the bones of old issues that may hold them back from greater self-acceptance. Restlessness may prove their greatest problem, yet as time goes on, they may well find themselves in search of greater inner peace and self-satisfaction. Generally speaking, these souls can easily become accustomed to the turmoil associated with this configuration without necessarily coming to terms with the fact that it's all in the eye of the beholder. They may also be resistant to the challenge of using their own power fully, since power can carry too much responsibility with it. Yet if they can rise to the challenge of accepting their infinite potential and acknowledge their own strengths, they will find the adventure and truth that beckons, along with a high degree of personal fulfillment.

CHALLENGE: **BEING RESPONSIBLE FOR THEMSELVES**

FULFILLMENT: **SEEKING THE SOURCE OF THE POWER THAT RESIDES WITHIN**

June 19–24
MAGIC
GEMINI–CANCER CUSP

Somewhat likely to be seduced by the power they will doubtless wield over others, those born on the Cusp of Magic who travel the Way of Empowerment can nevertheless expect great enlightenment. Two dangers present themselves here, the first being that these extraordinarily magnetic people will seek their validation from others through a series of stormy, passionate, and tempestuous relationships, the second that they will become caught up in other kinds of sensual excess in lieu of developing their inner sense of worth. Either way, these individuals may get caught up in a rather vicious circle where disappointments lead to further self-criticism and further self-criticism impels them to seek disappointment on an unconscious level. Yet they do possess the inclination to preserve a private world; if they can take that impulse and nurture their privacy in an effort to come to peace within themselves, taking up and using their own genuine power will prove no problem at all.

ROSS PEROT
Businessman; politician, presidential candidate for independent party ticket
———
6/27/1930
Cancer I

CHALLENGE: **NOT SEEKING SELF-VALIDATION IN OTHERS**
FULFILLMENT: **FINDING THE POWER OF UNCONDITIONAL LOVE IN THEMSELVES**

June 25–July 2
THE EMPATH
CANCER I

Inclined to lead rather melodramatic personal lives, those born in the Week of the Empath who negotiate the demands and challenges of the Way of Empowerment can realize great accomplishment and development, providing they learn to distinguish between themselves and others. Over time, this life journey will reveal much about themselves to themselves, though they may have to go through no small amount of sifting and winnowing to come to a place of peace and self-acceptance. Highly materialistic, these souls may amass considerable wealth and possessions before they find that true satisfaction lies elsewhere; some may also get caught up in excessively sensual or addictive behaviors. Yet if they get in touch with the fact that life is a casting off of the illusionary in a quest for the real and keep both their sensitivity and their more aggressive side under control, all will go smoothly.

CHALLENGE: **STRENGTHENING THEIR BOUNDARIES AND THEIR EGOS THROUGH NUMEROUS CONFRONTATIONS**
FULFILLMENT: **SPENDING SOME TIME IN RETREAT TO MARSHAL THEIR PERSONAL POWER**

July 3–10
THE UNCONVENTIONAL
CANCER II

Cancer II's who find themselves on the Way of Empowerment are likely to experience quite a few shake-ups along the road; nevertheless, they are promised considerable satisfaction. Much more magnetic and compelling than some Cancer II's, they will doubtless play out many of the life lessons of this karmic path through their attraction to the unusual, the bizarre, and the extraordinary. Yet they will come to accept those same qualities within themselves as they progress along this path, for these individuals may emerge from rather quiet and secure backgrounds into adult lives of amazing adventure and impact. Yet in the end, such transformations will be the result of imaginative, creative, and unusual people having accepted themselves in such a way that they need no one's permission to be who they really are.

GEORGE STEINBRENNER
Owner of the NY Yankees; controversial businessman
———
7/4/1930
Cancer II

CHALLENGE: **ACCEPTING THE IDEA THAT THERE IS A MORE SPIRITUAL PURPOSE TO THEIR CONFRONTATIONS: INNER GROWTH**
FULFILLMENT: **INDULGING IN THEIR ECCENTRICITY**

July 11–18
THE PERSUADER
CANCER III

Enterprising and often excessive, the souls born in this week who find themselves on the Way of Empowerment must take care that their desire for power does not express itself in worldly terms at the expense of their higher spiritual development and understanding. These personalities can in fact be so good at getting what they want that they may neglect the greater inner tasks required by this karmic path. Extremely observant, they are bound to discover and embrace their own strengths and weaknesses. Too, their propensity to invest themselves in any number of self-help programs or educational classes will bear fruit on this karmic path in the form of a strong sense of their own power. Still, they have the capacity for considerable self-control along with their ability to manage others, and if they learn to release their impulses toward overanalysis and hypercriticism in the interest of greater self-acceptance and enjoyment of life, their efforts are sure to be rewarded.

CHALLENGE: **TEMPERING THEIR DIRECTNESS WITH A DOSE OF CHARM**
FULFILLMENT: **DISCOVERING THEIR TALENTS AS THEY FULFILL THEIR AMBITIONS**

July 19–25

OSCILLATION
CANCER–LEO CUSP

Cancer–Leos' emotional extremes and rather manic aspect may interfere with the higher challenge of the Way of Empowerment, yet if they answer the soul's call to greater self-acceptance and tolerance, their journey is likely to be especially enlightening. It may take some time for these dramatic and rather formidable personalities to understand that their outer experience is but a reflection of their own inner attitudes and that the upsets, setbacks, and even triumphs of this road all have their origins in their own consciousness. Too, they may become overly preoccupied with the search for understanding and analyze or reanalyze their problems to such an extent that they lose sight of the bigger picture and larger objective. Yet if they embrace even their conflicts as opportunities for growth and increased understanding, the road to selfhood may be rocky, but it will never be dull.

CHALLENGE: **KNOWING ENOUGH NOT TO TRY TO FIND WHO THEY ARE THROUGH A SERIES OF ROMANTIC MISADVENTURES WITH OTHERS**

FULFILLMENT: **INTEGRATING THEIR ENERGIES AND EMBRACING THEIR STRENGTHS**

NOTABLES: **MATT LeBLANC (ACTOR, *FRIENDS*); CHUCK DALY (LEGENDARY BASKETBALL COACH)**

NEIL ARMSTRONG
Astronaut, 1st man on the moon

8/5/1930
Leo II

July 26–August 2

AUTHORITY
LEO I

Those born in the Week of Authority who travel the Way of Empowerment may well get considerably more than they bargained for in terms of worldly position, responsibility, and personal baggage. Thus, they will have to work not to be seduced by their own ability to reign with the monarch's sense of dignity and supremacy or otherwise to confuse authority with autocracy. Alternatively, the more private of these personalities may get caught up in personal dramatics and endless self-analysis and cling to a secret cynicism that can only feed their feelings of unworthiness. Too, they have a pronounced tendency to competitiveness and a need to assert themselves that may be frustrated until they come to understand the truth of philosopher Pierre Lecomte du Nouy's insight when he wrote, "Action follows conviction, not knowledge."

CHALLENGE: **NOT JUDGING OTHERS TOO HARSHLY**

FULFILLMENT: **TAPPING INTO THEIR MAGNETIC AND CREATIVE CAPACITIES**

NOTABLE: **GEOFFREY HOLDER (DANCER/CHOREOGRAPHER; PAINTER)**

August 3–10

BALANCED STRENGTH
LEO II

It is simply not in the nature of those born in the Week of Balanced Strength to back down from challenges, even if those challenges involve developing self-love and acceptance. Thus they are likely to do quite well on the Way of Empowerment, providing they avoid the tendency to negate themselves and their own achievements and remain open to the possibility of change. Change is the key word here, for once Leo II's have formed a particular set of beliefs, they can cling quite stubbornly to even the most negative or unproductive notions about themselves and what is possible. Yet their considerable insight and intuitive capacity are much enhanced on this karmic path; if they can employ those gifts in such a way that they view themselves in terms of their exceptional potential, rather than their faults and failings, they can expect extraordinary reward and affirmation from the world at large.

CHALLENGE: **WEEDING OUT THE ASSOCIATES AND INTIMATES WHO DISHONOR OR DISRESPECT THEM**

FULFILLMENT: **STANDING FIRM IN THEIR OWN DEFENSE**

NOTABLES: **HERBERT HOOVER (31ST U.S. PRESIDENT); RIDDICK BOWE (HEAVYWEIGHT BOXER); DEION SANDERS (FOOTBALL AND BASEBALL PLAYER)**

FRANK GIFFORD
Football great, Giants (seen here with wife Kathie Lee)

8/16/1930
Leo III

August 11–18

LEADERSHIP
LEO III

Turning their charismatic energy inward in an effort to develop self-love and appreciation will come a bit easier for Leo III's than for some others on this karmic path, as they will doubtless make the connection between gaining the respect of others and developing self-respect somewhat earlier than most. Thus they can expect considerable fulfillment on this life journey, providing they don't expend their energies in melodrama or set unrealistic goals for either themselves or others. Though they will doubtless display some rather aggressive or overly authoritarian attitudes, they are quite able to master the demons of self-doubt and self-criticism. All in all, this is a rather fortunate configuration, and their passage is likely to be marked by personal power, contentment, and an unusual amount of worldly achievement as well.

CHALLENGE: **OVERCOMING MEMORIES OF SUFFERING AT THE HANDS OF EARLY OPPRESSORS**

FULFILLMENT: **HAVING CULTIVATED SELF-WORTH, SHARING THE GLOW OF THEIR SELF-LOVE WITH OTHERS**

NOTABLES: **DON HO (SINGER, "TINY BUBBLES"); ROBERT CULP (ACTOR, *I SPY*); TED HUGHES (POET; MARRIED SYLVIA PLATH); LUCY STONE (FEMINIST)**

August 19–25

EXPOSURE
LEO–VIRGO CUSP

The highly observant and often rather calculating souls born on this cusp who travel the Way of Empowerment may experience a certain amount of tumult on this karmic path, yet they can nevertheless expect great success. Earthy and often quite sensual, some with this configuration may lose themselves in sexual peccadilloes, sensual overindulgence, and even the odd addiction, to the detriment of their higher development. Too, they will face the challenge of having some of their personal faults and failings exposed, either to themselves or to others. Yet as uncomfortable as such experiences may be, they are only a manifestation of their inner yearning for greater personal power and a sense of inner peace. If they come to accept, first of all, that even the most beautiful gardens must be weeded from time to time and even the best minds freed from outworn notions of self, their passage will be considerably eased and their way to success illuminated.

PRINCESS MARGARET
Sister of
Queen Elizabeth II

8/21/1930
Leo–Virgo Cusp

CHALLENGE: **PUTTING THEIR OUTSTANDING ABILITY TO JUDGE OTHERS' CHARACTER TO AN HONEST ASSESSMENT OF THEMSELVES**

FULFILLMENT: **FEELING EMPOWERED ENOUGH TO REVEAL THEMSELVES TO OTHERS**

NOTABLE: **LOLA MONTEZ (DANCER)**

August 26–September 2

SYSTEM BUILDERS
VIRGO I

Often motivated by unconscious drives and/or inexplicable behaviors, those born in this week may experience quite a few personal struggles until they get in touch with those qualities that hold them back from greater self-love and self-acceptance. The impulse to order the world and to impose structures and systems on those around them may arise from a rather chaotic inner life, and while their impulse to seek power is quite strong, it may manifest itself not outwardly but in an number of compulsive disorders or a rather neurotic attention to life's little melodramas. In relationships, those with this configuration may be all but exhausted by their choice of difficult partners. Still, once they learn to relax their standards for their own and others' behavior and cultivate greater personal security, they can attain a great psychological victory and open themselves to the opportunities for happiness that await them.

CHALLENGE: **BEING FAR LESS SELF-CRITICAL AND FAR MORE SELF-EMBRACING**

FULFILLMENT: **STANDING UP FOR THEMSELVES**

September 3–10

THE ENIGMA
VIRGO II

Though a sense of personal security and self-love will be rather hard won for those born in the Week of the Enigma, they can nevertheless take great strides along this karmic path. Perhaps the principal danger of this configuration is that these personalities may hesitate to enlist others in their quest for greater understanding of their own energies and that it will thus take them a bit longer than might really be necessary to come to terms with, and then to release, the problems that hold them back from a higher level of self-realization. Yet they are gifted with both great discernment and a thoughtful side that will stand them in good stead, as they are likely to choose their battles carefully and to educate themselves thoroughly in the workings of power before they attempt to wield it themselves.

CHALLENGE: **LOWERING THE HIGH STANDARDS THEY SET FOR THEMSELVES**

FULFILLMENT: **COMING TO A FIRM AND USEFUL UNDERSTANDING OF THE WORKINGS OF POWER**

NOTABLE: **EUELL GIBBONS (NATURALIST)**

September 11–18

THE LITERALIST
VIRGO III

Though their sense of inner oppression and frustration may have to grow great indeed before these practical souls attempt the journey of self-understanding and enlightenment required by this karmic path, they can nevertheless accomplish much on this road. Self-criticism can be a real personal demon, and Virgo III's will doubtless hold themselves to rather exacting standards before they allow themselves to really blossom. Yet they have a knack for discerning the truth and a dislike of pretension that will enable them to face their real problems as they encounter them. Keeping a sense of humor and avoiding those who push their emotional buttons will prove especially useful to these sometimes excitable people. But if they understand that their desire for harmony in their relationships is intimately linked to the desire to avoid internal conflict, all will progress nicely.

BILL MONROE
Country/bluegrass singer,
mandolin player

9/13/1911
Virgo III

CHALLENGE: **NOT ALLOWING THEIR POWER URGES TO RUN OUT OF CONTROL**

FULFILLMENT: **DOING SOMETHING FOR THE LOVE OF IT RATHER THAN TO SHORE UP THEIR SENSE OF SELF-WORTH**

NOTABLE: **HARRY CONNICK, JR. (JAZZ/POP MUSICIAN/SINGER/PIANIST; ACTOR)**

September 19–24

BEAUTY
VIRGO–LIBRA CUSP

Attraction to higher ideals is very much in keeping with the nature of those born to this karmic path, and the Way of Empowerment will provide no small number of opportunities for Virgo–Libras to explore their needs in greater depth. Yet their yearning for power may manifest itself in a fascination with its trappings rather than its substance until they cultivate the depth of self-awareness and self-understanding required by this karmic path. An excess of sensuality is rather common with this configuration, as Virgo–Libras are prone to seeking out any number of back doors and escape hatches before they confront the causes of their lack of fulfillment. Still, their free-spirited ways will aid them greatly in their quest for self-love and self-acceptance. If they do not fail the higher challenge of this karmic path and allow increased awareness to open the doors to power and freedom, all will go brilliantly for them.

CHALLENGE: **DEVELOPING THE ABILITY TO FIGHT FAIRLY**
FULFILLMENT: **FINDING OUT THAT THEY ARE MORE THAN ABLE TO STAND UP FOR THEMSELVES**

BONNIE PARKER
One half of the infamous
criminal team of
Bonnie and Clyde

10/1/1911
Libra I

September 25–October 2

THE PERFECTIONIST
LIBRA I

Those born in the Week of the Perfectionist who travel the Way of Empowerment are among those who will experience the greatest struggles on this karmic path yet at the same time have the potential to realize the greatest rewards. Yet identifying the cause of and cure for their rather difficult and exacting approach to themselves and the rest of the world will prove especially important to their success. Too often the underlying reason for their lack of self-worth is a rather strained relationship with an authority figure. Such experiences will have to be thoroughly analyzed and released before these individuals can make the progress toward self-empowerment that is promised by this karmic path. Nevertheless, they have the potential for a rare kind of personal triumph and an even rarer kind of worldly achievement, as long as they educate themselves to the difference between real power and mere control.

CHALLENGE: **NOT ITEMIZING EVERYTHING THAT'S WRONG WITH THEM**
FULFILLMENT: **OPERATING FROM THEIR OWN SENSE OF JUSTICE AND ETHICS**

October 3–10

SOCIETY
LIBRA II

Once they make the necessary journey within in order to address their underlying feelings of inadequacy, Libra II's can well take great strides along this karmic path. Until they do, however, they may expend too much energy on activities such as social climbing and vying for popularity. Not especially good at knowing what's really best for them, some of their more deeply personal problems may go untreated; others may find themselves more or less at the mercy of external turmoil without gaining a clear understanding of who they are and why they're here. Internal pressure can lead them to seek avenues of escape through excess sensuality and a concurrent tendency to deny or dull their own sense of ambition. Too, these personalities may become rather lazy or overly complacent when it comes to taking their capacity for power and using it to free others from oppression and injustice. Yet if they move beyond mere self-acceptance and into the realm of the universal, they can find both personal peace and worldly renown.

CHALLENGE: **NOT SACRIFICING THEIR SELF-ESTEEM TO THEIR NEED TO WIN**
FULFILLMENT: **TAKING BETTER CARE OF THEMSELVES**

TONI BRAXTON
R&B singer

10/7/1967
Libra II

October 11–18

THEATER
LIBRA III

Leaving worldly success and admiration behind to take a voyage of self-discovery may come as a result of experience with overreaching, overconfidence, or overly aggressive attitudes that can show up in those born in this week who travel the Way of Empowerment. Indeed, many of them will disguise their feelings of insecurity with chronic rebellion, overindulgence, and hubris, resulting in some fairly spectacular mistakes. And though they have an impulse to fool all the people all the time, they will have to withdraw from their struggles and stop trying to kid themselves if they are to meet the higher challenge of this karmic path. Developing a better sense of who they are will lead them to a greater understanding and empathy for others. Yet once acceptance is achieved and self-love manifested in greater interest in and understanding of their fellows, few are more adept at wielding power with grace, modesty, and wisdom.

CHALLENGE: **RECOGNIZING HOW TRULY FOND THEY ARE OF THE POWER STRUGGLES AND POLITICS IN THEIR LIVES**
FULFILLMENT: **BROADENING THEIR SENSE OF PERSONAL POWER BY RELATING TO OTHERS ON A FEELING LEVEL**

October 19–25

DRAMA AND CRITICISM
LIBRA–SCORPIO CUSP

Blessed with excellent insight and considerable potential, those born in this week who travel the Way of Empowerment may nevertheless be their own worst enemies. Their tendency to aggression or confrontation is especially strong, and many may become didactic, overbearing, or downright preachy in their attempts to shore up their egos by imposing their ideas on others. Whatever their outer circumstances, relinquishing a measure of personal power in the interest of higher development may not come easily, as these individuals are inclined to believe that their worldly status is hard won and well-deserved. Too, they may wage an internal war between their need for rational analysis and their search for emotional commitment and expression. Yet if they strive not to pin things down but rather to free up their options, they will realize that their quest offers a rare wholeness and understanding that few will find in this lifetime.

CHALLENGE: **REALIZING WHEN THEY ARE TILTING AT WIND-MILLS**

FULFILLMENT: **BASKING IN THE INNER PEACE THAT COMES FROM TAPPING INTO THE POWER WITHIN**

NOTABLES: **WILL ROGERS, JR. (ACTOR; HUMANIST; LECTURER); SONNY TERRY (BLUES SINGER; HARMONICA PLAYER)**

MAHALIA JACKSON
Gospel singer

10/26/1911
Scorpio I

October 26–November 2

INTENSITY
SCORPIO I

Those born in the Week of Intensity who travel the Way of Empowerment may have to work a bit to reconcile the darker and lighter aspects of their natures. Yet they are destined for wonderful fulfillment, for no matter what the depths or heights of their experience along the way, they are gifted with an innate ability to look themselves squarely in the eye. Issues of guilt may be the root of their feelings of unworthiness, and some on this road may swing from lighthearted and essentially escapist episodes to nadirs of depression until they find the emotional balance they seek. Yet the call to self-love and acceptance of their own and others' foibles will doubtless come as time serves to mellow and experience to instruct. If they in turn learn the lesson of giving back to the world, they will be spiritual survivors in the highest sense.

CHALLENGE: **LEARNING THE POWER OF FORGIVENESS**

FULFILLMENT: **COMBINING THEIR CHARM, MAGNETISM, AND VIRTUOSO ABILITIES**

November 3–11

DEPTH
SCORPIO II

Though quite capable of rising to the challenge of discovering the connections between their perceptions of themselves and their external reality, a number of Scorpio II's born to this karmic path may get mired in a need to shore up their sense of self with extremes of material acquisition and a quest for power at its most manipulative. These are people who like to pull the strings and set the stage, and though they may not be are onstage themselves, they will be rather formidable players behind the scenes. Extremes of emotion are likely to lead to any number of revelations about their true natures. If they can turn away from their preoccupation with others' motives and their chronic "What's in it for me?" attitude, they will realize great success—if only they come to understand that self-love is the greatest gift they can give themselves.

CHALLENGE: **KNOWING THAT POWER, SEX, OR MONEY WILL NEVER MAKE THEM HAPPY**

FULFILLMENT: **DISCOVERING THAT IN THEIR OWN LOVING NATURES THEY POSSESS THE GREATEST POWER OF ALL**

NOTABLES: **EUGENE V. DEBS (LABOR ORGANIZER; ORGANIZED SOCIAL DEMOCRATIC PARTY); MARTIN LUTHER (RELIGIOUS LEADER; LED PROTESTANT REFORMATION)**

JULIA ROBERTS
Actress, *Pretty Woman*

10/28/1967
Scorpio I

November 12–18

CHARM
SCORPIO III

The notion of self-love may manifest itself as mere self-indulgence until those born in the Week of Charm develop a more dedicated attitude toward their own higher development on this karmic path. Inclined to dissociate from rather than confront the more unpleasant aspects of their own psyches, some on this road may content themselves with living life on the surface, at the expense of the richer experience that beckons. Yet they have a realistic side that will stand them in good stead. Once they make the connection between their self-criticism and self-doubt and the lack of genuine fulfillment in their lives, they are finally likely to do something about it. If the resulting acceptance does not become mired in complacency or selfishness and they fulfill the higher challenge of using their power in service of others, they will make a memorable mark.

CHALLENGE: **NOT PLAGUING THEMSELVES WITH SELF-DOUBT**

FULFILLMENT: **OWNING UP TO THEIR OWN CHARM AND MAGNETISM**

NOTABLE: **PRINCE CHARLES (PRINCE OF WALES; HEIR APPARENT TO BRITISH THRONE)**

November 19–24
REVOLUTION
SCORPIO–SAGITTARIUS CUSP

Learning to cultivate self-control will mark the journey of those born on this cusp who travel the Way of Empowerment. Very prone to excess, extremes, and impulsiveness, these personalities will find it a bumpy ride and will have to work hard to develop a sense of equilibrium. Gifted with enormous powers of persuasion and the ability to inspire whole movements, they may well attract more attention than they know what to do with and create more problems than they solve when their ideals are not built on a solid foundation of self-acceptance. Yet they have a fine philosophical perspective that will stand them in good stead. If they are careful to mitigate their tendency to "shoot first and ask questions later" through perspective, planning, and a bit of emotional distance, their courage and ability to free themselves and others from oppression will be unmatched.

BURNE HOGARTH
Cartoonist, "Tarzan"
───────
11/25/1911
Sagittarius I

CHALLENGE: **NOT SUBCONSCIOUSLY BEATING THEMSELVES UP BY ENGAGING IN EVERY ARGUMENT, FIGHT, OR CONFRONTATION THAT COMES THEIR WAY**

FULFILLMENT: **UNCOVERING THEIR POWER TO CREATE THEIR OWN REALITY**

November 25–December 2
INDEPENDENCE
SAGITTARIUS I

Those born in the Week of Independence who navigate the Way of Empowerment may experience a number of struggles with its challenges, as they are rather prone to displays of authority and autocracy. Indeed, many of them will find that the road to their personal hell is paved with some very good intentions until they gain the necessary perspective on their own conflicts. They have a profound need to be loved and respected that will not, however, be met until they make a journey within to discover the shadow areas that hold them back from fulfillment. Yet as soon as they discover that the affirmation they seek from the world is to be found in their own hearts, accept that each of us has unique strengths and weaknesses, and give themselves the gifts of love and self-respect, they will be rewarded with personal liberation and worldly validation.

CHALLENGE: **STANDING UP FOR THEIR PRINCIPLES IN SUCH A WAY AS NOT TO WOUND THEIR SENSITIVITY**

FULFILLMENT: **ENJOYING GIVING OF THEMSELVES TO OTHERS, SAFE IN THE KNOWLEDGE THAT WHO THEY ARE IS INEXHAUSTIBLE**

NOTABLES: **T. CORAGHESSAN BOYLE (SATIRICAL FICTION WRITER, *THE ROAD TO WELLVILLE*); SAMUEL RECHEVSKY (7-TIME U.S. CHESS CHAMPION)**

December 3–10
THE ORIGINATOR
SAGITTARIUS II

Overcoming their defensive attitudes will be paramount to the success of Sagittarius II's who travel the Way of Empowerment. Lack of validation at an early age may lead to later problems, and the souls on this karmic path will have to accept and embrace their own unique gifts before they can progress in this life journey. Rebelliousness may be a special problem, and they would do well not to beat their heads against the brick walls of convention when greater self-acknowledgment is really what they seek. Yet at the core, these individuals are not afraid to stand up and show the world who they really are and what they're really made of, and with the right balance of self-awareness and self-control, they can reach the pinnacles of success and personal fulfillment.

CHET HUNTLEY
TV journalist
───────
12/10/1911
Sagittarius II

CHALLENGE: **TEMPERING THEIR TENDENCY TO FIGHT FIRST AND ASK QUESTIONS LATER**

FULFILLMENT: **BELIEVING IN THEMSELVES AND THEIR ABILITY TO MAKE ANYTHING HAPPEN**

December 11–18
THE TITAN
SAGITTARIUS III

Sometimes plagued by secret insecurities and a rather shaky ego, those born in the Week of the Titan who travel the Way of Empowerment will often be driven to overachieve. As they have a rather demanding attitude until they cultivate the fine art of self-love, many with this configuration would do well to follow the three Rs of spiritual advancement along this road: relaxing, reflecting, and releasing the inner anxieties that hold them back from happiness. Yet they are gifted with greater objectivity than they might otherwise have had, and that, combined with a natural generosity of spirit and philosophical turn of mind, will serve them especially well. If they can manage to avoid the traps of reaching for impossible challenges and unreachable stars without first cultivating the personal strength needed to see things through, they can expect great achievement and a sense of true personal triumph.

CHALLENGE: **KNOWING THAT A CHIP-ON-THE-SHOULDER ATTITUDE ONLY ATTRACTS MORE CHIPS**

FULFILLMENT: **OPERATING IN THE WORLD FROM A PLACE OF EMPOWERMENT**

NOTABLES: **JULES DASSIN (DIRECTOR, *THE NAKED CITY*); SPIKE JONES (BANDLEADER, JAZZ AND DIXIELAND); TED NUGENT (FLAMBOYANT ROCK GUITARIST)**

December 19–25
PROPHECY
SAGITTARIUS–CAPRICORN CUSP

Those born on the Cusp of Prophecy who find themselves on this karmic path can expect great fulfillment, providing they manage to banish some personal demons and nurture the qualities of intellect, intuition, and insight that beckon. Indeed, many of them will be less inclined to second-guess themselves than most and more able to rise above the obstacles to development that may arise along this life journey. If they can manage to embrace their own need for security without getting mired in purely material definitions of what security means, the sense of self-acceptance and personal power that emerges over time will shape some formidable personalities, some of whom may well give a whole new meaning to the concept of mind over matter.

GEORGE FOREMAN
Heavyweight boxer
───────────
1/10/1949
Capricorn III

CHALLENGE: **KNOWING WHEN THEY HAVE CALLED THEIR CALAMITIES ONTO THEMSELVES**

FULFILLMENT: **UNDERSTANDING THE POWER OF THEIR INTENTIONS**

NOTABLES: **STEVE GARVEY (BASEBALL PLAYER); SAMUEL L. JACKSON (ACTOR, *PULP FICTION*); SUSAN LUCCI (SOAP OPERA ACTRESS, *ALL MY CHILDREN*); BARBARA MANDRELL (COUNTRY MUSIC SINGER)**

December 26–January 2
THE RULER
CAPRICORN I

Marked by both extraordinary endurance and a strong sense of personal identity, those born in this week who make their way along this karmic path may find it at times arduous but always rewarding. In fact, their biggest problem may be an unwillingness to come to terms with outworn ideas or traditions that hinder the expanded notions of self demanded by this karmic path. Many have a rather rigid attitude toward getting their own way that will cause them no end of trouble until they begin to take stock of themselves and consider where they really want to be. Others will find that this path demands that they relinquish a measure of control and responsibility in order to be able to truly enjoy what life has to offer. Yet if they do not give in to self-doubt or the need to impose ideas that they do not truly believe on others, these individuals can achieve real triumph.

CHALLENGE: **REMEMBERING TO REWARD THEMSELVES NOW AND THEN**

FULFILLMENT: **BALANCING SELF-ASSERTION AND SELF-CONTROL**

NOTABLES: **GÉRARD DÉPARDIEU (FRENCH ACTOR); DONNA SUMMER (DISCO-ERA SINGER)**

January 3–9
DETERMINATION
CAPRICORN II

No matter what the exact nature of the fetters that hold them back from higher development and greater happiness, those born in the Week of Determination who travel the Way of Empowerment will find a way to break them. Natural strivers, they may well encounter some major personal challenges, yet the sheer magnitude of their struggle will in a curious way serve to reinforce their sense of self and what they're capable of achieving. Too, they have a natural inclination toward metaphysical and philosophical subjects that will be of great assistance on this life journey, as such studies and pursuits may help them to put any personal problems into a larger perspective. Yet inner peace, increased self-esteem, and emotional stability are all theirs for the asking. And though the road may be long, their rewards will be rich.

JOHN SINGER SARGENT
Painter, *Two Girls Fishing*
───────────
1/12/1856
Capricorn III

CHALLENGE: **NOT WEARING THEMSELVES OUT TRYING TO ASSERT THEMSELVES OR THEIR GOALS**

FULFILLMENT: **FEELING THE FREEDOM AND EMPOWERMENT OF ADMITTING A MISTAKE**

NOTABLE: **JOSÉ FERRER (ACTOR/DIRECTOR)**

January 10–16
DOMINANCE
CAPRICORN III

Stern taskmasters, those born with this configuration may have to avoid a tendency to internalize an early authority figure to the extent that they become their own worst enemies when it comes to self-negation or feelings of worthlessness. Though they are likely to be more charismatic and compelling than many others born in this week, some of their best qualities and talents may never see the light of day until they conquer some deeply personal issues and learn to give both themselves and others credit where credit is due. Though authority issues may be their biggest stumbling block, they also have a tendency to repress their emotions, which habit may in turn express itself in extremes of frustration. Still, if they adjust their focus only slightly from a preoccupation with their own rights to the right of others to be freed from both inner and outer oppression, all will go much more smoothly.

CHALLENGE: **NOT FLAGELLATING THEMSELVES BY REMAINING LOYAL TO THE NEGATIVE FIGURES IN THEIR LIVES**

FULFILLMENT: **DISCOVERING THE STEELY STRENGTH OF THEIR INNER CORE**

January 17–22

MYSTERY AND IMAGINATION
CAPRICORN–AQUARIUS CUSP

Learning to regulate their sometimes explosive emotional energies will prove paramount to the success of those born on the Cusp of Mystery and Imagination who travel the Way of Empowerment. These expressive and temperamental people are prone to externalizing their demons, and this configuration may result in any number of rather pointless personal battles and stormy scenes until they make a better connection between their beliefs about themselves and what has been referred to as "the answering universe." Though it will doubtless take time for them to turn their attention away from worldly struggles and look inward for their answers, the journey will prove rewarding as they learn to lay aside their weapons and make peace with the fascinating, ardent, and exciting being that dwells within.

ANDY KAUFMAN
Actor/comedian, *Taxi;*
outlandish characters

1/17/1949
Capricorn–Aquarius Cusp

CHALLENGE: **NOT BEING SEDUCED BY THE POWER OF THEIR FANTASIES AT THE EXPENSE OF THEIR SOUL**

FULFILLMENT: **PUTTING THEIR MAGNETISM AND POWER TO GOOD USE IN SERVICE TO OTHERS**

January 23–30

GENIUS
AQUARIUS I

Those born in the Week of Genius who find themselves on the Way of Empowerment can expect great success, as they are gifted both with a higher degree of natural objectivity and a broader sense of human freedom than other Aquarius I's. Though they may have a tendency to allow their vanity to be wounded, they are unlikely to get overly mired in undue emotionalism or sensuality. Issues of rebellion and authority may prove to be this karmic path's principal lesson, and the souls who make the trip would do well to recall the words of writer George Eliot, who wrote, "The strongest principle of human growth lies in human choice." If they choose carefully and realize that their resistance to personal empowerment is ultimately a product not of external circumstances but of personal choices, their progress and impact are all but assured.

CHALLENGE: **UNDERSTANDING THAT STRUCTURE AND LIMITATION ARE SOMETIMES NOT AS DISEMPOWERING AS ABSOLUTE FREEDOM**

FULFILLMENT: **RELAXING IN THE SERENITY BORN OF SELF-LOVE**

NOTABLE: **MADAME SUN YAT-SEN (WIDOW OF SUN YAT-SEN, POLITICAL LEADER; ARDENT COMMUNIST)**

January 31–February 7

YOUTH AND EASE
AQUARIUS II

The principal stumbling block of those born in the Week of Youth and Ease who find themselves on the Way of Empowerment is one of emotional immaturity. Yet there is also a promise of tremendous achievement, as these individuals can easily find the place of inner peace and self-satisfaction promised by this karmic path. Though they will have to divest themselves of troublesome personal problems and develop a bit more depth, the process of discovering their route to empowerment should prove relatively easy. If every journey begins with a single step, they have only to embrace the truth of who they are in an effort at enlightenment and self-discovery and stop looking for their answers in others. After that, their easygoing natures, natural virtuosity, and tremendous charisma will all but take care of the rest.

JOHN BELUSHI
Comedian/actor, *Saturday Night Live, Blues Brothers*

1/24/1949
Aquarius I

CHALLENGE: **ENDING THEIR FASCINATION WITH TRYING TO FIND THEMSELVES IN THE MIRRORS OTHERS PRESENT THEM**

FULFILLMENT: **REVELING IN THE SENSE OF ACCOMPLISHMENT THAT HAVING A FIRM GRIP ON WHO THEY ARE GIVES THEM**

NOTABLE: **NATALIE COLE (SINGER, "UNFORGETTABLE")**

February 8–15

ACCEPTANCE
AQUARIUS III

Though they probably experienced a certain amount of early repression or rejection, Aquarius III's can nevertheless expect great satisfaction and reward on this life journey. In fact, stubbornness may be their biggest problem. They also have a tendency to allow others to superimpose a set of beliefs on them, then to staunchly defend those beliefs as their own without fully evaluating them first. Thus, acknowledging the need for change as necessary and natural, and not merely as an admission of personal failure, will be especially important in their higher development. Yet the impulse toward freedom from oppression of any kind runs strong in the Aquarian psyche, and once they gain perspective and accept themselves for who and what they are, these remarkable and inspired people will have little trouble drawing the love of others and of the universe at large.

CHALLENGE: **MAKING THEIR OWN DECISIONS AND FORMING THEIR OWN OPINIONS**

FULFILLMENT: **STANDING UP FOR THE RIGHTS OF OTHERS AND THEREBY EMPOWERING THEMSELVES**

NOTABLES: **JUDITH LIGHT (ACTRESS, *WHO'S THE BOSS?*); WILLIAM TALBOT (DEVELOPED SEVERAL PHOTOGRAPHIC PROCESSES)**

February 16–22

SENSITIVITY
AQUARIUS–PISCES CUSP

Highly dramatic and prone to overreacting to the dilemmas and dramas of daily life, those born on this cusp who travel the Way of Empowerment will have to work hard not to cancel out their best efforts with self-doubt and second guesses. In many cases their impulse to protect their more sensitive side will interfere with their higher development, as many of them will continually be involved in attempts to enforce their wills and wield their personal power without first acknowledging their own deep need for emotional sustenance. Thus a willingness to admit their own need for love will be their first step toward higher development. If they can further recognize that their need for material success and achievement can be realized only when they pursue the things that nurture their spirits, their road to contentment will smooth considerably.

ANDRÉS SEGOVIA
Guitarist/composer

2/21/1893
Aquarius–Pisces Cusp

CHALLENGE: **TEMPERING THEIR BELLIGERENCE ENOUGH TO ASK WHY THEY'RE FIGHTING**

FULFILLMENT: **DELVING INTO THE CAUSE OF THEIR SUFFERING ONLY TO REALIZE THAT IT'S ONLY IN THEIR MINDS**

NOTABLES: **IVANA TRUMP (EX-WIFE OF MILLIONAIRE DONALD); RUSSELL CROUSE (MUSICAL DRAMATIST)**

February 23–March 2

SPIRIT
PISCES I

Those born in the Week of Spirit who embark on the Way of Empowerment are destined for a great deal of satisfaction along this road, as their interest in the nonmaterial makes a nice balance with the more solid achievements promised by this karmic path. In fact, the only real obstacle for these individuals might be their refusal to take responsibility for their emotional lives, as they have a tendency to blame and point fingers. Though they have little trouble identifying or analyzing the sources of their dissatisfaction, they may have a bit more trouble when it comes to releasing the issues that hold them back from greater fulfillment. Yet once they accept that they are not necessarily better nor worse than anyone else, their resulting peace and sense of inner worth is quite likely to manifest itself in the kind of personal power that can make a real impact when it comes to making the world a better place.

CHALLENGE: **NOT LETTING THEIR SPIRITUALITY KEEP THEM FROM KNOWING WHEN THEY ARE BEING STEPPED ON**

FULFILLMENT: **GETTING TO KNOW THEMSELVES A LITTLE BETTER**

NOTABLE: **RALPH LINTON (DEVELOPED CULTURAL ANTHROPOLOGY; WROTE THE TREE OF CULTURE)**

March 3–10

THE LONER
PISCES II

Gifted with an unassailable aesthetic and moral code, those born in the Week of the Loner who travel the Way of Empowerment may well develop the self-love and self-acceptance promised by this karmic path. Not likely to blame their troubles on others, they may nevertheless struggle a bit with a tendency to take things rather too much to heart and to blame themselves for others' failings. Yet this karmic path endows them with much more of an ability to relax and release than they might otherwise have had, and if they take care to nurture their often wounded spirits with aesthetics and open themselves to the true beauty that exists in the world, the avenue to self-acceptance and the ability to come into their own sense of power will surely follow. If they remember that love and acceptance spring first from a desire for self-fulfillment, they can surely find a measure of magic along this unusual road.

WILLIAM FRAWLEY
TV/radio actor,
I Love Lucy

2/26/1893
Pisces I

CHALLENGE: **CHANGING THEIR THINKING PATTERNS AWAY FROM NEGATIVITY**

FULFILLMENT: **COMING TO KNOW THE JOY OF ACCEPTING THEMSELVES**

March 11–18

DANCERS AND DREAMERS
PISCES III

Those born in this week are likely to infuse this karmic journey with not just self-acceptance and love but genuine spiritual awareness as well. Yet they will have to work to avoid a tendency to get caught up in melodrama or to believe themselves chronically at the mercy of forces beyond their control. Too, submerging their ego is part of their challenge, and they will have to be careful to distinguish between self-love and smug satisfaction. And while they may resist undertaking the psychological challenge to release old issues and will doubtless be tempted to "let things go" without first analyzing what impact their beliefs have on their lives, this karmic path promises to ground them in both spiritual reality and material accomplishment, as long as their great potential and power are neither abused nor carelessly discarded along the way.

CHALLENGE: **NOT MEASURING THEIR SELF-WORTH BY HOW MUCH THEY ARE NEEDED**

FULFILLMENT: **INVOKING THE PROMISE OF THE MAGNETISM OF THIS KARMIC PATH TO ACHIEVE MIRACLES**

NOTABLE: **GROVER CLEVELAND (22ND AND 24TH U.S. PRESIDENT)**

The Way of Satisfaction

SCORPIO I TO TAURUS I
Intensity to Manifestation

Powerful and creative individuals, the men and women born to the Way of Satisfaction believe that they came into this life to build something of lasting value. Indeed, many on this karmic path do contribute a body of work to the world. But these individuals must learn that their self-worth does not reside in their work or creativity. Rather, on this karmic path, they must learn to find a sense of satisfaction with themselves, independent of their achievements. Those on this karmic path are born with an intense, hard-driving nature. Demanding people, they expect the best of themselves and others. Learning when enough is enough and how to be satisfied with the results of their labors is crucial to this path. Though often quite successful, not every person born to this karmic path must leave behind a legacy on the order of, for example, John D. Rockefeller. However, this path does mean that whatever those born to it choose to do with their lives, they must find within themselves the capacity to be satisfied with their work and, as a corollary, with themselves. This requires that they do what is extremely difficult for them by learning the core lesson of this path: how to live and let live by adopting a generally more relaxed approach to life. If they do so successfully, they will be blessed with something for which many yearn: contentment.

"Formidable" is the word that best describes the men and women born to the Way of Satisfaction. There are few who can equal their attention to detail or capacity for concentration. When they invoke these traits to achieve a goal, there is nothing that can stand in their way. Their capacity for intense focus, combined with their discrimination and analytical ability, gives their minds a laserlike power to home in on the underlying truth of any issue, whether practical, financial, or psychological. They always know the real motivation for anyone's behavior.

While the aforementioned represent some of their past-life tools, this karmic path calls those on it to put them to some useful purpose. The point of destination of this path, Taurus I, is an energy that is oriented to the tangible, so those on this path have a great impulse to amass or build something of lasting value. Possessing virtuoso talents, those on this path are often not content unless they do something with those talents, and that something has to be tangible—and preferably big. This is because, on a certain level, those on this path are incapable of valuing themselves or their abilities unless they are actually able to see the physical manifestation of those abilities in the world. In other words, these people expect a lot of themselves.

However, not all people are moguls, nor are they meant to be. Many on this karmic path denigrate themselves horribly about their unfulfilled ambitions. They may belittle a perfectly nice job, house, mate, or life, with chronic dissatisfaction the result. Moreover, having such high aspirations means that it is difficult to be satisfied with the

---

GOAL
Experiencing a sense of contentment

CORE LESSON
To approach living in a more relaxed manner by releasing any identification with one's work or creative end products

---

GIFTS
Discerning, Productive, Sensuous

PITFALLS
Driven, Tense, Stubborn

fruits of one's labors. Possessing high standards, those on this path become bogged down by them. At work here is the fact that those on this path do not see their creative products as spiritually inspired or God-given; rather they view them from the perspective of the ego and see them as the proof of their self-worth. They identify with their work. If it is not perfect, that means they are imperfect or, even worse, no good. They can't seem to keep themselves from this particular form of self-flagellation. What's more, they drive themselves ceaselessly and intensely onward, amassing, producing, or achieving more and more to prove their worth to themselves and the world. The core lesson for the individuals on this path is to relax their Scorpio I intensity enough to stop identifying with what they do. After all, people are more than what they produce or do and are worth more to boot. But self-worth must come from within and cannot be found in an end product. Ego identification leads only to suffering. And until those on this path learn this lesson, they will be condemned to suffer.

The great promise of this karmic path is abundance and creative fulfillment. These individuals have the capacity to manifest both in their lives, in both large and small ways. But the real key is be satisfied with what they have. As they discover self-worth, it will be reflected onto the world, and they will begin to attract whatever they need. If, on the other hand, those

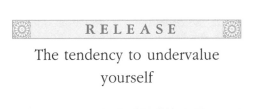

RELEASE

The tendency to undervalue yourself

REWARD

The joy of feeling content

on this path denigrate themselves, believing they are only as good as their last bit of good work, they will have to work all the harder to produce the good things life has to offer. They risk cutting themselves off from the flow of life and will find working a frustrating and dissatisfying experience. Taking satisfaction in a job well done and standing firm in the sense of their own worthiness can be extremely healing for those on this path.

A pitfall for the men and women on this karmic path is that often they will put themselves into situations where they are surrounded by people whose values are exactly opposite those they should be embracing. It seems these individuals like to make things difficult for themselves. For example, performers on this path tend to associate with those who evaluate them solely on the basis of their last performance. Businessmen might be considered only as good as their last deal. Others may find themselves evaluated on the basis of who their friends are or to whom they are married. Such judgments will prove difficult for those on this path since they do possess a sense of ethics and fairness that rebels against such a way of thinking. Until their innate morality rears up to foster an inner rebellion against such prejudice, superficiality, and snobbery, these sensitive souls are bound to be wounded by such attacks on their pride. All of which is designed to help them accept their destiny and move

SUGGESTION

Know that you are not only what you do. Seek out activities that promote relaxation. Cultivate a wide variety of friends from many walks of life. Honor your sense of ethics.

along their karmic path. Those on this path must learn to remember that their worth is intrinsic and depends only on how they feel about themselves. Feeling satisfied with and secure in who they are is all they need.

Those on the Way of Satisfaction, though possessing a great deal of awareness, must nevertheless slow down long enough to put it to use. Often tense, they would do well to move to the more Venusian or sensuous, Taurus I side of the axis and begin to enjoy life's pleasures a little more. Often for these individuals, allowing themselves creature comforts at all is a strong indication that they are moving to a place of greater satisfaction since it implies that they are finally valuing themselves and their needs. Many activities can help to promote relaxation: massage, using essential oils and aromatherapy, opening up new culinary horizons, practicing yoga or tai chi, playing sports, having a satisfying sexual relationship, and a host of other physical activities will serve to ground such individuals. Also, calming and healing spiritual activities such as inspirational reading and study or meditation are recommended. Spending time in the country or even living there will also serve to bring those on this karmic path to a state of contentment. Indeed, shunning the tension- and anxiety-producing aspects of city or corporate life may become a lifesaving imperative.

The karmic lessons of those on the Way of Satisfaction generally involve work in some fashion and, complimentarily, relationships. Some on this karmic path may be so obsessed with their careers or ambitions that even

BALANCE POINT

Approval and Self-worth

acknowledging that one's private life is important is a big step forward. A second step can be broadening the scope of their social contacts beyond those that are work-related or have some bearing on their career. Although they may view such relationships as frivolous at first, really getting away from it all to relax means eliminating shop talk from their leisure time. Moreover, friends from other walks of life will help these individuals feel valued for who they are, not what they do. Strengthening family ties can have a positive influence on those on this karmic path if they take advantage of the relaxation and altered perspective afforded by holiday festivities, marriages and births, educational and recreational involvement, and vacation trips. Love is the best medicine for those who suffer from Scorpio I sternness. A partner who can break through their armor with daily doses of kindness and affection may prove the greatest stimulus of all for a complete metamorphosis.

The journey of this karmic path can be likened to that of a hard-driving corporate executive, who, whether through some epiphany or by some other design, suddenly retires. With hours of time on his hands, such a person is now given the opportunity to indulge in relaxing and satisfying activities that are not tied up with stress and success. Personal goals become more important, as does the sharing of love and a variety of experiences with others. Older and wiser, such individuals are no longer driven to prove themselves, but rather are content to give themselves over to pursuing simple pleasures.

CRYSTALS AND GEMSTONES

Petrified Wood is a stone of being. While holding this stone the individual is reminded not to be distracted by superficial achievements but to merge with the pulse of creation.

NOTABLES ON THIS KARMIC PATH

Magician **Harry Houdini** used his extraordinary intensity and amazing feats of escape to gain recognition. However, his ability to relax was also key to his survival, as he often evaded the bonds and chains of his tricks by loosening tensed muscles. Yet on a personal level, Houdini never managed to truly unwind

HARRY HOUDINI

for a significant period of time. Like many on this path, he drove himself ceaselessly and identified completely with his illusionist persona. Dying young, it is unclear if he ever achieved the intention that is the destination of this karmic path.

LUCILLE BALL

Actress and comedian **Lucille Ball** came to be known for her drive and dynamic energy. She appeared in numerous films and radio shows to limited success before meeting and marrying Cuban-born bandleader Desi Arnaz. With Arnaz, Ball conceived of the TV series *I Love Lucy,* which they produced and starred in. This popular situation comedy became the vehicle for Ball's stardom and personal wealth. After buying out Arnaz's share of their company, Desilu Productions, she sold the corporation

for seventeen million dollars. Like many on the Way of Satisfaction, Lucille reached the top of her profession and was able to reap the rewards of her hard work.

Philanthropist **John D. Rockefeller, Jr.** represents those on this karmic path due to his embodiment of his personal ethics and sense of fair play. Unlike his father, who founded monopolistic Standard Oil, Rockefeller Jr. dedicated himself to creating major organizations whose sole purpose was helping humanity. As a patron of New York City, he not only brought about the construction of Rockefeller Center, he also donated the land for the United Nations, was chairman of the Rockefeller Institute of Medical Research, made major contributions to the Museum of Modern Art, and helped construct low-rent housing. Applying his intensity to the concrete goals of Manifestation, John D. Rockefeller Jr. used his abundance to achieve self-fulfillment.

JOHN D. ROCKEFELLER, JR.

Other Notables: David Mackenzie Ogilvy, Kathleen Deanne Battle, Christa McAuliffe, Mary Higgins Clark, Stephen Sondheim, Robert Frost, Sandra Day O'Connor, Karl Marx, John Emerson, Richard Simmons, Cat Stevens, Jane Wyatt, Tipper Gore, Phil Hartman, Jeremy Irons, Bryant Gumbel, Donna Karan, Berry Gordy, Jr., John Cassavetes, Francisco Franco, Gertrude Stein, Joanne Woodward

---

BIRTHDAYS ON KARMIC PATH 30

August 23, 1892–January 10, 1893 | April 5, 1911–August 24, 1911

November 14, 1929–April 4, 1930 | June 26, 1948–November 13, 1948 | February 5, 1967–June 26, 1967

September 16, 1985–February 4, 1986 | April 28, 2004–September 15, 2004

KARMIC PATH
30

March 19–24
REBIRTH
PISCES–ARIES CUSP

The souls born on this cusp who travel the Way of Satisfaction can experience wonderful rewards along this life's journey, providing they do not succumb to the notion that "too much is not enough" and find within themselves the capacity for enjoyment of pleasures in life that exist apart from their work or professional interests. Highly motivated and probably quite successful in worldly terms, they will nevertheless have to take care to cultivate their natural sensitivity. Though gifted with greater insight into their own and others' motives than they might otherwise be, they will need to stop and smell the roses in order to realize the higher challenge of this calling. And when one considers it, that can be a rewarding task indeed.

STEVE MCQUEEN
Actor, *The Great Escape*

3/24/1930
Pisces–Aries Cusp

CHALLENGE: **MEASURING THEIR WORDS AND ACTIONS MORE CAREFULLY**
FULFILLMENT: **HAVING FOUND SUCCESS ON SOME LEVEL, BEING ABLE TO INDULGE THEIR SENSUOUS SIDE**
NOTABLES: **STEPHEN SONDHEIM (COMPOSER/LYRICIST, "SUNDAY IN THE PARK WITH GEORGE"); HARRY HOUDINI (WORLD'S GREATEST MAGICIAN)**

March 25–April 2
THE CHILD
ARIES I

Those born in the Week of the Child who make their way along this karmic path should take care that their desire to be taken seriously does not turn into an obsession with making a mark on the world. Nevertheless, they are gifted with great enthusiasm and a playful side that will stand them in good stead here and allow them to enjoy life more. Likely to be rather physical, they will doubtless derive great joy from pursuing athletic or outdoor activities apart from their daily routine. Such pursuits will help to reduce their susceptibility to stress and at the same time keep them in tune with the rhythms of the earth and of their own bodies. This will be a relatively easy passage and one that promises great fulfillment, providing they lay aside ego issues and place themselves within a larger, more benevolent scheme.

CHALLENGE: **KEEPING THEIR TEMPERS IN CHECK**
FULFILLMENT: **CREATING SOLELY FOR PLEASURE OR AS A HOBBY**
NOTABLES: **JOHN ASTIN (ACTOR, *THE ADDAMS FAMILY*); CASANOVA (ADVENTURER; ROMANCER); ROBERT FROST (TEACHER; POET, *A GIFT OUTRIGHT*)**

April 3–10
THE STAR
ARIES II

Those born in the Week of the Star who find themselves on the Way of Satisfaction may find that their desire to be at the center of life's stage makes for more anxiety than it's ultimately worth. Ego issues and pride may be the single biggest obstacle to their advancement along this road, and they will have to release their more competitive instincts before they can realize the higher challenge of this karmic path. Possessiveness in all its forms may be a problem for these unstoppable types, and some will experience great difficulty with issues of jealousy, envy, or outright greed before they learn the gentle art of letting go and begin to more fully appreciate themselves for who they are, not what they can accomplish. Yet if they can come to terms with the simple fact that no one is indispensable and make time for the wealth of simple pleasures and well-earned rewards that beckon, life will be rich indeed.

SANDRA DAY O'CONNOR
U.S. Supreme Court justice; 1st woman to serve on court

3/26/1930
Aries I

CHALLENGE: **DEALING WITH THE NOTION THAT OTHERS VALUE THEM MORE FOR THEIR IMAGE AND LESS FOR WHO THEY ARE**
FULFILLMENT: **REACHING THE POINT WHERE THEY DON'T HAVE TO PROVE ANYTHING**
NOTABLE: **HELMUT KOHL (GERMAN CHANCELLOR; 1ST LEADER OF UNIFIED GERMANY)**

April 11–18
THE PIONEER
ARIES III

Those born in the Week of the Pioneer who find themselves on the Way of Satisfaction have a capacity for dynamic leadership that might exist at odds with the higher challenge here. Yet these people will certainly flourish on this karmic path, as their passion, optimism, and positive attitudes are certain to be of great help along the journey. They may be prone to control issues, however, and may put their own needs on the back burner as they continually strive for worldly success. In the area of personal relationships, these souls may encounter some rude awakenings should they fail to take time out for relaxation and sharing or to attach adequate meaning to their private life. Yet whatever the challenges of this karmic path, Aries III's will doubtless find a way to meet them, though the key will be their willingness to let themselves enjoy comfort and the pleasures of family and friends.

CHALLENGE: **NOT SACRIFICING THEIR PERSONAL LIFE TO AMBITION, EVEN IF STRIVING FOR A GREATER GOOD**
FULFILLMENT: **BECOMING A MODEL OF QUIET HUMILITY AND SELF-WORTH**

April 19–24
POWER
ARIES–TAURUS CUSP

Those born on the Cusp of Power who navigate the promise and challenge of the Way of Satisfaction can realize true happiness and contentment, providing they do not succumb to their workaholic tendencies and recognize that true power involves knowing when to turn the reins over to somebody else. They are likely to take real pleasure in what is generally known as "the good life," and their sensual side is bound to be given full expression on this karmic path. Releasing their identification with their product, whatever that may be, may be a bit difficult for these people, and they may also have difficulty with developing a more relaxed attitude toward life, especially if they feel their ambitions are not yet fulfilled. Nevertheless, they can expect personal and spiritual rewards, in more or less direct proportion to their ability to release their need for control.

GUGLIELMO MARCONI
Invented radio, 1909;
Nobel Prize for physics

4/25/1874
Taurus I

CHALLENGE: **DEVELOPING A LIVE-AND-LET-LIVE ATTITUDE**
FULFILLMENT: **EMBRACING THE ADAGE "LIVING WELL IS THE BEST REVENGE"**

April 25–May 2
MANIFESTATION
TAURUS I

Those born in the Week of Manifestation may be motivated by such a pronounced need to make their mark on the world that they fall prey to a kind of tunnel vision as they overfocus on their careers. Yet they have the possibility for wonderful fulfillment and real happiness, especially in the areas of family life and through their natural predisposition to enjoy beauty and sensual pleasure. Stubbornness may contribute to their failure to change, even when a change in their work habits is clearly indicated. Yet if they are careful to cultivate a genuine sense of self-worth, their need for validation in their careers and personal endeavors should abate somewhat, and they will find the freedom that comes with a true appreciation of all life has to offer.

CHALLENGE: **UNCOVERING AND RELEASING THE KERNEL OF INSECURITY THAT KEEPS THEM FROM ACHIEVING HAPPINESS**
FULFILLMENT: **NOURISHING THEIR PHYSICAL BEING WITH GOOD FOOD, EXERCISE, SEX, AND RECREATION**

May 3–10
THE TEACHER
TAURUS II

Taurus II's run the risk of becoming quite demanding, inflexible, and entrenched in the pursuit of worldly success on the Way of Satisfaction. However, their need to share their ideas and to nurture those close to them is likely to provide a nice balance here. If they can make the distinction between mere self-interest and true self-development, this passage is likely to be even easier. Freeing themselves from their notions of dignity and worldly image will also be important to their development, as some along this road may expend a great deal of energy in trying to maintain a reputation that they no longer want or need. Though they like to work, they may become quite comfortable with the idea that they can kick back and enjoy the finer things from time to time. If they combine a need for pleasure with their need for wider horizons and a broader range of possibilities for fulfillment, they will attain the highest levels of personal contentment.

KARL MARX
Socialist leader/
philosopher; originator of
modern communism,
Communist Manifesto

5/5/1818
Taurus II

CHALLENGE: **SHAKING OFF THE UNDERLYING ISSUE OF NOT BELIEVING THEY DESERVE TO HAVE PLEASURE**
FULFILLMENT: **SLOWING DOWN AND COMPLETELY INDULGING THEMSELVES NOW AND THEN**
NOTABLE: **FRANK CONRAD (RADIO BROADCASTER)**

May 11–18
THE NATURAL
TAURUS III

Once they understand that many of their more material ambitions are tied to a need for security that can come only from within, Taurus III's are likely to do quite well on the Way of Satisfaction. Much drawn to the natural world, simple pleasures, and physical and sensual activity, they are quite capable of detaching themselves from the rat race and finding the inner peace and contentment promised by this karmic path. While many will doubtless be distracted by the need to amass possessions and even fortunes in the search for self-affirmation, this will prove to be a dead end. If they are careful not to get caught up in issues of rebellion and ego and give themselves fully to their own need for beauty, a simpler life, and unspoiled pleasures, they are especially well suited to achieving security, calm, self-worth, and contentment.

CHALLENGE: **UNDERSTANDING THAT THEIR WORTH IS NOT ABOUT WHAT THEY EARN OR ACHIEVE**
FULFILLMENT: **RETREATING TO NATURE ON A REGULAR BASIS**
NOTABLE: **MAUREEN O'SULLIVAN (ACTRESS, "JANE" IN *TARZAN* MOVIES)**

May 19–24
ENERGY
TAURUS–GEMINI CUSP

Those born on this cusp may find this karmic path more of a struggle than it really needs to be until they develop the ability to slow down and take stock of both what they have and where they want to go. Intense and emotional almost to a fault, these souls are gifted with a greater focus than they might otherwise have had. Thus, they may experience more conflict when it comes to releasing their worldly ambitions and identification with career interests. Yet they are quite capable of attaining contentment and self-satisfaction, providing they allow themselves some necessary breaks and get into touch with the things that truly nourish their spirits and gladden their hearts.

VINCENT PRICE
Actor, known for horror roles, "Master of Menace," *House of Wax*
———
5/27/1911
Gemini I

CHALLENGE: **RELINQUISHING THE NOTION THAT THEY ARE A FORCE TO BE RECKONED WITH**

FULFILLMENT: **BENEFITING FROM MEDITATION, YOGA, SPORTS, AND ALL OTHER MIND/BODY/SPIRIT AVOCATIONS**

May 25–June 2
FREEDOM
GEMINI I

For Gemini I's on the Way of Satisfaction, the path of least resistance is likely to be the key to higher development. Rather confrontational by nature, they like to debate and, more important, to win and may experience quite a bit of difficulty releasing their more competitive side in the interest of increased security and self-satisfaction. Impatience with themselves and others may contribute to their troubles, as their naturally high standards can cause no end of frustration when things don't come to them as quickly or as easily as they feel they should. Yet they can derive great satisfaction, providing they cultivate their interest in intellectual and spiritual pursuits and make the time for study, rest, and meditation, all of which will offer them a wider perspective on the world of pleasurable possibilities that await them.

CHALLENGE: **LEARNING THE ART OF QUIET CONTEMPLATION**

FULFILLMENT: **ENJOYING A RICH FAMILY LIFE AND ITS GROUNDING INFLUENCE ON THEM**

NOTABLES: **RANDOLPH CHURCHILL (JOURNALIST); HUBERT H. HUMPHREY (VICE PRESIDENT UNDER LBJ)**

June 3–10
NEW LANGUAGE
GEMINI II

Learning to bring their considerable communicative and creative talents to bear in an atmosphere of trust and contentment may prove challenging for those born in the Week of New Language who navigate the Way of Satisfaction. This journey will require these compelling people to release their notions of worldly success and achievement in the interest of greater self-confidence and personal evolution. A pitfall for them may be their need to communicate effectively and to dazzle a wide audience with insight and perception; they will do better to turn to their nearest and dearest and open the channels of communication and understanding that exist close by. If they can avoid flagellating themselves and exacerbating their feelings of inadequacy through a need to bite off more than they can chew, professionally speaking, they will realize great personal evolution and enjoy many peaceful pleasures.

SHERRY STRINGFIELD
Actress, *ER*
———
6/12/1967
Gemini III

CHALLENGE: **GRAPPLING WITH THEIR SENSE THAT THEY ARE MISUNDERSTOOD BY OTHERS AND HOW THIS AFFECTS THEIR SELF-WORTH**

FULFILLMENT: **EXPRESSING THEMSELVES PHYSICALLY**

June 11–18
THE SEEKER
GEMINI III

The individuals born in the Week of the Seeker who negotiate the promise and challenge of the Way of Satisfaction may be the kind of people who travel far and wide in search of worldly affirmation and validation only to discover, as Dorothy so aptly conceded in the movie *The Wizard of Oz*, that "there's no place like home." Motivated by a need to push the envelope and seek adventure in even the most ordinary circumstances, they will find self-worth only if they nourish their spirits through not just quantity but quality of experience. Scattering their energies will only contribute to their lack of satisfaction with themselves, just as spreading themselves too thin will interfere with their ability to relax. Yet if they nourish their inner natures through study, meditation, and developing a love of truth, and learn the value of their own good company, all will go more smoothly.

CHALLENGE: **NOT PUSHING THEMSELVES ONWARD TO A BROADENING RANGE OF INTELLECTUAL INVOLVEMENTS AND OVER-THE-TOP ADVENTURES**

FULFILLMENT: **RESTING PEACEFULLY IN THE KNOWLEDGE AND APPRECIATION OF THEIR TALENTS**

NOTABLES: **ERWIN MUELLER (INVENTED FIELD MICROSCOPE); PRINCE ALI AKBAR KHAN (INDIAN MUSICIAN; DIRECTOR)**

June 19–24

MAGIC
GEMINI–CANCER CUSP

The often rather mellow, laid-back exteriors of those born on the Cusp of Magic who travel this path can sometimes disguise very intense personalities. They can derive great contentment through their ability to retreat into their intensely private inner world once they relinquish some of their formidable focus. The principal task for these people will be to make every effort to examine and release old emotional baggage. Issues of dependency and codependency can be problems, as they have a strong desire to please others before they get down to the business of acknowledging their own needs. Alternatively, they can become mired in this karmic path's Scorpio I origin and be demanding or suspicious of others, insisting on control instead of addressing their own deeper needs. Still, if they realize the value of letting go and nurturing themselves, their natural curiosity and intuition will guide them toward a higher level of fulfillment.

GINGER ROGERS
Actress/dancer, Fred Astaire's frequent dancing partner

———

7/16/1911
Cancer III

CHALLENGE: **NOT IDENTIFYING THEIR SELF-WORTH WITH WHOMEVER THEY ARE LINKED ROMANTICALLY WITH**
FULFILLMENT: **VALUING THEIR TALENTS AND BEING SECURE ENOUGH TO PUT THEM TO A HIGHER PURPOSE**
NOTABLES: **DAVID OGILVY (FOUNDED OGILVY, BENSON & MATHER); JUAN MANUEL FANGIO (SOUTH AMERICAN RACE CAR DRIVER)**

June 25–July 2

THE EMPATH
CANCER I

Though gifted with a better set of emotional boundaries than they might otherwise have had, those born in the Week of the Empath who travel the Way of Satisfaction may have to do a bit of work before they are able to distinguish their sources of true contentment and find the inner security and peace promised by this karmic path. Their impulse to identify with their work and especially their financial interests is especially strong, and any hint of failure may send them into a tailspin of self-negation. Yet they have the possibility of achieving great contentment, particularly if they acknowledge their need to withdraw from the world from time to time and use those moments to nourish their deeply spiritual sense of understanding and their own best notions and intuitions of what makes them happy.

CHALLENGE: **NOT ALLOWING THEIR SENSE OF SELF TO SWING ACCORDING TO FLUCTUATIONS IN THEIR CAREERS OR FINANCES**
FULFILLMENT: **GROUNDING THEMSELVES BY GETTING IN TOUCH WITH THEIR PHYSICALITY**
NOTABLES: **KATHY BATES (ACTRESS; OSCAR FOR *MISERY*); PRINCE LEOPOLD BERNHARD (PRINCE OF THE NETHERLANDS)**

July 3–10

THE UNCONVENTIONAL
CANCER II

These imaginative people may do very well when placed on the Way of Satisfaction, providing they are able to direct their rich fantasy lives in such a way as to free themselves from the drudgery of too much career responsibility. Apt to be quite lavish in their tastes and possessing a fondness for creature comforts, they can truly enjoy themselves on this karmic path, providing they give themselves permission to do so. Too, Cancer II's run the risk of becoming obsessive and even greedy in their search for material achievement and may fail to address the more fun-loving and lighthearted side of their natures. Nevertheless, family and domestic life, especially children, will almost certainly bring out the best in these personalities, as such secure interactions will serve to strengthen their sense of self while indulging their more playful, pleasurable, and imaginative aspects.

RICHARD SIMMONS
TV host; fitness guru

———

7/12/1948
Cancer III

CHALLENGE: **RESISTING THE INNER VOICE THAT TELLS THEM THAT THEY ARE A BORE**
FULFILLMENT: **FEELING CONTENT WITH THEIR DAY-TO-DAY LIVES**
NOTABLES: **MITCH MILLER (CONDUCTOR/PRODUCER; TV HOST; "YELLOW ROSE OF TEXAS"); GEORGES POMPIDOU (FRENCH PRESIDENT; HELPED DRAFT FIFTH REPUBLIC CONSTITUTION)**

July 11–18

THE PERSUADER
CANCER III

Highly materialistic, Cancer III's are likely to achieve success, though not necessarily happiness, on the Way of Satisfaction. Their workaholic tendencies will be quite pronounced, and they will doubtless have to undergo a major shift in priorities before they can recognize the higher promise of this karmic path. Controlling their personal needs is second nature to these stubborn people; they may have to learn to accept and appreciate the simple pleasures. The key here is to take special care to nourish the spiritual and social aspects of their personalities and, in short, learn when to take a vacation. A meaningful and lively social life will provide them with a more relaxed perspective and help them to avoid the pitfalls of "all work and no play." Yet if they take care to indulge in that which makes them feel good, rather than with that which they feel is good for them, they can experience great transformation.

CHALLENGE: **FORCING THEMSELVES TO ADDRESS THEIR OWN NEEDS**
FULFILLMENT: **FEELING GOOD ABOUT THEMSELVES FOR HOW THEY HAVE TOUCHED OTHERS, NOT FOR WHAT THEY HAVE ACHIEVED**
NOTABLES: **HUME CRONYN (ACTOR/DIRECTOR); PINCHAS ZUKERMAN (VIOLINIST)**

July 19–25
OSCILLATION
CANCER–LEO CUSP

If they can manage to balance the nurturing and aggressive energies of their personalities with spontaneity and free expression, those born in this week who travel the Way of Satisfaction can have a fine time. Though not likely to be among the more placid of the travelers here, they will derive great contentment from familiar environments and are able to find pleasure and even a measure of excitement in even relatively mundane circumstances. Though some may experience difficulty with the need to turn inward and address what, exactly, motivates their sense of ambition, most will find it rather easy to learn to live and let live. And while there are those who will choose to exploit their talent for intensity to the detriment of stability and joy, most will do very well when grounded in solid domestic and family relationships and may truly blossom when they undertake the task of raising or working with children, pursuing creative hobbies, or otherwise indulging their need for serenity.

CHALLENGE: **ALLOWING THEIR LIVES TO BE ROUTINE**
FULFILLMENT: **TEMPERING THEIR EXPECTATIONS OF THEMSELVES BY BEING CONTENT WITH THE ORDINARY**
NOTABLE: **CAT STEVENS (FOLK/POP SINGER, "MOONSHADOW"; BECAME DEVOUT MUSLIM)**

MARSHALL McLUHAN
English professor; writer; controversial views on the media, predicted the global village based on electronic interdependence in 1962

7/21/1911
Cancer–Leo Cusp

July 26–August 2
AUTHORITY
LEO I

These personalities will face their share of challenges along the Way of Satisfaction, as they are likely to have difficulty separating themselves from their professional endeavors and worldly reputation. Tenacious and opinionated, often in the extreme, these individuals may face some hard lessons in the area of personal relationships until they take stock of what they really want out of life and learn to enjoy themselves more. Authoritarian and hardworking, they can easily rise to a certain level of achievement, yet may back down from the need to take a personal inventory in the interest of greater happiness. Yet the tendency to self-flagellation is not much of a danger, as long as they learn to relax their standards and indulge their natural sense of generosity. Too, their great honesty, sensuality, and love of laughter will be of great assistance on this journey, and if they release their need to impress others through their worldly standing, they will consider themselves fortunate indeed.

CHALLENGE: **REALIZING THAT THEIR CREATIVE PRODUCTS ARE NOT EXTENSIONS OF THEMSELVES**
FULFILLMENT: **BEING SECURE ENOUGH TO POKE FUN AT THEMSELVES NOW AND THEN**
NOTABLE: **EMILY BRONTË (AUTHOR, *WUTHERING HEIGHTS*)**

August 3–10
BALANCED STRENGTH
LEO II

The principal problem for Leo II's who travel the Way of Satisfaction will be the fact that they are likely to be surrounded by people whose values differ so greatly from their own that they become enmeshed in the need to win or convince others of the rightness of their position. Thus, this configuration may in some way entail their making something of a break with their immediate environment as they go in search of the fulfillment they seek. This may be easier than it sounds for these stubborn people, however, as it is difficult for them to change their minds. Yet if they allow themselves enough latitude to understand that change and the yearning for greater enjoyment of the simple pleasures is not necessarily an admission of guilt, failure, or otherwise falling short of the mark, the result is likely to be both spiritually beneficial and personally liberating.

CHALLENGE: **PUTTING LIMITS ON THE DEGREE OF THEIR SACRIFICING FOR WORK**
FULFILLMENT: **CULTIVATING AND ENGAGING MORE SPIRITED, UPBEAT, AND JUST PLAIN FUN FRIENDS AND ASSOCIATES**
NOTABLES: **LUCILLE BALL (ACTRESS/COMEDIAN, *I LOVE LUCY*); WILLIAM DINES (INVENTED ATMOSPHERIC MEASURING DEVICES)**

KATHLEEN BATTLE
Opera singer

8/13/1948
Leo III

August 11–18
LEADERSHIP
LEO III

Likely to experience great material success on the Way of Satisfaction, Leo III's will nevertheless have to avoid a tendency to become so entrenched that they lose sight of everything but their goals. Especially prone to a narrow and materialistic view of life, they will have to do a bit of work to open themselves to the wide array of pleasures and the sense of satisfaction that beckon here. A real reevaluation of themselves and their values is likely to occur at some point in their lives, probably as the result of a career upset or a change in a relationship of long standing. And while they are quite capable of manipulating others through their financial power and worldly status, ultimately they will have to come to terms with the fact that control over others holds little possibility for personal gratification.

CHALLENGE: **KNOWING THAT THE RECOGNITION AND ACKNOWLEDGMENT OF OTHERS IS NOT A TRUE MEASURE OF SELF-WORTH**
FULFILLMENT: **FINDING WAYS TO RELAX AND GIVE THEMSELVES PLEASURE**
NOTABLES: **GEORGE IV (KING OF ENGLAND); JANE WYATT (ACTRESS, *FATHER KNOWS BEST*)**

August 19–25

EXPOSURE
LEO–VIRGO CUSP

Leo–Virgos may have a certain amount of difficulty in attaining the balance between their need for approval and their need for an increased sense of self-worth and acceptance that is called for by the Way of Satisfaction. In fact, those born in the Week of Exposure may become unduly suspicious and caught up in all sorts of intrigues and scandals when traveling this karmic path. Indeed, their intensity can be their undoing. Highly observant and perceptive, they may nevertheless find themselves confronted with a truly unmanageable level of conflict if they attempt to expand their worldly power base at the expense of their own deeper needs. In fact, "simplify" ought to be their mantra on this journey. Learning to trust and themselves and to indulge in more spontaneous forms of self-expression will keep them connected with the higher aspirations of this karmic path. Yet if they can manage to stay honest with themselves, their way will be greatly clarified.

ROBERT PLANT
Lead singer of Led Zeppelin, "Stairway to Heaven"

8/20/1948
Leo–Virgo Cusp

CHALLENGE: **DISENTANGLING THE MANY RUSES THEY HAVE USED TO HIDE WHO THEY REALLY ARE**

FULFILLMENT: **LETTING GO AND BEING COMPLETELY THEM-SELVES WITH TRUSTED FRIENDS OR MATES**

NOTABLE: **TIPPER GORE (WIFE OF VICE PRESIDENT AL GORE)**

August 26–September 2

SYSTEM BUILDERS
VIRGO I

Separating their notions of self-esteem from their job or profession may prove a rather arduous process for those born in the Week of System Builders who travel the Way of Satisfaction. Though there are few who can equal in their power of concentration or attention to detail, this usually comes at the expense of too much emotional repression, which may assume rather dangerous proportions. Yet they can achieve much by undertaking a journey inward in order to establish their true priorities and identify the routes to greater contentment. And while they may never turn out to be hedonists, they can derive a great sense of personal liberation by freeing themselves from those who fail to adequately nourish their spirit and by embracing activities, people, and interests that impart to them a sense of genuine joy .

CHALLENGE: **WORKING TO HEAL THEIR DIFFICULTY IN MAKING DECISIONS AND THEREBY THEIR SENSE OF SELF-WORTH**

FULFILLMENT: **NURTURING THEIR PHYSICAL AND EMOTIONAL NEEDS**

NOTABLES: **CHRISTA MCAULIFFE (1ST TEACHER IN SPACE; DIED IN *CHALLENGER* EXPLOSION); VALERIE SIMPSON (SONG-WRITER; SINGING PARTNER IN ASHFORD & SIMPSON)**

September 3–10

THE ENIGMA
VIRGO II

Those born in the Week of the Enigma who make their way along this karmic path can expect considerable reward and contentment, providing they loosen up a bit and allow themselves sufficient opportunities to pursue the things that make them really happy. These hardworking, discerning people do, however, run the risk of becoming too caught up in their worldly image and others' opinions of them to make the necessary attempts to look inward and get in touch with the feeling of inadequacy that may hold them back from greater fulfillment. Yet if they learn to indulge their fine tastes and open themselves to greater intimacy with others, they can experience a real flowering.

ALFRED A. KNOPF
Publisher; house included 16 Nobel laureates

9/12/1892
Virgo III

CHALLENGE: **LETTING GO OF A CERTAIN PICKINESS AND LEARNING HOW TO BE SATISFIED**

FULFILLMENT: **SURROUNDING THEMSELVES WITH FRIENDS AND LOVED ONES WHO ARE DEPENDABLE, LOYAL, AND, ABOVE ALL, KIND**

September 11–18

THE LITERALIST
VIRGO III

Diligent and goal-oriented, these intense personalities may experience a bit of struggle in the quest for greater personal satisfaction and contentment. In fact, they have a stubborn, even didactic, streak that may well manifest itself as a tendency to be much better at knowing what's good for everyone else than what's good for themselves. Too, they may get so caught up attending to the tasks and duties of the moment and putting out the small fires of daily life that they fail to grasp the connection between success and personal satisfaction. Yet they can much fulfillment and happiness, and if they are careful not to become ruthless or judgmental and instead nurture their sense of values and innate need for harmony, they will find great peace in both a job well done and the simpler and more earthy pleasures that beckon.

CHALLENGE: **CULTIVATING A MORE "GO WITH THE FLOW" APPROACH TO LIFE**

FULFILLMENT: **ENJOYING THE LEISURE-TIME ACTIVITIES THAT PROFESSIONAL SUCCESS AFFORDS**

NOTABLE: **JOHN RITTER (ACTOR, *THREE'S COMPANY*)**

September 19–24

BEAUTY
VIRGO–LIBRA CUSP

Though likely to have much greater powers of concentration, application, and, perhaps even depth of character than might ordinarily be the case, Virgo–Libras who travel the Way of Satisfaction can expect a journey marked by both a measure of success and personal harmony. The key to their development, however, will be learning to give up their preoccupation with superficial issues and go beneath the surface to access their truest sources of personal enlightenment. Despite their seeming self-confidence, they may harbor some deep-seated feelings of unworthiness that will require greater scrutiny. Yet in many ways the challenges of this karmic path are quite well suited to these sensuous, physical individuals; if they are careful not to ignore the higher challenge of acceptance of self and contentment with what they have, they are in for a comfortable trip.

BRYANT GUMBEL
TV journalist,
The Today Show

9/29/1948
Libra I

CHALLENGE: **NOT SLIPPING INTO A FORM OF SELF-SATISFACTION THAT IS MERELY SMUG**
FULFILLMENT: **REVELING IN AN EASY GIVE-AND-TAKE BETWEEN WORK AND PLAY**
NOTABLES: **PHIL HARTMAN (ACTOR/COMEDIAN, *SATURDAY NIGHT LIVE*); JEREMY IRONS (ACTOR, *REVERSAL OF FORTUNE*)**

September 25–October 2

THE PERFECTIONIST
LIBRA I

Not much inclined to sensuous self-indulgence or contentment with the simple pleasures, the intense personalities born in this week who navigate the Way of Satisfaction will have to do some reconstructing of their lives in order to realize their opportunities for happiness. Often quite cool and collected, they have a worldly, sophisticated exterior that can sometimes mask a wealth of emotional conflicts that beg for both acknowledgment and resolution. These individuals would do well to cultivate the fine art of simply letting go when people and events don't accord with their exacting standards. Yet if they open themselves to the possibility of a wide variety of personal relationships and increased rapport with others, and remember to reward themselves for their own accomplishments, the road to happiness and self-love will be considerably eased.

CHALLENGE: **OWNING THE IDEA THAT THEIR WORKAHOLISM IS MERELY AN ATTEMPT TO SHORE UP THEIR SHAKY SENSE OF SELF-WORTH**
FULFILLMENT: **FEELING TRULY SATISFIED NOT JUST WITH THEIR BODY OF WORK BUT WITH EACH INDIVIDUAL ELEMENT AS WELL**
NOTABLE: **OLIVIA NEWTON-JOHN (SINGER; ACTRESS, *GREASE*)**

October 3–10

SOCIETY
LIBRA II

The imaginative, rather romantic souls born in the Week of Society who travel the Way of Satisfaction are likely to be popular, insightful characters who will nevertheless have something of a problem releasing their tendency to undervalue themselves. Though certainly not as lackadaisical as some Libra II's when it comes to applying their considerable talents in a professional arena, they may be rather blind when it comes to knowing what will make them happy or will afford them greater opportunities to develop a secure and contented identity. Thus, the key to their advancement along this karmic path will be their ability to zone in on themselves and the things they really care about and to avoid the temptation to deceive themselves or to adopt a set of values not truly their own.

DONNA KARAN
Fashion designer

10/2/1948
Libra I

CHALLENGE: **TEMPERING A CERTAIN TENDENCY TO ELITISM OR SNOBBISHNESS BEFORE THEY LEARN A PAINFUL LESSON BY BEING THE VICTIM OF SAME**
FULFILLMENT: **PAMPERING THEMSELVES WITH ALL MANNER OF CREATURE COMFORTS**
NOTABLE: **JACKSON BROWNE (SINGER)**

October 11–18

THEATER
LIBRA III

Possessed of some truly virtuoso talents, those born in the Week of Theater who travel the Way of Satisfaction can expect quite a lot of success on this path, yet they may have to work a bit harder to achieve the levels of personal satisfaction and self-worth that beckon. Libra III's may get mired in their need for approval and lose sight of the deeper objectives of this karmic path. Self-examination does not come easily to them, in any event, and they may stick to the same course for years without adequately evaluating their own role in their personal development. Yet they have a capacity to manifest their fondest dreams in highly tangible ways. If they can harness their energy in such a way that their power to achieve coincides with their deepest desires, all will go well.

CHALLENGE: **BANISHING THE KIND OF DRAMATICS THEY USE TO GAIN A RATHER HOLLOW BRAND OF APPROVAL FROM OTHERS**
FULFILLMENT: **FIGURING OUT WHO THEIR FRIENDS ARE**
NOTABLE: **MARGOT KIDDER (ACTRESS, *SUPERMAN*)**

October 19–25

DRAMA AND CRITICISM
LIBRA–SCORPIO CUSP

Learning to mitigate their intensity with proper amounts of relaxation, enjoyment, and simple fun will doubtless prove the biggest problem for those born on the Cusp of Drama and Criticism who travel this karmic path. Inclined to be hypercritical, they are equally likely to be hard on themselves, especially when they fall short of their own ideas of accomplishment. Yet they are possessed of a sensuous side that, properly indulged, can do much to augment their tendency to live on the edge or push the envelope of accomplishment. If they cultivate greater versatility and self-acceptance though the wide variety of friends, associates, and experience available to them, they will realize the relatively rare combination of great success coupled with great happiness and peace.

ED ASNER
Actor, *The Mary Tyler Moore Show*

11/15/1929
Scorpio III

CHALLENGE: **DEFEATING THEIR PESSIMISM**

FULFILLMENT: **FINDING CONTENTMENT AND SATISFACTION IN A LOVE RELATIONSHIP**

NOTABLES: **LYDIA LOPOKOVA (RUSSIAN DANCER); JENNY AND ROSE DOLLY (TWINS; VAUDEVILLE STARS, *ZIEGFELD FOLLIES*)**

October 26–November 2

INTENSITY
SCORPIO I

Learning to relax will be of paramount importance to those born in the Week of Intensity who travel the Way of Satisfaction, as will be learning to forgive and forget. Highly likely to become masters of their professions no matter what they choose to do with their lives, these personalities may nevertheless find material success a rather meaningless experience until they give themselves permission to enjoy the fruits of their labors. And while these highly emotional people may never be entirely satisfied with themselves or others, they will do best when they surround themselves with a select group of family and friends whose more tolerant and indulgent attitudes will encourage them to accept their own humanity and capacity for pleasure and contentment. That, along with learning to laugh at themselves and the world at large, will be their key to contentment.

CHALLENGE: **TRYING NOT TO CRAVE APPROVAL FROM OTHERS BUT LEARNING TO GIVE IT TO THEMSELVES**

FULFILLMENT: **MATURING TO THE POINT WHERE THEY ARE LESS DEMANDING OF EVERYONE**

November 3–11

DEPTH
SCORPIO II

To fulfill the promise of abundance inherent to this karmic path, those born in the Week of Depth will have to work hard to release their identification with worldly achievement and attention to detail. Yet they are well suited to the inner journey required by this karmic path and will doubtless come to the realization that we are all more than the sum of our worldly achievements—and more, too, than the sum of our problems or psychological issues. The depth of understanding available to these people is the single ingredient that will enable them to rise to the higher challenge of developing a real sense of self-worth. And though many will struggle to overcome any number of tendencies toward self-destruction, self-doubt, and an overly materialistic view of the world, if they keep in mind that their reality is ultimately shaped by their attitudes and that this works both for good and for ill, they will find peace.

MCLEAN STEVENSON
Actor, *M*A*S*H*

11/14/1929
Scorpio III

CHALLENGE: **ENJOYING MONEY FOR THE PLEASURES IT AFFORDS, NOT FOR THE SELF-ESTEEM THEY MISTAKENLY THINK IT REPRESENTS**

FULFILLMENT: **RELAXING, LETTING LIFE TAKE ITS COURSE, WHILE PUTTING THEIR KIND, GENTLE, AND DEVOTED SIDE IN CONTROL**

November 12–18

CHARM
SCORPIO III

Those born in the Week of Charm who find themselves on the Way of Satisfaction can find wonderful fulfillment, yet they will have to make peace with their own inclination to self-negation before they can realize its promise. In fact, many of these charismatic people project a worldly image that has little to do with their innermost needs and desires. Thus, they may be curiously unable to achieve their goals due to a number of upheavals and upsets before they realize they are striving toward aims they don't necessarily want to achieve. Still, opportunities for tremendous personal growth abound with this configuration, and if they work to reconcile their innermost feelings with their outer reality, they are more than capable of enjoying a relaxed, tolerant, and ultimately more loving attitude toward themselves and others.

CHALLENGE: **SORTING OUT WHAT IT IS THEY TRULY WANT AND WHY**

FULFILLMENT: **KNOWING THAT THEY ARE WORTHY OF LOVE WITHOUT HAVING TO USE CHARM OR MANIPULATION TO GET IT**

NOTABLES: **HAROLD ROSS (FOUNDED *THE NEW YORKER*); WILLIAM SCHWENK GILBERT (ENGLISH DRAMATIST)**

November 19–24
REVOLUTION
SCORPIO–SAGITTARIUS CUSP

Likely to be more preoccupied with changing the world than they are with changing themselves, Scorpio–Sagittarians on this path can nevertheless realize the satisfaction and sense of triumph that comes with achieving their own private revolution. This is a configuration that points more to personal transformation than to effecting alterations or sweeping changes in their immediate environment. Cultivating the necessary sense of self-worth and contentment may not come easily for them, as they are more inclined to seek out peak or ecstatic experiences than they are to undertake the slower business of raising their own self-esteem. Yet they have the possibility of success, especially when they slow down, relax, and remember that Rome was not built in a day.

BERRY GORDY, JR.
Music executive; founded
Motown Records

———

11/28/1929
Sagittarius I

CHALLENGE: **TRANSFORMING THEIR GENERAL DISSATISFACTION WITH NEARLY ALL THEY ENCOUNTER**
FULFILLMENT: **DEVELOPING MORE CONTENTMENT WITH WHAT IS AND PATIENCE FOR WHAT MAY BE**
NOTABLE: **MARILYN FRENCH (AUTHOR, *THE WOMEN'S ROOM*)**

November 25–December 2
INDEPENDENCE
SAGITTARIUS I

Those born in the Week of Independence can experience quite a bit of personal fulfillment and happiness on the Way of Satisfaction, yet they will have to work hard to overcome their need to win at all costs. Though they are blessed with considerable insight, their stubbornness, fixation, and obsession with success or what others may think of them can all be real obstacles to their development, as can their tendency to assert their authority in all the wrong places and situations. Still, their innate need for greater freedom and natural love of life will be assets. Further, their keen insight will help steer them away from stifling routines and burdensome responsibilities. If they are careful to nurture their social side and focus their considerable energies on those things that augment and enhance their feelings of worthiness, these souls will shine.

CHALLENGE: **FOSTERING WITHIN THEMSELVES TRUE SELF-CONFIDENCE RATHER THAN JUST A GOOD ACTING JOB**
FULFILLMENT: **INDULGING THEIR LOVE OF TRAVEL, SPORTS, OR OTHER HOBBIES**
NOTABLE: **AMOS BRONSON ALCOTT (EDUCATOR; MYSTIC; WRITER)**

December 3–10
THE ORIGINATOR
SAGITTARIUS II

The Originators who travel the Way of Satisfaction may discover that some of their feelings of unworthiness stem from the fact that their natural talent and unusual brand of creativity are a bit ahead of their time. Apt to associate worldly success with self-worth, these original individuals will certainly take advantage of the promise of this karmic path to fulfill their ambitions; the question is, will they be happy? Yet when they set aside more worldly aspirations in order to pursue a greater degree of self-acceptance and happiness, that worldly validation of their efforts and contributions will follow. Finally, this life journey may present these individuals with opportunities to establish connections with soul mates that should not be ignored. For it is likely that they will find that their deepest satisfaction ultimately comes through the experience of genuine love.

DICK CLARK
Host of *American
Bandstand*

———

11/30/1929
Sagittarius I

CHALLENGE: **REALIZING THAT THEY CAN NEVER SATISFY EVERYONE AND FOCUSING ON SATISFYING THEMSELVES**
FULFILLMENT: **COMING TO TERMS WITH THEIR ECCENTRICITY**
NOTABLES: **FRANCISCO FRANCO (SPANISH DICTATOR); JOHN CASSAVETES (ACTOR/DIRECTOR)**

December 11–18
THE TITAN
SAGITTARIUS III

Those born in the Week of the Titan who negotiate the Way of Satisfaction may have to make a rather strenuous inward journey before they can successfully release their need to exercise authority over others, on the one hand, and their deep-seated and well-disguised feelings of unworthiness, on the other. Self-awareness is not likely to be their strong suit, and they will be challenged to reevaluate both their worldly ambitions and their sense of entitlement before they can make real progress. Broadening their social context, indulging their philosophical inclinations, and educating themselves in issues and experiences common to us all will prove especially beneficial, as will a conscious effort to develop greater peace of mind through living and letting live.

CHALLENGE: **NOT INFLICTING PICAYUNE TYRANNY ON OTHERS**
FULFILLMENT: **GETTING TO THE ROOT OF THEIR DISSATISFACTION AND LACK OF SELF-WORTH TO TRANSFORM THEM**
NOTABLES: **J. PAUL GETTY (OIL BILLIONAIRE); CHRISTOPHER PLUMMER (ACTOR, *THE SOUND OF MUSIC*); WILLIAM SAFIRE (JOURNALIST; WON PULITZER)**

December 19–25

PROPHECY
SAGITTARIUS–CAPRICORN CUSP

Those born on the Cusp of Prophecy who travel this karmic path may well have a relatively easy passage, as its energies are much in keeping with their natural inclinations. They will have to combat their tendency to get mired in purely material pursuits, however, as they may have pronounced acquisitive instincts. Some of them will also struggle with depression and a tendency to be antisocial. Yet no one is better at playing their hunches and getting in touch with their inner guidance system of intuition and self-awareness. If they bring those instincts to bear in their quest for greater self-worth, they will rarely be disappointed. They will, however, need to cultivate their social side and indulge themselves in those things that give them both sensual gratification and a sense of their place in the larger scheme.

CHALLENGE: **TEMPERING THEIR AMBITION AND TENDENCY TO WORK TOO HARD WITH SENSUOUS PLEASURES**

FULFILLMENT: **FEELING GREAT SATISFACTION IN A GOOD LOVE RELATIONSHIP**

NOTABLE: **DAME REBECCA WEST (NOVELIST; CRITIC, *THE BIRDS FALL DOWN*)**

MARY HIGGINS CLARK
Author,
Where Are the Children

12/24/1929
Sagittarius–Capricorn
Cusp

December 26–January 2

THE RULER
CAPRICORN I

The rather formidable souls born in the Week of the Ruler who make their way along this karmic path may achieve a high degree of worldly success, yet they will have some rather serious problems with learning to release their tendency to identify themselves totally with those same accomplishments. Thus, it is likely that most of the lessons of this karmic path will revolve around issues of personal enjoyment and the development of a more satisfying private life. Emotional expression does not come easily to these people, in any event, yet if they cultivate a network of close friends and family who will help them to release their feelings of self-doubt, unworthiness, or overly strict ideas of what and what is not acceptable, they will surely prosper.

CHALLENGE: **GRAPPLING WITH THEIR EGO AND ITS IDENTIFICATION WITH WORLDLY ACHIEVEMENT**

FULFILLMENT: **FEELING RELAXED AND CONTENT ENOUGH TO REVEAL THEIR EMOTIONS**

NOTABLES: **MILI BALAKIREV (RUSSIAN COMPOSER); JASON ROBARDS (ACTOR)**

January 3–9

DETERMINATION
CAPRICORN II

Encouraging their natural interest in metaphysical matters will be of great assistance to those born in the Week of Determination who travel the Way of Satisfaction. So highly motivated that they will often be tempted to ignore the challenge implied here and stretch their talents to the outermost limits, they have some workaholic aspects that will bear watching. Yet if they strive not only for worldly accomplishment but for spiritual satisfaction, this road is likely to be eased considerably. Especially important will be their choice of partner; if they can share the ups and downs of everyday existence with someone who will help them lighten them up a bit and appreciate them more for their idealism, humor, and sensitivity than they do for their material wealth, worldly status, and potential to leave the competition in the dust, they will realize great happiness.

CHALLENGE: **STEPPING BACK AND LOOKING AT WHAT THEIR DETERMINATION TO WIN MIGHT BE COSTING THEM**

FULFILLMENT: **HAVING PROVEN WHAT THEY NEED TO, DROPPING THE TOUGH-GUY ACT AND REVEALING THEIR SENSITIVE SIDE**

DON SHULA
Miami Dolphin head coach

1/4/1930
Capricorn II

January 10–16

DOMINANCE
CAPRICORN III

Since those born in the Week of Dominance often have a work ethic more or less equivalent to that of John Calvin, who believed that worldly success was direct evidence of God's love, their attitudes will likely need a bit of readjusting on this karmic path. The inner journey it requires will dictate that they come to terms with a secret inferiority complex that can hold them back from real enjoyment. Much prone to the need to prove themselves, they will have to recognize the value of private life and nurture close relationships with others in an atmosphere of mutual trust, rather than one of rigid boundaries. Yet many of these people have a strong sensual side that needs encouragement. If they can remember to reward themselves for their own considerable efforts, life will doubtless be easier for them.

CHALLENGE: **LOWERING THEIR EXPECTATIONS ENOUGH TO BE HAPPY WITH THEIR MANY ACCOMPLISHMENTS**

FULFILLMENT: **ALLOWING THEMSELVES DOWNTIME TO REDISCOVER WHO THEY ARE**

NOTABLE: **ROD TAYLOR (AUSTRALIAN ACTOR, *THE BIRDS*)**

January 17–22

MYSTERY AND IMAGINATION
CAPRICORN–AQUARIUS CUSP

Blessed with a naturally lighthearted outlook and a fine sense of humor, those born on this cusp will do very well on the Way of Satisfaction. If they are careful to keep their sense of perspective about their tendency to overidentify with their work or creative talents, these highly social and rather tempestuous personalities are sure to find both achievement and fun along this road. In fact, the only real danger is that they may become so wrapped up in the imaginative and creative side of existence that they fail to direct their energies in a productive fashion and come to expect more worldly reward before they put out the necessary effort. Emotional instability may also plague some of them. Yet all in all, their potential for happiness is great—providing they keep in mind that happiness has a way of attracting more of the same.

CHALLENGE: **KNOWING THE DIFFERENCE BETWEEN REWARD-
ING THEMSELVES WITH SENSUOUS PLEASURES AND GOING
HOG WILD**

FULFILLMENT: **COMBINING THEIR INVENTIVENESS WITH THE
PRAGMATISM OF THIS KARMIC PATH TO CREATE SOMETHING
OF SERVICE TO OTHERS**

**EDWIN "BUZZ"
ALDRIN**
Astronaut, 2d man to
walk on the moon

1/20/1930
Capricorn–Aquarius Cusp

January 23–30

GENIUS
AQUARIUS I

Likely to become so caught up in the manifestation of ideas, theories, and brilliant innovation that they fail to connect not only with the world of personal pleasure but with the human side of existence, those born in the Week of Genius who travel the Way of Satisfaction will require a bit of grounding before they can find real happiness. Yet they have a great potential for success as Aquarius I's are unlikely to get bogged down in a preoccupation with power structures, intrigues, or overidentification with their professional or creative products. In fact, there is much of the maverick about these souls, and if they employ their need for freedom in a quest for greater enjoyment, all will go brilliantly.

CHALLENGE: **KNOWING WHEN TO STOP PUSHING AND BE
SATISFIED**

FULFILLMENT: **FEEDING THEIR NEED FOR A VARIETY OF
EXPERIENCES AND PLEASURES**

NOTABLE: **JOHN D. ROCKEFELLER, JR. (PHILANTHROPIST)**

January 31–February 7

YOUTH AND EASE
AQUARIUS II

If they can control their tendency to harbor leftover feelings of self-doubt or unworthiness and open themselves to the world of reward and pleasure, those born in the Week of Youth and Ease are likely to have a positively cushy trip on the Way of Satisfaction. If the laws of reincarnation operate as is generally believed, these souls must have been very, very good in their past lives, for almost no one is better equipped to strike the right balance between concerted effort through their own virtuoso talents and a genuine ability to set aside conflicts in the interest of greater enjoyment of life. Though they may have a tendency to emotional immaturity or isolation resulting from a need for approval, their sheer popularity and love of the good life will ensures that with even a modicum of introspection, life will be good to them.

CHALLENGE: **BECOMING MORE SATISFIED WITH THEIR PHYSICAL
APPEARANCE, ESPECIALLY AS THEY AGE**

FULFILLMENT: **GOING ABOUT THEIR LIVES AND WORK WITH
AS FEW PROBLEMS AS POSSIBLE**

NOTABLE: **HUGO VON HOFMANNSTHAL (POET; PLAYWRIGHT)**

GERTRUDE STEIN
Writer; art patron;
hostess and inspiration
to Hemingway, Fitzgerald,
etc.

2/3/1874
Aquarius II

February 8–15

ACCEPTANCE
AQUARIUS III

Aquarius III's who travel they Way of Satisfaction may need to honor their sense of ethics and release the personal demons that hold them back from greater self-affirmation. Cutting loose old habits and opinions will prove to be very important, and they must be careful to embrace the opportunities for renewed self-esteem offered by this karmic path. The saving grace of this configuration is the simple fact that these individuals tend to bore easily. They can use that quality to get themselves unstuck from even the deepest workaholic ruts, for they will be quite conscious of the dangers of "all work and no play." Perhaps the principal danger is that these souls may misdirect their energies and exhaust their potential in approval seeking. If they take care to evaluate themselves and learn that self-worth is ultimately a question of allowing themselves to fail occasionally, all will go brilliantly.

CHALLENGE: **REMEDYING WHATEVER INNER DISSATISFACTION
IT IS THAT CAUSES THEM TO GET INTO NUMEROUS SCRAPES**

FULFILLMENT: **ARRIVING AT A POINT IN LIFE WHERE THEY
FEEL GOOD ABOUT THEIR ABILITY TO OFFER SOMETHING OR
SOMEONE A GOOD MEASURE OF DEDICATION**

NOTABLES: **ARLEN SPECTER (U.S. SENATOR FROM PENNSYL-
VANIA); AMY LOWELL (POET)**

KARMIC PATH
30

February 16–22

SENSITIVITY
AQUARIUS–PISCES CUSP

The individuals born in this week who travel the Way of Satisfaction may find life a bit difficult. They will have to learn to set aside some of their own rather self-protective attitudes and allow themselves to reconcile their inner and outer natures before they can achieve the levels of relaxation and enjoyment that beckon. It will help them to keep their focus directed on tangible things and creature comforts that allow them greater access to their inner lives in a nonthreatening way. Using their worldly success to make available the worlds of beauty, fine things, and a country hideaway, and most especially indulging their natural interest in music, will greatly aid them in their quest for personal affirmation and enjoyment of life.

JOANNE WOODWARD
Actress, *The Three Faces of Eve*; activist

2/27/1930
Pisces I

CHALLENGE: **GETTING A GRIP ON THEIR INSECURITY**
FULFILLMENT: **MAXIMIZING THEIR SATISFACTION IN LIFE BY PROTECTING AND NURTURING THEIR SENSE OF SELF-WORTH**

February 23–March 2

SPIRIT
PISCES I

The higher challenge of this path is bound to do much to ground these intensely emotional and highly spiritual people in the world of personal pleasure and enjoyment. Too much watery energy can get in the way of their success and lead them to flounder a bit, yet whatever their personal insecurities, they can mitigate them to some extent by indulging themselves in the sensual and more earthy aspects of this configuration. Otherwise, they run the risk of getting lost somewhere in the course of their inner journey, stuck in a world of introspection that is neither productive nor enjoyable. Thus they should take care to surround themselves with beautiful things, lighthearted friends, and substantial evidence of their achievements that indulge their senses and at the same time affirm their identities.

CHALLENGE: **LIMITING THE DEGREE TO WHICH THEY PURSUE THEIR SPIRITUAL AMBITIONS**
FULFILLMENT: **GROUNDING THEMSELVES IN THE DAY-TO-DAY WORLD OF PRACTICAL NECESSITIES AND RELATIONSHIPS**

March 3–10

THE LONER
PISCES II

The Loners who travel the Way of Satisfaction may find the peace they seek in a private inner world, yet they may fail the higher challenge to development presented by this karmic path by becoming mired in suspicious and pessimistic attitudes toward themselves and others. Broadening their social network will help them keep a perspective on both career and personal issues, as will being willing to indulge their fine sense of the aesthetic. Too much introspection can be as dangerous as too little. Yet if they embrace their sense of beauty and remember to congratulate themselves for having survived what will doubtless be a number of emotional extremes, they can make tremendous progress.

ANTONY ARMSTRONG-JONES
Photographer/socialite

3/7/1930
Pisces II

CHALLENGE: **RECOGNIZING THAT SOMETHING IS WRONG WHEN THEY FEEL LONELY IN A CROWD OF PEOPLE WHO ARE SUPPOSED TO BE THEIR FRIENDS**
FULFILLMENT: **INDULGING THEIR LOVE OF MUSIC AND BEAUTY**

March 11–18

DANCERS AND DREAMERS
PISCES III

A tendency to overidentify with their own unique brand of talent and creativity will mark the journey of those born in this week who travel the Way of Satisfaction. Yet this will be a generally easy passage, providing these individuals can strike the right balance between a true sense of self-worth and too much self-satisfaction and complacency. Too, the need to be needed can serve as a substitute for genuine self-esteem for a number of these personalities, and they will have to take care to evaluate their relationships more carefully. Yet there is nevertheless a great deal of joy and happiness to be discovered along this karmic path, especially when they begin to understand that pleasure shared is pleasure doubled.

CHALLENGE: **AVOIDING SMUGNESS BY INJECTING A DOSE OF HUMILITY INTO THEIR SELF-ESTEEM**
FULFILLMENT: **FINDING CONTENTMENT IN THEIR NATURAL SENSE OF WONDER**

The Way of Grace

SCORPIO II TO TAURUS II
Depth to Teacher

The life purpose for the men and women on the Way of Grace is to cultivate the delicacy, tact, and culture that are the nature of grace. Often this goes so far as to include an ease or suppleness of movement or of the physical body in general. It certainly includes a mastery of what has been popularly termed "grace under fire": the generosity of spirit, charm, and propriety in even the most difficult of circumstances. It is interesting that individuals on the Way of Grace are given many opportunities to develop this attribute, since it seems to be their fate to undergo challenges and trials in their lives. As a result of the strength and character that results from overcoming such episodes, their fullest potential blossoms and they find personal fulfillment. Often these men and women become leaders by example because others become attracted to their grace, charm, and great magnetism. This enables them to have a platform for their views. Sharing a message is important to those on the Way of Grace and, true to the nature of grace, this message usually concerns those less fortunate than themselves and other good causes.

The Scorpio II origin of the Way of Grace carries with it such profundity of feeling that the individuals on this path are easily wounded by criticism, other forms of carelessness, or life trauma—particularly the loss or death of loved ones. Thus, many on this path prefer to live behind the scenes or in some form of retreat from life. However, Scorpio

---

CORE LESSON

Detaching emotionally when times get tough

GOAL

To develop ease of living and movement, culture, and elegance

---

GIFTS
Steadfast, Magnetic, Fair

PITFALLS
Depressed, Prone to Worry, Inflexible

---

energy is also a blueprint for tremendous inner resources, including empathy, seriousness of purpose, and strength of character, which are often put to the test on this path. Ironically, accident or coincidence plays a large role in the lives of those on the Way of Grace and they are no strangers to tragedy. Under the gun, these individuals have two choices: to revert to their Scorpio II roots by becoming angry, defensive, resentful, jealous, or to rise gracefully above the fray, providing proof of their great inner strength. As conflict or tragedy arises, they remain calm, aware, concerned for others, and do not devolve into self-pity or self-involved hysterics. Initially, this may not always be the case and "keeping it together" is apt to be difficult for them because, as feeling oriented as they are, they take all their own troubles and those of their loved ones to heart.

Whether the individuals on this path, like Hamlet, chose to "suffer the slings and arrows of outrageous fortune," or to "take arms against a sea of troubles," it is important for them to be less attached emotionally to what is occurring, no matter how painful. Otherwise each parry or thrust in a battle could wound these sensitive souls irrevocably. Despite their sensitivity, these individuals are fighters by nature, and fiercely protective of their loved ones. They don't back down and will continue to the bloody end of any contretemps. Thus, on this karmic path, it is imperative for them to learn how to detach their feel-

ings from any fight if they are to keep their psychological health intact. Separating their feelings from what may be happening around them, controlling the urge to escape, and developing a philosophical approach will assist them in being detached. This core lesson, once learned, will have many ramifications since it allows those on this path to emerge gradually from their self-imposed retreat and to carry on a more public life.

Intensely sensuous individuals, those on the Way of Grace find that a combination of physical activity and surrounding themselves with beauty helps to keep them in possession of their feelings and gives them peace of mind. Throughout their lives, the men and women on the Way of Grace will find themselves attracted to the beauty of the physical form. In fact, movement of all kinds fascinates them, including dance, athletics, and horsemanship. The men and women on this path may even be noted for a certain suppleness in the way they move. Sometimes this is innate. Other times it has been consciously cultivated due to a long-held belief from childhood that they are in some way awkward. As they progress on this karmic path, the fact of becoming increasingly comfortable in their bodies and exhibiting greater ease of movement is often symbolic of their development of inner grace.

Quite by trial and error, the individuals on the Way of Grace will find those art objects, hobbies, and activities that give them a sense of balance. Often they are extremely unaware of how sensitive they are to their environments, but, in fact, the balance of the elements around them can have extreme consequences for their emotional states. Raucous sound, poor architecture, jarring design, or other disruptive influences will eventually be banished from their living space, quite unconsciously, because these elements don't "feel right" to them. Due to their instinct for physical proportion, they have a natural feel for *feng shui,* the Chinese art of placement, and will positively blossom in simpler settings, with well-thought-out designs, perhaps even those influenced by the principles of Zen Buddhism.

Without thinking about it too much, those on the Way of Grace will eventually find a way to surround themselves with all that calms, soothes, and heals. Perhaps this is their inner response to the often turbulent outer world to which they are subjected. Their inner world begins to mirror their outer life and they start to feel more serene. Their mode of dress, too, becomes more elegant. And they appear to others as graceful and cultured. The overall effect is one of confidence and presence. Venus, the ruler of their destination point of Taurus II, begins to take over, and these individuals begin to exhibit great charm and personal magnetism. Soon, they are discovered by such a host of admirers that they can virtually write their own ticket for whatever

RELEASE

The need to hide

REWARD

The joy of rising above it all

SUGGESTION

Don't fight your fate. Cultivate emotional detachment—this doesn't mean don't feel; just don't let it get to you. Surround yourself with what feels right. Trust your sense of beauty.

they wish to do with themselves.

Often, much like a butterfly emerging from its chrysalis, those on this karmic path spend quite a lot of time behind the scenes early in life only to undergo their metamorphosis and emerge into the spotlight. They become softer, perhaps kinder, and more refined with maturity. Some of those on the Way of Grace may involve themselves in fashion or the arts, given their finely honed aesthetic sensibilities. Others may be athletes since, on this karmic path, many perfect a certain grace of movement, not to mention their instinct for distance and measurement. Then there are a few whose great compassion and empathy will cause them to embrace their place in the spotlight as an opportunity to present their views or promote their favorite causes. As freethinkers committed to the truth, so that even their lives become more public, they will be true to themselves. Rarely overlooked, they will take their places with the movers and shakers of the world. Few would ever guess that their stars would rise as high as they often do. A true metamorphosis from introvert to extrovert occurs here, though rarely by design. Rather, those on this karmic path are presented with opportunities that, once accepted, lead to worldly recognition.

The social arena is the crucible for the metamorphosis of those on the Way of Grace. It is here that basically private, even escapist personalities learn to leave their worries behind and put their energies to work, often in the service of others. Their charm and grace motivate, inspire, and teach others by example. Ultimately, they may exhibit leadership skills, whether in

managing a family or professional group. Frequently known for their fairness, they will be sought out for their highly objective opinions and thus make particularly good consultants and troubleshooters. The magnetic qualities of those on the Way of Grace often places such individuals at the center of broad circles of friends or other social groups.

Choosing a suitable life partner is usually of paramount importance for those on this karmic path; a true partnership, one beneficial to the social and career advancement of both parties, would be the ideal. Raising children is also recommended for such a couple, whether their own or others'. The process of this path often transforms an intense sexuality into a more sensuous, more relaxed one. Such redirection is unlikely to come with any sense of regret or loss. In fact, sex can be an addiction to many on this path before they mature. Family ties are strong for those on this path, even to the point of establishing a kind of dynasty, which can continue for many generations. In terms of finances, the willingness to spend on objects of beauty does not mean that those on this path are extravagant. Quite the opposite, money minded, they have a keen sense of what something is worth. Moreover, their Scorpio I roots mean that they know how to attract money to them.

Reflecting on this karmic path reminds one of the children's fairy tale, "The Ugly Duckling." A young swan, mistaken for a young duck, is ridiculed by the other ducks as a misfit and labeled ugly. It is only with time that the "duckling" emerges as a full-grown swan, considered the most elegant and graceful of all waterfowl.

BALANCE POINT

Intensity and Ease

CRYSTALS AND GEMSTONES

*Luminous **Selenite** glows. The delicate radiance of this mineral shines upon any difficulty the individual encounters, motivating to move from the intensity of pain to the ease of joy.*

NOTABLES ON THIS KARMIC PATH

Typical of those on this path, **Jacqueline Kennedy Onassis** displayed great strength at a time of extreme duress. At the funeral of her slain husband, her stoic composure lent support to both her children and a grieving nation. As First Lady she contributed an unaccustomed grace to the White House, not only with her impeccable appearance, but also through her taste in furnishings and cultured manner. Inviting many artists to appear and perform at the Presidential residence, she rid her position of the dowdy connotations inherited from its predecessors. Throughout the rest of her life she maintained her glamorous image, marrying shipping magnate Aristotle Onassis in 1968 and later working in New York publishing.

JACQUELINE KENNEDY ONASSIS

Grace Kelly, who became Princess Grace of Monaco, clearly followed her eponymous path. After a wild adolescence in Philadelphia, Kelly embarked on a short but legendary acting career, lending her polished elegance to such films as *High Noon, High Society,* and *The Country Girl,* for which she won a Best Actress Oscar. She succeeded in surrounding

GRACE KELLY

herself with the beauty and serenity required by those born on this karmic path through her marriage to Prince Rainier III. This partnership was favorable for her in many ways; it greatly benefited her social standing and gave the opportunity to serve as a role model.

Vital to the Dallas Cowboys' three Superbowl victories, Quarterback **Troy Aikman** exemplifies the term "grace under fire." Overcoming a slight childhood physical disability to play football at age eight, he has excelled at his sport and the suppleness of movement characteristic of this path. Deeply caring like

TROY AIKMAN

many on the Way of Grace, Aikman is good with children. His time spent teaching children has reinforced his belief that kids should be allowed to follow their dreams. Troy modestly credits his coaches and parents for helping him to do just that.

Other Notables: Larry Gatlin, Ursula Kroeber LeGuin, Willa Cather, Sinead O'Connor, Andrew Lloyd Webber, Rhea Perlman, Steve Winwood, Stevie Nicks, Cole Porter, Phylicia Rashad, Mae West, Yasir Arafat, Bob Newhart, Arnold Palmer, Bert Stern, Cyril Cusack, Ronald Reagan, Kurt Cobain, Bernadette Peters, James Taylor, Dick Button, Steven Tyler

---

BIRTHDAYS ON KARMIC PATH 31

April 3, 1892–August 22, 1892 | November 14, 1910–April 4, 1911

June 26, 1929–November 13, 1929 | February 5, 1948–June 25, 1948 | September 16, 1966–February 4, 1967

April 28, 1985–September 15, 1985 | December 8, 2003–April 27, 2004

KARMIC PATH
31

March 19–24
REBIRTH
PISCES–ARIES CUSP

Those born in this period are promised a process of great personal refinement along this karmic path. Yet they will nevertheless have to do a certain amount of work when it comes to the better controlling of their emotions, as they have both a deeply sensitive emotional nature and the potential to respond in a purely aggressive fashion when the chips are down. It will be particularly important for them to off-load some early emotional baggage; hanging on to feelings of being misunderstood or mistreated early in life can establish response patterns that will need to be adjusted before these people can realize the potential for transformation. Yet their natural independence and resilience will be of utmost assistance here. If they are careful to cultivate patience and objectivity, their evolution on this path will be nothing short of miraculous.

CHALLENGE: **NOT DEVOLVING INTO THE VICTIM ROLE**
FULFILLMENT: **BECOMING MORE SOCIALLY ADEPT**
NOTABLE: **ANDREW W. MELLON (FINANCIER; PUBLIC OFFICIAL; PHILANTHROPIST; FORMED GULF OIL}**

ANDREW LLOYD WEBBER
Composer, *Evita, Cats, Phantom of the Opera*

3/22/1948
Pisces–Aries Cusp

March 25–April 2
THE CHILD
ARIES I

Gifted with greater depth and more emotional maturity than some born in this week, the Aries I person who travels the Way of Grace may have a rough start in life that may contribute to a tendency to isolation or a rather neurotic quest for security on this path. Though their rather unrefined approach to life may require some polishing, whatever their circumstances, Aries I's will have the ability to serve as teachers or role models to others. Though their partner choices are not inclined to be especially realistic, they are nevertheless destined to realize much of their potential for development through raising or working with children. In an atmosphere that provides them the chance to impart their experience and knowledge they will inspire others and gain needed respect.

CHALLENGE: **ROUNDING OFF THEIR ROUGHER EDGES**
FULFILLMENT: **STANDING THEIR GROUND**
NOTABLES: **AL GORE (U.S. VICE PRESIDENT); STEVEN TYLER (LEAD SINGER, AEROSMITH); RHEA PERLMAN (ACTRESS, CHEERS)**

April 3–10
THE STAR
ARIES II

Those born in the Week of the Star may have a rather extraordinary journey along this karmic path and will likely experience some degree of notoriety or even fame along the way. Thus, balancing the public and private sides of life may be especially difficult for these people, and they will have to take some care that their highly charged emotional natures do not find expression in either too much detachment or in extremes of depression. It will be important for them to align themselves with a social network or find a platform from which they can share their views on those things they perceive as issues. Frustration with or repression of their need to star is not likely to be an option for these souls. However, if they can better integrate that need with a more objective and enlightened awareness of their own emotions, they are sure to develop the great strength of character, formidable inner resources, and inner healing that are promised here.

CHALLENGE: **TEMPERING THE INTENSITY OF THEIR DESIRE TO BE AT THE CENTER OF THINGS**
FULFILLMENT: **EMERGING FROM THEIR TRIALS AS A KIND OF BEACON FOR OTHERS**

TENNESSEE WILLIAMS
Playwright; won 2 Pulitzer Prizes, *A Streetcar Named Desire*

3/26/1911
Aries I

April 11–18
THE PIONEER
ARIES III

Those born in the Week of the Pioneer may undergo a number of trials by fire along the Way of Grace, yet they are not only likely to emerge relatively unscathed, but considerably enlightened. Here some natural leadership abilities may take some time to emerge, but once evident, can be given full play. Moreover, Aries III's bring to this path an intensely positive attitude that will be of great benefit in their development, as they are unlikely to get bogged down in either the sense of isolation, or the tendency to depression that often occurs for some along this road. Thus, though this is a passage that is not without its ups and downs, there is nevertheless more potential for success than anything even resembling failure here.

CHALLENGE: **DEVELOPING A GREATER ABILITY TO HANDLE STRESS**
FULFILLMENT: **DISCOVERING THAT OTHERS WANT TO HEAR WHAT THEY HAVE TO SAY**

April 19–24

POWER
ARIES–TAURUS CUSP

It is rather difficult to identify anything that might go wrong for those born on the Cusp of Power who travel the Way of Grace. Though this may not be the easiest of journeys, the combination of inner strength, persuasive power, and the fine sense of both aesthetic and spiritual value that marks those on this road is almost certain to prove a recipe for real success. In fact, the only real danger indicated here is that these formidable people may withdraw from the higher challenge of serving as an example to others or to share themselves—whether in an atmosphere of social interaction or within the context of a family. Nonetheless, if they can overcome a tendency to be too long suffering for their own good, and learn the value of unconditional love, they can really shine along this road.

CHALLENGE: **LETTING GO OF THE TRAUMAS OF THE PAST**
FULFILLMENT: **STEPPING INTO THE ROLE OF BEING QUIETLY INFLUENTIAL**

BARON VON RICHTHOFEN
German fighter pilot in WWI, "The Red Baron," 80 aerial victories

5/2/1892
Taurus I

April 25–May 2

MANIFESTATION
TAURUS I

A fine combination of intellectual, emotional, and practical powers comes together in those born in the Week of Manifestation who navigate the Way of Grace. Indeed, their biggest stumbling block may lie in their tendency to cling to notions of hierarchy when the situation demands something more resembling heroism. Resistance to change when change is demanded of them may also prove difficult. Yet they are blessed with wonderful qualities of calm and are sure to exhibit a fine measure of grace under fire. Though it is not likely that Taurus I's will be much able to indulge their great need for peace and quiet with this configuration, they will nevertheless have the opportunity to reveal considerable courage, some astonishing leadership skills, and a sincere interest in bringing others together in an atmosphere of protection and nurture.

CHALLENGE: **RELEASING INFLEXIBILITY**
FULFILLMENT: **CULTIVATING A PEACEFUL, GRACEFUL HOME ENVIRONMENT**
NOTABLE: **LARRY GATLIN (COUNTRY MUSIC SINGER, THE GATLIN BROTHERS)**

May 3–10

THE TEACHER
TAURUS II

Of the myriad characteristics of those born with this configuration, perhaps the most identifiable will be that their sense of both the aesthetic world and the world of information will be marked by a passionate commitment to excellence along this karmic path. Real students of life, these personalities are blessed with a considerable empathy for the underdog. They are unlikely to encounter any adversities or personal setbacks in which they are unable to derive a sense of greater meaning. Once those insights are properly processed, Taurus II's will be impelled to share them with the world. And though they may have to fight to gain the spotlight, they are nevertheless unlikely to use their position in a selfish or undignified manner. Thus, though this may be a tumultuous life's journey, it also promises rich reward.

CHALLENGE: **DETACHING FROM CRITICISM INSTEAD OF FIGHTING**
FULFILLMENT: **INDULGING IN THEIR LOVE OF SENSUOUS PLEASURES AND SHEER PHYSICALITY**
NOTABLES: **ARCHIBALD MacLEISH (POET/WRITER; WON 3 PULITZERS); SIR GEORGE PAGET THOMSON (NOBEL WINNER IN PHYSICS, ELECTRON DIFFERENTIATION IN CRYSTALS)**

STEVE WINWOOD
Virtuoso rock keyboardist/songwriter, "Back in the High Life"

5/12/1948
Taurus III

May 11–18

THE NATURAL
TAURUS III

Those born in the Week of the Natural who navigate the promise and challenge of the Way of Grace have tremendous potential for self-realization, yet may nevertheless get knocked for a loop or two along this road. They may have to work hard to overcome feelings of anger, resentment, or rebellion—especially with regard to authority issues—that can waste their energies futilely in frustration or restlessness, when circumstances demand instead an attitude of calm and dignity. There is also a strong temptation to withdraw and refuse the higher challenge to share their knowledge with the world. Yet, they have a more lighthearted approach to life than many along this road, and if they are careful to recognize that real individualism is the product of self-knowledge rather than self-evasion, they can realize great success along the way.

CHALLENGE: **OVERCOMING THE SCARS OF EARLY REJECTION**
FULFILLMENT: **GIVING FULL RUN TO THEIR CHARM AND LOVE OF PLEASURE**
NOTABLE: **DAME MARGARET RUTHERFORD (STAGE/FILM ACTRESS, "MISS MARPLE")**

May 19–24

ENERGY
TAURUS–GEMINI CUSP

Blessed with a more discerning attitude and greater depth of feeling than many Taurus–Geminis, these souls will nevertheless have to work to reconcile their tempestuous approach to problems with the higher challenge to objectivity. Though this passage is likely to be exciting and even breathtaking at times, these people must avoid the pitfalls of recklessness, impulsiveness, and sheer stress, and cultivate some basic endurance when it comes their time to shine forth as an example for those they meet along the way. If they employ their considerable energy, brilliance, and versatility as they cope with the trials and triumphs of this road, and combine them with the empathy and understanding that are part of their endowment, they can have considerable impact along the Way of Grace.

CHALLENGE: **GRAPPLING WITH THE TENDENCY TO WORRY TOO MUCH**
FULFILLMENT: **STEADYING THEMSELVES WITH PHYSICAL ACTIVITY AND NATURAL BEAUTY**
NOTABLES: **JEAN PAUL MARAT (FRENCH REVOLUTIONARY POLITICIAN; ASSASSINATED); HONORÉ DE BALZAC (FRENCH AUTHOR; DEVELOPED THE REALISTIC NOVEL COMÉDIE HUMAINE)**

STEVIE NICKS
Singer, solo and with
Fleetwood Mac

5/26/1948
Gemini I

May 25–June 2

FREEDOM
GEMINI I

Gifted with a natural objectivity and a firm belief structure, Gemini I's will nevertheless have to control some combative tendencies as they travel this karmic path. Highly susceptible to stress, some will come unhinged easily, and they should be careful to monitor their levels of irritation. Too much energy and too much emotion can combine in a pressure cooker of experience that, if not controlled, can result in some explosive and even quite destructive episodes. Surrounding themselves with beautiful things and calming friends will prove especially useful, as will cultivating their natural interest in the rights of others. Yet even when crisis compels them to more aggressive action, they will do well to meditate from time to time on the wisdom contained in a line from the *I Ching*'s hexagram of Revolution which states: "On your own day, you are believed."

CHALLENGE: **ALLOWING THAT THEY MAY NEED TO CULTIVATE A MORE GRACEFUL SPEAKING MANNER**
FULFILLMENT: **DISCOVERING THEIR CAPACITY TO CHARM OTHERS**
NOTABLES: **JERRY MATHERS (TELEVISION ACTOR, LEAVE IT TO BEAVER); JACQUES FRANÇOIS HALÉVY (FRENCH COMPOSER)**

June 3–10

NEW LANGUAGE
GEMINI II

Some early conflicts or lack of understanding from family can contribute to an "ugly duckling" psychology for those born in the Week of New Language who travel the Way of Grace. Gemini II's will have to work hard to overcome some rather defensive attitudes about their own unique abilities as they travel this karmic path. Allowing themselves to be motivated by a need for acceptance will in many ways prove the path of most resistance here, resulting in wounded feelings, an impulse to withdraw, and a number of experiences with rejection. Yet if they set such emotions aside and develop their capacity to transcend trials with greater élan, they will be able to step into the role of teacher and to share their ideas with the world in a compelling style that is without rival along this road.

CHALLENGE: **OVERCOMING THEIR BELIEF IN THEIR OWN AWKWARDNESS**
FULFILLMENT: **GETTING TO THE POINT WHERE THEY DETACH THEMSELVES FROM ALL FORMS OF CRITICISM**

COLE PORTER
Composer/lyricist,
"Night and Day"

6/9/1892
Gemini II

June 11–18

THE SEEKER
GEMINI III

The personalities born in the Week of the Seeker who negotiate the trials and triumphs of the Way of Grace can expect considerable accomplishment here. They must not, however, allow their Scorpio origins to distort their objectivity with extremes of emotion, or go overboard with the idea that being "different" is somehow an end in itself. They are likely to be freethinkers but will have to watch a tendency to become controlling or manipulative as they assume the responsibility of imparting their ideas to others. Yet whatever the ups and down they encounter along this road, they are likely to transcend their troubles through their innate ability to take risks and to explore the frontiers of experience in a way that is neither too daring, nor too hesitant to progress.

CHALLENGE: **MODERATING THEIR RESTLESSNESS AND BECOMING MORE EASEFUL**
FULFILLMENT: **MOVING INTO THE ROLE OF EXTROVERT AND HAVING THEIR OPINIONS MATTER**
NOTABLE: **BASIL RATHBONE (ACTOR; OFTEN PLAYED SHERLOCK HOLMES)**

June 19–24
MAGIC
GEMINI–CANCER CUSP

The individuals born on the Cusp of Magic who find themselves on the Way of Grace can expect a most rewarding journey. The qualities of character that come together here are likely to make a nice mix of personal strength and necessary compassion. In times of trouble, however, they will have to learn to distinguish between sensitivity and mere self-pity or suffering. Moreover, the tendency to withdraw will be especially pronounced, as they have a strong inclination to withdraw into a private inner world. Yet they have fine evaluative instincts that should be encouraged as their natural insight and sense of a larger scheme will help them to better understand the role of upset and setback in their lives. If they are careful to nurture their sense of beauty with fine things and a peaceful personal space, yet do not withdraw from the challenge to impart their special brand of magic to others, they can truly blossom along this road.

PHYLICIA RASHAD
Actress, *The Cosby Show*
───────────
6/19/1948
Gemini–Cancer Cusp

CHALLENGE: **WEATHERING EARLY EMOTIONAL STORMS AND CONFLICTS**
FULFILLMENT: **ENCOURAGING THEIR INNATE SENSE OF MAGIC BY SURROUNDING THEMSELVES WITH BEAUTY**
NOTABLE: **CLARENCE THOMAS (U.S. SUPREME COURT JUSTICE)**

June 25–July 2
THE EMPATH
CANCER I

Those born in the Week of the Empath who find themselves on the Way of Grace will doubtless have an amazing grasp of the emotional context within which events take place. However, they will have to work hard to overcome a high degree of personal sensitivity before they can step into the role of teacher and impart their unique brand of knowledge to others. The tendency to withdraw into moodiness and even depression is quite pronounced here, as is the tendency toward self-protection. Yet if these personalities make conscious effort to cultivate greater objectivity and to put their personal troubles in a larger, more universal context, their rare gifts of understanding can provide real enlightenment for those they meet along the way.

CHALLENGE: **COUNTERING THE DESIRE TO RETREAT**
FULFILLMENT: **FINDING A MORE SOOTHING APPROACH TO LIFE**
NOTABLE: **PETER MAAS (INVESTIGATIVE REPORTER; AUTHOR, *VALACHI PAPERS*)**

July 3–10
THE UNCONVENTIONAL
CANCER II

Cancer II's have wonderful potential to rise above their personal troubles and sorrows, but there is a danger that they will have an overdeveloped sense of privacy that will cause them to withdraw into a private fantasy, rather than assume the role of teacher or example to others. Many of these souls have a lavish streak that will manifest in a wonderful sense of beauty, and they are likely to be astute collectors and lifelong students of culture. Though there are many here who will be characterized by a tendency to worry or even to obsess over their circumstances, they nevertheless bring a sense of fun and adventure to this path that is missing elsewhere. If they can overcome their more difficult aspects, they will doubtless derive great benefit from the objectivity, perspective, and freedom of thought that all beckon here.

PEARL S. BUCK
Writer; won Pulitzer and Nobel prizes
───────────
6/26/1892
Cancer I

CHALLENGE: **DEVELOPING THE EMOTIONAL BOUNDARIES TO DISENGAGE FROM CONFLICT**
FULFILLMENT: **STEPPING INTO THE LIMELIGHT TO SHARE THEIR MORE UNUSUAL IDEAS**
NOTABLE: **RICHARD ALDINGTON (ENGLISH WRITER)**

July 11–18
THE PERSUADER
CANCER III

Though this may not be the most comfortable or easy of journeys, there is much to indicate that Cancer III individuals will do wonderfully well on the Way of Grace. Highly observant of both the facts and the emotional impulses that come into play in any situation, these personalities are quite capable of developing the objectivity and strength to transcend even the toughest times and circumstances. Though they will doubtless become frustrated when things don't go their way, they will nevertheless discover tremendous inner resources when under the gun, though the more critical issue is that they will face circumstances that can neither be accurately predicted nor completely controlled. If these personalities leave themselves open to the possibility that such experiences can transform them, rather than cling to the notion that they must control or manipulate circumstances to their liking, this road holds great possibilities for enlightenment.

CHALLENGE: **BEING LESS FORCEFUL WHEN CONVINCED THEY ARE RIGHT**
FULFILLMENT: **DISCOVERING THEIR OWN STRENGTH AND CAPACITY FOR GRACE UNDER FIRE**
NOTABLE: **DICK BUTTON (5-TIME WORLD CHAMPION ICE SKATER; TV COMMENTATOR)**

July 19–25
OSCILLATION
CANCER–LEO CUSP

It will be of great benefit to those born in this week who navigate the ups and downs of the Way of Grace to surround themselves with calming influences and educational resources and to develop a measure of mental discipline along this road. Extremes of emotion can prove their biggest liability here, and while it is fair to say that these individuals have a rather manic side, they can experience much more in the way of downs than ups if they allow themselves to get mired in their Scorpio II origins, or to otherwise come to identify with their own sense of suffering. Yet they are nevertheless gifted with a strongly expressive nature; if they nurture their need to share their knowledge with others and are careful not to withdraw from the higher challenge here, their lives and experiences can serve as tremendous sources of inspiration and instruction for those they meet along the way.

CHALLENGE: **PUTTING A LID ON THEIR MORE AGGRESSIVE SIDE**
FULFILLMENT: **SHARING THEIR APPRECIATION OF BEAUTY WITH OTHERS**
NOTABLE: **CHARLES C. LITTLE (PUBLISHER; COFOUNDER, LITTLE, BROWN)**

HAILE SELASSIE
Former Ethiopian ruler

7/23/1892
Cancer–Leo Cusp

July 26–August 2
AUTHORITY
LEO I

Balancing what may prove to be an awesome set of responsibilities with a calm and nurturing home environment may be important for those born in the Week of Authority who travel the Way of Grace. Whatever their personal circumstances, people are likely to look up to these individuals in some fashion, and Leo I's will have to be careful not to abuse either their power or the privilege involved in serving as examples or role models for others. Yet though this path will not evolve without its share of personal drama or tribulation, these personalities are gifted with both the aesthetic inclinations and the deeper understanding to come through their trials unscathed. Strength, dignity, and loyalty are all in abundance here and will serve these people well as they step into the important roles that fate has in store.

CHALLENGE: **NOT RETREATING INTO A RIGID COCOON WHEN THE GOING GETS TOUGH**
FULFILLMENT: **WATCHING THEIR AESTHETIC UNDERSTANDING AND APPRECIATION UNFOLD**
NOTABLES: **JACQUELINE KENNEDY ONASSIS (FIRST LADY OF JFK; EDITOR); WILLIAM POWELL (ACTOR, *THE THIN MAN*); JACK WARNER (FILM EXECUTIVE/PRODUCER)**

August 3–10
BALANCED STRENGTH
LEO II

These tough customers are blessed with the natural strength and endurance to be able to handle just about anything life can throw their way. Yet they will have to be careful that they don't take themselves so seriously that they fail to enjoy the many gifts that the Way of Grace has to offer. Surrounding themselves with evidence of their accomplishments in the form of beautiful things, a serene home, and a sense of elegance will be especially important here, as the right atmosphere can do much to balance their feelings and remind them of just what they've been working for. They bring to this path a greater sense of emotional stability than might otherwise be the case, and if they are careful not to lose themselves in negative emotional patterns, a refusal to change, or by identifying too much with their own sense of suffering, all can go quite brilliantly here.

CHALLENGE: **BELIEVING THAT THEY DESERVE AN EASIER TIME OF IT**
FULFILLMENT: **LIVING LIFE WITH MODERATION AND ABUNDANCE**
NOTABLE: **JAMES GAMBLE (COFOUNDER, PROCTER & GAMBLE CO.)**

MAE WEST
Actress, mistress of comic timing, *My Little Chickadee*

8/17/1892
Leo III

August 11–18
LEADERSHIP
LEO III

Leo III's who travel the Way of Grace have a pronounced streak of what might best be called heroism, and their ability to rise above even the worst trials and setbacks will doubtless serve as an inspiration to those they meet along this road. In fact, the greatest pitfall for those with this configuration will lie in their tendency to maintain a rather selfish or narrow view of personal relationships, to the detriment of their capacity for happiness and fulfillment. Though their natural emotional intensity is not for everyone, those brave enough to weather the storms of a personal attachment to these dauntless and daunting personalities can be rewarded with tremendous loyalty and passion. Those born in the Week of Leadership who travel this karmic path will be happy here, especially when their shared knowledge results in the rewards of being honored and respected by those around them.

CHALLENGE: **TRANSFORMING THEMSELVES INTO COMMITTED MATES**
FULFILLMENT: **RESTING IN THE KNOWLEDGE THAT THEY WON THE FIGHT AND ROSE ABOVE IT ALL**
NOTABLE: **FRANCIS GARY POWERS (U2 PILOT; PLANE SHOT DOWN OVER USSR, 1960)**

August 19–25
EXPOSURE
LEO–VIRGO CUSP

Overcoming their tendencies to introversion may prove a challenge for those born in this week who travel the Way of Grace, yet they can realize a rich and ultimately rewarding passage here. Gifted with keen evaluative instincts and a strongly emotional nature, they may take a backseat early in life, only to emerge as flamboyant and inspiring role models later on. Likely to meet almost any trial or personal setback with real objectivity, they will still have to work on their tendency to employ their great insight as a purely manipulative tool. Learning to trust themselves will be especially important here as well. The outlook is good for the souls along this road as step into a developing sense of culture, education, and serenity with no trouble at all.

YASIR ARAFAT
Leader of Palestine
Liberation Organization
___
8/24/1929
Leo–Virgo Cusp

CHALLENGE: **TRANSFORMING THEMSELVES INTO EXTROVERTS**
FULFILLMENT: **ADOPTING A MORE COLORFUL, ALBEIT ELEGANT, STYLE**
NOTABLES: **BRET HARTE (WRITER OF STORIES OF OLD WEST); ALFRED LUNT (STAGE ACTOR); PETER THOMSON (GOLFER)**

August 26–September 2
THE SYSTEM BUILDER
VIRGO I

Though less likely to suffer the consequences of repressed personal needs and emotions than other Virgo I's, those who travel the Way of Grace can nevertheless expect a struggle with the necessity of allowing themselves permission to enjoy the fruits of their prodigious labors. Though blessed with real objectivity, they do not always extend that quality to themselves when evaluating their own needs and goals, and may thus get mired in depression or a misplaced sense of suffering. Yet if they work to develop their sense of the aesthetic and combine it with their natural flair for structure and service, they can rise to the higher challenge; the resulting manifestations of a wonderfully elegant and refined vision can serve as a great source of inspiration and instruction for others.

CHALLENGE: **BREAKING DOWN THE STRUCTURES THAT KEEP THEM FROM ENJOYING LIFE**
FULFILLMENT: **ARRIVING AT A POINT WHERE THEY CAN INDULGE THEMSELVES**
NOTABLE: **LEE DeFOREST (INVENTOR OF TRANSISTOR)**

September 3–10
THE ENIGMA
VIRGO II

Those born in the Week of the Enigma who find themselves on the Way of Grace can enjoy a wonderfully rewarding journey, providing they learn to leave their worries behind them on the road. Though some will manifest a tendency toward self-doubt in a chronically picky attitude, if they recognize their own high standards and reconcile them with an ability to reward themselves with the finer things of life, they will doubtless do quite well. In fact, the manifestations of this path may require these rather aloof individuals to share themselves with partners who will enable them to better comprehend their own deeply emotional side, yet will at the same time help them to rise on the social scene. But a real metamorphosis is possible here, one made all the sweeter by virtue of the fact that Virgo II's will be able to manifest their truest natures in an atmosphere of beauty and security.

CHALLENGE: **DROPPING THEIR AIR OF MYSTERY NOW AND AGAIN**
FULFILLMENT: **SURROUNDING THEMSELVES WITH ALL THAT PLEASES THEM TO FORM AN ATMOSPHERE OF TASTE AND SERENITY**
NOTABLE: **BOB NEWHART (TV ACTOR, *THE BOB NEWHART SHOW*)**

September 11–18
THE LITERALIST
VIRGO III

Those born in the Week of the Literalist who travel the Way of Grace can expect great success and a high degree of personal accomplishment and contentment here. Yet they may struggle to overcome some of the more negative traits of their Scorpio II origins, and will have to guard against a tendency to be entirely too long-suffering on the one hand or rather ruthless or judgmental on the other. Nevertheless, their shrewd evaluative instincts will serve them in especially good stead; if they are careful to augment their practical talents with a real appreciation of aesthetics and to recognize and cultivate their need for harmony and the finer things of life, they are sure to be rewarded with genuine appreciation and admiration for their efforts along this life's journey.

ARNOLD PALMER
Champion golfer
___
9/10/1929
Virgo II

CHALLENGE: **NOT BEING MIRED IN THE CONFLICTS OR TRAUMAS THAT BEFALL THEM**
FULFILLMENT: **UNLOCKING THEIR SELF-EXPRESSION THROUGH SPORTS OR PHYSICAL ACTIVITY**

September 19–24
BEAUTY
VIRGO–LIBRA CUSP

Blessed with a greater depth of emotion and understanding than might ordinarily be the case, Virgo–Libras who find themselves on the Way of Grace could not ask for a life path of greater promise or potential. There is little danger of failing the higher challenge implied on this path. Their sense of beauty will be quite pronounced and their knack for creating quality and harmony in their personal environment quite conducive to their emergence from a more introverted state and into roles where they can share their special aesthetic ideas with others. In fact, the principal pitfall will be the misuse of their great gifts in such a way that they escape from reality, as there is a pronounced predisposition to addictions and overindulgence with this configuration. Yet there is little that can go terribly wrong here, and if these personalities only exert the effort necessary to cultivate their natural inclinations, life will be good on the Way of Grace.

CHALLENGE: **DEVELOPING THE INTROSPECTION TO DEAL CONSTRUCTIVELY WITH LIFE TRAUMA**

FULFILLMENT: **INDULGING THEIR LOVE OF EXTERNALS**

NOTABLES: **ANNE MEARA (STAGE/TELEVISION/FILM ACTRESS); THOMAS EAGLETON (U.S. SENATOR; VICE PRESIDENTIAL CANDIDATE WITH GEORGE MCGOVERN; PSYCHIATRIC TREATMENT REVEALED)**

CHARLES RUDOLPH WALGREEN
Founded Walgreen
drugstore chain

10/9/1873
Libra II

September 25–October 2
THE PERFECTIONIST
LIBRA I

It will be of the utmost importance for those born in the Week of the Perfectionist who travel the Way of Grace to identify and allow themselves to gravitate toward those objects, activities, and pursuits that afford them a greater sense of harmony. Though blessed with great inner strength and a considerable potential for transformation, they may nevertheless fall prey to some of their own rigid patterns and suffer much more than is necessary from a sense that life is not what it "ought to be." Greater flexibility will be an asset here, as will the ability to detach without repressing their emotional responses to their circumstances. It can be a fine line to walk, and a difficult balance to find, yet if they keep in mind that the strongest trees are those that bend with the wind, they can realize great happiness along this road.

CHALLENGE: **CHOOSING, RATHER THAN MASTERING THEIR EMOTIONS IN ORDER TO RISE ABOVE THEM**

FULFILLMENT: **LEARNING HOW TO RELAX AND ENJOY LIFE MORE**

October 3–10
SOCIETY
LIBRA II

Blessed with a truly exquisite aesthetic sense, it is unlikely that those born in the Week of Society who travel the Way of Grace will fail the higher challenge here, unless they choose to actively practice the art of self-deception. Well-suited to the demands of this path, they are likely to be quite willing to step into the roles of teachers and aspire to share their knowledge, insight, and perceptions with others. Yet their considerable objectivity may cause them a certain amount of regret if their own needs and desires are neglected. However, if they allow themselves to be guided through their inner conflicts by a need to heal and to calm themselves inwardly through the outward experience of sensual and aesthetic pleasures, they are unlikely to stray very far from the path to fulfillment on the Way of Grace.

CHALLENGE: **GETTING MORE IN TOUCH WITH WHAT'S TRULY GOOD FOR THEM—AND THEN SURROUNDING THEMSELVES WITH IT**

FULFILLMENT: **COMING TO FULLY TRUST THEIR INSTINCT FOR THE BEAUTIFUL OR SPIRITUAL**

NOTABLE: **BERT STERN (PHOTOGRAPHER FAMOUS FOR IMAGES OF MARILYN MONROE)**

LUKE PERRY
Actor, *Beverly Hills 90210*

10/11/1966
Libra III

October 11–18
THEATER
LIBRA III

Those born in the Week of Theater who navigate the challenge and promise of the Way of Grace are gifted with tremendous emotional depth, a clear perspective, and the ability to give fullest expression to their worldly and aesthetic sensibilities. Thus, theirs may be a journey quite rich in blessings and reward, especially as these individuals develop necessary objectivity and distance from their own passions and ego drives. Though this road will not be without its trials and tribulations, each experience will hold meaning and a great opportunity for self-realization. Even the worst troubles can be grist for Libra III's creative mill, and if they do not burn themselves out in sheer intensity, nor succumb to careless overconfidence, the combination of energies here can be a real blueprint for success.

CHALLENGE: **DISTANCING THEMSELVES FROM THEIR MORE INTENSE OR NEGATIVE EMOTIONAL IMPULSES**

FULFILLMENT: **REVELLING IN THE GIFTS OF WORLDLY RECOGNITION**

October 19–25

DRAMA AND CRITICISM
LIBRA–SCORPIO CUSP

Though there are few personalities better equipped with the necessary objectivity and élan to navigate the demands of the Way of Grace, those born in this week may nevertheless experience a struggle to achieve the necessary degree of detachment required along this road. They may be inclined to get entirely too wrapped up in their own points of view, and their penchant for intensity will exist at decided odds with the need to rise above the fray and cultivate greater serenity. As crises emerge in their experiences, therefore, they will be challenged to practice better what they preach and to teach others through example rather than through criticism or conflict. There is a huge potential for successful metamorphosis along the way and, if they cultivate calm and a higher level of awareness, all will go brilliantly here.

URSULA LeGUIN
Science fiction writer
———
10/21/1929
Libra–Scorpio Cusp

CHALLENGE: **COMBATTING THEIR OWN FEISTINESS AND NEED TO FIGHT**

FULFILLMENT: **TRANSFORMING CHARISMA INTO GRACE**

October 26–November 2

INTENSITY
SCORPIO I

Blessed with virtuoso energies and great powers of concentration, those born in the Week of Intensity who travel the Way of Grace will have to learn to regulate their emotions and respond to upsets, setbacks, and crises with a greater degree of calm. These highly charged people may experience problems with loss, guilt, or an innate lack of confidence in themselves; this can turn them away from the higher challenge of sharing and imparting their considerable stores of knowledge to others. Though they are likely to be highly selective in any event, they can accomplish the higher goals, especially as they mellow and allow themselves the sense of freedom that comes with greater detachment. Their Scorpio ability to rise, phoenixlike, from the ashes of even the worst disasters is bound to serve as a source of both inspiration and instruction for those with whom they come into contact along this life's journey.

CHALLENGE: **COMING TO TERMS WITH THE GREATER PURPOSE OF THE CALAMITIES IN THEIR LIVES**

FULFILLMENT: **HAVING WEATHERED THE STORM, DISCOVERING THEY HAVE THE AFFECTION AND APPROVAL OF OTHERS**

NOTABLE: **DAVID SCHWIMMER (ACTOR, *FRIENDS*)**

November 3–11

DEPTH
SCORPIO II

Learning to release their tendencies to worry, depression, and emotional fixation will prove paramount to the success of those born in this week who find themselves on the Way of Grace. Though it cannot be said that life will be entirely kind to these souls, the challenges they encounter along this path are likely to provide them with excellent prospects for success and achievement. It should be remembered that in spite of their great empathy and passionate emotions, Scorpio II's also possess fine analytic abilities, which they would do well to cultivate and enhance. Their great talent for accumulation of material wealth will also be an asset as long as they take care to indulge themselves in those things that speak to their sense of beauty, harmony, and enjoyment. They must encourage in themselves the sense of security and graciousness that comes with finding their own level of elegance and cultural refinement.

JOAN PLOWRIGHT
Actress, *The Entertainer*
———
10/28/1929
Scorpio I

CHALLENGE: **NOT TURNING LIFE'S CHALLENGES INWARD INTO SELF-DESTRUCTION**

FULFILLMENT: **SPENDING THEIR HARD-EARNED MONEY ON OBJECTS OF BEAUTY**

NOTABLE: **MARILYN BERGMAN (OSCAR-WINNING MOVIE SCORE COMPOSER WITH HUSBAND, ALAN)**

November 12–18

CHARM
SCORPIO III

Though there may be a fatalistic aspect to the lives of those born in the Week of Charm who travel the Way of Grace, there is nonetheless the potential for wonderful accomplishment and success. Gifted with a natural talent for elegant presentation, an eye for valuable things, and a natural graciousness, these personalities are likely to have a fine time along this road, yet will by no means remain exempt from the kinds of transformative experiences that occur along the way. Coincidence, accident, and conflict may mark this journey, and these personalities must always keep in mind that their challenge is to use such events as a means of getting in touch with their truest feelings. By releasing those feelings through objectivity and analysis, their journey—though sometimes fraught with challenge—will also be marked by tremendous reward, comfort, and security.

CHALLENGE: **CONTROLLING THEIR PASSIONATE NATURE**

FULFILLMENT: **REALIZING THAT THEY ARE INDEED A SWAN AMONG DUCKS**

NOTABLE: **GRACE KELLY (PRINCESS OF MONACO; FILM ACTRESS)**

November 19–24
REVOLUTION
SCORPIO–SAGITTARIUS CUSP

Scorpio–Sagittarians who make their way along this karmic path may have the singular experience of discovering that many of the trials and tribulations experienced are ultimately of their own making until they come to better terms with their own need for harmony. Likely to be both passionate and excitable by nature, they can have difficulty regulating their passions. Yet what is called for is a quieter kind of personal revolution that entails more awareness of their own needs and less conviction that they know what's best for everyone else. There is nevertheless potential for great success here, though the key to their triumphs will lie in their willingness to rise above the conflicts, crises, and convictions of the moment; they must allow themselves the longer view, the wider perspective, and the deep security that comes with a harmonious sense of self and the willingness to share themselves with others as both students and teachers.

SINEAD O'CONNOR
Irish pop singer

12/8/1966
Sagittarius II

CHALLENGE: **RISING ABOVE THEIR PROBLEMS RATHER THAN BEING BOGGED DOWN BY THEM**
FULFILLMENT: **GIVING IN TO THEIR DESIRE FOR ALL THINGS TO BE TASTEFUL AND LOVELY**
NOTABLE: **TROY AIKMAN (DALLAS COWBOYS QUARTERBACK)**

November 25–December 2
INDEPENDENCE
SAGITTARIUS I

Freethinkers of the highest order, Sagittarius I's who travel the Way of Grace may nevertheless balk at the prospect of cultivating a greater aura of calm and serenity, since there is a part of these personalities that may relish challenge even at the expense of their own deepest needs. Yet they are blessed with considerable strength and formidable inner resources that will doubtless enable them to come through any number of trials here; if they are careful to overcome some of their more temperamental qualities and encourage their natural inclinations toward philosophy and aesthetic pursuits, they can enjoy wonderful success along this road. Able to inspire others through their charm, physical grace, and an innovative approach to new ideas, they can both break new ground and maintain a sense of what is classic as they travel this karmic path.

CHALLENGE: **MANAGING THEIR NEED TO WIN**
FULFILLMENT: **TAKING THE HIGH ROAD**
NOTABLE: **CYRIL CUSACK (ACTOR/DIRECTOR/PLAYWRIGHT)**

December 3–10
THE ORIGINATOR
SAGITTARIUS II

Likely to be creative in the extreme, Sagittarius II's who find themselves on the Way of Grace may nevertheless have to confront some issues of defensiveness, envy, or personal rejection before they learn the fine art of being comfortable within one's own skin. Despite their sensitivity, these people can manifest an aggressive or combative side that can spur them to the heights of personal achievement. Yet such accomplishments may prove cold comfort until they allow themselves a measure of personal indulgence in those things that make them truly happy and further cultivate a greater sense of inner security. Their biggest hurdle may be to realize that acceptance from others depends first on acceptance of themselves. Whatever the trials or troubles encountered here, these unusual and ardent people are more than capable of rising above them and bringing to their situations a perspective that is both unique and philosophically innovative.

WILLA CATHER
Writer, O Pioneers!; won Pulitzer Prize

12/7/1873
Sagittarius II

CHALLENGE: **GETTING OVER THEIR OWN SELF-CRITICISM AND THE SENSE THAT THEY ARE MISFITS**
FULFILLMENT: **LOOSENING UP AND BECOMING MORE GRACEFUL—THEN SEEING ALL THE DOORS THAT OPEN TO THEM**

December 11–18
THE TITAN
SAGITTARIUS III

Though gifted with a higher degree of self-confidence and assurance than many of those who travel the Way of Grace, those born in this week will have a lot of work to do in order to conquer the demons of moodiness and personal sensitivity in order to be most effective here. Though well suited to the challenge of inspiring others with their knowledge and their innate ability to teach by example, Sagittarius III's can sometimes be their own worst enemies when they feel that life is not affording them a broad enough canvas on which to display their vision. If they can cultivate an inner balance of emotion with a broader intellectual and aesthetic perspective, and realize that perhaps their need for harmony is greater than their need to beat the odds, all will go well along this road.

CHALLENGE: **REMEMBERING TO INDULGE THEMSELVES ONCE IN A WHILE**
FULFILLMENT: **ALLOWING OTHERS TO ENCHANT THEM**
NOTABLES: **JOHN H. HAMMOND (RECORD PRODUCER; IMPRESARIO; CIVIL RIGHTS ACTIVIST); CARLO PONTI (ITALIAN FILM PRODUCER; HUSBAND TO SOPHIA LOREN)**

December 19–25
PROPHECY
SAGITTARIUS–CAPRICORN CUSP

As long as they do not allow themselves to succumb to overt pessimism or a thoroughly antisocial attitude, those born on the Cusp of Prophecy who travel the Way of Grace can expect a very personal metamorphosis along this journey. They are likely to have an astonishing depth of insight and a real perspective on the events and issues that determine all our lives. They will nevertheless have to cultivate within themselves the willingness to share their unique brand of knowledge with others in order to realize the higher challenge here. Further, it may not always be easy for these souls to be good to themselves. When they recognize that their inclination to surround themselves with beauty and harmony in those things that afford them a sense of pleasure and nourishment for the spirit as well as for the senses, the resulting integration and refinement of their aesthetic inclinations with their intuition and insight can serve as an inspiration for us all.

PAUL BOWLES
Writer/composer

12/30/1910
Capricorn I

CHALLENGE: **LEARNING HOW TO DETACH THEMSELVES NOT JUST FROM THE NEED FOR APPROVAL BUT FROM EMOTIONS AS WELL**
FULFILLMENT: **DEVELOPING THEIR AESTHETIC INSTINCTS**
NOTABLE: **KIEFER SUTHERLAND (FILM ACTOR, *THE LOST BOYS*)**

December 26–January 2
THE RULER
CAPRICORN I

The powerful individuals born in this week who travel the Way of Grace can realize great success and personal accomplishment as they are especially well suited to both the challenges and potential rewards offered by this life's journey. Formidable strength, personal courage, and a highly developed sense of the aesthetic combine here. Capricorn I's will also benefit from the fact that this path endows them with a greater empathy for others than they might have otherwise. In fact, their principal struggle may lie only in the fact that they are inclined to be too hard on themselves. Though it may take some time for these individuals to truly come into their own—and this configuration points more to success later in life than in youth, like fine wines—they are bound to mellow and become more valuable with time.

CHALLENGE: **KNOWING WHEN TO BACK DOWN FROM A FIGHT**
FULFILLMENT: **APPLYING A CERTAIN GRACIOUSNESS TO THEIR LEADERSHIP STYLE**

January 3–9
DETERMINATION
CAPRICORN II

Those born in the Week of Determination who travel the Way of Grace may also take time emerging from their cocoons of self-protective instincts and into the roles that destiny has in store. Though these individuals are intensely sensitive, they are neither weak nor overly involved with personal ego issues. Thus they can enjoy considerable success, especially as their aesthetic sense is encouraged and refined over time. Their free-thinking ways are likely to blossom here and they will benefit especially from studies of the theoretical and philosophical ideas that will serve to shape their messages and world views by grounding them in a sense of context and tradition. If they are careful to nurture their own feelings of self-confidence, they can expect to assume the role of teacher-by-example with an admirable combination of modesty and authority.

DIZZY DEAN
Hall of Fame pitcher for St. Louis Cardinals' "Gas House Gang"; last 30-game winner in the National League; colorful broadcaster

1/16/1911
Capricorn III

CHALLENGE: **FORCING THEMSELVES TO KNOW THAT RISING ABOVE IT ALL IS NOT ADMITTING FAILURE—OR DEFEAT**
FULFILLMENT: **COMMENDING THEMSELVES ON THEIR FORTITUDE TO OVERCOME THEIR DIFFICULTIES**
NOTABLE: **BUTTERFLY MCQUEEN (ACTRESS, PLAYED "PRISSY" IN *GONE WITH THE WIND*)**

January 10–16
DOMINANCE
CAPRICORN III

Those born in the Week of Dominance who negotiate the demands of the Way of Grace may experience a struggle in learning to meet challenges without indulging in a need to rail against fate or the unfairness of it all. These are individuals who like to feel themselves in control of their immediate environments, and some of the personal or professional upsets indicated here may knock them for a loop until they begin to better understand that life is not about reward and punishment, nor about what we necessarily deserve for our efforts. Though there is much to indicate that this life's journey will tweak Capricorn IIIs' secret feelings of insecurity, if they understand that a world of material and spiritual opportunities awaits them, and if they are willing to open themselves to a wider variety of shared experience, all will go well along this road.

CHALLENGE: **TEMPERING THEIR PROPENSITY TO WORRY AND EXPECT THE WORST**
FULFILLMENT: **REACHING THE POINT WHERE THEY NO LONGER FEEL INFERIOR OR AWKWARD**
NOTABLE: **DIZZY DEAN (NATIONAL LEAGUE BASEBALL PITCHER)**

January 17–22
MYSTERY AND IMAGINATION
CAPRICORN–AQUARIUS CUSP

RONALD REAGAN
40th U.S. president;
former actor
———
2/6/1911
Aquarius II

Those born in this period are likely to experience a rich and fulfilling life along the Way of Grace, as their natural imaginative and creative energies are better grounded in the real, while their sensitivity and depth are only enhanced along this path. Though they are likely to be intense individuals, they are a bit more light-hearted than many along this road and, if they can control their own tendencies to extremes, can emerge intact from any number of personal trials. In fact, their fate is difficult to predict, except to say that many of the crucial experiences of their lives will arise from accidental or ultimately unpredictable twists of fate and fortune. If they simply cultivate the art of "keeping it together" and nourish their inner security through those things that ground them in a sense of peace and greater tranquillity, they are more than capable of showing the world, through their unique examples, how even trials by fire can serve to transform and enlighten us all.

CHALLENGE: **BACKING SOME OF THEIR INTENSITY OFF A BIT—ESPECIALLY IN REGARDS TO THEIR PET CAUSES**
FULFILLMENT: **SETTLING INTO A CALMER, MORE GRACEFUL WAY OF LIFE**
NOTABLE: **JOHN MOSES BROWNING (INVENTED AUTOMATIC RIFLE, MACHINE GUN)**

January 23–30
GENIUS
AQUARIUS I

The personalities born in the Week of Genius who find themselves on the Way of Grace are likely to experience an enjoyable trip, though they may have to work on achieving the inclination to share their ideas and experiences with the world. Capable of great perseverance and emotional detachment, they are likely to be self-taught individuals. Thus, they may turn from the higher challenge here and retreat from their ability to teach others, believing perhaps that when it comes to life experience, "it's every man for himself." Nonetheless, Aquarius I's are gifted with a greater degree of empathy and depth of emotion than might otherwise be the case. If they can only open themselves to the wider experiences of travel, art, and ideas and learn to better nurture their deep sense of beauty through fine things, their naturally elegant and even exquisite tastes are sure to be indulged along this road.

CHALLENGE: **DISENGAGING, NOT RUNNING, FROM LIFE'S DIFFICULTIES**
FULFILLMENT: **GROUNDING THEMSELVES IN MORE PHYSICAL PLEASURES**

January 31–February 7
YOUTH AND EASE
AQUARIUS II

The souls born in the Week of Youth and Ease who make their way along this karmic path may find it a difficult road in some respects, as they are apt to have more personal sensitivity than actual depth and less stamina than will be required here. Yet there is potential for great transformation along this road, especially as this path will demand that they develop within themselves a deeper and more abiding sense of values. Able to detach themselves emotionally and rise above the fray, they may nevertheless have to learn to respond to events with greater maturity and calm if they are to succeed. Though likely to be blessed with a highly developed aesthetic sense that will be given full play in such areas as fashion, design, or a considerable flair for trend spotting, these individuals will doubtless be asked to focus their virtuoso energies more on what is abiding and less on what is popular if they are to become effective teachers along this road.

CHALLENGE: **CULTIVATING GREATER STRENGTH OF CHARACTER**
FULFILLMENT: **APPROACHING MATURITY WITH GRACE AND EASE**
NOTABLE: **BARBARA HERSHEY (ACTRESS, *HANNAH AND HER SISTERS*)**

CHRISTOPHER GUEST
Comic actor/writer/
director/songwriter,
This Is Spinal Tap
———
2/5/1948
Aquarius II

February 8–15
ACCEPTANCE
AQUARIUS III

An interesting combination of energies come together for those born in the Week of Acceptance who travel the Way of Grace, and the result is likely to manifest in some highly satisfying experiences for those along this path. Detachment from their own emotions and sensitivities is likely to come quite easily for these souls, as will the inclination to balance their environments with objects of beauty and culture. Even so, it may take some time, or even some traumatic experiences before these personalities are able to shed old notions of themselves or the "right" way to behave. Likely to be marked by a love of physical activity, they will acquire elegance and élan over the years, which will only serve as an external manifestation of their greater sense of ease and acceptance of life itself. A wide variety of experience, considerable personal charm, and the richer rewards of tolerance and true understanding are all in store for Aquarius III's who travel the Way of Grace.

CHALLENGE: **LEARNING HOW TO SCREEN OUT UPSET RATHER THAN HANG ON TO IT**
FULFILLMENT: **ADOPTING AN EASY-GOING, MORE ELEGANT WAY OF LIFE**
NOTABLES: **ELIZABETH BISHOP (WRITER/POET); TELLER (PARTNER WITH PENN; ILLUSIONIST)**

February 16–22

SENSITIVITY
AQUARIUS–PISCES CUSP

Generally speaking, the two major pitfalls for those born in this Cusp Week who travel the Way of Grace will be those of aggression and of self-pity. Likely to be marked by feelings of early rejection or a sense of being outside the mainstream, these people will have to acknowledge the true nature of their responses before they can successfully disengage from their emotions in times of trouble or strife. Thus, though this can be a difficult road, the potential for personal transformation and emergence from a self-inflicted cocoon of suffering is especially promising. Key to their development will be their ability to avoid the temptation to take the odd turn of fortune personally and to develop a true understanding of the popular maxim, "stuff happens." Yet if they cultivate more of a sense of balance through creature comforts, and indulge their sense of the aesthetic in such a way that it can be of benefit to more than just themselves, they will reap the rewards of true contentment here.

CHALLENGE: **HEALING THEIR CHIP-ON-THE-SHOULDER ATTITUDE**

FULFILLMENT: **SPENDING TIME OUTDOORS IN NATURAL BEAUTY**

NOTABLES: **KURT COBAIN (SINGER, NIRVANA); ANDREW SHUE (ACTOR, MELROSE PLACE)**

BERNADETTE PETERS
Stage/film actress,
Young Frankenstein

2/28/1948
Pisces I

February 23–March 2

SPIRIT
PISCES I

Marked by a truly promising combination of aesthetic and spiritual inclinations, those born in this week who travel the Way of Grace may nevertheless have to work to develop the ability to remove themselves successfully from personal troubles. Likely to be self-sacrificing, they will also have a tendency to get overly invested in outcomes and may suffer some disappointments before they learn that sometimes even love just isn't enough. Grounding themselves in hobbies and pursuits that nurture their sense of beauty will be especially important to these personalities as they have a unique ability to access their spiritual side through both the world of nature and the world of art. Yet if they can manage to successfully detach themselves from their troubles without becoming either smug or self-satisfied, they can emerge as among the most enlightened and successful examples along the Way of Grace.

CHALLENGE: **RELYING ON THEIR SPIRITUALITY TO GET THEM THROUGH THE ROUGH PATCHES**

FULFILLMENT: **DISCOVERING THE GRACE OF A HIGHER SPIRITUAL BEING**

NOTABLE: **PIERRE AUGUSTE RENOIR (FRENCH IMPRESSIONIST PAINTER)**

March 3–10

THE LONER
PISCES II

Though some early traumas may have left their marks on the psychic natures of those born in the Week of the Loner, they can nevertheless experience great satisfaction. Gifted with an amazing aesthetic sense and a natural elegance, they may ask little from the world, save to be left in peace and accepted for themselves. Though a tendency to extremes of depression and withdrawal from life will be especially pronounced, they will do well to keep in mind that the higher challenge implied here demands that they emerge from a chrysalis of isolation in order to share their knowledge and ideas with the world, if only by virtue of example. If they cultivate within themselves the necessary detachment and natural virtuosity that is part of this path, their efforts at personal transformation will be celebrated and rewarded with both love and admiration.

CHALLENGE: **LETTING GO OF THE BELIEF THAT THEY ARE RESPONSIBLE FOR THEIR MISFORTUNES**

FULFILLMENT: **ENGAGING IN THEIR LOVE OF NATURE AND BEAUTY SIMULTANEOUSLY**

NOTABLE: **JEAN HARLOW (FILM ACTRESS, HELLS ANGELS)**

L. RON HUBBARD
Sci fi writer; founder
Church of Scientology

3/13/1911
Pisces III

March 11–18

DANCERS AND DREAMERS
PISCES III

The ups and downs on the Way of Grace may prove an arduous road in some respects for those born in the Week of Dancers and Dreamers. Though gifted with a fine sense of beauty and a fondness for sensual pursuits, they will nevertheless have to develop a greater degree of personal fortitude and endurance if they are to realize the higher challenge here. In fact, the sense of detachment implied on this path may well demand that Pisces III's detach themselves first from their own opinions, for they can sometimes be convinced of their own points of view without adequately considering the broader implications. Yet if they avoid the tendency to be too self-indulgent on the one hand, and too self-satisfied on the other, their unique gifts can serve as a beacons of inspiration for those they meet along the way.

CHALLENGE: **CONTINUING TO MOVE FORWARD DESPITE LIFE'S SETBACKS**

FULFILLMENT: **BECOMING A VOICE ON BEHALF OF THE ARTS**

NOTABLES: **PERCIVAL LOWELL (ASTRONOMER; PREDICTED PLUTO'S DISCOVERY); JAMES TAYLOR (FOLK/ROCK SINGER/ SONGWRITER, "SWEET BABY JAMES")**

The Way of Innocence

SCORPIO III TO TAURUS III
Charm to the Natural

Those individuals born on the Way of Innocence are here to drop the facade of their public persona in favor of a purer, unaffected approach to life, one where they express themselves as naturally and directly as possible. Born with an innate belief that they are unworthy of love, those on this path grapple with the fear of revealing their true selves to others. Adept at artfulness and getting what they want and need through nondirect means, they are extremely charming, albeit determined individuals. Often subjected to undue criticisms and unfair assessments of their characters, those on the Way of Innocence have learned to shield themselves from hurt by being guarded and secretive. As they overcome their feelings of unworthiness and learn to trust in a higher power to protect them, those on this path can begin to reveal who they are to the world. Becoming more colorful and fun loving, these men and women will surprise others as they adopt a devil-may-care attitude. Returning to a more innocent way of being in the world, with a more spontaneous expression of their creativity and zest for life, the men and women on this path will discover that they serve as an inspiration to many.

The most significant and difficult problem that must be overcome by those on the Way of Innocence is the fear of being themselves. Somewhere, the men and women on this karmic path have been given the impression that they are scary or unappealing individu-

---

CORE LESSON
Trusting that there is an abundance and love life

GOAL
Becoming more aligned with their own energies and more direct

---

GIFTS
Steady, Charming, Resourceful

PITFALLS
Rebellious, Repressed, Closed

---

als—in essence, that they are unlovable. They respond to this deep-seated message by hiding behind—facades rather serious and controlled ones at that. Born psychologists, the men and women on the Way of Innocence possess a deep understanding of the human condition and its capacity for both good and evil. In part because of this understanding and, in part, due to actual experience, they are all too aware of the dangers of opening themselves up, only to be misused or mistreated. Thus they tend to be reserved except with a select group of trusted intimates. Unfortunately, it seems to be the fate of these individuals to encounter quite a bit of criticism from those outside their intimate circles. As closed as they are, they become much like blank screens on which others project their worst characterizations. At times they might feel like carrion that vultures are picking apart. This of course only reinforces their belief that they are unlovable and that the world is a dangerous and threatening place. Though they would never reveal it, the men and women on the Way of Innocence take the hurt and criticism inflicted on them very hard. It is a testament to their capacity for self-control that most people rarely understand this about them. Their dignity is important to them and they would never compromise it.

Often those on this path try to prove that they are worthy of love by working very, very hard to get others to like them. The upside of this is that, in the process,

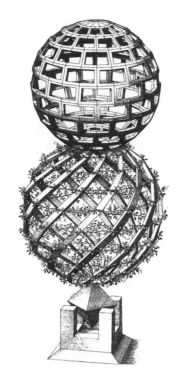

they learn how to capitalize on their innate charm. They rarely ask for anything directly, not only because in their hearts they believe that they deserve to receive it but for fear that by asking for what they need they will reveal too much about themselves, only to be rejected. Thus they are masters at backdoor politics, getting what they want by any means other than being direct. To describe them as manipulative is a tad strong, since it implies a lack of fairness or ethics. Actually, these individuals possess a highly refined sense of justice—they are just artful. People would want them on their side. Using their charm to get what they want, their determination is legendary. They fight for the underdog or disadvantaged both because they are highly empathetic and also because, subconsciously, it is a veiled attempt to be loved for their good works. Though they attempt to manage and control their environments, it is only because they are afraid that, if they do not, who they are and what really matters to them will not only be found out, but will be trampled on.

The core lesson for those on the Way of Innocence is to recreate a rather child-like trust in the process of life and in its abundance of love for all. Transforming their view of the world will be no easy matter, but well worth the effort. Approaching life in a trusting rather than mistrusting way will open up their lives and broaden their horizons immeasurably. If they can learn to trust themselves or

something greater than themselves to catch them when they fall, the men and women here will free their own energies rather than keeping them stuffed inside or masked in some way. They will begin to feel that it is safe to show who they are to the world. As their self-control starts to break up and wash away, so too will their reliance on controlling others or maneuvering to achieve their aims or to ensure the psychological or emotional safety of themselves or their loved ones.

Adopting a completely natural approach to themselves and life is the destiny of the individuals on the Way of Innocence. Nature is the perfect symbol for this path since most natural phenomena operate only according to innate patterns. Similarly, the Way of Innocence calls those born to it to listen only to the truth at their own cores. What creates the turning points in the lives of such individuals? Sometimes this occurs only when the men and women on this path have confronted the worst kinds of rejection. Suddenly, they realize that, no matter what they do, they can't make others approve of them or love them. Thus, they come to the conclusion that they may as well just be themselves and start having some fun. Often this happens at midlife, but, if they are fortunate, it can occur in adolescence or in the early twenties as well. Finally freeing themselves from trying to please or charm everyone and do the right thing, those

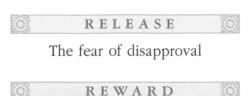

RELEASE

The fear of disapproval

REWARD

The joy of answering only
to themselves

SUGGESTION

Confront the fear of rejection. Be aware of how indirect you can be.
Try to become more attuned to nature's rhythms. Temper imagination
with practicality. Splash some color into your life.

on the Way of Innocence begin the process of uncovering and rediscovering their energies and abilities. One pitfall is that, in the joy and relief of asserting their true selves and dropping their facades, they may go overboard and throw all caution to the winds, becoming wild and rebellious even beyond the normal bounds set by society. Thus, the most successful individuals on this karmic path will meld their new found sense of self with some of the old control.

The recovery of lost innocence is marvelous to behold and can only be likened to Adam and Eve returning to the Garden. There's the feeling of springtime about the process, as hope returns. When they align their energies with the goal of this karmic path, the Natural, the men and women on the Way of Innocence become much more colorful, both in attitude and appearance. Drab or conservative clothing will be replaced with bright colors and more fashionable attire. They will begin to have more fun, and a zaniness or scathing humor emerges in them. Their masks are shed like old clothes and they stand naked, and very beautiful, before the audience. And the audience *roars* its approval! Suddenly the world wants what these individuals have to offer. Having let go of the need for approval, they discover that people suddenly seem to adore them. Innocence can be very beguiling, and those on this path aren't apt to ignore this—or fail to work it, just a little. The men and women on this karmic path will happily share the appeal of their innocence with the world, not as an act of manipulation, but as a gift to others. Because in so doing they are also celebrating the courage,

strength, and fortitude that they discovered in themselves to find a more honest way of being. Despite having been through so much themselves, their depth is such that they will always wish to help others, especially if it is to offer hope. "Hope springs eternal," is the message those on this path offer the rest of us.

Relationships may change radically for those on this path, some for the better. Changes in attitude, dress, and behavior may convince friends and family alike that such individuals may be ruining their lives. Threatened loved ones may place the blame on the change on someone outside the family circle. Usually, however, the change occurs within those born on this path, who then find themselves increasingly attracted to new, more unusual individuals. On the other hand, a mate who has had difficulty coping with the controlling nature of those on this path may experience great relief and joy when his or her spouse opens up to a more natural, fun-loving way of life. The blossoming of a stagnant marriage is not at all uncommon here, even at an advanced age. Friends usually weather such transformations more easily and are able to adjust to them with fewer problems.

An image that represents this karmic path may be that of a trustworthy servant, who has functioned perfectly for many years in a charming manner, quietly accomplishing his tasks and doing everything required of him. At some point, the individual decides to doff his uniform, don clothing more conducive to a free and independent lifestyle, and make his own way in the world as a freely functioning individual.

BALANCE POINT

Worldliness and
Innocence

CRYSTALS AND GEMSTONES

Angelite connects the individual to realms of unconditional love, allaying fears of rejection. This stone frees the heart to express inner truths with childlike joy and innocence.

NOTABLES ON THIS KARMIC PATH

Able to convey her naturalness of expression on the screen, film actress **Audrey Hepburn** became a symbol of beguiling inno-

AUDREY HEPBURN

cence. Born in Brussels, Belgium, she was featured in such films as *Sabrina, Breakfast at Tiffany's,* and *My Fair Lady.* Hepburn exhibited her concern for children in her work as goodwill ambassador for UNICEF, where she displayed her warmth, spontaneity and charm. Some doubt if there was ever any separation between Hepburn's screen persona and genuine self. Though she garnered five Oscar nominations, it has been said that "Audrey Hepburn didn't have to act, she just had to be."

Born Agnes Gonxha Bojaxhiu in Albania, **Mother Teresa** founded the sisterhood known as the Missionaries of Charity. Believing in life's abundance of love for all, the core lesson of the Way of Innocence, she pledged her life to helping the disadvantaged and be-

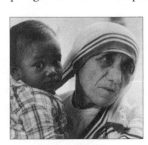
MOTHER TERESA

came revered because of her good works. Though she labored on behalf of innocents throughout the world, she is best known for her crusade to improve the plight of Calcutta's poor. Awarded both the Pope John Paul XXIII Peace Prize and the Nobel Peace Prize, Mother Teresa's work is carried on by followers who have established over 200 centers worldwide.

Employing visionary cinematic techniques to tap into the innocent core of his audience, **Steven Spielberg** has become the most commercially successful film director of all time. Like many on this path with Scorpio III energies, Spielberg possesses innate psychological astuteness, a gift that enables him to awaken collective themes and emotions in others. Perhaps the film that epitomizes his karmic path best is *E.T. the Extraterrestrial,* with its sense of the magical and theme of the recovery of lost innocence. Like many on this path, Spielberg came to a turning point in his career, and as a result he made *Schindler's List.* By being true to what matters to him, Spielberg began to make movies that not only entertain but also inform.

STEVEN SPIELBERG

Other Notables: Frank Gehry, André Previn, Burt Bacharach, Janet Jackson, Beverly Sills, Anne Frank, June Carter Cash, John Cusack, Mike Tyson, Henry David Thoreau, Salma Hayek, Adam Sandler, Stephen King, Chris Wallace, Kevin Kline, Arthur Rimbaud, John Philip Sousa, David Mamet, Johnny Bench, Ted Danson, Henry Miller, J. R. R. Tolkien, Benjamin Franklin, Mikhail Baryshnikov, Edna St. Vincent Millay

BIRTHDAYS ON KARMIC PATH 32

November 13, 1891–April 2, 1892 | June 26, 1910–November 13, 1910
February 4, 1929–June 25, 1929 | September 16, 1947–February 4, 1948 | April 28, 1966–September 15, 1966
December 7, 1984–April 27, 1985 | July 19, 2003–December 7, 2003

KARMIC PATH
32

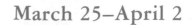

March 19–24
REBIRTH
PISCES–ARIES CUSP

The individuals born in this week are likely to be quite happy on this road as their natural energies are especially compatible with the higher challenge to adopt a more spontaneous attitude toward life and living. The endowment of their charm blesses them with considerable insight and self awareness. Though there are some here who will get bogged down in a sense of unworthiness or feeling that they are unloved, and bury their truest natures under a mountain of work and professional interests, their hunches, instincts, and natural spontaneity are sure to find wonderful expression here. Providing they do not channel their awesome energies into the need to compete, but keep themselves open, the opportunities for self-liberation, self-revelation, and self-realization will all be plentiful along the Way of Innocence.

MAX VON SYDOW
Actor, *The Exorcist*

4/10/1929
Aries II

CHALLENGE: **UNRAVELING SOME OF THEIR EMOTIONAL COMPLEXITY**

FULFILLMENT: **FINDING THAT THEIR DIRECTNESS OF AP-PROACH PAYS OFF FOR THEM**

March 25–April 2
THE CHILD
ARIES I

The souls born in the Week of the Child who travel the Way of Innocence are likely to have a fine time along this road, providing they take care to nurture their own spontaneity and do not allow themselves to be swayed from their course by an abundance of worldly concerns or the need for approval. In fact there are a number of individuals here who will repeat a pattern wherein they actively vie for acceptance and greater responsibility, only to rebel against those responsibilities later on. It is important that they tune out others' criticisms and tune in to their own needs for variety and new experiences without becoming overburdened by worry over what others might think of them. Thus they will enjoy both the benefits of an ever-increasing sense of faith in themselves, and the joy of being able to pursue their hearts' desires without needing anyone's permission to do so.

CHALLENGE: **HEALING CHILDHOOD ISSUES**

FULFILLMENT: **APPROACHING LIFE WITH A CHILDLIKE TRUST**

NOTABLE: **MILAN KUNDERA (AUTHOR,** *THE UNBEARABLE LIGHTNESS OF BEING***)**

April 3–10
THE STAR
ARIES II

Those born in the Week of the Star who navigate the challenge of the Way of Innocence are bound to encounter quite a bit of personal transformation along this karmic path. Their early experiences may lead them to compete for others' attention and approval and learn to successfully manipulate their environments in such a way that they remain at center stage. Yet as they proceed along this journey, they are likely to find that they are less interested in maintaining their star status and more interested in dropping their worldly masks. They will doubtless have to cultivate a less demanding and more trusting attitude in order to transform their world view so that it becomes easier to simply be themselves, have some fun, and align themselves with a more natural and less contrived pattern for living. This will prove to be the role of a lifetime for those born in the Week of the Star.

THOMAS JEFFERSON
3rd U.S. president;
founder of the University
of Virginia

4/13/1743
Aries III

CHALLENGE: **DROPPING THE NEED TO FEEL IMPORTANT**

FULFILLMENT: **FINDING APPROVAL ONCE THEY STOP SEEKING APPROVAL**

NOTABLE: **ANDRÉ PREVIN (CONDUCTOR/COMPOSER)**

April 11–18
THE PIONEER
ARIES III

The personalities born in the Week of the Pioneer who journey along the Way of Innocence will be blessed with a deep understanding of the human condition, combined with a powerful impulse toward expansion and exploration. The results can make for a fine mix along this path and many here will devote themselves wholeheartedly to improving social conditions, advocating the rights of others, or employing their talents in a political arena. Yet their impulses toward self-sacrifice will not go unrewarded, and it is certain that as they lose their fears of criticism or rejection by submerging themselves in a larger vision, they will find the courage, faith, and fortitude to rediscover a purer and more innocent sense of faith in themselves and the world at large. Thus, if they cultivate a naturally high sense of ideals and lose their fear of being themselves, they are in for a fine trip on the Way of Innocence.

CHALLENGE: **OVERCOMING THE COMPULSION FOR SECRECY**

FULFILLMENT: **ALIGNING THEMSELVES WITH THE NATURAL RHYTHMS OF LIFE**

April 19–24
POWER
ARIES–TAURUS CUSP

Establishing, nurturing, and protecting a personal power base as an outward manifestation of self-worth may mark the journeys of those born in this week who travel the Way of Innocence. Yet these personalities are bound to discover that worldly image and power are poor substitutes for genuine self-esteem and satisfaction. Though it is difficult to predict the circumstances that will provide turning points for these people, they are bound to discover somewhere along the road that power isn't everything. If they rise to the challenge to off-load the demands of worldly status and professional responsibility in the interests of cultivating a simpler lifestyle and a more complete sense of self, they can experience rich rewards along this journey. It is likely to be marked by both material success and a deep sense of spiritual enlightenment.

CHALLENGE: **RELEASING A CERTAIN KIND OF MANIPULATIVE CHARM THAT IS SECOND NATURE TO THEM**
FULFILLMENT: **RECOVERING THEIR LOST INNOCENCE**
NOTABLE: **AUGUSTUS D. JUILLIARD (MERCHANT; PHILANTHROPIST; HELPED ESTABLISH JUILLIARD SCHOOL OF MUSIC)**

April 25–May 2
MANIFESTATION
TAURUS I

Those born in the Week of Manifestation who find themselves on this karmic path are likely to experience a truly rewarding journey, yet they will have to avoid inflexibility and stubbornness if they are to realize the higher calling here. Nevertheless, these nurturing individuals are likely to have a fine intuitive grasp of life's inner rhythms and cycles, and respond beautifully to the burgeoning sense of faith and trust that comes with increased self-knowledge and understanding. Though they may take their share of lumps due to a lack of understanding from others, they are blessed with the natural strength and perception to rise above almost any obstacle. Much drawn to life's pleasures, if they do not close themselves off to the possibility of fulfillment because of mistrust or a dislike of change, and if they nurture their own need for harmony and sensual satisfaction, life will be rich along this road.

CHALLENGE: **BECOMING AWARE OF AND LOOSENING SOME OF THEIR RIGIDITY AND NEED FOR CONTROL**
FULFILLMENT: **INDULGING IN BEING MORE COLORFUL**

BURT BACHARACH
Songwriter/musician
———
5/12/1929
Taurus III

May 3–10
THE TEACHER
TAURUS II

Blessed with unique communication gifts and a rare curiosity, those born in the Week of the Teacher who make their way along this road are likely to experience great personal satisfaction and success. Much more energetic and open to new ideas than some of their fellow Taureans, this group will do especially well to explore their interests in other places, other cultures, or in a simpler, more natural lifestyle. On this karmic path, Taurus II's have a much more charming demeanor than these highly assertive and demanding people might have otherwise. If they take care not to become overly involved in the demands of worldly image, jockeying for position, or trying to please others at the expense of their own peace of mind, they are likely to be both very good at getting what they want, and very wise about making the right life choices along the Way of Innocence.

CHALLENGE: **COMING TO THE CONCLUSION THAT THEY DON'T HAVE TO PLEASE EVERYONE**
FULFILLMENT: **ADOPTING A NATURAL APPROACH TO THEMSELVES AND THEIR RELATIONSHIPS**
NOTABLE: **AUDREY HEPBURN (ACTRESS, *BREAKFAST AT TIFFANY'S*; UNICEF AMBASSADOR)**

May 11–18
THE NATURAL
TAURUS III

The people born in this week who travel the Way of Innocence may impart a new and entirely uplifting meaning to the phrase "noble savage" as they make their way along this path. Here Taurus III's are gifted with more worldly savvy than they might otherwise possess but they are also likely to be more easily satisfied with both themselves and their positions in life than some who travel this road. Though they may do a fair amount of hankering after the approval of others, they are rather unlikely to do much pining over lost loves and lost causes, and have a natural inclination toward freedom and fun that will be to their highest advantage here. They may discover, however, that greater stability goes hand in hand with increased simplicity. Still, they may well find what they seek in the great outdoors, unusual places, or a carefully cultivated and possibly secret personal retreat.

CHALLENGE: **NOT GETTING LOST IN SECOND-GUESSING THEMSELVES**
FULFILLMENT: **GETTING BACK TO BASICS**

JANET JACKSON
Pop singer/actress,
"What Have You Done for Me Lately"
———
5/16/1966
Taurus III

May 19–24
ENERGY
TAURUS–GEMINI CUSP

Those born in this period are likely to be more grounded on this karmic path than otherwise. Part of the process of dropping their facades will involve better channeling of their natural restlessness and energy. Yet these personalities will do well to make sure that their love of attention is not based in a deep-seated need for acceptance and approval. Nevertheless, they are bound to be compelling personalities who will doubtless draw a certain amount of fire for their wilder side. If they can maintain their courage and cultivate their sense of spontaneity without succumbing to the dangers of superficiality, thrill-seeking, or an utter lack of self-awareness, they can realize the highest levels of fulfillment. They will have a truly colorful, if controversial, life's journey along the Way of Innocence.

BEVERLY SILLS
Operatic soprano, later manager of NYC Opera

5/25/1929
Gemini I

CHALLENGE: **RELYING LESS ON CHARM AND ARTFULNESS TO GET THEM OUT OF SCRAPES**
FULFILLMENT: **MOVING THROUGH LIFE WITH THE PERFECT COMBINATION OF INNOCENCE AND WORLDLINESS**
NOTABLE: **MARVIN CHOMSKY (TELEVISION DIRECTOR, *ROOTS*, *GUNSMOKE*, *STAR TREK*)**

May 25–June 2
FREEDOM
GEMINI I

Those born in the Week of Freedom will doubtless be gifted with both a more refined outlook and a less abrasive character on this karmic path than they might have otherwise. Yet the downside is that they will also have to watch their manipulative tendencies if they are to find the fulfillment and authenticity promised along this road. They will be marked by a rather cynical attitude, and their wealth of plans and projects may further interfere with the call to simplicity and faith that is indicated here. Thus, they may get entangled in any number of games, intrigues, and psychodramas before they realize the value of a simpler and more trusting approach to the world. However, when they are able to strip away the camouflage of a worldly image that is not in keeping with their own deepest impulses toward freedom—particularly the freedom to be themselves—they can make great progress here.

CHALLENGE: **TEMPERING THEIR CYNICISM WITH A CHILDLIKE TRUST IN THE PROCESS OF LIFE**
FULFILLMENT: **ANSWERING ONLY TO THEMSELVES**

June 3–10
NEW LANGUAGE
GEMINI II

Those born in the Week of New Language who find themselves on the Way of Innocence may experience quite a struggle with the issue of feeling themselves rejected or misunderstood along this life's journey. Yet on this path, Gemini IIs' natural gifts are sure to be enhanced, making for some really brilliant communicators—at the very least, these personalities will be able to talk a good game. However, there is much about this configuration that suggests these individuals will have to avoid a tendency to "spin" the information or tinker with the truth out of defensiveness, distrust, or fear of reprisal. But there is the potential for wonderful success along this road, especially as these souls progress to the point where they are able to drop their disguises and personas and rediscover the freedom that comes with the confidence to be direct.

ANNE FRANK
Victim of the Holocaust; diary made famous

6/12/1929
Gemini III

CHALLENGE: **KNOWING HOW THEIR DEFENSIVENESS CAUSES THEM TO ATTRACT MISTRUST AND CRITICISM**
FULFILLMENT: **OPENING THEMSELVES; REVEALING THEIR UNUSUAL HUMOR AND UNIQUE EXPRESSIVENESS TO THE WORLD**
NOTABLE: **JULIANNA MARGULIES (ACTRESS, *ER*)**

June 11–18
THE SEEKER
GEMINI III

Simple disillusion and a cynical attitude may prove the biggest problems for those born in the Week of Freedom who travel the Way of Innocence. Though doubtless blessed with more than their share of charm, they will likely be so good at getting others to do what they want and at manipulating their environments, that they may neglect the higher task of attending to and nurturing a sense of self that is independent of others' approval or disapproval. Though it is likely that these people will push a few buttons as well as a few boundaries in their quests for self-fulfillment, they should find the material and spiritual rewards of this configuration well suited to their natural sense of adventure. If they are careful not to fall prey to their own chameleon-like abilities to do what the situation demands, and keep in touch with their own quests for self-transformation and enjoyment, all will go well along this life's journey.

CHALLENGE: **GRAPPLING WITH THE FRUSTRATING SENSE THAT THEY ARE NOT THE MASTERS OF THEIR FATE**
FULFILLMENT: **CELEBRATING THE FREEDOM THAT GOING THEIR OWN WAY GIVES THEM**
NOTABLE: **SANDY ALOMAR, JR. (BASEBALL PLAYER)**

June 19–24

MAGIC
GEMINI–CANCER CUSP

Those born on the Cusp of Magic who journey along the Way of Innocence can do very well along this path since they are inclined to embrace both the simplicity and innocence that are part of the higher calling here. Though they may well be puzzles to those around them, they are nevertheless likely to be well aware of their own deepest motivations and well equipped to free themselves from an overattachment to others' opinions of them, or to outworn worldly persons. They will have to be on guard against a tendency in themselves to manipulate others through purely emotional means, or to play games with feelings as a device for self-protection. Yet as the qualities of hope and resurrection of the self begin to manifest for these personalities, they will likely welcome them with wonderful enthusiasm and a renewed sense of faith in life itself.

CHALLENGE: **NOT USING WITHHOLDING AS AN INTER-PERSONAL TOOL FOR MANIPULATION AND CONTROL**
FULFILLMENT: **LIVING LIFE IN AN OPEN AND GRACIOUS MANNER**
NOTABLES: **JUNE CARTER CASH (COUNTRY MUSIC SINGER; MEMBER OF THE CARTER FAMILY); EDGAR BRONFMAN (FORMER CEO SEAGRAM, CO. LTD.)**

MIKE TYSON
Former heavyweight champion; life filled with scandals

———

6/30/1966
Cancer I

June 25–July 2

THE EMPATH
CANCER I

Those born in the Week of the Empath who travel the Way of Innocence may have to do a bit of soul-searching before they can successfully embrace the call to greater innocence and faith in themselves. In fact, these people can be oversensitive to the feelings of others, and some emotional setbacks and traumas can lead them to a certain wariness and fiercely self-protective stance. Overcoming feelings of unworthiness, the ability to forgive and forget, and to replace some fearful or aggressive attitudes with joy and acceptance will all play quite prominently in the life journeys of those born with this configuration. Yet if they can cultivate the willingness to turn loose old fears and personal slights and open themselves to the future with renewed confidence and hope, the rewards will be rich on this life's journey.

CHALLENGE: **RELEASING THE FEAR OF REJECTION AND LEARNING TO ASK FOR WHAT THEY NEED**
FULFILLMENT: **TRUSTING THAT IT'S OKAY TO REVEAL THEIR SOFT SIDE**
NOTABLES: **JOHN CUSACK (ACTOR, *THE GRIFTERS*, *GROSSE POINTE BLANK*); FRANK LOESSER (LYRICIST/COMPOSER, *GUYS AND DOLLS*); WILLIAM C. MELLON, JR. (PHYSICIAN; ESTABLISHED MISSION HOSPITAL IN HAITI)**

July 3–10

THE UNCONVENTIONAL
CANCER II

Those born in the Week of the Unconventional who find themselves on this karmic path may find the singular opportunity of revealing their rich inner lives to the world to be more of a challenge than they might have thought. Yet there is perhaps no more daunting personal accomplishment than to divulge one's fantasies and dreams to others. Nevertheless, the individuals on this path can realize true fulfillment here, as their fun-loving and imaginative energies are very much in keeping with the higher challenge of restored hope and personal freedom that beckon. If they can manage to risk the possibility of rejection or derision while refraining from the expectation of such responses, this journey will doubtless result in some colorful lives and rewarding adventures as they share themselves with the world.

CHALLENGE: **DARING TO REVEAL EVEN THEIR MOST UNUSUAL SIDES TO OTHERS**
FULFILLMENT: **INDULGING THEIR IMAGINATIONS AND CHARMING AN AUDIENCE**
NOTABLES: **GLORIA STUART (ACTRESS, *TITANIC*); MOISES ALOU (BASEBALL PLAYER)**

HENRY DAVID THOREAU
Writer/poet, transcendentalist, *Walden*

———

7/12/1817
Cancer III

July 11–18

THE PERSUADER
CANCER III

If the souls born in this week who find themselves on the Way of Innocence will only resist the need to prove themselves and concentrate instead on being themselves, all will go well along this life's journey. That may well be easier than it sounds, for it is likely that these souls will become so good at manipulating external circumstances to their satisfaction that they ignore or discount their deeper needs and inclinations. Personal insecurity may prove a big problem for many of these people as well, and they are likely to have a number of blind spots when it comes to seeing themselves as the world sees them. But if they learn better to separate from their immediate environment and go in search of those things that give them simplicity, security, and joy, their renewed vision and sense of attunement to the deeper rhythms and cycles of life can do much to restore their faith in themselves and the world at large.

CHALLENGE: **STRUGGLING WITH THEIR AMBITION AND EVALUATING ITS LONG-TERM CONSEQUENCES**
FULFILLMENT: **SIMPLIFYING THEIR LIVES AND BECOMING MORE GROUNDED IN THE NATURAL WORLD**
NOTABLE: **JOSIAH WEDGWOOD (POTTER; INVENTED UN-GLAZED BLACK BASALT WARE)**

July 19–25
OSCILLATION
CANCER–LEO CUSP

July 26–August 2
AUTHORITY
LEO I

Though blessed with considerably more stability and greater control than they might have otherwise, Cancer–Leos on this karmic path may undergo some rather spectacular personal transformations along the way. They are likely to have an irrepressible side in any event, and if they resist the temptation to disguise or deceive others in the interest of gaining love and approval, they are likely to find considerable fulfillment. Yet they are unlikely to have much patience with trying to be someone they are not, or attempting to live up to others' expectations. If they can avoid the emotional blockages that sometimes stand in the way of their creativity and zest for life, and never confuse the concept of innocence with a mere lack of self-awareness, their lives may well serve as inspiration for those they meet along the way.

DEAN CAIN
Actor, *Lois and Clark*

7/31/1966
Leo I

Learning not to take themselves and their intense level of ambition quite so seriously is likely to be the principal challenge to those born in the Week of Authority who travel the Way of Innocence. Quite capable of working toward any number of well-defined goals, these personalities may be easily seduced by a false set of aspirations until they come to better terms with their need to simply be themselves. Their natures are such that once they come into their own and release the need to be admired by those around them, they can willingly drop the masks of tiresome duty, personal insecurity, or undue responsibility to pursue a purely personal and less complicated set of goals. Though they may be perceived by others as selfish, eccentric, or even reclusive, once they come to terms with their need for greater fulfillment, they are likely to pursue an unwavering course to their happiness and will reveal themselves to the world without reservation or apology.

CHALLENGE: **CLEARING OUT THE BURIED EMOTIONS AND RESENTMENTS THAT ARE HOLDING THEM BACK**
FULFILLMENT: **PATTING THEMSELVES ON THE BACK FOR THEIR CAPACITY TO SURVIVE**

CHALLENGE: **LOOSENING THEIR GRIP ON THEIR ENVIRONMENT BY ALLOWING THEMSELVES TO GO WITH THE FLOW**
FULFILLMENT: **PRESENTING THEMSELVES TO THE WORLD WITH GREATER CONFIDENCE**

August 3–10
BALANCED STRENGTH
LEO II

August 11–18
LEADERSIIIP
LEO III

Learning to live a more balanced life and getting in touch with those things that make them truly happy will be important for the single-minded souls born in this week who travel the Way of Innocence. In fact there are many with this configuration who will have to abandon some deeply held beliefs about the value of keeping their heads down and their noses to the grindstone before they are able to realize the rich rewards of selfhood that beckon along this road. It will be especially helpful for these personalties to learn to adequately distinguish their own inclinations from what is expected of them, and to avoid the tendency to undue self-sacrifice or even masochism. Yet they will prove themselves survivors in the highest sense, and if they can further allow themselves the freedom that comes with personal resurrection and renewal, their priorities will doubtless become clear.

LEO SLEZAK
Famous opera tenor

8/18/1873
Leo III

A commanding and even heroic facade may disguise some deep-seated fears in the personalities of those born in this week who travel the Way of Innocence. Though they are likely to be worldly, sophisticated, and highly ambitious, true fulfillment may prove elusive until they release a deep sense of aggrievement and a fear of rejection. Very prone to shouldering huge responsibilities and attempting any number of daunting feats in order to gain respect and appreciation, they can succumb to some highly manipulative and even tyrannical tactics when things don't go as planned. Though likely to be quite social and even dazzlingly so at times, they will nevertheless manifest a rather closed attitude toward helpful interaction and may be self-sufficient to the point of neurosis. Relying less heavily on themselves alone and developing more confidence in life itself may well be the key to happiness and personal heroics for Leo III's.

CHALLENGE: **DROPPING THE NOTION THAT SOMEHOW CRITICISM AND DISAPPROVAL FROM OTHERS IS JUSTIFIED**
FULFILLMENT: **CREATING A BETTER BALANCE BETWEEN ALTRUISM AND SELF-INTEREST**

CHALLENGE: **KNOWING THE DIFFERENCE BETWEEN TAKING COMMAND AND PUSHING PEOPLE AROUND**
FULFILLMENT: **STEPPING MORE FEARLESSLY INTO THE LIMELIGHT ON PERSONAL MATTERS**

August 19–25

EXPOSURE
LEO–VIRGO CUSP

Some really interesting, if rather secretive, personalities are born on the Cusp of Exposure who travel the Way of Innocence. Yet they may find this a more difficult passage than it really needs to be, especially when their self-protective inclinations lead them to believe that it is not only useful, but necessary to conceal themselves behind a wall of worldly image. Formidable perception and keen awareness of others' motives can characterize this group. Most will face any number of issues that revolve around the themes of deception and revelation until they begin to better understand that truth is ultimately simple. Nevertheless, these individuals are well equipped to summon the courage to be themselves in the eyes of the world. Once they become less attached to their secrets and cultivate the willingness to trust and to make themselves worthy of trust in return, their natural charisma and flamboyance will make for some fascinating transformations along this life's journey.

CHALLENGE: **BEING LESS CONVINCED THAT THEY KNOW WHAT OTHERS ARE GOING TO DO**
FULFILLMENT: **PERMITTING THEMSELVES TO BE SPONTANEOUS**
NOTABLES: **EERO AND ELIEL SAARINEN (FATHER AND SON ARCHITECTS; SAME BIRTHDAY)**

JEAN LOUIS BARRAULT
French actor/producer;
member Comédie
Française

9/8/1910
Virgo II

August 26–September 2

SYSTEM BUILDERS
VIRGO I

Freeing themselves from the relative restrictions of their own carefully established rituals and routines may prove the principal challenge for those born in the Week of System Builders who travel the Way of Innocence. Indeed, awareness of their own inner emotional patterns and impulses may not be their strongest suit, yet there is nevertheless great potential for happiness and self-confidence here. They will have to take care, however, that their inclinations toward service and self-sacrifice do not distract them from the possibility of enjoyment or self-fulfillment. If these personalities can better learn to distinguish between spontaneity and disorder and refuse to allow themselves to be unduly threatened by external circumstances, life is sure to get easier along this road, especially when they learn the value of pleasing themselves before anyone else.

CHALLENGE: **SORTING THROUGH THE CONFUSING COMBINATION OF COMPLETE UNDERSTANDING OF THE PSYCHOLOGY OF OTHERS WITHOUT FULLY BEING AWARE OF THEIR OWN**
FULFILLMENT: **ALIGNING THEMSELVES WITH THEIR NEED FOR SIMPLER STRUCTURES AND LESS CHAOS**
NOTABLES: **MOTHER TERESA (CATHOLIC NUN; WON NOBEL PEACE PRIZE FOR MISSIONARIES OF CHARITY WORK IN INDIA); SALMA HAYEK (MEXICAN-BORN FILM ACTRESS, *WILD WILD WEST*)**

September 3–10

THE ENIGMA
VIRGO II

Blessed with more than their share of charm, refinement, and the subtler forms of social skill, those born in the Week of the Enigma may nevertheless encounter a struggle in their own processes of self discovery on this karmic path. Here it may not be so much a question of mistrusting others as it will be of mistrusting some of their own best impulses and inclinations. These personalities have some exacting standards that may prove far more of an obstacle to their fulfillment than anything the world might throw their way. It may take some time for these individuals to come to the realization that none of us is entirely perfect, and that perfection, ultimately, cannot be equated with happiness. Yet once they give themselves permission to live a little, life promises a lot along this karmic path.

CHALLENGE: **NOT ADHERING SO FIXEDLY TO THEIR OWN HIGH STANDARDS**
FULFILLMENT: **HAVING GIVEN UP ON TRYING TO PLEASE EVERYONE, FINDING WITHIN THEMSELVES A CHILDLIKE AND SPONTANEOUS KIND OF HAPPINESS**

ADAM SANDLER
Actor/comedian,
The Water Boy

9/9/1966
Virgo II

September 11–18

THE LITERALIST
VIRGO III

Those born in the Week of the Literalist are likely to do quite well along the Way of Innocence, as their natural dislike of phoniness and pretension will serve them very well along this road. Though considerably more charming than they might be otherwise, they may find that it is their own insistence on self-control that proves to be their biggest stumbling block here. Nurturing their deep need for harmony will be especially important and it is likely that they will find the peace and personal satisfaction they seek through the mastery of some craft or hands-on type of hobby. Though approval from others may prove elusive until they come more fully into their own, Virgo III's can expect great fulfillment here, as their natural love of truth is likely to keep them on a steadier course than many who travel this road.

CHALLENGE: **LETTING GO OF THEIR INSISTENCE ON HAVING THEIR WAY**
FULFILLMENT: **FINDING SELF-EXPRESSION THROUGH CREATIVITY, SUCH AS ARTS AND CRAFTS**
NOTABLE: **JEFF MacNELLY (CARTOONIST, "SHOE")**

September 19–24
BEAUTY
VIRGO–LIBRA CUSP

Gifted with greater stability and depth of emotional understanding than many others born in this period, the personalities who travel the Way of Innocence may wrestle with issues of approval and identity along this karmic path. Those on this path have an exalted idea of beauty that may prove difficult to reconcile with their inborn ability to perceive the less savory sides of humanity. The result may be a closed or repressed approach to life. Yet that aesthetic can serve them well if they embrace the artistry and innocence within themselves. Possessing formidable skills at getting the world to do their bidding will be an ultimately unsatisfying experience until they drop their worldly disguises and summon a more complete and authentic sense of self. Once that is accomplished, the fun and freedom that beckons will be more than worth the trip.

STEPHEN KING
Bestselling novelist, horror classics, *The Shining*

———

9/21/1947
Virgo–Libra Cusp

CHALLENGE: **NOT HIDING FROM THE GROSSNESS OF THE WORLD BY SURROUNDING THEMSELVES WITH OBJECTS OF BEAUTY**

FULFILLMENT: **WIELDING THEIR CHARM MORE COMFORTABLY AND NATURALLY**

September 25–October 2
THE PERFECTIONIST
LIBRA I

Those born in the Week of the Perfectionist who make their way along this karmic path may find it a rocky road until they come to better terms with some possible flaws in their own perceptions and learn to appreciate and accept themselves. Likely to project many of their own fears and insecurities onto others, they may have to work hard to develop the sense of trust that is part of the higher calling here. There is the potential for real transformation with this configuration, especially when these personalities let go of some of their more exacting standards and open themselves to a more flexible and easy-going attitude. If they can come to terms with the realities of their own accomplishments and realize that a renewed sense of innocence doesn't necessarily result in a loss of dignity, the world may well beat a path to their door.

CHALLENGE: **KNOWING THAT THEIR CRITICAL ATTITUDES ARE OFTEN REFLECTED BACK TO THEM**

FULFILLMENT: **FREEING THEMSELVES FROM THE CHAOS OF CONFLICTING EMOTIONS**

October 3–10
SOCIETY
LIBRA II

Though likely to be considerably less fearful of rejection than many along this road, those born in the Week of Society who find themselves on the Way of Innocence may discover that many of their fears of rejection or disapproval arise not so much from others' opinions of them, but are the result of unfortunate personal choices. These individuals are not especially astute when it comes to knowing what's good for them, and they may encounter a few rough spots before they develop higher expectations for their own personal fulfillment. Yet when they come to understand that it's much easier to get what one wants out of life once it has been identified the prospects for acceptance, fulfillment, and real joy in living will increase dramatically.

MEATLOAF
Pop/rock singer, "Paradise by the Dashboard Lights"

———

9/27/1947
Libra I

CHALLENGE: **NOT BECOMING BOGGED DOWN IN FASCINATION WITH THE INNER WORKINGS OF OTHERS AND INTERPERSONAL POLITICS**

FULFILLMENT: **BECOMING MORE ATTUNED TO THEIR OWN ESSENCE AND NEEDS**

NOTABLE: **LINDSAY BUCKINGHAM (FLEETWOOD MAC LEAD GUITARIST)**

October 11–18
THEATER
LIBRA III

Those born in the Week of Theater who find themselves on the Way of Innocence will adopt a number of roles and worldly disguises as they make their way along this karmic path. Blessed with an unusual amount of savvy, style, and perception, they may be quite adept at doing what is expected of them, and exhaust a fair amount of energy in trying to be all things to all people. While they are blessed with a much higher degree of interest and empathy for others than they might have otherwise, they will find that the fulfillment they seek is lacking until they come to better terms with who they are inside. Yet if they do not succumb to a rather suspicious or distrustful attitude toward the world, and summon the faith and courage to be more completely themselves, the rewards of fulfillment, spontaneity, and a renewed lust for life with be especially sweet here.

CHALLENGE: **DROPPING THE FACADE**

FULFILLMENT: **LIVING IN GREATER ALIGNMENT WITH NATURE'S RHYTHMS**

NOTABLES: **CHRIS WALLACE (TELEVISION JOURNALIST); JOSEPH ALSOP (REPORTER/COLUMNIST); LAURA NYRO (POP MUSIC WRITER/SINGER, "ELI'S COMING")**

KARMIC PATH
32

October 19–25

DRAMA AND CRITICISM
LIBRA–SCORPIO CUSP

The sensuous and dramatic personalities born in this period who travel the Way of Innocence may experience rejection until they come to understand better that their lack of approval from others may be a manifestation of their own careless attitudes toward fulfillment. Nevertheless, there is enormous potential for growth here, providing these charismatic and creative individuals refuse to allow themselves to sink into cynicism or misanthropy. In fact it is very likely that their own creative talents will provide the key to their enlightenment and sense of transformation as it will put them in touch with a sense of both themselves and the larger rhythms and patterns of life. Once they alter their perceptions of themselves and others in such a way as to provide for greater hope and faith, then the liberation, security, and simplicity that result will provide them ample rewards for their efforts.

CHALLENGE: **RELEASING AN OVERSERIOUS VIEW OF THINGS**
FULFILLMENT: **DECIDING JUST TO HAVE FUN AND DAMN THE REST**
NOTABLE: **ARTHUR RIMBAUD (FRENCH POET, *A SEASON IN HELL*)**

KEVIN KLINE
Actor/director; Oscar for
A Fish Called Wanda

10/24/1947
Libra–Scorpio Cusp

October 26–November 2

INTENSITY
SCORPIO I

Though in many ways material reward and external security will come easily to those born in the Week of Intensity, emotional satisfaction and freedom will be considerably harder to achieve. It will be critical to the fulfillment of these individuals to let go of a highly suspicious attitude toward others in order to find happiness here. Gifted with keen perception, these people are often highly manipulative and controlling in the extreme. Thus, overcoming their own defenses and cultivating their sense of humor will prove especially important. Yet once they understand how their own suspicions and fears serve to shape their reality, once they establish the possibility of truly being themselves without first considering others' opinions, motives, or hidden agendas, life will get much easier along this karmic path.

CHALLENGE: **GIVING UP ON THE NOTION THAT THROUGH IRON-WILLED CONTROL THEY CAN PROTECT THEMSELVES AND THEIR LOVED ONES**
FULFILLMENT: **TURNING ON TO THEIR OWN POSITIVE SUNNY SIDE AND REDISCOVERING WHAT GIVES THEM JOY**
NOTABLES: **A. J. AYER (PHILOSOPHER); C. W. POST (CEREAL MANUFACTURER; HEALTH FANATIC; ANTILABOR)**

November 3–11

DEPTH
SCORPIO II

Many of the souls born in the Week of Depth will struggle mightily to overcome a somewhat negative or even downright depressive attitude toward themselves and the world before they can realize the higher level of fulfillment promised here. There are a number of these individuals who will experience painful rejections or traumas that will profoundly affect both their self-images and their images of the world at large. Deep though they may be, they have a strong tendency to overidentify with their own sense of suffering—to the extent that they refuse to consider happiness as a worthwhile goal. Yet when they confront the possibility that much of their personal suffering may be self-inflicted, and thereby free themselves from the prisons of fear and self-protection, their resulting transformation and renewed sense of hope are sure to assume really inspiring proportions along the Way of Innocence.

CHALLENGE: **REFUSING TO USE ANY VARIETY OF FEEL-GOOD SUBSTITUTES FOR OWNING WHO THEY ARE**
FULFILLMENT: **REAPING THE REWARDS OF THEIR FINANCIAL ACUMEN AND ALLOWING IT TO BUY THEM FREEDOM**
NOTABLE: **JOHN PHILIP SOUSA (BAND MASTER; COMPOSER, "STARS AND STRIPES FOREVER")**

HILLARY RODHAM CLINTON
Attorney; child advocate;
First Lady

10/26/1947
Scorpio I

November 12–18

CHARM
SCORPIO III

As long as they do not allow their own sense of natural realism to become confused with the face they present to the world, there is the certainty of success for those born in the Week of Charm who travel this karmic path. Whatever their daily lives and responsibilities, it will be especially important for these worldlywise personalities to nurture and develop the qualities of creativity, spontaneity, and faith that lie within them. They may work very hard to get others to like or approve of them, and some may substitute the ability to manipulate others for a more genuine sense of fulfillment. Yet once they understand that it is indeed possible to change their lives simply by changing their perceptions, and successfully attune themselves to the sense of deeper belonging that is implied here, they can expect a joyous and bountiful life experience along this karmic path.

CHALLENGE: **REALIZING HOW HEAVILY THEY RELY ON CHARM AND SEXUAL POLITICS TO GET WHAT THEY WANT**
FULFILLMENT: **RELEASING THEIR EMOTIONAL CONFLICTS AND ADOPTING A MORE OPEN APPROACH TO LIFE**
NOTABLES: **ERWIN ROMMEL (GERMAN WW II FIELD MARSHAL, "THE DESERT FOX"; INVOLVED IN PLOT TO ASSASSINATE HITLER); AVERELL HARRIMAN (FINANCIER; DIPLOMAT; GOVERNOR OF NEW YORK); SIR FREDERICK BANTING (DISCOVERED INSULIN)**

November 19–24
REVOLUTION
SCORPIO–SAGITTARIUS CUSP

Though blessed with considerably more finesse and worldly savvy than they might have otherwise, the souls born on the Cusp of Revolution who make their way along this karmic path are assured of an enriching and fulfilling—if somewhat tumultuous—life experience. Likely to be less preoccupied with what others may think of them than many along this road, Scorpio–Sagittarians may express their personal insecurities in a more worldly arena. Their need for freedom is sure to be of utmost importance, whatever their life goals. If they do not become bogged down in tiresome rituals, endless intrigues, or fruitless battles in their quest for acceptance, then the rewards of self-renewal, greater faith, and the reawakening of a sense of hope will prove more than worth the sacrifice of their worldly image along this karmic path.

CHALLENGE: **COMING TO SOME REAL CONCLUSIONS ABOUT WHAT REALLY MATTERS**
FULFILLMENT: **EXPLODING THEIR OWN CAREFULLY CRAFTED PUBLIC PERSONAS**
NOTABLE: JOHN LARROQUETTE (TV ACTOR, *NIGHT COURT*)

DAVID MAMET
Playwright/screenwriter,
American Buffalo

11/30/1947
Sagittarius I

November 25–December 2
INDEPENDENCE
SAGITTARIUS I

Ironically, those born in the Week of Independence may well find that the biggest obstacle to their fulfillment lies in their ability to trust themselves and give proper credence to their own highest impulses. In fact, many along this road will put such a high priority on issues of honor and trust that they become the unwitting victims of their own moral codes. They may be considerably less direct than they believe themselves to be when it comes to asking for respect or acceptance from those around them. They must understand that others will only disappoint them until they develop a real and unvarnished sense of uniqueness that is free of the fear of personal rejection. Then they are wonderfully well equipped to cast off the shackles of hesitancy and conformity and will doubtless prove themselves worthy of their own desires.

CHALLENGE: **UNCOVERING THAT SMALL BUT INSIDIOUS SIDE OF THEMSELVES THAT IS INDIRECT AND ARTFUL AND PUTTING IT TO BETTER USE**
FULFILLMENT: **OFFERING HOPE TO OTHERS AS THEY SHARE WHO THEY ARE**
NOTABLES: PETRA KELLY (COFOUNDED GREEN PARTY IN GERMANY); CARLOS MERIDA (ABSTRACT EXPRESSIONIST ARTIST)

December 3–10
THE ORIGINATOR
SAGITTARIUS II

The inborn ability to do their own thing will prove the single greatest asset for those born in the Week of the Originator who travel the Way of Innocence. Nevertheless, they will have to take some care to cultivate a stronger sense of confidence and personal identity, and not to act out of neediness or the desire to impress. Indeed there can be found a number of "square pegs in round holes" among those with this configuration as they seek to conform to professional, personal, or worldly standards that are not their own. They may encounter quite a bit of personal frustration here, yet will be rescued from too many poor choices by their own wilder and more original impulses. If these souls can master the art of acknowledging their own sense of passion and avoid the pitfalls of self-pity or defensiveness, the prospects for spiritual, financial, and personal reward here will prove quite surprising to them and everyone else.

CHALLENGE: **CONTROLLING THE TENDENCY TO USE AGGRESSION AS A MASK**
FULFILLMENT: **ENJOYING THE SENSE OF REBIRTH ONCE THEY DROP THEIR BAGGAGE**
NOTABLES: JOHNNY BENCH (BASEBALL HALL OF FAME CATCHER); JIM MESSINA (FOLKSINGER)

GREGG ALLMAN
Musician/keyboardist,
The Allman Brothers Band

12/8/1947
Sagittarius II

December 11–18
THE TITAN
SAGITTARIUS III

Those born in the Week of the Titan who find themselves along the Way of Innocence may spend a great deal of time exhorting others to a more natural lifestyle until they come to realize that their sermonizing is more than likely a projection of their own unfulfilled needs. Much attracted by the themes of individual freedom versus the so-called restraints of society, those born in this week may find that their answers lie not so much in theory as in their willingness to confront personal issues. Often plagued by secret insecurities that they hide behind a blustery show of charm and bravado, they may have to reveal some genuine vulnerability before they can get what they need. Yet if they succeed in conquering the tendency to agonize or overwork problems to the point where solutions cease to be relevant, and instead allow themselves the freedom to pursue their wildest dreams, all will go well along this life's journey.

CHALLENGE: **FERRETING OUT THE DARKER, MORE CONTROLLING SIDES OF THEIR PERSONALITIES**
FULFILLMENT: **ENGAGING THEIR OWN SENSE OF ENCHANTMENT AND SHARING IT WITH OTHERS**
NOTABLE: STEVEN SPIELBERG (OSCAR-WINNING DIRECTOR/PRODUCER, *E.T., SCHINDLER'S LIST, SAVING PRIVATE RYAN*)

December 19–25

PROPHECY
SAGITTARIUS–CAPRICORN CUSP

Those born on the Cusp of Prophecy who travel they Way of Innocence are wonderfully well equipped to rise to the challenge and promise of this karmic path. Blessed with a more socially adept set of skills than they might have otherwise, these individuals are unlikely to be overtly troubled by the need for acceptance and approval. Their strong intuitions and extrasensory gifts are likely to emerge here, however. These individuals may have to come to terms with the clarity of their own insights before they can successfully free themselves from the bonds of convention or conformity and seek the color, excitement, and rich sense of personal reward that are all promised. Though their eventual success may well lie in their willingness to play hunches for everything they're worth, the resulting joy and renewal will be more than worth the risks along this karmic path.

TED DANSON
Actor, *Cheers*

12/29/1947
Capricorn I

CHALLENGE: **REALIZING HOW THEY WEAVE THEIR INTUITIVE INSIGHTS INTO A MACHIAVELLIAN POLITICAL AGENDA**

FULFILLMENT: **RECOVERING THEIR LOST INNOCENCE**

NOTABLES: **PETER CRISS (DRUMMER FOR ROCK GROUP KISS); BILL RODGERS (MARATHON RUNNER; WON N.Y. AND BOSTON 4 TIMES)**

December 26–January 2

THE RULER
CAPRICORN I

The commanding and closed personalities born in the Week of the Ruler who make their way along this karmic path may find this road less than fulfilling until they gain a better knowledge of their own capacity for happiness. Though many here will find their self-confidence augmented by their ability to shoulder responsibilities and assume authority over others, real satisfaction may prove rather elusive. Likely to be shrewd judges of character, they can nevertheless miscalculate their own needs. Many will fall victim to rigid or overly conventional notions of what is possible or socially acceptable. Though this may be a challenging journey in many respects, Capricorn I's are blessed with the strength of their own convictions. If they can simply adjust those convictions to include what is right for them, rather than holding on to ideas of what is right for everyone else, their strength, faith, and ability to change their lives for the better can serve as real sources of inspiration for many along the way.

CHALLENGE: **NOT HIDING THEIR LIGHT BEHIND WORK OR CORPORATE STRUCTURES**

FULFILLMENT: **FINDING RENEWAL THROUGH THE RECOVERY OF LOST INNOCENCE**

NOTABLES: **HENRY MILLER (AUTHOR, *TROPIC OF CANCER*); JOYCE HALL (FOUNDER OF HALLMARK CARDS)**

January 3–9

DETERMINATION
CAPRICORN II

Though their natural resilience and resourcefulness may well be put to the test along the Way of Innocence, Capricorn II's are wonderfully well equipped to realize the higher and more complete sense of reward and satisfaction that beckons here. In fact, some rejection in early years may have well contributed to deep-seated feelings of insecurity or unworthiness, as well as the impulse to do what others expect of them in an effort to gain approval. At the same time, there exists in these personalities both a strong sensitivity and an admirable, even naive sense of faith in a higher order of existence that will serve them extremely well. If they do not allow their sense of disappointment in the past to shape their vision of the future, they are assured of better times, broader horizons, and a whole lot more fun as they successfully navigate this path.

J.R.R. TOLKIEN
Philologist/writer,
Lord of the Rings

1/3/1892
Capricorn II

CHALLENGE: **BREAKING FREE OF PATTERNS INVOLVING BATTLES FOR CONTROL**

FULFILLMENT: **PLACING GREATER FAITH IN THE BOUNTY OF LIFE AND THEREBY REGAINING A SENSE OF JOY IN PURITY AND INNOCENCE**

NOTABLE: **KENNY LOGGINS (POP SINGER)**

January 10–16

DOMINANCE
CAPRICORN III

A combination of rebelliousness and repression may occur in the lives of those born in the Week of Dominance who travel this karmic path, and it is likely that their distrustful outlooks were shaped by less-than-accepting early environments. Yet as the Capricorn III individuals come into their own, they may find within themselves a tendency to re-create their former oppressors on the one hand or to become entirely too self-sacrificing on the other. As they mature, however, these personalities are likely to greatly enhance their ability to accept people as they are, and to accept themselves as well. If they can take that process one step further and find the courage to reveal their truest natures without too much concern over convention or tradition, the resulting sense of security that comes with genuineness, simplicity, and a renewed hope in the future will prove life's greatest reward for Capricorn III's.

CHALLENGE: **LEARNING HOW TO PREVENT ISSUES OF DOMINANCE AND CONTROL FROM SIDETRACKING THEM**

FULFILLMENT: **EMBRACING THEIR CLOSER RELATIONS IN OPENNESS AND DEVOTION**

NOTABLES: **HAL ROACH (FILM PRODUCER/DIRECTOR, *OUR GANG*, LAUREL & HARDY); JOHN CARPENTER (DIRECTOR, *STARMAN*)**

January 17–22

MYSTERY AND IMAGINATION
CAPRICORN–AQUARIUS CUSP

January 23–30

GENIUS
AQUARIUS I

Once they adequately make the connection between their sometimes manic emotional extremes and deep-seated needs for approval and acceptance, life is bound to get much easier for those born in this period who travel the Way of Innocence. Many of these souls will be very prone to leading Walter Mitty–like existences, until they summon the courage to reveal their rich and imaginative sides to the world, regardless of any perceived consequences. There is little danger of the Capricorn–Aquarian failing the higher challenge here. When it comes to those personal declarations of independence from all that is pretentious, stifling, or merely dull in favor of those things that are real, rewarding, and full of fun, they are certain to make the right choices along this life's journey.

BENJAMIN FRANKLIN
Statesman; writer;
scientist; inventor

1/17/1706
Capricorn–Aquarius Cusp

CHALLENGE: **NOT WEARING THEIR UNPREDICTABILITY AS A SHIELD**
FULFILLMENT: **INDULGING THEIR PROCLIVITY TO HAVING A GOOD TIME, PARTICULARLY OUT-OF-DOORS**
NOTABLES: **ANATOLY SHCHARANSKY (SOVIET DISSIDENT; IMPRISONED); OLIVER HARDY (FILM COMIC; PARTNER OF STAN LAUREL)**

Those born in the Week of Genius who travel this karmic path are likely to travel far and wide in the search for intellectual and spiritual validation and will surely relish the opportunities and challenges for greater self-realization. Though inclined to get caught up in purely theoretical or abstract pursuits and studies at the expense of their wilder inclinations and most basic drives, Aquarius I's have a naturally independent streak that is sure to manifest along this life's journey. Once they get in touch with the fact that their legendary dislike of authority is at least in part tied to their own need for acceptance, things will smooth considerably. A sense of what is truly important, valuable, and above all, pleasurable, will blossom in flamboyant and inspirational ways as they renew the sense of hope and confidence that is part of their souls' calling.

CHALLENGE: **BEING LESS STUDIED IN THEIR MANNER**
FULFILLMENT: **OVERCOMING THE FEAR OF BEING THEMSELVES**

January 31–February 7

YOUTH AND EASE
AQUARIUS II

February 8–15

ACCEPTANCE
AQUARIUS III

Charming and adaptable, sometimes to a fault, the individuals born in the Week of Youth and Ease who navigate the Way of Innocence may have to work hard to summon the courage to be more completely themselves. Likely to be motivated by a need to be loved and accepted, they may well fall in with the trends and views of the many in an attempt to belong. They will have to take care that they are not hampered in their process by simple emotional immaturity or through the refusal to identify just what it is that holds them back from a higher sense of pleasure and fulfillment. Nonetheless, there is the prospect of wonderful personal satisfaction here, and if they are careful to cultivate self-knowledge and to choose real happiness over mere gratification, and real individuality over popularity, they are sure to shine.

MIKHAIL BARYSHNIKOV
Russian dancer and actor

1/28/1948
Aquarius I

CHALLENGE: **ELIMINATING THE SELF-CONSCIOUSNESS THAT KEEPS THEM FROM OPERATING FROM A PURER SENSE OF SELF**
FULFILLMENT: **DOING SOMETHING SIMPLY BECAUSE IT'S FUN**
NOTABLE: **ALICE COOPER (ROCK SINGER, "SCHOOL'S OUT")**

Finding the courage to truly be themselves may take those born in the Week of Acceptance on a fascinating life's journey, especially as they divest themselves of outworn notions of worldliness and come to embrace the richness of simpler pleasures. In the meantime, however, some with this configuration may have to work especially hard to avoid a tendency to pull the wool over others' eyes, or to promise more than they can ever deliver in their attempts to gain approval. Still there is an appealing serendipity about this passage that is very much in keeping with Aquarius III's natural inclinations and instincts. If they do not repress their need for variety and hold to the idea that their truest colors contain a rainbow of possibilities for fulfillment, they are sure to realize a happy and fulfilling passage along the Way of Innocence.

CHALLENGE: **TEARING DOWN THE WALLS ERECTED DUE TO EARLY EXPERIENCES OF BEING REJECTED**
FULFILLMENT: **DEVELOPING A NATURAL RHYTHM AND FLOW FOR THEIR MOVEMENT THROUGH LIFE**

February 16–22
SENSITIVITY
AQUARIUS–PISCES CUSP

Personal sensitivity and a rather defensive attitude toward the world may mark the journeys of those born in this period who travel they Way of Innocence. Indeed there are a number with this position who will seek validation through the pursuit of professional goals yet fail to find what they need or want in their chosen arena. The key to success and fulfillment will lie in their willingness to remove the chips from their shoulders, lay down their weapons, and reveal their more sensitive and dreamy sides to the world. If they can cultivate regular communication with their intuition and allow themselves to be guided by a higher sense of purpose than merely being one of the gang, their energy and willingness to change their lives, have some fun, and attune themselves to the rhythms of life itself will serve them well along this karmic path.

CHALLENGE: **DROPPING THEIR TOUGH, RATHER AGGRESSIVE-SEEMING FACADE**
FULFILLMENT: **BEING THE COLORFUL, ROMANTIC SOULS THEY TRULY ARE**
NOTABLES: **MEYER ROTHSCHILD (FOUNDER OF BANKING DYNASTY); WENDELL WILLKIE (BUSINESSMAN; PRESIDENTIAL CANDIDATE)**

EDNA ST. VINCENT MILLAY

Poet/writer; used pen name Nancy Boyd

2/22/1892
Aquarius–Pisces Cusp

February 23–March 2
SPIRIT
PISCES I

Naturalness and spirituality will likely go hand in hand for those born in this week who travel the Way of Innocence, as they are possessed of a deeply intuitive nature combined with a rare sense of realism. Yet it is their very sensitivity that may prove the biggest obstacle to their fulfillment, as they are much inclined to take rejections or personal setbacks to heart. They will have to do some work to shore up their sometimes shaky egos and self-images. Once they free themselves from the idea that others' perceptions and reactions are more valid than their own and learn to stand up for what they truly believe in, including their own right to happiness, their feelings of unworthiness will fall away to reveal to the world soulful and sensuous beings, made all the more beautiful by their impulse to share themselves with others.

CHALLENGE: **ESCHEWING THE TENDENCY TO RETREAT FROM THE WORLD**
FULFILLMENT: **GROUNDING THEIR VISIONARY IDEALS IN SOME SENSE OF FORM OR STRUCTURE**

March 3–10
THE LONER
PISCES II

Loners born in this week who travel the Way of Innocence can enjoy some fine prospects for fulfillment and enlightenment, providing they allow themselves to do so. Though gifted with much more sociability and worldly inclinations than they might have otherwise, they will nevertheless have strongly self-protective sides that will beg for nurture and validation along this road. Yet their search for the natural, spontaneous, and uncomplicated will manifest itself in some highly idealistic and subjective pursuits. If they do not allow their personal insecurities to hold them back from getting what they require most from the world—to be accepted as they really are—and further realize that in order to be accepted on their own terms, they must first reveal themselves to others, all will go well on this journey.

CHALLENGE: **FORCING THEMSELVES TO SHOW OTHERS WHO THEY ARE**
FULFILLMENT: **TRUSTING IN SOMETHING GREATER THAN THEMSELVES TO SHIELD THEM**

March 11–18
DANCERS AND DREAMERS
PISCES III

Those born in this week who travel the Way of Innocence can expect a fine and fulfilling passage, providing they do not become mired in petty personal problems or confine their best impulses within a prison of uncomfortable conformity. There is something of a danger that these individuals will fall prey to their impulses to please all of the people, all of the time, even if it means weaving many a tangled web or employing any number of deceitful artifices to maintain their public images. Thus they can neglect their own needs for self-development and dwell in a rather self-satisfied illusion of fulfillment without ever attaining the real thing. Yet if they make an effort to stay honest, and don't fall victim to either their own or others' sensitivity, this path can serve to ground them in the real, and renew their sense of wonder at the same time.

CHALLENGE: **NOT CLOAKING THEMSELVES IN AN AIR OF MYSTERY SIMPLY AS A DEFENSE MECHANISM**
FULFILLMENT: **ENGAGING THEIR OWN PRACTICALITY TO SHARE WHAT THEY KNOW WITH OTHERS**

VITA SACKVILLE-WEST
English novelist and poet,
The Edwardians

3/9/1892
Pisces II

The Way of Modulation

SCORPIO–SAGITTARIUS CUSP TO TAURUS–GEMINI CUSP
Revolution to Energy

The feisty fighters who tread the Way of Modulation are here in this lifetime to learn to curb their rebellious impulses and steady their energies. Imbued with a passionate brand of inspiration, those on this path must learn how to harness it to maximum effect. Wrapped up in broad philosophies and big ideas, these individuals must move toward a greater focus on the details since their ultimate success lies in how they evaluate and present information. Gifted with restless, active minds, the individuals on the Way of Modulation tend to burn out easily, never accomplishing what they set out to do. They must learn to cultivate patience and to modulate their energies by slowing down and embracing the present rather than chasing after the past or what may lie ahead. Expansive individuals, those on this path will learn to harmonize their energies and, in so doing, will have a thing or two to teach the world about compromise.

The individuals on the Way of Modulation are destined to disseminate ideas and data in one form or another. Mentally agile individuals, they possess the quickness of mind to channel information to a broader audience whether through speaking, writing, or any media format. In fact, they may be wonderful storytellers with a true gift for the art of narrative. They are oriented toward spiritual ideas and broad philosophies, often searching for truth and justice. Passionate individuals, they yearn for a better world—and they are often willing to fight for it. All too aware of problems, their responses to what they see is a desire to overturn it, change it, or fix it. Often rebels or iconoclasts, their personalities are tumultuous, ranging from stubborn resistance to change to a desire to topple the existing order, caring little what is destroyed in the process. Their great gift is the dynamolike energy that pushes them forward. Unfortunately, this intensity is not often regulated in a productive way. Their interests are eclectic, and they can fly every which way, without accomplishing anything. Burning as brightly as they do, they burn out quite easily.

The individuals on this path are easily bored and rarely satisfied with whatever is going on in the moment. Because they are apt to chuck what they are doing to rush off in search of the next, latest thing, never leaving their marks anywhere, career success may elude them despite their high aspirations. They may tend to leave things unfinished as they flit from one cause or hobby to another, only to drop it as they chase the next butterfly. Also, their work may be sloppy since they tend not to check facts or double-check data. The core lesson for those on the Way of Modulation is to steady and regulate their own energies as well as their thinking. Slowing down and modulating emotional swings are crucial for any kind of achievement on this path. As simple as it sounds, these people need to stop and think before they act, or speak. Particularly since, being

---

CORE LESSON

Slowing down and steadying their energies

GOAL

To cultivate the patience to work with the information before them

---

GIFTS
Inspired, Expressive, Versatile

PITFALLS
Superficial, Rebellious, Dilettantish

combative types, they tend to overreact, and often vengefully. Tending to put their all into something, they often end up short of energy or interest when the time comes to finish what they started. Their dynamic energy is their gift, a font of endless inspiration for them. If they could only learn how to modulate their energy flow and focus, much like water or electricity, they would avoid getting bogged down in fruitless struggles and start to call upon this source at will, directing it to the successful achievement of a variety of goals.

Restless souls, the individuals on the Way of Modulation always seem to want more. This expansiveness and thirst for more input or ever larger plans and goals can be quite wearing on themselves and others. Part of the journey for those on the Way of Modulation is to develop more patience. Apt to be either forward seeking or backward looking, too often these individuals overlook what's right in front of their noses. It is important for them to practice taking the time to fully evaluate and understand the information, data, or input before them. Not only will making peace with what is in the present moment make them happier, it will cause them to become more observant and oriented toward facts as opposed to simply ideas. Gathering information in the right way will enable them to present it most effectively as well. Moreover, given that the men and women on this path are often overly focused on the big picture with big

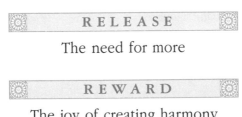

RELEASE

The need for more

REWARD

The joy of creating harmony

ideas in mind, they can be a bit judgmental. Developing more acceptance of the way things are wouldn't hurt them. It might even serve to temper their hunger for ever new forms of experience. On the Way of Modulation, these men and women may discover that taking a different route to the office can be just as fulfilling a new experience as jumping on a plane to join a protest in Paris.

There is a need to create harmony here in the sense of a pleasing or sympathetic arrangement or presentation of ideas and facts. Data is just data until you do something creative with it. Thus, how information is presented and expressed is important on this path. The individuals here are destined to learn how to package information as attractively as possible—how to give it grace and beauty of form—how to make it say something. Rather than inflicting their ideas fractiously and forcefully on others, the men and women on the Way of Modulation will learn how to put forth their thoughts without putting off their audience. Music, singing, chanting, or speaking may be particularly important for those on this path as a means of communicating. Learning how to modulate their voices for maximum effect will also be important. Harmony is a theme on the Way of Modulation for other reasons too. Having learned how to modulate a variety of divergent energies within themselves, those on this path may become adept at handling such energies in their environments. Combined with a talent for assessing

SUGGESTION

Learn to empty now and then. Practice stopping and thinking about what you are doing and saying at regular intervals. Cultivate patience for what's in front of you.

large amounts of information, they may find themselves later in life acting in the role of moderator. Encouraging negotiation and compromise, the men and women on this path may find themselves engineering peaceful resolutions to conflict. This talent comes from hard-won experience. Born feisty, the individuals on this journey have to learn to walk away from a fight. Those born on the Way of Modulation may one day be called to promote harmony by teaching others how to temper combative tendencies and express their views in a moderate yet effective manner.

People may view those on this karmic path as aloof and in some ways unapproachable, despite their considerable magnetism and charm, since they tend to fly off on a moment's notice or are often wrapped up in their own thoughts. Learning to release such elusiveness, and simply to slow down, will be essential to their business and social lives. However, as they progress on this path they will be more patient with people, more "present," and will put greater effort into harmonious relations with others. They will always be somewhat mercurial by nature, and will discover that loved ones, not to mention business associates and clients, will seem to need more of their time than they are prepared to give. Alternatively, others on the Way of Modulation may fritter their energy away on too many involvements or idle pursuits. Thus, monitoring and adjusting the energy given to relationships will also be required here if they are to find the middle ground between the extremes of selfishness and altruism.

Although those on this path may be most comfortable with just a few deep, intimate relationships, they seem destined to be surrounded by a variety of more superficial ones. Tending as they do to think the grass is always greener on the other side, the men and women on the Way of Modulation may be hard-pressed to stick to one partner. Commitment is not their forte. A problem for them may be promiscuity, particularly given their passionate nature. However, a stable family life is often the best form of grounding for these individuals. Even those who have a secret life away from their families will always depend heavily on them to provide the steadiness they so sorely need. These individuals should be encouraged to enroll in some type of formal higher education. Despite the fact that those on the Way of Modulation may feel the urge to rebel against authority and quit school to focus their energies on immediate social advancement or financial gain, it would be best if they took advantage of opportunities to sample a variety of philosophical, technical, or artistic pursuits. Going to a university, attending a community college, or simply taking a few adult education courses will also teach those on this path different methods of presenting information while holding them to exacting and rigorous standards for fact checking and attribution of sources.

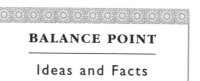

BALANCE POINT

Ideas and Facts

In terms of imagery, one could compare the process of this path to the workings of a series of canal locks that join bodies of water that are at two different levels. By constructively connecting the two, the locks permit boats to travel to areas that they would otherwise be unable to reach. In this extremely practical enterprise, however, patience is important—raising and lowering the water level can be a very slow and deliberate process.

CRYSTALS AND GEMSTONES

Stilbite holds a focused energy that assists the individual to harness the exuberance of creativity while honoring the present. This mineral guides one to witness the miracle in the moment.

 NOTABLES ON THIS KARMIC PATH

Undersea explorer **Jacques Cousteau** certainly learned the secret to success on this karmic path—analyzing, sorting, and presenting large amounts of data. By steadying his energies and learning great patience, Cousteau succeeded in elucidating many mysteries of the ocean.

JACQUES COUSTEAU

However, true to form, his restless mind was always on the lookout for new adventures and undiscovered frontiers. By balancing this energy with resolve and command, he was able to develop projects such as the aqualung and the underwater television. Because of Cousteau's remarkable work, we have a clearer collective vision of the richness contained in the seas around us.

DANIELLE STEEL

Romance novelist **Danielle Steel**'s amazing accomplishments attest to her ability to direct her prodigious energy into her work. Not only has she authored more than forty-five best-selling novels, she has also produced a series of books for young readers. In addition to her writing, Steel has raised nine children and contributed her time to The American Library Association, the National Committee for the Prevention of Child Abuse, and the American Humane Association. Danielle Steel's efficient organization of these many activities displays her success on the Way of Modulation.

Author Samuel Langhorne Clemens, better known as **Mark Twain**, worked as a printer, Mississippi riverboat pilot, miner, prospector, soldier, and editor before turning to writing as a career. Through his numerous occupations and extensive travels, Twain became acquainted with practically every personality type. Sifting through this wide breadth of experience, Twain was able to communicate his perception of humanity in an honest and un-

MARK TWAIN

affected manner. Among his most popular works are *The Adventures of Tom Sawyer, A Connecticut Yankee in King Arthur's Court,* and *The Adventures of Huckleberry Finn.*

Other Notables: David Hare, Betty Buckley, Alexander Gardner, Akira Kurosawa, Laurie Anderson, Mick Fleetwood, Salman Rushdie, Arlo Guthrie, Steve Forbes, Don Henley, Carlos Santana, Casey Stengel, Arnold Schwarzenegger, Betty Thomas, Jane Curtin, Sam Neill, Dr. Joyce Brothers, Camille Saint-Saëns, Alvin Toffler, Roger Moore, Fanny Brice, Chris Rock, Cindy Crawford, David Niven

---

BIRTHDAYS ON KARMIC PATH 33

June 25, 1891–November 12, 1891 | February 4, 1910–June 25, 1910

September 15, 1928–February 3, 1929 | April 28, 1947–September 15, 1947 | December 7, 1965–April 27, 1966

July 18, 1984–December 6, 1984 | February 28, 2003–July 18, 2003

KARMIC PATH
33

March 19–24
REBIRTH
PISCES–ARIES CUSP

The high-voltage personalities born on the Cusp of Rebirth who find themselves on the Way of Modulation will have to be careful that their energetic, dynamic, and direct approach to life is not allowed to overwhelm their subtler perceptions or more intuitive insights. Highly passionate and motivated, they will have to learn the value of looking before they leap and cultivating greater thoroughness in order to be most effective here. Temper and real aggression can be their biggest stumbling blocks, and some will manifest a pronounced tendency toward knocking over stone walls with their heads! Yet they are gifted with formidable powers of logic and a deep understanding of where the real issues lie. If they can avoid the dangers of merely skimming the surface, or of purely self-centered goals and objectives, they will doubtless realize a successful and exciting, if not entirely calm, life's journey.

AKIRA KUROSAWA
Film director,
Rhapsody in August

3/23/1910
Pisces–Aries Cusp

CHALLENGE: **ENCOURAGING THEIR ABILITY TO DO WHILE MODULATING THEIR PROPENSITY TO DREAM**

FULFILLMENT: **PRESENTING THEIR IDEAS IN AS STRAIGHTFORWARD A MANNER AS POSSIBLE**

March 25–April 2
THE CHILD
ARIES I

Those born in the Week of the Child who journey along the Way of Modulation may encounter a number of problems with the naive notion that there is no problem in life that cannot be solved through energetic progress. Change may well be a kind of god to these individuals, and they will have to take care that they do not throw out the baby with the bathwater as they attempt to improve their lives. *Stop, look, and listen* ought to be the mantra for this group, as they are quite easily excited at the prospect of anything new. Withdrawing from the action at given intervals will be especially useful, as will their ability to temper a tendency to be easily bored with pursuits that require concentration, application, and planning. If they do not scatter their attention on the one hand, nor get so caught up in their passions that they lose perspective on the other—neither their natural enthusiasm nor their prodigious energy is likely to desert them along this journey.

CHALLENGE: **CULTIVATING PATIENCE**

FULFILLMENT: **APPLYING THEIR ENERGY MORE CONSISTENTLY AND CONSTRUCTIVELY IN THEIR LIVES**

April 3–10
THE STAR
ARIES II

Those individuals born in the Week of the Star who travel the Way of Modulation may well discover just how difficult it is to gain perspective and patience when one is always at the center of the action. Simple irritability may be their biggest stumbling block, and many of these personalities will be marked by a hair-trigger temper that constantly gets them into hot water. Yet they are likely to be gifted with broader philosophical perspectives than some born in this week, and more altruistic impulses that can find dynamic expression here. If they can find a focus other than themselves, and channel their energies toward the attainment of realizable goals and objectives, their potential to shine as beacons of inspiration and transformation along the Way of Modulation is great indeed.

CHALLENGE: **SACRIFICING THEIR TEMPERS FOR THE SAKE OF GREATER HARMONY**

FULFILLMENT: **SERVING AS THE VOICE OF TEMPERANCE OR MODERATION IN A GROUP ENDEAVOR**

NOTABLES: **PETER DUCHIN (PIANIST); ROBIN WRIGHT-PENN (ACTRESS, *FORREST GUMP*)**

GREG MADDUX
Ranked among baseball's all-time greatest pitchers; won a record 4 consecutive Cy Young awards 1992–95

4/14/1966
Aries III

April 11–18
THE PIONEER
ARIES III

Fearless and visionary, those born in the Week of the Pioneer who travel the Way of Modulation will doubtless make their marks along this road. Blessed with a highly developed social sense, these dynamic leaders may be much inclined toward tearing down old altars and have a strong impulse to literally "change the world." Yet there is a significant danger of burnout with this configuration, as these personalities are much inclined to bite off more than any mortal might be expected to chew. They may have to learn to back up and gain some perspective, and the cultivation of real planning and management skills will be especially important to their success. Still, as maturity enhances their sense of patience, these achievement-oriented people are likely to go far, and their natural commitment and dedication to their ideals can very well manifest in ways that benefit us all.

CHALLENGE: **REMEMBERING TO MANAGE THE DETAILS WHEN PURSUING THEIR GOALS OR IDEALS**

FULFILLMENT: **DISCOVERING HOW MUCH MORE EFFECTIVE THEY CAN BE ONCE THEY DEVELOP THEIR MARKETING AND PRESENTATION SKILLS**

NOTABLE: **DAVID JUSTICE (BASEBALL FIELDER, MOSTLY WITH ATLANTA BRAVES)**

April 19–24
POWER
ARIES–TAURUS CUSP

While likely to be gifted with a greater sense of stability and purpose than many others who travel the Way of Modulation, those born on the Cusp of Power will have to be on guard against a tendency to become stuck in the notion that whatever they have, it will never be enough. Moderating their own needs and prodigious energies will be especially important, as these formidable personalities will surely grapple with problems of excess along the road. Yet at the same time, the elements that come together on this life's journey make for a fine mix, as the endowments of this path make Aries–Tauruses less likely to become lazy or complacent, while they in turn bring greater focus to this passage. Passionate and powerful, if they can avoid both the dangers of workaholism and judgementalism, their versatility, energy, and inspiration is likely to manifest in some tangible accomplishments and successes along the road.

CHALLENGE: **TAKING CARE NOT TO ENGAGE IN ONE POWER STRUGGLE AFTER ANOTHER TO THE DETRIMENT OF THEIR LONG-TERM GOALS**

FULFILLMENT: **ENJOYING THE SUCCESS THAT THE COMBINATION OF THE SHEER POWER OF THEIR LOGIC AND THEIR PERSUASIVENESS PROVIDES THEM**

LADY EMMA HAMILTON
Lord Nelson's mistress

4/26/1761
Taurus I

April 25–May 2
MANIFESTATION
TAURUS I

The dauntless individuals born in the Week of Manifestation who navigate the Way of Modulation can expect a fine and fulfilling passage, providing they back up their many interests and inclinations with solid planning and a sincere effort to avoid both self-involvement and excess—particularly of a physical kind. Yet they are likely to be uplifted by more mental and emotional flexibility on this karmic path than other Taurus I's, and the rare combination of stamina and versatility should make for a nice mix. Carefully nurturing their innate need for harmony will be especially important, as will the ability to back up and take a look at the bigger picture. For while it is unlikely that these souls will fall prey to scattered or superficial efforts, it will be difficult for them to backtrack once they have taken a wrong turn along the Way of Modulation.

CHALLENGE: **AVOIDING CONFRONTATION AND COMBATIVENESS**

FULFILLMENT: **ACHIEVING SOME OF THEIR OWN GRANDEST PLANS AND SCHEMES THROUGH SHEER FORCE OF WILL**

May 3–10
THE TEACHER
TAURUS II

Many of those born in the Week of the Teacher who journey along this karmic path may well find themselves in their glory along this road. Though they will certainly have as many lessons to be learned as the rest of us, there is nevertheless potential for huge accomplishments, especially in the areas of education, communication, and pure inspiration. Intense and interested in everything around them, they will nevertheless do well to delegate the grounded detail work to others, as they are likely to have little patience or understanding for the myriad of cogs and gears that turn the wheels of progress. Yet if these personalities carefully cultivate in themselves their impulses to share their highly progressive notions, their forward-thinking concepts and genuine interest in making the world a better place can find real expression here, especially when they also make patience their particular virtue.

CHALLENGE: **LOOKING BEFORE THEY LEAP—PARTICULARLY AS REGARDS ADDRESSING INJUSTICE**

FULFILLMENT: **ENGAGING THEIR ENTREPRENEURIAL SIDE TO PRESENT INFORMATION IN A WHOLLY UNIQUE AND USEFUL WAY**

DOUG HENNING
Magician, hosted numerous television specials

5/3/1947
Taurus II

May 11–18
THE NATURAL
TAURUS III

Though it is likely that issues of personal freedom and rebellion may assume the proportions of a moral crusade for those born in this week who travel the Way of Modulation, they will do better to occasionally let sleeping dogs lie. Easily aroused to anger and frustration, those born in the Week of the Natural may have to work to find that delicate balance between a sense of personal security and the seduction of ever greener pastures. Though likely to be a bit more easygoing than some who make this journey, Taurus III's may nevertheless find themselves expending far too much energy in trying to resist restriction or authority and not nearly enough to accomplish worthwhile goals. If they can learn not to allow circumstances or people to provoke them while cultivating the sense of calm within themselves that is often missing in the external world, they can make great progress here.

CHALLENGE: **GRAPPLING WITH ISSUES OF FREEDOM AND SECURITY AND THE EXPLOSIVE RESENTMENT THEY ENGENDER IN THEM**

FULFILLMENT: **TUNING IN TO THE MORE HARMONY-LOVING SIDE OF THEIR NATURES**

May 19–24

ENERGY
TAURUS–GEMINI CUSP

Those born on the Cusp of Energy who travel the Way of Modulation may discover that even the best intentions don't mean much when hindered by poor or careless execution. Learning to plan carefully will prove a great asset in their quest for advancement and greater stability, as will cultivating within themselves the capacity for personal satisfaction. Blessed with the ability to deal with problems in a dynamic and versatile fashion, they can nevertheless fall prey to a kind of crisis consciousness, or nagging feelings of unfulfillment until they better appreciate the value of the "the bird in the hand." Especially suited to jobs or pursuits that enable them to stay focused without stifling their natural brilliance and creativity, they will have a fine sense of both the up-to-date and of what is to come. Providing they cultivate greater self-awareness, endurance, and the ability to make peace with the present, the promise for the future is great for those who travel this road.

CHALLENGE: **REFINING THEIR CAPACITY TO REGULATE THEIR ENERGIES**
FULFILLMENT: **DISCOVERING THE GREATER INNER CALM THAT PATIENCE BRINGS THEM**
NOTABLE: **SCATMAN CROTHERS (FILM ACTOR, *THE SHINING*)**

ARTIE SHAW
Clarinet player and bandleader
___
5/23/1910
Taurus–Gemini Cusp

May 25–June 2

FREEDOM
GEMINI I

Once they understand that part of the challenge of the Way of Modulation is to recognize that their personal stress levels will rise in direct proportion to the number of unfinished projects on their mental drawing boards, progress will get easier along this road. Indeed, many of these information-hungry individuals will come to realize that the devil is in the details, once they find the means to focus in on those ideas, concerns, and pursuits that afford them a measure of calm. Likely to be wonderfully expressive, they will nevertheless struggle with an excess of nervous energy throughout their lives, and may be further prone to lash out at others as personal pressures become too much to bear. Yet these individuals can realize tremendous accomplishment as long as they channel their enthusiasms in such a way that their ideas manifest in results—not just debate.

CHALLENGE: **ADMITTING TO THEMSELVES THAT, INDEED, HASTE MAKES WASTE**
FULFILLMENT: **WORKING TO CREATE HARMONY**
NOTABLES: **JESSE COLTER (COUNTRY MUSIC SINGER); SONDRA LOCKE (ACTRESS); LAURENCE ROCKEFELLER (DONATED 33,000 ACRES TO GRAND TETON NATIONAL PARK)**

June 3–10

NEW LANGUAGE
GEMINI II

Brilliant and versatile communicators, those born in the Week of New Language will do especially well to pace themselves and not expect too much, too soon, as they travel this sometimes bumpy road to personal development. Likely to be intensely driven by the need to share their unique ideas and abilities with others, they will have to cultivate the necessary follow-through in order to enjoy the level of fulfillment that is promised here. Some early problems with an overly restrictive or traditional background may well fuel an impulse to burn their bridges behind them in a search for acceptance and understanding. Yet if they recognize that there is no inherent rejection involved in merely being misinterpreted, and augment their considerable gifts with training, pacing, and the ability to try and try again, they can make this a marvelously rewarding and uniquely creative journey.

CHALLENGE: **PAYING CLOSER ATTENTION TO PRACTICALITIES**
FULFILLMENT: **DEVELOPING A UNIQUE FORMAT FOR THE PRESENTATION OF THEIR IDEAS**
NOTABLES: **DAVE BRUBECK (JAZZ MUSICIAN); DAVID HARE (ENGLISH DRAMATIST, *PLENTY*)**

LAURIE ANDERSON
Performance artist/musician
___
6/5/1947
Gemini II

June 11–18

THE SEEKER
GEMINI III

Those born in the Week of the Seeker may end up manifesting some of the Revolutionary origins of this karmic path in a rather iconoclastic approach to the world. Yet they will find a measure of satisfaction here, as it is very much a part of their nature to explore the limitations imposed by society and overcome them if they can. Thus, these personalities will doubtless relish the energy, excitement, and opportunities for communication implied by this configuration, taking great delight in applying their talents to become involved in any number of causes and personal crusades. If they are careful not to scatter their attentions or spread themselves too thin, yet at the same time maintain a variety of interests outside their primary areas of focus, they can do quite well, though, as with most of the other travelers on this road, patience will be required to find the level of harmony implied.

CHALLENGE: **REINING IN THEIR DESIRE TO BE EVERYWHERE AT ONCE**
FULFILLMENT: **REGULATING THEIR CHARM FOR MAXIMUM EFFECT TO ACHIEVE THEIR RATHER LOFTY VISIONS**
NOTABLES: **JACQUES COUSTEAU (OCEANOGRAPHER; EXPLORER); E. G. MARSHALL (CHARACTER ACTOR)**

June 19–24

MAGIC
GEMINI–CANCER CUSP

Logic and feeling combine with high ideals and energy in those born on the Cusp of Magic who travel the Way of Modulation, and the result can be a dynamic and fascinating mix. Here it is likely that their objectivity will be a useful tool in regulating their passions and inspirations, and if these individuals can further take the step into focusing and channeling their drives toward some useful purpose, there will be almost nothing to stand in the way of their success. If they cultivate their innate need to withdraw into a private world from time to time in order to recharge and reevaluate their directions, and do not fail the higher challenge of sharing and communicating their insights and observations with others, they are sure to serve as sources of inspiration and enlightenment. They may even prove themselves to be the instruments of far-reaching change along this life's journey.

SALMAN RUSHDIE
Writer; forced into hiding due to Muslim anger over *Satanic Verses*

6/19/1947
Gemini–Cancer Cusp

CHALLENGE: **WORKING TO HARMONIZE THEIR MANY DIVERGENT ENERGIES**

FULFILLMENT: **DRENCHING THEMSELVES IN A KIND OF MAGICAL CREATIVITY FOR PACKAGING THEIR IDEAS**

June 25–July 2

THE EMPATH
CANCER I

A number of individuals born in this week who navigate the Way of Modulation will have to fight a tendency toward emotional extremes. However, there is potential for great success and enlightenment along this road. Blessed with a broader perspective than Cancer I's might have otherwise, these people bring a depth and diversity of feeling and perception to this journey that is lacking in some of their fellow travelers. Though their communication efforts will be based in the broader philosophies and concepts that are part of their Revolutionary origins, such efforts will always have a sense of the personal and attainable that can be highly appealing. Thus, if they are careful not to withdraw from others or retreat behind an impenetrable shell in an effort at self-protection, all will go beautifully for them.

CHALLENGE: **NOT PERMITTING THEMSELVES TO BE BUFFETED BY EMOTIONAL EXTREMES**

FULFILLMENT: **TRUSTING THEIR INTUITION TO TELL THEM WHAT IDEAS OR INFORMATION IS MOST IMPORTANT**

NOTABLE: **MARK HELPRIN (AUTHOR, *SOLDIER OF THE GREAT WAR*)**

July 3–10

THE UNCONVENTIONAL
CANCER II

Though there may be some bright stars born in the Week of the Unconventional who travel the Way of Modulation, they are in danger of burning out rather quickly unless they learn to regulate their often wild emotions and to separate their idealistic fantasies from reality. Frustration and scattered energies can put these highly imaginative individuals on emotional overload, and there is a high-strung quality to these people that can cause no end of trouble. Also, they may present a face to the world that is considerably different from what goes on in their tumultuous inner or private lives. Yet if they learn to focus their energies in such a way that they can concentrate on the information at hand, and not allow their imaginations to substitute for facts, their progress along this road is assured.

STEVE FORBES
Son of multimillionaire publisher Malcolm; ran for president

7/18/1947
Cancer III

CHALLENGE: **RELEASING THEIR REBELLIOUS QUALITIES IN FAVOR OF A MORE TEMPERATE APPROACH**

FULFILLMENT: **BECOMING STORYTELLERS**

NOTABLES: **BETTY BUCKLEY (STAGE/SCREEN ACTRESS, *CATS*); ARLO GUTHRIE (FOLKSINGER, "ALICE'S RESTAURANT")**

July 11–18

THE PERSUADER
CANCER III

Those born in the Week of the Persuader who travel the Way of Modulation are likely to enjoy an especially fulfilling life's journey, particularly when they use their communicative gifts for more than purely personal ends. Quite able to cultivate the qualities of focus and mental discipline necessary for self-realization, they will nevertheless have to regulate a tendency toward emotional extremes and overtaxing themselves by taking on an excess of responsibilities. Though there are a number of alarmists and zealots here, it is likely that Cancer III's on this path will be the kind of people admired not only for their fine minds and formidable energy, but for their keen perceptions and communicative skills. If they can fight the tendency to spring into action when action is not necessarily appropriate, they can realize tremendous fulfillment and self-realization along this road.

CHALLENGE: **ATTEMPTING TO BETTER REGULATE THEIR DRIVE**

FULFILLMENT: **PERSUADING OTHERS OF THEIR VIEWS AND IDEAS**

NOTABLES: **GEORGE EASTMAN (INVENTOR; FOUNDER OF KODAK); BELA SCHICK (PEDIATRICIAN; PIONEER IN STUDYING CHILDHOOD DISEASES)**

July 19–25

OSCILLATION
CANCER–LEO CUSP

Blessed with an extraordinary amount of moral courage and the strength to stand up for what they believe in, Cancer–Leos who travel the Way of Modulation may nevertheless have to choose their battles quite carefully before they can operate effectively here. Otherwise, their wilder energies can manifest in manic searches for stimulation and their idealism in mere windmill chasing. Learning the value of careful research, good planning, and personal calm will be important, as will their willingness to exorcise any psychological demons they are trying to outrun. Yet if they can surround themselves in an atmosphere of relative stability that at the same time does not hinder their thirst for knowledge and progress, their ability to communicate the big picture in a dazzling and dynamic style is sure to prove an inspiration for many along this karmic path.

DON HENLEY
Pop singer/drummer,
The Eagles
———
7/22/1947
Cancer–Leo Cusp

CHALLENGE: **WEAVING THE MANY DIFFERENT STRANDS OF THEIR PERSONALITIES INTO A COHERENT AND FOCUSED WHOLE**
FULFILLMENT: **SURROUNDING THEMSELVES WITH A WIDE VARIETY OF PEOPLE**
NOTABLES: **CARLOS SANTANA (GUITAR GREAT, "BLACK MAGIC WOMAN"); DANNY GLOVER (ACTOR, *LETHAL WEAPON*); ELY CULBERTSON (INVENTED CONTRACT BRIDGE)**

July 26–August 2

AUTHORITY
LEO I

Those born in the Week of Authority who find themselves on the Way of Modulation will doubtless enjoy great success along this road as their natural generosity of spirit, combined with their talent for self-assertion, is sure to get their message across. Though gifted with a much broader view of the issues and a much wider philosophical perspective than might otherwise be the case with other Leo I's there is nevertheless a danger that these personalities will fail the higher challenge here and collapse into self-interest or purely manipulative behaviors. Some rather fixed attitudes may exist, decidedly at odds with the impulse for change and reform that is implied here, yet that same quality will provide these souls with greater stability and thus increase their potential for effectiveness. If they channel their energies in a productive fashion and are careful not to succumb to the demands of ego, great happiness and real achievement will be in order along this road.

CHALLENGE: **BALANCING WORK AND PLAY**
FULFILLMENT: **USING THEIR AUTHORITY TO GET THEIR POINT OF VIEW ACROSS**
NOTABLES: **ARNOLD SCHWARZENEGGER (BODYBUILDER-TURNED-ACTOR, *THE TERMINATOR*); BETTY THOMAS (ACTRESS/FILM DIRECTOR, *DR. DOOLITTLE*)**

August 3–10

BALANCED STRENGTH
LEO II

These are personalities who so thrive on challenge that they may have to work to understand just why they always seem to be in the center of the fray. A certain amount of trial and error is indicated here, for these people have a tendency to get emotionally invested in things before they really understand what those things are about. Yet once they make the distinction between truly playing their hunches and merely playing with fire, things will improve considerably. In fact, the principle struggle on this path will lie in the fact that Leo II's are secretly unwilling to change, an aspect that will surely cause them a measure of conflict along this road. However, they are gifted with considerably more endurance, tenacity, and patience than some others here, and if they can avoid the tendency to push themselves too hard, and channel their energies in a direction that creates more harmony than it does conflict, there is little that can stand in the way of their personal progress.

CASEY STENGEL
Hall of Fame baseball
player/manager; won
7 World Series as
manager of the Yankees
———
7/30/1891
Leo I

CHALLENGE: **MODULATING THEIR ENERGIES LESS IN THE SENSE OF STEADYING THEM AND MORE IN TERMS OF JUMP-STARTING THEM**
FULFILLMENT: **WATCHING THE FRUITS OF THEIR SINGLE-MINDED DEVOTION AND PATIENCE GROW**
NOTABLE: **ADOLF BUSCH (VIOLINIST)**

August 11–18

LEADERSHIP
LEO III

Passionate and proud, the remarkable individuals born in the Week of Leadership who travel the Way of Modulation are gifted with the ability not only to implement plans, but to see them through to a fruitful and satisfying conclusion. For that reason alone, most will doubtless find quite a measure of happiness in this life's journey. They will, however, have to be on guard against the tendency to expect too much, too soon, and further, to expect more than might be offered in exchange for their efforts. Nevertheless, they will have to avoid a tendency toward burn-out or disillusionment when things don't go their way. Furthermore, they must keep in mind that sharing and communicating with others is part of the higher challenge here. Leo III's, like most others along this path, will have to cultivate the qualities of patience, endurance, and real diplomacy before they can find their niche. Once it is carved, however, their personal legacy may well be carved in stone.

CHALLENGE: **DEVELOPING A CAPACITY FOR DIPLOMACY, COMPROMISE, AND THE CREATION OF HARMONY**
FULFILLMENT: **SEEING THEIR LARGE-SCALE PLANS AND PROJECTS TO FRUITION**
NOTABLES: **DANIELLE STEEL (BESTSELLING NOVELIST); CAROL MOSELEY-BRAUN (U.S. SENATOR)**

August 19–25

EXPOSURE
LEO–VIRGO CUSP

Among the most powerful information brokers along this karmic path, those born on the Cusp of Exposure who travel the Way of Modulation will face a number of life's lessons revolving around issues of sharing and integrity. Keenly perceptive, these individuals are not so much superficial as they are inclined to simply gloss over those details and issues that might interfere with their goals or sense of progress. Thus, they may find many of their projects and plans don't come to flower, simply because they have neglected to impart significant portions of the truth, or were in too much of a hurry to consider the implications of their actions. Though likely to be very flamboyant and capable of attracting great amounts of attention, they will have to cultivate and maintain a measure of calm and a talent for planning that will insure their successful passage along the Way of Modulation.

JANE CURTIN
Comedian/actress,
Saturday Night Live

———

9/6/1947
Virgo II

CHALLENGE: **DEALING WITH THEIR TENDENCY TO BE OVER-WHELMED BY TOO MUCH DATA**

FULFILLMENT: **REVEALING WHAT THEY KNOW AT THE PERFECT MOMENT**

NOTABLES: **KEITH MOON (DRUMMER, THE WHO); CINDY WILLIAMS (ACTRESS, LAVERNE AND SHIRLEY)**

August 26–September 2

SYSTEM BUILDERS
VIRGO I

Though blessed with considerably more stability and concentration than many who travel the Way of Modulation, those born in the Week of the System Builders will nevertheless have to make an effort to get at the roots of their own lack of emotional objectivity. Otherwise, these souls can encounter any number of problems with outbursts of passion, fits of temper, and emotional dramas that will surely interfere with their progress toward their goals. Cultivating calm and the willingness to explore their own patterns will prove especially useful, as will the ability to share their thoughts and opinions with others. There is the potential here to succeed in almost any area of endeavor. If they avoid the dangers of hypervigilance, alarmist attitudes, or the tendency to be judgmental or over critical of traditions, institutions, and peoples, their success along this life's journey is assured.

CHALLENGE: **LIVING AS SIMPLY AS POSSIBLE IN ORDER TO AVOID A PSYCHOLOGICAL IMPLOSION DUE TO THEIR DIVERGENT ENERGIES**

FULFILLMENT: **REVEALING WHAT THEY KNOW AT THE PERFECT MOMENT**

NOTABLE: **PEGGY LIPTON (ACTRESS, THE MOD SQUAD)**

September 3–10

THE ENIGMA
VIRGO II

Blessed with amazing energy, endurance, and natural discrimination, those born in the Week of the Enigma are likely to find the Way of Modulation an interesting and rewarding passage. These personalities are likely to have higher standards and a greater sense of discernment than many who travel this road, and both their personal choices and their judgments of others will be reasonably sound. Their calm and collected exteriors can serve to hide passionate and tumultuous personal lives, however, and they will do well to better integrate their issues of involvement versus detachment, or risk developing real conflicts between their public and private selves. Gathering and sharing information is likely to come easily, provided it is not too personal. Still, the promise for achievement is very strong with this configuration, and if they allow themselves the luxury of honest self-expression and avoid the tendency toward purely material or superficial goals, happiness will be theirs.

ARTHUR HAYS SULZBURGER
Second-generation
publisher of
The New York Times

———

9/12/1891
Virgo III

CHALLENGE: **LEARNING TO PRESENT INFORMATION MORE OPENLY**

FULFILLMENT: **USING THEIR ANALYTICAL ABILITIES AND DISCERNMENT AS MODERATORS OF CONFLICT**

NOTABLE: **LIZ TILBERIS (EDITOR, HARPER'S BAZAAR)**

September 11–18

THE LITERALIST
VIRGO III

Motivated by an overriding need to see their plans come to tangible realization, those born in the Week of the Literalist can really shine along this road, providing they can overcome an early tendency to sensationalism and excitability. Their single greatest strength is their ability to focus, and they are further blessed with both keen powers of observation, a broader philosophical perspective, and a way with information that will all serve them especially well here. While selfishness and a ruthless attitude are to be avoided, their own abiding need for harmony should see them through. It will pave the way for greater composure and the intellectual and emotional clarity necessary to absorb and impart information in a way that is accessible to all.

CHALLENGE: **NOT DEVOLVING INTO RUTHLESSNESS OR TYRANNY IN ORDER TO ACHIEVE THEIR AIMS**

FULFILLMENT: **EMBRACING THEIR OWN LOVE OF TRUTH AND NEED FOR HARMONY**

NOTABLES: **PRINCE HARRY (SON OF CHARLES AND DIANA); RODDY McDOWALL (ACTOR, NATIONAL VELVET, PLANET OF THE APES); SAM NEILL (ACTOR, JURASSIC PARK)**

September 19–24
BEAUTY
VIRGO–LIBRA CUSP

The souls born in this period may find the yellow brick road to personal fulfillment hard to navigate until they learn to better insulate themselves against distraction and to manage their own flightiness. Though likely to be both creative and idealistic in the extreme, some fairly selfish tendencies can show up here. Virgo–Libras will doubtless encounter the challenge of really facing themselves before they can make significant progress, and it will be difficult for these personalities to focus their energies. If they overcome a natural disorganization, a tendency to minimize their own mistakes, and direct their talents toward professions or pursuits that demand self-discipline and yet nurtures their need for beauty, they will proceed along this life's journey with the relatively rare combination of both elegance and energy.

CHALLENGE: **NOT SUCCUMBING TO FLIGHTINESS OR DILETTANTISM**

FULFILLMENT: **ENGAGING THEIR FLAIR FOR DIPLOMACY TO CREATE A MORE HARMONIOUS ENVIRONMENT**

NOTABLE: **DR. JOYCE BROTHERS (PSYCHOLOGIST; POPULAR MEDIA PERSONALITY)**

ADAM WEST
Actor, best known for portraying Batman on television

9/19/1928
Virgo–Libra Cusp

September 25–October 2
THE PERFECTIONIST
LIBRA I

If they are careful not to mismanage their own formidable energies in bouts of pickiness, irritability, and hyperbolic emotional expressions, Libra I's can do quite well on the Way of Modulation. Their natural organizational abilities are a fine complement to the passionate dynamism that characterizes this path. Though simple lack of patience can be a huge obstacle to their development, they are gifted with broader philosophical perspectives than might otherwise be the case. The gifts of this path will serve to balance and mitigate some of Libra I's perfectionist tendencies. Thus these souls can expect real success and accomplishment on this journey, as they are both able to grasp the bigger picture and to home in on the details that illuminate the larger scheme.

CHALLENGE: **WORKING ON THEIR ISSUES SURROUNDING COMPULSIVENESS AND OBSESSIVENESS**

FULFILLMENT: **COMBINING THEIR SHARP WIT WITH THEIR TALENT FOR PRESENTING INFORMATION**

NOTABLE: **SPANKY MCFARLAND (CHILD ACTOR, *OUR GANG*)**

October 3–10
SOCIETY
LIBRA II

Those born in the Week of Society who travel the Way of Modulation will have to be careful to avoid spreading themselves too thin as they make their way along this road. Likely to be highly social, these butterflies can burn out rather quickly if they fall prey to superficiality or a lack of real awareness of who they are and where they want to go. Grounding themselves with steady habits and personal boundaries will be important as they tend to rely too much on others for input and inspiration. They will nevertheless have tremendous insight, and a fine grasp of the bigger picture. Objectivity will surely be among their greatest assets, as will their ability to present ideas diplomatically. If they can focus their energies so their talent for information is channeled into useful expression, their insights into current events and trends will be of great value to themselves and others.

CHALLENGE: **NOT DISSIPATING THEIR ENERGIES IN TOO MUCH SOCIAL ACTIVITY**

FULFILLMENT: **INVOLVING THEMSELVES IN CURRENT EVENTS AND THE MEDIA**

CAMILLE SAINT-SAËNS
French composer and musician, *Samson et Delila*

10/9/1835
Libra II

October 11–18
THEATER
LIBRA III

Those born in the Week of Theater who find themselves on the Way of Modulation may well experience an exciting and fulfilling journey. Likely to have greater depth and conviction than might otherwise be the case, they are bound to exceed even their own expectations of happiness and success on this path. Making the time to refine and recharge their personal power bases will prove important, however, as will the ability to establish and organize clear-cut priorities, They will do well to maintain and augment their sense of involvement with some necessary follow-through. Cultivating diplomacy in preference to hyperbole will work wonderfully well as they take up the challenge to get their messages across and share their ideas with the world. They are gifted with generous measures of pure life force that will doubtless help them as they mature, so long as they regulate and moderate their energies and talents along the way.

CHALLENGE: **PAYING MORE ATTENTION TO THE FACTS— AND STICKING TO THEM**

FULFILLMENT: **USING THEIR POWERS OF DIPLOMACY TO FURTHER THEIR PET PROJECTS OR TO SERVE OTHERS**

NOTABLE: **ROGER MOORE (ACTOR; KNOWN FOR ROLE OF JAMES BOND)**

October 19–25

DRAMA AND CRITICISM
LIBRA–SCORPIO CUSP

Passionate and inspiring, Libra–Scorpios who find themselves on the Way of Modulation will benefit from learning to moderate and regulate their considerable gifts. Controlling promiscuous and colorful private lives may be a good place to start as these charismatic and compelling individuals can quite successfully scatter their energies through the distraction of endless romances and too many social demands. The formation of mutually ambitious partnerships will also help ground them in the real world, although some may find that such partnerships require interested others to dwell in Libra–Scorpio's long shadow. Their gifts for discernment, information, and ideas are so pronounced that there is little possibility they will entirely fail the challenges encountered here. An often inimitable style of sharing and presenting ideas comes as second nature to these personalities, and if they cultivate and regulate their talents, their voices will not soon be forgotten along the Way of Modulation.

CHALLENGE: **TEMPERING THEIR FERVOR AND CULTIVATING THE ENDURANCE FOR THE LONG HAUL**

FULFILLMENT: **LIVING AND WORKING WITH GREATER BALANCE AND PEACE OF MIND**

NOTABLE: **ADLAI STEVENSON (VICE PRESIDENT TO GROVER CLEVELAND)**

TED SHAWN
Dancer/choreographer;
founded Jacob's Pillow
Festival

10/21/1891
Libra–Scorpio Cusp

October 26–November 2

INTENSITY
SCORPIO I

At once elusive and profound, the souls born in the Week of Intensity who find themselves on the Way of Modulation may wrestle with their tendencies to emotional extremes, and with their polarized personalities. On this path, Scorpio I's will be more discriminating and less likely to be swept up in the causes of the moment. Nevertheless, they have to be on guard against the pitfalls of fruitless struggles, selfishness, and suspicion in themselves if they are to realize the higher challenge. There is considerable potential for real success here, especially when Scorpio I gains greater perspective, a calmer center, and the particular brand of philosophical humor and tolerance that only come with the passage of time.

CHALLENGE: **APPLYING TO THE FACTS AT HAND THEIR FAMOUS ABILITY TO FOCUS**

FULFILLMENT: **THE SATISFACTION OF ENTERTAINING OTHERS AS THEY PRESENT THEIR IDEAS**

November 3–11

DEPTH
SCORPIO II

This combination of qualities can make for a fine mix along this life's journey as the endowments of the Way of Modulation are such that Scorpio II's will be less likely to get ensnared in their own sense of suffering. More likely, they will dedicate their talents toward making the world a better place. The ability to simply lighten up and not take things so personally will prove especially important to their success, as will conscious efforts to improve their objectivity. Their remarkable concentration and intellectual qualities are sure to come to the fore with this configuration, and their talents for assimilating, organizing, and imparting information to others will be among their prodigious abilities. If they can overcome the tendencies to secrecy, or to burn out their energies in worry or mere escapism, all can go wonderfully well along the way.

CHALLENGE: **LEARNING TO PERIODICALLY LET EVERYTHING GO**

FULFILLMENT: **FINDING FINANCIAL SUCCESS AS THEY APPLY THEIR POWERS OF CONCENTRATION TO THEIR LONG-TERM GOALS**

FANNY BRICE
Actress, *Ziegfeld Follies*

10/29/1891
Scorpio I

November 12–18

CHARM
SCORPIO III

Those born in the Week of Charm who find themselves on this karmic path are likely to enjoy a wonderfully successful and personally rewarding journey, as their natural talents are especially compatible with the challenge and promise implied here. Gifted with considerable diplomatic skills and the abilities to organize and focus, Scorpio III's have a natural realism fired by genuine passion and a sense of conviction along this road, but without the danger of the high-flown zealotry that can be found elsewhere. These individuals will not only be aware of their own needs, but will have a knack for presenting their ideas in such a way that they will be guaranteed the greatest acceptance. If they are only willing to complete the karmic task of rising above mere self-interest to share their views with the world, all can go quite brilliantly here.

CHALLENGE: **RELYING LESS ON CHARM AND MANIPULATION AND MORE ON THE PERSUASIVE POWER OF LOGIC AND WELL-ORGANIZED FACTS**

FULFILLMENT: **ENJOYING THE WIDE VARIETY OF INDIVIDUALS WHO WILL BE ATTRACTED TO THEM**

NOTABLE: **MICHEL GAUQUELIN (FRENCH STATISTICIAN; ASTROLOGER)**

November 19–24
REVOLUTION
SCORPIO–SAGITTARIUS CUSP

Like ancient depictions of the god Janus, who faced both the future and the past, Scorpio–Sagittarians who travel this karmic path may have to fight to find a focus in the present before they realize the highest levels of accomplishment along the Way of Modulation. Maybe the worst problem they will face is an inherent tendency to disperse their energies in less-than-worthy causes and concerns, or to confuse a sense of self with a sense of passion. If they can cultivate more objectivity and genuine detachment, this road will smooth out considerably. If they employ their boundless curiosities in a way that involves serious study, education, application, and focus on particular areas of interest, and accept as well that slower progress is often preferable to no progress at all, they can realize their finest dreams of being effective forces for change.

MARK TWAIN
Considered America's greatest writer, *Tom Sawyer, The Adventures of Huckleberry Finn*

11/30/1835
Sagittarius I

CHALLENGE: **CONTROLLING THEIR DESIRE TO OVERTURN ESTABLISHED SYSTEMS**

FULFILLMENT: **FINDING THE RIGHT COMBINATION OF PRESERVATION AND RELEASE TO ACHIEVE THEIR AIMS**

November 25–December 2
INDEPENDENCE
SAGITTARIUS I

Sagittarius I's are likely to make significant progress along the Way of Modulation, providing they can learn to distinguish between their need for meaningful stimulation and their tendency to act out of simple frustration or rebelliousness. Gifted with a high moral sense and a genuine grasp of philosophical issues, they will nevertheless have to fight a tendency to fly off the handle or to burn out in the search for expression of their ideals. They will do well to cultivate practicality and focus as they are prone to scatter their energies in ever-widening quests for freedom, resulting in a jack-of-all-trades dilettantism. Also, they can be prone to poor impulse control and an overcompetitiveness that can hinder their abilities to share their visions and talents in effective ways. Still, success will be theirs when they allow themselves to be guided by their considerable intuition and keep their passions in check with objectivity and a clear sense of the facts.

CHALLENGE: **LEARNING HOW TO REGULATE THEIR ACTIONS AND WORDS**

FULFILLMENT: **EXPRESSING THEMSELVES AND WHAT THEY KNOW THROUGH REPARTEE AND DEBATE**

December 3–10
THE ORIGINATOR
SAGITTARIUS II

An aloof and rather defensive quality may interfere with Sagittarius II's need to connect and share ideas with others along this karmic path. In fact many Sagittarius II's are so defensive regarding their own uniqueness and talents that they may well flit from one thing to another in an effort to avoid disappointment or the possibility of rejection. In general, poor attitudes can undermine their own best efforts, and the resulting lack of appreciation can in turn fuel their tendencies toward more aggressive evasion of the issues. Their unique style of communication will prove to be both their greatest strength and their greatest weakness until they simply slow down, think things through, and control their more ardent and emotional sides. As they do, they will find their frustration will be much eased and the way to success and enlightenment illuminated more clearly along the Way of Modulation.

CHALLENGE: **NOT PUSHING AHEAD OR TRYING TO RISE TO THE TOP AT ANY COST**

FULFILLMENT: **PRESENTING THEIR UNIQUE VIEWS IN A WELL-PACKAGED FORMAT**

HELEN FRANKENTHALER
Abstract expressionist artist

12/12/1928
Sagittarius III

December 11–18
THE TITAN
SAGITTARIUS III

Likely to be easily seduced by the grand plan, the big picture, or the need for sweeping and far-reaching changes and reforms, those born in the Week of the Titan may fail to find the joy and sense of connection available right in their own backyards. Excess will likely be their biggest weakness, as will a tendency toward irritability and frustration. Settling down, slowing down, and applying themselves to the need to better synthesize the ideas and information coming at them from without may also prove to be a problem. Still, they are blessed with the relatively rare combination of tremendous enthusiasm coupled with thoughtful and philosophical turns of mind. If they are careful to avoid aloofness and temper tantrums, and refine both their persons and their messages to the point where they are more easily understood, all will go much more smoothly along this life's journey.

CHALLENGE: **TEACHING THEMSELVES TO HAVE MORE PATIENCE FOR THE NITTY-GRITTY**

FULFILLMENT: **BECOMING THE VOICE FOR POSITIVE, YET PEACEFUL, CHANGE**

December 19–25

PROPHECY
SAGITTARIUS–CAPRICORN CUSP

The ability to share their considerable insight and understanding with others will doubtless figure prominently on the life journeys of those born in this cusp week who travel the Way of Modulation. Gifted with sometimes amazing powers of concentration and intuition, they will have a great talent for getting to the heart of the matter or the core of the problem that few will ever possess. The chief issue is that they may disdain the prospect of deeper involvement and hold themselves aloof from the challenge to impart their ideas to the world. Finding a comfortable space between self-interest and altruism may be especially difficult for these self-contained people. Yet if they understand that the resolution of that sense of conflict can be found in their willingness to open themselves up to greater intimacy and spirituality with those who will provide them with an avenue to the larger world, they can make their mark on the Way of Modulation.

BO DIDDLEY
Seminal rock 'n' roll
singer/guitarist, creator
of the "Bo Diddley beat"
———
12/30/1928
Capricorn I

CHALLENGE: **NOT LETTING THEMSELVES BE PULLED DOWN TO A PESSIMISTIC OR CYNICAL VIEW OF THINGS**
FULFILLMENT: **TRUSTING THEIR HUNCHES WHEN PRESENTING THEIR DATA**

December 26–January 2

THE RULER
CAPRICORN I

This combination of energies can make for some truly formidable and powerful personalities. Those born in the Week of the Ruler may have to work hard to avoid the pitfalls of forcing their ideas and methods on others or suffer some unpleasant consequences in the face of their lack of essential diplomacy. Gifted with a high moral sense, they may display a world view that is missing in some necessary shades of gray. Others of this type will be prone to believe that might makes right—or worse, to channel their prodigious strength and energy into purely selfish pursuits. Thus, cultivating their natural curiosity and working to expand their horizons will be especially useful in their advancement along this path; it will help them develop both greater tolerance and the sense of acceptance that is always implied in the free exchange of thoughts and ideas.

CHALLENGE: **BEING MORE REFLECTIVE OR MODERATE WHEN IT COMES TO THEIR OPINIONS OF THEIR OWN IDEAS**
FULFILLMENT: **ALLOWING THEMSELVES TO RECHARGE AND RELAX NOW AND THEN**

January 3–9

DETERMINATION
CAPRICORN II

Those born in the Week of Determination can utilize the gifts of the Way of Modulation in a unique fashion, providing they do not allow themselves to become overly radical or caught up in less than realistic causes and concerns. Much inclined to strive toward their goals, they can nevertheless be a bit uncomfortable with the natural versatility that is part of this path's energy. As a result, some will set themselves courses of action without first considering the implication or consequences, while others will become tied to traditions that have outlived their usefulness. Learning to share their views and opinions may prove to be the principal challenge here, as these sometimes reticent personalities can be hesitant to tip their hands. Finally, the simple ability to admit the occasional failure will be especially important, as will a willingness to take their attention away from loftier objectives and into the realms of the here and now.

CHALLENGE: **TAKING A HARD AND REALISTIC LOOK AT THE FACTS BEFORE THEM**
FULFILLMENT: **ALLOWING THEMSELVES TO LIGHTEN UP AND FLOW IN HARMONY WITH THEIR CIRCUMSTANCES**
NOTABLE: **ADOLPH ZUKOR (EARLY MOVIE MOGUL)**

January 10–16

DOMINANCE
CAPRICORN III

Those born in the Week of Dominance who find themselves on the Way of Modulation can expect considerable fulfillment and enjoyment of this life's journey as they are well suited to the challenge of focusing their considerable talents and energies toward attainable goals. Though not as expansive as some along this path, these personalities have fine talents for both information gathering and detail work, which will serve them in especially fine stead here. In fact, their principal failing will lie in their tendency to hold themselves aloof and fail to make the necessary efforts to share their ideas with others. Finally, they may pursue their own objectives rather heedlessly or tend to idolize higher causes at the expense of personal development. Yet if they can avoid a certain inclination to put the blinders on or to deal with themselves and others too severely, all can go quite well on this karmic path.

MARTIN LUTHER KING, JR.
Sixties' civil rights
activist; assassinated
———
1/15/1929
Capricorn III

CHALLENGE: **ALLOWING THEIR DEVOTION TO THEIR CAUSE TO BE THE TEMPERING AGENT FOR THEIR FEELINGS**
FULFILLMENT: **SOFTENING THEIR MORAL STANCE AND THEREBY ENHANCING ALL THEIR RELATIONS**

January 17–22

MYSTERY AND IMAGINATION
CAPRICORN–AQUARIUS CUSP

January 23–30

GENIUS
AQUARIUS I

The peaks and valleys that these souls experience will serve as sources of instruction and enlightenment for those born on this cusp who make their way along this karmic path. They are gifted with highly developed skills for not only getting what they want for themselves, but for applying their talents in such a way as to improve the lot of others. Their involvement with personal causes and crusades may be quite intense, but lacking in a certain level of commitment as their curious and passionate natures spur them ever onward. Slowing down and toning down their approach will be critical to their achievement, for they are often restless in the extreme and apt to believe that reality pales in comparison to their high-flown beliefs and passions. If they can direct themselves to the advancement and exchange of ideas and further develop a sense of greater peace with the realities of the moment, they will find their direction much clarified along the Way of Modulation.

STEFAN EDBERG
Tennis player
———
1/19/1966
Capricorn–Aquarius Cusp

CHALLENGE: **MODERATING AND CHANNELING THEIR UNIQUE AND ELECTRIC BRAND OF ENERGY**
FULFILLMENT: **UTILIZING THEIR EXPRESSIVE, CHARISMATIC STYLE TO HELP OTHERS**

Aquarius I's will take quite naturally to the Way of Modulation, providing they can draw upon some of their more fixed energies and apply their attention to particular areas of interest in a steadier fashion than might seem entirely comfortable to them. Restless and high-strung, they can succumb to simple rebelliousness and hamper their own progress by an extremely low frustration threshold. The demands of this karmic path will be expressed in a subtle drawing away from broad ideological pursuits and into a more practical and focused arena. They may struggle a bit with the reality that they can't accomplish their highest goals without some grounding in practical realities and will always be inclined to favor the future over the past. These quick minds will adjust to the need for regulation and modulation, however, if only because it will provide an interesting challenge for their problem-solving abilities.

CHALLENGE: **TAKING A FIRM AND STEADYING GRASP OF THEIR IMPATIENCE AND DISTRACTION**
FULFILLMENT: **TAKING TIME TO SIMPLY BE IN THE PRESENT MOMENT**
NOTABLE: **CLAES OLDENBURG (SCULPTOR; "POP" ART)**

January 31–February 7

YOUTH AND EASE
AQUARIUS II

February 8–15

ACCEPTANCE
AQUARIUS III

True focus and application of some highly developed creative abilities may prove elusive for those born in the Week of Youth and Ease who find themselves on the Way of Modulation. Though likely to be blessed with more of a sense of rebelliousness, passion, and conviction than they might have otherwise, these individuals may nevertheless experience some difficulty with their ability to slow down, settle down, and live more fully in the moment. Finding some avenue of creative or personal expression will likely prove the principal challenge for these talented people and they will further have to monitor their inclinations to be swept up in the tides of emotion that surround their pet causes or crusades. Yet if they can avoid superficiality, cultivate some necessary calm, and accept the task of developing greater discernment, they can realize considerable progress along the road.

CHRIS ROCK
Actor/comedian,
Chris Rock: Bring the Pain!
———
2/7/1966
Aquarius II

CHALLENGE: **TAKING CARE TO CALL ON THEIR PASSION AND ENDURANCE MORE OFTEN**
FULFILLMENT: **EXPRESSING THEIR VERSATILE MINDS IN A PUBLIC VENUE**

Finding the balance between freedom and restriction may be only one of the lessons presented to those born in the Week of Acceptance who negotiate the Way of Modulation, and some with this configuration may falter in their progress along this road. On the one hand, they can be prone to projecting their fears of confinement onto others; on the other hand, they can cling to unfair or intolerant attitudes that are better left behind. A number of real iconoclasts can be found on this karmic path, yet these individuals will have to take special care that they don't fight for freedom, only to turn into persecutors later in life. Still, mental agility is a real asset, as is their craving for a wide variety of experience. If they can manage to keep themselves open to the possibilities for change, stick to the facts, and still manage to explore their options in more measured and realistic ways, life can be quite kind to them along this karmic path.

CHALLENGE: **KNOWING WHEN TO STOP WANTING MORE**
FULFILLMENT: **REMAINING OPEN TO LIFE YET DEDICATED TO SOMETHING**

February 16–22

SENSITIVITY
AQUARIUS–PISCES CUSP

The more inspired and expressive tendencies of those born in this cusp week who travel the Way of Modulation can be wrongly spent in a belligerent and rebellious attitude toward the world. Aggression can take the place of patience here and sheer excitability can be these souls' undoing. Some fiercely self-protective and determined attitudes may well spur these people to success, yet the ability to find real satisfaction in their lives may prove hard to come by. Nevertheless, emotional depth and personal dynamism can coexist more peacefully, though fulfillment for these personalities may manifest in a more abstract set of commitments. However, if they better cultivate the art of being in the moment and work to integrate the highly divergent impulses at work here, all will go well along this most interesting road.

CINDY CRAWFORD
Supermodel
———————
2/20/1966
Aquarius–Pisces Cusp

CHALLENGE: **FERRETING OUT AND RELEASING THEIR MORE COMBATIVE TENDENCIES IN FAVOR OF MORE SERENITY**
FULFILLMENT: **SETTLING AND SLOWING DOWN TO INDULGE IN MORE OF THE SIMPLER THINGS**
NOTABLE: **JUSTINE BATEMAN (ACTRESS, *FAMILY TIES*)**

February 23–March 2

SPIRIT
PISCES I

Those born in the Week of Spirit may well experience a number of struggles with disorganization and a rather flighty attitude along the Way of Modulation. Though there is the potential for great accomplishment, most will have to work hard to develop the necessary perspective and personal discipline to harness some volatile emotions. Others of this type might be characterized by a chronic lack of depth, poor planning, or unrealistic quests for greener pastures. Living on a sense of unfulfilled expectation is often their worst vice. Yet as charming, talented, and charismatic as these people are, it is likely that the world will be forgiving of their faults. If they can employ their communicative talents in such a way that they have the opportunity to inspire, rather than be tied down to a specific set of rules or facts, they will doubtless find this road much easier.

CHALLENGE: **NOT LIVING IN THE WORLD OF HIGH CONCEPTS AND EXPECTATIONS**
FULFILLMENT: **DEVELOPING THE DISCIPLINE TO BE SATISFIED WITH EVERYDAY TASKS**

March 3–10

THE LONER
PISCES II

The introspective inclinations of those born in the Week of the Loner are likely to serve them rather well on this karmic path, providing these personalities do not allow their emotional sensitivity to run the show. Likely to be more lighthearted than some of their fellow Pisces II's, they will display a particular gift for examining and disseminating information. Sharing that information and their views with others will prove much more of a challenge since these individuals can be very recalcitrant when it comes to giving up their unique ideas. Though likely to become rather impassioned in the search for a higher set of ideals, the business of settling down to the here and now may prove difficult. Yet if they can moderate their intensity with periods of introspection, rest, and withdrawal, these sensitive and perceptive people will find both peace and a considerably brighter outlook along the Way of Modulation.

DAVID NIVEN
Actor; won Oscar for
Separate Tables
———————
3/1/1910
Pisces I

CHALLENGE: **REGULATING THEIR ENERGIES BY ALLOWING ENOUGH TIME FOR RETREAT AND QUIET**
FULFILLMENT: **CREATING A PEACEFUL AND HARMONIOUS HOME**
NOTABLE: **EDIE BRICKELL (SINGER)**

March 11–18

DANCERS AND DREAMERS
PISCES III

Practical matters and issues of stability can be real sticking points for those born in this week who travel the Way of Modulation. Though these truly gifted and creative individuals are likely to be talented and passionate in the extreme, there is a pronounced tendency here to skim the surfaces of problems and refuse the call to greater objectivity, common sense, and a more integrated sense of energy. While some may act out their searches for protection and stimulation through a string of friends, lovers, and marriages, others will manifest this path in a tendency to switch jobs, change careers, or become professional students. Yet if they can surround themselves with those who speak to their need for greater stability without demanding too much in turn, these souls will display amazing communicative gifts that will be all the more valuable for their ability to uplift the hearts of those they meet along the way.

CHALLENGE: **BEING MORE HUMBLE AND GROUNDED**
FULFILLMENT: **EXPLORING TECHNOLOGY AND SCIENCE**

The Way of Liberation

SAGITTARIUS I TO GEMINI I
Independence to Freedom

Those born on the Way of Liberation come into this lifetime to define what freedom means to them personally. Often, the individuals on this path will learn that freedom is a state of mind. Sometimes on this path, the individuals born to it will find themselves in situations where they feel limited in some way. This occurs in order for them to discover the nature of true liberation. Stubborn individualists, these are people who can become quite combative when they feel others are encroaching on their rights. While their intuition is their great strength, they may confuse what it is telling them due to their fear of restriction. Often they seem to think that everything around them is holding them back or keeping them down. Usually the limitations they perceive exist only in their very active imaginations. This path calls those born to it to discover how their thoughts affect their reality and to transform how they think from negative to positive. This requires them to adopt a more conscious awareness of how their minds work and to become more objective. Ultimately they will realize that they are, in fact, the masters of their own destinies. Here the way to liberation is in mastering one's thoughts.

The individuals on this karmic path are truly independent spirits. They like to be left alone to do things their own way in their own time. Among the most willful people in the personology system, the men and women on this path stick to their guns and like to win. Moreover, so set are they on following their own courses that they can be quite contentious when crossed, opposed, or criticized. Those born on the Way of Liberation are quite emotional. They are particularly passionate when it comes to their own independence and also that of others. They often stand up for the underdog and oppose injustice fiercely. Because of this viewpoint, many of the individuals on the Way of Liberation are more sensitive than the average person to being structured or limited in any way and often feel cooped up, trapped, and hemmed in by life. Failing to take responsibility for their own lives is a problem here, and it is common for these individuals to accuse those around them of hindering their freedom of movement or of holding them down or back. When convinced by their sense of fairness that they have been wronged in any way, they slip into the role of aggrieved victim quite easily. At such times, their innate obstinacy often kicks in and they can hold on to feelings of resentment for long periods of time. In fact, this rather insidious attitude hurts them although they often don't know it. Wrapping themselves in feeling wronged and hurt eventually becomes a form of imprisonment for them and keeps them from any true inner freedom.

The goal of this path is for the individuals on it to experience the kind of liberation that comes from feeling free within themselves as a result of releasing their re-

---

CORE LESSON
Learning to perceive limitations as the illusions that they are

GOAL
To become adept at transforming their thinking from negative to positive

---

GIFTS
Quick-minded, Intuitive, Charismatic

PITFALLS
Self-pitying, Tyrannical, Cynical

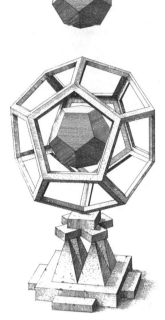

sentments and starting to perceive things more objectively. Ultimately, they will come to realize that whatever they think limits them is nothing more than the result of their own mental monkeys playing tricks on them. The chains that bind them or the walls that entrap them, whether unfulfilling jobs, demanding spouses, abusive bosses, or too much responsibility, can all be transformed. On a certain level such walls exist in their minds alone. They could just as well be made of paper as stone. Simply changing their perceptions would allow those on the Way of Liberation to walk right through them at any time. Thus, as mystics say, all of life is illusion, and limitation is just a mental construct that can be altered anytime.

Those on this path would do well to cultivate being consciously aware of their own thinking processes. In so doing they might catch themselves when they fall into the resentment trap or pity pot. The core lesson for the men and women on the Way of Liberation is to learn how to question their own perceptions and transform their thinking. Often, situations can be completely altered simply by looking at them from different perspectives. Falling into negativity can perpetuate unhappy circumstances because it can only breed and attract more misfortune. Those on this path must learn that they can in fact change their reality—or at least their experience of it—simply by changing their thinking from negative to positive. Norman Vincent

Peale caught on to this idea quite some time ago and wrote about it in his seminal book *The Power of Positive Thinking*. Developing a more conscious and objective approach will require them to do some work in the beginning. When things appear to be bleak, they must force themselves to repeat positive statements or other forms of affirmation several times. Often, wondrous changes for the better in affects or attitudes occur. As they practice this technique, over time they will be able to stop themselves before they become too dark or negative.

The men and women on the Way of Liberation will learn that having free will means that they can make any choices they wish for themselves. Ultimately they will see that whatever besets them comes from their own choices and that they in fact possess the freedom to chose something different for themselves. Truly believing that their horizons are bright and that ever new opportunities are available to them is crucial for these vibrant individuals, for their curiosity is unlimited, their intuitive strength unparalleled, and their hunger to learn and to be innovative almost insatiable.

There is no telling if an individual will succeed on this path. Only through raw experience will those on the Way of Liberation define what freedom means to them. Often they will truly experience some forms of prejudice or repression that will challenge them to reflect on the meaning of liberation and to re-

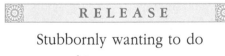

RELEASE

Stubbornly wanting to do
everything your own way

REWARD

The joy of inner freedom

SUGGESTION

Take responsibility for your actions. Understand that by changing your thinking, you can change your experience. Remember to indulge in reverie—daydreaming is very freeing.

vise their value systems. Those on this path can go either way. They can either feel repressed and put upon—a kind of minority of one—or they can opt to gleefully go about their lives in the full knowledge that they are perfectly free to create whatever realities or destinies they choose. Thus, this path will witness some genuinely unique individuals as well as some rather miserable and self-pitying souls. The former tend to be eclectic and creative, exhibiting an appealing ease in living since they give others the sense that they are wholly unfettered. Because of their concern for issues of freedom and justice, often those on this path will take up the cause of freedom generally, becoming involved in political causes. More often, the freedom with which they live their lives will cause them to be role models.

Often, those on this karmic path will be viewed by others as selfish or self-involved due to their drive toward freedom. Before maturity causes them to take more responsibility for them-

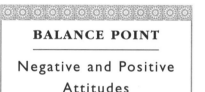

BALANCE POINT

Negative and Positive Attitudes

selves, their relationships are likely to be contentious until they realize that others are not the problem. Unfortunately, guaranteeing oneself freedom sometimes involves inhibiting someone else's. Thus, those on this path are likely to be targets of resentment within their social groups. Family relationships can be especially thorny for those on this karmic path. A paradoxical fact about those on the Way of Liberation is that they may be unusually fretful and may chafe under rules of any kind in their youth, but are capable of turning into true tyrants as adults, frequently suppressing their own chil-

dren. As far as friendships and love relationships are concerned, those on this path need warmth and affection but may have trouble accepting them, since they are suspicious that these are veiled forms of subjugation. Committing to marriage is a difficult proposition for them, but frequently one that provides them with true happiness and stability in the long run.

What is best for those on this path is to be left alone as much as possible to their own devices. Frequently their hobbies and other leisure-time activities are what interest them more than their principal professions. It is not at all unusual to find such individuals working in steady jobs, but really putting most of their energies and interests in their time away from them. Those on the Way of Liberation will fulfill their contractual and other business obligations to the letter, as long as they are free to pursue other nonprofessional activities without restriction. Probably the worst thing for them is to have a nagging partner or spouse; this can drive them to despair, drugs, drink, or actual illness.

This path could be likened to an old story of a captive who was held in a cage. Year in and year out the captive sat in the cage meekly accepting the hopelessness of his situation. One day, quite by accident the captive came to press on the door of the cage only for it to swing open. The door had never been locked, and the captive had been free to escape at any time all along. The moral, of course, is that the captive had only been a prisoner of his own thinking and nothing more.

CRYSTALS AND GEMSTONES

Polish Zincite sears through any confusion or illusion of limitation held within the solar plexus. This mineral forms a strong connection to the power and accuracy of instinctive or "gut" reactions.

 NOTABLES ON THIS KARMIC PATH

MAURICE SENDAK

The world that **Maurice Sendak** created in his children's books is unforgettable. In works such as *The Night Kitchen* and *Where the Wild Things Are,* Sendak created a nightmarish reality that is both scary and funny at once. Interestingly, in *Where the Wild Things Are,* Sendak writes of a little boy who longs for freedom and escapes from home—the perfect metaphor for his karmic path. Moreover, his characters, often taking the form of goblins and other scary creatures, could be considered symbolic of his own inner landscape. By liberating his characters from the recesses of his imagination—allowing them to emerge and become part of our everyday world—Sendak not only entertained his audience but also fulfilled his destiny.

Few American film directors have reached the rarefied levels of **Stanley Kubrick,** who produced such masterpieces as *2001: A Space Odyssey*

STANLEY KUBRICK

and *The Shining.* A truly independent spirit, Kubrick felt subject to no laws but his own, producing most of his films in Britain to avoid the commercial restrictions imposed by Hollywood. Like others on this path, it was difficult to cross, oppose, or criticize him. Able to alter circumstances by viewing them from another perspective, Kubrick made important intellectual inroads in film with his masterful irony. Keeping his negativity under control was a constant personal challenge, but humor, however dark, was his salvation.

PATTI SMITH

Unpredictable, impassioned, and sometimes combative, **Patti Smith** typifies the Way of Liberation. Following her own unique vision, she has invariably remained true to her aesthetic values. Both a poet and a musician, Smith set the power of the word to music, and credits Rimbaud and Bob Dylan among her early influences. Performing in both mainstream and avant-garde venues, she has successfully negotiated the literary and rock worlds. Her albums *Horses, Radio Ethiopia,* and *Easter* resist classification, but are pure idiosyncratic invention. Despite personal tragedy Smith's muse has brought her to the positive pole of her path, writing in *Paths That Cross,* "All Things Renew."

Other Notables: Camille Paglia, Glenn Close, Max Ernst, Emmylou Harris, Elton John, Tom Clancy, David Letterman, Billy Martin, Tony Richardson, Dr. Ruth Westheimer, James Brown, Chè Guevara, Sandra Bullock, Francis Scott Key, Shania Twain, Stanford White, Johnny Mercer, Ben Stiller, Michael Ovitz, Jimmy Buffett, Carol Bayer Sager, Farrah Fawcett, Billy Crystal

---

BIRTHDAYS ON KARMIC PATH 34

February 3, 1891–June 24, 1891 | September 15, 1909–February 3, 1910

April 27, 1928–September 14, 1928 | December 7, 1946–April 27, 1947 | July 18, 1965–December 6, 1965

February 28, 1984–July 17, 1984 | October 9, 2002–February 27, 2003 | May 21, 2021–October 8, 2021

KARMIC PATH
34

March 19–24

REBIRTH
PISCES–ARIES CUSP

A volatile combination of extreme directness and a hypersensitivity toward restriction may make the Way of Liberation a rocky road for those born in the Week of Rebirth. A sense of being misunderstood may contribute to some overly aggressive or contentious habits here, and these folks will do well to cultivate the objectivity and natural flair for analysis that is the calling of this karmic path. To offset these difficulties, however, these passionate people will have an easier time with the relationship aspects of this path than some. If they are careful to surround themselves with those who will accept their need for freedom without expecting too much by way of monogamy, ironclad commitments, or living by the rules, they can realize a fine level of happiness and some really positive growth along the way.

CHALLENGE: **WORKING HARD TO BECOME CLEARER AND MORE OBJECTIVE IN HOW THEY THINK**
FULFILLMENT: **HARNESSING THEIR GREAT INTUITIVE STRENGTH TO ACHIEVE CLEARLY DEFINED GOALS**
NOTABLES: **CHICO MARX (MEMBER OF THE MARX BROTHERS); GLENN CLOSE (FILM/STAGE ACTRESS, *FATAL ATTRACTION*)**

EMMYLOU HARRIS
Grammy-winning country music singer

4/2/1947
Aries I

March 25–April 2

THE CHILD
ARIES I

Those born in the Week of the Child who make their way along this karmic path are likely to have wonderfully exciting and expansive adventures, as their natural energies are very much in keeping with the call to greater freedom here. Though there is some danger of their becoming cynical or overly self-pitying, their biggest stumbling block will be an overly rebellious attitude toward authority that will exist at decided odds with the need to be taken seriously by those around them. Moreover, they can fail to take adequate responsibility for their own woes and get caught up in a tendency to project their fears and misplaced ideals onto others. Yet once they come to terms with the idea that a higher sense of freedom is formed by their own positive choices and not simply by the need to break away from those things that they find stifling, restrictive, or simply dull, all can go quite brilliantly here.

CHALLENGE: **LEARNING HOW TO RELEASE RESENTMENT AND PITY**
FULFILLMENT: **EXPERIENCING THE SENSE OF INNER LIBERATION THAT COMES FROM LETTING GO**
NOTABLES: **ELTON JOHN (POP/ROCK SINGER/COMPOSER, "ROCKET MAN"); CAMILLE PAGLIA (AUTHOR, *SEXUAL PERSONAE*)**

April 3–10

THE STAR
ARIES II

Those born in the Week of the Star who navigate the challenges and demands of the Way of Liberation can expect tremendous progress along this road, especially when they recognize that freedom, at its essence, is the ability to make positive choices and not merely the opportunity to do a multitude of things. Perhaps the single biggest danger for these energetic and passionate souls will be their tendency to place themselves in the center of the action, only to become unhappy and rebel against the responsibilities that arise from feeling themselves indispensable to the running of an organization, family, or other social unit. Thus, developing greater awareness of those things that really make them happy and at the same time serve to spark their curiosity and impulses toward expansion will be especially useful to their development and enlightenment along this road.

CHALLENGE: **RECOGNIZING THAT THE DEPENDENCY OF OTHERS IS OF THEIR OWN MAKING**
FULFILLMENT: **LETTING GO OF NEGATIVE FEELINGS BY GIVING THEMSELVES FULLY TO A CAUSE OR GOAL**
NOTABLE: **CHARLES WILKES (EXPLORER; NAMED ANTARCTICA A CONTINENT)**

DAVID LETTERMAN
Late night talk show host/comedian, *The Late Show with David Letterman*

4/12/1947
Aries III

April 11–18

THE PIONEER
ARIES III

The pioneers born in this week who find themselves on the Way of Liberation, are likely to have a fine time of it, providing they nurture their talents for abstraction and generosity. In fact, stubbornness can be their biggest failing, as they are quite prone to want to impose their ideas on others. While a sense of personal conviction is not necessarily inappropriate, it can become tiresomely didactic when Aries III's fall victim to the notion that their ways are the best or only ways to get things done. Still they should have little trouble rising to the higher challenge of positive thinking and perception that is offered here, and their naturally buoyant spirits, highly motivated attitudes, and powers of social persuasion are all likely to be tremendous assets as they access their need to rise above the limitations of ordinary life in a quest for personal freedom.

CHALLENGE: **NOT ENSLAVING THEMSELVES BY OVERADHERENCE TO ABSTRACT IDEAS OR THEORIES**
FULFILLMENT: **NOT REALIZING THAT, IN THEIR CASE, FREEDOM IS A STATE OF MIND**
NOTABLES: **KAREEM ABDUL-JABBAR (BASKETBALL PLAYER); TOM CLANCY (AUTHOR, *THE HUNT FOR RED OCTOBER*); LINDA BLOODWORTH-THOMASON (TELEVISION PRODUCER, *DESIGNING WOMEN*)**

KARMIC PATH
34

April 19–24
POWER
ARIES–TAURUS CUSP

Though the personalities born in the Week of Power who travel this karmic path may experience struggles with the notion that one can change reality simply by transforming one's thoughts and perceptions, they are nonetheless likely to do quite well along this road. There will be a pronounced tendency here to pursue personal goals at the expense of a wider perception or the development of broader spiritual horizons. Perhaps the principal danger for these personalities lies in their disposition to stay mired in purely materialistic concerns or to concentrate their efforts on gaining worldly recognition at the expense of a sense of idealism and hope. Yet if they can take time from the day to nurture a sense of reverie and a more mystical sense of what is possible, they have rare capabilities for bringing their dreams into reality.

TED SORENSEN
Assistant, special counsel to JFK; wrote
The Kennedy Legacy

5/8/1928
Taurus II

CHALLENGE: **SCALING BACK THEIR AMBITIONS IN FAVOR OF A SIMPLER, FREER LIFE**

FULFILLMENT: **USING THEIR OWN POWER TO HELP EMPOWER OTHERS**

NOTABLE: **SERGEI PROKOFIEV (RUSSIAN COMPOSER)**

April 25–May 2
MANIFESTATION
TAURUS I

Those born in this week who navigate the challenge of the Way of Liberation may find the journey uncomfortable at times as their sense of security may exist at odds with the call to find greater versatility and freedom through the cultivation of broader vision and more positive perceptions. Stubbornness and a tendency to exaggerate will be especially pronounced in those with this configuration. They will have to take care not to set themselves insurmountable obstacles to happiness by holding on to notions of self-sacrifice, a misplaced sense of duty, or a mistaken perception of their own limitations. Yet there is the potential for considerable success here, particularly when Taurus I's cultivate contact with nature in the form of hobbies and recreational activities. These will put them in touch with a larger view of the universe and its workings, while at the same time serving to nourish and comfort their more physical side.

CHALLENGE: **LEARNING HOW TO CHANGE THEIR PERCEPTION AT WILL**

FULFILLMENT: **FINDING GREAT INNER FREEDOM IN LETTING GO OF THEIR OWN RULES**

May 3–10
THE TEACHER
TAURUS II

The versatile and often brilliant individuals born in the Week of the Teacher who travel the Way of Liberation are likely to experience a fine and fulfilling journey, providing they do not allow some cynical or overly critical attitudes to limit their perceptions of all that is possible. In fact, the only real danger to higher development that presents itself here will lie in their tendencies to set themselves up as authorities on almost any subject and to impose their opinions on others without adequately considering alternative viewpoints. Likely to be blessed with formidable verbal skills, they can be prone to argumentative tendencies as well. Yet there is the prospect of great success here, as they bring to this path a grounded sense of character and a flair for conceptualization. If they cultivate some necessary flexibility and avoid negative or cynical patterns of thought, they can expect no small measure of personal success and freedom along the way, particularly through the exploration of other cultures or concepts outside their usual spheres.

BILLY MARTIN
Baseball player/manager, 5 stints as manager with the NY Yankees

5/16/1928
Taurus III

CHALLENGE: **SEEING PROBLEMS AS POTENTIAL OPPORTUNITIES**

FULFILLMENT: **OPENING UP THEIR INNER VISTAS TO EDUCATIONAL OPPORTUNITIES OF ALL KINDS**

May 11–18
THE NATURAL
TAURUS III

Those born in the Week of the Natural who travel the Way of Liberation can experience great fulfillment along this life's journey, providing they do not allow their struggles with authority to subsume or obscure the sense of mental and emotional freedom that is part of their higher calling. These individuals are likely to be so sensitive to feelings of limitation or restriction that they bolt at the first breath of responsibility, and some may thus get mired in a chronic sense of failure or dissatisfaction. If they can understand that independence from external restriction is only half the battle, and that what truly matters here is the freedom that comes with being able to change one's attitudes and perceptions, they will find their frustrations dissipate and their enjoyment of the world increase in proportion. Cultivating imagination and flexibility will prove especially important to their success, as will the willingness to accept that personal security, as well as personal freedom, ultimately come from within.

CHALLENGE: **NOT MISTAKING HIDING FROM RESPONSIBILITY FOR FREEDOM**

FULFILLMENT: **OVERCOMING INSECURITY AND SELF-DOUBT THROUGH POSITIVE ATTITUDES AND SELF-ENDORSEMENT**

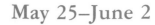

May 19–24
ENERGY
TAURUS–GEMINI CUSP

Those born on the Week of Energy who find themselves on the Way of Liberation are likely to find this a most rewarding journey, providing they do not spread themselves too thin, or misuse their vitality in resentments and aggression. In fact, these free spirits will do well to acquaint themselves with the value of certain limitations in their lives, or run the risks of rootlessness and superficiality as their quests for greater freedom can sometimes degenerate into searches for mere stimulation or simple thrill-seeking. If these versatile and brilliant individuals can cultivate greater awareness of their own self-defeating thought patterns, manage certain ego issues, and avoid both a sense of entitlement and of unfulfilled expectation, these personalities are destined to live life to its fullest and most dazzling along this karmic path.

JACK KEVORKIAN
Outspoken advocate of
euthanasia,
"Doctor Death"

5/26/1928
Gemini I

CHALLENGE: **DEVELOPING AN ABILITY TO KNOW WHEN THE RESTRICTIONS UNDER WHICH THEY CHAFE ARE MERELY IN THEIR OWN MINDS**

FULFILLMENT: **SHOWING OTHERS HOW ATTITUDE IS THE KEY TO TRUE FREEDOM**

NOTABLES: **ROSEMARY CLOONEY (POPULAR 50s SINGER); T. BOONE PICKENS, JR. (BUSINESS EXECUTIVE; FOUNDED MESA PETROLEUM CO.)**

May 25–June 2
FREEDOM
GEMINI I

The individuals born in this week who travel the Way of Liberation are likely to be gifted with a truly formidable and even quite intimidating verbal ability. Naturally witty, charismatic, and imaginative, they may nonetheless suffer from a rather abrasive streak that can be hard to manage. It may be evident that as compelling as these individuals can be, they can get on other people's nerves just as easily as others get on theirs. Impatience and excitability may be their principal failings, and they will do well to study relaxation techniques and cultivate greater personal stability, not so much in the name of structure as for the sake of their own mental health. A fear of domination can cause them to overreact to circumstances with tyrannical or manipulative tactics of their own. Still, there is the prospect of some brilliant success here, especially as they learn to release their negativity and come to terms with their own power to shape reality through the freedom of personal choice.

CHALLENGE: **REINING IN THE ANXIETY AND WORRY THAT ONLY CONTRIBUTE TO THEIR SENSE THAT THEY AREN'T FREE**

FULFILLMENT: **MANAGING THEIR IDEAS FOR GREATER PRODUCTIVITY AND HAPPINESS**

June 3–10
NEW LANGUAGE
GEMINI II

Blessed with unusual style and ability in the area of personal communication, these personalities may nevertheless experience a certain amount of struggle when it comes to coping with their own more rebellious or defensive attitudes. Authority issues can be a big stumbling block for these souls, as can a deep-seated need to be accepted by others—even at the expense of personal freedom. As a result, these individuals will alternate between vociferously venting their complaints and resentments, and keeping silent when they might do better to speak up. However, their natural flexibility and flair for innovation are bound to serve them well. If they can only recognize that their sometimes overly defensive or negative attitudes are of their own creation and choose the higher goals of self-realization and a workable definition of personal freedom, the road ahead will provide rich and ample opportunities for fulfillment.

CHÉ GUEVARA
South American
revolutionary leader,
helped Castro

6/14/1928
Gemini III

CHALLENGE: **UNDERSTANDING THEIR OWN POWER TO CREATE THEIR REALITY—ESPECIALLY WHEN THAT REALITY TAKES THE FORM OF ANOTHER PERSON**

FULFILLMENT: **COMING TO TERMS WITH THE ORIGINALITY OF THEIR THINKING**

NOTABLES: **JAMES IVORY (FILM DIRECTOR, IVORY-MERCHANT); DR. RUTH WESTHEIMER (SEX THERAPIST)**

June 11–18
THE SEEKER
GEMINI III

Blessed with a great sense of adventure and a yearning for wider experience, Gemini III's who travel this karmic path will eventually form a clear definition of just what freedom means to them. There may be potentially painful trials and errors involved in that process however, especially if they allow themselves to succumb to periodic bouts of disillusion or personal resentment. The yearning for freedom may manifest here as a refusal to take on some of the more ordinary challenges of life, and some may find the responsibilities of relationships, family, or profession burdensome. They may discover that their impulses to control or manipulate others are really only devices for keeping themselves as free from pressure as possible. Yet if they work to better understand and regulate their sometimes volatile and unpredictable impulses, these individuals can expect the highest level of personal fulfillment along this karmic path.

CHALLENGE: **TAKING CARE NOT TO ALLOW FRUSTRATION OF THEIR OWN SENSE OF FREEDOM TO TURN THEM INTO MINIATURE TYRANTS**

FULFILLMENT: **EXPERIENCING THE JOY OF FINDING LIBERATION WITHIN**

NOTABLES: **JAMES BROWN (GODFATHER OF SOUL); VIC DAMONE (SINGER/ENTERTAINER)**

June 19–24
MAGIC
GEMINI–CANCER CUSP

Some unusual energies come together in this configuration, and most born on the Cusp of Magic will find the Way of Liberation quite an instructive life's journey. Perhaps the principal difficulty here will be that these cusp people have a strong desire to place themselves in the service of causes or ideals that will exist at odds with their needs for personal freedom. Letting go of old resentments will be still another challenge, for as much as these individuals are able to express their feelings or air their grievances, they have an equal dislike of confrontation and can thus become quite manipulative as they work to turn situations or circumstances to their advantage. At worst, these people will be highly critical, emotionally demanding, and quite prone to complaining. Yet at their best, their sensitivity will be tempered with both objectivity and inspiration, and their deep capacity for love enhanced and fulfilled as they explore their strengths and find freedom in releasing the need for guarantees.

ROALD AMUNDSEN
Explorer; 1st man to
reach the South Pole

7/16/1872
Cancer III

CHALLENGE: **COMING TO UNDERSTAND HOW THEIR QUEST FOR LOVE ENSLAVES THEM**
FULFILLMENT: **LIBERATING THEMSELVES AS A RESULT OF TRANSFORMING NEEDINESS INTO GIVING**
NOTABLE: **FRANCIS CROWNINSHIELD (EDITOR, *VANITY FAIR*; COFOUNDER OF MOMA)**

June 25–July 2
THE EMPATH
CANCER I

Though the Way of Liberation is almost certain to give Cancer I Empaths much more objectivity and a better sense of personal boundaries than they might have otherwise, it is likely that many of these souls will stumble before finding their footing on this karmic path. The need for freedom and independence that goes with this configuration, combined with their extreme sensitivity, can drive many of these people to withdraw from the world and into a self-imposed isolation. Others will manifest a neurotic or aggressive self-reliance that can cause them to alienate those with whom they would most like to establish emotional bonds or connections. Affirmations, exercises in positive thinking, and the ability to give themselves a pat on the back from time to time will be especially important for these souls. Yet once they apply their formidable intuitions to overcoming their sense of limitation and work on the development of a stronger sense of self, freedom is sure to follow.

CHALLENGE: **REMAINING EVER WATCHFUL OF THEIR THOUGHTS AND NOT GIVING IN TO PURE FEELING**
FULFILLMENT: **BEING FREE OF THE EMOTIONAL TURMOIL IMPOSED ON THEM BY OTHERS**
NOTABLE: **MEL BROOKS (COMEDIAN/ACTOR/WRITER/ DIRECTOR, *HISTORY OF THE WORLD PART I*)**

July 3–10
THE UNCONVENTIONAL
CANCER II

Those born in the Week of the Unconventional who travel the Way of Liberation may be in for a wild time as they struggle first to confront, and then to vanquish issues of restriction versus independence. No matter what their chosen venues or professions, many of this type will find their freedom in retreat into admittedly fantasy-rich, yet often unrealistic emotional lives, while others will act out their rebellions against authority, sometimes with the help of less-than-desirable associates. This can be a rocky road at times, especially if Cancer II's choose to obsess over the flaws and imperfections in their lives and circumstances, then use some of their more unfortunate perceptions as excuses for not getting what they really want. Nonetheless, these unusual people are quite capable of acquiring the broader point of view and wider areas of interest indicated here, and if they are careful to cultivate a real sense of optimism, they are likely to find a wealth of opportunities for personal fulfillment.

CLEMENT CLARKE MOORE
Educator/poet, *The Night Before Christmas*

7/15/1779
Cancer III

CHALLENGE: **GIVING UP SELF-JUDGEMENT AND THE FEAR OF REVEALING WHO THEY ARE**
FULFILLMENT: **INDULGING THEIR UNUSUAL INTERESTS AND UNIQUE WAYS OF THINKING**
NOTABLES: **VINCE EDWARDS (ACTOR, *BEN CASEY*); GINA LOLLOBRIGIDA (ACTRESS, *SOLOMON AND SHEBA*; ITALIAN SEX SYMBOL)**

July 11–18
THE PERSUADER
CANCER III

Those born in the Week of the Persuader who navigate the challenge and promise of the Way of Liberation can expect considerable fulfillment along the way, providing they adequately manage a tendency to be overly demanding, and avoid expecting others to provide them with the sense of freedom they must find for themselves. Also, these people are likely to be direct to the point where they may appear threatening or intimidating to others, and their formidable ability to be articulate will have to be tempered with a measure of diplomacy in order to be most effective. There is nonetheless the possibility for great success along this road, providing they keep in touch with their own deepest needs and desires, and keep their minds open to the world of possibilities that await their further exploration.

CHALLENGE: **TEMPERING THEIR DRIVE BY ACKNOWLEDGING THEIR NEED FOR FREEDOM**
FULFILLMENT: **STANDING UP FOR THE RIGHTS OF OTHERS**
NOTABLE: **BOB CRANE (ACTOR, *HOGAN'S HEROES*)**

July 19–25

OSCILLATION
CANCER–LEO CUSP

Cusp personalities born in this week who travel the Way of Liberation may well founder a bit until they attune themselves to the measure of personal freedom that is possible once their sometimes unmanageable emotions are under better control. Gifted with great enthusiasm, and real moral courage, they can nevertheless defeat some of their own best impulses with indecision or negativity. Yet once they begin to understand that at least some of their fears of restriction or issues with authority may be projections of their own inner conflicts, their path to fulfillment will smooth considerably. These souls will discover ample and often delightful opportunities to indulge in a wide spectrum of emotions along this life's journey. If they are careful to maintain both the passion and the positiveness they bring to this life, true self-realization and the freedom to pursue their fondest dreams can be theirs.

CHALLENGE: **HAVING THE COURAGE TO FREE THEMSELVES FROM THEIR OWN SELF-IMPOSED RESTRICTIONS**
FULFILLMENT: **FINDING THE BALANCE BETWEEN FEELING AND OBJECTIVITY**
NOTABLE: **ORSON BEAN (ACTOR/COMEDIAN; PANELIST ON *TO TELL THE TRUTH*)**

SANDRA BULLOCK
Actress, *Speed*

7/26/1965
Leo I

July 26–August 2

AUTHORITY
LEO I

Passionate and truth-loving, the souls born in the Week of Authority who find themselves on the Way of Liberation can nevertheless be aggressive and competitive in the extreme. Some highly volatile tempers will have to be kept in careful check if these people are to be taken as seriously as they want to be, and there is much to indicate that theirs will be a lifelong struggle with authority issues. On the one hand, they are likely to resist anything that hints at restriction, and on the other, they can become overly controlling when they assume a commanding role. Yet there are fine minds and some wonderfully broad perspectives on life to be found here as well. If they do not misuse their energies through feeling themselves to be victims of forces beyond their control, and take care to develop and embrace the possibility of changing the world just by changing their attitudes, these souls will manifest a true understanding.

CHALLENGE: **KNOWING WHEN THEIR ADHERENCE TO THE RULES, STANDARDS, AND HIGHER PRINCIPLES KEEPS THEM AND THOSE AROUND THEM IMPRISONED**
FULFILLMENT: **SPENDING TIME ALONE AND ALLOWING THEMSELVES TO RELAX COMPLETELY**
NOTABLE: **ELISHA GRAY (INVENTOR; CLAIMED TO INVENT TELEPHONE BUT LOST PATENT TO BELL)**

August 3–10

BALANCED STRENGTH
LEO II

Impulsive and often reckless in the extreme, the rather touchy individuals born in this week who travel the Way of Liberation may expend untold amounts of energy in excitability, irritability, and an unwillingness to change. For some, this configuration will result in a "me against the world" attitude that will require some attention before these souls can fulfill the higher promise indicated here. Erratic emotions and unpredictable tempers will doubtless be their biggest stumbling blocks and they will do well to develop greater objectivity, and a real sense of humor to find success along the road. Blessed with great empathy and a need to employ their talents in the service and protection of the downtrodden, they can find fulfillment, providing they develop the simple knack of knowing when to give up on a particular course of action and get on to something else.

CHALLENGE: **FREEING THEMSELVES FROM THEIR OWN OVERBLOWN SENSE OF RESPONSIBILITY TO OTHERS**
FULFILLMENT: **TEARING DOWN THE IMAGINARY WALLS THEY BELIEVE RESTRICT THEM**
NOTABLES: **HAAKON VII (1ST KING OF INDEPENDENT NORWAY); BOB COUSY (BASKETBALL PLAYER, BOSTON CELTICS); BENJAMIN SILLIMAN (FOUNDED *AMERICAN JOURNAL OF SCIENCE*)**

FRANCIS SCOTT KEY
Poet, wrote "The Star-Spangled Banner"

8/1/1779
Leo I

August 11–18

LEADERSHIP
LEO III

The souls born in the Week of Leadership who navigate the ups and downs of the Way of Liberation are likely to experience wonderful fulfillment along this life's journey. Though these dynamic people thrive on challenge, and most will have a fine sense of personal direction, real freedom may be harder to come by until they learn to develop more self-awareness and learn to choose their battles more carefully. Though resentment and self-pity can both be problems for their often large egos, these people have an inborn ability to simply do their own thing, regardless of what the world may think, and thus the promise for success is quite pronounced here. If they rise to the challenge of greater objectivity and perspective and indulge their yearning for wider experience without oppressing others or becoming entangled in issues of ego, authority, or entitlement, all will go well.

CHALLENGE: **SEEING HOW THE STRENGTH OF THEIR RESENTMENTS HOLD THEM BACK**
FULFILLMENT: **FINDING GREATER SATISFACTION IN RELATIONSHIPS BY TRANSFORMING THEIR THINKING FROM SELF-CENTEREDNESS TO CONCERN FOR OTHERS**
NOTABLE: **LINA WERTMULLER (DIRECTOR, *SEVEN BEAUTIES*)**

August 19–25

EXPOSURE
LEO–VIRGO CUSP

The abiding need to overcome a sense of personal repression in the interest of greater freedom can manifest itself in spectacular turnabouts and revelations for many of those born in the Week of Exposure who travel the Way of Liberation. Though there is some danger here of their developing purely escapist secret lives or becoming people who pay mere lip service to the rules, most born with this configuration are well equipped to deal with the challenges offered here. Nevertheless, these personalities will have to take some care that they do not become dishonest in their dealings. Blessed with fine perceptions, great powers of observation, and considerable communicative talents, they will doubtless find unique and highly creative ways to turn even the most bleak situations to their own advantage. Yet attitude will be the key; if they can tone down the dramatics and a tendency to self-aggrandizement through self-pity, most will realize considerable success.

MARLEE MATLIN
Actress, *Children of a Lesser God*

8/24/1965
Leo–Virgo Cusp

CHALLENGE: **CONCLUDING THAT SECRECY IS A FORM OF IMPRISONMENT AND RELEASING THE NEED FOR IT**
FULFILLMENT: **BECOMING MORE DIRECT AND POSITIVE IN THEIR DEALINGS WITH OTHERS**
NOTABLES: **REGGIE MILLER (BASKETBALL PLAYER, INDIANA PACERS); KYRA SEDGWICK (ACTRESS, *PHENOMENON*)**

August 26–September 2

SYSTEM BUILDERS
VIRGO I

Virgo I's who travel the Way of Liberation have many chances for success and self-fulfillment here, yet they may have to work hard to develop both a broader vision and a greater sense of the power of their own perceptions to shape their lives. Learning to free themselves from guilt and repression and avoiding the tendency to sacrifice their own desires on the altar of duty will likely be issues that figure prominently in their development. They are gifted with greater imagination and intuition than they might have otherwise, but staying in touch with those qualities in the course of daily living will be crucial to their eventual success. If they can learn to follow their own impulses toward expansion and experience without first needing permission or sanction from those who would hold them back from their higher dreams, all can go quite nicely along the Way of Liberation.

CHALLENGE: **STRUGGLING TO FREE THEIR MENTAL PROCESSES FROM AN OVERDEPENDENCE ON STRUCTURE**
FULFILLMENT: **BECOMING FREER IN THEIR ABILITY TO MAKE DECISIONS**
NOTABLE: **JAMES COBURN (ACTOR; OSCAR FOR *AFFLICTION*)**

September 3–10

THE ENIGMA
VIRGO II

Here the impulse toward personal liberation is likely to have some very well-thought-out and practical aspects, though it may take time for those born in the Week of the Enigma to really blossom along this path. Nonetheless, they have a pronounced sense of both discernment and objectivity that will serve them well here, and the endowments of this journey will in turn bestow the gifts of humor, resilience, and a fine communicative edge. The resulting mix looks very much like a recipe for real success, and if these souls will only find the courage to cast off the restrictions of convention, repression, or an overly picky attitude, they can expect both worldly and spiritual expansion along this road. When they understand that here the deepest sources of self-fulfillment are often linked to fearless self-expression, their paths to freedom will doubtless become clear.

SHANIA TWAIN
Country music singer/songwriter

8/28/1965
Virgo I

CHALLENGE: **DISCERNING WHEN THEIR OWN MISGUIDED THINKING HAS CREATED DIFFICULT CIRCUMSTANCES FOR THEM**
FULFILLMENT: **USING THE POWER OF THEIR INTELLECT TO STAY UPBEAT AND OPEN**
NOTABLE: **CHARLIE SHEEN (ACTOR, *PLATOON*)**

September 11–18

THE LITERALIST
VIRGO III

A pronounced argumentative streak will bear some watching for those born in the Week of the Literalist who navigate the challenges and demands of the Way of Liberation. Highly demanding of themselves and others, some along this road may find this journey rather uncomfortable until they better establish the connection between their perceptions and their sense of limitation or restriction. Until that time, however, they can expend a great deal of energy trying to convince others of the rightness of their opinions, or indulging in endless debate. Developing a more conscious approach to their own attitudes will prove especially useful here, as will the willingness to simply set aside preconceived ideas or prejudices in the interest of truth and personal objectivity. Persistent and shrewd, if they take care to choose their paths to freedom carefully, they are likely to reach their goals.

CHALLENGE: **OVERCOMING THEIR OWN STUBBORNNESS AND INFLEXIBILITY**
FULFILLMENT: **RELEASING FEELINGS OF HAVING BEEN WRONGED**
NOTABLES: **AGNES DeMILLE (DANCER/CHOREOGRAPHER, *OKLAHOMA!*); JAMES RUSHMORE WOOD (FOUNDER, BELLEVUE HOSPITAL)**

September 19–24
BEAUTY
VIRGO–LIBRA CUSP

Those born on the Cusp of Beauty who travel the Way of Liberation are likely to experience a fine and fulfilling journey, providing they do not allow others to call the shots, or succumb to a sometimes overriding need for material security. Many along this road will manifest this destiny path by simply striving to be happy, without much thought or energy wasted on struggles with those who might be blocking their progress. Others will hinder their own higher development with unproductive relationships, self-pity, or a tendency to want things handed to them on the proverbial silver platter. Yet there is great potential for transformation here, and if they take care to cultivate the self-knowledge that will enable them to better understand their sometimes overly sensitive attitudes and release the need to be dominated by others, their progress on this destiny path is assured.

CHALLENGE: **NOT GLOSSING OVER THEIR DARK SIDE**
FULFILLMENT: **REVELING IN THEIR INSPIRATIONS**
NOTABLE: **KWAME NKRUMAH (OVERTHROWN PRESIDENT OF GHANA)**

SCOTTIE PIPPIN
Basketball player; won 6 championships alongside Michael Jordan on the Bulls

9/25/1965
Libra I

September 25–October 2
THE PERFECTIONIST
LIBRA I

Those born in the Week of the Perfectionist who travel this karmic path may have to work harder than most to cultivate and maintain the positive attitude that is part of the higher calling here. Expressive and perceptive, they may nevertheless be rather anxiety prone and are susceptible to all sorts of stress, both real and imagined, along this journey. Yet they are gifted with a much broader philosophical perspective than they might have otherwise, and if they can cultivate some necessary objectivity and learn to appreciate new concepts and ideas, there are prospects for considerable success here. Providing they do not waste their formidable energies and keen perceptions on petty or irrelevant concerns and learn to release any buildup of personal frustration when things don't go as planned, they can expect life to be rewarding, if not entirely smooth, along the Way of Liberation.

CHALLENGE: **UNDERSTANDING THAT THEIR HIGH STANDARDS AND NEED FOR PERFECTION ENSLAVE THEM**
FULFILLMENT: **EXPERIENCING THE JOY OF SEEING THINGS FROM WHOLLY NEW PERSPECTIVES**

October 3–10
SOCIETY
LIBRA II

Marked by considerable communicative skill and conversational talent, Libra II's who find themselves on the Way of Liberation will bring to this path more diplomatic skill than some of their fellow travelers will. With that gift comes the caveat, however, that these souls will have to work quite hard to free themselves from the demands and duties of an expansive network of social contacts in order to get in touch with a more defined sense of personal freedom. Though some may well succumb to the dangers of a sarcastic or derogatory wit in their dealings with others, most will find their diplomatic inclinations quite useful when it comes to realizing their deeper needs. If these individuals can only learn to take their impulses toward freedom more seriously, and get better acquainted with their own sense of curiosity, life will evolve quite effortlessly along this karmic path.

CHALLENGE: **TEMPERING A CERTAIN CONTENTIOUSNESS IN DEALING WITH OTHERS**
FULFILLMENT: **GETTING AWAY AND DAYDREAMING NOW AND THEN**

MARIO LEMIEUX
Center, Pittsburgh Penguins; 3-time MVP, led the NHL in scoring 5 times; member of hockey's hall of fame

10/5/1965
Libra II

October 11–18
THEATER
LIBRA III

Those born in this week who travel the Way of Liberation may have to work to overcome the tendency to dramatize their own troubles before they make the necessary progress toward personal liberty and fulfillment demanded by this karmic path. Hardheaded and marked by a tendency to blame the world for their own unhappiness, these souls may have to practice more introspecting and less performing in order to realize that the sense of freedom they seek may come only when they release their need to command attention. Moreover, they can become entangled in endless debates or arguments as they attempt to bring people around to their own ways of thinking. Yet there is nevertheless the prospect of great success here, as these serious people come into their own with the development of broader perspectives and more lighthearted and flexible approaches to the issues.

CHALLENGE: **LIBERATING THEMSELVES FROM RESENTMENT AND SELF-PITY**
FULFILLMENT: **CRAFTING A MORE DETACHED AND POSITIVE APPROACH TO LIVING**

October 19–25

DRAMA AND CRITICISM
LIBRA–SCORPIO CUSP

Likely to be very compelling speakers on almost any subject, those born in this week who make their way along this karmic path may be marked by pompous or overbearing tendencies. Real objectivity will prove a worthy goal for these individuals, who have a tendency to take the world too personally on the one hand or to entirely discount views and opinions not their own on the other. Yet there will likely be some truly brilliant minds here that will be matched by astute powers of observation and formidable powers of persuasion. If they come come to terms with those ideas or personal prejudices that hold them back from higher levels of fulfillment, and release the need to get revenge when they feel they have been wronged, there is no limit to their possible achievements along the Way of Liberation.

STANFORD WHITE
Architect, designed first
Madison Square Garden

11/9/1853
Scorpio II

CHALLENGE: **INVOKING THEIR OWN FORMIDABLE POWERS OF PERSUASION TO PERSUADE THEMSELVES TO CHANGE THEIR OWN WAY OF THINKING**

FULFILLMENT: **FREEING THEMSELVES FROM FEELING DISAPPOINTMENTS TOO DEEPLY**

October 26–November 2

INTENSITY
SCORPIO I

Scorpio I's who find themselves on the Way of Liberation can experience real transformation and fulfillment along the road, providing they do not allow dark impulses or negative thinking patterns to obscure a deeper set of needs. Cultivating their natural humor will be especially important to their success, as will the ability to release suspicion or a misplaced sense of martyrdom. Many here will likely find that the sense of freedom they seek will not arise from a stubborn insistence on doing things their own ways, or being islands unto the themselves, but through the willingness to be convinced of alternatives to their own sense of suffering. Greater trust and openness will be critical to their success, as will the ability to use their considerable insights, intuitions and investigative talents, not as defensive weapons, but as instruments of more objective understanding of themselves and others.

CHALLENGE: **CULTIVATING OBJECTIVITY AND RATIONAL THINKING TO OFFSET THEIR EMOTIONAL INTENSITY**

FULFILLMENT: **USING HUMOR TO LIGHTEN UP AND SEE THINGS DIFFERENTLY**

November 3–11

DEPTH
SCORPIO II

As long as they do not make the mistake of confusing profundity with simple unhappiness, those born in the Week of Depth can realize a high degree of personal fulfillment along this road. Yet their own sense of suffering can block their progress, and some will succumb to the dangers of self-pity and self-negation until they come to a better understanding of how their attitudes shape the reality of their experiences. Resentment and an ongoing sense of feeling wronged are real dangers here. However, this configuration can become evident in those who arrive at an almost mystical comprehension of the relationship between mind and matter. If they are careful to avoid the tendency to worry or become depressed, and explore instead the worlds of possibility and transformation that beckon, all will go well along the Way of Liberation.

JOHNNY MERCER
Lyricist, "Moon River";
founder of Capitol
Records

11/18/1909
Scorpio III

CHALLENGE: **LEARNING HOW TO SEE NEGATIVE EXPERIENCES AS OPPORTUNITIES FOR POSITIVE SOLUTIONS**

FULFILLMENT: **COMPREHENDING ON A DEEP SPIRITUAL LEVEL THE DEGREE TO WHICH THEIR THINKING CREATES THEIR REALITY**

November 12–18

CHARM
SCORPIO III

The principal pitfall for those born in the Week of Charm who travel the Way of Liberation will lie in their innate ability to manipulate people and circumstances. Skilled diplomats, they can ignore the higher challenge implied here and retreat into hurt feelings or aggrieved dissatisfaction when others fail to fulfill those needs that can only be fulfilled by themselves alone. Transformation of their attitudes will thus prove especially important to their development, for there is a certain sense of entitlement here that bears watching. Moreover, they can become so accustomed to restriction or repression that they fail to take responsibility for the part they play in their own unhappiness. Yet if they can relinquish the need for control in the interest of nurturing their curiosity, and embrace the possibilities for expansion and liberation that beckon, all will go well on this life's journey.

CHALLENGE: **GENERATING FAITH IN SOMETHING HIGHER THAN MANIPULATION IN ORDER TO MAKE THEMSELVES FEEL SECURE**

FULFILLMENT: **TAKING RESPONSIBILITY FOR THEIR OWN LIVES**

November 19–24
REVOLUTION
SCORPIO–SAGITTARIUS CUSP

Blessed with a natural sincerity and a genuine desire to free the world of all that is foolish, restrictive, or limiting, the volatile people born in this cusp week may discover that the challenge of freeing themselves from repressive attitudes or negative thinking patterns will be the key to their success along this road. Excitable by nature, they can scatter their energies in premature offensives against authority or in poorly conceived plans and ideas. The resulting failures and setbacks can serve to contribute to a sense of being victimized or badly used. These individuals will do well to apply their analytic and objective talents in ways that help them learn to examine their own attitudes and beliefs better before expending their energies in torrents of rhetoric or endless lists of their grievances. Nevertheless, these dauntless and progressive people can realize tremendous success providing they avoid cynicism or autocracy, and learn to temper their passions with simple common sense.

CHALLENGE: **NOT SUCCUMBING TO THEIR OWN TYRANNICAL STREAK AS THEY FIGHT FOR FREEDOM, WHETHER THEIR OWN OR OTHERS'**

FULFILLMENT: **REALIZING THAT THEY ARE ALREADY LIBERATED**

NOTABLE: **BAT MASTERSON (WESTERN LAW ENFORCER)**

BEN STILLER
Actor/writer, *There's Something About Mary*
———
11/30/1965
Sagittarius I

November 25–December 2
INDEPENDENCE
SAGITTARIUS I

The most difficult challenge for those born in the Week of Independence who travel the Way of Liberation will lie in just how willing they are to speak up for what they believe in. Furthermore, these souls are asked to broaden their sense of justice to include more than just themselves. How they go about that task will be as unpredictable as these rugged individualists themselves are, yet, generally speaking, their karmic tasks will revolve around a process of depersonalizing their views of the world. Deep within, these individuals may experience quite a lot of anxiety about their own abilities, which will in turn give rise to an often misplaced sense of personal limitation or restriction. Yet if they can come to understand the sense of adventure that is part of this path and nurture their own philosophical and intellectual curiosity, they can experience a rare level of personal evolution and a rare kind of freedom that arises from a sense of personal control and not merely resistance to external restraints.

CHALLENGE: **KNOWING THAT IT IS THEIR OWN INSECURITY THAT CAUSES THEM TO BOLT IN THE NAME OF FREEDOM**

FULFILLMENT: **FINDING FREEDOM IN EXPRESSION**

NOTABLE: **JAMES AGEE (WRITER/POET, *LET US NOW PRAISE FAMOUS MEN*)**

December 3–10
THE ORIGINATOR
SAGITTARIUS II

The ability to manage aggression can be the key to open the doors to freedom for those born in this week who travel the Way of Liberation. Gifted with some really unique abilities, these souls are destined to accomplish a great deal here, yet they will have to work hard to cultivate a more positive attitude toward themselves and their goals before they find a more secure footing along this road. A sense of rejection can drive these souls far from the mainstream, yet it is equally likely that many will find the liberty they seek the further they depart from the tried and true. For others, however, this path will be realized in an inward journey to set aside insecurity, sometimes with the aid of psychological professionals or spiritual teachers. If they can come to accept that genuine originality is always dependent upon new input, and not the result of stubbornly insisting on their own way of doing things, all can go well along this road.

CHALLENGE: **RELEASING COMBATIVENESS AND FEELING AGGRIEVED**

FULFILLMENT: **COMING TO TRULY BELIEVE THAT THEY ARE THE MASTERS OF THEIR OWN DESTINY**

NOTABLE: **DOUGLAS FAIRBANKS, JR. (ACTOR/WRITER/PRODUCER)**

MICHAEL OVITZ
Entertainment agent; cofounder Creative Artists Agency
———
12/14/1946
Sagittarius III

December 11–18
THE TITAN
SAGITTARIUS III

Those born in the Week of the Titan who travel the Way of Liberation can expect wonderful success and enlightenment along this road as their natural energies are very much in keeping with the higher calling implied here. These personalities are likely to have a wonderfully broad perspective and will have little trouble viewing life's limitations as the illusions that they are. Problems can arise however if they allow themselves to collapse into feelings of martyrdom or victimhood when things don't go their way, and they should remember to shore up their own egos when others won't or can't. Yet if they can control a tendency to be rather fussy on the one hand, or overly aggressive or resistant to authority on the other, there is little that can go wrong for these adventurous and talented souls along this karmic path.

CHALLENGE: **KNOWING THAT THE GREATEST THREAT TO THEIR PERSONAL FREEDOM IS IN TAKING ON TOO MUCH RESPONSIBILITY**

FULFILLMENT: **USING THEIR CAPACITY FOR GREAT INTUITIVE LEAPS IN CONCEPTUAL THOUGHT TO KEEP THEM FREE**

NOTABLES: **STEVE BIKO (SOUTH AFRICAN CIVIL RIGHTS LEADER); EMERSON FITTIPALDI (RACE CAR DRIVER); PATTY DUKE (ACTRESS, *THE MIRACLE WORKER*)**

December 19–25
PROPHECY
SAGITTARIUS–CAPRICORN CUSP

Those born on the Cusp of Prophecy who find themselves on the Way of Liberation may discover that many of their personal issues of freedom revolve around developing the ability to simply speak up and allow themselves to be heard. Naturally independent, these people are unlikely to be overly concerned with what others may think of them, yet they will have to take their independence a step further if they want to find real fulfillment here. Thus, self-expression will be the key that unlocks the doors to personal liberation. Some with this configuration may have dour outlooks that bear some attention, and they will need to be careful to avoid negative or pessimistic thought and behavior patterns. Yet there is the prospect of great self-realization for these unique individuals, as long as they do not equate freedom with isolation, or contentment with the acceptance of illusory restriction.

JIMMY BUFFETT
Pop songwriter/performer,
"Margaritaville"

12/25/1946
Sagittarius–Capricorn
Cusp

CHALLENGE: **COMBATTING PESSIMISM AND DEPRESSION**
FULFILLMENT: **BELIEVING IN THEIR OWN INTUITIVE AND MENTAL STRENGTHS**
NOTABLE: **LARRY CSONKA (FOOTBALL PLAYER)**

December 26–January 2
THE RULER
CAPRICORN I

Those born in the Week of the Ruler who travel the Way of Liberation may find that many of their principal issues will revolve around their need to divest themselves of too much responsibility. Protective and often nurturing, these souls can become overburdened as they take on duties and challenges as a ways of shoring up their self-images, only to feel victimized by the demands placed on them. An increased awareness of their deeper emotional needs will help enormously, as will cultivating the flexibility to simply go with the flow from time to time. Alternatively, tyranny and aggression can come to the fore as they attempt to impose their wills on others. If they keep in mind that emotions are best expressed rather than repressed, and that tolerance of themselves and others is always a worthy goal, things will smooth considerably as they make their way along the road.

CHALLENGE: **USING THEIR SHREWDNESS AND INSTINCT FOR TURNING A PROFIT TO TRANSFORM THEIR OUTLOOK FROM TIME TO TIME**
FULFILLMENT: **CREATING BALANCE BETWEEN WORK AND PLAY**
NOTABLES: **MARIANNE FAITHFULL (SINGER; ACTRESS); CALVIN HILL (FOOTBALL PLAYER, DALLAS COWBOYS); EDGAR WINTER (SINGER; MUSICIAN)**

January 3–9
DETERMINATION
CAPRICORN II

Negative self-perceptions will have to be significantly altered by Capricorn II's who find themselves on the Way of Liberation. Though blessed with stronger egos and a greater sense of independence than many of their fellows born in this week, these individuals may still have a problem with self-esteem. Yet their natural inclinations toward the theoretical and philosophical will be especially pronounced with this configuration, and if they use their ever-increasing knowledge to illuminate their personal strengths and weaknesses, the results can be much stronger and more optimistic perspectives. Nevertheless, there is much to indicate that they will gain a fine grasp of just what it means to change the world by altering one's perceptions and ways of thinking, and though it may take some time for them to spread their wings, they can nevertheless expect to soar to fulfillment in this life's journey.

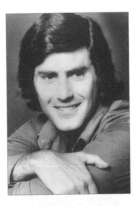

URI GELLER
Psychic

12/20/1946
Sagittarius–Capricorn
Cusp

CHALLENGE: **BEING SURE TO STRUCTURE PLENTY OF TIME FOR REVERIE AND DAYDREAMING**
FULFILLMENT: **BEING LEFT ALONE TO QUIETLY GO THEIR OWN WAY**
NOTABLES: **DAVID BOWIE (GROUNDBREAKING ROCK STAR); HENRY HOLT (PUBLISHER); CAROL BAYER SAGER (SINGER/ SONGWRITER, "THAT'S WHAT FRIENDS ARE FOR")**

January 10–16
DOMINANCE
CAPRICORN III

Simple stubbornness can well be the biggest pitfall for those born in the Week of Dominance who travel the Way of Liberation, and many along this road will have to work hard to cultivate the flexibility and sense of personal freedom that is part of the higher calling here. Many will be held back by negative attitudes or secret feelings of inferiority that can work to their detriment, especially if they cling to external restrictions or limitations as a means of enhancing feelings of safety and security. Yet they are infinitely more intuitive than many of their fellows born in this week, and if they can learn to consciously encourage their gifts, while at the same time be willing to develop an openness to the world of ideas, perceptions, and possibilities that await their exploration, all can go well—particularly as they learn to graciously accept the higher blessings of positivity, freedom, and fun that are all offered here.

CHALLENGE: **TAKING CARE THAT THEIR DEVOTION TO OTHERS OR THEIR CAUSES DOES NOT BEGIN TO FEEL LIKE A TRAP**
FULFILLMENT: **ENJOYING THE SELF-CONFIDENCE THAT A POSITIVE ATTITUDE BRINGS THEM**

January 17–22

MYSTERY AND IMAGINATION
CAPRICORN–AQUARIUS CUSP

The rugged and often eccentric individuals born in this week who navigate the Way of Liberation are likely to have a fine time along this road, as the energies here are especially compatible with the challenge of discovering a personal definition of freedom. Though many of these people will encounter a number of struggles with an overly rebellious attitude and may be rather volatile in the extreme, most are blessed with a naturally positive outlook and passion that should find their highest expressions in this life's journey. For some, freedom will be found in a rich, rewarding, and imaginative inner life, while others will seek their liberation in more tangible ways. Though it is difficult to predict their eventual directions, it is safe to say that all here will experience unusual and exciting passages, marked by great creativity, a sense of adventure, and quite a lot of fun.

PAUL AUSTER
Writer, *Smoke*

2/3/1947
Aquarius II

CHALLENGE: **CULTIVATING EVEN GREATER SERENITY BY EXPLORING METAPHYSICS**
FULFILLMENT: **DEFINING A PURELY PERSONAL APPROACH TO THEIR OWN FREEDOM**
NOTABLE: **JILL EIKENBERRY (ACTRESS, *LA LAW*)**

January 23–30

GENIUS
AQUARIUS I

Those born in the Week of Genius who find themselves on this karmic path can expect a relatively easy time of it as their own highly intellectual energies are very compatible with the sense of freedom and personal liberty that beckons here. The fiery energies of the Sagittarian origins of this path will likely imbue these people with more passion than they might have otherwise and help to mitigate their sometimes detached and unemotional attitudes. Nevertheless, they will have to avoid a tendency to scatter their energies or spread themselves too thin. Though stubbornness may be a problem, real aggression or competitiveness will not, as Aquarius I's will have little trouble at all doing their own thing. As a result, there is much to indicate that these will be unique and exciting people, gifted with both great brilliance and the courage to march to the beat of their own drums.

CHALLENGE: **STUDYING THE WORKINGS OF THEIR OWN MINDS**
FULFILLMENT: **ENGINEERING MOMENTS OF PURE BRILLIANCE BY LEARNING HOW TO OPEN THE DOORS OF PERCEPTION.**

January 31–February 7

YOUTH AND EASE
AQUARIUS II

Among the most lighthearted of those who travel this road, those born in the Week of Youth and Ease are likely to experience a wonderfully fulfilling passage, providing they do not fall prey to their own insecurities, or succumb to the need to be accepted by others, at the expense of their own deeper desires. Cultivating a greater awareness of their own thinking patterns and accepting responsibility for their own actions will prove crucial to their success, as these curiously passive personalities can sometimes go to great lengths to avoid acknowledging the roles they play in shaping their own realities. Yet there is little danger of their becoming chronically negative or self-defeating, and the occasional minor attitude adjustments should prove all they need to find happiness and liberty along this road.

FARRAH FAWCETT
Actress, *Charlie's Angels*,
The Apostle

2/2/1947
Aquarius II

CHALLENGE: **QUELLING THEIR OCCASIONAL IMPULSES TO ACT OUT AND BEING CONTENTIOUS OR STUBBORN SIMPLY TO PROVE THEY ARE THEIR OWN PERSONS**
FULFILLMENT: **FLOWING RATHER EASEFULLY THROUGH LIFE**
NOTABLE: **DAN QUAYLE (VICE PRESIDENT UNDER BUSH)**

February 8–15

ACCEPTANCE
AQUARIUS III

Marked by a pronounced tendency to irritability, those born in the Week of Acceptance who navigate the Way of Liberation may discover that their principal challenge involves the release of some overly didactic or prejudicial attitudes before they find real reward here. On the other hand, there are some with this configuration who will find a necessity to develop greater discernment before their paths to personal liberation are clarified. Either way, these individuals are well equipped to meet the challenge of learning to let their heads rule their hearts as they are blessed with great curiosity and a fine flair for the world of ideas and information. Thus, if they are careful to get the facts—including those that pertain to their own patterns of thinking and behavior—and draw their conclusions accordingly, these natural individualists are sure to find the freedom they need along this life's highway.

CHALLENGE: **DIGGING DEEPLY TO UNEARTH AND RELEASE THE SECRET PREJUDICES THAT HOLD THEM BACK**
FULFILLMENT: **APPROACHING LIFE IN A FREER, EASIER MANNER**
NOTABLE: **RONALD COLMAN (SCREEN ACTOR)**

February 16–22

SENSITIVITY
AQUARIUS–PISCES CUSP

Personal touchiness and an aggressive or defensive attitude can make this a troublesome journey for those born on the Cusp of Sensitivity. Combativeness and an overriding desire to succeed can serve to stifle some of their impulses to personal freedom, while a sense of victimization can further hamper their development. Thus, there will be a number of individuals along this road who will find themselves sounding a theme of "I coulda been a contender," until they gain a better sense of their own power to shape their lives through their perceptions. Overcoming emotionalism and turning their attention to more abstract and idealistic concerns will be especially helpful in their process, as will the ability to know when to back up and give up the fight—especially when the fight is unproductive, unworthy, or fails to contribute to a more positive and self-affirming attitude.

EDWARD JAMES OLMOS
Actor, *Stand and Deliver*

2/24/1947
Pisces I

CHALLENGE: **WORKING TO MOVE THEMSELVES AWAY FROM SELF-PITY AND TOWARD SELF-EMPOWERMENT**
FULFILLMENT: **GETTING A BETTER GRIP ON THEIR OWN EMOTIONAL SIDE**

February 23–March 2

SPIRIT
PISCES I

Those born in the Week of Spirit who find themselves along this karmic path will have to avoid a tendency to exalt their own emotions and passions and cultivate a more objective perspective if they are to find fulfillment along this journey. Yet there is the potential for great fulfillment with this configuration as Pisces I's are well acquainted with and quite comfortable in the realms of abstraction and the world of ideas that are part of the higher calling here. The key to their liberation will lie in their ability to rise above their own emotional dramas, and to take adequate responsibility for the parts they play in shaping their own destinies. Rather than lay blame upon others or bewail their fates, they will do well to cultivate a more proactive approach to personal satisfaction. If they are careful to avoid the traps of irresponsibility, emotional self-indulgence, and simple disillusion, all will progress quite nicely here.

CHALLENGE: **ENGAGING THEIR IDEALISM TO DIG THEMSELVES OUT OF ANY FUNKS THAT FAULTY THINKING CAN PRODUCE**
FULFILLMENT: **APPLYING THEIR SENSE OF JUSTICE TO HELP OTHERS**
NOTABLE: **DAVID SARNOFF (BROADCAST PIONEER/EXECUTIVE; FOUNDED NBC)**

March 3–10

THE LONER
PISCES II

Though highly independent and naturally individualistic, Pisces II's who travel the Way of Liberation may nevertheless find themselves prisoners of their own destructive emotional patterns. Basically quite gifted with a great capacity for inner freedom and a wonderful ability to go their own way, these personalities are nevertheless alarmingly negative in their outlook, and many will find the challenge to lighten up and adopt a breezier approach a bit daunting at times. Some may withdraw into self-imposed isolation in the mistaken belief that solitude and freedom are somehow the same. Yet if these souls can come to realize that the way to fulfillment involves altering their perceptions to include both a more positive view of the world and themselves, they can make tremendous progress along the way.

BILLY CRYSTAL
Actor/comedian,
City Slickers; frequent
Oscar host

3/14/1947
Pisces III

CHALLENGE: **COMPLETELY ELIMINATING FROM THEIR THINKING THE NOTION THAT THEY ARE VICTIMS**
FULFILLMENT: **STAYING POSITIVE BY FOCUSING ON HIGHER IDEALS**
NOTABLES: **SAMUEL BRONFMAN (DISTILLER, SEAGRAM & SONS); DAVID KENNEDY (PERSONAL PHOTOGRAPHER TO GERALD FORD)**

March 11–18

DANCERS AND DREAMERS
PISCES III

These extraordinary people are likely to experience a rich and rewarding journey along the Way of Liberation, yet may find that many of their problems arise more from the way that others perceive them than the way in which they view themselves. There is something of a danger that they will have their best intentions misunderstood or misinterpreted with this configuration, and their interactions with the people around them may devolve into conflict if they allow an omniscient or high-handed delivery to get in the way of their message. They are capable of appearing to others as much more passionate and in control than they really are, and will often promise much with little follow-through. Yet if they can come to terms with the idea that every freedom involves an equal measure of responsibility, all can go brilliantly along this karmic path, and their flair for real individuality can serve as a source of inspiration to many along the way.

CHALLENGE: **NOT ALLOWING THEIR OCCASIONAL BOUTS OF JEALOUSY AND RESENTMENT TO GET THE BETTER OF THEM**
FULFILLMENT: **EXPERIENCING THE JOY OF INNER FREEDOM**

The Way of Translation

SAGITTARIUS II TO GEMINI II
Originator to New Language

The life purpose of the individuals born on the Way of Translation is to find a way to communicate their unique thinking or unusual ideas. Blessed with a kind of genius, those on this path have a difficult time expressing what they know. Born with their own peculiar vernaculars, many on this karmic path may feel misunderstood by others because their patterns of thinking or speech are of their own making. This difficulty generates in them enormous frustration and a deep need to be understood and is the basis for many of their troubles since it causes them to be attention seeking and defensive. Others view them with suspicion and many of their relationships may be fraught with conflict. The life of purpose of the men and women on the Way of Translation is to work to build bridges of understanding. The first step is to give up being lone wolves and learn to cooperate with others. Learning how to speak their language is the second. Aligning themselves with the idioms of their times will help them put their ideas across in confidence. Ultimately, those on the Way of Translation may find themselves in the role of channel, fostering understanding, perhaps even teaching.

The individuals on the Way of Translation are extremely clever, original thinkers. Their strength is in making great creative leaps in conceptual thought. Seeing the big picture is their forte—but usually they see it in wholly personal ways. Often brilliant, a large measure of their creativity is due to the unusual way they think, allowing them to see solutions to problems or generate ideas when others would fail. In short, they think "outside of the box." However, they are often stymied in their abilities to then communicate their concepts or theories to others because their manners of speech are highly individualistic as well. They often interpret words differently from the ways others do and use certain terms well outside the realm of standard English. People sometimes accuse them of saying something other than what they intended, if not of outright lying. Because their minds are highly inventive and expansive, their ideas may fly from one topic to the next resulting in a barrage of verbiage. It is no wonder others can't keep up or become bewildered.

A certain assertiveness and aggression are innate to the men and women on the Way of Translation. Theirs is a competitive spirit with a real need for achievement and recognition. Thus, they strive for success, perhaps hoping to realize the acceptance that, deep down, they don't feel they have been given. Many on this path may go far as a result. Due to the passion of their convictions, they may seem belligerent and put others off. These men and women love action and, because they so crave acknowledgement, they will often place themselves at the center of things, grandstanding and trying to dazzle the audience. For those close to them, this may wear thin after a while. Deep down these individuals may never feel fully understood or believe their own press releases. There is a

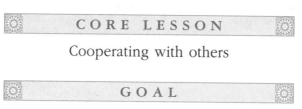

CORE LESSON
Cooperating with others

GOAL
Find a bridge to understanding

GIFTS
Ardent, Innovative, Mentally Agile

PITFALLS
Insecure, Inarticulate, Aggressive

curious lack of confidence here and, with it, no small amount of sensitivity. Yearning to be understood and admired, while feeling misunderstood, these men and women can be very defensive and attack others—in particular, verbally—without warning. Craving attention as they do, sometimes they create conflict since any kind of attention is better than none. Going overboard, these souls often only get themselves into hot water. Ultimately, they must learn that attention is not acceptance, success is not validation, and that neither buys you love.

Clearly, there is great danger here for these individuals to veer off and go down the wrong road, one filled with quarrels and conflict. However, with awareness, it is possible for these souls to change their life direction. In order to do so, it is imperative for the individuals on the Way of Translation to find ways to create and promote understanding in their relationships. This can be achieved by putting their ideas in terms that others can understand. The goal of the Way of Translation is for these individuals to educate themselves in the vernacular of the world. They must find a bridge between their forms of thinking and expression and that of others by clothing their ideas in the fashions of the times. Finding better ways to communicate is a tall order for these people because they, and their egos, are usually significantly invested in their natural modes of speech and thought. Their will to win

means that they prefer to insist on others' seeing things their way, rather than coming around to the ways of the rest of us.

Often the success or failure of those on the Way of Translation, both in terms of their spiritual lives and their worldly positions, is dependent on their willingness to compromise. Indeed, compromise is the core lesson of this path. Before one can bridge a communication gap, one must be able and willing to see things the way others do. Those on this path must learn how to put themselves in someone else's shoes, grasp how they think, and hear how they word things. Only then can they meet adversaries and loved ones alike halfway. They do, in fact, possess a great deal of psychological insight—if they choose to use it. Usually the result of their efforts to compromise is that they find the bridge to understanding that has eluded them all of their lives.

They will be able to put forth their ideas in more straightforward and conventional language, thus avoiding misunderstandings. Moreover, they will learn the value in fewer words. Often prattling on about things or saying too much is what gets them into hot water. These individuals would do well to remember, "the less said, the better." As they gain confidence in their ability to make themselves understood, their natural defensiveness will melt away, and others will become more open to what they have to say and trust them more.

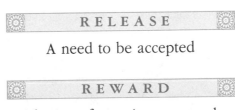

RELEASE

A need to be accepted

REWARD

The joy of easy interpersonal understanding

SUGGESTION

Seek validation within the self, rather than from others. Stay true to who you are by remaining more natural. Know that seeking compromise is not an admission of failure. Put yourself in others' shoes.

As they progress on this path, those on the Way of Translation will become more and more adept at couching their ideas in language that can be more readily accepted. Eventually, they may develop roles in the world at large actually serving as interpreters of sorts for others. Here their ability to penetrate to the hearts of issues and to quickly size up what others are saying stands them in good stead. Moreover, due to their ability to see larger issues and broader concepts, once they find their mediums for translating these ideas for others, they may find themselves highly in demand as writers or speakers. If they work hard, they may truly find fulfillment for their natural versatility and quickness of mind. All sorts of occupations involving language and communication—notably journalism, creative writing, law, and teaching, to name a few—are areas where those on this path may excel. Some on this karmic path may find metaphorical languages with which to touch people—for example, occupations that deal in visual imagery such as photography, painting, sculpture, or filmmaking.

Few individuals pay as much attention to their public images as those on this karmic path. Consequently, how others see them is a matter of the utmost importance to them. Initially on this path, as they attempt to reach out to others in a spirit of cooperation, they may miss the mark due to inexperience and spend too much time and energy trying to convince others of their worth rather than standing confident in themselves. Frequently these attempts merely backfire as they appear sycophantic and they are viewed, instead, with suspicion as to their real motives. In extreme cases, they may actually be labeled as con artists or panderers. All they really need is to cultivate some of the social graces. Learning this "language" will help them enormously along the way. Their nature is really very direct and natural; expressing it in some more socialized or reined in form is far preferable to discarding it in favor of a false front that is an attempt at sophistication.

Inevitably, those on this path are attracted to those who can help them achieve their ambitions but, deceived by self-interest, may cut themselves off from those who really love or care for them and whom they most need. There is no doubt that faithful life partners would be worth all the gold in the world to them, were they only to realize it. Blessed by friends or family members loyal to them through thick and thin, they will have the necessary emotional support to go far in implementing their visions. The question is, of course, how much they are willing to give in return, and how faithful they are willing to be. Those involved with such individuals will have to understand their need for action and change.

The importance of opening lines of communication is observed in the story of the Tower of Babel. The confusion engendered by people speaking different languages to each other was sufficient to put an end to the building of the edifice. Symbolically, it may be seen as putting a stop to unbridled egoism and stressing the importance of understanding. The more successful of those on the Way of Translation may be viewed as intermediaries who, working for the common good, facilitate the ability of others to communicate.

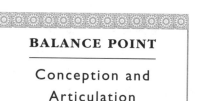

BALANCE POINT

Conception and
Articulation

CRYSTALS AND GEMSTONES

Prehnite is a bridge that links the individual to multidimensional realms of consciousness. This stone opens the throat chakra making it possible for complex thoughts to be shared with clarity.

NOTABLES ON THIS KARMIC PATH

Considered by some to be a master consensus builder and skilled policy craftsman, it seems that U.S. President **Bill Clinton** has well learned cooperation, the core lesson of this path. However, in building bridges with his opposition, Clinton often crosses the lines separating parties and claims the enemy's

BILL CLINTON

territory as his own. Those on the Way of Translation must learn to articulate their original ideas in the vernacular of their time rather than interpreting communications in their own way. Clinton, however, has often been accused of playing with semantics rather than coming to the point. Thus it would seem that the president may have some work to do on this path.

MARY SHELLEY

Born to two brilliant social reformers, **Mary Wollstonecraft Shelley** faced the task of making her own way in the world. She quickly found success in writing, creating her novel *Frankenstein,* as well as various travel logs and journals. As an author, she was well-suited to husband Percy Bysshe Shelley, and spent many years after his death editing and publishing his works. Typical of this path, she brought numerous ideas to the public's attention through her mastery of both literary language and the vernacular. This forward-looking writer anticipated several modern science-fiction themes in her work.

SUSAN SARANDON

One of the most feisty personalities in contemporary cinema, **Susan Sarandon** lives her life on and off the screen her own way. For years she was unable to project her strong ideas through the roles she was offered, and she rejected many parts. Her career began to flourish later in life, when she began to communicate her feminist views through films such as *The Witches of Eastwick* and *Thelma and Louise.* A master of the vernacular, her ability to play almost any role is evidenced in her portrayal of a Louisiana nun in *Dead Man Walking,* for which she won a Best Actress Oscar. Politically and socially active, she defines her stance in a most articulate fashion.

Other Notables: Maya Angelou, Gabriel Garcia Marquez, Byron Janis, Hans Küng, Helen Mirren, Sergei Diaghilev, Fred "Mr." Rogers, James Garner, Charlotte Brontë, Shirley Temple Black, Bertrand Russell, Jessica Tandy, Errol Flynn, Connie Chung, Freddie Mercury, Agatha Christie, Tommy Lee Jones, Oliver Stone, "Jelly Roll" Morton, Aimee Semple McPherson, Demond Wilson, Peter Martins, Sally Field, Robert Mapplethorpe, Edward Albee

---

BIRTHDAYS ON KARMIC PATH 35

September 14, 1890–February 2, 1891 | April 27, 1909–September 14, 1909

December 7, 1927–April 26, 1928 | July 18, 1946–December 6, 1946 | February 27, 1965–July 17, 1965

October 9, 1983–February 27, 1984 | May 21, 2002–October 8, 2002

KARMIC PATH
35

March 19–24
REBIRTH
PISCES–ARIES CUSP

The natural directness of the Pisces–Aries personality will be given an unusual twist on the Way of Translation. Likely to be full of opinions and ideas, these individuals will do well to carefully formulate their plans before giving them full expression, or run the risk of being chronically misunderstood and misinterpreted. Overassertiveness can be something of a problem here, and many with this configuration may manifest some rather belligerent attitudes that will serve to disguise their need for acceptance and fear of rejection. Though likely to be free and original thinkers, they will nevertheless face the challenge of refining their forms of personal expression and social interaction before they can realize their ability to bring the world around to their ways of thinking. Yet if they can cultivate calm and objectivity, and avoid the tendency to want to do everything themselves, success can be theirs along this path.

FRED "MR." ROGERS
TV producer/host,
Mr. Rogers Neighborhood

3/20/1928
Pisces–Aries Cusp

CHALLENGE: **BEING SURE TO KEEP THEIR EXPRESSION AS SIMPLE AS POSSIBLE**

FULFILLMENT: **FINDING SELF-ACCEPTANCE**

NOTABLES: **SERGEI DIAGHILEV (BALLET IMPRESARIO); BYRON JANIS (PIANIST; DISCOVERED UNKNOWN CHOPIN WALTZES); HANS KÜNG (OFFICIAL THEOLOGIAN OF SECOND VATICAN COUNCIL)**

March 25–April 2
THE CHILD
ARIES I

Though those born in the Week of the Child who travel the Way of Translation will never lack for inspiration and creative approaches to people and problems, their ability to verbalize their ideas in such a way that others can readily accept and understand them will prove key to their success. In fact, many of these individuals will have to overcome a naive style of perception and self-expression as their natural passion and enthusiasm can sometimes get in the way of the message here. The need to be taken seriously can sometimes lead to overcompetitiveness or a tendency to intimidate others with a barrage of words, when a more thoughtful presentation would better serve their purposes. Yet if they can overcome the tendency to scatter their energies, to need instant gratification, and to desire action rather than enlightenment, great progress is sure to come as they make their way along the road.

CHALLENGE: **TEMPERING THE TENDENCY TO EXPRESS THEMSELVES IN GREAT OUTBURSTS OF FEELING**

FULFILLMENT: **FEELING HAPPY IN RELATIONSHIP WITH THOSE WHO UNDERSTAND THEM**

NOTABLES: **JIM LOVELL (ASTRONAUT); SARAH JESSICA PARKER (ACTRESS, *HONEYMOON IN VEGAS*)**

April 3–10
THE STAR
ARIES II

When the Aries II personality on the Way of Translation speaks, people are likely to listen. These often compelling and unusual individuals will likely draw both a great deal of attention, and a certain amount of fire as they make their way along this road. And while they will have little problem gaining an audience, it is somewhat difficult to determine whether they will have an easy time making themselves understood. Blessed with the ability to take in enormous amounts of information and input, they will nevertheless have to work to distill their ideas down to their essentials. Dazzling personas and compelling verbal styles may not be enough to find success if these personalities are focused more upon getting attention than they are upon real accomplishments. Yet they have a fine talent for the big picture and the larger view. If they leave the detail work to others and concentrate upon putting their inspirations into more vernacular and accessible formats, they can inspire many along the way.

MAYA ANGELOU
Writer/director, *I Know Why the Caged Bird Sings*

4/4/1928
Aries II

CHALLENGE: **BEING LESS INVOLVED IN THEIR PUBLIC IMAGES AND MORE INVOLVED IN THE TRUTH OF WHAT THEY SAY**

FULFILLMENT: **USING LANGUAGE TO CONNECT TO A LARGER AUDIENCE**

NOTABLE: **ROBERT DOWNEY, JR. (ACTOR, *CHAPLIN*)**

April 11–18
THE PIONEER
ARIES III

The original and visionary individuals born in this week who travel the Way of Translation can be on the cutting edge of innovation and invention, yet they may fail to bring others around to their causes if they allow their more competitive instincts to override the need for more effective communication. There is a danger of their being too far-out or unusual to have their ideas be everyone's cup of tea. Yet there is the potential for enormous success and accomplishment along this road, especially when these inspired and inspiring people better learn to set ego aside and to take the world less personally. It will be critical for them to keep always in mind the larger picture and to avoid a tendency to impose their beliefs on others. Yet if they can meet the challenge, they are more than capable of fulfilling the promise of this karmic path.

CHALLENGE: **EXPRESSING THEIR BELIEFS WITHOUT FORCING THEM ON OTHERS**

FULFILLMENT: **PURSUING THEIR HIGHEST VISIONS AND GOALS**

NOTABLE: **ETHEL KENNEDY (WIDOW OF RFK)**

April 19–24

POWER
ARIES–TAURUS CUSP

Those born on the Cusp of Power who navigate the Way of Translation have both originality and considerable resources at their disposal. With this configuration, innovation and creativity are grounded in a more practical approach, yet the tendency to be blunt or verbally overbearing can prove their biggest stumbling block to real success. Further, theirs is an inclination to be self-centered in the extreme, and their goals and dreams will have to be mitigated by consideration of others, if only in the interest of garnering needed support. Likely to be mentally adept and quite shrewd, these gifted people must nevertheless gain a better grasp of what it means to compromise and cooperate. Yet their grasp of the bottom-line issues, combined with a certain universality of vision, speaks to real accomplishment and success, and their creative communication is likely to find great response from others along the way.

CHALLENGE: **RELENTING IN THEIR DEFENSE OF THEIR VIEWS IN ORDER TO REACH OUT TO OTHERS**

FULFILLMENT: **FEELING SECURE IN WHO THEY ARE AND WHAT THEY BELIEVE**

NOTABLE: **SHIRLEY TEMPLE BLACK (CHILD FILM STAR; LATER U.S. AMBASSADOR)**

CHARLOTTE BRONTË
Writer, *Jane Eyre*

4/21/1816
Aries–Taurus Cusp

April 25–May 2

MANIFESTATION
TAURUS I

The personalities born in this week may find that they wind up far more disorganized and unstructured than when they began in life, as there is much about this configuration to suggest that theirs will be a process of learning increased flexibility, broader vision, and the ongoing ability to speak their minds, regardless of the perceived consequences. Though stubbornness and a tendency to be overbearing may be present here, they are gifted with a much better ability to structure their thoughts and plan their verbal presentations than some others along this road. If they can bring themselves to accept the increased freedom indicated here and yet apply their unique gifts in such a way as to bring them to manifestation, they can realize rare accomplishment and long and productive careers.

CHALLENGE: **GRAPPLING WITH THEIR STUBBORNNESS AND DETERMINATION IN ORDER TO BETTER COOPERATE WITH OTHERS**

FULFILLMENT: **TAPPING INTO THEIR VENUSIAN LOVE OF HARMONY**

NOTABLE: **QUEEN JULIANA OF THE NETHERLANDS**

May 3–10

THE TEACHER
TAURUS II

There is a great deal to indicate that the brilliant communicators born in the Week of the Teacher who find themselves on the Way of Translation will find both their life's work and many of their life's lessons revolve around issues relating to cross-cultural or interracial studies and interpretations. While such issues may not present themselves in a strictly literal sense, these individuals are bound to be quite interested in not only their own unique ideas, but also in those of others. Finding the means within themselves to translate and relay the essence of the available information in a readily understandable way will figure prominently on this life's journey. Moreover, they have a real need for personal recognition and achievement that will serve them well in the pursuit of their ambitions, and if they take care not to give in to a need for instant gratification on the one hand, or pedantry and inflexibility on the other, they will doubtless travel far along this road.

CHALLENGE: **COMPROMISING THEIR MORAL STANCE NOW AND THEN**

FULFILLMENT: **HAVING FOUND A BETTER BRIDGE FOR COMMUNICATION AND SHARING IT WITH OTHERS**

NOTABLE: **EDWIN LAND (FOUNDED POLAROID CORP.)**

BERTRAND RUSSELL
Philosopher;
mathematician; won
Nobel Prize for Literature

5/18/1872
Taurus III

May 11–18

THE NATURAL
TAURUS III

Rebelliousness and the need for personal validation may be the biggest stumbling blocks for those born in the Week of the Natural who journey along the Way of Translation. Though likely to be more fun loving and lighthearted than many of their fellows along this road, there is a proportionate danger of their scattering their energies in frustration, dilettantism, and a tendency to talk a better game than they ever get down to actually playing. Thus, this configuration can make for a number of snake-oil salesmen and women, but it can also make for its share of orators, diplomats, and most especially—musicians. Depersonalizing their visions will be the key to success, yet there is much to indicate a wealth of natural talent and even the touch of genius here. If these individuals can gain a better grasp of themselves as the instruments and translators for a more universal source of inspiration, and abandon a preoccupation with personal security or public image, all can go brilliantly along this karmic path.

CHALLENGE: **USING THEIR CHARM FOR SOMETHING OF REAL VALUE AS OPPOSED TO MERE ICONOCLASM**

FULFILLMENT: **EXPERIENCING THE DEEPENING OF INNER WORTH AS THEY FIND THEMSELVES TO BE UNDERSTOOD**

NOTABLE: **JAMES MASON (ACTOR, *THE VERDICT*)**

May 19–24

ENERGY
TAURUS–GEMINI CUSP

Quite clever and on the cutting edge of innovation when it comes to matters of style, fashion, and presentation, those born on the Cusp of Energy who navigate the Way of Translation make wonderful performers, public speakers, and harbingers of fashion. Yet if they are to realize the fulfillment promised by this path, it is likely that they will also have to learn that the joy of genuine creative effort is in performing the task itself, not merely using their talents to win the admiration or attention of others. Though these dazzling people will surely evidence a certain preoccupation with public image, they will be faced with the challenge of exploring the person beneath the facade. Yet if they do not allow themselves to become overly self-absorbed or self-interested and nurture their grasp of the bigger picture and the larger trends, they are likely to be richly rewarded along this life's journey.

CHALLENGE: **ALLOWING THEIR THINKING TO BE MORE FO-CUSED, STRAIGHTFORWARD, AND RATIONAL**

FULFILLMENT: **LETTING GO OF THE FEAR THAT THEY ARE MERELY DILETTANTES**

NOTABLE: **TODD STOTTLEMEYER (BASEBALL PITCHER)**

CZARINA ALEXANDRA
Wife of Nicholas II

6/6/1872
Gemini II

May 25–June 2

FREEDOM
GEMINI I

Personal success and a measure of worldly recognition may surface quite early in the lives of those born in this week who find themselves on the Way of Translation, yet it may take some time for them to come into their own and display their unique gifts. Overcoming a tendency to be typecast or otherwise pigeonholed in the eyes of the world may well figure into this journey, as will abandoning some defensive attitudes toward being taken seriously. Restlessness may further hamper their ability to cultivate deeper understanding of the issues at hand. Yet if they can manage to focus and train their gifts in some productive way, they have a remarkable ability to put their fingers on the pulse of their times, and their talents for communication will strike chords of real response in the hearts and minds of those around them.

CHALLENGE: **SLOWING DOWN LONG ENOUGH TO PUT THEM-SELVES IN SOMEONE ELSE'S SHOES**

FULFILLMENT: **REACHING NEW LEVELS OF UNDERSTANDING WITH OTHERS**

NOTABLES: **BENNY GOODMAN (JAZZ MUSICIAN; "KING OF SWING"); BROOKE SHIELDS (MODEL; ACTRESS, SUDDENLY SUSAN)**

June 3–10

NEW LANGUAGE
GEMINI II

Originality and a unique style of communication will characterize the life experience of those born in this week who travel the Way of Translation, yet they will face the challenge of developing a broader, less personal view of the world. Learning to leave issues of defensiveness or fear of rejection by the side of the road will lighten and speed their passage here, as will the willingness to surround themselves with those who encourage and support their originality and individuality. There will doubtless be some concerns as to whether developing more refined or popular styles of communication constitutes "selling out" to the establishment or sinking to the lowest common denominator. If these personalities take a longer view and concentrate on developing a body of work, however, rather than a series of single accomplishments, their endurance and evolution are sure to find reward and appreciation along this life's highway.

CHALLENGE: **REALIZING THAT OTHERS CAN'T BE EXPECTED TO AUTOMATICALLY KNOW HOW UNIQUE THEY OR THEIR IDEAS ARE**

FULFILLMENT: **FINDING A WAY OF GETTING THEMSELVES ACROSS TO OTHERS**

NOTABLES: **GLORIA REUBEN (ACTRESS, ER); JESSICA TANDY (ACTRESS; OSCAR FOR DRIVING MISS DAISY)**

ELIZABETH HURLEY
Actress/model,
Austin Powers

6/10/1965
Gemini II

June 11–18

THE SEEKER
GEMINI III

The Seekers born in this week who travel the Way of Translation can experience a fine and fulfilling passage, providing they don't allow their sense of adventure and yearning for broader experience to substitute for developing the knack of a more vernacular and accessible style of communication. Likely to be interested in almost everything, these people may nevertheless find their opinions and views meet with unreasonable resistance or challenge until they settle down a bit and learn to plan their presentations more carefully. Until they do, they can find themselves in and out of a number of difficulties, all of which revolve around their unwillingness to grasp the simple fact that though they can express themselves with an awesome clarity, it does not necessarily guarantee others' understanding of their intentions. Thus, not a little frustration and impatience can be experienced here. Yet if they can learn to listen, analyze, and test the waters as well they they can think and articulate, all is sure to go smoothly if not always predictably.

CHALLENGE: **KEEPING THEIR FOCUS ON THE MATTER AT HAND RATHER THAN DREAMING OF FAR-OFF VISTAS**

FULFILLMENT: **TAKING UP THE CHALLENGE OF FORMULATING THEIR CONCEPTS MORE FULLY**

NOTABLE: **BURL IVES (ACTOR; FOLKSINGER)**

June 19–24

MAGIC
GEMINI–CANCER CUSP

Quick witted, creatively gifted, and insightful, those born on the Cusp of Magic who travel the Way of Translation are likely to realize real reward and fulfillment here, as originality is likely to be tempered with intuition and a fine grasp of the best way to get their ideas across. The principal danger is that these souls will retreat into a world of their own rather than face the higher challenge of effective communication. They may sacrifice genuine creativity and inspiration to the need to be accepted, resulting in a kind of "fake it till you make it," attitude toward success. Unrealistic dreams, a sense of unfulfilled expectation, and the fear of rejection can be problems to address along the way, yet if they reach out in a genuine effort to share their ideas and gifts with the world, they are likely to find not only acceptance, but adulation along this life's journey.

ERROL FLYNN
Adventure movie star,
Zorro

—————
6/20/1909
Gemini–Cancer Cusp

CHALLENGE: **TAPPING INTO THEIR UNIQUE BLEND OF LOGIC AND FEELING TO FIND THE BEST LANGUAGE FOR WHAT THEY HAVE TO SAY**

FULFILLMENT: **SHARING THEIR SENSE OF THE MAGIC AND MYTH IN EVERYDAY LIFE WITH OTHERS**

June 25–July 2

THE EMPATH
CANCER I

Building a bridge to more effective forms of communication may prove difficult at times for the Cancer I on the Way of Translation. Though gifted with extraordinary sensitivity and intuition, the fear of rejection and a hesitance to put either themselves or their ideas on the line may interfere with their growth along this road. Alternatively, they may present themselves in an overly aggressive manner, intent on winning, or at least debating, issues down to the smallest details. Indeed, their conversational styles can sometimes be quite exhausting as they seek to wear down the opposition in much the same fashion as "water weareth away the stone." In any event, a highly emotional quality can color their speech and written communications. Yet if they learn to channel their talents in ways that are less personal, less aggressive, and more universal in scope, they can become fine writers, musicians, and creative communicators of all kinds.

CHALLENGE: **WORKING TO OVERCOME THE DEFENSIVENESS, FEAR, AND ANXIETY OVER BEING ACCEPTED THAT EXISTS AT THEIR VERY CORE**

FULFILLMENT: **FINDING A SYMBOLIC LANGUAGE TO EXPRESS THEIR DEEP WELLS OF FEELING**

July 3–10

THE UNCONVENTIONAL
CANCER II

Originality can go to extremes for those born in this week who find themselves on the Way of Translation, and some may find this an especially challenging, if not downright arduous, journey. Here, strong and often brilliant creative ideas and impulses can either simmer for years on mental back burners without ever finding real outlets, or will be expressed in rather impassioned and aggressive bursts of enthusiasm that fail to find a hearing. Cancer II's may succumb to some of their own darker impulses as a certain fascination with sometimes unsavory people, practices, and substances can all surface here. Yet if they can come to terms with the need to control their own fantasies and to direct their prodigious creative and communicative gifts in a more effective fashion, the rewards of self-discipline and a positive direction for their will to win is sure to be found somewhere along this karmic path.

LISA RINNA
Actress, *Melrose Place*

—————
7/11/1965
Cancer III

CHALLENGE: **LEARNING HOW TO MANIFEST THEIR LARGER VISIONS AND VIVID FANTASIES IN THE WORLD OF FORM**

FULFILLMENT: **PUTTING THEIR ATTRACTION TO THE UNUSUAL IN A LANGUAGE OTHERS CAN UNDERSTAND**

NOTABLE: **ADOLPHUS BUSCH (BREWER; DEVELOPED A BEER BOTTLE THAT COULD WITHSTAND ALL TEMPERATURES)**

July 11–18

THE PERSUADER
CANCER III

Those born in the Week of the Persuader can realize great success along this karmic path providing they take care to cultivate a more objective, and less self-interested view of the world. Coming to terms with their own originality and uniqueness may figure prominently into this life's journey, and some here may waste their energies in merely trying to conform, when they would do better to actively advance their own ideas and projects. Approval seeking and simple defensiveness can also be stumbling blocks here. Yet if they can cultivate their unique communicative talents in such ways as to tone down their directness with diplomacy, their ambition with patience, and their passion with a greater degree of empathy for others, all can go brilliantly along this life's journey.

CHALLENGE: **STANDING FIRM IN HOW THEY VIEW THINGS AND WHAT THEY THINK**

FULFILLMENT: **USING THEIR GIFT FOR OBSERVATION IN ORDER TO MIMIC HOW OTHERS PRESENT THEIR IDEAS**

July 19–25

OSCILLATION
CANCER–LEO CUSP

The verbally gifted people born on the Cusp of Oscillation who travel the Way of Translation can be rather touchy when it comes to the simple give and take of interpersonal communication. They can be highly resistant to others' input or opinions, and may become quite alienated and even angry if their ideas are not met with the warm reception they feel they deserve. Others of this type will manifest their originality in a tendency to megalomania, and can hinder their higher development by refusing to admit mistakes or to accept that a measure of rejection comes as part and parcel of being an original. Yet if they can manage to control their more aggressive side, and cultivate self-confidence apart from the opinions of others, they will discover that the most brilliant communicators among us know how to listen as well as they know how to speak.

CHALLENGE: **NOT RETREATING INTO ANGER WHEN THEY FEEL MISUNDERSTOOD**

FULFILLMENT: **INVOKING THEIR MORAL COURAGE IN REACHING OUT TO OTHERS**

NOTABLES: **DAVID BELASCO (ACTOR; DRAMATIST; PRODUCER); ILIE NASTASE (ROMANIAN TENNIS PLAYER)**

KENNETH STARR
Lawyer/judge,
independent counsel
investigated President
Clinton

7/21/1946
Cancer–Leo Cusp

July 26–August 2

AUTHORITY
LEO I

Leo I's can realize tremendous success and personal accomplishment along the Way of Translation, providing they take care not to fall into the trap of believing that they have a corner on truth, or that theirs is the only way of doing things. The impulse to impose their ideas and beliefs on others is very strong here, and most will have a healthy dose of personal ambition to accompany their sometimes startlingly original concepts and ways of thinking. There is much about this configuration to suggest that these individuals will have a fine grasp of philosophical and spiritual precepts. If they are careful to align themselves with a larger and more universal sense of faith and seek validation for their ideas, more than for their identity, all can go beautifully along this karmic path.

CHALLENGE: **LOOSENING THEIR EGO'S GRIP IN IDENTIFYING WITH THEIR IDEAS**

FULFILLMENT: **COMMUNICATING THEIR LOVE OF PRINCIPLE AND HIGH IDEALS IN A SIMPLER, LESS AGGRESSIVE FASHION**

August 3–10

BALANCED STRENGTH
LEO II

Even geniuses make mistakes, and those born in this week who travel the Way of Translation may well experience the truth of that statement at more than one point along this karmic path, as once they have set themselves on a given course of action, it can be difficult for them to change their minds. Characterized by great personal determination and diligence, these souls may nevertheless have to learn to be less emotionally invested in their plans, inspirations, and projects, and above all to learn greater flexibility—both in their mental processes, and in their interactions with others. Yet if they can manage to steer clear of the need for ego gratification, and stay in touch with their considerable intuition and natural sense of timing, they are unlikely to make too many wrong turns along this road.

CHALLENGE: **RELAXING THE RIGIDITY OF THEIR APPROACH AND THE DEFENSIVENESS OF THEIR ATTITUDE**

FULFILLMENT: **ENJOYING THE FACT THAT OTHERS APPRECIATE THEM FOR THEIR BALANCED VIEWPOINT**

NOTABLES: **IAN ANDERSON (LEAD SINGER, JETHRO TULL); LONI ANDERSON (ACTRESS); SHIRLEY JACKSON (PHYSICIST; 1ST BLACK FEMALE TO EARN PH.D. AT MIT)**

HELEN MIRREN
British actress

7/26/1946
Leo I

August 11–18

LEADERSHIP
LEO III

Leo III's who travel the Way of Translation will have the kind of creativity and originality that has an almost mythic aspect, though these souls will nevertheless have to take care not to allow success to go to their heads, or to become overbearing or domineering in their attempts to share their inspirations with the world. Developing a less high-handed approach and a more common touch in their interpersonal communications will help a great deal, as will developing a more user-friendly style in management or administration. Above all, they will do well to view their own talents with a touch of humility, and to keep in mind the words of author Walter Mizner: "A good listener is not only popular everywhere, but after awhile he knows something."

CHALLENGE: **ATTEMPTING TO BECOME MORE APPROACHABLE AND OPEN TO OTHERS' IDEAS**

FULFILLMENT: **FINDING A FORMAT TO SHARE THEIR PHILOSOPHICAL PERSPECTIVES WITH A BROADER AUDIENCE**

NOTABLES: **JIM WEBB (COMPOSER); SUSAN SAINT JAMES (ACTRESS, MCMILLAN AND WIFE)**

August 19–25

EXPOSURE
LEO–VIRGO CUSP

Those born on the Cusp of Exposure who travel the Way of Translation are likely to be quite brilliant, yet rather difficult to fathom. Blessed with a unique talent for communication and interaction, they may have less difficulty with their ability to express themselves than some on this path, yet considerably more difficulty when it comes to their tendency to dissemble, obfuscate the issues, or otherwise manipulate the information. No matter how gifted they are as speakers and orators, people will find them difficult to trust, perhaps due to the fact that Leo–Virgos rarely tell all they know. High-handedness can be a problem, and they may be quite unwilling to reveal their best ideas, inspirations, or creative endeavors to those they feel are unworthy or unable to understand. Yet when they find the courage to stand on the strength of their ideas, rather than their charms, they reveal themselves to be inspiring individuals whose messages are made more meaningful by virtue of their accessibility and truth.

DAME AGATHA CHRISTIE
English mystery writer,
Murder on the Orient Express

9/15/1890
Virgo III

CHALLENGE: **TRYING TO COUCH THEIR LANGUAGE IN THE VERNACULAR OF THEIR TIME**
FULFILLMENT: **COMING TO UNDERSTAND THAT THERE IS NOTHING WRONG WITH THEM**
NOTABLES: **DAWN STEEL (PRODUCER; FILM EXECUTIVE); CONNIE CHUNG (TV JOURNALIST)**

August 26–September 2

SYSTEM BUILDERS
VIRGO I

Virgo I's may find themselves highly resistant to many of the challenges implied along the Way of Translation, especially when they allow their feelings of rejection and need for acceptance to become entangled with their more creative thoughts and impulses. In fact, these individuals may be unaware of how original their thoughts and inspirations are, and thus be confused when their ideas fail to gain immediate acceptance within established structures or institutions. Though their impulse to serve others is quite strong, it may thus fail to find an outlet, until Virgo I's hit upon the right way to present themselves to the world. Overcoming undue modesty or self-consciousness will be especially important here, as will the willingness to compromise. Yet if they can cultivate greater flexibility and set aside the need for validation, they can find great success and accomplishment, though it will doubtless be more of a process of slow building than of becoming overnight sensations.

CHALLENGE: **UTILIZING THEIR IMPULSE TO SERVE AS AN IMPETUS TO COOPERATE MORE FULLY WITH OTHERS**
FULFILLMENT: **DISCOVERING HOW TO STRUCTURE THEIR APPROACH SO THAT IT IS BETTER RECEIVED**
NOTABLE: **LESTER YOUNG (INNOVATIVE JAZZ SAXOPHONIST)**

September 3–10

THE ENIGMA
VIRGO II

The people born in the Week of the Enigma who travel the Way of Translation may encounter any number of issues and crises that revolve around their own carefully constructed public images. Though their lightning-fast wits and amazing verbal talents may well dazzle slower minds, and their powers of observation and analysis are truly formidable, they can hide their lights under a bushel in the interest of gaining acceptance and approval from the mainstream. Though a tendency to overcriticism or cynicism may appear in some of these individuals, others will find themselves caught in futile attempts to conform. Yet as they gain in confidence, they will feel less need to repress their own original impulses and inspirations in the interest of toeing the line or following the rules. Thus, learning to fearlessly display their more original and natural side will be of paramount importance here.

OLIVER STONE
Film director/writer,
Platoon, JFK; Oscar winner

9/15/1946
Virgo III

CHALLENGE: **DESISTING IN THEIR INNATE TENDENCY TO CREATE ELABORATE DEFENSES THAT ONLY KEEP THEIR REAL MEANING HIDDEN**
FULFILLMENT: **BEING WILLING TO SHARE THEIR MORE PROFOUND OR ESOTERIC NOTIONS**
NOTABLES: **FREDDIE MERCURY (LEAD SINGER, QUEEN); BILLY PRESTON (KEYBOARDIST; FEATURED WITH THE BEATLES)**

September 11–18

THE LITERALIST
VIRGO III

The individuals born in this week who navigate the challenges of the Way of Translation are blessed with an innate ability to hang in there for the duration—a quality that is bound to serve them well along this karmic path. An unusual combination of genuine originality and a grounded, practical approach is likely to insure that their gifts will come to fruition, and that their talents will not go unrecognized. There is a danger, however, that these dauntless souls may succumb to ruthlessness or some rather judgmental attitudes as they achieve success. Yet here the will to win is mitigated by modesty, and an ability to get to the bottom line. If they hone their creative and communicative talents in such a way as to effectively get their points across without too much emotion or undue oratory, so much the better.

CHALLENGE: **COMPROMISING THEIR POSITIONS OR VIEWPOINTS MORE OFTEN**
FULFILLMENT: **EXPERIENCING AN EASIER GIVE-AND-TAKE WITH OTHERS**
NOTABLE: **TOMMY LEE JONES (ACTOR, *THE FUGITIVE*)**

September 19–24
BEAUTY
VIRGO–LIBRA CUSP

Great idealism and sensitivity can make those born on the Cusp of Beauty blessed with unique verbal and communicative talents, yet they will nevertheless have to avoid a predisposition to long-windedness or "purple prose" in order to be most effective here. On the one hand, they can simply be the kind of people who fall in love with the sounds of their own voices; on the other, verbal skill can be expressed in a tendency to dissemble, evade, or otherwise obscure their meanings. Yet there is the prospect of great success here, especially as they free themselves from their fears of what others may think, and direct their talents to the expression of a wealth of original and creative ideas—and not merely use them as means to pull the wool over others' eyes.

JOHN PRINE
Storytelling songwriter,
"Bruised Orange"

10/10/1946
Libra II

CHALLENGE: **RELEASING THEIR MORE INTELLECTUAL PRE-TENSIONS OR AIRS IN FAVOR OF A COMMON TOUCH**
FULFILLMENT: **FINDING THE BRIDGE TO OTHERS FOR COMMUNICATING THEIR DEEP PASSION FOR BEAUTY**
NOTABLE: **JELLY ROLL MORTON (LEGENDARY JAZZ PIANIST)**

September 25–October 2
THE PERFECTIONIST
LIBRA I

Those born in the Week of the Perfectionist who travel the Way of Translation are blessed with amazing talent, considerable ambition, and the simple ability to get things done. Likely to be more flexible than might otherwise be the case, they can find great fulfillment here, providing they overcome some daunting personal insecurities and learn to better go with the flow. Opinionated and often downright argumentative, they will have little trouble getting their points across, but will run the risk of alienating or offending others until they hone the necessary diplomatic skills and a much needed sense of humor. Yet their great thirst for recognition and a solid sense of personal ambition are likely to be grounded in good organizational skills and an ability to keep up with the details. If they are careful to develop their more social impulses and keep their more abrasive tendencies under control, they are sure to make real progress along the Way of Translation.

CHALLENGE: **JUDGING THEMSELVES LESS WHEN OTHERS FAIL TO GRASP THEIR POINT**
FULFILLMENT: **USING HUMOR TO REACH OUT SOCIALLY**
NOTABLES: **GROUCHO MARX (COMEDIAN, MARX BROTHERS); CHRISTINE TODD WHITMAN (NEW JERSEY GOVERNOR)**

October 3–10
SOCIETY
LIBRA II

The fun loving attitude and social disposition of those born in the Week of Society will prove an enormous asset as they travel the Way of Translation. Here, natural diplomatic talent does much to mitigate some rather abrasive tendencies, while real originality is unlikely to be lost or obscured by the fear of rejection. Thus, there is little that can go wrong, save for a tendency to scatter their energies. These people can have such a wealth of plans and projects that they fail to bring their most cherished ambitions to satisfying fruition and they can fall down in their abilities to prioritize. Yet these souls are amazingly talented and further blessed with a will to win that is neither overbearing nor unduly combative. With only a modicum of focus and a little bit of luck, these individuals are likely to make their marks in great style along this karmic path.

CHALLENGE: **TAKING CARE TO PRESENT THEIR EMOTIONAL NEEDS OR DESIRES IN AS STRAIGHTFORWARD A MANNER AS POSSIBLE**
FULFILLMENT: **SERVING AS CHANNELS FOR LARGER ISSUES**
NOTABLES: **AIMEE SEMPLE MCPHERSON (EVANGELIST); EDDIE RICKENBACKER (AVIATOR; WON MEDAL OF HONOR); BEN VEEREN (ACTOR/ENTERTAINER, *ROOTS*)**

DWIGHT D. EISENHOWER
34th president; supreme commander of the Allied invasion of Normandy leading to German surrender in WWII

10/14/1890
Libra III

October 11–18
THEATER
LIBRA III

Those born in the Week of Theater who travel the Way of Translation may struggle to tone down a sometimes overly dramatic or even outrageous personal image before they can realize the higher degrees of creative fulfillment, versatility, and recognition promised here. Brilliant communicators by nature, they will be challenged to bring their ideas to the fore, and not simply bowl others over in attempts to gain acceptance and personal recognition. Though gifted with considerably more confidence in their own abilities than some of their fellow travelers, they may nevertheless fall prey to hyperbole at the expense of content. Still, if they do not succumb to the impulse to blame others for their own shortcomings or wallow in feelings of being misunderstood or misinterpreted, they can make their marks on the world with a rare and unusual talent for making themselves heard.

CHALLENGE: **REINING IN THEIR MORE DRAMATIC IMPULSES IN ORDER TO GET THEIR POINTS ACROSS BETTER**
FULFILLMENT: **HAVING FOUND THE RIGHT PLATFORM FOR THEIR IDEAS, BEING HEARD BY A LARGER AUDIENCE**
NOTABLES: **LILLIE LANGTRY (ACTRESS; MISTRESS TO KING EDWARD VII); SUZANNE SOMERS (ENTREPRENEUR; ACTRESS, *THREE'S COMPANY*)**

October 19–25
DRAMA AND CRITICISM
LIBRA–SCORPIO CUSP

Emotional insecurity and poor self-image can contribute to a tendency to be hypercritical of others, and the souls born in this week who travel the Way of Translation should avoid personal defensiveness, or a penchant for building themselves up by tearing others down. Nevertheless, these individuals are likely to be blessed with some unique talents and the ability to express their ideas volubly and well. Diplomacy and refinement of their verbal skills will prove the key to their success however, since temperamental and combative tendencies can be somewhat exacerbated here. Yet if they can channel their sense of ambition in constructive ways and maintain a fearless attitude toward failure, they can find astonishing success along this exciting, if somewhat controversial life's journey.

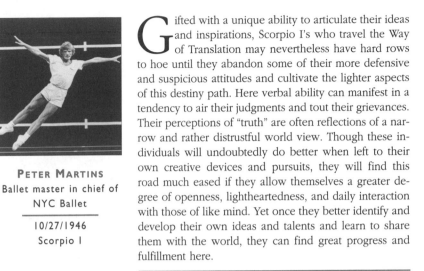

PETER MARTINS
Ballet master in chief of
NYC Ballet
10/27/1946
Scorpio I

CHALLENGE: **UNDERSTANDING THAT, SOMETIMES, THE SHEER PASSION OF THEIR CONVICTIONS UNDERMINES THEIR PRESENTATIONS**
FULFILLMENT: **PUTTING THEIR PENCHANT FOR DRAMA TO USE IN CRAFTING APPEALS FOR SUPPORT**
NOTABLE: **FLOYD BENNETT (AVIATOR, WITH ADMIRAL BYRD, 1ST FLIGHT TO NORTH POLE)**

October 26–November 2
INTENSITY
SCORPIO I

Gifted with a unique ability to articulate their ideas and inspirations, Scorpio I's who travel the Way of Translation may nevertheless have hard rows to hoe until they abandon some of their more defensive and suspicious attitudes and cultivate the lighter aspects of this destiny path. Here verbal ability can manifest in a tendency to air their judgments and tout their grievances. Their perceptions of "truth" are often reflections of a narrow and rather distrustful world view. Though these individuals will undoubtedly do better when left to their own creative devices and pursuits, they will find this road much eased if they allow themselves a greater degree of openness, lightheartedness, and daily interaction with those of like mind. Yet once they better identify and develop their own ideas and talents and learn to share them with the world, they can find great progress and fulfillment here.

CHALLENGE: **BEING LESS JUDGMENTAL AND CRITICAL IN THE INTEREST OF COOPERATION AND FAIRNESS**
FULFILLMENT: **PERSUADING OTHERS OF THEIR LARGER VISIONS**
NOTABLES: **IVAN REITMAN (DIRECTOR/PRODUCER, STRIPES, GHOSTBUSTERS); PAT SAJAK (GAME SHOW HOST, WHEEL OF FORTUNE)**

November 3–11
DEPTH
SCORPIO II

The individuals born in this week who find themselves on the Way of Translation can sometimes manifest some rather bizarre or downright peculiar inclinations. But even if they are the proverbial boy or girl next door, there is bound to be something different about them, and they may find this road difficult until they learn a greater willingness to open up and share their uniqueness with the world. Though their thoughts and emotions are likely to run much deeper than some others' along this path, they will nonetheless display a more engaging and social aspect than many of their Scorpio cousins born in this week. Thus, there exists the probability of great success along the road, and though it may take them a while to come to terms with the facts of their own accomplishments, real happiness can be theirs in the course of time.

SALLY FIELD
Actress, *Places in the Heart*
11/6/1946
Scorpio II

CHALLENGE: **FEELING LESS CONCERNED ABOUT WHETHER OTHERS LIKE OR ACCEPT THEM**
FULFILLMENT: **SHARING THEIR FEELINGS IN A MANNER THAT OTHERS CAN RELATE TO**
NOTABLES: **ROBERT MAPPLETHORPE (CONTROVERSIAL PHOTOGRAPHER); GRAM PARSONS (SINGER/SONGWRITER; BLENDED COUNTRY AND ROCK)**

November 12–18
CHARM
SCORPIO III

The individuals born in the Week of Charm who travel this path of destiny are among those who can also enjoy a fine degree of accomplishment, and the realization of some personal dreams. But again, originality and the sharing of their own inspirations through effective communication may take a backseat to a more comfortable and/or conventional lifestyle. Yet here aggression is tempered by marvelous diplomatic skills and some fine organizational talents that enable them to be excellent serving at the helms of projects or whole companies, or otherwise in the center of the action. Perhaps their principal pitfall will lie in their self-sufficiency. Believing themselves to be realistic, they can unnecessarily cut themselves off from those who would most support their efforts, resulting in loneliness and the extremes of cynicism.

CHALLENGE: **RELYING LESS ON EMOTIONAL MANIPULATION AND MORE ON STRAIGHTFORWARD DISCUSSION AND NEGOTIATION TO ACHIEVE THEIR AIMS**
FULFILLMENT: **HEALING THE DEEP-SEATED HURT THEY FEEL FOR NOT FITTING IN**
NOTABLE: **CHRIS DREJA (ORIGINAL MEMBER, THE YARDBIRDS)**

November 19–24
REVOLUTION
SCORPIO–SAGITTARIUS CUSP

Excitability and sheer aggression can be the principal stumbling blocks for those born in this week who travel the Way of Translation. Though they will never lack for inspiration, and can be counted upon to have unique visions of the world, their interactions with others can be characterized by a great deal of grandstanding, combativeness, and long-winded debate. They attempt to impose their ideas on others, not through the clarity or grace of their verbal presentation, but rather through sheer force of will. Moreover, change can be embraced more for its own sake, than for its tangible benefits. Yet if they take care to focus their prodigious energies and keep in mind that the higher task is not simply to express themselves, but to make themselves understood, the road ahead is bound to be an adventurous and exciting one.

CHALLENGE: **FORCING THEMSELVES DOWN OFF THEIR HIGH HORSES**

FULFILLMENT: **CONVINCING OTHERS OF THEIR REVOLUTIONARY APPROACH**

NOTABLE: **DUANE ALLMAN (GUITARIST; MEMBER OF THE ALLMAN BROTHERS BAND)**

CHARLES DE GAULLE
French general and 1st
president of 5th Republic
———
11/22/1890
Scorpio–Sagittarius Cusp

November 25–December 2
INDEPENDENCE
SAGITTARIUS I

Coming to terms with the fact that real independence and originality don't depend on validation from others is likely to be the principal task of those born in this week who find themselves on the Way of Translation. Yet once they come to terms with that much, Sagittarius I's are likely to find considerable fulfillment along this road. Though there are some of this type who may squander their energies in needless rebellion or unimportant contretemps with authority, most others will pursue their ambitions with tremendous willpower, sustained effort, and amazing endurance. Making themselves understood often amounts to a moral crusade for these people, and it is that quality alone that will lend integrity to their messages and communications and color their interactions with those around them with both honesty and inspiration. If they can avoid the tendency to be entangled in too much debate, long-winded discourse, or the simple need to win at any cost, their success is all but assured along this karmic path.

CHALLENGE: **NOT RETREATING TO THEIR OWN INNER WORLD WHEN OTHERS FAIL TO UNDERSTAND THEM**

FULFILLMENT: **FINDING COMFORT IN THE COMMONALITY OF CERTAIN MORAL VALUES AND HIGHER STANDARDS**

NOTABLE: **GAETANO DONIZETTI (ITALIAN COMPOSER)**

December 3–10
THE ORIGINATOR
SAGITTARIUS II

Learning the fine art of overcoming their personal defensiveness in the interest of putting their unique ideas and vision before others is critical to the success of those born in the Week of the Originator who travel the Way of Translation. Yet once they come to comprehend that the key to their success lies not in changing their natural energy, but simply in directing it through improved communication, all is likely to go brilliantly along this road. Overcoming insecurity can still prove a heavy burden for many of these souls, and the task of sharing their inner selves with others can be considerably more difficult than it sounds. Yet their extroverted and passionate souls will at some point demand effective expression. Then the task of keeping their originality under wraps may prove to be much more difficult than learning to voice their own opinions better and to stand up for those things that inspire and illuminate their world view.

CHALLENGE: **RECOGNIZING THAT THEIR AGGRESSIVENESS IS MERELY A MASK FOR INSECURITY AND DEFENSIVENESS AND THAT IT ONLY SERVES TO ALIENATE OTHERS**

FULFILLMENT: **SURROUNDING THEMSELVES WITH LOVED ONES WHO UNDERSTAND THEM**

NOTABLE: **JOHN MURRAY (FATHER OF AMERICAN UNIVERSALISM)**

JOSEPH HENRY
Invented electromagnetic
telegraph
———
12/17/1797
Sagittarius III

December 11–18
THE TITAN
SAGITTARIUS III

Here is another of the configurations in which the individuals are blessed with such original vision and talent that it seems the vision is tinged with an almost mythic quality. Those born in the Week of the Titan who travel the Way of Translation can find wonderful success and enlightenment, providing they avoid the tendency to take themselves too seriously. Ego can be rather inflated here, and a hidden insecurity may prove their undoing, especially if they allow their sense of worth to be determined by what others may think of them, rather than by what they think of themselves. Surrounding themselves with those who will indulge their tendencies to extravagance, yet enable them to refine their communicative style will prove especially helpful, as will an ability to avoid mere debate in the interest of real dialogue.

CHALLENGE: **EXAMINING THE SOURCE OF THEIR SECRET YET ENORMOUS INSECURITY**

FULFILLMENT: **OPERATING MORE ON THE LEVEL OF THE COMMON MAN TO COMMUNICATE THEIR VISION**

NOTABLE: **EDWIN ARMSTRONG (ENGINEER; INVENTOR; HIS WORK IN RADIO FREQUENCY MODULATION ELIMINATED STATIC)**

KARMIC PATH
35

December 19–25
PROPHECY
SAGITTARIUS–CAPRICORN CUSP

The only real challenge for those born in this week who travel the Way of Translation will lie in their willingness to communicate their ideas with others. Not much hindered by either a fear of rejection or a deep need for acceptance, many of these people will nevertheless be inclined to keep much of their uniqueness to themselves, thus failing the challenge to refine and employ their unusual, intuitive, and often amazingly inspired communicative gifts. Though not much inclined to the more combative tendencies indicated for some of their fellow travelers along this road, they are quite capable of turning a cold shoulder to those who don't readily understand them. Still these thoroughly original and even eccentric people are likely to do well here, especially when they lighten up a bit, avoid the traps of pure self-absorption, and maintain a variety of friends and interests.

CHALLENGE: **FORCING THEMSELVES TO AT LEAST ATTEMPT TO EXPRESS THE KNOWLEDGE THEIR PSYCHIC ABILITY GIVES THEM**

FULFILLMENT: **BUILDING BRIDGES OF HARMONY AND CO-OPERATION**

JUDITH KRANTZ
Author, *Scruples*

———

1/9/1928
Capricorn II

December 26–January 2
THE RULER
CAPRICORN I

Rulers who are born to the Way of Translation will doubtless be gifted with more original vision than many of their fellow Capricorns, yet they will nevertheless encounter some obstacles along this journey. Though the potential for finding practical outlets for their ideas is very pronounced here, they can rigorously repress their own uniqueness for many years in the interest of conforming to more conventional attitudes in an attempt to gain acceptance and career success. Still, maturity will tinge their creative efforts with lasting value, and if they learn not to be quite so hard on themselves and others, and to simply lighten up a bit, they will make tremendous strides along the way. Finding the balance between emotional detachment and mere repression will be especially important to their development, as will the process of discovering simple faith in their own abilities. If they can come to terms with the idea that winning does not always involve a battle, achievement can be theirs.

CHALLENGE: **NOT SUPPRESSING THEIR IDEAS AS MUCH AS CLOTHING THEM IN THE VERNACULAR OF THE DAY**

FULFILLMENT: **CREATING SOCIAL NETWORKS AND HARMONIOUS WORK TEAMS**

January 3–9
DETERMINATION
CAPRICORN II

Again, the struggle to conform or to gain acceptance from those around them can exist at decided odds with a sense of their own originality for those born in the Week of Determination who travel the Way of Translation. Many of these personalities may falter a bit on this path before they free themselves of the need to be like everybody else and develop the strength of their talents and convictions. Though many of these souls will show truly eccentric streaks, they can learn to turn them to their advantage through resilience, resourcefulness, and ever-increasing charm. Overcoming a kind of ugly duckling self-image and learning to acquaint themselves with their strengths rather than their weaknesses will be their principal lesson here. Yet once they learn it, the impulse to express themselves should not be long in following, and their astute insights, their sharp wits, and grasp of the simpler forms of social grace will all serve them wonderfully well along this road.

CHALLENGE: **RIPPING OFF THE MASK OF AUTHORITARIANISM AND DETERMINATION THAT HIDES THEIR INNER FEAR**

FULFILLMENT: **MEETING OTHERS HALFWAY**

NOTABLES: **ZULFIKAR ALI BHUTTO (PAKISTANI PRIME MINISTER; EXECUTED); W. M. KIPLINGER (FOUNDED KIPLINGER WASHINGTON EDITORS, INC.)**

WILLIAM PETER BLATTY
Author, *The Exorcist;*
wrote and produced the
film based on his novel

———

1/7/1928
Capricorn II

January 10–16
DOMINANCE
CAPRICORN III

Capricorn III's who travel the Way of Translation can find this journey uncomfortable and difficult until they overcome some of their more defensive attitudes and learn to open up and share their opinions and ideas with the rest of the world. Though much better planners and more highly organized than some others on this path, they can hold themselves back from the kinds of achievement and recognition they deserve through their own highly self-protective attitudes. Though there is much about this configuration to indicate that they will always be the kind of people who never tell all they know, they can nevertheless find success here, providing they come to better understand that flexibility and tolerance are the keys to their success, and that genius is never a liability.

CHALLENGE: **NOT HIDING THEIR WISDOM FOR FEAR OF REJECTION**

FULFILLMENT: **REALIZING THE VALUE OF THOSE WHO KNOW AND LOVE THEM**

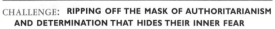

January 17–22

MYSTERY AND IMAGINATION
CAPRICORN–AQUARIUS CUSP

Blessed with a talent for the theoretical, conceptual, and abstract modes of thought, the individuals born on this cusp who travel the Way of Translation will doubtless find unique outlets for their unusual brand of creativity and originality. Yet there is an equal possibility that they will squander their energies in an abundance of talk that is backed up with very little in the way of substantive effort. At their core, however, they have fine reserves of humor and a lighthearted attitude toward personal troubles that can serve them extremely well. Though they will doubtless experience a number of emotional ups and downs and will have to guard against the demons of aggression and unrest, there is nonetheless the possibility of great success along this road as they learn to express themselves better and to use their considerable talents in ways that can serve to inspire many.

CHALLENGE: **MODERATING THE EXTREMES OF THEIR APPROACH IN ORDER TO BETTER REACH PEOPLE OF ORDINARY CONCERNS.**

FULFILLMENT: **USING HUMOR TO PROMOTE UNDERSTANDING**

NOTABLE: **VIDAL SASSOON (HAIRSTYLIST; FOUNDER AND CHAIRMAN, VIDAL SASSOON INC.)**

DESMOND MORRIS
Zoologist; writer; studied
human behavior,
The Naked Ape
─────────
1/24/1928
Aquarius I

January 23–30

GENIUS
AQUARIUS I

Those born in the Week of Genius who travel the Way of Translation can experience a fine and fulfilling passage, providing they learn to communicate their ideas in such a way that others can readily understand their value. These naturally independent souls are blessed with fine dispositions for ideas and abstractions yet may fail the higher challenge implied here when they allow themselves to become impatient or intolerant of slower minds and slower wits than their own. Though they are unlikely to fall victim to an overly personalized view of the world, their ego issues can nevertheless cause them to retreat into ivory towers of theory or speculation when their ideas fail to find a hearing. Yet there is potential for the highest success here and if they refine their communicative style in such a way that it never loses the common touch, all can go brilliantly along this path.

CHALLENGE: **GROUNDING SOME OF THEIR GENIUS IN MORE ORDINARY TERMS**

FULFILLMENT: **FINDING THE SELF-WORTH TO TRULY PROCLAIM WHAT THEY KNOW**

January 31–February 7

YOUTH AND EASE
AQUARIUS II

Much of the genuine originality and inspiration that are the gifts of this path may take a backseat to Aquarius II's overriding need for acceptance as they travel the Way of Translation. Yet there is nonetheless the potential for great recognition and accomplishment here, and they will doubtless have an easier time of things than many who travel this road. Vulnerability may be their biggest stumbling block and they will have to work hard to free themselves from the need for validation from others at the expense of their integrity, as there is a strong inclination to tell people what they want to hear, or even to dissemble with this configuration. They can fall victim to a fear of being able to fulfill others' expectations. Still, when they find within themselves the courage to be unique and divest themselves of the need to be merely popular, their ideas can gain a warm and wide reception along this karmic path.

CHALLENGE: **NOT SACRIFICING THEIR IDEAS OR INTEGRITY FOR FEAR OF ROCKING THE BOAT OR REJECTION**

FULFILLMENT: **TRUSTING IN THEIR INNATE ABILITY TO DO ALL THINGS WELL, EVEN RELATE ON A BASIC, DEEPER LEVEL**

ROGER MUDD
Television journalist, CBS
newscaster
─────────
2/9/1928
Aquarius III

February 8–15

ACCEPTANCE
AQUARIUS III

Gifted with tremendous talents for self-expression, those born in this week will nevertheless have to try to be less abrasive and more diplomatic as they travel the Way of Translation. Though these lively and affectionate people are well suited to the challenges implied here, they will have to develop a more objective and open attitude toward their own ideas in order to be most effective. They can become inordinately defensive and overbearing when misunderstood or misinterpreted and take flight in a careless and even defiant nonattachment to others. Yet if they can stay in touch with their most natural impulses, and develop a real awareness of their own constructive and destructive modes of thinking, and at the same time refuse to get caught up in issues of combativeness, denial or intolerance, their creativity will come to the fore and their unique talents can find the fullest expression here.

CHALLENGE: **DEDICATING THEMSELVES LESS TO SEEKING ACCEPTANCE AND MORE TO ACCEPTING OTHERS**

FULFILLMENT: **APPROACHING THE SEARCH FOR A BETTER WAY TO COMMUNICATE AS A COLORFUL KIND OF GAME**

February 16–22

SENSITIVITY
AQUARIUS–PISCES CUSP

Those born on the Cusp of Sensitivity who travel the Way of Translation are highly original and genuinely creative. Personal touchiness or an aggressive, chip-on-the-shoulder attitude can hinder their higher development, however. These individuals are much prone to feelings of isolation or being misunderstood, and a sense of chronic alienation can be their undoing. Though the impulse toward success and achievement is quite strong, they may fail the higher challenge here by refusing to share themselves with others, refine their communicative style, or to remain open to new ideas and greater flexibility. Keeping their eyes on the larger picture and learning to release old hurts and slights will be especially useful, as will maintaining a sense of humor and greater objectivity in their dealings with others.

CHALLENGE: **TRANSFORMING SENSITIVITY INTO EMPATHY**
FULFILLMENT: **SUCCEEDING IN BRIDGING CHASMS OF MIS-UNDERSTANDING IN BOTH THEIR PERSONAL AND OTHER RELATIONSHIPS**

GABRIEL GARCÍA MÁRQUEZ
Author, *Love in the Time of Cholera*

3/6/1928
Pisces II

February 23–March 2

SPIRIT
PISCES I

Some real social butterflies can show up among those born in the Week of Spirit who travel the Way of Translation. There is some danger, however, that their best ideas may fail to bear fruit if these people succumb to either their fears of rejection or high-handed, superior attitudes. Intense emotionalism can be a stumbling block, and they may well be prone to overreact in the face of ordinary misunderstanding. Cultivating greater objectivity will be key to their success, as will developing a greater awareness of just how big a part their own attitudes play in setbacks and upheavals. Yet if they can manage to effectively organize and prioritize their ideas, and learn to communicate to others in a clear and understandable style, they can realize considerable success along this path, especially in the fields of music or the more creative forms of writing.

CHALLENGE: **LETTING THEIR SPIRITUAL IMPULSES BE THEIR GUIDES AS THEY SEEK BETTER COOPERATION WITH OTHERS**
FULFILLMENT: **WATCHING THE CONFLICT IN THEIR LIVES LESSEN AS THEY DEVELOP MORE STRAIGHTFORWARD APPROACHES TO COMMUNICATING**

March 3–10

THE LONER
PISCES II

Some reclusive tendencies may well interfere with the higher development of those born in the Week of the Loner who travel the Way of Translation. Though likely to be extremely perceptive and able to penetrate to the heart of the matter, they may stumble in their inclination to share their unique and often artistic visions with the rest of the world. Though they are gifted with their share of ambition, and can be quite tough customers when it comes to getting what they want, communicating with others is not likely to be their greatest strength. Hampered by extremes of emotional sensitivity and an often defensive attitude, they may thus retreat into pure self-interest or an impenetrable and antisocial lifestyle. Cultivating a close circle of friends and associates will probably be most helpful here, and though they will never be among the more extroverted of the people who make this life's journey, they need not be the most disappointed.

CHALLENGE: **REALIZING THAT LANGUAGE IS ONLY ONE FORM OF REACHING OUT TO OTHERS**
FULFILLMENT: **LOOKING INWARD TO A HIGHER POWER OR SPIRIT FOR ACCEPTANCE**
NOTABLES: **PIET MONDRIAN (ARTIST; MAJOR INFLUENCE ON PURELY ABSTRACT PAINTERS); JAMES EARL RAY (CONVICTED ASSASSIN OF MARTIN LUTHER KING, JR.)**

EDWARD ALBEE
Pulitzer Prize-winning playwright

3/12/1928
Pisces III

March 11–18

DANCERS AND DREAMERS
PISCES III

Perhaps the greatest danger for those born in the Week of Dancers and Dreamers who travel they Way of Translation will lie in the fact that though they are perceptive and creative in the extreme, they are not likely to be blessed with an equally acute talent for judging other people. As a result, they may misjudge their best friends while seeking approval from those who would like to control or otherwise manipulate them. Cultivating greater objectivity and a less generally dependent attitude will be most beneficial to their development, as will finding the courage and personal strength to stand up for their ideas and conviction—even if it means risking rejection or reprisal. Yet if they refuse to allow their independence to devolve into mere wanderlust, or their great versatility into a shallow view of the world, they can recognize great accomplishment and even a measure of adulation along this life's highway.

CHALLENGE: **INVOKING THEIR GREAT NATURAL EMPATHY TO POSITION WHAT THEY THINK AND FEEL IN A MANNER THAT OTHERS WILL UNDERSTAND**
FULFILLMENT: **BEING A CHANNEL FOR DISSEMINATION OF INFORMATION, WISDOM, AND PHILOSOPHICAL CONSTRUCTS**
NOTABLE: **FRANK BORMAN (ASTRONAUT; CHAIRMAN OF EASTERN AIRLINES)**

The Way of Experience

SAGITTARIUS III TO GEMINI III
The Titan to The Seeker

The individuals born on the Way of Experience are called to open themselves to ordinary experience and the lessons it has to offer. Their destiny is to find themselves in the small things in life. So preoccupied are these ambitious and larger-than-life souls with their goals and mythic ways of living that often they never become acquainted with themselves. Scaling back, opening up, and experiencing life on a more basic level will teach those on this path everything they need to know. It may not be so easy for these men and women to live the simple life since everything they touch tends to take on a fantastic aspect. Keeping romanticism to a minimum, tempering a certain snobbishness, and getting their hands dirty as they join ordinary mortals in the business of living are the goals of this path. As they experience life on its own terms they will begin to know who and what they are and their experience of living will deepen in a wholly wonderful way.

The individuals on this karmic path are born with big personalities. Everything about them is huge: their ideas, their feelings, the way they live, and even their ambitions. Rarely do they do anything on less than a grand scale. When upset, it's an event of volcanic proportions. When depressed, they exist in the blackest of states. If they want something, nothing stops them from getting it. You can find them in the biggest homes and the fanciest cars or producing the most prolific creative output. The trouble is

that none of this bounty makes them especially happy. It all comes easily to them of course, but, eventually, those on this path will start to feel that something is missing. Usually what's missing is them! As imposing as these men and women may appear to the rest of us, the sad truth is that often they are clueless as to who they are or what makes them tick. They are so focused on the more titanic aspects of life that they forget to pay attention to the details, and one of those details is themselves.

It is the destiny of the individuals on this karmic path to redefine their essential selves. Accomplishing this involves embracing as many different experiences as life offers them. For it is in getting to know themselves through these experiences that they will come to better understand their own most basic natures. This karmic path is one of exploration. Testing, probing, trying, and failing will all provide invaluable opportunities for growth. Moreover, it is not necessary for these individuals to travel to faraway places or spend years at universities taking courses in order to experience themselves. Rather, it is in the most ordinary of circumstances and events that those on the Way of Experience will find the most illumination.

The core lesson of this karmic path is for the men and women on it to be as open and available as possible to whatever experience life hands them. There is something of the snob about these individuals, though it is rarely based in anything as conventional as prejudice or

CORE LESSON
To be open to a variety of experiences, no matter how small

GOAL
Redefining who they are

GIFTS
Big-Hearted, Warm, Aspiring

PITFALLS
Egotistical, Insecure, Unaware

status. They simply believe themselves to be inherently superior to others and therefore above it all. They don't like to get their hands dirty, so to speak. But they must if they are to fulfill their destiny. They need to experience what life is like for the ordinary man and to realize that they aren't too different from anyone else. By acknowledging such equality, those on this karmic path gain in their humanity and correspondingly in their humility. The most mundane circumstances can be lessons for them, whether pumping their own gas or riding a bus. In order to permit such scenarios to occur, those on this path must release some of their preconceived notions and relax. Tending to be rather driven and controlling types, they don't often adjust their agendas to make room for the unexpected. This is a path about going with the flow and seeing what life brings. Feeling less tense when something upsets the applecart could be a good start. Developing some natural curiosity about how things work in the workaday world would also be helpful here. Those on this karmic path are meant to seek the god of small things.

Not all individuals on the Way of Experience succeed in meeting its strict demands. Their big personalities tend to have big egos to match and their struggles to rein in their intensely egotistic attitudes can be monumental, with the possibility of failure lurking around every corner. The most successful on this path are able to gradually divest themselves of the ego's false and inflated sense of self and, in the process, build a secure and self-sufficient character little by little, without dramatic statements or precipitous actions. Such a process will be slow and organic, one that grows from being fully present in day-to-day life without huge agendas or the insertion of the mythic into every little detail. A pitfall here is that there is something of the drama queen about these individuals, men and women alike. When things don't go their way, they tend to withdraw to sulk. And what a royal sulk it is. They can stay hidden for weeks completely bogged down in their rage or self-pity or both. The only cure for their moods will be to engage in everyday life again.

Another problem on this path is that those on it tend to be very drawn to magical or ecstatic experiences. As they search for a better sense of self, they must take care not to become involved in cults or other dangerous and escapist activities such as any variety of addictions—alcohol, drugs, sex, and relationship dependencies all pose threats. Keeping their metaphysical yearnings to the more traditional or mundane would be wise. Moreover, though this path calls those on it to give up a measure of control, it does not mean surrendering to addiction. Rather, it is about surrendering to events beyond one's control. Having accepted life's events, those on the Way of Experience may begin to investigate who is in control if not them.

RELEASE

The identification with your image

REWARD

The joy of self-discovery

SUGGESTION

Get to know yourself at a deep level. Develop a more realistic assessment of your abilities. Take care not to become overly involved in your fantasies. Try to live life in terms of the ordinary.

Given that those on this path are called to live in a manner that is more elemental or basic, they may find themselves romanticizing simpler times; for example, becoming enamored with certain periods in history or even fixated on their own youth. Born romantics, those on this path must learn not to forget the present and everyday activities. It is extremely easy for them to become lost in their romantic illusions and fantasies. Sticking to the practical details of life and its responsibilities is important. Though this may seem a contradiction to the idea of being open to experience, the truth is that it is possible to fulfill obligations even while being flexible.

A large part of this karmic path is often conducted inwardly. Seeking on this path means searching within for life's answers and for a sense of self. While life experience provides the stage and opportunities for growth, understanding comes from time spent alone. Much of the work of this path will be in negotiating with the ego's grandiosity to scale back expectations to reasonable levels. The Way of Experience involves the deepening of feeling and thought, rather than an expansion in the magnitude of energies and goals. Quietude is vital to such a process, since by quieting the mind and abandoning a path of trying to impress others, such individuals may at last have the chance to come to peace with themselves and to tap into some of the most profound wellsprings of existence. Forming close friendships and love relationships can be crucial for those on this path to experience the lessons of intimacy. Raising children can prove to be the most illuminating experience of all for those on this path as it will serve to remind them of what really matters. Opening up a whole new world of deeper feelings can be one of the richest and fullest experiences that life has to offer.

What is best for those on this path is to accept the challenge of small, everyday projects, rather than pursuing the daunting difficulty of grandiose dreams and visions. Learning to live each day to the fullest, taking things as they come, moving forward step by gradual step—all of these will prove more than equal to ego-driven, titanic projects in both interest and reward. Adopting a Zen view that no event is any more significant than any other in itself will perhaps be helpful in deflating the grandiosity and megalomania of Sagittarius III origins and bringing things into proper perspective. Learning the small lessons in life—kindness, caring, service, reverence, helpfulness—is all-important for the spiritual development of those on the Way of Experience.

BALANCE POINT

Fantasy and Reality

Often in fairy tales, a monarch is served by a fool or court jester. These figures are actually highly evolved, and serve to remind the king or queen of the wisdom found in simplicity and to warn against overblown ego. The fool card in the tarot is a symbol of opening up all experience and in trusting the process of life. Thus, on the Way of Experience, the impressive individuals found here are called to allow themselves to adopt the role of fool.

CRYSTALS AND GEMSTONES

Seer stones form a window through which an individual can gaze at a miniature interior world. This quartz offers the opportunity to behold the beauty in what is seemingly insignificant.

NOTABLES ON THIS KARMIC PATH

VINCENT VAN GOGH

Dutch painter **Vincent van Gogh** openly admitted the difficulty of grounding himself in a meaningful daily existence apart from his dreams and visions. Yet we see his struggle to relate to ordinary people (a requirement of this karmic path) in both his early paintings of simple peasants and his work as a missionary to Belgian miners. Though he translated his mundane daily experiences into visual masterpieces, this did not make the mediocrity of life any easier for him. Perhaps ultimately van Gogh became lost in his fantasies, with his suicide perhaps betokening his failure to find himself, fulfill his soul, and revel in the commonplace.

Cher not only sounds great but looks terrific too. Though she has reached the heights of fame, Cher has experienced mediocrity as well. Through it all she inadvertently fulfilled her karmic destiny to redefine herself through experience—though in Cher's case the experiences may not be as ordinary as for others. However, Cher has shown her ability to at least play ordinary people in her triumphant acting career, portraying working-class women in films such as *Mask* and *Moon-*

CHER

struck. Despite relationship upheaval and career ups and downs, Cher has indeed taken up the challenge of self-discovery that is her destiny.

Because of his love of achievement and press coverage, businessman **Donald Trump** does not give the impression of someone whose top priority is becoming better acquainted with his inner humanity and the small experiences in life. Whether up

DONALD TRUMP

or down financially, Trump has shown the vigor that springs from passionate desire as well as the ability to forgo attachments and move on. His adherence to his larger-than-life persona does not speak well of his progress on this path and it is hard to say whether he attempts to better understand his inner self, but success on this spiritual path may be limited until he builds an inner life that appears to be less ego-driven.

Other Notables: Robert Johnson, Carl Olof Larsson, Paul Adolph Volcker, Zane Grey, Wallace Stegner, Eudora Welty, Candice Bergen, Reggie Jackson, Herbert Marshall, Barry Manilow, Gilda Radner, Sylvester Stallone, James Whistler, Jamie Wyeth, Linda Ronstadt, Edgar Degas, Andy Warhol, Harry F. Guggenheim, Calista Flockhart, Dwight Gooden, Elizabeth Cady Stanton, Barry Goldwater, Ethel Merman, Princess Stephanie of Monaco, Harry Helmsley, Liza Minnelli

BIRTHDAYS ON KARMIC PATH 36

April 26, 1890–September 13, 1890 | December 6, 1908–April 26, 1909

July 18, 1927–December 6, 1927 | February 27, 1946–July 17, 1946 | October 8, 1964–February 26, 1965

May 21, 1983–October 8, 1983 | December 30, 2001–May 20, 2002 | August 10, 2020–December 29, 2020

KARMIC PATH
36

March 19–24

REBIRTH
PISCES–ARIES CUSP

Those born in this week who travel the Way of Experience may find it a difficult road as it will be rather hard for them to come to terms with the idea that developing greater subtlety, nuance, and appreciation for the details is very much in order. Passions can interfere with good sense here, and an overly romantic or idealistic attitude can further hamper these souls' development. Likely to be motivated by the need to achieve, they are capable of some spectacular accomplishments though they will have to keep themselves open to greater objectivity, a wider variety of ordinary experience, and a more curious and enthusiastic way of dealing with the world. If they remember to embrace the everyday with the same elemental energy with which they see their own goals, life will be more rewarding and their road to redemption considerably eased by immersing themselves in such experiences as family and children.

CHALLENGE: **RECOGNIZING THEIR OWN ELEMENTAL NATURE FOR WHAT IT IS**

FULFILLMENT: **SOFTENING THEIR OVERALL APPROACH TO LIFE AND LOVE**

NOTABLES: **TIMOTHY DALTON (ACTOR, JAMES BOND); CLYDE BARROW (INFAMOUS MURDERER; BONNIE & CLYDE)**

ROBERT LOUIS JOHNSON
CEO BET television

4/8/1946
Aries II

March 25–April 2

THE CHILD
ARIES I

Maintaining their natural enthusiasm and curiosity about people, places, and concepts will be key to the successful navigation of the Way of Experience for those born in this week. A certain naïveté can be both a blessing and a curse with this configuration, however, since their dynamic and spontaneous approach to the world can result in some rather superficial views, and they can be easily seduced into a false set of values. Yet their need to retreat from the fray at given intervals should be encouraged here, since it is in these periods of introspection and reflection that they are most likely to explore the secrets of their own truest natures. Thus renewed, they will be able to face almost any challenge head-on, and if they are careful to balance their enthusiasms with a variety of experience, and to keep their passions grounded in realistic efforts, all well go beautifully along this road.

CHALLENGE: **SEEKING THEMSELVES IN THE MOST FUNDAMENTAL EXPERIENCES**

FULFILLMENT: **SEEING THEMSELVES IN THEIR CHILDREN OR CREATIVE OUTPUT**

April 3–10

THE STAR
ARIES II

Ego issues and the secret conviction that the rest of the world will somehow be unable to get along without them can hinder the journey of self-awareness and broader perspective for those born in the Week of the Star who travel the Way of Experience. Likely to be hugely successful in any event, they may have an unrealistic notion of their own talents and abilities, and will have to cultivate the fine art of taking themselves out of the action, if only to get in better touch with some unfulfilled aspects of their own natures. Frustrations and a sense of unrealized expectation can bring some difficult and irritable qualities to the fore here as well. Yet if they learn to simply calm down, chill out, and get some distance on troubling situations, they will discover the need within themselves for greater depth and subtlety, and will seek out those who can broaden their education accordingly.

CHALLENGE: **WRESTLING WITH THEIR EGOS IN ORDER TO CULTIVATE GREATER HUMILITY AND SIMPLICITY**

FULFILLMENT: **FINDING SUCCESS BY JUST BEING AN "ORDINARY JOE"**

NOTABLES: **BILL KREUTZMANN (ORIGINAL DRUMMER FOR THE GRATEFUL DEAD); CRAIG T. NELSON (ACTOR, COACH)**

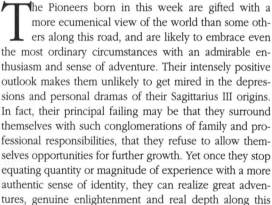

ALBERT "CUBBY" BROCCOLI
Film producer, known for James Bond films

4/5/1909
Aries II

April 11–18

THE PIONEER
ARIES III

The Pioneers born in this week are gifted with a more ecumenical view of the world than some others along this road, and are likely to embrace even the most ordinary circumstances with an admirable enthusiasm and sense of adventure. Their intensely positive outlook makes them unlikely to get mired in the depressions and personal dramas of their Sagittarius III origins. In fact, their principal failing may be that they surround themselves with such conglomerations of family and professional responsibilities, that they refuse to allow themselves opportunities for further growth. Yet once they stop equating quantity or magnitude of experience with a more authentic sense of identity, they can realize great adventures, genuine enlightenment and real depth along this life's journey.

CHALLENGE: **MAKING QUIET TIME FOR INTROSPECTION AND SELF-ANALYSIS**

FULFILLMENT: **ENGAGING IN THE ORDINARY RESPONSIBILITIES OF FAMILY AND FRIENDS**

NOTABLES: **BOBBY VINTON (SINGER); AL GREEN (SOUL SINGER); ED O'NEILL (ACTOR, MARRIED WITH CHILDREN); EUDORA WELTY (WRITER, THE OPTIMIST'S DAUGHTER)**

April 19–24
POWER
ARIES–TAURUS CUSP

Acquiring, establishing, and using their power over others may prove an ultimately unfulfilling experience for those born in this week who travel the Way of Experience. Inclined to pursue their goals with an awesome diligence and zeal, they may nevertheless fail to focus on the need for a more established sense of self and broader experience. Depending upon externals or material possessions to enhance their egos can be a particular failing here as well. Thus, learning to relinquish a certain amount of worldly power in the interest of more variety will doubtless figure prominently in this life's journey. If they can avoid the tendencies to laziness, complacency, and overindulgence and embrace instead the versatility, liveliness, and curiosity that are part of the higher calling here, they can expect not only great accomplishment, but great breadth of understanding along this road.

CHALLENGE: **NOT BEING SEDUCED BY THE GLAMOR AND EGO INFLATION OF POWER**

FULFILLMENT: **ALLOWING LOVE TO CARVE GREATER DEPTH IN THEIR HEARTS**

NOTABLE: **ERICK HAWKINS (MODERN DANCER/CHOREOGRAPHER)**

HEDDA HOPPER
Actress/journalist, gossip
columnist

5/2/1890
Taurus I

April 25–May 2
MANIFESTATION
TAURUS I

A distinct determination to bring even their most far-fetched dreams into concrete reality may mark the journey of those born in this week who navigate the Way of Experience. Yet they will doubtless encounter their shares of obstacles along this path until they better learn to accommodate others into their plans. Stubbornness and an unwillingness to compromise can be problems here. While details and structure are their forte, it will be necessary for them to develop a more flexible approach. Yet if they learn to enjoy the benefits of further education and at the same time suppress their innate abilities to exaggerate their woes and personal troubles, they can find considerable success and accomplishment along this life's journey, as they have both the ability to dream and the skills to see those dreams into realization.

CHALLENGE: **RELEASING THE NEED FOR CONTROL TO PERMIT A GREATER VARIETY OF LIFE EXPERIENCE TO TOUCH THEM**

FULFILLMENT: **FEELING MORE GROUNDED IN THEIR TRUE SELVES**

NOTABLES: **CARL GUSTAV XVI (KING OF SWEDEN; YOUNGEST REIGNING MONARCH); TALIA SHIRE (ACTRESS, *ROCKY*)**

May 3–10
THE TEACHER
TAURUS II

High ambition and lofty goals may characterize those born in the Week of the Teacher who travel the Way of Experience, yet they may have to come down to earth and cultivate more practicality if they are to find success. Likely to be didactic and often overbearing, they will have to work hard to see others' points of view and cultivate the openness to new ideas indicated here. The impulse toward ever-expanding horizons is especially strong, and there is much to indicate that these souls may do a fair amount of exploring other cultures and countries at some points in their lives. Nevertheless, this can be a fortunate configuration especially as these individuals gain in realism and learn to better appreciate the adventures and fulfillment available in their own backyards. Particularly suited to share their knowledge with others, they will likely shine as teachers, and most especially—parents.

CHALLENGE: **ENGAGING IN COURSES OF STUDY OF THEMSELVES**

FULFILLMENT: **GETTING BACK TO BASICS BY BECOMING TEACHERS OR MENTORS TO OTHERS**

NOTABLES: **DONOVAN (POP SINGER); GREG GUMBEL (NBC SPORTS JOURNALIST)**

CANDICE BERGEN
Actress, *Murphy Brown*

5/9/1946
Taurus II

May 11–18
THE NATURAL
TAURUS III

The fun loving and restless types born in the Week of the Natural who find themselves on the Way of Experience may be somewhat resistant to the challenges here, especially if they allow themselves to be sidetracked by issues of rebellion or undue restlessness. There is much to indicate success, however, as long as they take care to keep their tempers in check and leave their egos at the door. Plagued by insecurity, they may find themselves tied to particular courses of action, even when they themselves have ceased to find them productive or useful, and they can become slaves to habit, despite their love of freedom. If they can avoid obsessions and extremes of emotion, they can realize increasing depth of understanding, personal comfort, and a high degree of enlightenment, and will come to know just what it means to live every day to its fullest.

CHALLENGE: **NOT ALLOWING INSECURITY TO CAUSE THEM TO BUY INTO THEIR EGO'S DEMANDS FOR AGGRANDIZEMENT**

FULFILLMENT: **EXPERIENCING THE FREEDOM OF JUST BEING A PART OF THE FLOW OF LIFE**

NOTABLE: **REGGIE JACKSON (BASEBALL GREAT, MOST NOTABLY WITH YANKEES AND A'S)**

May 19–24

ENERGY
TAURUS–GEMINI CUSP

Though Taurus–Geminis will doubtless enjoy a wonderful degree of accomplishment and recognition for their efforts along this road, they may fail the higher challenge here, especially if they neglect to adequately ground themselves in the details of daily life or succumb to an inflated self-image. Too much energy badly directed can be their biggest stumbling block, and better learning the value of subtlety, the simple pleasures, and the ability to tone down their more grandiose visions in favor of more realistic goals will all prove important to their development. Yet if they simply slow down a bit and allow themselves to take things as they come, rather than trying to make them happen, all will go beautifully along this life's journey, providing they cultivate the qualities of empathy for others and a sense of their own roles in the everyday world,

CHALLENGE: **SLOWING DOWN TO TRULY SAVOR AND REFLECT ON EACH EXPERIENCE THAT COMES THEIR WAY**

FULFILLMENT: **DISCOVERING A GREATER TRUTH ABOUT THEMSELVES THROUGH A MORE THOUGHTFUL APPROACH**

NOTABLES: **BOBBY MURCER (BASEBALL OUTFIELDER, N.Y. YANKEES); HO CHI MINH (VIETNAMESE COMMUNIST LEADER)**

CARL LARSSON
Swedish illustrator/writer

5/28/1853
Gemini I

May 25–June 2

FREEDOM
GEMINI I

Those born in the Week of Freedom who navigate the challenge and promise of the Way of Experience are likely to do extremely well along the road, providing they don't succumb to the need to continually assert themselves, or get mired in fussiness and irritability. Blessed with an unusual degree of personal charisma, a certain combative quality may nevertheless prove their biggest downfall, and they may misuse their energies in trying to bully or manipulate those around them. If they refuse to become cynical, disillusioned, or simply depressed when their plans fail to come to fruition, and keep themselves open to the need to finish what they start, they will doubtless enjoy a wide variety of friends, jobs, and interests in the course of their development along this life's highway.

CHALLENGE: **TAKING FULL ADVANTAGE OF THE VARIETY OF EXPERIENCES THAT COME THEIR WAY RATHER THAN ONLY TOUCHING THEM BRIEFLY**

FULFILLMENT: **ENJOYING THE GREATER INNER PEACE FROM KEEPING IT SIMPLE**

NOTABLE: **RAINER FASSBINDER (GERMAN ACTOR; AUTHOR; DIRECTOR)**

June 3–10

NEW LANGUAGE
GEMINI II

The interesting and compelling people born in the Week of New Language who travel this karmic path may well enjoy this journey, as they are both genuinely talented and much more bighearted than they might be otherwise. Though personal defensiveness may well be a problem, this path imbues them with a greater sense of personal strength and far less fear of appearing foolish or inadequate. Yet these souls will have to keep a weather eye on their fascination with the darker forms of experience and most especially their own tendencies to extremes. They can recognize wonderful fulfillment along this road, especially when they choose to ground themselves with friends and associates whom they can embrace as real peers. Such close associates will be most helpful in refining their creative and communicative talents and assisting them in staying open to the value of life's smaller lessons.

CHALLENGE: **NOT ROMANTICIZING THE DARKER ELEMENTS BY LOOKING DOWN ON MORE BASIC, OR OLD-FASHIONED VALUES**

FULFILLMENT: **LIBERATING THEMSELVES FROM ANY CONCERN ABOUT THEIR IMAGES**

NOTABLE: **FREDDY STONE (MEMBER, SLY AND THE FAMILY STONE)**

BARRY MANILOW
Singer/songwriter,
"I Write the Songs"

6/17/1946
Gemini III

June 11–18

THE SEEKER
GEMINI III

The Seekers who travel the Way of Experience are likely to experience great personal evolution along this karmic path as their natural energies are very much in keeping with the higher tasks indicated here. Sparkling, witty, and not inclined to take themselves too seriously in any event, they will nevertheless have to be mindful of their predisposition to take huge and sometimes rather stupid risks, usually in the name of fun or adventure. For in fact, these individuals are gifted with a fine practical streak, as well as the ability to perceive the big picture. Yet they will have to control their very versatility and cultivate a measure of personal depth and self-understanding before they can realize many of the more substantive rewards offered here. However, they are well suited to the demands of this destiny path, and if they take care to ground themselves with the closer forms of relationship, and cultivate faithfulness and simple patience, all is likely to go well along this road.

CHALLENGE: **SCALING BACK THEIR NEED FOR ADVENTURE**

FULFILLMENT: **KEEPING THE HOME FIRES BURNING**

NOTABLES: **STAN LAUREL (ACTOR; COMEDY TEAM LAUREL & HARDY); EGON SCHIELE (AUSTRIAN EXPRESSIONIST PAINTER)**

KARMIC PATH
36

June 19–24
MAGIC
GEMINI–CANCER CUSP

Personal sensitivity combines with a common touch for those born on the Cusp of Magic who travel the Way of Experience, and there is everything to indicate the highest degree of spiritual enlightenment and a genuine enjoyment of life's rich experiences here. Likely to be both enchanting and inspirational people, their greatest pitfall will lie in an excess of idealism, most especially romantic idealism. Though they can yearn to connect with a soulmate, lover, marriage or business partner, they can also consider themselves a bit too good for anyone. Climbing down from their self-erected pedestals from time to time will be especially useful, as will the willingness to join with others in common efforts. And while applying their natural objectivity to themselves and developing a greater willingness to admit to some normal human failings may come hard for some of this group, as a whole they are likely to find considerable success on this road.

JAMIE WYETH
Painter/member of art
dynasty, realistic style,
Portrait of a Pig

7/6/1946
Cancer II

CHALLENGE: **BREAKING THEMSELVES OF THE HABIT OF OVER-INDULGING IN FANTASY**
FULFILLMENT: **LOOKING ORDINARY LIFE SQUARELY IN THE EYE AND TAKING IT FOR WHAT IT IS**
NOTABLES: **GUSTAVUS SWIFT (DEVELOPED REFRIGERATED RAILROAD CARS); MAURICE SAATCHI (COFOUNDER, ADVERTISING AGENCY SAATCHI & SAATCHI)**

June 25–July 2
THE EMPATH
CANCER I

Though much stronger individuals than some born in the Week of the Empath, these souls who travel the Way of Experience may fail the higher challenge here if they isolate themselves from others, or retreat into depression, hurt feelings, or a sense of chronically unfulfilled expectation. Highly prone to taking on other people's problems, petty disputes, and even personality traits, they may undergo a necessary process of self-review before they develop a truly secure sense of identity. The ability to extricate themselves from the dramas of the moment and get in touch with their places in the larger scheme will be at issue here, and they will do especially well to cultivate greater objectivity and self-esteem. Still, they are blessed with a much more developed sense of empathy and understanding of others than some along this road, and this quality alone is bound to ease their travels over the rougher spots along the Way of Experience.

CHALLENGE: **CURTAILING THE PROPENSITY TO HOLD ON TO SLIGHTS, EGO WOUNDS, AND HURT FEELINGS FOR TOO LONG**
FULFILLMENT: **WORKING OUT THE BUSINESS OF DAY-TO-DAY LIVING WITH LOVED ONES**
NOTABLE: **GILDA RADNER (ACTRESS/COMEDIAN, *SATURDAY NIGHT LIVE*)**

July 3–10
THE UNCONVENTIONAL
CANCER II

A penchant for the bizarre and unusual can reach titanic proportions for those born in the Week of the Unconventional who travel this karmic path, and there are many here who will seek self-fulfillment in any number of odd, ecstatic, or even cultlike experiences and affiliations. At best, they will find it hard to keep their more romantic imaginings tempered with truth and practical reasoning. At worst, they may be unable to adequately distinguish reality from fantasy, or truth from fiction. Yet the danger of overindulgence in fantasy, idealism, and escapism is nevertheless mitigated by their astute psychological insight. If they can learn to analyze and evaluate their own behavior with the same accuracy as they can often view others, life will become much easier. Once they cultivate greater objectivity and better discover the truth of who they are inside, they can find great fulfillment and not a little enlightenment along the way.

LINDA RONSTADT
Pop/country singer,
"Desperado"

7/15/1946
Cancer III

CHALLENGE: **KEEPING THEIR MINDS ON THE GOAL OF THIS PATH: SELF-KNOWLEDGE**
FULFILLMENT: **HAVING GIVEN UP THEIR PRETENSIONS, FEELING FREE TO INDULGE THEIR MORE NURTURING SIDE**
NOTABLES: **SYLVESTER STALLONE (ACTOR, *ROCKY*); JAMES WHISTLER (PAINTER, *WHISTLER'S MOTHER*; ETCHER)**

July 11–18
THE PERSUADER
CANCER III

Charismatic and persuasive in the extreme, those born in this week who travel they Way of Experience may in fact be so good at getting others to do their bidding, they lose track of themselves along this karmic path. In fact, these personalities may give way to any number of excesses and overindulgences in the process of trying to identify their own deeper needs, and a considerable degree of self-aggrandizement can hamper their higher development. Although the acquisition of fine professional and organizational skills will prove relatively easy, their need for validation may cause them to become relationship junkies or be drawn into cultlike activities and pursuits. Still, their special gifts give them the ability to work well with others, despite their more controlling inclinations. If they are careful not to succumb to tunnel vision, excesses of passion, or a tendency to bombast, they can be objective, capable, and quite enterprising in the pursuit of a more adventurous approach to life and living.

CHALLENGE: **SETTING ASIDE CAREER CONCERNS TO ALLOW FOR A GREATER VARIETY OF EXPERIENCES OF LIFE**
FULFILLMENT: **ENGAGING IN QUIET ACTIVITIES OR CREATIVE PURSUITS THAT HELP REVEAL THEIR TRUE NATURE TO THEMSELVES**
NOTABLE: **CHEECH MARIN (COMEDIAN, CHEECH & CHONG)**

July 19–25
OSCILLATION
CANCER–LEO CUSP

For those born on the Cusp of Oscillation who travel the Way of Experience, there is a strong tendency to exalt themselves in the areas where they should be most humble, and this inaccurate self-perception and lack of objectivity can really interfere with basic good judgment. As a result, pride can go before many a fall as their more egotistic impulses may obscure their intuition, and setbacks only exacerbate their tendencies to emotional dramatics. While histrionics and temper tantrums can allow them at times to turn a situation to advantage, they should keep in mind that spilling one's guts is ultimately about as attractive as it sounds. Still, for all their emotional highs and lows, they are blessed with a consuming curiosity that will serve them in fine stead here. While modesty, adaptability, and the willingness to ground themselves in the here and now will always prove challenging for these people, they will do well to keep in mind the truth of the precept "Seek, and ye shall find."

ROSE KENNEDY
Matriarch of the Kennedy family

7/22/1890
Cancer–Leo Cusp

CHALLENGE: **WORKING HARD TO EVEN OUT MOOD SWINGS FOR GREATER BALANCE AND NORMALCY IN THEIR LIVES**
FULFILLMENT: **INDULGING THEIR NATURAL CURIOSITY AS THEY SEEK OUT NEW ADVENTURES**
NOTABLE: **EDGAR DEGAS (FRENCH IMPRESSIONIST PAINTER/ SCULPTOR)**

July 26–August 2
AUTHORITY
LEO I

Those born in the Week of Authority who travel the Way of Experience may find this road a struggle since they can be loath to relinquish their sense of command in the interest of the mental adventure and expansion that are part of the higher promise here. Big egos abound among those with this configuration, and they may well have huge impacts as moguls and monarchs. They are unlikely to experience much in the way of personal fulfillment, however, until they trade in some of their grander schemes for more modest, yet more flexible attitudes and lifestyles. Cultivating a love of learning will be especially important to their success along this road, as staying in touch with the larger world of ideas and experience will help them keep their perspectives on problems and personal dramas and give them a sense of their places in the larger, more universal scheme.

CHALLENGE: **GIVING UP CONTROL AND ALLOWING THE NATURAL PROCESSES OF LIFE INTO THEIR LIVES**
FULFILLMENT: **ARRIVING AT A PLACE WHERE THEY HAVE NOTHING TO PROVE**

August 3–10
BALANCED STRENGTH
LEO II

Though much more grounded in realistic effort than some other Leos who travel the Way of Experience, those born in the Week of Balanced Strength who make their way along this road will nevertheless experience their share of trials and tribulations. Their principal failing will lie in their inability to admit mistakes or to abandon unproductive efforts or courses of action. They take such pride in their ability to simply endure that they are capable of throwing quite a lot of good money after bad, or otherwise wasting time and effort as they attempt to turn their high-flown plans into reality. They can keep themselves so occupied that they fail to access their considerable intuition or nurture their curiosity about themselves and others—and while they are likely to be generous and indulgent with others, they may not extend those same gifts to themselves. Yet if Leo II's can cultivate greater flexibility and intellectual curiosity and pay heed to the small, still voice within, they can really blossom along this path, though they will have to make some changes first.

ANDY WARHOL
Famed pop artist/painter/filmmaker

8/6/1927
Leo II

CHALLENGE: **SEEING THEIR ROLE AS LONG-SUFFERING VICTIM AS JUST ANOTHER FORM OF EGO DRAMA**
FULFILLMENT: **HAVING THE STRENGTH TO ALLOW THEM-SELVES SOME BASIC HAPPINESS**
NOTABLE: **ROBERT SHAW (AUTHOR; DRAMATIST/ACTOR, JAWS)**

August 11–18
LEADERSHIP
LEO III

Ego issues can be the principal stumbling block of those born in this week who travel the Way of Experience, not necessarily because they think so highly of themselves, but because they sometimes lack basic empathy for and understanding of others. As a result, people may well perceive them as heroic and authoritative, only to discover that they can be somewhat conceited or downright selfish underneath. When Leo III's fail to command respect, their sense of identity can suffer greatly, leading to all sorts of problems with depression and self-pity. Still, this path endows them with both finer intellects and broader yearnings for experience and adventure than they might have otherwise. If they are careful to nurture their inclinations toward self-discovery and greater flexibility, and to avoid the tendency to take themselves and their goals quite so seriously, they can realize not only great success, but great freedom along this life's journey.

CHALLENGE: **PERMITTING THEIR NATURAL CURIOSITY AND LOVE OF LEARNING TO OVERCOME THEIR CONCERN FOR THEIR IMAGES**
FULFILLMENT: **HAVING MORE FUN AS THEY GIVE UP TRYING SO HARD**
NOTABLE: **ROSALYNN CARTER (FIRST LADY OF JIMMY CARTER)**

August 19–25

EXPOSURE
LEO–VIRGO CUSP

Those born on the Cusp of Exposure who travel the Way of Experience are likely to do wonderfully well, as they have been blessed with a certain ability to keep their best ideas realistic and their sense of self more grounded than some who travel this road. Intensely analytical and objective, they can derive great satisfaction from merely being bigger fish in smaller ponds, rather than indulging in the kind of rainbow-chasing grandeur that is the lot of many on this karmic path. Though they will doubtless have a flamboyant streak, they have a naturally intellectual inclination that will serve them in wonderful stead here. While seeking immediate gratification or validation for their often shaky egos may be one of their principal vices, a grasp of the larger issues, and a fine sense empathy and insight into the quirks and quandaries of the human heart, will always rank among their virtues as they make their way along this life's journey.

CHALLENGE: **LETTING DOWN THE FACADES OF THEIR IMAGES**
FULFILLMENT: **ENJOYING THE PROCESS OF SELF-ANALYSIS AND OBSERVATION IN THE FACE OF EXPERIENCE**
NOTABLES: **ALTHEA GIBSON (TENNIS PLAYER; 1ST BLACK TO WIN WIMBLEDON); HOUARI BOUMEDIENNE (ALGERIAN POLITICAL LEADER; PRESIDENT)**

HARRY F. GUGGENHEIM
Publisher; philanthropist; cofounder of Long Island paper *Newsday*

8/23/1890
Leo–Virgo Cusp

August 26–September 2

SYSTEM BUILDERS
VIRGO I

A simple lack of self-awareness may prove the biggest stumbling block for those born in the Week of the System Builders who navigate the challenges of the Way of Experience. Motivated by a great need to keep the world in order, and to put reality into better alignment with the world of logical thought, they can do well here, especially when they cultivate within themselves their inclination to explore wider areas of interest and better learn the value of going with the flow. They have doubtless been gifted with a higher degree of versatility and a much broader vision than many of this group have, and if they can combine those talents with an eye for detail, determination and diligence, they can accomplish some really great things along this road. If they can guard against fussiness and personal insecurity and further develop a sense of identity quite apart from their ambitions and material accomplishments, so much the better.

CHALLENGE: **NOT ALLOWING THEIR NEED FOR STRUCTURE TO LIMIT THEIR OPENNESS OR EXPERIENCE OF LIFE**
FULFILLMENT: **REVELING IN A BIT OF IMPROMPTU ADVENTURE NOW AND THEN**

September 3–10

THE ENIGMA
VIRGO II

Well suited to the demands and challenges of the Way of Experience, these souls may nevertheless struggle a bit with the call to wider variety and adventure that beckons here. There are a number of these people who simply don't like to get their hands dirty, even if that might prove an ultimately educational and enlightening experience. The high-flown and romantic notions of their Sagittarius III origins can manifest in unrealistic ideas of perfection and personal accomplishment, or as an overpreoccupation with worldly image and material success. Nevertheless, there is a strong possibility of real spiritual progress here, especially when these individuals are willing to go within and address those personal issues that lie at the heart of their need for fulfillment. If they are careful to cultivate an openness to daily interactions and to others, they in turn will find great satisfaction in the process of self-discovery that follows.

CHALLENGE: **DISPENSING WITH A CERTAIN SUPERCILIOUS OR CONDESCENDING ATTITUDE ABOUT THE MUNDANE**
FULFILLMENT: **OPENING THE DOORS TO MORE ORDINARY TYPES OF EXPERIENCE**
NOTABLES: **PAUL VOLCKER (CHAIRMAN, FEDERAL RESERVE BOARD, 1979–97); FRANZ WERFEL (WRITER, *THE SONG OF BERNADETTE*)**

MAN RAY
Painter/photographer, inspired by Dadaism

8/27/1890
Virgo I

September 11–18

THE LITERALIST
VIRGO III

Practical in the extreme, the personalities born in this week are quite unlikely to succumb to the vices of unrealistic ambition or overly romanticized visions that can plague some of their fellow travelers along the Way of Experience. Yet these often powerful people may resist the call to a more flexible orientation and fail to cultivate the broader range of interaction and knowledge indicated here. Many of them can be dogged by a secret insecurity that may be expressed as chronic fussiness, ruthlessness, or even the occasional bout of megalomania. Though likely to rise to the tops of their chosen professions, cultivating a greater awareness of who they really are and learning to take things as they come will be paramount to their success. Once they learn to believe in themselves and stop trying so hard to prove their value to the world, an expanded and more relaxed attitude is sure to follow. Otherwise, they may have occasion to reflect upon the truth of the maxim: "Experience is what you get when you didn't get what you wanted."

CHALLENGE: **PRYING THEIR VISELIKE GRIPS OFF THE STEERING WHEELS OF THEIR LIVES**
FULFILLMENT: **LETTING A LITTLE ROMANCE OR FANTASY SEEP INTO THEIR EVERYDAY ACTIVITIES**
NOTABLE: **PETER FALK (ACTOR, *COLUMBO*)**

September 19–24
BEAUTY
VIRGO–LIBRA CUSP

Those born on the Cusp of Beauty who travel the Way of Experience will have to find ways to ground themselves in ordinary pursuits and activities, if only to find outlets for their enormous creativity. There is a danger here that these somewhat unstable people will fail to heed the call to greater experience and self-realization, however, and some may waste their energies in a never-ending cycle of sensation and immediate ego gratification. There is also a danger that they will believe themselves a bit more talented, accomplished, and refined than they actually are, and egos can blossom to some amazing proportions. Indeed, these souls will be forced to face themselves without illusion and to develop the necessary willingness to climb down from their idealistic ivory towers from time to time. Though well equipped to meet the challenge to exchange their high-flown fantasies for the illumination to be found in more ordinary life experience, they may have to confront their deeper needs in order to be most effective here.

TOMMY LASORDA
Famous baseball manager,
LA Dodgers

9/22/1927
Virgo–Libra Cusp

CHALLENGE: **CULTIVATING A BETTER SENSE OF REALITY BEFORE THEY SUCCUMB TO A ROMANTICIZED VERSION**
FULFILLMENT: **INDULGING IN A VARIETY OF SENSUAL EXPERIENCES**
NOTABLE: **JOHN DANKWORTH (JAZZ SAXOPHONIST)**

September 25–October 2
THE PERFECTIONIST
LIBRA I

The ability to stay grounded in the here and now and avoid a tendency to slide into preoccupation with their pet obsessions will doubtless be issues that figure prominently on the life journey of those born in the Week of the Perfectionist who travel the Way of Experience. Stern and demanding taskmasters, they will doubtless be as hard on themselves as they are on others, yet the endowments of this path will also give them greater intellectual inclinations, and a more philosophical attitude than they might otherwise possess. Here the combination of vision and practicality can make for a nice mix, and if these souls are careful not to repress their impulses toward greater self-knowledge and discovery, and to rise to the task of taking joy in the day-to-day working out of their projects and plans, all can go brilliantly along this road.

CHALLENGE: **BEING CAREFUL THAT THE CONTEMPLATION OF INNER LIFE DOESN'T TAKE THE PLACE OF EXPERIENCING IT IN ACTION**
FULFILLMENT: **BREAKING FREE FROM ROUTINE TO GO ON SMALL EXPLORATORY JAUNTS**
NOTABLE: **TOM BOSLEY (ACTOR, *HAPPY DAYS*)**

October 3–10
SOCIETY
LIBRA II

The personalities born in this week who find themselves on the Way of Experience may have to learn the value of separating from a well-entrenched family, social network, or professional organization, if only to make the necessary time to embark on a personal voyage of self-discovery. Though well equipped to meet the higher challenge implied here, they will nonetheless struggle when it comes to getting acquainted with their own deeper needs. In fact, there are many with this configuration who will be content with their measure of worldly power, and not much interested in seeking out abstractions like the meaning of life. Still there is the prospect of great success, and if they follow their more social instincts as a means to gain greater experience of the world, and at the same time use periods of solitude to gain a clearer understanding of themselves, they will make amazing progress along this life's journey.

CHALLENGE: **NOT SEEKING THEMSELVES THROUGH THE EYES OF OTHERS**
FULFILLMENT: **BECOMING REACQUAINTED WITH WHO THEY ARE THROUGH SOLITARY EXPERIENCES**

October 11–18
THEATER
LIBRA III

Though likely to be possessed of a rare and compelling kind of personal magnetism, Libra III's on the Way of Experience may nevertheless find this road a personal struggle until they develop a sense of identity and a measure of worldly experience apart from their images. The need to interact with others may be something they will need to cultivate, for as much as they may desire an audience, they are not likely to be especially long on qualities like empathy and understanding. It is not so much unkindness or even superficiality that is the problem here as it is a tendency to self-absorption. These souls may well become victims of their own intensity, so driven by worldly ambition, that they fail, not only to stop and smell the roses, but to notice there are roses at all. Thus, their willingness to open themselves to life's adventures, even those that might seem at first glance too pedestrian for their tastes, will be especially important, as will the ability to delve beneath their well-constructed facades to access the soul underneath.

GEORGE C. SCOTT
Actor, *Patton*

10/18/1927
Libra III

CHALLENGE: **REALIZING THAT THEIR PENCHANT FOR DRAMA IS KEEPING THEM FROM SELF-KNOWLEDGE**
FULFILLMENT: **INDULGING THEIR TENDER SIDE**
NOTABLE: **PIERRE CHODERLOS DE LACLOS (ARMY OFFICER; WROTE *LES LIAISONS DANGEREUSES*)**

October 19–25

DRAMA AND CRITICISM
LIBRA–SCORPIO CUSP

Though these larger-than-life individuals may never acquire what is generally known as a down-to-earth or common touch, they can nevertheless find fulfillment along this karmic path. What these souls will doubtless discover in the course of this life's journey is the relatively simple lesson that more is not always better. Libra–Scorpios must learn to regulate their considerable gifts in the interest of both greater refinement and broader experience. In some cases, that may require the exaltation of a particular ability at the seeming expense of other gifts. Other individuals here may be the insulated prodigies who wake up one day only to discover that they know very little of the world outside. By far the biggest challenge for those with this configuration will be to develop a sense of greater humility and understanding of their fellows that is neither overly critical nor patronizing. Yet if they can back up their astute talents for observation with a measure of understanding for life outside their usual spheres, all will go well along this road.

STEPHEN CRANE
Author,
The Red Badge of Courage

11/1/1871
Scorpio I

CHALLENGE: **NOT FALLING INTO THE ABYSS OF GIVING THEIR SENSUOUSNESS AND PASSION FREE REIN**
FULFILLMENT: **GROUNDING THEMSELVES IN FAMILY LIFE**

October 26–November 2

INTENSITY
SCORPIO I

Those born in the Week of Intensity who travel the Way of Experience will have to face down the demons of depression, self-pity, and suspicion before they can realize the higher challenge here. Though gifted with many more extroverted traits than some of their Scorpio fellows, these dramatic and intense people will always have problems with extremes of emotion, and they may have trouble seeing the world in more than shades of black and white. Keeping themselves open to new experiences can be a special problem, for setbacks and disillusionment can only serve to exacerbate some of their more negative traits in a kind of "that which I have feared hath come upon me" cycle of perception. They must learn to accentuate the positive, eliminate the negative, and reach for the broader range of experience, self-awareness, and groundedness in daily life indicated here. They can then realize great fulfillment—especially when they learn not to take themselves or the world quite so seriously, and above all, to keep their sense of humor.

CHALLENGE: **RELEASING THE INTENSITY OF THEIR APPROACH AND BEING LESS SELECTIVE**
FULFILLMENT: **FINDING OUT NEW THINGS ABOUT THEMSELVES AS THEY TRY SOMETHING DIFFERENT**
NOTABLE: **CLEO LAINE (JAZZ SINGER)**

November 3–11

DEPTH
SCORPIO II

Emotional extremes and tendencies to narcissistic fantasies can plague those born in the Week of Depth who travel the Way of Experience. Curiously enough, however, they have the potential for the rare kind of depth and self-knowledge that are part of the higher promise here, though broader experience of the world may not come quite so easily. Avoiding emotional dramas and screening out the influences and personal obsessions that can distract them from their higher quest for freedom or expanded knowledge will be of great benefit. For, in fact, these people can attain the highest levels of success, accomplishment, and worldly experience as they are never hesitant to get their hands dirty, to empathize with others, or to explore the outer reaches of what is possible. Thus, most will embrace the intellectual and spiritual challenges that present themselves along the Way of Experience.

DWIGHT GOODEN
Baseball pitcher,
superstar with the
NY Mets

11/16/1964
Scorpio III

CHALLENGE: **COMING TO TERMS WITH THE SOURCE OF THEIR PERIODIC BOUTS WITH DEPRESSION**
FULFILLMENT: **IMPOSING THE ORDINARY ON THEIR OTHERWISE EXTRAORDINARY LIVES**
NOTABLE: **CALISTA FLOCKHART (ACTRESS, *ALLY MCBEAL*)**

November 12–18

CHARM
SCORPIO III

Those born in the Week of Charm who travel the Way of Experience can find this life's journey to be a struggle since they are somewhat hesitant to broaden their knowledge and/or widen their perspective, especially if such activities should threaten to put their creature comforts at risk. The process of going within is not their first nor strongest inclination, and they can be highly resistant to the idea that external achievements are not enough. They can employ their natural diplomatic talents in such a way that they are exposed to different people, different views, and even different cultures, and further apply their realism to the search for genuine self knowledge, wider experience, and true enlightenment. Thus, they can find great satisfaction in attaining a more common touch. Releasing their worldly image and acquiring a more authentic and involved approach to life may well prove to be to the benefit of not only themselves, but the rest of us as well.

CHALLENGE: **ENGAGING THEIR CAPACITY FOR REALISTIC SELF-ASSESSMENT WHENEVER FANTASY OVERTAKES THEM**
FULFILLMENT: **RELAXING AND FLOWING WITH WHAT LIFE BRINGS**
NOTABLE: **ELIZABETH CADY STANTON (WOMEN'S RIGHTS LEADER)**

November 19–24
REVOLUTION
SCORPIO–SAGITTARIUS CUSP

Those born on the Cusp of Revolution who travel this karmic path are in fact very likely to find both considerable success and a broad education along this road. Well disposed and well suited to meet the challenges of this path, they will nevertheless have to fight a tendency to emotional extremes, overenthusiasm, or unrealistic goals. Making time and room in their lives for periods of quiet reflection, introspection, and a more grounded sense of their roles in the larger scheme will be of paramount importance here. It is likely that many of the issues and lessons they encounter will involve their ability to develop empathy and understanding of their fellows on a strictly personal, rather than a societal, political, or even universal level. Keeping their ambitions manageable, their goals realistic, and their dreams tinged with inspiration can ease their passage and smooth their way along this karmic path.

OTIS CHANDLER
Publisher of
Los Angeles Times
11/23/1927
Scorpio–Sagittarius Cusp

CHALLENGE: **RELEASING AN OVERATTACHMENT TO THE TRADITIONS OF THE PAST**
FULFILLMENT: **FINDING CONTENTMENT IN THE MUNDANE**

November 25–December 2
INDEPENDENCE
SAGITTARIUS I

Those born in the Week of Independence who journey along the Way of Experience may have a difficult time scaling down their expectations and their egos as they travel along this road. There is nevertheless the prospect of amazing personal growth as they evolve along this karmic path. Grounding themselves in day-to-day activities and interactions will prove especially important to their development, as will cultivating greater self-awareness and most especially, self-discipline. High-flown ideals, personal sensitivity, and an exaggerated need for freedom can cause these people to hold themselves aloof from the challenge of finding enlightenment or adventure in the more everyday kinds of experience implied here. Yet if they allow their yearning for true fellowship to inform their impulses, and cultivate a greater willingness to bond, all will progress nicely along this life's journey.

CHALLENGE: **NOT GOING OVERBOARD TO PURSUE THE LATEST ADVENTURE OR GRANDIOSE SCHEME**
FULFILLMENT: **COMING TO THE CONCLUSION THAT THERE'S NO PLACE LIKE HOME**

December 3–10
THE ORIGINATOR
SAGITTARIUS II

While a great need to be accepted lies at the core of the Sagittarius II born in this week who navigates the challenge and promise of the Way of Experience, he or she may nevertheless retreat into an attitude that is at once defiant and superior. Controlling aggression may be the principal challenge, as Sagittarius II's are often so uniquely gifted that they are fueled by the need to prove themselves at all costs. While it is safe to say that they will accomplish much in worldly terms, they may nevertheless find it difficult to admit or acknowledge the skeletons that often rattle in their psychological closets. Depression and disillusion can be problems here as well. Yet if they strive to connect with others in more intimate and meaningful ways than simply getting attention, and work to uncover more realistic goals and personal aspirations, their search for enlightenment and understanding will not go unrewarded along this life's journey.

TERI HATCHER
Actress, *Lois and Clark*
12/8/1964
Sagittarius II

CHALLENGE: **GRAPPLING WITH THE PERSONAL INSECURITY THAT MAY BE KEEPING THEM OVERINVOLVED WITH THEIR PUBLIC PERSONAS**
FULFILLMENT: **DEVELOPING A STRONG SENSE OF SELF**
NOTABLE: **OLIVIER MESSIAEN (COMPOSER AND ORGANIST)**

December 11–18
THE TITAN
SAGITTARIUS III

Discovering common ground between themselves and the rest of the world is likely to form the core of the quest for those born in this week who travel the Way of Experience. Though blessed with fine intelligence and a wonderfully philosophical turn of mind, they are likely nevertheless to be challenged to lose some of their more high-handed or superior attitudes as they make their way along this karmic path. Immersing themselves in the huge variety of experience and knowledge available in daily life will serve to take them out of their heads and into the real world. Further, a more tangible set of achievements will help to mitigate the secret insecurity that they are somehow ill-suited to life in the world. Though it is important that they do not neglect their creativity, imagination, or higher aspirations, it will serve them well to temper and balance their dreams in the smaller satisfactions of a job well done, the laughter of close friends, and the comforts of children and family ties.

CHALLENGE: **TAKING CARE TO TEMPER THEIR ATTRACTION TO THE MAGICAL AND ECSTATIC**
FULFILLMENT: **KNOWING THAT IT'S ALL RIGHT TO MAKE MISTAKES**
NOTABLES: **EDWARD BARNARD (ASTRONOMER; DEVELOPED CELESTIAL PHOTOGRAPHY); BILLY RIPKEN (BASEBALL PLAYER)**

KARMIC PATH
36

December 19–25
PROPHECY
SAGITTARIUS–CAPRICORN CUSP

Gifted with a combination of realism and inspiration, those born in this week who find themselves along the Way of Experience are likely to experience both great achievement and high levels of personal satisfaction along this road. These individuals have a rare ability to focus their talents and to home in on the aspects of themselves that require greater nurture and cultivation, though they may become frustrated when their efforts at expansion aren't met with instant acceptance or approval. As a result, feelings of unworthiness or insecurity can cause them to withdraw from or to question their own best impulses and intuitions. Yet they are blessed with a natural sense of independence and a yearning for wider experience that promises to serve them quite well along this journey. If their great curiosity, considerable intellect, and strong spiritual sense are given the free rein those qualities deserve, these souls can find that the microcosm of experience will illuminate the macrocosm of life.

BARRY GOLDWATER
U.S. senator, 1964
presidential candidate

1/1/1909
Capricorn I

CHALLENGE: **NOT ALLOWING THEIR MORE EXPANSIVE SIDE TO GET OUT OF CONTROL**
FULFILLMENT: **OPENING MORE TO RELATIONSHIP, EVEN IN ITS MOST ORDINARY ASPECTS**

December 26–January 2
THE RULER
CAPRICORN I

Though there will be any number of moguls, magnates, and monarchs born in this week who travel the Way of Experience, it may take them some time to divest themselves of a more worldly sense of accomplishment and rise to the challenge of greater self-knowledge that is indicated here. Gifted with the ability to focus their talents and energies on a path of genuine and lasting achievements, these people will nonetheless have trouble with issues of expansion, and may resist the call to broader interests. Thus they may find themselves confronted with a host of opportunities or turns of fortune for which they are seemingly unprepared. In fact, many of these people are tightly controlled or emotionally bottled up and may shut down entirely if their commanding attitudes are not met with warm response. Yet though they can well become prisoners of their own responsibilities, they have the tools to unlock the doors to self-realization and enlightenment.

CHALLENGE: **RESISTING THE SEDUCTION OF THEIR PUBLIC ROLES IN FAVOR OF THEIR PRIVATE ONES**
FULFILLMENT: **SETTLING INTO A MORE EXPERIENTIAL APPROACH TO LIFE**
NOTABLES: **LEW AYRES (ACTOR, ALL QUIET ON THE WESTERN FRONT); DANA ANDREWS (ACTOR, THE OX-BOW INCIDENT)**

January 3–9
DETERMINATION
CAPRICORN II

Personal modesty and high aspirations can combine in an interesting way for those born in the Week of Determination who find themselves on the Way of Experience. Inclinations to service, self-sacrifice, and achievement are all quite pronounced here, and this configuration can manifest in rich experience, considerable knowledge, and genuine self-awareness. Though depression and insecurity can be problems, and these souls may find it difficult to establish a balance between their highest dreams and actual reality, they are equally unlikely to suffer from the excesses of ego indicated elsewhere. If they can avoid the pitfalls of self-pity and pessimism, and embrace instead the promise of wide experience of fellowship with others, and the touch of adventure that beckons along this road, they can certainly find happiness here.

ETHEL MERMAN
Actress/singer,
Annie Get Your Gun

1/16/1909
Capricorn III

CHALLENGE: **ALLOWING SOME OF THEIR HIDDEN SENSITIVITY ROOM TO BREATHE**
FULFILLMENT: **EMBARKING ON A JOURNEY TO DISCOVER THE INNER LIFE AND ITS YEARNING FOR THE METAPHYSICAL**

January 10–16
DOMINANCE
CAPRICORN III

Quite capable of grounding their highest dreams and aspirations in practical, day-to-day reality, those born in the Week of Dominance who travel the Way of Experience are likely to do well along this road. Gifted with greater self-confidence than they might have otherwise, many of the lessons of this life's journey will nevertheless involve their willingness to open themselves up to attitudes, lifestyles, and points of view that are not necessarily their own. Tolerance, empathy, and understanding will be the keys to happiness here, though those traits will likely be acquired as they divest themselves of ego and gain more in the way of logic and objectivity. Yet if these individuals can manage their frustrations, control their more eccentric impulses, and be willing to go within on the voyage of self-discovery indicated here, they can encounter fine and fulfilling life experiences along this road.

CHALLENGE: **DIVESTING THEMSELVES OF PREJUDICE, INTOLERANCE, AND IMPOSSIBLY HIGH STANDARDS**
FULFILLMENT: **ALLOWING THEIR LIVES TO BE MORE ORDINARY, EVEN HUMDRUM**
NOTABLE: **GORDON CRAIG (DANCER; STAGE DESIGNER; AUTHOR)**

January 17–22

MYSTERY AND IMAGINATION
CAPRICORN–AQUARIUS CUSP

January 23–30

GENIUS
AQUARIUS I

Excesses of romanticism, imagination, and unrealistic dreams can hinder the higher development of those born in this week who find themselves on the Way of Experience. Yet they will be well disposed to the challenge of developing greater understanding of life's mysteries and most especially the mystery of self. Though these individuals will not be without their share of conflicts, and will have to work hard to develop greater stability, they have a fine ability not to take them themselves too seriously or to take life's woes too much to heart. If they can ground their sometimes chaotic energies in the more dependable pleasures of family, friends, and children, this process will insure increased self-knowledge, shared understanding, and a wide range of satisfying and enlightening experiences along this life's journey.

ZANE GREY
Author of bestselling westerns, *Riders of the Purple Sage*

1/31/1872
Aquarius II

CHALLENGE: **DEVELOPING THE FOCUS TO STICK TO EVERYDAY CONCERNS AND PRACTICAL DETAILS**
FULFILLMENT: **SAVORING THEIR EXPERIENCES RATHER THAN FOREVER LOOKING TO WHAT'S ON THE HORIZON**
NOTABLE: **U THANT (U.N. SECRETARY-GENERAL, 1962–72)**

Big ideas and grandiose visions must here be tempered by the willingness to put sustained effort behind their inspiration. For those born in the Week of Genius who find themselves on the Way of Experience may be hindered in their development by a distaste for grounded detail work on the one hand, or a rather snobbish or superior attitude on the other. Yet their inclinations to fellowship and natural curiosity will likely serve them in wonderful stead here, especially if they turn their attentions to humanitarian concerns. If they can curb some of their tendencies toward expansiveness that can lead them to becoming reckless, distracted, or unduly stressed out, and surround themselves with people who can keep them grounded in the here and now, they can realize amazing success and no small degree of personal satisfaction and fulfillment along this life's journey.

CHALLENGE: **RESISTING THE LURE OF WORLDLY EXCITEMENT**
FULFILLMENT: **FINDING SIMPLER, MORE PRACTICAL APPLICATIONS FOR THEIR UNIQUE MINDS**
NOTABLES: **JULIA MORGAN (ARCHITECT OF HEARST CASTLE); ANN TODD (ACTRESS, *THE SEVENTH VEIL*)**

January 31–February 7

YOUTH AND EASE
AQUARIUS II

February 8–15

ACCEPTANCE
AQUARIUS III

Though there is much to indicate that these personalities will be both talented and compelling, coming to terms with their real values, cultivating greater depth, and aligning themselves with a broader range of interests are indicated in their passage along this karmic path. There will be a number of rather inflated egos here, and a tendency to think big without the attendant ability backing up their efforts with realistic choices. They are nevertheless well disposed toward the challenge to wide experience and variety that beckons here. Some will struggle with issues of emotional immaturity and insecurity though they can avoid the tendency to get hooked on the applause and attentions of others and attend to the business of self-discovery, expanding their personal boundaries, and true personal growth. Thus they will make huge strides along the road, especially if those strides take them on a journey within.

DEAN RUSK
Secretary of state to Kennedy and Johnson

2/9/1909
Aquarius III

CHALLENGE: **NOT PERMITTING THE PATH OF LEAST RESISTANCE TO SHAPE WHO THEY ARE**
FULFILLMENT: **MAKING THE EFFORT TO SEEK OUT THEIR TRUE NATURE**
NOTABLES: **BRANDON LEE (SON OF BRUCE; ACTOR, *THE CROW*); PRINCESS STEPHANIE OF MONACO**

Allowing their visions and imaginative gifts to lead them to wider adventure will prove the principal karmic task of those born in the Week of Acceptance who travel the Way of Experience. Though many here may have establishment roles, they will nevertheless be possessed of a fine and admirable impulse to question the limits and push the boundaries of their personal experience in the search for truth and enlightenment. Though sheer restlessness can cause them to fail to back up their best impulses with necessary planning, they have the resourcefulness and resilience to overcome the obstacles of misinformation, intolerance, or bad judgment that may present themselves along this journey. If they take care to cultivate objectivity and a measure of self-awareness and never refuse the call to further exploration of the real issues, all can go brilliantly here.

CHALLENGE: **DEVELOPING A CAPACITY TO REFLECT ON THEIR EXPERIENCE AND WHAT IT MEANS FOR THEM ON AN INNER LEVEL**
FULFILLMENT: **FINDING OUT HOW BEAUTIFULLY A LIFE OF GOING WITH THE FLOW SUITS THEM**
NOTABLES: **JOSEPH MANKIEWICZ (PRODUCER/DIRECTOR, *ALL ABOUT EVE*); WILLIAM PICKERING (ASTRONOMER; PREDICTED EXISTENCE OF 9TH PLANET)**

February 16–22

SENSITIVITY
AQUARIUS–PISCES CUSP

Insecurity and pessimism can hinder the higher development of those born in this period who travel the Way of Experience. Their personal sensitivity can cause them to withdraw from the challenge to open themselves to wider life experience and explore the nature of their limitations versus their expectations. Though likely to be highly success oriented, they may be ignorant of some of their more self-destructive habits and tendencies and can at times prove themselves to be their own worst enemies when it comes to really getting what they want out of life. Tempering their idealism with objectivity and their sensitivity with simple optimism will prove especially important here. If they can overcome isolation, feelings of rejection, or a rather superior attitude that causes them to hold themselves aloof from greater involvement, risk-taking, or investigation of the issues, they can expect great progress and ever-increasing amounts of fulfillment along this life's journey.

WALLACE STEGNER
Author, wrote on the American West; won Pulitzer

2/18/1909
Aquarius–Pisces Cusp

CHALLENGE: **REMOVING THEMSELVES FROM THE ROLLER-COASTER RIDE OF THEIR EMOTIONAL LIVES BY GETTING BACK TO BASICS**

FULFILLMENT: **SETTLING INTO A SECURE LOVE RELATIONSHIP**

February 23–March 2

SPIRIT
PISCES I

A sense of the mythological and imaginative realms will likely mark the personalities of the people born in the Week of Spirit who travel the Way of Experience, though they will face the task of learning to test their visions in reality as they journey along this road. Overidealism and emotionalism may be problems here, and by far their biggest challenge will lie in their ability to back up their bighearted promises and generous impulses with necessary follow-through and delivery. They can be irresponsible, loftily ambitious, snobbish, or tending to believe themselves over the rest of us. There are nevertheless strong impulses toward emotional connection and bonding that may well prove their salvation. If they can learn to love others as well as they often love themselves, their way will be considerably clarified along the Way of Experience.

CHALLENGE: **GRAPPLING WITH THEIR LOVE OF PLEASURE AND KEEPING THEIR PASSIONS WITHIN LIMITS**

FULFILLMENT: **KEEPING THEIR FEET ON THE GROUND AND SERVING OTHERS IN THE MOST BASIC WAY POSSIBLE**

NOTABLE: **VERONICA WEBB (MODEL; ACTRESS)**

March 3–10

THE LONER
PISCES II

Those born in the Week of the Loner who find themselves on this karmic path may be flummoxed by the challenges presented here. Possessed of formidable intellects and great curiosity, they may nevertheless be quite prone to collapse into depression, feelings of being misunderstood, or overromanticizing their troubles. In fact, they may have quite a heroic sense of their own sufferings which can only serve to isolate them further from the mainstream. Still they have a great sense of the aesthetic that may well be their truest compass in the search for direction. If they can allow themselves to grow and expand their world views, and don't forget to test their own limits in reality, they have a fine flair for detail, nuance, and subtlety that will cause them to see many of the details that others might miss along this karmic path.

HARRY HELMSLEY
Hotel/real estate mogul

3/4/1909
Pisces II

CHALLENGE: **STOPPING LONG ENOUGH TO FIGURE OUT HOW THEIR LIVES TURNED OUT AS THEY DID**

FULFILLMENT: **LETTING SOMEONE ELSE SHOULDER THE BURDEN**

March 11–18

DANCERS AND DREAMERS
PISCES III

Marked by a sense of adventure and a certain lust for life, those born in this week who travel the Way of Experience can find great reward and fulfillment, if only they can be persuaded to venture out of their heads and into reality long enough to put down some necessary roots. Scattered energy and overly romanticized ideals are big problems here, as is a tendency to disconnect from demanding situations. Toning down the drama and increasing objectivity will prove especially important, as will their willingness to ground their talents in training and effort. While they may be rather loath to climb down from their ivory towers, they can do themselves and the world a great service on this path when they bring their special brand of magic into the real world and come to terms with the fact that opportunities for expansion and growth also imply dedication, involvement, and responsibility.

CHALLENGE: **NOT BELIEVING THAT THEY KNOW EVERYTHING**

FULFILLMENT: **UNDERSTANDING THAT THEY HAVE NOTHING TO PROVE**

NOTABLES: **BOBBY BONDS (BASEBALL PLAYER; OUTFIELDER); LIZA MINNELLI (SINGER; ACTRESS, *CABARET*)**

The Way of Enchantment

SAGITTARIUS–CAPRICORN CUSP TO GEMINI–CANCER CUSP
Prophecy to Magic

Those on the Way of Enchantment are destined to find a way to emerge from the shell they hide in and to express the more feminine side of their nature by becoming more compassionate, nurturing, and loving. Prone to emotional dormancy, the men and women on this karmic path must learn how to reach out to others, thereby allowing them to share their unique brand of inspiration and magic. Goal- and career-oriented, this karmic path calls those on it to let relationships be the center of their life. Thus they will learn lessons on love and loving, and as they learn, they will open to the enchantment of everyday life. As their emotional lives open and flow, they will blossom into individuals who give light and inspiration to others.

The Way of Enchantment symbolically links two of the most powerful points of the year, the winter and summer solstices. Ancient peoples recognized and celebrated these periods in the yearly cycle in order to harness their energy and magic. Thus there is something indescribable, even mystical, about this karmic path. Those born to it come into this lifetime with core energies that are at once deeply profound and difficult to embody, as well as express. Individuals on this karmic path begin their journey at the Cusp of Prophecy, the winter solstice, and thus have characteristics that reflect that time of the year. As the amount of available daylight is at its nadir, it is a time of contracting, going within, and preserving energy. This time

> ### CORE LESSON
> Moving into the light of a relationship from the shadows of a solitary life
>
> ### GOAL
> To reach out of themselves and touch those around them

is symbolized by seed energy. Within the seed exist all the power and potential of the plant, but in an extremely contracted form. The men and women on the Way of Enchantment tend to be withdrawn and to keep their inner beauty and considerable understanding under wraps. Born with what can be termed old souls, the individuals on this path are attracted to ancient philosophies and religions. They possess a profound depth of wisdom that seems to originate at their very core. Highly intuitive, even psychic, they prefer to keep what they know to themselves. However, their inscrutable and rather cool facade should not be mistaken for a lack of passion. Though never obvious to others, their profundity brings with it emotions that are deeply felt.

In early life, the individuals on the Way of Enchantment tend to be extremely focused on their careers and goals. Requiring little from others, they keep to themselves and are self-protective. It may be difficult for them to reach out to others, and they rarely allow others close enough to them to become true intimates. Quite shy and serious, few choose to try to cross the invisible barriers they throw up around themselves. They are solitary and like it that way. There is something wounded about these souls that doesn't seem to heal. And it is this that keeps them in retreat from the world and in a posture of defense. In some cases the wound originated in childhood, when they were criticized too severely or neglected in some

> ### GIFTS
> Psychic, Generous, Inspirational
>
> ### PITFALLS
> Withdrawn, Wounded, Workaholic

way. Or the simple fact may be that, as psychically sensitive as they are, as children it was difficult for them to handle the overload of impressions their gift gave them. Alternatively, perhaps no one believed them when they gave voice to their psychic awareness. Whatever the cause, those on this karmic path don't see the world as a particularly friendly place and prefer to make sure it can't hurt them in any way.

The goal for the individuals on this karmic path is to reach out of themselves to connect with others and show the world who they are and what they know. The Gemini–Cancer destination of this karmic path, the summer solstice, is a time of great fecundity. Thus, the men and women on the Way of Enchantment are called to allow their souls to blossom forth from the seed potential that they keep hidden from the world. There is much about these individuals that promises extraordinary spiritual and creative fulfillment. By nature, they are already plugged into the world of spirit. It is their task to begin to act as a conduit for it. But for this to occur, those on this path must embrace their feminine wisdom and the qualities it represents. Encouraging their own feelings and instincts and their nurturing, fertile, and creative side, as well as honoring their extraordinary intuitive faculties by giving them expression, will help those on this path to open up to others and to life. Those on the Way of Enchantment must learn to live from this feminine viewpoint and, in so doing, give their emotions expression. The verdant, chaotic profusion of summer cannot be denied. These souls' progress can be likened to the sap beginning to flow through trees as spring approaches or to the waters of springs and rivers starting to flow with the winter thaw. The waters of life, feeling, and inspiration must ultimately become a flow of love. True fulfillment will come to those on the Way of Enchantment only when they reveal their souls to others as they love. Loving from the very depths of their hearts will illuminate their lives with the miracle and magic of everyday enchantment.

The karmic journey for the men and women on the Way of Enchantment is to move out of the shadows into the light. By overcoming their shyness or fear and finding within themselves the ability to reach out to others and to express emotion, those on this karmic path will also reach within to draw on their own brand of charm. It should be remembered that the summer solstice is the most light-filled day of the year. Bringing their unique brand of magic to others by sharing their wisdom, depth of feeling, and ability to see the mystical or miraculous in everyday life is their way of drawing on the light of divine inspiration in order to reflect it back, moonlike, on others. As much as they may struggle with the inner wounds that hold them back, it is only in giving to others in loving kindness that

RELEASE
The need to be self-protective

REWARD
The joy of loving and being loved

SUGGESTION

Focus less on yourself. Move your orientation away from your inner life and out toward others. Even if it's hard in the beginning, free your emotions; as they flow, they will find their own level. Step out of the shadows and into the light.

these shamanic individuals will heal themselves. Though shy and withdrawn, those on the Way of Enchantment in truth possess an inherent generosity. They give quite willingly in backhanded or even anonymous ways. As they emerge from their shells, they become more and more oriented toward giving outwardly. Some on this karmic path may drop out of the corporate life to draw on their strengths, becoming intuitive healers, such as therapists, body workers, hypnotists, or workers in any other occupation that involves nurturing and supporting others, thus embodying the archetype of the wounded healer. Others will find useful ways to put their career success to work, for example by utilizing their influence to promote pet charities or service organizations. Over time, those on the Way of Enchantment will redirect the flow of their lives from objective to more personal or universal concerns in order to work for some greater good or for the good of their loved ones.

As they allow their inner light to shine forth, those on this karmic path will begin to attract others, and their lives, often so solitary in early years, will become filled with warm and loving relationships. Gradually, relationships will become the center of their lives. They will learn many lessons in this arena, since in some ways they are quite innocent in the ways of relating. Trial and error will guarantee that they'll experience a few knocks, but it is imperative that they not scurry back to isolationism or self-protection when hurt. The discovery and experience of love in its many forms are the destiny of these individuals. Truly, "it is better to have loved and lost than never to have loved at all." This karmic path calls those on it to discover and express the many forms of love: the love of friendship, the love of master and disciple, the love of parent for child, the love in romance and marriage, even the love found in devotion to God. Many on this karmic path will encounter soul mates on their journey. It will be quite obvious when people begin to do the work of this path. They will begin to appear to be lit from within by a soft, warm glow and the air around them will appear to contain light. In short, they will appear to be in love.

In fact, the story inherent in the journey of this karmic path can be compared to that of the Fisher King. In the tale, the king is wounded and, as a result, the kingdom of which he is a symbol is barren, a wasteland. The wound will not heal unless someone retrieves the Holy Grail, the cup or platter that symbolically holds the waters of life. Along comes a young hero, the Grail Knight, whose many adventures along the way include falling in love and failing in his first attempt to heal the king because he didn't listen to his inner voice. After further trials, Parsifal, the hero of the tale, renounces convention and acts from his heart and out of compassion, thus healing the king. Likewise, opening to the waters of love and expressing the compassion born of that love will heal those on this karmic path.

BALANCE POINT

Contraction and Expansion

CRYSTALS AND GEMSTONES

*The vibration of **Dioptase** calls forth a wild joy from deep within the soul. This stone guides the individual to re-create personal wounds into gifts that heal the planet.*

NOTABLES ON THIS KARMIC PATH

JOHANN SEBASTIAN BACH

Orphaned as a young boy, musical genius **Johann Sebastian Bach** was deeply religious. Like many on this path, his greatest challenge was to reveal his inner self and allow others to partake in his emotional life. Widowed in 1720, his second marriage to Anna Magdalena Wilcke furnished him with a soul mate and a family life. Though mainly known to his contemporaries as an organist, first as the Kapellmeister to Prince Leopold of Anhalt-Cöthen, then as cantor of the Thomasschule in Leipzig, he composed prolifically, producing complex and innovative music, most notably the *Brandenburg Concertos,* revealing both his genius and depth of spirit.

Television anchorwoman **Diane Sawyer's** assured poise belies the painful shyness and uncertainty that marked her teenage years. Like others on the Way of Enchantment, she gained her composed presence by developing a mature confidence and letting go

DIANE SAWYER

of insecurity. Sawyer worked as a press aide to President Nixon and cohosted the *Morning News* with Charles Kuralt before becoming the first woman correspondent on *60 Minutes*. She is now one of the best known of all investigative reporters, coanchoring ABC's *Primetime Live*. Sawyer's apparently successful marriage to brilliant director Mike Nichols reflects the tendency of many on this path to ultimately find great happiness in love.

MARCEL PROUST

One of the most introverted of modern novelists, **Marcel Proust** isolated himself through much of his adult life. Following the death of his mother in 1905, he secluded himself in a soundproof apartment and produced his magnum opus, *Remembrance of Things Past.* Although he never experienced consistent personal interaction, Proust successfully captured a complex social world in his numerous volumes, displaying his extraordinary imagination and powers of observation. Completely withdrawn from his community, he was thus able to creatively embrace humanity, thereby achieving a certain level of success on the Way of Enchantment.

Other Notables: John Wesley Powell, Cesar Chavez, Pat Conroy, Alistair Cooke, Sri Ramakrishna, Janeane Garofalo, Coretta Scott King, Ruth Prawer Jhabvala, Wynonna Judd, Darci Kistler, Courtney Cox, Bob Fosse, Bob "Captain Kangaroo" Keeshan, Ken Russell, Courtney Love, Orville Wright, Theodore Dreiser, Carole Lombard, John Kenneth Galbraith, Goldie Hawn, Bette Midler, Naomi Judd, Dolly Parton, Boris Pasternak, Harry Belafonte, Vaslav Nijinsky, George Plimpton

---

BIRTHDAYS ON KARMIC PATH 37

December 5, 1889–April 25, 1890 | July 17, 1908–December 5, 1908 | February 27, 1927–July 17, 1927

October 8, 1945–February 26, 1946 | May 20, 1964–October 7, 1964

December 30, 1982–May 20, 1983 | August 10, 2001–December 29, 2001 | March 22, 2020–August 9, 2020

KARMIC PATH
37

March 19–24

REBIRTH
PISCES–ARIES CUSP

The Way of Enchantment gifts those born on the Cusp of Rebirth with greater stores of understanding and insight than they might otherwise have possessed, and most with this configuration are likely to find great fulfillment, despite some difficult personality traits and sometimes rough edges to their personality. Perhaps their worst fault will be their unwillingness to connect in meaningful ways with others, as they can be rather prone to self-centered pursuits or subject to the stubborn conviction that they have to do everything themselves. Nevertheless, they can manifest amazing instincts and will be able to play their hunches. Further, if they allow their intuitive channels to stay open, there is a strong probability that they will realize the kind of transformative love relationship that will not only fulfill their highest dreams but provide them with opportunities for real spiritual rebirth. If they are brave enough, this lifetime provides them with the chance to live happily ever after.

JOHN POWELL
Anthropologist, classified
American Indian languages

3/24/1834
Pisces–Aries Cusp

CHALLENGE: **OVERCOMING THE SHYNESS THAT COMES FROM OVERSENSITIVITY**

FULFILLMENT: **EXPRESSING THEIR PASSION**

NOTABLES: **JOHANN SEBASTIAN BACH (GERMAN COMPOSER); WILLIAM MORRIS (CRAFTSMAN; POET; POLITICAL ACTIVIST)**

March 25–April 2

THE CHILD
ARIES I

Though the endowments of the Way of Enchantment will ensure that those born in the Week of the Child have greater stability and insight than some others born in this week, they may have to struggle a bit with the challenge to open themselves to a more profound level of awareness and experience. In fact, their principal life lessons will almost certainly revolve around issues of authority or wanting to be taken more seriously versus simply wanting to be taken care of by others. Yet they have a much more extroverted and willing attitude toward connecting and establishing relationships than some of the personalities who travel this road, and if they are careful to augment their considerable intuition with a measure of common sense, they will succeed in avoiding the pitfalls of overromanticizing people and circumstances and will thus enjoy great progress.

CHALLENGE: **LETTING GO OF CHILDHOOD WOUNDS**

FULFILLMENT: **ACTING ON BEHALF OF THEIR LOVED ONES**

NOTABLES: **MSTISLAV ROSTROPOVICH (CELLIST, COMPOSER); JOHN R. VANE (BIOCHEMIST; SHARED 1982 NOBEL)**

April 3–10

THE STAR
ARIES II

Those born in the Week of the Star who travel the Way of Enchantment may find this life experience imbued with either real magic or just plain luck. In short, they are destined for considerable success and a wealth of opportunities. Active, outgoing, and passionate, they may nevertheless experience some conflict as to whether they want to be noticed and appreciated or merely to be left alone. Yet the former desire will win out for most of these unusual personalities, and if they are careful to nurture within themselves the qualities of caring, inspiration, and a deep capacity for love to augment their already expansive, charismatic, and adventuresome natures, there will be little they cannot accomplish as they make their way along this spiritual highway.

CESAR CHAVEZ
Organized National Farm
Workers Association

3/31/1927
Aries I

CHALLENGE: **NOT ALLOWING THEIR NEED FOR EGO GRATIFICATION TO BE THEIR ARMOR AGAINST VULNERABILITY**

FULFILLMENT: **SURROUNDING THEMSELVES WITH LOVED ONES**

NOTABLES: **GERRY MULLIGAN (JAZZ SAXOPHONIST); M. W. NIRENBERG (BIOCHEMIST; WON NOBEL PRIZE); EFREM ZIMBALIST (VIOLINIST, COMPOSER)**

April 11–18

THE PIONEER
ARIES III

Those born in this week who travel the Way of Enchantment are likely to have a really unique vision of the future and were probably the kind of children who had a clear sense of themselves and what they wanted to be from a very early age. This karmic path imbues these individuals with a much more highly developed sense of empathy for their fellows than might otherwise be the case, and they will doubtless strike willing chords of response and support as they put themselves and their ideas out in the world. However, it can safely be said that they may experience a bit more of a struggle when it comes to their need for connection and emotional intimacy on a more personal level. Yet they are more positive by nature than some others on this karmic path, and their naturally high spirits, combined with their deep sensitivity and understanding, will allow them to transcend almost any obstacle to happiness and fulfillment that they encounter along the road.

CHALLENGE: **NOT NEGLECTING THOSE CLOSEST TO THEM AS THEY WORK ON BEHALF OF THOSE OUTSIDE THEIR CIRCLE**

FULFILLMENT: **REFLECTING THE BEAUTY OF THEIR LOVED ONES**

NOTABLE: **CHARLES WILSON PEALE (PAINTER; NATURALIST; FOUNDED PEALE MUSEUM)**

April 19–24
POWER
ARIES–TAURUS CUSP

Though the road to worldly success will be wide open to the dynamic personalities born on the Cusp of Power who travel the Way of Enchantment, the path to personal fulfillment may be a bit more obscure. These individuals have a pronounced tendency to overlook or ignore some of their deepest emotional needs and to keep themselves tied to purely material issues and concerns—sometimes at the expense of their higher emotional and spiritual development. Gifted with tremendous instincts and dynamic energy, they will nevertheless have to work a bit to open themselves to the wider possibilities of love and connection that present themselves along this karmic path. Yet if their need for control is not allowed to supersede their need for love and they can successfully put aside the hurts and slights of the past, they can look with great hope and anticipation toward the ultimate realization of their heart's desires.

CORETTA SCOTT KING
Civil rights activist; widow of Martin Luther King, Jr.

4/27/1927
Taurus I

CHALLENGE: **GIVING UP THE "WILL TO POWER" FOR THAT GREATER POWER, LOVE**

FULFILLMENT: **SURRENDERING TO THE ENCHANTMENT OF EVERYDAY LIFE**

April 25–May 2
MANIFESTATION
TAURUS I

It is likely that those born in the Week of Manifestation who find themselves on the Way of Enchantment will receive something of an education as they examine the power of love versus their need for security in the course of this life journey. Allowing themselves to remain open to the wealth of emotional and intuitive information available to them will be among their principal tasks, as these individuals have a strong impulse to withdraw in the face of conflict or to stubbornly refuse opportunities for change—even when that change promises greater fulfillment. Taking risks is not in their repertoire, and they may repress a great deal of creativity, inspiration, or imagination as they attempt to restructure their own and others' emotions. Yet if they do not allow themselves to retreat from the challenges of this karmic path to nurse their wounds, and instead cultivate the simple art of caring, all with go well for them.

CHALLENGE: **OVERCOMING THEIR RIGIDITY TO REACH OUT TO OTHERS IN A MORE NATURAL, FLUID MANNER**

FULFILLMENT: **DIRECTING THEIR CONCERNS FROM THE PERSONAL TO THE UNIVERSAL**

May 3–10
THE TEACHER
TAURUS II

As long as they don't allow themselves to become convinced of the idea that they know everything, those born in the Week of the Teacher are likely to do quite well on the Way of Enchantment. The task that presents itself will almost certainly involve these individuals' ability to step back from the facts and honor their stores of wisdom and intuition. Charismatic and sensual, these highly attractive and often compelling personalities will doubtless manifest the gifts of this karmic path in a unique ability to sway others to their way of thinking. Thus, a willingness to occasionally change the way they think will be especially useful. A more open approach to the spiritual and creative world will serve to keep their insights fresh and their sense of wonder intact. These often demanding people may nevertheless fail the challenges of this karmic path and retreat into isolation or demand guarantees before they give their hearts. Yet if they remain as willing to learn as they are to teach, opportunities for real fulfillment and genuine love will surely present themselves.

RUTH PRAWER JHABVALA
Screenwriter, Merchant-Ivory films, *Heat and Dust*

5/7/1927
Taurus II

CHALLENGE: **LEARNING TO IMPART INFORMATION LESS FOR OBJECTIVITY AND MORE FOR ENCHANTMENT**

FULFILLMENT: **SHARING THEIR DELIGHT IN BEAUTY WITH OTHERS**

May 11–18
THE NATURAL
TAURUS III

Though much more lighthearted and adventurous than many who travel the Way of Enchantment, the individuals born in this week may nevertheless have to face down a certain fear of commitment before they can realize its possibilities for growth. In relationships especially, they will struggle with issues of authority, and their need for connection may be greatly outweighed by their need for freedom. Too, some early conditioning and perhaps rejection may lead them to develop a rather defensive attitude toward others that will bear watching. Yet they have within themselves both the necessary wisdom and the capacity for caring that will enable them to transcend their difficulties, and if they can stay as alert to the possibilities for love as they are to the reality of frustration, they can take great strides along this road.

CHALLENGE: **EXTENDING THEMSELVES TOWARD OTHERS IN A MANNER THAT IS AT ONCE SINCERE AND CARING**

FULFILLMENT: **FINDING THEIR SOUL MATE**

NOTABLE: **HERBERT ROSS (DIRECTOR, *FOOTLOOSE*)**

May 19–24
ENERGY
TAURUS–GEMINI CUSP

Likely to be both creatively gifted and a bit more stable than they might otherwise be, Taurus–Geminis on the Way of Enchantment will nevertheless face the challenge of learning to acknowledge their more profound insights and instincts. Many of them will suffer from a tendency to deny or diminish their own gifts—yet at the same time they may be motivated by a need to connect with others that can manifest itself in an inclination to seek center stage. Some awesome yet rather divisive energies can make this a most interesting yet somewhat arduous life's journey, as they have some profound talents and instincts coupled with an impulse toward superficiality or a self-destructive "die young, stay pretty" refusal to mature. At best, these people will become spokespersons for some deeper collective knowledge, imparting their curious brand of wisdom in a lively, accessible style. At worst, they will retreat into irritability, frustration, or false glamour at the expense of emotional depth and spiritual generosity.

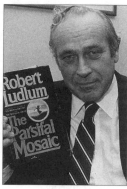

ROBERT LUDLUM
Writer/actor, suspense fiction

5/25/1927
Gemini I

CHALLENGE: **SLOWING DOWN LONG ENOUGH TO TRULY ENGAGE THEIR OWN WISDOM**

FULFILLMENT: **OFFERING MORE AND REQUIRING LESS IN RELATIONSHIPS**

May 25–June 2
FREEDOM
GEMINI I

Those born in the Week of Freedom who travel the Way of Enchantment can experience great growth and spiritual advancement, providing they do not succumb to an uncaring or unconcerned attitude toward others, on the one hand, or a compulsion to verbalize their complaints, on the other. In fact, many of these individuals will be so articulate that they will tend to rely more on what is said than what is felt. Thus, learning to trust their instincts and develop a more open attitude toward emotional forms of connection and expression will be especially useful. Yet if they can set aside some of their scrappier aspects and learn the value of surrender as opposed to the value of winning, they have a rare ability to imbue their ideas with the verbal magic necessary to communicate fully and completely with those around them, and that quality alone is sure to smooth their passage.

CHALLENGE: **CHECKING THEIR EMOTIONAL VOLATILITY IN FAVOR OF GENEROSITY**

FULFILLMENT: **WEAVING A WEB OF ENCHANTMENT AROUND THEMSELVES AND THEIR LOVED ONES**

NOTABLES: **WYNONNA JUDD (COUNTRY MUSIC SINGER); DMC (HALF OF RAP DUO RUN-DMC)**

June 3–10
NEW LANGUAGE
GEMINI II

Gifted with a unique and highly personal style of communication, Gemini II's may indeed find the emotional and spiritual connections they seek as they make their way along this karmic path. Yet they will have to venture out from a fairly defensive, rejected, and misunderstood frame of mind before they can find the fulfillment promised them. Though many of these individuals will profess not to care about what others may think of them, they may in fact work hard to curry the attention and favor of others. Yet they will be required to make a connection between their seeming lack of love and acceptance and their pronounced tendency to bury their real desires beneath a barrage of words before they can become really effective. Still, as they become more self-assured and venture to ask for the things their hearts truly desire, they may find, to their great surprise, that they are quite good at getting what they want. The key is being able to ask for it.

COURTNEY COX
Actress, *Friends*

6/15/1964
Gemini III

CHALLENGE: **GRAPPLING WITH THE EMOTIONAL BLOCKS THAT PREVENT THEM FROM FULLY ARTICULATING THEIR PROFOUND WISDOM**

FULFILLMENT: **FINDING THE PARTNER WITH WHOM VERBAL COMMUNICATION IS SUPERFLUOUS**

NOTABLE: **DARCI KISTLER (BALLET DANCER)**

June 11–18
THE SEEKER
GEMINI III

Well equipped to rise to the challenge and promise of the Way of Enchantment, those born in the Week of the Seeker can expect a fine and fulfilling life experience, providing they learn to appreciate the greater depth of experience offered by deep emotional connection. Love and affection may be important to many of these personalities, yet may be put on the back burner as they pursue a wide variety of other interests and enthusiasms. Though unlikely to be as shy and retiring as some of their fellow travelers on this road, they may take refuge in superficial connections or prefer to be the rolling stone that gathers no moss—at least when it comes to relationships. Overcoming their reluctance to commit will thus prove important, as will a willingness to seek out more than the obvious truths and experiences of life. Yet if they can open themselves to higher realms and embrace the possibilities for fulfillment and love they encounter, all will go wonderfully well.

CHALLENGE: **REACHING NOT JUST FOR A WIDE VARIETY OF EXPERIENCES BUT FOR DEPTH OF EXPERIENCE AS WELL**

FULFILLMENT: **FINDING THE INTUITIVE WISDOM AT THEIR CORE**

June 19–24

MAGIC
GEMINI–CANCER CUSP

Gifted with some really remarkable energies, those born on the Cusp of Magic who travel the Way of Enchantment are likely to enjoy an extraordinary passage, yet they will face some equally extraordinary challenges along the way. While it can safely be said that this journey may prove a bit easier for females with this configuration than for males, both sexes are likely to be what are generally called "incurable romantics." Yet they may have to work a bit to accept that quality in themselves. Overcoming their shyness, their tendency to be preoccupied with professional goals, and their stubborn refusal to acknowledge their need for deep connection will present opportunities for growth, as will learning to fully acknowledge, then act upon their insights, inspirations, and intuitions. If they keep in mind that they have within themselves the innate ability to turn their emotional scars into stars, their more magical side will surely shine forth through interaction with and love for others, and they can then bestow their gifts of wisdom, love, and forgiveness on the world.

BOB FOSSE
Choreographer/dancer,
All That Jazz
___
6/23/1927
Gemini–Cancer Cusp

CHALLENGE: **FORCING THEMSELVES TO REACH OUT TO OTHERS AND SHARE THEIR WISDOM IN A SPIRIT OF LOVINGNESS**
FULFILLMENT: **ACKNOWLEDGING THEIR NEED FOR OTHERS**

June 25–July 2

THE EMPATH
CANCER I

Revealing themselves to others and the world may seem like a daunting task for those born in the Week of the Empath who travel the Way of Enchantment, for many of these personalities have a tendency to submerge themselves in the attitudes and feelings of others without first establishing an identity apart from those around them. Often retiring and gentle, these people nevertheless have great stores of inner strength and the flexibility to bend, rather than break, under pressure. Likely to be gifted with extrasensory talents and amazing insights, they will face the challenge of finding a way to bring their wisdom to the world. Many of these personalities will manifest this need by choosing a life partner who paves their way to greater recognition, while others will find themselves unable to connect on an intimate level until they find the courage to emerge from their shells of isolation. Yet if they keep in mind that in this case at least, love is an answer rather than a question, all will go brilliantly.

CHALLENGE: **FIGHTING THEIR BOUTS OF DEPRESSION**
FULFILLMENT: **WORKING SOME OF THEIR UNIQUE MAGIC ON BEHALF OF OTHERS**
NOTABLE: **BOB KEESHAN (CAPTAIN KANGAROO)**

July 3–10

THE UNCONVENTIONAL
CANCER II

Those born in the Week of the Unconventional who find themselves on the Way of Enchantment are in for a stimulating and often exciting passage, providing they do not retreat from its challenge by refusing to share their gifts with the world. They have a strong inclination to retreat into fantasy or otherwise "live in their heads," and some may encounter difficulties with mood swings, paranoid tendencies, or leading a kind of double life, at least in the emotional sense. Too, some will go overboard in their search for connection and love and manifest darker inclinations toward obsession, possessiveness, and wholly unrealistic expectations of their relationships and partners. Yet if they take care to employ the more stable and self-disciplined endowments of this karmic path to channel and direct their imaginative and creative qualities, they will realize great personal and spiritual transformation in the course of this life journey.

KEN RUSSELL
Director, *The Rainbow*
___
7/3/1927
Cancer II

CHALLENGE: **ASSOCIATING WITH ONLY THOSE PEOPLE WHO ARE THEIR SPIRITUAL EQUALS**
FULFILLMENT: **UNDERSTANDING THAT THEY ARE NOT BIZARRE AS MUCH AS THEY ARE ENCHANTING**
NOTABLES: **JANET LEIGH (ACTRESS, *PSYCHO*); DOC SEVERINSEN (COLORFUL BANDLEADER OF *TONIGHT SHOW* ORCHESTRA); NEIL SIMON (PLAYWRIGHT; PULITZER FOR *LOST IN YONKERS*)**

July 11–18

THE PERSUADER
CANCER III

There is a touch of the miraculous about the insights and perceptions of those born in the Week of the Persuader who navigate the Way of Enchantment, yet they may lose track of its higher challenge if they confuse their ability to control others through emotional means with the experience of genuine love and spiritual connection. Learning to trust will be especially crucial to their development, and if they can come to terms with some rather daunting security issues and develop the openness needed to turn their deep need for connection into opportunities for growth and fulfillment, they are capable of showing the world who they really are. These individuals have the rare gift of being able to bring their most inspired visions to fruition and can find wonderful fulfillment as they divest themselves of objective and professional concerns and turn their talents instead to the personal, universal, and spiritual realms.

CHALLENGE: **SETTING THEIR DEEPER NEEDS FREE BY ALLOWING THEMSELVES TO LOVE**
FULFILLMENT: **SUPPORTING AND INSPIRING THEIR LOVED ONES**
NOTABLE: **LUPE VELEZ (ACTRESS; KNOWN AS MEXICAN SPITFIRE)**

July 19–25

OSCILLATION
CANCER–LEO CUSP

Cancer–Leos who make their way along this karmic path are likely to experience amazing rewards and enlightenment, providing they can learn to overcome extremes of emotional sensitivity, on the one hand, and complete emotional blockage, on the other. Though the deep creative and intuitive talents that are part of this karmic path are very much in keeping with these individuals' natural inclinations, many will experience more than their share of problems as they come to terms with their tendencies to excess and personal drama. Some may be inclined to exaggerate their own faults and failings, while others may have an almost manic sense of faith in their own abilities. Thus, while it is difficult to predict the twists and turns of this life journey, it is safe to say that these exciting and often profoundly gifted people will encounter many opportunities for personal, emotional, and spiritual development.

CHALLENGE: **NOT ALLOWING THEMSELVES TO RETREAT INTO SEETHING RESENTMENT**
FULFILLMENT: **FORMING A DEEPLY SPIRITUAL BOND WITH ANOTHER PERSON**
NOTABLE: **BARRY BONDS (BASEBALL OUTFIELDER, GIANTS GREAT)**

BRETT HULL
Hockey player

8/9/1964
Leo II

July 26–August 2

AUTHORITY
LEO I

Though likely to be considerably less shy or retiring than some others who travel this karmic path, those born in the Week of Authority will have to avoid becoming ensnared in their need for approval and acceptance in order to find real fulfillment. In short, their desire for love and a deeper sense of connection to others can manifest itself as attention seeking or a need to validate their methods and ideas. In fact, some of them will require constant reassurance from partners or friends. Yet this karmic path endows them with a much higher degree of empathy with and sensitivity to others than many of their fellows possess. If they can maintain their lofty aspirations and standards, their faith in the higher realms will not desert them, nor will their yearning for love and the deeper forms of connection and attachment go unrewarded as they make their way along the road.

CHALLENGE: **REINING IN THE DEMANDS OF THE EGO BY RECOGNIZING THAT IT ONLY HINDERS TRUE CREATIVITY**
FULFILLMENT: **SHARING THEIR INTUITIVE UNDERSTANDING OF ANCIENT PHILOSOPHIES OR DEEPER WISDOM**
NOTABLE: **VIVICA A. FOX (ACTRESS, *INDEPENDENCE DAY*)**

August 3–10

BALANCED STRENGTH
LEO II

Opening themselves to the flow of their feelings may not be easy for those born in this week who travel the Way of Enchantment, as they may find it more difficult than most to overcome the restrictions implied or imposed early in life in order to become more fully themselves. Single-mindedness may be their biggest enemy, and it is likely that once they have a chosen a particular avenue to personal fulfillment, they will be reluctant to change their course, even to realize their highest potential. Yet they are capable of great devotion and creative effort. If they take care to make choices based on their hunches, intuitions, and insights rather than on others' expectations, and to employ the sturdy independence and sense of self that are their gifts in the search for love and a deeper level of fulfillment, happiness is sure to be their reward.

CHALLENGE: **FORGIVING THEMSELVES WHEN THEY LET OTHERS DOWN**
FULFILLMENT: **CHOOSING TO LIVE IN THE LIGHT BY FORSAKING THE DARKNESS**

COURTNEY LOVE
Rock singer/actress;
widow of Kurt Cobain

8/9/1964
Leo II

August 11–18

LEADERSHIP
LEO III

The larger-than-life energies of those born in this week who travel the Way of Enchantment will find wonderful opportunities for fulfillment, as Leo III's who make their way along this road will be able to imbue the people, situations, and circumstances around them with the kind of magic that can transform the everyday into something truly special. Blessed with a marked ability to tap into the collective and archetypal aspects of consciousness, these souls will nevertheless have to collect and control themselves in order to direct their actions effectively. They should take care, as well, that their personal interests do not fail to include their need to bond with others or otherwise degenerate into selfish or self-centered drives. Yet their great generosity is sure to come to the fore, and with time these gifted people will develop the sense that personal power is strengthened through giving and that pleasure shared is pleasure doubled.

CHALLENGE: **ACHIEVING RESULTS THROUGH LOVING KINDNESS RATHER THAN AGGRESSION**
FULFILLMENT: **OFFERING OTHERS THE GIFT OF INSPIRATION**
NOTABLE: **KARL LIEBKNECHT (GERMAN POLITICIAN)**

August 19–25
EXPOSURE
LEO–VIRGO CUSP

August 26–September 2
SYSTEM BUILDERS
VIRGO I

Leo–Virgos who travel the Way of Enchantment may have a difficult time emerging from their shells and are likely to resist the need to share their lives in deeply committed relationships. Yet there is much to indicate that even if they run, they may not be able to hide from the higher challenge of this karmic path. In a good number of these individuals, shyness will conflict with their desire for self-expression, just as their desire to withdraw or isolate themselves will be met with opportunities to expand their influence and deepen their concepts of love. And while it may often seem that such opportunities are unwelcome or unexpected, these insightful, sensitive people are more than capable of finding and spreading their light in the world. If they can acknowledge their self-containment as an asset rather than as an end in itself, all will go brilliantly.

ORVILLE WRIGHT
Invented and flew 1st
airplane with brother

8/19/1871
Leo–Virgo Cusp

Though the Way of Enchantment can imbue Virgo I personalities with a much higher degree of emotional awareness and sensitivity than they might otherwise have had, they may need to struggle a bit with the challenge to reveal themselves and their souls to the world as the channels of higher insight and purpose. Indeed, this can be quite difficult for many of these souls, as they may find it extremely trying to overcome both their shyness and their need to impose order on the sometimes chaotic world of emotion and feeling. In fact, they may spend their energies in trying to control others' emotions rather than in exploring their own. Yet by no means will these people be devoid of talent or creativity. If they can successfully find a way to acknowledge and analyze their intuitions and insights and share them with the world in an atmosphere of mutual trust and inspiration, they will garner great support and enthusiasm from both their life partners and the wider world.

CHALLENGE: **GENERATING THE COURAGE TO FULLY REVEAL THEMSELVES TO THOSE THEY LOVE**

FULFILLMENT: **SHARING WHAT THEY KNOW IN A SPIRIT OF GENEROSITY**

CHALLENGE: **FIGHTING FEELINGS OF DEFEAT AND INADEQUACY**

FULFILLMENT: **CHANNELING THEIR WISDOM BY SERVING OTHERS**

NOTABLES: **LYNDON B. JOHNSON (36TH U.S. PRESIDENT); KEANU REEVES (ACTOR, *SPEED*)**

September 3–10
THE ENIGMA
VIRGO II

September 11–18
THE LITERALIST
VIRGO III

Those born in this week who travel the Way of Enchantment may find wider acceptance than they ever dreamed possible, yet they will have to struggle when it comes to acknowledging their deeper needs and more soulful inclinations. Self-sufficient to the point of neurosis, they may be as hesitant to share their insights as they are to ask for help or assistance. And while keeping open the channels between the conscious and unconscious may not prove especially difficult in itself, communicating with others about matters they consider to be deeply personal will be challenging in the extreme. Yet they have the possibility for wonderful enlightenment on this journey, and if they allow themselves to understand that ultimately we are all deserving of love, love will surely find them.

THEODORE DREISER
Writer, *Sister Carrie*

8/27/1871
Virgo I

The personalities born in this week may have an especially difficult time on the Way of Enchantment, as they will be loath to emerge from their shells and divest themselves of their more self-protective attitudes and inclinations. Some may manifest extreme defensiveness regarding their own emotional sensitivity and may further waste their energies by denying their highly developed intuition. Though deeply emotional, they may shy away from exploring their passions to the fullest. Yet they do have a more expressive side and a fine instinct for truth seeking. If they can come to terms with the idea that emotions and insights are not necessarily carved in stone and that there is much to be learned from simply immersing themselves fully in the experience of life and love, their quest for fulfillment will be rewarded with great happiness and some eye-opening insights as they make their way along this life's highway.

CHALLENGE: **EXPRESSING THEIR MOST PROFOUND THOUGHTS AND FEELINGS**

FULFILLMENT: **SURRENDERING COMPLETELY TO ROMANCE**

NOTABLES: **MICHAEL DEBAKEY (SURGEON; PERFORMED 1ST U.S. HEART TRANSPLANT); ROSIE PEREZ (ACTRESS, *DO THE RIGHT THING*); RICHARD WRIGHT (WRITER, POET, *BLACK BOY*)**

CHALLENGE: **LEAVING THEIR PRACTICALITY AND SHREWDNESS AT THE DOOR ONCE IN A WHILE**

FULFILLMENT: **RECOGNIZING THAT THEY POSSESS THE SAME CAPACITY FOR LOVE AS EVERYONE ELSE**

NOTABLE: **FAITH FORD (ACTRESS, *MURPHY BROWN*)**

September 19–24

BEAUTY
VIRGO–LIBRA CUSP

Those born on the Cusp of Beauty who travel the Way of Enchantment are likely to experience considerable success and wonderful fulfillment as they make their way along the road. Their inborn ability to commit themselves completely to an ideal is likely to find full expression, yet they will have to take care not to fall under the spell of domineering or unworthy partners in their search for higher love. Yet they are blessed with more stability and greater depth than they might otherwise have had, and if they can channel their talents, creativity, and impulses toward generous sharing of themselves with others and away from self-indulgence and overly romantic fantasies, there is little that can go wrong as they seek the highest realization of their ideals and dreams.

CHALLENGE: **WORKING HARD TO UNCOVER WHY THEY AVOID THE DEEPER SIDE OF LIFE**

FULFILLMENT: **INFUSING THEIR LOVE OF BEAUTY WITH A SENSE OF THE MYSTICAL**

NOTABLES: **WILLIAM HALSTEAD (SURGEON; ESTABLISHED 1ST SURGICAL RESIDENCY PROGRAM AND STERILE TECHNIQUES); JESSE LASKY, JR. (SCREENWRITER)**

CAROLE LOMBARD
Actress, *Twentieth Century*

10/6/1908
Libra II

September 25–October 2

THE PERFECTIONIST
LIBRA I

Those born in the Week of the Perfectionist who travel the Way of Enchantment may well experience an unusually enlightening passage as they seek to express their insights and emotions in more effective ways. Their search to free their emotions through greater self-expression will figure prominently along this life journey, and they would do well to examine their real motivations as they seek to reconcile reality with their ideals of perfection. Yet they are not without their more generous impulses and are quite capable of employing their insights and intuitions in such a way as to open the channels of communication between themselves and others. If they can learn to express their needs in ways that are neither too critical nor unduly exacting, they can realize wonderful progress and ever-increasing confidence through their ability to both give and receive love.

CHALLENGE: **UNDERSTANDING HOW THEIR PERFECTIONISM HURTS THEM**

FULFILLMENT: **REALIZING THAT THE GREATEST HEALING FORCE OF ALL IS LOVE**

NOTABLES: **JANEANE GAROFALO (ACTRESS, COMEDIAN); SAMUEL ADAMS (AMERICAN POLITICIAN; REVOLUTIONARY LEADER)**

October 3–10

SOCIETY
LIBRA II

Though gifted with greater wisdom, stability, and intuition than they might otherwise have had, those born in the Week of Society who travel the Way of Enchantment will have to explore the nature of real intimacy and connection as they make their way along this road. In fact, their lives may become quite cluttered with obligations and contacts, yet real fulfillment may be lacking until they find the courage to express their deepest needs. Many of these souls also have a tendency to deny both their need and capacity for love. As a result, some may retreat from the challenge of this karmic path in superficiality or popularity at the expense of more intimate and soulful connections. Yet if they can learn to take their feelings more seriously and choose their friends and associates more carefully, they not only will find great fulfillment in the experience of love on a personal level but will also find ways to share their magic through philanthropic and philosophical pursuits.

CHALLENGE: **GROUNDING THEMSELVES THROUGH DEEPER CONNECTIONS WITH OTHERS**

FULFILLMENT: **DISCOVERING THE ENCHANTMENT IN ACTUAL RELATIONSHIPS AS OPPOSED TO THOSE THAT ARE MERE FANTASY**

NOTABLE: **JOSH LOGAN (THEATER/FILM DIRECTOR, *SOUTH PACIFIC*)**

JOHN KENNETH GALBRAITH
Economist; adviser to
President Kennedy

10/15/1908
Libra III

October 11–18

THEATER
LIBRA III

Though much more extroverted and outgoing than some who travel this road, those born in the Week of Theater may have to avoid a tendency to obscure or discount their own desires and emotions in the search for acceptance. Many of these personalities have a strong inclination to tell others what they want to hear and to show others only what they expect to see, while at the same time keeping their deeper needs hidden and their deeper insights to themselves. Yet an amazing amount of creativity and passion goes with this configuration, and if Libra III's can learn to see life in less worldly and more personal terms without giving way to histrionics, emotionally demanding attitudes, and purely selfish drives, they have a rare capacity for sharing themselves with the world as true instruments of higher consciousness and inspiration.

CHALLENGE: **SOFTENING THEIR CYNICISM AND HEARTS HARDENED BY DISAPPOINTMENT**

FULFILLMENT: **FREEING THE FLOW OF THEIR EMOTIONAL EXPRESSION**

NOTABLE: **JIM PALMER (BASEBALL PITCHER; SPORTSCASTER)**

October 19–25

DRAMA AND CRITICISM
LIBRA–SCORPIO CUSP

"Think less, feel more" might well serve as the mantra for those born on this cusp who travel the Way of Enchantment. Though likely to be highly expressive and able to articulate their emotions and insights, they will have to guard against their tendency to repeatedly list their complaints or to alienate others with their often overwhelming style of loving. Too, worldliness may substitute for spirituality, and they may misuse their insightfulness by indulging in overanalysis, hypercriticism, and rigid points of view. Nevertheless, some powerful energies come together in this configuration, and these passionate people are more than equal to its challenges. If they can avoid romantic addictions and obsessions, use their great love of beauty to enhance their vision, and share their insights in a spirit of universal love, their sense of magic is sure to manifest itself as they make their way along this karmic path.

PAT CONROY
Author, *The Great Santini*

———

10/26/1945
Scorpio I

CHALLENGE: **NOT SUCCUMBING TO THEIR PROPENSITY TO OVERANALYZE**

FULFILLMENT: **DISCOVERING THE FONT OF INTUITIVE WISDOM THAT IS AT THEIR DISPOSAL**

NOTABLES: **DIVINE (ACTOR; FEATURED IN JOHN WATERS' FILMS AS FEMALE); ALEXANDER SCHNEIDER (2D VIOLIN IN BUDAPEST STRING QUARTET)**

October 26–November 2

INTENSITY
SCORPIO I

Shyness, suspicion, and a rather defensive attitude toward others may mark the journey of those born in this week who travel the Way of Enchantment. Yet for all of the obstacles that can present themselves, there is an equal potential for deep insight and an almost mystical understanding of themselves and others. A willingness to reveal their truest natures to another will likely be the critical element in their successful navigation of this road, and some will fail its higher challenge through refusing to open their hearts. Yet they have a deep need for connection and acceptance that can find fulfillment through the cultivation of their sunnier and more creative side. If they concentrate their energies in such a way that their passions and insights are conjoined with their deep commitment to others, all will go beautifully.

CHALLENGE: **STAYING IN THE SUNNY SIDE OF THEIR PERSONALITY BY FIGHTING THEIR ATTRACTION TO THE DARK SIDE**

FULFILLMENT: **BEING APPRECIATED FOR THEIR DEPTH OF FEELING**

NOTABLE: **LEE KRASNER (ARTIST; WIFE OF JACKSON POLLOCK)**

November 3–11

DEPTH
SCORPIO II

Those born in the Week of Depth who travel the Way of Enchantment may manifest extraordinary psychic talents and pronounced mystical inclinations. Soulfulness and sadness do not necessarily go hand in hand, however, and many of these personalities will have to avoid a tendency to confuse tragedy with creativity and suffering with love. Too, they may romanticize their relationships beyond all reason. The realization that not everyone is a soul mate may come especially hard for many of them as well. Yet if they refuse to allow depression to sap their energy and obscure their sense of purpose, and if they can cultivate within themselves the ability to lighten up and nurture a more positive attitude toward themselves and others, the light of their creativity and insight will shine through and their truest purpose will be illuminated.

BURGESS MEREDITH
Actor, *Rocky*, the Penguin
in TV show *Batman*

———

11/16/1908
Scorpio III

CHALLENGE: **NOT REPRESSING THEIR DEPTH OF FEELING FOR FEAR THAT IT WILL BRING THEM UNHAPPINESS**

FULFILLMENT: **UNDERSTANDING THAT, IN LOVE, THERE IS NO ROOM FOR RESENTMENT**

NOTABLE: **FRIEDRICH SCHILLER (PLAYWRIGHT, *STURM UND DRANG*)**

November 12–18

CHARM
SCORPIO III

Developing a greater sense of compassion to augment their already considerable insight will figure prominently in the life experience of those born in the Week of Charm who travel the Way of Enchantment. Blessed with both charisma and creative talent, as well as the ability to implement their fondest dreams, Scorpio III's will nevertheless have to face down the demon of self-interest or a preoccupation with convention if they are to be really successful. Though the personalities with this configuration have a rare awareness of just what it is that touches others' hearts, their special brand of understanding may end up taking a backseat to purely selfish drives. And though many things come quite easily to them, they will have to learn that their primary challenge is to show the world who they really are and not preoccupy themselves with merely getting what they want.

CHALLENGE: **RELEASING SELFISH EGO DRIVES BY REALIZING THAT THEIR LIVES ARE MORE THAN THAT**

FULFILLMENT: **ENJOYING THE LIGHTNESS OF SPIRIT THIS PATH CAN CONFER**

NOTABLES: **IMOGENE COCA (TV COMEDIAN, *SHOW OF SHOWS*); JOSEPH MCCARTHY (U.S. SENATOR; HOUNDED COMMUNISTS IN U.S. MCCARTHY HEARINGS)**

November 19–24
REVOLUTION
SCORPIO–SAGITTARIUS CUSP

Emotional extremes and an exalted sense of victim-hood are the two principal challenges for those born on this cusp who travel the Way of Enchantment. Yet there is much to indicate that these unusual and ardent personalities will have some ecstatic and even deeply mystical experiences in their process of enlightenment. Though well equipped to turn their attentions from self-interest toward increased awareness of others and the world, these rather excitable people may miss out on many of the subtleties of human interaction, and many will waste their energies in seeking "justice" or even revenge when they feel they have been wronged. Yet there is nevertheless a potential for great transformation, and if these individuals can release the tendency to replace excess with a calmer and more sustained sense of relationship, the love they seek is sure to find fulfillment and expression.

CHALLENGE: **BEING TAKEN SERIOUSLY WITHOUT RESORTING TO AN OVERSERIOUS APPROACH**

FULFILLMENT: **EXPLODING POPULAR IDEAS IN FAVOR OF OLD TRUTHS AND PROFOUND WISDOM**

NOTABLE: **GOLDIE HAWN (ACTRESS, *LAUGH IN; PRIVATE BENJAMIN*)**

ALISTAIR COOKE
Introduced *Masterpiece Theatre*

———

11/20/1908
Scorpio–Sagittarius Cusp

November 25–December 2
INDEPENDENCE
SAGITTARIUS I

Once they come to understand that needing love isn't necessarily a bad thing, the expansive and outgoing personalities born in this week can find wonderful fulfillment along the Way of Enchantment. It can safely be said that a somewhat repressive or unusual early life may have contributed to the compulsion of these individuals to overreact emotionally in later years. However, they are more than capable of rising to the challenge of transforming their potential in ways that will benefit and inspire the multitude. Further, there is a strong indication that these individuals are destined to find a real soul mate—and, strengthened by a primary relationship, will successfully heal not only themselves but others through the magic and transformative power of love.

CHALLENGE: **NOT FEARING THAT BY ATTRACTING OTHERS, THEY WILL LOSE THEMSELVES**

FULFILLMENT: **GIVING THEIR SENSITIVE AND INSPIRED INNER SELVES THE OPPORTUNITY TO SHINE FORTH**

NOTABLE: **JOHN MCVIE (FORMED ORIGINAL FLEETWOOD MAC)**

December 3–10
THE ORIGINATOR
SAGITTARIUS II

If the unusual personalities born in the Week of the Originator are careful not to retreat from the challenges presented by the Way of Enchantment, they can realize considerable progress as they make their way along this road. It is likely that a number of these individuals will, however, experience problems with poor self-esteem, self-pity, and depression and some will require considerable encouragement or even professional help before they can emerge from their shells and into the light. Yet this karmic path promises that they will find that encouragement, especially through a love relationship of a transformative kind. If Sagittarius II's can then bring themselves to share their good fortune with others in the form of insights, empathy, and their special brand of creativity, they can give many a new twist to some very old lessons, and their insights can serve to enlighten us all.

BETTE MIDLER
Actress/singer/comedian, *The Rose*

———

12/1/1945
Sagittarius I

CHALLENGE: **APPLYING THEIR INTUITIVE BRILLIANCE TO THE TASK OF FINDING A CURE FOR THEIR WOUNDED SENSE OF SELF**

FULFILLMENT: **HAVING FOUND SELF-ACCEPTANCE, OFFERING ACCEPTANCE TO OTHERS**

December 11–18
THE TITAN
SAGITTARIUS III

The generous and larger-than-life personalities born in the Week of the Titan who travel the Way of Enchantment have a thoughtful, introspective side that need not be a liability, providing they take care to align themselves with more mystical and philosophical studies and stay clear of endless ruminations over personal slights, romantic fantasies, or an exaggerated inventory of hurt feelings. Indeed, their biggest problem may be their inability to bring their ideals down to earth and imbue everyday experience with the sense of magic that is part of their higher calling. Though rarely selfish, these people may be somewhat self-centered and will have to work hard to open the channels of communication between themselves and others. Yet once they come to understand that the seeds of potential and fulfillment will remain only seeds until they open themselves to the freer flow of emotion and inspiration available to them, and begin to seek out others as they would themselves be sought, all will go well as they travel this life's highway.

CHALLENGE: **MOVING THEIR FOCUS FROM THE LARGER WORLD TO THE PERSONAL**

FULFILLMENT: **OPENING TO THE INSPIRATION THAT IS GAINED FROM LOVE**

December 19–25

PROPHECY
SAGITTARIUS–CAPRICORN CUSP

Learning to enhance their strengths and play down their weaknesses will figure prominently on the life journeys of those born on the Cusp of Prophecy who travel the Way of Enchantment. In fact, many of these personalities may find that their greatest insights and intuitions, as well as their sense of the future, revolve around an improved and enlightened vision of themselves. Thus their principal karmic task will be to bring their sense of self to fuller and more profound expression and to refuse to take refuge in false ambitions, overwhelming responsibilities, or a stubborn refusal to connect with others. In a way, they must give themselves permission to love and be loved and avoid settling for less. And while some will have occasion to recall the words of writer Cormac McCarthy, who wrote, "Between the wish and the thing, the world lies waiting," they can rest assured that they have the strength of character and depth of instinct to see that their wishes are realized, no matter what worldly obstacles may get in the way.

LILA BELL WALLACE
Cofounded *Reader's Digest*

12/25/1889
Sagittarius–Capricorn
Cusp

CHALLENGE: **BELIEVING IN THEMSELVES**
FULFILLMENT: **REDIRECTING THE FLOW OF THEIR LIVES FROM CAREER CONCERNS TO RELATIONSHIPS**
NOTABLE: **DIANE SAWYER (TV JOURNALIST)**

December 26–January 2

THE RULER
CAPRICORN I

If the personalities born in the Week of the Ruler who travel the Way of Enchantment can reconcile themselves to the notion that acceptance of themselves and others will pave the way to love and greater personal fulfillment, they can realize considerable progress along this karmic path. Yet that task may prove more difficult than it sounds, for these people are subject to a number of secret insecurities, coupled with a tendency toward ironclad convictions. In any event, an ability to express their emotions openly is not likely to come easily, and many will have to work hard to meet this challenge. Yet if they cultivate their more nurturing side and expand their capacity to experience love through a variety of friends, partners, and children, they can unleash their creativity and enhance their insight and, through loving others, will certainly come to love themselves a bit better.

CHALLENGE: **EMBRACING THEIR OWN FEMININE SIDE**
FULFILLMENT: **LETTING A BIT OF MAGIC INTO THEIR LIVES**
NOTABLE: **DAVY JONES (BRITISH SINGER, THE MONKEES)**

January 3–9

DETERMINATION
CAPRICORN II

There is a strong inclination toward spirituality that is likely to come to the fore for Capricorn II's who make their way along this karmic path, and though it may take them a while to blossom, they are sure to cultivate the seeds of potential and fulfillment that are part of its endowment. Essential to their process will be offloading some early emotional baggage or a sense of self that was forged by an unforgiving or unenlightened early background. Yet they are well equipped to appreciate and understand the magic that is inherent in everyday experience, and if they can learn to turn their attentions away from ambition and professional pursuits and toward the more personal and even romantic side of life, their search will be rewarded by the kind of long-lived, mutually fulfilling friendships, marriages, or partnerships that few will ever know.

MORDECAI WYATT JOHNSON,
seen here with President Hoover; 1st black president, Howard University

1/12/1890
Capricorn III

CHALLENGE: **LETTING GO OF THEIR FEAR OF THE METAPHYSICAL AND THEIR INTUITION**
FULFILLMENT: **HAVING A PARTNER WITH WHOM TO SHARE THE JOYS OF LIFE**
NOTABLE: **DIANE KEATON (ACTRESS, *ANNIE HALL*)**

January 10–16

DOMINANCE
CAPRICORN III

Though many Capricorn III's will find themselves somewhat uncomfortable with the demands and challenges presented by the Way of Enchantment, they nevertheless have a prospect of great success and personal fulfillment. How quickly that fulfillment will come will depend on their willingness to open themselves to a wider world of emotion and experience. Control issues can be a problem, as these personalities may act from a place of insecurity and a sense that they are somehow undeserving of affection, which in turn may lead them to withhold love from others. Too, their natural wisdom may cause them to set themselves up as authorities when in fact they would do better to immerse themselves in the free flow of experience and interaction. Yet their very willingness to seek the truth and their impulse toward self-sacrifice will serve them well in their search for fulfillment. And if they can encourage their more generous, nurturing side and at the same time expand their experience of relationships, they will make wonderful, if measured, progress.

CHALLENGE: **HEALING THEIR SECRET INFERIORITY COMPLEX**
FULFILLMENT: **GIVING OF THEMSELVES TO OTHERS AS FULLY AS POSSIBLE**
NOTABLE: **NAOMI JUDD (COUNTRY SINGER; MOTHER HALF OF THE JUDDS)**

January 17–22
MYSTERY AND IMAGINATION
CAPRICORN–AQUARIUS CUSP

Unlikely to be too encumbered by shyness or retiringness, those born on the Cusp of Mystery and Imagination who travel the Way of Enchantment are nonetheless in for an unusual and at times amazing life experience. Powerful energies come together here, yet these individuals' challenge will be learning to direct those energies outward rather than inward. Characterized by what might best be termed "seething id," these people are not as likely to emerge from their shells as they are to burst out of them. Too, they may often feel as though their emotions are out of their control and may thus remain more or less at the mercy of their impulses. Yet there is much to indicate that they are possessed of tremendous talent and creativity. If they can manage to ground their more chaotic impulses in the magic of everyday experience, their search for love and fulfillment will certainly be rewarded.

DOLLY PARTON
Country music
singer/songwriter, "I Will
Always Love You"

1/19/1946
Capricorn–Aquarius Cusp

CHALLENGE: **PUTTING THEIR CREATIVE AND INSPIRATIONAL TALENTS TO USE IN SERVICE TO OTHERS**
FULFILLMENT: **FINDING THE ONE PROFOUND CONNECTION OF A LIFETIME**
NOTABLE: **DAVID LYNCH (DIRECTOR, *BLUE VELVET*)**

January 23–30
GENIUS
AQUARIUS I

Faulty self-image or a poor sense of self-esteem can cause Aquarius I's who travel the Way of Enchantment to withdraw from the challenge to greater emotional fulfillment and into an ivory tower of professional preoccupations and abstract concerns. Cultivating empathy will be important, as will the stabilizing influence of a beloved life partner. Though reaching out to share their inspirations and ideas with others will be challenging in any event, there is much to indicate progress, especially when these gifted individuals take the time to connect with their own profound emotions. Once they do and begin to use those emotions to inform their sense of creativity, they will have a unique capacity to back up their hunches with just the right combination of effort and inspiration and will be able to share their sense of magic with the world.

CHALLENGE: **DEVELOPING A GREATER CAPACITY FOR EMPATHY**
FULFILLMENT: **SHARING THEIR ENTHUSIASMS AND SENSE OF THE ECSTATIC WITH A BROADER AUDIENCE**
NOTABLE: **GENE SISKEL (FILM CRITIC; HALF OF SISKEL AND EBERT)**

January 31–February 7
YOUTH AND EASE
AQUARIUS II

The principal task for those born in this week who travel the Way of Enchantment will be learning to set aside their need to be accepted and to reach for a more authentic sense of life and love. There is much to indicate that these people suffer from a certain degree of emotional immaturity, which may make them hesitant to rock the boat, especially if doing so might affect their sense of personal security. Yet they also have virtuoso talents and creative gifts that will demand to be shared, and their impulse to self-expression will at some point be sure to outweigh their need for self-protection. Once they make that leap and open themselves to the possibility of more profound relationships, they will find that their truest calling is to be not merely liked but truly loved.

BORIS PASTERNAK
Lyric poet/novelist/
translator, *Dr. Zhivago*

2/10/1890
Aquarius III

CHALLENGE: **OPENING TO THEIR DEEPER SIDE AND ITS WISDOM, NO MATTER WHAT IT TELLS THEM**
FULFILLMENT: **SEEING THE MIRACLES IN EVERYDAY LIFE**
NOTABLE: **LINDA WACHNER (OWNER AND CEO, WARNACO GROUP)**

February 8–15
ACCEPTANCE
AQUARIUS III

Independent to a fault, the restless souls born in this week who travel the Way of Enchantment may nevertheless resist some of its challenges and fail to share their deeper emotions or to cultivate the broader spiritual perspective this passage demands. While some, through a need for variety, may find themselves too busy or preoccupied to open themselves on a more intimate level, others will manifest a rather irritating neediness until they come to terms with the idea that one must be willing to give in order to receive. Once they become more confident of their ability to bring joy to others and to express their love of humanity in more personal forms of connection, they will discover a wealth of inner resources and strengths. And if they keep in mind that their profound emotions and insights are gifts meant to be shared with the world and not secrets to be kept, all will go brilliantly.

CHALLENGE: **LEARNING HOW TO OFFER SOMEONE THE GREATEST GIFT OF ALL—THAT OF COMMITMENT**
FULFILLMENT: **DISCOVERING THEIR ABILITY TO ACCEPT OTHERS UNCONDITIONALLY, PARTICULARLY THOSE THEY LOVE**
NOTABLE: **MARISA BERENSON (ACTRESS; INTERNATIONAL JET-SETTER)**

February 16–22
SENSITIVITY
AQUARIUS–PISCES CUSP

Integrating their great sensitivity and empathy into a more open and willing attitude toward the world will be especially important to those born on the Cusp of Sensitivity who travel the Way of Enchantment. They have a pronounced tendency not only to hide their light under a bushel but to allow themselves to be unduly affected by others' opinions. Too, some with this configuration may deny themselves opportunities for deeper fulfillment and submerge themselves in professional concerns at the expense of their higher development. Yet if they can overcome their defensive attitudes and take care that their natural sensitivity and understanding do not manifest in touchiness or an unwillingness to commit to others, their profound comprehension of life's mysterious and magical aspects will emerge in the light of acceptance and universal love.

HARRY BELAFONTE
Singer/performer, "Day-O"

3/1/1927
Pisces I

CHALLENGE: **NOT FALLING INTO THE TRAP OF THINKING NO ONE WILL UNDERSTAND THEM AND SO KEEPING WHAT THEY KNOW TO THEMSELVES**

FULFILLMENT: **OFFERING SOMEONE THEIR COMPLETE DEVOTION**

NOTABLES: **SRI RAMAKRISHNA (RELIGIOUS LEADER, SAINTED HINDU WISEMAN); TYNE DALY (ACTRESS, *CAGNEY AND LACEY*)**

February 23–March 2
SPIRIT
PISCES I

Especially well suited to the demands of the Way of Enchantment, those born in the Week of Spirit are likely to have a fine time, providing they do not succumb to the temptations of self-pity, introspection, and inability to deal with reality. Chances are, these deeply spiritual personalities will be quite preoccupied with the realms of the metaphysical, philosophical, or even religion, yet it is important for them to ground their sensitivities and stabilize their sense of magic in everyday experience. Otherwise, they may well fail to focus their insights and intuitions in such a way that they can be shared with others. It will be important for them to stay in touch with the more sensual sides of their natures and to avoid any inclination to escape into the realms of purely theoretical ideas of love. Yet if they never lose sight of the personal side of life and open themselves to the numerous opportunities for connection that will arise along this journey, they will realize their heart's desires and their fondest dreams.

CHALLENGE: **TEMPERING THEIR EMOTIONALITY WITH A DOSE OF PRACTICALITY**

FULFILLMENT: **SHARING THEIR SPIRITUAL LIGHT WITH OTHERS**

March 3–10
THE LONER
PISCES II

The call to greater self-expression and openness to others may be difficult for those born in the Week of the Loner who travel the Way of Enchantment. Likely to be gifted with profound and soulful insights, they may nevertheless do themselves a great disservice by withdrawing from the connection. In any event, they will need much encouragement and help to emerge from their shells, for though they may have a great desire for a sense of both personal and universal love, they may well lack the tools to express themselves, as their shyness can reach almost phobic proportions. Too, they will have to undergo a certain amount of trial and error as their capacity for devotion seeks fulfillment, as they are more vulnerable to illusion or seduction than some of their fellows on this road. Yet if they can manage to summon the courage to reveal themselves more fully to others and recognize that acceptance by others of who they truly are exists in proportion to their willingness to be open to the opportunities that come their way, things will be easier for them.

CHALLENGE: **TRUSTING THEIR SIXTH SENSE MORE AND THEIR DOOM-AND-GLOOM FEARS LESS**

FULFILLMENT: **FINDING SUCCESS BY REACHING OUT TO OTHERS TO DO GOOD DEEDS**

March 11–18
DANCERS AND DREAMERS
PISCES III

Marked by enormous psychic talent and a truly visionary side, those born in this week who travel the Way of Enchantment are blessed indeed. Grounded by a more profound level of insight and natural wisdom than they might otherwise have had, many with manifest an almost clairvoyant vision of human relationships. They may, however, distance themselves from the possibilities for greater personal fulfillment through refusing to come down to earth and will have to take care that their more defensive attitudes are not disguised by self-righteousness. Yet their insights into the myriad of human emotions and experience will be marked by rare understanding and true compassion. If they can avoid an addiction to romantic fantasies and instead concentrate on reality, these wonderfully talented and gifted people are more than capable of sharing not just their hearts but their souls with the world in a spirit of generosity and transcendence.

VASLAV NIJINSKY
Ballet dancer, considered one of the greatest among the men

3/12/1890
Pisces III

CHALLENGE: **BEING CAREFUL IN THEIR CHOICE OF ROMANTIC PARTNER**

FULFILLMENT: **FEELING THAT OTHERS NEED THEM**

NOTABLES: **GEORGE PLIMPTON (WRITER, EDITOR, ACTOR, *PAPER LION*); LILLIAN KATZ (FOUNDED MAIL-ORDER FIRM LILLIAN VERNON); GOTTLIEB DAIMLER (INVENTED INTERNAL COMBUSTION ENGINE)**

The Way of Tenderness

CAPRICORN I TO CANCER I
Ruler to Empath

Those on the Way of Tenderness are here to release their need to be in control and to go in search of their inner sensitivity. The individuals on this karmic path often spend most of their energy seeking career advancement, to the detriment of their emotional life. One day, they must open up to their own feeling nature. Learning to be tender with their burgeoning albeit inchoate emotional life will help them discover their capacity to offer tenderness to others. Being aware of and valuing emotional connections to others is the goal of this karmic path. Ultimately, building and caring for a family—whether a traditional one with a spouse and children or one made up of friends or coworkers—will be the fulfillment of those on this path.

The men and women on this karmic path are born executives. They take charge and like to be in control. Structure, standards, and ironclad rules are second nature to them. Though born to rule, they are not necessarily born to lead. While the men and women on this path lack the fiery, charismatic passion required for true leadership, they are excellent managers. They are adept at implementing the plans of others, understanding technological needs and how to put them into place, maximizing efficiency, and choosing the right people for the right jobs. In matters of finance and money management, they are especially gifted. More than committed, they will see whatever they dedicate themselves to through to the very end. Stead-

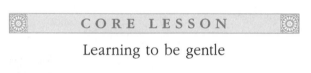

CORE LESSON
Learning to be gentle

GOAL
To achieve an awareness of their emotional connection to others

GIFTS
Capable, Dedicated, Involved

PITFALLS
Fearful, Tyrannical, Cold

fast in who they are, they rarely question themselves. So sure are they of themselves that they won't stand for criticism or resistance to their authority. They require and expect respect. Theirs is a rare no-nonsense, cool, yet capable approach to life. In fact, if unevolved, they can be ruthless.

While being in authority is second nature for the men and women on the Way of Tenderness, rarely do they take responsibility in the realm of feelings, whether their own or others. They can be hard on people, expecting much of them and rarely understanding when emotional needs get in the way of fulfilling what they consider to be duty. It is their nature to "manage" feelings. Not surprisingly, this cold, detached type of management only infuriates those close to them since it has little to do with the recognition and understanding—the empathy—that others crave. However, as tough as they are on others, they are hardest on themselves. They do not forgive their own mistakes or flaws and, true workaholics, push themselves relentlessly to achieve their lofty goals or ambitions, sacrificing their personal life along the way. So focused are the individuals on this karmic path that they have little patience for their own needs or moods, finding them inconvenient, and tend to ignore or repress their feelings rather than deal with them. Somewhere in the backgrounds of the men and women on this path is a stern disciplinarian, usually a father, who simply wouldn't put

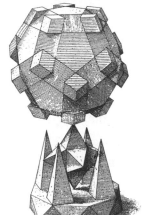

up with emotional displays, perceiving them to be weakness. Raised to disdain any expression of softness or tenderness, these men and women are often locked into a rather rigid approach to life, one that leaves both their emotional needs and those of their loved ones unmet.

The Way of Tenderness calls those on it to get in touch with their feelings. Becoming less demanding of themselves, and more understanding of the side of them that experiences life emotionally, and treating their feelings with honor as opposed to derision, will enable those on this karmic path to be tender with themselves. Opening up in this way is a whole new experience for them, one that initially won't feel particularly comfortable since their internal script tells them that the feeling realm is a dangerous quagmire, one best left buried within. The first order of business on this path is to conquer the fears associated with any expression of emotion. The second is to reawaken childhood memories and examine the patterns created then. As those on this path release the internalized figures of their parents and their scripts, they can re-create new, positive parental figures within themselves. Taking responsibility for their emotional lives and rebuilding their emotional foundations in this manner means that those on this path can begin to nurture, nourish, and protect their own more vulnerable, feeling side, thus allowing themselves to feel safe enough to allow the ex-

pression of this side of themselves. As they learn to connect with their feelings, they will come to understand how to connect with others as well.

The core lesson for those on the Way of Tenderness is to learn how to become gentle and tender, both to themselves and to others. Relaxing their rigidity, softening their demeanor and manner of expression, and worrying less about rules, rationality, and what's practical will help those on this karmic path give up their strict, uncompromising approach. As they place more value on feeling and instinct and become aware of its importance both for themselves and as a basis of connection to others, they can transform their role as authority figure from that of stern disciplinarian to loving parent. Supporting the growth of others, protecting them and their feelings, giving others the sense that they won't be judged or faulted for making mistakes, and not expecting people to be other than who they are, are the goals of this karmic path. Simply cultivating empathy and understanding will enable them to bow to its requirements. In return, the men and women on the Way of Tenderness will begin to feel a sense of belonging, of family, and of connectedness to human beings in general that they never experienced before. A great sense of joy will accompany this transformation, since, on an unconscious level, these individuals often feel very alone. Though it may sound like a cliché, the phrase "It's lonely

RELEASE

The fear of expressing feelings

REWARD

The joy of giving emotional
nourishment to others

SUGGESTION

Listen to the old scripts that may be playing in your mind. What are they telling you about your feelings? Allow yourself to express your emotions, no matter what the consequences. Realize the rewards of learning how to give.

at the top" never applied more to anyone. As they learn to give to others on an emotional level, their deep feelings of loneliness will fall away.

Since both Capricorn and Cancer are signs that prefer security to change, progress along this karmic path may be slow. Some may opt for material security and ambition rather than seeking emotional growth. Should this occur, they risk withdrawing further and further into an ivory tower, one where repressed feelings manifest themselves as fears and insecurities that take increasing control of their lives. Thus, on this path, it is sometimes necessary for some cataclysmic event to occur before those on it awaken to the feeling realm. Initially, such an event may be a debilitating depression, one that prevents those on this path from fulfilling their duties. Such an inward withdrawal is actually the first sign of renewal for these people. Such an experience may result in a flash of realization or another type of epiphany that hurtles them from their high detachment down into the soup of humanity. Another scenario may be an experience of passionate love that overwhelms their ego boundaries to become obsession. Having limited experience with how to handle their feelings, those on this path may certainly flounder in a sea of conflicting emotion once they give their feelings free rein. A caring and professional therapist or psychoanalyst could prove immeasurably useful.

It may be necessary for those on this karmic path to examine the nature of all their relationships, not just those with their family of origin. It is common for those on this path to create friendships or marry simply to increase their social standing or further their ambitions. Here we find the person who marries the boss's child to get ahead. This path calls those on it to transform their personal relationships into true intimacies, involving nurture, support, and the expression of affection. Moving in such a direction in their relationships will often cause their emotional life to blossom, and they will then shower those around them with positive energy and joy. Ultimately, those who have virtually abandoned their families to their career ambitions must return to the fold and find the right balance between work and home life. In fact, building their own family with a strong emotional core is crucial to those on this path as a symbol that they have left their personal history behind. Having evolved on this path and having come full circle, those on the Way of Tenderness will dedicate themselves not to fulfilling their ambitions, but, rather, to those they love. "Once again—with feeling" could be the directive here.

BALANCE POINT

Career and Family

Like Ebenezer Scrooge in Charles Dickens's tale *A Christmas Carol,* those on the Way of Tenderness are called to understand all the ways in which they have shut themselves off from human feelings and the effect this may have had on those around them. As those on this karmic path look back on their early lives and their own young selves with compassion, they will experience the softening that is the hallmark of this path. Ultimately, a wonderful tenderness will become their mode of being in the world and, in much the same way that Scrooge comes to care for Tiny Tim, so will those on this path learn to nurture, support, and respect those they love.

CRYSTALS AND GEMSTONES

Barite frees the individual to express the full range of emotions and supports the awareness that even while striving for external success, heartfelt connections are the true riches of life.

NOTABLES ON THIS KARMIC PATH

CALAMITY JANE

As a scout, gold prospector, Pony Express rider, and soldier, **Calamity Jane** lived an exciting and varied life. An expert markswoman and rider who dressed as a man, Jane had a tough nature and ability to hold her own in rough mining-town society, which typified her origins on the Way of Tenderness Capricorn I, the Ruler. However, she did eventually exhibit her feeling side as heroine of the smallpox epidemic in Deadwood, South Dakota, as companion to "Wild Bill" Hickok, and later by falling in love with Clinton Burk. The couple married, but Burk soon left Calamity Jane. Burned by love, Jane spent the final years of her life sharing her many wild frontier experiences with eager audiences, but died in poverty.

Singer/songwriter **Van Morrison** has consistently displayed the professional dedication common to those born on this path. Heeding his musical calling early on, he performed with various teenage groups before embarking on a highly successful solo career. Morrison has met the challenge of nurturing his emotional side (so crucial to the Way of Tenderness) by moving in the 1980s from more instinctive forms of blues and rock to highly spiritual

VAN MORRISON

and mystical arrangements. Though he has incorporated many influences into his work, Morrison has always managed to create his own unique sound, producing several hit records without giving in to crass commercialism.

GUTZON BORGLUM

American artist **Gutzon Borglum** is perhaps best known for his gigantic sculpture at Mount Rushmore. His transformation of solid rock into the faces of Washington, Jefferson, Lincoln, and Roosevelt serves as a fitting symbol for this karmic path, which moves from the hard structure of Capricorn I to the emotional expression of Cancer I. Borglum tackled this project with characteristic involvement and uncompromising dedication, laboring toward its completion until his death in 1941.

Other Notables: Louis L'Amour, Herbert von Karajan, Jessye Norman, Joan Crawford, Abraham Maslow, Bette Davis, Edward R. Murrow, Mary Wollstonecraft, Melissa Gilbert, Jimmy Stewart, Ian Fleming, John Fogerty, Carly Simon, Milton Berle, Erle Stanley Gardner, Edna Ferber, Steve Martin, Itzhak Perlman, LeAnn Rimes, Jose Feliciano, Phil Jackson, Rod Carew, Don McLean, Chuck Berry, James Boswell, Jawaharlal Nehru, Lee Salk, Nicolas Cage, Eartha Kitt, Lou Costello

---

BIRTHDAYS ON KARMIC PATH 38

July 16, 1889–December 4, 1889 | February 27, 1908–July 16, 1908

October 8, 1926–February 26, 1927 | May 20, 1945–October 7, 1945 | December 30, 1963–May 19, 1964

August 10, 1982–December 29, 1982 | March 22, 2001–August 9, 2001 | November 1, 2019–March 21, 2020

KARMIC PATH
38

March 19–24
REBIRTH
PISCES–ARIES CUSP

Those born on the Cusp of Rebirth who find themselves on the Way of Tenderness will doubtless find this an interesting journey, as they will be asked to release many of their more defensive attitudes toward human relationships and embrace the infinite opportunities for increased understanding available to them. In fact, some of their more straightforward aspects will need to be replaced with greater refinement and sensitivity, especially in their interactions and negotiations with others. Some will fail the higher challenge of this karmic path due to overambition, workaholism, or a failure to develop empathy and tolerance; others, on the other hand, will find great fulfillment as they turn their attentions away from themselves and their more entrenched attitudes and toward what may well be a wide and loving family circle.

TRACY CHAPMAN
Folksinger; Grammy
winner "Fast Car"

3/30/1964
Aries I

CHALLENGE: **NOT EXHIBITING A RUTHLESS STREAK AS THEY KNOCK OTHERS BACK WITH THE SHEER FORCE OF THEIR ARGUMENTS**
FULFILLMENT: **OPENING TO THEIR OWN SENSITIVE CORE**
NOTABLES: **LOUIS L'AMOUR (POPULAR WESTERN WRITER); JOAN CRAWFORD (ACTRESS; OSCAR FOR MILDRED PIERCE)**

March 25–April 2
THE CHILD
ARIES I

Gifted with far greater executive strength than might otherwise be the case, Aries I's can experience great satisfaction and contentment on the Way of Tenderness, providing they learn to take others' feelings as seriously as they take their own. Often rather resistant to the idea that others' views and opinions should play a role in the decisions they make, these highly individualistic personalities will have to consciously evolve their natural curiosity into a genuine understanding of others. Highly intent on making themselves understood, they may fail to put themselves in the other guy's shoes on a fairly regular basis. Yet if they can set aside their feelings of personal insecurity and perhaps some rather childish fears to reach out to those around them, and give themselves permission to be a bit more vulnerable, they can realize great progress.

CHALLENGE: **RECOGNIZING THAT RETREAT IS A FORM OF CONTROL**
FULFILLMENT: **INVOLVING THEMSELVES WITH THOSE WHO ARE NEEDY, SUCH AS PETS OR SMALL CHILDREN**
NOTABLES: **OTTO VON BISMARCK (CHANCELLOR OF GERMAN EMPIRE); GUTZON BORGLUM (SCULPTOR, MT. RUSHMORE); DAVID LEAN (DIRECTOR, LAWRENCE OF ARABIA)**

April 3–10
THE STAR
ARIES II

Those born in the Week of the Star who travel the Way of Tenderness may have to work hard to set aside the demands of ego and worldly ambition if they are to be successful in fulfilling their karmic tasks. Highly success-oriented and often motivated by a need to be at the center of the action, they may fail the higher challenge to develop greater empathy with and understanding of others. Thoroughly emotional and even passionate, they may successfully repress or overshadow some of their more nurturing and sympathetic characteristics through self-centeredness. Too, they may work hard to seek the attention of others yet hold themselves aloof when the opportunity for more intimate and emotional connection presents itself. Thus, though this may be a trying passage for some, if they examine their outworn patterns and rewrite their personal scripts to achieve greater emotional fulfillment, their efforts will not go unrewarded.

HERBERT VON KARAJAN
Conductor, Berlin
Philharmonic

4/5/1908
Aries II

CHALLENGE: **OPENING THEIR EYES TO THE NEEDS OF THEIR LOVED ONES**
FULFILLMENT: **BUILDING A FAMILY**
NOTABLE: **BETTE DAVIS (ACTRESS, JEZEBEL)**

April 11–18
THE PIONEER
ARIES III

Though they will have to guard carefully against their tendency to impose their ideas on others or to fall into the trap of believing they know what's best for everybody else, Aries III's can do quite well on the Way of Tenderness, as they have an ability to set their egos aside in the interest of a larger good. While many of these souls will struggle a bit with the challenge to release control, they are in fact quite well suited to living in groups and have an innate need to surround themselves with family and friends. If they can use this kind of contact to cultivate a greater sense of emotional connection and the tenderness necessary to nurture others into greater fulfillment, they will be rewarded with great contentment and a wide and willing support network as they make their way along this road.

CHALLENGE: **NOT THINKING THAT THEY ALWAYS KNOW WHAT'S BEST FOR EVERYONE**
FULFILLMENT: **BECOMING MORE SYMPATHETIC WITH WHAT'S REALLY GOING ON FOR OTHERS**

April 19–24
POWER
ARIES–TAURUS CUSP

The personalities born in this period can realize considerable progress along the Way of Tenderness, providing they do not allow their more ruthless or autocratic impulses to supersede or substitute for their inner desire to connect with others on an emotional level. Though likely to be passionate, they may also display some rather unpleasant fixations or obsessions. Childhood issues may plague some of the more extreme of this type, yet even at their worst they will display a rare ability to understand the emotions of others. If they are careful not to use that power for purely personal ends and always to keep in mind that empathy includes releasing control, they can realize both a high level of worldly success and a fine and fulfilling personal life as they make their way along this road.

EDWARD R. MURROW

Broadcast journalist,
Hear It Now

4/25/1908
Taurus I

CHALLENGE: **LEARNING WHEN THEY ARE REPRESSING THEIR FEELINGS THROUGH HARD WORK**

FULFILLMENT: **ALLOWING CONSIDERATION FOR OTHERS' FEELINGS TO GUIDE THEM**

NOTABLE: **LIONEL HAMPTON (JAZZ MUSICIAN)**

April 25–May 2
MANIFESTATION
TAURUS I

For the souls born in the Week of Manifestation who travel the Way of Tenderness, the challenge will lie in mitigating their natural sense of structure with the free flow of human feelings and emotions. Underneath their cool and often gruff exteriors, there runs an undercurrent of great sensitivity and vulnerability that is sure to stand them in good stead. If they can manage to combine their natural toughness, executive ability, and sense of realism with emotional connections and genuine empathy for others, their plans and goals may well result in the kinds of good works and lasting legacies that will benefit not only themselves but everyone else. On the downside, they have a tendency to be rather inflexible and even smothering. Yet if they are careful not to exploit the emotions of others in service to their own ends nor to overburden themselves with too much responsibility at the expense of real bonding, they can take huge strides along this life journey.

CHALLENGE: **NOT LETTING THEIR GRUFF FACADE KEEP THEM FROM BEING TENDER**

FULFILLMENT: **NURTURING THEIR OWN NEEDS AND FEELINGS ONCE IN A WHILE**

NOTABLE: **CALAMITY JANE (LEGENDARY FRONTIER FIGURE; DRESSED AS A MAN)**

May 3–10
THE TEACHER
TAURUS II

The strong tendency of Taurus II's to cultivate teacher-student type relationships is especially pronounced on the Way of Tenderness, as will their inclination to imbue those same relationships with all sorts of hidden emotional agendas until they come to better terms with their own emotional workings and their need to be needed. At the very least, these individuals will be fond of asserting their opinions but will doubtless have to overcome a rather severe and even authoritarian style before they can become most effective. Whatever their particular venue or area of expertise, however, their challenge is to divorce their egos and more demanding attitudes from the process of instruction—whether their own or someone else's. Yet if they always keep in mind that while one can control the messages and ideas that one shares with the world, it is ultimately impossible to control how others may receive the information—when such communications have to do with emotions.

MARY WOLLSTONECRAFT GODWIN

Early feminist; mother of Mary Shelley

4/27/1759
Taurus I

CHALLENGE: **LEARNING THEIR AUTHORITY WILL NOT BE UNDERMINED IF THEY SHOW SOME EMOTION NOW AND THEN**

FULFILLMENT: **UNDERSTANDING THAT THEIR DESTINY INVOLVES PROTECTING AND NURTURING OTHERS**

NOTABLE: **MELISSA GILBERT (ACTRESS, *LITTLE HOUSE ON THE PRAIRIE*)**

May 11–18
THE NATURAL
TAURUS III

The natural and, some might even say, exaggerated spontaneity of those born in this week who find themselves on the Way of Tenderness will certainly help to offset, or at least soften, many of the hard-boiled attitudes of the Capricorn I origins of this karmic path. Thus, many will find considerable contentment and fulfillment on this road, providing they do not allow their fear of commitment or authority issues to interfere with the call to greater understanding. In fact, these people are quite capable of turning into the kind of autocrats they most resent unless they examine themselves rather rigorously to find out what their real motives are. On the other hand, the prospect of genuine intimacy may panic them. While issues of both emotional and financial security will doubtless figure prominently in their lives, they would do well to keep in mind the sense of satisfaction they will achieve by giving themselves unselfishly to the nurture and education of others.

CHALLENGE: **REALIZING THAT TO OPEN TO THEIR EMOTIONAL SIDE, THEY MUST ALLOW DEEPER INVOLVEMENTS IN THEIR LIVES**

FULFILLMENT: **ENJOYING THE HARMONY THAT BEING IN TOUCH WITH THEIR FEELINGS BRINGS THEM**

May 19–24
ENERGY
TAURUS–GEMINI CUSP

Though blessed with much greater versatility and flexibility than some who travel the Way of Tenderness, those born on the Cusp of Energy who travel this karmic path will have to work hard to develop the sincerity, empathy, and nurturing ability it requires. In fact, they may pour their astounding energies into purely professional concerns and pursuits and live their lives on a rather detached or even superficial level, content to perform, perhaps, but reluctant to connect. Others of this type may succumb to overly demanding attitudes, requiring that all the giving come from their "better half" and all the taking be theirs. Thus, acquainting themselves with the ebb and flow of interaction and concentrating a bit less on their passions and more on the gentle art of love will be to their ultimate benefit and satisfaction.

JIMMY STEWART
Actor; Oscar for
Philadelphia Story

5/20/1908
Taurus–Gemini Cusp

CHALLENGE: **MOVING LESS QUICKLY OR FORCEFULLY, PARTICULARLY IN MATTERS OF LOVE**

FULFILLMENT: **ENGAGING IN MATURE RELATIONSHIPS, AS OPPOSED TO ROMANTIC FANTASIES**

May 25–June 2
FREEDOM
GEMINI I

The personalities born in the Week of Freedom can find much enrichment and connection as they make their way along this karmic path, yet they will have to avoid a tendency to irritability, combativeness, or "picking others to pieces" in an attempt to show off the elegance of their arguments. In fact, one of their principal challenges in the process of cultivating greater empathy and understanding may well be learning to shut up and let others do the talking. Yet they are blessed with a better ability to build for the long term and a greater sense of focus than some of their fellows born in this week. If they can control their tempers, manage their tendency to manipulate others, and turn their natural sociability into greater understanding and empathy, all will go well for them.

CHALLENGE: **NOT HIDING THEIR VULNERABILITY BY NEVER STAYING IN ONE PLACE TOO LONG**

FULFILLMENT: **RELAXING IN THE IDEA THAT IT'S OKAY TO HAVE FEELINGS**

June 3–10
NEW LANGUAGE
GEMINI II

Though perhaps there is no one better qualified to articulate the often mysterious and inexpressible worlds of emotion than those born in this week who travel the Way of Tenderness, they will find themselves inadequate to that task until they break down the barriers between their subconscious drives and their conscious forms of expression. Plagued by a sense of being misunderstood or misinterpreted, some with this configuration may allow their fears to harden into a rather armored and defensive approach to emotional expression and bonding. Yet if they give themselves permission to love and be loved, they will develop a more complete and confident sense of identity. That process will involve coming to terms with their darker inclinations and insecurities. If they are willing to rewrite old scripts and open themselves to the wealth of subtle impressions that flow from the world of the heart, they will find the connections and acceptance they seek as they travel the Way of Tenderness.

JOHN FOGERTY
Songwriter/guitarist,
Credence Clearwater
Revival

5/28/1945
Gemini I

CHALLENGE: **NOT MISTAKING THE DARK SIDE OF LIFE FOR EMOTIONAL DEPTH**

FULFILLMENT: **DISCOVERING THEIR OWN EMOTIONAL VOCABULARY**

NOTABLE: **BOB CUMMINGS (ACTOR, *DIAL M FOR MURDER*)**

June 11–18
THE SEEKER
GEMINI III

Emotional considerations may not rate especially high on these souls' list of priorities as they travel the Way of Tenderness, and many born in this week will flounder a bit as they make their way along this road. Cultivating an ability to address and examine their preoccupations with the new, with money and financial concerns, and with their reluctance to form lasting relationships may figure prominently in this life journey, and some may ignore, or at least defer rising to, its higher challenge. Too, some with this configuration will manifest this destiny in rather controlling or manipulative tendencies and will employ their considerable charms in emotional games and subtle power plays. Yet lasting love is likely to find them in the course of this life journey, and if they can manage to ground themselves in a primary relationship, they will widen their circle of affection through family, children, and friends.

CHALLENGE: **LEARNING TO ENJOY THE DEEPENING OF EMOTIONAL EXPERIENCE RATHER THAN NEEDING A VARIETY OF IT**

FULFILLMENT: **LETTING GO OF CONTROL**

NOTABLE: **ADRIENNE BARBEAU (ACTRESS, *MAUDE*; NOTED FOR GIVING BIRTH TO TWINS AT AGE 51)**

June 19–24
MAGIC
GEMINI–CANCER CUSP

Those born on the Cusp of Magic who travel the Way of Tenderness are likely to realize wonderful success along this life journey, as they are gifted with a bit more common sense than some others born in this week, as well as an astute and perceptive grasp of human emotion. They can, however, be rather cool customers, and they will have to take care to release their detachment as opportunities for love and fulfillment present themselves, or risk missing their chances through a tendency to make others work too hard to win their hearts. Yet they have an enormous capacity for love; if they can grant themselves the permission to receive love in return, they are destined for happiness and a sense of real belonging.

CHALLENGE: **RESPONDING TO OTHERS LESS OUT OF CALCULATION AND MORE FROM HEARTFELT TENDERNESS**

FULFILLMENT: **ENGAGING IN TRUE GIVE-AND-TAKE ON A FEELING LEVEL**

NOTABLES: **GEORGE PATAKI (NEW YORK GOVERNOR); ANNE MURRAY (POP AND COUNTRY SINGER); BEAUMONT NEWHALL (PHOTO HISTORIAN)**

June 25–July 2
THE EMPATH
CANCER I

Those born in the Week of the Empath who journey along the Way of Tenderness are destined for great happiness and fulfillment as they make their way through life, providing they can release their fear of their own and others' emotions and open themselves to the wider possibilities for love and connection that await them. Perhaps their principal challenge will be learning to relax and understand that emotions are meant to flow— not to be repressed or stifled in the interest of maintaining exterior calm or a sense of false control. Sensitive in the extreme, these personalities will suffer from shyness and a feeling of vulnerability, and many will have a difficult time summoning the strength to immerse themselves in what may prove to be deep emotional waters. Yet once they learn that there is an essential difference between establishing proper boundaries and erecting impenetrable walls, life will prove infinitely more sweet.

CARLY SIMON
Popular singer/songwriter,
"You're So Vain"

6/25/1945
Cancer I

CHALLENGE: **NOT BEING AFRAID OF LOSING THEMSELVES BY LOVING OTHERS**

FULFILLMENT: **SHARING THEIR SENSITIVITY AND THE INTUITIVE GIFTS IT BRINGS WITH OTHERS**

NOTABLES: **THURGOOD MARSHALL (U.S. SUPREME COURT JUSTICE; CIVIL RIGHTS ACTIVIST); ANTONIO GAUDÍ (CATALAN ARCHITECT)**

July 3–10
THE UNCONVENTIONAL
CANCER II

Those born in the Week of the Unconventional who make their way along this karmic path may experience some difficulty in coming to terms with their darker imaginings. Intent, on the one hand, on controlling their emotions, they may also have to deal with some deep-seated or unaddressed problems. Though likely to be a bit more lighthearted than many who travel this road, they may have problems with their ability to distinguish where reality leaves off and their imagination begins. Their shyness may turn to paranoia or control to autocratic obsession. And though they may be devoted to their family and friends, they would also do well to cultivate their taste for the unusual, as such associates and comrades can both indulge their need for fantasy and keep them open to a wider and farther-ranging variety of connection than these often rigid individuals might allow themselves.

ERLE STANLEY GARDNER
Writer/lawyer; created
Perry Mason

7/17/1889
Cancer III

CHALLENGE: **NOT RUNNING AWAY FROM FEELINGS INTO COLD DETACHMENT OR RUTHLESSNESS**

FULFILLMENT: **ADOPTING A LESS STRUCTURED APPROACH TO LIFE AND WATCHING AS IT FREES THEIR INNER FLOW**

NOTABLE: **NELSON ROCKEFELLER (NEW YORK GOVERNOR; VICE PRESIDENT TO GERALD FORD)**

July 11–18
THE PERSUADER
CANCER III

Repressed emotions and passions may prove the principal stumbling block for those born in the Week of the Persuader who travel the Way of Tenderness. Though these people have a deeply sensitive and emotional side, it may never see the light of day until they come to understand that the ability to control one's needs is not necessarily synonymous with total repression of one's feelings. Too, they may prove as hard on others as they often are on themselves and may doom very workable relationships with excess expectations or demanding attitudes. Others will go overboard in the experience of tenderness and love, and some may manifest overly romantic or smothering tendencies once they think they have found "the one." Yet if they can come to terms with the insecurities that often drive them and allow themselves to be vulnerable without being needy, they can realize great progress.

CHALLENGE: **GRAPPLING WITH THE RESENTMENT THAT COMES FROM THEIR IDEA THAT THEY GIVE MORE THAN THEY RECEIVE**

FULFILLMENT: **BONDING DEEPLY WITH A FEW CLOSE INTIMATES**

NOTABLES: **MILTON BERLE (ACTOR, COMEDIAN; "UNCLE MILTIE"); THOMAS BULFINCH (AUTHOR, *BULFINCH'S MYTHOLOGY*); MAX FLEISCHER (CARTOONIST, *POPEYE*)**

KARMIC PATH
38

July 19–25
OSCILLATION
CANCER–LEO CUSP

Blessed with more stability than they might otherwise have had, the unusual personalities born on the Cusp of Oscillation who navigate the Way of Tenderness will nevertheless have to delve deep to come to a better understanding of their inner workings and vulnerabilities. Though many with this configuration may quite easily achieve a sense of control or even mastery over their private domain, they run the risk of becoming rather dogmatic or emotionally blocked. Others will repeat a pattern of disappointing or unworkable relationships, leading to a sense of "déjà vu all over again" until they examine their old scripts and come to understand the part they play in their own emotional development or lack thereof. Yet they have the potential for great happiness. If they explore their need for variety in relationships and allow themselves the openness and sensitivity to be more tolerant of their own vulnerabilities, without succumbing to hopelessness or extremism, their travel along this road will become much easier.

CHALLENGE: **EXPLORING THE BROAD RANGE OF THEIR EMOTIONAL EXPRESSION—AND ATTEMPTING TO UNDERSTAND IT**
FULFILLMENT: **SETTLING INTO THE BOUNTY OF A RICH FAMILY LIFE**

DAVID SANBORN
Grammy Award-winning saxophonist; has recorded with scores of popular music's top artists

7/30/1945
Leo I

July 26–August 2
AUTHORITY
LEO I

Emotional sensitivity is not the strong suit of those born in the Week of Authority, and many born in this week who travel the Way of Tenderness will have to endure a number of disappointments before they figure out what is holding them back from a higher level of development. Competitiveness can be a problem for these individuals, as can their tendency to become extremely frustrated when things don't go their way. Too, they may be drawn to those who admire them more for their achievements and worldly power than for their empathy. Yet they have a fine generosity of spirit and can find wonderful fulfillment through their willingness to nurture and nourish themselves through a close relationship with family and, most especially, children.

CHALLENGE: **RECOGNIZING WHEN THEY ARE MERELY IMPOSING THEIR WILL, NOT CONCERN, ON OTHERS**
FULFILLMENT: **INVOKING THEIR GREAT GENEROSITY TO NURTURE AND PROTECT THEIR LOVED ONES**

August 3–10
BALANCED STRENGTH
LEO II

It may be a long, slow road for those born in this week who travel the Way of Tenderness as they may be somewhat resistant to its challenges. In fact, they may prove to be their own worst enemies when it comes to the area of emotional fulfillment, for they are unusually inflexible in many respects and are often willing to settle for less than they can have. Rather tough customers on the whole, they may define their strengths in terms more of the things they resist than of their willingness to embrace the new or untried. Yet if they can manage to be a bit less demanding of themselves and occasionally allow themselves to indulge their more sensitive and intuitive side, their empathy will blossom and their scope of opportunities for fulfillment will widen.

CHALLENGE: **NOT PERMITTING THEIR PROPENSITY TO SACRIFICE FOR OTHERS TO BECOME A MEANS OF CONTROL**
FULFILLMENT: **LOOKING OUT FOR THEIR OWN NEEDS AND FEELINGS**

STEVE MARTIN
Comedian/actor, *The Jerk*

8/14/1945
Leo III

August 11–18
LEADERSHIP
LEO III

The individuals born in the Week of Leadership who journey along the Way of Tenderness will experience numerous opportunities for fulfillment and happiness on this life journey, as long as they are willing to relinquish some of their perceived control in exchange for greater personal happiness. Hampered by an often rather closed attitude, they may seem unapproachable or unduly severe, and some will have to work to show that they are interested in and sensitive to the needs of others. Too, love and respect go hand in hand for these personalities. They will have to put a considerable effort into breaking down the barriers they erect between themselves and others here and consciously accept the need for compromise. Yet as long as they do not confuse the art of emotional expression with an insistence on getting their own way, they are capable of deep and abiding ties, and that quality alone is sure to bring them fulfillment.

CHALLENGE: **BEING LESS JUDGMENTAL AND MORE HONEST**
FULFILLMENT: **INSPIRING THE LOVE OF OTHERS**
NOTABLES: **SUZANNE FARRELL (BALLET DANCER); EDNA FERBER (WRITER; WON PULITZER, *SO BIG*)**

August 19–25

EXPOSURE
LEO–VIRGO CUSP

The art of being kind to themselves and others may not come especially easily for those born on this cusp who travel the Way of Tenderness. Though their hearts may be in the right place, they may suffer from an extreme need for privacy or desire to keep their innermost feelings to themselves, while outwardly projecting an image that is much at odds with their truest natures. Their ability to feel safe may also prove elusive. Yet their naturally astute insights and psychological flair will not be wasted. If they can turn their considerable powers of observation to the examination of their ingrained patterns and behaviors and be willing to rattle the emotional skeletons in the closet that hold them back from a higher level of fulfillment, their powers of observation will ripen into real understanding and their insights into empathy and compassion as they make their way along this life journey.

LeAnn Rimes
Country singer, "Blue";
child prodigy

8/28/1982
Virgo I

CHALLENGE: **OPENING THEIR HEARTS TO SHARE THEIR FEELINGS**

FULFILLMENT: **ENGAGING IN RELATIONSHIPS IN WHICH THE FLOW OF AFFECTION AND TRUST IS NATURAL AND EASY TO THEM**

NOTABLES: **STEVE KROFT (TV REPORTER, *60 MINUTES*); LILI BOULANGER (FRENCH COMPOSER)**

August 26–September 2

SYSTEM BUILDERS
VIRGO I

Though many of these personalities will be loath to turn their attention to emotional issues and to explore the more sensitive side of their nature, they are promised great, if rather measured, progress along the Way of Tenderness. Perhaps the principal challenge of Virgo I's on this karmic path will be to transform their impulse to service into the ability to reach out to others in more personal and emotional ways. They may, however, have problems overcoming their sense of structure and need for security, and some may content themselves with the appearance of committed relationships or caring that is devoid of content. In fact, some of these people may give a whole new meaning to concepts such as the institution of marriage, for example. Yet as difficult as this passage can be and as resistant as these personalities may be to the challenge of exploring the behavior patterns and emotional obstacles that stand in their way, the potential for a kinder, gentler future awaits.

CHALLENGE: **BECOMING AWARE OF THE CONNECTION BETWEEN THEIR NEED FOR SAFETY IN STRUCTURE AND THEIR EMOTIONAL LIFE**

FULFILLMENT: **ESTABLISHING A HARMONIOUS HOME LIFE**

NOTABLES: **VAN MORRISON (SINGER/SONGWRITER, "BROWN-EYED GIRL"); ITZHAK PERLMAN (POPULAR VIOLIN SOLOIST)**

September 3–10

THE ENIGMA
VIRGO II

Getting in touch with their feelings may be problematic for those born in the Week of the Enigma who find themselves on the Way of Tenderness, as they may be far more preoccupied with appearances and worldly ambitions than they are with acknowledging their deepest impulses and emotions. Aloofness and a certain sense of detachment may stand in the way of the higher development required by this karmic path, as may their conviction that they must work out their problems on their own. Yet they are blessed with the strength to face down even the worst personal demons and are more than capable of taking responsibility for their behavior. Once they successfully connect with their own feelings, they will be able to reach out to others in search of the interpersonal connections they seek.

Phil Jackson
Basketball coach,
Chicago Bulls

9/17/1945
Virgo III

CHALLENGE: **TEMPERING THEIR PERFECTIONISM AND JUDGMENTALISM**

FULFILLMENT: **ALLOWING THEIR KIND, THOUGHTFUL SIDE TO EXPRESS ITSELF**

NOTABLES: **JOSE FELICIANO (LATIN/POP SINGER); ROBERT A. TAFT (U.S. SENATOR FROM OHIO; "MR. REPUBLICAN")**

September 11–18

THE LITERALIST
VIRGO III

Overcoming a tendency to ruthless or judgmental tendencies will figure prominently in the life journey of those born in the Week of the Literalist who make their way along this karmic path. Though rather inflexible and often unwilling to change, they may spend their energies wrongfully by projecting their own faults and failings onto those around them, and their emphasis on practical matters may manifest itself in a preoccupation with material or professional concerns at the expense of a more complete sense of emotional connection. Yet they have some wonderful nurturing qualities that will serve them especially well. If they can learn to love themselves through the experience of genuinely caring for others, life will become vastly more rewarding.

CHALLENGE: **PLACING GREATER VALUE ON THE REALM OF FEELINGS**

FULFILLMENT: **NOT BEING AFRAID TO BE VULNERABLE**

NOTABLES: **ROBERT BENCHLEY (AUTHOR; OSCAR FOR *HOW TO SLEEP*); HERBERT HENRY ASQUITH (BRITISH PRIME MINISTER)**

September 19–24
BEAUTY
VIRGO–LIBRA CUSP

Those born on the Cusp of Beauty who travel the Way of Tenderness can find great fulfillment and happiness along the road as they are likely to be both strengthened and stabilized by the Capricorn I origins of this path. Moreover, they are likely to use the challenge of generating greater depth and sensitivity called for here. Though there is some danger that they may succumb to selfish or materialistic preoccupations at the expense of developing a greater sense of caring and compassion for those around them, their ideals of beauty and love will be unlikely to lead them down too many wrong turns as they make their way along their life journey. They will, however, derive great benefit from a rigorous self-examination of their behavior patterns and the release of any internalized feelings of unworthiness. If they can successfully commit their hearts in a spirit of compassion and emotional self-expression, they will find the sense of belonging and security they require.

MARTIN HEIDEGGER
German philosopher
———
9/26/1889
Libra I

CHALLENGE: **NOT LOSING THEMSELVES IN HIGH-MINDED NOTIONS OF ROMANCE WHEN A LITTLE TENDERNESS WILL DO**
FULFILLMENT: **UNDERSTANDING THAT LOVING KINDNESS IS THE HIGHEST IDEAL OF ALL**
NOTABLE: **WALTER LIPPMANN (WRITER, EDITOR; MOST INFLUENTIAL POLITICAL COMMENTATOR OF HIS TIME)**

September 25–October 2
THE PERFECTIONIST
LIBRA I

Often the victims of their own rigorously high standards, those born in the Week of the Perfectionist may find this a decidedly uncomfortable passage until they learn to relax and allow for the free flow of emotion in both themselves and others. Repression of their feelings may be a special problem here, as may a tendency to be both demanding and overexacting in their interactions with others. Cultivating a wider circle of social contacts and forming a variety of relationships will be especially constructive, as will allowing themselves permission to be less than perfect themselves. When they do, they will find their tolerance of others increasing in proportion and their opportunities for connection and love much increased.

CHALLENGE: **ACKNOWLEDGING THAT, DEEP DOWN, THEY POSSESS A SENSITIVE SIDE THAT NEEDS TO BE NURTURED**
FULFILLMENT: **TRUSTING AND USING THEIR EMOTIONAL RADAR**
NOTABLES: **ROD CAREW (HALL OF FAME BASEBALL PLAYER); DON MCLEAN (SINGER/SONGWRITER, "AMERICAN PIE"); BRIAN FERRY (SINGER, ROXY MUSIC)**

October 3–10
SOCIETY
LIBRA II

Though likely to be surrounded by a wide circle of friends, family, and social contacts, those born in this week who travel the Way of Tenderness may face the challenge of coming to terms with their deeper emotional levels. Often, hampered by a refusal to take their own emotions and impulses seriously, they run the risk of repressing their emotional needs or becoming mired in others' problems and concerns as a means of avoiding their own. Some of these personalities may even be quite severe or scathing in their dealings with others, and mood swings may cause them to withdraw from the seeming chaos or unmanageability of their feelings. Yet if they can avoid the dangers of fantasy and self-deception and utilize their more social impulses in their search for true belonging, they can take huge strides toward happiness in the course of this life journey.

CHUCK BERRY
Singer/guitarist,
"Johnny B. Goode"
———
10/18/1926
Libra III

CHALLENGE: **TAKING THE TIME TO ENJOY A HOT BATH, INDULGE IN FANTASY, AND LOVE THEMSELVES A BIT NOW AND THEN**
FULFILLMENT: **EXISTING AT THE CENTER OF A CIRCLE OF FRIENDS AND LOVED ONES**
NOTABLE: **KLAUS KINSKI (POLISH ACTOR)**

October 11–18
THEATER
LIBRA III

There may well be a great deal more acting out of their feelings than real awareness of their internal workings for the dramatic and compelling personalities born in this week who find themselves on the Way of Tenderness. Imbued with an aura of authority, they will feel their responsibilities strongly, yet they will have to guard against overconfidence and overdetachment as they make their way along the road. Putting themselves into another's place is not always their strongest suit, and some may well display some rather selfish or simply careless attitudes toward those around them. Especially uncomfortable when faced with the emotional expectations of others, some may withdraw from the challenges of this karmic path and take flight from opportunities to commit or belong. Yet if they allow themselves to remain open to higher levels of understanding, their sensitivity will blossom.

CHALLENGE: **NOT TAKING SUCH A STANCE OF INFORMED AUTHORITY THAT THEY FORGET HOW EMOTIONALLY VULNERABLE THEY CAN BE**
FULFILLMENT: **BEING THE PATRIARCH OR MATRIARCH OF A LARGE FAMILY**
NOTABLE: **JOHN SULLIVAN (SOLDIER IN AMERICAN REVOLUTION; GOVERNOR OF NEW HAMPSHIRE)**

October 19–25
DRAMA AND CRITICISM
LIBRA–SCORPIO CUSP

The natural magnetism and air of authority of those born in this period who travel the Way of Tenderness will stand them in wonderful stead, as others are likely to be drawn to them in considerable numbers, and the resulting opportunities for connection and contact will increase their chances to develop the sensitivity and nurturing attitudes required by this karmic path. Though likely to be quite emotional, even passionate, these souls may lack compassion and may even be quite careless and unfeeling in their dealings with others. They may often display a rather cold streak that will bear watching and may try to conquer hearts just because they can or seek to manipulate people for purely selfish ends. Yet if they can play down their more ruthless tendencies and capitalize on their need to connect with others in deep forms of emotional expression, they will make wonderful progress.

CHALLENGE: **NOT IMPOSING THEIR VIEWS AND WILLS ON OTHERS WHILE IGNORING THEIR WISHES**
FULFILLMENT: **LIVING A LIFE OF FEELING AND PASSION**
NOTABLES: **MARGARET DUMONT (ACTRESS, MARX BROTHERS FILMS); WILLIAM BUTCHER (CEO, CHASE MANHATTAN BANK)**

October 26–November 2
INTENSITY
SCORPIO I

H. R. HALDEMAN
Nixon chief of staff; involved in Watergate

——
10/27/1926
Scorpio I

Those born in the Week of Intensity who find themselves on this karmic path will have a fine and fulfilling journey, provided they do not allow their naturally suspicious attitude to hinder their higher development. Often plagued by a number of unresolved problems resulting from early childhood restrictions or an overemphasis on responsibility, they may neglect their deeper need for connection by withdrawing from more committed forms of relationship. They tend to have few close associates and may hold some intolerant and judgmental attitudes toward a wide range of people and interests. Too, they have a pronounced tendency to depression, and some may suffer from a kind of low-grade torment for years, until they come to better terms with their inner emotional workings. Yet if they can cultivate a genuine curiosity about people and allow it to blossom into real nurturing instincts, they will find themselves transformed.

CHALLENGE: **UNEARTHING THE FUNDAMENTAL KINDNESS THAT SO MUCH OF THEIR INTENSITY MASKS**
FULFILLMENT: **COMING TO TERMS WITH THEIR MOODS**
NOTABLES: **JAMES BOSWELL (WRITER, *LIFE OF SAMUEL JOHNSON*); JACK COHN (STARTED COLUMBIA PICTURES WITH BROTHER)**

November 3–11
DEPTH
SCORPIO II

Moving from a rather rigid upbringing or a preoccupation with material security and into the world of emotional exchange and expression will come rather easily for Scorpio II's who travel the Way of Tenderness. In fact, these highly sensitive and naturally empathetic people will have little trouble acquainting themselves with the deep compassion and strong emotional currents that run through their personalities, yet they may have a bit more trouble opening to others in an attitude of concern and nurture. Yet, like their emotions, their bonds tend to be deep and lasting. If they can avoid the temptation toward self-destructive behavior, an exalted sense of suffering, or a refusal to participate in everyday forms of interaction, they will find a real sense of metamorphosis as they move from pessimism to hope and from isolation to belonging.

CHALLENGE: **RELEASING THEIR TENDENCY TO CONDEMN OTHERS**
FULFILLMENT: **MANAGING THE AFFAIRS OF A LARGE ORGANIZATION OR FAMILY**

November 12–18
CHARM
SCORPIO III

JAWAHARLAL NEHRU
Indian prime minister 1947–64; father of Indira Gandhi

——
11/14/1889
Scorpio III

Those born in the Week of Charm who find themselves on this karmic path can find fulfillment along the way, providing they do not allow their natural realism and practicality to overwhelm their more emotional, empathetic side. Likely to be rather secretive and often manipulative, these souls may spend a great deal more time exploring and examining others' emotions than they do their own and will have to come to terms with the fact that much of their interest in others' motives is really a disguised desire for greater self-knowledge. In any event, these people will have to work especially hard to overcome their need for self-protection and to set aside control issues. Yet their yearning to be liked and accepted is especially strong and will doubtless serve them well in their quest for connection and belonging. Thus, there is the promise of great reward, particularly when they allow their natural sensitivity and perception to shine forth.

CHALLENGE: **DIFFERENTIATING BETWEEN THE GENEROSITY OF TENDERNESS AND A BID FOR CONTROL WITH MANIPULATION**
FULFILLMENT: **SEEKING TO USE THEIR INFLUENCE TO HELP OTHERS**
NOTABLES: **HUSSEIN TAHA (ISLAMIC SCHOLAR); EDWIN THOMAS BOOTH (SHAKESPEAREAN ACTOR); DeWITT WALLACE (PUBLISHER AND FOUNDER OF *READER'S DIGEST*)**

November 19–24

REVOLUTION
SCORPIO–SAGITTARIUS CUSP

Those born on the Cusp of Revolution who travel the Way of Tenderness will have a much more conservative streak than many of their fellows born on this cusp, and some of the less evolved of this type may literally spend their lives exalting old myths or out-of-date value systems. Though empathy and compassion will be present in these personalities, their autocratic inclinations may combine with their executive ability in a rather dangerous fashion. Some of these people have an uncomfortably pronounced tendency to set themselves up as judge, jury, and lynch mob, and all of them will have to work hard not to succumb to the notion that they know what's good for everybody else. On the plus side, however, they are well equipped to rise above old patterns and rebuild the foundations of their emotional lives if necessary. If they can turn their attentions to a more personal form of connection, concentrating a bit less on abstracts or perceived issues and a bit more on personalities, all will go well.

JEANE KIRKPATRICK
Diplomat

———
11/19/1926
Scorpio–Sagittarius Cusp

CHALLENGE: **LEARNING TO THINK BEFORE THEY SPEAK AND TO KEEP THEIR OPINIONS TO THEMSELVES**

FULFILLMENT: **REALIZING THAT OTHERS DON'T BUY THEIR ACT AND IN FACT SEE THEM AS SOFTIES UNDERNEATH**

November 25–December 2

INDEPENDENCE
SAGITTARIUS I

The inner sensitivity of the Sagittarius I personality will be sure to emerge on the Way of Tenderness, though these people will have to be careful that their emotional expressions evolve into genuine concern and compassion for others and must learn to release their chronic sense of insecurity. Often these restless souls will avoid connection in the name of freedom, even though deep inside they yearn to belong. Yet they have the potential for considerable success, especially when they allow themselves access to their considerable stores of intuition and learn to honor their feelings with the same fervor with which they honor their ideals. Generous by nature, they need to give themselves permission to be loved and open themselves to sharing their joys and sorrows in an atmosphere of mutual trust and respect; if they do so, they will find great happiness.

CHALLENGE: **PERCEIVING THAT HONOR, TRUST, AND FAIRNESS ARE NOT EQUIVALENT TO COMPASSION, TENDERNESS, AND LOVE**

FULFILLMENT: **FINDING SOMETHING OR SOMEONE THEY WANT TO RETURN HOME TO**

December 3–10

THE ORIGINATOR
SAGITTARIUS II

Likely to be far less conservative than many of their fellow travelers on the Way of Tenderness, those born in the Week of the Originator will nevertheless have to overcome some highly defensive attitudes toward emotional expression if they are to be truly successful. A restrictive or intolerant early life may have burdened them with enormous responsibilities and a desire to repress their own best talents and impulses. Often hindered by a concomitant rejection complex, they may play by the rules quite unsuccessfully until they come to understand that the rules won't necessarily get them where they want to go. Yet if they can manage to turn their need to be accepted into an effort at real communication with and compassion for other people, they will find their defenses considerably reduced and their potential for happiness increased in proportion.

WILLIE MAE THORNTON
Singer, "Big Mama"

———
12/11/1926
Sagittarius III

CHALLENGE: **CULTIVATING THE ABILITY TO MOVE BEYOND THEIR OWN CONCERNS, ESPECIALLY WHEN THE GOING GETS ROUGH**

FULFILLMENT: **EMBRACING THE SPIRITUAL LAW THAT YOU REAP WHAT YOU SOW**

NOTABLES: **PAUL BERN (DIRECTOR; MGM EXECUTIVE); THOMAS P. GORE (U.S. SENATOR)**

December 11–18

THE TITAN
SAGITTARIUS III

Empathy and generosity toward others may manifest itself in some rather judgmental or moralistic attitudes for those born in this week who find themselves on the Way of Tenderness, and some will have to work hard to overcome an unduly evangelical or authoritarian stance before they can find true fulfillment. Seemingly self-assured and confident, they may mask their insecurities and need for love under quite a few layers of false bravado. Marked by a tendency to withdraw and ruminate endlessly over slights, hurts, and problems, they will find their way much eased if only they can bring themselves to share their feelings trustingly. Learning to start small, nurture, and grow may prove a bit difficult for these souls, but if they keep their mind more on the process and less on the goal, they will find true happiness.

CHALLENGE: **BACKING OFF FROM CAREER AMBITIONS TO BE MORE INVOLVED WITH FRIENDS AND FAMILY**

FULFILLMENT: **LETTING LOVE LIGHTEN THEIR BURDEN**

December 19–25

PROPHECY
SAGITTARIUS–CAPRICORN CUSP

Not much inclined to share their insights, feelings, and intuitions, those born on this cusp who find themselves on the Way of Tenderness may project an image to the world that is stern, aloof, and uncaring—the irony being that their inner lives may be rich, emotional, and motivated by amazing insight and empathy. Simple antisocialness will prove their biggest barrier to fulfillment, and they would do well to cultivate their more nurturing side. Yet for all of that, they have a curious knack for making their feelings clear—though their form of expression may not always be verbal. If they can release the notion that it is their feelings that somehow set them apart from other people and give themselves permission to join in a community of those who appreciate their insight and comprehension, things will go much more smoothly as they travel this road.

LEE SALK
Scientist/psychologist

12/27/1926
Capricorn I

CHALLENGE: **NEEDING PEOPLE A LITTLE BIT MORE**
FULFILLMENT: **DEDICATING THEMSELVES TO SOMETHING OR SOMEONE**

December 26–January 2

THE RULER
CAPRICORN I

Likely to be highly success-oriented and motivated by the need to prove themselves to others, those born in this week may struggle a bit with the call to greater empathy and emotionalism this karmic path presents. The less evolved of this group will be rather bottled-up individuals whose emotional blockages cause them a great deal of trouble. Others, however, will respond wonderfully well to the challenges of this karmic path and be content to employ their talents for stability, solidity, and structure in creating nurturing environments for their children, employees, and loved ones. In any event, it will be essential for them to open their hearts and unbend their wills. If they can allow themselves to bond with others, others will be more than content to bond with them.

CHALLENGE: **STRUGGLING WITH THEIR PROPENSITY TO DICTATE TO, CONTROL, OR MANAGE OTHERS**
FULFILLMENT: **BUILDING A HAPPY FAMILY LIFE**
NOTABLE: **YURI GRIGOROVICH (DIRECTOR OF BOLSHOI BALLET)**

January 3–9

DETERMINATION
CAPRICORN II

Blessed with a highly astute perception of their own and others' often confusing emotions and motivations, Capricorn II's will likely enjoy this life journey greatly, though they will have to avoid a tendency to hide their real feelings or to submerge their own needs in hollow attempts at self-sacrifice. Too much responsibility and too many obligations early in life may cause them to neglect their own needs, and many will have to work especially hard to allow themselves freer personal and emotional expression. They may also be inclined to hide their light under a bushel or otherwise repress their feelings as they strive to achieve lofty professional goals and ambitions, to the detriment of their higher development. Yet they have a potential for great progress, and while they may never reach a stage where they might be called "touchy-feely," they should try to abandon their more defensive attitudes in the interest of sharing themselves with others.

NICOLAS CAGE
Actor, *Leaving Las Vegas*

1/7/1964
Capricorn II

CHALLENGE: **REALIZING THAT THEY OFTEN RUN AWAY FROM DEEPER EMOTIONAL ISSUES—ESPECIALLY WHEN RELATIONSHIPS AREN'T WORKING**
FULFILLMENT: **ENTERING INTO A RELATIONSHIP WITH A PARTNER WHO IS WILLING TO SHARE DAY-TO-DAY RESPONSIBILITIES**

January 10–16

DOMINANCE
CAPRICORN III

Those born in this week who find themselves on the Way of Tenderness may have to come to terms with some prominent control issues as they navigate this karmic path. Many of them will struggle to suppress their truest feelings and will have to cultivate a greater degree of awareness of their own motives and patterns as a means of coming to terms with the possibility that their impulse to control or dominate their immediate environment and close associates may in fact arise from their desire to repress their own passions. Owning up to and honoring their feelings will be especially important to these personalities, and they must learn to be kinder to themselves. Yet if they can become more flexible and consciously cultivate their more nurturing side, all will go well.

CHALLENGE: **NOT SEEKING LOVE TO PROVE TO THEMSELVES THAT THEY ARE WORTHWHILE**
FULFILLMENT: **FINDING THE PROPER BALANCE BETWEEN DEVOTION AND PRACTICALITY**
NOTABLES: **JOHNNIE RAY (SINGER, "CRY"); HENRY K. THAW (ARCHITECT)**

January 17–22

MYSTERY AND IMAGINATION
CAPRICORN–AQUARIUS CUSP

Those born in this period who find themselves on the Way of Tenderness may be much more light-hearted and flexible than some others on this road, yet they will have to work against their tendency to see the world and themselves in a less-than-favorable light. Nonetheless, they are blessed with a fine sense of concern and caring for others that is sure to find expression. Feelings of personal unworthiness can be a special burden for these personalities, and some of them may express hidden emotional conflicts in unpredictable ways. Coming to terms with old scripts and releasing old patterns may be difficult until they find ways to anchor themselves in a support network. Yet if they can manage to follow their hearts and reach out to others, their need to share will be rewarded with great emotional fulfillment.

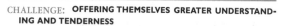

EARTHA KITT
Singer/actress, Catwoman
in TV show *Batman*
───
1/17/1927
Capricorn–Aquarius Cusp

CHALLENGE: **OFFERING THEMSELVES GREATER UNDERSTANDING AND TENDERNESS**

FULFILLMENT: **USING HUMOR TO LIGHTEN THE HEARTS OF OTHERS**

January 23–30

GENIUS
AQUARIUS I

A cool, analytical detachment characterizes the personalities born in this week who travel the Way of Tenderness, and some will fail its higher challenge through an unwillingness or inability to connect with others on an emotional level. Their fixed attitudes, coupled with a tendency toward emotional instability, can make this a trying journey until they learn to integrate their feelings with their mental and intellectual side. Until they do, their emotional expressions may take the form of emotional eruptions—and some will have rather bad tempers or suffer from bewildering mood swings. Yet they are characterized by a high sense of principle and a general empathy for the problems of the human condition. If they can allow those feelings to focus in more personal ways and learn to share them with others, they can make great progress.

CHALLENGE: **NOT HARDENING IN A RATHER COLD-BLOODED QUEST FOR SUCCESS**

FULFILLMENT: **ALLOWING LOVE TO FULLY IMBUE THEIR SOULS**

NOTABLE: **GRIGORI RASPUTIN (RELIGIOUS FIGURE KNOWN FOR STRONG INFLUENCE ON CZARINA ALEXANDRA)**

January 31–February 7

YOUTH AND EASE
AQUARIUS II

The individuals born in this week who travel the Way of Tenderness can have a highly successful and rewarding passage, as they are both well disposed toward living and working in a community of others and less overtly repressed than some of their fellows on the road. Still, emotional immaturity may plague some of these personalities, and they may spend their energies in trying to please others or to prove themselves at the expense of coming to terms with their feelings. Thus it may be difficult for these people to open up on more than a superficial level until they acquaint themselves with the issues and fears that hold them back from a higher level of fulfillment. Yet if they can learn more about themselves by reaching out to others and avoid their tendency to cut themselves off from deeper self-knowledge and emotional connections, all will go well.

BRIDGET FONDA
Actress,
Single White Female
───
1/27/1964
Aquarius I

CHALLENGE: **NOT DEVOLVING INTO LAZINESS OR TAKING SHORTCUTS WHEN IT COMES TO EMOTIONAL HONESTY**

FULFILLMENT: **PARENTING THEMSELVES BY IMPOSING BOTH STRUCTURE AND NURTURING ON THEIR INNER LIVES**

NOTABLE: **STAN GETZ (JAZZ SAXOPHONIST; EXPONENT OF COOL JAZZ)**

February 8–15

ACCEPTANCE
AQUARIUS III

While a number of the personalities born in the Week of Acceptance who travel the Way of Tenderness will make a rather superficial show of attending to others' needs, others may manifest this particular destiny as inflexibility, rigidity, or emotional repression as they attempt to come to terms with the issues of sensitivity and empathy that are part of its higher calling. Examining ingrained patterns of both thinking and feeling will be important for these people, and some will face the task of releasing old prejudices and patterns. Yet if they can manage to distinguish between vulnerability and neediness and open themselves to the wide variety of interaction and connection that awaits them, this is bound to be an ongoing education for them.

CHALLENGE: **HEALING THEIR SELF-ESTEEM ISSUES THROUGH TENDERNESS AND SELF-LOVE**

FULFILLMENT: **HAVING COME TO TERMS WITH THEIR EMOTIONAL PALETTE, BUILDING UPON IT**

NOTABLES: **CHRIS FARLEY (ACTOR, COMEDIAN; KNOWN FOR OBESITY AND PHYSICAL HUMOR; *TOMMY BOY*); LEONTYNE PRICE (OPERA SOPRANO, *PORGY AND BESS*)**

February 16–22
SENSITIVITY
AQUARIUS–PISCES CUSP

Likely to enhance some of the natural characteristics of those born in this week, the Way of Tenderness can result in a wonderfully empathetic nature or heightened sense of aggressive self-protection. The development of empathy and sensitivity will definitely be the higher road for these personalities. Hindered by a sometimes overwhelming fear of rejection, these people must develop appropriate forms of emotional expression and to channel their intensity away from professional interests or a need to prove themselves in worldly terms and toward more intimate and personal connections and contacts. Yet they have a great probability of success on this road, providing they can learn to reach out to others, overcome their fears and sense of isolation, and learn the value of deeper and more fulfilling involvements.

MATT DILLON
Actor, *The Outsiders*

2/18/1964
Aquarius–Pisces Cusp

CHALLENGE: **NOT DEALING WITH THEIR OVERSENSITIVITY WITH DEFENSIVENESS OR INTENSE EMOTIONAL DETACHMENT**

FULFILLMENT: **FINDING THE COURAGE TO BE KIND**

NOTABLES: **ROY COHN (CHIEF COUNSEL FOR MCCARTHY INVESTIGATIONS); SIR JOHN MILLS (ACTOR, DIRECTOR, *GANDHI*); REMBRANDT PEALE (ARTIST; HISTORICAL PAINTER)**

February 23–March 2
SPIRIT
PISCES I

Those born in the Week of Spirit who tread the Way of Tenderness may experience quite a bit of difficulty in learning to discern their own truest needs and emotions versus the expectations of others. Tremendously empathetic and naturally kind, they may nevertheless flounder a bit, especially if they have internalized the patterns of an unduly dominant parent or a carefully controlled childhood environment. Though they have a pronounced tendency to say what they think people want to hear, as opposed to expressing themselves more genuinely they will make wonderful progress as time goes on and they acquaint themselves with their feelings. If they can then reach out in honesty, rich rewards await them.

CHALLENGE: **STEPPING OUT OF THE WORLD OF CONCEPTS AND IDEAS INTO THE WORLD OF ONE-ON-ONE INTERACTION**

FULFILLMENT: **ENJOYING THE SATISFACTION OF EMOTIONAL RESPONSIBILITY**

March 3–10
THE LONER
PISCES II

Though likely to be emotional, empathetic, and possessed of genuine understanding, those born in the Week of the Loner who travel the Way of Tenderness may find expressing those qualities considerably more difficult. Early rejection or repression may have proven especially hard for these souls, and some may shut down their emotions as a means of self-protection in a harsh world. Alternatively, they may be so emotionally fragile that all of life is suffering for them. Too, their sensitivity may cause them to exaggerate the need for control of themselves and others. Yet it is likely that time will do much to mellow these people, and as they grow in self-confidence and understanding, their ability to connect and to express themselves will improve in proportion.

CHALLENGE: **INVOKING THEIR CAPACITY FOR STRUCTURE TO ERECT BETTER EMOTIONAL BOUNDARIES**

FULFILLMENT: **GIVING OF THEMSELVES TO PETS AND SMALL CHILDREN**

NOTABLES: **LOU COSTELLO (COMEDY TEAM, ABBOTT & COSTELLO); JULIETTE BINOCHE (FRENCH ACTRESS, *THE ENGLISH PATIENT*); BRET EASTON ELLIS (AUTHOR, *LESS THAN ZERO*); ROSA LUXEMBURG (GERMAN SOCIALIST LEADER OPPOSED TO WW I)**

March 11–18
DANCERS AND DREAMERS
PISCES III

The individuals born in this week who travel the Way of Tenderness are likely to realize great success and a fine sense of personal fulfillment, providing they can come to terms with the issues that hold them back from the freer forms of emotional expression. Their impulse to connect with others and their natural empathy are quite pronounced, yet they may do themselves great disservice by clinging to an aloof or high-handed approach to those with whom they would most like to share their thoughts and feelings. Yet once they come to terms with the idea that their tremendous need to be needed is hardly a liability, they will find wonderful rewards and happiness as they travel this karmic path.

REX HARRISON
Actor/singer, *My Fair Lady*

3/5/1908
Pisces II

CHALLENGE: **BEWARING OF APPEARING SO GLIB AND INDEPENDENT THAT NO ONE DARES TO LOVE THEM**

FULFILLMENT: **ALLOWING THEMSELVES TO NEED AS WELL AS BE NEEDED**

NOTABLES: **ROB LOWE (ACTOR, *ST. ELMO'S FIRE*; MEMBER OF THE "BRAT PACK"); EDWARD H. HEINEMANN (AIRCRAFT DESIGNER)**

The Way of Originality

CAPRICORN II TO CANCER II
Determination to the Unconventional

Those on the Way of Originality are here to delve into and assimilate the content that lies in the realms of their unconscious. As career-oriented and ambitious as they are, those on this karmic path must overcome their fear of being different from others in order to pursue their individuality. To do this, they must undergo a process of examining their inner life, dreams, fantasies, and imagination, as it is there that they will discover the wealth of inspiration that will allow them to live an authentic life. Swimming in the waters of the unconscious and discovering the fertile world of imagination that exists there in the form of metaphor, symbology, dreams, and reflections is a frightening prospect for those on this karmic path, even though it is this path's core lesson. Though they will never give up their orientation toward the practical, they must eventually use it to draw on the imagery found in their imagination and to give it material form.

The men and women on the Way of Originality come into this lifetime as rather literal-minded and materially oriented souls. Hardworking, they enjoy power and prestige and are often very concerned with status. They have little time for anything other than the pursuit of their goals. Possessing a philosophical bent, they are intrigued by the theoretical or technical. But it is facts and figures, not feelings, that most interest them. Gifted with tremendous patience, they will spend many years climbing the ladder of suc-

CORE LESSON

Vanquishing their fear of
their own unconscious

GOAL

To tap into their creative fertility

cess, rung by rung. Often those on this karmic path subscribe to the notion that the end justifies the means. This is partly because they do not deal well with failure or its consequences. Their thinking is so linear that anything that doesn't fit into the structure they have created for themselves frightens them. First and foremost, they are fearful that the more unusual side of their personality will come to light. Caught up in traditional notions of success, they're afraid it will knock them off the social register and leave them without the security of social or material resources. Thus they become quite adept at hiding their more unique personality traits and conforming to what's expected of them. These souls often use their tremendous determination to keep themselves squeezed into the little boxes in which they believe they must live. Of course, over time such repression can become quite stressful since it engenders a deep insecurity and a certain amount of inner pressure as unexpressed parts of the personality clamor for expression. These men and women often live out their own more peculiar sides by surrounding themselves with eccentric or even unstable individuals.

The great lesson of this karmic path is that these individuals must move past their fears to confront and come to terms with the shadow side of their personality—all that is unusual or unsavory—so that they can step more fully into their true selves. The watery realms of feeling and imagination that are the provenance of the sign of Cancer

---

GIFTS
Resourceful, Determined, Unique

PITFALLS
Hysterical, Fearful, Obsessive

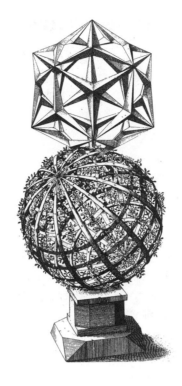

mean that they must come to grips with their great discomfort with anything that can't be defined, classified, or organized. The journey into the lunar world is a very threatening one for those on this karmic path, since they sense that their sense of self will be broken down in the process. This is both necessary and good for these individuals, given their tendency to cling to their identities so assiduously. The transformation of this path requires having the courage to probe into their peculiarities and bring them to light, thereby recreating their sense of self. Delving into the depths of who they are is not always easy for them, however. Often securely armored against deeper awareness, they may require years of work to break down their defenses so that their true natures may be revealed. The journey is well worth it, however, since ultimately the men and women on this karmic path will learn about symbols, metaphor, and the great rites and mysteries of being human: birth, life passages, and death.

There is a very real danger when those on this karmic path refuse to do its work. So powerful is the psychological content of those on this karmic path that, when repressed too severely, it can become quite twisted and explosive. If such content is allowed to fester too long, it may emerge in ways that are destructive not only to the individuals on this path but also to their loved ones, their social circle, and even society at large.

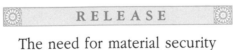

RELEASE

The need for material security

REWARD

The joy of unlocking one's inner resources

Those on this path are urged to work with a professional who can act as mediator with or guide to the underworld of psyche and feeling. Moreover, having taken the initial steps, those on this path will periodically need to return to their inner lives, both to check in with themselves and for renewal.

As those on the Way of Originality give themselves over to their process, they will succeed in mining gold from their unconscious that manifests itself as fresh and original ideas, inspired visions, and even a new approach to living. On this karmic path even a scientist or executive must become a poet. Delving into the ideas and images that lie buried within them can result in great bursts of creative energy. As those on this path progress, they will begin to manifest in the outer world what they have encountered by going into their inner world. Their homes and environments will suddenly be littered with all manner of symbolic and unusual imagery, objects, and artwork as their need for a material representation of what they have learned exhibits itself. Ideally, they also begin to explore their creativity, possibly beginning to write, paint, sculpt, create music, or experiment with photography, thus acting out an important aspect of the Cancer archetype—that of joining the conscious and unconscious realms by giving birth to new ideas. They can thus become the midwives of their own and others' artistic expression.

KARMIC PATH
39

SUGGESTION

Realize that not everything can be controlled. Chaos can be creative.
Never hesitate to ask for guidance. Awareness can be the highest calling.

Some on this path may find themselves drawn to illuminating the workings of the unconscious and may become guides to others as psychologists, therapists, or healers who journey to the nether regions of the psyche. True fulfillment will come to those on this path as they learn to give form or expression to the images found in the unconscious, thus blending their objective or material orientation with their newfound subjective understanding. They may even use their tremendous resourcefulness and business sense to manifest their creativity in physical forms that are commercially lucrative. Though they will never lack for ambition, those on the Way of Originality will find their ambitions transformed. Fear of losing the security of the corporate world can be a powerful force to keep them from doing the work of this path. However, by choosing freelance work or self-employment, they can in the end do work that is closer to their hearts.

Though many of the challenges of this karmic path will take place in the professional area of life, the real transformative process will occur on an inner level as the individuals on it feel their way toward a new self. Along the way they may have to grapple with the disapproval or discouragement of others. Consequently, a supportive and appreciative circle of friends and acquaintances is of vital importance. Of course, some on this path may go too far. Changing too radically and too quickly—whether lifestyle or hairstyle, clothing or speech—may cause those on the Way of Originality to risk rejection due to what is perceived as antisocial behavior. Often it works out best if their mates are a bit unusual or original as well, marrying someone who prefers a traditional lifestyle may hold those on this path back. It is better if, as a couple or family, they have the potential to live a nonconformist lifestyle, one that stresses personal expression. What is most important is that a polarization between Capricorn II roots and Cancer II goals does not result in a personality torn between workaholic dedication and self-destructive or hysterical revels. Balancing the material and the subjective is the real challenge of this path.

This karmic path is reminiscent of the Greek myth of the earth goddess Demeter. Demeter's creative progeny, her beloved daughter Persephone, was carried against her will into the underworld by its ruler, Hades. In her grief and despair, Demeter went in search of her daughter and neglected her duties, causing the earth to be barren. To save mankind from famine and to return fertility to the earth once more, the other gods brokered an agreement whereby Persephone spent one third of the year with Hades but the rest of the year with her mother. Symbolically, Persephone's return signifies the end of winter while she represents the seed that returns to grow in the earth at that time. But more than that, Persephone also represents her mother's creativity. Somehow this creativity was cut off or disowned by the mother, ruler of the material world, and it was only in seeking it in the underworld of the unconscious that it could be returned to her, accompanied by the seeds of fresh ideas. Thus, every year a return to the underworld must occur for the earth mother to renew her creative fertility.

BALANCE POINT

Objectivity and
Subjectivity

CRYSTALS AND GEMSTONES

Charoite aligns the upper chakras, opening the connection to "All That Is." Through this bridge the individual will find the courage and trust to live from the authentic self.

NOTABLES ON THIS KARMIC PATH

MILES DAVIS

Trumpeter **Miles Davis** epitomizes the Way of Originality. Reveling in the chaos of creativity, Davis employed his intensity to shape the face of music. After studying at the Juilliard School, Davis played until 1948 in Charlie Parker's legendary quintet. Acting as a leader of the jazz movement from 1949 to 1969, he partook in the development of such varied styles as cool jazz, hard bop, modal jazz, and fusion. Davis is also responsible for the introduction of several key players to the jazz scene; he recruited John Coltrane, Bill Evans, and Herbie Hancock for his band. Also known for his elegant style, Davis was voted one of the ten best dressed men in New York for many years.

DR. MARIA MONTESSORI

Dr. Maria Montessori became the first Italian woman to earn a medical degree, thereby displaying both her karmic path's roots in Capricorn II determination and her destination in Cancer II unconventionality. Her later work as a psychiatrist led her to establish the school system that today bears her name. Basing her educational method on freedom of movement and personal choice, she sought to encourage the very originality that characterizes her karmic path. She was consequently able to balance her Capricorn II feeling for structure with her Cancer II belief in idiosyncrasy. The many Montessori schools currently in existence continue to provide an alternative to standard education.

Jamaican reggae idol **Bob Marley** typified many aspects of the Way of Originality. Marley gave birth to his ideals in word and song, inspiring not only his countrymen but also young people of every nationality and race. Rising from the poorest of backgrounds, Marley taught others that it was possible to overcome restrictions and gain success through self-expression. Religiously inspired, he brought Rastafarianism to the world's attention and, with it, a passionate involvement with art and life. He tragically died of cancer at age 36.

BOB MARLEY

Other Notables: Pat Riley, Eric Clapton, Linda Hunt, Charlie Chaplin, F. W. Woolworth, Pete Townshend, Andy Griffith, Marilyn Monroe, Prince William, Norman Jewison, Anna Pacquin, Tony Bennett, Sir Edward Burne-Jones, Bobby Short, John Coltrane, Mark McGwire, Marla Maples, Brad Pitt, Simone de Beauvoir, Rod Stewart, Robert Burns, Tom Selleck, Mia Farrow, Mathilde Galland Krim, Rumer Godden, Frank J. Biondi, Jr., Paul Lynde, Tori Amos, Astrid Lindgren

---

BIRTHDAYS ON KARMIC PATH 39

February 25, 1889–July 15, 1889 | October 8, 1907–February 26, 1908 | May 20, 1926–October 7, 1926

December 29, 1944–May 19, 1945 | August 10, 1963–December 29, 1963

March 22, 1982–August 9, 1982 | October 31, 2000–March 21, 2001 | June 12, 2019–October 31, 2019

KARMIC PATH
39

March 19–24

REBIRTH
PISCES–ARIES CUSP

The personalities born in this week who travel the Way of Originality may well enjoy great success on this road, providing they do not shut themselves off from their powerfully intuitive and richly creative side. Though some on this path may be highly resistant to probing their own subconscious lives and will doubtless struggle with fears of being different or of rejection, others of this type who are more passionate will find they have little choice in the matter, as their more emotional aspects are sure to come to the fore, especially in their dealings with family and friends. Whether they are aware of it or not, they will be prone to "letting it all hang out." If they allow themselves the freedom to journey into the realms of a more creative and expressive way of life and refuse to take refuge from the turmoil of their own psyches in purely material concerns, adventure and rewards await them.

CHALLENGE: **DRUMMING UP THE COURAGE TO TURN INWARD**
FULFILLMENT: **FINDING THE FREEDOM THAT COMES FROM LETTING GO OF OLD WOUNDS AND SCRIPTS**
NOTABLE: **PAT RILEY (BASKETBALL COACH; 4 TITLES WITH LAKERS)**

ERIC CLAPTON
Guitarist/singer, blues master, "Layla"

3/30/1945
Aries I

March 25–April 2

THE CHILD
ARIES I

Those born in the Week of the Child who travel the Way of Originality will have great creative potential coupled with a much greater degree of spontaneity than some others on this karmic path. Yet they will have to work hard to overcome their need for approval and their need to be taken seriously before they can see that potential come to fruition. Some will also encounter problems in the arena of personal relationships, as they are inclined to manifest their need to explore their subconscious drives through some really bizarre choices of partner. Once they realize that many of their feelings and fears of being misunderstood will ease considerably once they understand themselves better, all will go well for them.

CHALLENGE: **DEALING WITH THE PAIN OF CHILDHOOD ISSUES**
FULFILLMENT: **WORKING ON THEIR OWN, FORMULATING ORIGINAL IDEAS OR PRODUCTS**
NOTABLES: **LINDA HUNT (ACTRESS; OSCAR WINNER FOR *THE YEAR OF LIVING DANGEROUSLY*); GABE KAPLAN (ACTOR, *WELCOME BACK, KOTTER*)**

April 3–10

THE STAR
ARIES II

Likely to be less afraid of what others may think of them yet a bit more afraid of themselves than their fellows on this highway, those born in the Week of the Star will have to develop the inclination to go into their inner worlds before they can find fulfillment. They are naturally quite extroverted, though much of their compulsion to be at center stage may be motivated by their need to please or be accepted by those around them. Yet their creative side will beg for expression as well. If they do not allow their sense of ambition to result in a ruthless attitude toward others, these success-oriented individuals can indeed dare to be different, as this journey requires, once they learn not to take its ups and downs so seriously. Assuming they succeed, they are likely to achieve great things and even receive acclaim for their creative efforts.

CHALLENGE: **OVERCOMING THEIR FEAR OF BEING DIFFERENT FROM OTHERS**
FULFILLMENT: **SHINING THE LIGHT OF THEIR INDIVIDUALITY AS BRIGHTLY AS POSSIBLE**

CHARLIE CHAPLIN
Actor/producer/director, "The Little Tramp"

4/16/1889
Aries III

April 11–18

THE PIONEER
ARIES III

The Pioneers who tread the Way of Originality are likely to realize considerable enlightenment, providing they allow their best ideas and imaginings full play. Gifted with a special genius for gathering other people to a cause and organizing their efforts, they may nevertheless neglect the fuller development and further exploration of their own psyches as they push toward the next horizon or goal. Yet their passionate natures will come to the fore, and though they may harbor fears of being labeled unrealistic, they will have the rare ability to ground their unique visions in the kind of solid and well-informed foundation that makes for real progress. If they take care to avoid forcing their ideas on others and concentrate on their creativity and inspiration, all will go beautifully.

CHALLENGE: **NOT BECOMING A PRISONER OF REPRESSED SUBCONSCIOUS CONTENT**
FULFILLMENT: **INSPIRING OR ENTERTAINING OTHERS WITH THEIR UNIQUE VISION**
NOTABLES: **F. W. WOOLWORTH (RETAILER; FOUNDED CHAIN); TONY DOW (ACTOR, *LEAVE IT TO BEAVER*); A. PHILIP RANDOLPH (LABOR LEADER; ACTIVIST)**

April 19–24
POWER
ARIES–TAURUS CUSP

Those born on the Cusp of Power who travel the Way of Originality will be preoccupied with personal achievement and success but will have to learn to value their own uniqueness before such achievement will manifest itself in its most creative form. Taking the risks associated with being different or mediating between the realms of the conscious and unconscious may also be a role they embrace for selfish reasons. Though gifted with a rare ability to tap into the subconscious and collective needs of humankind, they will be inclined to use their insights to manipulate others, and their thirst for personal acceptance and power may reach manic proportions. Yet if they are careful to examine their motives as they unlock their secret drives, they can realize lasting accomplishments.

CHALLENGE: **EXAMINING THEIR FEARS**
FULFILLMENT: **FINDING A WAY TO EXPRESS THEIR WELTER OF FEELINGS CREATIVELY**
NOTABLES: **G. DONALD HARRISON (DESIGNED 20TH-CENTURY CHURCH ORGANS); JOSÉ ECHEGARAY Y EIZAGUIRRE (STATESMAN; WRITER; NOBEL PRIZE FOR LITERATURE); ADOLF HITLER (NAZI DICTATOR)**

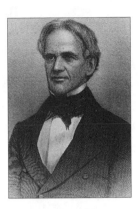

HORACE MANN
Father of American
public education

5/4/1796
Taurus II

April 25–May 2
MANIFESTATION
TAURUS I

This karmic path gives these rather practical people a greater degree of imagination than they might have otherwise but may enhance some of their more conventional leanings as well. Thus, this may not be an easy road for many Taurus I's, as they will have to do a certain amount of work to stay open to the subconscious and creative forces at their disposal. Too, their need for acceptance and approval may be pronounced, and some may harbor unreasonable fears of their more creative and unusual impulses. Yet if these personalities develop the courage to relinquish their need for security in search of greater variety and creativity and take care to develop their more playful and imaginative side, their inspirations can combine with their formidable energy and fine work ethic to create products of lasting value.

CHALLENGE: **NOT LETTING OVERDEPENDENCE ON STRUCTURE BLOCK THEIR EMOTIONAL FLOW**
FULFILLMENT: **GIVING SHAPE TO THE INSPIRATIONS THAT SPRING FROM THEIR EMOTIONAL LIFE**
NOTABLES: **BIANCA JAGGER (MODEL; EX-WIFE OF MICK); LUDWIG WITTGENSTEIN (PHILOSOPHER); RITA COOLIDGE (SINGER, ENTERTAINER)**

May 3–10
THE TEACHER
TAURUS II

Those born in the Week of the Teacher who navigate the promise and challenge of the Way of Originality can experience great fulfillment on this karmic path, providing they do not allow their fears of being different to overwhelm their need for fresh ideas and inspirations. Too, their need to share their vision with others is quite pronounced. Thus, the worst of this type will display a tendency to demagoguery or pedantry, stuck in their own narrow track, while the best of them will be able to infuse knowledge with inspiration and a sometimes astonishing grasp of universal precepts. The key to their development will be a willingness to explore their psyches with the same fervor that they search for other types of knowledge. If they can avoid holding themselves aloof from deeper awareness and be willing to talk about themselves with the same openness with which they talk about most other things, all will go beautifully.

CHALLENGE: **EMBRACING THE ADAGE "THE UNEXAMINED LIFE IS NOT WORTH LIVING."**
FULFILLMENT: **SETTING UP COMMERCIAL ENTERPRISES BASED ON THEIR CREATIVE INSPIRATIONS**
NOTABLE: **DANIEL BERRIGAN (POET; POLITICAL ACTIVIST; CLERGYMAN)**

JOHANNES BRAHMS
German composer

5/7/1833
Taurus II

May 11–18
THE NATURAL
TAURUS III

Divesting themselves of deep-seated security issues will figure prominently on the life journey of those born in the Week of the Natural who travel the Way of Originality. Though generally well suited to the challenge of accessing the higher forms of creativity, they may be a bit more reluctant when it comes to exploring their subconscious drives more deeply and may get mired in purely material concerns and stifling jobs or professions. Yet personal frustration is likely to impel them forward. If they can manage to release their ego concerns and embrace to the opportunities for self-realization available through new ideas, new pursuits, and renewed creative effort, they will achieve both great transformation and the ability to fearlessly pursue even their wildest dreams.

CHALLENGE: **MOVING RHYTHMICALLY IN TUNE TO A NATURAL CYCLE OF INTROVERSION AND EXTROVERSION**
FULFILLMENT: **FINDING SELF-EMPLOYMENT THROUGH ARTISTIC ACTIVITY**
NOTABLE: **OTTO FRANK (FATHER OF ANNE)**

May 19–24
ENERGY
TAURUS–GEMINI CUSP

If the souls born on the Cusp of Energy can summon the necessary strength to examine their own inclinations and avoid burning themselves out in an excess of superficial activities and pursuits, they can do marvelously well on this karmic path. Gifted with a knack for tapping into powerful collective energies, they may nevertheless get mired in a preoccupation with appearances or a rather compulsive attitude toward professional and material matters. Nevertheless, they are blessed with both the courage and the inclination to explore the worlds of the seen and unseen; if they can control their impulsiveness and develop the patience and personal depth necessary for self-discovery, they can create some genuine magic.

PETE TOWNSHEND
Songwriter/guitar great,
The Who

5/19/1945
Taurus–Gemini Cusp

CHALLENGE: **IMPOSING THE DISCIPLINE OF SELF-ANALYSIS ON THEMSELVES**
FULFILLMENT: **DELIBERATELY INVOKING COLLECTIVE ENERGIES**
NOTABLE: **CHRISTINE JORGENSEN (TRANSSEXUAL; 1ST PUBLICIZED SEX CHANGE BY AN AMERICAN)**

May 25–June 2
FREEDOM
GEMINI I

Though gifted with greater stability and strength than they might otherwise have had, those born in the Week of Freedom may nevertheless have a rather didactic streak that will have to be overcome if they are to shine their brightest on the Way of Originality. They will have to avoid overintellectualizing or overanalyzing their wilder and more expressive side, and some will do themselves a great disservice by talking themselves out of their own best impulses. When repressed, they may be prone to complaining and blaming until they realize that their dissatisfactions have a deeper cause. Yet once they come to terms with their originality and creative impulses, they will pursue their goals fearlessly and will be blessed with the ability to articulate the ephemeral and often indefinable world of spirit for anyone who cares to listen.

CHALLENGE: **LEARNING HOW TO INTERPRET THE WORLD OF SYMBOLS IN ORDER TO UNLOCK THEIR INNER SECRETS**
FULFILLMENT: **ARTICULATING THEIR UNIQUE FORM OF CREATIVITY AND HAVING IT UNDERSTOOD BY OTHERS**
NOTABLES: **ANDY GRIFFITH (ACTOR, *MATLOCK*); MILES DAVIS (JAZZ TRUMPETER, INNOVATOR, *KIND OF BLUE, BIRTH OF COAL*)**

June 3–10
NEW LANGUAGE
GEMINI II

Though defensiveness or a fear of being misunderstood may get things off to a rather slow start, those born in the Week of New Language who travel the Way of Originality are likely to find wonderful fulfillment as they make this life journey. Not greatly encumbered by the conventionality that can plague some others on this road, these souls have a unique gift for creative expression that is sure to come to the fore. Developing a sense of spiritual fluency may prove a bit more troublesome, however, as some may be disinclined to delve deeply into the creative force or image. Yet if they can come to better terms with their darker side and find the source from which their freshest inspirations spring, they will be more than able to translate the realms of the unconscious to the conscious world.

MARILYN MONROE
Model/actress,
*Some Like It Hot,
The Seven Year Itch*

6/1/1926
Gemini I

CHALLENGE: **ENJOYING THE ROLE OF BEING A COMPLETE ORIGINAL**
FULFILLMENT: **TAPPING INTO THE SOURCE OF THEIR MANY UNIQUE IDEAS AND CONCEPTS**
NOTABLES: **TARA LIPINSKY (OLYMPIC GOLD-WINNING FIGURE SKATING CHAMPION); ALLEN GINSBERG (BEAT POET, *HOWL*); COLLEEN DEWHURST (ACTRESS, *DESIRE UNDER THE ELMS*); JERRY STILLER (ACTOR/COMEDIAN, *SEINFELD*)**

June 11–18
THE SEEKER
GEMINI III

The personalities born in this week who travel the Way of Originality can realize considerable enlightenment, though they will have to develop a willingness to go within and examine their motives more closely before they can make real progress. Adventure-loving and much more willing to take risks than some others on this path, they may nevertheless spend their energies in an ever-widening search for more superficial forms of experience, rather than pursuing their inspirations back to the source—their font of creative impulse. Too, some with this configuration will have a rather deceptive or manipulative tendency that will bear watching. Yet if they can summon the strength to face down some of their darker impulses and at the same time resist becoming disillusioned, their creativity will blossom and they will find fulfillment.

CHALLENGE: **NOT SIDESTEPPING LOOKING AT THEIR DEEPER MOTIVATIONS BY PUTTING THOSE OF OTHERS UNDER GLASS**
FULFILLMENT: **ACCEPTING THAT INNER EXPLORATION IS JUST AS FASCINATING AS OUTER**
NOTABLE: **PAUL LYNDE (COMEDIAN; CENTER SQUARE ON *HOLLYWOOD SQUARES*)**

June 19–24

MAGIC
GEMINI–CANCER CUSP

Those born on the Cusp of Magic are well suited to the challenge of exploring the mystery of self, yet there is a danger that they may lose their way in the twists and turns of the Way of Originality. As they are naturally private people, perhaps their principal fault will be not the ability to face down their personal demons and extract the universal truths inherent in their experience but their willingness to turn their knowledge into creative activity and expression and share it with the world. Too, they may try to repress their truest impulses with logic or overanalysis. Yet if they can avoid the dangers of isolation and surround themselves with the objects and symbols that give rise to their highest creative impulses, they can realize brilliant rewards and certain fulfillment.

ELISABETH KÜBLER-ROSS
Wrote *On Death and Dying*

7/8/1926
Cancer II

CHALLENGE: **NOT ALLOWING REASON TO CAUSE THEM TO REPRESS THEIR INDIVIDUALITY**

FULFILLMENT: **DABBLING IN THE LARGE COLLECTIVE FORCES AND SYMBOLS THAT TOUCH THEIR PSYCHE**

NOTABLE: **ANNA AKHMATOVA (RUSSIAN POET)**

June 25–July 2

THE EMPATH
CANCER I

The personalities born in the Week of the Empath can experience a fine and fulfilling life journey, providing they acquaint themselves with the more universal and less personal truths of this karmic path. Highly sensitive and deeply emotional, they may have to work hard to overcome their early fear of disapproval or shyness about expressing a more authentic sense of self. Many of these people will have to face the fact that they have internalized an overly dominant or repressive parent or authority figure and will have to relinquish some old patterns in order to connect with the creative energy and inspiration to be found within themselves. On the one hand, their extreme sensitivity can pave the way for greater freedom; on the other, they may cling to old patterns and what has been termed "ghost memories" of pain or suffering and fail to find the release required for creative progress. Yet as they learn to heal themselves, they will turn out to be among those most able to heal others.

CHALLENGE: **TAKING TIME OUT FROM THE PURSUIT OF THEIR GOALS TO GET IN TOUCH WITH THE WORLDS OF THEIR FEELINGS AND UNCONSCIOUS**

FULFILLMENT: **FREEING THEMSELVES FROM ALL THE INNER VOICES THAT TELL THEM WHO THEY SHOULD BE**

July 3–10

THE UNCONVENTIONAL
CANCER II

Early repression or a harsh home environment may prove a difficult challenge for those born in this week who travel the Way of Originality, as it may cause them to retreat into a world of fantasy and imagination and to fail to develop the tools needed for creative self-expression. Many of these people will be quite fearful of their darker impulses and even harbor qualms about their sanity, while others may seek rather bizarre and unusual partners and friends as a means of offsetting their more unconventional leanings. Yet it is through facing down their fears that they will discover the value of "thinking differently." Once they find the courage to flout convention and be more eccentric, creative, and expressive, their potential for happiness is sure to flower as they integrate the best of their conscious and unconscious impulses.

MATHILDE KRIM
Founded AIDS medical foundation

7/9/1926
Cancer II

CHALLENGE: **DRAWING ON THEIR INNER STRENGTH TO FACE THEIR FEARS**

FULFILLMENT: **FINDING NONTRADITIONAL WAYS TO BE SUCCESSFUL**

NOTABLES: **JEAN COCTEAU (MODERNIST POET; FILMMAKER); FRED GWYNNE (ACTOR, *THE MUNSTERS*); NOBLE SISSLE (LYRICIST, SINGER, "I'M JUST WILD ABOUT HARRY")**

July 11–18

THE PERSUADER
CANCER III

Those born in the Week of the Persuader who find themselves on the Way of Originality can find considerable success and wonderful fulfillment, as their great personal strength endows them with the capacity to face down their fears and emerge from their shells to share their insights with the world. In fact, the principal failing of this group will be that if given a choice, they may choose gaining power over others over achieving a deeper level of self-awareness, or learning to control their needs over facing their personal problems. Yet this configuration can make for a nice mix of creative and executive ability; if they can avoid seeking excess professional responsibility and control their need for power, approval, and recognition, they will find the personal and creative freedom they seek.

CHALLENGE: **FINDING THE BASIS OF THEIR INSECURITY**

FULFILLMENT: **WORKING WITH OTHERS TO MANIFEST A CREATIVE VISION**

ORIGINALITY

July 19–25

OSCILLATION
CANCER–LEO CUSP

A need to face down their personal conflicts or problems and their sometimes overwhelming creative impulse may mark the lives of those born on this cusp who travel this karmic path. Yet their efforts to overcome their personal restrictions and their host of fears about the image they project to the world will not go unrewarded as they make their way along the road. Learning not to be so hard on themselves and to hang a bit less of their identity on what others may think of them will be paramount to their development, as will developing a willingness to give their powers of creative and emotional expression full play. Yet once they "break out"—and these individuals are almost certain to do so—they will discover the joys of a more integrated sense of self and further identify and create images that give form to the more ephemeral aspects of the human experience.

SYDNEY OMARR
Astrologer; journalist

8/5/1926
Leo II

CHALLENGE: **HAVING THE COURAGE TO LOOK AT THEIR INNER WORKINGS**

FULFILLMENT: **SETTLING INTO A CREATIVE RHYTHM**

NOTABLES: **NORMAN JEWISON (DIRECTOR, *FIDDLER ON THE ROOF*); ANNA PACQUIN (ACTRESS, *THE PIANO*)**

July 26–August 2

AUTHORITY
LEO I

Fears for their psychological health and sensitivity to "the rules" may hold a number of these personalities back from the higher challenge of the Way of Originality. Though they may be convinced that they are in charge, fate may intervene in their lives to widen their scope and offer them the opportunity to access the rich stores of knowledge available to them in the worlds of the subconscious and unconscious. Though the routes they take to that knowledge will be varied, in one way or another they may have to face down some personal demons and submerge themselves in the larger flow of experience. Thus, while some of the less evolved of this type will be content to live rather narrow lives as the proverbial big fish in a small pond, others will be more than willing to swim against the current to return to the source of their deepest creative drives. If they can dare to be different, they will have much to give.

CHALLENGE: **LEARNING THAT IT'S OKAY TO MAKE THEIR OWN RULES**

FULFILLMENT: **BEING FREE TO MEDITATE ON THEIR INNER LIVES**

August 3–10

BALANCED STRENGTH
LEO II

If they allow themselves to be aided by their fascination for unusual people and situations, Leo II's can do quite well on the Way of Originality. Yet they may bury their deepest inclinations and inspirations in a tendency to be too self-sacrificing or even masochistic, and they will have to work a bit to overcome their sometimes overwhelming sense of responsibility. They will need to divorce themselves from more conservative or careful individuals who threaten to hold them back and will have to own up to their more creative side if they are to really blossom. Yet once they summon the courage to break their bonds, they are likely to cut a dramatic figure as they undergo the process of transformation and emerge from their cocoon of self-doubt to spread their wings in the sunlight of creative expression and endeavor.

TONY BENNETT
Singer, "I Left My Heart in San Francisco"; painter

8/3/1926
Leo II

CHALLENGE: **EXAMINING THEIR MORE MASOCHISTIC TENDENCIES AND THEIR ORIGINS**

FULFILLMENT: **TURNING PAIN INTO GOLD AND PROFIT**

NOTABLES: **JACKIE PRESSER (LABOR UNION OFFICIAL); PER WAHLOO (SWEDISH AUTHOR); RICHARD ANDERSON (ACTOR, *SIX MILLION DOLLAR MAN*)**

August 11–18

LEADERSHIP
LEO III

If they refuse to allow a sense of defensiveness or fear of ridicule to hinder their higher development, Leo III's can find considerable reward on the Way of Originality. And while it may take some time for these often rigid and inflexible people to find their footing on this karmic path, the quest for greater happiness and fulfillment is important to them. Though blessed with the ability to do their own thing no matter what the consequences, they will need to explore the things in themselves that give rise to ultimately self-defeating behaviors. Yet their tastes for the unusual are sure to fuel the fires of their highly creative talents, and if they can come to understand that perhaps their principal fear is of themselves, all will go brilliantly for them.

CHALLENGE: **NOT LETTING SOMETHING AS SIMPLE AS PRIDE STAND IN THE WAY OF THE WORK OF THIS KARMIC PATH**

FULFILLMENT: **REAPING THE REWARDS OF EMOTIONAL INSIGHT**

NOTABLES: **JOHN DEREK (PHOTOGRAPHER; DIRECTOR); CLAUS VON BULOW (BRITISH BUSINESSMAN)**

August 19–25

EXPOSURE
LEO–VIRGO CUSP

Whether they like it or not, and despite their assiduous efforts to repress their true natures, the inner creativity and flamboyance of those born on the Cusp of Exposure will break out from time to time along the Way of Originality. Yet these talented people can achieve great success on this road, as they are blessed with amazing analytical skills and the ability to turn within to solve their problems. Yet they will not be without fear, and some will suffer exceedingly—and needlessly—from their anxieties over appearing to be or actually being quite different from everyone else. Yet they can experience great transformation and enlightenment in the course of this journey, and if they notice and celebrate those things in themselves that seem to capture the attention of others, they will find great fulfillment and real happiness as well.

CHALLENGE: **FEELING LESS AFRAID OF WHO THEY TRULY ARE**

FULFILLMENT: **BALANCING THE INTROVERTED AND EXTRO-VERTED SIDES OF THEIR PERSONALITIES TO ACHIEVE THE GREATEST ARTISTIC EFFECT**

NOTABLES: **TORI AMOS (SINGER/SONGWRITER, "CRUCIFY"); BENJAMIN HARRISON (23D U.S. PRESIDENT); JOHN STAMOS (ACTOR, *FULL HOUSE*)**

SIR EDWARD BURNE-JONES
Painter/designer, pre-Raphaelite artist

8/28/1833
Virgo I

August 26–September 2

SYSTEM BUILDERS
VIRGO I

The Way of Originality can be a rocky road for those born in the Week of System Builders. These often retiring people will have to overcome their fear of their truest nature, and some will retreat from their higher tasks in a stubborn refusal to venture outside their narrow world of self-imposed restrictions. Yet they have the potential for some really astonishing transformation, as these highly analytical and perceptive people are more than able to grasp the larger symbols and more universal truths inherent in human experience. If they can work through their emotions in such a way that they become better acquainted with their rich stores of knowledge, they will then be able to translate their findings in a way that will be useful to all.

CHALLENGE: **GOING SLOWLY ENOUGH ON THIS JOURNEY TO AVOID FALLING APART FROM FEAR**

FULFILLMENT: **INDULGING THEIR CAPACITY TO FIND THE UNIVERSAL TRUTHS RESIDING WITHIN THEM**

NOTABLE: **MARIA MONTESSORI (DOCTOR; EDUCATOR; DEVELOPED MONTESSORI SCHOOLS)**

September 3–10

THE ENIGMA
VIRGO II

Those born in the Week of the Enigma who make their life passage along the Way of Originality will doubtless have an interesting journey. By and large, these personalities tend to be very private people who will be well able to make the journey inward toward self-discovery. At the same time, they are hesitant to allow others into their private inner worlds and may have to develop quite a bit of courage to bring their increased self-knowledge into a larger arena of creative effort and public expression of their gifts. The danger is that they will be so needy of safety and hiding out that they never show the world who they are or what they can do. If they keep in mind that their natural good taste and discernment will not evaporate in the face of public opinion and that even their wildest impulses are tempered with common sense, they can find considerable fulfillment.

CHALLENGE: **REVEALING SOME DEEPLY HIDDEN TRUTHS TO THEMSELVES**

FULFILLMENT: **MINING THE WEALTH OF IMPRESSIONS FROM THEIR YEARS OF OBSERVING OTHERS**

NOTABLES: **SAM GOLDWYN, JR. (TOOK OVER UNIVERSAL STUDIOS FROM FATHER); WILLIAM H. DANFORTH (FOUNDED RALSTON PURINA); GEORGE HARTFORD (COFOUNDED GREAT ATLANTIC & PACIFIC TEA CO.)**

BOBBY SHORT
Singer/pianist

9/15/1926
Virgo III

September 11–18

THE LITERALIST
VIRGO III

Gifted with the strength and concentration to achieve even the most unlikely goals, Virgo III's who travel the Way of Originality will have their share of ups and downs. Though they are highly focused, they may find it difficult to focus on the nebulous and unpredictable world of their subconscious drives. Thus, these souls may resist or discount many of their own original or innovative ideas, especially if they think those ideas are colored by emotion. Nevertheless, at their core they are truth seekers; if their journey takes them on a search for self, they will emerge from their cocoon of restriction with a renewed sense of courage and creativity, plus the sense of ambition to make even the most far-fetched of their ideas fly.

CHALLENGE: **NOT FEARING THE EMOTIONS THEY HAVE KEPT LOCKED WITHIN**

FULFILLMENT: **BREAKING FREE FROM THE SELF-IMPOSED STRUCTURE OF A TRADITIONAL LIFESTYLE**

September 19–24
BEAUTY
VIRGO–LIBRA CUSP

Those born on the Cusp of Beauty who find themselves on the Way of Originality can experience a fine and fulfilling passage, providing they do not content themselves with superficial truths or fall into the trap of keeping up appearances at the expense of developing deeper awareness. Though some will be inspired to follow and embrace their more creative side, others will struggle with the internalized behavior patterns or sense of restriction imposed on them by an overly dominating parent or early authority figure and continue to act out their issues with partners of the same ilk. Yet the outlook is entirely favorable, if they will only answer the call of their deeper needs and explore the sense of beauty that is so much a part of who they are.

JOHN COLTRANE
Innovative saxophonist and jazz great

9/23/1926
Virgo–Libra Cusp

CHALLENGE: **DRAWING ON THEIR CREATIVITY, AS OPPOSED TO BEING DERIVATIVE**
FULFILLMENT: **FREEING THEMSELVES FROM THEIR ATTRACTION TO DARKER INTERESTS OR NEFARIOUS PURSUITS**
NOTABLE: **DUKE SNIDER (ONE OF BASEBALL'S GREATEST CENTER FIELDERS)**

October 3–10
SOCIETY
LIBRA II

Reaching for the courage and insight necessary to dare to be different will not come too easily for those born in the Week of Society. Though they have much creative potential, these individuals may fail the higher challenge of this karmic path by refusing to turn inward and ferret out the aspects of their psyches that hold them back from becoming more completely who they are. Though they are unlikely to suffer from the more fearful aspects of this path and not very inclined to worry about their image, they have a certain disinclination to take their own desires seriously. Yet if they can successfully emulate their more unconventional friends and associates and use their insights into others as means of self-discovery, they will discover a fine knack for creative expression and an unusual ability to bring their insights into the mainstream with diplomacy and style.

CHALLENGE: **NOT ALLOWING THEMSELVES TO BE SIDETRACKED BY THE LATEST ENTERTAINMENT**
FULFILLMENT: **HONORING THEIR INDIVIDUALITY**
NOTABLE: **ELIZABETH SHUE (ACTRESS, _LEAVING LAS VEGAS_)**

September 25–October 2
THE PERFECTIONIST
LIBRA I

Once they come to terms with the idea that their insistence on perfection and quest to impose order on an often disorderly universe may well be a projection of their deepest fears regarding their often messy emotions, this passage will doubtless go a bit more easily for Libra I's who travel the Way of Originality. Learning to release themselves from fear and owning up to their more creative and unconventional impulses may prove difficult, as they may be prone to being preoccupied with what others may think of them and projecting their worst fears about themselves onto the rest of the world. Thus, the most extreme of this type may be darkly paranoid and will have to take care to avoid the dangers of fanaticism. Yet if they can learn to release the ghosts of the past and glean that which is of value from their explorations into the unconscious, these personalities are blessed with the kind of dogged determination that will enable them to find real fulfillment.

CHALLENGE: **PUTTING AN END TO SELF-JUDGMENT AS THEY SORT THROUGH THEIR FEELINGS**
FULFILLMENT: **RETREATING PERIODICALLY FOR QUIET CONTEMPLATION**
NOTABLE: **JULIE LONDON (ACTRESS/SINGER, "CRY ME A RIVER")**

October 11–18
THEATER
LIBRA III

Reinventing the self in order to express their originality and creativity is unlikely to prove much of a problem for the talented people born in this week who travel the Way of Originality. In fact, their biggest problem may lie in their tendency to project a compelling personal image that serves as a disguise for the turmoil of inner insecurity. Yet they are blessed with a wonderful and flexible sort of strength, and that alone can carry them though many of the secret fears that plague those who find themselves on this road. Though they will have to delve deeply, their fine analytic qualities will stand them in wonderful stead, and they are likely to be able to free themselves from self-doubt through their love of the unconventional and innovative as well as to experience some rather graceful transformations along the way.

MARK McGWIRE
Baseball player; set single season record for home runs with 70 in 1998

10/1/1963
Libra I

CHALLENGE: **TAKING THE DRAMA OUT OF THEIR INNER EXPLORATIONS**
FULFILLMENT: **WORKING WITH COLLECTIVE FORCES AND SYMBOLS IN A NEW AND LUCRATIVE WAY**

KARMIC PATH
39

October 19–25

DRAMA AND CRITICISM
LIBRA–SCORPIO CUSP

These personalities are likely to experience few problems as they make their way along the Way of Originality, as their natural gifts and inclinations are very much in keeping with the call to freedom of expression and creativity that beckon. Though they will have to wrestle with issues of personal insecurity and do a bit of digging to unearth the notions that hold them back from a higher level of fulfillment, they will be more than willing to take the risks associated with daring to be different. Yet they will have to avoid a tendency to extremes as they cast off the ill-fitting garments of conformity. In fact, their principal fault may be a tendency to use power for their own ends or to manipulate knowledge and people. If they can manage to take the higher road of true creative expression and share their insights generously with others, all will go amazingly well for them.

CHALLENGE: **NOT BOGGING THEMSELVES DOWN TOO MUCH AS THEY EXPLORE THEIR PSYCHES**

FULFILLMENT: **EXPRESSING THEIR LOVE OF BEAUTY**

NOTABLES: **LORD ALFRED DOUGLAS (BRITISH POET); TRACY NELSON (ACTRESS)**

TATUM O'NEAL
Actress; youngest Oscar
winner in history for
Paper Moon

———

11/5/1963
Scorpio II

October 26–November 2

INTENSITY
SCORPIO I

Polarity of experience can mark the journey of those born in the Week of Intensity who travel the Way of Originality, yet with time and experience they can channel their highly charged emotional lives into appropriate channels for creative expression. Though they may well begin life in a much more ordered and restrained environment than where they wind up, these people may experience a number of extremes in between. Chief among their tasks will be to come to terms with their mood swings, as well as their tendency to fear and suspect everyone's motives but their own. Yet their intensity can be a great blessing, and if they can maintain a measure of objectivity as they encounter the bumps and potholes along the road, they are sure to find the joy of integration and a real sense of connection with the source from which all inspiration springs.

CHALLENGE: **LEARNING TO FORGIVE BOTH THEMSELVES AND OTHERS**

FULFILLMENT: **TRANSFORMING FEAR WITH HUMOR**

NOTABLES: **LAUREN HOLLY (ACTRESS, *PICKET FENCES*); MARLA MAPLES (MODEL)**

November 3–11

DEPTH
SCORPIO II

Though this can be a darker journey than most, those born in the Week of Depth who travel the Way of Originality are blessed with the strength and stamina to see them through even the most perilous twists and turns of this life passage. Emotionalism may thwart their best creative efforts, and some will prove to be their own worst enemies as they attempt to manipulate subconscious symbols to their own ends or otherwise seek to "own the magic" or exploit others' creative efforts. Yet more genuine forms of self-discovery and an impulse toward creative expression of their own will doubtless surface. If they can avoid depression, exalt transcendence, and rigorously avoid addiction or repetitive behavior, they can do as well as dream as they make their way along this karmic path.

CHALLENGE: **REFUSING TO REPRESS THEIR SHADOW SIDE OR ESCAPE INTO ADDICTIONS**

FULFILLMENT: **LIGHTENING THEIR SPIRIT THROUGH CREATIVE EXPRESSION**

NOTABLE: **FILIPPO TAGLIONI (ROMANTIC BALLET DANCER)**

ASTRID LINDGREN
Swedish writer,
Pippi Longstocking

———

11/14/1907
Scorpio III

November 12–18

CHARM
SCORPIO III

Those born in the Week of Charm who travel the Way of Originality may experience any number of struggles as they wrestle with issues of social acceptance and worldly power versus the need for creative and authentic self-expression. In fact, they may suffer much less early restriction or rejection than some of their fellow travelers along this road, but complacency and conventionality may prove troublesome, as they may be reluctant to venture out from a carefully constructed power base or worldly facade. Yet if they delve beneath the surface and open themselves to the richly imaginative and creative worlds that beckon, their efforts at greater originality, innovation, and increased consciousness will be fruitful and more often than not profitable.

CHALLENGE: **EXAMINING THEIR OWN INNER WORKINGS A BIT MORE AND THOSE OF OTHERS LESS**

FULFILLMENT: **APPLYING THEIR EXECUTIVE ABILITY TO A CAREER IN THE ARTS OR ARTS MANAGEMENT**

November 19–24
REVOLUTION
SCORPIO–SAGITTARIUS CUSP

Though they may have to face the fact that not every creative impulse is worthy of full expression, the individuals born on this cusp who find themselves on the Way of Originality are in for a series of rather astonishing personal transformations. Though some will be reluctant to do the inner work required and will have to face the reality of living for a time as square pegs in round holes, their natural disdain for the middle of the road is sure to come to their rescue. They are especially well suited to the higher challenge here of this karmic path, able to both cast off convention and stand up for their own and others' creative efforts and innovations. Still, they will have to be on guard against their tendency to indulge in some rather fanatic inclinations. But in the end, theirs is likely to be among the most successful and enriching of personal journeys.

CHALLENGE: **BUSYING THEMSELVES LESS WITH REVOLUTIONIZING THEIR OUTER WORLD AND MORE WITH THEIR INNER WORLD**
FULFILLMENT: **GIVING THEMSELVES PERMISSION TO BE WHOLLY ORIGINAL**

JANINE TURNER
Actress, *Northern Exposure*

12/6/1963
Sagittarius II

November 25–December 2
INDEPENDENCE
SAGITTARIUS I

Unencumbered by the shyness and insecurity that can plague many others on the Way of Originality, these dauntless, independent people will likely have an easy passage along this karmic path. The need for freedom and independence is innate to these individuals, and they should experience little trouble with the call to unearth and then to honor their own best creative and innovative impulses. While some will experience early repression and manifest their anxieties in endless emotional outbursts rather than cultivating the deeper degree of self-awareness required, such setbacks and psychological glitches are unlikely to get in their way much in their quest for independence, originality, and the freedom to be who they really are.

CHALLENGE: **GOING ON THE QUEST FOR SELF-DISCOVERY DESPITE FEARS OF WHAT THEY MIGHT DISCOVER**
FULFILLMENT: **USING THEIR INTUITIVE STRENGTHS TO LIVE LIFE THEIR OWN WAY**

December 3–10
THE ORIGINATOR
SAGITTARIUS II

Though they may have to unlearn a number of early lessons, those born in the Week of the Originator who navigate this karmic path can experience wonderful reward and achievement. For this group, it will become obvious early in life that they will have little success in disguising their creative and sometimes eccentric impulses at self-expression, and thus they will emerge much more rapidly from their shell of self-protection than some others on this road. Overcoming a defensive attitude toward others will be paramount to their success, however, and some may spend their energy rather unwisely in fruitless and rather manipulative attempts to "get in with the in crowd." Yet once they gain some perspective on their fears and develop a more detached attitude toward public opinion, their efforts are likely to be well rewarded and appreciated as a breath of fresh creative air.

CHALLENGE: **MAKING SURE THAT THEY REGULARLY ENGAGE A DEEPER LEVEL OF EMOTION OR UNDERSTANDING**
FULFILLMENT: **FINDING SUCCESS FOR THEIR ORIGINAL IDEAS**
NOTABLE: **CARRIE HAMILTON (ACTRESS)**

BRAD PITT
Actor, *Legends of the Fall*

12/18/1963
Sagittarius III

December 11–18
THE TITAN
SAGITTARIUS III

A rather exalted self-image can be both a blessing and a curse for those born in the Week of the Titan who find themselves on the Way of Originality. Though gifted with a much higher degree of self-assurance than many who make their way along this road, they will have to face down the demons of doubt and insecurity before they can find the success and freedom of expression they seek. Moreover, they would do well to come to terms with the idea that much of their own misfortune is the manifestation of unlived, unexpressed, or unloved parts of themselves. Alternatively, they may have to deal with a tendency to indulge in all manner of unrealistic fantasies before they can direct their prodigious energies in a more productive fashion. Yet if they can manage to overcome the inner insecurities that often plague them and avoid trying to wield power that has nothing real behind it, they will have some amazing and rather transcendent experiences on this karmic path.

CHALLENGE: **LEARNING THE TRUTH OF THE SPIRITUAL LAW "AS WITHIN, SO WITHOUT"**
FULFILLMENT: **INDULGING THEIR LOVE OF THE SYMBOLIC, LARGE COLLECTIVE TRENDS, AND ART FORMS OF ALL KINDS**

December 19–25
PROPHECY
SAGITTARIUS–CAPRICORN CUSP

Blessed with both great insight and a natural disdain for what people may think of them, those born on the Cusp of Prophecy who travel the Way of Originality may well have an extraordinary ability to detect both their own and others' emotional patterns. Thus they can do beautifully on this journey, though they will have to be on guard against a tendency toward antisocial behavior. Their highly developed intuitive faculties can contribute to a sense of being out of the mainstream. Some early psychic talents may have been rigorously repressed along with their spiritual and creative side, and many of these people will be positively loath to rely on anything as ephemeral as a hunch. Yet they have both the strength and the endurance to face down even the worst of personal problems and will likely experience a rediscovery or reawakening of their gifts as they make their way along the road. If they can avoid power plays, overindulgence, and misanthropy, they will enjoy great success.

SIMONE DE BEAUVOIR
French novelist
_____
1/9/1908
Capricorn II

CHALLENGE: **ENTRUSTING THEIR MANY INSIGHTS ABOUT THEMSELVES TO OTHERS**
FULFILLMENT: **RESTING SECURE IN WHO THEY ARE AND HOW THEY EXPRESS THEMSELVES**
NOTABLES: **CAB CALLOWAY (JAZZ MUSICIAN; PERFORMER); JENNIFER BEALS (ACTRESS, FLASHDANCE)**

January 3–9
DETERMINATION
CAPRICORN II

Due to an early sense of rejection, restriction, or repression, these personalities may take their time coming into their own on the Way of Originality. They may be inclined to self-sacrifice as well as self-doubt, which takes the form of paranoia. Exploring and expanding their natural inclination toward theoretical and spiritual concerns will do much to reassure them, however, by expanding their often naive perceptions of the world. Yet the gifts of this karmic path will allow them to draw on their considerable strength in their search for a more authentic sense of self. Thus, no matter how great or limited their talents, they are sure to find fullest expression if only these rugged individualists can find the courage to present their truest face to the world. These people will doubtless find that many of their creative leanings manifest themselves in a fascination with the outer edges of spiritual understanding, and some will find, or perhaps even found, whole new religions.

CHALLENGE: **UNDERSTANDING THAT EXPRESSING WHAT THEIR SUBCONSCIOUS TELLS THEM WON'T CAUSE THEIR LIVES TO CRUMBLE**
FULFILLMENT: **NOT THINKING THEY HAVE TO BE PERFECT**
NOTABLE: **FRANK BIONDI, JR. (MEDIA EXECUTIVE)**

December 26–January 2
THE RULER
CAPRICORN I

While finding the courage to flaunt convention and unearth their creative talents may not be easy for those born in the Week of the Ruler, they are more than capable of rising to the challenge to greater self-expression required by this karmic path. In fact, this path will encourage these souls to deal with their tendency to suppress their feelings, thus offering the potential for a more joyful outlook and relaxed approach to life. Until then, however, these people will not find what they're looking for, as this is a configuration that causes powerful executives to retire to sail around the world or mavens of society to move into a loft to take up sculpt or dance. Extreme as those examples may seem, they serve to illustrate that it is important for these rather controlled people to feel as though they have fulfilled their obligations before they can find the freedom to indulge their impulses.

CHALLENGE: **GIVING THEMSELVES PERMISSION TO FULFILL THEIR DREAMS**
FULFILLMENT: **CHOOSING TO PUT FAMILY LIFE AHEAD OF THEIR CAREER**
NOTABLE: **MADAME DE POMPADOUR (MISTRESS OF LOUIS XV)**

January 10–16
DOMINANCE
CAPRICORN III

Those born in the Week of Dominance may find that their principal spiritual challenges revolve around issues of tolerance, of both themselves and others. Their attraction to the unusual, the mysterious, and even the bizarre may be either rigorously and fearfully repressed or manifested in some deeply ambivalent relationships as these personalities seek to act out their urges through other people. Yet if they come to understand creativity and imagination as resources upon which they can draw, rather than as nameless threats to be conquered, this journey will be much easier. If they can learn to embrace their more outrageous inclinations and to love themselves through a process of increased understanding, they will doubtless both find fulfillment and achieve a measure of transformation.

ROD STEWART
British pop singer
_____
1/10/1945
Capricorn III

CHALLENGE: **LEARNING TO BALANCE THEIR MORAL VIEWPOINTS WITH A HEALTHY DOSE OF UNDERSTANDING**
FULFILLMENT: **FEELING THE SELF-CONFIDENCE TO ACCEPT WHO THEY ARE**
NOTABLES: **JOSE LIMON (MODERN DANCER/CHOREOGRAPHER); EDWARD TELLER (PHYSICIST; WORKED ON A AND H BOMBS)**

January 17–22

MYSTERY AND IMAGINATION
CAPRICORN–AQUARIUS CUSP

The individuals born on the Cusp of Mystery and Imagination who travel the Way of Originality can experience a truly fulfilling—which is not to say entirely smooth—passage. Until they cast off their protective armor and the chains of convention, they may find themselves in the midst of an internal war as their deeply creative natures struggle to emerge. It will also seem to many of them that they are at the mercy of so-called forces beyond their control. Yet once they come to understand that the ups and down of this passage are part of a larger design to free them from their sense of restriction and that their fears are not so much unfounded as they are inappropriate, they have the potential to indulge their creative impulses in sometimes astonishing and usually wonderful ways.

CHALLENGE: **CHOOSING TO SHARE THE TRUTHS THAT CAN BE FOUND IN THEIR INNER LIVES**

FULFILLMENT: **FINDING THAT THEIR ENERGIES ARE LESS CHAOTIC ONCE THEY GET IN TOUCH WITH THEIR SUBCONSCIOUS**

NOTABLE: **SUSAN ROTHENBERG (PAINTER; PRINTMAKER; EXPRESSIONIST)**

ROBERT BURNS
Scotland's national poet

1/25/1759
Aquarius I

January 23–30

GENIUS
AQUARIUS I

Those born in the Week of Genius who travel the Way of Originality can experience a fine and fulfilling life journey, as they are blessed with a greater belief in their right to independence than many on this road. They may have to take care not to go to extremes, however, for their disdain for convention can sometimes lead them to uncaring or even rather foolish behavior. It may be important for them to stop analyzing their thoughts and start observing their actions, feelings, even dreams a little more closely. Yet if they can manage to channel their uniquely creative talents and focus them in such a way that they are given full expression, their ideas, talent for utilizing symbols, and dramatic flair for innovation can manifest themselves in creative products that are not only unusual but tinged with more collective truth than is usual for their fellows born in this week.

CHALLENGE: **TEMPERING THEIR JUDGMENTALISM AND IMPATIENCE**

FULFILLMENT: **HAVING THE FREEDOM TO FULFILL THEIR CREATIVE VISION**

NOTABLE: **TOM SELLECK (ACTOR, *MAGNUM, P.I.*)**

January 31–February 7

YOUTH AND EASE
AQUARIUS II

The need for approval and tendency to bury their deepest fears in escapist activities will be pronounced in those born in the Week of Youth and Ease who travel the Way of Originality. Yet they have the potential for brilliant success, particularly since they are more apt than many to venture outside the mainstream and into the tributaries of genuine creative endeavor, if only because it comes easily to them. Yet many of these souls will display a particular leaning or creative gift that will steer them in the right direction. The biggest danger is that these souls may become so hooked on people's approval of their unique style that they fail to grow. Once they come to understand that the only real security to be found is that which comes from pursuing an ideal of self, they will find great happiness.

CHALLENGE: **NOT ATTRACTING TROUBLED OR DARK INDIVIDUALS WHO REPRESENT A PROJECTION OF THEIR UNCONSCIOUS**

FULFILLMENT: **TAPPING INTO THE COLLECTIVE AND WINNING ITS APPROVAL**

NOTABLES: **DAVID BRENNER (COMEDIAN); BOB MARLEY (REGGAE LEGEND; GUITARIST/SINGER)**

JACQUELINE DU PRÉ
Cellist

1/25/1945
Aquarius I

February 8–15

ACCEPTANCE
AQUARIUS III

Developing greater tolerance and understanding of those around them will be the first step toward higher development for those born in this week who travel the Way of Originality. Turning loose old fears and prejudices will be paramount to their development, and such exercises in understanding will allow them to understand themselves better. Though likely to be untroubled by what the world may think of them, these people may take some time to know what to think of themselves, and they may have to work to reveal their more vulnerable side. Yet if they indulge their thirst for broader experience and allow their inventive nature full play, they can reach the heights of personal fulfillment and happiness.

CHALLENGE: **INVESTING SOME TIME NOW AND THEN TO TRY TO UNDERSTAND WHAT MAKES THEM TICK**

FULFILLMENT: **ACKNOWLEDGING AND ACCEPTING THEIR UNIQUE INDIVIDUALITY**

NOTABLE: **MIA FARROW (ACTRESS, *ROSEMARY'S BABY*)**

February 16–22
SENSITIVITY
AQUARIUS–PISCES CUSP

Personal armor will be a big stumbling block for those born in this week who find themselves on the Way of Originality, yet they are gifted with the fortitude and endurance needed to overcome even the most overwhelming obstacles to their higher development. Most pronounced will be a tendency to shut down emotionally and concentrate on career interests at the expense of their deeper needs for creative expression. Such repression can sometimes manifest itself outwardly in a harsh or even ruthless attitude as these individuals seek to protect themselves against intrusions on their private inner worlds. Yet the secrets of sensitivity and creativity will definitely come out in the course of this passage, and their great challenge is to be able to risk greater integration of their own personality. When they find the courage to face their fears and learn to embrace the unusual and unconventional, they will be liberated from the bonds of self in a uniquely fulfilling way.

JOHN HEARD
Actor

3/7/1945
Pisces II

CHALLENGE: **FINDING THE RIGHT BALANCE BETWEEN THEIR WORLDLY IDEALISM AND DEEP INNER SENSITIVITY**
FULFILLMENT: **COMING TO TERMS WITH THEIR OWN DEPTH**

February 23–March 2
SPIRIT
PISCES I

Once they have successfully transcended the restrictions and fears of early life, the principal danger for those born in the Week of Spirit will be that they may fall victim to some far-out ideas or take some disastrously wrong turns. Fanaticism and a tendency to fall under the domination of others may be problems that repeatedly appear in the course of this life experience, and Pisces I's will have to draw upon the strength and practical talent that is part of the endowment of this karmic path if they are to stay grounded in the here and now. Indeed, some with this configuration may become spiritual or creative groupies, attaching themselves to all sorts of cults and movements, while others will have to avoid the traps of working out their issues in abusive relationships. Yet it is likely that their very spirituality will prove to be their greatest strength, and if they allow themselves the freedom to mine the gold of their subconscious drives, amazing transformation and productive creative effort will be the hallmarks of this journey.

CHALLENGE: **NOT LETTING THEMSELVES BE SWAMPED BY THEIR PSYCHOLOGICAL PROCESSES**
FULFILLMENT: **GIVING FORM TO THEIR UNIQUE VISION, IN PARTICULAR WHEN RELATED TO SPIRITUALITY OR RELIGION**

March 3–10
THE LONER
PISCES II

Fears of rejection and humiliation can reach almost phobic proportions for those born in the Week of the Loner who travel the Way of Originality. At the same time, their creative and unconventional side will be tinged with an admirable and spiritual aspect. And while they may find the strength to dare to be different and get into close touch with their abundant creative abilities, they may fail the higher challenge of this karmic path and keep their light under the proverbial bushel. If they can manage to connect with people who can be less fearful and more supportive of their strengths without indulging their fears and weakness, they will take great strides along this road, as they have a natural grasp of more universal truths and will emerge from the underworld of fear with ideas and symbols that will be of value to us all.

CHALLENGE: **NOT RETREATING INTO THEMSELVES OUT OF FEAR OF BEING DIFFERENT, BUT CHOOSING INSTEAD TO TACKLE SOME HEFTY SELF-ANALYSIS**
FULFILLMENT: **USING THEIR TALENT FOR BUSINESS TO BRING THEIR HARD-WON KNOWLEDGE TO A BROADER PUBLIC**
NOTABLE: **TRISH VAN DEVERE (ACTRESS, DAY OF THE DOLPHIN)**

ROB REINER
Actor/writer/producer/
director, All in the Family

3/6/1945
Pisces II

March 11–18
DANCERS AND DREAMERS
PISCES III

The natural gifts and creative strengths of those born in the Week of Dancers and Dreamers who travel the Way of Originality may be so pronounced that it will be hard for these people to hold themselves back or to consciously hinder their development. They will experience their share of ups and downs, however, especially when they neglect to nurture their talents and content themselves with trying to appear "normal" when in fact they are anything but. On the other hand, some of this group will be so far out that they disdain to share their talents with others and content themselves with dwelling in a world of unfulfilled expectations or the secret belief that they are a little bit better than anyone else. The key here is for these individuals to spend less time pondering philosophy or abstract notions of the meaning of life and more time examining their inner workings. Ultimately, if they can balance these two approaches, this journey promises wonderful rewards.

CHALLENGE: **APPLYING A BIT OF DISCIPLINE AND ELBOW GREASE TO THEIR PSYCHOLOGICAL PROCESSES**
FULFILLMENT: **MEDIATING BETWEEN THE COLLECTIVE UNCONSCIOUS AND THE MATERIAL WORLD**

The Way of Seduction

CAPRICORN III TO CANCER III
Dominance to the Persuader

Those born to the Way of Seduction are here to develop the ability to persuade others to their point of view rather than to dominate them. These career-oriented individuals have executive ability, but they also tend to be heavy-handed bosses with some dictatorial tendencies. In the course of both their professional and personal lives, the men and women on this karmic path are apt to discover that their approach to others could benefit from an overhaul. Thus, they will learn to temper their management style by learning how to seduce others to accede to their wishes rather than demanding they do so. Learning the art of seduction requires that they observe and relate to others' needs and desires, then position their own desires or wants in relation to theirs to strike a bargain. Much of this karmic path has to do with developing the skills of parenting; thus, those on it will learn to nurture and support coworkers and loved ones alike. It may shock them to discover how rich the benefits of their newfound approach can be in both business and pleasure.

Because of their heightened sense of responsibility, the individuals born to the Way of Seduction often tell others what to do or try to dominate them to achieve their aims. They impose their wills on those around them not so much as a hostile act but as an expression of their belief that they know best. In fact, those who have Capricorn III as their starting point have

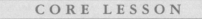

CORE LESSON
Supporting others by understanding
what they need or want

GOAL
To learn how to persuade others
to their point of view

GIFTS
Surmounting, Persuasive,
Observant

PITFALLS
Self-sacrificing, Dictatorial,
Detached

---

a great capacity for devotion and want to make a contribution to the lives of their fellow men. It's just that the way they go about achieving their aims seems a little hard. Possessing a tremendous capacity for emotional detachment, they often do not consider the effects of their actions on others. So responsible and hardworking are those on the Way of Seduction that they often do not bother to delegate their work, choosing to do it themselves to save trouble. The result is that they overburden themselves with work and worry.

The men and women on this karmic path have executive ability, though this does not necessarily translate into management ability. Their talents may lie more in the creation of efficient structures, financial budgets and forecasts, or strategic thinking. Their management style, however, leaves a lot to be desired, as it can be too direct for their own good. Coworkers and employees see them as being heavy-handed, barking orders and tending to be tyrannical. Of course, they themselves never see things this way. They view themselves as self-confident, capable, and having the courage and the heart to "be the responsible one." This attitude tends to give others offense since it implies that they are incompetent or, worse, moronic. Generally, the individuals on this path have good intentions and their hearts are in the right place; it's just that their methods need some work. On the Way of Seduction, they must learn how to persuade

others to do their bidding rather than demand it, in both their professional and personal lives.

Because both Capricorn III and Cancer III denote a need for control or influence, it is unlikely that those on this karmic path will give them up. However, they must transform the manner in which they attempt to control others, moving from domination to persuasion, from giving orders to seduction. The key differences in these approaches are consideration and egalitarianism. In an act of persuasion, the other party is treated as an equal rather than as an underling. Meanwhile, though seduction is often considered a bit unsavory, in truth the person being seduced is rarely duped and is usually perfectly aware of what is happening. In fact, he is often made happy by the act of seduction because he is being offered something he would like to have. There is an offer and an acceptance of that offer. Both sides achieve their aims, and a fair exchange has taken place. Another point is that the offeror takes the offeree's needs, desires, and even ego into account.

Reaching an understanding of what others desire is the core lesson of this karmic path. In the zodiac, Cancer is the sign of the mother. When children are small, they are rarely able to articulate what they want or need; thus, knowing and understanding their children's needs is second nature to mothers. The men and women on the Way of Seduction must develop this capacity as regards others. Though a certain coldness permeates these individuals, they must open their hearts enough to feel empathy and compassion more fully. By truly examining their fellows, these individuals can begin to develop a working understanding of what makes them tick. It's important, however, that they don't judge other people's needs. Often, people only want positive reinforcement or recognition. It never hurts to give someone a few ego strokes. As the saying goes, "You attract more flies with honey than with vinegar."

An interesting point about the art of seduction is that it requires proper timing. Many a relationship conflict has developed because a request was made at the wrong time. Those on the Way of Seduction would do well to think carefully before choosing the moment for action. Some of the wisdom of Cancer III lies in its understanding of timing. Moreover, due to its association with the moon, Cancer is also about the public and the collective unconscious. Thus, individuals who are successful on this karmic path may become adept at influencing the public at large. Eventually, these people will begin to invoke collective symbols and powerful imagery to persuade others. More frequently than not, those on this path will work behind the scenes, since rarely do those on the Way of Seduction enjoy being in the limelight. But they do have a message to share, and learning how to put that message across in a manner that will make others accept it more readily is

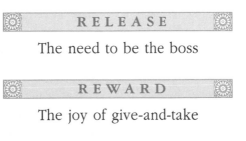

RELEASE
The need to be the boss

REWARD
The joy of give-and-take

SUGGESTION

*Become more observant generally. Study others and what they want.
Consider the right moment for action. Ask yourself if you are acting
out of kindness. Treat others with equality and respect.*

one result of this path. It may not be surprising to find that those on this path can be savvy marketers. The whole purpose of marketing is to identify a need in the marketplace, fill it, and then let everyone know about it, all of which require the skills this path confers.

It should be noted that those on this karmic path will rarely resort to moral shortcuts, lying, or telling half-truths to get what they want, as their sense of honor precludes doing so. They always win their arguments through hard work and preparation. They combine the logical reasoning and love of data of Capricorn III with the formidable powers of observation of Cancer III to make any case they present undefeatable. Attitude is an important consideration. Releasing the need to seem to be completely in control, allowing others to dominate now and then, or just showing some vulnerability can achieve tremendous results. As those on this path let go of their dictatorial tendencies and allow their relationships to become more democratic, networking can become a real talent. Few are as aware as these individuals that it's not what you know but who you know.

As they progress in the lessons of this karmic path, those on the Way of Seduction will find that the quality of all their relationships improves. Others will be more receptive to them as they soften their approach. These are individuals who hang on to what they've got. They often have friendships from all periods in their lives, going back even to childhood. Friends and family who have supported those on the Way of Seduction through thick and thin will delight in their newfound awareness

BALANCE POINT

Hierarchy and
Democracy

and understanding of their needs. In some ways, the real goal of this path—one that may be realized later in life—is for those on the Way of Seduction to become a source of support for others. Also, having spent many years pursuing their ambitions, those on this path might be ready for a little seduction themselves, that is, they may allow themselves to be seduced by the pleasures of relaxation, leisure-time activities, and the more passionate or sensuous side of their natures. This does not imply that they will suddenly become romantic predators—the men and women on this path stick to their mates. But it may be that their spouses will be surprised to discover that their mates have developed some new tricks!

In describing this path, one thinks of the old tale *A Thousand and One Nights*. The heroine, Scheherazade, found herself in the harem of the king of Samarkand. The policy was that, once visited by the king, each woman in the harem was to be put to death. Scheherazade considered her situation and cleverly realized that the king probably needed some entertainment more than he needed just another visit to a woman. Thus, on the first night of his visit, she began to tell him a story that not only whiled away the time they spent together but conveniently was not yet concluded by the time the sun came up and it was time for him to leave. Seduced by the tale, the king determined to return the next night, thus sparing Scheherazade's life. This continued for 1,001 nights, until finally the king decided he could not put Scheherazade to death. She had successfully seduced the ruler with both her wits and her wisdom.

CRYSTALS AND GEMSTONES

Pyrite allows an individual to witness the truth behind another's façade.
When this information is received with compassion,
it becomes possible to offer others what they truly want.

NOTABLES ON THIS KARMIC PATH

SIR LAURENCE OLIVIER

Portraying everyone from Heathcliff to Richard III, entertainer Archie Rice to Hamlet, **Sir Laurence Olivier** captivated audiences year after year. With a characteristic talent for getting his message across, Olivier acted with such skill that viewers were convinced of the authenticity of his characters, affording him both critical and popular acclaim. Olivier's directing work and ambition to be the world's greatest actor exhibits his Capricorn III origin and its affinity for dominance. However, this desire hardly inhibited him from fulfilling his destiny on the Way of Seduction, as he employed his gift of powerful persuasion to entertain audiences everywhere.

VLADIMIR LENIN

Marxist revolutionary **Vladimir Lenin** was born in a small town in Russia, studied at Kazan and St. Petersburg, and was initially exiled to Siberia for his participation in revolutionary activities. In 1917, leading a small group of dissenters, he succeeded in inspiring the Bolshevik Revolution and becoming ruler of his country. Characteristic of this path, he joined immense ambition, an indomitable will, managerial sensibilities, and finely tuned persuasiveness to touch the hearts and minds of his countrymen and convince them of the sanctity of his ideals.

Due to his strict Methodist upbringing, few would guess that **Hugh Hefner** would become the publisher of *Playboy* magazine. Creator of the "bunnies" and an entire chain of recreational clubs, he gave the concept of seduction a whole new meaning. Eschewing sleaziness, *Playboy* raised the standard of the pornography industry and brought sexuality into mainstream acceptance

HUGH HEFNER

through its unique blend of centerfolds, celebrity interviews, literary fiction, and essays. Since the mid-1980s, Hefner's daughter Christie has served as CEO of his media empire, which has expanded to include everything from CD-ROMs to motion picture production.

Other Notables: Robert Heinlein, Warren Burger, Alexandre Eiffel, Chico Mendes, H. L. Hunt, Sydney Chaplin, Natasha Richardson, Quentin Tarantino, Conan O'Brien, Queen Elizabeth II, David Attenborough, Mike Myers, John Wayne, George Michael, Barbara Stanwyck, Whitney Houston, Rajiv Gandhi, Barry White, Fay Wray, Gene Autry, Eugene O'Neill, Noah Webster, John Keats, Danny DeVito, George Martin, Valery Giscard d'Estaing

---

BIRTHDAYS ON KARMIC PATH 40

October 6, 1888–February 24, 1889 | May 20, 1907–October 7, 1907
December 29, 1925–May 19, 1926 | August 9, 1944–December 28, 1944 | March 22, 1963–August 9, 1963
October 31, 1981–March 21, 1982 | June 11, 2000–October 30, 2000 | January 22, 2019–June 11, 2019

KARMIC PATH
40

March 19–24
REBIRTH
PISCES–ARIES CUSP

Once they comprehend that the cultivation of greater refinement in their approach to others is necessary to their higher development, things will go well for those born in this period who travel the Way of Seduction. While they may believe themselves to be honest, straightforward, and forthright, others may see them as blunt, tactless, and utterly without consideration or empathy. Still, once they begin to view their relationships with other people as more of a game and less of a war, they can experience a wonderful sense of transformation and increased savvy in their dealings with others. Since family is so important to these souls, they are likely to encounter many of their life's lessons through the experience of learning to get along with and communicate with their children, though their professional ambitions will be pronounced as well.

CHALLENGE: **REFINING THEIR APPROACH TO OTHERS FROM A DIRECT ASSAULT TO A MORE TACTICAL MANEUVER**

FULFILLMENT: **PUTTING SOME OF THEIR PASSION INTO HOW THEY CARE FOR OTHERS**

GARRY KASPAROV
World chess champion
———
4/13/1963
Aries III

March 25–April 2
THE CHILD
ARIES I

If they allow themselves to develop the talent for strategy and refined communication skills called for by the Way of Seduction, Aries I's can go a long way toward the achievement of their personal and professional goals. Ego issues, overidealism, and perhaps a bit too much spontaneity will all be problems, and they will often refuse the higher challenge of this path by withdrawing from conflicts into isolation and disillusion. At least some of their journey may involve learning how to become more observant of the needs of others. They will have to do a great deal of work to release some deep-seated security issues and to understand that their effectiveness depends largely upon their willingness to negotiate, rather than command, the respect of others. Yet if they remain willing to grow, great enlightenment will come to them.

CHALLENGE: **CULTIVATING THE ART OF THINKING BEFORE THEY SPEAK**

FULFILLMENT: **REAPING THE REWARDS OF A SOFTER APPROACH IN RELATIONSHIPS**

NOTABLES: **QUENTIN TARANTINO (WRITER/DIRECTOR, *PULP FICTION*); RANDALL CUNNINGHAM (FOOTBALL QUARTERBACK)**

April 3–10
THE STAR
ARIES II

Going beyond their own point of view in order to perceive and then to acknowledge the needs of others may be difficult for those born in the Week of the Star who travel the Way of Seduction. Their natural charisma will go a long way toward winning people over; however, they may fail the higher challenge of this karmic path due to their refusal to release some self-centered notions or prima donna attitudes. If they can let go of their ego issues to the point where they develop a cannier approach to teamwork and at the same time avoid their inclinations to excess and emotional extremes, they will experience great personal and spiritual evolution and an ever-increasing sense of empathy and understanding of others.

CHALLENGE: **BEING LESS SELF-CENTERED AND MORE AWARE OF THE CONCERNS OF OTHERS**

FULFILLMENT: **EXPERIENCING THE SATISFACTION OF RELATIONSHIPS THAT ARE BASED ON GIVE-AND-TAKE**

NOTABLES: **ROGER CORMAN (HORROR MOVIE DIRECTOR); HUGH HEFNER (FOUNDER OF *PLAYBOY* MAGAZINE); JULIAN LENNON (SINGER/SONGWRITER; SON OF JOHN)**

CONAN O'BRIEN
Comedian/TV host,
Late Night with Conan O'Brien
———
4/18/1963
Aries III

April 11–18
THE PIONEER
ARIES III

Those born in the Week of the Pioneer who travel the Way of Seduction can do wonderfully well on this road, providing they do not allow their tendency to impose their ideas on others or their rather didactic approach to problem solving to hinder their progress. Though they are brilliant managers, they will have to learn to be better motivators if they are to succeed. Too, avoiding extremes or a tendency to view the world in black and white will be necessary. Yet if they can keep themselves open to a more empathetic approach and learn to temper their idealism with diplomacy and an awareness of others' needs, they will do beautifully.

CHALLENGE: **STEPPING OUT OF THE ROLE OF LEADER OR AUTOCRAT IN ORDER TO WORK WITH OTHERS AS EQUALS AND PEERS**

FULFILLMENT: **PERSUADING OTHERS TO THEIR POSITIVE VIEWPOINT**

KARMIC PATH
40

April 19–24
POWER
ARIES–TAURUS CUSP

Given that these personalities are vested with a certain amount of personal power, they are sure to find success on the Way of Seduction, provided they take the time to learn the lessons of this karmic path. Indeed, some pretty formidable players can be found with this configuration. Moreover, it is likely that most on this path possess both the natural savvy and the common sense to find their way around almost any obstacle that presents itself. Yet some may fail the higher challenge of this path by failing to develop a genuine sense of empathy for the needs of others and concentrating solely on their own. Too, they have a pronounced tendency to employ manipulative measures as opposed to persuasive ones when attempting the act of seduction. Yet if they can manage to keep their sense of personal responsibility intact and use it to illuminate the consequences of their actions, most of them will do brilliantly.

QUEEN ELIZABETH II
Current queen of England
———
4/21/1926
Aries–Taurus Cusp

CHALLENGE: **CONSIDERING THE NEEDS OF THOSE THEY WISH TO INFLUENCE**

FULFILLMENT: **ESTABLISHING THEIR POSITION THROUGH CHARM RATHER THAN DOMINATION**

NOTABLES: **DON ADAMS (ACTOR/COMEDIAN, *GET SMART*); VLADIMIR ILYICH LENIN (MARXIST; LED BOLSHEVIK REVOLUTION; 1ST LEADER OF USSR)**

April 25–May 2
MANIFESTATION
TAURUS I

Little prone to either the emotional excesses or the purely manipulative tendencies of some others on the Way of Seduction, Taurus I's are likely to do wonderfully well on this life journey. Well suited to the areas of planning, structure, and strategy, they will nevertheless have to do a bit of work to cultivate and encourage their more nurturing side. Stubbornness, too, will probably be the biggest problem for these individuals, since it prevents them from considering viewpoints other than their own and keeps them entrenched in their own. Yet if they can develop an openness to the needs of others and rise to the numerous occasions for connection, nurture, and heartfelt communication that will present themselves, all will go well in a process of steady development and increased awareness.

CHALLENGE: **GRAPPLING WITH THEIR NEED FOR HIERARCHICAL AS OPPOSED TO FLAT STRUCTURES**

FULFILLMENT: **ENJOYING THE HARMONY THAT PERSUASION AS OPPOSED TO DOMINATION BRINGS**

May 3–10
THE TEACHER
TAURUS II

Those born in the Week of the Teacher who find themselves on this karmic path will find that its lessons hold considerable importance for them. Compelled by their need to share with others, they may find their most cherished ideas and thoughts falling on more or less deaf ears until they cultivate and refine their methods of presentation to include a sense of empathy and alignment with others' needs. For example, if interested in enlightening others, they would do better to discuss than to lecture. Indeed, adjusting their own needs and desires to accommodate others may be a special sticking point for many of this group, and some will be loath to give up an inflexible or even somewhat pedantic stance, even if doing so will result in greater fulfillment of their own needs. Yet if they can bring themselves to give up a measure of security and control in exchange for a more-than-equal measure of fulfillment and accomplishment, they will take great strides along the road.

A. P. GIANNI
Banker, established branch banking system and radical lending policies
———
5/6/1870
Taurus II

CHALLENGE: **SHELVING THEIR MORAL STANCE LONG ENOUGH TO DEVELOP A TRUE UNDERSTANDING OF WHERE OTHERS ARE COMING FROM**

FULFILLMENT: **SEDUCING OTHERS WITH THE POWER AND ELEGANCE OF THEIR ARGUMENTS**

NOTABLES: **SIR DAVID ATTENBOROUGH (NATURALIST; BROADCASTER); MARCUS LOEW (THEATER OWNER)**

May 11–18
THE NATURAL
TAURUS III

Those born in the Week of the Natural who travel the Way of Seduction may experience a bit of difficulty, as they are prone to frustration and a sense of rebellion against the idea that they may have to adjust their freedom-loving ways in order to be most effective. In fact, many of this type can become so preoccupied with issues of security that when threatened, they drive others away with their strong, volatile, and sometimes tactless opinions. Cultivating greater sensitivity will prove especially important in their development, as will being willing to set aside or at least adjust their needs to those around them, whether or not they feel confident doing so. Once they begin to be open to establishing structure, rather than simply rebelling against it, they will successfully sway others to their causes with insight and even a sense of adventure.

CHALLENGE: **COMING TO TERMS WITH THE FACT THAT SOMETIMES THEY ACT JUST LIKE THE AUTHORITY FIGURES THEY REJECT**

FULFILLMENT: **USING THEIR UNIQUE CHARM TO WIN OTHERS TO THEIR POINT OF VIEW**

NOTABLE: **NATASHA RICHARDSON (ACTRESS, *THE HANDMAID'S TALE*)**

May 19–24
ENERGY
TAURUS–GEMINI CUSP

Though endowed with much more versatility and natural charm than some on this path, those born on the Cusp of Energy who travel the Way of Seduction will have to work hard to put their own needs aside in order to see and appreciate what others may need. Bargaining or compromising is not prominent in their makeup, and some will fail the higher challenge of this karmic path through selfishness or ill-considered demands. It is important for them to weigh their words carefully, particularly when making offers. Yet they have the potential for success and considerable accomplishment, as their natural energies can serve to lighten the more ponderous aspects of this karmic path while, at the same time, its higher calling will reward them with a depth of emotion and understanding.

JOHN WAYNE
Actor, quintessential mythical movie hero, westerns, *True Grit*

5/26/1907
Gemini I

CHALLENGE: **VIEWING OTHERS LESS AS THEIR AUDIENCE AND MORE AS PARTICIPANTS IN THEIR ADVENTURE**
FULFILLMENT: **NEGOTIATING SOLUTIONS TO LIFE'S MORE TRIVIAL PROBLEMS**
NOTABLES: **SIR LAURENCE OLIVIER (ACTOR/DIRECTOR; OSCAR FOR *HAMLET*); JOHN BARDEEN (NOBEL PRIZE FOR PHYSICS)**

May 25–June 2
FREEDOM
GEMINI I

The volatile personalities born in the Week of Freedom who travel the Way of Seduction can experience great success, yet they will have to avoid a tendency to indulging in emotional extremes and ververbalizing their objectives if they are to succeed. In fact, they are quite capable of blowing everybody out of the water with weapons from their formidable verbal arsenal, yet may fail to accomplish their goals until they gain a better grasp of others' needs. Yet they are infinitely more adaptable than some on this path, and if they can focus their powers of observation in such a way that they attune themselves to the psychology of seduction rather than intimidation, their success will be assured.

CHALLENGE: **RECOGNIZING THAT APPEARING IMPATIENT CAN RUIN THE BEST-THOUGHT-OUT ARGUMENTS**
FULFILLMENT: **INVOKING THEIR CONSIDERABLE NATURAL CHARM**
NOTABLE: **MIKE MYERS (ACTOR/COMEDIAN, *AUSTIN POWERS*)**

June 3–10
NEW LANGUAGE
GEMINI II

The curious combination of energies that come together for those born in the Week of New Language who travel the Way of Seduction can make for wonderful fulfillment, providing these souls are careful not to allow defensiveness to interfere with their need to make themselves understood. In fact, they are quite charming and able to home in on what others want to hear, as they are blessed with formidable powers of both persuasion and observation. Yet they will need to learn the art of controlling their tendency to employ sarcasm or wittiness at others' expense, as they can wound without intending to do so when they allow their communicative talents to run unchecked. Still, if they can first focus on their own needs and then align themselves with those around them, they will be able to strike the right bargains and find the road to happiness.

RACHEL CARSON
Biologist; wrote *Silent Spring*, warned of dangers of pesticides

5/27/1907
Gemini I

CHALLENGE: **NOT INSISTING ON USING THEIR HIGHLY PERSONAL LANGUAGE AT ALL COSTS**
FULFILLMENT: **FEELING THE WARM GLOW OF INTERRELATEDNESS AS THEY DEAL WITH OTHERS ON AN EQUAL FOOTING**
NOTABLE: **JOHNNY DEPP (ACTOR, *EDWARD SCISSORHANDS*)**

June 11–18
THE SEEKER
GEMINI III

Not very encumbered by the dictatorial tendencies of some others on this karmic path, those born in the Week of the Seeker who travel the Way of Seduction can realize wonderful success and considerable fulfillment in both the personal and professional areas of life. Often brilliant negotiators, they may nevertheless have a bit of trouble focusing on the needs of others and are inclined to take off for new adventures when the going gets rough, rather than hanging around to work things out. Yet they have the potential to have considerable insight and consideration for others; if only they take the time to follow their inclination for compromise and avoid their tendency to indulge in emotional outbursts, they are more than capable of bringing their charms to bear in such a way that many of their goals and objectives will be achieved in a win/win atmosphere.

CHALLENGE: **TEMPERING THEIR TENDENCY TO DREAM UP IDEAS OF WHAT OTHERS SHOULD DO**
FULFILLMENT: **ENJOYING THE FRUITS OF THE CLOSER OBSERVATION OF HUMANITY AS A WHOLE**
NOTABLE: **HELEN HUNT (ACTRESS; EMMY FOR *MAD ABOUT YOU*; OSCAR FOR *AS GOOD AS IT GETS*)**

June 19–24

MAGIC
GEMINI–CANCER CUSP

Particularly well suited to this karmic path, the souls born on the Cusp of Magic who find themselves on the Way of Seduction can realize truly extraordinary fulfillment. It is important for them to avoid taking things too personally or simply withdrawing when things don't go their way. Depression and a tendency to worry can be special problems for these people, and they will further also to avoid allowing themselves to become disillusioned in the face of disappointment. Yet they have a fine ability to attune themselves to others' needs and a rare capacity for empathy that will serve them well as they make their way along the road. If they can avoid emotional manipulation and turning their understanding of other people to their own ends, they will inspire mutual trust and kindness from many they meet in the course of this life journey.

CHALLENGE: **SOFTENING THE STEELY COLDNESS OF THEIR ARGUMENTS**
FULFILLMENT: **RELATING TO OTHERS FROM A PLACE OF GREATER EMPATHY**

FRIDA KAHLO
Mexican painter

7/6/1907
Cancer II

June 25–July 2

THE EMPATH
CANCER I

The highly sensitive individuals born in the Week of the Empath who navigate the challenge of the Way of Seduction are likely to do very well indeed, as they are gifted with more personal strength than might otherwise have been the case, together with a sensitivity to others' needs and emotions. Yet they will have to avoid their tendency to be rather too inclined to self-sacrifice, on the one hand, or to withdraw into self-imposed isolation, on the other. Yet the energies here can make for a fine combination. If they bring their forces to bear in a spirit of kindness and compromise, rather than in an insistence on having their own needs and feelings validated, all will go brilliantly for them, especially as they take on the challenges of truly committed relationships and acquire both nurturing and parenting skills.

CHALLENGE: **NOT BECOMING ADDICTED TO THE ACT OF SEDUCTION**
FULFILLMENT: **ENJOYING THE UNUSUAL DEGREE OF CAREER SUCCESS THIS PATH AFFORDS THEM**
NOTABLE: **GEORGE MICHAEL (POP SINGER; MEMBER OF WHAM!, "FAITH")**

July 3–10

THE UNCONVENTIONAL
CANCER II

Those born in this week will find an number of unexpected and rather interesting relationships on the Way of Seduction, providing they are careful to reach out to others in a genuine spirit of kindness and compromise and do not retreat from the higher challenge of this karmic path by succumbing to their darker fears and imaginings and retreating into a fantasy world. On the other side of the coin, many will engage in any number of passive-aggressive moves to bend others to their will, while their own deepest desires remain unfulfilled. Rather more fun-loving than many who travel this road, they may misuse their sensitivity to exploit others' desires. If they work to cultivate their capacity for devotion, while at the same time employ their considerable psychological insight to get those around them to accede to their wishes, they can see many of those wishes come true as they make their way along this karmic path.

CHALLENGE: **BECOMING MORE DIRECT IN THEIR APPROACH AND—THOUGH IT SEEMS A CONTRADICTION IN TERMS—EVEN IN SEDUCTION**
FULFILLMENT: **USING THEIR CAREFULLY CRAFTED VERNACULAR TO SEDUCE OTHERS**

ROBERT HEINLEIN
Science fiction author,
Stranger in a Strange Land

7/7/1907
Cancer II

July 11–18

THE PERSUADER
CANCER III

These souls can realize brilliant success and considerable accomplishment on this karmic path, yet they will have to learn that in order to seduce others, one must occasionally be willing to be seduced. Often loath to relinquish control, they may well retreat from the higher challenge of this karmic path, by developing an idea that they don't need anyone. Yet they will discover that, for the sake of their spiritual growth, developing more empathy is all-important, and while they are passionate, they may not always take others' feeling and desires into account. Yet if they learn the lesson that devotion does not always imply surrender and that their natural impulse to self-sacrifice is not something to be rigorously suppressed, they will open themselves to new worlds of fulfillment and happiness within the context of mutually rewarding personal and professional relationships.

CHALLENGE: **REALIZING THAT NOT EVERYONE CAN BE EXPECTED TO BE AS RESPONSIBLE AND HARDWORKING AS THEY ARE**
FULFILLMENT: **ACKNOWLEDGING THE CONSIDERABLE CHARM THAT IS THEIR BIRTHRIGHT**
NOTABLES: **PHOEBE CATES (ACTRESS, *FAST TIMES AT RIDGEMONT HIGH*); BARBARA STANWYCK (ACTRESS, *DOUBLE INDEMNITY*)**

July 19–25

OSCILLATION
CANCER–LEO CUSP

Those born on the Cusp of Oscillation who travel the Way of Seduction may be far too preoccupied with trying to understand themselves to develop the empathy needed to understand others. Though they are wonderful communicators, this karmic path holds some extreme possibilities that can cause them trouble in their search for compromise. Yet if they can control their tendencies to emotional outbursts, mood swings, and an emotionally blocked approach to others, they will find a measure of fulfillment and enlightenment. The key to their success will be in their willingness to nurture others. If they can bring forth the qualities of compassion and insight that are their birthright and leave behind their tendency to stress, depression, and anxiety, they will achieve wonderful expansion and great personal growth.

CHALLENGE: **ADAPTING TO A WIDE VARIETY OF PEOPLE AND THEIR CONCOMITANT PALETTE OF NEEDS**

FULFILLMENT: **ALLOWING THEIR DEPTH OF FEELING TO DOMINATE**

SAM ELLIOT
Actor, *Roadhouse*

8/9/1944
Leo II

July 26–August 2

AUTHORITY
LEO I

Those born in the Week of Authority who travel the Way of Seduction may experience a bit of difficulty with the challenge to relinquish control and step into the role of compassionate persuader. Yet many of them will rise to the challenge due to their innately generous and rather expansive disposition. Principal among their problems will be their inclination to try to sway others to their own opinions for purely personal ends, rather than to join with them in a spirit of mutual give-and-take. Too, stroking others' egos is not much in their line. Yet they have a capacity for devotion that is bound to find expression. Once they come to terms with the fact that the ability to command respect is not quite the same thing as the ability to engender love, they will absorb the rest of the lessons much more easily.

CHALLENGE: **REDUCING THEIR NEED FOR CONTROL OR ADHERENCE TO STANDARDS AS THEY NEGOTIATE LIFE**

FULFILLMENT: **DISCOVERING HOW MUCH THERE IS TO LEARN FROM BEING OBSERVANT**

NOTABLES: **LISA KUDROW (ACTRESS, *FRIENDS*); MELVIN BELLI (LAWYER; DEFENDED LENNY BRUCE)**

August 3–10

BALANCED STRENGTH
LEO II

Those born in this week have a fine chance for happiness on the Way of Seduction, as they are possessed of both the natural modesty and the honesty to rise to its higher challenge of compromise and kindness. They will, however, have to be on guard against their tendency to be too self-sacrificing or to take on too much personal responsibility as they make their way along this karmic path. Too-rigorous a repression of their own needs will result in depression and quite a lot of guilt, while too adamantly or single-mindedly maintaining their own point of view will lead to increased unhappiness and a sense of isolation. Yet if they can employ their considerable intuitive talents to learn more about others and their motivations, they will be more than able to achieve benevolent leadership and trusting interaction.

CHALLENGE: **DEVELOPING THE NUANCES OF TIMING TO A HIGH ART**

FULFILLMENT: **LOVING HOW THEY ARE TREATED ONCE THEY ADOPT AN EQUALITARIAN AND FAIR-MINDED APPROACH TO LIFE**

WHITNEY HOUSTON
Pop singer; actress,
The Bodyguard

8/9/1963
Leo II

August 11–18

LEADERSHIP
LEO III

Inclined to do their own thing and go their own way with or without the help of others, those born in the Week of Leadership who travel the Way of Seduction may experience great difficulty in coming to terms with the challenge and promise of this karmic path. Somewhat self-absorbed by nature, they may take quite a bit of time to recognize the need for greater compromise and negotiation in their dealings with others. Though dedicated and devoted, often in the extreme, they may be rather loath to relinquish their more commanding attitudes or, in extreme cases, thoroughly dictatorial style. Yet when they come to understand that their effectiveness will be enhanced by empathy and understanding of others, their kinder impulses will blossom and their progress be assured.

CHALLENGE: **APPROACHING LIFE LESS FROM A GOAL ORIENTATION AND MORE FROM A PROCESS ORIENTATION**

FULFILLMENT: **MANAGING OTHERS FROM A PLACE OF NEGOTIATION**

NOTABLE: **ROBYN SMITH (JOCKEY)**

August 19–25

EXPOSURE
LEO–VIRGO CUSP

Highly observant and insightful, these personalities can do wonderfully well on the Way of Seduction, providing they do not utilize manipulative methods or deceive others as they make their way along the road. Some with this configuration may develop a great understanding of their fellows, yet the qualities of genuine empathy may prove a bit harder to come by. Too, their willingness to compromise may not reach the necessary level of generosity. Yet if they can avoid their tendency to dissemble and control others through a knowledge of what makes them tick and instead join with them in an atmosphere of kindness, fellowship, and mutual respect, they will make excellent and inspiring leaders and may prove even more formidable as powers behind the thrones.

BARRY WHITE
American soul/pop/
R&B singer
———
9/12/1944
Virgo III

CHALLENGE: **NOT PERMITTING THEIR NEED FOR SECRECY TO DEFEAT THEIR PURPOSE**
FULFILLMENT: **WEAVING A SPELL OF SEDUCTION AROUND FRIENDS AND OTHER INTIMATES**
NOTABLE: **RAJIV GANDHI (INDIAN PRIME MINISTER)**

August 26–September 2

SYSTEM BUILDERS
VIRGO I

If they do not allow their fondness for structure to devolve into an insistence on ironclad rules and regulations, those born in this week can expect great evolution and fulfillment as they make their way along this karmic path. They may be controlling in the extreme, yet once they come to understand that their own disregard of others' needs may in fact be a reflection of the fact that they are neglectful of their own, their life journey will be smoothed considerably. Emotional repression may be their biggest problem, while the ability to compromise in the interest of a larger good or purpose will be their greatest strength. If they can cultivate their modesty and adaptability and play down their need for control at the expense of understanding, all will go beautifully.

CHALLENGE: **NOT LETTING THEIR FEARS CAUSE THEM TO LASH OUT IN DEMANDING OR DICTATORIAL WAYS**
FULFILLMENT: **ALLOWING THEIR NATURAL SENSE OF FAIR PLAY TO TAKE THE LEAD**
NOTABLES: **FRANK "TUG" McGRAW (BASEBALL PITCHER, MOSTLY WITH THE PHILLIES); WILLIAM SHAWN (LONGTIME EDITOR OF THE NEW YORKER)**

September 3–10

THE ENIGMA
VIRGO II

The personalities born in the Week of the Enigma who travel the Way of Seduction may experience great reward and fulfillment in the course of this passage, as they are well inclined to rise to the challenge of kindness and the more diplomatic and understanding forms of interaction that are necessary. A lack of awareness of their own emotions may interfere with their developing the compassion for others that is called for, but time is bound to unbend them a bit, and experience will prove a teacher in the course of this life journey. If they can avoid an excess of self-sufficiency, learn to delegate responsibility, and reach out to those with whom they work and live in a spirit of mutual respect, life will be as kind to them as they are to others.

FAY WRAY
Actress, *King Kong*
———
9/15/1907
Virgo III

CHALLENGE: **NOT ONLY UNDERSTANDING EMOTION IN OTHERS BUT SHOWING SOME OF THEIR OWN**
FULFILLMENT: **USING THEIR FINE DISCERNMENT TO BROKER SUCCESSFUL DEALS**

September 11–18

THE LITERALIST
VIRGO III

Tactlessness may be the single worst enemy of those born in the Week of the Literalist who travel the Way of Seduction. Many of these personalities fancy themselves truth seekers, yet they may experience considerable difficulty when they seek to impose their version of the truth on those around them without adequate concern for their feelings, views, and needs. Alternatively, some with this configuration may be self-sacrificing in the extreme, so devoted to harmony that they control others through any number of less obvious but equally destructive emotional devices. If they can manage to learn that the things they may consider phony, pretentious, or otherwise without practical value may seem to those around them to be beautiful, important, and good—and work on their tolerance as well as their presentation—they will accomplish much.

CHALLENGE: **TEMPERING THEIR NO-NONSENSE ATTITUDES SUFFICIENTLY TO ENGAGE IN THE DANCE OF SEDUCTION**
FULFILLMENT: **EXPERIENCING THE EPIPHANY THAT WITHHOLDING CERTAIN FACTS IS NOT NECESSARILY MANIPULATIVE, JUST SENSIBLE**
NOTABLES: **JACQUELINE BISSET (MODEL; ACTRESS, THE DEEP); WARREN BURGER (APPOINTED CHIEF JUSTICE OF THE U.S. SUPREME COURT BY NIXON); MICKEY HART (DRUMMER, THE GRATEFUL DEAD)**

September 19–24
BEAUTY
VIRGO–LIBRA CUSP

Gifted with better-grounded sensibilities than some of their fellow Virgo–Librans and much greater diplomatic skills than some on the Way of Seduction, these personalities can prove themselves to be formidable leaders and skillful managers as they make their way along the road. The key to their development, however, will be a willingness to give up their self-interested side. Some of them will manifest any number of unresolved security issues, causing them to go to extremes of supposed dedication and the attendant creation of guilt in others, while others will refuse the call to greater empathy and misuse their gifts in high-handed ways and a prima donna attitude toward coworkers and family. Yet as volatile as these energies can be, they can also synthesize into a powerful and effective formula for personal and professional success.

CHALLENGE: **SORTING THROUGH THE COMPLEXITY OF THEIR FEELINGS TO MAKE THEIR POINT**

FULFILLMENT: **CREATING ELEGANT DECISION TREES AND OUTLINES FOR THEIR ARGUMENTS**

EUGENE O'NEILL
Playwright, *The Iceman Cometh;* won Nobel Prize

10/16/1888
Libra III

September 25–October 2
THE PERFECTIONIST
LIBRA I

Learning to choose their moments carefully will be especially important for those born in the Week of the Perfectionist who travel the Way of Seduction, as they are inclined to air grievances and sound alarms without considering the feelings, obligations, and pressures of others. Highly motivated and hardworking in the extreme, they may learn to delegate responsibility, yet be perennially dissatisfied with the results. It will therefore be important for these personalities to understand the best way to motivate others and the fact that their impulse to criticize may well arise from their need for control. If they can rise to the challenge to greater empathy and learn that honey will do the job faster and more effectively than vinegar, success will be theirs.

CHALLENGE: **NOT OBSESSING TOO MUCH OVER THEIR NEED TO WIN**

FULFILLMENT: **MARSHALING INFORMATION, BOTH EMPIRICAL DATA AND INTUITIVE WISDOM, TO MAKE THEIR CASE**

NOTABLES: **GENE AUTRY ("SINGING COWBOY"); MICHAEL DOUGLAS (ACTOR, *WALL STREET*); LORD HORATIO NELSON (BRITISH ADMIRAL)**

October 3–10
SOCIETY
LIBRA II

Brilliantly suited to the promises and challenge of the Way of Seduction, Libra III's will find that their diplomatic talents and their powers of insight and observation all come into full play as they make their way along this road. The key to their development will be their willingness to adequately articulate their own needs and desires, as they have a certain tendency to couch their real requests in imprecise language and then become frustrated when things don't go as they had originally wanted. Yet they have much to look forward to as they make their way along this karmic path, and if they avoid their inclination to employ sharp witticisms at the expense of empathy or to go overboard in the search for compromise to the extent that they write themselves out of the script, life will be fine and full of rewards.

CHALLENGE: **REALIZING THAT BEING OVERCRITICAL ONLY HURTS THEMSELVES**

FULFILLMENT: **GLORYING IN THE PERSONAL AND PROFESSIONAL SUCCESS THIS PATH BRINGS**

NOTABLE: **JOHN ENTWHISTLE (BASS PLAYER, THE WHO)**

NOAH WEBSTER
Lexicographer,
Webster's Dictionary

10/16/1758
Libra III

October 11–18
THEATER
LIBRA III

Those born in the Week of Theater may need to face the fact that they are often rather overbearing and less mindful of others' needs than is appropriate for those on this karmic path. These charismatic people may indulge in any number of antics, manipulations, and power plays as they attempt to impose their will on others. Too, they may lack real empathy, as they fully expect those around them to roll with the punches—even if they happen to be the ones doing the punching. Yet these individuals can nevertheless be brilliant and even inspirational when it comes to bringing people together in the interest of larger ideas or efforts. If they can also find a way to be nurturing and kind, they will not only accomplish much but will find great personal and professional satisfaction.

CHALLENGE: **COMING DOWN OFF THEIR HIGH HORSE LONG ENOUGH TO DEAL WITH OTHERS ON AN EQUAL FOOTING**

FULFILLMENT: **ENJOYING THE INHERENT DRAMA IN THE ACT OF SEDUCTION**

October 19–25

DRAMA AND CRITICISM
LIBRA–SCORPIO CUSP

Though gifted with a great deal more confidence and natural charm than many born to this karmic path, Libra–Scorpios will have to do a bit of work to put themselves into the other guy's place in order to better understand and empathize with him. Their tendency to be overcritical and even rather overbearing is quite pronounced, and they will have to come to terms with the idea that sharp insight, considerable intellect, and the ability to call things as one sees them are talents, not weapons. And while they may overwhelm others, they will not experience relationships based on mutual trust, satisfaction, and reward until they examine their motives and learn the gentler arts of kindness, empathy, and real compassion. Yet if they can avoid power plays, examine their own motives, and use their enormous charm in constructive ways, they are sure to get what they want.

CHARLES HENRY DOW
Formed Dow Jones

11/6/1851
Scorpio II

CHALLENGE: **NOT ENGAGING IN ENDLESS DEBATE FOR DEBATE'S SAKE BUT TO ACHIEVE RESOLUTION**
FULFILLMENT: **DISCOVERING HOW GOOD THEY ARE AT BROKERING DEALS OR MEDIATING CONFLICTS**
NOTABLES: **RICHARD BYRD (MADE 1ST FLIGHT OVER NORTH POLE); PETER TOSH (REGGAE GREAT; WORKED WITH BOB MARLEY)**

October 26–November 2

INTENSITY
SCORPIO I

Likely to be quite calculating and discerning, those born in the Week of Intensity will nevertheless have to learn the art of forgiveness and compassion if they are to find real success on the Way of Seduction. Many of these personalities have a stern, unbending aspect that will get them into trouble again and again until they bring their powers of observation and insight to bear in such a way that they can attain their objectives without compromising their highly developed sense of justice. Too, they may withdraw from the higher challenge to kindness of this karmic path and withdraw into isolation and judgmentalism. Yet if they can manage to keep themselves open to understanding their fellows, develop a sense of timing, and reach out in kindness and reciprocity, they are destined to learn much about themselves and others as they make their way along the road.

CHALLENGE: **MODERATING THEIR SENSITIVITY BEFORE IT INTERFERES WITH THE GOALS OF THIS KARMIC PATH**
FULFILLMENT: **INDULGING THEIR INNATE TALENT FOR SPEAKING THE OTHER GUY'S LANGUAGE**
NOTABLES: **KINKY FRIEDMAN (OUTLAW COUNTRY MUSICIAN; NOVELIST, *JEWISH COWBOY*); JOHN KEATS (POET, "ODE ON A GRECIAN URN"); DENNIS FRANZ (ACTOR, *NYPD BLUE*)**

November 3–11

DEPTH
SCORPIO II

A sincere sense of empathy may not be much of a stumbling block for those born in the Week of Depth who travel the Way of Seduction, yet trust may be a bit harder for them to come by. It can safely be said that most of these people will have to struggle mightily with their tendencies to worry and depression and their fixed notion that they have to do everything themselves. Secrecy, too, may be a problem, as they are not especially fond of opening up and talking about what they want and need. Nevertheless, they have the possibility of success, and if they can manage to cultivate their more nurturing and emotional side without stirring up the demons of distrust and control, they will find this karmic path both rewarding and in many instances surprising as the opportunities for connection and compassion summon them to growth and awareness.

DANNY DeVITO
Actor/director/producer,
Taxi

11/17/1944
Scorpio III

CHALLENGE: **ROUTING OUT ALL REVENGE MOTIVES THEY MAY SECRETLY HARBOR**
FULFILLMENT: **DIGGING DEEPLY FOR THAT WELLSPRING OF COMPASSION AT THEIR CORE**
NOTABLES: **JOHN J. O'BRIEN (BASKETBALL REFEREE AND EXECUTIVE); JOE NIEKRO (BASEBALL PITCHING GREAT); TIM RICE (BROADCASTER; WRITER, LYRICIST, *EVITA*)**

November 12–18

CHARM
SCORPIO III

Brilliantly suited to the challenge and promise of the Way of Seduction, those born in the Week of Charm are likely to have a fine and fulfilling journey, providing they can manage to overcome some rather selfish tendencies and develop the higher sense of compassion and empathy it requires. A tendency to be manipulative will undoubtedly be their biggest problem, and though they are adept at getting others to do what they want, they may hold themselves aloof from the dynamics of everyday give-and-take and may become caught up in games or "keeping score." Yet once they come to understand that mutual respect and understanding are much easier to come by when one releases personal defensiveness and comes to terms with the idea that a need for control is often a thinly disguised attempt at self-protection, the rest will be easy.

CHALLENGE: **NOT GOING OVERBOARD SO THAT SEDUCTION BECOMES THEIR REASON FOR LIVING**
FULFILLMENT: **ENJOYING HOW GOOD THEY ARE AT WORKING WITH OTHERS TO ACHIEVE A COMMON GOAL**
NOTABLE: **LORNE MICHAELS (FOUNDER/PRODUCER, *SATURDAY NIGHT LIVE*)**

November 19–24

REVOLUTION
SCORPIO–SAGITTARIUS CUSP

Those born on the Cusp of Revolution who find themselves on the Way of Seduction may have considerable difficulty absorbing the life lessons and higher challenges it offers. These individuals will be wont to create havoc when they should stay calm, to give orders when they ought to negotiate, and to tear down structures when they ought to be building them. Too, these rather volatile people often allow their emotions to direct their choices, without adequately considering the needs of those around them. Yet they have the possibility of great enlightenment, as they are by no means closed off from a sense of compassion for others. If they can manage to refine their sense of timing, slow down and really listen to what others are trying to say, and perhaps be willing to change themselves before they attempt to change the rest of the world, they will be assured of great progress, wonderful enlightenment, and some fine and fulfilling relationships.

CHALLENGE: **OVERCOMING THEIR STUBBORN REFUSAL TO SEE ANY POINT OF VIEW OTHER THAN THEIR OWN**
FULFILLMENT: **USING THE TOOLS OF THIS KARMIC PATH TO ACHIEVE THEIR AIMS**
NOTABLE: **MARCIA CARSEY (PRODUCER, *THE COSBY SHOW*; *ROSEANNE*)**

CHICO MENDES
The Amazonian Gandhi; Brazilian fighter against deforestation of the Amazon

12/15/1944
Sagittarius III

November 25–December 2

INDEPENDENCE
SAGITTARIUS I

If they refuse to allow their more temperamental aspects to interfere with their intuitive grasp of others, things can go well for Sagittarius I's who travel the Way of Seduction. They may be fond of stirring things up in personal and professional matters yet become a bit bewildered when things get out of hand or people's feelings get hurt. Some will refuse the challenges of this karmic path altogether through a rather manic insistence on doing everything their own way. Too, they will have to come to an understanding of the fact that successful seduction in any form is the result of not impulse but of careful planning. Once they ground themselves in the need to negotiate and cultivate the finer arts of empathy and compassion, their natural sense of honor is sure to come to the fore, and their rewards will be ensured, especially as they take up roles as parents and authority figures.

CHALLENGE: **TEMPERING THEIR NEED TO WIN IN FAVOR OF LETTING EVERYBODY WIN**
FULFILLMENT: **ENJOYING THE REPARTEE AND DEBATE OF PERSUASION**

December 3–10

THE ORIGINATOR
SAGITTARIUS II

The Originators who travel the Way of Seduction are bound to have a truly unique approach to problem solving and administration, yet they will have to work a bit to develop the qualities of compassionate understanding and reciprocal effort that are part of their higher calling. Personal defensiveness may be their biggest obstacle to fulfillment, and some will refuse to develop a more open attitude toward give-and-take out of fear they may be the ones "taken" or deceived. Their tendency to become isolated or withdrawn is also quite pronounced, and they will have to work hard to avoid developing suspicious attitudes toward friends, coworkers, and life partners. Yet if they can display their uniqueness and originality in an atmosphere of trust, they are sure to return that favor to others, helping them to blossom, encouraging their individuality, and applauding their success.

CHALLENGE: **CULTIVATING THE SENSITIVITY TO OTHERS' NEEDS THAT IS NECESSARY TO SEDUCTION**
FULFILLMENT: **USING THEIR UNIQUE LANGUAGE TO SELL THEIR POINT OF VIEW OR PRODUCT**
NOTABLES: **THOMAS CARLYLE (SCOTTISH CRITIC; HISTORIAN); DENNIS WILSON (DRUMMER, THE BEACH BOYS)**

ROBERT MOSES
NYC Parks Commissioner 1934–60; public administrator responsible for setting aside millions of acres in parklands

12/18/1888
Sagittarius III

December 11–18

THE TITAN
SAGITTARIUS III

The Titans who travel the Way of Seduction may find this an uncomfortable passage, since there is a strong chance that they will have to swallow their considerable pride before they can develop the qualities of empathy and understanding it requires. Their tendency to try to do everything themselves and to shoulder unimaginable amounts of responsibility will be especially pronounced, as will be a certain moodiness and a pervading sense of isolation. Yet they have a natural compassion for others that is likely to stand them in good stead. If they can manage to come down to earth and adjust their own needs in accordance with the needs of those around them, these personalities can find wonderful fulfillment and a sense of personal power that is based neither on fantasy nor on a sense of domination but on their ability to join forces with others toward a sense of larger purpose and accomplishment. Cultivating humility and real respect for the talents and abilities of others will do much to ease their way.

CHALLENGE: **PAYING MORE ATTENTION TO THE DETAILS OF OTHERS' EXISTENCE**
FULFILLMENT: **INVOKING LARGER FORCES AND COLLECTIVE IMAGERY TO SEDUCE THE PUBLIC**
NOTABLE: **ALEXANDRE EIFFEL (FRENCH ENGINEER)**

December 19–25

PROPHECY
SAGITTARIUS–CAPRICORN CUSP

Though well equipped to answer the call to greater understanding of others' needs and desires, those born on the Cusp of Prophecy who travel the Way of Seduction may have a harder time coming to terms with the need for greater negotiation and diplomacy as they make their way along this road. In fact, these personalities may be quite independent and even rather disdainful of what others may think about them; as a result, they may persist in high-handed or unduly rigid methods of management or administration long after those methods have ceased to be productive or useful. Yet they have the possibility of great enlightenment and progress. If they are willing to open themselves to the world of give-and-take and avoid using their intuition and perception in attempts to control, rather than empathize with, those around them, success and a great degree of personal fulfillment will be theirs.

RICHARD LEAKEY
Anthropologist; writer,
Origins

—————

12/19/1944
Sagittarius–Capricorn
Cusp

CHALLENGE: **INFUSING THEIR ATTEMPTS TO WIN OTHERS OVER WITH A BIT OF REAL WARMTH**

FULFILLMENT: **FINDING A PRACTICAL USE FOR THEIR MANY INSIGHTS**

NOTABLES: **MICHAEL THOMAS (CONDUCTOR); TIM REID (ACTOR, *WKRP IN CINCINNATI*)**

December 26–January 2

THE RULER
CAPRICORN I

Those born in the Week of the Ruler who navigate the challenge and promise of the Way of Seduction may find themselves a bit bewildered by this journey until they come to a better understanding of just why their often dogmatic and dictatorial approaches don't work. In fact, such stern and rigid attitudes can often arise from the need of Capricorn I's to prove themselves, yet they will achieve little satisfaction unless they also cultivate a more nurturing and concerned approach to others. And while their emotions may be deeply felt, these personalities can never express them easily. Yet they have the potential for wonderful transformation, and if they can allow themselves to venture out of their armor and reach out to others in genuine caring and concern, they will find themselves much softened by love and enlightenment.

CHALLENGE: **PRYING LOOSE THEIR GRIP ON THE REINS OF POWER LONG ENOUGH TO BRING OTHERS ALONG ON THE RIDE**

FULFILLMENT: **DISCOVERING THAT THEIR INNATE CARING HAS A USEFUL PURPOSE**

January 3–9

DETERMINATION
CAPRICORN II

Blessed with a fine sensitivity and a much greater grasp of others' needs than some who make their way along this karmic path, those born in the Week of Determination can find wonderful fulfillment, as they have a nice mix of ambition and modesty, devotion and inspiration. Whether or not they will bring those qualities to bear in their dealings with others is a bit up in the air, however, since they are by nature rather solitary types who prefer individual effort to reciprocal understanding or group endeavor. Too, fear of rejection and an inability to relax can be problems to overcome. Yet they have a subtle side that will stand them in wonderful stead, and if they can allow themselves to aspire to more than they often feel they deserve, life will offer them a wide range of possibilities for fulfillment.

GEORGE MARTIN
Beatles producer

—————

1/3/1926
Capricorn II

CHALLENGE: **BECOMING A BIT MORE IMAGINATIVE IN HOW THEY INTERACT WITH OTHERS**

FULFILLMENT: **PERMITTING THEMSELVES A MEASURE OF RELAXATION AND PLEASURE AFTER LONG PERIODS OF HARD WORK**

January 10–16

DOMINANCE
CAPRICORN III

The ability to release their need to control their environment will be the special task of those born in this week who travel the Way of Seduction. Combining both the best and the worst aspects of this karmic path, these personalities are likely to be capable, competent, and responsible in the extreme yet will have enormous difficulty when faced with the challenge of being open and nurturing and using their charms to get their way. A willingness to overcome a secret inferiority complex may lie at the heart of their challenge, and much about this journey implies that they will have to give themselves permission to enjoy and fulfill themselves before they can gain a real perspective on what others need and want. Until they are better acquainted with their own needs, aligning their desires with those around them will be difficult. Yet if they can proceed from within in an attitude of mutual respect and compassion and learn not to be so hard on themselves, they will be kinder to others as they progress along the road.

CHALLENGE: **LETTING GO OF CAREER AMBITIONS AND THE DESIRE TO CLIMB THE LADDER OF SUCCESS**

FULFILLMENT: **REACHING A POINT WHERE THEY ARE CONFIDENT IN THEIR ABILITY TO BOTH PRODUCE AND SEDUCE**

NOTABLES: **GRANT TINKER (TV PRODUCER; NBC CHAIRMAN)**

January 17–22

MYSTERY AND IMAGINATION
CAPRICORN–AQUARIUS CUSP

Gifted with an unusual ability to tap into collective ideas and needs, the individuals born on this cusp who travel the Way of Seduction can experience a truly transformative life experience, as they have both highly developed instincts and the ability to inspire others. Perhaps their biggest problem will be their tendency to emotional extremes, and some are capable of periods of great planning and carefully constructed efforts that are then blown apart by sometimes uncontrollable fits of temper. Thus, they will have to be especially wary of their tendency to shoot themselves in the foot or otherwise sabotage their best efforts though inconsiderate or insensitive behavior. Yet if they can bring their considerable charm and knack for inspiration to bear in the search for mutual trust, understanding, and empathy, they will enjoy great personal and professional success as they convey their gifts to the larger world.

ARTHUR OCHS SULZBERGER

New York Times publisher

2/5/1926
Aquarius II

CHALLENGE: **NOT ALLOWING THEIR CHAOTIC ENERGIES TO SIDETRACK THEM FROM THEIR GOALS**
FULFILLMENT: **USING HUMOR TO OUTWIT OR CONVINCE OTHERS**
NOTABLES: **PATRICIA NEAL (ACTRESS; OSCAR FOR *HUD*); SOPHIE TAEUBER (SWISS ARTIST/SCULPTOR; ACTIVE IN DADA MOVEMENT)**

January 23–30

GENIUS
AQUARIUS I

Blessed with much more insight, focus, and sensitivity than they might otherwise have possessed, those born in the Week of Genius who travel the Way of Seduction will face the challenge of bringing others around to their way of thinking. They are likely to be serious and responsible, and much of their natural genius may manifest itself in the kind of "common touch" that is in tune with collective needs and a real source of inspiration to those around them. In fact, learning to care about and nurture others in a more personal and less abstract way can be a real sticking point for these people, as these are the kinds of Aquarians who are responsible for statements such as "I love humanity; it's people I can't stand." Yet if they can control their impatience and cultivate a nurturing attitude, their progress will be ensured.

CHALLENGE: **DEVELOPING SUFFICIENT PATIENCE FOR OTHERS TO WANT TO SEDUCE OR PLEASE THEM IN THE FIRST PLACE**
FULFILLMENT: **USING SMOOTH ARGUMENTS TO CONVINCE OTHERS OF THEIR NEED FOR FREEDOM—AND SUCCEEDING!**

January 31–February 7

YOUTH AND EASE
AQUARIUS II

Likely to be much more easygoing than some who make their way along the Way of Seduction, those born in the Week of Youth and Ease who travel this karmic path will nevertheless have to work a bit to avoid controlling others with their considerable charms and devolving into amoral or careless manipulations. Emotional immaturity can lead to selfishness and the sort of casual cruelty that damages themselves and others. Yet if they allow themselves to develop greater understanding and empathy for others and refuse to be drawn into superficial games and power plays to the detriment of their higher spiritual development, life will reward them with both a sense of power and a feeling of enlightenment.

PAUL BOCUSE

Restaurateur,
"Nouvelle Cuisine"

2/11/1926
Aquarius III

CHALLENGE: **ADHERING TO A STRICT CODE OF HONOR**
FULFILLMENT: **IMPRESSING OTHERS WITH THEIR MAGNETISM**
NOTABLE: **VALÉRY GISCARD D'ESTAING (FRENCH PRESIDENT)**

February 8–15

ACCEPTANCE
AQUARIUS III

The happiest of these individuals will be those who learn to accept others for what they are, as those born in this week who travel the Way of Seduction will have to learn to set aside some of their more intolerant attitudes in order to join with others in a mutually beneficial effort at understanding. Though commanding and competent, these people may fall victim to rather fixed attitudes that will require thorough scrutiny. Yet they are blessed with considerable charm and an innate ability to get others to do what they want them to do. If they can deepen their empathy and temper their need for control, and at the same time acknowledge their vulnerability without falling prey to neediness and irritability in their dealings with others, the world will open in a range of wider possibilities for connection and expansion.

CHALLENGE: **LEARNING TO AGREE TO DISAGREE**
FULFILLMENT: **USING THEIR TREMENDOUS RESOURCEFULNESS TO GET WHAT THEY WANT**
NOTABLES: **LESLIE NIELSEN (ACTOR/COMEDIAN, *NAKED GUN*); JOAN MITCHELL (ARTIST/ABSTRACT EXPRESSIONIST); CHARLES VAN DOREN (EDITOR; INVOLVED IN GAME SHOW SCANDAL)**

KARMIC PATH
40

February 16–22

SENSITIVITY
AQUARIUS–PISCES CUSP

Fine possibilities for success and expansion await those born on the Cusp of Sensitivity who travel the Way of Seduction. Gifted with the insight and understanding needed to navigate this path with considerable success, these people will nevertheless face the challenges of workaholism, personal touchiness, and pessimism. Too, they may find themselves more or less at the mercy of unresolved internal conflicts, which they may project onto others in unrealistic expectations of consistency or faithfulness. Yet if they can learn to set aside their fears of rejection and loss of control, and instead use their sensitivity to join with their associates in efforts at increased understanding and respect, they can quite successfully adjust their needs to complement, rather than conflict, with those of the people around them.

H. L. Hunt
Oil tycoon billionaire
—
2/17/1889
Aquarius–Pisces Cusp

CHALLENGE: **MAKING SURE THAT THEY AREN'T THROWING THEIR WEIGHT AROUND FOR FEAR NO ONE LIKES THEM**

FULFILLMENT: **DISCOVERING THEIR INNATE CHARM AND ABILITY TO DRAW OTHERS TO THEM**

NOTABLE: **NELSON BUNKER HUNT (BUSINESS EXECUTIVE; HAD ROLE IN 1980 SILVER CRASH)**

February 23–March 2

SPIRIT
PISCES I

Some really amazing people can be found among those born in the Week of Spirit who travel the Way of Seduction, as they are a rare combination of charm and ability. Their capacity to empathize is quite pronounced, yet they will have to be careful of a tendency to use others or to treat people carelessly. Yet they have considerably more natural confidence than many who travel this karmic path, as well as a profound grasp of the truths and inner needs that are common to us all. If they can avoid their tendency to be too self-sacrificing, on the one hand, and too manipulative, on the other, and instead bring their forces to bear in such a way that their gifts can be shared rather than hoarded, they will find wonderful fulfillment in their ability to inspire others and themselves to new levels of accomplishment and intimate connection as they tap into both personal and collective desires.

CHALLENGE: **AVOIDING A KNOW-IT-ALL ATTITUDE IN FAVOR OF ONE OF CONCERNED INTEREST**

FULFILLMENT: **OPERATING FROM SPIRITUAL PRINCIPLES AS THEY DEAL WITH OTHERS**

March 3–10

THE LONER
PISCES II

Though gifted with a great capacity for empathy and soulful understanding, those gifts might never be shared by the Loners who travel the Way of Seduction. Indeed, many with this configuration expect far too much of others and become entangled in the idea that friends, partners, and coworkers are supposed to be able to guess what they want or otherwise anticipate their needs. Such a path will only lead to disappointment and disillusionment, however, until they learn to charm those around them with directness rather than obscurity. Too, many of this group will fail the higher challenge of this karmic path if they cut themselves off from the possibility of more reciprocal relationships. Yet once they come to grips with the notion that it may be a fear of rejection that lies at the heart of their need to be alone and open themselves to the need for others, intimacy, empathy, and understanding will be their rewards.

ALAN GREENSPAN
Chairman of the
Federal Reserve
—
3/6/1926
Pisces II

CHALLENGE: **NOT FALLING INTO MANIPULATION WHEN THEY ARE ATTEMPTING SEDUCTION**

FULFILLMENT: **BELIEVING THAT THEY ARE UP TO THE INTELLECTUAL CHALLENGE OF MAKING A GOOD CASE FOR THEMSELVES**

March 11–18

DANCERS AND DREAMERS
PISCES III

True masters of the art of seduction, those born in the Week of Dancers and Dreamers are blessed with an unusual combination of inspiration and strength that can make for wonderful accomplishment as they make their way along this karmic path. Their sensitivity to others' needs is pronounced, yet along with that sensitivity they have an ability to manipulate others through emotion that will bear watching. Keeping their sights set on the more collective forms of inspiration and avoiding emotional games will be especially useful to their development. Yet if they can avoid making high-handed judgments or taking a rather holier-than-thou distance from others, and instead embrace their helpful and nurturing side, they will be able to fully experience the joys of doing good and bring a more transcendent perspective to those who join them on this life journey.

CHALLENGE: **REALIZING HOW EASY IT IS FOR THEM TO SLIP INTO THE ROLE OF DOMINATOR**

FULFILLMENT: **OPERATING FROM THEIR CORE OF SENSITIVITY AND COMPASSION AND SEEING MIRACLES THAT CAN RESULT**

NOTABLES: **RALPH ABERNATHY (BAPTIST CLERGYMAN; CIVIL RIGHTS ACTIVIST); PETER GRAVES (ACTOR, *MISSION: IMPOSSIBLE*); JERRY LEWIS (COMEDIAN; ZANY TV/FILM STAR, *THE NUTTY PROFESSOR*)**

The Way of Versatility

CAPRICORN–AQUARIUS CUSP TO CANCER–LEO CUSP
Mystery and Imagination to Oscillation

The intelligent individuals on the Way of Versatility come into life with an approach that is heavily dependent on logic and analysis. This karmic path calls the individuals born to it to cultivate the feeling and intuitive side of their personalities and, in so doing, to become more heart-centered. Innovative and questioning, those on the Way of Versatility are blessed with many aptitudes. But their objectivity may appear to others to be cold and some of their decisions heartless. They have all the intuitive and feeling gifts of anyone else; they just need to put them to better use. As they do so, they round out and balance their personalities. Eventually, having refined all their strengths, they will be able to switch back and forth between intuition and logic so smoothly and rapidly that they always seem to know the right thing to do or say. Maximizing their talents in this fashion means that they are not only agile but versatile. Though this karmic path promises considerable worldly success, the price for it is some hard work in the areas of relationship and feeling.

Quick-witted and intellectual, the men and women on the Way of Versatility possess many gifts. Their minds, while retentive, work rapidly and are capable of an extraordinary level of analysis, logic, and deductive reasoning. Because they approach life in a detached manner, they are completely objective when sizing up a problem or situation. They are often successful, not only because they are extremely clever but also because they are hardworking. Though highly dependable and responsible, they are not traditionalists—their talent for innovation means that they will break the established order if need be. Because they question everything, they are able to detect when something isn't working, much like the little boy who announced that the emperor was wearing no clothes, and then to tear down established systems only to rebuild them in a new, more efficient manner. Those on the Way of Versatility are both innovative enough to envision new concepts or methods and pragmatic enough to put their ideas into effect. They do not rebel so much as improve. Their thinking is never limited by a need to adhere to established methods or to do what everyone else is doing, yet they are not wildly independent types either, preferring to remain calm and rational.

Such a detached mental orientation means that those on this karmic path are a bit one-sided. Their masculine analytical side holds too much sway. They may become so immersed in the elegance of their mental constructs that they often seem both unconcerned and unaffected by the effects of their actions on others. It follows that people see them as emotionally cool, if not cold. Naturally, this doesn't win them any popularity contests. In truth, they do possess a great deal of concern for humanity, only in a rather abstract sort of way. The old saying "I love humanity; it's people I can't stand" ap-

---

CORE LESSON

Developing their
feeling/intuitive side

GOAL

To become heart-centered, combining both
logic and intuition

GIFTS
Innovative, Brilliant, Dauntless

PITFALLS
Cold, Superior, Aloof

plies to these individuals. Quite often when they are working out a new approach to something, they gain satisfaction from the idea that the results of their work will serve their group, society, or humanity in some way. However, on the whole, these individuals prefer to remain in a mental ivory tower, rather than engage in an intimate fashion with the roiling masses of humanity.

Because the men and women on the Way of Versatility prefer emotional detachment, they do not often give their feelings voice or their passion free rein. Doing so scares them. They don't feel particularly good at the feeling game, so they sidestep it and stick to what they are good at: logic. The trouble is, this does not serve them well because it keeps them out of balance. Without feeling or intuition, it is as though they are operating at half power or basing their decisions on incomplete information. Part of the problem may be that they are gun-shy. Early in life they may have made some bad decisions based on their feelings, causing them to decide to stick to cold, hard analysis. It is not so much that they repress their emotions, it's more that they ignore them. The result is that they appear aloof and unapproachable, particularly to those intimates who reach out to them for affection or warmth, only to be turned away at the door, and to those in their circle who find their chilliness unsettling if not downright frightening. Their intentions, of course,

are good; they just need to develop the one thing they are not good at: warmth.

Thus, the goal of this karmic path is for these individuals to combine their practical and mental abilities with emotion and intuition and, in so doing, to become more heart-centered. All of the mystic traditions speak of the necessity of "coming from the heart." It is from this place that one extends love and compassion, or warmth, to others. Learning how to open the heart is the core lesson of this path. Being open at the heart level means not only that one's feelings are expressed or extended outward but that one's heart is open to accept. Such receptivity is crucial to those on this path, because it is how the intuitive awareness that is located at the heart level is developed. Taking in impressions at the feeling level is a large part of the act of intuition. Such impressions are nonverbal and nonmental, sometimes appearing as visual images or feelings. Intuition means inner knowing. This kind of knowing may not be logical or necessarily sensible, but it is often true. So cultivating intuitive awareness is the first step. The second is learning to trust what this awareness is telling you. Finally, through trial and error, one must learn when the right course of action is to listen to one's inner voice or to an argument based on logical reasoning. Knowing, at a deep level, is the core lesson of this karmic path.

Once those on the Way of Versatility realize that they

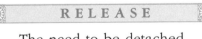

RELEASE

The need to be detached

REWARD

The joy of a fully
integrated approach

SUGGESTION

*Find a loving emotional basis in spiritual belief. Work to open your heart center.
Practice listening to your inner voice. Take some calculated risks.*

must begin to pay closer attention to what their hearts are telling them, they will undoubtedly learn its lessons quite quickly and will reap untold benefits in many areas of their lives. By rounding out their already awesome arsenal of talents by developing greater intuitive awareness, those on the Way of Versatility often become unstoppable. Whenever they need to take action or make a decision, they can either invoke their lightning-quick mental process or check in with their intuitive understanding. The result is that they rarely make the wrong move. Soon they are able to switch back and forth between the two functions so smoothly and effortlessly that the lines blur, forming a fully integrated mental/intuitive process that makes for formidable individuals indeed. Moreover, they make it all look easy!

Due to their many talents, and as they strengthen their intuitive muscle, those on this karmic path can be intimidating, to say the least. Therefore it is important for them to keep their hearts open and available to others. A little bit of warmth goes a long way. Their connection to others will deepen, and any loneliness that resulted from their aloof stance will begin to fall away. Not a few individuals on the Way of Versatility have based their relationship decisions, whether personal or business, on logic rather than on listening to their instincts, with disastrous results. When those on this karmic path become more intuitive and less mental about their relationships, they begin to attract a wider variety of people, and the quality of their relationships improves.

As calm, cool, and collected as those on this karmic path may appear, they do experience some personal in-

BALANCE POINT

Logic and Intuition

stability. Remember that they are beginners when it comes to managing deep emotions. Until they learn how to deal with their feelings, they may experience some mood swings or depression. Cultivating a more positive or sunnier outlook will help them combat their tendency toward negativity or cynicism. As coolly rational as these individuals are, they are easily bored and thus possess a wild streak. It is best if they make a point of taking a risk now and then to generate a little romance or drama in their lives. If they don't, they may find themselves breaking loose every once in a while only to go overboard. Moderately feeding their need for occasional excitement is the best antidote. They will be happiest in a profession or relationship where they can combine their many talents and skills, using a little bit of everything, and when surrounded by eclectic, passionate people. Otherwise, some unexpressed aspect of their personality may act up and act out, causing them some embarrassment.

Those who take up the challenge of the Way of Versatility can be likened to the Magician card in tarot decks. This card depicts a wizard and represents conscious awareness and the ability to ground the nonmaterial in the material world. The magician marshals unseen energies and forces without being overwhelmed by them. He both receives and directs. Most important, however, are the implements that are pictured at his disposal. Symbolically, they represent each of the major human functions: thought, sensation, feeling, and intuition. Having conquered and integrated them, all four are now at the magician's disposal, to be used at will as he makes his magic in the world.

CRYSTALS AND GEMSTONES

Lapis lazuli connects an individual to the celestial realms. This stone brings in expansive energy and holds the space for one to allow, honor, and perhaps merge with his intuitive voice.

NOTABLES ON THIS KARMIC PATH

A prototype of the cool, witty, and intellectual individuals born on the Way of Versatility, **Robert Kennedy** dazzled foes and followers alike. As council to the Hoover Commission, the Senate Permanent Subcommittee on Investigations, and the Senate Select Committee on Improper Activities in the Labor or Management

ROBERT KENNEDY

Field, Kennedy was described as calculating, ruthless, and overly ambitious by his detractors. However, as attorney general for his brother, John F. Kennedy, he used his position to support his strong idealistic stance for justice, honor, and integrity. His untimely death, assassinated as he ran for president in 1968, means it will never be clear whether he fully opened to his emotional/intuitive side.

MICHAEL JORDAN

Generally considered the greatest basketball player of all time, **Michael Jordan** has versatility beyond his undeniable excellence on the court. Not only has he led the Chicago Bulls to an unprecedented six NBA championships in eight years, but also his poise and skill at public speaking are apparent in his many commercial endorsements, and his lucrative business endeavors also attest to his amazing range of abil-

ity and intellectual gifts. Few may know the real Jordan. and, because of his godlike status in the eyes of many fans, Jordan sometimes appears cool and aloof under the intense glare of public scrutiny—as is characteristic of this path.

Though **Vanessa Williams** lost her Miss America crown, her versatility became apparent to the public when she embarked on a career in the entertainment industry. After nine Grammy nominations, a multiplatinum album, a number-one single, and an Oscar (for the song "Colors of the Wind"), Williams has more than

VANESSA WILLIAMS

proven her talent as a singer. She has also emerged as an actress of note, earning critical acclaim for her role in *Kiss of the Spider Woman* and later appearing in the box office hits *Eraser* and *Dance with Me.* Throughout this rise to fame, Williams has remained a devoted mother to her three children.

Other Notables: Diana Ross, Tony Orlando, Judith Jamison, George Lucas, Rudolph Giuliani, Marvin Hamlisch, Jim Thorpe, Raymond Chandler, Russell Baker, Mike Douglas, Oscar Peterson, Robert Rauschenberg, Joseph Kennedy, T. S. Eliot, Lenny Bruce, Johnny Carson, Demi Moore, Jodie Foster, Louisa May Alcott, Sammy Davis, Jr., Dick Van Dyke, Seal, Henri Matisse, Hakeem Olajuwon, James Michener, Sheryl Crow, W. H. Auden

---

BIRTHDAYS ON KARMIC PATH 41

May 18, 1888–October 5, 1888 | December 29, 1906–May 19, 1907

August 9, 1925–December 28, 1925 | March 21, 1944–August 8, 1944 | October 31, 1962–March 21, 1963

June 11, 1981–October 30, 1981 | January 22, 2000–June 10, 2000 | September 2, 2018–January 21, 2019

KARMIC PATH
41

March 19–24

REBIRTH
PISCES–ARIES CUSP

Those born in this period who travel the Way of Versatility are likely to be especially challenged by the call to open themselves to greater levels of feeling. Though passionate at the core, they may nevertheless spend a lot of time second-guessing themselves about what they truly feel and wind up canceling themselves out in the war between head and heart. Though this karmic path endows them with much talent and energy, they will have to learn the value of what might best be termed "irrational thought" before they can experience the creativity and versatility that are its reward. Yet if they cultivate their ability to play their hunches, develop faith in their inner guidance system, and learn to define fulfillment in terms not of what they are able to do without but what they are willing to risk in the interest of happiness, all will go well.

CHALLENGE: **NOT REPRESSING THEIR EMOTIONAL SENSITIVITY**
FULFILLMENT: **ALLOWING THEMSELVES A LITTLE ADVENTURE NOW AND THEN**

DIANA ROSS
Singer, solo and with
The Supremes

3/26/1944
Aries I

March 25–April 2

THE CHILD
ARIES I

Those born in this week who navigate the challenges of the Way of Versatility are likely to find considerable fulfillment, as they bring to this journey a certain spontaneity and enthusiasm that will serve them well in their search for greater emotional integration. Though they may be held back from a higher level of warmth through a tendency to maintain a rather superficial or overidealistic view of the world, they can successfully overcome whatever obstacles may present themselves in the course of this life journey by maintaining a positive attitude, spontaneity, and an ease in interacting with others in groups, relationships, and family. If they do not turn away from the call to greater emotionalism and retreat into feeling perennially misunderstood or unappreciated, life will be good for them.

CHALLENGE: **TEMPERING ANY MOODINESS WITH A DOSE OF POSITIVE THINKING**
FULFILLMENT: **THROWING THEMSELVES INTO THEIR MANY PROJECTS AND ENTHUSIASMS**

April 3–10

THE STAR
ARIES II

The personalities born in the Week of the Star who find themselves on the Way of Versatility can experience great fulfillment and happiness, providing they do not allow ego issues to stand in the way of their higher development. Likely to be wonderfully gifted and compelling individuals, they may yearn for the attention and applause of others yet hold back from real intimacy. Though some will retreat from the challenge to develop greater personal warmth through being preoccupied with success and achievement, they will find that life can indeed be lonely at the top. Yet if they allow themselves greater spontaneity, control their preoccupation with worldly image, and utilize their gifts of intuition and application, they will experience the best of all worlds as they make their way along this road.

CHALLENGE: **KNOWING WHEN TO LET GO OR GIVE IN**
FULFILLMENT: **ALLOWING OTHERS ACCESS TO THEIR INNER LIVES**

TONY ORLANDO
Singer/entertainer, Tony
Orlando and Dawn,
"Tie a Yellow Ribbon
Round the Old Oak Tree"

4/3/1944
Aries II

April 11–18

THE PIONEER
ARIES III

Often hindered by a pronounced tendency to impose their ideas on others without regard to their feelings, those born in the Week of the Pioneer who find themselves on the Way of Versatility will have to actively cultivate what has been referred to as "people skills" in order to find the happiness and connection they seek. Though gifted with formidable talents and the ability to inspire others to lofty goals and ideas, these individuals may nevertheless fall down in this karmic path's challenge to develop connection, empathy, and warmth. In fact, some of them will be much better at giving than receiving and may act out of the belief that they know what's best for everyone else, while ignoring or suppressing their own deepest needs. Yet if they allow their actions always to be informed by intuition and stay realistic in their expectations of others, life will get easier for them.

CHALLENGE: **BITING THEIR TONGUES WHEN THEY'D LIKE TO TELL OTHERS WHAT TO DO**
FULFILLMENT: **USING THEIR MANY TALENTS FOR A GOOD CAUSE**
NOTABLE: **"PAPA DOC" FRANÇOIS DUVALIER (HAITIAN DICTATOR)**

April 19–24
POWER
ARIES–TAURUS CUSP

Truly formidable energies come together for those born on this cusp who travel the Way of Versatility, yet they will have to be mindful of the fact that worldly success does not always make for personal happiness or fulfillment. Though likely to be unencumbered by too much ivory-tower idealism, they may nevertheless fail the call to develop warmth and connection that will put their highest plans and goals over the top. In fact, many of them will show a pronounced tendency to "use" others or bend them to their will. A measure of humanity will serve to temper both their ambitions and perceptions with insight and understanding. Yet this is a group who will doubtless learn well from any mistakes they may make along the road, and if they are willing to set aside the almost ruthless aspect of their ambitions in favor of a more nurturing approach to others, they will find and direct their personal powers in ways that can benefit all.

JUDITH JAMISON
Dancer, Alvin Ailey
Dance Theater

5/10/1944
Taurus II

CHALLENGE: **NOT OVERPOWERING OTHERS WITH THE SHEER FORCE OF THEIR ARGUMENTS**
FULFILLMENT: **SENSING THE PERSONAL POWER THAT RESULTS WHEN THEIR HEARTS AND MINDS ARE IN BALANCE**

April 25–May 2
MANIFESTATION
TAURUS I

This configuration can make for some truly accomplished people as those born in the Week of Manifestation journey along the Way of Versatility. The practicality and grounded physical energies of Taurus I's will do much to steady the highly charged energies of this karmic path, though these people will face the challenge to shake themselves up a bit by getting in touch with their sense of passion and excitement. Yet they have a much better grasp of what makes people tick than some others on this road, and if they can avoid the pitfalls of a damaging and often destructive temper and instead direct their formidable energies away from purely theoretical constructs and into the world of manifestation and personal and spiritual fulfillment, this combination can synthesize into a powerful and complete vision. It is likely that greater self-awareness will inspire them to take more risks, and if these personalities first acknowledge and then direct their passion in some constructive fashion, there will be little they cannot accomplish.

CHALLENGE: **NOT STICKING SO RIGIDLY TO THEIR INTELLECTUAL ARGUMENTS**
FULFILLMENT: **FEELING STRONG ENOUGH TO HANDLE THEIR EMOTIONAL COMPLEXITY**
NOTABLE: **JILL CLAYBURGH (ACTRESS, *AN UNMARRIED WOMAN*)**

May 3–10
THE TEACHER
TAURUS II

Much more volatile than some of their fellows born in the Week of the Teacher, those who travel the Way of Versatility are likely to find considerable enjoyment on this life journey, providing they can augment their intelligence and perception with a measure of compassion and generosity of spirit. There is a danger, however, that they will hold themselves aloof from the kind of committed and inspired relationships they long for and retreat into an ivory tower of cynicism or effete attitudes toward the world. Opening their hearts may prove a difficult task, as they can be so convinced of their own expertise and understanding that they ignore the attempts of others to reach them on a more emotional level. Yet if they can control their more aloof aspects and embrace the wealth of spontaneous and emotional interaction that awaits them along this road, they are sure to find the things they seek.

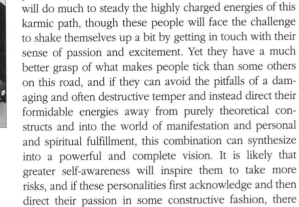

GEORGE LUCAS
Producer/director,
Star Wars

5/14/1944
Taurus III

CHALLENGE: **NOT DEVOLVING INTO PENDANTRY WHEN THEY ARE AFRAID**
FULFILLMENT: **DEVELOPING THE EMPATHY TO TRULY UNDERSTAND THOSE THEY TEACH OR SERVE**

May 11–18
THE NATURAL
TAURUS III

Much more logical than some of their fellows born in this week, Taurus II's bring to the Way of Versatility a natural inclination toward adventure and spontaneous expression that will serve them well. Nevertheless, they may well have to struggle a bit with security issues before they can release the need to prove themselves and embrace the challenge to become more completely who they are. Gifted with fine innovative talents, these inquiring minds may strike out in any number of odd or unusual directions in their search for higher levels of fulfillment. Thus, though they can be counted upon to break new ground in their chosen fields or even to change direction entirely, those same tendencies will bear watching when they come into play in the area of personal relationships, as these individuals can swing from one extreme to another in their choices of partners. Yet if they can learn to discern the difference between boredom and stability, they will have more fun than most.

CHALLENGE: **FINDING THE BALANCE BETWEEN THEIR NEED FOR STABILITY AND NATURAL IMPULSIVENESS**
FULFILLMENT: **SATISFYING THEIR SOUL'S YEARNING FOR NATURAL BEAUTY**
NOTABLE: **DAPHNE DU MAURIER (GOTHIC NOVELIST, *REBECCA*)**

KARMIC PATH
41

May 19–24
ENERGY
TAURUS–GEMINI CUSP

Gifted with some truly formidable talents for inspiration and innovation, the brilliant people born on this cusp who travel the Way of Versatility are likely to have a fine and fruitful journey. In fact, impatience may prove their biggest enemy, and they will have to work a bit to cultivate the greater degree of personal warmth and understanding this karmic path requires. Never inclined to suffer fools gladly, they will have to be on guard against their tendency to be too demanding and critical of others. Yet once they bring their powers to bear in such a way that includes, rather than precludes, the power of faith and intuitive strength and integrate those qualities with their intellectual brilliance and God-given talents, they are sure to make a formidable mark on the world.

EMILE BERLINER
Invented the microphone
and the gramophone

5/20/1851
Taurus–Gemini Cusp

CHALLENGE: **NOT QUESTING AFTER INTELLECTUAL STIMULATION WHILE NEGLECTING THE NEEDS OF THEIR HEARTS**
FULFILLMENT: **REVELING IN THEIR CAPACITY TO DO ANYTHING THEY SET THEIR HEARTS AND MINDS ON**
NOTABLES: **JOE COCKER (SINGER, BLUES STYLIST, "UP WHERE WE BELONG"); PATTI LaBELLE (POP, SOUL SINGER)**

May 25–June 2
FREEDOM
GEMINI I

Those born in the Week of Freedom who journey along the Way of Versatility have some considerable strengths in their favor, along with their share of weaknesses. Among their strengths are a formidable intellect, a rare gift for innovation, and the ability to be far more flexible than some others who travel this karmic path. Yet they may have a propensity for criticizing others or for grandstanding when diplomacy and negotiation would better serve their purposes. Too, they have a tendency to retreat from the more emotional approach to life this karmic path requires and into a world of ivory-tower theories and ideas that are doomed to fail. Yet they have remarkable minds and a need to know, and if they can avoid the dangers of scattering their energies and being irritable, and work to cultivate spiritual and emotional depth, they will realize great progress.

CHALLENGE: **BEING QUIET LONG ENOUGH TO LISTEN TO WHAT THEIR HEARTS ARE TELLING THEM**
FULFILLMENT: **PERFECTING THEIR SENSE OF TIMING**
NOTABLES: **RUDOLPH GIULIANI (NEW YORK CITY MAYOR); MARVIN HAMLISCH (COMPOSER, *A CHORUS LINE*); GLADYS KNIGHT (SINGER, "MIDNIGHT TRAIN TO GEORGIA")**

June 3–10
NEW LANGUAGE
GEMINI II

Their ability to communicate effectively will prove both a great blessing and something of a burden for those born in this week who travel the Way of Versatility. Much preoccupied with bringing others over to their way of thinking, those born in the Week of New Language may nevertheless fail the higher challenge of imbuing their ideas and inspirations with the measure of warmth and enthusiasm that is necessary to bring others around. In fact, many of their best concepts will be expressed in admittedly innovative yet rather idiosyncratic ways. Rejections and misunderstanding may then drive them further into a superior, critical, or overly aloof style of presentation that only fosters greater distance between themselves and others. Yet if they can learn to employ their considerable charms in their dealings, avoid impatience, and learn to be as receptive to those around them as they often expect others to be to them, they will find considerable fulfillment and increased happiness.

JIM THORPE
American sportsman,
Olympian, football player,
baseball player, called
"greatest athlete ever"

5/28/1888
Gemini I

CHALLENGE: **OVERFOCUSING ON THE SHEER ELEGANCE OF THEIR LINE OF REASONING**
FULFILLMENT: **DISCOVERING AND INTERPRETING THE MANY NONVERBAL FORMS OF COMMUNICATION**
NOTABLE: **BOZ SCAGGS (SINGER, *SILK DEGREES*)**

June 11–18
THE SEEKER
GEMINI III

Marked by a rare sense of adventure and the ability to take more risks than some others who travel the Way of Versatility, those born in the Week of the Seeker can expect to learn a great deal as they make their way along this road. Yet there is a danger that they will fail to develop the depth of perception and emotional connection required. Easily distracted and often preoccupied, these personalities will have to work a bit to come to terms with the fact that their emotional lives may be less than satisfactory. Too, they have a tendency to overthink or overwork problems to such an extent that they rob themselves of the capacity to act upon their deepest feelings and impulses. Disillusionment and cynicism may also be pitfalls for these people, yet if they work to stay in touch with their truest natures and avoid their inclination to indulge in mental gamesmanship, they can take great strides along this karmic path.

CHALLENGE: **ATTACHING THEMSELVES TO SOMETHING OR SOMEONE**
FULFILLMENT: **ALLOWING THEIR INTUITION TO GUIDE THEM**

KARMIC PATH
41

June 19–24

MAGIC
GEMINI–CANCER CUSP

JEFF BECK
Guitarist, The Yardbirds,
Jeff Beck Group, and as a
solo artist

6/24/1944
Gemini–Cancer Cusp

Personal objectivity and detachment may actually mask a wealth of deeply felt emotions in those born on the Cusp of Magic who travel the Way of Versatility, and they are likely to be blessed with a rare perception and insight into the more spiritual and intuitive sides of life. Yet though there is a promise of enormous success and fulfillment for them, they may experience problems with personal connection, especially if they turn from the challenge of this karmic path and retreat into an impenetrable private world. Much inclined to live in their heads, these souls will have to work hard to develop their receptivity to others and avoid their tendency to shut out those people or feelings that challenge their pet theories about the world. If they can muster the courage and personal strength to reveal themselves and their deeply felt emotions, there will be little that they cannot do in the course of this life journey.

CHALLENGE: **REALIZING THAT THEIR ICY APPROACH IS EXTREMELY REJECTING**

FULFILLMENT: **REVEALING THE WARMTH THAT IS THEIR BIRTHRIGHT**

NOTABLE: **PETER ASHER (MUSIC PRODUCER)**

June 25–July 2

THE EMPATH
CANCER I

Those born in the Week of the Empath who journey along the Way of Versatility can realize great progress and personal fulfillment, providing they divest themselves of some overly self-protective attitudes and learn to distinguish genuine intuition from passing moods. Much more intellectually inclined than they might otherwise have been, they may nevertheless fail the higher challenge of this karmic path if they allow personal disappointment or disillusionment to lead them to shut down their emotions. Too, some of them will have an overly aggressive insistence on getting their own way or achieving their goals at all costs, including that of their own happiness. Yet if they can avoid their tendency to self-imposed isolation and learn to integrate their formidable intuition with their equally formidable capacity for emotional bonding and connection, all will go brilliantly.

CHALLENGE: **RISKING SOME EMOTIONAL PAIN DESPITE EARLY NEGATIVE EXPERIENCES**

FULFILLMENT: **KNOWING THAT IT'S OKAY TO CARE EVEN WHEN IT DOESN'T MAKE SENSE**

July 3–10

THE UNCONVENTIONAL
CANCER II

RAY DAVIES
Founded rock group
The Kinks

6/23/1944
Gemini–Cancer Cusp

The conflict between head and heart may manifest itself outwardly in some rather unusual lifestyle choices for those born in this week who find themselves on the Way of Versatility. In fact, their principal problem may be that they may pride themselves on what they consider to be objective decisions when in reality their choices are emotionally based. A yearning for excitement may cause them to stir up the pot when things might be better left alone, or to open any number of cans of worms just for the sake of variety. Yet if they can manage to bring their considerable imaginative gifts together with their well-informed and curious intellect and to cultivate personal warmth over dramatic fireworks and committed emotional bonds over depressing or addictive obsessions, they will make a memorable impact as they travel this life's highway.

CHALLENGE: **KNOWING WHEN THEY ARE MASKING INTUITIVE INSIGHTS WITH LOGIC**

FULFILLMENT: **CUTTING LOOSE AND INDULGING THEIR FANTASIES**

NOTABLE: **ROBBIE ROBERTSON (MUSICIAN; CORE MEMBER OF THE BAND)**

July 11–18

THE PERSUADER
CANCER III

Those born in the Week of the Persuader can realize great success and worldly accomplishment on this karmic path, yet the personal side of their lives may languish as they pursue their intellectual and theoretical notions of how things (and people) ought to be rather than facing the reality of how things actually are. Though personally passionate and deeply emotional, they may fail to gain the support they need for their plans and projects if they refuse to take into account the desires and needs of those around them. Their empathy and capacity to nurture may be hidden behind mental or professional competitiveness or mired in a need for control. Yet if they can learn to open themselves to their needs and refuse to use their intelligence and perception solely to manipulate others, their intuitive strengths will blossom and their relationships will flourish.

CHALLENGE: **INVOKING THEIR DEEP EMPATHY TO BE BETTER TO THEMSELVES**

FULFILLMENT: **VIEWING THEIR FEELINGS AS ANOTHER ASSET RATHER THAN AS SOMETHING TO FEAR**

July 19–25

OSCILLATION
CANCER–LEO CUSP

Those born on this cusp who travel the Way of Versatility can experience an altogether thrilling life journey, providing they do not go overboard in their search for greater emotional integration and employ their considerable intellects in such a way that their personal reality manifests itself in a wide range of real experience—not just a succession of manic mood swings. Yet a rare kind of self-knowledge is likely to emerge among the peaks and valleys of some unusual and even extreme circumstances. Their flair for innovation, imagination, and observation will be highly pronounced as well. If they can come to understand that their considerable gifts and talents are the tools of self-discovery and not the burdens of fate or personality, they will open themselves willingly to their own and others' needs. Above all, the key to their progress will lie in their ability to clear themselves of an overabundance of distractions so that they can acquaint themselves with the clear small voice within.

CHALLENGE: **PROVIDING THE EXCITEMENT THEY CRAVE WITH-OUT INDULGING IN EXCESSES THAT MAKE THEM UNSTABLE**
FULFILLMENT: **FEELING CONFIDENT AND SECURE IN THEIR MANY TALENTS**
NOTABLE: **RAYMOND CHANDLER (MYSTERY NOVELIST; SCREEN-WRITER, *THE BIG SLEEP*)**

SHERRY LANSING
Film executive

7/31/1944
Leo I

July 26–August 2

AUTHORITY
LEO I

Those born in the Week of Authority who find themselves on the Way of Versatility can experience great personal and professional fulfillment, providing they appreciate their great gifts and do not succumb to a desire to "lord" themselves and their accomplishments over everyone else. Likely to be quite focused in the area of personal and professional ambition, they may nevertheless display a rather unpleasant tendency to detach themselves emotionally. In point of fact, they may be altogether too stubborn and will have to learn which situations in life require gentle understanding and which require the heavier hand of authority. And while it is entirely possible that they may be just a bit smarter or more gifted than those around them, those qualities amount to very little if one has only one's own companionship for comfort.

CHALLENGE: **COMING DOWN OFF THEIR HIGH HORSES TO EXTEND SOME HUMAN WARMTH TO THOSE AROUND THEM**
FULFILLMENT: **ALLOWING THEMSELVES TO BE VULNERABLE**

August 3–10

BALANCED STRENGTH
LEO II

If they do not fall prey to the dual threats of single-mindedness, on the one hand, and chronically repressed passion, on the other, those born in the Week of Balanced Strength who journey along the Way of Versatility have excellent chances for personal and professional accomplishment. Gifted with a more pronounced intellectual and analytical side than they might otherwise have had, these individuals can use it to detach from situations they find unfulfilling or emotionally compromising. The problem is that once devoted Leo II's detach emotionally, they may well stay that way for an alarmingly long period of time. In fact, there is much to suggest that these personalities will be prone to going a bit too far even in the right direction—for once their decisions are formed, it is often difficult for them to change their minds. Yet if they can nurture within themselves their yearning for greater variety, learn to open their hearts even in the face of uncertainty, and come to terms with the fact that no decision is carved in stone, they will make a great mark on the world.

CHALLENGE: **BEING LESS SINGLE-MINDED LONG ENOUGH TO DEVELOP THEIR TREMENDOUS INTUITIVE GIFTS**
FULFILLMENT: **SOFTENING ENOUGH TO ACCEPT KINDNESS FROM OTHERS**

RUSSELL BAKER
Author/columnist for
The New York Times

8/14/1925
Leo III

August 11–18

LEADERSHIP
LEO III

Brilliantly innovative and wonderfully competent, those born in this week who travel the Way of Versatility are likely to be forces to be reckoned with in the professional arena, yet they will have to work a bit harder to get in touch with their more emotional and intuitive side if they are to be really successful. In fact, they may be much more preoccupied with gaining the respect of others than they are with gaining their love, and that, coupled with a rather detached attitude toward relationships in general, can make for some long and lonely nights until they come to a better understanding of their own and others' needs. Yet if they can find the balance between mind and emotion and learn that love is a motivating force for everyone, they may well manage to give far more than they take as they make their way along this karmic path.

CHALLENGE: **THINKING MORE DEEPLY ABOUT THE "PUSH ME, PULL YOU" EFFECT THEY HAVE ON OTHERS**
FULFILLMENT: **LETTING THE REAL CHARM AND WARMTH AT THEIR CORE WIN THE DAY**
NOTABLES: **MIKE DOUGLAS (TELEVISION TALK/VARIETY SHOW HOST); NORRIS AND ROSS McWHIRTER (BRITISH TWIN BROTHERS FOUNDED INFORMATION SERVICE; *GUINNESS BOOK OF WORLD RECORDS*); OSCAR PETERSON (JAZZ MUSICIAN, PIANO VIRTUOSO)**

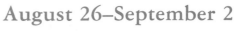

August 19–25

EXPOSURE
LEO–VIRGO CUSP

Sharing and a sense of interconnectedness with others are not likely to be the principal strengths of those born in the Week of Exposure who travel the Way of Versatility, and they may have to divest themselves of some deeply held beliefs about themselves and how the world works before they can make real personal progress. They have a strong tendency to both observation and analysis, yet they will have to avoid their inclination to use their knowledge of others for purely personal or manipulative ends. Though likely to have the "dirt" on just about anyone, they must develop their own capacity to play a hunch before they will be able to realize their fonder and more human desires. Nevertheless, they are possessed of a rabble-rousing streak that will prove most interesting, for it is just at the moment when they feel they have attained real mastery that they are likely to reveal their truest desires and head off into uncharted—and often deeply personal—territory.

JOSEPH KENNEDY
Patriarch; financier

9/6/1888
Virgo II

CHALLENGE: **TOSSING CAUTION TO THE WINDS BY REVEALING THEIR MORE HEARTFELT SIDE**
FULFILLMENT: **DELIGHTING IN THEIR ABILITY TO TURN ON A DIME**
NOTABLE: **PETER WEIR (FILM DIRECTOR, *THE YEAR OF LIVING DANGEROUSLY, WITNESS, THE TRUMAN SHOW*)**

September 3–10

THE ENIGMA
VIRGO II

The task of learning to admit and acknowledge their own needs will figure prominently in the lives of those born in the Week of the Enigma who journey along the Way of Versatility. Though likely to develop the personal strength and courage necessary to face down even the most daunting of personal demons, they will blanch a bit when it comes to sharing their needs and emotions with others. In any event, warmth is not their strongest suit. Though their intentions are invariably honorable, their means of expression may be rather high-handed, impersonal, or downright cold. Learning to relax, let their hair down, and cultivate the art of going with the flow will be especially important to their development. Yet if they allow themselves the privilege of simply being as human as everyone else, their efforts at gaining and receiving understanding will not go unrewarded.

B. B. KING
Legendary blues guitarist,
"The Thrill Is Gone"

9/16/1925
Virgo III

CHALLENGE: **RELYING LESS ON ANALYSIS AND MORE ON INTUITION WHEN MAKING DECISIONS**
FULFILLMENT: **LETTING OTHERS SEE THE DEPTH OF THEIR KINDNESS**
NOTABLES: **PETER SELLERS (ACTOR/COMEDIAN, *DR. STRANGELOVE, PINK PANTHER*); FRANCES WRIGHT (SOCIAL REFORMER; LECTURED ON BIRTH CONTROL AND WOMEN'S RIGHTS); JONATHAN TAYLOR THOMAS (ACTOR, *HOME IMPROVEMENT*)**

August 26–September 2

SYSTEM BUILDERS
VIRGO I

Those born in the Week of System Builders who make their way along this karmic path may well have to struggle a bit with their deep yearning for excitement and their deep need for connection. Still, they have the potential for wonderful accomplishment, providing they do not attempt to impose structure on a world of ever-changing emotional needs and learn to follow their hearts instead of their heads. Repressed passion and unfulfilled desires will throw a wrench into even their best-laid plans until they become better acquainted with and more receptive to the voice of their inner longings. Yet once they begin the quest for emotional connection and experience that lies at the heart of their journey and cultivate the warmth and depth of desire that is necessary to smooth their way, the fulfillment will prove well worth the risks.

CHALLENGE: **NOT RETREATING INTO LOGICAL STRUCTURES OR EFFICIENCY FOR EMOTIONAL SAFETY**
FULFILLMENT: **LOOSENING UP AND HAVING A GOOD TIME**
NOTABLE: **DONALD O'CONNOR (FILM ACTOR, *SINGIN' IN THE RAIN*)**

September 11–18

THE LITERALIST
VIRGO III

At first glance, the characteristics of the Virgo III personality appear to be at real odds with the challenge and promise of the Way of Versatility, yet these souls have the possibility of great advancement, especially if they apply their gifts for elegant construction to the business of understanding emotions. Imbuing their keen analyses of the human condition with a measure of empathy and warmth will prove a bit difficult, however, as they can be both judgmental and rather ruthless. Yet once they set aside their insistence on maintaining a purely practical perspective on life and embrace the challenge to connect and give proper reverence and acknowledgment to their higher intuitions, they will do quite well. Too, their knack for serving as an investigator of the truth and a catalyst for change may work for either good or ill, depending on whether they choose to assume a reactionary, protective, and rigid approach to innovation and improvement or instead take the higher road to spirituality, empathy, and love.

CHALLENGE: **CONVINCING THEMSELVES THAT PURE RATIONALITY ISN'T ALL IT'S CRACKED UP TO BE**
FULFILLMENT: **KNOWING THAT IT'S ALL RIGHT TO BE FALLIBLE**
NOTABLE: **MAURICE CHEVALIER (FRENCH SINGER, ACTOR, *GIGI*)**

September 19–24
BEAUTY
VIRGO–LIBRA CUSP

The energies that come together for those born on the Cusp of Beauty who travel the Way of Versatility make for a nice mix, providing these personalities can avoid the tendency to retreat from passion and emotion into an ivory tower of theory or speculation. Indecision may also be a lifelong problem for many of these people, as they are prone to overthinking or overworking problems to the point where they become ineffectual. Too, they may have a rather high-handed or snobbish approach to other people that will work to their detriment. Yet if they consciously cultivate real spirituality and allow their love of beauty to guide them, and if they come to terms with the fact that balance, in this particular case, requires their coming to terms with their emotions, all will go brilliantly for them.

CHALLENGE: **LEARNING TO MANAGE THEIR WILD SIDE BEFORE IT ACTS OUT**

FULFILLMENT: **ENGAGING THEIR PASSION AS THEY PURSUE THEIR IDEALIZED FORMS**

T. S. ELIOT
Poet/critic/playwright;
Nobel Prize for
Literature

9/26/1888
Libra I

September 25–October 2
THE PERFECTIONIST
LIBRA I

Frustration may plague those born in the Week of the Perfectionist who travel the Way of Versatility, as they may become so fixated on problems and details that they fail to take in the larger picture of what is possible. Though likely to be very goal-oriented and hugely successful on this road, their dealings with others may be marked by a decided lack of warmth or understanding. The art of give-and-take is something they will have to learn if they are to succeed, and some diplomatic skills wouldn't hurt either. At a deeper level, they would benefit enormously from acquainting themselves with their need for warmth. If they can learn that their goals will be achieved much more easily when they open themselves to a deeper level of awareness and receptivity, they will find both success and personal fulfillment as they travel this life's highway.

CHALLENGE: **NOT DRIVING THEMSELVES MAD TRYING TO SOLVE EVERY PROBLEM**

FULFILLMENT: **ACKNOWLEDGING THEIR FEELINGS**

NOTABLE: **CLAY FELKER (COFOUNDED *NEW YORK MAGAZINE*)**

October 3–10
SOCIETY
LIBRA II

Until they come to terms with their own feeling and intuitive side, those born in the Week of Society who find themselves on this karmic path may experience a bit of a struggle with their tendencies to be rather involved on the surface of life, yet detached from its deeper meaning. Though highly social and insightful in the extreme, they will have to learn to develop a greater awareness of their own needs and those of others before they can make real progress. Blessed with a keen intellect, they will doubtless be sought after for their wit, problem-solving skills, and insight, yet may languish in their own development through being unwilling to know what's best for them. Nevertheless, if they can answer the call to greater spiritual and emotional awareness and open their hearts to the possibility of a more passionate involvement in life, things will go wonderfully well for them.

CHALLENGE: **TAKING THEIR OWN NEEDS AND DESIRES MORE SERIOUSLY**

FULFILLMENT: **ENJOYING THEIR ABILITY TO BE FAIR DUE TO THEIR UNIQUE INTEGRATION OF MIND AND HEART**

NOTABLE: **GORE VIDAL (WRITER/CRITIC/ESSAYIST; *MYRA BRECKINRIDGE*; UNSUCCESSFULLY RAN FOR OFFICE)**

MARGARET THATCHER
British prime minister
1979–90

10/13/1925
Libra III

October 11–18
THEATER
LIBRA III

Those born in the Week of Theater who travel the Way of Versatility can experience wonderful fulfillment and happiness, providing they are able to overcome a rather heartless streak and learn to make their decisions based more on feeling than on the facts. They may have no small amount of difficulty when it comes to focusing their knack for logic and analysis on both human and higher spiritual objectives. Worldliness and natural savvy may prove to be great assets in the achievement of their goals, yet these sophisticated people may indulge more in melodrama than in genuine passion or commitment. One way or another, their challenge will be to attune themselves to a more human and less abstract set of values. Yet once they come to terms with the need for empathy, understanding, and integration of the emotional side of life, they can take great strides along this karmic path.

CHALLENGE: **FIGURING OUT HOW NOT TO BE SO INTIMIDATING**

FULFILLMENT: **FEELING THE SENSE OF FLOW THAT COMES WHEN FEELINGS AND INTUITIONS MESH WITH THOUGHTS**

NOTABLES: **ELMORE LEONARD (WESTERN AND CRIME NOVELIST); ANGELA LANSBURY (ACTRESS, *MURDER, SHE WROTE*); LENNY BRUCE (STAND-UP COMEDIAN KNOWN FOR PROFANITY AND OUTRAGEOUS HUMOR)**

KARMIC PATH
41

October 19–25

DRAMA AND CRITICISM
LIBRA–SCORPIO CUSP

Those born on the Cusp of Drama and Criticism are likely to do brilliantly on the Way of Versatility, providing they can reconcile some basic conflicts within their complex natures and learn not to cancel out their best impulses with excess analysis or an overdependence on logic. They will be aided in their quest for greater connection and warmth by their own passionate inclinations, though they will have to fight against their tendency to use others for their own gratification or to retreat from their challenge into isolation and snobbish or superior attitude. Learning to slow down and listen to their intuition will be especially important, as will developing the ability to identify the nature of their own deepest needs. Once they have succeeded in doing that much, the rest will be easy.

JOHNNY CARSON
TV host, *The Tonight Show*

10/23/1925
Libra–Scorpio Cusp

CHALLENGE: **NOT OVERINVOLVING THEMSELVES IN THEIR LOVE OF BEAUTY AND ATTRACTION TO THE DARK SIDE**
FULFILLMENT: **KNOWING THE DIFFERENCE BETWEEN ROMANTIC INCLINATION AND TRUE WARMTH**
NOTABLES: **ROBERT RAUSCHENBERG (ARTIST WHO OFTEN WORKED IN MIXED MEDIA); ART BUCHWALD (JOURNALIST; WIDELY SYNDICATED COLUMNIST)**

October 26–November 2

INTENSITY
SCORPIO I

The willingness to release suspicion, stop calculating, and avoid assuming the worst of others will figure prominently in the life journeys of those born in the Week of Intensity who travel the Way of Versatility. Likely to be intellectually gifted, insightful in the extreme, and deeply passionate at their core, these personalities will nevertheless face the challenge of learning to leave themselves open to emotion and connection before they can become more effective. Some early disappointments or rejections may have caused these individuals to retreat into isolation, a preoccupation with worldly achievements, or overly self-protective behavior. On the surface, they may also appear rather forbidding and unapproachable. Yet if they keep in mind that this configuration endows them with the saving grace of a brilliant sense of humor and cultivate their ability to charm others with laughter, they will do much to integrate the forces of emotion and intelligence as they navigate the twists and turns of the Way of Versatility.

CHALLENGE: **TAKING CARE NOT TO BE NEGATIVE OR DEPRESSIVE**
FULFILLMENT: **USING HUMOR TO COMPENSATE FOR THEIR OTHERWISE DETACHED APPROACH**

November 3–11

DEPTH
SCORPIO II

There may be a rather relentless quality to the intellect and insight of those born in the Week of Depth who travel the Way of Versatility, for their emotional natures are so strong and intense that they may choose to mask them with an equally intense insistence on cold logic and a rather heartless approach to the world. Yet they do themselves a great disservice by persisting in such attitudes, for underneath their often forbidding exteriors lie any number of spiritual truths as well as a great yearning and capacity for emotional bonding. Though they are sure to attain great worldly and financial success, the quality of their lives will largely be determined by their willingness to take emotional risks and to open themselves to the possibility of greater fulfillment, happiness, and connection. If they can avoid both pessimism and negativity and learn that the most genuine connections are often the result of spontaneous feeling rather than calculated campaigns, all will go well for them.

DEMI MOORE
Actress, *G.I. Jane, Ghost*

11/11/1962
Scorpio II

CHALLENGE: **LEARNING WHAT, EXACTLY, GIVES RISE TO THEIR COMPETITIVENESS AND ENVY**
FULFILLMENT: **LIVING FROM THE PHILOSOPHICAL POINT OF VIEW THAT COMING FROM THE HEART GIVES THEM**
NOTABLE: **RICHARD BURTON (WELSH-BORN STAGE AND FILM ACTOR, *CLEOPATRA*, *EQUUS*)**

November 12–18

CHARM
SCORPIO III

Those born in the Week of Charm who find themselves on the Way of Versatility can experience a really triumphant life journey, as they have a fine knack for knowing how to approach others and the warmth needed to generate enormous amounts of enthusiasm and support. Where they may well fail the challenge of this karmic path is by being unwilling to extend themselves to others in compassion or spontaneous expression of emotion. In fact, selfishness may be their biggest vice, with a certain laziness regarding their emotional development running a close second. If they can manage to embrace their opportunities to reach a higher spiritual awareness and bring themselves to show some vulnerability from time to time, they may be surprised and pleased by the responses of others to their honesty and heartfelt expressions of self.

CHALLENGE: **NOT ALLOWING THEMSELVES TO BE SATISFIED WITH RELATIONSHIPS THAT ARE LESS THAN HEARTFELT**
FULFILLMENT: **ENJOYING THE SATISFACTION OF TAKING CARE OF SOMEONE**
NOTABLES: **ROCK HUDSON (HOLLYWOOD LEADING MAN, ACTOR, *PILLOW TALK*); HOWARD BAKER (U.S. SENATOR; RANKING REPUBLICAN INVESTIGATING WATERGATE SCANDAL; PRESIDENT REAGAN'S CHIEF OF STAFF)**

November 19–24
REVOLUTION
SCORPIO–SAGITTARIUS CUSP

Those born on the Cusp of Revolution may experience some rather astonishing personal transformations as they make their way along this karmic path. Likely to be a fine mix of passion and instinct and of insight and empathy, these personalities may nevertheless have a bit of trouble regulating the powerful energies that come together here and may thus experience extremes of mood or behavior until they learn to allow intuition to inform their decisions. Inclined to be overidealistic at certain times and overly cynical at others, they will have to work hard to narrow their focus from broad philosophical concerns and concentrate more upon personal and spiritual development. Learning to slow down, to allow things to take their course, and to open themselves up to others in compassionate understanding will be big lessons, yet these individuals are likely to learn them well.

CHALLENGE: **TEMPERING THEIR TENDENCY TO SNOBBISM**
FULFILLMENT: **WARMING OTHERS WITH THEIR UNIQUE BRAND OF CHARM**
NOTABLES: **DALE CARNEGIE (AUTHOR, SPEAKER, HOW TO WIN FRIENDS AND INFLUENCE PEOPLE); WILLIAM F. BUCKLEY, JR. (JOURNALIST; CONSERVATIVE; LONGTIME EDITOR OF NATIONAL REVIEW)**

JODIE FOSTER
Actress, *Silence of the Lambs;* won 2 Oscars

11/19/1962
Scorpio–Sagittarius Cusp

November 25–December 2
INDEPENDENCE
SAGITTARIUS I

The highly individualistic people born in the Week of Independence who travel the Way of Versatility can experience wonderful fulfillment and accomplishment, though they may have to work a bit to gain the facility in human interaction it requires. Their biggest problem will be that they may have an overidealistic approach to life, and their high-flown theories may be rather offputting to more emotionally centered types. Too, they may be so insistent upon their personal independence that they simply drive others away. Yet their hearts are almost certainly in the right place, and if they can bring themselves to give voice to their deepest needs and desires in a spirit of warmth and generosity, their capacity for emotional fulfillment will not go undeveloped or their spirits unnourished as they travel along this road.

CHALLENGE: **REALIZING THAT THEIR FEAR OF COMMITMENT MAY BE HOLDING THEM BACK**
FULFILLMENT: **INVOKING THEIR SENSE OF JUSTICE AND COMPASSION TO IMPROVE THE LOT OF OTHERS**
NOTABLES: **"BO" JACKSON (FOOTBALL PLAYER); MARY WALKER EVANS (1ST WOMAN PHYSICIAN IN U.S.)**

December 3–10
THE ORIGINATOR
SAGITTARIUS II

Those born in the Week of the Originator may present a face to the world that is far removed from their ardent and emotional inner selves. The impulse toward self-protection may prove their biggest stumbling block, as these gifted people may have a rather defensive attitude toward the world that finds expression in an unusual or even peculiar approach to others. Likely to be rather mysterious at best, these people will surely display some amazing talents and aptitudes, yet they will have to work hard to learn to trust themselves and others if they are to be really successful in their quest for self-realization and fulfillment. Still, if they can overcome their pride and their tendency to overreact to rejection and disappointment, and never fear to tell the truth, their instincts for connection and real innovation are unlikely to mislead them in their quest for emotional and spiritual integration.

CHALLENGE: **NOT ALIENATING EVERYONE BY INSISTING ON THE LOGIC OF THEIR OWN VIEWS**
FULFILLMENT: **HEALING SOME OF THE WOUNDS OF THE PAST IN ORDER TO OPEN THEIR HEARTS AGAIN**
NOTABLE: **SAMMY DAVIS, JR. (SINGER, DANCER, LAS VEGAS ENTERTAINER; MEMBER OF THE "RAT PACK")**

LOUISA MAY ALCOTT
American writer,
Little Women

11/29/1832
Sagittarius I

December 11–18
THE TITAN
SAGITTARIUS III

So convinced are the individuals born in the Week of the Titan of the rightness of their own opinions that they may have a bit of difficulty when they find themselves on the Way of Versatility. Their rather lofty approach to their goals and ideals can actually interfere with the quest for integration of their intuitive side, and there may be a number of cases of what might best be termed stunted emotional development among those with this configuration. A lack of awareness of their own truest natures may in turn lead to a lack of awareness of or interest in the needs of others. Yet they are considerably aided by a natural generosity of spirit that will stand them in fine stead. If they can only learn to listen to their hearts, avoid setting unrealistic goals and indulging in too much inflated philosophy, and release their conviction of their innate superiority, things will go much more smoothly.

CHALLENGE: **HAVING NAILED DOWN THEIR INTUITIVE GIFT, TACKLING THEIR EMOTIONAL REALM**
FULFILLMENT: **DISCOVERING HOW GOOD THEY ARE AT WHAT THEY DO**
NOTABLES: **WILLIAM "REFRIGERATOR" PERRY (FOOTBALL GREAT FOR CHICAGO); DICK VAN DYKE (TELEVISION/MOVIE ACTOR, COMEDIAN; KNOWN FOR EPONYMOUS TV SHOW)**

December 19–25

PROPHECY

SAGITTARIUS–CAPRICORN CUSP

Those born on the Cusp of Prophecy will have some unusual and powerful energies, talents, and resources at their disposal as they make this life journey. Yet they may have a bit of a struggle coming to terms with what may well be their greatest asset: a powerful intuitive sense. Taking risks and acknowledging their deeper needs will not come easily to these people, and some will fail the higher challenge of this karmic path through refusing to come to terms with their special psychic talents and their essential spirituality. Too, they may be rather forbidding types, content to be entirely removed from involvement with others. Yet if they allow their passions and inclinations a bit more exercise and learn not to fear the mysteries within, they will be able to open their hearts and are sure to develop much more warmth and compassion with the passage of years.

CHALLENGE: **FORCING THEMSELVES OUT OF THEIR SELF-IMPOSED RETREAT**

FULFILLMENT: **BELIEVING IN THE VALUE OF THEIR INTUITIVE AND SENSITIVE SIDE**

NOTABLE: **RALPH FIENNES (ACTOR, SCHINDLER'S LIST, THE ENGLISH PATIENT)**

HENRI MATISSE
French painter, *Blue Nude*

12/31/1869
Capricorn I

December 26–January 2

THE RULER

CAPRICORN I

Those born in the Week of the Ruler may prove highly resistant to the challenges presented by the Way of Versatility, as they dislike things that threaten their sense of security, not the least of which is an awareness of their own deepest emotional levels. Though they are likely to be powerful and successful people, developing spontaneity is not high on their list of personal priorities, and their formidable sense of logic may well interfere with the growth and development of their more spiritual nature. Yet these rather cold and even forbidding people are sure to thaw a bit with the passage of time. If they can learn not to be quite so demanding of themselves and to develop a more tolerant attitude toward the emotions of others, they will recognize wonderful fulfillment, especially if they indulge their more nurturing and spontaneous side through interactions with children and grandchildren.

CHALLENGE: **LEARNING THAT IT IS POSSIBLE TO GET BOGGED DOWN IN INNOVATION AND IMPROVEMENT**

FULFILLMENT: **EXPERIENCING MOMENTS OF VIRTUOSITY**

January 3–9

DETERMINATION

CAPRICORN II

Those born in the Week of Determination who navigate the Way of Versatility may stumble a bit in the course of their higher development if they stick to a purely logical or rational perspective on reality. Though their emotional road may be rocky until they learn to release the burden of self-doubt, they will find that their real salvation lies in their inclination to study higher spiritual and metaphysical matters. Aided by a natural practicality, they are unlikely to be troubled by too much idealism or theory and have a knack for application of spiritual principles. Thus, many will find themselves quite happy on this karmic path, and though it may take a number of years for them to discover their real talent for innovation and invention, if they get in touch with their more radical side and learn to operate from the deepest levels of awareness and sincerity, they will be rewarded with great fulfillment and considerable accomplishment.

CHALLENGE: **TEMPERING THEIR SOMETIMES COLDHEARTED APPROACH TO HUMAN RELATIONS**

FULFILLMENT: **DISCOVERING THAT THEIR SENSITIVITY IS AN ASSET**

PIERRE DuPONT
Business executive;
philanthropist

1/15/1870
Capricorn III

January 10–16

DOMINANCE

CAPRICORN III

The souls born in the Week of Dominance who travel the Way of Versatility will become much happier as they gradually learn to relinquish their need to control their environment through logic and practicality and open themselves to the worlds of intuition and imagination that await them along this karmic path. For many of these people, however, that task will prove daunting indeed, as they may overburden themselves with daily responsibilities, obligations, and worries to such an extent that they tune out what their hearts are trying to say. Thus, cultivating time alone and allowing themselves periods of rest and what might best be termed "spiritual nourishment" will prove especially useful. If they do not succumb to worry, intolerance, or a tendency to exalt intelligence to the point where it obscures enlightenment, all will go well.

CHALLENGE: **NOT CONFUSING DEVOTED ATTENTION WITH CARING**

FULFILLMENT: **ENJOYING THE SATISFACTION OF GROWING THEIR TALENTS AND SKILLS**

January 17–22

MYSTERY AND IMAGINATION
CAPRICORN–AQUARIUS CUSP

Some rather difficult and elusive personalities are born with this configuration, and it's anyone's guess just how well they will do with this karmic path's call to develop a more open heart and a better-informed intuition. Perhaps their principal challenge will be learning to recognize that their need to order the world with logic is but a reflection of their fear of their more chaotic and disruptive side. The most successful of these personalities will learn to integrate their sense of fun, spontaneity, and intuition and use it to inform some highly intelligent decisions; the least successful will cling to an overly aloof and often overbearing attitude, yearning to "get out of their heads" but always unable to take the risks needed. Yet if they can manage to surround themselves with people who are their equals, the mutual respect inspired by such relationships will enable them to open up more completely and reap the emotional and spiritual rewards that await them.

JAMES MICHENER
Writer, historical fiction,
Space

———

2/3/1907
Aquarius II

CHALLENGE: **NOT CONFUSING ANY NUMBER OF ADDICTIONS OR UNHEALTHY BEHAVIORS WITH TRUE FEELING**

FULFILLMENT: **TAKING PRIDE IN HOW HARD THEY WORK TO KEEP THEIR HEARTS OPEN**

NOTABLE: **HAKEEM OLAJUWON (BASKETBALL CENTER)**

January 23–30

GENIUS
AQUARIUS I

Some truly startling intellectual gifts are sure to be present among those born in this week who travel the Way of Versatility. Yet these gifted people will run the risk of either dwelling too much in the realms of the mind, on the one hand, or indulging in too much recklessness and ill-considered action, on the other. Likely to question everything, they may prove to be a real thorn in the side of more established and traditional thinkers and will have to be careful not to expend needless energy in run-ins with authority. They will, however, need to familiarize themselves with their own emotions in order to realize the higher promise of this karmic path, and learning to listen to their hearts instead of their heads may prove to be a lifelong challenge. Yet if they cultivate and learn to respect the more intuitive forms of knowledge, and nurture their affection for humanity with some down-to-earth interactions, they will enjoy some amazing accomplishments in the course of this life's journey.

CHALLENGE: **NOT PERMITTING THEIR NEED FOR FREEDOM TO INTERFERE WITH THEIR SOUL'S GROWTH**

FULFILLMENT: **FINDING THAT THEY CAN REACH OUT AND TOUCH OTHERS**

NOTABLE: **HENRY MATHER GREENE (ARCHITECT, CONTRIBUTED TO THE DESIGN OF THE BUNGALOW)**

January 31–February 7

YOUTH AND EASE
AQUARIUS II

The personalities born in the Week of Youth and Ease are likely to have far more social skills and interactive talents than some others who travel this road, and by and large they can expect great success and happiness. In fact, their principal problem may be a lack of deeper awareness of the more spiritual and emotional side of life or a tendency to skim along the surface when deeper investigation of themselves and issues is required. For some a tendency to personal isolation may also be a problem, as may refusing to follow their best instincts and impulses for fear of rocking the boat. Nevertheless, they have the potential for the highest achievement, and if they are careful to cultivate sincerity and soulfulness, brilliant success and personal fulfillment can be theirs.

SHERYL CROW
Rock/pop star

———

2/11/1963
Aquarius III

CHALLENGE: **COUNTERACTING A CERTAIN INDIFFERENCE TO THE FEELINGS OF OTHERS**

FULFILLMENT: **SUCCEEDING IN ALL THEIR ENDEAVORS**

NOTABLES: **ALFRED ADLER (PSYCHOANALYST WHO REBELLED AGAINST FREUD'S TEACHING; COINED PHRASE "INFERIORITY COMPLEX"); NORTON SIMON (BUSINESS EXECUTIVE; FOUNDED FOOD CONGLOMERATE)**

February 8–15

ACCEPTANCE
AQUARIUS III

Providing they do not allow some of their more fixed or inflexible attitudes to cloud their better judgment or their intuitive sense of what is right, those born in the Week of Acceptance who travel the Way of Versatility can experience wonderful progress. Intellectual and always questioning, they may, however, fail to question some of their own more fixed opinions or to evaluate or reevaluate their pet theories and beliefs. Yet at their core, these truly progressive personalities have a fine sense of the larger picture. If they can narrow their focus to the point where they imbue their inspirations with warmth, tolerance for others, and respect for their own intuitive and emotional side, they will realize great advancement along this road, especially when they concentrate their energies upon changing themselves, rather than changing the world.

CHALLENGE: **QUESTIONING THEIR HIGHLY INGRAINED NEED FOR DETACHMENT**

FULFILLMENT: **TAKING RISKS—IN MEASURED DOSES**

NOTABLES: **SAMUEL TILDEN (ATTORNEY, HELPED BREAK UP BOSS TWEED'S RING; NEW YORK GOVERNOR); TRAVIS TRITT (COUNTRY MUSIC SINGER)**

February 16–22

SENSITIVITY
AQUARIUS–PISCES CUSP

In a way, emotional detachment may prove something of a gift for those born on the Cusp of Sensitivity who find themselves on the Way of Versatility, as their intellectual and logical powers will do much to mitigate some of their more self-defeating emotional problems. Yet for many this road will not always be an easy one, especially if they go overboard and allow eccentricity, escapism, or a runaway imagination to disturb their delicate emotional balance. Mood swings and repression of emotions are likely to be their biggest faults, yet they are possessed of a natural concern for others that will serve them well. If they work to overcome pessimism and insecurity and avoid the tendency to second-guess their best impulses or torture themselves with "could have, would have, should have" patterns of thought, their more spiritual side will open up.

W. H. AUDEN
Poet/writer

2/21/1907
Aquarius–Pisces Cusp

CHALLENGE: **KNOWING THAT THEY CAN WORK HARD TO INTEGRATE ALL THEIR FUNCTIONS BUT THAT IN THE END IT IS UP TO SPIRIT AND IS THEREFORE A MYSTERY**

FULFILLMENT: **USING THEIR IMAGINATIONS TO VISUALIZE AND ACHIEVE THEIR GOALS**

NOTABLES: **SEAL (POP SINGER); ROBERT YOUNG (TV ACTOR, *FATHER KNOWS BEST*; *MARCUS WELBY, M.D.*)**

February 23–March 2

SPIRIT
PISCES I

Those born in the Week of Spirit who navigate the challenge and promise of the Way of Versatility are likely to experience a wonderfully fulfilling life journey, providing they do not succumb to the dangers of ivory-tower idealism, on the one hand, or emotional eccentricity, on the other. Yet the gifts of this karmic path will do much to ground the flightier tendencies of this group, while their need for spiritual and emotional connection and nourishment is unlikely to go unacknowledged or ignored. Though they are capable of imbuing their experience with a rare kind of practical magic, controlling their expectations and cultivating a sense of responsibility for their behavior will prove especially important. Yet if they can cultivate within themselves the ability to take risks in the interests of happiness and integrate their intuition into daily life, there will be little they cannot accomplish.

CHALLENGE: **TONING DOWN THEIR KNOW-IT-ALL ATTITUDE**

FULFILLMENT: **WORKING WONDERS WITH JUST A MODICUM OF SIMPLE CHARM**

March 3–10

THE LONER
PISCES II

Those born in the Week of the Loner who journey along the Way of Versatility may well develop the faith and knowledge of their own highly intuitive and spiritual side but may fail the higher challenge of integrating their hearts and emotions into their dealings with others. Thus it may take these souls no small amount of work and a number of personal disappointments until they figure out just what they're doing wrong when it comes to dealing with others. Their formidable intellectual gifts may also exacerbate their tendency to withdraw into ivory towers of theory or speculation. Mood swings, unpredictability, and a perennially defensive outlook may all be problems. Yet if they learn to trust themselves, trust for others will not be long in coming, and the courage to act upon their deepest levels of knowledge and conviction will blossom.

CHARLES BARKLEY
Basketball player

2/20/1963
Aquarius–Pisces Cusp

CHALLENGE: **NOT USING INTELLECTUALISM TO HIDE FROM HURT**

FULFILLMENT: **INDULGING THEIR LOVE OF BEAUTY, PERHAPS THROUGH THEIR ARTISTIC TALENTS**

NOTABLES: **LOGAN WILSON (EDUCATIONAL INNOVATOR; INTRODUCED RACIAL INTEGRATION INTO HIGHER EDUCATION)**

March 11–18

DANCERS AND DREAMERS
PISCES III

Employing their considerable talent and intellect to justify some downright irresponsible behavior may well be a hallmark of those born in this week who travel the Way of Versatility. Though wonderfully gifted, amazingly competent, and often inspirational, many of these people will prefer others to take the risks or pick up the pieces. Flightiness and unrealistic expectations may hinder their higher development and many of them may hold themselves aloof from the challenge to adjust their rather superior attitudes toward others. Yet if they can manage to cultivate sincerity, self-knowledge, and openness, the integration of creative talent, keen intellect, and spiritual understanding will make for some amazing and inspirational personalities, capable of both practical innovation and the manifestation of a rare kind of personal magic.

CHALLENGE: **BEING SURE TO CULTIVATE HUMILITY LEST THEY PUT PEOPLE OFF**

FULFILLMENT: **PRESENTING THEIR GREAT GIFTS AND VERSATILITY ON A LARGER STAGE**

The Way of Study

AQUARIUS I TO LEO I
Genius to Authority

Those on the Way of Study are here to choose a field of endeavor or a craft and, through years of disciplined and determined effort, to become the authorities in their field. Blessed with brilliance, they grasp things so quickly that they often move from one topic to the next, avoiding the painstaking groundwork of thorough preparation. The individuals on this karmic path must rely less on their own cleverness and set about gaining the perspective that only serious study of all facets of a subject can give them. Only then can they hope to bring a unique point of view to the world. Moreover, those on the Way of Study are called to find principles or points of view in which they believe. Through identifying with principles or connecting with something greater than themselves, those on this karmic path not only fulfill their individuality but come to understand it. Their many years of solitary study or work on their craft will also provide the forum for many deep insights into their own natures.

The individuals born to the Way of Study spend much of their lives deep in thought. Considered by many to be brilliant, they find school easy, but they may not make the best students since they are restless and easily bored and will concoct elaborate schemes to emancipate themselves from routine. Freedom, especially mental freedom, is important to them. Their minds roam far and wide. They love to dream up wild theories and will flit from one preoccu-

pation to the next. Moreover, they often spend hours dreaming of romantic and far-off lands, glory, or visions of the future. A number of them are science fiction buffs. On the whole, those on this karmic path prefer solitary pursuits, though they do like to be surrounded by a group of unique and unusual friends as this provides endless hours of entertainment for them in the form of people watching.

As distracted or wacky as those on this karmic path may sometimes appear to be, underneath all their mad-professor posturing is a brain that operates a bit faster than the norm. Thus, many will listen to what they have to say. And as much as they like to be left alone to go their own way, those on the Way of Study truly enjoy both holding court and holding forth. What is ironic about them is that in early years, often what they have to say isn't particularly brilliant, nor is it well thought out. This is because their stubborn adherence to their own ideas and methods and their need for freedom keep them from doing the work of a real scholar. It may take being laughed out of the auditorium a few times before those on this path begin to realize that it is time to get serious. Unfortunately, such an experience may be the only thing that will help them shift their perspective and develop some goals. In their yearning for recognition, these men and women will finally settle into the self-imposed discipline required to be true lifelong students rather than mere dilettantes.

CORE LESSON
Choosing and identifying with a principle or point of view

GOAL
To understand who they are by dedicating themselves to a chosen field of endeavor

---

GIFTS
Unusual, Truth Loving, Passionate

PITFALLS
Egotistical, Autocratic, Closed-minded

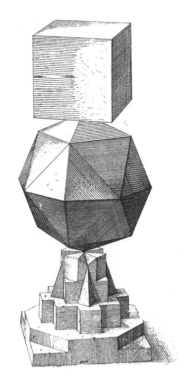

Those on the Way of Study are destined to devote themselves to an area of expertise and to learn about it slowly, deliberately, and carefully. Applying a bit of determination will be necessary, since these people are easily thrown off course. The men and women on this karmic path are called to study the work of those who have gone before, understand the underlying principles or laws of their field, and immerse themselves in their subject so that they make it their own. They are not expected to simply memorize material or swallow it whole but must cultivate the patience to do the groundwork before they can launch their own theories or make their own contributions. It is only then that these individuals will come to be viewed and respected as authorities on a given topic.

Often those on this karmic path are able to relate to many different points of view in an argument. While this gives them a tremendous ability to assimilate and integrate huge amounts of information, on this path they are called to choose one point of view. Happiness comes to the individuals on the Way of Study when they find principles or ideals that they can identify with and live their lives by. They must move out of their theories and fantasies and bring ideas into some sort of reality for themselves. In so doing, they move closer to the goal of this path, which is to come to understand who they are as individuals. Usually they are not really sure of who they are or what they stand for. By carefully considering what ideas or fields are attractive to them, choosing a subject or point of view, observing themselves as they engage in the process of study, and being self-aware throughout, these individuals will come to understand who they really are. In some ways, those on this path are, in reality, studying themselves. It is by looking in the mirror of the abstract truths they embrace that these individuals will come to see themselves, perhaps for the first time. Thus, this is a path of individuation through the process of acquiring knowledge. As they move from their universal concerns or ideas and learn to personalize them, they will discover their own myth. Their life's work will become their heroic quest as they reconnect their core self to some greater purpose. They will stop assuming the role of know-it-all and become the voice of quiet, confident authority. From such a stance, they are bound to attract attention.

For such self-confident, independent personalities, it may be torture to follow strict guidelines or rules, but their success on this karmic path depends on their developing the discipline required to do just that. What motivates them most powerfully is their need to master a topic or field. Many on this path are quiet, unassuming individuals who may not be consciously aware of where they are headed. Although many born to the Way of Study are self-taught, sooner or later they

RELEASE

The tendency to become
restless and bored

REWARD

The joy of being an authority
on a topic

SUGGESTION

Stay in touch with the world. Never forget to be self-aware. Detach once in a while from your work—insights or breakthroughs are likely to occur. What does what you do say about you?

will find it necessary to subject themselves to the rigorous requirements of a teacher, school, or other institution. It should be noted that those on this path can be found in all walks of life, not just academia. On the other hand, those who have difficulty forsaking their Aquarius I roots may find it difficult to buckle down to the absolute authority of a teacher or discipline. Instilling calm and respect for authority in themselves may prove daunting, but without these traits they will find it difficult or impossible to progress.

With maturity, those on this karmic path often enjoy the security that the group or institution to which they belong brings them. Often they forsake early radicalism and become quite traditional, even conservative. For many, the structure afforded them by an institution gives them the time and facilities they need to pursue their work without interruption. One danger, of course, for those on this path is that they may retreat from the world and become increasingly isolated from it. Stuffiness and pedantry are pitfalls to be avoided. Also, overblown ego and pride may be a problem, in the sense that those on this path identify with their expertise in a given field so much that they ignore other points of view and become increasingly rigid or conceited.

These individuals are likely to encounter at least one mentor or teacher in their lives, but ultimately such a figure, although revered, may have to be surpassed or re-

jected so that their own authority can be established without question. Feeling competitive with others, particularly when beginning their studies, will help them sharpen their ambitions but will have to be dropped at a certain point when it becomes counterproductive.

These people are rarely sidetracked from their studies by too much human interaction. Having one faithful friend, fellow student, or coworker with whom they can share their joys and sorrows is usually all they require. Their preoccupation with their work or craft may prove problematic in love affairs or marriages. Still, many may be able to develop a stable domestic situation with an understanding mate and children, as long as their autocratic tendencies do not run out of hand. The extended family unit may prove the significant social point of interaction for those on the Way of Study, and a lasting relationship with one parent or sibling can be highly beneficial and stabilizing.

In describing this path, there come to mind the lives of certain spiritual masters, such as Buddha or Mohammed, who gave up involvement with the material aspects of life to penetrate more deeply into the meaning of life through prayer, fasting, and meditation. Only then were they ready to receive their deepest and most profound revelations. Similarly, those on this karmic path must to an extent isolate themselves and go inward in order to devote themselves to mastering their subject, only to shine the more brightly when they emerge.

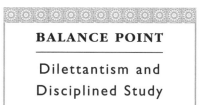

BALANCE POINT

Dilettantism and
Disciplined Study

CRYSTALS AND GEMSTONES

Optical calcite is a lens that shows the individual how to ground ideas with focus. This mineral illustrates how ideas remain abstract until they can be connected to the whole.

NOTABLES ON THIS KARMIC PATH

Mohandas K. Gandhi's patient mental discipline allowed him to realize his own life's purpose working for the liberation of his people. After studying law in London, he went to South Africa, where he opposed discriminatory legislation against Indians before returning to India in 1914 to support the Home Rule Movement against the British. His examination of the *Bhagavadgita,* as well as works by idealists such as Tolstoy, Ruskin, and Thoreau, led him to embrace the ideal of nonviolence, which he advocated as leader of the Indian National Congress. The effectiveness of these and other campaigns was evidenced by India's achievement of independence in 1947.

MOHANDAS K. GANDHI

An innovator in printing and engraving, a gifted painter, and an outstanding poet, **William Blake** studied each of his passions with devotion all his life. Unfortunately, he found little worldly success in these pursuits, though today his works are viewed as masterpieces.

WILLIAM BLAKE

A visionary and a mystic, Blake evaded the more commercial and material aspects of the world (which he detested), instead feeding his muse with London street life, where he picked up the local rhythms and rhymes found in his *Songs of Innocence* and *Songs of Experience.* Blake's elevation of imagination over experience leads some to proclaim him the first Romantic artist in England while his education of himself through experience makes him a fitting symbol on the Way of Study.

Joni Mitchell was first recognized as a gifted songwriter because of the popularization of her songs by other artists. She later emerged as a powerful performer in her own right. By early 1968 she had her own top-ten hit in "Both Sides Now" and the

JONI MITCHELL

next year she released her album *Clouds.* Each of her albums testifies to her widening musical horizons, expanding from her individual folk style to include jazz and pop elements. Like many on this path, Mitchell found her greatest success in introspective self-realization, writing words that expressed her most intimate feelings.

Other Notables: Leo Buscaglia, Irving Berlin, Yogi Berra, Malcolm X, Pierre Salinger, Paula Abdul, Medgar Evers, Tom Cruise, Horst P. Horst, Albert Sabin, Giuseppe Verdi, Sam Shepard, Robert Louis Stevenson, Billie Jean King, Otto Preminger, Keith Richards, Conrad Hilton, John Denver, Ben Kingsley, Joe Frazier, Stockard Channing, George Papandreou, Alice Walker, Roger Daltrey, Arthur M. Schlesinger, Tony Hillerman, Hannah Arendt, Soichiro Honda, Henry R. Kravis

---

BIRTHDAYS ON KARMIC PATH 42

December 28, 1887–May 17, 1888 | August 9, 1906–December 28, 1906 | March 21, 1925–August 8, 1925

October 31, 1943–March 20, 1944 | June 11, 1962–October 30, 1962

January 21, 1981–June 10, 1981 | September 2, 1999–January 21, 2000 | April 14, 2018–September 1, 2018

KARMIC PATH
42

March 19–24

REBIRTH
PISCES–ARIES CUSP

Those born in this period may experience a bit of difficulty in acquiring the level of interest, skill, and mastery of a particular subject that are required by the Way of Study. Passionate and straightforward, they may well resist the higher challenge of this karmic path and needlessly expend their energies in frustration, recklessness, or an insistence on independence. Cultivating steady learning habits and mental discipline will aid them in their quest for a higher level of self-realization and transformation. If they allow their sense of passion to guide them to an area of learning that will involve them on a mental, emotional, and spiritual level, they are more than capable of displaying the kind of heartfelt dedication and persistence that will allow this karmic path to provide a journey of real personal and spiritual transformation.

CHALLENGE: **QUELLING THEIR NEED FOR ACTIVITY AND DEVELOPING THE ABILITY TO SIT STILL**
FULFILLMENT: **DISCOVERING THE HIDDEN FACETS OF THEIR PERSONALITY THROUGH QUIET STUDY**
NOTABLE: **JOSEPH ALBERS (PAINTER; TEACHER; HELPED INTRODUCE BAUHAUS CONCEPTS TO U.S.)**

March 25–April 2

THE CHILD
ARIES I

Those born in the Week of the Child are certainly endowed with the intelligence and curiosity to make the Way of Study a success, but they may have trouble with the level of commitment and dedication to a particular principle or point of view that is required. Likely to be mentally facile and possessed of a certain sense of awe and wonder about the world, they will have to take care that they do not scatter their energies in superficial interests or less-than-productive attempts at buckling down. Still, they have a propensity to isolate themselves periodically and a need to be taken seriously that will serve them especially well in the course of this life journey. If they do not fall prey to the demons of impatience or unrealistic or premature efforts to bring their ideas to the world, a stronger sense of personal identity and a unique and beautifully coherent understanding of the larger themes of life can be theirs.

CHALLENGE: **NOT TAKING THE EASY WAY OUT BECAUSE IT IS MORE FUN**
FULFILLMENT: **DEVELOPING THEIR IDEAS FROM A SOLID BASE OF KNOWLEDGE**
NOTABLE: **JAMES E. CASEY (BUSINESS EXECUTIVE, FOUNDED UNITED PARCEL SERVICE)**

FLANNERY O'CONNOR
Southern author,
A Good Man Is Hard to Find

3/25/1925
Aries I

April 3–10

THE STAR
ARIES II

Those born in the Week of the Star who make their way along this karmic path may have to undertake quite a lot of soul-searching and evaluation before they come to terms with the fact that the center of the action is not always where their truest impulses and needs lie. There can be quite a lot of the performer about these people, and they will have to carefully control their impulse to gain gratification from others rather than to cultivate the necessary depth and concentration to become masters of their own points of view. Yet they have an enormous capacity for hard work that is sure to stand them in wonderful stead, and if they can direct their efforts toward a particular area of interest, infuse their explorations with real passion, and always remain open to the idea that there is much to be learned by even the most brilliant among us, they can make great progress.

CHALLENGE: **RELEASING THEIR NEED TO PROVE ANYTHING TO ANYONE BUT THEMSELVES**
FULFILLMENT: **FEELING PRIDE IN THE RESULTS OF THEIR HARD WORK**

April 11–18

THE PIONEER
ARIES III

Marked by a tendency to impose their ideas and will on others, those born in the Week of the Pioneer who navigate the challenge and promise of the Way of Study may have something of the idealistic autocrat about them. In fact, their sense of adventure may prove to be both their biggest blessing and their biggest curse as they make their way along this road, for they have the capacity to dream up really brilliant schemes and ideas but will have to work hard to develop the necessary follow-through to turn those ideas into reality. Restlessness may also be a big problem for many of these individuals, and some will chafe needlessly at the restrictions required in dedicating themselves to a highly focused course of study or area of endeavor. Nevertheless, they have a certain depth of character and conscience that are admirable assets. If they will only choose to motivate themselves as well as they can often motivate others, expertise, admiration, and true self-realization can be theirs.

CHALLENGE: **NOT JUMPING INTO TEACHING BEFORE THEY HAVE COMPLETED THEIR OWN COURSE OF STUDY**
FULFILLMENT: **ENJOYING THE PROCESS OF DISCOVERY THAT SELF-EDUCATION BRINGS**
NOTABLE: **ROD STEIGER (ACTOR, *IN THE HEAT OF THE NIGHT*)**

LEO BUSCAGLIA
Educator/author,
Living, Loving, and Learning

3/31/1925
Aries I

April 19–24
POWER
ARIES–TAURUS CUSP

Those born on the Cusp of Power who journey along the Way of Study can realize amazing success and accomplishment, providing they take care to define their definitions of power not in worldly terms but in more esoteric, philosophical, and intellectual ones. Though many will prove resistant to such notions and needlessly expend their energies in a rather autocratic and authoritarian approach to issues, others will be able to connect successfully with the idea that their life has a larger purpose than the mere acquisition of material goods or worldly influence. When they do, their keen mental aptitude, infinite patience, and unique sense of personal timing will prove invaluable in their quest for self-realization through the discovery and study of larger and more universal truths. If they take care that dedication does not turn into stubborn fixation or an insistence on asserting themselves before the time is right, they will have considerable impact.

CHALLENGE: **AVOIDING THE TENDENCY TO BE A PEDANT OR KNOW-IT-ALL**

FULFILLMENT: **DISCOVERING THE POTENCY OF THEIR ABILITY TO CONCENTRATE**

IRVING BERLIN
Russian-born U.S. composer, wrote countless popular songs, "God Bless America," "White Christmas"

5/11/1888
Taurus III

April 25–May 2
MANIFESTATION
TAURUS I

Those born in the Week of Manifestation who journey along the Way of Study are likely to find this a comfortable journey, as many of their natural inclinations are very much in keeping with its higher challenge. Likely to be far less distracted or reckless than many on this road, they are natural masters at giving shape and substance to even the most difficult concepts or abstractions. Indeed, closed-mindedness may prove to be their biggest enemy, as some with this configuration become so focused on a particular course of action that they neglect to acquaint themselves with the worlds of knowledge available on almost any given subject and may get lost in the details of or an overly pedantic approach to their subject. Yet if they can set their course, protect their sense of personal peace, and apply themselves diligently to those studies or subjects that never fail to fire their imaginations and larger sense of self, all will go brilliantly.

CHALLENGE: **NOT ADHERING TOO RIGIDLY TO THE RULES**
FULFILLMENT: **FINDING A CERTAIN PLEASURE IN THEIR STUBBORN PERSISTENCE IN THEIR WORK**
NOTABLE: **CHUCK BEDNARIK (FOOTBALL PLAYER; 8-TIME ALL-PRO LINEBACKER)**

May 3–10
THE TEACHER
TAURUS II

Though well suited to the call to deep and thorough study in a given area of interest, those born in the Week of the Teacher who travel this karmic path may become mired in the need to assert their brilliance at the expense of acquiring real authority. Yet they often become experts in their chosen fields, though they may experience a number of disappointments and disillusions until they become willing to buckle down and apply themselves. Indeed, that dynamic may spill over into their personal relationships, and they will have to struggle a bit to remain open to the notion that they are here to learn rather than to teach. Yet they have the possibility of great success, simply because their fine minds and intellects are imbued with a passion for self-discovery. If they can avoid the traps of scattered interests, on the one hand, and pedantry, on the other, they are more than capable of distilling their knack for knowledge into a unique message or vision that they will then share with the larger world.

CHALLENGE: **RELYING LESS ON TEACHERS AND MORE ON BEING SELF-TAUGHT**

FULFILLMENT: **SHARING THEIR VIEWS AND THEORIES WITH OTHERS**

YOGI BERRA
New York Yankees great, catcher and manager

5/12/1925
Taurus III

May 11–18
THE NATURAL
TAURUS III

Rebelliousness and frustration may stand in the way of the higher development of those born in the Week of the Natural who make their way along this karmic path. Though capable of finding the level of focus and dedication implied here, they will have to address their rather uncomfortable or ambiguous relationship with authority in general before they allow themselves to become authorities in a particular area. While they may fancy themselves entirely too fun-loving and adventurous to embark on a journey of apprenticeship or study in any given field, once they do so, they will find their efforts beautifully rewarded with a sense of security and grounding that may be otherwise lacking. Coming to better terms with their subject will surely put them into a better relationship with themselves, and once they allow illumination and enlightenment to shine through the lens of expertise, they are likely to enjoy the trip immensely.

CHALLENGE: **NOT FEELING EMBARRASSED BY THE LEVEL OF THEIR ERUDITION**

FULFILLMENT: **FINDING AREAS OF STUDY THAT TRULY ENGAGE AND FASCINATE THEM**

May 19–24
ENERGY
TAURUS–GEMINI CUSP

Those born in this period who travel the Way of Study may have to work harder than most to apply themselves to its higher challenge of devoting themselves and their curious minds to a particular field of endeavor. Wide-ranging interests and a pronounced tendency toward dilettantism may be their biggest faults. Too, they may fail to approach their intellectual infatuations with seriousness and depth and hence may suffer the consequences of ill-formed plans and poor preparation. Yet if they keep in mind that they have prodigious energy that can be successfully distributed between a particular field of study and a wide variety of social contacts, this karmic path will smooth considerably for them. Once they are reassured that dedication does not necessarily mean isolation and that, though genius may be a gift, it is diligence and dedication that make for real expertise and a sense of authority in a given field, all will go well.

CHALLENGE: **DISCIPLINING THEMSELVES TO FOCUS ON THEIR SUBJECT OF CHOICE**
FULFILLMENT: **REAPING THE REWARDS OF PATIENCE, PLANNING, AND GREATER SELF-UNDERSTANDING THAT STUDY GIVES THEM**
NOTABLE: **JOSHUA LEDERBERG (NOBEL PRIZE-WINNING GENETICIST)**

MALCOLM X
African American activist, Nation of Islam member; assassinated

5/19/1925
Taurus–Gemini Cusp

May 25–June 2
FREEDOM
GEMINI I

The self-imposed discipline and scholarship called for by the Way of Study are likely to be a bit difficult for those born in the Week of Freedom to achieve. Though brilliant, perceptive, and often technically gifted, they will battle the demons of distraction and dilettantism for much of their lives until they learn to settle down, buckle down, and apply themselves to a more thorough knowledge of a particular field or area of study. Rebelliousness may also be a problem for many of these individuals, and an exceedingly low frustration threshold may hold them back from a higher level of expertise. Yet if they can control their impatience, finish what they start, and understand that there is also a great deal of personal freedom and inner peace to be found in dedicated concentration, they will discover much about themselves in the course of this life journey.

CHALLENGE: **KNOWING WHEN IT'S TIME TO STOP TALKING AND START LISTENING**
FULFILLMENT: **GAINING THE RESPECT OF OTHERS FOR THEIR SERIOUS EFFORTS**
NOTABLES: **TONY HILLERMAN (MYSTERY NOVELIST, BOOKS SET IN SOUTHWEST); JULIAN BECK (COFOUNDED LIVING THEATER)**

June 3–10
NEW LANGUAGE
GEMINI II

Those born in the Week of New Language who travel the Way of Study have a fine potential for success and a higher level of self-realization, providing they do not succumb to the personal demons of disorganization, frustration, or the need to get their point of view across to others before they have fully educated themselves on a particular subject. Likely to be intellectually gifted, their quick minds are wont to jump to any number of conclusions, yet they will be faced with the challenge of learning that at times theirs is not the only point of view worth consideration. In fact, many of their more pompous attitudes may arise out of personal defensiveness until their journey requires them to take a closer look at themselves through the lens of a particular area of study or scholarship. If they allow themselves to grow through discipline, their success will be ensured and their opinions likely to be supported.

CHALLENGE: **DROPPING THEIR INSISTENCE ON ALWAYS DOING THINGS THEIR OWN WAY**
FULFILLMENT: **ASSIMILATING AND INTEGRATING LARGE AMOUNTS OF INFORMATION OR CONFLICTING VIEWS**
NOTABLES: **BARBARA BUSH (FIRST LADY TO GEORGE; LITERACY ADVOCATE); DENNIS WEAVER (ACTOR, McCLOUD; ENVIRONMENTAL ACTIVIST)**

PIERRE SALINGER
Journalist/author/press secretary for John F. Kennedy

6/14/1925
Gemini III

June 11–18
THE SEEKER
GEMINI III

Able to take in and understand enormous amounts of information, Gemini III's will nevertheless have to work hard to cultivate the level of personal discipline required by the Way of Study. Indeed, these personalities have a pronounced fondness for exploring the limits and pushing the frontiers of experience, yet it may take them some time to settle down and focus their energies in such a way that their yearning for experience manifests itself in some concrete accomplishments. Personal discipline and the willingness to remove themselves from a wealth of social contacts and responsibilities will prove especially important, as will the ability to understand scholarship and study as means of personal enlightenment. Nonetheless, they have the promise of great success, and as long as they manage to ground themselves in focused effort, their love of learning in all its forms is certain to hold sway.

CHALLENGE: **SELECTING PRINCIPLES OR VIEWPOINTS TO CALL THEIR OWN**
FULFILLMENT: **REALIZING THAT THE JOURNEY *IS* THE DESTINATION**
NOTABLE: **ALLY SHEEDY (ACTRESS, *HIGH ART*, MEMBER OF THE "BRAT PACK")**

June 19–24

MAGIC
GEMINI–CANCER CUSP

Though temperamentally and spiritually able to embrace a lifework as a heroic quest, those born on the Cusp of Magic who travel the Way of Study will have to endure a certain amount of trial and error before they discover their true calling. In fact, they will display a marked tendency to attach themselves to others, especially romantic partners, in an effort at self-discovery, and it may well be a series of disappointments with "the other" that throws them back on themselves in an effort at self-healing and self-realization. Yet once they turn their fine and intuitive minds to a particular area of interest, they are well suited to the challenges of thoroughness, scholarship, and concentration of this karmic path. Aligning themselves to a larger sense of purpose through study is highlighted here, and with time, effort, and experience these individuals can find wonderful fulfillment.

PAULA ABDUL
Dancer/pop music singer

6/19/1962
Gemini–Cancer Cusp

CHALLENGE: **TAKING CARE NOT TO NEGLECT BROADENING THEIR EXPERTISE**

FULFILLMENT: **INVOKING THEIR LOGICAL MINDS AND INTUITIVE INSIGHT AS THEY PURSUE A COURSE OF STUDY**

June 25–July 2

THE EMPATH
CANCER I

Though gifted with more emotional detachment than some of their fellows born in this week, Cancer I's who travel the Way of Study may have to work a bit to align themselves with the higher set of principles and ideals required by this karmic path. Prone to be buffeted about by others' emotions, they may have a great need for attention and affection, and some will have to endure great disappointment before they can successfully turn away from purely personal concerns and learn to embrace and identify more abstract truths as a means of self-knowledge. Yet they are likely to respond well to the sense of security that comes with aligning themselves with an institution or organization that will encourage and support their growing expertise and authority and allow their ideas and theories to manifest themselves in concrete and often quite comforting reality.

CHALLENGE: **DISCOVERING PRINCIPLES AND HIGHER AUTHORITIES BY WHICH THEY CAN LIVE**

FULFILLMENT: **PUTTING THEIR NATURAL AGGRESSIVENESS TO USE IN RESEARCH AND HIGHER EXPLORATION**

NOTABLES: **PATRICE LUMUMBA (1ST PRIME MINISTER OF REPUBLIC OF CONGO); MEDGAR EVERS (CIVIL RIGHTS LEADER; MURDERED)**

July 3–10

THE UNCONVENTIONAL
CANCER II

The process of greater individuation that comes through the acquisition of knowledge is likely to go rather smoothly for those born in the Week of the Unconventional who travel this karmic path. Yet they will have to work a bit to get out of their heads and turn their high-flown and rather fanciful ideas into reality. Keeping a tight rein on their imagination and sticking to facts rather than theories will be helpful to many of them, as they may have a propensity to get lost in their fantasies. Focusing their formidable intellects by studying a particular subject will be a real godsend to most of these individuals and help them to acquire the mental discipline they need to free themselves from some of their darker imaginings. Yet they will be blessed with a fine sense of history and a real vision of the future. If they can successfully train themselves to live comfortably in the present, all will go beautifully.

TOM CRUISE
Actor,
Top Gun, Jerry McGuire

7/3/1962
Cancer II

CHALLENGE: **BEING SURE TO CONNECT WITH OTHERS ONCE IN A WHILE TO COMPARE NOTES**

FULFILLMENT: **FOLLOWING A PERSON, VISION, OR THEORY TO ITS CONCLUSION**

July 11–18

THE PERSUADER
CANCER III

Somewhat freer spirits than many born in this week, Cancer III's who travel the Way of Study are likely to do wonderfully well, as their intellect and motivation can combine here in highly effective ways. The degree of mental discipline called for by this karmic path is likely to come rather naturally to these souls, and that, combined with their formidable ability to control their needs, should mark them for both success and considerable accomplishment. They may stumble a bit, however, when it comes to aligning themselves with a higher set of principles or ideals, and some may get mired in purely materialistic or ego-oriented pursuits at the expense of their higher spiritual awareness. Yet if they do not allow their inner insecurity to misdirect them to the need for personal recognition or indulge themselves in pompous displays of holding forth on their ideas, things will go quite easily for them.

CHALLENGE: **RELEASING THEIR NEED FOR RECOGNITION**

FULFILLMENT: **INVOKING THEIR POWERS OF FOCUS AND OBSERVATION AS THEY DELVE DEEPER INTO THE TOPICS THAT INTEREST THEM**

July 19–25

OSCILLATION
CANCER–LEO CUSP

Restlessness and recklessness may hinder the higher development of those born on the Cusp of Oscillation who travel the Way of Study. It will be especially important for this group to cultivate the mental discipline needed to order their thoughts and inspirations and use them as a stepping-stone to the acquisition of real knowledge and authority. Too, some on this karmic path may scatter their energies among an assortment of less-than-worthy interests and pursuits. A tendency to be a jack-of-all-trades and master of none will also be a problem. Yet once they grasp the fact that fits of temper, emotional displays, and personal melodramas will only interfere with their innate need for recognition and enlightenment, they will be able to tackle almost any subject with energy, courage, and a fine and abiding sense of curiosity.

ANTHONY EDWARDS
Actor, *ER*

7/19/1962
Cancer–Leo Cusp

CHALLENGE: **GETTING A GRIP ON THEIR TENDENCY TO VAC-ILLATE AND PROCRASTINATE**
FULFILLMENT: **DELVING INTO HERETOFORE UNCHARTED TERRITORY**
NOTABLE: **ROB MORROW (ACTOR, *NORTHERN EXPOSURE*, *QUIZ SHOW*)**

July 26–August 2

AUTHORITY
LEO I

Leo I's who travel the Way of Study are likely to do wonderfully well as they make their way along this road, as their natural brilliance, propensity to chart and then follow the course of their own interests, and far-reaching grasp of abstracts are all likely to come to the fore. Though prone to do a bit of grandstanding and blowing their own horns early on, their more egocentric qualities are likely to abate a bit with time as they devote themselves to more introspective and intellectual pursuits and inclinations. They will, however, have to take care that their fondness for their own company does not devolve into misanthropy or their penchant for solitude into loneliness. If they can keep in mind that the higher challenge of this karmic path is not just to discover their own unique point of view and sense of authority in the larger scheme but to share it with others in a spirit of generosity and a firm belief in the value of self, all will go beautifully.

CHALLENGE: **RELYING MORE ON SELF-WORTH AND LESS ON THE RECOGNITION OF OTHERS**
FULFILLMENT: **EXPERIENCING THE SATISFACTION OF HARD-WON ACHIEVEMENT**

August 3–10

BALANCED STRENGTH
LEO II

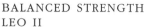

Those born in the Week of Balanced Strength who travel the Way of Study are likely to have a wonderful time, as their natural sense of devotion and single-mindedness will serve them well in the search for higher truths. They will, however, have to be on guard against a tendency to become too self-absorbed or so devoted to a particular set of ideals that it becomes all but impossible for them to change their minds. The key to their development will be a willingness to grow and continue to refresh their views and opinions through being open to innovation and enlightenment. If they can manage to keep in mind that knowledge is ultimately a flexible concept and to stay abreast of the world and its developments, they will never be disappointed in their search for truth.

WESLEY SNIPES
Actor,
White Men Can't Jump

7/31/1962
Leo I

CHALLENGE: **NOT BEING SIDETRACKED BY THE DEMANDS OF OTHERS**
FULFILLMENT: **INVOKING THEIR TREMENDOUS DETERMINATION TO ATTAIN MASTERY IN A SUBJECT**

August 11–18

LEADERSHIP
LEO III

It is likely that the single biggest key to the higher development of those born in the Week of Leadership who travel the Way of Study will be their ability and willingness to evaluate their growth processes and teach themselves some new tricks from time to time, rather than succumbing to complacency or even stagnating in the interest of maintaining a sense of control. Though likely to be much more focused than many others who travel this road, they will have to come to terms with the fact that simply believing oneself to be an expert or authority does not an expert make. Yet once they have settled down to their need for greater education in a specific field, they will be blessed with a singular ability to follow through on even the most arduous and painstaking tasks. For that reason alone, life is likely to reward their efforts.

CHALLENGE: **TAKING CARE NOT TO SACRIFICE TOO MANY OF THEIR DEEPER NEEDS FOR THE SAKE OF THEIR CRAFT**
FULFILLMENT: **HANGING IN FOR THE LONG HAUL IN ORDER TO MASTER THEIR FIELD OF STUDY**

August 19–25

EXPOSURE
LEO–VIRGO CUSP

Those born on the Cusp of Exposure who journey along the Way of Study are likely to be somewhat torn between a need to reveal what they know and an equal need to shut themselves away from the world to quietly pursue their own interests. Inclined to stay behind the scenes and well suited to the task of aligning themselves with a higher set of principles or ideals, these people may dedicate themselves for years to a particular subject or area of research, only to be "discovered" for their work or insights at seemingly inconvenient moments. Thus, there may well be a number of reluctant celebrities within this group; yet if they can manage to maintain their sense of integrity and balance their need for education with their need for revelation, life will be sweet.

CHALLENGE: **GRAPPLING WITH SHYNESS OR INSECURITY THAT MAY PREVENT THEM FROM BEING ACKNOWLEDGED AS AN AUTHORITY ON A TOPIC**
FULFILLMENT: **PUTTING THEIR PASSION INTO THEIR WORK**

August 26–September 2

SYSTEM BUILDERS
VIRGO I

The souls born in this week who travel the Way of Study can enjoy a wonderfully fulfilling life journey, as this karmic path imbues them with a much more generous imagination than they might otherwise have had, while their grounded and disciplined approach will serve them especially well. In fact, their principal failing will be that they may close themselves off from the world in their efforts to master a particular subject and refuse the higher challenge of allowing their subject to illuminate their sense of self. Yet they have a wonderful impulse to service that will aid them greatly and help them to overcome the sense of shyness or preoccupation that can hold them back from enjoying higher rewards. Thus there will be almost nothing they cannot accomplish, providing they take care to emerge from their shells and into the spotlight of recognition and real acceptance of their efforts.

ALBERT BRUCE SABIN
Immunologist; his polio vaccine replaced Salk's

8/26/1906
Virgo I

CHALLENGE: **RELEASING THEIR NEED TO BE ON TOP OF EVERY DETAIL OR FACT**
FULFILLMENT: **SERVING HUMANITY THROUGH THEIR WORK**

September 3–10

THE ENIGMA
VIRGO II

Thoughtful, discerning, and possessed of naturally high standards for themselves and others, those born in the Week of the Enigma who find themselves on the Way of Study are likely to enjoy an especially fulfilling life journey, providing they avoid the dangers of too much obsession with detail and too little recognition of the need for self-knowledge. Dedicated and conscientious by nature, they are unlikely to be overly troubled by restlessness or recklessness, yet some will shy away from the higher challenge to allow their avenues of interest to illuminate the self, broader philosophies, or deeper human truths. Nevertheless, true expertise can be theirs, since these naturally discriminating souls are prone to standing by their higher principles. If they can complement their natural sense of detachment with dashes of humor, flexibility, and a willingness not to take themselves too seriously, they will doubtless flourish.

CHALLENGE: **NOT RETREATING SO FAR INTO THEIR WORK THAT THEY LOSE THEIR SENSE OF SELF**
FULFILLMENT: **SOLVING PROBLEMS OR PUZZLING OUT SOLUTIONS DURING THE COURSE OF THEIR STUDIES**
NOTABLE: **LAWRENCE POWELL (BIBLIOPHILE, FOUNDED UCLA SCHOOL OF LIBRARY SCIENCE)**

September 11–18

THE LITERALIST
VIRGO III

Blessed with a more grounded energy than some others who travel this road, Virgo III's on the Way of Study will nevertheless have to avoid the tendency to become obsessed with getting others to see things their way. Nonetheless, the Aquarius I origins of this karmic path endow these personalities with much more imagination and vision than they might otherwise have had. Too, they have a fine sense of truth and a dislike of pretension that will serve them well on this journey, providing they allow their instincts to inform and illuminate their wealth of knowledge and take care to avoid the demons of pickiness, misanthropy, or a stubbornly judgmental attitude toward new developments. Their expertise is likely to blossom with the passage of time, and if they take care not to abuse the privilege of power, power and authority will be theirs.

KATHRYN MURRAY
Dancer, established dance studios with husband, Arthur

9/15/1906
Virgo III

CHALLENGE: **NEGOTIATING THE NEED FOR MORE THEORETICAL CONSIDERATIONS AND THEIR INHERENT PRACTICALITY**
FULFILLMENT: **APPLYING THEIR LOVE OF PRECISION TO A CRAFT**
NOTABLE: **KRISTY MCNICHOL (ACTRESS, *FAMILY*)**

September 19–24

BEAUTY
VIRGO–LIBRA CUSP

Indecision, restlessness, and a certain kind of laziness may hinder the higher development of those born in this period who travel the Way of Study. Blessed with highly creative instincts and a real flair for aesthetic pursuits, they will have to work hard to control some rather flighty attitudes and learn to discipline themselves to the extent that they can apply their energies to the sometimes painstaking and rather slow business of self-education. Though there may well be any number of perpetual students who have this configuration, their pursuit of knowledge is likely to be somewhat superficial and lacking in the kind of dedicated or sustained effort that is required, since more than most these individuals will take the easy way out. Interestingly enough, however, they do best when aligning themselves with an institution, organization, or particular mentor who can provide them with the tools needed to ground their energies and set them on the path to devoted learning.

CHALLENGE: **ELIMINATING THEIR VOCABULARY OF EXCUSES FOR AVOIDING MORE DIFFICULT TASKS**

FULFILLMENT: **APPLYING HIGHER STANDARDS OR IDEALS IN THEIR WORK**

GIUSEPPE VERDI
Composer dramatic opera,
Falstaff, La Traviata, Aïda

10/10/1813
Libra II

September 25–October 2

THE PERFECTIONIST
LIBRA I

Those born in the Week of the Perfectionist who journey along the Way of Study can enjoy great personal and professional fulfillment, as their dedication, drive, and devotion to thoroughness are likely to stand them in especially good stead. They will, however, run the risk of manifesting certain obsessive or compulsive tendencies that will bear a certain amount of watching. Too, some may refuse the higher challenge of allowing their field of expertise to illuminate their inner reality. There is also the danger that emotional repression will cause them difficulty in dealing with those around them. Still, they have the probability of wonderful success and accomplishment, and if they take care not to turn away from the world in defiance, discontent, or misanthropy, their faultless principles and high ideals can serve as an inspiration for many.

CHALLENGE: **TEMPERING THEIR GREAT RESTLESSNESS BY CULTIVATING A ZEN-LIKE APPROACH TO WORK**

FULFILLMENT: **SECURING THEIR SENSE OF THEMSELVES**

NOTABLES: **PAUL MILLER (JOURNALIST; BUSINESS EXECUTIVE, GANNETT CO., ASSOCIATED PRESS); WILLY LEY (PIONEER IN ROCKET RESEARCH); DMITRI SHOSTAKOVICH (COMPOSER)**

October 3–10

SOCIETY
LIBRA II

Disparate and rather superficial interests may hinder the higher development of those born in the Week of Society who travel this karmic path, and many will falter a bit until they come to a better understanding of where their truest interests lie. Though likely to be voluble and seemingly well versed in any number of subjects, deeper understanding or expertise may elude them until they make the connection between concerted personal effort, painstaking groundwork, and real authority in a particular field. Too, many of them will refuse to align themselves to a set of principles or ideals and fail to develop the kind of core philosophy or belief system that is part of the higher challenge of this karmic path. If they can successfully overcome the obstacles of self-deception and ground their sense of theory in effort and their visions in concrete reality, life will become much smoother and more fulfilling.

CHALLENGE: **GETTING A HANDLE ON AVOIDANCE BEHAVIOR AND OTHER FORMS OF ESCAPISM**

FULFILLMENT: **EXPERIENCING THE SELF-ESTEEM THAT COMES FROM PAINSTAKING EFFORT**

NOTABLE: **TOMMY LEE (ROCK DRUMMER, MÖTLEY CRÜE)**

JOAN CUSACK
Actress, *In and Out*

10/11/1962
Libra III

October 11–18

THEATER
LIBRA III

The compelling, versatile personalities born in the Week of Theater will have to work a bit to apply themselves to developing their craft or widening their body of knowledge in a given area before they will find real success on this karmic path. Yet they have the natural dedication and drive to accomplish almost anything they set out to do. Chief among their faults is a tendency to exalt the concept of mental freedom at the expense of painstaking effort. Ego issues or a need to hold forth on all sorts of subjects may also interfere with the process of individuation through education. Thus, there may be a number of blowhards and prima donnas in this group, yet there will also be a number of genuine artists and dedicated, deep thinkers. If they can avoid too much detachment, on the one hand, and too great a need for recognition, on the other, they will find both peace and real authority.

CHALLENGE: **GENERATING REAL PASSION OR CONVICTION**

FULFILLMENT: **ENLARGING AND DEEPENING THEIR SENSE OF SELF AS A RESULT OF CULTIVATING AN AREA OF EXPERTISE**

NOTABLES: **HANNAH ARENDT (HISTORIAN, POLITICAL PHILOSOPHER, *THE ORIGINS OF TOTALITARIANISM*); CHARLES REVSON (BUSINESS EXECUTIVE, FOUNDED REVLON, INC.)**

October 19–25

DRAMA AND CRITICISM
LIBRA–SCORPIO CUSP

A passion for learning may characterize the life journey of those born on the Cusp of Drama and Criticism who travel the Way of Study. Blessed with both far-reaching vision and a sense of standards, they may nevertheless fall down a bit when their penchant for espousing their views or grandstanding their opinions gets in the way of the kind of painstaking effort and focus that will be necessary to their success. Ego issues will be a lifelong problem for these often less-than-modest individuals, as will their tendency to distract themselves with tangential relationships and interests. Still, in many respects they are well suited to the concepts of self-education and eventual mastery of a particular subject or field, and if they can manage to focus their energies in such a way that their studies serve to illuminate the larger truths of self and its place in the universe, all will go brilliantly.

SAM SHEPARD
Playwright/actor; Pulitzer
for *Buried Child*

—————

11/5/1943
Scorpio II

CHALLENGE: **WEANING THEMSELVES FROM THEIR PENCHANT FOR PREACHING, ESPECIALLY BEFORE THEIR KNOWLEDGE BASE IS IN ORDER**
FULFILLMENT: **KNOWING THAT THEY ARE THE MASTERS OF THEIR DOMAIN**
NOTABLES: **EVANDER HOLYFIELD (HEAVYWEIGHT BOXING CHAMPION); B. D. WONG (STAGE AND SCREEN ACTOR, *M. BUTTERFLY*)**

October 26–November 2

INTENSITY
SCORPIO I

Though there may be a number of hermits and misanthropes born in this week, most Scorpio I's traveling the Way of Study will find this quite a fulfilling journey, as the energies that come together can make for a well-rounded approach to personal education and enlightenment. Few are their equals when it comes to focusing their powers of concentration or attending to the details at hand. Truly unique thinkers, they are promised tremendous success in whatever area of endeavor they choose to channel their energies into, and a touch of the performer enables them to be compelling, witty, and charismatic proponents of whatever principles and ideals they may hold. If they can open themselves to the worlds of higher understanding and development that await them along this road, they are bound to be rich in knowledge and blessed with a deep understanding of both themselves and the world around them.

CHALLENGE: **BEING SURE TO ENTERTAIN POINTS OF VIEW OTHER THAN THEIR OWN**
FULFILLMENT: **PUTTING THEIR CAPACITY TO FOCUS TO GOOD USE**

November 3–11

DEPTH
SCORPIO II

Sure to have a fine grasp of the concept that abstract truth often reveals the mystery of self, those born in the Week of Depth who make this karmic journey are likely to realize enormous enlightenment and transformation. Going into things deeply, with care and awareness, is often the hallmark of these highly individualistic personalities, and the Aquarius I origins of this karmic path further endow them with a greater ability to detach from their often tumultuous emotional lives. They will, however, have to cultivate a greater willingness to share their expertise with others, as these often secretive and controlling people may falter a bit when called to step into a role of authority and use their knowledge in purely manipulative or self-serving ways. Yet if they can overcome some self-interest in favor of true self-knowledge, all will go wonderfully well for them.

ROBERT LOUIS STEVENSON
Writer, *Treasure Island*

—————

11/13/1850
Scorpio III

CHALLENGE: **NOT GOING OVERBOARD ON AN OVERLY RIGID ADHERENCE TO CONCEPTS SUCH AS TRUTH OR JUSTICE**
FULFILLMENT: **DELVING DEEPLY INTO THEMSELVES AS THEY PURSUE THEIR CRAFT**

November 12–18

CHARM
SCORPIO III

Those born in the Week of Charm who travel the Way of Study are likely to find that their inclinations and intellectual interests are indissolubly bound to a sense of worldly ambition. Though likely to be more unique and visionary than some born in this week, these individuals will nevertheless have to overcome a tendency to too much complacency or a preoccupation with others' opinions—both of which will hinder their higher development. Too, it may take some time for them to settle down, gain a greater grasp of what it is they really want out of life, and find the courage to leave more conventional ideas of success and achievement by the wayside. Yet they are gifted with considerable intelligence, resourcefulness, and resiliency, and if their outer sense of ambition is aligned with their search for a firm set of personal beliefs, there is very little that will hold them back as they step into the role of authority.

CHALLENGE: **NOT RESORTING TO CHARM WHEN A FIRM GROUNDING IN PRINCIPLE, FACTS, OR THEORY IS NEEDED**
FULFILLMENT: **FINDING THE PRINCIPLES THEY CAN LIVE THEIR LIVES BY**
NOTABLES: **WALLACE SHAWN (ACTOR, *MY DINNER WITH ANDRÉ*); SOICHIRO HONDA (JAPANESE AUTO EXECUTIVE, FOUNDED HONDA MOTOR CO.); CURTIS LeMAY (AIR FORCE OFFICER; DIRECTED BERLIN AIRLIFT)**

November 19–24

REVOLUTION
SCORPIO–SAGITTARIUS CUSP

Characterized by fearless thinking and radical attitudes, the souls born on the Cusp of Revolution can do a great deal to change the world for the better—but they will have to do their homework first. Gifted with a natural talent and disposition for delving into broad philosophical concerns and abstractions, they may nevertheless have a bit of a problem focusing their energies in such a way that they attain both a sense of personal enlightenment and a sense of authority. They have a marked tendency to excitability, and they will display a tendency to go off half-cocked when espousing their latest theories. If they can slow down long enough to realize that education is the true key to their success, their innate love of learning is sure to come to the fore as they make their way along this road. Properly grounded in the details and research necessary to support their beliefs, they are sure to go far in the course of this life passage.

BILLIE JEAN KING
Tennis player, won 20
Wimbledon titles; famous
battle of the sexes
───
11/22/1943
Scorpio–Sagittarius Cusp

CHALLENGE: **CONCERNING THEMSELVES MORE WITH BUILDING ON EXISTING KNOWLEDGE THAN WITH TEARING IT DOWN**
FULFILLMENT: **THROWING OFF THE ROLE OF REACTIONARY AND BEING THEIR OWN PERSON WITH THEIR OWN BASE OF EXPERTISE**

November 25–December 2

INDEPENDENCE
SAGITTARIUS I

The personalities born in the Week of Independence who find themselves on the Way of Study can enjoy a fine and fulfilling life journey, providing they narrow their field of interest and pursuits and learn to direct their passion for mental freedom into a quest for real expertise. In any event, these quick-minded individuals are likely to have something of a love affair with learning itself and will pride themselves on the scope of their education. Much inclined to philosophical interests, they will, however, have to learn to ground their efforts and see their unique visions through to satisfying manifestation. If they can control their impulsiveness and distractibility and turn their energies to those subjects that fire their imaginations and fuel their search for higher truth, all will go well.

CHALLENGE: **TEMPERING THEIR DISAPPOINTMENT WHEN THE WORLD FAILS TO LIVE UP TO THEIR STANDARDS**
FULFILLMENT: **ENJOYING LEARNING FOR LEARNING'S SAKE**
NOTABLE: **BRUCE PALTROW (PRODUCER, ST. ELSEWHERE)**

December 3–10

THE ORIGINATOR
SAGITTARIUS II

Daring to be different, separating themselves from those who would reject them for their unique views, and being willing to dwell in the mind or live outside the norm will all be qualities that characterize the quest of those born in the Week of the Originator who travel the Way of Study. Though they will have to be on guard against some rather misanthropic inclinations in themselves, they will find that their karmic path becomes increasingly clear as they divest themselves of their need for approval and simply do their own thing and pursue their own interests. In their search for higher development, their often stunning and highly radical approach to a given subject may manifest itself in a truly rare grasp of both inner and outer realities. If they can use their education to broaden and nurture the gifts within and learn to embrace their unique point of view, the world may well beat a path to their door as they come into their own.

KEITH RICHARDS
Rolling Stone guitarist,
rock legend
───
12/18/1943
Sagittarius III

CHALLENGE: **WORRYING LESS ABOUT RECOGNITION OR PROVING THEMSELVES TO OTHERS**
FULFILLMENT: **LOSING THEMSELVES IN A LOVE OF THEIR SUBJECT**
NOTABLES: **OTTO PREMINGER (FILM DIRECTOR/PRODUCER, ANATOMY OF A MURDER); MICHAEL ONDAATJE (AUTHOR, THE ENGLISH PATIENT)**

December 11–18

THE TITAN
SAGITTARIUS III

Those born in the Week of the Titan who travel the Way of Study may have a rather arduous personal journey until they learn to apply themselves and their talents in a more focused fashion. Thinkers on a grand scale and often highly romantic, they will face the challenge of bringing some of their more far-fetched notions into concrete reality in order to be really effective. They will also have to work hard to divest themselves of their need for others' approval and perhaps consciously cultivate more of a fondness for solitary pursuits. Yet they have a fine inclination toward philosophical thought and an innate need to identify with higher principles and beliefs. If they refuse to allow their egos or a lack of self-awareness to hinder their higher development and accomplishment, they will be able to step into the role of authority and expert.

CHALLENGE: **FOCUSING ON THE WORK OR CRAFT AND LETTING THE IDEAS UNFOLD**
FULFILLMENT: **PRODUCING A BODY OF WORK**
NOTABLES: **STEVEN BOCHCO (TELEVISION PRODUCER, N.Y.P.D. BLUE, HILL STREET BLUES); GROVER WASHINGTON (JAZZ SAXOPHONIST)**

KARMIC PATH
42

December 19–25

PROPHECY
SAGITTARIUS–CAPRICORN CUSP

The unusual, interesting individuals born on the Cusp of Prophecy who travel the Way of Study are likely to experience a fine and fulfilling life journey. Their natural inclinations are very much in keeping with the higher calling to gain self-knowledge and awareness by directing their energies away from distracting or superficial concerns and toward greater mastery in a specific area of endeavor. They will have to be on guard in themselves against a bit too much isolation, however, for these naturally rather solitary personalities may fail the higher challenge of sharing their insights and expertise with the rest of us in some manifestation of their unique point of view. Nevertheless, they have the greatest auguries for success, and if they stand by their abilities to go within and follow their personal lodestar, it will surely illuminate their road to success.

CHALLENGE: **NOT ALLOWING THEIR PASSION FOR THEIR SUBJECT TO UNDERMINE THEIR SCHOLARSHIP**

FULFILLMENT: **ENTERTAINING LEAPS OF INTUITIVE REASONING TO FURTHER THEIR UNDERSTANDING OF THEIR FIELD**

NOTABLES: **LEONID BREZHNEV (COMMUNIST LEADER, HEAD OF SOVIET UNION); CONRAD HILTON (HOTEL EXECUTIVE, FOUNDED HILTON HOTEL CORP.)**

JOHN DENVER
Singer/songwriter, "Rocky Mountain High," pictured taping *The John Denver Show,* 1974

12/31/1943
Capricorn I

December 26–January 2

THE RULER
CAPRICORN I

Though gifted with far more originality and breadth of vision than many others born in the Week of the Ruler, those who travel the Way of Study will face the challenge of setting aside their need for recognition and authority until they have acquired a more thorough and complete education. Yet they are marked for wonderful success, as they possess both the patience and the diligence to see even the most arduous or demanding projects and plans through to successful conclusion. Likely to be grounded in a fine practical and moral sense, the self-imposed discipline necessary for scholarship and hard-won expertise is inherent in these dedicated people. If they allow their pursuits to illuminate the mystery of self, their place in the world and the cosmos is sure to become clear with the passage of time.

CHALLENGE: **BEING WILLING TO OPEN THEMSELVES TO THE ILLUMINATION THAT SERIOUS STUDY CAN PROVIDE**

FULFILLMENT: **LIVING UP TO THEIR OWN STANDARDS OF EXCELLENCE**

NOTABLES: **BEN KINGSLEY (ACTOR, *GANDHI*); JOHANNES KEPLER ("FATHER OF MODERN ASTRONOMY," DESCRIBED PLANETARY MOTION)**

January 3–9

DETERMINATION
CAPRICORN II

The process of discovering a core identity and a firm set of principles through the pursuit of a specific area of study will come rather easily to those born in this week who travel this karmic path. Characterized by a far-ranging intellect and a great ability for practical application, these individuals will have little trouble in their quest for greater expertise. Where they may fail, however, is through their tendency to blame circumstances or fate for their inability to follow their best ideas through to a satisfying conclusion. Yet they are marked by both considerable patience and a fine philosophical sense. If they can bring these capabilities to bear in such a way that their dedication is firm and their originality not lost in efforts at self-sacrifice, their efforts are certain to be well rewarded.

CHALLENGE: **STRIVING TO UNEARTH A SENSE OF SELF AS THEY REACH FOR GREATER KNOWLEDGE**

FULFILLMENT: **ALLOWING WORK TO BE THEIR TEACHER**

NOTABLE: **ANSELME PAYEN (CHEMIST, DISCOVERED CELLULOSE)**

HENRY KRAVIS
Partner in Kohlberg, Kravis, Roberts and Co.; record-setting leverage buyout of RJR Nabisco

1/6/1944
Capricorn II

January 10–16

DOMINANCE
CAPRICORN III

Likely to be rather modest and unassuming, the personalities born in the Week of Dominance who travel the Way of Study can nevertheless give a whole new meaning to the phrase "Still waters run deep." In fact, they are so well suited to the challenge and promise of the Way of Study that one can only wonder what they might have done right in a former life! For here stability combines with natural brilliance, and patience and thoroughness serve to augment and enhance their need to control or master an area of study. In any event, results are important to this group, and they are likely to do wonderfully well by attaching themselves to a group, institution, or organization that will support their work. If they will allow greater spiritual illumination to shine through their subject, very little will go wrong as they make their way along this karmic path.

CHALLENGE: **REFRAINING FROM POSTURING OR GRANDSTANDING**

FULFILLMENT: **STEPPING INTO THE ROLE OF QUIET AUTHORITY**

January 17–22

MYSTERY AND IMAGINATION
CAPRICORN–AQUARIUS CUSP

Perhaps the principal dangers for those born on the Cusp of Mystery and Imagination who travel the Way of Study will be their tendency to become rather too caught up in wild or unrealistic ideologies, on the one hand, or to become too self-sacrificing or withdrawn, on the other. Yet they are gifted with a natural inclination toward higher principles and ideals, and if they can find an area of study or endeavor that will bring them a clearer sense of self, all will go well. The problem is that these unpredictable people are inclined to lack personal discipline, become too enamored of their own ideas, and rather recklessly change horses in midstream. Yet their talent for innovation and their sheer intellectual curiosity will serve them well. If they take care to ground themselves in concentrated effort and to integrate their gifts of inspiration and imagination with hard work and stability, life will become much easier for them.

STOCKARD CHANNING
Film/stage actress, *Grease*

2/13/1944
Aquarius III

CHALLENGE: **KEEPING THEIR MORE CHAOTIC ENERGIES UNDER CONTROL IN ORDER TO DEVOTE THEMSELVES TO THEIR WORK**
FULFILLMENT: **INDULGING THEIR TALENT FOR INVENTION ONCE THEY HAVE GROUNDED THEMSELVES IN A FEW FUNDAMENTAL PRINCIPLES**
NOTABLE: **JOE FRAZIER (HEAVYWEIGHT BOXING CHAMPION)**

January 23–30

GENIUS
AQUARIUS I

Focus, focus, and more focus will have to be the watchwords for the brilliant, distracted, and rather far-out thinkers born in the Week of Genius who travel the Way of Study if they want to ensure that their tendency to being absent-minded professors does not devolve into their becoming flaky, disorganized "space cadets." Indeed, there is so much going on in the minds of these people at any given moment that it may be difficult for them to hone and direct their powers of concentration. Surrounding themselves with a stable support network will surely help to ground their energies, and while they may well resist aligning themselves with a group, institution, or organization, they would do well to do so, as it will serve to structure and discipline their intellectual and spiritual powers. If they keep in mind the maxim that in order to rule, one must first learn to serve, all will go wonderfully well.

CHALLENGE: **REALIZING THAT THERE ARE AS MANY AVENUES TO THE DEEP STUDY OF ONE SUBJECT AS THERE ARE TO THE SUPERFICIAL STUDY OF MANY**
FULFILLMENT: **ANSWERING ONLY TO THEMSELVES AND THEIR PRINCIPLES**
NOTABLE: **RUTGER HAUER (ACTOR, *LADYHAWKE*)**

January 31–February 7

YOUTH AND EASE
AQUARIUS II

Cultivating their virtuoso energies will prove especially important for those born in the Week of Youth and Ease who travel the Way of Study. Though the solitude called for may not prove a viable choice for many of these people, they will do well under the tutelage and support of an organization or institution that can help to structure their talents and efforts. The danger is that these easygoing types may fail to develop their own more original ideas and simply give up and go with the flow. Yet they will find their popularity hollow and lackluster until they answer the higher call to awakening a more developed sense of self and a higher set of principles through concentrated effort. If they develop the simple ability to throw themselves wholeheartedly into their work, that work is likely to be quite productive.

ALICE WALKER
Writer/poet,
The Color Purple; won
Pulitzer

2/9/1944
Aquarius III

CHALLENGE: **NOT CHOOSING THE PATH OF LEAST RESISTANCE**
FULFILLMENT: **MASTERING THEIR MEDIUM AND THROUGH IT FINDING THEMSELVES**
NOTABLE: **ANTONIO J. DeSUCRE (VENEZUELAN REVOLUTIONARY)**

February 8–15

ACCEPTANCE
AQUARIUS III

Those born in the Week of Acceptance who travel the Way of Study will find this an educating, enlightening journey. While some with this configuration will struggle with issues of tolerance, prejudice, and negative belief systems and be forced to change their minds and opinions through introspection and study, a number of others will have a rather lackadaisical or careless attitude toward personal development, remaining content to accept things pretty much as they are. Either set of beliefs is bound to come under fire, and both types would do well to heed the often disruptive call to evaluate and reevaluate where they stand. Yet once they realize that there is no guarantee they will receive authority and recognition and conscientiously apply themselves to those areas that will allow them to become experts in and proponents of their unique ideas, life will become much easier for them.

CHALLENGE: **APPLYING THEMSELVES WITH DEDICATION AND CONSISTENCY**
FULFILLMENT: **FINDING SELF-ESTEEM IN KNOWLEDGE**
NOTABLES: **GEORGE PAPANDREOAU (GREEK POLITICAL LEADER, 1ST SOCIALIST PRIME MINISTER OF GREECE); WILLIAM BARTRAM (BOTANIST); CARL BERNSTEIN (JOURNALIST, HELPED EXPOSE WATERGATE)**

February 16–22

SENSITIVITY
AQUARIUS–PISCES CUSP

Developing a willingness to become more self-aware through the pursuit of abstract truth is likely to be a relatively easy karmic task for those born on the Cusp of Sensitivity who travel the Way of Study. In fact, getting in touch with their deepest needs, principles, and sense of self will almost certainly involve divesting themselves of a preoccupation with personal issues or the need for recognition and settling down to a given field of study or area of endeavor. This is one group who will respond especially well to the promise that examining larger truths and developing an area of expertise or specialty will serve to illuminate many of the mysteries of soul and self. If these personalities can open themselves to that enlightenment, control their excess personal sensitivity, and avoid the pitfalls of distrust, rebellion, and frustration, they can expect the highest rewards for their efforts.

GEORGE PEABODY
Philanthropist, founded
Peabody Museum and
Peabody Institute

2/18/1795
Aquarius–Pisces Cusp

CHALLENGE: **NOT LOSING THEMSELVES IN ABSTRACTIONS OR IDEALISM**
FULFILLMENT: **GROUNDING THEMSELVES WITH DILIGENT STUDY AND INVESTIGATION**

February 23–March 2

SPIRIT
PISCES I

Two challenges will figure prominently in the lives of those born in the Week of the Spirit who journey on the Way of Study. The first is how to focus their highly mutable energies in such a way that they become capable of sustained effort and scholarship. The second is how to form a firm set of unassailable principles on which to hang a more assured sense of self.

Yet many of these souls will doubtless flourish on this road, as they are quite capable of facing the task of applying themselves and exploring those abstract truths that will serve as a springboard to self-realization. Armed with the knowledge and support they require to bring their unique ideas to manifestation in the world, their desire to do good will beautifully enhance their air of authority, and they will be able to share their ideas in such a way that all will benefit from their thoughtfulness.

CHALLENGE: **SUPPORTING THEIR JOURNEY THROUGH DAILY ROUTINE**
FULFILLMENT: **INVOLVING THEIR MYSTICAL ORIENTATION IN THEIR COURSE OF STUDY**
NOTABLE: **JOHN FOSTER DULLES (SECRETARY OF STATE FOR DWIGHT EISENHOWER; ADVOCATED DEVELOPMENT OF NUCLEAR POWER)**

March 3–10

THE LONER
PISCES II

Those born in the Week of the Loner who find themselves on the Way of Study are likely to do wonderfully well, as their sense of self and often fragile egos will be greatly bolstered by the call of this karmic path to focus and expertise. Likely to come upon both intellectual and spiritual truths in the course of their studies, these solitary figures will nevertheless have to take care that they do not withdraw from the world entirely. Though underlying emotional problems may trouble some of this group and cause them to collapse into pessimism and self-doubt, most will find themselves strengthened through knowledge. They would do especially well to align themselves with a group, institution, or organization that will support yet not intrude upon their efforts. Thus, considerable transformation and self-realization are possible for them, and these unique and rather blessed individuals are likely to find this a deeply rewarding and enlightening passage.

ROGER DALTREY
Rock star, lead singer of
The Who

3/1/1944
Pisces I

CHALLENGE: **REFUSING TO GIVE UP IN THE FACE OF DIFFICULTY**
FULFILLMENT: **ENJOYING A GREATER SENSE OF INDIVIDUATION AS THEY PURSUE THEIR INTERESTS**
NOTABLES: **KIRI TE KANAWA (OPERA SINGER); KNUT ROCKNE (LEGENDARY NOTRE DAME FOOTBALL COACH)**

March 11–18

DANCERS AND DREAMERS
PISCES III

Though it may well seem anathema to those born in the Week of Spirit to have to settle down, buckle down, and apply their considerable gifts in a directed and concentrated effort, they can realize great success on this life journey. Likely to be troubled by some rather superior attitudes, many of them will have to suffer a few setbacks as the result of poor planning or half-baked schemes and views. Disappointments may also knock them off balance and cause them to head off in a new direction when they would do better to pursue what they have started. Going into things deeply—with care, awareness, and deliberation—may seem daunting, but once they develop a more directed approach to their endeavors, the resulting spiritual and personal enlightenment will strengthen their natural talents, and they may turn into a source of inspiration to many they meet.

CHALLENGE: **ANSWERING THE CALL TO STUDY THEIR OWN LIFE NOW AND THEN**
FULFILLMENT: **EXPANDING THEIR LIFE AND WORLDVIEW THROUGH DEDICATION TO SOMETHING GREATER THAN THEMSELVES**
NOTABLE: **PATTI BOYD (MODEL; FAMOUS MARRIAGES WITH MUSICIANS)**

The Way of Resolve

AQUARIUS II TO LEO II
Youth and Ease to Balanced Strength

The life purpose of the individuals on the Way of Resolve is to learn how to face any challenge or problem without backing down. To accomplish this task, those on this karmic path must develop the ability to set their resolve and make a commitment. These individuals are often multifaceted, and on the surface life seems to come easily to them. However, they tend to lack resolve and prefer to take the path of least resistance. Thus, they are known to leave their associates and intimates in the lurch when push comes to shove. Moreover, as they often do not have the determination to see a job through to the end, the quality of their work may suffer, making it difficult for them to advance in their chosen career or profession. Those on this path often pay too much attention to what others think, preventing them from cultivating their own beliefs. Without a more fully developed value system, they may lack a sense of self. As those on this path learn to face challenges, they will come to understand what it is they themselves stand for.

The individuals on the Way of Resolve are, in some ways, blessed. Coming into this lifetime with Aquarius II characteristics, they often don't realize how easy certain skills or talents are for them compared to others. There is an aura that seems to surround these people; it's as though they were born under a lucky star. This is not to say that the men and women on the Way of Resolve are not hard-working; quite the contrary. It's just that they always seem so relaxed that they make what they do seem effortless. In truth, they do have a maddening habit of taking the easy way out, mainly because they don't believe in getting themselves too worked up over anything. Their approach to life is best defined by the phrase "going with the flow." While they have the potential to succeed in any area of life, many of those on this karmic path drift aimlessly without any clear goals.

Because they don't like to deal with problems or conflicts, they will usually sidestep any issue or simply do what they believe others expect of them. In fact, such a pattern, usually established in childhood or the teen years, may mark them for all their lives. The trouble is that since they never test their values in conflict or by facing challenges head-on, they rarely discover what it is they truly believe. Another way these people avoid conflict is by simply evading responsibility in relationships. Those on this karmic path have an innate propensity to move from one person to the next as soon as difficulties arise. These are true "commitmentphobes." Because they view people as disposable, many of their relationships are superficial. Thus, they do not experience the joy that intimacy can bring. In addition, in the workplace, their work or output is often viewed less positively than might be expected. This may be because, subconsciously, others sense that they do not put their own truth into what

CORE LESSON

Standing up for what they believe
in or for those they love

GOAL

To take up any challenge and
not back down

GIFTS
Tough, Action-oriented,
Accomplished

PITFALLS
Morally Weak, Self-absorbed,
Immature

they do but seek to please their superiors or the market.

The men and women on the Way of Resolve are called to develop a capacity to know what they believe in and to stand up for it. How can those on this karmic path do its work? How can they discover their inner strength, moral character, and value system? As is true of people following all the karmic paths, those on the Way of Resolve must do some work to develop an approach to life opposite that which is most natural to them: when their first reaction is to back down, they must stand up; what they would like to evade, they must confront; whomever they would rather avoid, they must face. As they take on challenges rather than sidestep them, these individuals will be forced to ask themselves what really matters to them. Slowly, with each successive situation, their belief system will begin to crystallize, developing into one that is independent of what others think. For some people, moral questions are resolved through soul-searching; for the individuals on this path, such questions are resolved through action. Only by being forced to stand up for themselves and others will they come to understand what they are made of and what the people closest to them mean to them. The word "resolve" has a number of meanings, and all of them apply. As a verb, it means to make a firm decision or to find a solution. Finally, as a noun, it means firmness of purpose or determination.

RELEASE

Caring about what others think

REWARD

The joy of a strong sense of self

Resolving to stick to what they start and hang in for the long haul, even when it is inconvenient to do so, will take those on this karmic path a long way toward their goal. Too often, these individuals back down from fights. However, they must learn what it means to fight to the end. Life will hand these men and women many opportunities for growth. One personal challenge after another will confront them, until they learn how to look problems squarely in the face and work out a solution. At times they may feel somewhat victimized or beset by problems. The sooner they learn the lessons of this path, the sooner their troubles will subside. This does not mean that they are not to utilize diplomacy or compromise; on the contrary, they must learn to become problem solvers by studying the art of negotiation and conflict resolution. In this way, they will acquire insight into the workings of power and politics. Such skills can be developed not only as a result of experience but also through reading, study, and thinking. Thus, those on this path frequently study history and philosophy in some depth.

As those on this karmic path learn to accept responsibility and challenge, not only will they begin to have a new sense of self, one that is not dependent on the opinions of others, but they will begin to feel a greater sense of self-worth as well. More than any other sign, Leo, the goal of this path, is about liking oneself on a core level, regardless of what others

SUGGESTION

Try to discern the underlying pattern in the challenges that confront you.
Reflect on what matters most to you. What do you respect? Seek to develop maturity.

may think. This involves knowing one's strengths and weaknesses, what one does and does not believe, and feeling that one has the strength of self to handle whatever comes along. As fundamental as this sounds, and as easily as many things come to those on this path, knowing the truth of who they are is not one of those things.

This karmic path also calls those on it to learn to value the people in their lives. Often those on this path take others for granted. Also, as they truly dislike dependency in any form—whether their own or others—they will go to great lengths to avoid commitment or responsibility, fearing that it will hold them back. The irony is that it is usually through the deepening connection of committed relationships that those on this path will grow. Often, it is in longer-term involvements that individuals learn how to resolve conflicts and problems day by day rather than running from them. As they engage more fully with others, accept the responsibilities of relationships, and allow others to be dependent on them, they will learn many of the lessons of this path. It will teach them about the virtues of loyalty and fidelity. Sometimes they may find their limits tested by someone's dependency, perhaps due to illness. Having the stick-to-itiveness to stay in the relationship when the going gets tough will say much about how far they have progressed in their karmic task.

What is best for these individuals is a full and active life that is replete with challenges. Long-range projects may be especially beneficial for them, as they will both develop their determination and give these busy individuals the ego boost of feeling that they really matter. A strong motivating factor in their development may be the idea of leaving behind a legacy of some kind, such as a fine family, a thriving business, or authorship or some other artistic achievement. As the men and women on the Way of Resolve progress along their karmic path, they will be best served by associating with freethinking yet responsible individuals who have achieved something for themselves through strength of purpose. In many cases, those on this path are afforded their greatest growth opportunities by the duties and responsibilities of marriage and children. Some may truly blossom in such circumstances, having found the most important thing of all to believe in: love, the crowning jewel of a good life.

BALANCE POINT

Giving Up
and Standing Firm

In describing this path, one thinks of young Prince Hal of England, the title character in Shakespeare's play *Henry V*. As a young man, he learns the pleasures of debauchery through his friend and adviser, Falstaff. Yet when he ascends the throne to become Henry V, he refuses to even recognize his old friend and in rejecting him seems to show great ingratitude. What he does is necessary, however, indicating that he has grown into manhood and accepted the responsibilities of his position with dignity and resolve.

CRYSTALS AND GEMSTONES

Chalcopyrite is an extraordinarily grounding mineral that holds all color rays. This stone strengthens resolve because it reflects the knowing that all accomplishments come from committing to the power within.

NOTABLES ON THIS KARMIC PATH

ROSIE O'DONNELL

Irrepressible **Rosie O'Donnell** fought her way up the entertainment ladder with great determination. Working the comedy club circuit for many years, Rosie finally got her big break on television's *Star Search*. She then moved to Los Angeles, where she applied her humor to both television and film. O'Donnell has since devoted her time to the eponymous, ever-popular variety/talk show for which she won an Emmy Award in 1997. Like many on the Way of Resolve, Rosie is not one to back down from a fight—particularly when defending someone else—but also has learned the importance of compromise and understanding.

Whether racing cars or acting in films, **Paul Newman** has found the perfect combination of flexibility and resolve. Consistently dedicated to his ideals, he served as a delegate to a United Nations disarmament conference in 1978 and currently donates the profits from his food products to a camp for children with terminal diseases. Despite the many activities that occupy his time, he has successfully made his marriage and family a top priority. Like many on this path, Newman

PAUL NEWMAN

has learned to accept personal and professional responsibility. His determination to create a strong and lasting legacy is also characteristic of the Way of Resolve.

Realizing her calling at age twelve, **Georgia O'Keeffe** worked steadily to develop her talent, achieving fame early on for her flower paintings and cityscapes. Her marriage to photographer Alfred Stieglitz furthered her personal growth, and his images created a distinct impression of her unusual character and strange beauty. After Stieglitz's death in 1946, O'Keeffe moved from New York to New Mexico, her inspiration for the symbolic southwestern landscapes that made up her later work. Georgia O'Keeffe saw her artistic vision through until the end of her life, which spanned nearly a century, thus becoming one of the greatest icons of her time.

GEORGIA O'KEEFFE

Other Notables: Matthew Broderick, Patrick Ewing, LeCorbusier, Shirley Chisholm, Alexander Haig, Yukio Mishima, Richard Wagner, Josephine Baker, Anne Morrow Lindbergh, Billy Wilder, Arthur Ashe, Leo Durocher, Mick Jagger, John Huston, Robert DeNiro, Mama Cass Elliot, Julio Iglesias, Catherine Deneuve, John Reed, Jane Austen, Edouard Manet, Garth Brooks, Robert Altman, Jon Bon Jovi, Soren Kierkegaard, Philip Johnson, Satchel Paige, Bill Bradley, Faye Wattleton, Robert Crumb

---

BIRTHDAYS ON KARMIC PATH 43

August 8, 1887–December 27, 1887 | March 21, 1906–August 8, 1906 | October 30, 1924–March 20, 1925

June 11, 1943–October 30, 1943 | January 21 1962–June 10, 1962

September 1, 1980–January 20, 1981 | April 14, 1999–September 1, 1999 | November 23, 2017–April 13, 2018

KARMIC PATH
43

March 19–24

REBIRTH
PISCES–ARIES CUSP

Those born in this period may experience their share of ups and downs on the Way of Resolve. Passionate and straightforward, they may well needlessly expend their energies in recklessness or an insistence on independence without ever developing an unshakable set of values or beliefs. Self-consciousness and deep-seated insecurities, probably resulting from early childhood conditioning, may plague this group, and they may further be troubled by a chronic emotional immaturity that will be difficult to overcome. Yet if they learn to play their hunches and allow the circumstances in their lives to inform and shape a higher set of values, they will have all the strength, energy, and courage needed to make this life journey a rousing success. If they can find activities, professions, and most especially family ties that will involve them on both an emotional and spiritual level and control their tendency to sidestep the real issues, all will evolve nicely for them.

DAVID LIVINGSTONE
Missionary/explorer,
discovered Victoria Falls
and sources of the Nile

3/19/1813
Pisces–Aries Cusp

CHALLENGE: **NOT LETTING INSECURITY CAUSE THEM TO TAKE THE EASY WAY OUT**
FULFILLMENT: **STANDING BY THEIR LOVED ONES**
NOTABLES: **JOHN EHRLICHMAN (DOMESTIC COUNSELOR TO PRESIDENT NIXON; JAILED FOR WATERGATE); JOHN D. ROCKEFELLER III (PHILANTHROPIST; HEAD OF THE ROCKEFELLER FOUNDATION)**

March 25–April 2

THE CHILD
ARIES I

Lively, curious, and talented, those born in the Week of the Child who navigate the challenge and promise of the Way of Resolve will experience a number of struggles with issues of emotional insecurity, immaturity, and an overriding need for approval. Nevertheless, at their core these individuals are likely to thrive on challenge and in the course of this journey can be counted on to create their own opportunities for enlightenment should it prove too easy or placid for their tastes. Rather too open for their own good, they will need to choose their friends wisely and well, for the wrong people can easily lead them astray. Though some will scatter or needlessly expend their energies in thrill seeking, sensationalism, or naivete, most will successfully develop the firmness of character, single-mindedness, and firm beliefs that are all part of their evolutionary path.

CHALLENGE: **SURROUNDING THEMSELVES WITH INDIVIDUALS OF SOUND MORAL CHARACTER**
FULFILLMENT: **DISCOVERING THE SATISFACTION OF WINNING THE GOOD FIGHT**
NOTABLE: **NATHAN CURRIER (LITHOGRAPHER; STARTED BUSINESS WITH JAMES IVES)**

April 3–10

THE STAR
ARIES II

Those born in the Week of the Star are likely to experience a fine and fulfilling journey along the Way of Resolve, as genuine talent and genuine ambition can come together here in extraordinary ways. They have an innate need to be at the center of the action and to indulge in the give-and-take of human interaction that will serve them especially well. Aries II intensity and energy will surely lead them into the kinds of situations that will encourage their karmic work. Though they will have a pronounced tendency to avoid confronting themselves and defining and redefining their beliefs, these personalities are sure to find all the opportunities they need for higher development in their contacts with others. If they refuse to allow themselves to be motivated solely by the need for approval and learn not to back down from confrontation, they are assured of great, if not always entirely comfortable, progress along this road.

MATTHEW BRODERICK
Actor,
Ferris Beuller's Day Off

3/21/1962
Pisces–Aries Cusp

CHALLENGE: **LEARNING HOW TO STICK TO COMMITMENTS**
FULFILLMENT: **KNOWING THAT OTHERS DEPEND ON THEM**
NOTABLE: **HARVEY W. CUSHING (NEUROSURGEON WHO MADE BRAIN SURGERY FEASIBLE)**

April 11–18

THE PIONEER
ARIES III

These popular and often inspirational people have a rare gift for bringing people together under a common flag or cause. The most important factor for those born in the Week of the Pioneer who travel the Way of Resolve will be how willing they are to give of themselves in the interest of those same causes. Dominant and capable of real self-sacrifice, they may nevertheless shy away from situations that demand too much confrontation. Yet in many ways they are happiest when involved in groups. If they develop a sense of attachment and allow others to be dependent upon them, they are capable of a greater depth of commitment than might at first be apparent. If they can retain a larger sense of purpose, a higher set of ideals, and a firmer grasp of their own beliefs and work to overcome their need to be liked at the expense of really liking themselves, all will go wonderfully well.

CHALLENGE: **NOT BEING DISTRACTED BY WHAT OTHERS THINK**
FULFILLMENT: **LEARNING HOW TO RESOLVE CONFLICTS**
NOTABLE: **SAMUEL BECKETT (IRISH DRAMATIST, *WAITING FOR GODOT*)**

April 19–24

POWER
ARIES–TAURUS CUSP

Gifted with the grace and tenacity to face the challenges that will come their way along the Way of Resolve, those born on the Cusp of Power are likely to do wonderfully well, as this karmic path will offset some of their more ruthless and manipulative aspects, while rewarding their great strength and personal fortitude. The result can make for a nice mix for these individuals, and they are unlikely to stumble too much in the course of this life journey. Though marked by a rather calculating and even mercenary streak, if they can manage to turn away from a purely materialistic viewpoint, avoid being too long-suffering or merely complacent, and allow the challenges they face to illuminate the larger spiritual truths of identity, belief, and character, there will be little they cannot accomplish.

AL UNSER, JR.
Race car driver

4/19/1962
Aries–Taurus Cusp

CHALLENGE: **KNOWING THE DIFFERENCE BETWEEN TAKING A STAND AND SIMPLY ASSERTING THEIR WILL**

FULFILLMENT: **BEING RESOLUTE IN ALL THEY DO**

NOTABLE: **STEPHEN DOUGLAS (POLITICIAN; "LITTLE GRANT"; KNOWN FOR DEBATES WITH LINCOLN)**

April 25–May 2

MANIFESTATION
TAURUS I

Those born in the Week of Manifestation who journey along the Way of Resolve may encounter a number of issues and problems revolving around their unwillingness to rock the boat of their personal habits and beliefs or otherwise risk upsetting the harmony they need. These souls have a tendency to evaluate their success in purely practical terms, and it may thus take some time for them to find adequate footing on this karmic path. Most are quite resistant to giving up their security in favor of abstractions such as principles and strength of character. As a result, they may encounter overwhelming problems or tumultuous turns of fortune in the course of their development. Yet if they can rouse themselves to accept the challenges to higher awareness that present themselves and find a balance between genuine inner peace and mere complacency, life will be much kinder to them.

CHALLENGE: **GIVING UP THEIR NEED FOR HARMONY IN FAVOR OF PRINCIPLE**

FULFILLMENT: **PROTECTING THOSE CLOSE TO THEM**

May 3–10

THE TEACHER
TAURUS II

Those born in the Week of the Teacher who find themselves on the Way of Resolve can do very well on this karmic path, as their natural tendency to be movers and shakers will prove a great asset in overcoming some of the more lackadaisical inclinations of their Aquarius II roots. Likely to be blessed with a natural flair for imparting their ideas and views, they have a self-confidence that will be important as well. If they nurture their natural inclination to side with the underdog, stand up for what they truly believe, and take care not to get caught up in the need to be popular, they can fight many a good fight as they make their way along this road. Though their more demanding and self-aggrandizing qualities may offer them their share of pitfalls, if they keep in mind that challenge can always serve as an opportunity for self-improvement and the development of a more cohesive identity, these souls can travel along this karmic path swiftly, easily, and with grace.

ROBBIE KNIEVEL
Motorcycle stuntman; son of Evel Knievel; jumped the Grand Canyon

5/7/1962
Taurus II

CHALLENGE: **STANDING BY A POINT OF VIEW RATHER THAN ENDLESSLY DISCUSSING ITS MERITS OR FLAWS**

FULFILLMENT: **HONORING THEIR INTERPERSONAL COMMITMENTS**

NOTABLES: **PATRICK EWING (BASKETBALL GREAT); SOREN KIERKEGAARD (PHILOSOPHER, FOUNDER OF EXISTENTIALISM)**

May 11–18

THE NATURAL
TAURUS III

A healthy streak of rebellion is likely to prove a wonderful asset for those born in the Week of the Natural who travel the Way of Resolve. Though gifted with more personal strength than they may be aware of, they may have to wrestle down some security issues before they can find their footing. The worst of this type will prove themselves to be true "commitmentphobes," while on the other end of the spectrum will be those who tie themselves to personally unsatisfactory jobs, relationships, and lifestyles in the interest of material comfort and so-called security. Yet once challenged by fate, circumstances, or their own need for growth, these people are likely to rise to their challenges with an abundance of energy, a fine sense of humor, and a wonderfully constructive attitude toward improvement. If they take care not to squander their energies in feeling frustrated, being unaware of their own deepest needs, or failing to formulate a real belief system, they can reach amazing levels of fulfillment and self-realization.

CHALLENGE: **REALIZING THAT THEIR DESIRE TO BE UNFETTERED IS MERELY A RESPONSE TO LONG-AGO EVENTS THAT ARE NO LONGER RELEVANT**

FULFILLMENT: **DISCOVERING WHAT TRULY MATTERS TO THEM**

May 19–24

ENERGY
TAURUS–GEMINI CUSP

Taurus–Geminis can find this a most interesting and highly unusual journey, yet the lessons of the Way of Resolve may be a bit tricky for them. Inclined to move through life on a more superficial plane than some who travel this karmic path, they may become entangled in merely acting out their anxieties and emotional burdens until they are forced, often by personal setbacks of some kind, to take the time to turn their energy to developing a set of core beliefs. Once these are discovered and properly formulated, however, they are less likely than some to back down from a fight or give up and go with the flow. In fact, they may have some peak experiences and real epiphanies of understanding when they meet their challenges head-on. If they can free themselves of the need to surround themselves with those who may well admire their talents yet fail to appreciate their strengths, all will go well, if not often smoothly, along this road.

RICHARD WAGNER
Composer, "Ring Cycle"

———

5/22/1813
Taurus–Gemini Cusp

CHALLENGE: **DEVELOPING THE ABILITY TO FINISH WHAT THEY START**

FULFILLMENT: **FEELING A GREATER SENSE OF PERSONAL PURPOSE**

May 25–June 2

FREEDOM
GEMINI I

Those born in the Week of Freedom who travel the Way of Resolve can experience great personal fulfillment, as they have a rather feisty side and most will rise willingly and well to its challenges. Though many things come easily to these often brilliant people, they will have to work diligently to cultivate their ability to follow through on plans and projects and to determine what their deepest beliefs and principles really are. Further, they have a pronounced tendency to control or manipulate others with their considerable charm and will have to avoid the tendency to be quite manipulative. Yet they can prove to be both highly principled and politically and diplomatically adept. If they can find the firmness of purpose to complement those qualities, they are destined to go far.

CHALLENGE: **ELIMINATING AVOIDANCE BEHAVIOR FROM THEIR BAG OF TRICKS**

FULFILLMENT: **OVERCOMING THEIR SECRET INSECURITY BY BEING MORE SURE OF THEMSELVES**

June 3–10

NEW LANGUAGE
GEMINI II

Those born in the Week of New Language who find themselves on the Way of Resolve can do quite well on this road, yet they will have to work a bit to set aside their need for approval, develop a set of values, and tone down their defensiveness. Prone to lashing out at those who misunderstand them, they may also develop the habit of obscuring their best talents, feelings, and principles through futile attempts to fit in with their environments. Too, they may have a rather disorganized inner life and will often have to struggle with indecision and a rather indeterminate belief system. Yet if they can develop inner strength and real self-knowledge and free themselves of their dependence on others' opinions, and realize that their unique talents and gifts are indissolubly bound to a core belief in themselves, they will realize great personal growth and expansion.

JOSEPHINE BAKER
Black entertainer

———

6/3/1906
Gemini II

CHALLENGE: **PERSISTING IN COMMUNICATING EVEN WHEN THEIR WORDS FALL ON DEAF EARS**

FULFILLMENT: **POSSESSING A SENSE OF PRIDE IN THEIR ACCOMPLISHMENTS**

NOTABLES: **KARL FERDINAND BRAUN (NOBEL PRIZE-WINNING GERMAN PHYSICIST); PAT GARRETT (LAWMAN; KILLED BILLY THE KID)**

June 11–18

THE SEEKER
GEMINI III

Learning to deal with the situations and circumstances that confront them, rather than striking out in ever-changing directions, will be prominent in the life journey of those born in the Week of the Seeker who navigate the challenge and promise of the Way of Resolve. Prone to pushing the limits of their experience, some on this road would much rather switch than fight and may be too chameleon-like for their own good. They will also need to overcome their restlessness and a certain cynicism before they can be really successful. Yet these personalities have a fine flair for objective evaluation and are more willing than some others to take the risks associated with standing up for their principles. If they can manage to find the focus, strength, and wisdom to complement their versatility, intelligence, and optimism, they will discover amazing opportunities for the kind of expansion that comes with a commitment to spiritual awareness, identity, and growth.

CHALLENGE: **NOT PRETENDING THAT RUNNING IS ACTUALLY SEEKING**

FULFILLMENT: **STAYING GROUNDED IN THEIR INTIMATE RELATIONSHIPS**

June 19–24

MAGIC
GEMINI–CANCER CUSP

Those born on the Cusp of Magic who travel the Way of Resolve can realize enormous personal and spiritual fulfillment, providing they do not hinder their own development by clinging to attitudes or people that work against the natural flow of their growth and clarification of their personal identity. Very well suited to immersing themselves in long-term projects, commitments, and relationships, they may nevertheless have a bit of trouble with childish, sycophantic, or irresponsible inclinations. Too, their ability to charm and enchant others can work against them if they don't temper their need for approval with some objective self-evaluation. If they make a concerted effort to get involved, stay involved, and devote themselves wholeheartedly to their self-development, they can take great strides along this karmic path.

ANNE MORROW LINDBERGH
Author/poet; wife of
Charles Lindbergh

6/22/1906
Gemini–Cancer Cusp

CHALLENGE: **RELYING LESS ON CHARM OR EMOTIONAL MANIPULATION TO GET WHAT THEY WANT**

FULFILLMENT: **GROWING UP AND TAKING ON RESPONSIBILITY, PARTICULARLY REGARDING OTHERS**

NOTABLES: **HENRY WARD BEECHER (CLERGYMAN; SPOKE OUT ON SOCIAL ISSUES—FOR TEMPERANCE, AGAINST SLAVERY); ERNEST CHAIN (BIOCHEMIST, HELPED DEVELOP PENICILLIN); BILLY WILDER (FILM DIRECTOR, *SUNSET BOULEVARD*)**

June 25–July 2

THE EMPATH
CANCER I

Many born in the Week of the Empath who travel the Way of Resolve will find this a difficult journey, until they gain a better understanding of how easily they are swayed by the emotions and feelings of others. Yet, at their core, Cancer I's are cardinal, or active, energy, and these personalities will doubtless discover within themselves their capacity for strength and even a measure of real aggression when their principles of family, philosophy, or justice are challenged. The key to their success will be refusing to allow themselves to be ruled by their need for love and approval or to collapse into self-negating patterns of behavior through emotional repression or isolation from others. Yet the Aquarius I roots of this karmic path will endow them with much more objectivity than they might otherwise have had, and if they can channel their talents and energies in a direction that will speak to both their emotional needs and their deepest beliefs, they will accomplish much.

CHALLENGE: **NOT MOLDING THEMSELVES BASED ON THE EXPECTATIONS OF OTHERS**

FULFILLMENT: **KNOWING THAT IT IS ALL RIGHT TO STAND UP FOR THEMSELVES**

July 3–10

THE UNCONVENTIONAL
CANCER II

A tendency to view the world through a rather distorted set of glasses may plague those born in the Week of the Unconventional who make this karmic journey. These souls' tendency to retreat into an unrealistic vision of how things ought to be, rather than to confront reality on its own terms, may prove their biggest vice, and they will have to guard carefully against flights of fancy. Too, these personalities may maintain an active fantasy life as a form of protection or a kind of hedge against the deeper commitment and firmer set of beliefs that are called for by this karmic path. At the same time, their fascination for the unusual and deep-seated willingness to fly in the face of convention can be great advantages. If they can find the balance between commitment and obsession, between nonattachment and mere evasion, all can go brilliantly here.

GERALDO RIVERA
TV journalist,
investigative reporter

7/4/1943
Cancer II

CHALLENGE: **KNOWING HOW THEY ENCOURAGE DEPENDENCY IN OTHERS**

FULFILLMENT: **BALANCING ATTACHMENT AND DETACHMENT**

NOTABLES: **ARTHUR ASHE (TENNIS PLAYER; AIDS SPOKESMAN); PHILIP JOHNSON (ARCHITECT; DESIGNED NEW YORK'S LINCOLN CENTER); "SATCHEL" PAIGE (BASEBALL GREAT, PITCHER)**

July 11–18

THE PERSUADER
CANCER III

A fine combination of dynamic action and virtuoso energy, those born in the Week of the Persuader who travel the Way of Resolve can expect great success and fulfillment. Not as inclined to be swayed or shaped by the opinions of others as some others on this karmic path, they have keen powers of observation as well as a knack for ferreting out others' purposes and agendas. Good problem solvers for the most part, they will nevertheless have to avoid their tendency to manipulate others through power plays or ego trips. This karmic path endows them with a more subtle approach than they might otherwise have had, and if they can keep in mind that its higher calling requires them to stand up for themselves and their beliefs and not just to gain attention for their accomplishments, they can realize a fine synthesis of creative gifts, real commitments, and heartfelt involvements.

CHALLENGE: **ACCEPTING FAILURE WITH EQUANIMITY**

FULFILLMENT: **MAKING PEACE WITH THEIR OWN DIRECTNESS**

NOTABLES: **CHRISTINE MCVIE (SINGER, FLEETWOOD MAC); CLIFFORD ODETS (DRAMATIST)**

July 19–25
OSCILLATION
CANCER–LEO CUSP

Emotional excitability and demanding attitudes may conceal a great deal of personal indecision in the personalities born in this period who travel the Way of Resolve. Wont to do a great deal of flip-flopping in the areas of commitment, some of them will disguise their inability to make decisions behind a smoke screen of emotional dramatics. Interested in a wide variety of people, they will have to do a fair amount of sampling and experimenting in their relationships before they can successfully develop the core set of beliefs and the capacity for devotion and dedication required by this karmic path. In fact, these people learn by doing rather than through mere study or speculation. Yet, though they will doubtless undergo a great deal of trial and error, once they have come to a firmer sense of self and personal principle, they will be able to meet almost any challenge with dynamic energy and heartfelt commitment.

CHALLENGE: **NOT CONFUSING RESOLVE WITH RISK TAKING**
FULFILLMENT: **STEADYING THEIR LIVES THROUGH STRUCTURE AND DETERMINED EFFORT**

BILL BRADLEY
Basketball player; senator
from N.J.
___
7/28/1943
Leo I

July 26–August 2
AUTHORITY
LEO I

Though much more accommodating and adaptable than many born in the Week of Authority, these unique and gifted individuals will have to learn not to take themselves and their talents quite so much for granted as they make their way along the Way of Resolve. Destined for personal and professional success, they will nevertheless find it difficult to sustain their efforts, and some will face the choice of dedicating themselves wholeheartedly and fiercely to maintaining their place at the top of the heap or contenting themselves with being the proverbial flash in the pan or flavor of the month. Though they have prodigious energy, dynamism, and plain horse sense, they will have to prove themselves again and again. Yet they have a real instinct for what works and what doesn't; if they do not fritter away their energies in indecision, self-destructive habits, or chronic immaturity, their rewards will be great and their legacy a lasting one.

CHALLENGE: **ELIMINATING A CERTAIN AUTOCRATIC STREAK FROM THEIR PERSONALITIES**
FULFILLMENT: **REMAINING FIRM IN THEIR SENSE OF SELF, YET ALSO BEING CONSIDERATE OF OTHERS**
NOTABLES: **MICK JAGGER (SINGER, THE ROLLING STONES); GRACIE ALLEN (COMEDIAN; STARRED WITH HUSBAND IN** BURNS AND ALLEN SHOW**); LEO DUROCHER (BASEBALL PLAYER/MANAGER; "NICE GUYS FINISH LAST")**

August 3–10
BALANCED STRENGTH
LEO II

Finding and settling down to what might best be termed a lifework will prove the salvation of those born in the Week of Balanced Strength who journey along the Way of Resolve. Charming, magnetic, and versatile in the extreme, they will nevertheless prove to be their own worst enemies if they fail to heed the call of their deepest instincts or allow themselves to be distracted from their true course by laziness, complacency, or the need to be popular. For this is indeed a configuration where it is ultimately not who they know but what they know that really counts. Yet these individuals have a pronounced ability to concentrate their energies in tough, single-minded efforts. If they can augment that ability with a clearer understanding of who they are and what they stand for, and realize that individuality is what gives rise to real originality, almost nothing will hold them back from higher fulfillment as they take on the challenges and rewards of this life journey.

CHALLENGE: **NOT SACRIFICING THEMSELVES FOR THE GOOD OF THE GROUP**
FULFILLMENT: **REAPING THE REWARDS OF HAVING A STRONG SENSE OF THEIR OWN VALUES**
NOTABLE: **FAYE WATTLETON (PRESIDENT, PLANNED PARENTHOOD FEDERATION; BUSINESS EXECUTIVE)**

ROBERT DeNIRO
Actor, Goodfellas,
The Godfather Part II;
Oscar winner
___
8/17/1943
Leo III

August 11–18
LEADERSHIP
LEO III

The personalities born in the Week of Leadership who journey along the Way of Resolve can expect a really rewarding passage, providing that their need to be liked never overrides their need for respect. Indeed, many of the upheavals and challenges of this journey will appear more on the personal than the professional front, and they may struggle with both issues of commitment, on the one hand, and lack of empathy, on the other. They will be able to measure their progress by just how well they're dealing with the challenge of leading others. They will therefore have to be especially watchful of their tendency to project their own failings or ambitions onto others, especially their children, or to win others' affections through manipulation or emotional bribery. If they come to terms with the fact that the ability to inspire the respect of others arises from self-respect, they will travel far.

CHALLENGE: **TENDERING OTHERS THE RESPECT THEY DEMAND FOR THEMSELVES**
FULFILLMENT: **INVOKING THEIR TREMENDOUS GENEROSITY AND MAGNANIMITY**

August 19–25

EXPOSURE
LEO–VIRGO CUSP

Developing and maintaining a sense of unassailable personal integrity will be particularly important for those born on the Cusp of Exposure who travel the Way of Resolve. Indeed, these charismatic and compelling personalities have so accurate a perception of what makes others tick and what others want to hear that they may well fail to evaluate their own views thoroughly or to put themselves into the equation as crises or opportunities for greater growth arise. Though blessed with great poise and self-containment, they may fail to show their hand when a situation calls for dedicated commitment. Likely to be real masters of observation, they will develop a fine grasp of the workings of power and diplomacy. Yet they will be forced, either by choice or by circumstance, to expand their sense of self in such a way that they aspire not only to work on behalf of harmony, but also, in doing so, to exceed the expectations of themselves and others in strength, faith, and devotion.

CHALLENGE: **NOT HIDING OUT THROUGH VACILLATION AND AVOIDANCE**

FULFILLMENT: **FEELING CONFIDENT IN WHAT THEIR EYES, HEARTS, AND MINDS TELL THEM**

ROBERT CRUMB
Cartoonist; self-portrait

8/30/1943
Virgo I

August 26–September 2

SYSTEM BUILDERS
VIRGO I

Indecision and an innate need to keep the peace at all costs, even that of their own self-respect, will hamper the development of Virgo I's who travel the Way of Resolve. Though on the surface dedicated, committed, and steady, these personalities may encounter great difficulties when it comes to the challenge of commanding attention and respect for their deepest and truest beliefs. Yet it is their own talent for creating structure and system that will come to their rescue, as they will have a much easier time of things when they allow themselves to approach their problems in a measured, disciplined fashion. Regular study and explorations of philosophical thought will be enormously beneficial, as it will enable these individuals to comprehend how others have managed to structure the problems of identity and commitment. If they can manage to overcome their dislike of confrontation and stand up for a set of beliefs that arise from passion and conviction, they will have little to fear and everything to gain.

CHALLENGE: **GRAPPLING WITH THE DIFFICULTY THEY HAVE IN MAKING DECISIONS**

FULFILLMENT: **MAKING THEIR RESOLVE AN ACT OF LOVE, BOTH FOR THEMSELVES AND FOR OTHERS**

NOTABLE: **BOB KERREY (POLITICIAN, GOVERNOR, SENATOR OF NEBRASKA; DECORATED FOR BRAVERY IN VIETNAM WAR)**

September 3–10

THE ENIGMA
VIRGO II

The highly discriminating and discerning personalities born in the Week of the Enigma who journey along the Way of Resolve can expect wonderful success and accomplishment, providing they do not allow their concern for public opinion to stand in the way of developing a higher set of beliefs and standards. Though they bring to this karmic path much more of the proverbial "iron will" than some others who travel this road do, they may shy away from standing up and fighting for what they truly believe. Still, they have a highly developed moral sense that will rarely lead them astray, and if they can put themselves in the forefront, their ideals and convictions can serve as a real rallying point for their families, organizations, and friends. If they can understand that even the bloodiest of conflicts are generally resolved not with arms but with words, their diplomatic skills, grasp of issues, and strength of conviction will lead them to fulfillment and self-confidence.

CHALLENGE: **GETTING DOWN AND DIRTY ONCE IN A WHILE**

FULFILLMENT: **SHOWING THEIR GREAT INNER STRENGTH TO THE WORLD**

NOTABLE: **ALF LANDON (BUSINESSMAN; POLITICIAN, LOST OVERWHELMINGLY TO ROOSEVELT)**

DAME EDITH SITWELL
Poet, *The Outcasts*

9/7/1887
Virgo II

September 11–18

THE LITERALIST
VIRGO III

Those born in the Week of the Literalist who journey along the Way of Resolve can expect the highest success and fulfillment once they divest themselves of their need to be liked or to maintain harmony at the expense of truth. Yet they bring to this karmic path a natural practicality that will stand them in good stead, as they have a gift for dedication and application that will make for long-term success and accomplishment. They will be asked in the course of this journey to take risks and get emotionally involved on a deeper level than is often their inclination. If they do not back down from the challenge to growth and enlightenment and remain willing to take a stand for their deeply held beliefs, they will find that they are able not only to fight for their own convictions, but also to turn their goals into satisfying reality.

CHALLENGE: **ACCEPTING THAT SOMETIMES CONFLICT IS NECESSARY**

FULFILLMENT: **BELIEVING IN THEMSELVES**

NOTABLES: **NADIA BOULANGER (FRENCH COMPOSER/CONDUCTOR; 1ST WOMAN TO TEACH AT PARIS CONSERVATORY); HANS ARP (FRENCH AUTHOR; SCULPTOR; FOUNDED DADAIST MOVEMENT)**

September 19–24

BEAUTY
VIRGO–LIBRA CUSP

The gentle and often rather indecisive people born on this cusp who find themselves on the Way of Resolve may have a rather difficult time, as many of their natural inclinations are at odds with the ability to successfully handle its challenges. Marked by what might most diplomatically be termed a desire to please, they may have a tendency to "just follow orders" even when a situation demands that they take an entirely different stand. Too, they may allow themselves to be buffeted about on the tide of public opinion, unsure of themselves and what they truly think or believe. Thus the ability to get in touch with a deeper level of feeling will prove most important. If they can come to consciously practice the art of making decisions and developing convictions in small ways, then the larger issues will fall into place. If they can also acknowledge that sins of omission can nonetheless be sins, life will be quite rewarding as they chart their rather indirect route along this karmic path.

CHALLENGE: **GUARDING AGAINST THEIR PROPENSITY FOR TAKING THE PATH OF LEAST RESISTANCE**

FULFILLMENT: **FINDING A MORAL COMPASS**

NOTABLES: **"MAMA" CASS ELLIOT (SINGER, THE MAMAS AND THE PAPAS); JULIO IGLESIAS (SPANISH SINGER/SONG-WRITER, "TO ALL THE GIRLS I'VE LOVED BEFORE")**

LECH WALESA
Polish trade union leader, president; Nobel Peace prize
─────
9/29/1943
Libra I

September 25–October 2

THE PERFECTIONIST
LIBRA I

Those born in the Week of the Perfectionist who travel the Way of Resolve can realize great fulfillment, providing they do not allow themselves to become distracted from their higher goals through insecurity, pickiness, or emotional immaturity. In fact, these dynamic and attractive personalities may present a face to the world that is decidedly at odds with their complex emotional nature. They do have their own brand of backbone, however, and the question is not so much whether they will rise to the challenges that present themselves but how they will choose to embrace those opportunities for growth. Once they come to understand that mastering one's emotions is not at all the same thing as repressing them, their indecision and insecurity will yield to the surer sense of self that is the product of committing oneself fully to the task of self-expansion and improvement.

CHALLENGE: **STRUGGLING TO FIND THE BALANCE BETWEEN BEING HARD ON THEMSELVES AND WANTING TO BE LET OFF EASILY**

FULFILLMENT: **TAKING PRINCIPLED ACTION AGAINST INJUSTICE**

NOTABLE: **MARILYN MCCOO (SINGER, THE FIFTH DIMENSION)**

October 3–10

SOCIETY
LIBRA II

Well liked and sought after, those born in the Week of Society who travel the Way of Resolve may have a difficult time rising to the challenge of developing a core set of beliefs. Though keen observers and analyzers of human nature in the abstract, these discerning and generally tasteful people will have a more arduous task in bringing their powers of analysis to bear in the business of self-examination and evaluation. They tend not to take their own needs very seriously, which can further hinder their development, and are somewhat hesitant to fight for themselves, much less their principles. Nevertheless, they can make great progress, especially if they take care to include in their network of friends and family a few challenging individuals who, as a result of their own strong natures, will demand from them an ever-higher level of achievement, awareness, and personal principle.

CHALLENGE: **NOT FLOUNDERING IN THE SEA OF PUBLIC OPINION**

FULFILLMENT: **CLARIFYING WHO THEY ARE AND WHO THEY WANT TO BE**

NOTABLES: **H. RAP BROWN (POLITICAL ACTIVIST; AUTHOR); CHEVY CHASE (ACTOR/COMEDIAN, *VACATION*)**

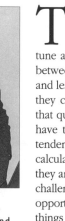

LECORBUSIER
Bauhaus architect and artist
─────
10/6/1887
Libra II

October 11–18

THEATER
LIBRA III

The unique, talented individuals born in the Week of Theater who find themselves traveling the Way of Resolve can enjoy much in the way of personal fortune and blessings, yet they will have to strike a balance between committing themselves to purely personal needs and learning to value the needs and rights of others. Once they commit themselves, they tend to give their all, and that quality alone is sure to serve them well. Yet they will have to face down the demon of self-absorption or the tendency to collapse into cynicism and a rather cold or calculating attitude in the face of disappointment. Still, they are gifted with the inner strength to rise to almost any challenge that may present itself. If they can meet their opportunities for growth with an awareness of those things that really matter and confront adversity with confidence and grace, they will accomplish much in the interest of higher development.

CHALLENGE: **CALLING UP SOME OLD-FASHIONED FIRE AND BRIMSTONE TO BACK UP THEIR BELIEFS**

FULFILLMENT: **LIVING FROM A CORE UNDERSTANDING OF WHO THEY REALLY ARE**

KARMIC PATH
43

October 19–25

DRAMA AND CRITICISM
LIBRA–SCORPIO CUSP

Gifted with a dramatic and often quite compelling public persona, the unique individuals born on the Cusp of Drama and Criticism who travel the Way of Resolve have a gift for airing their views and opinions. Nevertheless, they will face the challenge of developing some solid principles if they are to be truly successful on this karmic path. In fact, their biggest problem may be that they may display much more conviction than they actually feel and thus may have to fight against a reputation for phoniness, flightiness, or flakiness until they come to a firmer sense of their own principles. If they can rise to the opportunities for growth, not take shelter in trivial excuses for their own lapses of standard or behavior, and refuse to be swayed by either their need for attention or the vagaries of public opinion, their path will become considerably clarified.

JOHN REED
Journalist/activist;
Ten Days That Shook the World
─────────
10/20/1887
Libra–Scorpio Cusp

CHALLENGE: **BELIEVING IN THE POWER OF THEIR CONVICTIONS**
FULFILLMENT: **INVESTING THEIR PASSION IN A CODE OF HONOR**
NOTABLES: **BRIAN PICCOLO (FOOTBALL PLAYER; SUBJECT OF *BRIAN'S SONG*); SANDY ALOMAR, SR. (BASEBALL GREAT)**

October 26–November 2

INTENSITY
SCORPIO I

The personalities born in the Week of Intensity who travel the Way of Resolve are characterized by a phoenixlike quality that ensures that Scorpio I's not only will rise to the challenges that present themselves along this road but will be able to emerge from even the worst trials and setbacks to soar to new heights of self-awareness and personal achievement. The key to their development will be a willingness not just to take the easy way out or to blame their trials on others but to recognize that in many significant ways they are their own instruments of change and that seemingly unpleasant changes in circumstances are often the result of their deep-seated need for transformation and development. This may not be an entirely easy journey, for there is much to suggest a number of baptisms by fire. Yet out of those fires, Scorpio I's are sure to forge both solid principles and a sense of faith in who they are.

CHALLENGE: **REMEMBERING TO COUNT THEIR MANY BLESSINGS**
FULFILLMENT: **REALIZING THEIR CAPACITY TO TRANSFORM ANY CONDITION OR SITUATION BY CONFRONTING IT**
NOTABLE: **CHIANG KAI-SHEK (CHINESE REVOLUTIONARY LEADER; PRESIDED OVER TAIWAN'S "ECONOMIC MIRACLE")**

November 3–11

DEPTH
SCORPIO II

The emotionally complex and soulful personalities born in this week who travel the Way of Resolve are well suited to the higher challenge of formulating and fighting for beliefs and principles. They will, however, need to struggle a bit to develop greater self-confidence and self-respect. Overemotionalism may be their undoing, and the sense that life is unfair may cause them to collapse into self-negating habits and thought patterns. They have a pronounced unwillingness to share their problems with others or allow anyone into the secrets of their private world, and the tendency to create an easygoing facade that masks a maelstrom of emotions is very pronounced. Thus there will be a number of real *pagliacci* with this configuration, and though most of them will not lack the courage of their convictions, they may have a real struggle putting them on display. Yet if they keep in mind that fulfillment will come only with a willingness to reveal their deepest needs, strongest values, and true identity, their efforts will be well rewarded.

CHALLENGE: **NOT GETTING STUCK IN INDECISION OR REPRESSED EMOTION**
FULFILLMENT: **DEVELOPING CONFLICT RESOLUTION AND PROBLEM SOLVING INTO A HIGH ART**

CATHERINE DENEUVE
French actress,
Belle de Jour
─────────
10/22/1943
Libra–Scorpio Cusp

November 12–18

CHARM
SCORPIO III

Many things come easily to these often gifted people, yet the individuals born in the Week of Charm who travel the Way of Resolve will experience their share of struggles in the course of standing up for the things in which they truly believe. A tendency to complacency and comfort will prove their biggest stumbling blocks. Personal relationships may prove especially troublesome, as they may have a pronounced tendency to project their needs, desires, and even deficiencies onto others. This can all add up to a real capacity for self-deception until they come to a better psychological and spiritual understanding of their own patterns and habits. Yet if they remember to stretch themselves and their understanding and to continue to raise the bar of their aspirations and standards, their life can be wonderfully enlightening and satisfying.

CHALLENGE: **NOT PLEASING OTHERS TO THE POINT WHERE THEY HAVE NO SENSE OF SELF**
FULFILLMENT: **LETTING THEIR RELATIONSHIPS FLOW IN AN EASY GIVE-AND-TAKE**
NOTABLES: **JAMES MAXWELL (SCOTTISH MATHEMATICIAN, PHYSICIST; FOUND LIGHT TO BE ELECTROMAGNETIC); WILLIAM HERSCHEL (ASTRONOMER; DISCOVERED URANUS); VISCOUNT MONTGOMERY (BRITISH FIELD MARSHAL; LED ALLIED INVASION OF NORMANDY)**

November 19–24
REVOLUTION
SCORPIO–SAGITTARIUS CUSP

Though personal growth may well come in fits and starts for those born on the Cusp of Revolution who travel the Way of Resolve, these dauntless, courageous types are well suited to the challenges that present themselves along this road. In fact, their biggest problem will not be so much an ideological conflict as a practical one, and Scorpio–Sagittarians will have to work hard to develop the willingness to follow up their own philosophical epiphanies with dedication and long-term commitment. Surrounding themselves with more stable and matures types will certainly ease the burden, as will grounding themselves in learning and a study of philosophical constructs. If they can manage to organize their beliefs to form a system and rise to the challenge of seeing their projects through to a satisfying conclusion, their road will be considerably smoothed.

SHIRLEY CHISHOLM
1st black woman elected
to Congress

11/30/1924
Sagittarius I

CHALLENGE: **SPENDING LESS TIME CRITICIZING THE MORES AND VALUES OF OTHERS AND MORE TIME EXAMINING THEIR OWN**

FULFILLMENT: **BUILDING A BUSINESS OR RELATIONSHIP WITH TIME AND DEDICATION**

NOTABLES: **GERALDINE PAGE (ACTRESS, *A TRIP TO BOUNTIFUL*); BORIS KARLOFF (HORROR FILM ACTOR, *FRANKENSTEIN, THE MUMMY*)**

November 25–December 2
INDEPENDENCE
SAGITTARIUS I

The individuals born in the Week of Independence who journey along the Way of Resolve may have a genuine horror of commitment and indulge in quite a bit of posturing and espousing the concept of so-called personal freedom until they come to face the fact that they are actually running from themselves. Inclined to feel themselves the victims of circumstance or the prisoners of uptight society, these souls nevertheless possess enormous reserves of willpower and courage and a healthy respect for higher moral principles that will serve them well. Though they will have to do quite a bit of soul-searching before they can bring themselves to hang in for the longer haul, they can find great fulfillment once they overcome their natural skittishness and realize that true freedom and independence arise out of a secure sense of self and are ultimately based in mind, not in lifestyle.

CHALLENGE: **REALIZING THE DIFFERENCE BETWEEN HAVING AN HONOR CODE AND LIVING ONE**

FULFILLMENT: **GIVING OTHERS THE GREATEST GIFT OF ALL: THEMSELVES**

NOTABLES: **ALEXANDER HAIG (SECRETARY OF STATE FOR RONALD REAGAN); PAUL DESMOND (JAZZ MUSICIAN)**

December 3–10
THE ORIGINATOR
SAGITTARIUS II

Those born in the Week of the Originator who journey along the Way of Resolve may take a bit longer than some others born in this week to come to terms with and embrace their unique visions or talents. Often extraordinarily gifted, they may nevertheless hold themselves back from higher development if they become enmeshed in the need to be accepted and hanker after approval when they would do far better to find the courage to simply be themselves. Yet no matter what their efforts to the contrary, they are not likely to be as good at fitting in or going with the flow as they are at voicing their highly original opinions, pursuing their thoughts, and developing their beliefs. If they nurture their ardent and committed side, yet find the strength of character to give up on those who cannot accept them for who they are, life will become much sweeter for them.

JANE AUSTEN
Novelist,
Pride and Prejudice

12/15/1775
Sagittarius III

CHALLENGE: **RELEASING THEIR NEED FOR ACCEPTANCE OR APPROVAL**

FULFILLMENT: **STANDING BY THEIR UNIQUE VIEWS OR METHODS**

NOTABLE: **JOHN BACKUS (COMPUTER SCIENTIST; INVENTED COMPUTER LANGUAGE FORTRAN)**

December 11–18
THE TITAN
SAGITTARIUS III

Blessed with the ability to envision their lives on a grand scale, those born in the Week of the Titan who journey along the Way of Resolve can experience extraordinary success and fulfillment. They may, however, need to develop more realistic expectations if they are to find happiness. Though blessed with quite a bit of moral courage and a rather fearless approach to life, they will need to develop greater self-awareness and overcome some secret insecurities in the course of this life journey. "Follow up and follow through" might well serve as a mantra for their personal development, for while their vision is expansive and their ideas are heroic, they may have a pronounced dislike of getting their hands dirty, figuratively speaking, or otherwise carrying a fight through to the end. If they can manage to find the balance between hope and realism, all will go well for them.

CHALLENGE: **COASTING ON THEIR INNATE TALENTS A LITTLE LESS BY CHALLENGING THEMSELVES A LITTLE MORE**

FULFILLMENT: **COMING TO LIKE THEMSELVES FOR WHO THEY FUNDAMENTALLY ARE**

NOTABLES: **ED KOCH (NEW YORK MAYOR); "DOC" FELIX ANTHONY BLANCHARD (FOOTBALL PLAYER/COACH)**

December 19–25
PROPHECY
SAGITTARIUS–CAPRICORN CUSP

Getting in touch with what may best be termed "gut instinct" will figure prominently for those born on this cusp who travel the Way of Resolve. Likely to be much more social than some others born in this week, these souls will nevertheless have to learn the ins and outs of power and negotiation in the course of developing a clearer insight into their beliefs. Yet they can make wonderful progress along this road, especially when they allow themselves to be guided by solid principles and their well-developed extrasensory or spiritual insight. If they do not allow their more easygoing aspects to devolve into carelessness or their need for approval to erode their sense of right and wrong, they can expect marvelous success, considerable achievement, and a degree of popularity that they will doubtless find pleasing as they make their way toward confident self-realization.

ROD SERLING
Science fiction writer,
creator of
The Twilight Zone
────────
12/25/1924
Sagittarius–Capricorn
Cusp

CHALLENGE: **NOT LETTING THEIR STRENGTH OF PURPOSE BECOME A CROSS THEY HAVE TO BEAR**

FULFILLMENT: **ALLOWING OTHERS TO GET CLOSE TO THEM**

December 26–January 2
THE RULER
CAPRICORN I

Those born in the Week of the Ruler who travel the Way of Resolve are likely to experience a really rewarding life experience, as their natural tendencies toward sternness and autocracy are nicely mitigated by the natural charm and easygoing gifts of the Aquarius II origins of this karmic path. In fact, their principal stumbling block may be their inclination to cling stubbornly to convention when their hearts would lead them elsewhere—toward a different set of values or principles. Yet they have a fine sense of moral courage and a good understanding of what makes people happy. If they can bring themselves to better acquaint themselves with the person they are inside and act according to their deepest convictions rather than out of concern for what others may think of them, their hard work, high principles, and trustworthiness are sure to bring them success.

CHALLENGE: **TAKING THE TIME TO EXAMINE WHAT THEIR ACTIONS REFLECT ABOUT THEM**

FULFILLMENT: **ENJOYING THE SENSE OF EMPOWERMENT THAT COMES FROM FACING PROBLEMS HEAD-ON**

NOTABLE: **GLENN DAVIS (FOOTBALL PLAYER; "MR. OUTSIDE")**

January 3–9
DETERMINATION
CAPRICORN II

Though often too unassuming and self-effacing for their own good, those born in the Week of Determination who travel the Way of Resolve are possessed of a measure of "true grit" when it comes to accomplishing their higher goals or formulating a better-developed set of principles. Though they may sometimes delude themselves with the notion that self-sacrifice is their true motivation for turning away from conflict, sooner or later they will rise to any genuine challenge to their personal integrity. And while they may meet conflict with what might best be termed a slow burn or a long fuse, once engaged they will fight to the end. If they educate themselves to a larger sense of philosophy and ground their sense of inspiration in sustained effort, these individuals will make the best of friends and the most formidable of adversaries.

YUKIO MISHIMA
Wrote modern Kabuki
────────
1/14/1925
Capricorn III

CHALLENGE: **KNOWING WHEN TO QUIT AND SIMPLY REST ON THEIR LAURELS**

FULFILLMENT: **SLOUGHING OFF THEIR DEFENSES ONCE THEY HAVE ACHIEVED A SENSE OF THEIR INNER STRENGTH**

NOTABLE: **GERALD DURRELL (BRITISH ZOOLOGIST; WROTE ON ANIMALS)**

January 10–16
DOMINANCE
CAPRICORN III

Those born in the Week of Determination who travel the Way of Resolve can find wonderful fulfillment, as they have a natural talent for commitment and dedication that will serve them especially well. Overcoming their inborn feelings of inferiority and insecurity may figure prominently on this life journey, and they will have to take special care that in their search to prove themselves and please others, they do not also fail to develop a clear sense of their own values or to please themselves. Yet they have the ability to acquire great self-respect, enlightenment, and spiritual awakening in the course of this life journey. If they remember to nurture their less conservative, more eccentric side, they may even have a great deal of fun, especially as they take on the responsibilities of parenthood or some creative endeavor.

CHALLENGE: **CULTIVATING THE KIND OF SELF-RESPECT THAT IS INDEPENDENT OF THE OPINIONS OF OTHERS**

FULFILLMENT: **PRIDING THEMSELVES ON THEIR LOYALTY**

NOTABLE: **HORATIO ALGER (UNITARIAN MINISTER; WROTE INSPIRATIONAL NOVELS ABOUT YOUNG MEN GAINING SUCCESS THROUGH HARD WORK; GAVE HIS WEALTH TO THE POOR)**

January 17–22

MYSTERY AND IMAGINATION
CAPRICORN–AQUARIUS CUSP

Marked by a certain spiritual and intellectual restlessness, the personalities born on the Cusp of Mystery and Imagination who make their journey along the Way of Resolve may flounder a bit until they come to better terms with the need to direct and apply their prodigious energies in some productive direction. Their yearning for excitement may well lead them off on any number of tangents early in life, and it won't be until they get a better grip on themselves and their truest inclinations that they will begin to find what they're looking for. Nevertheless, they have an innate attraction to higher principles and the more philosophical forms of thought. Thus, they have the possibility of great success and accomplishment, though they will have to discover the balance between inspiration and application and learn that there does indeed lie a middle road between rebellion and resolve.

LEWIS CARROLL
Author,
Alice in Wonderland

1/27/1832
Aquarius I

CHALLENGE: **TEMPERING THEIR RESTLESSNESS AND NEED FOR EXCITEMENT**

FULFILLMENT: **EXPERIENCING THE SATISFACTION OF SEEING THROUGH THEIR COMMITMENTS TO HELP OTHERS**

NOTABLE: **BENNY HILL (BRITISH COMEDIAN; TELEVISION SHOW SYNDICATED INTERNATIONALLY)**

January 23–30

GENIUS
AQUARIUS I

Those born in the Week of Genius who navigate the challenge and promise of the Way of Resolve will be aided to some extent in their quest for enlightenment by their natural fixed energy that, while almost certainly intellectual and theoretical, does not preclude the possibility of dedication and application. Though they have a rather rebellious attitude and may chafe at some of the constraints and challenges of this karmic path, they also have high standards and principles. Though they will need to step down from the ivory towers of speculation and theory and learn to practice some of the things they are prone to preach, their willingness to do so will be the key to their development and growth. If they can commit themselves to their self-realization to the same extent that they are committed to their ideals, this karmic path will teach them a great deal about the value of diligence, dedication, and responsibility to oneself and others.

CHALLENGE: **IMPROVING THEIR CAREER PROSPECTS BY LEARNING TO SEE THINGS THROUGH TO A CONCLUSION**

FULFILLMENT: **PUTTING THEIR OWN TRUTH INTO THEIR WORK**

NOTABLE: **EDOUARD MANET (FRENCH PAINTER, IMPRESSIONIST)**

January 31–February 7

YOUTH AND EASE
AQUARIUS II

Those born in this week who travel the Way of Resolve will have a certain amount of soul work to do as they face down the demons of emotional immaturity, carelessness, and a pronounced tendency to take the easy way out of conflicts or confrontation. Lighthearted and rather lucky, many of this group will find themselves attracted to precisely those people or situations that will aid them in identifying their shadow side, or the places where their emotional and spiritual growth has been stunted or stalled. Youthfulness will be the hallmark of their attitude and approach toward the world, and they may be unfairly accused of immaturity when in fact they are merely open-minded and flexible. Yet they will have to prove their willingness to shoulder responsibility and get in touch with their sense of principle. When they understand that the challenges they face are actually opportunities to develop greater personal strength and authority, their life will be as easy and full of good fortune inside as it often appears on the outside.

GARTH BROOKS
Popular country singer,
"The Dance"

2/7/1962
Aquarius II

CHALLENGE: **EJECTING THEIR YOUTHFUL IMMATURITY IN FAVOR OF A MORE SERIOUS OR RESPONSIBLE APPROACH TO LIFE**

FULFILLMENT: **FINDING JOY IN BEING THERE FOR ANOTHER**

NOTABLE: **AXL ROSE (HEAVY METAL SINGER, GUNS N' ROSES)**

February 8–15

ACCEPTANCE
AQUARIUS III

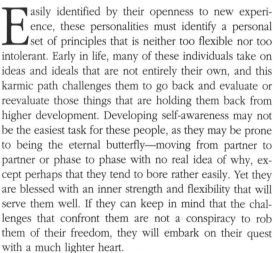

Easily identified by their openness to new experience, these personalities must identify a personal set of principles that is neither too flexible nor too intolerant. Early in life, many of these individuals take on ideas and ideals that are not entirely their own, and this karmic path challenges them to go back and evaluate or reevaluate those things that are holding them back from higher development. Developing self-awareness may not be the easiest task for these people, as they may be prone to being the eternal butterfly—moving from partner to partner or phase to phase with no real idea of why, except perhaps that they tend to bore rather easily. Yet they are blessed with an inner strength and flexibility that will serve them well. If they can keep in mind that the challenges that confront them are not a conspiracy to rob them of their freedom, they will embark on their quest with a much lighter heart.

CHALLENGE: **DISCOVERING THE PATTERNS OR THEMES IN THE CHALLENGES THEY ENCOUNTER**

FULFILLMENT: **LEARNING WHAT A RELIEF IT IS TO JUST STAY PUT NOW AND THEN**

NOTABLES: **JACK LEMMON (ACTOR, *MISTER ROBERTS*, *SAVE THE TIGER*); VIRGINIA JOHNSON (PSYCHOLOGIST, HUMAN SEXUALITY RESEARCHER, COWROTE *HUMAN SEXUAL RESPONSE*)**

February 16–22

SENSITIVITY
AQUARIUS–PISCES CUSP

Those born on the Cusp of Sensitivity who travel the Way of Resolve will have to work hard to avoid taking themselves and their circumstances too personally and not to believe that they are somehow victims of fate or circumstance when they are forced to face the music or fight the good fight in the name of principle. For all their easily hurt feelings and general touchiness, they are blessed with a feisty and even rather aggressive streak that will stand them in excellent stead on this life journey. In fact, the only real danger for those born with this configuration is that they may fail to integrate their inner and outer realities and may hold to one set of principles inwardly while outwardly appearing to go with the flow. Too, many of them may be haunted by a fear of rejection. Yet if they allow the ups and downs of their interactions with others to inform their sense of self and create a firmer set of principles, they will be capable of great commitment and forceful action in the service of what they believe is right.

ROBERT ALTMAN
Movie director, *Short Cuts*

2/20/1925
Aquarius–Pisces Cusp

CHALLENGE: **SEEING CONFLICT FOR THE LESSON THAT IT IS**
FULFILLMENT: **FINDING THE COURAGE TO BE VULNERABLE**
NOTABLE: **LOU DIAMOND PHILIPS (ACTOR, *LA BAMBA*)**

February 23–March 2

SPIRIT
PISCES I

Gifted with an enormous capacity for devotion and dedication, those born in the Week of Spirit who travel the Way of Resolve can experience wonderful fulfillment, though they may have to struggle with the challenge of directing their energies in such a way as to enhance their sense of identity. Scattered interests and a youthful attitude are hallmarks of these individuals, and some will find it especially difficult to take responsibility for their own action—or lack thereof. Likely to be much better at motivating other people than they are at motivating themselves, they may promise much more than they actually deliver and at some point will be called upon to pay the piper. Yet if they can learn the value of dedication and commitment, their more devotional and spiritual aspects will be awakened and their path to personal strength and firmer identity greatly clarified.

CHALLENGE: **COMBATING THEIR DESIRE TO LOSE THEMSELVES IN SENSUAL PLEASURES**
FULFILLMENT: **LETTING THEIR DESIRE TO DO GOOD BE THE PRINCIPLE BY WHICH THEY SET THEIR RESOLVE**

March 3–10

THE LONER
PISCES II

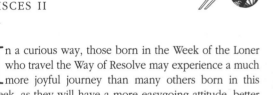

In a curious way, those born in the Week of the Loner who travel the Way of Resolve may experience a much more joyful journey than many others born in this week, as they will have a more easygoing attitude, better luck, and less of an exalted sense of suffering than many of their fellows. Though they are well acquainted with the need for self-awareness, some personal trauma or struggle may cause them to shut down or turn away from conflict if they cling to the fatalist belief that circumstances are beyond their control. Thus, they will face the challenge of assuming responsibility for many of their own choices and missed chances. A feeling of victimhood may hold them back as well. Yet if they can come to terms with the need to direct their energies in more effective ways and test their theories of life in practice, they will find greater enlightenment and a much stronger and more confident sense of self.

JON BON JOVI
Rock singer; actor

3/2/1962
Pisces I

CHALLENGE: **LEARNING TO STAND UP FOR THEMSELVES**
FULFILLMENT: **KNOWING THAT TO LIVE HONESTLY IS TO LIVE WELL**
NOTABLES: **HERSHEL WALKER (FOOTBALL PLAYER, RUNNING BACK); JACKIE JOYNER-KERSEE (OLYMPIC MEDALIST, TRACK ATHLETE)**

March 11–18

DANCERS AND DREAMERS
PISCES III

The individuals born in the Week of Dancers and Dreamers who journey along the Way of Resolve may appear as if they were born under the proverbial lucky star, yet they will have to learn to accept the responsibilities of their own giftedness as they make their way along this road. Commitment and responsibility are not their strong suits, and many will go through life rather blithely expecting others to clean up their messes and tie up their loose ends until they are forced to do so for themselves. Thus, the challenges of this karmic path may seem rather arduous until they come to understand the relationship between their attitudes and their circumstances and catch on to the power of belief to create reality. If they can release their emotional immaturity, divest themselves of their superior attitudes, and nurture their need to be effective, they will be able to stand up and be counted—both for their principles and for their actions.

CHALLENGE: **DISCIPLINING THEMSELVES TO SEE THINGS THROUGH**
FULFILLMENT: **DISCOVERING THAT WHAT MATTERS MOST TO THEM IS WHAT THEY HAVE HAD ALL ALONG**

The Way of Confidence

AQUARIUS III TO LEO III
Acceptance to Leadership

The Way of Confidence calls those born to it to develop the self-acceptance and self-assurance needed to step into the public spotlight and become leaders. Individuals on this karmic path often feel set apart from others in some way. Sensing that they are different, they surround themselves with friends for validation. Little can assuage their insecurity, however, until they believe in themselves and feel confident in their messages or missions. Only then can those on this path fulfill their destiny. Whether they become political leaders, the heads of business organizations, or simply the charismatic centers of groups of friends, those on this path are called to lead. However, they must base their desire to become leaders, not in a need for approval, but in the purest intention: the desire to further the highest good of their groups and society.

The individuals on this karmic path are unusual personalities. Since early childhood, they have known, deep down, that they march to the beat of a different drummer. This understanding seems to befuddle them a bit since they cannot quite grasp the reason for it. If you look closely at them, you can see a kind of hurt or haunted quality in their eyes. It's as if they don't feel they belong or that they are truly loved. Though they may have accepted that they are unusual, they may not have made peace with it. These men and women are quite social individuals and, consequently, surround themselves with people, forming more superficial relationships, in the hopes of blending in with the crowd and receiving the approval they crave. Quite deliberately, those on this path are extremely charming. First, it enables them to hide the fact they are different and, second, it serves to seduce people to become part of their circles. They are, in fact, good friends to others. Having grappled with the pain of feeling separate, there is little that shocks or frightens them, so they have the knack for making people feel accepted for who they are. They rarely let anyone in too close and do not remain in intimate relationships for too long, however, for fear that their idiosyncratic nature will be discovered—and rejected—thus fulfilling their worst fantasy.

The people born on the Way of Confidence truly do not think like the average Joe. Easily bored, they are dynamic individuals and change is a constant for them. Each of them is like a sun operating in a universe of its own making with many satellites revolving around it. Because of their sense that they are not like everyone else, they crave approval and acceptance, if not understanding. Somehow seeking it causes it to elude them. They suffer from low self-esteem as a result. Their sense of self-worth is built on a foundation of shifting sand because it often depends on what others think or on other ego-related issues such as job performance. More important, at their core, they don't believe that they are entitled to acceptance be-

---

CORE LESSON
Releasing insecurity and believing in oneself

GOAL
To step into the role of leader, whether by example or as an authority

---

GIFTS
Inventive, Lively, Commanding

PITFALLS
Insecure, Approval-seeking, Cold

cause they think something is fundamentally wrong with them. Where they might have gotten this idea often can't be traced to anything specific. Mom and Dad may have been unusual, which might have set those on this karmic path off from the other children at school. Or, they may carry wounds from other lifetimes when being different from one's culture was a far more dangerous proposition than it is in late twentieth-century industrialized society.

The key point is that those on the Way of Confidence are called to overcome their feelings of insecurity and low self-worth. The purpose of this karmic path is more than developing self-acceptance. These individuals must be willing to give up their anonymity (something that will never be entirely comfortable for them), put themselves forward into the public eye, and offer themselves and their innovative ideas or techniques to the world by stepping into leadership roles. Often leaders are those individuals who possess unique visions. If they were as ordinary as everyone else what would set them apart as leaders? In a way, those on this karmic path must begin to see that what they have always perceived as a weakness—that which makes them unusual—is, in fact, their greatest strength. Though many will become leaders on this path in the traditional sense of being in positions of authority, a number of individuals here may not enjoy being in command. Thus, some on this path will choose to lead by example.

RELEASE

The attachment to low self-worth

REWARD

The joy of acting for the greater good

Sometimes by simply acknowledging publicly how they are different, those on this path will inspire others. Cultivating self-acceptance is obviously the necessary first step in this process. However, equally as important is that those on this karmic path must believe they have "the right stuff" to be in charge.

With the confidence to share their views and ideas, these individuals have a lot to contribute since they possess a great deal of insight into the workings of both individuals and groups. Though they tend to simply want to fit in and live quiet lives, they must instead accept their destiny and learn how to be commanding, even heroic. To do so, their intentions must be pure and their natural generosity and desire to help others must come to the fore. Frequently, those on the Way of Confidence find themselves thrust into the spotlight, even if they are wholly unprepared for it. One day, quite suddenly, the universe may force them into leadership roles by creating power vacuums in their groups that only they can fill. Those on this karmic path may well hesitate or show signs of acute insecurity when it becomes obvious that they should step into the vacuum. However, whether in the family, job, or social sphere, those on this path must learn the skills of leadership, often in the form of on-the-job training. They will receive an education in the ins and outs of power and how to lead others with forcefulness and determination. Not fearing power, but using

KARMIC PATH
44

SUGGESTION

Realize being different doesn't mean there is something wrong with you. Own and embrace your individuality. Share your gifts with generosity. Risk being an example.

it as a tool to achieve common goals may require some battles at first, both inner and outer ones. Once established in leadership roles, however, those on this path can consolidate their groups, encouraging all members to work for the highest good and best interest. As their confidence grows, those on this path will become role models for others to emulate. Moreover, they are bound to use their psychological savvy to influence and persuade rather than dominate. Ultimately, those on this path will integrate the decisive and commanding energies symbolized by the Leo III destination of this path, fulfilling their destiny with passion, vigor, and pride.

Ironically, success will not come to those on this karmic path if they seek the limelight as a way to gain acceptance. This would make them ineffectual as leaders because their actions or decisions would be predicated on approval seeking. Rather, so confident must they be in who they are and what they think that they are wholly immune to issues of popularity. The greatest danger of the Way of Confidence is for those on it to become carried away by ego, hubris, or narcissism. All of which can result if those on this path have not eliminated all vestiges of insecurity or the need for approval or adulation from their psychological makeup. Dictatorial tendencies of those on this path can only harm their spiritual development and, worse, harm the people they are supposed to serve. A group led by someone of that bent will inevitably come unglued in times of crisis when the inadequacy of its leader becomes startlingly apparent. Alternatively, should their confidence in themselves be undermined in any way, those on this path may begin to question their every decision, thus weakening their capacity as leaders.

BALANCE POINT

Altruism and Egotism

Not surprisingly, the mate of someone on this karmic path may have to accept the role of foot soldier, carrying out day-to-day responsibilities while those on this path go about their work of leadership or command. However, partnerships of such inequality are not ideal for those on this path since their innate sense of fairness will cause them to feel guilty. Thus, for the men and women on the Way of Confidence friendships may always be preferable to more restrictive relationships like business partnerships, or familial or marital pairings since friendships leave them freer to act, with fewer binding expectations or fixed responsibilities. Those on this karmic path are not afraid of responsibility; it is just that their worldly goals leave little room for emotional investment in others.

An example from history that comes to mind is that of the Roman emperor Claudius. Early in his career as a politician, though quite intelligent, he was considered to be mentally deficient due to a physical disability and to his rather likeable, accepting nature. Not being taken seriously enabled him to survive the poisonous and homicidal atmosphere of Roman politics. Finally, he was manipulated into the role of emperor since everyone perceived him to be so weak as not to be a threat to their constituency. Claudius was a historian and an acute observer of all the political intrigue around him. Accepting the mantle of authority thrust upon him, he went on to become a capable, if not excellent emperor, ruling without exhibiting the tyrannical behavior that typified his forbears, taking the power conferred on him as leader of the greatest empire in the world at that time, and using it wisely.

CRYSTALS AND GEMSTONES

Jasper awakens the knowledge that each individual exists to fulfill his or her purpose. This stone commands the ego to move forth and carry out the soul's mission with confidence.

NOTABLES ON THIS KARMIC PATH

QUEEN ELIZABETH I

Daughter of Henry VIII who beheaded her mother Anne Boleyn, **Queen Elizabeth I** of England grew up in a dangerous atmosphere of intrigue that forced her to mask her true feelings in order to survive. She acceded to the throne after her sister Mary's death. More than fulfilling her destiny, Elizabeth was able to step into the spotlight and become a great leader, steering a skillful course in both foreign and domestic affairs, presiding over considerable economic growth and military victories during her reign. A truly unusual personality, Elizabeth enjoyed the affection of her people despite religious turmoil in England and her refusal to marry or produce an heir.

MADAME HELENA BLAVATSKY

Born in Ukraine, **Madame Helena Blavatsky** married a Russian general and attempted to settle down to life as a housewife. Before long, she was forced to realize how different she was from those around her, prompting her to leave her husband and travel for many years pursuing her interest in Eastern religions. In the United States, she cofounded the Theosophical Society. For years Blavatsky worked to express metaphysical principles, thereby acting as the forerunner of many twentieth-century New Age thinkers. A highly original thinker, her introduction of Egyptian, Tibetan, and Indian occultism into modern thought proved highly influential.

DAVID GEFFEN

Confident billionaire **David Geffen** boldly joined film director Steven Spielberg and former Disney executive David Katzenberg to form the highly controversial media conglomerate Dreamworks SKG. Geffen first founded Asylum Records and then in 1980, he founded his independent label, Geffen Records, and built the company with acts such as Aerosmith, Don Henley, Counting Crows, Beck, and Hole. He has shown great generosity and a strong desire to help others (as is characteristic of this path) through his support of the Gay Men's Health Crisis organization and by financing the construction of the David Geffen Center for HIV Prevention and Health Education.

Other Notables: James Clavell, Billy Kidd, Cornelius Vanderbilt, Leon Uris, Stephen Cannell, George Benson, Ozzie Nelson, John Major, Bob Woodward, Henry Cabot Lodge, Joe Namath, Harry F. Byrd, Charles Saatchi, Venus Williams, Tom Landry, Truman Capote, Jimmy Carter, Charlton Heston, Lee Iacocca, Wynton Marsalis, K. D. Lang, Nadia Comaneci, Scott Joplin, Meg Ryan, Howard Hughes, Aristotle Onassis, Jim Carrey, George Harrison, Bugsy Siegel, Bobby Fischer, Marc Chagall

BIRTHDAYS ON KARMIC PATH 44

March 20, 1887–August 7, 1887 | October 30, 1905–March 20, 1906 | June 10, 1924–October 29, 1924

January 21, 1943–June 10, 1943 | September 1, 1961–January 20, 1962

April 13, 1980–August 31, 1980 | November 23, 1998–April 13, 1999 | July 4, 2017–November 22, 2017

KARMIC PATH
44

March 19–24

REBIRTH
PISCES–ARIES CUSP

Those born in this period may experience difficulty in acquiring the level of personal confidence and self-esteem implied on this karmic path. Though they may well be passionate and straightforward, their inner lives can be marked be chronic self-suspicion, or what they may consider unrealistic dreams. Developing the strength and sense of self to follow their hearts and play their hunches will prove especially important for these people, as will the ability to serve as examples or role models for others. Most of all, they will have to work on resolving some inner conflicts before they really blossom here. Yet when they allow their sense of passion to guide them and take care to avoid personal touchiness, they gravitate quite naturally to the role of head of groups and family. Their sense of the larger issues, together with their ability to serve as loving examples to others, will allow them to shine as they make their way along this karmic path.

CHALLENGE: **BEING A LITTLE LESS OUTSPOKEN UNTIL THEY ARE MORE SURE OF THEMSELVES**

FULFILLMENT: **VIEWING THOSE THEY LEAD AS AN EXTENDED FAMILY**

NOTABLES: **FATTY ARBUCKLE (SILENT FILM STAR; COMEDIAN); GEORGE BENSON (JAZZ GUITARIST)**

**COMMODORE
MATTHEW PERRY**
U.S. naval officer opened
Japan to U.S. trade in 1854

4/10/1794
Aries II

March 25–April 2

THE CHILD
ARIES I

Those born in the Week of the Child who navigate the Way of Confidence can experience considerable success and fulfillment along the road as their naturally fiery energy and enthusiasm will be great assets in their quest to overcome personal insecurity. There is a danger, however, that these curious people will remain the eternal butterflies, always searching but never finding their truest roles. In fact, some can avoid commitments and the responsibility of leadership for fear that they will not be adequate to the demands placed upon them. Yet they have an innate need to be taken seriously that will serve them in wonderful stead along this path. Avoiding the dangers of isolation and fear of commitment and realizing that their eternal fascination for the unusual may lead them away from their real opportunities for growth and success will ensure that all will go brilliantly here.

CHALLENGE: **REJECTING THE NEGATIVE SCRIPTS FROM CHILDHOOD**

FULFILLMENT: **INITIATING CHANGE AND ACTION OR ESTABLISHING A VENTURE**

NOTABLES: **BOB WOODWARD (JOURNALIST; UNCOVERED WATERGATE SCANDAL); JOHN MAJOR (BRITISH PRIME MINISTER); CHRISTOPHER WALKEN (ACTOR; OSCAR FOR *THE DEER HUNTER*)**

April 3–10

THE STAR
ARIES II

If they can bring themselves to accept the responsibilities inherent in real leadership, Aries II individuals can expect wonderful success in the course of this life's journey. Blessed with considerable charisma, they may nevertheless have a few problems when it comes to really embracing their own individuality and may get caught up in trying to please others or the need to be accepted at any cost. Though hard workers, and capable of putting much effort into achieving their goals and aspirations, they may refuse the higher levels of both empathy and commitment that beckon here. Yet if they can manage to avoid extremes and cultivate within themselves the capacity for concentrated effort and at the same time nurture their need for others, they will successfully set aside their personal insecurities and be able to bask in the glow of their ability to lead others to the larger good.

CHALLENGE: **SETTING THE GOOD OF THE GROUP AHEAD OF SELFISH CONCERNS**

FULFILLMENT: **WORKING SIDE BY SIDE WITH OTHERS FOR A CAUSE**

NOTABLES: **WILLIAM WELCH (PATHOLOGIST, BACTERIOLOGIST; HELPED ESTABLISH ROCKEFELLER INSTITUTE); MICHAEL BENNETT (BROADWAY CHOREOGRAPHER, *A CHORUS LINE*)**

WILLIAM KIDD
1st American male to win
a medal in Alpine skiing,
1964 Olympics

4/13/1943
Aries III

April 11–18

THE PIONEER
ARIES III

Those born in the Week of the Pioneer who find themselves on the Way of Confidence are likely to experience wonderful success here, providing they do not fall into the trap of putting abstractions over personal considerations. These are idea people, easily caught up in the vision of the moment and much inclined to force their notions on others. Yet here they will doubtless receive an education in the workings of power when mere force of will fails to bring others around to their way of thinking. They will likely be social in the extreme, regularly aligning themselves with groups, families and larger networks. These individuals would do well to use their experience to give them the confidence to assume the roles of leadership this path requires. Even so, they have a rare combination of idealism and strength which will inspire many as they make their way along this karmic path.

CHALLENGE: **NOT LETTING OTHERS TAKE ADVANTAGE OF THEIR GENEROSITY**

FULFILLMENT: **CONVEYING THEIR CONSCIENCE AND DEPTH OF COMMITMENT TO OTHERS**

April 19–24
POWER
ARIES–TAURUS CUSP

Those born on the Cusp of Power who travel the Way of Confidence are likely to prove themselves real forces to be reckoned with in the course of this life's journey. Here the natural energies of the Aquarius III roots of this karmic path are considerably steadied, while at the same time it gives Aries–Tauruses a much more unique and original set of ambitions than they might have otherwise. The combination of strength and originality, along with a unique sense of timing can make for some truly powerful and accomplished individuals. Yet their amazing strengths will also indicate some weaknesses, principal of which will be their tendency to ruthless tactics, intolerant attitudes toward others, and an often overwhelming selfishness. The experience of love and being loved will do much to soften these rather crusty individuals. If they can avoid seeing their loved ones as mere extensions of their own egos, and learn to better empathize with others' needs, they can step into the roles that await them with self-assurance, self-knowledge, and considerable pride.

ROBERT C. WRIGHT
Chief executive officer,
NBC

4/23/1943
Aries–Taurus Cusp

CHALLENGE: **PUTTING THEIR NEED FOR POWER IN PERSPECTIVE BEFORE THEY ASSUME POSITIONS OF RESPONSIBILITY**
FULFILLMENT: **USING THEIR HIGHLY REFINED SENSE OF TIMING WHEN TAKING ACTIONS OR ISSUING ORDERS**
NOTABLES: **HERVÉ VILLECHAIZE (ACTOR, *FANTASY ISLAND*); TONY ESPOSITO (HOCKEY GOALIE)**

April 25–May 2
MANIFESTATION
TAURUS I

Those born in the Week of Manifestation who journey along the Way of Confidence may be loath to disturb their personal habits and routines to the extent that they may fail the higher challenge of committed leadership of others. Thus many here will prefer to serve as examples or role models rather than as authority figures. Blessed with a great gift for structure and organization, they can have brilliant organizational abilities, yet may leave the laurels for others. Some here will be especially reluctant to address the issues of their own originality and may exert needless energy in simply trying to be the proverbial square pegs in round holes or trying to preserve a largely illusory sense of "security." If these people can nurture their own inclinations to teamwork, group effort, and a more nurturing and less self-protective approach to life in general, they will accomplish both a high level of professional achievement and a measure of personal peace as well.

CHALLENGE: **COMPROMISING THEIR NEED FOR HARMONY IN ORDER TO MAKE DECISIONS OR EFFECT CHANGE**
FULFILLMENT: **FEELING SECURE ENOUGH TO WILLINGLY BE EXAMPLES FOR OTHERS**
NOTABLE: **VERNON CASTLE (CHAMPION BALLROOM DANCER; AVIATOR)**

May 3–10
THE TEACHER
TAURUS II

Those born in the Week of the Teacher who navigate the Way of Confidence can enjoy really brilliant success, providing they allow their own unique vision and sense of self to blossom and avoid the inclination to blend in with the crowd or otherwise keep up the pretense that they are ill-equipped for the role that fate provides them. Likely to be dynamic and magnetic individuals, they will display a deep desire to learn, and an equal desire to educate others. The key to their effectiveness in either role, however, will likely lie in their willingness to stand up and be counted for their own unique ideas and points of view and to refuse to be intimidated or corrupted by the need for approval. Yet there is the promise of enormous success with this configuration, and if they can successfully use their talents for communicating abstract ideas in practical terms, they can win the support and admiration of many they meet along the way.

MICHAEL PALIN
Writer; actor,
*Monty Python's Flying
Circus*

5/5/1943
Taurus II

CHALLENGE: **NOT ALLOWING INSECURITY TO BE THEIR DRIVING FORCE**
FULFILLMENT: **BEING THE CENTRAL AND MOST AUTHORITATIVE FIGURES IN THEIR GROUPS**
NOTABLES: **NICHOLAS ASHFORD (SINGER/SONGWRITER, ASHFORD AND SIMPSON, "REACH OUT AND TOUCH"); SIR THOMAS LIPTON (BROUGHT LIPTON TEA TO UNITED STATES FROM BRITAIN)**

May 11–18
THE NATURAL
TAURUS III

Though at their core the personalities born in the Week of the Natural who travel the Way of Confidence will always be rugged individualists, they may experience a struggle in the process of gathering the self-assurance to show their truest colors to the world. Security issues can be a big stumbling block here, and some may squander their energies in needless rebellion, while others will manifest a deep desire to "keep their heads down and their noses clean" in the interest of trying to fit in. In either case, there will be a strong predisposition to keep their relationships rather superficial, and most will have to work hard to develop trust in themselves and others. Yet if they nurture within themselves a flair for the unusual, a love of fun, and the ability to create and rise to their own challenges, their lives and abilities will doubtless serve as inspirations for others in the course of this life's journey.

CHALLENGE: **RECOGNIZING THAT SOME OF THEIR REBELLIOUSNESS AGAINST AUTHORITY MAY BE A DESIRE FOR SOME OF THEIR OWN**
FULFILLMENT: **TURNING WHAT IS UNIQUE ABOUT THEM TO THEIR ADVANTAGE**
NOTABLE: **HENRY CABOT LODGE (U.S. SENATOR; OPPOSED WWI PEACE TREATY)**

May 19–24
ENERGY
TAURUS–GEMINI CUSP

Charming and dynamic, those born on the Cusp of Energy who journey along the Way of Confidence have a brash and devil-may-care attitude that may well belie the true condition of their inner worlds, which can be in a constant state of psychic disarray. Though talented in the extreme, these people may nevertheless have a difficult time with the responsibilities of leadership and self-assurance and may display a rather manic resistance to fulfilling even the most mundane obligations. Others will scatter their energies in a wealth of superficial interests and contacts and concentrate on the need for approval at the expense of real sincerity. Yet if they come to understand that at the heart of their quest is the need to display their strengths and devotion to others, without regard to the need for validation, their travels will be considerably eased and their progress to fulfillment much clarified as they make their way along this karmic path.

GEORGE III
King of England during the American Revolution losing the British colonies

6/4/1738
Gemini II

CHALLENGE: **GROWING UP ENOUGH TO ASSUME SOME RESPONSIBILITY**
FULFILLMENT: **ENJOYING BEING EXAMPLES FOR OTHERS**
NOTABLES: **TOMMY JOHN (BASEBALL PITCHER); ELIZABETH WILLIAMS (IRISH CIVIL RIGHTS LEADER)**

May 25–June 2
FREEDOM
GEMINI I

The unique personalities born in the Week of Freedom who find themselves on this karmic path can do quite well along the Way of Confidence, providing they direct their natural dislike of oppression and exploitation into a broader sphere, and bring others to their cause with their talents for communication, charm, and inspiration. They will find themselves swimming against the current, however, if they allow personal touchiness or insecurity to surface in combative tendencies that will only to serve to alienate those they would most like to bring closer. Developing a more directed approach to their plans and schemes will enable them to develop greater self-confidence, as will the willingness to share their unique gifts in a spirit of generous understanding. Yet if they take care not to scatter their energies and manage to find the middle road between a sense of restriction and a larger sense of purpose, all will go well here.

CHALLENGE: **CULTIVATING STEADINESS AND CONSISTENCY OF PURPOSE**
FULFILLMENT: **INFLUENCING OTHERS THROUGH CHARM**
NOTABLES: **JOE NAMATH (JETS FOOTBALL QUARTERBACK; "BROADWAY JOE"); JOSEPH GUILLOTIN (FRENCH PHYSICIAN; PROPOSED EXECUTION BY DECAPITATION); CORNELIUS VANDERBILT (FINANCIER; MADE FORTUNE IN SHIPPING AND STOCK MARKET)**

June 3–10
NEW LANGUAGE
GEMINI II

Those born in the Week of New Language who find themselves on the Way of Confidence may be marked by a tendency to bury or obscure their original and compelling ideas in an excess of verbiage. They may sidestep the real issues and use their charms to win over people they could just as well do without. The need to communicate may be at war with an innate desire for self-protection here and the results can be people who are prone to speak a great deal, but who nevertheless reveal very little of their truest desires or inclinations. Though they will know how to dazzle, they may not necessarily know how to be themselves—even in the company of friends, family, or close associates. Yet if they cultivate real honesty, they may find that the less said, the better, as their best talents and unique sense of purpose begin to manifest.

VENUS WILLIAMS
Teen tennis champion

6/17/1980
Gemini III

CHALLENGE: **FIGURING OUT HOW TO ARTICULATE THEIR VISION IN WAYS THAT WILL CAUSE OTHERS TO FOLLOW THEM**
FULFILLMENT: **FINDING THAT THEY ARE COMFORTABLE IN THEIR OWN SKINS**
NOTABLES: **RUTH BENEDICT (ANTHROPOLOGIST); CHARLES SAATCHI (COFOUNDER ADVERTISING AGENCY SAATCHI & SAATCHI); HARRY F. BYRD (U.S. SENATOR AND GOVERNOR OF VIRGINIA)**

June 11–18
THE SEEKER
GEMINI III

Those born in the Week of the Seeker who navigate the challenge and promise of the Way of Confidence can be greatly aided in their quest for self-acceptance and self-assurance by an inborn sense of adventure. No matter what challenges confront them, they are possessed of an admirable ability to take risks—even when those risks involve revealing their truest natures and purposes to others. Highly versatile, they will nevertheless have to be on guard against the tendency to go off in a completely different direction just as they get ready to step into roles of leadership or greater responsibility. Indeed, they have a dislike of being tied down that may work against their higher development here. Yet if they can discover those things that awaken their sense of emotional or idealistic commitment while at the same time allowing them room to breathe, their sheer appetite for life can make for a memorable journey along this karmic path.

CHALLENGE: **POKING AROUND IN OTHERS' LIVES A BIT LESS**
FULFILLMENT: **TAKING OTHERS ALONG ON THEIR JOURNEYS AS GUESTS FOR ADVENTURE**
NOTABLES: **BARTOLOMEO VANZETTI (ITALIAN POLITICAL ACTIVIST; EXECUTED FOR MURDER); GEORGE BUSH (41ST U.S. PRESIDENT)**

June 19–24
MAGIC
GEMINI–CANCER CUSP

Those born on the Cusp of Magic are sure to be blessed with an undeniably unique vision that will require some encouragement and dedicated action before they really blossom along this karmic path. Yet all the indications here point to a really successful journey, as these personalities have a certain amount of natural faith that will serve them especially well here. Though the struggle to overcome personal insecurity will not be easy, they are blessed with a natural objectivity that can come to their aid in even the worst nadirs of depression or the most consuming of personal crises. The tendency to isolate themselves from others is a danger, for they will never learn the power of their own capacity for leadership if they shut themselves off from the possibility of acceptance. Learning to share their views in a spirit of generous and compassionate understanding will do much to reassure these sensitive people, as will nurturing within themselves their deepest need to dedicate their lives to a higher sense of purpose.

MARC CHAGALL
Artist, surrealist painter

7/7/1887
Cancer II

CHALLENGE: **VIEWING WHAT THEY PERCEIVE AS INADEQUACIES AS ASSETS**
FULFILLMENT: **MESMERIZING THEIR COHORTS AS THEY LEAD THEM TO THEIR GOAL**
NOTABLES: **CHET ATKINS (GUITAR PLAYER); AUDIE MURPHY (MOST DECORATED WWII U.S. SOLDIER-TURNED-ACTOR)**

June 25–July 2
THE EMPATH
CANCER I

The sensitive and trusting souls born in this week who journey along the Way of Confidence may have to overcome the tendency to be shrinking violets. Highly emotional, they will need to develop the personal strength to separate their opinions and feelings from others' in order to better analyze and control their own. Yet it is likely that they will eventually gain the confidence and sense of faith in themselves they require to step into roles of leadership, or if that proves too much, display a rare ability to lead by example, serving as inspiring role models for others. Cancer individuals with this configuration may have unreasonable fears of their own sensitivity. Yet once they comprehend that both their amazing capacity for empathy and their overall life experience are sources of great strength rather than weakness, they can display a rare and generous attitude toward others that is all the more valuable because it integrates strength and inspiration with real compassion.

CHALLENGE: **DESENSITIZING THEMSELVES TO WHAT OTHERS THINK**
FULFILLMENT: **FINDING AN OUTLET FOR THEIR NATURAL INITIATIVE AND ASSERTION**
NOTABLES: **GEORGE ABBOTT (PLAYWRIGHT, DIRECTOR); SIDNEY LUMET (FILM DIRECTOR, *NETWORK*)**

July 3–10
THE UNCONVENTIONAL
CANCER II

Those born in the Week of The Unconventional who find themselves on the Way of Confidence may prove to be their own worst enemies if they do not learn to share their more imaginative and creative gifts with the larger world. Too often these individuals can confine themselves to dull jobs or boring routines in vain attempts at conformity and hold back their best gifts in the mistaken belief that if anyone knew the truth about their fantasy-rich inner lives, acceptance would be impossible. Yet despite some rather self-destructive impulses to the contrary, they will doubtless come to terms with the fact that in the end, they must face the truth about themselves. Once they embrace and learn to celebrate their uniqueness and find the strength to stand up and be counted for who and what they are, they may well be surprised by the degree of admiration, acceptance, and authority they are able to inspire as they travel this karmic path.

MICHELLE KWAN
American Olympic skater

7/7/1980
Cancer II

CHALLENGE: **BECOMING BETTER STRATEGIC THINKERS IN ORDER TO PUT THEIR VISION INTO ACTION**
FULFILLMENT: **WORKING WITH OTHERS WHO SHARE THEIR GOALS OR ASPIRATIONS**
NOTABLE: **LOUIE BELLSON (JAZZ DRUMMER; BANDLEADER)**

July 11–18
THE PERSUADER
CANCER III

Persuaders who travel the Way of Confidence can enjoy some wonderful moments along this life's journey as here some natural talents for administration and leadership will find fulfillment. What they will have to be careful to avoid, however, is a tendency to project some of their more original and unique impulses onto others, or to let other people take the credit for their own accomplishments in an attempt to win approval or gain acceptance. The result can be their indulgence in a kind of chronic emotional blackmail that will work against their best interests and higher development. They are so able to control their own needs that they may be quite careless of the needs of other people and use their knowledge of human psychology and the workings of power as purely manipulative tools. Yet if they can manage to integrate self-respect and self-esteem into their individual game plans, the respect and admiration of others are sure to follow as they make their way to the sense of greater authority and leadership called for on this path.

CHALLENGE: **BELIEVING IN THEIR HEARTS THAT THEY DESERVE TO LEAD**
FULFILLMENT: **BEING RECOGNIZED AND REWARDED FOR THEIR EFFORTS**
NOTABLE: **BESS MYERSON (1ST JEWISH MISS AMERICA)**

July 19–25

OSCILLATION
CANCER–LEO CUSP

Those born on the Cusp of Oscillation who make their way along the Way of Confidence will have to work to accept their highly charged emotional natures and a tendency to wild swings of mood if they are to gain the levels of self-esteem and assurance that are implied here. Cultivating personal discipline will prove particularly important for these individuals, and they will do well to surround themselves with those who have a genuine faith in their ability to succeed on their own terms, rather than those who would diminish or disapprove of them for an inability to fit in. Once they understand that their greatest strengths lie in their dauntlessness and moral courage and not in their ability to suppress their emotions and passions under a mantle of dreary and unfulfilling conformity, they will be able to take up the higher challenge to leadership with grace, self-assurance, and a dash of genuine creative inspiration.

CHALLENGE: **TEMPERING THE PROPENSITY TO TAKE UNDUE RISKS OUT OF INSECURITY**

FULFILLMENT: **FINDING THE CONFIDENCE TO PURSUE THEIR CREATIVE VISION**

NOTABLE: **ELIAS SARKIS (PRESIDENT OF LEBANON)**

MARCEL DUCHAMP
Dada artist

7/28/1887
Leo I

July 26–August 2

AUTHORITY
LEO I

Those born in the Week of Authority who travel the Way of Confidence are likely to relish the process here, since their natural temperament and inclinations are very much in keeping with the path to leadership. Though it is unlikely that they will do much hand-wringing or agonizing over the fact that they are "different" from other people or their society, they will do well to keep in mind that such issues can hold them back from taking risks or raising the bar of their ambitions on a more unconscious level. Thus coming to terms with the restrictions and restraints of an early environment may prove important, as will their ability to be able to challenge themselves even when no one else will. If they can learn to acquaint themselves with their own vulnerabilities and at the same time share their inspirations and capacity for devotion with others, all will go brilliantly here.

CHALLENGE: **RESTRAINING THEIR NEED FOR ADMIRATION AND REINFORCEMENT**

FULFILLMENT: **FIRING THE ENGINES OF GROUP ENDEAVORS AND THEIR PARTICIPANTS**

NOTABLES: **VINCENT CANBY (NEW YORK TIMES FILM CRITIC); CARROLL O'CONNOR (ACTOR, ALL IN THE FAMILY)**

August 3–10

BALANCED STRENGTH
LEO II

The personalities born in the Week of Balanced Strength have the highest potential for self-realization and enlightenment as they make their way along this karmic path, yet they will have to be attentive to the higher calling to leadership that beckons here. Indeed many of these single-minded people may be so into doing their own thing or marching to the beat of their own drum that they fail to open up and share themselves in such a way that their talents and strengths can be recognized. Though some with this configuration will have no apparent concern for worldly success, others will be competitive in the extreme. In either case, the key to higher development will lie in their ability to devote themselves to those causes and principles that motivate them to get outside of their own interests and step into roles in which they can motivate and inspire others. If they can overcome the pitfalls of self-absorption and embrace the opportunities for self-enhancement and expansion that beckon here, they will go further than they ever believed possible in the course of this life's journey.

CHALLENGE: **DAMPING THEIR TENDENCY TO SACRIFICE THEMSELVES FOR OTHERS**

FULFILLMENT: **CHAMPIONING THOSE LESS FORTUNATE, THEIR FAVORITE CAUSES, OR PET PROJECTS**

JAMES BALDWIN
Black writer,
Blues for Mister Charlie

8/2/1924
Leo I

August 11–18

LEADERSHIP
LEO III

Blessed with an expansive, heroic, and original vision, those born in this week who travel the Way of Confidence are likely to experience a fruitful and fulfilling journey, so long as they do not turn away from the challenge to assume roles of leadership or seek to abuse their power over others. Charismatic, dynamic, and action oriented, these passionate people may have one principal fault—and that is a rather chronic failure to adequately consider the needs of others. These people may indeed be so intent on proving themselves that they become obsessed with their worldly image and ever-expanding power base, becoming autocratic, demanding, and dictatorial. Yet if they keep in mind that leadership is a fairly empty concept unless one has followers to inspire, and remember to indulge the impulse to include others in their plans, dreams, and schemes, they are assured of brilliant success and considerable accomplishment as they make their way along this road.

CHALLENGE: **DEALING WITH FEELINGS OF INADEQUACY RATHER THAN PROJECTING THEM**

FULFILLMENT: **SENSING THAT THEY MAKE A DIFFERENCE**

NOTABLES: **ROBERT BOLT (PLAYWRIGHT, SCREENWRITER; OSCAR FOR DR. ZHIVAGO; ANTINUCLEAR ACTIVIST); PHYLLIS SCHLAFLY (RIGHT-WING CONSERVATIVE ACTIVIST)**

August 19–25

EXPOSURE
LEO–VIRGO CUSP

Early feelings of insecurity and low self-worth may cause the individuals born on the Cusp of Exposure to withdraw from the higher challenge implied on the Way of Confidence into a secretive and nonsharing approach to the rest of the world. These souls are apt to try ferreting out other people's feelings and purposes before revealing their own. Yet it is likely that fate will step in to take a hand when they fail to accept the opportunities for command that present themselves along this journey, for this is a configuration that indicates any number of dark-horse candidates and meteoric rises to success. While no one can be promised fame or fortune, even the most retiring, unusual, or irascible of these highly private individuals can succeed in roles behind the scenes if they allow their natural sense of integrity, their unique vision, and their solid knowledge of the workings of power, politics, and ethics to serve as examples for other travelers whom they meet along the way.

CHALLENGE: **RISING TO THE OPPORTUNITIES PRESENTED TO THEM**

FULFILLMENT: **EMERGING FROM BEHIND THEIR DEFENSES IN A BLAZE OF GLORY**

NOTABLE: **LOUIS TEICHER (PIANIST, COMPOSER)**

MACAULAY CULKIN
Child actor, *Home Alone*

8/26/1980
Virgo I

August 26–September 2

SYSTEM BUILDERS
VIRGO I

Here some earthy and practical energies are enhanced and augmented by the unusually creative and abstract vision of the Aquarius III roots of this karmic path. Thus those born in the Week of System Builders will no doubt take great enjoyment from seeing their plans, inspirations, and schemes come into fruitful and productive manifestation. They may falter a bit, however, when it comes to the higher challenge of stepping into the role of confident leadership indicated here, as these rather modest people often incline to take a back seat or defer taking proper credit for their accomplishments. Yet they will do quite beautifully in groups and organizations and will do well to support their sometimes shaky egos with people, friends, and family who appreciate their dependability and sense of structure. If they accept the growing sense of confidence and command that will doubtless come with the passage of years, they can do a great deal to teach us all the truth of the maxim: "To rule is to serve."

CHALLENGE: **NOT SEEING THEMSELVES AS FLAWED**

FULFILLMENT: **SERVING AS EXAMPLES OR ROLE MODELS, PARTICULARLY WHEN DOING GOOD WORKS**

NOTABLE: **DINAH WASHINGTON (JAZZ VOCALIST)**

September 3–10

THE ENIGMA
VIRGO II

Those born in the Week of the Enigma who journey along the Way of Confidence can realize wonderful success and fulfillment in the course of this passage as they are a fine combination of charm, discernment, and strength of character. Much more inclined to implementation than initiation, however, they will have to work to overcome their need to conform and must divest themselves of a preoccupation with others' opinions if they are to be really successful here. Yet they are gifted with both personal strength and moral acuity. If they can access their deepest sources of inspiration and self-expression, they will accept the challenge to greater responsibility and leadership with a fair measure of grace, an insistence on high standards, and a flair for original planning that can take them to the top, should they care to go.

CHALLENGE: **FINDING THE CONFIDENCE TO REVEAL THEIR MORAL CENTER AND SHOW OTHERS THEIR OWN**

FULFILLMENT: **FEELING SOMEWHAT WARM AND PARENTAL TOWARD THEIR CHARGES**

NOTABLE: **DANIEL INOUYE (DEMOCRATIC SENATOR FROM HAWAII)**

TOM LANDRY
Legendary head coach of
Dallas Cowboys

9/11/1924
Virgo III

September 11–18

THE LITERALIST
VIRGO III

The need for greater self-realization, self-esteem, and a sense of control may well exist at odds with the Virgo III innate need for harmony and some rather self-effacing and defeatist attitudes toward fulfillment. Many here will shore up their sense of self through the mastery of craft or a growing dedication to a profession. On-the-job training and self-education are thus likely to figure prominently in their quest for self-fulfillment. Yet whatever their skills, when the call to assume a mantle of leadership comes and they are thrust into the spotlight in some fashion, most will be wholly unprepared, and some will shy away unless that role also offers them a practical advantage of some kind. If they take care to better acquaint themselves with the sometimes terrifying or unfamiliar landscape of their own emotions, they will find the strength to face down even the worst of personal demons as they make their way along this road.

CHALLENGE: **PROBING THEIR OWN SENSITIVITY TO CRITICISM BEFORE THEY ARE IN A POSITION TO CRITICIZE OTHERS**

FULFILLMENT: **DISCOVERING THEY POSSESS THE INNER STRENGTH TO LEAD**

NOTABLES: **LAUREN BACALL (ACTRESS, TONY FOR *WOMAN OF THE YEAR*); MAURICE JARRÉ (COMPOSER, SCORE FOR *DR. ZHIVAGO*)**

September 19–24
BEAUTY
VIRGO–LIBRA CUSP

The gifted and unique individuals who travel the Way of Confidence can enjoy both the best and the worst of times in the course of this life's journey. Likely to be lively, inventive, and thoroughly charming, these people may find this to be a configuration more oriented to socializing than it is to leading. In fact they may have a rather superficial side, and are inclined on the one hand to go with the flow, while on the other may yearn for the spotlight. Yet once they determine that the world is not necessarily going to beat a path to their door, and allow themselves to back up their natural talents with some dedicated effort, the devotion to a profession, talent, or creative endeavor is sure to meet with the stamp of approval. If they can better integrate aspiration and expectation with determination and sustained effort, their work will not go unrewarded as they make their way along this karmic path.

CHALLENGE: **CHECKING THEIR DESIRE TO FORCE THEIR OPINIONS ON OTHERS**

FULFILLMENT: **SHARING THEIR LOVE OF BEAUTY**

NOTABLES: **GAIL RUSSELL (ACTRESS; "HOLLYWOOD'S HAUNTED HEROINE"); ERIC STOLTZ (ACTOR, *MASK*); SHEILA MacRAE (ACTRESS; ORIGINAL ALICE KRAMDEN)**

CHARLTON HESTON
Actor, *Ten Commandments*;
president of NRA

10/4/1924
Libra II

September 25–October 2
THE PERFECTIONIST
LIBRA I

The souls born in this week who navigate the Way of Confidence can do quite well along this road, yet they will first have to face down not their notions of perfection, but their sense of personal imperfection before they can rise to the challenges indicated here. Likely to be highly goal and achievement oriented, they can nevertheless do themselves a great disservice if they project some personal anxieties onto the rest of the world and mask an essential indecisiveness under a barrage of criticism. Yet this path gifts them with both greater charm and more sociability than they might have otherwise. If they can learn to open up to others and share their emotions before their feelings reach "critical mass" and channel their natural energy into some larger purpose, rather than allowing themselves to get hung up on the details, life will be wonderfully rewarding here.

CHALLENGE: **ACCEPTING THE IDEA THAT SETTING THEMSELVES APART FROM OTHERS HOLDS THEM BACK**

FULFILLMENT: **DISCOVERING THE POWER RUSH THAT DECISIVENESS CAN BE**

NOTABLES: **TRUMAN CAPOTE (WRITER, *IN COLD BLOOD*); JIMMY CARTER (39TH U.S. PRESIDENT); HEATHER LOCKLEAR (ACTRESS, *MELROSE PLACE*); MARCELLO MASTROIANNI (ACTOR, *LA DOLCE VITA*)**

October 3–10
SOCIETY
LIBRA II

Those born in the Week of Society may have a rather difficult journey along the Way of Confidence until they come to better terms with the workings of their own psyches. In fact, some of this group will content themselves with being the proverbial "social butterflies" and squander their talents and energies in a rather superficial view of life. Others will be preoccupied with the need to conform or fit in with their environments to the detriment of their higher development. The tendency to approval seeking is also especially strong, and some of these individuals will deliberately allow themselves to be unduly dominated if they feel they are loved. Yet they have considerable insights into the follies and foibles of the human condition, and if they can only turn their capacity for insight into real self-knowledge and direct their energies to some coherent purpose, life is sure to reward them for their efforts as they make their way along this karmic path.

CHALLENGE: **BEING WILLING TO STEP OUT AHEAD OF THE PACK**

FULFILLMENT: **TAKING THEIR OWN DESIRES AND ASPIRATIONS MORE SERIOUSLY**

NOTABLE: **JAMES CLAVELL (AUTHOR, *SHŌGUN*)**

WYNTON MARSALIS
Jazz/classical trumpeter

10/18/1961
Libra III

October 11–18
THEATER
LIBRA III

Those born in the Week of Theater who navigate the challenge and promise of this destiny path can expect a fine and fulfilling journey, as these worldly and hard driving individuals aren't likely to lose much sleep over what others may think of them or falter too much in their quest for personal achievement and success. Where they will stumble, however, is in their tendency to be cold, unfeeling, and lacking in empathy for those around them. They can be rather loath to share their inner lives and shut people out without really intending to do so. Yet they have a fine ability to learn on their feet and adapt once they discern the error of their ways. If they do not allow themselves to collapse into cynicism on the one hand, or the need to dominate on the other, they can employ their fine persuasive talents and considerable vision to the tasks of leading others with vision, understanding, and a real sense of hope.

CHALLENGE: **ADMITTING TO THEIR MISTAKES RATHER THAN STICKING TO THEM**

FULFILLMENT: **PLAYING TO A BIGGER AUDIENCE OR ON A LARGER STAGE**

NOTABLES: **ISAAC MIZRAHI (FASHION DESIGNER); CHARLES SUMNER GREENE (AMERICAN ARCHITECT); LEE IACOCCA (CHAIRMAN OF CHRYSLER CORP.)**

October 19–25

DRAMA AND CRITICISM
LIBRA–SCORPIO CUSP

For those born on the Cusp of Drama and Criticism who travel the Way of Confidence, trying to keep their uniqueness under wraps will be much like trying to hide an elephant under a handkerchief. Like it or not, they will be noticed, celebrated, and occasionally even reviled as they make their way along this karmic path. Charming, versatile, and compelling in the extreme, what matters most to the higher development of these people will be their ability not to fall for their own press releases and keep a firm hold on some larger sense of purpose. They will face the additional challenge of learning to manage their tendencies to become rather cold and calculating in their dealings with others. Yet they have considerable personal, intellectual, and emotional powers at their disposal; if they are careful not to abuse them and hold always to a higher set of principles, their lives and efforts can make a real mark along this karmic path.

CHALLENGE: **DEALING WITH THE EMOTIONAL SENSITIVITY THAT CAN PREVENT THEIR LEADING OTHERS EFFECTIVELY**

FULFILLMENT: **INSPIRING OTHERS THROUGH WORDS OR EXAMPLE**

NOTABLE: **OSBORN ELLIOT (EDITOR, *NEWSWEEK*)**

ALEXANDRA DAVID-NEEL
French explorer to Tibet

10/24/1868
Libra–Scorpio Cusp

October 26–November 2

INTENSITY
SCORPIO I

Those born in the Week of Intensity who find themselves on the Way of Confidence may experience their share of struggles along this karmic path. Highly emotional and polarized personalities, they may swing from one extreme to another in the search for personal approval or validation on the one hand, and power on the other. Many of these individuals have an innate distrust of others, likely the result of their own insecurity. Nevertheless, they can build real walls in their efforts at self-protection and prove to be their own worst enemies when it comes to making friends and opening their hearts. Yet they have a fine grasp of the workings of power and politics and are likely to perceive patterns in behavior that others cannot. If they can divest themselves of some of the emotional shadow areas that hold them back from inspired leadership and keep both their sense of humor and a sense of honor intact, all will go well in the course of this life's journey.

CHALLENGE: **DIGGING AT AND HEALING THE ROOTS OF THEIR INSECURITY**

FULFILLMENT: **RADIATING CHARM TO INFLUENCE AND PERSUADE OTHERS**

NOTABLES: **DYLAN MCDERMOTT (ACTOR, *THE PRACTICE*); RUBY DEE (ACTRESS, *RAISIN IN THE SUN*)**

November 3–11

DEPTH
SCORPIO II

As well acquainted as they are with the depths and heights of human emotion, Scorpio IIs may nevertheless shy away from the challenge to expansion and larger purpose that is part of the path to true leadership. Personal anxiety may well prove their biggest stumbling block, for here they are not so much plagued by a fear of what others will think as they are worried about what may happen. Basically, they don't like to make mistakes and especially not in public. Thus when the opportunities for leadership come knocking, many will be reluctant to answer the door. Still, they have the strength of their convictions to aid them, and if their hearts or sense of principle is touched sufficiently by a cause or crusade, they can rise to the occasion with grace and élan. In the meanwhile they will do well to pursue their interests with the wholehearted dedication that is their trademark, and if they can learn to unbend and open up a bit in the process, so much the better.

CHALLENGE: **BECOMING MORE COMFORTABLE IN THE PUBLIC EYE**

FULFILLMENT: **KNOWING THAT WHAT THEY DO IS FOR THE GOOD OF OTHERS**

NOTABLES: **ERIKA MANN (GERMAN AUTHOR; ACTRESS; LECTURER); JOEL MCCREA (ACTOR, BEST KNOWN FOR WESTERNS)**

K. D. LANG
Country/pop singer

11/2/1961
Scorpio I

November 12–18

CHARM
SCORPIO III

Those born in the Week of Charm who find themselves traveling this karmic path can enjoy huge success and accomplishment, providing they do not content themselves with a shallow or superficial view of the world and overcome a rather unpleasantly pronounced tendency to self-interest. Their ability to charm, persuade, cajole, and manipulate other people will be both their blessing and their curse here, for they will be so good at getting what they want, they may not bother too much to develop any real sense of integrity or moral character. Repression of their own feelings may cause them to lose touch with the people they really are inside. Yet if they can cultivate their strengths and remember to set for themselves some necessary personal and professional challenges, they will prepare themselves for the role of leadership that beckons here and prove themselves both competent and beloved in the roles fate has in store.

CHALLENGE: **UNDERSTANDING THEIR OWN ASPIRATIONS OR DESIRES**

FULFILLMENT: **DISCOVERING THEIR OWN ALTRUISM, EVEN HEROISM**

NOTABLE: **NADIA COMANECI (ROMANIAN GYMNAST, 1976 OLYMPIC GOLD MEDALIST)**

November 19–24

REVOLUTION
SCORPIO–SAGITTARIUS CUSP

A sense of higher principle or purpose will come quite naturally to the highly individualistic people born on the Cusp of Revolution, yet they will have to work hard to better direct their sometimes chaotic energies in order to be most effective here. Personal insecurity can further cause them to respond with aggression when charm and diplomatic skills are called for, and they will have to cultivate a better understanding of the principles of self-acceptance before they develop greater tolerance for others. Yet at their core, these individuals have everything they need to assume the mantle of leadership and are sure to embrace the challenges with inspiration, determination and a fine sense of personal honor and responsibility.

SCOTT JOPLIN
Composer/pianist,
father of ragtime

─────────

11/21/1868
Scorpio–Sagittarius Cusp

CHALLENGE: **COMBATTING THE TENDENCY TO BE AUTOCRATS**
FULFILLMENT: **WARMING TO THEIR AUDIENCE WITH SOME SMALL AMOUNT OF MAGNANIMITY**
NOTABLE: **MARIEL HEMINGWAY (ACTRESS, *MANHATTAN*)**

November 25–December 2

INDEPENDENCE
SAGITTARIUS I

Those born in the Week of Independence who find themselves on the Way of Confidence can enjoy brilliant success as their natural energies are very much in keeping with the higher sense of challenge and purpose that is offered here. Though some with this configuration may needlessly squander their energies through a fear of commitment and refuse to be tied down to any perceived restrictions, most will manage to overcome their more temperamental and impulsive streak with an ever-increasing understanding and a fine sense of cooperation. They possess an enormous sense of willpower that will see them through even the most strenuous stretches of this road. Once they divest themselves of the need for validation and instead turn their sights to those things that they most value, their sense of fairness will shine through and their capacity for real leadership come into full flower as they travel this remarkable road.

CHALLENGE: **OVERCOMING THEIR FEAR THAT LEADERSHIP WILL TAKE AWAY THEIR FREEDOM**
FULFILLMENT: **OPERATING FROM THEIR CODE OF HONOR OR SENSE OF JUSTICE**

December 3–10

THE ORIGINATOR
SAGITTARIUS II

Providing they manage to overcome some early feelings of rejection or personal defensiveness, those born in the Week of the Originator who negotiate the challenge and promise of the Way of Confidence can expect a highly rewarding and interesting passage. It is important that they not translate their need for acceptance into a touchy attitude toward others or the impulse to hide their lights under a bushel. Unencumbered by much of the stubbornness and authoritarian tendencies of some of their fellows along this journey, these unique people are likely to also be blessed with a unique sense of philosophical perspective and personal vision that will serve them especially well here. If they refuse to allow their sense of higher purpose to be corrupted by their need to be accepted, they can emerge from the shadows of personal insecurity into the spotlight of leadership with their originality and sense of uniqueness fully intact.

MEG RYAN
Actress,
Sleepless in Seattle

─────────

11/19/1961
Scorpio–Sagittarius Cusp

CHALLENGE: **LETTING GO OF THE FEAR OF BEING DIFFERENT**
FULFILLMENT: **EMBRACING THEIR ORIGINALITY**
NOTABLE: **DALTON TRUMBO (SCREENWRITER; AUTHOR, *JOHNNY GOT HIS GUN*)**

December 11–18

THE TITAN
SAGITTARIUS III

Beautifully suited to the Way of Confidence, those born in the Week of the Titan can expect great rewards in the course of this life's journey. Indeed, these rather heroic types may be forced to do a great deal of soul-searching in order to discover just what it is that others may expect of them, for they are possessed of such a degree of natural confidence that they are often quite bewildered when things fail to go according to plan. Yet they will doubtless be aided on this journey by an interest in broader concepts and philosophical pursuits that will serve to enhance and augment their sense of purpose. If they do not scatter their resources in dilettantism and surround themselves with those who have a better eye for the details than they do themselves, they are in for a memorable and highly effective journey as they make their way along this karmic path.

CHALLENGE: **ROOTING OUT EVEN THE MOST OBSCURE SOURCES OF THEIR INSECURITY**
FULFILLMENT: **TAKING ON LARGE-SCALE CHALLENGES OR PROJECTS**

December 19–25

PROPHECY
SAGITTARIUS–CAPRICORN CUSP

Though well-suited to the higher challenge of purpose and leadership that beckons along this road, those born on the Cusp of Prophecy may nevertheless withdraw from the opportunities presented here in a somewhat sullen or misanthropic insistence on going their own way, regardless of the needs of others. Not much inclined to care what people think, they may fancy themselves so independent that they isolate themselves unnecessarily. Failing to share their unique vision with others may hinder their higher development as well. They will do well to remember that the fundamentals of human nature are the same in everyone. If they can bring themselves to teach, if only by example, that a sense of independence need not exist at odds with the need for love and validation, all will go much more smoothly as they make their way along this karmic path.

HOWARD HUGHES
Aircraft manufacturer;
movie mogul; eccentric

12/24/1905
Sagittarius–Capricorn
Cusp

CHALLENGE: **REMEMBERING TO NURTURE AND NOURISH A PERSONAL LIFE**

FULFILLMENT: **EXPERIENCING THE EASE WITH WHICH THEY STEP INTO POSITIONS OF POWER**

NOTABLE: **HARVEY FIRESTONE (MANUFACTURER, FOUNDER, PRESIDENT, FIRESTONE TIRE AND RUBBER CO.)**

December 26–January 2

THE RULER
CAPRICORN I

Though likely to be quite comfortable in the role of leadership, overcoming domineering and inflexible tendencies in the interest of developing greater empathy and understanding may prove somewhat arduous for Capricorn I's who journey along the Way of Confidence. It is difficult for these individuals to open up in any event, and some may have a real horror of nonconformity. They may encounter problems learning to accept and better tolerate their own peculiarities and those of others, not so much because they are innately intolerant or even insecure, but because they are convinced that the best methods are those that are tried and true. Yet, for all their seeming inflexibility, it is likely that these individuals will have their hearts in the right place. Highly moral and dependable, they will oppose injustice in all its forms. If they take care not to overburden themselves with undue responsibility or the need to be accepted at the expense of developing their own strengths and pursuing their own interests, all will go brilliantly here.

CHALLENGE: **RESISTING THE DESIRE TO BLEND IN WITH THE CROWD**

FULFILLMENT: **INDULGING IN THE DRAMATIC, NOT AS A GUILTY PLEASURE, BUT AS A MEANS TO AN END**

January 3–9

DETERMINATION
CAPRICORN II

Capricorn IIs can find themselves quite happy on the Way of Confidence, and though some of these individuals will get rather a slow start out of the gate when it comes to overcoming issues of personal insecurity, most will reach their goals quite successfully. Whatever the obstacles in their path to fulfillment, these are the kind of people who gain confidence through their personal struggles and will be able to shore up their sometimes shaky sense of self through their ability to take things one day or one step at a time. Key to their development will be their willingness to divest themselves of some unnecessarily self-sacrificing tendencies and to come to better terms with their own highly original viewpoints. Yet there is nonetheless the potential for wonderful success here, and if they learn the distinction between challenging themselves to higher levels of understanding and achievement and merely beating themselves up, they can realize their fondest dreams as they make their way along this karmic path.

ARISTOTLE ONASSIS
Millionaire shipping
executive; married Jackie
Kennedy

1/15/1906
Capricorn III

CHALLENGE: **NOT BEING SO HARD ON THEMSELVES—THIS IS A FORM OF EGO TOO**

FULFILLMENT: **SUSTAINING OTHERS WITH THEIR DETERMINATION AND PERSISTENCE**

January 10–16

DOMINANCE
CAPRICORN III

Those born in the Week of Dominance who negotiate the Way of Confidence may be so plagued by secret feelings of insecurity and inferiority that they try to hide under a mask of competence, focus, and dedication. Curiously enough, it is that same impulse to "keep it together" that will work to their advantage here, for sooner or later most with this configuration will come to realize that, strangely enough, the mask has become the reality, and they will understand that, in fact, there is nothing lacking in them at all. Once freed, they will be able to better embrace their own rather outrageous side and show their uniqueness to the world. Most will attain both a much-improved level of personal confidence and some formidable leadership skills in the course of this life's journey. If they can learn to be more tolerant of life outside the mainstream, their high principles and sense of purpose will come to the fore.

CHALLENGE: **BUILDING UP THE DEPTH OF EXPERIENCE THAT CREATES TRUE SELF-CONFIDENCE**

FULFILLMENT: **SETTING THEIR ECCENTRIC SIDE FREE AND WATCHING IT WORK FOR THEM**

NOTABLES: **WILLIAM BENDIX (ACTOR, *LIFE OF RILEY*); TEX RITTER (SINGING COWBOY); JOHN WELLBORN ROOT (ARCHITECT)**

January 17–22
MYSTERY AND IMAGINATION
CAPRICORN–AQUARIUS CUSP

January 23–30
GENIUS
AQUARIUS I

As long as they develop some necessary faith in their own abilities and vision, the gifted and inspiring people born in this period can expect considerable success and fulfillment in the course of this life's journey. Yet they will have to steady their energies somewhat in order to be most effective here. Theirs is a tendency to reverse their own decisions, and they may undermine their own abilities with too great an attachment to abstraction at the expense of their sense of humanity. If they can manage to counter a certain instability with concentration and effort and surround themselves with those individuals who would respond to their unique and original vision, they can prove themselves to be beloved in the roles of leadership. They have a rare gift for inspiration and know how to get the job done with a lighthearted and easygoing management style that is more valuable for its ongoing sense of the dream and real group effort than for individual deeds.

JIM CARREY
Actor/comedian,
Ace Ventura, The Truman Show

———

1/17/1962
Capricorn–Aquarius Cusp

CHALLENGE: **AVOIDING THE TENDENCY TO FIND OTHERS TO BE PARASITIC OR LIMITING**
FULFILLMENT: **STEERING A METAPHORIC SHIP WITH EASE AND COMMAND**
NOTABLE: **JOHN CHARLES FRÉMONT (MAPPED THE OREGON TRAIL)**

Great problem solvers and wonderful thinkers, those born in the Week of Genius who travel the Way of Confidence will nevertheless have to come to terms with the reality that human emotion does not always operate according to the same laws as their often inspired, yet ultimately scientific or systematic way of looking at the world. The lessons of this path may involve any number of run-ins with authority, most of which will provide them with an ongoing education in the workings of power. Several here will face the simple fact that many of their seemingly detached and distant attitudes are attempts to dissociate from their own insecurities, and that their choices in life are based upon their often neglected emotional nature. Yet their sense of higher principle and purpose is unusually strong, and if they can hit upon the thing that will enable them to embrace their own individuality, fire their passion, and fulfill their need for acceptance, all will go smoothly here.

CHALLENGE: **NOT BEING SEDUCED BY THE LATEST ADVENTURE BUT REMAINING TRUE TO THEIR CONVICTIONS**
FULFILLMENT: **REACHING OUT TO OTHERS IN A SPIRIT OF COOPERATION**
NOTABLE: **MARTY BALIN (FOUNDING MEMBER OF THE JEFFERSON AIRPLANE)**

January 31–February 7
YOUTH AND EASE
AQUARIUS II

February 8–15
ACCEPTANCE
AQUARIUS III

Those born in this week who travel the Way of Confidence will be unlikely to experience too much in the way of secret insecurity, as they will be the kind of people who can charm the birds right out of the trees. Despite all their seeming advantages, however, they may be rather complacent or morally lazy people who fail the higher challenge to purpose, principle, and dedicated leadership, unless of course someone hands it to them on the proverbial silver platter. They will have to take real care to develop standards and to align their lives to a higher sense of calling than merely being the belle of the ball or the happy-go-lucky Peter Pan. Still, there is marvelous potential for good fortune and amazing success with this configuration. If these individuals take care to cultivate the skills, dedication, and depth that go with the challenge to leadership, they will be well prepared when opportunities to step into the spotlight come their way.

JOHN CARRADINE
Actor

———

2/5/1906
Aquarius II

CHALLENGE: **FORCING THEMSELVES NOT TO MERELY GO ALONG WITH THE CROWD BUT TO FORGE THEIR OWN PATHS**
FULFILLMENT: **BEING FREE OF CARING WHAT OTHERS THINK**
NOTABLES: **STEPHEN CANNELL (PRODUCER, *ROCKFORD FILES*); BLYTHE DANNER (ACTRESS; TONY FOR *BUTTERFLIES ARE FREE*)**

Objectivity and a genuine knowledge of self will prove the keys to success for those born in this week who journey along the Way of Confidence. In fact, many of these individuals will struggle with identity issues, not sure of what to accept or what to reject and may be easily knocked off balance by rejection or an awareness of their own vulnerability. In fact, they have a real dislike of pretension, yet may be rather pretentious themselves in their search for approval. Some will exhibit prejudice or intolerance, while others may be easygoing in the extreme. Yet all will be motivated by both the need for affection and the need to prove they are made of sterner stuff than it sometimes appears. If they can back up these inclinations with dedication, concentrated effort, and a more devoted attitude toward their purpose, their lights are likely to shine brightly in the course of this life's journey.

CHALLENGE: **RELEASING THEIR YEARNING TO BE LOVED**
FULFILLMENT: **TURNING NONATTACHMENT INTO AN ASSET OF LEADERSHIP**
NOTABLE: **JOE PESCI (ACTOR, *GOODFELLAS*)**

February 16–22

SENSITIVITY
AQUARIUS–PISCES CUSP

These individuals can do beautifully on the Way of Confidence though they will have to do a bit of soul work in order to better integrate their ambitions with their sensitivity. Personally, they are likely to have little trouble developing the necessary empathy and compassion for others that is part of this destiny, yet professionally they may have to learn to release an attitude of defensive aggression before they can realize fulfillment here. Like many who travel this road, several of their core lessons will revolve around developing a firmer belief in themselves and not being afraid or defensive. Yet they will doubtless discover a certain amount of transcendence as they attach themselves to a larger sense of purpose, and if they allow their sensitivity to others to better inform their choices, all can go wonderfully well along this karmic path.

BUGSY SIEGEL
Notorious gangster, helped organize Murder Inc., began controlled gambling in Las Vegas

2/28/1906
Pisces I

CHALLENGE: **OVERCOMING THEIR DEEP-SEATED FEAR OF REJECTION**
FULFILLMENT: **BECOMING EXAMPLES OF LOVING KINDNESS**

February 23–March 2

SPIRIT
PISCES I

Those born in the Week of Spirit have an undeniable streak of vision and originality that will be hard to keep under wraps as they make their journey along the Way of Confidence. Blessed with a rare and unique understanding of others, they may nevertheless have to cultivate greater confidence in themselves in order to realize their highest potential. Though some may retreat into irresponsibility or a preoccupation with self-interest, most have an innate desire to make the world a better place and a sense of larger purpose that will doubtless serve them especially well here. If they can avoid the pitfall of allowing their talents to be exploited while developing their practical side, they can achieve the heights of fulfillment through their big-heartedness, generosity of spirit, and innate talent for doing right simply by doing good.

CHALLENGE: **GROUNDING SOME OF THEIR IDEALISM IN PRACTICAL APPROACHES AND GOOD MANAGEMENT**
FULFILLMENT: **GIVING THEIR ALTRUISM EXPRESSION**

March 3–10

THE LONER
PISCES II

Those born in the Week of the Loner who make their way along this karmic path can realize considerable progress and fulfillment in the course of their journey. This path gifts Pisces IIs with more social inclinations and ambition than they might have otherwise, yet they will encounter their share of obstacles and challenges, not the least of which will involve overcoming feelings of low self-worth, and a generally pessimistic or downright timid attitude toward human interaction. Yet there is a soulful, devotional quality that is most pronounced here. If they can turn their attention away from purely personal problems and pursuits, and align their lives to a greater sense of faith and a higher sense of purpose, their insecurities and feeling of rejection will fall away and they will find themselves transformed by confidence, able to step into the spotlight of self-realization and fulfillment.

BOBBY FISCHER
Chess prodigy, champion

3/9/1943
Pisces II

CHALLENGE: **OVERCOMING THEIR FEAR OF BEING OSTRACIZED**
FULFILLMENT: **ALIGNING THEIR NEED TO LEAD WITH A GREATER PURPOSE**
NOTABLE: **LYNN REDGRAVE (ACTRESS, *GEORGY GIRL*)**

March 11–18

DANCERS AND DREAMERS
PISCES III

The unique and gifted personalities who travel the Way of Confidence can enjoy a richly rewarding journey, providing they develop the necessary self-knowledge to confront their fears of rejection or disapproval. Charming in the extreme, they have a real gift of gab that may nevertheless fail to amount to much unless they back up their promises with some concentrated effort. Conversely, others of this group will have to be on guard in themselves against high-handed or superior attitudes which will only serve to alienate those who would rally round their cause. Yet they have a gift for inspiration and an ability to get in touch with collective needs and desires. If they guard against irresponsibility and watch their own tendency to become thoroughly unglued in the face of crisis, they can accomplish a great deal in the course of this life's passage.

CHALLENGE: **NOT THINKING THAT LEADERSHIP IS WRONG**
FULFILLMENT: **OWNING THEIR INNATE SELF-CONFIDENCE**
NOTABLES: **KEVIN DOBSON (ACTOR, *KNOTS LANDING*); LLOYD WANER (BASEBALL PLAYER FOR PITTSBURGH PIRATES; "LITTLE POISON")**

The Way of Trust

AQUARIUS–PISCES CUSP TO LEO–VIRGO CUSP
Sensitivity to Exposure

The individuals born on the Way of Trust are among the most deeply sensitive in the personology system. It may be difficult to discern, however, since crustacean-like, they cover up their soft underbelly with a hard shell of cool objectivism and ostensible rationality. Such a defense mechanism has grown over time, built in response to the myriad wounds, both large and small, inflicted on their delicate inner lives. Those born on this karmic path are called to reveal themselves to others and thereby become more balanced, mature, and psychologically whole as they integrate their inner and outer realities. Self-protective in the extreme, they may have experienced the betrayal of their trust. Thus, they must rebuild trust in themselves to be more discerning and better judges of character. Individuals on this path will learn how to evaluate others so that they know whom to trust and why. Only then will they fully show others what they are truly made of.

There is something otherworldly or even mystical about the individuals on the Way of Trust. They are, in fact, touched by forces far greater than themselves, and they are concerned with ideals, abstract notions of justice, and universal issues having to do with compassion and humanity. Their tremendous kindness is obvious in how much they care for small children and animals. Often these individuals are not even aware of their inherent mysticism themselves. Other people seem to sense it and are drawn to

them for it. Those on this path exhibit various defense mechanisms such as being secretive to preserve their inner world. Deep down, they know that their sensitivity is not only what makes them most human, but is like a golden thread connecting them to the divine. Though they are aware that they are a bit different from others, this doesn't disturb them much. However, they do pay a price for the delicacy of their inner lives, often suffering pain more acutely because of it. So as to protect their profound tenderness, rarely will they allow others a glimpse of it. They are not shy per se; they don't exhibit timidity; rather, they are extremely reserved and are often perceived to be cold by others. The men and women on this path defend their sensitivity differently. While the men will tend to be more withdrawn, the women are aggressive. Both sexes, however, are highly independent in both thought and action. Often they are taken up with spirituality in all forms and New Age topics such as astrology or mind power.

Those on the Way of Trust are notoriously bad judges of character. Since they tend to be psychic, they feel swamped by their extrasensory impressions and find it difficult to sort out what they are experiencing or sensing. Thus, they often feel confused and have a hard time making decisions. Many on this path experience others as lying or dissembling because they sense this to be true. With no basis in fact, people respond by telling them that they are "crazy" or "paranoid" and so they become insecure in

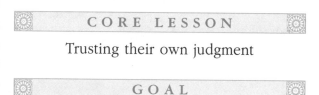

CORE LESSON

Trusting their own judgment

GOAL

To reveal their sensitive core to others

GIFTS
Service-oriented, Caring, Observant

PITFALLS
Narcissistic, Pessimistic, Escapist

their own ability to judge others. Not knowing what to believe, seeing untruths wherever they turn, they become distrustful and torn. Either they are super rational, making decisions based on pure logic with little intuition attached, or their tenderness—and neediness—hold sway in singularly irrational ways. Thus they are suspicious of those who might genuinely offer them love or, alternatively, they trust those who ultimately betray them so that their defensiveness is only compounded by life experience.

Recognizing their tendency to make poor judgements about others, those on this karmic path often retreat into social isolation. They are either withdrawn into their more spiritual or sensitive modes or wear their more public personas, the rational independent spirits who don't need or trust anybody. This split makes it difficult for them to truly connect with anyone. In addition, the core energy of these people is not particularly oriented to being in their bodies and is not well grounded, so one often finds body issues in those on this path. Out of touch with their own physicality, they yearn for touch and closeness yet find it difficult to reach out to receive the physical nurturing they crave. Though their acquaintances are many, their intimates are few. Sometimes those on this path are most comfortable with people who aren't in a position to be able to hurt them; thus one often sees the men and women on the Way of Trust ministering to the poor or sick.

RELEASE

The feeling of being a victim

REWARD

The joy of trusting themselves

Learning to be more spontaneous and free in their self-expression, reaching out of themselves to connect to others in relationships of true equality, and revealing the great beauty and compassion within them are the goals of this path. They have much to offer, but they must begin to risk allowing others to see their divine spark, even offering it to humanity in the form of service. In order for this to happen, those on this path must feel that they can trust their own judgment. They may need to heal old wounds arising from past bad decisions. They must first trust themselves before they can begin to trust others again. Working to improve their judgment, the first task and the core lesson of this path is to hone their discrimination in order to better evaluate their associates. The individuals on this karmic path must learn how to determine who is worthy of their trust and who is not. This requires the integration of their different strengths. Cultivating their intuition is the first step. Often this requires them to become more grounded in the body. Intuitive insight is often based in body wisdom. "Gut" feelings may actually be felt in the midsection of the body. It is important to begin to listen to what such sensations are communicating.

Tapping into their own psychic abilities will further bolster their judgment. Those on the Way of Trust are called to sift, sort, and weigh all types of information or impressions and, with a dose of objectivity, to reach

SUGGESTION

Learn to give without being taken advantage of. Avoid the tendency to retreat into an inner world. Trust in life and a higher power. Cultivate intuition and use your psychic ability—with discernment.

conclusions about the best courses of action or about the characters of individuals. They must learn when to pay attention to the little details that reveal so much about others. In time, those on the Way of Trust will develop a "testing" instinct. By observing people in different situations, they will learn how to test their integrity and trustworthiness. In addition, a knack for timing is crucial here since those on this path must learn not only whom to reveal themselves to, but when. (The goal of this path, Exposure, has to do with the right timing for revelation.) These individuals must develop wisdom— the understanding that is grounded in the body, in the heart, and not merely in rational thinking. By cultivating their own wisdom, those on this path will grow to trust themselves more and will be able to take more risks in revealing themselves to the world.

Ultimately, life circumstances will force those on this path out of their self-protective retreats because the world needs a dose of their sensitivity and caring. Allowing themselves to serve as examples to others is an important part of this karmic path. Those on it will learn how to relate in a more mature way, developing relationships based on mutual respect and trust rather than need or fear. What is best for those on this path is not necessarily to become wealthy or famous. This could necessitate hiding behind facades. Rather, they are quite happy working discreetly behind the scenes, revealing themselves in public now and then, all the while developing the skills necessary to open more to others on an intimate level. Although the spotlight can be turned on

BALANCE POINT

Suspicion and Trust

them occasionally, they will never be completely comfortable being in the public eye for long periods. They also need plenty of time to work on their private lives in peace and to nurture their physical side. It is highly recommended for these individuals to ground themselves through massage, yoga, or sports—anything that connects their spirit to their worldly shell. Also, such activities mean it is less likely that they will make disastrous relationship choices out of the pure need for physical affection. It is within the confines of one or two close friendships that those on this path receive lessons on judgment and trust and can practice becoming more transparent and emotionally honest. Those on the Way of Trust must take care to attract strong, independent, but kind souls, like themselves, rather than clingy or needy people.

In some ways this path can be likened to the teenage years in the human life cycle. Young maturing adults may be in the throes of emotional upheaval and hormonal changes. These years are a time of considerable inner growth as teens are testing limits and learning about relationships of all kinds. Most important, perhaps, teenagers are developing systems for evaluating and judging various situations and people. Leaving the safety of the family home, teenagers open to experience, only to return to the nest as need be. Similarly, those on this path are working hard to emerge from their shells to develop the emotional maturity to be discerning about others. Ultimately, trusting themselves, they will be able to show the world their great inner light.

CRYSTALS AND GEMSTONES

__Kunzite__ teaches the individual that by transforming the inner victim to love, he becomes safe and defense mechanisms such as suspicion can be released.

NOTABLES ON THIS KARMIC PATH

MARLON BRANDO

Displaying the sensitivity common to those on the Way of Trust, one of actor **Marlon Brando**'s most finely nuanced and charismatic performances was playing Stanley Kowalski in Tennessee Williams's *A Streetcar Named Desire*. A student of "method" acting, Brando became the leading male actor of his generation. His refusal of the Oscar awarded him for his work on *The Godfather* (to protest the film industry's treatment of Native Americans) epitomizes the idealism and keen sense of justice of those on this path. However, like many on the Way of Trust, he may be a poor judge of character as evidenced by some of the disasters in his personal life and he struggles to achieve a balance between his public and highly private life.

GRETA GARBO

Greta Garbo's intense drive toward stardom was matched only by her desire to flee it. Born in Sweden to an impoverished family, she rose to the heights of Hollywood fame only to retire abruptly at thirty-six and live in seclusion for her final decades. Garbo's nickname, "Swedish Sphinx," aptly reflects the Leo-Virgo destination of her path Exposure while the sensitivity of her Aquarius-Pisces origin is mirrored publicly in her characters' emotional struggles in films such as *Anna Karenina* and *Ninotchka*.

MARTIN SCORSESE

Film director **Martin Scorsese**'s early bouts with illness—such as asthma—displayed his sensitive constitution. Although he initially sought to isolate himself by entering a Catholic seminary, reflecting the deep spirituality common to those on this path, he ultimately rose to the challenge of his destiny, publicly emerging through his work as a film director. Casting his alter ego (Robert DeNiro) as his principal star, Scorsese examined the aggressive masculinity of his Italian-American heritage in films such as *Taxi Driver, Raging Bull,* and *Cape Fear.* Scorsese's work as a director may have helped him to rely on his own wisdom and intuition and develop the relationships of equality that are called for on his karmic path.

Other Notables: Princess Diana, Doris Day, Henry Mancini, George Clooney, Enya, Czar Nicolas II, Michael J. Fox, Lillian Hellman, Jean-Paul Sartre, Carl Lewis, Myrna Loy, David Duchovny, Linda Eastman McCartney, Annette Funicello, Larry Flynt, Stefanie Powers, Linda Evans, Calvin Klein, Jimi Hendrix, Janis Joplin, Christina Ricci, Sidney Poitier, Madeline Kahn, Red Smith, Michael Crichton, Frances Hodgson Burnett

---

BIRTHDAYS ON KARMIC PATH 45

October 29, 1886–March 19, 1887 | June 10, 1905–October 29, 1905 | January 21, 1924–June 9, 1924
September 1, 1942–January 20, 1943 | April 13, 1961–August 31, 1961
November 23, 1979–April 12, 1980 | July 4, 1998–November 22, 1998 | February 13, 2017–July 3, 2017

KARMIC PATH
45

March 19–24
REBIRTH
PISCES–ARIES CUSP

The Way of Trust endows the individuals born on the Cusp of Rebirth with greater natural refinement and sensitivity than they might have otherwise, though some here will wrestle with the ability to adequately integrate those qualities into their lives and world view. It's likely that these open and straightforward people will experience any number of drubbings for opening themselves to others early in their lives and, as a result, some will retreat behind a stubborn and ironclad facade of principle or habit in an attempt to cope. They can have a curious lack of self-awareness which may cause them to sometimes seem to be motivated by forces outside or beyond their control. Yet if they pay attention to their innate need to play their hunches and follow their instincts, if only through trial and error, this life experience will doubtless lead them to a better sense of trust in themselves, which in turn will emerge as the courage and enlightenment to trust others.

CHALLENGE: **LEARNING HOW THOUGHTLESS WORDS CAN BOOMERANG**

FULFILLMENT: **PLAYING THEIR SENSE OF TIMING TO PERFECTION**

DORIS DAY
Actress, *Pillow Talk*

4/3/1924
Aries II

March 25–April 2
THE CHILD
ARIES I

Those born in the Week of the Child who travel the Way of Trust have an interesting journey in store since they are naturally open-minded, curious and possess great enthusiasm, all of which will serve them in wonderful stead as they make their way along this road. Much more sensitive than some others born in this week, their principal stumbling block will lie in a tendency to withdraw in disappointment when life doesn't live up to their expectations, which in turn can foster attitudes of distrust and resentment of those who would intrude upon their private lives. They will, however, do well to keep in mind that perhaps their principal challenge will be to tread the fine line between ignorance and innocence by keeping their eyes on all that is good while retaining awareness of that which is not.

CHALLENGE: **RELEASING THE TENDENCY TO RETREAT IN ORDER TO NURSE THEIR WOUNDS**

FULFILLMENT: **KNOWING THAT THEY CAN ALWAYS MAKE A FRESH START**

NOTABLES: **PATTY HILL (EDUCATOR; CREATIVE APPROACH TO KINDERGARTEN); SARAH VAUGHN (JAZZ SINGER)**

April 3–10
THE STAR
ARIES II

If they can grapple with the tendency to be overly self-protective, and refuse to hold themselves aloof or apart from others, those born in the Week of the Star can do quite well along this karmic path. They may experience a certain amount of conflict with the higher challenge here, however, as their need to "star" may cause them to take advantage of the popularity this path confers, only to keep themselves aloof from their fans. As a result, some here may engage in vain attempts to shut down emotionally and content themselves with the pursuit of worldly ambitions, while others will swing from extremes of introversion and introspection to excesses of emotion, extroversion, and energy. They must understand that at the heart of their quest lies the potential to genuinely trust themselves and others as they express their deepest feelings. In the end, their kindness, generosity of spirit, and ability to motivate others are all sure to come to the fore in the course of this life's journey.

CHALLENGE: **NOT MERELY RELYING ON THEIR STAR QUALITY TO WIN FRIENDS FOR THEY'LL BE THE WRONG ONES**

FULFILLMENT: **FINDING RELATIONSHIPS OF MUTUAL SUPPORT**

NOTABLE: **FRANCIS CABOT LOWELL (FOUNDED 1ST COTTON-WEAVING MILL)**

HENRY MANCINI
Composer, "Moon River,"
"Victor/Victoria"

4/16/1924
Aries III

April 11–18
THE PIONEER
ARIES III

The individuals born in this week who negotiate the challenge and promise of the Way of Trust can experience untold fulfillment along this road. Their natural ability to join with others and expand the horizons of personal and ideological endeavors is sure to lead them in the right direction along this karmic path. Yet they may falter in the area of personal relationships as the energies here may make it especially difficult for them to open up on a one-to-one basis. There are some with this configuration who will be self-sacrificing in the extreme and may forfeit a more genuine awareness of themselves while they seek to fulfill the expectations of others. Despite their difficulties, they have the greatest potential for success along this path because they have both the sensitivity to inform their high ideals and the positivity to channel their more spiritual energies into practical and truly productive effort.

CHALLENGE: **BEING MORE DISCRIMINATING IN HOW THEY RESPOND TO WHAT OTHERS HAVE TO SAY**

FULFILLMENT: **CONVEYING THEIR DEPTH OF CONSCIENCE TO OTHERS**

NOTABLE: **PETER BEHRENS (ARCHITECT; DESIGNER)**

April 19–24
POWER
ARIES–TAURUS CUSP

Gifted with a much more "human touch" than some born on the Cusp of Power, these individuals can enjoy wonderful realization of their dreams and aspirations, though they will have to work to control a tendency to bury their best inclinations underneath a rigid or unapproachable exterior. Still, ambition is sure to come to the forefront here, and these individuals will be possessed of both a fine perception of their own strengths and weaknesses and a clear picture of what goes on in the hearts and minds of others. They will perhaps be at their best behind the scenes, pulling the strings or whispering into the ears of those in the forefront. Yet if they can learn to pay attention to their impressions and observations, while at the same time keep their suspicions from overriding their sense of integrity, they can prove themselves powerful individuals indeed as they make their way along this karmic path.

CHALLENGE: **NOT USING CONTROL AS A DISTANCING TOOL**
FULFILLMENT: **MASTERING THE TIMING FOR THEIR REVELATIONS**
NOTABLES: **J.M.W. TURNER (LANDSCAPE ARTIST, WATERCOLORIST); DON MATTINGLY (BASEBALL PLAYER, FIRST BASEMAN FOR YANKEES)**

April 25–May 2
MANIFESTATION
TAURUS I

The personalities born in the Week of Manifestation who find themselves on the Way of Trust can experience considerable happiness and fulfillment here. They will have to be on guard, however, so that their self-protective instincts do not cause them to withdraw from the higher challenge of being able to reveal themselves to others in a spirit of trust and understanding. They will doubtless spend no small amount of time in trying to structure their impressions and insights about the world in an attempt to make tangible their inner reality. It will be especially helpful for these people to engage in physical outlets for their energies and anxieties as well. Yet they will surely be kind in the extreme; if they indulge their more nurturing qualities without allowing themselves to become smothering, possessive, or immovable, they can find great depths of personal fulfillment and the heights of achievement in the course of this life's passage.

CZAR NICOLAS II
Last czar of Russia, disorganization led to revolution
5/18/1868
Taurus–Gemini Cusp

CHALLENGE: **REALIZING THAT THEIR STUBBORNNESS IS JUST A DEFENSE MECHANISM**
FULFILLMENT: **FEELING COMFORTABLE ENOUGH TO SHARE THEIR BURDENS WITH OTHERS**
NOTABLES: **SHELDON HARNICK (SONGWRITER, FIDDLER ON THE ROOF); ISAIAH THOMAS (BASKETBALL PLAYER, DETROIT PISTONS)**

May 3–10
THE TEACHER
TAURUS II

Blessed with a rare combination of native intelligence and great sensitivity, the danger for those born in the Week of the Teacher who travel the Way of Trust is that they will attempt to talk or think themselves out of their best intuitions, impulses, and sensibilities, burying their emotional side under heaps of abstraction. Yet they will have more than a touch of the "divine spark" about them, and their more charismatic qualities are sure to draw others who will offer innumerable opportunities for them to open up and reveal their truest natures. They will have to be careful not to evade that challenge, especially in the personal sphere, for there is a strong tendency to hold themselves apart from intimacy in the conviction that their role is to instruct others or to be instructed, rather than simply allowing themselves to love and be loved. Once they come to understand that it is possible to become emotionally involved without any sacrifice of personal dignity, all will go well here.

CHALLENGE: **ENTERING INTO RELATIONSHIPS BASED ON EQUALITY AND MUTUALITY OF RESPECT**
FULFILLMENT: **BEING ABLE TO FULLY TRUST THEIR OWN JUDGMENT IN INTIMATE MATTERS**

GEORGE CLOONEY
Actor, ER
5/6/1961
Taurus II

May 11–18
THE NATURAL
TAURUS III

For all that the souls born in this week may tout the virtues of rational thought and independence of spirit, they can have a number of hidden agendas. Some of this type may carry a sense of victimhood or the notion that they are somehow at the mercy of the establishment, which can hinder their ability to trust in their insights and can only contribute to their lack of trust in others. Yet they always have the ability to transcend those issues and learn better how to love, no matter what fears they may harbor about "security." If they are willing to seek out relationships with people whose ideas and philosophies are in keeping with their own, and take care not to withdraw from the world in defensive and unhealthy seclusion, life will become much easier along this karmic path. This will be especially true if they nurture their love of the natural world through physical contact with nature as experienced through the senses.

CHALLENGE: **REVEALING THEIR FUN-LOVING, ZANY SIDE TO OTHERS**
FULFILLMENT: **FEELING MORE GROUNDED AND SECURE IN WHO THEY ARE**
NOTABLES: **DENNIS RODMAN (BASKETBALL PLAYER; KNOWN FOR OUTLANDISH BEHAVIOR AND REBOUNDING; "THE WORM"); ENYA (NEW AGE MUSICIAN); TIM ROTH (ACTOR, RESERVOIR DOGS)**

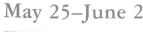

May 19–24

ENERGY
TAURUS–GEMINI CUSP

The individuals born in this week who find themselves on the Way of Trust may encounter a number of frustrations in their search for higher development and enlightenment. They may not be especially interested in reconciling their personal conflicts and may manifest hugely divergent and often bewildering energies. They can be secretive one moment, wildly extroverted the next—passionate then cold, extroverted then remote—and, it should be noted, not the slightest bit interested in explaining or exploring themselves. They are content to let the "devil take the hindmost" in their personal affairs and relationships. Coming to a deeper understanding of their own motivations will prove especially important here, and they will have to work hard to ground themselves and their efforts in reality. Otherwise, their natural emotional sensitivity may get mired in personal touchiness, high-handedness, or an inability to bond, which will only hold them back from their higher calling.

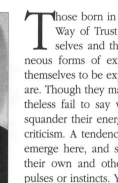

MELISSA ETHERIDGE
Pop/blues singer, musician

5/29/1961
Gemini I

CHALLENGE: **SETTLING DOWN LONG ENOUGH TO DO SOME REAL THINKING AND REFLECTION**
FULFILLMENT: **SHOWING THE WORLD THEIR UNIQUE IDEAS**

May 25–June 2

FREEDOM
GEMINI I

Those born in the Week of Freedom who travel the Way of Trust may balk at the call to open themselves and their sensitive natures to more spontaneous forms of expression. In fact, they can consider themselves to be expressive in the extreme, and probably are. Though they may talk a good game, they may nevertheless fail to say what they really mean or needlessly squander their energies in conflict, aggression, or hypercriticism. A tendency to be high strung and touchy may emerge here, and some will be inclined to overanalyze their own and others' more "irrational," emotional impulses or instincts. Yet if they can ground their often conflicting energies in directed effort and avoid too much unfinished emotional or professional business, they can achieve ever-increasing levels of personal confidence and enlightenment as they make their way along this road.

CHALLENGE: **HEALING THE WOUNDS FROM POOR RELATIONSHIP CHOICES**
FULFILLMENT: **FINDING SUPPORTIVE, NURTURING MATES**
NOTABLE: **LEA THOMPSON (ACTRESS, *CAROLINE IN THE CITY*)**

June 3–10

NEW LANGUAGE
GEMINI II

Those born in the Week of New Language may well experience tremendous conflicts between their innate need to express themselves and the impulse to keep a wealth of personal or emotional "secrets." Often troubled by a pronounced tendency to hide their lights under a bushel or to stay aloof from others in an overly defensive stance of self-protection, they may be rather haunted by their own darker side or some unusual fascinations and be further held back by a feeling of being misunderstood. There is a strong inclination to escapism, addiction, and a tendency to engage in emotional manipulations and deceptions to enhance their sense of "control." Indeed this configuration can manifest in many a tangled web if they attempt to conceal more than they reveal. Yet if they are careful to divest themselves of doubt and instead develop faith, they will find their efforts rewarded and their personal truth much simplified as they make their way along this karmic path.

MICHAEL J. FOX
Actor, *Family Ties, Back to the Future*

6/9/1961
Gemini II

CHALLENGE: **WORKING HARD TO ALWAYS BE HONEST**
FULFILLMENT: **HAVING COME TO TERMS WITH OLD MISTAKES, TRUSTING IN THEMSELVES ONCE MORE**

June 11–18

THE SEEKER
GEMINI III

Seekers who travel the Way of Trust are gifted with formidable intelligence, mental clarity, and considerable verbal ability. They will, however, find their rational approach somewhat limiting until they come to acknowledge their own sensitivity and its corollary, their intuition, and allow these tools to have a role in their decision-making process. It is likely for them to be preoccupied with material success and the sense of freedom it can represent. Their powers of observation can make them calculating people, who, though charming, may care more about manipulating others than opening their hearts. Still, it is not that they do not care about love, it is only that love may not rate as high as some other priorities. These people enjoy a challenge; if they can apply that single quality to the search for a more integrated and enlightened sense of self, and come to understand that their sensitivity and intuition are not meant to cancel out or interfere with their intellectual side, the result can be an enriching and rewarding journey along this karmic path.

CHALLENGE: **NOT FEARING THAT THEIR SENSITIVITY WILL SWAMP THEM**
FULFILLMENT: **USING THEIR WISDOM AND JUDGMENT TO BETTER FOCUS THEIR INTELLECTUAL EFFORTS**
NOTABLE: **BOY GEORGE (SINGER, CULTURE CLUB)**

June 19–24
MAGIC
GEMINI–CANCER CUSP

Here sensitivity and a highly refined intuition can assume mystical aspects in the course of the life journeys of those born on the Cusp of Magic who find themselves on the Way of Trust. Though there will be those in this group who try to suppress their sensitivity under a mountain of professional ambitions and endeavors, most will find happiness and fulfillment in a broader sense than mere material achievement. Perhaps their principal struggle will arise not so much out of an inability to trust themselves as it will be an inability to trust others with their feelings—particularly once they have been wounded in any way. Yet hiding behind a cool facade will only cause them unhappiness, and a tendency to be demanding or manipulative can only contribute to their woes. If they allow themselves to follow their instincts and keep harboring and nurturing their formidable capacity for love, all will go beautifully here.

CHALLENGE: **NOT TURNING ON THE FRIGID FACADE WHEN OTHERS DRAW TOO CLOSE**

FULFILLMENT: **BALANCING RATIONALITY WITH INTUITION TO GET WISDOM**

NOTABLES: LILLIAN HELLMAN (PLAYWRIGHT, *LITTLE FOXES*); JEAN-PAUL SARTRE (EXISTENTIALIST PHILOSOPHER, WRITER)

CARL LEWIS
Olympic gold medalist in track

7/1/1961
Cancer I

June 25–July 2
THE EMPATH
CANCER I

Some real shrinking violets can be found among those born in the Week of the Empath who travel the Way of Trust—at least in so much as that term applies to the more emotional side of life. Though likely to be kind and generous, many here will struggle to develop a sense of identity that is truly apart from others. Their tremendous sensitivity can forge some rather combative attitudes on the one hand, and some rather indecisive or wishy-washy habits on the other as they struggle to find the balance between separation and unity with others. Yet their need to connect will serve them well here, while at the same time, this path gifts them with a much greater degree of objectivity and observation than they might have otherwise. If they can avoid viewing people through rose-colored glasses and, further, discourage within themselves a tendency to withdraw in the face of conflict, they can find the right mix of action, emotion, and intellect.

CHALLENGE: **GRAPPLING WITH THEIR EMOTIONAL NEEDINESS BY FINDING WAYS TO NURTURE THEMSELVES**

FULFILLMENT: **MINISTERING TO THOSE LESS FORTUNATE OR OTHERWISE IN NEED**

NOTABLES: GEORGE HALE (ASTRONOMER; HELPED ORGANIZE AMERICAN ACADEMY OF SCIENCE); GREG LE MOND (BIKE RACER; 1ST AMERICAN TO WIN TOUR DE FRANCE)

July 3–10
THE UNCONVENTIONAL
CANCER II

Keeping control of pronounced escapist tendencies will doubtless figure prominently in the life journeys of those born in this week who find themselves on the Way of Trust, as some here will find it especially difficult to trust their own perceptions and reconcile some of their inner conflicts. Yet they bring to this journey a capacity for astute psychological insight that will hold them in wonderful stead here, as it will enable them to observe others from a more objective viewpoint than many who travel this road. It will be especially useful for these individuals to be able to give form to their richly imaginative natures through creative self-expression. Most often, they will choose to do so within a sacrosanct domestic space where they can play, dream, and indulge their most creative impulses. If they can keep in mind that their higher calling is to open up and share some of their inspiration with others, rather than to hoard their emotions in the extremes of self-protection, all can go well along this karmic path.

CHALLENGE: **TAKING CARE NOT TO OVERINDULGE IN SOLITARY PURSUITS AND THEIR RICH IMAGINATIVE LIFE**

FULFILLMENT: **FINDING THOSE WITH WHOM THEY CAN SAFELY SHARE THEIR INNER WORLD**

NOTABLES: FRANK GILBRETH (ENGINEER; EFFICIENCY EXPERT); LIONEL TRILLING (LITERARY CRITIC)

PRINCESS DIANA
Former wife of Prince Charles; beloved royalty

7/1/1961
Cancer I

July 11–18
THE PERSUADER
CANCER III

Persuaders who travel the Way of Trust can achieve a great deal in both their personal and professional lives along this path, yet they will have to work to get to the point where they don't feel quite such a necessity to control their feelings, set aside their needs, or obfuscate their truest desires. Highly observant, they have a fine knack for knowing what makes people tick, but may have more difficulty when it comes to turning their keen powers of insight upon themselves. Inclined to be rather controlling, they will want to make the rest of us jump through hoops in order to gain their trust. They can do a great deal of overanalyzing of their own best impulses and instincts and wind up "canceling themselves out." Yet if they keep in close touch with their passions and seek out those to whom they respond on a deep level, they will find their fears evaporating and their path to enlightenment considerably clarified.

CHALLENGE: **DENYING THEIR OWN DEEPEST NEEDS—IN PARTICULAR, PHYSICAL**

FULFILLMENT: **ENJOYING THE SELF-CONFIDENCE THAT COMES FROM EVOLVED POWERS OF DISCRIMINATION AND DISCERNMENT**

NOTABLES: FOREST WHITAKER (ACTOR, DIRECTOR, *WAITING TO EXHALE*); DOROTHY FIELDS (LYRICIST, "I CAN'T GIVE YOU ANYTHING BUT LOVE, BABY")

KARMIC PATH
45

July 19–25
OSCILLATION
CANCER–LEO CUSP

Though likely to be troubled in the course of their travels along the Way of Trust by no small amount of psychic upsets resulting from a division between their intuition and sensitivity and their more dynamic and rational side, the exciting individuals born on the Cusp of Oscillation are much more outgoing than some others on this road. Once they come to understand that it is necessary to their emotional and spiritual health to venture outward, then to retreat, then go outward again, they will succeed in gaining great insight into their personal rhythms and patterns that should considerably ease their passage. Ridding themselves of tension will be important, and they will do especially well to keep up some regular form of physical exercise or meditation practice. Though there are some who will actively attempt to repress their more emotional side and may fall out of touch with some of their best attributes, most will successfully integrate heart and mind and body and soul in the course of this most unusual journey.

MYRNA LOY
Actress, *Thin Man* series

8/2/1905
Leo I

CHALLENGE: **DEVELOPING THE UNDERSTANDING AND TOOLS TO MANAGE PSYCHIC STRESS**
FULFILLMENT: **FEELING A CERTAIN EXHILARATION IN THE RISK-TAKING ASPECT OF REVEALING THEMSELVES**
NOTABLES: **WOODY HARRELSON (ACTOR, *CHEERS*); DIANA TRILLING (AUTHOR, CRITIC)**

July 26–August 2
AUTHORITY
LEO I

Gifted with a natural generosity of spirit and a strong need to connect with others, those born in the Week of Authority who travel this karmic path can enjoy great success and personal enlightenment. This path endows them with a stronger altruistic impulse than they might have otherwise, and the result can make for a nice mix of kindness, natural compassion, and personal strength. Though there are some here who will get mired in ego issues or a sense of victimhood, most with this configuration will successfully divest themselves of an unnecessary sense of entitlement and be more than willing to open their hearts to others in a spirit of sharing and genuine empathy. In fact, if they don't turn away from the higher challenge in simple stubbornness and refusal to bond, they will be the kind of people who will be both much beloved and genuinely admired.

CHALLENGE: **PREOCCUPYING THEMSELVES LESS WITH HOW THEY APPEAR TO OTHERS**
FULFILLMENT: **BECOMING MORE SPONTANEOUS IN THEIR SELF-EXPRESSION**
NOTABLES: **CONSTANTINE I (KING OF GREECE DURING WWI); THELMA TODD (ACTRESS); CLARA BOW (SILENT FILM ACTRESS)**

August 3–10
BALANCED STRENGTH
LEO II

Getting in touch and staying in touch with their intuitive side will be the key to success for the individuals born in the Week of Balanced Strength who find themselves on this karmic path. They will have to work to cultivate that quality in themselves, however, and avoid the dangers of single-mindedness or stubbornness that can prove stumbling blocks to their development. There are some with this configuration for whom the impulse to altruism may devolve into a masochistic tendency, as once Leo II's have set themselves upon a particular course, they never give up. When it comes to problem solving, they like to be left alone to work things out for themselves—yet they will do much better when they allow themselves to be open with one or two close confidantes who can guide them in their decision making. Nevertheless, if they can learn to go with their "gut" feelings, their development is assured as they make their way along this road.

DAVID DUCHOVNY
Actor, *The X-Files*

8/7/1961
Leo II

CHALLENGE: **GETTING THEMSELVES OUT OF THE BAD RELATIONSHIPS THAT POOR JUDGMENT GOT THEM INTO**
FULFILLMENT: **PUTTING THEIR SENSITIVITY AND COMPASSION TO WORK AS THEY SERVE THOSE IN NEED**
NOTABLES: **PAUL CLAUDEL (CATHOLIC POET, PLAYWRIGHT); DAVE EVANS ("THE EDGE"; ROCK GUITARIST IN U2)**

August 11–18
LEADERSHIP
LEO III

The individuals born in this week who negotiate the ups and downs of they Way of Trust are likely to find great contentment here, as these are rather naturally open-hearted people at their core and will almost surely rise to the challenge of greater openness and self-expression. Not as likely to withdraw or shield their sensitivities as some who travel this road, their creative and commanding qualities are sure to hold a touch of the spirit as these people go about their personal and professional pursuits. Though it may be a struggle for them to become more approachable, if they do not succumb to a tendency to devolve into purely selfish interests, and cultivate their deeper levels of understanding and perception, their capacity for emotional bonding will result. Then there will be almost nothing to stand in the way of their highest personal and spiritual growth as they make their way along this road.

CHALLENGE: **STEPPING INTO THE LIMELIGHT TO SERVE AS EXAMPLES TO OTHERS**
FULFILLMENT: **TAKING A CERTAIN SATISFACTION IN THE EFFECT THEY HAVE ON OTHERS**

August 19–25

EXPOSURE
LEO–VIRGO CUSP

Those born on the Cusp of Exposure are blessed with the highest prospects for self-realization even as they face the daunting challenge of self-revelation along this karmic path. Born with faultless instincts and formidable powers of observation, they are a rare combination of intelligence and intuition. Discriminating, discerning, and ultimately very hard to fool, they are likely to hold themselves back not so much out of self-protective instinct or the need to feel safe, but out of the inner necessity of feeling like they have their emotional ducks in a row. In fact, what they may fear the most is not so much rejection, but the sheer power of their own passions. Much inclined to secrecy and a rather nonsharing approach to intimate interaction, they are nevertheless capable of displaying some passionate fireworks when they feel the time and place is right. Yet life is likely to provide them innumerable opportunities to show their stuff and find the freedom that comes with simply being understood.

RICHARD ROUNDTREE
Actor, *Shaft*

9/7/1942
Virgo II

CHALLENGE: **LEARNING HOW TO REVEAL WHO THEY ARE BEFORE THE TRUTH ABOUT THEM IS REVEALED FOR THEM**
FULFILLMENT: **KNOWING THEY CAN TRUST THEIR INTIMATES**
NOTABLE: **BILLY RAY CYRUS (COUNTRY POP SINGER, "ACHY-BREAKY HEART")**

August 26–September 2

SYSTEM BUILDERS
VIRGO I

Being emotionally unaware may be the principal pitfall for those born in the Week of System Builders who journey along the Way of Trust. Though likely to be quite giving and caring people, they may manifest the demands of this path in a tendency to take up more service-oriented professions, rather than in the pursuit of personal goals. Intimacy may scare them a bit, and they may further be quite prone to repress feelings due to their innate distaste for emotional pressure of any kind. Yet service to others will be sure to tap their deep reservoirs of kindness and allow them access to the worlds of spiritual and emotional connection that beckon here. If they can strike the right balance between altruism and self-interest, and further cultivate those relationships with people who ask nothing of them but simply allow them to be themselves, all will go well in the course of this life journey.

CHALLENGE: **KNOWING THAT SERVING OTHERS CAN BE A DEFENSE AGAINST GREATER CLOSENESS WITH OTHERS**
FULFILLMENT: **KNOWING HOW TO SEPARATE THE WHEAT FROM THE CHAFF WHEN JUDGING OTHERS**
NOTABLE: **DORE SCHARY (SCREENWRITER/PRODUCER, *BOYS TOWN*)**

September 3–10

THE ENIGMA
VIRGO II

The people born in this week who travel the Way of Trust may be enigmatic indeed, and will have to work hard to find a sense of personal and professional balance as they make their way along this road. Chief among their challenges will be their willingness to allow others into their more private worlds, as these people are rather loath to share their sensitive core. Though they will by no means be uncaring or entirely self-serving, they may nevertheless be uncomfortable with the idea and practice of emotional intimacy. While they will doubtless be sought after for their taste, discernment, and high personal standards, they may be inclined to shelter their own emotions from the scrutiny or analysis of those close to them. If they can open up, loosen up, and ante up their sense of what is possible within the emotional sphere, however, they can make great strides toward happiness and fulfillment as they travel this life's highway.

CHALLENGE: **TRUSTING LIFE'S PROCESS TO PROTECT THEIR SENSITIVE CORE**
FULFILLMENT: **KNOWING THAT THEY CAN UNRAVEL AND SOLVE ANY PROBLEM**
NOTABLES: **AL JARDINE (FOUNDING MEMBER OF THE BEACH BOYS); RICHARD ROUNDTREE (ACTOR, *SHAFT*)**

IVAN PAVLOV
Physiologist, discovered reflexive conditioning with experiments on dogs; won Nobel Prize

9/14/1849
Virgo III

September 11–18

THE LITERALIST
VIRGO III

Like many of their Virgo compatriots, those born in the Week of the Literalist who travel the Way of Trust may have a particularly difficult time with the struggle between head and heart. Gifted with a greater sensitivity and insight into others' motivations and feelings than they might have otherwise, they may have to work hard to overcome a naturally suspicious or defensive attitude toward interpersonal relations, and will likely display an overly rational approach to life in general. Highly resistant to others' attempts to analyze them, these individuals will mine their own feelings, psyches, and spirits for the gems of spiritual and emotional reward promised here. Despite their best attempts to resist or ignore the touch of the spirit that lingers about them, others will respond to their kindness, insight, and need for truth. If they can bring themselves to reciprocate that response and avoid the terror they feel about public displays of emotion or conflict, they can make great strides along this journey. While they may never be demonstrative, they will certainly find love.

CHALLENGE: **TAPPING INTO THEIR OWN INTUITIVE AND PSYCHIC ABILITIES**
FULFILLMENT: **FEELING SAFE IN INTIMACY**
NOTABLE: **EDDIE ANDERSON (ACTOR, JACK BENNY'S MAN-SERVANT ROCHESTER)**

September 19–24
BEAUTY
VIRGO–LIBRA CUSP

The souls born in this week who travel the Way of Trust will have great potential for success and personal fulfillment in the course of this life's journey, providing they do not content themselves with purely superficial concerns or attempt to bury their sensitivity through addiction, escapism, or a refusal to connect with the life of the spirit. Yet they are gifted with discernment, and their formidable powers of observation can work to their advantage, providing they do not preoccupy themselves too much with externals. Perhaps even more important is consciously working to make themselves more approachable to others, for these people disguise some of their best impulses under a haughty reserve or a snobbish, ivory tower approach to human involvement. If they can learn to nurture their love of beauty and at the same time come to better terms with the value of personal sacrifice and real trust, their path to growth and development is assured.

LINDA EASTMAN,
with Paul McCartney.
Photographer, married
Paul McCartney

9/24/1942
Virgo–Libra Cusp

CHALLENGE: **REJIGGERING THE BASIS ON WHICH THEY EVALUATE OTHERS**

FULFILLMENT: **SHARING WITH OTHERS THEIR TASTE IN AND SENSITIVITY FOR BEAUTY**

NOTABLE: **LEON JAWORSKI (LAWYER, PROSECUTOR AT WATERGATE AND NUREMBERG TRIALS)**

September 25–October 2
THE PERFECTIONIST
LIBRA I

Those born in the Week of the Perfectionist who find themselves on the Way of Trust may obscure a great deal of passion and emotional sensitivity underneath a facade of cynical and biting wit, or a tendency to keep themselves apart from others through hypercriticism or pickiness. Indecision can also be a problem for these individuals, as they can be torn between their impulse to reach out to others and the fear of being hurt or badly used. To make matters more complex, they can successfully hide a torrent of emotion beneath a rather cool and calculating facade. If they can come to better understand that the world of emotion and inspiration does not always operate by predictable or calculable laws, and learn as well that mastery of their feelings may not be nearly as important as being able to simply express them—things will prove infinitely easier as they travel this road to enlightenment.

CHALLENGE: **TEMPERING THEIR TENDENCY TO BE HYPERCRITICAL AND TAKING A MORE BALANCED APPROACH**

FULFILLMENT: **ACCEPTING THEIR FEELINGS**

NOTABLES: **MADELINE KAHN (ACTRESS, *BLAZING SADDLES*); RED SMITH (SPORTSWRITER; WON PULITZER PRIZE)**

October 3–10
SOCIETY
LIBRA II

Hampered by a tendency to be subsumed by superficial interests and pursuits, those born in the Week of Society can nevertheless experience considerable advancement and development in the course of this life's journey. They are much more socially inclined than many who travel this road, and more open to the idea of sharing their lives and hearts with their closest friends, partners, and associates. The problem is that they may well resist the call to deeper awareness of their own sensitivity that beckons here, and while they may have a genuine gift for inspiring others to trust them, they may be not at all willing to reciprocate in kind. Thus, they can drift indecisively through many shallow contacts, rather than allow themselves to risk being entirely "real" with any of them. If they can develop a greater understanding not just of their own sensitivity, but of their own deepest needs, life is sure to provide them with a host of opportunities to be inspired by genuine friendship and love.

PENNY MARSHALL
Actress/director,
Laverne and Shirley

10/15/1942
Libra III

CHALLENGE: **BECOMING MORE CAUTIOUS IN THEIR PERSONAL INVOLVEMENTS**

FULFILLMENT: **BOTH TRUSTING AND VALUING THEIR OWN INSIGHTFULNESS**

NOTABLES: **BRITT EKLAND (SWEDISH ACTRESS, *MAN WITH THE GOLDEN GUN*); ANDY DEVINE (ACTOR, ROY ROGERS' SIDEKICK)**

October 11–18
THEATER
LIBRA III

Some very adept and rather calculating performers will be among those born in this week who travel the Way of Trust, and some will experience real conflict between the need to gain the attention of those around them and the need to stay hidden in the interests of self-protection. Though this path endows them with much greater sensitivity than they might otherwise possess, they will nevertheless have to overcome a certain sense of detachment regarding the feelings of others if they are to be truly successful here. They can be considerably more concerned about their own feelings than they are about anyone else's. Yet they have great potential for success along this path, for once they give themselves to something or someone, they tend to give their all. If they observe closely and choose carefully, the result can be great fulfillment in the course of this life's journey.

CHALLENGE: **HEALING THE CYNICISM THAT COMES FROM OLD EMOTIONAL WOUNDS**

FULFILLMENT: **INCORPORATING THEIR FLAIR FOR DRAMA INTO THEIR REVELATIONS**

NOTABLES: **JEAN ARTHUR (ACTRESS, *SHANE*); JIM SEALS (FOLK/POP SINGER IN SEALS & CROFTS); BARON C. P. SNOW (PHYSICIST; NOVELIST, *STRANGERS AND BROTHERS*)**

October 19–25

DRAMA AND CRITICISM
LIBRA–SCORPIO CUSP

The highly charismatic and compelling individuals born on the Cusp of Drama and Criticism who find themselves along the Way of Trust may have a hard time keeping their emotions and inclinations a secret, no matter what defense mechanisms they may have in place. Marked by the need to express themselves, and the urge to protect their inner lives, they may find it difficult to comprehend just why it is that others keep wanting to connect with them, until they realize that such opportunities are of their own making, arising out of their deepest desires. Addictions of all kinds are to be avoided here, especially when the individuals in question erect their own bad habits as yet another wall in the way of enlightenment and love. Though they will doubtless experience more than their share of personal dramas, if they do not allow themselves to treat others carelessly and reach for greater spontaneity in personal expression, this can prove a highly rewarding passage.

CHALLENGE: **BEING WARY OF THEIR ADDICTIVE TENDENCIES IN RELATIONSHIPS**

FULFILLMENT: **CULTIVATING A CIRCLE OF TRUSTWORTHY ASSOCIATES**

NOTABLES: **MICHAEL CRICHTON (WRITER/PRODUCER, *JURASSIC PARK*); ANNETTE FUNICELLO (ACTRESS, SINGER; DISNEY MOUSEKETEER)**

November 3–11

DEPTH
SCORPIO II

Learning to trust will not come easily to those born in the Week of Depth who find themselves on this road, and indeed, there is a danger here that they will turn away from the higher challenge to open their hearts and minds in more spontaneous forms of expression. Though deeply soulful and spiritual, these profound individuals may shrink from the challenge of self-revelation and insist that others must somehow prove themselves and their worthiness. However, they will have to face the fact that their own defensive barriers are serving to hinder rather than insure their happiness. Overcoming their fears of betrayal will be especially important for this group as well. They will surely come to better understand that one tends to experience those things which one expects to experience, and that much of life is a self-fulfilling prophecy. Once they adjust their attitudes accordingly, things will get easier as they make their way along this karmic path.

CHALLENGE: **SETTING ASIDE THEIR COMPETITIVE INSTINCTS AND PROPENSITY FOR ENVY**

FULFILLMENT: **FEELING COMPASSION WITH DETACHMENT**

NOTABLE: **JEAN SHRIMPTON (POPULAR ENGLISH MODEL DURING THE 60s)**

LARRY FLYNT
Hustler magazine founder and owner

———

11/1/1942
Scorpio I

October 26–November 2

INTENSITY
SCORPIO I

The souls born in the Week of Intensity who make their way along this karmic path may be somewhat overburdened along this road by a suspicious and calculating attitude toward others that can at times border on the paranoid. Openness and sharing are not Scorpio's strongest traits in any event, and some will find this an especially difficult passage. Indeed, their obsession with privacy can result in impenetrable fortresses of self-protection, and their tendency to suspect the worst of others can be quite damaging to all concerned. Yet if they keep in mind that the key to their ultimate success will lie in their ability to manage their own darker side and to control their more negative perceptions of others, they will have a unique insight and a flair for analysis. If not wrongly used, these qualities can help them to release their fears and give them the ability to discover fulfilling relationships with a select group of comrades and friends.

CHALLENGE: **PRACTICING HARD TO DEVELOP THEIR "PEOPLE SKILLS"**

FULFILLMENT: **REVEALING THEIR NEAR VIRTUOSO TALENTS AT PRECISELY THE RIGHT MOMENT**

NOTABLES: **SHERE HITE (AUTHOR; CULTURAL RESEARCHER ON HUMAN SEXUALITY); STEFANIE POWERS (ACTRESS, *HART TO HART*; WILDLIFE ACTIVIST)**

November 12–18

CHARM
SCORPIO III

Those born in the Week of Charm who navigate the challenge and promise of the Way of Trust are more socially inclined and better able to open up than some of their Scorpio fellows along this road. Nonetheless, there will be a decidedly calculating streak in these individuals and, though they are likely to be real masters of observation and psychological insight, they will be much inclined to emotional manipulation. They may insist that others jump through all sorts of hoops in order to prove their devotion. There are a number of real heartbreakers here. Yet at their core, Scorpio III's have a realistic streak and are well able to face down the demons of personal distrust and defensiveness. If they can balance their sensitivity with that realism and avoid complacency, suspicion, or "looking out for number one" to the extent that no one else's needs really matter, they can realize great progress and will doubtless make their mark along this karmic path.

CHALLENGE: **FACING THEIR COMPULSIONS OR ADDICTIONS AS THE DEFENSES THEY ARE**

FULFILLMENT: **KNOWING INDIVIDUALS WELL ENOUGH TO TRUST THEM**

NOTABLE: **LINDA EVANS (ACTRESS, *DYNASTY*)**

DANIEL BARENBOIM
Pianist/conductor

———

11/15/1942
Scorpio III

November 19–24
REVOLUTION
SCORPIO–SAGITTARIUS CUSP

The individuals born in this period who make their way along this karmic path are likely to undergo some profound personal transformations in the course of this life's journey. While the exact nature of those transformations may remain hidden from others to a large extent, they can nevertheless be assured of great progress here. In fact, they may align themselves with philosophical movements, spiritual explorations, and the higher forms of art in an attempt to better understand themselves and their sensitivity. Likely to be motivated by an overriding desire to make the world a better place, they can attain great things, providing they can overcome emotional volatility and learn to place greater faith in their own impulses. Once they achieve more by way of self-acceptance and learn to complement their sense of inspiration with careful planning, success will be theirs on both the personal and professional planes.

CALVIN KLEIN
Fashion designer; known
for controversial ads

11/19/1942
Scorpio–Sagittarius Cusp

CHALLENGE: **REALIZING THAT PASSION AND SENSITIVITY MAKE FOR AN EXPLOSIVE MIX, DEVELOPING A LITTLE FORGIVENESS**

FULFILLMENT: **PURSUING THEIR MORE AVANT-GARDE INSPIRATIONS OR NEW AGE INTERESTS**

NOTABLES: **SIR HAROLD NICOLSON (BRITISH DIPLOMAT; WRITER, CRITIC); FRANCES HODGSON BURNETT (WRITER, *THE SECRET GARDEN*)**

November 25–December 2
INDEPENDENCE
SAGITTARIUS I

The personalities born in the Week of Independence who journey along the Way of Trust can realize a high degree of success and personal fulfillment, providing they find the balance between personal sensitivity and personal freedom. In fact, a sense of honor and trust rate quite high on their list of priorities, and it is doubtful that they will allow themselves to be drawn into dubious or compromising relationships. Yet at the same time, they will need to be sure that those same standards are not impossibly high. Overcoming their secret insecurities can be a big challenge for these people, and they will further have to make sure that their much-touted need for freedom isn't merely a cleverly fashioned defense against deeper personal interaction or openness. Learning to simply cooperate and not insist on having their own way will be the first step to success, and if they develop the same sense of faith in others that they often have in themselves, life will be much sweeter and more rewarding as they make their way along this karmic path.

CHALLENGE: **ACKNOWLEDGING PERSONAL INSECURITY**

FULFILLMENT: **FINDING THE SOUL MATES WHO LIVE UP TO THEIR ETHICAL STANDARDS**

NOTABLE: **ROBERT HAVELL, JR. (ENGRAVER; AQUATINTS FOR *AUDUBON'S BIRDS OF AMERICA*)**

December 3–10
THE ORIGINATOR
SAGITTARIUS II

Likely to be marked by a pronounced fear of rejection, those born in the Week of the Originator who travel the Way of Trust may experience a struggle along this road. On the one hand, they have a great need to be accepted, while on the other, they may manifest a rational, independent, and rather stubborn side that will insist they don't need anyone. Yet at their core, these individuals have a deep desire to show people who they really are and will work to manifest their wonderful originality and offbeat way of looking at the world. Gifted with an ardent nature, they are likely to succeed in that much, doing just that though they will have to overcome their own rather poor ability to judge others' characters. If they can develop greater discernment and express themselves only to those whom they can truly trust, instead of "casting their pearls before swine" or acting out of neediness and vulnerability, they will find their niche among those who appreciate their uniqueness in the course of this most interesting journey.

JIMI HENDRIX
Rock guitarist, "Purple
Haze"

11/27/1942
Sagittarius I

CHALLENGE: **TRYING TO DEVELOP SELF-ACCEPTANCE**

FULFILLMENT: **APPLYING INTUITIVE OR PRACTICAL WISDOM AS THEY USE THEIR TECHNICAL ABILITIES**

NOTABLES: **JOE McGINNISS (WRITER, *THE SELLING OF THE PRESIDENT*); HORACE LIVERIGHT (PUBLISHER, PRODUCER, *THE MODERN LIBRARY*)**

December 11–18
THE TITAN
SAGITTARIUS III

Big-thinking Sagittarius III's who make their way along this karmic path may find that their principal issues revolve around keeping their expectations of themselves and others on a realistic plane. These people are likely to be possessed of highly romantic natures and may chase quite a few windmills in their search for love and understanding. Not likely to be the best judges of character in any event, some of their problems will doubtless be mitigated by their willingness to develop more genuine self-awareness. There is an underlying streak of real insecurity in most of these individuals that will bear watching here. Yet there is the possibility of great progress, especially if they align themselves with those who will appreciate and understand the largesse of their vision, and at the same time, help them to understand the magic to be found in everyday experience.

CHALLENGE: **NOT FALLING PREY TO THEIR ROMANTIC VISIONS OR NEED FOR APPROVAL**

FULFILLMENT: **STANDING MORE FIRMLY ON THE WORLD STAGE**

NOTABLES: **DAVE CLARK (MUSICIAN; FORMED DAVE CLARK FIVE); WILLIAM K. VANDERBILT (BUSINESSMAN; SPORTSMAN); TY COBB (HALL OF FAME BASEBALL PLAYER, OUTFIELDER FOR DETROIT; "THE GEORGIA PEACH")**

December 19–25
PROPHECY
SAGITTARIUS–CAPRICORN CUSP

It's really anyone's guess how the life journeys of those born on the Cusp of Prophecy will manifest as they travel the Way of Trust, yet there is a number of factors that will distinguish these lives in significant ways. First, they will almost certainly experience real conflict between their formidable intuitive and even psychic tendencies and a need to order their world of perception with rational thought. Second, they will struggle with the call to open their hearts to others in a spirit of sensitive understanding, to the extent that some will withdraw from that challenge altogether, for here is where we can find some real hermits, recluses and misanthropes. Finally, these individuals will at some point during their journey face the relatively simple fact that their judgment is probably better that they ever believed. Once they come to terms with that much, their path to fulfillment will become much clearer as they make their way along this road.

MICHAEL NESMITH
Member of The Monkees;
director

12/30/1942
Capricorn I

CHALLENGE: **FINDING WAYS TO GROUND AND EXPRESS THEIR OTHERWORLDLY WISDOM AND PSYCHIC IMPRESSIONS**

FULFILLMENT: **TRUSTING WHAT THEY KNOW**

December 26–January 2
THE RULER
CAPRICORN I

Emotional repression will likely be the biggest stumbling block for those born in the Week of the Ruler who find themselves on the Way of Trust, and many here will have to work especially hard to rise to the challenge of more spontaneous self-expression. Though undoubtedly quite kind, and very prone to channel their self-protective instincts into protecting others, these travelers may fall down a bit when it comes to really opening their hearts. In fact, they may be rational in the extreme and much more prone to write checks to their favorite charities than they are to roll up their sleeves and become personally involved in the business of helping others. Some will manifest a curiously intolerant streak. Yet once they come to understand that their fear or refusal to accept the ways of others may in fact be a manifestation of their lack of self-acceptance, things will become much easier and they will find themselves adopting an infinitely more relaxed approach to life in general as they make their way along this karmic path.

CHALLENGE: **MAKING ROOM FOR THEIR SENSITIVITY IN THEIR LIVES**

FULFILLMENT: **DISCOVERING PEOPLE WHO ARE AS CARING, CONCERNED, AND TRUSTWORTHY AS THEY**

January 3–9
DETERMINATION
CAPRICORN II

Though it may take time for these people to develop the degree of confidence and faith in themselves required on the Way of Trust, the chances are good that those born in the Week of Determination will find fulfillment here. There will be something of a tendency to be too loyal and easily victimized by less sensitive types, but these resilient and resourceful people are equally likely to overcome those emotional issues that can stand in the way of real growth. Their fondness for metaphysical and spiritual studies is greatly enhanced with this configuration, and they will do well to educate themselves in such subjects, as those pursuits will help them to understand that a more "rational" approach to supposedly "irrational" subjects is quite possible and personally illuminating. They may prefer to stay behind the scenes, but at the same time should be careful not to withdraw from the opportunities for more spontaneous self-expression that present themselves in the personal sphere. If they can find the balance between openness and naïveté, all will go well along this road.

CHALLENGE: **BEING LESS HARD ON THEMSELVES FOR THEIR ERRORS IN JUDGMENT**

FULFILLMENT: **OPENING THEMSELVES TO SHARE THE JOYS AND SORROWS OF EVERYDAY LIFE WITH OTHERS**

JIM CROCE
Singer, "Time in a Bottle"

1/10/1943
Capricorn III

January 10–16
DOMINANCE
CAPRICORN III

Some rather suspicious and calculating people can be found among those born in this week who travel the Way of Trust, and most will have to work hard to rise to the higher challenge of emotional openness and confidence in themselves that presents itself here. Some of these people will manifest their inner uncertainties through a tendency to order or dominate their immediate environment in a mistaken notion that outer, or material, order creates inner serenity. Others may withdraw altogether in disappointment, frustration, or chronic pessimism. Yet if they refuse to give up on their own need for closeness and bonding, and don't expect so much of themselves, they will be able to forgive themselves for their mistakes or failures. Once they have mastered the art of being easier on themselves, they will find the world is much easier a place to be as they make their measured way along this karmic path.

CHALLENGE: **NOT RETREATING TOO MUCH INTO THEIR SHELLS**

FULFILLMENT: **DEVOTING THEMSELVES TO LOVED AND TRUSTED FRIENDS AND FAMILY MEMBERS**

NOTABLE: **HARVEY GANTT (AMERICAN ARCHITECT; POLITICIAN)**

January 17–22
MYSTERY AND IMAGINATION
CAPRICORN–AQUARIUS CUSP

Those born in this cusp week who find themselves on the Way of Trust are in for a rather exciting and unpredictable sort of journey. As much as they may try to shelter themselves from the scrutiny or insensitivity of a harsh world, it is likely the world will not entirely co-operate. This journey will be characterized by any number of unpredictable events and developments as the cosmic forces pull them out of their carefully erected internal worlds and back into the action. While they may well resist the challenge to develop greater trust and faith in themselves, it may be that the very unpredictability of their patterns is what scares them the most. Yet if they can avoid the dangers of escapism, self-negation, and chronic unrest, they can make wonderful spiritual and emotional progress in the course of this life's journey, as they are blessed with both lighter hearts and less baggage than some who travel this road.

JANIS JOPLIN
Rock superstar of 60s,
"Me and Bobby McGee"

1/19/1943
Capricorn–Aquarius Cusp

CHALLENGE: **ENCIRCLING THEMSELVES WITH A NETWORK OF TRUSTED SUPPORTERS TO HELP THEM THROUGH THEIR CHAOTIC LIVES**
FULFILLMENT: **KNOWING WHAT THEY NEED FROM OTHERS**
NOTABLE: **ALEXANDER WOOLLCOTT (AUTHOR, CRITIC)**

January 23–30
GENIUS
AQUARIUS I

Marked by a rather curious emotional detachment, those born in the Week of Genius who find themselves on the Way of Trust may be at a loss as to coping with the problems and issues that present themselves here. They may profess to be uninterested in concepts like safety, trust, and intimacy, yet they will yearn for a sense of more intimate, or higher connection. Their barriers to greater growth may be erected on the lofty concepts of personal freedom, intellectual expansion, and sticking to a misplaced sense of principle without considering the attendant human values. Personal defensiveness can take the form of preoccupation, absentmindedness, or super rationality. Yet if they take care to remain emotionally accessible and allow themselves the freedom that comes with insight into one's own need to be a part of something larger than themselves, their path to success will broaden.

CHALLENGE: **BOTHERING TO STOP AND TAKE A HARD LOOK AT THOSE AROUND THEM**
FULFILLMENT: **GETTING IN TOUCH WITH THEIR HEART AND BODY WISDOM**
NOTABLE: **ARTHUR RUBINSTEIN (PIANIST, SUPREME INTERPRETER OF CHOPIN)**

January 31–February 7
YOUTH AND EASE
AQUARIUS II

Blessed with a rare combination of spirit and heart, those born in this week who travel the Way of Trust will nevertheless have to learn to use their heads as they make their way along this karmic path. Naïveté and a tendency to become the victims of their own popularity will be especially pronounced in this group. Many here will undergo quite a lot of personal disappointment or emotional setbacks until they develop more strength, depth of understanding, and real compassion. Some here will isolate themselves from others out of fear that they will fail to live up to others' expectations. Yet if they find the courage to better manage their own sensitivity without retreating behind a facade of easygoing carelessness or refusing to address obviously emotional concerns, they can make great strides in growth, happiness, and fulfillment as they wend their way along this karmic path.

CHRISTINA RICCI
Actress,
The Addams Family

2/12/1980
Aquarius III

CHALLENGE: **REALIZING, THE HARD WAY, THAT THEY ARE TOO TRUSTING OF OTHERS**
FULFILLMENT: **CASTING A SPELL ON OTHERS WITH THEIR MAGNETISM**

February 8–15
ACCEPTANCE
AQUARIUS III

Guarding against the cynicism or intolerance that arises from personal disappointments will figure prominently in the life lessons of those born in this week who journey along the Way of Trust. Though they can believe themselves to be kind and compassionate in more universal ways, these individuals may nevertheless prefer not to have some of their best qualities put to the test in real life. There is a great fondness for abstraction here, and a tendency to withdraw into "principles" when in fact emotions are at issue. Yet if they can indulge their need for affection and come to understand that a sense of nonattachment need not exist at odds with honesty, integrity, and confidence, their path to personal liberation and enlightenment will become clear.

CHALLENGE: **BEING OPEN WHILE LEARNING DISCERNMENT**
FULFILLMENT: **FEELING AS THOUGH THEY BELONG**
NOTABLE: **AUDREY MEADOWS (ACTRESS, *THE HONEYMOONERS*)**

KARMIC PATH
45

February 16–22
SENSITIVITY
AQUARIUS–PISCES CUSP

Pessimism, isolation, and personal touchiness will prove the biggest stumbling blocks to higher development for those born in this week who travel the Way of Trust. Indeed, there are many here who will develop a chronically negative outlook on emotional interactions that may be expressed alternately as aggression and depression. There is a strong inclination to simply bury their sensitivity under a mountain of professional ambitions and responsibilities to the detriment of their emotional development. Yet these unusual people can set aside their defenses and come to better understand that so-called emotional scars are at best mere descriptions of past disappointments, and neither immutable facts nor inescapable conclusions. Then they will find themselves much freer to explore the worlds of spiritual expansion and confident emotional connection that beckon here.

SIDNEY POITIER
Actor, Oscar for
Lillies of the Field;
helped break Hollywood's
racial barrier

2/20/1924
Aquarius–Pisces Cusp

CHALLENGE: **DISMANTLING THE DEFENSE MECHANISMS THAT KEEP THEM BELLIGERENT OR WITHDRAWN**

FULFILLMENT: **BELIEVING THAT THEY ARE GOOD JUDGES OF CHARACTER**

NOTABLES: **GLORIA VANDERBILT (SOCIALITE; DESIGNER); MARGARET TRUMAN (DAUGHTER OF HARRY TRUMAN; AUTHOR, *LETTERS FROM FATHER*)**

February 23–March 2
SPIRIT
PISCES I

There may indeed be something quite otherworldly about those born in the Week of Spirit who travel the Way of Trust, and with even a small amount of personal and soul work, most will do wonderfully well as they make their way along this karmic path. In fact, their biggest single problem may be that they will tend to consider themselves victimized, or otherwise overreact emotionally to hurts, slights, or setbacks. Cultivating greater objectivity will be important here, as will the ability to apply their intuitive faculties and keen perceptions to the task of finding out just what it is that stands in the way of their fulfillment. They may retreat from the necessity of more confident self-expression and hide behind either an overly modest or an overly superior attitude, both of which will only serve to hinder their possibilities of connection with others. Yet the potential for success far outweighs the chances of failure, stagnation, or suspicion here, and their great kindness and desire to do good will lead them to the confidence they need.

CHALLENGE: **ADHERING TO THEIR INTENTIONS AND GENERALLY BEING MORE GROUNDED**

FULFILLMENT: **OFFERING THEIR KINDNESS AS AN EXAMPLE TO OTHERS**

March 3–10
THE LONER
PISCES II

Those born in the Week of the Loner may have a tough time in the course of this life's journey as they are marked by a sense of isolation that can be hard to conquer. Soulful and sincere, they may nevertheless have rather uninformed or unrealistic expectations of life; their resulting sense of disappointment can lead to depression, the extremes of secrecy, or a complete withdrawal from the mainstream. Yet when they come to terms with the relatively simple fact that their abiding need for acceptance arises not out of the failure of others to understand them, but out of their failure to stand up and be recognized for what they really are and what they really believe, things will doubtless improve. Faith and hope should be consciously cultivated here as well as the ability to simply pass over mistakes or problems. Though they will never be extroverts, they need not be disappointed or disillusioned in the course of this life's journey.

SYLVIA BEACH
Founded Shakespeare &
Co., published *Ulysses*

3/14/1887
Pisces III

CHALLENGE: **BRINGING THEIR ROMANTIC NOTIONS OF LIFE AND LOVE BACK DOWN TO EARTH**

FULFILLMENT: **EXPRESSING THEIR LOVE OF HUMANITY**

March 11–18
DANCERS AND DREAMERS
PISCES III

Revealing their inner beauty and compassion should not prove much of a problem for those born in this week who find themselves on the Way of Trust as they may well appear to lead rather blessed lives indeed. Principal among their problems will be a reluctance to take responsibility for the part they may play in their own disappointments, or cling to some rather unrealistic or naive notions in the interest of preserving their "innocence" or "freedom." Escapism can also be something of a stumbling block as this type is quite prone to various physical and emotional addictions. Yet most will do very well here, and if they can manage to stay grounded in the physical world though respect for the body, and connected to the world of the spirit through their deep reservoirs of emotion, they have nothing to fear. In fact, they have quite a lot to gain in the way of recognition, fulfillment, and happiness as they journey along this life's highway.

CHALLENGE: **OVERCOMING THE NEED TO BE NEEDED AND DEVELOPING THE NEED TO SHARE THEMSELVES**

FULFILLMENT: **COMBINING THEIR MYSTICAL SIDE WITH THEIR INHERENT PRACTICALITY**

NOTABLE: **MARJORIE MERRIWETHER POST (BUSINESS EXECUTIVE; PHILANTHROPIST)**

The Way of Structure

PISCES I TO VIRGO I
Spirit to System Builders

The Way of Structure calls those born to it to develop both the psychological and physical structures to maximize their health, work, and overall welfare. Spiritually idealistic, these individuals are challenged to develop their pragmatic side and eschew those elements that will distract them from the here and now. These individuals feel overwhelmed when they are called to make a decision and are daunted by large amounts of information. Those on this path will learn how to structure and arrange the details of life in a manner that enables them to be decisive. Taking their heads out of the clouds, paying attention to what is in front of their noses, and refusing to be carried away by metaphysical impulses will help those on this path to deal with and enjoy the tasks of everyday life. Eventually, they will find fulfillment by participating in the most mundane life experiences and will be grounded enough to put their compassion to work in service of their fellowman.

The individuals on this karmic path possess an inborn mysticism. Esoterically speaking, one could think of these souls as having spent many lifetimes pursuing a love of the divine, perhaps as monks or nuns, yogis or teachers. By nature they are devoted, caring, and inspired. There is a part of those born to the Way of Structure that exists in another dimension or another place. Yearning for a deeper connection to the divine, these individuals find it difficult to be wholly present in the now—or even in their own bodies

for that matter. Desiring transcendence and yearning for truth, beauty, and joy, they suffer from the harsh realities of life and the misfortunes of others. Often they want to do something to help others, but feel powerless to do so. They may feel a general dissatisfaction with the conditions of their time. Escapism runs rampant here as those on this path try to avoid dealing with the sorrows of the world. While the more evolved souls on this path will find solace in art, music, and the pursuit of a spiritual or inner life, others may choose more self-indulgent outlets such as sensual pleasure, or even mind-altering substances, and risk developing dangerous dependencies.

Those on this path may idealize romantic love, or abandon themselves in a relationship, attempting to merge with their love object only to be disappointed once the blinders of new love come off and they discover the "horrid reality" and sheer humanness of their loved one. Thus, they often move from one person to another forever searching for the unattainable.

The men and women on the Way of Structure may be some of the most impractical people in the personology system and rarely do they think logically. Making decisions is torture for them. They are so psychic they feel inundated with impressions much of the time and this causes them to feel disoriented and confused. They may not discern what is important or be able to pick out the details or facts that may enable them to draw conclusions. Their minds are

CORE LESSON
Creating structure in all aspects of their lives—physical, mental, and emotional

GOAL
To become decisive in practical and grounded ways

GIFTS
Spiritual, Compassionate, Psychic

PITFALLS
Ungrounded, Escapist, Unaware

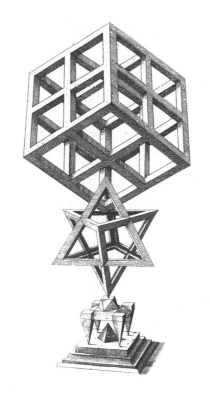

so adrift in spirit they often prefer to completely ignore anything having to do with the day-to-day practicalities, including taking care of their health. Often they are out of touch with their bodies and may be prone to exhibit emotional distress in physical ways. Part of the reason for this may be that on a deep spiritual level those on the Way of Structure may not wish to be embodied at all. Ambivalent about real life, it seems they would prefer to be elsewhere. It is important for those on the Way of Structure to connect to Earth energy and ground themselves in the here and now. They will enjoy life more once they figure out a way to deal with the world. It would help them to begin to learn how to make decisions. The first decision that they might choose is to get on with living by participating fully in life.

The goal of this path is for these individuals to become practical in their decision making. In order to become more decisive they must first create the structure for arranging information relevant to a question so that the answer or course of action they seek is made clear. Those on this path will learn to sift and weigh facts and data and learn how to analyze it by putting it into logical structures such as decision trees in order to help them make decisions. They must also work hard to learn how to create mental systems or hierarchies for ranking tasks or priorities. Believe it or not, such a simple and practi-

cal skill as putting things in order is somewhat foreign to these individuals.

Once they have trained their minds, the men and women on the Way of Structure can begin to establish better emotional boundaries between themselves and others. By recognizing that they have weak psychic boundaries and are frequently emotionally buffeted by the actions and feelings of others, those on this path can begin to create better internal and external structures to protect themselves from sensory overload. As those on this path become more adept at organizing their thoughts and crafting inner structure, they will also create outer regimens and routines all of which will serve to bring their lives into better balance. Moreover, they are likely to learn how to manage the connection between their minds and emotions and their bodies through sports, yoga, or martial arts. Those on this path will be immeasurably aided by a physical fitness regimen since it not only helps clear their thinking, but because it also clears the emotional or spirit body and brings it into alignment with the physical world.

By learning basic skills such as decision making and organization—in essence, dealing with life more effectively—those on this path will enjoy greater stability and inner peace though the process may be more difficult at first. With a more practical orientation, they will be better suited to help those around them. In

RELEASE

The yearning for a more idealized world

REWARD

The joy of knowing the right course of action

SUGGESTION

*Think of information as a tool. Realize that decision making is
about putting all considerations into perspective. Don't feel overwhelmed.
Get organized! Take one step at a time.*

fact, the inherent spirituality of those on the Way of Structure demands some commitment to serving others. Those on this path will never truly feel fulfilled unless they are able to help those in need, or contribute in some other way to making the world a better place. Thus, having injected some structure into their lives and getting a better grip on reality, many on this path may devote their spirituality to an art form, a craft, a skill, a field of endeavor, or even simply to their own form of service to others. Communication of all kinds, but writing, in particular, seems well suited to those on this path since they can pour their unique brand of inspiration and ability to craft an alternate reality in their minds onto the printed page. It should be noted that it is not uncommon for successful writers to have fixed schedules and routines for their writing.

Some on this path may go overboard, becoming so highly structured that they become rigid in their need for routine. In fact, as dependency oriented as they are, those on this path must take care not to become overly dependent on the structures they have erected. Organizing their lives too severely, they may cut themselves off from the creativity of random occurrence, epiphanies, and other serendipities that can initiate real change. An ancillary problem may be that they use their newly developed analytical skills to become too fault finding or pessimistic. Because of their yearning for a more beautiful way of life, both for themselves and others, those on this path often only see the negatives of the world and in others. The best prescription in such a scenario is

for those on the Way of Structure to invoke their capacity to forgive. A bottomless well of forgiveness is theirs for the asking since it comes naturally and easily to them. Forgiving others' failings, as well as their own and those of the world, will make those on this path much easier to live with and much happier in the long run.

The men and women on the Way of Structure might do well do cultivate some practical standards for what they are seeking in a partner and to separate the reality of living life day to day with someone from their desire for transcendence. Those on this path are happiest living a quiet, simple, even family, life. Eventually they will learn that it is best if they live far from noise and distraction since this interferes with their ability to be grounded.

BALANCE POINT

Spiritual and Physical

Leaving plenty of room for solitude, those on this path will structure a life that is satisfying in every respect, balanced between their devotion to something greater than themselves and mundane existence. In a sense, this karmic path offers nothing less than the promise that those on it may one day be the masters of both realms.

This karmic path calls to mind the Egyptian goddess Isis. In myth, Isis, among other things, ruled the practical arts of spinning, weaving, grinding, and healing, functioning as an earth goddess presiding over hearth and home. In the Egyptian pantheon, Isis was the daughter of Geb the earth god and Nut the sky goddess and was the mother of the race of Egyptian kings. As her family relations indicate, Isis is a fitting symbol for the Way of Structure since she acts as a mediator between the divine and earthly realms.

CRYSTALS AND GEMSTONES

Jade is a multidimensional stone infused with the knowledge of many realms. This mineral guides the soul to manifest, function, and find meaning on the earth plane.

NOTABLES ON THIS KARMIC PATH

MARIA CALLAS

As with many born to this path, opera soprano **Maria Callas** was impelled to find a strong physical basis for her life and work. In roles such as Medea and Norma, she brought a dramatic presence to the operatic stage, electrifying audiences with her performances. Equally dramatic was her romantic life (not surprising for someone whose karmic path originates in Pisces I Devotion), exemplified by her much publicized yet long-standing relationship with Greek shipping magnate Aristotle Onassis. Her commitment to structure can be found in her daily disciplined practice and ability to learn scripts for new characters both quickly and thoroughly.

English novelist **Charles Dickens** grounded his life by organizing his time between his writing and ten children. Structuring the release of his works as serials (published in periodical installments), Dickens guaranteed his regular work habits. However, common to this path, today he might be called a workaholic. Born with the social conscience of those on the Way of Structure, Dickens both illuminated and campaigned against the social ills of his time through his writ-

CHARLES DICKENS

ing. Talented as both speaker and actor, he gave many readings and lectures to an adoring public. Many now regard him as perhaps the greatest of all British novelists, second only to Shakespeare in character development.

Russian-born writer **Ayn Rand** was able to balance her Pisces I spiritual origins with her Virgo I destination. Leaving Russia shortly after her college graduation, Rand moved to the United States, where she developed her philosophy, "Objectivism," a seemingly Virgoan philosophy that focuses on reason, self-interest, and capitalism. In books such as *The Fountainhead* and *Atlas Shrugged,* she created protagonists who were able to revolutionize their immediate environment through genius and sheer force of will.

AYN RAND

Other Notables: Clara McBride Hale, Paul Tillich, Roy Lichtenstein, Alan Shepard, Jr., Nadja Salerno-Sonnenberg, Maria von Trapp, Barbra Streisand, Robert Penn Warren, Tammy Wynette, Henry Fonda, John Maynard Keynes, Curtis Mayfield, Paul McCartney, Harrison Ford, Jerry Garcia, Garrison Keillor, David Ben-Gurion, Dr. Marie Curie, John F. Kennedy, Jr., Kenneth Branagh, Emily Dickinson, Julia Louis-Dreyfus, Christian Dior, W.E.B. Du Bois

---

BIRTHDAYS ON KARMIC PATH 46

June 9, 1886–October 28, 1886 | January 20, 1905–June 9, 1905 | September 1, 1923–January 20, 1924

April 13, 1942–August 31, 1942 | November 22, 1960–April 12, 1961

July 4, 1979–November 22, 1979 | February 13, 1998–July 3, 1998 | September 24, 2016–February 12, 2017

KARMIC PATH
46

March 19–24

REBIRTH
PISCES–ARIES CUSP

The Way of Structure gifts the individuals born on the Cusp of Rebirth with quite a bit more natural sensitivity and spiritual leanings than they might have otherwise, though some here will experience problems putting their inner yearnings to practical use. Nevertheless, these open and straightforward people will likely succeed on this path, providing they immerse themselves fully in the experience of life and learn to channel their energies into productive pursuits. Nervousness and a tendency to be high strung are qualities that will have to be kept under control, and some may have to abandon their more unrealistic expectations or overweening desires for personal transformation. Most can experience considerable happiness and fulfillment along this road, however, especially when they immerse themselves in well-defined family and professional goals that hold them to a grand design and specific plans at the same time that they live their lives on a steady course and build on a secure foundation.

CLARA HALE
Founded Hale House in
Harlem for babies of
drug-addicted mothers

4/1/1905
Aries I

CHALLENGE: **TRAINING THEIR MINDS TO THINK MORE LOGICALLY**

FULFILLMENT: **PERSUADING OTHERS THROUGH WELL-FORMULATED ARGUMENTS**

March 25–April 2

THE CHILD
ARIES I

Those born in the Week of the Child who travel the Way of Structure have a natural love of life and a measure of enthusiasm for worldly experience that is likely to serve them well in the course of this journey. Yet they are infinitely more sensitive and spiritually oriented than some Aries I's, and they will have to guard carefully against an inclination to withdraw from the world in disappointment and isolation when "normal" life doesn't quite live up to their expectations. Escapism can be a real stumbling block here as well. Yet if they direct their energies in such a way that they can stay grounded in the physical without turning to the world of addiction, sensation, or unfulfilled dreams, they will find not only enlightenment, but a great measure of personal satisfaction as they make their way along this road.

CHALLENGE: **NOT VIEWING STRUCTURE TO BE LIMITATION**

FULFILLMENT: **FEELING IN CONTROL BY BEING ORGANIZED**

April 3–10

THE STAR
ARIES II

The individuals born in the Week of the Star who find themselves on the Way of Structure can experience great personal satisfaction and some significant career attainment, providing they do not allow themselves to go off on what might best be called "spiritual tangents" or hold themselves aloof from the call to stay fully grounded in the physical world. In fact, these people will have a tendency to take themselves more seriously than need be, and overidealism can also prove a problem. Yet there is a strong urge here to unite with groups and to stay at the center of things that will be to their benefit. If they can avoid the dangers of emotional excess or unrealistic expectations of themselves and others, and learn instead to direct their formidable energy to the attainment of tangible and practical goals, they are sure to make their mark along this karmic path.

BILL CONTI
Composer, *The Right Stuff*

4/13/1942
Aries III

CHALLENGE: **BECOMING MORE PRACTICAL IN MATTERS OF RELATIONSHIP**

FULFILLMENT: **GROUNDING THEIR INSPIRED APPROACH IN CREATIVITY**

April 11–18

THE PIONEER
ARIES III

Those born in the Week of the Pioneer who journey along this road may struggle to find the balance between their high ideals and effective execution of their plans. Though they will be blessed with broad and far-ranging vision, they can nevertheless experience conflict when it becomes obvious to them that there is more to getting a job done than lofty speeches or idle dreaming. Though they have the ability to inspire others, they will also need to demonstrate their willingness to roll up their sleeves and get their hands dirty in the interest of seeing their plans to conclusion, or risk promising much more than they ever deliver. Yet if they can develop personal discipline, and realign their sense of idealism to coincide more with what is "do-able" than what is merely "dreamable," they can realize great fulfillment and accomplishment along this karmic path.

CHALLENGE: **ROLLING UP THEIR SLEEVES AND GETTING DOWN TO WORK**

FULFILLMENT: **DOING SOMETHING OF SERVICE IN CONJUNCTION WITH OTHERS**

April 19–24

POWER
ARIES–TAURUS CUSP

A fine mix of spiritual leanings and physical energies come into play for those born on the Cusp of Power who travel the Way of Structure, and this configuration is likely to make for a number of real success stories. Gifted with a much more grounded and realistic approach to life than many who travel this road, these individuals are touched by inspiration that they might not otherwise possess. The resulting combination of imagination joined to a solid grasp of how the world works can make for enormous success and personal accomplishment. Though they will have to be careful of a certain tendency to overindulgence in physical pleasure, and a tendency to some rather manipulative or mercenary qualities, these individuals can nevertheless expect wonderful fulfillment in the course of this life's journey.

CHALLENGE: **NOT MASKING THE NEED FOR CONTROL AS A NEED FOR STRUCTURE**
FULFILLMENT: **USING DISCRIMINATION TO ACHIEVE ONLY THE BEST FOR THEMSELVES**
NOTABLES: **ROBERT PENN WARREN (POET, WRITER, *ALL THE KING'S MEN*); RICHARD DALEY, JR. (MAYOR, CHICAGO); PAT BROWN (CALIFORNIA GOVERNOR); SANDRA DEE (ACTRESS, SINGER, *GIDGET*)**

BARBRA STREISAND
Singer/actress/director,
Funny Girl, A Star Is Born;
won 2 Oscars

4/24/1942
Aries-Taurus Cusp

April 25–May 2

MANIFESTATION
TAURUS I

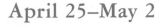 

The individuals born in the Week of Manifestation who are born to this destiny path are in little danger of being carried away by metaphysical impulses or inclinations, yet they will nevertheless have to be on guard in themselves against a tendency to a certain smugness or self-satisfaction that can work to their detriment here. In fact, they can seem rather fixed in their ideologies to the extent that others fail to recognize either the breadth of their vision or the scope of their practical talents. Thus, this configuration will require them to do much more in the way of self-starting than they might be inclined to do. Protective and nurturing, they will nevertheless experience little difficulty with the call to dedicated service and hands-on involvement that beckon here. If they can manage to control a lazy streak, and further avoid the dangers of self-satisfaction, they can enjoy the singular joy of seeing their vision materialize in tangible and structured reality as they make their way along this karmic path.

CHALLENGE: **GUARDING AGAINST THE TENDENCY FOR STRUCTURE TO BECOME RIGIDITY**
FULFILLMENT: **DEVOTING THEIR PRACTICALITY TO AIDING OTHERS**

May 3–10

THE TEACHER
TAURUS II

The challenge to develop greater structure in their lives may at times prove daunting for those born in the Week of the Teacher who journey along this karmic path as they are much caught up in the world of thoughts and ideas and may have little taste for mundane matters. Yet most of these souls will have a strong urge for physical expression in addition to their intellectual and spiritual endowments, and with a modicum of discipline they can realize great fulfillment here. Perhaps their principal problem will be only that they fail to properly channel their gifts in productive ways and retreat into high-handed, effete, or hypercritical attitudes. If they can remember not to take themselves too seriously and at the same time use their flair for knowledge and enterprise to best advantage, they will enjoy great fulfillment here, as they have a really remarkable gift for turning abstract ideals into practical and fruitful information.

CHALLENGE: **LEARNING BETTER WAYS TO RELAX**
FULFILLMENT: **STRUCTURING THEIR MENTAL PROCESSES THROUGH PHYSICAL ROUTINE AND VICE VERSA**
NOTABLE: **ROBERT BROWNING (ENGLISH POET)**

TAMMY WYNETTE
Country
singer/songwriter,
"D-I-V-O-R-C-E"

5/5/1942
Taurus II

May 11–18

THE NATURAL
TAURUS III

The highly individualistic souls born in this week who travel the Way of Structure may be resistant to some of the challenges, as there is a strongly rebellious streak in many of these people that can exist at decided odds with the higher calling to hands-on training and a more structured approach that is implied here. They are adventurous types who may dream more than they do, and some will have to work hard to divest themselves of phobic attitudes about restriction or the "chains" placed on them by society before they can be really effective. Grounding themselves in the world of nature, regular physical routines, and mental and emotional discipline will prove especially important, as will the ability to manage their tendency to change their friends and lovers and scene the way other people change clothes. Yet if they can come to better understand their own needs for security and immerse themselves fully into the experience of creating those things which really make them feel safe and centered, all will go well here.

CHALLENGE: **GETTING A HANDLE ON THEIR PROPENSITY TO BE BORED EASILY**
FULFILLMENT: **DISCOVERING THE INNER SENSE OF SECURITY THAT ROUTINE GIVES THEM**
NOTABLE: **HENRY FONDA (ACTOR, *GRAPES OF WRATH;* OSCAR FOR *ON GOLDEN POND*)**

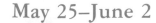

May 19–24
ENERGY
TAURUS–GEMINI CUSP

Those born on the Cusp of Energy who travel the Way of Structure may have their share of difficulties along this road as there is a pronounced tendency to somewhat scattered attentions and a general lack of discipline and groundedness that can give them trouble here. Though likely to have more personal depth than some travelers born in this week, they can nevertheless be rather flighty folk, whose attentions are all too easily swayed by the latest fad, fashion, or phase. Learning to slow down and ground themselves in measured and concerted effort will be especially important for these people, as theirs is a marked inclination to want to place themselves in the center of the action without first pausing to establish just where the action is. Dealing with the more mundane tasks and details of life will be important to their development and sense of accomplishment, and once they come to understand that more structured approaches result in more tangible results, they can make great progress along this road.

CHALLENGE: **DEVELOPING THE PATIENCE TO APPLY THEMSELVES MORE**

FULFILLMENT: **ENJOYING THE RESPECT OF OTHERS ONCE THEY HAVE SETTLED DOWN**

FELIX GRUCCI
Business executive,
fireworks

5/28/1905
Gemini I

May 25–June 2
FREEDOM
GEMINI I

Gemini I's who find themselves on the Way of Structure may be perplexed by the challenges until they come to a better understanding of the need to ground themselves in service to others and the joys of day-to-day reality. Highly strung and likely to be very susceptible to stress, they can suffer greatly when they feel themselves unduly restricted or constrained. Impatience with others can only exacerbate their tendency to fly off in new directions and leave things unfinished when things don't go according to plan. Yet while this road may not be an entirely easy one, these individuals can nevertheless come to understand the need to ground themselves in routines of their own choosing. They can surely make their mark by focusing their interests and understanding as they make their way along this karmic path.

CHALLENGE: **STRUCTURING THEIR THOUGHTS SO THAT THEY SAY AS MUCH WITH FEWER WORDS**

FULFILLMENT: **FEELING THE SATISFACTION OF COMPLETED PROJECTS**

June 3–10
NEW LANGUAGE
GEMINI II

Those born in this week who journey along the Way of Structure can realize great progress along this road. The individuals born in the Week of New Language, though talented and communicative, may nevertheless have a difficult time coming to terms with the higher challenges indicated here until they better learn to structure their ideas and put them forth in a more organized way. Gemini II's need to develop discipline; otherwise they may become mired in insecurity and may waste their gifts in unfulfilled longing for a more perfect world. Much inclined to scholarly and intellectual pursuits, they can expect particular success in fields that will allow them to display and exercise their special verbal skills within established systems and necessary structures. Writing and criticism are also good choices. Once they come to comprehend that the crux of their spiritual challenge is not just to overcome their personal defensiveness, but to help others better comprehend themselves, the path to enlightenment will be greatly clarified.

CHALLENGE: **NOT SLIPPING INTO FAULT FINDING, BEING OVERCRITICAL, OR A GENERAL SENSE OF DISSATISFACTION**

FULFILLMENT: **EFFECTING POSITIVE CHANGE IN THEIR LIVES AND THE LIVES OF OTHERS**

NOTABLE: **CURTIS MAYFIELD (POP/SOUL SINGER, SOLO AND WITH THE IMPRESSIONS)**

PAUL McCARTNEY
Legendary rock singer/
songwriter/multi-
instrumentalist; inducted
into the Rock and Roll
Hall of Fame with The
Beatles and as a solo
artist

6/18/1942
Gemini III

June 11–18
THE SEEKER
GEMINI III

Gemini III's who find themselves on the Way of Structure may experience a number of difficulties until they learn to better control their yearning for adventure and a tendency to jump the traces of established routines and conventions. Much prone to strike off in new directions, these individuals will have to come to learn the value of greater personal discipline and a more grounded approach to life in general. Rather easily disillusioned, they may need to guard against a tendency to find fault with themselves and the world. Their fondness for exploration and risk taking can cause them to set themselves unattainable or unrealistic goals, and the failures and setbacks that result can only contribute to their woes. Yet they are gifted with more analytic talents than many who travel this road, and if they are careful to organize the many aspects and levels of their personalities into a comprehensive and methodical approach to the world, they will find happiness here.

CHALLENGE: **TAKING THE TROUBLE TO APPLY THEIR FAR-REACHING MINDS TO MUNDANE DETAILS**

FULFILLMENT: **PURSUING THE TRUTH**

NOTABLES: **ROGER EBERT (FILM CRITIC, HALF OF SISKEL AND EBERT); PAUL McCARTNEY (SINGER/SONGWRITER, THE BEATLES, WINGS, "YESTERDAY")**

KARMIC PATH
46

June 19–24
MAGIC
GEMINI–CANCER CUSP

Extreme emotionalism can take its physical and spiritual toll on those born in this week until they better learn to use their inborn objectivity with a dose of personal discipline. Likely to be romantic and idealistic to the nth degree, they will need to work especially hard to keep themselves in the here and now and avoid putting themselves through the mill when life fails to live up to their expectations. Relaxation techniques and healthy exercise will be very useful as it will serve to ground them in their physical bodies and at the same time give them an outlet for stress or pent-up energy. Yet they will be blessed with tremendous compassion and a strong desire to make the world a better place. If they can avoid taking things too personally and learn to channel their action-oriented energy in realistic and well-defined ways, life will surely hold more than its share of practical magic for those who travel this road.

CHALLENGE: **NOT THROWING UP STRUCTURE MERELY TO MASK THEIR INNER LIVES**
FULFILLMENT: **FINDING GREATER EMOTIONAL BALANCE**
NOTABLES: **BRIAN WILSON (SONGWRITER; FOUNDER OF THE BEACH BOYS); MICHELLE LEE (DANCER; ACTRESS, *KNOT'S LANDING*)**

June 25–July 2
THE EMPATH
CANCER I

The personalities born in the Week of the Empath who travel the Way of Structure will have to work hard to come to terms with tangible and practical reality and develop better organizational skills if they are to realize the rewards that beckon here. Rather too sensitive for their own good, they are easily swayed by the thoughts and feelings of other people and may be wont to drift off on all manner of emotional and spiritual tangents until they develop better personal boundaries and concentrate on their own needs. Yet they are sure to recognize rather early on that keeping themselves on a more even keel will help to nurture their strong need for security. With that in mind, they can rise to the challenge to develop greater common sense and structure in their lives. Once they become more grounded, these individuals may further display a talent for life management skills many others would envy. Thus, if they can turn their attention away from the emotional and toward the practical life will be kind indeed.

CHALLENGE: **DEVELOPING PSYCHIC AND EMOTIONAL BOUNDARIES WITH OTHERS IN LIEU OF WITHDRAWING PHYSICALLY**
FULFILLMENT: **BECOMING BETTER MANAGERS**
NOTABLES: **ROBERT BALLARD (LOCATED THE *TITANIC*); ANDREA CROUCH (GRAMMY-WINNING GOSPEL SINGER)**

GEORGE MALLORY
Climbed Mt. Everest

6/18/1886
Gemini III

July 3–10
THE UNCONVENTIONAL
CANCER II

Cancer II's can experience some problems with the higher challenge implied by the Way of Structure, and their struggles may give a whole new meaning to "getting real." Highly imaginative and gifted with a strong spiritual inclination, these individuals may have a problem distinguishing fantasy from reality, and there is a genuine danger that they will fail the higher challenge of developing practical structure and groundedness here only to devolve into chronic escapism. Learning the value of objectivity and nonattachment will prove especially important to their development, as will increasing self-esteem through staying on a chosen career path, in a stable relationship, or pursuing an attainable set of personal goals. Surrounding themselves with tangible evidence of their success will also be helpful, as their homes will serve as a grounding influence for their more ethereal energies, and serve to remind them of the joys of solid achievement.

CHALLENGE: **PROVIDING AN OUTLET FOR THEIR YEARNING FOR TRANSCENDENCE**
FULFILLMENT: **CREATING A SAFE, ORGANIZED HAVEN FOR THEMSELVES**

July 11–18
THE PERSUADER
CANCER III

Those born in the Week of the Persuader are blessed with a rare combination of inspiration and common sense that can make for a fine and fulfilling life journey as they travel the Way of Structure. Likely to respond very well to the higher challenge to practical application of their talents and a more structured approach to life and living, most will do extremely well along this road. They will have to be careful, however, that they do not ignore or discount their own more imaginative and spiritual leanings as they pursue career or business goals. Highly emotional in any event, they will have to take care to control an innate tendency to excess as their need for grounding can manifest as addictive or compulsive behaviors if not properly regulated. Yet there is every indication of success along this road, providing they control their expectations and develop their natural ability to deal with facts and figures with insight and an eye to results.

CHALLENGE: **NOT ALLOWING THEIR ABILITY TO STRUCTURE AND CONTROL THEIR OWN NEEDS TO BECOME EXCESSIVE**
FULFILLMENT: **HONING THEIR POWERS OF OBSERVATION AND ATTENTION TO DETAIL TO A HIGH ART**

HARRISON FORD
Actor, *Indiana Jones,
The Fugitive*

7/13/1942
Cancer III

July 19–25
OSCILLATION
CANCER–LEO CUSP

Blessed with an enormous gift for innovation and more than a dash of real moral courage, those born in this cusp week who find themselves on the Way of Structure can enjoy great success, providing they do not allow some inner conflicts to get the best of them. Here the yearning for transcendence can surface as a tendency to create their own sense of crisis or emergency, and they will have to work a bit to balance the need for excitement against the necessity for structured thought and dedicated effort. Still, their capacity for inspiration can hold them in wonderful stead when they are put to use in the service of others, for this is a configuration that can make for true leaders. Learning to regulate emotions, attend to the details, and avoid their addictive side will all figure prominently, yet they are blessed with the courage to see them through the worst of times and the sense of hope to lead them to the best and most enjoyable life has to offer.

CHALLENGE: **GROUNDING THEMSELVES MORE FULLY IN THEIR BODIES THROUGH PHYSICAL ACTIVITY**

FULFILLMENT: **IMPROVING THEIR DAY-TO-DAY RELATIONS WITH OTHERS THROUGH A MORE BALANCED, MEASURED APPROACH**

NOTABLE: **CHRIS SARANDON (ACTOR, *DOG DAY AFTERNOON*)**

JERRY GARCIA
Songwriter/guitarist/singer,
founder of
The Grateful Dead
──────
8/1/1942
Leo I

July 26–August 2
AUTHORITY
LEO I

With even a modicum of training and personal discipline, those born in the Week of Authority who find themselves on the Way of Structure can expect a fine and fulfilling journey, for here ambition is tempered by sensitivity, and intuition fired by a sense of passion that is often missing in some others who travel this road. Though issues may arise with the willingness of Leo I's to take responsibility for their own follies and foibles, there is nevertheless the prospect of great success once these personalities come to terms with their tendency to expect too much, too soon. They will draw a number of fans and disciples and will have to take care not to allow their considerable impact on others to devolve into egotism or manipulation. Yet if they hold to ideals of service and devotion and at the same time direct their energies to tangible and realizable goals, they can accomplish much for themselves and others as they make their way along this life's highway.

CHALLENGE: **ADHERING LESS TO ABSTRACT NOTIONS AND MORE TO PRACTICALITIES**

FULFILLMENT: **FINDING MORE EMOTIONAL SATISFACTION BY BEING MORE FULLY PRESENT IN A RELATIONSHIP**

NOTABLE: **BOBBIE GENTRY (SINGER/SONGWRITER, "ODE TO BILLY JOE")**

August 3–10
BALANCED STRENGTH
LEO II

The individuals born in the Week of Balanced Strength who make their way along this karmic path are destined for considerable success and accomplishment as they have a natural ability to focus their attentions and direct their energies in highly productive ways. By no means as easily distracted as some who travel this road, this group has an admirable solidity that will serve these people well here. Some very devotional qualities will doubtless come to the fore as well, and their natural attraction to structure and single-minded effort is sure to show in a fine sense of groundedness and realism. If they are careful that their dedication does not become entangled with a sense of suffering and that their yearning for a better world does not devolve into victimhood, all can go beautifully along this karmic path.

CHALLENGE: **CREATING ADEQUATE BOUNDARIES SO THAT THEY MIGHT SERVE OTHERS WITHOUT HARMING THEMSELVES**

FULFILLMENT: **APPLYING THEIR POWERS OF CONCENTRATION**

NOTABLE: **BILLIE BURKE (ACTRESS, GLINDA, THE GOOD WITCH, IN *WIZARD OF OZ*)**

GARRISON KEILLOR
Writer/radio host,
Prairie Home Companion
──────
8/7/1942
Leo II

August 11–18
LEADERSHIP
LEO III

The commanding and even heroic people born in this week will surely bring a touch of the mythic to the Way of Structure, and no matter what their areas of personal or professional endeavor, they are capable of imbuing even the most mundane or practical concerns with a rare touch of spirituality and inspiration. They will have to be mindful of their tendencies to leave the details to others, however, and may further struggle with ego issues or an undue sense of entitlement. They will occasionally suffer setbacks due to a certain high-handedness in their dealings with others and will have to fight a tendency to take themselves and their ambitions too seriously. Once they begin to back up their sense of inspiration with dedicated and devoted effort, and turn an eye to what they can do for others, rather than what others might do for them, life will reward them richly along this road.

CHALLENGE: **LEARNING TO ATTEND TO THE DETAILS THEMSELVES RATHER THAN HANDING THEM OFF TO OTHERS**

FULFILLMENT: **TAKING ADVANTAGE OF RANDOM OCCURRENCE AND SERENDIPITY ONCE THEY START TO NOTICE THEM**

NOTABLE: **FRANCIS JOSEPH I, EMPEROR OF AUSTRIA (HIS ATTACK ON SERBIA PRECIPITATED WWI)**

August 19–25

EXPOSURE
LEO–VIRGO CUSP

The interesting and unusual individuals born in this period who negotiate the challenge and promise of the Way of Structure are likely to respond beautifully to the call for greater order in their lives, thoughts, and efforts. Indeed, they bring to this life's journey a rare combination of keen objectivity and spiritual understanding that can make for real success and satisfaction in the course of their development. Naturally dependable and reliable, they may nevertheless have to take some care to take responsibility for their own behaviors, rather than to blame the world for their troubles. Yet they are likely to be much more self-contained and grounded than some who travel this road, and if they do not allow their boundaries to be blurred by irrelevant or irrational concerns, they will inspire trust and devotion in others. Providing they keep a sense of personal integrity intact, there will be little they cannot accomplish in the course of this life's journey.

CHALLENGE: **BECOMING MORE REALISTIC IN LOVE**
FULFILLMENT: **RECORDING THEIR THOUGHTS OR IMPRESSIONS IN WORDS**
NOTABLES: **PATRICIA MCBRIDE (BALLET DANCER); ISAAC HAYES (SOUL/R&B SINGER/SONGWRITER, "SOUL MAN")**

PAUL TILLICH
Theologian, wrote
The Shaking of the Foundation

8/20/1886
Leo–Virgo Cusp

August 26–September 2

SYSTEM BUILDERS
VIRGO I

The naturally efficient and organized individuals born in this week who travel the Way of Structure can realize enviable success in the course of this life's journey, once they start not taking themselves quite so seriously. In fact there may be a naive aspect to many of these individuals and they will have to learn to take things more with a grain of salt as they make their way along this road. They will do well to take care when controlling their more imaginative and dreamy side, however, and remain mindful that this is one instance where too much control or repression of emotions and imagination is almost as treacherous as not enough control over same. Still, they will doubtless discover that their highest attainments will in some way reflect their unique ability to tap into their own vast reserves of spirit and in turn manifest their inspirations and faith through their practical and structured approach. If they can further relax a bit and set aside the need to impose their beliefs on others, they will surely accomplish great things through their ability to find God in the details of life.

CHALLENGE: **BALANCING THEIR DESIRE FOR A BETTER WORLD WITH AN ACKNOWLEDGMENT OF WHAT IS**
FULFILLMENT: **LIVING EACH DAY FULLY IN THE NOW**
NOTABLES: **DARYL DRAGON (POP SINGER, CAPTAIN IN DUO CAPTAIN AND TENNILLE)**

September 3–10

THE ENIGMA
VIRGO II

Giving shape and substance to their more spiritual and imaginative side is likely to come quite easily to those born in the Week of the Enigma who journey along the Way of Structure. Naturally discerning and blessed with keen powers of observation, these souls will have a certain immunity to the myriad of distractions, seductions, and addictions that can trouble so many who travel this highway. Yet they will nevertheless have to take some care that they do not go overboard in imposing their standards and structures on themselves and the world around them to the extent that they neglect to truly unite their spiritual and physical sides. Some here will rigorously suppress emotion and inspiration in favor of purely practical concerns, while others will exalt the material out of a fearful attitude toward their own subconscious leanings. Yet most will allow themselves to be guided to see their plans and dreams into tangible and rewarding reality.

CHALLENGE: **LEAVING ROOM FOR A LITTLE CREATIVE CHAOS IN THEIR LIVES**
FULFILLMENT: **LIVING A LIFE ACCORDING TO THEIR OWN EXACTING AND DISCERNING STANDARDS**
NOTABLES: **HILDA DOOLITTLE (MAJOR IMAGIST POET); PETER LAWFORD (ACTOR; MEMBER OF THE RAT PACK); FRÉDÉRIC MISTRAL (POET; 1904 NOBEL PRIZE)**

HANK WILLIAMS, SR.
Country singer,
"Your Cheatin' Heart"

9/17/1923
Virgo III

September 11–18

THE LITERALIST
VIRGO III

Though the individuals born in this week are promised great success and worldly accomplishment when traveling the Way of Structure, they may have to come to terms with the relatively simple fact that they may not be the super rational, super organized, and super practical individuals they fancy themselves to be. Learning to better compose themselves and order their own thoughts will be especially important for these people as they are rather prone to seize upon their inspirations as fact without doing the grounded detail and detective work. Easily frustrated, they may nevertheless have a certain distaste for confrontation, and the resulting sense of disappointment or chronic lack of fulfillment can result in judgmental or irrational attitudes about what is "supposed to happen" or what are "supposed" to be the facts. Yet if they can tap into rather than deny their deep reserves of spirit, compassion, and understanding and use them to inform their sense of reality, all will go brilliantly here.

CHALLENGE: **PAYING PARTICULAR ATTENTION TO THE MIND/BODY CONNECTION**
FULFILLMENT: **WORKING IN A STRUCTURED, THOROUGH, AND CRAFTSMANLIKE MANNER**
NOTABLES: **DOLORES COSTELLO (ACTRESS); BETSY DRAKE (ACTRESS; MARRIED TO CARY GRANT; *ROOM FOR ONE MORE*)**

September 19–24
BEAUTY
VIRGO–LIBRA CUSP

The sensitive souls born in this period who find themselves on the Way of Structure are likely to flounder a bit until they come to better terms with the need to become more grounded in physical and material reality. Easily swayed and far too susceptible to disappointment or disillusion, they may find that much of their confusion results from the failure to stick to their routines and apply themselves diligently to the tasks at hand. Escapism can be a big problem here and they will have to be careful that they do not attempt to ground their more ethereal energies with too much food, too much alcohol, or other substances in vain attempts to make themselves feel more "real." Their experiences with lovers and sexual partners may illustrate a similar lack of staying power, and many here will move from relationship to relationship in search of an impossible ideal. Yet if they learn the value of setting aside their own flightier inclinations in favor of peaceful routine, secure structure, and real service to others, their path will become much clearer as they make their way along the road.

CHALLENGE: **APPLYING A BIT OF DISCRIMINATION TO THEIR FANTASIES**

FULFILLMENT: **ENJOYING PURE PHYSICAL BEAUTY**

September 25–October 2
THE PERFECTIONIST
LIBRA I

The perfectionists who find themselves on the Way of Structure are likely to enjoy extraordinary success along the road so long as they do not allow themselves to be seduced by a sense of victimhood or embrace the notion that others are somehow responsible for their troubles. Indeed some here may fall prey to a certain preoccupation with the idea that the fault lies elsewhere and never come to terms with the reality that individuals are ultimately responsible for themselves and their happiness. There is a marked tendency to nagging, complaining, or laying the blame on others' doorsteps when life fails to meet their expectations. Indecision, too, can be a problem, and they can spend much time and effort trying to fix others' in an effort to avoid their own issues. Nonetheless there is the possibility for the highest achievement here, providing these personalities learn to better manage their own resources and adjust their attitudes accordingly.

CHALLENGE: **GUARDING AGAINST A GENERAL DISAPPOINTMENT IN LIFE**

FULFILLMENT: **BECOMING BETTER FRIENDS WITH THEIR OWN BODIES**

CHARLES PRATT
Oilman; established Pratt Institute and 1st free public library in NYC

10/2/1830
Libra I

October 3–10
SOCIETY
LIBRA II

The highly social and diplomatic people born in this week who journey along the Way of Structure may falter in the course of this life's journey through an inability to come to better terms with their own needs. Though blessed with a rare combination of keen insight and true compassion, they may become too caught up in a whirlwind of insubstantial obligations and distractions and thus fail the higher calling to ground their energies in the real world. Though sure to be popular with those around them, they will have to be careful not to see their ability to inspire others as a substitute for concerted and disciplined efforts of their own. If they can control their tendency to fantasize; avoid scattering their energies in speculative, unrealistic, or escapist pursuits; and, instead, turn their attentions toward those in need, they can find the fulfillment they seek through some form of service and will enjoy a satisfying and productive life's journey.

CHALLENGE: **DEVELOPING STRUCTURES TO MANAGE THEIR INTERACTIONS WITH THE MANY PEOPLE IN THEIR LIVES**

FULFILLMENT: **COMING TO ACCEPT THE MORE PHYSICAL SIDES OF LIFE**

NOTABLE: **PHILLIP BERRIGAN (CATHOLIC PRIEST; POLITICAL ACTIVIST; AUTHOR)**

October 11–18
THEATER
LIBRA III

Those born in the Week of Theater who find themselves on the Way of Structure can enjoy great success as they bring to this path a level of natural passion that, combined with a certain objectivity, can serve to keep them on a straighter road to fulfillment than many of their fellow travelers. Though they will manifest a richly imaginative side, there is also a healthy dose of self-interest and personal ambition that goes with this configuration. These personalities have a worldly disposition and a material side that are likely to keep them well grounded in the here and now. Thus, with only a modicum of personal discipline, the willingness to order their lives, and the release of their tendency to blame or point fingers when life falls short of their idealistic marks, these individuals will manifest both a high and inspired creativity and some extraordinary gifts for putting their talents to work as they make their way along this karmic path.

CHALLENGE: **NOT LETTING THEIR DESIRE FOR A BETTER WORLD TURN INTO CHRONIC *STURM UND DRANG***

FULFILLMENT: **FEELING A SENSE OF MASTERY AS THEY EFFICIENTLY ORGANIZE THEIR LIVES**

DAVID BEN-GURION
Israeli prime minister

10/16/1886
Libra III

October 19–25

DRAMA AND CRITICISM
LIBRA–SCORPIO CUSP

Though there are some born in this cusp week who travel the Way of Structure and will go through life feeling like square pegs in round holes, quite a few others will enjoy real achievement and success. With big personalities, they may chafe a bit at the call to ground themselves in the seemingly mundane issues of life and disdain the need for routine, structure, and personal discipline. Yet they have much greater objectivity than some who journey along this path, and their finely honed analytic talents will serve them in wonderful stead as they come to terms with physical and material reality. If they can be on guard in themselves against inflated opinions of their own talents and come to understand that their truest calling is to serve as channels for divine inspiration to manifest itself in the real world, they will take up their tasks more willingly as they make their way along this karmic path.

DR. MARIE CURIE
Physicist; 2 Nobel Prizes

11/7/1867
Scorpio II

CHALLENGE: **USING THEIR ANALYTICAL ABILITY TO THINK MORE STRATEGICALLY**

FULFILLMENT: **FINDING A PHYSICAL OUTLET FOR THEIR SPIRITUAL PASSION**

October 26–November 2

INTENSITY
SCORPIO I

If natural passion and intensity can serve as something of an antidote for unfulfilled yearnings and overly ethereal inclinations, Scorpio I travelers are likely to do quite well on the Way of Structure. Though they will almost certainly experience their share of mood swings, these highly polarized and emotional types nevertheless have great potential for success and accomplishment on this path, once they get more organized. Gifted with some truly virtuoso energies, they have a capacity for focus and formidable analytic abilities that will prove especially useful. Further, their strong physical and material needs should nicely balance the touch of the divine that is part of the endowment here. If they can avoid getting overly caught up in purely emotional concerns, better control a needy side, and learn not to be quite so thin-skinned, they can accomplish wonders as they make their way along this road.

CHALLENGE: **TEMPERING EMOTIONAL RESPONSES WITH A DOSE OF COMMON SENSE AND DISCRIMINATION**

FULFILLMENT: **USING THEIR TREMENDOUS ABILITY TO CONCENTRATE IN MEDITATION OR MIND/BODY PRACTICES**

NOTABLE: **ROY LICHTENSTEIN (ARTIST, POP ART)**

November 3–11

DEPTH
SCORPIO II

The souls born in the Week of Depth who journey along the Way of Structure have the highest potential for fulfillment and accomplishment along this road, provided they better cultivate their intellectual powers and learn to concentrate on life in the material world. In fact, escapism or getting bogged down in a sense of their own suffering can be problems for these people as they can express their need to connect in the physical world through sexual addictions, substance abuse, and even hypochondria. Worry and depression can be stumbling blocks as well, and some here will expend needless energy pondering the imponderables of existence. Yet if they focus and ground themselves through more constructive efforts in the physical, financial, and material structures of life, they can display wonderful dedication and concentration, resulting in great achievements and a sense of personal satisfaction.

CHALLENGE: **GETTING A GRIP ON THE REASONS THEY TEND TO BE DISAPPOINTED SO OFTEN**

FULFILLMENT: **ENJOYING THE SATISFACTION OF FEELING IN CONTROL**

NOTABLE: **DOROTHY DANDRIDGE (SINGER, ACTRESS, *CARMEN JONES*; 1ST AFRICAN AMERICAN WOMAN NOMINATED FOR OSCAR)**

November 12–18

CHARM
SCORPIO III

The individuals born the Week of Charm who navigate the Way of Structure are likely to have a fine and fulfilling journey as they have a natural gift for organization and analysis that is often lacking in those who make their way along this karmic path. Highly resourceful, they have keen powers of assessment and observation that will further hold them in good stead here. In fact their principal problems in this life's journey will be of a more personal and emotional nature than a question of material or professional concerns, for they may display a rather misplaced sense of idealism when it comes to finding "Mr. or Ms. Right" and drift through any number of less-than-satisfactory relationships in search of an impossible dream. Yet if they can manage to control a tendency to ground themselves through their ability to seduce others through charm and concentrate instead on those things which offer a more substantial reward, they will surely find happiness here.

ALAN SHEPARD
1st American to travel
in space

11/18/1923
Scorpio III

CHALLENGE: **BEING LESS BUFFETED BY THEIR ROMANTIC ILLUSIONS BY GETTING REAL**

FULFILLMENT: **MASTERING A SKILL OR CRAFT**

November 19–24

REVOLUTION
SCORPIO–SAGITTARIUS CUSP

Though a first glance at this configuration might indicate that Scorpio–Sagittarians may have a rough time on the Way of Structure, in fact, there are a number of indications to the contrary. Ideologically, these people may be a bit hard to take, for their aspirations are so high, their ideals so out of reach, and their dreams so lofty that bringing them down to earth may seem impossible. Yet at the same time, there is a strong indication that any number of these people might be able to do just that. The key to their success will lie in the willingness to turn their yearning for a better world into some form of organized action. To aid them in those ambitions, they have guts, determination, and loyalty to those causes they feel are just. If they can keep in mind that most revolutions are the result of a moment of true inspiration followed by years of dedicated, organized, and hands-on involvement, they may surprise both themselves and the rest of us as they make their way along this karmic path.

CHALLENGE: **REALIZING THE TRUE REASONS WHY THEY EM-BRACE THE COMMON MAN AND SCORN THE WEALTHY**

FULFILLMENT: **CREATING A STRATEGY FOR REACHING THEIR GOALS**

KENNETH BRANAGH
Actor/director, *Hamlet*

12/10/1960
Sagittarius II

November 25–December 2

INDEPENDENCE
SAGITTARIUS I

Sheer romanticism may be the biggest stumbling block for those born in the Week of Independence who travel the Way of Structure, and they may have a few rather hard lessons to learn as they make their way along this road. Chief among them is to control their impulses in order to be really effective. There is a pronounced tendency to follow their whims and change their plans to better conform with the innate need of Sagittarius I's for freedom, and they will have to develop a much more organized and efficient approach to life in order to display their gifts to best advantage. Keeping themselves grounded in some form of physical activity or routine will prove especially useful as it can give them an outlet for pent-up energies and help control a tendency to live solely in their heads. However, if they can manage to anchor themselves in the real by accepting personal responsibility and keep their high ideals grounded in hard work and dedicated effort, they will go far.

CHALLENGE: **RECOGNIZING THEIR NEED TO SHARE THE WORKLOAD**

FULFILLMENT: **ENJOYING DISCIPLINE AND THE SENSE OF STRUCTURE IT GIVES THEM**

NOTABLES: **AMY GRANT (POP SINGER, "FIND A WAY"); JOHN F. KENNEDY, JR. (SON OF JFK; FOUNDER OF *GEORGE* MAGAZINE); EFREM ZIMBALIST, JR. (ACTOR; COMPOSER)**

December 3–10

THE ORIGINATOR
SAGITTARIUS II

Practical, organized, and useful application of their inherent spirituality will likely come quite easily to those born in the Week of the Originator who travel the Way of Structure. Though they are unlikely to view the world the same way everyone else does, their uniqueness is by no means a liability here. However, they will have to overcome feelings of inferiority, defensiveness, and insecurity if they are to function at their most effective levels and further avoid a tendency to an exalted sense of martyrdom. Yet their technical gifts are most pronounced and if they organize themselves through training and discipline, they can well specialize in new approaches to old problems, or put an entirely different spin on old information. The potential for success is quite strong and it is likely that they will find their nameless yearnings assuaged by life in a secure and manageable environment. As long as they do not foster dependencies or escapism, they can make great progress especially within a scientific, religious, or research-oriented atmosphere.

CHALLENGE: **SETTING UP STRONGER EMOTIONAL BOUNDARIES**

FULFILLMENT: **APPLYING THEMSELVES TO A TECHNICAL SKILL OR HOBBY**

EMILY DICKINSON
Poet

12/10/1830
Sagittarius II

December 11–18

THE TITAN
SAGITTARIUS III

The souls born in the Week of the Titan who find themselves on the Way of Structure will have to face down the personal demons of overidealism, fretfulness, and plain hubris before they can operate at their most effective levels. Their attraction for magical and ecstatic experiences will be most pronounced here, and they will have to face some hard realities before they come to better terms with the necessity for training, grounding, and personal discipline. In fact, many will refuse the higher calling altogether and find themselves quite unable to adapt to the need for greater organization and structure. Yet if they can come to better understand that their big dreams and far-flung ambitions are not so much a liability but a challenge to imbue life with a sense of the mythic, and that training, discipline, and organization are simply the skills that are necessary to birth those dreams in reality, all will go much more smoothly here.

CHALLENGE: **PAYING BETTER ATTENTION TO THE DETAILS AND DEVELOPING A CAPACITY FOR ANALYZING THEM**

FULFILLMENT: **BECOMING INSPIRED COMMUNICATORS OR ORATORS**

NOTABLE: **BETSY BLAIR (ACTRESS, *MARTY*)**

December 19–25

PROPHECY
SAGITTARIUS–CAPRICORN CUSP

The personalities born on the Cusp of Prophecy who journey along the Way of Structure can experience great fulfillment and accomplishment along the way, providing they do not hold themselves aloof from the challenge to organize and train their sense of inspiration. On the one hand, many here will lose themselves in a preoccupation with their insights and intuitions and fail the higher challenge of sharing those gifts with the world through organized effort. On the other hand, there are those who will take themselves and their need for discipline so seriously that they shut down the channels between the worldly and higher self entirely. Neither of those alternatives will prove the way to salvation, however, and they will have to find the middle road that lies between organized effort and inspired concentration. If they can do that much, preferably through some form of service to others, the rest should go smoothly as they make their way along this karmic path.

NADJA SALERNO-SONNENBERG
Violinist

1/10/1961
Capricorn III

CHALLENGE: **MAKING CERTAIN THAT THE STRUCTURES THEY HAVE ESTABLISHED ARE FLUID**
FULFILLMENT: **IMBUING THEIR LIVES WITH ONGOING DOSES OF FORGIVENESS**
NOTABLES: **HAROLD MASURSKY (GEOLOGIST); DARYL HANNAH (ACTRESS, *SPLASH, HI LIFE*);**

December 26–January 2

THE RULER
CAPRICORN I

Those born in the Week of the Ruler who travel the Way of Structure are naturally dependable, pragmatic, and reliable in their steadfastness. They will be informed here by a higher sense of purpose and empathy for those in need. In fact, these rare individuals are capable of organizing their emotions and spiritual impulses in highly efficient and effective ways, though there is a danger that they will go overboard and display too much intolerance or a kind of missionary zeal for "saving" others or the world. Some strongly self-protective instincts can result in an unwillingness to leave themselves open to the wider world of experience, and repressed emotion can also be something of a problem. Yet at their best, these people will exhibit a profound understanding of the human condition, and the willingness to do something about it.

CHALLENGE: **RECOGNIZING THE LARGER STRUCTURES THEY NEED TO PUT INTO PLACE AT HOME AND AT WORK**
FULFILLMENT: **FINDING LOVE RELATIONSHIPS THAT ARE BALANCED AND DEPENDABLE**
NOTABLE: **DR. SAM SHEPPARD (ACCUSED OF KILLING HIS WIFE; *THE FUGITIVE* BASED ON HIS STORY)**

January 3–9

DETERMINATION
CAPRICORN II

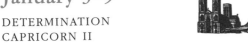

Those born in the Week of Determination who journey along the Way of Structure can realize great success and satisfying accomplishment along this road, though they will have to learn better to manage a naive or unstructured approach to life in order to be able to do so. In fact, there is much to indicate that their characters will be shaped by a tendency to be delicate or sickly in childhood, which can in turn lead them to escape from the harsher realities of life into a world of fantasy. Thus, it is likely that their sense of idealism and imagination may need a bit of adjustment here and there. Yet at their core, these are rather tough customers, endowed with considerable practical talent, a strong devotional quality, and a broader sense of vision. If they can unite all these qualities in such a way that they can effectively share their understanding with others, they will achieve wonderful things in the course of this life's journey.

JULIA LOUIS-DREYFUS
Actress, *Seinfeld*

1/13/1961
Capricorn III

CHALLENGE: **BEING MORE REALISTIC WHEN IT COMES TO RELATIONSHIPS**
FULFILLMENT: **COMBINING THEIR METAPHYSICAL LEANINGS WITH THEIR INNATE SPIRITUALITY**
NOTABLE: **EARL SCRUGGS (FATHER OF BLUEGRASS)**

January 10–16

DOMINANCE
CAPRICORN III

The naturally disciplined personalities born in the Week of Dominance who travel the Way of Structure are likely to quite enjoy this life's journey as their natural energies are very much in keeping with the higher calling to personal discipline, organized effort, and service to others that beckon here. The endowments of this path gift them with a much broader sense of spiritual insight and empathy than they might otherwise possess. Conversely, however, they will have to be on guard against a tendency to be entirely too self-sacrificing and careless of their own needs. Yet if they can manage a tendency to snobbishness or superiority, and further stay grounded in practical routines and organized efforts, they can enjoy great security, a high level of accomplishment, and the kind of life that reflects a nearly perfect balance of good planning and higher inspiration.

CHALLENGE: **BOLSTERING THEIR SELF-CONFIDENCE BY BEING ORGANIZED**
FULFILLMENT: **ENGAGING IN ACTIVITIES PROMOTING CHARITABLE CAUSES OR OTHER SERVICE**
NOTABLE: **KATY JURADO (MEXICAN ACTRESS, *BROKEN LANCE*)**

January 17–22
MYSTERY AND IMAGINATION
CAPRICORN–AQUARIUS CUSP

Though blessed with a great feeling for humanity and a wonderful compassion for the less fortunate, those born on the Cusp of Mystery and Imagination who travel the Way of Structure will nevertheless have to work hard to cultivate the stability and organization that is part of the higher calling here. In a word, the biggest fault of these individuals will be that they can refuse all manner of personal responsibility or go overboard in their yearnings for transcendence, while at the same time displaying a decided distaste for involvement in the day-to-day working out of their pet theories. Rather easily distracted in any event, they will have to work hard to train their minds, bodies, and emotions to the point where structure and routine become more of a habit and less of a chore. Yet if they avoid the tendency to scattered energy, stay grounded in the here and now, and learn to back up their lofty ideals with basic skills, they can make great progress here.

CHALLENGE: **NOT ATTACHING TOO MUCH TO THEIR VISIONS OF A BETTER WORLD**

FULFILLMENT: **EXPERIENCING GREATER STABILITY IN THEIR LIVES BY BECOMING MORE GROUNDED**

NOTABLES: **KARL WALLENDA (CIRCUS PERFORMER, HIGH-WIRE ACT); CHRISTIAN DIOR (FASHION DESIGNER)**

WAYNE GRETZKY
Hockey great
———
1/26/1961
Aquarius I

January 23–30
GENIUS
AQUARIUS I

Those born in the Week of Genius who find themselves on the Way of Structure have enormous potential for success, happiness, and achievement as their fixed Aquarian energy blesses them with a degree of necessary stability, natural objectivity, and the capacity to stick to even the most painstaking tasks and routines. Here the sense of spiritual yearning that is part of the Pisces I origin of this path is mitigated by strong intellectual inclinations of Aquarius I. While these individuals will almost certainly struggle with issues of rebellion or resistance to structure, there is an equal certainty that they will apply their minds to solving their problems. At their core, these are reasonable people in the best sense of that word. If they can also manage to be compassionate, organized, and grounded, they can do much to put their inspired theories into practice as they make their way along this karmic path.

CHALLENGE: **NOT ALLOWING THEIR NEED FOR FREEDOM TO INTERFERE WITH THEIR NEED FOR STRUCTURE**

FULFILLMENT: **GROUNDING THEIR GENIUS IN THEIR TALENT FOR TECHNOLOGY**

NOTABLE: **MARIA VON TRAPP (FLED NAZI-OCCUPIED AUSTRIA; FORMED TRAPP FAMILY SINGERS, SUBJECT OF *THE SOUND OF MUSIC*)**

January 31–February 7
YOUTH AND EASE
AQUARIUS II

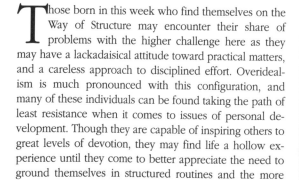

Those born in this week who find themselves on the Way of Structure may encounter their share of problems with the higher challenge here as they may have a lackadaisical attitude toward practical matters, and a careless approach to disciplined effort. Overidealism is much pronounced with this configuration, and many of these individuals can be found taking the path of least resistance when it comes to issues of personal development. Though they are capable of inspiring others to great levels of devotion, they may find life a hollow experience until they come to better appreciate the need to ground themselves in structured routines and the more disciplined forms of training and effort. Yet once they come to understand that their gifts are meant to be shared and that talent is indeed a terrible thing to waste, life will go much more smoothly here.

CHALLENGE: **RELEASING EMOTIONAL IMMATURITY AND ACCEPTING MORE RESPONSIBILITY**

FULFILLMENT: **PERFECTING THEIR TALENTS AND SKILLS**

CHARLES TIFFANY
Goldsmith and jeweler,
Tiffany and Co.
———
2/15/1812
Aquarius III

February 8–15
ACCEPTANCE
AQUARIUS III

Though gifted with a much higher degree of natural objectivity than some others who travel this road, those born in the Week of Acceptance, may nevertheless have to curb their need for variety and better discipline their flightier inclinations before they can become truly successful. Easily distracted and stressed out, they will need to find a rhythm for their activities in order to better regulate and direct the energies that come together here. In fact, they may manifest a needy side that is alternately expressed in extremes of vulnerability followed by extremes of freedom seeking and independence. Yet once they come to terms with the need for greater structure and organization in their lives and their approaches to problems, they can also see their more irritable tendencies evaporate, and their minds become much more able to embrace the challenge to live in the here and now.

CHALLENGE: **DECIDING TO STICK TO SOMETHING**

FULFILLMENT: **TAKING FULL ADVANTAGE OF THEIR RESOURCEFULNESS BY BECOMING MORE PRACTICAL**

NOTABLES: **CHARLES LAMB (ENGLISH ESSAYIST, AUTHOR); HAROLD ARLEN (SONGWRITER, "OVER THE RAINBOW")**

February 16–22

SENSITIVITY
AQUARIUS–PISCES CUSP

Personal sensitivity and an overriding sense of self-pity may prove the biggest stumbling blocks for those born on the Cusp of Sensitivity who travel the Way of Structure. Yet there is nevertheless the possibility of great success here, for these individuals are quite likely to derive a real sense of personal security and accomplishment from taking on the challenge to structure and order their lives through discipline, dedicated effort, and training their minds and bodies to some specific task or area of endeavor. There is a pronounced fear of rejection that can cause these people to either withdraw from the world of relationship or abandon themselves completely to the idea, rather than embrace the reality of love. Yet if they can control their idealism and learn to better manage their emotions, they can derive a great sense of safety, accomplishment, and satisfaction from keeping their "hands on the plow" and their feet on the ground.

W. E. B. Du Bois

Early black civil rights
activist

2/23/1868
Pisces I

CHALLENGE: **CHANNELING THEIR ENERGY INTO PHYSICAL ACTIVITIES AND GOAL-ORIENTED PURSUITS**
FULFILLMENT: **TAKING ACTION ON BEHALF OF OTHERS**

February 23–March 2

SPIRIT
PISCES I

Those born in the Week of Spirit who travel the Way of Structure can find their way on this life's journey, providing they attend to the dailiness of life and do not allow themselves to be overly distracted or encumbered by emotional, theoretical, or unduly abstract concerns. Learning to follow their hearts and at the same time using their heads will doubtless prove a big issue for these people, for they tend to have an exalted sense of their own inspiration and not much of a clue as to the relationship between theory or instinct and practical reality. Yet they do have a practical side, which if not neglected can really come to the fore. Also, their need to be of some service to others is especially pronounced. If they learn to back up their best impulses in such a way that they can keep their promises, give their hearts, and still manage to pay their bills, life will be rewarding here.

CHALLENGE: **OVERCOMING THEIR NATURAL TENDENCY TO WITHDRAW FROM THE DETAILS OF EVERYDAY LIFE AND, INSTEAD, ATTEND TO THEM**
FULFILLMENT: **SIFTING THROUGH MYRIAD INFORMATION FOR THE TRUTH**
NOTABLE: **FRANCHOT TONE (ACTOR, *MUTINY ON THE BOUNTY*)**

March 3–10

THE LONER
PISCES II

Though gifted with pronounced spirituality and tremendous empathy for others, those born in the Week of the Loner may nevertheless experience a certain amount of struggle on the Way of Structure. Loss or trauma may have shaped their identity, and they will have to work hard to ground themselves in contact with others and avoid their tendencies toward isolation, pessimism, and a negative outlook on life. They will do best when they surround themselves with beautiful things of lasting value and learn to better manage their escapist inclinations. Regular exercise will be most helpful and serve to offset depression. Friends and partners of a more practical nature will help them come down to earth a bit as well. Still, if they can learn to take their comfort from the sensual and physical joys that life has to offer and find safety in the sense of structure that beckons here, all will go well in the course of their development.

WILLIAM GODWIN

Political writer/novelist,
*The Adventures of
Caleb Williams*

3/3/1756
Pisces II

CHALLENGE: **RESTRUCTURING THEIR OWN MINDS TO BE MORE POSITIVE**
FULFILLMENT: **PURSUING THEIR LOVE OF BEAUTY THROUGH A CRAFT**

March 11–18

DANCERS AND DREAMERS
PISCES III

Impermanence and impulsiveness may be the biggest obstacles to the higher development of those born in this week who travel the Way of Structure, and some here may prove highly resistant to the challenge to greater organization and discipline in their personal and professional lives. Yet uniting the world of the spirit with the world of the physical need not be an impossible task, providing they discover the value in honing their special talents and creative impulses through some form of artistic or intellectual training. Even the most gifted ballerinas, for example, undergo rigorous and often grueling training as a means of honing their instrument, just as the same holds true for all who are blessed with special gifts or talents. Musicians practice, writers write, painters paint, and they do not expect to perfect themselves without dedicated effort. If these individuals can come to terms with that much, their path to achievement will be much clearer as they make their way along this life's highway.

CHALLENGE: **DETERMINING TO MAKE THE RIGHT DECISIONS FOR THEMSELVES**
FULFILLMENT: **REALIZING THEIR DREAMS IN THE HERE AND NOW**
NOTABLE: **FABIO (MODEL; POPULAR ON COVERS OF ROMANCE NOVELS)**

KARMIC PATH
46

779

The Way of Solution

LONER TO ENIGMA
Pisces II to Virgo II

The men and women born to the Way of Solution are sensitive souls who are sometimes overly aware of the harsh reality of life. Rather than retreat from this truth, however, those on this karmic path are called to engage in the world and actively seek solutions to the variety of problems or issues they may encounter in day-to-day living. To better enable this process, they are called to release their fatalism and to adopt a more optimistic approach. Throwing themselves into a variety of situations and crafting creative solutions, those on this karmic path will become adept at logistical planning and interpersonal relations that may lead them, ultimately, to considerable career success. However, their greatest challenge will be to apply their skills to themselves and their inner lives by addressing all that needs to be transformed within them on every level—mind, body, and spirit.

The individuals on the Way of Solution are soulful individuals. Creative, imaginative, and secretly romantic, those born to this karmic path are oriented to the material world for its beauty and the sensuous pleasure it might provide. Gifted with exquisite and discerning taste, they love the finer things, especially music. Coming in from Pisces II energy, the men and women on the Way of Solution are impressionable and feeling oriented. Because they see the world as a dangerous place, they tend to hide from it and are often loners. They turn their homes into impenetrable fortresses filled with all their most beautiful and favorite things to function as a haven from life. Prone to fantasy and wishful thinking, they wound easily and take all slights hard, frequently obsessing over them. Something has convinced these people that life is about suffering and that, in some way, it betokens devotion to God. Because they see it as inevitable, they are curiously passive. Having learned resignation and surrender from previous experiences, they tend to accept what comes their way—both good and bad. They hate conflict and prefer to indulge in pleasure and beauty rather than address their issues. A danger for them is to become caught in the spiral of materialism, sacrificing their creativity in order to make the money they need for the things that give them comfort.

Often one finds a curious refusal on the part of those on this karmic path to initiate change for the better. The men and women here must learn to release their attachment to suffering and to actively engage in addressing their problems. Becoming positive, realizing that anything is possible, and developing a can-do approach are the core lessons of this path. The goal of this path is for those on it to be willing to roll up their sleeves and set their minds to finding the solution to any problem. Only when they can tackle any issue, resolve it, and release it, will these individuals find true happiness. Moreover, they must invoke a certain amount of determination by going for broke and not resting until they have achieved a full resolution

---

CORE LESSON

Generating a positive attitude and can-do approach

GOAL

To become creative problem solvers

GIFTS
Soulful, Practical, Thoughtful

PITFALLS
Aloof, Self-pitying, Negative

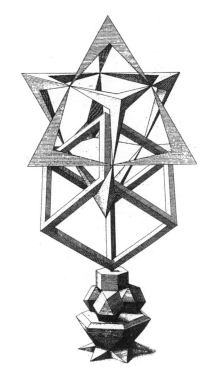

of all issues. It should be noted that those on this path tend to wear their hearts on their sleeves. Developing a more enigmatic facade or, colloquially, a poker face, will help them immeasurably to achieve their aims.

Coming from a place of decided introversion, those on the Way of Solution are naturally fascinated with puzzles of all kinds and can spend hours trying to figure out how things work. Particularly interested in matters of a technical nature, they can pore over operating manuals for hours on end. If they can take some of these inherent skills and apply them at work and in relationships, these men and women have the potential to become truly excellent problem solvers—able to throw themselves into the chaos of any situation, sort through it, and come to the right conclusion or best course of action. Many on this path will become adept at synthesizing large amounts of information and logistical planning. They may need to work on their verbal and writing skills since those on this path will need to communicate their findings and plans to others in an effective manner. Sharpening their minds and developing a craftsmanlike approach to work will also help those on this path. However, they needn't ignore their soulful side. In fact, often it will be their spiritual and intuitive strengths that provide them with creative breakthroughs when seeking solutions.

Much of the progress of those on this path, achieving the skills needed to create and effect solutions, oc-

curs in the workplace. As the individuals here progress, they are usually asked to move into positions of increasing responsibility. Gaining stature in their chosen fields, those on this path may need to remember that they are more likely to fulfill their destiny as they serve others. Creating efficiency and working through roadblocks are intended for a greater good. Remembering to go about their work with a dose of humility while keeping the larger goal in mind is important. Many on this path will be found behind the scenes in academia and business, quietly puzzling through their theories and creating more efficient work environments to benefit everyone.

Even though those on this path tend to really perfect their problem-solving abilities at work, it is important that they apply these same skills to themselves. A component of this path is purification and release. For example, some on this path may need to take a long, hard look at themselves to identify which aspects of their personality are no longer useful, such as being negative, and to work to transform them for the better or to eliminate them from their makeup entirely. Many on this path may need to clear up patterns or problems arising from childhood events. Though it may be traumatic for them to do so, this path calls them to address their issues. Speaking more metaphysically, some on this path may choose to resolve negative karma from past lives. Addressing health issues will also be im-

RELEASE

The propensity for passivity

REWARD

The joy of finding a solution

SUGGESTION

Roll up your sleeves and dive in. Perceive every problem to be an opportunity. The old saying is true: Every person we encounter is our teacher. Don't be afraid of life.

portant here. More than for others, those on this karmic path are prone to illnesses that are the result of emotional upset. Repressing their feelings may breed stomach ailments, lower back pain, headache, and other ailments. Not only do those on this path tend to ignore health warnings, they prefer to indulge themselves rather than develop healthy habits. Guarding against substance abuse and other dependencies such as workaholism may be in order here. Thus, applying their problem-solving approach to their own mind-body-spirit equation is an important part of this path.

The individuals on the Way of Solution are loners by nature, but, as is frequently the case, it is the area of interpersonal relations that will be the crucible for their greatest lessons. Those on this path blow hot and cold in intimate relations, usually not wanting to deal with issues and preferring to retreat into the safety of their inner lives or inner sanctum. Inevitably, they are bound to attract more than their share of difficult people, simply as a way for the universe to ensure that they are given ample opportunity to learn about negotiation and conflict resolution. The broad palette of individuals and relationship types encountered in the workplace will also be especially useful for growth. Because they are prone to isolating themselves, those on the Way of Solution must work hard to maintain contact with people. Friendships are the area in which emotional investment is most productive for those on this path. Having a small circle of intimate friends is generally enough for them, whether they have a life partner or not. The best people for these individuals are outgoing types who won't let them off the hook too easily. Surrounding themselves with individuals who possess optimism and initiative in

abundance will encourage the same energies in them. Early in their lives, love affairs tend to be short lived and highly passionate, but rarely productive or meaningful over the long haul. Due to their romanticism and sensitivity, it is generally they and not their partners who wind up most devastated from breakups. Ultimately, those on this path will become adept at forming mature relationships based on mutual respect and give and take rather than falling for more idealistic and less realistic choices that only leave them alone. In the final analysis, it is the negotiations of daily life and sharing everyday chores and activities, in living with someone, that will provide them the best opportunity for ongoing practice on their path.

The myth of Psyche reminds one of the individuals on this path. In Greek myth, Psyche symbolized the soul and her journey, that of transforming suffering into meaning. She fell in love with Eros, god of love and relationship. Before she was permitted union with her beloved, Psyche was set four problem-solving tasks. The first was to sort seeds, teaching her discrimination; the second to obtain golden fleece of rams, giving her courage; the third task called her to fill a goblet of water from the river Styx of the underworld, symbolizing the ability to manage emotions and spiritual life; and the final task was to go to the underworld and ask the goddess Persephone for some of her beauty ointment. This last task, representing the wisdom won from the journey into one's own inner depths, seemed the most daunting for Psyche, who at first retreated to a high tower in fear. Ultimately, Psyche completed all the tasks and was united with her love, heralding a new approach to both life and mature relationship.

BALANCE POINT

Thesis and Antithesis

CRYSTALS AND GEMSTONES

Citrine absorbs negativity and shines the golden ray of unconditional love on any wound or trauma. This stone leads to the knowledge that there is a solution to every problem.

NOTABLES ON THIS KARMIC PATH

With her feeling-oriented Pisces II roots, vocalist **Aretha Franklin** has consistently been able to express heartfelt emotion in song. She first began performing in her father's Baptist church in Detroit, later taking to the road with his traveling gospel revue. In 1966, Aretha joined Atlantic Records and began recording with rhythm-and-

blues masters, adding her own gospel roots to create the soulful sound that has captivated audiences for more than thirty years. Her career endured a slump during the late 1970s, but, characteristic of those on the Way of Solution, Aretha found her way back to the top, winning three Grammies in the 1980s.

ARETHA FRANKLIN

Typical of those on this path, statesman, diplomat, and political scientist **Henry Kissinger** forged solutions to a great variety of problems, principally in the international sphere. He served as adviser on foreign affairs to more than one U.S. president, and as secretary of state from 1971 to 1976, he engineered significant agreements with European, Middle Eastern, and Asian rulers. Negotiation and conflict resolution were his specialty and his policies emphasized dé-

HENRY KISSINGER

tente with China and the USSR and peace talks between the Arabs and Israelis. He was awarded the Nobel Peace Prize in 1973 for his role in the Vietnam cease-fire.

Actor **Richard Attenborough** gained stature through his accomplishments as a director and a producer. Characteristic of those on the Way of Solution, Attenborough was intrigued by the technical aspects of film and sought to understand the many difficulties associated with his craft. For twenty years, Attenbor-

RICHARD ATTENBOROUGH

ough pursued his dream to make a film about Mohandes Gandhi and ultimately overcame the daunting complexity of encapsulating his life on screen. He was decidedly successful, winning a best director Oscar for the resulting masterpiece.

Other Notables: Ludwig Mies van der Rohe, Wayne Newton, Aaron Spelling, Richard Avedon, Prince Rainier, Bob Dole, Antonio Banderas, Meriwether Lewis, Sean Penn, Shimon Peres, Hugh Grant, Vladimir Horowitz, Franz Liszt, Leslie Stahl, Dionne Warwick, Muhammad Ali, Wolfgang Amadeus Mozart, Carol King, Phil Esposito, Huey Newton, Lou Reed, Michael Eisner, Edward Easton, Barry Levinson, Sumner Redstone, Edith Hamilton, Graham Greene, Michael Crawford, Barry Diller, Roger Staubach, Oskar Kokoschka, Luther Burbank

BIRTHDAYS ON KARMIC PATH 47

January 19, 1886–June 8, 1886 | August 31, 1904–January 19, 1905 | April 13, 1923–August 31, 1923

November 22, 1941–April 12, 1942 | July 3, 1960–November 21, 1960

February 13, 1979–July 3, 1979 | September 24, 1997–February 12, 1998 | May 5, 2016–September 23, 2016

KARMIC PATH
47

March 19–24

REBIRTH
PISCES–ARIES CUSP

The inner emotional life of Pisces–Arians who travel the Way of Solution may be quite different from the more dynamic, competent, and ambitious facade they present to the world. Though likely to be extremely sensitive, rather thin skinned, and independent in the extreme, these souls are not likely to allow too much emotionalism to bleed through the fabric of a well-constructed worldly image. Yet they are gifted with a great deal more sensitivity and a much more developed sense of beauty than they might otherwise possess. If they can learn greater patience and the value of careful planning, they may well discover that their inner lives and outer images will meld into personalities that are assured, refined, and more than able to take up the challenge of finding positive solutions through a more detached and discerning viewpoint, along with ever increasing faith in their own capabilities.

EDWARD WESTON
Photographer

3/24/1886
Pisces–Aries Cusp

CHALLENGE: **NOT BACKING AWAY FROM PROBLEMS**
FULFILLMENT: **BEING PROACTIVE ABOUT THEIR HEALTH**
NOTABLE: **JESUS ALOU (DOMINICAN BASEBALL PLAYER)**

March 25–April 2

THE CHILD
ARIES I

Gifted with much more of an impulse to share their discoveries with others than some who travel this road, those born in the Week of the Child who find themselves on the Way of Solution may nevertheless encounter the need to evaluate and reevaluate some of their more deeply held beliefs about themselves as they make their way along this karmic path. It's likely that unfortunate early conditioning gave them an unstable sense of self and may have forged a sense of unworthiness or of being misunderstood. A tendency to isolate themselves may further contribute to an often negative outlook. Yet life will doubtless summon them to channel their energies into team and group endeavors, and such contact will do much to shore up and enhance a renewed sense of identity. If they can come to understand their own sensitivities and find the balance between natural passion and greater discernment, all will go well here.

CHALLENGE: **ADDRESSING THEIR CHILDHOOD ISSUES**
FULFILLMENT: **SURROUNDING THEMSELVES WITH HARMONIOUS RELATIONSHIPS**
NOTABLE: **ERICA JONG (WRITER, POET, *FEAR OF FLYING*)**

April 3–10

THE STAR
ARIES II

Though driven by a need to place themselves at the center of the action, those born in the Week of the Star who travel the Way of Solution may nevertheless hide a sensitive and rather fragile emotional nature under a carefully constructed and dynamic worldly image. Likely to have a fine understanding of the more soulful side of existence, they will nevertheless have to cultivate more objectivity and discernment and learn to view the world through less of an emotionally colored lens if they are to be truly successful here. They will do best when they refuse to hold themselves aloof from the challenges to connection and interaction that present themselves and use their special gifts to join with others in a spirit of genuine understanding. If they can exalt their sense of ethics and find the courage to be who they are without holding back in loneliness and disillusion, all will go well in the course of this life's journey.

**LUDWIG
MIES VAN DER ROHE**
Architect, Seagram
Building, NYC

3/27/1886
Aries I

CHALLENGE: **DISPELLING THEIR ROMANTIC ILLUSIONS**
FULFILLMENT: **ASSERTING THEIR SENSE OF THE POSSIBLE**
NOTABLES: **BARRY LEVINSON (DIRECTOR, *RAIN MAN*); MARSHA MASON (ACTRESS, *THE GOODBYE GIRL*); WAYNE NEWTON (POP SINGER, LAS VEGAS LOUNGE ACT, "DANKE SCHOEN")**

April 11–18

THE PIONEER
ARIES III

Blessed with a natural inclination to do good for others, those born in the Week of the Pioneer who travel the Way of Solution can realize great success and personal satisfaction along this karmic path. Here a sense of broader ideals is unlikely to be too tarnished by negative habits or an overly dour outlook on life, and they further are possessed with a certain fearlessness when it comes to pursuing their dreams and plans. However, they will have to avoid a tendency to need constant reassurance or to impose their will on others in an attempt to shore up their shakier areas of self. While the ability to interact in intimate, one-on-one relationships will never be their strongest suit, they can nevertheless find great expansion, satisfaction, and enlightenment in their ability to inspire others to a broader vision through their depth of conscience and deep sense of commitment to larger and less personal causes.

CHALLENGE: **WORKING ON LIVING WITH OTHERS AND SHARING CHORES IN THE DAY TO DAY**
FULFILLMENT: **FEELING THAT THEY ARE MAKING A MARK**
NOTABLES: **CLAIRE DANES (ACTRESS, *MY SO CALLED LIFE*); NIKOLAY STEPANOVICH GUMILEV (RUSSIAN POET); ANN MILLER (DANCER/ACTRESS/SINGER, *ON THE TOWN*)**

April 19–24
POWER
ARIES–TAURUS CUSP

Those born on the Cusp of Power who journey along the Way of Solution can expect great fulfillment along this road, as this path blesses them with more sensitivity than they might have otherwise, while their own powerful and controlled impulses are very much in keeping with the higher challenge to develop good personal and professional problem-solving skills. Perhaps their greatest asset will lie in their ability to be patient with themselves and others, and they will further display formidable communicative and persuasive powers. If they are careful not to burn their bridges, retreat into isolation or complacency, and regulate some strong materialistic leanings, they can thus realize a fruitful and satisfying passage, especially when they cultivate their inner strengths and release the idea of power as an instrument of control.

AARON SPELLING
TV producer,
*Charlie's Angels, Dynasty,
Beverly Hills 90210*

4/22/1923
Aries–Taurus Cusp

CHALLENGE: **FINDING MORE WAYS TO SHARE AND COOPERATE**
FULFILLMENT: **USING THEIR SUPERB SENSE OF TIMING TO SOLVE PROBLEMS**
NOTABLE: **JOHN MORTIMER (ATTORNEY; AUTHOR, HORACE RUMPOLE BOOKS; SCREENWRITER)**

April 25–May 2
MANIFESTATION
TAURUS I

The earthier energies of Taurus I will do much to ground the more ethereal and isolationist tendencies of this path, and the souls born in this week are likely to be characterized by a fine combination of deep emotion and practical talent. Perhaps their biggest fault will lie in their tendency to be too passive for their own good, however, and some will have to work hard to develop the sense of objectivity and detachment called for if they are to become effective here. They will have a pronounced resistance to change and may thus slip into some highly negative patterns of thought and feeling that will bear closer scrutiny and evaluation in the course of this journey. Yet if they better learn to simply release old grudges, concentrate on their advancement, and embrace the new, they can build solid and enduring evidence of their growth and contributions to mankind as they make their way along this karmic path.

CHALLENGE: **OVERCOMING THE RESISTANCE TO CHANGE TO SOLVE SOME OF THEIR BIGGER STUMBLING BLOCKS**
FULFILLMENT: **ADOPTING NURTURING ROLES TOWARD OTHERS**

May 3–10
THE TEACHER
TAURUS II

The individuals born in the Week of the Teacher who journey along the Way of Solution will have a far easier time of things than some along this road, as they have a natural predisposition to the kind of relationships that will serve to keep them spiritually and emotionally connected to the world. They have a strong impulse to share their many ideas with others, and are further helped by the fact that they can find a level of personal safety through relationships that are mutually rewarding yet often less than intimate. Strongly drawn to academic pursuits, they can also find satisfaction in any number of entrepreneurial ventures, and their love of physical activities and discipline will do much to offset a tendency to depression or worry. If they cultivate discernment and control a temperamental streak, their love of ideas, critical faculties, and practical aptitude are sure to find the fullest expression in the course of this life's journey.

RICHARD AVEDON
Personality photographer

5/15/1923
Taurus III

CHALLENGE: **FORCING THEMSELVES OUT INTO THE COMPANY OF OTHERS**
FULFILLMENT: **LETTING THEIR SENSE OF FAIRNESS WORK FOR THEM AS THEY RESOLVE INTERPERSONAL CONFLICT**
NOTABLES: **JOHN STETSON (HAT MANUFACTURER); ANNE BAXTER (ACTRESS, EAST OF EDEN)**

May 11–18
THE NATURAL
TAURUS III

Those born in the Week of the Natural who travel the Way of Solution are likely to be very unusual, even extreme individuals, who nevertheless have high principles and a fun-loving side that will serve them in excellent stead here. While there is some danger that they will shirk the higher spiritual task of problem solving and dedication to a lofty set of standards and instead become reclusive, isolated, or otherwise withdrawn from the world, they nevertheless have a deep understanding of the rhythms of life and an admirable reverence for nature and things of beauty. In fact, they will wrestle with any number of security issues, and there are those who will fail the higher challenge of negotiation and change their jobs, friends, or location with alarming speed if situations threatens too much involvement. Yet if they cultivate their easygoing side, avoid extremes of self-pity, and adhere to their own sense of principles, they can find a rare freedom through their ability to balance their need for sensual indulgence with the need for a more grounded, accomplished, and complete sense of self.

CHALLENGE: **NOT SACRIFICING THEIR CREATIVITY FOR THE SAKE OF EARNING MONEY**
FULFILLMENT: **ENJOYING THE SATISFACTION OF HANGING IN THERE AND WORKING THINGS OUT**
NOTABLE: **CHARLIE ROSE (TALK SHOW HOST)**

May 19–24

ENERGY
TAURUS–GEMINI CUSP

Though by no means as introverted as some along this road, those born on the Cusp of Energy who travel the Way of Solution will nevertheless have to work to manage their tendencies to emotional extremes and cultivate more of a practical side to their nature if they are to become truly effective here. This can be a journey fraught with many emotional ups and downs, and some will seek out avenues of escape as a means of dulling their pain or mitigating their sense of suffering. Learning about the creation of structure and the value of patience and planning will be especially important, as will the ability to simply back up from emotional trials in order to gain perspective. Yet even if they plunge to the depths now and then, they are unlikely to stay there for long, as their high energy and natural enthusiasm are a fine antidote for some of the more negative aspects of this path. If they can manage to detach and focus in such a way as to integrate their sense of inspiration with effective and well-planned action, all will go beautifully.

CHALLENGE: **FOCUSING LESS ON THEMSELVES AND THEIR RESENTMENTS**

FULFILLMENT: **FEELING APPRECIATED FOR THEIR SKILL**

SUMNER REDSTONE
Invented multiplex movie theaters; owner of Viacom

5/27/1923
Gemini I

May 25–June 2

FREEDOM
GEMINI I

The individuals born in this week who travel the Way of Solution can do very well along this road, though they will have to be on guard against a tendency toward emotional volatility or to indulge in the kind of "pity parties" that will only reinforce their insecurities. Nonetheless, they have a great deal of technical and analytic ability that, when applied to problem solving, organization, and administration, can serve to put them on the road to happiness and fulfillment. They have a combative streak which can conflict with the more timid or retiring aspect of their Pisces II roots, and the result can be explosions of temper followed by periods of pointless guilt and self-abnegation. Yet if they are careful to exalt their communicative talents and do not turn away from the higher calling to objectivity, detachment, and refinement that all beckon here, life promises to be rather sweet as they make their way along this road.

CHALLENGE: **CHOOSING THEIR WORDS WISELY AND TEMPERING IRRITABILITY**

FULFILLMENT: **TAKING THEIR SCHEMES TO THE NEXT LEVEL THROUGH EFFECTIVE PLANNING**

NOTABLES: **JAMES ARNESS (ACTOR, *GUNSMOKE*); PRINCE RAINIER III (MONARCH OF MONACO; MARRIED GRACE KELLY)**

June 3–10

NEW LANGUAGE
GEMINI II

The interesting and highly individualistic people born in this week who find themselves on the Way of Solution can do extremely well along this road, providing they do not succumb to feelings of being chronically misunderstood, or fall in love with their own darker side. Much more social than some who travel this road, they are also motivated by a strong need for acceptance that can actually work to their advantage here. Likely to have wonderful communicative talents or to be musically gifted, they will doubtless face the challenge of using their special gifts to open the avenues of connection between themselves and others. If they can manage to find ways to get their unique ideas, thoughts, and feelings across to others, and discover within themselves the release mechanism for their own defensiveness, the rest should fall quite easily into place as they make their way along this life's highway.

CHALLENGE: **CRAFTING WAYS TO USE LANGUAGE TO RESOLVE CONFLICT**

FULFILLMENT: **CHOOSING TO TACKLE THEIR OWN PROBLEMS**

AL JOLSON
Singer, Broadway theater; appeared in 1st talkie, *The Jazz Singer*

6/7/1886
Gemini II

June 11–18

THE SEEKER
GEMINI III

Here the impulse to push beyond the limitations imposed by society can get a bit out of hand if the souls born in this week who travel the Way of Solution use their own sense of adventure as a means to separate from others or to cling to their own sense of cynicism or disillusion. Yet there is nevertheless the potential for wonderful success and personal enlightenment along this highway, especially if these people take care to cultivate their formidable analytic and intellectual powers and to set aside feelings of self-pity and unworthiness. While it can be said that they will always like to keep others guessing and may consciously cultivate a mysterious side, they have a great desire to please others through their ability to charm. If they can only allow themselves to do so, life will be rewarding as they make their way along this karmic path.

CHALLENGE: **EXPRESSING THEIR EMOTIONS MORE GUARDEDLY OR INTELLIGENTLY**

FULFILLMENT: **APPLYING THEIR PENCHANT FOR SEEKING TO MORE PERSONAL MATTERS**

June 19–24
MAGIC
GEMINI–CANCER CUSP

Gemini–Cancers who make their way along the Way of Solution will face the challenge of maintaining their connections to the world and fighting a tendency to withdraw or isolate themselves in the face of hurt feelings, slights, or complications in their arduous emotional lives. Yet there is a great possibility of success here, providing they cultivate their highly astute powers of observation and perception and apply their talents to the business of finding solutions for their own and others' problems. Grounding some strong emotional energies will prove especially important on this road, as will simply gaining the life experience to better know when not to give their all or wear their hearts on their sleeves. While they will always tend to be rather private people, they have a fine willingness to negotiate, mediate, and come up with the right answers to the problems which may present themselves along this karmic path.

CAMILLE PISSARRO
Impressionist artist;
shown here, *rue St. Lazare*
—————
7/10/1830
Cancer II

CHALLENGE: **SAVING THEMSELVES FROM SELF-IMPOSED ISOLATION**

FULFILLMENT: **RELIEVING THEIR EFFORTS TO BE IN SERVICE OF A HIGHER CAUSE**

June 25–July 2
THE EMPATH
CANCER I

Empaths who journey along the Way of Solution will discover that their considerable sensitivity is both their greatest blessing and their greatest curse on this karmic path. On they one hand, it gives them a unique and undeniable sense of connection to those around them, and on the other, they will have to wrestle with the demons of self-doubt, a negative outlook, and a tendency to be entirely too thin skinned. Before they are free to realize the higher promise here, they will have to cultivate a more optimistic outlook and to grapple with their most deep-seated fears of loss and abandonment. Also, they will have to take special care not to overindulge in fantasy—particularly of the romantic variety. Yet if they can keep in mind that they have the natural strength and instinct to overcome almost any obstacle, their deep emotions need not be a liability.

CHALLENGE: **REFUSING TO ACCEPT THEIR OWN UNHAPPINESS OR SUFFERING**

FULFILLMENT: **DEALING WITH PEOPLE MORE EFFECTIVELY**

July 3–10
THE UNCONVENTIONAL
CANCER II

The unusual people born in this week who travel the Way of Solution may experience a struggle along this karmic path as there is a pronounced tendency to both personal isolation and escapism that goes with this configuration. Their biggest problem will lie in their inability to adequately manage emotions, and a strong obsessive streak having to do with hurts and slights can also be part of their makeup. Thus, finding the balance between enough detachment and too much isolation will prove a core lesson, as will their willingness to studiously avoid getting entrenched in their own fantasies. Yet as they venture out of their shells and into the world, they will discover their own potential for strong and astute psychological insight and an undeniable love of fun and humor. If they can learn to laugh at themselves and take care that their sense of privacy does not become a prison, they can find happiness here.

FRANCES LEAR
Editor, *Lear's*
—————
7/14/1923
Cancer III

CHALLENGE: **REALIZING THAT THEY MAY BE WILDLY OVERSPENDING ONLY TO FEATHER A JAIL CELL**

FULFILLMENT: **RISKING FINDING THE REASONS FOR SOME OF THEIR DARKER HABITS**

NOTABLE: **JEAN KERR (AUTHOR, DRAMATIST, *PLEASE DON'T EAT THE DAISIES*)**

July 11–18
THE PERSUADER
CANCER III

Cancer III's who find themselves on the Way of Solution are likely to enjoy a rather satisfying life's journey, providing they do not retreat into personal insecurity or unduly controlling or manipulative behaviors in attempts to protect their more sensitive and soulful side. In any event, there will be a pronounced tendency to worry, emotional excess, and concentration upon the details at the expense of the bigger picture. Yet there is the highest potential for success here, as these people are likely to be gifted both with great intuition and the communicative power to get their ideas across. If they can better learn to negotiate, rather than demand, and manage to mitigate an "all or nothing" view of compromise and personal interaction, all will go well along this road.

CHALLENGE: **REALIZING THAT MORE CAN BE ACHIEVED THROUGH COOPERATION AND NEGOTIATION**

FULFILLMENT: **UTILIZING THEIR CONSIDERABLE POWERS OF OBSERVATION TO FIND ANSWERS AND CRAFT SOLUTIONS**

NOTABLE: **DANIEL BARRY (CARTOONIST, *FLASH GORDON*)**

July 19–25
OSCILLATION
CANCER–LEO CUSP

Though blessed with considerably more optimism and energy than some who travel the Way of Solution, those born in this period will nevertheless have to work a bit to regulate some highly emotional energies and a pronounced tendency to go to extremes in their search for sensation and excitement. They possess great strength under fire and a fine measure of moral courage and principle that will serve them in good stead. Many of this type will manifest a fearful attitude toward their own emotionalism and may shut down in attempts to pursue worldly or material ambitions at the expense of their more soulful side. Yet if they can cultivate their more extroverted tendencies and work on their diplomatic skills, they are likely to assume the ever-increasing amounts of connection, personal interaction, and fulfillment implied here, and will be able to find viable answers to the problems of daily life as they make their way along this karmic path.

ANTONIO BANDERAS
Actor, *Desperado*

8/10/1960
Leo II

CHALLENGE: **CULTIVATING MORE OF A POKER FACE**
FULFILLMENT: **INVOKING THEIR RISK-TAKING ABILITIES TO DIVE INTO SITUATIONS THAT REQUIRE SOLUTIONS**
NOTABLE: **BOB DOLE (SENATOR FROM KANSAS, SENATE MAJORITY LEADER, PRESIDENTIAL CANDIDATE)**

July 26–August 2
AUTHORITY
LEO I

Those born in the Week of Authority who travel the Way of Solution are likely to have a much more introspective turn of mind than some of the travelers born in this week and will have to work hard to overcome a fatalistic streak or an exalted sense of personal suffering if they are to be truly successful here. Though gifted with fine administrative and diplomatic talents, they may get stuck in a submission to the idea that we are all ruled by forces beyond our control or see themselves as victims of "cruel fate" as a rationalization for their own fixed attitudes. Nevertheless they have a strong and abiding need for connection to others that will surely hold them in good stead, for no matter what obstacles may lie in their path to higher development, Leo I's are likely to recognize just how hollow life can be without people around them. Once they come to terms with that much, the rest will be easy as they make their way along this life's highway.

CHALLENGE: **TRAINING THEMSELVES TO SEE PROBLEMS AS OPPORTUNITIES FOR GROWTH AND NOT FATE**
FULFILLMENT: **INSPIRING OTHERS THROUGH THEIR OPTIMISTIC AND CAN-DO APPROACH**

August 3–10
BALANCED STRENGTH
LEO II

Though the souls born in the Week of Balanced Strength who make their way along this karmic path are likely to approach the business of their own development more in the manner of the tortoise than the hare, they are nevertheless promised a fine and fulfilling journey as they travel this life's highway. They will do well to remain mindful of their own tendencies to be too self-sacrificing, however, and some here will exalt a sense of personal suffering to the point of masochism. Depression or a misplaced sense of guilt can be a part of their emotional makeup as well. Yet at their core, these are tough customers indeed. If they can only call upon their great strength to analyze and evaluate those qualities of character that hold them back in isolation from higher development, they will be able to join with others in a spirit of understanding, mutual help, and extraordinary faithfulness as they make their way along this road.

MERIWETHER LEWIS
Explorer with Clark

8/18/1774
Leo III

CHALLENGE: **TAKING OFF THE HAIR SHIRT**
FULFILLMENT: **RECOGNIZING THAT WALKING AWAY IS A FORM OF SOLUTION**
NOTABLES: **ESTHER WILLIAMS (ACTRESS; SWIMMER; *NEPTUNE'S DAUGHTER*); ANNE KLEIN (FASHION DESIGNER); JAMES LOEB (BANKER; ENDOWED NYC'S INSTITUTE OF MUSICAL ART)**

August 11–18
LEADERSHIP
LEO III

The individuals born in this week who travel the Way of Solution can find great fulfillment and success in the course of this life's journey, yet they will have to work on their personal presentation and allow themselves to become more approachable. Likely to be extremely creative, they can do themselves a great disservice through a failure to share their best ideas, inspirations, and solutions to problems with others. Fine planners who are gifted with a broad and often inspired vision, they can hide their lights under a bushel if they refuse to delegate responsibility or insist on doing everything themselves. Yet they have considerably more personal strength and if they can cultivate their people skills and learn to join with others in negotiation, problem solving, and the crafting and execution of their plans and schemes, they can realize great personal satisfaction in the course of this life's journey.

CHALLENGE: **WORKING ON THEIR COMMUNICATION SKILLS AND INTERPERSONAL STYLE**
FULFILLMENT: **CRAFTING TRULY INSPIRED SOLUTIONS**
NOTABLES: **TIMOTHY HUTTON (ACTOR, DIRECTOR, *ORDINARY PEOPLE*); SEAN PENN (ACTOR, *DEAD MAN WALKING*); SHIMON PERES (ISRAELI PRIME MINISTER; 1994 NOBEL PEACE PRIZE); EDITH HAMILTON (MYTHOLOGY EXPERT)**

August 19–25
EXPOSURE
LEO–VIRGO CUSP

Those born on the Cusp of Exposure who travel the Way of Solution are likely to enjoy great success along this road, though they may find that fate often takes a hand in forcing them out of their private and self-protective worlds and into the limelight of leadership, administration, and even celebrity. Technically gifted and highly astute, they will make really formidable investigators or researchers in almost any field of endeavor. Secrecy and privacy may amount to something of an obsession with these individuals, and they will go to great lengths to avoid conflicts or confrontations. Yet others will doubtless come to depend on their insight and objectivity in the course of this passage. If they can bring themselves to reveal who they are and what they know even to a small circle of intimates, they are destined to find moments of true happiness in the course of this life's journey.

MONTY HALL
TV game show host,
Let's Make a Deal

8/25/1923
Leo–Virgo Cusp

CHALLENGE: **ACCEPTING THAT THEY NEED TO PUT THEIR CARDS ON THE TABLE ONCE IN A WHILE**

FULFILLMENT: **REVELING IN THEIR FASCINATION WITH MYSTERIES AND PUZZLES**

NOTABLE: **CAL RIPKEN, JR. (BASEBALL PLAYER, ORIOLES; IRON MAN HOLDS RECORD FOR MOST CONSECUTIVE GAMES PLAYED)**

August 26–September 2
SYSTEM BUILDERS
VIRGO I

Modest, dependable, and reliable in the extreme, Virgo I's who travel the Way of Solution are likely to have a fine talent for overcoming their emotionalism in favor of a more objective and discerning approach to problems. Nevertheless they may get mired in passivity or a refusal to change through their need to feel safe, or the conviction that their own fate is not necessarily a matter of personal choice. Though much more sensitive than many others born in this week, these individuals run the risk of compounding their sense of unhappiness through a reluctance to share their feelings with other people. Repressed emotion can manifest in all sorts of physical problems or a preoccupation with rigid routines. Yet if they can manage to release their feelings of distrust or unworthiness and apply themselves wholeheartedly to the crafting of solutions, they are sure to find recognition as they make their way along this karmic path.

CHALLENGE: **TAKING CARE TO MANAGE THEIR HEALTH THROUGH A REGULAR FITNESS PROGRAM**

FULFILLMENT: **OVERCOMING TIMIDITY TO STAND UP FOR WHAT THEY THINK**

NOTABLES: **SIR RICHARD ATTENBOROUGH (ACTOR; DIRECTOR, GANDHI); BRANFORD MARSALIS (JAZZ SAXOPHONIST)**

September 3–10
THE ENIGMA
VIRGO II

As mysterious and enigmatic as the personalities born in this week who find themselves on the Way of Solution can sometimes seem, they cry out for understanding from others and yearn to be accepted for who they really are. The problem is that they will have to work a bit to develop the necessary confidence to be able to reveal their more private nature to others. Indeed, their obsession with privacy may well arise out of the fear of what people will think of them, and many here will have worldly images that are very different from the persons they are inside. Yet there are the highest prospects for success and happiness, providing they apply their objectivity and powers of discernment to interpersonal relationships and avoid the dangers of too much introspection or an obsession with perfection. If they can learn to relax, go with the flow, and adjust their standards to allow for the unpredictability of human life, all will go brilliantly here.

HUGH GRANT
Actor, *Four Weddings and a Funeral*

9/9/1960
Virgo II

CHALLENGE: **UNLOCKING THE SECRETS TO THE SOURCE OF THEIR INSPIRATION**

FULFILLMENT: **PLAYING UP THEIR ENIGMATIC WAYS FOR MAXIMUM EFFECT**

NOTABLE: **J. P. MORGAN, JR. (FINANCIER)**

September 11–18
THE LITERALIST
VIRGO III

Those born in the Week of the Literalist who travel the Way of Solution can expect considerable accomplishment and fulfillment along this road, though they will have to take care to better allow their heads to rule their hearts. Gifted with some fine talents for observation, they have an innate dislike for emotional displays and will go out of their way to avoid confrontation. Yet they can shrink from the higher challenge to involvement, connection, and solution if they come to view all contacts with others with a suspicious or judgmental attitude. Conversely, some will prove themselves too self-sacrificing for their own good and exalt their sense of suffering to the point that they become insufferable. Still and all, results are important to these people; if they can come to the arena of personal and professional contacts with an eye to making things work, rather than the fear that they won't, all will go well in the course of this passage.

CHALLENGE: **FACING THE SOURCE OF THEIR SECRET INSECURITIES**

FULFILLMENT: **APPLYING CONCRETE PRACTICALITY TO THEIR QUEST FOR SOLUTIONS**

NOTABLES: **JOE MORRIS (FOOTBALL RUNNING BACK); TOM CONWAY (ACTOR, THE FALCON)**

September 19–24

BEAUTY
VIRGO–LIBRA CUSP

Those born on the Cusp of Beauty who navigate the challenge and promise of the Way of Solution will have to guard carefully against their tendency to retreat in the face of conflict or withdraw into an ivory tower of unrealistic expectation as they journey along this path. In fact, the tendencies to escapism are quite pronounced with this configuration, and some here may further develop a martyr complex in the face of disillusion or disappointment. However, at their core, these are highly social individuals with some formidable diplomatic talents at their disposal. If they can bring those gifts to bear in the sphere of human interaction and at the same time avoid the tendency to be dominated or easily controlled by those who would exploit their sensitivity and deep sense of beauty, they can find happiness and fulfillment in their travels along this road.

JOAN JETT
80s rock/pop star

9/22/1960
Virgo–Libra Cusp

CHALLENGE: **NOT AVOIDING PROBLEMS BY PRETENDING THEY DON'T EXIST**

FULFILLMENT: **TAPPING INTO THEIR FASHION AND BEAUTY SENSE TO PREDICT TRENDS**

NOTABLE: **JOHN LOMAX (FOLKLORIST)**

September 25–October 2

THE PERFECTIONIST
LIBRA I

Those born in the Week of the Perfectionist who find themselves on the Way of Solution can realize great fulfillment along this path, though they may have to better learn the value of compromise and negotiation first. In fact these people may have such high standards that they expend so much energy in pointing out those things that are wrong in life that they may never get around to turning their attention to workable solutions for improving the state of things. They may fail to focus their attention toward others and become preoccupied with their seeming lack of perfection or attainment in the physical or material realms of endeavor. It will be especially important for these people to learn not to be so hard on themselves or others. If they can thus avoid becoming the victims of their own impossibly high standards and learn instead to find paths to achievement and fulfillment by joining with others in a spirit of willing cooperation, they will find they are by no means alone in the quest for attainment of their high ideals.

CHALLENGE: **MISSING THE FOREST FOR THE TREES**

FULFILLMENT: **USING THEIR TECHNICAL KNOW-HOW TO PUT THINGS RIGHT AND FIX WHAT'S BROKEN**

NOTABLE: **GRAHAM GREENE (SPY NOVELIST)**

October 3–10

SOCIETY
LIBRA II

The personalities born in the Week of Society who journey along the Way of Solution can expect a great deal of personal fulfillment and happiness in the course of this life's journey, though they will have to develop greater discernment when it comes to identifying their own needs. In fact, they may appear to be people who lack for nothing, as they have fine social skills, wonderful powers of observation and insight, and diplomatic talents that many would envy. Add to that a wide and varied social circle and a rare ability to inspire trust in others and things look good indeed. Yet there is a darker side to these personalities and a tendency to mood swings and self-deception that can make for some disastrous personal choices. Thus, cultivating real self-knowledge and greater objectivity regarding their wishes and dreams will be especially useful, as will the ability to establish valid personal boundaries. If they can learn just when to say no, things will come quite easily here.

VLADIMIR HOROWITZ
Russian pianist

10/1/1904
Libra I

CHALLENGE: **KNOWING THAT THEY DON'T HAVE TO SOLVE EVERYONE'S PROBLEMS**

FULFILLMENT: **FEELING A SENSE OF PERSONAL POWER AS THEY GRAPPLE AND NEGOTIATE WITH A LARGE CIRCLE OF PEOPLE**

October 11–18

THEATER
LIBRA III

Libra III's who travel the Way of Solution can realize great progress in the course of this life's journey, providing they can keep the emotional drama to a minimum and cultivate their more objective side. Much more confident and savvy than some of their fellow travelers on this road, they may nevertheless be marked by a tendency to self-indulgence or exaggeration of their own troubles. Strongly sensual and even rather romantic, they can become cynical and even quite jaded as a result of disappointment. Yet they have a great potential for success as their emotions are regulated by a valuable detachment and formidable powers of observation. If they can put those gifts to use in the service of others, their leadership abilities are sure to come to the fore, and their worldliness can only help them as they apply themselves to the business of crafting solutions and learning to negotiate and compromise in both their personal and professional lives.

CHALLENGE: **CULTIVATING A LITTLE HUMILITY BY REFLECTING ON WHO THEY ARE ULTIMATELY SERVING**

FULFILLMENT: **BEING RECOGNIZED FOR THEIR TALENT FOR LARGE-SCALE PLANNING AND ORGANIZATIONAL STRUCTURE**

NOTABLE: **JEAN-CLAUDE VAN DAMME (BELGIAN ACTION STAR, MARTIAL-ARTS FILMS, *BLOODSPORT*)**

October 19–25

DRAMA AND CRITICISM
LIBRA–SCORPIO CUSP

If the individuals born on the cusp of Drama and Criticism can regulate a tendency to complain, they will do quite well along this karmic path. Much more dynamic than many who travel this road and passionate rather than purely emotional, they may nevertheless misuse their gifts for self-expression in pointing out all that is wrong with the world. Likely to be creative and artistic in the extreme, they will have to regulate their own prima donna attitudes and better learn the value of compromise if they are to step into the roles of greater responsibility and leadership that beckon here. There is an indication that many of these individuals will have worldly personae that are quite at odds with their private lives. Yet if they can manage to integrate discernment with passion and objectivity in a more trusting approach to others, all will go well in the course of this journey.

MARIE ANTOINETTE
Queen of France during
French Revolution;
executed

11/2/1755
Scorpio I

CHALLENGE: **NOT WALLOWING IN EMOTIONAL SENSITIVITY OR NEGATIVITY**

FULFILLMENT: **INSPIRING OTHERS TO EMBRACE THEIR SOLUTIONS**

NOTABLES: **MOSS HART (PLAYWRIGHT, DIRECTOR, *YOU CAN'T TAKE IT WITH YOU*); FRANZ LISZT (COMPOSER, PIANIST)**

October 26–November 2

INTENSITY
SCORPIO I

Those born in the Week of Intensity who journey along the Way of Solution may experience a less-than-satisfying passage characterized by early rejection, misunderstanding, and suffering until they realize that perhaps others' attitudes toward them are but outward manifestations of their own sense of dissatisfaction and unworthiness. Yet there will be an almost mystical aspect to many of these individuals that, if turned outward in sincere efforts at connection with their fellow travelers, can result in great and satisfying achievements, providing they do not couch their fears in a pious or rigid set of principles and gain a better grasp of what it means to live and let live. Learning not to take the world so personally and being able to release the feelings of being unloved, unwanted, and badly used will prove especially important, as will cultivating their unique gift for simply being able to laugh at themselves. If they can keep a sense of their larger goals, they can face what challenges may come as they make their way along this karmic path.

CHALLENGE: **REINFORCING THEIR SUNNIER, UPBEAT SIDE**
FULFILLMENT: **BECOMING CAUGHT UP IN PROBLEM SOLVING**
NOTABLE: **RIZA CYRUS PAHLEVI (SON OF SHAH OF IRAN; DECLARED HIMSELF RULER AFTER FATHER DIED)**

November 3–11

DEPTH
SCORPIO II

The intense individuals born in this week who travel the Way of Solution may exhibit some peculiar and even quite eccentric characteristics, and they will have to take special care not to succumb to their darker or more escapist side in the name of profundity. In any event, life is going to seem like a pretty serious business for these souls, and some may well turn away from the higher challenge to craft solutions to their problems and better learn to negotiate and compromise. Thus the ability to overcome selfishness, self-interest, and some of their more negative or suspicious attitudes toward humanity in general will prove especially important, as will the willingness to exchange their sense of suffering for a sense of tangible accomplishment. Once they come to understand that much of their misery is of their own choosing and that martyrs are not usually problem solvers, things will go more smoothly along this karmic path.

RuPAUL
TV host/entertainer;
famous cross dresser

11/17/1960
Scorpio III

CHALLENGE: **FORMULATING HEALTH AND FITNESS REGIMES TO HELP BURN OFF EMOTIONAL STRESS**

FULFILLMENT: **EMPLOYING THEIR LOVE OF RESEARCH AND PUZZLES IN WAYS THAT HELP OTHERS**

NOTABLES: **TOMMY DORSEY (BANDLEADER); ALGER HISS (GOVERNMENT OFFICIAL; ALLEGED SOVIET SPY)**

November 12–18

CHARM
SCORPIO III

Those born in the Week of Charm who travel the Way of Solution can expect a far easier life's journey than many of their Scorpio cousins on this path as they have a natural gift for diplomacy and a rare talent for negotiating even the most delicate of compromises. In fact, their biggest stumbling block can be a rather selfish or self-interested attitude, and some may fail the higher challenge to put their gifts in service to others. There are those here who will content themselves with purely material achievement and concentrate their energies in acquisition of creature comforts. Yet they have a resilience and resourcefulness that are admirable, and if they can cultivate their talent for making things work and turn their natural charm into a real impulse for connection with those around them, they will enjoy great reward and a genuine sense of accomplishment as they make their way along this road.

CHALLENGE: **NOT HIDING THEIR TRUE SELVES BEHIND A FACADE OF CHARM**

FULFILLMENT: **HELPING OTHERS WITH THEIR EMOTIONAL OR PSYCHOLOGICAL STUMBLING BLOCKS**

NOTABLES: **MARY PILLSBURY LORD (SOCIAL WORKER; HEIR TO PILLSBURY FORTUNE); ISAMU NOGUCHI (SCULPTOR, ARTIST, SET DESIGNER); DICK POWELL (ACTOR, DIRECTOR, TV HOST)**

November 19–24

REVOLUTION
SCORPIO–SAGITTARIUS CUSP

Though the ability to compromise may never be the strong suit of those born on the Cusp of Revolution who journey along the Way of Solution, they can nevertheless expect to make great progress here. Key to their development will be their willingness to put on the emotional brakes and instead direct their energies to careful planning, greater objectivity, and less of an exalted sense of their own martyrdom to their ideals. Though willing to risk everything on principle, these rather reckless types will have to learn when and where to direct their energies or risk burning themselves out in disappointment, misanthropy, and disillusion. Yet if they can cultivate a talent for working with others and nurture their need for real results, they can make wonderful strides, as a high sense of principle will be informed by deep emotion and, eventually, plain common sense.

LESLIE STAHL
TV journalist

12/16/1941
Sagittarius III

CHALLENGE: **RELEASING THE IDEA THAT IT IS HOLY OR EXALTED TO BE UNHAPPY**

FULFILLMENT: **LETTING THEIR REVOLUTIONARY ZEAL KICK IN**

NOTABLES: **COLEMAN HAWKINS (JAZZ SAXOPHONIST, "BODY AND SOUL"); NATHAN LEOPOLD, JR. (MILLIONAIRE'S SON; COMMITTED MURDER WITH LOEB, ATTEMPTED "PERFECT CRIME")**

November 25–December 2

INDEPENDENCE
SAGITTARIUS I

The natural independence of those born in this week is very much in keeping with the higher goals and challenges implied on the Way of Solution. Yet there are those here who will nevertheless struggle with some pervasive problems of personal insecurity and most will be rather skittish in the areas of relationship or interpersonal negotiation. In fact, what they fear is only that finding solutions to their problems will in some way impinge on their need for independence. Yet if they can cultivate greater objectivity, less personal touchiness, and a more steady and relaxed approach to connecting with others, their sense of greater responsibility will come to the fore and their gifts of leadership and wise administration will find the fullest expression in the course of this life's journey.

CHALLENGE: **NOT LIVING THEIR LIVES AS WANDERERS OR IN RETREAT**

FULFILLMENT: **SETTLING DOWN AND LIVING WITH OTHERS ON A DAY-TO-DAY BASIS**

December 3–10

THE ORIGINATOR
SAGITTARIUS II

Though they may well feel themselves misunderstood, maligned, or otherwise outside the mainstream as they travel the Way of Solution, the unique and compelling souls born in the Week of the Originator can nevertheless realize tremendous success and real achievement along this karmic path. Yet they will have to work hard to overcome some deep-seated feelings of mistrust and alienation and learn as well that being different is neither a liability nor an excuse to retreat into hopelessness and self-negation. In any event, these individuals will have to keep up their sense of humor in the course of their personal evolution. Yet they are motivated by a genuine yearning to be accepted that should work to their advantage. If they can learn to channel their ardent nature into careful and considerate negotiation with others and work to craft solutions to the dilemmas that present themselves along the way, life can be very good as they make their journey along this road.

DIONNE WARWICK
Pop singer, "Walk on By"

12/12/1941
Sagittarius III

CHALLENGE: **QUITTING THEIR TENDENCY TO NURSE HURTS AND GRUDGES**

FULFILLMENT: **RECEIVING RECOGNITION FOR THEIR ORIGINALITY OF THOUGHT**

NOTABLES: **BEAU BRIDGES (ACTOR, THE FABULOUS BAKER BOYS); BRUCE NAUMANN (SCULPTOR, FROM HAND TO MOUTH)**

December 11–18

THE TITAN
SAGITTARIUS III

Inclined to big plans, high ideals, and a rather romantic sense of the world, those born in the Week of the Titan may have to come down to earth a bit before they can be truly effective as they make their way along this road. Doubtless pegged as unrealistic dreamers early in life, or rejected for their more soulful inclinations, many of these people have a rather shaky self-image and a wide vein of well-disguised insecurity. They can be self-unaware, and unresolved emotional conflicts can result in mysterious physical problems or psychosomatic disorders. They may manifest some evangelical leanings, and may yearn for peak or ecstatic experience when careful planning and negotiation are what is called for. Yet whatever their faults or failings, these people are likely to have an unassailable vision of what is possible and a genuinely hopeful outlook that will serve them in good stead. If they can learn the value of compromise and the necessity for joining with others in the service of a common cause or goal, they will make inspiring and visionary leaders whose effectiveness can only be enhanced by their ability to be realistic.

CHALLENGE: **TAKING THE TIME TO LOOK WITHIN AND FIX A FEW THINGS THERE TOO**

FULFILLMENT: **INTEGRATING THEIR CAPACITY TO SEE THE BIG PICTURE WITH A DESIRE TO MAKE THINGS BETTER**

December 19–25
PROPHECY
SAGITTARIUS–CAPRICORN CUSP

Those born on the Cusp of Prophecy can find great fulfillment here, as they have a natural aptitude for practical matters and a rare capacity for discernment that will serve them especially well. Yet the impulse to really connect with others will be a big stumbling block to their development. Likely to be mysterious and intriguing personalities, they may nevertheless become alienated, isolated, or withdrawn to the extent that they are neither interested nor able to maintain the sense of connection to humankind, and there may be any number of recluses, hermits, and misanthropes here. Yet they are gifted with an unusual degree of independence, the capacity for detachment, and the ability to look the facts squarely in the eye. Much more grounded than some who travel this road, if they can avoid the dangers of personal frustration, overcome their sense of rejection, cultivate their people skills, and use their special gifts to craft solutions to their interpersonal problems, they will find a genuine sense of accomplishment in the course of this life's passage.

STEPHEN HAWKING
Physicist,
A Brief History of Time

1/8/1942
Capricorn II

CHALLENGE: **NOT ASSUMING THAT NO ONE IS INTERESTED IN WHAT THEY HAVE TO SAY**

FULFILLMENT: **FINDING RELATIONSHIPS THAT WORK FOR THEM**

NOTABLES: **SOPHIE LYONS (BANK ROBBER; AMERICA'S 1ST SOCIETY COLUMNIST); MAURICE WHITE (MUSICIAN; LEADER OF EARTH, WIND AND FIRE)**

December 26–January 2
THE RULER
CAPRICORN I

Marked by an emotional reserve that is likely to serve them well in the course of this life's journey, those born in the Week of the Ruler who travel the Way of Solution can expect great fulfillment and real rewards, providing they can control their fearful attitudes and keep their attention turned to the attainment of practical goals and objectives. The Loner origins of this path may cause these individuals to get mired in the conviction that they have to do everything themselves, and an unwillingness to delegate responsibility or to join with others in a spirit of compromise may be their principal pitfalls. Yet they have marvelous practical and administrative talents that are sure to be of use in the course of this journey, and if they can only develop the patience and understanding necessary to pave the way for smoother interpersonal relations, all will go brilliantly here.

CHALLENGE: **NOT NEGLECTING THEIR SOULFUL SIDE IN THEIR CLIMB UP THE LADDER**

FULFILLMENT: **FINDING THEMSELVES MAKING A REAL DIFFERENCE IN AN ORGANIZATION OR BUSINESS**

NOTABLES: **NATHAN MILSTEIN (CONCERT VIOLINIST NOTED FOR TECHNICAL MASTERY); COUNTRY JOE MacDONALD (ROCK SINGER KNOWN FOR WOODSTOCK PERFORMANCE)**

January 3–9
DETERMINATION
CAPRICORN II

The souls born in the Week of Determination who journey along the Way of Solution can expect great advancement and personal development in the course of this journey as the energies which come together here make for a fine mix of philosophical perspective, practical inclinations, and intuitive insight. Though many of these individuals may be marked by some introverted or even timid tendencies, they are nevertheless ambitious types who with time and patience can apply themselves to their goals. It is likely, however, that they will have to be on guard in themselves against an inclination to be too self-sacrificing or even quite naive when it comes to romantic or emotional matters. Yet they are possessed of great resourcefulness, wonderful stamina, and the realism necessary for great achievement and personal satisfaction as they make their way along this road.

LUCRETIA COFFIN MOTT
Organized 1st women's
rights convention in 1848

1/3/1793
Capricorn II

CHALLENGE: **ALLOWING THAT THEIR MORE RADICAL SIDE MAY BE JUST THE THING FOR CREATING THE BEST SOLUTIONS**

FULFILLMENT: **FORMING SOLID INTIMATE TIES WITH OTHERS**

January 10–16
DOMINANCE
CAPRICORN III

Worry, depression, and an overabundance of anxiety will have to be carefully controlled by the personalities born in the Week of Dominance who travel the Way of Solution. Indeed, they may be marked by a passive-aggressive approach to interpersonal relations, wanting to control on the one hand and to retreat from conflict or deep connection on the other. Though gifted with much more of a soulful and sensitive nature than some others born in this week, they may nevertheless use their energies wrongly in victimhood or even martyrdom. Thus the core lesson of this journey will be to develop a stronger and more flexible sense of self and to overcome those feelings of inferiority that hold them back from happiness. Yet time will provide them with both increasing self-control and self-confidence. If they can learn to release their need for dominance in the interest of negotiation and compromise, their solutions to problems are likely to be both functional and fair.

CHALLENGE: **BEING LESS FATALISTIC WHEN IT COMES TO HELPING OTHERS**

FULFILLMENT: **BALANCING MIND, BODY, AND SPIRIT**

January 17–22

MYSTERY AND IMAGINATION
CAPRICORN–AQUARIUS CUSP

Though there may be a certain amount of emotional chaos in the lives of those born on the Cusp of Mystery and Imagination, there will also be a great deal of reward and satisfaction as they learn to regulate their energies in the interest of realizing their goals. In many ways, this is a puzzling psychological journey, and these individuals will be called upon to explore their own and others' eccentricities as they work to solve the mysteries of human interaction. Yet it is a challenge they will doubtless embrace with a measure of enthusiasm as they are capable of crafting some truly unique and innovative approaches to even the most daunting of personal roadblocks or the most confusing conundrums of human relationship. If they can learn to value their sense of connection to others and manage a tendency to escape from conflict into the world of imagination, all will go well.

MUHAMMAD ALI
Heavyweight boxing
champion

1/17/1942
Capricorn–Aquarius Cusp

CHALLENGE: **BRINGING THEIR VISIONARY ENERGIES DOWN TO EARTH AND MAKING PRACTICAL USE OF THEM**
FULFILLMENT: **ALLOWING OTHERS CLOSE TO THEM**
NOTABLES: **MICHAEL CRAWFORD (ACTOR, LEAD IN *PHANTOM OF THE OPERA*); MAC DAVIS (COUNTRY MUSIC SINGER); AUGUST STRINDBERG (SWEDISH PLAYWRIGHT, FOREFRONT OF NATURALISTIC DRAMA)**

January 23–30

GENIUS
AQUARIUS I

While reining in their imaginations and devoting themselves to practical solutions may not be the forte of those born in the Week of Genius who find themselves on the Way of Solution, most can nevertheless make fine progress here as they hone and refine their more practical inclinations. Gifted with much more compassion and emotion than they might have otherwise, these people are likely to have a pronounced feeling for the human condition and a strong desire to put their mental powers to work in the service of some cause or idea. Highly idealistic as a rule, they will, however, have to learn to come down to Earth and get more specific when it comes to identifying both problems and goals. Yet their natural objectivity can serve them well here, and if they can bring their humanitarian instincts to bear in a more focused and less theoretical way, their creative problem-solving skills are likely to be unmatched.

CHALLENGE: **CURBING IMPULSIVENESS AND THE DESIRE TO RUN AT THE FIRST SIGN OF TROUBLE**
FULFILLMENT: **SENSING GREATER STABILITY IN THEIR LIVES AS A WHOLE ONCE THEY BEGIN TO TACKLE A FEW THINGS THAT NEED CHANGING**
NOTABLE: **WOLFGANG AMADEUS MOZART (FAMED COMPOSER, CHILD PRODIGY)**

January 31–February 7

YOUTH AND EASE
AQUARIUS II

Likely to be gifted with much more by way of social inclination than many who travel this road, those born in the Week of Youth and Ease who journey along the Way of Solution will nevertheless have to take care that they do not become the victims of their own strong desire to please. Yet they will be gifted diplomats and highly creative personalities whose principal failings may only be the reluctance to face down escapist tendencies or to devolve into pure self-interest. Others will manifest a careless or lackadaisical approach to practical matters and will have to work hard to focus their attentions not on what "ought" to be done, but what needs to be done in order to advance toward their goals. Yet if they can cultivate greater discernment and objectivity regarding personal issues and develop the willingness to put their talents in service of others, life promises much reward as they travel this interesting highway.

CAROLE KING
Singer/songwriter,
Tapestry

2/9/1942
Aquarius III

CHALLENGE: **GOING OUT INTO THE REAL WORLD NOW AND THEN**
FULFILLMENT: **SUBSTITUTING OBSESSIVE SELF-IMPROVEMENT FOR SERVICE TO OTHERS**
NOTABLES: **BARRY DILLER (FILM EXECUTIVE; QVC); ROGER STAUBACH (QUARTERBACK; WON HEISMAN TROPHY); AARON BURR (U.S. VICE PRESIDENT; KILLED ALEXANDER HAMILTON IN DUEL)**

February 8–15

ACCEPTANCE
AQUARIUS III

Those born in the Week of Acceptance may need to take a hard look at some of their core vulnerabilities before they can find ways to make necessary progress here. Indeed there is much about this configuration to indicate that these individuals may have taken on the burdens of inappropriate attitudes, poor self-images, or an overly negative outlook in childhood and will face the necessity of transforming early values into a more assured and cohesive sense of self. While some here will display intolerant or high-handed attitudes toward those around them, others can seem downright lazy or careless in their approach. Yet all will face the necessity of developing the emotional distance, discernment, and objectivity necessary to chart the path to fulfillment of their personal and professional ambitions. If they can come to understand that change is more a question of practical process than abrupt transformation, their way to enlightenment will be clear.

CHALLENGE: **OVERCOMING THEIR PROPENSITY TO LIVE LIFE IN FORCED RESIGNATION**
FULFILLMENT: **LETTING THEIR INNATELY AFFECTIONATE NATURE EMERGE**
NOTABLE: **LORD RANDOLPH CHURCHILL (BRITISH STATESMAN)**

February 16–22

SENSITIVITY
AQUARIUS–PISCES CUSP

Likely to be profoundly creative and emotional people, those born in this cusp week who travel the Way of Solution will nevertheless have to develop more of a practical and workable approach to problem solving as they journey along this path. Though ambitious and possessed of what might be termed a lofty idealism, they may allow themselves to be held back from the realization of their goals by a fear of rejection and a negative and pessimistic outlook. The inclination to isolation, self-pity, and feelings of being misunderstood are all prominent here. Yet their standards are undeniably high and their potential for success great. If they can control their defensiveness and channel their energies into ambitious pursuit of their goals, this position is sure to offer them innumerable opportunities to broaden their perspective and widen their sense of humanity.

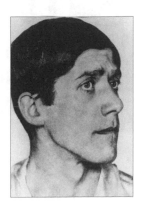

OSKAR KOKOSCHKA
Expressionist painter

3/1/1886
Pisces I

CHALLENGE: **BELIEVING THAT EVEN IN A SMALL WAY THEY HAVE THE ABILITY TO CHANGE SOME OF THE WORLD'S ILLS**

FULFILLMENT: **SOLIDIFYING THEIR SENSE OF SELF THROUGH ONGOING PROGRAMS OF SELF-IMPROVEMENT**

NOTABLES: **PHIL ESPOSITO (HOCKEY PLAYER; 1ST TO SCORE 100 POINTS IN A SEASON); HUEY NEWTON (COFOUNDED BLACK PANTHERS)**

February 23–March 2

SPIRIT
PISCES I

Those born in the Week of the Spirit who navigate the Way of Solution will doubtless be characterized by an elusive, mysterious, or even ethereal quality that can make life somewhat more difficult than necessary for these highly sensitive and emotional individuals. Yet the higher calling here indicates that they put their sense of inspiration to work in practical and effective ways. The result can be a truly winning combination as they use their talents to understand and craft solutions to even the most complex problems. Cultivating objectivity and releasing an irresponsible side will be important to that effort, however, as will the willingness to simply toughen up a bit and refuse to allow their insecurities to get the best of them. Still, these people have a great desire to do good and to place themselves in the service of others. If they can find ways to connect without allowing themselves to be exploited, and learn that life in this world is at best a balance of material concerns and spiritual impulses, all will go wonderfully well in the course of this passage.

CHALLENGE: **TRANSFORMING THEIR SPIRITUAL DEVOTION INTO ATTENTION TO WORLDLY MATTERS**

FULFILLMENT: **FINDING THEY ARE LESS DISSATISFIED ONCE THEY BRING EXPECTATIONS IN LINE WITH REALITY**

NOTABLE: **LOU REED (GUITARIST, SINGER, FOUNDER OF VELVET UNDERGROUND)**

March 3–10

THE LONER
PISCES II

Those born in the Week of the Loner who find themselves on the Way of Solution may be quite unusual people, characterized by profound insight, a deeply soulful quality, and, unfortunately, some problems that need to be dealt with. Early trauma, rejection, and crisis may have left a mark on these souls, and they will face the challenge of learning to release their sense of suffering. Though they will doubtless know a great deal about loss, they may need a great deal of help when it comes to the reality of forming viable relationships with others. Whatever their emotional scars, these souls also have a unique ability to transcend their trials through self-transformation. If they can understand that such transformation does not come through escape but through a process of objective self-evaluation and the willingness to work with others in a spirit of understanding, the path to enlightenment is sure to open into a world of possibilities here.

CHALLENGE: **ATTENDING TO THEIR PERSONAL DEMONS**

FULFILLMENT: **SHOWING THE WORLD THEIR UNIQUELY SOULFUL WAY OF SEEING THINGS**

NOTABLES: **LUTHER BURBANK (HORTICULTURIST); TAMMY FAYE BAKKER (EX-WIFE OF SCANDALOUS EVANGELIST JIM BAKKER); EDWARD KENDALL (1950 NOBEL PRIZE IN MEDICINE FOR CORTISONE)**

March 11–18

DANCERS AND DREAMERS
PISCES III

The truly gifted individuals born in the Week of Dancers and Dreamers who travel the Way of Solution will doubtless face the challenge of grounding both their emotions and their ambitions in the real world. In fact, the principal obstacle to their development may be a snobbish or high-handed attitude toward others, as some of this group will be marked by a pious or unduly superior attitude. Others will enter into codependent or even abusive relationships as a means of avoiding making their own way. Yet once they come to comprehend that the road to connection and realization of their personal and professional ambitions does not lie in their ability to hold themselves aloof from practical and mundane affairs, but to get better acquainted with the practical route to success, life will be much more rewarding as they travel this life's highway.

MICHAEL EISNER
Chairman,
Walt Disney Co.

3/7/1942
Pisces II

CHALLENGE: **TEMPERING A SUPERCILIOUS OR OMNISCIENT APPROACH TO THE PROBLEMS PRESENTED TO THEM**

FULFILLMENT: **EXPERIENCING THE MOMENT OF EPIPHANY WHEN THEY HAVE FOUND THEIR SOLUTION**

NOTABLES: **PAUL KANTNER (GUITARIST, SINGER, JEFFERSON AIRPLANE); EDWARD EVERETT HORTON (ACTOR, FRED ASTAIRE'S SIDEKICK); JERRY JEFF WALKER (COUNTRY SINGER/SONGWRITER)**

The Way of Grounding

DANCERS AND DREAMERS TO LITERALIST
Pisces III to Virgo III

The life purpose of those on this karmic path is to take the fertile imagination and visionary abilities symbolized by Pisces III energies and ground them in Virgo III pragmatism. Dreamers, the men and women on the Way of Grounding must develop the assurance and conviction to deal with the here and now. Because their minds are so highly philosophical, their struggle to ground their thoughts and make practical use of them is not an easy one. Many born to this path will be forced to become intensely pragmatic people, involving themselves in the financial and operating details of life, both at work and at home. Found in fields as diverse as accounting, the military, and the arts, the men and women on the Way of Grounding are called to develop a craftsmanlike and pragmatic mastery of their areas of expertise in order to provide something tangible to the world.

Whether it is their livelihood or not, the men and women on the Way of Grounding are the artists and poets of the personology system. On this path, they have been granted the ability to manifest some pretty big dreams. Not only are they born with great drive and persistence, but through their work on this path they will learn the art of making things happen. Their great blessing is their inherent belief that anything is possible. From past lives they have developed an abundance of faith, and it is the power of faith that aids them in this lifetime. Curiously, early in life they may not choose to make much of themselves, maddening their parents and friends. Others see them as unrealistic because they spend much of their time daydreaming or caught up in fantasy. They love to ponder the big questions in life such as the purpose and meaning of existence and the nature of the universe and mankind's role in it. Questioning everything and refusing to assume anything, they are rarely satisfied by a simple answer. They just "know that there is more to it than that" and will ponder and investigate a topic until they find what they are seeking. Accepting no preconceived ideas makes them wonderfully creative. They are often tinkerers since they are born with a gift for technology and science.

Content to live in their heads and dreams, those on this path often seem distracted or preoccupied and can be extremely ignorant of the practicalities of daily life. They can't be bothered with putting a meal on the table or tidying up when there are so many wonderful theories to work out and ideas to investigate. Moreover, because they are rarely plagued by doubt and believe in themselves and everything that they do, they aren't particularly compelled to prove the truth of their theories to anyone or make their dreams happen. It's enough that *they* know it works. This is due to their inherent faith. Also, they are usually quite spiritual, and their devotion to something greater than themselves, whether an idea, a vision, or a religion, is often enough for them. They don't need approval, ac-

---

CORE LESSON
Disciplining themselves to set tangible goals and adhere to them

GOAL
To literally manifest their visions and dreams in reality

GIFTS
Philosophical, Visionary, Brilliant

PITFALLS
Ineffectual, Arrogant, Absentminded

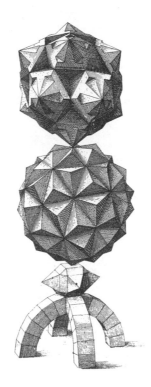

colades, or glory. This makes them both appealing to others and irritating since their omniscient manner can come off as egotism. They seem ineffectual and self-important all at the same time. There are those who will love them for their vision and find their distraction to be endearing. Rarely do they live their lives alone. However, their partners can expect to put up with a good deal of absenteeism as they are always preoccupied or on the move chasing their latest interest.

Though it would be nice for those on this path to simply live life following their hearts and passions, the Way of Grounding calls them, as their parents once did, "to make something of themselves." These men and women are blessed with the ability to see the theoretical or the possible in a tangible form in their mind's eye. Developing the knack for transforming this vision into the concrete is the goal of this path. Thus, they must ground their ideas and theories into something practical—perhaps even something the rest of the world can use. In many cases, this involves actually giving them physical form as a product or service. In a word, this is a path of harvesting. Those on it must harvest their knowledge and ideas, metaphorically separate the wheat from the chaff, and give their wisdom to the world. The destination of this path, the Literalist, represents some pretty practical and reality-based energies. Moving toward this pole of the karmic axis requires that those on this

RELEASE
The refusal to put down roots

REWARD
The joy of giving birth
to new ideas

path establish some truly tangible goals for themselves and then set out to achieve them. Often this path involves the mastery of a craft, whether in a creative, commercial, or other endeavor. But above all else, those on this path must learn to use some common sense and pay more attention to the details of life if they even hope to become more practical and thereby create something of lasting value.

The core lesson of the men and women on the Way of Grounding is to develop mental discipline and to realize that one can create structure and routine by becoming more organized and logical in one's thinking. In order to become more pragmatic, the people on the Way of Grounding must learn to impose some limitations, routines, and organization on themselves and to stick to them. It is particularly important if they are to rid themselves of any tendencies to sloppiness or a propensity to make mistakes by acting too quickly or glossing over the importance of details. Stern self-discipline will be needed initially since limiting their minds in any way is new to these individuals. In addition, through mental discipline, those on this path will learn to be more effective communicators. Presenting their plans with clarity can be crucial to garnering the necessary support from others to make things happen.

These individuals are in a position to leave their mark on the world permanently. However, it is important for those on this path to realize that this is a path not about

SUGGESTION

Realize that you already know how to make it happen, you just have to do it. Work on developing concentration and focus. Meditation is often an excellent tool for disciplining the mind.

fame or riches but about making the world a better place. Symbolically, a kind of sacrifice is called for here. Those on this karmic path give up some of their freedom and ethereal ways for the greater good of humankind, or even just for their families, by allowing themselves to be tied down to routines, schedules, and deadlines. By so allowing themselves to be limited, they are performing a service. The writer who sits down day after day gives pleasure to the reader; the scientist who spends hours in the laboratory testing hypotheses gives mankind the benefit of greater knowledge; and the artist who gropes within himself for higher ideals and studies his craft to ground abstraction in something the viewer can see or hear gives us understanding and inspiration. As they progress on this path, those on it will truly embody the Virgo archetype of their destination. Virgo represents the individual complete unto himself. Those on this path will not only experience the satisfaction of giving their ideas and visions form, but they will also find deep fulfillment and a sense of completion within themselves.

Although their instincts urge them to work alone, the individuals on the Way of Grounding will find that they are better able to give birth to their ideas in conjunction with others, particularly those whose strengths complement theirs. Accomplishing substantive results in a professional field will delight their parents but also their mates and offspring, to whom such achievement betokens increased commitment and security. Love is rarely the most important consideration for those on this path. However, since they are oriented primarily to matters of the mind and perception, the best partner for them is a person of intelligence, understanding, and indepen-

dence since any trace of possessiveness or cloying behavior will usually push those on this path away. On the whole, however, those on this karmic path do well in the stability of family life.

Grounding their minds is of course aided by grounding their bodies in physical activities (the discipline doesn't hurt them either). These individuals may have to force themselves to participate in sports or exercise of any kind, but running or other solitary forms of fitness may be just the thing since they provide time for the mind to wander freely. Of primary importance is for these individuals to remember to nurture the font of their inspiration and to nourish themselves with it. Should they fail to provide for this, those on this path may throw over all their efforts at discipline and unconsciously rebel in ways that are not only nonproductive but destructive. Building a need for solitude into their daily routine is important for those on this path in order to give them mental free time and plenty of space for daydreaming. Similarly, letting themselves go once in a while, letting the house grow untidy or the dishes undone, will provide the same psychological benefit.

As this karmic path calls for giving form to *logos* or the divine wisdom manifest in creation, one can only consider the Book of Genesis from the Bible wherein God gives form to all of creation. Moving his spirit upon the face of the waters, God ultimately formed man, Adam, from dust and gave him the breath of life so that he would become an embodied soul. Viewed as a metaphor, this story can inspire those on the Way of Grounding to invoke their deepest spiritual yearnings and give form to them.

BALANCE POINT

Theory and Practice

CRYSTALS AND GEMSTONES

Hematite is the master grounding stone. The energy in this mineral brings the daydreamer back to present reality with dreams intact and mind focused on creating something tangible.

NOTABLES ON THIS KARMIC PATH

Best known for his development of the atomic bomb at Los Alamos, physicist **J. Robert Oppenheimer** also achieved great distinction serving as director of Princeton's prestigious Institute of Advanced Study and as a UN and government adviser on nuclear power. Oppenheimer was able to ground his theoretical speculations, materi-

J. ROBERT OPPENHEIMER

alizing concrete realities—the goal of his karmic path, the Way of Grounding. Due to his later support of the regulation of nuclear power, he became the object of false accusations of disloyalty, which cost him his security clearance in 1953. However, he was vindicated when he received the Atomic Energy Commission's Fermi Award in 1963.

Few architects in history have been able to express their imaginative genius as fully as **Frank Lloyd Wright.** Wright began his career designing houses influenced by the Arts and Crafts movement, built with natural

FRANK LLOYD WRIGHT.

and regional materials and characterized by overhanging roofs and horizontal lines. These modern homes were both economically viable and aesthetically graceful. Later, Wright expanded on his theory of organic archi-

tecture, creating the Pennsylvania retreat Falling Water and Taliesin West in Arizona. During this period, he also planned the Guggenheim Museum, combining radical design with the practical needs of a great exhibition space. Wright assuredly met the challenge of this path, constantly manifesting his visions and dreams in reality.

Interior decorator and culinary authority **Martha Stewart** has built an empire on good taste. Beginning as a stockbroker, Stewart worked as a caterer and editor of *House Beautiful* before launching the many products that carry her name. Since that

MARTHA STEWART

time, she has come to author numerous cookbooks, create the magazine *Martha Stewart Living,* and produce several television programs. With such an extensive list of accomplishments, there is no doubt that Stewart was born with the kind of inherent faith in herself and her schemes typical of those on the Way of Grounding.

Other Notables: Marcel Marceau, Florenz Ziegfeld, Willem de Kooning, Salvador Dalí, Johnny Weismuller, Margaret Bourke-White, Deng Xiaoping, Robin Leach, D. H. Lawrence, Chubby Checker, Anne Rice, Paul Simon, Will Durant, Norman Mailer, Art Garfunkel, Ava Gardner, Carol Channing, Laura Ingalls Wilder, Chuck Yeager, Diane Arbus, Pablo Neruda, Don Hewitt, Laurence Tisch, Paddy Chayefsky, Thomas Paine, Dexter Gordon

---

BIRTHDAYS ON KARMIC PATH 48

August 30, 1885–January 18, 1886 | April 12, 1904–August 30, 1904 | November 22, 1922–April 12, 1923

July 3, 1941–November 21, 1941 | February 13, 1960–July 2, 1960

September 24, 1978–February 12, 1979 | May 5, 1997–September 23, 1997 | December 16, 2015–May 4, 2016

KARMIC PATH
48

March 19–24
REBIRTH
PISCES–ARIES CUSP

The individuals born in this week who travel the Way of Grounding are in for a fine life's journey as here the qualities of creativity, sensitivity, and imagination are nicely complemented by some dynamic energy and a straightforward approach to people, professional matters, and problem solving. Though they may have to learn to be a bit more blunt and even aggressive in the pursuit of their goals, they are apt to fulfill their yearnings to transform their dreams into reality. In fact, the quest for transformation and rebirth that is so much a part of their makeup is likely to revolve around their willingness to give birth to their inspirations and ideas in material ways. Thus, as long as their need for truth, and an innate need to win are not superseded by an unreasonable desire for harmony, undue impatience, or poor planning, these individuals can bring their fondest dreams and truest inspirations into tangible and rewarding manifestation as they make their way along this life's highway.

FLORENZ ZIEGFELD
Theater producer,
Ziegfeld Follies

3/21/1867
Pisces–Aries Cusp

CHALLENGE: **TEMPERING AN AGGRESSIVE NEED TO WIN IN FAVOR OF HIGHER GOALS**
FULFILLMENT: **GIVING BIRTH TO THEIR DREAMS**
NOTABLES: **MARCEL MARCEAU (FRENCH MIME ARTIST); AYRTON SENNA (BRAZILIAN AUTO RACER)**

March 25–April 2
THE CHILD
ARIES I

The enthusiastic and lively souls born in this week who travel the Way of Grounding may struggle with the challenge to bring their inspirations and theories down to earth in practical expression. There is a strong tendency to view the world in a naive way here, and some will find their faith and conviction under fire as they make their way along this karmic path. Yet the tests and trials they may encounter are not designed to dampen their great enthusiasm or contribute to a sense of disillusion, but are only a call to develop their talents for greater discipline and practical application of their gifts and talents. However, they will be aided along this journey by a strong desire to be taken seriously. Once they understand that it is far easier to achieve that end when one has solid evidence of one's accomplishments, all will go brilliantly here.

CHALLENGE: **BEING CAREFUL NOT TO RETREAT FROM THE WORLD TOO OFTEN**
FULFILLMENT: **UTILIZING THEIR NATURAL CREATIVITY IN CONJUNCTION WITH THEIR NEWFOUND PRAGMATISM**
NOTABLES: **ARTURO TOSCANINI (CONDUCTOR, LED NBC SYMPHONY); JENNIFER GREY (ACTRESS, *DIRTY DANCING*); KELLY LEBROCK (MODEL; ACTRESS)**

April 3–10
THE STAR
ARIES II

Tending to be goal and success oriented, those born in the Week of the Star who journey along the Way of Grounding are promised a really rewarding passage as here some truly inspired creative talents come together with a generous measure of worldly ambition and considerable drive. In fact, the principal danger for these souls will lie only in a tendency to retreat into wounded feelings or a rather high-handed attitude when the world demands that they indeed "put their money where their mouths are" and back up their theories with dedicated effort. There is an inclination to hold themselves aloof and fail to garner the support or resources they might need from others to really get their projects off the ground. Yet if they can manage to find the right balance between creative inspiration and concerted and practical effort, life is likely to be kind indeed as they make their way along this road.

MARCUS ALLEN
Football great, NFL's all-time rushing touchdown leader

3/26/1960
Aries I

CHALLENGE: **NOT LETTING THEMSELVES BE DISTRACTED BY OTHERS OR MORE PLAYFUL PURSUITS**
FULFILLMENT: **CHANNELING THEIR ENERGY INTO ACHIEVEMENT OF THEIR GOALS**
NOTABLE: **BUSTER DOUGLAS (HEAVYWEIGHT BOXER, DEFEATED MIKE TYSON FOR CHAMPIONSHIP)**

April 11–18
THE PIONEER
ARIES III

Learning to manifest their high ideals and dreams into real experience and tangible evidence of their accomplishment is well within the reach of those born in the Week of the Pioneer who travel the Way of Grounding as they have a fine gift for bringing others to their causes and a real yearning to push the frontiers of what is possible. Though there may be any number of these individuals who retreat from the higher challenge implied here and become mere "armchair travelers" on this road, content to live purely in their heads and theories, most will respond quite well to the challenge to make their dreams manifest in the real world. If they can control a certain tendency to impatience, avoid judgmentalism and arrogance, and nurture their yearning for truth, many here can indeed go where no one has gone before.

CHALLENGE: **GROUNDING THEMSELVES ENOUGH TO MANIFEST THEIR VISIONS**
FULFILLMENT: **WORKING IN CONJUNCTION WITH OTHERS OF LIKE MIND**
NOTABLES: **MICHAEL STUART BROWN (GENETICIST; WON NOBEL PRIZE); SIR JOHN GIELGUD (ACTOR, DIRECTOR, *ARTHUR*); WILBUR WRIGHT (INVENTED AND FLEW FIRST AIRPLANE WITH BROTHER ORVILLE)**

April 19–24
POWER
ARIES–TAURUS CUSP

A more grounded approach to aspiration will come quite naturally to those born on the Cusp of Power who journey along this karmic path, and some of these individuals are indeed destined to make a formidable mark on the world. Much less materialistic than some born in this week, these individuals are a fine mix of inspiration, investigation, and the kind of solid application necessary to see their goals to a satisfying, productive, and often lucrative conclusion. They have greater patience and a much more developed ability to carefully plan the route to solid achievement than many others along this road. If they can manage a rather arrogant attitude on the one hand, and control a lazy or complacent streak on the other, life will be good indeed.

WILLEM DeKooning
Painter, abstract
expressionist

4/24/1904
Aries–Taurus Cusp

CHALLENGE: **OVERCOMING A RUTHLESS STREAK AND CULTI-VATING GREATER HUMILITY**

FULFILLMENT: **GIVING THEIR LOVE TO THEIR DREAMS AND IDEAS**

NOTABLE: **VALERIE BERTINELLI (ACTRESS, *ONE DAY AT A TIME*)**

April 25–May 2
MANIFESTATION
TAURUS I

R ealism and practicality come quite naturally to those born in the Week of Manifestation who journey along the Way of Grounding, and most will enjoy great fulfillment here. Highly focused individuals for the most part, once they are seized by true inspiration, they are not likely to rest until they see their plans into some sort of practical implementation. The Pisces III origin of this path endows these individuals with a much higher degree of creativity, imagination, and breadth of vision than they might otherwise possess. Perhaps their principal pitfall will lie in in their emotionalism. They can succumb to hurt feelings, a sense of personal slight, or manifest a truly intractable stubbornness that can cause them to burn bridges when they would do better to concentrate on building them. If they can overcome that much, the rest will come quite easily as they make their way along this karmic path.

CHALLENGE: **DEVELOPING A TOUGHER SKIN**

FULFILLMENT: **SEEING THEIR PLANS AND IDEAS IMPLEMENTED**

NOTABLES: **BING CROSBY (SINGER, ACTOR, *WHITE CHRISTMAS*); CECIL DAY-LEWIS (BRITISH POET LAUREATE, AUTHOR); ARTHUR BURNS (CHAIRMAN FEDERAL RESERVE BOARD); STEVE CAUTHEN (JOCKEY; WON TRIPLE CROWN)**

May 3–10
THE TEACHER
TAURUS II

T he intellectually astute and creatively inspired individuals who make their journey along the Way of Grounding are promised great success, providing they can get out of their heads and learn to put their theories, plans, and schemes into practice as they make their way along this road. Though they will be much intrigued by the areas of abstraction, education, and information, they have a productive side and are quite fond of the kind of material manifestation indicated here. Though they will have to fight the tendency to smugness, high-handedness, or pedantry, they nevertheless have fine instincts for truth and a compulsion to bring their ideas to the world. If they can only cultivate a more practical approach, avoid a tendency to be critical of others' ideas and methods, and instead focus on the business of solid accomplishment, all will go well in the course of this life's journey.

SALVADOR DALÍ
Surrealist artist,
The Persistence of Memory

5/11/1904
Taurus III

CHALLENGE: **BEING ONE OF THOSE WHO DO, RATHER THAN ONE OF THOSE WHO TEACH**

FULFILLMENT: **KNOWING THAT THEY HAVE THE TALENTS NECESSARY TO MAKE ANYTHING HAPPEN**

NOTABLES: **J. B. JAY BECKER (GRAND MASTER BRIDGE PLAYER); GREGORY BATESON (CULTURAL ANTHROPOLOGIST); MAX MALLOWAN (ARCHAEOLOGIST; MARRIED AGATHA CHRISTIE); BONO VOX (LEAD SINGER OF U2)**

May 11–18
THE NATURAL
TAURUS III

T hose born in the Week of the Natural may hold a real disdain for the need for the practical application of their ideas, ideals, and theories, and some may falter a bit as they make their way along this karmic path. In fact, some irresponsible attitudes and a strong need for independence may exist at odds with the call to develop a more measured and pragmatic approach to seeing their plans to conclusion. Thus, these individuals can do a great deal of shadowboxing and obsessing over their lack of freedom until they come to better terms with the facts and demands of life in the world. Still, they have a strong need for security that will work very much to their advantage here; as soon as they stop expecting others to pave the way for their success, and settle down to the need for dedicated and devoted effort to their own ideals, they can find their path to comfort and contentment much improved.

CHALLENGE: **NOT BEING SATISFIED WITH THE KNOWLEDGE THAT THEY CAN MAKE THEIR FANTASIES REAL, BUT DOING IT**

FULFILLMENT: **EXPERIENCING THE SELF-ESTEEM THAT GIVING SOMETHING TANGIBLE FORM GIVES THEM**

NOTABLES: **JACOB JAVITS (LIBERAL REPUBLICAN SENATOR FROM N.Y.); JEAN GABIN (FRENCH CHARACTER ACTOR); JULIANNE PHILLIPS (ACTRESS)**

May 19–24
ENERGY
TAURUS–GEMINI CUSP

The lively and compelling personalities born on the Cusp of Energy who find themselves on the Way of Grounding may feel perplexed by the necessity to channel their formidable stores of inspiration and energy into practical or pragmatic approaches. Indeed, while few can match their brilliance and excitement, these individuals may fail to see the need for mental discipline. Cultivating the simple endurance to see their plans through to conclusion will be especially challenging as these souls have a decidedly flighty and easily distracted side that will have to be reined in a bit in order for them to become more effective. Learning the value of long-term planning and dedicated effort and taking up the task of training their creative abilities will be especially useful. Yet if they can be encouraged to set simple short-term goals and realize the gratification that comes with modest achievement, they can learn the value of more extended planning and set their eyes on the future with enthusiasm and confidence.

CHALLENGE: **TAKING THEIR HEADS OUT OF THE CLOUDS AND PLANTING THEIR FEET ON THE GROUND**

FULFILLMENT: **BUILDING A STRONGER SENSE OF SELF THROUGH DISCIPLINE**

NOTABLES: **FATS WALLER (JAZZ PIANIST, SINGER, COMPOSER, "AIN'T MISBEHAVIN' "); KRISTIN SCOTT THOMAS (ACTRESS, *THE ENGLISH PATIENT*)**

JOHNNY WEISMULLER
Gold medal Olympic swimmer-turned-actor, *Tarzan*

6/2/1904
Gemini I

May 25–June 2
FREEDOM
GEMINI I

Gifted with greater objectivity and more discernment than many who travel they Way of Grounding, the individuals born in the Week of Freedom may nevertheless chafe a bit at the higher challenge to practical effort and tangible manifestation of their ideas and dreams. In fact, there is a volatile side to these people that bears watching as they can misdirect their energies in endless debate, pointless speculation, and hypercriticism when things don't go according to their idealistic plans. On the other side of the coin, too much disillusion can manifest in cynicism and an unpleasant iconoclastic streak. Yet family life especially can have a valuable grounding influence, and if they are lucky enough to surround themselves with those individuals who will appreciate their brilliance and creativity, yet guide them toward a more realistic approach to tangible manifestation of their goals, all will go beautifully along this karmic path.

CHALLENGE: **TAKING UP THE CHALLENGE TO SELF-DISCIPLINE**

FULFILLMENT: **FINDING GROUNDING IN FAMILY LIFE**

June 3–10
NEW LANGUAGE
GEMINI II

Personal and professional disorganization can be a big stumbling block for those born in the Week of New Language who journey along the Way of Grounding, and they will have to work hard to find the most effective route to realization of their personal and professional goals. Yet they are blessed with some really formidable creative and communicative talents here, and they need only to cultivate some basic skills and learn to better appreciate the value of craft in bringing their message to others. The combination of sensitivity to rejection and a feeling of being misunderstood is greater than entirely appropriate in these somewhat thin-skinned people who can strike out at others in criticism, complaints, and personal sniping. Yet if they can learn to come to terms with the relatively simple fact that theories, ideas, and messages are only effective when they are understood by those with whom they are shared, they will have made the first big steps toward progress as they journey along this road.

CHALLENGE: **NOT GETTING LOST IN THEIR OWN REVERIES OR DREAMS**

FULFILLMENT: **ENJOYING THE TASK OF COMMUNICATING THEIR VISIONS AND THEIR IMPLEMENTATION TO OTHERS**

NOTABLE: **SIR JAMES YOUNG SIMPSON (OBSTETRICIAN; 1ST TO BRING ANESTHESIA TO CHILDBIRTH)**

MARGARET BOURKE-WHITE
WWII photojournalist, *Life* magazine

6/14/1904
Gemini III

June 11–18
THE SEEKER
GEMINI III

Gifted with a fine sense of adventure and a measure of faith, those born in the Week of the Seeker who journey along the Way of Grounding may discover that the practical application of their talents is neither entirely beyond their reach, nor entirely to their liking as they travel along this karmic path. Yet they can find happiness here, providing they allow themselves ample mental free time and the personal space to explore their ideas apart from the demands of daily life. There is a strong yearning for experience in these individuals that nicely complements the higher challenge, however, and once they come to terms with the fact that the ability to bring inspiration to manifestation is essentially experiential, they will doubtless find the right balance between adventure and perseverance as they make their way along this life's highway.

CHALLENGE: **NOT FLITTING FROM ONE INTEREST TO THE NEXT SO MUCH AS WORKING TO FULFILL THE POTENTIAL OF ONE**

FULFILLMENT: **GIVING THEMSELVES AMPLE ROOM TO DREAM THEIR DREAMS**

NOTABLES: **KEYE LUKE (ACTOR, 13 MOVIES AS CHARLIE CHAN'S "NUMBER ONE SON"); HARRIET BEECHER STOWE (WRITER, *UNCLE TOM'S CABIN*)**

June 19–24
MAGIC
GEMINI–CANCER CUSP

Characterized by a highly romantic and emotional approach to life, those born on the Cusp of Magic who journey along the Way of Grounding may have to work a bit to come down to earth and give real form to their talents and inspirations. Some will be characterized by extreme personal sensitivity, while others may withdraw into a private and isolated world. Yet there is a great deal of luck that goes with this configuration, and their journey will doubtless abound with opportunities to develop their capability, objectivity, and faith in a larger design. If these individuals can learn to better manage a rather needy side, and release the idea that they must depend on others to make their dreams come true, they can make great progress here. Thus, if they can master their emotional power and put it to use in a disciplined effort directed at realizing their goals, their efforts will be fired by passion and their dreams grounded in a wonderfully real world.

PETER LORRE
Actor, M, Casablanca

6/26/1904
Cancer I

CHALLENGE: **GETTING INVOLVED IN THE DAY-TO-DAY DETAILS OF OPERATING A BUSINESS**

FULFILLMENT: **PUTTING THEIR OWN UNIQUE IMPRINTS ON WHAT THEY CREATE**

NOTABLE: **TRACY POLLAN (ACTRESS, FAMILY TIES; MARRIED MICHAEL J. FOX)**

July 3–10
THE UNCONVENTIONAL
CANCER II

Some rather erratic tendencies may mark the lives of those born in this week who travel the Way of Grounding, and some will struggle mightily with the need to get out of their heads and bring their dreams into some form of concrete manifestation. Though creatively gifted and highly imaginative, they may founder a bit until they find more appropriate avenues for self-expression and discover the necessity of making their world a better place, not through fantasy, but through realistic effort. In many ways, these unique individuals can be easily led astray by their fascination with the unusual and some may go down any number of rabbit trails in the search for personal fulfillment. Yet they are blessed nonetheless with some formidable powers of observation and a fine sense of those attitudes and needs which are common to all human experience. If they cultivate the ability to tap into a higher source of inspiration, and find the discipline to bring their insight to the world in some form of concrete expression, they can accomplish great things as they make their way along this karmic path.

PABLO NERUDA
Surrealist poet

7/12/1904
Cancer III

CHALLENGE: **NOT FLOUNDERING IN FANTASY BUT FOCUSING ON WHAT IS PRACTICABLE**

FULFILLMENT: **REALIZING THEIR ABILITY TO TAP INTO COMMERCIALLY LUCRATIVE IDEAS**

June 25–July 2
THE EMPATH
CANCER I

If those born in the Week of the Empath can find the balance between their intuitive powers and the practical application of same, the results can be spectacular as they make their way along this karmic path. Yet that challenge may prove a bit more daunting than it sounds for these highly sensitive people, as their emotions tend to be rather delicately wired, and they are easily thrown off course by conflicts, setbacks, and personal disillusion. In fact, the principal danger here is Cancer I's will allow their fears to rule and learn to distrust their sense of higher inspiration. Many of these people will fail to garner the support they need from others through a tendency to display a clingy or needy side. Yet there are some strong practical talents in these individuals, and if they can channel their energies into dedicated effort, explore their own potential to make themselves secure, and learn to establish proper emotional boundaries between themselves and others, they will find security, contentment, and more than their share of accomplishment.

CHALLENGE: **BELIEVING IN THEMSELVES**

FULFILLMENT: **PUTTING THEIR PRACTICAL AND FINANCIAL ABILITIES TO WORK**

NOTABLE: **PAUL FRANÇOIS BARRAS (FRENCH REVOLUTIONARY, OVERTHROWN BY NAPOLEON)**

July 11–18
THE PERSUADER
CANCER III

The individuals born in the Week of the Persuader who find themselves on the Way of Grounding can expect great reward and accomplishment, providing they steer clear of emotional excess and turn their attention to better organizing, crafting, and disciplining their talents. In fact, these people have a wonderful gift for bringing others to a cause and a strongly inspirational streak that is sure to come to the fore here. Yet they can indulge in a tendency to be arrogant, so certain are they of their vision. They have a fine talent for facts and figures which will serve them well, yet they should take care to nurture their creativity with dream time. If they can realize the need for dedicated effort and avoid a tendency to manipulate others or to indulge in blaming the world for failing to recognize their genius, all can go quite well as they make their way along this karmic path.

CHALLENGE: **ACKNOWLEDGING THAT OFTEN WE NEED OTHERS TO MAKE OUR DREAMS REALITY**

FULFILLMENT: **OPERATING AS PART OF A TEAM TO PRODUCE SOMETHING OF TANGIBLE VALUE**

NOTABLES: **MARINA OSWALD (MARRIED TO ASSASSIN LEE HARVEY OSWALD)**

July 19–25

OSCILLATION
CANCER–LEO CUSP

Integrating emotion, dynamism, and inspiration into disciplined and directed action will prove the principal challenge for those born in this cusp week who travel the Way of Grounding. Indeed, the demands of this path can well exist at odds with their need to strike out in new directions or stir up the pot. In fact, the daily routines and discipline necessary for success in the real world can be arduous for these souls, and many here will chase any number of windmills and dream any number of "impossible" dreams before they settle down to the business of birthing their inspirations into manifestation. They will have to take care that their moral courage and deep sense of conviction does not emerge as an omniscient attitude, judgmentalism, or superiority. Yet if they can take up the challenge to a steadier and more reliable mode of living, surrounded by dependable people who will guide them without boring them to tears, life will doubtless become much easier as they make their way along this karmic path.

CHALLENGE: **DISCIPLINING THEIR EMOTIONAL SIDE**
FULFILLMENT: **STEADYING THEIR LIVES AS THEY FULFILL THEIR AMBITIONS**
NOTABLE: **NATALIA BESSMERTNOVA (RUSSIAN BALLERINA)**

PAUL ANKA
Songwriter/musician,
"You're Having My Baby"

7/30/1941
Leo I

July 26–August 2

AUTHORITY
LEO I

Learning to channel their sense of the infinite and strong capacity for faith into some form of tangible manifestation is likely to come quite easily for those born in the Week of Authority who travel the Way of Grounding. Though they may have to work hard to overcome a rather high-handed or superior approach, they nevertheless are blessed with considerably more personal strength than some who travel this road and can get where they want to go through steady application, personal willpower, and a willingness to look the facts squarely in the eye. Yet they like to be taken seriously, and these tough customers will pursue their goals with an awesome single-mindedness when they know they're on the right track. Thus, if they can use their gifts for leadership to bring others to their causes, overcome the limitations of egotism, and remain focused on their practical goals, they will doubtless leave their mark along this karmic path.

CHALLENGE: **DECIDING THAT ACHIEVING SOMETHING MATTERS TO THEM**
FULFILLMENT: **STANDING BY THEIR FAITH IN HIGHER PRINCIPLES**

August 3–10

BALANCED STRENGTH
LEO II

The forthright and unpretentious personalities born in the Week of Balanced Strength who journey along the Way of Grounding are likely to enjoy wonderful success and accomplishment, for here the ability to dream big is augmented by a real ability to plan well and apply themselves to their goals. And while early in life they may have a problem settling on desired goals, once they do, they have a natural endurance that is not always present in some others who travel this road, and an ability to dedicate themselves to their worldly tasks with something approaching real devotion. This path endows them with greater sensitivity and a broadness of perspective they might otherwise lack. The resulting combination will indeed result in a life's journey that is personally fulfilling and wonderfully inspirational as these fortunate and gifted people make their way along this karmic path.

CHALLENGE: **LETTING THEIR INTUITION LEAD THEM DESPITE THEIR "BETTER JUDGMENT" TO THE CONTRARY**
FULFILLMENT: **PROVING THEMSELVES TO OTHERS, EVEN KNOWING THAT THEY DON'T HAVE TO**

ELISHA OTIS
Developed first
passenger elevator

8/3/1811
Leo II

August 11–18

LEADERSHIP
LEO III

A fine combination of personal strength, breadth of vision and creative inspiration, most of those born in the Week of Leadership who journey along the Way of Grounding will enjoy a remarkable life's passage. This configuration is not without its stumbling blocks, however, and these individuals may struggle mightily to overcome the issues of ego in order to apply themselves to the business of manifesting their dreams. In short, there are a number of these personalities who may be so convinced of their superiority that they fail to trouble about practical matters or attend to those very details that will make their plans work. Approachability and the willingness to share their ideas can also be a problem here. Yet if they can climb down from some self-erected pedestals and gain a more realistic vision of their own place in the larger scheme, life is bound to reward their humility with happiness and their endurance with deep satisfaction as they travel this life's highway.

CHALLENGE: **NOT LETTING THEIR NEED FOR RECOGNITION INTERFERE WITH THEIR DESIRE TO MAKE A DIFFERENCE**
FULFILLMENT: **FINDING THEMSELVES LEADING A GROUP OF PEOPLE WORKING TOWARD A JOINT GOAL**
NOTABLE: **DAVID CROSBY (SINGER/SONGWRITER, CROSBY, STILLS AND NASH)**

August 19–25
EXPOSURE
LEO–VIRGO CUSP

If they can manage not to hoard their dreams and inspirations, but share them with the larger world, Leo–Virgos are likely to do beautifully on the Way of Grounding as they have a fine knack for practical application and dedicated effort that will doubtless serve them well as they make this journey. More keenly objective than many who travel this road, even the most high-flown of their inspirations will be tinged with some practical coloration. Yet for all of their powers of observation and investigation, they will have to learn to overcome their disposition to intrigues, secrets, and a private sense of psychodrama in order to manifest their best inspirations in reality. Facing the challenge of developing real integrity and honesty in their dealings with themselves and others will figure prominently in this life's journey. If they can regulate the flamboyant aspects of their characters in favor of a greater sense of humility and control a marked tendency to cynicism, their progress will be that much faster and their fulfillment more complete.

DENG XIAOPING
Leader of Chinese
Communist Party

8/24/1904
Leo–Virgo Cusp

CHALLENGE: **OVERCOMING A PROPENSITY TO KEEP THEIR IDEAS TO THEMSELVES**
FULFILLMENT: **CHOOSING THE RIGHT PEOPLE TO HELP FULFILL THEIR VISION**
NOTABLE: **COUNT BASIE (JAZZ MUSICIAN, BANDLEADER)**

August 26–September 2
SYSTEM BUILDERS
VIRGO I

Those born in the Week of the System Builders who find themselves on the Way of Grounding are likely to enjoy a really rewarding passage here as their natural gifts and aptitudes are very much in keeping with the higher challenge to practical application, modesty, and bringing their sense of inspiration to bear in the creation of tangibles. Gifted with a beautiful and elegant sense of structure and a healthy respect for training and craft, most will respond readily to the challenge to put their gifts to some practical use in the world. Though there is something of a danger here that these individuals will go a bit overboard in their material efforts and pragmatic attitudes and thus become rigid, most will enjoy the best of both the spiritual endowments and practical benefits of this path. If they can keep in mind that they already know all that they'll ever need to actualize their dreams, soon the liberation this idea gives them will ensure that they will enjoy great peace along the way.

CHALLENGE: **ALLOWING THEMSELVES BIGGER DREAMS**
FULFILLMENT: **BELIEVING THAT THEY ARE WORKING TOWARD A NOBLE CAUSE**
NOTABLES: **JOHN THOMPSON (BASKETBALL COACH, GEORGETOWN UNIVERSITY); CHRISTOPHER ISHERWOOD (NOVELIST; INSPIRED *CABARET*); ROBIN LEACH (TV HOST, *LIFESTYLES OF THE RICH AND FAMOUS*)**

September 3–10
THE ENIGMA
VIRGO II

Those born in the Week of the Enigma who journey along the Way of Grounding are likely to enjoy the trip as their natural powers of good taste, discernment, and objective analysis will be of great benefit in clearing away the cobwebs, fantasies, and less-than-useful ideas and inspirations to which those with Pisces III origins are sometimes prone. Though likely to lead rich inner lives and to be blessed with a measure of creative talent, these souls will nevertheless have a fine disposition for practical matters and will be drawn naturally to tangible manifestation and evidence of their accomplishment. Though they may run the risk of becoming rather snobbish, remote or high-handed, they have a gift for putting their talents to some larger purpose. If they can cultivate greater involvement and learn to serve others, they will enjoy the best life has to offer.

D. H. LAWRENCE
Writer; prosecuted for
obscenity,
Lady Chatterly's Lover

9/11/1885
Virgo III

CHALLENGE: **NOT RESISTING THE CALL TO MAKE SOMETHING OF THEMSELVES FOR FEAR THEY'LL LOSE THEIR PRIVACY**
FULFILLMENT: **UTILIZING THEIR FINE TASTE AND DISCRIMINATION TO PRODUCE ONLY THE BEST**
NOTABLES: **OTIS REDDING (SOUL SINGER, "DOCK OF THE BAY"); ELINOR WYLIE (POET, WRITER, *ANGELS AND EARTHLY CREATURES*); CHRISTOPHER HOGWOOD (FOUNDED ACADEMY OF ANCIENT MUSIC)**

September 11–18
THE LITERALIST
VIRGO III

Gifted with a fine sense of inspiration and a strongly realistic side, those born in this week who travel they Way of Grounding are likely to experience personal fulfillment and solid accomplishment, providing they do not go overboard in the pursuit of purely practical concerns and keep the channels open between the worlds of the mind and the world of tangible reality. In fact, there are some here who will do themselves a great disservice and fail to give themselves proper credit for their own insights and inspirations, discounting them as "irrational" or fanciful. Their need for harmony can often cause them to keep to themselves or otherwise fail to garner the support they need to get their plans and projects off the ground. Yet there is nevertheless a marvelous prospect of fulfillment here, and if these souls can come to realize their own gifts for making things happen, all will go well in the course of this life's journey.

CHALLENGE: **NOT UNDERMINING THEMSELVES OUT OF GUILT FOR THEIR GREAT BLESSINGS AND TALENTS**
FULFILLMENT: **HAVING THE SENSE THAT THEY ARE IN COMPLETE CONTROL**
NOTABLE: **KAREN HORNEY (PSYCHIATRIST, MAJOR FIGURE IN PSYCHOANALYTICAL MOVEMENT)**

September 19–24

BEAUTY
VIRGO–LIBRA CUSP

Those born on the Cusp of Beauty who journey along the Way of Grounding can find this a hard road in many respects, as they have little taste for practical matters. There is a rather snobbish streak in many of these personalities that will often work to their detriment here, and some with this configuration will hold themselves aloof from what they consider "mundane" practical interests. Though gifted with considerable creative talents and a strong feeling for progress and evolution in the world of ideas and trends, they may be rather helpless when it comes to putting those notions to work in the real world. They will do best when they consciously cultivate friends, partners, and associates who will ground their sense of inspiration and guide them to a set of tangible goals. If they can avoid the tendency to complacency on the one hand and superiority on the other, they will surely come to better terms with life as they travel this karmic path.

CHALLENGE: **AVOIDING THE PROPENSITY TO BE HAUGHTY OR ARROGANT**

FULFILLMENT: **GETTING SERIOUS AND SETTLING DOWN TO WORK**

NOTABLE: **ERICH VON STROHEIM (ACTOR; DIRECTOR, *INTOLERANCE*)**

September 25–October 2

THE PERFECTIONIST
LIBRA I

The individuals born in the Week of the Perfectionist who journey along the Way of Grounding can enjoy great achievement in the course of this life's journey, providing they keep their attention turned away from purely theoretical interests and toward the attainment of practical goals. In fact, there is a strongly inspirational streak in many of these people, along with a real ability to motivate themselves and others. While they may struggle with the necessity to bring their mercilessly high standards a bit more down to earth, they have a great deal of intensity and drive which will surely be of great value here. If they do not allow the demons of personal insecurity and indecisiveness to hinder their higher development, and instead work to develop focus, thoroughness, and the ability to take pride in a job well done, they will find joy and real accomplishment in the course of their travels.

CHALLENGE: **NOT PERMITTING THEIR PERFECTIONISM AND INDECISION TO DERAIL THEM FROM GETTING RESULTS**

FULFILLMENT: **SENSING THAT THEIR IDEAS AND VISIONS ARE UNDERSTOOD BY OTHERS**

REV. JESSE JACKSON
Civil rights activist; heads
Rainbow Coalition

10/8/1941
Libra II

October 3–10

SOCIETY
LIBRA II

Gifted with a highly creative impulse and some truly exquisite taste, Libra II's who travel the Way of Grounding may nevertheless experience a bit of difficulty in coming to terms with the higher challenge to material manifestation that is indicated here. In fact, there will be a number of what might best be termed "hothouse flowers" on this karmic path, who will require a rather sheltered or rarefied existence in order to be really functional. With a strong leaning toward self-deception, these people will manifest their frustration in criticism and some unfortunate escapist tendencies. Yet at their core, they possess both faith and inspiration. If they can only learn to channel those energies in such a way that they take themselves and their goals more seriously, the call to commitment, practical effort, and well-grounded creativity will be far easier to answer as they make their way along the road.

CHALLENGE: **TAKING THEIR OWN IDEALS OR DREAMS MORE SERIOUSLY**

FULFILLMENT: **USING THEIR INSIGHTFULNESS IN SERVICE TO A CAUSE**

NOTABLES: **PIERRE BONNARD (PAINTER, LITHOGRAPHER); NIELS BOHR (WORKED ON ATOMIC BOMB, MANHATTAN PROJECT); CHUBBY CHECKER (SINGER, "THE TWIST"); JACKIE COLLINS (BESTSELLING NOVELIST)**

October 11–18

THEATER
LIBRA III

Gifted with highly developed leadership abilities and considerable worldly ambition and drive, the individuals born in the Week of Theater who journey along the Way of Grounding can realize great achievement here, providing they remain willing to adjust their sense of ambition to better coincide with the real world. Highly perceptive and genuinely savvy, they can at times fall prey to overconfidence or fail to thoroughly plan the route to their goals. They will have to narrow their focus to include only those visions which promise tangible reward, for they have far more ideas than they do time on this earth. Yet making things happen is one of the things they do best; if they can only avoid the dangers of cynicism, high-handedness, or arrogance and apply themselves to crafting application and ultimate realization of their visions, life will be sweet as they journey along this road.

CHALLENGE: **BEING DRIVEN LESS BY WORLDLY AMBITION AND MORE BY INSPIRATION**

FULFILLMENT: **PRESENTING THE NEW AND UNIQUE TO THE WORLD**

NOTABLE: **PAUL SIMON (SINGER/SONGWRITER, WITH GARFUNKEL AND SOLO; GRAMMY FOR *GRACELAND*)**

ANNE RICE
Novelist,
The Vampire Chronicles

10/4/1941
Libra II

October 19–25

DRAMA AND CRITICISM
LIBRA–SCORPIO CUSP

The compelling and charismatic people born on the Cusp of Drama and Criticism who find themselves on the Way of Grounding can likewise expect accomplishment and satisfaction in the course of this life's journey, though they will doubtless have to work a bit to control a rather temperamental streak and learn to better practice what they preach. Wonderfully artistic, they may nevertheless manifest some snobbish or prima donna tendencies and may have an unrealistic vision of their talents as well. Yet life will surely prove a great teacher here. If they immerse themselves in the experiences of living, they will come to know what roads to pick since their strengths, opportunities, and preferences are sure to become clearer. Once they get out of their heads and into the real world, they will doubtless find it much to their liking as they make their way along this karmic path.

EZRA POUND
Poet/writer, *Cantos*;
indicted for treason, WWII
––––––––
10/30/1885
Scorpio I

CHALLENGE: **REALIZING IF THEY SPEND ALL THEIR TIME QUESTIONING EVERYTHING, THEY'LL NEVER PRODUCE ANYTHING**
FULFILLMENT: **CONTRIBUTING TO THE CREATION OF BEAUTY**
NOTABLE: **CHARLES MERRILL (FOUNDER, MERRILL LYNCH & CO., INC.)**

October 26–November 2

INTENSITY
SCORPIO I

Blessed with a fine sense of detail and unequaled powers of concentration, the personalities born in the Week of Intensity who journey along the Way of Grounding can expect great reward and fulfillment in the course of this passage. Perhaps their principal pitfall will only lie in their tendencies to an overly emotional outlook or too great an attachment to some idle hopes and dreams. These personalities can be rather thin-skinned when it comes to criticism and may shrink a bit from the idea of putting their creative inspirations "on the market," as it were. Yet they have some really brilliant investigative talents and a strong need for material security. If they can cultivate their more practical inclination and toughen up on an emotional level, there will be little they cannot accomplish in the course of this life's journey.

CHALLENGE: **CONCENTRATING ON HAVING GREATER MAGNANIMITY OF SPIRIT**
FULFILLMENT: **USING HUMOR TO CONVINCE OTHERS OF THEIR IDEAS**

November 3–11

DEPTH
SCORPIO II

The ability to stay grounded in practical effort and to develop a focus for their emotional and spiritual energies will be truly useful for those born in the Week of Depth who travel this karmic path. Yet getting out of their own heads and rising up from the pool of their highly emotional natures may prove more difficult than it sounds, for there are some strongly introverted tendencies here and the capacity to be literally swept away on tides of speculation, theory, and deep emotion. Nevertheless, these people have a strong need for money and material belongings that should be carefully cultivated, for their attraction to tangibles will serve to ground them in reality, and dedicated effort and routine will help to manage their emotions. Yet if they can avoid both escapism and anxiety and learn to take solace from their own ability to stay on a chosen course and see their plans through to satisfying conclusions, life will reward them richly as they make their way along this karmic path.

WILL DURANT
Historian (shown here
with wife, Ariel)
––––––––
11/5/1885
Scorpio II

CHALLENGE: **FORCING THEMSELVES TO GO OUT INTO THE "REAL" WORLD TO ACHIEVE THEIR AIMS**
FULFILLMENT: **COMING TO THE COMPLETION OF LONG-ABORNING PROJECTS**
NOTABLES: **GEORGE PATTON (WW II COMMANDER, "OLD BLOOD AND GUTS"); ART GARFUNKEL (SINGER, SIMON AND GARFUNKEL)**

November 12–18

CHARM
SCORPIO III

The fortunate individuals born in the Week of Charm who find themselves on the Way of Grounding are likely to enjoy real fulfillment and genuine accomplishment in the course of this life's journey, for here a higher sense of inspiration is well balanced by a strong sense of realism and personal resourcefulness. Indeed, their principal fault may only be that they are much more inclined to get others to do the work than they are to do it themselves. Laziness and complacency can also cause them to content themselves with less than they might achieve. Yet they are much more together than many who travel this road, and if they can cultivate their organizational abilities, nurture their vision, and keep a weather eye on the details, they are sure to get where they want to go as they travel this karmic path.

CHALLENGE: **RELEASING THE TENDENCY TO TAKE THE PATH OF LEAST RESISTANCE**
FULFILLMENT: **PUTTING THEIR CAPACITY TO FOCUS AND CONCENTRATE TO PRODUCTIVE USE**
NOTABLE: **MEL STOTTLEMEYER (BASEBALL PLAYER, YANKEES PITCHER, COACH)**

November 19–24
REVOLUTION
SCORPIO–SAGITTARIUS CUSP

Those born on the Cusp of Revolution who travel the Way of Grounding can run into a bit of trouble along this road as they are capable of some really big dreams and a fine sense of the big picture, but will have to work hard to ground that vision in reality. Follow-through and dedicated effort may not be their strongest suit, and they have a rather excitable side that can work to their detriment here. Yet at their core, results are important to these individuals; if they can learn to pursue a more tangible and less theoretical set of goals with the same zeal that they pursue their ideas, inspiration, and dreams, they have a rare ability to inspire others to their cause and a fine combination of determination and imagination that can lead them to the heights of success in the world.

CHARLES M. SCHULZ
Cartoonist, created
Peanuts comic strip

11/26/1922
Sagittarius I

CHALLENGE: **INVOKING DISCIPLINE, PERSISTENCE, AND DEDICATION TO FINISH WHAT THEY START**
FULFILLMENT: **HARVESTING THE FRUIT OF THEIR LABOR**
NOTABLE: **JULIET MILLS (ACTRESS, *NANNY AND THE PROFESSOR*)**

November 25–December 2
INDEPENDENCE
SAGITTARIUS I

The independent spirits born in this week who travel the Way of Grounding may find themselves a bit uncomfortable as they travel this road since their love of freedom can exist at odds with the need for a grounded and realistic effort toward manifesting their vision into tangible reality. A curious combination of willpower and rebellion, of honor and impulsiveness, can make this a rather unpredictable journey since their success will largely depend on how carefully they choose the dreams they wish to make manifest in the world and how carefully they apply themselves to the task of making it happen. Yet they like to win; if they can manage to arouse their more competitive side, and come to view the necessity of practical effort as more of a challenge than a chore, they will do quite well here.

CHALLENGE: **CHOOSING TO SETTLE DOWN**
FULFILLMENT: **FINDING THAT THEY CAN PUT THEIR ETHICS, MORALS, AND DREAMS INTO A FORM THAT WILL SERVE HUMANITY**

December 3–10
THE ORIGINATOR
SAGITTARIUS II

The personalities born in the Week of the Originator who travel the Way of Grounding are likely to be extraordinarily gifted individuals, blessed with both creative inspiration and a fine technical aptitude. Though likely to be extremely sensitive to rejection and possessed of a defensive side, they are nevertheless motivated by a strong need for acceptance. If they can channel that need into dedicated and concentrated effort to manifest their unique and original vision in reality, they will be able to approach the higher tasks here with an ardent dedication, the proper degree of humility, and a fervor than is often lacking elsewhere. If they can avoid emotional neediness, keep their feet on the ground and their heads in the stars, they can bring their unique talents to bear in ways that will serve to inspire many as they make their journey along this karmic path.

REDD FOXX
Bawdy comedian, pictured
in a wig as star of
television's *Sanford & Son*

12/9/1922
Sagittarius II

CHALLENGE: **OVERCOMING A CHIP ON THE SHOULDER ATTITUDE**
FULFILLMENT: **REVELING IN THE SHEER PLEASURE OF CREATION**

December 11–18
THE TITAN
SAGITTARIUS III

If they can come to terms with the fact that the Way of Grounding will ask them to come down to earth and put their talents to constructive use, those born in the Week of the Titan can realize some great things in the course of this life's journey. They may have to deal with some ego issues first, however, and some may struggle a bit with the call to greater humility and service that are part of the higher challenge here. Moodiness and instability can also pose problems for these individuals, yet directing their talents to grounded and practical concerns will serve to balance their inclination to emotional extremes. Thus if they employ their great energies, dauntless enthusiasm, and self-assurance in such a way that they never lose faith in what is possible, they are capable of shouldering huge responsibilities in the interest of bringing their ideas to manifestation in the course of this most interesting journey.

CHALLENGE: **STABILIZING THEIR INNER AND OUTER LIVES BEFORE THEY EMBARK ON ACHIEVING THEIR ASPIRATIONS**
FULFILLMENT: **REACHING FOR THE STARS AND PULLING ONE TO EARTH**
NOTABLE: **DON HEWITT (TV PRODUCER, *60 MINUTES*)**

December 19–25

PROPHECY
SAGITTARIUS–CAPRICORN CUSP

Highly suited to the call to grounded effort, personal dedication, and development of their practical talents, those born on the Cusp of Prophecy who travel this karmic path can enjoy a wonderfully fulfilling journey, providing they take care not to shut down or close themselves off from the source of their higher inspirations. Likely to be quite gifted, creative, and even clairvoyant, those born with this configuration are not highly social types and will be much inclined to the solitary aspects of an artistic or contemplative life. Yet they must remember the call to share their sense of inspiration with others and better understand that in some significant ways they are here to serve as a channel between the infinite and the material world. Thus, if they can better learn to give, there will be much to receive in the course of this life's journey.

VINCENT SARDI
Opened Sardi's restaurant in Manhattan's theater district

12/23/1885
Sagittarius–Capricorn Cusp

CHALLENGE: **CONVINCING THEMSELVES THAT OTHERS WILL WANT WHAT THEY HAVE TO SELL**
FULFILLMENT: **USING THEIR INTUITIVE STRENGTHS TO GET THINGS DONE**

December 26–January 2

THE RULER
CAPRICORN I

Hardworking and achievement oriented by nature, those born in the Week of the Ruler who find themselves on the Way of Grounding can expect really extraordinary success and accomplishment as their natural energies and inclination are very much in keeping with the higher challenge to tangible manifestation of their dreams and ideas. The problem is only that true inspiration and creative exploration may be given rather short shrift in the search for security and groundedness. Workaholic tendencies can surface here, as can a rather pronounced insecurity about their own creative gifts. Yet if they don't get lost in the details of life, and manage to find the time and space to nurture their sources of inspiration and innovation and idealism, there will be no one better or more capable of practical effort and tangible manifestation of their own divine spark than Capricorn I's who travel this road.

CHALLENGE: **STEPPING OFF THE TREADMILL NOW AND THEN TO RECHARGE THEIR PSYCHIC BATTERIES**
FULFILLMENT: **OFFERING THE WORLD A PRODUCT OR SERVICE IN WHICH THEY TRULY BELIEVE**
NOTABLE: **JOAN MCCRACKEN (ACTRESS, SINGER, BILLION DOLLAR BABY)**

January 3–9

DETERMINATION
CAPRICORN II

The dauntless and diligent souls born in this week who make their journey along the Way of Grounding are well suited to the challenges offered here and are likely to experience a truly satisfying passage. Natural strivers, these people will find it much in keeping with their energies and inclinations to give substantive form and shape to their ideas and dreams. Blessed with the patience to develop a craftsmanlike approach to their chosen fields of endeavor, they will find great peace and contentment in seeing their ideas brought to physical manifestation. Though they will have to avoid a tendency to personal insecurity and too much self-sacrifice, their strongly practical side, combined with a yearning to make their dreams real, is sure to pave the way to fulfillment and happiness here.

AVA GARDNER
Actress,
Night of the Iguana

12/24/1922
Sagittarius–Capricorn Cusp

CHALLENGE: **NOT BEING ASHAMED OF THEIR SPIRITUAL OR METAPHYSICAL LEANINGS**
FULFILLMENT: **RELAXING IN THE CONSIDERABLE SUCCESS THEY ARE CERTAIN TO ACHIEVE**
NOTABLE: **HANS VON BULOW (GERMAN PIANIST, CONDUCTOR)**

January 10–16

DOMINANCE
CAPRICORN III

Gifted with a fine sense of personal ambition and a rather modest approach to their own talents, those born in the Week of Dominance who make their way along this karmic path are sure to find the way to happiness and fulfillment of their dreams as they travel this road. Though they will have to avoid a tendency to go a bit overboard in the call to practical effort and may have to mitigate their highly focused approach with more in the way of fun and relaxation, they can nevertheless take wonderful satisfaction from the careful craftsmanship and tangible manifestation of their talents. While they may be short on patience when it comes to broadening their perspective or learning to include others in their efforts, their sense of direction, ambition, and dedication to their goals is sure to find the fullest expression here.

CHALLENGE: **NOT FULFILLING THEIR VISION BECAUSE THEY HAVE SOMETHING TO PROVE BUT BECAUSE THEY HAVE SOMETHING TO SAY**
FULFILLMENT: **MASTERING A FIELD OF ENDEAVOR**

January 17–22
MYSTERY AND IMAGINATION
CAPRICORN–AQUARIUS CUSP

Learning to better control their own chaotic energies will prove the core lesson for those born in this week who make their way along the Way of Grounding. Most likely these spirits will founder a bit until they come to a better understanding of the need for focus and direction of their considerable gifts. Choosing partners, friends, and associates of a more stable nature will prove especially helpful here, as will the ability to augment their personal routines with periods of freewheeling freedom when they can refresh their minds and nurture their sense of creative inspiration. Yet they have a strong sense of responsibility and an equally developed sense of their purpose in the larger scheme. As they come to understand, through training, discipline, and effort that they also have everything they need to bring their plans to fruition, all will go brilliantly here.

CHALLENGE: **UNDERSTANDING THAT IT IS NOT POSSIBLE TO LIVE IN A WORLD OF THEIR OWN MAKING**
FULFILLMENT: **HELPING THOSE LESS ADVANTAGED IN TANGIBLE WAYS**
NOTABLES: **TELLY SAVALAS (ACTOR, KOJAK); JEAN STAPLETON (ACTRESS, ALL IN THE FAMILY)**

LAURA INGALLS WILDER
Writer born into pioneer family, *Little House on the Prairie*

———
2/7/1867
Aquarius II

January 23–30
GENIUS
AQUARIUS I

Highly intellectual, inspirational, and theoretical, the individuals born in the Week of Genius who travel the Way of Grounding will have a somewhat harder time coming to terms with the need for a more pragmatic approach to reality. It is not so much that they are unwilling to learn the skills necessary to bring their talents to the fore or to manifest their plans in real world achievement; it is only that they may have to work quite hard to cultivate the qualities of dedication, patience, and devotion called for here. There is a strong streak of rebellion in these individuals when they come into conflict with authority or those who might be best able to aid them in realizing their goals. If they can get out of their heads a bit and learn to take pleasure in the process rather than the ultimate realization of their dreams, things will go more smoothly as they make their way along this road.

CHALLENGE: **COMING DOWN FROM THEIR IVORY TOWERS AND TREADING THE EARTH WITH THE REST OF US**
FULFILLMENT: **SEEING THEIR GENIUS IN MATERIAL FORM**
NOTABLES: **PADDY CHAYEFSKY (DRAMATIST, NETWORK); THOMAS PAINE (PHILOSOPHER; WROTE COMMON SENSE); JOHN HANCOCK (1ST MAN TO SIGN CONSTITUTION); DICK MARTIN (COHOST, LAUGH-IN)**

January 31–February 7
YOUTH AND EASE
AQUARIUS II

In many ways, life can be almost too easy for those born in this week who travel the Way of Grounding, and some may neglect their potential for higher development simply because they can be rather lazy about practical matters and unwilling to focus their talents in the interest of tangible achievement. Gifted with a strong ability to inspire others and to make themselves beloved by those around them, they can quite easily leave the more tedious details to others and content themselves with a superficial level of happiness and success. Still, they have strong virtuoso talents and remarkable creative gifts that will beg for expression. If they can only apply themselves to the discipline, training, and craftsmanship necessary to give form to their inspiration, the rest will fall into place as they make their way along this road.

CHALLENGE: **KICK-STARTING THEMSELVES**
FULFILLMENT: **EXPERIENCING THE SATISFACTION OF HANGING IN THERE FOR THE LONG HAUL**
NOTABLES: **CAROL CHANNING (ACTRESS, ENTERTAINER, HELLO, DOLLY); NORMAN MAILER (WRITER, THE NAKED AND THE DEAD)**

CHUCK YEAGER
Aviator/test pilot, 1st to break sound barrier

———
2/13/1923
Aquarius III

February 8–15
ACCEPTANCE
AQUARIUS III

Those born in the Week of Acceptance who find themselves on this karmic path may chafe a bit at the seeming restrictions and the call to more concerted effort that are implied on the Way of Grounding. Inventive and innovative, these individuals may nevertheless fail to find an outlet for their creative talents due to a rather restless streak that, if not properly controlled can cause them to be flighty, disorganized, and content with the more superficial forms of expression and experience. Developing simple consistency will be of great benefit here, as will their willingness to surround themselves with more stable types. Yet if they can learn to focus and still allow themselves the freedom to dream, they will find the right balance between creative ideas and practical effort as they travel along this road.

CHALLENGE: **PUTTING DOWN ROOTS LONG ENOUGH TO DO SOMETHING OF TANGIBLE VALUE**
FULFILLMENT: **FOLLOWING THEIR DREAMS AND WATCHING THEM COME TRUE**
NOTABLES: **FRANCO ZEFFIRELLI (ITALIAN DIRECTOR, ROMEO AND JULIET); JIM KELLY (QUARTERBACK, BUFFALO BILLS); YELENA BONNER (RUSSIAN SOCIAL REFORMER)**

February 16–22

SENSITIVITY
AQUARIUS–PISCES CUSP

Goal and result oriented, these individuals will have to overcome the demons of personal sensitivity and a fear of having their ideas rejected as they make their way along the Way of Grounding. Yet there is nevertheless the possibility of great success here, providing they learn the value of craftsmanlike dedication to a particular profession or area of endeavor and avoid the dangers of isolation and insecurity. Yet there is a healthy streak of aggression in many of these people that will serve them in good stead. If they can come to better understand that this path beckons them to a body of work rather than to the heights of fame and fortune, and develop the art of building on their achievements without allowing themselves to be defeated by their mistakes, all will go smoothly.

CHALLENGE: **STICKING TO WHAT THEY BELIEVE IN NO MATTER WHAT OTHERS MIGHT SAY**
FULFILLMENT: **FINDING THEY, IN FACT, POSSESS THE COURAGE TO EXPOSE THEIR IDEAS TO THE GLARE OF PUBLIC OPINION**
NOTABLE: **PRINCE ANDREW (DUKE OF YORK)**

DEXTER GORDON
Jazz saxophonist; received Best Actor nomination for role as jazz musician in *Round Midnight*, 1986

2/27/1923
Pisces I

February 23–March 2

SPIRIT
PISCES I

Practical matters and personal responsibility may be big stumbling blocks for those born in this week who travel they Way of Grounding, and while they may have more than their share of understanding, empathy, and creative inspiration, bringing those gifts to manifestation may be difficult for these souls. Stability in their surroundings and the development of personal discipline and steadier habit will be especially important to their success, as will the willingness to dedicate themselves fully to cause or primary relationship. Yet their is a practical and sensual side to these people that, if given proper encouragement and nurture, can enable them to really blossom in the course of this journey, especially within the context of a service-oriented profession or creative calling.

CHALLENGE: **RECOGNIZING THAT TO TRULY SERVE OTHERS, ONE MUST OPERATE IN THE DAY-TO-DAY WORLD**
FULFILLMENT: **KNOWING THAT THEY CAN LEAVE THE WORLD A BETTER PLACE**
NOTABLES: **CHARLES DURNING (ACTOR, *TOOTSIE*); DOROTHY STRATTEN (*PLAYBOY* MODEL; KILLED BY EX-LOVER)**

March 3–10

THE LONER
PISCES II

Because those born in the Week of the Loner who travel the Way of Grounding are inclined to work by themselves outside the confines of a structured organization, personal discipline will be especially important to them. They will do well to stick to organized routines and to schedule themselves with specific goals in mind. Some isolationist tendencies can interfere with their progress, as they often lack necessary input from others. Learning to bounce their ideas off friends and family who can help them sort through the pros and cons will be useful, as will those who can challenge their views without offending their sensitive natures. Yet they have all the ingredients for personal and professional achievement; if they can develop the tools and skills necessary to practical and consistent application of their gifts, all will go well here.

CHALLENGE: **LEAVING HARD TIMES BEHIND AND GETTING ON WITH THE BUSINESS OF LIVING**
FULFILLMENT: **BREAKING OUT OF THEIR SHELLS AND PUTTING THEIR VERY ESSENCE ON DISPLAY**
NOTABLES: **ED MCMAHON (JOHNNY CARSON'S RIGHT-HAND MAN ON *THE TONIGHT SHOW*; HOST *STAR SEARCH*); ANDRE COURREGES (FASHION DESIGNER, KNOWN FOR MINISKIRT); CYD CHARISSE (ACTRESS, DANCER, *BRIGADOON*)**

LAURENCE TISCH
Business executive; known for rescuing failing companies

3/15/1923
Pisces III

March 11–18

DANCERS AND DREAMERS
PISCES III

There will be much about these personalities that is inclined to "slip the surly bonds of earth," and some will struggle mightily with the call to develop greater practicality and focus. Though wonderfully creative and often truly inspired, they may scatter their energies or succumb to the yearning for a higher plane. Yet once they come to understand themselves as a channel for divine inspiration and train themselves as instruments to bring their talents to the world, they will take up their tasks much more easily. Developing the humility to understand that there is much they have yet to learn will be an important first step, as will developing the discernment and experience necessary to understand that following one's heart is not always the route to achievement. Yet there is the promise of real and lasting success. If they merely learn to do as well as they can dream, life will be rich indeed.

CHALLENGE: **NOT OVERCOMPENSATING BY BECOMING TOO DISCIPLINED OR RIGID**
FULFILLMENT: **DARING TO DREAM THE BIG DREAM AND MAKE IT COME TRUE**

Index of
Notables

Index

Boldface numbers indicate
pages with illustrations.

A

Aaron, Henry "Hank," 351, **362**
Aaron, Tommy, 116
Abbado, Claudio, 367
Abbott, Berenice, 275
Abbott, George, 739
Abdul, Paula, 703, **707**
Abdul-Jabbar, Kareem, 576
Abernathy, Ralph, 683
Abzug, Bella, 148
Acheson, Dean, 496
Acuff, Roy, 69
Adams, Abigail, 487
Adams, Ansel, 127, **139**
Adams, Don, 673
Adams, John, **87**
Adams, John Quincy, **307**
Adams, Samuel, 630
Adler, Alfred, 698
Adler, Stella, 186
Affleck, Ben, **292**
Agassi, André, 385
Agee, James, 584
Agnew, Spiro, 215
Aiello, Danny, 371
Aikman, Troy, 527, **527,** 536
Ailey, Alvin, 479, **489**
Aimée, Anouk, 417
Akhmatova, Anna, 659
Albee, Edward, 591, **603**
Albers, Joseph, 704
Albert, Prince, 469
Albrechtsberge, Johann, 74
Alcott, Amos Bronson, 520
Alcott, Louisa May, 687, **696**
Alda, Alan, 282
Aldington, Richard, 531
Aldrin, Edwin "Buzz," **522**
Alexander, Jason, **230**
Alexandra, Czarina of Russia, **594**
Alger, Horatio, 729
Ali, Muhammad, 783, **794**
Allen, Debbie, 447, 457
Allen, Gracie, 724
Allen, Marcus, **800**
Allen, Steve, **89**
Allen, Tim, **322**
Allen, Woody, 271, **280**
Alley, Kirstie, 265
Allison, Bobby, **200**
Allman, Duane, 600
Allman, Gregg, **552**
Alomar, Roberto, 490
Alomar, Sandy, Jr., 546
Alomar, Sandy, Sr., 727
Alou, Felipe, 289
Alou, Jesus, 784
Alou, Matty, 153
Alou, Moises, 547
Alpert, George, 288
Alpert, Herb, **304**
Alsop, Joseph, 550
Alsop, Stewart, 385
Altman, Robert, 719, **731**
Amis, Kingsley, 63
Amos, Tori, 655, 661
Amsterdam, Morey, 456
Andersen, Hans Christian, 287, **288**
Anderson, Eddie, 757
Anderson, Gillian, 447, **456**
Anderson, Ian, 596
Anderson, Jack, 55
Anderson, Laurie, 559, **562**
Anderson, Loni, 596
Anderson, Pamela, 463, **467**
Anderson, Richard, 660
Anderson, Sherwood, 421
Andress, Ursula, 256
Andretti, Mario, 107

Andrew, Prince (Duke of York), 811
Andrews, Dana, 617
Andrews, Julie, 271, **278**
Anfingen, Christian, 320
Angeli, Pier, 415, 419
Angelou, Maya, 591, **592**
Aniston, Jennifer, 431, **442**
Anka, Paul, **804**
Anne, Princess of England, 431, **436**
Ann-Margret, 47, **49**
Ant, Adam, 263
Anthony, Susan B., 447, 458
An Wang, **170**
Apple, Fiona, 79, **79**
Applegate, Christina, **328**
Aquino, Benigno, 408
Aquino, Corazon, **394**
Arafat, Yasir, 527, **533**
Araskog, Rand, 439
Arbuckle, Fatty, 736
Arbus, Diane, 799
Arendt, Hannah, 703, 710
Arlen, Harold, 778
Armani, Giorgio, 319, **323**
Armatrading, Joan, 424
Armstrong, Edwin, 600
Armstrong, Louis "Satchmo," 148
Armstrong, Neil, 495, **500**
Armstrong-Jones, Antony, **523**
Arnaz, Desi, 283
Arnaz, Desi, Jr., 346
Arness, James, 786
Arnold, Tom, 91
Arp, Hans, 725
Arquette, Patricia, 464
Arquette, Rosanna, **68**
Arthur, Jean, 758
Ashe, Arthur, 719, 723
Asher, Peter, 691
Ashford, Nicholas, 737
Asimov, Isaac, 159, **169**
Asner, Ed, **519**
Asquith, Herbert Henry, 645
Assante, Armand, 470
Astaire, Adele, 277
Astaire, Fred, 239, **239,** 241
Astin, John, 512
Astor, Lady Nancy, 306
Astor, Lord Waldorf, 306
Atkins, Chet, 739
Atkinson, Brooks, **440**
Attenborough, Sir David, 671, 673
Attenborough, Sir Richard, 783, **783,** 789
Auchincloss, Louis, 262
Auden, W. H., 687, **699**
Audubon, John James, 335, **337**
Auerbach, Red, **262**
Aung San, 378
Austen, Jane, 719, **728**
Auster, Paul, **586**
Autry, Gene, 671, 678
Avalon, Frankie, 79
Avedon, Richard, 783, **785**
Axson, Ellen, 321
Ayer, A. J., 551
Aykroyd, Dan, 351, **355**
Ayres, Lew, 617

B

Bacall, Lauren, 741
Bach, Johann Sebastian, 623, **623,** 624
Bach, Wilhelm Friedmann, 344
Bacharach, Burt, 543, **545**
Backus, Jim, 459
Backus, John, 728
Bacon, Francis, 378
Bacon, Kevin, 111, 115
Badu, Erykah, **363**
Baez, Joan, **73**
Bailey, David, 281
Bailey, Donald, 149
Bailey, F. Lee, 367, 370

Bailey, James, 83
Bailey, Pearl, **224**
Bailly, Jean Sylvain, 53
Baird, Spencer Fullerton, **330**
Baiul, Oksana, 111, 119
Baker, Ginger, 79, **85**
Baker, Howard, 695
Baker, James, 497
Baker, Josephine, 719, **722**
Baker, Louie, 739
Baker, Russell, 687, **692**
Bakker, Jim, 105
Bakker, Tammy Faye, 795
Bakshi, Ralph, **151**
Balakirev, Mili, 521
Balanchine, George, 47, 58
Baldwin, Alec, **112**
Baldwin, James, **740**
Balin, Marty, 746
Ball, Lucille, 511, **511,** 516
Ballard, Robert, 771
Balzac, Honoré de, 530
Bancroft, Anne, **453**
Bandaranaike, Sirimavo, **320**
Banderas, Antonio, 783, **788**
Bankhead, Tallulah, **106**
Banks, Dennis, **208**
Banks, Ernie, 474
Banting, Sir Frederick, 551
Barbeau, Adrienne, 642
Bardot, Brigitte, 319, **326**
Barenboim, Daniel, **759**
Barkley, Charles, **699**
Barnard, Edward, 616
Barnes, Edward, 353
Barnum, P. T., 63, **67**
Barras, Paul François, 803
Barrault, Jean Louis, **549**
Barrie, Sir James Matthew, 321
Barrow, Clyde, 608
Barry, Daniel, 787
Barry, Marion, 267
Barrymore, Drew, 191, **203**
Barrymore, Ethel, 292
Barrymore, John, 202
Barrymore, John Drew, 418
Barrymore, Lionel, **337**
Barthelme, Donald, 464
Bartók, Béla, 224
Bartram, William, 714
Baryshnikov, Mikhail, 543, **554**
Basie, Count, 805
Basinger, Kim, 287, 296
Bassett, Angela, 95, **100**
Bateman, Justine, 571
Bates, Kathy, 515
Bateson, Gregory, 801
Batista, Fulgencio, **185**
Battle, Kathleen Deanne, 511, **516**
Baudelaire, Charles Pierre, 399, 400
Baum, L. Frank, 479, **479,** 481
Baxter, Anne, 785
Beach, Alfred, 181
Beach, Sylvia, **763**
Beals, Jennifer, 665
Bean, Orson, 580
Beatty, Ned, 211
Beatty, Warren, 207, 208
Beauharnais, Joséphine de, 483
Beauvoir, Simone de, 655, **665**
Beck, 383, **387**
Beck, Jeff, **691**
Beck, Julian, 706
Becker, Boris, 488
Becker, J. B. Jay, 801
Beckett, Samuel, 720
Bednarik, Chuck, 705
Beecher, Henry Ward, 723
Beefheart, Captain, 73
Beery, Wallace, 368
Beethoven, Ludwig van, 175, **175,** 184
Begin, Menachem, 415, **420**
Begley, Ed, Jr., 469
Behrens, Peter, 752
Belafonte, Harry, 623, **635**
Belasco, David, 596
Bel Geddes, Barbara, 55

Bell, Alexander Graham, 95, **107**
Bell, Clive, 213
Bell, Derrick Albert, Jr., 487
Bell, Lawrence, 448
Bell, Vanessa, 306
Belli, Melvin, 676
Bellow, Saul, 351, 354
Bellson, Louie, 739
Belushi, Jim, 274
Belushi, John, **506**
Bemelmans, Ludwig, 287, **289**
Bench, Johnny, 543, 552
Benchley, Peter, 81
Benchley, Robert, 645
Bendix, William, 745
Benedict, Ruth, 738
Ben-Gurion, David, 767, **774**
Benitez, Jellybean, 135
Bennett, Floyd, 599
Bennett, Michael, 736
Bennett, Tony, 655, **660**
Benny, Jack, 474
Benson, George, 735, 736
Bentsen, Lloyd, Jr., 111, 122
Benz, Karl Friedrich, 200
Berenson, Marisa, 634
Bergen, Candace, 607, **609**
Bergen, Edgar, 79, **91**
Bergman, Ingmar, 223, **227**
Bergman, Ingrid, **309**
Bergman, Marilyn, 535
Bergstrom, Sune Karl, 329
Berkeley, Busby, 392
Berle, Milton, 639, 643
Berlin, Irving, 703, **705**
Berliner, Emile, **690**
Bern, Paul, 648
Bernhard, Leopold, Prince, 515
Bernhard, Sandra, 239, **242**
Bernsen, Corbin, 277
Bernstein, Carl, 714
Bernstein, Leonard, 213
Berra, Yogi, 703, **705**
Berrigan, Daniel, 657
Berrigan, Phillip, 774
Berry, Chuck, 639, **646**
Berry, Halle, 468
Bertinelli, Valerie, 801
Bertolucci, Bernardo, **107**
Bessmertnova, Natalia, 804
Best, Charles, 267
Beutel, Bill, 488
Bhutto, Benazir, 323
Bhutto, Zulfikar Ali, 601
Bibby, Thomas Geoffrey, 262
Big Bopper, **487**
Biko, Steve, 584
Billy the Kid, 344
Binoche, Juliette, 651
Biondi, Frank J., Jr., 655, 665
Bird, Larry, 175, **184**
Bishop, Elizabeth, 538
Bismarck, Otto von, 640
Bisset, Jacqueline, 677
Bixby, Bill, 362
Bizet, Georges, 431, 439
Black, Shirley Temple, 591, 593
Blair, Betsy, 776
Blair, Tony, 319, **321**
Blake, Eubie, **154**
Blake, William, 703, **703**
Blanchard, Felix Anthony "Doc," 728
Blatty, William Peter, **601**
Blavatsky, Madame Helena, 735, **735**
Bledsoe, Tempest, **260**
Bleeth, Yasmin, 418
Blige, Mary J., 351, 361
Bligh, Captain William, **69**
Bloodworth-Thomason, Linda, 576
Bloomingdale, Alfred S., 320
Blue, Vida, 484
Blume, Judy, 186
Boas, Franz, 387
Bochco, Steven, 712
Bocuse, Paul, **682**

Boeing, William Edward, 207, 214
Boesky, Ivan, 235
Bogart, Humphrey, 223, 233
Bogdanovich, Peter, 111, **116**
Bogosian, Eric, 321
Bohr, Aage Niels, 67
Bohr, Niels, 806
Bolger, Ray, 57
Bolívar, Simon, 420
Bolt, Robert, 740
Bolton, Michael, **331**
Bonaparte, Napoleon, 228
Bonds, Barry, 628
Bonds, Bobby, 619
Bonet, Lisa, 487
Bon Jovi, Jon, 719, **731**
Bonnard, Pierre, 806
Bonner, Yelena, 810
Bono, Chastity, **443**
Bono, Sonny, 303, **303,** 315
Bono Vox, 801
Boone, Debby, 175, **182**
Boone, Pat, 338
Booth, Catherine, 79
Booth, Edwin Thomas, 647
Booth, John Wilkes, 449
Booth, Shirley, 277
Booth, William, 64
Borden, Lizzie, 308
Borg, Björn, 191, 194
Borges, Jorge Luis, 223, **229**
Borglum, Gutzon, 639, **639, 640**
Borgnine, Ernest, 298
Borlaug, Norman, 400
Borman, Frank, 603
Born, Max, 200
Bosley, Tom, 614
Boswell, James, 639, 647
Botero, Fernando, 417
Boulanger, Lili, 645
Boulanger, Nadia, 725
Boulle, Pierre, 491
Boulton, Matthew, 373
Boumedienne, Houari, 613
Bourke-White, Margaret, 799, **802**
Bournonville, August, 277
Boutros-Ghali, Boutros, 55
Bow, Clara, 756
Bowe, Riddick, 500
Bowie, David, 585
Bowles, Paul, **537**
Boyd, Patti, 715
Boyer, Charles, 229
Boyle, Peter, 278
Boyle, T. Coraghessan, 504
Bracco, Lorraine, 230
Bradbury, Ray, 127, **133**
Bradlee, Ben, 95, **101**
Bradley, Bill, 719, **724**
Bradley, Ed, 47, **51**
Bradshaw, John Elliot, 367, **371**
Brady, Jim, 79, 85
Brady, Mathew, 329
Braestrup, Carl, 336
Brahe, Tycho, 200
Brahms, Johannes, **657**
Branagh, Kenneth, 767, **776**
Brandeis, Louis, 471
Brando, Marlon, 751, **751**
Brandt, Willy, 399
Braniff, Thomas Elmer, 111, 120
Branson, Richard, 431, **431, 435**
Braque, Georges, 175, **177**
Braun, Eva, 490
Braun, Karl Ferdinand, 722
Braun, Wernher von, 479, **480**
Braxton, Toni, 495, **502**
Brecht, Bertolt, 298
Brennan, Walter, 452
Brenner, David, 666
Breslin, Jimmy, 486
Brett, George, 321
Brezhnev, Leonid, 713
Briand, Aristide, 224

Brice, Fanny, 559, **567**
Brickell, Edie, 571
Bridges, Beau, 792
Bridges, Jeff, 463, 472
Bridges, Lloyd, 447, **457**
Brimley, Wilford, 326
Brinkley, Christy, 298
Brinkley, David, **147**
Britt, Mai, 256
Britten, Benjamin, 424
Broccoli, Albert "Cubby," **608**
Broderick, Matthew, 719, **720**
Brokaw, Tom, 95, 106
Bronfman, Edgar, 547
Bronfman, Samuel, 587
Bronson, Charles, **55**
Brontë, Anne, 458
Brontë, Charlotte, 591, **593**
Brontë, Emily, 516
Brook, Alexander, 275
Brooks, Garth, 719, **730**
Brooks, James L., **81**
Brooks, Mel, 579
Brosnan, Pierce, 353
Brothers, Joyce, Dr., 559, 566
Brown, Bobby, 399, 407
Brown, Clifford, 487
Brown, David, 308
Brown, Helen Gurley, 63, **75**
Brown, H. Rap, 726
Brown, James, 479, 482, 575, 578
Brown, Jerry, 175, **176**
Brown, John, **497**
Brown, Michael Stuart, 800
Brown, Pat, 769
Browne, Jackson, 518
Browning, Elizabeth Barrett, 239, **239**, 251
Browning, John Moses, 538
Browning, Robert, 769
Brubeck, Dave, **136**, 562
Bruce, Lenny, 687, 694
Bruce, Nigel, 405
Brunson, Dorothy, 187
Bryan, William Jennings, **320**
Bryant, Paul "Bear," 421
Brynner, Yul, **147**
Buatta, Mario, 279
Buchwald, Art, 695
Buck, Pearl S., **531**
Buckingham, Lindsay, 550
Buckley, Betty, 559, 563
Buckley, William F., Jr., 696
Buffalo Bill, 139
Buffett, Jimmy, 575, **585**
Bugatti, Ettore, 213
Bukowski, Charles, 132
Bulfinch, Charles, 468
Bulfinch, Thomas, 643
Bullock, Sandra, 575, **580**
Bulow, Claus von, 660
Bulow, Hans von, 809
Bundy, McGeorge, 192
Buñuel, Luis, 207, 219
Burbank, Luther, 783, 795
Burger, Warren, 671, 677
Burke, Billie, 772
Burke, Delta, 191
Burne-Jones, Sir Edward, 655, **661**
Burnett, Carol, 385
Burnett, Frances Hodgson, 751, 760
Burney, Fanny, 159, **162**
Burnham, Daniel Hudson, 117
Burns, Arthur, 801
Burns, Ed, 490
Burns, George, 383, **394**
Burns, Robert, 655, **666**
Burr, Aaron, 794
Burroughs, Edgar Rice, 447, **453**
Burroughs, William, 399, **410**
Burrows, James, 63, 73
Burton, Richard, 695
Burton, Sir Richard, 399
Buscaglia, Leo, 703, **704**
Busch, Adolf, 564
Busch, Adolphus, 595

Busfield, Timothy, **46**
Bush, Barbara, 706
Bush, George, 738
Bush, Kate, 100
Butcher, William, 647
Button, Dick, 531
Byatt, A. S., 239, 245
Byrd, Harry F., 735, 738
Byrd, Richard, 679
Byron, George Gordon, Lord, 223, **234**

C

Caesar, Sid, **53**
Cage, Nicholas, 639, **649**
Cagney, Jimmy, 243
Cain, Dean, **548**
Caine, Michael, 383
Calamity Jane, 639, **639**, 641
Calder, Alexander, 271, 276
Caldwell, Erskine, **56**
Caldwell, Zoe, 367, 373
Callas, Maria, 767, **767**
Calloway, Cab, 665
Cameron, James, 271, **276**
Campbell, Glen, 257
Campbell, Joseph, 47, 48
Campbell, Naomi, 383, **386**
Camus, Albert, 415, **415**
Canby, Vincent, 740
Candy, John, 415, 423
Cannell, Stephen, 735, 746
Capa, Robert, 423
Capone, Al, 266
Capote, Truman, 735, 742
Capra, Frank, 319, **321**
Capshaw, Kate, 311
Capucine, 313
Cara, Irene, 79
Cardin, Pierre, 47, 51
Carew, Rod, 639, 646
Carey, Drew, 111, 114
Carey, Mariah, 383, **384**
Carl Gustav XVI, King of Sweden, 609
Carlin, George, 207, **209**
Carlisle, Belinda, 100
Carlyle, Thomas, 680
Carmichael, Stokely, 51
Carne, Judy, 127
Carnegie, Dale, 696
Carney, Art, **215**
Caroline, Princess of Monaco, 159, 170
Caron, Leslie, **451**
Carpenter, John, 553
Carpenter, Karen, 447, **459**
Carradine, David, 232
Carradine, John, **746**
Carradine, Keith, 484
Carrey, Jim, 735, **746**
Carroll, Diahann, **291**
Carroll, Lewis, **730**
Carsey, Marcia, 680
Carson, Johnny, 687, **695**
Carson, Kit, 95, 105
Carson, Rachel, **674**
Carter, Dixie, 127, 130
Carter, Jimmy, 735
Carter, John Garnet, 154
Carter, Lynda, 404
Carter, Rosalynn, 612
Cartland, Barbara, 159, 163
Carver, George Washington, 271, **275**
Carvey, Dana, 240
Casals, Pablo, 399, **409**
Casanova, 512
Casey, James E., 704
Cash, Johnny, 431, **443**
Cash, June Carter, 543, 547
Cash, Roseanne, 239, 242
Cassatt, Mary, 207, **210**
Cassavetes, John, 511
Cassidy, Butch, 80
Cassidy, David, 447, 448
Cassidy, Shaun, 102
Cassini, Oleg, 431, **432**
Castle, Irene, 496

Castle, Vernon, 737
Cates, Phoebe, 675
Cather, Willa, 399, 527, **536**
Catherine the Great, 353
Catt, Carrie Chapman, 377
Caulfield, Maxwell, 56
Cauthen, Steve, 801
Cavett, Dick, 232
Cayce, Edgar, 383, **383**
Cerdan, Marcel, 308
Cerf, Bennett, 287, 290
Cézanne, Paul, 431, **442**
Chagall, Marc, 735, **739**
Chain, Ernest, 723
Chamberlain, Richard, 304
Chamberlain, Wilt, 239, 245
Chambers, Ann Cox, 168
Chambers, Whittaker, 160
Chandler, Harry, **145**
Chandler, Otis, **616**
Chandler, Raymond, 687, 692
Chanel, Coco, 159
Channing, Carol, 799, 810
Channing, Stockard, 703, **714**
Chaplin, Charlie, 655, **656**
Chaplin, Sydney, 671
Chapman, Tracy, **640**
Chardin, Pierre Teilhard de, 223, 225
Charisse, Cyd, 811
Charles, Prince of Wales, 495, **495**, 503
Charles, Ray, 479, **486**
Charles I, King of England, 216
Chase, Chevy, 726
Chavez, Cesar, 623, **624**
Chayefsky, Paddy, 799, 810
Checker, Chubby, 799, 806
Chekhov, Anton, 335, **346**
Cher, 607, **607**
Chevalier, Maurice, 693
Chiang Kai-Shek, 727
Chicago, Judy, 127, 132
Child, Julia, 463, **463**, 468
Chirac, Jacques, **408**
Chisholm, Shirley, 719, **728**
Chomsky, Marvin, 546
Chong, Tommy, 178
Chopin, Frédéric, 91
Chou En-lai, 299
Christie, Agatha, 591, **597**
Christie, Julie, 96
Christo, 287, 290
Chung, Connie, 591, 597
Churchill, Caryl, 165
Churchill, Lord Randolph, 794
Churchill, Randolph, 514
Churchill, Winston, 479, **488**
Claiborne, Craig, 133
Clancy, Tom, 575, 576
Clapton, Eric, 655, **656**
Clark, Dave, 760
Clark, Dick, **520**
Clark, Marcia, 309
Clark, Mary Higgins, 511, **521**
Clark, Petula, 407
Clark, William, **180**
Clarke, Arthur C., 239, **239**, 248
Claudel, Paul, 756
Clavell, James, 735, 742
Clayburgh, Jill, 689
Cleese, John, **119**
Cleveland, Grover, 507
Cliburn, Van, 323
Cline, Patsy, 399, **405**
Clinton, Bill, 591, **591**
Clinton, Hillary Rodham, **551**
Clooney, George, 751, **753**
Clooney, Rosemary, 578
Close, Glenn, 575, 576
Clurman, Harold, **149**
Cobain, Kurt, 527, 539
Cobb, Ty, 760
Coburn, James, 581
Coca, Imogene, 631
Cocker, Joe, 690
Cocteau, Jean, 659
Coen, Ethan, 95, 102
Coen, Joel, 264

Cohan, George M., 339
Cohen, Ben, 399, **399**, 411
Cohen, Leonard, 319, 326
Cohen, Mickey, 421
Cohn, Jack, 647
Cohn, Roy, 651
Cole, Natalie, 495, **495**, 506
Cole, Nat King, 191, **203**
Coleridge, Samuel Taylor, **103**
Collins, Jackie, 806
Collins, Joan, 367, **370**
Collins, Judy, 127, 129
Collins, Phil, 266
Colman, Ronald, 586
Colter, Jesse, 562
Coltrane, John, 655, **662**
Comaneci, Nadia, 735, 743
Combs, Sean "Puffy," 399, **407**
Comden, Betty, 353
Como, Perry, 481
Connery, Sean, 479, **485**
Connick, Harry, Jr., 495, 501
Connor, Bart, 112
Connors, Jimmy, 351, 357
Conrad, Frank, 513
Conrad, Joseph, **424**
Conrad, Robert, 315
Conroy, Pat, 623, **631**
Constantine I, King of Greece, 756
Conti, Bill, **768**
Conway, Tom, 789
Coogan, Jackie, 367, 375
Cook, Captain James, 375
Cook, Frederick, 114
Cooke, Alistair, 623, **632**
Cooke, Jack Kent, 463, 470
Cooke, Sam, **314**
Coolidge, Rita, 657
Cooney, Barbara, 308
Cooper, Alice, 554
Cooper, Gary, 159, **161**
Cooper, James Fenimore, 159, **165**
Cooper, Wilhelmina, 97
Coots, J. Fred, 321
Copland, Aaron, **183**
Copley, John Singleton, 67
Copperfield, David, 175, 181
Corbett, Gentleman Jim, 53
Corday, Charlotte, 260
Cori, Gerty Teresa, 356
Corman, Roger, 672
Cornelius, Don, 239
Cornell, Ezra, 217
Cornwell, Patricia, 191, 194
Cosby, Bill, 207, **207**, 211
Cosell, Howard, **144**
Costas, Bob, 367, **368**
Costello, Dolores, 773
Costello, Elvis, 271, **277**
Costello, Lou, 639, 651
Costner, Kevin, 266
Courbet, Gustave, 466
Couric, Katie, 159, **159**, 169
Courreges, Andre, 811
Cousins, Norman, 467
Cousteau, Jacques, 559, **559**, 562
Cousy, Bob, 580
Coward, Sir Noel, 223, 232
Cox, Archibald, 481
Cox, Courtney, 623, **626**
Craig, Gordon, 617
Crane, Bob, 579
Crane, Stephen, **615**
Crawford, Cindy, 559, **571**
Crawford, Joan, 639, 640
Crawford, Michael, 783, 794
Crichton, Michael, 751, 759
Crick, Francis, 306
Criss, Peter, 553
Crist, Judith, 66
Croce, Jim, **761**
Crofts, Dash, 164
Cronin, James, 454
Cronkite, Walter, 287, **287**, 295
Cronyn, Hume, 515
Crosby, Bing, 801

Crosby, David, 804
Cross, Christopher, **401**
Crothers, Scatman, 562
Crouch, Andrea, 771
Crouse, Russell, 507
Crow, Sheryl, 687, **698**
Crowe, Cameron, 147
Crowell, Luther, 357
Crowell, Rodney, 431, 436
Crowninshield, Francis, 579
Cruise, Tom, 703, 707
Crumb, Robert, 719, **725**
Crystal, Billy, 575, **587**
Csonka, Larry, 585
Cugat, Xavier, 233
Cukor, George, 239, 243
Culbertson, Ely, 564
Culkin, Macaulay, **741**
Culp, Robert, 500
Cummings, Bob, 642
cummings, e. e., 431, 438
Cunningham, Imogen, 144
Cunningham, Merce, **192**
Cunningham, Randall, 672
Cuomo, Mario, 415, 418
Curie, Jean Joliot, 208
Curie, Marie, 767, **775**
Currier, Nathan, 720
Curtin, Jane, 559, **565**
Curtis, Jamie Lee, 95, 104
Cusack, Cyril, 527, 536
Cusack, Joan, **710**
Cusack, John, 543, 547
Cushing, Harvey W., 720
Cuthbert, Betty, 177
Cuvier, Georges, 229
Cyrus, Billy Ray, 757

D

Daguerre, Louis Jacques, 239, **247**
Dahl, Roald, 287, **293**
Daimler, Gottlieb, 635
Daley, Richard, Jr., 769
Daley, Richard, Sr., **113**
Dalí, Salvador, 799, **801**
Dalton, Timothy, 608
Daltrey, Roger, 703, **715**
Daly, Chuck, 500
Daly, Marcus, 312
Daly, Tyne, 635
D'Amato, Alfonse, 212
Damon, Matt, 367, **374**
Damone, Vic, 578
Dandridge, Dorothy, 775
Danes, Clair, 784
Danforth, William H., 661
Dangerfield, Rodney, 79, **88**
Daniels, Jeff, 251
Daniken, Erich von, 304
Dankworth, John, 614
Danner, Blythe, 746
Danson, Ted, 543, **553**
Danza, Tony, 401
Darin, Bobby, **257**
Darrow, Clarence S., 447, **448**
Darwin, Charles, 127, **127**, 138
Darwin, Erasmus, 264
Dassin, Jules, 504
Dausset, Jean, 295
David, Hal, 98
David-Neel, Alexandra, **743**
Davies, Marion, 335, **345**
Davies, Ray, **691**
Davis, Benjamin, Jr., General, 456
Davis, Bette, 639, 640
Davis, Geena, 170
Davis, Glenn, 729
Davis, Jefferson, **162**
Davis, Mac, 794
Davis, Miles, 655, **655**, 658
Davis, Ossie, **248**
Davis, Patti Ann, 343
Davis, Sammy, Jr., 687, 696
Day, Doris, 751, **752**
Dayan, Moshe, 354
Day-Lewis, Cecil, 801
Day-Lewis, Daniel, 159, 161

Dean, Dizzy, **537**
Dean, James, 474
Dean, John, 159, 166
Debakey, Michael, 629
Debs, Eugene V., 503
Dee, Ruby, 743
Dee, Sandra, 769
DeForest, Lee, 533
Degas, Edgar, 607, 612
de Gaulle, Charles, **600**
DeGeneres, Ellen, 127
De Havilland, Olivia, 307
de Klerk, F. W., **267**
de Kooning, Elaine, 155
de Kooning, Willem, 799, **801**
Delaunay, Robert, 48
De Laurentiis, Dino, **180**
DeLillo, Don, 232
Delon, Alain, 279
Deluise, Dom, 372
DeMille, Agnes, 581
DeMille, Cecil B., 207, **207,** 212
Dempsey, Jack, 403
Dench, Judi, **312**
Deneuve, Catherine, 719, **727**
Deng Xiaoping, 799, **805**
DeNiro, Robert, 719, **724**
Dent, Bucky, **392**
Denver, Bob, **313**
Denver, John, 703, **713**
De Palma, Brian, 85
Dépardieu, Gérard, 505
Depp, Johnny, 674
Derek, Bo, **184**
Derek, John, 660
Dern, Bruce, **258**
Desmond, Paul, 728
DeSucre, Antonio J., 714
De Valera, Eamon, 159
Devine, Andy, 758
DeVito, Danny, 671, **679**
Dewey, Thomas E., 128
Dewhurst, Colleen, 658
DeWitt, Joyce, 481
Dey, Susan, 344
Diaghilev, Sergei, 591, 592
Diamond, Neil, 63, 74
Diana, Princess of Wales, 751, **755**
Diaz, Cameron, 287, **293**
DiCaprio, Leonardo, 191, **199**
Dickens, Charles, 767, **767**
Dickey, Herbert Spencer, 442
Dickinson, Angie, 447, 454
Dickinson, Emily, 767, **776**
Diddley, Bo, **569**
Didion, Joan, **312**
Dietrich, Marlene, 127, **137**
Diller, Barry, 783, **794**
Diller, Phyllis, 259
Dillinger, John, 115
Dillon, Matt, **651**
Dimaggio, Joe, 376
Dines, William, 516
Dinesen, Isak, 63
Dion, Celine, 479, 480
Dior, Christian, 767, **778**
Disney, Walt, **152**
Disraeli, Benjamin, 313
Ditka, Mike, 118
Divine, 631
Dix, Dorothea Lynde, 415, 416
DMC, 626
Dobson, Kevin, 747
Doctorow, E. L., 489
Dodington, Sven, 482
Dole, Bob, 783, **788**
Dole, Elizabeth, 239, 244
Dolly, Jenny, 519
Dolly, Rose, 519
Domingo, Plácido, 63, **74**
Donahue, Phil, **281**
Donahue, Troy, 282
Donaldson, Sam, 347
Donizetti, Gaetano, 600
Donovan, 609
Doolittle, Hilda, 773
Doolittle, James, 344
Doppler, Christian, 344

Dorfman, Dan, 407
Dorsey, Jimmy, 47, 59
Dorsey, Tommy, 791
Dos Passos, John, **393**
Doubleday, Frank Nelson, **249**
Douglas, Buster, 800
Douglas, Kirk, **296**
Douglas, Lord Alfred, 663
Douglas, Melvyn, 160
Douglas, Michael, 678
Douglas, Mike, 687, 692
Douglas, Stephen, 721
Dove, Heinrich, 358
Dow, Charles Henry, **679**
Dow, Herbert, 91
Dow, Tony, 656
Downey, Robert, Jr., 592
Downs, Hugh, 111
Doyle, Sir Arthur Conan, 351, **354**
Drabble, Margaret, 130
Dragon, Daryl, 773
Drake, Betsy, 773
Dreiser, Theodore, 623, **629**
Dreja, Chris, 599
Dreyfus, Alfred, **342**
Driver, Minnie, 362
Drysdale, Don, 244
DuBois, W. E. B., 767, **779**
Duchamp, Marcel, **740**
Duchin, Peter, 560
Duchovny, David, 751, **756**
Duff, Howard, 248
Dufy, Raoul, 386
Dukakis, Michael, 359
Duke, Doris, 456
Duke, Patti, 584
Dulles, John Foster, 715
Dumas, Alexandre, fils, **260**
Dumas, Alexandre, père, 399, **404**
Du Maurier, Daphne, 689
Dumont, Allen, 186
Dumont, Margaret, 647
Dunant, Jean Henri, 97
Dunaway, Faye, 63, **73**
Duncan, Isadora, **338**
Dunn, Alan, 196
du Pont, Eleuthère Irenée, 147
DuPont, Pierre, **697**
Du Pre, Jacqueline, **666**
Duran, Roberto, **402**
Durant, Will, 799, **807**
Durbin, Deanna, 88
Dürer, Albrecht, 239
Durning, Charles, 811
Durocher, Leo, 719, 724
Durrell, Gerald, 729
Durrell, Lawrence, 479, **491**
Dutton, Charles S., **426**
Duvalier, François "Papa Doc," 688
Duvalier, Jean-Claude, 403
Duvall, Robert, 489
Duvall, Shelley, 483
Dvořák, Antonín, 325
Dykes, John, 331
Dylan, Bob, 47, **47,** 50
Dylan, Jacob, 408

E

Eagleton, Thomas, 534
Earhart, Amelia, 271, **276**
Earp, Wyatt, 48
Eastman, George, 563
Easton, Edward, 783
Eastwood, Clint, 498
Ebert, Roger, 770
Echegaray y Eizaguirre, José, 657
Eco, Umberto, 431, **441**
Edberg, Stefan, **570**
Eddy, Mary Baker, 383, **383,** 387
Eddy, Nelson, **163**
Edelman, Marion Wright, 130
Eden, Barbara, 319, **325**
Edison, Thomas Alva, 95, **106**
Edwards, Anthony, **708**

Edwards, Blake, 52
Edwards, Douglas, 259
Edwards, Ralph, **434**
Edwards, Vince, 579
Edward VIII, King of England, **451**
Ehrlich, Paul, **418**
Ehrlichman, John, 720
Eiffel, Alexandre, 671, 680
Eikenberry, Jill, 586
Einstein, Albert, 303, **303,** 315
Eisenhower, Dwight D., **598**
Eisenhower, Mamie, 359
Eisenstadt, Alfred, 264
Eisner, Michael, 783, **795**
Ekland, Britt, 758
Eliot, George, 456
Eliot, T. S., 687, **694**
Elizabeth, Queen Mother, 196
Elizabeth I, Queen of England, 735, **735**
Elizabeth II, Queen of England, 671, **673**
Elizondo, Hector, 233
Ellington, Duke, 239, **241**
Elliot, Mama Cass, 719, 726
Elliot, Osborn, 743
Elliot, Sam, **676**
Ellis, Bret Easton, 651
Ellis, Havelock, 378
Ellison, Ralph, **411**
Ellsworth, Lincoln, 257
Emerson, John, 511
Emerson, Ralph Waldo, 367, **370**
Engels, Friedrich, 399, 408
Entwhistle, John, 678
Enya, 751, 753
Epstein, Brian, 326
Erasmus, Desiderius, **391**
Erickson, Erik, 114
Ernst, Max, 575
Ervin, Sam, 357
Erving, Julius "Dr. J.," **459**
Escher, M. C., 271, **274**
Esposito, Phil, 783, 795
Estaing, Valéry Giscard d', 671, 682
Estefan, Emilio, Jr., 331
Estefan, Gloria, 143, **143,** 149
Etheridge, Melissa, **754**
Eugenie, Princess, 336
Evans, Dale, 455
Evans, Dave, 756
Evans, Linda, 751, 759
Evans, Mary Walker, 696
Evans, Walker, **71**
Everly, Don, 234
Everly, Phil, 154
Evers, Medgar, 703, 707
Evert, Chris, **265**
Ewing, Patrick, 719, 721
Exner, Judith Campbell, 361

F

Fabergé, Peter Carl, 127, 130
Fabio, 779
Fairbanks, Douglas, **130**
Fairbanks, Douglas, Jr., 584
Fairchild, Morgan, 458
Faithfull, Marianne, 585
Falk, Peter, 613
Faludi, Susan, 79, 80
Falwell, Jerry, 367, **372**
Farley, Chris, 650
Farrakhan, Louis, 383, 385
Farrell, Mike, 154
Farrell, Suzanne, 644
Farrow, Mia, 655, 666
Fassbinder, Rainer, 610
Faulkner, William, **310**
Fawcett, Farrah, 575, **586**
Feldon, Barbara, **59**
Feliciano, Jose, 639, 645
Felker, Clay, 694
Fellini, Federico, 159, **170**
Ferber, Edna, 639, 644
Ferguson, Sarah, 47, **54**
Ferigno, Lou, 391

Fermi, Enrico, **150**
Ferraro, Geraldine, 293
Ferrer, José, 505
Ferrer, Mel, 261
Ferry, Brian, 646
Fiedler, Arthur, **440**
Field, Sally, 591, **599**
Fielding, Temple, 422
Fields, Dorothy, 755
Fields, W. C., **282**
Fiennes, Ralph, 697
Fierstein, Harvey, 274
Filene, Edward, 309
Finney, Albert, 257
Firestone, Harvey, 745
Fischer, Bobby, 735, **747**
Fisher, Carrie, 175, 183
Fittipaldi, Emerson, 584
Fitzgerald, Ella, 223, **225**
Fitzgerald, F. Scott, **358**
Fitzgerald, John "Honeyfitz," 218
Flack, Roberta, **155**
Flatley, Michael, 111
Flatt, Lester, 387
Flaubert, Gustave, 367
Fleetwood, Mick, 559
Fleischer, Max, 643
Fleming, Ian, 639
Fleming, Sir Alexander, **212**
Fletcher, Louise, **324**
Flockhart, Calista, 607, 615
Florey, Sir Howard, 278
Flynn, Errol, 591, **595**
Flynt, Larry, 751, **759**
Fogerty, John, 639, **642**
Fokine, Michel, 257
Follett, Ken, 479, **482**
Fonda, Bridget, 650
Fonda, Henry, 767, 769
Fonda, Jane, 191, **191,** 201
Fonda, Peter, **155**
Fontaine, Joan, 263
Fonteyn, Margot, 191, **193**
Foote, Horton, 319, 331
Forbes, Malcolm, 175, 181
Forbes, Steve, 559, **563**
Ford, Betty, 223, 224
Ford, Charlotte, 48
Ford, Edsel, 471
Ford, Eileen, 63
Ford, Faith, 629
Ford, Gerald R., 435
Ford, Glenn, **305**
Ford, Harrison, 767, **771**
Ford, Henry, 175, **175,** 180
Ford, Henry, II, 261
Ford, John, 399
Foreman, George, 495, **505**
Fortensky, Larry, 378
Fosse, Bob, 623, **627**
Fossey, Dian, 431, **441**
Foster, Jodie, 687, **696**
Fox, Michael J., 751, **754**
Fox, Vivica A., 628
Foxx, Redd, **808**
Foyt, A. J., **313**
Francis, Connie, 152
Francis Joseph I, Emperor of Austria, 772
Franco, Francisco, 511, 520
Frank, Anne, 543, **546**
Frank, Barney, 95, 96
Frank, Otto, 657
Frankenthaler, Helen, **568**
Franklin, Aretha, 783, **783**
Franklin, Benjamin, 543, **554**
Franz, Dennis, 679
Franz Ferdinand, Archduke of Austria, **168**
Fraser, Brendan, 447, **456**
Fraser, Lady Antonia, 399, **405**
Frawley, William, **507**
Frazier, Joe, 703, 714
Frederick the Great, 287, **287**
Frederika, Queen of Greece, **272**
Freed, Arthur, 437
Freeman, Morgan, 207, **210**
Frémont, John Charles, 746

French, Marilyn, 520
Freud, Anna, 392
Freud, Sigmund, 479, **479,** 481
Friedan, Betty, **122**
Friedkin, William, 111, **117**
Friedman, Kinky, 679
Friedman, Milton, 463, 468
Frost, Robert, 511, 512
Frost, Sir David, 127, **128**
Fujimoro, Alberto, 164
Fuller, R. Buckminster, 399
Fulton, Robert, **375**
Funicello, Annette, 751, 759
Funk, Isaac Kauffman, 405
Funt, Allen, 389

G

Gabin, Jean, 801
Gable, Clark, 175, **186**
Gabor, Eva, 122
Gabriel, Peter, 447, **458**
Gagarin, Yuri, 347
Galbraith, John Kenneth, 623, **630**
Galton, Sir Francis, 363
Galway, James, **120**
Gamble, James, 532
Gamow, George, 59
Gandhi, Indira, 239, **248**
Gandhi, Mohandas K., 703, **703**
Gandhi, Rajiv, 671, 677
Gantt, Harvey, 761
Garbo, Greta, 751, **751**
Garcia, Andy, 191, 192
Garcia, Jerry, 767, **772**
Gardner, Alexander, 559, **566**
Gardner, Ava, 799, **809**
Gardner, Erle Stanley, 639, **643**
Garfunkel, Art, 799, 807
Garland, Judy, 63, **63,** 66
Garner, James, 591
Garofalo, Janeane, 623, 630
Garr, Teri, 463, **472**
Garrison, Jim, **88**
Garrett, Pat, 722
Garvey, Steve, 505
Gates, Bill, 223, **223,** 231
Gatlin, Larry, 527, 529
Gaudí, Antonio, 643
Gauguelin, Michel, 567
Gauguin, Paul, 47, **47,** 50
Gaye, Marvin, 127, **128**
Gayle, Crystal, 265
Gazzara, Ben, 485
Gebel-Williams, Gunther, 319, 325
Geddes, James, 468
Geffen, David, 735, **735**
Gehrig, Lou, 79, **83**
Gehry, Frank, 543
Geldof, Bob, 255, **255,** 262
Geller, Uri, **585**
Gentile, Giovanni, 466
Gentry, Bobbie, 772
George, Boy, 754
George I, King of England, 399
George III, King of England, **738**
George IV, King of England, 516
George VI, King of England, **392**
Gerber, Daniel, 289
Gere, Richard, 463, 469
Gershwin, George, 271, 278
Gershwin, Ira, 280
Getty, J. Paul, 520
Getz, Stan, 650
Giamatti, Bartlett A., 176
Gianni, A. P., **673**
Gibb, Andy, 139
Gibb, Maurice, 473
Gibb, Robin, 473
Gibbons, Euell, 501
Gibbs, Josiah, 442
Gibran, Kahlil, 143, **143,** 153
Gibson, Althea, 613
Gibson, Edward, 231

Gibson, Mel, 207, **217**
Gielgud, Sir John, 800
Gifford, Frank, 495, **500**
Gifford, Kathy Lee, **308**
Gilbert, Melissa, 639, 641
Gilbert, Sara, 202
Gilbert, Sir John, 323
Gilbert, William Schwenk, 519
Gilberto, Astrud, 96
Gilbreth, Frank, 755
Gildersleeve, Virginia, 374
Gill, Brendan, 374
Gill, Vince, 159, 160
Gillespie, Dizzy, **263**
Gillett, George, Jr., 151
Gilliam, Terry, 63, 72
Gilot, François, 79, 88
Ginsberg, Allen, 658
Gish, Dorothy, 299
Gish, Lilian, 358
Giuliani, Rudolph, 687, 690
Gladstone, W. E., **105**
Gleason, Jackie, 319, **331**
Glenn, John, **99**
Glover, Danny, 564
Godard, Jean-Luc, **488**
Goddard, Robert, 166
Godden, Rumer, 655
Godfrey, Arthur, 69
Godwin, Mary Wollstonecraft,
   641
Godwin, William, **779**
Goebbels, Paul Joseph, 311
Goethe, Johann Wolfgang von,
   271, **277**
Goizueta, Roberto C., 439
Goldberg, Whoopi, 463, **471**
Goldblum, Jeff, 343
Golding, Sir William, 495
Goldman, Emma, 335, 339
Goldman, William, 452
Goldsboro, Bobby, 74
Goldwater, Barry, 607, **617**
Goldwater, Barry, Jr., 159
Goldwyn, Sam, Jr., 661
Goldwyn, Samuel, 159, 164
Gonne, Maude, 89
Goodall, Jane, 335, 336
Gooden, Dwight, 607, **615**
Gooding, Cuba, Jr., 489
Goodman, Benny, 594
Goodman, John, 355
Goodson, Mark, 378
Goodyear, Charles, 473
Gorbachev, Mikhail, 475
Gorbachev, Raisa, 441
Gordon, Dexter, 799, **811**
Gordon, Ruth, 351, **359**
Gordy, Berry, Jr., 511, **520**
Gore, Al, 528
Gore, Thomas P., 648
Gore, Tipper, 511, 517
Gorme, Eydie, 404
Gotti, John, 63, **71**
Gould, Elliot, 165
Gould, Glenn, 399, **399,** 406
Goulet, Robert, 360
Grable, Betty, 287, 296
Graf, Steffi, 415, **418**
Graham, Billy, 207, 215
Graham, Katharine, 271, **274**
Graham, Martha, 447, **447, 449**
Graham, Philip, 339
Grahame, Kenneth, 367
Grammer, Kelsey, 239, 251
Granger, Stewart, 433
Grant, Amy, 776
Grant, Cary, 47, **47,** 58
Grant, Hugh, 783, **789**
Grant, Ulysses S., 351, **353**
Graves, Michael, **339**
Graves, Peter, 683
Gray, Elisha, 580
Gray, Robert, 308
Graziano, Rocky, **66**
Green, Adolph, 328
Green, Al, 608
Green, Brian Austen, 259
Greene, Charles Sumner, 742
Greene, Graham, 783, **790**

Greene, Henry Mather, 698
Greene, Lorne, 367, **378**
Greenfield, Howard, 235
Greenfield, Jerry, 399, **399,** 411
Greenspan, Alan, **683**
Greenstreet, Sidney, 281
Greer, Germaine, 154
Greer, Roosevelt, 419
Gregory, Dick, **406**
Gretzky, Wayne, **778**
Grey, Jennifer, 800
Grey, Joel, 416
Grey, Zane, 607, **618**
Griffey, Ken, Jr., 408
Griffey, Ken, Sr., 448
Griffith, Andy, 655, 658
Griffith, D. W., **490**
Griffith, Melanie, **148**
Griffith-Joyner, Florence, 47, 57
Grigorovich, Yuri, 649
Grimm, Jakob, 473
Grimm, Wilhelm, **315**
Grisham, John, 239
Groening, Matt, 287, 298
Gropius, Walter, **129**
Grucci, Felix, **770**
Grumman, Leroy Randle, **425**
Guare, John, 175, 186
Guccione, Bob, 488
Gudonov, Alexander, 472
Guest, Christopher, **538**
Guevara, Chè, 575, **578**
Guggenheim, Daniel, 483
Guggenheim, Harry F., 607,
   613
Guggenheim, Solomon R., **298**
Guillaume, Robert, **200**
Guillotin, Joseph, 738
Guinness, Sir Alec, 399, **400**
Guisewite, Cathy, 431, 437
Gumbel, Bryant, 511, **518**
Gumbel, Greg, 609
Gumilev, Nikolay Stepanovich,
   784
Gurdjieff, 399
Guthrie, Arlo, 559, 563
Guthrie, Woody, 463, **467**
Gwathmey, Robert, 106
Gwynne, Fred, 659
Gyllenhammar, Pehr, 289

H

Haakon VII, King of Norway,
   580
Haas, Ernst, 123
Hackman, Gene, 463, **474**
Hagen, Uta, 178
Haggard, Merle, **208**
Hagman, Larry, 454
Haig, Alexander, 719, 728
Hailey, Arthur, 144
Halberstam, David, 335, 336
Haldeman, H. R., **647**
Hale, Clara McBride, 767, **768**
Hale, George, 755
Haley, Alex, 95, **100**
Hall, Arsenio, 239, 250
Hall, Daryl, 470
Hall, Jerry, 191, **195**
Hall, Joyce, 553
Hall, Monty, **789**
Halliburton, Richard, 217
Halstead, William, 630
Halston, 415, 417
Hamill, Dorothy, 196
Hamill, Mark, 390
Hamill, Pete, **291**
Hamilton, Alexander, 47, **57**
Hamilton, Carrie, 664
Hamilton, Edith, 783, 788
Hamilton, George, **116**
Hamilton, Lady Emma, **561**
Hamilton, Margaret, 104
Hamilton, Scott, 101
Hamlisch, Marvin, 687, 690
Hammerstein, Oscar, II, 403
Hammett, Dashiell, **450**
Hammond, John H., 536
Hampton, Lionel, 641

Hancock, Herbie, **96**
Hancock, John, 810
Hanks, Tom, 351, **351,** 355
Hannah, Daryl, 777
Hansbury, Lorraine, 495, **498**
Harburg, E. Y. "Yip," **368**
Harding, Tonya, 375
Harding, Warren G., 103
Hardwick, Elizabeth, 308
Hardy, Oliver, 554
Hardy, Thomas, 367
Hare, David, 559, 562
Hari, Mata, 420
Haring, Keith, **113**
Harlow, Jean, 539
Harmon, Tom, **182**
Harnick, Sheldon, 753
Harper, Fletcher, 266
Harper, Valerie, 79, 85
Harrelson, Woody, 756
Harriman, Averell, 551
Harriman, Pamela, 144
Harris, Emmylou, 575, **576**
Harris, Franco, 459
Harris, La Donna, 474
Harris, Richard, **406**
Harrison, Benjamin, 661
Harrison, G. Donald, 657
Harrison, George, 735
Harrison, Rex, **651**
Harrison, William Henry, 90
Harry, Prince, 565
Hart, Lorenz, 417
Hart, Mickey, 677
Hart, Moss, 791
Harte, Bret, 533
Hartford, George, 661
Hartley, Mariette, 79, 83
Hartman, Phil, 511, 518
Hartman-Black, Lisa, 194
Harvey, Paul, 207, **213**
Hasselhoff, David, 355
Hatcher, Teri, **616**
Hauer, Rutger, 714
Havel, Vaclav, 239, **246**
Havell, Robert, Jr., 760
Havlicek, John, 96
Hawke, Ethan, 375
Hawking, Stephen, **793**
Hawkins, Coleman, 792
Hawkins, Erick, 609
Hawn, Goldie, 623, 632
Hayden, Tom, 72
Haydn, Franz Joseph, 224
Hayek, Salma, 543, 549
Hayes, Helen, 191, **198**
Hayes, Isaac, 773
Hayes, Rutherford B., 342
Hayworth, Rita, 207, **214**
Headly, Glenne, 251
Heard, John, 667
Hearst, Patty, 299
Hearst, William Randolph, 191,
   191, 193
Heche, Anne, 431, **434**
Heckerling, Amy, 271, **273**
Hedren, Tippi, 314
Hefner, Hugh, 671, **671,** 672
Hegel, Georg Wilhelm
   Friedrich, 175, **181**
Heidegger, Martin, **646**
Heiden, Beth, 150
Heiden, Eric, 114
Heifetz, Jascha, **186**
Heinemann, Edward H., 651
Heinlein, Robert, 671, **675**
Heinz, Henry John, 191, 198
Hellman, Lillian, 751, 755
Helm, Levon, 82
Helms, Jesse, Jr., 79, 86
Helmsley, Harry, 607, **619**
Helmsley, Leona, 147
Helpern, David, 247
Helprin, Mark, 563
Hemingway, Ernest, 239, **244**
Hemingway, Mariel, 744
Hemsley, Sherman, 175
Henderson, Bruce, 353
Henderson, Florence, 362
Henderson, Skitch, 250

Hendrix, Jimi, 751, **760**
Henie, Sonja, 480
Henley, Don, 559, **564**
Henner, Marilu, 368
Henning, Doug, **561**
Henry, Joseph, **600**
Henry, O., 223, **229**
Henson, Jim, 239, **246**
Hepburn, Audrey, 543, **543,**
   545
Hepworth, Barbara, 105
Herbert, Frank, 134
Herman, Woody, **433**
Hernandez, Keith, **311**
Herrera, Caroline, 153
Herriot, James, 287, **294**
Herschel, John, 75
Herschel, William, 727
Hershey, Barbara, 538
Hershiser, Orel, IV, 101
Hesse, Hermann, 383, **383**
Heston, Charlton, 735, **742**
Hewitt, Abram Stevens, 340
Hewitt, Don, 799, 808
Heyerdahl, Thor, 367, **374**
Hickman, Dwayne, 337
Hickok, "Wild Bill," 495, 498
Hill, Anita, 191, **196**
Hill, Benny, 730
Hill, Calvin, 585
Hill, Grant, **294**
Hill, Patty, 752
Hillerman, Tony, 703, 706
Hilton, Conrad, 703, 713
Hilton, James, 191, **197**
Hirohito, Emperor of Japan,
   161
Hirsch, Judd, 315
Hirschfeld, Al, 79, 83
Hiss, Alger, 791
Hitchcock, Sir Alfred, 239, **244**
Hite, Shere, 759
Hitler, Adolf, 657
Ho, Don, 500
Hobbes, Leonard, 345
Ho Chi Minh, 610
Hoffa, Jimmy, 458
Hoffer, Eric, 116
Hoffman, Abbie, 232
Hoffman, Dustin, 207, **212**
Hoffs, Susannah, 90
Hofmannsthal, Hugo von, 522
Hogan, Ben, 468
Hogan, Paul, 118
Hogarth, Burne, **504**
Hogwood, Christopher, 805
Holden, William, 224
Holder, Geoffrey, 500
Holiday, Billie, 351, **352**
Holland, Brian, 58
Holley, Robert, **90**
Holly, Buddy, **245**
Holly, Lauren, 663
Holmes, Oliver Wendell, Jr.,
   335, **347**
Holt, Henry, 585
Holyfield, Evander, 711
Honda, Soichiro, 703, 711
Hooker, John Lee, **261**
Hoover, Herbert, 500
Hoover, J. Edgar, 415, **425**
Hope, Bob, 79, **82**
Hopkins, Sir Anthony, 191, **201**
Hopper, Dennis, 257
Hopper, Hedda, **609**
Horne, Lena, **259**
Horney, Karen, 805
Horowitz, Vladimir, 783, **790**
Horst, Horst P., 703
Horton, Edward Everett, 795
Horton, Peter, 309
Houdin, Robert Jean-Eugène,
   264
Houdini, Harry, 511, **511,** 512
Houghton, Henry, 305
Houseman, John, 118
Houston, Whitney, 671, **676**
Hoving, Thomas P., 473
Howard, Clint, 65
Howard, Leslie, 496

Howard, Ron, 287, 299
Howe, Elias, 463, 467
Howe, Julia Ward, 466
Howe, Viscount William, 340
Hubbard, L. Ron, **539**
Hudson, Rock, 695
Hughes, Howard, 735, **745**
Hughes, Langston, 138
Hughes, Ted, 500
Hull, Bobby, **153**
Hull, Brett, **628**
Humphrey, Doris, 390
Humphrey, Hubert H., 514
Humphrey, Muriel, 491
Hundley, Todd, 434
Hunt, E. Howard, 214
Hunt, Helen, 674
Hunt, H. L., 671, **683**
Hunt, Lamar, 404
Hunt, Linda, 655, 656
Hunt, Nelson Bunker, 683
Hunter, Alberta, 415, **416**
Hunter, Holly, **112**
Huntley, Chet, **504**
Hurley, Elizabeth, **594**
Hurt, John, 106
Hurt, William, 448
Hussein, King Ibn Talal, King
   of Jordan, **279**
Huston, Anjelica, 399, **403**
Huston, John, 719
Huston, Walter, **96**
Hutton, Barbara, 455
Hutton, Betty, 111
Hutton, Timothy, 788
Huxley, Aldous, 447, **452**
Hwang, David, 148
Hyatt, John Wesley, 479, 488
Hynde, Chrissie, 383, 389

I

Iacocca, Lee, 735, 742
Ian, Janis, 399, **400**
Ibsen, Henrik, 111, 112
Idol, Billy, 207, **216**
Iglesias, Julio, 719, 726
Iman, 223, **228**
Imus, Don, 84
Inouye, Daniel, 741
Ireland, Jill, 257
Irons, Jeremy, 511, 518
Irving, Amy, 309
Irving, Washington, 431, 432
Isaak, Chris, 195
Isherwood, Christopher, 805
Ito, Lance, Judge, **436**
Ives, Burl, 594
Ives, Herbert, 164
Ives, James, **283**
Ivory, James, 578

J

Jack, Wolfman, **154**
Jackson, Alan, 95
Jackson, Andrew, 319, **319**
Jackson, "Bo," 696
Jackson, Janet, 543, **545**
Jackson, Jesse, **806**
Jackson, Mahalia, 495, **503**
Jackson, Michael, 101
Jackson, Phil, 639, **645**
Jackson, Reggie, 607, 609
Jackson, Samuel L., 495, 505
Jackson, Shirley, 596
Jackson, Stonewall, 282
Jacobs, Walter, 370
Jagger, Bianca, 657
Jagger, Mick, 719, 724
James, Etta, 175
James, Frank, 265
James, Henry, **256**
James, William, 313
Jamison, Judith, 687, **689**
Janis, Byron, 591, 592
Jardine, Al, 757
Jarré, Maurice, 741
Jarreau, Al, 107
Jarriel, Tom, 313

Javits, Jacob, 801
Jaworski, Leon, 758
Jefferson, Thomas, **544**
Jenner, Bruce, 463, 471
Jennings, Paul, 240
Jennings, Peter, 159, **164**
Jennings, Waylon, 210
Jeter, Derek, 207, 211
Jett, Joan, **790**
Jewel, 223, **226**
Jewison, Norman, 655, 660
Jhabvala, Ruth Prawer, 623, **625**
Jillette, Penn, 251
Jobs, Steven, **251**
Joel, Billy, 479, **481**
Joffrey, Robert, 489
Johansson, Ingemar, 406
John, Elton, 575, 576
John, Tommy, 738
John Paul II, Pope, **145**
Johns, Jasper, 495, **497**
Johnson, Andrew, 127, 137, 331
Johnson, Don, 472
Johnson, Earvin "Magic," 63, 67
Johnson, Harold, 427
Johnson, Howard, 405
Johnson, Jack, 352
Johnson, Lady Bird, 457
Johnson, Lyndon B., 629
Johnson, Mordecai Wyatt, **633**
Johnson, Pamela, 482
Johnson, Philip, 719, 723
Johnson, Robert Louis, 607, **608**
Johnson, Samuel, 383, **389**
Johnson, Virginia, 730
Jolson, Al, **786**
Jones, Davy, 633
Jones, George, 453
Jones, Jack, 185
Jones, James Earl, 463, 474
Jones, Jennifer, 203
Jones, John Paul, **371**
Jones, Quincy, 383, **395**
Jones, Shirley, 336
Jones, Spike, 504
Jones, Tom, 82
Jones, Tommy Lee, 591, 597
Jong, Erica, 784
Joplin, Janis, 751, **762**
Joplin, Scott, 735, **744**
Jordan, Barbara, **267**
Jordan, Michael, 687, **687**
Jordan, Vernon, 287, 292
Jorgensen, Christine, 658
Joule, James Prescott, 479, 489
Jourdan, Louis, **179**
Joyce, James, 191, 202
Joyner-Kersee, Jackie, 731
Juan Carlos I, King of Spain, 201
Judd, Ashley, 465
Judd, Naomi, 623, 633
Judd, Wynonna, 623, 626
Juilliard, Augustus D., 545
Julia, Raul, 107
Juliana, Queen of the Netherlands, 593
Jung, Carl, 463, **468**
Jurado, Katy, 777
Justice, David, 560

K

Kael, Pauline, 179
Kaelin, Brian "Kato," 79, 91
Kafka, Franz, 127, **131**
Kahane, Meir, 420
Kahlo, Frida, **675**
Kahn, Madeline, 751, 758
Kanawa, Kiri Te, 715
Kandinsky, Wassily, 47, **56**
Kane, Carol, 354
Kanin, Garson, 456
Kantner, Paul, 795
Kaplan, Gabe, 656
Karajan, Herbert von, 639, **640**
Karan, Donna, 511, **518**

Karloff, Boris, 728
Karman, Theodore von, 223, 225
Karpov, Anatoli, 399, 402
Karras, Alex, 291
Kasem, Casey, 415, **417**
Kasparov, Garry, **672**
Katz, Lillian, 635
Kaufman, Andy, 495, **506**
Kavner, Julie, 389
Kay, Mary, 273
Kaye, Danny, 447, **447**, 458
Kazantzakis, Nikos, 120
Keach, Stacy, **50**
Keaton, Buster, 390
Keaton, Diane, 633
Keats, John, 671, 679
Keeshan, Bob "Captain Kangaroo," 623, 627
Keillor, Garrison, 767, **772**
Keitel, Harvey, 127, **129**
Keith, Brian, **87**
Keller, Arthur C., 148
Keller, Helen, 255, **255**, 259
Kelly, DeForest, 170
Kelly, Gene, 463, **469**
Kelly, Grace, 527, **527**, 535
Kelly, Jim, 810
Kelly, Petra, 552
Kelvin, Baron, 259
Kendall, Edward, 795
Kennedy, David, 587
Kennedy, Edward M., 431, 443
Kennedy, Ethel, 592
Kennedy, John F., Jr., 767, 776
Kennedy, John Fitzgerald, 271, **271**, 274
Kennedy, Joseph, 687, **693**
Kennedy, Joseph Patrick, II, 358
Kennedy, Robert, 687, **687**
Kennedy, Rose, **612**
Kensit, Patsy, 491
Kepler, Johannes, 713
Kerouac, Jack, **75**
Kerr, Graham, 362
Kerr, Jean, 787
Kerr, Walter, 435
Kerrey, Bob, 725
Kerrigan, Nancy, 422
Kesey, Ken, 271, 277
Kevorkian, Jack, **578**
Key, Francis Scott, 575, **580**
Keyes, Evelyn, **168**
Keynes, John Maynard, 767
Khan, Ali Akbar, Prince, 514
Khrushchev, Nikita, **448**
Kidd, Michael, 180
Kidd, William, 735, **736**
Kidder, Margot, 518
Kierkegaard, Soren, 719, 721
Kilgallen, Dorothy, 431, **435**
Kilmer, Val, 57
Kilpatrick, James J., Sr., 135
Kincaid, Jamaica, 482
King, B. B., **693**
King, Billie Jean, 703, **712**
King, Carole, 783, **794**
King, Coretta Scott, 623, **625**
King, Don, 399, **408**
King, Larry, 360
King, Martin Luther, Jr., **569**
King, Stephen, 543, **550**
Kingsley, Ben, 703, 713
Kinsey, Alfred, 451
Kinski, Klaus, 646
Kinski, Nastassja, 47, 58
Kipling, Rudyard, 79, **89**
Kiplinger, W. M., 601
Kirby, Durward, 469
Kirkland, Gelsey, 335, **345**
Kirkpatrick, Jeane, **648**
Kissinger, Henry, 783, **783**
Kistler, Darci, 623, 626
Kitt, Eartha, 639, **650**
Klein, Anne, 788
Klein, Calvin, 751, **760**
Klemperer, Otto, 49
Klimt, Gustav, 227
Kline, Kevin, 543, **551**

Klugman, Jack, **65**
Knievel, Evel, **150**
Knievel, Robbie, **721**
Knight, Bobby, 71
Knight, Gladys, 690
Knight, John, 439
Knight, Ray, 345
Knopf, Alfred A., **517**
Koch, Ed, 728
Koch, Robert, 280
Kodály, Zoltan, 152
Kohl, Helmut, 512
Kokoschka, Oskar, 783, **795**
Koppel, Ted, 106
Korda, Michael, 358
Korda, Sir Alexander, **485**
Kosinski, Jerzy, 367, 370
Kostelanetz, André, **137**
Kotto, Yaphet, 191, 199
Koufax, Sandy, 271, **281**
Krantz, Judith, **601**
Krasner, Lee, 631
Kravis, Henry R., 703, **713**
Kreskin, the Amazing, 313
Kreutzmann, Bill, 608
Krim, Mathilde Galland, 655, **659**
Krishnamurti, Jiddu, 399
Kristofferson, Kris, 239, **243**
Kroc, Ray, **102**
Kroft, Steve, 645
Krushnan, Lee, 631
Kübler-Ross, Elisabeth, **659**
Kubrick, Stanley, 575, **575**
Kudrow, Lisa, 676
Kundera, Milan, 544
Küng, Hans, 591, 592
Kunstler, William, 175, **178**
Kuralt, Charles, 319, 325
Kurosawa, Akira, 559, **560**
Kwan, Michelle, **739**

L

LaBelle, Patti, 690
Laclos, Pierre Choderlos de, 614
Ladd, Alan, Jr., 199
Ladd, Cheryl, 351, 355
Lahr, Bert, 404
Laine, Cleo, 615
LaLanne, Jack, 383, 390
Lalique, René, 320
Lamas, Fernando, 159
Lamb, Charles, 778
Lamour, Dorothy, **376**
L'Amour, Louis, 639, 640
Lancaster, Burt, **423**
Lanchester, Elsa, 103
Land, Edwin, 593
Landau, Martin, 339
Landers, Ann, **227**
Landon, Alf, 725
Landon, Michael, 191, 199
Landowska, Wanda, 387
Landry, Tom, 735, **741**
Lane, Nathan, 218
Lang, K. D., 735, **743**
Lange, Dorothea, 399, 402
Lange, Jessica, 481
Langtry, Lillie, 598
Lansbury, Angela, 694
Lansing, Sherry, **692**
Lansky, Meyer, 111
Lanza, Mario, 111, 122
Lardner, Ring, 75
Lardner, Ring, Jr., 335, **341**
La Rocque, Rod, 344
Larroquette, John, 552
Larson, Gary, 431, 436
Larson, Nicolette, 355
Larsson, Carl Olof, 607, **610**
Lasker, Albert, 257
Lasky, Jesse, Jr., 630
Lasorda, Tommy, **614**
Lasser, Louise, 128
Latifah, Queen, 383, 395
Lauer, Matt, 127, 137
Laughton, Charles, 243
Lauper, Cyndi, 319, **323**
Laurel, Stan, 610

Lauren, Ralph, 118
Laurent, Yves Saint, 244
Lavallade, Carmen de, 475
Lawford, Peter, 773
Lawless, Lucy, 479, 480
Lawlor, Richard, 404
Lawrence, Carol, 293
Lawrence, D. H., 799, **805**
Lawrence, Frieda Weekely, 287, **292**
Lawrence, Steve, 291
Leach, Robin, 799, 805
Leakey, Louis B., 63, **63**, 67
Leakey, Mary, 458
Leakey, Richard, **681**
Lean, David, 640
Lear, Frances, **787**
Lear, Norman, 47, **52**
Leary, Timothy, 135
LeBlanc, Matt, 500
LeBrock, Kelly, 800
LeCorbusier, 719, **726**
Lederberg, Joshua, 706
Lee, Brandon, 618
Lee, Bruce, 63, **72**
Lee, Gypsy Rose, 399, **410**
Lee, Michelle, 771
Lee, Richard Henry, 250
Lee, Robert E., 207, **218**
Lee, Spike, 159, **159**, 160
Lee, Tommy, 710
LeGuin, Ursula, 527, **535**
Lehmann-Haupt, Christopher, 338
Lehrer, Jim, 338
Leigh, Janet, 627
Leigh, Vivien, 415, 423
LeMay, Curtis, 711
Lemieux, Mario, •**582**
Lemmon, Jack, 730
Lemon, Meadowlark, 417
Le Mond, Greg, 755
L'Engle, Madeleine, 207, 216
Lenin, Vladimir Ilyich, 671, **671**, 673
Lennon, John, 63, **70**
Lennon, Julian, 672
Lennox, Annie, 265
Leno, Jay, 447, **449**
Leonard, Elmore, 694
Leonard, Sugar Ray, 193
Leonardo da Vinci, **256**
Leopold, Nathan, Jr., 792
Lerner, Alan Jay, 213
Lesh, Phil, 107
Lessing, Doris, 167
Letterman, David, 575, **576**
Levesque, René, **53**
Levin, Gerald, 127, 129
Levinson, Barry, 783, 784
Lewinsky, Monica, 255, **255**, 260
Lewis, Carl, 751, **755**
Lewis, C. S., **264**
Lewis, Huey, 399, 403
Lewis, Jerry, 683
Lewis, Jerry Lee, 63, 70
Lewis, Juliette, 259
Lewis, Meriwether, 783, **788**
Lewis, Shari, 362
Lewis, Sinclair, **74**
Ley, Willy, 710
Liberace, **193**
Lichtenstein, Roy, 767, 775
Liddy, G. Gordon, 488
Lieber, Jerome, 385
Lieberman, Nancy, 111, 115
Liebknecht, Karl, 628
Light, Judith, 506
Lightfoot, Gordon, 151
Lilly, Eli, 64
Limon, Jose, 665
Lin, Maya Ying, 47, 54
Lincoln, Abraham, 127, **138**
Lind, Jenny, 415, **422**
Lindbergh, Anne Morrow, 719, **723**
Lindbergh, Charles Augustus, 127, 138, 495
Lindgren, Astrid, 655, **663**

Lindsay, John V., 88
Lindsay, Vachel, 407
Linkletter, Art, 467
Linton, Ralph, 507
Lipinsky, Tara, 658
Lippmann, Walter, 646
Lipton, Peggy, 565
Lipton, Sir Thomas, 737
Liszt, Franz, 783, 791
Little, Charles C., 532
Little, Rich, 152
Little Richard, 408
Liveright, Horace, 760
Livingston, Robert R., 456
Livingstone, David, **720**
LL Cool J, 489
Lloyd, Harold, 497
Lloyd-George, David, 218
Locke, Sondra, 562
Locklear, Heather, 742
Lodge, Henry Cabot, 115, 735, 737
Loeb, James, 788
Loesser, Frank, 547
Loew, Marcus, 673
Loewe, Frederick, 159, 162
Logan, Josh, 630
Loggins, Kenny, 553
Lollobrigida, Gina, 579
Lomax, Alan, 377
Lomax, John, 790
Lombard, Carole, 623, **630**
Lombardo, Guy, 115
London, Jack, 431, **431**, 441
London, Julie, 662
Long, Huey P., Jr., 485
Long, Shelley, 485
Longfellow, Henry Wadsworth, **219**
Loos, Anita, 497
Lopez, Jennifer, **388**
Lopez, Nancy, 175, 185
Lopokova, Lydia, 519
Lorca, Federico García, 287, 290
Lord, Mary Pillsbury, 791
Lords, Traci, 465
Loren, Sophia, 319, **326**
Lorre, Peter, **803**
Louganis, Greg, 47, **58**
Louis, Earl of Mountbatten, 195
Louis, Joe, **385**
Louis-Dreyfus, Julia, 767, **777**
Louise, Tina, 362
Louis XIV, King of France, 245
Louis XV, King of France, 378
Louis XVI, King of France, **69**
Love, Courtney, 623, **628**
Love, Mike, 59
Lovejoy, Elijah Parish, 391
Lovell, Jim, 592
Lovett, Lyle, **135**
Lowe, Chad, 489
Lowe, Rob, 651
Lowell, Amy, 522
Lowell, Francis Cabot, 752
Lowell, Percival, 539
Lowell, Robert, Jr., 283
Loy, Myrna, 751, **756**
Lucas, George, 687, **689**
Lucci, Susan, 505
Luce, Claire Booth, **80**
Luce, Henry R., 288
Ludden, Allen, 214
Ludlum, Robert, **626**
Ludwig I, King of Bavaria, 293
Ludwig II, King of Bavaria, **165**
Lugosi, Bela, 159, **167**
Luke, Keye, 802
Lumet, Sidney, 739
Lumière, August, **215**
Lumière, Louis Jean, **134**
Lumumba, Patrice, 707
Lupino, Ida, 250
Lupone, Patti, 481
Luther, Martin, 495, 503
Luxemburg, Rosa, 651
Lynch, David, 634
Lynde, Paul, 658

Lynn, Loretta, **304**
Lyons, Sophie, 793

M

Ma, Yo Yo, 223, **230**
Maas, Peter, 531
MacArthur, Douglas, 271, **282**
McAuliffe, Christa, 511, 517
McBride, Patricia, 773
McBurney, Charles, 187
McCallum, David, 374
McCarthy, Eugene, 320
McCarthy, Jenny, 295
McCarthy, Joseph, 631
McCarthy, Mary, 467
McCartney, Linda Eastman, 751, **758**
McCoo, Marilyn, 726
McCormick, Cyrus, 138
McCovey, "Stretch," 201
McCracken, Joan, 809
McCrea, Joel, 743
McDermott, Dylan, 743
MacDonald, Country Joe, 793
McDormand, Frances, 147
McDowall, Roddy, 565
McDowell, Andie, 113
McEnroe, John, 79, 91
McEntire, Reba, 239, 240
McFarland, Spanky, 566
McFerrin, Bobby, 447, **447,** 459
McGhee, Brownie, 344
McGinniss, Joe, 760
MacGraw, Ali, 175, 176
McGraw, Donald Cushing, **322**
McGraw, Frank "Tug," 677
McGregor, Ewan, 352
McGwire, Mark, 655, **662**
McKay, Jim, 79, **86**
McKellar, Danica, 201
McKinley, William, 266
McLachlan, Sara, 479, 490
MacLaine, Shirley, 335, **335,** 337
McLean, Don, 639, 646
MacLeish, Archibald, 529
McLuhan, Marshall, **516**
McMahon, Ed, 811
McMahon, Jim, 69
McMillan, Terry, 390
McMurtry, Larry, 258
McNally, Terence, 111, 119
McNamara, Robert, **306**
MacNee, Patrick, 90
MacNeil, Robert, 474
McNelly, Jeff, 549
McNichol, Kristy, 709
McPherson, Aimee Semple, 591, 598
McQueen, Butterfly, 537
McQueen, Steve, **512**
MacRae, Gordon, 123
MacRae, Sheila, 742
McVie, Christine, 723
McVie, John, 632
McWhirter, Norris, 692
McWhirter, Ross, 692
Maddux, Greg, **560**
Madigan, Amy, **437**
Madison, Dolley, 111, 114
Madison, James, **219**
Madonna, 95, **95,** 100
Magliozzi, Ray, 496
Magritte, René, 264
Mahler, Gustav, **307**
Mahre, Phil, 161
Mahre, Steve, 161
Mailer, Norman, 799, 810
Major, John, 735, 736
Majors, Lee, 97
Makeba, Miriam, 431, 443
Malcolm X, 703, **706**
Malden, Karl, **432**
Malkovich, John, **296**
Mallarmé, Stéphane, 315
Malle, Louis, 399, 407
Mallory, George, **771**
Mallowan, Max, 801
Mamet, David, 543, **552**

Mancini, Henry, 751, **752**
Mandela, Nelson, 223, **223,** 227
Mandela, Winnie, 246
Mandrell, Barbara, 495, 505
Manet, Edouard, 719, 730
Mangano, Silvana, 497
Manilow, Barry, 607, **610**
Mankiewicz, Joseph, 618
Mann, Erika, 743
Mann, Horace, **657**
Mann, Thomas, 463, **466**
Mannes, David, 79, 91
Manson, Charles, 327
Mantle, Mickey, 447, **455**
Mao Zedong, **473**
Maples, Marla, 655, 663
Mapplethorpe, Robert, 591, 599
Marat, Jean Paul, 530
Marceau, Marcel, 799, 800
Marconi, Guglielmo, **513**
Marcos, Ferdinand, 261
Marcos, Imelda, 451
Marcuse, Herbert, 276
Margaret, Princess, 495, **501**
Margarethe II, Queen of Denmark, 96
Margulies, Julianna, 546
Maria Theresa, Archduchess of Austria, 81
Marie Antoinette, Queen of France, **791**
Marin, Cheech, 611
Maris, Roger, 319, **325**
Marisol, 498
Marley, Bob, 655, **655,** 666
Marley, Ziggy, 454
Marquez, Gabriel García, 591, **603**
Marsalis, Branford, 789
Marsalis, Wynton, 735, **742**
Marsh, Reginald, 299
Marshall, Alfred, 292
Marshall, E. G., 562
Marshall, Garry, 327
Marshall, Herbert, 607
Marshall, Penny, **758**
Marshall, Thurgood, 643
Martin, Billy, 575, **577**
Martin, Dean, 274
Martin, Dick, 810
Martin, George, 671, **681**
Martin, Mary, 415, **424**
Martin, Steve, 639, **644**
Martins, Peter, 591, **599**
Marx, Chico, 576
Marx, Groucho, 598
Marx, Harpo, 472
Marx, Karl, 511, **513**
Mary, Queen of Scots, 360
Masina, Giulietta, **123**
Maslow, Abraham, 639
Mason, James, 593
Mason, Marsha, 784
Masson, André, 393
Masters, William H., 319, **329**
Masterson, Bat, 584
Mastroianni, Marcello, 742
Masursky, Harold, 777
Mathers, Jerry, 530
Mathewson, Christy, 260
Mathis, Johnny, 271, 278
Matisse, Henri, 687, **697**
Matlin, Marlee, **581**
Matthau, Walter, 134
Mattingly, Don, 753
Mature, Victor, **330**
Maverick, Samuel Augustus, 356
Maxwell, James, 727
May, Elaine, 415, **417**
Mayer, Louis B., 47, **51**
Mayer, Oscar, 368
Mayfield, Curtis, 767, 770
Mayo, William, 275
Mays, Willie, 463, **465**
Mead, Margaret, 127, **127,** 136
Mead, William Rutherford, 127
Meadows, Audrey, 762
Meara, Anne, 534

Meatloaf, **550**
Mehta, Zubin, **257**
Meir, Golda, 287, **289**
Melcher, Frederic, 304
Mellencamp, John Cougar, 383, 390
Mellon, Andrew W., 528
Mellon, William C., Jr., 547
Melville, Herman, 463, 468
Mencken, H. L., **245**
Mendel, Gregor, 335, **340**
Mendes, Chico, 671, **680**
Mengers, Sue, 159, 165
Menken, Alan, 484
Menninger, Karl, 479, **484**
Menuhin, Yehudi, 305
Mercer, Johnny, 575, **583**
Merchant, Ismael, **233**
Mercury, Freddie, 591, 597
Meredith, Burgess, **631**
Meredith, Don, 176
Merida, Carlos, 552
Merman, Ethel, 607, **617**
Merrill, Charles, 807
Merton, Thomas, 367, **378**
Messiaen, Oliver, 16
Messina, Jim, 785
Metternich, Klemens Fürst von, 65
Michael, George, 671, 675
Michaels, Lorne, 679
Michener, James, 687, **698**
Midler, Bette, 623, 632
Midori, 319, 327
Mies van der Rohe, Ludwig, 783, **784**
Mifflin, George, 177
Mifune, Toshiro, **144**
Milken, Michael, 63
Millay, Edna St. Vincent, 543, **555**
Miller, Ann, 784
Miller, Arthur, 335, 342
Miller, Dennis, **311**
Miller, Glenn, 59
Miller, Henry, 543, 553
Miller, Mitch, 515
Miller, Paul, 710
Miller, Reggie, 581
Mills, Juliet, 808
Mills, Sir John, 651
Milne, A. A., 191, **202**
Milne, Christopher Robin, 127
Milstein, Nathan, 793
Mineo, Sal, **153**
Minnelli, Liza, 607, 619
Minnelli, Vincente, 447, 459
Mirabella, Grace, 495, 498
Mirren, Helen, 591, **596**
Mishima, Yukio, 719, **729**
Mistral, Frédéric, 773
Mitchell, Joan, 682
Mitchell, Joni, 703, **703**
Mitchell, Margaret, 175, **183**
Mitchell, Martha, 213
Mitterrand, François, 287, **295**
Mix, Tom, 281
Mizrahi, Isaac, 742
Modigliani, France, **226**
Modine, Matthew, **80**
Mondrian, Piet, 603
Monet, Claude, 367, **375**
Monk, Art, 127, 136
Monk, Thelonius, 262
Monroe, Bill, **501**
Monroe, Marilyn, 655, **658**
Montalban, Ricardo, 136
Montana, Joe, 191, **194**
Montand, Yves, 79, 86
Montebello, Guy-Philippe de, 257
Montessori, Maria, 655, **655,** 661
Montez, Lola, 501
Montgolfier, Jacques Etienne, 473
Montgomery, Elizabeth, **384**
Montgomery, Viscount, 727
Montoya, Carlos, 47, 56
Montreux, Pierre, 464

Moog, Robert A., 338
Moon, Keith, 565
Moore, Clayton, 389
Moore, Clement Clarke, **579**
Moore, Demi, 687, **695**
Moore, Henry, 271, 276
Moore, Mary Tyler, 223, **233**
Moore, Roger, 559, 566
More, Thomas, 63, 70
Morgan, J. P., **496**
Morgan, J. P., Jr., 789
Morgan, Julia, 618
Morgan, Marabel, 211
Morisot, Berthe, 361
Morissette, Alanis, 223, **223,** 226
Morris, Desmond, **602**
Morris, Greg, 326
Morris, Joe, 789
Morris, William, 624
Morris, William, Jr., 231
Morrison, Toni, 463, **475**
Morrison, Van, 639, **639,** 645
Morrow, Rob, 708
Morse, Robert, 465
Mortimer, Charles, 196
Mortimer, John, 785
Morton, "Jelly Roll," 591, 598
Moseley-Braun, Carol, 564
Moser, Barry, 63, 70
Moses, Edwin, 229
Moses, Grandma, **309**
Moses, Robert, **680**
Moss, Kate, **249**
Mostel, Zero, **363**
Mother Theresa, 543, **543,** 549
Motherwell, Robert, 378
Mott, Lucretia Coffin, **793**
Mowat, Farley, 97
Moyers, Bill, 335, **335,** 338
Mozart, Wolfgang Amadeus, 783, **794**
Mucha, Alphonse, 308
Mudd, Roger, **602**
Mueller, Erwin, 514
Muggeridge, Malcolm, 80
Muhammad, Elijah (Poole), 310
Muhammad, Wallace Poole, 359
Muir, John, **465**
Muller, Johannes, 435
Mulligan, Gerry, 624
Mulroney, Brian, 128
Munch, Edvard, 175, 184
Murcer, Bobby, 610
Murdoch, Iris, 175, **179**
Murdoch, Rupert, 463, **475**
Murphy, Audie, 739
Murray, Anne, 643
Murray, Arthur, 415, **416**
Murray, Bill, 431, **438**
Murray, John, 600
Murray, Kathryn, **709**
Murrow, Edward R., 639, **641**
Musberger, Brent, 130
Musial, Stan, 136
Mussolini, Benito, **132**
Mussolini, Rachelle, 432
Mussorgsky, Modest, 415, 416
Myers, Mike, 671, 674
Myerson, Bess, 739
Myrdal, Gunnar, 280

N

Nabokov, Vladimir, **241**
Nagano, Osami, 258
Namath, Joe, 735, 738
Nasser, Gamal Abdel, 249
Nast, Thomas, 358
Nastase, Ilie, 596
Nauman, Bruce, 792
Navratilova, Martina, 175, **175,** 182
Neal, Patricia, 682
Necson, Liam, 351, 354
Nehru, Jawaharlal, 639, **647**
Neill, Sam, 559, 565
Nelson, Craig T., 608
Nelson, Gunnar, **422**

Nelson, Harriet, 387
Nelson, Lord Horatio, 678
Nelson, Matthew, **422**
Nelson, Ozzie, 735
Nelson, Tracy, 663
Neruda, Pablo, 799, **803**
Nesmith, Michael, **761**
Ness, Eliot, **81**
Nevelson, Louise, 230
Neville, Aaron, 63, 74
Newhall, Beaumont, 643
Newhart, Bob, 527, 533
Newhouse, S. I., 402
Newley, Anthony, 447
Newman, Paul, 719, **719**
Newton, Helmut, 135
Newton, Huey, 783, 795
Newton, Sir Isaac, **121**
Newton, Wayne, 783, 784
Newton-John, Olivia, 518
Nicéphore, Joseph, 411
Nicholas II, Czar of Russia, 114
Nichols, Mike, 431, **439**
Nicholson, Jack, 207, **209**
Nicklaus, Jack, 95, **95,** 106
Nicks, Stevie, 527, **530**
Nicolas II, Czar of Russia, 751, **753**
Nicolson, Sir Harold, 760
Niekro, Joe, 679
Niekro, Phil, 128
Nielsen, Leslie, 682
Nightingale, Florence, 431, **433**
Nijinsky, Vaslav, 623, **635**
Nimoy, Leonard, 463, **464**
Nin, Anaïs, 79
Nirenberg, M. W., 624
Niven, David, 559, **571**
Nixon, Pat, 491
Nixon, Richard M., 447, **457**
Nkrumah, Kwame, 582
Noguchi, Isamu, 791
Nolte, Nick, 95
Noor, Queen, 383, **389**
Norman, Greg, 239, **250**
Norman, Jessye, 639
Normand, Mabel, 311
Novak, Kim, 394
Novak, Robert, 475
Nugent, Ted, 504
Nunn, Trevor, 105
Nureyev, Rudolf, 175, **187**
Nyro, Laura, 550

O

Oakley, Annie, **308**
Oates, John, 480
Oates, Joyce Carol, 159, 162
O'Brien, Conan, 671, **672**
O'Brien, John J., 679
Ocasek, Rick, 496
O'Casey, Sean, 256
Ochs, Arthur, 411
O'Connell, Jerry, **235**
O'Connor, Carroll, 740
O'Connor, Donald, 693
O'Connor, Flannery, **704**
O'Connor, Sandra Day, 511, **512**
O'Connor, Sinead, 527, **536**
Odets, Clifford, 723
Odetta, 489
O'Donnell, Chris, 387
O'Donnell, Rosie, 719, **719**
Ogilvy, David Mackenzie, 511, 515
O'Hara, Maureen, 127, **132**
Ohm, Georg Simon, 267
O'Keefe, Michael, 241
O'Keeffe, Georgia, 719, **719**
Olajuwon, Hakeem, 687, 698
Oldenburg, Claes, 570
Oldenburg, Richard, 374
Oldman, Gary, 111, 112
Olivier, Sir Laurence, 671, **671,** 674
Olmos, Edward James, **587**
Olmsted, Frederick Law, 351, 353

Olsen, Ashley, **498**
Olsen, Mary-Kate, **498**
Olsen, Merlin, 85
Omarr, Sydney, **660**
Onassis, Aristotle, 735, **745**
Onassis, Christina, 264
Onassis, Jacqueline Kennedy, 527, **527**, 532
Ondaatje, Michael, 712
O'Neal, Ryan, 49
O'Neal, Shaquille, **315**
O'Neal, Tatum, **663**
O'Neill, Ed, 608
O'Neill, Eugene, 671, **678**
Ono, Yoko, 383, **395**
Oppenheimer, J. Robert, 799, **799**
Orlando, Tony, 687, **688**
Ormandy, Eugene, **231**
Orton, Joe, 393
Orwell, George, 79, 83
Osmond, Marie, 54
O'Sullivan, Maureen, 513
Oswald, Lee Harvey, 111, **118**
Oswald, Marina, 803
Otis, Elisha, **804**
O'Toole, Peter, 399, **404**
Ovitz, Michael, 575, **584**
Owens, Jesse, 415, **421**
Ozawa, Seiji, 293

P

Paar, Jack, 223, 225
Pabst, G. W., 47
Pacino, Al, 95, **97**
Packard, David, 469
Pacquin, Anna, 655, 660
Paganini, Niccolo, 455
Page, Geraldine, 728
Page, Jimmy, 409
Paglia, Camille, 575, 576
Pahlevi, Riza Cyrus, 791
Paige, Satchel, 719, 723
Paine, Thomas, 799, 810
Paley, Bill, 150
Palin, Michael, **737**
Palmer, Arnold, 527, **533**
Palmer, Jim, 630
Palmer, Lilli, **386**
Paltrow, Bruce, 712
Paltrow, Gwyneth, 246
Papandreou, George, 703, 714
Papp, Joseph, 95, **99**
Parker, Bonnie, **502**
Parker, Charlie "Bird," 127, **127**, 133
Parker, Dorothy, 479, **479**, 485
Parker, Eleanor, **67**
Parker, Graham, 423
Parker, Sarah Jessica, 592
Parker, Theodore, 69
Parks, Bert, **377**
Parks, Gordon, 447, 455
Parks, Rosa, 447, **458**
Parsons, Elsie, 456
Parsons, Gram, 599
Parsons, Louella, 212
Parton, Dolly, 623, **634**
Passy, Frederic, 354
Pasternak, Boris, 623, **634**
Pasteur, Louis, **329**
Pataki, George, 643
Patinkin, Mandy, **344**
Patterson, Floyd, 313
Patton, George, 807
Pauley, Jane, 415, **423**
Pauling, Linus, 187
Pavarotti, Luciano, 271, **278**
Pavlov, Ivan, **757**
Pavlova, Anna, 223, **234**
Paycheck, Johnny, 50
Payen, Anselme, 713
Payne, James, 482
Paz, Octavio, 399, 400
Peabody, George, **715**
Peale, Charles Wilson, 624
Peale, Norman Vincent, 287, **290**
Peale, Rembrandt, 651

Pearl, Minnie, 447, 455
Pearson, Cyril Arthur, 79, 91
Peary, Robert E., 479, **481**
Peck, Gregory, 319, 320
Peebles, Mario Van, 159, 169
Peebles, Melvin Van, 399, 405
Pei, I. M., 271, **271**, 273
Pendergrass, Teddy, 448
Penn, Arthur, 47
Penn, Irving, 271, 274
Penn, Sean, 783, 788
Pepper, Claude, **197**
Perelman, S. J., 58
Peres, Shimon, 783, 788
Perez, Rosie, 629
Perkins, Anthony, 415
Perkins, Francis, 192
Perlman, Itzhak, 639, 645
Perlman, Rhea, 527, 528
Perón, Eva Duarte de, 191, **191**, 193
Perón, Juan, 383, 390
Perot, Ross, 495, **499**
Perry, Gaylord, 165
Perry, Luke, **534**
Perry, Matthew, Commodore, **736**
Perry, William "Refrigerator," 696
Pesci, Joe, 746
Petacci, Clara, 491
Peters, Bernadette, 527, **539**
Peterson, Oscar, 687, 692
Petty, Richard, **211**
Petty, Tom, 335, **343**
Pfeiffer, Michele, 159, 161
Philbin, Regis, 325
Philip, Prince of England, 95, 98
Philips, Lou Diamond, 731
Phillips, Chynna, 490
Phillips, John, 293
Phillips, Julianne, 801
Phoenix, River, 367, 373
Piaf, Edith, 319, **319**, 329
Piaget, Jean, 351, **356**
Piatigorsky, Gregor, 81
Picabia, Francis, 330
Picasso, Pablo, 191, **199**
Picasso, Paloma, 481
Piccard, Auguste, **122**
Piccard, Jean Felix, **122**
Piccolo, Brian, 727
Pickens, T. Boone, Jr., 578
Pickering, William, 618
Pickford, Mary, 495, **496**
Pierce, David Hyde, 80
Pillsbury, Charles, 280
Pinkerton, Allan, 469
Pinter, Harold, **486**
Pippin, Scottie, **582**
Pissarro, Camille, **787**
Pissarro, Lucien, 219
Pitt, Brad, 655, **664**
Pitt, William, the Elder, 423
Planck, Max, 399, 401
Plant, Robert, **517**
Plath, Sylvia, **407**
Player, Gary, 279
Pleshette, Suzanne, 234
Plimpton, George, 623, 635
Plowright, Joan, **535**
Plummer, Amanda, **160**
Plummer, Christopher, 520
Poe, Edgar Allen, **138**
Poitier, Sidney, 751, **763**
Polanski, Roman, 367, **372**
Pollan, Tracy, 803
Pompadour, Madame de, 665
Pompidou, Georges, 515
Ponti, Carlo, 536
Porter, Cole, 527, **530**
Porter, Eliot, 152
Post, C. W., 551
Post, Marjorie Merriwether, 763
Povich, Maury, 153
Powell, Colin, 207, 208
Powell, Dick, 791

Powell, John Wesley, 623, **624**
Powell, Lawrence, 709
Powell, William, 532
Power, Tyrone, 399, **401**
Powers, Francis Gary, 532
Powers, Stefanie, 751, 759
Praeger, Frederich A., 341
Pratt, Charles, **774**
Preminger, Otto, 703, 712
Prentiss, Paula, 155
Presley, Elvis, 303, **303**, 313
Presley, Lisa Marie, 490
Presser, Jackie, 660
Preston, Billy, 597
Previn, André, 543, 544
Previn, Soon-Yi, 319, 326
Revere, Paul, 111, **121**
Price, Leontyne, 650
Price, Vincent, **514**
Pride, Charlie, 175, **187**
Prima, Louis, 456
Prince, the artist formerly known as, 111, **114**
Prine, John, **598**
Prinze, Freddie, **275**
Pritchard, John M., Sr., 122
Pritikin, Nathan, 341
Procter, William C., 229
Prokofiev, Sergei, 577
Proulx, Annie, 293
Proust, Marcel, 623, **623**
Pryor, Richard, **72**
Puccini, Giacomo, 367, **377**
Pulitzer, Joseph, 64
Puzo, Mario, 127, **134**

Q

Quaid, Dennis, 288
Quaid, Randy, 438
Quant, Mary, 362
Quayle, Dan, 586
Quinn, Aidan, **91**
Quinn, Anthony, **305**

R

Rabe, David, 107
Rabin, Yitzhak, 63, 75
Radner, Gilda, 607, 611
Rainier III, Prince of Monaco, 783, 786
Raitt, Bonnie, 463, **471**
Ramakrishna, Sri, 623, 635
Rampal, Jean-Pierre, 265
Rand, Ayn, 767, **767**
Rand, Paul, **388**
Randall, Tony, **171**
Randolph, A. Philip, 656
Rashad, Ahmad, 472
Rashad, Phylicia, 527, **531**
Rasputin, Grigori, 650
Rathbone, Basil, 530
Rather, Dan, **439**
Rauschenberg, Robert, 687, 695
Ravel, Maurice, 479, **491**
Rawls, Lou, 223, **232**
Ray, Dixy Lee, 389
Ray, James Earl, 603
Ray, Johnnie, 649
Ray, Man, **613**
Ray, Satyajit, 113
Raye, Martha, 309
Reagan, Nancy, 95, 99
Reagan, Ronald, 527, **538**
Rechevsky, Samuel, 504
Redding, Otis, 805
Redford, Robert, 191
Redgrave, Lynn, 747
Redgrave, Vanessa, 223, 234
Redstone, Sumner, 783, **786**
Reed, Donna, 122
Reed, John, 719, **727**
Reed, John S., 154
Reed, Lou, 783, 795
Reed, Rex, **166**
Reed, Robert, 407
Reese, Della, 415, **415**, 419
Reeve, Christopher, 351, **358**
Reeves, George, 409
Reeves, Keanu, 629

Reichstein, Tadeusz, **324**
Reid, L. A., 146
Reiner, Carl, **64**
Reiner, Rob, **667**
Reinking, Ann, 471
Reiser, Paul, **160**
Reitman, Ivan, 599
Remarque, Erich Maria, 271, 275
Reno, Janet, 164
Renoir, Pierre Auguste, 539
Respighi, Ottorino, 291
Reuben, Gloria, 594
Reubens, Paul "Pee Wee Herman," 351, **357**
Revson, Charles, 710
Reynolds, Burt, **266**
Reynolds, Debbie, 415, **415**, 416
Rhine, Joseph B., 406
Ricci, Christina, 751, **762**
Rice, Anne, 799, **806**
Rice, Tim, 679
Rich, Buddy, 259
Rich, Charlie, 408
Richards, Keith, 703, **712**
Richards, Rene, 319, **319**, 325
Richardson, Natasha, 671, 673
Richardson, Patricia, 267
Richardson, Sir John, 247
Richardson, Tony, 575
Richie, Lionel, 483
Richter, Charles, 209
Richthofen, Baron von, **529**
Rickenbacker, Eddie, 598
Rickey, Branch, 201
Riddle, Nelson, **98**
Ride, Sally, 399, **399**, 402
Ridgway, Matthew Bunker, **427**
Riefenstahl, Leni, 111, **111**, 117
Rigby, Cathy, 344
Riggs, Bobby, 251
Riley, Pat, 655, 656
Rimbaud, Arthur, 543, 551
Rimes, LeAnn, 639, **645**
Rimsky-Korsakov, Nikolai, 219
Ringling, Charles, 184
Rinna, Lisa, **595**
Ripken, Billy, 616
Ripken, Cal, Jr., 789
Ripken, Cal, Sr., 271, **280**
Ripley, Robert, **473**
Ritchard, Cyril, 312
Ritter, John, 517
Ritter, Tex, 745
Rivera, Diego, 111, **111**, 120
Rivera, Geraldo, **723**
Rizzuto, Phil, 214
Roach, Hal, 553
Robards, Jason, 521
Robbins, Harold, **306**
Robbins, Jerome, 214
Robbins, Tim, **103**
Roberts, Eric, 192
Roberts, Julia, 495, **503**
Robertson, Robbie, 691
Robeson, Paul, 287, **288**
Robinson, Brooks, 209
Robinson, Edward G., **472**
Robinson, Frank, 293
Robinson, Jackie, 191, 202
Robinson, Smokey, 95
Robinson, Sugar Ray, 111
Rock, Chris, 559, **570**
Rockefeller, David, 351, 354
Rockefeller, John D., 415, **419**
Rockefeller, John D., III, 720
Rockefeller, John D., Jr., 511, **511**, 522
Rockefeller, Laurence, 562
Rockefeller, Nelson, 643
Rockefeller, Winthrop, 481
Rockne, Knute, 715
Rockwell, Norman, 463, **474**
Roddenberry, Gene, 95, **95**, 101
Rodgers, Bill, 553
Rodgers, Richard, **115**
Rodin, Auguste, 351, **359**

Rodman, Dennis, 753
Roebling, John, **242**
Roebling, Washington, 498
Rogers, Fred "Mr.," 591, **592**
Rogers, Ginger, **515**
Rogers, Kenny, 159, 165
Rogers, Mimi, 207, 218
Rogers, Roy, 447, 455
Rogers, Will, **295**
Rogers, Will, Jr., 495, 503
Rollins, Sonny, 485
Rolls, Charles Stewart, 373
Rommel, Erwin, 551
Ronstadt, Linda, 607, **611**
Rooney, Andy, 191, **201**
Rooney, Mickey, 134
Roosevelt, Eleanor, 79, **79**, 86
Roosevelt, Franklin D., 191, **202**
Roosevelt, Theodore (Teddy), 383, **391**
Root, John Wellborn, 745
Rorschach, Hermann, 87
Rose, Axl, 730
Rose, Billy, 229
Rose, Charlie, 785
Roseanne, 335, **335**, 343
Rosenberg, Ethel, **342**
Ross, Betsy, 175, **185**
Ross, Diana, 687, **688**
Ross, Harold, 519
Ross, Herbert, 625
Ross, John, 118
Ross, Sir James, 496
Rossellini, Isabella, **354**
Rossetti, Christina, 344
Rossetti, Dante Gabriel, 95, 97
Rossington, Gary, 392
Rostropovich, Mstislav, 624
Roth, David Lee, 230
Roth, Philip, 383, 384
Roth, Tim, 753
Rothenberg, Susan, 666
Rothschild, Meyer, 555
Rotten, Johnny, 218
Roundtree, Richard, 757, **757**
Rousseau, Jean-Jacques, 271, 275
Rowan, Dan, 67
Rowlands, Gena, **339**
Royce, Sir Frederick Henry, **192**
Rubenstein, Arthur, 762
Rubin, Jerry, **163**
Rudhyar, Dane, 415, 416
Rukeyser, Louis, 394
Rule, Janice, 452
RuPaul, **791**
Rushdie, Salman, 559, **563**
Rusk, Dean, **618**
Ruskin, John, 490
Russell, Bertrand, 591, **593**
Russell, Bill, **362**
Russell, Gail, 742
Russell, Honey, 82
Russell, Jane, 99
Russell, Ken, 623, **627**
Russell, Kurt, **411**
Russo, Rene, **299**
Ruth, Babe, 415, **426**
Rutherford, Dame Margaret, 529
Ryan, Meg, 735, **744**
Ryder, Winona, 319, **327**

S

Saarinen, Eero, 549
Saarinen, Eliel, 549
Saatchi, Charles, 735, 738
Saatchi, Maurice, 611
Sabin, Albert Bruce, 703, **709**
Sackville-West, Victoria, **555**
Sadat, Anwar, **217**
Sade, 89
Safer, Morley, 431, 439
Safire, William, 520
Sagal, Katie, 183
Sagan, Carl, 319, **327**
Sager, Carol Bayer, 575, 585

Saint-Exupéry, Antoine de, **195**
Saint James, Susan, 596
Saint-Saëns, Camille, 559, 566
Sajak, Pat, 599
Sakharov, Andrei, 95, **98**
Salerno-Sonnenberg, Nadja, 767, **777**
Salieri, Antonio, 244
Salinger, J. D., 207, **207**, 217
Salinger, Pierre, 703, **706**
Salk, Jonas, 367, 375
Salk, Lee, 639, **649**
Sambora, Richie, 115
Sampras, Pete, **340**
Samuelson, Paul, 353
Sanborn, David, **644**
Sanchez-Vicario, Arantxa, 328
Sand, George, 319, 323
Sandburg, Carl, 351, **361**
Sanders, Deion, 495, 500
Sandler, Adam, 543, **549**
Sands, Tommy, 197
Sanford, Isabel, **261**
Sanger, Margaret, **133**
Santana, Carlos, 559, 564
Sant'Angelo, Giorgio di, 257
Sarandon, Chris, 772
Sarandon, Susan, 591, **591**
Sardi, Vincent, **809**
Sargent, John Singer, **505**
Sarkis, Elias, 740
Sarnoff, David, 587
Sarnoff, Robert, 227
Sartre, Jean-Paul, 751, 755
Sassoon, Vidal, 602
Saura, Carlos, 441
Savage, Fred, 131
Savalas, Telly, 810
Sawyer, Diane, 623, **623,** 633
Sayers, Gale, **82**
Scaggs, Boz, 690
Scalia, Antonin, 267
Scarry, Richard, 175, 178
Schary, Dore, 757
Scheider, Roy, **279**
Schell, Maximillian, 488
Schiaparelli, Elsa, **357**
Schick, Bela, 563
Schiele, Egon, 610
Schiff, Dorothy, 91
Schiffer, Claudia, **373**
Schiller, Friedrich, 631
Schlafly, Phyllis, 740
Schlesinger, Arthur M., 703
Schlesinger, Arthur M., Jr., 262
Schlossberg, Caroline Kennedy, 136
Schmidt, Helmut, 217
Schnabel, Julian, 391
Schneider, Alexander, 631
Schopenhauer, Arthur, 223, 235
Schrieffer, John Robert, 466
Schulz, Charles M., **808**
Schumann, Clara, 469
Schur, Diane, 296
Schuster, Max Lincoln, 347
Schwarzenegger, Arnold, 559, 564
Schwarzkopf, H. Norman, 319, 325
Schweitzer, Albert, 479, **489**
Schwimmer, David, 535
Scialfa, Patti, 191
Scofield, Paul, 90
Scopes, Thomas, **196**
Scorsese, Martin, 751, **751**
Scott, George C., **614**
Scott, Randolph, 314
Scribner, Charles, Jr., 95, 99
Scruggs, Earl, 777
Sculley, John, 128
Seal, 687, 699
Seale, Bobby, **247**
Seals, Jim, 758
Sears, Richard W., 184
Sedaka, Neil, **139**
Sedgwick, Kyra, 581
Seeger, Pete, 191, 193
Segovia, Andrés, **507**

Seigel, Jerry, 374
Seinfeld, Jerry, 271, **271, 273**
Selassie, Haile, **532**
Seles, Monica, 248
Selleck, Tom, 655, 666
Sellers, Peter, 693
Selwyn, Edgar, 454
Selznick, David O., 113
Sendak, Maurice, 575, **575**
Senna, Ayrton, 800
Sennett, Mack, 282
Serkin, Rudolf, 80
Serling, Rod, **729**
Serpico, Frank, 256
Sese Seko, Mobuto, 487
Sessions, Roger, 345
Seurat, Georges, 335, **344**
Seuss, Dr., 47, **59**
Severinsen, Doc, 627
Seymour, Jane, 266
Shaffer, Paul, 472
Shahn, Ben, 277
Shah of Iran, **167**
Shakur, Tupac, 335, **338**
Shamir, Yitzhak, 375
Shandling, Gary, 472
Shankar, Ravi, 144
Shatner, William, 463, **464**
Shaw, Artie, **562**
Shaw, Bernard, 79, 82
Shaw, George Bernard, 479, **484**
Shaw, Robert, 612
Shawn, Ted, **567**
Shawn, Wallace, 711
Shcharansky, Anatoly, 554
Sheed, Frank, 322
Sheedy, Ally, 706
Sheen, Charlie, 581
Sheen, Fulton J., Bishop, 417
Sheen, Martin, **84**
Shelley, Mary, 591, **591**
Shelley, Percy Bysshe, 47, **52**
Shepard, Alan, Jr., 767, **775**
Shepard, Sam, 703, **711**
Shepherd, Cybill, 447, 459
Sheppard, Sam, 777
Sherman, William, 458
Shields, Brooke, 594
Shiner, David, 309
Shire, Talia, 609
Shoemaker, Willie, 454
Shore, Dinah, 271, 283
Shore, Pauly, 490
Short, Bobby, 655, **661**
Shostakovich, Dmitri, 710
Shostakovich, Maxim, 175, **177**
Shrimpton, Jean, 759
Shriver, Eunice Kennedy, 147
Shriver, Maria, 223, **231**
Shriver, Sargent, 343
Shubert, Jacob, 244
Shubert, Lee, 475
Shue, Andrew, 539
Shue, Elizabeth, 662
Shula, Don, **521**
Siegbahn, Manne, 376
Siegel, Bugsy, 735, **747**
Signoret, Simone, 111, 112
Silliman, Benjamin, 580
Sills, Beverly, 543, **546**
Silverheels, Jay, **194**
Silverstone, Alicia, 127, 134
Simmons, Gene, 469
Simmons, Richard, 511, **515**
Simon, Carly, 639, **643**
Simon, Neil, 627
Simon, Norton, 698
Simon, Paul, 799, 806
Simon, Richard (Leo), 267
Simpson, Nicole Brown, **66**
Simpson, Sir James Young, 802
Simpson, Valerie, 517
Simpson, Wallis Warfield, 367, **367, 371**
Sinatra, Frank, 319, **328**
Sinatra, Nancy, 82
Sinclair, Upton, 326
Sinise, Gary, 239, 251
Sirica, John J., **48**

Siskel, Gene, 634
Sissle, Noble, 659
Sitwell, Dame Edith, **725**
Skelton, Red, **435**
Skinner, Otis, 403
Skye, Ione, 341
Slater, Christian, **420**
Slater, Ellsworth, 183
Slezak, Leo, **548**
Slick, Grace, 111, **119**
Sliwa, Curtis, 288
Smith, Bessie, 448
Smith, Horace, 183
Smith, Jada Pinkett, 335, 341
Smith, Joseph, **265**
Smith, Keely, 443
Smith, Maggie, 313
Smith, Patti, 575, **575**
Smith, Red, 751, 758
Smith, Robin, 676
Smith, Will, 447, **454**
Smits, Jimmy, 111, 115
Smothers, Dick, 152
Smyth, Patty, 147
Snead, Sam, 402
Snider, Duke, 662
Snipes, Wesley, **708**
Snow, C. P., 758
Solzhenitsyn, Alexander, 207, **216**
Somers, Suzanne, 598
Somoza, Anastasio, 394
Sondheim, Stephen, 511, 512
Sontag, Susan, **393**
Soong, T. V., 440
Sorenson, Ted, **577**
Sosa, Sammy, 447, **455**
Sousa, John Philip, 543, 551
Souter, David, 117
Soyinka, Wole, 323
Spacek, Sissy, 463, 473
Spassky, Boris, 223, 234
Specter, Arlen, 522
Spector, Phil, 73
Speilberg, Steven, 543, **543, 552**
Spelling, Aaron, 783, **785**
Spinks, Leon, 307
Spock, Benjamin, 79, **79,** 81
Springfield, Rick, 485
Springsteen, Bruce, 463, **463, 470**
Stack, Robert, 201
Staël, Madame de, 353
Stafford, Jean, 355
Stahl, Leslie, 783, **792**
Stalin, Joseph, 281
Stallone, Sylvester, 607, 611
Stamos, John, 661
Stanislavsky, Konstantin, **218**
Stanley, Sir Henry Morton, 335, **346**
Stanton, Elizabeth Cady, 607, 615
Stanwyck, Barbara, 671, 675
Stark, Ray, 262
Starr, Belle, 58
Starr, Kenneth, **596**
Starr, Ringo, **83**
Staubach, Roger, 783, 794
Steel, Danielle, 564, 559, **559**
Steel, Dawn, 597
Steenburgen, Mary, 346
Stegner, Wallace, 607, **619**
Steichen, Edward, 304
Steiger, Rod, 704
Stein, Gertrude, 511, **522**
Stein, Leo, 177
Steinbeck, John, 127
Steinbrenner, George, 495, **499**
Steinem, Gloria, 335, **336**
Steiner, Rudolf, 287, **299**
Stengel, Casey, 559, **564**
Stephanie, Princess of Monaco, 607
Stern, Bert, 527, 534
Stern, Daniel, **149**
Stern, Howard, 287, **297**
Stern, Isaac, 148
Stern, Leonard, 176

Sternberg, Joseph von, 450
Stetson, John, 785
Steuben, Friedrich von, 293
Stevens, Cat, 511, 516
Stevens, Connie, 164
Stevens, John Paul, 145
Stevens, Robert Livingston, 246
Stevenson, Adlai, 567
Stevenson, McLean, **519**
Stevenson, Robert Louis, 703, **711**
Stewart, Andy, 186
Stewart, Jimmy, 639, **642**
Stewart, Martha, 799, **799**
Stewart, Patrick, 83
Stewart, Rod, 655, **665**
Stieglitz, Alfred, 159, **169**
Stiller, Ben, 575, **584**
Stiller, Jerry, 658
Stiller, Mauritz, 131
Sting, 383, **390**
Stipe, Michael, **57**
Stokes, William, 310
Stokowski, Leopold, 175, **176**
Stoller, Joseph, 395
Stoltz, Eric, 742
Stone, Freddy, 610
Stone, Irving, 63
Stone, Lucy, 500
Stone, Oliver, 591, **597**
Stone, Sharon, 111, **123**
Stoppard, Tom, 207, **211**
Stottlemeyer, Mel, 807
Stottlemeyer, Todd, 594
Stowe, Harriet Beecher, 802
Strachey, Lytton, 283
Strait, George, 351, 353
Strasberg, Lee, **151**
Strasberg, Susan, 175
Stratten, Dorothy, 811
Strauss, Johann, 215, 347
Strauss, Josef, 133
Strauss, Richard, 146
Stravinsky, Igor, **178**
Strayhorne, Billy, 344
Streep, Meryl, 479, **483**
Street, Picabo, 352
Streisand, Barbra, 767, **769**
Streseman, Gustav, 337
Strindberg, August, 794
Stringfield, Sherry, **514**
Stroheim, Erich von, 806
Stuart, Gloria, 547
Sturges, Preston, 271, 277
Sullivan, Margaret, 369
Sullivan, Anne, 63, **64**
Sullivan, Arthur Seymour, 289
Sullivan, Ed, 95, **102**
Sullivan, John, 646
Sullivan, Louis, 463, **469**
Sulzberger, Arthur Hays, **565**
Sulzberger, Arthur Ochs, **682**
Summer, Donna, 495, 505
Sun Yat-sen, Dr., **55**
Sun Yat-sen, Madame, 506
Susann, Jacqueline, 95, **101**
Sutherland, Donald, 323
Sutherland, Kiefer, 537
Swann, Lynn, **379**
Swanson, Gloria, **240**
Swayze, Patrick, 271, 276
Swift, Gustavus, 611
Swinburne, Algernon, 496
Sydow, Max von, **544**

━━━ T ━━━

Taft, Robert A., 645
Taft, William Howard, 437
Taglioni, Filippo, 663
Taha, Hussein, 647
Talbot, William, 506
Talese, Gay, 442
Talmadge, Norma, 322
Tan, Amy, **379**
Tandy, Jessica, 591, 594
Tange, Kenzo, 415, **421**
Tarantino, Quentin, 671, 672
Tarkenton, Fran, 106
Tarski, Alfred, 137

Tatiana, Duchess, 322
Taupin, Bernie, 447, **450**
Taylor, Elizabeth, 431, **431**, 443
Taylor, James, 527, 539
Taylor, Lawrence, 79, **90**
Taylor, Rod, 521
Tchaikovsky, Peter Ilyich, 367, **367, 369**
Teicher, Louis, 741
Teller, 538
Teller, Edward, 665
Tennant, Victoria, **310**
Tennyson, Alfred, Lord, 111, **111**
Terry, Dame Ellen, 107
Terry, Sonny, 503
Tesh, John, **355**
Tesla, Nikola, 479, **483**
Thalberg, Irving, 242
Thant, U, 618
Thatcher, Dennis, 353
Thatcher, Margaret, **694**
Thaw, Henry K., 649
Thomas, Betty, 559, 564
Thomas, Clarence, 531
Thomas, Dave, **419**
Thomas, Dylan, 367, **367**
Thomas, Helen A., 127, 132
Thomas, Henry, **341**
Thomas, Isaiah, 753
Thomas, Jonathan Taylor, 693
Thomas, Kristin Scott, 802
Thomas, Marlo, 152
Thomas, Martha, 457
Thomas, Michael, 681
Thomas, Philip Michael, 482
Thomas, Richard, 402
Thompson, Dorothy, 451
Thompson, Emma, 64
Thompson, Hunter S., 127, **131**
Thompson, John, 805
Thompson, Lea, 754
Thomson, Peter, 533
Thomson, Sir George Paget, 529
Thoreau, Henry David, 543, **547**
Thornton, Billy Bob, 223, **228**
Thornton, Willie Mae, **648**
Thorpe, Jim, 687, **690**
Thumb, Tom, 473
Thurman, Uma, 383, **385**
Thurmond, Strom, **104**
Tibaldi, Renata, 89
Tierney, Gene, 136
Tiffany, Charles, **778**
Tiffany, Louis Comfort, 47, 59
Tilberis, Liz, 565
Tilden, Samuel, 698
Tillich, Paul, 767, **773**
Tillis, Mel, 404
Tim, Tiny, 496
Tinker, Grant, 681
Tisch, Laurence, 799, **811**
Tocqueville, Alexis, Comte de, 276
Todd, Ann, 618
Todd, Thelma, 756
Toffler, Alvin, 559
Toklas, Alice B., 385
Tolkien, J.R.R., 543, **553**
Tomlin, Lily, 111, **117**
Tone, Franchot, 779
Torn, Rip, 474
Torre, Frank, 441
Torre, Joe, 83
Toscanini, Arturo, 800
Tosh, Peter, 678
Toulouse-Lautrec, Henri, 127, **136**
Townshend, Pete, 655, **658**
Tracy, Spencer, 208
Trapp, Maria von, 767, 778
Travers, Mary, 199
Travis, Randy, 63, **65**
Travolta, John, 287, **287**, 299
Trebek, Alex, **84**
Trench, Richard, 197
Trevino, Lee, 111, **120**
Trilling, Diana, 756

Trilling, Lionel, 755
Tritt, Travis, 698
Trotsky, Leon, 271, 279
Truffaut, François, 431, 442
Truman, Bess, 74
Truman, Harry S., 95, **97**
Truman, Margaret, 763
Trumbo, Dalton, 744
Trump, Donald, 607, **607**
Trump, Ivana, 495, **495,** 507
Tubman, Harriet, 203
Tuchman, Barbara, **490**
Tucker, Tanya, 102
Tully, Alice, 95, 102
Turlington, Christy, 457
Turner, Ike, 439
Turner, Janine, **664**
Turner, J.M.W., 753
Turner, Lana, 170
Turner, Ted, **152**
Turner, Tina, 143, **143,** 152
Tutu, Desmond, Bishop, 454
Twain, Mark, 559, **559, 568**
Twain, Shania, 575, **581**
Tweed, Boss, 304
Twiggy, **470**
Twitty, Conway, 367, **373**
Tyler, Liv, 95, 99
Tyson, Cicely, **361**
Tyson, Mike, 543, **547**

U

Udall, Morris, 66
Uecker, Bob, 314
Ullman, Liv, **104**
Ullman, Tracy, 57
Underwood, Tom, **297**
Undset, Sigrid, 175
Unitas, Johnny, 385
Unser, Al, Jr., **721**
Unser, Al, Sr., **130**
Unser, Bobby, 335, **347**
Updike, John, **427**
Uris, Leon, 735
Utrillo, Maurice, 121

V

Vaccaro, Brenda, 119
Vail, Alfred, 182
Valens, Richie, 47, **49**
Valenti, Jack, 95, 101
Valentino, Rudolph, 417
Vallee, Rudy, **148**
Valli, Frankie, 209
Van Buren, Abigail, **227**
Vance, Cyrus, **272**
Vance, Vivian, 468
Van Damme, Jean-Claude, 790
Vanderbilt, Cornelius, 735, 738
Vanderbilt, Gloria, 763
Vanderbilt, William Henry, 385

Vanderbilt, William K., 760
Van Devere, Trish, 667
Van Doren, Carl, 53
Van Doren, Charles, 682
Van Doren, Mark, 450
Van Dyke, Dick, 687, 696
Van Dyke, Jerry, 447, **452**
Vane, John R., 624
Van Gogh, Theo, 449
Van Gogh, Vincent, 607, **607**
Van Halen, Eddie, **266**
Vanzetti, Bartolomeo, 738
Vaughn, Robert, 408
Vaughn, Sarah, 752
Vaughn, Stevie Ray, 262
Vega, Suzanne, 67
Velez, Lupe, 627
Verdi, Giuseppe, 703, **710**
Vereen, Ben, 598
Verlaine, Paul, 207, 208
Verne, Jules, 122
Victoria, Queen of England, **466**
Vidal, Gore, 694
Villechaize, Hervé, 737
Vinton, Bobby, 608
Vlaminck, Maurice de, 432
Volcker, Paul Adolph, 607, 613
Vonnegut, Kurt, 55

W

Wachner, Linda, 634
Waggoner, Lyle, 304
Wagner, Jane, **314**
Wagner, Richard, 719, **722**
Wahlberg, Mark, 335, 338
Wahloo, Per, 660
Walesa, Lech, **726**
Walgreen, Charles Rudolph, **534**
Walken, Christopher, 736
Walker, Alice, 703, **714**
Walker, Hershel, 731
Walker, Jerry Jeff, 795
Walker, Robert, **214**
Wallace, Amy, 227
Wallace, Chris, 543, 550
Wallace, DeWitt, 647
Wallace, George C., **181**
Wallace, Lila Bell, **633**
Wallace, Mike, 223, **225**
Wallach, Eli, 328
Wallenberg, Raoul, 463, **468**
Wallenburg, Marcus, 223, 230
Wallenda, Karl, 778
Waller, Fats, 802
Waller, Robert James, 111, 116
Wallis, Hal, 229
Walston, Ray, 215
Walters, Barbara, 447, **454**
Walton, Bill, 335, **343**
Walton, Sam, 223, **224**

Walton, Tony, 327
Wambaugh, Joseph, 234
Wanamaker, John, 451
Waner, Lloyd, 747
Wang, Vera, 479, 483
Wapner, Joseph, 167
Warburg, J. P., **356**
Ward, Montgomery, 267
Warhol, Andy, 607, **612**
Warner, Jack, 532
Warner, Malcolm Jamal, 372
Warren, Robert Penn, 767, 769
Warwick, Dionne, 783, **792**
Washington, Booker T., 479, **480**
Washington, Denzel, 265
Washington, Dinah, 741
Washington, George, 223, **235**
Washington, Grover, 712
Washington, Martha, 258
Wasserstein, Wendy, 431, **438**
Waters, Maxine, 165
Watson, Tom, 469
Watt, James, 63, 74
Wattleton, Faye, 719, 724
Wayne, John, 671, **674**
Weaver, Dennis, 706
Weaver, Sigourney, 463, **470**
Webb, Jack, 144
Webb, Jim, 596
Webb, Sidney James, 355
Webb, Veronica, 619
Webber, Andrew Lloyd, 527, **528**
Webster, Daniel, 479, 490
Webster, Noah, 671, **678**
Wedgwood, Josiah, 547
Weicker, Lowell, 463, 465
Weill, Kurt, 219
Weill, Sanford I., 383, 395
Weir, Peter, 693
Weismuller, Johnny, 799, **802**
Welch, Raquel, 79, **85**
Welch, William, 736
Welk, Lawrence, 91
Welles, Orson, 351, **353**
Wellington, First Duke of, 241
Wells, Henry, **264**
Wells, H. G., 47, **54**
Welty, Eudora, 607, 608
Werfel, Franz, 613
Wertmuller, Lina, 580
Wesson, Daniel Baird, 225
West, Adam, **566**
West, Mae, 527, **532**
West, Rebecca, Dame, 521
Westheimer, Dr. Ruth, 575, 578
Westinghouse, George, 111, **118**
Weston, Edward, **784**
Wharton, Edith, **250**
Whistler, James, 607, 611

Whitaker, Forest, 755
White, Barry, 671, **677**
White, Betty, 298
White, E. B., 239, **243**
White, Jaleel, 111, 120
White, Maurice, 793
White, Richard Grant, 386
White, Stanford, 575, **583**
White, Vanna, 159, 171
Whitehead, Alfred North, 287, 298
Whitman, Christine Todd, 598
Whitman, Walt, 463, **463,** 466
Whitmore, James, 86
Whitney, C. V., 267
Whitney, Eli, 367, **376**
Wilder, Billy, 719, 723
Wilder, Gene, **290**
Wilder, Laura Ingalls, 799, **810**
Wilkes, Charles, 576
Wilkes, John, 310
Will, George F., 47, 49
William, Prince, 655
William IV, King of England, 389
Williams, Andy, 488
Williams, Billy Dee, 207
Williams, Cindy, 565
Williams, Elizabeth, 738
Williams, Esther, 788
Williams, Hank, Jr., **482**
Williams, Hank, Sr., **773**
Williams, John, 442
Williams, Paul, **70**
Williams, Robin, 351, **351,** 356
Williams, Ted, 207, **213**
Williams, Tennessee, **528**
Williams, Vanessa, 687, **687**
Williams, Venus, 735, **738**
Williamson, Marianne, 351, **351,** 355
Willis, Bruce, **240**
Willkie, Wendell, 555
Wilson, Brian, 771
Wilson, Dennis, 680
Wilson, Desmond, 591
Wilson, Flip, **360**
Wilson, Logan, 699
Wilson, Nancy, 223
Wilson, Woodrow, 457
Winfield, Dave, 383, 390
Winfield, Paul, 47, **50**
Winfrey, Oprah, 287, **298**
Winger, Debra, 241
Winslet, Kate, 159, **166**
Winter, Edgar, 585
Winters, Shelley, 52
Winwood, Steve, 527, **529**
Wittgenstein, Ludwig, 657
Wolfe, Thomas, **198**
Wollstonecraft, Mary, 639
Wonder, Stevie, 399, 401
Wong, B. D., 711

Wood, James Rushmore, 581
Wood, Natalie, 159, **164**
Woods, Tiger, 159, **159,** 169
Woodward, Bob, 735, 736
Woodward, Joanne, 511, **523**
Woolf, Leonard, 248
Woolf, Virginia, 191, 202
Woollcott, Alexander, 762
Woolworth, F. W., 655, 656
Wozniak, Steve, **403**
Wray, Fay, 671, **677**
Wright, Frances, 693
Wright, Frank Lloyd, 799, **799**
Wright, Orville, 623, **629**
Wright, Richard, 629
Wright, Robert C., **737**
Wright, Wilbur, 800
Wright-Penn, Robin, 560
Wrigley, William, Jr., 262
Wyatt, Jane, 511, 516
Wyeth, Andrew, **259**
Wyeth, Jamie, 607, **611**
Wyeth, N. C., 159, 167
Wyle, Noah, 335, 338
Wyler, William, **115**
Wylie, Elinor, 805
Wyman, Jane, **409**
Wynette, Tammy, 767, **769**

Y

Yamaguchi, Kristi, 339
Yanni, **263**
Yarrow, Peter, 162
Yeager, Chuck, 799, **810**
Yeats, William Butler, **114**
Yevtushenko, Yevgeny, 371
Young, Andrew Jackson, Jr., 431, 443
Young, Brigham, 450
Young, Lester, 597
Young, Loretta, 457
Young, Robert, 699
Younger, Cole, 233

Z

Zaharias, Babe Didrickson, **387**
Zahn, Paula, 139, 207
Zale, Tony, 434
Zanuck, Daryl, 117
Zanuck, Richard, 312
Zappa, Frank, 63
Zeffirelli, Franco, 810
Zemeckis, Robert, 401
Ziegfeld, Florenz, 799, **800**
Zimbalist, Efrem, 624
Zimbalist, Efrem, Jr., 776
Zimbalist, Stephanie, 182
Zola, Emile, 384
Zukerman, Pinchas, 515
Zukor, Adolph, 569

Picture Credits

YEAR	BIRTH DATE	KARMIC PATH NUMBER	NAME	PAGE
1880	January 1—March 25	15	Articulation	268
	March 26—August 14	14	Consolidation	252
	August 15—December 31	13	Expression	236
1881	January 1—January 3	13	Expression	236
	January 4—May 24	12	Amplification	220
	May 25—October 13	11	Inspiration	204
	October 14—December 31	10	Responsibility	188
1882	January 1—March 4	10	Responsibility	188
	March 5—July 23	9	Reform	172
	July 24—December 12	8	Influence	156
	December 13—December 31	7	Introspection	140
1883	January 1—May 2	7	Introspection	140
	May 3—September 21	6	Intention	124
	September 22—December 31	5	Awareness	108
1884	January 1—February 10	5	Awareness	108
	February 11—June 30	4	Instruction	92
	July 1—November 19	3	Compassion	76
	November 20—December 31	2	Discipline	60
1885	January 1—April 10	2	Discipline	60
	April 11—August 29	1	Artistry	44
	August 30—December 31	48	Grounding	796
1886	January 1—January 18	48	Grounding	796
	January 19—June 8	47	Solution	780
	June 9—October 28	46	Structure	764
	October 29—December 31	45	Trust	748
1887	January 1—March 19	45	Trust	748
	March 20—August 7	44	Confidence	732
	August 8—December 27	43	Resolve	716
	December 28—December 31	42	Study	700
1888	January 1—May 17	42	Study	700
	May 18—October 5	41	Versatility	684
	October 6—December 31	40	Seduction	668
1889	January 1—February 24	40	Seduction	668
	February 25—July 15	39	Originality	652
	July 16—December 4	38	Tenderness	636
	December 5—December 31	37	Enchantment	620
1890	January 1—April 25	37	Enchantment	620
	April 26—September 13	36	Experience	604
	September 14—December 31	35	Translation	588
1891	January 1—February 2	35	Translation	588
	February 3—June 24	34	Liberation	572
	June 25—November 12	33	Modulation	556
	November 13—December 31	32	Innocence	540
1892	January 1—April 2	32	Innocence	540
	April 3—August 22	31	Grace	524
	August 23—December 31	30	Satisfaction	508
1893	January 1—January 10	30	Satisfaction	508
	January 11—June 1	29	Empowerment	492
	June 2—October 20	28	Discovery	476
	October 21—December 31	27	Individuation	460
1894	January 1—March 11	27	Individuation	460
	March 12—July 31	26	Wonder	444
	August 1—December 19	25	Passion	428
	December 20—December 31	24	Transcendence	412
1895	January 1—May 10	24	Transcendence	412
	May 11—September 29	23	Devotion	396
	September 30—December 31	22	Extension	380
1896	January 1—February 17	22	Extension	380
	February 18—July 8	21	Revelation	364
	July 9—November 27	20	Consideration	348
	November 28—December 31	19	Release	332
1897	January 1—April 17	19	Release	332
	April 18—September 6	18	Freedom	316
	September 7—December 31	17	Electricity	300
1898	January 1—January 26	17	Electricity	300
	January 27—June 16	16	Mastery	284
	June 17—November 5	15	Articulation	268
	November 6—December 31	14	Consolidation	252
1899	January 1—March 26	14	Consolidation	252
	March 27—August 15	13	Expression	236
	August 16—December 31	12	Amplification	220
1900	January 1—January 4	12	Amplification	220
	January 5—May 25	11	Inspiration	204
	May 26—October 14	10	Responsibility	188
	October 15—December 31	9	Reform	172
1901	January 1—March 5	9	Reform	172
	March 6—July 24	8	Influence	156
	July 25—December 13	7	Introspection	140
	December 14—December 31	6	Intention	124
1902	January 1—May 3	6	Intention	124
	May 4—September 22	5	Awareness	108
	September 23—December 31	4	Instruction	92
1903	January 1—February 11	4	Instruction	92
	February 12—July 2	3	Compassion	76
	July 3—November 21	2	Discipline	60
	November 22—December 31	1	Artistry	44
1904	January 1—April 11	1	Artistry	44
	April 12—August 30	48	Grounding	796
	August 31—December 31	47	Solution	780
1905	January 1—January 19	47	Solution	780
	January 20—June 9	46	Structure	764
	June 10—October 29	45	Trust	748
	October 30—December 31	44	Confidence	732
1906	January 1—March 20	44	Confidence	732
	March 21—August 8	43	Resolve	716
	August 9—December 28	42	Study	700
	December 29—December 31	41	Versatility	684
1907	January 1—May 19	41	Versatility	684
	May 20—October 7	40	Seduction	668
	October 8—December 31	39	Originality	652
1908	January 1—February 26	39	Originality	652
	February 27—July 16	38	Tenderness	636
	July 17—December 5	37	Enchantment	620
	December 6—December 31	36	Experience	604
1909	January 1—April 26	36	Experience	604
	April 27—September 14	35	Translation	588
	September 15—December 31	34	Liberation	572
1910	January 1—February 3	34	Liberation	572
	February 4—June 25	33	Modulation	556
	June 26—November 13	32	Innocence	540
	November 14—December 31	31	Grace	524
1911	January 1—April 4	31	Grace	524
	April 5—August 24	30	Satisfaction	508
	August 25—December 31	29	Empowerment	492
1912	January 1—January 12	29	Empowerment	492
	January 13—June 2	28	Discovery	476
	June 3—October 21	27	Individuation	460
	October 22—December 31	26	Wonder	444
1913	January 1—March 12	26	Wonder	444
	March 13—August 1	25	Passion	428
	August 2—December 20	24	Transcendence	412
	December 21—December 31	23	Devotion	396
1914	January 1—May 11	23	Devotion	396
	May 12—September 30	22	Extension	380
	October 1—December 31	21	Revelation	364
1915	January 1—February 18	21	Revelation	364
	February 19—July 10	20	Consideration	348
	July 11—November 29	19	Release	332
	November 30—December 31	18	Freedom	316
1916	January 1—April 18	18	Freedom	316
	April 19—September 7	17	Electricity	300
	September 8—December 31	16	Mastery	284
1917	January 1—January 27	16	Mastery	284
	January 28—June 17	15	Articulation	268
	June 18—November 6	14	Consolidation	252
	November 7—December 31	13	Expression	236
1918	January 1—March 27	13	Expression	236
	March 28—August 16	12	Amplification	220
	August 17—December 31	11	Inspiration	204
1919	January 1—January 5	11	Inspiration	204
	January 6—May 26	10	Responsibility	188
	May 27—October 15	9	Reform	172
	October 16—December 31	8	Influence	156
1920	January 1—March 5	8	Influence	156
	March 6—July 24	7	Introspection	140
	July 25—December 13	6	Intention	124
	December 14—December 31	5	Awareness	108
1921	January 1—May 3	5	Awareness	108
	May 4—September 22	4	Instruction	92
	September 23—December 31	3	Compassion	76
1922	January 1—February 11	3	Compassion	76
	February 12—July 2	2	Discipline	60
	July 3—November 21	1	Artistry	44
	November 22—December 31	48	Grounding	796
1923	January 1—April 12	48	Grounding	796
	April 13—August 31	47	Solution	780
	September 1—December 31	46	Structure	764
1924	January 1—January 20	46	Structure	764
	January 21—June 9	45	Trust	748
	June 10—October 29	44	Confidence	732
	October 30—December 31	43	Resolve	716
1925	January 1—March 20	43	Resolve	716
	March 21—August 8	42	Study	700
	August 9—December 28	41	Versatility	684
	December 29—December 31	40	Seduction	668
1926	January 1—May 19	40	Seduction	668
	May 20—October 7	39	Originality	652
	October 8—December 31	38	Tenderness	636
1927	January 1—February 26	38	Tenderness	636
	February 27—July 17	37	Enchantment	620
	July 18—December 6	36	Experience	604
	December 7—December 31	35	Translation	588
1928	January 1—April 26	35	Translation	588
	April 27—September 14	34	Liberation	572
	September 15—December 31	33	Modulation	556
1929	January 1—February 3	33	Modulation	556
	February 4—June 25	32	Innocence	540
	June 26—November 13	31	Grace	524
	November 14—December 31	30	Satisfaction	508
1930	January 1—April 4	30	Satisfaction	508
	April 5—August 24	29	Empowerment	492
	August 25—December 31	28	Discovery	476
1931	January 1—January 12	28	Discovery	476
	January 13—June 3	27	Individuation	460
	June 4—October 22	26	Wonder	444
	October 23—December 31	25	Passion	428
1932	January 1—March 12	25	Passion	428
	March 13—August 1	24	Transcendence	412
	August 2—December 20	23	Devotion	396
	December 21—December 31	22	Extension	380
1933	January 1—May 11	22	Extension	380
	May 12—September 30	21	Revelation	364
	October 1—December 31	20	Consideration	348
1934	January 1—February 18	20	Consideration	348
	February 19—July 10	19	Release	332
	July 11—November 29	18	Freedom	316
	November 30—December 31	17	Electricity	300
1935	January 1—April 20	17	Electricity	300
	April 21—September 8	16	Mastery	284
	September 9—December 31	15	Articulation	268
1936	January 1—January 28	15	Articulation	268
	January 29—June 17	14	Consolidation	252
	June 18—November 6	13	Expression	236
	November 7—December 31	12	Amplification	220
1937	January 1—March 27	12	Amplification	220
	March 28—August 16	11	Inspiration	204
	August 17—December 31	10	Responsibility	188
1938	January 1—January 5	10	Responsibility	188
	January 6—May 26	9	Reform	172
	May 27—October 15	8	Influence	156
	October 16—December 31	7	Introspection	140
1939	January 1—March 6	7	Introspection	140
	March 7—July 25	6	Intention	124
	July 26—December 14	5	Awareness	108
	December 15—December 31	4	Instruction	92
1940	January 1—May 3	4	Instruction	92
	May 4—September 22	3	Compassion	76
	September 23—December 31	2	Discipline	60
1941	January 1—February 11	2	Discipline	60
	February 12—July 2	1	Artistry	44
	July 3—November 21	48	Grounding	796
	November 22—December 31	47	Solution	780
1942	January 1—April 12	47	Solution	780
	April 13—August 31	46	Structure	764
	September 1—December 31	45	Trust	748
1943	January 1—January 20	45	Trust	748
	January 21—June 10	44	Confidence	732
	June 11—October 30	43	Resolve	716
	October 31—December 31	42	Study	700
1944	January 1—March 20	42	Study	700
	March 21—August 8	41	Versatility	684
	August 9—December 28	40	Seduction	668
	December 29—December 31	39	Originality	652
1945	January 1—May 19	39	Originality	652
	May 20—October 7	38	Tenderness	636
	October 8—December 31	37	Enchantment	620
1946	January 1—February 26	37	Enchantment	620
	February 27—July 17	36	Experience	604
	July 18—December 6	35	Translation	588
	December 7—December 31	34	Liberation	572
1947	January 1—April 27	34	Liberation	572
	April 28—September 15	33	Modulation	556
	September 16—December 31	32	Innocence	540
1948	January 1—February 4	32	Innocence	540
	February 5—June 25	31	Grace	524
	June 26—November 13	30	Satisfaction	508
	November 14—December 31	29	Empowerment	492
1949	January 1—April 4	29	Empowerment	492
	April 5—August 24	28	Discovery	476
	August 25—December 31	27	Individuation	460
1950	January 1—January 12	27	Individuation	460
	January 13—June 3	26	Wonder	444
	June 4—October 22	25	Passion	428
	October 23—December 31	24	Transcendence	412
1951	January 1—March 13	24	Transcendence	412
	March 14—August 2	23	Devotion	396
	August 3—December 21	22	Extension	380
	December 22—December 31	21	Revelation	364